MACMILLAN
BIOGRAPHICAL ENCYCLOPEDIA
OF PHOTOGRAPHIC ARTISTS
& INNOVATORS

Also by Turner Browne

Louisiana Cajuns/Cajuns de la Louisiane

Also by Elaine Partnow

The Quotable Woman: 1800–1981
Breaking the Age Barrier

MACMILLAN BIOGRAPHICAL ENCYCLOPEDIA OF PHOTOGRAPHIC ARTISTS & INNOVATORS

TURNER BROWNE · ELAINE PARTNOW ·

MACMILLAN PUBLISHING COMPANY   New York

COLLIER MACMILLAN PUBLISHERS   London

To Clay

Macmillan Publishing Company
866 Third Avenue, New York, N.Y. 10022
Collier Macmillan Canada, Inc.

Library of Congress Cataloging in Publication Data

Browne, Turner.
Macmillan biographical encyclopedia of
photographic artists & innovators.

1. Photographers—Biography. I. Partnow,
Elaine. II. Title.
TR139.B767   1982   770′.92′2   [B]   82-4664
ISBN 0-02-517500-9

10 9 8 7 6 5 4 3 2 1

Designed by Jack Meserole

Printed in the United States of America

STAFF

Editors	TURNER BROWNE
	ELAINE PARTNOW
Assistant editor and proofreader	CHRIS KELEDJIAN
Senior writer	MICHELE KORT
Additional writers	SUSAN WITKOVSKY
	PAULINE HUERRE
	LINDA JACOBSEN
Proofreader and research assistant	RUTH SEAMAN
European correspondent	WENDY GRAD
File keeper	BETTE GLENN

Contents

Preface

The idea for this book was born of need and frustration. Several years ago one of the authors (Turner Browne), in attempting to ferret out information on Ernst Bloch (see Plate 46), could not, despite a thorough hunt, find one shred of biographical material on him: not in a who is who in art, not in a who is who in Belgium, not in any of the usual histories of photography. Bloch may not have been an especially famous artist, but his work is held in high esteem. Why should it be so difficult to find such basic information on so fine a photographer?

If the world of art could have its who's who (such as *Who's Who in American Art*), and the worlds of letters, music, architecture and science, and almost any country whose name can be pronounced, why shouldn't photography have a comprehensive biographical resource?

In answer to this question, we set out on a course that would eventually bring us into contact with photographic communities the world over. Beginning with correspondence to galleries, museums and photographic leaders across the globe, we eventually accumulated the names and addresses of about 7,000 photographers, all of whom were sent biographical questionnaires. As expected, about one to two percent of the mailings were returned "addressee unknown," and about 44 percent never responded, though we frequently sent out second and in some cases even third mailings. We were left with about 3,200 respondents, but they did not all meet the standards we had set for inclusion.

What would constitute qualification for a biographical entry in the *Macmillan Biographical Encyclopedia of Photographic Artists & Innovators?* This was the principal question that had to be answered in such a way as to be satisfactory not only to ourselves but to the needs of the photographic community. The uppermost attribute which sprang to mind was dedication: photography had to be a major passion if not the major pursuit in the biographee's life. Visibility was the second criterion, attained through appearances in important photographic journals, books, permanent collections in museums, or through grants and awards. It did not matter where the photographer came from (although we attempted to represent as many nations as we could), nor did it concern us if they were not well known. As long as the candidate fit both our major concerns, dedication and visibility, he or she would be included.

The function of this biographical resource is twofold: it strives to inform the reader about the world of photography as well as the photographers in it. It seemed only fitting, then, to include those persons, other than photographers, whose contributions to the field have proved vital to its growth and advancement, people such as important photographic curators, museum directors and gallery owners. Naturally, some flexibility in our criteria had to be exercised, for example, in the case of many inventors who, while never having been published or distinguished by awards and grants, are the bedrock upon which the state of the art rests. Photohistorians and photography critics, particularly via their bibliographical listings, are included so they can guide the researcher to additional information about artists and the art.

Once having ascertained who and on what basis candidates were to be chosen, it was time to move on to the next series of questions confronting us: What information should be included, what excluded? Basic biographical data was, of course, obligatory, but we wanted to go beyond fundamentals. We wanted to make this reference unique not only by placing the biographee within the context of his or her time but, by pinpointing specific influences—both familial and professional—shed some light on his or her personal style. Most photographers readily named their most important mentors and influences, and we found it fascinating to discover how many were the sons, daughters, mothers, fathers, husbands and wives of artists in other fields, especially the visual arts—as, for example, with Andreas Feininger whose late father was the painter Lyonel Feininger. Whenever possible we quoted the artist's description of his or her own work verbatim, departing from that practice only when sketchy notes or awkward grammar precluded it. We did not presume to describe the work of those little-known contemporary photographers who chose not to provide us with a description of their style; but with known contemporary photographers and, of course, those who are deceased, a simple statement describing their work has been supplied.

The publications section offers all monographs as well as selected books, anthologies and catalogs of the artist's work—the last category includes the museum or gallery that produced the catalog, as is done with original portfolios. In the interest both of space and usefulness, periodical listings have been limited to those journals that center upon photography and are reputable in the field. There are occasional exceptions, especially in the nineteenth-century entries when, perhaps, the only periodical in which to find a subject's work is *The Tucson Courier*, as with Buck Fly, or the *New York Times*, as with Karl Blossfeldt. Dates or volume numbers are included to make it possible to locate these publications, which come from all over the world, at libraries. For institutions and even individuals who maintain large collections of major photographic journals, this book will serve as the only necessary index to a specific photographer's work.

There was no question but to include a listing of permanent collections: it provides the reader with the locales that might give him or her the opportunity, in his own region or during some travels, to view original prints of the artist's work. The big question was whether or not to include a listing of exhibitions. Our answer was a somewhat long-winded no. The *Macmillan Biographical Encyclopedia of Photographic Artists & Innovators* has been designed to be a useful, practical reference book. Included is information that, specifically, can guide the reader to the practices of the photographer, the works of the photographer, and the photographer him/herself (thus the inclusion of addresses of the artists and their dealers and representatives, our desire being to establish a network for contacting one's colleagues). Exhibitions, important as they are, are transitory: once closed they exist no more except, perhaps, in catalogs (which have been included), memory, reviews and on résumés. To include listings of exhibitions, which often run into the many dozens, would at best serve only to impress and at worse cause the size of the book to be unwieldy and its consequent cost exorbitant.

Because this is the *first* who is who in photography, we needed to make this a who *was* who as well. Included among the more than 2,000 biographees are approximately 500 nineteenth- and early twentieth-century photographers. Among those of an earlier time are all the giants, all the initiators and innovators. Also appearing are many who never rose to fame or fortune either during their lifetime or afterward, but because of their dedication, their artistry, the visual heritage of cultures the world over is richer and more profound.

It seemed appropriate to provide the reader with the means of contacting the hundreds of museums and galleries referred to throughout the biographies, thus the geographical listing in the appendix.

Finally, what book on photographers would be complete without illustrations? Unfortunately, to have accompanied each of the more than 2,000 biographees with a sample of his or her work would have been prohibitive. Instead, we have chosen representative images spanning the birth and growth of photography and illustrating its many forms, techniques and development. Because it seemed stimulating to do so, we attempted to include many works of new or lesser known artists, artists whose photographs are not commonly reproduced in other major reference books and, in the case of the major artists, those images that, while still representing their style, have not been repeatedly reproduced.

Every effort has been made to keep the information in this book as current as possible. Because of the size of the work and the deadlines that had to be met, as well as the lively and ongoing activities of photography and its practitioners, the most current information available could not, naturally, always be included. We hope any individuals whose biographies may have suffered because of these limitations will understand and take comfort in the knowledge that their accomplishments will be enumerated in future revisions.

Acknowledgments

Putting together a book of this magnitude requires the tremendous cooperation and support of professionals not directly involved in its creation: the world photographic community did not let us down. Time and again we were amazed at the thoughtfulness and generosity of persons often thousands of miles away to whom we were unknown. They became our informational patrons, if you will. Our debt of gratitude is great and we feel obliged to single out those who went beyond the call of professional obligation: the list is long, which has been our good fortune.

Individuals who served as informal advisers from their countries are:

Australia Joyce Evans, Director; Church Street Photographic Center, Melbourne

Czechoslovakia Petr Tausk

Denmark Bjorn Oschner and Tage Poulsen

Italy Professor Giuliana Scima

Republic of South Africa Nat Cowan, Custodian; Bensusan Museum, Johannesburg

Spain Ms. Belen Agosti

U.S.S.R. Peeter Tooming, Estonia

The following professionals bent over backward to supply resources for our never-ending questions: Monica Cipnic, picture editor, *Popular Photography*; Nat Cowan, Johannesburg; Professor Peter C. Bunnell, Princeton University; James Enyeart, director, Terrence Pitts, curator, and the staff of the Center for Creative Photography in Tucson, Arizona; Robert D. Monroe (now retired), head of Special Collections Division of the University of Washington Libraries, Seattle; Nathan Lyons, director of the Visual Studies Workshop, Rochester; Cornell Capa, Anna Winand and Lee C. Sievan, International Center of Photography, New York City; Lillian Owens and the entire staff of Time, Inc.'s, Archives; the librarians at the International Museum of Photography/George Eastman House, Rochester.

Numerous unaffiliated individuals also gave generously of their time and resources, either because as photography buffs the book excited them . . .

Bevan Davies, New York City; Luis R. Nadeau, author of *History and Practice of Carbon Processes*, Fredericton, New Brunswick; Daryl Curran, Los Angeles; Rune Hassner, Stockholm; John and Sheryle Leekley, Los Angeles; Dorothea Jacobsen-Wenzel, Chicago; Ruth Lapin, Tucson; James Arthur Stewart, Los Angeles; John Oxley, Ambassador for South Africa in Australia; Sheila Pinkel, Los Angeles; Wilhelm Schürmann, Herzogenrath, West Germany; and Andrew Lanyon, a photographer from Cornwall with a special interest in Cornish photographers . . .

. . . or because as personal friends they wanted to lend their special abilities . . .

Ann and Burt Witkovsky, Laguna Hills, who provided office space at minimal cost; Rick Atwell, Joan Bell and Bette Glenn, for providing a roof over our heads while we did our research in New York City; Barry Ganapol in Tucson; Val Forslund, who did the Swedish translations; Kathleen Bender, who did the Italian translations; and Susan Partnow, who did the Spanish translations.

While many of the institutions and places of business we contacted were cooperative, certain of them, because of the special efforts of individual employees, were particularly helpful and magnanimous:

Museums and Libraries: The Alexander Turnbull Library of the National Library of New Zealand, John Sullivan, photograph librarian; Gibbes Art Gallery of the Carolina Art Association in Charleston, South Carolina, Jencie Steward, assistant curator; The Israel Museum in Jerusalem, Nissan Perez, associate curator of photography; Library of Congress, Prints and Photograph Division, Jerald C. Maddox, curator; Museum of Modern Art, Department of Photography; New Orleans Museum of Art, Tina Freeman, curator of photography; New York City Public Library; The Oakland Museum, Valliere Richard and Odet Meyers.

Magazines: Camera, Lucerne, Allan Porter, editor-in-chief; *European Photographer,* Gottingen, West Germany, Andreas Müller-Pohle, editor; *Life* Picture Service of Time, Inc., New York City, Pamela E. Kerr; *Nippon Camera,* Tokyo, Takao Kajiwara, editor; *print letter,* Zurich, Marco Misani, editor and publisher.

Galleries: The Photographers Gallery, London, Catharine Saunders; The Photographers Place, Derbyshire, Paul Hill; Simon Lowinsky Gallery, San Francisco, Betsy Evans, director; The Witkin Gallery, New York City, D. Bruce Cratsley.

Institutions and Organizations: Arts Council of Great Britain, London, Barry Lane; Creative Artists Public Service Program, New York City, Isabelle Fernandez, executive director, and Carol Greenberg, secretary; The French Institute, New York City, Jacqueline Chambord; John Simon Guggenheim Memorial Foundation, Arline Holden, editorial assistant; Los Angeles Center for Photographic Studies, Suda House and Bob Ketchum; National Endowment of the Arts, Visual Arts Program, Cathy Galuss; Overseas Press Club of America, Mary E. Novick, manager; Scottish Arts Council, Edinburgh, Sally Schofield; U.S. Department of Agriculture, Office of Governmental and Public Affairs, Washington, D.C., David F. Warren, Visual Information Officer; U.S. Department of the Interior, National Park Service at Yellowstone National Park, Timothy R. Manns, historian.

Universities: Columbia College, Chicago Center for Contemporary Photography, Steven Klindt, director; Princeton University; Marquand and Firestone Libraries; Royal Melbourne Institute of Technology, Brian Eric Gilkes; University of Nebraska, Sheldon Memorial Art Gallery, Lincoln, Norman A. Geske, director; University of Reading, Institute of Agricultural History and Museum of English Rural Life, Dr. Sadie B. Ward, photograph librarian.

Agencies and Businesses: Black Star Agency, New York City, Howard Chapnick; GAF Corporation, Jack Powell, Jr., senior public relations representative; l'Agence Rapho, Paris; Minolta Camera Company, Osaka, Richard Bryant; Pacific Press Service, Tokyo, Robert L. Kirschenbaum; and Photo Researchers, New York City, Suzanne Goldstein.

To all of the above, a deeply felt thank you.

Our wonderful and dedicated staff, listed in the front of this book, not only performed intelligently and competently, but helped to create an atmosphere of cooperation and ease that made the long hours and months pleasant and rewarding: Bette Glenn, Susan Witkovsky, Linda Jacobsen, Pauline Huerre, Wendy Grad, Ruth Seaman, and especially Chris Keledjian and Michele Kort, who hung in there for the duration and whose special knowledge and skills were invaluable.

We are also particularly grateful to our editor and our publisher for taking on so time-consuming and daring a venture as allowing the two of us to put together what is usually generated by specialty publishers who hire large, salaried staffs with computer access (we had none). Many were interested, but no others showed the foresight and enthusiasm, nor offered the support dealt to us by Charles Levine and the Macmillan Publishing Company. We'd also like to thank our agent, Harold Moskovitz, for his faith and perseverance in finding the right publisher.

It is our vision that this project be an ongoing one, that the *Macmillan Biographical Encyclopedia of Photographic Artists & Innovators* continue to be revised and reissued periodically. We therefore solicit you, reader and follower of photography, to submit to us, through the Macmillan Publishing Company, information that might be valuable to future editions: historical and contemporary information, address lists of photographers and announcements of new photographic galleries and museums would be welcome.

This project has sent us along a fascinating and multifarious road—one with no end in sight. To you the photographers, both living and deceased, we are most deeply indebted.

TURNER BROWNE
ELAINE PARTNOW

Hammond, Louisiana
February 1982

How to Use This Book

The organization of this book is simple and straightforward. The biographies appear in alphabetical order (all pseudonyms are cross-referenced); professions follow the name. The thrust of the biography, although following a specific order (place and date of birth, notable family members, education and strong influences, positions of employment, memberships, special achievements and awards, other media achievements and description of work, if any), has been written in prose style for ease and pleasure of reading, rather than the usual telegraphic, heavily abbreviated style of most who's who's. However, for the sake of space, it was necessary to use some abbreviations. Following this section, is a legend deciphering those abbreviations.

We chose to list publications and permanent collections in the telegraphic style as it seemed loquacious to do otherwise. Addresses of the entrant, representatives, dealers, and/or archives and estates always come at the close of each entry (of course, with most nineteenth-century biographees there usually is no information of this kind).

Under publications, the books listed have been fully authored by the biographee unless otherwise noted. If a book was authored by someone other than the biographee, that author's name follows the title of the book: in such cases it may be assumed that the biographee illustrated the cited work. Books published in the United States do not show publishers, as these are easily ascertained by checking *Books in Print* or the card catalogue at your local library. However, since books printed outside the United States are often difficult to find, we have included the names of publisher and/or the city of publication whenever we could obtain that information.

Locations of periodicals that appear frequently throughout the text are found in a legend following these pages.

Collections are listed alphabetically by the name of the larger institution, e.g. the Firestone Library at Princeton University, New Jersey, is alphabetized under Princeton, not Firestone. Where the name of the city or state appears in the name of the institution, it is not repeated at the end of that individual entry, thus in the entry University of Nebraska, Sheldon Memorial Gallery, Lincoln, Nebraska is not repeated; nor do we repeat the names of cities as with the San Francisco Museum of Modern Art or the New Orleans Museum of Art. States are listed at the end of an entry only when the city is not what we term an international city: Chicago, New York, Houston, Stockholm, London, Tokyo, etc., and—only because this is a book for the photographic community—Rochester, these cities, universally recognizable, have no need to be identified by state or country. Only obvious abbreviations have been used in this section and can be found in one of the following legends.

Portfolios, always contained in their own paragraph where they exist, are handled in the same manner as catalogs are under publications; publishers are always named.

Permanent collections located within the United States are listed first, alphabetically, each individual entry separated one from the next by a semicolon; a period closes the domestic entries. Then, again alphabetically by the name of institution, are listed the collections from other parts of the world. When several collections are in one country, they are lumped together in a clear fashion.

Occasionally you will find a biographee with only a country or city to identify his or her whereabouts: these occur when confidentiality of address was requested. Whenever possible we have posted alternate ways of contacting that person, as with dealers, representatives or at least a museum that possesses the artist's work. All domestic addresses are written in the style requested by the U.S. Post Office. Zip codes were provided wherever possible: unfortunately, due to national rezoning, national zip code directories have been unavailable for the past two years. Now with the new nine digit zip codes coming out, those we have provided will soon be obsolete. On foreign addresses we have written out each word of the address, as requested by the U.S. Postal System.

Several abbreviations were used for the sake of simplicity and space throughout both the collections and publications sections. We believe most of them are obvious and that you will not need the assistance of a key. However, for the one possibly obscure abbreviation we might have overlooked, a key is provided in the following pages.

In the appendices are listings of all photographic galleries and all museums with photography collections that we could garner on an international basis. The list is organized geographically, the United States appearing first, then, again in alphabetical order, by country, state or province and city. Once cities are located, institutions within it are listed alphabetically. Addresses are included.

We trust you will find the style in which we have presented the material clear and rewarding in your search for information.

Locations of Magazines

Afterimage: VSW	Rochester
Aperture	Millerton, New York
Art Week	Oakland, California
Aura	Washington, D.C.
Bombay Duck	San Francisco
Camera	Lucerne
Camera 35	New York City
Creative Camera	London
Creative Photography	New York City
Du	France
The Dumb Ox	Los Angeles
Exposure: SPE	Chicago
Foto	Amsterdam
Fotografia Italiana	Milan
Fotozoom	Mexico City
History of Photography	London
Il Diaframma	Italy
Image: IMP/GEH	Rochester
Infinity: ASMP	New York City
Journal: CCP (The Archive)	Tucson
Journal of Photography: RPS	London
Leica-Fotografie	Frankfurt
New Art Examiner	Chicago
Photo-Forum	New Zealand
Photographer's Forum	Santa Barbara
Photographis	Zurich
Photography Yearbook	London
Popular Photography	New York City
Portfolio	New York City
printletter	Zurich
Progresso Fotografico	Italy
U.S. Camera	New York City

Abbreviations

ORGANIZATIONS

American Society of Magazine Photographers	ASMP
College Art Associates	CAA
Creative Artists Public Service Program	CAPS
Center for Creative Photography	CCP
Deutsche Gesellschaft für Photographie	DGPh
Federation Internationale d'Art Photographique	FIAP

ORGANIZATIONS

Gesellschaft Deutscher
  Lichtbildner V.   GDL

International Alliance of Theatrical
  and Stage Employees   IATSE

International Center for Photography   ICP

International Museum of
  Photography/George Eastman
  House   IMP/GEH

Library of Congress   L/C

Massachusetts Institute of
  Technology   MIT

Museum of Modern Art   MOMA

National Association of Broadcast
  Employees and Technicians   NABET

National Endowment of the Arts   NEA

National Press Photographers
  Association   NPPA

Professional Photographers
  Association of America   PPA

Royal Photographic Society of
  Great Britain   RPS

Society for Photographic Education   SPE

State University of New York   SUNY

University of California at
  Los Angeles   UCLA

Visual Studies Workshop   VSW

UNDER COLLECTIONS

American	Amer.	History	Hist.
Center	Ctr.	Institution	Inst.
Collection	Cllctn.	International	Intl.
College	Coll.	Library	Lib.
Company	Co.	Metropolitan	Metro.
Corporation	Corp.	Museum	Mus.
Department	Dept.	National	Natl.
Foundation	Fndn.	Society	Soc.
Gallery	Gall.	University	Univ.
catalog	cat.	photograph	photo.
editor/edition	ed.	photographer/photography	photog.
illustration	illus.	publisher/publication	pub.
including	incl.	reprint	repr.
introduction	intro.	reproduction	repro.
monograph	mono.	volume	vol.
number	no.	with	w/

The Biographies

A

Mikkel F. Aaland *PHOTOGRAPHER · WRITER*
Born on June 3, 1952, in San Francisco, Aaland
studied at California State University in Chico,
California, where he received a BA in photojournalism in 1974. He has been mainly influenced by Harold Foote, Gordon Clark and Bill
Owens.

Aaland has worked as the part-time manager of
Foote Photos—a portable portrait studio—since
1971; since 1974 he has been working as a freelance photographer and writer. He founded and
organized the 1974 Northern California Photo-
Communications Conference, which has since
turned into an annual event.

From 1972 to 1974 Aaland distinguished himself in sports and was an All-American Swimmer.
He is a member of the NPPA and the Media Alliance.

The artist's work includes portraits in medium
formats and reportage in 35mm. He also writes
regularly for books, magazines and newspapers.

PUBLICATIONS Book: *Sweat: The Illustrated
History and Description of the Finnish
Sauna . . .*, incl. text, 1978. Periodicals: *Popular
Photography Annual*, 1980; *Foto*, 1979.

COLLECTIONS Oakland Mus., Calif. Bibliothèque Nationale, Paris; Muséet Moderne, Stockholm.

ADDRESS 290 Surrey St, San Francisco, CA
94131.

Ernst Abbe *PHYSICIST · PHOTOGRAPHIC EQUIP-
MENT MANUFACTURER* Born in Eisenach, Germany, on January 23, 1840, Abbe died on January
14, 1905, in Jena, Germany. He studied physics
and theoretical science.

In 1862 Abbe became a special instructor in
mathematics, physics and astronomy at the University of Jena. In 1866 he was asked by Carl
Zeiss for help in establishing the construction of
Zeiss microscopes, and from 1869 to 1871 Abbe
worked for Zeiss, setting up the bases for optical
calculations of these microscopes. The success of

the Zeiss microscopes led to Abbe's partnership
in the firm in 1875. In 1880 he recruited the German glassmaker Friederich Otto Schott to make
new forms of scientific glass, and in 1884 they
established the Glass Technical Laboratory of
Schott & Genossen in Jena, co-owned by Schott,
Abbe, Zeiss and Zeiss' son Roderich. Two years
later they issued their first price list for optical
glass. At that time Abbe hired Paul Rudolph to
help calculate apochromatic objectives. In 1890
Abbe and Rudolph introduced anastigmat lenses,
forerunners of the Protar and Tessar.

After Carl Zeiss died in 1888, Abbe bought out
Roderich's half of the business, set up the Carl
Zeiss Foundation and, in 1891, deeded the Zeiss
works (and later his interest in Schott & Genossen) to the foundation. Concerned with employee
welfare, he set up a profit-sharing plan and, in
1900, established an eight-hour work day for
Zeiss employees.

PUBLICATIONS Books: *Odyssey of 41 Glassmakers*, Walter Kiaulehn, 1959; *Ernst Abbe*, Norbert Gunther, 1946; *Zur Geschichte der
Zeissischen Werkstaette bis zum Tode Ernst
Abbes*, Morritz von Rohr, 1936 (Jena); *Ernst
Abbe: sein Leben und Wirken*, F. Auerbach, 1919
(Leipzig); *Ernst Abbe: Sein Leben, sein Wirken,
seine Personlichkeit*, 1918; *Die Lehre von der
Bildenstehung im Mikroskope*, Frederick Vieweg
u. Sohn, 1910 (Braunschweig); *Gesammelte Ab-
handlungen*, 2 vols., 1904–1906 (Jena); *Gedenk-
kreden und Ansprachen gehalten bei der
Trauerfeier für Ernst Abbe*, 1905 (Jena); *Über
Verbesserungen des Mikroskops mit Hilfe neuer
Arten optischen Gases*, 1886 (Jena); *Neue Appar-
ate zur Bestimmung des Brechungs*, 1874 (Jena).
Anthology: *Photography's Great Inventors*,
Louis W. Sipley, 1965. Periodicals: *Bild und Ton*,
1965, 1953.

James Abbé *PHOTOGRAPHER* Born in 1883 in
Alfred, Maine, Abbé died November 11, 1973, in
San Francisco. He grew up in Newport News, Vir-

ginia, where he received his first camera—a one-dollar box Brownie—at age fifteen.

The photographer's first news photo was of the battleship *Maine* in 1898. He worked as a reporter for the *Washington Post*, going to Europe on assignment in 1910, and in 1917 he established a studio in New York's Hotel des Artistes, where he did portraits of celebrities. Abbé returned to Europe in 1924, then covered the war in Mexico (1928), crime in Chicago (1929) and Hitler before he became chancellor (1932). He also was the first Western photographer to undertake a photo-interview with Stalin (1932), and he photographed the Spanish Civil War and the rise of Fascism in Germany and Italy. After the war Abbé moved to the San Francisco Bay Area, where he became a news commentator for radio station KLX and a television columnist for *The Oakland Tribune*, a job he held from 1950 until his retirement in 1961.

He was notable for both his photojournalism and his straightforward portraits of such celebrities as John Barrymore, Helen Hayes, Mae West, Mary Pickford, Rudolph Valentino and Irving Berlin.

PUBLICATIONS Monograph: *I Photograph Russia*, 1933. Book: *Around the World in Eleven Years*, bio., Abbé offspring, 1936. Anthology: *The Magic Image*, Cecil Beaton & Gail Buckland, 1975.

Berenice Abbott PHOTOGRAPHER Born July 17, 1898, in Springfield, Ohio, Abbott attended Ohio State University, Columbus (1918–21), and studied in Berlin and Paris with the sculptors Bourdelle and Brancusi. She worked as assistant to Man Ray in Paris, 1923–29.

Before returning to the United States in 1929, Abbott maintained her own Paris studio. Upon her return she began to document the changing face of New York City, partly funded by a WPA Federal Art Project grant. She has been a self-employed photographer since the late 1920s. The photographer has won honors from ASMP, the city of New York (1979), Smith College, University of Maine, the state of Maine and Bates College.

While in Paris, Abbott met the photographer Eugène Atget, shortly before his death in 1967. By acquiring his work after his death she brought his photographs to the attention of the world.

Working strictly in large-format black-and-white, Abbott is probably best known for her architectural and documentary images of New York City in the 1930s. She also took portraits of artists and personalities in Paris in the 1920s, and

in the 1940s began working on illustrating scientific principles. Throughout her career, she had a passion for documentation and continued to be "objective" in her approach.

PUBLICATIONS Monograph: *Berenice Abbott: Photographs*, David Vestal, 1970. Books: *The Attractive Universe*, E. G. Valens, 1969; *A Portrait of Maine*, w/Chenoweth Hall, 1968; *Motion*, E. G. Valens, 1965; *Magnet*, E. G. Valens, 1964; *The World of Atget*, 1964, repr. 1975; *Greenwich Village Today and Yesterday*, w/Henry W. Lanier, 1949; *The View Camera Made Simple*, 1948; *A Guide to Better Photography*, 1941, rev. ed., *A New Guide to Better Photography*, 1953; *Changing New York*, Elizabeth McCausland, 1939, repr. *New York in the Thirties*, 1973. Anthologies: *The Photograph Collector's Guide*, Lee D. Witkin & Barbara London, 1979; *Great Photographic Essays from Life*, Maitland Edey, 1978; *Photographs from the Julien Levy Collection*, David Travis, 1976; *The Magic Image*, Cecil Beaton & Gail Buckland, 1975; *Women of Photography*, Margery Mann & Ann Noggle, eds., 1975; *Looking at Photographs*, John Szarkowski, 1973; *The Woman's Eye*, Anne Tucker, ed., 1973; *Masters of Photography*, Beaumont & Nancy Newhall, 1969; *Photographers on Photography*, Nathan Lyons, ed., 1966. Catalog: *Photography*, 1977 (Univ. of Neb., Sheldon Mem. Art Gall.: Lincoln). Periodicals: *Camera*, Dec 1979, Nov 1975, Feb 1972; *Creative Camera*, Apr 1977; *Album*, no. 7, 1970.

PORTFOLIOS *Berenice Abbott's New York*, 1978 (Parasol Press: N.Y.); *Ten Photographs*, 1976 (Witkin-Berley: Roslyn Heights, N.Y.).

COLLECTIONS Allen Mem. Art Mus., Oberlin, Ohio; Art Inst. of Chicago; Chase Manhattan Bank, NYC; Detroit Inst. of Arts, Mich.; Harvard Univ., Fogg Art Mus., Cambridge, Mass.; High Mus. of Art, Atlanta, Ga.; Ind. Univ. Art Mus., Bloomington; IMP/GEH, Rochester, N.Y.; Kalamazoo Inst. of Arts, Mich.; L/C, Wash., D.C.; Menil Fndn., Houston, Tex.; Metro. Mus. of Art, NYC; Milwaukee Art Ctr., Wisc.; Minneapolis Inst. of Arts, Minn.; Mus. of the City of N.Y.; Mus. of Fine Arts, Boston; Mus. of Fine Arts, Houston; Mus. of Fine Arts of St. Petersburg, Fla.; MOMA, NYC; Natl. Cllctn. of Fine Arts, Wash., D.C.; Natl. Portrait Gall., Wash., D.C.; New Orleans Mus. of Art; Newark Mus., N.J.; Philadelphia Mus. of Art, Penn.; Princeton Univ. Lib., N.J.; R.I. School of Design, Providence; San Francisco Mus. of Modern Art; Seagrams Cllctn., N.Y.C.; Smith Coll., Mus. of Art, Northampton, Mass.; Smithsonian Inst., Wash., D.C.; Univ. of Ill., Krannert Art Mus., Urbana; Univ. of Mich.,

Ann Arbor; Univ. of Neb., Sheldon Mem. Art Gall., Lincoln; Univ. of N. Mex., Albuquerque; Univ. of Okla., Norman; Va. Mus. of Fine Art, Richmond; Westbrook Coll., Berenice Abbott Rm., Maine; Worcester Art Mus., Mass.; Yale Univ. Art Gall., New Haven, Conn. Natl. Gall. of Canada, Ottawa, Ontario.

DEALERS Lunn Gall., 3243 P St NW, Washington, D.C. 20007; Marlborough Gall., 40 W 57 St, New York, NY 10019; Witkin Gall., 41 E 57 St, New York, NY 10022.

ADDRESS Abbott Village, ME 04406.

Sam Abell PHOTOGRAPHER Born in Sylvania, Ohio, on February 19, 1945, Abell completed his BA at the University of Kentucky in 1969. His father, T. S. Abell, is a teacher of photography. Since 1970 the photographer has been doing contract work for *National Geographic.*

He does color photography "for editorial and artistic purposes."

PUBLICATIONS Books: *Still Waters, White Waters,* 1977; *Pacific Crest Trail,* 1975. Periodical: *Camera,* 1976.

REPRESENTATIVE Woodfin Camp, 222 W 83 St, New York, NY 10024.

ADDRESS Rt 2, Box 292, Crozet, VA 22932.

William de Wiveleslie Abney CHEMIST WRITER · TEACHER Born in Derby, England, on July 24, 1843, Abney died December 3, 1920, in Folkestone, Kent, England.

Abney became a lieutenant (1861) and then a captain (1873) in the Royal Engineers, later teaching chemistry for them at Chatham (until 1877). In 1877 he became active in London's Department for Science and Art, and in 1881 he retired from the army, becoming assistant director for science in the Science and Art Department of South Kensington in 1884. From 1900 Sir William directed secondary education for England and Wales. He served as president of RPS, 1892–94, 1896 and 1903–1905, and held posts at various learned societies as well as garnering numerous awards.

A specialist in the chemistry of photography, Abney was best known for the development of a photographic emulsion to map the solar spectrum far into the infrared. He was the first photographic investigator to make quantitative measurements of the relation between the transparency of the image and the exposure, according to C. E. K. Mees *(Theory of the Photographic Process),* and his other discoveries included copper bromide silver nitrate intensification (1877), the use of hydroquinone as a developer (1880) and

silver gelatin citrochloride emulsion for printing-out paper (known as P.O.P.) (1882). He wrote extensively in the field and was published in such periodicals as *Photography* and *Photographic News.*

PUBLICATIONS Books: *Quellendarstellungen zur Geschichte der Fotografie,* Wolfgang Baier, 1964; *The History of Three-Color Photography,* E. J. Wall, 1925; *Color Photography,* Wm. Burt Gamble, 1924; *The History of Photography,* Josef Maria Eder, 1905, repr. 1945; *Evening talks at the camera club on the action of light in photography,* 1897; *Instantaneous Photography,* 1895 (Low, Marston, London); *Platinotype; its preparation and manipulation,* w/Lyonel Clark, 1895; *Colour Measurement and Mixture,* 1891; *How to Become a Photographer,* 1891; *The Art and Practice of Silver Printing,* w/Harry P. Robinson, 2nd ed., 1888; *Negative Making,* 1887 (Piper & Carter: London); *Recent advances in photography,* 1882; *The practical working of the gelatine emulsion process,* 1880 (Piper & Carter: London); *A Treatise on Photography,* 1878, rev. ed., 1916 (Longmans, Green, London); *Science Lectures. Photography,* 1876 (London); *Instructions in Photography,* 1871, 11th ed., 1905 (Chatham); *Photography with Emulsions,* 1862. Anthology: *Photography's Great Inventors,* Louis W. Sipley, 1965. Catalogs: *Catalogue of Scientific Papers,* vol. 9, n.d., vol. 13, 1914 (Royal Society, London). Periodicals: "RPS of Great Britain: Library Catalogue," Sept 1939, "Sir William de Wiveleslie Abney," Chapman Jones, July 1921, Obituary, Jan 1921, *Photographic Journal* (RPS); *British Photographic Journal Almanac,* 1922; "Cantor Lectures on Photometry," vol. 42, 1894, "Cantor Lectures on Light and Colour," vol. 37, 1888, "Cantor Lectures on Photography and the Spectroscope," vol. 33, 1885, *Journal of the Society of Arts;* "Comparative Effects of Different Parts of the Spectrum on Silver Salts," *Proceedings of the Royal Society,* vol. 42, 1886; "Notes on Sensitometry," vol. 29, 1882, Obituary, Dec. 10, 1920, *British Journal of Photography;* "A New Developer," *Photography News,* vol. 24, 1880; "On the photographic method of mapping the least refrangible end of the solar spectrum," *Philosophical Transactions of the Royal Society of London,* vol. 171, 1880; "Photography at the least refrangible end of the spectrum and on some photographic phenomena," *Monographs of the Nottingham Royal Astronomical Society,* vol. 38, 1878.

Michael Henry Abramson PHOTOGRAPHER Born July 5, 1944, in Plainfield, New Jersey, Abramson earned a BA from Kenyon College,

Gambier, Ohio (1966), and an MA from the University of Chicago (1968).

A freelance photographer since 1970, he has had his work published in such periodicals as *Time, N.Y. Times, New Times, Look, Americana, New York, People, Us, Quick* and *Stern Manchete*. He has also worked on assignment for *Black Star*.

The ASMP member won a CAPS grant in 1974 and a Woodrow Wilson Fellowship in 1966 from the University of Chicago. In 1978 he received the silver medal in photography from the Art Directors Club of New Jersey.

A photojournalist, Abramson has covered such topics as political conventions and candidates, Northern Ireland, coal strikes, flooding of the Mississippi and street gangs of the South Bronx.

PUBLICATIONS Monograph: *Palante*, 1970. Books: *Inside Las Vegas*, Mario Puzo, 1977; *Our Portion of Hell*, 1971. Anthology: *The Eye of Conscience*, 1973.

ADDRESS 84 University Pl, New York, NY 10003.

Adál PHOTOGRAPHER · GALLERY DIRECTOR
Born Adál Maldonado in 1947 in Utuado, Puerto Rico, Adál earned an MFA from the San Francisco Art Institute in 1972.

He currently co-directs the gallery Foto in New York City. The photographer won an NEA Photographer's Fellowship in 1975.

PUBLICATIONS Monograph: *The Evidence of Things Not Seen*, 1975. Periodicals: *Creative Camera*, Jan 1975; *Camera*, Aug 1972.

COLLECTIONS San Francisco Mus. of Modern Art. Bibliothèque Nationale, Paris.

ADDRESS Da Capo Press, 277 W 17 St, New York, NY 10011.

Hans Christian Adam PHOTOGRAPHER · PHOTOHISTORIAN Born May 19, 1948, in Bad Münder, West Germany, Adam studied psychology and art history at Vienna and at Goettingen Universities (West Germany), receiving an MSc in psychology from the latter in 1975.

From 1979 to 1980 Adam was an intern at IMP/GEH in Rochester. He was a lecturer in History of Photography at Gesamthochschule Kassel in West Germany in 1978–79 and edited *Fotografie* magazine in Goettingen, 1977–79. From 1973 to 1975 Adam was a research assistant in the Audiovisual Department of the Physiological Institute, Goettingen University. He began doing photojournalism in 1963.

A member of DGPh, the photographer won a Canada Council photography fellowship in 1975.

He characterizes his work as "personal, environmental and documentary photography." He emphasizes the relationship between photo and text and also concentrates on "historical 'comparative' photography." His historical research centers on the relationship of photography and archaeology in the nineteenth century in the Near and Middle East.

PUBLICATIONS Catalog: *In unnachahmlicher Treue*, 1979 (Kunsthalle, Cologne). Periodical: *Fotografie*, no. 9, 1979.

COLLECTIONS Agfa-Gevaert Historama, Leverkusen, West Ger.; Bibliothèque Nationale, Paris.

ADDRESS Groner Str 15, D-3400 Goettingen, West Germany.

Robert Moyes Adam PHOTOGRAPHER · BOTANIST Born in 1885 in Carluke, Lanarkshire, Scotland, Adam died in November of 1967 in Edinburgh. He studied art at the Royal Institution in Edinburgh and at the College of Art at Luariston. He also took classes in science at Heriot-Watt College.

Adam began work for the Royal Botanical Gardens in 1907 and was promoted to its permanent staff in charge of the studio in 1914. He remained there until his retirement in 1949, widely publishing his work in books and such periodicals as *The Scots Magazines*. Adam was a member and official photographer of the Botanical Society of Edinburgh.

Both a botanical and landscape photographer, Adam worked solely with the heavy half-plate large format (6½ x 4¾) camera. In his book about Adam, George Oliver wrote that few of the photographer's contemporaries were able to match his "exalted standards of aesthetic awareness and technical accomplishment or to challenge for any length of time his singular ability to reveal the form and structure and changing aspect of Scottish . . . landscape with so much style and distinction." However, he received practically no recognition in his day.

PUBLICATIONS Books: *Hills and Glens*, Brenda G. Macrow, 1949 (Oliver & Boyd: Edinburgh); *Scotland, Rivers and Streams*, intro. by George Scott-Moncrieff, 1948 (Hopetown Press: Edinburgh); *Unto the Hills*, Brenda G. Macrow, 1947 (Oliver & Boyd: Edinburgh). Catalog: *Robert Moyes Adam: Photographer 1885–1967*, George Oliver, 1969 (Scottish Arts Council: Edinburgh). Periodical: Jeremy Bruce-Watt, *Scotland's Magazine*, Feb 1958.

COLLECTION D. C. Thomson & Co., Dundee, Scotland.

Ansel Easton Adams PHOTOGRAPHER TEACHER [See plate 72] Born February 20, 1902, in San Francisco, he is married to the author Virginia Best Adams. In his early years he received private tutoring at his home. His early education was slanted toward a career as a concert pianist. He chose photography as a profession in 1930.

Ansel Adams was founder and is now chairman of the board of the Friends of Photography (1967 to present), a founding member of the Group f.64 in 1932 and was on the board of directors of the Sierra Club, 1934–71. He also founded the Photography Department at California School of Fine Arts in San Francisco in 1946. A recipient of Guggenheim Fellowships in 1946, 1948 and 1958, he also received a Brehm Memorial Award from Rochester Institute of Technology in 1958, a John Muir Award from the Sierra Club in 1963, a Conservation Service Award from the Department of the Interior in 1968, a Progress Medal from PSA in 1969 and a Chubb Fellowship from Yale in 1970. He was made a Fellow of the Society of Photographic Scientists and Engineers in 1975. Adams also is the inventor of the Zone System of exposure, a system of measuring light and converting it into zones to make use of the maximum tonal range of film.

Ansel Adams—Photographer is a black-and-white film about the artist made in 1958.

Without question, he is the most well-known photographer in America, if not the world. He is most noted for his landscape images of the western United States and his contributions to photographic technology.

PUBLICATIONS Monographs: *The Camera*, 1980; *Yosemite and the Range of Light*, intro. by Paul Brooks, 1979; *Portfolios of Ansel Adams*, foreword by John Szarkowski, 1977; *Ansel Adams: Images 1923–1974*, foreword by Wallace Stegner, 1974; *Ansel Adams: Singular Images* w/ Land, McAlpin, Holmes, 1974; *Ansel Adams*, Liliane De Cock, ed., foreword by Minor White, 1972; *Ansel Adams: Volume I, The Eloquent Light*, Nancy Newhall, 1963; *My Camera in the National Parks*, w/Virginia Adams, 1950; *My Camera in Yosemite Valley*, w/Virginia Adams, 1950. Books: *Polaroid Land Photography Manual*, 1978; *Taos Pueblo*, Mary Austin, 1977; *Photographs of the Southwest*, Lawrence Clark Powell, 1976; *The Tetons and the Yellowstone*, Nancy Newhall, 1970; *Fiat Lux: The University of California*, Nancy Newhall, 1967; *An Intro-*duction to Hawaii, Edward Joesting, 1964; *Death Valley and the Creek Called Furnace*, Edwin Corle, 1962; *These We Inherit*, 1962; *This Is the American Earth*, Nancy Newhall, 1960; *Yosemite Valley*, Nancy Newhall, ed., 1959; *Artificial-Light Photography*, 1956; *Death Valley*, Nancy Newhall, 1954; *Mission San Xavier del Bac*, Nancy Newhall, 1954; *The Pageant of History in Northern California*, 1954; *Natural-Light Photography*, 1952; *The Land of Little Rain*, Mary Austin, 1950; *The Print*, 1950; *Camera and Lens*, 1948, rev. ed. 1970; *The Negative*, 1948; *Yosemite and the Sierra Nevada*, John Muir, Charlotte Mauk, eds., 1948; *Illustrated Guide to Yosemite Valley*, w/Virginia Adams, 1946, rev. ed., 1963; *Born Free and Equal: Photographs of the Loyal Japanese-Americans at Manzanar Relocation Center, Inyo County, California*, 1944; *Sierra Nevada: The John Muir Trail*, 1938; *Making a Photograph*, 1935; *Lights & Shadows of Yosemite*, K. A. Taylor, 1926. Anthologies: *The Photograph Collector's Guide*, Lee D. Witkin & Barbara London, 1979; *The Magic Image*, Cecil Beaton & Gail Buckland, 1975; *Looking at Photographs*, John Szarkowski, 1973.

PORTFOLIOS *Portfolio VII*, 1976, *Portfolio VI*, 1974, *Portfolio V*, 1971 (Parasol Press: N.Y.); *Portfolio IV: What Majestic Word*, 1963; *Portfolio III: Yosemite Valley*, 1960 (Sierra Club); *Portfolio II*, 1950; *Portfolio I*, 1948 (self-pub. w/ Grabhorn Press); *Parmelian Prints of the High Sierras*, 1927 (Jean Chambers Moore).

COLLECTIONS Most major museums in the U.S. Bibliothèque Nationale, Paris; RPS London; Victoria & Albert Mus., London.

ADDRESS Route 1, Box 181, Carmel, CA 93923.

Eddie Adams PHOTOGRAPHER · LECTURER Born June 12, 1933, in New Kensington, Pennsylvania, Adams worked for the *Philadelphia Bulletin*, 1958–62, as a photographer, later photographing for the Associated Press (1962–72), *Time* (1972–76) and special correspondent for the Associated Press in New York from 1976 to 1980. Since that time he has worked freelance. His work has also been seen in *Life* magazine, *Newsweek* and *Look*.

In 1969 Adams won a Pulitzer Prize as well as the World Press Photo Grand Award. He received Long Island University's George Polk Memorial Award in 1969, 1978 and 1979.

PUBLICATION Anthology: *Moments*, Sheryle & John Leekley, 1978.

REPRESENTATIVE Olden Camera, Herald Square, 33rd & Broadway, New York, NY 10001.

Robert Adams *PHOTOGRAPHER · WRITER* [See plate 127] Born May 8, 1937, in Orange, New Jersey, Adams earned a BA in English from the University of Redlands, California (1959), and a PhD in English from the University of Southern California, Los Angeles (1965).

A freelance photographer and writer since 1967, Adams was a lecturer and assistant professor of English at Colorado College, Colorado Springs, 1962–70.

The photographer won NEA Photography Fellowships in 1973 and 1978, a Guggenheim Fellowship in 1973 and the Award of Merit from the American Association of State and Local History in 1975.

Working in black-and-white, he has chosen as his main subject the current American West. He produces landscapes showing both the natural and man-made world.

PUBLICATIONS Monographs: *Prairie*, 1978; *Denver: A Photographic Survey of the Metropolitan Area*, 1977; *The New West*, 1974; *The Architecture and Art of Early Hispanic Colorado*, 1974; *White Churches of the Plains*, 1970. Anthologies: *American Images*, 1979; *The Photograph Collector's Guide*, Lee D. Witkin & Barbara London, 1979; *Mirrors and Windows*, John Szarkowski, 1978. Periodicals: "Recent American Photography," *Creative Camera*, Sept 1976; "Route 66 Revisited: The New Landscape Photography," *Art in America*, Jan/Feb 1976. Reviews: "Topographical Error," Charles Desmarais, *Afterimage: VSW*, Nov 1975; *Art in America*, Lewis Baltz, Mar/Apr 1975.

COLLECTIONS Ariz. State Univ., Tempe; Chase Manhattan Bank, NYC; Colorado Springs Fine Arts Ctr., Colo.; Colorado State Mus., Denver; Denver Art Mus., Colo.; Guggenheim Foundation Cllctn., NYC; IMP/GEH, Rochester; Metro. Mus. of Art, NYC; MOMA, NYC; Mus. of Fine Arts, Houston; N. Mex. State Univ., Las Cruces; Polaroid Cllctn., Cambridge, Mass.; Princeton Univ. Art Mus., N.J.; Univ. of Colo., Colo. Springs; Univ. of Neb., Sheldon Mem. Art Gall., Lincoln; Wheaton Coll., Wheaton, Ill. Australian Natl. Gall., Canberra.

ADDRESS 326 Lincoln St, Longmont, CO 80501.

Shelby Lee Adams *PHOTOGRAPHER* Born October 24, 1950, Adams earned a BFA in Photography (1974) from the Cleveland Institute of Art, Ohio, and an MA in Photography (1975) from the University of Iowa, Iowa City. Clarence John Laughlin is his mentor and personal friend.

Currently a freelance photographer, Adams taught photography in 1978–79 at the Cincinnati (Ohio) Art Academy and at Northern Kentucky University in Covington.

The photographer won an NEA grant in 1978 for book publication and a traveling exhibition, and in 1977 received an NEA Photography Survey grant to document eastern Kentucky. He has belonged to SPE since 1975.

Using a view camera and 35mm, he does "straight" documentary portraiture "with an interest in symbolism."

PUBLICATIONS Anthology: *Appalachia: A Self Portrait*, intro. by Robert Coles, 1979. Catalog: *Cincinnati Art Museum*, 1976. Periodical: *Photography Annual*, 1980.

COLLECTIONS Cincinnati Art Mus., Ohio; Cleveland Inst. of Art, Ohio; Univ. of Iowa, Iowa City; Univ. of Ky., Lexington.

ADDRESS 3 South Church St, Pittsfield, MA 01201.

Antoine Samuel Adam-Salomon *PHOTOGRAPHER · SCULPTOR* Adam-Salomon was born and died in France (1811–1881).

A successful sculptor working in Paris, he took up photography in 1858, giving it up in the 1870s due to failing eyesight.

Working in the painterly tradition, Adam-Salomon was noted for the high sidelight ("Rembrandt lighting") he used on his velvet-draped subjects. He became a master at the art of retouching.

PUBLICATIONS Book: *Pictorial Effect in Photography*, H. P. Robinson, 1869 (London). Anthologies: *The Magic Image*, Cecil Beaton & Gail Buckland, 1975; *Early Photographs & Early Photographers*, Oliver Mathews, 1973; *Galerie des Contemporains*, 7 vols., 1870. Periodicals: E. L. Wilson, *Philadelphia Photographer*, July 1881; *Cours familier de littérature*, A. de Lamartine, vol. 7, 1859.

Robert Adamson *PHOTOGRAPHER · CHEMIST* [See plate 3] Born in 1821 in Berunside, Scotland, Adamson died in 1848 in St. Andrews. He was influenced by William Henry Fox Talbot's calotypes (talbotypes).

Adamson worked as a camera operator and darkroom technician for David Octavius Hill, and prior to that was a chemist.

Strongly influenced by paintings, Hill and Adamson were considered by many to be the best portrait photographers of their day. They used calotypes for the greater part of their work; their portraits demonstrated a mastery of form, composition and lighting. They also produced cityscapes and landscapes.

PUBLICATIONS Books: *An Early Victorian Album: The Hill/Adamson Collection*, ed. & intro. by Colin Ford, commentary by Roy Strong, 1974; *Sun Pictures: The Hill-Adamson Calotypes*, David Bruce, 1974; *Hill and Adamson Photographs*, Graham Ovenden, ed., intro. by Marina Henderson, 1973; *A Centenary Exhibition of the Work of David Octavius Hill and Robert Adamson*, Katherine Michaelson, 1970; *Masters of Photography*, Beaumont & Nancy Newhall, 1958; *Calotypes by D. O. Hill & R. Adamson Illustrating an Early Stage in the Development of Photography, Selected from His Collection*, Andrew Elliot (pvt. prntg. of thirty-eight copies), 1928.

COLLECTIONS Albright-Knox Art Gall., Buffalo, N.Y.; Art Inst. of Chicago; IMP/GEH, Rochester; MOMA, NYC; Univ. of N. Mex. Art Mus., Albuquerque; Univ. of Tex., Gernsheim Coll., Humanities Research Ctr., Austin. Natl. Gall. of Canada, Ottawa, Ontario. In Scotland: Edinburgh Photographic Soc.; Edinburgh Pub. Lib.; Royal Scottish Mus., Edinburgh; Scottish Natl. Portrait Gall., Edinburgh; Glasgow Art Gall. & Mus.; Glasgow Univ. Lib. In London: British Mus.; Natl. Portrait Gall.; RPS; Science Mus.; Victoria & Albert Mus.

Peter Martin Addis *PHOTOJOURNALIST* Born March 9, 1948, in Chester, England, Addis studied at the Gwent Faculty of Art and Design's Department of Documentary Photography in Newport, South Wales, where he received a diploma in photography in 1978. He worked under David Hurn of Magnum, and also names, as mentors, John Charity, Ron McCormick and Keith Arnett.

Since 1978 he has worked as a freelance photojournalist in London. Addis belongs to the National Union of Journalists in Great Britain.

The photographer won grants from West Wales Association for the Arts in 1976 and 1978, from the Arts Council of Wales in 1978, and the Arts Council of Great Britain in 1980.

PUBLICATIONS Anthology: *New Britain Image*, Arts Council of Great Britain, 1977. Periodicals: *British Journal of Photography*, Feb 1979; *Zoom*, Jan 1979 (Paris).

COLLECTION Arts Council of Great Britain.

ADDRESS Flat 1, 130 Kew Rd, Richmond-upon-Thames, Surrey, England.

Adele (Sister) *PHOTOGRAPHER* Born December 4, 1915, in Massachusetts, Sister Adele studied at Carnegie-Mellon University in Pittsburgh, Pennsylvania (1934–35), before receiving her BS (1938) and MS (1940) from the University of Southern California, Los Angeles. She earned her PhD from the University of California, Berkeley, in 1949.

Sister Adele has been an artist-in-residence in photography at Dominican College, San Rafael, California since 1974. She was associate professor of humanities at that school from 1950 to 1974. She served as associate professor in English at California State University, Fresno, 1940–50.

Sister Adele belongs to SPE, RPS and Friends of Photography, and serves on the Board of Directors of San Francisco Women Artists.

PUBLICATIONS Periodicals: *Photo & Audio*, Aug 1979; *Photo-Revue*, Dec 1973.

COLLECTIONS L/C, Wash., D.C.; Oakland Art Mus., Calif. Bibliothèque Nationale, Paris; Dunedin Pub. Art Gall., New Zealand; Metro. Mus. of Modern Art, Manila, Philippines.

DEALERS Newman Gall., Bonaventure Hotel, 404 S Figueroa, Los Angeles, CA 90071; Larry Winn Gall., Design Center NW, 5701 6th Ave S #230, NW Seattle, WA 98108.

ADDRESS Dominican College, San Rafael, CA 94901.

Bob Adelman *PHOTOGRAPHER* Born on October 30, 1930, in New York City, he received a BA from Rutgers University, New Brunswick, New Jersey, in 1951 and an MA in Philosophy at Columbia University, New York City, in 1954. Later, in 1959, he studied with Alexey Brodovitch.

A freelance artist for twenty years, Adelman is a member of ASMP. He received a Guggenheim Fellowship in 1964, and his photographs have made the covers of *Time, Newsweek, Popular Photography, New York, Camera, Foto, Stern*, and *Esquire*, among others.

Mr. Adelman works strictly as a photojournalist and a documentarian.

PUBLICATIONS Books (all texts by Susan Hall): *Ladies of the Night*, 1974; *Gentleman of Leisure*, 1973; *Down Home*, 1972; *Street Smart*, 1972; *On and Off the Street*, 1970.

ADDRESS 119 Fifth Ave, New York, NY 10003.

G. Leslie Adkin *PHOTOGRAPHER · SCIENTIST · FARMER* Adkin lived in New Zealand from 1888 to 1964.

A farmer until 1946, he then worked for the Geological Survey, during which time he wrote thirty-two scientific papers and two books.

According to W. N. Wilson of the National Museum of New Zealand, "Leslie Adkins used his camera as a scientific recording instrument, as a means of logging the day-to-day activities of his family and friends, and to capture other scenes and incidents that either fascinated or amused him. His photographs are quite unpretentious and, when photographing people, his approach was always sensitive and sympathetic."

PUBLICATIONS Books: *Bibliographic Index of New Zealand Stratigraphic Names to 31 Dec 1950*, 1954 (New Zealand Geo. Survey, Wellington); *Horowhenna, Its Maori Place-names and Their Topographic and Historical Background*, 1948 (Dept. of Internal Affairs, Wellington).

COLLECTION Natl. Mus. of New Zealand, Wellington.

Will McGaffey Agar PHOTOGRAPHER
TEACHER · MUSICIAN Born September 7, 1950, in San Francisco, the artist earned a BA in 1973 and an MFA in 1979, both from the University of Minnesota. He was influenced in his work by Jerome Liebling, Robert Wilcox, Minor White and his father, Frank Agar, a teacher.

Having taught photography since 1975 at North Hennepin Community College in Minneapolis, he was a visiting artist in that city at the Metropolitan Community College in 1977 and, again, in 1979, at Wright State University in Dayton, Ohio.

Mr. Agar has been a member of the SPE since 1976.

In 1978 he did the sound track for the film *We're Number One*, sponsored by the American Lutheran Church.

The artist works in large format, producing "straight photography of both traditional genre and nontraditional, highly personalized statements [with] concern for the Fine Print as an end result."

PUBLICATIONS Catalogs: *Midwest Photo 80*, 1980; *Panorama of American Art 1979* (Midwest Mus. of American Art). Periodicals: *Photographers Forum*, Apr 1980; *Journal: PSA*, Feb 1975.

COLLECTIONS J. Hunt Gall., Minneapolis, Minn.; K-Mart Cllctn., Detroit, Mich.; Minneapolis Inst. of Art; N. Hennepin Community College, Minneapolis, Minn.

DEALER J. Hunt Gall., 2411 E 24 St, Minneapolis, MN 55441.

ADDRESS Agar Photography, Rt 5, Box 315, Maple Grove, MN 55369.

Lucien L. Aigner PHOTOGRAPHER · WRITER ·
FILM MAKER Aigner was born on September 14, 1901, in Ersekujvár, Hungary (now Novè Zámky, Czechoslovakia). He completed a law degree at the University of Budapest in 1924. In 1967 he attended the Winona School of Photography in Indiana.

Since 1972 Aigner has been making and exhibiting photos from his archives and lecturing about them. From 1954 to 1976 he operated a portrait and commercial studio in Great Barrington, Massachusetts. Previously he worked as a Paris correspondent and Bureau Chief of *Az Est* (Hungary) and as a Paris correspondent of the *London General Press*. He was also a contributor to *L'Illustration* and *Miroir du Monde* (Paris), the *Picture Post* (London) and *Muenchner Illustrierte* (Germany), among others, during the years 1925–39. He was also a contributor to *Look, The New York Times, Newsweek, Time Magazine*, etc. (1939–48), and was the producer-director of foreign language broadcasts at Voice of America (1946–53).

Aigner has been a member of the Great Barrington Rotary Club in Massachusetts since 1956, serving for six years as chairman of the International Student Exchange Committee. He is also a life member and Master of Photography of the Professional Photographers of America. Various distinctions were given to him: two grants for photography from NEA (1978, 1975), a New York Art Director Award (1941), a Leica Award (1936) and several awards from the Connecticut Professional Photographers Association. He has two documentary films to his credit: *Paintings for Halloween* (1972) and *Hong Kong Breakthrough* (1968).

Aigner has specialized in photojournalism, with emphasis on portraits of and essays on world leaders and celebrities, and has also been involved in pictorial chronicling of everyday life in Europe and, later, in the United States.

PUBLICATIONS Monographs: *Lucien Aigner*, autobio., 1979; *Between Two Worlds*, 1975 (Paris). Books: *Pictures with Meaning*, 1961; *What Prayer Can Do*, 1954; *Windows of Heaven*, Glenn Clark, 1954; *Are We to Disarm?*, 1932 (Geneva). Periodicals: *35mm Photography*, 1978; *The Professional Photographer*, 1973.

COLLECTIONS IMP/GEH, Rochester; L/C, Wash. D.C.; MOMA, NYC; Smithsonian Inst., Wash. D.C.. Bibliothèque Nationale, Paris; Landesbildstelle, Hamburg, Germany; Musée Nicéphore Niepce, Chalon-sur-Saône, France; Natl. Mus. of Photog., Helsinki, Finland.

REPRESENTATIVE   Stephen Rose, 23 Miner St, Boston, MA 02215.
ADDRESS   15 Dresser Ave, Great Barrington, MA 01230.

Roger Cushing Aikin   *ART HISTORIAN · PHOTOGRAPHER · TEACHER*   Born on May 19, 1947, in New York City, Aikin completed a BA in Art History and Photography at the University of Oregon, studying with Bernard Freemesser and Brett Weston, both of whom strongly influenced his work. In 1977 he completed a PhD in Art History at the University of California at Berkeley.

His teaching career spans Colorado College, the University of Colorado and the University of California at Davis.

He holds membership in SPE and the College Art Association. Aikin received an NDEA Title IV National Fellowship for the years 1971–74 and, in 1969, a Woodrow Wilson National Fellowship.

The photographer works with both an 11 x 14 view camera and in 2¼-inch format. He is also interested in multiple-image contact prints. His research is focused on Renaissance art and the West Coast regional school of photography.

PUBLICATIONS   Periodicals: "Brett Weston and Edward Weston: An Essay in Photographic Style," *Art Journal*, 1973; "Photography and Art History," *Exposure: SPE*, May 1975.

COLLECTIONS   Ansel Adams Cllctn., Carmel, Calif.; Univ. of Oregon Library, Eugene.

ADDRESS   1039 E College St, Iowa City, IA 52240.

Eugen Albert   *INVENTOR · PHOTOGRAPHIC EQUIPMENT MANUFACTURER*   Born in 1856, Albert died in 1929. He was the son of Josef Albert of Munich, who developed collotype reproduction. Eugen studied at the universities in Munich and Heidelberg, receiving his doctorate in 1882.

He opened his own company, the Münschner Kunst- und Verlagsanstalt/Dr. E. Albert & Co., to manufacture his first discovery—the isochromatic collodion emulsion for color reproduction. Considered superior to the best dry plates for a number of years, it was later used to produce color screen negatives. Albert overcame the moiré pattern in 3-color printing, introduced the use of masking to correct the black plate in 4-color printing, and in 1902 constructed a prototype 4-color press. His other important discoveries included: the Albert effect (1899)—that a fully exposed collodion plate treated with nitric acid and washed will produce a positive image when re-exposed to diffused light and developed; a halftone plate process in which the screen was separate from the negative; a bi-metallic plate for printing (1900); introduction of the lead matrix in electrotyping; and etching methods for photoengraved plates.

PUBLICATIONS   Books: *History of Photography*, J. M. Eder, 3rd ed., 1905, repr. 1945; *Lexikon für Photographie und Reproduktionstechnik*, G. H. Emmerich, 1910. Anthology: *Photography's Great Inventors*, Louis W. Sipley, 1965. Periodicals: *Bild und Ton*, 1957, 1955; *Photographic Journal*, 1939; *Photographische Correspondenz*, 1929, 1926; *Penrose's Annual*, 1901; *Jahrbuch für Photographie und Reproduktionstechnik*, J. M. Eder, 1889.

Josef Albert   *PHOTOGRAPHER · PRINTER · INVENTOR*   Born in 1825 in Munich, Germany, Albert died in 1886. He studied architecture until he learned of Daguerre's discovery, then pursued daguerreotypy under the instruction of Munich photographer Loccherer. His son was Dr. Eugen Albert.

In 1850 Albert opened his own portrait business in Augsburg. Eight years later he returned to Munich, where he became involved in the photographic reproduction of drawings and copperplate engravings, reproducing facsimiles of the work of German artists plus illustrations for scientific subjects.

In 1868 the inventor introduced Albertype—a glass support for collotype printing to which an undercoating fastened the relief emulsion. The process gave commercial viability to Poitevin's discovery, enabling the making of 1,000 or more copies from one plate. In 1873 Albert began operating a special high-speed press for collotype printing, and in 1876 he introduced color collotype.

PUBLICATIONS   Books: *Josef Albert: History of Photograph der Bayerischen Könige*, Winfried Ranke, 1977 (Schirmer/Mosel: Munich); *Quellendarstellungen zur Geschichte der Fotografie*, Wolfgang Baier, 1964; *History of Photography*, J. M. Eder, trans., E. Epstean, 1945; *Lexikon für Photographie und Reproduktionstechnik*, G. H. Emmerich, 1910; *Jahrbuch für Photographie und Reproduktionstechnik*, J. M. Eder, 1888. Anthology: *Early Photographs and Early Photographers*, Oliver Mathews, 1973; *Photography's Great Inventors*, Louis W. Sipley, 1965. Periodicals: *Photographische Correspondenz*, 1886, 1965; *Photographische Mittheilungen*, 1886, 1877.

Paul Albert *PHOTOGRAPHER* Born in New York City in 1947, Albert earned his BFA from Ohio University in 1968 and his MFA from the State University of Buffalo Visual Studies Workshop in 1973. Among others, he names as mentors Clarence White, Jr., Nathan Lyons, Syl Labrot and Aaron Siskind.

Since 1974 Albert has been a professor of photography at Dundas Valley School of Art in Ontario, Canada. From 1974 to 1977 he was instructor of photography at Mohawk College in Hamilton, Ontario.

A member of SPE, the photographer won Ontario Arts Council Grants, 1975–79, and a CAPS grant in 1974.

Albert describes his work as making silver prints using circular images and double exposures.

COLLECTION Art Gall. of Hamilton, Ontario, Canada.

ADDRESS 434 Market St, Santa Cruz, CA 95060.

Leopoldo Alinari *PHOTOGRAPHER* Born in Italy (probably in Florence) in 1832, Alinari died in 1865. His brothers, Romualdo (1830–1891) and Giuseppe (1836–1891), were also photographers.

The protégé of Giuseppe Bardi, a rich chalcographer (copper and brass engraver) in Florence, Alinari founded a photographic society in 1854 along with his brothers. He became quite well known, receiving prizes and awards from expositions in Florence (1861), Vienna (1873), Paris (1878) and Milan (1881).

Alinari's main subject matter was the monuments and buildings of Florence, Tuscany, Rome and Naples.

PUBLICATIONS Catalogs: *Gli Alinari fotografi a Firenze 1852–1920,* W. Settimelli & F. Zevi, 1977 (Florence); *Aspetti della fotografia toscana dell' Ottocento,* 1976 (Florence); *Centenario della fondazione,* 1955 (Florence); *Le Tre Venezie,* 1924 (Florence); *Cataloghi delle edizioni librarie,* 1922; *Rome,* 1912 (G. Barbèra: Florence); *Catalogo,* vols. 1–4, 1891–94 (Florence); *Relazioni dei Giurati: Fotografia Esposizione 1883* (Milan); *Industriale Italiana del 1881 in Milano,* A Montagna, 1883; *Elenco dei Premiati,* 1878 (Rome); *Esposizione Università di Parigi del 1878,* 1878 (Rome); *Esposizione Univ. di Vienna del 1873; Elenco degli Espositori Italiani,* 1873 (Rome); *Catalogo generale delle reproduzioni fotografiche,* 1873 (G. Barbèra: Florence); *La Esposizione Italiana del 1861,* 1862 (Florence).

Jim Alinder *PHOTOGRAPHER · ARTS ADMINISTRATOR · WRITER · EDITOR* Born March 31, 1941, in Glendale, California, Alinder earned a BA in 1962 from Macalester College, St. Paul, Minnesota, where he studied painting with Jerry Rudquist. He then studied photography at the University of Minnesota, Minneapolis, and took his MFA (1968) at the University of New Mexico, Albuquerque, where he studied photography with Van Deren Coke.

Alinder has been executive director of The Friends of Photography in Carmel, California, since 1977 and has been editor-in-chief of the organization's quarterly, *Untitled,* since 1978. He also is editor-in-chief of *Exposure: SPE* and previously directed the photography program at the University of Nebraska, Lincoln (1968–77). He served as a photography consultant to the Mid-America Arts Alliance, 1976–78, and since 1970 has been a visiting artist, workshop instructor and lecturer.

The SPE member has been the Society's secretary (1973–75), vice-chairman (1975–77) and chairman of the board (1977–79). Alinder won an NEA Photographer's Fellowship in 1973, a Woods Foundation Fellowship in 1974 and was a Kansas Bicentennial Photography Project participant in 1976.

Best known for his panoramic photographs and work with the Diana camera, he is interested in the "blending of formal values with socio-cultural concerns."

PUBLICATIONS Books: *Photographs of the Columbia River and Oregon,* ed., 1979; *Crying for a Vision,* ed. w/Don Doll, 1976. Anthologies: *The Photograph Collector's Guide,* Lee D. Witkin & Barbara London, 1979; *Self-Portrayal,* ed., 1978; *Kansas Album,* James L. Enyeart, ed., 1977; *The Photographer's Choice,* Kelly Wise, ed., 1975. Periodical: *U.S. Camera Annual,* 1970.

COLLECTIONS Art Inst. of Chicago; IMP/GEH, Rochester; MIT, Cambridge; MOMA, NYC; Mus. of Fine Arts, Houston; San Francisco Mus. of Modern Art; Smithsonian Inst., Wash., D.C.; VSW, Rochester. Bibliothèque Nationale, Paris; Natl. Gall. of Canada, Ottawa, Ont.; Victoria & Albert Mus., London.

DEALER Weston Gall., Box 655, Carmel, CA 93921.

ADDRESS 3079 Hermitage Rd, Pebble Beach, CA 93953.

Michele Margaret (Micky) Allan *PHOTOGRAPHER* Born January 4, 1944, in Melbourne, Australia, Allan received a BFA from the University of Melbourne in 1967 and a Diploma of Painting from the National Gallery School in Melbourne in 1968.

At the time of this writing, Allan is a tutor and artist-in-residence at the Art Workshop of the University of Sydney, Australia. She was a lecturer at the Art School, Preston Institute of Technology, Melbourne, 1975–76.

A member of the Art Workers Union as of 1979, Allan won Special Purpose Grants from the Visual Arts Board, Australia Council, in 1976 and 1978.

She works strictly in 35mm, producing black-and-white and hand-painted (oil, watercolor, gouache, pencil) photographs.

PUBLICATIONS Monograph: *My Trip*, 1976 (Melbourne). Book: *Cafe Sport*, w/Pamela Brown, 1979 (Seacruise Books: Sydney). Catalogs: *The Philip Morris Collection*, 1979 (Melbourne); *The CSR Pyrmont Refinery Centenary 1978 Photography Project*, 1978 (Sydney).

COLLECTIONS In Australia: Art Gall. of New South Wales; Art Gall. of South Australia; Australian Natl. Gall., Canberra; Ballarat Fine Art Gall., Victoria; Philip Morris Cllctn.; Univ. Art Mus., Queensland.

DEALER Frank Watters, 109 Riley St, East Sydney, NSW 2010, Australia.

ADDRESS Mountain Lagoon Rd, Bilpin, NSW 2758, Australia.

Alexander Alland, Sr. PHOTOGRAPHER · WRITER · HISTORIAN Born August 6, 1902, in Sevastopol, Russia, Alland attended Commerce School in Sevastopol and learned photography as a boy.

In 1920 he emigrated to Istanbul (formerly Constantinople) and set up a studio; in 1923 he traveled to New York City. Alland served as supervisor of the Mural Section of the Federal Art Project in 1936–38. In 1939 he was president of Exploration Photo Syndicate, and produced photomurals for the New York World's Fair ca. 1940. In 1940–41 he was photography editor of *Common Ground*. Alland directed exhibitions for the Council Against Intolerance in America in 1942–44. He is currently a freelancer.

Alland received the 50th Anniversary Commemorative Medal from the Museum of the City of New York for securing Jacob Riis' collection.

PUBLICATIONS Books: *Heinrich Tonnies, Cartes-de-Visite Photographer Extraordinaire*, 1978; *Jessie Tarbox Beals, First Woman News Photographer*, 1978; *Jacob A. Riis, Photographer & Citizen*, 1974; *My Dog Rinty*, 1946; *The Springfield Plan*, 1945; *American Counterpoint*, w/John Day, 1943; *Portrait of New York*, 1938.

COLLECTIONS MOMA, NYC; Mus. of the City of N.Y.; N.Y. Hist. Soc.; N.Y. Pub. Lib.

ADDRESS POB 267, North Salem, NY 10560.

Astrid Allard
See Astrid

(Harvey) Harold Allen PHOTOGRAPHER · TEACHER Born on June 29, 1912, in Portland, Oregon, Allen studied at, variously, the Art Institute of Chicago (1937–41), the School of Design, Chicago (1941), Life Magazine Photography School for the Armed Forces (1942), and the University of Chicago (1948–54). He has been influenced by the works of Atget, Edward Weston, Ansel Adams, Walker Evans and Berenice Abbott.

Retired in 1977, Allen was a professor, prior to then, at the School of the Art Institute of Chicago (1948–60 and 1966–77). He received an honorary Doctor of Fine Arts degree from the Art Institute in 1979. In 1978, at the Second Annual Chicago Art Awards, he received the "Special Artist Award: Body of Work." In 1971 the educator was awarded the Frederick Latimer Wells Professorship at the Art Institute.

Allen does documentary work with a 4 x 5 view camera. He concentrates on historical architecture and, in his words, has "the most extensive documentation of Egyptian-style American architecture in existence."

PUBLICATIONS Book: *Father Ravalli's Missions*, 1972. Periodicals (incl. text): "Egyptian Influences in Wedgwood Designs," 1962 (7th Wedgwood Internatl. Seminar); "Harold Allen: My Egypt," *Exposure: SPE*, Mar 1978; "Portrait of a Photographer as a Young Man," *The New Art Examiner*, June 1978.

COLLECTIONS American Telephone & Telegraph Co.; Art Inst. of Chicago; Chicago Historical Society; L/C, Wash., D.C.; Mass. Inst. of Tech., Cambridge; Metro. Mus. of Art, NYC, among others.

DEALER Douglas Kenyon, Inc., 155 E Ohio, Chicago, Il 60611.

ADDRESS 1725 S Desplaines St, Chicago, IL 60616.

Mariette Pathy Allen PHOTOGRAPHER Born in Alexandria, Egypt, on June 22, 1940, Allen received a BA at Vassar, Poughkeepsie, New York, and an MFA in Painting at the University of Pennsylvania, Philadelphia, 1965. She has studied photography with Harold Feinstein, Philippe Halsman and Lisette Model.

To date a freelance photographer, from 1972 to

1975 she was coordinator of documentation, NYC Dept. of Cultural Affairs; from 1967 to 1968 she worked as photographer, researcher and graphic designer for the State Museum of New Jersey, Trenton. She is a member of Professional Women Photographers, NYC.

Allen won a prize at the international "Phot-Univers 1978" Exhibit, and received a gubernatorial citation for her work exhibited in the 1979 "Celebration: New York in Color." She was also awarded the Thornton-Oakley Prize for Achievement in the Creative Arts by the University of Pennsylvania.

The artist works in both color and black-and-white. Her images concentrate on performances, events, people in their environments, and flowers. She is particularly interested in "surreal juxtapositions and painterly effects."

PUBLICATIONS Anthologies: *The Family of Woman*, 1979; *The Decade of Women*, 1979; *Women See Men*, 1977.

ADDRESS 211 Central Park West, #19K, New York, NY 10024.

Vance Bernard Allen PHOTOGRAPHER·EDITOR Born 1939 in Asbury Park, New Jersey, he received an AAS from Pratt Institute in Brooklyn, New York, in 1966. His major influences have been Walker Evans, Roy DeCarava and Gordon Parks.

Since 1974 Allen has been reviews editor and photographer for Garland Publishing, Inc. Previously, he was the assistant program director at James van Der Zee Institute in New York City, 1971–72, and teacher at the Stephen Gaynor School in New York City, 1969–71.

He is a member of NPPA and the American Society of Picture Professionals.

PUBLICATIONS Periodicals: *Popular Photography Annual*, 1975; *Black Photographers' Annual*, 1973.

REPRESENTATIVE Monkmeyer Press Photo Service, 15 E 48 St, New York, NY 10017.

ADDRESS POB 317, Peter Stuyvesant Station, New York, NY 10009.

David R. Allison PHOTOGRAPHER · TEACHER Born March 21, 1950, in Doylestown, Pennsylvania, at the time of this writing Allison is studying for an MFA in Photography at George Washington University in Washington, D.C. He received his BA in Visual Communications at Wilmington College (1972) and studied and worked with Michael A. Smith in 1971.

Since 1977 Allison has taught photography at both Northern Virginia Community College and

in the Smithsonian Institute's Resident Arts Program. He was a staff photographer for Staples & Charles Design Offices, 1975–78 and, in 1972, was editor of the *Wilmingtonian*.

George Washington University awarded Fellowships in Photography to Allison in both 1978 and 1979.

The artist works exclusively with an 8 x 10 view camera. His previous work concentrated on landscapes, abstractions and nudes, while more recent work deals with cityscapes and people.

COLLECTIONS Corcoran Gallery of Art, Wash., D.C.; L/C, Wash., D.C. Bibliothèque Nationale, Paris.

DEALER Kathleen Ewing Gall., 3020 K St NW, Wash., DC 20007.

ADDRESS 209 N Furman St, Alexandria, VA 22304.

George Alpert PHOTOGRAPHER · GALLERY DIRECTOR Born in New York City on April 3, 1922, Alpert studied at New York University, in New York City, North Carolina State University at Raleigh, Stanford University, Palo Alto, California, and the University of California at Berkeley.

Chairperson and president of the Soho Photo Foundation, Alpert has directed the Soho Photo Galleries in New York City since 1970, and since 1974 has worked at the New School for Social Research, also in New York City.

PUBLICATIONS Monograph: *The Queens*, 1975. Book: *Second Chance to Live: The Suicide Syndrome*, 1975.

ADDRESS 4 E 52 St, New York, NY 10022.

Manuel Alvarez Bravo PHOTOGRAPHER [See plate 77] Bravo was born February 4, 1902, in Mexico. His grandfather was Manuel Alvarez Rivas, a painter and photographer, and his father, Manuel Alvarez Garcia, was a writer and painter. He attended Catholic Brothers' School in Tlalpan, Mexico, from 1908 to 1914, and in 1918 he attended the Academia de San Carlos, where he studied painting and music. Self-taught in photography, he met German photographer Hugo Brehme in 1923, and began taking photographs in 1924.

Since 1959 he has been the director and chief photographer of the Fondo Editorial de la Plásticas Mexicana, which he founded. In 1943–59 he worked as photographer and camera operator at the Sindicado de Trabajadores de la Producción Cinematográfica de México (Mexican Film Workers Guild), of which he was a member. He also taught photography at the Escuela Central de Artes Plásticas (1929–30) and began freelance work in 1931, specializing in reproductions of paintings and other artworks.

In 1975 Bravo was a recipient of a Guggenheim Fellowship.

PUBLICATIONS Monographs: *Manuel Alvarez Bravo*, Jane Livingston et al, 1978; *Manuel Alvarez Bravo*, 1977 (La Photo Gallerie, Paris); *Manuel Alvarez Bravo*, Fred R. Parker, 1971; *Manuel Alvarez Bravo Fotografías 1928–68*, 1968 (Instituto Nacional de Bellas Artes, Mexico City); *Manuel Alvarez Bravo*, Luis Cardoza y Aragon, 1935. Books: *More Human Than Divine*, Wm. Philip Spratling, 1966 (Universidad Nacional Autonome de México, Mexico City); *Painted Walls of Mexico*, Emily Edwards, 1966; *Portrait of Mexico*, Bertram D. Wolfe & Diego Rivera, 1937. Anthologies: *The Photograph Collector's Guide*, Lee D. Witkin & Barbara London, 1979; *Photographs from the Julien Levy Collection*, David Travis, 1976; *The Magic Image*, Cecil Beaton & Gail Buckland, 1975; *Looking At Photographs*, John Szarkowski, 1973; *Great Photographers*, Time-Life Series, 1971; *Album*, No. 9, 1970; *Aperture*, 13: 4, 1968, 1:4, 1953. Periodicals: *Camera*, Dec 1979, Dec 1975, Dec 1972, Jan 1972; "The Indigenous Vision of Manuel Alvarez Bravo," A. D. Coleman, *Artforum*, Apr 1976; "The Labyrinth of Solitude—The Art of Manuel Alvarez Bravo," Gerry Badger, *British Journal of Photography*, May 21, 1976.

PORTFOLIOS *Untitled*, 1977 (Acorn Editions, London); *Fifteen Photographs*, 1975 (Double Elephant Press, New York).

COLLECTIONS Art Inst. of Chicago; IMP/GEH, Rochester; MOMA, NYC; New Orleans Mus. of Art; Norton Simon Mus. of Art, Pasadena, Calif.; Univ. of N. Mex., Albuquerque. Bibliothèque Nationale, Paris; Museo de Arte Moderno, Mexico City.

DEALER Witkin Gallery, 41 E 57 St, New York, NY 10022.

ADDRESS Espíritu Santo 83, Coyoacán, Mexico 21, DF.

Barry W. Andersen *PHOTOGRAPHER·TEACHER*
Born in New York on June 12, 1945, Andersen earned a BA from California State University at Northridge in 1973 and an MFA from the University of Florida in Gainesville in 1975, where he also taught as a graduate assistant. His major influences are Todd Walker, Jerry Uelsmann and Doug Prince.

Since 1975 he has been assistant professor of art at Northern Kentucky University (Highland Heights). He has been a member of SPE since 1974.

PUBLICATIONS Anthology: *Young American Photographers*, 1975. Catalogs: *20th Dixie Annual Catalogue*, 1979 (Montgomery Mus. of Fine Arts: Ala.); *Magic Silver Show Catalogue*, 1976 (Murray State Univ.: Ky.); *Southern Ethic Catalogue*, 1975 (Nexus Gall.: Atlanta, Ga.).

COLLECTIONS Cincinnati Art Mus., Ohio; Erie Ctr for the Arts, Erie, Pa.; Murray State Univ., Murray, Ky.; New Orleans Mus. of Art.

ADDRESS 227 Rosemont Ave, Fort Thomas, KY 41075.

C. Russell Anderson *PHOTOGRAPHY DEALER·HISTORIAN·PHOTOGRAPHER* Born May 18, 1946, in Quincy, Massachusetts, Anderson attended Indiana University, Bloomington, and studied under Henry Holmes Smith and Reginald Heron.

Since 1978 he has been general manager of The Weston Gallery, Inc. and previously operated Russ Anderson Ltd. in London (1972–77). In 1972 he worked for Sotheby's in London, was employed by Westminster Hospital in London from 1970 to 1972 and from 1967 to 1971 was a freelance cinematographer and still photographer.

A member of RPS, SPE and the American Society of Appraisers, he won the ADDI Award in 1971 as a motion picture camera operator.

Anderson's art history specialization is in British and French photography, 1839–1870, and the photographers P. H. Emerson, Paul Strand and F. H. Evans. He deals in nineteenth- and twentieth-century photographs.

PUBLICATIONS Book: *Carleton E. Watkins, Photographs of the Columbia River and Oregon*, James Alinder, ed., w/David Featherstone, 1979. Periodical: *Creative Camera*, Feb 1974.

COLLECTIONS Art Inst. of Chicago; Indiana Univ. Art Mus., Bloomington. Bibliothèque Nationale, Paris; Victoria & Albert Mus., London.

ADDRESS c/o Weston Gall., Inc, POB 655, Carmel, CA 93921.

Paul Lewis Anderson *PHOTOGRAPHER·AUTHOR* Born in 1880, Anderson died September 16, 1956, in Short Hills, New Jersey. He graduated from Lehigh University in Bethlehem, Pennsylvania, in 1901.

He worked for a time as an electrical engineer before studying and then teaching photography at the Clarence H. White School of Photography in New York City. He was an Associate of RPS.

A pictorial photographer and author of numerous articles for photographic magazines, Anderson also wrote several historical novels dealing with Roman history.

PUBLICATIONS Books: *The Technique of Pictorial Photography*, 1939; *The Fine Art of Photography*, 1919, repr. 1973; *Pictorial Photography*, 1917. Periodical: "Pictorial Landscape-Photography," *Photo-era, the American Journal of Photography*, 1914.

COLLECTION IMP/GEH, Rochester.

Momme Andresen CHEMIST Born in 1857 in Risum, Schleswig, Germany, Andresen died in 1951. He attended Technische Hochschule in Dresden, then studied physical science at the Universities of Jena and Genf until 1887.

After he graduated Andresen became a chemist at the Berlin firm of Aktiengesellschaft für Anilinfabrikation (AGFA), eventually rising to a directorial post. While there he made numerous discoveries in photochemistry, including the use of para-phenylene-diamine as a photographic developer (1888), Eikonogen (1889), a cartridge developer (1890) and the developer Rodinal (1891). The success of the latter encouraged AGFA, which heretofore had shown only a minor interest in photography, to build a small factory at Berlin-Treptow to manufacture photographic dry plates (1893). Andresen also discovered, concurrently with but independently of Lainer of Vienna, an acid fixing solution made from hypo solution and an acid sulphite (1889).

PUBLICATIONS Books: *Quellendarstellungen zur Geschichte der Fotografie*, Wolfgang Baier, 1964; *Lexikon für Photographie und Reproduktionstechnik*, G. H. Emmerich, 1910. Anthology: *Photography's Great Inventors*, Louis W. Sipley, 1965. Periodicals: *Bild und Ton*, 1959, 1957; *Jahrbuch für Photographie und Reproduktionstechnik*, 1899, 1895, 1892; *Photographic Times*, 1898; *Photographische Mittheilungen*, 1891.

Thorvald Andreas Rasmus Andresen PHOTOGRAPHER Born November 11, 1892, at Hjerting, Denmark, Andresen was a photographic apprentice from 1907 to 1910, and studied at the Copenhagen Institute of Technology in 1911.

Andresen operated his own photographic studio in Denmark from 1916 to 1936. He taught at the Professional School of the Danish Photographers' Association at Copenhagen Institute of Technology, 1928–34, and again in 1943, becoming the director from 1944 until 1947. From 1939 to 1960 he had his own studio in Copenhagen, specializing in portraits, interior decoration and architecture. From 1960 on he concentrated on gardens, architecture and arts and crafts, until 1970, when he retired to the island of Funen.

A member of the Danish Photographers' Association since 1914, Andresen organized the first Scandinavian course for master photographers in 1946. He was the recipient of a gold award in 1952 and a silver medal in 1933 from the Danish Photographers' Association.

The photographer's work, consisting of extensive coverage of Danish gardens, interior decoration, and Danish museums, has been widely published in magazines and books in Denmark, France, Germany, Switzerland, Italy, Norway and Sweden.

PUBLICATIONS Books: *Living in Scandinavia*, 1958; *Green Pleasures*, 1951; *Danish Castles and Manor Houses*, 1945.

ARCHIVE Royal Lib, Copenhagen.

ADDRESS Dauretoften 9, Svanninge, DK-5600 Faaborg, Denmark.

Mary Ellen Andrews PHOTOGRAPHER·WRITER Born in Reading, Pennsylvania, on June 18, 1937, Andrews studied with Lisette Model and Diane Arbus and was greatly influenced by the sculptor Louie Durchanek.

She is a freelance photographer and was the recipient of a Macdowell Fellowship for four consecutive years (1973–76).

At the time of this writing she was making color prints of the faces of transvestites and transsexuals.

PUBLICATIONS Anthologies: *Family of Children*, 1977; *Women Photograph Men*, 1977. Periodicals (text only): *Popular Photography*, winter 1978; *Camera 35*, Sept 1977, May 1977, Oct 1976, Apr 1975, Jan 1974.

DEALER Leslie-Lohman Gallery, 485 Broome St, New York, NY 10013.

ADDRESS 80 N Moore St, #17C, New York, NY 10013.

Ralph W. Andrews PHOTOHISTORIAN · AUTHOR Born January 12, 1897, in Denver, Colorado, Andrews attended the University of Minnesota in Minneapolis.

Since 1955 Andrews has freelanced as a copywriter and author. Prior to that he was an account executive with advertising agencies in Los Angeles and in Seattle, Washington (1925–41, 1950–55). From 1941 to 1945 he was a civilian employee of the U.S. Army—a port historian—in Seattle.

A trustee and former president of the Friends of Seattle Public Library, Andrews is also a member of the Jefferson Park Lawn and Sailing Club. The Seattle Historical Society gave him their annual award in 1955 for the best book by a Seattle author, and he received the Governor's Certificate of Recognition in 1966.

Having developed a strong interest in lumbering while working as a youthful saw salesman, Andrews made that industry a focal point of his photographic interests. His books on western photography have also covered seafaring, commercial fishing and Indians.

PUBLICATIONS Books: *Indian Leaders Who Helped Shape America*, 1971; *Timber: Toil and Trouble in the Big Woods*, 1968; *Historic Fires of the West*, 1966; *Photographers of the Frontier West: Their Lives and Their Works, 1875–1915*, 1965; *Picture Gallery Pioneers*, 1964; *The Seattle I Saw*, 1964; *Indians as the Westerners Saw Them*, 1963; *Curtis' Western Indians*, 1962; *Indian Primitive*, 1960; *Fish and Ships*, w/A. K. Larssen, 1959; *Heroes of the Western Woods*, 1959; *Redwood Classic*, 1958; *This Was Sawmilling*, 1957; *This Was Seafaring*, w/Harry A. Kirwin, 1956; *Glory Days of Logging*, 1955; *This Was Logging*, 1954.

ADDRESS 2405 S 122 St, Seattle, WA 98168.

Roswell Angier PHOTOGRAPHER · TEACHER
[See plate 114] Born December 2, 1940 in New Haven, Connecticut, he is married to painter Susan Hawley. He received an AB at Harvard, 1962, and an MA at the University of California at Berkeley, 1964. The artist reports that Robert Frank, William Klein, Baudelaire and Navajo witchcraft have strongly influenced his work.

At the time of this writing he was lecturing at the University of Massachusetts, Boston, and has taught at the Art Institute of Boston since 1975. He has also been photographer-in-residence at Eliot House, Harvard, since 1976. Prior to that he worked as a freelance photographer, beginning in 1972; was editor of *Fusion* magazine, Boston (1969–72); and was instructor in the Humanities Dept., Boston University (1968–72). Angier has also published poetry in *Quarterly Review of Literature* (1968) and *Quire* (1967), and an article he wrote on Baudelaire was in *Boston University Review* (1970).

Mr. Angier has been a member of the Boston Visual Artists' Union since 1974; in 1976 he was chairman of its Gallery Committee, and was alternate secretary-general in 1977. He has also served on the Artists' Advisory Council of the Massachusetts Arts and Humanities Foundation (1977–78), from which he received an Artist-in-Residence Grant (1977). A founding member of Voices Gallery (1978), he was also part of the "Works in Progress" NEA-sponsored Public Art Project (1975).

Working in both 35mm and with a view camera, the artist has produced work that is largely social documentation. He is currently working on a long-term project about the border towns of the Navajo Reservation in New Mexico and Arizona.

PUBLICATIONS Book: *A Kind of Life*, 1976. Anthology: *The Photographer's Choice*, 1976. Catalog: *14 New England Photographers*, 1978 (Mus. of Fine Arts: Boston). Periodical: *Photo*, May 1977.

COLLECTIONS Harvard Univ. Fogg Art Mus., Cambridge, Mass., Mus. of Fine Arts, Boston. Bibliothèque Nationale, Paris.

ADDRESS 65 Pleasant St, Cambridge, MA 02139.

James Craig Annan PHOTOGRAPHER Born in Hamilton, Scotland, on March 8, 1864, Annan died June 5, 1946, in Lenzie, Scotland. His father, Thomas Annan, was a photographer and copperplate engraver and a major influence on young Annan's career. James attended the Academy in Glasgow, Scotland, and studied chemistry and natural philosophy for two sessions in the 1880s at Anderson's College, Glasgow. Having studied with photogravurist-inventor Karl Klíč in Vienna in 1883, Annan was also influenced by David Octavius Hill, a friend of his father's, by the Glasgow Impressionist School, by Japanese prints, and by the painters Velásquez and Whistler.

Annan worked in his father's Glasgow printing factory and studio, T & R Annan & Sons, ca. 1879–1914. He joined The Linked Ring in 1895 and was the first president of the International Society of Pictorial Photographers in 1904. He was also a member of the Glasgow Art Club (1892), the Philosophical Society of Glasgow, the National Art Collections Fund and the Scottish Modern Arts Association, all 1888.

Annan was given a Royal Appointment "into the Place and Quality of Photographers & Photogravure Engravers to her Majesty in Glasgow" in 1889 and was made an Honorary Fellow of the RPS in 1924.

The photographer revived interest in David Octavius Hill and Robert Adamson's calotypes by producing photogravures from their negatives. He was a pioneer in experimentation with the hand-held camera. A pictorialist, Annan was considered a master of the photogravure process, specializing in portraits and genre scenes. He also did some carbon prints.

PUBLICATIONS Anthologies: *The Photograph Collector's Guide*, Lee D. Witkin & Barbara London, 1979; *The Collection of Alfred Stieglitz*,

Weston J. Naef, 1978; *Pictorial Photography in Britain*, Arts Council of Great Britain, 1978; *The Magic Image*, Cecil Beaton & Gail Buckland, 1975; *Camera Work: A Critical Anthology*, Jonathan Green, ed., 1973; *Early Photographs & Early Photographers*, Oliver Mathews, 1973. Catalog: *Glasgow Portraits*, 1967 (Scottish Arts Council: Glasgow). Periodicals: "J. Craig Annan," Joseph T. Keiley, vol. 8, Oct 1904, vol. 19, Jul 1907, vol. 26, Apr 1909, "Photography as a Means of Artistic Expression," vol. 32, Oct 1910, vol. 45, Jan 1914, *Camera Work*, facsimile repr. in 6 vols., 1969; "The Pictorial Work of J. Craig Annan," F. C. Lambert, *Practical Photographer*, no. 13, 1904.

PORTFOLIO *Venice and Lombardy: A Series of Original Photogravures*, 1898.

COLLECTIONS IMP/GEH, Rochester; Metro. Mus. of Art, NYC; Smithsonian Inst., Wash., D.C. Royal Photographic Soc., London; Scottish Arts Council Gall., Glasgow.

ARCHIVE Scottish Arts Council Gall., 19 Charlotte Sq, Edinburgh 2, Scotland.

Thomas Annan PHOTOGRAPHER [See plate 21] Annan lived from 1829 to 1887 in Scotland. His son, James Craig Annan, was also a photographer, and both were inspired by Annan's friend D. O. Hill to produce photogravures of Hill's and Adamson's calotypes.

The photographer operated T & R Annan & Sons in Glasgow, and was commissioned by Glasgow City Improvement Trust to document Glasgow slums (1868–77).

Known for his studio's photogravures, Annan also worked with calotypes, collodion wet-plate negatives, albumen prints and carbon prints. Besides documenting Glasgow's slums, architecture, citizens, etc., he reproduced works of art in photographs and shot portraits in a straightforward style.

PUBLICATIONS Books: *Thomas Annan's Old Streets and Closes of Glasgow*, intro. by Anita V. Mozley, 1977; *The Old Closes and Streets of Glasgow*, intro. by William Young, 1900; *Photographs of Old Closes, Streets, etc.*, 1868–1877, 1877; *The Old Country Houses of the Old Glasgow Gentry*, 1870, 2nd ed., 1878.

COLLECTIONS IMP/GEH, Rochester; L/C, Prints & Photographs Div., Wash., D.C. Mitchell Lib., Glasgow, Scotland.

ARCHIVE Scottish Arts Council Gall., 19 Charlotte Sq, Edinburgh 2, Scotland.

Edward Anthony PHOTOGRAPHER · MANUFACTURER [See plate 13] An American, Edward Anthony (1818–88) learned daguerreotypy from Samuel F. B. Morse, an inventor of the telegraph. His brother, Henry T. Anthony (1814–October 11, 1884—born and died in New York City), manufactured daguerreotype materials with him; his son, Richard Anthony, was involved in the same business.

In 1840 Edward Anthony participated in a survey of the U.S.-Canadian borders, making daguerreotypes of the terrain; this was the first such use of photography by the government. During the year 1847–48 he established a daguerreotype-supply business under his own name. In 1852 his brother joined the company, which was then renamed to include both their names. The firm eventually merged with Scovill & Adams (1901) which, in 1907, became known as Ansco (it later merged with Agfa [1928] but in 1943 dropped that name, henceforward to be known simply as Ansco). In 1881 the company introduced dry-plate outfits. With his brother Henry, Edward published *The Anthony Photographic Bulletin* (1870).

Anthony's was the world's first photographic supply house. With his brother, he pioneered the wet-plate process in the United States. He financed Thomas C. Roche and Mathew B. Brady to cover the Union armies (1861–65). In 1853 he established and financed the world's first photography contest; that same year, his portrait was used as the first photographic magazine illustration in the United States. He introduced celluloid cut film in 1888. In 1876 his firm received an award for "lanterns and graphascopes" at the Centennial Exhibition in Philadelphia.

Using daguerreotypes, collodion wet-plate negatives and albumen prints, Anthony is known for his portraits of government officials and other notables, his Civil War scenes and genre portraits, many of which he published as stereoscopes and *cartes de visite*.

PUBLICATIONS Book: *Photography and the American Scene: A Social History, 1839–1889*, Robert Taft, 1938. Catalogs: *New Catalogue of Stereoscopes & Views*, ca. 1867; *Comprehensive . . . Catalogue of Photographic Apparatus*, 1854.

COLLECTIONS IMP/GEH, Rochester; L/C, Wash., D.C.

Gordon Anthony PHOTOGRAPHER · BUSINESSMAN Born James Gordon Dawson Stannus on December 23, 1902, in Wicklow, Ireland, Anthony attended the School of the Royal Architectural Association in 1919.

From 1920 to 1932 he was on the managerial staff of Watney Combe Reide, Ltd., in London and for the next twenty years he freelanced as a photographer. He also served as the official portrait photographer for the Air Ministry in London, 1943–45. From 1952 to 1972 Anthony was an antiques dealer in London.

Anthony's 1948 book, *Studies of Dancers,* was the first book of color photographs to be published in England.

PUBLICATIONS Books: *A Camera at the Ballet: Pioneer Dancers of the Royal Ballet,* 1975 (David & Charles Newton Abbot); *Beryl Grey,* intro. by Arnold L. Haskell, 1952, *Dancers of the World,* 1952, *The Sadler's Wells Ballet,* 1952, *Alicia Markova,* 1951, *Margot Fonteyn,* 1950 (Phoenix House: London); *Studies of Dancers,* 1948, *Ballerina: Further Studies of Margot Fonteyn,* intro. by Eveleigh Leith, 1945, *Air Aces,* 1944 (Home & Van Thal: London); *The Sadler's Wells Ballet: Camera Studies,* intro. by Eveleigh Leith, 1942, 2nd ed., 1948 (G. Bles: London); *Sleeping Princess,* Nadia Benois, Arnold Haskell, Constant Lambert, 1942 (Routledge & Sons: London); *Russian Ballet,* 1939, *John Gielgud; Camera Studies by Gordon Anthony,* intro. by Michel Saint-Denis, 1938 (G. Bles: London); *The Vic-Wells Ballet,* intro. by Ninette de Valois, 1938 (Routledge & Sons: London); *Ballet,* intro. & notes by Arnold Haskell, 1937 (G. Bles: London); *Markova: a Collection of Photographic Studies,* foreword by Ninette de Valois, 1935 (Chatto & Windus: London); *Massine,* preface by Sacheverell Sitwell, n.d. (London).

COLLECTIONS Victoria & Albert Mus., Theatre Mus. Cllctn., London.

REPRESENTATIVE Herbert Van Thal, London Management, 235-41 Regent St, London WIA 2JT, England.

ADDRESS Garden Flat, Blue Willow, Landsdown Rd, Hove BN3 1FZ, England.

Henry T. Anthony
See Edward Anthony

Richard Anthony
See Edward Anthony

Taku Aramassa PHOTOGRAPHER Born August 15, 1936, in Tokyo, Japan, Aramassa earned a BA in Graphic Design from Musashino Art College, Musashino-shi, Tokyo, in 1960. His teachers were Hara Hiromu and Okai Mutsuaki.

A freelance photographer, he belongs to the Japan Photographers' Society (whose New Figure Prize he won in 1978) and Tokyo Designers' Space.

PUBLICATIONS Monographs: *To My Angels,* 1980 (Zenkou Shuppan Co.: Japan); *Carnaval,* 1979 (Cannon Co.: Japan); *American Parody,* 1978, *Patricia,* 1977 (Hokuto Kikaku Co., Ltd.: Japan); *Erika,* 1976 (Hokuo-sha Ltd.: Japan). Book: *Counterlight's a Coral Reef,* 1976 (Bunka Publishing Bureau: Japan).

COLLECTION Musashino Art College Art Mus., Tokyo.

ADDRESS Office Aramassa, #101 AOI-Apt 2-21-3 Nishiazabu, Minato-ku, Tokyo, Japan.

Diane Arbus PHOTOGRAPHER [See plate 106] Diane Arbus was born Diane Nemerov in New York City in 1923, and committed suicide in July 1971. She attended the Ethical Culture and Fieldston schools and studied photography with Lisette Model, 1955–57. She married Allan Arbus, who was a photographer and is now an actor, in 1941; their daughters, Doon and Amy, are in charge of the Diane Arbus Estate.

Her first published photographs, "Portraits of Eccentrics," appeared in *Harper's Bazaar* in 1961, and she subsequently worked as a freelance photographer for a number of magazines, including *Esquire, Show, The New York Times Magazine* and others. She taught photography courses at Parsons School of Design, Rhode Island School of Design, Cooper Union, and, in 1970–71, she gave a master class in New York City.

Arbus received Guggenheim Fellowships in 1963 and 1966. Her photographs appeared in three major museum exhibitions during her lifetime, all of them group shows. In 1970 she made a portfolio of ten photographs, printed, signed and annotated by her which were, the year after her death, chosen to be the first work of an American photographer exhibited at the Venice Biennale. Retrospective exhibitions devoted exclusively to her work traveled to museums throughout the United States, Canada, western Europe, Japan, Australia and New Zealand.

Although her early photographs were taken with a 35mm camera, her best known work was done in square format, which she began using in 1962. Most of her photographs were portraits—of circus performers, children, nudists and people she encountered on the street. As John Szarkowski, director of photography at the Museum of Modern Art, once wrote, "Her pictures . . . are concerned with private rather than social realities, with psychological rather than visual coherence. . . . Her real subject is no less than the unique interior lives of those she photographed."

PUBLICATIONS Monograph: *Diane Arbus,* 1972. Anthologies: *The History of Fashion Photography,* Nancy Hall-Duncan, 1979; *The Photograph*

Arbus

Collector's Guide, Lee D. Witkin & Barbara London, 1979; *Women of Photography*, Margery Mann & Ann Noggle, eds., 1975; *Looking at Photographs*, John Szarkowski, ed., 1973; *Photography Year 1973*, Time-Life Series; *The Woman's Eye*, Anne Tucker, ed., 1973; *Documentary Photography*, Time-Life Series, 1972; *Mirrors and Windows*, John Szarkowski, 1966. Catalog: *New Documents*, John Szarkowski, 1967 (MOMA: NYC). Periodicals: "The Diane Arbus Bibliography," *Exposure: SPE*, Sept 1977; "Freak Show," Susan Sontag, *New York Review of Books*, Nov 1973; "Diane Arbus," Peter C. Bunnell, *Print Collectors Newsletter*, Jan/Feb 1973.

PORTFOLIO   *A Box of Ten Photographs*, 1970.

REPRESENTATIVE   Estate of Diane Arbus, 55 W 68 St, New York, NY 10023.

Malcolm Arbuthnot   PHOTOGRAPHER · PAINTER   Arbuthnot was born in 1874 in London and died 1967 in Jersey, England. He was apprenticed to painter C. A. Brindley in Suffolk, England, and later studied painting under William Nicholson. His wife was a Kodak heiress.

In 1912 Arbuthnot managed Kodak's Liverpool, England, branch, then maintained his own London studio from 1914 to 1926. Published often in *London Illustrated News*, he quit photography in 1930 to devote himself to painting.

The artist belonged to The Linked Ring (1907), Photographic Society of Liverpool (ca. 1912), Royal Society of Arts (1939) and Royal Institute of Painters in Water Colors (1944).

He perfected a commercially successful gum process and marketed the Lento-pigment paper in the early 1900s.

He painted in a Post-Impressionist style, and also made a film, *London's Leading Photographer*.

Called "the most advanced of the moderns" in a 1909 *Amateur Photographer*, Arbuthnot's early interest in the pigment processes led him to create some remarkable gum and oil prints. Aside from commercial portraiture, his subjects were often entertainers. Most of his negatives were destroyed in a fire during World War I.

COLLECTION   RPS, London.

Frederick Scott Archer   INVENTOR   Born in 1813 in Bishop's Stortford, Hertforshire, England, Archer died May 2, 1857 in London. He was apprenticed to a silversmith in London.

Archer began his professional life as a portrait sculptor, experimenting with Talbot's calotype process in order to assist his sculpture. He invented the wet-collodion process (also known as

Archerotype or Archotype) in 1848, by which finely detailed glass negatives were produced. Archer also invented the ambrotype; introduced pyrogallic acid as a developer; devised a camera within which plates could be exposed, developed and fixed; came up with a method of whitening collodion positives upon glass; and constructed a triple lens to shorten the focus of a double combination lens.

Although Fox Talbot and Gustav Le Gray both attempted to sue Archer, claiming his was only a variant of their own inventions, the lawsuits came to nothing. Archer is generally accepted as the inventor of the process that replaced the daguerreotype and talbotype (or calotype) processes, and it was the first practical photographic process by which more than one copy of a picture could be made. Its popularity lasted from about 1855 to 1880, at which time the dry collodion process gained acceptance.

Archer also "invented the stripping of collodion films by coating the negative with a rubber solution, which enabled the negative films to be preserved without the glass plate" *(History of Photography)*. He patented this process in England on August 24, 1855.

Because he had neglected to patent his wet collodion process, Archer died a poor man, but the government granted an annual pension to his wife and children.

PUBLICATIONS   Monograph: *Photographic Views of Kenilworth*, 1851 (London). Books: *Cassell's Cyclopedia of Photography*, 1911, repr. 1973; *History of Photography*, Josef Maria Eder, 1905, repr. 1972; *A History of Photography*, Harrison, 1888; *Manual of the Collodion Photographic Process*, 1852, 2nd ed., *Collodion Process on Glass*, 1854 (London); *Photogenic Manipulation*, Robert J. Bingham, 1850. Periodicals: *British Journal of Photography*, Feb 26, 1875; *Liverpool and Manchester Photographic Journal*, 1857; *La Lumière*, 1852; *Athenaeum*, 1851; *The Chemist*, Mar 1851; *Humphrey's Journal*, 1851.

Jaime Ardila   PHOTOGRAPHER   Born December 22, 1942, in Bucaramanga, Colombia, Ardila received a diploma in architecture in 1966 from the University of Los Andes, Bogotá, Colombia. He studied photography at the Ansel Adams Workshop in Yosemite, California, in 1973 with Adams, Jerry Uelsmann, Jack Welpott, Judy Dater, David Muench and Wynn Bullock.

Ardila, a photography teacher at Museo de Arte Moderno in Bogotá, has also been a freelance photographer since 1972. He was an architectural designer in 1970–71 and head of editorial production at *El Espacio,* an evening newspaper, in 1966–69.

He does documentary work, both serially and sequentially, interrelating painting, photography, film, environment and written essays.

PUBLICATIONS Book: *Apuntes Para La Historia Extensa de Beatriz Gonzalez,* vol. 1, 1974 (Editores Tercer Mundo: Bogotá). Periodicals: *Arte en Colombia,* no. 2, no. 4, 1977.

COLLECTIONS Centre Culturel Municipal de Villeparisis, Paris; Centro de Arte Actual, Pereira, Colombia; Consejo Mexicano de Fotografía, Inba, Mexico; Mus. of Modern Art, Bogotá.

ADDRESS Apartado aéreo 90782, Bogotá, DE, Colombia.

Dick Arentz *PHOTOGRAPHER · TEACHER*
Born in Detroit, Michigan, on May 19, 1935, Arentz studied photography at the University of Michigan (1969–72), where he explored contact print processes with Phil Davis. He was greatly affected by the work and writings of Edward Weston.

Since 1979 he has been working as the Photographic Workshop Coordinator at the Museum of Northern Arizona and, since 1980, he has also been an instructor at Northern Arizona University.

He is a member of SPE.

Large-format photography is Arentz' central focus, and, at the time of this writing, he was working in the Four Corners area of the USA.

PUBLICATIONS Book: *Zion National Park,* w/ Stephen Jett, 1979. Periodical: "Death Valley," *Camera,* Nov 1973.

COLLECTIONS Gilmore Inst., Kalamazoo, Mich.; Monterey Peninsula Mus. of Art, Calif. Bibliothèque Nationale, Paris; Laenderbank, Vienna.

DEALER Photography Southwest Gallery, 4223 N Marshall Way, Scottsdale, AZ 85251.

ADDRESS 314 E David, Flagstaff, AZ 86001.

Merle Armitage *ART CRITIC · AUTHOR · EDITOR · PUBLISHER* Born in 1893, Armitage died on March 15, 1975, in Yucca Valley, California.

Originally a civil engineer, he switched careers to do modern stage design, then became a manager of touring artists. His last post was as editorial and art director for *Look* magazine.

Founder of the Los Angeles Grand Opera Association, he was its general manager from 1924 to 1930. He also was president of the American Institute of Graphic Arts (1950–51).

PUBLICATIONS Books: *Stella Dysart of Am-*

brosia Lake, 1959; *Fit for a Queen,* 1958; *Book Tradition,* 1955; *The Railroads of America,* 1952; *5 Essays on Klee,* et al., 1950; *Taos Quartet, in Three Movements,* 1950; *A Rendezvous with the Book,* 1949; *Igor Stravinsky,* Edwin Corle, ed., 1949; *Operations Santa Fe,* 1948; *Fifty Photographs: Edward Weston* et al., 1947; *Dance Memoranda,* Edwin Corle, ed., 1946; *Notes on Modern Printing,* 1945; *Accent on America,* 1944; *U.S. Navy,* 1940; *Fit for a King,* 1939; *Postcaviar: Barnstorming with Russian Grand Opera,* 1939; *So-Called Abstract Art,* 1939; *Book & Typography Designed by Merle Armitage,* 1938; *George Gershwin,* 1938; *Martha Graham,* ed., & foreword, 1937; *Sculpture of Boris Lovet-Lorski,* 1937; *Edward Weston,* 1932; *The Lithographs of Richard Day,* 1932; *Rockwell Kent,* 1932; *Warren Newcombe,* 1932; *The Work of Maier-Krieg,* 1932; *The Aristocracy of Art,* 1929.

Frank Armstrong *PHOTOGRAPHER* Born in Henderson, Texas, on September 10, 1935, Armstrong studied journalism at Kilgore College (1960–62) and the University of Texas at Austin (1962–65), where he subsequently taught photojournalism from 1969 to 1973. He also worked as chief photographer for the University News Service and the Texas Student Publications at his alma mater for that period of time.

In 1979 Armstrong received a Dobie-Paisano Fellowship for Visual Artists and Writers, granted by the University of Texas and the Texas Institute of Letters.

He works mainly in large format and deals with classical and social landscapes, focusing on the "interaction of man with the landscape, whether intentional or unintentional, through symbols placed on the land."

PUBLICATIONS Book: *Often in Different Landscapes,* poems by Leon Stokesbury, 1976. Periodical: *Photographic Portfolio Magazine,* June 1979.

COLLECTIONS Humanities Resrch. Ctr., Univ. of Tex., Austin; Texas Land Title Assoc., Austin.

DEALER Douglas Kenyon, 155 E Ohio St, Chicago, IL 60611

ADDRESS POB 4104, Austin, TX 78765.

Anthony C. R. Armstrong-Jones
See Lord Snowden

Eve Arnold *PHOTOJOURNALIST* [See plate 94]
Arnold was born in 1913. She is a member of Magnum. Her photoessays have appeared in *Life,* *Look* and the *London Sunday Times,* among

other journals. She established her career with sensitive essays in *Life* and *Look* on such subjects as childbirth, small-town America, Joan Crawford, and Clark Gable. Currently she is based in Europe and New York.

Arnold made a film in Arabia, *Behind the Veil*.

Her widely varied photographic subjects have included mental institutions, prisons for delinquent boys, divorce courts, little-known aspects of Russian life, the Queen of England, migratory potato pickers on Long Island, the Archbishop of Canterbury and Rudolf Nureyev.

PUBLICATIONS Monographs: *In China*, 1980; *Flashback: Eve Arnold's Fifties*, 1978; *The Unretouched Woman*, 1976.

COLLECTIONS Metro. Mus. of Art, NYC; MOMA, NYC.

REPRESENTATIVE Magnum Photos, Inc., 15 W 46 St, New York, NY 10036.

Jan Arnow PHOTOGRAPHER · AUTHOR · TEACHER · DESIGNER Arnow was born on November 14, 1947, in Chicago, Illinois, where she attended the Goodman School of Theater and the University of Illinois (1966–68) and completed a BFA at the School of the Art Institute (1973).

She has given numerous lectures and workshops in photography, design and textiles and, as of this writing, is an artist-in-residence at Saint Francis School in Louisville, Kentucky. She has also worked as a photography reviewer and columnist for the *Chicago New Art Examiner* (1976) and for two smaller local newspapers (1974). Since 1978 she has published a large number of articles in *American Home Crafts, Ladies' Home Journal, Country Living* and *Fiberarts* magazines, for which she has done the text as well as the design and the photography.

Arnow has been a member of SPE since 1976 and joined the Wisconsin Women in Publishing from 1975 to 1977.

In 1967 she received a scholarship from the Experiment in International Living to go to Japan, and in 1972–73, a scholarship from the School of the Art Institute of Chicago. She was selected for several awards: a Purchase Award from the Western Annual Juried Exhibition of Works on Paper (1974); a Gold Medal and a Merit Award from the Milwaukee Society of Communicating Arts (1975, 1976); and a Purchase Award from the Marine Bank Competition, Wisconsin (1976).

Arnow is deeply involved in obsolete and alternative photographic methods; she also does a great deal of photo textile work.

COLLECTIONS Allstate Insurance Co.; Amer. Hospital Assoc.; Marine Bank of Wisc., Milwaukee; Sears Roebuck & Co. Cllctn., Chicago; Standard Oil Co.; Western Ill. Univ., Macomb.

ADDRESS Rt 1, Box 101, Depauw, IN 47115.

Roger Arrandale-Williams PHOTOGRAPHER · TEACHER Born in Coventry, England, in 1946, the photographer studied at the Art Institute of Chicago before receiving his BFA (1968) and his MS (1970), both from Alfred University, Alfred, New York. He went on to earn an MFA at the University of Nebraska in Lincoln (1973). From 1975 to the present he has worked as an assistant professor at the State University of New York (SUNY) in Plattsburgh.

A member of the SPE and the Visual Studies Workshop since 1975, and Friends of Photography since 1977, Mr. Arrandale-Williams was the recipient of a SUNY grant-in-aid in 1979.

He works with large-format view cameras—specifically, 12 x 20 and 7 x 11—and his images focus on "the extended landscape."

PUBLICATIONS Anthologies: *Photography Year Book*, 1980; *Photography Year Book*, 1976 (Argo Press: England).

COLLECTIONS Dibert Gallery, Carmel, Calif.; Floating Fndtn. of Photography, NYC; Gallery f22, Santa Fe, N.M.; Humboldt State College, Arcata, Calif.; Sheldon Memorial Art Gall., Lincoln, Neb.

ADDRESS Art Dept, State Univ College, Plattsburgh, NY 12901.

Alan Gustav Artner CRITIC Born May 14, 1947, in Chicago, Artner studied English literature in his native city at Northwestern University, where he completed his BA (1968) and his MA (1969). Frederic Faverty, Richard Ellmann and Eric Heller were all his mentors.

He has been working as an art critic for the *Chicago Tribune* since 1973. From 1972 to 1973 he worked as an apprentice music critic for the same newspaper, after having received a Rockefeller Grant for the Training of Music Critics.

As a critic he specializes in art and photography.

ADDRESS c/o Chicago Tribune, 435 N Michigan Ave, Chicago, IL 60611.

Dana Asbury PHOTOGRAPHER · WRITER · TEACHER Born on May 25, 1953, in El Paso, Texas, Asbury completed her BA in Arts and Letters in 1975 at Wesleyan University in Middletown, Connecticut, where she studied with J. Seeley. In 1978 she obtained an MA and in 1980 an MFA in Photography from the University of New Mexico, where she studied under Betty Hahn and

Thomas Barrow and where she is currently teaching.

The teacher is a member of SPE. In 1980 she was recipient of a National Endowment of the Humanities Grant.

She works in 35mm and specializes in portraits done at night with long exposures.

PUBLICATIONS Books (text only): *Isolation and Intrustion*, intro., mono. by Tom Patton, 1979; *Self-Portrayal*, essay, James Alinder, ed., 1978. Periodicals (text only): "FSA revisited," Mar 1979, "Mums and Kitsch: New Work by Betty Hahn," summer 1979, "Solos by Linda Connor," Dec 1979, *Afterimage: VSW*; "Elusive, Familiar Mystery: Photos by Anne Noggle," *Exposure: SPE*, fall 1979; "New Faces," w/photos *American Photographer*, Feb 1979; "Photography in the Southwest," *Latent Image*, 1: 2/3, 1979; "Photography at the University of New Mexico," *Portfolio*, 1:2, 1979.

COLLECTIONS Univ. of New Mex. Art Mus., Albuquerque; Wesleyan Univ., Davison Art Ctr., Middletown, Conn.

ADDRESS 2734 Burton SE, Albuquerque, NM 87106.

Herbert Ascherman, Jr. *PHOTOGRAPHER · TEACHER · GALLERY DIRECTOR* Born in Boston on June 10, 1947, Ascherman received both a BA and an MAT from the University of Hartford, Connecticut; he did postgraduate work at the University of Connecticut.

Having taught photography in adult education at both Cleveland Heights High and John Carroll University, he lectures widely and does commercial freelance photography.

In 1977 he founded the Cleveland Photographic Workshop & Gallery, a nonprofit organization of which he is director. The Ohio Arts Council has awarded his workshop several grants.

Ascherman is a member of the New Organization Visual Arts in Cleveland, the SPE and the PPA.

He does both studio and location work in a medium format.

ADDRESS 1785 Coventry Rd, Cleveland Heights, OH 44118.

Astrid *PHOTOGRAPHER* Born in 1936 in Brussels, Astrid is the daughter of noted Belgian painter Antoine Allard. She spent the early part of her life in various African countries (Zaire, South Africa, Egypt), then obtained a BA at the French Lyceum in Brussels.

Astrid has worked in a variety of jobs—as a photographer's model, a nurse for three years at a Milanese hospital, and in various fashion houses and department stores. She undertook the art of collage while raising her four children and began photographing in 1974. She has exhibited her work since 1978 and her images have appeared in Spain's *Foto Zoom* and *Almanac Fotografare*.

Astrid strives to use photography as a means of transforming reality into a utopian vision of life. She calls her images "unrealistic" photographs, frequently using superimposition. Following "a path of transparent and fragile images," her chief subjects are eyes, hands, feet, clouds, children, sea gulls, doors and windows.

PUBLICATION Monograph (incl. poetry): *A comme . . . apprivoiser*, 1978 (Hachette: Paris).

ADDRESS Via Senato, 34, Milan, Italy.

Jean-Eugène-Auguste Atget *PHOTOGRAPHER · PAINTER · ACTOR · SAILOR* [See plate 40] Born in Libourne, France (near Bordeaux), in 1856 and died August 1927 in Paris, Atget was completely self-taught. He was encouraged by Georges Braque and Maurice Utrillo, who occasionally painted from his photographs, and was rescued from poverty and obscurity by Berenice Abbott just two years before his death.

Atget received one commission, in 1921, to document the brothels of Paris, but primarily made a meager living by selling his photographs to set designers and painters.

Eugene Atget, a black-and-white film of Atget's photographs with commentary, was made in 1963.

One of the most influential documentary photographers of the twentieth century, Atget worked with an 18 x 24-cm bellows camera and a set of rectilinear lenses with a wooden tripod. Using gelatin dry-plate negatives, he photographed more than 10,000 scenes of Paris—the architecture, monuments, prostitutes, fountains, trees, etc. Abbott called him "a lover of Paris, a Balzac of the camera."

PUBLICATIONS Books: *Atget: Magicien du Vieux Paris en son époque*, Jean Leroy, 1975 (Jean Balbo, Paris); *Les Metamorphoses de la Banlieue Parisienne*, Yvan Christ, 1969; *Les Metamorphoses de Paris*, 1967, Yvan Christ; *The World of Atget*, Berenice Abbott, 1964, repr. 1975; *A Vision of Paris*, Marcel Proust, A. D. Trottenberg, ed., 1963; *Atget, Photographie de Saint Germain des Près*, Yvan Christ, 1951 (Paris); *Atget, Photographe de Paris*, preface by Pierre MacOrlan, 1930 (Jonquières, Paris), U.S. ed., 1930; *Dans les rues de Paris au Temps des Fiacres*, Léon-Paul

Fargue Georges, n.d. (Pillement & Rene Coursaget: France). Anthologies: *Documentary Photography*, Time-Life Series, 1972; *Looking at Photographs*, John Szarkowski, 1973; *Photographs from the Julien Levy Collection*, David Travis, 1976; *The Julien Levy Collection*, 1977. Periodicals: *Camera*, Mar 1978; "Eugene Atget: A Chronological Bibliography," *Exposure: SPE*, May 1977; "Atget," John Szarkowski, *Album*, no. 3, 1970; *La Photographie Ancienne*, Emmanuel Sougez, no. 23, 1941; *Le Crapouillot*, May 1929; *La Révolution Surréaliste*, June & Dec 1926; *Paris-Quartiers*, 1924.

PORTFOLIO *Untitled*, 1956 (Berenice Abbott: New York).

COLLECTIONS Art Inst. of Chicago; IMP/GEH, Rochester; Metro. Mus. of Art, NYC; MOMA, NYC; New Orleans Mus. of Art; San Francisco Mus. of Modern Art; Univ. of N. Mex. Art Mus., Albuquerque. Archives Photographiques, Paris; Bibliothèque Nationale, Paris; Natl. Gall. of Canada, Ottawa, Ontario; Provinciaal Mus. voor Kunstambachten, Deurne (Antwerp), Belgium.

Louis Athol-Shmith *PHOTOGRAPHER · LECTURER* Born in Melbourne, Australia, on August 19, 1914, Athol-Shmith attended Wesley College in Bath, England.

Currently self-employed, he was a senior lecturer in photography from 1970 to 1979 at Prahran College in Australia. From 1934 to 1970 he operated his own studio, which dealt in illustrative and portrait photography.

The photographer is a Fellow of the Royal Society of Arts, London; a Fellow of RPS, and a member (1948) of the Fédération Internationale de l'Art Photographique (FIAP) in France.

In 1968 he founded the Department of Photography at the National Gallery of Victoria, and in 1945 co-founded the "Camera Graph" continuous-flow film system for accurately recording the finish of horse races and other sporting events.

Working in all formats, Athol-Shmith creates multimedia images as well as portraits, fashion photos and photo-reportage.

COLLECTIONS In Australia: Art Gall. of New South Wales; Australian Centre for Photography; Australian Natl. Gall., Canberra; Gryphon Gall., Melbourne; Philip Morris Cllctn. Bibliothèque Nationale, Paris.

ADDRESS 3/26 Powell St, South Yarra, Victoria, Australia 3141.

Benjamin Attas *PHOTOGRAPHER · TEACHER* Born in Manhattan on December 12, 1921, the photographer studied his craft at, variously, the New York Institute of Photography, the Clarence White School and the American Artists School, all during 1941–42. He has freelanced ever since.

From 1955 to 1957 he ran a commercial and portrait studio. Since 1957 he has worked as assistant manager and technical consultant for Modernage Photographic Services in Manhattan and has been an instructor for both, formerly, the New School for Social Research in New York, and, presently, Rockland Community College, Rockland County, New York.

A member of RPS, APS and SPE, Attas has written several training booklets and has functioned as consultant for several books on photography and its history.

He works mainly in color and has done color printing since 1940. He has also researched converting color to black-and-white for reproduction.

COLLECTIONS Brooklyn Main Lib., N.Y.; Brooklyn Mus., NY; IMP/GEH, Rochester; Rockland County Historical Society, NY.

ADDRESS 60 Kennedy Dr, West Haverstraw, NY 10993.

David Moses Attie *PHOTOGRAPHER* Born on November 30, 1920, in Brooklyn, New York, Attie attended the Kansas City Art Institute, Kansas, in 1940, and the Cooper Union School of Art in New York City, 1941–42. He also studied at the Alexey Brodovitch Design Laboratory at The New School for Social Research, New York City, from 1958 to 1962, and says that Brodovitch was a major influence in his work.

Attie is a freelance photographer and, since 1975, has also been teaching at the School of Visual Arts and The New School for Social Research, both in Manhattan. He has been a member of ASMP since 1962 and served on their board of governors in 1973–74.

Attie is the recipient of many awards; several were awarded him by the Art Directors Club: by the Metropolitan Washington Chapter, a Certificate of Merit (June 1973), a Gold Medal (June 1969), and a Distinctive Merit Award (June 1967); by the New Jersey Chapter, an Award for Excellence in Print (January 1970); and by the New York Chapter, a Certificate of Merit at the 49th Annual Exhibition (1969) and a Certificate of Merit (1966). For the years 1970 and 1972–73, the American Institute of Graphic Arts awarded the artist a Certificate of Excellence, and, in 1971 he received a Certificate of Merit from the Society of Publication Designers.

Attie's work, which includes both color and black-and-white, involves the use of multiple-image techniques. He does "straightforward photojournalist assignments," mainly in editorial illustration and in advertising.

PUBLICATIONS   Books: *Russian Self-Portraits,* 1977; *Teaching Hand Puppetry,* Larry Engler, 1973; *Saloon Society,* Bill Manville, 1960. Periodicals: *Progresso Photographico,* Apr 1978; *Popular Photography Annual,* 1978; *Smalfim Foto,* Jan 77; *Camera,* Feb 1969; *Creative Camera,* 1968; *Popular Photography,* incl. article, June 1965; *British Journal of Photography Annual,* 1964; *Photography of the World,* 1964; *US Camera Annual,* incl. text, 1964; *Camera,* July 1963; *Infinity: ASMP,* Mar 1963; *Popular Photography Annual,* 1962.

COLLECTION   MOMA, NYC.

ADDRESS   334 E 22 St, New York, NY 10010.

Otis A. Aultman   PHOTOGRAPHER · CAMERAMAN   The artist was born August 27, 1874, in Holden, Missouri, and died March 5, 1943, at El Paso, Texas. He received his education in Trinidad, Colorado, and learned photography from his brother, O. E. Aultman.

Aultman worked on architectural, archeological and historical finds from 1923 until the end of his career. He was a pioneer in motion picture work under contract with Pancho Villa and Obregon from 1916 to 1917. He worked with the International News Service and later Pathé News during the Mexican Revolution. Aultman was the official photographer of the Juárez Race Track. In 1909 he worked in partnership with Homer Scott in El Paso. Aultman co-founded the Adventurer's Club in El Paso.

During his years as a commercial photographer and news cameraman, Aultman covered extensively the events of the Mexican Revolution, including Pancho Villa's 1916 raid in Columbus, New Mexico. In addition to Villa, he photographed such notables as President William Howard Taft and Mexican President Porfirio Díaz. His work also includes the social life and architecture of El Paso in the early 1900s.

PUBLICATIONS   Books: *Photographs from the Border,* Mary A. Sarber, 1977; *Pancho Villa and the Columbus Raid,* Larry Harris, 1949.

ARCHIVES   El Paso Public Lib., Southwest Rm., El Paso, TX; Univ. of Tex. Library, El Paso, TX.

(Elizabeth) Alice Austen   PHOTOGRAPHER Alice Austen was born in Clifton on Staten Island, New York, in 1866. She died there on June 9, 1952. She was educated in private schools in Manhattan and Staten Island.

A hobbyist who was maintained by a family trust, she took up photography at the age of twelve and continued to take pictures until 1930, when the economic "crash" and crippling arthritis prohibited her from further photographic adventures.

During twenty-two trips she made abroad, she took pictures of palaces and historical scenes in France, England and Germany. She was this country's earliest and foremost woman photographer to work outside a studio. She worked with a Scovill 4 x 5 camera. All her prints were contact prints. She revealed an instinct for photojournalism eighty years before the word was coined, and is best known for her recording of national events and the genre views of her prosperous friends as well as the fishermen, blacksmiths and oyster shuckers of Staten Island. Of the approximately nine thousand negatives she made during her lifetime, thirty-five hundred survive.

PUBLICATIONS   Book: *Alice's World: The Life and Photography of an American Original: Alice Austen, 1866–1952,* 1976. Periodical: "Alice Austen," by Ann Novotny, *Camera 35,* May 1980.

COLLECTIONS   Alice Austen House, Staten Island, N.Y.; Staten Island Historical Mus., NY.

ARCHIVE   Friends of Alice Austen House, 315 W 78, New York, NY 10024.

Richard Avedon   PHOTOGRAPHER   Born May 15, 1923, in New York City, Avedon studied with Alexey Brodovitch at the Design Laboratory of the New School for Social Research in New York City from 1944 to 1950.

In 1966 Avedon was a staff photographer for *Vogue* magazine. Previously he was a staff photographer for both *Harper's Bazaar* (1945–65) and *Junior Bazaar* (1945–47). He now runs his own studio in New York City.

In 1978 Avedon was named President's Fellow by Rhode Island School of Design. Awards he has received are the Citation of Dedication to Fashion from Pratt Institute in 1976, the National Magazine Award for Visual Excellence in 1976 and the highest achievement medal award at the Art Directors' Show in 1950. *Popular Photography* voted him one of the world's ten greatest photographers in 1958. Avedon was also a visual consultant for the film *Funny Face,* produced by Paramount Studios.

The artist says of his work, "A photographic portrait is a picture of someone who knows he's being photographed, and what he does with this knowledge is as much a part of the photograph as what he's wearing or how he looks. He's implicated in what's happening, and he has a certain real power over the result. . . . We all perform. It's what we do for each other all the time, deliberately or unintentionally. It's a way of telling ourselves in the hope of being recognized as what we'd like to be. I trust performances. Stripping them away doesn't necessarily get you closer to anything. The way someone who's being photographed presents himself to the camera and the effect of the photographer's response on that presence is what the making of a portrait is about."

PUBLICATIONS Monographs: *Avedon: Photographs 1947–1977*, essay by Harold Brodkey, designed by Elizabeth Paul, 1978; *Portraits*, intro. by Harold Rosenberg, designed by Elizabeth Paul, 1976; *Alice in Wonderland: The Forming of a Company, The Making of a Play*, Doon Arbus, Merlin House, designed by Ruth Ansel, 1973; *Nothing Personal*, James Baldwin, designed by Marvin Israel; *Observations*, Truman Capote, designed by Alexey Brodovitch, 1959. Book: *Diary of a Century*, photographs by Jacques-Henri Lartigue, ed., 1970. Catalogs: *Photographer*, 1975 (Marlborough Gallery); *Avedon*, 1970 (Minneapolis Inst. of Arts). Anthology: *The Photograph Collector's Guide*, Lee D. Witkin & Barbara London, 1979.

PORTFOLIOS *Avedon*, 1978 (self-pub.); *Avedon*, 1970 (self-pub.).

COLLECTIONS Gilman Paper Co., NYC; Cincinnati Art Mus., Ohio; Hallmark Cards, Inc., Kansas City, Mo.; Houston Mus. of Fine Arts, Tex.; Metro. Mus. of Art, NYC; Middle Tenn. State Univ., Murfreesboro, Tenn.; MOMA, NYC; New Orleans Mus. of Art, La.; Rhode Island School of Design, Mus. of Art, Providence; San Francisco Mus. of Modern Art, Calif.; St. Louis Art Mus., St. Louis, Mo.; Smithsonian Inst., Wash., D.C. Contemporaneo, Caracas, Venezeula.

REPRESENTATIVE Norma Stevens, 1075 Park Ave, New York, NY 10028.

ADDRESS 407 E 75 St, New York, NY 10021.

David Avison PHOTOGRAPHER · TEACHER · PHYSICIST · DESIGNER Born on July 13, 1937, in Harrisonburg, Virginia, Avison received an ScB in 1959 from MIT, Cambridge, and a PhD in physics at Brown University in Providence, Rhode Island, in 1966. Three years later he decided to abandon his career in physics and commit himself totally to photography, which he then studied at the Institute of Design (Illinois Institute of Technology) in Chicago, earning an MS. He was predominantly influenced by the work of Garry Winogrand and Fredrick Sommer.

Since 1970 Avison has been teaching photography at Columbia College in Chicago. Prior to that he taught physics at Purdue University, Indiana (1967–69), and at Brown University (1960–66).

His several memberships include SPE, the Chicago Artists' Coalition, the Optical Society of Chicago, and the Society of Photographic Scientists and Engineers, for whom he has served as a board member.

When a physicist, Avison wrote several articles on acoustics and high-energy theory. During the years 1970–72 he invented and constructed a special panoramic camera. The NEA awarded him a Photographer's Fellowship in 1977.

For ten years Avison has been especially interested in the "possibility of the long-format/wide-angle image by photographing with the special panoramic cameras" which he designed and built for that purpose.

PUBLICATIONS Catalogs: *Panoramic Photography*, D. Edkins, 1977 (N.Y.U. Press); *70's Wide View*, E. A. King, 1978 (Northwestern Univ.: Chicago). Periodical: "Panorama," Andy Grundberg, *Modern Photography*, Aug 1978.

COLLECTIONS Art Inst. of Chicago; Exchange Natl. Bank, Chicago; IMP/GEH, Rochester; Midwest Mus. of Amer. Art, Elkhart, Ind.; Mus. of Fine Arts, Boston; MOMA, NYC.

DEALERS Douglas Kenyon, Chicago; The Afterimage, Dallas; Panopticon Gallery, Boston; Hills Gallery, Denver.

ADDRESS 1522 Davis St, Evanston, IL 60201.

Stephen Axelrad ATTORNEY · PHOTOGRAPHER · TEACHER Born in Washington, D.C., on September 12, 1943, Axelrad obtained a BA in English from the University of California at Berkeley (1965) and a JD from the University of Chicago's School of Law in 1969. He then became interested in photography and studied at Apeiron Workshop in Millerton, New York (1971), with Aaron Siskind, at UCLA Extension (1972–76) with Robert Heinecken, Jerry McMillan and Robert Cumming, and at California State in Fullerton (1977–79) with Darryl Curran, among others.

Axelrad has been a law instructor at the University of California in Los Angeles, at California State University in Northridge and at Western State University (1973–77). As of this writing he was teaching photography at Los Angeles Harbor College in San Pedro. He has also maintained his own legal practice in Los Angeles from 1971 to 1973 and from 1976 to the present.

He received the Juror's Purchase Award from the Kansas City Art Institute, Missouri, in 1979.

He specializes in Cibachrome color photographs. He is interested "in the interrelationship of creativity and art history" and structures his work "on legal reasoning based on many years of the practice of law."

COLLECTION   Kansas City Art Inst., MO.

ADDRESS   1813 Effie St, Los Angeles, CA 90026.

B

Clarence A. Bach *TEACHER · PHOTOGRAPHER* Born in Hollywood, California, in 1894, Bach died possibly around 1965–1970. An assistant to cameraman Frank Heisler at Fox Studios for twelve years, he then taught at John C. Fremont High School for thirty-five years, retiring in 1959.

Bach founded the first photojournalism course in the country in 1924. Nearly three hundred of his students became professional photographers, among them Mark Kauffman, Bob Landry, John Florea, Hank Walker, George Strook, John Wilkes and John Dominis (all of whom worked on staff for *Life* magazine), Art Rogers (of the *Los Angeles Times*) and John G. Zimmerman (of *Sports Illustrated*). Another 146 students became wartime photo-correspondents.

PUBLICATION Periodical: *Sports Illustrated*, June 15, 1958/59(?).

Karl Baden *PHOTOGRAPHER · TEACHER* Born June 24, 1952, in New York City, Baden received an MFA from the University of Illinois at Chicago Circle in 1979, where he studied with Joseph Jachna, and a BA in Fine Arts (Photography) from Syracuse University in 1975 (magna cum laude).

As of this date Baden was teaching photography at the Boston Center for Adult Education and Project Art Center. He has also developed a photography program for the disabled at the Walter E. Fernald School in Waltham, Massachusetts. Other teaching experience includes instructing photography at the University of Illinois at Chicago Circle 1978–79, and at Light Work in Syracuse, New York, 1976–77.

Baden was a recipient of a Light Work Fellowship for Photographers in 1975.

Working in 35mm black-and-white and sometimes adding hand coloring, Baden has been involved with a series of self-portraits entitled *Self-Images* since 1978.

PUBLICATIONS Periodicals (reviews): *Art Week*, Joan Murray, May 12, 1979; *New Art Ex-aminer*, Lynne Warren, Apr 1979, Devonna Pisiak, Feb 1979.

COLLECTIONS Light Work, Inc., Syracuse, N.Y.; Los Angeles Ctr. for Photographic Studies.

ADDRESS 3657 Woodbridge Ln, Wantagh, NY 11793.

Gerald David Badger *ARCHITECT · WRITER · PHOTOGRAPHER · TEACHER* Born June 13, 1948, in Northampton, England, Badger studied architecture at the Duncan of Jordanstone College of Art in Dundee in 1964–69, and photography with Joseph McKenzie in 1966–69. His major influences have been Roger Fenton, Eugene Atget, Walker Evans and Lee Friedlander.

Badger has been both an architect and a teacher of photography at the Stanhope Institute in London since 1976. Prior to that he worked at Peter Wood & Partners, architects, in London (1973–76).

A recipient of the Greater London Arts Association's Visual Arts Major Award in 1979, he also was awarded an Arts Council Grant for Photography in 1977.

Using a large format, he concentrates on urban landscapes and nudes.

PUBLICATIONS Catalogs (text only); *John Blakemore, British Image III*, 1977 (Arts Council of Great Britain); *New American Still Photography*, 1976 (Scottish Photography Group: Edinburgh). Periodicals: "Early Photography in Egypt," Dec 1979, "Walker Evans," Sept 1977, illus., Dec, Mar 1973, *Creative Camera*; *Artscribe*, no. 18, 1979; *Untitled*, no. 14, 1978 (Friends of Photography); *British Journal of Photography Annual*, 1978, 1975; *U.S. Camera Annual*, 1977; "Wynn Bullock," *The Photographic Journal*, May 1975; *Aktuell Fotografie*, 1975; *Spot*, 1975.

COLLECTIONS Arts Council of Great Britain, London; Bibliothèque Nationale, Paris; Dept. of the Environment, London; London Borough of Hounslow.

24 Clarence Rd, Croydon, Surrey, England.

Morley Baer   PHOTOGRAPHER   Born April 5, 1916, in Toledo, Ohio, Baer received a BA in 1936 and an MA in 1937 from the University of Michigan. His major influences have been Edward and Brett Weston.

Since 1946 he has done photography for many San Francisco and West Coast architects, architectural editors, and book publishers.

Baer is a member of ASMP and the Friends of Photography. In 1965 he was the recipient of an AIA Gold Medal for Photography and in 1980 a fellowship from the American Academy in Rome.

In his creative personal work Baer focuses on rural farm areas, as well as on the coast and hills of California.

PUBLICATIONS   Books: *Room and Time Enough*, 1979; *Painted Ladies*, 1978; *Bay Area Houses*, 1976; *Adobes in the Sun*, 1973; *Here Today*, 1968.

COLLECTIONS   M. H. de Young Mus., San Francisco; New Orleans Mus. of Art; San Francisco Mus. of Mod. Art; Univ. of Missouri Lib., Columbia.

ADDRESS   POB 2228, Monterey, CA 93940.

Oskar Baetschmann   CURATOR · TEACHER   Born in Lucerne, Switzerland, on September 15, 1943, Baetschmann studied at the Academy in Florence and at Zürich University, where he received his PhD in 1975. He then did postgraduate work in Rome, Paris and London.

He has been curator of the Kunstgewerbemuseum der Stadt in Zürich since 1978 and a lecturer at Universität Zürich since 1979. Baetschmann belongs to International Council of Museums (ICOM), Vereinigung der Kunsthistoriker in der Schweiz (currently chairman) and Comité National Suisse du CIHA.

PUBLICATIONS   Books: "Beiträgezu einem Übergang von der Ikonologie zu kunstgeschichtlicher Hermeneutik," *Ikonographie und Ikonologie. Theorien, Entwicklung, Probleme*, E. Kaemmerling, 1979 (Bildende Kunst als Zeichensystem: Cologne); "Pygmalion als Betrachter...," *Jahrbuch 1974–77 des Schweizerischen Instituts für Kunstwissenschaft*, 1978 (Zürich); *Bild-Diskurs. Die Schwierigkeit des "parler peinture*," 1977 (Handelsausgabe: Bern). Periodicals: "Zur Geschichte der Kunstgeschichte in Deutschland," Oct 1979, "Benennung oder Erfahrung," Sept 1978, *NZZ (Neue Züricher*

Zeitung, New Zurich newspaper); "Poussins 'Narziss und Echo' im Louvre...," *Zeitschrift für Kunstgeschichte*, no. 42, 1979; "Phillipe Junod, Transparence et Opacité. Réflexions autour de l'esthétique de Konrad Fiedler," *Revue de Théologie et de Philosophie*, no. 111, 1979.

ADDRESS   Kunstgewerbemuseum der Stadt Zürich, Ausstellungsstr 60, Postfach, CH-8031 Zürich, Switzerland.

David Bailey   PHOTOGRAPHER   Born in London in 1938, Bailey was an assistant to photographer John French in 1959, and his work was influenced by Josef von Sternberg's film *Shanghai Express*. At one time he was married to French actress Catherine Deneuve.

A freelance fashion photographer who lives in London, Bailey has been under contract to *Vogue* since 1960. His images have also appeared in such publications as *Sunday Times*, *Daily Telegraph*, *Elle* and *Glamour*. Michelangelo Antonioni's film *Blow-Up* was reportedly based loosely on Bailey's life.

Bailey made the films *Andy Warhol* (1973) and *Beaton by Bailey* (1971).

PUBLICATIONS   Books: *Mixed Moments*, 1976 (Olympus Optical Co.: London); *Andy Warhol/ Transcripts and Photographs*, 1973; *Beady Minces*, 1973; *Goodbye Baby and Amen*, 1969; *Box of Pin-ups*, 1965; *The Truth About Modelling*, Jean Shrimpton, 1963. Anthologies: *The History of Fashion Photography*, Nancy Hall-Duncan, 1979; *The Magic Image*, Cecil Beaton & Gail Buckland, 1975.

ADDRESS   39 Rokeby House, Lochinvar St, London SW 12, England.

James Bailey   PHOTOGRAPHER · TEACHER   Born in Vincennes, Indiana, on July 26, 1951, Bailey completed his bachelor's and master's degrees in fine arts at Ohio University, Athens (1973, 1976), where he also attended a Minor White residential workshop (1973–74). He is currently the owner of Precision Photographics in Hayward, California, where he has been teaching photography since 1977, both at Chabot College and at California State University.

Working in black-and-white as well as in color, and using large and medium formats, Bailey concentrates on "personal documentary and urban environment."

PUBLICATIONS   Book: *Contemporary California Photography*, 1978. Periodical: *Latent Image*, 1:2, 1979.

COLLECTIONS   L/C, Wash., D.C.; Oakland

Mus. of Art, Calif.; Princeton Univ., Minor White Archive, Princeton, N.J.

ADDRESS POB 3825, Hayward, CA 94540.

Oscar W. Bailey   TEACHER · PHOTOGRAPHER Born in 1925 in Barnesville, Ohio, Bailey completed his education in his home state, receiving his bachelor's degree from Wilmington College in 1951 and his Master of Fine Arts from Ohio University, Athens, in 1958. He has been a professor at the University of South Florida in Tampa since 1969. He had previously taught photography at the State University of New York in Buffalo (1958–69) and worked as a printer and a printing designer at the Coop. Recreation Service in Delaware, Ohio (1951–56).

The artist is a member of Friends of Photography, George Eastman House and SPE, of which he was a founding member. He was also awarded several grants: in 1967, a Faculty Research Fellowship from SUNY, Buffalo, for his "Work in Expressive Photography"; in 1974, a Research Council Grant from the University of South Florida; and in 1976, a Photographer's Fellowship Grant from NEA. In 1978 he was artist-in-residence at Art Park in Lewiston, New York.

Besides photography, Bailey has been interested in creating wind-supported sculptures.

Most of his photographic work falls into three categories: landscapes showing evidence of man, three-dimensional photo-constructions, and finally 8 x 48 contact prints produced with the antique CIRKUT camera.

PUBLICATIONS   Books: *Light and Lens*, 1973; *Photography 63*, 1963; *Photography at Mid-Century*, 1959. Periodicals: *Fotografi*, Sept 1978; *Aperture*, 8:2, 1961, 7:1, 1959; *Art in America*, 48:1, 1960.

COLLECTIONS   Boston Mus. of Fine Arts; Florida Ctr. for Arts, Tampa; Florida Office of Cultural Affairs, Tallahassee; IMP/GEH, Rochester; L/C, Wash., D.C.; MOMA, NYC; Mus. of Fine Arts, St. Petersburg, Fla.; New Orleans Mus. of Art; Ringling Mus. of Art, Sarasota, Fla.; Smithsonian Inst., Hist. of Photog. Cllctn., Wash., D.C.; Univ. of Oregon, Eugene.

ADDRESS   2004 Clement Rd, Lutz, FL 33549.

Joseph Armstrong Baird, Jr.   DEALER · COLLECTOR · HISTORIAN Born in Pittsburg, Pennsylvania, on November 22, 1922, Baird earned his bachelor's degree at Oberlin College in Ohio in 1944, and a master's degree and a doctorate at Harvard University, in 1947 and 1951. He is the owner of the North Point Gallery in San Fran-

cisco and is also a professor of art history at the University of California in Davis. He is a member of the Fine Arts Museum of San Francisco, the Oakland Museum, and also an honorary member of the California Historical Society, which granted him an Award of Merit.

As a photographer he is mainly interested in the art and the architecture of California.

PUBLICATIONS   Books: *The West Remembered*, 1973; *Historic Lithographs of San Francisco*, 1972; *California's Pictorial Lettersheets: 1849–1869*, 1967; *The Churches of Mexico*, 1962; *Time's Wondrous Changes*, 1962. Contributor: *Dictionary of World Art*, 1969; *Grolier Encyclopedia*, 1961. Catalogs: *Pre-Impressionism*, 1969 (Univ. of Calif.: Davis); *Catalogue of Original Paintings, Drawings and Watercolors in the Robert B. Honeyman, Jr., Collection*, 1968 (Friends of the Bancroft Lib.: Berkeley); *Samuel Marsden Brookes: 1816–1892*, 1962 (Calif. Hist. Soc.: San Francisco).

COLLECTIONS   Calif. Hist. Soc., San Francisco; Univ. of Calif., Baird Archive, Special Cllctn., Davis; Univ. of Calif., Bancroft Lib., Berkeley.

ADDRESS   North Point Gall., 872 N Point St, San Francisco, CA 94109.

Kenneth Winston Baird   TEACHER · PHOTOGRAPHER Born August 10, 1930, in Lancashire, England, he received an MA in Photography and Art History in 1977, and an MFA in 1980 from the University of New Mexico in Albuquerque. His main influences have been Thomas F. Barrow, Ann Noggle, Van Deren Coke and Beaumont Newhall.

Baird has been a freelance photographer since 1975. Prior to that he worked in England as a senior lecturer at the Manchester Education Committee 1970–75, and chairman of the Art Department at the Bristol Education Committee 1963–70.

In England he is a member of both the National Society for Art Education and the Committee for Aerial Archaeology, an Associate of RPS and a founding member of the Crescent Arts Workshop in Scarborough. In 1979 he received a Ford Foundation Grant. He has also been a recipient of the Arts Council of Great Britain award every year from 1975 to 1978, as well as the Award Fédération Internationale de l'Art Photographique (FIAP) in 1974, and the Goldsmiths Company of London's Art History Travel Award in 1968.

Baird also researched and printed the Tom Watson Collection in 1977–78 and produced a traveling show of Watson's work for Impressions Gallery in York, England.

Using various formats, in his work he focuses on social documentation, landscape, and aerial photography. He also does research on the history of photography of the North East Yorkshire Coast region of England.

PUBLICATIONS Anthologies: *History of Photography in New Mexico*, 1978; *Perspectives on Landscape*, 1978 (Arts Council of Great Britain). Periodicals: *Camera 35 Annual*, 1978, 1977.

COLLECTIONS Univ. of N. Mex., Art Mus., Albuquerque. Arts Council of Great Britain, London; Impressions Gall., York, England; Side Gall., Newcastle, England.

REPRESENTATIVE Single Images, 1204 Espanola, Albuquerque, NM 87110.

ADDRESS Photo Workshop, Heywood House, 3 Cliff St, Whitby, North Yorkshire, Y021 3DD England.

Deborah Frances Baker PHOTOGRAPHER · LECTURER Born April 19, 1954, in Honiton, Devon, England, Baker received a diploma in 1977 from Trent Polytechnic in Nottingham, England, where she studied with Thomas Cooper, Paul Hill, Raymond Moore and John Blakemore. She also attended the Maryland Institute in Baltimore, Maryland, in 1976.

As of this date Baker is a lecturer at the City of London Polytechnic. In 1980 she was a fellow in photography at Sheffield City Polytechnic. In 1979 she was the director of the Photographic Gallery in Cardiff, Wales, and worked as a lecturer at West Nottingham College in Mansfield, Nottinghamshire in 1978. She also worked as an assistant to both Paul Hill of The Photographer's Place in Bradbourne, Derbyshire (1978), and to Ralph Gibson in New York (1977–78).

The photographer defines her work as being "concerned with photography in its purest sense, translating the three-dimensional reality to a two-dimensional image. I am interested by the very nature of the city itself, the structure of the buildings, the illusions created by light on texture."

PUBLICATIONS Periodicals: *Open Eye Gallery Magazine*, June 1979; *Art and Artists*, Feb 1979; "Photographers," *Impressions Gallery Magazine*, Feb 1979; *News Reporter*, Dec 1978; *U.S. Camera Annual*, Dec 1977; *Nye Foto*, spring 1976.

COLLECTIONS Bibliothèque Nationale, Paris; Victoria & Albert Mus., London; Yorkshire Arts, England.

DEALERS David Dawson, B-2 Gall., Metropolitan Wharf, Wapping, London E1, England; Photographer's Gall., 8 Great Newport St, London WC1, England.

ADDRESS Daniel's Farm Cottage, Carlingcott, Bath, Avon BA2 8AL, England.

John Baldessari PHOTOGRAPHER · VIDEO ARTIST · TEACHER · PRINTMAKER Born June 17, 1931, Baldessari received a BA (1953) and an MA (1957) from San Diego State University, California. He also studied at the University of California, Berkeley (1957–58), and at Otis Art Institute in Los Angeles (1958–59).

Since 1970 he has taught at California Institute of the Arts, Valencia, California. Baldessari previously taught at the University of California, San Diego (1968–70).

He won NEA fellowships in 1973 and 1974. In 1973 he participated in a one-hour program (with video artist William Wegman) on KCET-TV in Los Angeles.

PUBLICATIONS Monographs: *A Sentence of Thirteen Parts (with Twelve Alternate Verbs), Ending in Fable*, 1977 (Anatol AV und Filmproduktion: Hamburg, Germany); *Brutus Killed Caesar*, 1976 (Univ. of Akron: Ohio); *Throwing a Ball Once to Get Three Melodies and Fifteen Chords*, 1975 (Univ. of Calif.: Irvine); *Throwing Three Balls in the Air to Get a Straight Line (Best of Thirty-Six Attempts)*, 1973 (Galleria Toselli: Milan); *Choosing: Green Beans*, 1972 (Galleria Toselli: Milan); *Ingres and Other Parables*, 1972 (Studio International Mag.: London). Books: *Artists and Photographers*, 1975; *Art History of Photography*, Volker Kahmen, 1973. Catalogs: *Photography & Language*, interview, 1976 (Camerawork Press); *Conceptual Art*, Ursula Myers, 1971. Periodical: *Artforum*, Oct 1973.

PORTFOLIO *Raw Prints*, 1976 (Cirrus Editions: Los Angeles).

COLLECTIONS Los Angeles County Mus. of Art; MOMA, NYC. Basel Mus., Switzerland.

DEALER Sonnabend Gall., 420 W Broadway, New York, NY 10012.

ADDRESS 3554 Beethoven St, Los Angeles, CA 90066.

Edouard-Denis Baldus PHOTOGRAPHER · PAINTER Born in France, Baldus lived from 1820 to 1882. Between 1851 and 1855 he fulfilled a commission by the Comité des Monuments Historiques to photograph monuments in Paris, Fontainebleau, Burgundy, the Dauphiné, Normandy, Auvergne and Provence. He was also commissioned by Baron James de Rothschild to photograph railroad lines in France. In 1854–55 he took extensive photographs of a new wing of the Louvre in Paris.

He was a founding member of the Société Héliographique in 1851. Baldus was also a pioneer in heliogravure, beginning in 1854, and he was the first to cover copper plates with a light-sensitive asphalt coating. In 1854 he etched such plates in a galvanic bath.

Baldus used the calotype process through 1851, and by 1852 was using the improved waxed-paper method. His negatives were transparent and almost devoid of grain. By 1856 he was working with collodion wet-plate negatives and albumen prints. Frequently using formats as large as 17½ x 23, Baldus mainly produced images of monuments and architecture throughout France, as well as "industrial landscapes."

PUBLICATIONS Albums: *Chemin de fer de Paris à Lyon et à la Mediterranée, Chemin de fer du nord: Ligne de Paris à Boulogne, Chemin de fer du nord: Ligne de Paris à Compiègne par Chantilly, Vues de Paris en Photographie,* ca. 1853–55 (Paris). Periodical: *La Lumière,* 1854.

COLLECTIONS IMP/GEH, Rochester; Univ. of N. Mex. Art Mus., Albuquerque. Académie des Beaux-Arts Archives, Paris; Bibliothèque Nationale, Paris.

Al Balinsky PHOTOGRAPHER·TEACHER Born on July 7, 1946, in New York City, Balinsky completed an MFA in Photography at Brooklyn College (1977), where he had also earned his bachelor's degree (1969). From 1970 to 1971 he studied at the Brooklyn Museum Art School in New York. Walter Rosenblum had a major influence on his artistic development.

Since 1977 he has been living in Wisconsin, where he is currently teaching at the Milwaukee Center for Photography and is also employed by the Inner City Arts Council to document Milwaukee's inner city. He worked previously in the same city as the coordinator of the Photography Program of the Children's Outing Association and as the founder and the exhibition committee member of the Perihelion Photographic Gallery. In 1977 he was artist-in-residence at the Mark Twain School for the Gifted and Talented in Brooklyn. The previous year he was hired by the Brooklyn Museum as an assistant curator for the Lewis Hine retrospective and was also research assistant for the Lewis Hine monograph that was published by Aperture. His experience covers some work in Mexico: in 1977 he was a photographer for the Tourist Board in Pátzcuaro, and in 1975 he documented the Purepecha Indians of Uruapan under the direction of the anthropologist Ricardo Reyes Cerda.

Balinsky is a founding member of the Perihelion Photo Gallery in Milwaukee, and in 1976–77 he served as the exhibition chairman and an executive board member of the Photographer's Forum in New York. He was the recipient of a grant from the Wisconsin Arts Board in 1979.

The artist specializes in documentary photography, using all formats, and has been focusing on Milwaukee's inner city for the last three years.

ADDRESS 1512 N Warren Ave, Milwaukee, WI 53202.

Val Baltkalns PHOTOGRAPHER · TEACHER Born November 23, 1921, in Moscow, Baltkalns studied at York University, Toronto, Canada, in 1969 and at Banff School of Fine Arts, Canada, in 1971. His mentor was Yousuf Karsh, for whom he worked as a technician in Ottawa around 1950.

A senior teaching master in photography at Loyalist College, Belleville, Ontario, since 1970, Baltkalns was formerly assistant general manager of the Canadian Weekly Newspapers Association 1966–69, and general manager of A. MacLean Newspapers, Ltd. He has also been an editor, advertising manager and photographer for various weeklies and dailies.

A Fellow of RPS since 1975, Baltkalns is a member of SPE and the National Association for Photographic Art in Canada. He was a member of the board of directors of Sigma Delta Chi in Toronto 1967–69.

Baltkalns works in a "conservatively formal style with an inclination to abstract," using grain as a pictorial element. His photographs usually portray movement in classical and modern ballet and the nude figure, and he also does pictorial landscapes.

PUBLICATIONS Monographs: *Sincerely Yours II,* 1979; *Sincerely Yours,* 1975. Books: *The Nude in Classroom,* 1975, *Basic Photography,* 1974 (Loyalist Coll.: Belleville, Ontario, Canada).

COLLECTION Loyalist Coll., Belleville, Ontario, Canada.

REPRESENTATIVE Art Frame Gall., POB 1537, Belleville, Ontario, Canada K8N 5J2.

ADDRESS 103 Everett St, Belleville, Ontario, Canada K8P 3K5.

Lewis Baltz PHOTOGRAPHER · TEACHER Born September 12, 1945, in Newport Beach, California, he received a BFA from the San Francisco Art Institute in 1969 and an MFA from Claremont Graduate School in California in 1971. He has been influenced by the work of Walker Evans.

Currently self-employed as a photographer, Baltz has given numerous lectures and workshops.

He is recipient of the United States-United Kingdom Exchange Fellowship, and also received a John Simon Guggenheim Memorial Fellowship in 1976 and NEA individual fellowships in 1973 and 1976.

Baltz works in 35mm black-and-white, and is known for his photographs of the new suburban and industrial landscapes.

PUBLICATIONS Monographs: *Park City*, 1980; *Nevada*, 1978; *The New Industrial Parks Near Irvine, California*, 1975. Book: *Maryland*, Jane Livingston, 1976. Anthologies: *Exploring Photography*, Bryant Campbell, 1979 (B.B.C. Pubs., London); *The Photograph Collector's Guide*, Lee D. Witkin & Barbara London, 1979; *Contemporary American Photographic Works*, ed., 1977; *The Photographer's Choice*, Kelly Wise, ed., 1975; *Untitled*, 2:7, 2:8, 1974 (Friends of Photography); *The Art of Photography*, Time-Life Series, 1971. Catalogs: *Photographs, Sheldon Memorial Art Gallery Collections*, 1977 (Univ. of Nebraska: Lincoln); *Lewis Baltz, Photographs 1967–75*, Janet Kardon, 1975 (Philadelphia Coll. of Art); *New Topographics*, William Jenkins, Oct 1975 (IMP/GEH, Rochester). Periodicals: *Camera*, Apr 1979, Nov 1975, Nov 1971; "Lewis Baltz's Formalism," Joan Murray, *Artweek*, Aug 27, 1977; "Route 66 Revisited: New Landscape Photography," Carter Ratcliff, *Art in America*, Jan/Feb 1976.

COLLECTIONS Art Inst. of Chicago; Baltimore Mus. of Art, Md.; Columbia Coll., Chicago; Corcoran Gall. of Art, Wash., D.C.; E. B. Crocker Art Mus., Sacramento, Calif.; Dallas Art Mus.; High Mus. of Art, Atlanta, Ga.; IMP/GEH, Rochester; La Jolla Mus. of Contemp. Art, Calif.; L/C, Wash., D.C.; Lincoln First Bank & Trust, Rochester; Miami-Dade Community Coll., Coral Gables, Fla.; Milwaukee Art Ctr., Wis.; Minneapolis Art Inst., Minn.; Mus. of Fine Arts, Boston; Mus. of Fine Arts, Houston; Mus. of Fine Arts, St. Petersburg, Fla.; MOMA, NYC; Natl. Cllctn. of Fine Art, Wash., D.C.; N. Mex. State Univ., Las Cruces; Norton Simon Mus., Pasadena, Calif.; Oakland Mus., Calif.; Philadelphia Mus. of Art, Penn.; Phillips Academy, Andover, Mass.; Pomona Coll., Claremont, Calif.; Princeton Univ. Art Mus., N.J.; San Diego State Univ., Calif.; San Francisco Mus. of Modern Art; Seagram Cllctn., N.Y.; Seattle Art Mus., Wash.; Stanford Univ. Art Mus., Calif.; Univ. of Calif. Art Mus., Berkeley; Univ. of Calif. at Davis; UCLA; Univ. of Calif. at Riverside; Univ. of Kansas, Spencer Art Mus., Lawrence; Univ. of Mass., Amherst; Univ. of Nebraska, Lincoln; Univ. of Nevada, Reno; Univ. of N. Mex., Albuquerque; Wesleyan Univ., Middle-town, Conn.; Williams Coll., Williamstown, Mass. Bibliothèque Nationale, Paris; Museo Civico e Gallerie d'Arte, Udine, Italy; Natl. Gall. of Australia, Canberra.

DEALER Castelli Graphics, 4 E 77 St, New York, NY 10021.

ADDRESS POB 366, Sausalito, CA 94966.

Anthony Bannon CRITIC · CURATOR · HISTORIAN · FILM MAKER Born December 6, 1942, in Hanover, New Hampshire, Bannon earned a BA in Biology from St. Bonaventure University, New York (1964), and an MA in Criticism from the State University of New York, Buffalo.

Since 1966 he has been the photography and art critic for the *Buffalo Evening News*. He previously taught science and English at Father Baker High School, Lackawanna, New York (1964–66). Bannon belongs to SPE, the Society of Professional Journalists, the Newspaper Guild and the Society of Aesthetics.

He won the Western New York Newspaper Guild Criticism Award in 1979 and the Newspaper Guild Page One Award in 1968, 1970, 1971, 1972, 1975, 1976 and 1977. He was a Critic Fellow of the Eugene O'Neill Memorial Theater Foundation and of the American Dance Conference in 1969, and a Fellow of the American Film Seminar in 1974–75.

His 16mm films include *Braves on the Rebound*, 1977; *Arteffects*, 1976; *Artpark Movie Process*, 1975; *UB/More to Come*, 1974; *Sourcework*, 1974; *A Celebration for the Troups*, 1972; *Citizen of What Country?*, 1971. He also made the 1974 videotape *Celebration*.

PUBLICATIONS Catalogs: *Painterly Photographs: Contemporary Handworked Images*, catalog essay, n.d. (Media Study/Buffalo & Wash. Project for the Arts); *Hallwalls Group Show*, 1976 (Hallwalls Gall.: Buffalo). Periodicals: "Letter from Buffalo," Sept 1980, *American Photographer*; "From Formal to Family: Donald Blumberg," Dec 1979, "John Pfahl's Picturesque Paradoxes," Feb 1979, "The Strategies of Signs & Seeing in the Criticism of Photography," Sept 1977, *Afterimage: VSW*.

ADDRESS *Buffalo Evening News*, One New Plaza, Buffalo, NY 14240.

David Lindbergh Barbour PHOTOGRAPHER Born in Winnipeg, Manitoba, Canada, on October 29, 1952, Barbour majored in geography and earned a BA in 1973 at the University of Saskatchewan. In 1976 he obtained a diploma in photography and visual communication at the

Banff School of Fine Arts in Alberta, where he had Randy Bradley, Bob Pfeiff and Bob Alexander as instructors.

He has been successively employed as a photographer by the National Historic Sites (1973) and the University of Regina (1974–75), both in Saskatchewan, by the Winnipeg Art Gallery in Manitoba (1976–79) and, since 1979, by Sparks and Associates in Kingston, Ontario. He also worked as a darkroom technician for the Saskatchewan government in Regina (1974) and as a film production assistant at the University of Manitoba in Winnipeg (1976). He was the recipient of several awards: a Canada Council short-term grant, a Manitoba Arts Council Award and a Mt. St. Vincent University Purchase Award, all in 1978; also two Saskatchewan Art Council awards, in 1976 and 1974.

Barbour is especially interested in "documentation of people and how they respond to the urban environment and to each other."

PUBLICATIONS   Catalogs: *Five Manitoba Photographers*, intro. by David McMillan, 1979 (Winnipeg Art Gall.: Manitoba); *Sweet Immortality*, 1978 (Edmonton Art Gall.: Alberta); *Canadians*, 1978 (Mt. St. Vincent Art Gall.: Halifax, Nova Scotia); *Three Manitoba Photographers*, 1977 (Winnipeg Art Gall.: Manitoba).

COLLECTIONS   Banff School of Fine Arts, Alberta; Edmonton Art Gall., Alberta; Mt. St. Vincent Univ. Art Gall., Halifax, Nova Scotia; Nat. Film Board of Canada, Ottawa, Ontario; Saskatoon Photographers' Gall., Saskatchewan.

ADDRESS   286 Barrie St, #2, Kingston, Ontario, Canada K7L 3K9.

Anthony Barboza   *PHOTOGRAPHER · PAINTER · POET · HISTORIAN*   Born on May 10, 1944, in New Bedford, Massachusetts, Barboza started photography in 1964 by attending a Kamoinge workshop with Roy DeCarava. From 1965 to 1968 he was a U.S. Navy photographer and since then has been working on a freelance basis.

In 1974 and 1976 Barboza received photography grants from the New York State Council of the Arts.

PUBLICATIONS (selected)   Anthologies: *SX-70 Art*, 1979; *Black Photographers Annual*, vol. 2, winter 1974, vol. 1, Sept 1973. Periodicals: *Picture Magazine #13*, Jan 1980; *Camera*, spring 1980; *Creative Camera*, Oct 1979, May 1975; *Popular Photography 35mm Photography*, spring 1977; *Popular Photography's Woman Annual*, fall 1970; *U.S. Camera*, Sept 1968.

COLLECTIONS   Howard Univ., Wash., D.C.; MOMA, NYC; Orleans Public Lib., Orleans,

N.Y.; Studio Mus. of Harlem, NYC. Univ. of Ghana, Africa; Univ. of Mexico, Mexico City.

ADDRESS   108 E 16 St, New York, NY 10003.

A. C. Barker   *PHYSICIAN · PHOTOGRAPHER*   Born in England in 1819, Barker died in Christchurch, New Zealand, in 1873. He reportedly learned photography from architect B. W. Mountfort.

Barker emigrated to New Zealand in 1850 (from London) to practice medicine in Christchurch. An ardent amateur photographer most of his life, he may have been an amateur naturalist as well, since he corresponded with Sir Richard Owen and Thomas Huxley. Dr. Barker was a founding member and onetime trustee of the Canterbury Philosophical Institute.

As a photographer he created an incomparable record of the first twenty years of development of Christchurch, New Zealand. He handcrafted his photographs, from cutting the glass to preparing his own egg emulsions. He was said to have even melted down the household silver and gold for use as sensitizing and fixing agents. Lucie-Smith says: "He is assured a privileged position among pioneer New Zealand photographers, though the aesthetic merit of his images has been only grudgingly acknowledged."

PUBLICATION   Anthology: *The Invented Eye*, Edward Lucie-Smith, 1975.

COLLECTIONS   Canterbury Mus., Christchurch, New Zealand; Natl. Mus. of New Zealand, Wellington.

ARCHIVE   Canterbury Museum, Christchurch, New Zealand.

William Edward Barksdale   *PHOTOGRAPHER · TEACHER*   Born December 26, 1927, in Welch, West Virginia, Barksdale received his BA in Fine Arts from the College of William and Mary, Williamsburg, Virginia (1950), and a Certificate in Theology from Nashotah House, Wisconsin (1954). He also studied with David Vestal, 1959–61.

Barksdale has been associate professor and coordinator of photography at Mercer County Community College, New York, since 1968. From 1961 to 1968 he taught photography at Brooklyn College, Queens College and Southampton College and did freelance photography. Barksdale was an Episcopal priest from 1956 to 1960.

He has belonged to SPE since 1969 and the National Education Association since 1970.

Working in small format, Barksdale does portraits and "romantic" landscapes.

PUBLICATIONS Book: *Modern American Gardens*, James Rose, 1967. Periodicals: *Popular Photography*, review, Feb 1973; *Infinity*, Aug 1968.

COLLECTION MOMA, NYC.

ADDRESS 20 Baldwin Rd, Shelter Island, NY 11964.

Oskar Barnack *INVENTOR · MECHANIC* Born November 1, 1879, in Lynow, Brandenburg, Germany, Barnack died on January 16, 1936, in Bad Nauheim, Germany. He attended school in Berlin-Steglitz, on a street renamed Barnackufer in 1961. He then studied to be a master mechanic.

After spending his journeyman years working in Vienna, Barnack went to Jena in 1902 to join the Palmos camera works (camera assembly department) of Zeiss. He joined Ernst Leitz at Wetzlar in 1911, heading the company's experimental department.

In 1906 Barnack had conceived of a panoramic camera using standard 9 x 18cm stereo glass plates, but could not find a manufacturer. However, from 1912 to 1914 he developed a prototype of the first small commercial camera, determining the size for 35mm film as well (24 x 36mm). Production of the instrument was delayed by World War I, but by 1924 the revolutionary Leica was on the market. Barnack was also partly responsible for designing the Leitz Elmar lens.

PUBLICATIONS Books: *Quellendarstellungen zur Geschichte der Fotografie*, Wolfgang Baier, 1964; *March of Photography*, Erich Stenger, 1958; *Ernst Leitz, Optische Werke Wetzlar 1849–1949*, 1949. Anthology: *Photography's Great Inventors*, Louis W. Sipley, 1965. Periodicals: *Foto Magazin*, Dec 1964, Jan 1961 (Munich); *Camera Industries of West Germany News*, Nov 1961; *Leica Photography*, no. 3, 1961; *Photographische Correspondenz*, 1937.

George N. Barnard *PHOTOGRAPHER* [See plate 7] Barnard was born and died in the United States, 1819–1920.

He was a news photographer prior to the Civil War, in which he was a photographer for the Union Army. He also worked in daguerreotypes and photographed genre scenes.

Like other war photographers of the day, Barnard recorded the devastation of battle rather than the battles themselves. The intricacies of the collodion wet-plate process barred him from working in the presence of actual confrontation. His series on Sherman's "March to the Sea," produced in 10 x 14, is an important document of American history.

PUBLICATIONS Books: *Gardner's Photographic Sketch Book of the War*, Alexander Gardner, 2 vols., 1866, repr. 1959; *Photographic Views of Sherman's Campaign*, 1866, repr. w/preface by Beaumont Newhall, 1977. Anthologies: *The Photograph Collector's Guide*, Lee D. Witkin & Barbara London, 1979; *Pioneers of Photography*, Aaron Scharf, 1975; *Looking at Photographs*, John Szarkowski, 1973; *Great Photographers*, Time-Life Series, 1971; *History of Photography*, Beaumont Newhall, 1964.

COLLECTIONS IMP/GEH, Rochester; L/C, Wash., D.C.; Univ. of N. Mex. Art Mus., Albuquerque. Natl. Gall. of Canada, Ottawa, Ontario.

Bruce Barnbaum *PHOTOGRAPHER* Born on October 27, 1943, in Chicago, Barnbaum specialized in mathematics at the University of California, Los Angeles, where he earned a BA (1965) and an MA (1967).

He has worked as a freelance photographer since 1970. In recent years he co-founded the Owens Valley Photography Workshop, where he also serves as an instructor. Prior to his work as a photographer he was a computer programmer/math analyst for Aerospace Corporation, 1967–70. He joined the Sierra Club in 1967, served as a photography instructor on many of its educational outings for six years and received its Ansel Adams Award for Photography in 1974.

Barnbaum works primarily in black-and-white in both medium and large formats. His images are predominantly comprised of nature and landscapes, man-made objects and found objects.

PORTFOLIO *Aftermath*, intro. & poems by Ben Maddow, 1979 (Stephen White Gall.: Los Angeles).

COLLECTIONS Amon Carter Mus., Fort Worth, Tex. Polaroid Corp., Amsterdam, The Netherlands; Preus-Laboratorium, Horten, Norway.

DEALER Stephen White Gall., 835 N La Cienega Blvd, Los Angeles, CA 90069.

ADDRESS 29322 Trailway Ln, Agoura, CA 91301.

Ed Willis Barnett *PHOTOGRAPHER · WRITER* Born May 8, 1899, in Birmingham, Alabama, Barnett was schooled at the University of Alabama and the United States Naval Academy, Annapolis, Maryland. He studied photographic processing with Adolf Fassbender and Otto Litzel.

A freelance photographer since 1967, Barnett was a senior partner of the Barnett & Barnett advertising agency 1929–67.

He is a Fellow of the Photographic Society of America and an honorary member of the Austrian Company of Photographers and the French Federation of Photographic Societies. He has been an Honorary Excellence of the International Federation of Photographic Art since 1971.

Barnett has won numerous awards, including the Litzel Gold Medal, 1974; Coupe de la Ville de Périgueux, Syndicat d'Initiative, Périgueux, France, 1969; and Spirit of Detroit Medal, 1966.

Barnett's work has focused mainly on the cathedrals and châteaux of France and England, "done in full scale and as tone-line mutations." He also photographs human-interest scenes, portraits, landscapes and cityscapes, using color and black-and-white, the latter often toned by gold processes.

COLLECTIONS Birmingham Mus. of Art, Ala.; Kodak Camera Club, Rochester; Mariners Mus., Newport News, Va.; Metro. Mus. of Art, NYC; MOMA, NYC; Seattle Mus. of Art, Wash.; private cllctns.

REPRESENTATIVE Martin Hames, Altamont School, 4801 Altamont Rd., Birmingham, AL 35222.

ADDRESS 4322 Glenwood Ave., Birmingham, AL 35222.

William Barraud PHOTOGRAPHER Born in 1810, Barraud died in England some time in the late nineteenth century.

A portrait photographer, with studios in both London and Liverpool, he seems to have been most active during the 1880s and 1890s.

PUBLICATIONS Books: *Men & Women of the Day*, 2 vols., 1899 & 1888; *London Medical Profession in all Countries*, w/Jerrard, 1873 (Churchill: London); *Sporting Embellished by Large Engravings & Vignettes Illustrative of British Field Sports from Pictures Painted by . . .*, Chas. J. Apperly, 1838 (Nimrod: London). Anthologies: *The Invented Eye*, Edward Lucie-Smith, 1975; *Early Photographs and Early Photographers*, Oliver Mathews, 1973.

Thomas F. Barrow PHOTOGRAPHER · HISTORIAN Born in Kansas City, Missouri, in 1938, Barrow earned a BFA in Graphic Design from Kansas City Art Institute in 1963 and an MS in 1967 from Illinois Institute of Technology, where he studied with Aaron Siskind. He took film courses with Jack Ellis at Northwestern University in 1965.

Barrow is currently an associate professor in the Department of Art at the University of New Mexico, Albuquerque. Prior to that (1973–76) he was associate director of the University's art mu-

seum. From 1965 to 1972 he held a number of positions at the George Eastman House in Rochester—assistant curator of exhibitions, associate curator of the Research Center, assistant director (1971–72) and editor of *Image* (1972).

A member of SPE since 1973, Barrow received NEA grants in 1973 and 1978 and was appointed to the NEA International Panel for a two-year term in 1979.

PUBLICATIONS (selected) *The Valiant Knights of Daguerre . . . by Sadakichi Hartmann*, foreword, 1978; "Three Photographers and Their Books," *A Hundred Years of Photographic History: Essays in Honor of Beaumont Newhall*, 1975; *Source and Resource*, intro., 1973; *Lewis Hine Portfolio*, intro., 1971. Anthologies: *The Photograph Collector's Guide*, Lee D. Witkin & Barbara London, 1979; *The Great West: Real/Ideal*, 1977; *The Photographer's Choice*, Kelly Wise, ed., 1975; *Light and Lens*, 1973. Catalogs: *Contemporary American Photographic Works*, 1977 (Mus. of Fine Arts: Houston); *The Light Gallery Catalogue of Contemporary Photographs*, 1976 (Light Gall.: NYC); *Catalogue of One Man Exhibition*, 1969 (Univ. of Calif.: Davis). Periodicals: "Some Thoughts on the Criticism of Photography," text only, *Northlight 8*, Nov 1978; "Footnotes," w/Peter Walch, text only, *New Mexico Studies in the Fine Arts*, vol. 2, 1977; "Thomas Barrow," Henri Man Barendse, *Artspace*, summer 1977; *Creative Camera*, Sept 1969.

PORTFOLIOS *Cracker Jacks*, 1977 (Art Inst. of Chicago); *The New Mexico Portfolio* (group), 1976; *Lewis Hine Portfolio*, intro, 1971 (IMP/GEH: Rochester).

COLLECTIONS Denver Art Mus., Colo.; Detroit Inst. of Art, Mich.; Harvard Univ., Fogg Art Mus., Cambridge, Mass.; IMP/GEH, Rochester; Lincoln Rochester Trust Co.; MIT, Cambridge; Minneapolis Inst. of Arts, Minn.; Mus. of Fine Arts, Houston; MOMA, NYC; New Orleans Mus. of Art; Newport Harbor Art Mus., Newport Beach, Calif.; Norton Simon Mus. of Art, Pasadena, Calif.; Philadelphia Mus. of Fine Arts, Pa.; Princeton Univ. Lib. Graphic Arts Cllctn., Princeton, N.J.; San Francisco Mus. of Modern Art; Sun Valley Ctr. for the Arts & Humanities Cllctn., Idaho; Univ. of Kans. Art Mus., Lawrence; Univ. of Neb., Sheldon Mem. Art Gall., Lincoln; Univ. of N. Mex., Art Mus., Albuquerque; Va. Mus. of Fine Arts, Richmond. Natl. Gall. of Australia, Canberra; Natl. Gall. of Canada, Ottawa, Ontario.

ADDRESS 624 Cedar NE, Albuquerque, NM 87106.

Miles Barth CURATOR Born in Chicago, Illinois, Barth received a BFA in Photography and the History of Photography jointly from the School of the Art Institute of Chicago and the University of Chicago. Hugh Edwards is his mentor.

Since 1979 he has been the curator of Archives and Collections at the International Center of Photography in New York City. Prior to that he was assistant curator of the Photography Department at the Art Institute of Chicago, 1971–77.

Barth received a Daniel D. Van de Grift Scholarship in 1971.

PUBLICATIONS Catalog: *Combattimento per un Immagine*, text only, 1973 (Galleria Civica d'Arte Moderna: Torino, Italy). Periodical: "Notes on Conservation and Restoration of Photographs," *The Print Collector's Newsletter*, text only, May/June 1976.

ADDRESS ICP, 1130 Fifth Ave, New York, NY 10028.

Frances Barthram
See Frances Evelegh

Jacques Z. Baruch ART DEALER · GALLERY OWNER · COLLECTOR · LECTURER Born on January 6, 1922, in Warsaw, Poland, Baruch received his education in his native city, completing a degree in fine arts at the Academy of Fine Arts and studying Architecture at the Polytechnica. He considers Le Corbusier his mentor.

Since 1967 he has been partner and co-director of the Jacques Baruch Gallery in Chicago. He is a member of the Print and Drawing Club of the Art Institute in Chicago and joined the Chicago Art Dealers Association in 1967 and the Association of International Photography Art Dealers in 1979. He was responsible for assembling the show "Contemporary Czechoslovakian Printmakers," by the Smithsonian Institution Traveling Exhibition Service (1979–81).

Baruch is a collector of outstanding prints, drawings, photographs and tapestries. As a dealer he specializes in Eastern European award-winning graphics, internationally renowned tapestry and fiber artworks from Europe and the United States, photography, paintings and Art Nouveau pieces.

PUBLICATIONS Catalogs (produced by Jacques Baruch Gallery): *The World of Jan Saudek, Photographs*, 1979; *Jiri Balcar*, 1979; *Albin Brunovsky-Vladimir Gazovic*, 1978; *Compositions in Fiber: Francoise Grossen-Jolanta Owidzka*, 1977. Periodicals: "Jacques Baruch," Barbara Varro, *Chicago Sun Times* "Chicago Style," Nov 26, 1978; "Separate but Equal," Candida Finkel, *The New Art Examiner*, 1978; "For Jacques & Anne Baruch, Home Is Where Art Is," Nory Miller, *Chicago Daily* "News-Panorama," 1974.

ADDRESS Jacques Baruch Gall., 900 N Michigan Ave, Suite 605, Chicago, Il 60611.

Ruth-Marion Baruch PHOTOGRAPHER · WRITER Born in Berlin, Germany, in 1922, Baruch received a BA in Creative Writing and Literary Criticism and a Bachelor of Journalism from the University of Missouri in Columbia in 1944. She earned an MFA in Photography from the School of Fine Arts, Ohio University, Athens, in 1946, and studied at the California School of Fine Arts in San Francisco under Ansel Adams, Minor White and Homer Page (1946–47).

Baruch is a self-employed photographer and writer, making "statements on the human condition . . . in a straightforward manner." She worked in 2¼ and 4 x 5 formats in the 1940s and 1950s and since 1961 has worked in 35mm.

PUBLICATIONS Books: *The Face of California*, 1970; *The Vanguard: A Photographic Essay on the Black Panthers*, w/Pirkle Jones, 1970; *Photography in the Twentieth Century*, Nathan Lyons, 1967. Anthology: *Photography Year Book*, 1958 (London). Catalogs: *Photography U.S.A.*, 1968 (De Cordova Mus.: Lincoln, Mass.); *Photography at Mid-Century*, 1959; *Family of Man*, Edward Steichen, ed., 1955 (MOMA: NYC). Periodicals: *British Journal of Photography*, June 1980; *Darkroom Photography*, Dec 1979; *American Photographer*, Aug 1978; *Artforum*, May 1964; *Photography*, June 1957; *U.S. Camera*, Aug 1954, July 1949.

COLLECTIONS CCP, Ansel Adams Cllctn., Tucson; IMP/GEH, Rochester; Oakland Mus. of Art, Calif.; Polaroid Corp., Cambridge, Mass.; San Francisco Mus. of Modern Art.

ADDRESS 663 Lovell Ave, Mill Valley, CA 94941.

Frédéric Barzilay PHOTOGRAPHER Barzilay was born April 16, 1917, in Salonique, Greece. His major influence was Harry Meerson.

Barzilay left Greece and moved to France in 1930 where he still resides. From 1952 to 1977 he was an international civil servant for UNESCO.

He has been a member of the Club des 30 x 40 since 1965 and of the Société Française de Photographie from 1960 to 1965.

Barzilay says of his work: "I have specialized since 1964 in the nude, with a tendency, for the past three or four years, to the abstraction of the forms, the lines being reduced to essential signs, almost ideograms. Part of my work is printed on aluminum and canvas."

PUBLICATIONS Books: *Tendres Parcours,* 1979; *Les Corps Illuminés,* André Pieyre de Mandiarques, 1965. Periodicals: *Photographe,* Oct/Nov 1966; *Planète,* Apr 1963; *Photography Year Book,* 1961.

COLLECTION Bibliothèque Nationale, Paris.

ADDRESS 8 rue Poliveau, 75005 Paris, France.

Gabriele Basilico PHOTOGRAPHER Born August 12, 1944, in Milan, Italy, Basilico earned a degree in architecture (1973) from Milan Polytechnic.

A freelance photographer since 1975, he has belonged to AFIP (Association of Italian Professional Photographers) since 1977.

Basilico made the film *Milano, Proletariato Giovanile* in 1976 for the Venice Biennale.

PUBLICATIONS Periodicals: *Zoom,* Aug 1980 (Germany); *Creative Camera,* Dec 1979; *Progresso Fotografico,* Feb 1979; *Fotografia Italiana,* no. 233, 1978, nos. 232 & 222, 1977.

COLLECTIONS Bibliothèque Nationale, Paris; Università di Parma, Archivio della Comunicazione.

ADDRESS Piazza Tricolore 4, Milan, Italy.

Claude Batho PHOTOGRAPHER Born June 1, 1935, in Chamalières in the Auvergne, France, Batho attended the Ecole des Beaux Arts de Paris 1955–57 and received a diploma in applied arts in 1956.

A professional photographer with the Archives Nationales since 1957, she became overseer in 1973. Batho was also awarded the Chevalier des Arts et Lettres.

PUBLICATION Book: *Le Moment des Choses,* T. Schavelzan, 1977 (Editions des Femmes: France).

PORTFOLIO *Portraits d'enfants,* Jean Claude Lemagny, 1975.

COLLECTIONS Bibliothèque Nationale, Paris; Musée d'Angoulême; Musée Nicéphore Niepce, Chalon-sur-Saône.

DEALER Galerie Agathe Gaillard, 3 rue du Pont Louis Philippe, 75003 Paris, France.

ADDRESS 5 rue des Minimes, 75003 Paris, France.

Carlo Bavagnoli PHOTOGRAPHER · FILM MAKER Born in Piacenza, Italy, on May 5, 1932, Bavagnoli studied humanities and art at Milan University. Since 1971 he has been working as an independent film maker for Italian and French television. Previously he worked as a freelance (1958–63), then as a staff photographer (1964–70) for *Life* magazine.

In 1978 he won the Prix Italia for his documentary *Estro Harmonico,* made for French television, and in 1969 he received first prize at the Venice Film Festival for his documentary *Vivaldi's Venice.*

He is mainly interested in landscapes and humanistic essays.

PUBLICATIONS Books: *Il Romanico e le Valli Piacentine,* 1978 (Pedrini Pub.); *Verdi e la sua Terra,* 1976 (Silva Pub.); *Cara Parma* 1962 (Pizzi Pub.); *Gente di Trastevere,* 1961 (Mondadori Pub.).

COLLECTIONS Bibliothèque Nationale, Paris; Biblioteca Giuseppe Verdi, Busseto, Italy.

ADDRESS 34 rue de Penthièvre, 75008 Paris, France.

Hippolyte Bayard PHOTOGRAPHER · INVENTOR [See plate 4] Born in Breteuil-sur-Noye, France, Bayard lived from 1801 to 1887. The Fox Talbot discoveries formed the basis for his work in photography, and Daguerre's invention inspired him to devise his own methods.

Bayard was a civil servant, a clerk with the Ministry of Finance. In the 1850s he was commissioned by the Comité des Monuments Historiques to record monuments in Normandy.

The photographer was a founding member of the Société Héliographique in 1851 and of the Société Française de Photographie in 1854.

During the winter and spring months of 1839 Bayard produced positive images in the camera on silver iodide paper. This invention was independent of and prior to Daguerre's experiments and was completely different from those of Talbot and Daguerre. Bayard also held the first known photographic exhibition (thirty of his photographs) on June 24, 1839.

In addition to producing the first positive paper prints in the camera, Bayard worked with calotypes, daguerreotypes, albumen-on-glass negatives, collodion wet-plate negatives and albumen prints. His subjects included cityscapes, landscapes and self-portraits.

PUBLICATIONS Book: *Hippolyte Bayard: Ein verkannter Erfinder und Meister der Photographie,* André Jammes, 1975. Catalogs: *Hippolyte Bayard, ein Erfinder der Photographie,* O. Steinert & P. Armant, 1960; *Bayard,* Lo Duca, 1943; *Histoire de la Découverte de la Photographie,* Georges Potonniée, 1925 (Paris), American ed. 1936. Anthology: *The Magic Image,* Cecil Beaton & Gail Buckland, 1975.

COLLECTIONS Art Inst. of Chicago; IMP/GEH,

Rochester. Société Française de Photographie, Paris.

ARCHIVE Société Française de Photographie, Paris.

Herbert Bayer *PHOTOGRAPHER · PAINTER · DE-SIGNER · ARCHITECT* [See plate 65] Born on April 5, 1900, in Haag, Austria, Bayer served his apprenticeship in architecture in 1919 with G. Schmidthammer in Linz (Austria). In Germany he studied in Darmstadt with Emanuel Margold (1920) and in Weimar at the Bauhaus (1921–23); he also studied mural painting with Vassily Kandinsky (1921).

Since 1965 Bayer has been employed as a consultant in architecture, art and design by Atlantic Richfield Company. Previously he was chairman of the Department of Design of the Container Corporation of America (1956–65) and consultant at the Aspen Institute of Humanistic Studies (1949). When he lived in Germany he was a master at the Bauhaus in Dessau, teaching typography (1925–28), and an art director at the Dorland Studio in Berlin (1928–38) and at *Vogue* in the same city (1929–30).

Bayer is a member of the American Institute of Architects, American Abstract Artists, the Aspen Institute of Humanistic Studies, the American Academy of Arts and Sciences and the Alliance Graphique Internationale.

In 1979 he received an honorary doctorate of fine arts from the Art Center College of Design in Pasadena, California, and in 1978 he was given the Austrian Honor Cross for Art and Science. He was appointed Honorary Fellow of the Hochschule für Kunstlerische und Industrielle Gestalung of Linz, Austria (1978) and of the Royal Academy of Fine Art in The Hague (1975), and was also selected as a member of the Art Director's Club Hall of Fame. He has been the recipient of several awards: the Adalbert Stifter Preis für Bildende Kunste, in Austria (1971), the Kulturpreis for photography in Cologne (1969) and the Ambassador's Award for Excellence, London (1968).

Bayer participated in the film *Bayer, the Man and His Work*, produced in 1975 by Atlantic Richfield Corporation. He also designed the "Beyond the Wall" mural and park at the Philadelphia College of Art (1977), the "Organ Fountain" in Linz (1977), the "Double Ascension" sculpture at the Arco Plaza in Los Angeles (1973), and the "Articulated Wall," a highway sculpture for the 1968 Olympics.

Bayer's specialty in photography is surreal photomontages. He was greatly influenced by the Bauhaus.

PUBLICATIONS Monographs: *Herbert Bayer, Painter/Designer/Architect*, 1967; *The Way Beyond Art*, Alexander Dorner, 1947. Books: *Book of Drawings*, 1961; *Bauhaus 1919–1928*, w/Ise & Walter Gropius, 1938. Anthology: *The Magic Image*, Cecil Beaton & Gail Buckland, 1975.

PORTFOLIOS *10 Fotoplastiken*, 1937 (self-published); *11 Photomontages*, 1932 (self-pub.).

COLLECTIONS Busch-Reisinger Mus., Cambridge, Mass.; Denver Mus. of Art, Colo.; Guggenheim Mus., NYC; Harvard Univ., Fogg Art Mus., Cambridge, Mass.; MOMA, NYC. Bauhaus-Archiv., Berlin; Bayerische Staatsgemäldesammlungen, Munich; Kunsthalle Mannheim, Germany; Mus. Essen, Germany; Mus. of Modern Art, Rome; National Galerie, Berlin; Neue Galerie, Linz, Austria; Staatsgalerie, Stuttgart, Germany.

DEALERS Marlborough Gall., NYC; Galerie Klihm, Munich, West Germany.

ADDRESS 184 Middle Rd, Montecito, CA 93108.

Jonathan Levy Bayer *PHOTOGRAPHER* Born March 28, 1936, in New York City, Bayer is the son of the collector Julien Levy; his stepfather is Herbert Bayer. He received an AB from Harvard University in Cambridge, Massachusetts, in 1958 and an MA from the University of Pennsylvania in Philadelphia in 1963.

Since 1971 he has been a freelance photographer. Previously he worked for the European Community Information Service (1967–71).

Bayer has been a member of the Greater London Arts Association (Visual Arts Panel) since 1977, and was a recipient of an award from the Arts Council of Great Britain in that same year.

PUBLICATIONS Book: *5*, 1974 (London). Anthology: *Reading Photographs*, 1978.

COLLECTIONS In London: Arts Council of Great Britain; Victoria & Albert Mus.

DEALERS Ian Birksted, 17 Flask Walk, London NW3, England; Parsons-Dreyfuss Gall., 24 W 57 St, New York, NY 10019.

ADDRESS Flat 1, 13 Leamington Rd Villas, London W11 1HS, England.

David Bayles *PHOTOGRAPHER* Born in Denver, Colorado, on June 13, 1948, Bayles obtained a BA from the University of Colorado in 1969 and an MA from the University of Oregon in 1973.

He has been working as a freelance photographer since 1973 and specializes in black-and-white photo-collage.

PUBLICATIONS Anthology: *Polaroid Manual*,

Ansel Adams, 1979. Periodical: *Camera*, Oct 1977, Sept 1975, Apr 1974.

COLLECTIONS   American Tel. & Tel. Boston; Chase Manhattan Bank, NYC; Oregon Arts Commission; Prestonwood Natl. Bank, Dallas; Rainier Natl. Bank, Seattle, Wash.

DEALER   Susan Spiritus, 3336 Via Lido, Newport Beach, CA 92660.

ADDRESS   85060 Spencer Hollow, Eugene, OR 97405.

Charles Bayliss   PHOTOGRAPHER   Born 1850 in Suffolk, England, Bayliss died in Australia in 1897. He was taken under the wing of Beaufoy Merlin while still a youngster and served as Merlin's assistant until his mentor's death in 1873.

Bayliss was brought to Australia in 1854 by his parents. Once apprenticed to Merlin, he traveled widely throughout Victoria and New South Wales. After Merlin's death, he continued to work under the patronage of Bernard Otto Holtermann, whose vision of ultralarge-format photography was executed by Bayliss in the following manner. From the tower of Holtermann's mansion in Sydney, Bayliss wielded an enormous camera, one that handled wet-plate glass sheets measuring over 3 x 5 feet, making panoramic views of the surrounding land that, when joined in a series, measured thirty-three feet.

With his mentor, Merlin, Bayliss created "superb photographic work" of the Tambaroora district of New South Wales. "His magnificent panoramas of Sydney, Melbourne, Ballarat and his views of many other town and country locations show that Bayliss had great confidence, technical ability and imagination. During the 1880s he photographed many major social and political events and was probably one of the pioneer process-engravers in Sydney," according to Andrew Hooper of the Royal Melbourne Institute of Technology.

PUBLICATIONS   Books: *Gold and Silver; an album of Hill End and Gulgong photographs from the Holtermann Collection*, Keast Burke, 1973 (Heinemann: Melbourne); *The Story of the Camera in Australia*, Jack Cato, 1955 (Georgian House: Australia).

COLLECTIONS   Mitchell Lib., Holtermann Cllctn., Sydney, Australia; Royal Melbourne Inst. of Tech., Australia.

ARCHIVE   Holtermann Collection, Mitchell Library, Sydney, Australia.

Douglas Carl Baz   PHOTOGRAPHER · TEACHER   Born on October 17, 1943, in Bayshore, New York, Baz received an MS from the Institute of

Design, Illinois Institute of Technology, where he studied with Aaron Siskind and Arthur Siegel. Since 1975 he has been Chairman of the Photography Dept., Bard College, Annandale, New York. In 1975–76 he worked as a contract photographer for Seagram's Bicentennial Project. Prior to that he was assistant professor of photography at Florida State University, Tallahassee, 1974, and from 1971 to 1974 Baz taught at Columbia College in Chicago.

A member of the SPE, the artist received a grant from NEA in 1980 and from New York State CAPS in 1979.

His major work has been in 4 x 5 format, silver prints, concentrating on landscapes and architectural images. Currently he is working in color in a 2¼ x 3¼ format and focusing on plant and animal forms.

PUBLICATIONS   Anthologies: *The New Vision*, 1980; *Courthouse*, Richard Pare, ed., 1978.

COLLECTIONS   L/C, Wash., D.C.; Mus. of Fine Arts, Boston.

DEALER   Visual Studies Workshop Gall., 31 Prince St, Rochester, NY 14607.

ADDRESS   Photography Dept, Bard College, Annandale-on-Hudson, NY 12504.

Jessie Tarbox Beals   PHOTOGRAPHER   Born December 23, 1870, in Hamilton, Ontario, Canada, Beals died May 30, 1942, in New York City. She received a Third Class Certificate of Qualification to teach at age seventeen. Her father, John Nathaniel Tarbox, was an inventor and sewing machine magnate.

Beals first taught in a one-room schoolhouse near Williamsburg, Massachusetts, and received her first camera as a subscription prize from *Youth's Companion*. She opened a neighborhood studio during summer vacations and worked as an itinerant photographer. In 1893 she moved to Greenfield, Massachusetts, to take another teaching job, but by 1900 she and her husband, Alfred T. Beals, had decided to become full-time itinerant photographers. Their first stop was a county fair at Brattleboro, Vermont, and from there they went to Buffalo, New York, where Jessie was hired by *The Buffalo Inquirer and Courier* (1902). In 1904 she was chosen to be the official photographer of the Louisiana Purchase Exposition in St. Louis, Missouri. Then she returned to New York about 1906, where she freelanced and established her own studio. About 1926 she ventured to Chicago and then to Southern California, where she photographed many of Hollywood's elite before returning to her beloved New York. Beals' work was widely published in such periodicals as the *New York American and Journal, New York Herald, Vogue, Harper's Bazaar, Town & Country* and *Better Homes and Gardens.*

She was probably the first woman press photographer, and her work ranged widely from portraiture to documentaries of New York's slum children (especially in 1910–12) to architecture, landscapes and gardens. Of her moody night images, Alexander Alland, Sr., wrote, "Her pictures of the Brooklyn Bridge under moonlight, Washington Square blanketed with a thick snowfall at dawn, and the towering spires of the city seen through winter mists became classics of the time."

PUBLICATIONS Monograph: *Jessie Tarbox Beals: First Woman News Photographer*, Alexander Alland, Sr., 1978. Catalog: *Women of Photography*, Margery Mann, 1975 (San Francisco Mus. of Art). Periodicals: "Jessie Tarbox Beals," Alexander Alland, Sr., *American Photographer*, Aug 1978; *The New York Sunday Times*, weekly, 1942; interview by Ralph Steiner, *PM*, Apr 1941; *The American Art News*, 17 consecutive issues beg. Dec 16, 1905.

COLLECTION Community Svc. Soc., NYC.

Michael James Beard PHOTOGRAPHER · TEACHER · PUBLISHER Born September 27, 1947, in Long Beach, California, Beard earned a BS in Chemistry in 1972 and an MFA in 1974. Wynn Bullock and Les Krims were his major influences.

Currently an art instructor at Stanford University, Palo Alto (since 1978), Beard is also editor/publisher of the fine art photography quarterly *Latent Image*. He taught art at Foothill College in Los Altos, California, from 1974 to 1978 and was assistant professor of photography at San Jose State University, California, 1972–74.

PUBLICATIONS Book: *Duet*, w/Jeff Shyshka, 1977. Periodicals: *Latent Image*, 1:2 & 3, 1979, 1:1, 1978.

ADDRESS POB 1695, Palo Alto, CA 94302.

Peter Hill Beard AUTHOR · PHOTOGRAPHER Born January 22, 1938, Beard graduated with a BA degree in 1961 from Yale University in New Haven, Connecticut.

Currently he is self-employed as a photographer.

He works predominantly in color and his subject matter is often dead and decaying animals of Africa. The photographer characterizes his work as "The documentation of the destruction of nature, and its replacement by human nature."

PUBLICATIONS Books: *The End of the Game*, 1977; *Longing for Darkness*, 1975; *Eyelids of Morning*, 1974; *The End of the Game*, 1963.

COLLECTIONS Blum & Helman Gall., NYC; ICP, NYC. Arles Photo Museum, Arles, France; Seibu Museum, Tokyo.

DEALER Blum & Helman Gall., 13 E 75 St, New York, NY 10021.

REPRESENTATIVES Peter Schub, 37 Beekman Pl, New York, NY 10022; Larry Goldman's Photo Artists, 157 E 57 St, New York, NY 10022.

ADDRESS POB 603 Montauk, Long Island, NY 11954.

Felice A. Beato PHOTOGRAPHER [See plates 12 and 15] Born in Venice, Italy (date unknown), Beato died in 1903. A naturalized British citizen, his work followed in the footsteps of war photographer Roger Fenton. He was partner to James Robertson from 1852 to 1865.

Under the rubric of Robertson Beato and Company, he and his partner were active photographers in the Middle and Far East, documenting such wartime efforts as the Crimean War and the Indian Mutiny. On his own, Beato photographed the Siege of Lucknow and the Opium War.

Initially using calotypes, and later the wet-collodion process, Beato was noted for his travel views of the Middle East as well as his war documentation. In later years he created panoramic landscapes of Japan and portraits and genre scenes of Japanese life.

PUBLICATIONS Books: *En Egypte au temps de Flaubert*, Marie-Thérèse & André Jammes, ca. 1976 (Kodak-Pathé: Paris); *Photographic Views and Costumes of Japan*, 1868 (Yokohama); *Indian Mutiny*, 1857–58; *Scenes of the Mutiny*, 1857. Catalog: *19th Century Photographs from the Collection*, preface by Van Deren Coke, 1976 (Univ. of Santa Fe Art Mus.: N. Mex.). Anthology: *The Invented Eye*, Edward Lucie-Smith, 1975. Periodical: "Robertson Beato & Co.: Camera Vision at Lucknow, 1857–58," Walter Chappell, *Image* 7, Feb 1958.

COLLECTIONS IMP/GEH, Rochester; MOMA, NYC; Univ. of N. Mex. Art Mus., Albuquerque. In London: Imperial War Mus.; Indian Record Office; Natl. Army Mus; Victoria & Albert Mus.

Cecil (Walter Hardy) Beaton PHOTOGRAPHER · DESIGNER · AUTHOR Born in London, England, on January 14, 1904, Sir Cecil Beaton died in that city on January 18, 1980. He was educated at Harrow and St. John's College, Cambridge, England, but never completed a degree. The self-taught photographer took up the medium as a hobby while at college. He was especially influenced in his youth by *cartes de visite* of society women.

Beaton was a staff photographer for *Vanity Fair* in the 1920s and for *Vogue* for several years, starting in 1930. He also freelanced for several other Condé Nast publications and later for *Harper's Bazaar*, as well as doing several covers for *Life*. He served in the British Ministry of Information as a photographer during World War II.

Sir Cecil designed sets and costumes for numerous ballets and theatrical productions, such as: *Follow the Sun* (1935, London stage), *Lady Windermere's Fan, Quadrille, The Grass Harp* (Broadway), *The School for Scandal* (Comédie Française in Paris), *Coco* (Broadway, 1971), *My Fair Lady* (1956), *The Second Mrs. Tanqueray, The Chalk Garden* and *Love's Labour's Lost*. He was scenic and costume designer for such ballets in London and New York as *Apparitions, Illuminations, Marguerite et Armand, Swan Lake, Picnic at Tintagel*; for Metropolitan Opera Company productions of *Vanessa, Turandot* and *La Traviata*; and for Hollywood films *Gigi* (1958), *The Doctor's Dilemma* (1958) and *My Fair Lady* (1964).

Beaton was knighted in 1972. He won Academy Awards for his costumes and design of *My Fair Lady* in 1965 (two awards) and *Gigi* in 1959.

Aside from his skills in theatrical design, Beaton also designed hotel lobbies and clubs, such as Raffles, a private club in New York's Sherry-Netherland Hotel.

One of the major fashion photographers of the 1930s, he became known in later years for his theatrical portraits of ballet and film stars as well as other notables. For years he was the favorite photographer of England's royal family. Beaton used both black-and-white and color, working in all formats. Though he always leaned toward the decorative, after his efforts as a wartime correspondent his photographs became less flamboyant.

PUBLICATIONS Monographs: *The Best of Beaton*, intro. by Truman Capote, 1968; *Beaton Portraits*, 1968; *Cecil Beaton's New York*, 1938, rev. ed., *Portrait of New York*, 1948; *Cecil Beaton's Scrapbook*, 1937. Books: *Cecil Beaton: Stage and Film Designs*, Charles Spencer, 1976; *Cecil Beaton's "Fair Lady"*, 1964; *Royal Portraits*, intro. by Peter Quennell, 1963; *Images*, preface by Edith Sitwell, intro. by Christopher Isherwood, 1963; *Japanese*, 1959; *The Face of the World*, 1957 (Weidenfeld & Nicolson: London); *It Gives Me Great Pleasure*, 1955, U.S. ed., *I Take Great Pleasure*, 1956; *Glass of Fashion* (no photos),

1954; *Persona Grata*, w/Kenneth Tynan, 1953; *Ballet*, 1951 (Wingate: London); *Photobiography*, 1951 (Odhams: London); *Ashcombe: The Story of a Fifteen-Year Lease*, 1949, *An Indian Album*, 1946, *Chinese Album*, 1946 (Batsford: London); *Face to Face with China*, Harold B. Rattenbury, 1945 (Harrap: London); *India*, 1945 (Thacker: Bombay); *Far East*, 1945, *Near East*, 1943 (Batsford: London); *Winged Squadrons*, 1942 (Hutchinson: London); *History Under Fire*, James Pope-Hennessy, 1941, *Time Exposure*, Peter Quennell, 1941 (Batsford: London); *Air of Glory*, 1941 (HMSO: London); *The Book of Beauty*, 1930. Anthologies: *The Photograph Collector's Guide*, Lee D. Witkin & Barbara London, 1979; *The Magic Image*, ed. w/Gail Buckland, 1975; *The Studio*, Time-Life Series, 1971; *Art and Technique of Color Photography*, Alexander Liberman, ed., 1951; *British Photographers*, 1944 (Collins: London). Diaries: *Self Portrait With Friends: The Selected Diaries of Cecil Beaton—1922–1974*, Richard Buckle, ed., 1979; *Cecil Beaton: Memoirs of the 40s*, 1972; *The Strenuous Years: 1948–55*, 1973, *The Happy Years: 1944–48*, 1972, *The Years Between: 1939–44*, 1965, *The Wandering Years: 1922–1939*, 1961 (Weidenfeld & Nicolson: London). Fiction: *My Bolivian Aunt*, 1971; *Quail in Aspic*, 1962; *The Gainsborough Girls*, play, produced in 1951; *"My Royal Past,"* by Baroness von Bulop, née Princess Theodora Louise Alexina Ludmilla Sophie von Eckermann-Waldstein, as told to Cecil Beaton, 1939.

COLLECTIONS New Orleans Art Mus.; Time-Life Cllctns., NYC. Imperial War Mus., London (approx. 40,000 World War II images); Natl. Portrait Gall., London.

Bernd Becher PHOTOGRAPHER Born in 1931 in Westphalia, Germany, Becher studied at the Staatliche Kunstakademie in Stuttgart (1953), and at the Staatliche Kunstakademie in Düsseldorf (1957), where he studied topography. His wife and collaborator is photographer Hilla Becher. They began their collaboration in 1959 and were married in 1961.

PUBLICATIONS Books (w/Hilla Becher): *Framework Houses of the Siegen Industrial Region*, 1977 (Schirmer Mosel: Munich); *Die Architektur der Förder- und Wassertürme*, 1971 (Prestel: Munich); *Anonyme Skulpturen*, 1970. Anthologies: *The Photograph Collector's Guide*, Lee D. Witkin & Barbara London, 1979; *The Magic Image*, Cecil Beaton & Gail Buckland, 1975; *Art History of Photography*, Volker Kahmen, 1974. Catalogs: *Deutsche Fotografie nach 1945*, Petra Benteler, 1979 (Fotoforum: Kassel,

Germany); *Kunst als Photographie, 1949–79,* 1979 (Innsbrucker Allerheiligenpresse: Austria); *(photo) (photo)[2] . . . (photo)[n]: Sequenced Photographs,* David Bourdon, 1975 (Univ. of Md. Art Gall.: College Park). Periodicals: "Unconscious Formalism: A Response to Andre's Notes on the Bechers," Joseph Masheck, Mar 1973, "A Note on Bernd and Hilla Becher," Dec 1972, *Artforum;* "Two Books of Ultra-Topography," Robert A. Sobieszek, *Image 14,* Sept 1971; *Kunst-Zeitung,* Jan 1969.

COLLECTIONS   MOMA, NYC; Oberlin Coll., Oberlin, Ohio. Wallraf-Richartz Mus., Cologne, Germany.

ADDRESS   Am Mühlenkamp 16, 4000 Düsseldorf-Wittlaer, West Germany.

Hilla Becher   *PHOTOGRAPHER*   Born in Potsdam, Germany, in 1934, Becher trained as a photographer at Düsseldorf Staatliche Kunstakademie (1957–61). Her husband and collaborator is photographer Bernd Becher.

See Bernd Becher

Tom Beck   *PHOTOGRAPHER · CURATOR · TEACHER*   Born April 25, 1947, in Baltimore, Maryland, Beck received a BA in 1969 and an MFA in 1972 from the University of Maryland, College Park, and another MFA in 1975 from Maryland Institute College of Art, Baltimore. He names Jacob Kainen and Jaromir Stephany as mentors.

In 1979 Beck became director of the Equitable Trust Company Photographic Survey of Maryland. Since 1974 he has been curator of the Edward L. Bafford Photography Collection, University of Maryland, Baltimore County, and he has lectured on photography at the Corcoran School of Art, Washington, D.C., since 1975.

A member of SPE, CAA, Washington Picture Group and Smithsonian Associates, Beck won NEA project grants in 1974 and 1977.

His most recent major body of work, entitled "Stanzas Made in Transit," consists of partially solarized images "which are a poem about riding a bus."

PUBLICATIONS   Books: *George M. Bretz: Photographer in the Mines,* 1977; *Extended Realism,* ed., 1976. Catalogs: *Roland Freeman, a Baltimore Portfolio 1968–1979,* 1979; *Lotte Jacobi Portraits and Photogenics,* 1978.

COLLECTION   Univ. of Md., Edward L. Bafford Photography Cllctn., College Park.

ADDRESS   1830 East-West Hwy, Silver Spring, MD 20910.

Howard S. Becker   *SOCIOLOGIST · PHOTOGRAPHER*   Born in Chicago on April 18, 1928, Becker obtained a doctorate in sociology from the University of Chicago in 1951. In 1970 he studied photography at the San Francisco Art Institute, where Phillip Perkiss and Saul Warkov were his principal teachers. He has been professor of sociology at Northwestern University since 1965. Previously he was employed as a researcher and an instructor at Stanford University (1962–65), the University of Illinois (1953–55) and the University of Chicago (1951–53).

In 1964 Becker was president of the Society for the Study of Social Problems, and, in 1978, of the Society for the Study of Symbolic Interaction. A Guggenheim fellowship was granted to him in 1978, and during the year 1969–70 he was a Fellow at the Center for Advanced Study in the Behavioral Sciences.

As a photographer, he specializes in social documentation and has written several articles on "methods of creating documentary projects."

PUBLICATIONS   Books: *Art Worlds,* 1980; *A Sociological Work,* 1970; *Outsiders,* 1963; *Boys in White,* w/Geer, Hughes & Strauss, 1961.

ADDRESS   Dept of Sociology, Northwestern Univ, Evanston, IL 60201.

(Alexandre) Edmond Becquerel   *PHYSICIST*   Born in Paris in 1820, Becquerel died in 1891. His father, Antoine César Becquerel, was a well-known physicist.

Young Edmond pursued a science career in the fields of electricity, magnetism, optics, meteorology and photography. He became interested in studying the photogalvanic effect in 1839, and in 1840 added to the 1839 discoveries about potassium bichromate made by Mungo Ponton. Becquerel experimented in color photography from 1847 to 1855, successfully obtaining the colors of the spectrum on a sensitized silver plate. His paper, "La Production des Couleurs sous l'action de la Lumière," read December 18, 1857, marks the beginning of color photography. The physicist was a founding member of La Société Héliographique in Paris in 1851, and in 1853 he became a professor at the Conservatoire des Arts et Métiers in Paris.

The "Becquerel effect" is the name given to his discovery that a second uniform exposure of colored light could strengthen the image on chloride print-out papers and also be used to create a print-out image in a silver gelatine bromide emulsion. His other optical researches included studies of irradiation, phosphorescence, construction of the solar spectrum, and the chemical action of light.

Becquerel

PUBLICATIONS Books: *Quellendarstellungen zur Geschichte der Fotografie*, Wolfgang Baier, 1964; *Encyclopedia voor Fotografie en Cinematografie*, Elsevier, 1958; *History of Photography*, Helmut & Alison Gernsheim, 1955; *Histoire de la Photographie*, Raymond Lécuyer, 1945; *La Lumière, Ses Causes et Ses Effets*, 2 vols., 1868, 1867. Anthology: *Photography's Great Inventors*, Louis W. Sipley, 1965. Periodicals: *Le Photographe*, 1963; *Photographic Times*, 1897; *Photographische Correspondenz*, 1891; *Photographic News Almanac*, 1890; *Year Book of Photography*, 1890; *Humphrey's Journal of Photography*, 1859.

Francis Bedford PHOTOGRAPHER · LITHOGRAPHER [See plate 8] Bedford, who lived in England from 1816 to 1894, was a co-founder of the Royal Photographic Society of Great Britain (1853). Upon the request of Queen Victoria, the photographer chaperoned the Prince of Wales (Edward VIII) on a tour of the Middle East in 1862 or 1863.

Bedford's photographic activities—chiefly architectural views and landscapes—were concentrated in Great Britain and the Middle East. Noted for the pastoral feeling of serenity in his work, he used both collodion wet- and dry-plate negatives and albumen prints in various sizes. He also produced many stereographs.

PUBLICATIONS Monographs: *Photographic Views of Chester*, 1865; *Photographic Views of Tintern Abbey and Chepstow*, 1865; *Tour in the East: Photographic Pictures Made by Mr. Frances Bedford [while accompanying] His Royal Highness, The Prince of Wales*, 1862 (Day: London); *Pictorial Illustrations of Torquay and Its Neighborhood*, ca. 1860 (Catherall & Pritchard: Chester, England). Books: *Cassell's Cyclopedia of Photography*, Bernard E. Jones, ed., 1911, repr. 1973; *The Holy Land, Egypt, Constantinople, Athens, etc.*, W. M. Thompson, 1866 (Day: London); *The Stones of Palestine*, Mrs. Mentor Mott, 1865; *The Wye: Its Ruined Abbeys and Castles*, 1863; *Ruined Abbeys and Castles of Great Britain*, Wm. & Mary Howitt, 1862 (Bennett: London); *The Sunbeam*, Philip Delamotte, ed., 1857 (London). Anthologies: *The Photograph Collector's Guide*, Lee D. Witkin & Barbara London, 1979; *The Invented Eye*, Edw. Lucie-Smith, 1975; *Early Photographs & Early Photographers*, Oliver Mathews, 1973.

COLLECTIONS Calif. Mus. of Photog., Riverside, Calif.; Kodak Mus., Rochester; Witkin Gall., NYC.

Daniel Manders Beere SURVEYOR · ENGINEER · PHOTOGRAPHER Born October 1, 1833, in Ballynacargy, West Meath, Ireland, Beere died in Melbourne, Australia, on September 26, 1909. The details of his schooling are unknown, but he probably learned photography in Canada, where he went at an early age to serve as a cadet to his uncle, Armstrong Beere, a bridge builder. His earliest photographs are dated to 1863, the year he arrived in New Zealand. Beere's father was Gerald Beere, prebendary of Limerick Cathedral, and his brother Gerald Butler Beere was captain of the Waikato Militia during the New Zealand Wars of the 1860s.

Beere was employed by the provincial government of Auckland as a surveyor in the Auckland and Waikato district (1864–67) and then worked as an engineer-surveyor on railways construction in North Island (1873–86). After that he traveled widely, finally settling in Melbourne.

The photographer was an amateur of considerable accomplishment, noted for his views of Auckland Province during the 1860s, including military encampments on the Waikato River, Maori settlements, and the houses and wharves of Waikato.

PUBLICATIONS Books: *Looking Back*, Keith Sinclair & Wendy Harrex, 1978 (Oxford: Wellington); *Inheritors of a Dream*, Dick Scott, 1962 (Ronald Riddell: Auckland). Anthology: *Maori in Focus*, William Main, 1976 (Millwood: Wellington).

COLLECTIONS Alexander Turnbull Lib., Wellington; Auckland Inst. & Mus.; Auckland Pub. Lib.

ARCHIVE Alexander Turnbull Library, POB 12–349, Wellington, New Zealand.

William Abraham Bell PHOTOGRAPHER · PHYSICIAN An Englishman (possibly lived 1839–1915), Bell received MA and MD degrees in England.

He is best known for his work (1867–72) in the New Mexico Territory. There he photographed the routes of the Palmer-Wright-Calhoun survey with Alexander Gardner in 1867 for the Union Pacific Eastern Division across New Mexico, Arizona and California. He also photographed for the Wheeler Survey in 1872 and for the Kansas Pacific Railway Company, to determine the best southern route to the Pacific.

PUBLICATIONS Books: *Echoes from the Mountains to the Plains*, 1907; *Photographs of the United States . . . West of the 100th Meridian*, w/ Timothy O'Sullivan, for seasons of 1871–73 (U.S. Army Corps of Engineers: Wash., D.C.); *The Colonies of Colorado in Their Relationship to En-*

glish *Enterprise and Settlement*, 1874 (Chapman & Hall: London); *Michel's Process for Removing External Tumours*, 1871 (London); *New Tracks in North America, A Journal of Travel and Adventure Whilst Engaged in the Survey for a Southern Railroad to the Pacific Ocean During 1867–1868*, 1869; *On the Medical Properties of Eucalyptus Globulus . . .*, 1869 (London). Catalog: *Alexander Gardner's Photographs Along the 35th Parallel*, intro. by Robert Sobieszek, 1971 (GEH: Rochester).

COLLECTION IMP/GEH, Rochester.

E. J. Bellocq PHOTOGRAPHER The American-born Bellocq lived from 1873 to 1949. He was active as a commercial photographer in New Orleans about 1895–1940. Besides a 1918 commission as company photographer with the Foundation Company, shipbuilders in New Orleans, little else is known about his professional work.

Bellocq is most recognized for his relaxed, realistic photographs of prostitutes in New Orleans' infamous red-light district, Storyville. Of this work, eighty-nine negatives survive. Bellocq also photographed the opium dens of New Orleans' Chinatown, but none of the plates or prints are known to have survived. Bellocq used a Bantam Special camera, which he apparently carted around with him day and night.

The photographer Lee Friedlander discovered Bellocq's work in 1958 and purchased the surviving plates in 1966. Bellocq's life and work, fictionalized, was the subject of Louis Malle's 1978 feature film, *Pretty Baby*.

PUBLICATIONS Books: *Storyville, New Orleans*, Al Rose, 1974; *E. J. Bellocq: Storyville Portraits*, John Szarkowski, ed., preface by Lee Friedlander, 1970. Anthologies: *Photography Rediscovered*, David Travis & Anne Kennedy, 1979; *Looking at Photographs*, John Szarkowski, 1973; *Caring for Photographs*, 1972.

COLLECTIONS MOMA, NYC; New Orleans Mus. of Art, La.

ARCHIVE Lee Friedlander, 44 S Mountain Rd, New City, NY 10956.

Cleveland Bellow PHOTOGRAPHER · TEACHER · GRAPHIC ARTIST Born on April 30, 1946, in San Francisco, California, Bellow studied at the California College of Arts and Crafts in Oakland where he earned a BFA in Graphic Design (1969) and an MA in Painting, Drawing and Education (1971). He also received his California Secondary Teaching and Community College Credentials (1971, 1972) and was an intern at the Fine Arts

Museums of San Francisco (1975–76). He was influenced by the work of Charles White and Roy DeCarava.

His professional experience is quite varied. Since 1972 he has been an art instructor at the Art Education and Training Program at the De Young Museum Art School in San Francisco; he has been working as exhibits curator and consultant to the Earth N' Arts Gallery in Oakland since 1976 and as graphic communication coordinator for OCCUR since 1979. In 1977 Bellow was appointed Alameda County Art Commissioner. He served as district organizer for the San Francisco Neighborhood Arts Program (1972–74) and as art director for the San Francisco Black Expo, a Cultural Exhibition (1972; 1974). He also taught art and art history at the following institutions: Laney College in Oakland (1973), Alcorn A&M College in Lorman, Mississippi (1971–72), and the Oakland Parks & Recreation Department (1968–71).

A former member of the Oakland Museum Contemporary Arts Council (1970) and of the Bay Area Rapid Transit (BART) Art Council (1973–75), Bellow has belonged to the Alameda County Art Commission, California, since 1977. He founded the Bay Area Black Artist Association (BABAA) in 1974.

Bellow describes his work in these words: "It has taken the shape of simple b&w photos to photo silkscreen paintings and prints. I'm now engaged in the use of photo-imagery in my drawings and employ color Xerox to produce new methods of reproducing images."

PUBLICATIONS Anthology: *Art: African American*, 1978. Periodical: *Black Arts International Quarterly*, 2:3, 1978.

COLLECTIONS In California: Broadway Federal Savings, Los Angeles; City of San Francisco; Calif. Coll. of Arts & Crafts, Oakland; Oakland Mus.; Oakland Public Schools; San Francisco Genl. Hospital; Stanford Univ. Gall. Other states: Alabama State Univ., Montgomery; Black Collegian Magazine, New Orleans; Jackson State Univ., Miss.; Johnson Pub. Co., Chicago.

DEALER Earth N' Arts Gall., 371 17 St, Oakland, Ca 94612.

ADDRESS 100 Rishell Dr, Oakland, CA 94619.

Rudy (Rudolph A.) Bender PHOTOGRAPHER · TEACHER · WRITER Born on February 22, 1937, in Miami, Florida, Bender obtained a BFA in Photography at the San Francisco Art Institute in 1965. He had previously studied sociology at Ohio State University (1961–63), advertising illustration at the Columbus College of Art and Design

(1958–60) and journalism at Ohio State University (1956–57). His mentors in photography include Mike Tatem, Morley Baer and Wynn Bullock.

He has been a freelance photographer since 1970 and a columnist and contributing editor with *Darkroom Photography Magazine* since 1979. From 1973 to 1979 he worked as an instructor in the Department of Photography at City College in San Francisco and from 1967 to 1970 was the lab manager for Eye Now in the same city.

Bender is a member of SPE, the Association for Multi-Image, and the American Federation of Teachers. In 1977 he received a grant from the Society for the Encouragement of Contemporary Art and in 1974, a Special Award at the Photography and Sculpture Competition organized by the Montalvo Center for the Arts in California. In 1972 he invented a variable interaxial stereoscopic camera system.

In 1979 the artist produced "A Study in Alternity," a stereoscopic multimedia production exploring dreams, hallucinations and visions, which premiered at the SPE National Conference.

His photographic work deals primarily with landscapes, executed in a formal superrealist style, and with hallucinatory dream imagery, executed in a surrealistic style in color. Bender is intensely involved in stereoscopic photography.

PUBLICATION   Periodical: *Popular Photography Annual*, 1978.

COLLECTIONS   Home Savings Cllctn., Los Angeles; San Francisco Mus. of Modern Art.

DEALER   Equivalents Gall., 1822 Broadway, Seattle, WA 98122.

ADDRESS   16058 Greenwood Ave N, Seattle, WA 98133.

Yaakov Ben Dov   *PHOTOGRAPHER · FILM MAKER*
Born in 1882 in Yekaterinoslav, Ukrania, Russia, Ben Dov died in 1968 in Jerusalem, Israel. He studied painting in Ukrania and at the Arts Academy in Odessa, then took up photography to earn a living. He is survived by his daughter, Hanna Ben-Dov, a notable painter residing in Paris.

A freelance mainly, the photographer taught at the newly founded (1906) Bezalel Art School in Jerusalem. He was a founder-member of the Union of Artisans of Eretz Israel and also helped establish Jerusalem's Savings and Loan Association.

Ben Dov received the "Worthy of Jerusalem" award for his cultural contributions to Israel.

Granted by the city's mayor, it bestows honorary citizenship in Jerusalem.

As a film maker, Ben Dov produced several documentaries for the Jewish Agency and the United Jewish Appeal about the land, the people, the settlements and the pioneers of Israel, including *The Return to Zion*, made in the 1920s.

His photographs, mostly documentary in nature, relate to the development of the land of Israel and the events that brought about the establishment of its statehood. Among other publications, he produced a series of postcards and stereo cards, and a portfolio of offset prints.

PUBLICATION   Monograph: *Yaakov Ben Dov*, Yona Fisher & Nissan Perez, eds., 1978 (Israel Mus.).

COLLECTIONS   Central Zionist Archives, Jerusalem; Israel Mus., Jerusalem.

ARCHIVES   The Israel Museum, POB 1299, Hakirya, Jerusalem 91000 Israel; Mme. Hanna Ben-Dov, Gît le Coeur, 75006 Paris, France.

Linda Benedict-Jones   *PHOTOGRAPHER · TEACHER*   Born October 21, 1947, in Beloit, Wisconsin, she received a BS degree from the University of Wisconsin at LaCrosse in 1969, and is currently a candidate for an MS degree at Massachusetts Institute of Technology. She also attended the Universidade de Lisboa, Portugal, in 1972, and the Alliance Française, Paris, in 1975.

As of this date, she is an instructor at the Creative Photo Lab, MIT, and has been a freelance photographer since 1969. Other work experience includes being a lecturer in photography at the London College of Printing (1977–79) and a teacher of English at both the Technip in Paris (1973–75) and the American Language Institute in Lisbon, Portugal (1972–73).

Benedict-Jones' work was featured in "Arena, Program of the Arts," by the BBC in November 1976, which was later included in the National Film Archives of England. In 1977 she received a grant from the Arts Council of Great Britain.

PUBLICATIONS   Anthologies: *In-Sights: Self-Portraits By Women*, Joyce T. Cohen, ed., 1978; *Women by Women*, 1978; *British Journal of Photography Annual*, 1977; *Creative Camera International Yearbook*, 1977; *La Photographie Actuelle en France*, 1977 (Editions Contrejour: Paris). Periodicals: *British Journal of Photography*, May 1978; *35mm Photography*, spring 1978; *Nueva Lente*, Oct 1977; *Foto*, Mar 1977 (The Netherlands).

COLLECTIONS   Bibliothèque Nationale, Paris; Dept. of the Environment, England; Musée Cantini, Marseilles, France; Musée d'Art et d'Histoire de Fribourg, Switzerland; Photographic Gall., Southampton, England.

DEALERS Photographer's Gallery, 8 Great Newport St, London, England; Galerie Fiolet, Herengracht 86, Amsterdam, The Netherlands; Viviane Esders Gallery, 12 rue Saint Merri, 75004 Paris, France.

ADDRESS 43 Royal Ave., Cambridge, MA 02138.

Jim Bengston PHOTOGRAPHER Born March 31, 1942, in Evanston, Illinois, Bengston received a BA in German Literature from Lake Forest College, Lake Forest, Illinois, in 1964. He also studied at Princeton University, Princeton, New Jersey, in 1964–65, and names Robert Frank, Dorothea Lange, Man Ray and Rodchenko as major influences.

A freelance commercial photographer in Oslo, Norway, since 1975, Bengston was a copywriter/translator/photographer with Young and Rubicam from 1971 to 1975. He served as photo editor for Associated Press in New York City, 1969–70.

A member of Forbundet Frie Fotografer since 1978, the photographer won first prize (color) in the Nikon International Photo contest in 1970.

Most of his work is black-and-white, small format, but recently he has been using Polaroid to document "my life, my friends and things which are close to me." He also takes landscapes in 8 x 10 format.

PUBLICATIONS Monograph: *Afterwords,* 1978 (self-published). Book: *"The Photographed Cat",* J. C. Suares, 1980. Periodicals: "Another Site Another Sight," *Camera,* Nov 1980; "Jim Bengston," *Fotoforum,* Nov 1980; "A Child's History of Photography," *Camera,* Dec 1979; "Pointers on Becoming an Author," Jack Manning, *N.Y. Times,* Mar 1979.

COLLECTIONS MOMA, NYC; Polaroid Cllctn., Cambridge, Mass. Bibliothèque Nationale, Paris; Heni Onstad Kunstsenter, Høvikodden, Oslo, Norway; Robert Meyer Cllctn., Oslo, Norway.

DEALER Fotogalleri, Oscarsgate 50b, Oslo 2, Norway.

ADDRESS Gråkamveien 7c, Oslo 3, Norway.

Martin Benjamin TEACHER · PHOTOGRAPHER Born on November 10, 1949, in Saugerties, New York, Benjamin specialized in studio art at the State University of New York in Albany, where he received a BA in 1971. Since 1979 he has been an assistant professor in art, teaching photography at Union College in Schenectady, New York,

and from 1972 to 1979 he lectured at the College of St. Rose in Albany.

Since 1978 he has been a member of SPE, the Catskill Center for Photography, and Friends of Photography. In 1979 he joined the Los Angeles Center for Photographic Studies. In both 1978 and 1979 he won first place in the faculty division of the Nikon/Nutshell College Photo Contest. In 1974 he was also the first place winner of the Time-Life Bicentennial Photography Contest.

The artist works in 35mm black-and-white and makes 16 x 20 silver prints.

PUBLICATION Periodical: *Time-Life Photography Annual,* 1974.

COLLECTIONS Murray State Univ., Murray, Ky.; SUNY, Albany.

ADDRESS 47 Raymo St, Albany, NY 12209.

Charles Harper Bennett CHEMIST Born in 1840 at Langdale Lodge in Clapham Park, London, Harper died in 1927 in Sydney, Australia. The son of a wealthy hat manufacturer, he attended King's College School in London, and later studied medicine.

His chemical experiments in photography resulted in production of a rapid gelatin dry plate, which he showed to the South London Photographic Society on March 7, 1878, along with a negative of a room interior taken by gaslight. Later that month he published a description of his method for increasing the speed of gelatin emulsion, a technique exceedingly important in the later development of modern emulsions and snapshot photography. Bennett did not patent his discovery. He later outlined conditions for eliminating fog in fast gelatin dry plates. After his father's death, Bennett settled in Australia (1894).

PUBLICATIONS Books: *History of Photography,* Beaumont Newhall, 1964; *History of Photography,* Helmut & Alison Gernsheim, 1955; *History of Photography,* W. Jerome Harrison, 1887. Anthology: *Photography's Great Inventors,* Louis W. Sipley, 1965. Periodicals: *British Journal of Photography,* Mar 21, 1879, Mar 29, 1878.

Derek Petersen Bennett PHOTOGRAPHER · CRITIC Born October 13, 1944, in Buffalo, New York, Petersen earned a BA in English literature from Sir George Williams University, Montreal, Canada (1969).

He is self-employed. His photography includes a series of street photographs and a long documentary project of German portraits.

PUBLICATIONS Periodicals: "Adams: 'Yosemite and the Range of Light,'" review, Nov 1979, interview w/Marco Misani & portfolio, July

1978, "Creative Camera Annual for 1978," review, Jan 1978, "'Real Dreams' by Duane Michals," review, May 1977, "Creative Camera Yearbook 1977," review, Nov 1977, *print letter; Fotografie,* Jan 1979.

COLLECTIONS Bibliothèque Nationale, Paris; Polaroid Cllctn., Amsterdam, The Netherlands.

DEALER Silver Image Gall., 92 S Washington St, Seattle, WA 98104.

ADDRESS Finsterwaldstrasse 23, 8200 Schaffhausen, Switzerland.

George Osborne Bennett, Jr. *PHOTOGRAPHER* Born in Philadelphia on October 30, 1945, Bennett attended Cornell University, where he received a BA in 1967.

Since 1974 he has lived in New York City, where he works as a freelance photographer. In 1973–74, he was J. Frederick Smith's studio manager. From 1967 to 1970 he served as an officer in the U.S. Navy.

Both his books (see below), which he photographed and designed, were honored with AIGA awards, and his images have been published in many American and European magazines.

Bennett specializes in "narrative serial photography" in his books, which he also designed, and in his editorial photographs.

PUBLICATIONS Books: *Fighters,* Peter Hamill, 1978; *Mannequins,* 1977.

COLLECTIONS Foto Gallery, NYC; Gallery 11, NYC.

REPRESENTATIVE Timothy Seldes, c/o Russell & Volkening, 551 Fifth Ave, New York, NY 10017.

ADDRESS George Bennett Studio, 40 W 29 St, New York, NY 10001.

Michael Bennett *PHOTOGRAPHER · ILLUSTRATOR* Born in Sevenoaks, Kent, England, Bennett received a BA in Fine Art from Leeds Polytechnic in Yorkshire, England, in 1975.

Since 1976 he has been self-employed as a photographer. Previously he was an instructor in photography at the Wildernesse Secondary School for Boys in Sevenoaks (1975–76).

A member of the National Union of Journalists, Bennett received an Arts Council of Great Britain award in 1975.

PUBLICATIONS Anthology: *About 70 Photographs,* William Messer, 1980. Periodicals: *Amateur Photographer,* Mar 1976; *British Journal of Photography,* Mar 1976; *Creative Camera,* Mar 1976.

COLLECTIONS In England: Arts Council of Gr. Brit.; Victoria & Albert Mus., London.

ADDRESS 3, Rookley Close, Tunbridge Wells, Kent, England.

Arthur David Bensusan *PHYSICIAN · PHOTOGRAPHER* Born June 13, 1921, in Johannesburg, South Africa, Dr. Bensusan earned Bachelor of Medicine and Bachelor of Surgery degrees from Rand School of Social Sciences in 1950.

For the past twenty-five years he has been director of photography at the Medical School in Johannesburg. He also founded and chairs the Bensusan Museum of Photography in Johannesburg and he founded Camera Pictorialists in that city as well. He is a past mayor of Johannesburg and has been a city councillor for sixteen years.

Bensusan is a fellow of the Photographic Society of America, RPS, Biological Photographers Association, and the Royal Society of Arts. He is also an Honorary Fellow of the Photographic Society of Southern Africa, an honorary member of the Photographic Society of America and a member of the London Salon of Photography.

His films include *Open Heart Surgery, Decompression Suit, Die Stem van S.A., Thatch Reflection Phenomenon, Rotary Afloat,* and *New Legs* (done approximately 1958–1964).

PUBLICATIONS Books: *Drug Exposure,* 1971 (Research Publications: Johannesburg); *Silver Images,* 1966; *South Africa: The Land, the People,* 1960 (Timmins: Cape Town); *A Short History of the Bensusan Family,* 1936(?) (Johannesburg); *The Exhibition Print,* n.d.; *Outdoor Photography,* n.d.; *Photography in South Africa,* n.d.; *Photography Simplified,* n.d.; *Pictorial Photographs,* n.d.; *South African Photogems of the Year,* n.d. (Johannesburg).

ADDRESS POB 1041, Port Shepstone, 4240 South Africa.

Stephen Anthony Benton *HOLOGRAPHER · PHYSICIST · INVENTOR* Born December 1, 1941, in San Francisco, Benton studied at the Massachusetts Institute of Technology, earning a BS in Electrical Engineering in 1963, and at Harvard University, where he received a PhD in Applied Physics in 1968. His mentors were Harold Edgerton and Edwin Land.

Benton worked with the Polaroid Corporation from 1961 to 1974, during which time (1968–73) he was also an assistant professor with the Division of Engineering and Applied Physics at Harvard University. Since 1974 he has been working with Polaroid in their research laboratories, doing three-dimensional photography, especially in practical forms of holography.

A director-at-large of the Optical Society of

America from 1977 to 1979, Benton is a member of the Society of Photographic Scientists and Engineers (SPSE), the Society of Photographic Instrumentation Engineers (SPIE) and the New York Academy of Science. He has been issued three patents, the first in 1972 for his "Method for Making Reduced Bandwidth Holograms," one in 1975 for "Light Filtering Arrangement for Holographic Displays," and another in 1980 for "Production of Volume Dielectric Holograms."

PUBLICATIONS Books: "Photographic Materials and their Handling," *Handbook of Optical Holography*, H. J. Caulfield, ed. 1979; "White-Light Transmission/Reflection Holographic Imaging," *Applications of Holography and Optical Data Processing*, E. Marom & A. A. Friesem, eds., 1977; "Prospects for Quasi-Holographic Three-Dimensional Displays in the Biomedical Sciences," *Holography in Medicine*, P. Greguss, ed., 1975. Periodicals: "Achromatic Images from White-Light Transmission Holograms" & "Distortions in Cylindrical Holographic Stereogram Images," Oct 1978, "Intra-Emulsion Diffusion-Transfer Processing of Volume Dielectric Holograms," Oct 1974, "On the Perception of Gradients of Retinal Disparity," Apr 1974, "Granularity Effects in Phase Holograms." "Properties of Granularity Wiener Spectra," W/ R. E. Kronauer, Apr 1971, "Multiple-Lens Parallax Panoramagraphy," Apr 1970, "Hologram Reconstructions with Extended Incoherent Sources," Oct 1969, "A Noise Analysis of Grainy Emulsions," W/R. E. Kronauer, Oct 1966, *Journal for the Optical Society of America*; "Approximations for Granularity Theory," *Photographic Science and Engineering*, July/Aug 1977; "Holography—The Second Decade," *Optics News*, summer 1977; "Holographic Displays—A Review," Sept/Oct 1975, "Simplified Talbot Interferometers for Lens Testing," *Optical Engineering*, July/Aug 1976; "Silhouette Holograms Without Vertical Parallax," *Applied Optics*, Dec 1970.

COLLECTIONS Franklin Inst, Philadelphia, Pa.; Mus. of Holography, NYC.

REPRESENTATIVES Mus. of Holography, New York City; Eve Ritscher Assoc., London.

ADDRESS Great Rd, Lincoln, MA 01773.

John Benton-Harris PHOTOGRAPHER · TEACHER · WRITER Born September 28, 1939, Benton-Harris studied at the Alexey Brodovitch Design Workshop in New York City. His major influences have been George Grosz, Edward Hopper, Ben Shahn and Jacob Riis.

Currently he is a self-employed photographer working in the field of photojournalism. He has also been a visiting lecturer at a variety of institutions, such as Trent Polytechnic in Nottingham (1973–76), West Surrey College of Art & Design in Farnham (1977, 1979) and the London College of Printing (1978 through 1980).

In 1978 Benton-Harris received three merit awards from the Art Directors Club of New York. He was also the recipient of Arts Council awards in 1972, 1973 and 1974.

Working in a documentary tradition, utilizing small-format black-and-white, he focuses on cultural and historical identities. In England he is interested in "making public the private spectacle of upper-class life and the belief in empire."

PUBLICATIONS Periodicals: *British Journal of Photography*, June 1980, Aug 1979; *Modern Photography*, Oct 1977; *Creative Camera*, Feb 1974, Sept 1971.

COLLECTIONS MOMA, NYC. Arts Council of Great Britain, London; Victoria & Albert Mus., London.

DEALER Wayne T. Stotts, Camera Work Gall., 326 Main St, Port Washington, NY 11050.

ADDRESS 25 Morland Ave, Croydon CRO-6EA, Surrey, England.

Roloff Beny PHOTOGRAPHER · AUTHOR Born January 7, 1924, in Medicine Hat, Alberta, Canada, Beny, also known as Roy Wilfred, earned a BFA in 1945 from Trinity College at the University of Toronto, Canada, and an MFA in 1947 from the State University of Iowa, Iowa City. He also undertook postgraduate studies at the University of New York (Institute of Fine Arts) and Columbia University, New York City, in 1947–48.

The self-employed photographer's photos have appeared in such publications as *Vogue, Harper's Bazaar* and *Time*.

Recipient of a Guggenheim Fellowship in 1953, Beny won a Canadian Council Visual Arts Award in 1968, and in that year his book *Japan in Colour* was selected as "the world's finest book" and was awarded a Gold Medal at the Leipzig International Book Fair. In 1967 he was elected Knight of Mark Twain, in 1973 was named a life member of the Royal Canadian Academy and in 1972 he received an LLD from the University of Lethbridge.

PUBLICATIONS Books: *Iran: Elements of Destiny*, 1978; *Persia: Bridge of Turquoise*, 1975; *In Italy*, 1974; *Island: Ceylon*, 1971; *India*, 1969; *Japan in Colour*, Anthony Thwaite, 1967; *To Every Thing There Is a Season*, 1967; *Pleasure of Ruins*, Rose Macaulay, 1964, rev. ed. 1977; *A*

Time of Gods, 1962; *The Thrones of Earth and Heaven*, Bernard Berenson, 1958. Anthology: *The Magic Image*, Cecil Beaton & Gail Buckland, 1975.

COLLECTIONS Harvard Univ., Fogg Art Mus., Cambridge, Mass.; MOMA, NYC; N.Y. Pub. Lib., NYC; Wesleyan Univ., Middletown, Conn.; Yale Univ. Mus., Conn. Art Gall. of Ontario, Canada; Bezalel Mus., Jerusalem, Israel; Milione Gall., Milan, Italy; Natl. Gall. of Canada, Ottawa; Redfern Gall., London.

DEALER Michael Shaw, Curtis Brown Ltd., 1 Craven Hall, London W2, England.

ADDRESS Lungotevere Ripa 3B, 00153 Rome, Italy.

Stephen Lynn Berens *CURATOR · PHOTOGRAPHER* Born September 28, 1952, in Fort Collins, Colorado, Berens received his BFA from the University of Nebraska, Lincoln, in 1974 and his MFA from Florida State University, Tallahassee, in 1977.

Gallery director of the Florida School of the Arts in Palatka since 1978, Berens belongs to SPE and the Florida Art Museum Directors Association. In 1979 he won an Individual Artist Grant from the Fine Arts Council of Florida.

Beren's photographic work "is concerned with the process of change." He makes 30 x 40 color prints from double- and triple-exposed negatives, the finished work realized through additional drawing and painting.

PUBLICATIONS Catalogs: *Cultural Artifacts*, ed., 1979; *Altered Landscapes*, ed. & photog., 1979; *Art Books: Books as Original Art*, ed., intro., 1978; *Tropical Landscapes*, intro., 1978 (Florida School of the Arts: Palatka); *Photographs*, 1977 (Univ. of Neb., Sheldon Memorial Art Gall.: Lincoln). Periodical: "An Offset Portfolio," *Exposure: SPE*, Dec 1977.

COLLECTIONS Fla. State Univ. Fine Arts Gall., Tallahassee; IMP/GEH, Rochester; Jacksonville Art Mus., Fla.; Mus. of Fine Arts, St. Petersburg, Fla.; Univ. of Neb., Sheldon Memorial Art Gall., Lincoln; Univ. of S. Fla. Art Bank, Tampa.

ADDRESS 571½ S Arizona Ave, Los Angeles, CA 90032.

Sara Betty Berenson *PHOTOGRAPHER · MANUSCRIPT EDITOR AND INDEXER* Born on February 5, 1937, in Brooklyn, New York, Berenson went to Antioch College in Ohio, where she received a BA in Literature and Philosophy in 1957. Her mentors were Aaron Siskind, Edward and Brett

Weston, Harry Callahan, Minor White and Paul Caponigro.

She works principally in black-and-white and specializes in abstract nature close-ups and silhouettes of plants.

PUBLICATION Periodical: *Modern Photography*, Oct 1968.

COLLECTIONS City of Dallas Cllctn.; Metro. Mus. of Art, NYC; Oakland Mus. of Art, Calif.: Univ. of Kan. Mus. of Art, Lawrence.

DEALER Focus Gall., 2146 Union St, San Francisco, CA 94123.

Eileen K. Berger *PHOTOGRAPHER* Born in New York City on November 5, 1943, Berger attended the University of Wisconsin, where she majored in philosophy and English literature (BA, 1965), and the Tyler School of Art, Philadelphia, where she specialized in photography (MFA, 1976). Wynn Bullock had a major influence on her development.

She has been teaching photography in various institutions: the Philadelphia College of Art since 1977, the Moore College of Art in 1977–78 and the Tyler School of Art in 1974–75, both in Philadelphia. In the fall of 1979 she was a guest artist at the Art Institute of Chicago. Previously Berger taught dance at Tennessee State University (1967–69) and at Vanderbilt University in Nashville (1965–66). She joined SPE in 1978. In 1980 Berger received a Photographer's Fellowship from the NEA.

The artist describes her work as being "basically autobiographical." She concentrates on the use of collage. For her "this stylistic device has become a logical way of integrating visual and verbal information, and allows for an exploration of complex psychological issues."

PUBLICATIONS Anthologies: *9 Critics/9 Photographers*, 1980; *In-Sights: Self-Portraits by Women*, Joyce T. Cohen, ed., 1978; *Women See Men*, 1977; *Women See Woman*, Annie Gottlieb, Cheryl Wiesenfeld, et al, eds., 1976.

ADDRESS 5900 Wayne Ave, Philadelphia, PA 19144.

Paul Eric Berger *PHOTOGRAPHER · TEACHER* Born on January 20, 1948, in The Dalles, Oregon, Berger completed an MFA from the Visual Studies Workshop in Rochester, where he was taught by Nathan Lyons and Syl Labrot. He received a BA from University of California at Los Angeles in 1970, where he studied under Robert Heinecken and Robert Fichter, and also attended the Art Center College of Design in Pasadena, California, from 1967 to 1969, where he had Todd Walker as a teacher.

The artist has been an assistant professor of art at the University of Washington in Seattle since 1978. He taught previously at the University of Illinois in Champaign (1974–78) and at the University of Northern Iowa in Cedar Falls (1973–74).

He has been a member of the SPE since 1974 and was recently elected to their board of directors. He was awarded an NEA Photographer's Fellowship in 1979, materials grants from the University of Illinois Research Board in 1975 and 1977 and a Young Photographer's Award at the sixth International Meeting of Photography in Arles, France.

In his work Berger concentrates on "multiple imagery in a structured sequence."

PUBLICATION Periodical: "Paul Berger's 'Mathematics' Photographs," Leroy F. Searle, *Afterimage: VSW*, Mar 1978.

COLLECTIONS Art Inst. of Chicago; IMP/GEH, Rochester; Princeton Univ. Art Mus., N.J.; Univ. of Calif., Davis; Univ. of Colorado, Boulder; Univ. of Mass., Amherst. Australian Natl. Gall., Canberra; Bibliothèque Nationale, Paris; Musée Réattu, Arles, France.

DEALER Light Gallery, 724 Fifth Ave, New York, NY 10019.

ADDRESS: 6712 Division NW, Seattle, WA 98117.

Maurizio Berlincioni PHOTOGRAPHER · JOURNALIST Born November 29, 1943, in Florence, Italy, Berlincioni attended the University of Florence, where he studied economics and political science.

He has been a freelance photographer since 1972.

A member of AIRF (Italian Association of Photojournalists) since 1978, he has also been a member of the Ordine Nazionale dei Giornalisti (National Journalists Guild) since 1979.

Berlincioni characterizes his work before 1977 as "almost exclusively reportage on the social scene, mostly urban." Since 1977 he has been doing research in different fields, such as industrial, architectural and still-life photography.

PUBLICATIONS Monograph: *Tuscania*, 1971 (Editphoto: Milan). Books: *Enciclopedia Pratica per Fotografare*, Arturo Carlo Quintavalle, 1979 (Fabbri Editori: Milan); *70 Anni di Fotografia in Italia*, Italo Zannier, 1978 (Punto e Virgola: Modena). Anthology: *2nd Almanacco Fotografico Italiano*, 1971 (Editphoto: Milan). Periodicals: *Il Fotografo*, Mar 1979; *Il Diaframma/Fotografia It-*

aliana, Oct 1975, June 1972; *Zoom*, Mar/Apr 1973 (France), Nov 1972 (Italy); *Popular Photography*, Dec, Jan 1970.

COLLECTION Centro Studi e Archivio Della Comunicazione Dell'Universita' Di Parma, Italy.

ADDRESS Via Il Prato 31, 50123 Florence, Italy.

Mieczysław Berman PHOTOGRAPHER · GRAPHIC ARTIST Born on July 7, 1903, in Warsaw, Berman died in 1975. He attended the School of Decorative Art in Warsaw (1921), and was strongly influenced by Dadaism.

Berman co-founded the Phrygiancap, an artists' group, in 1936. He was elected a corresponding member of the Deutsche Akademie der Künste zu Berlin (German Democratic Republic) in 1971.

Berman received a gold medal in 1937 at the International Exhibit of Artists and Technicians in Paris, and in 1950 Poland's national prize for political caricature.

His works are satirical photomontages with an emphasis on antifascist politics.

PUBLICATION Book: *Fifty Years of History in Berman's Photomontages*, 1973 (Galleria Schwarz: Milan).

COLLECTIONS Art Mus., Lodz, Poland; Historical Mus. of the Polish Revolutionary Movement; Natl Mus., Warsaw.

ARCHIVE Galleria Schwarz, Via Gesú 17, Milan, Italy.

Zeke Berman PHOTOGRAPHER Berman studied at Academia di Belli Arti in Florence, Italy (1972), and received a BFA in Sculpture from Philadelphia College of Art (1973).

A freelance photographer, Berman worked as a photo retoucher for Arton Associates in New York City in 1975–76. He won a CAPS grant in 1979, and a Residency grant from Lightwork in Syracuse, New York, in 1980.

Mainly photographing still lifes and interiors, the photographer is fascinated with the optical illusion of "linear elements laid out in three-dimensional space which also flip up to the two-dimensional 'picture plane' of the photograph's surface."

PUBLICATIONS Periodicals: *Artforum*, Mar 1980; review, Kay Larson, *Village Voice*, Dec 24, 1979.

COLLECTIONS Colgate Univ., Picker Art Gall., Hamilton, N.Y.; Everson Mus. of Art, Syracuse, N.Y.; Floating Fndn. of Photography, NYC; Metro. Mus. of Art, NYC; MOMA, NYC.

ADDRESS 20 Eldridge St, New York, NY 10002.

Jerry Berndt PHOTOGRAPHER Born November 11, 1943 in Milwaukee, Wisconsin, Berndt attended the University of Wisconsin in Madison 1963–67. He names Walker Evans, Robert Frank, Eugene Atget and Erich Saloman as major influences.

Currently a photography instructor at the Art Institute of Boston (since 1977), he was previously photography editor for the *Boston Phoenix* (1975–78). During that time he regularly had his photos published in *Time, Newsweek, Village Voice* and *Rolling Stone*. He was also staff photographer for the *Detroit Free Press* (1973) and photography editor for the *Detroit Area Weekly News* (1970–72). Berndt photographed the "Combat Zone" in Boston in 1968–70 for the Harvard University Laboratory of Community Psychiatry. From 1967 to 1969 he worked as a photographer and film maker for the Boston Children's Museum.

Since 1978 Berndt has belonged to the Boston Visual Artists Union and the Photographic Resource Center. He won a Kosciusko Foundation grant to photograph in Poland in 1976, and was awarded a Massachusetts Artists Foundation Fellowship in 1979. In 1980 Berndt was awarded a NEA Survey Project Fellowship.

Berndt has also made several 16mm films: *Forestry Camp* (1976, for the Commonwealth of Massachusetts), *The Kid* (1970, for the Boston Public Library), *The Weatherman* (1968, for the Boston Children's Museum) and *The Green Berets* (1967).

He uses all formats and his work is documentary in style. Berndt most recently has been photographing apparitions of the Virgin Mary.

COLLECTIONS Boston Mus. of Fine Arts; Boston Pub. Lib.; Harvard Univ., Lab. of Community Psychiatry; Kosciusko Fndn., NYC; Univ. of Wisc., Madison. Univ. of Warsaw, Poland.

ADDRESS 41 Magnolia Ave, Cambridge, MA 02138.

Jeff Berner PHOTOGRAPHER · AUTHOR Born on December 10, 1940, in Troy, New York, Berner completed his BA in English at San Francisco State University in 1966. He was greatly influenced by Alan Watts, a longtime personal friend and colleague.

He works mainly as a freelance photographer but has taught a survey of avant-garde art history at the University of California at Berkeley, at San Francisco State and at the San Francisco Art Institute (1965–70). During the year 1967–68 he was hired by the *San Francisco Chronicle*, for which he wrote the column "Astronauts of Inner Space."

Berner was awarded an honorable mention in the *Life* magazine photography contests in 1970 and 1971; he also won a First Award for Excellence by "DESI:GRAPHICS: USA 1979" for photography in design.

The artist works almost exclusively in color. He has photographed "a range of things from high-fashion nudes to open-heart surgery; world-class yacht-racing, landscapes, magazine illustration, etc." His specialty is "surreal sandwiches," which he calls "dreamspaces."

PUBLICATIONS Books: *The Holography Book*, 1980; *Uncarved Block, Unbleached Silk*, Alan Watts, 1979; *The Photographic Experience*, 1975; *The Innerspace Project*, 1972. *Aktual Art International*, 1967.

ADDRESS POB 503, Mill Valley, CA 94941.

Ruth Bernhard PHOTOGRAPHER [See plate 95] Born on October 14, 1905, in Berlin, Bernhard was the daughter of the noted and versatile artist Lucian Bernhard, often referred to as the "Father of the German Poster." She studied at the Academy of Art in her native town. Her works have been influenced by many photographers but especially by Edward Weston, Ansel Adams, Wynn Bullock and Dorothea Lange. She states that the music of Bach and Prokofiev and the poetry of Rainier Maria Rilke have also had an effect on her work.

Bernhard has taught numerous seminars and workshops. From 1968 to 1976 she was an instructor in creative photography at the University of California Extension in San Francisco. A member of Friends of Photography, she was granted a Certificate of Honor by the City of San Francisco in 1978 and a Dorothea Lange Award by California's Oakland Art Museum in 1975.

The artist describes her photographic production in these terms: "My work is primarily black-and-white view camera work, specializing in nudes, natural forms and still lifes. My philosophy: The celebration of the commonplace."

PUBLICATIONS Monograph: *Collecting Light*, 1979 (Friends of Photography: Carmel, Calif.). Books: *It's Only A Movie*, 1972; *Being Without Clothes*, 1970; *Light*[7], 1968; *The History of the Nude in Photography*, 1965; *The Big Heart*, w/ M. Van, 1957; *Poet's Camera*, 1946. Anthologies: *The Photograph Collector's Guide*, Lee D. Witkin & Barbara London, 1979; *Recollections: Ten Women of Photography*, Margaretta Mitchell, ed., 1979; *Photography in the 20th Century*,

1967. Catalogs: *Contemporary Trends*, 1976 (Columbia Coll., Chicago Photog. Gall.); *Women of Photography*, 1975 (San Francisco Mus. of Modern Art); *Through One's Eyes*, 1973 (Muckenthaler Cultural Ctr.: Fullerton, Calif.); *Photography USA*, 1968 (De Cordova Mus.: Lincoln, Mass.); *Photography in the Fine Arts*, 1967 (Metro. Mus. of Art: NYC); *An Exhibition of Contemporary Photography*, 1965 (Univ. of Illinois: Urbana); *The Photograph as Poetry*, 1960 (Pasadena Art Mus.: Calif.); *Creative Photography*, 1956 (Univ. of Kentucky: Lexington). Periodicals: *Exposure: SPE*, 1977; *Photography*, Mar 1972; *Creative Camera*, Oct, Apr 1971; *Popular Photography Annual*, 1962; *Aperture*, 1961, vol. 3, 1959, 4:1, 1956, 2: 3, 1953; *U.S. Camera*, 1952.

PORTFOLIOS *The Eternal Body, 1948–1970*, intro. by Wynn Bullock, 1976 (self-pub.); *The Gift of the Commonplace, 1935–1970*, intro. by Wynn Bullock, 1976 (self-pub.).

COLLECTIONS Columbia Coll. Gall. & Dept. of Photog., Chicago; Crocker Mus., Sacramento, Calif; De Cordova Mus., Lincoln, Mass.; IMP/GEH, Rochester; Indiana Univ. Mus. of Art, Bloomington; Metro. Mus. of Art, NYC; MIT, Dept. of Photog., Cambridge, Mass.; Mus. of Fine Arts, St. Petersburg, Fla.; MOMA, NYC; Oakland Mus. of Art, Calif.; Univ. of Illinois, Krannert Art Mus., Champaign; Univ. of Nebraska, Sheldon Memorial Art Gall., Lincoln; Univ. of Oregon, Eugene; Utah State Inst. of Fine Arts, Logan. Bibliothèque Nationale, Paris.

DEALER Stephen White Gall., 835 N La Cienega Blvd, Los Angeles, CA 90069.

ADDRESS 2982 Clay St, San Francisco, CA 94115.

David Martin Bernstein PHOTOGRAPHER · TEACHER Born December 25, 1936, in the Bronx, New York, he received a BPA degree from the Brooks Institute of Photographic Arts and Sciences in Santa Barbara, California, in 1956. He attended the University of Alaska in Anchorage 1958–60, was a student of aesthetic realism with Eli Siegel in New York City 1962–78, participated in photography workshops with Lou Bernstein 1968–71 and also attended the New School for Social Research in New York 1973–74.

Since 1979 Bernstein has been a freelance photographer. Previously he was a photography instructor at the High School of Fashion Industries in New York City (1978–79), a freelance photographer contributing to a variety of publications (1975–78), a photography instructor at the New York Institute of Photography in New York City (1972–75) and also a medical photographer at the Saint Albans Naval Hospital in New York (1968–72).

He has been a member of the American Society of Picture Professionals, Inc., since 1976, the Cinema Inquiry in New York City since 1975, the Society for Aesthetic Realism since 1962 and the Aesthetic Realism Photographers since 1963. Bernstein created a 16mm short film entitled *The Letterpress*.

PUBLICATIONS Books: *I Learned This About Photography*, 1976 (Sala de Cultura: Pamplona, Spain); *Aesthetic Realism: We Have Been There*, co-author, 1969; *Photography and Feeling: The American Indian*, 1965. Periodical: *Camera 35*, Nov 1969.

DEALER Terrain Gall., 141 Greene St, New York, NY 10013.

ADDRESS 67 Columbia St, New York, NY 10002.

Janet Belden Beyda PHOTOGRAPHER · SCULPTOR · WRITER Born October 24, 1917, in Manila, Philippine Islands, of American parents, Beyda studied sculpture and painting at Cooper Union School of Art (1934–38) and sculpture at the Art Students League (1938–41), both in New York City. She also studied sculpture on scholarship at Fontainebleau (France) School of Art in the summer of 1938.

Beyda has been in partnership with her photographer husband, Frank Beyda, since 1956, and previously was a freelance sculptor and painter. She belongs to ASMP (since 1979) and ANPPM (French advertising and fashion photographers, since 1961).

Since 1974 Beyda has used a "complicated technique of double exposure with graded masking" to record images "such as one sees in dreams and which people one's subconscious mind."

PUBLICATIONS Book: *Chers Amis*, 1977. Periodicals: *Zoom*, May 1980 (Paris); *Progresso Fotografico*, Mar 1975; *Photo*, July 1974.

COLLECTION Fribourg Mus. of Photography, Switzerland.

ADDRESS 2 rue Camille Tahan, Paris 75018, France.

Ken Biasco TEACHER · PHOTOGRAPHER/DESIGNER Born in Chicago, Illinois, on July 19, 1942, Biasco earned an MS (1969) and a BS (1968) from the Institute of Design at the Illinois Institute of Technology (Chicago), where he studied with Aaron Siskind and Wynn Bullock.

Since 1977 he has been the director of the photography program at the University of Texas in Dallas. Prior to that he was an assistant professor at the Institute of Design (1968–77) as well as the head of the Color Photography Department at the Chicago Academy of Fine Arts (1971–74). Concurrently with his teaching positions he has been working as a freelance photographer.

Biasco is a founding member of the south central chapter of SPE, a member of the Texas Arts Coalition and serves on the board of directors of the Allen Street Gallery in Dallas. He has been the recipient of a research grant from the University of Texas at Dallas and the President's Commission on Youth Award.

The artist experiments with color photography and solarization; he is also interested in multimedia slide presentations.

PUBLICATIONS Periodicals: *Vision Magazine*, interview, 1979; *Portfolio Magazine*, incl. interview, 1979; *Art Week*, interview, 1978.

COLLECTIONS City of Dallas Permanent Cllctn.; Rosner Cllctn. of Photography, Chicago.

DEALER Allen St Gall., 2817 Allen St, Dallas, TX 75204.

ADDRESS 417 Canyon Ridge, Richardson, TX 75080.

Israëlis Bidermanas ("Izis") PHOTOGRAPHER Born January 17, 1911, in Marijampole, Lithuania, Bidermanas died May 16, 1980, in Paris, France. He began to photograph at age thirteen in Lithuania.

Bidermanas left his native land for Paris when he was nineteen and worked as a laborer, retoucher and printer. He later ran a photographic portrait studio. In 1940 he had to hide from the Germans because he was Jewish; he took the name Izis, which he kept professionally. Izis ended up in Limoges, France, as a soldier in 1944 during the liberation of the town, where he photographed the French underground resistance fighters. These photographs were noticed by his superiors and exhibited in Limoges under the title "Ceux de Grammont." In 1949 Izis became a photo reporter at *Paris-Match*, where he remained until 1969.

In his work Izis strove for simplicity and an "invisible" technique. He wanted viewers to "forget the photographer" and not ask, "How did he do it?"

PUBLICATIONS Books: *Paris des Poêtes*, Jacques Prévert, preface, 1977; *The World of Marc Chagall*, Roy McMullen, 1969 (Aldus Books: London); *Le Cirque d'Izis*, Jacques Prévert, preface, 1965; *Israel*, André Malraux, preface, Nicolao Làzàr & Izis, eds., 1958; *Paradis*

Terrestre, w/Colette, 1953, *Charmes de Londres*, w/Jacques Prévert, 1952, *Grand Bal du Printemps*, w/Jacques Prévert, 1952 (La Guilde du Livre: Lausanne, Switzerland); *Paris des Rêves*, Jean Cocteau, preface, 1950 (Editions Clairfontaine: Lausanne).

COLLECTIONS Bibliothèque Historique de la Ville de Paris; Bibliothèque Nationale, Paris.

ARCHIVE Mme. Izis, 28 rue Henri Pape, 75074 Paris, France.

Dan Biferie PHOTOGRAPHER · TEACHER · GALLERY DIRECTOR Born in Miami, Florida, on December 17, 1950, Biferie attended Ohio University in Athens, where he completed bachelor's and master's degrees in fine arts (1972, 1974). He was influenced by Joe Crumley, Todd Walker, Jerry Uelsmann and Evon Streetman.

He has been employed as a photography instructor at Daytona Beach Community College in Florida since 1975 and has been the director of their Gallery of Fine Arts since 1978. Biferie is a member of the Florida Association of Museum Directors and president of Daytona Beach Community College Photographic Society. He also belongs to SPE, for which he serves as president of the southeast region.

Biferie works in black-and-white and is interested in "abstractions of light and space and documentary photographs of country people."

PUBLICATION Periodical: *Photographic Artist*, 1976.

COLLECTIONS Middle Tenn. State Univ., Murfreesboro; Mus. of Arts & Sciences, Daytona Beach, Fla.

DEALER Images Gall., Sarasota, FL 33578.

ADDRESS 22 Virginia Ave, Deland, FL 32720, or Daytona Beach Community Coll., POB 1111, Daytona Beach, FL 32015.

Michael (Selby John) Cerulli Billingsley PHOTOGRAPHER · TEACHER · EDITOR/PUBLISHER Born on June 6, 1946, in Kingston, Ontario, Canada, Billingsley obtained a BFA in Photography at the University of Delaware in 1967 and a Master's degree in Psychocommunications at Goddard College in Vermont in 1974. Besides studying photography with Minor White, he trained in Buddhist psychology and meditation with Trungpa Rinpoche for three years, and also studied mime with Walton, Warman and Aguilar.

As of this date Billingsley was the editor of the artists' magazine *Common Image*. Former founder, director, curator and magazine editor of the Image Co-op in Montpelier, Vermont, he also taught for five years at the Community College of Vermont.

He is a member of the Vermont Independent Film and Video Producers Guild and has been the recipient of several awards: a Project Costs Grant given by the Canada Council in 1980, three Artist Assistant grants given by the Polaroid Corporation (1979, 1978, 1977), one Publication Grant and one Individual Artist Assistance Grant by the Vermont Council on the Arts (1979, 1976) and two Project Assistance grants by the Polaroid Foundation (1978, 1977).

In addition to *Common Image*, Billingsley has published several tabloids, including *Image Co-op Newsletter*, *The International Free City Visionary* and *Heterodoxical Voice*.

The artist states: "My work is in the form of projects. Generally I am not concerned with image content. I use photographic images in groups, grids or juxtapositions to create a larger work, which may also incorporate videotape, audio, performance, sculpture."

COLLECTIONS Brattleboro Mus. Art Ctr., Vt.; Goddard Coll., Plainfield, Vt.; Photoworks Gall., Boston; Polaroid Corp., Cambridge, Mass.; Vermont Council on the Arts, Montpelier. Gallerie Optica, Montreal, Quebec, Canada.

REPRESENTATIVE Lumino Productions, 5 Kent St, Montpelier, VT 05602.

ADDRESS c/o *Common Image*, POB 1224, Montpelier, VT 05602.

Ilse Bing *PHOTOGRAPHER · POET* [See plate 63] Born March 23, 1899, in Frankfurt/Main, Germany, Bing studied history of art and mathematics at the universities of Frankfurt and Vienna until 1929. Self-taught as a photographer, she had close contact with the architect Mart Stam (for whom she made a photographic record of two building projects in 1930) and German painters Robert Michel and Ella Bergmann. Bing's husband, Konrad Wolff, is a professor of piano and an internationally known author of music books.

Bing has always worked as a freelance artist. Some of her assignments included: photographing painter Pavel Tchelitchew's staging of Ballanchine's *Errante* ballet at the Théâtre des Champs-Elysées, Paris, in 1933; a photographic survey of Pommery champagne in Reims and wine production in Burgundy following the end of prohibition (engaged by George Putnam); and regular fashion photography in Paris for *Harper's Bazaar* and Schiaparelli, 1933–35.

The photographer was among the first to use solarization (1934), electronic flash (1949), the 35mm camera (Leica) and to take photographs at night (since 1930).

Working in both black-and-white and color, Bing concentrates on pictorial photography: portraits, fashion, picture essays. Avoiding specialization, she has stressed the "abstract elements inherent in reality."

PUBLICATIONS Books: *Numbers in Images*, 1976; *Words as Visions*, drawings & poems, 1974; *Photography 1859–1937*, Beaumont Newhall, 1937; *L'Art Vivant—Living Art*, 1935. Anthologies: *Diverse Images*, 1979; *A Ten-Year Salute*, 1979; *The Photograph Collector's Guide*, Lee D. Witkin & Barbara London, 1979; *The Julien Levy Collection*, 1977; *Photographs from the Julien Levy Collection*, David Travis, 1976; *Documentation Photographique*, 1935 (Photo-Illustration: Paris); *Photographic*, *Arts-et-Métiers Graphiques*, 1933–34 (Paris). Periodical: *Creative Camera*, Nov 1978.

PORTFOLIO (group) *Fleeting Gestures*, 1979 (ICP, NYC).

COLLECTIONS Art Inst. of Chicago; Brooklyn Mus., N.Y.; CCP, Tucson; MOMA, NYC; New Orleans Mus. of Art; San Francisco Mus. of Modern Art; Stanford Mus., Calif.; Yale Univ. Art Gall., New Haven, Conn. Bibliothèque Nationale, Paris; Natl. Gall. of Can., Ottawa, Ont.

DEALERS Witkin Gall., 41 E 57 St, New York, NY 10022; Allan Frumkin Gall., 620 N Michigan Ave, Chicago, IL 60611; Galerie Zabriskie, 29 rue Aubrey le Boucher, Paris, France.

Ronald C. Binks *PHOTOGRAPHER · TEACHER* Born on October 20, 1934, in Oak Park, Illinois, Binks specialized in fine arts at the Rhode Island School of Design, where he earned a BFA in 1956, and studied at the Yale School of Design under Herbert Matter, completing an MFA in 1960. He also studied privately with Minor White.

For fourteen years Binks taught at the Rhode Island School of Design, and since 1976 he has been the director of the Division of Art & Design at the University of Texas in San Antonio.

Binks is a member of SPE and the CAA. In 1960 he received a Prix de Rome grant, and in 1956 a Fulbright grant, which he used for a two-year stay in Berlin. In 1968 he established the Department of Film Making at the Rhode Island School of Design.

The artist uses a large-format camera and concentrates on "straight photography, landscapes and environmental portraits."

PUBLICATIONS Periodicals: "Reading Photographs," *Aperture*, 1961; "New Photographers," *Art in America*, spring 1960.

COLLECTIONS Texas Tech. Univ., Mus. of Art, Lubbock; Witte Mus., San Antonio, Tex.
ADDRESS POB 404, Helotes, TX 78023.

Werner Adalbert Bischof *PHOTOGRAPHER*
Born 1916 in Zürich, Switzerland, Bischof died in a truck accident May 26, 1954, in the Peruvian Andes near Parcoy. He attended the teachers' seminar at Schiers, Graubunden, then the Zürich School of Arts and Crafts, where he studied photography with Hans Finsler.

A news photographer associated with Magnum Agency (beginning in 1949), Bischof headquartered in Zürich. He freelanced for such publications as *Du, Picture Post, Epoca, Paris-Match, Observer* and many American magazines, including *Life* and *Fortune*.

Bischof served as a war correspondent in France, Holland, Korea and Germany. In addition to his photojournalism, his personal work included detailed coverage of the culture and land of Japan.

PUBLICATIONS Monograph: *Werner Bischof*, Anna Farova, ed., 1968. Books: *The World of Werner Bischof*, Manuel Gasser, 1959; *From Incas to Indios*, w/Robert Frank & Pierre Verger, intro. by Manuel Tuñon de Lara, 1956; *Japan*, Robert Guillain, 1954; *Our Leave in Switzerland*, w/Arnold Kubler & Gottlieb Duttweiler, 1946; *24 Photos*, Manuel Gasser, 1946. Anthologies: *The Magic Image*, Cecil Beaton & Gail Buckland, 1975; *The Concerned Photographer*, Cornell Capa, ed., 1968; *Indiens Pas Mort*, Georges Arnaud, 1959.

COLLECTIONS Art Inst. of Chicago; IMP/GEH, Rochester; Metro. Mus. of Art, NYC; MOMA, NYC; Riverside Mus., NYC.

ARCHIVE Magnum Photos Inc., 15 W 46 St, New York, NY 10036.

Barbara Lee Bishop *PHOTOGRAPHER · TEACHER* Born on September 9, 1938, in Roanoke, Virginia, Bishop completed a bachelor's degree in art and education at Longwood College in Farmville, Virginia (1960), and an MFA in Painting and Graphic Arts at the University of North Carolina in Greensboro (1962). She also studied at the American Center for Students and Artists in Paris under Misch Kohn (1965) and at Columbia University in New York (1968–69).

Bishop has been teaching at Longwood College since 1965, first as an associate professor, and since 1970 as chairman of the Art Department; currently she serves as administrative director of its Fine Arts Center. Previously Bishop was chairman of the Art Department at Southern Semi-nary Junior College in Buena Vista, Virginia (1962–65).

She is a member of the Virginia Society for the Photographic Arts, the Richmond Artists Association, the Virginia Museum of Fine Arts, the National and the Virginia Art Education Associations and the Southeastern College Art Association. She received a Certificate of Distinction twice from the Virginia Museum in Richmond, one granted to Virginia Photographers (1971), the other to Virginia Artists (1979).

Bishop is currently working in SX-70 format. Her images generally consist of photo collages, and she also uses photography in photo-etching and silkscreen.

COLLECTIONS In Virginia: Ferrum Coll.; First & Merchants Bank; General Electric Co.; James Madison Univ.; Longwood Coll.; Phillip Morris, Inc.; Roanoke City Schools; Roanoke Fine Arts Ctr.; Southern Seminary Coll.; State Council of Higher Education; Va. Military Inst. Other states: Appalachian State Univ., N.C.; Lock Haven State Coll., Pa.

DEALERS Yeatts Gall., Walnut Ave SW, Roanoke, VA 24016; Art Sales Gall., Va. Mus. of Fine Arts, Richmond, VA.

ADDRESS Rt. 3, Box 568-B, Farmville, VA 73901.

Michael Bishop *PHOTOGRAPHER · TEACHER*
Born in 1946, Bishop studied with Henry Holmes Smith.

He has been on the adjunct faculty of the Visual Studies Workshop since 1975 and has taught at Rochester Institute of Technology (1977–78), University of California at Los Angeles (1972–75) and San Francisco Art Institute (1971–72). He is a founding member of Visual Dialogue Foundation in Carmel, California.

Using black-and-white, color and gum bichromate, Bishop photographs landscapes and commonplace objects. He also creates collages and photograms.

PUBLICATIONS Book: *Vision and Expression*, Nathan Lyons, ed., 1969. Anthology: *The Photograph Collector's Guide*, Lee D. Witkin & Barbara London, 1979. Catalogs: *Michael Bishop*, 1979 (Chicago Ctr. for Contemp. Photog.); *An Exhibition of Color Photography*, 1977 (Univ. of Conn., Jorgensen Gall.: Storrs); *American Photography: Past into Present*, Anita Ventura Mozley, 1976 (Seattle Art Mus./Univ. of Wash. Press: Seattle); *Peculiar to Photography*, 1976 (Univ. of N. Mex. Art Mus.: Albuquerque); *The Extended Document*, 1975 (IMP/GEH: Rochester); *12 Photographers*, 1975 (New Org. for the

Visual Arts at Park Centre: Cleveland, Ohio);
Light & Lens: Methods of Photography, 1973
(Morgan & Morgan & Hudson River Mus.: Yonkers, N.Y.); *60s Continuum*, Van Deren Coke,
1972 (IMP/GEH: Rochester); *Photo Media: Elements and Technics of Photography Experienced
as an Artistic Medium*, 1971 (Mus. of Contemp.
Crafts: NYC); *California Photographers 1970*,
1969 (Univ. of Calif.: Davis). Periodicals: "Michael Bishop at Light," Andy Grundberg, *Art in
America*, July/Aug 1977; "100 Years of Color,"
Julia Scully, Andy Grundberg & Mary O'Grady,
Christmas 1976, "Messages About the Medium,"
Julia Scully & Andy Grundberg, July 1976,
"Campus Boom!" Sept 1970, *Modern Photography*.

COLLECTIONS   Harvard Univ., Fogg Art Mus.,
Cambridge, Mass.; IMP/GEH, Rochester; Mus. of
Fine Arts, St. Petersburg, Fla.; Univ. of N. Mex.,
Albuquerque; Univ. of Tenn., Knoxville.

ADDRESS   72 N Union St, Rochester, NY
14603.

Sheila Maureen Bisilliat   *PHOTOGRAPHER*
Born February 16, 1931, in Surrey, England, Bisilliat is the daughter of painter Sheila Brannigan.
Bisilliat studied art with André Lhote in Paris
1953–54, and at the Art Students League in New
York City with Morris Kantor 1954–56.

She is currently a freelance photographer,
working in book publication, and a director of
documentary films. She worked for many years
as a photojournalist for Brazilian and foreign
magazines.

Bisilliat was a recipient of a Guggenheim Photography Grant in 1970 and received the Critics'
Grand Prix at the São Paulo (Brazil) XIII Bienal in
1976. She has also directed the documentary
films *Xingu Luta Epilogo* (1979), *Yaô/Initiation
Rituel* (1975) and *A João Guimarães Rosa* (1969).

PUBLICATIONS   Books: *Xingu*, 1979 (Editora
Raizes: São Paulo); *Xingu Tribal Territory*, Orlando & Cláudio Villas-Bôas, 1979 (William Collins: London); *A João Guimarães Rosa*, 1969
(Graficos Brunner: São Paulo).

REPRESENTATIVE   Nancy Palmer Agency, 129
Lexington Ave, New York, NY 10016.

ADDRESS   Rua Bela Cintra 2011, 01415 São
Paulo, Brazil.

Auguste-Rosalie Bisson   *PHOTOGRAPHER*
[See plate 14]   Bisson was born and died in Paris
(1826–1900). His father, Louis-François Bisson,
was a heraldic painter, and his brother, Louis-Auguste Bisson, was a photographer.

Auguste-Rosalie was an amateur heraldic

painter; for a time he was an inspector of measures and weights at Rambouillet. In 1841 he and
his brother opened a portrait studio in Paris,
which remained in business until 1865. The studio became a salon of sorts for artists and intellectuals.

Auguste daguerreotyped all the members of the
Chamber of Deputies and Senate, and these portraits were published as lithographs. In 1860,
with his brother, he accompanied Napoleon III
and the Empress Eugénie to the Swiss Alps, there
producing a dazzling array of mountain views. In
1861 he climbed Mount Blanc, along with
twenty-five carriers and guides, recording that
stark place with the use of the wet-collodion process. When their studio closed, Louis retired, but
Auguste went on to work for Léon and Levy, photographers, and then for the Adolphe Braun Studio. The brothers' work was exhibited in Paris,
Amsterdam, Berlin, Brussels, Edinburgh, London,
Manchester and Marseilles.

The Bisson brothers were founding members of
the Société Française de Photographie. In 1842
they proposed a better sensitizing method for daguerreotype plates and a method of electroplating
the plates with gold and silver; they also perfected the use of filters on the lens. In the same
year the Société d'Encouragement pour l'Industrie Nationale awarded the Bissons a medal for a
"nearly one metre"-long daguerreotype.

Working almost chiefly with collodion wet-plates—although he made some daguerreotypes
early in his career—Auguste is best known for
his Alpine views. However, the "Bisson fils," as
they are often referred to, also created a sizable
body of work concentrating on historical buildings in France, Italy and Belgium, as well as photographic reproductions of art works. They were
noted for the quality and the unusually large size
of their negatives, which often ranged up to
30¼ x 40 cm.

PUBLICATIONS   Books: *Le Mont Blanc et Ses
Glaciers*, 1860 (Paris); *L'Oeuvre de Rembrandt
reproduit par la Photographie*, Chas. Blanc, 3
vols., 1854–58 (Gide & Gide/J. Baudry: Paris);
*The Knight, Devil and Death: Oeuvre d'Albert
Dürer Photographié*, ca. 1854; *Monographie de
Notre Dame de Paris . . .*, ca. 1853–57 (A. Morel:
Paris); *Choix d'Ornements Arabes de l'Alhambra . . .*, 1853 (J. Baudry: Paris). Anthologies: *The
Photograph Collector's Guide*, Lee D. Witkin &
Barbara London, 1979; *Photography: The First
Eighty Years*, Valerie Lloyd, Colnaghi, et al, eds.,
1976 (London); *The Invented Eye*, Edward Lucie-Smith, 1975; *The Magic Image*, Cecil Beaton &
Gail Buckland, 1975; *Travel Photography*, 1972,

Great Photographers, 1971, Time-Life Series; *French Primitive Photography*, A. Jammes & R. Sobieszek, 1970. Catalogs: *L'Art en France sous le second Empire*, 1979 (Rénion des Musées Nationaux: Paris), *Une Invention du XIXᵉ Siècle*, Bernard Marbot, 1976 (Bibliothèque Nationale: Paris); *De Niepce à Man Ray*, André Jammes & Laurent Roosens, 1965 (Musée des Arts Décoratifs: Paris); *Hundert Jahre Photographie 1839–1939*, Helmut & Alison Gernsheim, 1959 (Cologne). Periodicals: *Le Moniteur de la photographie*, 1872, 1871, 1869, 1868, 1865, 1863, 1862, 1861; *Bulletin de la Société Française de Photographie*, 1871, 1860, 1858, 1857, 1856, 1855; *Comptes rendus hebdomadaires des séances de l'Académie des sciences*, 1865, 1862, 1858, 1855, 1854, 1853, 1844, 1843, 1842, 1841; *La Lumière*, 1865, 1862, 1861, 1860, 1859, 1858, 1857, 1856, 1855, 1854, 1853, 1851; *Revue Photographique*, 1863, 1862, 1861, 1859, 1858, 1856, 1855; *Cosmos*, Oct 26, 1855; *Revues des Deux Mondes*, Aug 1, 1855.
COLLECTIONS IMP/GEH, Rochester; MOMA, NYC; N.Y. Pub. Lib., NYC; Princeton Univ., Firestone Lib., N.J. Bibliothèque Nationale, Paris; Société Française, Paris; Victoria & Albert Mus., London.

Louis-Auguste Bisson PHOTOGRAPHER [See plate 14] Born in Paris in 1814, Bisson died there in 1876. He is the brother of Auguste-Rosalie Bisson, also a photographer.
Louis-Auguste's career followed the same path as his brother's with only a couple of exceptions: he retired in 1865, and he did not follow his brother up the arduous trail to Mont Blanc—that heroic adventure was Auguste's alone.
See Auguste-Rosalie Bisson

Laura Ann Blacklow PHOTOGRAPHER · TEACHER Born 1945 in Washington, D.C., Blacklow received a BFA from Boston University School of Fine Arts in 1967. She studied at the Visual Studies Workshop in Rochester, New York, 1973–75, and received an MFA there in 1977. Both Joan and Nathan Lyons were her teachers and major influences on her work.
Blacklow has been employed as a lecturer for a Visible Language Workshop at the Massachusetts Institute of Technology since 1979, and has also been an instructor at the School of the Boston Museum of Fine Arts since 1978. She was previously employed at the Massachusetts Institute of Technology as a research affiliate (1977–79) and as an instructor at Emerson College in Boston (1975–79).

A member of the Boston Visual Artists Union since 1977, she is also a founding member of the Pull Here Press, an artists' cooperative printshop in Boston that was founded in 1979. Blacklow was the recipient of a Massachusetts Artists Foundation Fellowship in Photography in 1978.
The photographer characterizes her work as being concerned "with the relationship of words to images, and of images to each other. I often work in the book format," she says, "and incorporate a variety of techniques. I think about the role of the woman artist in this society and how to integrate visible material with ideas and sensibilities."
PUBLICATIONS Books: *The Contemporary Quilt*, Pattie Chase, ed., 1978; *Innovative Printmaking*, Thelma R. Newman, ed., 1977; *Child's Version of "Beowulf,"* 1976; *The Long Way Around*, Carol Palmer, ed., 1976; *Where It's At*, 1974.
COLLECTIONS IMP/GEH, Rochester; Itek Corp., Rochester.
ADDRESS Cambridge, MA 02139.

James Pease Blair PHOTOGRAPHER Born April 14, 1931, in Philadelphia, Pennsylvania, Blair received a BS degree in Photography at the Institute of Design, Illinois Institute of Technology, Chicago, in 1954. He was taught and influenced by Harry Callahan, Aaron Siskind and Roy E. Stryker.
Since 1962 he has been a staff photographer for the National Geographic Society in Washington, D.C. Previously he worked as a freelance photojournalist (1959–62) and a film photographer at WIIC-TV in Pittsburgh, Pennsylvania (1958–59).
A member of the White House News Photographers Association, the NPPA and the Overseas Press Club, Blair was the recipient of the Overseas Press Club Best Photographic Reporting from Abroad Award in 1978. He was made a Yale University Poynter Fellow in 1977.
PUBLICATIONS Books: *As We Live and Breathe*, 1971; *Listen with the Eye*, 1964.
COLLECTION Yale Univ. Lib, New Haven, Conn.
ADDRESS Natl. Geographic Society, 1145 17 St NW, Washington, DC 20036.

Jonathan S. Blair PHOTOGRAPHER Born in Bryn Mawr, Pennsylvania, Blair studied at Northwestern University, Evanston, Illinois (1961–63), then (1965) earned a BFA in Photographic Illustration from Rochester Institute of Technology, New York, where he studied under Minor White.

His father, William M. Blair, is a writer and president of the National Press Club.

Since 1968 Blair has been a contract photographer for National Geographic Society, and since 1979 has been a guest lecturer at Maine Photographic Workshop. He also lectured in 1979 at the University of Southern Illinois, Carbondale, and at the University of Indiana, Bloomington. In 1963 he was a park photographer at Yosemite National Park and a staff photographer at Dearborn Observatory, Northwestern University.

PUBLICATIONS Periodicals: "The Quicksilver Galleons," Dec 1979, "The Mystery of Migration," Aug 1979, "Glass Treasure from the Aegean," June 1978, "The Leeward Islands: Hawaii's Wildlife Paradise," May 1978, "Bad Time to Be a Crocodile," Jan 1978, "Yellowstone's Hundredth Birthday," May 1972, "Stockholm: Where Quality Is a Way of Life," Jan 1976, "Cyprus Struggles for Unity," Mar 1973, *National Geographic*.

REPRESENTATIVE Woodfin Camp, 415 Madison Ave, New York, NY 10017.

ADDRESS POB 4849, Washington, DC 20008.

Michael Charles Blake   PHOTOGRAPHER · SCREENPRINTER Born in Waterford, Ireland, on January 28, 1950, Blake received a diploma in creative photography in 1974 from Trent Polytechnic School of Art, Nottingham. His principle influences have been Thomas Cooper, John Blakemore and Clive Adams.

Blake is currently a freelance photographer in Dublin, Ireland. Previously (in 1977) he was the director of Travelling Light Photography, Ltd., publishers and distributors of fine photography books, with Peter Turner and Heather Forbes. Prior to that (1976–77) he was coordinator of Co-Optic, a photographers' cooperative and publishing house.

Blake was awarded an Arts Council Grant to photograph Stonehenge and the Avebury Henge area in 1976.

PUBLICATION Anthology: *Perspectives of Landscape*, 1979 (Art Council of Great Britain).

COLLECTIONS In London: Arts Council of Great Britain Cllctn.; Dept. of the Environment Cllctn.

ADDRESS 24 Leeson Park, Dublin 6, Ireland.

John Blakemore   PHOTOGRAPHER · TEACHER Born July 15, 1936, in Coventry, England, Blakemore is a self-taught photographer, influenced by Minor White and Paul Caponigro.

Since 1970 he has been senior lecturer in photography at Derby Lonsdale College, Derby, England. In the previous ten years he worked as a photographer for various studios and industrial companies in London and The Midlands, England.

He won photography awards from the Arts Council of Great Britain in 1974 and 1976 and a Photography Bursary from the Council in 1979.

Blakemore's work was featured in the BBC-2 television program *Exploring Photography No. 3: The Landscape* in 1978.

Blakemore photographs the natural landscape in large-format black-and-white, "seeking to express . . . through richness of tone, quality of light, and detail . . . the spiritual and physical energy of nature."

PUBLICATIONS Monograph: *John Blakemore*, 1976 (Arts Council of Great Britain: London). Catalog: *Perspectives on Landscape*, intro. by Bill Gaskins, 1978 (Arts Council of Great Britain: London). Periodicals: *Creative Camera International Yearbook*, Feb 1977, *Yearbook*, 1976, *British Image 3*, 1977 (Arts Council of Great Britain); *British Journal of Photography Annual*, 1977; *Camera*, Aug 1976.

COLLECTIONS Los Angeles County Mus. of Art. Natl. Lib. of Wales; Fotografiska Muséet, Moderna Muséet, Stockholm. In England: Arts Council of Great Britain, London; Dept. of the Environment, London; East Midlands Art Assoc.; RPS, Bath; Victoria & Albert Mus., London; West Midlands Arts Assoc., England.

DEALER Visions Gall. Ltd, 7 Gate Mews, Rutland Gate, London SW7, England.

ADDRESS 62 Norman St, Cotmanhay, Ilkeston, Derbyshire, England.

Lazaro Blanco-Fuentes   TEACHER · PHOTOGRAPHER · AUTHOR Born April 1, 1938, in Ciudad Juárez, Chihuahua, Mexico, Blanco-Fuentes studied architecture and physics at the Universidad Nacional Autónoma de México (1958–63). He also attended Michigan State University, East Lansing (1967) and State University of New York (1971). Blanco-Fuentes is self-taught in photography.

Since 1964 he has been a science instructor and chairman of the Science Department at American School Foundation, Mexico City. He also teaches at the Photography Workshops, Casa del Lago, Universidad Nacional Autónoma de Mexico, which he initiated in 1973. He served as an adviser on photography to Museo Carillo Gil of the Instituto Nacional de Bellas Artes in Mexico in 1978, and he taught mathematics and physics at various schools in Mexico City in 1963.

A member of SPE, the photographer is a

founder (1976) and vice president of Consejo Mexicano de Fotografía. He won First Place in 1973 from the Departamento de Agrucultura, Exposición Nacional de Ganadería.

PUBLICATIONS   Anthology: *The Family of Woman*, 1979. Catalog: *El niño y la estructura*, 1979 (Caracas, Venezuela). Periodicals: *Zoom*, Mar 1979 (Paris); *Il Diaframma*, Feb 1979; *Camera*, Oct 1978; *Fotozoom Annual*, 1977; *Fotomundo Annual*, 1970; *Life* (Mexican, ed.), Oct 6, 1969.

COLLECTIONS   CCP, Tucson; Natl. Geographic Soc., Wash., D.C. Casa de Las Américas, Havana, Cuba; Consejo Mexicano de Fotografía, A.C., Mexico; Hartkampf Cllctn., Amsterdam, The Netherlands; Museo de Arte Moderno, Mexico City; U.N. Photo Archive, Geneva, Switzerland; Universidad Nacional Autónoma de Mexico, Mexico City.

DEALER   Prakapas Gall., 19 E 71 St, New York, NY 10021.

ADDRESS   Rep. Argentina 17-402, México 1, D.F., México.

Louis-Désiré Blanquart-Evrard   PHOTOGRA-
PHER · PRINTER · PUBLISHER · INVENTOR   [See plate 6]   Born in Lyons, France, in 1802, Blanquart-Evrard died in that city in April 1872.

He established the Imprimerie Photographique in Lille, France, in 1851, a printing house employing thirty to forty women to do assembly-line printing on a grand scale. He started a similar plant in Paris, and in 1855 began one on the Isle of Jersey in England, under the patronage of Prince Albert. The latter plant, which did permanent positive printing, was founded in conjunction with Thomas Sutton. Sutton and Blanquart-Evrard also co-founded and edited together the magazine *Photographic Notes* in 1856, which was published until 1867.

The photographer reported to the French Academy of Sciences on May 27, 1850, the invention of albumen paper. He contributed many other improvements to the printing and developing processes carried on in his business, such as introducing the process of developing silver chloride paper with gallic acid, resulting in the rapid printing that allows for large editions of silver prints; he invented the "amphitype" process; and he was able to reduce exposure time from minutes to seconds, among other improvements.

Most of his work was with the calotype, although he produced some albumen and salt prints. His work was described by his friend and co-editor Sutton as being "beautifully artistic: vigorous, without being glazed, and superb in color." Not only did the artist develop a fine and rapid printing process, but he fixed his prints in such a way that they retain their clarity to this day.

PUBLICATIONS   Books: *La Photographie: Ses origines, ses progrès, ses transformations*, 1869 (L. Daniel: Lille, France); *Intervention de l'Art dans la Photographie*, 1863 (L. Daniel: Lille, France); *Jerusalem*, Auguste Salzmann, 1856; *Le Nil: Monuments, paysages, explorations photographiques*, John B. Greene, 1854; *Egypt, Nubia, Palestine and Syria*, negatives by Maxime du Camp, 1852 (Lille, France); *Album photographique de l'artiste et de l'amateur*, w/Hippolyte Fockedey, 1851; *Traité de photographie sur papier*, 1851 (Roret: Paris); *Procédés employés pour obtenir les épreuves photographiques sur papier*, 1847 (Charles Chevalier: Paris). Anthologies: *The Photograph Collector's Guide*, Lee D. Witkin & Barbara London, 1979; *Une invention due XIXe siècle: Expression et technique de la photographie*, 1976 (Bibliothèque Nationale: Paris); *French Primitive Photography*, A. Jammes & Robt. Sobieszek, intro. by Minor White, 1970; *Art and Photography*, Aaron Scharf, 1969. Periodicals: Isabelle Jammes, *Camera*, Dec 1978; "Louis Désiré Blanquart-Evrard: The Gutenberg of Photography," Gerda Peterich, *Image 6*, Apr 1957; Thomas Sutton, *The British Journal of Photography*, vol. 19, 1872; *Bulletin Société Française Photographie*, 1860; *La Lumière*, Sept 3, 1856.

COLLECTIONS   IMP/GEH, Rochester. Bibliothèque Nationale, Paris; Lib. of Lille, France; Natl. Gall. of Can., Ottawa, Ontario.

Ernest Bloch   COMPOSER · PHOTOGRAPHER
[See plate 46]   Born July 24, 1880, in Geneva, Switzerland, Bloch died July 15, 1959, in Agate Beach, Oregon. He studied music first with Swiss composer Émile Jaques-Dalcroze, then with violinists Eugène Ysaye and Franz Schörg in Brussels (about 1899). He continued his studies with Ivan Knorr in Frankfurt and finally with Ludwig Thuille in Munich (1901–1903). Bloch first took an interest in photography in Brussels around 1896–97.

The composer taught at the Geneva Conservatory from 1911 to 1915, and in 1916 moved to the U.S., touring with Maud Allen's dance company. Bloch directed the Institute of Music in Cleveland (Ohio) from 1920 to 1925 and the San Francisco Conservatory from 1925 to 1930. Returning to Europe, he worked on several compositions there (1930–38), but with the rising tide of anti-Semitism, he moved back to the U.S., settling in

Oregon in 1943. For several summers he taught master classes in composition at the University of California, Berkeley.

Bloch received a number of awards for his musical compositions: the Coolidge Prize for *Suite for Viola and Piano* (1919), the Musical America Prize for *America* (1928), the first Gold Medal in Music from the American Academy of Arts and Letters (1942) and the Professor Emeritus of Music title from the University of California, Berkeley (1952).

Some of his other famed compositions are *Schelomo* (1916), *Israel Symphony* (1917), *Sacred Service* (1933), *Violin Concerto* (1938) and five string quartets. Bloch was an influential teacher, and his students included Roger Sessions, Leon Kirchner, Bernard Rogers, Quincy Porter, Randall Thompson and Eliot Carter.

Unconcerned with process, Bloch's forte in photography, as in music, lay in composition. "Beautifully orchestrated images of wilderness scenes, parks and shores illustrate Bloch's love of nature and comment on his sensitive awareness of light and the possible moods it commands," writes Bonnie Ford *(Ernest Bloch Archive)*. His more than 6,000 negatives and 2,000 prints also include many portraits, self-portraits and cityscapes.

PUBLICATIONS Books: *Ernest Bloch, Voice in the Wilderness*, Robert Strassburg, 1977; *Ernest Bloch: Creative Spirit*, Suzanne Bloch & Irene Heskes, 1976. Catalogs: *Ernest Bloch Archive*, Sharon Denton, intro. by Bonnie Ford, 1979 (CCP: Tucson); *Ernest Bloch: Photographer and Composer*, 1979 (CCP: Tucson). Periodicals: "Ernest Bloch," Eric Johnson, *Camera*, Feb 1976; "A Composer's Vision—Photographs by Ernest Bloch," Eric Johnson, *Aperture*, 16:3, 1972.

COLLECTION CCP, Tucson.

ARCHIVE Center for Creative Photography, University of Arizona, 843 E University Blvd, Tucson, AZ 85719.

Gay Shlenker Block PHOTOGRAPHER Born March 5, 1942, in Houston, Texas, Block attended Newcomb College, New Orleans, from 1959 to 1961 and the University of Houston School of Architecture (1971–73). She studied photography with Geoff Winningham (1974–76), Anne Tucker (1976–77) and Garry Winogrand (1976).

As of this writing she is a teacher of photography at the University of Houston Fine Arts School.

In 1978 Block received the NEA Photographer's Fellowship Grant. Also, she received a grant from Congregation Beth Israel, Houston, in 1975 to create a 16mm film entitled "A Tribute to Spirit: The Beth Israel Experience," completed in 1976.

Working with medium and large formats in black-and-white, she has made portraiture her main concern, focusing primarily on Jews in America. She began the series with her own community of origin, and has continued the work in other communities throughout the U.S.A.

PUBLICATIONS Anthology: *Self-Portrayal*, James Alinder, ed., 1978. Catalog: *Shot in Texas*, Mar 1977 (Ft. Worth Art Museum). Periodical: *Camera*, Aug 1977.

COLLECTIONS Ft. Worth Art Mus., Tex.; Mus. of Fine Arts, Houston, Tex.; Portland Art Mus., Maine.

DEALER Cronin Gall., 2008 Peden, Houston, TX 77019.

ADDRESS 443 Hunterwood, Houston, TX 77024

Barbara Blondeau PHOTOGRAPHER · TEACHER Born May 6, 1938, in Detroit, Michigan, Blondeau died December 24, 1974, in Philadelphia, Pennsylvania. She received a BFA from the School of the Art Institute of Chicago in 1961 and an MS from the Institute of Design of Illinois Institute of Technology, Chicago, in 1968, where she studied with Aaron Siskind and Joseph Jachna.

Her last post was as associate professor and chairperson of the Photo/Film Department at Philadelphia College of Art, and from 1970 to 1971 she was an assistant professor there. She also taught at Moore College of Art in Philadelphia (1968–70) and at St. Mary's College in Notre Dame, Indiana (1966–68).

Best known for the long strip prints she began producing in 1968, Blondeau worked in a wide variety of materials, processes, sizes and formats. "Whether she was working in black-and-white or color, whether the prints she made were on paper or on plastic, whether they were square in shape, or round, or long and narrow, Blondeau was refining and articulating ideas of transparence, of repetition, of patterning, and of narrative," wrote Charles Hagen *(Barbara Blondeau)*.

PUBLICATIONS Monograph: *Barbara Blondeau, 1938–74*, D. Lebe, J. Redmond, R. Walker, eds., 1976. Book: *Vision and Expression*, 1969. Anthologies: *Frontiers of Photography*, 1972, *The Print*, 1971, Time-Life Series; *Into the 70's*, 1970. Catalog: *The Multiple Image*, 1972. Periodicals: *Art in America*, Sept 1976; *Afterimage: VSW*, Mar 1976; *Camera*, Nov 1971; *Popular Photography Annual*, 1969.

COLLECTIONS VSW, Rochester. Natl. Gall. of Can., Ottawa, Ontario.

ARCHIVE Research Center, Visual Studies Workshop, 31 Prince St, Rochester, NY 14607.

Karl Blossfeldt *PHOTOGRAPHER · TEACHER* [See plate 39] Born in Schiele (Harz), Germany, in 1865, Blossfeldt died in Germany in 1932. Aside from pursuing his personal work in photography, he was a professor in the United States Schools of Free and Applied Art in Berlin.

With his meticulously produced studies of plant life, Professor Blossfeldt was attempting to prove his thesis that, though nature and art are widely differentiated in vital respects, the original forms of all art are to be found in nature. His enlarged images of the forms assumed by plants —buds, sprouts, leaves, stalks—are offered as evidence.

PUBLICATIONS Monographs: *Wunder in der Natur*, 1942 (Pantheon-verlag für Kunstwissenschaft); *Wundergarten der Natur*, 1932 (Verlag für Kunstwissenschaft: Berlin); *Konstformen i naturen*, 1930 (Bokförlaget natur och Kultur: Stockholm); *Urformen der Kunst*, intro. by Karl Nierendorf, 1925, U.S. ed., *Art Forms in Nature*, 1929; *First Forms of Art*, n.d. (Perleberg: Philadelphia). Periodical: "To Plants and Leaves We Can Go for Art Forms," H. L. Brock, *New York Times Magazine*, July 28, 1929.

PORTFOLIO *12 Fotografien*, intro. by Volker Kahmen, 1975 (Galerie Wilde: Cologne).

DEALER Galerie Wilde, auf dem Berlich 6, D-5000 Cologne 1, West Germany.

Elihu Blotnick *PHOTOGRAPHER · AUTHOR* Born in New York City on December 2, 1939, Blotnick earned a bachelor's degree in English at City College in his native city in 1962 and later joined the Master's Program in Literature at the University of California in Berkeley and at San Francisco State. Mark Linenthal was his mentor.

He has been a member of Mystery Writers of America since 1978, and the recipient of several awards granted to him by the American Institute of Graphic Arts (1976, 1973), the Northwest International Exhibition of Photography (1977, 1976) and the Art Director's Club of Washington D.C. (1976).

In 1976 the artist made, for Macmillan, *Webfooted Friends, a film that has nothing to do with ducks.* He has written several children's books.

Blotnick works in 35mm and is interested in documentary photography. His field of research is metaphor and visual equivalence.

PUBLICATIONS Books: *California Street 1*, incl. text, 1979; *Mysterious Mr. Blot*, 1979; *Never Distrust an Asparagus*, 1979; *Looking Up*, 1979; *Saltwater Flats*, incl. poems, 1974. Periodicals: *Camera*, 1974; *Communication Arts*, 1976.

COLLECTIONS Calif. Hist. Soc., San Francisco; LC, Wash., D.C.; Oakland Mus., Calif.

ADDRESS California Street, 723 Dwight Way, Berkeley, CA 94710.

Carroll Parrott Blue *PHOTOGRAPHER · FILM MAKER* Born August 23, 1943, in Houston, Texas, Blue went to Boston University, where she completed her bachelor's degree in 1964. She studied commercial photography at Los Angeles Trade Technical College from 1970 to 1972 and is currently a candidate for a Master of Fine Arts degree at the UCLA Film School. She has been greatly influenced by photographer Roy DeCarava and film maker Carlton Moss.

Blue is a member of the African Film Society, the American Film Institute, the Association of Independent Video and Filmmakers, the Friends of Photography, the Los Angeles Center for Photographic Studies and SPE. In 1979 she received an independent film maker's grant from the American Film Institute; she was awarded the Gold Hugo at the Chicago International Film Festival. In 1978 she won the third prize at the Second International Exhibition of Photography in Moscow.

Blue's most recent film was *Varnette's World: A Study of a Young Artist*, in 1980. Her film *Two Women* (1976) won second place in the 1977 Virgin Islands International Film Festival and a Certificate of Merit at the 1977 Chicago International Film Festival.

The artist describes herself as a documentary still photographer and a documentary film maker.

PUBLICATIONS Anthologies: *The Black Photographers Annual*, 1980; *Self Portrayal*, 1978; *Faces: USA*, 1978. Periodicals: *Black Art*, I:3, 1977; *The Black Photographer's Annual*, vol. 3, 1976.

COLLECTION E. Wash. State Coll., Cheney, Wash.

ADDRESS 2049½ S Holt Ave, Los Angeles, CA 90034, or POB 35532, Los Angeles, CA 90035.

Irena Blúhová *TEACHER · PHOTOGRAPHER · PUBLICIST* Born March 2, 1904, in Považská Bystrica, Czechoslovakia, Blúhová studied at the Bauhaus Academy of Arts in Dessau, Germany (1931–33), with Wassily Kandinsky and Josef Albers and at the School of Photography of the School of Artistic Craftsmanship, Bratislava, Czechoslovakia (1936–37), under Karol Plicka and Jaromir Funke. She later received an MA (1957) from the University of Pedagogics in Bratislava. Blühová's husband, Imro Weiner-Kráľ (1901–78), was a painter, graphic artist and theoretician.

Now retired, Blühová most recently founded and directed the Slovak Pedagogic Library in Bratislava (1951–65). Previously she directed the Folk Art Industry cooperative in Bratislava (1949–51) and both founded and headed the publishing and printing house Pravda (1945–48). From 1933 to 1941 she served as editor-in-chief of a publishing house at Bratislava.

Blühová co-founded and taught for Sociofoto, the society of progressive photographers at Bratislava, from 1933 to 1939. In 1976 she won the medal of the Building Academy of the German Democratic Republic on the fiftieth anniversary of the founding of the Bauhaus.

She calls her work "socially committed photography," and says she was "one of the first photographers to document the life of the toilers." Blühová has also done portraits and landscapes.

PUBLICATIONS Books: *No News for Kate*, 1966; *The First Steps*, Mladé letá, 1959 (Bratislava).

COLLECTIONS Bauhaus-Archiv, Berlin, West Germany; Bauhaus-Mus., Dessau, West Germany; Dokumentationsarchiv des Oesterreichischen Widerstandes, Vienna, Austria; Hochschule für Architektur und Bauwesen, Weimar, West Germany. In Czechoslovakia: Moravian Gall., Brno; Slovak Natl. Gall., Bratislava; Slovak Natl. Mus., Bratislava; Slovak Natl. Mus., Martin; Town Mus. of Bratislava.

REPRESENTATIVE Susan Blühova, 11A Hawthorn Rd, London N8 7LY, England.

ADDRESS Malá u. 17, 801 00 Bratislava, Czechoslovakia.

Donald Robert Blumberg PHOTOGRAPHER · TEACHER Born April 4, 1935, in Brooklyn, New York, Blumberg earned his BS in 1959 from Cornell University, Ithaca, New York, and his MS in 1961 from the University of Colorado, Boulder.

He taught at State University of New York at Buffalo (1965–72), first as an assistant (1965–69) and later as an associate professor of art. He also taught for Mobilization for Youth in New York City (1962–65), City College of New York (1963–64) and Brooklyn College (1962–63). Blumberg belongs to SPE and CAA.

The photographer won CAPS grants in 1975 and 1971; Summer Research Fellowships from SUNY in 1973, 1972, 1969, 1967 and 1966; and Institutional Funds Research Grants from SUNY Buffalo in 1975 and 1967.

He has made three films with Grace Blumberg: *Exorcise* (1968), *Buffalo to New York, New York to Buffalo* (1967) and *P.S. 32, Class 4A, 1907* (1966).

As of this date Blumberg is "working with collage concepts utilizing solely photographic material, or photographs in combination with found objects or a child's (my daughter) drawings."

PUBLICATIONS Monographs: *Photographs 1965–1978*, 1979; *In Front of St. Patrick's Cathedral*, intro. by Nathan Lyons, 1973. Books: *Coping with Television*, 1973; *The City: American Experience*, 1971. Anthologies: *Celebrations*, Minor White & Jonathan Green, eds., 1974; *Octave of Prayer*, Minor White, ed., 1972; *The Art of Photography*, Time-Life Series, 1971; *Vision and Expression*, 1969; *The Persistence of Vision*, 1967; *Photography in the Twentieth Century*, 1967. Catalogs: *In Western New York*, 1977, *32nd Western New York Exhibit Catalog*, 1968 (Albright-Knox Gall.: Buffalo); *Photography USA*, 1967 (De Cordova Mus.); *30th Annual Western New York Exhibit Catalog*, 1966 (Albright-Knox Gall.). Periodicals: *Photography Annual*, 1970, 1964.

PORTFOLIOS *Daily Photographs*, 1972, *Portraits of Students*, 1972 (Flower Mountain Press).

COLLECTIONS Alfred Univ., Picker Gall., Alfred, N.Y.; Art Inst. of Chicago; Colgate Univ., Hamilton, N.Y.; Cornell Univ., Johnson Mus. of Art, Ithaca, N.Y.; Cranbrook Acad. of Art, Bloomfield Hills, Mich.; Gall. Assoc. of N.Y., NYC; Harvard Univ., Carpenter Ctr. for the Visual Arts, Cambridge; IMP/GEH, Rochester; K-Mart Corp., Troy, Mich.; L/C, Wash., D.C.; MIT, Cambridge; Metro. Mus. of Art, NYC; Minneapolis Inst. of Art, Minn.; MOMA, NYC; Nassau Community Coll., Garden City, N.Y.; Norton Simon Mus. of Art, Pasadena, Calif.; Oakland Mus., Calif.; Charles Rand Penny Fndn., Olcott, N.Y.; Port Authority of N.Y., NYC; Pratt Inst., Brooklyn, N.Y.; St. Bonaventure Univ., NYC; UCLA; Univ. of Santa Clara, DeSaisset Art Gall. & Mus., Calif.; Vassar Coll. Art Gall., Poughkeepsie, N.Y.; VSW, Rochester; Worcester Art Mus., Mass. Natl. Gall. of Canada, Ottawa.

DEALERS Light Gall., 800 N La Cienega, Los Angeles, CA 90069; Visual Studies Workshop, 31 Prince St, Rochester, NY 14607.

ADDRESS 16918 Donna Ynez Ln, Pacific Palisades, CA 90272.

Erwin Blumenfeld PHOTOGRAPHER Born in Berlin in 1897, Blumenfeld died in Rome in 1969.

After the sudden death of his father in 1913, he started work as an assistant dress designer in a women's ready-to-wear store in Berlin. From 1916 to 1918 he was an ambulance driver in the German Army and from 1922 to 1935 he owned and operated a leather-goods shop in Amsterdam. He began photographing in 1922, often using his shop to display his works. When his store went bankrupt, he moved to Paris (1936) and established himself as a professional photographer.

He was first published in *Arts Graphiques* and *Verve*, then joined the Paris staff of *Vogue* in 1938 and *Harper's Bazaar* in 1939. After having been imprisoned in a Nazi camp in France in 1941, Blumenfeld emigrated to the United States. He freelanced for many important U.S. magazines—*Look*, *Cosmopolitan*, *Popular Photography*, etc.—and produced over a hundred color magazine covers.

Blumenfeld also painted and wrote, beginning at the time of the German Dada movement in the early 1900s. In his later years he wrote his autobiography (over the course of fourteen years) in German.

A highly successful fashion photographer, Blumenfeld worked in both black-and-white and, later, color. He did all his own darkroom work, using a variety of techniques such as double exposures and solarization, as well as using mirrors and reflectors. Blumenfeld is also known for his nudes and portraits.

PUBLICATIONS Book: *Durch Tausenjahrige Zeit*, autobio., 1976 (Huber, Frauenfeld: Switzerland). Anthologies: *The Magic Image*, Cecil Beaton & Gail Buckland, 1975; *Art and Technique of Color Photography*, Alexander Liberman, ed., 1951; *Seventeen American Photographers*, Ebria Feinblatt, 1948.

COLLECTIONS CCP, Tucson; Fashion Inst. of Tech. Lib., NYC; MOMA, NYC; New Orleans Art Mus.; Smith Coll. Mus. of Art, Northampton, Mass.; Univ. of N. Mex. Art Mus., Albuquerque; Witte Memorial Mus., San Antonio, Tex.

ARCHIVES Fashion Institute of Technology, 227 W 27 St, New York, NY 10001; Marina Schinz, 222 Central Park S, New York, NY 10020.

A. Aubrey Bodine PHOTOGRAPHER Born in 1906 in Baltimore, Maryland, Bodine died in that city on October 28, 1970. He was the chief photographer for the *Baltimore Sun* papers from 1927 to 1970.

He became a Fellow in the Photographic Society of America in 1946 and was elected an Honorary Fellow in 1965. A charter member and Fellow in the NPPA since 1953, he won first prize in *Popular Photography's* 1949 contest.

A pictorialist, he is best known for his images of the Chesapeake Bay Area. He loved to manipulate his negatives and was fascinated by the print quality that could be achieved.

PUBLICATIONS Books: *Bodine—A Legend in His Time* bio., Harold A. Williams, 1971; *The Face of Virginia*, 1963; *The Face of Maryland*, 1961; *A Guide To Baltimore and Annapolis*, 1957; *Chesapeake Bay and Tidewater*, 1954; *My Maryland*, 1952.

COLLECTIONS Baltimore Mus. of Art, Md.; Mariners' Mus., Newport News, Va.; Metro. Mus. of Art, NYC; Smithsonian Inst., Wash., D.C.

ARCHIVE Kathleen Ewing Gall., 3020 K St, Washington, DC 20007.

Dorothy Bohm PHOTOGRAPHER Born June 22, 1924, in Königsberg, Germany (then East Prussia), Bohm studied photographic technology at the University of Manchester (England), College of Technology, from 1940 to 1942, obtaining City and Guilds final Certificate in Photography, in addition to her graduate diploma. As a student Bohm admired Cartier-Bresson, Izis and Brandt.

Active at the Photographers' Gallery in London since its inception in 1971, she has served as its associate director since 1973. Previously she freelanced and traveled extensively (from 1960), and operated her own portrait studio in Manchester (1945–60). In 1945 she taught photography at the College of Technology in Manchester.

A member of the RPS, she is a trustee of the Hampstead Artists Council in London.

She primarily worked in small- and medium-format black-and-white in her earlier "human interest" photography. More recently Bohm has produced landscapes and still lifes with SX-70.

PUBLICATIONS Monograph: *A World Observed*, Hugh Evelyn, 1970 (London). Periodicals: *British Journal of Photography*, June 1980, Apr 1969; *British Journal of Photography Annual*, 1977, 1976, 1971, 1970, *Mussag*, Jan 1976; *Photographic Journal*, May 1975; *Amateur Photographer*, June 7, 1972, Feb 17, 1971; *Creative Camera*, Dec 1970, Apr 1969; *Camera Club Journal*, summer 1970; *Photography*, Oct 1955.

ADDRESS 16 Greenaway Gardens, London NW 3, England.

Walter Boje PHOTOJOURNALIST · TEACHER · EDITOR Born November 16, 1905, in Berlin,

Germany, Boje received a diploma in economics (1927) and a doctorate in political economy (1930) from the University of Berlin. He is self-taught in photography.

Currently editor of the magazine *Leica Fotographie*, Boje previously taught photography at the Institute for Art Education at the University of Munich (1973–76) and directed the Famous Photographers School in Munich (1969–72). From 1964 to 1969 he was co-editor of *Photoblätter*, and from 1954 to 1978 he taught at the German Institute for Publicity.

Boje belongs to GDL (since 1950), DGPh (since 1956) and Fédération Internationale de l'Art Photographique (since 1964). He won a gold medal for "The Magic of Color" exhibition at the Venice Biennale in 1960.

PUBLICATIONS Books: *Portraits im Farbe*, 1975 (Knapp Verlag: Düsseldorf); *Das grosse Hobby-Fotobuch*, 1970 (Ehapa-Verlag: Stuttgart); *Photographieren, mein Hobby*, 1965 (Ebenda); *Geliebte Camera*, 1965 (Südwest Verlag: Munich); *Mut zur Farbe*, 1963 (Umschau Verlag: Frankfurt); *Revolution im Unsichtbaren*, ed. w/ Otto Matschoss, 1963, *Die Welt der Photographie*, Peter Pollack, 1962, *Magie der Farbenphotographie*, 1961 (Econ Verlag: Düsseldorf); *Farbe überall*, 1960 (Umschau Verlag: Frankfurt); *Vom Photo zum Lichtbild*, 1956 (Knapp Verlag: Düsseldorf).

ADDRESS Johannisberg 4i, D-5653 Leichlingen, Germany.

Lee Boltin PHOTOGRAPHER Born November 19, 1917, in New York, Boltin was trained in photography under Thane Bierwert at the American Museum of Natural History in New York City.

Currently self-employed as a photographer, he was previously employed at the American Museum of Natural History in New York City from 1943 to 1950.

Boltin has been the recipient of awards from German Art Book Directors in 1979, Printing Industries in New York City in 1975 and 1977 and the National Urban League in 1961. He has also been involved in the films *Way of the Navaho*, *Jail Keys Made Here* and *So You're Going to Bulgaria*.

PUBLICATIONS Books (selected): *Masterpieces of Primitive Art*, 1978; *Thracian Treasure*, 1977; *Treasures of Irish Art*, 1977; *Tutankhamun*, 1976; *Beauty and Lore of Coins*, 1975; *Colorado*, 1975; *From the Land of the Scythians*, 1975; *Color Underground*, 1974; *Faces of Jesus*, 1974; *Ancient Mexico and Central America*, 1973; *The Gem Kingdom*, 1973; *The Mineral Kingdom*, 1972; *Art Before Columbus*, 1963.

COLLECTION Smithsonian Institutions, Wash., D.C.

ADDRESS 205 Albany Post Rd, Croton-on-Hudson, NY 10520.

Howard Bond PHOTOGRAPHER Born on July 23, 1931 in Napoleon, Ohio, Bond obtained a bachelor's degree in music from Bowling Green State University in Ohio (1953) and two masters from the University of Michigan, one in music (1958) and one in mathematics (1961). He says he has been considerably influenced by both Ansel Adams and Brett Weston.

He started working as a music teacher in Blissfield, Michigan (1953–58), and from 1961 to 1979 was employed as a computer programmer by General Motors, Bendix, the University of Michigan and Horiba Instruments. He currently works full time as a freelance photographer.

Bond has been a member of the Ann Arbor Art Association since 1968 and of Friends of Photography since 1970.

The artist uses view cameras up to 11 x 14 to make black-and-white photographs. He mainly focuses on "subjects from nature or architectural details" and is interested in "tonal gradations, texture and design."

PUBLICATION Periodical: *Creative Camera Annual*, 1976.

PORTFOLIOS *Portfolio I: Kings Canyon*, 1974; *Portfolio II: Austria*, 1978.

COLLECTIONS Amon Carter Mus., Fort Worth, Tex.; Fotomat Corp., San Diego, Calif.; Inst. of Arts, Kalamazoo, Mich.; Monterey Mus. of Art, Calif.; St. Louis Union Trust Cllctn., Mo. Bibliothèque Nationale, Paris; Sammlung Fotografis, Vienna.

DEALERS Blixt Gall., 229 Nickels Arcade, Ann Arbor, MI 48104; Halsted Gall., 560 N Woodward, Birmingham, MI 48011; Douglas Kenyon, Inc., 155 E Ohio St, Chicago, IL 60611; Gall. for Photographic Arts, 26777 Loraine Rd, N Olmstead, OH 44070; The Photography Gall., Inc., 132 S 17, Philadelphia, PA 19103; Photography Southwest, 4223 N Marshall Way, Scottsdale AZ 85251; Keystone Gall., 1213 State St., #F, Santa Barbara, CA 93101; Colorado Photographic Arts Ctr, 1301 Bannock St, Denver, CO 80204. Galerie Nagel, Fasanen Strasse 42, D-1000 Berlin 15, West Germany; Photogalerie Lange-Irschl, Türken Strasse 54, 8000 München 40, West Germany; Phototheque of Thessalonika, 1 Mitr Josif, Thessalonika, Greece; Photographic Ctr of Athens, Sina 52, Athens 135, Greece.

ADDRESS   1095 Harold Cir, Ann Arbor, MI
48103.

Inge Bondi   WRITER · CRITIC   Bondi was educated by twenty years of working at Magnum Photos, Inc., in New York City. She has been influenced by André Kertész (1970–72) and Ernst Haas, Robert Capa and David Seymour (from 1950).

Since 1969 she has been a freelance writer, and since 1976 a consulting editor for *printletter* magazine. Bondi was also president of Photography House Inge Bondi Ltd., dealers in photography (1970–72), taught contemporary history of photography at the Fairleigh Dickinson University in Teaneck, New Jersey (1970–72), and was secretary to the director for special projects at Magnum Photos Inc., New York City (1950–70).

Bondi writes about the creative process, time and place, as these shape photographers' lives. She is "largely interested in the twentieth century, outside of the U.S."

PUBLICATIONS   Books: *A Time to Play*, intro., Irwin Dermer, 1976 (I. Dermer: Zurich); *George Rodger*, intro., Arts Council of Great Britain, 1975. Periodicals: "Jakob Tuggoner", Sept 1980, "Collector Sam Wagstaff," Aug 1979, "Roman Vishniac," Sept 1978, "John Heartfield," Feb 1978; "Lucien Clergue," July 1977, "Ernst Haas," Oct 1976, *Die Weltwoche*; "Dan Berley Interview," Nov 1980, "Branchsi's Photographic Vision," July 1980, "Vision of Old Japan," May 1980, "Raoul Hausmann," no. 24, Nov 1979, "Christian Staub," no. 22, July 1979, "Metamorphosis of a Schadograph," no. 21, May 1979, "Robert Mapplethorpe," no. 19, Jan 1979, "Germaine Krull," no. 15, May 1978, "Paul Hill," no. 13, Jan 1978, "Herbert List," no. 6, Nov 1976, "Ray Metzker," no. 3, May 1976, "Renaissance of the Schadograph," no. 2, Jan 1976. *printletter*; "Chim's Way," *35mm Photography*, Jan 1970; "Ernst Haas," *Modern Photography*, July 1969.

ADDRESS   Berstr. 63, 8708 Maennedorf ZH, Switzerland.

James C. Bones, Jr.   PHOTOGRAPHER · WRITER Born November 1, 1943, in Monroe, Louisiana, Bones studied at the University of Texas, Austin, where he was an assistant to photographer Russell W. Lee from 1965 to 1967.

Self-employed since 1978 and prior to 1975, he served as a printing assistant to Eliot Porter from 1975 to 1978.

Bones received a J. Frank Dobie Fellowship of Residence in Austin (1972–73) and a Corporation for Public Broadcasting Fellowship in Dallas to produce the KERA-TV series *Images and Memories* (1970–71). In addition to that eight-part series, he worked on the KTBC-TV show *North Padre Island* in Austin in 1970.

He works in color, using a 4 x 5 view camera and producing dye transfer prints. His main subject is details of nature.

PUBLICATIONS   Monograph: *Texas Heartland, A Hill Country Year*, 1975. Books: *Faces and Facades*, 1977; *Texas Wild*, w/Richard Phelan, 1976; *The Wild Places*, 1975; *Texas Earth Surfaces*, 1970. Periodical: *Camera*, Aug 1977.

PORTFOLIOS   *A Wildflower Portfolio*, 1978, *A Texas Portfolio*, 1977 (Encino Press: Austin, Tex.).

COLLECTIONS   Amon Carter Mus. of Western Art, Fort Worth, Tex.; Univ. of Tex. Art Mus., Austin.

ADDRESS: POB 458, Tesuque, NM 87574.

Félix Bonfils   PHOTOGRAPHER   Born March 8, 1831, in St. Hippolyte du Fort (Gard), France, Bonfils died in 1885 in Alais, France. His wife, Marie Lydie Cabannis Bonfils (1837–1918), was a photographer and publisher; his son, Paul-Félix-Adrien Bonfils (1861–1929), was also a photographer.

A bookbinder as of 1858, Bonfils officially turned to photography in 1867. It is reported that he learned the craft from Abel Niepce de Saint-Victor around 1866–67 when he moved to Beirut, Lebanon. He established La Maison Bonfils there, a photographic publishing house that continued to operate well after his death under the direction of his wife and son. He also opened a studio in Alais (now Alès), France.

Bonfils' firm published tens of thousands of prints and lantern slides of Near East culture, more than any other studio. In 1871 he announced to the Société Française de Photographie, of which he was a member, that he had produced "15,000 prints and 9,000 stereoscopic views."

"Bonfils' photographs of the Near East—its landscapes, its cities, its architecture and its peoples—are some of the most telling and evocative traces of the Romantic Orient made in the last century," according to Robert A. Sobieszek and Carney E. S. •Gavin. The photographer's techniques included the use of the Dallmeyer triplet lens, wet collodion glass-plate negatives, and albumen prints. Many of the views in his photo albums were taken by other photographers, although no specific credits are given.

PUBLICATIONS   Books: *Majestic Inspirations, Incomparable Souvenirs*, Adam D. Weinberg,

1977; *Souvenir de Jerusalem*, ca. 1895 (Leipzig); *Nazareth et ses environs*, 1894 (St. Petersburg); *Souvenirs d'Orient, Album pittoresque des sites, villes et ruines . . .* , 4 vols., preface by Gratien Charvet, 1878 (Alais); *Album photographiques des sites les Plus Célèbres de l'Orient*, 1878 (Paris); *Catalogue des Vues Photographiques de l'Orient*, 1876 (Alais); *Architecture Antique: Égypte, Grèce, Asie Mineure, Album de photographies*, 1872 (Paris). Anthology: *The Photograph Collector's Guide*, Lee D. Witkin & Barbara London, 1979. Catalog: "*Remembrances of the Near East*", IMP/GEH 1980.

COLLECTIONS   Boston Pub. Lib., Mass.; Brandeis Univ., Waltham, Mass.; Harvard Univ., Cambridge, Mass.; IMP/GEH, Rochester; Metro. Mus. of Art, NYC; Semitic Mus., Cambridge, Mass.; Univ. of N. Mex. Art Mus., Albuquerque; and many libraries.

Lyle Bongé *PHOTOGRAPHER* Born November 5, 1929, in Biloxi, Mississippi, Bongé studied at Black Mountain College, Asheville, North Carolina, in 1947–48, where his mentor was M. C. Richards. He also attended the University of Southern Mississippi, Hattiesburg (1951), Tulane University, New Orleans (1951–52), and Mexico City College (1952). His father, Arch Bongé (1900–37), was a painter, as is his mother.

Bongé currently teaches at the New School for Social Research in New York City and is on the board of directors of Peoples Bank in Biloxi. In 1968 he broke the world's record for single-handed cross-gulf passages under sail.

PUBLICATIONS   Monograph: *The Sleep of Reason*, 1974. Anthology: *I Shall Save One Land Unvisited: 11 Southern Photographers*, J. Williams, 1978. Periodicals: *Aperture*, 1961; *Esquire*, Nov 1959.

COLLECTIONS   IMP/GEH, Rochester; Miss. Mus. of Art, Jackson; Mus. of Fine Arts, Houston; Pensacola Mus. of Art, Fla.

DEALER   Neikrug Gall., 224 E 68 St, New York, NY 10021.

ADDRESS   65 E 96 St, New York, NY 10028.

Susanne Bonge *PHOTO-ARCHIVIST·PHOTOHIS-TORIAN·LIBRARIAN·WRITER* Born September 9, 1912, in Bergen, Norway, Bonge took courses at Statens Bibliotekskole in Oslo, Norway, from 1965 to 1976, and attended the basic course in social anthropology at University of Bergen in 1968.

To date she is an archivist at the University Library in Bergen, where she has worked since 1947. Around 1964–65 she began to care for the library's collection of old photographs.

Bonge is a founding member (1975) of Norsk Fotohistorisk Forening and served as its first vice president in 1976–77. She received the Kongens Fortjentsmedalje i gull (King's medal of honor) in 1979.

In her work of collecting and preserving old photographs, she tries to "impress on writers, historians, and scientists the value of the photographs as *primary sources*" and not just illustrations. She is also interested in the life and working conditions of the historic photographers.

PUBLICATIONS   Books: "*Elder Norske Fotografer*," 1980 (The University Library of Bergen); *Photograf M. Selmers Bergensbilleder*, w/Ragna Sollied & Per Jonas Nordhagen, 1974 (B. Giertsens Forlag: Bergen, Nor.).

ADDRESS   Universitetsbiblioteket i Bergen, Billedsamlingen, Möhlenprisbakken 1, 5000 Bergen, Norway.

Sally Marie Boothe *CURATOR · PHOTOGRA-PHER · TEACHER* Born December 12, 1948, in Yoakum, Texas, she received a BA from Baylor University in Waco, Texas, in 1970, and an MFA from the University of Texas, at San Antonio in 1978. She also attended the University of Texas at Austin from 1972 to 1973.

Since 1978 she has been employed as both a curator of the San Antonio Museum Association in San Antonio, Texas, and an instructor at San Antonio College. Previously, she was a teaching assistant at the University of Texas at San Antonio in 1977, and an instructor at the Arkansas School for the Deaf in Little Rock from 1974 to 1975.

In 1980 she received the Mitchell A. Wilder Award from the Texas Association of Museums, and in 1979 she received the SAAF Addy Award from the San Antonio Designers Federation. She was also named one of the Outstanding Arkansas Artists by the Arkansas State Festival of the Arts in Little Rock in 1975.

PUBLICATIONS   Catalogs: *Paperworks: An Exhibition of Texas Artists*, 1979, *What's Up in Texas: New Lyricism and Straight Photography*, w/David Simpson, 1978 (San Antonio Mus. Assoc.: Tex.).

COLLECTIONS   Hawkes Gall., LaGrange, Ga.; San Antonio Mus. Assoc., San Antonio Mus. of Art, San Antonio, Tex.

ADDRESS   233 Lindell, San Antonio, TX 78212.

Howard Samuel Bossen *PHOTOGRAPHER · TEACHER · HISTORIAN* Born in Chicago on May

17, 1948, Bossen earned a doctorate and a master's degree in the history of photography at Ohio State University in Athens (1979, 1976). He studied photography under Barbara Blondeau, Thomas Porett and Leit Skoogfors at the Philadelphia College of Art, where he obtained his bachelor's degree in fine arts (1972), and under Aaron Siskind at the Institute of Design in Chicago (1968–69).

He has been an assistant professor in photojournalism at Michigan State University since 1979 and has also taught in the Art Department at Denison University in Granville, Ohio (1978–79), and at the Philadelphia College of Art (1974–75).

He joined SPE in 1976 and has been the recipient of two grants: one from the Ohio Arts Council (1976–77) and one from the Ohio State University Graduate School, from which, in the same year (1978), he also received a Fellowship.

Bossen describes his image-making as falling into "three broad categories: (1) Explorations of the human form. These images are primarily multiple exposures of male and female body parts. . . . (2) Personal documents. A detailed examination of the private and generally mundane moments in the lives of my family and friends . . . and, (3) Commercial work." His writing deals with historical and critical investigations of various aspects of photography.

PUBLICATIONS   Periodicals: *The Journal for Photographic Criticism*, Mar 1980; "Henry Holmes Smith," *Field of Vision*, Feb 1979; *Camera*, Sept 1972.

COLLECTION   Smithsonian Inst., Natl. Anthropological Archives, Wash., D.C.

ADDRESS   225 Collingwood Dr, East Lansing, MI 48823, or School of Journalism, Michigan State Univ, East Lansing, MI 48824.

Edouard Boubat   PHOTOGRAPHER   Born September 13, 1923, in Paris, Boubat studied bookprinting, design and typography at the Ecole Estienne in Paris from 1938 to 1942.

Since 1965 he has been a freelance photographer. Prior to that, he was employed as a staff photographer for *Réalités* magazine from 1951 to 1965.

Boubat was the recipient of the Kodak Prize at the Bibliothèque Nationale exhibition in Paris in 1947, and two films about him were created: *Chambre Noire*, for French television in 1966 and *Photo by Boubat* for Swedish television in 1967.

The photographer's work was described by Elaine A. King in 1977 in this way: "Unlike his fellow countrymen. French photographer Edouard Boubat's imagery is not dependent on intrinsic timing but, instead, his photographs purport to reflect timelessness and the lingering moment."

PUBLICATIONS   Monograph: *Édouard Boubat*, Bernard George, 1973. Books: *Preferées*, 1980 (Paris); *La Survivance*, 1976 (Mercure de France: Paris); *Anges*, Antoine Blondin, 1974 (Atelier d'Expression: Paris); *Miroirs, Autoportraits*, 1973 (Denoël: Paris); *Woman*, 1973. Anthologies: *The Photograph Collector's Guide*, Lee D. Witkin & Barbara London, 1979; *The Magic Image*, Cecil Beaton & Gail Buckland, 1975; *Album*, no. 12, 1970. Periodicals: *Camera*, Sept 1978, July 1975; "The Humanistic Eye: Édouard Boubat," Walter Rosenblum, *35mm Photography*, summer 1975.

COLLECTIONS   MOMA, NYC. In France: Musée d'Art Moderne, Paris; Musée Nicéphore Niepce, Chalon-sur-Saône.

REPRESENTATIVE   Rapho, 8 rue d'Alger, 75001 Paris, France.

Alice Boughton   PHOTOGRAPHER   [See plate 48]   Born in Brooklyn, New York, in 1865, Boughton died on June 22, 1943 in Brookhaven, Long Island, New York. She attended Miss Rounds' School in Brooklyn and studied painting in Paris. Boughton was associated with and possibly influenced by Gertrude Käsebier.

She opened a photo studio in New York in 1890, which she maintained for over forty years until her retirement. Boughton was a member of the Cosmopolitan Club in New York.

The photographer worked mainly in platinum prints but used some silver processes. She concentrated on portraiture, chiefly of prominent literary and theatrical persons, but also did female nudes in allegorical or natural settings and photographed children, frequently using her two daughters as models.

PUBLICATIONS   Books: *Photographing the Famous*, foreword by James L. Ford, 1928; *Household Arts and Social Lunches*, 1912; *The Servant in the House*, Charles Rann Kennedy, 1908. Anthologies: *The Photograph Collector's Guide*, Lee D. Witkin & Barbara London, 1979; *The Collection of Alfred Stieglitz*, Weston J. Naef, 1978; *Camera Work: A Critical Anthology*, Jonathan Green, ed., 1973. Periodical: "Photography, A Medium of Expression," *Camera Work*, Apr 1909.

COLLECTIONS   IMP/GEH, Rochester; Metr. Mus. of Art, NYC; MOMA, NYC. Duse Memorial Library, Asola, Italy.

Robert Charles Bourdeau PHOTOGRAPHER
Born on November 14, 1931, in Kingston, Ontario, Canada, he studied the arts at Queen's University in Kingston, Ontario, for a year, then attended the University of Toronto School of Architecture in Ontario.

Bourdeau works as a freelance photographer and has received grants from the Canada Council and the Ontario Arts Council.

Working with large format cameras, 8 x 10 up to 11 x 14, he focuses on landscape photography.

PUBLICATIONS Monograph: *Robert Bourdeau*, 1980 (Mintmark Press). Books: *The Banff Purchase*, 1979; *Canada, a Year of the Land*, 1967 (Natl. Film Board Book). Anthologies: *The Photographer's Choice*, Kelly Wise, ed., 1975; *Photography Year Book*, 1965 & 1964 (England). Periodical: *Photo Life*, July 1968.

COLLECTIONS Smithsonian Inst., Wash., D.C. In Canada: Banff Centre, Alberta; Canada Council Art Bank, Ottawa, Ontario; Jane Corkin Gall., Toronto, Ontario; Dept. of External Affairs, Cultural, Ottawa, Ontario; Edmonton Art Gall., Alberta; Mount Allison Univ., Sackville, New Brunswick; Natl. Film Board of Canada, Ottawa, Ontario; Natl. Gall. of Canada, Ottawa, Ontario; Ontario Inst. of Studies in Education, Toronto; Queens Univ., Kingston, Ontario; Univ. of Toronto, Ontario.

DEALER Jane Corkin Gall., 144 Front St W, Ste 620, Toronto, Ontario, Canada.

ADDRESS 1462 Chomley Crescent, Ottawa, Ontario KIG OVI, Canada.

Fergus Bourke PHOTOGRAPHER Born July 31, 1934, in Dublin, Ireland, Bourke is a self-taught photographer. His main influences have been André Kertész and Henri Cartier-Bresson.

A freelancer, Bourke is also official photographer of the National Theatre of Ireland (since 1971) and occasionally the stills photographer at the National Film Studios in Ireland. He belongs to the film section of the Irish Transport and General Workers Union.

Using small format, he has a "decisive moment" style, his main subject matter being Ireland. He also does theater and ballet photography.

PUBLICATIONS Books: *Irish Short Stories*, 1979 (Longman: London); *Mother Ireland*, Edna O'Brien, 1976. Periodicals: *U.S. Camera Annual*, 1972; *Modern Photography*, Apr 1972; *Leica Photography #3*, 1966.

COLLECTION MOMA, NYC.

REPRESENTATIVE Abbey Theatre, Dublin, Ireland.

ADDRESS 17 Strand Rd, Sandymount, Dublin, Ireland.

Margaret Bourke-White PHOTOGRAPHER
Born June 14, 1906, in New York City, Bourke-White died in Stamford, Connecticut, on August 27, 1971, after a courageous nineteen-year battle with Parkinson's disease. She studied biology and technology briefly before attending the Clarence White School of Photography at Columbia University, New York City. In 1927 she graduated from Cornell University, Ithaca, New York. Bourke-White's second husband (1942–45) was writer Erskine Caldwell.

She began her career as a freelance industrial and architectural photographer in Cleveland, Ohio, in 1927. She worked for Henry Luce's new *Fortune* magazine as a staff photographer from 1929 to 1933 and then was hired as one of the first four staff photographers for *Life* in 1933, remaining with the magazine until 1969.

Her photograph of Fort Peck Dam was the cover of *Life*'s first issue, and during her years with the magazine she was the first woman photographer attached to the U.S. armed forces. Among other events, she covered Buchenwald when General Patton arrived to release the prisoners, India during Gandhi's fight for independence, racial and labor unrest in South Africa and the Korean War.

Noted as an important innovator of the photoessay, Bourke-White's "special ability," according to Anne Tucker, "was to put news in context for people, to isolate that which was important in the values of her generation." Working with silver prints, her images include genre scenes and portraits taken during the Depression, industrial equipment, photoessays of various countries and events and some very large photomurals. She was admired as a dedicated photojournalist who believed it was her profession's responsibility to report whatever was seen and "pass it on to others."

PUBLICATIONS Monographs: *The Photographs of Margaret Bourke-White*, Sean Callahan, ed., 1972; *Margaret Bourke-White: Photojournalist*, Theodore M. Brown, 1972; *Portrait of Myself*, 1963. Books: *Documentary Expression and Thirties America*, William Stott, 1973; *A Report on the American Jesuits*, w/John La Farge, 1956; *Halfway to Freedom*, 1949; *Dear Fatherland, Rest Quietly*, 1946; *They Called It "Purple Heart Valley,"* 1944; *Shooting the Russian War*, 1942; *Say, Is This the U.S.A.*, Erskine Caldwell, 1941; *North of the Danube*, Erskine Caldwell, 1939; *You Have Seen Their Faces*, Erskine Caldwell,

1937, repr., 1975; *One Thing Leads to Another,* Fred C. Kelly, 1936; *Newsprint,* ca. 1935 (Internatl. Paper Sales: Montreal); *U.S.S.R. Photographs,* 1934; *Red Medicine,* Sir Arthur Newsholme & John Adams Kingsbury, 1933; *Eyes on Russia,* 1931, repr. 1968. Anthologies: *The Photograph Collector's Guide,* Lee D. Witkin & Barbara London, 1979; *Photography Rediscovered,* David Travis & Anne Kennedy, 1979; *Great Photographic Essays from LIFE,* Maitland Edey, 1978; *The Magic Image,* Cecil Beaton & Gail Buckland, 1975; *Women of Photography: An Historical Survey,* Margery Mann & Ann Noggle, eds., 1975; *Looking at Photographs,* John Szarkowski, 1973; *The Woman's Eye,* Anne Tucker, ed., 1973.

COLLECTIONS   Brooklyn Mus., N.Y.; Cleveland Mus. of Art, Ohio; IMP/GEH, Rochester; L/C, Wash., D.C.; LIFE Picture Cllctn., NYC; MOMA, NYC; New Orleans Mus. of Art; Syracuse Univ., George Argents Research Lib., N.Y. RPS, London.

ARCHIVE   Time, Inc., Time-Life Bldg, Rockefeller Ctr, New York, NY 10020.

Samuel Bourne   PHOTOGRAPHER   Born in Nottingham, England, Bourne lived from 1834 to 1912.

In 1863 he formed a partnership in Simla, India, with Charles Shepherd, who ran the oldest photographic firm in that country. Bourne led three expeditions to the Himalayas (1863, 1864 —for nine months—and 1866), during which he reached the Manirung Pass at a record height of 18,600 feet. He opened a branch of Bourne & Shepherd in Calcutta before returning to England in 1872, where he established S. Bourne & Co., a cotton and doubling manufacturing company. Bourne retired in the early 1900s to take up watercolor painting.

During his lonely treks in the Himalayas, he took to writing about his adventures, much of which was later published.

The photographer is reported to have made approximately 1,500 negatives in the Far East, most of which were of the Himalayas. Chiefly a landscape photographer, he was noted for the clarity of his images and the full range of tones expressed in his albumen prints (derived from the collodion wet-plate process). He also exhibited a sensitive hand in his portraits of native peoples in the places he visited.

PUBLICATIONS   Books: *The Photograph Collector's Guide,* Lee D. Witkin & Barbara London, 1979; *Pioneers of Photography,* Aaron Scharf, 1976; *The Magic Image,* Cecil Beaton & Gail Buckland, 1975; *Travels Among the Todas,* 1873 (Longmans, Green & Co.: London). Anthology: *The Last Empire: Photography in British India, 1855–1911,* Clark Worswick & Ainslee Embree, 1976. Periodicals: "Samuel Bourne: Photographer of India in the 1860s," Sean Sprague, Jan 14, 1977, "A Photographic Journey through the Higher Himalayas," installments, beg.. 1869, "Narrative of a Photographic Trip to Kashmir and Adjacent Districts," installments, beg. Oct 19, 1866, "Ten Weeks with the Camera in the Himalayas," installments, beg. Feb 1, 1864, *The British Journal of Photography.*

COLLECTIONS   Boston Public Lib., Mass.; Harvard Univ., Carpenter Ctr. for the Visual Arts, Cambridge; IMP/GEH, Rochester; N.Y. Public Lib., NYC; Univ. of N. Mex. Art Mus., Albuquerque; Univ. of Tex., Humanities Research Ctr., Austin. Natl. Gall. of Can., Ottawa, Ontario; In London: India Office Lib. & Records; Royal Geographical Soc.; RPS; Victoria & Albert Mus.

Robert Chandler Bowden   PHOTOJOURNALIST· AUTHOR   Born on August 30, 1941, in Fort Myers, Florida, Bowden studied at Florida Southern College where he received a BS in Journalism in 1963.

As of this date he works as a columnist for *The St. Petersburg Times,* where he served as bureau chief from 1968 to 1973 in his native Florida. He has also been employed as photography consultant for the Harte-Hanks newspaper chain (1977– 78) and as an editor for the *Manatee Times* (1973–78).

Bowden's work is totally centered on photojournalism.

PUBLICATIONS   Books: *Boss Wheels—End of the Supercar Era,* 1979; *Get That Picture,* 1978. Anthologies: *Best Pictures of 1979 & Best Pictures of 1978,* ed., writer.

ADDRESS   4907 22nd Ave W, Bradenton, FL 33505.

Harry Bowers   PHOTOGRAPHER · TEACHER Born in 1938 in Los Angeles, Bowers earned a BS in Engineering Physics from the University of California, Berkeley (1964), and an MFA in Photography from the San Francisco Art Institute (1974).

In 1979 he was a visiting artist-lecturer at the University of California, Santa Cruz, and at California College of Arts and Crafts, Oakland. From 1974 to 1979 he taught at the University of California, Berkeley, Extension Division. Bowers was instructor/chairperson of the Photography Department at San Francisco Art Institute in 1977–78.

He won an NEA Photographer's Fellowship in 1978 and 1980 and a National Science Foundation Fellowship in 1965.

PUBLICATIONS Anthology: *Photography Year: 1978*, Time-Life Series, 1977. Catalogs: *Some Twenty Odd Visions: A Book of Twenty-Four Unique Ways of Seeing the World*, 1978 (Univ. of Wash. Press, Blue Sky Gall.: Seattle); *Bent Photography, West Coast, USA*, 1977 (Australian Centre for Photography: Paddington). Periodicals: *Artforum*, May 1980; *Picture Magazine*, May 1979; *Artforum*, Sept 1978; *Artweek*, June 17, 1978, July 17, 1976.

DEALER Hansen Fuller Goldeen Gall., 228 Grant Ave, San Francisco, CA 94108.

ADDRESS 2021 10 St, Berkeley, CA 94710.

John F. Bowman PHOTOGRAPHER · TEACHER
Born on June 28, 1950, in Wichita, Kansas, Bowman has earned two MAs: one from Governors State University in Chicago, where he studied with Paul Schrawz, Brett Weston and Morley Baer, and one from Illinois University in Carbondale where he worked under Chuck Swedlund and David Gilmore. He obtained a BAE from Wichita State University as well.

From 1977 to the present he has been acting as the Coordinator of Photographic Studies at Prairie State College in Chicago. He also taught photography at the University of Dayton in Ohio (1976), at Southern Illinois University (1974–75), and at University City in St. Louis, Missouri (1972–73).

Bowman is a member of SPE, the American Association of Teachers, the National Education Association, and the United Teaching Profession. In 1974 he was awarded a Rockefeller Grant for the Arts, and in 1972, a Federal Project Grant to teach photography to the underprivileged in Wichita, Kansas.

The artist is currently involved with "mechanical design aspects of industrial sites in the Chicago area," and recently completed a group documentary project on Northern Illinois farm communities.

PUBLICATIONS Book: *Mechanical Man*, 1975 (self-published). Periodical: "Pin-hole Photography," *Popular Photography*, May 1976.

COLLECTIONS Governors State Univ., Chicago; Prairie State College, Chicago Hts.; Southern Illinois Univ., Carbondale; Univ. of Dayton, Ohio; Wichita State Univ., Ulrich Cllct., Kans.

DEALER Gallery 417, PSC, 202 S Halstead, Chicago Hts, IL 60411.

ADDRESS 4048 W 178 St, Country Club Hills, IL 60477.

Randy H. Bradley PHOTOGRAPHER · TEACHER
Born February 11, 1948, in Edmonton, Alberta, Canada, he studied photography at Northern Alberta Institute of Technology in Edmonton, and fine arts at both the University of Calgary and the Banff School of Fine Arts, both in Alberta.

Since 1976 he has been an instructor of photography at the Vancouver School of Art in British Columbia and of photographic aesthetics at Vancouver Community College. He conducted a workshop in photography for the National Parks of Canada at Haines Junction, Kluane National Park, Yukon Territory, in 1976, and from 1972 to 1976 taught photographic history at the Banff School of Fine Arts.

Bradley has been the recipient of four grants from the Canada Council: in 1979 he received a short-term grant for Cibachrome work in progress; in 1977, a project grant for work in progress; in 1974, a short-term grant for work in progress; and in 1973 a project grant for transfer processes.

PUBLICATION Book: *A Handbook and Collection of Early Photographic Recipes & Processes*, 1974 (Banff Centre Press, Alberta, Canada).

COLLECTIONS Alfred Univ. Art Cllctn., NY. Art Bank of Canada Council, Ottawa; Natl. Film Board of Canada, Ottawa; Red Deer Coll. of Art Gall., Alberta, Canada.

DEALER Nova Gall., 1972 W Fourth, Vancouver BC V6J 1M5, Canada.

ADDRESS 4590 Lions Ave, North Vancouver, British Columbia, Canada.

Mathew B. Brady PHOTOGRAPHER [See plate 18] Born near Lake George, New York, Brady lived from 1823 to 1896. Of Irish descent, he received art instruction from William Page, a friend of Samuel F. B. Morse, who was an early experimenter with daguerreotypes. Brady learned how to produce daguerreotypes from Morse, John W. Draper and a Professor Doremus.

Brady opened his first portrait studio in New York City in 1844, and by 1845 had decided to photograph all the distinguished and notable people of his day. He opened a second gallery in Washington, D.C., in 1858 and an opulent third one in New York in 1860.

Mathew Brady—Photographer of an Era is a black-and-white film about the artist made in 1953.

Known as "Mr. Lincoln's cameraman," Brady was the first photographer on the scene to record the American Civil War, 1861–65, during which he directed an extensive staff of photographers from his headquarters in Washington, D.C.

Though Brady was chiefly known for his documentation of the war, his most important contribution is as a historian. Since he worked with a large staff, many photos credited to Brady were in fact taken by others. Using daguerreotypes and collodion wet-plate negatives, Brady also photographed many of the country's best known public figures, such as Abraham Lincoln, Walt Whitman and P. T. Barnum. Many of the Civil War daguerreotypes were later copied onto glass plates. Despite his accomplishments, Brady died penniless.

PUBLICATIONS Books: *Mathew Brady and His World*, D. M. & P. B. Kunhardt, et al, 1977; *Mirror Image*, Richard Rudisill, 1971; *The Civil War in Pictures 1861–1865*, Donald H. Mugridge, 1961; *Civil War Photographs, 1861–65*, H. D. Milhollen & D. H. Mugridge, 1961; *The Daguerreotype in America*, Beaumont Newhall, 1961, repr. 1968; *Mathew Brady: Historian with a Camera*, J. D. Horan, 1955; *Mr. Lincoln's Contemporaries*, Roy Meredith, 1951; *Mr. Lincoln's Camera Man*, Roy Meredith, 1946, repr. 1974; *Photography and the American Scene*, Robert Taft, 1938; *The Photographic History of the Civil War*, Francis Trevelyan Miller, ed., 10 vols., 1911; *Brady's Collection of Historical Portraits*, 41st Congress, Report #46 Mar 1871 (U.S. House of Representatives, Wash., D.C.); *Metropolitan Fair, 1864*, 1864; *Gallery of Illustrious Americans*, C. Edwards Lester, 1850. Anthologies: *The Photograph Collector's Guide*, Lee D. Witkin & Barbara London 1979; *The Magic Image*, Cecil Beaton & Gail Buckland, 1975; *Great Photographers*, Time-Life Series, 1971.

COLLECTIONS Harvard Univ., Houghton Lib., Cambridge, Mass.; IMP/GEH, Rochester; Kalamazoo Inst. of Arts, Mich., L/C, Wash., D.C.; Natl. Archives, Wash., D.C.; N.Y. Public Lib., NYC; Smithsonian Inst., Wash., D.C.; Yale Univ., Beinecke Rare Book & Ms. Lib., New Haven, Conn.

James Bragge PHOTOGRAPHER Born 1833 in South Shields, England, he died July 17, 1908, in Wellington, New Zealand.

Bragge went to New Zealand in 1865 and opened a studio, the New Zealand Academy of Photographic Art, in Wellington. In 1880 he was commissioned by the Wellington City Corporation to photograph the city for the Melbourne International Exhibition.

Primarily a freelance, Bragge did studio portraits and city scenes in the style of the day.

PUBLICATION Anthology: *The Invented Eye*, Edward Lucie-Smith, 1975.
COLLECTION Natl. Mus. of New Zealand, Wellington.

Jeremiah O. Bragstad ARCHITECTURAL PHOTOGRAPHER · TEACHER Born November 24, 1932, in Boise, Idaho, Bragstad received a BA in Architecture from the University of California, Berkeley, in 1962. He took workshops with Morley Baer in 1962 and with Minor White in 1963.

A photography teacher at Cornell University, Ithaca, New York, since 1978, Bragstad was a self-employed architectural photographer in San Francisco from 1965 to 1978. He has been a member of SPE since 1976 and of ASMP since 1968. He presided over the San Francisco chapter of the latter from 1972 to 1974.

Using large and small formats, black-and-white and color, Bragstad photographs architectural exteriors and interiors for architecture texts, designers and publications.

PUBLICATION Book: *Converted Into Houses*, w/Charles Fraccia, 1976.
ADDRESS 72 German Cross Rd, Ithaca, NY 14850.

Brian Brake PHOTOGRAPHER Born June 27, 1927, in Wellington, New Zealand, Brake is a self-taught photographer, naming Karsh and Cartier-Bresson as major influences.

A freelance photographer since 1953, he has been associated with Rapho Agency since 1966. Brake served as a director of Zodiac Films in Hong Kong from 1970 to 1976, was a member of Magnum Photos from 1955 to 1966 and was cameraman-director in the New Zealand National Films Unit, 1949–53.

An Associate of RPS since 1947, Brake also belongs to ASMP (since 1956) and is an Honorary Fellow of New Zealand Professional Photographers Association. He won the Order of Merit from President Nasser of Egypt for his "Ancient Egypt" series in *Life* magazine.

The photographer's films include *Snows of Aorangi, Snowline Is Their Boundary*, and *Ancient Egypt—The Sun & The River*.

Brake's style varies from "classic landscape to photojournalist approach to people and their surroundings." He uses large and small format.

PUBLICATIONS Books: *The Sacred Image*, 1979; *Legend & Reality*, 1977; *New Zealand Potters*, 1976; *Form & Farbe*, 1972; *The Sculpture of Thailand*, 1972; *The House on the Klong*, 1968; *Peking—A Tale of Three Cities*, w/Nigel Cameron, 1965; *New Zealand—Gift of the Sea*, w/ Maurice Shadbolt, 1963.

COLLECTIONS   Dowse Art Gall., Lower Hutt, Wellington, New Zealand; Victoria & Albert Mus., London.

REPRESENTATIVES Photo Researchers Inc, 60 E 56 St, New York, NY 10022; John Hillelson Agency Ltd, 145 Fleet St, London EC4A 2BU, England; Agence de Presse Rapho, 8 rue d'Alger, 75001 Paris, France.

ADDRESS   POB 60 049, Titirangi, Auckland 7, New Zealand.

Jerri Bram   *PHOTOGRAPHER*   Born September 1, 1942, in Cross Plains, Wisconsin, she received a BA in 1965, and an MS in 1968 from the University of Wisconsin. Her mentor is Arthur Ollman.

To date Bram has worked as a freelance photographer.

Her latest work concentrates on the nude figure, particularly "pregnant women viewed aesthetically, symbolically and psychologically." She is also "very concerned with the evolution of body and spirit over a period of many years."

PUBLICATIONS   Monograph: *Transitions*, 1978 (Daniel Cointe: France). Periodical: *Photoreporter*, Aug 1978.

ADDRESS   75 Avenue Mozart, 75016 Paris, France.

Harrison Branch   *PHOTOGRAPHER · TEACHER* Born June 6, 1947, in New York City, Branch earned a BFA in 1970 from the San Francisco Art Institute and an MFA from Yale University's School of Art (New Haven, Connecticut) in 1972. His instructors included Jerry Burchard, Blair Stapp, Walker Evans and Paul Caponigro.

Joining the Department of Art at Oregon State University (Corvallis) in 1972, as an assistant professor, he became an associate professor in 1977 and currently holds that position. From 1970 to 1971 he was a photography lecturer at the University of Bridgeport in Connecticut.

A member of SPE since 1974, Crane received grants from Oregon State University Graduate School in 1976 and 1977 and from the Oregon State Foundation in 1974. In 1972 he won an Alice Kimball Traveling Fellowship from Yale University.

Working in a large format, Crane produces 8 x 10 and 11 x 14 contact prints using silver, platinum and palladium processes.

PUBLICATIONS   Periodicals: *Still 3*, 1973, *Still 2*, 1971 (Yale University).

COLLECTIONS Oakland Mus., Calif.; Shadow Gal., Oregon City, Ore. Bibliothèque Nationale, Paris.

DEALERS   Fifth Ave Gallery of Photography, 6960 Fifth Ave, Scottsdale, AZ 85251; Print Gallery, POB 7418, Carmel, CA 93921; Silver Image Gallery, 83 S Washington, Seattle, WA 98104.

ADDRESS   415 SW 11 St, Corvallis, OR 97330.

Constantin Brancusi   *SCULPTOR · PHOTOGRAPHER*   Born February 21, 1876, in Hobita, Pestisani, Romania, Brancusi died March 16, 1957, in Paris. The son of peasants, Brancusi did not attend primary school, but at the age of seven began work as a herdsman. During this period he learned woodcarving. He took many odd jobs, eventually attending the Craiova School of Arts and Crafts. In 1898 he entered the Bucharest School of Fine Arts.

In 1903 he fulfilled his first commission, the bust of a general. After serving in the military, he made his way to Paris and there entered the Ecole des Beaux-Arts, working at odd jobs to support his studies. He first exhibited in 1906. From about 1910 on, Brancusi utilized and developed the geometrization that would become his trademark in sculpture. On June 13, 1952, he became a naturalized French citizen. Brancusi photographed his work with great care, contributing to the field of photographic art reproduction.

PUBLICATIONS   Monographs: *Brancusi: The Sculptor as Photographer*, Hilton Kramer, 1979; *Brancuse: Photographe*, 1977 (Centre Georges Pompidou: Paris); *Brancusi*, Sidney Geist, 1968; *Brancusi*, Ionel Jianou, 1963; *Constantin Brancusi*, Carola Giedion-Welcker, ed., 1958, Eng. ed., 1959; *Constantin Brancusi*, David Lewis, 1957; *Constantin Brancusi*, Christian Zervos, 1957; *Brancusi*, V. G. Paleolog, 1947. Periodical: Essay, Ezra Pound, *The Little Review*, autumn 1921.

COLLECTIONS   Arts Club of Chicago; Guggenheim Mus., NYC; MOMA, NYC; Philadelphia Mus. of Art, Pa. Montparnasse Cemetery, Musée National d'Art Moderne, Paris; Muzeul de Arta, Craiova; Muzeul de Arta R.S.R., Bucharest; Tate Gall., London; and many other museums.

Bill Brandt   *PHOTOGRAPHER*   [See plate 64] Born in London in 1905, Brandt worked as an assistant to Man Ray in Paris in 1929–30.

When he returned to England in 1931, he began documenting the English way of life. His images appeared in *Harper's Bazaar, Lilliput, News Chronicle, Picture Post* and *Verve*. During World War II Brandt was a staff photographer for the

British Home Office, documenting the hard times of Londoners suffering through German bombing raids. After the war he began making landscape images, many of which were used in *Literary Britain* (1951). He is also known for his series of female nudes, particularly distinguished by his use of a wide-angle lens in close-up (causing the body shapes to appear distorted) and by the stark black-and-white tones with little middle range.

PUBLICATIONS Monographs: *Bill Brandt: Early Photographs 1930–1942*, 1975, *Bill Brandt: Photographs*, R. Campbell & Aaron Scharf, 1970 (Arts Council of Great Britain: London); *Shadow of Light*, 1966 (Bodley Head: London), rev. ed., 1977; *Perspective of Nudes*, 1961. Books: *Literary Britain*, 1951 (Cassell: London); *Camera in London*, 1948; *A Night in London*, 1938 (Country Life: London); *The English at Home*, 1936 (Batsford: London). Anthologies: *The Photograph Collector's Guide*, Lee D. Witkin & Barbara London, 1979; *The Magic Image*, Cecil Beaton & Gail Buckland, 1975; *Light and Lens*, Donald L. Werner, ed., 1973; *Looking at Photographs*, John Szarkowski, 1973; *Great Photographers*, Time-Life Series, 1971. Catalog: *Photographs*, 1977 (Univ. of Neb., Sheldon Mem. Art Gall.: Lincoln). Periodicals: *Camera*, Dec 1979, Sept 1978, Nov 1975, Dec 1972, May 1972; *Creative Camera*, Aug 1967, Dec 1966.

COLLECTIONS Art Inst. of Chicago; Boston Mus. of Fine Arts; Chase Manhattan Bank, NYC; Detroit Inst. of Arts, Mich.; Exchange Natl. Bank of Chicago; High Mus. of Art, Atlanta; IMP/GEH, Rochester; Minneapolis Inst. of Arts, Minn; MOMA, NYC; New Orleans Mus. of Art; Philadelphia Mus. of Art, Penn.; Princeton Univ., N.J.; San Francisco Mus. of Modern Art; Smithsonian Inst., Wash., D.C.; Univ. of Neb., Sheldon Mem. Art Gall., Lincoln; Univ. of N. Mex., Albuquerque; Univ. of Tex., Austin; Va. Mus. of Fine Arts, Richmond; Worcester Art Mus., Mass. Bibliothèque Nationale, Paris; Natl. Gall. of Can., Ottawa, Ontario; Victoria & Albert Mus., London.

DEALER Marlborough Fine Art Ltd, 6 Albemarle St., London WIX 3HF, England.

Brassaï *PHOTOGRAPHER · POET · SCULPTOR · DRAFTSMAN* [See plate 57] Born Gyula Halász on September 9, 1899, in Brassó, Hungary (now Braşov, Romania), Brassaï studied at the Académie des Beaux Arts in Budapest and the Academische Hochschule in Berlin-Charlottenburg, Germany. Influenced by his friend André Kertész, and using a small camera borrowed from him, Brassaï began photographing Paris at night.

He worked for *Minotaure* from 1933 to 1936 and for *Harper's Bazaar* from 1936 to 1965. A member of Pen Club and the Legion of Honor, he received the P. H. Emerson Medal in 1934, the Médaille d'Argent from the Centenaire de Daguerre Exposition in Budapest in 1937, an award from ASMP in 1966 and the Grand Prix National de la Photographie in France in 1978.

A sculptor and film maker as well as photographer, Brassaï made the film *Tant qu'il y aura des bêtes.*

PUBLICATIONS Monographs: *The Secret Paris of the 30s*, 1976; *Brassaï*, Lawrence Durrell, 1968; *Transmutations*, 1967; *Brassaï*, J. Adhemar et al., 1963 (Bibliothèque Nationale: Paris); *Brassaï*, Ludvic Soucek, 1962 (Editions d'Etat: Prague, Czechoslovakia); *Brassaï*, Henry Miller, 1952 (Edition Neuf); *Brassaï, Camera in Paris*, 1949 (The Focal Press: London); *Paris de Nuit*, Paul Morand, 1933 (Edition Les Arts et Métiers Graphiques: Paris). Books: *Henry Miller Rocher Heureux*, 1978 (Editions Gallimard: Paris); *Paroles en L'Air*, 1978 (Editions Jean-Claude Simoens: Paris); *Henry Miller Grandeur Nature*, 1975 (Editions Gallimard: Paris); *Picasso and Company*, 1966; *Conversations Avec Picasso*, 1964 (Editions Gallimard: Paris); *Graffiti*, w/Picasso, 1961 (Les Editions du Temps: Paris); *Paris*, John Russell, 1960; *Seville en Fete*, w/Henri de Montherlant, 1954 (Edition Neuf); *Histoire de Marie*, intro. by Henry Miller, 1949 (Editions du Point du Jour: Paris); *Les Sculptures de Picasso*, D. H. Kahnweiler, 1948 (Les Editions du Chêne: Paris); *Trente Dessins*, 1946 (Editions Pierre Tisné-Rombaldi). Anthologies: *The Photograph Collector's Guide*, Lee D. Witkin & Barbara London, 1979; *The Julien Levy Collection*, Witkin Gall., 1977; *Photography Year 1977*, 1977, *Great Photographers*, 1971, Time-Life Series; *Photographs from the Julien Levy Collection*, David Travis, 1976; *The Magic Image*, Cecil Beaton & Gail Buckland, 1975; *Looking At Photographs*, John Szarkowski, ed., 1973; *Images de Caméra*, ed., 1964 (Aldus: London).

PORTFOLIO *Portfolio Brassaï*, intro. by A. D. Coleman, foreword by Brassaï, 1973 (Witkin-Berley: N.Y.).

COLLECTIONS Ariz. State Univ., Tempe; Delgado Mus., New Orleans, La.; Detroit Inst. of the Arts, Mich.; Everson Mus., Syracuse, N.Y.; Exchange Natl. Bank of Chicago; IMP/GEH, Rochester; MOMA, NYC; New Orleans Mus. of Art, La.; R.I. School of Design, Providence; Univ. of Kans. Mus. of Art, Lawrence; Univ. of Mich., Ann Arbor; Univ. of Neb., Sheldon Mem. Art Gall., Lincoln; Univ. of N. Mex., Albuquerque;

Walker Art Ctr., Minneapolis, Minn.; Worcester Art Mus., Mass.; Yale Univ., New Haven, Conn. Bibliothèque Nationale, Paris; Israel Mus., Jerusalem; Musée Réattu, Arles, France; Natl. Gall. of Victoria, Melbourne, Australia; Provinciaal Mus. voor Kunstambachten, Antwerp, Belgium; Victoria & Albert Mus., London.

DEALER   Marlborough Gall., 40 W 57 St, New York, NY 10019.

ADDRESS   81 rue du Faubourg Saint-Jacques, Paris 75 (14e), France.

Adolphe Braun   PHOTOGRAPHER · TEXTILE DE-SIGNER   Born in France, Braun lived from 1811 to 1877. His son Gaston, born in 1845, was a photographer and color experimenter.

Adolphe worked as a designer-draftsman for a textile house in Alsace, France, in the 1850s and 1860s. He formed Adolphe Braun & Co. of Dornach (Switzerland) and Paris, which was later headed by his son. He was official photographer of the court of Napoleon III.

Along with his son, Braun was the first to introduce the orthochromatic process in the reproduction of paintings, a process he began work on about 1878. He introduced Sir Joseph Swan's carbon process into Belgium and France.

Braun's very early works were daguerreotypes, but he later switched to collodion wet-plate negatives and albumen prints. Working in both large format (about 9 x 19) and small *cartes de visite*, he was best known for his still lifes of flowers, photographed in direct sunlight with landscape lenses and a very small aperture opening, requiring exposures of as much as one-half hour. He was also well known for his color reproductions of artworks using the collodion process. Braun's images included Paris street life, portraits of well known people, mountain landscapes and a few nudes.

PUBLICATIONS   Book: *Vatican: Museo Vaticano*, 3 vols., ca. 1870. Anthology: *The Photograph Collector's Guide*, Lee D. Witkin & Barbara London, 1979; *The Magic Image*, Cecil Beaton & Gail Buckland, 1975; *French Primitive Photography*, Andre Jammes & Robt. Sobieszek, eds., intro. by Minor White, 1970. Catalog: *Catalogue général des photographies*, 1887 (Braun: Paris). Periodical: "Le Second Empire vous regard," Claude Roy, *Le Point*, Jan 1958.

COLLECTIONS   Boston Pub. Lib., Mass.; Harvard Univ., Carpenter Ctr for the Visual Arts, Cambridge, Mass.; IMP/GEH, Rochester; Metro. Mus. of Art, NYC; Temple Univ., Philadelphia, Pa.; Univ. of N. Mex. Art Mus., Albuquerque. Mulhouse Textile Mus., Mulhouse, France.

Benjamin Allen Breard   GALLERY OWNER   Born in Dallas, Texas, on July 4, 1946, Breard has an MS in Photojournalism from Syracuse University in New York (1971) and a BS in Journalism from Northwestern University in Chicago (1969).

He is the owner of The Afterimage Photograph Gallery in Dallas, founded in 1971.

Breard is a member of the Association of International Photography Art Dealers, Inc., and of the American Booksellers Association.

ADDRESS   The Afterimage Photograph Gallery, The Quadrangle #151, 2800 Routh St, Dallas, TX 75201.

David Brewster   PHYSICIST   Born December 11, 1781, in Jedburgh, Roxburghshire, Scotland, Brewster died February 10, 1868, in Allerly, Scotland. The son of a rector, he was educated for church work but ended up studying science at the University of Edinburgh, receiving an MA in the Ministry in 1800.

Brewster became principal of United College of St. Salvator and St. Leonard of the University of St. Andrews in 1838, and in 1859 took the same position at the University of Edinburgh.

Having studied optics, Sir David began investigating the nature of light in 1799 and became interested in photography by 1802. He is especially known for his experiments with lenses and polarized light (wherein all waves are in the same plane) and with metallic reflection and light absorption. In 1812 he suggested the construction of large lenses by using concentric zones, an idea later used in building lightweight, flat Fresnel lenses for lighthouses. He invented the kaleidoscope in 1816, and later began experimenting with the stereoscope, invented by Charles Wheatstone. In 1849 he announced two ideas that would soon be produced: a refracting stereoscope, built in 1851 by L. J. Duboscq of Paris, and a two-lens camera for taking stereoscopic pictures, built in 1853 by J. B. Dancer. In 1857 Brewster offered the notion of using microphotographs in pieces of jewelry. The inventor also gave his name to "Brewster's Law," which quantifies the relation between the polarizing angle and the refractive index of reflective substances.

Elected a Fellow of the Royal Society in 1815, Sir David received the decoration of the Hanoverian Guelphic Order in 1831 for his book on the life of Sir Isaac Newton, and he also helped form the British Association for the Advancement of Science in that year. In 1832 William IV knighted him.

PUBLICATIONS   Books: *Quellendarstellungen zur Geschichte der Fotografie*, Wolfgang Baier,

1964; *History of Photography*, Helmut & Alison Gernsheim, 1955; *Stereo Photography in Practice*, E. T. Linssen, 1952; *Principles of Stereoscopy*, H. C. McKay, 1948; *Cassell's Cyclopedia of Photography*, 1911, repr. 1973; *A History and Handbook of Photography*, Gaston Tissandier, 1876; *Memoirs of the Life, Writings and Discoveries of Sir Isaac Newton*, 1855; *Treatise of Optics*, 1831. Anthology: *Photography's Great Inventors*, Louis W. Sipley, 1965. Periodicals: *Bild und Ton*, 1951; *British Journal of Photography*, 1868; *Edinburgh Magazine*, Dec 1802.

Stephen Brigidi   *PHOTOGRAPHER · PAINTER* Born August 12, 1951, in Providence, Rhode Island, Brigidi earned a BA in 1973 from Providence College and an MFA in 1976 from the Rhode Island School of Design in Providence, where he studied with Harry Callahan and Aaron Siskind.

He is currently assistant professor of photography at the University of Hawaii at Manoa (since 1979), and previously taught photography at Rhode Island Junior College (1978–79) and Rhode Island School of Design (1975–76). Brigidi worked as a photographer for an industrial and advertising studio in 1976–77. He has belonged to SPE since 1978, Oriental Rug Society of New England since 1977 and Associazioni Artisti Versilia in Italy since 1977.

A MacDowell Colony Fellow (New York) in 1979, the photographer won an NEA Photographer's Fellowship in 1978, a Fulbright grant to Italy in 1977 and a Rhode Island State Council on the Arts Photographers' grant in 1975.

Brigidi has made two 16mm films, *Le Sacre* (1975) and *Tuesday* (1974).

PUBLICATIONS   Book: *The Nude*, 1980 (Contrejour, Paris). Catalog: *Witkin Gallery Catalogue*, 1976 (NYC). Periodical: *Fotografia Italiana*, Mar 1978.

COLLECTIONS   Corcoran Gall. of Art, Wash., D.C.; MOMA, NYC; New Orleans Mus. of Art; R.I. School of Design, Providence; Smithsonian Inst., Wash., D.C. Bibliothèque Nationale, Paris.

DEALER   Daniel Wolf, 30 W 57 St, New York, NY 10019.

ADDRESS   474 Thames St, Bristol, RI 02809.

Annie Brigman   *PHOTOGRAPHER · POET* Born Ann Wardrope Nott in 1868 in Honolulu, Hawaii, Brigman died in 1950 in Oakland, California. Her sister, Elizabeth Nott, was also a photographer.

Self-taught, Brigman freelanced during her entire career, which lasted until the 1930s. At that time, due to failing eyesight, she gave up photography and turned to writing.

She joined the Photo-Secession group in 1906.

Her first collection of poetry was published along with her photographs in *Songs of a Pagan*, and she was working on a second book of poetry at the time she died.

Brigman was a pictorial photographer. Her work was noted more for its poetry and abandon than its technique. She often used herself or her sister as a model, posed nude in the midst of nature. While working mainly with silver prints, she sometimes produced palladium or platinum prints.

PUBLICATIONS   Books: *Anne Brigman: Pictorial Photographer/Member of the Photo-Secession*, Therese Thau Heyman, 1974; *Songs of a Pagan*, incl. poetry, 1949. Anthologies: *The Photograph Collector's Guide*, Lee D. Witkin & Barbara London, 1979; *The Collection of Alfred Stieglitz*, 1978; *The Julien Levy Collection*, 1977; *Women of Photography: An Historical Survey*, Margery Mann & Ann Noggle, eds., 1975; *Camera Work: A Critical Anthology*, Jonathan Green, ed., 1973. Periodicals: "What 291 Means to Me," July 1914, "Mrs. Annie W. Brigman—A Comment," J. Nilsen Laurvik, Jan 1909, *Camera Work*.

COLLECTIONS   IMP/GEH, Rochester; Oakland Mus., Calif. RPS, London.

ARCHIVE   Oakland Museum, 1000 Oak St., Oakland, CA 94607.

Denis Brihat   *PHOTOGRAPHER* Born September 16, 1928, in Paris, Brihat is self-taught.

From 1952 to 1960 he worked for Rapho Agency in Paris, and since then has been a freelance and occasional teacher. He won the Prix Niepce in 1957.

Working with black-and-white originals, he adds color by toning processes. His subject matter is generally nature.

PUBLICATION   Catalog: *Photography Into Art*, 1972 (Arts Council of Great Britain: London).

COLLECTIONS   CCP, Tucson; MOMA, NYC. Bibliothèque Nationale, Paris; Musée d'Angoulême, France; Musée des Beaux-Arts, Toulon, France; Musée Nicéphore Niepce, Chalon-sur-Saône, France; Sterckof Mus., Belgium.

DEALER   Stephen White Gall., 835 N La Cienega Blvd, Los Angeles, CA 90069.

ADDRESS   84480 Bonnieux, France.

Alexey Brodovitch   *PHOTOGRAPHER · ART DIRECTOR · TEACHER* Born in Russia in 1895, Brodovitch died at Le Thor, near Avignon,

France, on April 15, 1971. He served in the White Imperial Army as a cavalry officer before fleeing to France after the Bolshevik Revolution. In 1932 he came to the United States, and two years later was made art director at *Harper's Bazaar*, a post he held until 1958.

Brodovitch conducted "design laboratories," which were sponsored by the Philadelphia Museum College and later by the New School for Social Research, the American Institute of Graphic Arts and ASMP. The latter, after Brodovitch's retirement, sponsored an Alexey Brodovitch Design Laboratory. Brodovitch was also art director of *Portfolio*, the layout and design magazine.

The most memorable of Brodovitch's photographs are of the ballet, in particular the Ballet Russe de Monte Carlo. But it is for his teaching that he is best remembered. Among his many pupils are Richard Avedon, Irving Penn, Hiro, Bruce Davidson and Art Kane. Ironically, the mentor did not believe in teaching. "I am a can opener," he would say. His aim was to provoke students into discovering themselves. In his role as art director, Brodovitch is credited with having revolutionized fashion photography.

PUBLICATION   Monograph: *Ballet*, 1945.

Michael Brodsky   PHOTOGRAPHER · TEACHER · GALLERY DIRECTOR   Born in Los Angeles, California, on September 26, 1953, Brodsky completed (with honors) a bachelor's degree in environmental studies, at the University of California in Santa Cruz (1975) and a master's degree in art and design at the California Institute of the Arts in Valencia (1978), where he studied under John Baldesarri, Robert Cumming and JoAnn Callis. He also attended various workshops with Peter Bunnell, Ansel Adams and others.

Since 1978 he has been working both as an art instructor and as the director of the New Image Gallery at the James Madison University in Harrisonburg, Virginia. Before that he was a photography instructor at the Orpheus Alternative University in San Francisco (1975–76) and at the Friends of Photography Members' Workshops (1975).

A member of SPE and CAA, Brodsky received a Study and Research Grant from the Academy of Art College in San Francisco (1975) and an Undergraduate Fellowship Grant to photograph in Indonesia when he was a student at the University of California in Santa Cruz. Since 1979 Brodsky has volunteered as assistant Curator for the Society for Photographic Artistic Change.

As of this date he is "working in the area of conceptual and environmental photography, combining installation-environments with photo documentation. [He is] investigating man and nature relationships and exploring new structural possibilities in nontraditional uses of photographs and other images."

PUBLICATIONS   Anthologies: *Collected Works*, 1978; *Eros and Photography*, 1978. Catalog: *Cleveland Self-Portrait*, Oct 1978.

COLLECTIONS   Cal. Arts, Valencia, Calif.; Southwest Ctr. of Photog., Taos, N. Mex.; Univ. of Calif., Special Cllctn. Lib., Santa Cruz. Kibbutz Lahovot Habashan, Israel; National Health Inst. of East Java, Indonesia.

ADDRESS   76 E Grattan St, Harrisonburg, VA 22801, or Art Dept, James Madison Univ, Harrisonburg, VA 22807.

Giacomo Brogi   PHOTOGRAPHER   Brogi was active in photography from 1860, and his work flourished from 1863 to 1896. His son, Carlo, with whom he collaborated, continued his father's career. Brogi toured Egypt and Palestine. He was founder of the Photographic Society of Italy, and its first vice-president. Brogi won awards at the Exposition in Milan (1881), the Universal Exposition in Vienna (1873) and the Exposition of Forli (1871).

His early work was almost exclusively portrait, turning later to views and reproductions of works of art.

PUBLICATIONS   Books: *Il ritratto in fotografia*, 1896 (Florence); *In proposito della protezione legale delle fotografie*, 1885 (Rome). Catalog: *Soggetti Artistici Eseguiti e Pubblicati del fotografo Giacomo Brogi*, 1863 (Florence).

John Brook   PHOTOGRAPHER · ASTROLOGER   Born in Woonsocket, Rhode Island, on August 29, 1924, Brook went to Harvard, where he completed a BS in 1945. He is completely self-educated in photography and has been self-employed since 1937, when he was still a boy.

In 1960 he won a Gold Medal at the Third Biennial in Milan. He was one of the twenty photographers chosen to exhibit at Kodak's "Universal Eye Gallery" at the 1970 Osaka World's Fair, and one of twenty included in *The Power of Seeing* portfolio published in the Thirtieth Anniversary issue of *Life* (December 23, 1966).

Brook's works consists of black-and-white "records of autobiographical events and color transparencies of visual events found in nature," both executed in medium format. He sometimes uses "self-designed lenses which embody common optical abberrations (positive or negative coma, positive spherical aberration, etc.)."

PUBLICATIONS Books: *Hold Me*, 1977; *Along the Riverrun*, 1970. Periodicals: *Aperture*, 1966; *Life*, Dec 23, 1966.

COLLECTIONS Art Inst. of Chicago; Boston Athenaeum; IMP/GEH, Rochester; Metro. Mus. of Art, NYC; MOMA, NYC; Phillips Academy, Addison Gall. of Amer. Art. Andover, Mass; Smithsonian Inst., Wash., D.C.; Univ. of Nebraska, Lincoln.

ADDRESS 166 Newbury St, Boston, MA 02116.

David B. Brooks PHOTOGRAPHER · AUTHOR · JOURNALIST · Born on May 7, 1933, in Regina, Saskatchewan, he first attended Oregon State University (1955–56), then the Brooks Institute of Photography in Santa Barbara, California (1956–57). He completed his bachelor's degree at California State University in Northridge in 1961.

From 1975 to 1978 he worked as a technical/feature editor for *Petersen's Photographic Magazine*, for which he is currently a contributing editor. He is a member of the Photographic Society of America, ASMP, NPPA, and SPE.

Since 1975 Brook's work has primarily consisted of "illustrative and experimental photography in conjunction with writing on technique. [His] personal work [is] limited to landscape, nature and figure photography."

PUBLICATIONS Books: *Photographic Materials and Processes*, 1979; *Guide to Small Camera Portraiture*, 1977; *Guide to Figure Photography*, 1974. Periodicals: *Petersen's Photographic Magazine*, monthly column since 1975 (Los Angeles).

ADDRESS 822 Inga Rd, Nipomo-Mesa, CA 93444.

Ellen Brooks PHOTOGRAPHER · TEACHER Born in Los Angeles on February 3, 1949, Brooks attended the University of Wisconsin from 1963 to 1965 and the University of California at Los Angeles from 1965 to 1971, where she studied under Bob Heinecken, Robert Fichter and Lynn Foulkes, among others.

She has been teaching at the San Francisco Art Institute since 1974; she also taught at the Chicago Art Institute (1976), the extension divisions of the University of California at Los Angeles and at Berkeley (1971–75) and Franconia College in New Hampshire (1974).

She is a member of SPE and of the Artist Committee at the San Francisco Art Institute. Brooks

has been the recipient of several awards: two grants from NEA (1976, 1979), the PHELAN Award (1971) and an Alumni Award from UCLA (1971).

The photographer specializes in "large-scale environmental pieces, indoor and outdoor installations dealing with the figure and its relation to the viewing audience."

PUBLICATION Anthology: *The Photograph Collector's Guide*, Lee D. Witkin & Barbara London, 1979.

COLLECTIONS UCLA. Natl. Gall., Ottawa, Canada.

ADDRESS 636 4 St, San Francisco, CA 94107.

Linda Brooks PHOTOGRAPHER · TEACHER Born in Brooklyn, New York, on June 7, 1951. Brooks obtained an MFA in 1976 and a BFA in painting in 1973, both from the State University of New York at Buffalo.

She has been employed as an assistant professor at the University of Minnesota in Minneapolis since 1976. She has also taught at SUNY, Buffalo (1975–76), and at Starpoint Central School in Lockport, New York (1973–75).

For the past several years, the artist has been a member of SPE, the St. Paul Art Collective in Minnesota, the George Eastman House and the Walker Art Center in Minneapolis. She had also joined the College Art Association (1976–78) and the Albright-Knox Art Gallery in Buffalo (1972–76). She was a recipient of the Minnesota State Art Board Project Grant in 1980 and in 1975 she won the first prize at the New York State Fair Photo Exhibit in Syracuse, New York.

Brooks works "primarily from interior sculptural installations or situations which [she sets] up specifically to photograph." She is also involved in "a series of small books of b&w contact prints and Cibachrome prints of sequential images of personal content."

PUBLICATIONS Catalogs: *In Situ*, co-designer, 1979 (St. Paul Art Collective; Landmark Ctr, Minn.); *Six Photographers*, 1978 (Cllctn. of St. Catherine: St. Paul, Minn.); *Studio Arts Faculty Exhibition*, 1977 (Univ. of Minnesota: Minneapolis).

COLLECTIONS Albright-Knox Art Gall., Buffalo, N.Y.; Cllctn. of St. Catherine, St. Paul, Minn.; IMP/GEH, Rochester; Minneapolis Inst. of the Arts., Minn.; Niagara Univ., Niagara Falls N.Y.; N. Hennepin Community Coll., Brooklyn Park, Minn.

ADDRESS 3213 16 Ave S, Minneapolis, MN 55407.

Milton E. (Pete) Brooks   *PHOTOJOURNALIST*
Born August 29, 1901, in St. Louis, Missouri, Brooks died September 3, 1956, in Detroit, Michigan. His father, James W. Brooks, was a reporter and desk man for the *St. Louis Globe-Democrat* and *Post-Dispatch.*

Brooks began newspaper work at the *Chicago Herald Examiner*, and then worked for the *Chicago Daily News, Paramount News Reel* and *New York Daily News.* He was employed by the *Detroit News* from 1928 to 1953, at which time he became a commercial photographer.

A member of Michigan Press Photographers Association, Brooks won the Pulitzer Prize in 1942 for Best News Photography. He also won first-prize awards from *Editor & Publisher*, the Michigan State/AP News Photo Contest and the Inland Daily Press Association Photo Contest.

His Pulitzer-winning photograph showed the confrontation between Ford Motor Company and the striking members of the United Auto Workers on April 2, 1941.

PUBLICATION   Anthology: *Moments*, Sheryle & John Leekley, 1978.

ARCHIVE   The Detroit News, 615 W. Lafayette, Detroit, MI 48231.

Lynn Brooks-Korn   *PHOTOGRAPHER*   Born on July 6, 1951, in Detroit, Michigan, Brooks-Korn completed an MFA in 1976 at the University of Michigan, where she had also obtained her bachelor's degree in the same field, magna cum laude, in 1973; her professor, David Reider, had a great impact on her work.

She has been employed as a photographic airbrush artist since 1977. She also worked as a photography instructor at Lansing Community College in Michigan in 1976–77, as a graduate assistant at the University of Michigan in 1976 and as an instructor at the Galliard Gallery in East Lansing in 1973.

Since 1977 she has been a member of CAA, SPE and the Women's Caucus for Art.

The artist has worked extensively in silver and alternative photographic processes, in gumbichromate and in color photography. She is currently working on a "series representing city and nature scapes which combine silver images, painting and airbrush techniques."

PUBLICATION   Book: *Lightworks*, Jan Arnow, 1980.

COLLECTION   Slide Cllctn., Univ. of Michigan, Ann Arbor.

ADDRESS   747 Edgemar Ave, Pacifica, CA 94044.

Dean Brown   *PHOTOGRAPHER*   Brown was born in 1936 and died July 8, 1973, in the White Mountains of New Hampshire. He is survived by his wife, formerly Carol Anderson, a painter. Brown received a BA from Brooklyn College, New York, in 1960 and an MA in Musicology from New York University in 1965.

Originally a music teacher, Brown then became a freelance photographer for such publications as *Opera News, New York*, Time-Life Books, *Holiday, Redbook* and *House & Garden.*

Brown worked with both dye-transfer color prints and silver prints, and did some black-and-white before 1969. His main concern, the subject, he represented clearly and faithfully. He is known chiefly for his color landscapes.

PUBLICATIONS   Books: *Photographs of the American Wilderness*, preface Robert Doty, intro. Carol Brown, 1976; *New England Wilds*, Ogden Tanner, 1974; *Wild Places: A Photographic Celebration of Unspoiled America*, Ann & Myron Sutton, 1973; *Cactus Country*, Edward Abbey, 1973; *Wild Alaska*, Dale Brown, 1972; *Landscape Gardening*, James U. Crockett, 1971. Anthology: *The Photograph Collector's Guide*, Lee D. Witkin & Barbara London, 1979. Periodicals: *Camera*, Jan 1974, Nov 1971, Oct 1971, Sept 1970.

COLLECTIONS   IMP/GEH, Rochester; Univ. of Kansas. Mus. of Art, Lawrence; Va. Mus. of Fine Arts, Richmond. Natl. Gall. of Canada, Ottawa.

Gillian Brown   *PHOTOGRAPHER · TEACHER*
Born in Manchester, New Hampshire, on April 25, 1951, Brown studied in Providence, Rhode Island, completing an AB in Art at Brown University in 1973 and an MAE at the Rhode Island School of Design in 1977. In 1980 she received an MFA from the University of California in Los Angeles, where she has worked as a teaching assistant since 1978. She also taught art for three years at the Mountain School in Vershire, Vermont.

A member of SPE and of the Los Angeles Center for Photographic Studies, she was the recipient of a Purchase Prize given by the Fleming Museum, UVM, in Burlington, Vermont. She also obtained several grants: a travel grant from the Ford Foundation (summer 1979), an Art Council grant from UCLA (1980 and 1978) and a grant for the individual artist by the Vermont Council on the Arts (1977).

She worked as the co-editor of the monthly publication of the Los Angeles Center for Photographic Studies.

Brown is "interested in conceptual issues in photography." Her work includes several "photographic installations."

PUBLICATIONS Anthologies: *Insights/Contemporary Female Self-Portraits*, 1978; *Tilt*, 1978. Catalog: *Biennial Juried Art*, 1978 (Municipal Art Gal.; Los Angeles).

COLLECTIONS California Inst. of the Arts, Valencia; Fleming Mus., Burlington, VT.

ADDRESS 1242 Harvard St, Santa Monica, CA 90405.

John Francis Brown *PHOTOGRAPHER · CURATOR* Born May 12, 1951, in Mol, Belgium, Brown attended Northampton School of Art (1972–73) and Trent Polytechnic (1973–76), both in England.

From 1979 to 1980 Brown was assistant to the curator of the RPS collection. He is currently a freelance photographer. From 1976 to 1977 he served as assistant to photographer Hugo Minnen in Geel, Belgium, as well as having worked for Sotheby's (Belgravia) on print production for auction catalogs. Brown is a member of Cyclists Touring Club.

"I work with grasses, panoramic landscapes and proverbs," says the photographer.

PUBLICATIONS Anthology: *New British Image*, 1978 (Arts Council of Great Britain). Periodical: *Camera*, Aug 1980.

COLLECTIONS Arts Council of Great Britain, London; Bibliothèque Nationale, Paris; RPS, London; Dept. of the Environment, London.

DEALERS The Photographers Gall., 8 Great Newport St, London WC2, England; David Dawson Gall., B2 Metropolitan Wharf, Wapping Wall, London E1, England; Viviane Esders, 12 rue St. Merrie, 75004 Paris, France.

ADDRESS 9 Tarbert Rd, London SE22, England.

Ken Brown *PHOTOGRAPHER · FILMMAKER · CARTOONIST* Born March 12, 1944, in Dayton, Ohio, Brown studied at the University of Massachusetts in Boston from 1962 to 1965.

Since 1977 Brown has been a film and animation instructor at Boston College in Massachusetts and has been self-employed in the postcard business since 1975. From 1977 to 1979 he was an artist-in-residence in Cambridge, Massachusetts. During the years 1970–75 he worked as a film instructor for the Boston area public schools.

He is a member of the Photographic Resource Center and the Boston Film/Video Foundation, and in 1977 was a recipient of both a Massachusetts Arts and Humanities Photography Fellowship and a Cambridge Arts Council Film Award. Films he has made are *Down to the Sea*, a documentary, and an animated film, *Stampede*.

Brown says of his work, "Coincidence, confluence, humor and irony—these are the things I love to look for in my photography. I love the populist tradition of postcards and have chosen the medium to disseminate my work."

PUBLICATIONS Anthology: *Art of the State*, 1978 (Mass. Arts & Humanities Fndn.). Periodicals: *Petersen's Photographic Magazine*, March 1980; *Lightwork Magazine*, 1978.

ADDRESS 65 Inman St, Cambridge, MA 02139.

Laurie Brown *PHOTOGRAPHER · TEACHER* Born in 1937 in Austin, Texas, Brown received a master's degree in fine arts from the California State University at Fullerton (1976) after having studied photography at Orange Coast College, Costa Mesa (1971–72). She also obtained her BA in California, at Scripps College in Claremont (1959).

She was an instructor in photography at Orange Coast College from 1976 to 1979. Since 1976 she has been a member of SPE and the Los Angeles Center for Photographic Studies. She was awarded a grant from the NEA for the year 1979.

Her work consists mainly of silver prints, "selectively toned—usually sequential pieces dealing with space and time." She is interested in "landforms, containing patterns and markings of earth-movers and tractors."

COLLECTIONS (selected) California State Univ., Long Beach; C.P, Tucson; Los Angeles County Mus. of Art; Minneapolis Inst. of the Arts, Minn.; New Orleans Mus. of Art; Newport Harbor Art Mus., Newport Beach, Calif.; Oakland Mus., Calif.; Santa Barbara Mus. of Art, Calif.; Security Pacific Bank, Los Angeles; Grünwald Cllctn., UCLA.

ADDRESS 539 Allview Terr, Laguna Beach, CA 92651.

Lawrie Brown *PHOTOGRAPHER · TEACHER* Born on March 11, 1949, in San Jose, California, Brown attended San Francisco State University, where she earned an MA in 1975, and San Jose State University, where she received her BA in the same field in 1972. She also took courses at the California College of Arts and Crafts in Oakland, California (1973; 1976), and at the University of Colorado in Boulder (1970–71).

Brown lives in California where she has held several teaching positions in photography. As of this writing she was the coordinator of the Photo

Department at Cabrillo College in Aptos. Previously she taught at Foothill College in Los Altos Hills (1979), at the Extension Programs of the University of California in Santa Cruz (1977) and of San Jose State University (1976–79), at the Friends of Photography Workshops in Carmel (1976; 1979) and at Merced College in Merced (1974–75).

Since 1973 she has been a member of SPE, VSW and the Friends of Photography. Brown received a Photographer's Fellowship from NEA in 1979 and a scholarship from the Academy of Arts College in San Francisco in 1973.

The artist works with silver and color prints. She is "mainly concerned with modifying the physical surface of the print and creating new relationships between the surface and the image."

PUBLICATIONS Monograph: *Banana No. 1*, 1975. Anthologies: *Contemporary California Photography*, 1978; *Untitled 6*, 1973. Periodical: *Popular Photography Annual*, 1976.

COLLECTIONS Metro. Mus. of Art, NYC; Mills Coll, Oakland, Calif.; Oakland Mus., Calif.; San Francisco Mus. of Modern Art. Bibliothèque Nationale, Paris.

DEALERS Marcuse Pfeifer Gall., 825 Madison Ave, New York, NY 10021; G. Ray Hawkins Gall., 7224 Melrose Ave, L.A., CA 90069; Focus Gall., 2146 Union St, San Francisco, CA 94123.

ADDRESS 424 Ocean View Ave, Santa Cruz, CA 95062.

Peter Thomson Brown PHOTOGRAPHER · TEACHER Born on June 5, 1948, in Northampton, Massachusetts, Brown studied photography at Stanford University in California, where he completed an MFA in 1977 and had Leo Holub, Keith Boyle and Geoff Winningham as teachers.

He has been a lecturer in photography at Rice University in Texas since 1978 and also taught at Stanford during the year 1977–78. A member of CAA and SPE, he received a Carnegie Foundation grant in 1977 and a Mileo Photo Award at the Bicentennial Commission Traveling Show.

Brown does medium-format photography, in black-and-white and color. "Light, space, beauty and mystery are [his] main concerns."

PUBLICATIONS Book: *Learning to Die/Learning to Live*, w/Robert Herhold, 1976. Periodical: *Popular Photography Annual*, 1976.

COLLECTIONS Mus. of Fine Arts, Houston; Stanford Univ. Mus. of Art, Calif.

DEALERS Smith-Andersen Gall., 200 Homer St, Palo Alto, CA 94301; Carson-Sapiro Gall., 1411 Market St, Denver, CO 80202.

ADDRESS 1113 Milford St, Houston, TX 77006.

Turner Browne PHOTOGRAPHER · CINEMATOGRAPHER · AUTHOR Born July 6, 1949, in Lake Charles, Louisiana, Browne attended Louisiana State University in Baton Rouge in 1968–69. As a photographer he is self-taught. He is married to author and actress Elaine Partnow.

A freelance photographer since 1969, Browne has also worked in the Hollywood film industry since 1972. From 1973 to 1975 he concentrated on a still photography documentation of the rural Cajuns of Louisiana. In the year 1975–76, he specialized in mural printing, including work from the original negatives of the John Kobal Collection, resulting in the traveling exhibit "Dreams for Sale"; these images include the work of Hollywood glamour photographers like Hurrell, Bull, Willinger, etc.

A member of the Friends of Photography and the Los Angeles Center for Photographic Studies, Browne received a photography grant from the Sunflower Foundation of Santa Barbara, California, in 1973.

Among his motion picture credits are director of photography on *Only Once in a Lifetime* (1978, produced by Sierra Madre Motion Picture Company of Los Angeles) and cameraman on *The New Klan*, a documentary aired on the national Public Broadcasting System in 1978.

Working in medium and large formats, Browne's personal work is mainly black-and-white. He concentrates on documentary, landscapes and found objects.

PUBLICATIONS Monograph: *Louisiana Cajuns/Cajuns de la Louisiane*, 1977. Book: *The Cajuns*, William Faulkner Rushton, 1979.

COLLECTIONS Jean LaFitte Natl. Park, New Orleans, La.; Louisiana Arts & Science Mus., Baton Rouge.

DEALER Nancy Moss, 1732 General Pershing, New Orleans, LA 70115.

AGENT Harold Moskovitz, 8921 Sunset Blvd, #2A, Los Angeles, CA 90069.

ADDRESS Route 4, Box 146 AJ, Hammond, LA 70401.

Anton Bruehl PHOTOGRAPHER [See plate 52] Born March 11, 1900, in South Australia, he received his first camera at the age of eight and, by fourteen, he was shooting and developing his own pictures. He graduated from an Australian school, having studied engineering. In 1924 he studied at the Clarence White School of Photography in New York.

Bruehl came to America in 1919. He taught at White's school, both in New York and in Canaan, Connecticut, in 1925. From 1926 to 1966 he had an advertising photography studio in New York. His pictures have appeared in *Vogue, Vanity Fair* and *House and Garden*, and he is considered one of the pioneers of color photography.

He was a recipient of the Harvard Award in 1929 and 1931.

PUBLICATIONS Books: *Tropic Patterns*, 1970, repr. 1973; *Magic Dials*, Lowell Thomas, 1939; *Photographs of Mexico*, 1933; *Form and Re-form*, Paul T. Frankl, 1930. Anthologies: *The Photograph Collector's Guide*, Lee D. Witkin & Barbara London, 1979; *Photographs From the Julien Levy Collection*, David Travis, 1976. Periodical: *Vogue*, June 1941.

COLLECTIONS Art Inst. of Chicago; CCP, Tucson; IMP/GEH, Rochester; MOMA, NYC; New Orleans Mus. of Art; Smith Coll., Northampton, Mass.; Univ. of N. Mex., Albuquerque; Univ. of Ariz., Tucson; Whitney Mus., NYC. Trois Siecles d'Art, Paris.

DEALER Witkin Gallery, 41 E 57 St, New York, NY 10022.

ADDRESS 2175 S Ocean Blvd, Delray Beach, Fl 33444.

Francis Bruguière PHOTOGRAPHER · PAINTER Born in San Francisco, California, on October 16, 1879; he died in May, 1945 in London, England. He was influenced by Frank Eugene.

A member of Photo-Secession (1905) and German Secession (1928), Bruguière created Britain's first abstract film in 1931, *Light Rhythms*, in co-operation with Oswell Blakeston. He was the official designer for the gateway to the British pavilion at the Paris Exposition in 1937.

Working mainly in silver prints but also using gum-bichromate and autochrome, Bruguière was one of the first photographers to explore extensively abstract photographic imagery. He produced purely abstract images by lighting cut paper; he also used solarization and solargrams. He also photographed architecture and stage actors.

PUBLICATIONS Monograph: *Bruguière: His Photographs and His Life*, James L. Enyeart, 1977. Books: *Few Are Chosen*, w/Oswell Blakeston, 1932; *Beyond This Point*, w/Lane Sieveking, 1929 (Duckworth, London); *A Project for the Theatrical Presentation of The Divine Comedy of Dante Alighieri*, Norman Bel Geddes, foreword by Max Reinhardt, 1924; *San .Francisco*, 1918; *The Evanescent City*, George Sterling, 1916. Anthology: *The Photograph Collector's*

Guide, Lee D. Witkin & Barbara London, 1979; *Photography Rediscovered*, David Travis & Anne Kennedy, 1979; *The Magic Image*, Cecil Beaton & Gail Buckland, 1975.

COLLECTIONS Art Inst. of Chicago, Julien Levy Cllctn.; IMP/GEH, Rochester; N.Y. Pub. Lib. at Lincoln Ctr., Bruguière Cllctn., Theatre Cllctn., NYC; Oakland Mus. of Art, Calif.; Univ. of Kansas. Mus. of Art, Lawrence; Univ. of Tex., Norman Bel Geddes Cllctn., Hoblitzelle Theatre Arts Cllctn., Humanities Research Ctr., Austin.

John Brumfield TEACHER · PHOTOGRAPHER · WRITER Born on April 1, 1934, in Los Angeles, Brumfield received his MFA in Photography at the California Institute of the Arts in 1972. He also earned an MA in Art from the University of California at Berkeley (1970), and both a BA and an MA in English Literature from California State University at Los Angeles in 1961 and 1962. His work has been influenced variously by Samuel Beckett, Wallace Stevens, Paul Bowles, John Keats and Winsor McCay, among others.

Presently Brumfield is both chairman of the Photography Program in the School of Art and Design at California Institute of the Arts and a visiting lecturer in the History of Contemporary Photography at The Art Center School of Design in Pasadena, California. Since 1962 he has held a variety of teaching positions at such schools as the University of Southern California, California State University at San Jose, California State College in Bakersfield; and from 1977 to 1979 he was associate dean of the School of Art and Design at California Institute of the Arts. Between the years 1963 and 1967 Brumfield worked as a commercial freelance photographer.

The teacher-photographer is a member of CAA, the United Professors of California and SPE. In 1979 he was a co-participant in an NEA Institutional Grant and in 1977 he was a participant in The Ryerson Symposium.

In describing his work, the artist states that he does "modular organizations of sequentially patterned 16 x 20 black-and-white photographs which, toying with the fictional nature of identity, show no concern whatsoever with 'photographic' esthetics."

PUBLICATIONS Books: *Language and Photography*, Lew Thomas, ed., 1977; *Eros and Photography*, Donna Lee Phillips, ed., 1978; *Structuralism and Photography*, Lew Thomas, ed., 1978. Periodical: "Br'er Camera and the Tar Baby," *the Dumb Ox*, 1977.

COLLECTIONS CCP, Tucson; L.A. County Museum; Minneapolis Inst. of the Arts, Minn.;

MOMA, NYC; San Francisco Mus. of Modern Art; Santa Barbara Museum of Art, Calif.; Grünwald Cllctn., UCLA.

DEALER   G. Ray Hawkins, 7224 Melrose Ave, L.A., CA 90046.

ADDRESS   c/o Calif. Inst. of the Arts, Valencia, CA 91355.

Helen M. Brunner   CURATOR · PHOTOGRAPHER
Born November 15, 1952, in Washington, D.C., Brunner earned an MFA in Photographic Studies (1977) from VSW (of SUNY, Buffalo), Rochester, New York.

Since 1975 she has been coordinator of the VSW Research Center. Brunner belongs to SPE, American Printing History Association, Center for Book Arts and American Association of Museums.

She won a Collaborations in Art, Science, and Technology Fellowship in 1978.

Her primary curatorial field is visual books and photo-printmaking, and her own work is concerned with "visual reinterpretation of early language systems." Although photographic, the pictures are manipulated.

ADDRESS   46 Kron St, Rochester, NY 14619.

Gail Susan Buckland   PHOTOHISTORIAN
Born in New York City on March 5, 1948, Buckland studied mainly at the University of Rochester, New York, where she obtained a bachelor's degree in history in 1970. She also took some courses at Columbia University in New York City (1967) and at Manchester University in England (1968–69). She spent the year 1970–71 at the London College of Printing studying photography.

Her work experience is quite varied. She taught photography at the Pratt Institute in Brooklyn (1977–78) and is currently both an adjunct assistant professor of photography at Cooper Union and a contributing editor to *Portfolio* (NYC). Previously she resided in Chicago, where she was both a faculty member at Columbia College (1975–77) and an assistant to the curator of photography at the Art Institute (1975–76). Prior to that, she spent four years in London, working as an exhibition organizer for the show "From Today Painting is Dead: The Beginnings of Photography" at the Victoria and Albert Museum (1971–72), as an archivist (1971–73) and a curator (1973–74) for the Royal Photographic Society of Great Britain and as an exhibition reviewer for the BBC Radio (1973–74).

Buckland is a member of the American Association of Picture Professionals, the Author's Guild and SPE. In 1976 she received a summer stipend from NEA.

Her books and articles deal with the history of photography, and mainly cover the nineteenth and early twentieth century.

PUBLICATIONS   Books: *First Photographs*, 1980; *The Magic Image* w/Cecil Beaton, 1975; *Reality Recorded*, 1974. Periodicals: "Fox Talbot," *Portfolio*, Apr/May 1979; "William Henry Fox Talbot," *American Photographer*, Jan 1979; "Another Fox Talbot," *Exposure: SPE*, fall 1978; "Riis: unable to be indifferent," *Afterimage: VSW*, Feb 1975; "Julia Margaret Cameron: An Exhibition at Leighton House," *The Photographic Journal*, May 1971.

ADDRESS   33 Riverside Dr, #14A1, New York, NY 10023.

Eugene Buechel, S.J.   PHOTOGRAPHER ·
TEACHER · PRIEST   Born in Schleida, Thuringia, near Fulda, Germany, on October 20, 1874, Buechel died on the Rosebud Reservation, South Dakota, October 27, 1954. He was schooled in Fulda between 1881 and 1897, when he entered the Society of Jesus in Blyenback, The Netherlands, where he remained until 1900. Buechel then attended St. Louis University in Missouri from 1904 to 1906, when he was ordained to the Jesuit priesthood. Buechel was possibly influenced by August Sander and/or John A. Anderson.

Buechel was a Jesuit teacher with the St. Francis Mission on the Rosebud Reservation in South Dakota from 1900 to 1904, where he made his first photographs with an 8 x 10 view camera. He then became a superior with the Holy Rosary Mission on the Pine Ridge Reservation in South Dakota from 1906 to 1916, transferring back to the St. Francis Mission from 1916 to 1923. From 1924 on, he served as a pastor, traveling to isolated Indian communities on the Rosebud Reservation.

A non-Indian authority on the Lakota language, he created 30,000 vocabulary cards that were the first written documents of that language. Buechel was a naturalist who preserved specimens of the flora of the upper plains of South Dakota, making identifications in English, Latin, and Lakota. He was a collector of Sioux artifacts, which he housed in the museum he founded in 1947—what was to become the Buechel Memorial Lakota Museum.

In a catalog on the artist-priest, David Wing writes that Buechel's "maturity and his distance from the technology of photography may explain the directness of his images. They are not in any aspect about the photographic process, but about his subjects and his relationship to them." He used simple adjustable cameras, estimated his exposures, and sent his exposed films to a commercial studio for processing and printing. Buechel was witness to the dramatic transitional period of white dominance on Indian reservations and "with his camera he chose and clearly rendered the people and landscapes he knew so well."

PUBLICATIONS Book: *Crying for a Vision*, Jim Alinder & Don Doll, eds., 1976. Language Books: *A Dictionary of the Teton Dakota Sioux Language*, Rev. Paul Manhart, 1970; *Grammar of Lakota*, 1939; *A Bible History in the Language of the Teton Sioux*, 1923. Catalog: *Eugene Buechel, S.J.: Rosebud and Pine Ridge Photographs, 1922–42*, David Wing et al, eds., 1974 (Buechel Memorial Lakota Mus.: St. Francis, S.D.).

ARCHIVE Buechel Memorial Lakota Mus., St Francis, SD.

Henry Buergel
See Henry Goodwin

Robb Casimir Alexander Buitenman *PHO-TOGRAPHER · PAINTER · WRITER · DESIGNER* Born March 30, 1946, Buitenman, self-taught, has been influenced by "Rembrandt, Picasso and nature."

A self-employed artist, Buitenman belongs to BBK (Dutch Art Union) and GKF (Dutch Union of Creative Photographers).

In 1978 he won the Golden Diaphragm Award as grand prize winner of the 2nd International Triennial Exhibition of Photography organized by the Museum for Art and History in Fribourg, Switzerland.

PUBLICATIONS Catalogs: *Dutch Landscape*, 1979 (Photogall. Canon: Amsterdam); *Art*, 1978 (Internatl. Art Fair: Basle); *2nd International Triennial Exhibition of Photography*, 1978 (Fribourg, Switzerland); *Fantastic Photography in Europe*, 1977 (Photogall. Canon: Amsterdam). Periodicals: *Foto*, July 1979, Apr 1979, Oct 1978, Dec 1977, Sept 1976 (The Netherlands); *Photographie*, Aug 1978.

COLLECTIONS Bibliothèque Nationale, Paris; Mus. of Art & History, Fribourg, Switzerland; Mus. of Modern Art, Amsterdam; Op-Art & Photographic Art Cllctn. of the Dutch Government, The Hague, The Netherlands; Polaroid Cllctn., Amsterdam.

DEALERS Galerie Jack Visser, Leidsegracht 74, 1016 CR, Amsterdam, The Netherlands; Canon Photogall. Geneva, rue St Léger 3, Geneva, Switzerland.

ADDRESS Stalden 30, 1700 Fribourg, Switzerland.

Jan Bułhak *PHOTOGRAPHER* Bułhak lived from 1876 to 1950 in Poland. He started photography in 1912 in the city of Wilno, and lectured frequently at Wilno University. After World War II he moved to Warsaw.

In 1927 Bułhak co-founded the Wilno Photographic Society, and in 1930 he initiated the birth of the Polish Photo-Club.

Noted for his "native photography," the influential Polish photographer made numerous views of several regions of his country.

PUBLICATIONS Books: *Fotografia ojczysta*, 1951 (Zakładu Narodowego im. Ossolińskich: Wrocław, Wydawn); *Wilno*, 1924 (J. Mortkowicza, W. Warszawie: Wydawn).

COLLECTION Muzeum Narodowe we Wrocławiu, Warsaw, Poland.

Clarence Sinclair Bull *PHOTOGRAPHER* Born in 1895 in Sun River, Montana, Bull died in 1979 in Los Angeles. He was apprenticed to the painter Charles Russell (1912) and attended the University of Michigan.

While in college Bull did some freelance work for a local paper. In 1918 he went to Hollywood and worked as an assistant camera operator at Metro Pictures. In 1920 Samuel Goldwyn hired him to do publicity stills, and when Goldwyn merged with Metro in 1924, Bull stayed on as head of the Metro-Goldwyn-Mayer stills department. He remained there until his retirement in 1960.

Considered one of the finest portrait photographers in the film industry, Bull photographed all the legendary stars who passed through MGM's gates during the studio's heyday. Said John Kobal of Bull, "Though he was experienced in every branch of his department, from printing to retouching, his fame rests on his photographic collaborations with Greta Garbo" (*The Art of the Great Hollywood Portrait Photographers*).

PUBLICATIONS Book: *The Faces of Hollywood*, w/Raymond Lee, 1968. Anthology: *Dreams for Sale*, 1976.

Wynn Bullock *PHOTOGRAPHER · TEACHER · INVENTOR* [See plate 90] Born Percy Wingfield Bullock on April 18, 1902, in Chicago, the photographer died on November 16, 1975, in Monterey, California. His mother was Judge Georgia P. Bullock. He studied music and voice in New

York City in preparation for a career as a concert singer, then attended Columbia University in New York City (1923) to further his general education. As a singer, he performed in Irving Berlin's *Music Box Revue* in New York City from 1921 to 1924. From 1928 to 1930 he studied voice, music and language in Europe and performed professionally. Bullock studied pre-law at West Virginia University, Morgantown, from 1933 to 1936 and enrolled as a law student at the University of Southern California, Los Angeles, in 1938. He left law school to study photography formally at Art Center in Los Angeles, where he was greatly influenced by Edward Kaminski. Then, in 1940–41, Bullock studied briefly with semanticist Alfred Korzybski and was deeply impressed by the man's basic principle that "the word as symbol is not the thing symbolized." Bullock was also strongly influenced by Edward Weston, whom he met in the late 1940s.

A freelance photographer from 1967 until his death, Bullock taught at Institute of Design in Chicago (1967), Monterey Peninsula College (1959–60), and San Francisco State College, where he headed the Photography Department from 1945 to 1958. He ran photo concessions at Ford Ord, California (1943–44), and at Camp Cooke, California (1942–43), and worked for Lockheed and then Connors-Joyce until the end of World War II. Bullock ran a commercial and portrait photography studio in Los Angeles in 1941.

Bullock belonged to ASMP, Carmel Camera Society, Professional Photographers of Northern California, Monterey Arts and Humanities Council, Masons, Camera Craftsmen and was a trustee and exhibition chairperson of Friends of Photography.

Between 1946 and 1948 he received patents in the United States, Canada and Great Britain for his "Photographic Process for Producing Line Image," a method of controlling the line effect of solarization. He also earned a second U.S. patent for "Methods and Means for Matching Opposing Densities in Film." Bullock won the Honor Medal for photographs from the Photo Ciné Club du Val de Bievre in 1957, the Award from the Professional Photographers of Northern California in 1960 and a Certificate of Excellence in the 26th Annual Exhibit of the Art Directors Club in Philadelphia in 1961.

Bullock was one of the subjects of the Fred Padula film, *Two Photographers—Wynn Bullock and Imogen Cunningham* (1966).

The photographer produced seascapes, landscapes and nudes—subjects that evoked for him symbolic meanings of a personal nature. He believed that, though an image is recorded for its own qualities, ultimately it "evokes a stream of consciousness about something that is not directly related to that thing. . . ." He further stated, "I think we have to evoke new symbols . . . that expand our minds so that we may be more at home in this scientific and terrifying age we live in."

PUBLICATIONS Monographs: *Wynn Bullock*, intro. by David Fuess, 1976; *Wynn Bullock; Photography, A Way of Life*, Barbara Bullock-Wilson, 1973; *Wynn Bullock*, Barbara Bullock, 1971. Books: *Dialogue with Photography*, Paul Hill & Thomas Cooper, 1979; *Darkroom 1*, Eleanor Lewis, ed., 1976; *The Photograph as Symbol*, 1976; *Photographers on Photography*, Nathan Lyons, ed., 1966; *The Widening Stream*, Richard Mack, 1965; *This is the American Earth*, Ansel Adams & Nancy Newhall, 1960; *The Big Sur— Highway One from Monterey to Morro Bay*, Emil White, ed., 1954. Anthologies: *The Photograph Collector's Guide*, Lee D. Witkin & Barbara London, 1979; *The Magic Image*, Cecil Beaton & Gail Buckland, 1975; *The Art of Photography*, 1971, *The Camera*, 1970, *The Great Themes*, 1970, Time-Life Series; *The Family of Man*, Edward Steichen, ed., 1955. Catalogs: *Wynn Bullock: Twenty Color Photographs*, 1972 (de Saisset Art Gall. & Mus., Univ. of Santa Clara: Calif.); *George Eastman House Collection*, 1968 (GEH: Rochester); *Photograph USA*, 1967 (De Cordova Mus.: Lincoln, Mass.); *American Photography: The Sixties*, 1966 (Sheldon Art Gall., Univ. of Neb.: Lincoln); *Photography in America 1850–1965*, 1965 (Yale Univ. Art Gall.: New Haven, Ct.); *Photography in the Fine Arts IV*, 1963 (Metro. Mus. of Art: NYC); *Way Out West Conference*, 1962 (Professional Photographers of N. Calif.); *Creative Photography 1956*, 1956 (Lexington Camera Club & Dept. of Art, Univ. of Ky.); *Danish International Salon of Photography*, 1956. Periodicals: *Camera*, Dec 1979, July 1975, Nov 1975, Dec 1972, Jan 1972; "Wynn Bullock, American Lyric Tenor," *CCP No. 2*, Sept 1976; *Artweek*, reviews, Oct 28, 1972, July 10, 1971; review, A. D. Coleman, *The Village Voice*, July 29, 1971; "Wynn Bullock, A Retrospective View," Colin Osman, ed., June 1971, "Wynn Bullock Nudes," June 1969, "Wynn Bullock," Lew Parrella, no. 87, 1958, *Creative Camera*; "Wynn Bullock: Tracing Man's Roots in Nature," Barbara Bullock & Jerry Uelsmann, *Modern Photography*, May 1970; "Photography Pristine and Pure," *Applied Photography*, no. 40, 1969; *Photography Italiana*, Mar 1969; Applied Photography, no. 35, 1967; *U.S. Camera Annual*, 1965, 1961, 1960, 1959, 1958, 1957, "Wynn Bullock," Lew Parella, 1956, 1955, 1952, 1943, 1942; *Photography Annual*, 1965, 1961, 1958, 1957; "The Nude in Nature," George Bush, no. 2, 1963, "Thoughts on Wynn Bullock," George Bush, no. 1, 1961, *International Photo Technik*; "Wynn Bullock: A Critical Appreciation," Nat Herz, *Infinity*, Nov 1961; "The Eyes of 3 Phantasts: Laughlin, Sommer, Bullock," Oct 1961, "The Sense of Abstraction in Contemporary Photography," Nathan Lyons, Apr 1960, "Creative Photography 1956," Van Deren Coke, Jan 1956, "Portfolio," Oct 1953, *Aperture; Camera Mainichi*, no. 12, 1961, no. 6, 1958; "Time's Vital Relationship to Photography," *Contemporary Photography* magazine, May/June 1960; "The Sense of Abstraction." *Contemporary Photographer*, July/Aug 1960;; *Sankei Camera*, no. 9, 1959; "Partial Reversal Line," *The Photographic Journal*, Apr 1955; *Asaki Camera*, no. 12, 1955; "Photographic Horizon," C. Weston Booth, *U.S. Camera*, Aug 1946.

PORTFOLIO *Photographs 1951–73*, 1973 (self-published: Monterey, Calif.).

COLLECTIONS Amon Carter Mus., Ft. Worth, Tex.; Art Assoc. of New England, Boston; Container Corp. of America, Chicago; E. B. Crocker Art Gall., Sacramento, Calif.; Exchange Natl. Bank of Chicago; Friends of Photography, Carmel, Calif.; IMP/GEH, Rochester; Indiana Univ., Dept. of Fine Arts, Bloomington; Kalamazoo Inst. of Art, Mich.; William H. Lane Fndn., Leominster, Mass.; Lincoln-Rochester Bank, Rochester; Metro. Mus. of Art, NYC; Mills College, Oakland, Calif.; Monterey Peninsula Coll., Monterey Calif.; MOMA, NYC; Mus. of Fine Arts, Boston; Mus. of Fine Arts, St. Petersburg, Fla.; Mus. of N. Mex., Santa Fe; Natl. Gall., Wash., D.C.; Norfolk Mus. of Art, Va.; Norton Simon Mus. of Art, Pasadena, Calif.; Oakland Mus. of Art, Calif.; Philadelphia Mus. of Art, Penn.; Phoenix Coll., Ariz.; Princeton Univ., N.J.; Rockford Art Assoc., Ill.; San Francisco Mus. of Modern Art, Calif.; Smith Coll., Northampton, Mass.; Smithsonian Inst., Wash., D.C.; UCLA; Univ. of Calif., Santa Cruz; Univ. of Fla., Fla Archives of Photography, Gainesville; Univ. of Ill., Urbana; Univ. of Neb., Lincoln; Univ. of Ore., Eugene; Univ. of Santa Clara, de Saisset Art Gall. & Mus., Calif.; Va. Mus. of Fine Arts, Richmond; Yale Univ. Art Mus., New Haven, Conn. Bibliothèque Nationale, Paris; Mus. of Photography, Paris; Natl. Gall., Ottawa, Canada; Rhodes Natl. Gall. of Art, Rhodes, South Africa.

ARCHIVES Center for Creative Photography,

University of Arizona, 843 E University Blvd, Tucson, AZ 85721; Edna Bullock, 155 Mar Vista Dr, Monterey, CA 93940.

Earle L. "Buddy" Bunker *. PHOTOJOURNALIST*
Born in 1912, Bunker died on January 22, 1975, in Omaha, Nebraska.

Known as Buddy or Bud to his friends, he entered the newspaper business with the *Omaha Bee-News* (1929–36). He then moved to the *World-Herald* of Omaha, where he remained until his death thirty-seven years later.

Bunker won the Pulitzer Prize for peacetime photojournalism in 1944, as well as the Associated Press Newsphoto Contest and other national awards.

His prize-winning photograph, "The Homecoming," showed a World War II veteran embracing his seven-year-old daughter while his wife stood nearby covering her face with her hands. The image has been reproduced in *Life, Time, Newsweek* and the *Readers' Digest*, among other publications, and has been called a wartime classic. A highly respected craftsman, Bunker concentrated on color reproduction for the last eighteen years of his life.

PUBLICATION Anthology: *Moments*, Sheryle & John Leekley, foreword by Dan Rather, 1978.

Peter C. Bunnell *TEACHER · CURATOR · HISTORIAN* Born in Poughkeepsie, New York, on October 25, 1937, Bunnell received his BFA from Rochester Institute of Technology in 1959, his MFA from Ohio University, 1961 and an MA from Yale University, 1965.

He is currently the McAlpin Professor of the History of Photography & Modern Art at Princeton University, where he has served in this capacity since 1972, as well as in his post as faculty curator of photography at The Art Museum there; previously (1973–78) he had served as The Art Museum's director. Prior positions have included curator of photography at The Museum of Modern Art (1966–72), staff assistant at George Eastman House (1958–65) and research associate at the Alfred Stieglitz Archive, Yale University (1961–66).

Bunnell has been a member of SPE since 1964 and has served as its director since 1969, functioning also as secretary (1970–72) and chairman (1973–76). He belongs to the Friends of Photography, serving on its Board of Trustees since 1974 and as its president since 1979. From 1975 to 1979 he served on the Board of Directors of CAA.

Mr. Bunnell was the recipient of a Guggenheim Foundation Fellowship in 1979. He was also director of the U.S. Exhibition, Venice Biennale, 1978.

His field of research includes twentieth-century photography from the Photo-Secession to the present, with monographic concentration on Alfred Stieglitz, Clarence H. White and Minor White.

PUBLICATIONS (selected) Books: *Sources of Modern Photography*, repr. series, w/R. Sobieszek, 1979; *Harry Callahan*, 1975; *Jerry N. Uelsmann/Silver Meditations*, intro., 1975; *Photographic Portraits*, 1972. Anthology: *The City/American Experience*, w/A Trachtenberg & P. Neill, 1971. Periodicals: "Why Photography Now," *the New Republic*, 1977; "Diane Arbus," *Print Collector's Newsletter*, 1973; "Photography into Sculpture," *Artscanada*, 1970; "Photography as Printmaking," *Artist's Proof*, 1969.

ADDRESS Dept of Art & Archeology, Princeton University, Princeton, NJ 08540.

Robert Wilhelm Bunsen CHEMIST Born March 31, 1811, in Göttingen, Germany, Bunsen died August 16, 1899, in Heidelberg.

Bunsen became professor of chemistry at the University of Heidelberg in 1852, and it was there he met the British student Henry Enfield Roscoe, who became his collaborator. They published a series of articles from 1854 to 1859 on the chemical action of light in photometry, actinometry and spectrum analysis. Considered by many historians to mark the foundation of photochemistry, their work resulted in the formulation of the Bunsen and Roscoe Law, or the Reciprocity Law. The law stated that the amount of a photochemical reaction depended upon the light energy absorbed, thus relating to the development of densities in a photographic emulsion. Later research by Schwarzschild, Sheppard, Mees and others showed that the rule applied chiefly to moderate intensities of illumination. Bunsen and Roscoe also discovered that magnesium wire or ribbon could be used as a source of photographic light, and presented papers on this work in 1859 and 1864. They invented an apparatus for burning magnesium wire wound on spools and moved by clockwork, the end of the wire being ignited by the flame of an alcohol lamp.

Bunsen's other inventions included a carbon-zinc electric cell (1841), grease-spot photometer (1844), filter pump (1868), ice calorimeter (1870) and vapor calorimeter (1887). He gave his name to the Bunsen burner, but contributed in only a minor way to its development.

PUBLICATIONS Books: *Quellendarstellungen zur Geschichte der Fotografie*, Wolfgang Baier, 1964; *History of Photography*, Helmut & Alison Gernsheim, 1955; *Lexikon für Photographie und Reproduktionstechnik*, G. H. Emmerich, 1910; *Gasometrische Methoden*, 1857. Anthology: *Photography's Great Inventors*, Louis W. Sipley, 1965. Periodicals: *Bild und Ton*, 1951, 1949; *Photographische Correspondenz*, 1899; *Photographic News*, 1864; *Poggendorffs Annalen der Physik und Chemie*, 1855–59.

Jerry Burchard PHOTOGRAPHER · TEACHER Born December 1, 1931, in Rochester, New York, Burchard earned a BFA in Photography from the California School of Fine Arts in San Francisco (1960).

Since 1966 Burchard has been professor of photography at San Francisco Art Institute and chaired the Photography Department in 1968–71 and 1978–79. Burchard won NEA Photographer's Fellowships in 1978 and 1976 and an NEA Photo Survey grant in 1979.

PUBLICATIONS Anthology: *Darkroom*, Eleanor Lewis, ed., 1977. Catalogs: *Attitudes: Photography in the 1970's*, 1979 (Santa Barbara Mus. of Art: Calif.); *Jerry Burchard, Ingeborg Gerdes, John Spence Weir: Photographic Viewpoints*, 1979 (San Francisco Mus. of Modern Art); *Jerry Burchard*, 1978 (Corcoran Gall. of Art: Wash., D.C.); *Auction*, 1977 (GEH:Rochester); *The Target Collection of American Photography*, 1977 (Mus. of Fine Arts: Houston); *A Kind of Beatness: Photographs of a North Beach Era, 1950–65*, 1975 (Focus Gall.: San Francisco); *Dimensional Light*, 1975 (Calif. State Univ.: Fullerton); *San Francisco Renaissance: Photographs of the 50's*, 1975 (Gotham Book Mart: NYC); *Recent Acquisitions*, 1969 (Pasadena Art Mus.: Calif.). Periodical: "Jerry Burchard Portfolio," *Infinity: ASMP*, 14:3, 1965.

PORTFOLIO (group) *New California Views 1979*, 1979 (Victor Landweber).

COLLECTIONS Addison Gall. of Art, Andover, Mass.; Corcoran Gall., Wash., D.C.; Harvard Univ., Fogg Art Mus., Cambridge, Mass.; Houston Mus. of Fine Art, Tex.; IMP/GEH, Rochester; L/C, Wash., D.C.; Minneapolis Art Inst., Minn.; Oakland Mus., Calif.; San Francisco Mus. of Modern Art; Seattle Art Mus., Wash.; VSW, Rochester; Sam Wagstaff Cllctn., NYC; Whatcom Mus., Bellingham, Wash. Univ. of Calgary, Nickel Arts Mus., Alberta, Canada.

ADDRESS 1014 Greenwich, San Francisco, CA 94133.

Jerry Burchfield   *PHOTOGRAPHER · TEACHER*
Born in Chicago, Illinois, on July 28, 1947, Burchfield attended California State University at Fullerton, where he earned a BA in Photocommunications in 1971 and an MA with an emphasis on photography in 1977. He participated in several workshops, with Paul Caponigro, Jerry Uelsmann, Dr. Donald Huntsman and Van Deren Coke. Darryl Curran had a direct influence on his development.

For the last few years he has been working as a part-time instructor at California State University in Fullerton, at Saddleback College in Mission Viejo, and at the Laguna Beach School of Art. Since 1976 he has been the co-owner and co-director of BC Space, a contemporary photography gallery and custom lab service in Laguna Beach.

Burchfield is a member of SPE, Friends of Photography and the Los Angeles Center for Photographic Studies. He received three awards in 1979: two Purchase Awards granted to him respectively by the Bellevue Art Museum in Washington and the Paul L. Schaeffer Memorial Photographic Foundation in Los Angeles, and a Glendale Federal Savings Award given at the Newport Beach Art Festival.

The artist works almost exclusively with color photography. His style has varied since 1974 but his concerns remain the same. He states: "I use photography as a tool to express my reactions to life and living. I am concerned with the nature of the photographic medium, color, light, its relationship to painting, and the way a photo is perceived."

PUBLICATIONS   Book: *The Basic Darkroom Book*, w/Tom Grim, 1978. Anthology: *Contemporary California Photography*, 1978. Periodical: *Photo Image Magazine*, 1:1, 1979.

PORTFOLIOS   *West Coast Now*, 1979 (Susan Spiritus Gall.: Newport Beach, Calif.); *L.A. Issue*, 1979 (L.A. Center for Photographic Studies).

COLLECTIONS   Bellevue Art Mus., Bellevue, Wash.; Chase Manhattan Bank, NYC; Denver Art Mus., Colo.; Eastern Washington Univ., Cheney; Gould Corp., Chicago; Newport Harbor Mus., Newport Beach, Calif.; Security Pacific Bank, Los Angeles; St. Louis Mus. of Art, Mo. Bibliothèque Nationale, Paris; Gakvin Coll., Tokyo.

DEALERS   G. Ray Hawkins Gall., Los Angeles, CA; Susan Spiritus Gall., Newport Beach, CA; BC Space, Laguna Beach, CA; Yuen Lui Gall., Seattle, WA; Foto Gall., NYC. Viviane Rudzinoff Gall., Paris; Ufficio dell Arte, Paris.

ADDRESS   POB 1502, Laguna Beach, CA 92652.

Shirley C. Burden   *PHOTOGRAPHER*   Born December 9, 1908, in New York City, Mr. Burden is brother of William A. M. Burden, U.S. Ambassador to Belgium from 1959 to 1961.

Presently teaching at the Art Center College of Design in Pasadena, California (since 1978), he continues to run a commercial studio, which he opened in 1946. In 1942 he produced training films for the army and air force through Trade Films, a company he formed. Burden co-produced the motion picture *She* with Merian C. Cooper in 1929, and was involved in production work his cousin W. Douglas Burden's *The Silent Enemy* in 1925.

A member of ASMP since 1959, he is chairman of the Department of Photography with the Museum of Modern Art in New York City, and a member of the advisory panel of the Santa Barbara Museum of Art in California. He has been a patron of Aperture, Inc. (Millerton, New York) since 1952.

Burden is interested in photographic essays, concentrating, usually, on people. He also does commercial work.

PUBLICATIONS   Monographs: *Behold Thy Mother*, 1965; *I Wonder Why*, 1963; *God Is My Life*, 1960. Anthology: *The Family of Man*, 1955. Periodicals: Photography Annual, 1966; *U.S. Camera Annual*, 1966.

COLLECTION   MOMA, NYC.

DEALER   Witkin Gall., Inc., 41 E. 57 St, New York, NY 10022.

ADDRESS   8826 Burton Way, Beverly Hills, CA 90211.

Victor Burgin   *PHOTOGRAPHER · WRITER · LECTURER*   Born July 24, 1941, in Sheffield, Yorkshire, England, he studied at the Royal College of Art, London, in 1965 and received an MFA degree from Yale University in New Haven, Connecticut, in 1967.

Burgin has been employed as senior lecturer in the history and theory of the visual arts at the Department of Film and Photographic Arts, School of Communication, Polytechnic of Central London, since 1973.

In 1980 he was made a Picker Professor of Arts by Colgate University in Hamilton, New York. From 1971 to 1976 he was a member of the Art Advisory Panel of the Arts Council of Great Britain. In 1978–79 he was made a Deutscher Akademischer Austauschdienst Fellow in Berlin, and in 1976–77 he became a US/UK Bicentennial Arts Exchange Fellow. He was also the creator of a film, *Concept*, for BBC-TV in 1971.

PUBLICATIONS   Books: *Two Essays on Art,*

Photography, and Semiotics, 1976 (Robert Self Pubs.); *Work and Commentary,* 1973 (Latimer: London). Periodicals: "Seeing Sense," *Artforum,* Feb 1980; "Looking at Photographs," *Tracks,* fall 1977; "Modernism in the Work of Art," *20th Century Studies,* 15/16, 1976; "Art, Common-Sense, and Photography," *Camerawork,* 3, 1976; "Photographic Practice and Art Theory," *Studio International* July/Aug 1975; "In Reply," *Art-Language,* summer 1972; "Situational Aesthetics," *Studio International,* Oct 1969.

COLLECTIONS Van Abbemuseum, Eindhoven, The Netherlands; Arts Council of Great Britain, London; Graves Art Gall., Sheffield; Tate Gall., London; Victoria & Albert Mus., London; Walker Art Gall., Liverpool. In France: Bibliothèque Nationale, Paris; Musée Grenoble, Grenoble; Musée National d'art Moderne, Centre Georges Pompidou, Paris; Ville de Lyon, Lyon.

DEALERS John Weber Gall., 420 W Broadway, New York, NY 10012; Liliane & Michel Durand-Dessert, 43 rue de Montmorency 75003, Paris.

ADDRESS 25 St. Mary-le-Park Court, Albert Bridge Road, London SW11 4 PJ, England.

J. Bradley Burns *PHOTOGRAPHER · MUSEUM CURATOR* Born December 7, 1951, in Chattanooga, Tennessee, Burns graduated in 1971 with a major in biology from the University of Tennessee at Chattanooga. He began his photography studies by attending the Ansel Adams Yosemite Workshops in 1973.

Since 1976 Burns has been coordinator of exhibitions at the Hunter Museum of Art in Chattanooga. He worked at the Ansel Adams Gallery and workshop as coordinator assistant in 1974. He also did freelance commercial photography from 1971 to 1973.

Burns is a member of the American Association of Museums, the Tennessee Association of Museums, Friends of Photography and the Sierra Club.

Working primarily in black-and-white, using all formats, he characterizes his work as "most images in the 'straight' style dealing with aspects of the landscape whether man-altered or natural, and the human figure. My work shows the influences of the 'West Coast/F-64' group."

PUBLICATIONS Catalogs: *At Mono Lake,* 1979 (Friends of the Earth); *Lightyear,* 1979 (Middle Tenn. State Univ.).

COLLECTIONS Amer. Telephone & Telegraph, Atlanta, Ga.; Dalton Creative Arts Guild, Dalton, Ga.; First Federal Savings & Loan, Jacksonville, Fla.; Hunter Mus. of Art, Chattanooga, Tenn.; Middle Tenn. State Univ., Photography Gall., Murfreesboro; Springfield Art Mus., Springfield, Mo. Univ. of Tokyo, Japan.

ADDRESS 45 Tunnel Blvd, Chattanooga, TN 37411.

Marsha Burns *PHOTOGRAPHER* Born in Seattle, Washington, on January 11, 1945, Burns, who studied at the University of Washington in Seattle and at the University of Massachusetts in Amherst, has been a freelance photographer since 1972. In 1978 she received a Photographer's Fellowship from NEA.

The artists says that her work "has for the most part been directorial toward the given subject, maintaining a 'fictive' distance with reference to a general theme of contemporary decadence."

PUBLICATIONS Periodicals (reviews): *The Seattle Sun,* Nancy Murry, Apr 25, 1979; *Popular Photography,* Natalie Canavor, May 1979.

COLLECTIONS Denver Art Mus., Colo.; Houston Mus. of Fine Arts; Minneapolis Inst. of Art, Minn.; MOMA, NYC; New Orleans Mus. of Art; Newport Harbor Art Mus., Calif.; Seattle Art Mus., Wash.; Springfield Art Mus., Mo.; Whatcom County Mus. of Art & History, Bellingham, Wash.

DEALERS Susan Spiritus, 3336 Via Lido, Newport Beach, CA 92660; Weston Gall., 6 & Dolores St, Carmel, CA 93921; Grapestake Gall., 2876 California St, San Francisco, CA 94115; The Silver Image, 83 S Washington St, Seattle, WA 98104; Halsted Gall., 560 N Woodward, Birmingham, MI 48011.

ADDRESS 627 First Ave, Seattle, WA 98104.

Michael Burns *PHOTOGRAPHER* Born in Lubbock, Texas, on January 31, 1942, Burns specialized in painting at the University of Washington in Seattle, where he obtained a BFA (1966), and at the University of Massachusetts in Amherst, where he completed an MFA (1969).

He has been working as a freelance photographer since 1972. Previously he held several teaching positions: he was an assistant professor at West Texas State University in Canyon (1971–72), a visiting artist at the University of Denver in Colorado (1970–71) and a visiting lecturer at the University of California in Berkeley (1969–70). Burns received a NEA Photographer's Fellowship in 1980.

Working with an 8 x 10 view camera, Burns has usually photographed landscapes, nudes and architecture. He says, "I am committed to clarity of perception, economy of seeing, and grace of presentation."

PUBLICATIONS Catalogs: *Attitudes: Photography in the 1970's*, May 1979 (Santa Barbara Mus. of Art: Calif.); *A Partial View: Young Photographers in the Northwest*, Mar 1979 (Mus. of Art, Washington State Univ.: Pullman). Periodical: *Popular Photography*, Oct 1979.

COLLECTIONS AT&T, Boston; Calif. State Mus., Long Beach; Chase Manhattan Bank, NYC; Detroit Mus. of Art, Mich.; Minneapolis Mus. of Art, Minn; New Orleans Mus. of Art; Oakland Mus., Calif.; Springfield Art Mus., Mo.; St. Louis Mus. of Art, Mo.; Washington State Arts Commission.

ADDRESS 627 First Ave, Seattle, WA 98104.

René Burri *PHOTOJOURNALIST · FILM MAKER* Burri was born in 1933 in Switzerland.

He is a member of Magnum. His photo-essays have appeared in *Look, Life, London Sunday Times* and *Stern*, among other magazines.

His film *What's It All About?* won the New York International Film and TV Festival Award in 1967, and he produced the film *Two Faces of China* with the BBC in 1972.

Based in Paris, Burri has covered stories in such places as Castro's Cuba, Nasser's Egypt, Japan, Thailand and Argentina. His most recent work includes extensive Middle East coverage, with stories on President Sadat of Egypt, the oil potentates, Oman and the emirates.

PUBLICATIONS Book: *The Germans*, 1962. Periodical: *Du*, May 1972.

REPRESENTATIVE Magnum Photos, Inc., 15 W 46 St, New York, NY 10036.

John Charles Burrow *PHOTOGRAPHER · PRINTER* Burrow was born and died in Cornwall, England (1850–1914). Little is known of his life.

He ran a printing works in Carnborne, Cornwall, and did portrait photography and photographs of disasters, but was chiefly known for his mining images.

One of Burrow's most famous pictures was of the wrecked ship *Escurial* at Hayle, with doomed sailors clinging to the rigging of the sinking vessel while the lifeboat rested helplessly in the soft sand in the foreground. "His most important work, however," writes photographer-historian Andrew Lanyon, "was his underground photography, carried out in the early 1890s in several Cornish tin and copper mines. This made him the British pioneer in underground photography." Burrow experimented with various sizes of camera, settling on a half-plate Kinnear with a Zeiss Anastigmat series III lens and Cadett lightning plates. He used exposures of 2 to 4 seconds.

PUBLICATION Monograph: *'Mongst Mines and Miners*, 1893 (England).

ARCHIVE Andrew Lanyon, 18 Farmers' Meadow, Newlyn/Perzance, Cornwall, England.

Larry Burrows *PHOTOJOURNALIST* Born May 29, 1926, in London, Burrows was killed in Laos on February 10, 1971 while photographing the Vietnam war.

After doing darkroom work for Keystone Photo Agency and *Life* magazine beginning in 1942 in London, he worked his way up to being one of *Life*'s most talented photographers, remaining with that publication till his death.

Burrows was twice awarded the Overseas Press Club's Robert Capa award, and in 1966 was named Magazine Photographer of the Year.

He was one of the subjects of the film biography *The Photographers* by Time-Life Productions in 1970.

The photographer was best known for his compassionate images of the Vietnam war, taken in small format in both black-and-white and color.

PUBLICATIONS Monograph: *Larry Burrows, Compassionate Photographer*, 1972. Anthology: *The Magic Image*, Cecil Beaton & Gail Buckland, 1975.

COLLECTION Time-Life Archives, NYC.

ARCHIVE Time-Life Pictures, Time & Life Bldg., Rockefeller Center, New York, NY 10020.

Gordon H. Burt *PHOTOGRAPHER · INVENTOR* Burt flourished in Wellington, New Zealand, from 1924 to 1965.

During those years, Burt worked as a commercial photographer in Wellington, dealing mainly with such things as posters and theater slides. He invented and developed a color photographic process that entailed a dye transfer process involving three-color separation negatives which combined to form a single color negative. That was then used to make a color print, which he called "Tru colour."

COLLECTION Natl. Mus. of New Zealand, Wellington.

Alfred Henry Burton *PHOTOGRAPHER* Born June 19, 1834 in Leicester, England, Burton died in 1914 in New Zealand. His father, John Burton, was an artist, photographer, bookseller and printer. His brother, Walter J. Burton (1836–80), was a photographer.

Burton emigrated in 1856 to Auckland, New

Zealand, where he worked as a printer, then returned to his homeland in 1862. He went back to New Zealand in 1867 to join his brother Walter, with whom he founded the firm of Burton Brothers in Dunedin (1868). Walter handled the studio's portraiture department, and Alfred toured the countryside, documenting the land and its people. In 1880 Walter committed suicide, and Alfred brought in Thomas Minto B. Muir to take over the portraiture. Around 1896 Burton sold the firm to Muir and George Moodie, then took up teaching elocution and English literature.

A Freemason, Burton was elected Grand Master of the Grand Lodge of New Zealand in 1904. He was also a fellow of the Royal Geographic Society.

The 1880s were Burton's most productive years, when he extensively photographed Maori life in the hitherto unexplored King Country. He is also noted for a rich series on the Coral Islands and Lakes Manapouri and Te Anau. These views were bound into albums, as well as sold individually.

PUBLICATION   Anthology: *The Invented Eye*, Edward Lucie-Smith, 1975.
COLLECTION   Natl. Mus. of New Zealand, Wellington.

Walter J. Burton
See Alfred Henry Burton

(Johan) Frederik Busch   PAINTER · PHOTOGRA- PHER · TEACHER   Born January, 1825, in Frederikvaerk, Denmark, he died January 14, 1883, in Frederiksberg, Denmark. Frederik was educated as a painter and studied with Eckersberg. His son, Peter Busch, was a writer.

Busch participated in making the decorations for the Museum of Thorvaldsen, Copenhagen. He worked with Eddelin in the Chapel of King Charles IV, but interrupted the job in 1848 to start work as a master painter in Naestved. In addition he painted portraits, and in 1859 started to support himself as a photographer. In 1875 he began teaching at the technical school of Frederiksberg and at the Royal Academy of Art in Copenhagen.

Considered one of Denmark's best outdoor photographers, he produced *cartes de visite*, landscapes and topographic photographs.

PUBLICATIONS   Books: *The Collection, Prospects from Denmark, Skaane & Sleswig*, n.d.; *Naestved in 12 Pictures*, n.d.; *Round the Earth in 80 Years*, Peter Busch, n.d. Anthology: *Photogra-*

phers in and from Denmark until 1900, Bjørn Ochsner, 1956, rev. ed., 1969.
COLLECTION   Royal Lib., Copenhagen.

George Tyssen Butler   PHOTOGRAPHER · WRITER · PRODUCER · DIRECTOR   Born in Chester, England, on October 12, 1943, Butler holds a BA with honors in Writing from the University of North Carolina (1966) and an MA from Hollins College in Virginia in English Writing (1968). He studied photography with Enrico Natali.

Since 1974 he has been president of White Mountain Films in New Hampshire. Between 1970 and 1974 he worked as a freelance photographer and in 1969 he was a Vista volunteer in Detroit. *Newsweek* hired him as a writer-reporter in 1968.

Butler produced and directed the highly acclaimed film documentary *Pumping Iron*, based on his book. The artist's images have appeared in most major magazines.

PUBLICATIONS   Books: *Pumping Iron*, w/ Charles Gaines, 1974; *The New Soldier*, w/David Thorne, 1971.
COLLECTION   Bibliothèque Nationale, Paris.
ADDRESS   True Farm, Holderness, NH 03245.

Jack Butler   PHOTOGRAPHER · TEACHER   [See plate 140]   Born on April 16, 1947, in Oswego, New York, Butler received a BA from California State College in Los Angeles in 1970 and an MA from California State University in the same city in 1972. In 1979 he completed an MFA at UCLA, where he studied under Karen Truax, Judith Golden, Robert Heinecken and Darryl Curran.

Butler currently teaches photography at East Los Angeles College, UCLA Extension, and Pasadena (California) City College (since 1976). He previously taught design at Pasadena City College (1976–77) and photography/art at Arcadia (California) High School (1971–76). A member of SPE, he was a board member of the Los Angeles Center for Photographic Studies.

The artist's work consists of Cibachrome prints with applied oil color. According to him, "this combination creates an aggressive and seductive surface. At first encounter, one is seduced by the beauty of the color and the tactility of the surface: then a secondary reaction takes place: the realization of pictorial content."

PUBLICATIONS   Anthology: *Photography and Language*, 1977. Catalogs: *Attitudes, Photography in the 70's*, 1979 (Santa Barbara Mus. of Art: Calif.); *Photographic Directions—Los Angeles 1979* (Security Pacific Bank, Los Angeles); *South-*

ern *California Invitation*, 1979 (Univ. of Southern Calif.: Los Angeles); *Polaroid Collaboration*, 1978 (Open Space Gall.: Victoria, B.C.).

COLLECTION Downey Mus. of Art, Calif.

ADDRESS 391 Cherry Dr, Pasadena, CA 91105.

Helen Buttfield PHOTOGRAPHER · DESIGNER · TEACHER Born February 27, 1929, Buttfield received a BA from Wellesley College, Wellesley, Massachusetts, in 1950, where she studied with John McAndrews, and in 1952 an MA from Ohio State University, studying with Mary Holmes. She also studied photography with David Vestal.

Since 1978 she has been an instructor in photography at the School of Visual Arts in New York City. Prior to that, she was a photographer for the New Zealand Department of Education from 1965 to 1968, the editor and art director for *Look* Book Division from 1962 to 1965 and also was a technical assistant at the American Museum of Natural History from 1960 to 1962 in New York.

Buttfield was the recipient of a CAPS Grant in photography in 1976, and was awarded a New York State Council Multi-Media Grant in 1973.

PUBLICATIONS Books: *The Way of Silence, Poetry & Prose of Basho*, w/Richard Lewis, 1970; *Of This World, A Poet's Life in Poetry*, Richard Lewis, 1968; *The Park*, Richard Lewis, 1968; *The Wind and the Rain*, 1968.

COLLECTIONS Field Mus. of Natural History, Chicago: L/C, Wash., D.C.; New York Pub. Lib., NYC. Bibliothèque Nationale, Paris.

DEALER Marcuse Pfeifer Gall., 825 Madison Ave, New York, NY 10022.

ADDRESS 212 E 14 St, New York, NY 10003.

Vitaly Butyrin PHOTOGRAPHER Born May 30, 1947, in Kaunas, Lithuania, S.S.R., Butyrin took up photography at age fifteen.

He has exhibited his work in more than 300 international shows and art photography salons in 45 countries, as well as in several one-person shows. Butyrin's photographs have been published in various photography magazines, and in the press more than 500 times.

His honorary memberships include KFK, Kaunas (1973); IFKP, Ploen, BRD (1972); NATRON, Maglaj, Yugoslavia (1974); Landerneau, France (1978); A.-74, Warsaw, Poland (1977); and Virton, Belgium. He has belonged to the International Federation of Photographic Art (FIAP) since 1976 and is a member of the Lithuanian Photography Art Society and its Art Council and Board. Butyrin has won more than 200 prizes, medals and diplomas at salons and exhibitions throughout the world.

Considered one of the world's leading science fiction photographers, Butyrin makes montages and collages that frequently consist of ten or more pieces. "In some of his pictures he fuses the world which has already been discovered with that which exists only in his imagination. . . . It is indeed a difficult task to create a world of allegory and symbols through photography, which is a document and testimonial of authenticity, and at the same time recreate a recognizable world full of realistic associations. And that is exactly what Butyrin does," writes Galina Nikulina in *Vitaly Butyrin*.

PUBLICATION Catalog: *Vitaly Butyrin*, 1979 (VAAP: Moscow).

COLLECTIONS Prakapas Photo Gall., NYC. Bibliothèque Nationale, Paris; Canon Photo Gall., Amsterdam; Musée Français de la Photographie, Bievres, France; Photography Mus., Šiauliai, Lithuanian SSR, USSR.

REPRESENTATIVE VAAP, 6a, Bolshaya Bronnaya Str., 103104 Moscow, USSR.

ADDRESS c/o The Photography Art Society of Lithuanian SSR, Pionieriu-8, 232600-Vilnius, Lithuanian SSR, USSR.

Joseph Byron PHOTOGRAPHER Born in Nottingham-on-the-Trent, England, in 1846, Byron died in New York City in 1923. He, and his son after him (Percy Claude Byron, 1879–1959), continued the family tradition in photography. He was taught by his father and grandfather in the studio his great-grandfather founded in Nottingham in 1844.

Byron worked in the family photographic firm from his youth onward. They had a growing chain of studios in four English cities. His early years in England were spent as a news photographer, preparing and developing his wet plates in a hansom cab, as well as specializing in *cartes de visite* in the family studio. He was employed by *The Graphic* of London and worked on a documentation of coal mines for the British government.

Byron came to the United States and established a studio in New York in 1888. His firm produced work for a variety of publications, among them *Once A Week* and *The Illustrated America*. In 1891, in New York, he pioneered the then new field of stage photography.

Throughout their careers, he and his son Percy documented life in New York, creating a monumental record (some 30,000 negatives) of the times in that city, especially notable for the period 1890 to 1910.

PUBLICATIONS Book: *Once Upon a City*, w/ Percy C. Byron, Grace M. Mayer, 1958. Anthology: *The Magic Image*, Cecil Beaton & Gail Buckland, 1975.

COLLECTION Mus. of the City of New York.

ARCHIVE The Byron Cllctn., Mus. of the City of New York, Fifth Ave & 103 St, New York, NY 10029.

Percy Claude Byron PHOTOGRAPHER Born in Nottingham-on-the-Trent, England, in 1879, Byron died in Cranford, New Jersey, on June 10, 1959. His father was photographer Joseph Byron (1846–1923). Although self-taught, Byron was heavily influenced by his father's work and studio. He began photographing regularly at the age of eleven.

When fourteen years old, he made his first sale to Arthur Brisbane, then managing editor of *The World*, thus beginning a busy freelance career for such publications as the *New York Recorder*, *The New York Herald*, *Once A Week* and *The Illustrated American*. He assisted his father in doing stage photography, and later in running their New York studio, which he and his mother continued operating after Joseph's death. The original firm had been founded in 1844 by his great-great grandfather in Nottingham.

Byron served as a Spanish-American War cam-era-correspondent for *The Journal* in 1898. He founded the first photoengraving plant in Edmonton, Alberta, Canada (1906–16). He returned to his father's studio in 1917, closing the firm's doors in 1942—it had been active ninety-eight years. He then became a staff photographer for Essex Art Engraving Company of Newark. Byron was the official photographer on the maiden voyage of the French liner *Norman*.

He won ten gold medals and diplomas for principal exhibitions in Europe and America, and first prize at the International Exposition of both 1931 and 1932. Byron also designed a camera that was a precursor of the Speed Graphic, as well as developing several minor innovations in the field.

With the use of an 11 x 14 camera, Percy Byron showed a sense of the newsworthy throughout his sixty-nine years as a photographer. He specialized in the photography of ships. He and his father's 30,000 genre scenes represent an important document of life in New York, especially between the years 1890 and 1910.

PUBLICATIONS Book: *Once Upon A City*, w/ Joseph Byron, Grace M. Mayer, 1958. Anthology: *The Magic Image*, Cecil Beaton & Gail Buckland, 1975.

COLLECTION Mus. of the City of New York.

ARCHIVE The Byron Cllctn., Mus. of the City of New York, Fifth Ave & 103 St, New York, NY 10029.

C

William Fleming Cadge *PHOTOGRAPHER · DE-SIGNER · ART DIRECTOR* Born in Philadelphia, Pennsylvania, on May 5, 1924, Cadge graduated from the Philadelphia College of Art.

He has concentrated on his own photography since 1976, but for fifteen years prior to that he was art director of *Redbook Magazine*. From 1957 to 1961 he was associate art director of *McCalls* and from 1956 to 1957 an art director for the advertising firm Doyle Dane Bernbach. He served as a designer for *Women's Home Companion* magazine, 1950–52, and for the *Philadelphia Evening Bulletin*, 1950–52.

Cadge has been a member of ASMP since 1976. He also belongs to the Art Directors Club of New York, and from 1958 to 1976 was a member of the Society of Illustrators. He has won numerous gold medals and awards throughout the years from the Art Directors Clubs of New York, New Jersey and Philadelphia, the Society of Publication Designers, and the Type Directors Club. He received Awards of Excellence at the C.A. Magazine Show in 1967 and 1968 and Gold Medals from the Society of Illustrators in 1971 and 1972.

Cadge's photographs serve as illustration for advertising, editorial and corporate clients. During his years at *Redbook*, he photographed over a hundred covers and took numerous photos to illustrate articles, features and fiction.

PUBLICATIONS Periodicals: *Print and Graphics Today*, 1977; *U.S. Camera*, 1965.

ADDRESS 33 Colonial Ave, Dobbs Ferry, NY 10522.

Charles Henry Caffin *ART CRITIC* Born in 1854 in Sittingbourne, Kent, England, Caffin died in 1918 in New York City. He received his BA from Oxford's Magdalen College and was influenced by Stieglitz.

Caffin worked in the theater about 1855–61. He emigrated to the United States in 1892 and did decorations for the Chicago World Columbia Exposition in 1893. He began writing reviews and art criticism about 1898, eventually publishing in *Cosmopolitan, St. Nicholas Magazine* and all the New York papers. He was also the American editor of *The Studio*.

Caffin's book *Photography as a Fine Art*, published in 1901, was "the first extensive examination of American expressive photography, a book that continues to have relevance into our own time" (Jonathan Green, *Camera Work*).

PUBLICATIONS Books: *How to Study Pictures . . .*, 1941; *American Masters of Sculpture*, 1913, repr. 1969; *Art for Life's Sake*, 1913; *Dancing and Dancers of Today*, w/Caroline Scurfield Caffin, 1912; *The Story of French Painting*, 1911; *The Story of Spanish Painting*, 1910; *The Story of Dutch Painting*, 1909; *The Appreciation of the Drama*, 1908; *Old Spanish Masters Engraved by Timothy Cole, 1907* (Macmillan: London); *The Story of American Painting*, 1907, repr. 1937; *Art in Photography*, ed. & contr., 1905; *American Masters of Painting*, 1902; *Photography as a Fine Art*, intro. by Thos. F. Barrow, 1901. Anthology: *Camera Work: A Critical Anthology*, Jonathan Green, ed., 1973.

Nicholas John Caire *PHOTOGRAPHER* Born February 28, 1837, in Guernsey, Channel Islands, Caire died February 13, 1918, in Melbourne, Australia. He learned photography from Townsend Duryea, an American-born photographer residing in Australia.

With his parents, Caire moved to Adelaide, Australia, about 1860, and by 1865 he was traveling widely around southeastern Australia. In the 1870s he established successful photography studios in both Melbourne and Victoria.

The photographer used the wet-plate process originally, then switched to the dry-plate process. He specialized in outdoor scenes, "doing his utmost to publicize the mountains and bush of Victoria: the country he loved dearly," wrote Andrew Hooper of the Royal Melbourne Institute of Technology. "Many of his photographs graphically recreate Australian pioneer life," added Hooper. Caire also took many views of aborigines.

PUBLICATIONS Books: *Gold and Silver; an album of Hill End and Gulgong photographs from the Holtermann Collection*, Keast Burke, 1973 (Heinemann: Melbourne); *The Story of the Camera in Australia*, Jack Cato, 1955 (Georgian House: Australia).

COLLECTIONS In Australia: Natl. Gall. of Victoria; Royal Melbourne Inst. of Tech.

Harry M. Callahan *PHOTOGRAPHER* [See plate 88] Born October 22, 1912, in Detroit, Michigan, Callahan studied engineering briefly at Michigan State College. His first interest in photography was as a hobbyist in 1938 when, with a Rolleicord, he taught himself the craft, though he was strongly influenced by the works of Ansel Adams.

He first worked as a processor in the photographic labs of General Motors Corp. in 1944. In 1946 he joined the faculty of the Institute of Design (formerly The New Bauhaus—later to become a part of the Illinois Institute of Technology); in 1949 he became head of the Department of Photography there. He resigned from that post in 1961 to head the same department at the Rhode Island School of Design in Providence, where, in 1964, he was appointed professor. Although Callahan relinquished that chairmanship in 1973, he continued to teach there until his retirement in 1977.

Mr. Callahan received a Graham Foundation Award for Advanced Studies in the Fine Arts in 1956. In 1963 he won the Photography Award at the Rhode Island Arts Festival and in 1969 he received the Governor's Award for Excellence in the Arts for that state. A citation for distinguished contributions as an artist, photographer and educator was awarded him in 1972 by the National Association of Schools and, in that same year, the artist received a Guggenheim Memorial Foundation Fellowship. The NEA awarded him a grant in 1977, and in 1979 he was given an honorary doctor's degree in fine arts by the Rhode Island School of Design.

His only membership was with the Detroit Photo Guild as a young hobbyist in 1940.

Harry Callahan is the subject of numerous articles, commentaries and reviews in various magazines and journals. The artist works predominantly in black-and-white, although he does some color as well. Images center on landscapes, cityscapes and portraits. His wife Eleanor is included in much of his best-known work.

PUBLICATIONS (selected) Monographs: *Harry Callahan: Color*, 1980; *Callahan*, John Szarkowski, ed., 1976; *Harry Callahan*, essay by Sherman Paul, preface by John Szarkowski, 1967; *Photographs: Harry Callahan*, essay by Hugo Weber, 1964; *The Multiple Image: Photographs by Harry Callahan*, essay by Jonathan Williams, 1961. Anthology: *The Photograph Collector's Guide*, Lee D. Witkin & Barbara London, 1979; *The Magic Image*, Cecil Beaton & Gail Buckland, 1975; *The Photographer's Choice*, Kelly Wise, ed., 1975. Periodical: "Portfolio—Harry Callahan—Eleanor—City—Landscape," *Camera*, Apr 1968.

PORTFOLIO *Landscapes, 1941–1971*, 1972 (Light Gallery: New York).

COLLECTIONS Art Institute of Chicago; Baltimore Museum of Art, Md; CCP, Tucson; CIBA-GEIGY, Ardsley-on-Hudson, N.Y.; Delaware Art Mus., Wilmington; Exchange Natl. Bank, Chicago; Hallmark Cards, Kansas City, Mo; Harvard Univ., Fogg Art Mus., Cambridge, Mass.; IMP-GEH, Rochester; Joseph E. Seagram & Sons, NYC; Metro. Mus. of Art, NYC; Minneapolis Inst. of Art, Minn.; MIT, Hayden Gall., Cambridge, Mass.; Mus. of Fine Arts, Boston; Mus. of Fine Arts, Houston; Mus. of Fine Arts, St. Petersburg, Fla.; MOMA, NYC; New Orleans Mus. of Art; Princeton Univ., Art Mus., N.J.; Rhode Island School of Design, Mus. of Art, Providence; Smith Coll. Mus. of Art, Northampton, Mass; St. Louis Union Trust Co., Mo.; UCLA Frederick S. Wight Art Gall.; Univ. of Mass., Univ. Gall., Amherst; Univ. of Neb., Sheldon Memorial Art Gall., Lincoln; Univ. of New Mexico, Univ. Art Mus., Albuquerque; Univ. of N. Carolina, Wm. Hayes Ackland Art Ctr., Chapel Hill; Vassar Coll. Art Gall., Poughkeepsie, N.Y.; Virginia Mus. of Fine Arts, Richmond; Yale Univ. Art Gall., New Haven, Conn. Bibliothèque Nationale, Paris; National Gall. of Canada, Ottawa; Victoria & Albert Mus., London.

DEALER Light Gallery, 724 Fifth Ave, New York, NY 10019.

Jo Ann Callis *PHOTOGRAPHER · TEACHER* [See plate 122] Born November 25, 1940, in Cincinnati, Ohio, Callis earned both her BA (1974) and MFA (1977) from UCLA. She cites as her major influence Robert Heinecken.

Callis has taught at California Institute of the Arts in Valencia from 1976 to the present, and since 1978 has also taught photography through University of California at Los Angeles Extension. From 1977 to 1978 she was a teacher at California State University in Fullerton.

A member of SPE since 1976, Callis received an NEA Fellowship in 1980 and was awarded the Ferguson Grant by the Friends of Photography in 1978.

Usually printing in 16 x 20 format, Callis works primarily in color. She fabricates tableaus "which often give the viewer a feeling that something is amiss." The images, she adds, "seem tactile and sensuous."

PUBLICATIONS Periodicals: *Journal*, 1979 (L.A. Inst. of Contemporary Art); *Photo*, 1978; *Popular Photography Annual*, 1978; *Glass Eye*, 1975, 1977; *Creative Camera Annual*, 1976.

COLLECTIONS CCP, Tucson; Denver Mus. of Art, Colo.; Harvard Univ., Fogg Art Mus., Cambridge, Mass.; Illinois State Univ., Normal; MOMA, NYC; New Orleans Mus. of Art; San Francisco Mus. of Modern Art; Univ. of Nebraska, Lincoln. Tasmanian Mus. of Art, Australia.

DEALERS G. Ray Hawkins Gall., 9002 Melrose Ave, Los Angeles, CA 90069; Susan Spiritus Gall., 3336 Via Lido, Newport Beach, CA 92663.

ADDRESS 2817 Glendon Ave, Los Angeles, CA 90064.

Julia Margaret Cameron   PHOTOGRAPHER
[See plate 22] Born June 11, 1815, in Calcutta, India, Cameron died in Kalutara, Ceylon—now Sri Lanka—on January 26, 1879. She was self-taught and greatly inspired by painter George Frederic Watts, a friend and mentor for twenty years.

Cameron moved to England in 1848, settling on the Isle of Wight in 1859. Around 1863, at the age of forty-eight, she received a camera from her daughter, took up the craft, and maintained her own private studio until 1875 when she returned to Ceylon.

Using the cumbersome collodion wet-plate process, Cameron achieved a mastery, if not in technique then in spiritual depth. Her portraits are considered among the finest in the medium. She also executed allegorical photographs influenced by pre-Raphaelite painting, as well as some genre scenes of native workers in Ceylon. Her friends, servants and neighbors were among her subjects, which included the likes of Thomas Carlyle, the poets Tennyson and Longfellow, Sir John Herschel, and Charles Darwin.

PUBLICATIONS Monographs: *A Victorian Album: Julia Margaret Cameron and Her Circle*, Graham Ovenden, ed., 1975; *Mrs. Cameron's Photographs from the Life*, Anita Ventura Mozely, 1974; *Julia Margaret Cameron: A Victorian Family Portrait*, Brian Hill, 1973; *Julia*

Margaret Cameron: Her Life and Photographic Work, Helmut Gernsheim, 1948, repr. 1975. Books: *Victorian Photographs of Famous Men and Fair Women*, intro. by Virginia Woolf & Roger Fry, 1926, rev. ed., Tristram Powell, ed., 1973; *Alfred, Lord Tennyson and His Friends*, Anne T. Ritchie & H. H. H. Cameron, 1893 (Unwin: London); *Idylls of the King and Other Poems*, 2 vols., Alfred Tennyson, 1875. Anthologies: *The Photograph Collector's Guide*, Lee D. Witkin & Gail London, 1979; *The Collection of Alfred Stieglitz*, Weston J. Naef, 1978; *The Invented Eye*, Edward Lucie-Smith, 1973; *The Magic Image*, Cecil Beaton & Gail Buckland, 1975; *Women of Photography*, Margery Mann & Ann Noggle, eds., 1975; *Camera Work: A Critical Anthology*, Jonathan Green, ed., 1973; *Looking at Photographs*, John Szarkowski, 1973; *Great Photographers*, 1971, *The Camera*, 1970, Time-Life Series; *Masters of Photography*, Beaumont & Nancy Newhall, 1969. Periodicals: "The Annals of My Glass House," autobio., *Photographic Journal*, vol. 67, 1927; *Camera Work*, Jan 1913.

COLLECTIONS IMP/GEH, Rochester; Metro. Mus. of Art, NYC; MOMA, NYC. In London: Natl. Portrait Gall., RPS, Victoria & Albert Mus.

Morrie Camhi   PHOTOGRAPHER · TEACHER · EDITOR Born in August 1928, in New York City, Camhi received his BA in Literature from UCLA in 1955. Wynn Bullock was a friend and influence.

An associate editor of *Photoshow* magazine since 1979, Camhi has been on the photography faculty of San Francisco City College from 1969 to the present. He owned Camhi Photography, an advertising firm, from 1964 to 1969 and was a partner in Camhi/Bardovi Photography from 1961 to 1964. He was manager and photographer for Donn-Maur Photography from 1955 to 1961 and a photographer for the U.S. Army Signal Corps, 1953–55.

Camhi has been a member of SPE since 1975 and is an officer/director of Professional Photographers West. He won NEA survey grants through MALDEF in 1977 and 1978 and the Aurora Award from Professional Photographers West in 1965, 1967 and 1969. He has also received various awards from foundations, including Columbia and Zellerbach.

Using various formats, Camhi generally deals with social documentary or environmental portrayal in a "straight and frontal style."

PUBLICATIONS (selected) Book: *Eye of Conscience*, 1973. Periodicals: *American Pho-*

tographer, 1979; *Picture*, 1979, 1978; *Popular Photography*, 1979.

COLLECTIONS Floating Foundation of Photography, NYC; Johnstone/Focus Gall., San Francisco; Los Angeles County Mus. of Art; Oakland Mus., Calif.; San Francisco Mus. of Modern Art; and private collections.

ADDRESS 95 Marshall Ave, Petaluma, CA 94952.

Roger Camp PHOTOGRAPHER · TEACHER · POET
Born on February 19, 1945, Camp received his BA in 1967 from the University of California at Santa Barbara, where he studied with William Rohrbach. He earned an MA from the University of Texas, Austin (1969), and both an MA and an MFA from the University of Iowa in Iowa City (1973, 1974), where he studied with John Schultz.

Since 1976 Camp has been head of photography at Golden West College in Huntington Beach, California. Previous to that he was an instructor of photography and literature at Columbus College of Art and Design in Ohio (1974–76) and a literature instructor at Eastern Illinois University in Charleston (1969–70). He is a member of SPE.

Camp was a Faculty Fellow in the History of Photography at Golden West College in 1977, a Grahame Fellow in Art at the University of Iowa in 1973 and a Danforth Fellow at the University of Texas' Black Studies Institute in 1969. Besides being a photographer, he is also a poet whose work has been published in various journals and quarterlies.

Printed in color, Camp's landscapes and female nudes are "variously described as abstract, formal, painterly."

COLLECTIONS Atkinson Gall., Santa Barbara City Cllctn., Calif.; Edison St. Gall., Salt Lake City, Utah; Middle Tennessee State Univ., Murfreesboro; Schaeffer Memorial Foundation, Beverly Hills, Calif. United Nations, Geneva, Switzerland.

ADDRESS POB 494, Corona del Mar, CA 92625.

Bryn Campbell PHOTOGRAPHER · WRITER
Born May 20, 1933, in the United Kingdom, Campbell studied at Manchester University in England.

As of this writing Campbell was self-employed. He was previously employed as picture editor for *The Observer* (1964–66), associate editor for *The British Journal of Photography* and picture editor for the *Journal*'s annual (1962–63), editor of *Cameras* (1960–61) and assistant editor

of *Practical Photography* and *Photo News Weekly* (1959–60).

Campbell has been a member of the Institute of Incorporated Photographers since 1969, of RPS since 1971, and of the Photography Committee (since 1978) and the Art Panel of the Arts Council of Great Britain. He has also been a trustee of the Photographers' Gallery, London, since 1974, and was awarded a fellowship from RPS in 1971 and a Kodak Bursary award in 1973.

Campbell is involved in photojournalism and also does experimental color photography, editing and photo-criticism.

PUBLICATIONS Books: *Exploring Photography*, ed., 1979; *European Colour Photography*, 1978; *Goalkeepers Are Crazy*, 1977; *Newspaper Dragon*, 1977; *Children and Language*, 1976; *British Image 1*, 1975; *The Camera & The Craftsman*, 1975; *The Experience of Sport*, 1975; *The Headless Valley*, 1973; *Loneliness*, 1973.

COLLECTIONS In London: Arts Council of Gr. Brit.; Victoria & Albert Mus.

DEALER Photographers' Gall., 8 Great Newport St, London WC2, England.

ADDRESS 11 Belsize Park Mews, London NW3 5BL, England.

Fredrich Cantor PHOTOGRAPHER · PAINTER · TEACHER Born July 8, 1944, in New York City, Cantor studied at the Pratt Institute in Brooklyn, New York (1962–64, 1966–67), at San Francisco Art Institute (1966), at Cooper Union in New York City (1969) and at Art Students' League in Woodstock, New York (1962, 1963). His teachers included Gloria Longval, Dick Ralph and Philip Pearlstein.

A freelance photographer since 1970, he has taught at Parsons School of Design (1977–78) and at the School of Visual Arts (1975–76) in New York City; at Brooklyn College (1974–76); and at Bucks County Community College, Pennsylvania (1973–74).

Cantor received a fellowship to the MacDowell Colony in 1980, also to Yaddo in 1978 and 1979 and to the Virginia Center for the Creative Arts in 1979. In that year he also won an award from the American Institute of Graphic Arts.

The photographer produces black-and-white and color images of people and landscapes and has worked with strobe lighting since 1975. His work has been described as having "a modern sensibility that loves clean design as well as the rapport between commonplace objects and monuments that are eternal" (Daniela Palazzoli, *L'Europeo*, June 1977).

PUBLICATIONS Monograph: *Rome: Volume 1,*

1977 (self-published). Periodicals: *Photo-Journal*, Dec & Nov 1979; *Foto*, Feb 1979; *Progresso Fotografico*, Dec 1978; *Le Nouveau Photocinema*, Feb 1977; *Creative Camera*, Mar 1975; *Zoom*, April 1980 (Paris), May/Jun 1973 (Paris); *British Journal of Photography*, Nov 12, 1971.

COLLECTIONS   New Orleans Mus. of Art; Univ. of Mass. Mus. of Art, Amherst; Univ. of Neb., Sheldon Mem. Art Gall., Lincoln. Bibliothèque Nationale, Paris; Polaroid Europa Cllctn., Amsterdam.

DEALERS   Marcuse Pfeifer Gall., 825 Madison Ave, New York, NY 10021; Galerie Delpire, 13 rue de l'Abbaye, 75006, Paris, France.

ADDRESS   338 W 11 St, New York, NY 10014.

Cornell Capa   PHOTOGRAPHER · EDITOR · MUSEUM DIRECTOR   Born April 10, 1918, in Budapest, Hungary, Capa received his baccalaureate in 1936 from Madach Imre Gymnasium in Budapest. His brother was the late photographer Robert Capa.

Founder and executive director of The International Center of Photography (ICP) in New York City since 1974, Capa was previously director of the Fund for Concerned Photography in New York City from 1966 to 1974. He was a staff photographer for *Life* magazine, 1946–54, then a contributing photographer until 1967. In 1954 he joined Magnum Photos. From 1938 to 1946 Capa was a darkroom technician for Time Inc.

A member of ASMP, the Overseas Press Club and the Authors League, Capa won the Morris Gordon Memorial Award in 1972 from Photographic Administrators, Inc., and the Robert Leavitt Award in 1968 from ASMP. In 1956 he was cited with a Page One Award for his "Retarded Children" essay.

Capa has been a frequent lecturer and workshop leader and has made three films: *Toward the Margin of Life* (Scholastic Magazines, Inc., 1972), *Who Am I? A photographic essay* (NBC/TV, 1971), and *Now God Speaks Tzeltal* (Magnum, 1965).

Capa's work as a photojournalist/documentary photographer has included magazine essays on the "Great Supersonic Transport Race," "Six Day War—Israel," JFK's "First Hundred Days in Washington," "Argentina Revolution" and the "Somoza Assassination."

PUBLICATIONS   Books: *ICP Library of Photographers*, ed. of first 6 titles, 1974; *Jerusalem: City of Mankind*, ed., 1974; *Margin of Life*, w/J. Mayone Stycos, 1974; *The Concerned Photographer 2*, ed., 1972; *The Concerned Photographer 1*, ed.,

1969; *Adlai E. Stevenson's Public Years*, w/Morath & Stevenson, 1966; *Language and Faith*, ed. & photos, 1972; *Israel: The Reality*, ed., 1969; *New Breed on Wall Street*, w/Martin Mayer, 1969; *The Andean Republics*, 1966; *The Emergent Decade of South American Painting*, w/ Thomas Messer, 1966; *Farewell to Eden*, w/Matthew Huxley, 1964; *Savage My Kinsman*, w/Elisabeth Elliot, 1959; *Through Gates of Splendor*, w/Elisabeth Elliot, 1957; *Let Us Begin . . .*, ed., 1961; *Retarded Children Can Be Helped*, w/ Maya Pines, 1957. Anthology: *Swift Sword*, 1967.

REPRESENTATIVE   Magnum Photos New York/ Paris, 15 W 46 St, New York, NY 10036.

ADDRESS   275 Fifth Ave, New York, NY 10016.

Robert Capa   PHOTOGRAPHER   Born Andrei Friedmann in Budapest, Hungary, in 1913, Capa was killed by a mine in Hanoi, Vietnam, on May 25, 1954, while doing a story for *Life* on the war in the Red River Delta. His wife, Gerda Taro, was his photography partner in Spain, where she died after being crushed by a Loyalist tank in the confusion of a retreat. His brother, Cornell Capa, is a photographer and founder and executive director of the International Center of Photography.

Capa studied sociology and journalism in Berlin and went to work for Deutscher Film Dienst in 1931 as a darkroom assistant. From 1932 on, he was a freelance photographer on assignment for *Life*, *Time* and various other U.S. magazines, as well as *Illustrated London News*. He was associated with Magnum Photos, which he co-founded in 1947.

The photographer won the U.S. Medal of Freedom in 1947, and the Croix de Guerre with Palm, Order of the Army, in 1954. The Overseas Press Club created the Robert Capa Medal in 1954, awarded each year for "superlative photography requiring exceptional courage and enterprise abroad."

Capa was probably the first war photographer to get dramatic close-ups of action. His motto— "the closer the better"—"made veteran combat troops blink in uneasy disbelief," according to *The New York Times*.

PUBLICATIONS   Books: *Front Populaire*, w/ David Seymour, text by Georgette Elgey, 1976 (Chene/Magnum: Paris); *Images of War*, 1964; *Report on Israel*, w/Irwin Shaw, 1950; *Russian Journal*, John Steinbeck, 1948; *This Is Israel*, w/ Jerry Cooke & Tim Gidal, foreword by Bartley C. Crum, 1948; *Slightly Out of Focus*, 1947; *Inva-*

sion!, Wertenbaker, 1944; *The Battle of Waterloo Road*, w/Diana Forbes-Robertson, 1941; *Death in the Making*, w/Gerda Taro, preface by Jay Allen, 1938. Anthologies: *The Magic Image*, Cecil Beaton & Gail Buckland, 1975; *Life Photographers: Their Careers & Favorite Pictures*, Stanley Rayfield, 1957.

COLLECTIONS   IMP/GEH, Rochester; Metro. Mus. of Art, NYC; MOMA, NYC; Natl. Gall. of Art, Wash., D.C.; Smithsonian Inst., Wash., D.C.; Univ. of Calif., Riverside Mus., Riverside. Bibliothèque Nationale, Paris.

ARCHIVE   Magnum Photos, Inc., 15 W 46 St, New York, NY 10036.

Paul Caponigro   *PHOTOGRAPHER · TEACHER*
[See plate 103]   Born in Boston, Massachusetts, on December 7, 1932, Caponigro studied music at Boston University (1950–51, 1955–56, 1958–59). His mentors in photography were Benjamin Chin and Minor White.

Currently self-employed, Caponigro taught at Yale University in New Haven, Connecticut (1970–71), at New York University in New York City (1967–70), at Boston University (1960–61) and at Minor White's Creative Photography Workshop (summer, 1959). He worked as a consultant to the Polaroid Corporation, 1960–65. The photographer is a founding member of the Association of Heliographers and their Gallery Archive in New York City.

Caponigro won Guggenheim Fellowships in 1975 and 1966, NEA Photography Fellowships in 1975 and 1971, and a first prize in the Tenth Boston Arts Festival in 1961.

Using large formats, he generally produces images derived from nature: flowers, water, leaves and images of the French and English landscape, including Stonehenge. He often abstracts details of nature by shooting in close-up.

PUBLICATIONS   Monographs: *Landscape*, 1975; *Sunflower*, 1974; *Paul Caponigro*, 1967, rev. ed., 1972. Anthologies: *The Photograph Collector's Guide*, Lee D. Witkin & Barbara London, 1979; *Mirrors & Windows*, John Szarkowski, ed., 1978; *The Great West: Real/Ideal*, Sandy Hume et al, eds., 1977; *The Magic Image*, Cecil Beaton & Gail Buckland, 1975; *Looking at Photographs*, John Szarkowski, 1973; *The Art of Photography*, 1971, *The Studio*, 1971, *The Camera*, 1970, *The Print*, 1970, Time-Life Series; *The Picture History of Photography*, Peter Pollack, 1969. Catalogs: *Photographs*, 1977 (Univ. of Neb., Sheldon Mem. Art Gall.: Lincoln); *Aspects of American Photography*, 1976 (Univ. of Mo.: St. Louis);

American Photography: The Sixties, 1966 (Univ. of Neb., Sheldon Mem. Art Gall.: Lincoln). Periodicals: *Creative Camera*, Nov 1978, June 1976, July 1973, May 1972; *Printletter 13*, Jan/Feb 1978; *Camera*, Dec 1975, Oct 1974, Jan 1973, Jan 1963; *Modern Photography*, Jan 1967, Aug 1959; *Contemporary Photographer*, summer 1963; *Aperture*, no. 3, 1958.

PORTFOLIOS   (all self-pub.) *Stonehenge*, 1978 (Santa Fe, N. Mex.); *Portfolio Two*, 1973, *Portfolio One*, 1960 (Redding, Conn.).

COLLECTIONS   Art Inst. of Chicago; Boston Athenaeum, Mass.; Boston Pub. Lib.; CCP, Tucson; Cornell Univ., Johnson Mus. of Art, Ithaca, N.Y.; Detroit Inst. of the Arts, Mich.; Exchange Natl. Bank of Chicago; Harvard Univ., Fogg Art Mus., Cambridge, Mass.; High Mus. of Art, Atlanta, Ga.; IMP/GEH, Rochester; Kalamazoo Inst. of Arts, Kalamazoo, Mich.; Katonah Gall., Katonah, N.Y.; L/C, Wash., D.C.; Menil Fndn., Houston, Tex.; Metro. Mus. of Art, NYC; MOMA, NYC; Mus. of Fine Art, Houston; Mus. of Fine Arts of St. Petersburg, Fla.; New Orleans Mus. of Art; Norton Simon Mus. of Art, Pasadena, Calif.; Philadelphia Mus. of Art, Penn.; R.I. School of Design, Providence; Seattle Art Mus., Wash.; Smith Coll. Mus. of Art, Northampton, Mass.; Smithsonian Inst., Wash., D.C.; UCLA; Univ. of Ill., Krannert Art Mus., Urbana; Univ. of Louisville, Ky.; Univ. of Neb., Sheldon Mem. Art Gall., Lincoln; Univ. of N. Mex., Albuquerque; Univ. of Ore., Eugene; Va. Mus. of Fine Arts, Richmond; VSW, Rochester; Yale Univ., New Haven, Conn. Bibliothèque Nationale, Paris; Natl. Gall. of Can., Ottawa, Ontario; Victoria & Albert Mus., London.

ADDRESS   Route 3, Box 960, Santa Fe, NM 87501.

Héctor M. Méndez Caratini   *PHOTOGRAPHER*
Born August 5, 1949, in San Juan, Puerto Rico, he received a BA from the University of Puerto Rico. He attended a photography course at the Germain School of Photography (N.Y.C.), and also workshops at the Friends of Photography with Arnold Newman, George Tice and Duane Michals.

Since 1973 Caratini has been a freelance photographer and a medical photographer at the School of Medicine, University of Puerto Rico, in the Ophthalmology Department.

He has been a member and president of the Asociación Fotográfica de Puerto Rico, and a founding member of the Consejo Latinoamericano de Fotografía since 1978.

Caratini's work photodocuments the history of Puerto Rico, its people, cultural heritage and changing landscape. He has documented hundreds of "lost" enigmatic Indian petroglyphs all over the island of Puerto Rico.

PORTFOLIO *Petroglifos de Boriquén*, 1978.

COLLECTIONS CCP, Tucson; Metro. Mus. of Art, NYC; Museo del Barrio, NYC. Museo de Arquitectura Colonial, Instituto de Cultura Puertorriqueña, Puerto Rico; Museo de Arte de Ponce, Puerto Rico; Museo de Arte Moderno, Consejo Mexicano de Fotografía, Mexico City.

ADDRESS Calle Mirsonia #1513, Santurce, Puerto Rico 00911.

John Carbutt *PHOTOGRAPHER · PHOTO-GRAPHIC EQUIPMENT MANUFACTURER · INVENTOR* Born in 1832 in Sheffield, England, Carbutt died in Philadelphia in 1905.

Having emigrated to the United States in 1853, he became a well-known local photographer in Chicago and the official photographer for the building of the Canadian Pacific Railway. After seeing woodburytypes in 1869, he purchased the American rights to the process in 1870 and established American Photo-Relief Printing Co. in Philadelphia, the city where he remained throughout his life. He began producing gelatin dry plates and, in 1879, established the first commercially successful factory for the plates in America. He also produced plates with positive emulsions for use as transparencies and lantern slides, and is chiefly credited with establishing the standard American size of 3¼ x 4 for lantern slides. In 1888 he began selling celluloid cut films; the first film strips Thomas Edison used for his Kinetoscope were obtained from Carbutt. The manufacturer also pioneered production of orthochromatic plates and filters, including those used in 1893 to cut haze in aerial photography, and produced plates for graphic arts and X-rays (1896). Finally he introduced cemented glass filters in 1897.

Carbutt was elected first president of the Photographers Association of America, a group that superseded the National Photographers Association in 1880.

PUBLICATIONS Books: *Edison Motion Picture Myth*, Gordon Hendricks, 1961; *Photography and the American Scene*, Robert Taft, 1938; *Lexikon für Photographie und Reproduktionstechnik*, G. H. Emmerich, 1910. Anthology: *Photography's Great Inventors*, Louis W. Shipley, 1965. Periodicals: *Camera*, 1905; *Journal of the Franklin Institute*, 1905, 1888; *Photographic Times*, 1897, 1896; *American Amateur Photog-*rapher, 1896; *American Annual of Photography and Photographic Times Almanac*, 1891, 1890; *Jahrbuch für Photographie und Reproduktionstechnik*, Josef Maria Eder, 1890; *Philadelphia Photography*, 1888, 1884, 1879, 1872, 1870; *Photo Miniature*, #37.

Ellen Carey *PHOTOGRAPHER* Born June 18, 1952, in New York City, she received a BFA in Printmaking from the Kansas City Art Institute in Missouri in 1975 and an MFA in Photography from the State University of New York at Buffalo in 1978. Carey also attended the Art Students League in New York City in 1970.

As of this writing she is a self-employed photographer. Previously she was a teacher at York College in Queens, New York, in 1979.

A member of VSW, Rochester, she was awarded a CAPS grant in photography in 1979.

Using large format, she creates one-of-a-kind photographs with applied paint, and is known for radical alterations on the photographs, using an airbrush, paint and various other mark-making tools.

PUBLICATIONS Anthologies: *The Grotesque in Photography*, A. D. Coleman, 1977; *Young American Photographers: Volume 1*, 1974. Periodicals: *Popular Photography Annual 1979*, fall 1979; *Bombay Duck*, No. 4, 1976.

COLLECTIONS Albright-Knox Art Gall., Buffalo, N.Y.; Colgate Univ., Picker Art Gall., Hamilton, N.Y.; Univ. of Colo., Boulder.

DEALER Texas Gall., 2012 Peden Ave, Houston, TX 77019.

ADDRESS 17 Cleveland Pl, New York, NY 10012.

Etienne Carjat *PHOTOGRAPHER · WRITER · CARICATURIST · EDITOR* Carjat was born in France in 1828, and died there in 1906. In addition to his work as a journalist, caricaturist, actor and playwright, Carjat established a photographic business which he ran from 1855 to 1867. He continued doing photography through 1875, his portraits appearing in several periodicals of the day, especially those related to theater, arts and letters.

Though he was one of the best French portrait photographers, his memory has been eclipsed by that of his better-known contemporary, Nadar. Carjat's portraits were noteworthy for their directness and simplicity. He used the collodion process, producing albumen prints, and some *cartes de visite*.

PUBLICATIONS Anthologies: *The Photograph*

Collector's Guide, Lee D. Witkin & Barbara London, 1979; *The Invented Eye,* Edward Lucie-Smith, 1975; *The Magic Image,* Cecil Beaton & Gail Buckland, 1975; *Great Photographers,* Time-Life Series, 1970; *Galerie de Contemporaine,* 7 vols., 1876–1885. Periodicals: "Carjat," J. Adhémar, *Gazette des Beaux-Arts,* July 1972; *Paris-Artiste,* no. 43, 1885.

COLLECTIONS Boston Public Lib.; IMP/GEH, Rochester; MOMA, NYC; Univ. of New Mexico Art Mus., Albuquerque. British Mus., London; Bibliothèque Nationale, Paris; Caisse Nationale des Monuments Historiques et des Sites, Paris; Natl. Gall. of Canada, Ottawa, Ontario.

John William Carnell PHOTOGRAPHER · TEACHER Born in Chicago on April 19, 1952, Carnell earned a BFA from the University of New Mexico in Albuquerque (1974) and an MFA from the Tyler School of Art at Temple University in Philadelphia (1976). He cites as the most notable influences on his work Steve Foster, John Gould, Thomas Barrow and William Larson.

Since 1976 he has been a photography instructor at both the Philadelphia College of Art and the Community College of Philadelphia. He has also taught photography at the Cheltenham Art Center in Pennsylvania (1976–77) and has been a member of SPE since 1977.

He received an NEA Photographer's Fellowship in 1980. Carnell also received an Exhibition Award at the Central Pennsylvania Festival of the Arts at Pennsylvania State in University Park (1979), and a First Place Award in the 2nd Annual Joseph Nicéphore Niepce Plastic Camera Competition (1977). In 1975 he won a Summer Fellowship Award from Temple University in Philadelphia.

Carnell works in both color and black-and-white, using small hand-held cameras and view cameras. He says, "My photographs range in appearance from imitations of casual snapshots to studied visual investigations of the urban landscape. My favorite theme is the role of nature in man's environment."

PUBLICATIONS Catalog: *Spectrum: New Directions in Color Photography,* Donna Nakao, 1979 (Univ. of Hawaii). Periodical: *Quiver,* vol. 1, no. 4, 1978 (Tyler School of Art, Temple Univ.: Philadelphia).

COLLECTIONS Calif. Inst. of the Arts, Valencia; MOMA, NYC. Mus. of Art and Hist., Fribourg, Switzerland.

ADDRESS 445 Hillside Ave, Jenkintown, PA 19046.

Samuel Carnell PHOTOGRAPHER · POLITICIAN Carnell was born in Nottinghamshire, England, in 1832 and died on October 14, 1920, in Napier, New Zealand. He was educated at Old Lenton, trained as a mechanic in the lace industry, and began photography after the invention of the collodion process.

In 1860 he moved to New Zealand, where he was employed for several years by Crombie and Webster. He opened a studio at Nelson and, in 1869, in the town of Napier, he managed the business of Swan and Wrigglesworth, which he soon purchased and then sold in 1905. After having occupied a parliamentary seat in Napier as a Liberal (1894–96), he was elected mayor of the city from 1904 to 1907. He also served his community as a member of the harbor board, the Hawkes Bay hospital board, the land board and the school committee.

Utilizing the wet collodion process, Carnell did studio portraiture in a very straightforward manner, concentrating much of his efforts on the aborigines.

COLLECTIONS Natl. Lib. of New Zealand, Alexander Turnbull Lib., Wellington.

Bobbi Carrey PHOTOGRAPHER · PHOTO ARCHIVIST · TEACHER Born in New York City on May 7, 1946, Carrey earned a BA in Spanish from Jackson College for Women, Tufts University in Medford, Massachusetts, in 1968. In 1970 she received an MAT in Visual Studies from Harvard University, Cambridge, Massachusetts.

A member of SPE, the American Society of Picture Professionals, the New York Photographic Historical Society and Boston Visual Artists Union, Carrey was awarded artist-in-residence status from the Massachusetts Council on the Arts (Boston) in 1979. She received an artist-in-residence award in 1978 from the Iowa Arts Council (Des Moines) and a residence grant from the New York State Council on the Arts in 1977. She was artist-in-residence with the Wiscasset School System (Maine) on award from the Alaska State Council on the Arts (Juneau) in 1972.

Of her work she says, "Through the use of multiple images, collages, and three-dimensional constructions, I attempt to construct and reconstruct my own reality. Ultimately, I am creating an autobiography." Carrey superimposes self-portraits over other photographs or graphics.

PUBLICATIONS Anthologies: *Insights: Self-Portraits by Women,* 1978; *Self Portrayal,* 1978; *Women Photograph Men,* 1977; *Women See Woman,* 1976; *The Photographers' Choice,* 1975; *Women of Photography,* 1975.

COLLECTIONS Antioch Coll., Inst. of Open Educ., Boston; Gemini Gall., Palm Beach, Fla.; Harvard Univ., Fogg Art Mus., Cambridge, Mass.; Internatl. Communication Agency, Wash. D.C.; Kalamazoo Inst. of the Arts, Mich.; MOMA, NYC; Marjorie Neikrug Gall., NYC; San Francisco Mus. of Art, Calif.; Witkin Gall., NYC.

DEALERS Marcuse Pfeifer Gall., 825 Madison Ave, New York NY 10021; Jeb Gall., 342 S Main St, Providence, RI 02901.

ADDRESS 16 Mt Auburn St, Cambridge, MA 02138.

James Carroll PHOTOGRAPHER · VIDEO TECHNICIAN Born February 26, 1940, in Salt Lake City, Carroll studied under Albert Freed from 1965 to 1969. Since 1968 he has been self-employed as a freelance photographer.

Carroll received a CAPS grant in 1973 and a technical-assistant grant in 1971, both from the New York State Council on the Arts.

The photographer's work, primarily in a 35mm format, can be characterized as photojournalism with an emphasis on human relations and human psychology.

PUBLICATIONS Catalogs: *Coming of Age in America,* 1975 (Midtown Y Gallery, NYC); *Visual Artists of N.Y. State,* 1973 (CAPS & NY State Council on the Arts: N.Y.). Periodicals: *Camera Mainichi,* No. 6, June 1978; *Lightwork,* Vol. 3, Apr 1975.

COLLECTIONS Richard Dry Lib. Buffalo, N.Y.; Charles Rand Penney Fndn., Olean, N.Y. Bibliothèque Nationale, Paris.

ADDRESS 382 Central Pk W, New York, NY 10025.

Lewis Carroll
See Charles Lutwidge Dodgson

Patty Carroll PHOTOGRAPHER The photographer was born December 30, 1946, in Chicago. Her father is John W. Carroll, an Illinois state senator. Carroll attended the University of Illinois in Urbana, receiving a BFA in 1968, and in 1972 she received an MS from the Institute of Design at Illinois Institute of Technology in Chicago. Art Sinsabaugh, Garry Winogrand and Arthur Siegel were her teachers.

Since 1977 she has been assistant professor at the Institute of Design in Chicago, and has also been designer for *Exposure,* Journal of the SPE, since 1978. Previously she had been an instructor at the University of Michigan in Ann Arbor

(1974–76) and Pennsylvania State University, University Park (1973–74).

Carroll is a member of SPE and CAA. She was the recipient of an award from the Illinois Arts Council in 1977, the Arts & Riverwoods Award from the Art Institute of Chicago (1977) and a Faculty Research Grant from Pennsylvania State University (1974).

PUBLICATIONS Anthologies: *Second Generation of Color,* 1977; *Women Photograph Men,* 1977; *The Multiple Image,* 1974.

PORTFOLIO *Sunset After Dark,* 1979 (Frumkin Gall.: NYC).

COLLECTIONS Ill. State Mus., Springfield; L/C, Wash., D.C.; Mus. of Contemporary Art, Chicago; Smithsonian Inst., Wash., D.C.

DEALER Frumkin Gall. Photographs, Inc., 620 N Michigan Ave, Chicago, IL 60611.

ADDRESS 3950 N Lincoln Ave, Chicago, IL 60613.

Kate Carter PHOTOGRAPHER · TEACHER Born in White Plains, New York, on September 20, 1946, Carter received both a BA (in English, 1968) and an MA (in American Thought and Civilization, 1970) from George Washington University in Washington, D.C.

She has served as associate director of the Maine Photographic Workshop, Rockport, since 1976. From 1972 to 1976 she was an assistant professor at Northern Virginia Community College in Alexandria.

A member of SPE, Carter is on the board of directors of the Maine Photographic Workshop and a vice president of the Rockport Institute of Photographic Education.

Carter works in 16 x 20 silver prints, "usually polytonal." Since 1974 she has photographically documented her daughter Aileen.

PUBLICATION Periodical: *35MM Photography,* fall 1979.

REPRESENTATIVE The Maine Photography Workshop, Rockport, ME 04856.

J. S. Cartier PHOTOGRAPHER Born October 31, 1932, in Paris, Cartier received a DEPP degree at Lycée Hoche in Versailles, France (1949), and a BEPC at Collège d'Altitude, Briançon, France (1950). He also studied at École des Arts Appliqués in Paris (1950–51) and at Ruskin School of Drawing and Fine Arts, Oxford, England (1957–60).

A freelance photographer since 1977, Cartier served as director of the Photography Department of French Cultural Services in New York from 1970 to 1977. He won a scholarship from ICP in New York City in 1976 and a CAPS grant in 1977.

His work is concerned with aspects of nature and the human environment "not apparent at first glance."

PUBLICATION   Periodical: *Le Nouveau Photocinéma*, Feb 1978.

COLLECTIONS   Metro. Mus. of Art, NYC. Bibliothèque Nationale, Paris.

DEALERS   Marcuse Pfeifer Gall., 825 Madison Ave, New York NY 10021; Witkin Gall., 41 E 57 St, New York, NY 10022.

ADDRESS   162 E 90 St, New York, NY 10028.

Henri Cartier-Bresson   *PHOTOGRAPHER*   Born August 22, 1908, in Chanteloup (near Paris), France, Cartier-Bresson studied painting with the artist Cottenet during 1922–23. In 1927 he went to Paris to study painting with André Lhote for two years, and in 1929 studied literature and painting at Cambridge University, England. His first influences were motion pictures, then Eugène Atget and Man Ray and later André Kertész.

Cartier-Bresson took up photography seriously in 1930, and in the following year made the first of many international excursions that he would take over the next forty years. His travels have been to places such as the Ivory Coast, Spain, the United States, Mexico, India, Burma, Pakistan, Japan, the Soviet Union, China, Cuba and Canada. He was first exhibited (at the Julien Levy Gallery in New York City) and published in 1932, and since then has contributed to hundreds of periodicals. In 1940 the photographer was captured by the Germans and held prisoner until his escape in 1943. He then joined a resistance group (MNPGD) to help prisoners and escapees, during which time he made photographic portraits of known artists for the publisher Braun. In 1947 he co-founded, along with Capa, Seymour and Rodger, the cooperative agency Magnum. Since 1973 he has photographed very little, instead concentrating on drawing and on making motion pictures.

He has received four Overseas Press Club awards: in 1948 for his reportage on the death of Gandhi; and for his reportage on Russia, China and Cuba in 1954, 1960 and 1964, respectively. He also received an honorary degree of Doctor of Letters from Oxford (1975), the Prix de la Société Française de Photographie, and the Prix de la Culture de la Société Allemande de Photographie.

Passionate about film since his youth and a student of the form with Paul Strand in 1935, Cartier-Bresson has made several documentaries, including *Victoire de la vie* (1937) and *Le retour* (1944). He also assisted Jean Renoir on the feature *Partie de Campagne* (1936).

Of the artist, Aaron Scharf has written, "The use of the 35-millimeter Leica was particularly relevant to Cartier-Bresson. It lent itself not only to spontaneity but to anonymity as well," a position preferred by the reticent photographer. Scharf explains that the title of Cartier-Bresson's book *The Decisive Moment* "refers to a central idea in his work—the elusive instant, when, with brilliant clarity, the appearance of the subject reveals in its essence the significance of the event of which it is a part, the most telling organization of forms." Cartier-Bresson has worked almost exclusively in black-and-white.

PUBLICATIONS   Monographs: *Henri Cartier-Bresson: Photographer*, Yves Bonnefoy, 1979; *Henri Cartier-Bresson*, 1976; *À propos de l'U.R.S.S.*, 1973, U.S. ed., *About Russia*, 1974; *The Face of Asia*, intro. by Robert Shaplen, 1972; *Vive la France*, Françoise Nourissier, 1970, U.S. ed., *Cartier-Bresson's France*, 1970; *Flagrants délits*, 1968, U.S. ed., *The World of Henri Cartier-Bresson*, 1968; *L'homme et la machine*, intro. by Etiemble, U.S. ed., *Man and Machine*, 1968; *China*, 1964; *Photographies de Henri Cartier-Bresson*, U.S. ed., *Photographs by Cartier-Bresson*, intro. by Lincoln Kirstein & Beaumont Newhall, 1963; *Les Européens*, U.S. ed., *The Europeans*, 1955; *Moscou, vu par Henri Cartier-Bresson*, U.S. ed., *The People of Moscow*, 1955; *D'une Chine à l'autre*, preface by Jean-Paul Sartre, 1954, U.S. ed., *From One China to the Other*, Han Suyin, 1956; *Images à la sauvette*, U.S. ed., *The Decisive Moment*, 1952. Book: *The Galveston That Was*, Howard Barnstone, 1966. Anthologies: *Dialogue with Photography*, Paul Hill & Thomas Cooper, 1979; *The Photograph Collector's Guide*, Lee D. Witkin & Barbara London, 1979; *Photographie als Kunst 1879–1979*, 1979 (Innsbrucker Allerheilengenpresse: Innsbruck); *Great Photographic Essays from LIFE*, Maitland Edey, 1978; *The Julien Levy Collection*, Witkin Gallery, 1977; *Photographs from the Julien Levy Collection*, David Travis, 1976; *The Magic Image*, Cecil Beaton & Gail Buckland, 1975; *Photography Year 1975*, Time-Life Series; *Looking at Photographs*, John Szarkowski, 1973; *Documentary Photography*, 1972, *Travel Photography*, 1972, *The Art of Photography*, 1971, *Great Photographers*, 1971, *Photographing Children*, 1971, *The Camera*, 1970, Time-Life Series; *Photographers on Photography*, Nathan Lyons, ed.,

1966; *Masters of Photography*, Beaumont & Nancy Newhall, 1958; *The Picture History of Photography*, Peter Pollack, 1958. Periodicals (selected): Entire issue, July 1976, "The Instant Vision of Henri Cartier-Bresson," Beaumont Newhall, Oct 1955, *Camera*.

COLLECTIONS Art Inst. of Chicago; ICP, NYC; IMP/GEH, Rochester; Julien Levy Cllctn., NYC; Menil Fndn., Houston, Tex.; Mus. of Fine Arts, Houston; MOMA, NYC; Graham Nash Cllctn., Los Angeles; Worcester Art Mus., Mass. Bibliothèque Nationale, Paris.

ADDRESS 198 rue de Rivoli, 75001 Paris, France.

Elizabeth Luther Cary ART CRITIC · AUTHOR Born May 18, 1867, in Brooklyn, New York, Cary died there on July 13, 1936. Her father, Edward Cary (died 1917), was editor of the *Brooklyn Union* and later on the staff of *The New York Times*. She was educated at home by her father, and later studied art for ten years under Charles Melville and Eleanor E. Sisnister.

Between 1893 and 1897 Cary undertook several translations from the French of nonfiction works. She wrote several original works from 1898 to 1907, and designed, wrote, edited and published a monthly art magazine called *The Scrip* from 1905 to 1908. It was this magazine that prompted the offer for her to join *The New York Times* as its only art critic (March 21, 1908), a post she held until her death. Her criticism also sometimes appeared in *Camera Work*.

Cary wrote on many aspects of art, ancient and modern, and, according to her obituary in *The New York Times*, "always kept a fresh point of view.... Without losing sight of the validity of tradition, she was yet able to find beauty and significance in the many departures."

PUBLICATIONS Books: *George Luks*, 1931; *Honoré Daumier*, 1907; *The Works of James McNeill Whistler*, 1907; *The Novels of Henry James*, 1905; *Books Are My Food*, w/Annie M. Jones, 1904; *Poems of Dante Gabriel Rosetti*, ed., 1903; *William Morris, Poet, Craftsman, Socialist*, 1902; *Ralph Waldo Emerson, Poet and Thinker*, 1900; *The Rosettis, Dante, Gabriel and Christina*, 1900; *Robert Browning, Poet and Man*, 1899; *Alfred Tennyson, His Homes, His Friends and His Work*, 1898. Translations: *The Land of Tawny Beasts*, 1895; *Russian Portraits*, E. Melchior, 1895; *Recollections of Middle Life*, Francisque Sarcey, 1893. Anthology: *Camera Work*, Jonathan Green, 1973. Periodicals: "The French Estimate of Emerson," *Literary Digest*, Jan 7,

1905; "Lowell the Man," *The Book Buyer*, July 1899.

Harriet Casdin-Silver HOLOGRAPHER · TEACHER Born in Worcester, Massachusetts, Casdin-Silver earned a BA from the University of Vermont, Burlington, and did graduate work at Columbia University and the New School for Social Research in New York City, at the Worcester Art Museum and at Cambridge Goddard Graduate School for Social Change, Massachusetts.

Since 1976 she has been a fellow at the Center for Advanced Visual Studies at MIT in Cambridge. From 1974 to 1978 she served as assistant professor (research) of physics at Brown University, Providence, Rhode Island, and from 1969 to 1973 she was artist-in-residence at American Optical Research Laboratories, Department of Optical Physics. Casdin-Silver taught at Clark University in Worcester from 1969 to 1974 and at the Worcester Art Museum in 1969–71.

The holographer won Rockefeller Foundation Fellowships in 1978 and 1979, an MIT Council for the Arts grant in 1978, an NEA grant in 1975 and Cabin Creek Grants from the New York State Council for the Arts in 1978 and 1979.

She considers holography "sculpture of light ... shaping imaginary spaces ... fantasy, reality, politics, change." She feels that her content "derives from humanistic sociological orientation," and "though technique is secondary to concept, research is an important aspect of my work."

PUBLICATIONS Book: "On Art, Technology and Holography," *New Spaces: The Holographer's Vision*, 1979. Catalogs: "Concept of Holography," *Expansion*, 1979 (Universitäbsbüchdrucherie for the Internationale Biennale: Vienna); "HC-S Holography," *5 Artists/5 Technologies*, 1979 (Grand Rapids Art Mus.: Mich.); "Holography, the most viable way toward 3 dimensional imagery ...," *Harriet Casdin-Silver Holography*, 1977 (Mus. of Holography: NYC). Periodicals: "Centerbeam Documenta 6," *Centerbeam*, 1980 (MIT Press); *ARTTRANSITION*, 1975 (MIT Press).

COLLECTIONS Brown Univ., Providence, R.I.; Mus. of Holography, NYC; Mus. of Science & Industry, ARTSCIENCE Gall., Chicago. Musée Français de l'Holographie, Paris; Mus. für Holographie, Cologne, Ger.; Richard Payne Cllctn., London; Societá Olographica Italiana, Rome.

ADDRESS Center for Advanced Visual Studies, MIT, Bldg WII, 40 Massachusetts Ave, Cambridge, MA 02139.

Jack Cyril Cato *PHOTOGRAPHER · WRITER*
Born in 1889 in Launceston, Tasmania, Cato died in Melbourne, Australia, in 1971. The photographer John Cato is his son. Cato was apprenticed in Tasmania to his cousin John Watt Beatti, a renowned topographical photographer, and studied art at the Launceston Art School with Lucien Dechanoux and portrait photography under Percy Whitelaw.

From 1909 to 1913 Cato worked in London, first for H. Walter Barnett, an Australian, in his popular society portrait studio, and then with Claude Harris, who specialized in theatrical personalities. He then worked as a freelance theatrical photographer, assisted by Nellie Melba, the famous singer, as a patron. The photographer moved to South Africa in 1913, working as an expedition photographer for Professor Cory of Grahamstown University before enlisting for war service. After the war he returned to Tasmania and set up a studio in Hobart in 1920. Seven years later he moved his studio to Melbourne, again with the assistance of Nellie Melba, and his studio became a leader in social portraiture until 1947, when he retired to concentrate on writing. He was nominated a fellow of RPS in 1917.

Cato specialized in theater photography, ethnographic portraiture and pictorial landscapes. He contributed some of the best portrait work in the pictorial era.

PUBLICATIONS   Books: *Melbourne*, 1949; *I Can Take It*, autobio., 1947 (Georgia House: Australia). Anthology: *The Story of the Camera in Australia*, 1955, repr. 1977 (Georgia House: Australia).

COLLECTIONS   In Australia: John Cato Cllctn., Melbourne; Latrobe Lib., Melbourne.

ARCHIVE   John Cato, Melbourne, Australia.

John Chester Cato *PHOTOGRAPHER · TEACHER*
Born November 2, 1926, in Hobart, Tasmania, Australia, Cato is the son of Jack Cato, who was a photographer, historian, and a fellow of the Royal Photographic Society. He apprenticed under his father and names Athol-Shmith as a major influence.

As of this writing Cato was head of photography at Prahran College of Advanced Education in Melbourne, Australia, where he lectured in 1975–76. He was a senior lecturer at Photography Studies College in Melbourne in 1977–79. From 1950 to 1974 Cato was director and photographer for Athol-Shmith, John Cato Pty. Ltd. He was a photojournalist for *The Argus* in Melbourne

(1947–50) and was in the Royal Australian Navy (1944–46).

The photographer is an Associate of the Institute of Australian Photography.

His work is in essay form, using the landscape as symbol.

PUBLICATIONS   Book: *The Story of the Camera in Australia*, research asst., Jack Cato, 1955, rev. ed., 1977. Periodicals: *Light Vision*, no. 1, 1977, "John Cato—Proteus," *Folio*, 1977 (Church Street Photographic Center: Richmond, Victoria, Australia).

COLLECTIONS   Bibliothèque Nationale, Paris. In Australia: Horsham Art Gall., Victoria; Natl. Gall. of Victoria; Mus. & Art Gall. of Tasmania, Hobart; Philip Morris Cllctn., Melbourne.

ADDRESS   23 Cannes Ave, Carrum, Victoria, Australia 3197.

Paul Cava (Cavalluzzi) *PHOTOGRAPHER · GALLERY OWNER*   Born May 15, 1949, in Brooklyn, New York, Cava received a BA degree from Richmond College in New York City (1972) and an MFA degree from Rochester Institute of Technology (1975). He studied visual arts and the history of art both academically and informally.

Since 1979 Cava has been the owner of Paul Cava Gallery in Philadelphia. He has also been the publisher of photographic posters since 1977.

PUBLICATIONS   Periodicals: "The Landscape Photographs of Gustave Le Gray," *The History of Photography*, text only, 2:4, 1978; "Interview with George Krause," *Philadelphia Arts Exchange*, text only, Jan 1977; "Interview with Owen Butler," *The Philadelphia Photo Review*, text only, Sept 1976; "A Conversation with Paul Cava," *The Philadelphia Photo Review*, Aug 1976.

COLLECTIONS   Free Lib. of Philadelphia; IMP/GEH, Rochester; MOMA, NYC; Carlton Willers Coll., NYC. Bibliothèque Nationale, Paris.

DEALER   Pfeiffer Gall., 825 Madison Ave, New York, NY 10021.

ADDRESS   1715 Spruce St, Philadelphia, PA 19103.

Vojtěch Čech
See Jiří Sever

Gusmano Cesaretti *PHOTOGRAPHER*   Born July 29, 1946 in Florence, Italy, Cesaretti is a self-taught photographer who cites film maker Pier Paolo Pasolini as a major influence.

Recently a special photographer for a United

Cesaretti

Artists film, Cesaretti has been a freelance photographer since 1974. From 1971 to 1973 he was staff photographer for the H. E. Huntington Library Art Gallery in San Marino, California, and from 1978 to 1979 he was curator of the Cityscape Foto Gallery in Pasadena, California, which he founded.

In 1973 Cesaretti won honors for "superior achievement in sculpture" at Pasadena City College, and in 1971 earned an ASMP/Art Directors Club of Los Angeles Award.

Cesaretti's work focuses on documentaries and graphics.

PUBLICATIONS   Monographs: *5 x 5 = 24*, 1979; *Street Writers: A Guided Tour of Chicano Graffiti*, 1975. Periodicals: *Camerart*, 1979, 1976; *Rolling Stone Magazine*, 1977; *Picture Magazine*, 1976.

COLLECTION   Ital-Carton Corp., Lucca, Italy.

REPRESENTATIVE   Rosa Castro, 97 E Colorado Blvd, Pasadena, CA 91105.

Samuel Emery Chamberlain   *PHOTOGRAPHER · AUTHOR · ETCHER*   Born in the United States in 1895, Chamberlain died in Marblehead, Massachusetts, on January 10, 1975. Sometimes known as Phineas Beck, he studied architecture at MIT in Cambridge and received a scholarship to study etching under Edouard Léon in Paris and Malcolm Osborne in London. His wife, Narcissa Gellaly, was his frequent co-author.

Chamberlain served with the American Army Ambulance Service of the French Army during World War I and was a major in photo-intelligence during World War II. He wrote and illustrated many articles in the 1920s for *Century*, *American Architect*, *Pencil Points*, *Art and Decoration*, *Architectural Record* and others. He was also an assistant professor of architecture at the University of Michigan, Ann Arbor, and the official etcher of the Williamsburg restoration in Virginia.

A gourmet, Chamberlain wrote articles for *Gourmet* magazine and wrote two books on cooking. During World War I he won the Croix de Guerre.

An architectural and scenic photographer, he photographed the American countryside and the landscapes of France, Britain and Spain.

PUBLICATIONS   Books: *Historic Deerfield*, w/ Henry N. Flynt, 1972; *Longfellow's New England*, Harry Hansen, 1972; *A Tour of Old Sturbridge Village*, 1972; *Yale, A Pictorial History*, Reuben A. Holden, 1967; *New England Legends & Folklore*, Harry Hansen ed. & intro., 1967; *My Confession*, incl. text, intro. by Roger Butterfield,

1956; *Italian Bouquet*, w/Narcissa Gellaly Chamberlain, 1958; *Old Rooms for New Living*, w/Narcissa Gellaly Chamberlain, 1953; *Soft Skies of France*, 1953; *Bouquet de France, an Epicurean Tour of the French Provinces*, w/Narcissa Gellaly Chamberlain, 1952; *Fair Harvard*, Donald Moffat, 1948; *Behold Williamsburg*, 1947; *Churches of Old New England*, Geo. Francis Marlowe, 1947; *Rockefeller Center*, 1947; *Springtime in Virginia*, intro. by Virginius Dabney, 1947; *Boston Landmarks*, M. A. De Wolfe Howe, 1946; *Ever New England*, intro. by Donald Moffat, 1944; *Clémentine in the Kitchen*, w/ Henry Stalhut, 1943; *Fair is Our Land*, 1942; *Historic Cambridge in Four Seasons*, 1942; *Coast of Maine*, 1941; *Martha's Vineyard*, 1941; *This Realm, This England*, intro. by Donald Moffat, 1941; *France Will Live Again*, intro. by Donald Moffat, 1940; *Old Marblehead*, 1940; *Portsmouth, New Hampshire*, 1940; *Nantucket*, 1939; *Gloucester and Cape Ann*, 1938; *Historic Boston in Four Seasons*, 1938; *Historic Salem in Four Seasons*, 1938; *Longfellow's Wayside Inn*, 1938; *Beyond New England Thresholds*, 1937; *Cape Cod in the Sun*, 1937; *Open House in New England*, 1937; *Through France With a Sketchbook*, 1929; *Domestic Architecture in Rural France*, 1928.

COLLECTION   IMP/GEH, Rochester.

Martín Chambi   *PHOTOGRAPHER*   [See plate 59]   Born in 1891 in Coaza, near Lake Titicaca, Peru, Chambi died in 1973 in Cuzco, Peru. His son and daughter, Victor and Julia Chambi, are Peruvian photographers and maintain his old studio in Cuzco. Chambi first worked with his father for the Santa Domingo Mining Company, an English firm looking for gold (1900). While there he met company photographer Max T. Vargas and went with him to the city of Arequipa as his apprentice for nine years (1908–1917).

In 1920 Chambi established a portrait studio in Cuzco, Peru, where he remained for the rest of his life. His studio was immensely popular. Widely published in various periodicals, his work appeared in *El Sol*, Cuzco's newspaper, *la Crónica*, a Lima newspaper, *La Nación* and *La Prensa*, newspapers of Buenos Aires, and the magazines *Kosko* and *Variadades*. His work was frequently exhibited in Chile, Argentina and Peru in the 1920s and '30s.

In 1917 Chambi's work was awarded a medal in a competition held by the Arequipa Cultura Center in Peru. He received numerous silver and gold medals from local competitions. Co-founder of Cuzco's Instituto Americano de Arte (1927–

28), he was also involved in establishing the city's Academia de Artes Plásticas. His work was shown at the first American Convention of the International Federation of Photographic Art in Mexico City (1964), and he was designated "patron" of the first graduating class of professional photographers at the National School of Graphic Arts in Lima (1971). Chambi's image "The Indian and the Llama" was used for an airmail postage stamp issued by the Peruvian government (without remuneration or credit). In 1979 an NEA grant was awarded, under the auspices of Earthwatch, to prepare a traveling show of the artist's work.

More important to Chambi than his studio work was his ongoing documentation of the Indian heritage of the highlands where he lived, both its current life and its architectural remains. Edward Ranney wrote in the *Earthwatch Newsletter* that what Atget was to Paris and Sander to Germany, so Chambi was to Cuzco before the 1950 earthquake. "Chambi was a portrait photographer with an unusual understanding of light . . . the pervasive quality of his work is a sensitive, unprejudiced receptivity to the human qualities of his subjects, a way of seeing which let their personalities speak for themselves."

PUBLICATIONS Books: *Documental del Perú*, 1968 (Cusco); *Cusco Pre-Hispánico y Cusco Virreynal*, Martín Noél (Univ. of Buenos Aires: Argentina); *Cuadernos de Arte Histórico de América*, Martín Noél; *Cusco, Capital Arqueológica de América del Sur*, Luis H. Valcárcel, 1951 (Edit. Pampa: Buenos Aires); *Pueblos y Paisajes Surperuanos*, J. Uriel García, 1937; *Cusco Monumental*, Luis H. Valcárcel, 1934 (Bco. Italiano); *Cusco Histórico*, Rafael Larco Herrera, 1934 (Lima, Peru); *La Ciudad de los Incas*, J. Uriel García, 1930 (Cusco); *Pintura Colonial*, Felipe Cossío del Pomar, 1928 (H. G. Rosas: Cusco). Catalog: *Martín Chambi*, 1978 (Secuenda Fotogalería: Lima). Periodicals: "Chambi of Cuzco," Max Kozloff, *Art in America*, Dec 1979; *Quest*, June 1979; *Popular Photography*, May 1979; "Pioneer Photographer of Peru," Roderick Camp, *Americas*, Mar 1979; "Martín Chambi, Photographer of the Andes," Roderick Camp, *Latin American Research Review*, 13:2, 1978; "Martín Chambi, Poet of Light," Edw. Ranney, *Earthwatch Newsletter* (Belmont, Mass.), 1977.

COLLECTIONS MOMA, NYC; Tulane Univ., Latin American Photographic Archive, New Orleans, La.; Univ. of N. Mex. Art Mus., Albuquerque.

ARCHIVES Edward Ranney, Rt 2, Box 299, Santa Fe, NM 87501; Foto Victor Chambi, Las Higueras G-2, Residencial Monterrico, Lima 3, Perú.

Victor Chambi Lopez PHOTOGRAPHER Born August 26, 1917, in Arequipa, Peru, Lopez attended the Instituto de Artes Gráficas in Buenos Aires, Argentina (1938–41), then studied painting and drawing with Lino E. Espilimbergo, Emilio Petorutti and Raul Soldi in Argentina (1938–45). His father, Martín Chambi Jimenez, was a photographer, and his sister, Julia Chambi, also became a photographer and archivist of her father's studio.

Since 1945 Chambi has been a freelance photographer. He has a studio and laboratory in his own home in Cuzco, Peru, where he teaches courses in the techniques and aesthetics of photography. In 1956 he returned to Peru from Buenos Aires, where he had also become a cinematographer (1947). Before that Chambi was his father's assistant, from 1932 to 1937. His work has been widely exhibited and published in books, magazines and on tourist posters, both in his home country and abroad.

The photographer is an associate of the Foto Club of Buenos Aires, having founded the first Foto Club in Peru in 1957 in Cuzco. He is also affiliated with FIAP and the Federación de Fotografía Americana.

In his personal work Chambi is especially interested in capturing the ethnological and anthropological aspects of humanity. He concentrates on the countryside, particularly the architectural and aesthetic values of the archaeological sites in Peru.

ADDRESS Foto Victor Chambi, Las Higueras G-2, Residencial Monterrico, Lima 3, Peru.

Koldo Chamorro de Aranzadi PHOTOGRAPHER · CRITIC Born August 20, 1949, in Vitoria (Alava), Spain, Chamorro studied economic management at the University of Navarra-Este, Spain, in 1971 and marketing at Aleph-3 in Pamplona, Spain, in 1971–72. Self-taught in photography, he began shooting pictures at age thirteen.

A publicity photographer with Cover-Press Agency in Madrid, Spain, since 1979, Chamorro was photography critic for the magazine *Agrupación Cinematografica Fotografica de Navarra* from 1973 to 1979. He has also been a freelance editorial and illustration photographer since 1970 and taught photography at Elisava Vocational Art School in Barcelona, Spain, in 1974–75.

From 1974 to 1976, with a grant from the Fun-

Chamorro de Aranzadi

dación de Arte Castellblanch in Barcelona, Chamorro studied abroad.

The photographer uses small format to produce photo-reportages of "human communities and sociological happenings." He also shoots portraits in medium format.

PUBLICATIONS Periodicals: *European Photography*, No. 2, 1980; *Photo-Reporter*, Mar 6, 1979; *Agrupación Cinematografica Fotografica de Navarra, passim*, 1973–79; *Agrupación Fotografica de Almeria*, 1974, 1973.

COLLECTIONS Bibliothèque Nationale, Paris; Fundación Argibide, Pamplona, Spain; Musée Réattu, Arles, France.

REPRESENTATIVE Barry Fellman, 1449 Brickell Ave, Miami, FL 33131.

ADDRESS Fuente del Hierro no. 19–8º B, Pamplona, Navarra, Spain.

Chris Chapman PHOTOGRAPHER Born October 8, 1952, in Wigan, Lancashire, England, Chapman received a BA from the Newport College of Art and Design, in Newport, England, in 1975.

Currently self-employed as a freelance photographer, Chapman has received awards from South West Arts in 1979, and the British Arts Council in 1976 and 1977.

PUBLICATIONS Book: *The Right Side of the Hedge*, 1977. Periodical: *Nye Foto*, 1976.

COLLECTION Arts Council of Great Britain, England.

REPRESENTATIVE Paul Henderson, Gidleigh Park Hotel, Chagford, Devon, England.

ADDRESS Tythe Barn Studio, Throwleigh nr. Okehampton, Devon, England.

Walter Chappell PHOTOGRAPHER [See plate 96] Born June 8, 1925, in Portland, Oregon, Chappell studied at Benson Polytechnical School and Portland School of Music, Oregon (1938–42). He was apprenticed to Frank Lloyd Wright in 1953–54 under a Taliesin Fellowship in Scottsdale, Arizona, and studied at IMP/GEH in 1957–60 with Beaumont Newhall and Minor White. He met Edward Weston while living in Monterey and Big Sur (1948–51); Weston and White were major influences.

A self-employed photographer since 1961, Chappell is also an interior and graphic designer. He founded and directed the Association of Heliographers Gallery in New York City (1962–65) and was curator of exhibitions and prints at IMP/GEH from 1957 to 1961. Chappell served as associate director of the Photography Workshop in Denver in 1955–57. In 1977 and 1980 he won an NEA Photographer's Fellowship.

In medium and large formats, the photographer has been working in four categories: "abstract vision of nature" (since 1954), "landscapes and objects portraiture" (since 1960), "gestures of the nude human form" (since 1957) and "metaflora series" (since 1974).

PUBLICATIONS Monograph: *Gestures of Infinity*, foreword by Minor White, 1957. Books: *Under the Sun*, w/Nathan Lyons & Syl Labrot, 1960, 2nd ed. 1971; *Logue and Glyphs 1943–1949* (poems), 1951. Anthologies: *Mirrors and Windows*, John Szarkowski, ed., 1978; *The Photographers' Choice*, Kelly Wise, ed., 1975; *Celebrations*, Minor White & Jonathan Green, eds., 1974; *Be-ing Without Clothes*, Minor White, ed., 1970; *Light⁷*, Minor White, ed., 1968; *Photography in the Twentieth Century*, 1963; *Photography Yearbook*, 1962 (London). Catalog: *Photographs*, 1977 (Univ. of Neb., Sheldon Mem. Art Gall.: Lincoln). Periodicals: *Photography Annual*, 1962; *Aperture*, 8:2, 1980, 9:1, 1961, 8:4, 1960, 8:2, 1960, 7:2, 1959, 5:4, 1957, 5:3, 1957.

PORTFOLIOS *Edmond Kara Sculpture*, 1971; *Edmond Kara Portfolio of Elizabeth Taylor Sculpture*, 1964; *Edmond Kara Portfolio One*, 1964; *Sharon Tate Portfolio*, 1964.

COLLECTIONS CCP Tucson; Colorado Photographic Art Ctr., Denver; Exchange Natl. Bank of Chicago; Harvard Univ., Fogg Art Mus., Cambridge, Mass.; IMP/GEH, Rochester; Ind. Univ. Art Dept., Bloomington; MGM Studios, Los Angeles; Metro Mus. of Art, NYC; MIT, Cambridge, Mass.; Mus. of Modern Art, Houston, Tex.; MOMA, NYC; Philadelphia Mus., Penn.; Polaroid Corp. Lib., Cambridge, Mass; Princeton Univ. Art Mus., Princeton, N.J.; R.I. School of Design, Providence; Roswell Mus., Roswell, N.Mex.; San Francisco State Univ., Calif.; Smithsonian Inst., Wash., D.C.; Stanford Univ. Mus., Palo Alto, Calif.; UCLA; Univ. of Neb., Sheldon Mem. Art Gall., Lincoln; Univ. of N.C., Ackland Mem. Art Mus., Chapel Hill; VSW, Rochester; Whitney Mus. of Amer. Art, NYC.

ADDRESS Box 18, Cordova, NM 87523.

Jean-Philippe Charbonnier PHOTOGRAPHER · TEACHER Born on August 28, 1921, in Paris, Charbonnier was a staff photographer for the French magazine *Réalités* from 1950 to 1974. Since 1976 he has been teaching photography at the ESAG (Ecole Supérieure d'Arts Graphiques) in Paris.

He describes his work as "human interest photojournalism." This style is exemplified in his series of portraits of VIPs from all over the world, which he produced for *Réalités*.

PUBLICATIONS Books: *Un Photographe vous parle*, 1961; *Les Chemins de la Vie*, 1957.

REPRESENTATIVES TOP Agency, 1 rue St Georges, 75009 Paris, France; Galerie Agathe Gaillard, 3 rue du Pont Louis Philippe, 75004 Paris, France.

ADDRESS 1 rue du Pont Louis Philippe, 75004 Paris, France.

Charles Louis Chevalier OPTICIAN · PHOTOGRAPHIC EQUIPMENT MANUFACTURER Born in 1804, Chevalier died in 1859. He lived in Paris.

In 1826 the optician gave a camera he had made to Nicéphore Niepce, advising him that Daguerre was also conducting similar photographic experiments. Chevalier also supplied Daguerre with photographic apparatuses and counseled him in his experiments. In 1828 he provided Niepce with two new lenses and in 1834 made a lens for astronomical use which he adapted to his camera, "the Photographe," in 1840. Chevalier is also reported to have supplied Fox Talbot with equipment after 1839. The manufacturer's early cameras consisted of two boxes, but in 1840 he introduced a wooden folding camera. Later productions included a problematic Megascope (1838), a lens with changeable front element (1844) and a complete daguerreotype-making outfit (1840). In 1840 he also made photomicrographs on daguerreotypes, and one of his last cameras was used for topographic photography. Chevalier was one of the founders of the Société Héliographique in 1851.

PUBLICATIONS Books: *Photographie im Wandel*, Rudolf Skopec, Aschner, 1964; *Quellendarstellungen zur Geschichte der Fotografie*, Wolfgang Baier, 1964; *Photographic Literature*, Albert Boni, 1962; *Focal Encylcopedia of Photography*, 1957, 1956 (Focal Press); *L. J. M. Daguerre*, 1956; *History of Photography*, Helmut & Alison Gernsheim, 1955; *Histoire de la Photographie*, Raymond Lécuyer, 1945; *Photography Principles & Practice*, 3rd ed., C. B. Neblette, 1939; *A History and Handbook of Photography*, Gaston Tissandier, 1876; *Notice sur l'usage des Chambres Obscures et des Chambres Claires*, 1829, repub. 1833. Anthology: *Photography's Great Inventors*, Louis W. Sipley, 1965. Periodical: *Humphrey's Journal of Photography*, 1859.

Carl Chiarenza PHOTOGRAPHER · ART HISTORIAN Born in Rochester, New York, on September 5, 1935, Chiarenza earned a BFA from his hometown's Institute of Technology in 1957. He continued his studies at Boston University, receiving an MS in 1959 and an AM in 1964. Harvard University awarded him a PhD in 1973.

Chiarenza has been on the art history faculty of Boston University since 1963, and from 1976 to the present has served as department chairman as well as associate professor. In 1973–74 he was an adjunct visiting professor at VSW in Rochester. Chiarenza has also worked as associate editor (1963–66) and editor (1966–69) of the magazine *Contemporary Photographer*.

Co-founder of the Society of Heliographers (1962–64) and of Imageworks (1971–73), Dr. Chiarenza is currently a member of the board of trustees of VSW (since 1975) and the Photographic Resource Center (since 1978). He has been on the Advisory Council of ICP from 1970 to the present and was on the SPE board of directors from 1968 to 1972.

Chiarenza received Danforth Teacher Grants in 1966–67 and 1967–68. He won Artist's Fellowships from the Massachusetts Arts and Humanities Foundation in 1975–76 and from the NEA in 1977–78. In 1971 he was awarded a Kress Foundation Grant.

As a photographer, Chiarenza uses black-and-white silver prints to convey an "abstract interpretation of the ideas of modern life in relation to the tradition of the imaginary landscape." His art historical research focuses on the modern period, with a concentration on twentieth-century American photography.

PUBLICATIONS (selected) Book: *One Hundred Years of Photograhic History*, Van Deren Coke, ed., 1975. Anthologies: *Object and Image*, George M. Craven, 1975; *Celebrations*, Minor White, 1974; *Octave of Prayer*, Minor White, 1972; *Light⁷*, Minor White, 1968; *Photography in the Twentieth Century*, Nathan Lyons, 1967. Catalog: *Photographs by Aaron Siskind in Homage to Franz Kline*, 1975 (David & Alfred Smart Gallery, Univ. of Chicago). Periodicals: "Siskind's Critics," *Journal of the Center for Creative Photography*, July 8, 1978; "Who Cares?—Concern, Protest and Action in Photography," *Contemporary Photographer*, 6:2, 1969; "Carl Chiarenza, A Portfolio," Lee Lockwood, *Contemporary Photographer*, 5:2, 1965; "Carl Chiarenza," Ralph Hattersley, *Infinity*, 11:9, 1962; "Discovery No. 35: Carl Chiarenza," Patricia Caulfield, *Modern Photography*, 22:6, 1958; "Stereotypes: Barriers to the Experience of Photographs," *Aperture*, 6:2, 1958.

COLLECTIONS CCP, Tucson; Harvard Univ., Fogg Art Mus., Cambridge, Mass.; IMP/GEH, Rochester; Mass. Inst. of Technology; Minneapolis Inst. of Arts; Mus. of Fine Arts, Houston;

UCLA; Worcester Art Mus., Mass. Polaroid-Europa Cllctn., Amsterdam.

DEALERS Cronin Gallery, 2008 Peden, Houston, TX 77019; Carl Siembab Gall., 162 Newbury St, Boston, MA 02116.

ADDRESS Room 301, 725 Commonwealth Ave, Boston, MA 02215.

Václav Chochola PHOTOGRAPHER Born January 30, 1923, in Prague, Czechoslovakia, Chochola learned photography as an apprentice in the Studio Otto Erban in Prague from 1941 to 1945. He was influenced by the work of Brassaï, Bill Brandt, Erwin Blumenfeld and Man Ray.

A freelance photographer, Chochola also writes essays and critiques on photography. He has belonged to the Union of Czechoslovak Fine Artists since 1949.

Chochola won the bronze medal at Expo '58 in Brussels, Belgium.

PUBLICATIONS (all Prague) Monograph: *Václav Chochola—Photographs 1940–60*, Jiří Kolář, 1961 (Odeon). Books: *Spring of Prague*, V. Holzknecht, 1970 (Obelisk); *Meisterfotografien*, Jiří Kolář, 1961 (Odeon); *Memory in Black and White*, Prošek & Řezáč, 1961 (Artia); *Painter František Tichý*, Fr. Dvořák, 1961 (Odeon); *Horses*, intro. by Matyašová, 1958 (Artia).

COLLECTIONS Moravian Gall., Brno, Czech.; Mus. of Decorative Arts, Prague; Polaroid Cllctn., Amsterdam, The Netherlands; Rudolf Kicken Gall., Cologne, Ger.; Univ. Gall., Mexico City.

ADDRESS Prosecká 47, CS-180 00, Prague 8, Czechoslovakia.

William Christenberry PHOTOGRAPHER · SCULPTOR Born in Tuscaloosa, Alabama, on November 5, 1936, Christenberry attended the University of Alabama, where he completed a BFA in 1958 and an MA in Painting in 1959.

Since 1974 he has been an art professor at the Corcoran School of Art in Washington, D.C., where he taught as an associate professor (1968–74).

In 1976 he was granted an NEA Fellowship in Photography, and in 1978 the Art-in-Architecture Program of the U.S. General Services Administration commissioned him to create a wall work for the Federal Building in Jackson, Mississippi.

Christenberry uses Brownie cameras and, since 1977, works in 35mm and up to 8 x 10.

PUBLICATIONS Book: *Beale Street*, ltd. ed., 1979. Periodical: *Camera*, Apr 1980.

COLLECTIONS Atlanta Mus., Ga.; Corcoran Gall. of Art, Wash., D.C.; L/C, Wash., D.C.; MOMA, NYC; Montgomery Mus. of Art, Ala.; New Orleans Mus. of Art; Yale Univ. Art Gall., New Haven, Conn. Stedelijk Mus., Amsterdam.

DEALERS Caldecot Chubb, 249 W 29 St, New York, NY; Sander Gall., 2604 Connecticut Ave NW, Washington, D.C. 20008.

ADDRESS 2739 Macomb St, Washington, D.C. 20008.

Henning Christoph PHOTOJOURNALIST Born May 6, 1944, in Leipzig, Germany, Christoph earned a BS in Journalism and Anthropology from the University of Maryland, College Park, in 1967. He then studied at the Folkwangschule in Essen, Germany (1967–69), under Professor Otto Steinert.

Christoph has been a freelance photographer since 1969. He belongs to ASMP and RPS.

In 1979 the photographer won the Otto Steinert Photographic Achievement Award and the Deutscher Wirtschaftsfotopreis. He received three World Press Photo Awards, in 1970, 1973 and 1977.

"My specialty," he says, "is the photo essay and picture story dealing with people in conflict with their environment and each other."

PUBLICATIONS Book: *Irrland-Irland*, 1978 (Spee Verlag). Anthologies: *The Family of Woman*, 1979; *The Family of Children*, 1977. Periodicals: *Photo*, Mar 1980; *The Art Annual*, 1980, 1977.

ADDRESS Kotumstrasse 61, 4300 Essen 1, West Germany.

Monica Cipnic PICTURE EDITOR · WRITER · PHOTOGRAPHER Born September 12, 1950, in Poughkeepsie, New York, Cipnic earned a BA in Government, English and History from Skidmore College, Saratoga Springs, New York (1972). Her late brother, Dennis Cipnic, was a photographer.

She is currently associate picture editor for *Popular Photography* and *Camera Arts* magazines, having started as assistant picture editor in 1973; she was promoted to her current position in 1974. She is responsible for all covers and major portfolios that appear in *Popular Photography*, *Photography Annual*, *Camera Arts* and *Photography Directory and Buying Guide*. Previously she was a production assistant for Alden Films and photographic assistant to her brother, Dennis Cipnic, both in New Orleans, 1972–73. She belongs to Women in Communications and the American Society of Picture Professionals.

ADDRESS 305 E 24 St, New York, NY 10016.

S. E. Ciriclio *PHOTOGRAPHER · TEACHER*
Born in New York City on November 27, 1946, Ciriclio earned a BFA from California College of Arts and Crafts in Oakland (1971) and an MFA from Oakland's Mills College (1974).

Ciriclio currently teaches photography at the San Francisco Art Institute (since 1979), California College of Arts and Crafts (since 1976) and Chabot College in Hayward, California (since 1972). Ciriclio has also been a guest lecturer, visiting artist and freelance photo consultant since 1972.

A member of SPE and CAA, the photographer won an NEA Photographer's Fellowship in 1979.

Ciriclio does "non-traditional work, generally on a large scale, using the super-eight movie, the color snapshot, and the found image as the basic core of my visual vocabulary. Formats have included unique books, albums, blueprint environments, mailings, and floor pieces."

COLLECTIONS Mills College, Oakland, Calif.; Oakland Mus.; San Francisco Mus. of Modern Art.

ADDRESS 535 Haddon Rd, Oakland, CA 94606.

Ed Cismondi *PHOTOGRAPHER · TEACHER*
Born on October 14, 1917, in San Jose, California, Cismondi has been "greatly" influenced by the works of Alfred Stieglitz, Paul Strand and Henri Cartier-Bresson.

He has been a photography instructor at San Jose State University since 1973 and regularly teaches workshops in photography. He is a member of SPE, the San Francisco Museum of Modern Art and Friends of Photography.

In 1959 Cismondi created a 16mm color film entitled *Photographer's Notebook*, later represented in the U.S. State Department's Art in the Embassies program (1967).

The artist says about his work: "I take a very literal approach, doing what photography does best . . . the rendering of fine detail, delineation of line and form, and nuances of tone. . . . My most significant images are abstractions of organic forms and geometric design."

PUBLICATIONS Books: *The Face of California*, 1971; *Photo Maxima*, 1958. Anthology: *Object and Image*, Craven, 1975.

COLLECTIONS Jacksonville Mus. of Art, Fla.; Monterey Peninsula Mus. of Art, Calif.; Oakland Mus. of Art, Calif.

DEALERS Focus Gall., 2146 Union St, San Francisco, CA 94123; Markham Gall., 1990 The Alameda, San Jose, CA 95126; Photography

Southwest Gall., 4223 N Marshall Way, Scottsdale, AZ 85251.

ADDRESS 120 College Ave, Los Gatos, CA 95030.

Larry Clark *PHOTOGRAPHER* Born in Tulsa, Oklahoma, in 1943, Clark, mainly self-taught, attended the Layton School of Art in Milwaukee in the 1961–62 school year.

A frequent lecturer on photography, at this writing he was teaching at Museo del Barrio in New York. Previously he lectured at the Floating Foundation of Photography, New York, CEPA Gallery, Buffalo, MIT, Cambridge, Rutgers University, New Jersey (all 1979), Apeiron Workshops, Millerton, New York, and Pratt Institute, Brooklyn (1978), and, in 1969, gave a series of lectures at the Art Institute of San Francisco. In 1973 he was awarded an NEA grant.

Clark is especially noted for his realistic documentation of the drug culture of the 1960s. More recently he is concentrating on the young street people of New York's Forty-second Street.

PUBLICATIONS Monograph: *Tulsa*, 1971. Book: "Larry Clark: Tulsa," *Light Reading*, A. D. Coleman, 1971. Anthologies: *The Photograph Collector's Guide*, Lee D. Witkin & Barbara London, 1979; *Darkroom 1*, Eleanor Lewis, ed., 1976. Periodicals: "The Tulsa Connection," Owen Edwards, *American Photographer*, Dec 1979; "Larry Clark at Robert Freidus," John Yau, *Art in America*, Dec 1979; "Proof Sheet," Jim Hughes, *Popular Photography*, Dec 1979; "Larry Clark," Allen Porter, *Camera*, Sept 1979; "The Ten 'Toughest' Photographs of 1975," Douglas Davis, *Esquire*, Feb 1976; "Personal Encounters," Gene Thornton, *The Saturday Review*, Dec 1972; "Tulsa: Death Is the Unconscious Goal," Alex Sweetman, *After-image*, Apr 1972; "Tulsa," Jim Hughes, *Camera 35*, Jan/Feb 1972.

PORTFOLIOS *Tulsa*, 1975 (Lustrum Press: New York); *Teen Lust*, 1974 (self-published: Tulsa, Okla.).

COLLECTIONS Brooklyn Mus., N.Y.; Chrysler Mus., Norfolk, Va.; ICP, NYC; IMP/GEH, Rochester; Metro. Mus. of Art, NYC; Minneapolis Inst. of Arts, Minnesota; Mt. Holyoke Coll. Art Mus., S. Hadley, Mass.; MOMA, NYC; New Orleans Mus. of Art; Philadelphia Mus. of Art, Pa.; Princeton Univ., Art Mus., New Jersey; R.I. School of Design, Art Mus., Providence; Samuel Wagstaff Cllctn., NYC; San Francisco Mus. of Modern Art; Smith Coll. Art Mus., Northampton, Mass.; St. Louis Art Mus., Mo. Australian Natl. Gall., Canberra.

DEALER Robert Freidus Gall., 158 Lafayette St, New York, NY 10013.

William Edward Clark PHOTOGRAPHER · CONTRACTOR Clark was born July 3, 1911, in Bedford County, Tennessee.

He served as a staff photographer for the *Nashville Tennessean* from 1929 to 1941 and for *Life* magazine from 1941 to 1962. Since 1964 he has presided over Clark Construction Corporation in Washington, D.C.

The photographer has specialized in political documentation, covering every Democratic and Republican presidential campaign from 1944 to 1960. He also covered the Nuremberg Trials and was the first American photographer to be admitted to Russia (1955) after Stalin's death.

PUBLICATIONS Books: *The Freedom Train*, 1976; *Days to Remember*, John Gunther & Bernard Quint, 1956. Anthology: *The Family of Man*, Edward Steichen, ed., 1955.

COLLECTION MOMA, NYC.

REPRESENTATIVES Time-Life Pictures, Time-Life Bldg, Rockefeller Ctr, New York, NY 10020; Camera Press Ltd, 400 Russell Ct, Coram St, London WC1 England.

ADDRESS 6671 MacArthur Blvd, Washington, DC 20016.

Richard C. Clarkson PHOTOGRAPHER Born August 11, 1932, in Oklahoma City, Oklahoma, Clarkson studied journalism at the University of Kansas in Lawrence in 1955.

Currently he is director of photography at *The Topeka Capital-Journal* in Topeka, Kansas, and lecturer at the School of Journalism at the University of Kansas in Lawrence. Clarkson is also a contributing contract photographer for *Sports Illustrated* in New York.

A member of ASMP, he has been education chairman since 1977, and was president in 1976 and vice-president in 1975 of the National Press Photographers Association. Clarkson was a recipient of NPPA's Sprague (1972) and Joseph Costa (1970) awards.

PUBLICATIONS Books: *Montreal '76*, w/Bill Bruns 1976; *Knight With the Hoosiers*, w/Bob Hammel, 1975; *Sooner*, w/Bill Bruns, 1974; *The Jim Ryun Story*, w/Cordner Nelson, 1967.

ADDRESS 2227 DeSousa Ct, Topeka, KS 66611.

Antoine-François-Jean Claudet PHOTOGRAPHER · BANKER · GLASS MERCHANT · INVENTOR Born in Lyons, France, in 1798; died in 1867.

Claudet worked with and later improved upon processes taught by Daguerre. Claudet was in the banking business in the years around 1819, moving into glass-making as director of a firm from about 1825 to 1838. He opened the first daguerreotype portrait studio in London with Richard Beard in 1840. In 1851 he opened his "Temple of Photography."

Of his many achievements, Claudet reduced the exposure time necessary for making daguerreotypes, and patented the use of red lighting in the darkroom. In 1841 he began the use of artificial lighting and painted backgrounds for portraiture. Claudet invented the focimenter, used to test the degree of achromatism in lenses, in 1844, and four years later invented the photographometer, a device which measures the sensitivity of a daguerreotype plate. In 1853 he patented a device that creates an illusion of movement in stereo-daguerreotype. One of England's earliest daguerreotypists, Claudet is credited with making the first daguerreotype stereographs, for which he invented many related devices and processes.

He was appointed official photographer to Queen Victoria in 1853. In 1863 he was awarded Chevalier of the Légion d'Honneur by the Emperor of France.

Working chiefly with daguerreotypes, particularly as used in stereoscope, Claudet made great use of painted backgrounds, dummied curtained windows and other props. He hand-colored much of his work, using a combination of dry color mixed with finely powdered gum. He also used calotypes, collodion wet-plate negatives, and albumen prints. His subjects were chiefly portraits, but he also did genre scenes.

PUBLICATIONS Books: *Du Stéréoscope et de ses Applications à la Photographie*, 1853 (Lerebours et Secretan: Paris); *Nouvelles Recherches sur la Différence Entre les Foyers Visuels et Photogéniques*, 1851 (Lerebours et Secretan: Paris); *Recherches sur la Theorie des Principaux Phénomènes de Photographie dans le Procédé du Daguerreotype*, 1850 (Lerebours: Paris); *History of Photography*, Josef Maria Eder, 1905, rev. 1932, repr. 1972. Anthologies: *Photography: the First Eighty Years*, P. & D. Colnaghi et al, 1976 (London); *The Photograph Collector's Guide*, Lee D. Witkin & Barbara London, 1975; *Photographing Children*, 1971; *Stereo Views: A History of Stereographs in America and Their Collection*, Wm. Culp Darrah, 1964. Periodical: "Antoine François Jean Claudet, 1797–1867," Arthur T. Gill, *Photographic Journal*, no. 107, 1967.

COLLECTIONS IMP/GEH, Rochester; several historical collections.

Lucien G. Clergue *PHOTOGRAPHER* ·
CINEMATOGRAPHER [See plate 104] Born in
Arles, France, on August 14, 1934, Clergue received a PhD in Letters from the University of
Provence, Marseille, France, in 1979. He also received a musical education, concentrating on the
violin.

Clergue currently divides his time between
teaching at the New School for Social Research
in New York City and the University of Provence
in Marseille. He has been a guest lecturer, at various times, at the Ansel Adams Workshops, Yosemite; the Friends of Photography Workshops,
Carmel; the University of Arizona, Tucson; and
UCLA, among others. His work has appeared in
such publications as *Vogue, Harper's Bazaar, Esquire, American Photographer, Camera 35, U.S.
Camera, Camera* and *Oui.*

In 1970 he founded the Recontres Internationales de la Photographie in Arles, and in 1966
Clergue was awarded the Lumière Prize.

He has been a cinematographer on several
short films and two feature-length films, *Manitas
de Plata* and *Picasso, War, Love and Peace*, both
for Universal Pictures.

Working in both black-and-white and color in
all formats, his subjects include nudes, bullfighting, landscapes, seascapes, Gypsies, the area of
Provence, Pablo Picasso, Jean Cocteau and the
poet St. John Perse.

PUBLICATIONS Monographs: *Language des
Sables*, 1980 (Agep: Marseille); *Saltimbanques*,
1980 (Agep: Marseille); *La Camargue est au bout
des Chemins*, 1978 (Agep: Marseille); *Camargue
Secrète*, 1976 (P. Belfond: Paris); *Lucien Clergue*,
1974 (Perceval: Paris). Books: *Mystique aux
Doigts*, 1976 (R. Laffont: Paris); *Genèse*, St. John
Perse, 1973 (P. Belfond: Paris); *Née de la Vague*,
1968, repr. 1978 (Belfond: Paris); *El Cordobes*,
J. M. Magnan et al., 1965 (Jeune Parque: Paris);
Birth of Aphrodite, F. G. Lorca, 1963; *Poesie der
Photographie*, w/J. M. Magnan, 1960 (Du Mont
Schauberg: Cologne); *Corps Mémorable*, Paul Elvard, 1957 (Seghers: Paris). Anthologies: *The
Photograph Collector's Guide*, Lee D. Witkin &
Barbara London, 1979; *The Picture History of
Photography*, Peter Pollack, 1958.

COLLECTIONS Art Inst. of Chicago; CCP, Tucson; Chase Manhattan Bank, NYC; L/C, Wash.,
D.C.; Metro. Mus. of Art, NYC; MOMA, NYC;
New Orleans Mus. of Art; Provincetown Art
Mus., R.I.; Ringling Mus., Sarasota, Fla.; Smithsonian Inst., Wash., D.C.; Worcester Art Mus.,
Mass. Bibliothèque Nationale, Paris; Folkwang
Mus., Essen, West Germany; Fndn. Sonja Henie,
Oslo, Norway; Israel Mus., Jerusalem; Kurstgewerbe Mus., Zurich, Switzerland; Musée Cantini, Marseille, France; Musee d'Ixelles, Brussels,
Belgium; Musée Georges Pompidou, Paris;
Musée Nicéphore Niepce, Chalon-sur-Saône;
Musée Reattu, Arles, France; Moderna Museet,
Stockholm; Munchner Mus., Munich, W. Ger.;
Oxford Coll. Gall., England; Royal Lib., Brussels,
Belgium; Royal Lib.; Copenhagen; Shadai Coll.,
Tokyo, Japan; Ulmer Mus., Ulm, West Germany;
Victoria Gall., Melbourne, Australia.

DEALERS Witkin Gall., 41 E 57 St, New York,
NY 10022; Jacques Baruch Gall., 900 N Michigan
Ave, #605, Chicago, IL 60611; G. Ray Hawkins
Gall., 7224 Melrose Ave, Los Angeles, CA 90046.

ADDRESS B.P. 84, 13632 Arles, France.

William Brooks Clift III *PHOTOGRAPHER*
Born in Boston on January 5, 1944, Clift is the
nephew of the late actor Montgomery Clift.

A self-taught freelance photographer, he has
received a Guggenheim Fellowship, an NEA
Fellowship (1972) and a commission from the
Massachusetts Arts Council (1971).

His work focuses on architecture, landscapes
and portraiture.

PUBLICATIONS Books: *Great West, Real/
Ideal*, 1977; *The Darkness and The Light: Photographs by Doris Ulmann*, ed., 1974. Anthologies: *American Images*, Renato Danese, ed.,
1979; *Court House: A Photographic Document*,
Richard Pare, ed., 1978; *Mirrors and Windows*,
John Szarkowski, 1978.

COLLECTIONS Amon Carter Mus., Fort Worth,
Tex.; Art Institute of Chicago; CCP, Tucson;
Mus. of Fine Arts, Boston; MOMA, NYC.

ADDRESS POB 6035, Santa Fe, NM 87502.

Alvin Langdon Coburn *PHOTOGRAPHER*
Born in Boston, Massachusetts, on June 11, 1882,
Coburn died November 23, 1966 in North Wales.
His early influences were his cousin, photographer Fred Holland Day, Edward Steichen, Whistler and the Impressionists. Later, works of the
ancient Japanese painter Sesshū had an impact on
him. Still later, the English Vorticists, who had
been influenced by Cubism and Futurism, affected his work.

Coburn received his first camera, a 4 x 5 Kodak
box, at age eight. By 1898 he had become a serious photographer, opening his first studio in New
York City in 1902. He worked in the Gertrude
Käsebier studio for a year and in 1904 emigrated
to London on a commission to photograph celebrities. He became a British subject in 1932. For
the years between 1910 and 1913, he traveled to
California, the Grand Canyon and New York.

Coburn became a member of the Photo-Secession in 1902 and The Linked Ring in 1903. He received an honorary fellowship from RPS in 1931. Coburn devised what he dubbed a Vortograph in 1917, a kaleidoscopic mirror apparatus that enabled him to produce what are considered by some to be the first purely abstract photographs.

A diverse photographic artist, Langdon produced the photogravure illustrations—83 plates and over 40,000 prints—for his books. His earlier years were dominated by the portraiture of the famous—Auguste Rodin, Henry James, George Bernard Shaw—as well as developing a unique style of impressionist scenes that embodied abstract forms. His later years were devoted to the purely abstract. In the catalog from his 1913 one-man show at the Goupil Gallery in London, he asked why the camera artist should not be permitted to "break away from the worn-out conventions . . . and claim the freedom of expression which any art must have to be alive?"

PUBLICATIONS Monograph: *A Portfolio of Sixteen Photographs by Alvin Langdon Coburn*, Nancy Newhall, 1962. Books: *Alvin Langdon Coburn, Photographer: An Autobiography*, Helmut & Alison Gernsheim, eds., 1966; *Edinburgh, Picturesque Notes*, Robert Louis Stevenson, 1954 (Hart-Davis: London); *More Men of Mark*, 1922 (Duckworth: London); *The Book of Harlech*, 1920 (Parry: Harlech, Wales); *London*, G. K. Chesterton, 1914 (pvt. prtg.: Minneapolis, Minn.); *Moor Park*, Rickmansworth, 1914 (Mathews: London); *Men of Mark*, 1913; *The Cloud*, Percy Bysshe Shelley, 1912; *The Door in the Wall and Other Stories*, H. G. Wells, 1911; *New York*, essay by H. G. Wells, 1910; *Mark Twain*, 1910; *London*, intro. by Hilaire Belloc, 1909; *Novels and Tales*, 24 vols., Henry James, 1907–1909; *The Intelligence of the Flowers*, Maurice Maeterlinck, 1907; *The Blue Grass Cook Book*, Minnie Fox, 1904. Anthologies: *The Photograph Collector's Guide*, Lee D. Witkin & Barbara London, 1979; *Photography Rediscovered*, David Travis & Anne Kennedy, 1979; *The Collection of Alfred Stieglitz*, Weston J. Naef, 1978; *Pictorial Photography in Britain 1900–1920*, 1978; *The Valiant Knights of Daguerre: Selected Critical Essays . . . by Sadakichi Hartmann*, Harry W. Lawton & George Know, eds., 1978; *The Julien Levy Collection*, Witkin Gall., 1977; *The Invented Eye*, Edward Lucie-Smith, 1975; *The Magic Image*, Cecil Beaton & Gail Buckland, 1975; *Camera Work: A Critical Anthology*, Jonathan Green, ed., 1973; *Looking at Photographs*, John Szarkowski, 1973; *Great Photographers*, 1971, *The Print*, 1970,

Time-Life Series; *Photographers on Photography*, Nathan Lyons, ed., 1966. Periodicals: *Camera Work*, Oct 1910, Oct 1909, Jan 1908, July 1906, Oct 1904, Apr 1904, July 1903.

PORTFOLIOS *A Limited Edition Portfolio*, intro. by William Jenkins, printed by Michaela Murphy, 1977 (Light Impressions & IMP/GEH; Rochester); *A Portfolio of 16 Photographs*, Nancy Newhall, 1962.

COLLECTIONS Art Inst. of Chicago, Ill.; Detroit Inst. of Arts, Mich.; IMP/GEH, Rochester, N.Y.; MOMA, NYC; Univ. of Kansas Mus. of Art, Lawrence; Univ. of Louisville, Photographic Archives, Ky.; Univ. of Maryland, Baltimore County Lib.; Univ. of New Mexico Art Mus., Albuquerque; New Orleans Mus. of Art; Wellesley Coll. Mus., Mass. RPS, London.

ARCHIVE IMP/GEH, Rochester.

Brian Walter Coe CURATOR Born December 27, 1930, in Cambridge, England, Coe attended University College in Hull, England, from 1949 to 1952.

He has been employed by Kodak Ltd. since 1952 in a variety of positions. Since 1969 he has been curator of the Kodak Museum. Previously he was a lecturer in the Kodak Education Service (1961–69), a lecturer for Kodak Lecture Service (1955–61), and worked for Kodak Research Laboratory (1953–55) and Kodak Standards Laboratory (1952–53).

Coe is an honorary member of New York Photo Historical Society (since 1978) and an honorary corresponding member of DGPh (since 1979). He was named a fellow of British Kinematography, Sound, and Television Society in 1973 and the Royal Society of Arts in 1980.

He made three films between 1962 and 1965, a series entitled *The Fundamentals of Film Making*.

PUBLICATIONS Books: *Cameras—From Daguerreotype to Instant Picture*, 1978 (Nordbok: England); *Colour Photography—The First Hundred Years*, 1978, *The Snapshot Photograph*, w/Paul Gates, 1977, *The Birth of Photography*, 1976 (Ash & Grant: England); *Victorian Townscape—The Work of Samuel Smith*, w/Michael Millward, 1974 (Wardlock: England); *George Eastman and the Early Photographers*, 1973 (Priory Press, England).

ADDRESS Kodak Museum, Headstone Dr., Harrow, Middlesex, England.

Alan Barry Cohen PHOTOGRAPHER · CRITIC · TEACHER Born August 28, 1943, in Harrisburg, Pennsylvania, Cohen received a BS in Nuclear

Engineering from North Carolina State University in Raleigh (1966) and an MS from Illinois Institute of Technology's Institute of Design in Chicago (1972), where he studied with Aaron Siskind, Arthur Siegel, Garry Winogrand and Charles Swedlund. He also attended the School of the Art Institute of Chicago in 1972, where he studied with Ken Josephson.

Since 1976 Cohen has taught at Columbia College in Chicago, and previously taught at Barat College in Lake Forest, Illinois (1978), Northern Virginia Community College, Alexandria (1975–76), and Illinois Institute of Technology's Institute of Design (1972–74). He worked at Argonne National Laboratory in Argonne, Illinois, from 1966 to 1969. Cohen has written criticism for *Aperture* (1876–78) and for the *Washington Star* (1979).

He belongs to CCP, VSW, GEH, CAA and Friends of Photography. Cohen won a NEA Art Critic Fellowship and an NEH Summer Seminar Fellowship in 1978.

Working in black-and-white, 35mm and 6 x 6cm formats, he chooses as his primary subjects the natural landscape and the nude. The photographer makes extensive use of electronic flash coupled to slow shutter speeds.

PUBLICATIONS Catalog: *DeuxièmeTriennale Internationale de la Photographie*, 1978 (France). Periodical: *Friends of Photography Newsletter*, July 1979.

COLLECTIONS Art Inst. of Chicago; CIBA-GEIGY Corporate Art Cllctn., Ardsley, N.Y.,; Corcoran Gall. of Art, Wash., D.C.; Ill. Inst. of Tech., Chicago; IMP/GEH, Rochester; Smithsonian Inst., Wash., D.C.; Univ. of Louisville, Ky. Bibliothèque Nationale, Paris; Musée d'art et d'histoire, Fribourg, Switzerland.

ADDRESS 5825 S Dorchester Ave, Chicago, IL 60637.

Joan Lebold Cohen ART HISTORIAN · PHOTOGRAPHER Born in Highland Park, Illinois, on August 19, 1932, Cohen received her AB from Smith College, Northampton, Mass., in 1954. Since 1960 she has studied Asian art and culture informally at the University of California, Berkeley, and at Harvard University, Cambridge, Mass. She considers her Asian art studies to be the most important influence on her work.

Since 1979 Cohen has been a freelance photographer and writer in Beijing, China. Previous to that time she lectured in Art History at Tufts University, Medford, Massachusetts (since 1968). From 1965 to 1972 she was a gallery instructor in the Department of Public Education at the Mu-

seum of Fine Arts, Boston, and from 1955 to 1956 was registrar at the Corcoran Gallery of Art in Washington, D.C. Cohen assisted with the slide and photograph collections of the Yale University Department of Fine Arts, New Haven, Connecticut, in 1954–55.

Cohen has been on the Smith College Alumnae Quarterly Editorial Board since 1978 and on the college's Museum of Art Visiting Committee since 1974. She is also on the board of directors of the Artists' Foundation in Massachusetts.

Cohen created shows for the television programs "Images" (WGBH-TV, Boston, 1965–66) and "Classroom 5" (WHDH-TV, 1966). She also produced filmstrips on "Art and Politics in China 1978" for Mass Communications, Inc., Westport, Connecticut.

Cohen describes her work as "mountain mist photographs in the manner of Chinese and Japanese painting." She also photographs the people of Asia and does photojournalism for newspapers and magazines.

PUBLICATIONS Books: *Angkor, Monuments of the God-Kings*, w/Bela Kalman, 1975; *China Today and Her Ancient Treasures*, w/Jerome Alan Cohen, 1974; *Buddha*, illus. by Mary Frank, 1969.

PORTFOLIO *Mountain Mists*, 1980 (Daniel Wolf Press, Inc, New York).

COLLECTIONS Harvard Univ. Law School, Cambridge, Mass.; Smith College Mus. of Art, Northampton, Mass.; and private collections.

REPRESENTATIVES Photo Researchers, 60 E 56 St, New York, NY; Daniel Wolf Press, Inc., 30 W 57 St, New York, NY; Art Asia, 8 Newbury St, Boston, MA.

ADDRESS c/o Coudert Brothers, 20 Chater Rd, Alexandra House, Hong Kong.

Joyce Tenneson Cohen PHOTOGRAPHER · AUTHOR Born May 29, 1945, in Boston, Massachusetts, Cohen earned a BA in 1967 from Regis College, Weston, Massachusetts, an MA from George Washington University, Washington, D.C., in 1969, and a PhD in 1978 from Union Graduate School, Antioch College, Yellow Springs, Ohio.

An associate professor of art at Northern Virginia Community College, Annandale, since 1970, she has also taught at the Corcoran School of Art in Washington, D.C., since 1978 and at the Smithsonian Institution in 1979. She belongs to SPE and CAA.

PUBLICATION Anthology: *In-Sights: Self-Portraits by Women*, ed., 1978.

COLLECTIONS Corcoran Gall. of Art, Wash.,

D.C.; L/C, Wash., D.C.; Smithsonian Inst., Wash., D.C. Bibliothèque Nationale, Paris.

DEALER Marcuse Pfeifer Gall., 825 Madison Ave, New York, NY 10022.

ADDRESS 1915 Biltmore St NW, Washington, DC 20009.

Lynne Cohen PHOTOGRAPHER · TEACHER · FILMMAKER Born in 1944, Cohen attended Slade School of Art of the University College, London (1964–65), and Ox-Bow Summer School of Painting in Saugatuck, Michigan (1964–65), then went on to receive a BS in Fine Arts and Art Education at the University of Wisconsin, Madison (1967). She earned an MA in Fine Art (1968) from Eastern Michigan University, Ypsilanti, and also studied at the University of Michigan, Ann Arbor (1968).

Currently an instructor at University of Ottawa, Canada (since 1974), Cohen also taught at Algonquin College (1973–75) and at Eastern Michigan University (1968–73).

Cohen won grants from the Canada Council in 1979 (Arts), 1978 (Travel), and 1975 (Project Cost). She received an Ontario Arts Council Special Projects Grant in 1978.

PUBLICATIONS Anthologies: *The Female Eye*, 1975 (Natl. Film Board of Can.: Ottawa); *The Photographers' Choice*, Kelly Wise, ed., 1975. Periodicals: *Photo Communiqué*, Sept-Oct 1979; *Art Magazine*, May/June 1979; review, Penny Cousineau, *Arts Canada*, Sept 1978; *Creative Camera*, Apr 1978.

COLLECTIONS Art Inst. of Chicago; IMP/GEH, Rochester; Light Work Gall., Syracuse, N.Y.; New Orleans Art Mus., La.; Univ. of N. Mex. Art Mus., Albuquerque. Bibliothèque Nationale, Paris. In Canada: Art Bank; Dept. of External Affairs, Ottawa, Ontario; Edmonston Art Gall., Alberta; Mt. Allison Univ., Sackville, New Brunswick; Natl. Film Board of Canada, Ottawa; Natl. Gall. of Canada, Ottawa; Natl. Pub. Archives of Canada, Ottawa; Walter Phillips Gall., Banff, British Columbia.

DEALERS Witkin Gall., 41 E 57 St, New York, NY 10022; Yajima Gall., 1434 Sherbrooke St W, Montreal, Quebec H36 1K4, Canada; Yarlow/Salzman Gall., 211 Avenue Rd, Toronto, Ontario, Canada.

ADDRESS 90 Wilbrod, University of Ottawa, Ottawa, Ontario KIN 6N5, Canada.

Mark Cohen PHOTOGRAPHER Born August 24, 1943, in Wilkes-Barre, Pennsylvania, Cohen studied at Pennsylvania State University, Uni-

versity Park (1961–63), and at Wilkes College, Wilkes-Barre, Pennsylvania (1963–65).

A self-employed photographer since 1967, Cohen has also taught photography at Princeton University, Princeton, New Jersey (1975), Wilkes College (1973–77) and Kings College, Wilkes-Barre (1968–72).

Cohen won Guggenheim Fellowships in 1971 and 1976 and an NEA Photographer's Fellowship in 1975.

PUBLICATIONS Books: *Photography in America*, Robert Doty, ed., 1975; *Vision and Expression*, Nathan Lyons, ed., 1968. Anthologies: *The Photograph Collector's Guide*, Lee D. Witkin & Barbara London, 1979; *Faces*, Ben Maddow, ed., 1977. Periodicals: *Modern Photography*, Nov 1979; reviews, Sally Eauclaire, June 1979, Andy Grundberg, Mar 1976, *Art in America*; article, Carol Squiers, Mar 1978, review, James Collins, Mar 1974, *Artforum*; *Camera*, Nov 1977; "Persistance of a Vision," Kenneth Poli, *Popular Photography*, Apr 1977; *Creative Camera Yearbook*, Peter Turner, ed., 1976 (London); "Mark Cohen's Works," Dennis Longwell, *Camera Mainichi*, Oct 1974.

COLLECTIONS Art Inst. of Chicago; Hofstra Univ., Emily Lowe Gall., Hempstead, N.Y.; Harvard Univ., Fogg Art Mus., Cambridge; IMP/GEH, Rochester; Minneapolis Inst. of Arts, Minn.; MOMA, NYC; Seagram Cllctn., NYC; Univ. of Mass., Amherst; Univ. of N. Mex. Art Mus., Albuquerque. Arts Council of Great Britain, London; Australian Natl. Gall., Canberra, New South Wales; Natl. Gall. of Canada, Ottawa, Ontario; Natl. Gall. of Victoria, Melbourne, Australia.

ADDRESS 32 W South St, Wilkes-Barre, PA 18702.

Van Deren Coke TEACHER · PHOTOGRAPHER · MUSEUM DIRECTOR · PHOTOHISTORIAN Born in Lexington, Kentucky, on July 1, 1921, Coke studied photography with Ansel Adams and Nicholas Haz. He received his BA from the University of Kentucky in 1956 and his MFA from Indiana University in 1958. He also undertook postgraduate studies at Harvard University in 1957–58.

Currently director of the Department of Photography at the San Francisco Museum of Modern Art, Coke was director of the Art Museum and professor of art at the University of New Mexico from 1962 to 1966 and 1973 to 1979. From 1963 to 1970 he also chaired the university's Department of Art. Coke was deputy director (1970–71) and director (1971–72) of the

International Museum of Photography at George Eastman House in Rochester, N.Y. In 1961–62 he was an associate professor at Arizona State University.

A member of CAA and SPE, Coke was on the board of directors of the former from 1975 to 1978 and of the latter from 1963 to 1965. He received awards in the following competitions: *Photography International*, 1955, 1956, 1957; *Modern Photography*, 1956; *U.S. Camera*, 1957, 1958, 1960; and *Art in America* "New Talent USA," 1960. He won research grants from the University of New Mexico in 1972–76 and a Guggenheim Fellowship in 1975.

Coke's photography is "in the surreal mode." As a historian of art and photography, he specializes in twentieth-century photography, American art and the influence of photography on painting.

PUBLICATIONS   Books: *Photography in New Mexico: From the Daguerreotype to the Present*, 1979, *One Hundred Years of Photographic History*, ed., 1975, *The Painter and the Photograph: From Delacroix to Warhol*, 1974, *Light and Substance*, 1974 (Univ. of N. Mex. Press; Albuquerque). Catalogs: *Fabricated to be Photographed*, 1980 (San Francisco Museum of Modern Art); *Photographs, Photographically Illustrated Books and Albums in University of New Mexico Libraries 1843–1933*, 1977, *Nineteenth Century Photographs from the Collection*, 1976, *Young Photographers*, 1968 (Univ. of N. Mex. Art Mus.: Albuquerque). Anthology: *The Photograph Collector's Guide*, Lee D. Witkin & Barbara London, 1979.

COLLECTIONS   Addison Gall. of Amer. Art, Andover, Mass.; Arizona State Univ. Cllctn. of Amer. Art, Tempe; Denver Art Museum; IMP/GEH, Rochester; MOMA, NYC; San Francisco Mus. of Modern Art; Sheldon Memorial Art Gall., Lincoln, Neb.; Smithsonian Inst., Wash., D.C.; Univ. of Kentucky Art Mus., Lexington; Univ. of New Mexico Art Mus., Albuquerque. Bibliothèque Nationale, Paris; Natl. Gall. of Canada, Ottawa, Ontario.

ADDRESS   San Francisco Museum of Modern Art, McAllister St at Van Ness Ave, San Francisco, CA 94102.

A. D. (Allan Douglass) Coleman   CRITIC · LECTURER · TEACHER   Born in New York City, Coleman majored in English literature obtaining a BA from Hunter College in the Bronx, New York (1964). In 1967 he completed an MA in the same subject and in creative writing at San Francisco State College. He was mainly influenced by the works of William Ivins, Marshall McLuhan, Minor White and Ralph Hattersley.

As of this writing he was holding several positions in New York City: he has been contributing editor for *Camera 35* since 1976, vice-president of the Photography Media Institute since 1977, photography instructor at New York University's Department of Film and Television since 1978 and since 1979 he has also been on the faculty of the New School for Social Research, where he had taught from 1969 to 1971. Before that he worked as a columnist for the *New York Times* (1970–74) and the *Village Voice* (1968–73).

He has been a member of SPE since 1972. In 1976 he received an NEA Art Critic's Fellowship and, in the same year, founded and organized a conference on photography criticism.

A. D. Coleman specializes in "freelance critical writing on photography directed toward a general audience, with specific pertinence to photographers, photography teachers and students and educators in all fields."

PUBLICATIONS   Monographs: *Confirmation*, 1975; *Carbon Copy*, 1973. Books (text only): *Light Readings*, 1979; *Lee/Model/Parks/Samaras/Turner: Five Interviews Before the Fact*, 1979; *The Grotesque in Photography*, 1977; *Edward S. Curtis: Portraits from North American Indian Life*, 1972.

ADDRESS   465 Van Duzer St, Staten Island, NY 10304.

Henry Keith Howard Hobbs Collie   PHOTOGRAPHER   Born July 21, 1948, in London, England, Collie earned an MA in 1973 from Royal College of Art, London.

A freelance photographer, he won scholarships from *Vogue* and *Telegraph* magazines in 1974.

PUBLICATIONS   Periodicals: *Camera*, Sept 1978, Apr 1978, Apr 1975.

COLLECTIONS   UCLA. Amsterdam Mus., The Netherlands; Bibliothèque Nationale, Paris; Victoria & Albert Mus., London.

DEALER   Robert Herschkowitz, 5 Kynance Mews, London SW7, England.

ADDRESS   2A Seagrave Rd, W Brompton, London SW6, England.

Norman B. Colp   PHOTOGRAPHER · BOOK MAKER · CURATOR   Born September 3, 1944, in the Bronx, New York, Colp earned a BA in Art from Queens College, Flushing, New York, in 1967. He also studied at Pratt Institute in Brooklyn, New York, and at Parsons School of Design in New York City. Colp names Eadweard Muy-bridge and Duane Michals as major influences.

Colp was curator at the Alternative Center for International Arts, in New York City from October 1979 to March 1980. He was a gallery assistant for the Greengrass Media Art Gallery in New York City in 1975–76 and for The Once Gallery in New York City from 1974 to 1975. In 1973 Colp served as curatorial assistant and exhibit coordinator for the Queens Museum in Flushing.

His photography deals with "the compression of time and documents that which we usually see daily but never take the opportunity to observe." Using black-and-white, color, and hand-coloring, he currently employs several display formats—small-scale flipbooks, wall-mounted portfolio books, and casebound books.

PUBLICATIONS Monographs (self-published): *Steam: My View from P.S. 1*, 1978; *The Last Hundred Acres*, 1978.

COLLECTIONS MOMA Lib. of Bookworks, NYC; Otis Art Inst. Lib., Los Angeles; 2nd St. Gall., Charlottesville, Va.

DEALER O. K. Harris, 383 W Broadway, New York, NY 10012.

ADDRESS 126 W 83 St, New York, NY 10024.

Eduardo Comesaña PHOTOJOURNALIST·PRESS AGENCY DIRECTOR Born in Buenos Aires on March 14, 1940, Comesaña completed a master's degree in film-making at La Plata University School of Fine Arts in 1962. A technically self-taught photographer, he held a deep appreciation during his formative years for the works of Henri Cartier-Bresson, Ansel Adams and W. Eugene Smith.

Since 1977 he has been working as a freelance photographer and founded a picture agency representing various foreign agencies such as Camera Press in London and Black Star and Pictorial Parade in New York. Previously he was employed as a staff photographer for the following magazines in Buenos Aires: *Primera Plana* (1964–66), *Confirmado* (1966–68) and *Editorial Abril* (1968–77).

Since 1964 he has been a member of the Asociación de Reporteros Gráficos de la Argentina for which he served as a vice-president during the year 1970-71. In 1979 he was a founding member of the Consejo Argentino de Fotografía. He also belongs to the following American societies: ASMP, SPE and Friends of Photography.

In 1972 he received the S.I.P-Mergenthaler Award in Photography in Miami and, in 1970, won the ADEPA-RIZZUTO First Prize in Photojournalism in Buenos Aires.

Comesaña specializes in journalistic and documentary work, and in candid portraits of famous people, all of which he executes in both black-and-white and color. He uses an unobstrusive small-camera technique.

PUBLICATIONS Periodicals: *Foco*, 1979; *Siete Días Ilustrados*, 1976; *Diafragma*, 1976; *Fotografía Universal*, 1970–71.

PORTFOLIO *Fotos Poco Conocidas de Gente Muy Conocida*, 1972 (Fondo Nacional de las Artes: Buenos Aires).

ADDRESS Casilla de Carrero 141, Suc. 26, 1426 Buenos Aires, Argentina.

Brian Condron PHOTOGRAPHER Born November 23, 1949, in Toronto, Ontario, Canada, Condron earned a photography diploma from Sheridan College, Oakville, Ontario, in 1971 and a BFA from York University, Toronto, in 1976.

Currently a photography instructor at Sir Sandford Fleming College, Lindsay, Ontario, he has won awards from the Ontario Arts Council in 1972, 1973, 1975 and 1976, and Canada Council Arts awards in 1976 and 1978.

Working in small format, Condron produces photographs of "social realism/irony." He has done a series on contemporary tourist reactions to Niagara Falls which has been described as "humorous and socially revealing."

PUBLICATIONS Catalog: *Exposure: Canadian Contemporary Photography*, 1975 (Gage Publishing: Toronto). Periodicals: review, Gary Michael Dault, *Saturday Night Magazine*, Jan/Feb 1978; "Photographs from Niagara Falls," *Impressions*, no. 22/23, 1979.

COLLECTIONS Art Bank, The Canada Council, Ottawa, Ontario; Natl. Film Board of Canada, Ottawa; Natl. Photography Cllctn., Pub. Archives, Ottawa; Ontario Arts Council, Toronto.

ADDRESS 123 Braemar Ave, Toronto, Ontario, Canada M5P 2L3.

Nancy Ford Cones PHOTOGRAPHER [See plate 38] Born September 11, 1869, in Milan, Ohio, Cones died January 3, 1962, in Loveland, Ohio. Her husband, James Cones (1861–1939), was a darkroom technician. Nancy learned retouching at a studio in Fostoria, Indiana, in 1895.

With her family, Nancy Ford settled in Indiana, where her father bought her a half-interest in a studio in Mechanicsburg. She returned to the family homesite of Lebanon in 1897 and met James Cones, a self-taught photographer, whom she married three years later. Together they bought a photo studio in Covington and for five years did mostly commercial and portrait work.

In 1905 they moved to a small farm near Loveland, Ohio, and remained there for the rest of their lives. James meticulously printed Nancy's photographs by the tedious gum-bichromate process and, when he died in 1939, she gave up photography except for occasional work in color slides. Her work was widely exhibited, including the London Salon of Photography Exhibitions in 1912 and 1928 and the First Rochester International Salon of Photography in 1920.

A member of the Women's Art Club of Loveland, Cones won numerous awards, including the Grand Prize at *Photo-Era*'s 1907 competition, and second place in Kodak's Progress Competition in 1902 and Bausch & Lomb's photography contest in 1903. In 1905 she won second place in the Souvenir Kodak Competition—a contest of 28,000 entrants in which first prize went to Edward Steichen and third to Alfred Stieglitz.

Her photographs, of which 15,000 glass plates and 3,000 gum prints remain, are mostly portraits of rural life, allegorical studies, "fairy tales," and illustrations of literary characters. "Personality—both the photographer's and her subjects—is a translucent, almost transparent ingredient in her photographs," writes James D. Scott (*Cincinnati Enquirer*, Nov 9, 1980). "Many of her pictures, in fact, are nakedly sentimental."

PUBLICATIONS Book: *Complete Self-Instructing Library of Practical Photography*, vol. 5, 1908. Catalog: *The Pictorial Work of the Royal Photographic Society*, 71st Annual Exhibition, 1929 (RPS: London). Periodicals: *Camera Craft*, Dec 1930, July 1926, Sept 1921, July 1921, May 1919, Apr 1919; "Why I Am a Pictorial Photographer," June 1930, "First Rochester International Salon of Photography," A. H. Beardsley, Apr 1930, "The Story of an Unopened Package," A. H. Beardsley, Nov 1928, article, Apr 1920, article, Mar 1914, article, Nov 1912, "The Eastman Advertising Competition," Malcolm Dean Miller, Feb 1911, article, May 1909, "Our Annual Contest," Wilfred A. French, Feb 1908, article, Jan 1904, *Photo-Era Magazine*; "Types in Photography," Dec 1929, "Art in Photography," Feb 1919, both by Elizabeth K. White, *Cincinnati Fine Arts Journal*; article, Aug 1929, "American Work at the London Exhibitions," Dec 1927, "The Development of Pictorial Photography in the United States," Paul L. Anderson, June 1914, *American Photography*; *The Camera*, Aug 1929, Dec 1913; *Revue du Vrai et du Beau*, Feb 25, 1928; *National Geographic*, Nov 1923; *Camera*, Feb 1923; *American Annual of Photography*, 1921, 1920, 1919; "The Exploits of Women in Photography," Leslie Curlis, *Abel's Photographic*

Weekly, July 3, 1915; Nancy Ford Cones, "The Work and Personality of a Remarkable Woman," Sigismund Blumann, *Wilson's Photographic Magazine*, Nov 1914; *Country Life in America*, June 1914, Sept 1, 1911; *Photograms of the Year*, 1910, 1908, 1907; *The Youth's Companion*, 1906, 1905, Dec 1903; "Genre Photography," J. P. Chalmers, *Camera and Dark Room*, Jan/Dec 1906; *Woman's Home Companion*, Feb 1904; *Browning's Magazine*, 1902.

REPRESENTATIVE Walt Burton Galls., 344 W 4 St, Cincinnati, OH 45202.

Gregory Conniff PHOTOGRAPHER Born May 3, 1944, Conniff earned a BA in government (1966) from Columbia University in New York City and an LLB (1969) from the University of Virginia School of Law in Charlottesville. He did postgraduate study at Montclair State Teachers College in New Jersey (1969), an independent apprenticeship with William Weege at Jones Road Print Shop in Barneveld, Wisconsin (1971), and studied typography and book design with Walter Hamady at the University of Wisconsin Graduate School of Art, Madison (1977).

Currently a self-employed photographer, Conniff practiced law from 1972 to 1978. He was a VISTA volunteer with Lawyers Committee for Civil Rights in Atlanta, Georgia, in 1969–70.

Conniff received Wisconsin Arts Board grants in 1979, 1977 and 1976, and a Fellowship in Photography from the Board in 1979.

PUBLICATIONS Catalog: *Gregory Conniff*, Jane Livingston, 1979 (Corcoran Gall. of Art: Wash., D.C.). Periodicals: "Gregory Conniff," summer 1980, *Art in America*; "Visual Metaphysics," Jim Sullivan, Dec 1979, "Inviting Invitational," Robert Muffoletto, Mar 1979, *Wisconsin Photographer*.

COLLECTIONS CCP, Tucson; Corcoran Gall. of Art, Wash., D.C.; High Mus. of Art, Atlanta, Ga.; Madison Art Ctr., Wis.; Milwaukee Art Ctr., Wis.; MOMA, NYC; Mus. of Fine Arts, Baltimore, Md.; Mus. of Fine Arts, Boston; Toledo Mus., Ohio.

ADDRESS 218 State St, Madison, WI 53703.

Linda Connor PHOTOGRAPHER · TEACHER Born in New York in 1944, Connor obtained a BFA from Rhode Island School of Design in 1967 and an MS in Photography from the Institute of Design at Illinois Institute of Technology in 1969. Right after completion of her graduate degree she was hired as instructor by San Francisco Art Institute, where she is still teaching and acted as co-chairperson of the Photography Department (1973–75). Concurrently she held temporary teaching appointments at California College of Arts & Crafts (summer 1970; spring 1973), the Extension Program of the University of California at Berkeley (1973) and the School of the Museum of Fine Arts in Boston (fall 1978). She was the recipient of several grants: a Guggenheim Fellowship (1979), an A.T.T. Photography Project Grant (1978), an NEA Individual Grant (1976) and a UCLA Faculty Grant (1973).

PUBLICATIONS (selected) Monograph: *Solos*, 1979. Anthologies: *American Images*, 1979; *Mirrors and Windows*, John Szarkowski, 1978; *Darkroom*, 1977; *Photography*, 1976; *Light and Substance*, 1974; *Private Realities*, 1974; *Light and Lens*, 1973 (Morgan & Morgan); *Be-ing Without Clothes*, Minor White, ed., 1970; *Vision and Expression*, 1969. Periodical: *Creative Camera*, 1971.

PORTFOLIOS *New Californians*, group, 1979; *Under Wear*, 1976 (Art Inst. of Chicago); *Apeiron Portfolio #1*, group, 1974.

COLLECTIONS Art Inst. of Chicago; Boston Mus. of Fine Arts; CCP, Tucson; Crocker Art Gall., Sacramento, Calif.; Dallas Mus. of Fine Arts; IMP/GEH, Rochester; Harvard Univ., Fogg Art Mus., Cambridge; Home Savings & Loans; MOMA, NYC; Mus. of Fine Arts, Houston; New Orleans Mus. of Art; Polaroid Corp. Collctn.; R.I. School of Design, Providence; San Francisco Mus. of Modern Art; J. B. Speed Art Mus., Louisville, Ky.; Stanford Art Mus., Calif.; Univ. of N. Mex. Mus., Albuquerque; Va. Mus. of Fine Arts, Richmond; VSW, Rochester; Yale Art Mus., New Haven, Conn. Musée Réattu, Arles, France; Natl. Gall. of Canada; Ryerson Inst., Canada; Victoria & Albert Mus., London.

REPRESENTATIVE Light Gall., 724 Fifth Ave, New York, NY 10019.

ADDRESS 1007 Haight St, San Francisco, CA 94117.

Ron Cooper PHOTOGRAPHER · PAINTER · GRAPHIC ARTIST Born on July 24, 1943, in New York City, Cooper attended the Chouinard Art Institute in Los Angeles from 1962 to 1964. From 1979 through 1980 he was a lecturer at the Art Center College of Design in Pasadena, California. Previously he lectured at the Otis Art Institute in Los Angeles (1978), at UCLA (1977), and at Claremont College in Claremont, California (1976).

He is a member of the Los Angeles Chapter of the Artist Equity Association and serves on their board of directors. He has been the recipient of several awards: one grant in photography (1979) and one in painting (1970) from NEA, a Theo-

doran Purchase Award from the Guggenheim Museum in New York (1971) and a Young Talent Purchase Grant from the Los Angeles County Museum of Art (1968).

His achievements in other media include a 16mm motion picture entitled *Ball Drop* (1969) and a sculpture, "Floating Volume of Light," completed in 1971.

Cooper's work "has been focused on two main ideas: the first is concerned with the manipulation of light; the second is maintaining the obvious characteristics of the material or process."

COLLECTIONS Art Inst., Chicago; Atlantic Richfield Corp., Los Angeles; Guggenheim Mus., NYC; Los Angeles County Mus. of Art; Security Pacific Natl. Bank, Los Angeles; Whitney Mus. of American Art, NYC. Neue Galerie, Aachen, West Germany; Kaiser Wilhelm Mus., Krefeld, West Germany; Stedelijk Mus., Amsterdam, The Netherlands.

DEALER Rosamund Felsen Gall., Los Angeles, CA 90069; Maggie Kress Gall., Taos, NM 87571.

ADDRESS Ron Cooper Studio, 1310 Main St, Venice, CA 90291.

Ruffin Cooper, Jr. PRINTMAKER · PHOTOGRAPHER Born January 4, 1942, in Washington, D.C., Cooper earned a BFA in 1964 from Boston University and studied at the San Francisco Art Institute in 1975.

A self-employed artist, he photographs abstract details of architecture, monuments and landscapes, producing 32 x 48 and 48 x 72 color prints.

PUBLICATIONS Periodicals: *Art Insight*, May/Jun 1979; *Popular Photography*, Dec 1974.

COLLECTIONS Bank of America; Chase Manhattan Bank; Gilman Paper Co.; IBM; Manufacturer's Hanover Trust; Metro. Life Insurance; Pennsoil.

DEALERS Lonny Gans, 21 Market St, Venice, CA 90291; O. K. Harris Gall., 383 W Broadway, New York, NY 10012.

ADDRESS 285 Chestnut St, Telegraph Hill, San Francisco, CA 94133.

Thomas Joshua Cooper PHOTOGRAPHER · TEACHER · CRITIC Born December 19, 1946, Cooper earned a BA in 1969 from Humboldt State University in Arcata, California, and an MA in Photography from the University of New Mexico, Albuquerque, in 1972. As of this writing he is an MFA candidate at the University of New Mexico.

Cooper was most recently a visiting assistant professor of art at Humboldt State University, and previously taught workshops at Sheffield Polytechnic of Sheffield, England (1975–79). From 1973 to 1976 he was course director for photographic studies and senior lecturer in photography and the history of photography at Trent Polytechnic in Nottingham, England.

Named a photography bursar (1976–77) for the Arts Council of Great Britain, Cooper won an NEA Photographer's Fellowship in 1978. In 1976 he co-wrote "Paul Strand—An Appreciation" for the BBC television program *Arena*.

Concerned with early primitive myths and rituals from North America and the British Isles, the photographer states that his photographs "are meditations."

PUBLICATIONS Anthologies: *Contemporary Images of Derbyshire*, James Hadfield, ed., 1979 (Derbyshire Festival Pub.: England); *Dialogue with Photography*, w/Paul Hill, 1979 (from "21 interviews w/Masters of Photography," first pub. in *Camera* 1975–79); *Photography in New Mexico*, Van Deren Coke, 1979 (Univ. of N. Mex. Press: Albuquerque); *Perspectives on Landscape —British Image 5*, Bill Gaskins, ed., 1978 (Arts Council of Great Britain: London). Catalogs: *Three Perspectives on Photography—Recent Photography in Britain*, 1979 (Arts Council of Great Britain: London); *Critics Choice*, John McEwen, 1978 (Inst. of Contemporary Arts: London); *Photomiscellany—120 Years of International Photographic History*, Angus Stokes, 1978 (Angus Stokes Gall.: Derbyshire, England); *Other Eyes*, 1976 (Arts Council of Great Britain: London); *Open Photography*, 1976 (Nottingham, England); *New Photography*, 1974 (Nottingham, England); *University of New Mexico Photographs*, 1970 (Univ. of N. Mex. Press: Albuquerque). Periodicals: review, John McEwen, *Arts Canada*, Feb/Mar 1978; *British Journal of Photography Annual*, 1978, 1976; article, Oct 7, 1977, review, Aug 5, 1977, "Paul Strand—An Appreciation," w/Paul Hill, Feb 13, 1976, *British Journal of Photography*; review, *Arts Review*, Sept 30, 1977; *Nye Foto*, July 1977; *U.S. Camera Annual*, 1977; review, *Popular Photography*, Nov 1976; *Fotografia Italiana*, Oct 1976; *Nueva Lente*, July/Aug 1976; *Camera*, Jan 1975; "Can British Photography Emerge from the Dark Ages?" w/Paul Hill, Sept 1974, Aug 1974, *Creative Camera*.

COLLECTIONS CCP, Tucson; College of the Redwoods, Eureka, Calif.; Humboldt State Univ., Arcata, Calif.; Monterey Peninsula Mus., Monterey, Calif.; Oakland Mus., Calif.; State Mus. of Fine Art, Santa Fe, N. Mex.; Univ. of N. Mex. Fine Art Mus., Albuquerque; Sam Wagstaff Cllctn., NYC, Arts Council of Great Britain, London; Bibliothèque Nationale, Paris; Natl. Gall. of Can., Ottawa; Open Univ., London; Trent Polytechnic, Nottingham, England; Victoria & Albert Mus., London.

ADDRESS POB 265, Arcata, CA 95521.

Pierre Cordier PHOTOGRAPHER · CINEMATOGRAPHER · TEACHER Born January 28, 1933, in Brussels, Belgium, Cordier studied with Otto Steinert in Saarbrücken, Germany, in 1958.

Since 1965 Cordier has been a teacher at the Ecole Nationale Supérieure d'Arts Visuels in Brussels.

He has been a member of the DGPh since 1971. On March 25, 1963, Cordier invented the "photochemigram," and on November 10, 1956, invented the "chemi-gram." Films Cordier created are *Start*, with Marc Lobet, 35mm (1974), *Chimigrammes*, 35mm (1963), Ministery of Culture, Belgium, and *Chimigrammes*, 16mm (1962), France.

PUBLICATIONS Books: *Photography without a Camera*, Patra Holter, 1972; *Selbstporträts*, Otto Steinert, 1961. Anthologies: *Time-Life Photography Year*, 1979; *The Picture History of Photography*, Peter Pollack, 1969. Periodicals: *Zoom*, June 1979 (Paris), Mar 1975 (Paris); *Progresso Fotografico*, Nov 1978; *Modern Photography*, Sept 1976; *Camera*, Dec, Feb 1975, Oct 1972, May, Feb 1971, Oct 1958; *Foto*, Sept 1970 (The Netherlands).

COLLECTIONS CCP, Tucson; Harvard Univ., Fogg Art Mus., Cambridge; IMP/GEH, Rochester; MOMA, NYC; Univ. of Austin, Gernsheim Cllctn., Texas. Bibliothèque Nationale, Paris; Folkwang Mus., Essen, Germany. In Belgium: Ministère de la Culture; Musée d'Ixelles; Musées Royaux des Beaux-Arts de Belgique; Sterckshof Mus., Antwerp.

DEALERS Galerie Paule Pia, Kammenstraat 57, B-2000 Antwerp, Belgium; Galerie d'Art Actuel Anne Van Horenbeeck, chausée de Charleroi 183, B-1060, Brussels, Belgium.

ADDRESS rue Reigersvliet 20, B-1040, Brussels, Belgium.

Jane Corkin GALLERY OWNER AND DIRECTOR Born December 14, 1949, in the United States, Corkin earned a BA in Art History and Political Science from Queen's University, Kingston, Ontario, Canada (1971). She also studied Venetian Settecento art in Venice, Italy, in the summer of 1969 (through the University of British Columbia) under Professor George Knox, and she studied Italian Renaissance art with Professor

Michael McCarthy (through the University of Toronto) in Rome, Florence, Venice and Milan during the summer of 1968.

Currently the owner and director of Jane Corkin Gallery in Toronto (since 1978), she taught at the Banff School of Fine Arts in 1979. From 1975 to 1978 she directed the Photography Department of David Mirvish Gallery, and from 1973 to 1975 she was a photographer and assistant to the director at the Mirvish Gallery. She was a freelance commercial photographer from 1970 to 1977. Corkin is a trustee of the Canadian Centre of Photography and Film (since 1979).

ADDRESS   Jane Corkin Gall., 144 Front St W, Suite 620, Toronto, Ontario M5J 1G2, Canada.

James H. Cornfield   *PHOTOGRAPHER · WRITER*
Born on November 6, 1945, in Chicago, Illinois, Cornfield completed a bachelor's degree at the University of California at Los Angeles in 1967. He was influenced by Bert Stern and Lawrence Schiller, with whom he worked in 1974 and 1975, also by Anthony Edgeworth and Irving Penn.

He worked as a feature editor for *Petersen's Photographic Magazine* (1972–75), served on the Editorial Advisory Board of *Horizon Magazine* in New York, and was director of photography for *East/West Network* in Los Angeles (1975–78); since 1978, he has been freelancing. He has been a member of ASMP since 1976.

Cornfield works in all formats and specializes in editorial, portrait, industrial and commercial-product photography.

PUBLICATIONS   Books: *Petersen's Guide to Electronic Flash Photography*, incl. text, 1975; *Bert Stern: the Photo Illustration*, text only, 1974. Periodicals: *Popular Photography Annual*, 1976, 1979.

PORTFOLIO   *Fat Tuesday*, 1976 (Wm. Dailey Pub.: Los Angeles).

ADDRESS   13836 Bora Bora Way, # 111, Marina Del Rey, CA 90291.

Carlotta M. Corpron   *PHOTOGRAPHER   · TEACHER*   Born on December 9, 1901, in Blue Earth, Minnesota, Corpron completed an MSc at East Michigan State University in Ypsilanti in 1925 and, the following year, an MA from Columbia University in New York City. In 1944 she studied photography with Gyorgy Kepes.

She taught art at the following institutions: Huntington College in Montgomery, Alabama (1926–28), the University of Cincinnati in Ohio (1928–35) and Texas Women's University in

Denton (1935–67). She is a member of the National Retired Teachers Association.

The artist is particularly interested in the study of light and specializes in experimental and abstract photography.

PUBLICATIONS   Anthology: *Recollections: 10 Women in Photography*, by Margaretta K. Mitchell, 1979. Catalogs: *Works on Paper*, by Robert Murdoch, 1978 (Dallas Mus. of Fine Arts); *Women of Photography*, Mann & Naggle, eds., 1975 (San Francisco Mus. of Art).

COLLECTIONS   Amon Carter Mus., Fort Worth, Tex.; Art Inst. of Chicago; CCP, Tucson; Dallas Mus. of Fine Arts; MOMA, NYC; Mus. of Fine Arts, St. Petersburg, Fla.; New Orleans Mus. of Art; San Francisco Mus. of Art.

DEALER   Marcuse Pfeifer Gall., 825 Madison Ave, New York, NY 10021.

ADDRESS   206 Forest, Denton, TX 76201.

Marie Cosindas   *PHOTOGRAPHER*   Born in Boston, Massachusetts, in 1925, Cosindas attended the Modern School of Fashion Design in Boston and the Boston Museum School. She also studied with Paul Caponigro (1961), Ansel Adams (1962) and Minor White (1963–64).

A freelance photographer, Cosindas won a Guggenheim Fellowship in 1967.

One of the first photographers to use Polaroid color film as her principal medium, Cosindas photographs mainly still lifes and portraits. To achieve a Rembrandt-like color quality, she alters the color through filters, development time and temperature.

PUBLICATIONS   Monographs: *Marie Cosindas: Color Photographs*, 1978; *Faces and Facades*, L. Fritz Gruber & Peter C. Bunnell, 1977. Book: *Polaroid Land Photography*, Ansel Adams, 1978. Anthologies: *The Photograph Collector's Guide*, Lee D. Witkin & Barbara London, 1979; *Mirrors & Windows*, John Szarkowski, ed., 1978; *Photographing Children*, 1971, *The Camera*, 1970, *Color*, 1970, *Light and Film*, 1970, Time-Life Series. Catalog: *Photographs*, 1977 (Univ. of Neb., Sheldon Mem. Art Gall.: Lincoln). Periodical: *Camera*, Nov 1974.

COLLECTIONS   Addison Gall. of Amer. Art, Andover, Mass.; Art Inst. of Chicago; Dartmouth Coll. Mus. Galls., Hanover, N. Hampshire; IMP/GEH, Rochester; Metro. Mus. of Art, NYC; MOMA, NYC; Mus. of Fine Arts, Boston; Polaroid Cllctn., Cambridge, Mass.; Univ. of Kansas, Lawrence; Univ. of Neb., Sheldon Mem. Art Gall., Lincoln. Natl. Gall. of Canada, Ottawa, Ontario.

ADDRESS   770 Boylston St, Boston, MA 02199.

Howard (Sydney Musgrave) Coster *PHOTOG-RAPHER* Born in 1885 in Ventnor, Isle of Wight, Coster died November 17, 1959, in London. Educated at Ventnor, he learned photography from his uncle, for whom he served as an assistant.

Coster traveled to South Africa in 1904, where he photographed farmers, livestock, and local events and later served in the photographic division of the Royal Air Force (1918–19). He ran studios in Bloemfontein and Johannesburg before returning to London and establishing a studio there in 1926.

A self-proclaimed "photographer of men," Coster was noted for his sincere, dignified portraits. The *London Times* wrote in his obituary: "Probably much of his success was due to his scrupulous study of his sitter beforehand—he had the true photographer's gift for appraisal—and to his shrewd and intuitive use of lighting."

PUBLICATION Anthology: *The Magic Image*, Cecil Beaton & Gail Buckland, 1975.

COLLECTIONS In London: Central Office of Info.; Natl. Portrait Gall.; RPS.

Samuel Laurence Coulthurst *BOOKSELLER · PHOTOGRAPHER* Born in England in 1867, Coulthurst died in November 1937, in Helsby, Cheshire, England. He was a bookseller in Manchester until he retired to Helsby in 1925. He was influenced by the works of Paul Martin.

Coulthurst joined the Manchester Amateur Photographic Society (MAPS) in 1889, becoming honorary secretary of its *Record and Survey* group in 1892. By 1901 he had led the group in amassing an album of 232 prints of Manchester and its surroundings, of which three copies were made. He remained active with MAPS until shortly before World War I.

With his brother-in-law, James Higson, Coulthurst would frequently disguise himself as a junkman, hiding his camera in a barrow, and thus capture some unique candid shots of the inhabitants and street life of Manchester, particularly the Flat Iron Market area of 1889–94. Sandra Martin has written (*Creative Camera*, July/Aug 1980), "These varied images, capturing actual moments in time, are remarkable for their realistic and convincing portrayal of attitudes and behavior." While he experimented with many processes and paper, Coulthurst preferred the platinotype.

COLLECTIONS Manchester City Art Gall., Rutherston Cllctn, England; Manchester Reference Lib.; MAPS, Manchester; Salford Reference Lib.

Penny Vickers Cousineau *PHOTOGRAPHER · TEACHER · WRITER* Born March 31, 1947, Cousineau received a BA in English Literature from the University of Manitoba in Winnipeg, Manitoba, in 1969, and a Post BA Certificate in Communications from Loyola of Montréal, in Montréal, Québec, in 1970. She received an MFA in Photography from the Visual Studies Workshop of SUNY in Rochester, in 1976.

Since 1977 Cousineau has been employed as a lecturer in the Department of Visual Arts at the University of Ottawa, Ontario.

She was awarded a research grant by the Canada Council in 1978.

PUBLICATIONS Catalog (text only): *The Female Eye*, winter 1975 (Natl. Film Board of Canada). Periodicals: "New Work by Robert Frank," Dec 1978/Jan 1979, review, Oct/Nov 1978, *Artscanada*, text only; "Robert Frank's Postcards from Everywhere," Feb 1978, "Too Much Exposure, not Enough Development," Feb 1976, "Readings in Zen and Photography," Mar 1974, "Earth Visions," Judith Egglington, Feb 1974, "*John Max's Open Passport*," Feb 1973, *Afterimage*, text only; "Vagabond," Gaylord Herron, summer/fall 1976, "Notations in Passing," Nathan Lyons, spring 1976, "Photography and Film," text only, fall 1975, "Michael Semack/Monograph," text only, May/June 1975, "Catharsis 3," Barbara Bruck, Sept/Oct 1974, *Ovo Photo*.

ADDRESS 39 Western Ave, Ottawa, Ontario, Canada.

Nat Cowan *CURATOR · PHOTOGRAPHER* Born February 1, 1903, in Hermon Cape Colony, South Africa, Cowan has been curator of the Bensusan Museum of Photography in Johannesburg, a branch of the city's Africana Museum, since 1968.

A fellow of RPS since 1940, he has also been an associate of the Photographic Society of America since 1944. Other memberships include being an associate of the Chartered Institute of Secretaries since 1946, and a fellow since 1952. He is also a founding member of the Photographic Society of Southern Africa (1954), and an honorary member of the South African Institute of Photographers, the Johannesburg Photographic Society and the Johannesburg Camera Club.

PUBLICATIONS Book: *The Old Transvaal 1839–1899*, w/A. P. Cartwright, 1978 (Purnells). Periodicals: *Creative Photography*, regular contributor.

COLLECTION Bensusan Museum of Photography, Johannesburg, South Africa.

ADDRESS POB 18956, 2038 Hillbrow, Rep. of South Africa.

Adger W. Cowans *PHOTOGRAPHER* Born September 19, 1936, in Columbus, Ohio, Cowans earned a BFA in 1958 from Ohio University, Athens, where he studied under Clarence H. White, Jr. He also names Edward Weston and Gordon Parks, Sr., as important influences.

A freelance photographer since 1963, Cowans served as an assistant to Gordon Parks at *Life* magazine in 1961–62 and was a U.S. Navy Photographer, 1958–60.

The photographer belongs to Local 644 of the International Association of Theatrical and Stage Employees (IATSE) and is a board member of International Black Photographers. He received a John Hay Whitney Foundation grant in 1962.

PUBLICATIONS Anthology: *Black Photographer's Annual*, 1976, 1974, 1973. Periodical: *Popular Photography Annual*, 1968, 1966.

COLLECTIONS IBM Corp., Rochester; IMP/GEH, Rochester; Shado Gall., Oregon City, Ore.; State Office Bldg., Harlem, NYC.

REPRESENTATIVE Roz Allen, 142 W 13 St, New York, NY 10011.

ADDRESS 136 W Broadway, New York, NY 10013.

Eileen Cowin *PHOTOGRAPHER · TEACHER* Born August 17, 1947, in Brooklyn, New York, Cowin received a BS in 1968 from the State University College of New York at New Paltz, and an MS in 1970 from the Illinois Institute of Technology in Chicago. She studied with Aaron Siskind and Arthur Segal.

Since 1975 Cowin has been associate professor at California State University in Fullerton, California. Her previous teaching experience was as instructor at Franconia College in Franconia, New Hampshire, from 1971 to 1975.

A member of SPE, she was a recipient of an NEA Fellowship Award in 1979.

PUBLICATIONS Books: *Light and Substance*, 1974; *The Art of Photography*, Time-Life Series, 1971.

COLLECTIONS Harvard Univ., Fogg Mus., Cambridge, Mass.; Minnesota Inst. of Art, Minneapolis, MOMA, NYC; Univ. of Kansas Art Mus., Lawrence. Natl. Gall. of Canada, Ottawa.

DEALER G. Ray Hawkins Gall., 7224 Melrose Ave., Los Angeles, CA 90046.

ADDRESS c/o Brecker, 653 Milwood Ave, Venice, CA 90291.

Paul Cox *PHOTOGRAPHER · FILM MAKER* Born April 16, 1940, in Venlo, The Netherlands, Cox studied at the Dutch School for Professional Photography and in 1960 worked for a short time with his father, film director/photographer Wim Cox. In 1966 he studied at Melbourne University, Australia.

Cox has lectured in photography and cinematography at Prahran College in Melbourne since 1970, and also freelances.

His films include the features *Kostas* (1979), *Inside Looking Out* (1977) and *Illuminations* (1976).

About his photography Cox says, "After years of experimentation I have returned to the simplest and most satisfying form of photography—I am now again a pictorialist."

PUBLICATIONS Books: *Mirka*, 1980; *Human Still Lives from Nepal*, 1975 (self-published); *Home of Man—The People of New Guinea*, 1971 (Nelson: Australia). Periodicals: *Creative Camera Annual*, 1975; *Camera*, Sept 1971, Feb 1971.

COLLECTIONS MOMA, NYC. Bibliothèque Nationale, Paris; Phillip Morris Cllctn., Melbourne, Australia; Natl. Gall., Canberra, Australia.; Natl. Gall. of South Australia, Adelaide; Stedelijk Mus., Amsterdam, The Netherlands.

DEALER Church St Gall., 384 Church St, Richmond, Melbourne, Australia.

ADDRESS 40 Murray St, Prahran, Melbourne, Australia.

Frank A. Coxhead *PHOTOGRAPHER* Coxhead is known for his work in the 1860s in Dunedin, New Zealand. His brother, H. Coxhead, was also a photographer of the same period.

Frank practiced photography in Dunedin by himself before forming a partnership with his brother. The two then opened branch studios in Invercargill and Timaru. Frank may also have been a partner to Le Seur of Dunedin.

A prolific landscape photographer, Coxhead captured the environs of Dunedin with his large-format equipment.

. PUBLICATIONS Book: *Dunedin in 1860*, ca. 1860 (New Zealand). Anthology: *19th Century New Zealand Photographers*, John B. Turner, 1970.

John Dean Craig *PHOTOGRAPHER · TEACHER* Born August 20, 1947, in Los Angeles, Craig earned his BA from the University of California at Los Angeles in 1970 and his MFA from the University of Florida, Gainesville, in 1972.

In 1979 he became an assistant professor at the

University of Connecticut in Storrs. Earlier that year the photographer had served as a visiting artist at the Art Institute of Chicago and at the University of Michigan in Ann Arbor. From 1975 to 1978 Craig was a photography instructor at Franconia College in New Hampshire and from 1972 to 1975 held the same position at Pensacola Junior College in Florida. At his alma mater, the University of Florida, he was a teaching assistant from 1970 to 1972.

A member of SPE, Friends of Photography and the American Association of University Professors, Craig was awarded an NEA Photographer's Fellowship in 1976.

Craig uses nonsilver processes such as photogravure etching and obsolete color processes like dye-coupler color to produce "multimedia photographics" with an emphasis on landscapes.

PUBLICATION   Book: *Darkroom Dynamics, A Guide to Creative Darkroom Techniques*, contr., Jim Stone, ed., 1979.

COLLECTIONS   J. B. Speed Art Mus., Louisville, Ky.; Mus. of Fine Arts, St. Petersburg, Fla.; Univ. of N.C., Chapel Hill; Univ. of Notre Dame, South Bend, Ind.

DEALERS   G. Ray Hawkins Gall., 7224 Melrose Ave, Los Angeles, CA 90046; Siembab Gallery, 162 Newberry St, Boston, MA 02116.

ADDRESS   Mansfield Apts 14, South Eagleville Rd, Storrs, CT 06268.

Barbara Bachmann Crane   PHOTOGRAPHER · TEACHER   Born March 19, 1928, in Chicago, Illinois, Crane received a BA in Art History from New York University, New York City, in 1950, and an MS from the Institute of Design, Illinois Institute of Technology, Chicago, in 1966, where she studied with Aaron Siskind. She also studied art history at Mills College in Oakland, California, from 1945 to 1948.

Working as a freelance commercial photographer off and on since 1960, Crane is also employed as an educator. Since 1967 she has taught at the School of the Art Institute of Chicago, and has been employed as a visiting artist in photography at the School of the Museum of Fine Arts of Boston (1979), a visiting lecturer in the history of photography at Tufts University Medford, Massachusetts (1979), a visiting professor of photography at Philadelphia College of Art (1977) and a lecturer in the history of photography at Illinois Institute of Technology in Chicago (1969).

Crane has been a trustee of Friends of Photography in Carmel, California, since 1975 and is a member of VSW, Rochester. From 1972 to 1976 she was a board member of SPE. A recipient of a Guggenheim Fellowship in Photography in 1979, she also received an NEA Photography Grant in 1974.

PUBLICATIONS   Books: *Object and Image*, George M. Craven, 1975; *Photography, Source and Resource*, Lewis, McQuaid & Tait, 1973; *Being Without Clothes*, Minor White, ed., 1970. Catalog: "Tar Findings," "Just Married," & "Neon Cowboy," *Contemporary Trends*, 1975 (Columbia College: Chicago). Periodicals: *Camera 35*, Dec 1979; *Photography Annual*, 1974, 1970, 1967; *Creative Camera*, Aug 1974; *Lightwork*, Oct 1974; *Ovo Photo*, Oct 1974; *The Professional Photographer*, May 1973.

PORTFOLIOS   *Tucson Portfolio I*, 1979; *Tucson Portfolio II*, 1980; *Student Independent* (group), 1978, 1976, 1974, 1969 (School of the Art Inst. of Chicago: Illinois); *The Photographer and the City*, 1976 (Mus. of Contemporary Art: Chicago); *Underware* (group), 1976 (School of the Art Inst. of Chicago: Illinois); *Independent for Houlihan*, 1972 (Chicago); *Student Independent* (group), 1966 (Illinois Inst. of Technology, Inst. of Design).

COLLECTIONS   Art Inst. of Chicago; CCP, Tucson; Chicago Bank of Commerce, Standard Oil Bldg., Chicago; Exchange Natl. Bank, Chicago; IMP/GEH, Rochester; L/C, Wash., D.C.; MIT, Hayden Gall., Cambridge, Mass.; Middle Tennessee State Univ., Murfreesboro; MOMA, NYC; Norton Simon Mus., Pasadena, Calif.; Univ. of Illinois, Krannert Mus., Champaign; Sam Wagstaff Cllctn., NYC.

ADDRESS   3164 N Hudson, Chicago, IL 60657.

Michael Patrick Crane   PHOTOGRAPHER · TEACHER · ARTS ADMINISTRATOR   Born December 24, 1948, in St. Louis, Missouri, Crane received an MFA from the School of the Art Institute of Chicago in 1976. He names as mentors Joyce Niemanas, Phil Hitchcock, Tom Jaremba, Bob Peters and Jim Ostler.

Presently gallery director and lecturer at San Jose State University in California, Crane held the same positions at California State University, Sacramento, 1978–79. He produced the radio program "New Title" at station KXPR in Sacramento in 1978–79. Crane administered the Ch'go Fog Performance Gallery in Chicago in 1975–76 and co-directed the N.A.M.E. Gallery in Chicago (which he co-founded), 1973–74. From 1974 to 1979 he was an editor/publisher of RDP Publications in Chicago, St. Louis and San Diego.

In 1977 Crane won a research fellowship from

the Institute for Advanced Studies in Contemporary Art in San Diego.

Crane's work explores the "interface between words and photographs; photographs and actions." He creates books, conceptual pieces, and live performances, as well as "photo-visual poems incorporating serial imagery" and "landscapes and topographic maps."

PUBLICATIONS Books: *Landscapes I'd Love to Do*, 1976; *Fill In This Space*, 1975. Anthologies: *Humanistic Perspectives in Contemporary Art*, 1978 (Galerie s:t Petri & Dept. of Art Hist., Univ. of Lund: Sweden); *Anti-Object Art*, Tri-Quarterly 32, fall 1974.
· COLLECTIONS Fluxus West Archive, San Diego, Calif.; Jean Brown Archive, Shaker Seed House, Tyringham, Mass. Archiv Sohm, Markgroningen, West Germany; Moderna Muséet, Stockholm, Sweden; Mus. of Contemporary Art, São Paulo, Brazil.
ADDRESS 180 Clareview Ave, San Jose, CA 95127.

David Bruce Cratsley GALLERY ADMINISTRA-TOR · PHOTOGRAPHER Born December 24, 1944, in Canton, New York, Cratsley is the son of Edward K. Cratsley (1914–78) who was, for several years, president of Swarthmore College in Swarthmore, Pennsylvania. He received a BA degree from Swarthmore in 1966, and did graduate study in art history at the University of Pennsylvania in Philadelphia from 1966 to 1967. Attending a master class with Lisette Model at the New School for Social Research in 1972, he subsequently studied privately with her and maintained a friendship that has been a major influence in his life.

Since 1977 he has been assistant to the director of Witkin Gallery, Inc., in New York City. Previously, Cratsley had been gallery manager (1976–77) and administrative assistant to the director of library at Magnum Photos (1972–73 and 1975) in New York City. He worked for the Parke-Bernet Galleries in New York as a consultant to their silver department, and also in their Houston, Texas, office, 1970–71, and for Sotheby & Co., London, as a silver and heraldry specialist, 1967–69.

Working in a 2¼" format, Cratsley has made photographs primarily of New York City, objects of art (in museums, etc.), family members and landscaped gardens.
PUBLICATIONS Anthology: *The Photograph Collector's Guide* (researcher), Lee D. Witkin & Barbara London, 1979. Periodical: *Photophile*, summer 1976.

Portfolios (all self-published): *David Bruce Cratsley 1980, Kelso Through the Locks*, 1980; *Bahama Witkin*, 1979; *Flea Market*, 1979; *Mr. Sweet at the Craft Fair*, 1979; *Robin Hood in Loudon County*, 1979; *With My Father in Mind*, 1978; *Witkin After Hours*, 1978; *Walking Through the Salad*, 1977; *Ms. Mutfit and the Dream of Open Windows*, 1976.
COLLECTIONS Brookdale Community Coll., Brookdale, N.Y.; Philip H. & A. S. W. Rosenbach Fndn., Philadelphia, Pa. Australian Natl. Gall, Canberra.
DEALERS Witkin Gall., Inc., 41 E 57 St, New York, NY 10022; Photographers' Gall., 8 Great Newport St, London WC2, England.
ADDRESS 129 E 29 St, New York, NY 10016.

George M. Craven TEACHER · WRITER · PHO-TOGRAPHER Born in Philadelphia, Pennsylvania, in 1929, Craven was educated at Ohio University (BFA, 1953; MFA, 1958) and received a diploma from the Radio-Film-TV Institute at Stanford University in 1964. He names Clarence H. White, Jr., as his mentor.

Since 1967 Craven has been professor of photography at De Anza College in Cupertino, Calif. From 1962 to 1967 he held the same title at Foothill College. He was an instructor at Everett Community College in Washington, 1960–62, and at Massachusetts College of Art, 1958–60. A member of SPE since 1963, he was the society's director in 1968–69.

Craven taught in England during 1969 under a Fulbright Exchange Grant, and he received Foothill-De Anza Professional Recognition Awards in 1971, 1974, 1977 and 1980.

Photographing mainly in color, Craven often works in dye transfer printmaking.
PUBLICATIONS Book: *Object and Image*, 1975. PERIODICAL "New Light on Photography," *Choice*, Feb 1978.
COLLECTION Oakland Art Museum, Calif.
ADDRESS De Anza College, Cupertino, CA 95014.

Mario Cresci PHOTOGRAPHER · VISUAL DESIGNER Born February 26, 1942, in Chiavari, Italy, Cresci received an MA in Design/Photography at the Institute of Art in Chiavari (1954) and studied industrial design in Venice (1962–66). His influences were Ugo Mulas, Jean Dibbets, Luigi Veronesi and Silvio Ceccato.

As of this writing Cresci is a consultant researcher for artistic handicrafts at IASM in Rome (since 1979). Previously he was a photographer and visual designer for Olivetti Systems in Milan

(1970–72), a designer for MAFIA agency in Paris (1969) and a photographer and designer for Milano Centro FLY Casa (1967). He joined AIAP in Milan in 1967.

He won the Italian Niepce Award in 1967, the Diomira Carlo Cardazzo Award in 1963, and the Bolaffi Award for Photography in Torino, Italy, in 1977.

In 1972 Cresci made the 16mm film *Analogue* for Review of Experimental Films of Ivrea.

The photographer sees his work as anthropological research and research into photographic language at an experimental level. His area of interest has been Fuglia Basilicata and the southern regions of Italy.

PUBLICATIONS Monographs: *Misurazioni: Segni e Analogie*, 1979 *(Meta Matera)*; *Mario Cresci: Due Dimensioni (Two Dimensions)*, 1977 (Nava: Milan); *Mario Cresci: Fotografia come Pratica Analitica (Photographs as Analytical Practice)*, 1977 (Il Diaframma: Milan); *Matera: Immagini e Documenti (Images & Documents)*, 1975 (Meta).

COLLECTIONS MOMA, NYC. Bibliothèque Nationale, Paris; Galleria Rondanini, Rome; Università di Parma, Archivio della Comunicazione, Italy; Work Gall., Zurich, Switzerland.

DEALERS Il Diaframma, Via Brera 10, Milan, Italy; Work Gall., Trittiglasse 24, Ch. 8001 Zurich, Switzerland.

ADDRESS Via Conservatorio 3, 75100 Matera, Italy.

Anthony Crickmay PHOTOGRAPHER Born 1937 in Woking, England, Crickmay apprenticed with Lotte Meitner, a Viennese photographer working in London.

Self-employed as a freelance photographer since 1956, he primarily contributes fashion work to the English *Vogue* magazine.

PUBLICATIONS Books: *Collected Dance Photographs*, 1980 (Collins, London); *Lynn Seymour*, 1980 (Studio Vista, London); *Art of Classical Dance*, 1979. Anthology: *The Magic Image*, Cecil Beaton & Gail Buckland, 1975.

ADDRESS 32 Donne Place, London SW3, England

Harry G. Critchfield TEACHER · PHOTOGRAPHER · MEDIA CENTER DIRECTOR Born on September 16, 1940, in Washington, D.C., Critchfield studied at San Francisco State University, where he obtained both a bachelor's (1962) and a master's (1967) degree. He was influenced by Jack Welpott, Don Worth, John Gutmann, Henry Holmes Smith and Robert Forth.

He was a photography instructor and director of the Media Center (1972) at the California College of Arts and Crafts in Oakland and has been head of their Photography Department since 1975. Previously he taught photography at Sam Houston State University in Huntsville, Texas (1970–72), and at Fort Bragg High School in California (1967–68).

In 1966 he joined SPE and in 1973 the Professional Photographers of San Francisco, serving on their board of directors during the year 1974.

Critchfield works in 4 x 5 and concentrates on landscapes.

ADDRESS 5212 Broadway, Oakland, CA 94618.

Charles Emile-Hortensius Cros INVENTOR · POET Born in Fabrezan, France, on October 1, 1842, Cros died August 10, 1888, in Paris. At fourteen he was studying Sanskrit at the College of France, and also was concerned with the synthesis of precious gems, writing literary monologs and scientific studies on such subjects as color photography.

Cros and Louis Ducos du Hauron simultaneously but independently discovered and published the basic principles of three-color photography. Their work was presented in 1869 to the Société Française de Photographie, but Cros had indicated his discovery two years earlier in a letter to the Académie des Sciences. Both processes suggested separating the color image through the use of filters and recombining them with red, blue, and yellow pigments. Cros suggested the use of a phenakistoscope or zoetrope to effect the synthesis, using the principle of the persistence of vision. The discoveries were variously critized as being "works of luck if not frauds" and "purely theoretical procedures."

Cros' other discoveries included a Chromometre (chromoscope) in 1879 for use in the optical synthesis of color, an inhibition color process called Hydrotypie in 1880, and a bleach-out color process in 1881. He also invented a phonograph (paleograph) in 1877.

PUBLICATIONS Books: *Quellendarstellungen zur Geschichte der Fotografie*, Wolfgang Baier, 1964; *Histoire de la Photographie*, Raymond Lécuyer, 1945; *Poèmes et Proses*, Henri Pansor, ed., 1944; *History of 3-Color Photography*, E. J. Wall, 1925; *Book of Photography*, Paul N. Hasluck, 1905; *Le Coffret de Santal (The Sandalwood Chest*, poetry), 1873; *Etudes sur les moyens de communication avec les planètes*, 1869. Anthology: *Photography's Great Inventors*, Louis W. Sipley, 1965. Periodicals: *Revue du Son*, Nov 1953;

Le Moniteur de la Photographie, 1881; *Photographic News,* 1879; *Bulletin de la Société Française de Photographie,* 1869; *Les Mondes,* Feb 25, 1869 (Abbé Moigno).

Suzanne Camp Crosby   *PHOTOGRAPHER · TEACHER*   Born May 20, 1948, in Roanoke, Virginia, Crosby earned her BFA in Painting (1970) from the University of Florida, Gainesville, and her MFA in Photography (1976) from the University of South Florida, Tampa. In 1979 she also studied in workshops under Ralph Gibson and George A. Tice.

From 1977 to the present Crosby has taught photography at Hillsborough Community College in Tampa. She was a visiting lecturer/instructor at Florida Technological University, Orlando (1977–78), and a photography instructor at Tampa Bay Art Center (1978–79). From 1972 to 1977 she was a photographer for the University of South Florida, Division of Educational Resources.

A member of SPE and Friends of Photography, Crosby won a Florida Fine Arts Council fellowship in 1979 and an NEA/Southeastern Center for Contemporary Art fellowship in 1978.

Crosby describes her images as "a composite of personal impressions and experiences, . . . a direct result and acknowledgment of details of my daily life. Ideally," she says, "the photographic image will serve as a point of departure for viewer interpretation and response, and provides a means of sharing individual perception."

PUBLICATIONS   Anthology: *In/Sights: Self-Portraits by Women,* Joyce Tenneson Cohen, ed., 1978. Periodical: *Petersen's Photographic Magazine,* Jan 1976.

REPRESENTATIVE   Atlanta Gallery of Photography, 3077 E Shadowlawn Ave NE, Atlanta, GA 30305.

John L. (Jay) Crouse, Jr.   *GALLERY OWNER · ART DEALER*   Born on April 13, 1949 in Lima, Ohio, Crouse obtained a BA in Economics from Denison University in Granville, Ohio, in 1971, and an MBA with a specialization in finance from George Washington University in Washington, D.C., in 1975. During the year 1975–76, he attended the Maine Photographic Workshop in Rockport.

He first worked as the manager of the Crouse Lumber Company in Lima, Ohio (1971–73). Since 1976 he has owned the Atlanta Gallery of Photography. He joined the High Museum of Art in Atlanta in 1976; in 1978 the Atlanta Historical

Society; and in 1979 the Association of International Photography Art Dealers.

Crouse specializes in the exhibition and sale of twentieth-century well-known and contemporary photographers.

PUBLICATION   Periodical: *American Photographer,* Mar 1980.

ADDRESS   3077 E Shadowlawn Ave NE, Atlanta, GA 30305.

François Crouton-La Fortune   *LIBRARIAN · PHOTOGRAPHER*   Born in Montreal, Quebec, on March 9, 1921, Crouton-LaFortune completed a BA and a Doctorate in Librarianship at the College of Montreal. He has been curator of the Quebec Museum since 1975. Previously he worked as a librarian at the Municipal Library of Montreal (1948–52), as chief librarian for the Canadian Institute of Quebec (1953–60) and as an assistant director for Quebec's Public Library Services (1960–75).

His photographic images are of street life, old houses, landscapes and children.

PUBLICATION   Book: *Où la Lumière Chante,* 1966 (Laval & Toronto Univs.).

COLLECTION   Musée Nicéphore Niepce, Châlon-sur-Saône, France.

ADDRESS   809 Av. Levis, Quebec PQ, Canada.

Patrick Shay Crowe   *PHOTOJOURNALIST*   Born March 25, 1941, in Corning, New York, Crowe is self-taught, influenced by W. Eugene Smith.

Since 1969 Crowe has been a photographer for the News-Journal Co. in Wilmington, Delaware. He has also worked at Cornell University in Ithaca, New York (1969), for Gannett Newspapers in Rochester, New York (1967–69), and at the *Corning Leader* in Corning, New York (1964–67). He has belonged to the NPPA since 1964.

In 1975 Crowe was named National Photographer of the Year and in 1972, Southern Photographer of the Year.

PUBLICATIONS   Anthologies: *The Family of Children,* 1977; *Photography Year,* Time-Life Series, 1976. Periodicals: *Popular Photography Annual,* 1976; *Modern Photography,* Jan 1974; *Camera 35 Annual,* 1973.

ADDRESS   2510 Cedartree Dr 1B, Wilmington, DE 19810.

Robert H. Cumming   *PHOTOGRAPHER · PAINTER · SCULPTOR · WRITER*   [See plate 118] Born in 1943 in Worcester, Massachusetts, Cumming earned his BFA (Massachusetts College of

Art, Boston, 1965) and MFA (University of Illinois, Champaign, 1967) in painting.

He has taught at the following schools: Hartford Art School, W. Hartford, Connecticut (1978 to the present); University of California, Irvine (1977–78); California Institute of the Arts, Valencia (1976–77); Otis Art Institute, Los Angeles (1975–76); University of California, Los Angeles (1974–77); and University of California, Riverside (1973).

Cumming received NEA grants in 1972 and 1975 and the Frank Logan Prize (for sculpture) at the Chicago Art Institute in 1969.

Primarily known as a painter, Cumming also works in drawing, sculpture, written narratives and video.

PUBLICATIONS Monographs: *Robert Cumming Photographs*, 1979; *Interruptions in Landscape and Logic*, 1977, *Discourse on Domestic Disorder*, 1975, *Training in the Arts*, 1973, *The Weight of Franchise Meat*, 1971, *Picture Fictions*, 1971 (self-published). Catalog: *Nation's Capitol in Photographs* series, 1976 (Corcoran Gall.: Wash., D.C.). Periodicals: "Robert Cumming: Trucage; Falsehoods," J. Hugunin, *Afterimage*, Dec 1978; "The Photographer and the Drawing," w/Fitch & Misrach, *Creative Camera*, Aug 1977; "The Directorial Mode," A. D. Coleman, Sept 1976, "Robert Cumming's Eccentric Illusions," P. Foschi, June 1975, *Artforum*.

COLLECTIONS Chicago Art Inst.; Cornell Univ., Johnson Lib., Ithaca, N.Y.; Corcoran Gall., Wash., D.C.; MOMA, NYC; Mus. of Fine Arts, Houston, Tex.

DEALER Gilbert Gallery, 218 E Ontario, Chicago, IL 60611.

ADDRESS 1604 N Grand, W Suffield, CT 06093.

Imogen Cunningham PHOTOGRAPHER [See plate 42] Born in Portland, Oregon, on April 12, 1883, Cunningham passed away on June 23, 1976, in San Francisco, California. Her former husband, Roi Partridge, is an etcher. Cunningham entered the University of Washington, in Seattle, in 1903 and earned a BS in Chemistry. Under a Phi Beta Phi scholarship, she went to Dresden, Germany, in 1909 to study at the Technische Hochschule with the famed photoscientist Robert Luther. Cunningham considered Gertrude Käsebier and Utamaro as major influences.

She took her first photograph in 1901, sixty-two years after the invention of the medium. She printed platinum-process photos for Edward S. Curtis' Seattle studio, 1907–1909, and opened her own studio in Seattle in 1910. She was a freelance photographer for the next sixty-six years, doing portraits, commercial assignments and teaching, in addition to her own work. In the mid-1930s she was a photographer for *Vanity Fair* and *Sunset* magazines.

In 1923 Cunningham joined the Pictorial Photographers of America, and in 1932 became a member of Group f.64, which included Edward Weston, Ansel Adams and Willard Van Dyke. In 1955 Cunningham joined the Bay Area Photographers.

Named a Fellow of the National Academy of Arts and Sciences in 1967, Cunningham received an honorary Doctor of Fine Arts degree from the California College of Arts and Crafts in Oakland. In 1970 she won a Guggenheim Fellowship; in 1971 she was the first recipient of the Dorothea Lange Award and in 1973 was named Artist of the Year by the San Francisco Art Commission. She set up the Imogen Cunningham Trust in 1975 to preserve and reproduce her work.

Cunningham appeared in several films, including Fred Padula's *Two Photographers: Imogen Cunningham and Wynn Bullock* (1966) and Ann Hershey's *Never Give Up: Imogen Cunningham* (1973).

Her work spanned half the history of photography, and, according to her Trust, "defies simple classification." Her early work was romantic and allegorical. She has encompassed "the various styles of pictorialism on into the f.64 [straight] style, always with a special awareness and acknowledgment for the individual subject at hand." Her photographs feature "very strong composition applied to portraits, plant forms, nudes and miscellaneous subject matter."

PUBLICATIONS Monographs: *Imogen Cunningham*, Judy Dater, 1979; *After Ninety*, intro. by Margaretta Mitchell, 1977; *Imogen!*, intro. by Margery Mann, 1974; *Imogen Cunningham: Photographs*, intro. by Margery Mann, 1970. Catalog: *Women of Photography: An Historical Survey*, Mann & Noggle, eds., 1975 (San Francisco Mus. of Modern Art). Anthologies (selected): *The Photograph Collector's Guide*, Lee D. Witkin & Barbara London, 1979; *Photography Rediscovered*, David Travis & Anne Kennedy, 1979; *Interviews with Master Photographers*, Danziger & Conrad, 1977; *The Magic Image*, Cecil Beaton & Gail Buckland, 1975; *Looking at Photographs*, John Szarkowski, 1973. Periodicals (selected): *Camera*, Oct 1975; "Imogen Cunningham," *Album*, no. 5, 1970; "Imogen Cunningham," George M. Craven, *Aperture*, 11:4, 1964; "Imogen Cunningham—An Appreciation," Flora

Huntley Maschmedt, *Wilson's Photographic Magazine*, Mar 1914. Transcript: "Imogen Cunningham: Portraits, Ideas, and Design," interviews by Edna Tartaul Daniel, foreword by Beaumont Newhall, 1961 (Regional Cultural History Project Interview, Univ. of Calif.: Berkeley).

COLLECTIONS Art Inst. of Chicago; CCP, Tucson; IMP/GEH, Rochester; Kalamazoo Inst. of Arts, Mich.; Metro. Mus. of Art, NYC; MOMA, NYC; New Orleans Mus. of Art, La.; Oakland Mus., Calif.; San Francisco Mus. of Modern Art; Seattle Art Mus., Wash.; Smithsonian Inst., Wash., D.C.; Stanford Univ., Palo Alto, Calif.; Tacoma Art Mus., Wash.; UCLA; Univ. of Wash. Libraries, Seattle. Provinciaal Mus. voor Kunstambachten, Antwerp, Belgium.

REPRESENTATIVE The Imogen Cunningham Trust, 1713 Grove St, Berkeley, CA 94709.

William Henry Cupit PHOTOGRAPHER · DESIGNER · TEACHER Born in Vancouver, British Columbia, on April 16, 1946, Cupit is a 1968 graduate of the Vancouver School of Art, where he majored in architectural design and photography.

Since 1978 he has been supervisor of the Photo Department at the Emily Carr College of Art. Previously he worked as a technical assistant in the Department of Photography at the Vancouver School of Art (1973–78), as a photographer and designer for the University of British Columbia (1972–73) and as a freelance architectural designer and photographer (1969–72).

In 1977 he received an Award of Excellence from the American Institute of Graphic Arts in New York.

Cupit's work consists of "silver and nonsilver images used in conjunction with mixed media such as oil paints, acrylics, pencil, etc."

PUBLICATION Anthology: *Exposure—Canadian Contemporary Photographers*, 1972 (Ottawa, Canada).

COLLECTIONS Bolivian Embassy, La Paz, Bolivia; Mus. of Art & History, Fribourg, Switzerland; Natl. Film Board Gall., Ottawa, Canada.

ADDRESS 3372 Viewmount Pl, Port Moody B.C. V3H 2L5, Canada.

Darryl J. Curran PHOTOGRAPHER · TEACHER [See plate 139] Born on October 19, 1935, in Santa Barbara, California, Curran holds a bachelor's and a master's degree from the University of California at Los Angeles (1960, 1964) where he studied with Don Chipperfield and Robert Heinecken. He was influenced by the work of Joseph Cornell, Franz Kline, Jean Tinguely and Robert Rauschenberg.

He started working at the UCLA Art Gallery (1963–65), then worked as a freelance photographer and designer (1965–67). Since 1967 he has been a professor of art at the California State University at Fullerton. In 1975 he was a visiting artist at the School of the Art Institute of Chicago.

Curran joined SPE in 1968 and served on their board of directors from 1975 to 1979. He is also a charter member of the Los Angeles Center for Photographic Studies, for whom he served, and still serves, on the board of directors (1973–77; 1979 to the present). In 1980 he received an NEA Photographer's Fellowship.

The artist has "worked generally in the area of collage, image association and mixed media photography as described by Jerry Uelsmann as 'post-visualization.' Many cameras and film formats have been explored, including the Diana plastic camera, Widelux, 6 x 6 range finder," etc.

PUBLICATIONS Catalogs: *Uniquely Photographic*, 1979 (Honolulu Academy of Fine Arts); *Translations: Photographic Images with New Forms*, 1979 (Herbert F. Johnson Mus. of Art, Cornell Univ.: Ithaca, N.Y.); *Photographic Directions: Los Angeles*, 1979 (Security Natl. Bank); *New Blues*, Che du Puich, 1976 (Ariz. State Univ.: Flagstaff); *Exposing: Photographic Definitions*, R. Mautner, 1976 (Los Angeles Inst. & Ctr. for Arts); *12 Photographers*, 1975 (New Organization for the Visual Arts: Cleveland, Ohio); *National Photography Invitational*, 1974 (Va. Commonwealth Univ., Anderson Gall.); *Photography Unlimited*, David Pratt, 1974 (Harvard Univ., Fogg Art Mus.: Cambridge, Mass.); *Light and Substance*, Van Deren Coke & Tom Barrow, 1974 (Univ. of N. Mex. Press: Albuquerque); *Photo Phantasists*, (Fla. State Univ.: Tallahassee); *Three Photographers*, 1971 (San Fernando Valley State Coll.: Calif.); *Photomedia U.S.A.*, 1971 (San Diego State Coll.: Calif.); *Continuum*, 1969 (Downey Mus. of Art: Calif.); *California Photographers*, 1970 (Univ. of Calif.: Davis); *Recent Acquisitions*, 1969 (Pasadena Art Mus.: Calif.); *Vision and Expression*, Nathan Lyons, 1969 (IMP/GEH: Rochester). Catalogs (text only): *Object, Illusion, Reality*, 1979 (Los Angeles Ctr. for Photog. Studies); *Emerging Los Angeles Photographers*, 1976 (Friends of Photog.: Carmel, Calif.); *24 from L.A.*, 1973 (San Francisco Mus. of Modern Art); *Graphic/Photographic*, 1971 (Calif. State Univ.: Fullerton).

COLLECTIONS Exchange Natl. Bank, Chicago; Harvard Univ., Fogg Art Mus., Cambridge, Mass.;

Los Angeles County Mus. of Art; Minneapolis Inst. of the Arts, Minn.; MOMA, NYC; Oakland Mus., Calif.; Pasadena Art Mus., Calif.; Seagram Corp. Collctn., NYC; UCLA; Univ. of N. Mex. Art Mus., Albuquerque. Natl. Gall. of Canada, Ottawa; RPS, London.

DEALERS   G. Ray Hawkins, 7224 Melrose Ave, Los Angeles, CA 90069; Geffrey Fuller Fine Art, 2108 Spruce St, Philadelphia, PA 19103.

ADDRESS   10537 Dunleer Dr, Los Angeles, CA 90064.

David Garfield Currie   TEACHER · PHOTOG-
RAPHER Born in Cleveland, Ohio, on December 26, 1941, Currie received a BFA (1963) and an MFA (1966) from Ohio University in Athens. He considers his mentors to be Minor White, Peter C. Bunnell and Clarence H. White, Jr.

Currie has been self-employed as a photographer since 1969 in addition to teaching photography at New Trier West High School in Northfield, Ill. (since 1966). He also taught part-time at the School of the Art Institute of Chicago in 1968. From 1964 to 1966 Currie was a graduate assistant at Ohio University and from 1963 to 1964 worked for Photographics, Inc., in Cleveland.

The photographer holds memberships in SPE, National Education Association, George Eastman House, and the Art Institute of Chicago.

Currie produces mainly black-and-white silver prints, using all format cameras. "I am intrigued," he says, "with the range of possibilities that photography offers, particularly in the areas of teaching and learning about perception, vision and sensitivity."

PUBLICATIONS   Books: *See for yourself*, 1979; "Notes Toward the Advocacy of Photography in the High School Curriculum," *Photography: Source/Resource*, Lewis, McQuaid & Tait, eds., 1973.

COLLECTIONS   Exchange Natl. Bank, Chicago; Houghton Mifflin, Inc., Boston; MOMA, NYC; Ohio Univ. Dept. Cllctn., Athens; Ohio Univ. Faculty Private Cllctn; Time-Life, Inc., NYC.

ADDRESS   1218 St. Johns Ave, Highland Park, IL 60035.

Asahel Curtis   PHOTOGRAPHER Born in Minnesota in 1874, Curtis died in Seattle, Washington, in 1941. A self-taught photographer, he began as a teenage hobbyist in 1887. He was a brother of photographer Edward S. Curtis (1868–1952).

Curtis became a professional in 1894 when he established a commercial photography studio in Seattle. His commissions carried him throughout the greater Northwest, to Alaska and British Columbia and the Yukon Territory, as well as Oregon, Idaho and especially Washington. His pictures were extensively used in advertisements, in local magazines such as *Argus, Sunset* and *The Coast,* as well as national periodicals such as *National Geographic.*

A founding member of the Seattle Mountaineers, Curtis was active in the Seattle Chamber of Commerce. A seasoned mountain climber, he was the first professional guide on Mount Rainier.

He left nearly 60,000 images of the life and times of the Northwest region. He photographed people—at work, at play, in the street—during an economic boom. Murray Morgan says, "Asahel did not rearrange, he recorded." According to David Sucher, his "pictures were used as tools to encourage further development of the region, foreshadowing the 'political photography' of today which is designed to move people to action."

PUBLICATION   Monograph: *The Asahel Curtis Sampler: Photographs of Puget Sound Past,* David Sucher, ed., foreword by Murray Morgan, afterword by Wes Uhlman, 1973.

COLLECTIONS   Ferry Mus., Tacoma, Wash.; Univ. of Washington, Suzzallo Lib., Seattle; Washington State Historical Society, Tacoma.

Edward Sheriff Curtis   PHOTOGRAPHER [See plate 36] Born near White Water, Wisconsin, in 1868, Curtis died October 21, 1954, in Los Angeles, California. His brother, Asahel Curtis (1874–1941) was a photographer of the Northwest. Self-taught, Edward Curtis built his first camera when still a child. Later he met George Bird Grinnell, a man with an extensive knowledge of Native Americans, who was a major influence in giving Curtis' work direction.

Curtis worked as an assistant to a commercial photographer before moving to Seattle with his family in 1887, where he had part interest in a studio. He first photographed an American Indian in 1896, was commissioned to Edward H. Harriman's two-month expedition to Alaska in 1899 and spent the summer of 1900 on a Montana Indian reservation, after which he began his methodical study of Native American tribes west of the Mississippi.

From 1906 to 1927 he traveled more broadly throughout the United States as well as British Columbia and continued to record, both on paper and with his camera, the North American Indian life-styles.

President Theodore Roosevelt, having viewed an exhibit of Curtis' work in Washington, D.C., introduced him to J. P. Morgan, who awarded the photographer an advance of $75,000 to complete his Indian study and publish the results. These negotiations occurred around 1905, and by 1930 Curtis had accomplished the remarkable task of creating a twenty-volume illustrated encyclopedia of North American Indian life which included about 1,500 photographic images.

Curtis achieved exceptional technical expertise for his day. Although his style was straightforward, he tended to romanticize his subjects by posing them with various props and even wigs. He first used a 7 x 14 view camera, later an 11 x 14, and then finally, a 6 x 8 reflex. He made platinum and silver prints as well as orotones, which were direct positives on glass plates.

PUBLICATIONS Monographs: *Edward Sheriff Curtis: Visions of a Vanishing Race*, Florence Curtis Graybill & Victor Boesen, 1976; *Portraits from North American Indian Life*, intros. by A. D. Coleman & T. C. McLuhan, 1972; *Curtis' Western Indians*, Ralph W. Andrews, 1962. Books: *The Kwakiutl, 1910–1914*, 1976; *In a Sacred Manner We Live*, Don D. Fowler, 1972; *The North American Indians*, Joseph Epes Brown, 1972; *Touch the Earth*, T. C. McLuhan, ed. 1971; *Indian Love Letters*, Marah Ellis Ryan, 1920; *In the Land of the Head-Hunters*, 1915; *Indian Days of Long Ago*, 1914; *The Flute of the Gods*, Marah Ellis Ryan, 1909; *The North American Indian*, 20 vols., Frederick Webb Hodge, 1907–30; *Harriman Alaska Series*, 14 vols., C. Merriam, ed., illus. w/D.G. Inverarity, 1901/2–33. Anthologies: *The Photograph Collector's Guide*, Lee D. Witkin & Barbara London, 1979; *Photography Rediscovered*, David Travis & Anne Kennedy, 1979; *The Valiant Knights of Daguerre . . . by Sadakichi Hartmann*, Harry W. Lawton & George Know, eds., 1978; *The Invented Eye*, Edward Lucie-Smith, 1975; *The Magic Image*, Cecil Beaton & Gail Buckland, 1975. Periodicals: "The Splendid Indians of Edward S. Curtis," Alvin M. Josephy, Jr., *American Heritage*, Feb 1974; *Camera*, Dec 1973.

COLLECTIONS Art Inst. of Chicago; L/C, Wash. D.C.; Pierpont Morgan Lib., NYC; Philadelphia Mus. of Art; UCLA; Univ. of New Mexico Art Mus., Albuquerque; Univ. of Washington Libs., Seattle. British Mus., London; Univ. of Exeter Lib., Exeter, England; and many others.

ARCHIVE Pierpont Morgan Lib., 29 E 36 St, New York, NY 10016.

William R. Curtsinger PHOTOGRAPHER Born in Philadelphia, Pennsylvania, on January 23, 1946, the self-taught Curtsinger has been a contract photographer for *National Geographic* from 1971 to the present. From 1967 to 1970 he served as a U.S. Navy photographer's mate.

Working with various formats in both color and black-and-white, Curtsinger describes himself as a photographer of natural history and "of people whom I get to know and like and relate to." For the past ten years he has photographed marine mammals of the world (whales, seals, dolphins) from both above and below the water.

PUBLICATIONS Book: *Wake of the Whale*, Kenneth Brower, 1979. Periodical: *Life*, incl. cover, July 1979.

REPRESENTATIVE Photo Researchers, 60 E 56 St. NYC.

ADDRESS Biddeford Pool, ME 04006.

Frank Cushing PHOTOJOURNALIST Born Francis W. Cushing in 1916, "Cush," as he was known to his friends, died on March 17, 1975, in Quincy, Massachusetts.

Cushing began employment at the *Boston Herald and Traveler* on October 1, 1932, where he worked at the display desk. He later became a staff photographer, retiring May 13, 1968. After his retirement from the paper he went to work as a painter for the Fore River Shipyard, where he became a foreman shortly before his retirement from there. During World War II he flew a string of combat missions with the Army Air Corps as an aerial photographer.

During his years as a photojournalist, he belonged to the Boston Press Photographers Association. Cushing was awarded the Pulitzer Prize in 1948 for his picture of a teenaged boy holding police at bay by threatening another youngster with a gun in the Roxbury district of Boston in June 1947.

PUBLICATION Anthology: *Moments*, Sheryl & John Leekley, foreword by Dan Rather, 1978.

D

Dean Dablow   *TEACHER · PHOTOGRAPHER*
Born on August 26, 1946, in Superior, Wisconsin, Dablow earned a BS at the University of Wisconsin in Stevens Point (1969). In 1974 he completed an MA and an MFA at the University of Iowa, where Professor John Schulze had a major influence on his development as a photographer.

Since 1976 he has been teaching at Louisiana Tech University in Ruston, first as an assistant professor and, since 1979, as an associate professor. He also taught at Coe College in Cedar Rapids, Iowa (1974–76).

He belongs to SPE and Friends of Photography.

Dablow received a Purchase Award granted by the Contemporary Art Center in New Orleans (1979) and won the Best of Show Prize in Painting at the Wausau Art Festival in Wisconsin (1969). He was also given a Purchase Award in Painting by Sentry Insurance in Stevens Point, Wisconsin (1968).

The artist, "presently concerned with the photograph as misrepresenting reality, [is] doing a series called 'Photographs Out of Context' which involves two identical photographs with differing captions."

PUBLICATIONS   Catalog: *Photography as a Fine Art*, 1974 (U.S. Info. Agy. Exhibition for American Embassies). Periodical: *Creative Camera International Yearbook*, 1977.

COLLECTIONS   Arkansas Art Ctr., Little Rock; Consolidated Paper Co., Port Edwards, Wis.; Contemporary Art Ctr., New Orleans; Golden West Coll., Huntington Beach, Calif.; Kansas City Art Inst., Mo.; LaGrange Coll., La Grange, Ga.; Marine Banks Art Collctn., Milwaukee, Wis.; Masur Mus. of Art, Monroe, La.; New Orleans Mus. of Art; Sentry Insurance Co., Stevens Point, Wis.

DEALER   Afterimage, The Quadrangle #151, 2800 Routh St, Dallas, TX 75201.

ADDRESS   1202 Greenwood Dr, Ruston, LA 71270.

Louis-Jacques-Mandé Daguerre   *PHYSICIST · PAINTER*   Born November 18, 1787, in Cormeilles, France (near Paris), Daguerre died July 10, 1851, in Bry-sur-Marne, France.

Daguerre first worked as an inland revenue officer, then became a rather successful scene painter and designer for the stage. He collaborated on his photography research with Joseph Niepce from 1829 until the latter's death in 1833, then continued experimentation on his own. His daguerreotype process was announced to the French Academy of Sciences by astronomer-physicist D. François J. Arago on January 9, 1839. Daguerre made few improvements on his invention and eventually returned to painting.

The daguerreotype process developed by the physicist—the first widespread, practical photographic process—earned Daguerre the Legion of Honor award in 1839 as well as a lifetime annuity from the French government in return for the publication of his invention "free to the world." The process used mercury vapor to develop the photographic image and a concentrated solution of sodium thiosulfate to fix it (by washing out unexposed silver iodide), thus reducing the necessary exposure time from seven or eight hours to about twenty minutes.

Daguerre also introduced to the stage the diorama—a display of views painted on transparent canvas which achieved various effects through subtle changes in lighting. Although short-lived on the stage, the device remained popular for both "peep shows" and three-dimensional museum reconstructions.

As a photographer, Daguerre generally shot still lifes and scenes of Paris.

PUBLICATIONS   Books (selected): *Latent Image*, Beaumont Newhall, 1967; *Daguerre (1787–1851) et les première daguerréotypes français*, 1961 (Bibliothèque Nationale: Paris); *L. J. M. Daguerre: The History of the Diorama and the Daguerreotype*, Helmut & Alison Gernsheim, 1956 (London), U.S. ed. 1968; *Cassell's Cyclopedia of Photography*, Bernard E. Jones, ed., 1911, repr. 1973; *History of Photography*, Josef Maria Eder, 1902, rev. 1932, repr. 1972; *History and Practice of Photogenic Drawing on the True Principles of the Daguerreotype with the New Method of Dioramic Painting*, 1838, repr. w/ intro. by Beaumont Newhall, 1971. Anthologies: *The Photograph Collector's Guide*, Lee D. Witkin & Barbara London, 1979; *The Magic Image*, Cecil Beaton & Gail Buckland, 1975.

COLLECTIONS IMP/GEH, Rochester; Univ. of Tex., Gernsheim Cllctn., Austin, Tex. Musée du Conservatoire Nationale des Arts et Métiers, Paris; Société Française de Photographie, Paris.

Louise Dahl-Wolfe PHOTOGRAPHER Born in San Francisco, California, in 1895, Dahl-Wolfe attended the California School of Fine Arts (now the San Francisco Art Institute) where she studied design with Rudolph Schaeffer who, along with Anne Brigman, were major influences.

A fashion and portrait photographer for *Harper's Bazaar* from 1936 to 1958, she has, since that time, pursued her personal work.

Along with her fashion photography, she is noted for her documentary work of life in the Great Smoky Mountains, 1931–33.

PUBLICATIONS Anthologies: *The History of Fashion Photography*, Nancy Hall-Duncan, 1979; *The Photograph Collector's Guide*, Lee D. Witkin & Barbara London, 1979; *Women of Photography*, Margery Mann & Ann Noggle, eds., 1975; *The Studio*, Time-Life Series, 1971. Periodical: *Vanity Fair*, Nov 1933.

COLLECTIONS Fashion Inst. of Technology Lib., NYC; MOMA, NYC.

REPRESENTATIVE Calloway Editions, 421 Hudson St., New York, NY 10014.

Richard Daintree PHOTOGRAPHER · GEOLOGIST Born in 1832 in England, Daintree died in Australia in 1878. He trained as a geologist at Cambridge, England.

Daintree emigrated to Australia in 1852 during its great gold rush. After little success as a miner, he became an assistant geologist in the Selwyn Geological Survey of Victoria (1854), then returned to England briefly, during which time he learned photography. On his return to Melbourne in 1857 he may have collaborated with Antoine Fauchery to publish a series of photographic albums entitled *Australia*. From 1858 to 1865 he used photography extensively in his continued work with the Geological Survey. After his resignation, he performed independently and dili-

gently as a geologist in northern Queensland, where he discovered deposits of copper and gold. Several of his images were shown at the Exhibition of Art and Industry in London (1871), and from 1872 to 1876 he was agent-general in London for Queensland. Daintree prepared and appeared in numerous exhibitions during his career.

The photographer helped develop the use of photography in geological field work, a difficult task in Australia's tropical zones, especially in the days of the wet-plate process. "His surviving photographs are superb specimens of art and recreate well the early settlement of Queensland," writes Andrew Hooper of the Royal Melbourne Institute of Technology.

PUBLICATIONS Monographs: *Queensland in the 1860's*, I. G. Sanker, 1977 (Queensland Mus.); *Richard Daintree: A Photographic Memoir*, G. C. Bolton, 1965 (ANU: Jacaranda); *Queensland, 1872* (Australia). Book: *Gold and Silver; an album of Hill End and Gulgong photographs from the Holtermann Collection*, Keast Burke, 1973 (Heinemann: Melbourne).

PORTFOLIOS *Twelve Illustrations of Life and Scenery in Queensland*, 1972; *Australia*, 1957.

COLLECTIONS All in Australia: La Trobe & Oxley Libs.; Natl. Gall. of Victoria; Queensland Hist. Soc.; Queensland Mus.; Royal Melbourne Inst. of Tech.

Robert D'Alessandro PHOTOGRAPHER · TEACHER Born in 1942, D'Alessandro earned a BFA in Graphic Design from Pratt Institute in Brooklyn, New York, in 1965 and an MFA in Photography from Brooklyn College in 1971. Robert Frank and Walker Evans are his major influences.

A freelance photographer since 1968, D'Alessandro has also held a number of teaching positions: assistant professor of photography, Brooklyn College (1974–present); photographer-in-residence, University of New Mexico, Albuquerque (1973); adjunct instructor in basic photography and art, Brooklyn College (1970–72); associate adjunct professor in graduate photography, New York University School of Education, New York City (1972); and instructor in advanced and basic photography, New School for Social Research, New York City (1970–72).

D'Alessandro won an NEA grant in 1975 and a CAPS grant in 1971. He also earned first prize at the Mount Holyoke College Art Museum Exhibition in 1971 and the judges' prize at the "City of Man" Exhibit of the University of Chicago in 1970.

PUBLICATIONS Monograph: *Glory*, 1973. Anthologies: *Family of Woman*, 1979; *Light Readings*, A. D. Coleman, 1979; *Photographers Cookbook*, Deborah Barsel, 1979; *Photography in New Mexico From Daguerreotype to the Present*, Van Deren Coke, 1979. Periodicals (selected): "Artists' Post Cards," *Portfolio Magazine*, 1979; *Popular Photography Annual*, incl. interview, 1976; *Popular Photography Annual—International Edition*, 1969.

COLLECTIONS IMP/GEH, Rochester; Lincoln First Bank of Rochester; New School for Social Research, NYC; Ryerson Polytechnical Inst.; Univ. of N. Mex. Fine Arts Mus., Albuquerque; James Van Der Zee Inst., New York. Bibliothèque Nationale, Paris; Natl. Museums of Canada, Ottawa.

ADDRESS 60 Washington Ave, Brooklyn, NY 11205.

John Henry Dallmeyer OPTICIAN · LENS MANUFACTURER Born September 6, 1830, in Loxton, Westphalia, Germany, Dallmeyer died December 30, 1883, in New Zealand. He left school at sixteen, then moved to England in 1851 where he learned the optical profession in the factory of his father-in-law, Andrew Ross. Dallmeyer's son, Thomas Rudolf Dallmeyer, was also an optician and carried on his father's business.

In 1858 Dallmeyer made lenses for Thomas Skaife's camera, the Pistolgraph, and a year later, after Ross' death, he opened his own business to manufacture photographic and telescope lenses. The lenses he produced included a rapid Petzval-type lens, a triple achromatic lens (1860), a stereoscopic lens, a wide-angle landscape lens (1866), a portrait lens allowing a sharp flat field or a diffusion of focus (1866), an aplanat lens which became world-popular (1866) and a wide-angle (100 degree) rectilinear lens.

Dallmeyer received numerous honors, including the Cross of the Legion of Honor and the Russian Order of St. Stanislaus. He served on the Council of RPS and of the Royal Astronomical Society.

PUBLICATIONS Books: *Cassell's Cyclopedia of Photography*, 1912; *Telephotography*, Thomas R. Dallmeyer, 1899. Anthology: *Photography's Great Inventors*, Louis W. Sipley, 1965. Periodicals: *Jahrbuch für Photographie und Reproduktionstechnik*, Josef Maria Eder, 1891; *Photographic News*, 1889, 1864; *British Journal of Photography*, 1884.

Thomas Rudolph Dallmeyer OPTICIAN · LENS MANUFACTURER Born in 1859, Dallmeyer died in 1906. His father, John Henry Dallmeyer (1830–

83), was also an optician, and founded the lens company that Thomas eventually took over.

For some years prior to his father's death, the younger Dallmeyer actively managed the family business. He patented the first practical telephoto lens in 1891, for which he received the 1896 Progress Medal of RPS. His other inventions included a mirror reflex camera (1893), a camera with an internal rotatable mirror capable of making four negatives (1898), an astigmatic corrector for residual errors in older-type lenses (1895) and a mirror reflecting camera (1900).

He served as president of RPS from 1900 to 1902.

PUBLICATIONS Books: *Cassell's Cyclopedia of Photography*, 1912; *Telephotography*, 1899. Anthology: *Photography's Great Inventors*, Louis W. Sipley, 1965. Periodicals: *Jahrbuch für Photographie und Reproduktionstechnik*, Josef Maria Eder, 1891; *Photographic News*, 1889, 1864; *British Journal of Photography*, 1884.

Stephen Neale Dalton PHOTOGRAPHER · NATURALIST · AUTHOR Dalton was born October 2, 1937.

A freelancer, he concentrates on the photography of wildlife.

He is a Fellow of the Institute of Incorporated Photographers, and won both an Honorary Fellowship and a Silver Progress Medal from London's Royal Photographic Society in 1978. His other honors include: Nikon Award (1977), Animal Photographer of the Year (1972), Hood Medal of the Royal Photographic Society (1971), and a Kodak Scholarship in Advanced Photography (1962). In 1970 he received a Kodak Award for having developed a system and technique for photographing insects in free flight.

One of Dalton's photographs of a wasp in flight was sent into space on board the Voyager I spacecraft. He was the subject of a BBC television documentary, "The World About Us," in 1978.

PUBLICATIONS Books: *The Miracle of Flight*, 1978; *Borne on the Wind, the Extraordinary World of Insect Flight*, 1975; *Bees from Close-Up*, 1968; *Ants from Close-Up*, 1967.

COLLECTION RPS, London.

ADDRESS Holly Farmhouse, Cob Lane, Ardingly, Sussex, England.

Bill Zulpo Dane PHOTOGRAPHER · TEACHER Born in Pasadena, California, in 1938, Dane earned his BA in Art and Political Science from the University of California, Berkeley, in 1964 and his MA in Painting from that school in 1968. He studied with Diane Arbus and Lee Friedlander in 1971 at Hampshire College, Amherst, Massachusetts.

From 1966 to the present he has taught art and photography in the Berkeley, California, public schools.

Dane won NEA Photographer's Fellowships in 1976 and 1977 and a Guggenheim Fellowship in 1973.

The photographer has mailed over 15,000 of his photographs as postcards to "relatives, friends, acquaintances, presidents, directors, galleries and museums."

PUBLICATIONS Anthology: *The Snapshot*, 1975. Catalog: *Mirrors and Windows*, 1978 (MOMA: NYC). Periodicals: "Love/Hate Relationships," *Artforum*, summer 1978; *Creative Camera*, Sept 1976.

ADDRESS POB 331, Richmond, CA 94801.

Jerry Dantzic PHOTOGRAPHER Born in 1925 in Baltimore, Maryland, Dantzic received a BA in English and Journalism from Kent State University in Kent, Ohio, in 1950, and attended the Alexey Brodovitch Workshop at the New School for Social Research in New York City (1954–55).

Dantzic has been self-employed as a freelance photojournalist and illustrator working out of his studio in New York since 1956. He also has been teaching courses in beginning and advanced photography at Long Island University Brooklyn Center in New York City since 1967.

Since 1954 Dantzic has been a member of ASMP and was the recipient of several awards, including a Guggenheim Fellowship in 1977, an NEA grant in 1975 and an Advertising Club of New York Distinctive Merit Award in 1967.

PUBLICATIONS Periodicals: *American Photographer*, Sept 1978; *Modern Photography*, Aug 1978; *Time*, May 29, 1978; *Du*, Feb 1977.

COLLECTIONS MOMA, NYC; N.Y. Historical Society, NYC; Smithsonian Inst., Wash., D.C.

ADDRESS 910 President St, Brooklyn, NY 11215.

Avery Coffey Danziger PHOTOGRAPHER Born in 1953 in Chapel Hill, North Carolina, Danziger studied at the University of North Carolina in Chapel Hill, Eisenhower College in Seneca Falls, New York, and the Instituto Allende in San Miguel de Allende, Mexico. He attended workshops at Penland School of Crafts in Penland, North Carolina, the Visual Studies Workshop in Rochester and New England School of Photography in Boston.

Danziger is currently a self-employed photographer.

He was the recipient of an NEA Photographer's Fellowship in 1979 and a teaching fellowship in photography at the Instituto Allende.

Danziger uses strobe in daylight and selective camera motion to produce color prints of dogs, plants and statues.

PUBLICATIONS Catalogs: *Perspectives*, 1979 (R. J. Reynolds Press: Winston-Salem, N.C.); *39th Annual North Carolina Artists Exhibition*, Dec 1976 (North Carolina Mus. of Art Press). Periodicals: "A Selection of Color Photographs—1979," Hunter Drohojowska, Apr 21, 1979, "Los Angeles Enters '79," Dinah Portner, Jan 27, 1979, *Artweek*; *Picture Magazine*, no. 13, Dec 1979.

COLLECTIONS MOMA, NYC; San Francisco Mus. of Modern Art. Bibliothèque Nationale, Paris.

ADDRESS 937 N Harper, W Hollywood, CA 90046.

Edward F. D'Arms, Jr. PHOTOGRAPHER · ACTOR · DIRECTOR Born May 20, 1937, in Minneapolis, Minnesota, D'Arms was influenced by W. Eugene Smith, Minor White, Joseph Sudek and Paul Strand. His father, Edward F. D'Arms (1904–), an educator, was one-time dean of the University of Colorado (1943) and has been an executive administrator for both the Rockefeller Foundation and the National Endowment for the Humanities.

Edward, Jr., has worked in the theater in Seattle, Washington, since 1969 as an actor, director and teacher, pursuing photography "exclusively on a personal basis." He writes on photography for *The Weekly*, a Seattle newspaper, and taught aesthetics at the University of Washington in 1974–75. D'Arms won an NEA Photographer's Fellowship in 1972.

Working in black-and-white and color, he produces abstractions, landscapes and portraits, attempting to record "personal revelation that has universal appeal."

PUBLICATIONS Periodicals: *Aperture* 17:2, 1973; *Camera*, May 1971; *U.S. Camera Annual*, 1971.

COLLECTIONS Northwest Pacific Bell Cllctn., Seattle; Rainier Bank Cllctn., Seattle; Seattle Arts Commission.

DEALER Marcuse Pfeifer Gall., 825 Madison Ave, New York, NY 10021.

ADDRESS 3211 40 W, Seattle, WA 98199.

Judy Dater PHOTOGRAPHER Born on June 21, 1941, in Hollywood, California, Dater attended the University of California at Los Angeles

(1959–62) and completed a bachelor's (1963) and a master's degree (1966) at San Francisco State University. She was formerly married to photographer Jack Welpott. Imogen Cunningham was her mentor.

Since 1978 she has been self-employed. Previously she taught at the University of California Extension (1966–75) and at the San Francisco Art Institute (1975–78).

She is a member of the San Francisco Camerawork Gallery and serves on their board of directors. She was the recipient of a Guggenheim Fellowship (1978), an NEA grant (1976) and a Dorothea Lange Award (1974).

Until 1979 the artist's work consisted mainly of black-and-white photographs. Since then she has started using color negative materials. She specializes in portraits and nudes, but is also interested in landscapes and miscellaneous subjects.

PUBLICATIONS Books: *Imogen Cunningham*, 1978; *Women and Other Visions*, w/Jack Welpott, 1975. Anthologies: *The Photograph Collector's Guide*, Lee D. Witkin & Barbara London, 1979; *Darkroom II*, Jain Kelly, 1978; *Faces*, Ben Maddow, 1977; *The Woman's Eye*, Anne Tucker, 1973; *Photography Year 1973*. Catalogs: *Private Realities—Recent American Photography*, Clifford S. Ackley, 1975 (Boston Mus. of Fine Arts).

COLLECTIONS CCP, Tucson; MOMA, NYC; San Francisco Mus. of Modern Art; Oakland Mus., Calif. Bibliothèque Nationale, Paris.

DEALERS Witkin Gall., 41 E 57 St, New York, NY 10022; Grapestake Gall., 2876 California St, San Francisco, CA 94115.

ADDRESS POB 79, San Anselmo, CA 94960.

Alma Davenport PHOTOGRAPHER Born October 5, 1949, in Gary, Indiana, Davenport earned a BFA (1970) and an MFA (1975) from the Rhode Island School of Design in Providence, where she studied with Harry Callahan, Aaron Siskind and Minor White.

As of this date she was writing a book on SX-70 photography for Van Nostrand/Curtin and London Publishers. She is also the acting director of arts education for the State of Rhode Island. In 1978–79 she was artist-in-residence and co-director of photographic workshops at the Department of Corrections, Adult Correctional Institute, Men's Maximum Security Prison. Davenport was associate professor of photography and head of the Photography Department at Rhode Island Junior College, Warwick, from 1976 to 1978, and taught photography at Brown University in Providence, Rhode Island (1975–76).

She has belonged to SPE since 1977, and serves on the Media Advisory Panel of the Rhode Island State Council on the Arts.

In 1978 she received a photographer-in-residence grant from the Rhode Island State Council on the Arts.

PUBLICATIONS Anthologies: *Faces and Facades*, 1980; *Family of Woman*, 1979; *Celebrations*, Minor White & Jonathan Green, eds., 1974.

COLLECTIONS ICP, NYC; L/C, Wash., D.C.; R.I. School of Design Mus., Providence; Tyler School of Art, Philadelphia. Natl. Gall. of Can., Ottawa, Ontario; Polaroid Intl. Cllctn., Amsterdam, The Netherlands.

DEALERS O.K. Harris Gall., 383 W Broadway, New York, NY 10012; Jeb Gall., S Main St, Providence, RI 02901.

ADDRESS 18 Creighton St, Providence, RI 02906.

Bruce Davidson PHOTOGRAPHER · FILM DIRECTOR Born September 5, 1933, in Chicago, Illinois, Davidson studied at Rochester Institute of Technology and at Yale University's School of Design in New Haven, Connecticut.

A freelance photographer and film maker, Davidson worked a year for *Life* magazine before joining Magnum Photos in 1958.

In 1962 Davidson received a Guggenheim Fellowship to photograph the civil rights movement, and in 1966 received the first photography grant from the NEA.

His first film, *Living Off the Land* (1970), was shown on CBS-TV and received the Critics Award from the American Film Festival. His 1973 film, *Isaac Singer's Nightmare and Mrs. Pupko's Beard*, won first prize in fiction at the American Film Festival. As of this writing he is working on a feature film.

Davidson describes his work as "a personal study of the contemporary world." He creates mainly portraits, combined with essays, that show a close rapport between Davidson and the people he photographs.

PUBLICATIONS Monographs: *Bruce Davidson Photographs*, 1979; *East 100th Street*, 1970. Anthology: *The Photograph Collector's Guide*, Lee D. Witkin & Barbara London, 1979.

COLLECTIONS Art Inst. of Chicago; Harvard Univ., Carpenter Ctr. for the Visual Arts, Cambridge, Mass.; Harvard Univ., Fogg Art Mus.; Metro. Mus. of Art, NYC; MOMA, NYC; Smithsonian Inst.; Univ. of Kans. Mus. of Art, Lawrence; Univ. of Nebr., Sheldon Mem. Art Gall., Lincoln; Yale Univ. Art Gall., New Haven, Conn.

REPRESENTATIVE Magnum Photos Inc., 15 W 46 St, New York, NY 10036.
ADDRESS 209 W 86 St, New York, NY 10024.

Bevan O. Davies PHOTOGRAPHER Born in Chicago on October 8, 1941, Davies attended for two years the University of Chicago, where he studied under Bruce Davidson. He works as a freelance photographer specializing in copying artworks. In 1978 he received an NEA grant and in 1979 a Traveling Fellowship to Scotland.

Davies focuses on architectural photography, using a large-format camera.

PUBLICATIONS Anthologies: *American Images*, Renato Danese, ed., 1979; *Photographie als Kunst*, Peter Weiermair, ed., 1979 (Vienna, Austria). Catalog: *Contemporary American Photographic Works*, Lewis Baltz, ed., 1977 (Mus. of Fine Arts: Houston).

COLLECTIONS Art Inst. of Chicago; IMP/GEH, Rochester; Mus. of Fine Arts, Houston.

DEALER Sonnabend Gall., 420 W Broadway, New York, NY 10012.

ADDRESS 431 W Broadway, New York, NY 10012.

George Christopher Davies PHOTOGRAPHER · GOVERNMENT OFFICIAL · SEAMAN Born in 1849 in Norwich, Norfolk County, England, Davies died there on November 29, 1922. His father, David Christopher Davies, was a noted Shropshire geologist.

George Davies served for many years as clerk of the peace and clerk of the Norfolk County Council.

A nature lover, he did much to popularize Norfolk Broads with his photographic images of the area's rivers and broads.

PUBLICATIONS Books: *Our Home in Aveyron*, 1890 (Blackwood: London); *The Swan and her Crew*, 5th ed., 1890(?) (Warne: London); *The Handbook to the Rivers and Broads of Norfolk and Suffolk*, 1887(?), *On Dutch Waterways*, 1886 (Jarrold: London); *Peter Penniless*, 1884 (Warne: London); *Practical Boat-Sailing for Amateurs*, 1880; *Wildcat Tower*, 1877 (Warne: London); *Angling Idylls*, 1876 (Chapman & Hall: London); *Rambles and Adventures of the School Field Club*, 1875; *Mountain, Meadow and Mere*, 1874 (King: London).

John Arthur Davies TEACHER · PHOTOGRAPHER Born December 11, 1949, in Sedgefield, England, Davies received a diploma in creative photography in 1974 from Trent Polytechnic, Nottingham, England.

A photography lecturer at Blackpool College of Art since 1978, he was a photographer at Sotheby's, Belgravia, London, in 1976. He joined the Visual Arts Committee at North West Arts in 1979.

Davies won Arts Council of Great Britain awards in 1975, 1976, 1977 and 1978, and was recently named a Photographic Fellow at Sheffield Polytechnic.

The photographer is concerned with the effects of the elements and land formations on the rural landscape.

PUBLICATIONS Periodicals: *Photoflash*, Nov 1979; "Perspectives on Landscape," *British Image* V, 1978; *British Journal of Photography Annual*, 1978, 1977; *Photo Technique*, 1977; *Aggie Westons*, summer 1976; *Creative Camera*, May 1976; *British Journal of Photography*, Feb 1976.

COLLECTIONS Arts Council of Great Britain, London; Dept. of the Environment, London; Southampton Univ., England; West Midland Arts Assoc., Stafford, England. Bibliothèque Nationale, Paris.

ADDRESS 2 Laurel Rd, Heaton Moor, Stockport, Chesire, England.

Theodore Peter Davies PHOTOGRAPHER · PAINTER · MIXED-MEDIA ARTIST Born on October 9, 1928, in Brooklyn, New York, Davies obtained a BA from the New York University School of Commerce in 1950. He pursued his education in New York City, attending the School of Modern Photography (1953–54) and the Art Students League (1957–60), and studied with George Grosz and Harry Sternberg.

He is currently working as Visual Arts Coordinator on the Queens Council on the Arts, as an instructor in photo-serigraphy at the Jamaica Arts Center in New York, and as a freelance photographer.

Davies is a member of two New York societies: the Queens Artists Association and the Art Students League, for which he has served as a recording secretary. In 1958 he won a John Sloan Merit Scholarship from the Art Students League of New York and, in 1973, a CAPS Fellowship in Printmaking.

Davies collaborated with Harry Sternberg on a short film entitled *The Many Worlds of Art*.

Besides specializing in photograms and photo-serigraphy, the artist "uses photography extensively in printmaking, collage, painting and mixed-media works."

PUBLICATIONS Periodicals: *Popular Photogra-*

phy Annual, 1961, 1956; *Aperture*, 8:2, 1960; *Popular Photography*, Nov 1955.

COLLECTIONS   Art Students League of N.Y., NYC; Brigham Young Univ., Provo, Utah; MOMA, NYC; Natl. Gall. of Art, Wash. D.C. (woodcuts); N.Y. Stock Exchange; Philadelphia Mus. of Art (woodcuts).

REPRESENTATIVE   Assoc. of American Artists, 663 Fifth Ave, New York, NY 10022.

ADDRESS   87-38 Santiago St, Hollis, NY 11423.

Thomas Landon Davies   *PHOTOGRAPHER · TEACHER · GALLERY DIRECTOR*   Born September 15, 1943, in Bryn Mawr, Pennsylvania, Davies received a BA in Psychology in 1965 and an MA in Art in 1976. He took workshops with Ansel Adams in 1966 and 1975 and with Minor White in 1971.

Davis co-founded The Photography Place, a complete photographic facility and gallery, in Philadelphia, in 1971, and has co-directed it since then. He has also been a photography lecturer at Rosemont College, Pennsylvania, since 1973 and was an instructor in photography at the University of Delaware, Newark (1973–76).

A member of SPE since 1972, Davies won a Connelly Foundation grant in 1979 for the study of pre-1850 photographic equipment and materials. In 1973 he invented the Davies focusing tunnel, "a major innovation in dark-cloth technology." In 1978 his camera obscura was included in *Fine Woodworking's Biennial Design Book Two*.

Davies works in large-format platinum, palladium, and silver printing, using selenium and sepia toning.

PUBLICATIONS   Book: *Shoots: A Guide to Your Family's Photographic Heritage*, 1977. Periodical: *Photographers Forum*, May 1980.

PORTFOLIO   *The Cow Portfolio*, 1974.

COLLECTIONS   Miller Plummer Cllctn., Philadelphia, Pa.; Philadelphia Mus. of Art. Photogalerie Die Brücke, Vienna, Austria.

REPRESENTATIVE   The Photography Place, 132 S 17 St, Philadelphia, PA 19103.

Bob Davis   *PHOTOGRAPHER*   Born in Melbourne, Australia, on August 8, 1944, Davis studied film production in Hobart, Tasmania, in 1963–64.

A freelance photographer, he is a member of AMPAS, the Hong Kong Foreign Correspondents' Club and, in 1973, joined the National Union of Journalists in London.

Davis works only in small format, his personal style being mainly black-and-white reportage. He also does commercial travel photographs in color.

PUBLICATIONS   Book: *Faces of Japan*, 1978 (Kodansha Internatl.: Japan). Periodicals: *Zoom*, 1979 (Paris); *British Journal of Photography*, 1979, 1973, 1971; *Camera Mainichi*, 1978; *Photo Technique*, 1974; *Image Magazine*, 1972.

COLLECTION   Natl. Gall. of Victoria, Melbourne, Australia.

REPRESENTATIVES   Aspect Picture Library, 73 Kingsmead Ave, Worcester Park, Surrey KT4, 8UZ, England; Pacific Press Services, Tokyo Central POB 2051, Tokyo, Japan; Woodfin Camp & Associates, 415 Madison Ave, New York, NY 10017.

ADDRESS   7th Floor, 69 Wyndham St, Hong Kong.

Keith F. Davis   *CURATOR · PHOTOGRAPHIC HISTORIAN*   Born in Middletown, Connecticut, on June 29, 1952, Davis received a BS in Cinema and Photography from Southern Illinois University, Carbondale, in 1974. He studied with Charles Swedlund. At the University of New Mexico, Albuquerque, where Davis received an MA in Art History in 1978, he was influenced by Beaumont Newhall, Van Deren Coke and Tom Barrow.

In 1979 Davis became curator of Hallmark Collections, the photo and art holdings of Hallmark Cards, Inc., in Kansas City, Missouri. From 1978 to 1979 he was a research intern at IMP/GEH, Rochester, and in 1978 was a teaching associate in the Art Department at the University of New Mexico, Albuquerque.

Davis belongs to Friends of Photography, George Eastman House, SPE, National Stereoscopic Association and CCP. He won the University of New Mexico's first Beaumont Newhall History of Photography Award in 1977.

Davis is interested in "the entire history of photography, with a specialty in nineteenth-century expeditionary work."

PUBLICATIONS   Periodicals: "History in Words and History in Photographs," *Image*, Sept 1979; "Photography at the University of New Mexico," *Artspace*, summer 1977.

ADDRESS   4850 Oak #4, Kansas City, MO 64112.

Margo Ann Davis   *PHOTOGRAPHER · TEACHER · EDUCATION ADMINISTRATOR*   Born in New York City on January 15, 1944, Davis earned her BA in French Language and Literature from the University of California, Berkeley, in 1965. She attended photography workshops with Minor White in Boston (1965–66) and apprenticed with Dave Bohn at the ASUC Studio, Berkeley (1966–69). She has also studied at the Sorbonne in France (1963–64) and is an MA candidate at San Jose State University, California.

Since 1978 Davis has been assistant director of the Center for Research on Women at Stanford University, Palo Alto, California. In 1975 she taught at the Friends of Photography Spring Workshop and at the Ansel Adams Yosemite Portrait Workshop. She has also lectured in photography for Stanford's Freshman Seminar Program (since 1972), has taught documentary photography at the University of California, Berkeley's Extension Center (1969–70) and taught at the San Francisco Art Institute Summer Workshop (1968). In 1967–68 she was researcher and photographer for the Sausalito (California) Teacher Education Project and has been a research assistant at two Centers for Research and Development in Higher Education—Berkeley (1967) and Harvard University (1966).

Davis won a grant from the Center for Research on Women at Stanford University in 1978 for an oral/visual history project on Stanford women. She also won a grant from the Grant B. Schley Foundation (1970) and received an honorable mention in the 1970 *Life* magazine photography contest.

Her work as a documentary photographer included a seven-year project, which began in 1967, on the island of Antigua in the West Indies and led to publication of a book.

PUBLICATIONS Book: *Antigua Black; Portrait of an Island People*, w/Gregson Davis, 1973. Periodical: *Creative Camera*, Oct 1973.

COLLECTIONS Stanford Univ. Mus., Palo Alto, Calif. Bibliothèque Nationale, Paris; and private collections.

ADDRESS c/o Center for Research on Women, Serra House, Serra St, Stanford University, Stanford, CA 94305.

Myron Hoff Davis   PHOTOJOURNALIST · TEACHER Born July 3, 1919, in Chicago, Illinois, Davis received a BA in English Language and Literature from the University of Chicago.

Since 1978 he has been teaching at Columbia College in Chicago. He previously worked as a photojournalist for *Life* magazine from 1940 to 1945.

Davis is a member of ASMP.

PUBLICATIONS Books: *Life Goes to War*, David E. Scherman, ed., 1977; *Life Goes to the Movies*, David E. Scherman, ed., 1975; *Weather*,

Time-Life Books, 1968; *Sandburg*, Edward Steichen, 1966; *The Land and Wildlife of South America*, 1964, *Machines*, 1964, *The Scientist*, 1964, *The Desert*, 1961, Time-Life Books; *Days to Remember, America 1945–1955*, John Gunther & Bernard Quint, 1956; *World Theatre in Pictures*, Tom Prideaux, 1953.

ADDRESS 5722 Stony Island, Chicago, IL 60637.

Robert Hobart Davis   EDITOR · DRAMATIST · PHOTOGRAPHER Born March 23, 1869, in Brownsville, Nebraska, Davis died in 1942, probably in New York.

In his youth Davis worked as a compositor on the *Carson Appeal* and later was a reporter for the *San Francisco Examiner, Call* and *Chronicle*. He founded and edited *Chic*, a San Francisco fortnightly (1894). Davis then moved to New York and worked for the *Journal* and *American* (1895–1903) and *N.Y. Sunday World* (1903), and was managing editor of *N.Y. Sunday News* (1904). He also served as associate editor of *Munsey's Magazine* and was founder and first managing editor of *All-Story Magazine, Scrap Book, Railroad Man's Magazine, Woman, The Ocean, The Live Wire* and *The Cavalier*. He wrote the "Bob Davis Reveals" column for the *New York Sun* for fifteen years. Davis belonged to the Overseas Press Club.

A prolific writer and widely traveled reporter, Davis made some 3,000 portraits of prominent people during his career. He used his images of foreign people and places to illustrate his many books.

PUBLICATIONS Monograph: *Man Makes His Own Mask*, 1932. Books: *Canada Cavalcade*, 1937; *Oriental Odyssey*, 1937; *The More I Admire Dogs—True Tales of Man's Best Friend*, 1936; *People, People Everywhere*, 1936; *Tree Toad, The Autobiography of a Small Boy*, 1935; *Bob Davis at Large*, 1934; *Islands Far and Near*, 1933; *Bob Davis Hither and Yon*, 1931; *Let's Go With Bob Davis, The Caliph of Bagdad—Life of O. Henry*, w/Arthur B. Maurice, 1931; *On Home Soil with Bob Davis*, 1930; *Bob Davis Abroad*, 1929; *Bob Davis Again—In Many Moods*, preface by Fannie Hurst, 1928; *Bob Davis Recalls*, 1927; *Over My Left Shoulder*, 1926; *Ruby Robert—Alias Bob Fitzsimmons*, 1926; *We Are French*, w/Perley P. Sheehan, 1914. Plays: *Efficiency and Laughter*, 1917; *The Family*, 191?.

George Davison   PHOTOGRAPHER · BUSINESS ADMINISTRATOR Born in 1854 in Lowestoft, England, Davison died in 1930 in Antibes, France. He was influenced by Peter Henry Emerson.

First employed as an audit clerk at England's Treasury, Davis became associated with the Kodak Company in that country in 1897 and quickly became its managing director in 1898. He served on Kodak's board of directors until 1913, when he failed to be reelected due to his anarchist activities. Having been one of the company's early shareholders, however, he left the firm as a wealthy man.

One of the first members of the London Camera Club (1885), Davison served as its secretary in 1886, the year he joined RPS. He won RPS Society Medal in 1890 and was a founding member of The Linked Ring in 1892.

Davison has been attributed with the founding of the impressionist school of photography in 1890. He was particularly skilled at producing photogravure prints (which he frequently sold as Christmas cards). His work would sometimes swing radically from pictorialism to journalism.

PUBLICATIONS Anthologies: *Pictorial Photography in Great Britain 1900–1920*, Arts Council of Great Britain, 1978; *The Magic Image*, Cecil Beaton & Gail Buckland, 1975; *Camera Work: A Critical Anthology*, Jonathan Green, ed., 1973.

COLLECTIONS Kodak Mus., Harrow, England; RPS, London.

Dawid (Björn Dawidsson) *PHOTOGRAPHER* Born July 6, 1949, in Örebro, Sweden, Dawid attended Fotoskolan (The Photoschool) (1969–70) and Beckman School of Advertising (1970–71), both in Stockholm.

A freelance photographer, Dawid also teaches photography occasionally at the Beckman School of Advertising. He received a Culture Grant from the government of Sweden in 1979, and a writers grant from the Swedish state in 1980.

Using various large formats, the photographer works with "found and made objects arranged in a collage/still-life style." He contact-prints his negatives and tones prints individually.

PUBLICATIONS Books: *Bilsamhället*, Magnus Mörk, 1978; *Verkligen*, w/Måkan Lind, 1978; *Så bleu mitl Liv*, Lars Ulvenstam, 1976. Periodicals: *Svensk Fotografi*, no. 2, 1980; *Interi*, no. 3/4, 1979; *Foto*, Feb 1976, Dec 1971; *Ord & Bild*, no. 4, 1975; *Aktuell Fotografi*, Mar 1974.

COLLECTION Fotografiska Muséet, Stockholm.

DEALER Camera Obscura Gall., Kåkrinken 5, 11127 Stockholm, Sweden.

ADDRESS Geijersvägen 25, 11244 Stockholm, Sweden.

Fred Holland Day *PHOTOGRAPHER · PUBLISHER* Born July 8, 1864, in Norwood, Massachusetts, Day died in his home town on November 2, 1933. He was educated at Chauncy Hall, a private school in Boston. He was a distant cousin of photographer Alvin Langdon Coburn.

Day began doing photography about 1887. With Harvard professor Herbert Copeland he established the publishing company of Copeland & Day (1893–99). Having been born into a wealthy family, Day was free to pursue his craft and spent much effort in convincing the art world that it should embrace photography. Through his publishing firm he produced very fine books of poetry and other literary works, notably several illustrated books by Aubrey Beardsley, including *The Chap Book*. He was an admirer of Keats, and his collection of the poet's letters, manuscripts and first editions was the finest of its day.

Day joined The Linked Ring in 1896. He carried on an active correspondence with Stieglitz, but was at odds with him and refused to join the Photo-Secessionists. He was also an accomplished painter.

As a pictorialist, Day found his chief interest in recreating legendary and Biblical scenes. He is most remembered for the remarkable series of about 250 photographs of the last days of Christ, in which Day himself portrayed the Savior. He worked with medium and large format; most of his prints were platinum. He also did many male nude studies and portraits of friends and servants, with an emphasis on the exotic.

PUBLICATIONS Books: *The Photographic Work of F. Holland Day*, Ellen Fritz Clattenburg, 1975; *Keats and the Bostonians*, Edw. Rollins Hyder & Stephen Maxfield Parrish, 1951. Anthologies: *The Photograph Collector's Guide*, Lee D. Witkin & Barbara London, 1979; *Photography Rediscovered*, David Travis & Anne Kennedy, 1979; *The Collection of Alfred Stieglitz*, Weston J. Naef, 1978; *Pictorial Photography in Great Britain, 1900–1920*, 1978; *The Valiant Knights of Daguerre . . .*, Sadakichi Hartmann, Harry W. Lawton & George Know, eds., 1978; *The Invented Eye*, Edward Lucie-Smith, 1975; *The Magic Image*, Cecil Beaton & Gail Buckland, 1975.

COLLECTIONS Art Inst. of Chicago; IMP/GEH, Rochester; L/C, Wash., D.C.; Metro. Mus. of Art, NYC; Norwood Historical Society, Mass. RPS, London.

Joe Deal *PHOTOGRAPHER · TEACHER* Born August 12, 1947, in Topeka, Kansas, Deal earned a BFA from the Kansas City [Missouri] Art Institute (1970) and an MA (1974) and MFA (1978) from the University of New Mexico, Albuquerque.

An assistant professor at the University of California, Riverside, since 1976, he previously served as director of exhibitions at IMP/GEH in Rochester (1974–75).

Deal received an NEA Photographer's Fellowship in 1976 and 1980.

PUBLICATIONS Anthologies: *The History of Photography in New Mexico*, Van Deren Coke, 1979; *Photographers' Choice*, Kelly Wise, ed., 1975. Catalogs: *Attitudes: Photography in the 1970's*, Fred Parker, 1979 (Santa Barbara Mus. of Art: Calif.); *Contemporary American Photographic Works*, Lewis Baltz, ed., 1977 (Mus. of Fine Arts: Houston); *The Great West: Real/Ideal*, 1977 (Univ. of Colo.: Boulder); *New Topographics: Photographs of a Man-Altered Landscape*, 1975 (IMP/GEH: Rochester). Periodicals: *Modern Photography*, May 1979; "Joe Deal's Optical Democracy," review, James Hugunin, *Afterimage: VSW*, Feb 1979; *DuMont Foto 1: Fotokunst und Fotodesign International*, 1978; "Joe Deal: New Topographics," *Northlight 4*, 1977.

PORTFOLIOS *New California Views* (group), 1979 (Landweber Artists: Los Angeles); *Interior Details Portfolio*, 1974 (self-pub.: Albuquerque).

COLLECTIONS Ariz. State Univ., Tempe; CCP, Tucson; IMP/GEH, Rochester; Minneapolis Inst. of Art, Minn.; MOMA, NYC; Mus. of Fine Arts, Boston; Mus. of Fine Arts, Houston; Seagram Cllctn., NYC; Univ. of Colo., Boulder; Univ. of Louisville, Ky.; Univ. of N. Mex., Albuquerque. Neue Sammlung, Munich, West Germany.

DEALER Light Gall., 724 Fifth Ave, New York, NY 10019.

ADDRESS 3007 Chestnut, Riverside, CA 92501.

Nicholas Dean   PHOTOGRAPHER · WRITER · GRAPHIC DESIGNER   Born July 20, 1933, in Huntington, New York, Dean attended Dartmouth and Harvard colleges. He studied with Ansel Adams and Minor White.

Presently a freelance photographer, writer and graphic designer, Dean was a member of the National Maritime Historical Society Falkland Islands Expedition in 1979. He taught at the Haystack Mountain School of Crafts, Deer Isle, Maine, in 1972, 1978 and 1979, and has taught summers at the Penland School of Crafts in North Carolina since 1969. He was a resident craftsman at Penland in 1972–73 and an artist-in-residence at Sandhills Community College, Southern Pines, North Carolina, in 1974.

Dean belongs to the Friends of the Wiscasset Schooners and is a member of the National Maritime Historical Society.

The photographer generally works in "large-format silver prints dealing with New England landscape." Since 1978 he has been especially concerned with nineteenth- and early twentieth-century sailing vessels.

PUBLICATIONS Books: *Portland*, Martin Dibner, ed., 1972; *Blues & Roots/Rue & Bluets*, w/ Jonathan Williams, 1971; *Lubec*, intro. by Ansel Adams, 1967.

COLLECTIONS Addison Gall. of American Art, Andover, Mass.; Harvard Univ., Cambridge, Mass,; IMP/GEH, Rochester; MIT, Cambridge; MOMA, NYC; Portland Mus. of Art, Maine; UCLA; Univ. of Maine, Augusta; Univ. of Minn., Minneapolis.

REPRESENTATIVE Ocean Science Associates, POB 187, Wiscasset, ME 04578.

ADDRESS River Road, RFD 1, Box 242, N Edgecomb, ME 04556.

Roy Rudolph DeCarava   PHOTOGRAPHER   [See plate 84]   Born December 9, 1919, in New York City, DeCarava studied painting with Byron Thomas and Morris Kantor at Cooper Union Institute (1938–40), painting with Elton Fax at Harlem Art Center (1940–42), and drawing and painting with Charles White at George Washington Carver Art School (1944–45), all in New York City.

He was appointed associate professor of art at Hunter College in New York City in 1975, and in 1979 became a full professor. Previously he was an adjunct instructor in photography at Cooper Union (1969–72) and a contract photographer for *Sports Illustrated* magazine, 1968–75. De-Carava's photographs have also appeared in such publications as *Look*, *Newsweek*, *Time* and *Life*.

A member of ASMP from 1963 to 1966, he chaired its Committee to End Discrimination Against Black Photographers. He also founded and directed A Photographers Gallery in New York City (1954–56) and was a member of the National Serigraph Society (1944–46).

DeCarava was the first black artist to win a Guggenheim Fellowship (1952). He has also received a Certificate of Recognition from the Mt. Morris United Presbyterian Church and Community Life Center in New York City (1969) and the Benin Award (1972).

Working in black-and-white, the photographer began shooting New York life, mainly Harlem, in 1946. He also is known for his portraits of jazz artists.

PUBLICATIONS Monograph: *Roy DeCarava, Photographer*, Jim Alinder, 1970. Books: *Light Readings*, A. D. Coleman, 1979; *Seventeen Black Artists*, Elton Fax, 1973; *Photography in America*, Robert Doty, 1974; *The Movement*, Lorraine Hansberry, 1964; *The Sweet Flypaper of Life*, w/ Langston Hughes, 1955; *The Columbia Historical Portrait of New York*, John A. Kouwenhoven, 1953. Anthologies: *American Images*, Renato Danese, 1980; *Photography of the Fifties*, Helen Gee, 1980; *The Photograph Collector's Guide*, Lee D. Witkin & Barbara London, 1979; *Mirrors and Windows*, John Szarkowski, 1978; *Looking at Photographs*, John Szarkowski, 1973; *Photography in the Twentieth Century*, Nathan Lyons, 1967; *The Photographer's Eye*, John Szarkowski, 1966; *The Family of Man*, Edward Steichen, ed., 1955. Catalogs: *Roy DeCarava, The Nation's Capital in Photographs, 1976*, 1976 (Corcoran Gall. of Art: Wash., D.C.); *Roy DeCarava: Photographs*, Alvia Wardlaw Short, 1975 (Mus. of Fine Arts: Houston). Periodicals: *Black Photographers Annual*, vol. 3, 1975, vol. 2, 1974, 1973; *Creative Camera*, Mar 1972; *Popular Photography*, Apr 1970; *Infinity: ASMP*, Apr 1964, Sept 1955; *Camera*, Jan 1960; *U.S. Camera Annual*, 1953; *Popular Photography Annual*, 1953.

PORTFOLIO *Untitled*, 1977 (self-pub.: NYC).

COLLECTIONS Andover Art Gall., Andover-Phillips Academy, Mass.; Art Inst. of Chicago; Atlanta Univ., Ga.; Belafonte Enterprises, Inc., NYC; CCP, Tucson; Corcoran Gall. of Art, Wash., D.C.; Harlem Art Cllctn., N.Y. State Office Bldg., NYC; Metro. Mus. of Art, NYC; Menil Fndn., Inc., Houston, Tex.; MOMA, NYC; Museum of Fine Arts, Houston, Tex.; Olden Camera, NYC; Seagram Cllctn., NYC; Univ. of Neb., Sheldon Mem. Art Gall., Lincoln.

ADDRESS 81 Halsey St, Brooklyn, NY 11216.

Friederich Wilhelm Deckel *INVENTOR · PHOTOGRAPHIC EQUIPMENT MANUFACTURER* Born in Jungingen, Germany, in 1871, Deckel died in 1948. He was apprenticed for three years in a mechanical workshop.

Deckel first worked for a company manufacturing hydrographic and cartographic instruments and, in the early 1890s, went to Jena for a couple of years to work under Professor Abbe at the Zeiss factory. After having been a journeyman with various manufacturers of precision optical instruments in Germany, The Netherlands and England, Deckel moved to Munich and worked for the Steinheil firm in 1897–98. Becoming familiar with the photographic industry, he opened his own workshop to produce camera shutters and, after two years, expanded into the sale of optical instruments. He started the firm of Bruns & Deckel in 1903 to manufacture the Compound shutter, conceived by Christian Bruns and constructed by Deckel. They dissolved their partnership in 1905, whereupon Deckel incorporated his company, which continued until 1916. During World War I his factory was used by the military and, during World War II, a great portion of it was destroyed; but at the time of Deckel's death it was under reconstruction.

The inventor was especially known for his internationally successful Compur shutter, designed in 1912. Deckel received an honorary Doctor of Technical Science degree from the Technical College of Munich in 1928.

PUBLICATIONS Books: *Encyclopedia of Photography*, 1963 (Greystone Press); *Die Photographische Kamera*, Josef Stuper, 1962; *March of Photography*, Erich Stenger, 1958; *Encyclopedie voor Fotografie en Cinemagrafie*, Elsevier, 1958; *Fünfzig Jahre*, Friederich Deckel, 1953. Anthology: *Photography's Great Inventors*, Louis W. Sipley, 1965. Periodical: *Photographische Correspondenz*, 1932.

Joel DeGrand *TEACHER* Born in Kittanning, Pennsylvania, November 16, 1944, DeGrand earned a BS from Indiana University of Pennsylvania (Indiana, Pennsylvania) in 1968 and an MFA from the University of Oregon, Eugene, in 1973, where he studied with Bernard Freemesser.

Currently on the staff of Pittsburgh Film-Makers, DeGrand has been department head of the School of Cinema and Photography at the University of Pittsburgh since 1977. He was a visiting lecturer in the Department of Cinema and Photography at Southern Illinois University, Carbondale, in 1974–75.

DeGrand won an artist-in-residence grant from Pittsburgh Film-Makers in 1977 and an NEA Photographic Survey Grant in 1980. He is a member of SPE and CAA.

Using primarily large-format cameras, the photographer produces color landscapes and experiments in silver and nonsilver processes.

PUBLICATIONS Books: *Field of Vision*, 1979; *Handbook for Silver/Non-Silver Processes*, 1977 (self-pub.).

PORTFOLIO *Pittsburgh Portfolio 1*, designer, 1979.

COLLECTION Pittsburgh Film-Makers, Pittsburgh, Pa.

ADDRESS 247 N Grant Ave, Kittanning, PA 16201.

A. Michael Degtjarewsky   *PHOTOGRAPHER*
Born on December 16, 1938, in Rostov in the Soviet Union, Degtjarewsky attended California State University at Los Angeles, where he earned a BS in Mechanical Engineering in 1965. In 1969 he studied photography with Ansel Adams and Pirkle Jones. He was also influenced by Minor White and Edward Weston.

He has been a photography instructor in California at Orange Coast College in Orange since 1974, at Mount Saint Antonio College in Pomona since 1979 and at several workshops in Yosemite. During the years 1975–76 and 1978 he taught at Santa Ana College. He also works as a contributing U.S. correspondent for *Color Foto Journal* in Munich, Germany.

He is a member of SPE, Friends of Photography, the Los Angeles Center for Photographic Studies and Cameravision in Los Angeles.

Degtjarewsky considers his work to fall within the tradition of Stieglitz and Minor White. In his recent work he became "interested in making images that are metaphors for the mythic and archetypal."

PUBLICATIONS   Periodicals: *Popular Photography Annual 1979; Picture Magazine*, no. 7, 1978; *Petersen's Photographic Magazine*, Mar 1974; *Camera*, July 1973; *Creative Photography*, Oct 1970.

COLLECTIONS   South Shores Management Inc., Torrance, Calif.; Polaroid Corp. of Europe.

DEALER   Stephen White Gall., 835 La Cienega Blvd, Los Angeles, CA 90069.

ADDRESS   452 N Oxford Ave, Los Angeles, CA 90004.

Charles De Kay   *POET · ART CRITIC · AUTHOR*
Born July 25, 1848, in Washington, De Kay died May 23, 1935, in New York City. His father, Commodore George C. De Kay, was a military hero. The younger De Kay attended a military academy in Connecticut, then Yale University in New Haven, Connecticut, where he graduated in 1868. After college he returned to Europe, where he had spent several childhood years (in Dresden), and, while visiting Paris and Venice, met Robert Browning, James McNeill Whistler and Henry James.

De Kay wrote poetry and critical pieces on art for numerous magazines and newspapers, joining the staff of *The New York Times* in 1876. He worked for that paper as literary editor, art editor and editorial writer until 1894, when President Grover Cleveland appointed him consul general to Berlin. On his return to the United States after three years he became associate editor of *Art World*. He continued writing for periodicals, translated and wrote several books and was a regular contributor to *The New York Times Book Review* until he became ill in 1928.

A member of the Century Club, the New York Historical Society and the National Institute of Arts and Letters, De Kay organized the Fencers Club in New York (1880) and, in Berlin, Der Berliner Fecht Klub. In 1882 he founded the Authors Club, in 1892 the National Sculpture Society, and in 1899 the National Arts Club, for which he served many years as managing director.

The critic was an expert fencer and, as master of a half-dozen languages, a book translator.

Of his criticism, Jonathan Creek wrote in *Camera Work*, "His assessments of photography and modern art were very guarded in tone and almost always flippant in style."

PUBLICATIONS   Books: *The Grisaille Glass of Paris & Wiley*, 1930; *The Califano Collection of Italian and Dutch Paintings*, 1917; *Schools of Painting*, ed., Mary Innes, 1911; *The Works of Alphonse Daudet*, 1900; *Bird Gods*, 1898; *Old Poetic Guild of Ireland*, 1890; *Side Light on Greek Art*, 1890; *Bayre: Life and Works . . .*, 1889; *Early Heroes of Ireland*, 1889; *Women in Early Ireland*, 1889; *The Bohemian*, 1878; *Life and Works of Louis Comfort Tiffany*, n.d. Poetry: *Love Poems of Louis Barneval*, ed. & intro., 1883; *The Vision of Esther*, 1882; *The Vision of Nimrod*, 1881; *Hesperus and Other Poems*, 1880. Anthology: *Camera Work: A Critical Anthology*, Jonathan Green, 1973.

Philip Henry Delamotte   *PHOTOGRAPHER ·*
GRAPHIC ARTIST · TEACHER   Delamotte was born (1821) and died (1889) in England. He trained with his father, William Delamotte (1775–1863), a painter.

From 1855 to 1879 he was a professor of drawing and perspective at King's College, London, then became a professor of fine art there until 1887. Delamotte also taught drawing to members of the royal family and was a photography instructor at the Photographic Institution, London. From 1851 to 1854 he was commissioned by the Crystal Palace Company to document the rebuilding of the Palace in Sydenham, his views serving as the basis for engravings in the *Illustrated News*, London.

A calotypist, Delamotte was one of the earliest photographers to use the medium for documentary purposes. Especially noted for his series on the Crystal Palace, he also did landscapes and some stereographs. In his later work he adopted the waxed paper negative and collodion processes.

PUBLICATIONS Books: *Holland House*, Princess Marie Liechenstein, 1874; *The Sunbeam*, ed., illus. w/F. Bedford, J. Cundall, Geo. W. Wilson, 1858; *Views of Oxford*, 1857 (Colnaghi & Co.; London); *The Oxymel Process in Photography*, 1856 (Chapman & Hall: London); *Photographic Reports of the Progress of the Works of the Crystal Palace and Gardens*, 2 vols., 1855; *Practice of Photography*, 1853. Anthologies: *The Invented Eye*, Edward Lucie-Smith, 1975; *The Magic Image*, Cecil Beaton & Gail Buckland, 1975; *Early Photographs & Early Photographers*, Oliver Mathews, 1973. Periodical: *Photographic Journal*, Feb 21, 1857.

COLLECTIONS Corning Mus. of Glass, Corning, N.Y. County Hall Members' Lib., London.

Jack Delano PHOTOGRAPHER · ILLUSTRATOR · FILMMAKER [See plate 71] Born August 1, 1914, Delano studied at Settlement Music School, Philadelphia, Pennsylvania, from 1925 to 1935 and at the Pennsylvania Academy of Fine Arts, Philadelphia, from 1932 to 1939.

A freelance photographer, book illustrator, and film and television director since 1969, Delano, prior to that time, held several posts in the Puerto Rican government's film and television services: general manager of TV and radio service (1964–69); program director for the educational TV station in San Juan (1957–64); and director/producer for educational film services (1946–52). He was also a freelance photographer and film maker from 1952 to 1957 and a photographer for the Farm Security Administration (FSA) in 1941–43.

Delano belongs to the Puerto Rico Atheneum, the Puerto Rico Society of Contemporary Music, and ASCAP. He received a National Endowment for the Humanities grant in 1979, a Guggenheim Photography Fellowship in 1946, a UNESCO Fellowship for Educational TV in 1961, and a Cresson Traveling Scholarship from the Pennsylvania Academy of Art in 1937.

Mainly known for his FSA photographs, Delano has done documentary photography and film work in Puerto Rico.

PUBLICATIONS Books: *The Iron Horse at War*, James Valle, 1977; *A Vision Shared*, Hank O'Neal, 1976; *In This Proud Land*, Roy E. Stryker & Nancy Wood, 1973; *Portrait of a Decade*, Jack Hurley, 1972; *The Emperor's Clothes*, drawings, w/Irene Delano, 1971; *Tenants of the Almighty*, Arthur Roper, 1943. Anthology: *The Photograph Collector's Guide*, Lee D. Witkin & Barbara London, 1979.

COLLECTIONS Harvard Univ., Visual Arts Ctr., Cambridge, Mass.; L/C, Wash., D.C.; MOMA, NYC; N.Y. Pub. Lib. Picture Cllctn.; Univ. of Louisville, Ky.; Univ. of Minn., Minneapolis.

DEALER Sonnabend Gall., 420 W Broadway, New York, NY 10012.

ADDRESS RFD #2, Box 8-BB, Rio Piedras, Puerto Rico 00928.

Eugène Delcroix PHOTOGRAPHER Born in 1891 in New Orleans, Delcroix died in 1967.

A commercial photographer in New Orleans, Delcroix worked for C. Bennett Moore and regularly contributed to the *Jefferson Review* from 1940 to the 1960s.

Delcroix's 2,000 surviving prints and negatives consist of French-quarter and bayou scenes in Louisiana.

COLLECTION New Orleans Mus. of Art.

ARCHIVE New Orleans Museum of Art, Lelong Ave City Park, New Orleans, LA 70119.

Geri Della Rocca de Candal PHOTOGRAPHER Born May 17, 1942, in Rome, Della Rocca de Candal is a self-taught photographer who became seriously involved in the art in 1968.

Working in black-and-white, the photographer "started working in the media doing 'reportage' photography and photojournalism. "At present," he says, "my main interest as well as field of research is toward the 'urban landscape' seen through an abstract interpretation."

PUBLICATIONS Book: *Effects and Experiments in Photography*, 1973 (Focal Press: London). Periodicals: *British Journal of Photography Annual*, 1979, 1976, 1970; *Photography Year Book*, 1972–80; *Photographie*, July 1978, July 1977; *Creative Camera*, July 1974.

COLLECTIONS Amon Carter Mus., Ft. Worth, Tex.; Lehigh Univ., Bethlehem, Pa.; L/C, Wash., D.C.; Polaroid Cllctn., Cambridge; Smithsonian Inst., Wash., D.C.; Univ. of Kansas Mus. of Art, Lawrence; Univ. of Missouri/Columbia, Mus. of Art & Archaeology; Univ. of N. Mex., Albuquerque. Art Mus. of São Paulo, São Paulo, Brazil; Bibliothèque Nationale, Paris; Musée Réattu, Arles, France; Photographic Museum of Finland, Helsinki.

ADDRESS Via Cappuccio n. 18, 20123 Milan, Italy.

Peter de Lory PHOTOGRAPHER · TEACHER · AUTO MECHANIC Born in Orleans, Massachusetts, on October 2, 1948, de Lory received his

BFA from the San Francisco Art Institute in 1971. From 1968 to 1972 he also studied at the Center of the Eye Photography Workshop in Aspen, Colorado. He received his MFA in Photography in 1974 from the University of Colorado, Boulder. De Lory names Minor White as a major influence.

From 1974 to the present, De Lory has taught workshops at the Sun Valley (Idaho) Center for the Arts and Humanities, and from 1976 to 1978 he directed the Photography Department at the Center. In 1979 he was a visiting artist at the School of the Art Institute of Chicago. De Lory has also taught at the Apeiron Workshop in Millerton, New York (1976), the University of Colorado (1973) and at the Center of the Eye Photography Workshop in Aspen, Colorado (1969–72). In 1973 he was a teaching assistant to Minor White in Hotchkiss, Connecticut.

A member of SPE, De Lory won a Western States Arts Foundation Fellowship in 1976 and an NEA Photographer's Fellowship in 1978.

PUBLICATIONS Book: *Self-Portrayal, The Photographer's Image*, 1978. Periodicals: *Afterimage: VSW*, Nov 1976; *Creative Camera*, Dec 1973; *Modern Photography*, June 1973.

PORTFOLIO *Landscapes One Portfolio*, 1978 (self-published).

ADDRESS 3105 S. Lucile Seattle, WA 98108.

(Léon) Robert Demachy PHOTOGRAPHER · PAINTER · BANKER · WRITER

Born in 1859 near Paris, Demachy died in 1936 near Hennequeville, near Trouville, France. His father was Charles Adolphe Demachy, founder of the Banque Demachy. He was educated at a Jesuit school.

With C. Puyo, Demachy founded the Photo-Club de Paris and was a member of The Linked Ring (1905) and an honorary fellow of the Royal Photographic Society in the same year. After serving a year as an army volunteer, the financially independent Demachy freely pursued his interest in art—in which he was influenced by the Impressionists—music and the automobile. He began making prints with the gum-bichromate process in 1894. He introduced the modern transfer method in oil printing in Paris in the spring of 1911, having earlier experimented with the Rawlins oil process. In 1914 he gave up photography. Demachy wrote more than 1,000 articles on photographic techniques and aesthetics.

Demachy worked chiefly in the impressionistic style, using all manner of manipulative techniques. Josef Maria Eder says he "brought gum printing to high perfection." His chief subjects were portraits and landscapes. He considered photography an art only when the photographer's hand altered the image in some way.

PUBLICATIONS Monographs: *Robert Demachy: Un Portfolio de seize photographies rares*, Roméo Martinez, 1975 (Videografic: Lausanne, Switzerland); *Robert Demachy 1859–1936*, Bill Jay, 1974; *The Pictorial Work of Robert Demachy*, F. C. Lambert, 1904 (Practical Photographer Lib. Series: London) *Esthétique de la Photographie*, Paul Bourgeois, ed., 1900 (Photo-Club de Paris). Books: *Le Report des épreuves à l'huile*, 1912; *In and Out of Three Normandy Inns*, Anna Bowman Dodd, 1910; *How to Make Oil and Bromoil Prints*, w/C. H. Hewitt, 1908; *Les Procédés d'art en photographie*, w/C. Puyo, 1906 (Photo-Club de Paris); *How to Make Oil Prints—The Rawlins Process*, 1905, 5th ed., 1914; *Photo-aquatint or the Gum Bichromate Process*, w/ Alfred Maskell, 1897 (Hazell, Watson & Viney: London). Anthologies: *The Photograph Collector's Guide*, Lee D. Witkin & Barbara London, 1979; *The Collection of Alfred Stieglitz*, Weston J. Naef, 1978; *Pictorial Photography in Britain 1900–1920*, Arts Council of Great Britain, 1978; *The Magic Image*, Cecil Beaton & Gail Buckland, 1975; *Camera Work: A Critical Anthology*, Jonathan Green, ed., 1973; *Great Photographers*, Time-Life Series, 1971. Periodicals: *Camera*, entire issue, Dec 1974; *Camera Work*, July 1907, Apr 1907, Oct 1906, July 1905, July 1904, Jan 1904; "Le Procédé Ozotype," *Bulletin du Photo-Club de Paris*, Feb 1901.

COLLECTIONS Metro. Mus. of Art, NYC. In Paris: Bibliothèque Nationale; Photo-Club de Paris, Société Française. RFS, London.

Adolf (Gayne) de Meyer PHOTOGRAPHER

Born in 1868 in Paris, De Meyer died in 1949 in Hollywood, California. Donna Olga Alberta Caraccio, an artist's model, was his wife and the goddaughter (and reportedly the illegitimate daughter) of King Edward VII.

A man of independent means, De Meyer and his wife were active promoters of the arts. He began photographing in the early 1900s. Traveling to America from London at the outbreak of World War I, he joined the staff of Condé Naste, photographing for *Vogue* and *Vanity Fair*. In 1923 he was contracted to *Harper's Bazaar*, where he remained until 1935. He returned to London, then Paris, when his contract with *Harper's* was dissolved. Due to his German heritage and title, World War II forced him to leave for America again, where he died in obscurity.

He was made a German baron in 1901, and was a member of The Linked Ring (1903).

Cecil Beaton has referred to him as "the Debussy of photography." Lee Witkin says he was "the first great fashion photographer." There is no doubt that De Meyer's style—encompassing halolike backlighting, starry highlights and poses of ultracasual sophistication—still shows its influence on today's fashion photography. He is especially noted for a series he did on the ballet star Nijinsky. He worked in platinum and silver prints.

PUBLICATIONS Monograph: *De Meyer*, Robt. Brandau, ed., bio by Philippe Julian, 1976. Book: *L'Aprés-midi d'un faune*, Auguste Rodin, Jacques-Emile Blanche & Jean Cocteau, 1914 (Paul Iribe: London). Anthologies: *The Photograph Collector's Guide*, Lee D. Witkin & Barbara London, 1979; *The Collection of Alfred Stieglitz*, Weston J. Naef, 1978; *Pictorial Photography in Britain 1900–1920*, Arts Council of Great Britain, 1978; *Camera Work: A Critical Anthology*, Jonathan Green, ed., 1973; *Looking at Photographs*, John Szarkowski, 1973; *The Studio*, Time-Life Series, 1971. Periodicals: "Women as Objets d'Art," *Photo World*, Apr/May 1977; *Vogue*, Apr 1976; *Camera Work*, Oct 1912, Oct 1908.

PORTFOLIO *L'Aprés-midi d'un faune*, printed by Richard Benson, notes by Sergei Diaghilev, Auguste Rodin, Jacques-Emile Blanche, 1978 (Eakins Press: N.Y.).

COLLECTIONS IMP/GEH, Rochester; Metro. Mus. of Art, NYC; New York Public Lib., Lincoln Cntr. Branch, NYC. Bibliothèque Nationale, Paris.

Henri De Monfreid ADVENTURER · AUTHOR · PHOTOGRAPHER Born in 1879 in La Franqui, France, De Monfreid died in 1974 at Ingrandes in the south of France. He studied in Paris.

Unable to settle down as a businessman, De Monfreid made his first trip to the Red Sea coast in 1911. He left France again in 1917 for a permanent vocation as an arms trader and pearl diver in and around the Red Sea, settling first in Djibouti with his wife and children. In later years he was exiled from Ethiopia because of his writings, but he returned in 1936 as a war correspondent. Arrested by the British Army in 1940 and sent to Kenya, he stayed there as a farmer until 1948, when he returned to France. At the age of seventy-nine he sailed his boat from Reunion Island to Mauritius, disappearing for two weeks along the way.

A great adventurer and prodigious writer, De Monfried produced photographs which, while not aesthetically outstanding, illustrate well the toughness of a very precarious existence. He hand-painted lantern slides and printed by the Fresson process. Most of the surviving views are of rather horrific scenes that were probably part of his everyday life.

PUBLICATIONS Books: *Le Feu de Saint-Elme*, 1973, *Un Amour de Pintade*, 1975 (Laffont: Paris); *Chasseur d'Isards*, 1971, *Les Deux Frères*, 1969 (Grasset: Paris); *Abdi, Enfant Sauvage*, 1968 (Editions de l'Amitié: Paris); *La Croix de Fer Forgé*, 1966, *L'Homme aux Yeux de Verre*, 1965, *La Chute Imprévue*, 1964, *Combat*, 1963, *Testament de Pirate*, 1962 (Grasset: Paris); *La Sirène de Rio Pongo*, 1961, *Le Récif Maudit*, 1959 (Flammarion: Paris); *Mon Aventure à l'Ile des Forbans*, 1958 (Grasset: Paris); *Pilleurs d'Epaves*, 1955 (Flammarion: Paris); *Ménélik tel qu'il fut*, 1954, *L'Envers de l'Aventure*, 1953 (Grasset: Paris); *Le Cimetière des Eléphants*, 1952, *Djalia*, 1951 (Table Ronde: Paris); *La Poursuite du Kaïpan*, 2 vols., 1934–51; *Le Naufrageur*, 1950 (Table Ronde: Paris); *Du Harrar au Kénia à la Poursuite de la Liberté*, 1949 (Editions du Triolet: Paris); *La Triolette*, 1948 (Table Ronde: Paris); *Charas*, 1947 (Editions du Pavois: Paris); *Le Drame de la Pologne*, 1945 (La Colombe: Paris); *Sir Henry Middleton*, 1941, *Le Secret du Lac Noir*, 1940 (Gallimard: Paris); *L'Enfant Sauvage*, 1938 (Grasset: Paris); *Sea Adventures*, 1937 (Methuen: London); *L'Avion Noir*, 1936, *Le Naufrage de la Marietta*, 1934 (Grasset: Paris); *The Book of Vagabonds*, 1933; *Vers les Terres Hostiles de l'Ethiopie*, 1933, *Aventures de Mer*, 1932 (Grasset: Paris); *Les Secrets de la Mer Rouge*, 1931, Eng. ed., 1934 (Faber & Faber: London); *Pearls, Arms and Hashish*, foreword & conclusion by Ida Treat, 1930.

DEALER The Photographers' Gall., 8 Gr Newport St, London WC2, England.

Dena PHOTOGRAPHER Born in Viborg, Finland, Dena earned an MA in Psychology from the University of Kansas, Lawrence, in 1952. She studied photography in the late 1950s and early 1960s with David Vestal, Alexey Brodovitch and Lisette Model.

A member of Professional Women Photographers since 1975, she has taught photography at the School of Visual Arts in New York City since 1973.

The photographer describes her style as "expressionistic but close to reality," with a "strongly defined structure." Her images include portraits of internationally known artists, children in their own environments and street scenes from different countries.

PUBLICATIONS Books: *Human Behavior: Status & Conformity*, 1976, *Human Behavior: How We Learn*, 1975, *Human Behavior: The Individual*, 1974 (Time-Life Books); *Leica Manual*, 1973. Anthologies: *The Family of Woman*, 1979; *Women: Images by 12 Women Photographers*, 1978; *The Family of Children*, 1977; *Women See Men*, 1977; *Women See Woman*, 1976; *Celebrations*, Minor White & Jonathan Green, eds., 1974; *Photographing Children*, 1971, Time-Life Series. Periodicals: *Popular Photography Annual*, 1977; *Zoom*, Oct 1977 (Paris); *Camera*, June 1975; *Popular Photography's Invitation to Photography*, 1973; *U.S. Camera Annual*, 1972; *Modern Photography Annual*, 1970; *Aperture*, 12:4, 1965.

COLLECTIONS Albright-Knox Gall., Buffalo, N.Y.; Archives of Amer. Art, NYC; Art Inst. of Chicago; Chrysler Mus., Norfolk, Va.; Ind. Univ. Art Mus., Bloomington; Metro. Mus. of Art, NYC; MOMA, NYC; Univ. of Syracuse, N.Y. Bibliothèque Nationale, Paris.

ADDRESS 35 E 85 St, New York, NY 10028.

Irwin D. Dermer PHOTOGRAPHER Born December 29, 1925, in Baltimore, Maryland, Dermer received a BA in Liberal Arts from the University of Maryland, College Park, in 1951 and studied photography at New York University in New York City (1971). He was influenced by the work of Constantine Brancusi.

A freelance photographer, Dermer also made the film *Threads of Life* in 1973 (a documentary about Iran and Afghanistan).

PUBLICATIONS Books: *A Time to Play*, 1976 (self-published); *The Witch's Hat*, 1975; *Light & Film*, Time-Life Series, 1970. Periodicals: *Camera*, Oct 1969, May 1968, Feb 1967.

COLLECTIONS Metro. Mus. of Art, NYC; Smithsonian Inst., Wash., D.C. Bibliothèque Nationale, Paris; Ministry of Education, Brussels, Belgium.

ADDRESS Postfach 5009 CH/8022, Zurich, Switzerland.

Bernard Descamps PHOTOGRAPHER Born January 16, 1947, in Paris, Descamps earned a doctorate in Biology, but abandoned his scientific studies in 1975 for photography.

A freelance photographer since 1975, Descamps created l'Atelier Studio, which organizes workshops, in that year.

His work includes both personal studies and commissions of an "artistic or cultural character."

PUBLICATIONS Monographs: *B. Descamps, photographies*, 1976 (Ed. Musé de Leverkusen RFA); *Rencontres*, 1976 (Ed. Contre Jour: Paris). Periodicals: *Camera*, 1979; *Fotografie*, 1979; *Creative Camera*, 1979.

COLLECTIONS Bibliothèque Nationale, Paris; Bibliothèque Publique d'Information, Paris; Centre Pompidou, Musée Nationale d'Art Moderne, Paris; Musée Réattu, Arles, France.

ADDRESS De Pressoir, 37500 Chinon, France.

Max Desfor EDITOR · PHOTOGRAPHER Born November 8, 1913, in New York City, Desfor is self-taught. His brother Sid was head of the NBC Photo Department and his brother Irving was a photography writer and photographer.

In 1979 Desfor became photo editor, then photo director of *U.S. News & World Report*. He worked for the Associated Press from 1933 to 1978, as a photographer, photo editor, foreign and war correspondent, and as head of Wide World photos. He also was Asia photo editor, based in Tokyo.

Desfor is president of the Foreign Correspondents Club of Japan and belongs to the NPPA, White House News Photographers Association and White House Correspondents Association.

He won the Pulitzer Prize for Photography in 1951.

PUBLICATION Anthology: *Moments*, Sheryle & John Leekley, 1978.

Charles Joseph Desmarais CURATOR · CRITIC · EDITOR Born April 21, 1949, in New York City, Desmarais earned his BS from the State University of New York, Buffalo, and his MFA from that school's Visual Studies Workshop in 1977. He lists Nathan Lyons, Charles Hagen and Peter Thompson as major influences.

He is currently director of the California Museum of Photography at Riverside. Since 1977 Desmarais has been editor of *Exposure: SPE*, and from 1977 to 1979 served as director/curator of the Chicago Center for Contemporary Photography. He was assistant editor of *Afterimage: VSW* from 1975 to 1977, and an intern for the NEA in 1976. In 1973–74 he was a curator for Friends of Photography in Carmel, California.

Desmarais is currently on the board of directors of SPE and is a member of the Photographic Historical Society of New York. He received an NEA Art Critic's Fellowship in 1979.

PUBLICATIONS Catalogs: *Michael Bishop*, ed. & intro., 1979, *Roger Mertin: Records 1976–78*, ed. & afterword, 1978, *A Directory: Critics of Photography*, ed. w/Tae Terumoto, 1977 (Chicago Ctr. for Contemporary Photography); *Photographic Works by Fred Endsley*, intro., 1977

(Chicago: Two Illinois Ctr). Periodicals: *Afterimage: VSW*, 2: 8–10, 3: 3–7, 9, 10, 4: 4, 5, 7–10, 5: 1, 2; *Art in America*, May/June 1977; *Artweek*, Mar, May 1974; *Exposure: SPE*, 15: 3.

PORTFOLIO *Sunset After Dark: Patty Carroll*, intro., 1979 (Frumkin Gall. Photographs, Chicago).

ADDRESS California Museum of Photography, U.C. Riverside, 3425 7 St, Riverside, CA 92502.

Theophilus Hope D'Estrella *TEACHER · PHOTOGRAPHER · LECTURER* Born February 6, 1851, in San Francisco, California, D'Estrella died October 29, 1929, in Berkeley, California. A deaf orphan, he attended California School for the Deaf in Berkeley from 1860 to 1873, then the University of California, Berkeley, from 1873 to 1876. D'Estrella completed his studies at the School of Design of the San Francisco Art Association (1879–84).

A teacher at the California School for the Deaf (1876–79 and 1884–1929), he inaugurated the school's art program, including photography. Using sign language, he gave lectures to deaf groups illustrating them with lantern slides, especially about his Hopi Indian trip of 1902.

D'Estrella belonged to the San Francisco Art Association, California Camera Club, which he joined in 1891 (and for which he served on its lantern-slide committee), Sierra Club, California Association of the Deaf and National Association of the Deaf.

He won first prize, animal section, at the First Photographic Salon in San Francisco in 1901 and the second-place Alvord award in drawing from the School of Design in 1881. The California School for the Deaf awarded him a three-month study tour of Europe in 1889. D'Estrella also exhibited small oils and watercolors in several annual Spring Exhibitions at M.H.A.I.

The photographer produced pictorial and documentary images of deaf children at work, play and fantasy at the California School for the Deaf, printing in small sizes for albums. He also created albums of his holiday trips with the Camera Club and the Sierra Club as well as his solo tramps in the Sierra Nevada.

COLLECTIONS Calif. Hist. Soc., San Francisco; Calif. School for the Deaf Archives, Fremont; Univ. of Calif., Bancroft Lib., Berkeley.

REPRESENTATIVE Mildred Albronda, 1400 Geary Blvd #303, San Francisco, CA 94109.

J. E. Devine *PHOTOGRAPHER · TEACHER* Born on August 31, 1944, in Mt. Kisco, New York, Devine earned his BA from Yale University, New Haven, Connecticut, in 1967 and his MFA from Yale's School of Art and Architecture in 1972.

The photographer has been an assistant professor at the State University of New York, Purchase, since 1977.

Devine works in 8 x 10 format, producing palladium prints in the "straight" genre.

COLLECTIONS Metro. Mus. of Art, NYC; MOMA, NYC; Seagram Cllctn., NYC.

DEALER Daniel Wolf, Inc., 30 W 57 St, New York, NY 10019.

ADDRESS 131 Duane St, New York, NY 10013.

John De Visser *PHOTOGRAPHER* Born February 8, 1930, in Veghel, North Brabant, The Netherlands, De Visser is self-taught, with major influences being Walker Evans, Henri Cartier-Bresson and Ernst Haas.

A freelance for twenty-three years, the photographer belongs to the Royal Canadian Academy of Fine Arts and the Canadian Association of Photographers and Illustrators.

PUBLICATIONS Books: *Newfoundland*, 1980; *Between Friends*, 1976; *Rivers of Canada*, 1974; *Heritage, a Romantic Look at Early Canadian Furniture*, 1971; *This Rock Within the Sea, A Heritage Lost*, 1968; *Canada, A Year of the Land*, 1967.

COLLECTION Natl. Film Board of Canada.

DEALER A Moment in Time Gall., 398 King St E, Toronto, Ontario, Canada.

ADDRESS 2 Hagerman St, Port Hope, Ontario, Canada L1A 3G9.

Lucinda Alice Devlin *PHOTOGRAPHER · TEACHER* Born December 18, 1947, in Ann Arbor, Michigan, Devlin received her BS in English Literature/Art from Eastern Michigan University, Ypsilanti, in 1971 and her MFA in Photography from the same school in 1974.

From 1977 to the present she has been adjunct professor of photography at Syracuse University, New York. She was the director of photographic and illustration services at Eastern Michigan University in 1973–74.

A member of SPE from 1975 to 1978, Devlin won a CAPS Photography Fellowship in 1979 and a Light Work Photography Grant through the New York State Council for the Arts in 1978.

Her color work consists of "contemporary interior environments" in a medium-format, documentary style.

COLLECTIONS Colgate Univ., Picker Art Gall., Gary M. Hoeffer Cllctn., Hamilton, N.Y.; Light Work, Syracuse, N.Y.

David L. DeVries   PHOTOGRAPHER · TEACHER
DeVries obtained a BA in Art from the University
of Southern Colorado in Pueblo in 1973. He specialized in photography at the University of Iowa's School of Art in Iowa City, where he
completed an MA (1975) and an MFA (1976),
studying under John Schulze.

Since 1978 he has been an assistant professor
in photography at Bemidji State University in
Minnesota. Previously he taught in Canada at the
University of Manitoba's School of Art in Winnipeg (1976–77) and was acting head of the Photography Department from 1977 to 1978.

He belongs to SPE, CAA and Friends of Photography. He was the recipient of a scholarship given
by the Ford Foundation (1975–76) and of a research grant awarded by the Canada Council and
the University of Manitoba (1976).

As of this writing the artist was "investigating
creative portraiture as an interchange between
subject and photographer." He is also working on
"a separate series of multiple-panel photographs
exploring the polyptych format in photography."
DeVries says: "I am interested in the linkage and
collisions between photographs, and between
people."

PUBLICATIONS   Periodicals: *Northlight*, Mar
1980; *Rocky Mountain Creative Arts Journal*,
spring 1975.

COLLECTIONS   Univ. of Iowa, Iowa City; Univ.
of Minn. Art Gall., Minneapolis; Sheldon Me-
morial Art Gall., Lincoln, Nebr.; Sioux City Art
Ctr., Iowa. London Regional Art Gall., London,
Ont., Canada; Univ. of Manitoba, School of Art,
Winnipeg, Canada.

ADDRESS   1203 Lake Ave, Pueblo, CO 81004.

Hugh Welch Diamond   PHYSICIAN · PHOTOGRA-
PHER   Born in Kent, England, in 1809, Diamond
died in 1886. He was admitted to the Royal College of Surgeons in 1824. Upon graduating, he
was appointed house surgeon to West Kent Infir-
mary at Maidstone.

Diamond later began a private practice in Soho,
then, after deciding to specialize in mental disorders, was appointed superintendent of the
Women's Department of the Surrey County Asylum, where he practiced from 1848 to 1858. During that time he was actively engaged in
photography and was editor of the *Photographic
Journal*. Upon his resignation from the asylum
he returned to private practice.

Diamond became a member of the Photographic Society in 1853 and served as its secretary for many years. He was also a member of the
Board of Health.

Diamond produced calotypes, concentrating
his images on the mental patients he treated.
While he also photographed topography of surrounding areas, he is noted for the several series
of sympathetic portraits of the mentally ill he
produced while at the Surrey County Asylum.

PUBLICATIONS   Anthologies: *The Invented
Eye*, Edw. Lucie-Smith, 1975; *The Magic Im-
age*, Cecil Beaton & Gail Buckland, 1975; *Early
Photographs and Early Photographers*, Oliver
Mathews, 1973 (Reedminster Pubs.: London).

COLLECTIONS   In England: Norwich County
Record Office; Norwich City Lib.; RPS; Royal Society of Medicine.

Paul Diamond   PHOTOGRAPHER   Born June
20, 1942, in Brooklyn, New York, Diamond
earned a BFA from Pratt Institute in Brooklyn in
1965.

Diamond was guest lecturer at the University
of Colorado in Boulder in 1977. He then taught
photography at California College of Arts and
Crafts in Oakland in 1977–78.

A member of SPE, he won a Guggenheim Fellowship in 1975 and an NEA Photographer's Fellowship in 1978.

PUBLICATIONS   Anthologies: *The Photograph
Collector's Guide*, Lee D. Witkin & Barbara London, 1979; *The Great West: Real/Ideal*, Sandy
Hume, et al., eds., 1977; *The Grotesque in Photography*, A. D. Coleman, ed., 1977; *The Photographer's Choice*, Kelly Wise, ed., 1975. Catalog:
Peculiar to Photography, 1976 (Univ. of N. Mex.:
Albuquerque). Periodical: *CCP Journal*, vol. 4,
1977.

COLLECTIONS   Addison Gall. of Amer. Art,
Andover, Mass.; Harvard Univ., Fogg Art Mus.,
Cambridge, Mass.; IMP/GEH, Rochester; Ohio
Wesleyan Univ., Delaware, Ohio. Natl. Gall. of
Canada, Ottawa, Ontario.

DEALER   Witkin Gall., 41 E 57 St, New York,
NY 10022.

ADDRESS   21 St James Pl, Brooklyn, NY 11205.

Claudette Bargreen Dibert   PHOTOGRAPHER ·
TEACHER   Born in Everett, Washington, in February 1942, she died in December 1982. Her father is Senator Howard Bargreen. She received
her BA in 1964 from the University of Washington, Seattle, and did graduate work at the University of Hawaii, Honolulu, 1970–73.

A photography instructor at Monterey Peninsula College in California since 1979, Dibert was a private art instructor in Hawaii from 1965 to 1970.

Dibert won first-place awards for her photographs at the W.A.G. Annual Show, Kailua, Hawaii, in 1974 and at the Camera 73 Exhibit in Honolulu in 1973.

As of this writing Dibert concentrates on night photography, using available light. She makes long exposures and uses camera movement to create abstract effects, and prints her color transparencies directly onto 20 x 24 Cibachrome paper. "My previous color work," she says, "dealt with realistic color and design images. Previous to the color work I did silver prints; documentary photographs of children, nature and figure studies."

PUBLICATION Book: *Photography Three Generations: 1933–1975*, Ken Dibert, 1975.

COLLECTION Seattle Art Commission, Wash.

DEALERS Print Gallery, Suvecino Ct, Carmel, CA 93921; Collectors Gall., 311 B Forest Ave, Pacific Grove, CA 93950; Equivalent Gall., 1822 Broadway, Seattle, WA 98122.

ADDRESS 9883 Holt Rd, Carmel Valley, CA 93923.

George Chalmers Dibert *ADVERTISING EXECUTIVE · PHOTOGRAPHER* Born December 1, 1901, in Johnstown, Pennsylvania, Dibert died in 1974. His major influence was his father, photographer Louis de Sauque Dibert (1878–1936). His son Ken Dibert (born 1945) also became a photographer.

Dibert retired in 1963 as vice-president of J. Walter Thompson and Company, having worked there since 1950. For the preceding twenty years he was an executive with the same company, and prior to that did media research for Young and Rubicam Advertising Company (1925–30). He was chairman of the Audit Bureau of Circulations in 1961.

Dibert worked in black-and-white medium format, doing studies of street scenes in the United State and Europe. His pictures were notably whimsical or philosophically amusing. He also did architectural studies.

PUBLICATION Book: *Photography, Three Generations: 1933–1975*, Ken Dibert, 1975.

REPRESENTATIVE The Dibert Gall., POB 7044, Carmel, CA 93921.

Kenneth D. Dibert *PHOTOGRAPHER · GALLERY DIRECTOR* Born February 19, 1945, in New York City, Dibert learned photography from his father,

George C. Dibert, 1959–65, and from photographer Jim Braddy, 1962–64.

Dibert has managed the Dibert Gallery in Carmel, California, since 1976, serving as gallery show curator, 1976–79. He has also worked as a freelance fashion and fine-arts photographer since 1979. He was president of Colorprints, Inc., in Honolulu (1971–75) and owner of Arte Fotográfico in Mexico (1967–70).

The photographer belongs to Friends of Photography.

Using small- and medium-format color, Dibert shoots mainly street scenes of "vanishing America" and nudes.

PUBLICATIONS Book: *Photography, Three Generations: 1933–1975*, Ken Dibert, 1975. Periodical: *Petersens Photographic Magazine*, Sept 1980.

COLLECTIONS Hawaii Fndn. of Culture & the Arts, Honolulu; Honolulu Acad. of Arts.

ADDRESS The Dibert Gall., POB 7044, Carmel, CA 93921.

Louis De Sauque Dibert *STRUCTURAL ENGINEER · PHOTOGRAPHER* Born August 27, 1878, Dibert died in 1936. His son George C. Dibert (1901–74) and grandson Ken Dibert (born 1945) also became photographers.

Dibert worked as a structural engineer from 1900 to 1921, then turned photographer, working as a freelance professional from 1921 to 1936. He was a member of the Philadelphia Photographic Society from 1930 to 1936. From 1929 to 1936 his works were widely exhibited from state to state in the photographic "salons" of the day.

He worked in 5 x 7 format, doing animated studies of people. He shunned the pictorialist trend of his era and dealt with sharply rendered, realistic subjects.

PUBLICATION Book: *Photography, Three Generations: 1933–1975*, Ken Dibert, 1975.

REPRESENTATIVE The Dibert Gall., POB 7044, Carmel, CA 93921.

Michael Di Biase *PHOTOGRAPHER* Born on September 8, 1925, in Brooklyn, New York, Di Biase taught at C. W. Post College in Greenvale, New York (1969–70). Since 1976 he has been a photography instructor at the School of Visual Arts in New York City.

He belongs to the C. G. Jung Foundation, SPE and Friends of Photography. In 1974 he was the recipient of a Guggenheim Fellowship.

The artist states: "My aim is to gather a body of work that will bring about a deeper understanding of psychic imagery. These will be used towards a meaningful visual context."

PUBLICATIONS Books: *Art of Photography*, vol. 10, 1971; *Photography U.S.A.*, 1967. Anthologies: *Self-Portrayal*, 1979; *Octave of Prayer*, 1972; *Photography in the 20th Century*, 1967; *Photography '63*, 1963. Periodical: *San Francisco Camera*, 1:5.

COLLECTIONS IMP/GEH, Rochester; MIT, Cambridge, Mass.; Pasadena Art Mus., Calif.; Polaroid Corp., Cambridge, Mass.

ADDRESS 1931 52 St, Brooklyn, NY 11204.

Willem Diepraam *PHOTOGRAPHER* Born April 13, 1944, in Amsterdam, The Netherlands, he was influenced by Edward van der Elskem.

Diepraam is a freelance photographer who has worked in photojournalism.

PUBLICATIONS Books (all The Netherlands): *The Dutch Caribbean*, 1978; *The Dutch Landscape*, 1977; *Frimamgrom*, 1975.

COLLECTIONS Ryils Pretenkabinet, Leiden, The Netherlands; Stedelijk Mus., Amsterdam.

DEALERS Galerie Fiolet, Herengracht 86, Amsterdam, The Netherlands; Photographers Gallery, 8 Gr Newport St, London, England.

ADDRESS Oydezydsvoorburgwal 247, Amsterdam 1012E2, The Netherlands.

Ann Espe Dietz *GALLERY AND BOOKSHOP OWNER* Born November 28, 1916, in Salt Lake City, Utah, Dietz received her BA from the University of New Mexico. Her great-grandfather was New Hampshire Senator Jacob H. Gallinger.

In 1964 she opened the bookshop Quivira (Albuquerque, New Mexico), and the next year added a gallery, one of the first private galleries for photography in the United States.

Dietz is a member of the Pan-American Round Table.

ADDRESS POB 4147, Albuquerque, NM 87196.

Jean Dieuzaide *PHOTOGRAPHER · ART DIRECTOR* [See plate 115] Born in 1921 in Grenade-sur-Garonne, France, Dieuzaide is self-taught in photography.

Currently art director of Galerie Municipale du Château d'Eau in Toulouse, France, he was chairman of the Art Photography International in 1970 and winner of the following awards: Knight of the Merit Order (1966), Nadar Prize (1961), and Niepce Prize (1955).

In addition to his photographs, Dieuzaide has made tapestries and was the subject of a 1958 television program, *Jean Dieuzaide, the Photographer*.

PUBLICATION Monograph: *Dialogue with Light*, 1979 (Crédit Commercial de France).

COLLECTIONS Metro. Mus. of Art, NYC; Va. Mus., Norfolk. In France: Bibliothèque Nationale, Paris; Cantini Mus., Marseilles; Musée Nicéphore Niepce, Châlon-sur-Saône; Musée Réattu, Arles. Sterckshof Mus., Antwerp, Belgium.

DEALER Paule Pia Photo Galerij, Kammenstraat 57, Antwerp 2000, Belgium.

ADDRESS 7 rue Erasme, Toulouse 31.400, France.

Lou Brown DiGiulio *MIXED-MEDIA PHOTOGRAPHER* Born on April 1, 1933, in Georgia, she attended Hunter College in New York City and California State University at Northridge, where she studied under Jerry McMillan.

She is presently working full time as a freelance photographer. Previously she was a photographic model (1953–62) and the co-owner of The Merry Hearts in Los Angeles, where she designed and manufactured children's wear (1963–65).

In 1976 she received an NEA grant to be an artist-in-residence at the University of Kansas in Lawrence.

Her work includes photo sculpture and photo silkscreen on fabric. The material is sewn, stuffed, wired and assembled to form a sculpture.

PUBLICATIONS Catalog: *A Ten Year Salute*, Lee D. Witkin, 1979 (Witkin Gall.: NYC). Anthology: *The Photograph Collector's Guide*, Lee D. Witkin & Barbara London, 1979.

ADDRESS 21900 Briarbluff Rd, Malibu, CA 90265.

Clyde H. Dilley *TEACHER · PHOTOGRAPHER* Born January 5, 1939, in Modesto, California, Dilley received a BA in Film and an MA in Creative Arts from San Francisco State College (1967, 1968), where he studied with Jack Welpott and Don Worth. As of 1979 he was a PhD candidate in art history at the University of New Mexico, working with Beaumont Newhall.

Since 1969 Dilley has been a professor in the Department of Photography and Cinema at Ohio State University, Columbus. In 1968–69 he taught at San Jacinto College in Pasadena, Texas. Dilley belongs to SPE, IMP/GEH and Friends of Photography.

The photographer describes his work as "monochromatic, . . . presently inclined to formal, straight renditions of nature and edifices." His academic work focuses on twentieth-century photo history and contemporary criticism.

PUBLICATIONS Anthologies: *Photography*, Phil Davis, 2d ed., 1972, 3d ed., 1975. Catalogs: *Nine Photographers*, 1975 (Akron Art Inst.: Ohio); *130 Years of Ohio Photography*, 1978 (Columbus Mus. of Fine Arts: Ohio); *Photographs by Clyde Dilley*, 1970 (Dallas Mus. of Fine Arts); *Exploring the Arts*, 1969 (Jewett Creative Arts Ctr.), *Vision and Expression*, Nathan Lyons, ed., 1969 (GEH: Rochester).

COLLECTIONS IMP/GEH, Rochester; Mass. Inst. of Tech., Cambridge; Smith Coll. Mus. of Art, Nancy Newhall Mem. Cllctn., Northampton, Mass.; Univ. of Santa Clara, Dept. of Art and Arch., Calif. Univ. of Exeter, American Arts Documentation Centre, England.

ADDRESS 156 W 19 Ave, Columbus, OH 43210.

Phillip Rick Dingus   PHOTOGRAPHER · TEACHER   Born January 3, 1951, in Appleton City, Missouri, Dingus received his BA in Fine Arts from the University of California, Santa Barbara, in 1973 and his MA and MFA in Studio Art—Photography from the University of New Mexico, Albuquerque, in 1977.

A lecturer in photography and drawing at New Mexico Tech, Socorro, since 1979, Dingus was also a guest lecturer at the Santa Fe Gallery of Photography in New Mexico, and a visiting artist at the School of Fine Arts, University of California, Irvine, in 1979. He was a field photographer for both the "Rephotographic Survey" of Southwest sites originally photographed by nineteenth-century expeditionary photographers and the National Park Service (1977–78).

A member of SPE, Dingus won a Special Projects Grant from the Graduate School of the University of New Mexico in 1979 and Ford Foundation grants-in-aid in 1977, 1978 and 1979.

PUBLICATIONS Anthologies: *Photography in New Mexico*, Van Deren Coke, 1979; *Photo Year 1979*. Periodicals: *Modern Photography*, May 1979; *British Journal of Photography*, July 14, 1978.

COLLECTIONS Mus. of Fine Arts, Santa Fe, N. Mex.; Univ. of N. Mex. Art Mus., Albuquerque.

ADDRESS 949 Buena Vista SE, J210, Albuquerque, NM 87106.

Stephanie Dinkins   PHOTOGRAPHER · WRITER   Born in St. Mary Parish, Louisiana, Dinkins received her BA from Newcomb College in New Orleans, Louisiana.

Since 1955 she has been a freelance photographer and writer. In 1954–57 she was a roving radio reporter in Africa and the Middle East for NBC, Canadian Broadcasting Corporation, United Nations and specialized agencies. She is a member of ASMP.

She does photojournalism, portraits and illustrations, often for travel books, concerning numerous countries around the world.

PUBLICATIONS Periodicals: *National Geographic*, Jan 1969; *Popular Photography Annual*, 1968, 1965; *U.S. Camera Annual*, 1965. Reviews: *Camera 35*, Oct 1975, July 1974, Oct 1964; *Popular Photography*, Nov 1974.

COLLECTIONS Amer. Tel. & Tel. Co., Boston; Historic New Orleans Cllctn.; ICP, NYC; Metro. Opera, NYC; New Orleans Mus. of Art; Tulane Univ., New Orleans.

REPRESENTATIVE Photo Researchers, 60 E 56 St, New York, NY 10022.

ADDRESS 7912 Willow St, New Orleans, LA 70118.

Frank P. DiPerna   PHOTOGRAPHER · TEACHER   Born on February 4, 1947, in Pittsburg, Pennsylvania, DiPerna earned a BS in Mechanical Engineering at the Virginia Polytechnic Institute in Blacksburg (1970). He specialized in photography at Goddard College in Plainfield, Vermont, where he completed a master's degree in 1971; he also attended a Center of the Eye Workshop in Aspen, Colorado, studying under Gary Winogrand (1971), and a Visual Studies Workshop in Rochester, where his instructors were Ralph Gibson, Nathan Lyons and Alice Wells (1971–72).

Since 1974 DiPerna has been teaching at the Corcoran School of Art in Washington, D.C., first as an instructor and, since 1978, as an assistant professor and chairman of the Photography Department. Previously he taught at the Northern Virginia Community College in Alexandria (1973–78); from 1969 to 1971 he was a marine engineer/naval architect for the U.S. Coast Guard in Washington, D.C.

In 1975 he was granted a Graduate Fellowship by the Virginia Museum of Fine Arts in Richmond.

Until 1978 the artist worked mainly in 35mm black-and-white and in 8 x 10 palladium prints. At present he is more interested in using the Polaroid SX-70 as well as producing Type C color prints. His subject matters are urban and natural landscapes, and constructed still lifes.

PUBLICATIONS Anthologies: *SX-70 Art*, Ralph Gibson, ed., 1979; *One of a Kind: Recent Polaroid Color Photography*, 1979. Catalog: *Color*

Photographs, 1977 (Corcoran Gall. of Art: Wash., D.C.).

COLLECTIONS Corcoran Gall. of Art, Wash., D.C.; L/C, Wash., D.C.; Smithsonian Inst., Wash., D.C.; Va. Mus. of Fine Arts, Richmond. Polaroid Cllctn., Amsterdam, The Netherlands.

DEALER Diane Brown Gall., 2028 P St NW, Washington, D.C. 20036.

ADDRESS 1744 Lamont St NW, Washington, D.C. 20010.

André Adolphe-Eugène Disdéri PHOTOGRA-PHER · INVENTOR · WRITER Disdéri was born in 1819 and died in 1889 or 1890 in France. He started out his career as a daguerreotypist with a studio in Brest, later opening a studio in Nîmes. In 1854 he opened a studio in Paris, where he produced *cartes de visite* so successfully that he soon opened a second Paris studio (1863), and then branch studios in London (1868), Madrid and Toulon. He was appointed official photographer to the imperial courts of Spain, England, France and Russia in 1861. And in the same year, under orders from the minister of war, he instructed French army officers in photography. From 1880 until his death, he worked in Nice as a beach photographer. Despite the great wealth he amassed during his successful years, he died in obscurity.

The probable inventor of the *carte de visite*, Disdéri received a patent for the process from the French government on November 27, 1854, and was certainly responsible for popularizing the fad. He devised systems by which he could expose eight or a dozen poses on one negative. He also invented multiple cameras with four and twelve lenses in 1862, so that he could make several exposures at one time.

Remembered for having been the first to establish photography as a business as well as an artistic craft, he was considered the outstanding portrait photographer of his day.

PUBLICATIONS Books: "Photography and the Theory of Realism," Robt. Sobieszek, *One Hundred Years of Photographic History*, Van Deren Coke, ed., 1975; *Art and Photography*, Aaron Scharf, 1969; *Creative Photography*, Helmut Gernsheim, 1962 (Faber & Faber: London); *Universal Textbook of Photography*, 2nd ed., 1864 (London); *L'Art de la photographie*, intro. by Lafon de Camarsac, 1862 (Paris); *Application de la photographie à la reproduction des oeuvres d'art*, 1861 (Paris); *Renseignements photographiques indispensables à tous*, 1855 (Paris); *Manuel Operatoire de photographie*, 1853 (Nîmes). Anthologies: *The Photograph Collector's Guide*,

Lee D. Witkin & Barbara London, 1979; *The Invented Eye*, Edw. Lucie-Smith, 1975; *Early Photographs & Early Photographers*, Oliver Mathews, 1973; *Immortal Portraits*, Alex Strasser, 1941.

COLLECTIONS IMP/GEH, Rochester; Metro. Mus. of Art, NYC; Smithsonian Inst., Wash., D.C.; Univ. of N. Mex. Art Mus., Albuquerque. Bibliothèque Nationale, Paris; Provinciall Museum voor Kunstambachten, Deurne (Antwerp), Belgium; and other museum collections.

Michael Disfarmer PHOTOGRAPHER Born Mike Meyer in 1884 in Indiana, Disfarmer died in Heber Springs, Arkansas, in 1959. He was probably a self-taught photographer.

Disfarmer moved with his family to Arkansas in the late 1800s and, later, after his father's death, to Heber Springs with his mother (1914), with whom he lived. About this time he set up his first studio, on the back porch of their home. There, about 1930, a tornado destroyed his home and killed his mother. He adopted the name Disfarmer, built a studio with a large north skylight, and became the unofficial town photographer, leading a hermitlike existence until his death. During 1973 his work was published in *The Arkansas Sun*, the Heber Springs weekly, and has also appeared in *Modern Photography*.

A musician skilled on many instruments, he was especially fond of fiddling.

Disfarmer's work stands as a historical and sociological document of the rugged farm life and the small-town culture of Mid-America, especially during the 1930s and 1940s. Making contact prints from 5 x 7 (early years) and 3¼ x 5½ (later years), he always used glass plates, even after sheet film was available. "With directness and simplicity, he achieved a revelation of character that more sophisticated photographers have attempted with greater technique but perhaps no greater success," wrote Julia Scully.

PUBLICATION Monograph: *Disfarmer: The Heber Springs Portraits 1939–46*, Julia Scully, 1976.

ARCHIVE Arkansas Arts Ctr., Little Rock.

Charles Lutwidge Dodgson NOVELIST · PHO-TOGRAPHER · LOGICIAN · MATHEMATICIAN Charles Lutwidge Dodgson, better known under the pseudonym of Lewis Carroll, was born in England on January 27, 1832, in Daresbury, Cheshire, and died on January 14, 1898, in Guildford, Surrey. His father, Rev. Charles Dodgson, was archdeacon of Richmond and canon of Ripon Cathedral. Dodgson received his secondary education at Richmond School (1844–45) and at Rugby School (1846–50). Then he attended Christ Church College in Oxford, where he completed a bachelor's degree in 1854, and remained on the faculty as a lecturer in mathematics during most of his life (1855–81). Dodgson was also a deacon in the Church of England (ordained on December 22, 1861).

Photography was his hobby from 1855 to 1880. His subjects were children and adults, including notables such as the actress Ellen Terry, the poet Lord Alfred Tennyson and the poet-painter Dante Gabriele Rossetti. The children were photographed nude, partially nude or costumed, and he posed them in various tableaux. His favorite child model was Alice Liddell, the namesake of his famous *Alice's Adventures in Wonderland*. Dodgson is often considered the best photographer of children in the nineteenth century. He used collodion wet-plate negatives and made albumen prints.

PUBLICATIONS Books: *Lewis Carroll: Fragments of a Looking Glass*, Jean Gattégno, 1976; *Le Bambine di Carroll: Foto e Lettere di Lewis Carroll a Mary, Alice, Irene, Agnese . . .* , Guido Almansi, ed., notes by Brassaï & Gernsheim, 1974 (Ricci: Parma, Italy), U.S. ed. entitled *Photos and Letters of Lewis Carroll to his Child Friends*, 1975; *Lewis Carroll at Christ Church*, 1974 (Natl Portrait Gall.; London); *Lewis Carroll: Photographer*, Helmut Gernsheim, 1949 (Parrish: London), rev. U.S. ed., 1969. Children's books: *Through the Looking-Glass and What Alice Found There*, 1872; *Alice's Adventures in Wonderland*, 1865. Verse: *The Collected Verse*, 1929; *Rhyme? and Reason?*, 1883; *The Hunting of the Snark*, 1876; *Phantasmagoria and Other Poems*, 1869. Novel: *Sylvie and Bruno*, 2 vol., 1889–93. Mathematical books: *Curiosa Mathematica*, 1888–93; *Euclid and His Modern Rivals*, 1879; *A Syllabus of Plane Algebraical Geometry*, 1860. Periodical (photography): "Hiawatha's Photographing," *The Train*, 1857.

COLLECTIONS Humanities Research Ctr., Gernsheim Collctn., Austin, Tex.; Princeton Univ., Firestone Lib., N.J. Natl. Portrait Gall., London.

Robert John Doherty MUSEUM DIRECTOR · TEACHER Born January 16, 1924, in Everett, Massachusetts, Doherty earned a BFA in 1951 from the Rhode Island School of Design, Providence, where he studied with Edwin LaFarge, James Pfeuffer and Matlack Price. He received his MFA in 1954 from Yale University, New Haven, Connecticut, and studied there with Alvin Eisenman, Alvin Lustig and Herbert Matter.

From 1972 to 1979 Doherty was director of the International Museum of Photography at George Eastman House, Rochester. Since 1973 he has also been adjunct professor at the University of Rochester and at Rochester Institute of Technology. He was director/chairman of the Allen R. Hite Art Institute and Fine Arts Department, University of Louisville, Kentucky (1967–72), a professor in that department (1965–72) and an associate professor (1959–64). Doherty founded the University of Louisville's Photographic Archives and was its curator from 1962 to 1965. At the Rhode Island School of Design (1957–59), Doherty was director of development, and he directed graphic design at the Reynolds Metals Co. from 1953 to 1957. His other work experience includes being a tool engineer for U.S. Motors Company (1952–53) and a production manager for Halladay Inc., printers (1949–51).

A member of RPS, DGP and the Advisory Council of Princeton University's Department of Art and Archaeology, Doherty was given the Photographic Administrators Award for Education in Photography in 1979. He won a Fulbright Travel Grant in 1965–66. He has also received awards from the Lithographers and Printers National Association (for Excellence in Design, 1960), American Institute for Graphic Arts (1957) and the American Institute of Architects (Award for Outstanding Architectural Literature, 1956).

PUBLICATIONS Books: *Social Documentary Photography in the USA*, 1974 (C. J. Bucher: Lucerne); *Louisville Architecture*, w/T. M. Brown, 1960 (Louisville Central Area, Inc.: Ky.); *Aluminum Foil Design*, 1959 (Anaconda Aluminum Co.: Louisville, Ky.).

ADDRESS 11 Hawthorne St, Rochester, NY 14610.

Robert Doisneau PHOTOGRAPHER [See plate 79] Born in 1912 in Gentilly, near Paris, France, Doisneau studied lithography at Ecole Estienne in Paris, 1926–29. In 1931 he served as an assistant to sculptor/photographer André Vigneau.

After returning from military service, Doisneau worked as an industrial photographer at the Renault car factory in France (1934–39). Since the 1940s, he has been a freelance photographer whose pictures have appeared in *Vogue*, *Life* and the English *Picture Post* magazines. Doisneau won the Prix Niepce in 1956 and the Prix Kodak in 1947.

His work was featured in the 1973 film *Le Paris de Robert Doisneau*.

Best known for his oftentimes amusing images of Parisian street life, Doisneau has said: "We must always remember that a picture is also made up of the person who looks at it. . . . That walk that one takes with the picture when experiencing it. I think that this is what counts. . . . You offer the seed, and then the viewer grows it inside himself."

PUBLICATIONS Monographs: *Le Mal de Paris*, Clement Lepidis, 1980 (Arthaud: Paris); *Le Paris de Robert Doisneau*, Max-Pol Fouchet, 1974 (Les Editeurs Français Réunis: Paris). Books: *The Boy and the Dove*, James Sage, 1978; *La Loire: Journal d'un Voyage—2*, 1978 (Denoël-Filipacchi: Paris); *Mon Paris*, Maurice Chevalier, 1970; *Epouvantables Epouvantails*, 1965 (Editions Hors Mesure: Paris); *Enfants*, 1957 (Heibon-sha: Tokyo); *Gosses de Paris*, 1956 (Edition Jeheber: Paris); *Paris Parade*, 1956 (Thames & Hudson: London); *Pour Que Paris Soit*, Elsa Triolet, 1956 (Editions Cercle d'Art: Paris); *Compter en S'Amusant*, 1955 (Editions Clairfontaine: Lausanne, Switzerland); *Instantanés de Paris*, 1955 (Editions Arthaud: Paris); *1,2,3,4,5*, 1955 (Editions Clairefontaine; Lausanne); *Les Parisiens Tels Qu'Ils Sont*, 1954 (Editions Delpire: Paris); *La Banlieue de Paris*, Blaise Cendrars, 1949 (Editions Pierre Seghers: Paris). Anthologies: *The Photograph Collector's Guide*, Lee D. Witkin & Barbara London, 1979; *The Magic Image*, Cecil Beaton & Gail Buckland, 1975; *Photography Year 1975*, Time-Life Series, 1975; *Looking at Photographs*, John Szarkowski, ed., 1973. Periodicals: *Camera*, Dec 1979, Nov 1975, Feb 1972.

PORTFOLIO *Doisneau*, 1979 (Hyperion, N.Y.).

COLLECTIONS Art Inst. of Chicago; CCP, Tucson; IMP/GEH, Rochester; MOMA, NYC; New Orleans Mus. of Art, La.; Univ. of New Mex., Albuquerque. Bibliothèque Nationale, Paris; Musé Réattu, Arles, France; Musée d'Art Moderne, Paris; Musée Nicéphore Niepce, Châlon-sur-Saône, France.

REPRESENTATIVE Rapho, 8 rue d'Alger, 75001 Paris, France.

Donald Arthur Doll, S.J. PHOTOGRAPHER Born July 15, 1937, in Milwaukee, Wisconsin, Doll, a Jesuit, earned a BA in Philosophy (1961) and an MA in Psychology (1962).

He has taught at Creighton University, Omaha, Nebraska, since 1969. A member of SPE and NPPA, he received a Special Citation in the 1976 Pictures of the Year Competition at the University of Missouri.

PUBLICATION Book: *Crying for a Vision*, 1976.

COLLECTIONS Rochester Inst. of Tech., N.Y.; Univ. of Neb., Sheldon Mem. Art Ctr., Lincoln.

ADDRESS Creighton University, 2500 California, Omaha, NE 68178,

Zoë Dominic PHOTOGRAPHER Born on the Fourth of July, 1920, in London, Dominic received no formal photographic training.

A freelance, the photographer is a Fellow of the RPS and also belongs to the National Union of Journalists and the British Association of Picture Libraries and Agencies.

Working in medium and small formats, Dominic specializes in theatre, opera, ballet and film photography.

PUBLICATIONS Books: *Frederick Ashton*, 1971 (Harrap); *Cranko and the Stuttgart Ballet*, 1973 (Gunther Neske Verlag). Anthologies: *The Magic Image*, Cecil Beaton & Gail Buckland, 1975.

COLLECTIONS Lincoln Center Archives, NYC. Victoria & Albert Mus., Theatre Mus., London.

REPRESENTATIVES Franz Furst, 420 E 55 St, New York, NY 10022; Camera Press, Russell Ct, Coram St, London WC1, England.

ADDRESS Dominic Photography, 9a Netherton Grove, London SW10 9TQ, England.

John Dominis PHOTOGRAPHER Born June 27, 1921, in Los Angeles, California, Dominis studied cinematography at the University of Southern California, 1941–43.

Since 1978 he has been employed as picture editor of *Sports Illustrated*. Previously he worked as the picture editor for *People* magazine (1974–78), and as a staff photographer for *Life* magazine (1950–73).

A member of ASMP, Dominis was named the Magazine Photographer of the Year in 1966 by the University of Missouri, and also the White House Press Photographer of the Year in 1963.

PUBLICATIONS Books: *The Best of Life*, 1973; *Great Dinners from Life*, 1969.

ADDRESS Time-Life Bldg, Rockefeller Center, New York, NY 10020.

W. F. Donkin PHOTOGRAPHER · MOUNTAINEER Born in England, Donkin died in 1889 in the Caucasus Mountains in Russia.

He belonged to the Alpine Club and RPS.

An Alpinist, the photographer was well respected for his mountain photographs, which the *London Times* (March 18, 1889) called "masterpieces of the photographic art . . . They are perfectly clear, the outline sharply defined, the details of feature distinct and easily recognizable

". . . all stand out with realistic clearness, and recall to the mountaineer that awful joy, the perfect peace which possesses him when he finds himself in those lofty solitudes."

Bonnie J. Donohue PHOTOGRAPHER · TEACHER · FILM MAKER Born on June 24, 1946, in Philadelphia, Pennsylvania, Donohue completed a BFA in Sculpture at the Tyler School of Art in her native city (1969) and an MFA in Photography and Film Making at the Visual Studies Workshop in Rochester, New York (1973). She studied under Keith Smith, Robert Frank, Wynn Bullock and Nathan Lyons, and was influenced by their work.

She is currently teaching photography at the Boston Museum School. Previously, she was an assistant professor in photography and film making at the School of the Art Institute of Chicago (1972–76) and a visiting faculty member at Alfred University in Alfred, New York (1976), and at the University of Colorado in Boulder (1977–79).

The artist, a member of VSW, SPE and CAA, was the recipient of two film maker's grants, one awarded by the American Film Institute (1971), the other by the Illinois Arts Council (1975). In 1974 she won the first prize for the best nonnarrative film, *Refocus: Womanview '75*, at the University of Iowa Film Festival.

Donohue's work always deals with a personal narrative. She uses nonsilver, collage, color multiples, multiple frames and, most recently, a highly patterned form in color and black-and-white.

PUBLICATIONS Anthology: *Image Nation Eleven*, 1973 (Coach House Press: Toronto, Ont.). Catalogs: *The Invented Landscape*, 1979 (New Museum: NYC); *Women's International Film Festival*, 1975 (Midwest Film Ctr, Art Inst. of Chicago); *Photomedia*, 1972 (Mus. of Contemporary Crafts: NYC). Periodicals: *Quiver #4*, 1979 (Tyler School of Art: Philadelphia); *Modern Photography Annual*, 1971.

ADDRESS 153 Westville St, Boston, MA 02122.

A. Doren PHOTOGRAPHER · TEACHER · GALLERY OWNER · COLLECTOR Born in Chicago, Illinois, in 1935, Doren received an AAS and a BFA from Rochester Institute of Technology, New York, where he studied with Minor White and Ralph Hattersley.

He is currently assistant professor of photography at the University of North Carolina, Greensboro, and owns his own gallery, A Personal Gallery.

PUBLICATIONS Book: *Search for Meaning*, 1962. Anthologies: *Celebrations*, Minor White & Jonathan Green, eds., 1974; *Octave of Prayer*, Minor White, ed., 1972; *Photographing Children*, Time-Life Series, 1971; *Be-ing Without Clothes*, Minor White, ed., 1970. Periodical: *Aperture* 10:3, 1962.

COLLECTIONS Ctr. for Creative Leadership, Greensboro, N.C.; The Camera Shop Quintessence Studio Gall., Nantucket, Mass.; Dallas Mus. of Fine Art, Tex.; IMP/GEH, Rochester; M.I.T., Cambridge; MOMA, NYC; NYU, NYC; R. J. Reynolds Cllctn., Winston-Salem, N.C.; R. I. School of Design, Providence.

ADDRESS 902 Silver Ave, Greensboro, NC 27403.

Elsa Dorfman PHOTOGRAPHER Born on April 26, 1937, in Cambridge, Massachusetts, Dorfman earned a BA in French Literature at Tufts University (1959) and an MA in Education at Boston College (1962). From 1972 to 1974 she was a fellow at Harvard University's Bunting Institute.

She takes photographs mainly of her family and friends; also self-portraits and portraits of women. The artist is known for her portraits of the American poets Allen Ginsberg and Robert Creeley. She "uses an informal snapshot style that belies the sense of composition and aesthetic concerns [and] always has a long descriptive title in longhand and a black line around the image."

PUBLICATIONS Books: *Three Afternoons with Charles Olson*, 1980; *Elsa's Housebook—A Woman's Photojournal*, 1974; *His Idea*, w/Robert Creeley, 1973 (Coach House Press: Toronto, Ont.). Anthology: *The Photograph Collector's Guide*, Lee D. Witkin & Barbara London, 1979.

COLLECTIONS Boston Mus. of Fine Arts; Colby Coll. Art Mus., Portland, Maine; Princeton Univ., N.J.; San Francisco Mus. of Modern Art; Univ. Art Mus., Berkeley.

DEALER Witkin Gall., 41 E 57 St, New York, NY 10022.

Robert Dorman PHOTOGRAPHER Born in 1885, Dorman died March 5, 1958, in Rutherford, New Jersey.

As a young man, Dorman was a soldier of fortune, fighting in several Latin-American revolutions and riding with Pancho Villa and his Mexican revolutionaries as a photo-correspondent. He served for many years (until his 1951 retirement) as manager of Acme Newspictures, at that time an affiliate of NEA Service, now of United Press Newspictures. Dorman was one of the first photographers to use airplanes to get more effective images.

A photojournalist whose heyday was in the twenties, Dorman notably covered such events as the Dempsey-Gibbons prizefight in 1923 at Shelby, Montana; the Labrador landing of the U.S. round-the-world flyers in 1924; the flight of the German dirigible *ZR-3* to the U.S.; and aerial shots over the Lake Denmark, New Jersey, arsenal in 1926 while ammunition sheds and shells were exploding into the sky.

Vero Charles Driffield *INDUSTRIAL CHEMIST · INVENTOR* Born on May 7, 1848, in Prescott, Lancashire, Great Britain, Driffield died November 14, 1915. Driffield studied science under a Dr. Knecht in Southport. He was apprenticed to photographer Henry Sampson in 1865. In 1871 he was employed as an engineer in Widens, for Gaskell, Deacon & Co., which later became United Alkali Co. He was a member of the Royal Photographic Society (RPS) of Great Britain.

With Ferdinand Hurter he laid the groundwork for what is now known as sensitometry (commonly called the H&D curve). In 1915 the RPS established the Hurter & Driffield Memorial. In 1888, with Hurter, he published the "Actinograph," a very thorough set of exposure tables.

PUBLICATIONS Book: *The Photographic Researches of Ferdinand Hurter and Vero Charles Driffield*, W. B. Ferguson, ed., 1920 (RPS: Great Britain), repr. 1974. Periodical: "Photochemical Investigations and a Method of Determination of the Sensitiveness of Photographic Plates," *Journal of the Society of Chemical Industry*, May 7, 1890.

ARCHIVE Royal Photographic Society of Great Britain, 14 S Audley St, London W1Y 5DP, England.

Russell Drisch *PHOTOGRAPHER · SCULPTOR* Born August 6, 1944, in Rock Island, Illinois, Drisch studied at Marquette University in Milwaukee, Wisconsin, and at Bradley University in Peoria, Illinois.

Self-employed for the past ten years, Drisch won a CAPS grant in 1978 and an NEA Photographer's Fellowship in 1976. He also had residencies at Yaddo in Saratoga Springs, New York, in 1976 and 1977.

Drisch's photographic work uses representational, photographically derived images in com-

bination with elements of painting, drawing and collage. His primary concern is in the "establishing of various planes and how our perceptions are altered when seeing/looking through foreground, through middleground and into the background."

PUBLICATIONS Anthology: "Russell Drisch," *Aperture*, 1978. Periodicals: "Handful of Color," Howard Millard, *Modern Photography*, Feb 1979; "A is for Artpark," Lucy Lippard, *Art in America*, Nov/Dec 1974.

PORTFOLIO *Palm Series*, 1975 (self-pub.).

COLLECTIONS Baltimore Mus. of Art., Md.; Canton Art Inst., Ohio; Chase Manhattan Bank, NYC; IMP/GEH, Rochester; Niagara Univ., Niagara Falls, N.Y.; Charles Rand Penney Cllctn., Rochester; Prudential Insurance Co. of Amer., Newark, N.J.; Psychiatric Inst., Wash., D.C.; R. J. Reynolds Industries, Winston-Salem, N.C.; Roosevelt Pub. Lib. & Gall., N.Y.; Rockefeller Art Ctr., Fredonia, N.Y.; SUNY Buffalo, N.Y.; Yaddo, Saratoga Springs, N.Y. Natl. Gall. of Canada, Ottawa, Ontario; York Univ. Art Gall., Toronto, Ontario, Canada.

DEALERS Kornblee Gall., 20 W 57 St, New York, NY 10019; Marianne Friedland Gall., 122 Scollard St, Toronto, Canada; Nina Freudenheim Gall., 560 Franklin St, Buffalo, NY; A. J. Wood Gall., 1630 Locust St, Philadelphia, PA 19103; Hokin Gall., 200 E Ontario, Chicago, IL 60611.

ADDRESS 134 Broadway, Brooklyn, NY 11211.

Carol Marie Drobek *PHOTOGRAPHER* Born August 6, 1949, in Philadelphia, Pennsylvania, Drobek received a BFA in Photography from Moore College of Art in Philadelphia in 1971, and an MFA from VSW/SUNY in Rochester in 1973, studying there with Nathan Lyons.

She is currently self-employed as a photographer.

The recipient of an NEA fellowship in photography in 1976, she also received a grant in photography from the New York State Council on the Arts in 1975.

The photographer describes her work as branching "from a concern with the photogram. It involves pure photograms, photographs, magnifications, producing unique images that challenge the imagination as well as most photographic concerns. These works take the form of one-of-a-kind images."

COLLECTIONS Colgate Univ., Hamilton, N.Y.; Phoenix Coll., Phoenix, Ariz.; VSW, Rochester.

REPRESENTATIVE Visual Studies Workshop, 31 Prince St, Rochester, NY 14607.

ADDRESS 1260 Broadway, San Francisco, CA 94109.

František Drtikol *PHOTOGRAPHER* Born in 1883 in Pribram, Czechoslovakia, Drtikol died in Prague in 1961. He served as an apprentice at a portrait studio in Pribram before attending (1901–1903) the Munich Lehr- und Versuchsanstalt für Photographie, a teaching and research institute for photography in Munich. Here he worked under the tutelage of G. H. Emmerich and Hans Spürl. He was strongly influenced by Jugendstil, or Art Nouveau.

After his schooling, Drtikol returned to Czechoslovakia and earned his living as a photographer, working for various studios, then opened his own studio in Prague, where he specialized in portraits of writers and artists. He joined the Prague Cooperative Artel, lectured and continued to paint, making backdrops for his photographs. Eventually he devoted himself completely to his painting. He was an influential figure in the European Bauhaus movement.

Drtikol is most noted for his "uniquely modernistic imagery through the use of harsh lighting and strangely contorted forms and backdrops. His primary subject was the female nude" (Light Impressions). Most of these images were made between 1900 and 1935.

PUBLICATIONS Monographs: *Zena na svetle (Women in Light)*, 1940; *Les nus de Drtikol*, A. Calvas, 1929. Book: *Prager Höfe und Hinterhöfe (Prague Courts and Backyards)* w/Augustin Skarda, 1911. Anthologies: *Photographie als Kunst, 1879–1979*, 1979 (Innsbrucker Allerheiligenpresse: Innsbruck); *The Magic Image*, Cecil Beaton & Gail Buckland, 1975. Catalog: *František Drtikol*, Anna Fárová, 1972 (Kunstgewerbemuseums: Prague).

PORTFOLIO František Drtikol Portfolio, 1979 (Light Impressions: Rochester).

COLLECTIONS IMP/GEH, Rochester. Mus. of Decorative Arts, Prague.

Alan Beckman Du Bois *MUSEUM DIRECTOR* Born on December 14, 1935 in Forest Glen, New York, Du Bois obtained a bachelor's degree in art education (1958) at New York's State University in New Paltz, where he studied under Robert Forth. In 1966 he completed an MFA in Photography and Related Arts at Indiana University, where Henry Holmes Smith was his mentor. In 1970 he attended a Summer Institute for Arts Administration at Harvard University.

Since 1966 he has been assistant director of the Museum of Fine Arts in St. Petersburg, Florida. Prior to that he was director of the Washington County Museum of Fine Arts in Hagerstown, Maryland. Before being associated with museums, he worked as an art teacher in the Public School System in Newburg, New York (1958–60; 1963–64), and as a graduate assistant in the Art Department at Indiana University (1960–63).

He is a member of CAA, the American Association of Museums and the Florida Art Museum Directors Association. He also belongs to SPE and has been serving as the secretary/treasurer of their Southeast Region since 1977. In 1972 and in 1975 he was granted an NEA Museum Professional Fellowship.

Du Bois' field of research is twentieth-century American photography. Since 1971 he has been building a collection of works by living American photographers at the Museum of Fine Arts in St. Petersburg.

PUBLICATIONS Catalogs: *On Assignment: Photographs by Sam Shere*, intro., 1978; *City and Machine*, 1973. Periodical: *Pharos 1978*, intro., XV: 2, 1978.

COLLECTION Ringling Mus. of Art, Sarasota, Fla.

ADDRESSES (bus.) 255 Beach Dr N, St Petersburg, FL 33701; (home) 6351 2nd Ave S, St Petersburg, FL 33707.

Louis Jules Duboscq *OPTICIAN · PHOTOGRAPHER* Duboscq (1817–86) was born and died in France.

He was responsible for a number of progressive steps in the field of photography, among them: the construction of automatic projection arc lamps with Foucault in 1849; construction of the "polyconograph" in 1861, a camera attachment containing a row of five double plateholders that were movable, making it possible for fifteen exposures to be made on one plate; the manufacture of Sir David Brewster's lenticular stereoscopic lens; and construction of an apparatus for enlarging by electric light, presented before the Paris Photographic Society on February 15, 1861.

Duboscq became involved with microphotography, collaborating with Léon Foucault and the optician Nachet. He also "produced a series of most beautiful stereoscopic daguerreotypes of persons, statues, bouquets of flowers, and objects of natural history, which thousands of persons flocked to see" (Eder).

PUBLICATIONS Books: *History of Photography*, Josef Maria Eder, 1905, repr. 1945; *Pratique du Saccarimètre soleil et du saccharimètre a penombres*, w/A. Duboscq, 1881 (Paris); *Description de l'appareil régulateur de la lumière électrique de Léon Foucault*, 1868 (Paris); *Instruction sur la pile à acide nitrique*, 18?? (Paris); *Pratique du Saccharimètre soleil*, 1866 (Hennuyer & fils:

Paris); *Règles pratiques de la photographie sur plaque, papier, albumine et collodion*, 1853 (self-pub.: Paris).

David L. DuBuque *PHOTOGRAPHER · TEACHER* Born in Northfield Falls, Vermont, on August 9, 1949, DuBuque is married to photographer De Ann Jennings. He studied photography at Orange Coast College in Orange, California (1972–75), and journalism at California State University in Northridge, where he completed his bachelor's degree in 1979. He studied under John Upton and Jerry McMillan, both of whom had a major influence on his development.

As of this writing he is holding several jobs: besides being a freelance photographer, he works as a photo instructor at Harbor College in San Pedro, California, and as a photographer for 20th Century Fox, Inc., in Los Angeles. From 1975 to 1978 he was a portrait photographer for Ed Lyn Studio in Los Angeles.

He belongs to the Los Angeles Institute of Contemporary Arts, the Los Angeles Center for Photographic Studies, the International Association of Business Communicators, the Southern California Business Communicators, and Cameravision Gallery in Los Angeles, for which he served as a board member in 1979.

DuBuque's work includes black-and-white and color, usually in small format. Whereas his black-and-white production is conceptual, his color work is humorous and is mainly made up of portraits.

PUBLICATIONS Catalog: *Attitudes: Photography in the 70s*, 1979 (Santa Barbara Art Mus.: Calif.). Periodical: *New West*, Nov 1978.

COLLECTION Laguna Beach Mus. of Art, Calif.

ADDRESS 1546 Lucretia Ave, Los Angeles, CA 90026.

Maxime Du Camp *PHOTOGRAPHER · WRITER* [See plate 5] Born February 8, 1822, in Paris, Du Camp died February 9, 1894, in Baden-Baden (now in West Germany).

Du Camp traveled widely throughout the Middle East with his companion, novelist Gustave Flaubert, in the years 1844–45 and 1849–51. He fought in France as a counterrevolutionist and was wounded and decorated in 1848. He also fought with Garibaldi in Italy. Founder of the *Revue de Paris* in 1851 in which he published Flaubert's *Madame Bovary*, Du Camp continued writing throughout his life.

Also an accomplished poet, novelist and art critic, he contributed to many publications.

A calotypist, he concentrated on the Middle East, photographing especially the pyramids, sphinx and other structures. His book of Middle Eastern photographs was the first of its kind to be illustrated with actual photographs.

PUBLICATIONS Monographs: *Egypte, Nubie, Palestine et Syrie*, 1852 (Gide et Baudry: Paris; E. Gambert & Co.: London); *Souvenirs et Paysages d'Orient*, 1851. Books: *Flaubert in Egypt*, Francis Steegmuller, ed. & trans., 1972; *Souvenirs d'un Demi-Siècle*, memoirs, 2 vols., 1949 (Paris); *Voyageurs et Ecrivains Françaises en Egypte*, vol. 2, J. M. Carré, 1932 (Cairo); *Souvenirs littéraires*, 1882 (Paris); *Paris, ses Organes, ses Fonctions et sa Vie*, 6 vols., 1869–75; *Expédition des deux-Siciles*, 1861; *Les chantes modernes*, poetry, 1855; *Le Nil, Egypte et Nubie*, 1854 (Librairie Nouvelle: Paris). Anthologies: *The Photograph Collector's Guide*, Lee D. Witkin & Barbara London, 1979; *Early Photographs & Early Photographers*, Oliver Mathews, 1973; *Great Photographers*, Time-Life Series, 1971; *French Primitive Photography*, André Jammes & Robt. Sobieszek, intro. by Minor White, 1969.

COLLECTIONS Art Inst. of Chicago; IMP/GEH, Rochester; MOMA, NYC; N.Y. Public Lib., Rare Book Div., NYC; UCLA. Bibliothèque Nationale, Paris.

Gillaume-Benjamin Amant Duchenne de Boulogne *PHYSICIAN · PHOTOGRAPHER* Born September 17, 1806, in Boulogne, France, Duchenne died in Paris, September 15, 1875. He maintained a lifelong medical practice, first in Boulogne (1831–42) and later in Paris (1842–75), during which time he pioneered several neurological advancements. To accompany his explorations on the effects of electrical stimulation on diseased nerves and muscles, he made photographic studies of the faces of his patients. Duchenne rendered the first accounts of several types of muscular atrophy and paralysis caused by nerve disorders. He also invented an instrument, now known as Duchenne's trocar, that enabled the diagnostic practice of biopsy to develop.

In photographing the faces of his patients, his "aim was to examine each muscle separately to determine its role in the play of facial expression. From 1852 to 1856 he took collodion photographs of every reaction of a mentally debilitated patient" *(French Primitive Photography)*.

PUBLICATIONS Books: *The Expressions of the Emotions in Man and Animals*, Charles Darwin, 1872; *Iconographie photographique pour servir à l'étude de la structure intime du système nerveux de l'homme*, 1869 (Pougin: Paris); *Album* de Photographies Pathologiques, 1862 (Baillière: Paris); Mécanisme de la physionomie humaine ou analyse électro-physiologique de l'expression des passions, 1862 (J. Renouard: Paris); De l'Electrisation localisée, 1855, U.S. ed., Localized Electricity, 1871 (Lindsay & Blakiston: Philadelphia); Physiologie des mouvements, 1867, U.S. ed., Physiology of Motion, 1949 (Lippincott: Philadelphia); Exposition d'une nouvelle méthode de galvanisation, 1850 (Rignoux: Paris). Anthologies: Early Photographs & Early Photographers, Oliver Mathews, 1973; French Primitive Photography, André Jammes & Robert Sobieszek, intro. by Minor White, 1970.

(Arthur) Louis Ducos du Hauron   INVENTOR · PHYSICIST   [See plates 32 and 134]   Born in 1837 in Langon, France, Ducos du Hauron died in October 1920 in Agen, France. Brother of scientist Alcide Ducos du Hauron, Louis was influenced by Sir David Brewster's theory of color.

On March 1, 1864, Ducos du Hauron patented, but did not build, a device for taking and projecting motion pictures. He was one of the first to conceive the three-color process of photography (and to actually produce a three-color print), for which he applied and received a patent from the French government on November 23, 1868. The physicist's theories formed the basis for later processes and had a tremendous influence on orthochromatic photography. He also developed a three-color camera which, using light filters, could simultaneously make three-color separations with one exposure. Called a "caméra héliochromatique," he received a patent for it in 1874, then patented a device for three-dimensional photography called an anaglyph in 1891. By 1897 Ducos du Hauron had invented a process for producing three-color negatives in a single exposure.

The inventor was also an accomplished pianist.

He received a gift from the Vienna Photographic Society in December 1904, the Chevalier of the French Légion d'Honneur in 1912 and a modest pension from the French government.

PUBLICATIONS   Books: History of Photography, Josef M. Eder, 1905, rev. 1932, repr. 1972; History of Three-Color Photography, E. J. Wall, 1925; Photographie indirecte des couleurs, 1900 (Paris); Traité pratique de photographie des couleurs, 1878 (Paris); Les Couleurs reproduites en photographie, Eugène Dumoulin, 1876 (Paris); L'Héliochromie, 1875 (Paris); Les Couleurs en photographie, 1869 (Paris).

COLLECTION   IMP/GEH, Rochester.

Thomas Dugan   PHOTOGRAPHER · PHOTO BOOK MAKER   Born September 5, 1938, in Bayonne, New Jersey, Dugan received an MA from Goddard College in Plainfield, Vermont. Among his influences are Richard Avedon, Irving Penn, Diane Arbus, Frederick Wiseman and the poet Arthur Rimbaud.

The self-employed artist is a member of SPE, Friends of Photography and VSW.

A "photo picture book maker" and photohistorian, Dugan, at this writing, was conducting a second series of interviews for Photography Between Covers.

PUBLICATIONS   Monographs: Self-Death Ritual Fantasy, 1979; Nantucket, 1978. Anthologies: Photography Between Covers: Interviews with Photo-Bookmakers, 1979; Self-Portrayal, 1978.

REPRESENTATIVE   Bayonne Publishing Co, 106 W 53 St, Bayonne, NJ 07002.

Alfred Martin Duggan-Cronin   PHOTOGRAPHER   Born May 17, 1874, in Ireland, Duggan-Cronin died in 1954 in Kamfersdam, near Kimberley, South Africa.

He went to South Africa in 1897, working as a night watchman for the DeBeers Company, returning in 1904 to Ireland, where he purchased a box camera. Upon his second venture to South Africa, he worked as a guard and dispenser at a convict hospital and began photographing tribal members with whom he came in contact. Duggan-Cronin then started traveling the countryside in order to photograph tribespeople in their natural habitat, covering 80,000 miles by about 1938. In 1924 Richard Madela, a Fingo tribesman and student teacher, became, first, his servant and, for seventeen years, his friend and assistant. The photographer went to London for exhibitions of his work in 1924 and 1931 and continued his other travels, including trips to Rhodesia and Portuguese East Africa, all the while photographing.

He received many grants to finance his travels: from McGregor Museum in Kimberley (1919), the Union Research Grant Board (several), Carnegie Trust Fund (several), the DeBeers Company (several). He established South Africa's first Bantu Picture Gallery (1924) and created a unique collection of native beadwork, leather work, implements, dresses and bows and arrows. With funding and housing provided by the DeBeers Company, he donated the collection and 750 framed photographs of tribespeople to the City of Kimberley.

The photographer worked with Imperial Sovereign glass plates, contact-printing his negatives on "Seltona." For a darkroom he variously used a tent, native huts, lean-to shelters made around his car, and finally, as a gift from DeBeers in 1938, a portable darkroom. His goal was "to record for posterity the primitive habits and dress, environment and customs of all the major groups of Bantu tribes living in Southern Africa." His 4,000 surviving negatives and his collections attest to his accomplishments.

PUBLICATIONS Books: *Silver Images*, A. D. Bensusan, 1966 (Howard Timmins: Cape Town); *The Bushman Tribes of Southern Africa*, intro. by D. F. Bleck, 1942 (Alex. McGregor Mus.: Kimberley, South Africa); *The Bantu Tribes of South Africa*, 4 vols., 1928–35 (Deighton/Bell: Cambridge, England). Catalog: *Catalog of the Permanent Collection of Native Studies in the Duggan-Cronin Bantu Gallery*, 194? (Alex. McGregor Mem. Mus.: Kimberley, South Africa).

COLLECTIONS City of Kimberley Archives, South Africa; Duggan-Cronin Bantu Art Gall., Kimberley; McGregor Mus., Kimberley; Papal Univ., Inst. of Roman Studies, Rome.

ARCHIVE Duggan-Cronin Bantu Art Gall., Kimberley, South Africa.

Rudolph Dührkoop *PHOTOGRAPHER* Born in 1848 in Hamburg, Germany, Dührkoop died there in 1918.

The photographer worked as a retail tradesman initially, then served in the army during the Franco-Prussian War (1870–71). He took up photography about 1880 and, in 1883, opened his own studio. Dührkoop traveled to Paris in 1900 and to London in 1901. In 1904 he attended the St. Louis Exposition and there he made the acquaintance of Gertrude Käsebier. He opened a second studio in Berlin while still maintaining his Hamburg operation. Dührkoop's work was widely exhibited.

During his lifetime he received many awards at exhibitions, among them a gold medal in 1899 from the city of Hamburg.

A portrait photographer, Dührkoop abandoned conventional studio portraiture about 1886 and, instead, visited subjects in their homes and photographed them in the open air. He eventually preferred printing on matte surfaces. In 1909 Hoppé referred to him as "the pioneer of artistic portrait photography on the Continent" (*Pictorial Photography*).

PUBLICATIONS Books: "and Minja Diez-Dührkoop," *Bildnis-Almanach für 1915 und 1916* (Berlin); *Das Kamerabildnis und seine kulturelle Bedeutung*, 1907 (Hamburg); *Kamera*, 1906 (Bild-

nisse: Berlin). Anthologies: *Pictorial Photography in Britain 1900–1920*, Arts Council of Great Britain, 1978; *Early Photographs & Early Photographers*, Oliver Mathews, 1973. Periodicals: *British Journal of Photography*, June 21, 1918; "Seven Portraits of Children," *Photo-Miniature*, Sept 1907.

COLLECTION Lib. of the Graphischen Lehrund Versuchsanstalt, Vienna.

David Douglas Duncan *PHOTOJOURNALIST · ART HISTORIAN* Born in Kansas City, Missouri, on January 23, 1916, Duncan earned a BA in 1938 in marine zoology at the University of Miami, Coral Gables, Florida, where he also studied Spanish. From 1933 to 1935 he attended the University of Arizona at Tucson.

Duncan took up photography as a hobby during his college years. He began freelancing in 1938, selling his pictures to newspapers. In 1940 he received his first assignment as photographer for the Chile-Peru Expedition of the American Museum of Natural History. He also furnished Pan American Airways with publicity photographs that year. Beginning in December 1941 he supplied photographs of Mexico and Central American countries to the Office of the Coordinator of Inter-American Affairs of the U.S. Department of Commerce. In February 1943 he entered the U.S. Marine Corps and was initially stationed at Ewa, near Honolulu, to command a photographic laboratory. Soon he was photographing operations of the South Pacific Air Transport Command, covering the guerrilla fighting of the Fijians against the Japanese (1944), Marine combat aviation on Okinawa, and, aboard the *USS Missouri* in 1945, he photographed the official surrender of Japan. After the war Duncan worked on staff for *Life* magazine (1946–56), covering the Korean War, South Africa, French Guinea, Morocco and King Farouk's departure from Egypt. He also covered the Vietnam War for *Life* and ABC-TV News. He then became a special correspondent for *Collier's*, after resigning from *Life,* and contributed to other magazines as well. In 1968 he covered the Republican and Democratic Conventions for NBC-TV News.

During his career he has received the Overseas Press Club Award twice, *U.S. Camera*'s Gold Medal for the book *This Is War!* (Duncan contributed royalties from the book to a Marine Corps fund for widows and children of the dead), a Legion of Merit, a Purple Heart, two distinguished flying crosses, six battle stars and three air medals.

Duncan's "world-ranging camera has recorded

many of the major events of the past thirty-five years. Whatever his subject—Caribbean turtles, Irish sheep, the U.S. Marines in three wars, the Near East conflict . . . Picasso, the treasures of the Kremlin—Duncan's photographs extract the essence of violence or beauty or way of life, often catching the episodic details that sum up a moment of history" (*Current Biography*).

PUBLICATIONS Monographs: *The Silent Studio*, 1976; *Prismatics: Exploring a New World*, 1973 (Collins: London); *War Without Heroes*, 1970; *Self-portrait, U.S.A.*, 1969; *I Protest*, 1968; *Yankee Nomad*, autobio., 1966 (Elsevier: Amsterdam); *Picasso's Picassos*, 1961; *The Kremlin*, 1960, repr. as *Great Treasures of the Kremlin*, 1968; *The Private World of Pablo Picasso*, 1958. Anthologies: *The Magic Image*, Cecil Beaton & Gail Buckland, 1975; *Famous Photographers*, Aylesa Forsee, 1968; *12 at War*, Robert E. Hood, 1967. Periodicals (selected): "Intimate Portfolio of Richard Nixon," *Newsweek*, Aug 19, 1968; *Life*, Feb 23, 1968, Oct 27, 1967; "Yap Meets the Yanks," Mar 1946, "Okinawa, Threshold to Japan," Oct 1945, "Fiji Patrol on Bougainville," Jan 1945, *National Geographic*.

COLLECTION Time-Life, Inc., NYC.

ADDRESS h. Castellaras 53, Mouans Sartoux, Alps Maritime, France.

Max Dupain (Maxwell Spencer) PHOTOGRAPHER Born in 1911 in Sydney, Australia, Dupain served a three-year apprenticeship in the studio of Cecil Bostock, beginning in 1930. He was later influenced by the German New Objectivity movement.

In 1943 he established his own studio, becoming a partner in 1947 with process engravers Hartland and Hyde, a partnership that continues to this day. Dupain was frequently published in *The Home* magazine, and by 1938 was a leading commercial photographer in fashion, advertising and portraiture. In 1943–44 he served in the army as a photographer in the camouflage unit, spending time in New Guinea before transferring to the Department of Information in 1945 to undertake the assignment of photographing Australia for promotional purposes. He returned to his studio in 1947, switching his emphasis to industrial and architectural work, although he continued in landscapes and portraiture. His work has been widely exhibited in Australia. Dupain is a founding member of the Contemporary Camera Group (1938), an affiliate of the Royal Australian Institute of Architects.

Gael Newton has written about Dupain (*Silver and Grey*, 1980), "His early work was in the pic-

torial style, but in 1933 Dupain began to photograph industrial forms such as silos in a way totally alien to the pictorialists. The new images stressed geometric form and were outlined and accentuated by clear hard light rather than romanticised by atmospheric effects. . . . Dupain rejected the romantic preoccupation with picturesque subjects and turned to developing a style in tune with contemporary life in the machine age." His work has continued toward the abstract.

PUBLICATIONS Book: *Silver and Grey*, Gael Newton, 1980. Periodical: *Art in Australia*, 1935.

ADDRESS Dupain, Hartland & Hyde, Artarmon St, Sydney, Australia.

Lennart Durehed PHOTOGRAPHER · GALLERY DIRECTOR Born January 2, 1950 in Gothenburg, Sweden, Durehed attended the School of Photography in Gothenburg (1967–69) and served as an assistant to Irving Penn in New York (1973–76).

He has managed Camera Obscura Gallery in Stockholm, Sweden, since 1977, previously working as a freelance photographer (1976–77) and a photographer at Picture Agency in Gothenburg (1970–73).

Durehed received a grant from the Swedish Photography Association in 1974 to study photography in the United States.

DEALER Camera Obscura, Kåkbrinken 5, S-111 27, Stockholm, Sweden.

ADDRESS Rådjursstigen 17, S-191 46, Sollentuna, Sweden.

(Jean-Louis-Marie) Eugène Durieu PHOTOGRAPHER · ADMINISTRATOR Born in 1800 at Nîmes, France, Durieu died in Paris in 1874. Durieu helped create a corps of diocesan architects in his capacity as administrator. In 1848 he was appointed general director of churches.

Durieu was a founding member of both the Société Héliographique and the Société Française de Photographie, holding office as the first president of the latter.

Durieu frequently collaborated with Eugène Delacroix, who used the photographs as models for his paintings. His main themes were nudes and astronomical studies, made in collaboration with Baron Gros. Durieu made daguerreotypes and salt prints. It was Durieu who stated, "The future of photography lies in paper."

PUBLICATIONS Book: *Tableau analytique des pièces justificative des comptes et des droits de timbre*, 1854 (Bureau du Mémonal: Paris). Catalog: *Une Invention du XIXᵉ siècle: La photographie*, Bernard Marbot, 1976 (Bibliothèque Nationale: Paris). Periodicals: *Bulletin de la So-*

ciété Française de Photographie, 1857, 1856, May 1855; *La Lumière*, 1856, 1855,

COLLECTIONS IMP/GEH, Rochester. Bibliothèque Nationale, Paris.

Jay Dusard PHOTOGRAPHER [See plate 109] Born in St. Louis, Missouri, on February 18, 1937, Dusard took a BA in Architecture from the University of Florida in Gainesville. From 1967 to the present he has been involved with informal studies with Frederick Sommer in Prescott, Arizona.

Presently a self-employed photographer, Dusard has taught at Prescott College (1968–74) and Prescott Center College (1975).

Known for his landscape photographs of massive Southwest rock formations, Dusard often toys with scale in his images in order to manipulate the viewer's spatial orientation.

PUBLICATIONS Book: *Land of Living Rock*, C. Gregory Crampton, 1972. Periodicals: "Visions from the Southwest," 52:3, 1980, "The Petrified Forest," 51:4, 1979, *Plateau* (Mus. of Northern Ariz.: Flagstaff); *Popular Photography*, Sept 1974; *Aperture*, 16:3, 1972.

COLLECTIONS Apeiron Workshops, Millerton, N.Y.; New Orleans Mus. of Art; Phoenix College, Ariz.; Photography Gall., Philadelphia.

REPRESENTATIVES Fifth Ave. Gall. of Photography, 6960 5 Ave, Scottsdale, AZ 85251; Stephen White Gall., 835 N La Cienega Blvd, Los Angeles, CA 90069.

ADDRESS 2221 View Dr, Prescott, AZ 86301.

Allen A. Dutton PHOTOGRAPHER · TEACHER Born in Kingman, Arizona, on April 13, 1922, Dutton earned an MA at Arizona State University in Tempe (1947). He also attended the Art Center School in Pasadena, California, in 1940 and studied with Minor White during 1963–64.

Since 1961 Dutton has been chairperson of the Photography Department at Phoenix College, Arizona. He previously taught art and photography at Phoenix Union High School from 1950 to 1961, after having worked as an entomologist for Arizona Agronomy Chemicals (1946–49).

A member of SPE, he received a John Hay Fellowship in 1960.

The artist specializes in surrealistic photomontages. He also makes "large-format photographs of desert landscapes that hide nudes."

PUBLICATIONS Monographs: *A. A. Dutton's Compendium*, 1977; *Great Stone Tit*, 1974. Books: *Darkroom Dynamics*, Jim Stone, ed., 1979; *The Grotesque in Photography*, A. D. Coleman, 1977. Anthology: *Self-Portrayal*, 1978. Periodicals: *Aperture*, 18:2, 1974, 17:1, 1972, 15:3, 1970, 14:1, 1968.

COLLECTIONS Ariz. State Univ., Northlight Gall., Tempe; MOMA, NYC; Robert Friedus Gall., NYC; Univ. of Ky., Lexington; Univ. of N. Mex., Albuquerque. Bibliothèque Nationale, Paris; Gall. Shunju, Tokyo; Il Diaframma, Milan, Italy.

DEALERS Vision Gall., 216 Newbury St, Boston, MA 02116; Photography Southwest Gall., 4223 N Marshall Wy, Scottsdale, AZ 85251.

ADDRESS 4925 W Banff Ln, Glendale, AZ 85306.

Jack Dykinga PHOTOGRAPHER Born in Chicago on January 2, 1943, Dykinga studied at St. Procopius College in Lisle, Illinois (1965), and at Elmhurst College, Illinois (1966). A self-taught photographer, he was influenced by the photojournalists of the *Chicago Sun Times*.

He is currently freelancing, and recently organized his company, Southwestern Wilderness Travel, which holds workshops in wilderness areas. He has worked at the *Arizona Daily Star* (since 1976), and at the *Chicago Tribune* (1964, picture editor, 1974–75) and the *Chicago Sun-Times* (1966–74). His work has also been published in such magazines as *Time, Newsweek, Life* and *U.S. News & World Report*.

Dykinga won the Pulitzer Prize in 1971; he has also won five "Pictures of the Year" awards from the NPPA/University of Missouri. He is a member of the Sierra Club.

The photographer pursues "honest storytelling" in his work. "I'm a great admirer of simple statements," he says, "clean and succinct images." Working mainly in small-format black-and-white, though recently with color transparencies, he has covered such subjects as petroleum development in Mexico and the Tarahuamara Indians.

PUBLICATION Anthology: *Moments*, Sheryle & John Leekley, intro. by Dan Rather, 1978.

ADDRESS Southwestern Wilderness Travel, 3808 Calle Barcelona, Tucson, AZ 85716.

E

Thomas Eakins   *PAINTER · PHOTOGRAPHER*
Born in Philadelphia, Pennsylvania, on July 25, 1844, Eakins died there on June 25, 1916. He attended the Pennsylvania Academy of Fine Arts, and anatomy classes at Jefferson Medical College. From 1866 to 1869 he studied at the Ecole des Beaux-Arts under painter Jean-Léon Gérôme. When in Spain in 1969 he was greatly influenced by the seventeenth-century paintings of Diego Velázquez and Jusepe de Ribera. His interest in photography was greatly influenced by Muybridge's motion studies.

Eakins taught at the Pennsylvania Academy of Fine Arts in the late 1870s, where he became a professor of drawing and painting in 1879. His insistence on nude models in his painting and drawing classes was a controversy of the day, and led to his forced resignation in 1886. He continued teaching intermittently at the Art Students League in Philadelphia, and at the National Academy of Design in New York City. During his active years he received several commissions for paintings. He was a member of the Philadelphia Sketch Club.

Eakins devised a variation of Etienne Marey's stop-motion wheel (around 1884), making studies of models in motion. The work of one of the greatest American painters of the nineteenth century, Eakins' paintings can be seen in most major museums. Eakins was a sculptor as well.

While he was little known for his photography, he used his photographic portraits and multiple-image studies of moving athletes and animals as a guide for his realist paintings, and the images, particularly his portraits, are fine in their own right. He used gelatin dry-plate negatives and made platinum prints taken with a 4 x 5 box camera.

PUBLICATIONS Books: *The Life and Work of Thomas Eakins*, Gordon Hendricks, 1974; *The Photographs of Thomas Eakins*, Gordon Hendricks, 1972; *Eakins*, Sylvan Schendler, 1967; *The Painter and the Photograph*, Van Deren Coke, 1964, rev. ed. 1972; *Thomas Eakins*, Fairfield Porter, 1959; *Thomas Eakins: His Life and Works*, Lloyd Goodrich, 1933. Anthologies: *The Photograph Collector's Guide*, Lee D. Witkin & Barbara London, 1979; *The Invented Eye*, Edward Lucie-Smith, 1975; *The Magic Image*, Cecil Beaton & Gail Buckland, 1975. Catalogs: *Thomas Eakins Photographs*, Nov 10, 1977 (Sotheby Parke Bernet: NYC); *Thomas Eakins: His Photographic Works*, Gordon Hendricks, 1969 (Penn. Acad. of Fine Arts: Phil.). Periodicals: "Photography and Teaching: Eakins at the Academy," Ronald J. Onorato, *American Art Review*, July/Aug 1976; "Some Recently Discovered Thomas Eakins Photographs," Garnett McCoy, *Archives of American Art Journal*, 12:4, 1972; "Walt Whitman and Thomas Eakins: A Poet's and a Painter's Camera-Eye," Lincoln Kirstein, *Aperture*, 16:3, 1972; "Eakins, Muybridge and the Motion Picture Process," William I. Homer, *Art Quarterly*, summer 1963.

COLLECTIONS Hirshhorn Mus. & Sculpture Garden, Wash., D.C.; Metro. Mus. of Art, NYC; Philadelphia Mus. of Art, Penn.

George Eastman   *INVENTOR · MANUFACTURER*
Eastman was born July 12, 1854, in Waterville, New York, and died by his own hand on March 14, 1934, in Rochester, New York. He was educated in the public schools of Rochester.

Eastman worked briefly in banking and insurance, then began manufacturing and marketing dry photographic plates in 1880. Initially called Eastman Dry Plate and Film Company, the business' name was changed to Eastman Kodak Company in 1892.

The invention of flexible roll film (celluloid) by Eastman made amateur photography a possibility for the first time and also contributed to the development of motion picture cinematography (with nitrocellulose film). In 1888 Eastman put the famous Kodak box camera on the market, containing film for 100 exposures. When the film was exposed, the camera was returned to the company intact for development of the emulsion. He also introduced the Brownie camera in 1890 to enable children to do photography.

Eastman introduced several mass-production methods in his factories long before Henry Ford's assembly line came into being, and he was one of the first employers to provide profit-sharing as an employee incentive. He contributed more than $75 million to educational organizations such as the University of Rochester (of which the Eastman School of Music is a part) and MIT, among others. His home is now the George Eastman House of Rochester.

PUBLICATION Book: *George Eastman*, Carl W. Ackerman, intro. by Edwin R. A. Seligman, 1930.

COLLECTION IMP/GEH, Rochester.

ARCHIVE International Museum of Photography, George Eastman House, 900 East Ave, Rochester, NY 14607.

Sally Eauclaire CRITIC · CURATOR · LECTURER Born August 15, 1950, in Cornwall, New York, Eauclaire earned a BA in 1972 and an MS in 1980 from the University of Rochester.

Since 1979 Eauclaire has written freelance criticism for *Art in America*, *Afterimage: VSW*, *Modern Photography* and other publications, especially about contemporary color photography as an art form. In 1979 she was organizing an exhibition, "The New Color: Color Photography of the 1970s," for the Everson Museum in Syracuse, New York. From 1973 to 1979 she was art critic for the *Democrat & Chronicle* in Rochester.

A member of SPE, Eauclaire won a National Endowment for the Humanities Journalist Fellowship in 1978.

ADDRESS 180 St. Paul St, Rochester, NY 14604.

José Ortiz Echagüe PHOTOGRAPHER · ENGINEER Born in 1886 in Guadalajara, Spain, Echagüe died in 1980 in Madrid. He received an engineering degree at Academia de Ingenieros Militares de Guadalajara. His first contact with photography was at age twelve.

Echagüe became a balloon pilot in the early 1900s and in 1910 was commissioned as an airplane pilot. He founded and was president of CASA, an aeronautical factory, and SEAT, a car-manufacturing company. His first photographs were published in *Photograms of the Year*, and in 1915 he started doing photography on a professional basis. His work was widely exhibited in Europe and the United States.

An honorary fellow of RPS and the Photographic Society of America, Echagüe won the Gold Medal of the Real Sociedad Fotográfica (Royal Society of Photography) of Madrid in 1975 and the Gold Medal of Labor in Spain for his photography books in 1958/59. He received a silver medal from the California Pacific International Exposition in 1935 and first prizes at the American Photographic Competition in Boston (1925) and the Frederick and Nelson Competition in Washington, D.C. (1924).

"The superb beauty of his prints, combined with his poignant subject matter, made his work accepted in hundreds of exhibits and magazines," according to Luis Nadeau. His international reputation began in 1907 when his work appeared in *Photograms of the Year*, edited by Mortimer in London. For thirty years he was the only Spaniard to be represented in this annual. Echagüe employed the exclusive Fresson process, manufacturing his own paper, which he called Carbondir (carbon direct), after 1965. His main subject was always Spain: its people, its landscapes and villages. Also, from 1909 to 1915, he specialized in aerial photography.

PUBLICATIONS Monographs: *José Ortiz-Euchagüe: Photographies*, 1979 (Ed. du Chene: Paris); *José Ortiz-Euchagüe: Photographs*, 1979 (Gordon Fraser: London); *José Ortiz-Echagüe, Spanien: Landschaften und Portraits*, 1979 (Schirmer Mosel: Munich); *José Ortiz-Echagüe: sus fotografías*, 1978 (Editorial Incafo: Madrid); *Espana, Castillos y Alcázares*, intro. by Justo Pérez de Urbel, 1956 (Ortiz-Echagüe: Madrid), English ed., *Castles and Fortresses*, 1971; *España, Mística*, intro. by Miguel Merrero-García, ed., 1943, *España, Pueblos y Paisajes*, intro. by J. Martínez Ruiz, 1938, *España, Tipos y Trajes*, 1933 (Publicaciones Ortiz-Echagüe: Madrid); *Espagne: Types et Costumes*, 1930 (Espasa-Calpe, S.A.: Madrid); *Spanische Köpfe*, 1930 (Editorial Wasmuth: Germany). Book: *Estampas Cartujanas*, Antonio Gonzales, 1956 (Editorial Vizcaina: Bilbao, Spain). Anthologies: *Pictorial Photography of Britain*, 1978 (Arts Council of Great Britain: London); *The Magic Image*, Cecil Beaton & Gail Buckland, 1975. Catalog: *José Ortiz-Echagüe*, Ignacio Barcelo, May 1962 (Sala de Exposiciones de la Dirección General de Bellas Artes: Madrid). Periodicals: Article, Italo Zannier, *Foto Italiana*, Nov 1978; article, Italo Zannier, *Foto Film*, Feb 1968; "Ortiz-Echagüe; el último pictorialista," Daniel Masclet, *Photo Cinema*, Oct 1965; "Lo que no cuenta el artista," May 1962, article, Livio Fusco, Apr 1961, *Arte Fotográfico*; "Medio siglo de actividad fotografica," *American Annual of Photography*, 1950; article, Paul L. Anderson, *The Camera*, Aug 1935.

COLLECTION RPS, London.

ARCHIVE Ornz Echagüe, 1 Tutor, 24 Madrid, Spain.

Richard Paul Edelman PHOTOGRAPHER · TEACHER · CONSERVATOR Born in Long Beach, New York, on August 31, 1951, Edelman obtained a BFA from the Rochester Institute of Technology (1972) and an MFA from the Pratt Institute in Brooklyn (1979). Since 1974 he has been doing freelance work as a photographer and photographic conservator. He has held several positions in New York, as a faculty member at the New School for Social Research (1977, 1979), as a producer and coordinator of a lecture series at the Floating Foundation of Photography in New York City (1979) and as an illustrator and consultant for a new series of textbooks put out by the New York Institute of Photography (1977–79).

He belonged to CAA (1977–79) and has been a member of SPE since 1977.

Edelman works in 35mm black-and-white and focuses on "psycho-historical portraits of the urban setting as a living organism." He also specializes in the presentation of photographic artwork.

PUBLICATION Periodical: *Print*, May/June 1977.

ADDRESS 361 W 36 St, 5th fl, New York, NY 10018.

Mary Beth Edelson PHOTOGRAPHER · CONCEPTUAL ARTIST · LECTURER Born in East Chicago, Indiana, Edelson received a BA from DePauw University in Greencastle, Indiana (1955), and an MA from New York University in New York City (1959).

Since 1971 Edelson has been giving many lectures and workshops and organizing panels and performances throughout the country. In 1979 she was a visiting artist at Chico University in California and in 1978 an artist-in-residence at Iowa University's Multi-Media Department and at San Jose State University in California. She has been a member of A.I.R. Gallery in New York City since 1975.

The artist makes the following statement about her work: "My involvement with the photograph began as a means to an end; the concept or idea leads the way. The open-ended possibilities of photography, i.e., multiplicity of choices, instant accessibility to content, collaging, juggling sequences, and later the manipulation of perceived reality to register as information what our eyes and mind tell us cannot happen—all helped to rivet me to the medium." Edelson also works in sculpture, video, painting, performance and making books.

PUBLICATIONS (selected) Anthologies: *The Decade of Woman*, 1980; *Performance*, Hans Breder, 1979; *The Tent Book*, E. M. Hatton, 1979; *American Women Artists*, Charlotte S. Rubinstein, 1979; *Earth Rites*, Sherry Mestel, 1978; *In/Sights, Self-portraits by Women*, Joyce Tenneson Cohen, 1978; *Women Artists*, Karen Peterson & J. J. Wilson, 1976. Catalogs: *Visual and Sculptural Bookworks*, 1979 (Seibu Mus.: Tokyo; Montclair Art Mus.: N.J.); *Private Icons*, 1979 (Bronx Mus.: N.Y.); *Contemporary Issues: Works on Paper by Women*, 1977 (Women's Building: Los Angeles); *Painting and Sculpture Today: 1974*, 1974 (Indianapolis Mus. of Art: Ind.); *Contemporary Religious Imagery in America*, 1974 (Ringling Mus. of Art: Sarasota, Fla.); *Six from Washington*, 1972 (Corcoran Gall. of Art: Wash., D.C.). Periodicals: "Complexes: Architectural Sculpture in Nature," Lucy R. Lippard, *Art in America*, Jan/Feb 1979; *American Photographer*, 1978.

REPRESENTATIVES A.I.R. Gall., 97 Wooster St, New York, NY 10012; Joann Dobrick, 216 E Ontario, Chicago, IL 60611.

ADDRESS 110 Mercer St, New York, NY 10012.

Josef Maria Eder CHEMIST · AUTHOR · HISTORIAN · TEACHER Born March 16, 1855, at Krems on the Danube, Eder died in Austria in 1944. He studied at the University of Vienna, specializing in the study of natural sciences.

Eder worked in the Austria State Mining Laboratory for a time and then became assistant to J. J. Pohl, professor of chemical technology in Vienna. For one year he was a substitute professor of chemistry at the technical high school at Troppau. In June 1880 he was appointed associate professor of photochemistry and scientific photography at the technical high school in Vienna. By 1882 his status changed to professor of chemistry and physics. In 1889 Eder was appointed director of the newly founded Graphische Lehr- und Versuchsanstalt, a post he held for many years, retiring in 1923.

Eder assisted the Austrian legislature in drafting a bill for the protection of the rights of inventors in the field of photography that went into effect in 1895. His efforts resulted in a government appointment as court expert in the field of the graphic industry and chairman of the government department of experts on patent rights, a position he retained for several years and from which he retired in 1925.

A member of the Vienna Photographic Society, the Kaiserlich Leopoldinisch-Carolinischen deutschen Akademie der Naturforscher and the Academy of Sciences at Vienna, he also served as honorary president of the Photographic Society, Vienna, and honorary member of the Association of Austrian Chemists. Additionally, he was a member of the First International Congress on Astrophotography and of many more associations throughout Europe.

Eder won first prize at the Photographic Society of Vienna competition (1878) and received an honorary degree of Doctor of Philosophy and Science at the technical high school of Vienna (1930). He was a Knight of the Imperial Austrian Order of the Iron Cross and of the Leopold Order, Commander of the Austrian Francis-Joseph Order, Commander of the Saxon Albrecht Order with Star, an officer in the French Foreign Legion of Honor, and commander of the Swedish Wasa Order. During World War I he was decorated by Emperor Carl with the gold war cross for civil services, and awarded the great decoration for distinction by the Austrian Republic. Among his numerous medals of honor are the Elliot Cresson gold medal of the Franklin Institute in Philadelphia, the gold medal of the Vienna Photographic Society, also their Voigtländer medal, the gold Swedish Adelsköld medal, the Petzval medal, the Plösl medal, the Maria Theresa medal of the Vienna Camera Club, the Daguerre gold medal of the Photographic Society of Berlin, the Senefelder medal of the Gremium of Lithographers and Copper Printers of Vienna, the progress medal of RPS, the Peligot medal of the Société Française de Photographie and the Japanese medal of honor of the Friends of Photography in Tokyo. On its twenty-fifth anniversary, the Graphische Lehr- und Versuchsanstalt presented Eder with a silver plaque bearing his portrait.

It would be impossible to enumerate all of Eder's accomplishments in the field of photographic research. A few of the more outstanding advancements have been his studies of the chemical foundation of photography and investigations of the double salts of cadmium bromide and iodide in their relation to negative collodion. With Captain Victor Tóth, he announced a lead intensifier and investigated the methods of dyeing photographic silver plates with the aid of ferricyanides, which were later to become very important. Eder investigated the composition and method of pro-

ducing iron oxalate and its compounds, then little known, which later became important in connection with platinotype and other iron-printing processes. He was the first to establish the dominating sensitiveness of the ultraviolet and the coefficient of light reaction. With Giuseppe Pizzighelli, he developed a silver chloride gelatine process, and he discovered the silver chloride bromide gelatine process. These latter two discoveries became the basis for the industry of the manufacture of photographic art paper and of positive films for motion pictures. Eder researched the reaction of silver halide compounds to the solar spectrum and the action of dyes and other substances on photographic emulsions. He constructed a quartz spectograph in 1889, through which he was the first to establish the ultraviolet emission spectrum of burning carbohydrates and that of the ammonium oxygen flame (1890–92). (Source: Hinricus Lüppo-Cramer's biography of Eder in *The History of Photography*.) Eder was active and instrumental in bringing the application of photography to all branches of science. His particular interest lay in the fields of sensitometry, actinometry, spectral analysis and spectography.

PUBLICATIONS Books: *Josef Maria Eder Bibliography*, Robert Zahlbrecht, preface by Luis Kuhn, 1955 (Vienna); *Josef Maria Eder, 1855–1944*, F. D. Dworschak & O. Krumpel, 1955 (Vienna); *Johann Heinrich Schulze*, 1917 (Vienna); *Über Schloss Münichau bei Kitzbühel in Tirol*, 1915; *Quellenschriften zu den frühesten Anfängen der Photographie*, 1913; *Atlas typischer Spektren*, w/Eduard Valenta, 1911, 3rd ed., 1928 (Academy of Sciences: Vienna); *History of Photography*, 3rd ed., 1905, repr. 1945; *Beitrage zur Photochemie und Spektralanalyse*, w/Eduard Valenta, 1904 (Vienna: Halle); *Rezepte, Tabellen und Arbeitsvorschriften für Photographie und Reproduktionstechnik*, 1889 (W. Knapp: Halle); *Jahrbuch für Photographie und Reproduktionstechnik*, 1887; *Ausfuhrliches Handbuch der Photographie*, 1884; *Photographische Korrespondenz*, 1880, rev. ed., *Theorie und Praxis der Photographie mit Bromsilbergelatine*; *Die Momentphotographie*, 1880; *Die chemischen Wirkungen des farbigen Lichtes*, 1879; *Über die Reaktionen der Chromasäure und Chromate auf Gelatine, Gummi, Zucker und andere Substanzen organischen Ursprunges in ihren Beziehungen zur Chromatphotographie*, 1878; *Die Bestimmung der Salpetersäure*, 1876; *Beitrage zur Kenntnis des Einflusses der chemischen Lichtintensität auf die Vegetation*, n.d.; *Unter-*

suchungen über Nitrozellulose, n.d. Contributor: *Der Siegeslauf der Technik*, Max Geitel, 3rd ed., 1928; *Grosses Konversations-Lexikon*, Meyer, 6th ed., 1902–1908; "Licht, chemische Wirkungen," *Neues Handwörterbuch der Chemie*, Fehling, vol. 4, 1886; "Analysen des chinesischen Tees," *Polytechnisches Journal*, n.d.; *Lexikon der gesamten Technik*, Otto Lueger, 1st & 3rd eds., n.d. Anthology: *Photography's Great Inventors*, Louis W. Sipley, 1965. Catalog: *Catalogue of the Austrian Exhibit at the World's Fair in Paris*, contr. & assoc. ed., 1900. Periodicals: "Sensitization: In Memory of Josef Maria Eder," A. Maschka, vol. 91, 1955, "Zum 75. Geburtstage Eder's," Alfred Hay, Apr 1930, *Photographische Korrespondenz*; "Dr. J. M. Eder: 80th Anniversary," *Photographic Journal*, Apr 1935.

Susan Beth Eder CALLIGRAPHER · ILLUSTRATOR · PHOTOGRAPHER · TEACHER Born April 8, 1950, in St. Louis, Missouri, Eder received her BA in 1972 from the University of Michigan in Ann Arbor and an MA from Ohio State University in 1974.

Currently Eder is a freelance calligrapher and illustrator. Previously she was employed as an instructor at Williams College in Williamstown, Massachusetts, in 1979, and in 1977–79 she was a part-time lecturer at North Adams State College in North Adams, Massachusetts. She also worked as a part-time instructor for SUNY at Morrisville from 1975 to 1977.

The recipient of an NEA Photography Grant in 1979, she was also awarded a CAPS Fellowship in Photography in 1977.

Utilizing 35mm and 110 formats, the photographer uses "photographic images as signs for objects rather than as aesthetically pleasing compositions, often cropping and splicing the photos to remove extraneous information." She goes on to say, "My works are content-oriented explorations of the relationship between internal and external realities, between human mental structures and natural systems." The processing and printing of her work are done commercially.

PUBLICATIONS Reviews: *Arts Magazine*, Mar 7, 1979, Dec 1975; *Village Voice*, Feb 21, 1977.

REPRESENTATIVE Marian Goodman, 38 E 57 St, New York, NY 10022.

ADDRESS 100 Hoxsey St, Williamstown, MA 01267.

Harold Eugene Edgerton TEACHER · INVENTOR · SCIENTIST [See plate 83] Born on April 6, 1903, in Fremont, Nebraska, Edgerton received his BS from the University of Nebraska, Lincoln, in 1925. From the Massachusetts Institute of Technology, Cambridge, he earned both his MS (1927) and his DSc (1931).

He worked for General Electric in 1925–26, but since 1927 he has been teaching at Massachusetts Institute of Technology. A professor of electrical engineering for many years, he is currently institute professor, emeritus.

Dr. Edgerton is a fellow of the Institute of Electrical and Electronic Engineers, Photographic Society of America, RPS and Society of Motion Picture & TV Engineers. He is also a member of the Academy of Applied Science, Academy of Underwater Arts & Sciences, American Academy of Arts & Sciences, American Philosophical Society, Boston Camera Club (Hon.), Marine Technology Society, Boston Museum of Science, National Academy of Engineering, National Academy of Sciences, Photographers Association of New England, Society of Photographic Engineers and Woods Hole Oceanographic Institution.

The scientist has received numerous awards and honors during his long career, among them four honorary degrees (two LLD degrees, one DSc, and one DEng) from four different universities. A selection of his other awards are: Lockheed Award for Marine Science and Engineering, Marine Technology Society, 1978; National Medal of Science, 1973; Holley Medal, American Society of Mechanical Engineers, 1973; NOGI Award, Underwater Society of America, 1971; Albert A. Michelson Medal, 1969, and Potts Medal, 1941, Franklin Institute; Alan Gordon Memorial Award, SPIE, 1969; John Oliver La-Gorce Gold Medal, 1968, and Franklin L. Burr Prize, 1953, National Geographic Society; Richardson Medal, Optical Society of America, 1968; Technical Achievement Award, ASMP, 1965; Silver Progress Medal, 1964, and Medal, 1936, Royal Photographic Society of London; Industrial Photographers Association, National Award, 1963; E. I. duPont Gold Medal Award, 1962, and Progress Award, 1959, SMPTE; Gordon Y. Billard Award, MIT, 1962; Boston Sea Rovers Award, 1960; New England Engineer of the Year Award, Eng. Societies of New England, 1959; 75th Anniversary Citation, 1955, and Master of Photography, 1949, Photographers Association of America; Photography Magazine Award, 1952; U.S. Camera Achievement Gold Medal Award, 1951; Joseph A. Sprague Memorial Award, National Press Photographic Association, 1949; Medal of Freedom, 1946; Modern Pioneers Award, National Association of Manufacturers,

1940; Citation for Operation Sandstone, University of California, Los Alamos Scientific Lab, (n.d.); Certificate of Appreciation from the War Department, 1946.

Dr. Edgerton's pioneering research in stroboscopic photography laid the foundation for the development of modern electronic speed flash. In 1931 at MIT he developed a lamp that produced a brilliant light with a duration of less than one-millionth of a second. He perfected the use of stroboscopic lights in both ultra-high speed motion and still photography, thus enabling photographers to capture activities beyond the perceptive capacity of the human eye—bullets in flight, light bulbs shattering, etc. He has also made significant contributions to underwater exploration by designing watertight cameras, strobes and side-scan sonar. He has worked aboard the boat *Calypso* with Jacques-Yves Cousteau exploring sea floors, and assisted in finding the sunken ships *USS Monitor* and *HRM Britannic*. During World War II, Edgerton photographed nuclear test explosions. His recent efforts have been in the area of sonar uses for archaeology and geology. Dr. Edgerton was a founding partner of EG&G, Inc., in Wellesley, Massachusetts, a company specializing in electronic technology.

PUBLICATIONS Books: *Moments of Vision*, w/ J. R. Killian, 1979; *Electronic Flash, Strobe*, 1979; *The Encyclopedia of Photography*, 1963; *Flash, Seeing the Unseen*, w/J. R. Killian, 1939, repr. 1954. Anthologies: *The Photograph Collector's Guide*, Lee D. Witkin & Barbara London, 1979; *The Magic Image*, Cecil Beaton & Gail Buckland, 1975; *Photography's Great Inventors*, Louis W. Sipley, 1965. Periodicals: *Industrial Photography*, Nov 1961; *Photographic Science & Engineering*, 1959; *Research Film*, 1958; *Progress in Photography*, 1940–1950; *Photo Technique*, Oct 1940, Oct, Aug 1939.
COLLECTIONS IMP/GEH, Rochester; MIT, Cambridge, Mass.; MOMA, NYC; Plainsman Mus., Aurora, Neb.; Smithsonian Inst., Wash., D.C. Bibliothèque Nationale, Paris; Fotografiska Muséet, Stockholm, Sweden; Georges Pompidou Centre, Paris; Science Mus., London.
REPRESENTATIVE Science Photo Lib., 2 Bleinheim Crescent, London W11 1NN, England.
DEALER Vision Gall., 216 Newbury St, Boston, MA 02116.
ADDRESS MIT, Rm 4-405, Cambridge, MA 02139.

Ellender Victorine Edwards PHOTOGRAPHER · TEACHER Born in Hagerstown, Maryland, Edwards received a BFA from the Maryland Institute, College of Art, in Baltimore in 1958. She also studied with Jean Liberté, Victor D'Amico and Reuben Kramer.

Since 1968 she has been an instructor for the Montgomery County Public Schools in Rockville, Maryland. She has also worked as an artist-in-residence and as director of children's "Paint-In" at Glen Echo National Park in Maryland from 1974 to 1976.

Edwards is a member of the Montgomery County Art Educators Association and the Independent Press Association.

In her photographs Edwards superimposes female nudes, one upon another, over landscapes to create a new abstract image. She also photographs people in newsworthy situations and has recently photographed Senator Edward Kennedy and Elizabeth Taylor.
ADDRESS Box 106, Rockville, MD 20850.

Ann Christine Eek PHOTOGRAPHER · CRITIC Born October 5, 1948, in Falun, Sweden, Eek studied at Fotoskolan (The Photoschool) of Stockholm, 1968–71. Her husband, Per Torgersen, is also a photographer and critic.

Eek works as a freelance photographer and writer, currently writing for *Aftenposten*, a newspaper on photography in Norway. She has also contributed to the Swedish photo magazines *Aktuell Fotografi*, *Fotografiskt Album*, *Foto*, and *Fotograficentrums Bildtidning*, and has illustrated school books since 1971. In 1971 and 1973 she taught at the Fotoskolan.

The photographer belonged to the Stockholm reportage group SAFTRA from 1969 to 1979 and currently belongs to Fotograficentrum [Photography Center] Sweden (since 1974, committee member 1974–75) and Svenska Fotografernas Förbund (Association of Swedish Photographers) since 1967. She was on the latter's authors' and illustrators' section committee between 1975 and 1978. Eek was also a member of Sweden's Fotografiska Muséets Vänner (Friends of the Photographic Museum) from 1973 to 1978 (on the committee 1973–76) and belongs to Forbundet Frie Fotografer (Association of Free Photographers) in Norway.

Eek won a five-year work grant from the Writers Fund of Sweden in 1977 as well as a memorial grant from Anna Riwkin Brick (1976), work (1974) and travel (1976) grants from the Writers Fund (Författarfonden) of Sweden, a culture award from the City of Stockholm (1974) and a government artist grant (1973).

In 1977 the film *Vi bär inte slöja längre (We*

don't wear veils anymore), based on Eek's still photographs, was produced for Swedish TV-2. Made with social anthropologist Berit Backer of Oslo, it concerned Albanian women in Yugoslavia.

Eek has photographed landscapes since 1966 and done reportage since 1967. She did documentary photography from 1972 to 1979 and currently does "subjective" photography.

PUBLICATIONS Books: *Växelbruk*, Siv Arb, 1977 (Författarförlaget: Stockholm); *Arbeta—inte slita ut sig!*, w/Ann Mårtens & Kajsa Ohrlander, 1974 (Ordfront: Stockholm). Periodicals: *Fotografiskt Album*, no. 1, 1979; *Fotografi*, Mar 1978; *Creative Camera International Year Book*, 1975; *British Journal of Photography*, 1972.

COLLECTIONS Bibliothèque Nationale, Paris; Fotografiska Muséet, Stockholm; Robert Meyer Cllctns., Oslo, Norway; Västerbottens Mus., Umeå, Sweden.

REPRESENTATIVE MIRA Bildarkiv, Kungsgatan 66, S-111 22 Stockholm, Sweden.

ADDRESS Deichmans gate 25, Oslo 1, Norway.

Ole Ege PHOTOGRAPHER Born May 23, 1934, in Hobro, Denmark, Ege completed commercial school in 1954.

A freelance photographer since 1967, he was formerly editor and publisher of the magazines *Ekko* (1967) and *Focus* (1963–64). He also edited *Foto-Magasinet* from 1959 to 1963.

Ege won an award from the Copenhagen City Art Fund and one from Århus City Art Fund in 1978.

Also a film maker, Ege was both director and cinematographer for the features *Bordello*, 1972, and *Pornography*, 1971. He won a Grand Prix Award for his documentary *A Summer Day* (with sculptor Shinkichi Tajiri) in Amsterdam in 1970.

Ege works in medium- and small-format still photography. He describes his subjects as being nudes, glamour, erotic pornography, landscapes, architecture, portraits and circus scenes.

PUBLICATIONS Book: *Aerø*, 1974. Periodicals: *Dansk Fotografisk Tidsskrift*, 1979; *Fotografish Årsbok Sweden*, 1964.

COLLECTION Royal Library, Copenhagen.

ADDRESS Reykjaviksgade 3, 1–2300 Copenhagen, S. Denmark.

William Eggleston PHOTOGRAPHER Born in 1939 in Memphis, Tennessee, Eggleston attended Vanderbilt University in Nashville, Tennessee, Delta State College in Cleveland, Mississippi, and the University of Mississippi, Oxford. He was influenced by the work of Henri Cartier-Bresson.

A self-employed photographer, he was a lecturer in visual and environmental studies at Harvard University in Cambridge, Massachusetts, in 1974. Eggleston won an MIT Research Fellowship in 1979, an NEA Photographer's Fellowship in 1975, and a Guggenheim Fellowship in 1974.

The photographer is known for his work in color, which he began using exclusively in 1966.

PUBLICATIONS Monographs: *Wedgwood Blue*, 1979; *Flowers*, 1978; *Morals of Vision*, 1978; *Election Eve*, 1977. Book: *Photography*, Barbara & John Upton, eds., 1976. Anthologies: *American Images*, Renato Danese, ed., 1979; *One of a Kind*, Belinda Rathbone & Eugenia Parry Janis, eds., 1979; *The Photograph Collector's Guide*, Lee D. Witkin & Barbara London, 1979; *Photography, Venice '79*, 1979; *Mirrors and Windows*, John Szarkowski, 1978; *Masters of the Camera*, Gene Thornton, 1976; *Photography Year 1976*, Time-Life Series; *The City*, Alan Trachtenberg, Peter Neill & Peter Bunnell, eds., 1971. Catalogs: *Aspects of American Photography*, 1976 (Univ. of Mo.: St. Louis); *William Eggleston's Guide*, John Szarkowski, 1976 (MOMA: NYC); *14 American Photographers*, Renato Danese, 1974 (Baltimore Mus. of Art: Md.). Periodicals: *Modern Photography*, Sept 1978, Aug 1976; *Picture Magazine*, 1:5, 1978; "The Second Generation of Color Photographers," Allan Porter, July 1977, "Choice: A Gallery Without Walls," Nov 1976, *Camera*; "MOMA Shows Her Colors," Michael Edelson, *Camera 35*, Oct 1976; "Reviews: Color Me MOMA," Dan Meinwald, *Afterimage: VSW*, Sept 1976; "How to Mystify Color Photography," Max Kozloff, *Artforum*, Nov 1976; *Camera Mainichi*, Dec 1974.

PORTFOLIO *Troubled Waters*, 1980 (Caldecot Chubb, N.Y.C.).

COLLECTIONS Brooks Mem. Art Gall., Memphis, Tenn.; Corcoran Gall. of Art, Wash., D.C.; MOMA, NYC; Natl. Cllctn. of Fine Arts, Wash., D.C.; New Orleans Mus. of Art.

ADDRESS c/o Lunn Gall., 406 Seventh St NW, Washington, DC 20004.

Judith Eglington PHOTOGRAPHER · FILM MAKER Born June 13, 1945, in Montreal, Canada, Eglington received a diploma from the Ecole des Beaux Arts in Montreal (1961) and later attended film school at Simon Frazer University in Vancouver, Canada (1969–71). She also studied with the Belgian surrealist painter Jan Cox (1964–65) and with Robert Frank (1967).

The self-employed photographer received Ontario Arts grants in 1975 and 1976; Canada Council Arts Photography Bursaries in 1969, 1970 and 1971; a Canadian Film Development Grant in 1972 and 1973; Donner Foundation video grants in 1971 and 1972 and Quebec Arts grants in 1961 and 1962.

Her theatrical films include: *Stallers Farm*, 1977; *View*, 1977; *The Dance*, 1975/76; *Earth Visions*, 1974; *Short Strokes*, 1974; *Help*, 1973; *Here's to You*, 1973; and the documentary *Barrier Free Housing*, 1979.

PUBLICATIONS Monographs: *Golden Apples of My Mind*, 1977; *The Athletes*, 1976; *Earth Visions*, 1972/73; *I Am a Living Creature*, 1969. Anthologies: *SX-70 Art*, Ralph Gibson, ed., 1979; *Instant Images*, 1978.

REPRESENTATIVE National Film Board, Stills Division, Tunneys Pasture, Ottawa, Ontario, Canada.

ADDRESS POB 397, Aylmer East, Quebec, Canada J9H 5E7.

Josef Ehm PHOTOGRAPHER Born August 1, 1909, in Habartov, Czechoslovakia, Ehm was apprenticed in the portrait studio of K. Podlipný in Poděbrady (1923–27). Largely self-taught, he was especially influenced by Albert Renger Patzsch and Man Ray.

A freelance photographer 1946–60 and from 1967 to the present, Ehm previously taught at the State Graphic School in Prague (1934–46, 1960–67). From 1927 to 1934 he worked as a photographer in various Prague studios. Ehm belongs to the Union of Czechoslovak Creative Artists (since 1947).

Ehm has won silver medals at the International Exhibition of Photography in Budapest (1958), at Bifota, Berlin (1958), at the International Exhibition in Poland (1956), and at the Exhibition of Professional Photographers in Prague (1938).

PUBLICATIONS Books (all Prague): *Prague*, J. Janáček, 1979 (Panorama); *Prague's Interiors*, E. Poche, 1973 (Odeon); *Czech Castles and Chateaus*, J. Wagner, 1971 (Orbis); *Czech Gothic Sculpture*, A. Kutal, 1962 (Odeon); *Jiří Mašín*, 1961 (SNKL); *Bohemian Porcelain*, E. Poche, 1956, *Italian Majolica*, J. Vydrová, 1955 (Artia); *Prague*, V. V. Stech, 1948; *St. George Church*, Cibulka, 1936 (Graphic School).

COLLECTIONS Moravian Gall., Brno, Czechoslovakia; Mus. of Decorative Arts, Prague, Czechoslovakia; Rudolf Kicken Gall., Cologne, Germany.

ADDRESS U Smaltovny 20 E, CS-170 00, Prague 7, Czechoslovakia.

Rudolf Eickemeyer, Jr. PHOTOGRAPHER · AUTHOR [See plate 34] Born in Yonkers, New York, on August 7, 1862, Eickemeyer died there on April 25, 1932. His father, Rudolf, Sr., was a noted inventor, and his sister, Eva E. Rowland, was a poet. The junior Eickemeyer attended Hoboken Academy but was a self-taught photographer.

He went to work as a draftsman for his father's firm, Osterhell & Eickemeyer (1884–1895), and began photographing on his own in 1893. In 1895 he became associated with James L. Breese of the Carbon Studio in New York and in 1900 became art manager of the Campbell Art Studio. He founded that company's New York branch and was an executive with the Campbell studio from 1911 to 1915, with a stint from 1905 to 1911 in his own studio, David & Eickemeyer.

After leaving Campbell, Eickemeyer worked independently until his retirement (which was shortly before he died). Remaining active in community affairs, the photographer was appointed chairman of the Yonkers Municipal Art Commission in 1911, commissioner of the Yonkers Museum of Art and Science (now the Hudson River Museum) in 1922, and was a director of the First National Bank and a trustee of the Yonkers Savings Bank. He also was elected to the Yonkers School Board in 1895 and served there until 1919.

Eickemeyer's myriad memberships included the RPS, which he joined in 1898, winning its Alberts Medal in 1894; the London Salon of Photography, 1898; the Camera Club of Vienna (1898), which awarded him their Silver Medal; the Hamburg Salon (1899); the Daguerre Club, of which he was a life member from 1903; The Linked Ring of London, which awarded him a medal in 1895; the New York Camera Club; and the Salon Club of America, of which he was art director. He was also an honorary member of Columbia University's Photographic Society, president of the Yonkers Art Association, vice-president of the Yonkers chapter of the Westchester County Historical Association, associate member of the Art Centre in New York, and a member of the Old English Sheepdog Club of America.

In addition to the awards already mentioned, among the nearly 100 Eickemeyer received were the Viceroy Gold Medal from the International Exhibition of the Photographic Society of Calcutta, India (1895), the gold medal of the St. Louis Exposition and a special gold medal from the Hamburg Senate.

He was a leader in the pictorial movement, and

his work included genre scenes, landscapes and portraits of notable persons taken in his native New York and abroad, where he traveled many times. Eickemeyer used every printing process available over the course of his career.

PUBLICATIONS Monograph: *Photography of Rudolph Eickemeyer*, 1972. Books: *In the Open*, 1908; *The Ministry of Beauty*, Stanton Davis Kirkham, 1907; *Nature and Culture*, Hamilton Wright Mabie, 1904; *Winter* (text only), 1903; *The Old Farm*, 1901; *In and Out of the Nursery*, verse by Eva Eickmeyer Rowland, 1900; *Down South*, 1900; *How to Make a Picture*, 1898; *Letters from the Southwest*, intro. by Sadakichi Hartmann, illus. by E. W. Deming, 1894.

COLLECTIONS Hudson River Mus., Yonkers, N.Y.; IMP/GEH, Rochester; Smithsonian Inst., Wash., D.C.

Terrill (Terry) E. Eiler   *PHOTOGRAPHER TEACHER*   Born August 11, 1944, in Boston, Massachusetts, Eiler earned both her BFA (1966) and MFA (1969) from Ohio University, Athens. Her major adviser on her master's degree was Arnold Gassan. She also studied in 1966 with Cliff Edom at the University of Missouri, Columbia, and lists as her mentors Winfield Parks and Robert Gilka.

She has been associate director of the Institute of Visual Communication at Ohio University since 1978. She has also been an assignment contract photographer for *National Geographic* since 1970 and a freelance photographer and co-owner of Mugwump, a stock photo agency, during the same period.

A member of ASMP, NPPA, SPE and the Society of Professional Journalists, Eiler received Ohio University's outstanding "University Professor" award in 1979.

"I am a documentarian," she describes herself, "concerned with photographing people and their environment . . . an interpreter of visual facts and a visual commentator." Much of her work has dealt with the American Indian.

PUBLICATIONS Books: *The Fun of Basketball Is Winning*, 1980; *Blue Ridge Harvest*, 1978; *Life in a Narrow Place*, Stephen Hirst, 1974; *Indian Shangri-la*, 1970; *Vanishing People of North America*, 1969. Periodicals: "Ohio's Forgotten Islands," Mar 1978, "The Navajo," Dec 1971, *National Geographic*.

COLLECTIONS Environmental Protection Agency, Wash., D.C.; Herd Mus., Phoenix, Ariz. L/C, Amer. Folklife Ctr., Wash., D.C.; Mus. of N. Ariz., Flagstaff; Natl. Geographic Soc., Wash., D.C.; Ohio Univ., Athens.

REPRESENTATIVE Mugwump, 330 B Barker Rd, Rt 2, Athens, OH 45701.

Alfred Eisenstaedt   *PHOTOGRAPHER*   Eisenstaedt was born December 6, 1898, in Dirschau, West Prussia (now Tczew, Poland).

He moved with his family to Berlin in 1906 and served in the German Army during World War I. He began doing freelance photography in the early 1920s while employed as a button and belt salesman, and received numerous assignments from various German publications. Photojournalism became a full-time profession for Eisenstaedt in 1929 when he was assigned to cover the Nobel Prize ceremony in Stockholm. He then worked for Pacific & Atlantic Photos Berlin office until he came to the United States in 1935. The following year he became one of *Life*'s original four photographers (along with Margaret Bourke-White, Peter Stackpole and Thomas McAvoy). His photographs have appeared in almost every major photography and news magazine over the years.

Eisenstaedt's more than 2,000 photographic assignments include more than ninety *Life* covers. His honors include: International Understanding Award for Outstanding Achievement (1967); Photographic Society of America achievement award (1967); Culture Prize in Photography from the German Society for Photography in Cologne (1962), and Photographer of the Year (Encyclopaedia Britannica and the University of Missouri, 1951). He belongs to the New York Press Photographers Association and Overseas Press Photographers.

"Especially recognized for his photographs of people—Winston Churchill, Charlie Chaplin, Richard Strauss, Gerhart Hauptmann, Sophia Loren, John F. Kennedy—Eisenstaedt has always treated the famous and the anonymous with equal care and perception," writes Gregory Vitiello. His work has vividly chronicled people and events since the early 1930s. Adds Vitiello, "Frequently described as the father of photojournalism, he was one of a handful of pioneers who developed photoreportage in the late 1920s and early 1930s, coincident with the emergence of high-speed Leica cameras." Eisenstaedt has said that the photojournalist's job is "to find and catch the storytelling moment."

PUBLICATIONS Monographs: *Eisenstaedt's Album*, 1976; *People*, 1973; *Witness to Nature*, 1971; *Martha's Vineyard*, 1970; *The Eye of Eisenstaedt*, 1969; *Witness to Our Time*, 1966. Books: *Eisenstaedt's Guide to Photography*, 1978; *Wimbledon: A Celebration*, John A. McPhee, 1972.

Anthologies: *The Photograph Collector's Guide*, Lee D. Witkin & Barbara London, 1979; *Great Photographic Essays from Life*, Maitland Edey, 1978; *The Magic Image*, Cecil Beaton & Gail Buckland, 1975; *Travel Photography*, 1972, *Photojournalism*, 1971, Time-Life Series.

COLLECTIONS Time-Life Inc., NYC; United Technologies Corp., NYC. RPS, London.

REPRESENTATIVE Time-Life Inc., Time-Life Bldg, Rockefeller Ctr, New York, NY 10020.

ADDRESS 72-15 37 Ave, Jackson Heights, NY 11372.

Peter Lars Elfeldt PHOTOGRAPHER Born January 1, 1866, in Elsinore, Denmark, Elfeldt died February 18, 1931, in Copenhagen. At age thirteen he became a messenger for the photographer Ratschack in Hilleroed, and by age seventeen he had become the photographer's assistant.

In 1890 Elfeldt was self-employed in Østergade, Copenhagen, and later become photographer to the royal court. He served as president of the Association of Danish Photographers from 1906 to 1918 and was a member of the board of the Association of Trade Guilds of Copenhagen from 1918 to 1923.

Elfeldt was best known for his photographs of the royal family, especially those taken at the castle of Fredensborg. He was the first to photograph public events in Denmark, and also photographed street life in Copenhagen and produced many stereographs.

COLLECTION Danish Television Cllctn.

Eliot Elisofon PHOTOGRAPHER · PAINTER · WRITER · ART COLLECTOR · LECTURER [See plate 137] Born in New York City on April 17, 1911, Elisofon died in his native city on April 8, 1973. He attended Fordham University, receiving a BA in 1933, and was influenced in his development by painters such as Picasso and Orozco.

His professional experience is varied. After having been employed as a social worker by the New York State Labor Department, he ran a commercial photography studio (1935–38), taught photography at the American Artists School (1938–42) and was on the staff of the Museum of Modern Art (1939). In 1938 he started his career as a freelance photographer, working on assignment for magazines such as *Fortune, U.S. Camera, Foto* and *Scribner's*. He also worked regularly for *Life* magazine, as a war correspondent during World War II, on and off as a staff photographer and on various assignments (1942–73). He also did the still photography for the motion pictures *Warlord, Khartoum* and *Dr. Doolittle*.

Elisofon belonged to ASMP, to the Royal Anthropological Society, the Overseas Press Club and the Explorers Club. In 1958 the Peabody Museum of Archaeology and Ethnology of Harvard University in Cambridge granted him a Research Fellowship in primitive art.

Elisofon proved to be an extremely versatile artist. Throughout his career he lectured at museums and colleges across America, and wrote articles and essays for a variety of magazines. He organized and wrote the catalog for "Masterpieces of Primitive Art," an exhibit at the Boston Museum of Fine Arts, and was also responsible for assembling the show "Understanding African Sculpture" (1953) at the Art Institute of Chicago, which then toured for three years, showing at several museums, including the Museum of Modern Art in New York.

Inventor of a method of filter control that alters and distorts color for mood, he served as a color consultant for the following Hollywood films: John Huston's *Moulin Rouge* (1952), *Bell, Book and Candle* (1956) and *The Greatest Story Ever Told* (1962). He also directed the prologue of the feature *Khartoum* (1966) and completed the film *Akan Gold* (1973). His work for television includes the cinematography for the American Institute of Architects series entitled *Man Builds* (NET); producing, directing and editing two segments of *Africa* (1967), an ABC documentary for which he also did the cinematography; contributing to the two parts of *Camera III: African Sculpture* (1970) for CBS; and producing, writing and directing four one-hour segments of *Black African Heritage* (1972) for Group W/Westinghouse Broadcasting.

Elisofon was a renowned watercolor artist, and his paintings are included in several collections all over the world.

A master of both color and black-and-white photography, Elisofon was a very prolific artist. As a photojournalist he excelled in action shots as well as pictures of quiet landscapes and objets d'art. He is also known for his special interest in primitive cultures.

PUBLICATIONS Monograph: *Tribute to Africa: The Photography and the Collection of Eliot Elisofon*, 1974. Books: *A Week in Joseph's World: Zaire*, 1973; *Erotic Spirituality: The Vision of Konarek*, Alan Watts, 1971; *A Week in Leonora's World: Puerto Rico*, 1971; *A Week in Agata's World: Poland*, 1970; *The Cooking of India*, Santha Rama Rau, 1970; *The Cooking of Japan*, Rafael Steinberg, 1970; *Java Diary*, 1969; *The Hollywood Style*, Arthur Knight, 1969; *Africa's Animals*, w/Marvin Newman, 1967; *The Nile*, intro. by Laurens van der Post, 1964; *Color Photography*, 1961; *The Art of Indian Asia*, Heinrich Zimmer, Joseph Campbell, ed., 1960; *The Sculpture of Africa*, Wm. Fagg, preface by Ralph Linton, 1958, repr. 1978; *African Folktales and Sculpture*, Paul Radin, ed., 1952; *Food Is a Four Letter Word*, foreword by Gypsy Rose Lee, 1948. Periodicals: "Color Control," *Popular Photography*, 1958; "War Photography," *U.S. Camera*, Mar 1944.

COLLECTIONS   Art Inst. of Chicago; Dallas Mus. of Contemporary Art; MOMA, NYC; Mus. of African Art, Wash., D.C.; Time-Life Archives, N.Y.

ARCHIVE   Museum of African Art, 316-318 A St NW, Wash., D.C. 20002.

Arthur Elliott   *PHOTOGRAPHER · COLLECTOR* Born in 1870 in New York, Elliott died in November 1938, in Cape Town, South Africa.

A jack-of-all-trades, Elliott worked his way to Great Britain as a captain's boy on a steamer, then traveled to South Africa in the late 1880s. He continued his helter-skelter career there until 1900, when he took up photography. Between 1910 and 1938 he produced five major photographic exhibitions that included the work of other photographers as well as his own. Early in his career he practiced in Pretoria and worked briefly as a staff photographer with the *Cape Times*, but in 1905 he opened a studio in Cape Town and remained there the rest of his life. Elliott was frequently published in South African books, newspapers and magazines as well as in publications outside that country.

Elliott was elected an honorary member of the National Society for the Preservation of Objects of Historic Interest and Natural Beauty in South Africa (1911). His most famous photograph, "The Sandpipers" (ca. 1908), was published in almost every country in the world, appearing in more than 300 newspapers and on innumerable calendars and Christmas cards. Its ubiquitousness led writer Conrad Lighton to describe Elliott as "surely as immortal as Peter Pan."

Generally using half-plate camera equipment, Elliott assiduously documented historic events in South Africa. He also collected images from other photographers so that he could preserve "for future South Africans—records which, when brought together, would form as nearly as possible an unbroken history of the Cape from its earliest days" (A. D. Bensusan, *Silver Images*).

PUBLICATIONS   Monographs: *Arthur Elliott*, Conrad Lighton, 1956 (Balkema: Cape Town); *South Africa through the Centuries*, notes by W. R. Morrison, 1930 (M. Miller: Cape Town); *Arthur Elliott, A Sentimental Appreciation*, Dr. P. W. Laidler, n.d. (Hist. Soc. of S. Africa). Book: *Silver Images*, Dr. A. D. Bensusan, 1966 (Howard Timmins: Cape Town). Catalogs: *The Cape Quaint and Beautiful*, 1938 (Cape Town); *The Story of South Africa*, 1913 (Pretoria). Periodicals: "Photographic Negatives Unique Africana," Denis Godfrey, *Sunday Chronicle*, July 6, 1964; A. G. Loxton, *Cape Argus*, Nov 11, 1938.

COLLECTIONS   All in South Africa: Bensusan Mus. of Photography, Johannesburg; Cape Arch., Cape Town; Photographic Fndn. Mus., Johannesburg.

David Elliott   *WRITER · CRITIC*   Born in Lexington, Kentucky, on December 24, 1944, Elliott received his BA magna cum laude in 1967 from Lawrence University in Appleton, Wisconsin.

He has been the photography critic and arts writer for the *Chicago Sun-Times* since 1978 and is also the Chicago art correspondent for *Artnews* magazine in New York. From 1971 to 1978 he was film critic for the *Chicago Daily News*, and in 1976 was a staff writer for the American Conservatory Theater in San Francisco. He wrote features for the *Chicago Daily News* from 1969 to 1971.

Elliott notes that he "instigated" the role of photography critic at the *Sun-Times* and is now "the most frequently published writer in Chicago dealing with photography as a serious art form." He also writes about art, theater and films.

ADDRESS   Chicago Sun-Times, 401 N Wabash, Chicago, IL 60611.

Rennie Ellis   *PHOTOGRAPHER · WRITER · FILM MAKER · GALLERY DIRECTOR*   Born November 11, 1940, in Melbourne, Australia, Ellis studied at Melbourne University and Royal Melbourne Institute of Technology from 1959 to 1963.

Ellis works as a freelance photographer, writer and film maker, as well as operating Scoopix Photo Library and Pentax Brummels Gallery of Photography.

He is a member of the Australian Journalists Association, Australian Society of Authors and Melbourne Cricket Club. In 1976 he was awarded a grant from the Visual Arts Board of the Australia Council and in 1972 won a silver medallion for his book *Kings Cross Sydney* from the Art Directors' Club of Melbourne. Ellis also directed and wrote two documentary films, *Escape to Cairns* and *Outback Australia*.

The photographer is best known for his erotic photography and his "documentation of pop culture and nonconformist, fringe people and unusual subcultures."

PUBLICATIONS Books: *Ketut Lives in Bali*, w/ Stan Marks, 1977; *Australian Graffiti*, 1975; *Kings Cross Sydney*, w/Wesley Stacey, 1971. Anthologies: *Australian Photography—A Contemporary View*, 1978; *New Photography Australia*, 1974. Catalog: *Australian Photographers—The Philip Morris Collection*, 1979.

COLLECTIONS Australian Ctr. for Photography; Bibliothèque Nationale, Paris; Natl. Gall. of Victoria; Tasmanian Mus. & Art Gall.

ADDRESS 154 Greville Street, Prahran, Victoria 3181, Australia.

Nancy Ellison PHOTOJOURNALIST · PAINTER · POET Born on May 12, 1936, in Los Angeles, California, Ellison, née Harrell, is married to producer-director Jerome Hellman. She obtained a BS in Fine Arts at Finch College in New York City in 1959. She was influenced by the work of De Kooning and the New York School of Abstract Expressionists and by the photographers Stieglitz, Man Ray, George Hurrell and Robert Frank.

She is a freelance photojournalist for magazines such as *Time, Vogue, Newsweek, People, Paris-Match*, etc. She also worked as a special photographer on the following motion pictures: *Coming Home, The Champ, Promises in the Dark, China Syndrome, The Day of the Locust, Oh God, Oh God* and *Coast to Coast*, among others. In 1956 she won the Leon Kroll Award for Painting.

Ellison is also a poet. Besides having published in American and international poetry anthologies and underground journals, she is the author of two books of poetry: *Come Late 1962* and *Head Fifth Poetry*.

A photojournalist, she works in 35mm format. On film sets she shoots rehearsals, action and exclusive reenactments. Her area of specialty is character studies and portraits of Hollywood stars, writers, directors, etc.

COLLECTION Allen Memorial Art Mus. (paintings), Oberlin, Ohio.

REPRESENTATIVE Gamma-Liaison: 150 E 58 St, New York, NY 10022 and 6606 Sunset Blvd, Hollywood, CA 90028.

ADDRESS 68 Malibu Colony, Malibu, CA 90265.

Dwight Lathrop Elmendorf WRITER · LECTURER · PHOTOGRAPHER · TEACHER Born in Brooklyn, New York, on March 13, 1859, Elmendorf died in New York on May 7, 1929. He received his AB degree from Princeton University,

Princeton, New Jersey, in 1882 and an AM degree in 1885.

Elmendorf was a teacher of the deaf from 1885 to 1897, a lecturer beginning in 1897, and a war correspondent from 1897 until the end of the Spanish-American War.

Elmendorf belonged to the Kane Lodge, F. & A.M., the Order of Foreign Wars, the Holland Society, the Players, and the University, Princeton and Arcola clubs. He also was a member of the New York Microscopic Society.

The travel photographer took views of landscapes and architecture in the Middle East and American West, with which he illustrated his books and lectures. He shot almost 200 photographs of Theodore Roosevelt and his Rough Riders.

PUBLICATIONS Books: *Madeira and the Mediterranean*, 1924; *A Trip to Puerto Rico with Dwight Lathrop Elmendorf*, 1921; *The Yosemite Valley*, 1916; *China*, 1915; *Grand Canyon of Arizona*, 1915; *The Holy Land*, 1915; *Yellowstone National Park*, 1915; *A Camera Crusade through the Holy Land*, 1912; *Lantern Slides, How to Make and Color Them*, 1895.

COLLECTION Roosevelt House, N.Y.

Paco Elvira PHOTOGRAPHER Born October 30, 1948, in Barcelona, Spain, Elvira studied economics at Barcelona University.

A freelance photographer since 1971, Elvira publishes his work in such magazines as *Mundo, Gaceta Ilustrada, Primera Plana* and *Interviu*.

He has been a member of the Spanish photo agencies Foto S.A., Barcelona (1977–78), and Cover (1979).

"I am a concerned photographer," says Elvira. "I photograph people and their relationship with other people and the land around them."

PUBLICATIONS Periodicals: "Paco Elvira, La Foto como Testimonio Social" *Tele Expres*, Nov 30, 1979; "Paco Elvira," *Flash Foto*, Apr 1979; "Paco Elvira's Londonderry," 1974, "Paco Elvira's Portugal," 1974, *Imagen y Sonido*.

ADDRESS Mandri-30, Barcelona 22, Spain.

Peter Henry Emerson PHOTOGRAPHER · WRITER [See plate 27] Born May 13, 1856, in Cuba, Emerson died May 12, 1936, in Falmouth, Cornwall, England. He attended Cranleigh School, King's College Hospital, London, and Clare College, Cambridge, where he studied the natural sciences and took a medical degree in 1885. He was influenced by Turner, Whistler and the French Impressionists.

Emerson first began to photograph as an aid to

an anthropological study of the peasants and fishermen of East Anglia. He later abandoned his medical training to pursue both the practice and artistic theories of photography.

Elected to the council of RPS in 1886, he had won its Progress Medal in 1895, as well as many other prizes and medals. Emerson was the first photographer to promote the craft as an independent art and the first to formulate an aesthetic theory about it. He established the Emerson medal, which he issued to such photographers as Stieglitz, Cameron and Nadar.

Working exclusively in platinum prints and gravures, Emerson pioneered "naturalistic" photography, becoming its leading advocate, theoretician and practitioner. In order to replicate scenes as he believed the human eye saw them, he advised sharp focus only at the center of the image, allowing the background to be soft-focused. Largely due to his theories, he was considered one of the leading photographers of his time, but he later rescinded his philosophy in his book *The Death of Naturalistic Photography*. His work was well executed, with subtle tonalities, evoking a naturalness unusual in his generation.

PUBLICATIONS Monographs: *Peter Henry Emerson: The Fight for Photography as a Fine Art*, Nancy Newhall, 1975; *Peter Henry Emerson: Photographer of Norfolk*, Peter Turner & Richard Wood, 1975. Books: *The History of Photography*, Beaumont Newhall, 1972; *Marsh Leaves*, 1895; *Birds, Beast and Fishes of the Norfolk Broadland*, incl. text, halftones by T. A. Cotton, 1895 (London); *On English Lagoons*, deluxe ed., 1893 (London); *Wild Life on a Tidal Water*, incl. text w/T. F. Goodall, 1890; *The Death of Naturalistic Photography*, no illus., text only, 1890, repr. 1973; *Naturalistic Photography for Students of the Art*, no illus., text only, 1889, repr. 1973; *The Compleat Angler*, vol. 1, Izaak Walton & Chas. Cotton, 1888 (London); *Idyls of the Norfolk Broads*, 1888 (Autotype: London); *Pictures of East Anglian Life*, 1888 (London); *Pictures from Life in Field and Fen*, 1887 (London); *Life and Landscape on the Norfolk Broads*, incl. text w/T. F. Goodall, 1886 (London). Anthologies: *The Photograph Collector's Guide*, Lee D. Witkin & Barbara London, 1979; *The Invented Eye*, Edward Lucie-Smith, 1975; *The Magic Image*, Cecil Beaton & Gail Buckland, 1975; *Looking at Photographs*, John Szarkowski, 1973; *Great Photographers*, Time-Life Series, 1971; *Masters of Photography*, Beaumont & Nancy Newhall, 1969; *Photographers on Photography*, Nathan Lyons, ed., 1966. Periodicals: *International Annual of Anthony's Photographic Bulle-*

tin, 1888; "Julia Margaret Cameron," text only, *Sun Artists*, Oct 1900.

COLLECTIONS IMP/GEH, Rochester; MOMA, NYC; N.Y. Pub. Lib., NYC; Univ. of N. Mex. Art Mus., Albuquerque; Univ. of Tex., Humanities Research Ctr., Gernsheim Cllctn., Austin. Colman & Rye Libs. of Local Hist., Norwich, England; RPS, London.

Chansonette Stanley Emmons PHOTOGRAPHER · HOUSEWIFE Born in Kingfield, Maine, on December 30, 1858, Emmons died in 1937. She was educated in Kingfield's one-room schoolhouse and went to Western Maine Normal School in Farmington in 1876. Her brothers, F. E. and F. O. Stanley, were the inventors of the Stanley photographic dry plate and the Stanley Steamer automobile.

Emmons was a self-employed photographer from 1898 until her death. She was a member of the Boston Society of Arts and Crafts and the Society's Guild of Photographers. A total listing of her awards is unavailable, but she did win prizes in several Boston-area photography exhibits during her lifetime.

A painter as well as a photographer, she was one of the pioneering women of photography, leaving a matchless record of rural New England at the turn of the century. Her greatest strength was in portraying young children and in capturing people at work, at play and in naturally lit interiors.

PUBLICATION Monograph: *Chansonetta*, Marius B. Peládeau, 1977.

COLLECTIONS Colby College Art Cntr, Waterville, Me.; Wm. A. Farnsworth Lib. & Art. Mus., Rockland, Me.

ARCHIVE Marius B. Peládeau, Four Rod Rd, Warren, ME 04864.

Morris Engel PHOTOGRAPHER Born in 1918, Engel was influenced by the photographers of New York's Photo League, particularly member Paul Strand. During World War II he served in the U.S. Navy under Edward Steichen, who was then director of naval combat photography. Engel received a citation from Steichen for his combat work.

A regular contributor to *PM* newspaper, Engel is best known for his photographic essays of New York City life.

PUBLICATIONS Monograph: *Photographs of People by Morris Engel*, 1939. Anthologies: *The Photograph Collector's Guide*, Lee D. Witkin & Barbara London, 1979; *Documentary Photography*, Time-Life Series, 1972. Periodicals: *U.S.*

Camera Annual, 1941; PM Picture Gallery, July 21, 1940.

COLLECTIONS Metro. Mus. of Art, NYC; MOMA, NYC; Univ. of N. Mex. Art Mus., Albuquerque; Worcester Art Mus., Mass.

REPRESENTATIVE Witkin Gallery, 41 E 57 St, New York, NY 10022.

ADDRESS 65 Central Park West, New York, NY 10023.

Scott D. Engel *PHOTOGRAPHER · TEACHER* Born in Portland, Oregon, on February 20, 1948, Engel obtained a BFA from the San Francisco Art Institute (1973) and an MFA from the University of Colorado in Boulder (1978).

He has been teaching photography at Arapahoe Community College in Littleton, Colorado, since 1979. Previously he was a photography instructor at the Community College of Denver (1979) and at the University of Colorado (1976–77), where he also worked as the director of their Fine Arts Center (1977–78).

A member of SPE, VSW and Friends of Photography, he was the recipient of a Purchase Award from the Bellevue Art Museum in Bellevue, Washington (1979), and of an Award of Merit from the Denver Art Museum (1976).

PUBLICATIONS Catalogs: *Photoworks 79*, 1979 (Bellevue Art Mus.: Wash.); *Self-Portrayal*, 1979 (Friends of Photography: Carmel); *20 Colorado Artists*, 1977 (Denver Art Mus.: Colo.).

COLLECTION Bellevue Art Mus., Wash.

ADDRESS 2550 S Williams, Denver, CO 80210.

Edmund Engelman *ENGINEER · PHOTOGRA-PHER* Born on May 21, 1907, in Vienna, Austria, Engelman attended the Technical University in Vienna where he completed a master's degree in electrical and mechanical engineering in 1932.

He has worked professionally as a consultant in photographic processing technology and in the design of photographic equipment, enlargers and control equipment for processors and silver-recovery systems.

He has been a member of the Society of Photographic Scientists and Engineers since 1944. In 1970 he patented a silver-recovery system, and in 1977 he received the Carey-Thomas award from *Publishers Weekly* for his book *Berggasse 19*.

Engelman also made a 16mm documentary movie with photographs and film clips from 1938, narrated by Eli Wallach and distributed by Filmmakers Library in New York City.

His interest is documentary photography. He has also worked with bromoil and gum prints.

PUBLICATION Monograph: *Berggasse 19, the Home and Offices of Sigmund Freud, Vienna 1938*, intro. by Peter Gay, 1976.

COLLECTION Guild Hall, East Hampton, N.Y. 11937.

ADDRESS 205 West End Ave, New York, NY 10023.

Chris Enos *PHOTOGRAPHER · ARTS ADMINIS-TRATOR · TEACHER* Born on August 21, 1944, Enos obtained a BA in Sculpture from San Francisco State University in 1969 and an MFA in Photography from the San Francisco Art Institute in 1971.

Since 1976 she has been president and director of the Photographic Resource Center in Boston. Her working experience includes teaching photography, both as instructor and as assistant professor at the following institutions: New England School of Photography, Boston (1977–78), Harvard University, Cambridge, Massachusetts (1977), Hampshire College, Amherst, Massachusetts (1974–75), and Windham College, Putney, Vermont (1974). She also taught at the University of California in San Francisco, at San Francisco Academy of Art (1972–73), at the Let A Dark Photo Laboratory in San Rafael and at Sonoma State University (1971–73), all in California.

Enos is a member of VSW, the Institute of Contemporary Art in Boston and the International Center for Photography in New York City. In addition, she belongs to SPE, for whom she serves on the board of directors. In Boston she received grants in photography from Massachusetts Council on the Arts and Humanities (1978), Cutler deLong West Foundation (1977) and The Artists Foundation (1975).

In 1978 she printed *Georgy Kepes Portfolio*, which was published by Vision Gallery in Boston.

PUBLICATIONS (selected) Anthologies: *Photography Annual*, 1979; *State of the Art*, 1978; *In/Sights*, 1978; *Eros in Photography*, 1978; *Women See Woman*, 1977; *Octave of Prayer*, 1972; *Be-ing Without Clothes*, 1971. Catalogs: *Self-Portrayal*, 1979 (Friends of Photography: Carmel, Calif.); *Images of Women*, 1977 (Portland Mus. of Art: Maine); *Women Artists in America*, 1973 (Univ. of Tenn.: Chattanooga). Periodicals: *Camera*, 1979, 1975; *Creative Camera Annual*, 1975; *Camera 35*, 1973.

COLLECTIONS Harvard Univ., Fogg Art Mus., Cambridge; Mus. of Fine Arts, Boston; Portland Mus. of Art, Maine; Sam Wagstaff Cllctn., NYC; San Francisco Art Inst.; Wellesley Coll., Mass.;

and private collections. Bibliothèque Nationale, Paris.

ADDRESS   POB 507, Boston, MA 02102.

James L. Enyeart *MUSEUM DIRECTOR · WRITER · PHOTOGRAPHER* Born January 13, 1943, in Auburn, Washington, Enyeart received a BFA from Kansas City Art Institute in Missouri in 1966 and an MFA from the University of Kansas in Lawrence in 1972.

Currently director for the Center for Creative Photography at the University of Arizona in Tucson, Enyeart previously worked as executive director for the Friends of Photography in Carmel, California (1976–77), and as curator of photography at the Museum of Art as well as professor in the Department of Art History at the University of Kansas (1968–76).

Enyeart has been vice-president of the board of directors of the Friends of Photography in Carmel, California, since 1978, as well as a member of SPE, VSW and RPS. He has been the recipient of numerous grants and fellowships, including, from NEA, a fellowship and grant in 1975, an individual grant in 1974, and a visiting-artist and lecturer's grant in 1973. He also received grants from Kansas Endowment for the Humanities in 1973 (through NEH), University of Kansas General Research Fund in 1971, University of Kansas Endowment Association in 1970 and 1972, University of Kansas Endowment Association in 1970 and 1972, Kansas Geological Survey in 1971, and a fellowship from the Organization of American States through the University of Chile, Santiago, in 1966. He was named an Honorary Research Fellow by the University of Exeter, England, in 1974.

PUBLICATIONS   Book (text only): *Francis Bruguière*, 1977. Anthology (text only): *Kansas Album*, ed., 1977. Catalogs: *The Architecture of St. Joseph*, 1974 (Albrecht Art Mus.: St. Joseph, Mo.). (Text only): *No Mountains in the Way*, 1975, "Oscar Gustav Rejlander," *The Paden Collection of Nineteenth Century Photographs*, 1974, *Language of Light*, 1974, *Invisible in America*, 1973, *Kansas Landscape*, 1971, *Karsh*, 1970, *Main Street Studio*, 1970 (Univ. of Kans., Mus. of Art: Lawrence). Periodicals: *Creative Camera*, Feb 1976. (Text only): "Cleaning Glass Plate Negatives," May 1974, "Marion Palfi—Social Research Photographer," Aug 1973, "Teaching the History of Photography," Aug 1973, *Exposure: SPE*; "Saving a Daguerreotype," *Journal of Photography: RPS*, Sept 1970.

COLLECTIONS   Albrecht Gall., St. Joseph, Mo.; IMP/GEH, Rochester; Univ. of Kans., Mus. of

Art; Univ. of Neb., Sheldon Mem. Gall., Lincoln. Bibliothèque Nationale, Paris.

ADDRESS   Center for Creative Photography, 843 E University Blvd, Tucson, AZ 85719.

Mitchell Epstein *PHOTOGRAPHER · TEACHER* Born August 23, 1952, in Holyoke, Massachusetts, Epstein attended Union College in Schenectady, New York (1970–71), Rhode Island School of Design (1971–72) and Cooper Union in New York City (1972–74).

He has been employed as an instructor of photography since 1977 at the Harvard University Carpenter Center for the Visual Arts.

Epstein was a recipient of a CAPS grant in 1980 and an NEA Individual Photography Grant in 1978.

PUBLICATIONS   Periodical: *Modern Photography*, June 1980. Reviews: *Afterimage: VSW*, summer 1979; *Village Voice*, Apr 23, 1979.

COLLECTIONS   Amoco Cllctn., Denver, Colo.; Corcoran Mus. of Art, Wash., D.C.; Le Moyne Art Fndn., Tallahassee, Fla.; Mus. of Fine Arts, Boston; Vassar Coll. Art Mus., Poughkeepsie, N.Y. Australian Natl. Gall., Canberra; Bibliothèque Nationale, Paris.

REPRESENTATIVE   Light Gall., 724 Fifth Ave, New York, NY 10019.

ADDRESS   424 W 119 St, Apt 67, New York, NY 10027.

Hugo Erfurth *PHOTOGRAPHER · TEACHER* Born in Halle, Germany, in 1874, Erfurth died in Gaienhofen, on Lake Constance. He studied photography at Höffert Atelier, Dresden. He also studied painting briefly.

Erfurth took over the studio of Dresden's court photographer, Schröder. He later established a studio that was to become a meeting place for artists and other notables during the 1920s. He taught photography at the Book Trade Academy in Leipzig under Professor Tieman until World War I. Erfurth moved to Cologne in 1934, where most of his work was destroyed in an air raid in 1943.

He was the co-founder and chairman for many years of the Gesellschaft Deutscher Lichtbildner (GDL), the German Photographers' Society, 1919. Erfurth was also a member of the London Salon of Photography. In 1904 he designed a special photography section at the Dresden Exhibition.

"In Hugo Erfurth," wrote Professor Dr. Otto Steinert, "we see one of the few great portraitists produced by photography." His oil-pigment prints exhibited an "impressive manner of rendering the human countenance and the essence of a personality."

PUBLICATIONS Monographs: *Hugo Erfurth, 1874–1948*, Bernd Lohse, 1977 (Seebruck); *Hugo Erfurth Sechsunddreissig Kunstlerbildnisse*, notes by Hermann Schardt, Otto Steinert, J. A. Schmoll, 1960. Anthologies: *Pictorial Photography in Great Britain 1900–1920*, Arts Council of Great Britain, 1978; *The Magic Image*, Cecil Beaton & Gail Buckland, 1975.

COLLECTIONS Agfa-Gevaert Photo-Historama, Leverkusen, West Germany; L. Fritz Gruber Cllctn., Cologne.

Elliott R. Erwitt PHOTOGRAPHER [See plate 89] Born on July 26, 1928, in Paris, Erwitt was mainly influenced by Robert Capa, Roy Stryker and Edward Steichen. He started working as a freelance photographer at age sixteen. Since 1953 he has been a member of Magnum Photos, for which he served as president from 1962 to 1966. He received an Art in Public Places grant from NEA in 1976 and a grant from the American Film Institute in 1973.

Erwitt also made several films, such as *Arthur Penn: the Director, Beauty Knows No Pain* (1973), *Red, White and Bluegrass* and *Beautiful, Baby, Beautiful*, among others.

Specializing in photojournalism and commercial photography, Erwitt is best known for his personal work, which mainly consists of humorous shots of dogs and people.

PUBLICATIONS Monographs: *Recent Developments*, intro. by Wilfred Sheed, 1979; *Observations on American Architecture*, w/Ivan Chermayeff, 1974; *Son of Bitch*, 1974; *The Private Experience*, Sean Callahan, ed., 1974; *Photographs and Anti-Photographs*, Sam Holmes & John Szarkowski, 1972. Anthology: *The Photograph Collector's Guide*, Lee D. Witkin & Barbara London, 1979; *The Magic Image*, Cecil Beaton & Gail Buckland, 1975.

PORTFOLIOS *15 Photographers*, 1977 (Acorn Ed.: Geneva, Switzerland); *Untitled*, intro. by Peter Bunnell, 1974 (Witkin-Burley: Roslyn Heights, N.Y.).

COLLECTIONS (selected) Art Inst. of Chicago; MOMA, NYC; New Orleans Mus. of Art; Smithsonian Inst., Wash., D.C.. Bibliothèque Nationale, Paris.

ADDRESS c/o Magnum Photos, 15 W 46 St, New York, NY 10023.

Manel Esclusa Canals TEACHER · PHOTOGRAPHER Born April 13, 1952, in Barcelona, Spain, Esclusa attended workshops with Ansel Adams,

Neal White, Susan Felter and Jean Dieuzaide in 1974.

Since 1977 Esclusa has taught photography at the Escuela de Diseño in Barcelona and at the Escuela Nikon since 1979. He previously taught group workshops at Taller d'Art Fotogràfic in Barcelona (1975–76).

A photographic scholarship from the Dotación de Arte Casetellblanch, a foundation in Barcelona, was awarded to him in 1974.

PUBLICATIONS Books: *La Photographie Fantastique*, 1979 (Contrejour: Paris); *Fantastic Photography in Europe*, 1978 (The Netherlands); *Manel Esclusa, Fotografíes*, 1977 (Spain); *Foto Arte 75*, 1975 (Spain). Periodicals: *Flash Foto*, July 1980; *European Photography*, #2, 1980; *Creative Camera*, Sept 1978; *Il Progresso Fotografico*, Sept 1975; *Anuario Cotecflash*, 1975, 1974; *Anuario de la Fotografía Española*, 1974, 1973.

COLLECTIONS Bibliothèque Nationale, Paris; Musée Réattu, Arles, France; Museu del Paper, Capellades, Barcelona, Spain.

ADDRESS GURB, 29 VIC, Barcelona, Spain.

Ute Eskildsen PHOTOGRAPHER · CURATOR Born February 2, 1947, in Itzehoe, Federal Republic of Germany, Eskildsen studied at a school for languages (1963–67) and was apprenticed in a portrait photography studio. From 1967 to 1969 he studied photography and photohistory at the Folkwang Schule für Gestaltung in Essen, Germany, under Otto Steinert and Erich vom Endt.

Since 1978 Eskilden has been curator of photography at the Museum Folkwang in Essen. In 1976–77 he served an internship at IMP in Rochester. He previously was assistant curator for photography exhibitions at the Museum Folkwang, an assistant in the Photography Department at the University of Essen (1972–74) and did freelance photography for periodicals and for a publishing house (1970–72).

Eskildsen has belonged to DGPh since 1975.

PUBLICATIONS Catalogs (text only): *Film und Foto der zwanziger Jahre*, 1979, *Neue Sachlichkeit and German Realism*, 1978/79, *Heinrich Kühn 1866–1944*, 1978 (Mus. Folkwang: Essen).

ADDRESS Haus Fuhr 13, 4300 Essen 16, Federal Republic of Germany.

Reed Estabrook PHOTOGRAPHER · TEACHER Born in Boston, Massachusetts, on May 31, 1944, Estabrook studied with Harry Callahan at the Rhode Island School of Design (BFA, 1969) and with Ken Josephson at the School of the Art Institute of Chicago (MFA, 1971). His wife is photographer Gwen Widmer.

Estabrook has taught photography at the University of Northern Iowa, Cedar Falls, since 1974, first as an assistant professor and from 1978 to the present as an associate professor. He was an instructor of photography at the University of Illinois from 1971 to 1974.

A member of SPE, he won an NEA Photographer's Fellowship in 1976 and a Nikon Research Award from Nikon Camera, Garden City, New York, in 1977. In 1971 Estabrook was awarded a William R. French Traveling Fellowship.

Estabrook usually works in applied color, generally oil, on silver prints.

PUBLICATIONS Anthologies (selected): *Self-Portrayal*, 1979; *The Art of Photography*, 1971. Catalogs: *Great West: Real/Ideal*, 1977 (Univ. of Colo., Boulder); *1007:1 Portfolio of Midwest Photographers*, 1972 (1007 Photo. Art Gall,; Urbana, Ill.). Periodical: *Creative Camera*, no. 153, 1977.

COLLECTIONS Art Inst. of Chicago; Concord Art Ctr., Calif.; Humboldt State Univ., Arcata, Calif.; IMP/GEH, Rochester; MOMA, NYC; R.I. School of Design, Providence; Univ. of W. Va., Morganstown.

ADDRESS 703 Iowa St, Cedar Falls, IA 50613.

Mary Lloyd Estrin PHOTOGRAPHER Born in Chicago, Illinois, on September 30, 1944, Estrin completed a BA at the University of California at Berkeley in 1966 and an MA (1975) at the Illinois Institute of Technology, where she studied under Arthur Siegel.

The artist specializes in black-and-white portrait photography and also in hand-painted photographs.

PUBLICATIONS Monograph: *To the Manor Born*, 1979. Periodicals: *Picture Magazine*, 1979; *Popular Photography Annual*, 1978.

COLLECTIONS Art Inst. of Chicago; CCP, Tucson; Mus. of Art, Santa Barbara, Calif.; Polaroid Cllctn., Cambridge, Mass.; Seagram Cllctn., N.Y.C.; Standard Oil of Ind.

DEALER G. Ray Hawkins Gall., 7224 Melrose St, Los Angeles, CA 90046.

ADDRESS 4865 Glencairn Rd, Los Angeles, CA 90027.

Frank Eugene PHOTOGRAPHER · PAINTER · TEACHER Born in New York City in 1865 as Frank Eugene Smith, Eugene died in 1936, probably in Germany. He studied at City College of New York and in 1886 he attended the Bayrische Akademie der Bildenden Kunste (Bavarian Academy of Graphic Arts), Munich.

Also in Munich, Eugene lectured at Lehr- und Versuchsanstalt für Photographie (Teaching and Research Institute for Photography) in 1907. About 1913 he was appointed royal professor of pictorial photography at the Royal Academy of Graphic Arts in Leipzig, which constituted the world's first notable academic position in the field. He was a member of The Linked Ring in 1900 and a founder-member of the Photo-Secession in 1902.

He was a talented etcher as well as a painter, and his photographs often show use of the etcher's needle. His style may be likened to Jugendstil, the south German and Austrian equivalent of Art Nouveau. An early exponent of the autochrome process, he produced platinum, gumbichromate and salt prints.

PUBLICATIONS Book: *Photo-Secession: Photography as a Fine Art*, Robert Doty, 1960, rev. ed., 1978. Anthologies: *The Photograph Collector's Guide*, Lee D. Witkin & Barbara London, 1979; *The Collection of Alfred Stieglitz*, Weston J. Naef, 1978; *Pictorial Photography in Britain 1900–1920*, Arts Council of Great Britain, 1978; *The Valiant Knights of Daguerre . . . by Sadakichi Hartmann*, Harry W. Lawton & Geo. Know, 1978; *The Magic Image*, Cecil Beaton & Gail Buckland, 1975; *Camera Work: A Critical Anthology*, Jonathan Green, ed., 1973; *The Great Themes & The Print*, Time-Life Series, 1970. Periodicals: *Camera Work*, Oct 1916, July 1910, Apr 1910, Jan 1909, Jan 1904; "American Photographers in London," Alvin Langdon Coburn, *Photo-Era*, Jan 1901; "Frank Eugene: Painter-Photographer," Sadakichi Hartmann, *The Photographic Times*, Oct 1899.

COLLECTIONS Art Inst. of Chicago; Metro. Mus. of Art. RPS, London.

Barnaby Evans PHOTOGRAPHER Born March 15, 1953, in Berkeley, California, Evans earned a BSc in Biology from Brown University, Providence, Rhode Island (1975).

A freelance photographer since 1978, he has been a technical consultant for Colorlab, Ltd., since 1976.

Usually working with an 8 x 10 view camera and printing his own 20 x 24 color prints, Evans explores "the formal and spatial possibilities of the urban and suburban landscape."

PUBLICATIONS Periodicals: *Popular Photography Annual*, 1980; *Camera*, Nov 1978, May 1978, July 1977; *Photographie*, June 1978; *Schweizerische Photorundschau*, June 10, 1978.

COLLECTIONS Addison Gall. of Amer. Art, Andover, Mass.; Polaroid Corp., Cambridge, Mass; R.I. School of Design, Mus. of Art, Providence. Bibliothèque Nationale, Paris; Polaroid

Europa Cllctn., Amsterdam, The Netherlands; Victoria & Albert Mus., London.

DEALER Elise Meyer, Inc., 410 W Broadway, New York, NY 10006.

ADDRESS 97 Wayland Ave, Providence, RI 02906.

Frederick H. Evans PHOTOGRAPHER · BOOK-SELLER [See plate 43] Born June 26, 1853, in Whitechapel, London, England, Evans died June 24, 1943, in London.

His bookshop in London, which catered to working people, became known as "the university of the city clerk" because of Evans' knowledge and stimulating conversation. After his retirement from bookselling in 1898, he devoted himself to photography and wrote articles for the leading photographic magazines of the day, such as *Photogram*. Evans went to work for *Country Life* magazine in 1906, and also organized several exhibits.

Evans joined The Linked Ring in 1900 and was named an Honorary Fellow of RPS in 1925.

Best known for his architectural photography, Evans portrayed the cathedrals of England and the chateaux of France as places of great beauty, accenting space and the infinite variety of light. These photos are considered among the finest in the genre. Without manipulating either negative or print, Evans produced mainly platinum prints and some silver. He created a few photographic portraits, the most noted being one of his friend Aubrey Beardsley.

PUBLICATIONS Monograph: *Frederick H. Evans*, Beaumont Newhall, 1964. Book: *The Dance of Death by Hans Holbein . . . Wood Engravings . . .* , 1913 (pvt. prntg.). Anthologies: *The Photograph Collector's Guide*, Lee D. Witkin & Barbara London, 1979; *Pictorial Photography in Great Britain, 1900–1920*, 1978 (Arts Council of Great Britain); *The Collection of Alfred Stieglitz*, Weston J. Naef, 1978; *The Magic Image*, Cecil Beaton & Gail Buckland, 1975; *Camera Work: A Critical Anthology*, Jonathan Green, ed., 1973; *Looking at Photographs*, John Szarkowski, 1973; *Caring for Photographs*, 1972; *The Print*, Time-Life Series, 1970. Catalog: *Frederick H. Evans*, Beaumont Newhall, 1964 (IMP/GEH: Rochester). Periodicals: "Evans—An Appreciation," George Bernard Shaw, *Camera Work*, illus. only, Oct 1903.

PORTFOLIO *F. H. Evans, 1853–1943: Ten Photographs*, preface & printed by George Tice, intro. by Evan Evans, 1971 (Witkin Gall.: NYC).

COLLECTIONS Boston Mus. of Fine Arts, Mass.; Harvard Univ., Carpenter Ctr. for the Visual Arts, Cambridge, Mass.; L/C, Wash., D.C.; New Orleans Mus. of Art, La.; Philadelphia Mus. of Art, Penn. Natl. Gall. of Canada, Ottawa, Ont.; RPS, London.

Terry Hoyt Evans PHOTOGRAPHER Born on August 30, 1944, in Kansas City, Missouri, Evans completed a BFA at the University of Kansas in Lawrence in 1968. She was influenced by Charles Harbutt and Jim Enyeart.

Since 1979 she has been working as an arts associate at The Land Institute in Salina, Kansas; she has also been teaching summer workshops in Abiquiu, New Mexico, since 1977. In 1976 she originated the *Kansas Album* project.

She is a member of SPE and has been awarded a Survey Grant by NEA in 1974 and a grant from the Kansas Committee for the Humanities in 1979.

The artist uses a medium-format camera. She specializes in documentary photography, related to people and land. Evans has been specifically interested in Kansas prairie and farm people as well as in poor people in India and China. She is also working on a continuing series on her family and herself.

PUBLICATIONS Monographs: *No Mountains in the Way*, 1975; *If . . . A Big Word With the Poor*, 1975. Anthologies: *Self-Portrayal*, 1979; *Family of Children*, 1977; *Kansas Album*, 1977.

COLLECTION Univ. of Kans., Lawrence.

ADDRESS 740 Highland, Salina, KS 67401.

Walker Evans PHOTOGRAPHER · WRITER [See plate 60] Born November 3, 1903, in St. Louis, Missouri, Evans died April 10, 1975, in New Haven, Connecticut. He studied at Phillips Academy, Andover, Massachusetts, and at Williams College, Williamstown, Massachusetts (1922–23), and audited classes at the Sorbonne in Paris (1926). His major influence was Eugène Atget.

Evans began photographing in 1927, using a vest pocket camera, and later worked for New York's General Education Board, photographing African Black art. He was a photographer for the Farm Security Administration (FSA) (1935–38), a writer for *Time* magazine (1943–45) and a writer and photographer for *Fortune* (1945–65). A professor of graphic design at Yale University, New Haven, Connecticut (1965–71), Evans continued to give occasional seminars until his death.

Winner of a Guggenheim Fellowship in 1940, the photographer was best known for his images of Depression-struck America, shot when he worked with the FSA. Using both silver and color prints (including some SX-70 pictures), Evans also documented Cuba and the American landscape and produced portraiture. Jerry Tallmer of the *New York Post* described him as "the man who used essential sparseness and flat reportage to create an altogether new photography."

PUBLICATIONS Monographs: *First and Last*, 1978; *Walker Evans: Photographs for the Farm Security Administration, 1935–38*, intro. by Jerald C. Maddox, 1973; *Many Are Called*, intro. by James Agee, 1966; *Message from the Interior*, afterword by John Szarkowski, 1966; *American Photographs*, essay by Lincoln Kirstein, 1938, repr. 1975. Books: *Images of the South: Visits with Eudora Welty and Walker Evans*, Carol Lynn Yellin, ed., 1977; *A Vision Shared*, Hank O'Neal, 1976; *The Years of Bitterness and Pride*, Hiag Akmakjian, 1975; *In This Proud Land*, Roy Emerson Stryker & Nancy Wood, 1973; *Portrait of a Decade*, F. Jack Hurley, 1972; "Photography," *Quality*, Louis Kronenberger, ed., 1969; *Just Before the War*, Rothstein, Vachon & Stryker, w/Thomas Garver, ed., 1968; *The Bitter Years: 1935–41*, Edward Steichen, ed., 1962; *African Folktales and Sculpture*, Paul Radin & James Johnson Sweeney, 1952, rev. ed., 1964; *Poems of the Midwest*, Carl Sandburg, 1946; *The Mangrove Coast*, Karl Bickel, 1942; *Let Us Now Praise Famous Men*, James Agee, 1941, rev. ed. 1960; *12 Million Black Voices*, Richard Wright & Edwin Rosskam, 1941; *Wheaton College Photographs*, 1941; *The Face of America: Home Town*, Sherwood Anderson, 1940; *Land of the Free*, Archibald MacLeish, 1938; *African Negro Art*, 1935; *The Crime of Cuba*, Carleton Beals, 1933, repr. 1970; *The Bridge*, Hart Crane, 1930. Anthologies: *The Photograph Collector's Guide*, Lee D. Witkin & Barbara London, 1979; *Photography Rediscovered*, David Travis & Anne Kennedy, 1979; *The Julien Levy Collection*, Witkin Gallery, 1977; *Photographs from the Julien Levy Collection*, David Travis, 1976; *The Magic Image*, Cecil Beaton & Gail Buckland, 1975; *Looking at Photographs*, John Szarkowski, 1973; *Great Photographers*, Time-Life Series, 1971; *Masters of Photography*, Beaumont & Nancy Newhall, 1969. Catalogs: *The Presence of Walker Evans*, Alan Trachtenberg, 1978 (Inst. of Contemporary Arts, Boston); *Walker Evans at Fortune*, Lesley K. Baier, 1978 (Wellesley Coll., Mass.); *14 American Photographers*, Renato Danese, 1974 (Baltimore Mus. of Art); *Photography Unlimited*, 1974 (Harvard Univ., Fogg Art Mus.: Cambridge); *Walker Evans*, intro. by John Szarkowski, 1971 (MOMA: NYC). Periodicals: "Walker Evans," Sidney Tillim, *Artforum*, Mar

1967; "Photographic Studies," *Architectural Record*, Sept 1930.

PORTFOLIOS *I. Selected Images, 1929–71*, printed by Thomas A. Brown & Baldwin Lee, 1977 (Graphics Intl.: Wash., D.C.); *Selected Photographs*, intro. by Lionel Trilling, printed by Richard Benson, John Deeks, & Lee Friedlander, 1974 (Double Elephant Press: NYC); *14 Photographs*, intro. by Robert Penn Warren, essay by Evans, printed by Thomas A. Brown, 1971 (Ives-Sillman: New Haven, Conn.).

COLLECTIONS Arnold H. Crane Cllctn, Chicago; Ctr. for Southern Folklore, Memphis, Tenn.; Gilma Paper Co. Cllctn., NYC; Harvard Univ., Fogg Art Mus., Cambridge; IMP/GEH, Rochester; L/C, Wash., D.C.; Metro. Mus. of Art, NYC; MOMA, NYC; New Orleans Art Mus.; San Francisco Mus. of Modern Art; Smithsonian Inst., Wash., D.C.; Univ. of N. Mex. Art Mus., Albuquerque; Wadsworth Atheneum, Hartford, Conn.; Yale Univ. Art Gall., New Haven, Conn. Natl. Gall. of Canada, Ottawa, Ontario.

Wendy Taylor Ewald   PHOTOGRAPHER · TEACHER   Born in Detroit, Michigan, Ewald received her BA in 1974 from Antioch College, Yellow Springs, Ohio. She also studied at Massachusetts Institute of Technology with Minor White in 1970–71, and with Wendy S. MacNeil and Bruce Davidson.

Since 1976 the photographer has directed the Mountain Photography Workshop at Appalshop in Whitesburg, Kentucky. From 1976 to 1979 she was an artist-in-residence for the Kentucky Arts Commission, teaching photography and filmmaking in three Appalachian schools. In 1971 she started (and operated, until 1973) the Half Moon Gallery (now the Half Moon Photography Workshop) in London, one of the first galleries in England devoted to photography.

Ewald is a member of SPE and has been on the Appalshop board of directors since 1976. She received individual grants in 1978 from Joint Foundation Support for Women and from the Kentucky Arts Commission and was awarded an NEA Photography Exhibition Aid grant in 1977, and an NEA Photographic Survey grant in 1976.

Working with a large-format camera, Ewald is "most interested in creating deep, sequential portraits of my intimate friends and family (in the last few years, older Appalachian women)." She sets up her photographs to "symbolically trace my subjects' lives."

PUBLICATIONS Book: *Grants: How to Get Them*, 1978. Anthologies: *Appalachia: A Self-*

Portrait, ed. & photo., 1979; *Women See Men,* 1977.

COLLECTION Univ. of Ky. Appalachian Cllctn., Lexington.

ADDRESS Appalshop, POB 743, Whitesburg, KY 41858.

Kathleen M. H. Ewing GALLERY OWNER Born in Washington, D.C., on June 5, 1947, Ewing received her BA in 1969 from Randolph-Macon Woman's College, Lynchburg, Virginia.

From 1971 to 1976 she was coordinator of photography at the National Gallery of Art, Washington, D.C., and in 1976 started her own gallery, Kathleen Ewing Gallery/Quindacqua, Ltd. She is a member of the Washington Professional Women's Cooperative.

Ewing's gallery represents contemporary photographers from both Washington, D.C., and various areas of the United States and Europe. It also carries an inventory of nineteenth-century vintage material.

PORTFOLIO (publisher) *The Eastern Shore,* Steve Szabo, 1976.

ADDRESS 3020 K St NW, Washington, DC 20007.

J. R. Eyerman PHOTOGRAPHER Born in Butte, Montana, on November 9, 1906, Eyerman received a BS in Civil Engineering from the University of Washington, Seattle, in 1932.

Currently a contract photographer and consultant to *Life* magazine (as well as to other magazines and to space and aviation firms), Eyerman was a staff photographer for *Life* from 1941 to 1961. During that time he spent four years as a war correspondent (1942–46) and almost two years (1946–47) as *Life*'s chief photographer. Previous to that time he had worked for the Engineering Department of Seattle (1929–34) and owned his own photography studio in Tacoma, Washington (1934–41). Since 1962 he has been a freelance photographer and since 1964 has owned Tech. Photomation Instruments in Santa Monica, California.

Eyerman is a member of ASMP, NPPA, Society of Photographic Scientists and Engineers, Society of Instrumentation Engineers and California Press Photographic Association.

Most of Eyerman's photographic work has been as a photojournalist. He has also developed photo technology, such as radio camera controls, a motor-driven 35mm camera, an interchangeable lens system for twin-lens reflex cameras and a prefogging technique that advanced the speed of color films.

ADDRESS 475 17 St, Santa Monica, CA 90403.

F

Sara Facio *PHOTOGRAPHER* Born in Buenos Aires, Argentina, on April 18, 1932, Facio studied in her native city at the National School of Fine Arts with Manuel Belgrano (1947–50), at the Pueyrredón (1951–54) and with the Annemarie Heinrich Photographic Studio (1960–62).

In 1960 Facio began both to manage the photographic studio Sara Facio/Alicia d'Amico and to head a monthly section, "Behind the Visor," for Buenos Aires' *Auto Club Magazine.* She maintains both these positions today. Additionally, she directed the weekly section "Photo Time" of the daily paper *La Nación* (1966–74), and, as of this writing, is artistic director for Azotea Publishers, a position she undertook in 1973.

An honorary member and exhibitor in the Photo Club of Buenos Aires, Facio is also a member of the Fédération International de l'Art Photographique (FIAP). She won a medal at the Argentine Federation of Photography (1963), Argentina's Olivetti prize for journalism (1968), and that country's FAF prize for journalism and writing (1970 and 1972).

Working predominantly in black-and-white, she makes her major theme people, in both portraits and genre scenes.

PUBLICATIONS Books: *Actos de Fé en Guatemala,* 1980 (Argentina); *Cómo tomar fotografías,* 1977 (Argentina); *Humanario,* 1976 (Argentina); *Retratos y Autorretratos,* 1974 (Argentina); *Geografía de Pablo Neruda,* 1973 (Spain).

COLLECTION Bibliothèque Nationale, Paris.

ADDRESS Juncal 1470, (1062) Buenos Aires, Argentina.

Marion Faller *PHOTOGRAPHER · TEACHER* Born on November 5, 1941, in Wallington, New Jersey, Faller obtained a BA in Art and Education from Hunter College in New York City in 1971 and attended the Visual Studies Workshop in Rochester, New York, completing an MFA in Photography through the State University of New York at Buffalo in 1979.

She is currently employed as a photography instructor at Colgate University in Hamilton, New York, where she has been teaching since 1974. Previously, she was a photography lecturer in New York City at Hunter College (1971–74) and Marymount Manhattan College (1973–74).

She served on the Photographic Advisory Committee of the Everson Museum of Art in Syracuse, New York (1976–79), and has been affiliated with SPE since 1974 and with the Photographic Historical Society of New York since 1972. Colgate University gave her a Development Award every year from 1975 to 1979; she also received a Photographer's Fellowship from CAPS, New York (1977), and a Photographer's Grant from Light Work, Visual Studies Inc., in Syracuse, New York (1976).

The artist's work, whether in black-and-white, color or nonsilver, often consists of groups of images exploring a specific context. "Each series of pictures has its own structure and limitations and utilizes whatever photographic process is necessary to best investigate and explicate the original idea."

PUBLICATIONS Book: *A Resurrection of the Exquisite Corpse,* 1978. Periodicals: "Marion Faller (A Portfolio of Photographs)," *Creative Camera,* July 1974; "Marion Faller (Gallery 35)," *35mm Photography,* summer 1973.

COLLECTIONS Carnegie Inst. Mus. of Art, Pittsburgh, Pa; Colgate Univ., Picker Art Gall., Hamilton, N.Y.; IMP/GEH, Rochester; Light Work, Community Darkrooms, Syracuse, N.Y.; Univ. of Louisville, Photog. Archives, Ky.; VSW Research Ctr., Rochester, N.Y. Natl. Gall. of Canada Ottawa.

DEALER Visual Studies Workshop Gall., 31 Prince St, Rochester, NY 14607.

ADDRESS Box 42, River Rd, Eaton, NY 13334.

Daniel Farber *MANUFACTURER · PHOTOGRAPHER* Born in Worcester, Massachusetts, on April 14, 1906, Farber is self-taught.

He co-founded and is vice-president of L. Farber Company (since 1924), and is a photographic associate in the Department of Decorative Arts at the Museum of Fine Arts in Boston (since 1978). Farber has belonged to the American Antiquarian Society since 1970.

He describes himself as "a businessman who pursues photography as a serious avocation."

PUBLICATIONS Books: *American Pewter in the Museum of Fine Arts, Boston*, 1974; *Location of Graves on Worcester Common*, w/Bouley, 1966 (self-pub.). Catalog: *Paul Revere's Boston* (Mus. of Fine Arts: Boston). Periodicals: *PSA Journal*, May 1968; *Popular Photography*, June 1960, Feb 1960, Oct 1959; *Modern Photography*, Apr 1958.

COLLECTIONS (selected) Akron Inst. of Art, Ohio; Amherst Coll., Mead Art Gall., Mass.; Art Inst. of Chicago; Boston Mus. of Fine Arts; Dallas Mus. of Fine Arts, Tex.; Denver Art Mus., Colo.; Kalamazoo Inst. of Art, Mich.; L/C, Wash., D.C.; Metro. Mus. of Art, NYC; MOMA, NYC; Norton Simon Mus. of Art, Pasadena, Calif.; Santa Barbara Mus. of Art, Calif.; Smithsonian Inst., Wash., D.C.; Univ. of Neb., Sheldon Mem. Art Gall., Lincoln.

ADDRESS 31 Hickory Dr, Worcester, MA 01609.

James Andrew Farber PHOTOGRAPHER Born August 27, 1946, in Los Angeles, Farber earned his BA in Theater Arts from San Francisco State University (1968) and also studied with Linda Connor at the San Francisco Art Institute (1971).

Farber has been displays coordinator of the Los Angeles International Film Exposition since 1976. He was a project photographer for the International Fund for Monuments, Venice, Italy, in 1975, and from 1969 to 1972 was staff photographer at KQED-TV, San Francisco. In 1972 he was associate producer/photographer for the national public television series *Critic At Large*.

A member of National Association of Broadcast Employees and Technicians, Soho/Cameraworks Gallery (1977–79) and Los Angeles Center for Photographic Studies (since 1979), Farber received a National Endowment for the Humanities grant in 1976 as a photographer for a project on the architectural history of America.

In 1972 Farber co-produced "An Hour With Pink Floyd," a special for national public television.

He terms his rephotographed collages of photography and printed images "dreamscapes . . . visualizations of my own psyche."

PUBLICATION Periodical: *Popular Photography*, Jan 1978.
ADDRESS 2022 Veteran Ave, Los Angeles, CA 90025.

Anna Fárová CRITIC·PHOTOHISTORIAN Born June 1, 1928, in Paris, Fárová studied at Charles University of Prague (1947–51) and received her PhD in Art History in 1973.

Currently doing criticism on the history of photography, Fárová was curator of photography in the Museum of Applied Arts in Prague from 1970 to 1974, a collection she founded. She belonged to the Union of the Artist in Prague (1965–69) and served on the advisory committee of the Eugene Smith Memorial Fund.

In 1978 she won the Humanitarian Award from ASMP.

PUBLICATIONS Books: *Sudek*, preface only, text by Sonja Bullaty, 1978; *Gypsies*, intro. only, 1975. Periodicals (text): *Camera*, Apr 1976, June 1973.

ADDRESS Anny Lettencke 17, 120-00 Prague 2, Czechoslovakia.

Antoine Fauchery PHOTOGRAPHER Born ca. 1827 in Paris, Fauchery died in April 1861 in Japan.

Fauchery dabbled in painting and literature for some years, and traveled with Nadar for a time. In 1852 he left France for Melbourne, Australia, to join the great gold rush. Returning to Europe in 1856, he applied for an official photographic mission to Australia, India and China (April 1857) and, with some assistance from the French government, departed again for Melbourne, where he worked throughout 1858. In 1860 he traveled through Manila and China, then on to Japan, where he died.

Said Andrew Hooper of the Royal Melbourne Institute of Technology: "Fauchery's photographic work in Australia was outstanding, considering the difficulties of working with the early wet-plate medium. Surviving photographs include some of the earliest views of Melbourne, portraits of aborigines, and imaginative 'action' pictures of gold-miners at work."

PUBLICATIONS Books: *Gold and Silver; an album of Hill End and Gulgong photographs from the Holtermann Collection*, Keast Burke, 1973 (Heinemann: Melbourne); *The Story of the Camera in Australia*, Jack Cato, 1955 (Georgian House: Australia); *Lettres d'un mineur en Australie*, 1856 (Europe).

COLLECTIONS In Australia: Natl. Gall. of Victoria; Royal Melbourne Inst. of Tech.

Douglas Faulkner PHOTOGRAPHER · WRITER
Born October 13, 1937, in Cincinnati, Ohio,
Faulkner studied English and creative writing at
the University of Miami, Coral Gables, Florida
(1957–60). His father was the renowned chemical
engineer Seymour Faulkner (1903–56).

A freelance photographer and writer since
1962, Faulkner served as a consultant to Time-
Life Books' Nature Series in 1962, and was a photographer's assistant in New York in 1960–62.
He has belonged to ASMP since 1962.

Working in color, the photographer finds his
main interest in dream life.

PUBLICATIONS Books: *Living Corals*, w/Rich-
ard Chesher, 1979; *Dwellers in the Sea*, w/B. Fell,
1976; *This Living Reef*, 1974; *Aquarium Fishes,
Their Beauty, History and Care*, w/James Atz,
1971; *The Hidden Sea*, w/Smith, 1970. Periodicals: *Creative Camera*, Mar 1971; *Camera*, Jan
1971.

COLLECTION Sea World, San Diego, Calif.
ADDRESS 5 W 8 St, New York, NY 10011.

Louis Faurer PHOTOGRAPHER Born August
28, 1916, in Philadelphia, Pennsylvania, Faurer is
a self-taught photographer who lists as his major
influences Henri Cartier-Bresson, Walker Evans
and Robert Frank, but especially Ben Rose and
Ben Somoroff.

Introduced to photography in 1937, Faurer
helped initiate Ben Rose's New York studio in
1946–47. From 1947 to 1969 he was a commercial photographer for such periodicals and publishing companies as Hearst, *Harpers Bazaar,*
Condé Nast, *Vogue*, Time-Life and *Fortune.*
From 1969 to 1974 he lived and worked in London and Paris, focusing on his personal photography, as he has continued to do since returning
to the United States. In 1977 he was on the faculty of the Parsons School of Design in New York
City.

Faurer is a member of SPE, Artists Equity Association of New York and Visual Artists & Galleries Association, New York. He won a
Guggenheim Fellowship in 1979 and in 1978 was
awarded both CAPS and NEA fellowships.

Faurer works in both black-and-white and
color, employing a variety of formats "in accord
with content, construction, and feeling of the
'frame.'" He likes to describe his work as a
"transformation of adversities into victories of
life and love."

PUBLICATIONS Books: *Aperture*, 1978, *Flair
Annual*, 1952; *Local Color*, Truman Capote,
1950. Anthologies: *The Camera as Witness*, 1967
(Southam Press Ltd.: Toronto, Canada); *100*

Years of the American Female, 1967; *Family of
Man*, Edward Steichen, ed., 1955. Periodical:
Camera 35, 1977.

COLLECTIONS Graphics Internatl. Ltd., Wash.,
D.C.; MOMA, NYC; New Orleans Mus. of Art;
Seagram Cllctn., NYC.

DEALER Light Gall., 724 Fifth Ave, New York,
NY 10019.

ADDRESS 463 West St, H-520, New York, NY
10014.

Lynn Gray Fayman PHOTOGRAPHER Born in
Kansas City, Missouri, on May 14, 1904, Fayman
died in San Diego, California, in June 1968. He
received his BA in Landscape Architecture from
Kansas State University, Manhattan, Kansas,
then did graduate work in photography at Art
Center School in Los Angeles, graduating in
1943.

Fayman worked for Convair in San Diego from
1943 to 1945, then was self-employed. His work
was widely exhibited during the 1960s.

A Fellow of the Photographic Society of America (1963), he served three terms as president of
the La Jolla Museum of Contemporary Art in
California.

His film *Color in Motion II, The Red Spot* was
shown at Cannes International Film Festival,
France, in 1954 and was chosen one of the ten
best films of 1955 in the PSA International Cinema Competition.

Fayman began experimenting with color materials when they became available after World
War II, translating his interest in stage lighting to
the photographic medium. His work coincided
with the Abstract Expressionist period of art and
had much in common with it. He used the Flex-
ichrome process extensively in his work (until it
was withdrawn from the market by Kodak), producing photograms and other abstract images.

PUBLICATIONS Books (all w/Helen Geisel):
Why I Built the Boogle House, 1964; *Do You
Know What I'm Going to Do Next Saturday?*,
1963; *I Was Kissed By a Seal at the Zoo*, 1962.

COLLECTIONS Ctr. for Photographic Arts, San
Diego; La Jolla Mus. of Contemporary Art, Calif.;
State of Calif., Sacramento.

ARCHIVE Danah Fayman, POB 625, La Jolla,
CA 92038.

Daniel E. Fear GALLERY OWNER Born March
28, 1949, in Tacoma, Washington, Fear has
owned and directed the Silver Image Gallery,
Inc., in Seattle since 1973.

Fear is a member of SPE and the Photography
Council of the Seattle Art Museum. He is a

founding member of the International Association of Photography Art Dealers and, as of this writing, is on its board of directors.

ADDRESS   92 S Washington St, Seattle, WA 98104.

David Featherstone   *PHOTOGRAPHER · CRITIC · ARTS ADMINISTRATOR*   Born in Iowa City, Iowa, on January 23, 1945, Featherstone studied folklore and mythology at the University of California in Los Angeles and attended the School of Oriental and African Studies at the University of London. He earned an AB in Anthropology at the University of California at Berkeley (1967) and an MA at the University of Oregon in Eugene (1971), where Bernard Freemesser and Robert Kostka were his teachers.

Since 1977 Featherstone has been working for the Friends of Photography in Carmel, California, as an executive associate and has been writing book reviews for their newsletter. His previous working experience includes being curator of the Historical Photograph Collection of the University of Oregon Library in Eugene (1974–76) and teaching photography at the Maude I. Kerns Art Center in the same city.

He belongs to SPE and VSW and was awarded an NEA Art Critic's Fellowship in both 1977 and 1979.

As an art critic, he focuses "on photographers who work from an inner need and whose work expresses archetypal forms." His photographs are "black-and-white documents of psychological states."

PUBLICATIONS   Books: *Vilem Kriz, Photographs (Untitled 19)*, text only, 1979; *Photographs from the Columbia River Expedition*, Carleton E. Watkins, intro., 1979.

ADDRESS   POB 2142, Carmel, CA 93921.

Gertrude Fehr   *PHOTOGRAPHER · TEACHER · JOURNALIST*   Born March 5, 1900, in St. Gallen, Switzerland, Fehr earned a degree from the Art & Craft Shop in Munich, Germany, and also studied at Atelier Wasow in Munich. Her husband was Swiss painter Jules Fehr.

Since 1960 Fehr has been a freelance photographer. Previously, she was headmaster of photography at Art & Craft School in Vevey, Switzerland (1945–60), and at School of Photography Fehr in Lausanne, Switzerland (1940–45), and head manager of Publiphot School, Photography and Applied Photography, in Paris (1933–37). She operated Studio G. Fehr in Munich from 1918 to 1932, specializing in portraiture and theater photography.

Fehr belongs to Union Suisse de Photography and DGPh. She has won numerous diplomas and medals, including the National State Medal of the French World Exhibition as well as diploma and medals of French Syndicate (1937) and the Golden Medal of the Triennale Milano (1933).

The photographer has taken portraits of many famous writers, painters and musicians as well as theatrical stills. She has also experimented with solarization and montage.

PUBLICATION   Catalog: *Gertrude Fehr, Fotografie Seit 1918* (Stadtmuseum: Munich, Germany).

COLLECTIONS   MOMA, NYC. German Theatre Mus., Munich; Kunsthaus of Zurich, Switzerland; Mus. of Munich (photomuseum), Germany; Univ. of Essen Mus., Germany.

DEALER   Karl Lipp, K. G. graph, Betriebe, Lautensackstrasse 2, 8000 Munich 21, Germany.

ADDRESS   Riant Chateau, 1820 Territet, Switzerland.

Jo Alison Feiler   *PHOTOGRAPHER*   Born in Los Angeles on April 16, 1951, Feiler received her BFA and MFA in Photography from California Institute of the Arts, Valencia (1970, 1975). She also studied at UCLA (1968–69) and Art Center College of Design, Los Angeles (1971–72).

Her most recent position (1977–79) was as a photographer of filmstrips for CRM/McGraw-Hill Productions in Santa Monica, California. Previously, she did publicity stills for Warner Brothers Records (1972) and still photography for Hawk Films and Warner Brothers Films in England (1974). She was photography editor of *Coast Environment Magazine* in Los Angeles (1970–72) and on the design staff of *Box* at California Institute of the Arts in 1971. She has also done freelance photography for a variety of magazines.

A member of RPS and the Los Angeles Center for Photographic Studies, Feiler won a cash award at the 2nd All California Photography Show, Laguna Beach Museum of Art, 1976. She won a scholarship grant in photography from California Institute of the Arts in 1974 and a Certificate of Art Excellence from the Los Angeles County Museum of Art in 1968.

Feiler takes small-format black-and-white photographs of people and describes her work as "not about an outward world which one sees with his eyes, but the inward world which we experience through feelings."

PUBLICATIONS   Anthologies: *The Nude 1980*, 1980 (Les Editions Contrejour: Paris); *Women on Women*, Katharine Holabird, 1978 (Aurum Press,

Ltd.: London). Periodicals: *Creative Camera*, Oct 1979; *Zoom*, Mar/Apr 1979 (Paris); *Popular Photography*, Apr 1978; *British Journal of Photography*, Apr 1977, Nov 1975, Aug 1974.

PORTFOLIO *Portfolio One* (group), Museum Edition Portfolio, July 1976 (G. Ray Hawkins Gall.: Los Angeles).

COLLECTIONS Crocker Natl. Bank, San Francisco; Elvehjem Art Ctr., Madison, Wis.; Fluor Corp., Irvine, Calif.; New Orleans Mus. of Art, La.; Security Pacific Natl. Bank, Los Angeles; Smithsonian Inst., Wash., D.C.

DEALERS G. Ray Hawkins Gall., 7224 Melrose Ave, Los Angeles, CA 90046; Photographers' Gall., 8 Great Newport St, London WC2, England.

ADDRESS 132-C San Vicente Blvd, Santa Monica, CA 90402.

Andreas B. L. Feininger PHOTOGRAPHER · WRITER Born December 27, 1906, in Paris, Feininger is the son of the painter Lyonel Feininger. He graduated summa cum laude from the Bauhaus in Weimar, Germany, where he studied from 1922 to 1925.

A freelance photographer and writer since 1963, Feininger was a staff photographer for *Life* magazine (1943–62). He worked for Black Star Picture Agency (1940–41) and was an architect in Germany (1929–31). Before that he was a cabinetmaker's apprentice. It was in Sweden in 1933 that Feininger decided to devote himself completely to photography.

A member of ASMP and a charter member of the Explorer's Club, Feininger won ASMP's Robert Leavitt Award in 1966 and the Gold Medal Award from the Art Directors Club of Metropolitan Washington in 1965. He also won medals from Fotografiska Föreningen, Stockholm, Sweden, in 1938 and 1939.

Using black-and-white and color, Feininger has done extensive work in the fields of telephoto and close-up photography, including many detailed nature studies, as well as concentrating on architectural forms and street scenes. "I am known for my documentary approach," he says, "clarity of presentation being of the greatest importance to me."

PUBLICATIONS Monograph: *Andreas Feininger*, Ralph Hattersley, 1973. Books: *Experimental Work*, 1978; *New York in the Forties*, 1978; *The Mountains of the Mind*, 1977; *Light and Lighting in Photography*, 1976; *Roots of Art*, 1975; *The Perfect Photograph*, 1974; *Darkroom Techniques*, 1974; *Principles of Composition in Photography*, 1973; *Photographic Seeing*, 1973;

Shells, Dr. W. Emerson, 1972; *Basic Color Photography*, 1972; *The Color Photo Book*, 1969; *Trees*, 1968, repr. 1978; *Forms of Nature and Life*, 1966; *Lyonel Feininger: City at the Edge of the World*, T. Lux Feininger, 1965; *The Complete Photographer*, 1965, rev. 1978; *New York*, Kate Simon, 1964; *The World Through My Eyes*, 1963; *Total Picture Control*, 1961, repr. 1970; *Maids, Madonnas and Witches*, Henry Miller & J. Bon, 1961; *Man and Stone*, 1961, repr. as *Stone and Man*, 1979; *The Anatomy of Nature*, 1956, repr. 1979; *Changing America*, Patricia Dyett, 1955; *The Creative Photographer*, 1955, rev. 1975; *Successful Color Photography*, 1954; *Successful Photography*, 1954, rev. 1975; *The Face of New York*, Susan E. Lyman, 1954; *Advanced Photography*, 1952; *Feininger on Photography*, 1949; *New York*, John Erskin & Jacqueline Judge, 1945; *New Paths in Photography*, 1939. Anthologies: *The Photograph Collector's Guide*, Lee D. Witkin & Barbara London, 1979; *The Magic Image*, Cecil Beaton & Gail Buckland, 1975.

COLLECTIONS Baltimore Mus. of Art, Md.; Carnegie-Mellon Univ., Hunt Inst. for Botanical Documentation, Pittsburgh, Pa.; City Library, Springfield, Mass.; Delaware Art Mus., Wilmington; Harvard Univ., Carpenter Ctr. for the Visual Arts, Cambridge, Mass.; ICP, NYC; IMP/GEH, Rochester; Metro. Mus. of Art, NYC; MOMA, NYC; Mus. of the City of N.Y.; New Orleans Mus. of Art, La.; N.Y. Historical Soc., NYC; Newark Mus., N.J.; Smithsonian Inst., Wash., D.C.; Time, Inc., NYC; Univ. of Delaware, Newark; Wellesley Coll., Mass.; Worcester Art Mus., Mass. Bibliothèque Nationale, Paris; Mus. Folkwang, Essen, Ger.; Mus. für Kunst und Gewerbe, Hamburg, Ger.; Victoria & Albert Mus., London.

ARCHIVE CCP, Univ. of Arizona, Tucson, AZ 85719.

ADDRESS 18 Elizabeth Lane, New Milford, CT 06776.

Mark Feldstein PHOTOGRAPHER Born March 5, 1937, in Milan, Italy, Feldstein received a BFA (1958) and MA (1960) from Hunter College in New York City. He also studied fine art at the Sculpture Center (1958–60) and at New York University (1960–62).

An associate professor of art at Hunter College since 1961, he has also been a visiting artist at the International Center for Photography, New York City, since 1978 and was an adjunct assistant professor at La Guardia City College in New York (1971–75).

He belongs to SPE and CAA.

Using 4 x 5 and 6 x 6 formats, the photographer produces surreal images, landscapes and still lifes.

PUBLICATIONS Monographs: *Sightings*, 1977; *Unseen New York*, 1975. Anthology: *Diverse Images*, 1980. Catalog: *Contemporary Photography*, 1979 (New Orleans Mus. of Art).

DEALERS Castelli Graphics, 4 E 77 St, New York, NY 10021; Galerie Zabriskie, 29 Aubry Le Bouche, Paris, France 75004.

ADDRESS 39 Bond St, New York, NY 10012.

Arthur Fellig
See Weegee

Sandra (Sandi) Lee Fellman PHOTOGRAPHER · TEACHER Born on January 24, 1952, in Detroit, Michigan, Fellman attended Sir John Cass College of Fine Arts in London (1972) and the University of Wisconsin at Madison, where she earned a BS in Art (1973) and an MFA with a specialization in photography and typography (1976). While at Madison she studied under Cavalliere Ketchum.

Since 1979 she has been an assistant professor of art at Rutgers University in New Brunswick, New Jersey. Prior to that she taught at the University of New Mexico in Albuquerque (1978–79), at Bemidji State University in Minnesota (1976–78) and also gave numerous workshops and lectures.

She has been a member of CAA, SPE, and George Eastman House in Rochester since 1973, and received a project grant from the Minnesota State Arts Board in 1978.

The artist works with a square-format camera. She "began in 1973, documenting prostitutes working at the Mustang Ranch in Nevada, in black-and-white. [Her] current work (large color prints) continues to be involved with the sensuous, the tactile and what might be characterized as 'female rituals' in a more nonspecific, abstract manner."

PUBLICATIONS Anthologies: *Multiples*, 1980 (Creatis, Paris); *Insights/Self Portraits by Women*, 1978. Catalog: *Photography Collection: Minneapolis Institute of Art*, 1980, Minnesota. Periodical: "How to Get Your Work Into Print" (review), *Popular Photography*, Mar 1977.

COLLECTIONS Bemidji State Univ. Lib., Minn.; CCP, Tucson; Columbus Public Lib., Wis.; Floating Foundation of Photog., NYC; L/C, Wash. D.C.; Minneapolis Inst. of Arts, Minn.; MOMA, NYC; Northland Community Coll., Thief River Falls, Minn.; Otis Art Inst., Los Angeles; Portland Mus. of Art, Maine; Princeton Univ. Lib., Graphic Arts Cllctn., N.J.; Security

Pacific Bank, Los Angeles; State Historical Soc. of Wis., Madison; Univ. of Md., Baltimore County; Univ. of Nev., Reno; Univ. of N. Mex., Fine Arts Mus., Albuquerque; Univ. of Wis. Memorial Union, Madison. Bibliothèque Nationale, Paris.

DEALERS Witkin Gall., 41 E 57 St, New York, NY 10022; Susan Spiritus Gall., 3336 Via Lido, Newport Beach, CA 92663; Albert Champeau/Ufficio dell'arte, 44 rue Quincampoix, 75004, Paris.

ADDRESS 548 Broadway #4E, New York, NY 10012.

Rosella L. Felsenfeld WRITER · EDITOR · TEACHER Born June 6, 1941, in Chicago, Illinois, Felsenfeld received a BA in English from Roosevelt University in Chicago (1962) and an MA in English from Northwestern University in Evanston, Illinois (1967). She earned an Abd PhD in English at the University of Wisconsin, Madison, in 1975. She names Jerome Rothenberg and Diane Wakowski as influences on her poetry and perception.

A freelance writer and researcher, Felsenfeld has edited *Camerawork Newsletter* since 1977, is West Coast correspondent for *American Photographer* and writes for *Darkroom* magazine. She taught writing at San Francisco Art Institute in 1977 and literature at Dominican College, San Raphael, in the same year. She was a researcher for the University of California Department of Pediatrics in 1978–79.

A founding member of Camerawork Gallery in San Francisco, Felsenfeld has been on its board of directors since 1976. She won an NEA photo research grant in 1978 and a California Arts Council grant in photography research in 1976.

Her poetry has been published in *Poetry From Violence* and *Saying Yes*, the latter being in the Artists' Book Collection of the Art Institute of San Francisco. She also has created, with Arthur Ollman, a series of eight videotapes on older California photographers (1976).

PUBLICATION Catalog: *Contemporary California Photography*, co-ed, 1978 (Camerawork Press: San Francisco).

ADDRESS 6509 Raymond St, Oakland, CA 94609.

Albert Fenn PHOTOGRAPHER Fenn was born July 10, 1912, in New York City. His uncle was the actor Paul Muni (1895–1967). He earned a BS in Chemistry from Polytechnic Institute of Brooklyn, New York, and names, as his major influences, Edward Weston, Paul Strand, Man Ray and Alfred Eisenstaedt.

As of this writing Fenn was living in Spain and freelancing for Time, Inc., magazines. Fenn has freelanced his photographs to numerous outlets, such as *Look, Time, Newsweek, Collier's, Saturday Evening Post,* etc., since 1962. From 1962 to 1972 he was also a contract photographer for Time, Inc., and worked for *Life* magazine from 1941 to 1962, first as a contract photographer (1941–46), then as a staff photographer.

Fenn is a member of the Overseas Press Club and was a member of the New York Newspaper Guild (1946–62).

A photojournalist, Fenn has covered all types of news events, political conventions, politicians, diplomats, presidents, foreign rulers and the United Nations. He specializes in scientific and medical photography.

COLLECTION MOMA, NYC.

ADDRESS c/o Mrs. Margot Spiro, 17 Kingfisher Dr, Middletown, NJ 07748.

Roger Fenton PHOTOGRAPHER · LAWYER Born 1819 in Heywood, Lancashire, England, Fenton died in England in 1869. He received an MA from University College, London, and studied painting with Paul Delaroche in Paris.

A solicitor from 1852 to 1854, Fenton worked as a professional photographer (1854–62), then returned to the practice of law. During his years as a photographer, he was commissioned to photograph the construction of a suspension bridge over the Dnieper River, in Russia (1852), to portray domestic scenes of the royal family, to record art treasures of the British Museum, and (with royal sanction) to photograph the Crimean War under the commission of publisher Thomas Agnew (1855). Wood engravings from some of the 300 to 400 images he shot during the war were published in *The Illustrated London News.*

Fenton helped form the Photographic Club in 1847 and co-founded the Photographic Society (later RPS) in 1853, serving as its secretary that year.

The photographer is especially noted for his coverage of the Crimean War, the first extensive photographic documentation of a war. Also notable were his portraiture and still lifes. Working with several different cameras (including a stereoscopic one) and using both calotypes and collodion wet-plates, he produced salt prints, albumen prints, photogalvanographics and carbon prints.

PUBLICATIONS Monographs: *Roger Fenton of Crimble Hall,* John Hannavy, 1976; *Roger Fenton: Photographer of the Crimean War,* Helmut & Alison Gernsheim, 1954, repr. 1973. Books: *Ruined Abbeys and Castles of Great Britain and Ireland,* vol. 1, Wm. & Mary Howitt, 1862; *The Conway in the Stereoscope,* J. B. Davidson, 1860; *Photographic Art Treasures,* 1856. Anthologies: *The Photograph Collector's Guide,* Lee D. Witkin & Barbara London, 1979; *The Invented Eye,* Edward Lucie-Smith, 1975; *The Magic Image,* Cecil Beaton & Gail Buckland, 1975; *Great Photographers,* 1971; *Light and Film,* 1970. Periodicals: *Stereoscopic Magazine,* 1858–63; "Narrative of a Photographic Trip to the Seat of the War in the Crimea," *Journal of the Photographic Society,* Jan 21, 1856.

COLLECTIONS Art Inst. of Chicago, Ill.; Harvard Univ., Carpenter Ctr. for the Visual Arts, Cambridge, Mass.; IMP/GEH, Rochester; L/C, Wash., D.C.; Univ. of N. Mex. Art Mus., Albuquerque; Univ. of Texas, Gernsheim Cllctn., Austin. In Great Britain: Cambridge Univ.; Liverpool City Libs.; Manchester City Libs.; Natl. Army Mus., London; Royal Lib., Windsor Park; RPS, London; Science Mus., London; Scottish Utd. Svc. Mus., Edinburgh; Stonyhurst Coll., Clitheroe; Victoria & Albert Mus., London.

Jim Ferguson PHOTOGRAPHER · VIDEO ARTIST Born June 4, 1954, in Ypsilanti, Michigan, Ferguson studied from 1972 to 1974 at Colorado State University, Fort Collins, and received his BFA from the San Francisco Art Institute in 1976. He earned an MFA in 1979 from the School of the Art Institute of Chicago.

A photography instructor at Northwestern University, Evanston, Illinois, in 1979, Ferguson previously was a photographer for Chicago Architecture Foundation (1978–79) and a photo archivist for the Museum of Albuquerque, New Mexico (1977–78).

He is a founding member of the Santa Fe Gallery of Photography, New Mexico. In 1980 he received a grant from the Illinois Art Council.

"My photographs often deal with juxtapositions which create spatial ambiguities," says Ferguson. "This requires the viewer to define the objects and spaces for themselves."

COLLECTIONS Amon Carter Mus. of Western Art, Ft. Worth, Tex.; Dallas Mus. of Fine Art, Tex.; Seattle Art Mus., Wash. Natl. Mus. of Anthropology, Mexico City.

REPRESENTATIVES The Afterimage, The Quadrangle #151, 2800 Routh St, Dallas, TX 75201; Peter M. David Gall., 430 Oak Grove St, Minneapolis, MN 55403.

ADDRESS 642 W Cornelia, Chicago, IL 60657.

Larry S. Ferguson *PHOTOGRAPHER · CURATOR*
Born in North Platte, Nebraska, on May 16, 1954, Ferguson earned a BFA at the University of Nebraska in Lincoln in 1977 and also attended an Archival Photography Seminar at the Rochester Institute in 1978. He was influenced by photographers Jim Alinder and Lawrence McFarland.

In 1978 he was appointed artist-in-residence-in-the-community for the Nebraska Arts Council and Western Heritage Museum in Omaha. He also works as curator of photographs for that museum's Bostwick-Frohardt Collection (also since 1978). In 1977–78 he was curator of photography at the Adams County Historical Society, Hastings, Nebraska.

A member of VSW, SPE and Friends of Photography, Ferguson was awarded two artist-in-residence grants and two exhibition grants (1978 & 1979) from the Nebraska Arts Council.

His work consists of medium- and large-format silver and color prints. He uses extreme-wide-angle lenses and chooses as his subjects people, landscapes and cityscapes.

PUBLICATIONS   Anthologies: *Pictures Through a Plastic Lens*, David Featherstone, 1980; *Object and Image*, George Craven, 1980; *Self-Portrayal*, 1978. Catalog: *Twelve Photographers: A Contemporary Mid-America Document*, 1978 (Mid-America Arts Alliance Touring Exhibition).

COLLECTIONS   Adams County Historical Soc., Hastings, Neb.; Blair Telephone Co., Neb.; Hastings Mus., Neb.; L/C, Wash. D.C.; Metro. Arts Council, Omaha, Neb.; Murray State Univ., Ky.; Omaha Airport Authority, Neb.; Second St. Gall., Charlottesville, Va.; Sheldon Memorial Art Gall., Lincoln, Neb.; Western Heritage Mus., Omaha, Neb.

ADDRESS   Western Heritage Mus., 801 10 St, Omaha, NE 68108.

Benedict J. Fernandez *PHOTOGRAPHER · TEACHER* Fernandez studied at Columbia University in New York City (1954–56). He also studied photography with Alexey Brodovitch, Minor White, Richard Avedon and at the Leica School of 35mm Photography.

Since 1970 he has been chairman of the Photography Department at the New School for Social Research in New York City. Previously, he was employed as an instructor of Puerto Rican Studies at Rutgers University (1973–74) in New Brunswick, New Jersey, and of photography at the Parsons School of Design in New York City (1965–70). He also worked as a resident color photographer for Joseph Papp's Public Theater in New York City (1966–72).

Fernandez has been a member of the Massachusetts Council on the Arts since 1975, and of Alexey Brodovitch's Design Laboratory since 1968. A recipient of an NEA grant in 1973, he also received a Guggenheim Fellowship in 1970.

The photographer's point of view, or opinion, is that "the camera is the vehicle which interprets. My style is confrontation," he states, "and the format is 35mm. The field of research is the social environment and its effect upon our society."

PUBLICATIONS   Books: *Four Generations*, 1977; *In Opposition: The Right to Dissent*, 1968; *Trumpet of Freedom*, 1967 (Canadian Broadcasting Co. Pubs.).

COLLECTIONS   Boston Mus. of Fine Arts, Mass.; MOMA, NYC; Mus. of the City of N.Y.; Smithsonian Inst., Wash., D.C. Arles Festival Cllctn., France; Bibliothèque Nationale, Paris.

ADDRESS   1432 37 St, North Bergen, NJ 07047.

Robert W. Fichter *PHOTOGRAPHER · TEACHER* Born in Fort Meyers, Florida, in 1939, Fichter earned a BFA in 1963 from Indiana University in Bloomington, where he studied photography and printmaking under Henry Holmes Smith. He earned an MFA in 1966 from the University of Florida in Gainesville, where he studied painting and printmaking.

An assistant curator of exhibitions for George Eastman House in Rochester (1966–68), he then moved west, working for UCLA as an assistant professor (1968–70), a lecturer (1971) and visiting associate professor (1971). Since 1972 he has been working as associate professor in the Department of Art at Florida State University in Tallahassee.

PUBLICATIONS   Book: *Light & Lens*, Donald Werner & Dennis Longwell, 1973. Anthologies: *The Photograph Collector's Guide*, Lee D. Witkin & Barbara London, 1979; *The Great West: Real/Ideal*, Sandy Hume et al., eds., 1977. Catalogs: *New Blues*, 1976 (Ariz. State Univ., Memorial Union Art Gall: Tempe); *New Images in Photography*, 1974 (Univ. of Miami, Lowe Art Mus.: Fla.); *Photography Unlimited*, 1974 (Harvard Univ., Fogg Art Mus.: Cambridge); *Photography Into Art*, 1972 (Arts Council of Great Britain: London); *60's Continuum*, Van Deren Coke, 1972 (GEH: Rochester); *Graphic/Photographic*, 1971 (Calif. State Coll.: Fullerton); *Into the 70's*, Tom Muir Wilson, Orrel E. Thompson & Robert M. Doty, 1970 (Akron Art Inst.: Ohio); *California Photographers 1970*, 1969 (Univ. of Calif., Memorial Union Art Gall.: Davis).

COLLECTIONS   Boston Mus. of Fine Arts; IMP/GEH, Rochester; Norton Simon Mus. of Art, Pasadena, Calif.; UCLA; Univ. of New Mexico, Albuquerque; VSW, Rochester. Natl. Gall. of Canada, Ottawa, Ontario.

DEALER   Robert Freidus Gall., 158 Lafayette St, New York, NY 10013.

ADDRESS   603 W Eighth Ave, Tallahassee, FL 32303.

Felice L. Fike   *PHOTOGRAPHER · TEACHER*
Born August 25, 1947, in Wausau, Wisconsin, Fike received her BA from Humboldt State University in Arcata, California (1976), and her MFA from Arizona State University, Tempe (1979).

In 1979 she became an instructor and coordinator of Darkroom Programs at the International Center of Photography in New York City.

A member of SPE, Visual Studies Workshop and Los Angeles Center for Photographic Studies, Fike received research grants in 1979 from both the Arizona Commission on the Arts & Humanities and the Arizona Historical Society.

Fike works mainly in nonsilver processes such as cyanotypes, printing all her images in negative, approximately 8 x 10. Many of the hand-sensitized papers she uses are first printed with verbal information and problem-solving data before receiving an image.

PUBLICATIONS   Periodicals: *Photographer's Forum Magazine*, text only, 1979; *Afterimage: VSW*, text only, 1979; *Artweek*, 1978.

COLLECTION   Ariz. State Univ. Art Mus. & Northlight Gall., Tempe.

ADDRESS   Internatl. Ctr. of Photography, 1130 Fifth Ave, New York, NY 10028.

Frank Filan   *PHOTOJOURNALIST*   Born in 1905 in Brooklyn, New York, Filan died July 23, 1952, in Los Angeles. His brother, Harold Filan, was a photojournalist with Associated Press.

Frank Filan also worked for Associated Press, from 1930 until his death, serving three years in the Pacific as a war photographer. During this time he made sixteen amphibious landings.

He won a Pulitzer Prize in 1944, shared with Earle Bunker, for his wartime picture of Japanese bodies strewn on bomb-gutted Tarawa. He also received commendation from Admiral Chester Nimitz for having rescued scores of wounded Marines in the face of Japanese fire.

PUBLICATION   Anthology: *Moments*, Sheryle & John Leekley, foreword by Dan Rather, 1978.

John Filo   *PHOTOJOURNALIST*   Born in Natrona Heights, Pennsylvania, on August 21, 1948, Filo earned a BS from Kent State University,

Kent, Ohio, in photo illustration in 1971. He learned photography from Eddie Adams, who had a strong influence on Filo's work.

He has been with Associated Press in Chicago since 1971 and opened their Springfield, Kansas, bureau. He has also done slide shows for the American Health Institute.

In 1971 Filo won the Pulitzer Prize for his photograph of a student who was shot at Kent State University. He also won the Keystone Press Award in 1970.

PUBLICATIONS   Book: *Kent State: What Happened and Why*, James Michener, 1975. Anthology: *Moments*, Sheryle & John Leekley, foreword by Dan Rather, 1978.

COLLECTION   MOMA, NYC.

ADDRESS   11810 W 66 St, Shawneee, KA 66203.

Laurence Fink   *PHOTOGRAPHER · TEACHER*
Born March 11, 1941, in Brooklyn, New York, Fink studied with Lisette Model. An assistant professor at Parsons School of Design in New York City (1967–72), he was assistant professor at the City University of New York from 1972 to 1976. For a year (1977–78) he taught at Yale University, returning to New York City to teach at Cooper Union, where he is presently working.

The recipient of an NEA grant in 1978, Fink was awarded CAPS grants in 1971 and 1974, as well as Guggenheim fellowships in 1976 and 1979.

PUBLICATION   Periodical: *Camera*, Nov 1977.

COLLECTIONS   Corcoran Gall. of Art, Wash., D.C.; L/C, Wash., D.C.; MOMA, NYC.

DEALERS   Light Gall., 724 Fifth Ave, New York, NY 10019; Sander Gall., 2604 Connecticut Ave NW, Wash., D.C. 20008.

ADDRESS   POB 295, Martins Creek, PA 18003.

Candida Finkel   *CRITIC*   Born February 25, 1947, in Chicago, Illinois, Finkel earned a BA in English from the University of Michigan, Ann Arbor (1968). She then studied at Columbia College in Chicago and at the School of the Art Institute of Chicago, where her major influence was Alex Sweetman. She received an MA in Speech Communication at Northwestern University in Evanston, Illinois, in 1980.

Finkel has been the photography editor of the *New Art Examiner* in Chicago since 1977, and has been a contributing editor of *Exposure* since 1978. She was Chicago correspondent for *Afterimage: VSW* (1977–79).

The critic belongs to SPE and Speech Communication Education. She was awarded an NEA critics grant in 1980.

PUBLICATIONS Periodicals: "Modernism in Photography," *The New Art Examiner*, Jan 1980; "Chicago Photography at the Art Institute," *Afterimage: VSW*, Apr 1979; "Photographs as Symbols and Non-Symbols," winter 1978, "Eros and Photography," fall 1978, "Space, Time, and the Syzygy," Dec 1977, *Exposure: SPE*.

ADDRESS 2917 Orchard Lane, Wilmette, IL 60091.

Hans Finsler PHOTOGRAPHER · TEACHER Born 1891 in Zurich, Switzerland, Finsler died in Switzerland in 1972. First studying architecture in Munich, he later studied art history and was deeply influenced by both Fritz Burger and Heinrich Wölfflin.

Finsler taught art history at Burg Giebichenstein in Halle, Germany, in 1922, where he was also librarian. Later he taught a course in the photography of objects at Zurich's School of Arts and Crafts, although he had no background in photography. This was during the time of the Bauhaus. He was himself the mentor of René Burri, Emil Schulthess and Werner Bischof, among others.

A. D. Coleman of *The New York Times* wrote that "Finsler is one of the handful who have reached the frontier of photographic psychology." Along with his landscapes and portraits, Finsler "began to develop and codify what might be called the psychomechanics of photography; the rules which determine how photographs affect the eye, and through it the intellect and emotions." This he accomplished in his "object" studies. He is considered one of the medium's more cogent philosophers.

PUBLICATIONS Monographs: *My Way to Photography*, 1971; *30 Aufnahmen aus den zwanziger Jahren*, 1970. Book: *Foto-auge*, Franz Roh & Jan Tschichold, 1929. Anthology: *The Magic Image*, Cecil Beaton & Gail Buckland, 1975. Periodicals: Review, A. D. Coleman, *New York Times*, II:20, Apr 26, 1970; *Du*, Mar 1964.

Carl Fischer PHOTOGRAPHER · ART DIRECTOR Born May 3, 1924, in New York City, Fischer studied at New York City's Cooper Union in 1948 and at the Central School of Arts in London in 1952, earning a BFA from the former in 1975.

Since 1958 he has operated Carl Fischer Photography, Inc. He previously was an art director with Grey Advertising (1956–58) and Sudler & Hennessey (1954–56) and an assistant art director with William H. Weintraub & Co. (1952–54). Fischer was a designer for *Look* (1949–51) and for

Columbia Records in 1948. He belongs to the Art Directors Club of New York, American Institute of Graphic Arts and the Directors Guild of America.

From the Art Directors Club, Fischer received a silver medal in 1975 and a gold medal in 1960. He received a Mark Twain Journalism Award in 1971, the St. Gaudens Medal from Cooper Union in 1969 and their professional achievement citation in 1966. He also won a Fulbright grant in 1951.

PUBLICATIONS Periodicals: *Camera 35*, 1978; *Commercial Photo*, 1975; *Communication Arts*, 1975; *Progresso Fotografico*, 1974; *Photo*, 1973.

COLLECTIONS Metro. Mus. of Art, NYC; Rose Art Mus., Amherst, Mass.

ADDRESS 121 E 83 St, New York, NY 10028.

Hal Fischer PHOTOGRAPHER · TEACHER · CRITIC Born on December 18, 1950, in Kansas City, Missouri, Fischer studied at the London School of Film. He also attended the University of Illinois in Urbana, where he earned a BFA (1973), and San Francisco State University, where he completed an MA in 1976. He has been teaching at California College of Arts and Crafts in Oakland since 1978 and at the City College of San Francisco since 1979. In 1977 he started working for *Artweek* (Oakland) as a contributing editor and in 1978 for *Artforum* (New York City) as a reviewer.

NEA awarded him an Art Critics Fellowship in 1977 and a Photographer's Fellowship in 1980.

As a critic Fischer deals with contemporary photography. His own photographic work combines images with the written word.

PUBLICATIONS Monographs: *18th Near Castro St. x 24*, 1979, *Gay Semiotics*, 1978 (NFS Press: San Francisco).

DEALER Robert Samuel Gall., 795 Broadway, New York, NY 10003.

ADDRESS 10 Lyon St, #211, San Francisco, CA 94117.

Rudolf Fischer CHEMIST Fischer was born (1881) and died (1957) in Berlin, Germany. He attended the Gymnasium in the Steglitz section of Berlin, then studied chemistry at Strassburg and the University of Berlin.

After graduation Fischer spent a year as an assistant at the Chemical Institute of the University of Berlin, a year in the army and a year as an assistant at the university's Pharmaceutical Institute. In 1906 he became a chemist and manager of the Neue Photographische Gesellschaft in

Steglitz, which specialized in photographic papers. From 1912 to 1914 Fischer worked with Swiss chemist Johann Wilhelm Siegrist, then entered the German Army during World War I. After the war he worked as a chemist for the Schering firm in Berlin until 1927, when he founded his own company, Technophot Dr. Rudolf Fischer. Located in Berlin-Neukoelln, it prosperously manufactured photographic papers for technical purposes.

Fischer received the Liebnitz Medal from the Prussian Academy of Science in 1944. In his early researches at Neue Photographische Gesellschaft, Fischer worked on print toning and patented ideas for three-color films and color coupler plates (1913–14). From 1929 to 1938 he obtained four patents for photographic materials, one being for a process to make natural-color copies.

PUBLICATIONS Books: *Quellendarstellungen zur Geschichte der Fotografie*, Wolfgang Baier, 1964; *Memoirs of a Photochemist*, Fritz Wentzel, 1960; *March of Photography*, Erich Stenger, 1958; *Encyclopedie voor Fotografie en Cinematografie*, Elsevier, 1958; *History of Color Photography*, Joseph S. Friedman, 1944; *History of 3-Color Photography*, E. J. Wall, 1925. Anthology: *Photography's Great Inventors*, Louis W. Sipley, 1965. Periodicals: *Bild und Ton*, 1960; *Zeitschrift für wissenschaftliche Photographie*, 1951; *British Journal of Photography*, 1914, 1913; *Photographische Correspondenz*, 1914.

Alida Livingston Fish PHOTOGRAPHER · TEACHER Born on May 2, 1944, in New London, Connecticut, Alida Fish is the sister of painter Janet Fish. She completed a BA at Smith College, in Northampton, Massachusetts, in 1967 and an MFA at the Rochester Institute of Photography in 1976. Her mentors were Evon Streetman, Betty Hahn and John Pfahl.

She has been teaching at the State University of New York in Buffalo since 1979 and also taught at the University of Rochester (1979), at Goddard College in Plainfield, Vermont (1978), and at Penland School in North Carolina (1973, 1977–78).

She belongs to SPE.

The artist combines gum-bichromate, nonsilver and Polaroid materials with drawing. Her pictorial style is characterized by preconceived and staged shooting, producing fantasy photographs.

PUBLICATIONS Anthologies: *The Family of Woman*, 1976; *Women See Woman*, 1976. Periodical: *Camera*, Feb 1979.

COLLECTIONS Humboldt State Univ., Arcata,

Calif.; Murray State Univ., Ky.; Rochester Inst. of Technology, N.Y.; Standard Oil of Ind.

ADDRESS c/o Nadal, RD 3, Canandaigua, NY 14424.

Elaine (Baunhuber) Fisher PHOTOGRAPHER · TEACHER Born on July 17, 1939, in Newark, New Jersey, Fisher obtained a BFA from Carnegie Mellon University in Pittsburg, Pennsylvania, in 1961 and also studied photography under Minor White (1966, 1968, 1973).

Since 1976 she has been an associate professor at Southeastern Massachusetts University in Dartmouth, where she started teaching in 1973. Prior to that she was an instructor at various private workshops in Massachusetts, Virginia and New York State (1970–72) and at the School of Fashion Design in Boston (1969–70).

Since 1974 she has been a member of SPE, serving as the first president of their Northeast Region from 1976 to 1978. In 1972 NEA granted her a Fellowship in Photography, and "Photovision '72 of New England Photographers" selected her work for first prize.

The artist, working in black-and-white in both small and large formats and using single and multiple negatives, deals mainly with "emotional and psychological expression."

PUBLICATIONS Anthologies: *Self-Portrayal*, J. Alinder, ed., 1979; *InSights—Self-Portraits by Women*, J. Cohen, ed., 1978; *Women See Woman*, 1976; *Light⁷*, Minor White, ed., 1968.

COLLECTION Chrysler Mus., Norfolk, Va.

ADDRESS Visual Design Dept., Southeastern Mass. Univ., N Dartmouth, MA 02747.

Jay McKean Fisher CURATOR Born June 3, 1949 in Portland, Oregon, Fisher received a BA from Occidental College, Los Angeles (1971), and an MA from the Clark Art Institute of Williams College, Williamstown, Massachusetts (1975). His early interest in photography was sparked by Charles Millard.

Since 1975 Fisher has been associate curator of prints, drawings, and photographs at the Baltimore (Maryland) Museum of Art. Previously, he served as an assistant in the Department of Prints and Drawings at the Sterling and Francine Clark Art Institute, Williamstown (1974–75), and as a curatorial aide at the J. Paul Getty Museum, Malibu, California (1971).

Fisher belongs to the Print Council of America, International Council of Museums, American Association of Museums, Washington Print Club, and, since 1978, has been president of the Print and Drawing Society of Baltimore. The curator won a Samuel H. Kress Foundation Fellowship in 1975 and Clark Art Institute fellowships in 1974 and 1973.

His curatorial interests include nineteenth-century French photography, twentieth-century American photography and a special concentration on photographers in the Baltimore and Washington, D.C., areas.

PUBLICATIONS Catalogs: *Five Maryland Photographers*, 1980; *The Hand of Man: Railroads in American Prints and Photographs*, 1978 (Baltimore Mus. of Art).

ADDRESS Dept of Prints, Drawings and Photographs, Baltimore Museum of Art, Art Museum Dr, Baltimore, MD 21218.

Shirley I. Fisher *PHOTOGRAPHER · TEACHER* Born in Cleveland, Ohio, Fisher received her BFA and MFA (1959) in Photography from Ohio University, Athens. She names Betty Truxell and Walter Allen as mentors.

A photography instructor at De Anza College in Cupertino, California, since 1967, she has been chairman of the school's Photography Department since 1975. At San Jose State University, California, she was a photography instructor in 1966 and college photographer from 1963 to 1970. She has also taught photography at Foothill College (1965–67) and Detroit Community Center (1960–63). Fisher was a photographer at Ford Hospital from 1961 to 1963 and a commercial photographer from 1959 to 1961.

A member of SPE, Friends of Photography and San Francisco Women Artists, and a former member of Biological Photographic Association (1961–63), Fisher won several grants for photographic research from De Anza College in 1970. Her work was included in the film *New Photographics, '71*, produced by Central Washington State College.

The photographer's major thrust since 1958 has been "inner-landscape post-visualization, multiple black-and-white printing, experimental explorations." She also has done traditional black-and-white landscapes since 1954 and is interested in traditional and experimental use of color.

PUBLICATIONS Books: *The Rug Book*, 1979; *To Discover, To Delight*, Bolton & Wilson, 1977; *Psychology for a Changing World*, P. Smith, 1965. Anthologies: *Petersen's Big Book of Photography*, Nov 1977; *Object and Image*, G. M. Craven, 1975; *Octave of Prayer*, 1972; *Young California Photographers*, 1972. Periodical: *Petersen's PhotoGraphic*, Mar 1978.

COLLECTIONS Norfolk Mus. of Art, Va.; Ohio Univ., Athens. Bibliothèque Nationale, Paris; and private collections.

DEALERS Focus Gall., 2146 Union St, San Francisco, CA 94123; Print Gall., Delores & 6 St, Carmel, CA 93921; Status Gall., Box 1786, Park City, UT 84060.

ADDRESS POB 1081, Cupertino, CA 95015.

Katherine Fishman *PHOTOGRAPHER · PAINTER · TEACHER* Born February 4, 1951, in Fort Wayne, Indiana, Fishman received her AB in Art from Kenyon College, Gambier, Ohio (1973), and her MFA from Indiana University, Bloomington (1976), where she studied with Henry Holmes Smith.

Since 1978 she has been assistant professor of Art at Wright State University, Dayton, Ohio. In 1977–78 she was a CETA artist for the Dayton City Beautiful Council, photographing women in historic architectural interiors.

Fishman is a member of SPE, CAA and Popular Culture Association. She received a Research Incentive Grant from the Research Council, Wright State University, in 1979 and a Doctoral Grant-in-Aid for Research from Indiana University in 1976.

She describes her work as "large painted photographs."

PUBLICATIONS Periodicals: "Midwest Art: A Special Report, Indianapolis, Cincinnati, Dayton," Holiday T. Day, *Art in America*, July/Aug 1979; "Images: Katherine Fishman," *Le Nouveau Photocinéma*, May 1977.

COLLECTIONS Corcoran Gall. of Art, Wash., D.C.; Dayton Art Inst., Dayton, Ohio; Ind. Univ., Bloomington.

DEALERS Andover Gall., 91 N Main, Andover, MA 01810; Foto, 492 Broome St, New York, NY 10013; Nancy Lurie Gall., 1632 N LaSalle St, Chicago, IL 60614.

ADDRESS c/o Betty Oettel, 2405 Cedar Canyons Rd, Fort Wayne, IN 46825.

George Fiske *PHOTOGRAPHER* Born in Amherst, New Hampshire, on October 22, 1835, Fiske died at Yosemite, California, on October 20, 1918. Fiske left home and traveled to Sacramento in 1858, where he worked as a banker, a clerk, a farmer (in San Jose) and finally as an assistant photographer, first to Carleton Watkins at his Yo-Semite Gallery (1868), then to Thomas Houseworth, both of San Francisco. In 1874 he returned to work for Watkins, who had changed his business name to Yosemite Art Gallery. In 1875 Fiske went with Watkins to Yosemite Valley, photographing there through the summer and fall. When Watkins lost his gallery, Fiske went into partnership with Charles Staples, running a boardinghouse (1876–77). From the time of its dissolution he remained in the photographic trade, working in Marin and Santa Clara counties. He probably traveled through Sequoia Valley with Eadweard Muybridge in 1872, and for many years was close friends with Yosemite's caretaker, the conservationist Galen Clark. In 1879 he moved to Yosemite Valley, where he resided for nearly forty years, all year round.

He received a silver medal at the Eighteenth Industrial Exhibition held at the pavilion of the Mechanics' Institute of San Francisco in 1883. Mainly known for his landscape views of Yosemite, views that "present eloquent visual testimony that he was a pantheistic worshipper of nature," Fiske also produced images of California's elegant seaside resorts, crumbling Franciscan missions and, predating Edward Weston by forty years, the pounding surf off Point Lobos. He was seen winters, his equipment loaded onto a sled, and summers, pushing his "cloud-chasing chariot," a wheelbarrow, loaded down with his 11 x 14 plate camera.

PUBLICATIONS Books: *The Big Trees of California*, Galen Clark, 1907; *In the Heart of the Sierras*, J. M. Hutchings, 1886; *Yosemite and the Big Trees of California*, 1881; *Pacific Coast Scenery*, 1872. Periodical: "Fiske's Views of Yosemite and Big Trees," *The Sentinel of Yosemite*, 1885.

COLLECTION CCP, Tucson.

Judith Anne Fiskin PHOTOGRAPHER Born April 1, 1945, Fiskin received her MA from University of California at Los Angeles in 1969, having also done graduate work at University of California, Berkeley (1966–67). She earned her BA from Pomona College in 1966 and studied at the University of Paris' Institute of Art and Archaeology in 1964–65.

Fiskin became associate dean of art and design at the California Institute of the Arts, Valencia, in 1979, and since 1977 has been an instructor in photography at the college. In 1973 she was co-director of Womanspace Gallery in Los Angeles and from 1969 to 1970 edited the *Notebooks* of architect Richard Neutra.

The photographer won an NEA photo survey grant in 1979 for a project about Long Beach, California.

Her work focuses on the landscape and architecture of Southern California. She uses small- and medium-format black-and-white images.

PUBLICATIONS Monograph: *31 Views of San Bernardino*, 1975. Periodicals (criticism): "Judy

Fiskin's Photographs," Richard Armstrong, *Journal: So. Calif. Art Magazine*, Sept/Oct 1979; *Art News*, Janet Kutner, Dec 1977, Hazlitt Gordon, Jan 1976.

COLLECTIONS Calif. Inst. of the Arts, Valencia; Calif. State Univ., Los Angeles; Dallas Mus. of Fine Art; La Jolla Mus. of Contemporary Art, Calif.; Natl. Archive, Wash., D.C.

DEALER Castelli Graphics, 4 E 77 St, New York, NY 10021.

ADDRESS 629 N Harper Ave, Los Angeles, CA 90048.

Steven Ralph Fitch PHOTOGRAPHER · TEACHER Born in Tucson, Arizona, on August 16, 1949, Fitch earned a BA in Anthropology from University of California, Berkeley, in 1971 and an MA in Photography from University of New Mexico, Albuquerque, in 1978. He names Roger Minick as his mentor.

A guest lecturer at the University of Colorado, Boulder, in 1979, Fitch was a photography instructor at the University of New Mexico, Albuquerque (1978–79). He was a teacher/supervisor at the ASUC Studio at University of California, Berkeley (1971–77).

A member of SPE, Fitch won NEA photography grants in 1973 and 1975. In the film medium, he made a one-minute television spot for the Society of Nutritional Education, Berkeley, California, in 1976.

Fitch's primary photographic interest is the American landscape, in particular the highway and urban-strip environment. Much of his work is done at dusk or night.

PUBLICATIONS Monograph: *Diesels and Dinosaurs*, 1976. Catalogs: *Beyond Color*, 1980 (San Francisco Museum of Modern Art: Calif.); *Attitudes: Photography in the Seventies*, 1979 (Santa Barbara Mus. of Modern Art: Calif.); *The Aesthetics of Graffiti*, 1978 (San Francisco Mus. of Modern Art: Calif.); *130 Years of Ohio Photography*, 1978 (Columbus Mus. of Art: Oh.); *Young American Photographers*, 1975 (Kalamazoo Inst. of Arts: Mich.); *Light & Substance*, 1973 (Univ. of N. Mex. Art Mus.: Albuquerque). Periodicals: *Picture Magazine*, Apr 1979; *Popular Photography Annual*, 1977; *Exposure: SPE*, May 1975.

PORTFOLIO *New California Views* (group), 1979 (Landweber/Artists: Los Angeles).

COLLECTIONS Atlantic Richfield Corp., Los Angeles; Calif. Mus. of Photography, Riverside; CCP, Tucson; Denver Art Mus., Colo.; Harvard Univ., Fogg Art Mus., Cambridge, Mass.; Houston Mus. of Fine Arts; Kalamazoo Inst. of Arts, Mich.; La Jolla Mus. of Art, Calif.; Lincoln First

Bank, Rochester; Miami-Dade Jr. Coll., Fla.; Minneapolis Inst. of the Arts, Minn.; MOMA, NYC; Mus. of Fine Arts, Boston; N. Mex. State Univ., Las Cruces; Newport Harbor Art Mus., Newport Beach, Calif.; Oakland Mus., Calif.; R.I. School of Design Art Mus., Providence; Security Pacific Natl. Bank, Los Angeles; Tyler Mus. of Art, Tex.; UCLA, Grunwald Ctr. for the Graphic Arts; Univ. of Neb., Sheldon Art Gall, Lincoln; Univ. of N. Mex. Art Mus., Albuquerque; Univ. of Okla. Mus. of Art, Norman. Australian Natl. Gall., Canberra, New South Wales.

REPRESENTATIVES Simon Lowinsky Gall., 228 Grant Ave, San Francisco, CA 94108; Susan Spiritus Gall., 3336 Via Lido, Newport Beach, CA 92660.

ADDRESS POB 4626, Berkeley, CA 94704.

Armand Hippolyte Louis Fizeau PHYSICIST Born in Paris on September 23, 1819, Fizeau died on September 18, 1896, in Nanteiulle-Haudoulin, France.

Intrigued by Daguerre's process after its announcement in 1839, Fizeau spent the next few years working with Alfred Donné on the conversion of daguerreotypes into intaglio printing plates. In August 1840 he introduced a major improvement in the daguerreotype process: gold-toning, which protected the daguerreotype from abrasion and tarnishing. On March 1, 1841, Fizeau announced the production of electrotype printing plates from daguerreotypes, and two of his etched plates were reproduced in *Excursions Daguerriennes* in 1842. The physicist unsuccessfully tried to produce stereo daguerreotypes in 1842, but in 1844, working in collaboration with J. B. Léon Foucault, he discovered the reciprocity failure of daguerreotypes. In the same year he made studies in the field of photographic photometry, and on April 2, 1845, along with Foucault, made the first daguerreotype photographs of the sun.

Fizeau became a member of the French Academy in 1860 and was appointed superintendent of physics at the Ecole Polytechnique, Paris, in 1863.

PUBLICATIONS Books: *Quellendarstellungen zur Geschichte der Fotografie*, Wolfgang Baier, 1964; *Encyclopedia of Photography*, 1963 (Greystone Press); *Brevets d'Invention Français 1791–1902*, 1958; *March of Photography*, Erich Stenger, 1958; *History of Photography*, Helmut & Alison Gernsheim, 1955; *Histoire de la Photographie*, Raymond Lécuyer, 1945; *A History and Handbook of Photography*, Gaston Tissandier, 1876. Anthology: *Photography's Great Inventors*, Louis W. Sipley, 1965. Periodicals: *Image*, May 1952; *Bild und Ton*, 1951, 1949; *British Journal of Photography*, 1926; *Photographic News*, 1895.

Frances Hubbard Flaherty FILM MAKER · PHOTOGRAPHER · LECTURER Born ca. 1886 in Cambridge, Massachusetts, Flaherty died on June 22, 1972, in Dummerston, Vermont. Her husband, Robert Joseph Flaherty (1884–1951), was a documentary film maker and photographer. Frances graduated from Bryn Mawr College in Bryn Mawr, Pa., in 1905.

She collaborated with her husband, whom she married in 1914, assisting him on many of his films while documenting the films' production in still photographs. After his death she lectured on his work at universities and film clubs. She co-founded the Robert J. Flaherty Foundation (now International Film Seminars) in 1951.

She co-edited *Moana* (1926), served as assistant scenarist and photographer on *Man of Aran* (1934) and co-wrote *Louisiana Story* (1948), all documentary films by Robert Flaherty.

Flaherty's silver prints were dramatic documents of the places and people she and her husband lived in and among while making their documentary films. The photographs embody the starkness and dignity of working-class people and of primitive peoples doing battle with the elements.

PUBLICATIONS Books: *The Odyssey of a Film-Maker: Robert Flaherty's Story*, 1960, repr. 1972 (Arno Press); *Sabu, the Elephant Boy*, w/Ursula Leacock, 1938 (J. M. Dent: London); *Elephant Dance*, preface by John Collier, 1937; *My Eskimo Friends, "Nanook of the North,"* w/Robert Flaherty, 1924.

Robert Joseph Flaherty FILM MAKER · PHOTOGRAPHER Born February 16, 1884, in Iron Mountain, Michigan, Flaherty died July 23, 1951, in Dunnerston, Vermont. His wife, Frances Hubbard Flaherty, was also a photographer and film maker. He studied at Upper Canada College, Toronto, and the Michigan College of Mines.

Flaherty first worked with his father, searching out iron deposits in Canada for the U.S. Steel Corp., and also worked in a Michigan iron mine. He then spent two years exploring the Canadian wilds before finding expedition sponsorship from Sir William Mackenzie, builder of the Canadian Northern Railroad. During expeditions from 1910 to 1916, Flaherty mapped the Baffin Land, northern Ungava and the Belcher's Island areas. In appreciation, Canada named one of the islands after Flaherty. In 1920–21 he filmed Eskimo life, under the sponsorship of the fur company Revillon Frères, which resulted in his first documentary film, *Nanook of the North*. Flaherty continued to make films and photograph native peoples until his death.

Acknowledged as the "father of the documentary," Flaherty produced, wrote and directed the following films: *Louisiana Story*, 1948; *The Land*, 1942; *Elephant Boy*, 1937; *Man of Aran*, 1934; *Tabu* and *Industrial Britain*, 1933; *White Shadows of the South Seas*, 1928; *The Twenty-Four Dollar Island*, 1927; *Moana*, 1926; *The Pottery-Maker*, 1925; *Nanook of the North*, 1922.

His still photographs, like his films, are powerful documents of the struggle of primitive peoples against the hostile forces of nature. At the same time they capture the aesthetic beauty of the exotic peoples he photographed and the places where they lived.

PUBLICATIONS Monographs: *Nanook of the North*, Robert Kraus, ed., 1971; *Robert Joseph Flaherty, Présentation*, Henri Agel, 1965 (Seghers: Paris); *Robert Flaherty*, Wolfgang Klane, ed., 1964 (Henschelverlag: Berlin); *The Innocent Eye*, P. Rotha & B. Wright, 1963 (Allen: London); *The Odyssey of a Film-Maker: Robert Flaherty's Story*, Frances Flaherty, 1960, repr. 1972 (Arno Press); *The World of Robert Flaherty*, Richard Griffith, 1953; *Robert Flaherty, Nota Biografica, Filmografia e Bibliografia*, Mario Gromp, 1952 (Guanda: Parma). Books: *Robert Flaherty: A Guide to References and Resources*, Wm. T. Murphy, 1978; *The Captain's Chair, a Story of the North*, 1938 (Hodder & Stoughton: London); *Samoa*, 1932 (R. Hobbing: Berlin); *My Eskimo Friends, "Nanook of the North,"* w/Frances Flaherty, 1924.

COLLECTION IMP/GEH, Rochester.

Robbert Flick PHOTOGRAPHER · TEACHER
Born November 15, 1939, in Amersfoort, The Netherlands, Flick received his BA from the University of British Columbia, Vancouver, Canada (1967), and his MA and MFA (1970, 1971) from University of California, Los Angeles, where he studied with Robert Heineken.

From 1976 to 1978 Flick taught photography at the University of Southern California, Los Angeles, as assistant professor, and as of this writing is an associate professor of art. He previously taught at the University of Illinois, Urbana-Champaign (1971–76), as instructor until 1973 and then as assistant professor.

Flick belongs to SPE, CAA, the Graphic Arts Council in Los Angeles and the Los Angeles Center for Photographic Studies. He received Canada Council bursaries in 1967 and 1969 and was named a fellow at the Center for Advanced Studies of the University of Illinois in 1973.

The photographer works mainly in black-and-white and is "predominately involved in landscape photography." Some of his series of photographs have been entitled "L.A. Diary," "Midwest Diary," "Wall Series" and "Inglewood Diary."

PUBLICATIONS Book: *Three Ring Circus Songs*, w/Hulcoop, 1968. Anthology: *Photographer's Choice*, 1975. Periodicals: *Afterimage*, vol. 8, 1980; *Light Vision 8*, Nov 1978.

PORTFOLIO *Silver see* (group), 1977 (Los Angeles Ctr. for Photographic Studies).

COLLECTIONS Addison Gall. of Amer. Art, Andover, Mass.; Art Inst. of Chicago; CCP, Tucson; Florida Ctr. for the Arts, Tampa; Harvard Univ., Fogg Art Mus., Cambridge; IMP/GEH, Rochester; Jacksonville Art Mus., Fla.; Norton Simon Mus., Pasadena, Calif.; UCLA, Frederick S. Wight Galls.; VSW, Rochester. Natl. Film Board of Canada.

DEALER Light Gall., 800 N La Cienega, Los Angeles, CA 90069.

ADDRESS 707 E Hyde Park Blvd, Inglewood, CA 90302.

Camillus Sidney (Buck) Fly PHOTOGRAPHER
Born in Andrew County, Missouri, in 1849, Fly died October 12, 1901, in Bisbee, Arizona. His wife, Mary E. (Mollie) Goodrich Fly, was also a photographer.

The self-taught Fly was raised in California; he and his wife moved to Tombstone, Arizona, in 1879, during the silver strike. First setting up shop in a tent, they built a combination boarding-house and photographic studio. Mollie operated the shop during Camillus' frequent field trips, on which he combined photography with prospecting. In 1892 he was commissioned by an English syndicate to take a series of pictures of the Chiricahua Mountains, which were later displayed in London. From 1894 to 1896 he served as sheriff of Cochise County. From 1880 on he was frequently published in the *Tombstone Epitaph*.

The state of Arizona named one of its highest mountains—Fly Peak in the Chiricahua range—in the photographer's honor. He was a member of the Ancient Order of United Workers.

Fly documented daily life and growth of Tombstone on his glass plate negatives, as well as photographing the surrounding mountains and deserts, which he loved. Accompanying General George Crook, he was able to photograph Geronimo before his capture. The pioneering photographer gained a fair amount of fame in the southeastern territory during his lifetime.

PUBLICATIONS Anthology: *Photographers of the Frontier West*, Ralph Andrews, 1965. Periodicals: *Tombstone Epitaph National Edition*, Apr 1979; *Harper's Weekly*, Apr 24, 1886.

Neil H. Folberg PHOTOGRAPHER Born April 7, 1950, in San Francisco, California, Folberg earned a BA in Photographic Field Studies (1972) from the University of California, Berkeley, under the supervision of William Garnett. From 1966 to 1976 he studied privately with Ansel Adams.

He was awarded a President's Undergraduate Fellowship at University of California, Berkeley, for photographic field work in Macedonia.

Folberg has been self-employed since 1972. Before 1976 he did work of a documentary nature, including studies of Yugoslav Macedonia and Lubavitcher Hasidic Jews in the U.S. and Canada. His most recent photographs have been of Jerusalem and color landscapes of the Sinai.

PUBLICATION Monograph: *Portfolio One: Glimpses of Lubavitcher Life*, 1975 (Bet-Alpha Press: Berkeley).

COLLECTIONS Sam Wagstaff Cllctn., NYC; Smithsonian Inst., Wash., D.C.; Israel Mus., Jerusalem; Mus. für Kunst, Hamburg, Germany; Stedelijk Mus., Amsterdam, The Netherlands.

DEALERS Douglas Elliott Gall., 1151 Mission St, San Francisco, CA 94103; Daniel Wolf, 30 W 57 St, New York, NY 10019; Galerie Fiolet, Herengracht 86, Amsterdam, The Netherlands.

ADDRESS Ma'alot Dafna 139/13, Jerusalem, Israel.

Harvey V. Fondiller EDITOR · WRITER · PHOTOGRAPHER Born on December 24, 1920, in New York City, Fondiller received his education in his native city, earning a BA (1940) and an MFA (1962) from Columbia University.

Since 1971 he has been a contributing editor and critic for *Popular Photography*, where he started working as an associate editor and movie/video editor. Previously, he was hired as a staff writer for the National Broadcasting Company (1955–60), an associate editor for *U.S. Camera* magazine (1948–49) and a writer-photographer for the U.S. Army Berlin District (1946). In addition, he has been involved in teaching in New York City at City University of New York (1974–78), New School for Social Research (1972–73) and Columbia University School of the Arts (1971–72).

Fondiller belongs to SPE and to the Historical Society of New York, for which he served on the board of directors (1972–79) and was nominated a fellow (1978). In 1962 he received the Samuel French Award in Playwriting, and has to his credit four plays published by Drama Book Shop in New York City (1962–63). His achievements also include 70 film segments made for NBC-TV (1953–54) and a 16mm film, *Audubon the Naturalist* which he directed for the Photo Library (1955). In addition, from 1948 to 1979 he wrote approximately 400 articles that appeared in photographic magazines.

PUBLICATIONS (editor) Books: *The Popular Photography Answer Book*, 1980; *The Encyclopedia of Photography*, 1974; *Invitation to Photography* & *35mm Photography* (four editions), 1967–74. Anthology: *The Best of Popular Photography*, 1979.

ADDRESS 915 West End Ave, New York, NY 10025.

Franco Fontana PHOTOGRAPHER Born December 9, 1933, in Modena, Italy, Fontana is a self-taught freelance photographer.

Working strictly in color, he is a "minimalist landscape photographer," wrote Sean Callahan. "Fontana distills the essence of a photograph into lines of color," he added (*American Photographer*, October 1978).

PUBLICATIONS Monograph: *Franco Fontana*, 1976 (Univ. of Parma: Italy). Books: *Paesaggio urbano*, 1980; *Presenze veneziane*, 1980; *Skyline*, 1978; *Laggiù gli uomini*, 1977; *Bologna il volto della città*, 1975; *Terra da leggere*, 1974; *Modena una città*, 1971.

COLLECTIONS IMP/GEH, Rochester; MOMA, NYC; San Francisco Mus. of Modern Art; Univ. of N. Mex. Art Mus., Albuquerque; Univ. of Tex., Austin. Australian Natl. Gall., Canberra; Bibliothèque Nationale, Paris; Israel Art Book Mus., Jerusalem; Kunsthaus Mus., Zurich, Switzerland; Musée d'Art et d'Histoire, Fribourg, Switzerland; Musée de la Photographie Réattu, Arles, France; Natl. Gall. of Victoria, Melbourne, Australia; Photographic Mus. of Finland, Helsinki; Tasmanian Mus. & Art Gall., Australia; Università di Parma, Museo della Fotografia, Italy; York Univ., Downsview, Canada.

ADDRESS Via R. Benzi # 40, 41010 Cognento (Modena), Italy.

Joan Fontcuberta PHOTOGRAPHER · WRITER · TEACHER [See plate 128] Born February 24, 1955, in Barcelona, Spain, the self-taught photographer graduated from the Faculty of Communications,

University of Barcelona, in 1977, having studied journalism and advertising.

Currently a teacher at his alma mater's Faculty of Fine Arts and at the Center for Image Studies in Barcelona (since 1978), he also directs a bi-weekly photography section in Spain's largest newspaper, *La Vanguardia* (since 1979). From 1977 to 1978 Fontcuberta wrote a weekly column on photography in the Barcelona newspaper *El Correo Catalan* and taught photography at the Department of Technology, Faculty of Communications, Barcelona. He has been a freelance photographer since 1976.

Fontcuberta founded the Alabern Group of Spanish creative photographers in 1976.

Using black-and-white and selenium-toned prints, Fontcuberta describes his work as "anti-documentalistic aesthetics." He says, "Not worried about objects by themselves, I try to find the absurd between objects' relations." He has a strong interest in textures and sensual images.

PUBLICATIONS Books: *Pintades*, 1977 (Ed. La Gaia Ciència: Barcelona); *Duchamp no ha comprendido Rembrandt*, 1976 (Galería "G": Barcelona). Periodicals: *Camera*, Nov 1980; *Zoom*, no. 67, 1979 (Paris); *Creative Camera Year Book 1978*; *Zoom*, Josep Rigol, no. 20, 1978 (Madrid); *Fotografie*, Sept 1978; *Fotografia Italiana*, June 1978; *Progresso Fotografico*, Roberto Salbitani, June 1977; *Flash-Foto*, no. 6, 1975.

COLLECTIONS Metro. Mus. of Art, NYC. Bibliothèque Nationale, Paris; Centro Cultural Hidalgo, Mexico; Fundació Joan Miró, Barcelona; Musée Réattu, Arles, France.

REPRESENTATIVES Canon Photo Gallery, 3 rue St. Leger, Geneva, Switzerland; Canon Photo Gallery, Amsterdam, The Netherlands; Galerie Agathe Gaillard, 3 rue de Pont-Louis-Philippe, Paris, France; Galeria Tretze, Valencia, Spain; Paule Pia Fotogaleri, Kammenstraat 57, Antwerp, Belgium; The Photographers' Gall., 8 Great Newport St, London WC2, England; Work Gall., Zurich, Switzerland.

ADDRESS Avda Infanta Carlota, 113 4º, Barcelona 29, Spain.

Heather Mary Forbes · PUBLISHER · PHOTOGRAPHER Born December 21, 1948, in Christchurch, New Zealand, Forbes earned a diploma in photography (1975) from Trent Polytechnic, Nottingham, England. Her major influences were John Mulvany and Thomas Cooper. Forbes' grandfather, George Forbes, was Prime Minister of New Zealand from 1930 to 1935.

Since 1978 Forbes has been director of Travelling Light, a publishing and distributing company based in London, and has done production management for the Arts Council of Great Britain's photography books. Previously (1975–76) Forbes was a bookshop assistant at The Photographers' Gallery in London.

She received a New Zealand Arts Council Grant for photography and photohistory research in 1977.

PUBLICATIONS Anthology: *New British Image*, 1977 (Arts Council of Great Britain: London). Periodicals: *British Journal of Photography Annual*, 1977; *Creative Camera International Yearbook*, 1977; *Foto*, Jan 1977; *Nueva Lente*, July/Aug 1976.

DEALER The Photographers' Gall., 8 Great Newport St, London, WC2 England.

ADDRESS 14 Cromford Rd, London SW18 INX, England.

Bonnie Ford CURATOR · PHOTOGRAPHER · TEACHER Born February 24, 1945, in Salt Lake City, Utah, Ford received a BS in Mathematics from the University of Utah, Salt Lake City (1967), and received an MFA in Fine Arts from the University of Arizona, Tucson, in 1980. She has studied with Ruth Bernhard, Paul Caponigro, Al Weber and Arnold Gassan.

Currently curator and registrar at the Weston Gallery in Carmel, California, Ford taught photography at the University of Utah (1976–77). She has been a member of SPE since 1978.

Ford won graduate academic scholarships from the University of Arizona in 1978 and 1979 and a Polaroid Fellowship and Curatorial Traineeship in 1978 from the Center for Creative Photography, Tucson, Arizona.

PUBLICATIONS Anthology: *Self-Portrayal*, Jim Alinder, ed., 1978. Catalogs: *Ernest Bloch Archive*, intro., 1979 (CCP: Tucson); *Ernest Bloch: Photographer and Composer*, 1979 (CCP: Tucson).

COLLECTION Utah State Div. of Fine Arts, Salt Lake City.

ADDRESS POB 6414, Carmel, CA 93921.

Trevor Nelson Ford PHOTOGRAPHER · WRITER Born June 14, 1953, in Northampton, England, Ford attended the West Sussex College of Design (1970–71) and the Swansea College of Art (1971–75), both in England. His major influences have been Henri Cartier-Bresson, Diane Arbus and Don McCullin.

Currently Ford is an assistant photographer for London Borough of Lambeth. He previously worked as a color technician at Elficolor/Woodmansterne Colourslides 1977–79.

Ford is a licentiate of the Society of the Industrial Artists and Designers and a member of the National and Local Government Offices Association, both in London. He was the recipient of an award from the Arts Council of Great Britain in May 1976.

PUBLICATIONS Anthology: *New British Image*, 1977 (Arts Council of Great Britain). Periodicals: *Photography Yearbook*, 1978; *Photo Technique Magazine*, July 1975.

ADDRESS 5 Sunnymead Close, Selsey, Chichester, West Sussex P020 ODB, England.

Oscar-Louis Forel *PSYCHIATRIST · PHOTOGRAPHER · WRITER · NATURALIST* Born September 20, 1891, in Zurich, Switzerland, Forel studied literature at the Sorbonne in Paris (1911–12) and medicine under César Roux at Lausanne (1912–18). His father, Auguste Forel (1848–1931), was a well known entomologist, anatomist and psychiatrist. Oscar's uncles were also prominent figures: François-Alphonse Forel (1841–1912) was an anatomist and founder of limnology, and Alexis Forel (1851–1922) was a chemist and founder of Musée Alexis Forel at Morges, Switzerland.

Oscar-Louis Forel directed the psychiatric clinic La Métairie in Nyon from 1924 to 1929, then founded and directed the psychiatric clinic Les Rives de Prangins in Nyon (1929–46). From 1925 to 1953 he taught at the University of Geneva.

Forel was president of La Société Suisse de Psychiatric, and was awarded the Legion of Honor by Charles de Gaulle in 1945.

As a photographer, he makes color prints of tree bark and wood, viewed extremely close up and framed to look like nonrepresentational painting. He calls his well-structured compositions "synchromies."

PUBLICATIONS Monographs: *Synchromies*, n.d. (du Temps: Paris; Edita: Lausanne), U.S. ed., *Hidden Art in Nature*, 1972; *Etude sur le Rythme*, 1920. Books: *F. -C. de Laharpe*, w/ Boethlink, 1969 (La Baconnière: Neuchâtel); *L'Accord des sexes*, 1953; *Mémoires*, ed., 1941 (La Baconnière: Neuchâtel); *Manuel de Psychiatrie*, 1940; *La psychologie des névroses*, 1925; *Visions secrétes*, w/David Douglas Duncan.

COLLECTION Le Manoir de St. Prex, Vaud, Switzerland.

REPRESENTATIVE Edita S. A. Lausanne, Le Manoir de St. Prex, Switzerland.

ADDRESS Le Manoir de St. Prex, rue Forel 15, St. Prex, Switzerland.

Stanley J. Forman *PHOTOGRAPHER* Born July 10, 1945, in Winthrop, Massachusetts, Forman studied at Franklin Institute Photography Department in 1965. He was a Nieman Fellow in Journalism at Harvard University, Cambridge, in 1979.

Since 1966 he has been a photographer for the *Boston Herald American* and from 1964 to 1966 was a freelance photographer. His photographs have appeared in such periodicals as *Newsweek*, *Time* and *Life*.

Forman is vice-president of the Boston Press Photographers Association and belongs to the NPA. He has won numerous awards, including the Pulitzer Prize in feature photography, staff award, in 1979, Boston Press Photographer of the year in 1978, American Academy of Achievement "Golden Plate" Award in 1977, the Pulitzer Prize for news photography in 1976 and 1977, the University of Missouri "News Photo of the Year" in 1976 and 1977, Headliners Club "Picture of the Year" in 1976 and 1977, World Press "Photo of the Year" in 1976 (The Hague), United Press International "Picture of the Year" in 1976, 1977, and 1978, International Firefighters Award in 1976 and 1977 and Associated Press "Spot News Picture of the Year" in 1967 and 1976. Forman was a National Press Photographer of the Year regional winner in 1973 and 1978.

PUBLICATION Anthology: *Moments*, Sheryle & John Leekley, 1978.

ADDRESS c/o *Boston Herald American*, 300 Harrison Ave, Boston, MA 02106.

Ellen Valworth Foscue-Johnson *PHOTOGRAPHER · TEACHER* Born in High Point, North Carolina, on August 18, 1938, Foscue-Johnson earned her BA magna cum laude from Duke University, Durham, North Carolina, in 1960. She received her MA in 1964 from Columbia University, New York City, majoring in English and comparative literature.

A freelance photographer, she also has given workshops or guest lectures on photography at the International Center of Photography, New York City; Peters Valley Craftsmen, Layton, New Jersey; Wellesley College, Massachusetts; and the University of Vermont, Burlington, among others.

The photographer works in large format, printing with platinum and palladium processes.

PUBLICATIONS Monograph: *The Garden Way Bread Book*, 1979. Book: *Childhood Development Research*, James J. Gallagher, ed., 1975. Anthologies: *Women See Men*, 1977; *The Rights of Children*, 1974.

COLLECTIONS Addison Gall. of Amer. Art, Andover, Mass.; Dartmouth Coll., Hopkins Art Ctr., Hanover, N.H.

REPRESENTATIVE Southern Vermont Art Center, Manchester, VT.

ADDRESS Terrible Mountain, Weston, VT 05161.

Janet Green Foster *TV COMMENTATOR · PHOTOGRAPHER · WRITER · HISTORIAN* Born 1940 in Ottawa, Canada, Foster received her BA in 1969, MA in 1970 and PhD in 1976 from York University, Toronto.

As of this writing Foster was doing freelance work.

Foster is a member of the Association of Canadian Radio and Television Artists, and was co-host and narrator of twenty-three CBC-TV specials entitled "Wild Canada" and "To the Wild Country."

Her photography focuses on nature and wildlife, including all aspects of Canadian wilderness, rural life and scenery.

PUBLICATIONS Books: *Cabin Full of Mice*, 1980; *Working for Wildlife*, 1978; *To the Wild Country*, 1975.

COLLECTION National Film Board of Canada, Ottawa.

REPRESENTATIVE Image Bank of Canada, Carlton St, Ste 901 Toronto, Canada.

Jean Bernard Léon Foucault *PHYSICIST* Foucault was born September 18, 1819, and died February 11, 1868, in Paris. He was educated in the medical profession.

The physicist's first published essay on any subject concerned the best method of using bromine in making daguerreotypes (November 1841). His other daguerreotype researches included collaboration with Hippolyte Fizeau on the reciprocity failure of daguerreotypes (1844), and he and Fizeau made a daguerreotype of the sun in 1845 with a "guillotine" type of shutter. With Alfred Donne, Foucault experimented with photomicrography and published the first photomicrographic reproductions (copper engravings made from daguerreotypes) in the book *Atlas du Cours de Microscopie*, in 1845. In 1846 Foucault published his experiments on the effects of red rays on daguerreotype plates and light-sensitive surfaces, and wrote on photometry and light interference. Appointed an astronomer at the Paris Observatory in 1855, he developed a method for photographing a solar eclipse, devised in 1860; this was used by others in 1870 and 1871. Albert Londe used Foucault's invention of a governor to control the operation of a chronophotographic apparatus in 1880.

One of the founders of the Société Française de Photographie, on November 15, 1854, Foucault was best known for his researches on the pendulum, the measurement of air velocities and production of the first mirror telescope. He also wrote on stereoscopic vision and optics. The "Foucault pendulum" received the Copley Medal of the Royal Society of London in 1855, and he gave his name to "Foucault [eddy] currents."

PUBLICATIONS Books: *Encyclopedie voor Fotografie en Cinematografie*, Elsevier, 1958; *March of Photography*, Erich Stenger, 1958; *Histoire de la Photographie*, Raymond Lécuyer, 1945; *Lexikon für Photographie und Reproduktionstechnik*, G. H. Emmerich, 1910; *Rescueil des Travaux Scientifiques de Léon Foucault*, Gabriel & Bertrand, 1878. Anthology: *Photography's Great Inventors*, Louis W. Sipley, 1965. Periodicals: *Bild und Ton*, 1951; *Photographic News*, 1895.

Flo Fox *PHOTOGRAPHER · STYLIST · TEACHER* Born September 26, 1945, in Miami, Florida, Fox considers her major influences to be Bill Brandt, Brassaï, Diane Arbus and Lisette Model.

Currently a teacher of photography at The Lighthouse for the Blind in New York City, she taught at Human Resources Center, Albertson, Long Island, New York, in 1979. She was an advertising stylist and tailor from 1971 to 1976 and made costumes for the New York Shakespeare Festival in 1973, 1974 and 1976.

Fox was a winner in the *Village Voice* Photography Contest in 1976, and won a Clio Award in 1971 as a stylist for a Revlon commercial.

She describes her work as reportage that looks "for the ironic . . . a touch of humor or hard-core reality." Her photographs include "street people, phallic symbols, reflections, cemeteries, and signs of the times."

PUBLICATIONS Anthologies: *Decade of Women*, 1980; *Women Photograph Men*, 1977; *Women See Men*, 1977; *Women See Woman*, 1976. Periodicals: *Camera 35*, July & Mar, 1978; *Popular Photography's 35mm Photography*, 1974.

ADDRESS 30 Perry St, New York, NY 10014.

Sharon Lee Fox *PHOTOGRAPHER · TEACHER* Born June 3, 1946, in Mt. Vernon, New York, Fox received a BA in Fine Arts from the American University, Washington, D.C., in 1968 and an MS in Art Education from Massachusetts College of Art, Boston, in 1973. She earned an MFA in Photography from Lone Mountain College, San Francisco, California, in 1978.

In 1979 she became a photography instructor at the Art Institute of Boston and since 1978 has been summer resident photography instructor at the Main Photographic Workshops, Rockport. From 1976 to 1977 she was in the Artist-in-Schools program at Bethel Regional High School, Bethel, Alaska, and from 1973 to 1976 she was director of photography at Project Art Center, Cambridge, Massachusetts.

The photographer is a member of SPE and the Polaroid Collection. As of this writing she was working in small-format black-and-white, using infrared film.

PUBLICATION Periodical: *Popular Photography's 35mm Photography*, winter 1979.

ADDRESS 4 Cambridge Terrace, Cambridge, MA 02140.

Jeffrey Fraenkel PHOTOGRAPHY DEALER Born January 28, 1955, Fraenkel earned a BFA from Antioch College (1977) in Yellow Springs, Ohio.

Currently director of Fraenkel Gallery in San Francisco, he worked for Grapestake Gallery in San Francisco (1977–79) and for Anschel Gallery in London in 1976. In 1979 he joined the Association of International Photography Art Dealers.

Fraenkel Gallery deals exclusively in photographs, covering both nineteenth and twentieth centuries.

ADDRESS Fraenkel Gall., 55 Grant Ave, San Francisco, CA 94108.

Klaus Frahm PHOTOGRAPHER Born August 23, 1953, in Boernsen, near Hamburg, Germany, Frahm studied communications and social anthropology at Mainz University, West Germany (1974–76), and is self-taught in photography. His major influences have been Walker Evans, C. J. Laughlin, Edward Weston, Emmett Gowin and Larry Fink.

A freelance photographer since 1977, he has worked for McCann-Erickson, GGK and ECM Records. In 1976–77 he was a photography instructor for U.S. forces in Mainz.

After turning from small- to large-format in 1978, Frahm began photographing the man-made landscape of Germany, including a documentation of Brickstone architecture in Hamburg and of the Hamburg suburbs.

PUBLICATIONS Periodicals: *Camera*, Nov 1979; *Creative Camera Collection 5*, 1978; *Fotografie*, Mar 1977.

COLLECTIONS Mus. für Kunst und Gewerbe, Hamburg, Germany; Mus. of Mod. Art, Tokyo; Stedelijk Mus., Amsterdam, The Netherlands.

ADDRESS Boernsenerstrasse 26, D-2050 Boernsen, West Germany.

Abraham (Abe) Samuel Frajndlich PHOTOGRAPHER Born May 28, 1946, in Frankfurt, Germany, Frajndlich received his BA (1968) and MA (1970) in English Literature from Northwestern University, Chicago. He studied with Minor White at a live-in workshop (1970–71) and worked with White from 1975 until White's death in 1976. Frajndlich also worked with Nathan Lyons in 1974–75.

A freelance photographer since 1970, Frajndlich does some commissioned portraiture and annual reports, along with his own work.

A member of SPE and the New Organization of the Visual Arts, Cleveland, Ohio, the photographer was chosen to represent the state of Ohio before the U.S. Senate in 1974.

Using his background in literature, Frajndlich was concerned in his early photographs with sequential literary issues. Recently his work addresses "more abstract and purely visual issues."

PUBLICATION Book: *Figments*, 1975 (self-pub.: Boston).

PORTFOLIOS *Homage to Yukio Mishima*, 1980; *Lives I've Never Lived*, 1979; *Private Figments*, 1975.

COLLECTIONS Cleveland Mus. of Art, Ohio; Exchange Natl., Bank of Chicago; IMP/GEH, Rochester; Princeton Mus. of Art, N.J.; Visual Studies Workshop, Rochester. Nicéphore Niepce Internatl. Mus. of Photography, Châlon-sur-Saône, France.

REPRESENTATIVE Arc Press, Box 4243, Euclid, OH 44132.

Martine Franck PHOTOGRAPHER Born February 4, 1938, in Antwerp, Belgium, Franck studied at the Ecole du Louvre in Paris from 1958 to 1962. She was an assistant to Eliot Elisofon and Gjon Mili, who were major influences.

A freelance photographer who has worked for several photo news agencies, Franck won a 1979 grant from the City of Paris and a 1976 grant from Fondation Nationale de la Photographie.

PUBLICATIONS Monographs: *Le Tempsde Vieillir*, 1980 (Editions Filipacchi-Denoël: Paris); *Martine Franck*, preface by Ariane Mnouchkine, 1976 (Editions Contrejour: Paris). Books: *Les Lubérons*, Yves Berger, 1978 (Editions du Chêne: Paris); *Quartier Beaubourg*, 1977 (Centre Georges Pompidou: Paris); *Le Théâtre du Soleil: 1793*, 1972, *Le Théâtre du Soleil: 1789*, 1971,

"Théâtre Ouvert" Collection (Editions Stock: Paris); *La Sculpture de Cardenas*, José Pierre, 1971 (Editions La Connaissance: Brussels, Belgium); *Etienne Martin, Sculpteur*, Michel Ragon, 1970 (Editions La Connaissance: Brussels, Belgium). Periodicals (selected): *Nippon Camera*, July 1980; *Zoom*, Aug-Sept 1978, Nov 1977 (Paris); *Camera*, June 1976; *Photo*, no. 104, May 1976; *Creative Camera*, Nov 1974; *Ovo Photo*, no. 17–18, 1974.

COLLECTIONS Bibliothèque Nationale, Paris; Georges Pompidou Library, Paris; Musée Cantini, Marseilles.

REPRESENTATIVE: Magnum Photos, 2 rue Christine, 75006, Paris, France.

JoAnn L. Frank PHOTOGRAPHER Born April 11, 1947, in Philadelphia, Pennsylvania, Moore received her BFA in Fashion Design from Moore College of Art (1968), where she studied photography with Leif Skoogfors.

A freelance photographer, Frank is a member of SPE.

Shooting only black-and-white and using small and medium formats, Frank mainly photographs interiors and some portraits. She spent four years working with photograms.

PUBLICATIONS Book: *3 Dozen*, 1977. Catalogs: *A Ten Year Salute*, 1980 (Witkin Gallery: NYC); *Women of Photography*, 1975 (San Francisco Mus. of Modern Art). Periodicals: *American Photographer*, Jan 1979; *Camera*, May 1975, Aug 1971; *Ovo Photo*, Oct 1974; "Invitation to Photography," *Popular Photography*, 1973.

COLLECTIONS Addison Gall. of Amer. Art, Andover, Mass.; Brookdale Community Coll., Lincroft, N.J.; CCP, Tucson; Metro. Mus. of Art, NYC; New Orleans Mus. of Art, La.; San Francisco Mus. of Modern Art; Univ. of Kansas Mus. of Art, Lawrence; Witkin Gall., NYC. Inst. of Photography, Tokyo; Tasmanian Mus. and Art Gall., Australia.

DEALER Witkin Gall., Inc., 41 E 57 St, New York, NY 10022

ADDRESS 308 E 94 St, New York, NY 10028.

Robert Frank PHOTOGRAPHER · FILM MAKER Born November 9, 1924, in Zurich, Switzerland, Frank was apprenticed to Hermann Eidenbenz in Basel, Switzerland, and Michael Wolfgensinger in Zurich (1942).

Frank was a photographer for Gloria Films in Zurich (1943–44) and for *Harper's Bazaar*, Paris, through the 1940s. He came to the United States about 1948 and freelanced for *Fortune, Junior Ba-*

zaar, *Life, Look, McCall's* and *The New York Times* through 1955. He began making films in 1958, and dropped still photography in 1966 to concentrate totally on that medium.

Recipient of a Guggenheim Fellowship in 1955, Frank was the first European photographer to be so honored.

Frank worked strictly in small format, producing silver prints. His best-known images are those of everyday life in America during the 1950s. In addition to subjective documentary, he has also been involved in fashion photography.

His films are: *About Me—A Musical*, 1971; *Conversations in Vermont*, ca. 1969; *Me and My Brother*, ca. 1965–68; *Kaddish*, ca. 1965–66; and *Pull My Daisy*, 1959.

PUBLICATIONS Books: *Robert Frank*, intro. by Rudolph Wurlitzer, 1976; *The Lines of My Hand*, 1971 (Kazuhiko Motomura; Tokyo), U.S. ed., 1972; *Zero Mostel Reads a Book*, 1963; *Pull My Daisy*, w/Jack Kerouac & Alfred Leslie, 1961; *Les Américains*, Alain Bosquet, ed., 1958 (Delpire: Paris), U.S. ed., *The Americans*, intro. by Jack Kerouac, 1959, rev. eds. 1978, 1969; *Indiens pas morts*, Georges Arnaud, 1956 (Delpire: Paris), U.S. ed., *From Incas to Indias*, intro. by Manuel Tuñan de Lara, 1956; *New York Is*, ca. 1950. Anthologies: *The Photograph Collector's Guide*, Lee D. Witkin & Barbara London, 1979; *The Magic Image*, Cecil Beaton & Gail Buckland, 1975; Time-Life Series; *Looking at Photographs*, John Szarkowski, 1973; *Documentary Photography*, 1972; *The Art of Photography*, 1971. Catalogs: *12 Photographers of the American Social Landscape*, Thomas H. Garver, 1967 (Brandeis Univ., Waltham, Mass.); *American Photography: The Sixties*, 1966 (Univ. of Neb. Sheldon Mem Art Gall., Lincoln). Periodicals: "Black and White Are the Colors of Robert Frank," Edna Bennett, *Aperture 9*, no. 1, 1961; "Robert Frank, Walker Evans," *U.S. Camera Annual* 1958.

COLLECTIONS Art Inst. of Chicago; IMP/GEH, Rochester; MOMA, NYC; Philadelphia Mus. of Art, Penn.; Smithsonian Inst., Wash., D.C. Natl. Gall. of Canada, Ottawa, Ontario.

DEALER Yajima Galerie, 1434 Sherbrooke Ouest, Montreal H3G 1K4, Canada.

Joseph von Fraunhofer PHYSICIST Born March 6, 1787, in Straubing on the Danube, Germany, Fraunhofer died on June 7, 1826, in Munich. The son of a master glazier, he served an apprenticeship with a mirror maker in Munich from the age of twelve while he completed his education. He studied mathematics and lens grinding under Ulrich Schiegg.

In 1806 Fraunhofer joined the firm of Utzschneider, Reichenbach und Liebherr, manufacturers of telescopes, microscopes and theodolites. He aided the company in the calculation of parabolic and hyperbolic surfaces for mirrors and grinding machines, and gradually mastered the manufacture of glass for scientific use, replacing the glassmaker in charge of the melts. In 1809 Fraunhofer became a partner of the firm, now known as Utzschneider, Reichenbach und Fraunhofer, in Benedictbeuern. From 1812 to 1814 the physicist studied the effect of various types of glass on the spectral colors of light, resulting in a spherically and chromatically corrected objective (lens). From 1814 to 1817 he studied the effects of sunlight through a prism, discovering the dark lines in the spectrum which bear his name and setting the stage for spectroscopy. He was also credited with being the first to study diffraction with a grating; his work on the refractive and color dispersive character of glass was presented to the Royal Bavarian Academy of Science on April 12, 1817.

PUBLICATIONS Books: *Quellendarstellungen zur Geschichte der Fotografie*, Wolfgang Baier, 1965; *Joseph von Fraunhofer und die Glashuette in Benediktbeuren*, H. Jebsen-Marwedel, 1963; *Aus Physik und Technik*, J. Zenneck, 1930; *Joseph Fraunhofer*, Monitz von Rohr, 1929. Anthology: *Photography's Great Inventors*, Louis W. Sipley, 1965. Periodicals: *Optik*, 1963; *Bild und Ton*, 1948.

Tony Frederick PHOTOGRAPHER · TEACHER
Born June 19, 1955, in Hutchinson, Kansas, Frederick received a BFA from the University of New Mexico in 1977. While there he worked with Thomas Barrow and Betty Hahn, who influenced his work. Frederick received an MFA at the University of Colorado, where he studied with Charles Reitz and Gary Metz.

Frederick worked at the University of Colorado as a graduate instructor from 1978 to 1979 and is currently with Illinois State University in Normal as an assistant professor of art.

He is a member of SPE and the College Art Association of America. In 1979 he received two Juror's awards, one "Perception: Field of View," and the other, "Exposure: Ideas and Images in Contemporary Photography." Frederick also received a "Teaching Excellence Award" from the University of Colorado that same year.

Of his work the artist says: "... recent work has been small color prints of people's homes, paired with short, fictional writings about the residents. The purpose is to visually document

and compare them with stories about their everyday concerns."

PUBLICATIONS Books: *A Handbook of Photographic Alternatives for the Photographer and Surface Designer*, Jan Arnow, 1980; *Photo-Art Processes*, Nancy Howell-Koehler, 1980.

COLLECTIONS Chrysler Mus., Norfolk, Va.; Michigan State Univ., Kresge Art Gallery, E. Lansing; Los Angeles Center for Photographic Studies.

ADDRESS 1112 E Grove St, Bloomington, IL 61701.

Hermine Freed PHOTOGRAPHER · VIDEO ARTIST Born May 29, 1940, in New York City, Freed received a BA from Cornell University in Ithaca, New York, in 1961 and an MA from New York University, New York City, in 1967.

Since 1974 Freed has been an instructor in video art at the School of Visual Arts in New York. Her former teaching experience includes an associate professorship at the School of the Chicago Art Institute (1976), the position of visiting artist at the University of Illinois in Chicago Circle (1974–75) and instructor at the 92nd Street Y.M.C.A. (1972–75), Five Towns Music and Art Foundation (1970–74), North Shore Community Art Center (1968–71) and New York University School of Continuing Education (1965–67).

Freed was the recipient of grants from CAPS and the Rockefeller Foundation in 1978, the New York State Council on the Arts in 1972 and 1974 and the NEA in 1974.

PUBLICATIONS Book: *Video Art*, 1976. Periodicals: Review, Nov/Dec 1979, "Collecting Video," 1977, *Print Collector's Newsletter*; *Arts Magazine*, Feb 1979; "In Time, Of Time," text only, *Arts*, Dec 1974; *Afterimage: VSW*, Apr 1968.

COLLECTIONS Art Inst. of Chicago; Calif. Inst. of the Arts, Oakland, Calif.; Denver Art Mus., Colo.; Grossmont Coll., El Cajon, Calif.; Hartwick Coll., Oneonta, N.Y.; InterCommunications Agcy., Wash., D.C.; Otis Art Inst., Los Angeles; Smith Coll., Northampton, Mass.; Univ. of Georgia, Atlanta; Univ. of Illinois, Chicago; Univ. of Mass., Amherst; Univ. of North Carolina, Chapel Hill; Univ. of Santa Clara, De Saisset Art Mus., Calif.; Virginia Commonwealth Univ., Richmond. Berlin Film Festival; Govt. of Austria; Hamburger Kunsthaller, Germany; ITF Interfindings, Milan; Natl. Gall. of Victoria, Melbourne, Australia; Newcastle upon Tyne Polytechnic Inst., England; Tehran Mus. of Contemporary Art; Queens Univ., Kingston, Canada; Wentworth-Melbourne Hotel, Australia.

DEALERS Castelli Gall., 420 W Broadway, New York, NY 10013; Sonnabend, 142 Greene St, New York, NY 10012; Steffanotti Gall., 30 W 57 St, New York, NY 10019.

ADDRESS 140 Fifth Ave, New York, NY 10011.

Leonard Freed PHOTOGRAPHER Born October 23, 1929, in Brooklyn, New York, Freed is a self-taught freelance photographer, handling assignments for such publications as *Paris-Match, GEO* (German and American), *London Sunday Times Magazine* and *Der Stern*. Freed belongs to Magnum Photos.

In 1963 he produced *Dansende Bromen* for Dutch television, a film about the Hasidic Jews of New York and Jerusalem.

"Curiosity is the most important aspect of my work," says Freed. "To photograph, you have to keep a childlike wonder at the world around you. If you lose that, you lose your vision."

PUBLICATIONS Monographs: *Made in Germany*, 1970; *Seltsame Spiele*, 1970 (Bärmèrer & Nikel: Germany); *Deutsche Juden Heute*, 1965 (Rütten & Loening: Germany); *Black and White America*, n.d.; *Joden van Amsterdam*, 1958 (De Dezige hij: Amsterdam). Anthologies: *The Magic Image*, Cecil Beaton & Gail Buckland, 1975; *Celebrations*, preface by Gyorgy Kepes, 1974; *The Concerned Photographer*, 1968.

COLLECTIONS MOMA, NYC. Bibliothèque Nationale, Paris; Leiden Univ., The Netherlands; Staatlich Mus., Amsterdam, The Netherlands.

REPRESENTATIVE Magnum Photos, Inc, 15 W 46 St, New York, NY 10036.

Jill Freedman PHOTOGRAPHER Born in Pittsburgh, Pennsylvania, on October 19, 1939, Freedman earned a BA in Sociology from the University of Pittsburgh in 1961. She has worked as a freelance documentary photographer since that time.

Recipient of an NEA grant in 1973 and a CAPS grant in 1974, Freedman took first prize in *New York Magazine*'s photo contest in 1973.

PUBLICATIONS Monographs: *Firehouse*, 1977; *Circus Days*, 1975; *Old News: Resurrection City*, 1971. Book: *Jerusalem: City of Mankind*, Cornell Capa, ed., 1974. Anthologies: *The Family of Woman*, 1979; "This Year's Books: A Fiery Season," *Time-Life Photography Year*, 1978; *The Family of Children*, 1977; *Women See Woman*, 1976; *Vision and Expression*, Nathan Lyons, ed., 1969. Periodicals: *Camera 35 Photo World*, Apr 1979, Sept 1978; *Creative Camera*, May 1978; *Popular*

Photography, June 1976; *Photo*, July 1977, June 1974; *Revue Suisse de Photographie*, Nov 1976; *Nikon News*, Nov 1976; *Zoom*, July/Aug 1975 (Paris); *Revue Fotografie*, spring 1975; *Camera 35*, Nov 1973, *Annual*, 1972; *35mm Photography*, Nov 1973; Camera Mainichi, Nov 1972, Mar 1972.

COLLECTIONS IMP/GEH, Rochester; Internatl. Ctr. for Photography, NYC; MOMA/NYC; Seagram Cllctn., NYC. Bibliothèque Nationale, Paris; Mus. of Applied Arts, Prague.

ADDRESS 181 Sullivan St, New York, NY 10012.

Roger Freeman PHOTOGRAPHER Born June 4, 1945, in Chicago, Illinois, Freeman received his BA from the University of Wisconsin, Madison, in 1967 and his MS from the Institute of Design, Illinois Institute of Technology, Chicago, in 1976.

He has been an assistant professor of photography at New York State College of Ceramics at Alfred University since 1977. In 1976 Freeman was an instructor for the Chicago City College System.

A member of SPE, Freeman won the Pauline Palmer Award from the Chicago Art Institute for the "Chicago & Vicinity" show in 1977.

Freeman uses small-format, black-and-white infrared film to create "images dealing with mundane objects/situations/landscapes." His work "avoids the bizarre effects of the film and concentrates on the transformation of glowing whites and rich shadow areas."

PUBLICATION Periodical: *Popular Photography Annual*, 1978.

COLLECTIONS Exchange Natl. Bank, Chicago; New Orleans Mus. of Art, La.; Rainier Bank, Seattle, Wash.

ADDRESS 58 S Main St, Alfred, NY 14802.

Roland Leon Freeman PHOTOGRAPHER Born July 27, 1936, in Baltimore, Maryland, Freeman lists as mentors Gordon Parks and Burk Uzzle.

Since 1968 he has been a freelance photographer whose works have appeared in *Time, Newsweek, Paris-Match* and *Der Stern*.

A member of the White House News Photographers Association and the U.S. Senate Press Photographers Gallery since 1970, he has also been a member of ASMP since 1972. Awarded a Young Humanist Fellowship in 1970 and a Senior Fellowship in 1972 by the National Endowment for the Humanities, he was also a photographer-in-residence and research associate at the Insti-

207

tute for the Arts and Humanities at Howard University in Washington, D.C., in 1978.

Freeman says of his work: "I am best known for my many photo essays on the different subcultures in America, especially my in-depth documentary studies of African-American expressive culture."

PUBLICATIONS Monographs: *A Baltimore Portfolio, 1968–1979,* 1979; *City Pavements/Country Roads,* 1978; *Folkroots: Images of Mississippi Black Folklife (1974–76),* 1977. Book: *Captive Capitol: Colonial Life in Modern Washington,* Sam Smith, 1974. Periodicals: "End of an Era," *35mm Photography,* summer 1975; "Room for One More: Roland Freeman," Julia Scully, *Modern Photography,* Nov 1971.

COLLECTIONS County Lib., Catonsville, Md.; Mississippi Dept. of Archives & History, State Historical Mus., Jackson; Natl. Mus. of History & Technology, Smithsonian Inst., Wash., D.C.; Univ. of Maryland, Edward L. Bafford Photography Cllctn., Baltimore.

REPRESENTATIVE Magnum Photos Inc., 15 W 46 St, New York, NY 10036.

DEALER Douglas Kenyon, Inc., 155 E Ohio St, Chicago, IL 60611.

ADDRESS 117 Ingraham St NW, Washington, DC 20011.

Tina Freeman PHOTOGRAPHER · CURATOR Born in New Orleans, Louisiana, on May 5, 1951, Freeman earned her BFA from Art Center College of Design in Los Angeles (1972). She studied with Helmut Gernsheim in 1978–79.

A freelance photographer since 1972, she has also been curator of photography at the New Orleans Museum of Art since 1973. Freeman is a member of SPE, for which she served as president in 1974, and RPS.

Working in both silver and platinum, Freeman mainly shoots interiors and portraits. Her field of research is early twentieth-century mid-European photography.

PUBLICATION Book: *Diverse Images, Photographs from the New Orleans Museum of Art,* ed., 1979.

DEALERS Betty Cuningham, 94 Prince St, New York, NY 10012; Galerie Simonne Stern, 2727 Prytania, New Orleans, LA 70130.

ADDRESS 2113 Decatur St, New Orleans, LA 70116.

Vida Freeman PHOTOGRAPHER · CERAMIST · TEACHER Born July 14, 1937, in Los Angeles, California, Freeman studied art at University of California at Los Angeles and received an MA in ceramics and photography at California State University, Northridge. She names as influences Robert Morris, Marcel Duchamp, John Cage and Ellsworth Kelly.

She has taught photography at California State University since 1973 and has taught ceramics at Los Angeles Valley College since 1977. From 1972 to 1975 she owned a gallery.

A member of SPE since 1978 and of the Los Angeles Center for Photographic Studies since 1976, she won a First Place Purchase Award from California Polytechnic University, Pomona, in 1976 and was a *Life* magazine photo contest winner in 1970. She works in ceramic art and sculpture as well as photography.

"My art work deals primarily with the earth . . . physically, geologically, and as the earth relates to its human inhabitants (past and present)," Freeman says. She uses a variety of techniques, incorporating palladium prints and text, straight black-and-white or toned photographs, photo-etching, and a combination of photo and ceramic materials.

PUBLICATION Periodical: *Modern Photography,* Jan 1972.

PORTFOLIOS *Death Valley: Palladium Prints and Text,* 1979; *L.A. Issues* (group), 1979.

COLLECTIONS Calif. State Poly. Univ., Pomona; CCP, Tucson; Los Angeles County Mus. of Art; Minneapolis Inst. of Arts, Minn.; Santa Barbara Mus. of Art, Calif.; Security Pacific Natl. Bank, Los Angeles; UCLA; Wells Fargo Bank, Los Angeles; Witkin Gall., NYC.

DEALERS G. Ray Hawkins Gall., 7224 Melrose Ave, Los Angeles, CA 90046; Witkin Gall., 41 E 57 St., New York NY 10022.

ADDRESS 18238 Septo St, Northridge, CA 91325.

Bernard Lawrence Freemesser TEACHER · PHOTOGRAPHER Born November 15, 1926, in Rochester, New York, Freemesser died in 1977. He received a BA in 1950 from San Diego State College and an MS in Photography in 1952 from the University of Oregon in Eugene. His photographic work was influenced greatly by his association with Brett Weston, W. Eugene Smith and Merle Armitage, as well as by the work of Edward Weston.

Freemesser was a professor of fine arts at the University of Oregon (1973–77), where he began teaching full time in 1965. Prior to that he was director of the university's Photographic Bureau (1955) and technical director of Northwest Photographic Illustrators (1953–55).

President of the Oregon Press Photographers

Association, Freemesser was also national chairman of SPE (1968–70) and a member of its board of directors (1968–73). He was also a trustee of Friends of Photography (1976–77). He received two grants from the University of Oregon. Producer of a TV series entitled "The Art of Seeing," which was shown twice weekly over an educational TV station, he also produced films entitled *Hey! Follow Me; A University and Its People; John Burton, His Art and His Philosophy* and *Eugene 66, A Community Environmental Portrait.*

Freemesser's early work utilized black-and-white in an 8 x 10 format and contact negatives, concentrating on landscapes. From 1972 on he worked in color, still with 8 x 10 contact prints, creating many abstractions. There was no retouching or manipulating of his work.

PUBLICATIONS Monograph: *An Oregon Experience,* 1974. Book: *The Literature of Photography,* w/George Carver, 1966.

COLLECTIONS Citizens Bank, Eugene, Oreg.; Equivalents Gall., Seattle, Wash.; Exchange Natl. Bank, Chicago; Univ. of Oregon, Mus. of Art.

REPRESENTATIVE Shirley Freemesser, 3241 Donald St, Eugene, OR 97405.

Robert French PHOTOGRAPHER Born November 11, 1841, in Dublin, Ireland, French died there on June 24, 1917.

He was in the Royal Irish Constabulary in 1860 and became a printer in a photography studio in 1863. He was next employed as a printer in William Lawrence's photographic studio in 1865 and, during the next forty-nine years (until his retirement in 1914), worked his way to colorist, to assistant photographer and eventually to chief photographer.

French's photographs provide a unique documentary of Irish life from approximately 1870 to 1913. Many have been wrongly attributed to his employer, William Mervin Lawrence.

PUBLICATIONS Books: *The Light of Other Days,* Kieran Hickey, 1903, repr. 1975; *The Emerald Isle Series,* w/other photographers, ca. 1900; *Ireland in the Magic Lantern,* 1890.

COLLECTIONS Natl. Lib. of Ireland, Lawrence Cllctn.; Natl. Lib. of Ireland, Dublin.

Théodore-Henri Fresson CHEMIST · AGRONOMIST · MILITARY ENGINEER · ELECTRONICS SPECIALIST Fresson lived from 1865 to 1951 in France. His sons Pierre (1904–) and Edmond (1898–1965) and grandsons Michel (1935–) and Jacques (1922?–) were all involved in the use of the Fresson photographic printing process.

Théodore-Henri was educated in chemistry and agronomy.

His most famous invention, developed between 1893 and 1900, is a direct carbon pigment process that produces beautiful permanent images in black-and-white. The monochrome paper was available commercially in the United States from 1927 to 1939. The chemist's sons and grandsons all used the process, which was strictly kept within the family. After 1950 Edmond and his son Jacques worked separately from the rest of the family, but Jacques abandoned all photographic activities after Edmond's death and could no longer supply paper to the famous pictorialist José O. Echagüe, the most prominent user of the process. The Fresson process was subsequently sold to Echagüe without the knowledge of the rest of the family, and shortly before his own death Echagüe sold it to Luis Nadeau in Canada, currently the only user of the process outside the family. In 1951 Pierre Fresson adapted it to color work, for which it is quite well known today because of its permanence and unique effect.

(Frank) David Freund PHOTOGRAPHER · TEACHER Born July 16, 1937, in Anderson, Indiana, Freund studied at the University of California at Berkeley in 1955–56, then went on to earn a BA in Theater from the University of California at Davis (1963) and an MFA in Photography from Visual Studies Workshop (SUNY) in Rochester, New York (1971). He names Nathan Lyons and John Wood as mentors.

Currently a Dayton-Hudson Distinguished Visiting Teacher/Artist at Carleton College in Northfield, Minnesota, Freund has been teaching photography as an adjunct professor at the Pratt Institute in Brooklyn since 1971 and as an assistant professor at Ramapo College in Mahwah, New Jersey, since 1973. He has also been involved in several summer workshops, including the Center of the Eye in Aspen, Colorado, and the Maine Photography Workshops in Rockport.

The photographer belongs to SPE and the American Federation of Teachers. He won an NEA fellowship in 1978, a grant from the Institute for Art and Urban Resources in New York City to photograph Long Island City in 1977 and a CAPS grant in 1971.

Freund works in 35mm, producing 7 x 10 silver-print images on 11 x 14 paper.

PUBLICATIONS Anthology: *The Great West: Real/Ideal,* Sandy Hume et al., eds., 1977. Catalog: *Attitudes: Photography in the 1970's,* 1979 (Santa Barbara Mus. of Art: Calif.). Periodicals:

Creative Camera Collection 5, 1978; *Exposure: SPE*, 14:3, 1976.

PORTFOLIO *CAPS Portfolio* (group), 1973.

COLLECTIONS Colgate Univ., Hamilton, N.J.; Corcoran Gall. of Art, Wash., D.C.; Crocker Art Gall., Sacramento, Calif.; IMP/GEH, Rochester; L/C, Wash., D.C.; Metro. Mus. of Art, NYC; MOMA, NYC; Mus. of Fine Arts, Houston; Univ. of Ariz., Northlight Gall., Tucson; Univ. of Colo., Boulder; Univ. of N. Mex. Art Gall., Albuquerque; VSW, Rochester. Bibliothèque Nationale, Paris.

REPRESENTATIVES Photocollect, Alan Klotz, 740 West End Ave, New York, NY 10024; Visual Studies Workshop Gall. 31 Prince St, Rochester, NY 14607.

ADDRESS 233 Fifth Ave, Brooklyn, NY 11215.

Gisele Freund JOURNALIST · PHOTOGRAPHER [See plate 82] Born December 19, 1912, in Berlin, Germany, Freund earned a PhD in Sociology and Art History from the Sorbonne in Paris, France. Her father, Julius Freund, was an art collector.

A freelance, she has been president of the Federation of French Art Photographers since 1977 and is also a member of the Fondation Nationale de la Photographie and the Council of the Syndicate of Art Critics of France.

In addition to her still photography, Freund made a 16mm color film, *The Last Survivors: Indians of Tierra del Fuego*.

A photojournalist, she has done work that has appeared in numerous magazines in the United States, England and France. She has shot picture stories and portraits of famous artists, writers and other persons, including Virginia Woolf, Eva Perón and James Joyce.

PUBLICATIONS Monograph: *Gisele Freund: Fotografien 1932–1977*, 1977 (Geraldine Fabrikant, Bonn). Books: *Mémoires de l'Oeil*, 1978 (Paris & Germany); *Photographie et Société*, 1974 (Editions du Seuil: Paris); *Le Monde et ma Caméra*, 1974; *Au Pays des Visages: 1938–1968*, 1968 (Musée d'Art Moderne, Paris); *James Joyce in Paris, His "Final Years,"* 1965, repr. 1966; *Mexique Précolombien*, 1954 (Monnies: Germany), repr. 1955; *La Photographie en France au 19ᵉ Siècle*, 1936 (France), 1940 (Spain), 1968 (Germany). Anthology: *The Photograph Collector's Guide*, Lee D. Witkin & Barbara London, 1979. Periodical: *Fotografia Italiana*, July/Aug 1969.

PORTFOLIO *Untitled*, 1978 (Graphics Internatl., Wash., D.C.).

COLLECTIONS CCP, Tucson; IMP/GEH, Rochester. Bibliothèque Nationale, Paris; Musée

de Toulon, France; Musée Réattu, Arles, France; Mus. Stockholm, Sweden; Stedelijk Mus., Amsterdam, The Netherlands.

REPRESENTATIVE Photo Researchers Inc., 60 E 56 St, New York, NY 10022.

ADDRESS B.P. 509, 75666 Paris Cedex 14, France.

Anthony Enton Friedkin PHOTOGRAPHER Friedkin was born May 26, 1949, in Los Angeles, California. His father, David Friedkin, was an award-winning film writer and director (d. 1976). Anthony Friedkin studied at the Art Center College of Design in Pasadena, California (1969–70), and was a visiting student at the London Royal College of Art in 1971. He also attended Aperion Workshops in Millerton, New York, in 1972.

Currently Friedkin is a professor of photography at both the University of California Extension Department in Los Angeles and the California Institute of the Arts in Valencia. In 1970 he worked as a correspondent for Magnum Photos in New York City.

He was the recipient of an NEA grant in 1977.

The photographer characterizes his work as being "in the tradition of Cartier-Bresson, Joseph Kouldelka and Robert Frank—down the line black-and-white full frame. The photograph has a strong sense of an event, the fate of the moment."

PUBLICATIONS Periodicals: *Photoshow*, Mar 1980; *Zoom*, Apr 1980, Aug 1976 (Paris); *Camera*, May 1974, Aug 1970.

COLLECTIONS Academy of Motion Picture Arts & Sciences, Los Angeles; Los Angeles County Mus. of Art; MOMA, NYC; Seagram Cllctn., NYC.

DEALER G. Ray Hawkins Gall., 7224 Melrose Ave, Los Angeles, CA 90046.

ADDRESS 828 12 St #A, Santa Monica, CA 90403.

Lee Friedlander PHOTOGRAPHER Born in 1934 in Aberdeen, Washington, Friedlander studied with Edward Kaminski at Art Center School in Los Angeles (1953–55).

Friedlander is a freelance photographer, and his images have appeared in such publications as *Esquire*, *McCall's*, *Collier's*, *Seventeen*, *Sports Illustrated* and *Art in America*. He won Guggenheim fellowships in 1960 and 1962 and an NEA Photographer's Fellowship in 1972.

In addition to his own photography, Friedlander is credited with rescuing the work of New Orleans photographer E. J. Bellocq from oblivion.

PUBLICATIONS Monographs: *Lee Friedlander Photographs*, 1978; *The American Monument*, Leslie George Katz, 1976; *Self-Portrait*, 1970. Books: *E. J. Bellocq: Storyville Portraits*, 1970; *Work from the Same House*, w/Jim Dine, 1969. Anthologies; *The Photograph Collector's Guide*, Lee D. Witkin & Barbara London, 1979; *Mirrors and Windows*, John Szarkowski, 1978; *American Photographers*, Manfred Willmann, ed., 1977 (Fotogalerie im Forum Stadtpark: Graz); *The Great West: Real/Ideal*, Sandy Hume et al., eds., 1977; *The Magic Image*, Cecil Beaton & Gail Buckland, 1975; *Looking at Photographs*, John Szarkowski, 1973; *Documentary Photography*, 1972, *The Camera*, 1970, Time-Life Series; *Contemporary Photographers*, Nathan Lyons, 1966. Catalogs: *The Nation's Capitol in Photographs*, 1976 (Corcoran Gall. of Art: Wash., D.C.); *Graphic/Photographic*, 1971 (Calif. State Coll.: Fullerton); *New Documents*, John Szarkowski, 1967 (MOMA: NYC); *12 Photographers of the American Social Landscape*, 1967 (Brandeis Univ.: Waltham, Mass.). Periodicals: *Creative Camera Annual*, 1978; "Lee Friedlander," Gerry Badger, *The British Journal of Photography*, Mar 5, 1976; *Camera*, Dec 1975, Dec 1971, Jan 1969, Apr 1966; *Creative Camera*, Sept 1971, May 1969.
PORTFOLIOS *Photographs of Flowers*, 1975 (Graphic Studio: Tampa, Fla.; Haywire Press: NYC); *Fifteen Photographs*, intro. by Walker Evans, 1973 (Double Elephant Press: N.Y.); *Photographs and Etchings*, 1969 (Petersburg Press: London).
COLLECTIONS Baltimore Mus. of Art, Md.; Boston Mus. of Fine Arts; CCP, Tucson; Corcoran Gall. of Art, Wash., D.C.; Detroit Inst. of Arts, Mich.; Harvard Univ., Fogg Art Mus., Cambridge, Mass.; IMP/GEH, Rochester; L/C, Wash., D.C.; Minneapolis Inst. of Arts, Minn.; MOMA, NYC; Mus. of Fine Arts, Houston; New Orleans Mus. of Art; Princeton Univ. Art Mus., N.J.; R.I. School of Design, Providence; San Francisco Mus. of Modern Art; Seagram Cllctn., NYC; Smithsonian Inst., Wash., D.C.; St. Petersburg Mus. of Fine Arts, Fla.; UCLA; Univ. of Kans. Mus. of Art, Lawrence; Univ. of Neb., Sheldon Mem. Art Gall., Lincoln; Univ. of N. Mex. Art Mus., Albuquerque; Va. Mus. of Fine Arts, Richmond; VSW, Rochester; Yale Univ., New Haven, Conn. Bibliothèque Nationale, Paris; Natl. Gall. of Canada, Ottawa, Ontario; Stedlijk Mus., Amsterdam, The Netherlands; Victoria & Albert Mus., London.
ADDRESS 44 S Mountain Rd, New City, NY 10956.

Benno Friedman PHOTOGRAPHER Born March 28, 1945, in New York City, Friedman received a BA in 1966 from Brandeis University, Waltham, Massachusetts.
He is a self-employed photographer, and his work has appeared in such publications as *Esquire*, *Asahi Camera*, *Camera 35*, *Popular Photography* and *Aperture.*
Friedman won a CAPS grant in 1978 and a Massachusetts Council on the Arts and Humanities Fellowship Grant in 1975.
The photographer produces hand-worked, toned, altered, one-of-a-kind prints.
PUBLICATIONS Anthologies: *Darkroom Dynamics*, Jim Stone, ed., 1979; *Octave of Prayer*, Minor White, ed., 1972; *Be-ing Without Clothes*, Minor White, ed., 1970. Periodical: *Art in America*, Feb/Mar 1970.
PORTFOLIO *White Sands*, 1976 (Light Gall.: NYC).
COLLECTIONS Boston Mus. of Fine Arts; Harvard Univ., Fogg Art Mus., Cambridge, Mass.; MIT, Cambridge, Mass.; MOMA, NYC; Santa Barbara Mus. of Art, Calif.; Vassar Coll. Mus., Poughkeepsie, N.Y.; Virginia Mus., Richmond; Wertheim & Co., NYC. Australian Natl. Gall., Canberra, New South Wales.
DEALER Light Gall., 724 Fifth Ave, New York, NY 10019.
ADDRESS 26 W 20 St, New York, NY 10011.

Susan Friedman PHOTOGRAPHER · TEACHER Born in Rochester, New York, Friedman received her BA and BEd in 1968 from the University of Buffalo, New York. She cites Marc Kaczmarek as a major influence.
Since 1968 she has been a freelance photographer, has taught workshops privately and has been an instructor at the University of California, Santa Cruz. She has also lectured at Friends of Photography, Carmel, California, and Cabrillo College, Aptos, California, among others.
She became a member of SPE in 1978.
Using medium format and silver prints, Friedman produces exotic images of women, often placing figures in desolate, primordial settings. The female form "becomes an expression of human sensuality and spirit" in her photographs.
PUBLICATIONS Books: *Nude 1980*, Claude Nori, 1980 (Paris); *Landscape for Two Figures*, poetry by Robert Durand, 1975; *A Separate Place*, 1974. Anthology: *Self-Portrayal*, 1979. Periodicals: *Popular Photography's 35mm Photography*, winter 1979; *Creative Camera*, May 1978.
COLLECTIONS MOMA, NYC; Oakland Mus.,

Calif. Canon Gall., Amsterdam, The Netherlands; Gall. Fiolet, Amsterdam.

DEALERS   Douglas Elliott Gall., 1151 Mission St, San Francisco, CA 94103; Canon Gall., Amsterdam, The Netherlands.

ADDRESS   POB 25, Pescadero, CA 94060.

Janet Fries   PHOTOGRAPHER · TEACHER   Born May 2, 1949, in Scranton, Pennsylvania, Fries received her BA in Art from Smith College, Northampton, Massachusetts (1971), and her MA in Photography from San Francisco State University (1976).

She has been a freelance photographer since 1973, specializing in photojournalism. Fries also teaches at City College of San Francisco (since 1977) and at the University of California Extension Center in San Francisco (since 1978). She taught at San Francisco State University from 1977 to 1979.

Fries is a member of ASMP and the Center for the Visual Arts and was a board member of Cameraworks Gallery (1977–79).

Working exclusively in small format, Fries has used both black-and-white and color. Many of her images are offshoots of her photojournalism assignments, but she also makes experimental color prints from hand-painted black-and-white negatives.

PUBLICATIONS   Anthology: *Photography & Language*, 1976. Periodicals: *Popular Photography*, Feb 1979; *ArtWeek* (review), Joan Murray, Jan 1977; *WestArt* (review), John Marlowe, Dec 20, 1974.

COLLECTIONS   Mills College, Oakland, Calif.; Oakland Mus., Calif.

ADDRESS   289 Crescent Ave, San Francisco, CA 94110.

William Friese-Greene   INVENTOR · PHOTOGRAPHER   Born in 1855 in Bristol, England, Friese-Greene died in 1921. He studied at the Blue Coat School in Clifton.

After his schooling he opened a photography studio in Bath. He became interested in animated screen pictures in the early 1880s after meeting a Bath mechanic, John Arthur Roebuck Rudge, who made magic lanterns and movable lantern slides. In 1885 he opened a London studio.

In the same year (1885) Friese-Greene joined RPS.

The inventor was involved in the development of motion pictures throughout his life. His first patent (with London engineer Mortimer Evans) was for a primitive motion picture camera using a roll of transparent flexible film (1889). In 1890

he and F. H. Varley patented a photometer and a rapid printing and processing machine, and in 1893 Friese-Green patented a camera that would produce magic-lantern animated images. His other patents included photographic printing machines using rolls of sensitized material (1895), a camera and projector "taking photographs in rapid succession" (1895), a camera to print positive films from negatives (1896, with J. A. Prestwich), a projector (1896) and a 3-color camera (1898).

PUBLICATIONS   Books: *William Friese-Greene and the Origin of Kinematography*, Brian Coe, 1962; *Der Weg des Films*, F. von Zglinicki, 1956; *Friese-Greene—Close-up of an Inventor*, Ray Allister, 1948; *The Cinema*, M. Jackson-Wrigley & Eric Leyland, 1939; *Histoire du Cinématographie*, G.-Michel Coissac, 1925; *Lexikon für Photographie und Reproduktionstechnik*, G. H. Emmerich, 1910. Anthology: *Photography's Great Inventors*, Louis W. Sipley, 1965. Periodicals: *Bild und Ton*, 1962, 1955; "William Friese-Greene and the Origin of Kinematography," Brian Coe, *Photographic Journal*, Mar & Apr 1962; *British Journal of Photography*, 1955; *British Journal Photographic Almanac*, 1922; *Optical Magic Lantern*, 1898, Apr 1890, Nov 1889.

Toni Frissel   PHOTOGRAPHER   Frissell was born in 1907 in New York City.

Before becoming a photographer Frissell trained as an actress, worked for a painter and was employed in advertising for Stern Brothers. Her brother Varick, a documentary film maker, introduced her to photography, and she became seriously committed to the field after he died while filming off the coast of Labrador in 1929. Her images soon began to appear in *Vogue*, and later in *Sports Illustrated*, *Look* and *Life*.

PUBLICATION   Anthology: *The Magic Image*, Cecil Beaton & Gail Buckland, 1975.

COLLECTIONS   L/C (Bureau of Prints & Photography, Toni Frissell Cllctn.), Wash., D.C.; Metro. Mus. of Art, NYC.

ADDRESS   25 Broad St, New York, NY 10004.

Francis Frith   PHOTOGRAPHER · PUBLISHER   [See plate 17]   Born in 1822 in Chesterfield, Derbyshire, England, Frith died in England in 1898. He attended Ackworth School and Quaker Camp Hill School in Birmingham ca. 1828–34.

Frith served an apprenticeship to Sheffield, the cutlery house, from 1838 to 1843, then conducted a successful wholesale grocery business from 1845 to 1856. He took up photography around 1850 and between 1856 and 1860 made three trips to the Middle East. In 1859 he established F. Frith and Company in Reigate, Surrey, a photographic publishing house that eventually specialized in popular postcard scenes of the Middle East and the British Isles. The company, which employed numerous photographers and printers, far outlived its founder (it closed its doors in the 1960s).

A prolific landscape and topographical photographer, Frith was particularly noted for the postcards produced by his firm. On his many expeditions to the Middle East and throughout Europe, he carried the bulky accouterments of the collodion wet-plate process, shooting in formats ranging from 6 x 8 to 16 x 20. He also produced stereographs.

PUBLICATIONS Books: *Victorian Cameraman*, Bill Jay, 1973 (David & Charles: Newton Abbot, England); *Lorna Doone*, 2 vols., R. D. Blackmore, ca. 1882–95; *Liverpool: Its Public Buildings, Docks, Churches, Etc.*, ca. 1870 (Liverpool); *The Book of the Thames from Its Rise to Its Fall*, M/M Samuel Carter Hall, 1867 (London); *Hyperion: A Romance*, Henry Wadsworth Longfellow, 1865; *The Gossiping Photographer on the Rhine*, 1864 (Reigate); *The Gossiping Photographer at Hastings*, 1864 (Reigate); *Photo-Views of Canterbury*, 1863 (Canterbury); *The Holy Bible*, 1862 (London); *Egypt, Nubia and Ethiopia*, Samuel Sharpe, engravings by Joseph Bonami, 1862 (London); *Views of Sinai, Palestine, Egypt, Ethiopia*, 8 vols., 1860–63 (London); *Cairo, Sinai, Jerusalem and the Pyramids of Egypt*, M/M Reginald Poole, 1860; *Memorials of Cambridge*, 2 vols., Chas. Henry Cooper, 1858. Anthologies: *The Photograph Collector's Guide*, Lee D. Witkin & Barbara London, 1979; *The Invented Eye*, Edward Lucie-Smith, 1975; *The Magic Image*, Cecil Beaton & Gail Buckland, 1975; *Great Photographers*, Time-Life Series, 1970.

COLLECTIONS Art Inst. of Chicago, Ill.; IMP/GEH, Rochester; Metro. Mus. of Art, NYC; N.Y. Pub. Lib., NYC; Princeton Univ., N.J.; UCLA; Univ. of N. Mex. Art Mus., Albuquerque; Worcester Art Mus., Mass. British Mus., London; Provinciaal Mus. voor Kunstambachten, Deurne (Antwerp), Belgium; RPS, London; Victoria & Albert Mus., London; and many libraries.

Shinya Fujiwara PHOTOGRAPHER Born March 4, 1944, in Fukuoka, Japan, Fujiwara studied oil painting for one year at Tokyo Art University.

A freelance photographer, he works primarily in the documentary mode. His major subjects are women and the eastern part of the world. In 1979 he designed the stage setting for the *Modern Noh Play of Mishima*.

PUBLICATIONS Books: *Lotos in Forest*, 1979 (Parco); *My India*, 1979 (Asahi Newspaper); *Spector Women*, 1977 (Parco). Novels: *Wandering in South East Asia*, 1978; *Wandering in Tibet*, 1977; *Wandering in India*, 1972.

ADDRESS 4-13-12-806 Shibaura Minatoku, Tokyo, Japan.

Eva Fuka PHOTOGRAPHER·DESIGNER Born in Prague, Czechoslovakia, Fuka received diplomas in photography at the State Graphic College in Prague (1945) and in painting at the Academy of Fine Arts, Prague (1950). Her late husband, Vladimir Fuka, was a graphic artist and illustrator.

Maintaining her own photo studio for the past several years, she previously did freelance photography in West Germany and Switzerland (1972–75). She worked in the photo studio at the Metropolitan Museum of Art in New York City in 1971–72 and was a darkroom technician at K + L, Berkey Co., New York, from 1967 to 1971. Fuka freelanced from 1952 to 1967 as well.

The photographer joined the Silvermine Guild of Artists in Connecticut in 1979. In 1980 she received a grant from the Connecticut Commission on the Arts.

Fuka works in collage, using black-and-white, color and some hand-tinting. In her recent work she serializes images, arranging them in grids of four or five rows within an over-all format, usually 30 x 40. She also works in portrait photography and as a commercial artist.

PUBLICATIONS Monograph: *Eva Fuka*, 1963 (Odeon: Prague). Books: *New York*, 1967, *The House of Seven Floors*, Jiri Weiss, 1964 (Mlada Fronta: Prague); *Poetry for Children*, 1963 (Albatros: Prague); *The Life of a Composer*, Karel Čapek, 1961 (CS: Prague).

COLLECTIONS MOMA, NYC. Natl. Gall., Prague, Czechoslovakia.

ADDRESS 160 Pacific St, Bridgeport, CT 06604.

Katsuji Fukuda PHOTOGRAPHER Born January 17, 1898, in Mitajiri, Yamaguchi-Ken, Japan, Fukuda is self-taught.

Since 1933 he has been a freelance photographer.

In 1955 Fukuda won the first prize of the Canon Contest and the Photographic Society of Japan award.

PUBLICATIONS Books: *Kyoto*, 1958 (Iwasaki Book Store); *Ginza*, 1952, *The Reality of Photography*, 1952 (ARS); *The Art of Color and Light*,

1951, *How to Take Easily Understood Photographs*, 1951, *Our Kimonos*, 1951 (Yukei-sha); *Photographic Art*, 1949 (Koga-so); *Flowers and Nude Women*, 1947 (Evening Star Co.); *How to Photograph Women*, 1947 (Seiun-sha); *Five Nude Poses*, 1946 (Evening Star Co.); *Departure*, 1942 (Koga-so); *Jingugaien*, 1942 (Nihon Shashin Kogeisha); *The Elementary School That Keeps Cows*, 1941, *Ginza*, 1941 (Genko-sha); *Female Expressions*, 1939, *How to Photograph Flowers*, 1939, *How to Photograph Women, Part 2*, 1939, *My Works*, 1938, *Photographic Techniques for Spring*, 1938, *How to Photograph Women*, 1937 (ARS).

COLLECTION Nihon Univ., Faculty of Art, Tokyo, Japan.

DEALER Zeit-Foto Co., Ltd, Yagicho-Bild. 5F, 1–4 Nihonbashi-Muromachi, Chuo-Ku Tokyo, Japan.

ADDRESS 1-15-5 Iwato-Kita, Komae-Shi, Tokyo 201, Japan.

John Charles Fuller TEACHER · PHOTOGRAPHER Born on October 7, 1937, in Laconia, New Hampshire, Fuller attended Syracuse University in New York State, where he earned an AB (1962) and an MA (1964), both in Art History. He then completed a PhD in Comparative Arts (1968) at Ohio University in Athens, where he studied under Clarence White, Jr.

Since 1967 Fuller has been teaching art history and photography at the State University of New York in Oswego, where he is currently an associate professor of art. Previously, he was a teaching fellow in the Department of Comparative Arts at Ohio University (1964–67) and served as a U.S. Navy photographer's mate (1956–58).

A member of CAA, George Eastman House and the Society of Architectural Historians, Fuller has been the recipient of several grants: a stipend for a seminar for college teachers from the National Endowment for the Humanities (1976), a SUNY Faculty Research Fellowship (1970) and a research grant from the U.S. Department of Education (1968).

Fuller's areas of scholarly research include nineteenth-century British photography and painting, as well as Surrealism and visual and verbal media. In his photography he works in silver prints and often includes architecture as part of his subject.

PUBLICATIONS Book: *The Camera Viewed: Writings on Twentieth-Century Photography*, Peninah R. Petruck, ed., vol 1, 1979. Periodicals: "O. G. Rejlander: From Philistine to Forerunner," text only, *Exposure: SPE*, Dec 1976;

"Frederick H. Evans as Late Victorian: Cathedral Amid the Fin de Siècle," text only, *Afterimage: VSW*, Oct 1976; "A View Through a Window," text only, *Photographic Journal: RPS*, Oct 1970; "Yearbook Photography," photos & text, *Camera 35*, Oct/Nov 1961.

COLLECTIONS Eastman Kodak Co., Rochester; Ohio Univ., Athens; Rochester Inst. of Technology; SUNY, Oswego; Univ. of the South, Sewanee, Tenn.

ADDRESS Box 373, Fancher Ave, Fair Haven, NY 13064.

Kathleen Collins Fuller PHOTOGRAPHER · HISTORIAN Born October 24, 1947, in Seattle, Washington, Fuller received a BA in Literature and an MA in Teaching from Reed College, Portland, Oregon, in 1971. She studied with Oliver Gagliani in Virginia City, Nevada, in 1976 and is a PhD candidate in the History of Photography at Pennsylvania State University at State College.

Fuller is a freelance photographer and editorial assistant for the journal *History of Photography* edited by Heinz Henisch.

The photographer belongs to Friends of Photography and RPS.

Fuller works in documentary reportage. Past projects have been on high schools and rural Pennsylvania, and she is currently documenting one Amish dairy farm family in Pennsylvania.

PUBLICATIONS Periodicals: "The 'Picture Takin' Lady,'" review of *Jessie Tarbox Beals*, 1979, and "The Darkroom Abolished," text only, 1979, *History of Photography*; *Lightyear*, vol. 8, 1978; *Aura*, Sept 1976.

COLLECTIONS Middle Tennessee State Univ., Murfreesboro. Bibliothèque Nationale, Paris; and many private collections.

ADDRESS 142 W South Hills Ave, State College, PA 16801.

Hamish Fulton PHOTOGRAPHER · SCULPTOR Born in 1946 in London, England, Fulton studied sculpture at three London schools between 1966 and 1969: Hammersmith College of Art, St. Martins School of Art and the Royal College of Art.

He has been self-employed since 1970.

The photographer's work consist of wood-framed, mounted photographs and text that relates to walks taken in various landscapes. In these works the words and photographs are of equal importance.

PUBLICATIONS Monographs: *Roads and Paths*, 1978 (Schirmer Mosel: Munich, Germany); *Nepal*, 1975 (Van Abbe Mus.: Eindhoven, The Netherlands); *Hollow Lane*, 1971 (Situation

Publications: London); *The Sweet Grass Hills of Montana*, 1971 (Sperone Editore: Torino, Italy). Catalog: *Hamish Fulton*, 1974 (Galleria Toselli: Milan, Italy).

COLLECTIONS Milwaukee Art Ctr., HHK Fndn., Wisc.; MOMA, NYC. Art Gall. of South Australia, Adelaide; Basel Kunstmus., Switzerland; Musée Nationale d'Art Moderne, Paris; Natl. Gall., Ottawa, Ont., Canada; Natl. Gall. of New South Wales, Australia; Scottish Natl. Gall., Edinburgh; Stedelijk Mus., Amsterdam, The Netherlands; Tate Gall., London; Van Abbe Mus., Eindhoven, The Netherlands.

DEALERS Thackrey & Robertson, 2266 Union St, San Francisco, CA 94123; Waddington Galleries, Cork St, London W1, England.

Jack Fulton *PHOTOGRAPHER · TEACHER* Born June 30, 1939, in San Francisco, Fulton is a self-taught photographer influenced by André Kertész, Bill Brandt, Peter Breughel the elder and Albrecht Dürer.

He has taught at the San Francisco Art Institute since 1969 and was chairman of his department from 1973 to 1977.

A member of SPE, Fulton won a NEA Fellowship in 1980 and an award from the American Society of Graphic Arts in 1975.

In 1978 he wrote and acted in a half-hour PBS television program on portraits, "Close Exposures of the Best Kind."

Fulton's photography consists mainly of visual and verbal puns. He also attaches "written, drawn and collaged materials to or upon other prints."

PUBLICATION Catalogs: *Attitudes: Photography in the 70's*, 1979 (Santa Barbara Mus. of Art); *Jack Fulton's Puns & Anagrammatic Photographs*, Van Deren Coke, 1979 (San Francisco Mus. of Modern Art); *First Light*, 1975 (Humboldt State Univ.: Arcata, Calif.).

COLLECTION San Francisco Mus. of Modern Art.

DEALERS Robert Freidus, 158 Lafayette St, New York, NY 10013; Silver Image Gall., 92 S Washington St, Seattle, WA 98104.

ADDRESS 109 Orange St, San Rafael, CA 94901.

Mitchell Funk *PHOTOGRAPHER* Born February 25, 1950, in New York City, the self-taught Funk has been a freelance photographer since 1969.

A member of ASMP since 1974, he won a Gubernatorial Citation from Governor Hugh Carey of New York in 1979 and an Award of Distinctive Merit in 1973 from the Society of Publication Designers.

Funk's specialty is sandwiching color transparencies to create strongly graphic, unreal landscapes.

PUBLICATIONS Periodicals: *Photo*, Dec 1979; *Popular Photography*, Nov 1979, Apr 1976, Dec 1970; *Fotografi*, Oct 1979; *Photo*, Oct 1979; *German Colorfoto Journal*, Nov 1978, Sept 1976, Apr 1976; *Foto*, July 1977; *Camera 35*, Feb 1980, Aug 1976, Mar 1971.

COLLECTION Chase Manhattan Bank, NYC.

ADDRESS 500 E 77 St, New York, NY 10021.

G

Dennis Gabor *PHYSICIST* Born June 5, 1900, in Budapest, Hungary, Gabor died February 9, 1979, in London. He studied electrical engineering in Germany and earned a doctorate.

Gabor worked as a research engineer for the firm of Siemens and Halske in Berlin from 1917 until 1933, when he fled Nazi Germany. He then worked with Thomson-Houston Company of Rugby, Warwickshire, England, and later joined the staff of the Imperial College of Science and Technology at the University of London. From 1949 to 1958 he was a reader in electronics there, then a professor of applied electronics from 1958 until 1967, when he joined Columbia Broadcasting System Laboratories at Stamford, Connecticut, as a staff scientist.

Gabor's greatest achievement was the invention of holography, a method of three-dimensional photography that allows the viewer to study an object as if seeing it through a window rather than on an ordinary two-dimensional surface. In recognition of his invention of the holographic process, made in 1947 while doing work on an electron microscope, Gabor was awarded the 1971 Nobel Prize for Physics. Holography has been applied in the fields of art, medicine, topographic map making, communications and computer technology.

Some of Gabor's other work includes research on high-speed oscilloscopes, communication theory, physical optics and television.

PUBLICATIONS Books: *Beyond the Age of Waste*, 1978; *Holographie 1973*, 1973? (Carl Friedrich von Siemens Stiftung: Munich); *The Mature Society*, 1972; *The Proper Priorities of Science and Technology*, 1972 (Univ. of Southampton: England); *Thoughts on the Future*, 1972; *Innovations: Scientific, Technological, and Social*, 1970; *Redundancy or Redeployment: Economic & Social Implications*, 1968 (Marlow Fndn.: London); *The Dangers of Inertia—Planning for Adaptability*, 1967; *An Introduction to Coherent Optics and Holography*, George W.

Stroke, 1966; *Inventing the Future*, 1963; *Electronic Inventions and Their Impact on Civilization*, 1959 (Imperial Coll. of Science & Tech.: London); *The Electron Microscope*, 1946; *Theory of Communication*, 1945; *Electron Optics*, 1943. Periodicals: "Interference Microscope with Total Wavefront Reconstruction," w/W. P. Goss, *Journal of the Optical Society of America*, July 1966; "Holography, or the 'Whole Picture,'" *New Scientist*, Jan 13, 1966; "Microscopy by Reconstructed Wavefronts," *Proceedings of the Physics Society*, no. 64B 449, 1951; "Microscopy by Wavefront Reconstruction," *Proceedings of the Royal Society*, no. A197, 1949; "A New Microscopic Principle," *Nature*, no. 161, 1948.

COLLECTION Mus. of Holography, NYC.

Verena von Gagern *PHOTOGRAPHER · ARCHITECT* Born December 1, 1946 in Bonn, Germany, von Gagern received an MA in Architecture at Pennsylvania State University, University Park, and, in 1974, attended workshops in Arles, France.

Von Gagern has taught photography at Salzburg College, Austria, since 1975.

In 1975 the photographer won first prize of the International Prize for Young Photographers in Arles.

PUBLICATIONS Anthologies: *Vorstellungen und Wirklichkeit*, 1980 (Wienand Verlag, Munich); *Fotosymposion Düsseldorf*, 1980 (Mahnert Verlag, Munich). Catalogs: *Die Neue Sammlung Museum*, 1979 (Munich, Germany); *Catalogue of Photokina*, 1967 (Cologne, Germany). Periodicals: *Actuell Fotografi*, Oct 1980; *Photo*, May 1978; *Camera*, Sept 1978, Oct 1977; *Zoom*, Sept 1977 (Paris); *Nueva Lente*, Dec 1976; *Popular Photography*, Oct 1976; *Nueva Fotografía*, Sept 1976.

COLLECTIONS Die Neue Sammlung, Munich, Germany; Kunstgewerbe-Mus., Hamburg, Germany; Musée Réattu, Arles, France.

ADDRESS 8000 München 40, Genterstr 13, Germany.

Oliver L. Gagliani *PHOTOGRAPHER · TEACHER*
Born February 11, 1917, in Placerville, California, Gagliani studied at the California State University at San Francisco (1940–42) and at the Heald Engineering College in San Francisco (1951–53). He later received an MFA from the California College of Arts and Crafts in Oakland (1972).

He has been an instructor of photography at the University of California Extension in San Francisco since 1969 and at Image Circle in Berkeley, California, since 1970.

Gagliani was the recipient of a Fisher grant in 1977 and an NEA grant in 1976.

PUBLICATIONS Monograph: *Oliver Gagliani*, 1975. Anthologies: *The Photograph Collector's Guide*, Lee D. Witkin & Barbara London, 1979; *Vision and Expression*, Nathan Lyons, ed., 1969; *Light⁷*, Minor White, 1968. Catalog: *Light and Substance*, 1974 (Univ. of N. Mex. Art Mus.: Albuquerque). Periodical: *Petersen's Photographic*, Nov 1979.

DEALERS Susan Spiritus, 3336 Via Lido, Newport Beach, CA 92660; Weston Gall., POB 655, Carmel, CA 93921; The Print Gall., Delores & 6th, Carmel, CA 93921.

ADDRESS 605 Rocca Ave, S San Francisco, CA 94080.

Charles Gagnon *PAINTER · PHOTOGRAPHER · FILM MAKER* Born May 23, 1934, in Montreal, Quebec, Canada, Gagnon studied at the Art Students League, New York University and Parsons School of Design, all in New York City.

Since 1975 he has been professor of visual arts at the University of Ottawa, Canada. From 1967 to 1974 he taught for the Communication Arts Department at Concordia University in Montreal.

Gagnon is a member of the Royal Canadian Academy and received grants from the Canada Council in 1979, 1969 and 1962.

PUBLICATIONS Catalogs: *The Banff Purchase*, P. Cousineau, 1979 (Banff Centre: Canada); *Charles Gagnon*, Phillip Frye, 1978 (Montreal Mus. of Fine Arts: Canada); *Camerart*, 1974 (Optica Gall.: Montreal, Canada); *Five Photographers*, 1974 (Mt. Allison Univ., Owens Art Gall.: Sackville, New Brunswick, Canada). Periodicals: *Artscanada*, Mar/Apr 1977, Dec 1974; *Ovo*, June 1974.

PORTFOLIO *Banff Purchase*, 1979 (Banff Centre, Alberta, Canada).

COLLECTIONS Hirshhorn Mus., Wash., D.C.

In Canada: Art Gall. of Ontario; Art Gall. of Vancouver; Canadian Govt. External Affairs, Ottawa; Montreal Mus. of Fine Arts; Mt. Allison Univ., Sackville, New Brunswick; Musée d'Art Contemporain, Montreal; Natl. Gall. of Canada, Ottawa; Toronto Dominion Bank.

DEALER Yajima/Galerie, 307 St. Catherine St W, Ste 515, Montreal, Quebec, Canada H2X 2A3.

ADDRESS 3510 Addington St, Montreal, Quebec, Canada H4A 3G6.

Phyllis Galembo *PHOTOGRAPHER · TEACHER*
Born in Freeport, New York, on April 2, 1952, Galembo received her MFA from the University of Wisconsin in Madison in 1977.

She is currently an assistant professor of art and photography at the State University of New York in Albany. She was an instructor of art in 1977 to 1978 at the State University College at Oswego in New York, and worked as a photography instructor from 1974 to 1976 at the Oregon Middle School in Wisconsin.

Since 1975 Galembo has been a member of SPE and Friends of Photography. She was the recipient of a 1979 CAPS grant and has received several purchase awards.

The photographer's works are color portraits in a fabricated environment.

PUBLICATIONS Anthologies: *Insights, Self Portraits by Women*, 1978; *Women See Men*, 1977; *Women See Woman*, 1976.

COLLECTIONS Floating Fndn. of Photography, NYC; Univ. of Wisconsin, Madison. Univ. of Moncton, New Brunswick, Canada.

ADDRESS 85 S Lake St, Albany, NY 12203.

William M. Gallagher *PHOTOGRAPHER* Born February 26, 1923, in Hiawatha, Kansas, Gallagher died September 28, 1975 in Flint, Michigan. He graduated from St. Matthew's High School in 1943 and is self-taught in photography.

Gallagher won his first (box) camera for selling magazines during high school years. One of the first pictures he snapped, of the Detroit skyline, won him $5 in a local contest, which he invested in a home developing kit. From 1943 to 1945 he served in the U.S. Army, and in 1946 he worked on the staff of the Flint *Sporting Digest*, a weekly covering sports events. The following year he joined the staff of the Flint *Journal*, a daily, working as a wirephoto operator before being made a staff photographer in 1947. He remained at that post until his death.

Gallagher was a member of the NPPA and the Michigan Press Photographers Association and was a counselor in photography for the Boy

Scouts of America. In 1953 he won the Pulitzer Prize for his photograph of then-Democratic candidate Adlai E. Stevenson showing a hole in the sole of his shoe. Among several other awards garnered for that image were the Michigan Associated Press Contact (first place and best in show, 1953) and the Michigan Press Photography Contest (first place, 1953).

PUBLICATION   Anthology: *Moments,* Sheryle & John Leekley, foreword by Dan Rather, 1978.

Linda K. Gammell   PHOTOGRAPHER   Born January 14, 1948, in Austin, Minnesota, Gammell received a BA in Journalism and Mass Communication (1972) and an MFA in Photography/Art History (1978) from the University of Minnesota, Minneapolis. Her advisers were Gary Hallman and James Henkel.

As of this writing Gammell is a visiting artist and a photography instructor at the Minneapolis College of Art and Design. She also has taught photography for Film in the Cities (Minneapolis) since 1978. She was a photography instructor at the University of Minnesota in 1976–77.

A member of SPE, the photographer has belonged to the Women's Art Registry of Minnesota since 1975. The Minnesota State Arts Board awarded her a fellowship in 1979 and project grants in 1978 and 1976.

Her work "is about fragments of life, often suggesting a narrative. The images usually comprise like or disparate objects or materials which are combined, often in layers, to suggest new meanings or thoughts."

PUBLICATIONS   Catalogs: *Minnesota Energy,* 1980 (Tweed Museum of Art, Duluth, Minn); *Electroworks,* 1979 (IMP/GEH: Rochester); *Spectrum—New Directions in Color Photography,* 1979 (Univ. of Hawaii: Manao).

COLLECTIONS   In Minnesota: Federal Reserve Bank, Minneapolis; Minneapolis Inst. of Arts; Minneapolis Star & Tribune Co.; Univ. of Minn. Galls., Minneapolis; Walker Art Ctr., Minneapolis.

ADDRESS   126 Warwick St SE, Minneapolis, MN 55414.

John B. Ganis   PHOTOGRAPHER · TEACHER Born July 15, 1951, in Evanston, Illinois, Ganis earned a BA from Ohio Wesleyan University, Delaware, Ohio, in 1972 and received an MFA in 1980 from the University of Arizona, Tucson. He was a studio assistant to Irving Penn in 1971, took a workshop with Lisette Model in 1972 and studied with Laurence Fink from 1973 to 1975.

Ganis has been a graduate teaching assistant at the University of Arizona, Tucson, since 1978 and worked there as coordinator and instructor of a summer arts workshop in photography in 1979. In 1978 he was a special assistant to W. Eugene Smith at the university; from 1974 to 1977 he was adjunct lecturer at Kingsborough Community College, Brooklyn, New York.

He is a member of SPE and the Shins-Yi Chuan Association in New York City.

Ganis has concentrated his photography in and around water since 1974. He says: "My work involves the interpretation of human form, gesture, and movement in interaction with water."

PUBLICATIONS   Periodicals: *Photographer's Forum,* Nov/Dec 1979; *Popular Photography Annual,* 1976.

COLLECTION   Lehigh Univ., Bethlehem, Pa.

ADDRESS   333 N Tucson Blvd, Tucson, AZ 85716.

Wifredo Garcia   PHOTOGRAPHER · TEACHER Born June 15, 1935, in Barcelona, Spain, Garcia earned a Doctorate in Chemistry and Pharmacy at Universidad de Santo Domingo, Dominican Republic. He also undertook two years of postgraduate study at Kansas State University, Manhattan.

Garcia is currently a professor of photography at the Universidad Autónoma de Santo Domingo and at the Universidad Nacional Pedro Henriquez Urena, both in Santo Domingo. Formerly he was a professor of chemistry at the Universidad Católica Madre y Maestra in Santiago, Chile.

A member and former administrator of Casa de Teatro, he is president of Fotogrupo in Santo Domingo. In 1979 he won first prize at the National Artistic Photography Contest in Santo Domingo.

Garcia considers himself a naturalist and his work is designed to "make our people know the values of nature and its need to be preserved." He also investigates primitive cultures in the Antilles, relating them to current behavior of peasants and country peoples.

PUBLICATIONS   Books: *Fotografía,* 1978; *Algo de Mi,* 1976 (self-pub.).

COLLECTIONS   Galería de Arte Moderno, Santo Domingo; Museo de las Casas Reales, Santo Domingo; Museo del Hombre Dominican, Santo Domingo; Mus. of Anthropology, Phototec, Paris.

ADDRESS   POB 1003, Santo Domingo, Dominican Republic.

Alberto Schommer Garcia de la Peña   PHOTOGRAPHER · CINEMATOGRAPHER   Born in Victoria, Spain, on September 8, 1928, Garcia studied at the School of Color in Hamburg, Germany, under Dr. Schmid in 1960.

Since 1955 he has been a self-employed photographer in Madrid, and since 1975 has operated a private studio. From 1965 to 1975 he worked at the private studio Hilarión Eslava and from 1963 to 1965 worked at the private studio Ferraz. Garcia has belonged to the Real Sociedad Fotográfica of Madrid since 1965 and to Sociedad Fotográfica de Guipuzcoa since 1975.

He was named best photographer in Spain by *Blanco y Negro* magazine in 1979 and most popular photographer in Spain by *Flash-Foto* magazine in 1975, 1976 and 1978. In 1967 and 1971 he won first prize for documentary cinematography in Barcelona.

Using various formats, Garcia creates surrealistic collages in his personal work. He also does advertising and journalistic photography.

PUBLICATIONS Monograph: *Psychological Photos*, 1975 (Nueva Lente: Spain). Books (all in Spain): *Alava Abierta*, 1979 (Caja Provincial de Ahorros de Alava); *Los Reyes Viajan*, 1978 (Fidusora de Seix Barral); *El Grito de un Pueblo*, 1977 (Editiones Vascas). Anthologies: *Nude 1980*, 1980; *Fantastic Photography in the World*, 1979.

COLLECTIONS Canon Gall., Amsterdam, The Netherlands; Gall. Château D'eau, Toulouse, France; Shadai Gall., Tokyo.

ADDRESS Estudio Zurbano, 84-bajo, Madrid 3, Spain.

Victor Gardaya PHOTOGRAPHER · TEACHER · WRITER Born in Port Chester, New York, on May 9, 1945, Gardaya received his BA in Philosophy from the City College of New York in 1968. He is self-taught in photography. Major influences on the artist are André Kertész, Duane Michals, Susan Sontag and Roger Fry.

A freelance photographer since 1973, Gardaya is also an instructor in photography at Seattle Central Community College, where he has been since 1977. In 1979 he became affiliated with the Factory of Visual Arts, Seattle, as an instructor of photography, where he continues as of this writing. In 1979 Gardaya also began to work with *Art Week*, *Argus* and *Northwest Photography* as a writer, photographer and film critic.

The artist is a member of the Seattle Photography Council and Friends of Photography. In 1979 he received an NEA grant to produce his book, *Art Deco Seattle*, with Allied Arts of Seattle. That same year the Washington State Arts Commission awarded him a special commendation in the Honors Program for Visual Artists.

"My principal concern is with documenting the human condition," says Gardaya. Technically he is interested in "the fine print"; philosophically, the "surreal, humanist, existential."

PUBLICATION Monograph: *Art Deco Seattle*, 1979.

COLLECTIONS In Seattle, Washington: Bank of Tokyo; SAFECO Coll.; Seattle Art Mus., Mus. of History & Industry.

DEALER Equivalents Gall., 1822 Broadway, Seattle, WA 98122.

ADDRESS 2517 E Miller, Seattle, WA 98112.

Bernard Gardel PHOTOGRAPHER Born September 2, 1951, in Lausanne, Switzerland, Gardel was influenced by the paintings of Paul Klee, the photos of Bill Brandt and the poetry of Rimbaud, Poe and Céline.

A freelance photographer since 1977, he was a commercial photographer from 1974 to 1977 and a reproduction photographer from 1971 to 1974.

Gardel won awards at the International Triennial Exhibition of Photography, Basel, Switzerland, and at the Great Prize of Swiss Photography exhibit in 1978. He was awarded Swiss Confederation grants in 1975 and 1976.

Working in large-format black-and-white, Gardel considers his photographs to be subjective interpretations of reality.

PUBLICATIONS Monographs: *Audio-Visual*, 1979 (Arles, France); *Fotografische Meditationen*, 1976. Periodicals: *Foto-Ciné-Expert*, May 1979; *Fotographie*, no. 9, 1979; *Professionelle Camera*, Jan 1979; *Photo*, Dec 1978; *Fotografie*, nos. 7 & 8, 1978; *Photographie*, Nov 1978; *Printletter*, Jan 1976; *Photoamateur*, May 1975.

COLLECTIONS Canon Gall., Geneva, Switzerland; Jean Dieuzaide Gall., Toulouse, France; Dieter Krebaum Gall., Weiheim/Mannheim, Germany; Lange-Irschl Gall., Munich, Germany; Moreno Gall, Geneva; Mus. of Art & Hist., Fribourg, Switzerland; Nikon Gall., Zurich, Switzerland; Photo Art Basel, Basel, Switzerland; Portfolio Gall., Lausanne, Switzerland; RES Gall., Hamburg, Germany; Trockenpresse Gall., Berlin, Germany; Work Gall., Zurich, Switzerland.

DEALERS Lange-Irschl, Türkenstrasse 54, 8000 Munich 40, Germany; Andreas Müller-Pohle Stargarder, Weg 18 D-3400, Göttingen, Germany.

ADDRESS Ebnetstr 106, 5504 Othmarsingen, Switzerland.

Alexander Gardner *PHOTOGRAPHER* Born 1821 in Paisley, Renfrew, Scotland, Gardner died in 1882 in Washington, D.C. A jeweler's apprentice from about 1835 to 1843, he pursued, on his own, interests in chemistry, optics and astronomy. He was self-taught in photography, but his years with Mathew Brady clearly had an impact on Gardner's work. His son, James Gardner, also became a photographer.

Before coming to America and working as Mathew Brady's assistant in 1856, Gardner was employed as a reporter and editor for the Glasgow *Sentinel.* He opened and operated Brady's Washington, D.C., studio in 1858, but resigned from Brady's stable of photographers in 1863 to operate his own studio. He felt that Brady did not give individual photographers both the credit and monetary gain that were due them, and other of Brady's best photographers, such as Timothy O'Sullivan, joined Gardner's mutiny. Gardner was named an official photographer for the Army of the Potomac and, in 1867, became the official photographer for the Union Pacific Railroad.

The photographer reportedly experimented with studio lighting by electricity around 1858 to 1862.

Noted especially for his Civil War photographs, Gardner also documented many other important scenes of U.S. history, including the execution of the conspirators against Lincoln, and Lincoln's funeral procession. He took many portraits of the sixteenth president, including the last ever taken, and he also photographed President Andrew Jackson, the trial and execution of the Andersonville Commandant Wirz and the life of the Great Plains Indians. He worked chiefly in stereoscopes, using the collodion wet-plate process.

PUBLICATIONS Books: *Gardner's Photographic Sketch Book of the War*, 2 vols, 1866; *Rays of Sunlight from South America*, printer, negatives by Henry Moulton, 1865. Anthologies: *The Photograph Collector's Guide*, Lee D. Witkin & Barbara London, 1979; *The Invented Eye*, Edward Lucie-Smith, 1975; *The Magic Image*, Cecil Beaton & Gail Buckland, 1975; *Looking at Photographs*, John Szarkowski, 1973; *Masters of Photography*, Beaumont & Nancy Newhall, 1969; *Photography and the American Scene*, Robert Taft, 1938. Periodicals: "Alexander Gardner's Photographs Along the 35th Parallel," Robert Sobieszek, *Image*, June 1971; "Alexander Gardner," J. Cobb, *Image*, June 1958.

COLLECTIONS Art Inst. of Chicago; Boston Pub. Lib.; Harvard Univ., Houghton Lib., Cambridge, Mass.; IMP/GEH, Rochester; Kansas Hist. Soc., Topeka; L/C, Wash., D.C.; Mo. Hist. Soc., St. Louis; MOMA, NYC; Natl. Archives, Wash., D.C.; Princeton Univ., N.J.; Smithsonian Inst., Wash., D.C.; Univ. of N. Mex. Art Mus., Albuquerque; Univ. of Penn., Philadelphia. British Mus., London; Natl. Gall. of Canada, Ottawa, Ontario.

George W. Gardner *PHOTOGRAPHER* Born July 22, 1940, in Albany, New York, Gardner received a BA in Anthropology from the University of Missouri in 1965. He studied with Paul Fisher.

Since 1962 Gardner has been a freelance editorial photographer.

Working primarily in black-and-white, Gardner focuses on images of America in which "opposites sardonically collide."

PUBLICATIONS Book: *Classic Country Inns of America*, w/Lilo Raymond, pub., 1978. Periodicals: *Popular Photography Annual*, 1980; *Creative Camera*, Feb 1972; *U.S. Camera Annual*, 1970; *Famous Photographer's Annual*, 1969.

COLLECTIONS A.T.T. Inc., NYC; Chicago Art Inst.; ICP, NYC; MOMA, NYC.

DEALER Douglas Kenyon Inc., 155 E Ohio St, Chicago, IL 60611.

ADDRESS POB 298, Hillsdale, NY 12529.

Richard Milton Garrod *CITY PLANNER · PHOTOGRAPHER* Born June 10, 1924, in Los Angeles, Garrod majored in photography at Pasadena City College, California (1941–42), and earned a BA from the University of California, Santa Barbara (1948). He then took an MA at the University of California, Berkeley (1952). The photographer studied with Ansel Adams, Brett Weston and Minor White.

Since 1962 Garrod has been planning director for the city of Monterey, a position he held for the city of Fontana from 1954 to 1962. He was also a city planner for the city of San Bernardino from 1949 to 1954. (All three are in California.)

A member of SPE, he is an advisory trustee for Friends of Photography (since 1979); he served on their board of trustees from 1968 to 1979, and was secretary from 1975 to 1978.

PUBLICATIONS Book: *Garrod-Gilpin Photographs*, w/Henry Gilpin, intro. by Ansel Adams & Glenn Wessels, n.d. Periodicals: *Popular Photography Annual*, 1969; *Contemporary Photographer*, 1961.

COLLECTIONS Brand Art Ctr., Glendale, Calif.; IMP/GEH, Rochester; Oakland Mus., Calif.; Smithsonian Inst., Wash., D.C.; Utah State Univ., Logan.

DEALER   The Print Gall., Dolores & Sixth, POB 7418, Carmel, CA 93921.

ADDRESS   2121 San Vito Circle, Monterey, CA 93940.

Jeffrey S. Gates   PHOTOGRAPHER · TEACHER Born in Los Angeles, California, on July 17, 1949, Gates completed his BA in Political Science at Michigan State University, East Lansing (1971), and his MA (1973) and MFA (1975) in Photography and Design at UCLA.

Gates currently teaches photography at a number of colleges in the Los Angeles area: Chaffey (since 1976), Pasadena City (since 1976), Cerritos (since 1977) and UCLA Extension (since 1977). He also became co-director of the gallery at Los Angeles Harbor College in 1979 and in 1978–79 was senior photographer for the Neuropsychiatric Institute at University of California at Los Angeles. He taught photography at Santa Ana College (California) from 1975 to 1979.

Gates is a member of SPE, CAA and the Los Angeles Center for Photographic Studies, where he is also on the board of trustees.

Gates describes his work as "a personal statement which is meant to convey the ambiguity that shapes and deforms all that exists."

PUBLICATIONS   Anthologies: *Self-Portrayal*, 1979; *Fantastic Photographs*, 1979. Periodicals: *Picture Magazine*, no. 10, 1979; *Creative Camera*, Oct 1979; *Printletter*, no. 17, 1978; *Progresso Fotografico*, May 1977; *Picture Magazine*, no. 4, 1977; *Untitled II*, 1976 (Friends of Photography); *Le Nouveau Photocinéma*, no. 52, 1976.

PORTFOLIO   *L.A. Issue* (group), 1979 (Los Angeles Ctr. for Photographic Studies).

COLLECTIONS   CCP, Tucson; Los Angeles County Mus. of Art; Minneapolis Inst. of the Arts, Minn.; Oakland Mus., Calif.; Santa Barbara Mus. of Art, Calif. Bibliothèque Nationale, Paris; Victoria & Albert Mus., London.

DEALER   G. Ray Hawkins Gall., 7224 Melrose Ave, Los Angeles, CA 90046.

Charles Robert Gatewood   PHOTOGRAPHER · TEACHER   Born November 8, 1942, in Chicago, Gatewood received a BA in Anthropology from the University of Missouri, Columbia, in 1963. He studied photography with George W. Gardner.

Since 1977 Gatewood has published *The Flash*, a photographic tabloid. He taught at ICP (1975–78), The New School for Social Research (1978) and NYU (1977), all in New York City. He also taught at San Francisco Art Institute in 1977, was an artist-in-residence at Light Work in Syracuse, New York, in 1976 and from 1969 to 1973 was a staff photographer for the *Manhattan Tribune*.

The photographer won CAPS fellowships in 1974 and 1977.

His photographic themes have included deviant behavior, the Mardi Gras and the Wall Street area of New York City.

PUBLICATIONS   Books: *Pushing Ink: The Fine Art of Tattooing*, w/Spider Webb & Marco Vassi, 1979; *X-1000*, w/Spider Webb & Marco Vassi, 1977; *Sidetripping*, w/William S. Burroughs, 1975 (New York). Anthologies: *The Grotesque in Photography*, A. D. Coleman, ed., 1977; *The Family of Children*, 1977; *People in Focus*, 1977; *Celebrations*, Minor White & Jonathan Green, eds., 1974; *Octave of Prayer*, Minor White, ed., 1972. Periodicals: *Camera 35*, Mar 1980; *Petersen's Photographic Magazine*, Jan 1979, Dec 1978; *Creative Camera*, Apr 1977, Mar 1975; *Popular Photography Annual*, 1977, 1967; *35mm Photography*, winter 1976, summer 1973, spring 1972, spring 1970; *Color Photography Annual*, 1970; *Popular Photography Woman*, winter, fall, spring 1970, 1969, 1968; *Modern Photography Annual*, 1969; *U.S. Camera Annual*, 1969.

COLLECTIONS   ICP, NYC; Light Gall., NYC; Light Work, Syracuse, N.Y.; Neikrug Gall., NYC; Portland Mus. of Art, Maine. Musée Français de la Photographie, Bievres, France.

ADDRESS   50 W 22 St, New York, NY 10010.

Pierre Gaudard   PHOTOGRAPHER   Born October 5, 1927, in Marvelise (Doubs), France, Gaudard was educated at Ecole Estienne in Paris.

A freelance photographer, Gaudard was the recipient of two grants from the Arts Council of Canada (1969 and 1973).

PUBLICATIONS   Monographs: *Les Prisons*, 1976; *Les ouvriers*, 1972. Periodicals: *Zoom*, 1980 (Paris); *Ovo*, 1978, 1976.

COLLECTIONS   Bibliothèque Nationale, Paris; Bibliothèque Nationale, Ottawa, Canada; Natl. Film Board, Ottawa, Canada.

DEALER   Yajima Gall., Montreal, Quebec, Canada.

ADDRESS   10255 rue Jeanne Mance, Montréal, Québec, H3L3B7 Canada.

Jean Claude Gautrand   PHOTOJOURNALIST · PHOTOHISTORIAN   Born in Sains en Gohelle, Pas de Calais, France, on December 19, 1932, Gautrand has worked for the French postal service for the last twenty years. Concurrently he has written for such publications as *Photo-Journal*, *Nouveau Photo Cinéma* and *Photo Ciné Revue*.

A founding member of Libre Expression (1959), Gautrand also belongs to the Conseil Artistique de la Fondation Nationale de la Photographie, the Conseil des Journées Internationales d'Arles, and George Eastman House. The artist has won the Grand Prize of Arts de la Ville Marseille, Musée Cantini (1969), the Grand Prize d'Avant Garde of Spain (1967), and the Grand Prize of the Fédération Internationale d'Art Photographique (1965).

PUBLICATIONS Monographs: *Forteresses du Dérisoire*, 1977 (Presse de la Connaissance: Paris); *Assassinat de Baltard*, 1972 (Formule 13); *Les Murs de Mai*, 1968 (Pensée et Action). Book: *Histoire de la Photographie Française*, Claude Nori, 1980. Catalogs: *Catalogue Monographie du Musée Nicéphore Niepce à Châlon-sur-Saône*, 1978; *J. C. Gautrand*, 1977 (Galerie Municipale du Chateau d'Eau: France). Periodicals: *Progresso Fotografico*, July 1977, Aug 1972; *Camera*, Apr 1977, Oct 1972; *Modern Photography*, June 1976, May 1972; *Photo Ciné Revue*, Sept 1972, June 1967; *Photo*, Sept 1972; *Nouveau Photo Cinéma*, May 1972, Apr 1967; *Arte Fotográfico*, Nov 1969; *Fotografia Italiana*, Jan 1968.

COLLECTIONS IMP/GEH, Rochester. In France: Bibliothèque Nationale, Paris; Cllctn. des Affaires Culturelles de la Ville de Paris; Musée Cantini, Marseille; Musée du Chateau d'Eau, Toulouse; Musée Nicéphore Niepce, Châlon-sur-Saône; Musée Réattu, Arles; Musée Toulon, Toulon.

ADDRESS 45 rue d'Avron, 75020 Paris, France.

Robert George Gauvreau PHOTOGRAPHER · TEACHER Born August 14, 1948, in Renton, Washington, Gauvreau earned a BA in 1970 from Central Washington State University, Ellensburg, and an MFA in 1973 in Photography from Arizona State University, Flagstaff. His major influences were Jack Stuler, Eric Kronengold and James Sahlstrand.

Gauvreau has been a photography instructor at Modesto Junior College, Modesto, California, since 1974. In 1973–74 he was a lecturer in photography at State University of New York, New Paltz, and from 1972 to 1973 he was a photography lab manager at Arizona State University.

A member of SPE since 1971, Gauvreau also belonged to Friends of Photography from 1971 to 1976.

Gauvreau works exclusively in large-format color, producing Ektachrome and Cibachrome prints. He mainly photographs modified natural scenes.

COLLECTIONS Coos Art Mus., Coos Bay, Ore.;

Creative Eye Gall., Sonoma, Calif.; Lucas Gall., San Francisco; Va. Intermont Coll., Bristol, Va.

ADDRESS 1425 Glenhaven Dr, Modesto, CA 95355.

Carney E. S. Gavin ARCHAEOLOGIST · MUSEUM CURATOR Born March 28, 1939, in Boston, Massachusetts, Gavin received an AB in Classics from Boston College in 1959. He was a Fulbright Scholar at Jesus College, Oxford University, from 1959 to 1961 and received a Bachelor of Sacred Theology degree from the University of Innsbruck in 1963, and a PhD in Near Eastern Languages and Civilizations in 1973 at Harvard University.

Since 1975 Gavin has been curator of the Harvard Semitic Museum. He was their assistant curator from 1973 to 1975.

Gavin has been assistant to the president of the American Schools of Oriental Research since 1973, director of the Goethe Society of New England since 1978, and a member of the International Committee for the Restoration of Babylon since 1978. Gavin was the recipient of an honorary diploma from the University of Damascus in 1978 for research in regional history. He was also the creator of a television film using early Middle Eastern documentary photographs, entitled *Petra, Jerash, and Damascus*, in 1978.

Gavin is involved with historical investigations, interdisciplinary research and the international coordination of various projects to preserve and share surviving early Middle Eastern photographs. He is also the director of photohistorical exhibitions and film projects.

PUBLICATIONS Book: *Remembrances of the Middle East*, w/Robert Sobleszek, 1980. Periodical: "Bonfils and the Early Photography of the Near East," *Harvard Library Bulletin*, Oct 1978.

ADDRESS Harvard Semitic Mus., 6 Divinity Ave, Cambridge, MA 02138.

Hans Gedda PHOTOGRAPHER Gedda was born July 8, 1942, in Flen, Sweden.

Since 1973 he has been a freelance photographer. Previously, he worked for Rolf Winquist at his studio (1963–73), where he learned photography.

Gedda was a recipient of a grant from the Stockholm Photographic Museum in 1974.

PUBLICATIONS Book: *Gedda's Pictures*, w/ Lars Forssell. Anthology: *SX-70 Art*, 1979.

COLLECTION Camera Obscura, Stockholm, Sweden.

ADDRESS Hantverkargatan 44, 11221 Stockholm, Sweden.

William Gedney PHOTOGRAPHER Born in Albany, New York, on October 29, 1932, Gedney studied at Pratt Institute in Brooklyn, New York, earning a BFA in 1955.

Recipient of a Guggenheim Foundation grant in 1966, Gedney was also awarded a Fulbright Fellowship in 1969, a CAPS grant in 1972, and an NEA grant in 1975.

PUBLICATION Anthology: *Vision & Expression*, Nathan Lyons, ed. 1969.

COLLECTIONS IMP/GEH, Rochester; MOMA, NYC.

ADDRESS 476 Myrtle Ave, Brooklyn, NY 11205.

Judith Michelman Gefter PHOTOGRAPHER Born April 4, 1922, in Gloversville, New York, Gefter earned a certificate from the Art School at Pratt Institute, Brooklyn, New York, in 1943. Since 1953 she has attended courses at the New York University School of Education, University of Florida, University of Miami, and the Wilson Hicks Conferences on the Communication Arts. She studied with William E. Parker and names Morris Gordon as her mentor.

A freelance photographer since 1958, she was a studio photographer from 1948 to 1958. Gefter was an artist/illustrator at the Office of War Information, Film Strip Division, in New York from 1943 to 1945, working with the Farm Security Administration files and with those of Edward Steichen from World War II.

Gefter has belonged to ASMP since 1958. She was featured in an audiovisual program completed in 1980, "Judith Gefter—The Challenge of Freelance Photography," produced by Media Loft Inc., Minneapolis, Minnesota.

Gefter shoots varied photographic series using color and silver images. She experiments in non-image color and storytelling as well as illustrative abstractions.

PUBLICATIONS Book: *Jacksonville Bicentennial*, 1976. Periodical: *Penthouse Photo World*, 1975.

COLLECTIONS Jacksonville Art Mus., Fla.; Mint Mus., Charlotte, N.C.; and private collections.

DEALER Russell B. Hicken, Fine Arts Ltd., 4201 Bayshore, Tampa, FL 33611.

ADDRESS 1725 Clemson Rd, Jacksonville, FL 32217.

Herbert Gehr
See Edmund Bert Gerard

Rene Guillermo Gelpi PHOTOGRAPHER [See plate 107] Born on June 4, 1946, in Brooklyn, New York, Gelpi currently works as night manager of Jack Ward Color Services, also in New York.

In 1978 he received the Robert F. Kennedy Journalism Award in Photography, Society of Publication Designers Award of Merit (1975), a CAPS grant in photography (1974) and a CAPS grant from the state of New York (1972).

Gelpi is known for his documentary portraits, and his work is described thus by Edward Bryant, Director of Picker Art Gallery: "His straightforward photographs go far beyond a merely sociological documentation or an exploitation of the unusual. To these individuals, with whom he achieves a remarkable responsive interaction, he gives persuasive, emblematic form as part of the human fabric of the city."

PUBLICATIONS Periodicals: *Nippon Camera*, Feb 1980; *Progresso Fotografico*, Apr 1979; *News Reporter*, Oct/Nov 1976; *Infinity*, Mar 1973; *Popular Photography*, June 1972.

COLLECTIONS Univ. of Kansas Mus. of Art; Charles Penny Fndn.

ADDRESS 675 Lincoln Ave, Brooklyn, NY 11208.

André Gelpke PHOTOGRAPHER Born March 15, 1947, in Beienrode, Gifhorn, Germany, Gelpke studied at Folkwangschule in Essen with Dr. Otto Steinert (1969–75).

He was co-founder of Bildagentur VISUM in Essen, where he worked from 1975 to 1978. Gelpke has been a member of DGPh since 1978.

PUBLICATIONS Books: *Dumont Foto* no. 1, 1979, *Die Geschichte der Fotografie im 20 Jahrhundert (History of Photography in the 20th Century)*, 1977 (Dumont Buchverlag: Cologne, Germany). Catalogs: *Deutsche Fotografie nach 1945*, 1979 (Fotoforum Kassel); *Essener Kunstszene*, 1979 (Gruga: Essen); *Sander Gallery*, 1979 (Wash., D.C.); *Venezia '79—La Fotografia*, 1979 (Venedig); *Aktion, Illustration, Feature*, 1978 (Folkwangmuseum: Essen); *Spectrum Galerie*, 1975 (Hannover). Periodicals: *Zoom*, nos. 55, 46 (Paris); *Professional Camera*, Sept/Oct 1979; *Schweizerische Photorundschau*, Aug 1979, Apr/May 1977; *Foto*, July 1979, June 1974; *Arte Fotográfico*, no. 314, 1978; *Camera*, Sept 1978, Apr 1977, Nov 1970; *Fotografie*, Aug 1978, May 1978; *Fotografia Italiana*, no. 205, 1975, no. 179, 1973;

Creative Camera, May 1974, July 1972; *Popular Photography Annual*, 1974, 1973; *Modern Photography Annual*, 1974.

COLLECTIONS Bibliothèque Nationale, Paris; Folkwang Mus., Essen, Germany; Neue Sammlung, Munich, Germany; Stedelijk Mus., Amsterdam, The Netherlands.

DEALERS Sander Gall., 2600 Connecticut Ave, Washington, DC 20008; Work Gall., Trittligasse 24, CH 8001, Zurich, Switzerland.

ADDRESS Meisenburgstr. 49, 4300 Essen 1, West Germany.

Arnold Genthe PHOTOGRAPHER Born in Berlin in 1869, Genthe died in New Milford, Connecticut, on August 9, 1942. He attended Wilhelm Gymnasium in Hamburg, Germany, then studied classical philology, archaeology, and philosophy at the Universities of Berlin and Jena, receiving a PhD in 1894. He studied at the Sorbonne in Paris from 1894 to 1895.

Genthe came to San Francisco in 1895 as a tutor to a German baron's son, and later opened his first portrait studio. In 1911 he moved to New York and opened another portrait studio, becoming a U.S. citizen in 1918.

The photographer belonged to the Bohemian Club in San Francisco, a circle of artists and writers. A linguist, Genthe was proficient in eight modern and ancient languages, writing his doctoral thesis in Latin. He received several university scholarships.

A collector of paintings, sculpture, old books, tapestries, furniture and Chinese porcelains, he also published several short stories and poems.

Genthe photographed hundreds of celebrities of the stage, dance, society, finance and politics, including Presidents Theodore Roosevelt, William Howard Taft and Woodrow Wilson. His series of photographs of Isadora Duncan and her dancers is frequently published, and he is also particularly known for his candid shots of San Francisco's Chinatown and the great San Francisco earthquake and fire of 1906. Initially working with gelatin dry-plate negatives and film negatives in platinum and silver prints, Genthe began using color in 1908 and produced many well-known autochromes.

PUBLICATIONS Books: *Walt Whitman in Camden*, preface by Christopher Morley, 1938; *As I Remember*, autobio., 1936; *Isadora Duncan*, foreword by Max Eastman, 1929; *Impressions of Old New Orleans*, foreword by Grace King, 1926; *Japanese Color Prints*, 1917; *The Book of the Dance*, 1916; *Sanctuary: A Bird Masque*, Percy MacKaye, 1913; *The Yellow Jacket: A Chinese Play Done in a Chinese Manner*, George C. Hazelton, Jr., & J. Harry Benrimo, 1913; *Old Chinatown*, Will Irwin, 1908, rev. ed. 1913; *De Lucani Codice Erlangensi*, 1894; *Deutsches Slang*, 1892. Anthologies: *The Photograph Collector's Guide*, Lee D. Witkin & Barbara London, 1979; *Photography Rediscovered*, David Travis & Anne Kennedy, 1979; *The Valiant Knights of Daguerre . . . by Sadakichi Hartmann*, Harry W. Lawton & George Know, eds., 1978; *The Collection of Alfred Stieglitz*, Weston J. Naef, 1978; *The Invented Eye*, Edward Lucie-Smith, 1975; *The Magic Image*, Cecil Beaton & Gail Buckland, 1975; *Looking at Photographs*, John Szarkowski, 1973; *The Picture History of Photography*, Peter Pollack, 1958; *Highlights and Shadows*, 1937. Periodicals: "Arnold Genthe," Will Irwin, *Wilson's Photography Magazine*, 50, 1913; "A Photographer of Japan—Arnold Genthe," Sidney Allen, *Photographic Times*, 42, 1910.

COLLECTIONS Art Inst. of Chicago; Calif. Palace of the Legion of Honor, San Francisco; IMP/GEH, Rochester; L/C, Wash., D.C.; Metro. Mus. of Art, NYC; New Orleans Mus. of Art; N.Y. Hist. Soc., NYC; Oakland Mus., Calif.; Smithsonian Inst., Wash., D.C.

Lowell Georgia PHOTOGRAPHER Born March 19, 1933, in Green Bay, Wisconsin, Georgia received a BA in English from St. Norbert College in DePere, Wisconsin.

Since 1969 he has been a freelance photographer. In the past he has worked for the National Geographic Society (1967–68), was picture editor for the *Denver Post* (1960–67) and worked for the *Green Bay Press Gazette* (1949–60).

Georgia was named National Press Photographer of the Year in 1963, was awarded the Inland Newspaper Association Trophy in 1960, and was named the Wisconsin Press Photographer of the Year in 1959.

PUBLICATIONS Books: *Trails West*, 1979; *Into the Wilderness*, 1978; *Children's Dolphins Book*, 1976. Periodicals: "Arctic Wildlife Range, Alaska," 1979, "Natural Gas," 1978, "Edmonton, Frontier of the North," 1976, *National Geographic*.

REPRESENTATIVE Photo Researchers, 60 E 56 St, New York, NY 10022.

ADDRESS 8665 W 67 Pl, Arvada, CO 80004.

Tyrone Georgiou PHOTOGRAPHER · TEACHER Born in New York City, Georgiou attended Yale School of Art and Architecture from 1969 to 1972; here he received a BFA and MFA.

He has been associate professor of art at State

University of New York, Buffalo, since 1972. From 1967 to 1970 he was a photographer and designer for the Architects' Renewal Committee in Harlem, New York City.

Georgiou won an NEA Photographer's Fellowship in 1979 and a fellowship from the Research Foundation, State University of New York, in 1975.

PUBLICATION   Periodical: *Still 3*, 1973.

COLLECTIONS   IMP/GEH, Rochester; Polaroid Clctn., Cambridge, Mass.

ADDRESS   123 Ashland Ave, Buffalo, NY 14222.

Edmund Bert Gerard   *PHOTOJOURNALIST · CINEMATOGRAPHER*   Born March 28, 1910, in Berlin, Germany, Gerard received a BA in 1929 from Lette Institute of Photography in Berlin. His mentor was cinematographer Karl Freund. In his work as a still photographer, Gerard is known as Herbert Gehr.

Since 1950 Gerard has been self-employed as a freelance cinematographer. Previously, he worked as a staff photographer for *Life* magazine (1944–50) after working under an exclusive contract with *Life* as a photographer (1939–44). In 1944 he was assigned by the United States government as motion picture photo-director of overseas operations. In 1938 he worked for *Life* through the Black Star Picture Agency. In Cairo, Egypt, he worked for both *The New York Times* as a staff photoreporter and for Fox Movietone news as a freelance cameraman (1937).

Currently a member of the International Alliance of Theatrical and Stage Engineers, local 644, he has also been a member of the National Academy of Television Arts and Sciences since 1954. Gerard has been the recipient of Emmy Awards in Cinematography for *This Is Edward Steichen* (1965), *Superfluous People* (1962), and *Junkyard by the Sea* (1960).

He was the first to photograph a color essay for *Life* (September 1939).

PUBLICATIONS   Periodical: *American Cinematographer*, July 1971, May 1969, Feb 1968.

ADDRESS   2 Ramsey Rd, Great Neck, NY 11023.

Ingeborg Gerdes   *PHOTOGRAPHER*   Born in Merseburg, Germany, on July 20, 1938, Gerdes earned an MFA in Photography from the San Francisco Art Institute in 1970. She has been a freelance photographer since 1970, and taught photography at the University of California Extension from 1976 to 1979, and at the San Francisco Art Institute in 1978.

Gerdes received two NEA fellowships (1975, 1977), and an NEA Survey Grant (1978). Her work is documentary.

PUBLICATIONS   Anthologies: *Some Twenty Odd Visions*, 1978; *Eros and Photography*, 1977; *Women of Photography*, 1975. Catalog: *California Photographers*, 1970 (Univ. of California: Davis). Periodicals: *Latent Image*, 1:1, 1978; *Camera*, Jan 1975.

COLLECTIONS   Harvard Univ., Fogg Art Mus., Cambridge, Mass.; Pasadena Art Mus., Calif.; San Francisco Mus. of Modern Art; Smith College Mus. of Art, Northampton, Mass. Bibliothèque Nationale, Paris.

ADDRESS   2015 Stockton St, San Francisco, CA 94133.

Robert R. Gerhart, III   *TEACHER · PHOTOGRAPHER · PAINTER*   Born October 24, 1943, in Reading, Pennsylvania, Gerhart earned a BFA from Pratt Institute, Brooklyn, New York, in 1965 and an MFA from Tyler School of Art, Temple University, Philadelphia, Pennsylvania, in 1969.

Since 1973 he has been assistant professor of art at University of North Carolina, Greensboro. From 1969 to 1973 he was an instructor at the School of the Dayton Art Institute, Ohio.

A member of the United Arts Council in Greensboro, Gerhart won University of North Carolina faculty grants in 1975, 1977 and 1978 and a Mint Museum Biennial Purchase Award, Charlotte, North Carolina, in 1975. At the Spring Mills Art Show in Lancaster, South Carolina, in 1979, he was named Best in Category.

Gerhart has produced books that are "serial works combining collage, montage, copy work, and repainting directly over photographs." He has used offset lithography and some duotone.

PUBLICATIONS   Books (self-pub.): *Turnpike Trip*, 1978; *Night Trains*, 1975; *The Wink*, 1974; *Eyes at Waterlevel*, 1972. Periodical: *Latent Image 3*, 1976.

COLLECTIONS   Duke Hospital, Durham, N.C.; Rausch Industries, N.C.; Springs Mills, Inc., Lancaster, S.C.; Univ. of N.C., Weatherspoon Gall., Greensboro.

DEALERS   Light Impressions, Box 3012, Rochester, NY 14614; Printed Matter, 7 Lispenard St, New York, NY 10013.

ADDRESS   Art Dept., University of North Carolina, Greensboro, NC 27412.

Monte H. Gerlach   *PHOTOGRAPHER · TEACHER*   Born January 1, 1950, in Hastings, Nebraska, Gerlach studied with Jim Alinder at the University of Nebraska, Lincoln (BA, 1972), and with Arthur

Siegel at Illinois Institute of Technology, Chicago (MS in Photography, 1975).

Currently a photography instructor at Ithaca College, Ithaca, New York (since 1978), he held the same position at Northern Illinois University, De Kalb, from 1976 to 1979. He was an assistant photographer for *Playboy* magazine in Chicago (1975–76).

A member of SPE, CAA, Friends of Photography and IMP/GEH, Gerlach won first place in the Image Gallery Photo Talent Search in New York City in 1979, and the Critic's Award of the Young Photographer's Competition in Arles, France, in 1978. He has also made a children's film, *Becoming Me*, for educational television in Lincoln, Nebraska.

Gerlach's work has included three types of images: distortions of nudes done with a slit camera and a strobe; street photographs exploring visual humor and the "mask" people wear in large cities; and light effects on parts of buildings and other artifacts.

PUBLICATIONS Anthologies: *Family of Woman*, 1979; *Young American Photographers*, 1974. Periodicals: *Exposure: SPE*, Mar 1978; *Aura*, June 1977, June 1976.

COLLECTION Univ. of Neb., Sheldon Art Mus., Lincoln.

ADDRESS 205 S Titus, Ithaca, NY 14850.

Thomas Roma Germano PHOTOGRAPHER · TEACHER Born in Brooklyn, New York, on June 14, 1950, Germano works as a freelance photographer as well as a photography instructor with United Cerebral Palsy in Brooklyn. From 1971 to 1974 he taught photography at the Pratt Institute, also in Brooklyn.

In 1975 he designed and manufactured a limited edition of 6 x 9 Siciliano hand cameras. Germano was awarded a CAPS grant in 1974.

His work is of views of middle-class neighborhoods, using the 6 x 9 Siciliano hand camera.

COLLECTION MOMA, NYC.

ADDRESS 431 18 St, Brooklyn, NY 11215.

Helmut Erich Robert Gernsheim PHOTOHISTORIAN · WRITER · COLLECTOR · PHOTOGRAPHER Gernsheim was born on March 1, 1913, in Germany. His father, Karl, was a literary historian at the University of Munich and his wife, Alison, was his frequent co-author and fellow photohistorian. Gernsheim matriculated at St. Anna College in Augsburg, Germany (1933). From 1934 to 1936 he studied the history of art at Munich University, and photography at State School of Photography, Munich.

When an opportunity to leave Germany arose, Gernsheim, who is half-Jewish, took it and began a career as a freelance photographer in England (1937). After the outbreak of war with Germany, he was interned as an enemy alien and sent to Australia (1940–41). From 1942 to 1945 he was photographer to the Warburg Institute of Art, University of London. In 1945 he founded the Gernsheim Photographic Collection, housed since 1964 at the University of Texas, Austin. Gernsheim represented Britain at the World Exhibition of Photography in Lucerne, Switzerland, in 1952 and at the UNESCO Conference on Photography and Film in Paris, 1955. He co-edited *Photography Year Book* in London from 1953 to 1955, and in 1968 was adviser on photography to the editor of the *Encyclopaedia Britannica*. In 1971–72 he was a lecturer at Franklin College, Lugano, Switzerland, and in 1979 was a Distinguished Visiting Professor at the University of Texas, Austin.

Gernsheim was responsible for the rediscovery of both Lewis Carroll's photographic work in 1948 and of the world's first camera photograph (1827) by Niepce in 1952. He won the 1955 Award of the American Photographers' Association, the 1959 German Kulturpreis Award, the 1969 Knight of Mark Twain and the 1970 Order of Merit of the German Federal Republic. In 1975 he was named a trustee of the Swiss Foundation and in 1978 an Honorary Fellow of the Photohistorical Society of New York.

The internationally recognized photographic historian is best known for his book *The History of Photography*, written with his wife Alison. He has also exhibited his own photographs around the world.

PUBLICATIONS Books: *Alvin Langdon Coburn, Photographer*, w/Alison Gernsheim, 1966, rev. ed., 1978; *A Concise History of Photography*, w/A. Gernsheim, 1965, new ed., 1971; *Fashion and Reality 1840–1914*, w/A. Gernsheim, 1963; *Edward VII and Queen Alexandra: A Biography in Word and Picture*, w/A. Gernsheim, 1962; *Creative Photography, Aesthetic Trends 1839–1960*, 1962, repr 1974; *The Recording Eye: A Hundred Years of Great Events*, w/A. Gernsheim, 1960; *Victoria R.*, w/A. Gernsheim, 1959; *L. J. M. Daguerre, the History of the Diorama and of the Daguerreotype*, w/A. Gernsheim, 1956; *Churchill, His Life in Photographs*, Randolph Churchill, 1955; *The History of Photography*, w/A. Gernsheim, 1955, rev. ed. 1969; *Roger Fenton, Photographer of the Crimean War*, 1954, repr. 1973; *Those Impossible English*, Quentin Bell, 1952; *Masterpieces of Victorian Photography*,

1951; *Beautiful London*, 1950; *Lewis Carroll, Photographer*, 1949, rev. ed., 1969; *Focus on Architecture and Sculpture*, 1949; *The Man Behind the Camera*, 1948, repr, 1979; *Julia Margaret Cameron*, 1948, rev. ed. 1975; *Twelfth Century Wall Paintings at Hardham and Clayton*, 1946; *New Photo Vision*, 1942. Anthology: *Dialogue with Photography* (interview), Paul Hill & Thomas Cooper, 1979. Articles and contributions: *Encyclopaedia Brittanica*, *Colliers Encyclopedia*, *Focal Encyclopedia*, *Oxford History of Technology* and many dictionaries.

PORTFOLIOS (ed.) *Werner Bischof, Erich Salomon, Felix H. Man, & Masterpieces in the Gernsheim Collection*, 1970–73 (Photo-Graphic Editions: London).

COLLECTIONS IMP/GEH, Rochester; MOMA, NYC; Univ. of Tex., Gernsheim Cllctn., Austin.

ADDRESS Via Tamporiva 28, CH 6976 Castagnola-Lugano, Switzerland.

Stephen B. Gersh PHOTOGRAPHER · TEACHER · CONSULTANT Born March 31, 1942, in Boston, Massachusetts, Gersh received an MA in Creative Photography from Goddard College, Plainfield, Vermont, in 1976. He also studied at Syracuse University, New York (1959–62), was an assistant to Ansel Adams in Carmel, California (1962–64), and undertook individual study with Minor White in Rochester (1964).

In 1975 Gersh co-founded and became director of Essex Photographic Workshop, Inc., Essex, Massachusetts. He also directed the Goddard Master's Program at Essex Photographic Workshop (1976–78) and has been a consultant to Polaroid Corporation's Marketing Division since 1975. He previously was director of the New England School of Photography in Boston (1972–75) and taught photography at M.I.T., Cambridge (1966–67).

PUBLICATIONS Book: *Polaroid Land Photography*, Ansel Adams, 1978. Periodical: *Camera*, June 1975.

PORTFOLIO *Peruvian Portfolio*, intro. by Carl Siembab, 1975 (self-pub.).

COLLECTIONS Boston Fine Arts Mus.; Exchange Bank of Chicago; Metro. Mus. of Art, NYC; Polaroid Cllctn., Cambridge, Mass.; Springfield Mus. of Art, Mass.; Stanford Univ., Stanford, Calif.; Univ. of Ariz., Tucson; Univ. of Ver., Robert Fleming Mus., Burlington; Wellesley Coll., Mass. Bibliothèque Nationale, Paris; Natl. Gall. of Canada, Ottawa.

ADDRESS Conomo Point Rd, Essex, MA 01929.

Georg Gerster PHOTOGRAPHER · WRITER · EDITOR Born April 30, 1928, in Winterthur, Switzerland, Gerster earned a PhD in German literature and philology from the University of Zürich.

Since 1956 he has been a freelance writer and photographer, specializing in science reports and frequently contributing to *National Geographic*, *GEO*, *Paris-Match*, and *Neue Zuercher Zeitung*. From 1950 to 1956 he was science editor of the *Weltwoche*, a Zürich-based weekly.

He has received the Anerkennungsgabe der Stadt Winterthur (1977), World Understanding Through Photography award (1976), Pictures of the Year award (1976), Prix Nadar in Paris (1976), Ehrengabe des Kts. Zuerich (1974), and Die Goldene Blende from Germany (1973).

PUBLICATIONS Books: *Flights of Discovery*, 1978; *Grand Design*, 1976; *Aethiopien*, 1974 (Zürich); *The Nubians*, Robert A. Fernea, 1973; *Churches in Rock*, 1970; *The World Saves Abu Simbel*, 1968 (Berlin/Vienna); *Nubien*, 1964 (Zürich); *Desert of Destiny*, 1961; *Sinai*, 1961 (Berlin/Frankfurt, Vienna); *Aus der Werkstatt des Wissens*, 2, 1958 (Folge/Frankfurt/Berlin).

REPRESENTATIVE Photo Researchers, Inc., 60 E 56 St, New York, NY 10022.

ADDRESS Tobelhusstr. 24, 8126 Zumikon-Zürich, Switzerland.

Alfred Gescheidt PHOTOGRAPHER Born December 19, 1926, in New York City, the photographer received his BFA from the University of New Mexico, Albuquerque, in 1950. He also studied at the Art Students League in New York, beginning in 1943, and at Art Center School of Design in Los Angeles in 1951.

A freelance photographer, Gescheidt was on the staff of Black Star Publishing Co. from 1952 to 1954. He has been a member of ASMP since 1978 and is on its board of governors. He is also a life member of the Art Students League in New York.

Gescheidt labels his work "photographic humor," directed mainly toward editorial magazine and newspaper illustration. He often uses multiple printing techniques.

PUBLICATION Book: *30 Ways to Stop Smoking*, 1964.

COLLECTIONS MOMA, NYC; Univ. of N. Mex., Raymond Jonson Gall., Albuquerque.

REPRESENTATIVES Felix Shagin Management, Inc., 1 Rockefeller Plaza, New York, NY 10020; Image Bank, 88 Vanderbilt Ave, The Penthouse, New York, NY 10017; Camera Press, Ltd., 400 Russell Ct, Coram St, London WC1, England.

Lieven Gevaert   PHOTOGRAPHIC EQUIPMENT MANUFACTURER · INVENTOR · PHOTOGRAPHER Born in Antwerp, Belgium, in 1863, Gevaert died in 1935.

Having become interested in photography at sixteen, he first tried to produce photographic plates commercially, then opened his own studio after a short training period. He soon invented a successful device for coating paper with emulsion and joined with Belgian businessman Armand Seegers to form a company that manufactured collodion photographic printing-out paper (1894). An immediate success, they opened a Paris office the next year and, by 1900, the firm had been incorporated and supported thirty employees. The Antwerp factory closed in 1905 and the company moved to Mortsel. The Germans took over the plant during World War I, but Gevaert resumed operations after the war's end.

The Gevaert company's other products included a world-famous collodion matte paper (1901), an extra-hard grade of development paper called Ridax (1905), a casein paper produced from milk protein, developed by Dr. Otto Buss (1905) and the developing-out papers Artos and Orthobrom. After the war Gevaert also manufactured plates (1920), roll films and film packs (1923), motion picture films (1924) and X-ray and sound motion picture films (1929).

PUBLICATIONS   Books: *Memoirs of a Photochemist*, Fritz Wentzel, 1960; *Encyclopedie voor Fotografie en Cinematografie*, Elsevier, 1958; *Focal Encyclopedia of Photography*, 1957, 1956 (Focal Press). Anthology: *Photography's Great Inventors*, Louis W. Sipley, 1965. Periodicals: *Perspective*, 1960; *Camera*, Mar 1935; *Photographische Correspondenz*, 1935.

Mario Giacomelli   PHOTOGRAPHER · POET · PAINTER   Born August 1, 1925, in Senigallia, Italy, Giacomelli began studying photography in 1954 with Giuseppe Cavalli, who was a member of the photographic group La Bussola in Venice.

A self-employed photographer since 1954, Giacomelli began work at age thirteen in a typography shop, later owning his own shop, Tipografia Marchigianna. In about 1954 he belonged to the photographic group Misa with Cavalli, Vincenzo Balocchi, Ferriccio Ferroni, Pierogiorgi Branzi and others. He has received numerous photographic awards in Italy, including honors at the 1978 Venice Bienniale and the Primo Premo, Mostra di Verona in 1958, 1959 and 1960.

A film of his work was made by Italian film maker M. Gadin in 1972. In addition to photography, Giacomelli writes poetry.

Using a large-format camera, the photographer creates a "free pure style of abstraction of landscape and figure" in both silver and color.

PUBLICATIONS   Monograph: *Mario Giacomelli*, 1980 (Parma Press, Italy). Anthologies: *The Magic Image*, Cecil Beaton & Gail Buckland, 1975; *Looking at Photographs*, John Szarkowski, ed., 1973; *The Art of Photography*, 1971; *The Print*, 1970, Time-Life Series. Periodicals: *Fotografia Italiana*, May 1978, 1975, 1972; *Popular Photography Annual*, 1965; *U.S. Camera International Annual*, 1964, 1963; *Progresso Fotografico*, Dec 1959; *Camera*, Sept 1958.

COLLECTIONS   Boston Mus. of Fine Arts, Mass.; Commonwealth Mus. of the Fine Arts of Va., Richmond; IMP/GEH, Rochester; MOMA, NYC; R.I. School of Design Mus., Providence; VSW, Rochester. Amer. Acad., Rome; Bibliothèque Nationale, Paris; Gabinetto Delle Fotografie, Rome; Natl. Gall. of Australia, Canberra; Victoria & Albert Mus., London.

ADDRESS   c/o Stephen Brigidi, 120 Commodore St, Providence, RI 02809; c/o Tipografia Marchigianna, via Mastai 24, Senigallia (Ancona), Italy 60019.

Ralph H. Gibson   PHOTOGRAPHER   [See plate 119]   Born January 16, 1939, in New York City, Gibson studied photography while serving in the U.S. Navy from 1956 to 1960 and at the San Francisco Art Institute in 1960–61.

Gibson founded Lustrum Press in 1969. He has given numerous lectures nationally and internationally since 1975.

Honored with a D.A.A.D. in Berlin, West Germany, in 1979, Gibson has received a CAPS grant (1977) and two NEA fellowships (1973, 1975).

Gibson's early work was in small-format black-and-white, and he is best known for his surreal, minimal style. In his current photographs, color is the predominant subject.

PUBLICATIONS   Monographs: *Days at Sea*, 1975; *Déjà-vu*, 1973; *The Somnambulist*, 1970; *The American Civil Liberties Union Calendar*, 1969; *The Hawk*, 1968; *The Strip*, 1966. Anthology: *The Photograph Collector's Guide*, Lee D. Witkin & Barbara London, 1979. Periodicals (selected): *Camera*, Apr 1979; *Popular Photography*, Apr 1977; *Popular Photography*, Feb 1976, Apr 1977; *Modern Photography*, Julia Scully, June 1975; *Creative Camera Yearbook*, 1975.

COLLECTIONS Art Mus. of the City of Sacramento, Calif.; CCP, Tucson; Dallas Mus., Fort Worth, Tex.; Harvard Univ., Fogg Art Mus., Boston; High Mus. of Art, Atlanta, Ga.; IMP/GEH, Rochester; Metro. Mus. of Art, NYC; MOMA, NYC; Mus. of Fine Arts, Houston, Tex.; Mus. of Fine Arts, St. Petersburg, Fla.; Oberlin Coll., Allen Mem. Art Mus., Oberlin, Oh.; Norton Simon Mus., Pasadena, Calif.; San Francisco Mus. of Modern Art, Calif.; Seattle Art Mus., Wash.; UCLA; Univ. of Fla., Miami; Univ. of N. Mex., Albuquerque; Va. Mus. of Fine Art, Richmond; VSW, Rochester. Art Gall. of South Australia; Australian Natl. Gall., Canberra; Bibliothèque Nationale, Paris; Contini, Marseilles, France; Fotografiska Muséet, Moderna Muséet, Stockholm, Sweden; Musée Réattu, Arles, France; Mus. of Modern Art, Brisbane, Australia; Natl. Gall. of Ottawa, Canada; Natl. Gall. of Victoria, Australia; Victoria & Albert Mus., London.

DEALER Castelli Graphics, 4 E 77 St, New York, NY 10021.

ADDRESS 331 W Broadway, New York, NY 10013.

Tim N. (Nachum) Gidal *PHOTOJOURNALIST · TEACHER · WRITER* Born May 18, 1909, in Munich, Germany, Gidal was educated at the University of Berlin and the University of Munich, receiving a PhD insigni cum laude in 1935. His major influences have been Judaism, Kafka, Hermann Hesse and Rogers and Hammerstein.

Currently an associate professor in the Department of Communication at the Hebrew University in Jerusalem, Israel, Gidal has also been a senior lecturer in visual communication since 1971. Previously, he was a senior lecturer at The New School for Social Research in New York City from 1955 to 1958, and worked as chief photoreporter for *Picture Post* from 1938 to 1940 and as a photoreporter for various German magazines until 1933.

Gidal has been a Fellow of RPS since 1970, and a member of DGPh since 1972.

PUBLICATIONS Monograph: *Eternal Jerusalem*, 1980 (Lucerne, Switzerland). Books: *Origin and Development of Modern Photojournalism*, 1973; *Everyone Lives in Communities*, 1972; *Picture Reporting and the Press*, 1935 (Tübingen, Germany). Anthologies: *The Photograph Collector's Guide*, Lee D. Witkin & Barbara London, 1979; *The Magic Image*, Cecil Beaton & Gail Buckland, 1975. Periodicals: *Camera*, Jan 1975; *Creative Camera*, Sept 1974.

COLLECTIONS IMP/GEH, Rochester; Univ. of Texas, Gernsheim Cllctn., Austin. Berlinsche Galerie, Berlin; Israel Mus., Jerusalem; Neue Sammlung, Munich, Germany; Victoria & Albert Mus., London.

DEALERS Witkin Gallery, 41 E 57 St, New York, NY 10022; Janet Lehr, 45 E 85 St, New York, NY 10028.

ADDRESS 16 Nili St, Jerusalem, Israel.

Sebastian Giefer-Bastel *PHOTOGRAPHER* Born February 11, 1949, in Frankfurt, West Germany, Giefer-Bastel attended the School for Graphic Design (Werkkunstschule) in Offenbach (1968) and studied architecture at Technische Universität in Munich (1971–76).

A freelance photographer, Giefer-Bastel won a gold medal in 1978 from the German Art Directors' Club.

He does documentary and fashion work, as well as research on laser photography, computer animation and new light forms.

PUBLICATIONS Periodicals: *Photo Italy*, Mar 1980; *Omni*, Aug 1979; *Photo France*, July 1979; *Stern*, no. 46, 1979, no. 51, 1978.

ADDRESS 3132 Hollyridge Dr, Hollywood, CA 90068.

Douglas R. Gilbert *PHOTOGRAPHER · TEACHER* Born August 14, 1942, in Muskegon, Michigan, Gilbert received his BA in Social Sciences from Michigan State University, East Lansing (1964), and his MS in Photography at the Institute of Design, Illinois Institute of Technology, Chicago (1972). At the latter school he studied with Aaron Siskind, Garry Winogrand and Arthur Siegel. Gilbert also studied with Bruce Davidson in 1965 in New York City and, from 1966 to 1969, at the New York Theological Seminary.

An assistant professor of art at Wheaton College, Illinois, since 1972, Gilbert was a staff photographer for *Look* magazine from 1964 to 1966.

Gilbert is a member of IMP/GEH, SPE, and the American Film Institute. In 1974 he won the John G. Curtis, Jr., Award from the Art Institute of Chicago, and in the same year won the Chicago Book Clinic Award of Merit for his book *C. S. Lewis: Images of His World*. In 1965 Gilbert received the Page One Award for "Magazine Photography of the Year" from the Newspaper Guild of New York.

The photographer describes his work as an "investigation of various aspects of the suburban landscape."

PUBLICATIONS Books: *C. S. Lewis: Images of His World*, w/Clyde S. Kilby, 1973; *The Steps of*

Bonhoeffer, w/J. Martin Bailey, 1969. Periodical: "Potpourri," *Camera*, July 1970.

COLLECTIONS Art Inst. of Chicago; High Mus. of Art, Atlanta, Ga.; Wheaton Coll. Amer. Art Coll., Wheaton, Ill.

ADDRESS 726 N Irving Ave, Wheaton, IL 60187.

Lynn Gilbert PHOTOGRAPHER Born January 7, 1938, in New York City, Gilbert received a BA from Sarah Lawrence College in Bronxville, New York, in 1959 and a BS from the Fashion Institute of Technology in 1962 in New York City.

She is self-employed as a freelance photographer.

Gilbert characterizes her work as "primarily black-and-white formal portraits of women and children in their own setting. They are studies that try to capture a distinctive characteristic with dignity."

PUBLICATIONS Books: *Originals: American Women Artists*, Eleanor Munroe, 1979; *The Russians in America*, Nancy Eubank, 1979; *Louise Nevelson*, Arnold Glimcher, 1976.

ADDRESS 880 Fifth Ave, New York, NY 10021.

Ruth Mayerson Gilbert PHOTOGRAPHER Born December 10, 1909, in the United States, Gilbert earned a BA at the University of Pennsylvania, Philadelphia, in 1931. She considers that her life in Europe since 1949, especially among the artists and musicians of Paris and Basel, is the major influence on her photography.

A self-taught freelance photographer, Gilbert began to photograph in 1972.

Her work is a "personal interpretation of scenes concerning men at work," mainly taken on the streets of Paris.

PUBLICATIONS Periodicals: *British Journal of Photography Annual*, 1980; *Nippon Camera*, Feb 1979; *Zoom*, Nov 1978 (Spain), Oct-Nov 1978 (England), Aug 1978 (France).

COLLECTION Bibliothèque Nationale, Paris.

DEALERS Neikrug Gall., 224 E 68 St, New York, NY 10021; Photo Art, Basel, Switzerland.

ADDRESS 1661 Crescent Pl NW, #405, Washington, DC 20009.

Bruce Gilden PHOTOGRAPHER Born October 16, 1946, in New York City, Gilden attended Pennsylvania State University, University Park (1964–65), New York University (1965–67) and the School of Visual Arts (1967), the latter two in New York City. He studied with Ralph Hatters-

ley and Ken Heyman, and his major influence was William Klein.

He has been a freelance photographer for various publishing companies since 1975, and gives lectures and workshops at Apeiron, the Catskill Center for Photography and other places.

In 1980 Gilden received an NEA Fellowship and a CAPS Grant.

Working in small and medium format, Gilden's aim is to photograph "scenes of people in existing environmental situations, taking the photograph at the moment the people and landscape are in unison." His major essays include Coney Island, Mardi Gras, disco, and New York street scenes.

PUBLICATIONS Book: *Dressing Up*, Peter Ackroyd, 1979. Anthology: *Family of Woman*, 1979. Periodicals: *Modern Photography*, July 1980; *35mm Photography*, spring 1979; *Creative Camera Annual*, 1978; *British Journal of Photography*, Jan 1977; *Nouveau Photo Cinema*, Oct 1977; *Photo Technique*, Jan 1977; *Ovo*, spring 1976; *U.S. Camera Annual*, 1972; *Popular Photography's Woman*, spring 1972; *Popular Photography's Annual*, 1971.

COLLECTIONS L/C, Wash., D.C. Bibliothèque Nationale, Paris.

DEALER O. K. Harris Gall., 383 W Broadway, New York, NY 10013.

ADDRESS 25 Mercer St, 5R, New York, NY 10013.

William B. Giles PHOTOGRAPHER Born March 5, 1934, in Boston, Massachusetts, Giles earned a BS in Agriculture from Cornell University, Ithaca, New York, in 1956, then did graduate work with Ralph Hattersley and Minor White at Rochester Institute of Technology, New York (1958–59). He took his MFA in 1962 from the University of Rochester.

A freelance photographer since 1973, Giles built the Light Works Lab in Santa Cruz, California, in 1979. He directed the Neary Gallery in Santa Cruz in 1976, and from 1969 to 1973 was a freelance lecturer, teacher and exhibition organizer. In 1968 he was director of the Rochester Photographic Workshop and in 1963 was a curatorial exhibit assistant at George Eastman House in Rochester, N.Y.

Giles established the first photographic teaching program at the University of Rochester in 1966. In addition to his photographic work, he has produced the video programs *Transformations* and *Snapshots of the Mind* (1979) and designed *The Magic Gem*, a children's book, for the Sri Rama Foundation in Santa Cruz (1976).

Currently producing large-format landscapes, Giles' earlier work involved portraiture and photojournalism.

PUBLICATIONS Books: *Reflections*, 1977 (self-pub.); *Buddha Is the Center of Gravity*, Sasaki Roshi, 1975. Periodicals: *Darkroom*, Phiz Mezey, 1:5, 1979; *Print Letter #20*, Marco Misano, 1979.

PORTFOLIOS *Mother of Pearls*, 1976 (self-pub.); *Oregon Rainbow #6*, Paul Caponigro, intro., 1977 (self-pub.: Portland, Ore.).

DEALER G. Ray Hawkins Gall., 7224 Melrose Ave, Los Angeles, CA 90046.

ADDRESS 513 Ocean View, Santa Cruz, CA 95060.

Henry E. Gilpin PHOTOGRAPHER · TEACHER · PEACE OFFICER Born November 10, 1922, in Cleveland, Ohio, Gilpin studied engineering at Los Angeles City College (1946–48) and at UCLA (1949). He studied ceramics at Cleveland Institute of Art, Ohio (1950), and photography at Ansel Adams' Yosemite Workshop (1959) and with Wynn Bullock (1963). The photographer Laura Gilpin was his cousin.

A teacher at Monterey Peninsula College, Monterey, California, since 1965, he taught at Ansel Adams' Yosemite Workshop from 1968 to 1973. Gilpin was a peace officer with the Monterey County Sheriff's Department (1951–76), retiring as captain of detectives. He spent nine of those years in forensic photography.

Currently an advisory trustee for Friends of Photography (since 1978), he was a trustee from 1969 to 1978.

PUBLICATIONS Book: *Garrod/Gilpin Photographs*, 1970. Anthologies: *International Photography Yearbook*, 1967, 1965. Periodicals: *British Journal of Photography*, Nov 1973; *Creative Camera*, Oct 1973; *Hasselblad Magazine*, vol. 4, 1972.

COLLECTIONS Currier Gall. of Art, Manchester, N.H.; Monterey Peninsula Mus. of Art, Calif.; Shaklee Corp., San Francisco; Utah State Univ. Gall., Logan. Oriental Photo Trading Co., Ltd., Tokyo.

DEALERS Josephus Daniels Gall., POB 7418, Carmel, CA 93921; International Ctr. of Photography, 1130 Fifth Ave, New York, NY 10028; Stephen White Gall., 835 La Cienega Blvd, Los Angeles, CA 90069.

ADDRESS 1353 Jacks Rd, Monterey, CA 93940.

Laura Gilpin PHOTOGRAPHER [See plate 73] Born April 22, 1891, in Colorado Springs, Colorado, Gilpin died November 30, 1979 in Santa Fe, New Mexico. She studied at the Clarence H. White School of Photography in New York in 1916–17. She was cousin to photographer Henry Gilpin.

Gilpin was given a Kodak "Brownie" camera on her twelfth birthday. By 1918 she had opened a portrait studio. She first traveled to the Southwest, the area of the country where she did her most famous work, in 1920. She was commissioned to Central City Theatre by the Robert Edmond Jones Production Company in Colorado (1932–36). She did public-relations photography for Boeing Airplane Company in Wichita, Kansas (1942–45), during which time her photos appeared in their monthly magazine.

A member of the Society of Women Geographers and Industrial Photographers of the Southwest, Gilpin won a Guggenheim Fellowship in 1975. She was also honored with the First Annual Governor's Award from the New Mexico Arts Commission in 1974; U.S. Indian Arts & Crafts Board Certificate; and Hon.D.Litt., University of New Mexico, 1970.

Ansel Adams called Gilpin "one of the most important photographers of our time." She documented the Navajo life-style and their special relationship with the land in a straightforward style. Working chiefly with platinum prints (and occasionally silver), she is noted for both her intimate portraits and panoramic landscapes, with an emphasis on the quality of light.

PUBLICATIONS Books: *A Taos Mosaic*, Claire Morrill, 1973; *The Enduring Navajo*, 1968; *The Rio Grande*, 1949; *Temples of Yucatan*, 1948; *The Pueblos*, 1941; *New Mexico: A Guide to the Colorful State*, 1940. Anthologies: *The Photograph Collector's Guide*, Lee D. Witkin & Barbara London, 1979; *Photography Rediscovered*, David Travis & Anne Kennedy, 1979; *The Great West: Real/Ideal*, Sandy Hume et al., eds., 1977; *Women of Photography*, M. Mann & A. Noggle, eds., 1975. Catalogs: *Aspects of American Photography*, 1976 (Univ. of Mo., St. Louis); *Laura Gilpin Retrospective*, 1974 (Mus. of N. Mex., Santa Fe). Periodicals: "Laura Gilpin, Photographer," *New America*, spring 1975; *Platinum Print: A Journal of Personal Expression*, several issues, 1913–16.

COLLECTIONS L/C, Washington, D.C.; Mus. of N. Mex., Santa Fe; New Orleans Art Mus., La.; Univ. of N. Mex. Art Mus., Albuquerque; Yale Univ. Art Mus., New Haven, Ct.

DEALERS Witkin Gall., 41 East 57 St, New York, NY 10022; Onivira Book Shop & Gall., 11 Cornell St SE, Albuquerque, NM 87106.

John Gintoff PHOTOGRAPHER Born December 13, 1947, in the U.S., Gintoff earned a BA in French from Franklin & Marshall College, Lancaster, Pennsylvania (1969), and an MFA in Photography from Tyler School of Art, Philadelphia (1977). He names Walker Evans, Lee Friedlander, Marcel Duchamp and James Joyce as major influences.

A freelance photographer, Gintoff taught at Philadelphia Community College, Pennsylvania, in 1977–78 and at Tyler School of Art, Philadelphia, in 1976–77.

He is a member of SPE, Artists' Equity and Asylum Hill Artists' Cooperative, Hartford, Connecticut (president, 1979).

In 1979 he won an individual artist's grant from the Connecticut Commission on the Arts as well as a Polaroid Corporation Honorarium. He also won a Polaroid Corporation grant in 1978.

Gintoff works in color photography, using 35mm and Polaroid SX-70.
PUBLICATIONS Anthologies: *SX-70 Art*, 1979; *One-of-a-Kind*, 1979.
COLLECTION Tyler School of Art, Philadelphia, Pa.
ADDRESS 40 Cottage St, Meriden, CT 06450.

Conrad Joseph Gleber, Jr. MIXED-MEDIA PHOTOGRAPHER · TEACHER · PUBLICATIONS MANAGER Born October 4, 1949, in Baton Rouge, Louisiana, Gleber completed his BFA at Florida State University, Tallahassee, and his MFA at the School of the Art Institute of Chicago. He studied with Evon Streeman, Robert Fichter, Todd Walker and Keith Smith.

Gleber has been director of publications for the School of the Art Institute of Chicago since 1977, and since 1975 has taught offset production at the school. In 1977 he co-founded Chicago Books, an artists' press, which he also directs. Gleber became a journeyman in the International Typographical Union in 1974. From 1976 to 1979 he was a visiting artist at several universities.

An NEA Photography Fellowship winner in 1979, Gleber received an Illinois Arts Council project grant (for Chicago Books) in 1978 and an Edward L. Ryerson Traveling Fellowship from the Art Institute of Chicago in 1976.

Gleber's work, although based on photographic images and ideas, is realized through the use of offset printing, commercial halftones and color separations. He creates traditional offset prints and artists' books, which are conceptual in content, and produces sculptures of photographic images printed on large stacks of paper held together by steel, wood or plastic.
PUBLICATIONS Periodicals: "Chicago Books," *Afterimage: VSW*, Apr 1978; "McLuhan's Mistake, The Book Is Back," *New Art Examiner*, Mar 1978; "The Art of Offset Technology," *Exposure*, Dec 1977.
COLLECTIONS Art Inst. of Chicago; Franklin Furnace, NYC; MOMA (artists' books cllctn.), NYC; Northwestern Univ., Special Cllctns., Chicago.
ADDRESS 123 W Hubbard, Chicago, IL 60610.

Peter Glendinning PHOTOGRAPHER · TEACHER Born September 23, 1951, in New York City, Glendinning received a BA in Photojournalism/Political Science (1973), a BFA (1976) and an MFA (1978) from Syracuse University, New York. He also attended law school there (1975–76), and studied with Lisette Model at the New School for Social Research in New York City (1974).

Since 1978 he has been assistant professor and head of photography in the Art Department at Michigan State University, East Lansing. In 1977 he taught color photography at Community Darkrooms in Syracuse.

A member of SPE and Friends of Photography, Glendinning won a Ford Foundation grant in 1978 and a Photographer's Grant in 1977 from Light Work, Inc. in Syracuse.

His most recent photographs "show oddly colored leafless trees, painted with large white numbers . . . made at night using many different colored light sources."
PORTFOLIO *Tablescapes*, 1978 (self-pub.).
COLLECTIONS Clara M. Eagle Gall., Murray, Ky.; Everson Mus., Syracuse; IMP/GEH, Rochester; K-Mart Corp., Detroit, Mich.; Light Work, Inc., Syracuse.
REPRESENTATIVE Mary Dennison, 651 Oak, Birmingham, MI 48009.
ADDRESS Art Department, Michigan State University, East Lansing, MI 48824.

Wilhelm von Gloeden PHOTOGRAPHER · PAINTER [See plate 35] Born in 1856 in Mecklenburg, Germany, Von Gloeden died in 1931 in Taormina, Sicily. His cousin, Baron von Pluschkow, was also a photographer.

Von Gloeden, who was a baron, started out to be a painter but soon switched to photography and remained at the discipline throughout his life.

Of some 3,000 glass plates he exposed, only a few hundred remain, the others having been destroyed by Mussolini's Fascist police. The baron used a handmade view camera with specially ground lenses for his lyrical essays on the male nude. Jean-Claude Lemagny refers to his "meticulous reconstructions and subtly erotic overtones," adding that "the ridiculous and the poetic are inseparable in these images." The photographer also produced travel books on Sicily and Taormina.

PUBLICATIONS Monograph: *Photographs of the Classic Male Nude,* preface by Jean-Claude Lemagny, 1975, U.S. ed., 1977. Book: *Les Amours Singulières,* Roger Peyrefitte, n.d.

COLLECTIONS IMP/GEH, Rochester; Natl. Geographic Society, Wash., D.C.

Leopold Godowsky, Jr. CHEMIST · VIOLINIST Born in Chicago in 1900, Godowsky spent his youth in Europe before settling with his parents in New York. Trained as a musician, he attended the Riverdale School in New York (ca. 1916), then studied chemistry, physics and mathematics at the University of California. His father was a renowned pianist, composer and developer of advanced piano techniques.

Godowsky worked as a professional violinist in California and then in New York, pursuing photographic experiments as a hobby with his friend Leopold D. Mannes, another musician, whom he had met at the Riverdale School. They first used the kitchen and bathroom as laboratories, but in 1924 and 1929 they rented space in office buildings. Their earliest attempts to improve color processes centered on the use of optical devices, and they patented a special lens movement. With the aid of C. E. K. Mees at Eastman Kodak, they experimented with direct color-plate and film processes. Their ideas took a new direction when they learned of the Fischer theory of color couplers. Thanks to Dr. Mees, they were allowed to continue their experiments at Eastman Kodak's Rochester laboratories from 1931 to 1939. In 1965 they received the Progress Medal of RPS.

The most important result of their work was the development of Kodachrome film in 1935, and their basic research led to Kodacolor film and prints (1941), Ektacolor film (1949) and Eastman color negative 35mm film (1949).

PUBLICATIONS Books: *From Dry Plates to Ektachrome Film,* C. E. K. Mees, 1961; *A Half Century of Color,* Louis W. Sipley, 1951; *History of Color Photography,* Joseph S. Friedman, 1944. Anthology: *Photography's Great Inventors,* Louis W. Sipley, 1965. Periodicals: *Photographic Journal,* 1964; *Bild und Ton,* 1961; *Journal of the Photographic Society of America,* Oct 1955.

Fay Godwin PHOTOGRAPHER Born in Berlin, but of British citizenship, Godwin is a self-taught freelance photographer.

She won an Arts Council of Great Britain award in 1978.

Her work consists mainly of landscapes in the British Isles, portraits of British and American writers and photojournalism.

PUBLICATIONS Books: *Remains of Elmet,* w/ Ted Hughes, 1979; *Islands,* w/John Fowles, 1978 (Cape: England); *The Drovers' Roads of Wales,* w/Shirley Toulson, 1977 (Wildwood: England); *The Oil Rush,* w/Mervyn Jones, 1976 (Quartet: England); *The Oldest Road—The Ridgeway,* w/ Jill Anderson, 1975 (Wildwood: England).

COLLECTIONS Bibliothèque Nationale, Paris; City Art Galls., Sheffield, England; Natl. Portrait Gall., London; Royal Lib., Copenhagen, Denmark; Victoria & Albert Mus., London.

DEALERS Anthony Stokes, 3 Langley Ct, London WC2, England; The Photographers' Gall., 8 Great Newport St, London WC2, England.

Carl Paul Goerz PHOTOGRAPHIC EQUIPMENT MANUFACTURER · INVENTOR Born in 1854 in Brandenburg, Germany, Goerz died in 1923.

He started a business selling drawing instruments, slide rules and similar apparatus in Berlin in 1886, adding photographic apparatus the next year. In 1888 he started a photographic workshop, where he built the first Goerz plate camera and aplanat lens. In 1891 Goerz constructed a focal plane camera based on Ottomar Anschuetz' patent, and the next year he made the famous Goerz Double Anastigmat, thanks to an idea from Emil von Hoegh. A folding Goerz-Anschuetz box camera was marketed in 1894, the same year in which Goerz established an eight-hour day for his employees.

The camera maker set up a small factory in Winterstein, Thuringia, in 1895 to grind lenses, and a large factory in Friedenau in 1898. In the next few years Goerz brought out a photographic stereo binocular (1899), the famous wide-angle Hypergon lens (1900) and a Pantar lens (1902). Goerz set up an optical plant in New York in 1902, and in 1903 he built a triple projector for Miethe's 3-color pictures, as well as making a reproduction anastigmat lens and changing the company name to A. G. C. P. Goerz. Before World War I, Goerz became involved in the manufacture of a large number of optical items for the German armed forces, such as periscopes and telescopes. But after the war, only Carl Zeiss of Jena was allowed to make military optical items, and the slack work at the Goerz plant led to its incorporation with Zeiss Ikon A. G.

PUBLICATIONS Books: *Quellendarstellungen zur Geschichte der Fotografie*, Wolfgang Baier, 1964; *Die Photographische Kamera*, Josef Stuper, 1962; *March of Photography*, Erich Stenger, 1958; *Lexikon für Photographie und Reproduks-tionstechnik*, G. H. Emmerich, 1910. Anthology: *Photography's Great Inventors*, Louis W. Sipley, 1965. Periodicals: *Foto Magazin*, 1964; *Bild und Ton*, 1962, 1959, 1956, 1951; *British Journal of Photography*, 1911.

Frank William Gohlke PHOTOGRAPHER Born April 3, 1942, in Wichita Falls, Texas, Gohlke received his BA in English from the University of Texas, Austin, in 1964 and his MA in English from Yale University, New Haven, Connecticut, in 1966. He "met and was encouraged by" Walker Evans in 1967 and studied with Paul Caponigro in 1967–68.

Since 1977 Gohlke has been a visiting artist for a month each year at Colorado College, Colorado Springs. He taught photography at Blake Schools from 1973 to 1975.

Gohlke won a Bush Foundation Artist's Fellowship for 1979–80, an NEA Photographer's Fellowship in 1978 and a Guggenheim Fellowship in 1975.

The photographer co-directed and wrote (with Mark Lowry) a half-hour television special for KTCA-TV2 in Minneapolis/St. Paul, entitled "Prairie Castles."

Working with large-format and 16 x 20 silver prints, Gohlke is "concerned with precise description and clarity of structure." His subject matter is primarily landscape and man-made structures and their interaction.

PUBLICATIONS Anthologies: *American Images*, Renato Danese, ed., 1979; *Darkroom 2*, Jain Kelly, ed., 1978; *Court House*, Richard Pare, ed., 1978. Periodicals: *Camera*, May 1976; "Route 66 Revisited," Carter Ratcliff, *Art in America*, Jan/Feb 1976; "Report from the Provinces," Stephen West, Feb 10, 1975, "Latent Image," A. D. Coleman, Oct 28, 1971, *Village Voice*.

COLLECTIONS Amon Carter Mus. of Western Art, Fort Worth, Tex.; Art Inst. of Chicago; Exchange Natl. Bank of Chicago; Federal Reserve Bank, Minneapolis, Minn.; IMP/GEH, Rochester; Kalamazoo Inst. of the Arts, Mich.; Minneapolis Inst. of Arts, Minn.; MOMA, NYC; Polaroid Corp, Cambridge, Mass.; Seagram Cllctn., NYC; Univ. of Kans. Art Mus., Lawrence; Univ. of Mass., Amherst; Univ. of Neb., Sheldon Memorial Art Gall., Lincoln; Univ. of N. Mex., Albu-querque. Natl. Gall. of Australia, Canberra; Staatliches Mus. für Angewandte Kunst, Die Neue Sammlung, Munich, Germany.

DEALER Light Gall., 724 Fifth Ave, New York, NY 10019.

ADDRESS 1322 Adams NE, Minneapolis, MN 55413.

Beryl M. Goldberg PHOTOGRAPHER · WRITER Born October 5, 1942, in New Jersey, Goldberg received a BA from Douglass College and did graduate study at New York University. She also attended workshops with Harold Feinstein, Lisette Model and John Morris.

Goldberg is a freelance photographer for magazines and book publishers.

She is a member of ASPP.

Working in 35mm, the artist is "interested in portraying man in his environment in this country and in the third world." She has done extensive work in South America and Africa.

PUBLICATIONS Anthologies: *Family of Children*, 1977; *Women See Men*, 1977. Periodical: *Popular Photography*, summer 1975.

COLLECTIONS Portland Mus. of Art, Portland, Maine. M. J. Paster Cllctn., London.

ADDRESS 845 West End Ave, Apt 6A, New York, NY 10025.

Emanuel Goldberg CHEMIST Born in 1881 in Germany, Goldberg later left his homeland because of Hitler and settled in Tel Aviv, Israel.

Goldberg served as assistant to Professor Adolf Miethe at Charlottenberg in 1906–1907, and subsequently as professor at Academy of Graphic Arts in Leipzig, at Technische Hochschule in Dresden and as director of Zeiss-Ikon. In Tel Aviv he established an optical business.

In 1910 Goldberg introduced wedges of pigmented gelatin for use in sensitometry. He also made one of the earliest quantitative investigations of the turbidity of photographic emulsions, reported in 1912. His other important work included studies of the causes of lens flare and of the multiple reflection of light in a lens from glass-air surfaces of its elements, and he invented an apparatus for measuring the specific brilliance of a lens. His major work on tone reproduction was published in 1922, and in 1926 he developed a grainless silver collodion emulsion for microphotographic reduction use. Goldberg and Robert Luther headed the German Committee for Sensitometry, which introduced the DIN method for determining emulsion speed, reported at the 8th International Congress of Scientific and Applied Photography in Dresden.

PUBLICATIONS Books: *Photographie im Wandel*, Rudolf Skopec, 1964; *Quellendarstellungen zur Geschichte der Fotografie*, Wolfgang Baier, 1964; *Memoirs of a Photochemist*, Fritz Wentzel, 1960; *Encyclopedia voor Fotografie en Cinematografie*, Elsevier, 1958; *Theory of the Photographic Process*, C. E. K. Mees, 1944; *Der Aufbau des Photographischen Bildes*, 1922; *Lexikon für Photographie und Reproduktionstechnik*, G. H. Emmerich, 1910. Anthology: *Photography's Great Inventors*, Louis W. Sipley, 1965. Periodicals: *Progress in Photography*, 1940–50; *Photographische Korrespondenz*, 1931, 1910; *British Journal of Photography*, 1926, 1910; *Photographic Journal*, 1912; *Jahrbuch für Photographie und Reproduktionstechnik*, J. M. Eder, 1910.

Gary Michael Goldberg PHOTOGRAPHER Born November 23, 1952, in San Jose, California, Goldberg earned a BFA from Arizona State University, Tempe (1975), and an MFA from University of Nebraska, Lincoln (1979).

As of this writing Goldberg was visual arts assistant at Mid-America Arts Alliance in Kansas City, Missouri. He previously was a museum fellow at Sheldon Memorial Art Gallery at the University of Nebraska (1976–79) and a photographer for Media Research and Development at Arizona State University (1975–76).

Goldberg belongs to SPE, CAA and American Association of Museums. He won Sheldon fellowships in 1976, 1977 and 1978.

PUBLICATIONS Books: *Photography for Kids*, 1976; *Creative Photography: Camera & Darkroom Manual*, 2nd ed. n.d. Anthology: *The Family of Woman*, 1979.

COLLECTIONS Univ. of Neb., Sheldon Mem. Art Gall., Lincoln; Western Heritage Mus., Omaha, Neb.

DEALER Morgan Art Gall., 5006 State Line, Shawnee Mission, KS 66208.

ADDRESS 4015 Charlotte #6, Kansas City, MO 64110.

Vicki Goldberg WRITER · CRITIC Born in St. Louis, Missouri, Goldberg earned an MA at the Institute of Fine Arts of New York University.

In addition to her freelance writing Goldberg lectures at the Metropolitan Museum of Art. She has taught at Queens College (1975), Brooklyn College (1974) and New York University (1973), all in New York City.

Goldberg's articles on photography and art have appeared in *American Photographer, Saturday Review, Village Voice, Photograph, Art Quarterly, Réalités* and others.

ADDRESS 1225 Park Ave, New York, NY 10028.

David Goldblatt PHOTOGRAPHER Born November 29, 1930, in Randontein, South Africa, Goldblatt received a bachelor of commerce degree from the University of Witwatersrand, South Africa, in 1956. His major influences were the writings of Bertrand Russell and Ludwig von Mises and the photographs of Dorothea Lange, Walker Evans and Norman Hall.

A freelance photographer since 1963, Goldblatt's work deals with South Africa.

PUBLICATIONS Books: *Some Afrikaners Photographed*, 1975; *On the Mines*, w/Nadine Gordimer, 1973. Anthologies: *Creative Camera International Year Book*, 1977; *Photography Year Book*, 1966. Periodicals: *Camera*, Apr 1973, June 1969.

COLLECTIONS MOMA, NYC. Bibliothèque Nationale, Paris; Durban Art Gall., Durban, South Africa; Natl. Gall. of South Africa, Cape Town; Natl. Gall. of Victoria, Melbourne, Australia.

ADDRESS Box 1464, Johannesburg, South Africa.

Judith Golden PHOTOGRAPHER · TEACHER Born November 29, 1934, in Chicago, Golden received her BFA from the School of the Art Institute of Chicago in 1973 and her MFA from the University of California at Davis in 1975.

As of this writing she is instructing at both California College of Arts and Crafts in Oakland and University of California at Davis. Her prior teaching experience was as lecturer in art at University of California at Los Angeles from 1975 to 1979.

Since 1975 Golden has been a member of SPE, and from 1976 to 1979 she was a member of the Los Angeles Center for Photographic Studies, serving as trustee from 1977 to 1979. She is also a member of Friends of Photography, Los Angeles Institute of Contemporary Art, CAA, Association of Academic Women and Women's Caucus for the Arts. Golden was the recipient of an NEA Photographer's Fellowship in 1979, a Regents Faculty Grant from UCLA in 1977 and a Chancellor's Graduate Fellowship from University of California at Davis in 1974. She was also featured in a sound filmstrip by Harcourt Brace Jovanovich in 1979, entitled "Photographers: Contemporary Artists at Work."

From 1975 to 1979 Golden did a series of self-portraits that were black-and-white toned photographs combined with collage and hand-colored.

Recently she has been creating Cibachrome color print portraits. She often uses her own image in her work.

PUBLICATIONS Anthologies: *In-Sights: Self Portraits by Women*, Joyce T. Cohen, ed., 1978; *Photography Year*, Time-Life Series, 1978; *Self-Portrayal*, Jim Alinder, ed., 1978; "Emerging L.A. Photographers," *Untitled*, 1976 (Friends of Photography). Catalogs: *Attitudes: Photography in the 1970's*, 1979 (Santa Barbara Mus. of Art); *Photographic Directions: Los Angeles 1979*, 1979 (Security Pacific Bank); *Southern California Invitational 1979—A Photographic Survey*, 1979 (Univ. of Southern California). Periodicals (reviews): "Shows We've Seen," *Popular Photography*, Dec 1977; "Judith Golden's Explorations of Self," Joan Murray, *Artweek*, Mar 26, 1977.

COLLECTIONS CCP, Tucson; E. B. Crocker Art Gall., Sacramento, Calif.; Harvard Univ., Fogg Mus. of Art, Cambridge; IMP/GEH, Rochester; Los Angeles County Mus. of Art; Minneapolis Inst. of the Arts, Minn.; MOMA, NYC; Oakland Mus., Calif.; Portland Mus. of Art, Portland, Maine; San Francisco Mus. of Modern Art, Calif.; UCLA, Frederick Wight Gall., Calif.; Univ. of Calif., Davis; Univ. of Colo., Boulder; Univ. of N. Mex. Art Mus., Albuquerque.

DEALER G. Ray Hawkins Gall., 7224 Melrose Ave, Los Angeles, CA 90046.

ADDRESS 773 Minna St, San Francisco, CA 94103.

David Goldes PHOTOGRAPHER · TEACHER Born January 25, 1947, in New York City, Goldes earned an MA in Microbiology and Molecular Genetics from Harvard University, Cambridge, Massachusetts, in 1971 and an MFA from the Visual Studies Workshop in Rochester, New York, in 1977. He studied at the latter with Nathan Lyons.

Currently an assistant professor of art at the University of Minnesota, Minneapolis, Goldes held the same position in 1979 at the University of Rhode Island, Providence.

PUBLICATION Periodical: *Camera*, vol. 8, 1974.

COLLECTIONS IMP/GEH, Rochester; Visual Studies Workshop, Rochester; Yale Univ. Art Mus., New Haven, Conn.

ADDRESS 809 SE Fourth St, Minneapolis, MN 55414.

Louis Goldman PHOTOGRAPHER Born June 8, 1925, in Germany, Goldman was self-taught in photography, influenced by Cartier-Bresson, W. Eugene Smith and Art Kane.

A freelance photographer, he belongs to Local 644 of the International Alliance of Theatrical and Stage Employees in New York City.

PUBLICATIONS Monograph: *A Week in Samil's World, Turkey*, 1973. Books: *A Week in Hagar's World, Israel*, Seymour Reit, 1969; *The Burning Bush*, Uri Kessary, 1957.

COLLECTIONS IMP/GEH, Rochester; MOMA, NYC.

REPRESENTATIVE Photo Researchers, 60 E 56 St, New York, NY 10022.

ADDRESS 352 W 56 St, New York, NY 10019.

Arthur Austin Goldsmith EDITOR · WRITER · TEACHER Born July 7, 1926, in Merrimack, Massachusetts, Goldsmith studied at the University of New Hampshire, Durham, in 1947–48, then completed his BS in 1951 at the Medill School of Journalism at Northwestern University, Evanston, Illinois. He earned an MS in 1972 from Fairfield University Graduate School of Communications, Fairfield, Connecticut.

Goldsmith has been editorial director of *Popular Photography* and *Camera Arts* magazines since 1972. Previously he was president and director of the Famous Photographers School (1961–72), picture editor of *This Week* (1960–61) and executive editor of *Popular Photography* (1951–60). He has written numerous magazine articles on practical, social and aesthetic aspects of photography and has been the editor of several Famous Photographers School textbooks.

Goldsmith is a member of ASMP, Photographic Administrators, Inc., RPS and DGP (corresponding member). He has won a Harrington Award and an Art Directors Club Merit Award, among others.

PUBLICATIONS Books: *The Camera and its Image*, 1979; *The Nude in Photography*, 1975; *The Photography Game*, 1971; *The Eye of Eisenstaedt*, w/Alfred Eisenstaedt, 1969; *How to Take Better Pictures*, 1956.

ADDRESS Popular Photography, One Park Ave, New York, NY 10016.

Rick S. Golt PHOTOGRAPHER · WRITER Born October 2, 1937, Golt is the grandnephew of Wilbur and Orville Wright and of Charles Kettering. He received a BA in English Letters in 1959 from Miami University, Ohio, and graduated from the Famous Photographers School in 1968. Golt also studied under Ansel Adams and Minor White.

The photographer has been president of Golt Photographic Art since 1970, and previous to that was creative director of N. W. Ayer & Son (1967–

70). Golt was staff photographer for *Camera Hawaii* and a pilot for Pan Am in 1966–67.

He received three grants between 1967 and 1972 from the State Foundation on Culture and Arts, Hawaii, and won the Famous Photographers Contest in 1968.

Golt's primary photographic subjects have been "people in their captured moments of visual portrayal" and "studies of form and line . . . as they appear in nature, buildings and certain activities."

PUBLICATIONS Books: *Nature's Palette*, 1979; *The Hawaii Garden*, vols. 1 & 2, 1978; *Sculptures in Sun*, 1977; *Hawaiian Reflections*, 1975; *Inside Waikiki*, 1974; *Betrayal* (fiction), 1964.

COLLECTIONS Amfac Corp., San Francisco; Fluke Fndn., San Francisco; Honolulu Academy of Art, Hawaii; Honolulu Medical Group, Fronk Clinic; Lutheran Genl. Hospital, Chicago; MOMA, NYC; Oasis Oil Corp., Los Angeles. EKORP Ltd, London; Southern Pacific Corp., Fiji Islands & Sydney Australia; Triad Corp., Riyadh, Saudi Arabia.

REPRESENTATIVE Photo Researchers, Inc., 60 E 56 St, New York, NY 10022.

DEALER Nu Art Galls., Ward Warehouse, Ward & Ala Moana, Honolulu, HI 96814.

ADDRESS POB 10020, Honolulu, HI 96816.

Ricardo Gomez Perez PHOTOGRAPHER Born May 27, 1952, in Caracas, Venezuela, Gomez Perez received a Higher Diploma in Creative Photography at London College in 1979. He also attended workshops with Charles Harbutt in 1976. Manuel Alvarez Bravo, Brian Griffin and Charles Harbutt have been his major influences.

Currently a freelance photographer, Gomez Perez was the recipient of a grant from the Department of Education and Science in England in 1979.

The artist does black-and-white photography in two specific areas: one series documents the "Teds in London" (since 1976), the other records the personal development of his way of seeing by the use of the electronic flash and movement (since 1978).

PUBLICATIONS Catalog: *Open Photography Midland Show*, 1978 (Nottingham, Great Britain). Periodicals: *British Journal of Photography*, Apr 1979; *Zoom*, no. 6 (England).

COLLECTION Manchester Polytechnic, Manchester, England.

DEALERS Work Gall., 24 Trittligasse, CH-8001 Zurich, Switzerland; Viviane Esders Galerie, 12 rue Saint Merri, Paris, France.

ADDRESSES 14 Jasmine Grove, London, England; Qta. Amelita, 10 Transversal Ave, Sucre Los Dos Caminos, Caracas, Venezuela.

Mark Goodman PHOTOGRAPHER · TEACHER Born in 1946 in Boston, Massachusetts, Goodman earned a BA in Anthropology from Boston University in 1970. He took photography workshops with Minor White in 1970, Bruce Davidson in 1971 and Berenice Abbott in 1974.

As of this writing Goodman was a lecturer at the University of Texas, Austin. He was an artist-in-residence at Apeiron Workshops, Inc., Millerton, New York, from 1972 to 1975.

Goodman won a Guggenheim Fellowship in 1977 and an NEA Photographer's Fellowship in 1973.

Working in various formats, Goodman specializes in portraits and documentary work.

PUBLICATIONS Anthology: *Kansas Album*, 1977. Periodical: *Aperture*, 19:4, 1975.

COLLECTIONS MOMA, NYC; Mus. of Fine Arts, Boston; Philadelphia Mus. of Art, Penn.; Univ. of Kansas, Spencer Mus. of Art, Lawrence; Univ. of Okla., Mus. of Art, Norman; Vassar Coll. Art Gall., Poughkeepsie, N.Y.

ADDRESS c/o Art Dept., Univ. of Texas at Austin, Austin, TX 78712.

Henry Goodwin PHILOLOGIST · LEXICOGRAPHER · PHOTOGRAPHER Born in 1878 in Germany, Goodwin died in 1931 in Sweden. He attended universities in Leipzig, Munich and Copenhagen as well as Oxford. In his youth the German portrait photographer Nicola Perscheid was his mentor; in later years he was influenced by Albert Renger-Patzsch.

Goodwin went to Sweden in 1908 and taught Old Scandinavian languages at the University of Uppsala. Several years later he began work as a lexicographer for the firm of Norstedt & Söner, but in 1915 he left the field of languages to set up a portrait studio in Stockholm, and he changed his name from the original Buergel. His studio, Kamerabilden (the Camera Picture), became quite successful.

A member of the Photographic Society (Stockholm) and RPS, Goodwin served as Scandinavian correspondent for the latter and for *Photograms of the Year*.

Goodwin took up horticulture in his later years, corresponding with persons around the world about the best method for growing roses.

Leif Wigh of the Fotografiska Muséet writes: "Dr. Henry Buergel Goodwin's photographs can be divided into three different periods. His earliest works, in the pictorial manner, mark him as one of the predecessors of Swedish pictorialism during the years of the First World War. His pictures from this period have characteristic softness, a lack of sharpness, and a not uninteresting elevated air in typical pictorialist manner. His second picture period was more down-to-earth; it was during this period that he left the studio to take pictures outdoors (though he kept the studio as a means of support). Toward the latter part of the 1920s he came in contact with the new objectivity during a visit to Germany . . . and subsequently began to photograph the vegetation in his garden in Saltsjöbaden. . . . Now Goodwin's photographs, fifty years after his death, stand out as some of the most eminent from the pictorial era in Sweden."

PUBLICATIONS   Books: *Kamerabilden*, 1929; *Anders de Wahl: En festskrift*, 1919; *Konstnärsporträtt*, 1917.

ARCHIVE   Fotografiska Muséet, Moderna Muséet, Skeppsholmen, Box 16382, 10327 Stockholm, Sweden.

Bonnie Gordon   TEACHER · PHOTOGRAPHER
Born 1941 in New York State, Gordon received a BFA in Illustration at Syracuse University in New York in 1962 and an MFA in Printmaking at the Rochester Institute of Technology in New York in 1970.

Since 1970 she has been an assistant professor of design at the State University of New York at Buffalo. Previously Gordon had been a designer and illustrator at E. S. & J. Studio in Rochester in 1969, and for Barlow Johnson in Syracuse from 1967 to 1969.

Gordon has been a recipient of a CAPS grant in 1978, an NEA grant in graphics in 1977 and a CAPS grant in graphics in 1975.

The photographer says of her work: "Each of my prints is part of a larger effort to translate the figurative subjects in Webster's Unabridged Dictionary into their pictorial counterparts in order to expose the latent myths and attitudes that underlie the literal meanings of English words."

COLLECTIONS   Colgate Univ. Art Cllctn., Hamilton, N.Y.; Everson Mus., Syracuse, N.Y.; Rochester Inst. of Technology, N.Y.

REPRESENTATIVE   Visual Studies Workshop Gall., 31 Prince St, Rochester, NY 14607.

ADDRESS   797 Potomac Ave, Buffalo, NY 14209.

Jerome J. Gordon II   PHOTOGRAPHER   Born January 18, 1949, in Chicago, Gordon earned a BA in English in 1971 from Washington University in St. Louis, Missouri, and an MS in Photog-

raphy from the Institute of Design at the Illinois Institute of Technology in 1976.

He has worked as a part-time instructor at Columbia College in Chicago since 1977.

Gordon joined SPE in 1975, and is a member of the International Photographers of the Motion Picture Industry, Local 666.

The artist works in 16 x 20 Cibachrome prints from Kodachrome. He concentrates on images of people in various bodies of water.

PUBLICATION   Periodical: *Popular Photography Annual*, 1979.

COLLECTIONS   Corcoran Gall. of Art, Wash. D.C.; L/C, Wash., D.C.

DEALER   Douglas Kenyon, Inc., 155 E Ohio, Chicago, IL 60611.

ADDRESS   845 W Belden, Chicago, IL 60614.

Tom Gore   PHOTOGRAPHER · EDUCATOR · CURATOR   Born August 7, 1946, in Victoria, British Columbia, Gore studied at the University of Victoria and was influenced by the writings of Camus and Kafka.

Gore has been an instructor at the University of Victoria since 1972, a curator of the Open Space Gallery since 1976 and a contributing editor of *Photo Communique*, in Toronto, Ontario, since 1979. Previously he was an instructor at Camosun College (1975–78) and a correspondent for *Arts West* (1976–78).

Northwest chairman of SPE since 1977, Gore was also treasurer of the Communication Arts Society from 1977 to 1978. Since 1976 he has been a member of the Open Space Gallery, and served as their chairman from 1978 to 1979. Gore was the recipient of travel grants from the Canada Council in 1977 and 1978.

Working in collage and occasionally Polaroid, he creates metaphoric sequences concerning the relationship of life and politics.

PUBLICATIONS   Books: *Photographic Education in the North West*, ed., 1978; *A Critical Bibliography of Photography*, 1977. Anthologies: *Photographs 1978*, ed., 1978; *B. C. Photography*, ed., 1977.

COLLECTIONS   In British Columbia, Canada: Univ. of Victoria; Vancouver Art Gall.

ADDRESS   POB 5207, Station B, Victoria, British Columbia, V8R 6N4, Canada.

Ulrich Görlich   PHOTOGRAPHER · TEACHER
Born May 23, 1952, in Alfeld, West Germany, Görlich studied with Michael Schmidt in Berlin from 1972 to 1976.

She has taught photography since 1979 at the Pädagogische Hochschule in Berlin, and since

1976 at Werkstatt für Photographie der VHS Kreuzberg, which she has headed since 1978.

A landscape photographer, she works in black-and-white only, with an 8 x 10 camera.

PUBLICATION   Periodical: *Camera*, Mar 1979.

COLLECTION   Berlinische Galerie, Berlin.

DEALER   Galerie Rudolf Kicken, Albertusstr 47, 5000 Cologne 1, Germany.

ADDRESS   Mussehlstr 23, 1000 Berlin 42, Germany.

John R. Gossage   PHOTOGRAPHER   Born in 1946 in New York City, Gossage studied there with Lisette Model, Alexey Brodovitch and Bruce Davidson from 1962 to 1964.

A self-employed photographer, he also teaches photography at the University of Maryland, College Park.

Gossage won NEA grants in 1978, 1974 and 1973, a Stern Family Foundation Grant in 1974 and grants from the Washington Gallery of Modern Art Fund in 1970 and 1969.

PUBLICATIONS   Monograph: *Gardens*, Walter Hopps, 1978. Book: *Time-Life Textbook of Photography*, John & Barbara Upton, eds., 1976. Anthology: *American Images*, 1979. Catalogs: *Better Neighborhoods of Greater Washington*, Jane Livingston, 1976 (Corcoran Gall. of Art: Wash., D.C.); *14 American Photographers*, Renato Danese, 1975 (Baltimore Mus. of Art: Md.); *photography 2*, 1975 (Glenn Smith Gall.: Newport Beach, Calif.); *Photography Here and Now*, 1972 (Univ. of Md. Art Gall.: College Park); *Joe Cameron—John Gossage*, intro. by Walter Hopps, 1969 (Corcoran Gall. of Art: Wash., D.C.). Periodicals: "Washington: Photography at the Corcoran," James Cassell, Oct 1979, "14 American Photographers," Mar 1975, *Afterimage: VSW*; "Art in Washington," *Art in America*, July/Aug 1978; *Arts Magazine*, May 1978; *Camera*, Mar 1977, Sept 1973, Aug 1970; *Artspace*, winter 1976–77; "Review: New York," Phil Patton, *Artforum*, Apr 1976; *Creative Camera*, Feb 1973; *Asahi Camera*, Jan 1965.

COLLECTIONS   Addison Gall. of Amer. Art, Andover, Mass.; Colgate Univ., Hamilton, N.Y.; Corcoran Gall. of Art, Wash., D.C.; Houston Mus. of Fine Art, Tex.; IMP/GEH, Rochester; L/C, Wash., D.C.; Miami Dade Coll., Miami, Fla; MOMA, NYC; Mus. of Fine Arts, St. Petersburg, Fla.; Norton Simon Mus. of Art, Pasadena, Calif.; Pan Amer. Union, Wash., D.C.; Philadelphia Mus. of Art, Penn.; Princeton Univ., N.J.; Seattle Arts Commission, Wash.; Smithsonian Inst., Wash., D.C.; Univ. of Mass. Art Gall., Amherst; Univ. of N. Mex. Art Gall., Albuquerque; Whea-

ton Coll., Wheaton, Ill. Australia Natl. Gall., Canberra; Bibliothèque Nationale, Paris; Walker Art Ctr., Liverpool, Eng.

DEALERS   Leo Castelli Graphics, 4 E 77 St., New York, NY 10021; Richard Hines Gall., 2030 Fifth Ave, Seattle, WA 98121; Light Gall., 800 N La Cienega Blvd, Los Angeles, CA 90069; Lunn Gall./Graphics Internatl., 3243 P St NW, Wash., D.C. 20007.

ADDRESS   1875 Mintwood Pl NW, #23, Washington, DC 20009.

Hal D. Gould   PHOTOGRAPHER · CURATOR   Born February 29, 1920, in Clarke, Wyoming, Gould studied at the Art Institute of Chicago from 1946 to 1948 and the Ray-Vogue School in Chicago in 1949. He became a "Master" of Photography from the Professional Photographers of America in 1962.

The artist is curator and executive director of the Colorado Photographic Arts Center in Denver, a nonprofit photography museum, where he has been since 1963. From 1955 to 1979 he was owner of the House of Photography in Denver.

Gould is a member of the Photographic Society of America in Philadelphia, the PPA in Des Plains, Illinois, and the Colorado Photographic Arts Center, Denver. In 1964 he received the National Award from the Professional Photographers of America.

Gould's works are large-format portraits and nature studies.

COLLECTIONS   Art Inst. of Chicago; Colorado Photographic Arts Ctr., Denver; Photographic Society of America, Philadelphia, Pa.; Pittsburg Mus., Pa.; Professional Photographers of America, Des Plains, Ill.

ADDRESS   1309 Bannock St, Denver, CO 80204.

Geoffrey R. Gove   PHOTOGRAPHER   Born in San Mateo, California, on August 13, 1943, Gove received his BA in Film from San Francisco State College in 1967. He attended a photo workshop led by Ansel Adams and Wynn Bullock in the summer of 1965 at the San Francisco Art Institute. He also took graphic arts and photography courses at New York University in 1971, 1973 and 1976.

Gove has been a freelance photographer since 1970. From 1972 to 1976 he did freelance photo research for Magnum, Photo Trends, Appleton-Century and other companies. He was a photo editor/researcher for Grolier Publishing in 1970–71 and a photo editor for *Pageant* magazine in 1968–69.

The photographer has been a member of SPE since 1978, ASMP since 1975 and the American Society of Picture Professionals since 1970. He won "Creativity" awards from *Art Direction* magazine in 1975, 1977, 1978 (2) and 1979 (2) and a Best of Year award for a 1974 *New Times* magazine cover. He also received the Grand Prize from KINSA, 1967.

Since 1973 Gove has worked with refracted-light photography, based mainly on objective imagery, and in 1974 began to experiment with the color Xerox process, especially with black-and-white to color conversions. He has also made a film, the 16mm documentary short *Squadron 74,* in 1967.

Gove works in all formats, concentrating mostly on small-format color. Currently experimenting in color video and super 8mm, he is "most interested in levels of perception that border on abstraction."

PUBLICATIONS Periodicals: *Nouveau Photo-Cinema,* Mar 1978; *Camera 35,* July 1975.

COLLECTIONS Imagebank, NYC; Images Gall., NYC; K & L Gall., NYC. Musée Calvet, Avignon, France.

DEALER Images Gall., 11 E 57 St, New York, NY 10022.

ADDRESS 117 Waverly Pl, New York, NY 10011.

Emmet Gowin PHOTOGRAPHER Born in Danville, West Virginia, in 1941, Gowin earned a BFA at Richmond Professional Institute in Richmond, Virginia (1965), and an MFA at the Rhode Island School of Design in Providence (1967), where he studied with Harry Callahan.

Currently he teaches at Princeton University in New Jersey and works as a freelance photographer.

"Emmet Gowin often uses his family and relatives as models [in his work]. They are, however, posed and recorded in such a way that the individual is made to represent broader aspects of human experience or the natural world," writes Clifford Ackley (*Private Realities*). He adds: "Much of the impact of Gowin's images derives, in fact, from an intensified recording of the drama of light and shadow. This drama is enhanced by the richly modulated tonalities of the photographic print itself."

PUBLICATIONS Monograph: *Emmet Gowin: Photographs,* 1976. Anthologies: *The Photograph Collector's Guide,* Lee D. Witkin & Barbara London, 1979; *Darkroom 2,* Jain Kelly, ed., 1978; *Mirrors and Windows,* John Szarkowski, ed., 1978; *Celebrations,* Minor White & Jonathan Green, eds., 1974; *The Art of Photography,* 1971, *Photographing Children,* 1971, Time-Life Series; *Be-ing Without Clothes,* Minor White, ed., 1970; *Vision and Expression,* Nathan Lyons, ed., 1969. Catalogs: *Aspects of American Photography,* 1976 (Univ. of Mo.: St. Louis); *New Images in Photography,* 1974 (Univ. of Miami, Lowe Art Mus.: Fla); *Private Realities,* Clifford Ackley, ed., 1974 (Boston Mus. of Fine Arts: Mass.); *Art in Virginia,* 1972 (Mus. of Fine Arts: Richmond); *60's Continuum,* Van Deren Coke, 1972 (GEH: Rochester); *Photography Invitational,* 1971 (Arkansas Arts Ctr.: Little Rock); *12 x 12,* 1970 (R.I. School of Design: Providence). Periodicals: *Creative Camera Annual,* 1977; *Camera,* Oct 1974; *Camera Mainichi,* Oct 1972; *Aperture,* 16:2, 1971; *Album,* nos. 5 & 6, 1970.

COLLECTIONS Art Inst. of Chicago; Cincinnati Art Mus., Ohio; Dayton Art Inst., Ohio; Harvard Univ., Fogg Art Mus., Cambridge, Mass.; Minneapolis Inst. of Arts, Minn.; MOMA, NYC; Rhode Island School of Design, Providence; Univ. of Kansas, Lawrence; Univ. of N. Mex., Albuquerque. Natl. Gall. of Canada, Ottawa, Ontario.

ADDRESS 212 N Chancellor St, Newton, PA 18940.

Peter Gowland PHOTOGRAPHER · CAMERA MANUFACTURER, · CINEMATOGRAPHER Born in Los Angeles, California, on April 3, 1916, Gowland was the son of Gibson Gowland, who starred in the classic Eric Von Stroheim film *Greed;* his mother was actress/poet Sylvia Andrew. Gowland learned about lighting and cameras while working as an extra in the film industry. He also studied with Jack Thomas, a Hollywood portrait photographer.

Self-employed since 1947, Gowland was in the Air Force from 1945 to 1946 and was a movie extra from 1933 to 1943. He belongs to the Screen Actors Guild and the American Federation of Television and Radio Artists.

In 1957 Gowland designed and manufactured the Gowlandflex twin-lens camera. As a cinematographer he has worked for *Wide World of Sports* and also made the films *Save Our Stream* (1965) and *Save Our Beach* (1968).

Gowland specializes in photographing women and is particularly known for his nude studies.

PUBLICATIONS Books: *Gowland's Guide to Glamour,* 1977; *How to Photograph Women,* 1955; and numerous "how to" books.

REPRESENTATIVE Freelance Photographers Guild, 251 Park Ave S, New York, NY 10010.

ADDRESS   609 Hightree Rd, Santa Monica, CA 90402.

Wendy Susan Grad   PHOTOGRAPHER   Born in Philadelphia, Pennsylvania, on September 13, 1955, Grad earned a BA in Cinema at the University of Southern California, Los Angeles, in 1977. Her major influences have been Magritte, Edward Steichen, Jerry Uelsmann and Irving Penn.

Since 1971 she has been a freelance photographer, specializing in advertising, public relations, travel and photojournalism.

A charter member of ICP, Grad also belongs to Friends of Photography (since 1975) and George Eastman House (since 1978). In 1970–71 Grad was the American representative to the Paris Opera Ballet in France.

Grad's work consists of pre-manipulated, pre-exposed Polaroid SX-70 portraits and abstract images. She has been making an ongoing series of portraits of poets since 1977. The artist states: "My chief interest is to define photography as painting through the use of non-traditional approaches." She also does straight color photographs in large format.

REPRESENTATIVE   Jane Jordan Browne, 410 S Michigan Ave., #828, Chicago, IL 60605.

DEALER   Mme Michelle Chomette, 240 bis Blvd St. Germain, 75005 Paris, France.

ADDRESS   439½ N Stanley Dr, Los Angeles, CA 90036.

Martus Granirer   PHOTOGRAPHER · TEACHER   Born February 19, 1933, in New York City, Granirer is self-taught in photography. He attended Harvard University (1950–52), Columbia School of General Studies as a philosophy major (1953–55), Brooklyn Law School (1955–57) and Columbia University Graduate School's MFA program in motion pictures (1956–57).

Self-employed as a freelance photographer as of this writing, Granirer previously taught at Wright State University in Dayton, Ohio, as artist-in-residence (1976), and at Moore College of Art in Philadelphia, Pennsylvania, as a visiting professor (1971–72). He was a lecturer at Manhattanville College in Purchase, New York, from 1968 to 1969, where he founded their photography program. From 1965 to 1969 he was an instructor and later an associate professor at the Philadelphia College of Art.

Granirer is currently a member of SPE, Society of Motion Picture and Television Engineers, Society of Photographic Scientists and Engineers, and Illuminating Engineering Society. He was also cameraman on the "Loops" project of USIA for the Brussels World's Fair of 1957.

The photographer says of his work: "I prefer to seek out or construct circumstances that in my photographs will present a sort of dry paradox that I hope will demonstrate or reveal something about the process of vision."

PUBLICATIONS   Book: *The Art of Photography*, consultant, 1971. Periodical: *Aperture*, 13:5, 1966.

COLLECTIONS   Addison Gall. of American Art, Andover, Mass.; MOMA, NYC.

ADDRESS   100 S Mountain Rd, New City, NY 10956.

Susan Kae Grant   PHOTOGRAPHER · TEACHER · BOOKMAKER   Born on July 29, 1954, in Fort Atkinson, Wisconsin, Grant received her BS in Art and Art Education at the University of Wisconsin in Madison in 1976. Working with Cavalliere Ketchum, Phil Hamilton and Walter Hamady, she received her MFA in Photography and Graphics also from the University of Wisconsin, in 1979.

In 1979 Grant became an instructor of photography at Wayne State University in Detroit, Michigan, where, as of this date, she continues to teach.

She maintains membership in the Association of University Professors, SPE, Wisconsin Women in the Arts and Women's Caucus of the Arts.

In 1976, with the aid of a summer art grant from the Madison Cultural Affairs Committee, Grant wrote the book *Retailing, Wrinkles and Wisdom*. She established The Black Rose Press for the production of handmade limited-edition books.

The artist says: "The main emphasis of my work is on pre-visualized black-and-white photography, influenced a great deal by the Surrealists." She has produced several handmade limited-edition books combining hand-set letterpress type, handmade papers and silver and non-silver images.

PUBLICATIONS   Books (private press): *An Alphabet Book*, 1979; *Backwards and Forwards*, 1979; *One Sunday I Became the Virgin Mary*, 1979; *Portrait of an Artist and Her Mother*, 1978; *Retailing, Wrinkles and Wisdom*, 1976.

PORTFOLIO   *Ten Below Zero* (group), 1978.

COLLECTIONS   CCP, Tucson; Minneapolis Art Inst., Minn.; Scottsdale Community Coll., Ariz.; Univ. of Iowa, Iowa City; Univ. of Wisc., Women's Studies Dept., Madison. Bibliothèque Nationale, Paris.

ADDRESS   2330 Rochester Rd, #203, Royal Oak, MI 48073.

Kenneth Robert Graves PHOTOGRAPHER · TEACHER Born June 27, 1942, in Portland, Oregon, Graves earned an MFA in Photography from the San Francisco Art Institute in 1971. He studied with Richard Conrat, John Collier and Jerry Burchard, and also worked and photographed with the late Tony Ray-Jones.

Graves has been assistant professor of photography in the Department of Visual Arts of Pennsylvania State University, University Park, since 1977. He taught at the San Francisco Art Institute in 1975 and at Film Center West in Berkeley, California, in 1972.

A member of the photographic agency Jeroboam, Inc., Graves won a Pennsylvania State University Faculty Research Grant in 1980, an NEA grant in 1974 and a Ferguson Grant from the Friends of Photography in Carmel, California, in 1973. His photo essay "Montgomery Street" was seen on KQED-TV in San Francisco in 1969.

He has been photographing at public festivals and events for the past ten years, "always hoping to see what is invisible, never describing a place, but rather seeing a special moment or situation."

PUBLICATIONS Books: *American Snapshots,* w/Mitchell Payne, 1977; *Time-Life Photography Year 1975.* Periodicals: *35mm Camera,* winter 1978; *Creative Camera,* Jan 1971; *Camera,* Apr 1970.

COLLECTION San Francisco Mus. of Modern Art.

REPRESENTATIVE Jeroboam, Inc., 1041 Folsom St, San Francisco, CA 94103.

ADDRESS 332 W Prospect Ave, State College, PA 16801.

Edward Grazda PHOTOGRAPHER Born March 27, 1947, in Queens, New York, Grazda attended the Rhode Island School of Design, receiving a BFA in Photography in 1969. He studied with Harry Callahan and Emmit Gowin.

A freelance photographer, he won an NEA award for 1979–80 and received CAPS grants in 1973 and 1975.

Grazda works in black-and-white, and says: "My work is about the real world, the surreal, and the unreal world of a photograph." From 1972 to 1978 he photographed in Latin America, and he worked with multiple images until 1974. In 1980 he began photographing in Asia.

PUBLICATIONS Periodicals: *Camera 35,* Apr 1980; *Camera,* July 1978, May 1974; *Art Forum,* Feb 1976; *Modern Photography,* July 1976, Feb 1975; *Creative Camera,* Aug 1975.

COLLECTIONS Art Inst. of Chicago; Bard College, Annandale-on-Hudson, N.Y.; Charles Rand Penney Foundation, Olcott, N.Y.; MOMA, NYC; Mus. of Art, Providence, R.I.; Mus. of Fine Arts, Houston, Tex.; New Orleans Mus. of Art. Musée Réattu, Arles, France.

DEALERS Cronin Gall., 2008 Peden, Houston, TX 77019; A Gall. for Fine Photography, 5432 Magazine St, New Orleans, LA 70115.

ADDRESS 17 Bleecker St, New York, NY 10012.

Mladen Grčević PHOTOGRAPHER · ART- & PHOTOHISTORIAN Born October 8, 1918, in Zagreb, Yugoslavia, Grčević earned a BL in Law (1942) and a BA and MA in Art History (1960, 1965) from the University of Zagreb. His mentor was Grgo Gamulin. Grčević's wife, Nada Grčević, is also an art- and photohistorian.

A freelance photographer, art- and photohistorian since 1954, Grčević formerly was professor at the Academy of Applied Arts (1952–54) and instructor in the School of Graphic Arts (1946–52), both in Zagreb.

The photographer belongs to Yugoslav Federation of Photography (since 1948), Association of Application Artists in Zagreb (since 1950) and Association of Art Historians in Zagreb (since 1960). He is an honorary member of the National Federation of Photo Societies of France (since 1955) and a member of the Art Commission of the International Federation of Photographic Art (FIAP, since 1972).

From 1939 to 1953 he concentrated on pictorial photography in his home country, but after 1954 he began traveling around the world, especially in Asia, and "came to the documentary (*LIFE*) photography with an accent on humanity." His research is on the early days of photography as an art form.

PUBLICATIONS Books: *Zadar,* V. Cestarić, 1978 (Zadar); *Early Croatian Heritage,* S. Gunjača, 1976 (Zagreb); *Gold and Silver of Zadar,* M. Krleža, 1971 (Zagreb); *Situla Art,* foreword by J. Kastelic, 1965; *Dalmatien,* foreword by K. Edschmid, 1961 (Andermann: Munich); *Yougoslavie,* foreword by L. Peillard, 1955 (Hachette: Paris). Anthology: *Zagrebačka fotografija,* w/ Nada Grčević & Zdenko Kuzmić, 1978 (Zagreb). Periodicals: "Za jednu univerzalnu povijest fotografije", *Zivot umjetnosti,* no. 6, 1968; "Grand Succès de la Photographie Française à Zagreb," *Photo Cinema,* July 1955.

COLLECTIONS Mariners Mus., Newport News, Va.; Smithsonian Inst., Wash., D.C. Arts & Crafts Mus., Zagreb, Yugoslavia; City of Havdrup Cllctn. of Photography, Denmark; Photographic Assoc. of Bengal, Calcutta, India.

ADDRESS Dvorničićeva 19, 41000 Zagreb, Yugoslavia.

Nada Grčević ART- & PHOTOHISTORIAN · CRITIC Born April 1, 1922, in Zagreb, Yugoslavia, Grčević earned a BA (1960) and MA (1965) in Art History from the University of Zagreb, Yugoslavia. Her mentor was Dr. Grgo Gamulin; her husband, Mladen Grčević, is a photographer as well as an art- and photohistorian.

Self-employed, Grčević has worked with the Yugoslav Lexicographic Institution since 1964, and with the Zagreb Center for Photography, Film and Television since 1977.

Grčević belongs to the European Society for the History of Photography and the Association of Art-Historians in Zagreb (since 1960), and has been a member of the advisory board of *History of Photography* magazine since 1977.

She has studied the interaction between photography and modern painting, and since 1960 has devoted her research to the history of photography, with special attention to early photography in Croatia (Yugoslavia).

PUBLICATIONS Anthology: *Zagrebačka fotografija*, w/Mladen Grčević & Zdenko Kuzmić, 1978 (Zagreb). Periodicals: "Sun Pictures by Dragutin Parčić: Early Scientific Calotypes in Croatia," no. 2/3, 1978, "Early Photography in Eastern Europe—Croatia," no. 2, 1977, *History of Photography*; "Early Photography in Zadar," *Zadarska Revija*, no. 2/3, 1978; "F. Pommer, the First Zagreb Photographer," *Iz storog i novog Zagreba*, vol. 5, 1974; "The Photographic Legacy of Dragutin Parčić," *Acta instituti Academiae Jugoslavicae*, vol. 19, 1972; "The beginnings of Photography in Croatia," *Život umjetnosti*, no. 6, 1968.

ADDRESS Dvorničiećeva 19, 41000 Zagreb, Yugoslavia.

Jonathan W. Green PHOTOGRAPHER · CRITIC · EDITOR · TEACHER Born in Troy, New York, on September 26, 1939, Green received his BA from Brandeis University in 1963, graduating Phi Beta Kappa. A Danforth Fellow, he earned an MA in 1967 from Harvard University. As an undergraduate he also studied at MIT and Hebrew University in Jerusalem. He worked with Ezra Stoller from 1967 to 1968, and taught photography with Minor White at MIT from 1968 to 1976.

Green is currently an associate professor of photography at Ohio State University in Columbus, where he has taught since 1976. Since 1977 he has also worked as editorial consultant and writer for Oxford University Press in New York City. Between 1968 and 1976 Green worked at MIT, first as an instructor, then assistant professor, and then as associate professor and director of the Creative Photography Laboratory. As an editorial consultant and associate editor he was at *Aperture* from 1972 to 1976.

Green is a member of SPE, VSW, Friends of Photography and the Center for Creative Photography. Between 1967 and 1976 he was a member of ASMP.

The artist was awarded AT&T's Bell System grant, "American Images" (1978) and an NEA Photographer's Fellowship in 1977. The New York Type Directors Club gave him an award for his book *The Snapshot* in 1974, and in 1973 Green received a Best Art Book award from the Art Librarians Society for another of his books, *Camera Work*.

Describing his style as "straight," Green worked in black-and-white prior to 1976, and now works in color. As a critic his interest lies in issues concerning the relationship of photography and American culture.

PUBLICATIONS Anthologies: *American Images*, 1979; *The Snapshot*, 1974; *Celebrations*, co-ed. w/Minor White, 1974; *Camera Work: A Critical Anthology*, ed. 1973. Periodicals (text only): "Aperture in the 50's: The Word and the Way," *Afterimage: VSW*, Mar 1979; "Bruce Davidson's East 100th Street," winter 1971, "The Photographs of Harry Callahan," winter 1968, *Aperture*. Periodicals: *Aperture*, 18:1, 2, 17:1, 3, 4.

COLLECTIONS Cleveland Mus. of Art, Ohio; MIT, Boston; Mus. of Fine Arts, Boston; Princeton Univ. Art Mus., N.J.; Univ. of Santa Clara, De Saisset Art Gall. & Mus., Calif; Virginia Mus. of Fine Arts, Richmond. In Stockholm: Fotografiska Muséet; Moderna Muséet.

DEALER Carl Siembab Gall., 162 Newbury St, Boston, MA.

ADDRESS 1430 S Galena Rd, Galena, OH 43021.

Robert Frederick Green PSYCHIATRIST · PHOTOGRAPHER · GALLERY OWNER Born October 13, 1923, in Newark, New Jersey, Green earned an MD from College of Medicine, State University of New York, in 1952, and interned at Brooklyn Hospital in New York in 1952–53.

Green is currently self-employed and president/owner of Gallery 614. He was an assistant in psychiatry at Tufts University, Medford, Massachusetts (1955–57), and served medical residencies at Worcester State Hospital, Massachusetts (1954–57), and at Peter Bent

Brigham Hospital in Boston, Massachusetts (1953–54).

He belongs to the New York Academy of Science, American Association for the Advancement of Science and the American Medical Association.

Green has revived and improved the classic carbro-carbon printing pigments and methods and conducts intensive workshops for monochrome and tricolor carbro printing. He is also the sole supplier of carbro materials in the United States and Canada.

PUBLICATIONS Book: *Carbro-Monochrome-Tricolor Monograph*, 1973, rev. 1975, 1979. Periodicals: "Tri-Color Carbro," *Petersen's Photographic Magazine*, May 1977; "Sans Silver," *Camera 35*, May 1975; "Neo-Carbro Printing," *The Range Finder*, Mar 1973.

ADDRESS Gallery 614, 614 W Berry St, Fort Wayne, IN 46802.

John B. Greene PHOTOGRAPHER Born in 1832 in Paris, France, of American parents, Greene died in 1856, probably in North Africa.

He began to take photographs in Egypt about 1852 and continued to work there and in other areas of northern Africa until his death. His photographs were exhibited in Paris in 1855 and 1857 and in Brussels in 1856.

Greene was a founding member of the Société Française de Photographie (November 15, 1854).

The photographer made salt prints from paper negatives, his subject matter including landscapes and architecture of Egypt and North Africa between 1852 and 1856.

PUBLICATION Monograph: *Le Nil: Monuments, Paysages, Exploitations Photographiques*, 1854 (Blanquart-Evrard: Paris).

COLLECTIONS Lunn Gall., Wash., D.C. Société Française de Photographie, Paris.

Stanley Norman Greene, Jr. PHOTOGRAPHER · CURATOR Born in Brooklyn, New York, on February 14, 1949, Greene studied at the School of Visual Arts in New York City (1971–72), Imageworks in Cambridge, Massachusetts (1972–74), and the San Francisco Art Institute, where he received his BFA in photography in 1978. His mentors were W. Eugene Smith, Judy Dater and Jerry Burchard.

As of this writing Greene was a contributing photographer for Ciardella Design Associations and Griswald Designs in San Mateo, California, and a fashion photographer for the Mistress Store in San Francisco, Greene was a founder and curator of exhibitions by San Francisco Urban En-

vironmentalists, 1976–77. From 1972 to 1975 he produced multimedia slide presentations for Imageworks, of which he was a founding member. In 1970–71 Greene was a photo assistant to W. Eugene Smith in New York City.

Greene is on the board of directors of Camerawork Gallery in San Francisco and on the board of trustees and college committee of the San Francisco Art Institute.

He has also made a 16mm film on the dance entitled *The Letter* (1976) and a videotape, *Prostitution in Boston*, commissioned by WGBH in Boston (1972).

Greene works in small-format photography, doing mostly reportage and surrealistic imagery.

PUBLICATION Anthology: *Photo-Erotica: Eros in Photography*, 1977.

COLLECTIONS Camerawork Gall., San Francisco; San Francisco Art Inst.; San Francisco Genl. Hospital. Bibliothèque Nationale, Paris.

REPRESENTATIVE Claire Mawe Holman, 2662 Russell St, Berkeley, CA 94705.

ADDRESS 16 Salmon Alley, #3, San Francisco, CA 94133.

B. Colin Greenly PHOTOGRAPHER · SCULPTOR · TEACHER Born January 21, 1928, in London, Greenly received an AB from Harvard in 1948, and studied at both Columbia University School of Painting and Sculpture in New York City from 1951 to 1953 and the American University Graduate School of Fine Arts in 1956.

A self-employed photographer, he taught art at State University of New York in New York City (1974–75). An artist-in-residence at Finch College Museum in New York City (1974), at Cazenovia College in Cazenovia, New York, and at Everson Museum School of Art (1972), he also was a Dana Professor of Fine Arts at Colgate University in Hamilton, New York (1972–73).

Greenly was the recipient of CAPS fellowships in photography in 1977 and 1972, and was awarded a grant from the Committee for the Visual Arts in New York City in 1974.

Besides his photography, he created an architectural design for the restoration and adaptation of the 1878 Hulse Basilican Plan Bank Barn at Campbell Hall in New York, and works in sculpture, drawings, paintings and woodcuts.

The artist characterizes his work as "a conceptual image, thought of as intangible and derived from previous art, geologic, biologic and philosophic interests which are incorporated into photographic presentations of sites and antiquities."

COLLECTIONS Albright Knox Art Gall., Buffalo, N.Y.; City of Baltimore Cllctn., Md.; Corcoran Gall. of Art, Wash., D.C.; Des Moines Art Center, Des Moines, Iowa; Everson Mus., Syracuse, N.Y.; High Mus. of Art, Atlanta, Ga.; Herbert F. Johnson Mus., Ithaca, N.Y.; Langlet School, McLean, Va.; Manufacturers & Traders Trust Co., Buffalo, N.Y.; MOMA, NYC; Natl. Cllctn. of Fine Arts, Wash., D.C.; Natl Gall., Rosenwald Cllctn., Wash., D.C.; Philadelphia Mus. of Art, Penn.; Potomac School, McLean, Va.; Virginia Natl. Bank, Norfolk; City of Wash., D.C., Cllctn. City of Toronto Cllctn., Canada.

ADDRESS RD 1, POB 118, Campbell Hall, NY 10916.

Larry Gregory *PHOTOGRAPHER · TEACHER*
Born in St. Louis, Missouri, December 1943, Gregory received his BS in Photography from Southern Illinois University, Carbondale (1965), and his MFA in Photography from Ohio University, Athens (1972). He names Clarence H. White, Jr., and Arnold Gassan as mentors.

Gregory has been an assistant professor in the Art Department of Northern Illinois University, De Kalb, since 1973. He was in the U.S. Navy from 1968 to 1972 and before that worked for Savage Communications, Toledo, Ohio (1968), and Neil Saver & Associates, St. Louis, Missouri (1966).

He is a member of SPE and Professional Photographers of America.

Concentrating on landscapes in both black-and-white and color, Gregory is "concerned with the . . . land and its forms, and man's manipulation of it."

PUBLICATION Book: *Architecture Evolving*, William Brown, 1976.

COLLECTIONS Davenport Mus. (slide cllctn.); L/C, Wash., D.C.; Northern Ky. State Univ., Highland; Va. Mus. of Fine Arts (slide cllctn.); private collections.

ADDRESS 221 Delcy, De Kalb, IL 60115.

Art (Arthur David) Grice *GENERAL CONTRACTOR · PHOTOGRAPHER · ILLUSTRATOR* Grice was born in Taunton, Massachusetts, on July 22, 1942. He is married to Emily K. Grice, a commercial photographer and co-owner of the Mind's Eye Gallery in Vancouver, British Columbia. Grice studied briefly in 1961–62 at Diablo Valley College and the California College of Arts and Crafts, both in the Bay Area of California. He is basically self-taught.

Since 1971 Grice has worked as a freelance photographer and self-employed contractor. He teaches and lectures occasionally.

Grice is a member of the Northwest Chapter of SPE and the Vancouver Image Exploration Workshops, having served as its president from 1974 to 1975. In 1975 he was awarded a Canada Council grant to develop basic technology for a 3-D camera, and in 1971 he received a grant from the Vancouver Community Arts Council for a Historic Sites Project.

The artist's work is "traditional" silver photography.

PUBLICATIONS Monograph: *Landscapes*, 1976. Book: *The Photographer*, 1975. Periodicals: *Camera*, July 1975; *Camera Canada*, Mar & Oct, 1973; *B.C. Photographer*, 1972.

COLLECTIONS In Canada: Bank of B.C., Vancouver; Insurance Corp. of B.C., Vancouver; Natl. Archives of Canada; Natl. Film Board of Canada, Ottawa, Ontario; Vancouver City Archives; Vancouver City Art Cllctn.; Vancouver Pub. Lib., Historic Photographs Cllctn.

ADDRESS POB 10071, Bainbridge Is., WA 98110.

Jennifer Griffiths *PHOTOGRAPHER* Born September 9, 1950, in Los Angeles, California, Griffiths received her BFA from California State University, Northridge, in 1974. She studied with Edwin Sievers.

A freelance photographer since 1976, she was a photographer's assistant for Charles Bush in 1975–76 and a Xerox processor for Hanna-Barbera Productions from 1968 to 1973.

A member of SPE, she won the Paul L. Schaffer Memorial Foundation Award in 1979.

Besides her photography, Griffiths has published a poetry book, *Bongo Chalice* (1977).

Working with small- and medium-format color transparencies, she produces color prints up to 16 x 20. She usually shoots at twilight.

PUBLICATIONS Book: *My Bed*, ltd. ed., 1976. Periodicals: *Print Magazine*, Dec 1978; *Picture Magazine*, no. 7, 1978; *Petersens Photographic Magazine*, Oct 1977; *Picture Magazine*, no. 4, 1977.

COLLECTIONS CCP, Tucson; New York Univ., Natl. Artists Alliance; Security Pacific Bank, Los Angeles; and private collections.

DEALER Mirage Gall., 1662 12 St, Santa Monica, CA 90404.

ADDRESS 201 San Juan, Venice, CA 90291.

Jan Groover *PHOTOGRAPHER · TEACHER* Born in Plainfield, New Jersey, in 1943, Groover studied painting and drawing at Pratt Institute in Brooklyn, New York (BA, 1965), and earned an MA in 1973 from Ohio State University, Columbus.

Groover is currently teaching at the University of Hartford, Connecticut.

She won a Guggenheim Fellowship in 1978, an NEA grant in 1978 and CAPS grants in 1977 and 1974.

PUBLICATIONS Anthologies: *The Photograph Collector's Guide*, Lee D. Witkin & Barbara London, 1979; *The Photographers' Choice*, Kelly Wise, ed., 1975; *Mirrors & Windows*, John Szarkowski, ed., 1960. Catalogs: *Jan Groover*, 1976 (Corcoran Gall. of Art: Wash., D.C.); *The Nation's Capital in Photographs*, 1976 (Corcoran Gall. of Art: Wash., D.C.); *(photo) (photo)*[2] ... *(photo)*[n]: *Sequenced Photographs*, David Bourdon, 1975 (Univ. of Md. Art Gall.: College Park). Periodicals: "Post Modern Photography: It Doesn't Look Modern at All," Gene Thorton, Apr 1979, review, Barbara Zucker, Apr 1976, *Artnews*; *Artforum*, Jan 1979, Apr 1976, Feb 1976, Nov 1973; "One + One = One," Andy Grunberg, *Modern Photography*, Mar 1978; "Uses and Misuses of Sequential Images," Robert W. Woolard, May 22, 1976, "Photographs in Sequence," Joan Murray, Oct 4, 1975, *Artweek*; review, Charlotte Thorp, "Entries," Robert Pincus-Witten, *Arts Magazine*, Mar 1976.

COLLECTIONS IMP/GEH, Rochester. Centre Georges Pompidou, Paris.

DEALER Sonnabend Gall., 420 W Broadway, New York, NY 10012.

H. F. Gros *PHOTOGRAPHER · COLLECTOR* Born in Switzerland, Gros probably died there, the last known photo of him being taken at his Geneva home in 1903. His career flourished from 1869, primarily in South Africa.

Gros first went to South Africa about 1869, opening a studio in Burghersdorp and then (1872) in Bloemfontein. He traveled to the Lydenburg gold field in 1874–75, and early in 1877 moved to Pretoria, capital of the Transvaal, and set up a studio. At that time very little cultural activity existed in the area. About 1903 Gros explored the new gold field in eastern Transvaal, traveling over the undeveloped land in a covered wagon drawn by oxen, and sometime later he returned to Geneva.

The photographer was an honorary member of the Photographic Society of Geneva.

Gros was a portraitist of such as Chief Sekukuni, and a documentary photographer who recorded "landscapes, native life, mining activity, town views and street scenes" of Transvaal life. His photographic albums "provide a comprehensive, socially significant document of life and conditions in the Zuid-Afrikaansche Republiek

during the years from about 1882 to 1892," according to Nat Cowan in *Africana Notes & News*. "His photographic technique," Cowan adds, "was nothing short of perfection. . . . It is not possible to improve on the tonal range of Mr. Gros' original prints."

PUBLICATIONS Books: *Secure the Shadow*, M. Bull & J. Denfield, 1970 (Terence McNally: Cape Town, S. Africa); *Picturesque Aspects of the Transvaal*, ca. 1888. Periodicals: "The Photograficana of H. F. Gros," Nat Cowan, *Africana Notes & News*, Sept 1978; *The Graphic*, May 28, 1881; *The Courier*, Jan 1, 1880.

COLLECTIONS In South Africa: Africana Mus., Johannesburg; Bensusan Mus. of Photography, Johannesburg; Johannesburg Pub. Lib.; Strange Lib. of Africana, Johannesburg.

Lori Gross *GALLERY DIRECTOR* Born July 23, 1953, Gross earned a BA from Colgate University, Hamilton, New York, in 1975 and an MA and MLS from Case Western University, Cleveland, Ohio, in 1978.

In 1979 she became director of the Daniel Wolf Gallery in New York City. Previously she was assistant curator/registrar at the Akron Art Institute, Ohio (1978–79), and an instructor at the Cleveland Museum of Art (1975–78).

PUBLICATIONS Catalog: *Acquisitions 1979*, 1979 (Akron Art Institute: Ohio). Periodical: "Guitar and Bottle of Marc on a Table," *The Bulletin of the Cleveland Museum of Art*, Apr 1977.

ADDRESS c/o Daniel Wolf, Inc., 30 W 57 St, New York, NY 10019.

L. Fritz Gruber *PHOTO-PROMOTER · EXHIBITION DIRECTOR · AUTHOR · COLLECTOR* Born on June 7, 1908, in Cologne, Germany, Gruber studied at the Abitur Realgymnasium in Cologne-Lindenthal (1926), then undertook art studies at Kölner Werkschulen. From 1926 to 1930 he studied art history, languages, literature and ethnology at Cologne University.

Since 1960 Gruber has organized Photokina cultural exhibitions—over 300 international shows. Previously he worked for Photokina in a general promoting capacity (from 1949). He lived in England (1933–39) for political reasons, working as a photo, photostat and microfilm expert. While a student at Cologne he had edited the anti-Nazi weeklies *Kölner Kurier* and *Westdeutscher Kurier*, which were suppressed in 1933.

Gruber was a founder (1951) and is now vice-president of DGPh. He is also an honorary fellow of RPS and an Honorary Excellence of Fédération

Internationale de Photographie. He received the Kulturpreis of DGPh (1970) and the First Class Order of Merit of the Federal Republic of Germany. He also was honored with the David Octavius Hill Medal of GDL (1968), the Progress Medal of RPS (1966) and the International Understanding Through Photography Award from the Photographic Society of America (1964).

The Gruber Collection of Photographs, about 1,000 pieces, mainly from the twentieth century, was acquired by the city of Cologne in 1977 and is now housed in the Cologne Art Museum, Ludwig.

PUBLICATIONS Books: *Wir zwei*, 1966; *Des Menschen Menschlichkeit*, 1963; *Bildschopfer unserer Zeit—Die grossen Photographen* (trilogy), 1963; *Stärker als Worte—Das Pressephoto*, 1962. Periodicals: *Photography Annual*, 1974; *Popular Photography*, Sept 1970, Aug 1966; *British Journal of Photography Annual*, 1965.

ADDRESS Paulistrasse 10, D-5000 Cologne 41, Germany.

Lois R. Gruberger PHOTOGRAPHER · PAINTER Born June 3, 1951, in New York City, Gruberger completed her BFA at Cooper Union in New York City (1973) and her MFA at the Art Institute of Chicago (1976). She studied with Garry Winogrand, Tod Papageorge and Charles Harbutt.

Since 1976 she has been a fine-arts instructor in photography at Ohio University, Athens.

Gruberger has been a member of SPE since 1975. She won an Ohio Arts Council grant in 1979 and in 1977 was artist-in-residence at Apeiron Workshops, Millerton, New York.

Working in small and medium format, black-and-white and color, the photographer mainly does portraiture. She completed a series on middle-aged women in 1977 and since then has focused on middle-aged men of differing occupations.

PUBLICATION Book: *Three Photographic Visions*, 1977.

COLLECTIONS Apeiron Workshops, Millerton, N.Y.; Brunswick Corp., Chicago; Northwest Mich. Coll., Traverse City, Mich.

DEALER Joy Horwich Gall., 226 E Ontario, Chicago, IL 60611.

ADDRESS 2058 Myrtle Ave, Baton Rouge, LA 70806.

Dorien Grunbaum PHOTOGRAPHER · TEACHER · CONSULTANT Born August 28, 1942, in Rotterdam, The Netherlands, Grunbaum received a BA in Anthropology from Syracuse University, New York (1964), and an MA from Teachers College,

Columbia University, in New York City (1970). In 1972 she was a student of Harold Feinstein.

A freelance photographer since 1973, Grunbaum has been a communications consultant for Morgan Guaranty Trust Co. in New York City since 1979. From 1972 to 1978 she was an assistant professor at Borough of Manhattan Community College in New York City. Grunbaum worked as a Peace Corps volunteer in Turkey from 1964 to 1966.

The photographer was a co-founder and member of Other Eyes Photography Collective from 1972 to 1978. She has also worked as a radio producer for an interview series about career change for WBAI-FM, New York (1979).

Grunbaum is interested in "documenting lives in transition," using small-format black-and-white film.

PUBLICATIONS Anthologies: *Women See Men*, 1977; *The Family of Children*, 1977; *Women Photograph Men*, 1977.

COLLECTIONS ICP, NYC; Metro. Mus. of Art (slide lib.), NYC.

ADDRESS 245 W 104 St, 12E, New York, NY 10025.

Jorge Guerra EDITOR · PHOTOGRAPHER · FILM MAKER Born in Lisbon, Portugal, on February 25, 1936, Guerra earned a degree in history and philosophy at Lisbon University, and studied for two years at the London Film School.

Since 1974 he has been co-director of *Ovo* magazine. He did freelance work as a gaffer (motion picture lighting technician) and cameraman in London from 1965 to 1970, moving to Montreal, Canada, that year to work as an assistant director at the Conservatory of Cinematographic Art until 1974.

Guerra received a grant from the Calouste Gulbenkian Foundation in Lisbon to study at the London Film School (1964), and later received a grant from the Arts Council of Canada to pursue research with Polaroid SX-70 film (1979). Guerra directed a documentary about the Royal Ballet School in London (1966).

A reportage photographer working in the documentary tradition, he has recently been working in Polaroid SX-70.

COLLECTIONS Calouste Gulbenkian Fndn., Lisbon, Portugal; Mus. of Contemporary Art, Montreal, Canada.

ADDRESS 307 Quest, rue ste-Catherine, Montreal, Quebec H2X 2A3, Canada.

Ara Güler PHOTOJOURNALIST Born in Istanbul, Turkey, on August 16, 1928, Güler passed his entrance exams to the Istanbul Drama School in 1948 and Istanbul University's Faculty of Economy in 1951.

Following military service, Güler worked for *Hayat* magazine until 1961 as their chief photographer. He also contributed to American Heritage's *Horizon* magazine and books. Then he became a Near East photo correspondent for *Life,* and later for *Paris-Match* and *Der Stern:* he still holds these positions. For several years he worked as an assistant cameraman in several Turkish film studios. He began his journalism career with the daily *Yeni Istanbul* in 1950.

Güler is a member of the Federation of International Journalism, the Turkish Journalist Syndicate, and the Turkish Journalists Association, whose First Award he received in 1979. He was also awarded Germany's Master of Leica in 1962.

Aside from the political aspects of Güler's journalistic work, his other subjects entail archaeology, important people in art, Islamic and Christian art and human interest.

PUBLICATIONS Books: *Splendor of Islamic Calligraphy,* 1976 (Thames & Hudson: London); *Saint Sophia,* 1971; *Turkei,* 1970 (Terra Magica: Germany); *Treasures of Turkey,* 1966 (Edition d'Art Albert Skira: Switzerland); *Young Turkey,* 1964; *Öster am* Eufrates, 1960 (Tidens Ferlag: Sweden).

COLLECTIONS Univ. of Nebr., Sheldon Memorial Art Gall., Lincoln. Bibliothèque Nationale, Paris.

ADDRESS Beyoğlu, Galatasaray Tosbağa Sok. 10/7, Istanbul, Turkey.

Neil Gulliver PHOTOGRAPHER Born July 13, 1944, in Beaconsfield, Buckinghamshire, England, Gulliver studied civil engineering at Kings College, London University, from 1963 to 1966, and received a Teacher's Certificate from Bede College, Durham University.

Since 1973 he has been a freelance photographer and was previously a lecturer in photography at North East London Polytechnic (1974–76).

Gulliver was a member of the National Union of Teachers from 1968 to 1972.

Working in a black-and-white 35mm format, the photographer concentrates on landscape and documentary depiction of rural areas, people and customs.

PUBLICATIONS Periodicals: *British Journal of Photography,* June 1976, Apr 1975, Jan 1975, Mar 1973.

COLLECTIONS Chelmsford & Essex Mus., Oak Park, Chelmsford, Essex, England; Bibliothèque Nationale, Paris.

ADDRESS 35A Lansdowne Gardens, London SW8 2EL, England.

Judith Mara Gutman HISTORIAN · CRITIC · LECTURER Born May 22, 1928, in New York City, Gutman received a BA from Queens College, Flushing, New York, in 1949 and an MS from Bank Street College, New York City, in 1959.

As of this writing she was a guest curator at the International Center of Photography (ICP) in New York City, and since 1976 has directed the ICP-sponsored project "The Photograph as a Cultural Artifact: 1850–1920, India." A lecturer at museums and colleges internationally since 1975, Gutman co-produced current-affairs films of Educational Film Strips from 1975 to 1979.

She belongs to the Authors Guild (since 1966) and SPE (since 1976). In 1979 she received a post-doctoral fellowship from the Social Science Research Council in New York City; in 1978 she was given a Ford Foundation grant for study in Scotland and England. In 1976 she received an award from the American Institute of Indian Studies and the Smithsonian Institution for the study of photography by Indian photographers in nineteenth-century India.

Involved in a major research project on photography in India, Gutman is "interested in the cultural and aethetic ties which photographs establish with each other." In her research she explores "the many layers of life which directly contribute to any one person's conscious and unconscious moves and thoughts."

PUBLICATIONS Books: *Lewis W. Hine: Two Perspectives,* 1974; *Is America Used Up?,* 1973; *The Making of American Society,* w/Edwin Rozwenc, 1972; *Lewis W. Hine and the American Social Conscience,* 1967.

ADDRESS 97 Sixth Ave, Nyack, NY 10960.

John Gutmann PHOTOGRAPHER · TEACHER · PAINTER Born May 28, 1905, in Breslau, Germany, Gutmann received a BA in 1923 from State Academy of Arts and Crafts, Breslau, where he studied with Otto Mueller. He attended the University of Breslau in 1926–27, then earned an MA in 1928 from the State Institute for Higher Education in Berlin. Gutmann undertook postgraduate work at the University of Berlin and State Academy of Arts, Berlin.

A professor of art and photography at San Francisco State University from 1938 to 1973, he remains a professor emeritus at that school. He previously served as a still photographer and motion picture camera operator for the U.S. Signal Corps (1943–45) and was a photojournalist for Pix, Inc., in New York City (1936–63) and for Presse-Photo in Berlin (1933–36). His photographs have been published in such periodicals as the *Saturday Evening Post, Life, Time, Look, National Geographic* and *Harper's Bazaar.*

Gutmann has been a member of CAA since 1946 and belonged to the American Association of University Professors from 1946 to 1963. He won a Guggenheim Fellowship in 1978 and received the Honor Award for Distinguished Teaching by the California State Colleges in 1968.

Since the 1930s Gutmann has worked in photojournalism, documentary, surrealism, symbolism, human interest and serial photography.

PUBLICATIONS Anthology: *Photography and Language,* 1977. Periodicals: *Art Forum,* Jan 1980; *35mm Photography,* winter 1977.

COLLECTIONS Amon Carter Mus., Ft. Worth, Tex.; Boston Mus. of Fine Arts; Crocker Art Gall., Sacramento, Calif.; Houston Mus. of Fine Arts; Lehigh Univ. Art Cllctn., Bethlehem, Pa.; Mills Coll. Art Cllctn., Oakland, Calif.; MOMA, NYC; Graham Nash Cllctn., San Francisco; New Orleans Fine Arts Mus., La.; San Francisco Mus. of Modern Art; Seagram Bicentennial Cllctn., NYC.

DEALERS Castelli Graphics, 4 E 77 St, New York, NY 10021; Fraenkel Gall., 55 Grant Ave, San Francisco, CA 94108.

ADDRESS 1543 Cole St, San Francisco, CA 94117.

Clara Gutsche PHOTOGRAPHER · TEACHER Born in 1949 in St. Louis, Missouri, Gutsche studied at Oberlin College, Ohio, from 1967 to 1969.

She has been a freelance photographer since 1970, and currently teaches photography at the University of Ottawa, Ontario, Canada (since 1979), and at Dawson College (since 1978). She was a photography instructor at Saidye Bronfman Centre from 1974 to 1978, and in 1975 was a photo editor at the National Film Board of Canada's Still Photography Division.

Gutsche won short-term grants from the Canada Council in 1978 and 1975 and arts grants from them in 1976 and 1973. In 1980 she received an Exhibition Grant from the Minister of Cultural Affairs in Quebec.

PUBLICATIONS Book: *Photography 1975 Photographie* (Natl. Film Board of Canada). Periodical: "Photographs of Women by Women," *Image Nation,* 1972.

COLLECTIONS In Canada: Canada Council Art Bank, Ottawa; Edmonton Gall., Alberta; McCord Mus., Notman Archives, Montreal; Musée d'Art Contemporain, Montreal; Natl. Film Board Still Photography Div., Ottawa; Photographer's Gall., Saskatoon, Saskatchewan; Pub. Archives of Canada, Ottawa.

ADDRESS c/o Univ. of Ottawa Photography Dept., Ottawa, Ontario, Canada.

H

Francis Haar *PHOTOGRAPHER · FILM MAKER · CALLIGRAPHER* Haar was born July 19, 1908, in Czernatfalu, Hungary. His wife is the ceramic artist Irene Haar, and his son, Tom Haar, is a photographer. He received a Master of Photography degree from the National Academy of Industrial Arts in Budapest, Hungary.

A lecturer in photography at the Art Department of the University of Hawaii (1964–75), he was previously owner of Haar Photo, an art and motion picture production studio in Tokyo (1940–56). He also owned Haar Studio in Paris (1937–39) and Budapest, Hungary (1934–37).

Haar is a member of both Honolulu Printmakers and Artists of Hawaii. A recipient of Golden Eagle awards from Washington, D.C., for films (1963, 1966), he also won first prize at both the Metropolitan Improvement Photo Contest in Chicago (1959) and the Hungarian National Photo Contest in 1933 and 1935. He has made several films, including *Holaulea*, Honolulu Academy of Arts (1961), *Ukiyoe, Japanese Print*, for the Art Institute of Chicago (1959), and *The Arts of Japan*, for the U.S. Information Agency in Tokyo (1953).

PUBLICATIONS Books: *The Artists of Hawaii*, vols. 1 & 2, w/Neogy & Turnbull; *Legends of Hawaii*, w/Paki, 1974; *Japanese Theatre in Highlights*, 1952, *Best of Old Japan*, 1950 (Charles Tuttle Co.: Tokyo); *Hungarian Picture Book*, 1941 (Benrido Publishing Co.: Kyoto, Japan); *Around Mount Fuji*, 1940 (Benrido Publishing Co.: Kyoto, Japan); *Way to the Orient*, 1940 (Arts Publishing Co.: Tokyo).

COLLECTIONS MOMA, NYC; State Fndn. on Culture & the Arts, Honolulu, Hawaii. Hungarian Natl. Archive, Budapest, Hungary; Victoria & Albert Mus., London.

ADDRESS 4236 Carnation Pl, Honolulu, HI 96816.

Ernst Haas *PHOTOGRAPHER* Born March 2, 1921, in Vienna, Austria, Haas attended medical school for one year and studied photography at Graphischen Lehr- und Versuchsanstalt in Vienna (1943–44). He was influenced by Cartier-Bresson and the books of Edward Weston.

A freelance throughout his career, Haas has served as a visiting lecturer in photography at Maine Photography Workshop, Rockport, and at Anderson Ranch Foundation, Aspen, Colorado. He currently is an adviser for *Stern* and *Geo*. He worked as a still photographer for such motion pictures as *The Bible, Little Big Man, The Misfits, Hello Dolly, West Side Story* and *Moby Dick*. Haas also served as a consultant on *The Bible*. In 1962 he worked on the *Art of Seeing* for NET-TV. From 1952 to 1960 he did photo essays for *Life, Paris-Match, Esquire* and *Holiday*. Previously he worked on assignment for *Heate* (1946), and in 1945 worked for the American Red Cross and occupation forces in Vienna.

Haas joined Magnum Photos in 1949 (until 1962), and was president of ASMP in 1960. He received the Kultur Preis from the German government in 1978 and the Newhouse Award from Syracuse University in 1958.

Haas works primarily in color, small format, but prefers audiovisual shows. "I love music," he says, "and with my audiovisual presentation I can combine music and photography—this is what I like to do best."

PUBLICATIONS Monographs: *In Germany*, 1977; *In America*, 1975; *The Creation*, 1971. Book: *Concerned Photographer*, Cornell Capa, ed., 1972. Anthologies: *The Magic Image*, Cecil Beaton & Gail Buckland, 1975; *Great Photographers*, Fritz Gruber, 1960 (Deutsch Buch-Gemeinshaft). Periodicals: *Camera*, Dec 1975, Oct 1970; *Creative Camera*, Feb 1973, Mar 1969, Sept 1967.

COLLECTIONS MOMA, NYC; Kodak Mus., Rochester, N.Y. Ctr. of Photography, Bath, England; Mus. of 20th Cent., Vienna.

ADDRESS 853 Seventh Ave, New York, NY 10019.

Jim Haberman *PHOTOGRAPHER · TEACHER* Born March 16, 1949, in Madison, Wisconsin, Haberman earned his BA in English from the University of Wisconsin, Madison (1971), and his MFA in Photographic Design from Goddard College, Plainfield, Vermont (1974). He considers Ralph Gibson, Emmet Gowin and Minor White as major influences.

Since 1976 Haberman has been a photography instructor at New England School of Art and Design in Boston. In 1978–79 he also served as artist-in-residence at Freedom House, Boston. He has given guest lectures and workshops at Boston's Museum of Fine Arts, the Rhode Island School of Design and the Maine Photo Workshops (among others) since 1976. From 1975 to 1977 he taught photography at Cambridge Center for Adult Education, De Cordova Museum School and Insight Workshops. He was a darkroom assistant for Minor White from 1974 to 1975.

Haberman has been a member of the Visual Studies Workshop in Rochester, New York, and the Photographic Resource Center in Boston since 1978 and a member of the Polaroid Foundation's Portfolio Program since 1972. He won a Photographer's Fellowship from the Massachusetts Council on the Arts and Humanities in 1979.

The photographer has completed two long-term projects: a group of pinhole photographic portraits (1974–76) and a series of hand-colored nude self-portraits (1976–79). As of this writing he was photographing mannequins and cast human body parts placed in unusual environments for a project entitled "Silver Fantasies."

PUBLICATIONS Books: *Popular Photography How-to Guide*, Jim Hughes, ed., 1978; *The Zone System Manual*, Minor White, Richard Zakia & Peter Lorenz, 1976. Periodicals: *35mm Photography*, summer 1979; *Modern Photography*, July 1979; *Darkhorse Magazine*, Nov, Aug 1977. COLLECTIONS Polaroid Cllctn., Cambridge, Mass.; Wodehouse Cllctn., Boston. Bibliothèque Nationale, Paris. REPRESENTATIVE Tony Decaneas, Panopticon, Inc., 187 Bay State Rd, Boston, MA 02215. ADDRESS 15 Cleveland St, Arlington, MA 02174.

Conrad Oswald Hafenrichter *PHOTOGRAPHER · TEACHER* Born December 31, 1948, in London, England, Hafenrichter received a diploma in art and design in 1972, and a BA in 1980.

He has been a lecturer in photography at Wimbledon School of Art since 1975. He was also a lecturer in photography at the Watford School of Art in 1975, and has been a freelance photographer since 1972.

From the Arts Council of Great Britain, he received a grant to document and exhibit photographs on "The Structured Theater," in 1976, and an award in 1975.

The artist says of his work: "I have tried to reflect through photography the paradoxical world in which we live, where the isolated irony becomes almost surrealistic and the mild absurdities a common feature of life."

PUBLICATIONS Periodicals: *British Journal of Photography*, June 1979, Dec 1978, Nov 1975; *Amateur Photographer*, June 1978, Sept 1975, July 1973; *Le Nouveau Photocinéma*, Mar 1977; *Creative Camera*, Nov 1975; *Photo Technique*, Nov 1975; *Photography*, Feb 1974. COLLECTIONS In London: Arts Council of Great Britain; Dept. of the Environment; Morton Morris & Co. Fine Art; Photographers Gall.; Victoria & Albert Mus. ADDRESS 37 Hartington Rd, Chiswick, London W4 3TL, England.

Otto Hagel *PHOTOGRAPHER* Born on March 12, 1909, in Fellbach, Germany, Hagel died in San Francisco, California, on January 18, 1973. Beethoven, Jack London and Steichen had a great influence on his development.

He worked as a freelance photographer and from 1936 to 1972 was employed by Time, Inc.

A member of ASMP, Hagel participated in the 1955 "The Family of Man" exhibit. He also has two films to his credit—one on Pond Farm potter Marguerite Wildenhain (1960), and the other, entitled *Century of Progress* (1934), dealing with the early labor struggles during the Depression.

Specializing in photojournalism and portraiture, the artist, exploring the "human condition," focused mainly on people in the news, in science and industry, in music and in politics and labor.

PUBLICATIONS Book: *Pottery Form and Expression*, 1962. Pamphlets: *Men and Machines*, 1963 (Pacific Maritime Assoc.: San Francisco); *Men and Ships Pictorial*, 1936 (Maritime Federation: San Francisco). COLLECTION West Coast Waterfront Maritime Bldg., San Francisco. ARCHIVE Mrs. Otto Hagel (Hansel Mieth), 2660 Porter Creek Rd, Santa Rosa, CA 95404.

Johan Hagemeyer *PHOTOGRAPHER · HORTICULTURIST* Born June 1, 1884, in Amsterdam, The Netherlands, Hagemeyer died in 1962 in

Berkeley, California. He studied horticulture, and was apprenticed in Berkeley to McCullagh, a commercial portrait photographer.

Hagemeyer worked as an insurance broker in The Netherlands until 1911, when he came to California, took up photography, and worked as a horticulturist until 1917. Having met Steichen on a trip to New York, he became serious about photography and began to work as an assistant to Edward Weston before establishing his own San Francisco studio. He later moved to Carmel, where he also ran a small gallery, and then to Berkeley.

PUBLICATIONS Anthology: *Photography Rediscovered*, David Travis & Ann Kennedy, 1979. Taped interview: *Johan Hagemeyer, Photographer*, Corinne L. Gilb, 1956 (Univ. of Calif., Regional Oral History, Bancroft Lib.: Berkeley).

COLLECTION Art Inst. of Chicago.

Betty Hahn PHOTOGRAPHER · TEACHER Born October 11, 1940, in Chicago, Illinois, Hahn attended Indiana University in Bloomington where she received a BA in Studio Art in 1963 and an MFA in Photography in 1966. She studied there with Henry Holmes Smith.

Hahn has been employed as an associate professor of art at the University of New Mexico in Albuquerque since 1976. Prior to that she was an assistant professor of photography at Rochester Institute of Technology (1969–76).

A member of SPE and CAA, Hahn was a recipient of an NEA Photographer's Fellowship in 1978, a University of New Mexico Research Allocations grant in 1977, a CAPS grant in 1976 and an NEA Visiting Artist grant in 1974 at Franconia College in New Hampshire.

Robert A. Sobiezek says of her work: "The photographic work of Betty Hahn is a contemporary reapplication of a good many of these fin-de-siècle predilections for the decorative image-making. Hers is very much, although quite unconsciously, an amalgamation of popular folk tradition and the elitist aestheticism of the pictorialists."

PUBLICATIONS Book: *Photography*, Phil Davis, 1972. Anthologies: *The Photograph Collector's Guide*, Lee D. Witkin & Barbara London, 1979; *Darkroom*, Eleanor Lewis, ed., 1977; *Innovative Printmaking*, Thelma R. Newman, 1977; *Women of Photography*, 1975; *The Print*, Time-Life Series, 1970; *Vision and Expression*, Nathan Lyons, ed., 1969; *Photography in the Twentieth Century*, Nathan Lyons, ed., 1967. Catalogs: *Photographs*, 1977 (Sheldon Art Gall., Univ. of Nebr.: Lincoln); *The Great West*, 1977 (Univ. of

Colo.: Boulder); *New Images in Photography*; *Object and Illusion*, 1974 (Lowe Art Mus.: Miami, Fla.); *Photography Into Art*, 1972 (Camden Arts Centre: London). Periodical: *Czechoslovakia Photographie*, vol. 2, 1973.

COLLECTIONS Akron Art Inst., Ohio; Art Inst. of Chicago; Ctr. for Photographic Studies, Louisville, Ky.; Chase Manhattan Bank, N.Y.; Colgate Univ., Hamilton, N.Y.; E. B. Crocker Mus., Sacramento, Calif.; Exchange Natl. Bank, Chicago; IMP/GEH, Rochester, N.Y.; Ind. Univ. Fine Arts Mus., Bloomington; Lincoln Rochester Bank Cllctn., Rochester, N.Y.; MOMA, NYC; Norton Simon Mus. of Art, Pasadena, Calif.; San Francisco Mus. of Modern Art, Calif.; San Jose State Coll., San Jose, Calif.; Smithsonian Inst., Wash., D.C.; UCLA; Univ. of Kans. Art Mus., Lawrence; Univ. of Nebr., Sheldon Art Gall., Lincoln; Univ. of N. Mex. Art Mus., Albuquerque; Vassar Coll. Art Gall., Poughkeepsie, N.Y.; Virginia Mus., Richmond, Va.; VSW, Rochester. Bibliothèque Nationale, Paris; Natl. Gall. of Canada, Ottawa; Ryerson Polytechnic Inst., Toronto, Canada.

DEALER Witkin Gall., 41 E 57 St, New York, NY 10019.

ADDRESS Art Dept, Univ. of N. Mex., Albuquerque, NM 87131.

James Hajicek PHOTOGRAPHER · TEACHER Born April 21, 1947, in St. Paul, Minnesota, Hajicek earned a BFA in 1970 from Kansas City Art Institute and School of Design, Missouri, and an MFA in 1978 from the University of New Mexico, Albuquerque.

Currently an assistant professor of art (since 1979) at Arizona State University, Tempe, he has taught there since 1976 and been managing editor of the school's *Northlight* magazine since 1976.

A recent recipient of a faculty grant-in-aid to research the woodburytype printing process in England, Hajicek won an NEA Photographer's Fellowship in 1979, an NEA Photographic Survey grant in 1979, an Arizona Commission on the Arts and Humanities organizational grant for Northlight Gallery in 1978 and a Ford Foundation Fellowship at the University of New Mexico in 1976.

From large-format contact prints (12 x 16 and 16 x 20), the photographer produces cyanotype landscapes.

PUBLICATIONS Anthology: *History of Photography in New Mexico*, Van Deren Coke, ed., 1979. Periodical: *Art Space*, spring 1978.

COLLECTIONS Apeiron Workshop, Millerton, N.Y.; Calif. State Univ., Long Beach; CCP, Tucson; Houston Mus. of Fine Arts, Tex.; IMP/GEH,

Rochester; New Orleans Mus. of Art, La.; Oakland Mus., Calif.; San Francisco Mus. of Modern Art; Security Pacific Bank, Los Angeles; Univ. of Calif., Riverside; Univ. of Colo., Boulder; Univ. of N. Mex., Albuquerque; Zesti Trust Internatl., Boston. Bibliothèque Nationale, Paris; Eikoh Hosoe Workshop, Tokyo.

DEALER Susan Spiritus Gall., 3336 Via Lido, Newport Beach, CA 92663.

ADDRESS 766 N Robson, Mesa, AZ 85201.

Miroslav Hák PHOTOGRAPHER Born in 1911 in Nová Paka, Czechoslovakia, Hák died in 1977 in Prague. He learned photography as an apprentice in his father's portrait studio in Nová Paka.

In 1928 Hák was employed as photographer in the portrait studio Langhans in Prague and in 1931 at Horn studio in Bratislava. He established his own studio in Prague in 1939, and from 1954 worked as a photographer in the Institute for Theory and History of Art in Prague.

According to Petr Tausk, Hák was "a keen experimenter who . . . explored various approaches in photography," using the camera in the traditional sense as well as doing experiments in the darkroom.

PUBLICATIONS Monograph: *Miroslav Hák*, intro. by Jiří Kolář, 1959 (SNKLHU: Prague). Book: *Očima (Through the Eyes)*, intro. by L. Linhart, 1947 (Filmové nakladatelství: Prague).

COLLECTION Mus. of Decorative Arts, Prague, Czechoslovakia.

Ernst Halberstadt PHOTOGRAPHER · PAINTER · SCULPTOR · TEACHER Born August 26, 1910, in Büdingen, Germany, Halberstadt is a self-taught photographer who served as assistant to painters Ezra Winter in 1932 and Diego Rivera in 1933.

Currently self-employed, Halberstadt taught drawing and painting at Massachusetts Maritime Academy in Buzzards Bay in 1974 and was visiting instructor in photography at Penland School of Crafts of North Carolina in 1973.

Halberstadt received the Art Directors Club of Boston Medal in 1956 and a fellowship in painting from New England Area Pepsi-Cola Competition in 1946.

PUBLICATIONS Books: *Rites of Spring*, 1973; *Shore Road to Ogunquit*, illus., 1969.

COLLECTIONS Addison Gall. of Amer. Art, Andover, Mass.; Brandeis Univ., Rose Art Mus., Waltham, Mass.; Brockton, Mass. Art Mus.; Chase Manhattan Bank Cllctn., NYC; Cleveland Mus. of Art, Ohio; DeCordova Mus., Lincoln, Mass.; Harvard Univ., Fogg Mus. of Art, Cambridge, Mass.; Metro. Mus. of Art, NYC; MOMA,

NYC; Mus. of Springdale Art Assoc., Utah; New Britain Mus., Conn.; Univ. of Ga. Mus., Athens.

DEALERS Steven Rose, 23 Minor St, Boston, MA; Daniel Wolf, 30 W 57 St, New York, NY 10019.

ADDRESS Sunset Island, Onset, MA 02558.

Marcus Halevi PHOTOGRAPHER Born January 17, 1942, in Croton-on-Hudson, New York, Halevi earned a BA in Architecture and Design in 1965 from the University of Michigan, Ann Arbor. His major influences were Eric Hegg's turn-of-the-century documentation of the Alaskan gold rush and the work of Darius Kinsey.

A freelance photographer since 1972, he was previously an architect (1968–72).

In 1978 Halevi won first prize from Boston Photo Arts.

Working in black-and-white in various formats, he calls his photographs a "continuing documentation of Alaska's people and its changing landscape."

PUBLICATIONS Book: *Alaska Crude: Visions of the Last Frontier*, Kenneth Andrasko, 1977. Periodical: *Popular Photography Annual*, 1978.

COLLECTION Anchorage Hist. & Fine Arts Mus., Alaska.

DEALER Betsy Van Buren Gall., 290 Concord Ave, Cambridge, MA 02138.

ADDRESS Box 803, Manchester, VT 05255.

Gary Lee Hallman PHOTOGRAPHER · TEACHER Born August 7, 1940, in St. Paul, Minnesota, Hallman received a BA (1966) and an MFA from the University of Minnesota, Minneapolis, where he studied under Jerome Liebling.

Hallman has taught photography at the University of Minnesota since 1970, first as an assistant professor (until 1976) and then as associate professor. He was a visiting adjunct professor of photography at Rhode Island School of Design in Providence in 1977 and a visiting artist at Southampton College of Long Island University in New York in 1972–73.

Hallman belongs to SPE. He was the recipient of a Bush Foundation Fellowship for Artists in 1976 and an NEA Photographer's Fellowship in 1975.

PUBLICATIONS Book: *Light and Lens*, Danald L. Werner, ed., text by Werner & Dennis Longwell, 1973. Anthologies: *The Photograph Collector's Guide*, Lee D. Witkin & Barbara London, 1979; *Mirrors and Windows*, John Szarkowski, ed., 1978. Catalogs: *The Less than Sharp Show*, 1977 (Columbia Coll. Photographic Gall.: Chicago); *Photography Unlimited*, 1974 (Harvard

Univ., Fogg Art Mus.: Cambridge, Mass.); *Photographers' Midwest Invitational*, 1973 (Walker Art Ctr.: Minneapolis); *60's Continuum*, Van Deren Coke, 1972 (GEH: Rochester); *Young Photographers*, Van Deren Coke, 1968 (Univ. of N. Mex.: Albuquerque). Periodical: *Image 17*, Sept 1974.

COLLECTIONS IMP/GEH, Rochester; MOMA, NYC; Univ. of N. Mex., Albuquerque.

DEALER Light Gall., 724 Fifth Ave, New York, NY 10019.

ADDRESS 2932 Pierce St NE, Minneapolis, MN 55418.

Philippe Halsman PHOTOGRAPHER Born in 1901 in Riga, Latvia, Halsman died in 1979 in New York City. He majored in electrical engineering at the Technische Hochschule in Dresden, Germany, from ca. 1924 to 1927. He started his career as a freelance photographer in Paris, where he lived from 1930 to 1940. He then moved to New York City, where he worked for the Black Star Agency until the end of his life. He also taught at the New School for Social Research in New York after 1971.

He was the first president of ASMP in 1945 and served as their president again in 1954. Around 1941 he received the Art Directors Club of New York Award and in 1975 a Life Achievement Award from ASMP.

Halsman has to his credit more than one hundred covers for *Life* magazine. He is also the designer of the Fairchild-Halsman camera, a 4 x 5 twin-lens reflex camera, which was never marketed but was copied by others.

Noted for his honest realism in portraiture, the photographer posed famous people in settings natural to their profession. Frequently he requested they jump first in order to relax. Just as frequently he captured those jumps with his camera. "His sharpness of image, careful delineation of tonal values, mastery of lighting and the revelation of both principal and contrasting textures made his technical standards legendary," stated *The New York Times* in his obituary. Halsman was very innovative in flash and studio techniques and managed always to arrive at animated portrayals of his subjects.

PUBLICATIONS *Sight and Insight*, 1972; *Halsman on the Creation of Photographic Ideas*, 1961; *Jump Book*, 1959; *Dali's Mustache: A Photographic Interview with Salvador Dali*, 1954; *Piccoli*, 1953; *The Candidate*, 1952; *The Frenchman: A Photographic Interview with Fernandel*, 1949. Anthologies: *The Photograph Collector's Guide*, Lee D. Witkin & Barbara London, 1979;

The Magic Image, Cecil Beaton & Gail Buckland, 1975; *Great Photographers*, 1971; *The Great Themes*, 1970. Periodical: "Philippe Halsman," Ruth Spencer, *The British Journal of Photography*, Oct 10 1975.

COLLECTIONS Life Picture Cllctn, NYC; Metro. Mus. of Art, NYC; MOMA, NYC; New Orleans Art Mus., La.; Smithsonian Inst., Wash., D.C. RPS, London.

Dirck Halstead PHOTOJOURNALIST Born December 24, 1936, in Huntington, New York, Halstead was educated at Haverford College in Pennsylvania.

Currently president of Dirck Halstead, Inc., he is a contract photographer for *Time* magazine. Halstead has covered major news events of the world for the past twenty years, and worked as the White House photographer for *Time* (1972–77). He previously worked as a staff photagapher out of the Dallas, Philadelphia and Washington bureaus of UPI from 1956 to 1971, and was appointed UPI's first roving staff photographer, working out of New York in 1967. From 1965 to 1967 he set up the UPI Photo Bureau in Saigon, where he doubled as picture bureau chief and combat photographer. He worked as the Newspicture bureau manager of the Philadelphia bureau (1963–65). Employed as a special roving photographer for the Department of the Army in Washington, D.C. (1960–62), he also worked as a Washington photographer for Black Star (1960–63). He started with coverage of the Guatemalan Revolution in 1954 for *Life* when he was seventeen years old.

Halstead is a member of Shooters III, Liaison-Gamma, ASMP, White House News Photographers Association, New York Press Photographers Association, NPPA, National Press Club and the Overseas Press Club. He has been the recipient of awards from NPPA's Pictures of the Year Competition in 1978 and 1973, each year from 1974 to 1978 from the New York Press Photographers Association, from the American Newspaper Guild (Front Page Award) in 1977, 1976 and 1975, and from the White House News Photographers Association in 1977 and 1976. Halstead has twenty-nine *Time* magazine cover photographs to his credit.

The photographer concentrates on photojournalism, corporate communication, annual reports and advertising.

REPRESENTATIVE FSM Inc., 1 Rockefeller Ctr., New York, NY 10020.

ADDRESS Rm 2850, Time-Life Bldg, New York, NY 10020.

Siegfried Halus PHOTOGRAPHER Born April 8, 1943, in Salzburg, Austria, Halus studied at the Pennsylvania Academy of Fine Arts from 1962 to 1966, then earned a BFA from the University of Pennsylvania in 1966. He studied with Wolfgang Behl at the Hartford Art School, West Hartford, Connecticut, where he received an MFA in 1968.

As of this writing he was teaching at Tufts University, Medford, Massachusetts. Halus taught at the University of Connecticut School of Fine Arts, Storrs, from 1974 to 1979 and at the University of Hartford Art School from 1966 to 1969.

He has been a member of SPE since 1970, Asylum Hill Artists Co-op in Hartford since 1974, Friends of Photography since 1975, the board of directors of the Greater Hartford Arts Council since 1978 and the Photographic Resource Center in Boston. Halus was awarded Individual Artist fellowships from the Connecticut Commission on the Arts in 1974 and 1979.

Before committing himself to photography in 1968, he had made sculpture his primary artistic activity. Halus' early photographic work was in small and medium formats, but he now works exclusively with a 4 x 5 view camera and has experimented with the use of the flashlight and lengthy exposures at night.

PUBLICATIONS Anthologies: *Time-Life Annual*, 1975; *Celebrations*, 1974; *Octave of Prayer*, 1972. Catalog: *Perspective 1964–77*, 1977 (New Britain Mus. of Amer. Art: Conn.). Periodicals: *Popular Photography Annual*, 1977; *Aperture*, no. 82. 1980.

COLLECTIONS Metro. Mus. of Art, NYC; MIT, Hayden Gall., Cambridge, Mass.; New Britain Mus. of Amer. Art, Conn.; N. Mex. Mus., Santa Fe; Philadelphia Mus. of Art, Penn.; Portland Mus. of Art, Maine.

ADDRESS POB 158, Andover, CT 06232.

Andre Haluska PHOTOGRAPHER Born May 4, 1947, in Trenton, New Jersey, Haluska obtained his BFA in Graphic Design from Tyler School of Art of Temple University, Elkins Park, Pennsylvania, and his MFA in Photography from the Visual Studies Workshop of the State University of New York, Rochester. He has studied with William G. Larson, Nathan Lyons and Syl Labrot.

Since 1978 he has been visiting lecturer at the University of Delaware, Newark. From 1974 to 1978 he was assistant professor of photography at the University of South Dakota, Vermillion, and from 1973 to 1974 was instructor of photography at Ocean County College, Toms River, New Jersey. He was an instructor at the Ashbourne School for emotionally disturbed children in Elkins Park, Pennsylvania, at various times from 1969 to 1972.

A member of SPE and Friends of Photography, Haluska won an NEA Photographer's Fellowship in 1979 and a New Jersey State Arts Council Grant in 1974. In 1980 he received a materials grant from Polaroid.

Working in color, Haluska has lately been involved in portraiture with mixed light sources and time exposures. He has also been investigating SX-70 materials through a grant from Polaroid.

PUBLICATIONS Book: *Innovative Printmaking*, 1977. Anthologies: *Self-Portrayal*, J. Alinder, ed., 1979; *The Art of Photography*, 1971. Periodicals: *Popular Photography Annual* 1979; *Quiver*, 1:4, 1979.

COLLECTIONS Colgate Univ., Hamilton, N.Y.; Corcoran Gall. of Art, Wash., D.C.; N.J. State Mus., Trenton; Univ. of S. Dak. Art Gall., Vermillion.

ADDRESS 2325 Pulaski Hwy, Newark, DE 19702.

Hiroshi Hamaya PHOTOGRAPHER Born March 28, 1915, in Tokyo, Hamaya is self-taught in photography.

He took his first photograph in 1931 and has worked freelance since 1937; he has been a contributing photographer for Magnum Photos since 1960. Between 1940 and 1967 he traveled to Manchuria, China, Europe, North America and Mexico.

Hamaya's work is chiefly concerned with the relationship of people to their surroundings. He does documentary work, with an emphasis on folklore, his most recent theme being "Nature of the World."

PUBLICATIONS Books (selected): *Summer Shots Antarctic Peninsula*, 1979, *Mt. Fuji: A Lone Peak*, 1978, *Landscape of Japan—National Park*, 1975, *A Treasury of Japanese Poetry*, 1972, *Landscapes of Japan*, 1964 (Japan); *Det Gomda Japan*, 1960 (Bonniers: Sweden); *The Document of Grief and Anger*, 1960, *Children in Japan*, 1959, *Red China I Saw*, 1958, *Japan's Back Coast*, 1957, *Urumch-Hsinchiang China*, 1957, *Snow Land*, 1956 (Japan). Anthology: *The Magic Image*, Cecil Beaton & Gail Buckland, 1975. Periodical: *Showa Nyonin Shu*, passim, 24 issues, 1977–78.

COLLECTIONS IMP/GEH, Rochester; MOMA, NYC. Bibliothèque Nationale, Paris; Modern Art Mus. of Japan, Tokyo.

ADDRESS 534, Higashikoiso, Oiso-Machi, Kanagawa-Ken, Japan 255.

James Hamilton *PHOTOGRAPHER* Born November 20, 1946, in Baltimore, Maryland, Hamilton studied at Pratt Institute in Brooklyn, New York, from 1964 to 1966.

He has been staff photographer for a number of magazines: *Village Voice* (1976 to present), *Harper's Bazaar* (1971–72), *The Herald* (1971), and *Crawdaddy!* (1969–70). Hamilton has also freelanced for numerous periodicals.

PUBLICATION Book: *Pinball!*, Roger C. Sharpe, 1976.

ADDRESS 70 University Pl, New York, NY 10003.

Hans Hammarskiöld *PHOTOGRAPHER* Born May 17, 1925, in Stockholm, Sweden, Hammarskiöld is primarily self-educated but was apprenticed in 1948 at Studio Uggla in Stockholm to photographer Rofl Wingvist.

He has been a freelance photographer since 1950, with the exception of the year 1955–56, when he served as a staff photographer for London *Vogue*.

A member of the Swedish group Tio since its founding in 1958, Hammarskiöld joined Friends of Photography in 1979. He won the *Svenska Dagbladets* (a Swedish newspaper) Photographic Award in 1951, the gold medal from Palazzo di Brera in Milan in 1951, the Swedish Tourist Association's silver medal in 1965, a Swedish Writers Foundation grant in 1974 and a Swedish government's artist grant in 1978.

Hammarskiöld mainly works with slide shows in Sweden, using between nine and forty carousel projectors. He also does industrial and nature photography, and, earlier in his career, produced picture stories, portraits, architecture shots and images for fashion and advertising.

PUBLICATIONS Monographs: *Hans Hammarskiöld*, w/Rune Jonsson, 1979 (Aktuell Fotolitteratur: Helsingborg, Sweden); *Objektivt sett*, 1955 (Nordisk Rotogravyr: Stockholm). Books: *Laser*, w/Carl Fredrik Reuterswärd, 1969 (Wahlström & Widstrand: Sweden); *Forna dagars Sverige*, vol. 3, w/Gustaf Näsström, 1962; *Lillasyster och jag*, 1960, *Billa och jag*, 1959 (Bonniers: Stockholm); *Stockholmskärlek*, w/Marianne Höök, 1953, *Värmland det sköna*, w/Eva Wennerström, 1951 (Wahlström & Widstrand).

COLLECTIONS L/C, Wash., D.C. Bibliothèque Nationale, Paris; Fotografiska Muséet, Stockholm.

DEALERS Camera Obscura, 5 Kåkbrinken, Stockholm, Sweden; Stephen White Gall., 835 N La Cienega Blvd, Los Angeles, CA 90069.

ADDRESS 7, Östermalmsgatan, 114 24 Stockholm, Sweden.

Wanda Lee Hammerbeck *PHOTOGRAPHER* Born March 24, 1945, in Lincoln, Nebraska, Hammerbeck earned a BA in Psychology from the University of North Carolina, Chapel Hill (1967), and an MFA in Photography from San Francisco Art Institute, California (1976).

Since 1976 she has been a lecturer in photography at Holy Names College in Oakland, California. During 1971–72 she was director of the graduate center at the University of North Carolina, and from 1969 to 1971 she was assistant to that college's dean of women.

Hammerbeck is on the board of directors and is director of the West Coast Visual Arts Archive for Camerawork Gallery in San Francisco and a member of SPE. She won the Juror's Award, first place, for her MFA exhibition at San Francisco Art Institute in 1977 and a Photographer's Fellowship from NEA in 1979.

Working in black-and-white and color, she has "consistently investigated the land and man's relationship to the land." Hammerbeck is concerned with "the way in which the camera records spatial information from the third to the second dimension."

PUBLICATIONS Monograph: *Depositions*, 1978 (NFS/Studebaker Press). Catalogs: *Object, Illusion & Reality*, 1979 (Calif. State Univ.: Fullerton); *Contemporary California Photography*, 1978 (Camerawork, Inc.: San Francisco).

PORTFOLIOS *Text and Context*, (self-published), 1980; *California Views* (group), 1979 (Landweber/Artist: Los Angeles).

COLLECTIONS Atlantic Richfield Cllctn., Los Angeles; CCP, Tucson; Denver Art Mus., Colo.; Harvard Univ., Fogg Mus. of Art, Cambridge, Mass.; Indianapolis Inst. of Art, Ind.; Miami Dade Coll., Miami, Fla.; MOMA, NYC; N. Mex. State Coll., Las Cruces; Oakland Mus., Calif.; R.I. School of Design, Providence; Santa Barbara Mus. of Art, Calif.; Tyler Mus. of Art, Tyler, Tex.; UCLA; Univ. of Calif., Calif. Mus. of Photography, Riverside; Univ. of Okla., Norman. Australian Natl. Gall., Canberra.

ADDRESS POB 5367, Berkeley, CA 94705.

Hella Hammid *PHOTOGRAPHER* Born July 15, 1921, in Germany, Hammid studied at the now defunct Black Mountain College in Asheville, North Carolina, in 1940–41. She names Galka E. Scheyer as her mentor.

She is a freelance photojournalist, her work having appeared in such publications as *Life, Ebony, Town & Country* and *The New York Times*.

She also handled camerawork for several films of Maya Deren: *A Study in Choreography for the Camera* (1945), *Ritual in Transfigured Time* (1945) and *At Land* (1944).

PUBLICATIONS Books: *Teaching My Wings to Fly*, Barlin, 1978; *Sensible Book*, Barbara K. Polland, 1973. Anthology: *Family of Man*, Edward Steichen, ed., 1955.

COLLECTIONS Blue Cross Headquarters, Los Angeles; MOMA, NYC; Security Pacific Bank, Los Angeles.

REPRESENTATIVE Photo Researchers, 60 E 56 St, New York, NY 10022.

ADDRESS 10256 Chrysanthemum Ln, Los Angeles, CA 90024.

Mary Sayer Hammond PHOTOGRAPHER TEACHER Born October 1, 1946, in Bellingham, Washington, Hammond received a BFA in Art Education (1967), Master of Art Education (1969), EdS (1973) and MFA in Photographic Design (1977) from the University of Georgia, Athens. As of this writing she is a PhD candidate in History of Photography at Ohio State University, Columbus.

Hammond has been an assistant professor of art at Valdosta State College, Valdosta, Georgia, since 1979 (and also 1976–77). She was administrative associate to the Department Chairman, Art Education, at Ohio State University in 1977–79 and a photography instructor at the University of Georgia in 1975–76. In 1973–74 she was a photography consultant at the National Italian Television Studios in Rome, and in 1969–71 was art supervisor for Madison County Schools, Georgia.

Since 1975 Hammond has been a member of SPE, RPS and Société Française de Photographie. She won a Fulbright-Hays Research Grant to study in Italy in 1973.

Hammond works in large-format color and black-and-white, using self-sensitized emulsions such as platinum, kallitype, calotype, cyanotype and argentotype. She combines drawings and photo images.

COLLECTIONS Univ. of Ga. Dept. of Art, Athens. Bibliothèque Nationale, Paris; Commissione per Gli Scambi Culturali fra L'Italia e Gli State Uniti, Rome.

ADDRESS 1904½ Williams St, Apt B, Valdosta, GA 31601.

Tim Handfield PHOTOGRAPHER Born March 12, 1952, in Melbourne, Australia, Handfield earned a BS in Physics from Latrobe University, Melbourne, in 1973. The self-taught photographer attended a Ralph Gibson workshop in 1977.

A freelance photographer since 1974, Handfield has operated a color printing laboratory in Melbourne since 1979.

Handfield has explored "the aesthetic possibilities of colour photography" since 1975, concentrating on images of the urban environment.

PUBLICATION Anthology: *Australian Photographers*, 1979 (Australia).

COLLECTIONS In Australia: Cllctn. of the High Court of Australia, Canberra; Horsham Regional Art Gall., Horsham, Victoria; Melbourne State Coll.; Natl. Gall. of Australia, Canberra; Phillip Morris Cllctn.; Swinburne Technical Coll., Melbourne.

DEALER Photographers Gall., 344 Punt Rd, South Yarra 3141, Victoria, Australia.

ADDRESS 7 Orchard St, Armadale 3143, Victoria, Australia.

Forman Hanna PHOTOGRAPHER · PHARMACIST Born 1882 in Anson, Texas, Hanna died in 1950 in Globe, Arizona. He studied pharmacy at the University of Texas in Galveston.

After his first trip to the Hopi Mesas by covered wagon in 1917, he photographed that area as well as the Apache Reservation until about 1940.

Hanna was a member of RPS.

The photographer's style can be described as pictorialist, using soft focus, soft contrast and painterly composition. The subjects he concentrated on were ranching portraits, landscapes, nudes and photographs of Indians in their homes and environment.

PUBLICATION Periodical: "Photography of the Nude," *Camera Craft*, Apr 1935.

COLLECTIONS Ariz. Historical Ctr., Tucson; Ariz. State Mus., Tucson; Brooklyn Mus., N.Y.; Mus. of Northern Ariz., Flagstaff; Smithsonian Inst., Natl. Mus. of History & Technology, Wash., D.C.

ARCHIVE Photographic Collections, Ariz. State Mus., Univ. of Ariz., Tucson, AZ 85721.

Georg E. Hansen PHOTOGRAPHER Born May 12, 1833, in Naestved, Denmark, Hansen died December 21, 1891, in Frederiksberg, Denmark. He was educated in Germany. His father was the daguerreotypist C. C. Hansen.

Hansen was established in Copenhagen in 1854. He was the first photographer in Denmark to prepare gelatine glass plates and to use a solar camera for enlargements. He exhibited his photographic works in Malmö (1865), Stockholm (1866), Paris (1867) and Copenhagen (1872).

A member of the Association of Photographers in 1865, Hansen was photographer to the Royal Danish, Russian, English and Greek courts. He was the recipient of exhibition medals in Berlin (1865) and London (1862).

In 1865 the first Danish magazine for photographers, *Alfen,* stated that his was "the newest, greatest and most beautiful photographic establishment in Copenhagen."

PUBLICATION   Anthology: *Photographers in and from Denmark,* Bjørn Ochsner, 1956, rev. ed. 1969.

COLLECTION   Royal Lib., Copenhagen, Denmark.

Cristobal Hara   PHOTOGRAPHER   Born in Madrid, Spain, in 1946, Hara studied economics at universities in Hamburg and Munich. Influenced by the work of Henri Cartier-Bresson, he has been a freelance photographer since 1969.

PUBLICATIONS   Periodicals: *Creative Camera,* Aug 1978; *Camera,* June 1976, Sept 1971; "Diary of a Soldier," *Du,* Dec 1972.

PORTFOLIOS   *English Clochards,* 1979; *English Pedigree,* 1976.

ADDRESS   Bailen, Madrid, Spain.

Charles Harbutt   PHOTOGRAPHER   Born July 29, 1935, in Camden, New Jersey, Harbutt received a BS degree in Journalism from Marquette University in Milwaukee, Wisconsin, in 1956.

Harbutt has been affiliated with Magnum Photos, Inc., since 1963. He has been a guest artist at MIT Creative Photography Lab (1978–79), Rhode Island School of Design (1976) and the Art Institute of Chicago (1975). In 1970 he was a faculty member of Cooper Union and Pratt Institute School of Visual Arts, both in New York City. Prior to that he was a consultant for the NYC Planning Commission (1968–70), a freelance magazine photographer (1959–63) and an associate editor of *Jubilee Magazine* (1956–59).

A member of the board of governors of ASMP in 1970–71, he also served as vice-president in the same year. He was awarded the Arles Prize for the best photographic book in 1974, *Travelog,* and in 1972 was the recipient of a CAPS grant. *America,* an eight-minute animated film, directed with Phil Gittelman, won a gold special award at the Atlanta International Film Festival in 1970.

Known for his uniquely composed black-and-white images, often using unusual perspectives to convey the desired emotion of loneliness, desolation, fear, etc., he has also covered elections, wars and the peace movement, among other subjects. He works in 35mm.

PUBLICATIONS   Monograph: *Travelog,* 1973. Book: *America in Crisis,* w/Lee Jones, ed., 1969. Anthology: *The Photograph Collector's Guide,* Lee D. Witkin & Barbara London, 1979. Periodicals (selected): *Modern Photography,* July 1979, July 1976, Mar 1959; *Creative Camera,* Feb 1978, Sept 1968; *Photo,* Mar 1975; *Zoom,* spring 1974 (Paris); *Camera,* May 1973; *Modern Photography Annual,* 1973; *Popular Photography Annual,* 1968; *Aperture,* 12:3, 1965; *Camera 35,* Mar 1962.

COLLECTIONS   Art Institute, Chicago; Columbus Mus. of Art, Ohio; Exchange Natl. Bank, Chicago; IMP/GEH, Rochester; Kalamazoo Inst. of Arts, Mich.; Marquette Univ., Milwaukee, Wisc.; Metro. Mus. of Art, NYC; MOMA, NYC; New Orleans Mus. of Art, La.; Plains Art Mus., Fargo, N. Dak.; Princeton Univ., Art Mus., N.J.; Rhode Island School of Design, Providence; San Francisco Mus. of Modern Art, Calif.; Smithsonian Inst., Wash., D.C.; Univ. of Iowa Mus. of Art, Iowa City; Univ. of Nebr., Sheldon Memorial Art Gall., Lincoln. British Arts Council, London; Moderna Muséet, Stockholm, Sweden; Stedlijk Mus., Amsterdam, The Netherlands. In France: Bibliothèque Nationale, Paris; Musée Réattu, Arles.

REPRESENTATIVE   Magnum Photos, Inc., 15 W 46 St, New York, NY 10036.

Goodwin Warner Harding   PHOTOGRAPHER   Born February 20, 1947, in Boston, Massachusetts, Harding earned a BA at Harvard College, Cambridge, Massachusetts, in 1969 and took advanced studies at MIT, Cambridge, with Minor White in 1968–70.

A freelance photographer since 1974, Harding was commissioned to take photographs for the NEA-sponsored project "Seven Photographers: The Delaware Valley" in 1976.

He works in large-format black-and-white.

PUBLICATIONS   Anthologies: *Octave of Prayer,* Minor White, ed., 1972; *Being Without Clothes,* Minor White, ed., 1970. Catalog: *Seven Photographers: The Delaware Valley,* W. Holmes, ed., 1979.

DEALERS   Equivalents Gall., 1822 Broadway, Seattle, WA 98122; Marcuse Pfeifer Gall., 825 Madison Ave, New York, NY 10021.

ADDRESS   45055 Highway 101 S, Neskowin, OR 97149.

Lewis Harding   *PHOTOGRAPHER · TEACHER*
Born in 1806 in Cornwall, England, Harding died in 1893. He was a descendant of the Trelawny line, an old and famous Cornish family.

Harding taught at a Roman Catholic Seminary in Sydney, Australia, for eleven years, including a term at the notorious penal settlement on Norfolk Island. He returned from Australia in 1847 suffering from a nervous breakdown. Under the care of a well known ichthyologist and natural historian, Dr. Jonathan Couch, Harding may have taken up photography as extended therapy and to illustrate a work Couch was involved with during the early 1850s, *The History of Polperro.*

"Harding's photographs span the wet-plate period and are a mixture of portrait and genre," writes historian/photographer Andrew Lanyon. Over 150 of Harding's prints survive, mostly of Polperro fishermen and their families. These "remarkable compositions" show him to be "the first and one of the best Cornish photographers."

PUBLICATION   Book: *The Rooks of Trelawne,* Gordon Fraser, 1976 (Photographers' Gall.: London).

COLLECTION   Royal Inst. of Cornwall, Truro, England.

ARCHIVE   Andrew Lanyon, 18 Farmers' Meadow, Newlyn/Penzance, Cornwall, England.

William James Harding   *PHOTOGRAPHER·CARPENTER*   Born in London in 1826, Harding died in Sydney, Australia, in 1899.

He went to New Zealand in 1855 to work as a cabinetmaker. That enterprise failing, he opened a photographic studio to practice the craft he had learned in London. The studio operated until 1889, at which time Harding left for Sydney.

The photographer created more than 6,000 commissioned *cartes de visite,* as well as studies of urban and rural scenes, often depicting the rigors of colonial life. His portraits have a directness not normally associated with the Victorian period. Using the collodion process, he maintained a traveling darkroom in which he coated and developed his own plates.

COLLECTION   Alexander Turnbull Lib., Wellington, New Zealand.

E. (Edward Fitzmaurice) Chambré Hardman
PHOTOGRAPHER   Born November 25, 1898, in Foxrock, County Dublin, Ireland, Hardman studied at St. Columba's College in Rathfarnham, County Dublin, and in 1917 entered Royal Military College in Sandhurst, England. He began photographing at age twelve.

Hardman was commissioned as an officer in the 8th Gurkha Rifles of the Indian Army, for which he served until 1923. In that year he and Kenneth Burrell started their own portrait studio, Burrell & Hardman Ltd, in Liverpool, England. Hardman opened a branch studio in Chester, England, in 1938, and carried on as managing director of the firm for over fifty years.

The photographer became a Fellow of RPS in 1925 and of the Institute of Incorporated Photographers in London in the early 1930s. Around that time he also joined the London Salon of Photography, and around 1930 he won first prize in the world competition organized by *American Photography.*

Hardman's main subject matter has been "illustrative and pictorial portraits and landscapes." Peter Hagerty writes of Hardman's work: "Chambré Hardman's photographs have become increasingly more concerned with the stark and barren landscape of the far north of Scotland. No less evocative than his earlier work, they have a natural beauty reminiscent of the remote and spectacularly sited lake of his childhood" (*Open Eye,* Nov/Dec 1980).

PUBLICATIONS   "Landscape: Another Personal View," Aug 1966, article, Oct 1955, *Photographic Journal* (RPS: London).

ARCHIVE   Liverpool City Lib., William Brown St, Liverpool, England.

ADDRESS   59 Rodney St, Liverpool 1, England.

Rex Hardy   *RESEARCH SCIENTIST · WRITER · PHOTOGRAPHER · AVIATOR*   Born August 9, 1915, in Los Angeles, California, Hardy studied history at Stanford University in 1937 and attended the U.S. Naval Flying School, Officer Training, in Pensacola, Florida, in 1941.

Since 1978 he has been principal research scientist for NASA Aviation Safety Reporting System. From 1946 to 1977 he was director of flight operations and chief pilot for Northrop Aircraft Co., Lockheed Missiles & Space Co., as well as an aviation consultant. Hardy was a combat pilot, squadron officer and commander in the U.S. Navy (1941–46). Before the war he was a freelance photographer for *Life, Time, Fortune* and *Colliers* (1939–41), and a *Life* staff photographer (1936–39).

Hardy belongs to the Aviation/Space Writers Association and is a past member of the American Society of Photogrammetry and the Institute of Aeronautical Sciences. He won a Distinguished Flying Cross, an Air Medal with Gold Star and other decorations for aerial photo reconnaissance missions in combat in the South Pacific during World War II.

The photographer was one of the original group of eight staff photographers for *Life*'s first issue. With the outbreak of World War II he became an officer and pilot in the navy's first photo reconnaissance squadron, and served for a time in Edward Steichen's Navy Photographic Unit.

PUBLICATIONS Anthology: *Life—The First Decade*, 1979. Periodical: *U.S. Camera Annual*, 1941.

ADDRESS 66 Mt Hamilton Ave, Los Altos, CA 94022.

Guillermo Hare *PHOTOGRAPHER · TEACHER* Born in Lima, Peru, on May 2, 1946, Hare studied art in 1964–65 but is a self-taught photographer. He worked with Minor White in Peru in 1973–74 and was also influenced by Aaron Siskind. He attended the Rhode Island School of Design MFA program in 1977–78.

Hare currently teaches photography at the Universidad de Lima and has also taught at the Universidad Católica, Lima, since 1975. He has been active as a freelance commercial photographer since 1971.

Hare is a founding member of Secuencia Fotogaleria. He received a Fulbright Grant in 1977 to study at the Rhode Island School of Design.

The photographer shoots images of man-made landscapes, urban and rural, using large-format film with extreme wide-angle lenses.

ADDRESS Francisco del Castillo 556, Lima 18, Peru.

James H. Hare *PHOTOJOURNALIST* Born October 3, 1856, in London, Hare died June 24, 1946, in Teaneck, New Jersey. The son of a camera maker, he was self-taught in the photographic arts.

After arriving in the United States in 1889, Hare became a news photographer. At that time, in order to reproduce a photograph for publication, the artist had first to make a line drawing of it. He later was photographer and editor of *The Illustrated American,* and in 1898 became a war correspondent for newspaper publisher Robert J. Collier. Hare covered five wars between that year and 1918, and continued photography until his retirement in 1931.

He had been an honorary president of the Overseas Press Club, and was awarded a medal and citation from the Emperor of Japan in 1907.

The photojournalist was credited with many firsts: the first air view of Manhattan from a balloon (1906), the first picture from an airplane (1911), the first photograph of a plane in flight during the early experiments of the Wright Brothers and the first serial shots of a football game. He is also said to have invented the snapshot when, unable to keep a swaying hot air balloon in focus, he lifted both camera and tripod and, pointing in the direction of the ascending balloon, snapped the shutter.

PUBLICATIONS Monograph: *Photojournalist: The Career of Jimmy Hare*, Lewis L. Gould & Richard Greffe, 1977; *Jimmy Hare, News Photographer*, Cecil Carnes, 1940. Book: *A Photographic Record of the Russo-Japanese War*, ed. only, notes by Capt. A. T. Mahan, 1905.

Margaret F. Harker *PHOTOHISTORIAN · TEACHER · AUTHOR · PHOTOGRAPHER* Born January 17, 1920, in Southport, Lancashire, England, Harker studied history of art and design at Southport School of Art (1938–39) and photography at the Polytechnic (Regent Street), London (1939–42).

Harker recently retired as professor and assistant director of the Polytechnic of Central London (formerly the Regent Street Polytechnic), where she also had served as dean of the School of Communication (1974–75) and head of the School of Photography (1959–74). She was a self-employed architectural photographer as well as a lecturer at the Polytechnic from 1943 to 1959.

Harker is a member of the council of the Royal Society of Arts and was also on the council of RPS (1951–76, president 1958–60) and of the Institute of Incorporated Photographers (1957–72, president 1964–65). She has been an honorary corresponding member of DGPh since 1960, an Honorary Fellow of the British Kinematograph, Sound and Television Society since 1969, and vice-president of the European Society for the History of Photography since 1977.

A winner of the Hood Medal of RPS for architectural photography in 1945 and 1948, Harker also won a Kodak Scholarship in 1968 and the President's Award from the Institute of Incorporated Photographers in 1975.

Despite her retirement, Harker continues to lecture on the history of photography and take photographs, with an emphasis on design.

PUBLICATIONS Books: *The Linked Ring: The Secession Movement in Photography, 1892–1910*, 1979 (Heinemanns: England); *Victorian and Edwardian Photography*, Collectors' Guides series, 1975 (Charles Letts: England); *Education and Training in Photography and Cinematography: Focal Encyclopedia of Photography*, 1965 (Focal Press); *Photographing Architecture*, 1951 (Fountain Press). Periodicals: "The Development of Professional Photography in Britain," Mar 26

& Apr 2, 1976, "Photography—Mirror of Society," Aug 30, 1974, "Annan of Glasgow, A Historical Review," Oct 1973, "The Secession Movement in Photography, 1892–1910," Dec 1972, *British Journal of Photography*; "Robert Demachy, 1859–1937," July 1973, "The First Seventy Years of Photography: 1840–1910—A Review," May 1971, "The Society's Collection—A Review of the Archives," Mar 1971, "Sense and Perception—An Historical Review, Jouhar Memorial Lecture 1967," June 1968, "The Place of Education in the Development of Professional Photography," Feb 1963, "Education in Photography," Dec 1962, "The Life and Work of Edward J. Steichen," Jan 1962, "Photography in the Service of Mankind," Jan 1960, *RPS Journal.*

ADDRESS Egdean House, Egdean, nr. Pulborough, West Sussex RH2o 1JU, England.

Thom W. Harney PHOTOGRAPHER Born October 14, 1946, in Chicago, Illinois, Harney received a BA in Business from Michigan State University, Lansing, in 1968. He names Henri Cartier-Bresson as a major influence.

Harney has been a freelance photographer since 1968.

Working strictly with a 35mm camera in black-and-white, Harney "reacts with it when I feel something special taking place."

PUBLICATIONS Periodicals: *Popular Photography Invitation to Photography*, 1974; *Color Annual*, 1974.

COLLECTIONS CCP, Tucson; Chicago Art Institute; Exchange Natl. Bank, Chicago.

ADDRESS 4947 N Leavitt, Chicago, IL 60625.

Steve Harper PHOTOGRAPHER · TEACHER · EDITOR Born August 26, 1944, in Newton, Kansas, Harper earned a Bachelor of Professional Arts degree in Motion Pictures from Brooks Institute of Photography in Santa Barbara, California. His minor field of study was illustrative photography.

Currently the photography editor for the *Wichita Eagle & Beacon*, he taught photojournalism at Wichita State University, Kansas, from 1973 to 1979.

Harper is a member of SPE, NPPA and International Frisbee Association. He won a grant in 1976 from Wichita State University for a project on the Flint Hills.

Working in large format up to 12 x 20, Harper photographs landscapes, primarily in Kansas and New Mexico. He has done extensive Polaroid photography using 4 x 5 as well as Super Shooter and Reporter SE cameras.

PUBLICATION Periodical: *Camera*, Sept 1975.
DEALER The Arts Works, 2906 E Central, Wichita, KS 67202.
ADDRESS 213 SW Fifth St, Newton, KS 67114.

Pamela Harris PHOTOGRAPHER · EDITOR · TEACHER Born June 10, 1940, in Erie, Pennsylvania, Harris received a BA in English Literature in 1962 from Pomona College in Pomona, California. She also studied briefly with Stephen Gersh in 1966 and attended two workshops with Minor White. The work of Dorothea Lange has been a major influence on Harris.

As of this writing she was a lecturer at Ontario College of Art in Toronto. She previously was employed as a lecturer at the University of California, Santa Cruz, in the spring of 1979.

Harris was a recipient of grants from Ontario Arts Council in 1978, 1976 and 1975. She also received bursaries in 1973 and 1971, and a short-term grant in 1969 from the Canada Council.

In 1973 she produced *The Women's Kit*, including photography, writing, taped material and art. She also built a community darkroom in an Arctic community and taught photographic skills to Inuit craftswomen in 1972.

In her work the artist is "interested in photography's possibilities as an activating medium that records and is involved with social movements, community groups, etc." As of 1980 she was photographing the United Farm Workers in Watsonville, California. She works in a 35mm format, producing silver prints.

PUBLICATIONS Monograph: *Another Way of Being*, 1976. Books: *To See Ourselves*, 1975; *Art, A Woman's Sensibility*, 1974. Anthologies: *Women See Woman*, 1976; *The Female Eye*, 1975; *Vision and Expression*, 1969. Periodical: *Arts Canada*, Jan 1973.

COLLECTIONS In Canada: Art Bank, Canada Council, Ottawa, Ontario; Mt. St. Vincent Univ. Gall., Halifax, Nova Scotia; Natl. Film Board Still Division, Ottawa; Ontario Arts Council, Toronto.

ADDRESS 306 Glen Rd, Toronto, Ontario, Canada M4W 2X3.

Alex Harsley PHOTOGRAPHER · TEACHER · GALLERY DIRECTOR Born in 1938 in Rockhill, South Carolina, Harsley studied privately with Lloyd Varden, a scientific adviser to the photographic industry.

Harsley is a founding director of Minority Photographers, Inc., and Fourth Street Photo Gallery (1971) and has administered and organized photographic and public programs at Fourth Street

Photo Gallery since 1975. In 1971 he published the newsletter *Person, Camera & the Image.*

Harsley organized a special collection of photographs taken in China during the period of 1927–31 by G. W. Mecham.

The photographer's own work is of an experimental nature.

PUBLICATIONS Anthology: *Looking Ahead,* 1975. Periodicals (reviews): *Popular Photography,* A. D. Coleman, July 1971; *Village Voice,* A. D. Coleman, July 1971.

DEALER Fourth St Photo Gall., 67 E Fourth St, New York, NY 10003.

ADDRESS 155 Essex St, New York, NY 10002.

William P. Hart *PHOTOGRAPHER* Hart flourished as a photographer in the 1880s in New Zealand; the date and place of his death are unknown.

Based in Queenstown, Hart was in partnership with a Mr. Campbell of Invercargill, at least through the 1880s. He apparently accompanied various explorers on their treks, such as Quinton McKinnon and Donald Sutherland (after whom Hart named Sutherland Falls).

Hart claims to have been the first to photograph Sutherland Falls, on March 9, 1883. Mount Hart was named after the photographer by Donald Sutherland.

Despite the fact that his photographs were mainly used to assist explorers in gathering information, Hart brought an aesthetic tone to his depictions of the New Zealand countryside.

PUBLICATION Anthology: *19th Century New Zealand Photographers,* John B. Turner, 1970.

Donald Scott Harter *PHOTOGRAPHER · GRAPHIC DESIGNER · TEACHER* Born January 10, 1950, in West Bend, Wisconsin, Harter earned a BS, MA and MFA in Art from the University of Wisconsin in Madison, where he studied under Cavallier Ketchum and Phil Hamilton.

Since 1977 he has been assistant professor at Midwestern State University, Wichita Falls, Texas. He previously was a visiting lecturer at the University of Wisconsin, Madison, in 1977, a graphic artist for the city of Madison in 1976–77, a workshop leader at the Arrowmont School of Crafts in 1976 and a visiting artist at Illinois Wesleyan University in Bloomington in 1976. In 1974–75 he taught at Rhode Island College in Providence.

A member of SPE, CAA and American Professional Graphic Artists, Harter won a grant from the Midwestern State University Humanities and Social Science Research Fund in 1979.

Harter describes his black-and-white work as "formalistic," and recently he has been "exploring organic shapes rather than more straight geometric shapes in landscapes."

PUBLICATIONS Periodicals: *Camera,* Aug 1975, Aug 1974.

COLLECTIONS Arkansas Art Ctr., Little Rock; Art Inst. of Chicago; CCP, Tucson; Minneapolis Inst. of Arts, Minn.; VSW, Rochester.

ADDRESS 4700 Taft Blvd, Apt 267, Wichita Falls, TX 76308.

Ilka Maria Hartmann *PHOTOGRAPHER* Born January 23, 1942, in Hamburg, Germany, Hartmann received an Abitur degree in 1963 from the German Gymnasium. She studied theology at universities in Berlin and Hamburg (1963–64) and emigrated to the United States in 1964, where she studied photography with Edward E. Schwyn and received a BA in Religion from University of the Pacific, Stockton, California, in 1966. Hartmann earned an MA in German Language and Literature from the University of California, Berkeley, in 1969. She names W. Eugene Smith, Dorothea Lange, Lewis Hine and Henri Cartier-Bresson as influences on her photography.

As of this writing Hartmann was a photography instructor at New College of San Francisco. She held the same position at Faultline Institute, Bolinas, California, in 1975–78, and was a teaching assistant in German at the University of California, Berkeley, in 1968–69.

Hartmann co-founded Jeroboam, a San Francisco photographers' cooperative, in 1972. She received a Woodrow Wilson Foundation fellowship in 1968 to study German language and literature.

A photojournalist, Hartmann works in small format, primarily in black-and-white. Since 1971 she has photographed American Indians in the San Francisco Bay Area, the Southwest and the Northwest, and the Huicholes in Mexico. She has also documented the events in a small California town since 1969 and has photographed harbor seals (1978), the Chinese community in Oakland, California (1972), Black Panthers in the San Francisco Bay Area (1967–70) and the San Francisco Bay oil spill of 1971.

PUBLICATIONS Books: *Pearson, A Harbor Seal Pup,* text by Susan Meyers, 1980; *The Town That Fought to Save Itself,* Orville Schell, 1976.

COLLECTION Oakland Mus., Calif.

DEALERS William M. Lyons Gall., 20th Century Photography, 3041 Grand Ave, Coconut Grove, FL 33133; Fotogalerie Trockenpresse, 1000 Berlin 12, Charlottenburg, Schlüterstrasse 70, Fed. Rep. of Germany.

ADDRESS POB 182, Bolinas, CA 94924.

(Carl) Sadakichi Hartmann *ART CRITIC · WRITER · POET · PAINTER* Born November 8, 1867, in Nagasaki, Japan, Hartmann (aka Sidney H. Allen) died November 22, 1944, in St. Petersburg, Florida. He was influenced by French Symbolism, the work of his poet friends Stéphane Mallarmé and Walt Whitman, and by Alfred Steiglitz.

Hartmann served as a secretary and helper to Walt Whitman in 1882 and did freelance writing for Boston and New York newspapers in the 1880s and 1890s. He founded *Art Critic* in 1893 and was a contributing editor to *Camera Work* from 1903 to 1917 (fifty issues).

A poet and fiction writer as well as a critic, Hartmann wrote numerous books. He also was a painter who specialized in pastels, and he toured the country with his lecture "Encouragement of American Art."

Considered one of the first photography critics, Hartmann was an influential figure in the world of visual arts. A leader of Greenwich Village's bohemian colony in his early days, he lived in Hollywood the last quarter century of his life, declaring, "Artists must not become too respectable because their mission is to teach the play phase of life."

PUBLICATIONS Books: *The Valiant Knights of Daguerre . . . by Sadakichi Hartmann*, Harry W. Lawton & George Knox, eds., 1978; *The Life and Times of Sadakichi Hartmann, 1867–1944*, 1970, repr. 1978; *Minutes of the Last Meeting*, bio., Gene Fowler, 1954; *Strands and Ravelings of the Art Fabric*, 1940; *A Note on the Portraits of Walt Whitman*, 1921; *The Last Thirty Days of Christ*, 1920 (pvt. prntg.); *The Elements of Pictorial Composition*, n.d.; *Esthetic Verities*, 1913, rev. 1926; *The Whistler Book: A Monograph of . . . James McNeill Whistler*, 1910, repr. 1924; *Landscape and Figure Composition*, 1910; *Composition in Portraiture*, 1909; *Winter*, photos by Rudolph Eickmeyer, 1903; *Japanese Art*, 1903, repr. 1971; *Modern American Sculpture*, 1902, repr. 1918; *A History of American Art*, 2 vols., 1901, rev. ed. 1938; *Conversations with Walt Whitman*, 1894, repr. 1972. Plays and Poetry: *Buddha, Confucius, Christ: Three Prophetic Plays*, Harry Lawton & George Knox, eds., 1971; *Moses*, 1934; *Tanka and Haiku: 14 Japanese*

Rhythms, 1915; *My Rubaiyat*, 1913; *Drifting Flowers of the Sea*, 1904; *A Tragedy in a New York Flat*, 1896. Periodical: *Sadakichi Hartmann Newsletter*, fall 1969 (Univ. of Calif.: Riverside).

COLLECTIONS Ridgway Lib., Philadelphia, Pa.; Univ. of Calif., Hartmann Archives, Riverside.

ARCHIVE Hartmann Archives, Univ. of Calif., Riverside, CA 92502.

Rune Hassner *PHOTOGRAPHER · WRITER · PHOTOHISTORIAN · TEACHER · TELEVISION PRODUCER* Born August 13, 1928, in Östersund, Sweden, Hassner studied photography with Rolf Winquist at Studio Uggla in Stockholm (1946–49).

Currently a freelance photographer, film maker and writer, Hassner was visiting professor in 1973 at the School of Mass Communications of the University of Minnesota, Minneapolis. He has also lectured in photohistory at the universities of Stockholm, Uppsala, Lund and Gothenburg since 1972.

Hassner belongs to Svenska Fotografernas Förbund (since 1966) and Fotografiska Muséets Vänner (since 1969), serving as the latter's chairman in 1973–75 and as a board member from 1972 to 1975. He has also been chairman of Tio Fotografer (1970, 1975), which he has belonged to since 1958.

The photographer won the Photo Prize of *Svenska Dagbladet* (Stockholm) in 1957, a Swedish government artist grant in 1968, Writer's Funds annual grants since 1975 (Sweden) and Swedish Film Institute prizes for documentary films in 1967 and 1969.

For television he made the eleven-part series *Bilder för miljoner* on photohistory (1969–70, Stockholm), and an English version, *Images for Millions*, produced for the University of Minnesota in 1973. He also made the series *China Towards the Year 2000* and *The Image as a Weapon*, both with Jan Myrdal in 1978. In addition, Hassner has made two feature films for Swedish TV, *Myglaren* in 1966 and *Hjälparen* in 1968.

PUBLICATIONS Books (in Stockholm): *Bilder för miljoner*, 1977 (Rabén & Sjögren); *Jacob Riis —reporter med kamera i New Yorks slum*, 1970 (Norstedts); *Rolf Winquist*, 1970 (Liljevalchs Konsthall); *Vår indiska by*, Sven o Andersson, 1962 (Rabén & Sjögren); *Det nya Kina*, 1957 (Nordisk Rotogravyr). Catalogs (Fotografiska Muséet: Stockholm): *Felix H. Man*, 1975; *Erich Salomon*, 1974; *André Kertész*, 1971.

COLLECTIONS L/C, Wash., D.C. Bibliothèque Nationale, Paris; Fotografiska Muséet, Stockholm; Fotografiska Muséet, Helsinki, Finland; Norsk Fotohistorisk Forening, Oslo, Norway.

REPRESENTATIVE Tiofoto AB, Drottninggatan 88 c, 111 36 Stockholm, Sweden.

ADDRESS Bastugatan 12 b, 117 20 Stockholm, Sweden.

Ralph Marshall Hattersley, Jr. *PHOTOGRA-PHER · WRITER · TEACHER* Born March 31, 1921, in Conrad, Montana, Hattersley studied at the University of Washington (Seattle), Montana State College (Bozeman), Rochester Institute of Technology (New York) and the University of Chicago.

A contributing editor to *Popular Photography* since 1970, he has taught at Maryland Institute College of Art (Baltimore), Smithsonian Institution (Washington, D.C.), School of Visual Arts (New York City) and Pratt Institute (Brooklyn, New York), among other places.

Hattersley has been a member of SPE since 1976.

His main activity is writing and illustrating books and articles for beginners in photography.

PUBLICATIONS Books: *Beginner's Guide to Photographing People*, 1978; *Photographic Lighting*, 1978; *Photographic Printing*, 1977; *Beginner's Guide to Darkroom Techniques*, 1976; *Beginner's Guide to Photography*, 1974.

ADDRESS 542 Collicello St, Harrisonburg, VA 22801.

Raoul Hausmann *PAINTER · SCULPTOR · POET · MIXED-MEDIA PHOTOGRAPHER* Born in Vienna, Austria, in 1886, Hausmann died on February 2, 1971, in Limoges, France.

He was one of the founders of the Dada movement in Berlin in 1918 along with Tzara, Huelsenbeck, Grosz and Janco. He thoroughly chronicled the movement, and was the inventor of phonetic poetry (about 1918), which influenced the concrete poetry style of the 1950s and 1960s.

Hausmann's originality lay in his integration of sound with the visual arts, in much the same way as contemporary music now utilizes visual effects in performance.

PUBLICATIONS Monograph: *Je ne suis pas un photographe*, 1975 (Paris). Book: *Hurra! Hurra! Hurra!*, 1921 (Der Malik: Berlin). Poetry: *Pin*, w/ Kurt Schwitters, n.d. (England).

Robert Häusser *PHOTOGRAPHER* Born in Stuttgart on November 8, 1924, Häusser received his master's degree in 1950 from the Meister-

schule für Handwerk und Kunst in Weimar, where he studied with Professor Hege. He has been self-employed since 1952.

The photographer is a member of GDL, DGPh, Deutscher Journalsitenverband, Deutscher Werkbund, Deutscher Künstlerbund and Neue Darmstädter Sezession. He won Schiller Plaque from the city of Mannheim in 1977, a gold medal at the Venice Bienniale in 1961 and the silver medal at the Swedish Master Competition in Stockholm, 1950.

Häusser has been the subject of two television programs: "Sprache aus Licht und Zeit—Ein Film über Robert Häusser" (1976) and "Robert Häusser—Ausstellung und Preisträger Schillerplakette" (1978), both for German TV. He also designed the scenery for the stage production of *So eine Liebe*, by Pavel Kohut, performed in 1973 at the Luzerner Festwochen in Lucerne, Switzerland, and at the National Theater in Mannheim, Germany.

PUBLICATIONS Books (in West Germany): *History of Photography in the 20th Century*, Petr Tausk, 1980 (London), 1977 (Cologne); *Die Welt der Oper*, 1977 (Verlag G. Braun: Karlsruhe); *Mannheim*, 1975 (Südwestdeutsche Verlagsanstalt: Mannheim); *Der Maler K. F. Dahmen*, 1972 (Bruckmann: Munich); *Der Bildhauer Hans Nagel*, 1971 (Institut für Moderne Kunst: Nuremberg); *Gelsenkirchen*, 1970 (Econ Verlag: Düsseldorf); *Ladenburg*, 1970 (Südwestdeutsche Verlagsanstalt: Mannheim); *Weinland Baden*, 1969 (Südwestdeutsche Verlagsanstalt: Mannheim); *Welt am Oberrhein*, 1963, 1962, 1961 (Verlag G. Braun: Karlsruhe); *Das Elsass*, 1962 (Verlag G. Braun: Karlsruhe); *Aus unseren Fenstern*, 1962 (Verlag Strohmeyer: Mannheim); *Heidelberg*, 1961 (Verlag Thorbeke: Konstanz); Ein Fotograf sieht Mannheim, 1957 (Bibliographisches Institut: Mannheim). Periodicals: "Spuren und Zeichen im Um-Raum," July 1978, "Robert Häusser—Meister der Leica," Fritz Kempe, June 1971, *Leica-Fotografie*; "Robert Häusser," Hans Christian Adam, *Fotografie*, Apr 1977; "Robert Häusser—Erfüllung durch Fotografie und Lebenskunst," Günther Lensch, *Foto-Magazin*, Dec 1974; "Robert Häusser," *Das Deutsche Lichtbild*, 1959; "Robert Häusser," Robert d'Hooghe, *Foto-Prisma*, Oct 1958.

COLLECTIONS IMP/GEH, Rochester; MOMA, NYC; Univ. of Texas, Humanities Resource Ctr., Gernsheim Cllctn., Austin. Stedelijk Van Abbe-Mus., Eindhoven, The Netherlands. In Germany: Folkwang Mus., Essen; Kunsthalle, Mannheim; Leopold-Hoesch-Mus., Düren; Neue Sammlung,

Munich; Staatliches Mus. für Kunst und Gewerbe, Hamburg; Wilhelm Hack-Mus., Ludwig-
shafen.

DEALERS   Galerie Kicken, Alberstrusstrasse
47–49, 5000 Cologne 1, West Germany; Galerie
Petra Benteler, 3830 University, Houston, TX
77005.

ADDRESS   Ladenburgerstrasse 23, 68 Mann-
heim-41, West Germany.

Josepha Haveman   *PHOTOGRAPHER · TEACHER ·
PRINTMAKER*   Born March 19, 1931, in The Netherlands, Haveman earned her BA in Art (1956)
and MA in Photography (1966) from San Francisco State University, California. She also did
graduate work in anthropology at the University
of California, Berkeley, from 1958 to 1961. She
cites Don Worth and Aaron Siskind as major influences.

Haveman has been associate professor at California College of Arts and Crafts, Oakland, since
1968. From 1978 to 1979 she taught at the University of Haifa and the Avni Art Institute, Tel
Aviv (both in Israel). In the summers of 1969 and
1970 she taught at Portland State University, Oregon, and from 1958 to 1961 was museum pho-
tographer/artist at the Museum of Anthropology,
University of California, Berkeley.

Haveman is president of Image Circle, Inc., and
a member of IMP/GEH, SPE, Friends of Photography, San Francisco Women Artists and the
American Association of University Professors.

Shooting in all formats, Haveman produces silver prints that emphasize form, structure and
high printing quality. She also does experimental
color photography and printmaking.

PUBLICATION   Book: *Workbook in Creative
Photography*, 1976.

COLLECTIONS   Art Inst. of Chicago; IMP/GEH,
Rochester; Oakland Art Mus., Calif.; Polaroid
Cllctn., Cambridge, Mass.; Walnut Creek Art
Ctr., Walnut Creek, Calif. White Gall., Tel Aviv,
Israel.

DEALER   Focus Gall., 2146 Union St, San Francisco, CA 94123.

ADDRESS   POB 9063, Berkeley, CA 94709.

Clementina Elphinstone Hawarden   *PHOTOG-
RAPHER*   Born June 1, 1822, near Glasgow, Scot-
land, Hawarden died January 19, 1865, in South
Kensington, England. Her husband, Cornwallis
Maude, was Fourth Viscount Hawarden and
Baron de Montalt of Hawarden. Lady Hawarden
was a self-taught photographer, influenced by the
Pre-Raphaelite movement.

A member of the Photographic Society of London in 1863, she won a medal at the Dublin Exhibition of 1865.

Essentially a Victorian in outlook, Lady Hawarden was noted for her compositional abilities
and for her groupings of carefully dressed and
posed female subjects. Bordering on mannerism
and pictorialism, her photographs, many stereoscopic, have been described by some historians as
"slightly strange" or "disturbing."

PUBLICATIONS   Book: *Clementina: Lady Hawarden*, Graham Ovenden, ed., 1974. Anthologies: *The Invented Eye*, Edward Lucie-Smith,
1975; *The Magic Image*, Cecil Beaton & Gail
Buckland, 1975; *Early Photographs & Early Photographers*, Oliver Mathews, 1973.

COLLECTION   Victoria & Albert Mus., London.

Josiah Johnson Hawes   *PHOTOGRAPHER ·
PAINTER*   Born on February 20, 1808, in East Sud-
bury (now Wayland), Massachusetts, Hawes died
on August 7, 1908, at Crawford's Notch, New
Hampshire. Hawes' brother-in-law and partner
was Albert Sands Southworth (1811–94), and his
wife was Nancy Southworth Hawes, a hand-
colorist at Southworth & Hawes.

Hawes, apprenticed to a carpenter, was a part-
time oil painter when he learned daguerreotypy
from François Gouraud, who represented Daguerre in America. He joined in partnership with
Southworth and Joseph Pennell in Boston in
1840, becoming a full partner on the latter's
death in 1845. The partnership lasted until 1862.
Hawes also sold daguerreotype supplies in the
1840s and 1850s.

Hawes and Southworth discovered a way in
which to reduce exposure time. They also devised a number of photographic devices, for
which they received patents, such as the Grand
Parlor Stereoscope, a viewer for large full-plate
stereo daguerreotypes.

Hawes and Southworth were noted as two of
the finest daguerreotypists of their day. According to Newhall, Hawes was the more artistic of
the two, as some of the studio's best renderings
were accomplished while Southworth was in
California (1849–51). Their portraits were sensitive and more natural than those in the typical
style of the times.

PUBLICATIONS   Books: *The Spirit of Fact*, Rob-
ert A. Sobieszek & Odette M. Appel, 1976; *The
Legacy of Josiah Johnson Hawes*, ed. & intro. by
Rachel Johnston Homer, 1972; *Mirror Image:
The Influence of the Daguerreotype on American
Society*, Richard Rudisill, 1971; *The Daguerreo-*

type in America, 1961, rev. 1968, Beaumont Newhall. Anthologies: *The Photograph Collector's Guide*, Lee D. Witkin & Barbara London, 1979; *The Invented Eye*, Edward Lucie-Smith, 1975; *The Magic Image*, Cecil Beaton & Gail Buckland, 1975; *Great Photographers*, Time-Life Series, 1971; *Masters of Photography*, Beaumont & Nancy Newhall, 1969. Catalog: *The Hawes-Stokes Collection of American Daguerreotypes . . .*, I. N. Phelps Stokes, 1939 (Metro. Mus. of Art: NYC).

COLLECTIONS Boston Athenaeum; Boston Pub. Lib.; Bostonian Soc; IMP/GEH, Rochester; Metro. Mus. of Art, NYC; Mus. of Fine Arts, Boston.

ARCHIVE Metro. Mus. of Art, Fifth Ave & 82 St, New York, NY.

David Haxton PHOTOGRAPHER · FILM MAKER Born January 6, 1943, in Indianapolis, Indiana, Haxton received his BA in 1965 from the University of South Florida, Tampa, and his MA in 1967 from the University of Michigan, East Lansing.

He has been assistant professor at William Paterson College, Wayne, New Jersey, since 1974. Previously he was a lecturer at San Diego State University, California, from 1969 to 1972.

Also a film maker, Haxton won film grants from the NEA in 1980 and 1978 and from the New York State Council on the Arts in 1977.

The photographer works in color, using standard photographic background paper and fluorescent lights or floodlights on stands. His visual concern is with the lights behind and in front of the manipulated (layered, torn, etc.) paper.

PUBLICATIONS Anthology: *One of a Kind*, Belinda Rathbone, 1979. Periodicals: "The Instant Still Life," Don Leavitt, *Popular Photography*, Dec 1979; "David Haxton," Philip Rand Smith, *Arts Magazine*, Feb 1979; "David Haxton," Ben Lifson, *Village Voice*, Jan 29, 1979; *Soho News*, Amy Taubin, Dec 22, 1977.

COLLECTIONS Denver Art Mus., Colo; MOMA, NYC (films); Whitney Mus. of Amer Art, NYC.

DEALER Sonnabend Gall., 420 W Broadway, New York, NY 10012.

ADDRESS 139 Spring St, New York, NY 10012.

Maria Eugenia Haya PHOTOGRAPHER · HISTORIAN Born June 5, 1944, in Havana, Cuba, Haya studied philology at Havana University (1972–78), graphic design with painter Raul Martinez (1965–66), photographic evaluation under Adelaida de Juan at José Martí National Library (1964–65) and history of photography under Mario Rodriguez Alemán at the Cuban Institute of Film Art and Industry (1962–63), all in Havana. Her husband, Mario Garcia Joya, is director of photography at the Cuban Institute of Film and Industry.

As of this writing she was a researcher for the History of Cuban Photography in Havana (since 1978). Haya organized the History of Cuban Photography exhibition in Mexico in 1979. She has also been a researcher and script supervisor with film maker Tomás Gutierrez Alea (1975, 1978), a photographer for the Chamber of Commerce (1970–78) and the Exhibitions Department of Exposicuba (1966–70) and a cartoon artist and animator with the Cuban Institute of Film Art and Industry (1962–64).

A member of the Cuban Union of Writers and Artists, Haya won first prize in the union's National Salon in 1978, and in the same year won first prize at the National Salon at University of Havana.

PUBLICATIONS Books: *Breve Historia de la Fotografía Cubana*, 1980 (Havana); *Carifesta*, 1979 (Havana); *Hecho en Latinoamerica*, 1979 (Mexico City); *Diana Habañera o la Fotografía Cubana*, 1971 (Havana). Anthologies: *Fotos de Cuba*, 1979 (Havana); *Photography Year*, 1979, Time-Life Series; *XX Aniversario Casa de las Americas: Obra Gráfica*, 1979 (Mexico City). Periodical: *La Gaceta de Cuba*, no. 170, 1978.

COLLECTIONS House of Culture, Prague, Czechoslovakia; Mexican Council of Photography, Mexico City. In Havana, Cuba: House of the Americas; Natl. Lib. of José Martí; Natl. Mus.; Natl. Union of Writers & Artists of Cuba; School of Philology, Univ. of Havana.

ADDRESS c/o Union de Escritores y Artistas, 17 y H, Vedado, Havana, Cuba.

Masumi Hayashi (Keesey) PHOTOGRAPHER Born September 3, 1945, at Gila Bend Relocation Center in Rivers, Arizona, the photographer received an MFA in 1977 from Florida State University, Tallahassee. Hayashi names Robert Fichter as her mentor.

A freelance photographer and graphic artist, Hayashi has operated her own company, Custom Picture Post Card Co., since 1977. She was an adjunct instructor at Florida State University in 1977 and an artist-in-the-schools in 1979, sponsored by LeMoyne Art Foundation, Tallahassee.

Hayashi is a member of SPE and Art Foundation, Inc., a Tallahassee artists' cooperative. In 1976 she won a Florida Craftsman Award.

The photographer works in nonsilver processes, using graphic arts, blueprinting, gum printing, photo silk screen and Inkodye.

PUBLICATIONS Books: *Akira: Sun & Moon*, 1979 (pvt. pub.); *Photo Images in Art*, Nancy Howell-Koehler, 1979; *Color Separations with Polaroid*, George C. Floersch, 1979 (Florida A & M Univ.: Tallahassee).

COLLECTIONS Florida State Univ., Tallahassee; Gulf Coast Photo Gall., Tampa, Fla.; IMP/GEH, Rochester; Jacksonville Fine Arts Mus., Fla.; Leon County Pub. Lib., Tallahassee, Fla.; Southern Exposure, Meridian, Miss.; State of Fla., Internatl. Year of the Child Committee, Tallahassee; St. Petersburg Fine Arts Mus., Fla.; Univ. of S. Fla., Tampa.

ADDRESS 412 Margaret Ct, Tallahassee, FL 32301.

Dannielle Beverley Hayes *PHOTOGRAPHER · ILLUSTRATOR · AUTHOR* Born March 24, 1943, in Quebec, Canada, Hayes received a Fine Arts Certificate from Cooper Union in New York City (1971) and also studied at the New School for Social Research in New York City. She was a friend of, and influenced by, Diane Arbus.

As of this writing she was adjunct professor of photography at New Jersey Institute of Technology Architectural School. Hayes has been a freelance photographer/illustrator since 1968. She was a staff photographer and illustrator for Fairchild Publications from 1965 to 1969.

She is a member of the International Center for Photography, Catskill Center of Photography and SPE, and is founder/director of Professional Women Photographers.

Hayes was photography chairwoman for the International Women's Art Festival in New York City in 1976. She designed costumes for the Academy Award-nominated film *The Dove* in 1965.

The photographer does commercial work and photojournalism, as well as working with very large negatives and the Kwik-Print process on flag nylon.

PUBLICATIONS Anthologies: *Women Photograph Men*, ed. & contr., 1977; *Women, Women, Women*, Leta Clark, 1977.

COLLECTIONS ICP, NYC; Metro. Mus. of Art, NYC.

DEALER K & L Color Gall, 222 E 44 St, New York, NY 10017.

ADDRESS 156 Second Ave, New York, NY 10003.

Frank Jay Haynes *PHOTOGRAPHER* Born October 20, 1853, in Saline, Michigan, Haynes died March 10, 1921, in St. Paul, Minnesota. He attended school in Saline. His son, Jack Ellis Haynes, was also a photographer.

Haynes was a photographer of western life and the early days of Yellowstone National Park. He came to Yellowstone in the 1880s, and accompanied expeditions into the park as official photographer. In 1886 he was employed by the *New York World* as a photographer for the winter expedition into the park, led by famed arctic explorer Frederick Schwatka. He also photographed President Chester A. Arthur's 1883 trip through Yellowstone. Previously he had opened a photographic studio in Moorehead, Minnesota (1876), and another in Fargo, Dakota Territory (1879). Employed by the Northern Pacific Railroad as official photographer, he was given a special pullman car for his shop.

In 1884 Haynes was given a lease by the Department of the Interior to open a studio in Yellowstone National Park, and he became its official photographer for the next thirty-two years, although he was not an employee of the government. With George W. Wakefield, Haynes was co-founder of the Yellowstone Park Stage Company. In 1895 he opened a studio in St. Paul, Minnesota. He retired from business in 1916. Throughout his life his work was published in numerous newspapers and magazines.

Haynes photographed the entire Northwest, from the Black Hills of South Dakota, the Twin Cities of Minnesota and the early development of the Canadian Pacific Railroad to the West Coast and Alaska. He took pictures of early forts, Indians, surveying parties, towns, ranching and agricultural pioneering, steamboats, railroads and equipment and battlefields.

PUBLICATIONS Monographs: *Following the Frontier with F. Jay Haynes, Pioneer Photographer of the Old West*, Tilden Freeman, 1964; *Yellowstone National Park in Photo Gravure*, 1891. Books: *Photography and the American Scene*, Robt. Taft, 1938; *Yellowstone Geysers*, Clyde Max Bauer, 1937, rev. 1947; *The Yellowstone National Park*, Hiram Martin Chittenden, 1895; *All About Yellowstone Park*, Albert Brewer Guptill, *Haynes Guide Book*, 1890, rev. annually through 1909. Catalog: *Catalogues of Stereoscopic Views*, 1879. Periodicals: "The First Winter Trip Through Yellowstone National Park," Apr 1942, "The Expedition of President Chester A. Arthur to Yellowstone National Park in 1883," Jan 1942, *Annals of Wyoming*; "Yellowstone Pictureland," *Photo Art Monthly*, June 1935; "Safeguarding

Scenic Photographs," *Abels Photographic Weekly*, Mar 3, 1923; *Haynes' Bulletins*, passim, Feb 1922–Dec 1924.

COLLECTIONS Montana State Historical Soc., Helena; Montana State Univ., Bozeman; Yellowstone Natl. Park, Wyoming.

Jack Ellis Haynes PHOTOGRAPHER · INVENTOR
Born September 27, 1884, in Fargo, Dakota Territory, Haynes died May 12, 1962, in Livingston, Montana. He studied to be a mining engineer at the University of Minnesota, from which he was graduated in 1908. His father was the photographer Frank Jay Haynes.

In 1921 Haynes took over his father's concession at Yellowstone National Park, making available to the public books, pamphlets, souvenirs and memorabilia of Yellowstone. He acted as director of a museum in the park headquarters, and worked for his father from 1897 on, becoming president of Haynes, Inc., and eventually taking over the company. He gave various lectures concerning Yellowstone, including one entitled "The Evolution of Photography in Yellowstone National Park."

Haynes invented a quick-acting tripod with a semispherical head and suspension cam leg clamps, and a slide rule to calculate salaries, meals, lodgings and sales tax. He also made miniature geyser models, which have been displayed at expositions in the U.S. A talented musician, he played the mandolin skillfully.

Having learned photography early in life, Haynes photographed the park's scenic wonders and captured many historical events. His work was sold in the park gift shops in the form of postcards, lithographs and souvenir folders. He often used pen and ink to make sketches of scenes for the *Haynes Guide Book*.

PUBLICATION Book: *Haynes Guide to Yellowstone National Park*, ca. 1921, rev. annually through 1948.

John Heartfield PHOTOGRAPHER · DESIGNER
Born in 1891, Heartfield died in Berlin in 1968. He anglicized his original name, Helmut Herzfelde, in protest over Germany's anti-British campaign. Heartfield studied at the School of Applied Arts in Munich (1907–10) and at Arts and Crafts School in Berlin (1912–14).

First working as a commercial artist for a paper manufacturer in Mannheim (1911–12), he served in the military from 1912 to 1914. With his brother Wieland Herzfelde, Heartfield established the publishing house Malik Verlag and the periodical *Neue Jugend* (ca. 1917), both catering to left-wing artists and writers. He co-edited the satirical magazines *Jedermann sein eigener Fussball* and *Die Pleite* with his brother and artist George Grosz, and with Grosz and Raoul Hausmann he edited *Dada 3* (1919–20).

From 1921 to 1923 Heartfield was the scenic director for Max Reinhardt in Berlin and from 1923 to 1927 he edited the satirical magazine *Der Knuppel*. He designed covers for and contributed to *Arbeiter-Illustrierten-Zeitung (AIZ)* in Berlin in 1929–33 and in Prague, Czechoslovakia, in 1933–38. He moved to Prague for political reasons, then emigrated to London in 1938, and was finally able to return to Germany in 1950. While an expatriate he designed book covers and illustrations, work he continued in his homeland, along with the design of posters and theatrical scenery. In 1960 he became a professor at Deutsche Akademie der Kunst.

Heartfield joined the Communist party in 1918 and was a founder-member of the Berlin Dadaists in 1919.

He was known for his meticulous, satirical political photomontages.

PUBLICATIONS Monographs: In Germany: *Montage: John Heartfield*, Echard Siepmann, 1977 (Elefanten Press Galerie); *Photomontages of the Nazi Period*, 1977; *John Heartfield: 33 Photomontages*, 1974 (VEB: Dresden); *John Heartfield, Krieg im Frieden*, 1972 (K. Hanser: Munich); *John Heartfield*, 1970 (VEB: Dresden); *John Heartfield: Leben und Werk*, Wieland Herzfelde, 1962 (Verlag der Kunst: Dresden). Elsewhere: *John Heartfield: Photomontagen zur Zeitgeschichte*, Konrad Farner, ed., 1945 (Kultur und Volk: Zurich, Switzerland); *John Heartfield: Eine Monographie*, Sergei Tretyakov, 1936 (Moscow). Books: *Photomontage*, Dawn Ades, 1976; *John Heartfield und die Kunst der Fotomontage*, Bodo Uhse, 1957 (Deutsche Akademie der Künste: Berlin); *Deutschland, Deutschland, über Alles*, Kurt Tucholsky, 1929, U.S. ed., 1972; *Gebrauchsgraphik*, vol. 7, H. K. Frenzel, 1927. Anthologies: *The Photograph Collector's Guide*, Lee D. Witkin & Barbara London, 1979; *The Magic Image*, Cecil Beaton & Gail Buckland, 1975; *The Print*, Time-Life Series, 1970. Catalogs: *Heartfield*, intro. by Roland Marz, 1976 (Staatliche Mus.: Berlin); *John Heartfield 1891–1968*, 1975 (Abbemuseum: Eindhoven, The Netherlands); *John Heartfield: Photomontages*, 1969 (Inst. of Contemporary Arts: London); *John Heartfield, Fotomontör*, 1967 (Moderna Muséet: Stockholm, Sweden).

COLLECTIONS Akademie der Künste der DDR,

East Berlin; Nationalgalerie, Staatliche Mus., West Berlin.

David Martin Heath *PHOTOGRAPHER · TEACHER* Born June 27, 1931, in Philadelphia, Pennsylvania, Heath studied art at the Philadelphia College of Art (1954–55) and photography under Richard Nickel at the Institute of Design, Illinois Institute of Technology, Chicago (1955–56). He further studied photography under W. Eugene Smith at the New School for Social Research in New York City (1959) and in Smith's Photo Workshop in New York (1961).

Since 1970 Heath has been professor of photography at Ryerson Polytechnical Institute, Toronto, Canada. He previously was an assistant professor at Moore College of Art, Philadelphia (1967–70), and an instructor in photography at the School of the Dayton Art Institute, Ohio (1965–67). He has been an artist-in-residence at the International Center of Photography in New York City (1978), Visual Studies Workshop (1976–77) and the University of Minnesota, Minneapolis (1965). Heath assisted photographers Wingate Paine, Carl Fischer and Bert Stern in New York from 1957 to 1963.

A member of SPE since 1965, the photographer received Guggenheim fellowships in 1963 and 1965.

PUBLICATIONS Book: *A Dialogue with Solitude*, 1965. Periodicals: *National Gallery of Canada Journal*, Oct 1979; "Le Grand Album Ordinaire," Charles Hagen, *Afterimage: VSW*, Feb 1974; review of *A Dialogue with Solitude*, Linda Knox, *Aperture*, no. 4, 1966; "Portfolio '64," *Contemporary Photographer*, fall 1964.

COLLECTIONS Art Inst. of Chicago; IMP/GEH, Rochester; Minneapolis Art Gall., Minn.; MOMA, NYC; Philadelphia Mus. of Art, Penn.; UCLA; Univ. of Rochester, N.Y.; Yeshiva Univ., NYC. Natl. Film Board of Canada, Ottawa; Natl. Gall. of Canada, Ottawa.

ADDRESS Ryerson Polytechnical Institute, Dept of Film and Photography, 122 Bond St, Toronto, Ontario M5B 1E8, Canada.

Vilém Heckel *PHOTOGRAPHER · MOUNTAINEER* Born May 21, 1918 in Plzeň, Czechoslovakia, Heckel died in an avalanche on May 31, 1970, near the mountain Huascarán in Peru. He learned photography as an apprentice in the portrait studio of Alois Chmelík in Plzeň (1932–36).

Heckel worked as a photographer in various firms from 1937 to 1956, mainly doing industrial and advertising photography. After 1956 he freelanced, primarily photographing in the mountains.

He became a member of the Union of Czechoslovak Creative Artists in 1949.

An excellent skier and mountaineer, Heckel successfully specialized in mountain photographs, with "quite unusual results," according to photohistorian Petr Tausk. He was a member of Czechoslovakian mountaineering expeditions to the Caucasus, Hindukush, the Himalayas, and the Cordilleras in Peru, where he perished with his whole party.

PUBLICATIONS Books (in Prague): *The Beauties of Czechoslovakia*, 1968 (Orbis); *Hindukush*, 1967; *Mountains and People*, 1964 (Orbis); *Climbing in the Caucasus*, 1960 (Artia); *Our Mountains*, 1956.

Eric A. Hegg *PHOTOGRAPHER* Born in 1868 in Bollnäs (near Stockholm), Sweden, Hegg died in California on December 13, 1948. He attended grade school in Wisconsin, where he was apprenticed to a local practitioner of art and photography.

Hegg opened a studio in Washburn, Wisconsin, at age fifteen, then moved to Tacoma, Washington, in 1888. Soon afterward he opened a studio in the Bellingham Bay area, then a second studio in nearby Fairhaven. He remained there until 1897, when he journeyed to Alaska on an old riverboat during the height of the gold rush days. Hegg lived in Alaska for twenty years and was the official photographer for the Guggenheim mining interests during part of that time. After his return to the forty-eight states he operated an art store in San Diego, California, for a while, then a studio in Fresno, California, for seven years. He spent six months in Hawaii on assignment for a California newspaper to draw illustrations, and returned to Bellingham in 1930, again to operate a studio.

Hegg was also an accomplished oil painter and illustrator.

The photographer's "greatest interest lay in recording scenes that showed men in contest with nature," according to Murray Morgan, *One Man's Gold Rush*. Hegg photographed the Lummi Indians in their annual runs for sockeye salmon, took some of the first photographs of white fishermen installing commercial traps, documented the industrialization of the Puget Sound salmon fishery and recorded the mechanization of logging. He also brought back photographs from almost every town of Alaska's gold district.

PUBLICATIONS Book: *One Man's Gold Rush*,

Murray Morgan, 1967. Anthology: *Alaskans*, Keith Wheeler, 1977.

COLLECTIONS   Alaska Hist. Soc., Juneau; Univ. of Calif., Bancroft Lib., Berkeley; Univ. of Wash., Suzzallo Lib., Seattle.

Robert Heinecken   *PHOTOGRAPHER · TEACHER* Born October 29, 1931, in Denver, Colorado, Heinecken completed his BA and MA at University of California at Los Angeles (1959, 1960).

He has taught at UCLA since 1960 as well as at the following schools: Harvard University (1972), San Francisco Art Institute (1971), School of the Art Institute of Chicago (1970), State University of New York, Buffalo (1969), and George Eastman House, Rochester (1967).

Heinecken has belonged to SPE since 1963, was its national chairman in 1971–72 and has been on the board of directors since 1972. He has also been on the board of trustees of Friends of Photography since 1974.

The photographer won an NEA Photographer's Fellowship in 1977 and a Guggenheim Fellowship in 1976.

Heinecken's work typically involves the figure, and he uses various photographic processes, including nonsilver, etching, lithography, collage, montage, large-scale, three-dimensional and emulsion on canvas.

PUBLICATIONS   Books: *Heinecken*, James L. Enyeart, 1979; *Are You Rea, 1964–68*, 1968 (self-pub.). Catalog: *Minor White, Robert Heinecken, Robert Cumming*, John Upton, 1973 (Calif. State Univ. Fine Arts Gall., Long Beach). Anthology: *The Photograph Collector's Guide*, Lee D. Witkin & Barbara London, 1979. Periodicals: "Robert Heinecken: An Interview," Charles Hagen, *Afterimage: VSW*, Apr 1976; "I Am Involved in Learning to Perceive and Use Light," *Untitled* no. 7/8, 1974; "Robert Heinecken," Carl I. Belz, *Camera*, Jan 1968.

COLLECTIONS (selected) CCP, Tucson; Harvard Univ., Fogg Art Mus., Cambridge, Mass.; IMP/GEH, Rochester; MOMA, NYC; Mus. of Fine Arts, Houston, Tex.; Norton Simon Mus., Pasadena, Calif.; San Francisco Mus. of Modern Art; Univ. of Nebr. Sheldon Mem. Gall., Lincoln; Univ. of N. Mex., Albuquerque.

DEALER   Light Gall., 724 Fifth Ave, New York, NY 10019.

ADDRESS   UCLA Dept of Art, 405 Hilgard Ave, Los Angeles, CA 90024.

Manfred Heiting   *DESIGNER · PHOTOGRAPHIC CONSULTANT*   Born February 2, 1943, in Detmold,

Germany, Heiting studied at the School for Arts and Crafts in Düsseldorf (1959–61) and at the School for Design, Ulm, Germany (1962).

Since 1968 he has been director of the International Polaroid Collection in Amsterdam, and since 1966 has also directed Design and Creative Services for Polaroid International.

Heiting has been a member of AIGA since 1967, DGPh since 1979 and the Photokina Executive Committee since 1978.

He maintains a private collection of photographs from 1900 to the present, as well as having charge of the Polaroid Collection of works from 1968 to the present. Heiting is also responsible for organizing commercial and cultural exhibitions by Polaroid throughout the world.

ADDRESS   Sarphatipark 82, Amsterdam, The Netherlands.

Nancy Hellebrand   *PHOTOGRAPHER*   Born in Philadelphia, Pennsylvania, in 1944, Hellebrand studied privately with Bill Brandt in London from 1971 to 1974.

As of this writing she was an assistant professor at Bucks County Community College, where she has been since 1975.

She has worked in black-and-white and is currently working in platinum. She does mostly portraits, her special interest being working-class people.

PUBLICATION   Monograph: *Londoners*, 1974.

COLLECTIONS   MOMA, NYC. Natl Portrait Gallery, London.

ADDRESS   2210 Delancey St, Philadelphia, PA 19103.

Keld Helmer-Petersen   *PHOTOGRAPHER · TEACHER*   Born August 23, 1920, in Copenhagen, Denmark, Helmer-Petersen is primarily self-taught in photography but studied under Harry Callahan at the Institute of Design in Chicago in 1950–51. He names Albert Renger-Patzsch, Walker Evans and Aaron Siskind as strong influences, among others.

Since 1955 the photographer has run his own studio, specializing in architecture, design and industrial photography. He has also taught photography at the Royal Academy of Art, Copenhagen, since 1964, and at the Department of Art History, University of Lund, Sweden (1978–79). In the 1950s Helmer-Petersen lectured at several schools of design, graphic art, and arts and crafts in Copenhagen.

He received a grant from the American-Scandinavian Foundation in 1950 to study at the Institute of Design, Chicago.

As a film maker Helmer-Petersen has done (in 16mm) *Falling Water; The Designer & Industrial Society*, 1951; *Chicago Light Motion Study*, 1951; and *Copenhagen Boogie;* and in 35mm, *Red and White*, 1968. He has written numerous articles for Danish, German and Japanese magazines.

Using various formats, Helmer-Petersen shows in his photographs "a strong leaning towards extreme simplicity and graphic clarity in carefully composed compositions, often silhouetted, but more often than not containing subtle greys in contrast to pure black and white." He occasionally produces photograms, light drawings and prints from paper negatives.

PUBLICATIONS Monographs: *Fragments of a City*, 1960; *122 Colour Photographs*, 1949. Books: *Romanesque Sculpture in Danish Churches*, 1962 (Viborg); *Danish Chairs*, 1954 (Copenhagen); *Colour Before the Camera*, 1952 (London).

COLLECTIONS MOMA, NYC. Royal Lib., Copenhagen, Denmark.

DEALERS Rudolf Kicken, Cologne, West Germany; André Wauters Fine Arts, 1100 Madison Ave, New York, NY 10028.

ADDRESS Kristiniagade 14, 2100 Copenhagen Ø, Denmark.

Hermann Ludwig Ferdinand von Helmholtz *PHYSIOLOGIST · PHYSICIST · TEACHER* Born August 31, 1821, in Potsdam, Germany, Helmholtz died September 8, 1894, in Charlottenburg, Berlin. He studied physiology and physics in Berlin, graduating from Friedrich Wilhelm Medical Institute in 1843.

Helmholtz first taught anatomy at the Academy of Fine Arts in Berlin, becoming professor of physiology at Koenigsberg in 1849. In 1855 he took the same position at Bonn, and transferred to the University of Heidelberg's chair of physiology in 1858. He next was appointed chairman of physics at the University of Berlin in 1871, and in 1887 also became director of the Physico Technical Institute at Charlottenburg. He was knighted by the German emperor in 1883.

The scientist developed the ophthalmoscope in 1851, and the telestereoscope in 1857, an instrument similar to the stereoreflector but made for direct visual use. Author of the important book *Physiological Optics*, he also did studies on color theory, photographed the solar spectrum and researched sound (physiological acoustics), electrical oscillations and electrodynamics. His work on Thomas Young's color theory led to its name being amended to the Young-Helmholtz theory.

PUBLICATIONS Books: *Stereo Photography in Practice*, E. T. Lingsen, 1952; *Principles of Stereoscopy*, H. C. McKay, 1948; *History of 3-Color Photography*, E. J. Wall, 1925; *History and Handbook of Photography*, Gaston Tissandier, 1876; *Handbook of Physiological Optics*, 1867 (Univ. of Heidelberg; Germany); *On the Sensations of Tone as a Physiological Basis for the Theory of Music*, 1862, Eng. ed., 1875. Anthology: *Photography's Great Inventors*, Louis W. Sipley, 1965. Periodicals: *Bild und Ton*, 1952; *Photographische Mittheilungen*, 1898.

Arnold Clayton Henderson *PHOTOGRAPHER · TEACHER* Born April 10, 1938, in Madison, Wisconsin, Henderson was the son of poet Ruth Gordon Henderson. He earned his AB in English at Cornell University, Ithaca, New York (1960), and his MA (1963) and PhD (1973) in English from the University of California, Berkeley. He also studied at the University of Nebraska, Lincoln (1960–61), and the University of Paris (1965–66). He names Dave Bohn and Vilem Kriz as mentors.

Henderson has been assistant professor of English and art at Rutgers University, New Brunswick, New Jersey, since 1970. He was a photography instructor at the Associated Students of the University of California Studio, Berkeley, from 1965 to 1969.

A member of SPE and Friends of Photography since 1977, Henderson also belongs to the CAA and Modern Language Association. He won a photography grant from Rutgers University in 1978. He has also won an award for poetry from the Academy of American Poets in 1968.

Working largely in black-and-white, Henderson creates photographs with "poetic or psychological implications." One series uses multiple printing "to explore the possibilities for growth of a young girl, juxtaposing her to ancestral women . . ."; another explores attitudes toward the nude.

PUBLICATIONS Anthologies: *Fantastic Photographs*, Attilio Colombo, 1979 (Contrejour: Paris); *Fantastic Photography in the USA*, Lorenzo Merlo, ed., text by Roman Cieslewicz, 1978 (Barcelona, Spain); *The Nude in Photography*, Arthur Goldsmith, ed., 1975; *Be-ing Without Clothes*, 1970; *Light*[7], 1968. Periodicals (selected): *Camera 35*, text & photos, Jan 1978; *Camera*, text & photos, Sept 1973; *Popular Photography Annual*, 1973.

COLLECTION MIT, Cambridge, Mass.

DEALERS Marjorie Neikrug Gall., 224 E 68 St, New York, NY 10021; Galerie Fiolet, Herengracht 86, Amsterdam, The Netherlands.

ADDRESS   322 Harper Pl, Highland Park, NY 08904.

Heinz K. Henisch   PHOTOHISTORIAN · PHYSICIST   Born April 21, 1922, in Neudek, Czechoslovakia, Henisch earned a BS (1942), PhD (1949) and DS (1948) from the University of Reading, England. His wife, Bridget A. Henisch, is a medievalist and writer.

Since 1974 Henisch has been professor of the history of photography, Department of Art History, Pennsylvania State University, University Park. Concurrently he has been a fellow of the Institute for the Arts and Humanistic Studies (since 1978) and professor of physics (since 1963). He was a lecturer at the University of Reading, England, from 1948 to 1963.

Henisch has been a member of SPE since 1977 and of RPS since 1950. He was named a fellow of the Photographic Historical Society of New York in 1978 and a fellow of RPS in 1976. He became a corresponding member of Deutsche Gesellschaft für Photographie in 1977 and an Honorary Fellow of "74 Group" in Warsaw, Poland, in 1976.

Henisch holds eight patents, all in the field of solid-state technology (1958–73). He has written numerous articles on photohistorical themes and, in 1977, founded the British journal *History of Photography*, of which he has been editor ever since. His photohistorical research has focused on James Robertson, the iconography of daguerreotype cases, early photomontage, early photography in eastern Europe, and the concept of photographic style. He collects antique photographs, literature and ephemera, and his personal photography emphasizes photomontage.

PUBLICATIONS   Books: *Crystal Growth in Gels*, 1973; *Chipmunk Portrait*, w/B. A. Henisch, 1970 (Carnation Press: England).

ADDRESS   249 Materials Research Laboratory, University Park, PA 16802.

Fritz Henle   PHOTOGRAPHER   Born June 9, 1909, in Dortmund, Germany, Henle earned a diploma in 1931 from the School of Photography in Munich. His mentor was Hannah Seewald. Henle's grandfather was the anatomist Jacob Henle.

Since 1959 Henle has been a freelance photographer, creating an archive of images of western Europe, Israel, the Mediterranean, and the Caribbean Islands. He also has written the column "Twin Lens" in *Popular Photography*. He freelanced for such journals as *Harper's Bazaar*, *Town & Country* and *Holiday* (1945–59), and previously worked for the Office of War Information (1942–45) and *Life* (1937–42). Henle was the photographer for the Italian (Sea) Line to India, China and Japan (1934–36), and in 1931–32 was an assistant to Professor Clarence Kennedy in Florence, Italy, on a Guggenheim Fellowship. In 1980 he received an NEA Photographer's Fellowship.

A founding member and trustee of ASMP, he also belongs to the Overseas Press Club.

With Geoffrey Holder, Henle has made the films *Shango* (1954) and *Yan Vallou* (1954). He also made *The Trinidad Carnival* (1952) and *Virgin Islands, U.S.A.* (1950).

PUBLICATIONS   Monograph: *Fritz Henle*, 1973 (self-pub.). Books: *Casals*, 1975; *A New Guide to Rollei Photography*, 1965; *With the Eyes of a Rollei Photographer*, 1964 (Heering Verlage: Munich); *Holiday in Europe*, Anne Freemantle, 1963; *Photography for Everyone*, Mike Kinzer, 1959; *The Caribbean: A Journey with Pictures*, w/P. E. Knapp, 1957; *Fritz Henle's Guide to Rollei Photography*, 1956; *Fritz Henle's Figure Studies*, 1954; *Fritz Henle's Rollei*, Winterry, 1950; *The Virgin Islands*, 1949; *Hawaii*, Norman Wright, 1948; *Paris*, Elliot Paul, 1947; *Mexico*, 1945; *China*, Kwok Ying Fund, 1943. Anthology: *The Photograph Collector's Guide*, Lee D. Witkin & Barbara London, 1979. Periodicals: *Modern Photography*, Mar 1972; *Infinity: ASMP*, Mar 1968; *Popular Photography*, Mar 1964; *Life*, Mar 1938.

COLLECTIONS   CCP, Tucson; IMP/GEH, Rochester; Lehigh Univ. Art Mus., Allentown, Penn.; MOMA, NYC; Univ. of Tex., Gernsheim Cllctn., Austin. In Germany: Agfa-Gevaert, Historama, Leverkusen; Fritz Gruber Cllctn., Cologne; Landesbildstelle, Hamburg.

DEALER   Witkin Gall., 41 E 57 St, New York, NY 10022.

ADDRESS   POB 723, Christiansted, St. Croix, U.S. Virgin Islands 00820.

Florence Henri   PAINTER · PHOTOGRAPHER   [See plate 54]   Born June 28, 1893 in New York, Henri studied piano with Busoni and Petri in Rome and Berlin. She studied painting with Hans Hofmann at the Art School in Munich (1914), with Archipenko in Berlin (1918–22), with Léger and Ozenfant in Paris at Académie Moderne, and with Moholy-Nagy at the Bauhaus, Dessau, in 1927, where she started photography. She later studied portraiture with Ivan Puni, in 1934.

In 1929 Henri opened a photographic studio in Paris, giving lessons and helping to launch a new generation of photographers. Her work has been published in such leading journals as *Vogue*, *Art*

Henisch   272

et *Décoration*, *Image Bravo*, *Votre Beauté*, *Réalisme* and *Varietà*, and she has exhibited internationally. She still lives in Paris.

Originally a pianist, she played concertos in major British and German theaters until 1918.

Henri's early art work was abstract, and her painting also explored Cubist ideas. Her photographs included still lifes and portraiture, and she also was interested in industrial photography. After 1945 she resumed painting primarily, and lived in Italy for some time.

PUBLICATIONS Monograph: *Florence Henri, una riflessione sulla fotografia*, Maurizio Fagiolo, 1975 (Turin). Catalogs: *Florence Henri, aspetti di un percorso 1910/1940*, Giuseppi Marcenaro, G. B. Martini & Alberto Ronchetti, 1979 (Banco di Chiavari: Genoa); *Florence Henri*, Suzanne Page & Herbert Molderings, 1978 (ARC Paris/Musée d'Art Moderne de la ville de Paris); *Florence Henri, Aspekte der Photographie der 20 er Jahre*, Herbert Molderings, 1976 (Westfalischer Kunstverein & Staatliche Kunsthalle: Munster & Baden-Baden); *De Miro d'Ajeta, Ester Carla, Florence Henri*, 1974 (Galleria Martini & Ronchetti: Genoa/N.Y.). Periodicals: "Florence Henri," *Du*, Nov 1978; *Photo*, Nov 1978; "Florence Henri," Akira Kokubo, *Camera Mainichi*, no. 6, 1975; "Florence Henri," De Miro d'Ajeta & Ester Carla, *Fotografare*, no. 5, 1975; "Le fotografie di Florence Henri," Germano Beringheli, *Il Lavoro*, Dec 31, 1974; "Florence Henri," Klaus-Jurgen Senback, *Galerie Wilde* 1974; "Florence Henri," D. Seylan, *Creative Camera*, July 1972; *Camera*, Sept 1967; "Florence Henri," H. K. Freuzef, *Gebrauchsgraphik*, no. 6, 1936; "Florence Henri," Jacques Guenne, *L'Intransigeant*, May 21, 1934; "The Studio Annual," *Modern Photography*, 1932.

COLLECTIONS IMP/GEH, Rochester; MOMA, NYC; San Francisco Mus. of Modern Art. Bibliothèque Nationale, Paris; Centre Georges Pompidou, Paris; Mus. Folkwang, Essen, Germany; Università di Parma, Museo della Fotografia, Italy.

DEALER Galleria Martini & Ronchetti, Via Roma 9, 16121 Genoa, Italy.

Diana Mara Henry PHOTOGRAPHER · TEACHER Born June 20, 1948, in Cincinnati, Ohio, Henry received her BA from Radcliffe College, Cambridge, Massachusetts, in 1969. She studied at the International Center of Photography (ICP) in New York City from 1974 to 1976 and cites as major influences Ernst Haas, Bea Nettles and Lucas Samaras.

She taught photography at ICP in 1975–79 and originated and directed ICP's Community Workshop Program in 1975–77.

Henry is a member of ASMP, American Society of Picture Professionals and SPE and has been a board member of Friends of the Alice Austen House since 1976.

Henry practices photojournalism, using small format and silver prints. She considers her work "lucid interpretation of the human cycle and straightforward representation of women's roles."

PUBLICATIONS Book: *What Women Want*, 1979. Anthologies: *The Decade of Women*, 1980; *Spirit of Houston*, 1978; *Women Photograph Men*, 1977.

COLLECTIONS Arthur & Elizabeth Schlesinger Lib., Cambridge, Mass.; L/C, Wash., D.C.; Natl. Archives, Wash., D.C.

DEALER Chisholm Gall., 13198 Forest Hill Blvd, West Palm Beach, FL 33411.

ADDRESS 1160 Fifth Ave, #411, New York, NY 10029.

Claire Henze PHOTOGRAPHER · TEACHER Born in Pasadena, California, on August 29, 1945, Henze earned her BA from Mills College, Oakland, California, in 1967 and studied at Art Center College of Design in Los Angeles in 1967–69.

A freelance photographer, she was co-director of Ohio Silver Gallery in Los Angeles in 1975 and a lecturer in photography at Immaculate Heart College in Los Angeles in 1973–75.

Henze is a member of SPE and was on the board of trustees of the Los Angeles Center for Photographic Studies in 1974.

Using silver prints, she expresses social commentary in her work.

PUBLICATIONS Anthology: *Women See Woman*, 1976. Periodical: *Journal*, no. 1, June 1974 (Los Angeles Inst. of Contemporary Art).

PORTFOLIO *Silver See* (group), 1977 (Los Angeles Ctr. for Photographic Studies).

COLLECTIONS CCP, Tucson; Harvard Univ., Fogg Art Mus., Cambridge, Mass.; IMP/GEH, Rochester; Los Angeles County Mus. of Art; Minneapolis Inst. of Art, Minn.; MOMA, NYC; Oakland Mus., Calif.; UCLA, Frederick Wight Galls.; Univ. of N. Mex. Art Mus., Albuquerque.

ADDRESS 1671 Poppy Peak Dr, Pasadena, CA 91105.

Anthony Hernandez PHOTOGRAPHER Born July 7, 1947, in Los Angeles, California, Hernandez studied at East Los Angeles College in 1966–67.

He is currently a freelance photographer.

Hernandez

Awarded a Photographer's Fellowship from NEA in 1975, 1978 and 1980, he was also the recipient of the Ferguson Grant by the Friends of Photography in Carmel, California, 1972.

PUBLICATIONS Catalogs: *Attitudes: Photography in the 1970's*, 1979 (Santa Barbara Mus. of Art: Santa Barbara, Calif.); *Peculiar to Photography*, 1976 (Univ. of N. Mex.: Albuquerque); *Language of Light*, 1974 (Univ. of Kansas Mus. of Art: Lawrence); *Photography 1/Recent Photographs by 7 Artists*, 1974 (Jack Glenn Gall.: Corona del Mar, Calif.); *24 From L.A.*, 1973 (San Francisco Mus. of Art); *The Crowded Vacancy*, 1971, *California Photographers*, 1970 (Univ. of California at Davis). Periodicals: "Washington," Mark Power, *Afterimage: VSW*, Feb 1977; "Los Angeles," Peter Plagens, *Artforum*, Oct 1971; *Untitled*, Fred Parker, no. 2, Oct 1972, no. 3, Jan 1973, no. 4, Apr 1973; "The Last L.A. Landscape," Robert Mautner, *Artweek*, Nov 13, 1976.

COLLECTIONS Corcoran Gall. of Art, Wash., D.C.; IMP/GEH, Rochester; Mus. of Fine Arts, Houston, Tex.; MOMA, NYC; Norton Simon Mus., Pasadena, Calif.; Seagram Cllctn., NYC; Seattle Art Commission, Wash.; Univ. of Calif., Davis; Univ. of Kans. Mus. of Art, Lawrence. Bibliothèque Nationale, Paris.

ADDRESS 255½ S Carondelet Ave, Los Angeles, CA 90057.

Gaylord Oscar Herron DESIGNER · CARPENTER · PAINTER · PHOTOGRAPHER Born April 11, 1942, in Tulsa, Oklahoma, Herron is a self-taught photographer influenced by Atget, Walker Evans, Henri Rousseau and Albert Pinkham Ryder.

Now a designer and builder of furniture, Herron was chief photographer for the University of Tulsa, Oklahoma, in 1977–78. He was a feature reporter for KOTU-TV, Tulsa, in 1969–74 and a feature photographer for the *Tulsa Tribune* in 1966–69.

Herron won a Brotherhood Award from the National Conference of Christians and Jews in 1970. In addition to doing photography, he also paints and writes poetry.

Herron has worked in all photographic formats, using mostly black-and-white, but recently he switched to Fotomat processing and simple plastic cameras and scrapbook presentation.

PUBLICATION Monograph: *Vagabond*, 1975.

ADDRESS 106 E 25 St, Tulsa, OK 74114.

Sir John Herschel ASTRONOMER · MATHEMATICIAN · SCIENTIST Born March 7, 1792, in Slough, near Windsor, England, Herschel died May 11, 1871 in Collingwood, Kent, England. His father,

Sir William Herschel (1738–1822) was an astronomer and inventor, and his aunt, Caroline Lucretia Herschel (1750–1848), was also an astronomer. Sir John studied at Cambridge University from 1809 to 1813, specializing in mathematics. He also studied law briefly.

Herschel taught mathematics at Cambridge 1815–16, then became his father's assistant in 1817 and carried on Sir William's work. In his later years he was appointed Master of the Mint (1850–56), and was scientific and technical director of the Great Exhibition of 1851 in London.

Herschel co-founded the Analytical Society of Cambridge (1812) and the Royal Astronomy Society, London (1820). He was secretary of the latter in 1824–27. Herschel won the Copley Medal of the Royal Society in 1821, the Gold Medal of the Royal Astronomical Society in 1824 and the Lalande Prize of the Paris Academy of Sciences in 1825. He was knighted in 1831 and earned a baronetcy about 1839.

Sir John discovered the use of alkaline hyposulphates of soda in 1819 and realized their application to photography when he heard of Daguerre's and Talbot's work in 1839. He published important studies on the subject of photochemistry in that year, and on February 20, 1840, he read a paper on his work before the Royal Society. Herschel is also reported to be the first to use the term "photography," in 1839, and conducted the first experiments on the effect of the color spectrum on photographic emulsion in 1840.

As an astronomer, Herschel's cataloguing of stars and the accurate information he gathered on multiple stars have been among astronomy's most significant contributions. He wrote numerous papers and catalogs for professional journals and societies.

PUBLICATIONS Books: *Outlines of Astronomy*, 1849; *Results of Astronomical Observations, Made During the Years 1834–38 at the Cape of Good Hope*, 1847.

Benjamin Hertzberg PHOTOGRAPHER Born August 29, 1910, in Richmond, Virginia, Hertzberg received an AB in 1931 from Cornell University, Ithaca, New York, and an MBA from the Harvard Graduate School of Business Administration, Cambridge, Massachusetts, in 1933.

Hertzberg has focused on photography full time since 1973. From 1933 to 1972 he was president of Champale, Inc., and treasurer of the U.S. Brewers Association from 1965 to 1972.

Using only black-and-white, Hertzberg produces photo essays "documenting the human condition."

PUBLICATIONS Anthology: *Family of Woman*, 1979. Catalog: *The Selective Eye*, 1977 (Herbert F. Johnson Mus.: Ithaca, N.Y.).

COLLECTIONS Harvard Univ. Carpenter Ctr. for the Visual Arts, Cambridge, Mass.; Lexington School for the Deaf, Queens, N.Y. (murals); Town Hall, Pound Ridge, N.Y. Bibliothèque Nationale, Paris.

ADDRESS 60 E 42 St, Rm 1514, New York, NY 10165.

Paul B. Herzoff *PHOTOGRAPHER · TEACHER* Born August 21, 1946, in Hollywood, California, Herzoff studied documentary social science and philosophy at the University of California, Berkeley, from 1964 to 1972. A self-taught photographer, he worked at the Associated Students of University of California Studio, Berkeley, with Dave Bohn and Roger Minick.

In 1979 Herzoff became an instructor at the California College of Arts and Crafts, Oakland, and he has been head of the Photography Department at the ASUC Studio since 1976. He was the studio's darkroom manager 1970–76, and was an instructor for the John Swett School District, Crockett, California, 1971–72.

A member of SPE since 1978, Herzoff won the NEA Photographer's Fellowship in 1972 and 1973.

Since 1977 Herzoff has done stereoscopic color photography—portraits, fantasy costumes, food sculpture, etc. Since 1973 he has also done commercial illustration and portraiture, and from 1970 to 1976 he did documentary photography.

PUBLICATIONS Book: *Roll Your Own*, J. Pallidini & B. Dubin, 1976. Periodicals: *Popular Photography*, Dec 1978; *Artweek*, review, Joan Murray, Apr 1975.

DEALER Foto Gall., 492 Broome St, New York, NY 10012.

ADDRESS 1420 45 St, #7, Emeryville, CA 94608.

Alexander Hesler *PHOTOGRAPHER* Hesler was born in 1823 in the United States and died there in 1895.

Initially headquartered in Galena, Illinois, he established a studio in Chicago around 1852— Hesler's Photographic & Fine Art Gallery.

A daguerreotypist, Hesler is most noted for his landscapes and for his portrait of Abraham Lincoln. He also made ambrotypes. It was Hesler's images of the Minnehaha Falls in Minnesota that inspired Longfellow to write the epic poem *Hiawatha*. The poet, who had never visited the falls, sent Hesler a signed copy of the first edition in January 1856 with his personal thanks inscribed within.

PUBLICATIONS Anthology: *Early Photographs & Early Photographers*, Oliver Mathews, 1973. Periodical: *New York Times Magazine*, Oct 25, 1925.

George M. Hester *PHOTOGRAPHER · ORCHARDIST* Hester was born September 1, 1925, in Wildwood, New Jersey.

Self-employed as a photographer in New York City, he also owns Heald Orchards and previously worked as an art director for Bonwit Teller in New York City.

Hester is a member of the Metropolitan Opera Guild and the Authors Guild.

Working in black-and-white and color, he does nude studies in his studio, often using family situations and children.

PUBLICATIONS Monographs: *Man and Woman*, 1977; *The Classic Nude*, 1970.

ADDRESS 171 W 71 St, New York, NY 10023.

Paul Willingham Hewson *PHOTOGRAPHER · GALLERY OWNER* Born May 31, 1948, in Feilding, New Zealand. Hewson is self-taught in photography.

Currently Hewson is director of Real Pictures Ltd, a custom color laboratory that also maintains a photography gallery and acts as facilitator for photographers wishing to publish photographic monographs or books. Previously he was assistant editor of *Photo-Forum* magazine from 1974 to 1977.

Since 1974 he has been a committee member of Photo-Forum Inc. Hewson was the recipient of a Queen Elizabeth II Arts Council grant in 1977.

COLLECTIONS Univ. of Queensland Art Mus., Brisbane, Queensland, Australia. In New Zealand: Alexander Turnbull Lib., Wellington; Auckland City Art Gall., Auckland; Manawatu Art Gall., Palmerston North; Waikato Art Mus., Hamilton.

ADDRESS Real Pictures Ltd, POB 7195, Auckland, New Zealand.

Varvara Hasselbalch Heyd *PHOTOGRAPHER* Born April 16, 1920, in Copenhagen, Denmark, Heyd studied photography at D'Ora Portrait Studio in Paris (1938–39) and at Uggla Portrait Studio in Stockholm, Sweden (1943).

She opened a society portrait studio, Varvara Foto, in Copenhagen in 1943, and a similar studio, Varvara, in Knightsbridge, London, in 1946. Heyd has belonged to Dansk Fotografisk Forening in Copenhagen since 1943 and has contributed to such magazines as *Berlingske Tidende, Panorama* and *Tidens Kvinder*.

PUBLICATIONS Monograph: *Menig 5277, Varvara*, 1944. Book: *Madeira*, 1955 (Ides & Caldendes: Switzerland).

REPRESENTATIVE Nordisk Foto Teknik, Lergravsvej 61, 2300 Copenhagen S, Denmark.

ADDRESS Grönningen 15, 1270 Copenhagen K, Denmark.

Ken Heyman PHOTOGRAPHER Born 1930 in New York City, Heyman received a BA from Columbia University in New York City in 1956. He studied with the anthropologist Margaret Mead.

Currently Heyman is a freelance photographer. After graduation from the university, Mead invited him to take pictures to document her fieldwork in Bali. Thereafter followed a friendship and collaboration of more than twenty years. After his initial work with Dr. Mead, Heyman began doing photo essays for *Life* as well as for other magazines. From 1958 to 1962 he was the New York representative of the Rapho Guillumette Agency. In 1963–64 he was affiliated with Magnum.

In 1976 Heyman was the recipient of the World Understanding Award, sponsored by the School of Journalism, University of Missouri, the NPPA, and Nikon, Inc.

PUBLICATIONS Books: *The Family of Children*, ed., 1977; *World Enough*, w/Margaret Mead, 1976; *They Became What They Beheld*, w/Edmund Carpenter, 1970; *Color of Man*, w/Robert Cohen, 1968; *The Private World of Leonard Bernstein*, w/John Gruen, 1968; *This America*, w/Lyndon B. Johnson, 1966; *Family*, w/Margaret Mead, 1965; *Pop Art*, w/John Rublowsky, 1965.

ADDRESS 64 E 55 St, New York, NY 10022.

Chester Archer Higgins, Jr. PHOTOGRAPHER Born in Lexington, Kentucky, on November 6, 1946, Higgins earned a BS at Tuskegee Institute in Alabama. His mentors are P. H. Polk, Arthur Rothstein and Romare Bearden.

Since 1975 Higgins has been on staff at *The New York Times*. In 1974 he received an NEA grant and a United Nations Medal, and in 1973 he won the American Graphic Design Award and the New York Metropolitan Printers Award. Higgins was the recipient of Ford Foundation fellowships in 1974, 1973 and 1972.

The photographer invented KULAKA, a mind game based on Egyptian theology (1978).

Using an unobtrusive style, Higgins attempts to document "the behavior of people and things."

PUBLICATIONS Books: *Drums of Life*, 1980; *Black Woman*, 1974; *Student Unrest*, 1969.

COLLECTIONS ICP, NYC; MOMA, NYC; Tuskegee Inst., Ala.; Vassar Coll., Poughkeepsie, N.Y.

REPRESENTATIVE Photo Researchers, 60 E 56 St, New York, NY 10022.

ADDRESS 575 Main St, Roosevelt Island, NY 10044.

Daniel W. Higgins PHOTOGRAPHER · PRINTMAKER · TEACHER Born March 1942 in Detroit, Michigan, Higgins received a BA in Anthropology (1964) and an MFA (1968) from the University of Michigan, Ann Arbor.

He has taught in the Art Department at the University of Vermont in Burlington since 1969. In 1973 he produced "Vernacular Art in Vermont," a visual documentation of shrines, murals and roadside art, sponsored by the Vermont Council of Arts.

His work combines photography and photo-offset printing. He produces portfolios and postcard prints.

PUBLICATIONS Monographs: *The Incredible Onion Portraits*, 1978; *The Forgotten Trash Can Photos*, 1975 (self-pub.).

COLLECTIONS Catskill Ctr. for Photography, N.Y.; Cornell Univ. Lib., Ithaca, N.Y.; Franklin Furnace, NYC; Half Moon Photography Workshop; Robert Hull Fleming Mus.; VSW, Rochester.

DEALER Patagraphics, Box 204, Winooski, VT 05404.

Michael Hiley WRITER · LECTURER Born in Halifax, Yorkshire, England, on September 28, 1945, Hiley earned an MA in English at the University of Cambridge in 1967.

Since 1979 he has been senior lecturer in the history of photography at Leicester Polytechnic's School of Art History. Prior to that he lectured at the same institution's School of Fine Art (1968–79).

Hiley is an associate member of RPS. His articles have appeared in *Creative Camera, Studio International, The Photographic Journal* and *History of Photography*.

PUBLICATIONS Books: *Bill Brandt: Nudes 1945–1980*, 1980; *Frank Meadow Sutcliffe*, 1979; *Victorian Working Women*, 1979; *Frank Sutcliffe, Photographer of Whitby*, 1974.

ADDRESS c/o Gordon Fraser Gall. Ltd, Fitzroy Rd, London NW1, England.

David Octavius Hill *PHOTOGRAPHER · PAINTER* [See plate 3] Born in Perth, Scotland, in 1802, Hill died May 17, 1870, in Newington. He attended Perth Academy and probably the School of Design in Edinburgh. Influenced by Fox Talbot's techniques, he was the artistic partner of Robert Adamson.

Commissioned to paint 474 ministers of the Church of Scotland in 1843, Hill sought out photographic assistance, and thus began his partnership with Adamson. He founded and was secretary of the Royal Scottish Academy (1830–69). A pioneer in lithography, Hill published a series of landscapes at age nineteen.

Hill and Adamson used calotypes and were especially known for the masterful form, composition and dramatic lighting of their portraits. They also photographed cityscapes, landscapes and architectural monuments.

PUBLICATIONS Monographs: *An Early Victorian Album*, Colin Ford, ed. & intro., commentary by Roy Strong, 1974; *Sun Pictures*, David Bruce, 1974; *Hill and Adamson Photographs*, Graham Ovenden, ed., intro. by Marina Henderson, 1973; *A Centenary Exhibition of the Work of David Octavius Hill and Robert Adamson*, Katherine Michaelson 1970; *David Octavius Hill*, Heinrich Schwarz, 1931; *Calotypes by D. O. Hill & R. Adamson Illustrating an Early Stage in the Development of Photography*, Andrew Elliot, 1928 (pvt. prntg., only 38 copies). Books: *Masters of Photography*, Beaumont & Nancy Newhall, 1958; *A Series of Calotype Views of St. Andrews*, 1846 (Edinburgh). Anthologies: *The Photograph Collector's Guide*, Lee D. Witkin & Barbara London, 1979; *The Magic Image*, Cecil Beaton & Gail Buckland, 1975. Periodicals: "The First Victorian Photographer," *Metro. Mus. of Art Bulletin*, Dec 1958; "David Octavius Hill," Heinrich Schwarz, *Complete Photographer*, no. 31.

COLLECTIONS Albright-Knox Gall., Buffalo, N.Y.; Art Inst. of Chicago; IMP/GEH, Rochester; Metro. Mus. of Art, NYC; Univ. of N. Mex. Art Mus., Albuquerque; Univ. of Tex., Gernsheim Coll., Humanities Research Ctr., Austin. In Edinburgh: Edinburgh Photographic Soc.; Edinburgh Pub. Lib.; Royal Scottish Mus.; Scottish Natl. Portrait Gall. In Glasgow: Glasgow Art Gall. & Mus.; Glasgow Univ. Lib. In London: British Mus.; Natl. Portrait Gall.; RPS; Science Mus.; Victoria & Albert Mus. Natl. Gall. of Can.

Douglas Hill *PHOTOGRAPHER* Born February 18, 1950, in London, England, Hill is the son of actor Arthur Hill. He studied at the University of California at Los Angeles in 1971–73 with Robert Heinecken, Darryl Curran, Jerry McMillan and Leland Rice, and at the California Institute of the Arts, Valencia, in 1973–74 with Ben Lifson.

Hill has been a freelance photographer since 1970.

He has belonged to Cameravision since 1977 (president, 1977–78) and the Los Angeles Center for Photographic Studies. The photographer, as of this writing is working on the Los Angeles Bicentennial Documentary Project, funded in part by an NEA grant.

Using large- and small-format color, Hill concentrates on the urban landscape, predominantly architecture, people and foliage.

PUBLICATION Periodical: *Camera*, May 1978
COLLECTION Seagram Cllctn. NYC.
REPRESENTATIVE Ufficio dell'Arte-Creatis, 44 rue Quincampoix, 75004 Paris, France.
ADDRESS 1400¼ Laurel Ave, Hollywood, CA 90046.

Paul Hill *PHOTOGRAPHER · AUTHOR · TEACHER · WORKSHOP DIRECTOR* Hill was born December 15, 1941, in Ludlow, England.

As of this writing he is a visiting professor at Sheffield Polytechnic and Derby Lonsdale College of Higher Education, both in England. He has also been director of the Photographers' Place since 1976. Previously he was a lecturer in photography (1974–78) at Trent Polytechnic. He was also a freelance photographer for various British and international publications and industries from 1964 to 1974.

Hill has been a member of the Arts Council of Great Britain since 1978 and is also a member of the Society of Industrial Artists. In 1967 he was named Midland Photographer of the Year. Hill has also lectured on three BBC-TV programs: "Exploring Photography" (1978–79); "Grass is Greener" (1977); and a profile of Paul Strand on "Arena" (1976).

PUBLICATIONS Books: *Dialogue with Photography*, w/Thomas Cooper, 1979; *Fotografie als Kunst*, Floris Neusüss, ed., 1979; *Three Perspectives on Photography*, w/A. Kelly & J. Tagg, 1979; *Exploring Photography*, Bryn Campbell, 1978. Periodicals: *Printletter*, Jan 1978; *British Journal of Photography Annual*, 1978, 1970; *U.S. Camera Annual*, 1977; *Camera 35*, Nov 1977;

Fotografi, Apr 1976; *Camera*, Aug 1976; *Creative Camera*, Apr 1975.
COLLECTIONS VSW, Rochester. Bibliothèque Nationale, Paris; Mus. of Modern Art, Stockholm. In England: Arts Council of Great Britain, London; British Council, London; East Midlands Arts Assoc., Loughborough; Graves Art Gall., Sheffield; West Midlands Arts Assoc., Stafford; Victoria & Albert Mus., London.
REPRESENTATIVE Photographers' Place, Bradbourne, Ashbourne, Derbyshire DE6 1PB, England.

John K. Hillers PHOTOGRAPHER [See plate 24] Born in Germany in 1843, Hillers died in the United States in 1925.

From 1871 to 1873 Hillers traveled with Major John Wesley Powell's survey of the Colorado River, first as an oarsman, then as a survey photographer in 1872. He continued to photograph on various Powell-led expeditions, and was later hired by the U.S. Bureau of Ethnology and the U.S. Geological Survey, working for the latter until at least 1919. His images were printed in various publications of the day.

Noted for his albumen prints of landscapes and Indians of the Southwest, Hillers also made glass transparencies, some of which were hand-colored. All were carefully catalogued, resulting in a body of work with great ethnographic value.

PUBLICATIONS Monographs: *"Photographed All the Best Scenery": Jack Hillers' Diary of the Powell Expeditions, 1971–75*, Don D. Fowler, ed., 1972; *Notes on Hillers' Photographs of the Paiute and Ute Indians*, Julian H. Steward, 1939; *Photographs Made by John K. Hillers of Zuni, Hopi and Navaho Country*, 188?. Books: *Photography and the American Scene*, Robert Taft, 1938; *A Canyon Voyage*, Frederick S. Dellenbaugh, 1926; *The Romance of the Colorado River*, Frederick S. Dellenbaugh, 1902. Anthology: *Picture Gallery Pioneers*, Ralph Andrews, 1964.
COLLECTIONS Boston Pub. Lib.; Denver Pub. Lib., Colo.; IMP/GEH, Rochester; L/C, Wash., D.C.; Mus. of N. Mex., Santa Fe; Natl. Archives, Wash., D.C.; N.Y. Pub. Lib., NYC; Smithsonian Inst., Anthropological Archives, Wash., D.C.; Univ. of Calif., Bancroft Lib., Berkeley; Univ. of N. Mex. Art Mus., Albuquerque; Utah State Hist. Soc., Salt Lake City.

Lewis Wickes Hine PHOTOGRAPHER · TEACHER · SOCIAL REFORMER [See plate 41] Born September 26, 1874, in Oshkosh, Wisconsin, Hine died November 3, 1940, in Hastings-on-Hudson, New York. The self-taught photographer studied sporadically at the University of Chicago, Illinois (ca. 1898), and at Columbia and New York universities in New York City, earning a master's degree in sociology at the latter in 1905. He was influenced by his friend and teacher, Frank A. Manny.

Hine taught botany and nature studies at the Ethical Culture School in New York (1901–1908), and prior to that held a variety of jobs as a laborer. He began the first of his many social documentaries in 1905, photographing the immigrants on Ellis Island. It was the first photographic documentary to combine text with story, and was published in 1908 by *Charities and the Commons* (later *Survey*), which hired him as a staff photographer. Hine was appointed official photographer of the National Child Labor Committee in 1911 to do extensive exploration of child labor conditions in the United States, and remained at that post until 1916. During World War I he served as a photographer with the Red Cross in Europe. Hine photographed the construction of the Empire State Building (1930–31), was chief photographer for the National Research Project of the Works Progress Administration (1936) and documented the Tennessee Valley Authority project.

Trained as a sociologist, Hine used photography as a documentary tool to inspire social reform. His early photographs were printed from gelatin dry-plate negatives in a 5 x 7 format; his later ones were silver prints of 4 x 5 Graflex negatives. Oblivious to danger, he hid notes of conversations with factory children in his coat pockets and kept careful records of all he observed. His documentation of child labor conditions was instrumental in the passage of child labor laws. Hine's work revealed both the horror of exploitative conditions and the dignity of work, as illustrated by his photos of the construction of the Empire State Building. He was published in many periodicals besides those already mentioned, including *Red Cross Magazine* and *Survey Graphic*.

PUBLICATIONS Monographs: *America & Lewis Hine: Photographs 1904–1940*, Walter & Naomi Rosenblum & Alan Trachtenberg, 1976; *Lewis W. Hine, 1874–1940*, Judith Mara Gutman, 1974; *In Ordering Use This Number 1756 Hine Photo Company*, Thomas F. Barrow, 1970. Books: *Lewis W. Hine and the American Social Conscience*, Judith Mara Gutman, 1967; *Skyscraper*, Naumburg, Lambert & Mitchell, 1933; *Through the Threads*, 1933; *Men at Work*, 1932, rev. ed., 1977; *The Human Cost of War*, Homer

Folks, 1920; *The Pittsburgh Survey: Findings in Six Volumes*, Paul U. Kellog, ed., ca. 1911. Anthologies: *The Photograph Collector's Guide*, Lee D. Witkin & Barbara London, 1979; *Photography Rediscovered*, David Travis & Anne Kennedy, 1979; *The Magic Image*, Cecil Beaton & Gail Buckland, 1975; *Looking at Photographs*, John Szarkowski, 1973; *Documentary Photography*, 1972; *Great Photographers*, Time-Life Series, 1971. Catalog: *The Lewis W. Hine Document*, intro. by Naomi Rosenblum, 1977 (Brooklyn Mus.: N.Y.).

PORTFOLIOS *Portfolio 1*, printed by Gerry Dartt, 1974 (IMP/GEH: Rochester); *Untitled* (2), intro. by Maryann Older, 1942 (Photo League: NYC).

COLLECTIONS Amer. Red Cross Headquarters, Wash., D.C.; Art Inst. of Chicago; Columbia Univ., Avery Architectural Lib., NYC; Detroit Inst. of Arts, Mich.; Exchange Natl. Bank of Chicago; IMP/GEH, Rochester; L/C, Wash., D.C.; Minneapolis Inst. of the Arts, Minn.; MOMA, NYC; Natl. Archives (WPA), Wash., D.C.; New Orleans Mus. of Art; N.Y. Pub. Lib., Hine Cllctn., Local Hist. & Genealogy Div., NYC; Princeton Univ., N.J.; Smithsonian Inst., Wash., D.C.; Tennessee Valley Authority, Knoxville; Univ. of Md., Baltimore County Lib.; Univ. of Minn., Social Welfare Hist. Archives, Minneapolis.

Sherman Hines PHOTOGRAPHER Born November 22, 1941, in Liverpool, Nova Scotia, Canada, Hines graduated from Brooks Institute of Photography in Santa Barbara, California, with a BPA degree in 1968.

Hines has been a freelance photographer since 1968.

A member of Camera Craftsmen, he was recently made a fellow of the American Society of Photographers.

PUBLICATIONS Books: *Nova Scotia: Lighthouse Route & Annapolis Valley*, 1980; *Atlantic Canada*, 1979; *Outhouses of the East*, 1978; *Nova Scotia*, 1975.

COLLECTION Photographic Arts & Sciences Fndn., Inc., Santa Barbara, Calif.

DEALER Keystone Gall., 1213 State St, Ste "F", Santa Barbara, CA 93101.

ADDRESS 2319 Brunswick St, Halifax, Nova Scotia, Canada B3K2Y9.

Alfred Horsley Hinton PHOTOGRAPHER · EDITOR Born in 1863 in England, Hinton died there in 1906. He studied painting with the artist John Peel.

After leaving school he worked in a London photographic materials warehouse, where he became interested in photography. By 1890 he was exhibiting his own images, and from 1888 to 1891 he edited the short-lived *Photographic Art Journal*. Then Ralph Robinson hired him to manage his Guildford Studios, and in 1893 he became editor of *The Amateur Photographer*, a post he held until his death.

Hinton lectured frequently and was an early member of The Linked Ring and the Photographic Salon.

A pictorialist, the photographer was most noted for his landscapes. He wrote extensively and did much to popularize pictorial photography.

PUBLICATIONS Books: *Kuntslerische Landschafts—Photographie in Studium und Praxis*, 1920 (Union Deutsche: Berlin); *Art in Photography*, Charles Holme, ed., 1905; *Practical Pictorial Photography*, 1902 (Hazell: London). Anthologies: *Pictorial Photography in Britain, 1900–1920*, Arts Council of Great Britain, 1978 (London); *Landscape Photographer*, no. 11, 1904 (London). Periodicals: "Methods of Control in Pictorial Photography," Apr 1904, "Combination Printing in Pictorial Photography," Feb 1904, *Photo-Miniature.*

Hiro (Yasuhiro Wakabayashi) PHOTOGRAPHER Born in Shanghai on November 3, 1930, Hiro attended the American Institute of Graphic Arts in New York City from 1956 to 1964. He studied with Alexey Brodovitch at the New School for Social Research (1956–58) and worked as Brodovitch's assistant in 1958–60. In 1956–57 he worked as assistant to Richard Avedon.

Currently a self-employed fashion photographer, Hiro was on staff for *Harper's Bazaar* from 1966 to 1974 (he started photographing for them in 1958). From 1963 to 1966 he photographed major opera singers for *Opera News*.

A member of ASMP and the Directors Guild of America, Hiro has won several awards: Society of Publication Designers Award (1979), Syracuse University's Newhouse Citation (1972), ASMP's Photographer of the Year (1969) and the New York Art Directors Club Gold Medal Award (1968).

PUBLICATIONS Anthologies: *The History of Fashion Photography*, Nancy Hall-Duncan, 1978; *The Magic Image*, Cecil Beaton & Gail Buckland, 1975. Periodicals: "Hiro," *Zoom*, Nov 1972 (Paris); "Hiro," Richard Avedon, *Camera*, 1965.

COLLECTION IMP/GEH, Rochester.

REPRESENTATIVE Norma Stevens, 1075 Park Ave, New York, NY 10028.

ADDRESS 50 Central Park West, New York, NY 10023.

Steven Hirsch PHOTOGRAPHER Born June 5, 1948, in Brooklyn, New York, Hirsch studied with Philippe Halsman at the New School for Social Research in New York City in 1971 and with Charles Harbutt in 1974.

As of this writing he was teaching photography at the School of Visual Arts, New School for Social Research and Parsons School of Design, all in New York City.

"Hirsch is best known for his work in a genre called 'street photography,' " writes Don Leavitt in *Popular Photography*, "which he describes as the recording of the spontaneous interaction of people with the man-made environment of the great city." Using mainly SX-70, he has also done a series on stuffed animals, displayed at museums of natural history.

PUBLICATIONS Anthology: *SX-70 Art*, Ralph Gibson, ed., 1979. Periodicals: *Camera 35*, Nov 1979; "The Instant & Beyond," Jim Hughes, *Popular Photography*, Jan 1979; *Popular Photography Annual*, 1978, 1977; "The Harbutt Workshop," Charles Harbutt, *Modern Photography*, Apr 1976.

COLLECTIONS New Orleans Mus. of Art; Polaroid Cllctn., Cambridge, Mass.

DEALER Bertha Urdang Gall., 23 E 74 St, New York, NY 10021.

ADDRESS 83-46 118 St, Kew Gardens, NY 11415.

Walter Hirsch PHOTOGRAPHER Born April 12, 1935, in Leningrad, U.S.S.R., Hirsch is a self-taught photographer.

Currently a freelancer, he is connected with the Bildhuset in Stockholm, Sweden.

Hirsch is a member of the Swedish Photographers Association and the Press Photographers Association. Named Photographer of the Year in 1979, he has been the recipient of artistic scholarships from the Swedish state in 1977–78, 1974 and 1968. He has also created films and radio plays.

PUBLICATIONS Periodicals: *Zoom*, Mar 1980 (England), July/Aug 1975 (Paris).

COLLECTIONS IMP/GEH, Rochester. Bibliothèque Nationale, Paris. In Stockholm: Fotografiska Muséet; Moderna Muséet.

REPRESENTATIVE Bilhuset, Birger Jarlsgatan 15, 111 45 Stockholm, Sweden.

ADDRESS Bergsrådsvägen 16, 12158 Johanneshov, Sweden.

Orval Hixon PHOTOGRAPHER [See plate 49] Born February 4, 1884, near Richmond, Missouri, Hixon got his first camera in 1898 through a sales gimmick promising equipment in return for selling bluing. He built his first darkroom from a pine organ crate. Years later he took night classes in drawing at Kansas City Art Institute, and he read, watched, listened and followed developments announced by national photographic associations.

His first job (1902) was as a printer's devil for *The Missourian*, the local newspaper. About a year later he moved to Kansas City and went into partnership in an advertising and printing business, during which time he was commissioned by the Union Pacific to record all their railroad lines in the state of Kansas. When the business dissolved, around 1906, Hixon apprenticed himself to Lyman Studebaker, proprietor of a successful portrait studio, for whom he worked until 1914, when he opened his own Main Street Studio. He briefly took on a business manager/partner, James Hargis Connelly, in 1915, and moved his studio to the Baltimore Hotel in 1920. Hixon also maintained branch studios in Liberty, Missouri, and Manhattan, Kansas, then moved his entire operation to Lawrence, Kansas, in 1930, and has remained there ever since. His studio is now in his home.

Hixon is a photographer of celebrities, and his approximately 37,000 images include an incomparable record of vaudeville performers such as Al Jolson, Ruth St. Denis, Eddie Cantor and Fanny Brice. Because he refused to relocate in Hollywood, he did not enjoy the fame of some of his counterparts until the recent rediscovery of his works. James Enyeart (*Main Street Studio*) described his work as "widely known and admired within the theater world," and "not dependent upon radical innovations. Rather, it is the result of the sensitive and intelligent application of conventional techniques." And John Tibbetts (*American Classic Screen*) wrote that the color-blind Hixon's glass plates "demonstrate the elusive union of the artist's brush and the mechanical fidelity of the plate. All of which accounts for the unique mixture of dream and reality in Hixon's best work."

PUBLICATIONS Catalog: *Main Street Studio*, James Enyeart, intro. by Joe Page, 1971 (Univ. of Kans. Mus. of Art: Lawrence). Periodical: "Coming to Light," John Tibbetts, *American Classic Screen*, Mar/Apr 1978.

COLLECTION   Univ. of Kans., Lawrence.
ARCHIVE   Univ. of Kans., Lawrence, KA 66044.
ADDRESS   2613 Harvard Rd, Lawrence, KA 66044.

Nicholas C. Hlobeczy   *PHOTOGRAPHER · CURATOR · TEACHER*   Born September 9, 1927, in Swissvale, Pennsylvania, Hlobeczy earned his BFA in Painting from the Cleveland Institute of Art, Ohio, in 1952. He was a friend and student of Minor White from 1961 to 1976.

Hlobeczy has been head of the Photography Department at the Cleveland Museum of Art since 1968. He also taught photography at Case Western Reserve University, Cleveland, 1969–73, and has taught private workshops since 1973. He coordinated photo workshops for Minor White in Cleveland from 1963 to 1966 and assisted White at two Hotchkiss, New York, workshops. From 1955 to 1967 Hlobeczy worked as a lithographer for Photo Litho Plate Company in Cleveland.

The photographer has won several awards at the annual May show of the Cleveland Museum of Art since 1952, and won first prize at Yolo International in 1964.

His silver prints detail nature, his aim being "the exploration of the creative process and a study of myself through the craft of photography."

PUBLICATIONS   Anthologies: *The Great West*, 1977; *Photography in the Twentieth Century*, Nathan Lyons, 1967. Periodicals: *Aperture*, 17:2, 1973, 17:1, 1972, 14:1, 1968, 11:2, 1964.

COLLECTIONS   Cleveland Mus. of Art, Ohio; MIT, Cambridge, Mass.; Princeton Univ., Minor White Cllctn., N.J.; Rochester Inst. of Technology, Rochester, N.Y.

ADDRESS   1796 Cadwell Rd, Cleveland Hts, OH 44118.

Rick McKee Hock   *PHOTOGRAPHER · EXHIBITION DIRECTOR*   Born December 13, 1947, in Roswell, New Mexico, Hock received his BFA in Printmaking from the University of Connecticut, Storrs, in 1977 and his MFA in Photographic Studies from the Visual Studies Workshop at State University of New York, Buffalo, in 1979.

Hock has been director of exhibitions at IMP/GEH, Rochester, N.Y., since 1978, and previously supervised book and framing sales at Light Impressions Corporation in Rochester (1977–78). He taught photography for the Inner College at the University of Connecticut in 1975.

Hock won a research grant from the State University of New York in 1980 and an NEA Photographer's Fellowship in 1979.

Using an 8 x 10 camera, Hock concentrates on landscape photography.

ADDRESS   51 B Prince St, Rochester, NY 14607.

Ernst Hoeltzer   *ENGINEER · PHOTOGRAPHER*   Born in 1835 in Thuringia, Germany, Hoeltzer died July 3, 1911, in Isfahan, Iran (then Persia). He learned photography in Germany about 1870–71.

Hoeltzer worked as an engineer in the eastern Mediterranean and Black Sea regions before becoming an employee of the Persian Telegraph Department, for which he worked from 1863 to 1890. After his retirement he lived in Berlin for a while (1897–1908), but returned to Isfahan, the city he had worked in for twenty-seven years, where he died.

The photographer's documentary work was concentrated on subjects in the area around Isfahan. "The themes of his photographs include portraits of eminent personalities in both Persian and Armenian communities ... carefully observed views of the historical monuments of Isfahan, scenes of local life and festivals and a series illustrating the crafts for which Isfahan was famous," writes Helmut Wietz *(Isfahan in Camera)*. The more than one thousand surviving plates taken between 1873 and 1897 are "characterized by his great capacity for both objectivity and technical excellence."

PUBLICATION   Monograph: *Isfahan in Camera*, Jennifer Scarce, foreword by Helmut Wietz, 1976.

Marta Hoepffner   *PHOTOGRAPHER*   Born January 4, 1912, in Pirmasens/Pfalz, Germany, Hoepffner studied painting, graphics and photography under Professor Willi Baumeister at Frankfurt/Main Art College in 1929–33.

A freelancer since 1934, Hoepffner taught photography privately from 1950 to 1975. She belongs to Bund Freischaffender Fotodesigner (since 1970) and Budesverband Bildender Künstler (since 1956).

PUBLICATIONS   Monograph: *Ausdruck und Gestaltung*, intro. by Willi Baumeister, 1947 (H. E. Günter: Stuttgart). Books: *Kunst kontra Technik*, Herbert W. Franke, 1978 (Fischer: Frankfurt); *Farbe, Ursprung, Systematik*, Harald Küppers, 1977 (Munich); *Die Kinetische Kunst*, Frank Popper, 1975 (DuMont: Cologne); *Solarisation*, 1956 (Der Grosse Brockhaus). Catalogs: *Marta Hoepffner*, intro. by J. H. Muller & Willy Rotzler, 1979

Hoepffner

(K. E. Osthaus-Mus.: Hagen, Germany); *Das Experimentelle Photo in Deutschland 1918–1940*, intro. by Emilio Bertonati, 1978 (Galleria del Levante: Munich); *Licht, Bewegung, Farbe*, intro. by Dietrich Mahlow, 1967 (Kunsthalle: Nuremberg); *Marta Hoepffner*, intro. by William Simmat, 1966 (Galerie R. Springer: Berlin); *Marta Hoepffner*, intro. by Adam Seide, 1965 (Galerie Dorothea Loehr: Frankfurt).

COLLECTIONS Bibliothèque Nationale, Paris; Fürstliche Kunstsammlungen, Vaduz, Liechtenstein; Mus. d. 20 Jahrhunderts, Vienna, Austria; Neue Galerie am Landesmus., Graz, Austria. In West Germany: Bauhaus-Archiv, Berlin; Fotohistorama Leverkusen Cllctn., Stenger; Fotomus., Munich; Kaiser-Wilhelm-Mus., Krefeld; Karl-Ernst-Osthaus-Mus., Hagen; Kunsthalle, Recklinghausen; Ministry for Culture, Wiesbaden; Mus. am Ostwall, Dortmund; Mus. für Kunst und Gewerbe, Hamburg; Neue Sammlung, Munich; Städt Kunstsammlung, Gelsenkirchen.

DEALERS Benteler Galls., 3830 University Blvd, Houston, TX 77005; Sander Gall., 2604 Connecticut Ave, Washington, DC 20008; Galeri Alvensleben, Arcisstrasse 58, D-8000 Munich 40, West Germany; Galerie Seebacher, A-6700 Bludenz, Austria; Galleria del Levante, via Spiga 1, I-20100 Milan, Italy.

ADDRESS Eichendorffweg 56/58, D-7993 Kressbronn, West Germany.

Thomas M. Hoepker PHOTOGRAPHER · EDITOR Born June 10, 1936, in Munich, Germany, Hoepker studied history of art and archaeology at University of Munich from 1957 to 1960.

As of this writing Hoepker was executive editor of *Geo* in New York City (since 1978), he was photographer/correspondent for *Stern* magazine in the United States (1976–78) and in East Germany (1974–76). From 1969 to 1973 he was a freelance photographer and film maker in West Germany, and from 1963 to 1968 he was a staff photographer for *Stern* in Hamburg, Germany.

Hoepker belongs to Bund Freischaffender Fotodesigner (since 1972) and DGPh (since 1969). He won the latter's Kulturpreis in Köln in 1964.

PUBLICATIONS Books: *Vienna*, 1979; *Sculpture Safaris*, 1976; *Berliner Wände*, 1975; *Leben in der DDR*, 1975; *Yatun Papa*, 1962.

COLLECTION Bibliothèque Nationale, Paris.

REPRESENTATIVE Woodfin Camp Associates, 415 Madison Ave, New York, NY 10017.

ADDRESS 250 E 63 St, New York, NY 10021.

Evelyn Hofer PHOTOGRAPHER Born in Germany, Hofer learned photography by serving as apprentice in two commercial studios in Switzerland.

In 1947 she came to the United States and began working as a fashion photographer for *Harper's Bazaar* under Alexey Brodovitch. She later worked for *Vogue*. Her collaboration with Mary McCarthy on the book *The Stones of Florence* led to other books on famous cities of the world.

PUBLICATIONS Books: *The Bayous*, Peter S. Feibleman, 1973; *The World of Turner*, Diana Hirsh, 1969; *Barbarian Europe*, Gerald Simons, 1968; *The District of Columbia*, 1968; *Age of Kings*, Charles Blitzer, 1967; *Dublin: A Portrait*, V. S. Pritchett, 1967; *The Evidence of Washington*, William Walton, 1966; *New York Proclaimed*, V. S. Pritchett, 1965; *The Presence of Spain*, James Morris, 1964; *London Perceived*, V. S. Pritchett, 1962; *The Stones of Florence*, Mary McCarthy, 1959. Anthologies: *The Photograph Collector's Guide*, Lee D. Witkin & Barbara London, 1979; *Color*, Time-Life Series, 1970.

COLLECTIONS Indiana Univ. Art Mus., Bloomington; Metro. Mus. of Art, NYC; Smith Coll. Mus. of Art, Northhampton, Mass.

DEALER Witkin Gall., 41 E 57 St, New York, NY 10022.

ADDRESS 55 Bethune St, 1005-D, New York, NY 10014.

Oskar Hofmeister PHOTOGRAPHER Hofmeister was born (1869) and died (1937) in Hamburg, Germany. His brother Theodor was also a photographer.

First employed as a secretary of the county court, Hofmeister took up photography with his brother in 1895. Their careers followed a parallel course, except that Oskar was not involved with the production of Theodor's two booklets on printing techniques.

See Theodor Hofmeister

Theodor Hofmeister PHOTOGRAPHER Hofmeister was born and died in Hamburg, Germany (1868–1943). His brother Oskar was also a photographer.

First employed as a wholesale merchant, he took up photography in 1895. Along with his brother they produced their first exhibit the following year, and in 1902 Theodor began teaching photography.

Hofmeister belonged to Die Gesellschaft zur Forderung die Amateur Photographie. Until 1914 he and his brother were at the center of the Hamburg school of photography.

Working chiefly with gum-bichromate prints, Theodor and Oskar took views of landscapes, fishermen, the seashore and other genre scenes. In their earliest days they produced postcards, then carbon pigment prints. Later Theodor handled most of the printing and Oskar made the exposures, although they always discussed compositions together.

PUBLICATIONS Anthologies: *Pictorial Photography in Britain, 1900–1920*, Arts Council of Great Britain, 1978; *Camera Work: A Critical Anthology*, Jonathan Green, ed., 1973; *Early Photographs & Early Photographers*, Oliver Mathews, 1973. Periodical: *Camera Work*, July 1904.

COLLECTIONS In Germany: Dresden Kupferstichkabinette; Hamburg Kunsthalle; Kaiser Wilhelm Mus., Krefeld.

Jacob Holdt AUTHOR · PHOTOGRAPHER Born in Copenhagen, Denmark, on April 29, 1947, Holdt took up photography while vagabonding in America. He documented his five-year trip through the States, with particular emphasis on black communities.

In addition to his photographic production, he put together a five-hour multimedia show consisting of 3,000 slides, with music, interviews and commentaries, which has a permanent base and theater in Copenhagen, where it has been running since 1975. The production has also been presented by black Americans in European schools, institutions and theaters. In 1979 the show was made into a four-and-a-half-hour film to be shown in theaters and on television; the project was financed by a grant from the Danish State Television and by American Pictures Foundation, established for humanitarian aid to Africa.

Holdt's work, executed in 35mm and color, focuses on destitute black Americans, indirectly making a strong criticism of American and Western affluent society.

PUBLICATION Monograph: *American Pictures*, 1977 (Information Pub.: Copenhagen).

ADDRESS Købmagergade 43, 1150 Copenhagen K, Denmark.

Douglas Holleley PHOTOGRAPHER Born May 29, 1949, in Sydney, Australia, Holleley received a BA from Macquarie University in Sydney (1971) and an MFA from the Visual Studies Workshop, State University of New York at Buffalo (1976), where his major influence was Nathan Lyons.

As of this writing Holleley was a freelance photographer. In 1979 he taught workshops in Sydney and Melbourne, Australia. In 1978 he led workshops at Apeiron and the International Center of Photography in New York and at Artists for the Environment in New Jersey. Holleley was Visiting Picker Professor of Fine Arts at Colgate University, Hamilton, New York, in 1977.

A member of VSW and the Australian Centre for Photography, he received grants from the Australia Council/Visual Arts Board in 1974, 1975 and 1979.

The photographer's main area of interest is instant imaging systems, especially Polaroid SX-70 and 8 x 10, as well as color Xerox and Xerox Telecopiers.

PUBLICATIONS Books: *Bridal Sweet*, 1976, *The Ray Gun Catalog*, 1976 (self-pub.); *Far Fetched at the Visual Studies Workshop*, 1976; *A Passing Show*, 1973 (Macquarie Univ.: Sydney, Australia). Anthologies: *SX-70 Art*, 1979; *Australian Photographers*, 1979 (Philip Morris Cllctn.: Canberra, Australia); *Australian Photography Annual*, 1976 (Sydney); *New Photography Australia*, 1974 (Australian Centre for Photog.: Sydney). Catalog: *Electroworks*, 1979 (IMP/GEH: Rochester). Periodicals: *Australian Photography Annual*, 1978; *Popular Photography Annual*, 1977.

COLLECTIONS CCP, Tucson; Colgate Univ., Hamilton, N.Y.; IMP/GEH, Rochester; VSW, Rochester. In Australia: Art Gall. of New South Wales, Sydney; Art Gall. of S. Australia; Australian Centre for Photography, Sydney; Philip Morris Cllctn., Canberra.

ADDRESS Rockcorry 1, Old Bathurst Rd, Woodford 2778, Australia.

Fred Hollyer PHOTOGRAPHER Born in 1837, Hollyer died November 21, 1933, in England. He was greatly influenced by the pre-Raphaelites, whom he met in 1860.

Hollyer established a studio on Pembroke Square, Kensington, England, which became a haven for artists and writers.

A fine landscape and portrait photographer, he is best known for his reproductions of paintings. In Hollyer's obituary the London *Times* wrote: "Hollyer stood to mass reproduction in the relation of the 'private press' to commercial printing. . . . In workmanship he was extremely fastidious, giving personal attention to every stage of the process, so that the final result was not so much a photograph of a painting as a translation of its qualities in photographic terms." His work did much to popularize the paintings of such pre-Raphaelites as Rossetti, Albert Moore, Sir W. B. Richmond, Burne-Jones and Watts.

PUBLICATIONS Anthologies: *The Invented Eye*, Edward Lucie-Smith, 1975; *Early Photo-*

graphs & Early Photographers, Oliver Mathews, 1973.

Wendy Holmes PHOTOGRAPHER Born October 21, 1946, in New York City, Holmes received a BA from Smith College, Northampton, Massachusetts, in 1968, and undertook special studies with Minor White at MIT, Cambridge, Massachusetts, in 1969.

As of 1979 she was resident photographer at Peters Valley, Layton, New Jersey (since 1976), and an instructor at the International Center of Photography in New York City. From 1973 to 1975 she was a freelance photographer, and from 1970 to 1973 staff photographer at Wave Hill Center, Bronx, New York.

Holmes won an NEA grant to coordinate the exhibition "Seven Photographers: The Delaware Valley" in 1976 and a New York State Council on the Arts grant in 1980 and 1970.

The photographer produces 4 x 5 palladium prints.

PUBLICATIONS Monograph: *Hudson City*, 1971. Book: *Brother Can You Spare a Dime*, w/ Susan Winslow, 1978. Catalog: *Seven Photographers: The Delaware Valley*, intro., 1979.

COLLECTIONS Addison Gall. of Amer. Art, Andover, Mass.; N.J. State Mus., Trenton. Bibliothèque Nationale, Paris.

ADDRESS Peters Valley, Star Rt, Layton, NJ 07851.

Robert Everett Holmgren PHOTOGRAPHER Born in Chicago, Illinois, on January 31, 1946, Holmgren attended Southern Illinois University in Carbondale, earning a BS in 1972.

A freelance photographer, he concentrates on "portraits of unusual people or normal people in unusual situations, confusing landscapes and close-ups blown up to twice the size of the subject."

PUBLICATIONS Periodicals: *Glass Eye*, Sept 1976; *Camera*, Aug 1974, Aug 1972.

COLLECTIONS Film in the Cities, St. Paul, Minn.; IMP/GEH, Rochester; MOMA, NYC.

ADDRESS 239 Cotter, San Francisco, CA 94112.

Thyra Holt PHOTOGRAPHER Born June 10, 1890, in Sindal, Denmark, Holt studied photography in her hometown about 1909, then for a short time in Dresden, Germany. She worked at the Munich photographic studio of Wanda v. Debschitz, who had a large influence on Holt's development as a photographer. She also served as apprentice for a year with Francis de Jongh in Lausanne, Switzerland.

Holt established herself as a photographer in Kolding, Denmark, in 1921, and from 1928 to 1958 operated a studio at Arnagerterv, Copenhagen, with Margrethe Madsen.

She is a member of the Danish Photographic Society, the Zonta Club in Copenhagen, and the Grundtrig Society in Copenhagen.

Primarily a portrait photographer, Holt and her partner photographed a number of authors, such as Pearl S. Buck and Rabindranath Tagore. She also created images of Danish manors and folk high schools.

PUBLICATION Book: *Minderige Steder Grundtvigs Liv*, 1954 (Denmark).

COLLECTIONS Den Permanente, Copenhagen; Royal Lib., Copenhagen.

ADDRESS Esthersvej 17, Dk-2900, Hellerup, Denmark.

Bernard Otto Holtermann COLLECTOR · MINER · BUSINESSMAN Born April 29, 1838, in Hamburg, Germany, Holtermann died April 29, 1885, in New South Wales, Australia.

Holtermann joined Australia's gold rush in 1858, thus avoiding military service in Germany, and spent years mining around Tambaroora, New South Wales, before he and his partners struck a large and lucrative vein in their Star of Hope mine. An enthusiast of the relatively new field of photography, Holtermann acted as patron to H. B. Merlin and Charles Bayliss. He moved to Sydney in 1874, where he had a mansion built for himself and from whose tower Bayliss created some famous images. In 1876 and 1878 he exhibited photographs at the Philadelphia Centennial Exhibition and at the Paris Exposition Universelle Internationale, respectively. For the two years prior to his death he served as a Member of Parliament in New South Wales.

In the 1870s Holtermann innovatively conceived of "ultra-large format photography." Andrew Hooper of the Royal Melbourne Institute of Technology has written: "He may be remembered as a visionary in the development of photography in Australia (perhaps the world). He liked the art of photography for its own sake, yet realized its great 'documentary possibilities.' Photographs from the Holtermann Collection are probably the most comprehensive photographic coverage of a community in the nineteenth century ever done."

PUBLICATIONS Books: *Gold and Silver: An Album of Hill End and Gulgong Photographs from the Holtermann Collection*, Keast Burke,

1973 (Heinemann: Melbourne); *The Story of the Camera in Australia*, Jack Cato, 1955 (Georgian House: Austria).

ARCHIVE Holtermann Collection, Mitchell Library, Sydney, Australia.

Leo M. Holub *PHOTOGRAPHER · TEACHER* Born in Decatur, Arkansas, on November 25, 1916, Holub studied at the Chicago Art Institute in 1936–37 and at the California School of Fine Arts, San Francisco, in 1938–39.

He has been a senior lecturer in art at Stanford University, Stanford, California, since 1960, and before that taught drawing at the California School of Fine Arts (1956–58).

He belongs to the Czechoslovak Society of Arts & Sciences.

Holub works in straight photography, documenting people and places. He is interested in continuing the photographic traditions of the past.

PUBLICATION Book: *Stanford Seen*, Stanford Art Book #1, 1964.

COLLECTIONS San Francisco Mus. of Modern Art; Stanford Mus. of Art, Calif.

DEALERS Focus Gall., 2146 Union St, San Francisco, CA 94123; Smith Anderson Gall., 200 Homer St, Palo Alto, CA 94301.

ADDRESS 3663 21 St, San Francisco, CA 94114.

Jesper Hōm *PHOTOGRAPHER · CINEMATOG-RAPHER* Born October 5, 1931, in Copenhagen, Denmark, Hōm was the son of painter Paul Hōm. He served his apprenticeship at the photographic department of Gutenberghus Printers and Publishers in Copenhagen from 1948 to 1951.

Currently a freelance photographer, from 1963 to 1970 Hōm worked with freelance photojournalists in Copenhagen who, together, founded the Delta-Group. He freelanced in San Francisco (1959–61) and in Paris (1952–54), and operated his own studio in Copenhagen from 1954 to 1959.

Hōm was director of photography on the 1967 film *Quite Days in Clichy*. In 1969 he directed, wrote and photographed his own feature film, *Smile Emil*, for which he won the Danish Film Institute award for directing and camerawork in 1970.

For the past few years the photographer has concentrated on photojournalism and architectural photography, mainly in color. He also does studio portraits.

PUBLICATIONS Books (in Copenhagen): *For Kids Only*, w/Groenlykke, 1975, U. S. ed., 1977;

Glaedespiger, Rosenkild & Bagger, 1975; *What a Child Needs*, Gjellerup, 1967; *Meet the Danes*, Rhodos, 1965; *Bravo Pjerrot*, Rhodos, 1965; *Roses Never Strike*, Fogtdal, 1964. *Say Cheese*, Mobilia, 1959 (Denmark). Periodicals: *Popular Photography Annual*, 1971; *Photography Year-book*, 1967.

COLLECTIONS Hamburger Bildstelle, Hamburg, Germany. In Denmark: Louis Paulsen Fndn., Copenhagen; Louisiana Mus. of Modern Art, Humlebaek; Mus. of Arts & Crafts, Copenhagen; Royal Lib., Copenhagen.

ADDRESS: c/o Brask, 12 W 69 St, New York, NY 10023.

Benno Homolka *CHEMIST* Born in Chrusteniz, Bohemia, in 1860, Homolka died in 1925. He studied at universities in Prague and Munich.

After graduation he worked for four years as an assistant at Royal Bavarian Academy of Science, then joined the Farbwerke vorm Meister, Lucius & Bruening at Hoechst am Main near Frankfurt. Originally engaged in the development of new dyes, he later began work in the photographic department with Ernst Koenig. Together they developed the Pinachrome color process, based on leuco dyes, which was unsuccessfully marketed in 1904 but set the stage for later work by Fischer and Siegrist and for modern color-coupler photography. Homolka discovered the sensitometer Pinacyanol in 1905, and in 1907 worked with leuco bases as color developers. He was the author of numerous articles on photographic developers, solarization and photographic emulsions.

PUBLICATIONS Books: *Photographic Chemistry*, 2 vols., Pierre Glafkides, 1960, 1958 (Fountain Press); *March of Photography*, Erich Stenger, 1958; *History of Color Photography*, Joseph S. Friedman, 1944; *Theory of the Photographic Process*, C. E. K. Mees, 1944; *History of 3-Color Photography*, E. J. Wall, 1925; *Lexikon für Photographie und Reproduktionstechnik*, G. H. Emmerich, 1910; *Book of Photography*, Paul N. Hasluck 1905. Anthology: *Photography's Great Inventors*, Louis W. Sipley, 1965. Periodicals: *Bild und Ton*, 1964; *Zeitschrift für Angewandte Chemie*, 1924; *Photographische Correspondenz*, 1922, 1907; *Photographische Kunst*, Apr 1903; *Poggendorffs Handbuch*, no. 6.

Klaus Honnef *MUSEUM CURATOR* Born October 14, 1939, in Tilsit, Russia, Honnef studied sociology with René König at the University of Cologne (1965). He was influenced by Eugen Rosenstock-Huessy, avant-garde artists and essays by Walter Benjamin, Siegfried Krakauer, Andre Bazin and Erwin Panofsky.

Honnef has been the curator for changing exhibitions at the Rheinisches Landesmuseum in Bonn, Germany, since 1974, and is currently a professor at the University at Kassel. Previously he was director of the Westfälischer Kunstverein Münster (1970–75) and chief of culture and entertainment at Aachener Nachrichten (1968–70).

Honnef is a member of DGPh, the Association Internationale des Critiques d'Art, the Internationale Kunstausstellungsleiter Tagung and the International Council of Museums.

PUBLICATIONS Book: *Eisenstaedts' Germany*, 1980. Catalogs: *In Deutschland*, 1979 (Bonn); *Lichtbildnerische Wirklichkeiten*, 1979 (Vienna); *Eugène Atget*, 1978 (Bonn); *Werner Mantz*, 1978 (Bonn); *Wilhelm Schürmann*, 1978 (Cologne); *Germaine Krull*, 1977 (Bonn); *Gisèle Freund*, 1977 (Bonn); *Liselotte Strelow*, 1977 (Bonn); *150 Jahre Fotografie*, 1977 (Mainz-Frankfurt); *Sektion Fotografie: Einführung*, 1977 (Kassel); *Werner Mantz*, 1977 (Bonn); *Albert Renger-Patzsch*, 1976 (Bonn); *Kark Blossfeldt*, 1976 (Bonn); *Modellbilder*, 1976 (Bonn); *Hilla und Bernd Becher*, 1975 (Bonn).

ADDRESS Klaus Honnef, Kaufmannstrasse 41, D-5300 Bonn 1, Germany.

Brian Robert Hope *PHOTOGRAPHER · TEACHER · LANDSCAPE GARDENER* Born August 21, 1954, in Henley-on-Thames, England, Hope attended Banbury College of Art (1972–73), Trent Polytechnic in Nottingham (1973–75) and Derby College of Art (1975–76), all in England. His major influences were Thomas Cooper, Paul Hill, Ray Moore and John Blakemore.

As of this writing he was teaching photography at West Oxfordshire Technical College as well as doing freelance photography and landscaping. From 1977 to 1978 he did photography and carpentry in Hollywood, California.

Hope received grants from the Arts Council of Great Britain and from the Southern Arts Council in 1977.

Working in 35mm and 4 x 5 formats, the photographer uses "the existing . . . circumstances and coincidences that surround us to determine the pictures, [with] quality of light a primary consideration."

PUBLICATION Periodical: *Creative Camera*, Nov 1977.

Godfrey Thurston Hopkins *PHOTOJOURNALIST* Born April 16, 1913, in London, England, Hopkins trained as a graphic illustrator at Brigh-

ton School of Art in Brighton, England, during the 1930s.

After leaving school he worked in London as a staff photographer for *Picture Post*, and later freelanced for the British and European press. Since retiring from photojournalism Hopkins has devoted his time exclusively to painting.

PUBLICATION Monograph: *Thurston Hopkins*, 1977 (Arts Council of Great Britain).

COLLECTIONS In London: Arts Council of Great Britain Clltn.; Victoria & Albert Mus.

REPRESENTATIVE Folkwang, 43 Essen-Werden, Abtel, Germany.

ADDRESS Cambridge Lodge, London Rd, Uckfield, E. Sussex, England TN22-1HA.

(Henry) Thomas Hopkinson *WRITER · TEACHER* Born April 19, 1905, in Manchester, England, Sir Thomas earned his BA in 1927 and his MA in 1930 from Pembroke College, Oxford, England.

He directed the Centre for Journalism Studies at University College, Cardiff, England, from 1970 to 1975, and before that was Senior Fellow in Press Studies at the University of Sussex, England, 1967–69, and visiting professor of journalism at the University of Minnesota, Minneapolis, 1968–69. He was director for Africa, International Press Institute (1962–66); editor of *Drum* magazine in South Africa (1958–61); feature editor of the *News Chronicle* (1954–56); and editor of *Picture Post*, 1940–50, and *Lilliput*, 1941–46.

Hopkinson was knighted in 1978 and in 1978 he was named an Honorary Fellow of Pembroke College and Honorary Professor Fellow at University College.

Hopkinson writes and edits photographic magazines and books.

PUBLICATIONS Books: *David Hurn, Photographs 1956–76*, 1979; *Bert Hardy, Photojournalist*, 1975; *Picture Post, 1938–50*, ed., 1970, repr. 1979 (Treasures of RPS: London); *South Africa*, 1964, repr. 1969.

ADDRESS 6 Marine Parade, Penarth, S Glamorgan, United Kingdom.

Emil Otto Hoppé *PHOTOGRAPHER · BANKER · WRITER* Born in Munich in 1878, Hoppé died in 1972. He was educated in Vienna.

A banker with the Lombard Bank, London, in about 1900–1907, Hoppé first established a London studio in 1907, then another, larger one in 1913, where he remained until 1933. Hoppé was a world traveler and was an official representative of Great Britain at the International Exhibition at Dresden in 1909.

He was a founding member of the London Salon of Photography in 1910 and became a member of RPS in 1903. Hoppé was also a graphic artist, whose black-and-white drawings frequently appeared in magazines.

He chiefly made portraits and travel views with a reflex camera, working in silver and platinum prints. Although he used soft focus and retouched his work, the aesthetic qualities of his portraits went beyond the sentimental approach of most of the work of his day.

PUBLICATIONS Monograph: *Camera Portraits by E. O. Hoppé,* Terence Pepper, 1978 (Natl. Portrait Gall.: London). Books: *Hundred Thousand Exposures,* intro. by Cecil Beaton, 1945 (Focal Press: London); *The London of George VI,* 1937; *A Camera on Unknown London,* 1936 (Dent: London); *The Image of London,* 1935 (Chatto & Windus: London); *Round the World with a Camera,* 1934 (Hutchinson: London); *London,* 1932 (Medici Society: London); *The Fifth Continent* [Australia], 1931; *Deutsche Arbeit: Bilder von Wiederaufstieg Deutschlands,* 1930 (Ullstein: Berlin); *Romantik der Kleinstadt,* ca. 1929; *The United States of America,* 1927, U.S. ed. entitled *Romantic America,* 1927; *London Types Taken from Life,* Wm. P. Ridge, 1926; *Picturesque Great Britain,* intro. by Chas. F. G. Masterman, 1926; *In Gipsy Camp and Royal Palace,* 1924; *The Book of Fair Women,* intro. by Richard King, 1922; *Taken from Life,* w/J. D. Beresford, 1922 (Collins: London); *Gods of Modern Grub Street,* Arthur St. John Adcock, 1913 (Sampson Low, Marston: London); *Studies from the Russian Ballet,* 1911. Anthologies: *The Photograph Collector's Guide,* Lee D. Witkin & Barbara London, 1979; *Pictorial Photography of Britain 1900–1920,* Arts Council of Great Britain, 1978; *The Magic Image,* Cecil Beaton & Gail Buckland, 1975; *Creative Photography,* Helmut Gernsheim, 1962 (Faber & Faber: London); *E. O. Hoppé and Others: Photography,* 1911 (London).

COLLECTIONS IMP/GEH, Rochester; Univ. of Tex., Gernsheim Cllctn., Austin. In England: Kodak Mus., Harrow; Mansell Cllctn., London; RPS, London.

Bruce David Horowitz YOUTH WORKER · PHOTOGRAPHER Born February 2, 1949, in Philadelphia, Pennsylvania, Horowitz received a BA in General Arts from Pennsylvania State University, University Park, in 1970, studying photography with Marc Hessel. In 1974 Horowitz earned his MFA in Photography from the Visual Studies Workshop, State University of New York at Buffalo, where he studied with Nathan Lyons and Beaumont Newhall.

Horowitz has been a youth worker since 1971 at the Nineteenth Ward Youth Project Convalescent Hospital for Children in Rochester. He taught in the photography department at Pennsylvania State University, University Park, in 1976–77.

A member of Friends of Photography and the Association of Child Care Workers, Horowitz won photography fellowships from NEA in 1975 and from CAPS in 1976.

The photographer's images are "about life, style, culture and the quality of people's emotional existence in America." He says that people present themselves to his camera "in a way that reveals much about their humanity and specialness."

PUBLICATIONS Catalog: *Photographs,* 1977 (Sheldon Art Gall., Univ. of Neb.: Lincoln). Periodicals: *Camera,* Oct 1971, Feb 1971.

COLLECTIONS Colgate Univ., Picker Art Gall., Hamilton, N.Y.; IMP/GEH, Rochester; MOMA, NYC; Univ. of Nebr., Sheldon Art Gall., Lincoln; VSW Cllctn., Rochester.

DEALER Visual Studies Workshop Gall., 31 Prince St, Rochester, NY 14607.

ADDRESS 274 Berkeley St, Rochester, NY 14607.

Horst P. Horst PHOTOGRAPHER Born in Weissenfels, Germany, in 1906, Horst studied art at Kunstgewerbeschule, an applied arts school in Hamburg, and in the studio of renowned architect Le Corbusier, with the purpose of becoming an architect. He switched career goals when he began studying photography with Hoyningen-Huené.

A freelance photographer, Horst has worked for Condé Nast publications since 1932. He became the chief photographer for *Vogue* in 1934.

PUBLICATIONS Books: *Salute to the Thirties,* 1971; *Vogue's Book of Houses, Gardens, People,* 1968; *Patterns from Nature,* J. J. Augustin, 1946; *Orientals,* 1945; *Photographs of a Decade,* J. J. Augustin, 1944. Anthologies: *Vogue Book of Fashion Photography 1919–1979,* Polly Devlin, 1979; *History of Fashion Photography,* Nancy Hall-Duncan, 1979.

ADDRESS 166 E 63 St, Apt 10B, New York, NY 10021.

P. David Horton PHOTOGRAPHER Born February 4, 1939, in Jackson, Ohio, Horton received a BFA (1962) and an MA (1964) from Ohio State University, Columbus, where he studied with Minor White and Peter C. Bunnell.

A visiting instructor at Pratt Institute, Brooklyn, New York, since 1977, Horton taught at William Paterson College, Wayne, New Jersey, from 1973 to 1978. He also was an assistant professor of art at Linfield College, McMinnville, Oregon (1968–70), and taught at Seattle Community College, Washington (1966–67), and Everett Junior College, Washington (1965–66).

A member of SPE, Horton won a CAPS grant in 1977 and a faculty research grant from William Paterson College in 1978.

His present work is large-format black-and-white photographs of "large scale abstract all-white constructed environments," while his work from 1976 to 1979 consisted of "dyptichs comparing semi-abstract high-key landscapes and interiors to altered landscapes and interiors."

ADDRESS   RFD #1, Wawayanda Rd, Warwick, NY 10990.

Frank Horvat   PHOTOGRAPHER   Born in Abbazia, Italy, on April 28, 1928, Horvat studied at the Lycée in Lugano, Switzerland, until 1947 and at the Accademia di Brera, Milan, Italy, until 1949.

He is currently a contributing photographer to the French *Vogue* (since 1963), *Glamour* (since 1958) and *Elle* (since 1958). He has also freelanced for *Harper's Bazaar* (1961–67), *Réalités* (1956–65) and *Life* (1954–56).

He was a member of Magnum Photos from 1958 to 1961.

In addition to still photography, Horvat has done documentary films for the French government.

His work consists of reportage, fashion, advertising and essays on nature. In the late 1950s Horvat was one of the first to introduce 35mm techniques to fashion photography.

PUBLICATION   Book: *The Tree*, John Fowles, 1979 (London); U.S. ed. 1980.

COLLECTION   Bibliothèque Nationale, Paris.

DEALER   Daniel Wolf, Inc., 30 W 57 St, New York, NY 10019.

ADDRESS   5 rue de l'Ancienne Mairie, 92100 Boulogne, France.

Eric Hosking   PHOTOGRAPHER   Hosking was born October 2, 1909, in London, England.

Since 1929 he has been a freelance photographer.

Hosking has been a member of RPS since 1930 and of the Institute of Professional Photographers since 1939. He was awarded an Order of the British Empire.

The photographer concentrates on all forms of wildlife, focusing particularly on birds. As of this writing he was experimenting with an infrared heat unit for photographing birds and insects in flight.

PUBLICATIONS   Books: *Wildlife Photography*, 1976; *An Eye for a Bird*, 1974. Anthology: *The Magic Image*, Cecil Beaton & Gail Buckland, 1975.

COLLECTIONS   Australian Mus., Sydney; Nature Conservancy Council, England; Royal Photographic Society, London; Singapore Mus., Singapore.

ADDRESS   20 Crouch Hall Rd, London N8 8HX, England.

Eikoh Hosoe   PHOTOGRAPHER   Born March 18, 1933, in Yonezawa City, Yamagata-Ken, Japan, Hosoe graduated from Tokyo College of Photography in 1954.

He has been a professor at Tokyo Kogei Daigaku (Tokyo Institute of Polytechnics) since 1975.

Hosoe is a member of Japan Professional Photographers Society and Photographic Society of Japan. He won the Minister of Education Award of Arts in 1970 and awards from the Japan Photo Critic Society in 1961 and 1963.

In addition to still photography, he produced and directed a 16mm black-and-white film in 1960, *Naval and Atomic Bomb*, and directed the segments "Judo" and "Modern Pentathalon" for the 1966 film *Tokyo Olympic Games.*

Working in black-and-white, often in high contrast, Hosoe produces abstractions of the human form and surreal landscapes.

PUBLICATIONS   Monographs (Japan): *Embrace*, 1971; *Ordeal by Roses*, 1971; *Kamaitachi*, 1969; *Killed by Roses*, 1963; *Man and Woman*, 1961. Books (w/Betty Jean Lifton): *Return to Hiroshima*, 1970; *A Dog's Guide to Tokyo*, 1969 (Japan); *Taka-Chan and I*, 1967 (Japan). Anthology: *The Photograph Collector's Guide*, Lee D. Witkin & Barbara London, 1979.

COLLECTIONS   IMP/GEH, Rochester; MOMA, NYC. Bibliothèque Nationale, Paris; Natl. Gall. of Canada, Ottawa; Natl. Gall. of Victoria, Melbourne, Australia; Nihon Univ., Tokyo; Tokyo Inst. of Polytechnics; Victoria & Albert Mus., London.

DEALER   Light Gall., 724 Fifth Ave, New York, NY 10019.

ADDRESS 5, Aizumicho, Shinjuku-Ku, Tokyo, Japan 160.

Sue Houle PHOTOGRAPHER Born in Lowell, Massachusetts, on November 27, 1940, Houle earned a BFA from Boston University School of Fine & Applied Arts, Massachusetts, in 1963. She also studied aerial photography in the Archaeology Department of Oxford University, England, in 1973. Houle names Tom Kelley as her major influence.

A freelance photographer, Houle belongs to ASMP (since 1973), the Hollywood Women's Press Club (since 1975) and RPS (since 1977).

Houle won a Dewar's Achievement Award in 1978, the Hollywood Women's Press Club's Carol Channing Diamond Award in 1977 and a Levin Foundation Exhibit Grant for her show "Africa Portraits" in 1969. She did a TV special, "Talk About Pictures," in 1975.

Houle does "anthropological photodocumentary work, with an emphasis on photographic analyses of tribal groupings." She also photographs personalities, animals, children and aerial scenes.

PUBLICATIONS Periodicals: "The Eyes of Modern Psychics," Oct 1979, "The Eyes of Ancient New Guinea," June 1977, "Amazon Images," Dec 1973, "Portrait Studies on Photographers," July 1972, "Africa Portraits," winter quarterly, 1970, *Petersen's Photographic Magazine;* "New Guinea Notebook," *U.S. Camera Annual,* 1977; "Images and Concepts," *Popular Photography,* Oct 1975; *Popular Photography's Women,* fall ed., 1971.

ADDRESS 9040 Harratt St, Los Angeles, CA 90069.

Suda Kay House PHOTOGRAPHER · TEACHER [See plate 143] Born January 31, 1951, in Duquoin, Illinois, House earned a BFA in 1973 from University of Southern California, Los Angeles, and an MFA in 1976 from California State University, Fullerton. She studied with Phillip Melnick at the former and with Darryl Curran and Eileen Cowin at the latter.

Currently a photography instructor at Grossmont College, San Diego, California, House has also taught at East Los Angeles College (1979), Los Angeles Southwestern (1977–79), Cerritos College in Norwalk, California (1977–79), Rio Hondo College in Whittier, California (1977), and University of California at Los Angeles Extension (1979).

A former president of the Los Angeles Center for Photographic Studies (1974–76), she is a member of SPE. House won an NEA photography exhibition grant in 1979.

PUBLICATIONS Books: *Time-Life Photography Annual,* 1980; *Alternative Photographic Processes,* Kent Wade, 1978. Catalogs: *Alternative Imaging Systems,* 1979 (Everson Mus.: Syracuse, N.Y.); *Approaches to Xerography,* 1979 (Los Angeles Municipal Art Gall.); *Attitudes: Photography in the 1970s,* 1979 (Santa Barbara Mus. of Art: Calif.); *Photographic Directions: Los Angeles, 1979,* 1979 (Security Pacific Bank: Los Angeles); *Untitled 11: Emerging Los Angeles Photographers,* Aug 1976 (Friends of Photography: Carmel, Calif.).

COLLECTIONS CCP, Tucson; Calif. State Univ., Fullerton; Los Angeles County Mus. of Art; Minneapolis Inst. of the Arts, Minn.

ADDRESS 8420 Fanita Dr # 38, San Diego, CA 92071.

Robert Houston PHOTOGRAPHER Born November 13, 1935, in Baltimore, Maryland, Houston received a BS degree from the University of Maryland. His major influence has been Gordon Parks.

Since 1979 Houston has been employed in Baltimore as both a staff photographer for *Metropolitan* magazine and as a film-making instructor for the Cultural Arts Program. He has also been a freelance photographer, working in advertising, editorial, illustration and fashion photography since 1968. In 1972, at the Boston Institute of Art, he was employed as an instructor of documentary photography.

A member of the Freelance Photographers Guild in New York, Houston was a recipient of an award from Eastman Kodak for photographic excellence in 1967.

PUBLICATION Monograph: *Legacy to an Unborn Son,* 1970.

REPRESENTATIVE c/o Black Star, 450 Park Ave S, New York, NY 10022.

ADDRESS 1512 Chase St, Baltimore, MD 21213.

David Howard PHOTOGRAPHER · TEACHER Born January 25, 1948, in Brooklyn, New York, Howard attended Ohio University, Athens, from 1969 to 1971 and earned his MFA from San Francisco Art Institute in 1975. He studied with Robert Frank, Jerry Uelsmann and Ansel Adams.

A freelance photographer since 1974, Howard was director and an instructor at San Francisco Center for Visual Studies, California (1976–79), and a visiting artist at San Francisco City College in 1975.

Working in black-and-white, often using multiple printing techniques, Howard explores the "objective reality of illusionistic perceptions."

PUBLICATIONS Monographs: *Perspectives*, 1978; *Realities*, 1976. Anthology: *Photography for Visual Communications*, 1976.

COLLECTIONS City of San Francisco, MOMA, NYC; Oakland Mus., Calif.; San Francisco Mus. of Modern Art; Univ. of Santa Clara, De Saisset Art Gall. & Mus., Calif.

REPRESENTATIVE Phillip Hardgrave, 232-B Cole St, San Francisco, CA 94117.

ADDRESS 49 Rivoli, San Francisco, CA 94117.

Graham Howe PHOTOGRAPHER · CURATOR · PUBLISHER [See plate 130] Born April 18, 1950, in Sydney, Australia, Howe received a diploma in art and design from Prahran C.A.E., Melbourne, Australia, in 1971 and an MA (1978) and MFA (1979) in Photography from University of California at Los Angeles.

Since 1976 Howe has been curator of the Graham Nash Collection, Los Angeles. From 1977 to 1978 he was a teaching assistant at UCLA. He directed the Australian Centre for Photography in Sydney 1974–75, was a research assistant at RPS in London 1973–74 and was an exhibitions designer for the Photographers Gallery London in 1972–73.

A member of SPE since 1975, Howe received a UCLA Art Council Scholarship in 1977 and a Ford Foundation Travel Grant in 1978.

His photography is concerned with the "ambiguity and multiplicity in photographic perception" and how they modify our own perception.

PUBLICATIONS Books: *The Graham Nash Collection*, 1978; *Two Views of Manzanar*, essay & ed., Ansel Adams/Toyo Miyatake, 1978. Catalogs: *Paul Outerbridge*, 1976 (Los Angeles Ctr. for Photographic Studies); *New Photography Australia—A Selective Survey*, 1974; *Aspects of Australian Photography*, 1974 (Australian Centre for Photography). Periodicals: *Creative Camera International Yearbook*, 1978; *Fotographie 5*, 1978; *Light Vision*, no. 3, 1978; *The Dumb Ox*, no. 6/7, 1977.

COLLECTIONS CCP, Tucson; Houston Mus. of Fine Art, Tex.; ICP, NYC; Los Angeles County Mus. of Art; Metro. Mus. of Art, NYC; Minneapolis Inst. of Arts, Minn.; MOMA, NYC; Newport Harbor Mus. of Art, Newport Beach, Calif.; Santa Barbara Mus. of Art, Calif.; UCLA Cllctns. Bibliothèque Nationale, Paris. In Australia: Natl. Gall. of Victoria, Melbourne; Tasmanian Art Gall. & Mus., Hobart, Tasmania.

ADDRESS 9358 Culver Blvd, Culver City, CA 90230.

George Hoyningen-Huené PHOTOGRAPHER [See plate 56] Hoyningen-Huené was born in 1900 in Saint Petersburg, Russia (now Leningrad), and died in Los Angeles on September 13, 1968. His maternal grandfather, George V. N. Lathrop, was the United States Ambassador to Saint Petersburg, and his father, Baron Barthold von Hoyningen-Huené, was chief equerry to the czar. A baron himself—although he did not use the title—he fought in the Russian counterrevolution after having fled to Sweden. He studied with Cubist painter André Lhote and was influenced by Steichen.

In 1925 Hoyningen-Huené started working in Paris with *Vogue* magazine and became their chief photographer. He was also a leading photographer for *Harper's Bazaar*, and moved to New York to work for it in 1935. In 1946 he went to Hollywood, serving as a color consultant on many films, such as *A Star Is Born*, *Les Girls* and *Heller in Pink Tights*, and achieving success as a fashion photographer for such renowned beauties as Greta Garbo, Katherine Hepburn, Marlene Dietrich, Sophia Loren and Ava Gardner, among others. In addition, he taught at the Edward Kaminski School of Creative Photography in Los Angeles and at the Art Center School in Pasadena.

The artist used an 8 x 10 studio camera. While his books focused on travel and architectural photography, he is best known for the glamour photographs he took of Hollywood stars and high society, wherein he often brought much sculpture, draperies and other decoration into play. His initial claim to fame rests on the work he did for the great fashion magazines. Orville Prescott, reviewing his book *Hellas* for *The New York Times*, writes that his photographs are "Magnificent, lovely as pictures and extraordinarily evocative in their capacity to stir the imagination."

PUBLICATIONS Books: *Baalbek, Palmyra*, David M. Robinson, 1946; *Mexican Heritage*, Alfonso Reyes, 1946; *Egypt*, George Steindorff, 1943; *Hellas: A Tribute to Classical Greece*, Hugh J. Chisholm, ed., 1943; *African Mirage, the Record of a Journey*, 1938; *Meisterbildnisse, Frauen, Mode, Sport, Künstler*, 1932 (D. Reiner: Berlin). Anthology: *The Magic Image*, Cecil Beaton & Gail Buckland, 1975.

COLLECTION IMP/GEH, Rochester.

Kurt Hubschmann
See Kurt Hutton

Arthur Freiherr von Huebl CHEMIST · WRITER · MILITARY OFFICER Born in 1852 in Hungary, Von Huebl died in 1932. He attended military academy and Technische Hochschule in Vienna.

First serving as an artillery officer, then as chemist of the artillery arsenal, Von Huebl went on to become director of the technical group in the Royal Military Geographical Institute in Vienna. He was responsible for the development of photogrammetry and stereophotogrammetry for map-making and topography, publishing numerous articles on the subject. His photographic inventions included work on the platinotype process and photomechanical reproduction (late 1890s), invention of the multiple gum printing process (1898), improvements on Thomas Manly's pigmented gelatin process, Ozotype (1903), and work on light filters (1921).

Among the many honors he received were honorary membership in the Royal Photographic Society of Camera and Photographic Clubs of Vienna, RPS and the Photographic Society of Florence. He also received the Voigtlaender Gold Medal and the Gold Medal of Photographische Gesellschaft in Vienna. A member of many famous national orders, Von Huebl rose to the rank of major general and was knighted by Emperor Franz Josef.

PUBLICATIONS Books: *History of Photography*, J. M. Eder, 1945; *History of 3-Color Photography*, E. J. Wall, 1925; *Lexikon für Photographie und Reproduktionstechnik*, G. H. Emmerich, 1910; *Die Dreifarbenphotographie*, 1897, rev. 1902, 1912; *Der Platindruk*, 1895. Anthology: *Photography's Great Inventors*, Louis W. Sipley, 1965. Periodicals: *Bild und Ton*, 1963, 1962, 1959; *Photographische Correspondenz*, 1932, 1911; *Photographische Mittheilungen*, 1894; *Photographic Times*, 1894; *Jahrbuch für Photographie und Reproduktionstechnik*, 1890.

Carol Huebner PHOTOGRAPHER · TEACHER Born September 28, 1947, in Minneapolis, Minnesota, Huebner received a BA in 1970 from Antioch College, Yellow Springs, Ohio, and an MFA in 1978 from Rochester Institute of Technology. She also served as an assistant to Robert Sobieszek.

Huebner is currently an instructor of photography and offset printing at William Paterson College, Wayne, New Jersey.

She has belonged to SPE since 1976. In 1976 she won an Aperture Publications First Place Award, and in 1975 she was given a Kodak Snapshot Award in Sacramento, California.

As a curator Huebner organized the shows "Small Press Books," at the University of Rochester's Rush Rhees Gallery, in 1979, and "Photographs by David Levinthal," at George Eastman House, in 1978.

The photographer works in large format, making 16 x 20 hand-colored silver prints. She also does research on 19th-century photographic history, including original research on the Thomas Brumby Johnston Album.

PUBLICATION Periodical: "East Meets West; Photography Current Trends," *West Art*, Dec 1978.

COLLECTION Nassau Community Coll., N.Y.

ADDRESS 20 N Moore St, New York, NY 10013.

Laton Alton Huffman PHOTOGRAPHER Born October 31, 1854, in Castalia, Iowa, Huffman died December 28, 1931, in Billings, Montana. He learned photography by assisting his father in the elder's studio (1864).

In 1878 Huffman went to Fort Keogh in Yellowstone Territory as an army post photographer, working there until 1882. He later set up a studio in nearby Miles City. He lived in Montana until his death.

On long exploring trips Huffman recorded life in the Old West, from the Indian, the soldier and the buffalo hunter to bull trains (freight wagons pulled by oxen). He also took portraits of notable Indians and even of Calamity Jane. He is particularly noted for his documentation of the indiscriminate slaughter of buffalo.

First using a stereographic camera that utilized 5 x 8 glass negatives, in the mid-1880s, Huffman switched to a single-lens camera with 6½ x 8½ format. Like many of his contemporaries, he used a portable darkroom tent.

PUBLICATIONS Monograph: *The Frontier Years*, Mark H. Brown & W. R. Felton, 1955. Book: *Before Barbed Wire*, Mark H. Brown & W. R. Felton, 1956. Anthology: *Early Photographs & Early Photographers*, Oliver Mathews, 1973. Catalog: *Fine 19th and 20th Century Prints and Photographs*, no. 242, Feb 1979 (Sotheby Parke Bernet: Los Angeles). Periodical: "Dimming Trails of the Old West," *New York Times*, IV: 28–29, Oct 23, 1955.

Diane Hopkins Hughs TEACHER · PHOTOGRAPHER Born in 1935 in Mesa, Arizona, Hughs earned her BFA from the University of Texas, Austin, in 1957 and her BS from Indiana University, Bloomington, in 1965. She studied at a University of Oregon, Eugene, workshop in 1968 with Brett Weston, Bernard Freemesser and

Merle Armitage, and at a Center of the Eye workshop in Aspen, Colorado, in 1969 with Paul Caponigro.

As of this writing Hughs was an Instructor of photography and art at Schreiner College, Kerrville, Texas (since 1975). Previously she was director of the museum school and curator of education at Wichita Falls Museum, Texas (1970–74); assistant professor of art at Southern Methodist University, Dallas (1965–70); crafts director/instructor for the U.S. Army Special Services in Italy and Germany (1962–64); an English teacher at Lincoln School, San Jose, Costa Rica (1962), and an art teacher in the Dallas public schools (1958–61).

Hughs has belonged to SPE since 1969 and the National Art Education Association since 1958.

Her work is in black-and-white, "basically straight, in the formal sense," and she also has produced a large body of work using the collage/grid format.

PUBLICATIONS Anthology: *Observations and Reflections,* 1972. Catalog: *Middle Tennessee State University Photographic Annual,* 1971.

COLLECTIONS Amon Carter Mus., Fort Worth, Tex.; Middle Tenn. State Univ., Murfreesboro; Permian Basin Oil Mus., Midland, Tex.

ADDRESS 709 Galbraith, Kerryville, TX 78028.

James Richard Hugunin PHOTOGRAPHER · CRITIC · EDITOR Born June 20, 1947, in Milwaukee, Wisconsin, Hugunin attended Art Center College of Design in Los Angeles (1971), earned a BA in Art from California State University, Northridge (1973), and received an MFA from University of California at Los Angeles (1975), where he studied with Jerry McMillan and Robert Heinecken.

Hugunin is the editor of *The Dumb Ox,* a quarterly art journal in Los Angeles which he co-founded in 1976. He also has taught art at California Lutheran College in Thousand Oaks since 1977, and has been director of the Graphic Camera Department at Mid-Ocean Motion Pictures in Hollywood since 1979. In 1979 he directed the Graphic Camera Department at Capitol Records in Hollywood, and in 1978–79 was a graphic arts photographer (special effects) for Robert Abel and Associates on the feature film *Star Trek.*

He is a member of the International Art Critics Association, Film Technicians Local 683 in Los Angeles and Associated Art Publishers in San Francisco.

PUBLICATIONS Periodicals: "Broken Mirrors and Dirty Windows," *Journal,* Sept/Oct 1979;

"Tarnished Meditations: Thoughts on Jerry Uelsmann's Photographs," May 1979, "Joe Deal's Optical Democracy," Feb 1979, *Afterimage: VSW.*

COLLECTIONS Franklin Furnace Archive, NYC; La Mamelle Video Archive & Microfiche Records, San Francisco; UCLA Art Lib., Special Cllctns. Other Books and So Archives, Amsterdam, The Netherlands; Royal Coll. of Art, Art Lib., London.

ADDRESS 901½ S Berendo St, Los Angeles, CA 90006.

Peter Hujar PHOTOGRAPHER Born October 11, 1934, in Trenton, New Jersey, Hujar is a free-lance photographer who is self-taught.

He won an NEA grant in 1980 and 1977, a CAPS grant in 1976 and a Fulbright Fellowship to Italy in 1962–63.

Most recently he has been working in a square format on 16 x 20 paper. His unmanipulated silver prints are portraits and nudes of artists, writers and friends, and he also photographs found objects.

PUBLICATIONS Monograph: *Portraits in Life and Death,* intro. by Susan Sontag, 1976. Anthologies: *The Grotesque in Photography,* 1977; *The Photograph Collector's Guide,* Lee D. Witkin & Barbara London, 1979.

COLLECTIONS Fordham Univ., St. Thomas More Chapel, Bronx, N.Y.; New Orleans Mus. of Art, La.; Princeton Mus., N.J.; San Francisco Mus. of Modern Art.

DEALERS Marcuse Pfeifer Gall., 825 Madison Ave, New York, NY 10021; La Remise du Parc, 2 Impasse des Bourdonnais, 75001 Paris, France.

ADDRESS 189 Second Ave, New York, NY 10003.

Diana Emery Hulick PHOTOGRAPHER · ART HISTORIAN Born in Boston, Massachusetts, in 1950, Hulick received an AB from Bryn Mawr College, Bryn Mawr, Pennsylvania, in 1971 and an MFA in Photography from Ohio University, Athens, where she studied with Arnold Gassan. She also earned an MFA in Modern Art and History of Photography in 1978 from Princeton University, New Jersey.

Hulick taught history of photography at Nova Scotia College of Art and Design, Halifax, Canada, in 1979, and she taught photography at the University of Manitoba, Winnipeg, Canada, in 1975. She instituted and developed a photography program at Stephen's College in Columbia, Missouri, during 1973–76.

She is a member of SPE and CAA. In 1979 she won a McCormick Fellowship from Princeton, and in 1978 and 1979 she was awarded Spears Dissertation Research grants.

Hulick works with 35mm color slides and hand-painted color Xerox collages that combine words and images. She has done research in the general history of photography with a special interest in Diane Arbus, and she has also studied archival preservation and conservation.

PUBLICATION   Book: *El Quatre Gats, Art in Barcelona Around 1900*, contributor, 1978.

COLLECTIONS   Ohio Univ., Athens; Photoworks, Boston, Mass.; Shado Gall., Ore.; Stephens Coll., Columbia, Mo.

ADDRESS   Dept of Art & Archaeology, Princeton Univ., Princeton, NJ 08544.

John Humble   PHOTOGRAPHER · TEACHER
Born February 24, 1944, in Washington, D.C., Humble received his BA in Philosophy in 1970 from University of Maryland, College Park, and his MFA in Photography in 1972 from the San Francisco Art Institute, California.

Humble is a photography instructor at University of California, Los Angeles Extension (since 1979), Santa Monica College, California (since 1978), Fullerton College, California (since 1977), and California State University, Long Beach (since 1976). He also taught photography at California State University, Los Angeles, in 1976.

A member of SPE, Visual Studies Workshop and the San Francisco Art Institute, Humble won an NEA Photography Survey Grant in 1979 to work on the Los Angeles Documentary Project.

Humble works in a documentary style, printing 4 x 5 Ektachrome on Cibachrome paper.

COLLECTIONS   Corcoran Gall. of Art, Wash., D.C.; Indiana State Univ., Terre Haute; L/C, Wash., D.C.; Smithsonian Inst., Wash., D.C.

ADDRESS   3781 Boise Ave, Los Angeles, CA 90066.

Richard (Sandy) Hume   PHOTOGRAPHER ·
TEACHER   Born March 5, 1946, in Boulder, Colorado, Hume received a BA in Political Science (1973) and an MFA (1975) from the University of Colorado, Boulder.

A photography instructor at the University of Colorado, Denver, since 1978, he taught photography at the school's Boulder campus from 1974 to 1977.

Hume has belonged to SPE since 1975. He was the recipient of NEA fellowships in 1978 and 1976 and of a Guggenheim Fellowship in 1977–78.

PUBLICATIONS   Anthologies: *Mirrors and Windows*, 1978; *Self-Portrayal*, 1978. Catalogs: *Pe-*

culiar to Photography, 1977 (Univ. of N. Mex.: Albuquerque); *Flash*, 1977 (Miami-Dade Community Coll.). Periodicals: *Afterimage: VSW*, summer 1979; *Exposure: SPE*, May 1977, May 1976.

COLLECTIONS   Atlantic Richfield Corp., Los Angeles; Avila Coll., Kansas City, Mo.; CCP, Tucson; Ctr. for Arts & Humanities, Sun Valley, Ida.; Colo. Mountain Coll., Breckenridge; Corcoran Gall. of Art, Wash., D.C.; Denver Art Mus., Colo.; Free Lib., Philadelphia, Penn.; IMP/GEH, Rochester; Los Angeles County Mus. of Art; Md. Art Inst., Baltimore; MOMA, NYC; Oakland Mus., Calif.; Smithsonian Inst., Wash., D.C.; Univ. of Kans., Lawrence; Univ. of N. Mex., Albuquerque; Univ. of Northern Iowa, Cedar Falls; VSW, Rochester.

ADDRESS   1179 Ravenwood Rd, Boulder, CO 80303.

Robert Hunt   INVENTOR · PHOTOHISTORIAN
Born in Plymouth Dock, England, in 1807, Hunt died in 1887.

Beginning in 1829 and continuing into the 1880s, Hunt was a scientific writer, with interests in many fields. As early as 1840 he was writing about photography and conducting his own photographic researches. In 1841 he published the first English treatise on photography, and during the same year he delivered a paper to the Chemical Section of the British Association on the photographic effect of ferrocyanate of potash on silver iodide. In 1842 he devised the photographic process of chromatype, used in later photographic methods.

Hunt also experimented with the influence of light on chemical compounds and the uses of iron sulphate in developing photographic images, a discovery of great value to the later collodion process. In other writings of the 1840s Hunt described the Energiatype and Chromo-Cyanatype processes, and in 1844 his major work, *Researches on Light*, appeared. In 1845 he devised an actinograph along the lines of Herschel's, and in 1850 he delivered his paper "On the Present State of Our Knowledge of the Chemical Action of the Solar Radiations," an important historical account.

Hunt was a founder, in 1853, of the Photographic Society of London.

PUBLICATIONS   Books: *Quellendarstellungen zur Geschichte der Fotografie*, Wolfgang Baier, 1964; *History of Photography*, Helmut & Alison Gernsheim, 1955; *Historie de la Photographie*, Raymond Lécuyer, 1945; *Cassell's Cyclopedia of Photography*, 1911, repr. 1973; *History of Pho-*

tography, W. Jerome Harrison, 1887; *Researches on Light*, 1844, 2nd ed. 1854; *Popular Treatise on the Art of Photography*, 1841. Anthology: *Photography's Great Inventors*, Louis W. Sipley, 1965. Periodicals: *Photographic Quarterly*, Apr 1892; "Photographic Researches Before Daguerre," *Photography Year Book*, 1882; *Chemist*, vol. 5, 1844; *Philosophical Magazine*, 1844, Feb 1840 and 1840, passim.

Debora Hunter   PHOTOGRAPHER · TEACHER
Born June 16, 1950, in Chicago, Illinois, Hunter earned a BA in English Literature from Northwestern University, Chicago (1972), and an MFA in Photography from Rhode Island School of Design, Providence (1976), where she studied with Harry Callahan and Aaron Siskind.

Since 1976 she has been assistant professor of photography at Meadows School of the Arts, Southern Methodist University, Dallas, Texas. Previously she taught photography at Swain School of Design in New Bedford, Massachusetts, and at Rhode Island School of Design (1975–76).

In 1973–74 Hunter edited and archived the work of photographer Wallace Kirkland under a research grant from ICP in New York City.

PUBLICATIONS   Anthologies: *A Ten Year Salute: A Selection of Photographs in Celebration, The Witkin Gallery 1969–79*, Lee Witkin, 1979; *Women See Woman*, 1976. Periodicals: *Camera*, Sept & Aug 1975.

PORTFOLIOS   *R.I.S.D. Annual Photographic Portfolio* (group), 1976, 1975.

COLLECTIONS   Dallas Mus. of Fine Arts, Tex.; R.I. School of Design Art Mus., Providence; Wesleyan Univ. Art Mus., Middletown, Conn.; Witkin Cllctn., NYC; Yale Univ. Art Mus., New Haven, Conn.

DEALERS   Witkin Gall., 41 E 57 St, New York, NY 10022; Sander Gall., 2600 Connecticut Ave NW, Washington, DC 20008; Delahunty Gall., 2611 Cedar Springs, Dallas, TX 75201.

ADDRESSES   5811 Martel Ave, Dallas, TX 75206; Dept of Art, Meadows School of the Arts, Southern Methodist Univ, PO Box 296, Dallas, TX 75275.

(James Francis) Frank Hurley PHOTOGRAPHER ·
FILM MAKER · EXPLORER   Born October 15, 1885 (or 1890?), in Sydney, Australia, Hurley died in Australia in 1962. Unschooled, he learned photography from Harry Cave around 1905.

Hurley produced picture postcards with Cave until 1910, when he took over the business. From 1911 to 1912 he was the official photographer for the Australian Antarctic Expedition, led by Sir Douglas Mawson. In 1913, with the proceeds from a film he had produced *(Home of the Blizzard)*, he returned to the Antarctic to rescue Mawson, who had been stranded there. Hurley went on to film in Java, Australia's Northern Territory, where he recorded aboriginal ceremonies, and in the Gulf of Carpentaris. In 1914 he served as official photographer with Sir Earnest Shackleton's Antarctic Expedition and became trapped in Weddell Sea for a year before he, Shackleton and five others rowed 800 miles to South Georgia Island.

Hurley was made the official Australian war photographer around 1917, recording battles at Ypres, Menin Road and Passhenduck. During the next several years he traveled to Egypt, New Guinea, America and England. In 1927 he worked as picture editor for *The Sun*, a Melbourne newspaper, before heading for Antarctica again, this time with Sir Douglas Mawson's 1929–30 expedition. He later worked eight months as chief cinematographer for Cinesound Studios, where he made ten films and numerous documentaries. In 1939 Hurley headed the Australian Imperial Forces Photographic Unit. From 1943 to 1946 he worked as director of British Army Features and Propaganda, returning to Sydney in 1946, after which he toured Australia and wrote many books.

In 1943 Hurley received the Order of the British Empire.

A prolific film maker, Hurley produced, among others: *The Holy Land* (ca. 1943), *Siege at Tobruk* (ca. 1941), *Advance into Libya* (ca. 1939), *Pearls and Savages* (U.S. title, *The Lost Tribe*), *With Head Hunters in Papua* (which took eight months to hand-color) and *Siege of the South* (ca. 1931), *The Ross Smith Flight* (1918), *With Allenby in Palestine* (1917) and *In the Grip of the Polar Ice* (1917).

Always carrying his camera equipment with him, Hurley recorded subjects as far-ranging as the battle at Jericho (Arabia), in 1922, landscapes and aerial views. He traveled more than 250,000 miles to make his dozens of films, documentaries and still images, and he was widely exhibited.

PUBLICATIONS   Monographs: *Australia: A Camera Study*, rev. ed., 1961 (Angus & Robertson: Sydney); *Canberra: A Camera Study*, 1961? (John Sands Pty); *The Snowy Mountains*, 1961?; *The South Coast from Stanwell Park to Kiama, New South Wales*, 1961; *Western Australia*, 1953, *The Blue Mountains and Jenolan Caves*, 1952, *Sydney from the Sky*, 1952, *Queensland, A Camera Study*, 1950, *Shackleton's Argonauts*,

n.d. (Angus & Robertson: Sydney); *Pearls & Savages*, 1924.
COLLECTIONS In Australia: Natl. Archives, Canberra; Royal Melbourne Inst. of Tech.

David Hurn PHOTOGRAPHER·TEACHER Born in 1934 in Redhill, England, Hurn developed an interest in photography while studying at the Royal Military Academy.

Since 1973 Hurn has been head of the school of film and photography at Gwent College of Higher Education in Newport. In 1967 he joined Magnum Photos. Hurn has freelanced since 1955, his first major assignment being to cover the Hungarian revolution.

In 1979 Hurn was chosen to be a Distinguished Visiting Artist at Arizona State University, Tempe, under funding by a United Kingdom-United States Bicentennial Arts Fellowship program. He also received a bursary from Kodak of England in 1975 and an award from the Welsh Arts Council in 1971.

PUBLICATIONS Catalogs: *Catalogue*, Apr/May 1977 (Galerie Municipale en Chateau d'Eau); *Personal Views*, 1972 (British Council). Periodicals: *Zoom*, May/June 1977, Nov/Dec 1972 (Paris); *Amateur Photographer*, 150:24, 1974, 143:13, 1971; *Creative Camera*, Dec 1974, Apr 1971; *British Journal of Photography*, 121:48, 1974, 118:22, 1971; *Photography*, 13:4, 1958.
REPRESENTATIVE Magnum Photos Inc, 15 W 46 St, New York, NY 10036.
DEALER Fifth Ave Gall. of Photography, 6960 Fifth Ave, Scottsdale, AZ 95251.

George Hurrell PHOTOGRAPHER Born in 1904 in Cincinnati, Ohio, Hurrell attended the Chicago Art Institute in 1920 and assisted portrait photographer Eugene Hutchinson in 1922.

From 1960 to 1975 Hurrell was a freelance production and publicity still photographer for movies and television. Before that he was with Walt Disney Studios (1954–56), and was a staff photographer for the Pentagon (1942–46), which position he left to work for Columbia Pictures. In 1935–38 he worked for Warner Brothers; in 1932–34 he was with 20th Century-Fox while running his own studio in Hollywood (until 1934). Hurrell began as a freelance photographer for Metro-Goldwyn-Mayer Film Studios (1930–32).

PUBLICATIONS Monograph: *The Hurrell Style*, 1977. Anthology: *Dreams for Sale*, 1976.
PORTFOLIO *Hurrell*, 1979, intro. by Helmut Newton (Creative Art Investments: Los Angeles).

COLLECTIONS MOMA, NYC. Kobal Cllctn., London.
DEALER Creative Art Images, 10889 Wilshire Blvd, #1166, Los Angeles, CA 90024.

Ferdinand Hurter INDUSTRIAL CHEMIST Born March 15, 1844, in Schaffhausen, Switzerland, Hurter died March 5, 1898, in either Widnes or Manchester, England. His father, Alderman Tobias Hurter, was a famous artistic bookbinder. Hurter studied at Zurich Polytechnic, ca. 1864, and with Bunsen, Kirchoff and Helmholz in Heidelberg, where he gained his PhD summa cum laude.

Hurter worked for United Alkalai Company in England (originally Gaskill, Deacon & Co. in Widnes) from 1867 to 1898. He was appointed chief chemist and technical adviser in 1890.

Along with that of V. C. Driffield, Hurter's experimentation laid the groundwork for photographic sensitometry. Driffield and Hurter developed what is commonly called the "H & D curve." In 1881 the partners also patented an actinometer.

A Hurter & Driffield Memorial was established by RPS in 1915.
PUBLICATIONS Book: *The Photographic Researches of Ferdinand Hurter and V. C. Driffield*, W. B. Ferguson, ed., 1920, repr. 1974. Periodical: "Photochemical Investigations and a Method of Determination of the Sensitiveness of Photographic Plates," *Journal of the Society of Chemical Industry*, May 1890.
ARCHIVE RPS of Great Britain, 14 S Audley St, London W1Y 5DP, England.

Terry L. Husebye PHOTOGRAPHER Born in El Paso, Texas, on March 16, 1945, Husebye received a BA in American Institutions (1968), an MA in Photography and Graphics (1973) and an MFA in Photography (1979) from the University of Wisconsin, Madison. He studied with Cavalliere Ketchum at Wisconsin and with Van Deren Coke and Beaumont Newhall at the University of New Mexico, Albuquerque (1973–74, 1978).

Husebye was a visiting lecturer at the University of Wisconsin Art Department in 1979 and a graduate teaching assistant at the University of New Mexico in 1973–74. He worked on the Trans-Alaska pipeline from 1974–76. In 1971–72 he was photography coordinator for the Madison Art Center in Wisconsin.

Husebye belongs to SPE.

The artist prints large color photographs from medium-format negatives.

PUBLICATIONS Catalog: *Light and Substance*,

text only, 1974 (Univ. of N. Mex. Press). Periodicals: *Le Nouveau Photocinéma*, Dec 1976; *Camera*, Aug 1974; *35mm Photography*, spring 1973; *Popular Photography Annual*, 1973.

COLLECTIONS Art Inst. of Chicago, Ill.; Center of Photographic Arts, Chicago; L/C, Wash., D.C.; Madison Art Ctr., Wisc.; Minneapolis Art Inst., Minn.; Mus. of N. Mex., Santa Fe; Northwestern Univ. Lib., Evanston, Ill.; Pa. State Hist. Soc., Harrisburg.

ADDRESS 203 Alamo Dr, Santa Fe, NM 87501.

W. John Huss *PHOTOGRAPHER · TEACHER* Born September 11, 1942, in Hartford, Connecticut, Huss attended Dartmouth College, Hanover, New Hampshire, from 1961 to 1964 then earned his BA in Political Science from the University of Hartford, Connecticut, in 1973. He also studied at the Maine Photographic Workshop in 1974 with John Loengard. Huss has been influenced by W. Eugene Smith, Peter Gowland and Lucien Clergue.

He is currently president and director of the New England Photography Center, Inc., in East Hartford, Connecticut, and director of photography at Elmwood Community Center in West Hartford. Huss taught photography at the Connecticut School of Fine Arts, Wethersfield, in 1977–79 and in 1972. He has also done freelance photography from 1967 to 1979.

Huss has belonged to ASMP since 1972. He writes a weekly column on photography for the *East Hartford Gazette* (Connecticut).

His personal work is in black-and-white and centers around two themes—the figure and studies of motion and space relationships. He also does general commercial photography.

REPRESENTATIVE New England Photography Center, Inc., POB 18371 Charter Oak Mall, East Hartford, CT 06118.

Kurt Hutton *PHOTOGRAPHER* Born (and also known as) Kurt Hubschmann in Strasbourg, Alsace, in 1893, Hutton died in Aldeburgh, England, in 1960. He studied law at the University of Oxford, England, and was a self-taught photographer.

Hutton served as a cavalry officer during World War I and won an Iron Cross (2nd Class) for bravery at the battle of Verdun in 1918. In that year he left the service because of tuberculosis, and recovered at a sanatorium in St. Moritz, Switzerland. In 1923 he became a portrait photographer in partnership with Frau Engelhardt, and in 1930

started photographing for *Dephot* and *Weltrundschau*. In 1934 he served as a photographer for *Weekly Illustrated*, then went to work as a photographer for *Picture Post* in 1938, remaining there until the magazine's demise in 1957. In that year he photographed the Aldeburgh Festival and its leading figure, Benjamin Britten. He also contributed to *Photography Yearbook* and *Photography* magazine during the 1950s.

Working with a 35mm Leica and a Contax, Hutton was considered a "humanistic photographer." In *Creative Camera Yearbook*, 1976, Colin Osman stated, "Kurt Hutton was one of the few building a new concerned journalism; he brought to it integrity and charity."

PUBLICATIONS Monograph: *Birth and Life of a Foal*, 1972. Book: *Kurt Hutton—Speaking Likeness*, 1947. Anthology: *Picture Post 1938–1950*, Tom Hopkinson, ed., 1970. Periodical: *Creative Camera International Year Book*, 1976, Colin Osman.

COLLECTIONS Univ. of Tex. Humanities Research Ctr., Gernsheim Cllctn., Austin. Colin Osman Cllctn., London.

ARCHIVE Photography Collection, Humanities Research Ctr., Univ. of Texas, POB 7219, Austin, TX 78712.

Ut Cong Huynh *PHOTOJOURNALIST* Huynh was born March 29, 1951, in Saigon, Vietnam. His older brother, also a photojournalist, was killed while on assignment for AP in 1965.

Huynh has been with the Associated Press since 1966. He names the Vietnam war as his major influence.

A member of the Wire Service Guild since 1977, the photographer won a number of major awards in 1973, including the Pulitzer Prize. Some others were: World Press Photo Award, George Polk Memorial Award from Long Island University, Overseas Press Club Award and National Press Club Award.

Huynh's Pulitzer Prize-winning photograph was the moving image of several small children, one naked, all crying as they ran away from their burning, napalmed village twenty-five miles west of Saigon.

PUBLICATION Anthology: *Moments*, Sheryle & John Leekley, 1978.

COLLECTION Vietnam War Photo Cllctn., Asahi Shimbun Bldg., Tokyo.

REPRESENTATIVE Associated Press, 50 Rockefeller Plaza, New York, NY 10020.

ADDRESS 2505 Baltusrol Dr, Alhambra, CA 91803.

Philip Hyde *PHOTOGRAPHER* Born August 15, 1921, in San Francisco, California, Hyde studied at San Francisco City College (1942–43), the University of California Berkeley (1946) and the California School of Fine Arts, San Francisco (1947–50). At the latter he was taught by Ansel Adams and Minor White. He names Adams and Edward Weston as major influences and David Brower as his mentor.

Hyde has been a freelance photographer since 1950. He is a member of Sierra Club, Wilderness Society and Friends of the Earth. In 1962 he won a Merit Award from the California Conservation Council, and in 1951 he received the Albert M. Bender Award in Photography from the San Francisco Art Association.

Using large format, Hyde emphasizes the natural scene—landscape and details, with a concern for conservation. His early work was in black-and-white, but more recently he has been using color, with an emphasis on dye-transfer prints.

PUBLICATIONS Books (selected): *Alaska: The Great Land*, Miller & Wayburn, 1974; *Slickrock: Canyon Country of Southeast Utah*, w/Edward Abbey, 1971; *The Wilderness World of the Grand Canyon*, Ann & Myron Sutton, 1971; *Navajo Wildlands*, w/Stephen Jett, 1967; *Time and the River Flowing: Grand Canyon*, François Leydet, 1964; *Island in Time: The Point Reyes Peninsula*, Harold Gilliam, 1962; *Wilderness, America's Living Heritage*, David Brower, ed., 1961; *This Is Dinosaur*, Wallace Stegner, ed., 1955. Periodicals: *Darkroom*, Mar 1980; *Modern Photography*, Nov 1976.

PORTFOLIOS *There Was a River: Glen Canyon*, Bruce Berger, Aug 1979 (Northland Press: Flagstaff, Ariz.); *Mountain and Desert; Sierra Club Gallery*, 1973.

COLLECTIONS CCP, Tucson; IMP/GEH, Rochester; Oakland Mus., Calif.; Polaroid Cllctn., Cambridge, Mass.

ADDRESS Box 205, Taylorsville, CA 95983.

Scott Hyde *PHOTOGRAPHER* Born in Montevideo, Minnesota, in 1926, Hyde studied in New York City at the Art Students League (1947–49), at Pratt Graphics Center and at Columbia University. Later, in Pasadena, California, he studied at the Art Center College of Design.

From 1947 to 1949 Hyde worked with Condé Nast Publications, and in 1950 began a freelance career that has continued into the present.

Hyde was awarded a Guggenheim Fellowship in 1965 and CAPS grants in 1972 and 1974.

PUBLICATIONS Monograph: *CAPS Book*, 1975 (self-pub.). Anthologies: *The Photograph Collector's Guide*, Lee D. Witkin & Barbara London, 1979; *Mirrors and Windows*, John Szarkowski, ed., 1978; *On the Offset Press*, 1977. Periodicals: *Modern Photography Annual*, 1974; *Aperture 15*, no. 2, 1970.

COLLECTIONS Cooper-Hewitt Mus., NYC; Colgate Univ., Hamilton, N.Y.; Everson Mus. of Art, Syracuse, N.Y.; High Mus., Atlanta, Ga.; IMP/GEH, Rochester; Metro. Mus. of Art, NYC; MOMA, NYC; Mus. of the City of New York; Norton Simon Mus. of Art, Pasadena, Calif.; Smithsonian Inst., Wash. D.C.; UCLA. Bibliothèque Nationale, Paris; Musée Française de la Photographie, Bievres, France.

ADDRESS 215 E Fourth St, New York, NY 10009.

I

Paul Ickovic *PHOTOGRAPHER* Born in Kettering, England, on March 16, 1944, Ickovic earned a BA at Goddard College in Plainfield, Vermont (1972). He was greatly influenced by the work of Louis Faurer, Henri Cartier-Bresson and Robert Frank.

Since 1964 Ickovic has been working as a free-lance photographer. From 1976 to 1979 he was director of photographic development for Thomas Todd Printers in Boston; in 1971 he taught photography at Goddard College.

Ickovic belongs to SPE, and was awarded a Photographers Fellowship by the Vermont Council on the Arts in 1976. He has made a documentary film on sculptor Arnaldo Pomodoro.

The artist, working in 35mm format, specializes in "street photography, with primary focus on people in urban settings, their symbols and artifacts."

PUBLICATIONS Monograph: *In Transit*, 1977. Anthology: *Soul of Vermont*, 1972.

COLLECTIONS Gilbert Cllctn., Chicago; MOMA, NYC. Bibliothèque Nationale, Paris; and private collections.

REPRESENTATIVE Panopticon, 187 Bay State Rd, Boston, MA 02215.

ADDRESS 183 Marlborough St, Boston, MA 02116.

Ikko (Narahara) *PHOTOGRAPHER* Born November 3, 1931, in Fukuoka, Japan, Ikko earned a BA in Law from Chuo University, Tokyo (1954), and an MA in Art History from Waseda University, Tokyo (1959).

Ikko is a self-employed photographer.

He belongs to the Japan Professional Photographers Society, and has received the Minister of Education Award of Arts, Japan (1968), Mainichi Art Award, from Mainichi Newspapers (1967), the Photographer of the Year Award (1967) and Most Promising Photographer Award, from Japan Photo Critics Association (1958).

PUBLICATIONS Books (all Tokyo): *Light and Waves*, 1980 (Parco Shuppan); *Journey to 'A Land Near and Yet so Far,'* 1979 (Shuei-sha); *Domains*, 1978 (Asahi Sonorama); *Where Time Has Vanished*, 1975 (Asahi Shimbun-sha); *Celebration of Life*, 1972 (Mainichi Newspapers); *Man and his Land*, 1971 (Chuokoron-sha); *Japanesque*, 1970 (Mainichi Newspapers); *España Gran Tarde*, 1969, *The World of Kazuo Yagi*, 1969 (Kyuryudo); *Where Time Has Stopped*, 1967 (Kajima Shuppankai).

PORTFOLIO *Seven from Ikko*, 1977 (Unac: Tokyo).

COLLECTIONS Boston Mus. of Fine Arts; IMP:GEH, Rochester; MOMA, NYC. In Tokyo: Kyushu Sangyo Univ.; Nihon Univ.; Tokyo Inst. of Polytechnics. Bibliothèque Nationale, Paris.

ADDRESS Villa Fresca 702, 2-30-16 Jingumae Shibuya-ku, Tokyo, Japan.

Eleonore Roberts Ines *PHOTOGRAPHER · TEACHER* Born July 15, 1934, in Danzig, Poland (née Labunski), Ines is self-taught in photography.

She has conducted workshops for the Santa Barbara Photography Gallery in California since 1978 and also taught at the University of California, Santa Barbara, in 1978. Between 1969 and 1972 she taught at the Laguna Blanca School and was co-director and founder of the Visible Light Gallery, also in Santa Barbara.

A member of RPS and Friends of Photography, Ines won the 1973 Nature Nate Award at the International Exhibition of Photography and produced multimedia slide programs featured in the same year at the International Convention of Photographers in San Francisco. In 1966 she took first prize in the All British Competition, a photography contest.

Her early work is in black-and-white, but she has worked in color since 1975. Producing multimedia programs utilizing music and slides, Ines says that "the sound dictates the use of visual images, which not only relates closely to the music but harmonizes in color, form and subject matter with each other."

PUBLICATIONS Periodicals: *Popular Photography*, May 1980; *Popular Photography Annual*, 1974; *Popular Photography's Color*, 1974.

COLLECTIONS Chase Manhattan Bank, NYC; Chrysler Mus., Norfolk, Va.; Eastern Washington State Coll., Cheney.

DEALER London Photographers' Gall., 8 Newport St, London, England.

ADDRESS 3340 Cliff Dr, Santa Barbara, CA 93109.

Deborah Irmas PHOTOHISTORIAN Born in Los Angeles, California, on June 29, 1950, Irmas earned a BFA (1973) at the University of Southern California in her native city. She also attended Boston University, where she completed an MA (1975) and as of this writing was a PhD candidate in Art History.

Irmas taught art history at Boston University (1974–75) and has been a lecturer in the history of photography at the University of California at Los Angeles since 1978. She was also the curator of two exhibitions: "Historical Photographs," from the Boni Collection, which she organized with Tom Barrow at the Frederick S. Wight Gallery at UCLA in 1975, and "The Photographic Magic of William Mortensen" (1979), sponsored by the Los Angeles Center for Photographic Studies and the National Endowment for the Arts. Her professional experience includes coordinating a symposium, "Collecting Photography" (1978), at the Los Angeles Center for Photographic Studies and working as a picture editor for the college textbook division of Harcourt, Brace Jovanovich (1976–77). In addition, she is co-owner and director of Photologue International Inc., a worldwide source for photography exhibition catalogs through mail order.

Irmas belongs to SPE and the Los Angeles Center for Photographic Studies.

Commercial and pictorial photography of California in the thirties and contemporary photography are Irmas' areas of interest. She is also versed in nineteenth-century French photography.

PUBLICATIONS Catalog: *The Photographic Magic of William Mortensen*, intro., 1979 (Los Angeles Center for Photographic Studies). Periodicals: "Thoughts on the Last Ten Light Years," *Journal*, Sept/Oct 1979; "An Interview with Shelley Rice," *The Dumb Ox*, fall 1977 & spring 1978; "Monsters and Madonnas," *Photograph*, summer 1977.

PORTFOLIO *Portfolio # 1* by Jerry McMillan, intro. by Deborah Irmas, 1978 (self-pub.).

ADDRESS POB 29087, Los Angeles, CA 90029.

Shyla L. Irving PHOTOGRAPHER Born on April 30, 1943, in New Haven Connecticut, Irving is married to writer John Irving. She attended the Convent of the Sacred Heart in New Haven, and the University of Iowa in Iowa City, where she completed a BFA in 1975.

Currently working as a freelance photographer, she has had her work published in *Rolling Stone*, *Time* and *The New York Times Magazine*. From 1975 to 1979 she was director of photography at the Brattleboro Museum and Art Center in Vermont.

A member of the Photographic Resource Center in Boston, Irving received a Vermont Arts Council grant in 1979 and a Vermont Historical Society Grant in 1977.

The artist, working strictly in color, photographs people, landscapes and still lifes of food.

REPRESENTATIVE Robbins & Covey Assocs., 10 Fifth Ave, New York, NY 10021.

DEALER Marcuse Pfeifer, 825 Madison Ave, New York, NY 10021.

Yasuhiro Ishimoto PHOTOGRAPHER Born in San Francisco on June 14, 1921, Ishimoto studied with Harry Callahan and Aaron Siskind at the Chicago Institute of Design, graduating from their photography department in 1952. He has worked exclusively as a freelance photographer.

In 1978 Ishimoto won Japan's Minister of Education Prize, in 1970 he was given the Mainichi Art Award and in 1958 he received the Japan Photo Critic Association Award. He won the Moholy-Nagy award in 1951 and 1952; in 1950 he was winner of the Young Photographers' Contest, sponsored by *Life* magazine.

PUBLICATIONS Books: *Journey to Kunisaki*, 1978; *The Mandalas of the Two Worlds*, 1977; *World of Kenmochi Isamu*, 1976; *The City*, 1971; *Chicago, Chicago*, Bijutsu Shuppan-Sha, 1969; *Someday Somewhere*, 1960.

COLLECTIONS Chicago Mus. of Fine Art; MOMA, NYC.

DEALER Gilbert Gall., Ltd, 218 E Ontario St, Chicago, Il 60611.

ADDRESS 6-7-11 Kitashinagaw, Shinagawa-ku, Tokyo, Japan.

Barry Lee Iverson *PHOTOGRAPHER · TEACHER*
Born in Stanley, North Dakota, on June 21, 1956,
Iverson received a BS (1979) from the University
of Colorado in Boulder, where he studied under
Gary Metz and Bonnie Donahue. In Boulder he
was also influenced by Hal Gould and Rick Koop-
man.

A freelance photographer, Iverson is working
for GAMMA in Cairo, Egypt, as of this writing.
Previously he was employed as a photographer
for the *Colorado Daily* (1979) and taught photography: in Thorpe, England, and Athens, Greece
(1979), working for TASIS; in Switzerland, at the
Leysin American School (1978) and at the Summer Art Workshop in Lugano (1977).

He belongs to SPE, the Colorado Photographic
Arts Center and RPS.

Iverson is engaged in an "ongoing documentary
of the aged," begun in 1977, and is "also concerned with objects as structures—structural
compositions in two dimensions." Another of his
interests is research in the history of photogravure.

PUBLICATION   *Fotografi*, June 1978.

COLLECTIONS   Colo. Photog. Arts Ctr., Denver; Michigan State Univ., East Lansing; Univ. of
Colo., Boulder.

ADDRESS   c/o American Express, 15 Sharia
Kasr El Nil, POB 2160, Cairo, Egypt.

Frederick Eugene Ives *INVENTOR · PHOTOG-
RAPHER · PRINTER*   Born February 17, 1856, in
Litchfield, Connecticut, Ives died May 27, 1937,
in Philadelphia, Pennsylvania. His son, Herbert
Eugene Ives (1882–1953), was an award-winning
physicist who pioneered in long-range color television transmission.

At age thirteen Ives was apprenticed as a
printer on the *Litchfield Enquirer*. He took it
upon himself to do an intensive study of photography. In 1874 he was appointed the official photographer of Cornell University in Ithaca, New
York. There he established and conducted a department devoted to photographic work and research, remaining until 1878. Turning more and
more to the further development of photomechanical processes, he went to work for Crosscup
& West Engraving Company in Philadelphia,
where he continued his work on halftone plates
for printing. He later went to England and Vienna
to confer with colleagues, but returnd to and remained in Philadelphia.

Ives was a fellow of a dozen or more scientific
societies in this country and Europe. As the inventor of the halftone engraving process, in universal use today, Ives revolutionized the field of
magazine and newspaper illustration. He also developed the "first practical and successful color
projection of three diapositives on a screen
(1888)," according to Joseph Eder *(History of Photography)*. This apparatus he called a "triple projection lantern." Ives is the acknowledged
inventor of the American enamel process (used
with Levy screens in printing). He developed a 3-
color camera, the chromoscope, patented in 1892
—the first of its kind to achieve practical results,
according to Eder; Ives later refined the camera,
calling it a photochromoscope (1894 patent). It
was Ives' work that made 3-color projection possible for motion picture photography (1897).
Other inventions include the parallex stereogram
and the modern short-tube single-objective mon-
ocular microscope.

For his brilliant pioneering work Ives received
many honors and awards. Among them are eight
medals from the Franklin Institute; the Rumford
Medal from the American Academy of Arts and
Sciences, 1912; the Medal of Honor of the United
Typothetae of America, 1926; and similar honors
from societies in London, Edinburgh and
Vienna.

In 1928 his son established an honor medal to
be awarded in his name by the American Optical
Society for distinguished work in the field of optics.

Because he failed to patent many of his inventions and processes, Ives made little money.
Commenting on this situation, he once said: "I
have myself been deprived of any material reward
for inventions which ultimately proved of great
commercial value, but I am thankful that I could
find some contentment in the pleasure of accomplishment" *(New York Times*, May 28,
1937).

PUBLICATIONS   Books: *Early Photographs &
Early Photographers*, Oliver Reed, 1973; *History
of Photography*, Josef Maria Eder, 1945, repr.
1978; *Autobiography of an Amateur Inventor*,
1928; *Color Photography*, William B. Gamble,
1923; *Cassell's Cyclopedia of Photography*,
1911, repr. 1973. Pamphlets & periodicals: *Frederick E. Ives*, L. W. Sipley, 1956 (Amer. Mus. of
Photography: Philadelphia); "Frederic Eugene
Ives," Edward Epstean & J. A. Tennant, *Applied
Physics*, Apr 1938; "The Work of Frederic E.
Ives," W. B. Hislop, *Penrose's Annual*, no. 40,
1938; "Pioneering Inventions by an Amateur,"
*Journal of the Society of Motion Picture Engi-
neering*, Sept 1934; *A Few Words About Halftone, Trichromatic Process Printing, and
Rotogravure*, July 1925 (Philadelphia); "An Ap-

preciation of Mr. F. E. Ives," C. H. Claudy, *British Journal of Photography, Color Supplement*, Sept 3, 1920; "Photography in the Colors of Nature," *British Journal of Photography*, Jan 23, Feb 13, 20, 27, 1891, and also *Smithsonian Institute Annual Report 1893*, 1894 (Wash., D.C.); *A New Principle in Heliochromy*, 1889 (Philadelphia); "Chlorophyl and Gelatine-Bromide Plates," *Journal of the Franklin Institute*, June 1888.

COLLECTIONS   IMP/GEH, Rochester; Smithsonian Institute., Wash., D.C.

Izis
See Israëlis Bidermanas

J

Joseph David Jachna   *PHOTOGRAPHER* ·
TEACHER   Born in Chicago on September 12, 1935,
Jachna earned a BS in Art Education (1958) and
an MS in Photography (1961) from the Institute
of Design, Illinois Institute of Technology, Chicago. He studied with Harry Callahan and Aaron
Siskind.

Since 1969 he has been teaching photography
at the University of Illinois, Chicago Circle.

Jachna received a Project Completion Grant
from the Illinois Arts Council in 1979, an NEA
Photographer's Fellowship in 1976, the Silver
Circle Award for Excellence in Teaching from
the University of Illinois at Chicago Circle in
1974 and a Ferguson grant in 1973. He also was
awarded two grants from the University of Illinois, Chicago, in 1972, and a faculty research
grant from Illinois Institute of Technology in
1969.

PUBLICATIONS   Books: *Juxtapositions*, 1974;
Searchlights on Literature, 1968; *Photography in
the Twentieth Century*, Nathan Lyons, 1967. Anthologies: *Photography Year 1974*, Time-Life Series, 1974; *Be-ing Without Clothes*, Minor White,
ed., 1970. Catalogs: *The Photographer and the
City*, 1977 (Mus. of Contemporary Art: Chicago);
The Target Collection of American Photography,
Anne Tucker, ed., 1977 (Mus. of Fine Arts: Hous-
ton); *Language of Light*, 1974 (Univ. of Kans.
Mus. of Art: Lawrence); *Catalog of Prints Sale*,
1974 (VSW: Rochester); *Photography: Midwest
Invitational*, 1973 (Walker Art Ctr.: Minneapo-
lis); *Photography in the Twentieth Century*, 1967
(GEH: Rochester); *Photography USA '67*, 1967
(DeCordova Mus.: Lincoln, Mass.); *Photography
'63, An International Exhibition*, 1963 (N.Y.
State Exposition & GEH: Rochester). Periodicals:
Review, *Afterimage: VSW*, June 1977; "Joseph D.
Jachna: Door County Landscapes," *Photo-Forum*,
no. 26, June/July, 1975; *Asahi Camera*, Apr 1975;
Camera Mainichi, Sept 1974; *Exposure: SPE*,
Nov 1973; *Untitled* no. 4, June 1973 (Friends of
Photography: Carmel, Calif.); *Modern Photogra-*
phy, Mar 1971; *1969 Photography Annual*, 1968;
Aperture, 9:2, 1961; *Photography*, Nov 1959.

COLLECTIONS   Art Inst. of Chicago; Burpee Art
Mus., Rockford, Ill.; CCP, Tucson; Ctr. for Pho-
tographic Studies, Louisville, Ky.; Exchange
Natl. Bank of Chicago; Friends of Photography,
Carmel, Calif.; Ill. Inst. of Tech., Chicago; IMP/
GEH, Rochester; Reva & David Logan Fndn.,
Chicago; Minneapolis Inst. of Arts, Minn.; MIT,
Cambridge, Mass.; MOMA, NYC; Mus. of Con-
temporary Art, Chicago; Princeton Univ., N.J.;
Univ. of Kans. Mus. of Art, Lawrence; Univ. of
Louisville, Ky. Ryerson Polytechnic Inst., To-
ronto.

DEALERS   Visual Studies Workshop Gall., 31
Prince St, Rochester, NY 14607; Jeffrey Gilbert
Gall., 218 E Ontario, Chicago, IL 60611.

ADDRESS   5707 W 89 Pl, Oak Lawn, IL 60453.

William Henry Jackson   *PHOTOGRAPHER* ·
PAINTER · WRITER   [See plate 30]   Born April 4,
1843, in Keesville, New York, Jackson died June
30, 1942, in New York City. His son, Clarence S.
Jackson, was a photographer, writer and biographer. Jackson's only known education was at the
Fourth Ward school in 1853.

In 1858 Jackson went to work as a retoucher
and colorist in C. C. Schoonmaker's photographic portrait studio in Troy, New York, and in
1861 he worked for the Mowrey Studio, Rutland,
Vermont. A Union soldier in the Civil War, he
became a staff artist for the 12th Vermont Infantry, Company K, in 1862. In 1866 Jackson traveled to the West as a trail drover for a Mormon
wagon train. He and his brother established a
photographic portrait studio in Omaha, Nebraska, in 1867. From 1870 to 1878 he was the
official photographer for the U.S. Geological &
Geographical Survey of the Territories (the Hayden Survey), working in the Wyoming area in
1870–72 and in Colorado in 1873. At the Centennial Exposition in Philadelphia in 1876 he acted
as a guide with the Hayden Survey exhibit.

In 1879 Jackson opened a studio in Denver, the Jackson Photographic Company, specializing in commissioned landscapes for the railroads. He was official photographer at the Chicago World's Columbian Exposition in 1893, and in 1894–96 *Harper's Weekly* commissioned him to travel around the world on assignment for the World Transportation Commission. Jackson was director of the Photochrom Company from 1897 to 1924 and became part owner of the Detroit Publishing Company in 1898. From 1929 to 1942 he was research secretary for the Oregon Trail Memorial Association. At the age of ninety-two, in 1935, the artist was commissioned by the Department of the Interior to do a series of murals for a new building.

Jackson was a member of the Explorers Club, a life member of the National Photographers Association (from 1873), president of the Colorado Camera Club in 1900 and an Honorary Fellow of RPS (1938). He won a bronze medal from the Centennial Commission in 1893 and earned an honorary DL from the University of Wyoming. The National Park Service paid homage to the photographer by having him buried in Arlington, Virginia, since it was his photographic works that inspired the government to establish Yellowstone, Grand Teton and Mesa Verde National parks.

Jackson was noted for his landscape photographs of the American West. In the early days of his long career he worked with collodion wet-plate negatives and albumen prints, exploring every format from stereoscopic views to enormous 20 x 24 glass-plate negatives. Later he worked with gelatin dry-plate and film negatives and silver prints. He was especially noted for his views of the Yellowstone area, though he photographed scenes from all over the world and did many portraits of Indians as well. The technical quality of his images was probably the best of his day, and he is considered by many to be the premier "frontier" photographer.

PUBLICATIONS Books: *William Henry Jackson's Colorado*, William C. Jones & Elizabeth Jones, 1975; *William Henry Jackson*, Beaumont Newhall & Diana E. Edkins, 1974; *Lens on the West*, Helen Markley Miller, 1966; *William Henry Jackson: Pioneer Photographer of the West*, Aylsea Forsee, 1964; *The Diaries of William Henry Jackson, Frontier Photographer*, bio., LeRoy R. & Ann W. Hafen, 1959; *Pageant of the Pioneers*, Clarence S. Jackson, 1958; *Picture Maker of the Old West*, bio., Clarence S. Jackson, 1947; *Time Exposure*, autobio., 1940, repr. 1970; *Drawings of the Oregon Trail*, 1929/30; *The Pioneer Photographer: Rocky Mountain Adventures with a Camera*, w/Howard R. Driggs, 1929; *The Cañons of Colorado*, 1900; *Among the Rockies*, 1900; *Jackson's Famous Pictures of the World's Fair*, 1893, 1895; *Wonder-Places*, 1894; *The White City (as it was . . .)*, 1894; *Catalog of Standard & Panoramic Photographs*, 1894 (self-pub.); *Grand Cañon of the Arkansas*, 1880?; *Denver & the Rio Grande Railroad Co. Rocky Mountain Scenery*, ca. 1885 (American Bank Note Co.: N.Y.); *Portraits of American Indians*, 1876 (pvt. prntg.); *Photographs of the Yellowstone National Park and Views in Montana and Wyoming Territories*, 1873, and *View of the Yellowstone*, 1871 (U.S. Dept. of the Interior, U.S. Geological Survey). Anthologies: *The Photograph Collector's Guide*, Lee D. Witkin & Barbara London, 1979; *Era of Exploration . . . 1860–1885*, Weston J. Naef & James N. Wood, 1975; *The Magic Image*, Cecil Beaton & Gail Buckland, 1975; *Looking at Photographs*, John Szarkowski, 1973; *Great Photographers*, Time-Life Series, 1970; *Picture Gallery Pioneers, 1850–1875*, Ralph W. Andrews, 1964; *Photography and the American Scene . . . 1839–1889*, Robert Taft, 1938.

PORTFOLIOS 3 albums: *West Indies, Bahama Islands & Venezuela*, 1900–1905.

COLLECTIONS Acad. of Natural Sciences, Philadelphia; Amer. Antiquarian Soc., Worcester, Mass.; Amon Carter Mus. of Western Art, Ft. Worth, Tex.; Boston Pub. Lib., Mass.; Bureau of Ethnology, Wash., D.C.; Denver Pub. Lib., Colo.; Eastman Kodak Co., Rochester; Edison Inst., Dearborn, Mich.; Harvard Univ., Cambridge, Mass.; IMP/GEH, Rochester; L/C, Wash., D.C.; Mus. of N. Mex., Santa Fe; Natl. Archives (Hayden Survey), Wash., D.C.; Princeton Univ., Firestone Lib., N.J.; Smithsonian Inst., Wash., D.C.; State Hist. Soc. of Colo., Denver; Union Pacific Hist. Mus., Omaha, Neb.; Univ. of Calif., Bancroft Lib., Berkeley; Univ. of N. Mex. Art Mus., Albuquerque; Yale Univ., Beinecke Rare Book & Ms. Lib., New Haven, Conn.

J. Lotte Jacobi PHOTOGRAPHER Born August 17, 1896, in Thorn, West Prussia, Germany, Jacobi attended the Bavarian State Academy of Photography and the University of Munich (1925–27). She also studied at the University of New Hampshire in Durham from 1961 to 1962, from which she received an honorary DFA in 1974. Her father, grandfather and great-grandfather were all photographers, the latter's teacher having been Daguerre.

The photographer has run a studio in Deering,

New Hampshire, since she closed her New York studio in 1955. She fled to the U.S. in 1935 from Germany, having operated her father's Berlin studio from 1927 until that time.

A member of Professional Photographers of New Hampshire, Jacobi won first prize from the New Hampshire Art Association in 1970, first prize in the British War Relief Photography Competiton of 1941 (*Life* magazine) and a silver medal from the Royal Photography Salon in Tokyo in 1931.

A recognized portrait photographer since the early days of her career in Germany, Jacobi's sitters have included Einstein, Thomas Mann and Alfred Stieglitz. She is also known for her abstract images and landscapes, and has worked in silver, bromoil-transfer and platinum.

PUBLICATIONS Monograph: *Lotte Jacobi*, 1978. Book: *Albert Einstein: 100th Anniversary*, 1979 (self-pub.). Anthologies: *The Photograph Collector's Guide*, Lee D. Witkin & Barbara London, 1979; *Recollection, 10 Women Photographers*, 1979; *Women of Photography*, Mann & Noggle, eds., 1975; *Light*[7], Minor White, ed., 1968. Catalog: *Lotte Jacobi*, 1973 (Mus. Folkwang: Essen, Germany). Periodicals: *Popular Photography*, July 1967; *Camera*, Apr 1967; *Foto*, Oct 1965 (Munich); *Aperture*, 10:1, 1962, 8:2, 1960; *Infinity: ASMP*, Apr 1960.

PORTFOLIO *Portfolio I*, 1978 (self-pub.).

REPRESENTATIVE Doris Bry, 11 E 73 St, New York, NY 10021.

ADDRESS Old Country Rd, Box 228, Deering, NH 03244.

Mark Jacobs AUTHOR · TEACHER · PHOTOGRAPHER Jacobs was born in Chicago, Illinois, on February 23, 1951. Since 1966 he has been the owner of Foto-Tek Camera in his native city. He has also been writing books on photography for National Textbook Company since 1975.

He belongs to SPE.

Jacobs' personal work, executed in black-and-white large format, "is primarily directed at the illusion and reality of space and perception." As a researcher he is interested in the history of color processes.

PUBLICATIONS Books: *Toward a History of Color Photography*, 1980; *Curriculum Guide for Photography*, 1977; *Teachers Guide for Photography*, 1975; *Photography in Focus*, 1975.

COLLECTION Art Inst. of Chicago.

ADDRESS 7002 N Western Ave, Chicago, Il 60645.

N. Keith Jacobshagen II PHOTOGRAPHER · TEACHER Born September 8, 1941, in Wichita, Kansas, Jacobshagen earned a BFA in 1965 from Kansas City Art Institute, Missouri, an MFA in 1968 from the University of Kansas, Lawrence, and also studied one year at Art Center College of Design in Los Angeles.

He has been associate professor at University of Nebraska, Lincoln, since 1968.

A member of SPE from 1970 to 1975, the photographer received a Tulsa (Oklahoma) Art Directors Club Award in 1970 and a Woods Fellowship in 1974.

PUBLICATIONS Anthology: *Young American Photography: Volume 1*, 1974. Catalogs: *Twelve Photographers, A Contemporary Mid-America Document*, 1978 (Mid-America Arts Alliance: Kansas City, Mo.); *Photographs, Sheldon Memorial Art Gallery Collection*, 1977 (Univ. of Neb. Press: Lincoln). Periodicals: *Art in America*, July/Aug 1979; *Camera*, Nov 1971; *Creative Camera*, Nov 1970; *Popular Photography's Woman*, 1970.

COLLECTIONS Brandeis Univ., Rose Art Mus., Waltham, Mass.; Honeywell Corp., Minneapolis, Minn.; IBM, Kansas City, Mo.; Natl. Bank of Commerce, Lincoln, Nebr.; Norton Simon Mus. of Art, Pasadena, Calif.; Oakland Mus., Calif.; Penn. Academy of Fine Arts, Philadelphia; Pennzoil Co., Houston, Tex.; Sioux City Art Ctr., Iowa; Univ. of Kans. Mus. of Art, Lawrence; Univ. of Nebr., Sheldon Mem. Art Gall., Lincoln; Univ. of Okla. Mus. of Art, Norman.

DEALERS Dorry Gates Inc., 5321 Belleview Ave, Kansas City, MO 64112; Robert Schoelkopf Gall., 825 Madison Ave, New York, NY 10021.

ADDRESS Dept of Art, Woods Hall, University of Nebraska, Lincoln, NE 68588.

Max Jacoby PHOTOJOURNALIST Born June 8, 1919, in Koblenz, Germany, Jacoby is self-taught, influenced by visual arts, classical and jazz music and the photography of Weston, Strand and Cartier-Bresson. He is a freelance photojournalist. His wife, Hilla Jacoby, is also a photographer.

Jacoby belongs to ASMP and DGPh.

PUBLICATIONS Books: *The Land of Israel*, w/ Hilla Jacoby, 1978 (Hoffman & Campe; Hamburg); *Sweden*, w/Hilla Jacoby, 1978 (Bucher: Switzerland); *Confrontation*, n.d., *Impressionen*, n.d., *Joseph Karsch*, n.d. (Gebr. Hartmann: Berlin); *Käthe Kollwitz*, n.d., *Riemenschneider*, n.d. (Christian Wegner: Hamburg); *Marcel Marceau*, n.d. (Renate Gerhard: Berlin); *Theater*, vols. 1 & 2, n.d., (Buenos Aires, Argentina).

ADDRESS Spessartstrasse 15, 1000 Berlin 33, Germany.

Barbara Jaffe *PHOTOGRAPHER* Born June 3, 1942, Jaffe earned her BA at Post College, Long Island, New York, in 1964 and her MA at the New School for Social Research, New York City, in 1979.

She has taught photography at the New School since 1974, and also currently teaches at New York University in Manhattan, Stockton State College, Pomona, New Jersey, and Wagner College, Staten Island, New York. She taught at Manhattanville College in New York City in 1975.

Jaffe has been a member of SPE since 1975.

Using large-format color, Jaffe is concerned in her work with "issues of illusion, layering, transparency, translucency, interaction and ambiguity of picture planes."

PUBLICATIONS Anthology: *Women See Woman*, 1976. Periodicals: *Popular Photography's 35mm Photography*, 1978; *Feminist Art Journal*, fall 1976; *Popular Photography*, Feb 1976.

ADDRESS 240 Waverly Pl, New York, NY 10014.

N. Jay Jaffee *PHOTOGRAPHER* Born on March 8, 1921, in Brooklyn, New York, Jaffee received no formal training in photography. He started using a camera in 1947, and met Sid Grossman at the Photo League in 1948 and Steichen in 1950. He works as a freelance photographer, a printing and graphic arts consultant, and also sells prints to collectors and museums.

Jaffee received a Combat Infantry Badge and Bronze Star during World War II and was granted a New York Art Directors Award in 1978.

His work, in black-and-white small and medium formats, is personal and subjective. His early production is documentary in style. He describes his photographic technique as reflecting "a sense of discovery and spontaneity."

PUBLICATION *Photographs, 1947–55*, 1976.

COLLECTIONS Brooklyn Mus., N.Y.; Brooklyn Public Lib., N.Y.; Franklin Stainless Corp., Port Washington, N.Y.; L/C, Wash., D.C.; Metro Mus. of Art, N.Y.; MOMA, NYC; Newport Harbor Art Mus., Calif.; Olden Camera, NYC; Symbax, NYC. Bibliothèque Nationale, Paris.

REPRESENTATIVE Nouvel Observateur Gallery, Paris, France.

ADDRESS POB 52, Glen Oaks, NY 11004.

Gottfried Jäger *TEACHER · PHOTOGRAPHER* Born May 13, 1937, in Burg/Magdeburg, Germany, Jäger graduated in photo-engineering from the State Technical School of Photography in Cologne in 1960. His mentor was Dr. Herbert W. Franke of Munich; his father is photographer Ernst Jäger.

A professor of photography and photographic art at Fachhochschule Bielefeld, Fachbereich Design, since 1973, he previously taught photographic technology at Werkkunstschule Bielefeld, Germany (1960–73). He also conducts private workshops on photographic and graphic art and design.

Jäger belongs to the Union of Fine Arts, DGPh, GDL, Federation of Independent Photographic Designers, Council of the Professional Photographers of Europe, German Computer Graphics and Computer Art Society.

The photographer is especially concerned with investigating "graphic light effects achieved with multi-lens." Says Jäger: "For me, photography is not a medium of reproduction but a medium of production."

PUBLICATIONS Books (in Germany): *Generative Fotografie—Theoretische Grundlegung, Kompendium und Beispiele einer fotografischen Bildgestaltung*, w/Karl M. Holzhauser, 1975 (Otto Maier Verlag: Ravensburg); *Apparative Kunst—Vom Kaleidoskop zum Computer*, w/ Herbert W. Franke, 1973 (DuMont Schauberg: Cologne).

COLLECTIONS In Germany: Fotomuseum der Stadt, Munich; Kestner Mus., Hannover; Landesbildstelle/Mus. Für Kunst und Gewerbe, Hamburg; Mus. Mönchengladbach.

DEALER Galerie Jesse, Niederwall 38, D-4800 Bielefeld 1, Germany.

ADDRESS Barnhausen Nr. 48, D-4807 Borgholzhausen, Germany.

Christopher James *PHOTOGRAPHER · TEACHER* James was born in Boston, Massachusetts, on May 8, 1947. His great-grandfather was philosopher William James, his great-uncle writer Henry James and his grandfather printer Alexander James. He received a BFA (1969) from the Massachusetts College of Art in Boston and an MA (1971) from the Rhode Island School of Design in Providence.

As of this writing he was teaching in Massachusetts, both at Harvard University in Cambridge and at the Worcester Art Museum School. Previously he taught at Keene State College in New York State (1977–78) and at Greenfield Community College in Massachusetts (1971–78).

A member of SPE since 1974, James was awarded a Massachusetts Arts Foundation Fellowship in 1978 and an NEA Artist-in-Residence Grant at Keene State College in 1977.

The artist, working in black-and-white, specializes in "manipulated prints that are selectively toned, dyed with silver, replacing mordant dyes, and painted with tinted and transparent enamel paints."

PUBLICATIONS Periodicals: *Camera*, 1979; *Popular Photography*, 1979; *American Photographer*, 1978; *Photography Annual*, 1977, 1975; *Camera 35*, 1973.

COLLECTIONS Boston Mus. of Fine Arts; Denver Art Mus., Colo.; Detroit Inst. of Arts, Mich.; IMP/GEH, Rochester; Minneapolis Inst. of Arts Mus., Minn.; MOMA, NYC; R.I. School of Design Mus., Providence; Worcester Art Mus., Mass. Bibliothèque Nationale, Paris.

DEALERS Witkin Gall., 41 E 57 St, New York, NY 10022; Harcus Krakow Gall., 7 Newbury St, Boston, MA 02116.

ADDRESS 116 Commonwealth Ave, Boston, MA 02116.

Joaquim Pla Janini PHYSICIAN · PHOTOGRAPHER Born in Tarragona, Spain, March 23, 1879, Janini died in Barcelona on February 11, 1970. He studied medicine in the Philippines at the University of Santo Tomás and in Spain at the University of Barcelona, graduating in 1903. He began to photograph when he was fourteen.

Janini was co-founder, in 1923, and several times president of the Agrupació Fotográfica de Catalunya (Barcelona). His awards include gold medals from several international photography competitions, including Prague, Vienna, Tokyo and Berlin. In 1963 he received the gold medal from the Químicas Sindicato in Madrid.

His work is neopictorialist in style, concentrating on still life, landscape and fantasy. He used Fresson, bromoil and transfer bromoil processes.

PUBLICATIONS Periodicals: *Arte Fotográfico*, no. 142, Oct 1963; *Art de la Llum*, Oct 1934.

REPRESENTATIVE Joan Fontcuberta, Avenida Infanta Carlota 113 4°, Barcelona-29 Spain.

Eugenia Parry Janis ART HISTORIAN · TEACHER · WRITER Born July 28, 1940, in Chicago, Illinois, Janis earned a BA from the University of Michigan, Ann Arbor (1961), and an MA (1963) and PhD (1971) from Harvard University, Cambridge, Massachusetts.

Since 1968 she has been an art history professor at Wellesley College, Wellesley, Massachusetts, and has also taught courses at Brandeis University in Waltham, Massachusetts, University of Massachusetts in Amherst and Harvard University in Cambridge.

Currently a member of the Visiting Committee of IMP/GEH, Rochester, in 1980 she won an award from the American Council of Learned Societies. In 1973 she won a Guggenheim Fellowship to study the history of photography.

She is interested in the incorporation of photography into general art history, her own main research concern being early French photography.

PUBLICATIONS Book: *Photography Within the Humanities*, ed. w/Wendy MacNeil, 1977. Anthology: "The Color Photographer as Epicurean," *One of a Kind*, 1979. Catalogs: *The Second Empire (1852–1870), Art in France Under Napoléon III*, 1978–79 (Philadelphia Mus. of Art & Musées Nationaux: Paris); *The Monotypes of Edgar Degas*, 1968 (Harvard Univ., Fogg Art Mus.: Cambridge). Periodical: "The Man on the Tower of Notre Dame: New Light on Henri Le Secq," *Image*, Dec 1976.

ADDRESS Jewett Arts Center, Wellesley College, Wellesley, MA 02181.

Arno Jansen PHOTOGRAPHER Born February 13, 1938, in Aachen, Germany, Jansen studied photography at Folkwangschule in Essen, Germany, 1959–63, under Professor Otto Steinert.

Since 1973 Jansen has been professor in the Art Department at Fachhochschule in Cologne, Germany. He was appointed head of photographic studies at the Kölner Werkschulen in 1965. Prior to that he worked as a photojournalist and commercial artist as well as a lecturer in the Photography Department at the School of Fine Arts in Braunschweig, Germany (1964).

Jansen has been a member of the GDL since 1978 and the DGPh since 1971.

In the last five years the photographer has focused on "arranged still lifes, which are engaged in reflections about fear, aggression, sexuality, death and decay."

PUBLICATIONS Periodicals: *Zoom*, Nov 1979 (Germany); *Fotografie*, Sept 1979, June 1978.

COLLECTIONS In Germany: Staatliche Landesbildstelle Cllctn., Hamburg; Wallraf-Richartz-Museum, Gruber Cllctn., Cologne. Bibliothèque Nationale, Paris.

ADDRESS Ubierring 40, 5000 Cologne 1, West Germany.

Bernd Jansen PHOTOGRAPHER Born November 20, 1945, in Bedburg, West Germany, Jansen studied photography from 1966 to 1971 at the Folkwang School, Essen, Germany, under Dr.

Otto Steinert. He has been a freelance photographer since 1971.

Jansen has belonged to GDL since 1970 and DGPh since 1973. He won the Heinrich Heine Prize of the city of Düsseldorf, Germany, in 1972.

PUBLICATIONS Catalogs (in West Germany): *Kunstmuseum Catalog*, (Düsseldorf); *Gallery Spectrum Catalog*, 1973 (Hannover).

COLLECTIONS IMP/GEH, Rochester. Bibliothèque Nationale, Paris; Pentax Mus., Tokyo. In West Germany: Mus. Folkwang, Essen; Staatliche Landesbildstelle, Hamburg; Stadtmuseum, Düsseldorf.

ADDRESS Talweg 15, 4 Düsseldorf 31, Germany.

Catherine S. Jansen TEACHER [See plate 138] Born in New York City on December 14, 1945, Jansen is the wife of photographer William G. Larson. After having completed a BFA at the Cranbrook Academy of Art in Bloomfield Hills, Michigan (1968), she earned an MFA from Temple University in Philadelphia (1973).

Since 1973 she has been working at Bucks County Community College in Newton, Pennsylvania, where she is an assistant professor and the coordinator of the Photography Department. Previously she was an instructor at the Philadelphia Museum of Art (1971–73).

The artist experiments with three-dimensional photography, Kirlian photography on cloth and color Xerox, and produces life-size cloth photographic room environments.

PUBLICATIONS Books: *Alternative Photographic Processes*, Kent Wade, 1978; *Innovative Printmaking*, Thelma Newman, 1977; *Design Through Discovery*, Margorie Elliot, 1977. Anthologies: *Photography '77*, 1977; *Frontiers in Photography*, 1973.

COLLECTIONS Honolulu Academy of Art, Hawaii; Philadelphia Mus. of Art, Pa.

ADDRESS 152 Heacock Ln, Wyncote, PA 19095.

Pierre Jules César Janssen ASTRONOMER · PHYSICIST Born February 22, 1824, in Paris, Janssen died December 23, 1923, in Meudon, France. He was educated as an astrophysicist in Paris.

In 1865 he became professor of general science in the school of architecture at the University of Paris. He was also the first director of the observatory at Meudon.

Janssen belonged to the Paris Academy, the Bureau of Longitude, and La Société Française, of which he served as president.

Janssen's first important photographic contribution was the development of an apparatus in 1874 to photograph the transit of Venus across the sun. The instrument, which produced forty-eight photographs around the edge of a circular daguerreotype plate, influenced Etienne-Jules Marey's later chronographic cameras. Janssen's photographs of the sun in 1877—he was the first to photograph it regularly—were considered the finest of the nineteenth century. Earlier (1868) he had invented a method for observing solar prominences without benefit of an eclipse.

His other discoveries included the existence of increasing densities beyond the point at which blackening had decreased to nothing (1880) and the principle of reciprocity failure. He also photographed the moon by earth-reflected light (1880), a comet (1881) and the nebulae in Orion (1881). In 1881 he constructed a photometric apparatus for measuring the sensitivity of photographic plates

Janssen, for whom a moon crater was named, was quoted as saying: "The photographic plate is the retina of the scientist, but a retina far superior to the human eye because, for one thing, it keeps the record of the phenomena which it sees, and for another it sees more."

PUBLICATIONS Books: *March of Photography*, Eric Stenger, 1958; *Histoire de la Photographie*, Raymond Lécuyer, 1945; *Photography Theory and Practice*, L. P. Clerc, 1937; *Histoire du Cinématographie*, G-Michel Coissac, 1925; *Atlas des Photographies Solaires*, 1904; *La Photographie Animée*, Eugene Trutat, 1899. Anthology: *Photography's Great Inventors*, Louis W. Sipley, 1965. Periodicals: *Bild und Ton*, 1954; *Photographic Times*, Aug 1895; *Jahrbuch für Photographie und Reproduktionstechnik*, Josef Maria Eder, 1890; *Photographic News*, 1881; *British Journal of Photography*, 1880.

James Jarché PHOTOGRAPHER · LECTURER Born in September 1890 in London, Jarché died in that city on August 6, 1965. He was apprenticed to his father, an immigrant French photographer, beginning at age nine.

He worked for Argent Archer, a magazine picture agency, in 1907, and later worked for Warhurst, the "pioneer of Fleet Street photography." He was connected with Odhams Press for many years and was frequently published in *Illustrated London News*. He left Odhams in 1953 for Associated Press, and later worked six years on the *Daily Mail* before retiring.

One of the most distinguished British press photographers, Jarché preferred the carefully conceived magazine set piece to the quick-shot newspaper picture. He photographed events that serve well as an illustrative commentary on English life and shot portraits of such notables as George Bernard Shaw, Sir Alexander Fleming and Albert Einstein. In a career that spanned nearly half a century he contributed notably to the technical advance and physical expansion of illustrative technique as applied to newspapers and magazines.

Stephen Barlow Jareckie CURATOR Born in Orange, New Jersey, on February 18, 1929, Jareckie obtained a BA from Lehigh University in Bethlehem, Pennsylvania (1951), and an MA form Syracuse University, New York (1961).

He has been working at the Worcester Art Museum in Massachusetts as curator of photography (since 1973), associate curator (1969–73) and assistant to the administrator (1967–71). Jareckie belongs to the New England Museum Association and the George Eastman House in Rochester and is an associate member of the U.S. Naval Institute.

PUBLICATIONS Catalogs: *American Photography*, 1976 (Worcester Art Museum: Mass.); *Three European Photographers: Bill Brandt, Lucien Clergue and Paolo Monti*, 1965; *Brassaï*, 1963; *Reflections: Color Photographs by Daniel Farber*, 1963. Periodicals: "Photography at the Worcester Art Museum," Feb 1974, "Thomas Eakins: His Photographic Works," Dec 1970, "The Photography Collection Grows: Gifts and Purchases, 1968–1969," Jan 1970, "Cartier-Bresson: Recent Photographs" (MOMA exhibition), Oct 1968, "Photographs by Dorothea Lange" (MOMA exhibition), Oct 1966, *News Bulletin and Calendar* (Worcester Art Museum: Mass.).

ADDRESS Worcester Art Mus., 55 Salisbury St, Worcester, MA 01608.

Bill Jay PHOTOHISTORIAN · ART CRITIC Born in Maidenhead, Berkshire, England, on August 12, 1940, Jay received his diploma at Berkshire College of Art. He earned both an MA and an MFA at the University of New Mexico in Albuquerque, where he studied with Van Deren Coke and Beaumont Newhall.

Since 1974 Jay has taught the history of photography at Arizona State University in Tempe, currently as an associate professor. Prior to that time he worked at several photographic archives, among them IMP/GEH, the University of New Mexico Art Museum and the Bibliothèque Nationale in Paris. In London, Jay was editor-director of the magazines *Album* (1969–71) and *Creative Camera* and picture editor of *Daily Telegraph* magazine. He was director of photography of the Institute of Contemporary Arts (1969–71) and arranged the British Documentary Photograph 1850–1970 Collection for the Arts Council of Great Britain. He has published over 200 articles in a wide variety of journals over the past fifteen years and delivered scores of papers at major symposia and conferences.

Jay is a member of SPE, having served on its board of directors from 1974 to 1978, and RPS, serving on its Royal Committee in 1972.

His field of research covers both the nineteenth and twentieth centuries, but he specializes in the wet-plate era of British topographical work.

PUBLICATIONS Books: "Julia Margaret Cameron," *Appraisals*, 1979; *Negative/Postive: A Philosophy of Photography*, 1979; "The Romantic Machine," *Photography: Current Perspectives*, 1979; *Models, Messages, Manipulations*, 1976 (self-pub.); *Essays and Photographs: Robert Demachy 1859–1936*, 1974; *Victorian Candid Camera; Paul Martin 1864–1944*, 1973; *Victorian Cameraman: Francis Frith's Views of Rural England 1850–1898*, 1973 (David & Charles: Devon, England); *Customs and Faces: Sir Benjamin Stone 1838–1914*, 1972; *Views on Nudes*, 1972 (Focal Press: London).

COLLECTION Univ. of N. Mex. Art Mus., Albuquerque.

ADDRESSES 5626 S Sailor's Reef, Tempe, AZ 85283; Art Dept, Arizona State University, Tempe, AZ 85281.

De Ann Jennings PHOTOGRAPHER · TEACHER Born in Manti, Utah, on May 14, 1945, Jennings is married to photographer David Dubuque. She earned her BS at the University of Utah, Salt Lake City, in 1967 and her MA in Art/Photography in 1976 at California State University, Fullerton.

She became an instructor at Harbor College, San Pedro, California, in 1979. Previously she taught at El Camino College, California (1977–79), California State University, Los Angeles (1978–79), and Los Angeles Valley College, Van Nuys, California (1977–78).

She is a board member of the Los Angeles Center for Photographic Studies and Cameraworks Gallery and is a member of the Los Angeles Institute of Contemporary Art.

Jennings works in black-and-white and color, dealing with personal erotic and humorous fantasies.

PUBLICATIONS Books: *Eros and Photography*, 1978; *Photography Today*, Lou Jacobs, 1976. Anthologies: *Expressive Photography*, Lou Jacobs, 1979; *Self-Portrayal*, Jim Alinder, ed., 1979; *Insights: Self-Portraits by Women*, Joyce T. Cohen, ed., 1978. Periodicals: *Camera 35*, Oct 1979, spring 1977; *American Photographer*, Sept 1978, Jan 1978; review, Robert Mautner, *Art Week*, May 20, 1978; *35mm Photography*, spring 1977; review, Joan Murray, *Popular Photography*, June 1976; review, Nancy Marmer, *Artforum*, April 1976; *The Dumb Ox*, fall 1976.

PORTFOLIO *L.A. Issue* (group), 1979 (Los Angeles Ctr. for Photographic Studies).

COLLECTIONS CCP, Tucson; Los Angeles County Mus. of Art; Minneapolis Inst. of Arts, Minn.; Newport Harbor Art Mus., Newport Beach, Calif.; Santa Barbara Art Mus., Calif.; UCLA, Grunwald Gall.; Univ. of Calif., Irvine.

ADDRESS 1546 Lucretia Ave, Los Angeles, CA 90026.

Andrea Jennison PHOTOGRAPHER · TEACHER
Born December 24, 1944, in Portland, Maine, Jennison earned a BA in French Literature and Art History from Colby College, Waterville, Maine (1967), and did graduate work in photography at Rhode Island School of Design, Providence (1972–73), where she studied with Aaron Siskind. She earned an MFA in Photography and Printmaking from the University of Colorado, Boulder (1975), studying with Gary Metz and Charlie Roitz.

Since 1978 Jennison has been director of photography programs and instructor of photography at Colorado Mountain College, Breckenridge. She taught photography at Laramie City Community College, Cheyenne, Wyoming, in 1978, and in that year also served as artist-in-residence at Hebard School, Cheyenne. From 1975 to 1977 she taught photography at Metropolitan State College, Denver, Colorado, and was a media technician at Laredo School, Denver, in 1976–77.

A member of SPE since 1975, Jennison won an NEA/Wyoming Arts Council Artist-in-Schools grant in 1978.

COLLECTIONS Ariz. State Univ., Tempe; Colo. Mountain Coll., Breckenridge; Denver Art Mus., Colo; Md. Art Inst., Baltimore; Univ. of Colo., Boulder.

ADDRESS Colorado Mountain College, Box 2208, Breckenridge, CO 80424.

Yale Joel PHOTOGRAPHER · TEACHER Born February 21, 1919, in New York City, Joel began to learn photography by working as an assistant to photojournalists at *Life* magazine in 1936 and with graphic artist/photographer Herbert Matter.

A staff photographer for *Life* from 1947 to 1972, Joel has done freelance photojournalism for such magazines as *Smithsonian*, *Time* and *People*. During World War II he was a combat photographer for the U.S. Army. He currently holds photography workshops in Croton-on-Hudson, New York.

A member of ASMP and the New York Press Photographers Association, Joel was named Photographer of the Year in 1953.

Primarily a photojournalist, Joel also works in advertising and industrial photography.

PUBLICATIONS Books: *Creative Camera Techniques*, 10 vols., 1979; *Danny Goes to the Hospital*, 1970; *What Musical Instrument Shall I Play?*, 1969; *Firehouse*, 1966. Anthology: *The Print—Images Created in the Darkroom—What the Camera Never Saw*, 1970.

ADDRESS Woodybrook Lane, Croton-on-Hudson, NY 10520.

Eric B. Johnson PHOTOGRAPHER · TEACHER
Born August 5, 1949, in Portland, Oregon, Johnson earned a BA from the University of Oregon Honors College, Eugene, in 1971, his major influence being Bernard Freemesser. He earned an MA (1975) and MFA (1978) in Photography from the University of New Mexico, Albuquerque, citing Thomas Barrow, Van Deren Coke and Betty Hahn as major influences.

In 1979 Johnson was a visiting assistant professor in the Department of Photography and Cinema at Ohio State University, Columbus. He taught photography at Western Washington University, Bellingham, in 1978–79 and was a graduate teaching fellow at the University of New Mexico from 1975 to 1977.

Johnson belongs to SPE and CAA.

The recent series of photograms made by Johnson on printing-out paper, "Templates," used architectural engineering templates as negatives combined with ordinary photographic negatives. The photographer also works with silver prints, using extremely wide-angle lenses.

PUBLICATIONS Periodicals: *Creative Camera*, Sept 1979; *Camera*, Aug 1979; "The Photographs of Ernest Bloch," *Camera*, Feb 1976; "A Composer's Vison: The Photographs of Ernest Bloch," *Aperture*, 16:3, 1972.

PORTFOLIO *Ground Management (Golf)*, 1978.

COLLECTIONS R. Joseph Monsen Cllctn., Seattle, Wash.; San Francisco Mus. of Modern Art;

St. Louis Mus. of Art, Mo.; Univ. of N. Mex. Mus. of Art, Albuquerque. Bibliothèque Nationale, Paris; Moderna Muséet, Stockholm, Sweden.
ADDRESS   486 Euclid St, Ashland, OR 97520.

Joanne Jackson Johnson   PHOTOGRAPHER · TEACHER   Born October 17, 1943, in Winnipeg, Manitoba, Canada, Johnson received a BS from the University of Manitoba in 1965 and an MFA in Film and Photography from the University of Minnesota in 1972, where she studied with Jerome Liebling and Allen Downs.

Since 1977 Johnson has been employed as assistant professor of photography at the School of Art of the University of Manitoba. She previously did freelance film work for the National Film Board and commercial companies in Winnipeg (1974–77).

A founding member of the Winnipeg Film Group in Manitoba, Johnson has also been a member of its board of directors since 1974. She received Manitoba Arts Council project grants in 1978, 1979 and 1980.

PUBLICATIONS   Catalogs: *Clayton Bailey, Joanne Jackson Johnson, David McMillan,* 1977 (Winnipeg Art Gall.); *Exposure: SPE,* 1975 (Art Gall. of Ontario: Toronto).

COLLECTION   Natl. Film Board of Canada Stills Division, Ottawa, Ontario, Canada.

ADDRESS   164 Armstrong Ave, Winnipeg, Manitoba, Canada R2V 1P5.

Thor Anders Johnson   TEACHER · PHOTOGRAM-METRIST · PHOTOGRAPHER   Born March 12, 1947, in Seattle, Washington, Johnson received a BA (1976) and an MA (1978) in Art from San Francisco State University, California. His mentors were Jack Welpott, Don Worth, Ralph Putzker and Neal White.

Currently a photo instructor at Mesa College in San Diego, California, he also works as a gallery technician (since 1979) and a photo instructor (since 1978) at Southwestern College in San Diego. Johnson has been an arts consultant for the Chula Vista City School District in San Diego since 1978.

He has been a member of the Center for Photographic Arts since 1979 and of SPE since 1978.

Primarily working in black-and-white, Johnson uses "evacuated landscapes to discuss subjective relationships between myself and the viewers of my photographs."

PUBLICATIONS   Anthologies: *Contemporary California Photography,* 1978; *Untitled,* no. 14; *Aperture '77,* Apr 1977.

DEALER   Gallery Graphics, 3847 Fifth Ave, San Diego, CA 92103.
ADDRESS   853 Elm Ave, Chula Vista, CA 92011.   .

Tore Yngve Johnson   PHOTOGRAPHER   Born August 1, 1928, in Paris, Johnson died May 14, 1980, in Stockholm. His father was the writer Eyvind Johnson (1900–76), who won the 1974 Nobel Prize in Literature.

A freelance photographer, Johnson was widely exhibited in his home country of Sweden.

PUBLICATIONS   Books (in Sweden): *Hallarna i Paris,* Sven Aurén, 1967 (Wahlström & Widstrand); *Färdmän på isarna,* Jan Sundfeldt, 1964 (Forum); *Skulptur,* 1958 (Bok-Konsum); *Okänt Paris,* Ivar Lo-Johansson, 1954 (Rabén & Sjögren); *Paris hemliga tecken,* Goran Schildt, 1952 (Wahlström & Widstrand).

COLLECTIONS   L/C, Wash., D.C. Bibliothèque Nationale, Paris; Fotografiska Muséet, Stockholm; Norsk Fotohistorisk Förening, Oslo; Photo Mus. of Finland, Helsinki.

DEALER   Tio Foto, Drottninggatan 88 c, 111 36 Stockholm, Sweden.

ARCHIVE   Anita Waxell, Stora Gungans, Väg 6, 122 31, Enskede, Sweden.

Frances Benjamin Johnston   PHOTOGRAPHER · WRITER   Born in 1864 in Grafton, West Virginia, Johnston died in 1952 in New Orleans, Louisiana. After attending Notre-Dame Convent, Govanston, Maryland, she studied painting and drawing at the Académie Julien, Paris (1883–85), then at the Art Students League in Washington, D.C. She served an apprenticeship with Dr. Thomas William Smillie, director of the Smithsonian Institution's Photography Division.

Johnston first worked as a magazine correspondent, ca. 1889, illustrating her articles first with her drawings, then later with her photographs. Her many commissions included photographing the Washington, D.C., school system for the Paris Exposition of 1900, Admiral Dewey's victorious return from Manila (in Naples), construction of the New Theatre in New York (1909), the architecture of Fredericksburg, Virginia, and its environs (1927) and numerous important buildings and homes of wealth. In the early 1890s she opened a portrait studio in Washington, D.C., and around the turn of the century took on a partner for a few years, Mattie Edward Hewitt. Johnston was the unofficial White House photographer through the administrations of Cleveland, Harrison, McKinley, Roosevelt and Taft. She also traveled widely and continued to write for such publications as *Lester's Magazine* and *Town and Country*.

The photographer was an out-of-town member of the New York Camera Club and an honorary member of the American Institute of Architects (1945). She won a gold medal at the Paris Exposition of 1900, the Grand Prix at the Third International Photographic Congress in 1900 and Carnegie Foundation grants in 1933, 1934, 1935 and 1936 totaling over $26,000.

Known as the first woman press photographer, Johnston worked mainly in straightforward reportage, using medium- to large-format gelatin dry-plate negatives and producing platinum and silver prints. Ann Tucker in *The Woman's Eye* notes: "Even if her photographs were not as beautiful as they unquestionably are, her careful, expansive documentation of the events and customs of her day would be invaluable to historians."

PUBLICATIONS   Books: *A Talent for Detail*, Pete Daniel & Raymond Smock, 1974; *The Hampton Album*, Lincoln Kirstein, 1966; *The Early Architecture of Georgia*, w/Frederick Doveton Nichols, 1957; *The Dwellings of Colonial America*, Thomas Tileston Waterman, 1950; *The Mansions of Virginia, 1706–1776*, T. T. Waterman, 1945; *The Early Architecture of North Carolina*, w/T. T. Waterman, 1941; *Plantations of the Carolina Low Country*, Samuel Gaillard Stoney, 1939; *Colonial Churches in Virginia*, w/ Henry Irving Brock, 1930; *Working with the Hands*, Booker T. Washington, 1904. Anthologies: *The Photograph Collector's Guide*, Lee D. Witkin & Barbara London, 1979; *Photography Rediscovered*, David Travis & Anne Kennedy, 1979; *The Invented Eye*, Edward Lucie-Smith, 1975; *The Magic Image*, Cecil Beaton & Gail Buckland, 1975; *Women of Photography*, Margery Mann & Ann Noggle, eds., 1975; *The Woman's Eye*, Ann Tucker, ed., 1973; *Looking at Photographs*, John Szarkowski, 1973. Periodicals: "The Foremost Women Photographers in America," 6-pt. series, 1901, "What a Woman Can Do with a Camera," 1897, *Ladies' Home Journal*; *Demorest's Family Magazine*, Jan 1890, Dec 1889.

COLLECTIONS   Carnegie Inst., Pittsburgh, Pa.; Harvard Univ., Carpenter Ctr. for the Visual Arts, Cambridge, Mass.; Henry E. Huntington Lib. & Art Gall., San Marino, Calif.; L/C, Wash., D.C.; Metro. Mus. of Art, NYC; MOMA, NYC.

Frank B. Johnston   *PHOTOGRAPHER · NEWS-PAPER REPORTER*   Born in 1904, Johnston died May 24, 1956, in Philadelphia, Pennsylvania.

He worked for the Philadelphia Electric Company, Times Wide World Photos (now a division of Associated Press) and the *Philadelphia Daily News* before joining the staff of *The Philadelphia Inquirer* about 1936. He became head of its photographic department shortly before World War II and remained in that post until his death. He also served in the U.S. Navy.

Johnston served as president of the Philadelphia Press Photographers Association and vice-president of Region No. 3 of the NPPA. He was also a member of the Pen and Pencil Club and a Mason.

Johnston won many awards for his photographs and was noted for his successful effort to admit photographers into the courtroom.

A news photographer and photographic editor, Johnston pioneered in many fields of newspaper photography.

Helen Head Johnston   *GALLERY OWNER*   Born in Atlanta, Georgia, Johnston received an AB in Journalism from the University of Georgia, Athens.

She has owned and directed Focus Gallery in San Francisco since 1966. Previous to that she was publicity representative for the M. H. de Young Memorial Museum in San Francisco from 1953 to 1965.

Johnston belongs to the San Francisco Art Dealers Association, Western Association of Art Museums, and Women in Communication. Recipient of the Dorothea Lange Award in 1972, given by the Oakland Museum for outstanding contribution to photography, she also received the Honor Award for outstanding contribution to professional photography from Professional Photographers of Northern California in 1968.

ADDRESS   Focus Gall., 2146 Union St, San Francisco, CA 94123.

J. Dudley Johnston   *PHOTOGRAPHER · CURATOR*   Born in 1868 in Liverpool, Johnston died in London in 1955. He was a businessman in Liverpool and moved to London in 1911. A frequent contributor to the *Photographic Journal*, Johnston began his involvement with photography in 1880, with a real commitment occurring about 1904.

Johnston became a member of the Liverpool Photographic Society in 1904 and was president from 1909 to 1911. He joined The Linked Ring and RPS about 1907. He served on the RPS council from 1916 and acted as its president in 1923 and 1929–31. From 1923 until his death he was curator of the RPS Print Collection and was elected an Honorary Fellow in 1923. He was an important historian of RPS. In 1947 he was awarded the Order of the British Empire for his service to photography.

A pictorialist, Johnston included in his subjects landscapes and cityscapes. Initially he worked in gum-bichromate and platinum prints; in the 1930s he mastered the complicated thiocarbamide process used in making transparencies, becoming an acknowledged expert.

PUBLICATIONS Book: *Pictorial Photography, 1904–1940,* 1952 (RPS: London). Anthologies: *Pictorial Photography in Britain 1900–1920,* 1978 (Arts Council of Great Britain); *The Magic Image,* Cecil Beaton & Gail Buckland, 1975. Periodicals: "Wm. Henry Fox Talbot, F.R.S., Pt. II," w/R. C. Smith, Dec 1968, "Wm. Henry Fox Talbot, F.R.S., Pt. I," Jan 1947, "Sidelights on Fox-Talbot," Jan 1941, "The Facts About Nicéphore Niepce," vol. 80, 1940, "Some Episodes in the Society's History," Dec 1924, *Photographic Journal* (RPS: London); *Studio,* 1908.

COLLECTION RPS, London.

Mark David Johnstone   PHOTOGRAPHER · CRITIC · TEACHER   Born 1953 in St. Louis, Missouri, Johnstone received a BA from Colorado College in Colorada Springs in 1975 and an MFA from the University of Southern California in Los Angeles in 1979.

As of this writing, Johnstone is a visiting professor at the Color Photography Institute of Colorado College. He is also a critic and contributing editor for *Artweek* and the Los Angeles correspondent for *Afterimage.* He was previously a visiting instructor at the Photography Institute of Colorado College (1979, 1976) and an instructor at the College of Continuing Education at the University of Southern California in Los Angeles (1977).

Since 1978 Johnstone has been a member of Friends of Photography, and since 1976 a member of SPE. Johnstone was the recipient of Ford Foundation Venture grants in 1972 and 1973.

COLLECTIONS   Calif. Mus. of Photography, Riverside; Downey Mus. of Art, Downey, Calif.

ADDRESS   POB 1279, Inglewood, CA 90308.

Darryl Deuischer Jones   PHOTOGRAPHER   Born in Fort Wayne, Indiana, on March 29, 1948, Jones completed a BA in Psychology at Indiana University (1970), where he studied photography under Henry Holmes Smith and Reginald Heron. In Fort Wayne he learned carbon and carbro printing with Dr. Robert F. Green (1973–74).

For the last few years Jones has been working as a freelance photographer and teaching carbon and carbro printing techniques at the Maine Photographic Workshops. He is also an instructor at the Herron School of Art in Indianapolis; previously he taught at the Indiana Vocational Technical College (1978–79).

Jones belongs to RPS.

The artist, specializing in carbon and carbro printing, works in small to large format and also uses a Kodak Cirkut camera.

PUBLICATIONS   Periodicals: "Home-made Color: Tri-color Carbon and Carbro," *How-to Photography,* summer 1978; "Carbonated Prints —Carbon and Carbro," *35mm Photography,* summer 1976; "Carbro: The Royal Path," *Petersen's Photographic Magazine,* July 1975.

COLLECTIONS   In Indiana: Baker & Daniels, Indianapolis; Crown Hill Cemetery, Indianapolis; Gallery 614, Fort Wayne. IMP/GEH, Rochester.

DEALERS   Gall. 614, 614 W Berry, Fort Wayne, IN 46802; Neikrug Gall., 224 E 68th St, New York, NY 10021.

ADDRESS   2918 Highwoods Dr E, Indianapolis, IN 46222.

Dewitt Lane Jones III   PHOTOGRAPHER · FILM MAKER · LECTURER   Born on July 26, 1943, in Tampa, Florida, Jones completed a BA in Drama at Dartmouth College in Hanover, New Hampshire (1965), and an MFA in Film-making at the University of California at Los Angeles (1967).

Since 1971 Jones has been employed as the president of Dewitt Jones Productions Inc. in Bolinas, California. From 1969 to 1971 he was a partner of The New Film Company in Boston. Previously he worked in Los Angeles as a film director for Desort-Fisher Productions (1968–69) and as a producer for Leo Burnett Advertising (1967–68).

A member of the Academy of Motion Pictures Arts and Sciences since 1975, Jones received a Picture of the Year Award from the National Press Photographers Association (1977), a Grand Prize at the Cortina International Sports Film Festival (1974) and also won four Cine Golden Eagles.

Jones' stills are 35mm exclusively. His main interests are photojournalism, landscape and adventure photography.

PUBLICATIONS   Books: *Robert Frost: A Tribute to the Source,* David Bradley, poems by Robert Frost, 1979; *What the Road Passes By,* Ellie Huggins, ed., 1978; *John Muir's America,* T. H. Watkins, 1976. Periodicals: "California's Redwood Coast," Sept 1977, "Robert Frost—His Beloved

Land," Apr 1976, "John Muir's Wild America," Apr 1973, *National Geographic.*

REPRESENTATIVE Woodfin Camp, 415 Madison Ave, New York, NY 10017.

ADDRESS Box 116, Bolinas, CA 94924.

Harold Henry Jones *TEACHER · ART ADMINIS-TRATOR · PHOTOGRAPHER* Born September 29, 1940, in Morristown, New Jersey, Jones earned a diploma from the Newark School of Fine and Industrial Art, New Jersey, in 1963, a BFA from Maryland Institute of Art, Baltimore, in 1965 and an MFA in Photography/Art History from University of New Mexico, Albuquerque, in 1972.

Currently the coordinator of the Photography Program, Department of Art, University of Arizona, Tucson (since 1977), he was the founding director of the Center for Creative Photography at the university (1975–77). Jones was adjunct associate professor of art history at Queens College, New York City, in 1974–75, and director of Light Gallery in New York City from 1971 to 1975. He was first associate then assistant curator of George Eastman House in Rochester, New York, during 1968–71.

A member of Photography Instructors Association and SPE, Jones was on the board of the latter in 1971–75. He received an NEA Photographer's Fellowship in 1977 and an NEA exhibition grant in the same year. He also won the Gold Award in 1977 from the National Design Competition, Rochester, for designing the program for the Center for Creative Photography.

Besides photography Jones draws and does historic research.

PUBLICATIONS Anthology: "The 50s—A Renaissance in Photography," *The Photographers' Choice*, 1975. Catalogs: *Contemporary California Photography*, intro., 1978 (Camerawork Gall.: San Francisco); "Photography," intro., *Twenty Arizona Artists*, Aug 1978 (Ariz Commission of Arts/Humanities & Phoenix Art Mus.); *Figure in Landscape*, 1971 (IMP/GEH: Rochester). Periodical: "Five Quotations," *Northlight*, Nov 1978.

COLLECTIONS Ariz. State Univ., Northlight Gall., Tempe; CCP, Tucson; IMP/GEH, Rochester; MOMA, NYC; Norton Simon Mus. of Art, Pasadena, Calif.; R.I. School of Design, Providence; Santa Fe Mus., N. Mex.; UCLA Art Mus.; Univ. of Colo., Boulder. Natl. Gall. of Canada, Ottawa, Ontario.

DEALERS Light Gall., 724 Fifth Ave, New York, NY 10019; Si Lowinsky Gall., 228 Grant Ave, San Francisco, CA 94108.

ADDRESS Art Dept, Univ of Arizona, Tucson, AZ 85721.

Pirkle Jones *PHOTOGRAPHER · TEACHER* Born January 2, 1914, in Shreveport, Louisiana, Jones graduated from the California School of Fine Arts (now the San Francisco Art Institute). He studied with Ansel Adams and Minor White in 1949, and cites them as major influences along with Dorothea Lange, Edward Weston and Alfred Stieglitz.

He has taught photography at the San Francisco Art Institute since 1970 and freelanced from 1949 to 1970. He was a professional assistant to Ansel Adams in 1949–52, and from 1941 to 1946 was in the U.S. Army Signal Corps.

Jones is a member of Friends of Photography. He won an NEA photography grant in 1977 and a certificate of recognition from the National Urban League for photographic excellence and participation in "America's Many Faces" (chairman, Edward Steichen) in 1961.

Using small and large formats, Jones prints his unmanipulated images up to 16 x 20, usually in silver, selenium-toned. He is interested in photographs as both documents and works of art.

PUBLICATIONS Anthologies: *Octave of Prayer*, Minor White, 1972; *Photography in the Twentieth Century*, 1964; *Photography at Mid-Century*, 1960; *Photography Yearbook*, 1956. Periodicals: "Masters of the Darkroom," Phiz Mezy, *Darkroom*, 1979; *U.S. Camera Annual*, 1963, 1961, 1959, 1953, 1940; "Death of a Valley," w/Dorothea Lange, *Aperture*, 1960; *Popular Photography's Photography Annual*, 1960; Minor White, *Image*, no. 49, 1957; Nancy Newhall, *Aperture*, 4: 2, 1956.

PORTFOLIO *Portfolio Two*, foreword by Ansel Adams, 1968 (self-pub.).

COLLECTIONS: Amon Carter Mus. of Western Art, Ft. Worth, Tex.; Art Inst. of Chicago; Dominican Coll. Lib., San Rafael, Calif.; IMP/GEH, Rochester; L/C, Wash., D.C.; Metro. Mus. of Art, NYC; Mills Coll., Albert Bender Cllctn., Oakland, Calif.; MIT, Cambridge, Mass.; MOMA, NYC; New Orleans Mus. of Art; Oakland Mus. of Art, Calif.; San Francisco Art Inst. Lib.; San Francisco Mus. of Modern Art; Univ. of Ariz., Ansel Adams Cllctn., Tucson: Univ. of Calif., Bancroft Lib., Berkeley; Univ. of N. Mex. Art Mus., Albuquerque. Victoria & Albert Mus., London.

DEALERS Weston Gall., Sixth & Delores, POB 655, Carmel, CA 93921; Photo Gall. Internatl., 2-5-18 Toranomom Minato-ku, Tokyo 105, Japan.

ADDRESS 663 Lovell Ave, Mill Valley, CA 94941.

Kenneth Josephson PHOTOGRAPHER · TEACHER
Born July 1, 1932, in Detroit, Michigan, Josephson received a BFA in 1957 from the Rochester Institute of Technology in New York and an MS from the Institute of Design at Illinois Institute of Technology in Chicago in 1960.

Since 1961 Josephson has been employed as a professor at the School of the Art Institute of Chicago, and has been a freelance photographer since 1958. Previously he was employed as a visiting professor at the Institute of Design in Chicago (1969), an associate professor at the University of Hawaii (1967–68) and an exchange teacher at Konstfackskolan in Stockholm (1966–67). He also worked as a photographer for the Chrysler Corporation (1957–58).

Josephson was a recipient of NEA grants in 1979 and 1975. He also received a Guggenheim Fellowship in 1972.

He works in black-and-white and also produces assemblages and photocollages. His work contains an extensive use of juxtaposition, exploring the differences between photography and reality. He describes his work as both humorous and surreal.

PUBLICATIONS Monographs: *Kenneth Josephson: The Illusion of the Picture*, Floris M. Neüsuss, 1978 (Fotoforum; Kassel, Germany); *The Bread Book*, 1973 (self-pub.). Anthologies: *Nude: Theory*, Jain Kelly, ed., 1979; *The Photograph Collector's Guide*, Lee D. Witkin & Barbara London, 1979; *Self-Portrayal*, Jim Alinder, ed., 1978; *Mirrors and Windows*, John Szarkowski, 1978; *A Thousand and One Pictures*, 1978 (Moderna Muséet; Stockholm); *The Great West Real/Ideal*, 1977; *The Photographers' Choice*, 1975; *Looking at Photographs*, John Szarkowski, 1973; *Photography in the Twentieth Century*, 1967; *The Photographer's Eye*, John Szarkowski, 1966. Catalogs: *Chicago: The City and Its Artists, 1945–78*, 1978 (Univ. of Mich. Mus. of Art); *Spaces*, 1978 (Rhode Island School of Design Mus. of Art); *The Photographer and the City*, 1977 (Mus. of Contemporary Art: Chicago). Periodicals: *Modern Photography*, 40:7, 1976, 25:5, 1961; "Photos Within Photographs," Max Kozloff, *Artforum 14*, Feb 1976; *Creative Camera*, Aug 1974; *Camera*, May 1974; *Photography Yearbook*, 1968; *Aperture*, 9:2, 1961.

PORTFOLIOS *Kenneth Josephson*, intro. by Alex Sweetman, 1975 (Ctr. for Photographic Studies: Louisville); *Underware* (group), 1977 (School of the Art Inst. of Chicago).

COLLECTIONS Art Inst. of Chicago; CCP, Tucson; E. B. Crocker Gall., Sacramento, Calif.; Exchange Natl. Bank of Chicago; Fla. Ctr. for the Arts, Tampa, Fla.; Harvard Univ., Fogg Art Mus., Cambridge, Mass.; IMP/GEH, Rochester; Charles Levy Co., Chicago; MOMA, NYC; Mus. of Contemporary Art, Chicago; Mus. of Fine Arts, Boston; Mus. of Fine Arts, Houston, Tex., Norton Simon Mus., Pasadena, Calif.; R.I. School of Design, Mus. of Art, Providence; Seagram Cllctn., NYC; Southern Ill. Univ., Edwardsville; UCLA; Univ. of Fla., Gainesville; Univ. of Iowa Mus. of Art, Iowa City; Univ. of Louisville, Ky.; Univ. of Neb., Sheldon Memorial Art Gall., Lincoln; Univ. of N. Mex., Albuquerque; Virginia Mus. of Fine Arts, Richmond. Bibliothèque Nationale, Paris; Fotografiska Muséet, Stockholm; Natl. Gall. of Canada, Ottawa, Ontario.

REPRESENTATIVE Workshop Gall., Visual Studies Workshop, 31 Prince St, Rochester, NY 14607.

ADDRESS 2648 w 21 Pl, Chicago, IL 60608.

Mario Garcia Joya CURATOR · PHOTOGRAPHER · CINEMATOGRAPHER Born July 28, 1938, in Havana, Cuba, Garcia Joya has been doing graduate work in philology at Havana University since 1978, specializing in Cuban studies. He previously studied photographic evaluation with Adelaida de Juan at the National Library (1965–66), history of photography with Mario Rodriguez Aleman at the Cuban Institute of Film, Art and Industry (1963–64), graphic design with painter Raul Martinez (1957–58) and fine arts at San Alejandro Fine Arts Academy (1955–57), all in Havana. His wife, Maria Eugenia Haya, is a photographer and historian.

Currently director of photography at the Cuban Institute of Film and Industry in Havana (since 1961), Garcia Joya organized the Cuban exhibitions "Recontres Internationales de Photographie" in Arles, France (1978), and the first Latin-American sampling of contemporary photography in Mexico (1977). In 1967 he worked as a photographer at the Cuban Pavillion Exhibition at Expo '67 in Montreal, Canada, and from 1963 to 1965 he was a photographer for *Cuba* magazine.

Garcia Joya has belonged to the Cuban Union of Writers and Artists since 1960, in 1980 serving as its secretary; he was previously president of the photography section (1978–80). He won First International Prize from the Ministries of Culture of the Socialist Countries in Budapest, Hungary (1979), and a photographic diploma for his book *Un Mundo amasado por los Trabajadores* at the 1977 International Book Exposition in Germany. He also won first prize at the 1966 Havana Carnival, the photojournalist prize from the

Cuban Union of Writers and Artists in 1964 and the Komsomolskaya Pravda Prize from Czechoslovakia in 1961.

PUBLICATIONS Books: *Pintura cubana: Temas y variaciones*, Adelaida de Juan, 1978 (UNEAC: Cuba); *Un Mundo amasado por los Trabajadores*, 1974, *A la Plaza con Fidel*, 1970 (Book Institution: Havana); *Las Artes Plasticas*, Adelaida de Juan, 1968 (Cuadernos Populares: Cuba); *Diez Años de Arquitectura Revolucionaria*, Roberto Segre, 1968 (UNEAC: Cuba); *La Histoia, la Provincia, La Revolución, LAS VILLAS*, 1965 (Venceremos Editions: Havana); *Páginas de Memorias*, 1964 (Book's Inst.: Havana). Anthologies: *XX Aniversario Casa de las Americas*, Maria E. Haya, 1979 (INBA: Mexico City); *Fotos de Cuba*, 1975 (Book's Inst.: Havana). Periodicals: *El Caimán Barbudo*, no. 113, 1978, no. 112, 1977; *Fototécnica Año IX*, no. 1, 1978; *Revolución y Cultura*, no. 56, 1977.

COLLECTIONS In Havana: House of the Americas; Natl. Lib. of Jose Martí; Natl. Mus. of Havana; Natl. Union of Writers & Artists; Univ. of Havana, School of Philology. House of Culture, Prague, Czechoslovakia; Mexican Council of Photography, Mexico D.F.; Mus. of Santiago de Cuba, Oriente, Cuba.

ADDRESS % Union de Escritores y Artistas, 17 y H, Vedado, Havana, Cuba.

Estelle Jussim TEACHER · WRITER Born March 18, 1927, in New York City, Jussim studied at Queens College in New York, receiving a BA in 1947, and at Columbia University in New York, where she earned an MS in 1963 and a PhD in 1970.

In 1972 Jussim assumed her current position as professor of visual communication at Simmons College in Boston. From 1969 to 1972 she was assistant professor of communications media at Hampshire College in Amherst, Massachusetts. In 1965–66 she held the position of executive assistant to the director of educational resources for the Borough of Manhattan; before that she was employed by the Columbia University libraries from 1963 to 1965.

A member of SPE, the Popular Culture Association and the Society for the Anthropology of Visual Communication, Jussim is also on the board of trustees of VSW and on the international board of advisers of *History of Photography* magazine in London. She was awarded an honorary membership in DGPh.

Her work deals with the history and criticism of photography and communication theory and the psychology of popular arts. Among other activities, she serves as a consultant to photographic archives.

PUBLICATIONS Books (text only): *Jerome Liebling*, 1978; *Visual Communication and the Graphic Arts*, 1974. Periodicals: "Icons or Ideology: Stieglitz and Hine," *Massachusetts Review*, winter 1978–79; "Technology or Aesthetics: Alfred Stieglizt & Photogravure," Jan 1978, "From the Studio to the Snapshot," July 1977, *History of Photography*.

ADDRESS POB 132, Granby, MA 01033.

K

Fritz Kaeser *PHOTOGRAPHER* Born in Greenville, Illinois, on July 3, 1910, Kaeser studied art education at the University of Illinois, Champaign-Urbana (1928–30), and the University of Wisconsin, Madison (1930–31). He studied at the Chicago Art Institute in 1931–32, and was apprenticed to as well as studied with William Mortensen in 1932. Kaeser took a study work course with Ansel Adams at the San Francisco School of Fine Arts in 1946, and worked in lithography at Colorado Springs Art Center in 1948.

Presently self-employed, the photographer had his own studio gallery in Tucson, Arizona (1951–58), and studios in Aspen, Colorado (1946–51), and Madison, Wisconsin (1933–43).

Kaeser won the Jay Sternberg Award in 1960 from the Tucson Art Center, and served as president of the Tucson Fine Arts association in 1956.

He has exhibited his lapidary work, "Designs in Stone," at the Tucson Gem and Mineral International Exhibition, 1970–76.

Most recently Kaeser has been painting on film with solarizations (since 1975) and has also worked in bromoil transfers and carbo prints. From 1955 to 1975 he concentrated on "subjective image and form," and from 1940 to 1955 he primarily produced ski, mountain and desert landscapes.

PUBLICATIONS Periodicals: "Desert Textures," *Arizona Highways*, Jan 1955; *U.S. Camera Annual*, 1943; *U.S. Camera*, Feb 1943, Nov. 1941; *American Annual of Photography* 1936, 1935, 1934.

COLLECTIONS CCP, Tucson; Palm Springs Desert Mus., Calif.; Univ. of Notre Dame, Snite Mus. of Art, Ind.

DEALER America West Gall., 363 S Meyer, Barrio Viejo, Tucson, AZ 85701.

ADDRESS 3030 N Camino del Oeste, Tucson, AZ 85705.

Manfred Paul Kage *PHOTOGRAPHER · PHOTO-DESIGNER* Born October 4, 1935, in Delitzsch, Germany, Kage has been founder and owner of the Institut für Wissenschaftliche Fotographie und Kinematographie since 1960.

He belongs to GDL, DGPh, BFF and Künstlerhaus Wien.

Kage works with diapositives, kaleidoscope-photography, photomicrography, SEM-color, Kirlian photography and video.

PUBLICATIONS Book: *Kunstformen der Technik*, 1979. Periodical: *Camera*, Feb 1975.

REPRESENTATIVE Peter Arnold Agency, 1500 Broadway, New York, NY 10036.

ADDRESS Schloss Weissenstein, D-7321 Lauterstein, West Germany.

Steve Kahn *PHOTOGRAPHER* Born in 1943 in Los Angeles, Kahn earned a BA in 1966 from Reed College, Portland, Oregon. His wife is visual artist Lita Albuquerque.

A freelance photographer, Kahn taught at California Institute of the Arts, Valencia, in 1978–79.

In 1980 he received a Photographer's Fellowship from the NEA.

PUBLICATIONS Monograph: *Stasis*, 1973 pub.). Catalogs: *Attitudes: Photography in the 1970's*, 1979 (Santa Barbara Mus. of Art: Calif.); *Contemporary California Photography*, 1978 (Camerawork Gall.: San Francisco); *Interchange*, 1978 (Mt. St. Mary's College: Los Angeles); *Emerging L.A. Photographers*, 1977 (Friends of Photography/ICP: Carmel & NYC); *Contemporary American Photography*, 1976 (UCLA); *Exposing: Photographic Definitions*, 1976 (Los Angeles Inst. of Contemporary Art); *Light and Substance*, 1974 (Univ. of N. Mex.: Albuquerque); *24 from L.A.*, 1973 (San Francisco Mus. of Modern Art).

COLLECTIONS Dallas Mus. of Fine Arts, Tex.; Houston Mus. of Fine Arts, Tex.; Los Angeles County Mus. of Art; San Francisco Mus. of Modern Art; UCLA; Univ. of N. Mex., Albuquerque.

Bibliothèque Nationale, Paris; Univ. of Sydney, Australia.

DEALERS Rosamund Felsen, 669 N La Cienega Blvd, Los Angeles, CA 90069; Emmy de Martelaere, 11 rue de Marignan, Paris, 75008 France.

ADDRESS 622 Rose Ave, Venice, CA 90291.

Clemens Kalischer PHOTOGRAPHER · GALLERY DIRECTOR Born March 30, 1921, in Hoyren, Bavaria, Kalischer studied at Lycée Michelet in Paris, at Cooper Union and at the New School for Social Research, both in New York City. His early influences were André Kertész, Paul Strand and Henri Cartier-Bresson.

Self-employed since 1949, Kalischer directs Image Gallery, Stockbridge, Massachusetts. He also teaches photography at Berkshire Community College and Williams College, Williamstown, Massachusetts. He previously worked for *Coronet* magazine (1948–49) and for France Press News Agency (1947–48).

Kalischer belongs to the Laurel Hill Association (since 1952) and the American Society of Picture Professionals. He has been president of the Edna St. Vincent Millay Art Colony in Austerlitz, New York, since 1975, and in that year served with the New York Governor's Task Force on the Arts. In 1980 he received a grant from the Institute for Urban Design in Cambridge, Mass.

Besides his personal work Kalischer does photojournalism, commercial, portrait and architectural photography. His "Image Photos" Library consists of 500,000 pictures.

COLLECTIONS Brooklyn Mus., N.Y.; L/C, Wash., D.C.; Metro. Mus. of Art, NYC; Williams Coll. Mus., Williamstown, Mass.

ADDRESS Main St, Stockbridge, MA 01262.

Richard Kalvar PHOTOGRAPHER Born November 14, 1944, in New York, Kalvar earned a BA in English from Cornell University, Ithaca, New York, in 1968. An important influence was Jerome Ducrot, for whom he worked as an assistant in 1965–66.

Kalvar has been a member of Magnum Photos since 1977 and was an associate member from 1975 to 1977. He was a founder and member of the Visa Agency in Paris, 1972–75.

The photographer shoots unposed black-and-white images.

PUBLICATIONS Anthology: *Album Photographique*, 1979 (Centre Pompidou: Paris). Periodicals: *American Photographer*, Mar 1979; *Creative Camera*, Nov 1971; *Zoom*, May 1971 (France).

COLLECTION MOMA, NYC.

REPRESENTATIVE Magnum Photos, 251 Park Ave, New York, NY 10036.

ADDRESS 2 rue Christine, Paris, France 75006.

Jonas Kalvelis PHOTOGRAPHER Born in the Kupiškis district of Lithuanian SSR on March 2, 1925, Kalvelis studied land organization at the Agricultural Training College in Kaunas, Lithuanian SSR, from 1953 to 1958.

Since 1954 Kalvelis has been head of the photo laboratory of the Institute of Planning of Water Resources in Kaunas. Prior to that he was a technician for the Institute of Forestry in Kaunas, 1948–54.

Kalvelis has been a member of the Photography Art Society of Lithuanian SSR since 1970 and an associate of the Fédération Internationale d'Art Photographique (FIAP) since 1976.

Of his work Kalvelis states: "Nature is by itself the author of its own art. The only remaining thing is to be able to notice it and convey it to others."

PUBLICATIONS Book: *Lietuvos Fotografija*, 1978 (Vilnius). Catalog: *Jonas Kalvelis*, intro. by Algirdas Gaižutis, 1975 (Kaunas). Periodical: *Sovietskoye Photo*, Dec 1978.

COLLECTIONS Musée Français de la Photographie, Bièvres, France; Photography Mus., Šiauliai, Lithuanian SSR.

REPRESENTATIVE Photography Art Society, Pionieriu 8, 232600 Vilnius, Lithuanian SSR, USSR.

ADDRESS Rotušės I, 233000 Kaunas, Lithuanian SSR, USSR.

Toshimi Kamiya PHOTOGRAPHER · EDITOR Born May 16, 1946, in Tokoname, Aichi-ken, Japan, Kamiya received a Bachelor of Japanese Literature degree from Seikei University in 1969. His mentor is Yoshiro Sakurai.

Currently Kamiya is editor of *Design Atelier*, a photography magazine.

Working in 35mm black-and-white, Kamiya describes his style as a "journey through the spirit of Japanese traditional beauty." He likens his work to that of the famous hokku poet Basho (1644–94).

PUBLICATION Periodical: *Camera*, Oct 1977.

PORTFOLIOS *Sourei-Fu*, 1979; *Sankai-Zu*, 1976; *Privates*, 1975; *Museum-One*, 1974; *Yamaguchi*, 1973; *Discussion with Private Times*, 1972.

COLLECTIONS Forum Stadtpark, Graz, Steiermark, Austria; Yama-Roku Cllctns., Kawakita, Yamagata, Japan.

REPRESENTATIVE UNAC Tokyo, Azabudai Uni-House 112, 1-1-20 Azabudai Minatoku, Tokyo 106, Japan.
ADDRESS 1-29-36 Hamadayama Suginami-ku, Tokyo 168, Japan.

Klaus Wilhelm Kammerichs *PHOTOGRAPHER·TEACHER·SCULPTOR* Born December 1, 1933, in Iserlohn, Westfalen, Germany, Kammerichs studied at Werkkunstschule in Düsseldorf, Germany (1954–56), and at Staatliche Kunstakademie in Düsseldorf under Professor Otto Coester (1956–59). He also served an apprenticeship in photography in Iserlohn (1951–54).

Since 1962 he has taught photography at the Technical College in Düsseldorf and has been a design professor at Fachhochschule in Düsseldorf since 1973, heading the design faculty there since 1978. He previously ran the photo studio at Die Werbegesellschaft in Essen (1960–61) and at Gramm & Grey Advertising Agency in Düsseldorf (1959–60).

Kammerichs belongs to Westdeutscher Künstlerbund (since 1977), Bund Freischaffender Fotodesigner (since 1974), GDL (since 1977) and DGPh.

The photographer creates photo sculptures "for a 'kinetic' public," said J. J. de Lucie-Meyer in *Novum*, June 1976. He added: "After the first surrealistic impression the viewer instinctively looks for a point of view which will yield a realistic picture."

PUBLICATIONS Catalogs: *Westdeutscher Künstlerbund*, 1979 (Karl-Ernst-Osthaus-Mus.: Hagen, Germany); *Westdeutscher Künstlerbund in der Stadthalle Wilhelmshaven*, 1979; *Thema Heidelberg*, 1978 (Kurpfälz Mus. & Kunstverein); *Westdeutscher Künstlerbund*, 1977 (Karl-Ernst-Osthaus-Mus.: Hagen); *De Fiets*, 1977 (Mus. Boymans-van Beuningen: Rotterdam, The Netherlands); *Photography as Art—Art as Photography*, 1975 (House of European Photography: Chalon-sur-Saône, France); *Klaus Kammerichs, Photoskulpturen*, 1975 (Kunstverein dur die Rheinlande und Westfalen: Düsseldorf). Periodicals: *Camera*, Feb 1975; *Photographis* 1970, 1966; *Modern Photography*, 23:1, 1959.

COLLECTIONS In West Germany: Karl-Ernst-Osthaus-Mus., Hagen; State of North Rhine-Westphalia, Düsseldorf.

DEALER Galerie Niepel, Grabenstr 72, 4000 Düsseldorf, West Germany.

ADDRESS Am Oberbach 14, 4005 Meerbusch 3, West Germany.

Consuelo Kanaga *PHOTOGRAPHER* Born May 25, 1894, in Astoria, Oregon, Kanaga died on February 28, 1978, in Mt. Kisco, New York. She was influenced by Steichen and Stieglitz, and in 1927 traveled in Europe with Louise Dahl-Wolfe. Kanaga's second husband was the painter Wallace Putnam.

Kanaga became a reporter and feature writer, then a photographer, for the *San Francisco Chronicle* (1915). In 1926 she joined the *New York American* as a news photographer, and in 1934 she was a contract photographer for the *Daily Worker* and *New Masses*. She participated in the Works Progress Administration Arts Program in 1936, and in the 1940s she freelanced for *Woman's Day*.

Kanaga was a member of Group f.64.

PUBLICATIONS Anthology: *Family of Man*, Edward Steichen, ed., 1955. Catalogs: *Recollections: Ten Women of Photography*, Margaretta K. Mitchell, 1978 (ICP: NYC); *Photographs: A Retrospective*, 1974 (Lerner-Heller Gall.: NYC).

COLLECTIONS IMP/GEH, Rochester; Metro. Mus. of Art, NYC; MOMA, NYC.

Art Kane *PHOTOGRAPHER* Born Arthur Kanofsky in New York City on April 9, 1925, Kane graduated from Cooper Union, New York City, in 1950. From 1954 to 1957 he studied with Alexey Brodovitch.

A freelance photographer since 1959, Kane has also been the corporate design director of Penthouse International since 1973. He was the art director for a fashion advertising agency (1957–59) and for *Seventeen* magazine (1950–57). Before that he was a designer at *Esquire* magazine (1949–50). His images have appeared in *Look*, *Life*, *Vogue*, *McCall's* and *Esquire*.

A member of the Directors Guild of America and ASMP, he was awarded the ASMP Photographer of the Year distinction in 1963. He has also been the recipient of a Newhouse Citation from Syracuse University, New York (1961), the Page One Award from the Newspaper Guild of America (1966) and the Augustus Saint-Gaudens Medal for Distinguished Achievement given by Cooper Union (1967).

PUBLICATIONS Periodicals: *Camera*, Dec 1975, Oct 1974, Apr 1970.

COLLECTIONS Metro. Mus. of Art, NYC; MOMA, NYC.

ADDRESS Penthouse Int. Ltd, 909 Third Ave, New York, NY 10022.

Kenji Kanesaka *PHOTOGRAPHER · REPORTER · CRITIC* Born September 22, 1934, Kanesaka graduated in English from Keio University, Tokyo (1956). He later attended the Harvard International Seminar on Culture (Cambridge, Massachusetts) in the summer of 1961, and was a visiting scholar at Northwestern University Film Department, Evanston, Illinois (1964–65).

Currently a freelancer, Kanesaka was a reporter for *Asahi Graph Magazine* in the late 1960s and early 1970s. He has belonged to Japan Film Pen Club since the early 1960s.

The photographer won a Japan Society grant in 1966, a Fulbright Fund travel grant in 1964 and the top Fred A. Niles prize from the Hull House International Experimental Film Festival in Chicago (1965) for the film *The Burning Ear*.

His other films include *Hopscotch* (1967) and *Super Up* (1966).

PUBLICATIONS Books (in Tokyo): *Photographing America*, 1979 (Asahi Sonorama Co.); *Super American Dream*, 1976 (Kodan-Sha); *Republic of Fantasy*, 1971 (Shobun-Sha); *Underground Generation*, ed., 1968 (Noble Shobo); *Will the Movies Collapse?*, 1968 (Sanichi-Shobo); *Underground America*, 1967 (Gakugei-Sha).

REPRESENTATIVE Junichiro Tamada, Rokkor Club, Toyokawa Bldg, 8-12-13 Ginza, Chuo-ku, Tokyo, Japan.

ADDRESS 4-21-12 Takinogawa, Kita-ku, Tokyo 114, Japan.

James H. Karales *PHOTOJOURNALIST* Born in Canton, Ohio, on July 15, 1930, Karales earned his BFA at Ohio University, Athens, in 1955.

He has been freelancing since 1971 (also in the years 1958–60), but from 1960 to 1971 he was a staff photographer for *Look* magazine. His images have appeared in the pages of *Life, Saturday Review, Art in America, America Illustrated, Popular Photography, Modern Photography* and *Camera 35*.

Karales has been the recipient of numerous awards, among them: the Art Directors Club, New Jersey chapter (1974) and New York chapter (1969, 1968, 1966); a CAPS grant (1974) and Picture of the Year (1965).

Some of his more important picture essays have been on New York's lower East Side (1975, 1970), East Germany (1970), Selma, Alabama (1965), Vietnam (1964–66), Geel, Belgium (1961), the logging industry (1958) and Rendville, Ohio (1956).

COLLECTION MOMA, NYC.

ADDRESS 147 W 79 St, New York, NY 10024.

Barbara E. Karant *PHOTOGRAPHER · TEACHER* Born August 18, 1952, in Chicago, Illinois, Karant earned a BFA from the Rhode Island School of Design, Providence, in 1974 and an MFA from the School of the Art Institute of Chicago in 1977. Major influences were Harold Allen, Joy Neimanas, Karen Savage and Aaron Siskind.

Karant has lectured in the Department of Fine Arts, Loyola University, Chicago, since 1978 and has been a freelance architectural photographer since 1977. In 1976 she was assistant to the curator of photography at the New Orleans Museum of Art.

Karant became a member of SPE in 1977.

The photographer works exclusively in color, using an 8 x 10 Deardorf view camera. Her work "centers on the architectural complexities of interior spaces."

PUBLICATIONS Periodicals: *Afterimage*, Apr 1980; *Popular Photography's 35mm Photography*, winter 1978.

COLLECTIONS Chrysler Mus., Norfolk, Va.; Ill. State Mus., Springfield; St. Louis Mus. of Art, Mo.

DEALER Allan Frumkin Gall., 620 N Michigan Ave, Chicago, IL 60611.

ADDRESS 2107 N Dayton St, Chicago, IL 60614.

Malak Karsh *PHOTOGRAPHER* Born March 1, 1915, in Mardin, Armenia (now Turkey), Karsh attended American College in Aleppo, Syria, and then studied two years with his famed brother, photographer Yousuf Karsh.

He has been self-employed since 1945 under the name of Malak Photographs Ltd in Ottawa, Canada.

A member of ASMP, Ottawa Board of Trade and Professional Photographers of Canada (PPOC), Karsh served for many years as director of the Eastern Ontario branch of PPOC. He received designations of Craftsman Photographic Arts and Master of Photographic Arts from PPOC, and was awarded the gold medal for excellence from the National Film Board of Canada in 1977.

PUBLICATION Book: *Stones of History*, Canada.

COLLECTIONS Dept. of External Affairs, Canada; Natl. Film Board of Canada.

ADDRESS 292 Laurier Ave E, Ottawa, Ontario K1N 6P5 Canada.

Yousuf Karsh *PHOTOGRAPHER* [plate 87] Karsh was born December 23, 1908, in Mardin,

Armenia (now Turkey). After suffering the horrors of the Armenian massacres by the Turks, he emigrated to Canada at age sixteen with the help of his uncle, a photographer in Sherbrooke, Quebec. From 1928 to 1931 Karsh was apprenticed to painter and photographer John Garo in Boston. His brother Malak is also a photographer.

Karsh returned to Canada in 1932 and soon opened his own studio in Ottawa, Ontario. He was appointed official portrait photographer of the Canadian government in 1935, and gained international prominence with his portrait of Winston Churchill, which appeared on the cover of *Life* magazine in December 1941.

Karsh is a trustee of the Photographic Arts and Sciences Foundation, was elected to the Royal Canadian Academy of Arts in 1975 and is a corporate member of the Muscular Dystrophy Associations of America. Named an Honorary Fellow of RPS in 1970, he also received a U.S. Presidential Citation for meritorious service on behalf of the handicapped in 1971, a Canada Council Medal in 1969 and a Medal of Service of the Order of Canada in 1968. In 1970 Karsh was designated Master of Photographic Arts by the Professional Photographers Association of Canada.

Karsh is best known for his portraits of such illustrious people as Ernest Hemingway, Albert Einstein, John F. Kennedy, Pablo Picasso, Georgia O'Keeffe, Edward Steichen, Pablo Casals and Elizabeth II.

PUBLICATIONS Monographs: *Karsh Canadians*, 1978 (Univ. of Toronto Press); *Karsh Portraits*, 1976; *Faces of Our Time*, 1971 (Univ. of Toronto Press); *Karsh Portfolio*, 1967; *Portraits of Greatness*, 1959; *Faces of Destiny*, 1946. Books: *The Warren Court*, w/John P. Frank, 1965; *In Search of Greatness*, autobio., 1962; *These Are the Sacraments*, w/Bishop Fulton J. Sheen 1962; *Canada*, J. Fisher, 1960; *This Is the Holy Land*, w/Bishop Fulton J. Sheen & H. V. Morton, 1960; *This Is Rome*, w/Bishop Fulton J. Sheen & H. V. Morton, 1959; *This Is the Mass*, w/Bishop Fulton J. Sheen & Henri Daniel-Rops, 1958. Anthologies: *The Photograph Collector's Guide*, Lee D. Witkin & Barbara London, 1979; *Interviews with Master Photographers*, James Danziger & Barnaby Conrad, 1977; *The Magic Image*, Cecil Beaton & Gail Buckland, 1975; *Great Photographers*, 1971, *The Great Themes*, 1970, Time-Life Series.

COLLECTIONS Art Inst. of Chicago; IMP/GEH, Rochester; Metro. Mus. of Art, NYC; MOMA, NYC; St. Louis Art Mus., Mo. Natl. Gall. of Canada, Ottawa, Ontario; Natl. Portrait Gall., London.

ADDRESS Chateau Laurier Hotel, Suite 660, Ottawa, Canada KIN 857.

Gertrude Käsebier PHOTOGRAPHER Born Gertrude Stanton in Des Moines, Iowa, in 1852, Käsebier died in New York in 1934. She attended the Moravian Seminary for Girls in Bethlehem, Pennsylvania, and studied painting at Pratt Institute, Brooklyn, in 1888. She apprenticed herself to a German chemist in 1893 and a few years later to a commercial portrait photographer in Brooklyn for six months.

Establishing a studio in New York in 1897, she did portrait work and undertook magazine assignments for such journals as *McClure's*, *Scribner's*, *Camera Notes*, *The Craftsman*, *The Monthly Illustrator* and *The Photographic Times*.

Käsebier was the first woman elected to The Linked Ring (1900), a founding member of the Photo-Secession (1902), and co-founder, with Coburn and White, of the Pictorial Photographers of America (1916).

Considered one of America's most eminent photographers, Käsebier was a subjective artist. Her purpose, according to Ann Tucker in *The Woman's Eye* "was not to inform, but to share an experience, to evoke an emotional response from the viewer." Considered a radical in her day, she departed from the artificial settings and flat lighting of accepted portrait photography. Using wet plates, she printed her naturalistic images in platinum and silver, as well as working with gum-bichromate, gum-platinum and bromoil.

PUBLICATIONS Anthologies: *The Photograph Collector's Guide*, Lee D. Witkin & Barbara London, 1979; *Photography Rediscovered*, David Travis & Anne Kennedy, 1979; *The Collection of Alfred Stieglitz*, Weston J. Naef, 1978; *Pictorial Photography in Britain 1900–1920*, 1978 (Arts Council of G.B.:London); *The Valiant Knights of Daguerre . . . by Sadakichi Hartmann*, Harry W. Lawton & George Know, eds., 1978; *The Julien Levy Collection*, Witkin Gallery, 1977; *The Invented Eye*, Edward Lucie-Smith, 1975; *The Magic Image*, Cecil Beaton & Gail Buckland, 1975; *Women of Photography*, Margery Mann & Ann Noggle, eds., 1975; *Camera Work: A Critical Anthology*, Jonathan Green, ed., 1973; *The Woman's Eye*, Ann Tucker, ed., 1973; *The Print*, Time-Life Series, 1970. Periodicals: "Gertrude Käsebier Lost and Found," Mary Ann Tighe, *Art in America*, Mar/Apr 1977; "Rediscovering Gertrude Käsebier," Barbara L. Michaels, *Image*, June 1976; "Gertrude Käsebier," Joseph T. Keiley, *Camera Work*, Oct 1907; "Photography as an

Käsebier

320

Emotional Art," Giles Edgerton, *The Craftsman*, 1907, repr. *Image*, Dec 1972; *Camera Work*, no. 10, Apr 1905; "Mrs. Käsebier's Work—An Appreciation," Charles H. Caffin, and "Gertrude Käsebier, Professional Photographer," Frances B. Johnston, *Camera Work*, no. 1, Jan 1903.

COLLECTIONS Art Inst. of Chicago; IMP/GEH, Rochester; L/C, Wash., D.C.; Metro. Mus. of Art, NYC; MOMA, NYC; New Orleans Mus. of Art; Princeton Univ., N.J.; Smithsonian Inst., Wash., D.C.; Univ. of Kansas Mus. of Art, Lawrence; Univ. of N. Mex. Art Mus., Albuquerque. RPS, London.

Barbara Kasten PHOTOGRAPHER · TEACHER
Born in Chicago, Illinois, Kasten received a BFA from the University of Arizona, Tucson, in 1959 and an MFA from California College of Arts and Crafts, Oakland, in 1970.

She has been assistant division chairperson of the Photography Department at Orange Coast College, Costa Mesa, California, since 1975.

A member of SPE, Kasten won an NEA Services to the Field grant in 1980, also a Fulbright-Hays grant in 1971 and an NEA Photographer's Fellowship in 1978.

The photographer uses various multimedia techniques, as well as cyanotype and Polaroid.

COLLECTIONS Art Inst. of Chicago; CCP, Tucson; IMP/GEH, Rochester; Monterey Mus. of Art, Calif.; San Francisco Mus. of Modern Art; Univ. of N. Mex. Art Mus., Albuquerque.

ADDRESS Box 4231, Inglewood, CA 90309.

Sonia Katchian PHOTOGRAPHER Born December 20, 1947, in Beirut, Lebanon, Katchian earned a BA in 1968 from Barnard College, New York City, where she studied under W. Eugene Smith and Arthur Tcholakian.

Katchian is a freelance magazine photographer.

She has belonged to ASMP since 1972 and the Newspaper Guild of New York since 1977.

She considers her photography to be "inquiries into the nature of people." Subjects have included American politics, heavyweight boxing, Middle East politics and women.

PUBLICATIONS Book: *Muhammad Ali*, 1977. Anthology: *Women See Woman*, 1976.

COLLECTIONS Apeiron Workshop, Millerton, N.Y.; Metro. Mus. of Art, NYC. Julien Levy Cllctn., Paris.

REPRESENTATIVE Black Star, 450 Park Ave S, New York, NY 10016.

ADDRESS 478 W Broadway, New York, NY 10012.

Bruce F. Katsiff PHOTOGRAPHER Born December 10, 1945, in Philadelphia, Pennsylvania, Katsiff earned a BFA from Rochester Institute of Technology, New York, in 1968 and an MFA from Pratt Institute, Brooklyn, New York, in 1973.

He has been chairman of the Fine Arts Department of Bucks County Community College, Pennsylvania, since 1973, and from 1968 to 1973 was an associate professor of photography at the school.

Katsiff is a member of CAA and a board member of the Arts Alliance of Bucks County (since 1978). He received a Pennsylvania Bicentennial Commission grant in 1976 and a Pennsylvania Arts Council grant for a photo documentation project in 1968.

Currently working in large format, black-and-white, he has also done nonsilver work with photo silk screen.

PUBLICATION Catalog: *Vision and Expression*, 1969 (IMP/GEH: Rochester).

COLLECTIONS IMP/GEH, Rochester; Pratt Inst., Brooklyn, N.Y.; Rochester Inst. of Tech., N.Y.; Underground Gall., NYC. Amer. Arts Documentation Ctr., Exeter, England.

ADDRESS River Rd, Lumberville, PA 18933.

Susan Lorkid Katz PHOTOGRAPHER · TEACHER
Born December 4, 1947, in Brooklyn, New York, Katz received a BA in Psychology from the State University of New York at Stony Brook (1969), an MS in Counseling from Hunter College, New York City (1973), and an MFA in Photography from Brooklyn College, New York (1979).

As of this writing she is teaching photography as an adjunct assistant professor at Pace University at the College of White Plains, New York, an adjunct instructor at Jersey City State College, New Jersey, and at the New School for Social Research in New York City.

Katz belongs to the Foundation for the Community of Artists (since 1979), SPE and CAA (since 1977), and is president of Photographers Forum (since 1978). She won grants from ICP in 1976 and from Haystack Mountain School of Crafts, Deer Isle, Maine, in 1974.

A documentary photographer, Katz is concerned with expressing "reactions and perceptions about the human experience."

PUBLICATIONS Catalog: *Devastation/Resurrection*, 1979 (Bronx Mus.: N.Y.). Periodicals (text only): *Photography*, 1:4, 1977, 1:2, 1976; *Village Voice*, July 12, 1976.

COLLECTION L/C, Wash., D.C.

ADDRESS 509 Cathedral Parkway #3B, New York, NY 10025.

Louise E. Katzman CURATORIAL ASSISTANT · PHOTOGRAPHER Born in New York in 1949, Katzman studied in 1969 at the School of Visual Arts in New York City and in 1970 at the University of Copenhagen, Denmark. She then earned her BA (1971) from Harpur College, State University of New York at Binghamton, where she took studio art under Don Bell and Ken Jacobs, and received an MFA in photography (1975) from the California College of Arts and Crafts, Oakland, where she studied with Robert Forth. Her father is film director/producer Sam Katzman.

A curatorial assistant at the San Francisco Museum of Modern Art since 1977, she previously was assistant director of the World Print Council in San Francisco (1975–77). She served museum internships at the San Francisco office of the Smithsonian Institution's Archives of American Art (1974–75), and at the Richmond Art Center (1973), where she was the curator's assistant. In 1972–73 she was a photographer for the Media Center at the California College of Arts and Crafts.

Katzman has belonged to SPE since 1976.

Besides organizing and acting as curator of exhibitions, she does research on recent California photographic history.

PUBLICATIONS Catalogs (text only): *Jim Dong, Jim Goldberg, Chris Huie, Kate Kline May, Danuta Otfinowski: Photographs*, 1979, *Photographic Works: Lawrie Brown, Wanda Hammerbeck*, 1978 (San Francisco Mus. of Modern Art); (research only) *California Pictorialism*, 1977.

BUSINESS San Francisco Mus. of Modern Art, Van Ness at McAllister St, San Francisco, CA 94102.

ADDRESS 67 Lippard, San Francisco, CA 94131.

Steven Edward Katzman PHOTOGRAPHER · GALLERY DIRECTOR Born December 8, 1950, in Omaha, Nebraska, Katzman earned a degree in political science from the University of Wisconsin at Green Bay in 1973. His major influence was Jerry Uelsmann.

A freelance photographer since 1973, Katzman founded Image of Sarasota, Inc. in 1977.

He has belonged to SPE since 1979. In 1979 he received a Florida Arts Council Grant to publish a catalog for a show at the Loch Haven Art Center, Orlando, Florida.

As a gallery director Katzman promotes and encourages photography as a fine art form in the Southeast and advises local museums. His gallery serves as a resource center for photographic education and workshops. As a photographer he works in a surreal genre, dealing with subject matter indigenous to Florida and the South.

PUBLICATION Catalog: *Florida Light*, 1979.

COLLECTION Mint Mus., Charlotte, N.C.

ADDRESSES Image of Sarasota, Inc., 1323 Main St, Sarasota, FL 33577; 1230 Sea Plume Wy, Sarasota, Fl 33581.

Walter Kaufmann TEACHER · PHOTOGRAPHER Born July 1, 1921, in Freiburg, Germany, Kaufmann received his BA from Williams College, Williamstown, Massachusetts, in 1941 and his MA (1942) and PhD (1947) from Harvard University, Cambridge, Massachusetts.

He has been a member of the Philosophy Department of Princeton University, Princeton, New Jersey, since 1947, a professor since 1962 and a Stuart Professor of Philosophy since 1979. He was a visiting fellow at Australian National University in 1974 and has been a visiting professor at Columbia, Cornell, New School for Social Research, University of Michigan and University of Washington, among other schools. He was a Fulbright professor at Jerusalem University (1962–63) and at Heidelberg University, Germany (1955–56).

A member of American Philosophical Association and American Association of University Professors, Kaufmann won the International Leo Baeck Prize in 1961.

His photography is small-format in black-and-white and color.

PUBLICATIONS Monographs: *Man's Lot: A Trilogy*, 1978; *What Is Man?*, 1978; *Time Is an Artist*, 1978; *Life at the Limits*, 1978; *Religions in Four Dimensions*, 1976. Books (selected): *The Future of the Humanities*, 1977; *Existentialism, Religion, and Death*, 1976; *Tragedy and Philosophy*, 1968, repr. w/new preface 1979; *Goethe's Faust*, 1961; *Existentialism from Dostoevsky to Sartre*, 1956; *Nietzsche: Philosopher, Psychologist, Antichrist*, 1950, 4th ed. 1974.

ADDRESS Dept of Philosophy, Princeton Univ., Princeton, NJ 08544.

Daniel Kazimierski PHOTOGRAPHER Born November 14, 1949, in Warsaw, Poland, Kazimierski received an MA in Theology from the Catholic Academy of Theology in Poland. He also studied at Vancouver School of Art, Canada

(1975–77), Ontario College of Art, Toronto, Canada (1977–78), and York University, Toronto, where he earned an MFA in 1980.

Currently working at the International Center of Photography, Kazimierski was an instructor at York University in 1979.

Kazimierski is a member of SPE. He won an Ontario Arts Council Project Grant in 1978 and an Ontario Graduate Scholarship in 1979.

The photographer's current work deals with eroticism, sexuality and voyeurism. He is especially interested in nonsilver processes, particularly multiple gum printing. His previous work included photojournalism, street photography and series on Mardi Gras in New Orleans and the Hutterite colony in Saskatchewan, Canada.

PUBLICATIONS Periodicals: *Portfolio*, no. 2, 1979; *Image Nation*, no. 18, 1978.

COLLECTIONS In Canada: McCord Mus., Norman Photographic Archives, Montreal; Mt. St. Vincent Univ. Art Gall., Halifax, Nova Scotia; Natl. Film Board of Canada, Stills Div., Ottawa, Ont.; Saskatchewan Archives Board, Regina, Sask. Bibliothèque Nationale, Paris.

DEALER Déjà Vue Gall., 122 Scollard St, Toronto, Ontario, Canada.

ADDRESS Intl. Ctr. of Photography, 1130 Fifth Ave, New York, NY 10028.

Cherry Kearton *PHOTOGRAPHER · NATURALIST · AUTHOR* Born in 1871 in Thwaite, Swaledale, Yorkshire, England, Kearton died September 28, 1940, in London. A self-taught photographer, he was educated at Muker National School and Birkbeck College. His brother, Richard Kearton, was also a photographer and naturalist, and his niece, Grace Kearton, entered the photography field as well.

Cherry Kearton's first job was at Cassell Publishers in London, and in 1892 he began collaborating with his brother on books and articles. In 1905 he made the first aerial photographic record of London from a balloon. During World War I, with the rank of captain, Kearton served as official photographer for the British Expeditionary Force in France. He later traveled widely in Africa, Australia and elsewhere, filming big game and natural wildlife as well as taking still photographs. During one five-month period he and his wife lived on an island inhabited only by penguins, where he photographed the birds and wrote a dissertation on their group habits.

Kearton and his brothers claimed to be the first to illustrate a book on nature studies totally with photographs. Among the several films he shot in India, Burma, Borneo and Malaya were *Dassan*

(about penguins) and *Tembi* (about crocodiles). He also invented a "gun" camera.

Noted for his photographs of wildlife in its natural habitat, Kearton created book illustrations that were "a sharp contrast to the stilted, though accurate, bird-drawings of the 19th century. His work revealed to the public the charm of bird photography as a means of catching the attitudes and revealing the intimate habits of birds. They played a considerable part in the great popularization of nature study . . ." (London *Times*, Sept 30, 1940).

PUBLICATIONS Monographs: *Cherry Kearton's Travels*, 1941 (R. Hale: London); *My Woodland Home*, 1938; *I Visit the Antipodes*, 1937 (Jarrolds: London); *Adventures with Animals and Men*, 1935; *The Lion's Roar*, 1934; *The Animals Came to Drink*, 1932; *The Island of Penguins*, 1930 (Longmans, Green & Co.: London); *In the Land of the Lion*, 1929 (Arrowsmith: Bristol, England); *My Animal Friendships*, 1928; *My Happy Chimpanzee*, 1927; *My Happy Family*, 1927; *My Dog Simba*, 1926 (Arrowsmith: London); *My Friend Toto*, preface by Sir Gilbert Parker, 1925; *The Shifting Sands of Algeria*, 1924 (Arrowsmith: London); *Photographing Wild Life Across the World*, 1923 (Arrowsmith: London); *Wild Life Across the World*, intro. by Theodore Roosevelt, 1913. Books: *The Natural History of Selborne*, Gilbert White, 1925; *Through Central Africa*, w/James Barnes, 1915 (Cassell: London). With Richard Kearton: *Kearton's Nature Pictures*, 2 vols., 1910; *The Fairyland of Living Things*, 1908; *Nature's Carol Singers*, 1906; *Pictures from Nature*, 1905; *Strange Adventures in Dicky-bird Land*, 1901; *Our Bird Friends*, 1900; *At Home with Wild Nature*, 1900?; *With Nature and a Camera*, 1897; *British Birds' Nests*, 1895. Anthology: *The Magic Image*, Cecil Beaton & Gail Buckland, 1975.

Richard Kearton *PHOTOGRAPHER · ORNITHOLOGIST · AUTHOR* Born January 2, 1862, in Thwaite, Swaledale, Yorkshire, Kearton died February 8, 1928, in Caterham Valley, England. Photographer and naturalist Cherry Kearton was his brother, and photographer Grace Kearton was his daughter. He was educated at Birkbeck College and was self-taught in photography.

Kearton spent many years working on his father's farm. He obtained employment at the publishing house of Cassell in London (about 1883–98), and while there produced several natural history books. He also gave numerous lantern-slide lectures.

He introduced the use of the "hide" method of

323

bird-watching. Since avian creatures take little or no notice of most other animals, the use of an animal skin makes an excellent disguise for close-up viewing.

Kearton became an expert "in obtaining 'close-up' pictures of wild creatures of all descriptions in their natural haunts. . . . The work involved no small risk, and demanded also a mastery of the art of disguise, as well as almost inexhaustible patience," wrote the London *Times* (Feb 10, 1928). It added that it was often impossible to distinguish the contributions of Richard from those of his brother Cherry but that they both "did a great deal to spread a knowledge and love of natural history, and to encourage habits of careful and accurate observation."

PUBLICATIONS Monographs: *At Home with Wild Nature*, w/Cherry Kearton, 1922; *Wonders of Wild Nature*, 1915; *Wild Nature's Ways*, 1903; *Our Bird Friends*, 1900; *Wild Life at Home: How to Study and Photograph It*, 1898; *Birds' Nests, Eggs, and Egg Collecting*, 1896, rev. & repr. 1915. Books w/Cherry Kearton: *Kearton's Nature Pictures*, 2 vols., 1910; *The Fairyland of Living Things*, 1908; *Nature's Carol Singers*, 1906; *Pictures from Nature*, 1905; *The Adventures of Cock Robin and his Mate*, 1904; *Wild Nature's Ways*, 1903; *Strange Adventures in Dicky-bird Land*, 1901; *Our Bird Friends*, 1900; *Our Rarer British Breeding Birds*, 1899; *With Nature and a Camera*, 1898. Other Books: *A Naturalist's Pilgrimage*, 1926; *Wonders of Wild Nature*, w/ Grace Kearton, 1915; *Baby Birds at Home*, w/ Grace & Cherry Kearton, 1912; *The Adventures of Jack Rabbit*, w/Grace Kearton, 1911; *The Natural History of Selbourne*, Gilbert White, 1903; *British Birds' Nests*, intro. by R. B. Sharpe, 1895, repr. 1908. Anthology: *The Magic Image*, Cecil Beaton & Gail Buckland, 1975.

Marcia Keegan   *PHOTOGRAPHER · AUTHOR* Born May 23, 1942, Keegan received a BA from the University of New Mexico, Albuquerque, and was an assistant to art director Alexey Brodovitch in New York City.

Currently a freelance photographer and writer, she was a photographer for Associated Press in 1974–75 and an editor and photographer for the *Albuquerque Journal* in 1966–69.

Keegan belongs to ASMP, Authors Guild, American Pen Women and Women in Communication. She won a CAPS grant in 1971 and a New Mexico Press Award in 1967.

Her work focuses on the Southwest Indian tribes and landscape.

PUBLICATIONS   Monographs: *Oklahoma,*

1979; *Pueblo and Navajo Cookery*, 1978; *Mother Earth Father Sky*, 1975; *We Can Still Hear Them Clapping*, 1974; *The Taos Indians and Their Sacred Blue Lake*, 1972.

COLLECTIONS Kansas City Art Mus., Kansas.; L/C, Wash., D.C.; Lincoln Ctr. Mus. of Performing Arts, NYC; Metro. Mus. of Art, NYC; Philbrock Art Mus., Tulsa, Okla.

ADDRESS 140 E 46 St, New York, NY 10017.

Larry (Lawrence Alexander) Keenan, Jr.   *PHOTOGRAPHER* Born in San Francisco on November 20, 1943, Keenan attended the California College of Arts and Crafts in Oakland, where he earned a BFA (1965) and a BAA with distinction (1967).

Since 1964 Keenan has been a freelance photographer, working for record companies and book publishers and doing various commercial assignments. From 1967 to 1970 he taught photography and art at Concord High School in Concord, California, and lectured at the California College of Arts and Crafts and the University of California at Berkeley.

A member of SPE, ASMP and the San Francisco Society of Communicating Arts, he received seven "Creativity" awards from *Art Direction Magazine* (1973–79).

Keenan has a particular interest in "the bizarre juxtaposition of images, real or imagined, in life and death." He also claims to have documented the "Beat Generation."

PUBLICATIONS Periodicals: *Camera 35*, 1974; *Popular Photography, Color Annual*, 1972, 1971; *Popular Photography, 35mm Annual*, 1971.

COLLECTIONS Smithsonian Inst., Wash., D.C.; DeYoung Mus., San Francisco.

REPRESENTATIVE David Freidberg, 49 Potomac St, San Francisco, CA 94117.

ADDRESS 7101 Saroni Dr, Oakland, CA 94611.

Peter Keetman   *PHOTOGRAPHER · PHOTODESIGNER* Born in Wuppertal-Elberfeld, Germany, on April 27, 1916, Keetman received his master's credentials in photography in Munich after having studied at the master school of Adolf Lazi in Stuttgart (1950). From 1935 to 1937 he attended the Bavarian State Instructional Institution for Photography in Munich.

A freelance since 1952, Keetman has been closely associated with commercial photographer Nikolai Borg in Munich for the past eighteen years.

Keetman is a founding member of Fotoforum,

begun in 1949, and has been a member of GDL since 1957 as well as DGPh, Stuttgarter Photographische Gesellschaft and Bund Freischaffender Fotodesigners.

Keetman describes his experimental photography as "the making visible of things which move, which can be portrayed only by means of photography."

PUBLICATIONS Books: *Spiele mit dem Orff Schulwerk*, 1975 (Metzler Press); *Berchtesgaden, Reichenhall, Salzburg*, 1959, *Bavarian Lakeland*, 1957, *Munich*, 1955 (Thorbecke Press). Anthologies: *The History of Photography in the 20th Century*, Petr Tausk, 1977; *A Concise History of Photography*, Helmut & Alison Gernsheim, 1965; *Creative Photography*, Helmut Gernsheim, 1962; *The Picture History of Photography*, Peter Pollack, 1958.

ADDRESS Seestrasse 17, D-8211 Breitbrunn/Chiemsee, West Germany.

Dorothea Kehaya PHOTOGRAPHER · TEACHER Born May 25, 1925, in New York City, Kehaya is a self-taught photographer.

Besides being a freelance photographer, she has taught privately since 1976. In 1971 she taught photography at the School of Visual Arts in New York City.

Kehaya belonged to the Association of Heliographers in New York City from 1963 to 1965.

Jacob Deschin (*New York Times*, Nov. 10, 1968) described Kehaya's color nature studies as "cross[ing] nature and art to accomplish a personal synthesis in each print." She uses color filters to control color paper and light, he added, "as a painter mixes colors on a palette." Kehaya herself says: "If I could articulate in words, I wouldn't make pictures—therefore all the pictures I make are an expression about my feelings of life."

PUBLICATIONS Book: *Photography*, Barbara & John Upton, 1977. Anthology: *Color*, Time-Life Series, 1970. Periodicals: *Photography Annual*, 1979, 1973, 1972, 1970; "Between Teacher and Student," Jacob Deschin, summer 1974, "35mm, The Nature Camera," spring 1970, *35mm Photography: Popular Photography's Color Photography*, 1974, 1973; "Adventures in 110," Sept 1973, "Color Off the Beaten Path," Hugh Birnbaum, Apr 1972, *Popular Photography*; *U.S. Camera Annual*, 1971; *Life*, Oct 8, 1971; *Nikon World*, fall/winter 1970; "Do It All Yourself!—A Personal Prejudice," *Invitation to Photography*, 1970.

COLLECTIONS Exchange Natl. Bank, Chicago; L/C, Wash., D.C.; Metro. Mus. of Art, NYC;

Mus. of the City of N.Y.; Univ. of Va. Mus., Charlottesville.

DEALER Neikrug Galls., 224 E 68 St, New York, NY 10021.

ADDRESS RFD 3, 164 West Rd, Putney, VT 05346.

Alexander Keighley PHOTOGRAPHER Born in Keighley, Yorkshire, England, in 1861, the photographer died in Yorkshire on August 2, 1947. He received a scholarship to the School of Mines (now Royal College of Science) in 1877, where he studied under T. H. Huxley. Painting and photography were initially leisure-time activities. His work was influenced by H. P. Robinson.

Keighley was director of Sugden Keighley & Co., a textile manufacturer, until 1932, when he left to devote himself to photography, which he had first taken an interest in about 1883.

He served as president of the Bradford Photographic Society, was elected an Honorary Fellow of RPS (1911) and was a founding member of The Linked Ring (1892). Once chosen as "world pictorial photographer No. 1" by American photographers, he twice won the Prix d'Honneur of the International Salon of Photography. After an exhibit in 1901 he was acknowledged as a leader of British pictorial photography.

A multitalented artist, Keighley used crayon, watercolors and chalk, spraying, stippling and heavily retouching his carbon prints to make them resemble reproductions of paintings. Finishing with a coat of varnish, the photographer often added animals, trees, heavenly bodies and other fanciful elements to his very popular, commercially successful images.

PUBLICATIONS Book: *Alexander Keighley: A Memorial*, 1947 (RPS: London). Anthologies: *Pictorial Photography in Britain 1900–1920*, Arts Council of Great Britain, 1978; *The Magic Image*, Cecil Beaton & Gail Buckland, 1975.

COLLECTIONS IMP/GEH, Rochester; Natl. Mus. of Hist. & Tech., Wash., D.C. RPS, London.

Joseph T. Keiley LAWYER · EDITOR · PHOTOGRAPHER Born July 16, 1869, in New York, Keiley died on January 21, 1914, probably in Brooklyn, New York. A Wall Street lawyer, he was the associate editor of *Camera Notes* and then *Camera Work*.

Keiley joined the Camera Club in 1899 and was the fourth American to be elected to The Linked Ring. A member of the Photo-Secession, he was acknowledged to be its historian.

With Alfred Stieglitz, he developed a refinement of the glycerine process for local development of the platinum print. An art photographer as well as a historian, Keiley employed the platinotype process with a variation arrived at through his researches with Stieglitz.

PUBLICATIONS Anthologies: *Camera Work: A Critical Anthology*, Jonathan Green, ed., 1973; *Early Photographs & Early Photographers*, Oliver Mathews, 1973. Periodicals: "J. Craig Annan," *Camera Work*, Oct 1904; "Improved Glycerine Process for the Development of Platinum Prints," w/Alfred Stieglitz, *Camera Notes*, Nov 8, 1900.

COLLECTION IMP/GEH, Rochester.

Robert W. Kelley PHOTOGRAPHER Born in Fort Dodge, Iowa, on February 3, 1920, Kelley studied journalism at the University of Washington in 1937.

Kelley has been a freelance magazine photographer since 1969. From 1966 to 1969 he worked for Time Inc., as a contract photographer. He was a staff photographer with *Life* magazine from 1950 to 1966, during which time his photographs were used on sixteen covers of the magazine. Before that he was a contract photographer for *Life* from 1947 to 1950. His editorial photographs have seen print in dozens of *Life* picture essays. In earlier years he worked for the *Seattle Times* (1946–47) and the *Seattle Post Intelligencer* (1938–42).

A member of the White House News Photographers Association and the NPPA, Kelley received a Best News Picture award from the latter organization in 1955.

PUBLICATIONS Book: *Anatomy of a Fisherman*, w/Robert Traver, 1978. Periodicals (selected): "Pictorial Summation of a Tragicomic Mistrial," May 21, 1965, "An Island's Awakening," July 20, 1959, "Elvis—A Different Kind of Idol," Aug 27, 1956, "A New Revivalist," May 7, 1951, "Life Looks at the Habits of U.S. Executives," June 28, 1948, *Life*.

ADDRESS POB 13, Edmonds, WA 98020.

Angela Mary Kelly TEACHER · PHOTOGRAPHER Born October 25, 1950, Kelly received a diploma in education from Mary Ward College of Education in Nottingham, England (1972), and a diploma in creative photography from Trent Polytechnic in Nottingham (1975).

She has been a photography lecturer at Manchester Polytechnic since 1978, and previously taught photography at Nelson & Colne College, Lancaster, England (1975–78).

A member of the photography panel of the Arts Council of Great Britain in 1979, she won a Minor Award from the Council in 1978.

Kelly works in various formats of black-and-white, focusing on the urban landscape and self-portraiture. "The approach," she says, "is analytical and conceptual."

PUBLICATIONS Book: *Three Perspectives on Photography, Recent British Photography*, text only, 1979. Periodicals: *U.S. Camera Annual*, 1978; *Camera Work*, no. 12, 1978 (Half Moon Photo Workshop: London); "The State of Photographic Education," text only, *British Journal of Photography*, 1977.

COLLECTIONS Arts Council of Great Britain, London; Dept. of the Environment, London.

ADDRESS 2 Laurel Rd, Heaton Moor, Stockport, Cheshire, England.

Thomas J. Kelly III PHOTOJOURNALIST Kelly was born August 8, 1947, in Hackensack, New Jersey.

Since 1974 he has been the director of photography at *The Mercury* in Pottstown, Pennsylvania. Prior to that he was chief photographer for *Today's Post* in King of Prussia, Pennsylvania (1971–74), and a freelance photographer for the *Montgomery Post* and the *Times Herald* in Norristown, Pennsylvania (1969–71).

Kelly has been both the associate director of the NPPA and the president of the Pennsylvania Press Photographers Association since 1973. Awarded the Pulitzer Prize for Spot News Photography in 1979 from Columbia University in New York City, he was also named Newspaper Photographer of the Year by the NPPA Region III in 1975, 1976 and 1979, and Pennsylvania Photographer of the Year in 1976. In 1980 he received the Robert F. Kennedy award for photojournalism.

PUBLICATIONS Anthology: *Photoyear 80*, Time-Life Series, 1980. Periodicals: *American Photographer*, Nov 1980; *Life*, June 1980.

ADDRESSES POB 208 Sanatoga, PA 19464; Hanover & King Sts, Pottstown, PA 19464.

Fritz (Max Kurt) Kempe PHOTOGRAPHER · AUTHOR · PHOTOHISTORIAN · COLLECTOR Born in Greifswald, Germany, on October 22, 1909, Kempe learned photography from his father, Max Kempe. In 1938 Fritz Kempe passed his master's examination.

Since 1977 Kempe has been the honorary director of the Sammlung der Geschichte der Photographie in the Museum für Kunst in Hamburg. From 1949 to 1974 he was director of the State

Regional Photo Office/Agency in Hamburg, and during the years 1946–68 he was editor of the *Hamburger Allgemeine Zeitung.* Prior to that he was press chief/supervisor of a Hamburg welfare Organization (1945–49); before that had his own studios—an advertising and industrial studio in Berlin (1938–39) and Photo-Kempe in Greifswald (1929–38).

Kempe belongs to a number of professional organizations, among them DGPh, GDL and Bundes Freischaffender Fotodesigner (BFF). He also has an Honoraire Excellence in the Fédération Internationale de l'Art Photographique (FIAP) and an honorary membership in the Photographic Historical Society of New York. The History Section of the DGPh awarded Kempe the Erich Stenger Prize in 1979; in 1974 he was the recipient of the David Octavius Hill Medal from the GDL; in 1964 he received the Culture Prize from the DGPh.

The artist was involved with the films *Laterna Magica Hamburgensis* (1959) and *Werkstatt des Friedens* (1950).

Since 1949 Kempe has photographed Hamburg personalities, including politicians, merchants, scientists and artists. "Everything that I have photographed, researched, collected and written, is determined by my historical interest in photography," he states.

PUBLICATIONS Books: *Albert Renger-Patzsch —100 Photographien 1928,* 1979 (Schürmann & Kicken: Cologne); *Daguerreotypie in Duetschland,* 1979 (Heering-Verlag Seebruck: Munich); *Photographie-Zwischen Daguerreotypie und Kunstphotographie,* 1977 (Mus. für Kunst & Gewerbe: Hamburg); *Vor der Camera—Zur Geschichte der Photographie in Hamburg,* 1976 (Christians: Hamburg); *One Hundred Years of Photographic History,* 1975 (Univ. of N. Mex.: Albuquerque); *Das Bild und die Wirklichkeit,* 1974 (Inst. für Film & Bild: Munich); *Hamburger, Bernhard Meyer-Marwitz,* 1963 (H. G. Imlau: Hamburg); *Die Welt der Photographie,* w/Von Zwei Kapiteln, 1962 (Econ: Düsseldorf); *Film: Technik-Gestaltung-Wirkung,* 1958 (Westermann: Braunschweig); *Der Film in der Jugend- und Erwachsenenbildung,* 1952 (Heering-Verlag: Seebruk: Munich).

COLLECTIONS IMP/GEH, Rochester; San Francisco Mus. of Art; Univ. of N. Mex. Art Mus., Albuquerque. Det Kongelike Bibliotek, Copenhagen; Folkwang Mus., Essen, W. Ger. Fotografiske Muséet, Stockholm; Mus. of Art & Crafts, Hamburg W. Ger.

DEALER PPS Galerie, 1 Feldstrasse/Hochhaus, D-2000 Hamburg 4, West Germany.

ADDRESS Eilbeker Weg 65 a, D-2000 Hamburg 76, West Germany.

Michel Kempf PHOTOGRAPHER · WRITER · TEACHER Kempf was born April 3, 1946, in Paris; his wife is photographer Christiane Barrier. He is self-taught in photography, and began working as a portraitist in St. Tropez, France, in 1968.

Kempf has written several hundred articles about photography as a fine art for various magazines, including *Photo Revue.* Since 1977 he has taught photography at l'Ecole Supérieure d'Arts Graphiques in Paris as well as working in his own studio in Paris since 1974.

Kempf was the recipient of the New York Art Directors Club Award in 1973 and the Obelisk of Photokina in Cologne, Germany, in 1968.

Working in large-format black-and-white, Kempf makes landscapes in what he calls "a classical way." He also works on the technical problems of conservation and has written several articles on the subject. As of this writing he was engaged in the restoration of plates by Atget for the National Collection of France.

COLLECTIONS In France: Bibliothèque Nationale, Paris; Musée Réattu, Arles.

DEALER Galerie Agathe Gaillard, 3 rue du Pont Louis Phillipe, 75004 Paris, France.

ADDRESS 52 rue de Paradis, 75010 Paris, France.

Clarence Kennedy PHOTOGRAPHER · ART HISTORIAN · TEACHER Born September 4, 1892, in Philadelphia, Pennsylvania, Kennedy died in 1972. His wife, Ruth Wedgwood Doggett Kennedy, whom he married in 1921, was his frequent collaborator. Kennedy earned a BS (1914) and an MA in Architecture (1915) from the University of Pennsylvania. He studied with Professor Franz Studniczka, restoring and photographing sculpture in 1920–21, and completed his PhD at Harvard, Cambridge, Massachusetts, in 1924.

Kennedy held a number of teaching positions at Smith College, Northampton, Massachusetts. He was an instructor in art history (1917), assistant professor (1921), associate professor (1925; director of a graduate-study program in Paris and Florence) full professor (1930–31) and chairman of the Art Department (1952–54). He conducted the Smith College seminar in Florence with his wife in 1957–60 (summers only), after which he retired from Smith. Kennedy was also a Charles Eliot Norton Fellow at Harvard in 1920–21, a visiting professor of Fine Arts at New York University in 1932 and the Annual Carnegie Professor at Toledo Museum of Art, 1938–39. He conducted a summer course for the Intercollegiate Council for Summer Study Abroad in 1956, and he was Resident Art Historian with his wife at the American Academy in Rome, 1960–61.

Kennedy won a Carnegie Scholarship for study in Florence in 1927, a Guggenheim Fellowship in 1930 and a College Art Association Research Fellowship in 1931–32. He became a member of the Society of Motion Picture and Television Engineers in 1952 and of Sigma Xi in 1960.

He developed a special stereoscopic camera in 1938–39, collaborated with the Meriden Gravure Company on the development of collotype, offset processes and other photographic technology in 1938–39, formed the Cantina Press in 1938 and developed stereo-photography for aerial mapping. With Edwin Land he devised a system for projecting stereoscope slides using Land's Polaroid filters over the lenses of a double projector. Land established the Clarence and Ruth Wedgwood Kennedy Art Fund for the Smith College Art Department in 1959.

Kennedy is best known for his revealing studies of sculptures and other pieces of art.

PUBLICATIONS Books: *Photographs by Clarence Kennedy*, 1967; *Four Portrait Busts by Francesco Laurance*, 1962; *Gehenna Essays in Art*, 1962; *The Renaissance Painter's Garden*, 1948; *Duveen Sculpture in Private Collections of Americans: Italian Renaissance*, 1944; *Romanesque Sculptures of the Pilgrimage Roads*, 1923. Catalog: *Italian Drawings 1330–1780*, 1941.

ARCHIVE Smith Coll Mus of Art, Northampton, MA 01060.

Martha Hoeprich Kennedy CURATOR · LIBRARIAN Born March 18, 1951, in Boston, Massachusetts, Kennedy earned her BA and MA in History of Art (1973, 1976) and her MLS (1979) from the University of California, Berkeley.

Kennedy is currently photographs curator at the California Historical Society in San Francisco, where she is in charge of a photograph collection of approximately 200,000 images relating to California history. She was formerly assistant librarian at the California College of Arts and Crafts in Oakland (1979).

She is a member of the Art Librarians Society of North America and Photo Archivists of the Bay Area.

The photographer's own research interest is in cased images.

PUBLICATION Catalog: *Three Centuries of French Art*, vol. 3, 1975 (Fine Arts Museums of San Francisco).

ADDRESS Calif. Historical Soc., Photographs Dept, 2090 Jackson St, San Francisco, CA 94109.

David Hume Kennerly PHOTOGRAPHER Born in Oregon on March 9, 1947, Kennerly names photography instructor Darrell Greenlee and news photographers David Falconer, Larry Burrows and John Dominis as major influences.

A freelance photographer since 1977, primarily with *Time* magazine, Kennerly was personal photographer to President Gerald R. Ford from 1974 to 1977. Prior to that he was a contract photographer for *Life* and *Time* (1972–74), United Press International staff photographer (1967–72), staff photographer for *Oregon Journal* and *Portland Oregonian* (1966–67) and staff photographer for *The Lake Oswego Review* (1965–66).

Kennerly is a member of the White House Press Photographers Association. In 1976 he was awarded a first prize for features and general news in the World Press Photo Contest and also a Special Citation from NPPA. In 1975 he was given the Wilson Hicks Award for excellence in reporting with camera. In 1972 he won a Pulitzer Prize for feature photography of the Vietnam war.

Primarily a news photographer, Kennerly received wide recognition for his extensive coverage of Gerald Ford during his presidency and for his coverage of the Vietnam conflict.

PUBLICATION Monograph: *Shooter*, 1979.

REPRESENTATIVE Robert Pledge, Contact Press Images, 135 Central Park West, New York, NY 10023.

ADDRESS 3332 P St, NW, Washington, DC 20007.

Colleen Frances Kenyon PHOTOGRAPHER · TEACHER Born August 6, 1951, in Dunkirk, New York, Kenyon received a BS from Skidmore College, Saratoga Springs (1973), and an MFA from Indiana University, Bloomington (1976), where she studied with Henry Holmes Smith. Her twin sister is photographer Kathleen Kenyon.

She is currently director of education (since 1978) and exhibitions coordinator at Catskill Center for Photography, New York. She taught photography in 1977 at Slippery Rock State College, Pennsylvania.

A past member of the CAA and Women's Caucus for Art, she serves as secretary of the board of directors of the Catskill Center for Photography (since 1978), and has belonged to SPE since 1976.

Kenyon won a CAPS grant in 1979 and an artist-in-residence grant from the New York State

Council on the Arts at the Catskill Center for Photography in 1978.

The photographer creates black-and-white, sepia-toned, hand-colored images printed on 16 x 20 paper. Her ongoing project is photographing herself and her twin sister.

PUBLICATIONS Book: *Alternative Photographic Processes*, Kent Wade, ed., 1978. Anthology: *Self-Portrayal*, Jim Alinder, ed., 1978. Periodicals: *Afterimage: VSW*, Jan 1980; *Darkroom*, May 1980; *Popular Photography Annual*, 1979.

COLLECTIONS IMP/GEH, Rochester; Ind. Univ., Bloomington; MOMA, NYC; Skidmore Coll., Saratoga Springs, N.Y.

ADDRESS Box 77, Route 212, Shady, NY 12479.

Douglas M. Kenyon GALLERY OWNER Kenyon was born in Chicago, Illinois, on September 1, 1942.

He has been president and director of his own gallery, Douglas Kenyon, Inc., since 1969. He was a conservator in the prints and drawings department of the Art Institute of Chicago from 1970 to 1978 and remains a consulting conservator there. From 1965 to 1970 he was a photography collection assistant at the institute.

Kenyon is a member of the Chicago Art Dealers Association, Association of International Photography Art Dealers and American Institute for Conservation of Historic and Artistic Works.

PUBLICATION Book: *Framing and Conservation of Works of Art on Paper*, 1975.

ADDRESS Douglas Kenyon, Inc., 155 E Ohio St, Chicago, IL 60611.

Kathleen Kenyon PHOTOGRAPHER · TEACHER Born August 6, 1951, in Dunkirk, New York, Kenyon earned a BS from Skidmore College, Saratoga Springs, New York (1973), and an MFA from Indiana University, Bloomington (1976), where she studied with Henry Holmes Smith. Her twin sister is photographer Colleen Kenyon.

Most recently she has been a visiting assistant professor of photography at Bard College, Annandale-on-Hudson, New York, and director of the Woodstock Photography Workshops Program in Woodstock, New York. From 1976 to 1979 she taught photography at the University of Southern California School of Fine Arts, Los Angeles.

Kenyon has been a member since 1976 of the CAA, SPE, Women's Caucus for Art, Los Angeles Institute of Contemporary Art and Los Angeles Printmaking Society, serving on the executive board of the last in 1977–78. She joined the Los Angeles Center for Photographic Studies in 1978, and the Southern California Chapter of the Women's Caucus for Art in 1977, serving as its vice-president in 1977–78 and its president in 1978–79. In 1979 she received grants from the Visiting Artists Program, Committee for the Visual Arts, New York, and from the Catskill Center for Photography, Woodstock, New York.

The photographer produces Type C color images, 7½ x 7½, in various series. In 1977–78 the series "Fitting" investigated the ritual of dressing and undressing, and in 1978 she began a series of photographs entitled "Sacred Children," consisting of images of herself alone, her twin sister, and both together.

PUBLICATIONS Books: *High Contrast*, J. Seeley 1980; *Alternative Photographic Processes*, Kent Wade, ed., 1978. Periodicals: *Darkroom*, May 1980; *LAICA Journal*, Jan 1979; *Afterimage: VSW*, May/June 1975.

COLLECTIONS Ind. Univ., Bloomington; Skidmore Coll., Saratoga Springs, N.Y.

ADDRESS Box 68, Route 212, Shady, NY 12479.

Gyorgy Kepes PAINTER · DESIGNER · PHOTOGRAPHER Born in 1906 in Selyp, Hungary, Kepes collaborated with Moholy-Nagy on light and design experiments in Berlin and London from 1930 to 1936. It was at this time that Kepes began making photograms.

In 1937 Kepes came to the United States to join Moholy-Nagy at the New Bauhaus in Chicago—later the Institute of Design—where he headed the Light and Color Department. Since 1946 he has been at the Massachusetts Institute of Technology, where he is now director emeritus of the Center for Advanced Visual Studies. For a time he was editor of *Visual Arts Today*.

In his work with photograms, or lensless images—made on photographic paper by interposing objects between it and a light source and by manipulating light and shadow—Kepes has been able to achieve an even freer imagery than was possible with film.

PUBLICATIONS Books: *Arts of the Environment*, ed., 1972; *The Man-Made Object*, ed., 1966; *Sign Image Symbol*, ed. 1966; *Education of Vision*, ed., 1965; *The Nature and Art of Motion*, ed., 1965; *Structure in Art and in Science*, ed., 1965; *the New Landscape in Art and Science*, 1956; *Language of Vision*, 1944.

REPRESENTATIVE Prakapas Gall., 19 E 71 St, New York, NY 10021.

Margot Kernan PHOTOGRAPHER · TEACHER · FILM CRITIC Born in Cambridge, Massachusetts, on September 11, 1927, Kernan received a BA in 1948 from Bennington College, Vermont. She studied at the Stanford University (California) Radio-Television-Film Institute in 1963, then took her MA in Creative Arts from San Francisco State College, California, in 1966. She is the daughter of photographer Nina Howell Starr.

Since 1975 Kernan has been professor of Speech and Drama and faculty associate for Film Studies at George Washington University, Washington, D.C. She was academic director of the Antioch College Centre for British Studies in London in 1974–75 and associate professor of Urban Media at Antioch's Washington-Baltimore campus from 1970 to 1975. Kernan served as U.S. correspondent for the *International Film Guide* in London from 1966 to 1975.

A member of SPE since 1968, she also belongs to the Society for the Anthropology of Visual Communication (since 1972) and Women in Film.

The photographer describes her work as "personal investigations of the relationships between human beings and light." She works in 35mm black-and-white and color, and in Instamatic 110 color.

PUBLICATIONS Books (text only): *The Politics of Revolution*, 1973; *Racism*, 1973; *Radical Voices*, 1973. Periodicals: *British Journal of Photography*, Apr 1979; *Arts in Society*, 10:2, 1973.

COLLECTIONS Corcoran Gall. of Art, Wash., D.C.; Phillips Cllctn., Wash., D.C.

DEALERS Foundry Gall., 2121 P St NW, Washington, DC 20037; Anne Winkelman, 8009 Overhill Rd, Bethesda, MD 20014.

ADDRESS 1601 38 St NW, Washington, DC 20007.

Sean Kernan PHOTOGRAPHER Born June 19, 1942, in New York City, Kernan earned a BA in English from the University of Pennsylvania, Philadelphia, in 1965. He is self-taught as a photographer.

Since 1975 he has been a faculty member at the New School for Social Research in New York City, and from 1973 to 1978 he taught at Manhattanville College, Purchase, New York.

A member of ASMP, Kernan won a grant from the Connecticut Commission on the Arts in 1975 and a fellowship from the Eugene O'Neill Foundation in 1968.

He conceived and was associate producer for "To America," a CBS-TV special, in 1976.

PUBLICATIONS Periodicals: *Camera*, June 1975, Nov 1970; *Popular Photography Annual*, 1974; *Creative Camera*, Mar 1974.

DEALER Witkin Gall., 41 W 57 St, New York, NY 10019.

ADDRESS 5 White St, New York, NY 10013.

André Kertész PHOTOGRAPHER · REPORTER [See plate 50] Born July 2, 1894, in Budapest, Hungary, Kertész studied at the Academy of Commerce in Budapest ca. 1912.

A freelance photographer since 1925, when he began his photography career in Paris, Kertész came to the United States in 1937.

Kertész is a member of ASMP. In 1977 he won the New York City Mayor's Award, and in the same year he was named Commander of the Order of Arts and Letters in France. He received a gold medal at the 1963 Venice Biennale.

Called "the creator of the literary reportage" by Tim N. Gidal in *Modern Photo Journalism*, Kertész is one of the pioneers in the use of the 35mm camera in photojournalism. His images are mainly taken from everyday life, although he also is known for his distorted nudes and has done commercial work. Says Kertész: "I made my first photos in 1912, and my reportage was always an interpretation of my feelings about what I had seen."

PUBLICATIONS Monographs: *André Kertész*, intro. by Carole Kismaric, 1977; *Distortions*, intro. by Hilton Kramer, 1976; *Of New York*, 1976; *Washington Square*, intro by Brendan Gill, 1975; *J'Aime Paris: Photographs Since the Twenties*, Nicolas Ducrot, ed.,1974; *André Kertész: Sixty Years of Photography, 1912–1972*, Nicolas Ducrot, ed., 1972, repr. 1978; *Foto*, 1972 (Corvina: Hungary); *On Reading*, 1971; *The Photographs of André Kertész*, 1967; *Paragraphic*, 1966; *André Kertész, Photographer*, intro. by John Szarkowski 1964; *Day of Paris*, George Davis, ed., 1945; "Caricatures and Distortions," *Complete Photographer*, vol. 10/11, 1941–43; *Les Cathédrals du vin*, Pierre Hamp, 1937 (Sainrapt et Brice: Paris); *Nos Amies les Bêtes*, Jaboune, 1936, *Paris vu par André Kertész*, Pierre MacOrlan, 1934, *Enfants*, Jaboune, 1933 (Editions d'Histoire et d'Art: Paris). Anthologies: *The Photograph Collector's Guide*, Lee D. Witkin & Barbara London, 1979; *The Magic Image*, Cecil Beaton & Gail Buckland, 1975. Periodicals: "André Kertész," Ruth Spencer, *The British Journal of Photography*, Apr 5, 1975; "My Friend Kertész," Brassaï, *Camera*, Apr 1963.

COLLECTIONS Detroit Inst. of Arts, Mich.; Harvard Univ., Carpenter Ctr. for the Visual Arts, Cambridge, Mass.; Mint Mus. of Art, Charlotte,

N.C.; MOMA, NYC; New Orleans Mus. of Art, La.; Smithsonian Inst., Wash., D.C.; Univ. of Kansas. Mus. of Art, Lawrence; Univ. of Nebr., Sheldon Mem. Art Gall., Lincoln; Wellesley Coll. Mus., Wellesley, Mass.; Worcester Art Mus., Mass. Centre Georges Pompidou, Paris.

ADDRESS 2 Fifth Ave, New York, NY 10011.

Dmitri Kessel PHOTOJOURNALIST Born August 20, 1902, in Kiev, Russia, Kessel studied at the Poltava Staff Officers' School in Russia and at Rabinovitch School of Photography in New York City.

Since 1972 he has freelanced for various publications, including *Smithsonian*, Time-Life Books and *Life*. He worked on contract for Time Inc., from 1967 to 1972, and previous to that was a staff photographer for *Life* (1944–67) and a war correspondent (1942–44). Kessel's assignments have included recording Greek liberation and the civil war in 1944–45 and photographing Czechoslovakia in 1937, before the German occupation.

The photographer was decorated by the Shah of Iran in 1967, knighted by the Italian government in 1965 with the title of Cavaliere, awarded the medal of the City of Ravenna in 1959 and granted the award of Spanish Morocco (The Order of Excellence) in 1949.

Kessel specializes in the fields of industrial photography and photographing architecture and fine arts.

PUBLICATION Book: *Splendors of Christendom* (Edita of Lausanne: Switzerland). Anthology: *The Magic Image*, Cecil Beaton & Gail Buckland, 1975.

COLLECTIONS MOMA, Family of Man Cllctn., NYC; Photography in the Fine Arts, NYC.

ADDRESS 36 Ave Gabriel, 75008 Paris, France.

Edmund Kesting PHOTOGRAPHER · COLLAGIST Born in 1892 in Dresden, Germany, Kesting died October 21, 1970, in Birkenwerder, near Berlin, Germany. He studied at the Akademie der Kunste in Dresden (1911–16), and, after serving in the armed services (1916–18), he studied with Richard Muller and Otto Gussmann. During that time he was appointed chairperson of the Student Counsel at the Akademie.

Kesting exhibited pictures and collages of the war at a one-man show in Dresden in 1918, and in 1919 he founded the Der Weg School for training in composition in Dresden, where he taught nature study. In 1920 he met Herwarth Walden, with whom he began a longstanding friendship

and collaboration. In 1923 Kesting had a one-man exhibit, "Sturm," and was published in *Der Sturm* magazine. He exhibited in New York and Moscow in 1926, and in 1927 participated in the "Great Berlin Art Show." Walden, his fellow member of the "Sturm-circle," left for the USSR in 1932, which ended their relationship, and the next year Kesting joined with Leitung von Lothar Schreyer of Berlin's Wegschule to publish material on the "Degenerate Art" school of photography ("Entarteten Kunst" Zuwendung zur Fotografie). With Will Gorham, Kesting set up the first German Art Show in Dresden, including pieces from the "Entarteten Kunst." He later taught for several years, and in 1955 was a professor at the Deutschen Hochschule für Filmkunst.

Known for his collages and montages as well as his photography, Kesting was at the helm of the German avant-garde in the 1920s. During the Third Reich, however, he was not allowed either to work or exhibit.

PUBLICATIONS Books: (In Germany) *Prachtgefasse, Geschmeide, Kabinettstücke*, Walter Holzhausen (Wasmuth: Tübingen); *Chorin: Gestafte und Geschichte . . .*, 1962 (St. Benno: Leipzig); *Ein Maler sicht durch's Objektiv*, 1958 (Fotokino Verlag: Halle); *Dresden wie es war*, 1955 (Rembrandt Verlag: Berlin).

Robert Glenn Ketchum PHOTOGRAPHER · CURATOR · ADMINISTRATOR Born on December 1, 1947, Ketchum received a BA in Design at the University of California at Los Angeles, studying under Teske, Fichter and Heinecken. He also attended Brooks Institute in Santa Barbara and the California Institute of the Arts in Valencia, where he completed an MFA in 1973.

Since 1979 he has been curator at the National Park Foundation in Washington, D.C., and contributing photographer for *Powder Magazine*. His professional experience also includes serving as a curator for the Security Pacific Bank (1979) and teaching photography at the California Institute of the Arts, Valencia (1975), and in workshops that he started at the Sun Valley Center for the Arts and Humanities in Sun Valley, Idaho (1971–73).

He belongs to SPE, Friends of Photography in Carmel, the Sierra Club and the Los Angeles Center for Photographic Studies, for which he served as president in 1979. The National Park Foundation awarded him two grants for curatorial research (1978 and 1979) and he received a Ciba-Geigy materials grant for Cibachrome printing and masking research (1979).

The artist, working in 35mm and 4 x 5, produced black-and-white prints as well as Cibachrome color prints. He is involved in "presenting conceptual ideas through photographs of the natural environments."

PUBLICATIONS Catalogs (text only): *Landscape Photographers and America's National Parks*, 1979; *Photographic Directions: Los Angeles*, 1979, Outerbridge, w/Graham Howe, 1976. Periodical: *Popular Photography*, Mar 1980.

COLLECTIONS Calif. Inst. of the Arts, Valencia; CCP, Tuscon; Harvard Univ., Fogg Art Mus., Cambridge; IMP/GEH, Rochester; Los Angeles County Mus. of Art; Minneapolis Inst. of the Arts, Minn.; MOMA, NYC; Oakland Mus. of Art, Calif.; UCLA, Frederick S. Wight Gall., Calif.; Univ. of N. Mex. Art Mus., Albuquerque.

DEALERS Silver Image Gall., 83 S Washington, Seattle, WA 98104; Susan Spiritus Gall., 3336 Via Lido, Newport Beach, CA 92663.

ADDRESS 696 Stone Canyon Rd, Los Angeles, CA 90024.

Jay A. Keystone GALLERY OWNER · PHYSICIAN Born October 6, 1937, in Detroit, Michigan, Keystone earned a BA from the University of Michigan, Ann Arbor, in 1958 and an MD from that school in 1962. He served a residency in 1966–68 and had an Allergy-Immunology Fellowship at the University in 1968–70.

Specializing as an allergist, Keystone has been a partner in the Santa Barbara Medical Clinic since 1970. He is also a partner in Keystone Gallery with his wife Lanie. He belongs to the AMA and the American Academy of Allergists.

ADDRESS Keystone Gall., 1213 State St, # F, Santa Barbara, CA 93101.

Lanie Keystone GALLERY OWNER · DANCE SPECIALIST Born March 31, 1942, in Detroit, Michigan, Keystone earned a BA in Theater and Education from the University of Michigan, Ann Arbor, in 1970. She studied dance at her alma mater as well as at the University of Southern California (Los Angeles) and San Francisco State University.

Since 1971 Keystone has been a dance educator for Goleta and Montecito (California) public schools and a member of Valerie Huston Dance Theater. She is currently a partner in the Keystone Gallery with her husband Jay Keystone. She belongs to the California Dance Educators Association and the Junior League of Santa Barbara.

ADDRESS Keystone Gall., 1213 State St., #F, Santa Barbara, CA 93101.

Algimantas Kezys PRIEST · PHOTOGRAPHER · GALLERY OWNER Born October 28, 1928 in Vistytis, Lithuania, Kezys, a Roman Catholic priest, received an MA in Philosophy in 1956 from Loyola University of Chicago, Illinois.

He recently founded, and owns, the Galerija art gallery in Chicago. He also founded the Lithuanian Photo Library and has served as its president since 1966, and he founded and directs (since 1976) the Lithuanian Library Press in Chicago. From 1974 to 1977 he directed the Lithuanian Youth Center in Chicago.

PUBLICATIONS Monographs: *A Lithuanian Cemetery*, 1976; *Form and Content*, 1972; *I Fled Him Down the Nights and Down the Days*, 1970; *Photographs/Algimantas Kezys, S.J.*, 1966.

COLLECTIONS Art Inst. of Chicago; Carnegie Inst. of Pittsburgh, Mus. of Art, Pa.; Los Angeles County Mus. of Art.

DEALERS Gall. of Photographic Art, 26777 Lorain Rd N, Olmsted, OH 44070; Douglas Kenyon, Inc., 155 E Ohio St, Chicago, IL 60611.

ADDRESS 5620 S Claremont Ave, Chicago, Il 60636.

Erika Kiffl PHOTOGRAPHER Born December 19, 1939, in Karlsbad, Czechoslovakia, Kiffl studied at Fach Hochschule in Krefeld under Josef Fassbender and at Kunstakademie in Düsseldorf under Walter Breker. Her main Influence has been the work of André Kertész.

PUBLICATIONS Book: *Künstler in imrem atelier*, 1979 (Mahnert-Lueg Verlag: Munich). Periodicals: *Zoom*, March 1980 (Germany); *Professional Camera*, Feb 1979.

COLLECTIONS In Germany: Institut für Moderne Kunst, Nürnberg; Kunsthalle, Hamburg; Kunstmuseum, Düsseldorf; Neue Sammlung, Munich.

DEALER Photographer's Gall., 8 Great Newport St, London WC2, England.

ADDRESS Lindemannstrasse 3, D-4000, Düsseldorf, West Germany.

Helmmo R. Kindermann PHOTOGRAPHER Born October 11, 1947, in Lancaster, Pennsylvania, Kindermann received his BFA in 1969 from Tyler School of Art, Philadelphia, Pennsylvania, where he studied with William G. Larson. He studied with Nathan Lyons and Keith Smith at the Visual Studies Workshop in Rochester and earned his MFA there in 1973.

Since 1973 Kindermann has been Photography Department chairman at Lake Placid School of Art, Fawn Ridge, Lake Placid, New York. In 1979 he was curator of photography for the XIII Olympic Winter Games, National Fine Arts Committee, U.S. Eye exhibition in Lake Placid.

He has belonged to SPE since 1973, Friends of Photography since 1975 and CAA since 1977.

The photographer uses color and black-and-white, combining nonsilver techniques with painterly concerns.

The greater part of his work deals with humorous content from found photographic sources, each photograph including additions and color applied by hand.

PUBLICATIONS Books: *Innovative Printmaking Techniques*, Thelma Newman, 1977; *Light and Lens—Methods of Photography*, 1973; *Frontiers of Photography*, 1972; *Photo/Synthesis*, n.d. Periodicals: *American Photographer*, 3:2; *Camera 35*, 18:5; *Quiver*, no. 4 (Tyler School of Art: Philadelphia, Pa.).

COLLECTIONS Mississippi Art Assoc., Jackson; VSW, Rochester, N.Y.

REPRESENTATIVE Visual Studies Workshop Gall., 31 Prince St, Rochester, NY 14607.

ADDRESS Wardner Rd, Rainbow Lake, NY 12976.

Bruce Anthony King PHOTOGRAPHER · BUSINESSMAN Born in Toronto, Ontario, on February 23, 1934, King earned an AB from Hamilton College in Clinton, New York, in 1956. He attended it also from 1951 to 1954. From 1954 to 1955 he attended the Sorbonne in Paris, where he received a Degré Superieur from Cours de Civilisation. He also earned a diploma from Saint Andrews College at Autoro, Ontario, in 1951.

King is the president of several businesses: Washburn-Garfield Company (since 1956), Black Ice Publishers (since 1972) and Waites Industrial (since 1979). He has also been on the board of directors of Wyman-Gordon Company since 1979. His images appear regularly in *Natural History*, *Country Journal* and *The Worcester Telegram and Gazette*.

Twice, in 1978 and 1973, King was given the Certificate of Award from the Printing Industries of America. Also in 1978, he won the Medaille Préfet des Yvelines at Photo Univers in Bievres, France, and and Award of Merit from the Advertising Club of New York.

King photographs everyday events and ordinary objects. What interests him is "where and how man fits on the land and in nature."

PUBLICATIONS Books: *My Maine Thing*, 1980; *Criss-Cross Applesauce*, Tomie de Paola, 1979; *The Faces of the Great Lakes*, Jonathan Ela, 1977; *A Place to Begin*, *The New England Experience*, Hal Borland, 1976; *Ojibwa Summer*, James

Houston, 1972. Periodicals: *Popular Photography Annual*, 1978; *The Gallery*, Aug 1973; *The British Journal of Photography*, Dec 29, 1972.

COLLECTIONS Harvard Univ., Fogg Art Mus., Cambridge, Mass.; Minneapolis Inst. of Art, Minn.; MOMA, NYC; Worcester Art Mus., Mass. Natl. Film Board of Canada, Still Div., Toronto, Ontario.

ADDRESS Box 298, Southboro, MA 01772.

Darius Reynold Kinsey PHOTOGRAPHER Born July 23, 1869, in Maryville, Nodaway County, Missouri, Kinsey died May 13, 1945, in Sedro-Woolley, Washington. His wife, Tabitha May Kinsey (1875–1963), was a photoprinter.

Kinsey arrived in Snowqualmie, Washington Territory, in 1889, where he obtained his first camera, a 6½ x 8½, and began photographing. He later added an 8 x 10 and a 4½ x 6½ to his collection. By 1894 he was traveling through the countryside, and he soon formed a partnership with his brother Clark, establishing a studio in Sedro-Woolley. He married Tabitha on October 8, 1896, and she ran Kinsey Photo Studio's darkroom from 1899. Between 1897 and 1906 Kinsey organized seven major photo expeditions, including ones to Mt. Baker and Mt. Rainier. He traveled widely in the western United States, and exhibited at the St. Louis Exposition of 1904. In 1906 he relocated in Seattle and worked until an accident in 1940 caused him to stop.

"Darius Kinsey at his best nudged genius," wrote David Bohn. He exhibited "a remarkable consistency of work—the smooth tonal range and tight control of contrast, the delicacy of so many of the pictures." With his 11 x 14 Empire State camera, among others, he produced a monumental body of work: some 4500 surviving negatives and plates in eleven different formats (he switched from glass to film in 1914). With his heavy equipment he followed the timber from the forests to the mills to the docks, where schooners freighted away their cargo. Thus he depicted all aspects of the logging industry. He also did other industrial photography, taking a special interest in dam construction.

PUBLICATIONS Monograph: *Kinsey, Photographer*, 2 vols., David Bohn & Rodolfo Petschek, eds., w/contr. by Darius Kinsey, Jr. & Dorothea Kinsey Parcheski, 1975. Books: *The Way Life Was*, 1974; *Chechacos All*; *The Pioneering of Skagit*, Margaret Willis, ed., 1973; *The Shay Locomotive*; *Titan of the Timber*, Michael Koch, 1971; *American Album*, O. Jensen & J. Kerr, 1968; *Photographers of the Frontier West*, Ralph W. Andrews, 1965; *Pacific Coast Shay: Strong*

Man of the Woods, Dan Ranger Jr., 1964; *Logging Railroads of the West*, Kramer Adams, 1961; *Climax—An Unusual Steam Locomotive*, Thomas Taber & Walter Casler, 1960; *This Was Sawmilling*, 1957, *Glory Days of Logging*, 1956, Ralph W. Andrews; *Down on the Farm*, Stewart H. Holbrook, 1954; *This Was Logging!*, Ralph W. Andrews, 1954; *18 Men and a Horse*, Donald H. Clark, 1949, repr. 1969; *An Illustrated History of Skagit and Snohomish Counties*, brief bio., 1906. Anthology: *The Photographer's Eye*, John Szarkowski, 1966. Catalogs: *Green Gold Harvest*, Susan H. L. Barrow & J. Allan Evans, 1969 (Whatcom Mus. of Hist. & Art: Bellingham, Wash.); *The Photographer and the American Landscape*, John Szarkowski, 1963 (MOMA: NYC); *Catalogue of Washington Timber and Scenic Views*, 1916. Periodicals: "Kinsey, Photographer," Dave Bohn, May 1975, "Shakespeare in the Logging Camp," Thomas Emerson Ripley, May 1967, *The American West*; "The Enduring Legacy of Darius Kinsey," Frank Denman, *Seattle*, Jan 1970; "Daylight in the Swamp," Stewart H. Holbrook, *American Heritage*, Oct 1958; "Speaking of Pictures: Work of Forgotten Photographers . . . ," *Life*, Sept 10, 1951; "Dempsey Logging Camp at Hamilton Has Unique Features," *West Coast Lumberman*, Oct 1, 1918; *The Yellow Strand*, Jan–Mar 1916, Nov & Dec 1915; "Logging in the Northwest," *Scientific American*, D. A. Willey, Dec 19, 1900.

COLLECTIONS   MOMA, NYC; Snoqualmie Valley Hist. Soc., North Bend, Wash.

Tabitha May Pritts Kinsey   *DARKROOM ASSISTANT · STUDIO MANAGER*   Born May 24, 1875, in Waverly Mills, Minnesota, Kinsey died on November 23, 1963, in Bellingham, Washington. Her husband was photographer Darius Kinsey.

Tabitha ran her husband's studio and did all his printing for about fifty years, beginning in 1896. She can be considered as much a part of the monumental work produced by Kinsey as he was himself.

See Darius Kinsey.

Kent Bruce Kirby   *PHOTOGRAPHER · TEACHER*   Born December 31, 1934, in Fargo, North Dakota, Kirby received a BA in 1956 from Carleton College, Northfield, Minnesota, an MA in 1959 from University of North Dakota, Grand Forks, and an MFA in 1970 from University of Michigan, Ann Arbor.

He has been professor and chairman of the department of Art and Design at Alma College, Alma, Michigan, since 1962. Previously he was

an instructor at Wilkes College, Wilkes-Barre, Pennsylvania (1961–62), and an art instructor and acting department head at Muskingum College, New Concord, Oregon (1959–61).

Kirby is a member of American Association of University Professors, CAA, National Council of Art Administrators, Mid-Michigan Association of Working Artists and the Mt. Pleasant Art Guild. A Michigan Council for the Arts grantee in 1975 and 1978, he won an NEA Fellowship in 1976. He was a Charles A. Dana Professor of Art at Alma College in 1976 and was named a research fellow at the Newberry Library, Chicago, in 1974.

Kirby works in hand-printed collotype, one of the earliest photomechanical, ink-to-paper printing processes.

COLLECTIONS   Art Inst. of Chicago; Cranbrook Academy of Art Mus., Bloomfield Hills, Mich.; Guggenheim Mus., NYC; Metro. Mus. of Art, NYC; Mich. State Univ., East Lansing; Philadelphia Mus. of Art, Pa.

ADDRESS   4100 Riverview Dr, Alma, MI 48801.

Wallace W. Kirkland   *PHOTOGRAPHER · AUTHOR*   Born on August 4, 1891, at Retreat Plantation, Orange Bay, Jamaica, in the British West Indies, Kirkland died September 14, 1979, in Oak Park, Illinois. He received a degree in sociology from George Williams College, Chicago, Illinois, in 1923.

The young Kirkland was an apprentice for the Jamaican Government Railway in 1904, then worked in a hard-rubber factory in New Jersey in 1905. He worked for five years in a small-town grocery store, and was in charge of the explosives department at DuPont in Pompton Lakes. Kirkland served for a time as a YMCA outpost secretary, traveling the Mexican border during the Pancho Villa uprising (World War I). After completing his schooling, he became Boys' Club Director for Jane Addams' Hull House in Chicago (1921–36), during which time he became interested in photography. He freelanced for such publications as *Field and Stream*, *Outdoor Life*, *Ranger Rick's Nature Magazine*, *Country Beautiful*, the New York *Herald Tribune* and *Life*. He did school, farm and industrial photography for *Life* from 1937 until he became a staff photographer for the magazine in 1942, where he remained until 1967. Kirkland also taught photography at a Saugatuck, Michigan, art school and at Fish Creek, Door County, Wisconsin.

He was active in many press photography groups in Chicago and New York. Kirkland's photo of Jane Addams is at the U.S. Children's Bureau in Washington, D.C. Fourteen of his photographs of the poorhouse in Evansville, Indiana, won him an honorable mention for picture sequence at the *Encyclopaedia Brittanica* annual contest in 1951. They were also shown by the Milwaukee Art Institute in its "Seven States Show" and purchased by the institute for its collection.

Kirkland was known for his *Life* photographs of famous personages such as Gandhi, Franklin Roosevelt, General MacArthur, Harry Truman and Paul Robeson. As a World War II correspondent, he traveled throughout the South Pacific. Early in his career he did photographs for private-school catalogs, but his more artistic efforts were of nature.

PUBLICATIONS Books: *A Walk by the Pond, A Walk in the Woods, A Walk in the Fields, A Walk by the Seashore* (four books), 1971; *The Lure of the Pond,* 1969; *Recollections of a Life Photographer,* 1954; *Shenshoo, the Story of a Moose,* 1929. Catalog: *50 Photographs by Wallace Kirkland, Life Photographer,* 1952 (Art Inst. of Chicago).

COLLECTIONS Milwaukee Art Inst., Wisc.; State Historical Soc. of Wisc., Madison; Univ. of Ill., Jane Addams Mem. Cllctn., Urbana.

ARCHIVE Dr. Wallace W. Kirkland, 141 S Scoville Ave, Oak Park, IL 60302.

Semyon Davidovitch Kirlian & Valentina Chrisanfovna Kirlian *ELECTRICIAN · INVENTOR / TEACHER · JOURNALIST · INVENTOR* Both inventors were born in Krasnodar, Russia (the dates are unknown). In 1939, in his native town, Semyon Kirlian began investigating energy fields surrounding living organisms. Inadvertently he discovered corona-discharge photography, now commonly known as Kirlian photography. With his wife's assistance, Kirlian (pronounced Keer-lee-an) began experiments in the field, first using himself as a guinea pig by placing a photographic plate between the skin of his hand and a metal electrode, and using a high-frequency instrument employed in electrotherapy. By 1949 the pair had perfected this entirely new method of photography (covered by fourteen different patents) that did not require a camera, but, instead, a high-frequency-spark generator or oscillator, and presented it to the Presidium of the Academy of Sciences in the USSR.

After a period of time they received some research monies through the Ministry of Public Health, and later, in the 1960s, the Kirlians obtained full funding through the government.

Their images—some static, some moving—show brilliant colors and patterns of light radiating from living organisms. Through their work it has been possible to diagnose diseased plants. There is speculation today that the changing colors and patterns of light demonstrated in these images are only reflections of levels of moisture retention and dryness. But the controversial process is believed by others to reflect disease and the varying states of emotional upheaval and calm in a living thing.

PUBLICATIONS Books: *The Kirlian Aura,* Stanley Krippner & Daniel Rubin (1974); *Psychic Discoveries by the Russians,* Mark Ebon, ed., 1971; *Psychic Discoveries Behind the Iron Curtain,* Sheila Ostrander & Lynn Schroeder, 1970; "The Biological Essence of the Kirlian Effect," *The Concept of Biological Plasma,* G. Inyushin, et al, 1968 (Kirov State University: Kazakhstan); *Electromagnetic Fields and Living Nature,* A. S. Pressman, 1968 (Science: Moscow). Periodicals: *Science Digest,* Jan 1977, May 1974; *Popular Electricity,* Jan 1975; *Modern Photography,* Apr 1974; *Science News,* Sept 29, 1973; *Popular Photography,* Feb 1973; "The Borders of the Unknown," I. Belov, *Inventor,* no. 6, 1964; "Russians Photograph Life and Death," *Fate,* Sept 1962; "Signals—Of What?" I. Leonidov, *Soviet Union,* no. 145, 1962; "Photography and Visual Observation by Means of High-Frequency Currents," *Journal of Science & Applied Photography,* 6:6, 1961.

Sardi Klein *PHOTOGRAPHER · TEACHER* Born in New York City on February 25, 1949, Klein studied photography with Lisette Model, Tad Yamashiro, Diane Arbus and Ralph Hattersley at the School of Visual Arts in New York City, graduating in 1970.

Since 1974 she has taught photography at the Bedford Hills Correctional Facility and the Bayview Correctional Facility for the Floating Foundation of Photography in New York City. Klein also teaches photography at the School of Visual Arts, a position she has held since 1975. She was a staff photographer with *Free Enterprise* magazine (1974–78). Her photographs appeared in the Claudia Wiles film *Girl Friends.* Her personal photographs are environmental portraiture.

PUBLICATIONS Anthologies: *The Family of Woman,* 1979; *Women Photograph Men,* Danielle B. Hayes, ed., intro. by Molly Haskell, 1977; *Women See Men,* Yvonne Kalmus et al., eds., 1977; *Women See Woman,* Annie Gottlieb, Cheryl Wiesenfeld, et al., eds., 1976.

ADDRESS 558 Second St, Brooklyn, NY 11215.

William Klein *PAINTER · PHOTOGRAPHER ·
FILM MAKER* [See plate 99] Born in 1928 in New
York, Klein received a Bachelor of Social Science
degree from the City College of New York and a
License in Literature from the Sorbonne in Paris.

Currently self-employed, he was under contract to *Vogue* magazine from 1955 to 1965. In
1965 he gave up professional still photography to
make movies, but returned to still photography
in 1978–79.

His book *New York* won the Prix Nadar in
France in 1957.

As a painter Klein worked with Fernand Léger
upon arriving in Paris, exhibited throughout Eu-
rope, and executed numerous abstract murals for
French and Italian architects. As a film maker,
Klein created the following: *The Little Richard
Story* (1979), *Music City* (1978), *Maydays*, (1978),
Hollywood, California (1977), *The Model Couple*
(1975–76), *Muhammad Ali The Greatest* (1974),
Le Grand Café (1972), *Eldridge Cleaver Black
Panther* (1970), *Panafrican Cultural Festival*
(1969), *Mr. Freedom* (1967–68), *Qui Etes-Vous
Polly Maggoo?* (1966, which won the Prix Jean
Vigo), *Cassius the Great* (1964–65, won the
Grand Prix at the International Festival, Tours)
and *Broadway By Light*, 1959.

PUBLICATIONS Books: *Mr. Freedom*, 1968
(Eric Losfeld: Paris); *Tokyo*, 1964, *Moscow*, 1962,
Rome, 1958, *New York*, 1956 (Editions du Seuil:
Paris). Anthology: *The Magic Image*, Cecil Bea-
ton & Gail Buckland, 1975.

PORTFOLIO *New York 54/55*, 1978 (Atelier J.
M. Bustamante/Bernard Saint-Genes: Paris).

COLLECTIONS MOMA, NYC. Centre Georges
Pompidou, Paris; French Fndn. of Photography,
Lyon; Victoria & Albert Mus., London.

DEALERS Light Gall., 724 Fifth Ave, New
York, NY 10019; Zabriskie Gall., 29 rue Aubry le
Boucher, Paris, France; Canon Gall., 3 rue Saint
Leger, Geneva 1205, Switzerland; Photographer's
Gall., 8 Great Newport St, London WC2, En-
gland.

ADDRESS 5 rue de Medicis, 75006 Paris,
France.

Mark Klett *PHOTOGRAPHER · TEACHER* Born
September 9, 1952, in Albany, New York, Klett
earned his BS in Geology (1974) from St. Lawrence University, Canton, New York, and his
MFA in Photography (1977) from the Visual Studies Workshop, Rochester, New York. He studied
with Michael Bishop, Nathan Lyons and Linda
Parry.

He has been assistant director of photography
at Sun Valley Center for the Arts and Humanities, Idaho, since 1978. He is also chief photographer on the Rephotographic Survey Project (since
1977), sponsored by the Colorado Mountain College and Sun Valley Center for the Arts and Humanities. Klett was a geologist and geologist field
assistant for the U.S. Geological Survey, Branch
of Energy Resources, in 1974–76.

A member of SPE since 1977, Klett won an
Emerging Artist Fellowship from the NEA in
1979.

Klett works in small and large formats, and in
black-and-white and color. He is especially interested in color and formal relationships. For the
Rephotographic Survey Project he has been photographing sites of nineteenth-century western
landscapes.

PUBLICATIONS Anthology: *Photo Year*, 1979.
Periodicals: "Rephotographing Jackson," w/Jo
Ann Verburg, *Afterimage: VSW*, text only, sum-
mer 1978; "Subject, Vantage Point, View Point:
Factors in Rephotography," *Exposure: SPE*, fall
1979.

COLLECTIONS IMP/GEH, Rochester; St. Lawrence Univ., Canton, N.Y.; Sun Valley Ctr. for
the Arts & Humanities, Idaho; Univ. of Kans.,
Spencer Mus., Lawrence.

ADDRESS Box 656, Sun Valley, ID 83353.

Karel Václav Klič *INVENTOR · GRAPHIC ARTIST ·
PRINTER* Born in 1841 in Arnau, Bohemia, Klič
studied art at the Academy of Arts in Prague,
Czechoslovakia. He died in 1926 in Vienna, Austria.

Klič worked in his father's photographic studio
for a while, then began making drawings and
woodcuts for publications. To improve the typical woodcut reproduction, he began photochemical experiments, opening his own shop,
Photochemische Werkstaette, in Vienna in 1871.
He made zinc plates by an asphalt process, then
studied halftone screens and the use of carbon
tissue as a photoresist in copper plates and in
photointaglio reproduction.

In 1878 Klič invented the most precise (though
slow) commercial photogravure printing method.
He sold the process in Vienna, Brussels and Paris
in 1881, and, in 1883, to Annan and Swan in London and to a firm in Munich. Then, in 1890, he
sold it to Storey Brothers & Co. Ltd. of Lancaster,
Lancashire, England. The first commercial operation of the process is considered to have oc-
curred on October 11, 1893. The Storeys formed
Rembrandt Intaglio Printing Company, Ltd., in
1895, the first rotogravure firm, and Klič was put
in charge of the technical aspects of the business.
He also joined as a partner in the firm, waiving

his right to sell the process to anyone else. He returned to Vienna in 1897, making frequent trips to the Rembrandt plant until World War I.

PUBLICATIONS Books: *Geschichte des Tiefdruckes*, 1963, 1959; *Photomechanical Halftone*, Louis W. Sipley, 1958; *Evolution of Rotogravure*, J. S. Mertle, 1957; *Karl Klietch: Der Erfinder der Heliogravure und des Rakeltiefdruck*, Karl Albert, 1927; *Lexikon für Photographie und Reproduktionstechnik*, G. H. Emmerich, 1910; *Bilderbuch für hagestolm*, w/Spitzer, 1874 (Vienna). Anthologies: *Early Photographs and Early Photographers*, Oliver Mathews, 1973; *Photography's Great Inventors*, Louis W. Sipley, 1965. Periodicals: *Bild und Ton*, 1958, 1954; *Photoengravers' Bulletin*, June 1945; *Photographische Correspondenz*, 1931, 1927, 1911, 1880, 1877; *Photogram*, 1894.

Stuart D. Klipper   *PHOTOGRAPHER · TEACHER*
Born August 27, 1941, in the Bronx, New York, Klipper received a BA in Psychology from the University of Michigan, Ann Arbor (1962).

Most recently a visiting artist at Colorado College, Colorado Springs (1978–79), he taught photography at Minneapolis College of Art and Design in 1970, 1972, 1974 and 1978. In 1975–76 Klipper was a photography instructor at University of Minnesota, Minneapolis, and at The Blake School, Minneapolis.

The photographer won a Guggenheim Fellowship in 1979, an NEA Photographer's Fellowship in 1979, an NEA Photo Survey grant in 1976, a Minnesota State Arts Board Technical Assistance Grant in 1976, and a Minnesota State Arts Council Grant in 1974.

Klipper handled still photography, cinematography, interviewing and editing for the BBC production "D. H. Lawrence in New Mexico" in 1969.

PUBLICATIONS Book: *Photography*, Michael Simon, 1978. Catalog: *Mid-West Invitational Catalogue*, 1974 (Walker Art Ctr.: Minneapolis).

COLLECTIONS Art Inst. of Chicago; Chase Manhattan Bank Art Program, NYC; Exchange Natl. Bank, Chicago; First Natl. Bank of Minneapolis; Kray Research, Inc., St. Paul, Minn.; David & Reva Logan Fndn. Cllctn., Chicago; Minneapolis Inst. of Arts, Minn.; Minn. Mus. of Art, St. Paul; Signode Corp., Chicago; Univ. of Kans. Mus. of Art, Lawrence; Univ. of Minn. Gall., Minneapolis; Walker Art Ctr., Minneapolis; Weil Cllctn., Minneapolis, N.Y. & Wash., D.C.

DEALERS Peter M. David Gall., 430 Oak Grove, Minneapolis MN 55403; O. K. Harris, 383 W Broadway, New York, NY 10012; Douglas Kenyon Gall., 155 E Ohio St, Chicago, IL 60611.

ADDRESS 614 W 27 St, Minneapolis, MN 55408.

Richard Allan Knapp   *PHOTOGRAPHER ·*
TEACHER Born in Rochester, New York, on July 18, 1942, Knapp received a BA from the University of Rochester (1964) and an MLS from Rutgers University in New Jersey (1966). He also completed an MFA at the University of New Mexico in Albuquerque (1974), writing his thesis on "Spirit and Psychic Photography." He studied under Ray Metzker, William Giles, Van Deren Coke and Beaumont Newhall.

Since 1975 Knapp has been employed as a photography instructor, first at the University of New Mexico (1975–78) and as of this writing at the University of Albuquerque. Previously he worked as a librarian for the Peace Corps in Nepal (1966–67) and at the University of Rochester (1967–70).

In 1978 NEA awarded him a Photographer's Fellowship.

Knapp specializes in photo-collage and altered photographs, and describes his technique in these terms: "Among other things, I scratch, cut and tear my black-and-white photos, sometimes chemically toned, and reassemble the pieces into collages."

COLLECTION Univ. of N. Mex. Art Mus., Albuquerque.

DEALER Meridian Gall., 220 Central Ave SW, Albuquerque, NM 87102.

ADDRESS 136 57 St SW, Albuquerque, NM 87105.

Frederic Hardwicke Knight   *PHOTOGRAPHER ·*
AUTHOR · PUBLISHER Born July 12, 1911, in Stoke Newington, London, Knight studied with Professor Oakley at the Académie Française in 1930.

Since 1976 Knight has been writing and publishing, and previously served as director of medical photography at the University of Otago Medical School and Dunedin Hospital, New Zealand (1957–77), and at Enfield Group Hospitals in England (1948–57). During World War II he was chief photographer for the Plastic Surgery Unit in Gloucester with Sir Harold Gillies. In 1936 Knight did ethnographic documentary work in the Caucasus (Daghestan), and in 1935 did photography for a French archaeological team in northern Iran and Armenia.

A fellow of the New Zealand Institute of Medical and Biological Illustration (since 1970) and of the New Zealand Institute of Medical Photographers (since 1966), he is president of the latter. He also presides over the Dunedin Film Society and Otago Anthropological Society and is vice-president of the Archives Association.

Knight has done pioneering work in the use of autoradiography in the detection of nuclear contamination (1956) and in fluorescein angiography and retinal photography.

He takes documentary photographs "of social and ethnographic significance" and collects work of local historical importance or excellence and researches the photographers' lives.

PUBLICATIONS Book: *Burton Brothers: Photographers*, 1980 (McIndoe); *Cutten*, w/Dr. Grief, 1979, *Otago Peninsula*, 1978, 2nd ed., 1979 (HK: Dunedin, N.Z.); *History of Broad Bay School*, 1977 (Allied Press); *Princes Street by Gaslight (The Photography of D. L. Mundy)*, 1976, *Matanaka*, w/Dr. Coutts, 1975, *Dunedin Then*, 1974, *Photography in New Zealand: A Social & Technical Study*, 1971 (McIndoe: Dunedin). Periodicals: "Burton Brothers of New Zealand," Apr 1979, *Otago Peninsula*, 1978, 2nd ed., 1979 (HK: Dunedin, N.Z.); *History of Broad Bay School*, 1977 (Allied Press); *Princes Street by Gaslight of Photography*; "The Background to and Present State of Medical Photography in New Zealand," *British Journal of Photography*, 1970; "Retinal Photography," *New Zealand Medical Journal*, Mar 1965.

COLLECTION Otago Mus., Dunedin, New Zealand.

ARCHIVE Hocken Lib., University of Otago, Dunedin, New Zealand.

ADDRESS 15 King George St, Broad Bay, Dunedin, New Zealand.

Paul Steven Knotter   *PHOTOGRAPHER ·*
TEACHER · PERFORMANCE ARTIST Born May 3, 1952 in Globe, Arizona, Knotter earned a BFA in 1976 from Arizona State University, Tempe, and an MFA from University of California at Los Angeles in 1979. He studied with Robert Heinecken, Judith Golden, James Antonie and Allen Dutton.

In 1979 Knotter taught photography for UCLA's Extension program and at the Fernald School at UCLA. He was also a set decorator for NBC and CBS in that year, and from 1978 to 1979 he was curator and director of the G.O. Gallery in Los Angeles.

He became a member of SPE in 1978.

Knotter won the UCLA Art Council's Anna Bing Arnold award in 1979, the UCLA Art Department's Alfred Orselli Memorial Award in 1978, and a Ford Foundation Travel Grant in

1978. He co-founded *The Dumb Ox* magazine with Theron Kelley in 1976.

A performance artist, Knotter performed "This Is Living" in 1978 at UCLA and "The Performist" in 1976 at Arizona State University.

The photographer is concerned with "the adaptation of photography to sculptural applications" and "the objectification of objects through contextual reorganization in photography." He produces large-format Cibachrome prints.

PUBLICATIONS Catalog: *Light II*, 1977. Periodicals: *Afterimage: VSW*, review, Nov 1979; *The Dumb Ox*, no. 5, 1978, no. 4, 1977.

COLLECTION Humboldt State Univ., Arcata, Calif.

DEALER Joni Gordon, Newspace, 5015 Melrose, Los Angeles, CA 90042.

ADDRESS 7777 Santa Monica Blvd, #1, Los Angeles, CA 90046.

Gustav Raphael Koegel   *MONK · CHEMIST · INVENTOR* Born in 1882, Koegel died in 1945.

Little is known about Koegel's early years, except that he served as a Benedictine monk in the Beuron Cloister, Baden-Württemberg, Germany. While there he became interested in deciphering palimpsests—parchments from which original writings had been removed chemically or by mechanical abrasion in order to permit new writing. Koegel employed chemical means and photographic methods to bring out the old writings, developing the use of ultraviolet light, which caused the erased writing to fluoresce and thus show up on photographic negatives. He used diazo dyes as well, and became an authority on this light-sensitive material. From 1916 to 1921 he perfected a diazo paper developable by exposure to ammonia vapor and, by 1921, had interested Kalle & Co. A.G. at Wiesbaden-Biebrich in the process. The diazo copying paper they marketed four years later, the first to compete with blueprint paper, was named Ozalid—the reverse spelling of "diazo" with an added "l."

Koegel later withdrew from the cloister and continued his photochemistry research at Kalle & Co. He also was named an honorary professor at the Technische Hochschule in Karlsruhe.

PUBLICATIONS Books: *Encyclopedia of Photography*, 1963 (Greystone Press); *Reprographie*, 1963 (1st Internatl. Congress: Cologne); *From Dry Plates to Ektachrome Film*, C. E. K. Mees, 1961; *Encyclopedie voor Photographie und Reproduktionstechnik*, Elsevier, 1958; *March of Photography*, Erich Stenger, 1958; *History of Color Photography*, Joseph S. Friedman, 1944; *Photography Theory and Practice*, L. P. Clerc,

1937. Anthology: *Photography's Great Inventors*, Louis W. Sipley, 1965. Periodicals: *Bild und Ton*, 1955; *Photographische Correspondenz*, 1926.

Ernst Koenig CHEMIST Born in 1869 in Flensburg, Germany, Koenig died in 1924. He studied medicine at the University of Kiel, then chemistry at the University of Leipzig.

After completing his studies in 1893 Koenig joined the Farbwerke vorm Meister, Lucius & Bruening at Hoechst am Main near Frankfurt. He instigated the development of a photographic department there, which produced plates and the prepared rapid developer Pinakol.

Koenig had made his first photochemical discoveries as a student, developing a Kallitype paper. At Farbwerke he collaborated with Benno Homolka to develop the color process using pinachrome. Based on leuco dyes, it was marketed unsuccessfully in 1904, but set the stage for later work by Fischer and Siegrist and for modern color coupler photography. Koenig also contributed to the development of panchromatic emulsions through isocyanine dyes, and extended plate sensitivity from yellow into the extreme red and rear infrared of the spectrum through the use of such dyes as Pinaverdol, Orthochrome, Pinachrome, and Pinacyanol blue.

PUBLICATIONS Books: *Photographic Chemistry*, 2 vols., Pierre Glafkides, 1960, 1958 (Fountain Press); *March of Photography*, Ewrich Stenger, 1958; *History of Color Photography*, Joseph S. Friedman, 1944; *Theory of the Photographic Process*, C. E. K. Mees, 1944; *History of 3-Color Photography*, E. J. Wall, 1925; *Lexikon für Photographie und Reproduktionstechnik*, G. H. Emmerich, 1910; *Das Arbeiten Mit Farbempfindlichen Platten*, 1909; *Die Autochromphotographie*, 1908; *Book of Photography*, Paul N. Hasluck, 1905; *Die Dreifarbenphotographie*, 1904. Anthology: *Photography's Great Inventors*, Louis W. Sipley, 1965. Periodicals: *Bild und Ton*, 1964; *Zeitschrift für Angewandte Chemie*, 1924; *Photographische Correspondenz*, 1922, 1907; *Photographische Kunst*, Apr 1903; *Poggendorffs Handbuch*, no. 6.

Walter Koenig CHEMIST · INVENTOR Born in 1878 in Annaberg, Germany, Koenig died in 1964. He was educated at Leipzig University and the Technische Hochschule in Dresden, receiving from the latter an engineer's degree in 1902 and a doctorate in 1903.

After graduation Koenig worked as a chemist in the Farbenfabriken vorm Friedr. Bayer & Co. in Elberfeld (until 1908). He also served as an as-

sistant at the Technische Hochschule in Dresden from 1906 until 1908, when he became a special instructor there. From 1913 to 1945, and from 1949 to 1957, Koenig was professor of color chemistry and dye technique at the Hochschule, also assuming directorship of the laboratory of color and textile chemistry in 1926.

During 1922–24, Koenig devised an improved method of preparing carbocyanine spectral sensitizers for photographic emulsions, and in 1924–25 described the indocyanines and the preparation of quinoline. In 1925 he patented a method of preparing dicarbocyanines that are efficient as deep-red and infrared sensitizers, and he proceeded to develop polymethine dyes for sensitizing photographic emulsions for infrared—a spectral field invisible to the human eye. These emulsions are valuable in the photography of distant scenes, penetration of mist and fog and aerial photography. The chemist also developed the green and yellow sensitizer thiazole purple, and patented other color sensitizers for infrared in 1935.

PUBLICATIONS Books: *Photographic Chemistry*, 2 vols., Pierre Glafkides, 1960, 1958 (Fountain Press); *March of Photography*, Erich Stenger, trans. E. Epstean, 1958; *Theory of the Photographic Process*, C. E. K. Mees, 1944; *Photography Principles and Practice*, 3rd ed., C. B. Neblette, 1939. Anthology: *Photography's Great Inventors*, Louis W. Sipley, 1965. Periodicals: *Wissenshaftliche Zeitschrift der Technischen Universitaet Dresden*, 1963; *Zeitschrift für wissenschaftliche Photographie*, 1936, "Die Chemie der Sensibilisatoren," 1935; *Berichte der Deutschen Chemiken Gesellschaft*, 1934, 1928, 1922.

Mary Koga PHOTOGRAPHER Born in Sacramento, California, on August 10, 1920, Koga earned a BA from the University of California at Berkeley in 1942 and an MA from the University of Chicago in 1947. Later she took up photography and completed an MFA at the School of the Art Institute of Chicago (1973).

Since then she has been teaching photography at Columbia College in Chicago. Her first career was devoted to the social sciences: initially a social worker for the Family Service Bureau of United Charities of Chicago (1947–52), she then worked as a faculty member and chief psychologist at the Medical School of Northwestern University in Chicago (1952–58), and as assistant professor in the School of Social Service Administration at the University of Chicago (1959–69).

She belongs to SPE, the Artists' League of the

Midwest and the National Association of Social Workers.

Koga works in black-and-white and color. She is interested in photographing people in their own environment and in exploring abstractions from natural subjects, such as plant and flower forms.

PUBLICATIONS Anthologies: *Family of Children*, 1977; *Women of Photography*, 1975. Catalog: *Chicago: The City and Its Artists, 1945–78*, 1978 (Univ. of Mich., Mus. of Art: Ann Arbor). Periodical: *Camera 35*, 1975.

COLLECTIONS Exchange Natl. Bank, Chicago; Kimberly-Clark, Chicago; Seagram Cllctn., NYC; San Francisco Mus. of Modern Art.

DEALER Douglas Kenyon, Inc., 155 E Ohio St, Chicago, IL 60611.

ADDRESS 1254 Elmdale Ave, Chicago, IL 60660.

Dr. Kyō Koike PHOTOGRAPHER · PHYSICIAN · POET · NATURALIST Born in 1878 in Shimane Prefecture, Japan, Koike died March 31, 1947, in Seattle, Washington. Trained as a physician in Japan, he taught himself photography after receiving a camera as a gift about 1918. He was influenced by Japanese woodblock prints and *sumi* painting.

Dr. Koike set up medical offices in Seattle upon his arrival there in 1917. He soon took up photography and from then on devoted himself to the craft. Incarcerated in a Japanese internment camp in Minidoka, Idaho, after Pearl Harbor, he served as the camp doctor. After returning to Seattle, Koike continued to practice both medicine and photography. He published his photographs in various journals in Germany, The Netherlands, France, Poland, England and America, including *American Photographer, Camera, American Annual of Photography, Salon Internationale d'Art, Pictorial Photography of America* and *Photofreund*.

He founded the still-functioning Rainier Ginsha, a haiku society, in 1934, and served as a teacher and poet. In 1923 Koike co-founded the Seattle Camera Club, editing its bilingual monthly bulletin, *Notan* ("dark and light"), from 1923 to 1929, when the club ceased to exist. He was also an associate of RPS.

Under the pen name of Banjin, Koike contributed poetry to Japanese publications. He also translated some thirty volumes of Japanese literature into English between 1919 and 1924, was a stamp collector and collected and classified wildflowers from the Cascades and Mt. Rainier area.

Koike was a pictorialist whose work was close to that of the modernists. His photography was exhibited in salons all over the European continent and the United States. He chose natural subjects, especially landscapes, and made judicious use of soft focus. Koike's simple, spare photographs exemplified the qualities of haiku poetry.

PUBLICATIONS Catalog: *Photographic Work*, 1929 (Art Inst. of Seattle: Wash.). Periodicals: "The Seattle Camera Club," Oct 1925, "Why I Am a Pictorial Photographer," Sept 1928, *Photo-Era Magazine*.

COLLECTION Univ. of Wash., Suzzallo Lib., Seattle.

Rudolf Koppitz PHOTOGRAPHER · TEACHER Born in Austria, Koppitz died in 1936. For twenty years he taught at the famed Graphischen Lehr- und Versuchsanstalt in Vienna, as well as teaching private students at his home.

In his personal work he concentrated on landscapes, portraits, nudes and country life, using gum-bichromate, bromoil and bromoil transfer processes.

PUBLICATIONS Monograph: *Rudolf Koppitz*, 1937. Anthology: *The Magic Image*, Cecil Beaton & Gail Buckland, 1975.

COLLECTIONS RPS, London; Sammlung Fotografis Landerbank, Vienna.

Robert Koslowsky CHEMIST Born in Kiel, Germany, in 1901, Koslowsky attended the Hebbelschule and studied chemistry at Kiel University, returning after 1925 for doctoral studies.

Koslowsky joined Agfa in Wolfen, Germany, in 1928. He first worked in the scientific laboratory for a year, then transferred to film manufacture and to the sensitization laboratory. Koslowsky's discoveries included the use of complex gold salts to increase emulsion sensitivity without graininess (1936) and new classes of panchromatic sensitizers (1931), resulting in the progress of high-speed, fine-grain photo emulsions. The 1936 invention was kept as a trade secret and not patented. After World War II the British and Americans disclosed it while publishing German patents and trade secrets. From 1923 to 1925 Koslowsky worked as a laboratory assistant in the Gesellschaft für Chemische Industrie in Basel, Switzerland.

Koslowsky received the Gold Medal of the Photographische Gesellschaft in Vienna in 1953.

PUBLICATIONS Books: *Quellendarstellungen zur Geschichte der Fotografie*, Wolfgang Baier, 1964; *From Dry Plates to Ektachrome Film*, C. E. K. Mees, 1961 (Ziff-Davis: NYC). Anthology: *Photography's Great Inventors*, Louis W. Sipley,

1965. Periodicals: *Photographische Correspondenz*, 1953; *Science et Industries Photographiques*, 1951; *Zeitschrift für wissenschaftliche Photographie*, 1951.

Josef Koudelka PHOTOGRAPHER Born in 1938 in Boskovice, Czechoslovakia, Koudelka earned a degree in engineering from the university of Prague in 1961. As a photographer, he is self-taught.

In 1971 he became affiliated with Magnum Photos, freelancing for that agency. During the years 1962–70 he was the photographer for the Divadlo Theater in Prague.

Koudelka is a member of the Czechoslovakian Union of Artists, which he joined in 1964.

PUBLICATIONS Book: *Gypsies*, Willy Guy, 1975. Anthologies: *The Photograph Collector's Guide*, Lee D. Witkin & Barbara London, 1979; *Photography Year*, Time-Life Series, 1976; *The Magic Image*, Cecil Beaton & Gail Buckland, 1975; *Celebrations*, Minor White & Jonathan Green, eds., 1974; *Looking at Photographs*, John Szarkowski, 1973. Periodicals: *Camera*, Dec 1979, Aug 1979, Dec 1975, Feb 1972, Mar 1970, Nov 1967; *Creative Camera*, Feb 1976, Apr 1973.

COLLECTIONS MOMA, NYC. RPS, London.

REPRESENTATIVE Magnum Photos, Inc., 15 W 46 St, New York, NY 10036.

Cal Kowal PHOTOGRAPHER · TEACHER Born in Chicago, Illinois, in 1944, Kowal received his BA in Art/Architectural History from the University of Illinois, Chicago (1967), and his MS from the Institute of Design, Illinois Institute of Technology, Chicago (1971), where he studied with Aaron Siskind, Arthur Siegel and Joe Jachna. His brother, Dennis Kowal, is a sculptor.

Currently head of the photography department at the Art Academy of Cincinnati, Ohio (since 1971), he was a guest professor in the Architecture Department at Miami University, Oxford, Ohio, in 1976–78. In 1975 he founded Rose/Pose Publishing, a press for limited-edition artists' books.

Kowal belongs to SPE, the Graphic Arts Society, Cincinnati Art Museum, and is on the board of trustees of the Contemporary Art Center in Cincinnati. He won an artist-in-residence grant from NEA in 1976 to work at the Light Work gallery, Syracuse University, New York.

Besides his personal photography, Kowal publishes small-press photography books and produces limited-edition portfolios of original photographs.

PUBLICATIONS Monographs: *This Space Re-*
served, 1979; *T-Shirts Are Tacky*, 1976; *A Book Full of Spoons*, 1975 (self-pub.). Periodical: *Fotografia*, review by Szymon Bojko, 1978.

PORTFOLIOS *Fractured White Light* 1980 (self-published); *Portfolio I*, 1979 (self-published).

COLLECTIONS Art Institute of Chicago; Cincinnati Art Mus., Ohio; IMP/GEH, Rochester; Miami Univ. Art Mus., Oxford, Ohio; New Orleans Mus. of Art; J. B. Speed Art Mus., Louisville, Ky.

DEALERS Gilbert Gall., 218 E Ontario St, Chicago, IL 60611; Steve Rose Gall., 23 Minor St, Boston, MA 02215.

ADDRESS Photography Dept, Art Academy—Eden-Park, Cincinnati, OH 45202.

Ivan Kozáček PHOTOGRAPHER · EDITOR Born December 24, 1923, in Dolné Srnie, Czechoslovakia, Kozáček is a self-taught photographer.

Since 1955 Kozáček has been technical and graphic editor in the Institute of Health Education in Bratislava, Czechoslovakia. Previously he was art editor in the publishing house Tvar in Bratislava (1949–55) and a clerk in the Corn-Trust in Bratislava (1945–47).

Kozáček has belonged to the photographic group Pictus since 1964. He became a member of the Union of Slovakian Photographers in 1968, serving as its secretary from 1968 to 1978 and its president since 1978. He won gold medals in 1969 and 1979 from the Union of Czech Photographers, and medals from the Educational Institute in Bratislava in 1965 and 1970.

PUBLICATIONS Books: *Child and His Health*, co-author, 1979; *Two Poles of Photography*, L. Noel, 1976; *Landscape in Photography*, L. Paule, 1975; *Creative Photography*, A. Gregorová, 1972 (Osveta: Martin); *Encyclopedia of Practical Photography*, P. Tausk et al., 1972 (SNTL: Prague).

COLLECTIONS In Czechoslovakia: Cllctn. of Union of Slovakian Photographers, Bratislava; Mus. of J. M. Petzval, Spišská Belá.

ADDRESS Murgašova 5, CS-801 00, Bratislava, Czechoslovakia.

Max Kozloff PHOTOGRAPHER · WRITER · CRITIC Born June 21, 1933, in Chicago, Kozloff earned a BA (1953) and an MA (Art History, 1958) from the University of Chicago. He also studied at the Institute of Fine Arts of New York University in New York City from 1960 to 1964. His wife, Joyce Kozloff, is a painter.

Currently a self-employed photographer and writer, Kozloff has lectured at the Art Institute of Chicago, University of New Mexico, Albuquerque (1978), California Institute of Arts, Valencia

(1970), Queens College of City University of New York (1973) and Washington Square College of New York University (1961). He has also been contributing editor of *Artforum* (1963–76), art critic for *The Nation* (1961–69) and New York editor of *Art International* (1961–64).

Kozloff has won an NEA Fellowship for Art Criticism (1972), Guggenheim Fellowship (1969), Pulitzer Award for Criticism (1962), Fulbright Fellowship (1962), Frank Jewett Mather Prize for Art Criticism (1965) and Ingram-Merril Foundation Award (1965).

"I am a color photographer working in the tradition of Atget," says Kozloff. "For me, the possibilities of color negative material have barely been explored. My subject matter is of the streets, the store windows particularly." Kozloff also works in portraiture.

PUBLICATIONS Books: *Photography and Fascination*, 1979; *Cubism/Futurism*, 1972; *Jasper Johns*, 1969, repr. 1972; *Renderings, Critical Essays on a Century of Modern*, 1969.

DEALER Holly Solomon Editions, 24 W 57 St, New York, NY 10019.

ADDRESS 152 Wooster St, New York, NY 10012.

Thomas Neergaard Krabbe PHYSICIAN · ORNITHOLOGIST · PHOTOGRAPHER Born August 2, 1861, in Kirke Hvalsø, Denmark, Krabbe died January 9, 1936, in Copenhagen. Finishing his general education in 1879, he then earned a Bachelor of Medicine degree in 1889.

Krabbe worked as a medical doctor in Greenland from 1889 to 1909. He also participated in animal-preservation work.

A co-founder of the Association of Ornithology, he was a member of its executive committee from 1921 to 1929. He was also honorary member of the Association for Preservation of Animals, "The Swallow" and the Association for Defenseless Animals and a member of the executive committee in the Greenland Society.

PUBLICATION Book: *Greenland, Its Nature, Inhabitants, and History*, 1930 (Eng. & Dan. Ed.).

COLLECTIONS In Copenhagen: National Mus.; Royal Lib.

Arnold Kramer PHOTOGRAPHER Born December 31, 1944, in Cambridge, Massachusetts, Kramer earned a BS (1966) and MS (1968) from Massachusetts Institute of Technology in Cambridge. He studied photography with Minor White from 1967 to 1972.

Since 1970 Kramer has been a lecturer in photography at the School of Architecture, University of Maryland, College Park.

He won NEA Photographer's Fellowships in 1975 and 1979 and grants from the Creative and Performing Arts Board of the University of Maryland in 1972 and 1976.

His work is "in the manner of cultural and emotional documentation primarily through portraiture." Since 1978 he has exclusively produced color prints.

PUBLICATION Catalog: *Interior Views*, 1978 (Corcoran Gall. of Art: Wash., D.C.).

COLLECTIONS Corcoran Gall., Wash., D.C.; Seagram Cllctn., NYC.

DEALER Sander Gall., 2600 Connecticut Ave NW, Washington, DC 20008.

ADDRESS 1839 Ingleside Terrace NW, Washington, DC 20010.

George Krause PHOTOGRAPHER · TEACHER Born in Philadelphia on January 24, 1937, Krause attended the Philadelphia College of Art in the fifties.

A professor of photography at the University of Houston since 1975, he previously taught at Bucks County Community College in Newtown, Pennsylvania (1972–75), and at Brooklyn College in New York (1970). From 1964 to 1972 he worked as a freelance photographer.

A member of the Society of Fellows of the American Academy in Rome, he has received many distinctions. In 1976 he won the Prix de Rome (first in photography); NEA gave him two grants (1979, 1971) and the Philadelphia College of Art an Alumni Award (1970); in addition, he was awarded two Guggenheim fellowships (1976, 1967) and a Fulbright Fellowship to Spain (1963).

The artist specializes in surreal imagery exploring fantasies. Much of his work implies a change or metamorphosis. He has made a series of photographs on gravestones, another on religious statues.

PUBLICATIONS (selected) Monograph: *George Krause*, 1972. Anthology: *The Photograph Collector's Guide*, Lee D. Witkin & Barbara London, 1979. Periodicals: *Camera*, Jan 1966, Aug 1964; *Art in America*, Dec 1964, June 1963.

PORTFOLIOS *George Krause 1960–1970*, 1980 (Mancini Gall., NYC); *Saints and Martyrs*, intro. by Carole Kismaric, 1975 (Photopia Gall.: Philadelphia).

COLLECTIONS Addison Gall. of American Art, Andover, Mass.; Harvard Univ., Fogg Mus., Cambridge, Mass.; IMP/GEH, Rochester; L/C, Wash., D.C.; Mus. of Fine Arts, Boston; Mus. of Fine Arts, Houston; MOMA, NYC; Philadelphia Mus.

of Art, Pa. Bibliothèque Nationale, Paris; Muséo de Bellas Artes, Caracas, Venezuela.

DEALER David Mancini, 1728 Spruce St, Philadelphia, PA 19103.

ADDRESS 420 E 25, Houston, TX 77008.

Rolf H. Krauss HISTORIAN · BUSINESSMAN Born December 13, 1930, in Stuttgart, Germany, Krauss studied at the University of Munich receiving, in 1952, a diploma in both business and political economics; in 1956 he received his doctorate.

He belongs to DGPh.

PUBLICATIONS Books: *Die Fotografie in der Karikatur*, 1978 (Heering-Verlag: Germany); *Collection Dr. R. H. Krauss, Bücher und andere Dokumente über Photographie*, 1975 (Stuttgart). Periodicals: "Travel Reports and Photography in Early Photographically Illustrated Books," Jan 1979, "Photographs as Early Scientific Book Illustrations," Oct 1978, *History of Photography*.

ADDRESS Hasenbergstrasse 95–97, D 7000, Stuttgart 1, Germany.

Jill Krementz PHOTOGRAPHER · AUTHOR Born February 19, 1940, in New York, Krementz studied at Drew University, Madison, New Jersey (1958–59), and the Art Students League in New York City. She also studied anthropology with Dr. Margaret Mead at Columbia University in New York City. She is married to novelist Kurt Vonnegut.

Krementz has been a contributing photographer to *People* magazine since 1974. She was an associate editor of *Status-Diplomat* magazine in 1966–67, a contributing editor to *New York* magazine in 1967–68 and a correspondent for Time-Life, Inc., in 1969–70. In 1964–65 she was a staff photographer for the *New York Herald Tribune* and photographed in Vietnam in 1965–66. She worked as a reporter for *Show* magazine (1962–64), and as an editorial assistant for *Glamour* magazine in 1960–61.

Krementz in on the board of directors of ASMP. She was awarded an honorary doctorate from Caldwell College, Caldwell, New Jersey, in 1979, and also in that year was chosen to take official photographs of four members of the U.S. Cabinet.

The photographer specializes in portraits, photojournalism and books for children. She is known for her numerous portraits of authors, among them Vladimir Nabakov, Tennessee Williams and Norman Mailer.

PUBLICATIONS Monographs: *A Very Young Skater*, 1979; *A Very Young Circus Flyer*, 1979; *A Very Young Gymnast*, 1978; *A Very Young*

Rider, 1977; *A Very Young Dancer*, 1976; *Sweet Pea—A Black Girl Growing Up in the Rural South*, foreword by Margaret Mead, 1969. Books: *Words and Their Masters*, Israel Shanker, 1974; *The Face of South Vietnam*, Dean Brelis, 1968.

COLLECTIONS Delaware Art Mus., Wilmington; L/C, Wash., D.C.; MOMA, NYC.

ADDRESS c/o Donald Farber, 600 Madison Ave, New York, NY 10022.

Jörg Krichbaum PHOTOGRAPHER · CRITIC · TEACHER Born in Dortmund, West Germany, on November 2, 1945, Krichbaum studied German philology and art history at the University of Göttingen from 1972 to 1979. From 1961 to 1963 he studied photography at the Vogelsänger Studios in Bielefeld.

Since 1979 Krichbaum has worked as photographer, critic, author and lecturer at the Universities of Munich and Göttingen.

He is a member of DGPh.

PUBLICATIONS Books (text only): *Abenteuer Malverini*, 1980 (Hanser: Munich); *Female Artists*, 1979, *Albrecht Altdorfer*, 1978 (DuMont: Cologne); *Heinrich Riebesehl*, 1978 (Riesweiler); *Lexicon of Imaginative Painting*, 1977 (DuMont: Cologne).

COLLECTIONS Bibliothèque Nationale, Paris; Leverkusen Mus., Germany; Moderna Muséet, Stockholm.

ADDRESS Roman-Strasse 21, D-8000 Munich 19, West Germany.

Les Krims PHOTOGRAPHER · TEACHER Born August 16, 1943, in New York City, Krims earned a BFA from Cooper Union in New York City (1964) and an MFA from Pratt Institute in Brooklyn, New York (1967).

Currently a full professor at State University of New York at Buffalo, he previously taught at Rochester Institute of Technology in New York (1967–69) and was assistant instructor in photography and printmaking at Pratt Institute (1966–67).

Krims won NEA fellowships in 1976, 1972 and 1971 as well as CAPS grants in 1975 and 1973. He received a grant and a grant-in-aid from the Research Foundation of SUNY in 1970 and 1971, a New York State Council on the Arts grant in 1971, and an Artistic Decorators Incorporated Award in 1969.

PUBLICATIONS Monographs: *Nude in Photography*, 1975; *Making Chicken Soup*, 1972 (Humpy Press); *Eight Photographs: Leslie Krims*, 1970. Anthologies: *Das Sofortbild Polaroid*, 1977 (Der Löwe, Aktionsgalerie: Bern, Switzerland);

The Photographers' Choice, Kelly Wise, ed., 1975; *Photography in America*, Robert Doty, ed., 1974. Anthology: *The Photograph Collector's Guide*, Lee D. Witkin & Barbara London, 1979. Periodicals: *Camera Magazine*, Sept 1978, Dec 1975, Feb 1972, Dec 1971; *French Photo*, Nov 1976; "Violated Instants," A. D. Coleman, *Camera 35*, July 1976; *Afterimage: VSW*, May/June 1976; *Zoom*, Sept/Oct 1975 (Paris); *Creative Camera International Yearbook 1975*, 1975; *Foto*, Mar 1974, Apr 1973; *Popular Photography Italiana*, 1970; *Camera Mainichi*, Aug 1970; *Album #4*, spring 1970; *Aperture*, 13:3, 1967.

PORTFOLIOS *Les Krims Kodalith Images 1968–1975*, 1976 (Galerie Die Brücke: Vienna); *Kidnapping Portfolio*, 1971 (Light Gall.: NYC); *The Deerslayers*, 1972, *The Incredible Case of the Stack O'Wheats Murders*, 1972, *The Little People of America 1971*, 1972 (Humpy Press: Buffalo, NY).

COLLECTIONS Amarillo Art Ctr., Tex.; Catskill Art Society, Inc., N.Y.; Boston Mus. of Fine Art, Mass.; Colgate Univ., Picker Gall., Hamilton, N.Y.; Cornell Univ., Herbert F. Johnson Mus. of Art, Ithaca, N.Y.; Erie Community Coll. No., Dry Mem. Lib., N.Y.; IMP/GEH, Rochester; L/C, Wash., D.C.; Minneapolis Inst. of Arts, Minn.; MOMA, NYC; Mus. of Fine Art, Houston, Tex.; Nassau Community Coll., Garden City, Long Island, N.Y.; Ohio Wesleyan Univ., Delaware; Pratt Inst. Lib., Brooklyn, N.Y.; R.I. School of Design Mus. of Art, Providence; St. Bonaventure Univ., St. Bonaventure, N.Y.; San Francisco Mus. of Modern Art; SUNY, Geneseo; Univ. of Kansas Mus. of Art, Lawrence; Univ. of N. Mex., Albuquerque; Vassar Coll. Art Gall., Poughkeepsie, N.Y.; VSW, Rochester; Wellesley Coll., Wellesley, Mass. Australian Natl. Gall., Canberra; Georges Pompidou Centre, Paris; Natl. Gall. of Canada, Ottawa, Ontario; Tokyo Coll. of Photography.

DEALERS Witkin Gall., 41 E 57 St, New York, NY 10022; Light Gall.; 1018 Madison Ave, New York, NY 10021; Visual Studies Workshop, 31 Prince St, Rochester, NY 14607.

ADDRESS 187 Linwood Ave, Buffalo, NY 14209.

Vilem Kriz PHOTOGRAPHER [See plate 105] Born in Prague, Czechoslovakia, on October 4, 1921, Kriz began working in photography before receiving a university education. He attended the School of Graphic Arts in Prague and studied with Jaromir Funke, Josef Ehm and Frantisek Drtikol. Living in Paris from 1946 to 1952, he attended the Ecole Cinématographique et Photographique, worked with Jean Cocteau and was associated with many other artists. When in Prague and in Paris he was active in the Surrealist movement. Since then his photography has remained rooted in a Surrealist sensibility.

In 1952 he moved to the United States and, as of this writing, is teaching Surrealism and photography at the California College of Arts and Crafts in Oakland.

Kriz makes his original prints on 11 x 4 paper, toning them individually with chemical solutions of his own formulation. Commenting on his work, Thomas Albright, art critic for the *San Francisco Chronicle*, says, "Vilem Kriz is one of the last of the true Surrealists. His work is a masterful demonstration of the grand-style Surrealist spirit."

PUBLICATIONS Books: *Seance*, 1979; *Vilem Kriz, Surrealist*, David Featherstone, 1979; *The Grotesque in Photography*, A. D. Coleman, 1977; *Sirague City*, 1975; *Conversation*, 1963; *Vision of the Times*, 1949 (Paris); *In Another Time*, 1940 (Prague); *They Come Alive Again*, 1940 (Prague); *Everlasting Beauty*, 1939 (Prague). Periodical: *Creative Camera*, 1970.

COLLECTIONS Art Mus. of the City of Sacramento, Calif.; Cincinnati Art Mus., Ohio; Dallas Mus. of Fine Arts; IMP/GEH, Rochester; Metro. Mus. of Art, NYC; MOMA, NYC; Mus. of Fine Arts, Boston; Oakland Mus. of Art, Calif.; San Francisco Mus. of Modern Art; Santa Barbara Mus. of Art, Calif. Arts & Crafts Mus., Prague, Czechoslovakia.

DEALERS Gilbert Gall., 218 E Ontario, Chicago, IL 60611; Focus Gall., 2146 Union St, San Francisco, CA 94123.

ADDRESS 1905 Bonita Ave, Berkeley, CA 94704.

Eric David Kroll PHOTOJOURNALIST Born October 23, 1946, in New York City, Kroll earned a BA in Cultural Anthropology from the University of Colorado, Boulder, in 1969.

Kroll, a freelance photojournalist for the past eleven years, was a "specials" photographer for Paul Schrader's Columbia Pictures film *Hardcore* (1978) and was an adjunct lecturer at Hunter College in New York City (1976). In 1973–75 he was assistant professor of photography at Antioch College, Baltimore, Maryland. Kroll owned and operated One Loose Eye Gallery of Photography in Taos, New Mexico, in 1969–70.

He won a CAPS fellowship in photography in 1975.

Originally a photographer of "one of a kind" art images, he now mainly photographs a variety of people, from "portraits of prostitutes to a shot of Balanchine at a dance rehearsal."

PUBLICATIONS Monograph: *Sex Objects, An American Photodocumentary*, 1977. Periodicals: *Popular Photography*, June 1980; "Eric Kroll: La Grande Misère Des Marginaux," *Photo-Reporter*, Apr 1979; "Filles à Louer," *Photo*, June 1978.

ADDRESS Box 4184, Grand Central Sta., New York, NY 10017.

Eric Adolph Kronengold PHOTOGRAPHER · TEACHER Born June 29, 1935, in Long Island City, New York, Kronengold studied at Tulane University, New Orleans (1960-62), then at San Francisco State University, where he received a BA (1965) and MA (1970). He names John Guttman, Don Worth and Jack Welpott as mentors. His father, Adolph Kronengold (born 1900), is an illustrator.

Since 1970 Kronengold has been professor of art at Arizona State University in Tempe. Previously Kronengold was a graphic designer for Stilten Graphics, San Carlos, California (1969-70), and a custom color printer for Jones Photocolor Lab, San Francisco (1966-69).

He has belonged to SPE since 1972. The photographer received an Arizona State University faculty grant-in-aid in 1972.

PUBLICATIONS Anthologies: *Octave of Prayer*, Minor White, ed., 1972; *Young Photographers*, 1968. Periodicals: *New America, A Review*, spring 1977; *Modern Photography*, Sept 1970.

COLLECTIONS Ariz. Commission on the Arts, Phoenix; CCP, Tucson; Chicago Art Inst.; MIT, Hayden Gall., Cambridge, Mass.; Univ. of Colo., Boulder; Univ. of the South, Gall. of Fine Arts, Sewanee, Tenn. Bibliothèque Nationale, Paris.

DEALER Fifth Avenue Gall. of Photography, 6960 Fifth Ave, Scottsdale, AZ 85251.

ADDRESS 1136 W 10 St, Tempe, AZ 85281.

Michel Szulc Krzyzanowski PHOTOGRAPHER Born April 23, 1949, in Oosterhout, The Netherlands, Krzyzanowski studied at the Dutch academies of St. Joost in Breda and Koninklijke in 's Hertogenbosch.

A freelance, Krzyzanowski belongs to Vakvereniging voor Fotografen and won the Award Triennale in Fribourg, Switzerland, in 1975.

PUBLICATIONS Monograph: *Neem Nou Henny*, 1977 (The Netherlands). Periodicals: *Zoom*, Aug 1976, Apr 1974 (Paris); *Creative Camera*, Jan 1973.

COLLECTIONS MOMA, NYC; Univ. of N. Mex., Albuquerque. In The Netherlands: Prentenkabinet, Leiden; Stedelijk Mus., Amsterdam.

Bibliothèque Nationale, Paris; Musée Cantini, Marseille, France; Musée d'Art, Fribourg, Switzerland; Natl. Portrait Gall., London.

DEALER Lunn Gall., 3243 P St NW, Washington, DC 20007.

ADDRESS Luybenstraat 28, 's Hertogenbosch, The Netherlands.

Gernot Kuehn PHOTOGRAPHER · FILM EDITOR Born August 31, 1940, in Frankfurt am Main, West Germany, Kuehn studied at California State University, Los Angeles (American studies), and at the University of Southern California, Los Angeles (cinema).

Kuehn is a freelance film editor and photographer. He does documentary photography, emphasizing "the human element and changes affected by it." He has done a series on nocturnal Hollywood and another on aging in various European countries.

He belongs to Motion Picture Film Editors Local 776 in Hollywood and to the Los Angeles Center for Photographic Studies.

PUBLICATION Monograph: *Views of Los Angeles*, 1978.

COLLECTIONS Brooks Inst. of Photography, Santa Barbara, Calif.; Univ. of Notre Dame, Notre Dame, Ind.

DEALERS Alonzo Gall. Inc., 30 W 57 St, New York, NY 10019; Susan Spiritus Gall., 3336 Via Lido, Newport Beach, CA 92663.

ADDRESS 2740 Pitcher Rd, Los Angeles, CA 90068.

Heinrich Kühn PHOTOGRAPHER · INVENTOR Born in 1866 in Dresden, Kühn died in 1944, probably in Innsbruck. He studied medicine in Innsbruck around 1880, after which he became completely engrossed in photography. He did experiments in the field and met Hugo Henneberg and Professor Hans Watzek, with whom he published important works. Kühn founded a school of photography in Innsbruck (1912-16). He also contributed to many publications of the day, including *Photographischen Rundschau* and *Das Deutsche Lichtbild*.

With Watzek and Henneberg, Kühn formed Das Kleeblatt (The Trifolium) and was a member of Vienna Camera Club and The Linked Ring in 1895.

Through his work on lenses he produced the Kühn Tieferbilden-Rodenstock-Imagon. He also developed a movable-back camera and, in the 1930s, a double-emulsion film. He was awarded an Honorary Doctorate of Philosophy from the

University of Innsbruck for services to the scientific and artistic aspects of photography in 1937.

With his two cohorts, Kühn was a founder-leader of the German-Austrian school of photography, which embodied a pictorial trend. Having evolved the multiple gum printing technique for color prints, his portraits, landscapes and genre scenes were produced also as oil-transfer and platinum prints. He also did some work with autochromes. In his later years he relinquished the manipulated print for a more straightforward approach to photography.

PUBLICATIONS Monograph: *Heinrich Kühn (1866-1944), Photography*, Peter Weiermair, 1978 (Allerheiligen Presse, Innsbruck). Book: *Technik der Lichtbildnerei*, 1921 (Knapp, Halle, Prussia). Anthologies: *The Photograph Collector's Guide*, Lee D. Witkin & Barbara London, 1979; *The Collection of Alfred Stieglitz*, Weston J. Naef, 1978; *Pictorial Photography in Britain 1900-1920*, Arts Council of Great Britain, 1978; *The Magic Image*, Cecil Beaton & Gail Buckland, 1975; *Camera Work: A Critical Anthology*, Jonathan Green, ed., 1973; *The Art of Photography*, Time-Life Series, 1971. Catalog: *Heinrich Kühn 1866-1944*, von H. Speer, 1976 (Innsbruck). Periodicals: *Camera*, entire issue, June 1977; "Heinrich Kühn," Robt. A. Sobieszek, *Image*, Dec 1971; *Camera Work*, Jan 1911, Jan 1906.

COLLECTIONS Art Inst. of Chicago; IMP/GEH, Rochester; Metro. Mus. of Art, NYC; Smithsonian Inst., Wash, D.C.; Univ. of Tex., Gernsheim Cllctn., Austin; Yale Univ., Beinecke Rare Book & Ms. Lib., New Haven, Conn. Natl. Gall. of Canada, Ottawa, Ontario.

Kipton C. Kumler PHOTOGRAPHER · ACCOUNTANT [See plate 112] Born in 1940 in Cleveland, Ohio, Kumler earned a BEEng (1963) and a MEEng (1967) from Cornell University, Ithaca, New York, and an MBA from Harvard University, Cambridge, Massachusetts (1969). He studied photography with Minor White and Paul Caponigro.

Kumler is employed by the Lexington Consulting Group, Lexington, Massachusetts.

He won a Massachusetts Artists Foundation grant in 1977 and an NEA survey grant in 1980 and 1976.

Kumler describes his work as "natural symbolism." He works in large format, producing silver and platinum prints.

PUBLICATIONS Monographs: *The Platinum Print*, 1979; *Plant Leaves*, 1978; *A Portfolio of Plants*, 1977 (self-pub.); *Kipton Kumler: Photographs*, 1975.

COLLECTIONS Amon Carter Mus., Fort Worth, Tex.; Boston Mus. of Fine Arts; Cornell Univ., Ithaca, N.Y.; Houston Mus. of Fine Arts, IMP/GEH, Rochester; Metro. Mus. of Art, NYC; R. I. School of Design, Johnson Mus., Providence; Univ. of Nebr., Lincoln; Worcester Art Mus., Mass. Bibliothèque Nationale, Paris; Victoria & Albert Mus., London.
DEALER Marcuse Pfeifer, 825 Madison Ave, New York, NY 10022.
ADDRESS 34 Grant St, Lexington, MA 02173.

Frank Asakichi Kunishige PHOTOGRAPHER Born in Japan in 1878, Kunishige died April 9, 1960, in Seattle, Washington. He graduated from a school of photography in Illinois in 1911.

Kunishige arrived in San Francisco, California, in 1896, and opened a studio there around 1912. He moved to Seattle, working for the Ella McBride Studio in 1917 and freelancing, which he did for most of his remaining years. In 1941 he moved to Twin Falls, Idaho, working in a studio there. He was interned during World War II and returned to Seattle after the war. He also taught photography.

Kunishige was a member of the Seattle Buddhist Church, the Bocho Club, and the Seattle Camera Club. He developed a printing-out paper manufactured and sold under the trade name *Textura Tissue*, a softly textured, warm-tone paper. He was the recipient of many awards and prizes.

His principal subject matter was the human figure, particularly as expressed in dance. Never fully revealing the body, his images touched gently on the erotic. "He had a keen sense for the formal architectural elements in which the figure was contained" (*Northwest Photography*, Mar 1980).

COLLECTION Univ. of Washington, Suzzallo Lib., Seattle.

Satoshi Kuribayashi PHOTOGRAPHER Born May 2, 1939, in China, Kuribayashi studied at Tokyo General Photographic College in Yokohama City, Japan.

A freelance photographer since 1969, he worked for Taiyo Life Insurance Co. Ltd. (1964-69) and for Japan Ground Self-Defense Force (1960-64).

He has belonged to Japan Professional Photographers Society (JPPS) since 1975.

Kuribayashi won the Recommendation Prize of Asahi Pentex International Photo Contest in 1965, the Most Excellent Award of ANSCO

Color Photo Contest in 1965, the New Talent Prize of JPPS in 1978, and the Nobuo INA's Prize in 1979.

He specializes in insect ecology photography, taking photos of insects in flight with equipment he invented. "I like to challenge the areas that have been regarded impossible to take pictures of," he says.

PUBLICATIONS Books (in Japan): *Insects Ecology Photographing Technique*, 1979 (Asahi Sonorama Co.); *Fire Flies*, 1978 (Nature Books Co.); *Insects Records I and II*, 1977 (Shakai-Shisou-Sha Co.; *Insects in Okinawa*, 1973 (Gakushu-Kenkyu-Sha Co.); *Science Album Series*, 1971 (Akane Bookstore).

ADDRESS 751 Shimoderamen, Tabira-machi, Kita-matsuura-gun, Nagasaki Pref. 859-48, Japan.

Hans-Martin Küsters *TEACHER · PHOTOGRAPHER* Born December 22, 1946, in Aachen, Germany, Küsters is a self-taught photographer who previously studied at Aachen University (1966–69) and at Cologne University (1970–72), Germany, passing the state examination at both.

Currently a photography instructor at Aachen University, he taught photography at the adult college at Aachen (1976–78) and taught in a school for the handicapped in 1972.

Küsters won first prize in the Kunstverein Hamburg in 1977.

His work is concerned with the social landscape: "man in conflict between social norms and realization of the self; modern architectural effects upon man."

PUBLICATIONS Book: *Photo-Métro*, 1978 (Contrejour: Paris). Anthology: *A Collection of Photographic Essays*, 1979. Catalogs: *Fotografen in Aachen*, 1979 (Neueen Galerie/Sammlung Ludwig: Aachen; *In Deutschland*, 1979 (Rheinischen Landesmuseums: Bonn). Periodicals: *Professional Camera*, Jan 1979; *Fotografia Italiana*, Jan 1979; *Arte Fotografico*, Aug 1978; *Foto*, Aug 1978; *Arbeiterfotografie*, Mar 1978; *Fotografie*, Apr 1978.

COLLECTIONS Univ. of N. Mex. Art Mus., Albuquerque. In Germany: Münchner Stadtmuseum, Munich; Die Neue Sammlung, Munich; Rheinisches Landesmuseum, Bonn. Bibliothèque Nationale, Paris.

DEALER Galerie Rudolf Kicken, Albertusstrasse 47/49, D-5000 Cologne 1, Germany.

ADDRESS Neustrasse 103, D-5120, Herzogenrath, Germany.

Kineo Kuwabara *PHOTOGRAPHER · CRITIC* Born December 9, 1913, Kuwabara has been a professor at Tokyo College of Photography in Yokohama since 1972.

A member of Japan Photocritics Association (since 1970) and Japan Photographic Association (since 1972), he won the Prize of the Year from the latter in 1975.

PUBLICATIONS Books: *Tokyo Days*, 1978 (Asahi Sonorama Co., Ltd.: Japan); *Fantastic City*, 1977, *Memories of My Photographic Life*, 1977, *Manchuria 1940*, 1974, *Tokyo 1936*, 1974 (Shobun-sha: Japan). Periodical: "Memory of Photography After the World War II," *Asahi Camera*, July 1979.

REPRESENTATIVE Zeit-Foto Co., Ltd (Z-F Salon), Yagicho-bild, 5F, 1-4, Nihonbashi-Muromachi, Cho-Ku, Tokyo, Japan.

ADDRESS 2-711, 2-Chome 5, Kamiyoga, Setagaya-Ku, Tokyo, Japan.

L

Syl (Sylvester Welch) Labrot *PHOTOGRAPHER · PAINTER · GRAPHIC ARTIST* Born November 12, 1929, in New Orleans, Labrot died July 14, 1977, in New York City. He attended the University of Colorado, Boulder, from 1947 to 1951, and during that time enrolled in the New York Institute of Photography correspondence course. He was impressed by Edward Weston's works and career.

Labrot began freelancing as a color photographer while still in college, and almost immediately began selling to major publications, including *Life, Saturday Evening Post* and *Ladies' Home Journal.* His photographs also appeared on billboards, greeting cards, calendars and in many small publications.

Labrot taught at VSW from 1971 to 1973. He joined the Boulder Camera Club while in college, serving as its president one year, and won a CAPS grant in 1976. In 1959 Labrot took up painting and in 1965 he had a one-man exhibit in New York City. He twice won awards in the New England Annual at Silvermine and, in 1969, received a commission from the Bridgeport Museum to produce the mixed-media work, "Vision and Reality."

The photographer always worked in color, developing his own Ansco images. In his early career he photographed architecture, but by 1957 he began to investigate abstract color photography. He incorporated offset printing, screen printing and painting in his work.

PUBLICATIONS Monograph: *Pleasure Beach,* 1976 (self-pub.: NYC). Books: *Encyclopedia of Photography,* contr., vol. 4, 1977; *Under the Sun,* w/Nathan Lyons & Walter Chappell, 1960. Anthology: *Photography Year 1973,* Time-Life Books, 1973. Catalogs: *Photography Unlimited,* 1974 (Fogg Art Mus.: Cambridge, Mass.); *Synthetic Color,* 1974 (S. Ill. Univ.: Carbondale). Periodical: "Color and the Creative Image," *Aperture,* spring 1971.

COLLECTIONS Exchange Natl. Bank of Chicago; IMP/GEH, Rochester; MOMA, NYC; Philadelphia Mus. of Art, Pa.; VSW, Rochester; and many private collections.

REPRESENTATIVE Visual Studies Workshop, 31 Prince St, Rochester, NY 14607.

ARCHIVE Barbara Wilson Labrot, 298 Fifth Ave, New York, NY 10016.

Fritz Lachmund *PHOTOGRAPHER · AUTHOR · ARCHIVIST* Born on February 23, 1911, in Hamburg, West Germany, Lachmund attended Landeskunstschule, a regional art school now called Hansische Hochschule für Bildende Kunste (1930–32). Prior to that he attended Industrial Arts School (1926–29) and the Volsschule (1917–26).

Aside from his photographic activities, Lachmund frequently lectures on the history of Hamburg and its surrounding area, organizes exhibitions, and serves, more or less, as the foundation for contemporary and historical photography in his native area.

A freelance photographer, he is a member of the Historical Society of Hamburg (Verein für Hamburgische Geschicte), a friend of the Altonaer Museum, and, since 1960, a member of the Society for Hamburg Collectors (Vereinigung der Hamburgensien-Sammler).

His personal work centers again on his native country, with particular attention to Hamburg, including portraits of public life and genre scenes. In his photographic collection he has approximately 200,000 views of the city and its surrounding areas, some images dating back to 1843.

PUBLICATIONS Books (in Germany): *Von Mottenburg nach Blankenese,* 1979, *Das Alte Barmbek,* 1976 (Christians); *Hamburg zu Kaisers Zeiten,* 1976 (Hoffmann & Campe); *Mein Eimsbüttel (als Bildautor),* 1975, *Altona und Ottensen,* 1974, *Liebes schönes Harburg (als Bildautor),* 1973, *Alt-Hamburg durch die Camera,* 1971 (Christians); *Die Alstadt Hamburgs in Bilddokumenten,* 1968 (Dörling); *Das alte Blan-*

kenese, 1968 (Koetz); *Alt-Altona*, 1964 (Friba); *Seinerzeit zur Kaiserzeit*, 1962 (Topographikon).

REPRESENTATIVE Zur Hauptsache Verlag Hans Christians, Kleine Theaterstrasse 9/10, 2000 Hamburg 36, West Germany.

ADDRESS Am Sorgfeld 97, 2000 Hamburg 55, West Germany.

Herbert Lambert *PHOTOGRAPHER · MUSICIAN · CRAFTSMAN* Born in 1881, Lambert died March 7, 1936, in England. His father, Henry Lambert, was also a photographer.

The younger Lambert worked with his father and brother in a studio in Bath, succeeding them in 1900. He also was managing director of the London firm Elliot & Fry, and contributed to photography as a lecturer and writer as well as a practitioner.

A member of RPS and Professional Photographic Association, Lambert was also an accomplished musician on both the harpsichord and the clavichord, spending many years designing finely adjusted clavichords.

The photographer was primarily a portraitist, with many notable musicians of his day serving as subjects. He also copied Fox Talbot's works for posterity.

PUBLICATIONS Book: *Studio Portrait Lighting*, 1930 (I. Pitman: London). Anthology: *The Magic Image*, Cecil Beaton & Gail Buckland, 1975.

Maureen Lambray *PHOTOGRAPHER* Born in Coral Gables, Florida, Lambray is self-employed.

A member of ASMP and the International Alliance of Theatrical and Stage Engineers (IATSE), she received two awards in 1977 for the photography and design for her monograph, *The American Film Directors*.

PUBLICATION Monograph: *The American Film Directors*, 1976.

DEALER G. Ray Hawkins Gall., 7224 Melrose, Los Angeles, CA 90046.

ADDRESS 52 E 81 St, New York, NY 10028.

Vladimír Lammer *PHOTOJOURNALIST* Born December 8, 1930, in Prague, Czechoslovakia, Lammer worked in a portrait photo studio, then studied photography for three years at Prague Graphic School.

A photojournalist for *Květy* weekly magazine since 1971, he previously worked as its picture editor (1968–70) and as chief of the photo department of the daily paper *Obrana lidu* (1952–58).

Since 1952 Lammer has been a member of the Union of Czechoslovak Journalists, and he joined the Union of Czechoslovak Artists in 1979. He

won first prizes in 1970 and 1965 in a nationwide exhibition of Czech photographers, and since 1964 has won several honorary diplomas from World Press Photo in Haag.

Two short films have been made from Lammer's photographs, one for Prague television about Arab countries (1972), and one for Finland TV about Vietnam (1967).

The photojournalist works in medium format, his chief interests being circus photography and the humor of everyday life.

PUBLICATIONS Books: *Die Geschichte der Fotografie in 20. Jahrhundert*, 1977 (Du Mont Buch Verlag: Cologne); *Practical Photography*, 1972 (SNTL: Prague); *Terra Magica*, 1966 (Hanns Reich Verlag: Munich); *1st Czechoslovak Spartakiade*, 1961, 1956 (Olympia). Periodical: *British Journal of Photography Annual*, 1970.

COLLECTION Moravian State Mus., Brno, Czechoslovakia.

ADDRESS Svidnická 507, 181 00 Prague 8, Troja, Czechoslovakia.

David John Lampson *POET · PHOTOGRAPHER* Born July 22, 1940, in London, Lampson was influenced by the imagist poets, pictorialists and the painters Munch, Ensor and Velásquez.

Currently director of photography for Empress Productions in Los Angeles, Lampson directed about thirty documentary films for the Ford Motor Co. in Europe between 1971 and 1975.

The 1978 syndicated television series, "America Still," produced by Metro Productions in Los Angeles, was based on Lampson's photographs.

About his work the photographer says: "I constantly juxtapose pen and camera. The good poems and the lasting images are lean and hostile to manipulation."

PUBLICATIONS Periodicals: *Popular Photography*, May 1977; *Village Voice*, Feb 14, 1977; *New York Times*, Feb 11, 1977; *Petersen's Photographic Magazine*, Feb 1976.

REPRESENTATIVE Carol Sheff, 3629 Grand View Blvd, Los Angeles, CA 90066.

ADDRESS 1032 Second St #205, Santa Monica, CA 90403.

Edwin Herbert Land *INVENTOR · PHYSICIST* Born May 7, 1909, in Bridgeport, Connecticut, Land attended Norwich Academy and Harvard University, Cambridge, Massachusetts.

Land, the inventor of the Polaroid process, was a Ford Foundation trustee from 1967 to 1975. He was a member of the President's Committee on the National Medal of Science (1969–72) and of the Carnegie Commission on Educational Television (1966–67). He has been a member of the President's Foreign Intelligence Advisory Board since 1961, and was on the National Commission on Technology, Automation, and Economic Progress (1964–66). In 1960–73 he acted as consultant-at-large for the President's Science Advisory Committee, on which he served from 1957 to 1959.

Concurrent with his many years of research, Land has taught at Harvard University (1949–68, 1974) and at MIT, Cambridge (since 1956). In 1937 he established the Polaroid Corporation in Cambridge. In 1932 Land founded Land-Wheelwright Laboratories in Boston along with George Wheelwright III, a Harvard physics instructor.

The inventor has received fourteen honorary degrees from ten universities, including an ScD, LLD and LHD. He was director of the Optical Society of America in 1950–51 and became an honorary member in 1972. He was named a fellow of the Photographic Society of America in 1950, the American Academy of Arts & Sciences in 1943 (president 1951–53), the National Academy of Sciences in 1953 and RPS in 1958. He became a member of the New York Academy of Sciences in 1957. Among his honorary fellowships are ones with the Society of Photographic Scientists and Engineers (1957), the German Photographic Society (1963) and the Society of Photographic Science and Technology of Japan (1975).

Land's numerous awards include: Hood Medal (1935) and Progress Medal (1957) from RPS; Rumford Medal of the American Academy of Arts & Sciences (1945); Certificate of Appreciation from the Army-Navy (1947); Duddell Medal from the Physical Society of Great Britain (1949); Progress Medal from the Society of Photographic Engineers (1955); Progress Medal of the Photographic Society of America (1960); Presidential Medal of Freedom (1963); Popular Science Award (1966); Optical Society of America's Frederic Ives Medal (1967); Photographic Society of Germany's Kulturpreis (1967); National Medal of Science (1967); Photographic Science & Engineering Journal Award (1971); ASMP's Technical Achievement Award (1975); and Franklin Institute of Philadelphia's Cresson Medal (1937), Potts Medal (1956) and Vermilye Medal (1974). Land was named to the National Inventors Hall of Fame in 1977.

The invention of the Polaroid process by Land —a one-step technology for developing and printing photographs within the camera unit—is regarded as the single most important advance in photographic technology since George Eastman's flexible roll film. Land produced the first synthetic sheet polarizer (the Polaroid J sheet) in 1932, and then devised further uses for his invention, such as Polarizing filters for sunglasses and other optical devices (1936) and military hardware for World War II (infrared filters, lightweight range finders, night-adaptation goggles, etc.). In 1941 he discovered a way to make three-dimensional motion picture film.

He produced the Polaroid Land camera in 1947 and in 1963 introduced the Polacolor process, a multilayer instant color film that can provide a stable, full-color print in sixty seconds. Further innovations in chemistry, electronics and optics led to the SX-70 system, presented to the public in 1972, which allows the entire developing process to take place without timing or peeling layers apart. In 1977 Land announced Polavision, the first system for instant motion pictures, and introduced Polaroid's system for 8 x 10 color prints. Land has received more than 160 patents for his innovations in light and plastics, and his interest in light and color has brought about a new theory of color perception, which he revealed in a series of experiments.

PUBLICATIONS   Books: *The Instant Image: Edwin Land and the Polaroid Experience*, Mark Olshaker, 1978; *Singular Images*, photos by Ansel Adams, 1962; *Generation of Greatness; the Idea of a University in an Age of Science*, 1957. Periodicals: *Proceedings of the Natl Academy of Science*, 45:115, 1959; "Vectographs," *Journal of the Optical Society of America*, Sept 1940.

COLLECTION   Polaroid Corp., Cambridge.

ADDRESS   Polaroid Corp., Cambridge, MA 02139.

Mark Steven Landsberg   ARCHITECT · PHOTOGRAPHER · TEACHER   Born February 18, 1954, in Miami, Florida, Landsberg earned a BA in Design from the University of Florida, Gainesville, in 1976, where he studied with Jerry Uelsmann, Todd Walker and Doug Prince.

Since 1976 he has been a partner of the Design Guild in Boston and taught various visual studies courses at the Boston Architectural Center. Previously Landsberg freelanced as an architectural/commercial photographer.

He belongs to SPE, the Photographic Resource Center in Boston, the Society for Commercial Archaeology and the Miami Design Preservation League. He has been the photographer on a project tracing "vernacular traditions in American architecture," funded by several NEA grants, and won his own NEA Design Fellowship in 1979.

Integrating his photography with his architectural career, Landsberg has attempted in his urban landscapes "to capture the interaction of people with buildings, structures, and forms, with a high degree of graphic complexity."

COLLECTIONS Coral Gables Federal Savings, Fla; Rouse Corp., Boston, Mass.; Univ. of Fla., Gainesville.

ADDRESS 98 Oxford St, Somerville, MA 02143.

Ellen Land-Weber PHOTOGRAPHER · TEACHER Born March 16, 1943 in Rochester, New York, Land-Weber received her BA (1965) and MFA (1968) from the University of Iowa, Iowa City. She studied with John Schulze.

She has taught at Humboldt State University, Arcata, California, since 1974.

A member of SPE, she was elected to its board and became its treasurer in 1979. Land-Weber won an NEA Photographer's Fellowship in 1974 and in 1979.

She produces straightforward black-and-white portraits and still lifes as well as collage and color Xeroxes, using natural forms and materials directly in the copying machine.

PUBLICATION Book: *The Passionate Collector,* 1980.

COLLECTIONS IMP/GEH, Rochester; New Orleans Mus. of Art; San Francisco Mus. of Modern Art; Univ. of Nebr., Sheldon Mem. Art Gall., Lincoln: Natl. Gall. of Canada, Ottawa, Ontario.

ADDRESS 790 Park Pl, Arcata, CA 95521.

Victor Landweber PHOTOGRAPHER · PUBLISHER Born September 11, 1943, in Washington, D.C., Landweber received his BA in 1966 from the University of Iowa, Iowa City, and his MFA in 1976 from UCLA. He studied with John Schulze at the former, Robert Heinecken at the latter.

A self-employed photographer and art publisher (Landweber/Artists), he has taught part-time at UCLA Extension since 1971 and at Orange Coast College, Costa Mesa, California (1973–76).

He has been a member of the board of trustees of the Los Angeles Center for Photographic Studies since 1976, was chairman of its Portfolio Committee in 1976–77, and director of exhibitions in 1978–79.

Landweber produced monochrome prints from 1966 to 1975, Polaroid prints in the studio from 1975 to 1978, and as of this writing was doing color prints.

PUBLICATIONS Books: *Photography & Lan-*

guage, 1976; *Travel Photography,* 1972. Catalog: *California Photographers 1970,* 1970 (Univ. of Calif.: Davis). Periodicals: *Popular Photography's Annual,* 1977; *Untitled,* no. 6, 1974, no. 7/8, 1975, no. 11, 1976; *Currant Art Magazine,* 2:2, 1976; *The Dumb Ox,* 1:1, 1976; *35mm Photography,* spring 1975; *Glass Eye,* 2:2, 1975; *Exposure: SPE,* 13:2, 1975.

PORTFOLIOS *New California Views,* ed., 1979 (Landweber/Artists); *Silver See—A Portfolio of Photography from Los Angeles,* producer, 1977 (Los Angeles Center for Photographic Studies).

COLLECTIONS Addison Gall. of Amer. Art, Andover, Md; Atlantic Richfield Co., Los Angeles; CCP, Tucson; Corcoran Gall. of Art, Wash., D.C.; Dallas Mus. of Art, Tex.; Denver Art Mus., Colo.; Harvard Univ., Fogg Mus. of Art, Cambridge, Mass.; Houston Mus. of Art, Tex.; ICP, NYC; IMP/GEH, Rochester; La Jolla Mus. of Art, Calif.; Los Angeles County Mus. of Art; Metro. Mus. of Art, NYC; Milwaukee Art Mus., Wisc.; Minneapolis Inst. of Arts, Minn.; MOMA, NYC; N. Mex. State Univ., Las Cruces; New Orleans Mus. of Art; Newport Harbor Mus. of Art, Newport Beach, Calif.; Norton Simon Mus. of Art, Pasadena, Calif.; Oakland Mus., Calif.; Phoenix Coll. Mus., Ariz.; Polaroid Cllctn., Cambridge, Mass.; R. I. School of Design, Providence; San Francisco Mus. of Modern Art; Security Pacific Natl. Bank, Los Angeles; Standard Oil of Ohio; Sun Valley Ctr. for the Arts & Humanities, Idaho; Tyler Mus. of Art, Tex.; UCLA; Univ. of Calif. Mus. of Photography, Riverside; Univ. of Iowa Mus. of Art, Iowa City; Univ. of Kans., Lawrence; Univ. of N. Mex. Art Mus., Albuquerque; Univ. of Okla., Norman; VSW, Rochester. Australian Natl. Gall., Canberra; Musée Française de la Photographie, Bièvres, France; Polaroid Internatl. Cllctn., Amsterdam; Tokyo Cllctn. of Photog., Shadai Gall.

DEALERS Janus Gall., 8000 Melrose Ave, Los Angeles, CA 90046; Magnuson-Lee Gall., 8 Newbury St, Boston, MA 02116,

ADDRESS 2207 Stanley Hills Dr, Los Angeles, CA 90046.

Barry John Lane ARTS ADMINISTRATOR Born March 22, 1944, in Watford, England, Lane received a BA in Philosophy and Psychology from Oxford University, England, in 1967. He gained an interest in photography from *Creative Camera* and *Album* magazines and their editor, Bill Jay.

A photography officer with the Arts Council of Great Britain since 1973, he was previously regional art officer for the council (1970–73) and exhibitions director for the Museum of Modern Art, Oxford (1967–70).

A member of RPS and SPE, Lane received a Kodak Award in 1972 to investigate public funding of photography in the United States and Canada.

At the Arts Council he oversees photography publication and exhibition programs as well as grant programs for photographers, museums, galleries and other organizations.

PUBLICATIONS Books: *About 70 Photographs*, 1980; *Isle of Man*, 1980; *David Hurn—Photographs 1956–1976*, 1979; *Germany—the New Photography 1927–33*, 1978; *Perspectives on Landscape*, 1978; *British Image 2*, 1977, *John Blakemore*, 1977; *New British Image*, 1977; *British Image 1*, 1975, ed. (Arts Council of Great Britain Photography Publications: London); *Thurston Hopkins*, 1977, *Bert Hardy*, co-ed., 1975, *George Rodger*, 1975 (Fordon Fraser Photographic Monographs, in assoc. w/Arts Council of Great Britain).

ADDRESS Arts Council of Great Britain, 105 Piccadilly, London W1V OAU, England.

Gerald Lang PHOTOGRAPHER Born May 25, 1939, in St. Paul, Minnesota, Lang earned a BA in 1962 and an MFA in 1966 from the University of Minnesota, Minneapolis. As an undergraduate he studied photography with Jerome Liebling and Allen Downs.

Lang became an associate professor in the Department of Art at Pennsylvania State University, University Park, in 1977, became an assistant professor there in 1972, having begun as an instructor in the department in 1969. In 1966 and 1968 he was an instructor in the Department of Art at the University of Minnesota.

Lang is a member of SPE and Friends of Photography. Awarded first place at the Pennsylvania Festival of the Arts (State College) in 1970, Lang has earned grants from the Institute for Arts and Humanistic Studies for "Parklands" in 1975, from the Central Fund for Research, the NEA and the Pennsylvania Council on the Arts, all in 1976, and the Institute for the Arts and Humanistic Studies in 1978. In 1979 he received a Faculty Research Grant from the Pennsylvania State University College of Arts and Architecture in Middletown.

His other achievements include the films *Is There Art Around You?*, which he filmed and edited in 1970 for WPSX-TV of University Park, Pennsylvania, and *Geometric Vector Addition*, a short animated film he made for the University of Minnesota in 1966.

His work, in large format, "deals with the figure and environmental relationships." He does some work with platinum.

PUBLICATIONS Catalogs: *Photography: The Selected Image*, 1978 (Mus. of Fine Arts: Houston); *Images of Woman*, 1977 (Portland Mus. of Art: Portland, Me.); *Young Photographers*, 1968 (Purdue Univ.: Lafayette, Ind.). Periodical: *Image*, 15/1 (IMP/GEH: Rochester).

COLLECTIONS Carl Siembab Gall., Boston; Chicago Art Inst., Ill.; IMP/GEH, Rochester; Juniata Coll., Huntingdon, Penn.; L/C, Wash., D.C.; Minneapolis Inst. of Art, Minn.; Mus. of N. Mex., Santa Fe; Penn. State Univ. Mus. of Art, University Park; Portland Mus. of Art, Maine; Stout State Univ., Menomonie, Wisc.; Univ. of Minn., Univ. Gall., Minn. Natl Gall. of Canada, Ottawa.

DEALER Witkin Gall., 41 E 57 St, New York, NY 10022.

ADDRESS POB 112, Lemont, PA 16851.

Wendy F. Lang PHOTOGRAPHER · CONSULTANT Born February 15, 1938, in Cleveland, Ohio, Lang received a BA in Design from Antioch College, Antioch, Ohio, in 1961, and an MA in Latin American Studies from Stanford University, Palo Alto, California, in 1963. She considers her major influences to be Lucas Samaras, Duane Michals, Jerry Uelsmann and Max Waldman.

As of this writing Lang was with the University of California, Riverside, as coordinator of the photography museum there. She also teaches photography at Los Angeles City College. Working in New York City from 1966 to 1969, she was an administrator and consultant with the Head Start and Model Cities programs.

A member of the Los Angeles Center for Photographic Studies since 1978, Lang is a member of the board of trustees of Cameravision. She is also a member of SPE, ICP and Friends of Photography.

Her subject matter varies, and she works with the SX-70 making images that are mounted together.

PUBLICATIONS Periodicals: "Baptism of Eros II," *Petersen's Photographic Magazine*, June 1979; *Communication Arts*, Dec 1974.

COLLECTIONS G. Ray Hawkins Gall., Los Angeles, Calif. Nara Mus., Japan.

ADDRESS 1231 Kipling Ave, Los Angeles, CA 90041.

Dorothea Lange PHOTOGRAPHER [See plate 61] Born in 1895 in Hoboken, New Jersey, Lange died October 13, 1965, in San Francisco, California. She attended the New York Training School for Teachers from 1914 to 1917, studying photography with Arnold Genthe in 1915. She then studied with Clarence White at Columbia University in New York City (1917–18). Lange's first husband was painter Maynard Dixon; her second, economist/author Paul Taylor. Her son, Daniel Dixon, is a newspaper reporter.

After moving to San Francisco from the East Coast in 1918, Lange first worked as a photofinisher, then opened her own portrait studio (1919), which she operated for more than twelve years. She was commissioned by the California State Emergency Relief Administration to photograph migrant agricultural workers in 1935, and from 1935 to 1942 photographed for Roy Stryker's Farm Security Administration (FSA). She worked for the War Relocation Authority (1941–43), then for the Office of War Information until 1945. Lange photographed on assignment for *Life* in 1954 and traveled abroad several times.

A member of Group f.64, Lange received a Guggenheim Fellowship in 1941, from which she resigned in order to document the Japanese internment camps in the United States. Lange's work is said to have been highly instrumental in establishing decent camps for migrant workers, and her work with the California State Emergency Relief Administration encouraged the formation of the FSA. In 1971 the Oakland Museum in California established the Dorothea Lange Award, its first recipient being Imogen Cunningham.

KQED-TV, part of the Public Broadcasting Service, produced two films on Lange in 1965 by Philip Green and Robert Katz: *Dorothea Lange, Part 1: Under the Trees* and *Part 2: The Closer for Me.*

She is best remembered for her black-and-white FSA photographs of migrant workers. Edward Steichen called Lange the greatest documentary photographer in the United States. As her work matured, Anne Tucker commented in *The Woman's Eye* that Lange would "photograph people in relation to one another and to their immediate environment. To Lange," added Tucker, "an object's value was not necessarily measurable by its uniqueness or its monetary worth, but in time and energy invested, hopes and failures involved."

PUBLICATIONS Monographs: *Dorothea Lange: A Photographer's Life*, Milton Meltzer, 1978; *Dorothea Lange Looks at the American Country Woman*, Beaumont Newhall, 1967. Books: *The American Farm: A Photographic History*, 1977; *A Vision Shared*, Hank O'Neal, 1976; *The Years of Bitterness and Pride*, Hiag Akmakjian, 1975;

In This Proud Lane, Roy Emerson Stryker & Nancy Wood, 1973; *To a Cabin*, w/Margaretta K. Mitchell, 1973; *Executive Order 9066*, Maisie & Richard Conrat, 1972; *Portrait of a Decade*, F. Jack Hurley, 1972; *Just Before the War*, Rothstein, Vachon & Stryker, w/Thomas Garver, ed., 1968; *The Making of a Documentary Photographer*, Suzanne Reiss, 1968; *The Bitter Years*, Edward Steichen, ed., 1962; *Poems of the Midwest*, Carl Sandburg, 1946; *12 Million Black Voices*, Richard Wright & E. Rosskam, 1941; *The Face of America*, Sherwood Anderson, 1940; *An American Exodus*, w/Paul S. Taylor, 1939, rev. 1969, repr. 1975; *Land of the Free*, Archibald MacLeish, ed., 1938. Anthologies: *The Photograph Collector's Guide*, Lee D. Witkin & Barbara London, 1979; *Great Photographic Essays from LIFE*, Maitland Edey, 1978; *The Magic Image*, Cecil Beaton & Gail Buckland, 1975; *Women of Photography*, Margery Mann & Ann Noggle, eds., 1975; *The Woman's Eye*, Anne Tucker, 1973; *Great Photographers*, Time-Life Series, 1971; *Photographers on Photography*, Nathan Lyons, ed., 1966. Catalog: *Dorothea Lange*, intro. by George P. Elliott, 1966 (MOMA, NYC). Periodicals: "The Assignment I'll Never Forget," *Popular Photography*, Feb 1960; "Death of a Valley," w/Pirkle Jones, 8:3, 1960, "Photographing the Family," w/Daniel Dixon, 1:2, 1952, *Aperture*; "Dorothea Lange," Daniel Dixon, *Modern Photography*, Dec 1952; "Dorothea Lange: Camera with a Purpose," Pare Lorentz, *U.S. Camera*, no. 1, 1941.

COLLECTIONS Amon Carter Mus. of Western Art, Ft. Worth, Tex.; IMP/GEH, Rochester; L/C, Wash., D.C.; Mint Mus. of Art, Charlotte, N.C.; MOMA, NYC; Natl. Archives, Wash., D.C.; N.Y. Pub. Lib., NYC; San Francisco Mus. of Modern Art; Smithsonian Inst., Wash., D.C.; Univ. of Louisville, Ky.; Univ. of Minn., Minneapolis; Univ. of Nebr., Sheldon Mem. Art Gall., Lincoln; Univ. of N. Mex. Art Mus., Albuquerque; Worcester Art Mus., Mass.

ARCHIVE Oakland Museum, 1000 Oak St, Oakland, CA 94607.

Vidie Lange PHOTOGRAPHER Born in Dubuque, Iowa, Lange studied at the Art Students League in New York City.

From 1977 to 1979 she was an originator of, and teacher at, Lumina Workshop in Boulder, Colorado. Lange served as curator of prints and photographs and organized shows at Womanspace in 1976, and in 1972 she taught photography at Lac Court Oreilles Indian Reservation in Wisconsin.

The artist is a member of SPE.

As of this writing she was working on a series of hand-painted photographs of Las Vegas.

PUBLICATION   Periodical: *Camera*, Nov 1979.

COLLECTIONS   Ariz. State Univ., Northlight Gall., Tempe; Art Inst. of Chicago; Denver Art Mus., Colo.; L/C, Wash., D.C.; Philadelphia Art Mus., Penn.; Univ. of N. Mex. Art Mus., Albuquerque. Bibliothèque Nationale, Paris.

DEALERS   Susan Spiritus Gall., 8336 Via Lido, Newport Beach, CA 92663; Sebastian-Moore, 14 & Market, Denver, CO 80202.

ADDRESS   3732 Wonderland Hill Ave, Boulder, CO 80302.

Frederick Langenheim   PHOTOGRAPHER   Born 1809 in Germany, Langenheim died 1897 in the U.S., probably in Philadelphia. The photographer William Langenheim was his brother, and Friederich Voigtländer (1812–78), optical manufacturer, a distant cousin.

Having emigrated from Germany, Frederick and his brother William, along with another German, G. F. Schreiber, opened a daguerreotype studio in Philadelphia in the early 1840s. Shortly thereafter they enlisted and fought in the Mexican War. About 1845–46, they made several five-panel panoramas of Niagara Falls, sending copies to the heads of various European governments, for which they received several gold medals. The brothers established the American Stereoscopic Company, which became a major producer of stereo views; they sold it to E. & H. T. Anthony & Company in 1861.

Langenheim and his brother introduced the Petzval-Voigtländer lens to the U.S. in 1842–43, and they were the first to introduce glass transparencies for projection (usually known as lantern slides) in 1846. In 1849, for £1000, they purchased from Fox Talbot the U.S. rights to his calotype process. In that same year they produced stereoscopic slides on glass or paper based on Niepce de Saint-Victor's albumen process, calling them "hyalotypes."

A daguerrotypist and calotypist, Langenheim produced portraits and landscapes as well as his various photographic inventions.

PUBLICATIONS   Books: *The Daguerreotype in America*, Beaumont Newhall, 1961, rev. ed., 1968; *Photography and the American Scene*, Robt. Taft, 1938. Anthologies: *The Photograph Collector's Guide*, Lee D. Witkin & Barbara London, 1979; *Early Photographs & Early Photographers*, Oliver Mathews, 1973. Catalog: *Photographic Magic Lantern Slides*, 1850. Periodicals: *British Journal of Photography*, 1865; *Daguerreian Journal*, Apr 15, 1851.

COLLECTIONS   IMP/GEH, Rochester; L/C, Wash., D.C.; Missouri Historical Soc., St. Louis.

William Langenheim   PHOTOGRAPHER · MANUFACTURER AND SUPPLIER   Born in 1807 in Germany, he died in 1874 in the U.S., probably in Philadelphia. Frederick Langenheim the photographer was his brother, and Friederich Voigtländer (1812–78), an optical manufacturer, was a distant cousin.

See Frederick Langenheim.

Andrew Lanyon   PAINTER · AUTHOR · PHOTOGRAPHER   Lanyon was born May 24, 1947, in Penzance, Cornwall, England. His father was the painter Peter Lanyon. He studied at the London School of Film Technique and lists as his major influences Piero della Francesca and Buster Keaton.

Lanyon works as a self-employed photographer.

His main photographic concern is with "what a camera does to reality." He is involved with reportage, collage, paintings about photography and early Cornish photography.

PUBLICATIONS   Catalogs: *The Rooks of Trelawne*, 1976 (Gordon Fraser, Matthews, Miller, Dunbar & Photographer's Gall.); *Snap!*, 1976 (Gordon Fraser); *The Casual Eye*, intro. by Bill Jay, 1968 (Northern Arts); *The Durham Surrealist Festival*, Ian Barker, 1967.

COLLECTIONS   In England: Arts Council of Great Britain; Contemporary Arts Society of Great Britain (painting); St. Ives Mus., Cornwall.

ADDRESS   18 Farmers Meadow, Newlyn, Penzance, Cornwall, England.

Louis Lanzano   PHOTOGRAPHER   Born in New York City on June 28, 1947, Lanzano studied at the New School for Social Research in New York City. His major influence was Lisette Model.

Currently an instructor of photography at the School of Visual Arts in Manhattan, Lanzano was the recipient of an NEA fellowship and a medal from the Centre National du Cinéma at Phot-Univers in Paris, both in 1978.

PUBLICATIONS   Periodicals: *Camera*, July 1980; *Camera 35*, July 1979; *Photo*, Jan 1979; *Creative Camera*, Dec 1978; *Petersen's Photographic Magazine*, Dec 1978; *Picture*, Oct 1978; *Modern Photography*, Sept 1978; *35mm Photography*, Nov 1975.

COLLECTIONS   Boston Mus. of Fine Art; ICP, NYC; Minneapolis Inst. of Arts, Minn.; Mus. of

Fine Art, St. Petersburg, Fla.; MOMA, NYC; New Orleans Mus. of Art. Bibliothèque Nationale, Paris; Centre Georges Pompidou, Paris; French Mus. of Photography, Bièvres, France.

DEALER   Kiva Gall., 231 Newbury St, Boston, MA 02115.

ADDRESS   49 W 19 St, New York, NY 10011.

Harry Lapow   *PHOTOGRAPHER · DESIGNER* Born in Newark, New Jersey, on February 6, 1909, Lapow studied at Fawcett Art School in Newark and took courses at Columbia College and Brooklyn College, New York.

Most recently he was manager of creative packaging for Jos. E. Seagram & Co., New York City (1971–72), and was corporate design director for Sterling Drug Co., Montvale, New Jersey (1962–69). He operated Harry Lapow Associates from 1941 to 1962.

Lapow was a founding member, director and fellow of the Package Designers Council (1952–75). He won a Popular Photography competition in 1955 and received a CAPS grant in 1973.

He photographs mainly people, but also animals, landscapes and tree torsos.

PUBLICATIONS   Monograph: *Coney Island Beach People*, 1978. Anthologies: *Family of Woman*, 1979; *Family of Man*, 1955.

COLLECTIONS   Metro. Mus. of Art, NYC; MOMA, NYC.

DEALER   G. Ray Hawkins Gall., 7224 Melrose Ave, Los Angeles CA 90046.

ADDRESS   40 E Ninth St, New York, NY 10003.

Fernando La Rosa   *PHOTOGRAPHER*   Born May 28, 1943, in Arequipa, Peru, La Rosa earned a BA (1964) from Escuela Nacional Superior de Bellas Artes in Lima, Peru. In 1973 he studied at MIT and took a workshop with Minor White.

La Rosa currently is president of Secuencia Cultural Association and director of Secuencia Foto Galeria in Lima, Peru (both since 1976). He also taught photography at the Galeria from 1975 to 1979 and at the Armando Robles Godoy Filmmakers School in Lima in 1977. La Rosa was editor and a monthly contributor to *Secuencia Textos* (1976–79). He has been a member of the Secuencia Cultural Association since 1974.

Using a 4 x 5 format, the photographer experiments with "the juxtaposition of geometrical 'frames' and how they alter the urban landscape."

PUBLICATIONS   Books: *Previ*, 1976 (State Housing Dept., Lima); *Huella 10*, 1973 (Lima).

COLLECTIONS   Art Mus. of R.I., Providence; Brooklyn Mus., N.Y.; Columbia Univ., NYC; Dumbarton Oaks Mus., Wash., D.C.; Metro.

Mus. of Art, NYC. Art 45 Gall., Montreal, Canada; Bibliothèque Nationale, Paris.

DEALER   Secuencia Foto Galeria, Lima, Peru.

ADDRESS   77 St Marks Pl, New York, NY 10003.

Gilles Michel Léon Larraín   *ARCHITECT-DE-SIGNER · PHOTOGRAPHER*   Born December 5, 1938, in Da Lat, South Vietnam, Larraín received a BS in 1957 from the Lycée Français de New York, studied at New York University in New York City (1957–58), and at École Nationale des Beaux-Arts in Paris (architecture, 1960–64). He studied city planning and architecture at "AT.URB.A." in Paris in 1964–65.

He has been president of Gilles Larraín, Inc., since 1973, and from 1974 to 1977 was U.S. correspondent for the French magazine *Architecture d'Interieur/Cree*. From 1972 to 1975 he was correspondent for *Atlas Air France* magazine and from 1971 to 1973 he was a freelance photographer and technical assistant for Office de Radiodiffusion Télévision Française. Prior to 1970 Larraín practiced architecture and design in Paris and New York.

He has been a member of ASMP since 1973.

The photographer was the subject of a one-hour color television documentary in 1975, *Gilles Larraín, Un Photographe à New York*.

Larrain does advertising, general and studio photography. He mainly photographs people—"idols," transvestites, motorcycle club members, youth gangs and American Indians—in their own environments.

PUBLICATIONS   Books: *Idols*, Ralph Gibson, ed., 1973; *Design and the New Aesthetics*, Nicholas Polites, ed., 1972. Periodicals: *Zoom*, June 1980 (Germany), Dec 1973 (France), Nov 1973 (Italy).

COLLECTIONS   Bibliothèque Nationale, Paris; Centre Georges Pompidou, Paris; Galerie Baecker, Bochum, West Germany; Modern Art Mus., Munich, West Germany; Palais des Beaux Arts, Brussels, Belgium.

ADDRESS   95 Grand St, New York, NY 10013.

Jean Claude Larrieu   *PHOTOGRAPHER · CINE-MATOGRAPHER · FILM MAKER*   Born September 20, 1943, in Montastruc, France, Larrieu is a self-taught photographer.

He has been a still photographer since 1970 and, since 1967, has been a director of photography in films and television. Larrieu has made two 35mm films, *Montastruc* (1979) and *Quand Meurent Les Ephémères* (1972).

His photography focuses on families, isolated individuals and large groups.

COLLECTION Bibliothèque Nationale, Paris.

DEALER Agathe Gaillard, 3, rue du Pont Louis Philippe, 75004 Paris, France.

ADDRESS 16, rue de la Goutte D'Or, 75018 Paris, France.

Lisa Larsen PHOTOGRAPHER Born in Germany in 1925, Larsen died in New York City on March 8, 1959. Her husband, Niels Rasmussen, was also a photographer.

Initially apprenticing with *Vogue*, she later freelanced for several years through Graphics House agency. As a freelance, she had assignments from *New York Times Magazine, Parade, Glamour, Vogue, Charm* and *Holiday*. Larsen served on the staff of *Life* from 1949 to 1959.

Named Woman Photographer of the Year in 1953 by the NPPA and Encyclopaedia Brittanica, she also won the Mathew Brady Award from the University of Missouri in that year. She was named Magazine Photographer of the Year in 1958 by those same three organizations, the first woman to receive that title. Also in 1958, the Overseas Press Club of America honored her for best overseas camera reporting. Fluent in French, English, German and some Danish and Russian, Larsen was the first American photographer in ten years to be admitted to Outer Mongolia (in 1956) and is remembered particularly for her pictures of Premier Khrushchev.

Working with a Leica in color and black-and-white, Larsen produced warm, realistic, sympathetic portraits. She put great emotional intensity in her photographs, which ranged in subject matter from political figures to fashion to landscapes and architecture. Her major interest, though, was traveling to remote regions of the world.

COLLECTION Life Picture Archives, NYC.

William Larson TEACHER · PHOTOGRAPHER Born October 14, 1942, in North Tonawanda, New York, Larson studied art and history at the University of Siena, Italy, in 1963, then received a BS in Art from the State University of New York, Buffalo, in 1964. He earned an MS in Photography from the Institute of Design, Illinois Institute of Technology, Chicago, in 1968.

Larson has taught numerous workshops since 1973, and is currently professor and chairman of the Department of Photography at the Tyler School of Art, Temple University, Philadelphia, Pennsylvania. He edits *Quiver*, the bi-annual

photographic publication of the Tyler School of Art.

He won a Polaroid grant in 1979 and an NEA Photographer's Fellowship in 1979 and in 1971.

Larson produces sequential and narrative work in both black-and-white and color. Having a special interest in technological image-processing systems, he makes electro-carbon prints that are transmitted by telephone, and he has also worked with holographs since 1977.

PUBLICATIONS Monographs: *Big Pictures, Little Pictures*, 1980; *Euclids Vacation*, 1980; *Fireflies*, 1976. Anthologies: *One of a Kind*, 1979; *Spaces*, Aaron Siskind, ed., 1978; *Photographers Choice*, 1975; *The Great Themes*, Time-Life Series, 1970. Catalog: *Moholy-Nagy Photographs*, picture ed., 1975 (Claremont Colls.: Calif.). Periodicals: "William Larson: Time and Structure," Skip Atwater, *Afterimage: VSW*, Dec 1976; "New Frontiers in Color," Rourke & Davis, *Newsweek*, Apr 19, 1976; *Modern Photography*, Feb 1972, Sept 1971, Apr 1971 (incl. text; *Modern Photography Annual*, 1970; *Camera* (incl. text), Apr 1970.

COLLECTIONS Kalamazoo Inst. of Art, Mich.; MOMA, NYC; New Orleans Mus. of Art; Philadelphia Mus. of Art, Penn.; R.I. School of Design Mus. of Art, Providence; Sun Valley Ctr. for the Arts & Humanities, Sun Valley, Idaho; Univ. of Hartford Mus., Conn.; Univ. of Louisville, Ky.; Univ. of Tenn., Knoxville. Australian Natl. Gall., Canberra; Mus. of Art & Hist., Freibourg, Switzerland; Univ. of Exeter, American Arts Documentation Ctr., Exeter, England.

DEALER Light Gall., 724 Fifth Ave, New York, NY 10019.

ADDRESS 152 Heacock Ln, Wyncote, PA 19095.

Jacques Henri Lartigue PAINTER · PHOTOGRAPHER [See plate 44] Born June 29, 1894, in Courbevoie, France, Lartigue studied art and painting at the Académie Julien. Lartigue received his first camera around 1901, at age seven.

The artist divided his time between painting and photography, his photographs appearing in numerous periodicals, including *Life, Photo* and *Camera*, from the early 1900s to the present day. He received a Médaille d'Argent de la ville de Paris and a Chevalier de la Légion d'Honneur.

Using a range of cameras, 35mm to large-format view, and working in both black-and-white and color, Lartigue photographs "all that I have seen during my life." His subjects have included cars, family, friends and sports. He is especially noted for the sense of movement he captures.

Some of his most memorable images were taken during his childhood.

PUBLICATIONS Monographs: *Mon Livre de Photographie*, 1977 (Flammarion); *Histoire de la Photographie*, 1976 (Delpire); *Jacques-Henri Lartigue*, intro. by Ezra Bowen, 1976; *Mémoires sans Mémoire*, 1975 (Laffont: Paris); *J.H.L. et les Autos*, 1974, *Instants de ma Vie*, 1973, *J.H.L. et les Femmes*, 1973 (Chène: Paris); *Boyhood of J. H. Lartigue*, 1971 (Edita); *Diary of a Century*, Richard Avedon, ed., 1970, repr. 1978; *Boyhood Photos of J. H. Lartigue*, 1966 (Guichard: Lausanne, Switzerland). Anthologies: *The Photograph Collector's Guide*, Lee D. Witkin & Barbara London, 1979; *The Magic Image*, Cecil Beaton & Gail Buckland, 1975; *Looking at Photographs*, John Szarkowski, 1973. Catalog: *Lartigue 8 x 80*, Michel Frigot, 1975 (Musée des Arts Décoratifs: Paris). Periodicals: *Camera*, Dec 1979, Nov 1975, Feb, Dec 1972, Sept 1970; "The Photographs of Jacques Henri Lartigue," John Szarkowski, *MOMA Bulletin*, 30:1, 1963.

PORTFOLIOS *The Jacques-Henri Lartigue Portfolio*, printed by Time-Life Books Photography Lab., 1977 (Time-Life: NYC); *Untitled, Selected Images, 1905–1929*, intro by Anaïs Nin, printed by Jean Yves du Barre, 1972 (Witkin-Berley: Roslyn Hts., N.Y.).

COLLECTIONS MOMA, NYC; New Orleans Mus. of Art, La.; San Francisco Mus. of Modern Art. Bibliothèque Nationale, Paris; Grand Palais, Paris; and many other collections.

REPRESENTATIVE Isabelle Jammes, curator of Association des Amis de J. H. Lartigue, Grand Palais, Portel, Av F Roosevelt, 75008 Paris, France.

ADDRESS 102 rue de Longchamp, 75116 Paris, France.

Joan Clarence Latchford PHOTOGRAPHER · WRITER Also known as John Latchford, she was born in Toronto, Ontario, Canada, on December 18, 1926. Latchford earned a teaching certificate in 1953 from Digby-Stuart Training College in London and since 1976 has studied anthropology at the University-Without-Walls, Howard University, Washington, D.C. She names Dr. Jane Philips as her mentor.

A freelance writer and documentary photographer since 1960, she previously worked as a field supervisor for Blankenship-Gruneau Research in Toronto (1959–60).

Latchford has won two Canada Council Grants.

PUBLICATIONS Books: *The Immigrant Experience*, Leuba Bailey, 1975, *Isolation in Canadian Literature*, David Arnason & Alice K. Hale, 1975, *The Role of Women in Canadian Literature*, Elizabeth McCullough, 1975, all from the series "Themes in Canadian Literature" (Macmillan: Canada); *Dimensions of Man*, 1972 (Macmillan: Canada); *In and Out of Love*, Bruce Vance, ed., 1971; *Canada, A Year of the Land*, 1967 (Natl. Film Bd. of Canada); *Call Them Canadians*, 1967 (Natl. Film Bd. of Canada: Ottawa, Ontario).

COLLECTION Natl. Film Bd. of Canada, Ottawa, Ontario.

ADDRESS 7 Summerhill Gardens, Toronto M4T 1B3, Ontario, Canada.

Clarence John Laughlin PHOTOGRAPHER [See plate 80] Born in Lake Charles, Louisiana, in 1905, Laughlin is a self-taught photographer who was influenced by Baudelaire and the French Symbolists. He moved with his family to New Orleans in 1910 and had to leave school to support his family after his father's death in 1918.

In 1968 Laughlin was named an associate of research at the University of Louisville, Kentucky. Currently he lives in New Orleans. In 1942 he was with the Photography Department of the National Archives in Washington, D.C., and in 1941 he worked in fashion for *Vogue*. In 1940 he was a civil service photographer for the U.S. Corps of Engineers in Louisiana. Laughlin did not begin photography until 1934, when he started freelancing, primarily in the field of architecture.

PUBLICATIONS Monograph: *Clarence John Laughlin: The Personal Eye*, 1973. Books: *Ghosts Along the Mississippi*, 1948, repr. 1962; *New Orleans and Its Living Past*, David L. Cohn, 1941. Anthologies: *The Photograph Collector's Guide*, Lee D. Witkin & Barbara London, 1979; *Great Photographic Essays from Life*, Maitland Edey, 1978; *The Julien Levy Collection*, Witkin Gall., 1977; *Photographs from the Julien Levy Collection*, David Travis, 1976; *The Magic Image*, Cecil Beaton & Gail Buckland, 1975; *Photography Year 1975*, Time-Life Series; *Looking at Photographs*, John Szarkowski, ed., 1973; *The Photographer's Eye*, John Szarkowski, ed., 1966. Catalogs: *Photographs*, 1977 (Univ. of Neb., Sheldon Memorial Art Gall.: Lincoln); *Photographs of Victorian Chicago*, 1968 (Corcoran Gall. of Art: Wash., D.C.). Periodicals: "Clarence John Laughlin: Phantoms and Metaphors," Mary Louise Tucker, *Modern Photography*, Apr 1977; *Creative Camera*, May 1975, Feb 1971; *Camera* July 1968, Aug 1950; "Three Phantasts: Laughlin, Sommer, Bullock," Jonathan Williams, *Aperture* 9, no. 3, 1961.

357

Laughlin

COLLECTIONS Art Inst. of Chicago; Exchange Natl. Bank, Chicago; Harvard Univ., Fogg Art Mus., Cambridge, Mass.; IMP/GEH, Rochester; Metro. Mus. of Art, NYC; MOMA, NYC; New Orleans Mus. of Art; Philadelphia Mus. of Art, Penn.; Philips Gall., Wash., D.C.; Smithsonian Inst., Wash., D.C.; Univ. of Louisville, Ky.; Univ. of Nebr., Sheldon Memorial Art Gall., Lincoln. Bibliothèque Nationale, Paris.

ARCHIVE University of Louisville, Louisville KY 40208.

DEALER A Gallery for Fine Photography, 5432 Magazine St, New Orleans, LA 70115; Nancy R. Moss 1732 General Pershing, New Orleans, LA 70115.

John Launois PHOTOJOURNALIST Born November 23, 1928, in France, Launois studied at French CEP. He names as mentors the photographer Joe Pazen, Black Star Agency president Howard Chapnick, Curtis Prendergast of *Time* and *National Geographic* editor W. E. Garrett.

As of this writing Launois was a freelance photographer exclusively for Black Star. Launois was a contract contributor to *Saturday Evening Post* (1963–69) and a photo-correspondent for *Life* and Black Star in the Far East (1956–63).

The photographer received the World Understanding Award from the University of Missouri School of Journalism in 1973 for his photographs of the Tasaday people. He belonged to the Foreign Correspondent Club of Japan from 1957 to 1963.

PUBLICATIONS Periodicals: "The Tasaday—A True Stone Age Tribe," *National Geographic,* Aug 1972; "50 Years of Communism," *Saturday Evening Post*, Oct 1967; "The Trans-Siberian Express," *Life*, June 1960.

REPRESENTATIVE Black Star, 450 Park Ave So, New York, NY 10016.

Julie Rasmine Marie Laurberg PHOTOGRAPHER Born September 7, 1856, in Grenå, Denmark, she died June 29, 1925, in Ordrup. Laurberg apprenticed with the portrait painter and photographer Leopold Hartmann, then traveled to Paris and Italy.

In 1905 she established herself as a photographer in Copenhagen, and opened a studio with Fransiska Gad in 1907 that shortly won great recognition. She was appointed photographer to the Royal Court in 1910, and during her career co-edited teaching books on photography and wrote articles on the trade.

Very active in the feminist movement, Laurberg was among the co-founders of the Women's Building Society. She also served on the board of

the Photographers Trade School of the Association of Danish Photographers, and was the school's treasurer until her death.

PUBLICATION Book: *Johannes Poulsen, 1901–1926*, Edward Brandes, 1926 (Hasselbach: Copenhagen).

COLLECTION Royal Lib., Copenhagen, Denmark.

Michel Laurent PHOTOJOURNALIST Born in 1945 in France, Laurent died April 28, 1975, near Saigon, Vietnam.

Employed by Associated Press for a number of years, Laurent later became associated with the Gamma Photo Agency in Paris. His photographic work took him to Africa, the Middle East and Asia, where he covered such events as hunger in Biafra, the civil war in Jordan and the war in South Vietnam.

He won the Pulitzer Prize in 1972, shared with Horst Faas of Associated Press, for his photograph of soldiers bayonetting turncoats after the 1971 India-Pakistan war. His work with Faas was also incorporated in a widely used photo essay, "Death in Dacca," which won them a number of awards, including the World Press Photo Contest and a citation from the George Polk Memorial Awards of the Overseas Press Club. Laurent was the last journalist or photographer to be killed covering the 30-year Indochina war.

PUBLICATION Anthology: *Moments: The Pulitzer Prize Photographs*, Sheryle & John Leekley, 1978.

John Nilson Laurvik ART CRITIC · PHOTOGRAPHER Born in Norway in 1876, Laurvik died May 2, 1953, in New York City. He studied at the University of Antwerp, Belgium.

Laurvik wrote criticism of art and photography for numerous periodicals during his career, including *Camera Work, Century,* and *International Studio*. In 1909 his photographs were exhibited at Little Galleries and he helped hang the International Exhibition of Photography in New York. In that year he also edited *Photographic Progress*, a short-lived periodical out of Philadelphia, and a year later was a principal lecturer at the Buffalo Show. In 1915 Laurvik served on the art commission for the Panama-Pacific International Exposition in San Francisco, where he functioned as art director for the Palace of Fine Arts. He also wrote many literary translations from Danish.

Laurvik was a member of the Photo-Secession.

In *Camera Work*, Jonathan Green wrote that Laurvik "was among the most informed and least partisan defenders of modernism." He used the autochrome process for his own photographs.

PUBLICATIONS Books: *Per and the Fisherman*, illus. by William Siegal, 1939; *The Graphic Work of Cadwallader*, 1916; *The Etchings of J. André Smith*, 1914; *Anders Zorn, Painter-Etcher*, 1913; *Post-Impressionism, Futurism, Cubism*, 1913; *René Lalique*, 1912. Anthology: *Camera Work: A Critical Anthology*, Jonathan Green, 1973. Catalogs: *Catalogue of the Loan Exhibition of Drawings and Etchings by Rembrandt from the J. Pierpont Morgan Collection*, 1920 (San Francisco Art Assoc.); *Catalogue of the Loan Exhibition of Paintings by Old Masters*, 1920 (Palace of Fine Arts: San Francisco); *The Netherlands*, 1916 (San Francisco); *Catalogue Deluxe of the Department of Fine Arts, Panama-Pacific International Exposition*, ed. w/John E. D. Trask, 1915. Periodical: "John W. Alexander, An Analysis," *Metropolitan*, Dec 1909.

Alma Lavenson PHOTOGRAPHER [See plate 93] Born in San Francisco, California, in 1897, Lavenson received a BA in 1919 from the University of California at Berkeley. She had no formal training in photography, but was acquainted with and influenced by Edward Weston, Ansel Adams and especially Imogen Cunningham.

In 1979 she received two awards, one from NEA for a retrospective show, and a Dorothea Lange Award as an outstanding woman photographer. Lavenson has made an extensive record of the Mother Lode country of California. Her present work is of miscellaneous subjects in the California environment. In her extensive travels she has photographed people in their natural environments.

PUBLICATION Catalog: *Alma Lavenson*, 1979 (Univ. of Calif.: Riverside).

COLLECTIONS Metro. Mus. of Art, NYC; Mills Coll. Mus., Oakland, Calif.; MOMA, NYC; Natl. Gall. of Art, Wash. D.C.; Oakland Mus., Calif.; San Francisco Art Commission; San Francisco Mus. of Modern Art; Seattle Art Mus., Wash.

ADDRESS 58 Wildwood Gardens, Piedmont, CA 94611.

Richard Alan Lawson PHOTOGRAPHER · TEACHER Born April 10, 1946, in Moline, Illinois, Lawson earned a BS in Photography in 1974 from Southern Illinois University, Carbondale, where his mentors were Charles Swedlund and David Gilmore. In 1976 he received an MFA in Photography from University of Illinois, Urbana-Champaign, his mentors being Art Sinsabaugh, Robert Flick and Luther Smith.

Since 1977 he has been a visiting assistant professor of photography in the Department of Cinema and Photography at Southern Illinois University. He was a lab technician for Colorprints (Film Division) in Chicago, Illinois, in 1972, and held the same position at Gamma Photo Labs in Chicago in 1971.

A member of Friends of Photography (1979) and SPE (1977), Lawson received a Project Director's Grant in 1979 from the Illinois Humanities Council. In 1978 he won a Special Research Grant from the board of trustees of Southern Illinois University.

The photographer's dominant style is large black-and-white prints from medium-format negatives "shot entirely with electronic flash to create a mutation between surrealistic imagery and documentary concerns." Also working in experimental color, his photography deals with man-made symbols, social landscape, and ironic humor. He has also conducted research on "The Preservation, Printing, Exhibition, and Publication of Historical Negatives from Illinois Prisons."

PUBLICATIONS Monograph: *Apparitions: Halloween 1974*, 1975 (self-published: Champaign, Ill.). Anthologies: *Photo-Art Processes*, Nancy Howell-Koehler, 1979; *High-Contrast: Student Photographs, Number One*, Charles Swedlund, 1973.

COLLECTIONS Ill. State Mus., Springfield; L/C, Wash., D.C.; Princeton Univ. Lib., N.J.; Southern Ill. Univ. Mus., Carbondale, Ill.

ADDRESS 606 Skyline Dr, Carbondale, IL 62901.

Peter Laytin PHOTOGRAPHER · TEACHER · CRITIC Born December 6, 1949, in New York City, Laytin received a BA from the University of Wisconsin, Madison, in 1971 and a Master of Arts and Humanities degree from the State University of New York, Buffalo, in 1976.

A photography critic for *Views* magazine since 1979, the freelance photographer also is an assistant professor at Fitchburg State College, Fitchburg, Massachusetts (since 1977). He was instructor and lecturer (1973–76) and assistant professor (1976–77) at the MIT Creative Photography Lab. From 1975 to 1977 he also co-directed the MIT Creative Photography Gallery. Since 1972 Laytin has taught in the Cambridge Center for Adult Education.

He is a member of SPE (since 1976), Friends of Photography (since 1978) and the National Education Association (since 1978).

Laytin uses a variety of formats in black-and-white and color and has done extensive work with black-and-white-infrared film.

PUBLICATIONS Book: "Infrared Photography," *Darkroom Dynamics*, Jim Stone, ed., 1979. Periodicals: *American Photographer*, Mar 1980; *British Journal of Photography*, Aug 1978; *Aperture*, 18:2, 1974, 17:1, 1973.

COLLECTIONS Harvard Univ., Fogg Art Mus., Cambridge, Mass.; MIT Cllctn., Cambridge; Polaroid Corp., Cambridge, Mass. Bibliothèque Nationale, Paris; Polaroid Europa, Amsterdam, The Netherlands; Victoria & Albert Mus., London.

DEALER Carl Siembab Gall., 162 Newbury St, Boston, MA 02116.

ADDRESS 19 Westmoreland Ave, Arlington, MA 02174.

Marvin P. Lazarus LAWYER · PHOTOGRAPHER Born June 1, 1918, in Albany, New York, Lazarus earned a BA from Union College in Schenectady, New York, in 1940 and an LLB from Harvard Law School, Cambridge, Massachusetts, in 1943.

He has been resident counsel at Martin E. Segal Co. since 1974, and from 1962 to 1974 was a freelance photographer. He was resident counsel for Eagle Industries from 1950 to 1962 and assistant attorney general for New York State from 1943 to 1950.

Lazarus specializes in portraits of American and European painters and sculptors that reflect their styles of painting.

PUBLICATION Periodical: *Popular Photography Annual*, 1964.

COLLECTIONS Chrysler Mus., Norfolk, Va.; MOMA, NYC.

DEALER Marilyn Pearl Gall., 29 W 57 St, New York, NY 10019.

ADDRESS 16 Sherman Ave, White Plains, NY 10605.

Wayne Rod Lazorik PHOTOGRAPHER · TEACHER Born May 8, 1939, Minneapolis, Minnesota, Lazorik received a BS (1962) and MFA (1965) at the University of Minnesota, Minneapolis.

He has taught in the Department of Art at the University of New Mexico, Albuquerque, since 1966 and as of this writing was an associate professor and the department chairperson (since 1978). He directed the Westbank Gallery in Minneapolis from 1962 to 1965.

Lazorik belongs to CAA and SPE and has been treasurer of the latter's board of directors (1973–77). He won an NEA Photographer's Fellowship in 1976.

In 1964–66 the photographer worked on the film *Minnamath*, a National Science Foundation project.

PUBLICATIONS Catalog: *Attitudes: Photography in the 1970s*, 1979 (Santa Barbara Mus. of Art: Calif.). Periodicals: *Creative Camera*, June 1973; *Il Diaframma Fotografia Italiana*, May 1972; *Image*, Mar 1972.

PORTFOLIOS *The New Mexico Portfolio*, 1976 (Center of the Eye Photography Collaborative: Santa Fe, N. Mex.); *Views* (group), 1963 (Westbank Gall.).

COLLECTIONS Art Inst. of Chicago; IMP/GEH, Rochester; Minneapolis Art Inst., Minn.; Mus. of Fine Arts, San Francisco; Mus. of N. Mex., Santa Fe; Portland Mus. of Art, Ore.; Univ. of Minn. Fine Arts Gall., Minneapolis; Univ. of N. Mex., Albuquerque; Yale Univ. Art Gall., New Haven, Conn. Natl. Mus. of Canada, Ottawa, Ontario.

ADDRESS 2707 Eighth St NW, Albuquerque, NM 87107.

Mathew Carey Lea CHEMIST · WRITER Born in 1823 in Philadelphia, Lea died in 1897. His father, Isaac Lea, was a naturalist. Mathew was tutored privately in law (admitted to the bar in 1847) and later studied chemical research in James C. Booth's Philadelphia laboratory.

Ill health forced Lea to give up his legal career, and he spent the next several years traveling in Europe before turning his interest to the scientific field. He made numerous contributions to photographic chemistry, including a methodology for making mordant dye pictures (1865), research on the effect of colors on the sensitivity of photographic plates (1865), a plate-cleaning solution of bichromate of potash and sulphuric acid, a ferrous oxalate developer modified two years later by Eder for use with silver emulsions (1877), and the discovery of the allotropic forms of silver (1889–91). He also wrote *Manual of Photography*, which became a valued handbook for the wet-collodion photographer; recommended the use of green glass for the darkroom (in 1870); and described the photo-bromide and photo-iodide of silver and their relation to the latent photo image (1887).

Lea published frequently in American and European scientific and photographic publications, including *The Philadelphia Photographer* and *American Journal of Science*.

He was elected to the National Academy of Sciences after 1891.

PUBLICATIONS Books: *Quellendarstellungen zur Geschichte der Fotografie*, Wolfgang Baier, 1964; *History of Color Photography*, Joseph S. Friedman, 1944; *Lexikon für Photographie und*

Reproduktionstechnik, G. H. Emmerich, 1910; *Kolloides Silber und die photohaloide*, 1908 (T. Steinkopff: Dresden); *Book of Photography*, Paul N. Hasluck, 1905; *Chemistry of Photography*, W. Jerome Harrison, 1892; *A Manual of Photography*, 1868, 2nd ed., 1871; *Newman's Manual of Harmonious Coloring*, ed., 1866 (Benerman & Wilson: Philadelphia). Anthology: *Photography's Great Inventors*, Louis W. Sipley, 1965. Periodicals: "Memorial Address with Bibliography," *National Academy of Science Biographical Memoirs*, vol. 5, 1905; *Journal of the Franklin Institute*, Feb 1898; *Photographische Mittheilungen*, 1897; Obituary, 1897, "On Some New Developers," 27:280, 1880, "Developing Powers of Cuprous Salts," 25:276, 1878, "New Developers & Modes of Development," 24:292, 1877, "Dr. Vogel's Theory," 23:28, 1876, 22:245, 1875, "On the Reduction by Light as Influenced by Colour," 21:109, 121, 1874, *British Journal of Photography*; "Identity of the Photosalts of Silver with the Material of the Latent Photographic Image," 33:480, 1887, "On Red and Purple Chloride, Bromide, and Iodide of Silver," 33:349, 1887, *American Journal of Science*.

Kermit Lee PHOTOGRAPHER · TEACHER Born October 23, 1950, in Phoenix, Arizona, Lee earned a BFA from Rochester Institute of Technology, New York, in 1972, and an MA and MFA from the University of New Mexico, Albuquerque (1973, 1975).

He has taught at both Arizona State University, Tempe, and Scottsdale Community College, Arizona, since 1978. He has been editor of *Northlight Magazine* in Tempe since 1979. Lee taught at the University of New Mexico, Albuquerque, in 1973–75.

A member of SPE, he received an NEA Photographer's Fellowship in 1979 and a grant from the University of New Mexico in 1974.

The photographer deals with "the similarity between the ritual of making music and the making of photographs" in his work. He explores music theory "realized in the construction of still life arrangements."

PUBLICATIONS Periodicals: *Bombay Duck*, Apr 1976; reviews, *Artweek*, Oct 9, 1976, Apr 17, 1976.

COLLECTIONS Ariz. State Univ., Tempe; Exchange Natl. Bank, Chicago; Lincoln First Bank, Rochester; Los Angeles County Mus. of Art, Calif.; Northlight Gall., Tempe, Ariz.; Phoenix Gall., San Francisco; San Francisco Mus. of Modern Art; Univ. of N.Mex, Albuquerque.

ADDRESS 2227 W Cortez, Phoenix, AZ 85029.

Russell Lee PHOTOGRAPHER · TEACHER [See plate 67] Born July 21, 1903, in Ottawa, Illinois, Lee received a degree in chemical engineering from Lehigh University in Bethlehem, Pennsylvania, in 1925. He studied painting from 1929 to 1935 and then began photography.

Since 1947 he has been a freelance photographer, and from 1965 to 1973 he was a lecturer in the Art Department of the University of Texas. Previously he had worked at the U.S. Department of Interior Coal Mines Administration (1946–47), for the Air Transport Command, U.S. Army (1943–45) and for the Farm Security Administration (1936–43). He also worked as a plant manager and chemist from 1925 to 1929.

Lee has been a member of ASMP since 1950.

PUBLICATIONS Monograph: *Russell Lee: Photographer*, F. Jack Hurley, 1978. Books: *Executive Order 9066: The Internment of 110,000 Japanese Americans*, Maisie & Richard Conrat, 1972; *A Medical Survey of the Bituminous Coal Industry*, J. T. Boone, 1947 (U.S. Dept. of the Interior: Wash., D.C.). Anthology: *The Photograph Collector's Guide*, Lee D. Witkin & Barbara London, 1979. Catalog: *Russell Lee: Retrospective Exhibition 1934–1964*, 1965 (Huntington Art Gall., Univ. of Tex: Austin). Periodicals: "Russell Lee," F. Jack Hurley, *Image 16*, Sept 1973; "Image of Italy," *Texas Quarterly*, no. 4, 1961.

COLLECTIONS Boston Mus. of Fine Art; CCP, Tucson; L/C, Wash., D.C.; Mus. of Fine Arts, St. Petersburg, Fla.; MOMA, NYC; Natl. Archives, Wash., D.C.; Univ. of Louisville Photo Lib., Ky.; Univ. of Minn., Minneapolis; Univ. of Tex. Austin.

DEALER Witkin Gall., 41 E 57 St, New York, NY 10022.

ADDRESS 3110 West Ave, Austin, TX 78705.

David Lees PHOTOGRAPHER Born September 21, 1917, in Pisa, Italy, Lees received a degree from the Florence School of the Arts, Italy, in 1938. His father, Edward Gordon Craig, was the renowned theatrical stage designer.

Currently a freelance doing mainly industrial work, Lees photographed for Time-Life from 1952 to 1972.

The photographer has taken portraits of such notables as Ezra Pound, Henry Moore and Emilio Pucci. He is primarily a photojournalist, and his photo essays have included records of major events at the Vatican.

PUBLICATIONS Monograph: *Photographing with David Lees*, 1978 (Italy). Book: *The Food of the Middle East*, 1969. Catalog: *David Lees*, 1971 (La Strozzina Gall.: Florence, Italy).

ADDRESS Via Cappellini 20, 20124 Milan, Italy.

Gustave Le Gray PHOTOGRAPHER · PAINTER
[See plate 9] Born in 1820 in France, Le Gray died in approximately 1882 in Cairo. He studied painting with Delaroche in Paris and his photographic work was influenced by Alphonse Louis Poitevin.

Le Gray operated a portrait studio at the Barrière de Clichy in Paris from 1848 to 1859. His whereabouts were unaccounted for from 1859 to 1864, when he is known to have left Paris. In 1865 he had resettled in Cairo, where he painted and taught drawing.

A founder-member of the Société Héliographique in 1851, Le Gray was the first to introduce the possibilities of the use of collodion in photography (in 1850); with collodion he eventually succeeded in producing pictures with relatively short exposure time.

A landscape and seascape photographer who also did some portraiture, Le Gray was most noted for having initiated combination printing. The cloud effects he achieved with his waxed-paper negative and collodion wet-plate negatives and his salt-and-albumen prints caused a sensation in his day. He also recorded architecture and scenes of military life.

PUBLICATIONS Books: *Photography: The First Eighty Years*, Valerie Lloyd, 1976 (P. & D. Colnaghi: London); *Une Invention de XIXe siècle*, Bernard Marbot, 1976 (Bibliothèque Nationale: Paris); *Creative Photography: Aesthetic Trends, 1838–1960*, Helmut Gernsheim, 1962 (Faber & Faber: London); *History of Photography*, Josef Maria Eder, 1945; *Traité nouveau théorique et pratique*, 1853, 2nd ed., 1854; *Photographie: Traité pratique de photographie sur papier et sur verre*, 1850, rev. 1852, 1854 (Ballière: Paris). Anthologies: *The Photograph Collector's Guide*, Lee D. Witkin & Barbara London, 1979; *The Invented Eye*, Edw. Lucie-Smith, 1975; *The Magic Image*, Cecil Beaton & Gail Buckland, 1975; *Early Photographs & Early Photographers*, Oliver Mathews, 1973 (Reedminster: London); *French Primitive Photography*, André Jammes & Robt. Sobieszek, intro. by Minor White, 1969.

COLLECTIONS Art Inst. of Chicago; IMP/GEH, Rochester; Metro. Mus. of Art, NYC; Smithsonian Inst., Wash., D.C.; Univ. of N. Mex. Art Mus., Albuquerque; Univ. of Tex., Gernsheim Cllctn., Austin. Société Française de Photographie, Paris.

Laurence Le Guay PHOTOGRAPHER · EDITOR · PUBLISHER · CRITIC Born in Sydney, Australia, in 1917, Le Guay began photographing in 1935 as an assistant in Dayne Portrait Studios.

From 1936 he began exhibiting in local and overseas salons, opening his own studio in Martin Place in 1938. During World War II Le Guay served in the RAAF as a war photographer and spent a brief time in London documenting plastic surgery for burn victims. He returned to Sydney and established a new studio in 1946. Soon he was involved with running a photography school, then he founded the magazine *Contemporary Photography*, the first Australian journal not published by a photo-supply firm. In 1947 he went into partnership with John Nisbett; although their studio specialized in fashion and commercial illustration, Le Guay also took assignments for the Geographical Society in northern and central Australia. In 1948 he served as photographer for the first postwar Australian Antarctica expedition, sponsored by the Department of Information. He and Nisbett closed their studio in 1972, but Le Guay continued his own photography and also did editing. He spent much of 1974 sailing around the world in a yacht, recording the trip for a book.

A member of the Sydney Camera Circle and the Contemporary Camera Groupe, the photographer was awarded the Commonwealth Medal in 1963 for his services to photography. He is a Fellow of RPS and a founding member of the Australian Centre for Photography.

Le Guay made a film on the Sydney Harbour Bridge ca. 1948.

Primarily a photojournalist, he also does fashion and portrait photography, for the last ten years working solely in color.

PUBLICATIONS Book: *Sailing Free*, 1975. Anthologies: *Australian Photography—A Contemporary View*, ed., 1978; *Australian Photography 76*, ed., 1977.

COLLECTIONS MOMA, NYC. In Australia: Australian Centre for Photography, New South Wales; Church St. Gall., Melbourne; Natl. Gall. of Victoria, Melbourne. RPS, London.

ADDRESS 163 Crown St, Sydney, New South Wales 2010, Australia.

Janet Lehr ATTORNEY · ART DEALER · AUTHOR · BOOK REVIEWER Born June 7, 1937, in New York City, Lehr earned an LLB from Brooklyn Law School, New York, in 1959.

Since 1972 she has directed Janet Lehr, Inc., and from 1962 to 1972 she was co-director of Gallery 6M in New York City. She writes reviews for the New York Photographic Historical Society's publication, *Photographica*, and for the

Maine Antique Digest; she also publishes annual catalogs of her holdings.

Lehr is a founding member of the International Association of Photographic Art Dealers (1979); she served on its board of directors in its first year. She is also on the board of directors of The New York Photographic Historical Society, and is a member of Antiquarian Bookman Association.

PUBLICATION Periodical: "Talbot's Role in the History of Photography," *AB Bookman's Weekly,* Jan 1978.

ADDRESS POB 617, Gracie Sq Sta, New York, NY 10028.

Ingeborg Theresia Leijerzapf PHOTOGRAPHY CURATOR Born March 3, 1946, in Wassenaar, The Netherlands, Leijerzapf studied art history at the University of Leiden, The Netherlands, receiving a doctorate in 1972.

Leijerzapf has been curator of the photography department of the Prentenkabinet van de Rijksuniversiteit (University of Leiden) since 1972.

A member of the European Society for the History of Photography since its inception in 1977, Leijerzapf serves as the group's treasurer.

Her field of research is Dutch photography, especially from the turn of the century.

PUBLICATIONS Books: *Fotografie in Nederland 1920–1940,* 1979, *Fotografie in Nederland 1839–1920,* 1978, *Fotografie in Nederland 1945–1975,* 1978 (Staatsuitg, The Hague).

COLLECTION Prentenkabinet van de Rijksuniversiteit Leiden, The Netherlands.

ADDRESS Rapenburg 65, 2311 GJ Leiden, The Netherlands.

Arthur Leipzig PHOTOGRAPHER · TEACHER Born October 25, 1918, in the United States, Leipzig studied with Sid Grossman in 1942 and with Paul Strand in 1946 at the Photo League in New York City.

A freelance photographer since 1947, Leipzig has also been professor of art (since 1968) and director of photography (since 1972) at C. W. Post College, Long Island University, New York. He was a staff photographer for *P.M.* newspaper in New York City from 1942 to 1946.

A member of ASMP and SPE, the photographer won a Long Island University Research Grant in 1979 to photograph the black Jews of Northern Ethiopia, and he received the National Urban League Photography Award in 1962.

COLLECTIONS Brooklyn Mus., N.Y.; IMP/GEH, Rochester; Midtown Y Gall., NYC;

MOMA, NYC; VSW, Rochester. Natl. Gall. of Art, Ottawa, Canada.

ADDRESS 378 Glen Ave, Sea Cliff, NY 11579.

Jean-Claude Lemagny PHOTOGRAPHY CURATOR Born November 24, 1931, in Versailles, France, Lemagny received his Agrégé de l'Uniersité in 1962.

In 1969 he became curator of photography at the Bibliothèque Nationale in Paris, concentrating on the area of twentieth-century photography since 1972. He was curator of the Print Department at the Bibliothèque from 1963 to 1968, his duties including the cataloging of art books and French engravings of the eighteenth century.

ADDRESS c/o Bibliothèque Nationale, Department des Estampes et de la Photographie, 58 rue Richelieu, 75084 Paris, France.

Elizabeth Anne Lennard PHOTOGRAPHER · FILM MAKER Born March 14, 1953, in New York City, Lennard studied at the San Francisco Art Institute with Tony Ray Jones (1971) and at the University of California in Santa Cruz and in Los Angeles (1972–74). Her father is sociologist Dr. Henry Lennard, and her sister, Erica Lennard, is a photographer.

A freelance photographer, Lennard won an NEA Photographer's Fellowship in 1979.

She has made two short films, *Mardi Gras* (16mm black-and-white, 1979) and *The Wonderful Travelers* w/Erica Lennard (35mm color, 1977).

For the past seven years the photographer has produced most of her work on 16 x 20 prints, hand-painted in oil colors. Her "connections are often intellectual rather than visual." She is currently interested in architectural subjects shot abstractly, a concern also demonstrated in her film *Mardi Gras.*

PUBLICATIONS Books: *Les Femmes, Les Soeurs,* text only, w/photos by Erica Lennard, 1976, U.S. ed., *Women, Sisters,* 1978; *Sunday,* w/Erica Lennard, 1973. Periodicals: *Picture,* June 1980; Reviews, *Artweek,* Apr 1979; *Color Photography Annual,* 1979; *Camera 35 PhotoWorld,* Feb 1979; *Zoom,* Dec 1977 (Paris).

COLLECTIONS Moderna Muséet, Stockholm, Sweden; Musée d'Art Moderne, Centre Georges Pompidou, Paris; and private collections.

DEALER Thackeray & Robertson Gall., 2266 Union St, San Francisco, CA 94123.

ADDRESS 23 E 22 St, New York, NY 10010.

Erica Lennard PHOTOGRAPHER Born in New York City on November 11, 1950, Lennard earned a BFA in 1972 at the San Francisco Art Institute. Her sister, Elizabeth, is also a photographer.

A freelance photographer, Erica Lennard specializes in fashion, portraits and glamour for a variety of magazines, including *Mademoiselle, Interview, Seventeen, Ms.,* German *Vogue,* Italian *Vogue, Marie Claire* and others. She has been widely exhibited, and portfolios of her work have appeared in *Camera 35, U.S. Camera Annual* and *Popular Photography.*

In 1977 Lennard was the recipient of an NEA grant. With Elizabeth Lennard she made a short 35mm film, *The Wonderful Travelers,* produced by French television.

PUBLICATIONS Monographs: *Les Femmes, Les Soeurs,* 1976, U.S. ed., *Women, Sisters,* 1978; *Sunday,* w/Elizabeth Lennard, 1973.

COLLECTIONS IMP/GEH, Rochester. Bibliothèque Nationale, Paris; Centre Georges Pompidou, Paris; Moderna Muséet, Stockholm; Stedelijk Mus., Amsterdam, The Netherlands.

REPRESENTATIVE Photo Artists, 157 W 57 St, New York, NY 10019.

DEALER Sonnabend Gall., 420 W Broadway, New York NY 10013.

Lynn Lennon PHOTOGRAPHER Born July 12, 1931, in Dallas, Texas, Lennon earned a BA in Art from Baylor University, Waco, Texas.

A freelance photographer, she currently serves on the board of directors of the Center for Visual Communications in Dallas and is a member of the Photographic Advisory Committee at the University of Texas, Dallas (since 1979).

Her work has included documentary series on the Big Thicket area of Southeast Texas and on the sugar cane industry in Louisiana, as well as a series of forty fantasy self-portraits, many using multiple negatives.

PUBLICATIONS Anthology: *Self-Portrayal,* Jim Alinder, ed., 1978. Periodicals: Review, *Art Week,* Apr 22, 1978; *Visions,* Mar 1978.

COLLECTIONS La. Arts & Science Ctr., Baton Rouge; La. State Univ., Rural Life Mus., Baton Rouge; Marcuse Pfeifer, NYC; Riverside Mus., Baton Rouge, La.; Univ. of Ark., Fayetteville.

DEALER Afterimage Gall., The Quadrangle, Dallas, TX 75201.

ADDRESS 4000 Buena Vista, Dallas, TX 75204.

Joanne Leonard PHOTOGRAPHER · TEACHER Born September 8, 1940, in Los Angeles, Leonard earned a BA from the University of California, Berkeley, in 1962, then studied photography at San Francisco State College, California, in 1963–64. She considers John Collier, Jr., a major influence.

A teacher at the University of Michigan, Ann Arbor, since 1978, Leonard gave a workshop at Cornell University, Ithaca, New York, in 1977, and taught photography at Mills College, Oakland, California, from 1975 to 1977. She has also been an instructor at both the University of California's Berkeley Extension (1974–77) and at the Davis campus (1976), at California State University, Hayward (1974–75) and at San Francisco Art Institute (1970–75).

A member of SPE and CAA since 1977, Leonard was the official photographer for the American Olympic Team in 1972 in Sapporo, Japan. She received a Rackham grant and fellowship from the University of Michigan in 1979, and two NEA grants in 1977 (for a photo survey and for a special book course at Mills College).

The photographer produces "humanistic and sometimes feminist" images, occasionally using collage.

PUBLICATIONS Anthologies: *Family of Children,* 1977; *Women See Men,* 1977; *American Photography: Past into Present,* 1976; *Women See Woman,* Wiesenfeld et al, eds., 1976; *From the Center,* Lucy Lippard, 1976; *Frontiers of Photography,* 1972, *The Great Themes,* 1970 Time-Life Series; *Vision and Expression, Contemporary Photographers,* 1969; *Women by Three,* 1969. Catalogs: *Photo/Synthesis,* 1976 (Cornell Univ.: Ithaca, N.Y.); *Art: A Woman's Sensibility,* 1975, *Anonymous Was a Woman,* 1974 (Calif. Inst. of the Arts: Valencia). Periodicals: "Women in the Arts," *Arts and Society,* spring/summer 1974; *Creative Camera,* Jan 1973; *Life,* Dec 25, 1970.

COLLECTIONS IMP/GEH, Rochester; Graham Nash Cllctn.; San Francisco Mus. of Modern Art; Stanford Univ. Mus., Palo Alto, Calif.; U.S. State Dept., Art in Embassies Cllctn.; Witkin Gall., NYC. Univ. of Exeter, Amer. Arts Documentation Centre, England.

DEALERS Focus Gall., 2146 Union St, San Francisco, CA 94123; Paula Anglim Gall., 710 Montgomery St, San Francisco, CA 94111; Blixt Gall., 229 Nichols Arc, Ann Arbor, MI 48106.

ADDRESS 1319 Pomona Rd, Ann Arbor, MI 48103.

Jean-Marc Le Pechoux PHOTOGRAPHER · EDITOR · PUBLISHER Born October 5, 1953, in Nancy, France, Le Pechoux studied with Jean-Pierre Sudre at Stage Experimental Photographique in Paris, 1970–71.

As of this writing Le Pechoux was director of Light House Studios in Melbourne, Australia. He was also editor/publisher of *Light Vision*, an Australian photography magazine, from 1977 to 1979. He taught at Photography Studies College in Melbourne from 1974 to 1976, and from 1971 to 1974 was a freelance photographer in Paris.

A member of the Institute of Australian Photographers, Le Pechoux won a grant in 1978 from the Visual Arts Board of the Australia Council.

COLLECTIONS In Australia: Natl. Gall. of Victoria, Melbourne; Philip Morris Cllctn. of Australian Natl. Gall., Canberra.

DEALER Light Quest Pty Ltd, 12A Kingsway, Armadale 3143, Victoria, Australia.

ADDRESS 75 Wilson St, South Yarra 3141, Victoria, Australia.

Markus J. Leppo PHOTOGRAPHER · JOURNALIST · PUBLISHER Born September 22, 1934, in Wiborg, Finland, Leppo is a self-taught photographer. His father, Jaakko Leppo, was a journalist and author.

Since 1978 Markus has been managing director of Oy Valokuvakirja-Photobook Ltd. publishing company and director of the Photobook Gallery in Helsinki. He is also a freelance journalist and photographer for various magazines (since 1959). From 1957 to 1958 he was picture editor for *Helsingin Sanomat*.

A founding member of the Society of Finland's Museum of Photographic Art (1969), Leppo won a Project Grant from the Nordic Cultural Foundation in 1979, State Project grants in 1977 and 1971, a grant from Iceland-Finland Cultural Foundation in 1977, a State Grant for Artists in 1974, Finnish-Swedish Cultural Foundation grants in 1971 and 1969, and grants from the Kordelin Foundation of Helsinki in 1968, 1966 and 1965.

He made the film *Vaivaisveistokset* in 1970.

Working in formats from 35mm to 5 x 7, the photographer does reportage, urban landscapes and simple realism that borders on the abstract. He also carries out research on Finnish folk art, especially wood carvings.

PUBLICATIONS Books: *Finland's Wooden Men-at-Alms*, 1979, *Vanha Helsinki*, 1979 (Photobook: Helsinki); *Talonpoikaistalot*, 1973, *Helsinki*, 1972, *Vaivaisukot*, 1967 (WSOY: Helsinki).

COLLECTIONS In Finland: Amos Anderson Art Mus., Helsinki; Borås Art Mus., Boras; City of Helsinki Art Cllctn.; Västerbottens Mus., Umeå. Hans Wagner Cllctn., London; Huhtamäki Art Cllctn., Sweden.

DEALER Photobook Gall., Tehtaankatu 13, Helsinki, Finland.

ADDRESS Merikatu 9 A, SF-00140, Helsinki 14, Finland.

Nathan Bernard Lerner PHOTOGRAPHER · PAINTER Born March 30, 1913, in Chicago, Lerner received a BS degree from the New Bauhaus School of Design in Chicago, where he studied with Moholy-Nagy, Georgy Kepes and Alexander Archipenko. He also studied at the Art Institute of Chicago and with painter Samuel Ostrovsky.

Professor at the University of Illinois Department of Art from 1967 to 1972, he also worked as head of Lerner Design Associates from 1949 to 1973. Prior to that he was head of production design and dean of faculty and students (1945–49), acting educational director (1946–47) and head of photography (1941–43) at the Institute of Design in Chicago.

A member of the Artist Guild of Chicago, he received a grant in 1978 from the Illinois Arts Council/NEA. He was also the creator of special effects for the UNESCO film *Chopin*, by Genya Cenkalski, for the Polish government.

The artist says of his work: "Starting in 1932 it was strongly humanistic, becoming very experimental in 1937 to 1942 at the School of Design, and combining these elements in later work. In all the work there is a strong interest and concern for light."

PUBLICATIONS Book: "Light as a Creative Medium," w/Georgy Kepes, *Encyclopaedia of the Arts*, 1944. Periodical: "Space in Your Pictures," *Minicam Magazine*, 1942.

COLLECTIONS Amon Carter Mus., Ft. Worth, Tex.; Art Inst. of Chicago; Burpee Mus., Rockford, Ill.; Exchange Natl. Bank, Chicago; IMP/GEH, Rochester; Ind. State Univ., Terre Haute; Inst. of Contemporary Art, Boston; Inst. of Contemporary Art, Chicago; Metro. Mus. of Art, NYC; Minneapolis Art Inst., Minn.; MOMA, NYC; Monterey Inst. of Art, Calif.; Mus. of Contemporary Art, Chicago; St. Louis Mus., Mo.; Seattle Mus. of Art, Wash.; Univ. of Ill., Chicago. Bauhaus-Archive, Berlin, Germany; Bibliothèque Nationale, Paris; Mus. of Modern Art, Paris. In Japan: Nihon Univ., Tokyo; Pentax Mus., Tokyo.

DEALER Light Gall., 724 Fifth Ave, New York, NY 10019; Freidus Gall., 158 Lafayette St, New York, NY 10013.

ADDRESS 849 Webster St, Chicago, IL 60614.

Henry Le Secq PHOTOGRAPHER · PAINTER [See plate 11] Born 1818 in France, Le Secq died in 1882. He studied painting with Paul Delaroche.

While he directed his main career energies toward painting, in 1851 he was commissioned by the Comité des Monuments Historique, along with Bayard, Baldus, Le Gray and Mestral, to document the historic architecture of France.

In 1851 Le Secq became a founder-member of the Société Héliographique.

Working with waxed-paper negatives and calotypes, Le Secq did still lifes, genre views, landscapes and architecture. He was noted for his use of light and mass.

PUBLICATIONS Monograph: *Amiens: Recueil de Photographies*, 1852. Book: *Une Invention de XIXe siècle: Expression et technique de la photographie*, Bernard Marbot, 1976 (Bibliothèque Nationale: Paris). Anthologies: *The Invented Eye*, Edward Lucie-Smith, 1975; *The Magic Image*, Cecil Beaton & Gail Buckland, 1975; *Early Photographs & Early Photographers*, Oliver Mathews, 1973 (Reedminster Pubs.: London); *French Primitive Photography*, André James & Robt. Sobieszek, intro. by Minor White, 1969. Periodicals: "The Man on the Tower of Notre Dame," Eugenia Parry Janis, *Image*, Dec 1976; *Camera*, 1974; "Henry Le Secq," G. Cromer, *Bulletin de la Société Française de Photographie*, 1930; H. de Lacretelle, *La Lumière*, Mar 20, 1852.

COLLECTIONS IMP/GEH, Rochester. In Paris: Bibliothèque Nationale; Direction de l'Architecture, Photography Office; Musée des Arts Decoratifs.

Henry M. Lester PHOTOGRAPHER · PUBLISHER · EDITOR Born in 1899 in Poland, Lester died in 1972 in New York City. His wife, Ruth Lester, is curatorial associate at the International Center of Photography in New York City. Lester studied engineering at the Universities of Warsaw and Moscow (1918–21) and at City College and Columbia University in New York City (1921–23).

A freelance photographer from 1940 to 1972, he was also conservator of the Film Collection of the American Museum of Natural History in New York City (1968–72), editor of the *Journal of Abstracts of Photographic Science and Engineering* (1961–63) and evaluation manager of foreign scientific and technical literature at McGraw-Hill Publishers (1959–61). He was cofounder/editor of Morgan & Lester Photographic Book Publishers from 1934 to 1956 and worked in scientific, medical, industrial and high-speed motion picture photography from 1930 to 1959.

Lester was a founding member of Circle of Confusion (1933), a founder and first president of the Miniature Camera Club of New York (1933), a member of the Oval Table Society (1946), a Fellow of the Photographic Society of America (1948) and of RPS (1949). He was also a Fellow of the New York Microscopical Society (1951), the Society of Photographic Scientists & Engineers (1956—as well as the founder and first president of its New York chapter) and the Biological Photographic Association (1963).

In 1947 Lester received a patent for his invention of a continuous-flash lighting unit (developed in 1941).

Lester specialized in high-speed still and motion picture photography of such subjects as hummingbirds in flight or a rattlesnake striking. He also worked in scientific, medical and industrial motion picture photography, and was a publisher, editor, writer and consultant.

PUBLICATIONS Books (publisher): *Stereo Realist Manual*, 1954; *Ansel Adams Basic Photographic Series*, 1948–56; *Graphic Graflex Photography*, 1st ed., 1940; *Photo-Lab Index*, ed., 1939; *Miniature Camera Work*, 1938; *Leica Photo Annual* 1937, ed., 1936; *Leica Manual*, 1st ed., 1935.

COLLECTIONS Amer. Mus. of Natural Hist., NYC; IMP/GEH, Rochester; N.Y. Zoological Soc., NYC; Sperry Gyroscope, NYC.

ARCHIVE c/o Ruth Lester, 270 West End Ave, New York, NY 10023.

Marc B. Levey COUNSELOR · TEACHER · WRITER Born May 29, 1938, in Wilkes-Barre, Pennsylvania, Levey earned his BA in 1965 from the University of Nebraska, Lincoln, and his MA in Communications in 1973 from Pennsylvania State University, University Park. He has done doctoral work in adult education and names as his major influences Freeman Patterson and Harald Mante.

Levey has been coordinator of counseling, Office of Special Programs, Pennsylvania State, since 1970 and was previously associate professor of aerospace studies at Lawrence University, Appleton, Wisconsin (1968–70). He was assistant director of aircraft maintenance, 18th Tactical Fighter Wing from 1965 to 1968.

A member of SPE, Pennsylvania Human Relations Commission and, since 1976, the American Association of University Professors, Levey won an Irish Government Tourist Board Travel Grant in 1979.

Mixing counseling and teaching, he conducts research in the area of evaluation and photo education, especially for adults. For the past two years he has been concentrating on photographs dealing with the nature of work and its relationship to how people define themselves.

PUBLICATIONS Books: *Photography: Buying, Choosing and Using*, 1979; *Photography: Composition, Color and Display*, 1979. Periodical: *Petersen's Photographic Magazine*, Feb 1977.

COLLECTIONS Penn. State Univ., Hazleton; Univ. of N.C. Imperial Galls., Dublin, Ireland.

ADDRESS 1120 S Allen St, State College, PA 16801.

Hans Leopold Levi *PHOTOGRAPHER · EDUCATOR · CRITIC* Born July 20, 1935, in Mainz, Germany, Levi earned an MA in 1972 from San Francisco State University. He names Henry Holmes-Smith, Jack Welpott and Don Worth as his mentors.

Since 1977 Levi has taught at St. Louis Community College at Florissant Valley and at Lindenwood College, St. Charles, Missouri. He also taught at the former from 1972 to 1974.

A member of SPE, Friends of Photography and IMP/GEH, the Photographer won First Portfolio Award for best photography at California College of Arts and Crafts, Oakland, in 1969.

PUBLICATIONS Book: *Street Jesus*, 1972. Periodicals: *New Art Examiner*, criticism, Dec & Nov 1979; review, *Artweek*, Apr 1975; review, *Camera 35*, Aug 1973; *Photography Annual*, 1972 (Middle Tenn. State Univ.: Murfreesboro); *Modern Photography*, Sept 1970.

COLLECTIONS Art Inst. of Chicago; Columbus Art Mus., Mo.; IMP/GEH, Rochester; MOMA, NYC; New Orleans Mus., La.; Norton Simon Mus. of Art, Pasadena, Calif.; Oakland Mus., Calif.; St. Louis Mus. of Art, Mo.; San Francisco State Univ.; Univ. of Kans., Lawrence; Univ. of Md. Mus., College Park; Univ. of Mo., St. Louis.

DEALER Kamp Gall., 339 N Euclid, St Louis, MO 63108.

ADDRESS 3 Cardigan Ln, St Louis, MO 63135.

Michael Grayson Levine *PHOTOGRAPHER* Born May 27, 1952, in Newark, New Jersey, Levine received a BFA in 1975 from Ithaca College in Ithaca, New York, and an MFA in Photography from Florida State University in Tallahassee in 1977, where his major influence was Jim Roche. He also studied at Rochester Institute of Technology (1973–75), where he was influenced by Betty Hahn, Owen Butler and Tom Wilson.

Levine has been self-employed as a photographer, specializing in photographing artworks, since 1978. Prior to that he was a member of the Artist in Residency Program at the Los Angeles Institute of Contemporary Art (1978–79), and a photographer for the city of Los Angeles, for which he documented the performing and visual arts (1978).

He is currently a member of the Citizens' Party, Environmental Action, and the Cousteau Society, and was the recipient of an NEA Photographer's Fellowship in 1978.

COLLECTIONS CCP, Tucson; Foto Gall., NYC; IMP/GEH, Rochester; Jacksonville Fine Arts Mus., Fla.; Mus. of Fine Arts, St. Petersburg, Fla.; UCLA, Grunwald Ctr. for Graphic Arts; Witkin Gall., NYC.

ADDRESS 133 N Union Ave, Los Angeles, CA 90026.

David Joshua Levinson *PHOTOGRAPHER · TEACHER* Born on July 5, 1944, in New York City, Levinson earned both a BFA (1972) and an MFA (1974) from the Rochester Institute of Technology in New York. He studied with Bea Nettles, Betty Hahn, John Pfahl, Aaron Siskind and Harry Callahan.

Since 1975 Levinson has been an assistant professor of art at Thomas Nelson Community College in Hampton, Virginia. In 1968 he went to work as color printer at Berkey K & L Gallery of Photographic Arts. Before that he was studio manager for Bob Richardson Fashion Studio from 1965 to 1968. In 1964 he worked as a technician for Stewart Color Laboratory.

Levinson is a member of SPE and Friends of Photography.

Most of his work is in color, often with the use of multiple printing. He is "concerned with isolating form, separating nonhuman subject matter from its environment."

PUBLICATIONS Periodicals: *Color Photography*, 1977; *Modern Photography*, Mar 1977, Feb 1975; *Popular Photography*, Dec. 1976.

COLLECTIONS Chrysler Mus., Norfolk, Va.; R.I. School of Design, Providence; Rochester Institute of Technology, N.Y.

ADDRESS 549 Logan Pl, #31, Newport News, VA 23601.

Joel D. Levinson *PHOTOGRAPHER* Born in Bridgeport, Connecticut, Levinson earned a BA in Communications (1975) and an MA in Visual Design (1978) from the University of California, Berkeley.

He taught at the Neary Gallery workshops in 1979, San Francisco Center for Visual Studies in 1977–78 and workshops at University of California, Berkeley, in 1976–77. Levinson presided over the University of California photography organization from 1975 to 1977.

The photographer won the Eisner Award in 1978 from the University of California for achievement in photography.

Levinson produced a series of photographs on "California Flea Markets" from 1975 to 1977 and is currently working on a "Self-Indulgence" series.

PUBLICATIONS Periodicals: *Picture,* Dec 1979; *Darkroom,* 1:6, 2:1/2; *Latent Image,* May 1979; *Printletter-International,* Mar/Apr 1979; *Artweek,* Mar 1979; *Photographics,* Oct 1978; *New Age,* Apr 1978, Jan 1977.

COLLECTIONS Brandeis Univ., Waltham, Mass.; Yale Univ. Art Gall., New Haven, Conn.

ADDRESS 8352 Kent Dr, El Cerrito, CA 94530.

Helen Levitt PHOTOGRAPHER Born in New York City, Levitt studied with Walker Evans in 1938–39 and at the Art Students League in New York City in 1956–57. Her small-camera street photography was influenced by Henri Cartier-Bresson.

A freelance, her work has appeared in *Time, New York Post, Fortune* and *Harper's Bazaar,* among other periodicals. She won Guggenheim fellowships in 1959 and 1960.

Levitt made two films, *The Quiet One* (1949), with James Agee, and *In the Street* (1952), with Agee and Janice Loeb.

PUBLICATIONS Monograph: *A Way of Seeing,* 1965. Anthologies: *The Photograph Collector's Guide,* Lee D. Witkin & Barbara London, 1979; *Mirrors and Windows,* John Szarkowski, 1978; *Faces: A Narrative History of the Portrait in Photography,* Ben Maddow, 1977; *The Magic Image,* Cecil Beaton & Gail Buckland, 1975; *Looking at Photographs,* John Szarkowski, 1973; *The Family of Man,* Edward Steichen, ed., 1955; *The History of Photography,* Beaumont Newhall, 1949. Catalogs: *Helen Levitt,* 1980 (Sidney Janis Gall.: NYC); *Curators Choice: Contemporary American Photography,* 1979 (Venezia La Fotografia: Venice, Italy); *The Target Collection of American Photography,* 1977 (Mus. of Fine Arts: Houston, Tex.); *Harlem on My Mind,* 1968 (Metro. Mus. of Art: NYC); *Photography in the 20th Century,* 1967 (Natl. Gall. of Canada: Ottawa, Ontario); *Guggenheim Fellows in Photography,* 1966 (Philadelphia Coll. of Arts: Pa.); "A Way of Seeing," *Photography in America, 1850–1965,* 1965 (Yale Univ. Art Gall.: New Haven, Conn.); *Contemporary American Photography,* 1953 (Natl. Mus. of Mod. Art: Tokyo); *Photography Mid-Century,* 1950 (Los Angeles County Mus.). Periodicals: "The City's Lively Beat," Lloyd Fonvielle, no. 81, 1978, "New York City," Ben Mad-

dow, 19:4, 1975, *Aperture;* "Women," Anne Tucker, Feb 1972, "A Portfolio of Photographs by the John Simon Guggenheim Fellows," Allan Porter, ed., Apr 1966, *Camera; U.S. Camera Annual,* 1971; *Modern Photography,* Mar 1967; "Helen Levitt's Photographs: Children of New York and Mexico," Edna Bennett, *U.S. Camera,* 6:4, May 1943.

COLLECTIONS Metro. Mus. of Art, NYC; MOMA, NYC; N.Y. Pub. Lib., NYC; Springfield Art Mus., Mo.

DEALER Prakapas Gall., 19 E 71 St, New York, NY 10021.

ADDRESS 4 E 12 St, New York, NY 10003.

Barry Anthony Lewis PHOTOGRAPHER Born July 23, 1948, in London, Lewis earned a degree in chemistry in 1969 from Leicester University, a certificate in education in 1971 and an MA in photography from Royal College of Art in 1977. He names Bill Brandt, his tutor, as a strong influence.

A freelance photographer, Lewis publishes his work in London *Sunday Times Magazine, Vogue, Quest* and *Time,* among other periodicals.

Lewis received an Arts Council of Great Britain Award in 1979, a travel grant to Rome from RCA in 1977 and the Young Scientist of the Year first prize award in 1966. He is a member of the National Union of Journalists.

PUBLICATIONS Books: *Have Wheels Will Travel,* n.d.; *Working Lives,* n.d.

COLLECTIONS In London: Arts Council of Great Britain; British Council; Mus. of London; Victoria & Albert Mus.

REPRESENTATIVE Network, 271 Kentish Town Rd, London NW5 2JS, England.

ADDRESS 37 Womersley Rd, London N8 9AP, England.

Cynthia Gano Lewis PHOTOGRAPHER · PICTURE FRAMER Born April 5, 1950, in Berkeley, California, Lewis attended Bard College, Annandale-on-Hudson, New York (1967–69), and received her BA in Studio Art from the University of Arizona, Tucson, in 1979. She studied with Harold Jones and Jack Welpott.

She currently operates Lewis Framing Studio with her husband and has worked at the Center for Creative Photography in Tucson since its beginning in 1975.

Lewis belongs to SPE, Friends of Photography and VSW.

Working in medium-format black-and-white, the photographer uses long exposures and works with a small, flattened space. "My photographs," she says, "are about human emotions and relationships, usually employing the nude, abstractions, self-portraiture, and occasionally landscape."

PUBLICATIONS Catalogs: *Photoworks '79*, 1979 (Bellevue Art Mus.: Bellevue, Wash.); *Arizona Outlook '78*, 1978 (Tucson Mus. of Art: Ariz.). Periodicals (text only): "Ralph Gibson's Early Work," *Center for Creative Photography, No. 10*, Oct 1979; "Snapshots," *Southwestern Art*, summer 1977.

COLLECTIONS Bellevue Art Mus., Wash.; CCP, Tucson; Erie Art Ctr., Pa.

ADDRESS 521 N. Treat, Tucson, AZ 85716.

Robert Lewis PHOTOGRAPHER · TEACHER Born March 21, 1940, in Westford, Massachusetts, Lewis received a BS from New England College in Henniker, New Hampshire, in 1961, and an MFA in Photography from Ohio University in 1971.

Since 1975 Lewis has been director of the Milwaukee Center for Photography in Wisconsin, of which he was co-founder. He was the co-founder and director of the Creative Photography Workshop in Milwaukee in 1974, and was an instructor of photography in the Graphic and Applied Arts Division of Milwaukee Area Technical College (1973–74). He also was instructor of Photography at the University of Wisconsin Extension in Milwaukee and at the Milwaukee Area Technical College (1972).

A member of SPE since 1975, Lewis was responsible for co-founding Photography Collectors, Inc., in Milwaukee in 1977. He was the recipient of a Wisconsin Arts Board/NEA grant in 1979 as well as a Paul Schutzer Memorial Internship in Visual Communication, sponsored by *Life* magazine, in 1971.

COLLECTION Milwaukee Art Center, Wis.

ADDRESS 3265 N Summit Ave, Milwaukee, WI 53211.

Steven A. Lewis PHOTOGRAPHER · TEACHER · HISTORIAN Born April 16, 1947, in Cleveland, Ohio, Lewis received a BA from the University of Wisconsin, Madison, in 1969. He was a Graduate Special Student with Minor White at MIT, Cambridge, Massachusetts, in 1970–71, and received his MFA from Ohio University, Athens, where he was a student of Arnold Gassan (1971).

He has taught at Allan Hancock College, Santa Maria, California, since 1974, and previously taught at Denison University, Granville, Ohio (1974), and Ohio University, Athens (1973).

Lewis won National Endowment for the Humanities grants in 1977 and 1976 for the establishment of the first oral history project in photography, based at George Eastman House, for which he functions as research associate. He also won grants from the Polaroid Foundation (1974) and SPE (1973) for the book *Photography: Source & Resource*. He was awarded an NEA Artists Service Grant in 1973. He is a member of SPE, CAA and Friends of Photography.

The greater part of the photographer's work is in small-format black-and-white, investigating random serial and sequential relationships. He places sequential imagery side by side on a single print.

PUBLICATIONS Book: *Photography: Source & Resource*, w/McQuaid & Tait, 1973. Periodicals: "Interview with Max Yavno," *Photo Bulletin*, 1:2; "Oral History Materials on Photography: A Bibliography," *Image*, 18:2, 1975.

COLLECTIONS Milwaukee Art Ctr., Wisc.; U.S. Information Agency, Wash. D.C.

ADDRESS 904 S Speed St, Santa Maria, CA 93454.

Alexander Liberman EDITOR · SCULPTOR · PAINTER Born in 1912 in Kiev, Russia, Liberman studied painting with André Lhote (1929–31) and architecture with Auguste Peret (1930–32). He also studied at L'Ecole des Beaux Arts in Paris (1931–32).

Liberman has been editorial director of the Condé Nast magazines—among them *Vogue*, *Glamour* and *Gentlemen's Quarterly*—since 1962. He joined Condé Nast Publications in 1941, and in 1943 became art director of *Vogue*. In 1932–36 he was art director and managing editor of the Paris magazine *Vu*. Liberman received a gold medal for design at the International Exhibition in Paris, 1937.

PUBLICATIONS Books: *Greece, Gods, and Art*, 1968; *The Artist in His Studio*, 1960. Anthology: *The Magic Image*, Cecil Beaton & Gail Buckland, 1975.

ADDRESS 173 E 70 St, New York, NY 10021.

Jerome Liebling PHOTOGRAPHER · FILM MAKER · TEACHER Born April 16, 1924, in New York City, Liebling was educated at Brooklyn College in Brooklyn, New York (1942, 1946–48), and attended film workshops at the New School of Social Research in New York City (1948–49). His teachers were Walter Rosenblum, Paul Strand and Lewis Jacobs.

Liebling has been employed as a professor since 1970 at Hampshire College in Amherst, Massachusetts. He has taught photography in the Art and Architecture Department of Yale University, where he worked with Walker Evans (1976–77), the Art Department of the University of Minnesota in Duluth (1949–70) and at the State University of New York in New Paltz, New York (1957–58).

A founding member of SPE, he was also a member of the Photo League from 1946 to 1948. Liebling was a recipient of an NEA Survey Grant in 1980 and a fellowship in 1979, a Guggenheim Fellowship in 1976, and a fellowship from the Massachusetts Council of the Arts in 1975.

Also involved in film making, Liebling has been the producer and director of several films, including *89 Years* (1978), and, with Allen Downs, *The Old Men* (1965), *Pow-Wow* (1961) and *The Tree Is Dead* (1956).

The photographer describes his work as being in the documentary tradition of Eugene Atget, August Sander, Paul Strand and Walker Evans, "broad-ranging 'straight' photography emphasizing photography's ability to deal with meaningful recording of events in time."

PUBLICATIONS Monograph: *The Photography of Jerome Liebling, 1947–1977*, 1978. Books: *Photography Current Perspectives*, Jan 1978; *The Photography Catalog*, 1976. Anthology: *Mirrors and Widows*, John Szarkowski, 1978. Periodical: *Aperture*, no. 79, 1977.

COLLECTIONS Boston Mus. of Fine Arts; Harvard Univ., Fogg Art Mus., Cambridge, Mass.; ICP, Rochester, N.Y.; L/C, Wash., D.C.; Minneapolis Inst. of Art, Minn.; MOMA, NYC; Sheldon Memorial Gall., Lincoln, Nebr.; Univ. of Ariz., Photography Ctr., Tucson; UCLA Art Gall., Los Angeles; Yale Univ. Art Gall., New Haven, Conn.

DEALERS Vision Gall., 216 Newbury St, Boston, MA 02126; Susan Spiritus Gall., 3336 Via Lido, Newport Beach, CA 92663.

ADDRESS: 39 Dana St, Amherst, MA 01002.

Benjamin M. Lifson CRITIC · WRITER · PHOTOGRAPHER · TEACHER Born in Minneapolis, Minnesota, on February 19, 1941, Lifson attended Oberlin College, Oberlin, Ohio (1958–60), transferring to the University of Minnesota in Minneapolis, where he earned a BA in English Literature in 1962. His MA, also in English Literature, was completed in 1967 at Yale University, New Haven, Connecticut.

Lifson is now simultaneously teaching at Yale University and the Lincoln Center campus of Fordham University, New York City. He was a visiting instructor of photography at Harvard University, Cambridge, Massachusetts, for the year 1976–77, and an instructor of photography at the California Institute of Arts in 1970–74, serving also as chairperson of its photographic program. Lifson is senior photography critic at New York's *Village Voice*, with which he has been associated since 1977. He writes variously for *Popular Photography, Art In America, Portfolio, Creative Camera, Professional Photographer* and *Aperture.*

Awarded NEA grants in 1971 and 1977 for photography, and in 1979 for criticism, he also received a Guggenheim Fellowship for photography in 1978.

COLLECTIONS Akron Art Institute, Ohio; IMP/GEH, Rochester; Minneapolis Art Institute, Minn.

ADDRESS 124 W 93 St, New York, NY 10025.

Joan Liftin PHOTOGRAPHER · EDITOR Born November 1, 1935, in Teaneck, New Jersey, Liftin received a BA in Journalism from Ohio State University, Columbus, in 1957.

She has directed Magnum Library since 1975, and previously served as photo editor for UNICEF (1970–75).

Liftin is a member of ASMP.

A large number of her photographs appeared in the film *Girlfriends*, about a fictional woman photographer.

PUBLICATIONS Anthologies: *Family of Woman*, 1979; *Family of Children*, 1978. Periodicals: *Creative Camera 10 Year Annual*, 1977; *Creative Camera*, May 1976; *Modern Photography Annual*, 1975.

COLLECTION IMP/GEH, Rochester.

REPRESENTATIVE Woodfin Camp, 415 Madison Ave, New York, NY 10017.

ADDRESS One Fifth Ave, New York, NY 10003.

Wulf Ligges PHOTOGRAPHER Born January 21, 1939, in Bregenz, Austria, Ligges was an engineering graduate (1962) of Staatlich Höhere Fachschule für Fotografie in Cologne, Germany.

A freelance photographer, Ligges' main subject is landscape. He produces photo books and calendars.

PUBLICATIONS Books: *Niederrhein*, 1979, *Norwegen*, 1977, *Westfalen*, 1974, *Bonn*, 1971, *Die Nordfriesischen Inseln*, 1970, *Die Lüneburger Heide*, 1968 (DuMont Buchverlag: Cologne, Germany).

COLLECTIONS In Germany: Bildagentur Mauritius Frankfurt; City of Duisburg. In Austria: Galerie Annasäule, Innsbruck; Galerie Elefant,

Plate 1   Joseph Nicéphore Niepce,
"Table Laid for a Meal," ca. 1830.

Plate 2   Carl Ferdinand Stelzner,
"Runge and Wife Wilhelmine," 1840–44.

Plate 4   Hippolyte Bayard,
"Chair in a Garden," ca. 1847.

OPPOSITE
Plate 3   David Octavius Hill
and Robert Adamson,
"A Medical Visit," 1845.

Plate 5   Maxime Du Camp,
"The Sphinx," ca. 1850.

Plate 7   George N. Barnard,
"Mills Burning in Oswego," 1853.

*Plate 8 Francis Bedford,
Untitled, ca. 1850–60.*

*Plate 9 Gustave Le Gray,
"Seascape," ca. 1856.*

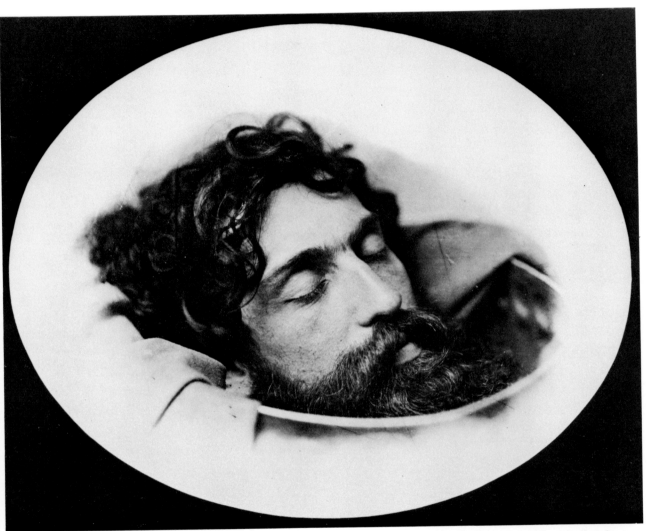

Plate 10   Oscar Gustav Rejlander,
"Head of St. John the Baptist," 1858.

Plate 11 Henry Le Secq,
"Fishing Boats on Beach," ca. 1852.

*Plate 12   Felice A. Beato,
"The Fish Boat and King's Yacht,"
ca. 1859.*

*Plate 13   Edward Anthony & Co.,
Stereoscopic image, "Vendue Range,
Charleston, South Carolina," ca. 1850–74.*

Plate 14   Auguste-Rosalie Bisson and
Louis-Auguste Bisson, "Sea of Ice,
View from Flégére," ca. late 1850s.

Plate 15   Felice A. Beato,
"The Capture of Fort Talsu
in North China," 1860.

Plate 16 Napoleon Sarony & Co.,
"Portrait, Female," ca. 1860.

*Plate 18   Mathew B. Brady,
"Magazine in Battery Rodgers," 1863.*

*Plate 21   Thomas Annan,
Untitled, ca. 1868.*

Plate 20   Carleton Eugene Watkins,
"Washington Column," ca. 1862.

Plate 19   Henry Peach Robinson,
"Ye Ladye of Shalott," 1862.

from life registered photograph copy right Julia Margaret Cameron 1869

Plate 23   Timothy H. O'Sullivan,
"Mt. Agassiz-Unitah Mountains,"
1869.

OPPOSITE
Plate 22
Julia Margaret Cameron,
"The Kiss of Peace," 1869.

Plate 24   John K. Hillers,
Untitled, ca. 1873.

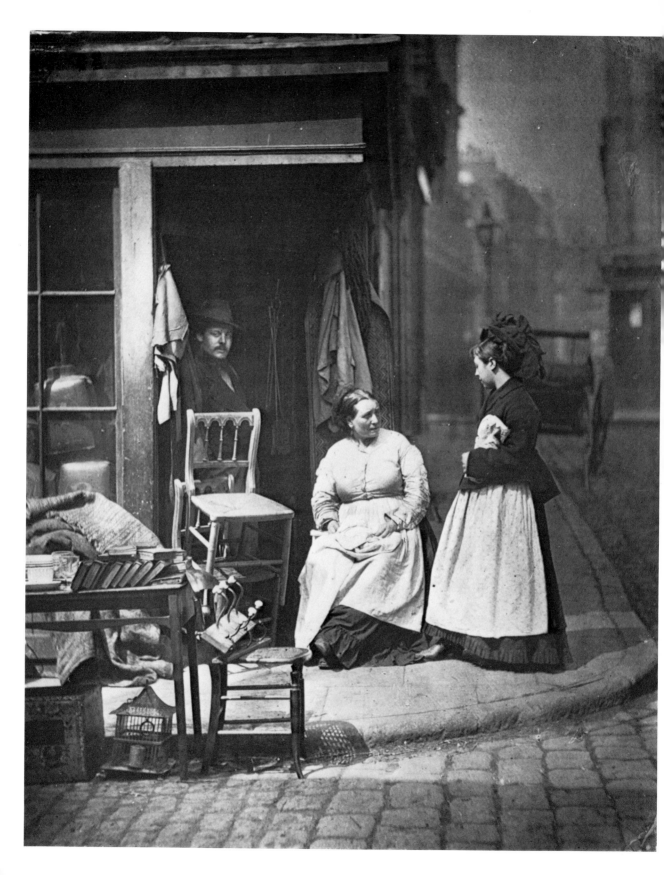

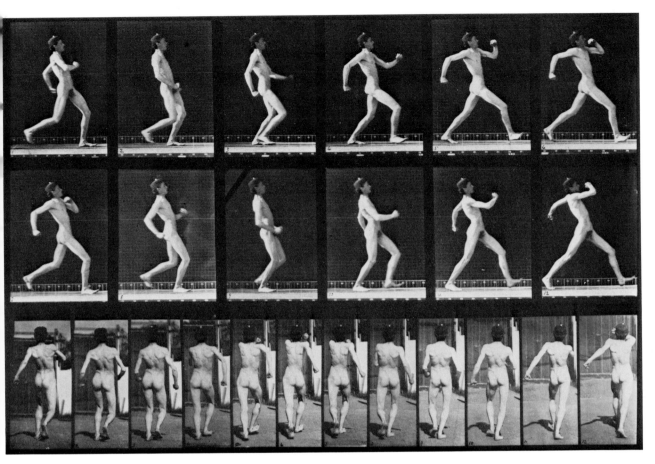

Plate 26
Eadweard Muybridge,
"Walking," 1885.

Plate 27
Peter Henry Emerson,
"During the Reed-Harvest,"
ca. 1885.

OPPOSITE
Plate 25 John Thomson,
"Old Furniture," ca. 1876.

Plate 29 Nadar (Gaspard Félix Tournachon),
Untitled, ca. 1886

Plate 28 George François Mugnier,
"Moss Covered Live Oaks," ca. 1885.

*Plate 30   William Henry Jackson,
Untitled, ca. 1880s.*

Plate 32   (Arthur) Louis Ducos du Hauron,
"Self-Portrait with Distorting Camera,"
ca. 1889–90.

OPPOSITE
Plate 33   Alfred Stieglitz,
Untitled, ca. 1896–99.

Plate 35   Wilhelm von Gloeden,
Untitled, ca. 1900.

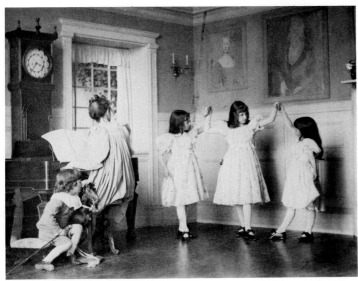

Plate 34   Rudolf Eickemeyer, Jr.,
"The Dance," ca. 1896.

Plate 38 Nancy Ford Cones,
"Threading the Needle," ca. 1905.

OPPOSITE
Plate 37 *Adam Clark Vroman,*
"Three Hopi's," 1901.

Plate 36 *Edward Sheriff Curtis,*
Untitled, ca. 1900.

Plate 39   Karl Blossfeldt,
"Papaver Orientale," ca. 1900–28.

OPPOSITE
Plate 40   Jean-Eugène-Auguste Atget,
"Cabaret Bar," ca. 1910.

Plate 41   Lewis Wickes Hine,
"Street Urchins," 1910.

OPPOSITE
Plate 42   Imogen Cunningham,
"The Plea," 1910.

Plate 44   Jacques Henri Lartigue,
"Zissou in His Tire Boat,
Chateau de Rouzat," 1911.

OPPOSITE
Plate 43   Frederick H. Evans,
"South Nave Aisle, Westminster Abbey,"
ca. 1911.

Plate 45 Karl Struss,
"Penn Station, New York," 1911.

OPPOSITE
Plate 46 Ernest Bloch,
"Old Woman with Mushrooms, Satigny,
Switzerland," 1912.

Plate 47   James Augustus Joseph Van Der Zee, "Nude, Harlem," 1923.

Plate 48   Alice Boughton, "Eurydice Returning to Hades," ca. 1925.

OPPOSITE
Plate 49   Orval Hixon, "Ole Olson," ca. 1925.

Plate 50   André Kertész,
"Crossroads," ca. 1926.

Plate 52   Anton Bruehl,
Untitled, 1927.

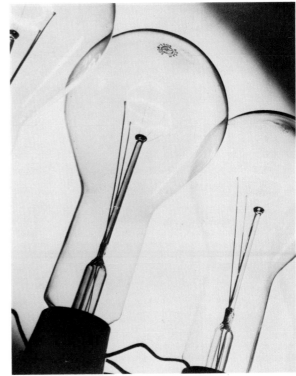

OPPOSITE
Plate 51   Edward Weston,
Untitled, 1927.

Plate 53   László Moholy-Nagy,
Untitled, ca. 1928.

Plate 55   Felix H. Man, "Home of
Handweaver in Upper Silesia During
the Depression in Germany," 1930.

Plate 54   Florence Henri,
"Obst" (Fruit), 1929.

Plate 56   George Hoyningen-Huené,
"Mrs. Michael Arlen," 1930.

Plate 57   Brassaï,
"Girl Playing Snooker," 1933.

Plate 58   William Mortensen,
"Venus and Vulcan," 1934.

Plate 59   Martín Chambi,
"Indian Woman and Child
from Keromarca," ca. 1934.

Plate 60   Walker Evans,
"Moundsville, Alabama," 1936.

Plate 61   Dorothea Lange,
"Plantation Owner and Field
Hands," 1936.

*Plate 63 Ilse Bing,
"The Trocadero Seen from Pont
Alexandre III with Lamppost,"
1935.*

OPPOSITE
*Plate 64 Bill Brandt,
"Hornton Street, London,"
ca. 1930s.*

*Plate 62 Lisette Model,
"French Gambler, Promenade
des Anglais, Riviera," n.d.*

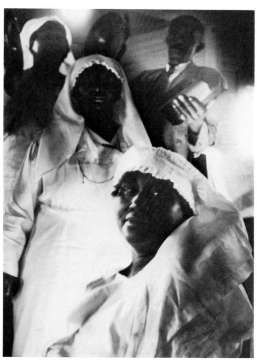

Plate 66   Eudora Welty,
"Preacher and Leaders of the Holiness
Church," 1939.

*Plate 65   Herbert Bayer,
"Metamorphosis," 1936.*

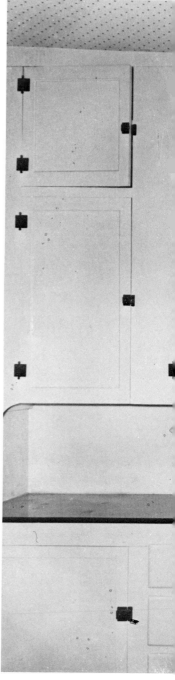

Plate 68   Arthur Rothstein,
"Mr. & Mrs. A. B. on Their Farm
Near Kersey, Colorado," 1939.

*Plate 67   Russell Lee,
"Kitchen of Tenant Client,
Hidalgo, Texas," 1939.*

Plate 69   John Felix Vachon,
"Grain Elevators and Freight Car,"
ca. 1940.

Plate 70   Lou Stouman,
"Times Square in the Rain," 1940.

Plate 71   Jack Delano,
"Interior of Rural House," 1941.

Plate 72
Ansel Easton Adams,
"Winter Sunrise," ca. 1944.

Plate 73   Laura Gilpin,
"Navaho Ethel Kellerwood,"
ca. 1940s.

Plate 74
Minor Martin White, From
"Sequence 17, 2nd Movement," n.d.

Plate 75 Arnold Newman,
"Max Ernst," 1942.

Plate 76 Wright Morris,
"Dresser Drawer," 1947.

Plate 78   Weegee,
"At the Palace Theatre," n.d.

Plate 79   Robert Doisneau,
"The Innocent," 1949.

OPPOSITE
Plate 77   Manuel Alvarez Bravo,
"Threshold," 1947.

OPPOSITE
Plate 81   Frederick Sommer,
"Idée et Orchidée," 1949.

Plate 82   Gisele Freund,
"Evita Peron," 1950.

Plate 80   Clarence John Laughlin,
"The Elder Worship," 1949.

Plate 83   Harold Eugene Edgerton, "Tennis Serve," 1952.

OPPOSITE
Plate 85   Jean-Pierre Sudre, "The Basket of Eggs," 1953.

Plate 84   Roy Rudolph DeCarava, "Boy Looking in Doorway," n.d.

Plate 86   Paul Strand,
"The Family, Luzzara, Italy," 1953.

Plate 87   Yousuf Karsh,
"Portrait of Schweitzer," n.d.

Plate 88   Harry M. Callahan,
"Environs of Chicago," ca. 1953.

Plate 92   Aaron Siskind,
"Arizpe 21," 1961.

*Plate 93 Alma Lavenson,
"Man with Sickle, Spain," 1962.*

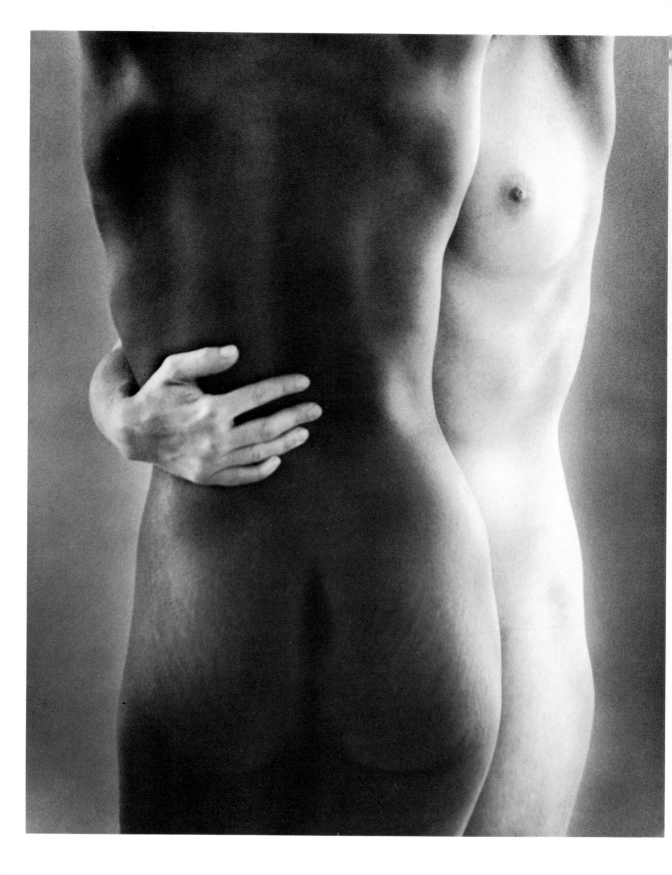

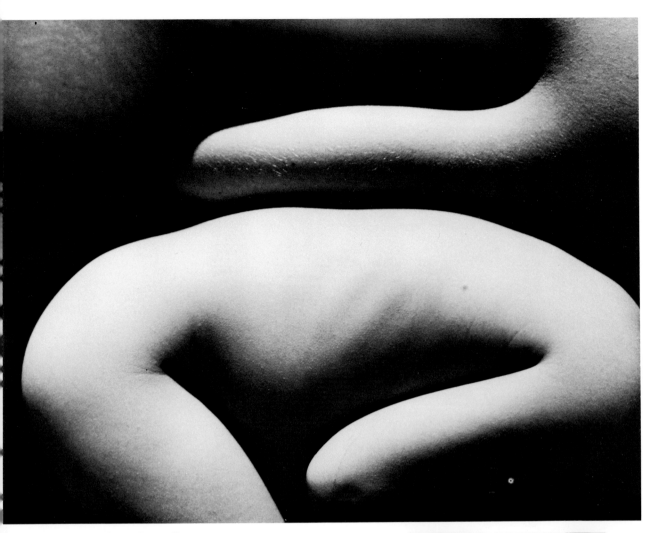

Plate 96   Walter Chappell,
"Mother/Child, Tassa Harra
Hot Springs, California," 1963.

Plate 94   Eve Arnold,
"London," 1962.

OPPOSITE
Plate 95   Ruth Bernhard,
"Two Forms," 1963.

Plate 97   Ralph Eugene Meatyard,
"Caroling, Caroling," 1964.

*Plate 98 Garry Winogrand,
"American Legion
Convention, Dallas, Texas,"
1964.*

*Plate 99 William Klein,
"Armistice Day," n.d.*

*Plate 100   Ralph Steiner,
"Hanging Sheets," 1965.*

*Plate 102   George A. Tice,
"Waterfall," n.d.*

*Plate 101   Danny Lyon,
"Prisoners Picking Cotton," 1967–69.*

*Plate 103   Paul Caponigro,
"White Deer," 1967.*

*Plate 104   Lucien G. Clergue,
Untitled, n.d.*

Plate 105   Vilem Kriz,
"Sirague City," 1970.

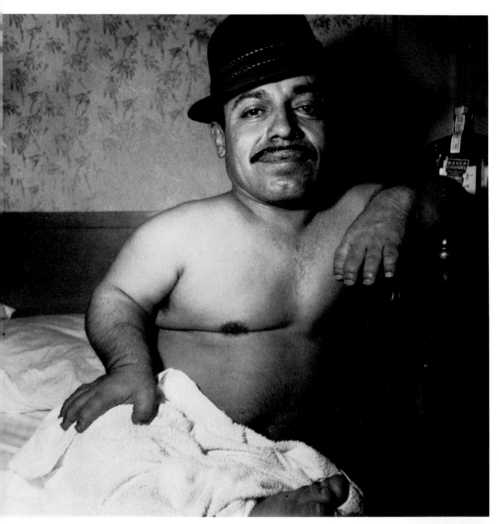

Plate 106   Diane Arbus,
"Mexican Midget," 1970.

Plate 108   William (Bill) Elmo Owens,
From "Suburbia," 1971.

OPPOSITE
Plate 107   Rene Guillermo Gelpi,
"Street Gang Member, Brooklyn," 1970.

Plate 109   Jay Dusard,
"Canyon de Chelly, Arizona," 1971.

*Plate 110   Jesús Sánchez Uribe,
Untitled, 1972.*

*Plate 111   Josef Sudek,
"Lillies of the Valley," 1971–72.*

Plate 113   Eva Rubinstein,
"Bed in Mirror," 1972.

Plate 114   Roswell Angier,
"Mr. & Mrs. Steve Mills,
Pilgrim Theater," 1973.

OPPOSITE
Plate 112   Kipton C. Kumler,
"Fronds, Wellesley," 1972.

Plate 116 *Arno Rafael Minkkinen,*
"Flam, Norway," 1973.

OPPOSITE
Plate 115 *Jean Dieuzaide,*
"La Fleur Fanée," 1973.

Plate 117 *Jack Welpott,*
"Sabine, Arles," 1973.

Plate 118   Robert H. Cumming,
"Fast and Slow Rain," 1974.

Plate 119   Ralph H. Gibson,
From "Quadrants," 1975.

OPPOSITE
Plate 120   Don Worth,
"Tropical Leaves," 1975.

Plate 121   Peeter Tooming,
"Because. . . ," ca. 1975.

Plate 122   Jo Ann Callis,
From "Morphe Series," 1976.

Plate 124 Suzanne Opton,
Untitled, 1976.

Plate 125 J. Seeley,
Untitled, 1977.

Plate 123   Starr Ockenga,
Untitled, 1976.

Plate 127   Robert Adams,
From "Denver Series," 1977.

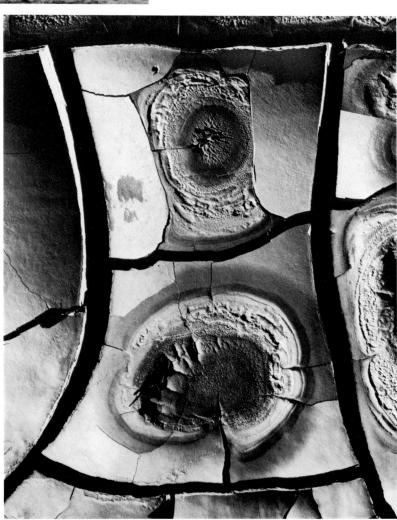

Plate 126   Brett Weston,
"Mud Cracks," 1977.

Plate 128 Joan Fontcuberta,
Untitled, 1978.

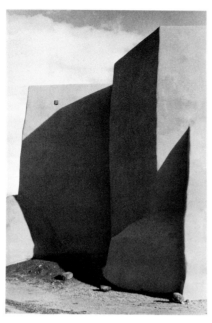

Plate 129   Bernard Plossu,
"Ranchos de Taos," 1978.

Plate 130   Graham Howe,
"Stakes in Ground," 1978.

Plate 131   Jerry N. Uelsmann,
Untitled, 1980.

Plate 133   Tom McNease,
Untitled, 1980.

Plate 132   Dazhen Wu,
"Waiting Room, China,"
1980.

Plate 134 (Arthur) Louis Ducos du Hauron,
Untitled, ca. 1889.

Plate 135 Alfred Stieglitz,
Untitled, ca. 1910
(reproduced from Camerawork*).*

Plate 136 Eliot Furness Porter,
"Red Osier, Near Great Barrington,
Massachusetts," 1957.

Plate 137 Eliot Elisofon,
"Initiation at Muela Buandu
Village, Yaka, Zaire," 1959.

Plate 138 Catherine S. Jansen,
"Blue Room," 1972.

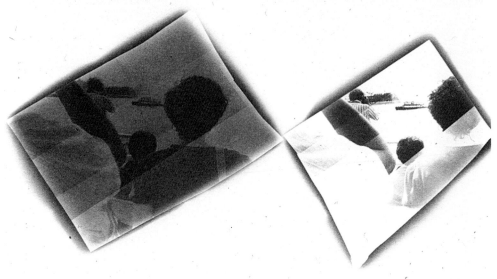

Plate 139 Darryl J. Curran
"Revisions," 1976.

Plate 140 Jack Butler,
"Excitable Pages #19," 1979.

Plate 141 Gail Skoff,
"Caribbean Storm," 1979.

*Plate 142 Gregory Allen MacGregor,
"Water Train," 1979.*

*Plate 143 Suda Kay House,
Untitled, 1980.*

Plate 144 Joel Peter Sternfeld,
"Elkmont Campground, Great Smoky
Mountain National Park," 1980.

Landeck; Galerie Taxipalais, Innsbruck; IBM, Bregenz.

REPRESENTATIVES Pacific Press Service, CPO Box 2051, Tokyo, Japan; Bildagentur Mauritius, D8102 Mittenwald, Pf 209, Germany.

ADDRESS A 6403 Flaurling 34, Austria.

Ken Light PHOTOGRAPHER · FILM MAKER Born in New York City on March 16, 1951, Light received a BGS from Ohio University, Athens, in 1973.

He has worked with the Labor Occupational Health Program at the University of California, Berkeley, since 1975, and has been an instructor at Contra Costa College, San Pablo, California, since 1974. Light was visual arts coordinator of Alameda County Neighborhood Arts from 1970 to 1975.

He is a member of SPE and NABET, Local 532.

Light received an American Film Institute independent film-maker grant in 1979 and a grant from the Film Fund in 1978 (with the Labor Occupational Health Program). He won a California Arts Commission grant in 1975.

He has made three 16mm documentary films: *The Woodworkers Film*, 1979 (30 min., color); *Working for Your Life*, 1979 (55 min., color); and *Working Steel*, 1976 (20 min., b/w).

Light works in social documentary in both films and still photography. His early work focused on antiwar and "New Left" activities, and he usually concentrates on the subject of workers.

PUBLICATIONS Catalog: *Images of Work*, 1978 (San Jose Mus. of Art: Calif.). Periodicals: *Film Library Quarterly*, 12: 2/3, 1979; "Hands of the Nation," *American Photographer*, 1:5; "22 Top Photographers," *Modern Photography Annual*, 1974.

COLLECTIONS Calif. Historical Soc., San Francisco; ICP, NYC; Oakland Mus., Calif.; San Francisco Mus. of Modern Art.

DEALER Lowinsky & Ari, 228 Grant Ave, San Francisco, CA 94108, & 542 S Alameda, Los Angeles, CA 94501.

ADDRESS 836 Contra Costa Ave, Berkeley, CA 94707.

Greer H. Lile PHOTOGRAPHER · COLLECTOR Lile was born February 21, 1925, in El Dorado, Arkansas. His wife, Mary Lile, is his partner in their photography-collection work and is also a retoucher.

A self-employed photographer, Lile began collecting photography materials about 1950. In 1974 he established the Gallery of Photographic History, a nonprofit public museum.

Lile has collected a wide range of photographic memorabilia, including over 4,000 cameras and pieces of equipment, more than 3,000 books and magazines and numerous photographs. As a photographer, Lile does large-format portraiture.

PUBLICATION Periodical: *Kodak Studio Light*, no. 2, 1975.

ADDRESS 310 Lanehart Rd, Little Rock, AR 72204.

Edwin Hale Lincoln PHOTOGRAPHER Lincoln lived from 1848 to 1938 in New England.

He took up photography in 1877, and in 1883 he went to the Berkshires of New England, where he photographed the grounds and interiors of many of its great estates. He also began to photograph wildflowers, which he continued to do from 1893.

Lincoln was a charter member of the American Orchid Society.

Best known for his flower images, "Lincoln also photographed local Berkshire landmarks, special events, and landscapes. For his nature studies he used a number of cameras, none using a negative smaller than 8 x 10 inches. . . . He printed his work on platinum paper only. . . . Because of the long exposures needed, he often carried his flower subjects, their roots wrapped in moss, back to his studio. There, by natural light, he could compose them and photograph them unhindered by breezes" (William F. Robinson, *A Certain Slant of Light*).

PUBLICATION Monograph: *Wild Flowers of New England*, 3 vols., 1904, rev. to 8 vols., 1914.

PORTFOLIO *Wild Flowers of New England*, 1914 (E. H. L. [self-pub.] Pittsfield: Mass.).

Daniel Allen Lindley, Jr. TEACHER · PHOTOGRAPHER Born in New Haven, Connecticut, on August 28, 1933, Lindley received a BA in 1955 from Yale University (New Haven, Connecticut), an EdM from Harvard University (Cambridge, Massachusetts) in 1959 and a PhD from Florida State University (Tallahassee) in 1970. His friendship with Walker Evans was a major influence on his work.

A member of the National Council of Teachers of English, Lindley prepared multimedia presentations for them in 1976 and 1977. He received a fellowship from the National Endowment for the Humanities in 1976. Lindley is a member of SPE.

His work is large-format representational photography. He is also documenting connections between writing and ways of living. Lindley's academic interests are in the relationship between rhetoric and image photography.

PUBLICATIONS Periodicals: "Photography and the Way of the Self," *Kansas Quarterly*, 11:4, fall 1979; "Walker Evans, Rhetoric and Photography," text only, *Exposure: SPE*, Mar 1978.

COLLECTION Art Inst. of Chicago.

ADDRESS 1217 Ridge Ave, Evanston, IL 60202.

Therold S. L. Lindquist *TEACHER · PHOTOGRA-PHER* Born February 28, 1932, in Jamestown, New York, Lindquist earned a BFA in 1957 from Rochester Institute of Technology, New York, an MFA in 1959 from Ohio University, Athens, and a PhD in 1977 from Walden University. He studied with Minor White, Beaumont Newhall, Ralph Hattersley and Wilson Hicks.

Since 1966 Lindquist has taught at State University College of New York, Fredonia. He previously taught at the University of Miami in Coral Gables, Florida (1959–66).

A member of SPE, the photographer won an NEA grant in 1975.

His early photographic work consists of black-and-white nature studies, but his recent work is in Cibachrome color. As of this writing Lindquist is documenting Copper Canyon and the Tarahumara Indians in Mexico.

Lindquist is also a sculptor, and his sculpture is in the Gustave Ring Collection in Washington, D.C., and the Alex Renault Collection in Miami.

PUBLICATIONS Books: *Born of the Sun*, 1975; *The Human Image: Sociology and Photography*, 1975; *Architecture in Westfield*, 1974; *The Beginner and the Wheel*, 1964.

ADDRESS 227 Chestnut St, Fredonia, NY 14063.

Linda Lindroth *PHOTOGRAPHER · PICTURE EDITOR · WRITER · RESEARCHER* Born in Miami, Florida, on September 4, 1946, Lindroth earned a BA in Studio Art from Douglass College, New Brunswick, New Jersey, in 1968 and an MFA in Art from Rutgers University, New Brunswick, in 1979. She has studied with Garry Winogrand, Peter Bunnell, Leon Golub and John Goodyear.

A freelance photographer since 1972, Lindroth was a teaching assistant at Douglass College in 1977–79. She was a picture researcher at the publishers Harcourt Brace Jovanovich (1974–77) and Holt, Rinehart and Winston (1973–74). She was a Harcourt art editor in 1969–72 and an advertising copywriter for WCTC Radio, New Brunswick, in 1968–69.

A member of SPE since 1977, and the American Society of Picture Professionals since 1973,

Lindroth won an American Institute of Graphic Arts Certificate of Excellence in 1975 and an award for documentary photography in the 1974 exhibition "New Jersey Photography." She received a New Jersey State Council on the Arts Fellowship in Photography in 1974.

The photographer's early work was in small format documentary pictures, but as of this writing she uses medium format for urban and social landscapes and "a series of psychological portraits including narrative statements" (the latter blown up to 4 x 5 feet on photolinen).

PUBLICATIONS Book: *Innovative Printmaking*, Thelma R. Newman, 1977. Anthology: *In/Sights: Self-Portraits by Women*, Joyce Tennyson Cohen, 1978. Catalogs: *Artists' Books USA*, 1978 (Independent Curators, Inc.: NYC); *Photo/Synthesis*, Jason Wong, ed., 1976 (Cornell Univ.: Ithaca, N.Y.); *Photographic Process as Medium*, Rosanne T. Livingston, ed., 1976 (Rutgers Univ.: New Brunswick, N.J.); *Die Innere Landschaft: Acht Amerikanische Photographinnen*, 1975 (Germany); *International Triennial of Photography*, 1975 (Fribourg, Switzerland); *New Jersey Photography*, 1974 (Rutgers Univ.: New Brunswick, N.J.). Periodicals: *Creative Camera*, Nov 1975; *Feminist Art Journal*, fall 1974.

COLLECTIONS Metro. Mus. of Art, NYC; MOMA, NYC; N.J. State Mus., Trenton. Bibliothèque Nationale, Paris; Musée d'Art et d'Histoire, Fribourg, Switzerland.

ADDRESS 95 Watchung Ave, Chatham, NJ 07928.

John William Lindt *PHOTOGRAPHER · BUSINESS-MAN* Born in 1845 in Germany, Lindt died February 19, 1926, at his home, "The Hermitage," near Melbourne, Australia.

Lindt ran away to sea at an early age, deserting the ship in Queensland, Australia, in 1865, whereupon he traveled the "outback" for several months. Around 1867 he apprenticed himself to a photographer in Graffon, North South Wales.

Shortly after the end of his apprenticeship he opened a studio, then moved to Melbourne in 1876 and established a successful studio there that catered mainly to businesses and society families. He also became an importer and dealer in cameras and accessories. From 1885 to 1889 Lindt went on several expeditions to New Guinea, the New Hebrides and Fiji, and in 1895 he built his country retreat, "The Hermitage," which became a well known guest house as well as serving as his studio.

From the time he opened his first studio Lindt enjoyed a growing reputation. He exhibited large prints, made directly from 20 x 26 wet-plate negatives, in various industrial exhibitions throughout the world. His dry-plate photographs of his travels became internationally popular through travel books and lantern-slide shows.

PUBLICATIONS Monograph: *Picturesque New Guinea*, 1887 (Longmans, Green & Co.: London). Books: *Gold and Silver: An Album of Hill End and Gulgong Photographs from the Holtermann Collection*, Keast Burke, 1973 (Heinemann: Melbourne, Australia); *The Story of the Camera in Australia*, Jack Cato, 1955 (Georgian House: Australia); *Australian Aboriginals*, 1880? (Melbourne, Australia).

COLLECTIONS In Australia: Natl. Gall. of Victoria; Royal Melbourne Inst. of Tech.

Gabriel Lippmann PHYSICIST Born August 16, 1845, in Hallerich, Luxemburg, Lippmann died on July 13, 1921, while en route by boat from France to the United States. The son of French parents, he was educated at a French normal school and at Heidelberg University, where he studied physics under Kuehne and Kirchoff.

From 1883 on he was a physics professor at the Sorbonne in Paris, and belonged to the Académie des Sciences. As part of his research in optics he experimented with producing a photographic plate with a transparent grainless emulsion on which he could make records of colors. In 1891 he announced his interference method of color photography, which involved a reflecting coat of mercury behind the emulsion of a photographic plate. It marked the beginning of direct color photography, although it was not commercially successful. In 1892 Lippmann made color photographs of the French countryside. His other photographic discoveries involved the use of light filters, the development of various photographic testing and picture-taking processes and the construction of lenticular film material in 1908.

Lippmann won the Nobel prize in physics in 1908 for producing the first color photographic plate.

He also made important contributions in electricity, acoustics and optics, including the 1873 invention of the capillary electrometer to measure very small voltages (used in early electrocardiographs).

PUBLICATIONS Books: *Quellendarstellungen zur Geschichte der Fotografie*, Wolfgang Baier, 1964; *March of Photography*, Erich Stenger, 1958; *Histoire de la Photographie*, Raymond Lécuyer, 1945; *History of Color Photography*, Joseph S. Friedman, 1944; *History of 3-Color Photography*, E. J. Wall, 1925; *Cassell's Cyclopedia of Photography*, 1912; *Lexikon für Photographie und Reproduktionstechnik*, G. H. Emmerich, 1910; *Book of Photography*, Paul N. Hasluck, 1905; *Rapport sur les titres de M. Lippmann au Grand Prix de 12,000 francs*, Louis Alphonse Davanne, 1895 (RPS: London). Anthology: *Photography's Great Inventors*, Louis W. Sipley, 1965. Periodicals: *Foto Magazin*, Sept 1961; *Bild und Ton*, 1961, 1955; *Image*, June 1956; *Photographische Correspondenz*, 1945; *British Journal Photographic Almanac*, 1922; *Bulletin de la Société Française de Photographie*, 1921; obituary, July 22, 1921, "The Principles of Direct Colour Photography by Prismatic Dispersion," Aug 17, 1906, "Colour Photography," Jan 7, 1898, *British Journal of Photography*; "Colour Photography" *Proceedings of the Royal Institute of Great Britain*, Apr 17, 1896; "On Colour Photography by the Inferential Method," *Proceedings of the Royal Society, Jahrbuch für Photographie und Reproduktionstechnik*, 1892; "La Photographie des couleurs," *Comptes Rendus*, Feb 2, 1891; "Photographie des couleurs du spectre solaire," *L'Astronomie*, vol. 10, 1891.

Herbert List PHOTOGRAPHER Born October 7, 1907, List died April 4, 1975. He studied at Heidelberg University in Germany and learned photography from Andreas Feininger in 1929. He was later influenced by such Surrealist artists as Man Ray, De Chirico and Max Ernst.

List freelanced after he left his family coffee-importing business in 1935. In the 1930s his work was published in such places as *Verve, Arts et Métiers Graphiques, Photographie, Harper's Bazaar, Life, Look, Epoca* and several German magazines.

List won the David Octavius Hill medal in 1960.

Creating surrealist "metaphysical" photography and travel images in the 1930s, List concentrated on portraits of European artists in the 1940s and 1950s. He also specialized in photographing works of art.

PUBLICATIONS Books: *Napoli e i suoi personaggi*, w/Vittorio de Sica, 1968 (Rizzoli: Milan, Italy); *Caribia*, 1963; *Bildwerke aus Nigeria*, William B. Fagg, Brit. ed., *Nigerian Images* (Lund Humphries: London); *Roma*, 1955; *Licht über Hellas*, 1953. Anthology: *The Magic Image*, Cecil Beaton & Gail Buckland, 1975. Periodical: *Du*, Apr 1973.

PORTFOLIO *Zeitlude Null* (PPS Galerie: Hamburg, Germany).

COLLECTIONS Boston Mus. of Fine Art;

MOMA, NYC; New Orleans Mus. of Art, La.; San Francisco Mus. of Modern Art. In Germany: Munich Photomus.; Mus. für Kunst und Gewerbe, Hamburg.

DEALERS Light Gall., 724 Fifth Ave, New York, NY 10019; Sander Gall., 2604 Connecticut Ave, Washington, DC 20008; PPS Galerie, Feldstrasse, Hochhaus, Hamburg, West Germany 2000.

ARCHIVE Max Scheler, Bellevue 39a, 2 Hamburg 60, West Germany.

Jacqueline Livingston *PHOTOGRAPHER · TEACHER* Born in August 1943, in Phoenix, Arizona, Livingston earned a BA (1964) and MA (1965) in Art, Secondary Education, from Arizona State University, Tempe.

From 1975 to 1978 she was assistant professor of architecture and art at Cornell University, Ithaca, New York. She has also taught photography at University of California Extension at Berkeley and San Francisco (1973–75) and at Arizona State University (1965–67).

Livingston has belonged to SPE since 1974. She won Humanities Faculty Research grants from Cornell in 1975 and 1976.

"My work deals largely with changing female and male roles in American culture," she says. Using portraits of herself and her family, many images show "staged, often surreal landscapes of anxiety, alienation and frustration." Most recently Livingston has produced a controversial series of nude photographs of her son, husband and father-in-law.

PUBLICATIONS Anthologies: *In-Sights: Self-Portraits by Women*, Joyce Tenneson Cohen, ed., 1978; *Vision and Expression*, Nathan Lyons, ed., 1969. Catalogs: *The Male Nude*, 1978 (Marcuse Pfeifer Gall.: NYC); *Young American Photographers*, 1975 (Kalamazoo Inst. of Arts: Mich.); *Young Photographers*, 1968 (Univ. of N. Mex.: Albuquerque). Periodicals: *Camera 35*, June 1980; "Feminism and Photography: Trouble in Paradise," Shelley Rice, Mar 1979, "Livingston Firing Sparks Controversy," Apr 1978, *Afterimage: VSW*; "The Male Nude at Marcuse Pfeifer," Rene Ricard, *Art in America*, Sept–Oct 1978; "Livingston vs. Cornell," *Women Artist News*, Apr 1978; "The Erotic Eye," Joseph Czarnecki, *Artweek*, Jan 25, 1975.

COLLECTIONS IMP/GEH, Rochester; Kalamazoo Inst. of Arts, Mich.; Metro Mus. of Art, NYC; MOMA, NYC; Oakland Mus., Calif.; San Francisco Mus. of Modern Art; Univ. of N. Mex. Art Mus., Albuquerque. Bibliothèque Nationale, Paris.

DEALER Robert Samuel Gall., 795 Broadway, New York, NY 10003.
ADDRESS 327 N Albany St, Ithaca, NY 14850.

Camilo Lleras *PHOTOGRAPHER* Born December 22, 1949, in Bogotá, Colombia, Lleras studied architecture and fine arts from 1969 to 1971. He is a self-taught photographer.

A freelance since 1972, Lleras currently teaches photography and art history. He taught photography and experimental film and headed the program on photography and graphic design at Taller 5, School of Design, in Bogotá in 1976–79.

The photographer is a founding member (1978) of Consejo Latino Americano de Fotografía in Mexico.

His work involves serial and sequential self-portraiture and experimentation with techniques such as solarization, high contrast and multiple images.

PUBLICATIONS Book: *Hecho en Latinoamerica*, w/Jaime Ardila, 1978 (Consejo Mexico de Fotografía: Mexico). Periodical: "Obra Fotográfica de Camilo Lleras," *Arte en Colombia*, no. 2, 1977.

COLLECTIONS In Colombia: Atenas Publicidad, Bogotá; Centro de Arte Actual, Pereira; Luis Angel Arango Pub. Lib., Bogotá; Mus. of Modern Art, Bogotá. Centre Culturel Municipal de Villeparisis, Paris; Consejo Mexicano de Fotografía, INBA, Mexico.

ADDRESS Apartado aéreo 90782, Bogotá, D.E., Colombia.

Chris Locke *PHOTOGRAPHER · LECTURER* Born in 1950 at Shoreham-by-Sea, England, Locke studied at the Guildford School of Photography in 1968–71 and continued to study photography at Trent Polytechnic in 1971–72.

Since 1979 he has been employed at West Notts College, and has worked as a freelance photographer since 1972. Previously he lectured at Lanchester Polytechnic (1978–79) and Sheffield Polytechnic (1977–78).

In 1974 Locke received a grant from the Arts Council of Great Britain, and a Materials Grant from Ilford Ltd.

The photographer describes his work as being "large format and 35mm landscape concerned with the exploration of the compositional and emotive aspects normally found in family snapshot albums."

PUBLICATIONS Anthology: *Perspectives on Landscape*, 1978. Periodicals: *British Journal of*

Photography, Oct 1977, Dec 1975, July 1973; *Creative Camera*, June 1975.

PORTFOLIO *Untitled*, 1974 (self-pub.).

COLLECTIONS In London: Arts Council of Great Britain; Dept. of the Environment.

ADDRESS 36 Linden St, Mansfield, Nottinghamshire, England.

John Borg Loengard *PHOTOGRAPHER · EDITOR*
Born in New York City in 1934, Loengard received a BA from Harvard University, Cambridge, Massachusetts, in 1956.

In 1978 Loengard became picture editor for *Life* magazine, a position he now holds. From 1973 to 1978 he held the same position for *Life Special Reports,* and for *People* magazine in 1973–74. From 1961 to 1972 he was a staff photographer with *Life.*

PUBLICATIONS Periodicals: "The Vanishing Cowboys," Mar 1970, "Georgia O'Keeffe," Mar 1968, "The Shakers," Mar 1967, *Life.*

ADDRESS 322 W 77 St, New York, NY 10024.

Bernd Lohse *PHOTOJOURNALIST · WRITER*
Born October 5, 1911, in Dresden, Germany, Lohse studied languages, history and journalism at Frankfurt and Berlin universities (1930–32).

Though retired since 1975, Lohse is still active as a writer, critic, translator and lecturer on photography. From 1965 to 1975 he was editor of *Photoblätter* in Leverkusen, and from 1955 to 1965 was book editor at Umschau Verlag in Frankfurt. He was a photographer for *Neue Illustrierte* in Cologne in 1950–53, and edited *Photo-Magazin* in Munich in 1949–50. He also edited *Foto-Spiegel* in 1947–49.

Lohse has belonged to the Association of German Journalists since 1932, GDL since 1950 and DGPh since 1951 (board member since 1966).

PUBLICATIONS Books: *Hugo Erfurth, Photograph der Goldenen 20er Jahre,* 1977; *Kanada— Land von Morgen?,* 1954; *Australien und Südsee Heute,* 1953; *Cameras from Germany,* 1950. Periodical: *Camera,* Oct 1976.

ADDRESS Neuenkamp 64, D-5090 Leverkusen 31, West Germany.

Steven Richard Lojewski *PHOTOGRAPHER · TEACHER* Born June 23, 1952, in London, England, Lojewski earned a diploma in art and design from Prahran College, Melbourne, Australia, in 1975.

Since 1978 he has been a photography lecturer at Sydney College of Art, Sydney, Australia. He taught at Photographers' Gallery, Preston Institute and Prahran College, all in Melbourne, between 1975 and 1977, and was a freelance photojournalist in 1973–75. Lojewski worked as a printer and assistant in commercial photography studios from 1972 to 1975. Prior to 1971 he was a gardener.

In 1979 he became a member of the Executive Committee of the Australian Center for Photography, and in 1976 he won a grant from the Australian Visual Arts Board.

He produces selenium-toned silver prints, using small and medium formats.

PUBLICATIONS Anthology: *Time-Life Annual,* 1979. Catalog: *Phillip Morris Collection* (Australia). Periodicals: *Print Letter,* Jan 1980; *Creative Camera,* Mar 1978.

COLLECTIONS In Australia: Art Gall. of New South Wales, Sydney; Australian Natl. Gall., Phillip Morris Cllctns., Canberra; Horsham Art Gall., Horsham, Victoria; Natl. Gall. of Victoria, Melbourne; S. Australian Art Gall., Adelaide; Swinburne Coll., Melbourne; Tasmanian Art Gall., Hobart.

DEALERS Australian Centre for Photography, 76 A Paddington St, Paddington H.S.W., Australia; Photographers Gallery, 344 Pont Rd, South Yarra, Victoria, Australia.

ADDRESS 6/78 Louisa Rd, Birchgrove, H.S.W., 2041 Australia.

Donald Peter Lokuta *PHOTOGRAPHER · TEACHER* Born October 6, 1946, in Elizabeth, New Jersey, Lokuta earned a BA in 1968 from Newark State College, Union, New Jersey, an MA in 1971 from Montclair State College, New Jersey, and a PhD in 1975 from Ohio State University, Columbus.

Since 1975 he has been associate professor of photography at Kean College in Union, New Jersey, and he recently established Lokuta Graphics. From 1972 to 1975 he taught in the Photography Department of Ohio State University.

A member of SPE, he also belongs to the Summit Art Center in Summit, New Jersey, and to City Without Walls Gallery in Newark. He won a fellowship from the New Jersey State Council on the Arts in 1980 and a survey grant in 1974 from Ohio State University.

Working in black-and-white, Lokuta does work that ranges from environmental portraiture to semiabstract images concerned with design. He also produces silk-screened photographic prints.

PUBLICATIONS Book: *History of Photography Instruction,* 1976. Periodicals: *History of Photography: An International Quarterly,* July 1977; *Exposure: SPE,* Feb 1977; *The New Daguerreian Journal,* Feb 1975, Jan 1974, Oct 1973.

COLLECTIONS In N.J.: IBM Corp.; N.J. State

Mus., Trenton; Newark Mus.; Morris Mus. of Arts & Science, Morristown.

DEALER Woodman Gall., 8 Dehart St, Morristown, NJ 07960.

ADDRESS 980 Salem Rd, Union, NJ 07083.

Fred Spencer Lonidier *PHOTOGRAPHER* · *TEACHER* Born February 19, 1942, in Lakeview, California, Lonidier received a BA in Sociology from San Francisco State College (1966) and an MFA in Photo/Mixed Media from University of California, San Diego (UCSD), in La Jolla (1972).

Since 1975 he has been an assistant professor at UCSD. He received Academic Senate Research grants from UCSD in 1978 and 1975, a Ford Foundation Leave Grant in 1977 and a Regents Fellowship from UCSD in 1971.

PUBLICATION Books: *Photography: Current Perspectives*, Allan Secula, 1978; *Photography and Language*, Lew Thomas, ed., 1976. Catalogs: *Dialogue/Discourse/Research*, William Spurlock, 1979 (Santa Barbara Mus. of Art: Calif.); *Social Works*, Ruth Iskin, 1979 (Los Angeles Inst. of Contemporary Art). Periodicals: *Artweek*, Judith Dunham, Oct 14, 1978; *Camera 35*, Lou Stettner, Aug & Feb 1978; *Afterimage: VSW*, James Hugunin, summer 1978; *LAICA Journal*, Aug/Sept 1975.

COLLECTIONS In Calif.: Long Beach Mus. of Art; Oakland Mus.

ADDRESS Univ. of California, San Diego, B-027, La Jolla, CA 92093.

Victor Lopez Chambi
See Victor Chambi Lopez

Catherine Agard Loughran *PHOTOGRAPHER* · *COUNSELOR* Born November 20, 1946, in Green Bay, Wisconsin, Loughran received her BS (1973), MA (1974) and MFA (1975) from the University of Wisconsin, Madison.

Presently doing counseling and photography in Madison, she taught photography and drawing at Kansas State College, Emporia (1976–77), and photography at University of Wisconsin Extension (1976).

Loughran has undertaken work in three major areas: portraiture, Cibachrome prints of "found symbolism" and painted photographs of formal abstractions.

PUBLICATIONS Periodicals: *New Art Examiner*, Dec 1978, May 1977.

COLLECTIONS Art Inst. of Chicago; Burpee Art Mus., Rockford, Ill.; Friends of Photography, Carmel, Calif.; Governor State Univ., Park Forest South, Ill.; Madison Art Ctr., Wisc.; Portland Mus., Maine.

DEALER Jacques Baruch Gall., 900 N Michigan Ave, Chicago, IL 60611.

ADDRESS 1127 Sherman Ave, Madison, WI 53703.

Lynn Lown *PHOTOGRAPHER* Born October 17, 1947, in Iowa Falls, Lown earned a BFA from the University of Iowa, Iowa City, in 1971, and an MFA in 1973 from the University of Oregon, Eugene.

He taught at New Mexico Community College in Santa Fe from 1977 to 1979, and as of this writing he teaches at Texas Christian University in Fort Worth and freelances as a photographer.

PUBLICATION Periodical: *El Palacio*, fall 1979.

COLLECTIONS CCP, Tucson; Dallas Fine Arts Mus., Tex.; New Mex. State Univ. Fine Arts Mus., Las Cruces; Univ. of Iowa Mus. of Art, Iowa City; Univ. of Nebr. Sheldon Memorial Gall., Lincoln; Univ. of New Mex. Art Mus., Albuquerque; Western New Mex. Univ., Silver City.

REPRESENTATIVES Douglas Kenyon Gall., 155 E Ohio St, Chicago, IL 60611; The Afterimage Gall., Quadrangle #151, 2800 Routh St, Dallas, TX 75201; G. Ray Hawkins, 7224 Melrose Ave, Los Angeles, CA 90046; Maggie Kress Gall., Box 2241, Taos, NM 87571; Sebastian Moore Gall., 1411 Market St, Denver, CO 80202; A Gall. for Fine Photography, 5432 Magazine St, New Orleans, LA 70115; Witkin Gall., 41 E 57 St, New York, NY 10022.

ADDRESS POB 32047, Fort Worth, TX 76714.

Ben Judah Lubschez *ARCHITECT* · *PHOTOGRAPHER* Born in 1881 in Odessa, Russia, Lubschez died August 17, 1963, in New York City. In 1884, he emigrated with his family to Kansas City, Missouri, and he received his schooling there.

Lubschez worked in Kansas City until 1918, when he moved to New York to work for H. Van Buren Magonigle. He later opened his own offices, and in 1944 he joined the firm of Voorhees, Walker, Foley, Smith, where he remained until his 1961 retirement.

In 1911 the architect founded the Kansas City chapter of the American Institute of Architects (AIA), and was its president for five years. He was also a member of AIA's New York chapter, the New York chapter of the Society for Ethical Culture and the Amateur Astronomers Association of the Museum of Natural History in New York City.

Lubschez photographed city life from 1900 to 1920 and also did architectural photography, his images appearing in several architectural and photographic magazines.

PUBLICATIONS Monograph: *Manhattan—the Magic Island*, 1927. Books: *Plantations of the Carolina Low Country*, 1938; *Over the Drawing Board*, 1920; *Perspective*, 1913.

Allan I. Ludwig PHOTOGRAPHER · HISTORIAN Born June 9, 1933 in Yonkers, New York, Ludwig earned a BFA (1956), an MA and PhD (1964, History of Art) from Yale University, New Haven, Connecticut. He studied painting with Josef Albers, James Brooks and Bernard Chaet, and photography with Herbert Matter.

Ludwig has been Derendinger Professor of Art at Bloomfield College, Bloomfield, New Jersey, since 1975, and before that was president of Automated Communications, Inc. (1968–75). He was an associate professor of art at Syracuse University, New York (1968–69), an associate professor of fine arts at Dickinson College, Carlisle, Pennsylvania (1964–68), an assistant instructor at Yale University (1958–64) and a founder and instructor in the Rhode Island School of Design's photography program (1956–58).

A member of CAA since 1956, he is on its board of directors, and is a member of the acquisitions committee of the Alternative Museum in New York City. Ludwig won a National Endowment for the Humanities summer fellowship in 1967, an American Council of Learned Societies fellowship in 1967, American Philosophical Society fellowships in 1964–66, the John Addison Porter Prize at Yale University in 1964 and a Bollingen Foundation Fellowship for 1961–63.

His work is primarily in black-and-white, and he usually produces 11 x 14 archival selenium-toned silver prints. He recently has been experimenting with photo-fusion and mixed media.

PUBLICATIONS Monograph: *Graven Images*, 1966. Periodicals (text only): "Richard Lytle," Mar 1977, "Lawrence Fane," Nov 1976, "Philip Grousman," Nov 1974, *Arts Magazine*.

COLLECTIONS Alternative Mus., NYC; Archives of Amer. Art, NYC; José Limon Foundation, NYC; L/C, Wash., D.C.; Moravian Coll., Bethlehem, Pa.; MOMA, NYC; Polaroid Fndn., Cambridge, Mass.; Roland Gibson Cllctn. of Modern Art; Smithsonian Inst., Wash., D.C.; State Univ. of N.Y., Potsdam; Univ. of Notre Dame, Notre Dame, Ind.; Walker Art Ctr., Minneapolis, Minn; Yale Univ., New Haven, Conn.

DEALER Alonzo Gall., 30 W 57 St, New York, NY 10019.

ADDRESS 141 Upper Mountain Ave, Montclair, NJ 07042.

Karel Ludwig PHOTOGRAPHER · GRAPHIC ARTIST Born September 27, 1919, in Prague, Czechoslovakia, Ludwig died there on July 4, 1977.

After receiving a basic education, he went to work as an assistant in the graphic workshop for advertising drawings in the shoe factory of Baťa in Zlín, Czechoslovakia (1938–39). At this time he began photography, and on returning to Prague worked in theater and motion picture publicity.

Ludwig was known for his nudes, according to Petr Tausk. Also an outstanding portraitist, he was one of the genre's most important representatives in the 1940s in Czechoslovakia. Recently a portfolio of his work was published in Prague.

PUBLICATIONS Monograph: *Fotografie Karla Ludwiga: Filmové nakladatelství*, 1948 (Prague). Book: *Memory in Black and White*, intro. by J. Řezáč, 1961 (Artia: Prague).

COLLECTION Mus. of Decorative Arts, Prague, Czechoslovakia.

Hinricus Lueppo-Cramer CHEMIST · WRITER Born Lueppo Hinricus Cramer in Leer, Ostfriesland, in 1871, Lueppo-Cramer died in 1943. He attended the Gymnasium in his hometown, then specialized in chemistry studies at Munich, Heidelberg and Berlin.

Upon finishing his studies in 1884, Lueppo-Cramer joined the Berlin chemical firm of Schering, which he left in 1902 to serve as director of Dr. Schleussner's dry-plate factory in Frankfurt am Main (until 1918). Lueppo-Cramer next went to work for the Kranseder & Company dry-plate factory in Munich, and in 1922 took charge of the research department of the Deutsche Gelatinefabriken A.G. at Schweinfurt, where he stayed until 1932.

While working at Schering the chemist invented the intermediate developer Adurol (1899). He continued to study chemical development, contributing greatly to the discovery of new hydroquinone developers. His other experiments concerned such areas as solarization, the Herschel Effect, the Albert Effect, the desensitizing action of most developers (1901), and the desensitization of emulsions, which permitted development under comparatively bright light (1920). He wrote hundreds of articles and papers and a number of books.

Among the honors Lueppo-Cramer won were the gold medal of the Photographische Gesellschaft in Vienna and the Progress Medal of RPS.

PUBLICATIONS Books: *Quellendarstellungen*

zur Geschichte der Fotografie, Wolfgang Baier, 1964; Memoirs of a Photochemist, Fritz Wentzel, 1960; Focal Encyclopedia of Photography, 1957, 1956 (Focal Press); Theory of the Photographic Process, C. E. K. Mees, 1944; History of 3-Color Photography, E. J. Wall, 1925; Das Latente Bild, 1911; Lexikon für Photographie und Reproduktionstechnik, G. H. Emmerich, 1910; Die Roentgen-Photographie, 1909; Kolloidchemie und Photographie, 1908; Photographische Probleme, 1907. Anthology: Photography's Great Inventors, Louis W. Sipley, 1965. Periodicals: Monthly Abstract Bulletin, 1944; Zeitschrifte für wissenschaftliche Photographie, 1926, 1925, 1924; Photographische Correspondenz, 1920, 1901.

Auguste Lumière   INVENTOR · SCIENTIST
Born October 19, 1862, in Bensançon, France, Lumière died April 10, 1954, in Lyon, France. His brother, Louis, was also an inventor and scientist, and his father, Antoine, was a painter and pioneer photographer. Auguste was educated at Martinière industrial school in Lyon.

Lumière ran a photographic-plate factory in Lyon with his brother, which, by 1894, produced 15,000,000 plates a year. He had first worked in his father's laboratory with his brother, specializing in studies of chemistry and biology.

He belonged to the French Medical Academy.

Along with Louis, Auguste Lumière invented the first popular color photographic process, autochrome, in 1904, using a type of positive color transparency. The process was used in experiments by the Photo-Secessionists. The Lumières also invented the cinématographe, a motion picture camera and projector, patented on February 13, 1895, and introduced to the public on December 28 of that year at the Grand Café in Paris. It was the first public film showing. The brothers produced several film shorts, such as La Sortie des Usines Lumière and L'Arroseur arrosé in 1895, as well as the first newsreel and documentary films.

Also a physician, physicist, chemist, and botanist, Auguste did considerable scientific research and writing covering tuberculosis, cancer, X-ray techniques and pharmaceutical developments. His principal early studies, on blood and the lymphatic and interstitial fluids, resulted in the development of many new medicines. He was credited with helpful discoveries about the healing of wounds and invented a system of non-adhering bandages, vital to the prevention of hemorrhages. His work with hyposulphite of magnesium proved effective in the treatment of many chronic diseases, and he developed a vaccine for the gastrointestinal system to prevent typhoid fever.

PUBLICATIONS   Books: Les Frères Lumière, Henri Kubnick, 1938 (Librairie Plon; Paris); La Vie, la Maladie, et la Mort; Phénomènes Colloïdaux, 1928 (Masson: Paris); "Autochrome," La Photographie des couleurs et les plaques autochrome, E. Wallon, 1907 (Gauthier-Villars: Paris). Periodical: "The Story of Lumière," Claude Walter, Ciba Journal, spring 1964.

COLLECTION   IMP/GEH, Rochester.

Louis Lumière   INVENTOR · SCIENTIST   Born October 5, 1864, in Bensançon, France, Lumière died June 6, 1948, in Bandol, France. His brother, Auguste, was a fellow inventor and scientist, and his father, Antoine, was a painter and pioneer photographer. Louis was educated at Martinière industrial school in Lyon, France, but quit at age sixteen due to ill health. He was then tutored by a family friend who was a professor of Greek.

In 1880 Louis went to work in his father's laboratory, and soon after, he and his brother cofounded a photographic-plate factory that also manufactured paper and related products.

He was honorary president of the French Chamber of Cinema, president of the council of the French Society of Physics and a member of the National Conservatory of Arts & Trades, National Office of Inventions, Institute of Optics and the French Academy of Sciences. Lumière was named a grand officer in the French Legion of Honor in 1935.

Devoted to the problems of photography, he discovered a way of making bromide of silver emulsions for photographic plates by treating oxide of silver with bromide of ammonia. He later invented an improved process, which remains a family secret to this day. With Auguste he invented the first color process, autochrome, which used a positive color transparency.

The brothers Lumière also devised the cinématographe, a motion picture camera and projector, which they patented on February 13, 1895. They are credited with having made the first movie in 1895, La Sortie des Usines Lumière, showing workers leaving their factory, and gave the first public motion picture showing on December 28 of that year at the Grand Café in Paris. The Lumières produced several short films and were considered responsible for the first newsreel and documentary films.

PUBLICATIONS   Books: Louis Lumière: Choix de Textes et Propos de Louis Lumière, George Sadoul, 1964 (Seghers: Paris); Louis Lumière, Inventeur, Maurice Berry & Lo Duca, 1948 (Editions Prisma: Paris); *Les Frères Lumière*, Henri Kudnick 1938 (Librairie Plon: Paris); *Jubilé Louis Lumière, 6 Novembre 1935*, 1936; *Hommage à Louis Lumière, le Cinématographe Appliqué a l'Education . . .* , 1935 (Musée Galliéra: Ville de Paris). Periodicals: "The Story of Lumière," Claude Walter, *Ciba Journal*, spring 1964; "Hommage de la Cinématographie Française, Louis Lumière, Quarante;" *La Cinématographie Française*, Nov. 1935; "The work of Louis Lumière," E. Wallon, *Bulletin Société Française Photographie*, vol. 8, 1921.

COLLECTION IMP/GEH, Rochester.

Christian G. Lund *PHOTOGRAPHER* Born July 2, 1923, in Ottawa, Ontario, Canada, Lund was influenced by Harry Rowed, Nick Morant and Ronnie and Louis Jacques of the National Film Board of Canada.

Lund has been the photo editor of the National Film Board of Canada since 1975. Previously he worked as the photo editor for Information Canada (1971–75) and as a photojournalist (1942–71).

He is a member of Professional Photographers of Canada and Professional Photographers of Ontario. A recipient of a Gold Medal for photographic excellence in 1971 from the National Film Board of Canada, he was also awarded a Master of Photographic Arts from the Professional Photographers of Canada in 1968.

PUBLICATIONS Monograph: *Stones of History*, 1967 (Natl. Film Board of Canada). Periodicals: *British Photography Yearbook*, 1965, 1964, 1963; *Canadian Art*, Nov/Dec 1961.

COLLECTION Natl. Film Board of Canada, Still Photo Div., Ottawa, Ontario, Canada.

ADDRESS 191 Wilshire Ave, Ottawa, Ontario, Canada K2C OE6.

Harry H. Lunn, Jr. *ART DEALER* Born April 29, 1933, in Detroit, Michigan, Lunn earned a BA in Economics from the University of Michigan, Ann Arbor.

He has been president of Lunn Gallery/Graphics International Ltd. since 1968.

Lunn belongs to RPS, International Association of Photography Dealers and Art Dealers Association of America.

His gallery specializes in nineteenth- and twentieth-century prints and drawings and rare photographs. He handles the estates of Milton Avery and George Grosz.

PUBLICATION Catalog: *Milton Avery—Prints*, 1973.

ADDRESS 3243 P St NW, Washington, DC 20007.

Markéta Luskačová *PHOTOGRAPHER* Born August 29, 1944, in Prague, Czechoslovakia, Luskačová received a degree in Cultural Sociology from Prague University in 1967.

A freelance photographer, she is a member of Magnum Photos (since 1977) and was also a member of the Czechoslovakian Arts Union 1969 to 1975.

PUBLICATIONS Catalog: *Women with Camera*, 1975 (Mus. of Art: San Francisco). Periodicals: *Creative Camera Yearbook*, 1976; *Creative Camera*, Nov 1973, Oct 1971; *Camera*, 1969.

COLLECTIONS San Francisco Mus. of Art. Bibliothèque Nationale, Paris; British Arts Council, Great Britain; Moravian Gall., Brno, Czechoslovakia; Mus. of Decorative Arts, Prague, Czechoslovakia; Side Gall., Newcastle, Great Britain; Victoria & Albert Mus., London.

ADDRESS 63 Blenheim Crescent, London W11, England.

Robert Luther *CHEMIST* Born in 1868 in Moscow of German parents, Luther died in 1945. He attended grammar school in Moscow and studied chemistry at the University of Dorpat. He then studied with Wilhelm Ostwald in Leipzig from 1894 to 1896.

From 1890 to 1891 Luther was an assistant to Prof. Fr. Beilstein in St. Petersburg, Russia, and, in 1896, became an assistant to Ostwald in Leipzig. In 1901 he was named subdirector of the Institute for Physical Chemistry, which Ostwald had established, and from 1906 to 1908 Luther directed the institute. He then became professor of photography and director of the newly established Scientific Photography Institute of the Technische Hochschule in Dresden (until 1936), during which time the Dresden photographic industry grew considerably, due to his leadership. Luther wrote and co-wrote (with such researchers as Goldberg, Weigert and Waentig) numerous articles on his studies in photochemistry.

He was an important organizer of DGPh and its first director in 1930.

Luther introduced a simple method for obtaining the characteristic curve of a photographic material (1910), and later developed the Luther theory concerning the spectral transmission of filters. His other research interests included three-dimensional photography (ca. World War I). In 1931, along with Goldberg, he presented the DIN sensitometry theory to the International Congress for Scientific and Applied Photography at Dresden.

PUBLICATIONS Books: *Quellendarstellungen zur Geschichte der Fotografie*, Wolfgang Baier,

1964; *Memoirs of a Photochemist*, Fritz Wentzel, 1960; *March of Photography*, Erich Stenger, 1958; *Memorial Publication by the Deutsche Gesellschaft für Photographie*, Dec 1955; *Theory of the Photographic Process*, C. E. K. Mees, 1944; *Lexikon für Photographie und Reproduktionstechnik*, G. H. Emmerich, 1910. Anthology: *Photography's Great Inventors*, Louis W. Sipley, 1965. Periodicals: *Photographische Correspondenz*, 1938, 1933, 1928.

David Hollis Lyman   PHOTOGRAPHER · WORKSHOP DIRECTOR · WRITER · EDITOR   Born in Houston, Texas, Lyman is self-taught in photography.

Lyman founded the Maine Photographic Workshop in 1973, and has continued to work as the director. He is also the editor of various magazines—*The Student Skier, Goose City Gazette, Cape Resorter, The Mount Snow Valley News* and *The Transit* (a U.S. Navy monthly)—and has been a freelance photojournalist since 1967. Previously he worked as a U.S. Navy journalist (1965–67), as a staff photographer for Magnum Film Production in Boston (1964–65) and as a freelance photographer (1962–64).

Lyman was the recipient of a U.S. Navy Commendation Medal for coverage of the Seabees' achievements in Vietnam in 1967.

ADDRESS   Maine Photographic Workshop, Rockport, ME 04856.

Mary Ann Bruchac Lynch   WRITER · EDITOR · PHOTOGRAPHER   Born May 8, 1944, in Saratoga Springs, New York, she received an AB in English from Cornell University, Ithaca, New York (1966), and an MA in English from the University of California at Berkeley (1967). She names Robert Heinecken and Margaretta Mitchell as influences. Her brother, Joseph Bruchac, is a poet, editor and writer.

A self-employed media and editorial services consultant since 1976, Lynch has edited and published *Combinations, A Journal of Photography* since 1977. In 1978 she was executive director of Art Resources Open to Women (AROW) in Schenectady, New York, and from 1974 to 1976 she was executive director of the Hawaii Film Board in Honolulu. Lynch served as media specialist for the College of Education, University of Hawaii, Honolulu, in 1973, and from 1968 to 1973 taught English and was an academic advisor at the university.

The photographer belongs to SPE (since 1975), Hawaii Film Board (since 1974), and Image Foundation (of which she was a founding board member in 1975). Lynch received a publication grant from the New York State Council on the Arts in 1979, and grants from the University of Hawaii in 1973 and 1974 and from the National Science Foundation in 1971. She also won the Special Achievement Award in photography from the City and County in Honolulu in 1974.

A screenwriter as well, she wrote *Kohala Una Paa*, produced by Tip Davis Films in Honolulu in 1975.

Working primarily in black-and-white with some hand-coloring, Lynch does documentary studies of people in relation to their cultural ties (such as native Hawaiians, isolated communities, and country places) and autobiographical imagery, often combined with words.

PUBLICATIONS   Anthologies: *Women Artists in America*, J. L. Collins; *Manna-Mana*, Leonard Lueras, ed., 1973.

COLLECTIONS   City of Honolulu, Hawaii; State Fndn. on Culture & the Arts, Honolulu; Sun Valley Ctr. for the Arts & Humanities, Ida.; Univ. of Hawaii, Honolulu.

ADDRESS   Middle Grove Rd, Greenfield Ctr, NY 12833.

George Platt Lynes   PHOTOGRAPHER · PUBLISHER   The American-born Lynes (1907–55) was a self-taught photographer.

Beginning in 1926, his publishing company, As Stable Publications, produced small books by such authors as Gertrude Stein and Ernest Hemingway. He began doing portraiture in the mid-1920s, opening a New York studio in 1933 and spending three years in Hollywood in the mid-1940s. Lynes contributed photographs to such publications as *Town and Country, Harper's Bazaar, Vogue* and *Camera*.

Often collaborating with the painter Pavel Tchelitchev, who would provide unusual backgrounds, Lynes devoted his personal work to male nudes, the ballet and surrealistic still lifes. He made his living doing advertising and fashion images as well as portraits, and sometimes worked with Julien Levy. Working in large format, he "showed striking ingenuity in working out poses and new uses of materials to express the character of the sitter," according to Beaumont Newhall in *The History of Photography*.

PUBLICATIONS   Books: *Surrealism and American Art*, 1931–1947, Jeffrey Weschler, 1977; *The New York City Ballet*, w/Martha Swope, text by Lincoln Kirstein, 1973. Anthologies: *The Photograph Collector's Guide*, Lee D. Witkin & Barbara London, 1979; *The Julien Levy Collection*, Witkin Gallery, 1977; *Photographs from the Julien Levy Collection*, David Travis, 1976; *The*

Magic Image, Cecil Beaton & Gail Buckland, 1975. Catalogs: *Seventeen American Photographers,* Ebria Feinblatt, 1948 (Los Angeles County Mus.); *International Photographers,* 1932 (Brooklyn Mus.: N.Y.); *Murals by American Painters and Photographers,* 1932 (MOMA: NYC). Periodicals: "George Platt Lynes," *Camera,* Feb 1956; *Dance Index,* entire issue, Dec 1944; "Studio Fashions," Philip Andrews, *The Complete Photographer,* 6:26, 1942.

COLLECTIONS Art Inst. of Chicago; IMP/GEH, Rochester; Inst. for Sex Research, Bloomington, Ind.; Metro. Mus. of Art, NYC; MOMA, NYC; N.Y. Pub. Lib., Lincoln Ctr., NYC; Smithsonian Inst., Wash., D.C.

ARCHIVE Magda Vasillov, 325 E 77 St, New York, NY 10021

Danny Lyon PHOTOGRAPHER · FILM MAKER [See plate 101] Born March 16, 1942, in Brooklyn, New York, Lyon received a BA in 1973 from the University of Chicago.

A freelance, Lyon documented the civil rights movement in 1962–64 and was on the staff of the Student Non-Violent Coordinating Committee (SNCC) at the University of Chicago.

He received a Guggenheim Fellowship in 1978 (film) and in 1969 (photography), and NEA grants in 1976 (film), 1974 and 1972 (photography).

Lyon's films include: *Little Boy,* 1977; *Los Niños Abandonados,* 1975; *El Mojado,* 1974; *Llanito,* 1971; and *Social Sciences 127,* 1969.

PUBLICATIONS Monographs: *The Paper Negative,* 1980; *Conversation with the Dead,* 1971; *The Destruction of Lower Manhattan,* 1969; *The Bikeriders,* 1968. Book: *The Movement,* Lorraine Hansberry, 1964. Anthologies: *The Photograph Collector's Guide,* Lee D. Witkin & Barbara London, 1979; *The Magic Image,* Cecil Beaton & Gail Buckland, 1975. Catalog: *Danny Lyon: Ten Years of Photographs,* 1973 (Newport Harbor Art Mus.: Newport Beach, Calif.). Periodicals: *Camera,* Feb 1977; *Creative Camera,* Dec 1969, Sept 1969.

PORTFOLIO *The First Portfolio* (group), 1975 (Apeiron Workshops: Millerton, N.Y.).

DEALER Simon Lowinsky Gall., 228 Grant Ave, San Francisco, Ca 94108.

David Matthew Lyons PHOTOGRAPHER Born March 4, 1954, in Bushmills, Northern Ireland, Lyons studied archaeology and classics at University College in Cardiff, Wales (1972–73), and creative photography at Trent Polytechnic/Derby College of Art and Technology (1973–76) under Thomas Cooper, John Blakemore and Paul Hill.

As of this writing Lyons was photographer/designer of the new Wordsworth Museum at Dove Cottage in Grasmere, Cumbria, primarily responsible for photographs interpreting the poems of William Wordsworth. Previously (since 1976) he was picture editor of *Ballymena Guardian* in Northern Ireland.

From 1977 to 1979 Lyons served as an advisor to the Photography, Film, and Video Panel of the Northern Arts Association of England and, during the same years, held a fellowship in creative photography from Northern Gas/Northern Arts.

Working in 35mm and 6 x 7cm formats, the photographer works in documentary and landscape, his main interests being in atmosphere, surrealism and visual experimentation "without resort to manipulation of subject."

PUBLICATIONS Periodicals: "Against American Domination," July 11, 1979, "Stranger in Shetland," Dec 13, 1978, *Amateur Photographer;* "The Scottish Photography Group," w/Sue Green, Oct 13, 1978, "Photography: The Mass Media and Their Society," Feb 25, 1977, *British Journal of Photography.*

COLLECTIONS Northern Gas, Newcastle-upon-Tyne, England; Scottish Arts Council, Edinburgh; Wordsworth Mus., Trustees of Dove Cottage, Grasmere, Cumbria, England.

REPRESENTATIVE South Yorkshire Photographic Projects, 173–175 Howard Rd, Walkley, Sheffield S63RU, England.

ADDRESS Ballylough, Bushmills, Co. Antrim, Northern Ireland.

Nathan Lyons PHOTOGRAPHER · TEACHER · WRITER · EDITOR Born in 1930 in the United States, Lyons received a BA from Alfred University, Alfred, New York, in 1957.

He currently holds a number of positions: director of Visual Studies Workshop in Rochester, New York (and editor of its publication *Afterimage* since 1972); professor of art and director of the Program in Photographic Studies at State University of New York, Buffalo; and adjunct professor at Rochester Institute of Technology and at SUNY, Albany. Lyons founded VSW in 1969 after having worked at George Eastman House from 1957. He had previously worked as senior photographer for the U.S. Air Force (1950–54).

Lyons founded and served as first chairperson of SPE (1963). He was on the board of directors of Center of the Eye in Aspen, Colorado (1970–73), a member of the CAPS Committee Review Board (1971–75), appointed to New York Governor Carey's Task Force on the Arts (1975), and he was chairperson of the New York State Foundation for the Arts in 1976. Lyons also serves on NEA's Visual Arts Policy Committee.

PUBLICATIONS Books: *Notations in Passing,* 1974; *Vision and Expression,* 1969; *The Persistence of Vision,* 1967; *Photography in the Twentieth Century,* 1967; *Toward a Social Landscape,* 1966; *Aaron Siskind, Photographer,* 1965; "Landscape Photography," vol. 11, 1963, "Photographic Books," vol. 14, 1963, *The Encyclopedia of Photography; Under the Sun* w/Syl Labrot & Walter Chappell, 1960, 2nd ed., 1972. Anthologies: *The Photograph Collector's Guide,* Lee D. Witkin & Barbara London, 1979; *Photographers on Photography,* 1966; *Photography 64,* 1964; *Photography 63,* 1963. Periodicals: "Weston on Photography," *Afterimage: VSW,* 3:1, 1975; *35mm Photography,* spring 1970; *Portfolio,* 16:2, 1971; "The Workshop Idea in Photography," 9:4, 1961, "Form in Art and Nature," 9:1, 1961, "To the Spirit of a Time: In Consideration," 8:2, 1960, *Aperture.*

COLLECTIONS Addison Gall. of Amer. Art, Andover, Mass.; Glendale Coll., Calif.; IMP/GEH, Rochester; MOMA, NYC; Norton Simon Mus. of Art, Pasadena, Calif.; Phoenix Coll., Ariz.; UCLA; Univ. of Ill., Krannert Art Mus., Urbana-Champaign; Univ. of Minn., Minneapolis; Va. Mus., Richmond. Bibliothèque Nationale, Paris; Natl. Gall. of Canada, Ottawa.

ADDRESS Visual Studies Workshop, 31 Prince St, Rochester, NY 14607.

Robert A. Lyons *PHOTOGRAPHER · PRINTER*
Born August 17, 1954, in Malden, Massachusetts, Lyons earned a BA from Hampshire College, Amherst, Massachusetts, and an MFA from Yale University, New Haven, Connecticut.

He is currently a freelance photographer and director of Solio, a workshop for the conservation and restoration of photographic materials (since 1977). In 1976 he printed Roberta Neiman's photographs for her book *Ever Since Durango,* in 1975 he printed a portfolio for Helen Levitt of New York City and in 1972 he served as director of photography for Tel El Gezer Archaeological Excavations in Israel, funded by Hebrew Union College in Cincinnati, Ohio.

Lyons won Ford Foundation grants in 1977 and 1978, and in 1980 he received an NEA Survey Grant.

PUBLICATIONS Periodicals: *Camera,* Sept 1975, Sept 1974.

PORTFOLIO *Pioneer Valley Poems,* 1979 (Hampshire Typothetae: Northampton, Mass.).

COLLECTIONS Portland Mus. of Art, Maine; Princeton Univ. Art Mus., Minor White Estate, N.J.; Yale Univ., Sterling Lib., New Haven, Conn.

ADDRESS 30 N Maple St, Florence, MA 01060.

M

Cynthia MacAdams *PHOTOGRAPHER · ACTRESS* Born in Webster, South Dakota, on September 5, 1939, MacAdams earned a BA in 1961 from Northwestern University in Evanston, Illinois. She began her work as a photographer in 1974, after having devoted time to acting in such films as *Me and My Brother* (1966), *Wild in the Streets* (1968), *The Last Movie* (1970) and *The Mad Bomber* (1972).

She concentrates her images on women—nudes, portraits and all other aspects.

PUBLICATIONS Monograph: *Emergence*, 1977. Periodical: *Camera 35*, June 1978.

DEALERS Graphic Gall., 141 E Alameda, Santa Fe, NM 87501; Marjorie Neikrug Photographica Ltd., 224 E 68 St, New York, NY 10021.

ADDRESS 734 N Sweetzer, Los Angeles, CA 90069.

(Ian) Pirie MacDonald *PHOTOGRAPHER* Born January 27, 1867, in Chicago, MacDonald died April 22, 1942, in New York City. The self-taught photographer took up the medium shortly after quitting school at age eleven, then served an apprenticeship with Forshew Studio in New York from 1883 to 1888.

A freelance for sixty years, MacDonald opened his own studios in Albany, New York, in 1889 and in New York City in 1900. He belonged to the Rotary Club of New York (president, 1926–27), Adirondack Mountain Club (president), Fifth Avenue Association, St. Andrews Society, Pilgrims, Professional Photographers Society of New York (served as first & third presidents), Chambre Syndicat Française de la Photographie, RPS and the Oval Table Society (president in 1937).

MacDonald won dozens of prizes and awards internationally, including: Cramer Grand Prize Cup, numerous medals and awards from the Photographers Association of America, gold medal at the St. Louis Exposition, decorated as Officier d'Académie by the French Republic in 1906,

Palmes Académique first class. He was also very active with the Boy Scouts of America and was elected its chief emeritus in 1920.

A portrait photographer, MacDonald exclusively portrayed men from 1900. His subjects included more than 60,000 prominent members of government and industry, Theodore Roosevelt among them. He posed his sitters without expression, dramatizing them, instead with lighting effects and a soft-focus look.

COLLECTIONS IMP/GEH, Rochester; N.Y. Hist. Soc., NYC. RPS, London.

Gregory Allen MacGregor *PHOTOGRAPHER* [See plate 142] Born February 13, 1941, in La Crosse, Wisconsin, MacGregor earned an MA in Photography/Art in 1970 from California State University, San Francisco. He studied with Jack Wellpot, Don Worth and Jerry Uelsmann. From 1965 to 1967 he studied with Ruth Bernard.

He was assistant professor and co-chairman of the Photography Department at Lone Mountain College in San Francisco (1970–78) and as of this writing is a contributing editor to *Exposure* and *Darkroom Dynamics*. MacGregor is also teaching art at California State University at Hayward. He was a research physicist at the Lawrence Radiation Lab in Berkeley, California, in 1966–70 and an instructor at Wisconsin State University, Whitewater (1964–66).

MacGregor was a member of the American Association of University Professors (1970–78) and has belonged to SPE since 1970. He has been chairman of SPE's western region since 1976.

The central idea in the photographer's work is "the intersection and cross influence of technology." He works in color and black-and-white, often hand-painting and toning the latter prints.

PUBLICATIONS Monograph: *Deus Ex Machina*, 1975. Book: *Darkroom Dynamics*, contr. ed., 1979. Anthology: *Fantastic Photography*, 1979. Catalog: *Fantastic Photography in the USA*, 1978 (Cannon Photo Gall: Amsterdam). Periodicals: *Popular Photography*, June 1980; *Latent Image*, vols. 2 & 3, 1979.

PORTFOLIOS (group) *Out of State*, 1979; *Text & Context*, 1979; *Meridian 122*, 1972.

COLLECTIONS Art Inst. of Chicago; IMP/GEH, Rochester; Graham Nash Cllctn., Los Angeles; Grapestake Gall., San Francisco; Houston Art Mus., Tex.; Middle Tenn. State Univ., Murfreesboro; MOMA, NYC; Norton Simon Mus., Pasadena, Calif.; Oakland Mus., Calif.; San Francisco Mus. of Modern Art; Southwestern Cllctn., Chula Vista, Calif.; Whitney Mus. of Amer. Art, NYC.

DEALERS Equivalents Gall., 1822 Broadway, Seattle, WA 98102; Foster Goldstrom Gall., 257 Grant Ave, San Francisco, CA 94108; O.K. Harris Gall., 383 W Broadway, New York NY 10006; Susan Spiritus Gall., 3336 Via Lido, Newport Beach, CA 92663.

ADDRESS 2829 Eleventh Ave, Oakland, CA 94610.

BUSINESS Lone Mt. College, 2800 Tuck Blvd, San Francisco, CA 94118.

Ernst Mach   SCIENTIST · INVENTOR · WRITER
Born in 1838 in Turas, Persia, Mach died in Munich, Germany, in 1916. He studied science.

In 1861 Mach became a mathematics lecturer at the Vienna technical school and, in 1864, received a full professorship at the University of Graz. Later he became professor of physics at the University of Prague, moving to Vienna in 1894 to become professor of history and theory of inductive science at the University of Vienna. He moved to Munich for the last three years of his life.

Mach was the first to use an electric spark to record a bullet in flight (1884) and, in 1888, proposed the use of time-lapse photography to study the growth of plants, embryos and even human life from cradle to grave. He invented stereo X-rays in 1896, which were produced by Eder and Valenta at the Graphische Lehr- und Versuchsanstalt in Vienna.

PUBLICATIONS Books: *Quellendarstellungen zur Geschichte der Fotografie*, Wolfgang Baier, 1964; *History of Photography*, Helmut & Alison Gernsheim, 1955. Anthology: *Photography's Great Inventors*, Louis W. Sipley, 1965. Periodicals: *Bild und Ton*, 1961; *Photographische Correspondenz*, 1916, 1886, 1884; *Jahrbuch für Photographie und Reproduktionstechnik*, Joseph Maria Eder, 1891, 1888; *Photographische Mittheilungen*, 1884.

Aleksandras Macijauskas   PHOTOGRAPHER
Born May 16, 1938, in Kaunas, Lithuania, Macijauskas completed Kaunas Secondary School in 1962 and later studied with the Faculty of Philosophy at the University of Marxism-Leninism (1976–77).

Macijauskas worked as a photojournalist for the *Evening News* in Kaunas (1967–73) and as a worker in a machine-tool plant in Kaunas (1956–67).

He has been a member of the Photography Art Society of Lithuanian SSR since 1969 and executive secretary since 1973. He has belonged to the Journalist Union since 1971. Macijauskas won the Grand Prize at Golden Eye-73 in Novy Sad, Yugoslavia, and at Ružomberok, Czechoslovakia, in 1969.

PUBLICATIONS Catalogs: *Veterinary Clinic*, 1979 (Phot. Art Soc. of Lith. SSR/Academy of Veterinary Medicine: Kaunas); Catalog, 1977 (Phot. Art Soc. of Lith. SSR); Catalog, 1977 (Mus. Dolnickeho Knut i Brnenska: Brno); *A. Macijauskas*, 1976 (Zwiazek Polskich Artystow Fotografikow); *A. Macijauskas*, 1971 (Photo. Art Soc. of Lith. SSR). Periodicals: *Soviet Photo*, Feb 1978; *Foto Kino Revija*, Oct 1973; *Fotografie*, Jan 1969.

COLLECTIONS Prakapas Photo Gall., NYC; San Francisco Mus. of Modern Art; Univ. of N. Mex. Art Mus., Albuquerque. In France: Bibliothèque Nationale, Paris; Musée Française de la Photographie, Bièvres; Musée Réattu, Arles. Canon Photo Gall., Amsterdam, The Netherlands; Musée D'Art et Histoire, Fribourg, Switzerland; Photography Mus., Šiauliai, Lithuanian SSR.

REPRESENTATIVE Photography Art Society of Lithuanian SSR, Pionierių 8, 232600 Vilnius, Lithuanian SSR, USSR.

ADDRESS Taikos pr. 63-56, Kaunas, Lithuanian SSR, USSR.

Ulrich B. Mack   PHOTOGRAPHER   Born July 19, 1934 in Glasehausen, Eichsfeld, Germany, Mack studied at Hochschule für Bildende Kunste in Hamburg under A. Mahlau (graphic arts), and later studied photography under E. T. Roeger. Married to painter Katrin Mack, he was influenced by Thomas Höpker, Henri Cartier-Bresson, August Sander and A. Renger-Patzsch.

A teacher of photography at Fach Hochschule in Dortmund since 1975, he freelanced from 1971 to 1975. Previously he was a staff photographer at *Stern* magazine in Hamburg (1968–71) and at *Quick* in Munich (1963–66).

Since 1968 a member of DGPh, Mack won the

World Press Award in 1964 at The Hague, Netherlands.

He has made television films for Norddeutscher Rundfunk in Hamburg on fencing and pole-vaulting.

Using Polaroid positive/negative film in all formats, but mainly 8 x 10, the photographer has recorded images of the small German island of Pellworm since 1970.

PUBLICATIONS Books: *Faces & Façades*, 1977 (Polaroid); *Mackpferde* 1966 (Hallwag-Verlag: Bern, Switzerland). Periodicals: *Creative Camera*, Nov 1979; *Leica-Fotografie*, Feb 1978, Feb 1969, May 1965; *Camera*, July 1977, Dec 1975, Oct 1974, May 1973, Oct 1972, Nov 1971, Sept 1971, Nov 1970, Sept 1969; *Du*, June 1970, Dec 1965.

PORTFOLIO *Stille*, 1979 (Westermann Edition: Hamburg).

DEALER Photographers Gall., 8 Great Newport St, London WC2, England.

ADDRESS Isestrasse 111, D2000 Hamburg 13, Germany.

David S. Maclay, Jr. *PHOTOGRAPHER · CARPENTER · SCULPTOR* Born June 27, 1946, in Boston, Massachusetts, Maclay received a BFA from San Francisco Art Institute in 1968. He also attended the School of Boston Museum of Fine Arts from 1964 to 1967.

A member of Camerawork Gallery (since 1979) and Branan Street Cultural Center (1977–78), he was also president of Open Studios South of Market in 1976–79. Maclay has been the recipient of an NEA Grant in 1980 and of The Furgeson Grant from Friends of Photography in Carmel, California, in 1979, and a Southern Educational Communications Association grant in 1976.

The photographer works in black-and-white and color, producing "photographs of sculptural material, usually large-scale, found objects arranged in an architectural format." He also does urban industrial documentation.

DEALER Grapestake Gall., 2876 California St, San Francisco, CA 94115.

ADDRESS 83 Converse St, San Francisco, CA 94103.

Robert MacPherson *PHOTOGRAPHER · SURGEON* The British MacPherson was born in 1811 and died in 1872. A surgeon in Edinburgh, he went to Rome in 1840. Influenced by a medical colleague who was also a photographer, MacPherson developed an interest in the new art

form. His own work soon surpassed that of his friend and fellow countryman, James Anderson.

In 1853 MacPherson obtained a patent from the Minister of Commerce, Art, Industry and Agriculture for a method of making lithographic copies using lithographic stone and steel plates.

He is especially remembered for his photographs of architecture and sculpture.

PUBLICATIONS Books: *The History of Photography*, Helmut & Alison Gernsheim, 1955; *The Resurrection of Jesus Christ*, 1867 (Wm. Blackwood & Sons: Edinburgh & London); *The Perpetual Obligation of the Revealed Moral Law and of the Day of Holy Rest*, 1866 (Edinburgh); *Vatican Sculptures*, 1860 (Chapman & Hall: London).

Wendell Scott MacRae *PHOTOGRAPHER* Born July 10, 1896, in Metropolis, Illinois, MacRae died November 30, 1980, in State College, Pennsylvania. He attended Macalester College in St. Paul, Minnesota (1914–16), and graduated from the University of Minnesota, Minneapolis (1920).

MacRae went to work for the research department of Paramount Studios in Astoria, Long Island City, New York, in 1924, and in 1926 worked for Roland Rogers Productions as a film editor. He moved to Hollywood in 1927 to find work in motion pictures but by 1928 had returned to New York and taken a position with Ewing Galloway, a photo agency. MacRae started his own photography business in 1930, which he operated until 1949. From then until 1960 he was publications production manager for Pennsylvania State University, University Park. From 1960 to 1965 MacRae worked for the university as historical collection curator.

In his review of MacRae's book *Willingly to School*, Christopher Morley wrote: "Here . . . appears a book, mostly photographs, so fresh, so sane, so truly touching and healthy, so beautiful with the beauty of the commonplace . . . who touches it touches the meaning of man" (*Saturday Review*, February 9, 1935).

PUBLICATIONS Books: *America's Williamsburg*, Gerald Horton Bath, 1946 (Colonial Williamsburg); *Willingly to School*, 1934. Catalog: *Photographs: 1927 to 1949*, 1980 (Witkin Gall.: NYC). Periodical: "Wendell MacRae: Expression in Commercial Photography of the 1930s," Charles W. Mann, Jr., *History of Photography 2*, Apr 1978.

COLLECTIONS CCP, Tucson; Metro. Mus. of Art, NYC; New Orleans Mus. of Art; Seagram

Cllctn., NYC; Yale Univ. Art Gall., New Haven, Conn.

DEALER   Wendell S. MacRae Trust, Witkin Gall., Inc., 41 E 57 St, New York, NY 10022.

Alen Brasil MacWeeney   PHOTOGRAPHER Born September 1, 1939, in Dublin, Ireland, MacWeeney began an apprenticeship as a press photographer at age sixteen. His early influences were Anthony Armstrong-Jones, William Klein, Irving Penn and Richard Avedon. MacWeeney came to the United States as the latter's assistant in 1961 and in that year studied at Alexey Brodovitch's Design Lab.

Since 1964 he has done commercial photography, including editorial work for *Esquire, Life, Look, New York Times, Mademoiselle, Time-Life Books* and *Harper's Bazaar.*

A member of ASMP since 1974, MacWeeney belonged to the National Photographic Society of Ireland in 1954–57. He won the American Institute of Graphic Arts Certificate of Excellence in 1972 and Certificates of Merit from the Art Directors Club of New York in 1966, 1970 and 1971.

In addition to his photography, MacWeeney has done fieldwork in Ireland with Artelia Court from 1966 to 1973, collecting and recording Irish folklore, traditional literature and music. In 1968 he recorded an album, *The Traveling People of Ireland.*

Using mainly small- and medium-format black-and-white, the photographer takes "psychological portraits of people, animals, and landscapes," as well as nudes. His personal work has included New York portraits (1970–present), New York subways (1977–78), conflict in Northern Ireland (1971), Irish landscapes (1969–72), Irish tinkers (1965–70), Yeats in Ireland (1965–66), Mexico (1964), and Dublin streets (1963).

PUBLICATIONS   Periodicals: *Aperture* no. 82, 1980; *Leica Photography,* no. 1, 1977; *Techniques Graphiques,* Sept 1969; *Creative Camera,* May 1969; *Modern Photography,* May 1968; *U.S. Camera,* Apr 1967; *Life Gallery of Photography,* Mar 1967; *Asahi Camera,* 1966.

COLLECTIONS   MOMA, NYC; Philadelphia Mus. of Art, Pa.; Va. Mus. of Fine Art, Richmond.

REPRESENTATIVE   Peter Jones, Inc., 125 E 84 St, New York, NY 10028.

ADDRESS   36 Gramercy Park, New York, NY 10003.

Richard Leach Maddox   PHOTOGRAPHER · PHYSICIAN · INVENTOR   Born in 1816 in Bath, England, Maddox died May 11, 1902, in Southampton. He studied medicine in England.

After a world voyage in 1839–40, Maddox settled in Constantinople, Turkey, for several years and practiced medicine. In 1875 he moved to Ajaccio, Corsica, then to Bordighera, Italy, and later returned to England. Maddox was especially interested in photomicroscopy, having been trained in microscopy as a physician. The discomfort caused him by the use of collodion sparked experiments that led to Maddox's recognition as "the inventor of the first serviceable gelatine silver bromide emulsion" (Eder, *History of Photography*). He wrote many articles for the *British Journal of Photography.*

Maddox received numerous awards and medals, among them the Progress Medal of RPS (1901), from the Photographic Society of London (1853) and the Dublin International Exhibition (1865). He was elected to honorary fellowship in the Royal Microscopical Society, and in 1892 was awarded a special grant of more than 500 pounds by photographers from England, France, Germany and America who wished to recognize his achievements.

As a photographer Maddox was most noted for his photomicrographs. He also made portraits and landscape views.

PUBLICATIONS   Books: *The History of Photography,* Helmut & Alison Gernsheim, 1955; *Cassell's Cyclopedia,* 1911, repr. 1973; *History of Photography,* Josef Maria Eder, 1905, repr. 1972; *History of Photography,* W. J. Harrison, 1887. Anthologies: *Early Photographs & Early Photographers,* Oliver Mathews, 1973; *Photography's Great Inventors,* L. W. Sipley, 1965. Periodicals: *British Almanac,* 1902; *British Journal of Photography,* 1902; *Scientific American,* July 26, 1902; "An Experiment with Gelatino-Bromide," *British Journal of Photography,* Sept 8, 1871, repr. in *Image,* Dec 1954.

Shinzo Maeda   PHOTOGRAPHER   Born June 3, 1922 in Tokyo, Maeda graduated in 1943 from Takushoku University.

Since 1967 he has been president of Tankei Co. Ltd., a photo agency. He is a member of the Japan Photographers Society, the Natural Science Photography Society, the Japan Photo Agency Association, and is subchairman of the Nippon Alpin Photograph Society.

Primarily a photographer of Japanese landscapes, he tries to "incorporate the feeling of traditional Japanese painting" in his photographs.

PUBLICATIONS   (All Japan) Books: *The Four Seasons,* 1978 (Internatl. Info. Co.); *The Color of*

Japan, 1976 (Travel Yomiuri Pub.); *Mountains and Rivers of Japan*, 1976, *Poetry of Nature*, 1976, *The Outline of Modern Japanese Prints*, 3 vols., 1975, *Four Seasons of Japan*, 1974 (Mainichi Pubs.).

ADDRESS   Mezon-Aoyama No.402, 2-7-26 Kitaaoyama, Minato-ku, Tokyo 107, Japan.

David Maestro   PHOTOGRAPHER · PAINTER
Born January 18, 1927 in Sarajevo, Yugoslavia, Maestro received a BA in Humanities at Haifa University of Israel in 1976. He also studied at the Art Institute in Israel under the painter Marcel Janco in 1955–58.

Maestro has been head of the Photography Unit at Technion Israel Institute of Technology in Haifa since 1972. Prior to that he worked for Israel TV from 1968 to 1972.

He is a member of RPS, Professional Photographers of America, Professional Photographers of Israel and Painters' and Sculptors' Association in Israel.

PUBLICATIONS   Book: *Israel—The Reality*, 1969. Periodicals: *The British Journal of Photography*, no. 33, 1977, *Annual*, 1976; *Creative Camera International Year Book*, 1976; *Israel Annual of Art Photography*, 1974, 1965.

COLLECTIONS   Jewish Mus. of NYC. In Israel: Israel Mus., Jerusalem; Mus. of Modern Art, Haifa; Tel Aviv Mus. Mus. of Art and History, Fribourg, Switzerland.

ADDRESS   9 Oren St, Haifa, Israel.

William Maguire   PHOTOGRAPHER · TEACHER
Born in Ft. Bragg, North Carolina, on September 8, 1943, Maguire received a BA (1961) and an MAT (1967) from the University of Notre Dame in Indiana. He also earned an MS at the Institute of Design in Chicago (1972), where he studied with Garry Winogrand, Aaron Siskind, Arthur Siegel and Chuck Swedlund.

Since 1975 he has been an assistant professor at Florida International University in Miami. Before that he taught at the University of Miami (1974–75) and at Marymount College in Salina, Kansas (1968–70).

The photographer was awarded an NEA Photographer's Fellowship in 1977 and in 1979, and a Florida Fine Arts Council Artist's Fellowship in 1978.

COLLECTION   St. Petersburg Mus. of Fine Arts, Fla.

DEALER   Gallery Exposures, 357 Alcazar, Coral Gables, FL 33134.

ADDRESS   POB 1015, Homestead, FL 33030.

Christopher Brian Maher   PHOTOGRAPHER
Born June 2, 1952, in New York City, Maher received his BFA in Photographic Illustration from Rochester Institute of Technology, New York, in 1974. He studied nonsilver photography and video at the Visual Studies Workshop in Rochester in 1975, and studied with William Jenkens at the University of Rochester in 1976. Maher completed graduate course work in public visual communications at Southern Illinois University, Carbondale, in 1979.

A freelance photographer, Maher was a photographic technician for the Eastman Kodak Co. in Rochester from 1973 to 1979.

He has been a member of SPE since 1978.

In 1979 the photographer designed a chemical contrast control system for Cibachrome Type A material with a modified P-12 process.

Working primarily in small-format color, he makes photographs that are a "surreal interpretation of relationships through visual juxtaposition."

PUBLICATION   Monograph: *Modified P-12 Process for Cibachrome Contrast Control*, 1979 (self-pub.).

COLLECTION   ICP, NYC.

REPRESENTATIVE   Vision/Art, Box 361, Syosset, NY 11791.

ADDRESS   7703 Camino Real, Apt A-108, Miami, FL 33143.

Tony Maine   PHOTOGRAPHER   Born October 20, 1941, in Detroit, Michigan, Maine earned a BA in 1963 from Eastern Michigan University, Ypsilanti.

A freelance photographer, he most recently worked on a photography project for the University of California. In 1980 he received an NEA Folk Arts Grant.

PUBLICATIONS   Monograph: *Two Eggs Any Style*, 1976. Periodicals: *Off the Wall*, July 1979; *Village Voice*, Aug 1977.

COLLECTIONS   K-Mart Cllctn., Troy, Mich.; Security Savings Bank, Oakland, Calif.

REPRESENTATIVE   Magnum Photos Inc, 15 W 46 St, New York, NY 10036.

DEALER   O. K. Harris Gall., 383 W Broadway, New York, NY 10012.

ADDRESS   22527 Morley, Dearborn, MI 48124.

Jay Maisel   PHOTOGRAPHER   Born January 18, 1931, in Brooklyn, New York, Maisel studied painting with Joseph Hirsch in 1949, then at the Cooper Union in New York City in 1952. He received his BFA from Yale University, New Haven, Connecticut, in 1953, studying color with

Josef Albers. He took photography courses with Herbert Matter in 1954 and with Alexey Brodovitch in 1956.

A freelance photographer since 1954, he taught color photography at Cooper Union (1969–74) and at the School of Visual Arts (1967), both in New York City.

He received ASMP's Outstanding Achievement in Photography Award in 1978 and Cooper Union's Saint-Gaudens Medal in 1977.

PUBLICATIONS Books: *San Francisco*, 1979, *New York*, 1976, *Jerusalem*, 1976, Time-Life Great City Series; *Photography Year 1975*; *Snake River Country*, 1974; *Baja California*, 1972; *The Greatest Jewish City in the World*, 1972. Anthology: *Photographers on Photography*, 1978. Catalog: *Harlem on My Mind*, 1968. Periodicals: "Sunlight Art," *Life*, Oct 1979; interview, *American Photographer*, June 1979; *Photo*, Nov 1978; Apr 1978, Mar 1977, Aug & June 1976, June 1975, Dec 1974; *Camera 35*; *Modern Photography*, Sept 1972, Oct 1970, Apr 1960; *Camera*, Nov 1969; *Popular Photography*, Mar 1969; *Photo Techniques*, May 1966.

ADDRESS 190 The Bowery, New York, NY 10012.

Christopher E. Makos PHOTOGRAPHER Born January 4, 1948, in Lowell, Massachusetts, Makos studied at the City College of New York. The major influences on his work have been by Man Ray, Weegee and Brassaï.

Currently Makos is art director for a new photo book on Debbie Harry and Chris Stein. He was previously art director for the Andy Warhol photo book *Exposures* in 1979, and has been staff photographer for *Interview* magazine since 1975.

In 1978 Makos was the recipient of the Bonn Photo Award in Bonn, Germany.

PUBLICATIONS Monograph: *White Trash*, 1977. Book: *Terrorist Chic*, Michael Selzer, 1979. Anthologies: *Contact Theory*, 1980; *SX-70 Art*, 1979. Catalog: *Makos*, 1976 (Luciano Anselmino: Milan, Italy). Periodical: *Photo*, Feb 1978.

DEALER G. Ray Hawkins, 7224 Melrose Ave, Los Angeles, CA 90060.

ADDRESS 227 Waverly Pl, New York, NY 10014

Adál Maldonado
See Adál

Mati Maldre PHOTOGRAPHER · TEACHER Born April 3, 1947, in Geestacht, Germany, Maldre received a BA in Design (1969) from the University of Illinois at Chicago Circle, where he studied with Joseph Jachna, Hans Schaal, Robert Stiegler and Wayne Boyer. He then took an MS in Photography from the Institute of Design at Illinois Institute of Technology, Chicago, where he studied with Aaron Siskind, Arthur Siegal and Charles Swedlund (1972).

Since 1972 Maldre has been an associate professor of art at Chicago State University. He has also taught photography at Beverly Art Center School of the Arts, Chicago (since 1973). In 1974 he was a photographer and lab technician for Encyclopaedia Britannica in Chicago.

Maldre belongs to SPE, CAA, IMP/GEH, VSW, Chicago Center for Contemporary Photography and Friends of Photography. He won a Chicago State University Grant for Faculty Research in 1977, an Illinois Humanities Council Grant in 1976, and five Encyclopaedia Britannica educational assistance grants between 1969 and 1972. He also received a Merit Award from Radius 76 at Burpee Museum, Rockford, Illinois, and the Grand Award from Photo Images 76 in Springfield, Illinois.

In 1969 Maldre edited the documentary film *The Paint In*, sponsored by the Mayor's Beautiful Chicago Committee and aired on PBS in Chicago.

Maldre produces large-format Cibachrome prints, and uses color-separation filters while photographing architecture to highlight "the documentation of time and the recording of motion."

PUBLICATIONS Catalogs: *Photography: Smile of the Birdie*, 1979 (Art Inst. of Chicago, Junior Mus.); *Illinois Photographers*, 1978 (Ill. State Mus.: Springfield); *First Light*, 1975 (Humboldt Arts Council: Eureka, Calif.).

COLLECTIONS Chicago State Univ. Gall.; Humboldt Arts Council, Eureka, Calif.; Ill. State Mus., Springfield; Kalamazoo Inst. of the Arts, Mich.

ADDRESS 3036 W 114 Pl, Merrionette Park, IL 60655.

Joe Maloney PHOTOGRAPHER Born in Worcester, Massachusetts, on October 28, 1949, Maloney earned a BA in 1976 from Ramapo College, Mahwah, New Jersey.

A freelance photographer since 1976, he taught color printing at the International Center of Photography in New York City in 1979 and has been a shipping clerk at Pace Editions in New York City since 1978. He worked at Light Gallery in New York City (1976–78) as a student intern and part-time shipping clerk.

Maloney won an NEA Photographer's Fellowship in 1979.

He works in large-format color, primarily shooting landscapes.

PUBLICATIONS Catalogs: *Presences: The Figure and Manmade Environments*, 1980 (Albright College: Reading, Pa.); *American Landscape Photography 1860–1978*, 1979 (Mus. Die Neue Sammlung: Germany). Periodical: *Modern Photography*, June 1980.

COLLECTIONS IMP/GEH, Rochester; Lehigh Univ., Bethlehem, Pa.; Univ. of Colo., Denver; Univ. of Mass., Amherst. Australian Natl. Gall., Melbourne; Mus. Die Neue Sammlung, Munich, Germany.

DEALER Light Gall., 724 Fifth Ave, New York, NY 10019.

ADDRESS 145 E 26 St, New York, NY 10010.

Felix H. Man *PHOTOGRAPHER · JOURNALIST · AUTHOR · EDITOR* [See plate 55] Born Hans Baumann on November 30, 1893, in Freiburg, Breisgau, Germany, Man studied art at Freiburg University, and later in Munich and Berlin about 1912.

His photographs have appeared in *Harper's Bazaar*, *Life* and *Sports Illustrated*, among other journals. He edited *Europaeische Graphic* (1962–75) and was a contributing photographer to *Picture Post* in London (1938–45, 1948–51), *Weekly Illustrated* London (1934), *Berliner Illustrierte* (1932–33) and *Munchner Illustrierte Presse* (1929–32).

A member of DGPh, Man received the Verdienstkreuz First Class from the Federal Republic of Germany in 1968 and the 1965 Kulturpreis of DGPh as a pioneer of pictorial journalism.

Known for his pictorial essays, the photographer worked originally with an Ermanox and later with a Leica.

PUBLICATIONS Monograph: *Felix H. Man—Photo Classics IV*, Helmut Gernsheim, ed., 1972 (London). Books (text only): *The Complete Graphic Work of Graham Sutherland 1922–68*, 1971 (Monaco); *Artist Lithographs, a World History from Senefelder to the Present Day*, 1970; *Lithography in England, 1801–10*, 1962; *Eight European Artists*, 1954; *150 Years of Artists' Lithographs*, 1953 (Heinemann: London). Anthology: *The Magic Image*, Cecil Beaton & Gail Buckland, 1975.

COLLECTIONS IMP/GEH, Rochester; Univ. of Tex., Gernsheim Cllctn., Austin. Natl. Gall. of Australia, Canberra; Natl. Portrait Gall., London.

ADDRESSES 30 via Giubbonari, 00186 Rome, Italy; 306 Keyes House, Dolphin Sq, London SW1, England.

David Mandel *PHOTO ARCHIVIST · PHOTOGRAPHER* Born March 19, 1947, in Port Arthur, Texas, Mandel received a BA in Psychology from Brandeis University, Waltham, Massachusetts (1969), and an MFA in Photography from the University of Nebraska, Lincoln (1976). He names Egon Schiele, George Fanning and George Talbot as major influences.

Since 1977 he has been photo archivist for the State Historical Society of Wisconsin and has also taught in the communications program at University of Wisconsin, Extension Division. In 1977 he taught photography and history of photography at Beloit College, Beloit, Wisconsin.

Mandel received an NEA Survey Grant in 1980 and a Wisconsin Humanities Committee Grant in 1979.

His photographic work is large-format, documentary, monumental landscapes. He does research in the archival preservation of historical photographs and also researches nineteenth-century photography, especially itinerant landscape photographers in the Midwest.

COLLECTIONS Barry Coll., Miami, Fla.; Burpee Art Mus., Rockford, Ill.; State Hist. Soc. of Wisconsin, Madison; Univ. of Nebr., Sheldon Memorial Art Gall., Lincoln.

ADDRESS 1104 Garfield St, Madison, WI 53711.

Michael S. Mandel *PHOTOGRAPHER · FILM MAKER* Born in Los Angeles on November 24, 1950, Mandel received his BA in Philosophy from California State University, Northridge, in 1972 and his MFA in Photography from San Francisco Art Institute in 1974. He names Ed Sievers and Robert Heinecken as mentors.

In 1979 he became a photography instructor at Hartnell College, Salinas, California, and in 1976 taught photography at the San Francisco Museum of Modern Art and at University of California Extension in San Francisco.

Mandel, with Larry Sultan, received several grants: from the California Arts Council, 1978; an NEA Photographer's Fellowship, 1976; and an NEA Works of Art in Public Places grant, 1975. Alone he won an NEA Photographer's Fellowship in 1973, grants from the U.S. Department of Interior, 1972, and San Fernando Valley State College Foundation, 1970.

His "foremost interest is the influence of photography on the development of culture."

PUBLICATIONS Books (self-publ.): *S.F. Giants: An Oral History*, 1979; *Evidence*, w/Larry Sultan, 1977; *Baseball-Photographer Trading Cards*, 1975; *How to Read Music in One Evening*, w/

Larry Sultan, 1974; *Seven Never Before Published Portraits of Edward Weston*, 1974; *Myself: Timed Exposures*, 1972.

COLLECTIONS Atlantic Richfield Co., Los Angeles; CCP, Tucson; Mus. of Fine Arts, Houston, Tex.; Univ. of Alaska, Geophysical Inst., Fairbanks; UCLA, Frederick S. Wight Gall.

ADDRESS 111½ Riverview St, Santa Cruz, CA 95062.

Ann Mandelbaum PHOTOGRAPHER · TEACHER
Born July 16, 1945, in Wilkes-Barre, Pennsylvania, Mandelbaum earned a BA from Connecticut College, New London, in 1967, and an MA in Media Studies from Antioch College, Ohio, in 1976.

Since 1977 she has taught photography both at the Pratt Institute of Brooklyn, New York, and the New School for Social Research in New York City.

She is a member of SPE.

Mandelbaum's work is traditional 35mm silver images concentrating on gesture and body language. She makes some use of macrophotography to interpret body parts.

PUBLICATIONS Anthologies: *Insights*, 1978; *Women Photograph Men*, 1977; *Women See Men*, 1977. Periodical: *Popular Photography Annual*, 1979.

DEALER O. K. Harris Gall., 383 W Broadway, New York, NY 10012.

ADDRESS 389 4 St, Brooklyn, NY 11215.

Thomas Manly PHOTOGRAPHER · INVENTOR
Manly died in 1932 in England.

He worked on the development of ozotype, a pigmented gelatin process that he patented in 1899. He also developed the ozobrome method of producing carbon pictures from bromide prints, patented in 1905, which allowed them to be produced in other than daylight.

PUBLICATIONS Books: "Ozobrome" & "Ozotype," *Cassell's Cyclopaedia of Photography*, 1911, repr. 1973; *Lessons in ozotype . . . Pigmented gelatine printing . . . pigmented gum printing*, 190-? (Ozotype Co.: London); *Ozotype, the new carbon printing process without transfer, actinometer or safe edge*, Amateur Photographic Lib., no. 20, 1900 (Hazell, Watson & Viney: London). Anthology: *Early Photographs & Early Photographers*, Oliver Mathews, 1973.

Jimmie Mannas FILM MAKER · PHOTOGRAPHER
Born September 15, 1941, in Newark, New Jersey, Mannas received degrees from New York Institute of Photography in 1960, School of Visual Arts (in film editing) in 1964, and New York University (in film and television) in 1969. He lists as mentors Roy DeCarava and Robert Frank.

Since 1976 Mannas has been director of a film cooperative entitled New Images. The managing director of Gillham Productions (1974–76), he also served as consultant to the Ministry of Information in Guyana (1971–74), and was director of the photography department of Youth in Action in Brooklyn, New York (1965–67).

As of this writing Mannas was the president of the International Black Photographers. He has also been a member of the Association of Video and Filmmakers since 1977. Awarded NEA grants for film-making in 1977 and 1978, he was also the recipient of an American Film Institute Fellowship in 1968 and a grant from the New York State Council on the Arts in 1970. Mannas also created two feature-length films: in 1976 he produced, directed and wrote *Aggro Seizeman*, and in 1971 he was producer and cameraman for *The Fight*, which was the first Ali–Frazier fight film.

PUBLICATIONS Periodicals: *Black Photographers Annual*, 1978, 1977, 1966, 1965, 1963.

COLLECTIONS Black History Lib., Schomburg Cllctn., NYC; Howard Univ., Communications Dept., Wash., D.C.; New York State Office Bldg., NYC.

ADDRESS 394 Waverly Ave, Brooklyn, NY 11238.

Leopold D. Mannes CHEMIST · PHYSICIST · MUSICIAN Born in 1899 in New York, Mannes died in 1964. His father conducted a music school, and he was trained as a musician, with photography as a hobby. After attending New York's Riverdale School (ca. 1916) he went to Harvard University in Cambridge, Massachusetts, earning a degree in physics in 1920.

Mannes was working as a professional musician in New York when he began photographic experiments in 1921 with fellow musician Leopold Godowsky, Jr., whom he had met at the Riverdale School. They first used a kitchen and a bathroom as laboratories, renting space in office buildings in 1924 and 1929. Their earliest attempts to improve color processes involved the use of optical devices and they patented a special lens movement. With the aid of C. E. K. Mees at Eastman Kodak, they experimented with direct color plate and film processes, and their ideas took a new direction when they learned of the Fischer theory of color couplers. Thanks to Dr. Mees, they continued their experiments at Eastman Kodak's Rochester laboratories from 1931 to

1939. In 1965 they received the Progress Medal of the RPS.

The most important result of their work was the development of Kodachrome film in 1935, and their basic research led to Kodacolor film and prints (1941), Ektacolor film (1949) and Eastman color negative 35mm film (1949).

PUBLICATIONS Books: *From Dry Plates to Ektachrome Film*, C. E. K. Mees, 1961; *A Half Century of Color*, Louis W. Sipley, 1951; *History of Color Photography*, Joseph S. Friedman, 1944. Anthology: *Photography's Great Inventors*, Louis W. Sipley, 1965. Periodicals: *Photographic Journal*, 1964; *Bild und Ton*, 1961; *Journal of the Photographic Society of America*, Oct 1955.

Constantine Manos   *PHOTOJOURNALIST*
Born in Columbia, South Carolina, Manos developed an interest in photography at age thirteen through a school camera club in his hometown. He earned a BA in English from the University of South Carolina, Columbia.

Manos became a working professional photographer at age fifteen, covering the efforts of Martin Luther King, Jr., to desegregate public transportation in Montgomery, Alabama. At nineteen he became the official photographer for the Boston Symphony Orchestra. In 1964 Manos joined Magnum, and his photos subsequently appeared in *Look, Life, Esquire* and *Sports Illustrated*. He now lives in Boston.

Manos' *Look* picture essay, "Funeral of a Soldier," won the New York Art Directors Club award in 1966. In 1974 he was commissioned to produce mural-size photographs of the people of Boston for the Bicentennial Pavilion, "Where's Boston?" which are on display at Boston's Faneuil Hall.

PUBLICATIONS Books: *A Greek Portfolio*, 1972; *Portrait of a Symphony*, 1961.
COLLECTION MOMA, NYC.
REPRESENTATIVE Magnum Photos, Inc, 15 W 46 St, New York, NY 10036.

Man Ray   *PHOTOGRAPHER · PAINTER · FILM MAKER* Born August 27, 1890, in Philadelphia, Pennsylvania, Man Ray (Emmanuel Rudnitsky) died November 18, 1976, in Paris, France. Self-taught, he may have attended classes at the Academy of Art in New York City (1908–12). He was introduced to photography by Alfred Stieglitz and was strongly influenced by Marcel Duchamp and the Dada movement, as well as by Cézanne, Picasso, Brancusi, Robert Henri and George Bellows.

Prior to 1920 Man Ray did odd jobs in advertising while he freelanced as a painter. From 1921 to 1939 he was a portrait and commercial photographer in Paris, then moved to Hollywood, where he continued his art, taught photography and lectured for ten years. He returned to Paris in 1950 and devoted himself to his art.

Man Ray received the gold medal from the Venice Foto Biennale in 1961 and the DGPh Cultural Award in 1966.

He rediscovered the photogram, calling it a Rayogram or Rayograph, and innovated aesthetic uses of solarization. He experimented with fusing photography and painting. Among the first to combine objects and paintings, he became known for his assemblages. He also developed and was noted for an automatic technique of painting that he called "natural painting."

Man Ray made several avant-garde films, including *L'Etoile de Mer* (1928–29), *Emak Bakia* (1927), *Anemic Cinema* (1924), *La Retour à la Raison* (1923) and *Les Mystères de Chateau de Dé*. He also directed parts of Hans Richter's film *Dreams That Money Can Buy* (1944).

Called "the poet of the darkroom" by Jean Cocteau, Man Ray pioneered the aesthetic use of such darkroom techniques as photograms, solarization, granulation, distortion and other manipulations. These he used with "a keen sense of mockery" in order to "poke fun at the serious ideas of art long before op and pop art were accepted categories," according to *The New York Times*. First a Dadaist, then a Surrealist, in his later years the artist said, "If I contradict myself, if I move from style to style, so does nature."

PUBLICATIONS Books: *Man Ray: The Rigour of Imagination*, Arturo Schwarz, 1977; *Man Ray's Photography*, Janus, 1977 (Electa: Milan, Italy); *Man Ray*, Roland Penrose, 1975; *Man Ray*, 1973; *Man Ray: 60 Years of Liberties*, Arturo Schwarz, 1971; *Ogetti d'Affezione*, 1970 (Einaudi: Turin, Italy); *Rayograph*, Giulio Carlo Argan, 1970; *Les Invendables*, ltd. ed., 1969 (Galerie Alphonse-Chave: Vence, France); *Man Ray*, intro. by Jules Langsner, 1966; *Man Ray: Portraits*, 1963; *Self-Portrait*, 1963, French ed., *Autoportrait*, 1964; *12 Rayographs/1921–1928*, 1963; *Les Main Libres*, 1937; *La Photographie n'est pas l'art*, foreword by André Breton, 1937; *Facile*, poems by Paul Eluard, 1935 (G.L.M.: Paris); *Photographies, 1920–1934*, 1934, essays & poems by Breton, Eluard, Duchamp, Tzara & Ray, repr. as *Man Ray Photographs 1920–1934*, intro. by A. D. Coleman, 1975; *Kiki Souvenirs*, 1929 (Henri Broca: Paris); *Revolving Doors*, 1926; *Man Ray*, Georges Ribemont-Dessaignes, 1924 (Gallimard: Paris); *Les Champs Délicieux:*

Album de Photographies, preface by Tristan Tzara, 1922 (Société Générale d'Imprimerie et d'Edition: Paris); *A Book of Diverse Writings*, 1915. Anthologies: *The Photograph Collector's Guide*, Lee D. Witkin & Barbara London, 1979; *Photography Rediscovered*, David Travis Anne Kennedy, 1979; *The Julien Levy Collection*, Witkin Gall., 1977; *Photographs from the Julien Levy Collection, Starting with Atget*, David Travis, 1976; *The Magic Image*, Cecil Beaton & Gail Buckland, 1975; *Photography Year 1974*, Time-Life Series, 1974; *Looking at Photographs*, John Szarkowski, 1973; *Great Photographers*, 1971, *The Studio*, 1971, Time-Life Series. Catalogs: *Man Ray*, 1974 (Galleria il Fauno: Italy); *Man Ray*, 1974 (Alexander Iolas Gall.: NYC); *Man Ray*, intro. by Alain Jouffroy, 1972 (Musée National d'Art Moderne: Paris).

PORTFOLIOS *Mr. and Mrs. Woodman*, 1979 (Unida: The Netherlands); *Electricité*, intro. by Pierre Bost, 1931 (La Compagnie Parisienne de Distribution d'Electricité: Paris).

COLLECTIONS Art Inst. of Chicago; IMP/GEH, Rochester; MOMA, NYC; New Orleans Art Mus., La.; Oakland Mus., Calif.; R.I. School of Design, Mus. of Art, Providence; Univ. of N. Mex. Art Mus., Albuquerque; Yale Univ. Art Gall., New Haven, Conn. Provinciaal Mus. voor Kunstambachten, Antwerp, Belgium.

Louis-Amédée Mante *INVENTOR · PHOTOGRAPHER · CHEMIST · MUSICIAN* Born in 1826 in France, Mante died in 1913 in Seine-Port near Paris. His son-in-law, Edmond Goldschmidt, who died in 1933, was a photographer and Mante's collaborator.

Self-taught as a musician, photographer and chemist, Mante built his own darkroom and laboratory at age sixteen. By 1844 he was a bassist with the orchestra of the Opéra in Paris and he remained a professional musician for fifty years. In the photography field, he recently has been named as the possible inventor of the autochrome. Several of his recently uncovered images were evidently taken prior to 1900, years before the Lumières patented their autochrome plate in 1904.

Mante experimented with several photographic and photomechanical processes, resulting in a number of inventions: a process for using false ivory as a photographic support for the negative (1851); one of the first successful attempts at mechanical photoreproduction (1853); refinements of heliographic engraving (1860s, early 1870s), a process for phototypography (reported to the Société Française de la Photographie in 1872); and possibly, production of a trichrome color photograph (1856, thirteen years prior to its official recognition). Much of his photographic work was done in collaboration with Goldschmidt. Several books and articles on Mante are currently being researched.

It is difficult to attribute the autochromes specifically to Mante or Goldschmidt, although it seems that Goldschmidt's sophistication and self-consciousness (he was a bit of a dandy), as well as his travels to Algeria and the south of France, identify certain images as his. Mante's landscapes, on the other hand, "are devoid of pictorial references and effects; instead, they are sharply focused, and intense in color" (A. S. Godeau, *Portfolio*, Jan/Feb 1981).

ARCHIVE Mme. Jacqueline Millet, c/o Editions Créatis, Paris, France.

Martin Manz *PHOTOGRAPHER · FILM MAKER* Born May 15, 1954, in Freiburg, West Germany, Manz studied art at the Professional College (Fach Hochschule) in Cologne, where he also worked in photography. After that he worked in a photo studio for advertising and fashion. He has been studying at the German Academy for Film and Television in Berlin since 1978. His photographic work has been influenced by several film makers, particularly Wim Wenders.

Manz is currently a freelance photographer and film maker.

PUBLICATIONS Catalogs: *Deutsche Fotografie nach 1945*, 1979 (Fotoforum: Kassel); *In Deutschland*, 1979 (Landesmuseum: Bonn). Periodicals: *Camera*, May 1980, Apr 1978.

COLLECTION Landesmuseum, Bonn, West Germany.

ADDRESS Postrasse 3, D-7814 Breisach am Rhein, West Germany.

Robert Mapplethorpe *PHOTOGRAPHER* Born November 4, 1946, Mapplethorpe studied at the Pratt Institute from 1963 to 1970.

The photographer was awarded a CAPS grant in 1978.

The subjects of Mapplethorpe's works are portraits, still lifes, nudes and landscapes.

PUBLICATIONS Catalogs: *Jurka Gallery*, 1979 (Amsterdam); *Chrysler Museum*, 1978 (Norfolk, Va.). Periodicals: *Picture Magazine*, no. 12, 1979; interview, Inge Bonde, *Printletter*, no. 19, Jan/Feb 1979; *Créatis*, no.7, 1978; *Camera*, Sept 1977.

COLLECTIONS Metro. Mus. of Art, NYC; MOMA, NYC.

DEALER Robert Miller Gall., 724 Fifth Ave, New York, NY 10019.
ADDRESS 24 Bond St, New York, NY 10012.

Elli Marcus *PHOTOGRAPHER · GRAPHOLOGIST*
Born in 1899 in Berlin, Marcus died on August 8, 1977, in New York City.

She worked as a theatrical photographer in Berlin until forced to flee the Nazis around 1931–33. She opened a studio in Paris, but then had to escape Nazi occupation again and went to the United States in March 1941. Here she continued her photography until 1957, when she became a full-time graphologist.

Her work appeared in numerous German periodicals in the 1920s and 30s, such as *Welt Spiegel*, *Berliner Illustrierte Zeitung*, *Die Dame* and *Elegante Welt*. In the U.S. she was frequently published in *U.S. Camera* during the 1940s and 50s.

Marcus was primarily a theatrical photographer, claiming to be the first female photographer to work on the stage. She captured such notable theatrical personages as Max Reinhardt, Marlene Dietrich and Bertolt Brecht. She also did some fashion and advertising work, always using silver prints. Her later interest in graphology led her to experiment with enlarged photographs of the handwriting of her subjects, combining them in her portraits through photomontage.

PUBLICATION Anthology: *The Photograph Collector's Guide*, Lee D. Witkin & Barbara London, 1979.

COLLECTIONS IMP/GEH, Rochester; Natl. Portrait Gall., Wash., D.C.; Princeton Univ. Art Mus., N.J.

Etienne-Jules Marey *PHYSIOLOGIST · INVENTOR · PHOTOGRAPHER* Born March 5, 1830, in Béaune, France, Marey died May 15, 1904, in Paris. He received his M.D. in Paris in 1859 and was influenced by the photographic inventions of French astronomer Jules Janssen (1824–1907).

Marey began his career as an assistant surgeon in a Paris hospital in 1855. He then studied human and animal physiology and the animated motion of the body, later becoming professor of medicine at the University of Paris. In 1867 Marey was appointed to the chair of natural history at Collège de France.

A member of the Academy of Medicine (1872) and the Academy of Sciences (1876), he was for many years the president of the Société Française de Photographie, as well as the founder of the Institute for Physiology (Institut Marey) in Paris.

He was the inventor of the "chronophotograph" (1888), from which modern cinematography was developed, and some considered Marey and not the Lumière brothers the true father of cinematography. But since Marey's apparatus used no transparent film, no perforation of film strips, no intermittent forward movement, and an insufficient picture size, he cannot be so considered, according to many others.

The inventor also devised a photographic gun (1882), equipped with a sight and a clock movement, for taking serial pictures. Josef Eder *(History of Photography)* tells us that "he invented a series of registering appliances to serve as exact aids independent of the individuality of the observer, for the analysis of very complicated and fleeting physiological functions; for instance, the heart action, with the aid of the sphygmograph (an instrument for recording graphically the features of the pulse and variations in blood pressure. Invented by Marey, it is still used today, with some modifications), the gait of horses and dogs, the flight of birds, and so forth." In addition, he constructed an instrument for making serial photomicrographs and, subsequently, also high-frequency-current serial negatives, with electric arc lamps, at the rate of 120 pictures a second.

Marey made many improvements on his chronophotograph, some with the assistance of George Demeny (1850–1917), who worked for him from 1882 to 1894. He used a new serial apparatus, the photochronograph (as he later called it), in which a strip of negative paper wound continuously from spool to spool.

Because his report to the Academy of Sciences in 1890 made public the principle of animated photography, he was denied the patent he applied for in 1893 since French law at that time denied ownership of any invention made public before application for a patent.

Marey employed serial photography systematically in all his researches after 1882. With his chronographic devices he photographed jellyfish, fish, insects and the movements of blood corpuscles in the capillary vessels. His photographs of humans in motion are characterized by their being draped in either black suits with metal strips or white lines and dots drawn along their limbs as they passed in front of black backdrops. Sometimes the costumes used were half white and half black so that only one side of the body was visible. His motion studies were particularly remarkable in that his invention allowed the serial to be imprinted on one negative. In addition to his inventions, Marey wrote extensively on the circulation of the blood, cholera, terrestrial and aerial locomotion, experimental physiology and graphic methods of physiology.

PUBLICATIONS Books: *The History of Photography*, Beaumont Newhall, 1964; *Cassell's Cyclopedia*, Bernard E. Jones, ed., 1911, repr. 1973; *History of Photography*, Joseph Maria Eder, 1904, repr. 1972; *Institut Marey*, 1902 (Paris); *La Chronophotographie*, 1899 (Paris); *Le Mouvement*, 1894, Eng. ed. 1895 (RPS: London); *La Photographie du Mouvement*, 1892 (Paris); *Le vol des oiseaux*, 1890 (Masson: Paris); *La Locomotion et la Photographie*, 1886 (Paris); *Du Mouvement dans les Fonctions de la Vie*, 1868 (Paris). Anthologies: *The Invented Eye*, Edward Lucie-Smith, 1975; *Pioneers of Photography*, Aaron Schark, 1975; *Early Photographs & Early Photographers*, Oliver Mathews, 1973. Pamphlets: *Fonctions et organes*, 1902 (Paris); *Exposition l'Histoire de la Chronophotographie*, 1900 (Paris Universal Exhibition, Musée Retrospectif); *Nouveaux développements de la chronophotographie*, 1897 (Imprimerie Nationale: Paris); *Conditions de la rapidité des images dans la chronophotographie*, 1886 (Paris); *Développement de la méthode graphique par l'emploi de la photographie*, 1885 (Paris); *Emploi de la photographie instantanée pour l'analyse des mouvements chez les animaux . . .* , 1882 (Paris); *La Méthode Graphique dans les Sciences Expérimentales et principalement en Physiologie et en Médecine*, no, 19, 1878 (Paris). Periodicals: "Marey—Physiologist and First Cinematographer," A. R. Michaelis, Dec 2, 1955, "The Marey Museum," A. R. Michaelis, Feb 10, 1956, *British Journal of Photography*; "The History of Chronophotography," *Smithsonian Institution Annual Report*, 1901; "La Chronophotographie," *Annales*, 1:3, 1893 (RPS: London).

COLLECTIONS Kingston-upon-Thames Mus., England; Lib. of the Graphischen Lehrund Versuchsanstalt, Vienna; Marey Inst., Paris; Musée des Beaux-Arts, Béaune, France; RPS, London.

ARCHIVES Musée des Beaux-Arts, Béaune, France; Institut Marey, Paris.

John Margolies PHOTOGRAPHER · LECTURER · CRITIC Born May 16, 1940, in New York City, Margolies received his BA from the University of Pennsylvania, Philadelphia, in 1962 and his MA from the Annenberg School of Communications in Philadelphia in 1964.

Margolies was a visiting instructor at the University of California, Santa Barbara, in 1972; a resident thinker at the American Federation of Arts, New York City (1969–70); and assistant ed-

itor of *Architectural Record* (1964–68). He was on the executive board of the Architectural League of New York (1968–70 and 1976–79).

Margolies received a Guggenheim Fellowship (architectural criticism) in 1978; grants from NEH (1978) and the New York Council for the Humanities (1977) through the Gallery Association of New York State, Hamilton, for the Catskill project; NEA project grants in 1972, 1973, and 1977; a New York State Council on the Arts Architecture Program grant in 1976; and a grant from the Graham Foundation/Walker Art Center Program in Architectural Criticism in 1970.

In addition to still photography, Margolies has worked on commercial television productions and produced several videotapes: *Telethon: The Television Environment* (projected photographs and videotape collage), *House Tour* (black-and-white, 1974), and *Resorts of the Catskills* (color, 1977).

Margolies produces color slides and prints about twentieth-century commercial, vernacular architecture, including roadside architecture and mountain and seaside resorts.

PUBLICATIONS Monograph: *Resorts of the Catskills*, 1979. Catalog (text only): *Recorded Activities*, 1970 (Moore Coll. of Art: Philadelphia, Pa.). Periodicals: "Remembering What We've Forgotten," *Show* magazine, Aug 6, 1970; "Three New Theaters," *Art in America*, May/June 1970. Text only: "TV—The Next Medium," *Art in America*, Sept/Oct 1969; "Triennale—It's Not Only What You See But How You See," June/summer, 1968, "Michael Steiner—From Stark Simplicity to Sensual Complexity," Apr 1968, art reviews & criticism, May/summer, Sept/Oct 1967, Dec/Jan, Feb, Mar 1968, *Arts Magazine*; "Denver: Museum for Architect and Curator," *Arts Yearbook 9*, 1967. Reviews: *Artforum*, Dec 1977; "TV: The Whitney Shows New 'Projected Video,' " John J. O'Connor, *N.Y. Times*, June 6, 1975; "Architecture of Joy," Douglas Davis, *Newsweek*, Nov 2, 1970.

COLLECTIONS Everson Mus. of Art, Syracuse, N.Y.; N.Y. Pub. Lib., NYC.

ADDRESS 222 W 72 St, #3-A, New York, NY 10023.

Richard Margolis PHOTOGRAPHER Born June 10, 1943, in Lorain, Ohio, Margolis earned a BS in Photo-illustration from Kent State University, Kent, Ohio, in 1969 and an MFA from Rochester Institute of Technology, New York, in 1978.

An instructor at Nazareth College, Rochester, since 1978, he has also done commercial photography since 1968.

Margolis is a member of SPE. He won a CAPS grant in 1978.

Working in black-and-white, the photographer produces "subjective or personal landscapes, emphasizing form and composition as symbolist elements."

PUBLICATIONS Book: *Photography—How-to Guide*, 1979. Catalogs: *130 Years of Ohio Photography*, 1979; *Some 20 Odd Visions*, 1978. Periodicals: *American Photographer*, Aug 1979; *Creative Camera Annual*, Dec 1978; *Picture Magazine*, Apr 1977; *Fotofolio*, Jan 1976. Reviews: *Saturday Review*, Owen Edwards, Apr 28, 1979; *Village Voice*, Apr 16, 1979.

COLLECTIONS Addison Gall. of Amer. Art, Andover, Mass.; IMP/GEH, Rochester; L/C, Wash., D.C.; MOMA, NYC; Yale Univ. Art Gall., New Haven, Conn. Bibliothèque Nationale, Paris; Victoria & Albert Mus., London.

DEALERS Foto, 492 Broome St, New York, NY 10013; Kathleen Ewing Gall., 3020 K St, Washington, DC 20007.

ADDRESS 113 Cypress St, Rochester, NY 14620.

Mary Ellen Mark PHOTOGRAPHER · TEACHER Mark earned a BFA in Painting and Art History (1962) and an MA in Photojournalism (Annenberg School of Communications, 1964) from the University of Pennsylvania in Philadelphia.

A self-employed photographer, Mark has taught at Ansel Adams Workshop in Yosemite (1978), Maine Photographic Workshop in Rockport, Maine (1974–78), and Apeiron Photography Workshop in Millerton, New York (1975). She has also lectured at MIT in Cambridge, Yale University in New Haven, Connecticut, the New School in New York City and Brooks Institute in Santa Barbara, California.

Mark won an NEA Fellowship in 1979 and in 1977, a commission for the Bell System Photography Project in 1978, a CAPS grant in 1977, a U.S. Information Agency grant to lecture and exhibit in Yugoslavia in 1975 and a Fulbright Scholarship to photograph in Turkey in 1965.

PUBLICATIONS Monographs: *Ward 81*, 1979; *Passport*, 1974. Books: *The Photojournalist: Two Women Explore the Modern World and the Emotions of Individuals*, w/Annie Liebovitz, 1974; *America in Crisis*, 1969. Anthologies: *American Images*, 1979; *Photography Year 1977*, Time-Life Series; *Great Themes*, 1971, *Photographing Children*, 1971, Time-Life Series; *Vision and Expression*, Nathan Lyons, ed., 1969. Periodicals: *Life*, July 1980; *American Photographer*, June 1978; *Photo*, Aug 1980, Apr 1978, June 1977; *Camera*,

Sept 1977; *British Journal of Photography Annual*, 1972.

COLLECTIONS Bibliothèque Nationale, Paris; Natl. Gall. of Australia, Canberra, New South Wales.

REPRESENTATIVE Magnum Photos, Inc, 251 Park Ave So, New York, NY 10010.

ADDRESS 143 Prince St, New York, NY 10012.

Tom Marotta PHOTOGRAPHER · JOURNALIST · AUTHOR Born in Paris, France, on March 24, 1943, Marotta studied fine arts at the School of Visual Arts in New York City in 1966 and later took a BS in Photography from City College in New York (1975). He received a BA in English from Hunter College in New York City in 1978. His mother, Florence Vicari, is a designer.

A freelance photographer since 1959, Marotta is a contributing editor to *Lens* and *Lens on Campus* magazines in Garden City, New York.

He won the Goodman Fiction Writing Award from City College in 1977 and a Polaroid educational grant in 1976.

Marotta describes himself as a "reportage photographer" who tries to portray people "as they are, without props or posing." He uses mainly a 35mm lens "so that I can get my subject involved with the camera."

PUBLICATIONS Monograph: *For They Are My Friends*, 1975. Anthology: *Who Needs Parks*, 1974. Periodicals: *Camera 35*, Mar 1979; *Lens on Campus*, Nov, Feb 1979; *Lens*, Nov/Dec, Sept/Oct 1978, Sept/Oct, Jul/Aug 1977; *35mm Photography*, spring 1977; *Photo*, winter special, 1977–78; *Popular Photography*, spring 1978; *Camera*, Sept 1975.

COLLECTIONS L/C, Wash., D.C.; SHADO Gall., Portland, Ore. Bibliothèque Nationale, Paris.

REPRESENTATIVE FPG, 251 Park Ave So, New York, NY 10010.

ADDRESS 680 West End Ave, New York, NY 10025.

Simon Nevile Lewellyn Marsden PHOTOGRAPHER · WRITER Born December 1, 1948, in Lincoln, England, Marsden learned photography by assisting a professional photographer. He also studied at Ampleforth College in England and the Sorbonne University in Paris.

A freelance, Marsden received British Arts Council Awards in 1975 and 1976. As of this writing he was working on photographs and stories concerning hauntings and legends in England.

PUBLICATIONS Periodicals: *Creative Camera*,

Apr 1980; *Modern Photography*, Feb 1979; "Perspectives on Landscape," *British Image No. 5*, 1978; *The British Journal of Photography Annual*, 1976; *Creative Camera Annual*, 1976; *The British Journal of Photography*, Jan 1975.

COLLECTIONS N.Y. Art Alliance Inc., NYC; Univ. of Nebr., Lincoln; Sam Wagstaff Cllctn., NYC. Arts Council of Great Britain, London; Bibliothèque Nationale, Paris; Victoria & Albert Mus., London.

ADDRESS Flat 3, 294 Fulham Rd, London SW10, England.

Adolphe Alexandre Martin   PHOTOGRAPHER · TEACHER · INVENTOR   Living from 1824 to 1896 in France, Martin studied with Léon Foucault.

A Parisian college professor, Martin originated the ferrotype, or tintype—images produced on black lacquered tinned iron by the wet-collodion process. He described the process in 1852 and 1853 in memoirs he presented to the Académie des Sciences. Martin also experimented in the production of guncotton (pyroxylin), and, in aiding the Paris Observatory, he constructed "a reflection mirror of greater dimensions than had been achieved before that time" (Eder). He also developed a procedure for silver-plating mirror surfaces with invert sugar and silver nitrate, and he was concerned with the calculation of photographic lenses.

PUBLICATIONS Books: *History of Photography*, Josef Maria Eder, 3rd ed., 1905, repr. 1945; *Détermination des courbures de l'objectif grand-anulair pour vues*, 1892 (Gauthier-Villars: Paris); *Sur une méthode d'autocollimation directe des objectifs astronomique . . . .*, 1881(?) (Gauthier-Villars: Paris); *Photographie nouvelle*, 1852 (Chevalier: Paris). Anthology: *Early Photographs & Early Photographers*, Oliver Mathews, 1973. Periodicals: *La Lumière*, 1853, 1852; *Bulletin Société Française de Photographie*, 1896.

Josiah Martin   PHOTOGRAPHER · TEACHER   Martin lived from 1843 to 1916. He established the first model training school in Auckland, New Zealand, and was president of Auckland Institute and Museum in 1889. Martin edited *Sharland's New Zealand Photographer* for several years ca. 1901 and maintained a partnership for some time with W. H. T. Partington in Auckland.

A member of the Geological Society in London (ca. 1883), Martin won a gold medal at the Paris Exhibition in 1889.

The photographer made nature studies of the area surrounding Auckland and other parts of New Zealand, paying particular attention to the thermal region. His work was in the traditional landscape style of the day.

PUBLICATIONS Book: *The Terraces of Rotomahana*, poem by Frank Cowan, 1885 (Wilson & Horton; Geological Society: London). Anthology: *19th Century New Zealand Photographers*, John B. Turner, 1970 (New Zealand).

COLLECTION Auckland Inst. and Mus., New Zealand.

Paul Martin   PHOTOGRAPHER   Born in Alsace-Lorraine, France, in 1864, Martin died in England in 1944. He attended school in London from 1873 to 1878, then at Ecole Gosserez, Châlons-sur-Marne, France, from 1878 to 1880. He was apprenticed to a wood-engraver at the age of sixteen for three years, and took up photography as a hobby in 1884.

Martin began to do serious work in 1892 and with H. G. Dorrett, opened a photographic studio that they ran from 1899 to 1926. He wrote articles for various journals of the day as well as presenting lectures during which he used his photographs for slide shows. He was a member of the West Sussex Photographic Society and The Linked Ring.

Martin was a pioneer of what we know today as "candid photography," using a Facile camera that he kept concealed to avoid making his subjects self-conscious. He hand-held the camera to capture spontaneous genre views of life in London, Brittany, Cornwall and Switzerland. He was also one of the earliest experimenters in night photography. While Martin was known to have made carbon and platinum prints as well as lantern slides, his chief process was printing silver prints from gelatin dry-plate negatives. In his later years he did some pictorial work, but he is remembered for his snapshot-type images of Victorian life.

PUBLICATIONS Books: *Paul Martin: Victorian Photographers*, Roy Flukinger et al, 1977; *Victorian Candid Camera: Paul Martin 1864–1944*, Bill Jay, intro. by Cecil Beaton, 1973 (David & Charles, Newton Abbot, England); *Victorian Snapshots*, 1939, repr. 1973. Anthologies: *The Invented Eye*, Edw. Lucie-Smith, 1975; *Early Photographs & Early Photographers*, Oliver Mathews, 1973 (Reedminster Pubs., London); *Great Photographers*, Time-Life Series, 1971. Periodical: "Paul Martin," *Album*, 7, 1970.

COLLECTIONS Art. Inst. of Chicago; Univ. of Tex., Gernsheim Collctn., Austin. In England: Kodak Mus., Harrow; Radio Times Hulton Picture Lib., London; RPS, London; Victoria & Albert Mus., London.

Martin Martinček *PHOTOGRAPHER · LAWYER*
Born January 30, 1913, in Liptovský Sv. Peter, Slovakia, Czechoslovakia, Martinček's wife is the painter Ester M. Šimerová-Martinčeková. He received a Doctor Juris (1937) from the Komeneský University in Bratislava, Slovakia, and has continued to study photography privately since 1932.

Martinček has been a professional photographer since 1961 in Liptovský Mikuláš, Slovakia. Previously he was director of the Museum of Literature and History at Liptovský Mikuláš (1957–61), a lawyer in Komunálny podnik, Liptovský Mikuláš (1951–57), and a judge in Bratislava, Slovakia (1937–51).

A member of the Slovak Union of Artists since 1957, he won the Excellence de la Féderation de l'Art Photographique in Berne, Switzerland, from the International Federation of Photographic Art, and was named Artist of Merit by the Czechoslovak government, both in 1970. He also was awarded the Golden Medal by the Musée des Nations International Competition at Neuchâtel, Switzerland, in 1958, and was the subject of a Czechoslovakian film entitled *M. Martinček, a Man with a Camera*, made in Bratislava (1968).

Working in 24 x 30cm up to 50 x 60cm format in black-and-white, he photographs "the people and landscape of Slovakia, wood structures, water, ice, stone, earth and sunlight."

PUBLICATIONS Monographs: *Martin Martinček*, Karel Dvořák, 1979 (Press Photo: Prague); *Martinček*, Ľudovít Hlaváč, 1978 (Osveta, Martin: Slovakia); *Martin Martinček*, Zora Rampáková, 1976 (FAMU: Prague). Books: *The Mountain*, 1978 (Osveta, Martin: Slovakia); *Hill People*, 1975 (Osveta, Martin: Slovakia); *Lights in Waves*, 1972 (Pallas: Bratislava); *People in the Mountains*, 1969 (Tatran: Bratislava); *The Undiscovered World*, 1964 (Tatran: Bratislava); *The Uninvestigated World*, 1964 (Artia: Prague). Periodicals: *Praha*, Nov 1978; *Foto Magazin*, Oct 1978, Aug 1970; *Fotografie*, Sept 1975; *Photo-Ciné-Revue*, No. 12, 1971; *Fotomüvészet*, Mar 1968; *Rolleigrafie*, June 1965; *Photography*, Nov 1964, July 1963; *Foto*, No. 12, 1961 (Budapest).

COLLECTIONS In Czechoslovakia: Banská Bystrica Gall.; Liptovský Mikuláš Gall.; Natl. Gall. Prague; Poprad Gall.; Slovak Natl. Gall., Bratislava.

ADDRESS Kukučínova 9, 031 01 Liptovský Mikuláš, Czechoslovakia.

Michael Martone *PHOTOGRAPHER · AUTHOR*
Born November 8, 1941, in New York City, Martone studied photography at the High School of Performing Arts in New York City in 1956. His father was WPA artist Jack Martone.

As of this writing Martone was a lecturer in the New Masters Series at the Smithsonian Institute (since 1979). He was artist-in-residence at Syracuse University, New York, in 1978. In 1977 he was a graduate lecturer at the Maryland Institute of Fine Arts in Baltimore.

Martone was recipient of an NEA photography grant in 1975. His work is either autobiographical and/or surreal or one-of-a-kind chemically manipulated images. A. D. Coleman of the *Village Voice* (April 29, 1971) says: "He is a master of postexposure manipulation."

PUBLICATIONS Monograph: *Dark Light*, 1974. Anthologies: *Light Readings*, A. D. Coleman, 1979; *The Grotesque in Photography*, A. D. Coleman, 1977. Catalog: *The Multiple Image*, 1972 (MIT & Univ. of Rhode Island). Periodical: *Creative Camera*, Sept 1973.

COLLECTIONS Harvard Univ., Fogg Mus., Cambridge, Mass.; High Mus. of Art, Atlanta Ga; MOMA, NYC.

ADDRESS 342 E 15 St, New York, NY 10003.

Charles Marville *PHOTOGRAPHER* Marville was born and died in France (1816–ca. 1880). Little is known about his life besides his work of documenting the buildings of Paris for the French government's Commission for Monumental Historical Monuments.

Although he was also a painter and lithographic artist, Marville is remembered for his photographs of old Paris. Beaumont Newhall (in *History of Photography*) says: "Marville's pictures of streets and houses, worn by human use but emptied of people, have the melancholy beauty of a vanished past." The photographer made calotypes, as well as salt and albumen prints from collodion wet plates.

PUBLICATIONS Books: *Une Invention du XIXe siècle*, Bernard Marbot, 1976 (Bibliothèque Nationale: Paris); *The History of Photography*, Beaumont Newhall, 1964. Anthologies: *The Photograph Collector's Guide*, Lee D. Witkin & Barbara London, 1979; *The Magic Image*, Cecil Beaton & Gail Buckland, 1975; *Early Photographs & Early Photographers*, Oliver Mathews, 1973; *French Primitive Photography*, André Jammes & Robert Sobieszek, intro. by Minor White, 1969.

ALBUMS (all by Louis-Désiré Blanquart-Evrard: Lille, France): *Etude et Paysages*, 1854–55, *Bords du Rhin*, 1854, *Variétés photographiques*, 1854–55, *Art religieux*, 1854–55, *Souvenirs photographiques*, 1853–54, *Etudes photographiques*,

1853–54, *Paris photographique*, 1852–54, *Mélanges photographiques*, 1852–54, *Album photographique de l'artiste et de l'amateur*, 1851.

COLLECTIONS IMP/GEH, Rochester; Univ. of N. Mex. Art Mus., Albuquerque; Witkin Cllctn., NYC. In Paris, France: Bibliothèque Nationale; Société Française de Photographie; V. Barthélemy Cllctn.

Ivan Massar PHOTOGRAPHER Born June 12, 1924, in Columbus, Ohio, Massar studied at the Art Center School in Los Angeles, California, in 1947 and in Paris at the Académie André Lhote in 1949. Working with Roy Stryker, his mentor, he documented the "Story of Steel," coal mining and riverboat transportation in 1951–52.

A freelance photojournalist and industrial photographer, Massar has worked on assignment for most major magazines since 1950. His work also appears in several Time-Life books and the *World Book Encyclopedia.*

Massar is a member of ASMP.

The photographer works with a 35mm camera for his photojournalism and documentary images.

PUBLICATIONS Books: *The Illustrated World of Thoreau,* Howard Chapnick, ed., 1974; *The Illustrated Leaves of Grass,* 1971.

COLLECTIONS Metro. Mus. of Art, NYC; Smithsonian Inst., Wash., D.C.

REPRESENTATIVE Black Star Pub. Co., 450 Park Ave So, New York, NY 10016.

ADDRESS 296 Bedford St, Concord, MA 10742.

Jay B. Mather PHOTOJOURNALIST Born April 22, 1946, in Denver, Colorado, Mather received a BA from the University of Colorado, Boulder (1969). He names Robert Rhode, Charles Freestone and David Cupp as major influences.

Since 1977 he has been a staff photographer for the *Courier-Journal and Louisville Times* and previously was a staff photographer for the *Denver Sentinel* (1972–77).

Mather has been a member of NPPA since 1972. He was named Southern Photographer of the Year in 1978 and runner-up Newspaper Photographer of the Year in the Pictures of the Year Competition of 1976.

His major projects during his newspaper career include essays on Colorado plains dirt farmers, the demise of the Amtrak Floridian passenger train, Cambodian refugees and a Mennonite community in Kentucky.

PUBLICATIONS Books: *Photojournalism 2* and *Photojournalism 5.* Anthology: *The Family of Woman,* 1979.

ADDRESSES Courier-Journal & Louisville Times, 525 W Broadway, Louisville, KY 40202; 310 Monohan Dr, Louisville, KY 40207.

Margrethe Mather PHOTOGRAPHER · ANTIQUE DEALER Born in 1885 in Salt Lake City, Utah, Mather died in 1952 in Glendale, California. She was influenced by the anarchist philosopher Emma Goldman, whose lectures she attended.

Prior to taking up photography Mather, an orphan, earned her living as a prostitute. An accomplished photographer by the time she met Edward Weston, in 1912, she influenced him greatly, and they became partners in a studio in the Hollywood-Pasadena area. Her photographs appeared in various photography periodicals, and her image appeared frequently in Weston's photographs. From 1934 until her death Mather dealt in antiques and occasionally photographed friends.

Working with an 8 x 10 view camera, Mather almost always contact-printed her silver and platinum photographs. She made portraits of friends and celebrities, such as Sadakichi Hartmann, Johan Hagemeyer and, of course, Weston. She was a classicist, tending toward patterned images and the abstract. She never used a light meter in her work.

PUBLICATIONS Monograph: *Margrethe Mather,* 1979. Books: *Edward Weston: Fifty Years,* Ben Maddow, 1973; *The Daybooks,* 2 vols., Edward Weston, 1971. Anthologies: *The Photograph Collector's Guide,* Lee D. Witkin & Barbara London, 1979; *Photography Rediscovered,* David Travis & Anne Kennedy, 1979; *California Pictorialism,* Margery Mann, 1977.

COLLECTIONS CCP, Tucson; IMP/GEH, Rochester; MOMA, NYC; New Orleans Mus. of Art; San Francisco Mus. of Modern Art; Univ. of N. Mex. Art Mus., Albuquerque.

ARCHIVE CCP, Tucson.

Elizabeth Matheson PHOTOGRAPHER · EDITORIAL ASSISTANT Born in 1942 in Hillsborough, North Carolina, Matheson received an AB in 1964 from Sweet Briar College, Sweet Briar, Virginia. She began photographing in 1972 and studied at Penland School, North Carolina, in 1973 with John Menapace.

Matheson has worked in the publications office of Duke University, Durham, North Carolina, since 1976. From 1966 to 1969 she was a copywriter for Harper & Row, Publishers, in New York City.

The photographer won an NEA grant through the Southeastern Center of Contemporary Arts in 1977.

Working in small- and medium-format black-and-white, Matheson photographs straight urban and suburban landscapes.

PUBLICATIONS Anthology: *Women See Men*, 1977. Periodicals: *Latent Image*, IV, 1978, III, 1976, II, 1975.

COLLECTIONS Duke Hospital, Durham, N.C.; N.C. Mus. of Art, Raleigh; N.C. Natl. Bank, Durham; Southeastern Ctr. of Contemporary Art, Winston-Salem, N.C.

ADDRESS 1204 Roosevelt Dr, Chapel Hill, NC 27514.

G(ästgifvar) Eric Matson *PHOTOGRAPHER* Born June 16, 1888, in Nås Parish in Dalarna, Sweden, Matson died on December 9, 1977, in the United States. His wife and partner, Edith Yantiss, died in 1966.

Matson's family emigrated to Palestine in 1896 to join a small American commune founded in 1881. In 1898 Wilhelm II of Germany visited the colony, and the American Colony Photo Department was formed to meet the demand for photographic mementos of the state visit. It was there that Matson and his Kansas-born wife-to-be worked and learned. They married in 1924, and took over the photo department in 1934, renaming it the Matson Photo Service. Terrorist activities caused them to flee to the United States in 1946, where they continued working together until Edith Matson's death.

Matson successfully used oil paints for hand-coloring and pioneered the use of both the Finlay and Lumière color processes. Five thousand of his photographs have survived, showing the dramatic changes that swept over Palestine and the Middle East during World War I. An exceptional series documents the disastrous locust plagues of 1915 and 1930. The photographer's meticulous attention to technique, artistic quality and technological innovation, according to Rune Hassner *(The Middle East)*, should place him "among the foremost documentary photographers of his time."

PUBLICATIONS Book: *The Middle East*, 1980. Periodicals: "The Matson Collection," George S. Hobart, *The Quarterly Journal of the Library of Congress*, Jan 1973; "Multi-colored Cones of Cappadocia," Dec 1939, "The Rose-red City of Rock," Feb 1935, *National Geographic*.

ARCHIVE L/C, Matson Cllctn., Documentary Photography, Prints and Photographs Division, Wash., D.C.

Gordon Matta-Clark *PHOTOGRAPHER · SCULPTOR · FILM MAKER* Born in 1945 in New York City, Matta-Clark died in August 1978 in Nyack, New York. He studied for a year at the Sorbonne in Paris, and received an MA in Architecture from Cornell University, Ithaca, New York.

A freelance artist, Matta-Clark saw his works widely exhibited under the sponsorship of various individuals, museums and other groups in the United States and Europe. In 1974 he was an artist-in-residence at Art Park in Lewiston, New York.

A Guggenheim Fellowship recipient in 1977, the artist also won two CAPS grants (for sculpture, 1976, and in multimedia, 1974) and an NEA fellowship (1975).

From 1971 to 1977 Matta-Clark made sixteen short films in both 16mm and super-8, some in black-and-white and some in color. They include *Tree Dance*, 1971, *Automation House*, 1972, and *Conical Intersect, Paris*, 1975. These experimental efforts attempt to document visually spaces not otherwise accessible to the viewer.

Matta-Clark's photography initially grew out of his desire to document his architectural sculptures. At first producing straight large-format black-and-white (later, Cibachrome) prints, he eventually began cutting his negatives and rearranging them before printing in order to best illustrate his concepts of "expanding space."

PUBLICATIONS Books: *Art Park: Program in Visual Arts*, 1976; *Splitting*, 1974; *Walls Paper*, 1973. Anthology: *Twentieth Century Artists*, Sam Hunter, 1972. Periodicals (reviews): *Artforum*, Apr 1978, Nov 1975, April Kingsley, Jan 1973, Robert Pincus-Witten, Sept 1970; Giancarlo Politi, *Flash Art*, June 1976; Dale McConathy, *Vogue*, Mar 1970. Other periodicals: *Artforum*, July/Aug 1977, "P.S. 1's Inaugural Installations," Nov 1976; "Manhattan Seven: Gordon Matta-Clark," Hayden Herrera, July/Aug 1977, "The Great Divide: 'Anarchitecture' by Gordon Matta-Clark," Al Brunnel, Sept 1974, "The Alchemist and the Phenomenologist," Cindy Nemser, Mar 1971, *Art in America*; "Documenta 77," *Stern*, June 1977.

COLLECTION Mus. of Contemporary Art, Chicago.

DEALER Young Hoffman Gall., 215 W Superior St, Chicago, IL 60610.

ARCHIVE Jane Crawford, 20 E 20 St, New York, NY 10003.

Herbert Matter *PHOTOGRAPHER · DESIGNER* Born in Engelberg, Switzerland, in 1907, Matter studied painting at the Ecole des Beaux-Arts in

Geneva from 1925 to 1927. The following two years he studied under Fernand Léger and Amédée Ozenfant at the Académie Moderne in Paris. There he became interested in photography and design.

Currently living in the United States, Matter worked with the Graphics Program for the New York Studio School (1964–78). From 1958 to 1968 he worked as design consultant for the Guggenheim Museum in New York City and the Museum of Fine Arts in Houston. In 1954–55 he did design work for the New Haven Railroad. Matter was a professor of photography at Yale University, New Haven, from 1952 to 1976. Prior to that (1946–66) he was a design consultant for Knoll International. When he first arrived in the United States (New York, 1936), he freelanced, doing many assignments for *Harper's Bazaar* and *Vogue*. Before that he worked as a photographer and designer at Studio Deberny & Peignot in Paris while simultaneously freelancing, then returned to Switzerland (1932–36).

In 1932 the Swiss Office of Traffic in Zurich awarded him a plaque.

In 1949 he made a color film on the works of Calder for the Museum of Modern Art in New York City. He also worked on documenting the works of Giacometti from 1960 to 1977. Yale University showed a retrospective of Matter's work in 1978.

PUBLICATION Anthology: *Photographie als Kunst*, 1979.

PORTFOLIO *13 Photographs: Alberto Giacometti and Sculptures*, 1978 (Ives-Sillman, Inc.: Hamden, Ct.).

Klaus Peter Matthes PHOTOGRAPHER Born February 19, 1929, in Bargteheide, Holstein, Germany, Matthes attended Ahrensburg High School until 1949, then until 1952 did advanced studies in commerce and science in Hamburg, Germany. His wife, Mia Gautheir Matthes, is a photographer and his collaborator.

A freelance photographer, Matthes previously worked in decoration and window display in Montreal (1955–58) and in the advertising department of Deutsche Maizenawerke AG in Hamburg (until 1955).

Matthes received a Canada Council of Arts grant in 1969, and in 1965 was named Photographer of the Year by Quebec Provincial Photographers Association.

PUBLICATIONS Books (all w/Mia Matthes): *Musique d'été*, 1976 (Editions Fides: Montreal); *Le Corps secret*, 1969 (Editions du Jour: Montreal); *Québec et l'Ile d'Orléans*, Gatien La-

pointe, 1968 (Editions du Pélican: Quebec); *Bonjour Québec*, 1967 (McClelland & Stewart: Toronto).

ADDRESS 4582 Des Cageux, Chomedey, Laval, Quebec H7W 2F7, Canada.

Mia Gautheir Matthes PHOTOGRAPHER Born May 19, 1920, in Montreal, Canada, Matthes studied at the Ecole Normale, Mont Laurier, Quebec (1934–38). Her husband, Klaus, is a photographer and her collaborator.

A freelance photographer since 1958, she previously taught fashion design at Ecole Ménagère Provinciale and designed window displays.

Matthes was elected president of the Montreal section of Quebec Provincial Photographers Association in 1965, and in 1969 received a Canada Council of Arts grant.

PUBLICATIONS Books (all w/Klaus Matthes): *Musique d'été*, 1976 (Editions Fides: Montreal); *Le Corps secret*, 1969 (Editions du Jour: Montreal); *Québec et l'Ile d'Orléans*, Gatien Lapointe, 1968 (Editions du Pélican: Quebec); *Bonjour Québec*, 1967 (McClelland & Stewart: Toronto).

ADDRESS 4582 Des Cageux, Chomedey, Laval, Quebec H7W 2F7, Canada.

Neil Maurer PHOTOGRAPHER Born January 12, 1941, in New York City, Maurer earned a BA in Sociology from Brown University, Providence, Rhode Island (1962), and an MFA in Photography from Rhode Island School of Design, Providence (1975).

As of this writing an assistant professor of art at the University of Texas at San Antonio (since 1978), he previously taught at University of Bridgeport (Connecticut), Ocean County Community College, Toms River, New Jersey (1977–78), and Corcoran School of Art, Washington, D.C. (1975).

Maurer is a member of SPE and a recipient of a Fulbright-Hays photography grant for work in Peru (1975).

COLLECTIONS Chase Manhattan Bank, NYC; Corcoran Gall. of Art, Wash., D.C.; MOMA, NYC; R. I. School of Design Mus. of Art, Providence; Smithsonian Inst., Wash., D.C.

DEALER Prakapas Gall., 19 E 71 St, New York, NY 10021.

ADDRESS 723 E Woodlawn, San Antonio, TX 78212.

Holly Maxson PAPER CONSERVATIONIST · PHOTOGRAPHER Born November 11, 1952, in Abington, Pennsylvania, Maxson earned a BFA in

Photography/Printmaking from Tyler School of Art in Philadelphia (1975). She names André Kertész as a major influence.

In 1979 she became conservation technician at the Historical Society of Pennsylvania in Philadelphia, and previously served as assistant to the director of the Photopia Gallery in Philadelphia (1978). Maxson was associate editor and sales representative for Contact Press Images, Inc., in New York City in 1977 and director of photography for Dickinson College in Pennsylvania in 1976.

The photographer won first place in the Central Pennsylvania Festival of the Arts in 1976 and 1975.

PUBLICATION Anthology: *Women Photograph Men*, 1977. Periodical: *Popular Photography Annual*, 1980.

COLLECTIONS Alfred Stieglitz Cllctn., Metro. Mus. of Art, NYC; Philadelphia Mus. of Art, Pa.

ADDRESS 2012 Spruce St, Philadelphia, PA 19103.

James Clerk Maxwell PHYSICIST Born November 13, 1831, in Edinburgh, Scotland, Maxwell died on November 5, 1879, in Cambridge, England. He studied for three years at the University of Edinburgh, and earned a mathematics degree in 1854 from Trinity College in Cambridge.

In 1856 Maxwell became a professor of natural philosophy at Marischal College in Aberdeen, Scotland, and, in 1860, went to King's College in London. He later became the first Cavendish Professor of Physics at Cambridge.

By 1855 Maxwell had discovered a system for photographically recording colors and reproducing them by making separation negatives through red, green and violet glasses and projecting them from "magic lanterns" onto a screen. Around 1860 he collaborated with Dr. Thomas Sutton on putting his theories into practice, and in 1861 he demonstrated his process before the Royal Society of Edinburgh, which later awarded him their Rumford Medal.

The outstanding physicist of his day, Maxwell made tremendous achievements in electricity and magnetism. Besides contributions to color vision and production of one of the first color photographs, he developed a theory of Saturn's rings, worked out the mechanics and kinetic theory of gases, and showed that light is an electromagnetic wave.

PUBLICATIONS Books: *Quellendarstellungen zur Geschichte der Fotografie*, Wolfgang Baier, 1964; *History of Color Photography*, Joseph S. Friedman, 1944; *History of 3-Color Photography*, E. J. Wall, 1925; *Book of Photography*, Paul N. Hasluck, 1905; *La Photographie Animée*, Eugene Trutat, 1899; *Theory of Heat*, 1877; *Treatise on Electricity and Magnetism*, 1873. Anthology: *Photography's Great Inventors*, Louis W. Sipley, 1965. Periodicals: *Journal of Photography Science*, 1961; *Photoengravers' Bulletin*, Mar 1939; *British Journal of Photography*, 1902, 1861; *Photo Miniature*, no. 183; *Penrose's Annual*, 1901; "Theory of Compound Colours," 1860, "Experiments on Colour," 1855, *Transactions of the Royal Society* (Edinburgh).

John Jabez Edwin Mayall PHOTOGRAPHER Born 1810 in Philadelphia, Pennsylvania, Mayall died 1901 in England.

In addition to lecturing on chemistry, Mayall ran a daguerreotype studio with Marcus A. Root from 1842 to 1846 in Philadelphia. He moved to London shortly thereafter, first managing the studio of Antoine Claudet. In April 1847 he opened the American Daguerreotype Institution, later opening an additional studio in Brighton, Sussex.

A daguerreotypist, Mayall managed to make his portrait studio one of the most successful, on a commercial basis, in London. He produced many albumen prints which were the basis for engravings appearing in *Illustrated Times* and *Illustrated London News*, a series illustrating the Lord's Prayer, and a large-format collection for the Great Exhibition of 1851. From his studio he produced mainly *cartes de visite* and cabinet portraits.

PUBLICATIONS Book: *Tallis' History and Description of the Crystal Palace and the Exhibition of the World's Industry in 1851*, 1851. Anthologies: *The Magic Image*, Cecil Beaton & Gail Buckland, 1975; *Early Photographs & Early Photographers*, Oliver Mathews, 1973 (Reedminster: London).

John Clark Mayden PHOTOGRAPHER Born May 16, 1951, in Baltimore, Maryland, Mayden earned a BA in Fine Arts, Politics and Government from Ohio Wesleyan University, Delaware, Ohio (1974), and attended Graduate University of Baltimore School of Law, Maryland (1978). He names Lawrence Siegall, Lawrence Fink and Harold Jones as mentors.

As of this writing Mayden was hired to participate in a photographic survey of the State of Maryland. He has been a photography instructor at Dundalk Community College, Baltimore, since 1975. In 1974–75 he was center director and photography instructor for the Urban Services Cultural Arts Project in Baltimore.

Mayden received a Baltimore Camera Club Service Award in 1979, a Maryland Arts Council grant in 1978 and a Sally Thomas Humphrey Art Award from Ohio Wesleyan University in 1973 and in 1974.

He works in small and medium format. His main subjects are black urban dwellers. "I strive to convey feelings of dignity, pride and qualities common to all people," he says.

PUBLICATIONS Book: *Literature Lives*, 1975. Periodicals: *Black Photographers Annual*, 1976, 1974.

COLLECTIONS Equitable Trust Bank, Baltimore; Md. Inst. of Art, Baltimore; Ohio Wesleyan Univ., Delaware, Ohio.

ADDRESS 2068 Linden Ave, Baltimore, MD 21217.

Marshall Mayer CARPENTER · PHOTOGRAPHER Born May 26, 1952, in Des Moines, Iowa, Mayer earned a BA in 1974 from Colorado College in Colorado Springs and also studied at the University of New Mexico, Albuquerque (1975), and at the University of Colorado, Boulder (1976). In 1980 he received his MFA from the University of California, San Diego. He names as influences Mark Mayer, Mark Johnstone, Bonnie Lambert and Gary Metz, among others.

Currently a carpenter and freelance photographer in Los Angeles, he worked as a cook and waiter in that city in 1979. He was an instructor at the University of California, San Diego, in 1978–79, also working as a cook in that city.

A member of Hotel and Restaurant Employees and Bartenders Union of San Diego, Local #30, in 1978–79, Mayer has belonged to the New American Movement in Los Angeles since 1979. He was awarded a Leon F. Goodman Scholarship from the University of California, San Diego, in 1979 and a Regents Fellowship from that school in 1978.

As of this date he is photographing different types of historic sites in Los Angeles as part of a Los Angeles Bicentennial project on the city's history.

PUBLICATIONS Anthologies: *Contemporary California Photography*, 1978; *Great West, Real/ Ideal*, 1977. Periodical: *The Dumb Ox*, no. 6/7, 1978.

ADDRESS 1463 Scott Ave, Los Angeles, CA 90026.

Elaine Mayes PHOTOGRAPHER · FILM MAKER Born October 1, 1938, in Berkeley, California, Mayes earned a BA from Stanford University, Palo Alto, California, in 1959. She also studied at the San Francisco Art Institute with Paul Hassel, John Collier and Minor White.

She has been associate professor of film and photography at Hampshire College in Amherst, Massachusetts, since 1971, and previously taught photography and film-making at the University of Minnesota, Minneapolis (1968–70).

A member of SPE and CAA, Mayes won a grant from the NEA in 1978 to participate in a photographic survey project (of Long Island, New York) sponsored by Apeiron Workshop and Olympus Camera Corporation. She also received an NEA fellowship in 1978 and in 1971. In 1975 and 1971 she received Hampshire College Funds for Research to complete films, and in 1974 a grant from the Royal Film Archive of Belgium, which was also film-related. Grants from the University of Minnesota Graduate School (1969), America the Beautiful Foundation in Washington, D.C. (1966), and Federal Bureau of Public Roads in D.C. (1966) supported photographic projects.

PUBLICATIONS Monograph: *When I Dance*, 1969. Books: *Faces*, 1977; *Fashion*, 1977; *The Sixties*, 1977; *The City*, Alan Trachtenberg, Peter Neill & Peter Bunnell, 1971; *Love Needs Care*, David Smith & John Luce, 1971. Anthologies: *A Book of Photographs*, Sam Wagstaff, 1978; *Darkroom I*, 1977. Periodicals: *Modern Photography*, July & Feb 1979, Feb 1978; *Popular Photography Annual*, 1975; *Camera*, Feb 1972; *Aperture*, 15:2, 1970.

COLLECTIONS Boston Mus. of Fine Arts; Corcoran Gall., Wash., D.C.; Dallas Mus. of Fine Arts, Tex.; Harvard Univ., Fogg Art Mus., Cambridge, Mass.; IMP/GEH, Rochester; Metro. Mus. of Art, NYC; Minneapolis Inst. of Arts, Minn.; MOMA, NYC; Oakland Mus., Calif.; Philadelphia Mus. of Art, Pa.; San Francisco Art Inst.; Smith Coll. Art Mus., Northampton, Mass.; Univ. of Mass. Class of 1928 Photography Cllctn., Amherst; Sam Wagstaff Cllctn., NYC.

ADDRESS c/o Film & Photography Dept, Hampshire College, Amherst, MA 01002.

Thomas Dowell (Tom) McAvoy PHOTOGRAPHER Born November 6, 1905, in Baltimore, Maryland, McAvoy died February 12, 1966, in Alexandria, Virginia. He graduated from Calvert Hall College in 1924.

The photographer worked for the *Baltimore News* in 1924, the *Baltimore Sun* (1925–26), the *Washington Herald* (1926–28) and the *Washington Daily News* (1928–35). He freelanced for *Time* (1935–36) and served on the staff of *Life* (1936–61).

McAvoy belonged to ASMP, White House

News Photographers Association, Catholic Club, Capital Yacht Club of Washington and Dallas Press Club. He was one of four staff photographers for *Life*'s premier issue in 1936.

Noted for his candid news shots, McAvoy was one of the first photographers to use a Leica for news coverage. He chronicled Franklin D. Roosevelt, Juan Perón and other political figures, often disguising himself to obtain intimate portraits. His work strongly influenced contemporary U.S. photojournalism.

PUBLICATION Anthology: *Life Photographers: Their Careers & Favorite Pictures*, Stanley Rayfield, 1957.

COLLECTIONS IMP/GEH, Rochester; Time-Life Archives, NYC.

Angus Rowland McBean *PHOTOGRAPHER* Born June 8, 1904, in Newbridge, Monmouthshire, South Wales, McBean attended numerous schools during the time of World War I.

After a stint as a bank clerk, at the age of twenty he went to work in the antiques and decorating departments of Liberty & Company in London, and left their employ seven years later. Self-employed ever since, McBean opened a studio in London in 1935 that has specialized in theater photography, selling to such periodicals as *Sketch* and covering almost all London stage shows until 1971.

McBean is a Fellow of the Institute of British Photographers, and has been written about in numerous photography magazines.

Early in his career McBean was a maskmaker. He designs and prints wallpaper as well as doing interior decoration and restoration.

A photographer of British theater for forty years (1930–70), McBean says about his work: "My life's work has been given to add a minute scrap to the gaiety of nations and their strife, and to record what little beauty and happiness and achievement we have. . . . I don't believe that atrocity photographs do anything to relieve the world malaise: photography can only prettify even violent death and, by repetition, make ordinary and everyday such horrors."

PUBLICATIONS Anthology: *The Magic Image*, Cecil Beaton & Gail Buckland, 1975. Catalog: *A Darker Side of the Moon*, 1976 (Impressions Gall.: London). Periodicals: *Creative Camera*, Feb 1980; *British Journal of Photography*, Aug 17, 1979.

COLLECTIONS Harvard Univ., Theatre Lib., Cambridge, Mass. In England: British Theatre Mus.; Impressions Gall., York; Kodak Mus., Hemmel, Hemstead; Natl. Portrait Gall., Lon-

don; RPS, London; Victoria & Albert Mus., London. Natl. Gall., Canberra, Australia.

ARCHIVE Harvard Univ. Theatre Lib., Cambridge, Mass.

ADDRESS Flemings Hall, Bedingfield, Eye, Suffolk, England 1P23 7QF.

Wayne McCall *PHOTOGRAPHER · GALLERY DIRECTOR* Born June 11, 1942, in Glendale, California, McCall attended Glendale College in 1960–61 and the University of Arizona, Tucson, in 1966–68. Fred Parker was his major influence.

As of this writing McCall was photography coordinator for Visible Light Gallery in Santa Barbara, California. He was previously co-director of Santa Barbara Photography Gallery (since 1977). He has also been a freelance photographer since 1969 and is a staff photographer at the Santa Barbara Museum of Art (since 1972).

Working in all formats, and primarily in black-and-white, McCall's professional photography involves art and architecture; his personal work is an exploration of fears and fantasies.

PUBLICATIONS Books: *Rescued Buildings*, 1977; *Mud, Space & Spirit*, 1976; *Santa Barbara Architecture*, 1975; *Hot Tub*, 1973.

COLLECTION Santa Barbara Mus. of Art, Calif.

DEALER M. Shore & Son Gall., 12 W Anapamu St, Santa Barbara, CA 93101.

ADDRESS 281 Oak Rd, Santa Barbara, CA 93108.

Linda Louise McCartney *MUSICIAN · PHOTOGRAPHER* Born September 24, 1942, in New York, McCartney attended the University of Arizona in Tucson and began studying photography at Arts Centre of Tucson. She is married to musician Paul McCartney.

A member of the rock band Wings since 1971, McCartney has also been a freelance photographer since the mid-1960s. She began working at *Town and Country* magazine in New York after college, and at one time was official staff photographer at New York's Fillmore East concert hall. Her photographs have been published in numerous magazines and on Wings' album covers.

She has also composed and performed the music for two animated films, *Seaside Woman* (1979) and *Oriental Nightfish* (1977). The former won the Palm D'Or at the Cannes Film Festival.

McCartney is best known for her images of rock music personalities, such as the Rolling Stones, Bob Dylan, the Beatles and especially of her husband and family.

PUBLICATION Monograph: *Linda's Pictures*, 1976.

ADDRESS MPL Communications Ltd., 1 Soho Sq, London W1, England.

Dan McCormack *PHOTOGRAPHER · TEACHER · CURATOR · SURVEYOR* Born January 22, 1944, in Chicago, Illinois, McCormack received a BS in Photography from the Illinois Institute of Technology in Chicago in 1967, where he studied with Aaron Siskind, Joe Jachna and Art Siegal. He then received an MFA in Photography from the School of the Art Institute of Chicago in 1969, where he studied with Ken Josephson, Barbara Crane and Frank Barsotti.

He has been a photography instructor at the Junior College of Albany, New York, since 1979 and at Somerset County College, Somerville, New York, since 1976. From 1972 to 1979 he was assistant professor of photography at Columbia-Greene Community College, Hudson, New York, and was a photography and film instructor at the State University of New York, New Paltz, in 1970–71.

McCormack has belonged to SPE since 1965, and the Catskill Center for Photography since 1977. At the latter he has been associate curator and vice-president of the board of directors since 1978.

His early work was with multiple images, then he did landscapes and worked with a plastic camera. Since 1977 he has used infrared and color and has done surreal imagery.

PUBLICATIONS Anthologies: *Celebrations*, 1974; *Octave of Prayer*, 1972; *Be-ing Without Clothes*, 1970. Catalogs: *The Diana Show*, Mar 1980 (Friends of Photography: Carmel, Ca.); *The Multiple Image*, Apr 1972 (Univ. of R. I.: Providence). Periodical: "Off the Wall," *Flash*, May 1979.

COLLECTION Art Inst. of Chicago.
ADDRESS RD 1, Box 69, Accord, NY 12404.

Donald McCullin *PHOTOJOURNALIST* Born October 9, 1935, in King's Cross, London, McCullin won a Trade Arts Scholarship in painting to Hammersmith School of Arts and Crafts, which he attended from 1948 to 1950.

Forced to earn a living at age fifteen due to the death of his father, he worked at several odd jobs, including that of a color mixer and messenger boy for Larkins, cartoon makers. About 1954 he joined the Royal Air Force, where he was made a photographer's assistant working on aerial reconnaissance printing. After the service he returned to Larkins, working in their darkroom for three years while pursuing his own serious interest in photography. Eventually his work found its way

into print in such publications as London's *The Observer*, for which he did contract work. When not on assignment he resides in Hertfordshire, England.

McCullin was a recipient of the World Press Photographers Award and the Warsaw Gold Medal for the war photography he did in Cyprus in 1964.

Author John le Carré has written (*American Photographer*, May 1981) of McCullin's "refusal to let distance intervene; his refusal to switch off, to compromise in any way in the relation between himself and his subject" in his "haunted and at times unearthly" images.

PUBLICATIONS Monographs: *Homecoming*, 1979; *The Destruction Business*, 1971 (Open Gate Books: London). Periodical: "Homecoming," *American Photographer*, Nov 1979.

ADDRESS c/o Sunday Times Magazine, 200 Gray's Inn Rd, London WC 1, England.

John Chang McCurdy *PHOTOGRAPHER* Born August 1, 1940, in Korea, McCurdy received a BA in 1964 from California State University at San Francisco, and did graduate work at the Uppsala University in Sweden from 1964 to 1968.

A self-employed photographer, McCurdy previously worked as a member of the faculty at Uppsala University in Sweden from 1970 to 1973.

A member of ASMP, he was the recipient of a grant from the American Scandinavian Foundation in 1979.

PUBLICATIONS Books: *Iceland*, Almenna Bokafelagid, 1979; *Of All Things Most Yielding*, 1974.

ADDRESS 156 Fifth Ave, New York, NY 10010.

Fred W. McDarrah *PHOTOGRAPHER · WRITER · EDITOR* Born November 5, 1926, in Brooklyn, New York, McDarrah received a BA in Journalism from New York University, New York City, in 1954.

On the staff of *Village Voice* since 1959, he has been picture editor of the weekly newspaper since 1971.

McDarrah is a member of the American Society of Picture Professionals, ASMP, NPPA, New York Press Club, New York Press Photographers Association, Photographic Historical Society of New York, Photographic Society of America, SPE and the Authors Guild. He won a Guggenheim Fellowship in 1972.

McDarrah does documentary work and photojournalism for *Village Voice* and various magazines.

PUBLICATIONS Books: *Stock Photo & Assignment Sourcebook*, ed., 1977; *Photography Marketplace*, ed., 1975, 2nd ed. 1977; *Museums in New York*, 2nd ed. 1973, 3rd ed., 1978; *Guide for Ecumenical Discussion*, 1970; *The New Bohemia*, 1966; *New York, New York*, 1964; *Greenwich Village*, 1963; *The Artist's World in Pictures*, 1961; *The Beat Scene*, 1960. Catalogs: *Summer Catalogue*, 1973 (New School for Social Research: N.Y.); *Sculpture in Environment*, 1967 (N.Y.C. Parks Dept.); *Art USA Now*, 2 vols., 1962 (C. J. Bucher: Switzerland). Periodicals: "Politicalization of the Avant Garde," *Art in America*, Feb 1974; "Eyes of the Voice," *Camera 35*, Nov 1972.

ADDRESS 505 La Guardia Pl, New York, NY 10012.

Michaelin Daphne McDermott PHOTOGRAPHER Born May 17, 1947, in Brantford, Ontario, Canada, McDermott earned a BA from the University of Manitoba, Winnipeg, Canada.

A freelance photographer from 1975 to 1979, she has been a photographer for the Winnipeg Art Gallery since 1979.

She received a Manitoba Art Council grant in 1980 and a Canada Council grant in 1978.

McDermott does black-and-white portraiture, using a 6 x 7 format.

PUBLICATIONS Anthology: *Self-Portrayal*, 1978. Catalog: *Five Manitoba Photographers*, 1979 (Winnipeg Art Gallery: Canada).

COLLECTION Mt. St. Vincent Art Gall., Halifax, Nova Scotia, Canada.

ADDRESS 11-176 Rue Thomas Berry, St. Boniface, Manitoba R2HOP7, Canada.

Paul A. McDonough PHOTOGRAPHER Born February 18, 1941, in Portsmouth, New Hampshire, McDonough studied at the New England School of Art, Boston, Massachusetts (1958–61), and at a Garry Winogrand workshop in New York City (1967).

He has been an adjunct assistant professor at Pratt Institute, Brooklyn, New York, since 1973 and also taught at Cooper Union in New York City in 1975–76. He was a photography instructor at Parsons School of Design in New York City in 1970–71.

The photographer won an NEA fellowship in 1977.

Working in small- and medium-format black-and-white, McDonough photographs "contemporary life."

COLLECTIONS MOMA, NYC; Seagrams Cllctn., NYC.

ADDRESS 1623 Second Ave, New York, NY 10028.

Elliott McDowell PHOTOGRAPHER · PUBLISHER Born in Evansville, Indiana, McDowell graduated in 1970 from Southern Methodist University, Dallas, Texas, with a degree in advertising and marketing. He attended summer workshops with Ansel Adams in 1973–75.

Self-employed as a fine-art photographer and publisher since 1975, he worked in advertising and public relations for American Gypsum Company from 1971 to 1974.

He is a member of Friends of Photography, and won the Kaffie Gallery Invitational in 1976.

Using everything from miniature negatives (Minox) to large format, the photographer produces "elegant absurdities as well as classical 1930s style, redone with what is available today."

PUBLICATIONS Monographs: *Moonrise Over Rolls Royce*, 1978, *Room Service*, 1978, *Boots and Wurlitzer*, 1977 (self-pub.).

COLLECTIONS Albrecht Art Mus., St. Joseph, Mo.; CCP, Tucson; Mus. of Fine Arts, Santa Fe, N.M.; Mus. of S. Tex., Corpus Christi.

DEALERS Afterimage Gall., The Quadrangle No. 151, 2800 Route St, Dallas, TX 75201; Fifth Ave Gall. of Photography, 6960 Fifth Ave, Scottsdale, AZ 85251.

ADDRESS Box 21F, Route 4, Santa Fe, NM 87501.

D. Keith McElroy ART HISTORIAN Born May 30, 1948, in Dallas, Texas, McElroy earned his BA in Art and Sociology from North Texas State University, Denton (1965), an MLA in Anthropology from Southern Methodist University, Dallas, Texas (1970), and a PhD in History of Photography from the University of New Mexico, Albuquerque (1977), where he studied with Beaumont Newhall and Van Deren Coke.

Currently an assistant professor at the University of Arizona, Tucson (since 1977), he was previously an instructor at the University of New Mexico (1975–77) and at Southern Methodist University (1965–70), where he also directed the Student Center.

McElroy is a member of the Association for Latin American Art, the Latin American Studies Association and SPE.

His primary research area is the history of photography in Latin America, especially in nineteenth-century Peru.

PUBLICATIONS Catalog: *Fotografía en el Perú: Siglo XIX*, 1975 (Banco Continental: Lima). Periodicals: "Benjamin Franklin Pease, An American Photographer in Lima, Peru," July 1979, "The Daguerrean Era in Peru, 1839–1859," *History of Photography, An International Quarterly*, Apr 1979; "Foreign Photographers Before the Revolution," *Artes, Visuales*, vol. 12, 1976 (Museo de Arte Moderno: Mexico D.F.); "Evolution of the Interior of Santa María Magdalena, Lima, Peru," *New Mexico Studies in the Fine Arts*, vol. I, 1976; "Santa María Magdalena, una iglesia con sorpreseas," *Siete Dias*, June 1975.

ADDRESS Dept of Art, Univ of Ariz, Tucson, AZ 85721.

Lawrence Dean McFarland *PHOTOGRAPHER · TEACHER* Born September 1, 1942, in Wichita, Kansas, McFarland earned a BFA from Kansas City Art Institute, Missouri (1973), and an MFA from the University of Nebraska, Lincoln (1976).

He was an assistant professor at Colorado Mountain College at Leadville (1976–79) and at Vail (1976–77). McFarland taught at Apeiron Workshops, Inc., Millerton, New York, in 1977–78, where he was also artist-in-residence (1977).

A member of SPE since 1974, McFarland won an NEA Photographer's Fellowship in 1979.

PUBLICATIONS Anthologies: *The Great West —Real/Ideal*, 1977; *Kansas Album*, James L. Enyeart, ed., 1977; *Young American Photography*, vol. 1, 1974. Catalog: *Photographs*, 1977 (Univ. of Nebr., Sheldon Mem. Art Gall.: Lincoln).

COLLECTIONS CCP, Tucson; IMP/GEH, Rochester; L/C, Wash., D.C.; Minneapolis Inst. of Art, Minn.; Univ. of Colo., Boulder; Univ. of Kans., Helen Foresman Spencer Mus. of Art, Lawrence.

ADDRESS POB 788, Beaver, OK 73932.

Kenneth McGowan *PHOTOGRAPHER* Born December 3, 1940, in Ogden, Utah, McGowan began working in photography in 1959 in Utah, then studied at University of California at Los Angeles, where he earned an MA in 1966. He served as an assistant to Robert Heinecken and Edmund Teske at UCLA, but names "movies" as his major influence. The photographer's father is painter John Thomas McGowan.

A freelance since college, McGowan has done special effects for films as well as portraits of film, recording and television personalities.

His recent work has been in color, which he taught himself beginning in 1968. He uses medium format and prints in large Cibachrome.

PUBLICATIONS Anthology: *One of a Kind*, 1979. Periodicals: Review, *Artforum*, Nov 1978;

Foto, Oct 1978; review, *Afterimage: VSW*, Feb 1978; *Camera Mainichi*, Jan 1978; *Popular Photography Annual*, 1977; *Zoom*, Mar 1976 (Paris).

COLLECTIONS Academy of Motion Picture Arts & Sciences, Los Angeles; Denver Art Mus., Colo.; Harvard Univ., Fogg Art Mus., Cambridge, Mass.; Houston Mus. of Fine Arts, Tex.; Metro. Mus. of Art, NYC; MOMA, NYC; Seagram Cllctn., Los Angeles; UCLA. Australian Natl. Gall., Canberra.

DEALER Leo Castelli Uptown, 4 E 77 St, New York, NY 10021.

ADDRESS 744 N La Cienega Blvd, Los Angeles, CA 90069.

John McKee *PHOTOGRAPHER · EDUCATOR* Born October 20, 1936, in Evanston, Illinois, McKee earned an AB in Music from Dartmouth College, Hanover, New Hampshire (1958), and an MA in French from Princeton University, Princeton, New Jersey (1961).

McKee has been employed in various positions at Bowdoin College, Brunswick, Maine, since 1962: lecturer in photography (since 1969); director, Center for Resource Studies (1966–67); instructor in French (1962–66).

He won a Maine State Award in 1973 and a Silver Award from the San Francisco International Film Festival in 1962 for *Princeton Contexts*.

McKee uses small format for street photography and large format for landscapes.

PUBLICATIONS Books: *Photographs: John McKee*, 1973; *Hands to Work and Hearts to God*, w/Theodore Johnson, 1969; *Report on the Wildlands*, 1968; *As Maine Goes*, 1966.

COLLECTION Bowdoin Coll. Mus. of Art, Brunswick, Maine.

ADDRESS RD 1, Box 1419, Brunswick, ME 04011.

Donald McLeish *PHOTOGRAPHER · MOUNTAINEER · TRAVELER* Born March 11, 1879, in London, England, McLeish died there on January 4, 1950.

During World War I McLeish was a naval aerial photo-pioneer and the official POW photographer. Between wars he freelanced as a photo-illustrator of world publications such as *National Geographic*. He was also employed by Newman Travel Talks, giving film and slide lectures in the United States between the years 1909 and 1914, and in 1898 he taught photography at Regent Street Polytechnic in London.

McLeish both designed and built a 4 x 5 plate

camera that is now in the permanent collection of the Science Museum in Kensington, London.

PUBLICATIONS Books: *Wonderful London*, 1924 (London); *Wonders of the Past*, ca. 1924 (London). Periodical: Review, *Ciba-Geigy Photo Journal*, July 1979.

ARCHIVE Gordon McLeish, 2 Avebury Rd, Wimbledon, London SW19 3RA, England.

Jerry McMillan PHOTOGRAPHER Born December 7, 1936, in Oklahoma City, Oklahoma, McMillan studied at the Chouinard Art Institute in Los Angeles, California, from 1958 to 1960.

Currently employed as a teacher at Art Center College of Design in Pasadena, California, he previously taught at University of California at Los Angeles (1973, 1971 and 1970) and at California State University at Northridge (1970).

In his work McMillan uses paper, metal and glass to produce photo sculpture and drawings.

PUBLICATIONS Catalogs: *Attitudes: Photography in the 1970's*, 1979 (Santa Barbara Mus. of Art: Calif.); *Photographic Directions: Los Angeles, 1979*, Robert Glenn Ketchum, 1979 (Security Pacific Bank: Los Angeles); *The Lyon Collection: Modern and Contemporary Works on Paper*, Jane K. Bledsoe, 1976 (The Art Galls., Calif. State Univ. at Long Beach); *Photo/Synthesis*, Jason D. Wong, 1975 (Herbert F. Johnson Mus. of Art, Cornell Univ.: Ithaca, N.Y.); *Acquisitions 1972/ 1973*, Elwyn Lynn, 1973 (Art Gall. of New South Wales: Australia); *Surrealism Is Alive and Well in the West*, 1972 (Baxter Art Gall., Calif. Inst. of Technology: Pasadena). Periodicals: "California Cut-ups," James Hugunin, *Afterimage: VSW*, Oct 1979; "Contemporary Photographs—Recent Acquisitions," Joan Murray, Apr 7, 1979, "Exploratory Photographic Visions," Suzanne Muchnic, Nov 20, 1977, "Frank Stella and Jerry McMillan," Martha Spelman, Oct 22, 1977, *Artweek*; "Look Through a Peephole and Discover a Landscape," Margery Mann, *Popular Photography*, Sept 1971; *Modern Photography*, July 1970; "Photography into Sculpture," Peter C. Bunnell, *ArtsCanada*, June 1970; "Photographs as Sculpture and Prints," Peter C. Bunnell, *Art in America*, Sept/ Oct 1969; review, Fidel A. Danieli, *Artforum*, Mar 1967.

PORTFOLIO *Silver See* (group), 1977 (Los Angeles Ctr. for Photographic Studies).

COLLECTIONS ARCO Cllctn., Los Angeles; Art Inst. of Chicago; Bank of Boston, Los Angeles; Blue Cross of Southern Calif., Los Angeles; Calif. State Univ. at Long Beach, Lyon Cllctn.; CCP, Tucson; Claremont Colleges, Claremont, Calif.; Des Moines Art Mus., Iowa; Fort Worth Art Mus., Tex.; General Services Administration Project, Oklahoma City, Okla.; Harvard Univ., Fogg Art Mus., Cambridge, Mass.; IMP/GEH, Rochester; La Jolla Mus. of Contemporary Art, La Jolla, Calif.; Long Beach City Coll., Calif.; Los Angeles County Mus. of Art; Los Angeles Inst. of Contemporary Art; Minneapolis Inst. of Arts, Minn.; MOMA, NYC; Newport Harbor Art Mus., Newport Beach, Calif.; Norton Simon Mus., Pasadena, Calif.; Oakland Mus., Calif.; Pall Corp., Glen Cove, Long Island, N.Y.; Palomar Coll., San Marcos, Calif.; San Francisco Mus. of Modern Art; UCLA, Frederick S. Wight Gall., Los Angeles; Univ. of N. Mex., Art Mus., Albuquerque. Power Art Inst., Sydney, Australia.

DEALER Grapestake Gall., 2876 California St, San Francisco, CA 94115.

ADDRESS 1024¼ N Western Ave, Los Angeles, CA 90029.

Tom McNease PHOTOGRAPHER·TEACHER·EDITOR [See plate 133] Born November 2, 1946, in Meridian, Mississippi, McNease earned a BS in Zoology from Southeastern University in Hammond, Louisiana. He is a self-employed photographer.

PUBLICATIONS Periodicals: *Camera*, Mar 1975, Sept 1974.

Portfolio *Illuminations*, 1978 (A Gallery for Fine Photography: New Orleans).

COLLECTIONS Exchange Natl. Bank of Chicago; La. Arts & Science Ctr., Baton Rouge; New Orleans Mus. of Art; Prestonwood Cllctn. of Photographic Art, Dallas, Tex.

DEALERS Hills Gall., 3113 E Third Ave, Denver, CO 80206; Afterimage, The Quadrangle #151, 2800 Routh St, Dallas, TX 75201; A Gall. for Fine Photography, 5432 Magazine St, New Orleans, LA 70115; Fourth St Photo Gall., 67 E 4 St, New York, NY 10003.

ADDRESS POB 481, Madisonville, LA 70447.

Larry E. McPherson PHOTOGRAPHER · TEACHER Born May 1, 1943, in Newark, Ohio, McPherson received a BA in 1976 from Columbia College, Chicago, Illinois, having previously studied at Ohio State University, Newark, and Rochester Institute of Technology, New York. He earned an MA in 1978 from Northern Illinois University, DeKalb.

An assistant professor of art since 1978 at Memphis State University, Tennessee, McPherson previously taught at Columbia College (1971–76) and at the School of the Art Institute of Chicago (1972). He has also been an architectural and advertising photographer.

He won a Guggenheim Fellowship in 1980 and NEA Photographer's Fellowships in 1979 and in 1975; in 1977 he received an Illinois Arts Council photography project grant.

McPherson specializes in printing his own dye transfer images of landscapes, nature and cows.

PUBLICATIONS Anthology: *Vision and Expression*, Nathan Lyons, ed., 1969. Periodicals: *Art Voices South*, Gary Witt, July/Aug 1979; review, Candida Finkel, *Afterimage: VSW*, Oct 1978.

COLLECTIONS Art Inst. of Chicago; IMP/GEH, Rochester; MOMA, NYC.

ADDRESS 4595 Buffer Dr, Memphis, TN 38128.

Jim McQuaid *PHOTOGRAPHER · TEACHER · HISTORIAN · WRITER* Born in Detroit, Michigan, on September 17, 1946, McQuaid earned a BA in Political Science from the University of Michigan, Ann Arbor (1968). He was a special student at Maryland Institute College of Art in Baltimore in 1968–69, where he studied with Jaromir Stephany.

McQuaid has been visiting assistant professor at the University of Massachusetts, Boston, since 1978 and was director of the Oral History Project at IMP/GEH (1976–78). He has been an instructor at Western Michigan University, Kalamazoo (1975–76); Denison University, Granville, Ohio (1974–75); and at Central Michigan University, Mt. Pleasant (1974).

He is a member of SPE (since 1971) and the Oral History Association (since 1975). He became a member of the board of directors of Massachusetts' Dorchester Arts Council in 1979.

McQuaid won a grant from NEA in 1978 to direct the project "Index to Photographic Collections." As project director of "Oral History in Photography," he received grants from New York State Council on the Arts in 1977 and from NEA in 1976. In 1975 he was awarded a Trebor Rettetsoh Memorial Fellowship. He was a co-recipient of three grants supporting research on the project "Photography: Source & Resource"—from the Polaroid Foundation in 1974, from NEA in 1973 and from SPE in 1972.

His photographic work is technically straightforward, black-and-white, "concerned with basic issues of seeing, not subject-oriented." His previous photography has included documentary work and color. McQuaid's research has focused on recording and making available previously inaccessible photographic resources.

PUBLICATIONS Book: *Photography: Source & Resource*, co-author, 1973. Periodicals: "Chronology of the Life of Lisette Model," *Journal from the Center*, no. 4, May 1977; "Review of Twenty-Seven Photo Textbooks," *Exposure: SPE*, fall 1975; *Invitation to Photography*, summer 1975; "A Survey of Oral History Materials on Photography," *Image*, summer 1975; "Initial Results of a Survey of Photographic Educators," *Exposure: SPE*, Dec 1972.

COLLECTIONS Middle Tenn. State Univ., Murfreesboro; Rettetsoh Family Fund, State College, Pa.

ADDRESS 14 Moseley St, #2, Dorchester, MA 02125.

Daniel Meadows *PHOTOGRAPHER* Born January 28, 1952, in Gloucestershire, England, Meadows studied at Manchester Polytechnic, Manchester, England from 1970 to 1973.

A freelance photographer since 1973, he was artist-in-residence to Nelson & Corne College, Lancashire, England (1975–77).

Meadows belongs to the National Union of Journalists and the Association of Cinematograph, Television & Allied Technicians. He received an Arts Council of Great Britain grant award in 1973.

Working in documentary photos and photojournalism, the photographer is mainly concerned with life in the north of England. His major project has been a record of the textile industry in Lancashire.

PUBLICATIONS Monograph: *Living Like This*, 1975 (Arrow Books: England). Anthology: *British Image One*, 1975 (Arts Council of Great Britain: London).

ADDRESS 45 Bank St, Barnoldswick, Lancashire BB86AU, England.

Lorran Robles Meares *MEDIA PRODUCTION SPECIALIST · PHOTOGRAPHER* Born August 18, 1947, in Tampa, Florida, Meares studied at the University of South Florida, Tampa, in 1967–69 and earned a BA in Art from the University of Central Florida, Orlando, in 1975.

As of this writing Meares was a photography instructor at Crealde Art Center, Winter Park, Florida, and at Valencia Community College, Orlando, as well as being educational media production specialist for the University of Central Florida in Orlando. From 1971 to 1979 Meares was Photography Department supervisor in the University of Central Florida's Department of Instructional Resources, and from 1969 to 1971 was a freelance photographer. In 1967–69 the Floridian was a photographer for the Department of Educational Resources, University of South Florida, Tampa.

A member of SPE, the photographer won an individual artist's fellowship from the Florida Fine Arts Council in 1978.

Meares produces black-and-white stereo silver prints mounted on oak photo boxes with stereo viewers in a style self-described as "light paintings." The artist also does research in stereoscopic multi-image projected animation sequences.

PUBLICATION Periodical: "Stereoscopy," H. A. Layer, *Exposure: SPE*, fall 1979.

COLLECTIONS Maryland Inst., Coll. of Art, Wilgus Cllctn., Baltimore; Ramapo Coll., Mahwah, N.J.; Univ. of Central Fla., Orlando; Witkin Gall., NYC.

DEALER Image, 1323 Main St, Sarasota, FL 33577.

ADDRESS 28 Palermo Ave, Orlando, FL 32807.

Ralph Eugene Meatyard *PHOTOGRAPHER · OPTICIAN* [See plate 97] Born May 15, 1925, in Normal, Illinois, Meatyard died May 7, 1972, in Lexington, Kentucky. He participated in the navy V-12 program at Williams College in Williamstown, Massachusetts, in 1943–44, then attended Illinois Wesleyan University in Bloomington in 1950. In 1954 Meatyard studied photography with Van Deren Coke; he also studied briefly with Minor White and Henry Holmes Smith.

In 1949 Meatyard became a licensed optician and went to work for Gailey Eye Clinic. The next year he took a job as optician for Tinder-Krauss-Tinder in Lexington, and in 1967 he opened his own optical business there, which he called Eyeglasses of Kentucky.

He joined the Lexington Camera Club in 1954 and was also a member of the Photographic Society of America.

PUBLICATIONS Monographs: *Ralph Eugene Meatyard*, James Baker Hall, 1974; *Ralph Eugene Meatyard*, 1970. Books: *The Family Album of Lucybelle Crater*, Jonathan Williams et al, 1974; *The Unforeseen Wilderness*, Wendell Berry, 1971. Anthologies: *The Photograph Collector's Guide*, Lee D. Witkin & Barbara London, 1979; *The Grotesque in Photography*, A. D. Coleman, 1977; *The Magic Image*, Cecil Beaton & Gail Buckland, 1975; *Photography Year*, 1973, *The Art of Photography*, 1971, *Photographing Children*, 1971, Time-Life Series; *Be-ing Without Clothes*, Minor White, ed., 1970; *Light⁷*, Minor White, ed., 1968. Catalog: *Photographs*, 1977 (Univ. of Nebr., Sheldon Mem. Art Gall.: Lincoln). Periodicals: *Creative Camera*, June 1975, Apr 1974; *Camera*, July 1974; *Photo Reporter*, Mar 1973; *Popular Photography*, July 1969; *Art-*

forum, June 1966; "The Photographs of Ralph Eugene Meatyard," Van Deren Coke, *Aperture* 7:4, winter; *Image*, 15:2.

COLLECTIONS Addison Gall. of Art, Andover, Mass.; Art Inst. of Chicago; Ctr. for Photographic Studies, Louisville, Ky.; Cincinnati Art Mus., Ohio; IMP/GEH, Rochester; MIT, Cambridge, Mass.; Metro. Mus. of Art, NYC; MOMA, NYC; Norton Simon Mus. of Art, Pasadena, Calif.; Philadelphia Mus. of Art, Pa.; Smithsonian Inst., Wash., D.C.; Thomas Merton Studies Ctr., Louisville, Ky.; UCLA; Univ. of Louisville, Ky.; Univ. of Nebr., Sheldon Mem. Art Gall., Lincoln; Univ. of N. Mex., Albuquerque; VSW, Rochester.

ARCHIVE Madelyn Meatyard, 418 Kingsway Dr, Lexington, KY 40507.

A. J. Meek *PHOTOGRAPHER · EDUCATOR* Born August 29, 1941, in Beatrice, Nebraska, Meek earned a BFA from Art Center College of Design in Los Angeles, California (1970), and an MFA from Ohio University, Athens (1972).

He has been head of photography/film at Louisiana State University, Baton Rouge, since 1977, and from 1972 to 1977 was assistant professor in the Art Department of Utah State University, Logan. He was a guest instructor at the College of Marin, Kentfield, California, in 1975, and a teaching assistant at Ohio University in 1970–72.

Meek has belonged to SPE since 1969, Friends of Photography since 1978, and the George Eastman House since 1970. He won an NEA fellowship in 1975 and an exhibition aid grant from Utah State University.

Working in small and large formats, Meek does photography that is "straight" and project-oriented.

PUBLICATIONS Book: *Spirit of Utah 1860–1976*, ed., 1976 (self-pub.). Periodicals: *Stonecloud*, no. 5; *Bombay Duck*, no. 2; *Exposure: SPE*, 12:4. Reviews: *Artweek*, 9:12, 16:26.

COLLECTIONS Chrysler Mus. at Norfolk, Va.; New Orleans Mus. of Art. In Scotland: Inverness Art Mus. & Gall., Inverness; Royal Commission of Ancient Monuments of Scotland, Edinburgh; Tankerness Mus., Kirkwall, Orkney.

ADDRESS 1278 Sharlo Ave, Baton Rouge, LA 70808.

Richard A. Meek *PHOTOGRAPHER* Born November 12, 1923, in Richmond, Indiana, Meek has been a freelance photographer since 1958.

He worked as a contract photographer for Time-Life (1958–70) and was a staff photographer for *Life* (1951–54), after which he joined the original staff of *Sports Illustrated* in 1954 (until 1958). He worked with Victor Keppler (1949–50) and maintained his own studio in Richmond from 1942 to 1949.

A member of ASMP, Meek has won numerous awards from various chapters of the Art Directors Club: Metropolitan Washington (1974, 1973, 1967), New York (1968) and Detroit (1961, 1960). He has also been honored by Society of Publication Designers (1969), Graphic Design of Germany (1967) and National Press Photographers of America & Encyclopaedia Britannica 14th Annual News Pictures of the Year.

Meek does photojournalism, sports photography and illustrative food photography.

PUBLICATIONS   Books: *Bill Cosby's Personal Guide to Tennis Power*, 1975; *Melting Pot*, 1971, *Great West*, 1971, *Northwest*, 1970, *Caribbean*, 1970, *Scandinavia*, 1968 (Time-Life Books, Foods of the World); *Greece*, 1963, *West Indies*, 1963 (Time-Life Books, World Library). Periodical: *Popular Photography*, incl. text, Sept 1966.

ADDRESS   8 Skyline Dr, Huntington, NY 11743.

Charles Edward Kenneth Mees   CHEMIST · INVENTOR · WRITER   Born in Wellingborough, England, in 1882, Mees died in 1960. He studied chemistry at St. Dunstan's College (BSc, 1903) and at University College, London (doctorate).

At St. Dunstan's, Mees began a friendship and collaboration with fellow student Samuel E. Sheppard, which led to their joint BSc thesis introducing the idea of gamma infinity. Their researches of the next three years were published in a book in 1907, one of the most valuable references on the photographic process. After receiving his doctorate Mees spent six years with the firm of Wratten and Wainwright, producing a series of light filters, darkroom safelights and dye-sensitized panchromatic plates. In 1912 he was asked to organize and direct Eastman Kodak's new research laboratory in Rochester, New York, and George Eastman purchased Mees' former firm as part of the bargain.

During World War I, Mees put together the first school of aerial photography and added a department of synthetic organic chemistry to the laboratory. After the war he started departments for developing photographic apparatus, emulsion research and cellulose ester yarn and plastics. In 1923 he introduced 16mm amateur motion picture film, and later encouraged Mannes and Godowsky in their development of Kodachrome. A prolific writer, Mees produced over 200 articles in scientific publications as well as more than 10 books.

He was a Fellow of RPS and an honorary member of the Photographic Society of America.

PUBLICATIONS   Books: *From Dry Plates to Ektachrome Film*, 1961; *The Theory of the Photographic Process*, 1942, rev. 1954; *Investigations on the Theory of the Photographic Process*, w/ Samuel Sheppard, 1907. Anthology: *Photography's Great Inventors*, Louis W. Sipley, 1965. Periodicals: "Charles Edward Kenneth Mees, 1882–1960," Walter Clark, *Biographical Memoirs of Fellows of the Royal Society*, Nov 1961; *Perspective*, 3:1, 1961; "C. E. Kenneth Mees, 1882–1960," T. H. James, *Photographic Science & Engineering*, Nov/Dec 1960; *Journal of the Optical Society of America*, Nov 1960; *Nature*, Oct 1, 1960; *Photographic Journal*, Oct 1960; *Photography*, Oct 1960; *Radiography*, Oct 1960; *Science et Industries Photographiques*, Sept 1960; *Process*, July 1960; *Image*, Oct 1954; *Journal of the Franklin Institute*, 1954; *Saturday Evening Post*, Oct 25, 1947; "Charles Edward Kenneth Mees: Hon. F.P.S.A.," Walter Clark, *Journal of the Photographic Society of America*, Oct 1943; *Photoengravers Bulletin*, Sept 1935.

Lotte Meitner-Graf   PHOTOGRAPHER   Born in Vienna, Austria (date unknown), Meitner-Graf died in London in May 1973. She was married to a chemist, Dr. Walter Meitner, who died in 1959. Her studies were at the Graphische Lehr- und Versuchsanstalt in Vienna.

Meitner-Graf was a freelance photographer in Vienna until 1938, when Hitler's occupation forced her to seek asylum in London. There she remained the rest of her life. During the war she managed the Fayer Studio, signing all her photographs with Fayer's name. In the early 1950s she opened her own studio.

Principally a portrait photographer, she earned her living taking photographs of famous personalities, and many such portraits were used on book and album jackets. But she did not limit her interest to people of fame or wealth. In addition to her portraits, her work also showed her fascination with the human hand and with details of everyday nature, such as dewdrops and dandelions. An exacting printer, she worked strictly in black-and-white.

PUBLICATION   Anthology: *The Magic Image*, Cecil Beaton & Gail Buckland, 1975.

Israel Berendt Melchior   MANUFACTURER · ENGINEER · PHOTOGRAPHER   Born May 12, 1827, in

Copenhagen, Denmark, Melchior also died there September 7, 1893. He received a bachelor's degree in engineering.

Melchior was a member of the Association of Photographers in 1865.

The photographer concentrated on stereoscopic photographs taken at Rolighed, Villa Maria, Villa Melchior and other places in Denmark and abroad, as well as on portraits of the Danish author H. C. Andersen.

PUBLICATIONS Anthology: *Photographers in and from Denmark Until 1900*, Bjørn Ochsner, 1956, rev. ed. 1969. Periodical: *Danske Museer*, no. 3, 1952.

COLLECTIONS In Denmark: Hegels Cllctn., Øregård; Mus. of Textiles, Aarhus; Royal Lib., Copenhagen.

Philip Albert Melnick PHOTOGRAPHER · TEACHER Born May 7, 1935, in Chicago, Illinois, Melnick earned a BA (1966) and MFA (1969) at University of California in Los Angeles, where he studied photography with Robert Heinecken.

An assistant professor at Northern Illinois University, DeKalb, since 1977, he previously was a visiting photography lecturer at Orange Coast College, Costa Mesa, California (1976–77), and an assistant professor (1972–76) and instructor (1969–72) at the University of Southern California, Los Angeles.

Melnick belongs to SPE (since 1972) and is a founding charter member of the Los Angeles Center for Photographic Studies. He was its trustee in 1974–77, treasurer in 1974–75 and vice-president/secretary in 1976–77. The photographer earned an Illinois Arts Council grant in 1979.

He uses mainly black-and-white in medium format. Melnick's current work ranges "from architectural details and formal plantings in the urban landscape to examination of formal room arrangements (interiors) in California and in the Midwest."

PUBLICATIONS Anthology: *Emerging Los Angeles Photographers*, 1976. Catalog: *Photographic Directions, Los Angeles 1979*, 1979 (Security Pacific Bank: Los Angeles). Periodical: *Popular Photography Annual*, 1979.

PORTFOLIO *Silver See* (Group), Victor Landweber, ed., 1977 (Los Angeles).

COLLECTIONS Seagram Ill. State Mus., Springfield; Minneapolis Inst. of Arts, Minn.; Mus. of Fine Arts, Boston; Seagram Cllctn., NYC; UCLA.

DEALERS O. K. Harris, 383 W Broadway, New York, NY 10012; G. Ray Hawkins, 7224 Melrose Ave, Los Angeles, CA 90069.

ADDRESS Dept of Art, Northern Ill. Univ, DeKalb, IL 60115.

John Menapace PHOTOGRAPHER · TEACHER · BOOK DESIGNER Born in Shamokin, Pennsylvania, in 1927, Menapace attended Yale University for three years (until 1949) and started as a self-taught photographer in 1957. He participated in workshops with Ansel Adams and Beaumont Newhall in 1969, with Minor White in 1970 and with Nathan Lyons in 1977.

As of this writing Menapace was an instructor in photography for the Art Department of Duke University, Durham, North Carolina (since 1972). He has also been design/production manager of Duke University Press since 1957. He was a visiting artist at the University of North Carolina, Chapel Hill, in 1979 and conducted workshops at Penland School of Crafts in Durham in 1979, 1977, 1975, 1974 and 1972.

Menapace is a member of SPE.

Menapace's work is described thus by Donald Kuspit: "[He] breaks down his world into pure forms, yet they seem also semantic fragments . . . uses abstraction . . . as a means of emphasis, rather than as a reductionist assertion of independent primary form."

PUBLICATION Anthology: *I Shall Save One Land Unvisited: Eleven Southern Photographers*, Jonathan Williams, ed., 1978.

COLLECTIONS Duke Univ. Mus. of Art, Durham, N.C.; Milwaukee Art Mus., Wisc.; N.C. Mus. of Art, Raleigh; R. J. Reynolds, Inc., Winston-Salem, N.C.; Univ. of N.C., Ackland Art Ctr., Chapel Hill.

DEALERS Osuna Gall., 2121 P St NW, Washington, DC 20037; Witkin Gall., 41 E 57 St, New York, NY 10022.

ADDRESS 3425-A Randolph Rd, Durham, NC 27705.

Antonio Mendoza PHOTOGRAPHER Born July 21, 1941, in Havana, Cuba, Mendoza received an MA in Architecture from Harvard's School of Design in 1968.

Mendoza is a freelance photographer.

In his work he concentrates on photographs of animals, using flash in a 35mm format.

PUBLICATIONS Periodicals: *Popular Photography*, Aug 1980; *35mm Photography*, winter 1979; *Print*, Summer 1978; *Camera 35*, June 1977.

COLLECTIONS Addison Gall. of American Art, Andover, Mass.; Harvard Univ., Fogg Art Mus., Cambridge, Mass.; MOMA, NYC; Mus. of Fine Arts, Boston.

DEALER   Light Gall., 800 N La Cienega Blvd, Los Angeles, CA 90069.

ADDRESS   145 W Broadway, New York, NY 10013.

John Douglas Mercer   PHOTOGRAPHER   Born July 31, 1945, in Des Moines, Iowa, Mercer received a BS from Northwest Missouri State University, Maryville, in 1970 and an MA and MFA from Arizona State University, Tempe, in 1972 and 1973.

In 1978 Mercer was a guest lecturer at Sonoma State University, Sonoma, California, and in 1976 he taught photo workshops at the University of California, Berkeley, and at Modesto Junior College, California. From 1973 to 1974 he was photography instructor at Napa Junior College, California. He founded the Creative Eye Gallery in Sonoma in 1974 and directed it till 1977; he also co-founded the Northlight Gallery in Tempe in 1971.

The photographer was awarded a California Arts Council grant in 1977.

Using black-and-white, Mercer photographs nudes and nature, and he uses color for documentary and multiple exposures.

PUBLICATIONS   Monograph: *Island of the Pelicans*, 1976. Anthology: *Young American Photographers*, 1974.

COLLECTIONS   Erie Art Ctr., Pa.; Oakland Mus., Calif.; San Francisco City Cllctn.; San Francisco Mus. of Modern Art.

DEALER   Annex Gall., 604 College Ave., Santa Rosa, CA 95404.

ADDRESS   POB 620, Sonoma, CA 95476.

Henry Beaufoy Merlin   PHOTOGRAPHER   Born 1830 in England, Merlin died in 1873 in Australia. The son of an English chemist, he was sponsored in his photographic work by the Australian collector Bernard Otto Holtermann.

Merlin emigrated to Australia in 1849, and by 1866 he had established himself as a traveling photographer, working under the trade name of American and Australian Photographic Company. In 1871 he was selected as the official photographer for the Victorian-New South Wales Eclipse Expedition to the tropics of northern Queensland. Merlin hired Charles Bayliss as an assistant in his work in the gold field of the Hill End/Tambaroora district in New South Wales (where he met Holtermann, about 1872). Holtermann appointed him as photographer for a traveling exposition that he had planned to illustrate the sights of New South Wales and Sydney. Merlin died of potassium cyanide poisoning, a result of his work with the collodion wet-plate process.

Andrew Hooper of the Royal Melbourne Institute of Technology says of Merlin's work: "The thousands [of images] taken in the Tambaroora district are distinctive in their eye for detail and wry social commentary."

PUBLICATIONS   Books: *Gold and Silver: An Album of Hill End and Gulgong Photographs from the Holtermann Collection*, Keast Burke, 1973 (Heinemann: Melbourne); *The Story of the Camera in Australia*, Jack Cato, 1955 (Georgian House: Australia).

COLLECTIONS   In Australia: Mitchell Lib., Holtermann Cllctn., Sydney; Royal Melbourne Inst. of Tech.

ARCHIVE   Holtermann Cllctn, Mitchell Lib, Sydney, Australia.

Roger Mertin   PHOTOGRAPHER   Born December 9, 1942, in Bridgeport, Connecticut, Mertin earned a BFA in 1965 from Rochester (New York) Institute of Technology and an MFA in 1972 from Visual Studies Workshop in Rochester.

Since 1973 Mertin has been assistant professor of fine arts and photography at the University of Rochester. He also teaches at VSW.

The photographer won a Guggenheim Fellowship in 1974 and an NEA Photographer's Fellowship in 1976.

PUBLICATIONS   Anthologies: *The Photograph Collector's Guide*, Lee D. Witkin & Barbara London, 1979; *Mirrors and Windows*, John Szarkowski, ed., 1978; *The Great West: Real/Ideal*, Sandy Hume et al, eds., 1977; *Be-ing Without Clothes*, Minor White, ed., 1970; *The Print*, Time-Life Series, 1970; *Vision and Expression*, Nathan Lyons, ed., 1969; *Light[7]*, Minor White, ed., 1968; *Photography in the 20th Century*, Nathan Lyons, ed., 1967. Catalogs: *Records 1976–78*, 1978 (Chicago Ctr. for Creative Photography, Columbia Coll.); *Peculiar to Photography*, 1976, *Light and Substance*, 1974 (Univ. of N. Mex.: Albuquerque); *Photography Unlimited*, 1974 (Harvard Univ., Fogg Art Mus.: Cambridge, Mass.); *Photograph, U.S.A.*, 1967 (De Cordova Mus.: Lincoln, Mass.). Periodicals: *Album*, no. 8, 1970; *Camera*, Sept 1959.

COLLECTIONS   Art Inst. of Chicago; Baltimore Mus. of Art, Md.; IMP/GEH, Rochester; MIT, Cambridge, Mass.; MOMA, NYC; Univ. of Nebr., Sheldon Mem. Art Gall., Lincoln; Univ. of N. Mex., Albuquerque; VSW, Rochester. Natl. Gall. of Canada, Ottawa, Ontario.

DEALER Stephen Rose Gall., 216 Newbury St, Boston, MA 02116.

ADDRESS c/o Visual Studies Workshop, 31 Prince St, Rochester, NY 14607.

Susanne Mertz PHOTOGRAPHER Born February 4, 1946, in Copenhagen, Denmark, Mertz studied photography at the Mydtskov-Rønne Studios in Copenhagen (1963–67). The photographer's father is the painter Albert Mertz.

Mertz has been a freelance photographer since 1971, taking pictures of theater groups, musicians, feminist groups and old shops in Copenhagen. She also makes photographic backgrounds for television cartoons. Previously she worked in Copenhagen for two years at Ole Bjork Studio (1969–71), and in Paris at Claude Rodriguez Studio (1967–68).

PUBLICATION Book: *Happiness Is Being a Woman*, 1975.

ADDRESS Dronningensgade 6, 1420 Copenhagen, Denmark.

Ronald Malcolm Mesaros PHOTOGRAPHER Born September 6, 1942, in Rahway, New Jersey, Mesaros earned a BFA from Rochester Institute of Technology, New York (1965), and an MS from Illinois Institute of Technology, Chicago, in 1967. He has studied with Aaron Siskind, Arthur Siegel, Minor White and Nathan Lyons.

He has been a freelance photographer since 1967, concentrating on people, sports and travel.

PUBLICATIONS Anthologies: *Photographing Children*, 1971; *Art of Photography*, 1971; *Light & Film*, 1970; *Vision & Expression*, 1969.

COLLECTION IMP/GEH, Rochester.

ADDRESS POB 87, Topanga, CA 90290.

John Messina PHOTOGRAPHER · TEACHER · ARCHITECT Born September 17, 1940, in New Orleans, Louisiana, Messina earned a Bachelor of Architecture degree from Louisiana State University, Baton Rouge, in 1965 and a Master of Architecture (with emphasis on photography) from Massachusetts Institute of Technology, Cambridge, Massachusetts, in 1977.

He has taught at Wellesley College, Wellesley, Massachusetts, since 1978 and at Boston University in Massachusetts since 1976.

Winner of the American Institute of Architects Medal in the Study of Architecture in 1965, Messina was a member of SPE from 1976 to 1978.

PUBLICATIONS Periodicals: *Saturday Review*, Nov 1972; *Camera 35*, Sept 1972; *Look*, June 15, 1971.

COLLECTIONS Harvard Univ., Fogg Art Mus., Cambridge, Mass.; New Orleans Mus. of Art.

ADDRESS POB 534, Concord, MA 01742.

Ray K. Metzker PHOTOGRAPHER · TEACHER Born September 10, 1931, in Milwaukee, Wisconsin, Metzker earned a BA from Beloit College, Beloit, Wisconsin, in 1953 and an MS from the Institute of Design, Illinois Institute of Technology, Chicago, in 1959. He studied there with Harry Callahan and Aaron Siskind.

He has taught at Philadelphia College of Art, Pennsylvania, since 1962, and also taught at the Rhode Island School of Design, Providence (1977), and at the University of New Mexico, Albuquerque, in 1970–72.

Metzker won Guggenheim fellowships in 1966 and 1979 and an NEA fellowship in 1974.

Most widely known for work in cumulative imagery, Metzker has "the formalist's sensibility which is applied to exploring phenomena and issues confined to black-and-white photography."

PUBLICATIONS Monograph: *Sand Creatures*, 1979. Anthologies: *The Photograph Collector's Guide*, Lee D. Witkin & Barbara London, 1979; *Mirrors and Windows*, John Szarkowski, ed., 1978; *The Photographer's Choice*, Kelly Wise, 1975; *Looking at Photographs*, John Szarkowski, 1973; *The Persistence of Vision*, Nathan Lyons, 1967. Periodicals: *Aperture* 13: 2, 1967; 9: 2, 1961.

COLLECTIONS Art Inst. of Chicago; Boston Mus. of Fine Arts; Harvard Univ., Fogg Art Mus., Cambridge, Mass.; IMP/GEH, Rochester; Metro. Mus. af Art, NYC; Milwaukee Art Ctr., Wisc.; MOMA, NYC; Mus. of Fine Arts, Houston, Tex.; Philadelphia Mus. of Art, Pa.; Smithsonian Inst., Wash., D.C.; Wesleyan Univ., Davidson Art Ctr., Middletown, Conn. Australian Natl. Gall., Canberra; Bibliothèque Nationale, Paris; Natl. Gall. of Canada, Ottawa, Ontario.

DEALER Light Gall., 724 Fifth Ave, New York, NY 10019.

ADDRESS 733 S Sixth St, Philadelphia, PA 19147.

Douglas William Metzler PHOTOGRAPHER · PAINTER Born February 4, 1947, in New York City, Metzler attended the School of Visual Arts in New York City (1967–68). His major influences were the artist Brice Marden, Marden's wife Helen, Bob Roca, Balthus and New York City in the late 1960s.

A self-employed photographer/painter since 1976, Metzler was a staff photographer for United Artists Records in Los Angeles from 1974 to

1976. He worked for Delta Presse in Paris and Dakar, Senegal, West Africa, in 1972–73, and from 1969 to 1972 assisted New York photographers Garry Gross, Carl Fischer and William Helburn.

Metzler has mainly done portraiture, especially diptychs, since 1974. In 1976 he began the series "Shooting Down"—images photographed from above that have a 3-D effect or "float"—and began painting on his photographs.

PUBLICATIONS Catalog: *Attitudes in Photography in the Seventies*, Fred Parker (Santa Barbara Mus. of Art, Calif.). Periodicals: *New West*, July 1978, June 7, 1976, May 1976; "Direct Views of the Simple: Photography of Doug Metzler," James Welling, *Art Week*, Nov 1977; *Esquire*, Mar 1977; *Rolling Stone*, Sept 26, 1974.

COLLECTIONS Parasol Press, NYC; Security Pacific Bank Cllctn., Los Angeles.

REPRESENTATIVE Modernism, 326 Eighth St, San Francisco, CA 94103.

ADDRESS 1 Sheridan Sq, New York, NY 10014.

Sheila Metzner ART DIRECTOR · DESIGNER · PHOTOGRAPHER Born in New York City on January 4, 1939, Metzner received a BFA from Pratt Institute in Brooklyn, New York, in 1960.

The freelance photographer works in black-and-white and color, her color prints being made by the Fresson process in Paris from 35mm transparencies. "Their glamour," says Alexandra Anderson in *Camera Arts*, "comes from the photographer's reverent use of objects that refer to the now-established elegance of art nouveau and art deco, her paraphrase of the decor of a highly selective, nostalgic vision of the past."

PUBLICATIONS Periodicals: *Art in America*, Sept 1980; "The Portrait Traditions and Transitions," Howard Millard, *Modern Photography*, Aug 1979; "Post Modern Photography—It Doesn't Look Modern at All," Gene Thornton, *Artnews*, Apr 1979.

COLLECTION MOMA, NYC.

DEALER Daniel Wolf, 30 W 57 St, New York, NY 10019.

ADDRESS 924 West End Ave, New York, NY 10025.

Pedro Meyer PHOTOGRAPHER Born October 6, 1935, in Madrid, Spain, Meyer is self-taught in photography but received a BS in Business Administration from Babson College, Wellesley, Massachusetts, in 1956.

A freelance photographer, Meyer is president of the Mexican Council of Photography, as well as a founding member of the following groups: Consejo Latinoamericano de Fotografía (1978); Consejo Mexicano de Fotografía (also president, 1977); Grupo Arte Fotográfico (1963); Escuela Secundaria del Colegio Montessori de la Ciudad de México (also president, 1974); and Colegio Montessori de la Ciudad de México (1968).

Meyer organized the First Exhibition of Contemporary Latin American Photography at the Museum of Modern Art in Mexico City in 1978.

His photography is done mainly in small format and deals with portraiture and social documentation.

PUBLICATIONS Anthologies: *The Photographer's Choice*, 1975; *La Noche de Tlaltelolco*, 1971 (Ediciones ERA, S.A.: Mexico). Periodicals: *Camera*, Oct 1979; *Fotografía Italiana*, 1977; *Foto Zoom Anuario*, 1977; "La Mujer," *Fotomundo Anuario*, 1970; *Fotomundo*, 1970.

PORTFOLIOS *Negromex en Blanco y Negro, Seis Abstracciones en Concreto*, intro. by Raquel Tibol, 1977 (Negromex, S.A.: Mex.); *Y las cosas que le pasan al hombre*, 1977 (Ingenio Mostzorongo, S.A.: Mexico).

COLLECTIONS Addison Gall. of Amer. Art., Andover, Mass.; Babson Coll., Wellesley, Mass.; Boston Mus. of Fine Arts; CCP, Tucson. Casa de las Américas, Havana, Cuba; Casa del Lago, Universidad Nacional Autónoma de México, México D.F.

DEALER Witkin Gall., 41 E 57 St, New York, NY 10022.

ADDRESS Apartado 10–670, Mexico 10, D.F., Mexico.

Joel Meyerowitz PHOTOGRAPHER Born in New York City in 1938, Meyerowitz graduated from Ohio State University, Columbus, in 1959. He works as a freelance photographer.

In 1978 and 1970 he received a Guggenheim Photographers' Fellowship; he also won an NEA grant in 1978 and a CAPS grant in 1975.

PUBLICATIONS Monograph: *Cape Light*, 1978. Book: *The City: American Experience*, Alan Trachtenberg, Peter Neill & Peter C. Bunnell, eds., 1971. Anthologies: *The Photograph Collector's Guide*, Lee D. Witkin & Barbara London, 1979; *Mirrors and Windows*, John Szarkowski, ed., 1978; *The Snapshot*, Jonathan Green, ed., 1974; *Looking at Photographs*, John Szarkowski, 1973; *Photography Year 1973*, Time-Life Series; *Vision and Expression*, Nathan Lyons, ed., 1969; *Photography in the Twentieth Century*, Nathan Lyons, ed., 1967. Periodicals: *Camera*, Sept 1978, Sept 1977, July 1977; *American Photographer*,

Aug 1978; *Aperture*, no. 78, 1977; *Artforum*, Jan 1975.

PORTFOLIO *The Cape*, 1977 (self-pub.: NYC).

COLLECTIONS Boston Mus. of Fine Arts; IMP/GEH, Rochester; MOMA, NYC; Philadelphia Mus. of Art, Pa.; St. Louis Art Mus., Mo.; Virginia Mus. of Fine Arts, Richmond.

DEALERS Witkin Gall., 41 E 57 St, New York, NY 10022; Harcus Krakow Gall., 7 Newbury St, Boston, MA 02116; Nancy R. Moss Represents, 1732 Gen. Pershing St, New Orleans, LA 70115; Grapestake Gall., 2876 California St, San Francisco, CA 94115.

ADDRESS 817 West End Ave, New York, NY 10025.

Steven J. Meyers PHOTOGRAPHER Born October 5, 1948, in Newark, New Jersey, Meyers earned a BA in Psychology from Wheaton College, Wheaton, Illinois (1970), and an MS in Photography from the Institute of Design at Illinois Institute of Technology, Chicago (1976), where he studied with Arthur Siegel, Edward Ranney and Arthur Lazar.

A freelance photographer and designer since 1977, Meyers was director of photography for Sundance Publications, Ltd, of Denver and Silverton, Colorado, in 1975–77.

Meyers belongs to SPE.

The photographer produces "primarily large-format ambiguous images of western landscape." Most of his recent work is paired images of desert formations, "largely selected for their metaphorical possibilities."

PUBLICATIONS Books: *Earth Wisdom*, Dolores LaChapelle, 1978; *Evaluation and Prediction of Avalanche Hazard, San Juan Mountains, Colorado*, 1978 (Inst. of Arctic & Alpine Research Snow & Avalanche Project: Boulder, Colo.); *Avalanche Atlas, Ouray County, Colorado*, 1977 (Univ. of Colo., Inst. of Alpine & Arctic Research: Silverton, Colo.).

DEALER Alonzo Gall., Inc, 30 W 57 St, New York, NY 10019.

ADDRESS POB 481, Silverton, CO 81433.

Phiz Mezey PHOTOGRAPHER · TEACHER · WRITER Born August 25, 1925, in New York City, Mezey received her BA from Reed College, Portland, Oregon, in 1948 and her MA from San Francisco State University, California, in 1971. She studied with Lloyd Reynolds at Reed.

Currently professor of educational technology at San Francisco State University, she has been a contributing editor of *Darkroom Photography* *Magazine* since 1978. Mezey was a photography instructor at San Francisco City College (1973–78) and a media specialist for the Sausalito (California) Teacher Education Project (1966–69). An editor and writer in the Office of War Information Overseas Bureau in 1944–46, she was a freelance writer and photographer for the next twenty-five years.

Mezey has been a member of SPE since 1978. She won the America's Many Faces Award from the National Urban League in 1961. Articles by the writer have appeared in such publications as *The Nation, The New Republic, The New York Times* and *Aperture.*

Mezey began as a photo-essayist and currently concentrates on portraits. Using small format, she works in an informal style, focusing on the communication between photographer and subject.

PUBLICATIONS Books: *Something That's Happening*, 1968; *Our San Francisco*, 1965.

COLLECTION San Francisco Art Commission.

ADDRESS 209 Upper Terrace, San Francisco, CA 94117.

Barbara L. Michaels ART HISTORIAN Born October 4, 1935, in New York City, Michaels earned her BA in 1957 from Cornell University, Ithaca, New York, and her MA in 1962 from the Institute of Fine Arts, New York University, New York City. As of this writing she was a PhD candidate at the Graduate Center, City University of New York.

Since 1976 Michaels has been a lecturer at New York University, and she was an adjunct assistant professor at College of New Rochelle, New York, in 1978. She was assistant curator of the Atget Collection, Photography Department, at the Museum of Modern Art in New York City from 1973 to 1976. In 1971 she taught at the New School for Social Research in New York City; from 1967 to 1968 she was executive secretary at the Studio Museum in Harlem, New York; from 1958 to 1963 she was a gallery assistant at Samuel M. Kootz Gallery, Inc., in New York City.

Her field of art history is the history of photography.

PUBLICATIONS Periodicals: "An Introduction to the Dating and Organization of Eugène Atget's Photographs," *The Art Bulletin*, Sept 1979; "Dating Atget," *Exposure: SPE*, May 1977; "Rediscovering Gertrude Käsebier," *Image*, Aug 1976.

ADDRESS Fine Arts Dept, Main Bldg, New York Univ, Washington Square E, New York, NY 10003.

Chester Michalik TEACHER Born February 21, 1935, in Holyoke, Massachusetts, Michalik received a BS from Massachusetts College of Art, Boston, in 1960 and an MFA from Boston University in 1964.

An assistant professor at Smith College, Northampton, Massachusetts, since 1978, Michalik was an associate professor at Rhode Island School of Design, Providence, from 1964 to 1978. He has also taught at, among other schools, Imageworks School of Photography, Cambridge, Massachusetts (1970–72).

Recipient of a Massachusetts Art and Humanities grant in 1976, Michalik won a Fulbright Fellowship in 1967.

Working in black-and-white, medium format, Michalik takes photographs in urban environments, generally without people. His intent, he says, is "to try to produce personal interpretations of the psychological qualities of cities."

COLLECTIONS Amon Carter Mus. of Art, Fort Worth, Tex.; Art Inst. of Chicago; IMP/GEH, Rochester; Kansas City Mus. of Art, Kans.; L/C, Wash., D.C.; Mus. of Fine Art, Houston, Tex.; Old Stone Bank, Providence, R.I.; R.I. School of Design Mus., Providence; VSW, Rochester; Wellesley Coll., Mass.; Worcester Mus. of Art, Mass. Arts Mus., Toronto, Canada.

DEALER Carl Siembab Gall., 162 Newbury St, Boston, MA 02116.

ADDRESS 108 South St 14-B, Northampton, MA 01060.

Duane Michals PHOTOGRAPHER Born February 18, 1932, in McKeesport, Pennsylvania, Michals received a BA from the University of Denver in Colorado in 1953.

Michals has been a freelance photographer since 1958.

The artist is best known for his "sequences," which he began in 1969, usually depicting a surreal transition in small-format black-and-white. He also does portraits and some commercial work.

PUBLICATIONS Monographs: *Changes*, 1980; *Real Dreams*, 1977; *Vrais Rêves*, 1977 (Editions Chêne, Paris); *Take One and See Mt. Fujiyama*, 1976; *Chance Meeting*, 1973, *Paradise Regained*, 1973, *Things are Queer*, 1973 (Fotogalerie Wilde: Cologne, Germany); *The Journey of the Spirit After Death*, 1971; *Sequences*, 1970. Books: *Light Readings*, A. D. Coleman, 1979; *Nude: Theory*, Jain Kelly, ed., 1979; *Photography Between the Covers*, Thomas Dugan, 1979; *Homage to Cavafy*, 1978; *The Wonders of Egypt*, 1978 (DeNoel: Paris); *Darkroom I*, Eleanor Lewis, ed.,

1977; *Fotografie im 20 Jahrhundert*, Peter Tausk, 1977 (Dumont: Germany); *Theater of the Mind*, Arthur Tress, intro. by Duane Michals, 1976; *The Photographic Illusion*, Ronald H. Bailey, 1975; *Vision and Expression*, Nathan Lyons, ed., 1969. Anthologies: *The Photograph Collector's Guide*, Lee D. Witkin & Barbara London, 1979; *American Photographers*, Manfred Willmann, ed., 1977 (Fotogalerie im Forum Stadtpark: Graz, Austria); *Art as Photography as Art*, Lee Battaglia, no. 10, 1975; *The Magic Image*, Cecil Beaton & Gail Buckland, 1975; *The Photographer's Choice*, Kelly Wise, 1975; *The Art of Photography*, 1971, *The Camera*, 1970, *The Print*, 1970, Time-Life Series. Catalogs: *Sequenced Photographs*, 1976 (Univ. of Missouri: St. Louis); *Das Technische Bild und Dokumentationsmittel Fotografie*, 1973 (Mus. Folkwang: Essen, Germany); *12 Photographers of the American Social Landscape*, 1967 (Brandeis Univ.; Waltham, Mass.); *American Photography: The 60's*, 1966 (Univ. of Nebr.: Lincoln); *Contemporary Photographers*, 1966 (GEH: Rochester). Periodicals: *Photography Forum*, Aug 1979; *American Photographer*, Apr 1979; *Camera 35*, Mar 1979, Oct 1976, Dec 1972, Oct 1971; *Modern Photography*, Mar 1979, Feb 1973, Jan 1971; "Duane Michals," *Nueva Lenta*, no. 28, 1979, June 1974; "Collection 5," 1978, Oct 1976, Oct 1969, *Creative Camera*; *Popular Photography*, Oct 1977, "Annual," 1974, Nov 1973, Dec & Feb 1971; *Kunstforum*, no. 18, 1976; *Village Voice*, Nov. 8, 1976; *Zoom*, Oct 1976 (Paris); *Photo*, Sept & July 1976 (Paris), nos. 53, 58, 61, 64, 66, 1971; "Seeing in Sequence," *Art and Man*, 6:6, 1976 (Natl. Gall. of Art); *Camera*, May 1975, Oct 1970, July 1969; *Photo World*, June 1974, Dec 1973; *Progresso Fotografico*, Jan 1974; *Photo Cine Review*, Sept 1973; *Foto*, Aug 1973, Aug 1972 (Sweden); *Camera Mainichi*, May 1972; *Album*, no. 7, Aug 1970; *Art Scene*, June 1968; *Art In America*, June 1967; *Contemporary Photographer*, spring 1964.

PORTFOLIOS *Ten Photographers* (group), 1978 (Women's Campaign Fund: Wash., D.C.); *The First Portfolio*, 1975 (Apeiron: Millerton, N.Y.); *10 Fotografien*, 1975 (Galerie Wilde: Cologne, Germany); *Untitled*, 1972 (self-pub.).

COLLECTIONS Akron Art Inst., Ohio; Art Inst. of Chicago; Boston Mus. of Fine Arts; Carnegie Inst., Pittsburgh, Pa.; Cincinnati Art Mus., Ohio; Exchange Bank of Chicago; IMP/GEH, Rochester; Hofstra Univ., Emily Lowe Gall., W. Hempstead, Long Island, N.Y.; Metro. Mus. of Art, NYC; MOMA, NYC; Mus. of N. Mex., Santa Fe; William Rockhill Nelson Gall., Kansas City, Mo.; New Orleans Mus.; Norton Simon Mus.,

Pasadena, Calif.; Ohio State Univ. Cllctn.; Philadelphia Lib., Pa.; R.I. School of Design, Providence; Smithsonian Inst., Wash., D.C.; UCLA; Univ. of Delaware, Wilmington; Univ. of Maryland, College Park; Univ. of Miami, Lowe Art Mus., Fla.; Vassar Coll., Poughkeepsie, N.Y.; Wesleyan Univ. Cllctn., Middletown, Conn.; Worcester Art Mus., Worcester, Mass. Bibliothèque Nationale, Paris; Israel Mus., Jerusalem; Moderna Muséet, Stockholm; Natl. Mus. of Canada, Ottawa; Stedelijk Mus., Amsterdam.
DEALER Sidney Janis Gall., 6 W 57 St, New York, NY 10019.
ADDRESS 109 E 19 St, New York, NY 10003.

Francesco Paolo Michetti *PHOTOGRAPHER · PAINTER* Born in Tocco Casauria, Abruzzo, Italy, on October 2, 1851, Michetti died in the town of Francovilla a Mare in 1929. He became interested in photography when he made his first trip to Paris in 1871. The painter Manono Fortuny greatly influenced Michetti's work. The photographer won first prize in the first Biennial of Modern Art held in Venice in 1895.

Known especially for his *cartes de visite* and the use of color-tone (a technique that was later popularized), Michetti paid particular attention to documenting rural life in Italy. Becoming convinced that art was only an imitation of nature, Michetti abandoned painting and devoted the latter part of his career to producing straight photography. Two of his photographic essays include the amputees in Casalbordino (1895–1900) and the tuna slaughter in Acireale, about 1907.

PUBLICATION Monograph: *Francesco Paolo Michetti*, Marina Miraglia, 1975 (Giulio Einaud: Torino, Italy).

Hansel Mieth *PHOTOGRAPHER · WRITER* Mieth was born April 9, 1909, in Fillback, Germany; her husband was photographer Otto Hagel. She names as major influences her mother and the artists Käthe Kollwitz and Vincent van Gogh.

Mieth worked for Time Inc., after moving to California in 1941, having been a staff photographer for *Life* magazine from 1937 to 1941. From 1934 to 1936 she was a WPA photographer in the West Coast project.

She belongs to the American Newspaper Guild. The photojournalist specializes in medical research stories, but she "had to go on any story *Life* sent me, from Southern mansions to Hell Hole swamp to Japanese relocation camps."

PUBLICATION Anthology: *Best of Life*, 1973.

COLLECTION L/C, Wash., D.C.
REPRESENTATIVE Time-Life Pictures, Time & Life Bldg, Rockefeller Ctr, New York, NY 10020.
ADDRESS 2660 Porter Creek Rd, Santa Rosa, CA 95404.

Adolf Miethe *CHEMIST · PHYSICIST* Born Christian Heinrich Emil Adolf Miethe in Potsdam in 1862, Miethe died in 1927. He attended the Potsdam Gymnasium and the Universities of Berlin and Göttingen.

In 1887 he promoted magnesium flashlight photography in Germany together with Johannes Gaedicke. Joining Dr. Hartnack's firm in Potsdam in 1889, he first developed new microscope and photographic lenses; later he developed a telephoto lens while working with Schulze & Bartels in Rathenow from 1891 to 1894. Then Miethe joined Voigtländer & Sohn as a research scientist, becoming one of its first directors upon its incorporation. The scientist took over as professor of photochemistry at the Technische Hochschule in Berlin in 1899 after Hermann Vogel died, and the department expanded under his direction to include photomechanical reproduction and spectrophotometry. Miethe directed the Photographisches Wochenblatt from 1889, and in 1894 founded Das Atelier des Photographen and Photographische Chronik, which he directed for the next twenty-five years. In 1904 he became head of the Technische Hochschule in Berlin.

Miethe helped pioneer the production of panchromatic emulsions for color photography by his discovery, with Arthur Traube in 1902, of ethyl red, the first color sensitizer of the isocyanine series. His final set of experiments, in 1926, explored the use of ultraviolet light in photographing fossils.

An honorary member of numerous photographic societies, he was a founder of Deutsche Kinotechnische Gesellschaft in 1919.

PUBLICATIONS Books: *Quellendarstellungen zur Geschichte der Fotografie*, Wolfgang Baier, 1964; *Festschrift*, 1963 (100 Jahre Institute für ange wandre Photochemie und Filmtechnik); *History of Photography*, J. M. Eder, 3rd ed., 1905, repr. 1945; *Lexikon für Photographie und Reproduktionstechnik*, G. H. Emmerich, 1910; *Dreifarbenphotographie nach der Natur*, 1904. Anthology: *Photography's Great Inventors*, Louis W. Sipley, 1965. Periodicals: *Fotografie*, Feb 1963; *Photographische Correspondenz*, 1927; *History of 3-Color Photography*, E. J. Wall, 1925.

Jun Miki *PHOTOGRAPHER* Born September 14, 1919, in Kurashiki City, Japan, Miki graduated from the Faculty of Economy, Keio University.

Since 1957 Miki has been self-employed as a freelance photographer. Previously he worked as a photographer for Time-Life (1949–56). As of this writing Miki was also a professor at Nihon University in Japan.

He is chairman of the Nikkor Club, and vice-president of Japan Professional Photographers' Society. He has been the recipient of awards from Japan Professional Photographers' Association (1962), from KODANSHA (1960) and from the Japan Photographic Critics' Association (1959).

PUBLICATIONS Books: *Keio Gijuku*, 1979; *Sokagakkai*, 1970; *Samba Samba Brasil*, 1967; *Mexico*, 1961.

ADDRESS Shirogane Mansion 301, 4–10–18, Shirogane, Minato-Ku, Tokyo, Japan.

Henryk Mikolasch *PHOTOGRAPHER* Born in 1876 in Poland, Mikolasch died there in 1931.

Working as a photographer in the city of Lwów from 1921 on, Mikolasch also lectured on photography at Lwów Polytechnic.

In 1903 he became a member of the Lwów Photographic Society and served as its chairman for many years.

Famous in his country for his gum prints, Mikolasch made many photographs of wild animals.

PUBLICATION Book: *Album of Polish Photographers*, ed., 1905.

COLLECTION Muzeum Narodowe we Wrocławiu, Warsaw, Poland.

Tom Millea *PHOTOGRAPHER* Born September 30, 1944, in Bridgeport, Connecticut, Millea earned a BA in History with emphasis on anthropology and sociology. He studied with Jonathan Greenwald and Paul Caponigro (1966–73) in Bethel, Connecticut, then moved to California.

As of this writing Millea was a self-employed photographer; he taught photography at Monterey Peninsula College, California, and at the University of California at Santa Cruz and at Santa Barbara (Extension) from 1975 to 1979. He also served as an instructor and independent counselor for Antioch College in 1976–79. Millea was director of photography in 1973 at Photo-Graphic Workshop in New Canaan, Connecticut, and co-director of the Underground Gallery of Photography in New York City in 1969–70.

He works mainly in platinum and palladium processes, using small- and large-format cameras. His subjects include nudes and landscapes.

PUBLICATIONS Books: *The Platinum Print*, 1980; *Freewheeling Meditations*, 1974.

PORTFOLIOS *Image Continuum*, Ted Orland & Sally Mann, eds., 1976; *Portfolio One*, 1975 (self-pub.).

COLLECTIONS CCP, Tucson; Floating Fndn. of Photography, NYC; Oakland Mus., Calif.; Seagram Corp., Los Angeles; Stanford Univ. Mus., Calif. Victoria & Albert Mus., London.

DEALERS Weston Gall., Box 655, Carmel, CA 93921; Smith Andersen Gall., 200 Homer St, Palo Alto, CA 94301; G. Ray Hawkins Gall., 7224 Melrose Ave, Los Angeles, CA 90046.

ADDRESS Box 4212, Carmel, CA 93921.

Brian Charles Miller *PHOTOGRAPHER · TEACHER* Born July 29, 1947, in Framingham, Massachusetts, Miller earned a BA in Ceramics and Design (Photography) in 1971 and an MA in Design (Photography) in 1972 from California State University, Fullerton.

He currently teaches photography and art at Orange Coast College, Costa Mesa (since 1973), and at Saddleback College, Mission Viejo (since 1976), as well as being a photographer and technician at Surfer Publishing Group, Dana Point, all in California. Miller taught photography at Santa Ana College, California, from 1972 to 1979.

A member of SPE, Los Angeles Institute of Contemporary Art (LAICA), Friends of Photography and National Association of Underwater Instructors, he is a founding member of Los Angeles Center for Photographic Studies. Winner of an Art Scholarship from the Costa Mesa Art League in 1967, he received a State University Research Grant in photo-ceramics from California State University, Fullerton, in 1971.

He works in photo-assemblage.

PUBLICATIONS Periodicals: "The Primacy of Idea," Dinah Porter, *Artweek*, Mar 10, 1979; "Narrative Landscape on the Continental Shelf: Notes on Southern California," Kim Levin, *Arts Magazine*, Oct 1976; *Journal*, Aug-Sept 1975 (LAICA).

COLLECTIONS IMP/GEH, Rochester; Newport Harbor Art Mus., Newport Beach, Calif.

ADDRESS POB 703, S Laguna, CA 92677.

Laurence Glenn Miller *PHOTOGRAPHER · TEACHER* Born October 8, 1948, in New York City, Miller earned a BS (1972) and an MA (1973) from the University of Wisconsin, Madison, where he studied with Cavalliere Ketchum. He later attended the University of New Mexico, Albuquerque (1973–74), where he studied with

Beaumont Newhall, Van Deren Coke and Tom Barrow.

As of this writing Miller is teaching history of photography at the New School for Social Research (since 1977) and is associate director of Light Gallery (since 1974), both in New York City.

A member of SPE (since 1977) and CAA, he won a CAPS grant in 1977.

Miller curated the exhibit, "The Book—A New Direction for Photography," at the Quivira Gallery in Albuquerque in 1974.

PUBLICATIONS Catalogs: *An Exhibition of Color Photography*, 1977 (Univ. of Conn., Jorgensen Gall.: Storrs); *Light and Substance*, 1974 (Univ. of N. Mex. Art Mus.: Albuquerque).

COLLECTIONS Art Inst. of Chicago; C. W. Post Coll., Greenvale, N.Y.; Madison Art Ctr., Wisc.; Northwestern Univ., Evanston, Ill. Bibliothèque Nationale, Paris.

ADDRESS 113 Willow Ave, Hoboken, NJ 07030.

Lee Miller *PHOTOGRAPHER · MODEL · PAINTER*
Born in the United States ca. 1906, Miller died in 1977 in London. Her husband, Sir Roland Penrose (1900–), is an art critic and collector. She studied art in Paris in 1925 and painting at the Art Students League in New York City from 1926 to 1929, then returned to Paris to study with Man Ray in 1929–32.

Miller began work as a model in New York for Edward Steichen ca. 1922 and later worked as an assistant and model for Man Ray in Paris (1929–32). She opened her own studio in Paris in 1930, occasionally teaching photography as well, then opened a New York studio in 1932. She joined the London War Correspondents Corps (1939–45), publishing her descriptions and photographs from the front in *Vogue*.

Also an actress, Miller played the lead role in Jean Cocteau's film *Le Sang d'un Poète* in Paris in 1930.

Miller was especially noted for her fashion photography during World War II, which, in a straight, documentary style, showed women coping with war conditions.

PUBLICATIONS Book: *Wrens in Camera*, K. M. Palmer, 1945 (Hollis & Carter: London). Anthology: *The History of Fashion Photography*, Nancy Hall-Duncan, 1979.

Neil Allen Miller *TEACHER · PHOTOGRAPHER*
Born April 26, 1945, in Cleveland, Ohio, Miller earned a BFA in Photography from Ohio University, Athens, in 1969, and an MFA in 1977 from Arizona State University, Tempe. He attended a workshop with Ansel Adams in 1973.

Miller is, as of this date, Visual Communications Design Program coordinator for Arizona State University; he has been part-time news photographer and editor for KOOL-TV in Phoenix, Arizona, since 1971. He lectured at Arizona State University on media production from 1971 to 1978.

Miller is a member of SPE, Friends of Photography, IMP/GEH and the University Film Association. Between 1973 and 1979 he developed a file of tape recordings of various photographers' lectures, most of which are included in the Center for Creative Photography, Tucson.

Miller works in black-and-white, using various formats. His 35mm work, using on-camera flash, concentrates on gatherings of people. His medium-format work is mainly landscapes and studies of his children.

PUBLICATION Periodical: *Camera*, Aug 1974.

COLLECTIONS Arizona Bank, Phoenix; Arizona State Univ., Tempe; CCP, Tucson; F22 Gall., Santa Fe, N.M.; Univ. of New Mexico, Albuquerque.

ADDRESS 5124 E Toniko Dr, Phoenix, AZ 85044.

James Oliver Milmoe *PHOTOGRAPHER* Born April 21, 1927, in Pittsburgh, Pennsylvania, Milmoe received a BA from Colorado College, Colorado Springs, in 1949 and an MFA from the University of Denver, Colorado, in 1978.

A freelance photographer and photographic consultant since 1961, he has also taught in the Fine Art Department (since 1969) and in Continuing University Studies (since 1959) at the University of Colorado, Denver.

A member of ASMP, SPE and the Association for Gravestone Studies, he was elected a fellow of the Photographic Society of America in 1973. In that year he also won the Governor's Award from the Colorado Council on the Arts and Humanities.

The photographer works in black-and-white and color in a variety of formats, including stereoscopic. He applies photography to printmaking, including photo-intaglio with aquatint, silk screen, photolithography, xerography and cyanotypes. He is interested in "a personal photographic interpretation of the aspen tree and the sculpture and folk art of the cemetery."

PUBLICATIONS Book: *Guide to Good Exposure*, 1964, 2nd ed., 1966. Periodical: *Communication Arts*, 13:3, 1971.

PORTFOLIO *Colorado Portfolio* (Colorado State Bank).

COLLECTIONS Chicago Art Inst.; Colorado State Bank; Denver Art Mus., Colo.; MOMA, NYC; United Banks of Colo.

ADDRESS 14900 Cactus Circle, Golden, CO 80401.

Jacques Minassian *PHOTOGRAPHER* Minassian was born September 12, 1946, in Paris.

He is currently employed as a freelance photographer.

A member of VIVA (1975–78), Minassian was the recipient of grants from the Gulbenkian Foundation in Lisbon, Portugal, and the Fondation Nationale de la Photographie in Lyon, France, in 1977.

PUBLICATIONS Periodicals: *Nouveau Photocinéma*, Mar 1979, Nov 1977; *News Reporter*, Nov 1977; *Progresso Fotografico*, May 1977.

COLLECTIONS In France: Bibliothèque Nationale, Paris; Centre Georges Pompidou, Paris; Fondation Nationale de la Photographie, Lyon.

ADDRESS 74 rue d'Hauteville, 75010 Paris, France.

Leigh Richmond Miner *PHOTOGRAPHER · TEACHER · CRAFTSMAN · COLLECTOR · BOTANIST* Miner was born in Cornwall, Connecticut, on August 5, 1864, and died in Hampton, Connecticut, on June 9, 1935. He studied applied arts at the Academy of Design in New York City and did graduate work at the Pennsylvania Museum in Philadelphia.

Miner became an instructor at Hampton Institute in 1898, eventually serving as director of applied art. He maintained his own studio in New York City ca. 1904–1907.

The photographer worked with glass negatives, superbly executing a compassionate record of the lives of blacks on St. Helena Island.

PUBLICATIONS Books: *Face of an Island*, Edith M. Dobbs, 1971; *Home Decoration*, 1921.

Roger Minick *PHOTOGRAPHER · TEACHER* Born July 13, 1944, in Ramona, Oklahoma, Minick earned a BA in History from the University of California, Berkeley, in 1969. He also apprenticed in photography at the Associated Students of the University of California (ASUC) Studio on the Berkeley campus from 1964 to 1969. His wife, Joyce Minick, is a writer.

Minick was a photographer for the Mexican American Legal Defense and Educational Fund's (MALDEF) Photo Survey in 1977–79. He directed the ASUC Studio from 1970 to 1975.

Winner of a Guggenheim Fellowship in 1972, the photographer participated in two NEA-sponsored photo surveys, the first for MALDEF and another for the Oakland Museum in 1979.

Using small or large format, Minick works in an interpretive, documentary mode, often emphasizing people, their landscape and life-style. His recent work has been more urban than rural and more personal in nature.

PUBLICATIONS Monographs: *Hills of Home, The Rural Ozarks of Arkansas*, Bob Minick, 1975; *Delta West, The Land and People of the Sacramento–San Joaquin River Delta*, 1969. Periodicals: *Creative Camera*, Jan 1980; *Photoshow*, Mar 1980; *Camera*, summer 1980; *Popular Photography*, Feb 1979; *American Photographer*, Jan 1979; *Picture Magazine*, nos. 8 & 9, fall 1978.

PORTFOLIOS *Delta Portfolio*, 1976, *The Ozark Portfolio*, 1976 (self-pub.).

COLLECTIONS CCP, Tucson; Exchange Bank of Chicago; Harvard Univ., Fogg Art Mus., Cambridge, Mass.; Guggenheim Memorial Fndn., NYC; Houston Mus. of Fine Arts, Tex.; Hunter Mus. of Art, Chattanooga, Tenn.; Mid-America Ctr. Mus., Hot Springs, Ark.; MOMA, NYC; Oakland Mus., Calif.; San Francisco Mus. of Modern Art, Calif.; Seagram Cllctn., NYC.

DEALERS Grapestake Gall., 2876 California St, San Francisco, CA 94115; Douglas Kenyon Gall., 155 E Ohio St, Chicago, IL 60611.

ADDRESS 950 Stannage Ave, Albany, CA 94706.

Arno Rafael Minkkinen *PHOTOGRAPHER · TEACHER · WRITER* [See plate 116] Born June 4, 1945, in Helsinki, Finland, Minkkinen earned a BA in English (1967) from Wagner College, Staten Island, New York, and an MFA in Photography (1974) from Rhode Island School of Design, Providence. His major influences were Harry Callahan, Aaron Siskind, John Benson and Ralph Hattersley.

Minkkinen has been assistant professor of photography at MIT, Cambridge, Massachusetts, since 1977. From 1976 to 1977 and from 1967 to 1972 he was an advertising copywriter in New York, and in 1974–76 he taught at the Helsinki Institute of Industrial Design.

He is a member of SPE, Friends of Photography and the Photographic Resource Center in Boston, Massachusetts.

Working in small format, the photographer produces unmanipulated self-portraits and nudes against natural landscapes, often in and around lakes and rivers.

PUBLICATIONS Monograph: *Frostbite*, 1978.

Anthologies: *Fantastic Photographs*, 1979; *Self-Portrayal*, 1978. Periodical: *Popular Photography Annual*, 1978.

COLLECTIONS Addison Gall. of Amer. Art, Andover, Mass.; CCP, Tucson; R.I. School of Design, Providence. Fotografiska Muséet at Moderna Muséet, Stockholm, Sweden; Wämo Aaltosen Museo, Turku, Finland.

DEALER Yuen Lui Gall., 906 Pine St, Seattle, WA 98101.

ADDRESS 95 Lowell St, Andover, MA 01810.

Marco Misani EDITOR · PUBLISHER · PHOTOGRAPHER Born October 11, 1949, Misani is a self-taught journalist and photographer.

Since 1976 he has been editor and publisher of *printletter*.

PUBLICATIONS Periodicals: "Silence," Nov 1975, "European Scenes," June 1973, *Camerart*; *Creative Camera*, Mar 1975.

ADDRESS POB 250, CH-8046 Zurich, Switzerland.

Clark Mishler PHOTOGRAPHER Born August 31, 1948, in Trenton, Michigan, Mishler attended Ferris State College, Big Rapids, Michigan (Associate Degree, 1968), Art Center College of Design, Los Angeles (1970), and the Missouri Photo Workshop, Columbia (1976).

Since 1979 he has done freelance photography in Anchorage, Alaska, which he did also in 1973–77. From 1977 to 1979 he was layout editor for *National Geographic Magazine* in Washington, D.C., and from 1973 to 1977 he was publisher of *The Alaska Catalog*. In 1971–73 Mishler was a member of the Skyriver documentary film project in Anchorage.

A member of SPE and the Alaskan Photographers Guild, he won first prize in the All Alaska Juried Art Exhibition in 1976.

Mishler works in abstract color photojournalism.

PUBLICATIONS Periodicals: *National Geographic Magazine*, June 1979; *Aura Magazine*, 1976.

COLLECTION Alaska Contemporary Art Bank, Anchorage.

REPRESENTATIVE Alaskaphoto, 1431 W Ninth Ave, Anchorage, AK 99501.

ADDRESS 1238 G St, Anchorage, AK 99501.

Léonard Misonne PHOTOGRAPHER Born in 1870 in Gilly (Charleroi), Belgium, Misonne died in 1943. He received a diploma in engineering at the University of Lowen in 1895.

Misonne became interested in photography during his student days, and since he came from a comfortable financial background he was free to pursue his interest throughout his life.

He was a member of the London Salon.

A pictorialist, the photographer once wrote, "The theme is nothing in itself, light is all," according to Carolyn Bloore *(Pictorial Photography in Britain)*. He used a variety of processes to record his atmospheric landscapes and street scenes—gum-bichromate, carbon, bromoil, oil prints, Fresson and bromide.

PUBLICATIONS Books: *Introduction à l'oeuvre photographique de Léonard Misonne*, Maurice Misonne, 1971; *Twenty-four photographs*, 1934; *Tableaux Photographiques*, 1927. Anthologies: *Pictorial Photography in Britain, 1900–1920*, Arts Council of Great Britain, 1978; *The Magic Image*, Cecil Beaton & Gail Buckland, 1975; *Early Photographs & Early Photographers*, Oliver Mathews, 1973.

COLLECTIONS Het Sterckshof, Deurne, Antwerp, Belgium; Mus. Agfa-Gevaert, Leverkusen, Germany.

ARCHIVE L. Misonne Family, Charleroi, Belgium.

Richard Laurence Misrach PHOTOGRAPHER Born July 11, 1949, in Los Angeles, California, Misrach earned a BA in Psychology from the University of California, Berkeley, in 1971.

He was on the photography staff of the Associated Students of the University of California Studio, Berkeley, from 1971 to 1977.

Misrach won a Guggenheim Fellowship in 1978, NEA fellowships in 1977 and 1973, and a Ferguson Grant in 1976.

In black-and-white, and more recently color, the photographer's work has included a documentary of street life in Berkeley and photographs of the desert at dusk, for which he used flash.

PUBLICATIONS Monographs: *A Photographic Book*, 1979; *Telegraph 3 A.M.: The Street People of Telegraph Avenue, Berkeley*, 1974. Anthologies: *American Images* Renato Danese, ed., 1979; *Mirrors & Windows*, John Szarkowski, ed., 1978. Periodicals: *Picture Magazine*, Apr 1979; "The Photographer and the Drawing," ed., *Creative Camera*, Aug 1977; *Popular Photography Annual*, 1977; *Photo Magazine*, Mar 1977. Review: "Stopping the World: Photographs as Myth," Irene Borger, *Exposure*: SPE, fall 1979.

COLLECTIONS ARCO Ctr. for Visual Arts, Los Angeles; Crocker Art Ctr., Sacramento, Calif.; Houston Mus. of Fine Arts; Kalamazoo Inst. for the Arts, Mich.; L/C, Wash., D.C.; Madison Art Ctr., Wisc.; MOMA, NYC; Oakland Mus., Calif.; San Francisco Mus. of Modern Art, Calif.; Smithsonian Inst., Wash., D.C.; Springfield Art Mus., Mo. Centre Georges Pompidou, Musée d'Art Moderne, Paris.

DEALER Grapestake Gall., 2876 California St, San Francisco, CA 94115.

ADDRESS 1420 45 St, Emeryville, CA 94608.

Margaretta K. Mitchell *PHOTOGRAPHER · WRITER · PHOTOHISTORIAN · TEACHER* Born May 27, 1935, in Brooklyn, New York, Mitchell graduated in 1957 from Smith College, Northampton, Massachusetts, where she studied with Leonard Baskin, Ruth and Clarence Kennedy and Phyllis Lehmann. She also studied etching at the Boston Museum School (1958–59), and attended Escuela de Bellas Artes in Madrid (1959–60).

Most recently she has been teaching photography for the Civic Arts Program in Walnut Creek, California, and for City College of San Francisco. She taught photography from 1976 to 1978 at University of California Extension, San Francisco and Berkeley, and from 1973 to 1976 at Head-Royce Schools in Oakland, California. From 1974 to 1978 she also taught private workshops and seminars. In 1975 Mitchell served on the staff of the Photography Workshop in Volcano, Hawaii, and in 1973 was an assistant at Ansel Adams Yosemite Workshop. She worked as a research assistant to Dr. Edwin Land in 1957–59.

Mitchell belongs to ASMP, SPE and San Francisco Women Artists.

In 1978 she created the slide/film presentation, *Dance for Life* for the San Francisco Art Commission at the San Francisco Museum of Modern Art.

About her portraiture, Mitchell writes, "I am careful not to call forth the darkness, which is easy enough because we live in a dark age. I attempt to share in the humanity, not the vanity of the sitter."

PUBLICATIONS Books: *To a Cabin*, w/Dorothea Lange, 1973; *Gift of Place*, 1969. Anthology: *Recollections: Ten Women of Photography*, ed., 1979. Periodicals: *Popular Photography*, July 1979, July 1976, July & Mar 1975; *35mm Photography*, Nov 1976.

COLLECTIONS Archive of the Performing Arts, San Francisco; Exchange Natl. Bank of Chicago; ICP, NYC; Pennzoil Corp., Houston, Tex.; Smith Coll. Mus., Northampton, Mass.; Univ. of Calif., Bancroft Lib., Berkeley.

ADDRESS 280 Hillcrest Rd, Berkeley, CA 94705.

Toyo Miyatake *PHOTOGRAPHER* Born in 1895 on the island of Shikoku, Japan, Miyatake died in Los Angeles in 1979. He learned photography from, and was greatly influenced by, Mr. Shigeta, a teacher in Los Angeles.

Miyatake moved to San Francisco with his family in 1909 and worked in his father's bakery and confectionery store. In 1923 he set up a studio in San Francisco's Little Tokyo, but moved to Japan to care for his ailing father (1933–36). He then returned to the same area and established another studio, but was relocated to Manzanar, a Japanese internment camp, during World War II. He remained there until the end of the war and was eventually allowed to be the official camp photographer. Upon his release, he established a studio in Los Angeles' Little Tokyo.

Most noted for his documentation of the people and life of Manzanar and Little Tokyo, Miyatake always worked in large format and was clearly influenced by traditional Japanese artists. He used dramatic lighting in his portraits of such personalities as the Japanese dancer Michio Ito, Thomas Mann, and Crown Prince Akihito. He also produced abstract images.

COLLECTION Los Angeles County Mus. of Natural Hist.

Lisette Model *PHOTOGRAPHER* [See plate 62] Born in Vienna, Model received early training in music as a student of Arnold Schönberg. In 1922 she went to Paris to study music and painting, beginning photography in 1937. She moved to the U.S. in 1938 with her husband, the painter Evsa Model. She died in May 1983.

In 1940 Model applied for a job in the photographic lab of the newspaper *P.M.* in New York City, but instead of hiring her, the picture editor, Ralph Steiner, published her Promenade des Anglais images: taken on the French Riviera in 1937, they made her a critical success. From 1941 to 1953 she worked for *Harper's Bazaar*, and since 1951 the photographer has taught at the New School for Social Research in New York City.

Working in small- and medium-format black-and-white, Model is known for her stark images of isolated individuals, often large individuals who fill most of the frame and create a sense of mass. She has also done an ongoing series on reflections.

PUBLICATIONS Monograph: *Lisette Model*, essay by Berenice Abbott, 1979. Books: *The History of Photography from 1839 to the Present Day*, Beaumont Newhall, 1949, 4th ed., 1964; *A Guide to Better Photography*, Berenice Abbott,

1941. Anthologies: *The Snapshot,* Jonathan Greene, 1974; *Looking at Photographs,* John Szarkowski, 1973; *Hundred Years of the American Female,* Nancy White, ed., 1967; *Photography in the Twentieth Century,* Nathan Lyons, 1967; *Photography of the World,* 1958 (Heibonsha: Tokyo); *The Family of Man,* Edward Steichen, ed., 1955. Catalogs: *Model Photographs,* 1976 (Sander Gall.: Wash., D.C.); *Women of Photography: An Historical Survey,* Margery Mann, 1975 (San Francisco Mus. of Modern Art). Periodicals: *Camera,* Dec 1979, Sept 1978, Dec 1977, Nov 1975, Dec 1972, Feb 1972, Mar 1971; "Lisette Model: Re-Emergence from Legend," *Aperture,* no. 78, 1977; "Lisette Model," *Center for Creative Photography Bulletin,* May 1977; *Creative Camera,* Yearbook 1976, Nov 1974, Nov 1969; "Lisette Model: Keeping the Legend Intact," *Infinity: ASMP,* Jan 1973; "Gallagher's People . . . Photographed by Lisette Model," Apr 1945, "Lisette Model: Pictures By a Great Refugee Photographer," Tom Maloney, Oct 1942, *U.S. Camera; U.S. Camera Annual,* 1943, 1942; "Candid Photography," Phillip Andrews, *Complete Photographer,* Dec 20, 1941.

PORTFOLIO *Lisette Model,* 1976 (Lunn Gall./ Graphics Internatl. Ltd.: Wash., D.C.).

COLLECTIONS IMP/GEH, Rochester; MOMA, NYC; New Orleans Mus. of Art; Smithsonian Inst., Wash., D.C.

ADDRESS 137 Seventh Ave S, New York, NY 10014.

Tina Modotti *PHOTOGRAPHER · MODEL · REVOLUTIONARY* Born Assunta Adelaide Luigia Modotti on August 16, 1896, in Udine, Italy, she died January 5, 1942, in Mexico City. She was married to Roubaix (Robo) de L'Abrie Richéy (1890–1922), an American poet and painter. Edward Weston was her teacher and most important influence.

Modotti began work at the age of ten in a textile factory, and after emigrating to San Francisco in 1913, worked again in a textile mill before setting herself up as a dressmaker. After marrying, she moved to Los Angeles in 1917 and was featured in several Hollywood films (1920). She met Weston in 1921 and lived with him in Mexico from 1923 to 1926, where she took up photography and also modeled for such renowned muralists as Diego Rivera and José Orozco, as well as for Weston. Becoming deeply involved with revolutionary politics, she joined the Communist Party in 1927. While residing in Mexico she contributed frequently to *Mexican Folkways* magazine and the newspaper *El Machete,* the

revolutionary organ for which she served as the Italian-Spanish translator. She was deported in 1929, staying briefly in Berlin before moving on to Moscow. While in Europe she contributed to such publications as the *British Journal of Photography* and the *Revue Mensuelle Illustré.* She relinquished photography in 1931 to devote herself completely to revolutionary causes and was instrumental in maintaining the Soviet International Red Aid in 1932. She worked as a reporter (not a photographer) for the Spanish paper *Ayuda.* Known simply as "Maria" in her revolutionary work, Modotti returned to Mexico on April 19, 1939, resumed her true name, and once again picked up the camera.

During a brief stay in Germany in 1930, she became a member of Unionfoto GmbH.

Working exclusively in silver and platinum prints, she made her work "highly personal and distinct," said Gustavo Ortiz Hernán in Constantine's *Tina Modotti: A Fragile Life.* "Ideologically she belongs to the avant garde. . . . Her photographs can be easily classified: works of pure composition in which concerns for perspective, construction, and dimension reveal the skill of the artist in handling her medium." Her most frequent subjects were portraits of artist friends, Mexican peasants, frescoes and abstract compositions.

PUBLICATIONS Monographs: *Tina Modotti: A Fragile Life,* Mildred Constantine, 1975; *Tina Modotti, Garibaldina e artista,* 1973 (Circolo Culturale: Udine, Italy). Books: *The Daybooks of Edward Weston,* vol. 1 & 2, Nancy Newhall, ed., 1961; *Portrait of Mexico,* Bertram D. Wolfe & Diego Rivera, w/Bravo & Lupercio, 1937; *The Frescoes of Diego Rivera,* intro. by Ernestine Evans, 1929; *Idols behind Altars,* Anita Brenner, w/Edw. Weston, 1929; *The Book of Robo,* intro. by John Cowper Powys, 1923. Anthologies: *The Photograph Collector's Guide,* Lee D. Witkin & Barbara London, 1979; *Women of Photography,* Margery Mann & Ann Noggle, eds., 1975; *Looking at Photographs,* John Szarkowski, 1973. Periodicals: "Sesso, Arte, Violenza e Marxismo," *Bolaffiarte,* special issue, 1977; "Tina's Trajectory," David Vestal, *Infinity: ASMP,* Feb 1966; *Creative Arts,* Carleton Beal, Feb 1929; *Transition,* Feb 1929.

COLLECTIONS IMP/GEH, Rochester; MOMA, NYC; Oakland Mus., Calif. Natl. Lib., Mexico City.

Denny R. Moers *PHOTOGRAPHER* Born in Detroit, Michigan, Moers earned a BFA in 1973 at Empire State College, Rochester, New York, where he studied poetry with Robert Creeley, and an MFA in 1977 from VSW in Rochester, where he studied with Nathan Lyons.

A freelance photographer, he has also assisted photographer Aaron Siskind since 1978.

Moers won a Rhode Island Aid to Individual Artists grant in 1979.

His "trademark" is using a fogging process to achieve various colors in black-and-white silver prints. The one-of-a-kind prints have a visual quality "characteristic of watercolors, pastels and washes."

COLLECTIONS Del. Art Mus.; Graham Nash Cllctn., Los Angeles; R.I. Mus. of Art, Providence.

DEALERS O. K. Harris Gall., 383 W Broadway, New York, NY 10012; G. Ray Hawkins Gall., 7224 Melrose Ave, Los Angeles, CA 90060; Kathleen Ewing Gall., 3020 K St NW, Washington, DC 20007.

ADDRESS 141 Ivy St, Providence, RI 02906.

Curtis E. Moffat   *PHOTOGRAPHER · PAINTER*
Born in New York in 1887, Moffat died February 15, 1949, in Edgartown, Martha's Vineyard, Massachusetts. His father-in-law was the noted English actor Sir Herbert Beerbohm Tree. Moffat attended St. Mark's School, Southborough, Massachusetts, ca. 1913–14 and later studied art at the Ecole des Beaux Arts in Paris. He collaborated with Man Ray and Freddie May and was influenced by Braque, De Chirico and Picasso.

He began his professional photographic career in Paris after World War I and opened a studio in London in 1925. He remained in that city for the greater part of the next thirty-four years, occasionally returning to New York. He also established his own interior decorating firm, Curtis Moffat, Inc., and designed furniture.

He belonged to the Edgartown Yacht Club and the Reading Room of Edgartown.

As a painter, Moffat concentrated mainly on still lifes. He also was a collector of Chinese objects and African sculpture.

The artist's concerns ranged from the abstract and avant-garde to the decorative and commercial. Experimenting a great deal with color, he also worked on photograms with Man Ray and took portraits of friends and various literati and artists for weekly magazines.

PUBLICATION Anthology: *The Magic Image*, Cecil Beaton & Gail Buckland, 1975.

John Moffat   *ENGRAVER · PHOTOGRAPHER*
Born in Aberdeen, Scotland, on August 26, 1819, Moffat died in Edinburgh in April 1894. His son

Frank Pelham (1854–1914) was president of Professional Photographers Association and another son, Arthur Elwell (1860–1943), was a painter.

Moffat's father moved the family to Edinburgh in 1826. In 1847 he began a business as a portrait engraver and in 1853 began a photography business. He became quite successful, and by 1887 was employing twenty assistants. His son Frank joined the firm, and his son Arthur, who had won a silver medal at Edinburgh, evidently produced oil portraits based on his father's photographs. Frank took over the business upon Moffat's death.

The photographer belonged to the Edinburgh Photographic Society and was a council member of the Photographic Society of Scotland (1865).

In addition to his photography, he was also an amateur violinist and an amateur landscape watercolorist.

A portrait photographer, Moffat used the collodion wet-plate process and produced stereographs. He took photographs of many nineteenth-century notables, including Henry Fox Talbot, Sir David Brewster, Lord Moseberry and Mr. and Mrs. Gladstone.

PUBLICATION Anthology: *Early Photographs & Early Photographers*, Oliver Mathews, 1973.

COLLECTIONS All England: Fox Talbot Mus., Lacock, Wiltshire; J. S. Moffat Cllctn., Berkhamsted, Herts; Kodak Mus., Harrow.

ARCHIVE J. S. Moffat, Dial House, Hudnall Lane, Little Gaddesden, Berkhamsted, Herts, England.

Susan Roberta Mogul   *PHOTOGRAPHER · VIDEO ARTIST* Born August 15, 1949, Mogul studied at the University of Wisconsin, Madison (1967–69), and received a BFA from Tufts University/Boston Museum School of Fine Arts, Massachusetts (1972). She also attended California Institute of the Arts, Valencia (1973), and the Feminist Studio Workshop, Los Angeles (1973–75). Mogul is currently an MFA candidate at the University of California at San Diego, La Jolla. She names artist Judy Chicago and designer Sheila de Bretteville as major influences.

A freelance photographer and video artist, she has taught at the Feminist Studio Workshop's Summer Art Program at the Woman's Building, Los Angeles, and has given numerous guest lectures at colleges and art schools.

Mogul won a Louis B. Mayer grant in 1979 to carry out the video project *Waiting at Columbia*.

She works with photography and video performance, specializing in photomontage and photo-environments. Mogul displays her images and tableaus in the everyday environment, such as the "Waiting at Columbia" project, which took place in a Hollywood drugstore and included mural-sized photomontages, custom photo placements, and life-sized photo cutouts. Characteristic of her work is its humor, its focus on women's experience and its commitment to making art accessible to many people.

PUBLICATIONS Anthology: *Women See Woman*, 1976. Periodicals: "Susan Mogul: Moving the Goods," Martha Rosler, *Artweek*, Aug 1976; *Art in America*, May 1976. Reviews: "Mogul Goes Hollywood," Ruth Askey, *Artweek*, Jul 14, 1979; *Artforum*, Leon Rubinfein, Dec 1976.

COLLECTIONS Video: Anthology Film Archive, NYC; Donnell Lib., NYC; Long Beach Mus. of Art, Calif.; SUNY, Old Westbury, N.Y. Photography: Folkwang Mus., Essen, Germany.

ADDRESS 9244 Regents Rd, #G, La Jolla, CA 92037.

Lucia Moholy ART HISTORIAN · PHOTOHISTORIAN · PHOTOGRAPHER · WRITER Born in Austria, Lucia Moholy was married to artist and photographer László Moholy-Nagy. She studied English language and literature at Prague University in Czechoslovakia, photography and history of photography at the Academy of Graphic Art in Leipzig, Germany, and design and photography at the Bauhaus in Weimar/Dessau, Germany.

She has been living in Switzerland since 1960. Her professional career has consisted of teaching language, history of art and history of photography. She was, at one time, head teacher of photography at Itten School of Art in Berlin. For a time she was the stage photographer at the State Opera in Berlin (until 1931). In 1934 Moholy moved to England, where she established a portrait studio. With Dr. Arundell Esdaile she organized the British Microfilm Service. She later served as a UNESCO consultant in the Middle East, then as a consultant for medical libraries for World Health Organization. For several years Moholy was a contributor to London's *Burlington Magazine* and Switzerland's *Werk* and *Archithese*.

The historian is a member of several professional organizations, among them RPS (since 1948), Association Internationale des Critiques d'Art (since 1975), the European Society for the History of Photography, Schweizerisches Institut für Kunstwissenschaft, etc.

PUBLICATIONS Books: *Moholy-Nagy Marginal Notes*, 1972 (Krefeld: Germany; England); *A Hundred Years of Photography*, 1939. Periodical: *Camera*, Feb 1978.

COLLECTIONS Julien Levy Cllctn., Chicago; San Francisco Mus. of Modern Art. Die Neue Sammlung, Munich; Mus. Ludwig, Cologne; Natl. Portrait Gall., London.

ADDRESS Rotfluhstrasse 10, 8702 Zollikon, Switzerland.

László Moholy-Nagy PHOTOGRAPHER · STAGE DESIGNER · PAINTER [See plate 53] Born in Bacsborsod, Hungary, on July 20, 1895, Moholy-Nagy died in Chicago on November 24, 1946. He is survived by a daughter, Hattula Moholy-Nagy, the executor of his estate. His second wife, Sibyl Pietzsch Moholy-Nagy, a writer and architectural historian, died January 8, 1971. His first wife, Lucia Moholy, is a photographer and lives in Switzerland. Moholy-Nagy attended the University of Budapest. He served in the Austro-Hungarian Army (1915–18).

He was influenced by Kasimir Malevich, El Lissitzsky and the Dada group. He arrived in Berlin in 1920, and served on the faculty at the Staatliche Bauhaus in Weimar and Dessau (1923–28). He was a stage designer at the Piscator Theater in Berlin (1928–33). Then he was art adviser for Simpson's, the Royal Air Lines and London Transport in London between 1935 and 1937. In 1937 he came to Chicago as director of the New Bauhaus. He founded the School of Design in Chicago—later the Institute of Design—in 1938. In those years he was also a design adviser for Spiegel, Inc., the Baltimore & Ohio Railroad, Parker Pen Co. and others.

Moholy-Nagy became a member of the Hungarian art group *Ma* in 1919, and American Abstract Artists in 1941. Among his many accomplishments, Moholy-Nagy, with Ludwig Kassák, co-edited an anthology of modern art and poetry, *Buch Neuer Künstler*, in 1922. With Walter Gropius he co-edited and designed fourteen volumes of *Bauhaus Bücher*, a journal, in the 1920s. Moholy-Nagy was also a contributor to *i 10*, an art monthly published in Amsterdam in 1927. Between 1930 and 1936 he made several films, including *Light Display Black, White, Grey*, and *Life of the Lobster*. He created the special effects for the motion picture *The Shape of Things to Come*, based on H. G. Wells' novel, in 1936, but they do not appear in the commercial version.

Moholy-Nagy is noted for creating images from widely varied points of view and for his photograms and "photoplastics" (montages). He strongly believed that the conventions of photography should not limit its use and even today his work stands as a pacemaker in photographic experimentation. His photographic images were in both black-and-white and color (transparencies).

PUBLICATIONS Monographs: *Moholy-Nagy: Marginal Notes; Documentary Absurdities,* Lucia Moholy, 1972 (Scherpe: Krefeld, Germany); *Moholy-Nagy,* Richard Kostenlanetz, ed., 1970; *Moholy-Nagy,* 1967 (Eindhoven: The Netherlands); *Moholy-Nagy, Experiment in Totality* (bio.), intro. by Walter Gropius, Sibyl Moholy-Nagy, 1950, repr. 1969; *Vison in Motion,* 1947, repr. 1965; *Eton Portrait,* intro. by Bernard Fergusson, 1937, repr. 1949 (J. Miles: London); *L. Moholy-Nagy,* Franz Roh, ed. 1936; *László Moholy-Nagy,* Siegfried Giedon, 1936; *L. Moholy-Nagy: 60 Fotos,* Franz Roh, ed., 1930 (Klinkhardt & Bierman: Berlin). Books: *An Oxford University Chest,* John Betjeman, 1938 (J. Miles: London); *The Street Markets of London,* Mary Benedetta, 1936, repr. 1972; *Fototek,* 1929; *Von Material zu Architektur,* 1929, U.S. ed., *The New Vision,* 1930, repr. as *The New Vision and Abstract of an Artist,* 1964; *Die Bühne im Bauhaus,* foreword by Walter Gropius, w/Oskar Schlemmer, 1925, repr. 1965 (Mainz: Berlin); *Malerei, Fotographie, Film,* 1925, U.S. ed., *Painting, Photography, Film,* note by Hans M. Wingler, 1969. Anthologies: *The Photograph Collector's Guide,* Lee D. Witkin & Barbara London, 1979; *The Julien Levy Collection,* Witkin Gallery, 1977; *Photographs from the Julien Levy Collection,* David Travis, 1976; *The Magic Image,* Cecil Beaton & Gail Buckland, 1975; *Great Photographers,* 1971, *The Print,* 1970, Time-Life Series; *Photographers on Photography,* Nathan Lyons, ed., 1966; *The Picture History of Photography,* Peter Pollack, 1958. Catalogs: *László Moholy-Nagy,* 1976 (Centre Nationale d'Art et de Culture: Paris); *Photographs of Moholy-Nagy from the Collection of Wm. Larsen,* Leland D. Rice & David W. Steadman, eds., 1975 (Galls. of Claremont Colls.: Claremont, Calif.); *László Moholy-Nagy,* Hans Maria Wingler, 1972 (Bauhaus-Archiv: Berlin); *László Moholy-Nagy,* 1969 (Mus. of Contemporary Art: Chicago). Periodicals: "Photography and Moholy-Nagy's Do-it-Yourself Aesthetic," Caroline Fawkes, *Studio International,* July 1975; "The Photographs of Moholy-Nagy," Beaumont Newhall, *Kenyon Review,* summer 1941; *Telehor: The International Review for New Vision,* special issue, 1936; *De Stijl,* July 1932; *Broom,* Mar 1923; *Bauhaus Bücher,* no. 7, 1923.

COLLECTIONS Art Inst. of Chicago; Dayton Art Inst., Ohio; Detroit Inst. of Arts, Mich.; IMP/GEH, Rochester; Jacksonville Art Mus., Fla; Los Angeles County Mus. of Art; MOMA, NYC. Bauhaus-Archiv, West Berlin; Provinciaal Mus. voor Kunstambachten, Deurne (Antwerp), Belgium.

ESTATE Hattula Moholy-Nagy, 1204 Gardner, Ann Arbor, MI 48104.

Pablo Ortiz Monasterio   *PHOTOGRAPHER · GRAPHIC DESIGNER · TEACHER* Born June 2, 1952, in Mexico City, Monasterio studied economics at the National University of Mexico for three years, then photography at Ealing Technical College, London, for a year, earning a diploma in photography from London College of Printing.

In 1979 Monasterio became chief editor of the Archivo Etnografico Audiovisual in Mexico City, and since 1977 he has taught at the Metropolitan University of Mexico.

Monasterio belongs to Consejo Mexicano de Fotografía (since 1977).

PUBLICATIONS Books: *El Desnudo Fotografico,* 1980 (Mexico City); *El Mundo Interior,* 1979 (Mexico). Periodicals: *Foto-Zoom,* July 1980; *Anuario de Foto-Zoom,* 1977; *British Journal of Photography Annual,* 1977; *Creative Camera,* Nov 1976; *Nueva Lente,* Sept 1976; *British Journal of Photography,* July 1976, July 1975; *Revista de Bellas Artes,* July 1976 (Mex. City).

COLLECTIONS Carlton Gall., NYC. Bibliothèque Nationale, Paris; Casa de Las Americas, Havana, Cuba. In Mexico City: Consejo Mexicano de Fotografía; Galería Juan Martín; Instituto Nacional de Bellas Artes.

ADDRESS Magnolia 38, San Angel Inn, Mexico 20 D.F., Mexico.

Désiré Charles Emanuel Van Monckhoven *SCIENTIST · INVENTOR* Born in 1834 in Ghent, Belgium, Van Monckhoven died in 1882.

A prolific researcher in scientific and applied photography, Van Monckhoven also did work in chemistry, optics, astronomy and spectroscopy. His photographic inventions included an enlarging apparatus (1869), an improvement in the Drummond light (1869) and a collodion dry-plate process (1871). In 1878–79 he devised a new method of developing silver bromide gelatin emulsions and introduced the use of ammonia for sensitizing an emulsion without heat or cooking. His researches into the carbon printing process in the late 1870s led to his establishment of factories for manufacturing carbon tissue and gelatin. Van Monckhoven later made gelatin dry plates and sold gelatin emulsions to other dry-plate manufacturers. A prolific writer, the scientist published his first book at age eighteen. One of his last books, *Lehrbuch der Photographie,* appeared in French, German, Italian and Russian editions.

Among many honors, Van Monckhoven received the medal of the Photographische Gesellschaft in Vienna. The private astronomical observatory he had built was purchased by the Belgian government after Van Monckhoven's death.

PUBLICATIONS Books: *Photographie im Wandel*, Rudolf Skopec, 1964; *Encyclopedie voor Fotografie en Cinematografie*, Elsevier, 1958; *Focal Encyclopedia of Photography*, 1957, 1956 (Focal Press); *History of Photography*, W. Jerome Harrison, 1887; *Traité d'Optique Photographique*, 1866 (Paris); *Traité General de Photographie*, 1852. Anthology: *Photography's Great Inventors*, Louis W. Sipley, 1965. Periodicals: *Bild und Ton*, 1954; *Photographische Mittheilungen*, 1882; *British Journal of Photography*, 1882, 1879, 1874; *Photographische Correspondenz*, 1879.

Lorraine Monk   CURATOR · WRITER   Born in Montreal, Quebec, Canada, Monk earned her BA (1944) and MA (1946) from McGill Univeristy in Montreal.

Having joined the National Film Board of Canada as a writer in 1957, she has served as head of its Still Photography Division since 1960. In 1967 she started the Film Board's Photo Gallery in Ottawa and also inaugurated a program of traveling exhibitions across Canada and around the world.

Her book *Between Friends/Entre Amis* won Monk many awards, including the 1977 Gold Medal at the International Book Fair in Leipzig, Germany, and the "best printed book" award at International Gallery of Superb Printing (U.S.) in 1976. Monk received the Canadian ESFIAP award in 1966 for excellence in service from the Fédération Internationale de l'Art Photographique.

PUBLICATIONS *Signature Two*, producer, Robert Bourdeau, 1979 (Mintmark Press); *Between Friends/Entre Amis*, 1976, *A Time to Dream*, 1971 (McClelland & Stewart Ltd.: Toronto); *Stones of History, Call Them Canadians, Canada/ A Year of the Land*, for Canadian Centennial, n.d. (Natl. Film Board of Canada); *Canada*, 1973 (Clarke, Irwin & Co. Ltd.).

ADDRESS National Film Board, Still Photography Division, 150 Kent St, Ottawa, Ontario, Canada.

Gary Monroe   PHOTOGRAPHER   Born September 6, 1951, in Miami Beach, Florida, Monroe received a BA in 1975 from the University of South Florida, Tampa, and an MFA in 1977 from the University of Colorado, Denver.

As of this date Monroe was a photographer for the Miami Beach Photographic Project, sponsored by NEA and Miami Beach Community Development, and an adjunct photography instructor at Miami-Dade Community College (since 1975).

A member of SPE, Monroe received an NEA Aid to Publication Grant in 1980 and a Photo Survey Grant in 1979.

The photographer, as of this writing, was producing a documentary film on life in South Beach and curating a vintage collection of photographs of Miami for the Miami Public Library.

Using small-format black-and-white, Monroe is currently documenting the ethnic concentration of elderly Jewish people in South Beach, Miami Beach.

PUBLICATIONS Catalogs: *Florida Light*, Oct 1979; *Photographs of Miami Beach*, 1978.

COLLECTIONS Bass Mus., Miami Beach, Fla.; Corcoran Gall., Wash., D.C.; Miami-Dade Community Coll., Miami.

DEALER Gall. 24, 2399 NE Second Ave, Miami, FL 33137.

ADDRESS 1340 Flamingo Way, Miami Beach, FL 33139.

Robert Monroe   PHOTOGRAPHER   Born in New York, the self-taught photographer has been a freelance for over thirty years.

A member of ASMP, he developed a prismatic lens in 1960.

Monroe mainly uses black-and-white, some with applied color. His primary subject matter is the human form and nature.

PUBLICATIONS Periodicals: *Kodak International*, 1977; *Popular Photography*, 1977; *Popular Photography's Woman*, 1972; *U. S. Camera Annual*, 1951, 1950.

COLLECTIONS Neikrug Gall., NYC; Ulster County Community Coll., Stone Ridge, N.Y. Bibliothèque Nationale, Paris.

DEALER Neikrug Gall., 224 E 68 St, New York, NY 10021.

ADDRESS 255 W 90 St, New York, NY 10024.

Tomás Montserrat   PRIEST · PHOTOGRAPHER   Born July 8, 1873, in Llucmajor, near Mallorca, Spain, Montserrat died in that town on February 13, 1944. Montserrat attended a seminary in Palma de Mallorca from 1888 to 1898 and, while there, taught himself photography.

After being ordained a priest in 1898, Montserrat returned to Llucmajor, where he spent his life as both parish priest and town photographer.

Using a primitive open-air studio behind the church, the photographer left a "portrait of a people more primitive, tougher, but more humane than the ones we live with now," wrote Helena Srakocie.

PUBLICATIONS Monograph: *Tomás Montserrat, 1873–1944*, Helena Srakocie, 1977 (Spectrum Editions/Bolopie, London).

George Moodie
See Alfred Henry Burton

Sarah Moon PHOTOGRAPHER · FILM MAKER
Currently living in Paris, Moon is a self-employed photographer whose images have appeared in *Vogue, Nova,* Italian *Bazaar, Elle, Photo, Zoom* and *Graphis.* She received the J. Arthur Rank Gold Award in London (1971), the Gold Screen Award in Italy (1979) and the Grand Prix at the International Advertising Festival in Cannes (1979).

PUBLICATIONS Periodicals: *Camera,* Sept 1978, Dec 1975, Feb 1970.

REPRESENTATIVE Push Pin Studios, Inc., 67 Irving Pl, New York, NY 10003.

David Murray Moore PHOTOGRAPHER
Moore was born in April 1927, in Sydney, Australia, the son of architect/painter John D. Moore (1888–1958). He served as an assistant in the Max Dupain Studio in Sydney (1947–51) and in the Russell Roberts Studio of Sydney (1946–47). He considers Dupain his mentor.

Since 1951 Moore has been a photojournalist and industrial photographer.

He belongs to the Institute of Australian Photography (since 1958) and the Australian Centre for Photography (since 1973).

In 1971 Moore won first prize in the Color Section of the Nikon International Photographic Competition and in 1967 won five first prizes at the Pacific Photographic Fair in Melbourne, Australia. He received a special award in 1965 at "The World and its People" exhibition of the New York World's Fair.

PUBLICATIONS Monograph: *David Moore,* 1980 (Richmond Hill Press). Books: *Living and Partly Living,* 1971 (Thomas Nelson); *Camera in Australia,* 1970 (A. H. & A. W. Reed); *In the Making,* w/David Beal, 1969 (Thomas Nelson); *The U.S. Overseas,* Time-Life Series, 1969; *Isles of the South Pacific,* 1968 (Natl. Geographic Soc.); *Life in Australia,* 1968 (Southern Cross); *Australia and New Zealand,* Time-Life Series, 1964. Anthologies: *Australian Photography,* 1976 (Globe Publishing Co.); *Photography Year 1967* (Fountain Press). Catalog: *New Photography Australia,* 1974 (Australian Centre for Photography).

COLLECTIONS MOMA, NYC; Smithsonian Inst., Wash., D.C. Australian Natl. Gall., Canberra; Bibliothèque Nationale, Paris; Natl. Gall. of Victoria, Melbourne, Australia; Phillip Morris Cllctn., Melbourne, Australia.

DEALERS In Australia: Australian Centre for Photography, 257 Oxford St, Paddington, New South Wales; Axiom Gall., 29 Gipps St, Richmond, Victoria; MacQuarie Galls., 40 King St, Sydney, New South Wales.

ADDRESS 58 Middle St, McMahon's Point, New South Wales 2060, Australia.

Raymond Moore PHOTOGRAPHER Born August 26, 1920, in Wallasey, Cheshire, England, Moore studied painting at the Wallasey College of Art (1937–40) and at the Royal College of Art in London (1947–50).

Moore is currently self-employed as a freelance photographer.

In 1978 he was a recipient of a Major Bursary from the Arts Council of Great Britain.

PUBLICATIONS Books: *Penrose Annual,* Minor White, 1971; *Colour Photography,* Eric de Maré. Anthology: *The Magic Image,* Cecil Beaton & Gail Buckland, 1975. Periodicals: *Camera,* Aug 1976; *Creative Camera,* June 1973, June 1972, June 1969, Nov 1968, June 1967.

COLLECTIONS Art Inst. of Chicago; Gernsheim Cllctn., Austin, Tex.; Univ. of N. Mex., Albuquerque. Bibliothèque Nationale, Paris; Contemporary Art Society for Wales; Univ. Coll., Aberystwyth, Wales; Victoria & Albert Mus., London; Welsh Arts Council.

ADDRESS 30 Eden St, Stanwix, Carlisle CA3 GLR, Cumbria, England.

Inge Morath PHOTOGRAPHER · WRITER Born May 27, 1923, in Graz, Austria, Morath received a BA from the University of Berlin. Her husband is playwright and author Arthur Miller.

A freelance photographer and writer, Morath worked as an assistant to Henri Cartier-Bresson at one time. She has been guest instructor at Cooper Union in New York City, among other schools.

Morath joined Magnum Photos in 1953 and belongs to ASMP. In 1976 she won the Great Photographers Award for Photographic Excellence at Stuttgart Bookworks in Switzerland.

Morath works in both black-and-white and

color in small format, producing travelogues, reportage and portraits.

PUBLICATIONS Monograph: *Inge Morath*, Olga Carlisle, 1975 (Bucher Verlag: Lucerne, Switzerland). Books: *Chinese Encounters*, Arthur Miller, 1979; *In the Country*, Arthur Miller, 1977; *Boris Pasternak: My Sister Life*, Olga Carlisle, 1975; *East-West Exercises*, Ruth Bluestone Simon, 1973; *In Russia*, Arthur Miller, 1969; *Le Masque*, 1967 (Maeght: Paris); *Tunisia*, Claude Roy & Paul Sebag, 1961; *Bring Forth the Children*, w/ Yul Brynner, 1960; *From Persia to Iran*, Eduard Sablier, 1961; *Venice Observed*, Mary McCarthy, 1956; *Fiesta in Pamplona*, 1956. Anthology: *Great Photographers of Our Time*, Olga Carlisle, 1975 (Bucher: Switzerland). Periodicals: "Inge Morath," Allen Porter, *Camera*, Nov 1969; article, Saul Steinberg, *Creative Camera*, Feb 1969.

PORTFOLIOS *Ten Photographers*, 1978 (Women's Campaign Fund: Wash., D.C.); *Untitled*, 1977 (Neikrug Gall.: NYC).

COLLECTIONS Art Inst. of Chicago; Boston Mus. of Fine Arts; Harvard Univ., Fogg Art Mus., Cambridge, Mass.; ICP, NYC; Metro. Mus. of Art, NYC; R.I. School of Design, Providence. Bibliothèque Nationale, Paris; Kunsthaus Zürich, Stiftung für Photographie, Switzerland; Art Mus. Prague, Czechoslovakia.

REPRESENTATIVE Magnum Photos, 15 W 46 St, New York, NY 10036.

DEALER Marjorie Neikrug, 224 E 68 St, New York, NY 10021.

ADDRESS Tophet Rd, Roxbury, CT 06783.

Craig H. Morey PHOTOGRAPHER · GALLERY DIRECTOR Born July 23, 1952, in Fort Wayne, Indiana, Morey studied photography at Indiana University in Bloomington, earning a BA in 1974. His primary influence is Henry Holmes Smith.

Currently the director of Camerawork Gallery in San Francisco, he was with the Palace of the Legion of Honor in San Francisco as an installation assistant in 1977, worked with the M. H. de Young Museum in the same city in 1976, and assisted Christo Javacheff in 1976 with his Running Fence Project.

A member of SPE, Morey won a Special Jury Prize at the International Triennial of Photography in Fribourg (1978).

His work is in black-and-white and color, dealing primarily with sexuality and design.

PUBLICATIONS Anthologies: *Photography for Collectors*, 1980; *Self-Portrayal*, 1979; *Eros and Photography*, 1977. Periodicals: *Darkroom Photography*, May 1979; *Northwest Photography*, July 1979; *Picture Magazine*, no. 8, 1978. Reviews: *Popular Photography*, 85:4, 1979; *New Art Examiner*, May 1979; *Artweek*, Dec 17, 1977.

COLLECTIONS Princeton Art Mus., N.J. Mus. of Art & History, Fribourg, Switzerland.

DEALER Stuart Wilber, 2943 N Halsted, Chicago, IL 60657.

ADDRESS 180 Carl St, San Francisco, CA 94117.

Barbara Brooks Morgan PHOTOGRAPHER · WRITER Born July 8, 1900, in Buffalo, Kansas, Morgan is married to Willard D. Morgan, a writer, photographer and publisher. She studied at University of California in Los Angeles, from 1919 to 1923.

Morgan is co-owner of the publishing company Morgan & Morgan, Inc., and was an instructor of art at UCLA from 1925 to 1930.

She was elected a fellow of the Philadelphia Museum of Art in 1970.

Working strictly in black-and-white, the artist is best known for her photographs of dancers. She has also created photomontages and light drawings as well as portraits and candid photographs of children.

PUBLICATIONS Monographs: *Barbara Morgan: Photomontage*, 1980; *Barbara Morgan*, intro. by Peter Bunnell, 1972; *Summer's Children*, 1951. Books: *Prestini's Art in Wood*, Edgar Kaufmann Jr., 1950; *Martha Graham: Sixteen Dances in Photographs*, 1941. Anthologies: *The Photograph Collector's Guide*, Lee D. Witkin & Barbara London, 1979; *Recollections: Ten Women of Photography*, Margaretta Mitchell, 1979; *The Magic Image*, Cecil Beaton & Gail Buckland, 1975; *Women in Photography*, Margery Mann & Ann Noggle, eds., 1975; *Looking at Photographs*, John Szarkowski, ed., 1973; *The Woman's Eye*, Ann Tucker, ed., 1973; *Art of Photography*, 1971; *Photographing Children*, 1971, *The Studio*, 1971, *Photography as a Tool*, Time-Life Series, 1970. Periodicals: *British Journal of Photography*, June 13, 1975; *Foto*, July 1972 (The Netherlands), July 1965 (Munich); "My Creative Experience with Photomontage," *Image*, 14:5–6, 1971; *Popular Photography*, Aug 1969, Oct 1951, June 1945; *Camera*, Feb 1952; *Aperture* 11:1, 1964, 1:4, 1953; *U.S. Camera*, Feb 1944, Dec 1941; "Barbara Morgan: Painter Turned Photographer," Etna M. Kelley, *Photography*, Sept 1938.

PORTFOLIO *Barbara Morgan Dance Portfolio*, 1977 (Morgan & Morgan).

COLLECTIONS Addison Gall. of America Art, Andover, Mass.; Bennington Coll., Vermont; IMP/GEH, Rochester; L/C, Wash., D.C.; Marquette Univ., Milwaukee Wis.; MIT, Cambridge,

Mass.; Metro. Mus. of Art, NYC; MOMA, NYC; Mus. of Fine Arts, St. Petersburg, Fla.; Natl. Portrait Gall., Wash., D.C.; N.Y. Pub. Lib.; Philadelphia Mus. of Art, Penn.; Phoenix Coll., Ariz.; Princeton Univ. Art Mus., N.J.; Smithsonian Inst., Wash., D.C.; UCLA; Utah State Univ., Logan. Fotografiska Muséet, Stockholm, Sweden; Natl. Gall. of Canada, Ottawa, Ontario.

ADDRESS   120 High Point Rd, Scarsdale, NY 10584.

Hiromitsu Morimoto   PHOTOGRAPHER   Born April 30, 1942, in Japan, Morimoto received a BA in 1967 from California State University, Long Beach, and also studied at the Art Students League in New York City (1967–68).

He taught at Westbeth Graphic Workshop (1975–78) and Cooper Union (1975–76), and also served as master printer for Bank Street Atelier (1975–77), all in New York City.

The photographer won an NEA grant in 1980 and a CAPS grant in 1978.

He uses liquid silver emulsion on rag paper in the production of his photographs.

PUBLICATIONS   Anthology: *The Photographer's Choice*, 1975. Periodicals: *Modern Photography*, Mar 1979; *Print Collector's Newsletter*, Sept 1979, Mar/Apr 1977, Sept 1976.

COLLECTIONS   MOMA, NYC. Mus. of Modern Art, Tokyo.

DEALERS   Marcuse Pfeifer Gall., 825 Madison Ave, New York, NY 10021; Nishimura Gall., Ginza, Tokyo, Japan.

ADDRESS   463 West St, (Studio 356-G), New York, NY 10014.

Wright Morris   PHOTOGRAPHER · WRITER   [See plate 76]   Born January 6, 1910, in Central City, Nebraska, Morris studied at Pomona College, Claremont, California, from 1930 to 1933.

He was a professor of literature at San Francisco State University, California, from 1962 to 1974. He has given numerous lectures, including ones at Bennington College, Vermont, in 1979 and at the University of Nebraska, Lincoln, in 1975.

Morris belongs to the National Institute of Arts and Letters and the American Academy of Arts & Sciences. He received Guggenheim Fellowships in 1942, 1946 and 1954. He also won a Rockefeller grant in 1967 and a National Book Award in 1957.

The photographer produces images of structures and artifacts without people—"habitations without the inhabitants"—and characterizes them in the facing text.

PUBLICATIONS   Books: *Conversations with Wright Morris*, Robert E. Knoll, ed., 1977; *The Cat's Meow*, 1975 (ltd. ed.); *Structures and Artifacts*, 1975; *Love Affair: A Venetian Journal*, 1972; *God's Country and My People*, 1968; *The Home Place*, 1948, repr. 1968; *The Inhabitants*, 1945, repr. 1973. Novels: *Plains Song*, 1980; *A Life*, 1973; *Fire Sermon*, 1971; *In Orbit*, 1967; *Ceremony in Lone Tree*, 1960; *The Field of Vision*, 1956. Literary criticism: *Earthly Delights, Unearthly Adornments*, 1978; *About Fiction*, 1975; *The Territory Ahead*, 1958. Anthology: *The Photograph Collector's Guide*, Lee D. Witkin & Barbara London, 1979. Periodicals: *Modern Photography*, Mar 1978; *Exposure: SPE*, James Alinder, Feb 1976.

COLLECTIONS   Boston Mus. of Fine Arts, Mass.; MOMA, NYC; Mus. of Fine Arts, Houston; Princeton Univ., Princeton, N.J.; San Francisco Mus. of Modern Art, Calif.; Univ. of Calif. Art Mus., Berkeley; Univ. of Neb., Sheldon Memorial Gall., Lincoln.

DEALERS   Prakapas Gall., 19 E 71 St, New York, NY 10021; Witkin Gall., 41 E 57 St, New York, NY 10022.

ADDRESS   341 Laurel Way, Mill Valley, CA 94941.

Samuel Finley Breese Morse   PAINTER · INVENTOR · PHOTOGRAPHER   Born April 27, 1791, in Charlestown, Massachusetts, Morse died April 2, 1872, in New York City. His father, Jedidiah Morse, was a geographer and clergyman. After studying at Phillips Academy, Andover, Massachusetts, Samuel Morse went to Yale University, graduating in 1810. From 1811 to 1813 he studied in England under the direction of Benjamin West.

Morse painted miniature portraits to earn his living, traveling throughout New England, New York and South Carolina, and finally settling in New York City in 1825. In 1932 he was made a professor of drawing at what is now New York University. He began experimenting with the development of a telegraph in 1832 and in 1837 turned his full attention to it. He created the Morse code in 1838 and sent his first successful message in 1839. During his 1838 visit to France, Morse met Daguerre and they became good friends. The inventor then became one of the first practitioners of the daguerreotype in the United States, sharing a studio with John W. Draper, a professor of chemistry. On that New York City studio rooftop in September 1839 he began making images, and his 1840 picture of his class reunion was evidently the first group portrait made.

Morse became a generous philanthropist in his later years. The artist organized and founded the National Academy of Arts in 1825 and served as its president from 1826 to 1845. For the invention of his form of telegraph and the Morse code, he was awarded numerous medals and decorations as well as a 100,000-franc stipend from a coalition of countries, sponsored by the Emperor of France. He was also made an honorary member of several art and science societies. In 1942 the Morse Telegraph Club was founded, an association of former American and Canadian telegraph operators that perpetuates the memory of Morse.

Although Morse relinquished his interest in photography to devote himself to the telegraph and his painting, he was one of the field's early experimenters, attempting to fix the image of the camera obscura as early as 1812. One of the most respected painters of his day, Morse in his work "combined technical competence and a bold rendering of his subjects' character with a touch of the Romanticism he had imbibed in England" (Carleton Mabee, *The American Leonardo*).

PUBLICATIONS Monograph: *Samuel F. B. Morse, American Painter*, 1932. Books: *Samuel F. B. Morse and American Democratic Art*, Oliver W. Larkin, 1954; *History of Photography*, Josef Maria Eder, 1945, repr. 1972; *The American Leonardo*, Carleton Mabee, 1943, repr. 1969. Anthology: *Early Photographs and Early Photographers*, Oliver Mathews, 1973. Catalog: *Paintings by Samuel F. B. Morse*, 1932 (Metro. Mus. of Art/ Syracuse Mus. of Fine Arts: N.Y.). Periodicals: "Fulton & Morse: Two Yankee Inventor-Painters," James T. Flexner, *Artnews Annual*, no. xxvii, 1958; "What Samuel Wrought," Marshall B. Davidson, *American Heritage*, no. 12, 1961.

COLLECTIONS Locust Grove, nr. Poughkeepsie, N.Y.; Metro. Mus. of Art, NYC; U.S. Natl. Mus. of Hist. & Tech., Wash., D.C.

ARCHIVE Locust Grove, nr. Poughkeepsie, NY 12601.

William Mortensen PHOTOGRAPHER · WRITER
[See plate 58] Born on January 27, 1897, in Park City, Utah, Mortensen died of leukemia on August 12, 1965, in Laguna Beach, California. He studied drawing and painting at the Art Students League in New York City and was taught personally by Arthur Kales, the "Bromoil King." He was influenced by Cecil B. De Mille and inspired by Myrdith Monaghan, whom he married and photographed continually. His travels in Europe also had a great effect on his development.

After serving in the U.S. Army (1918–19), he taught at his alma mater, the East Side High School in Salt Lake City (1920). He then did photography for the Western Costume Company in Los Angeles, opened his own studio on Hollywood Boulevard in 1925 and worked as a still photographer for De Mille's *The King of Kings* (1926). In 1930 he founded the Mortensen School of Photography in Laguna Beach, which he operated for thirty years.

In 1935 Mortensen began experimenting with the Metalchrome process which, along with pigment printing, he perfected. The former transformed black-and-white images into color; the latter, a nonsilver process, transformed the image into ink renderings. Also, he was the first to shoot movie stills with a small-format camera.

In 1949 he received the Hood Award from RPS.

Mortensen's photographs fall into three main groups: Hollywood glamour portraits, studies of female nudes and sensational narrative subjects or illustrations. According to Deborah Irmas, curator, "Mortensen was a novelist photographer; all of his photographs were products of his imagination. Also, any alteration of that image through chemical, optical, or manufactured means was perfectly legitimate. The final criteria for judgement was on the total visual result, not the process."

PUBLICATIONS Books: *The Mortensen Collection of the Photographic Society of America*, pamphlet, Myrdith Mortensen, June 1970; *Flash in Modern Photography*, 1941; *Outdoor Portraiture*, 1940; *Mortensen on the Negative*, 1940; *Print Finishing*, 1938; *The Model*, 1937; *The Command to Look*, 1937; *Monsters and Madonnas*, 1936; *Pictorial Lighting*, 1935; *Projection Control*, 1934. Anthology: "Control in Photography," *The Complete Photographer*, Willard D. Morgan, ed., vol 3, 1942–43. Periodicals (by the artist): "The Hermits of Baltimore," *Camera*, Feb 1953; "Talking About Photography with Mortensen," *American Photography*, Aug 1950; "Portraiture: Surface and Substance," *Camera Craft*, Aug 1940; "How to Make Abrasion-Tone Prints," *Popular Photography*, Aug 1938; "Color in Photography," part I, May 1938, part II, June 1938, part III, July 1938, "The Bromoil Transfer Factors in Inking," June 1936, "Venus and Vulcan," part I, Mar 1934, part II, Apr 1934, part III, May 1934, part IV, June 1934, *Camera Craft*. Periodicals (about the artist): "Pictorialism—Bodine and Mortensen: Two Extremes of this Approach," Ed Scully, *Modern Photography*, Jan 1971; "The Metalchrome Story," Grey L. Silva, *Photographic Society of America Journal*, Mar 1970.

COLLECTIONS Photog. Soc. of America, Philadelphia; UCLA, Special Cllctns Lib.; Court of England; Vatican Lib., Rome.

Francis J. Mortimer *PHOTOGRAPHER · POSTER DESIGNER* Born ca. 1874–76 in Portsmouth, England, Mortimer was killed by a bomb in London on July 31, 1944. He attended Portsmouth Grammar School, then studied law and journalism.

After passing his law examination, Mortimer turned to journalism and poster design. He was on the staff of the *British Journal of Photography* in 1940, editor of *Amateur Photographer* (1908–44) and editor of *Photograms of the Year* for several years beginning in 1912.

He joined RPS in 1905 and was president in 1940–42. He also belonged to The Linked Ring (1907) and was active in the London Camera Club from 1942 on.

Mortimer won more than 400 medals and other awards for his photographic work, including RPS's Honorary Fellowship in 1932 and Progress Medal in 1944. He also won silver and bronze medals for his poster designs at the Crystal Palace Exhibitions in London in 1899 and 1900.

The photographer worked in photojournalism and pictorialism, specializing in marine scenes.

PUBLICATIONS Books: *The Photographer Speaks*, w/Dr. Olaf Bloch et al., 1940 (Allen & Unwin: London); *The Dictionary of Photography*, 1926, 14th ed., 1937; *The Oil and Bromoil Processes*, w/S. L. Coulthurst, 1909, 2nd ed., 1912 (London); *Photograms of the Year*, 1895 (Iliffe: London).

Charles Delevan Mosher *PHOTOGRAPHER* Born on a farm in New York State on February 10, 1829, Mosher died in Chicago, Illinois, on June 7, 1897. He was apprenticed to an Albany, New York, cabinetmaker from 1845 to 1849. From his uncle, photographic entrepreneur Nathaniel Smith, he learned daguerreotypy.

Mosher operated a portable studio in various small towns covering western New York, Pennsylvania, Ohio and Illinois in the years 1850–62. He opened a Chicago portrait studio in 1863 where he specialized first in *cartes de visite*, then in cabinet photographs.

Mosher received the Medal of Honor at the Philadelphia Centennial Exposition in 1876. On May 18, 1889, Mosher deposited about 8,000 photographs of prominent Chicago citizens in the City Hall vault, to be opened at that city's 1976 bicentennial. He was a member of the Chicago Photographers Association.

Portraits of prominent citizens in the style of the day were the specialty of Charles Mosher. His clientele included such persons as President Lincoln, Generals Grant, Sherman and Sheridan and suffragettes Elizabeth Cady Stanton and Susan B. Anthony. He imported his cameras and lenses from England's famous Dallmeyer optical works, and instituted improved skylights in his studios, adopted by gallery owners in Europe and the United States.

PUBLICATION Periodical: "Chicago's Bicentennial Photographer," *Chicago History*, summer 1976.

COLLECTIONS Chicago Historical Soc.; City Hall, Chicago.

Kim Mosley *PHOTOGRAPHER · TEACHER · SCULPTOR · PAINTER* Born June 6, 1946, in Chicago, Illinois, Mosley earned a BFA in 1969 from the University of Illinois, Normal (studying with Art Sinsabaugh and Peter Bodnar), and an MFA from Bradley University, Peoria, Illinois (studying with Ron Linden, Robin Mayor and Dow Mitchell).

Mosley has been assistant professor in art at St. Louis Community College at Florissant Valley, Missouri, since 1975. Previously Mosley taught art at Southern Methodist University, Dallas, Texas (1972–75), and at Bradley University (1971–72).

A member of SPE since 1972 and NEA since 1977, the artist was commissioned by the Dallas Museum of Fine Arts to do a painting about Dallas in 1975.

Mosley's work is self-described as "nudes, alterations of other photographers' works and found images, street scenes, suburbia at night, discount stores and shopping malls."

COLLECTIONS Dallas Mus. of Fine Arts, Tex.; Kalamazoo Inst. of Art, Mich.; Masur Mus. of Art, Monroe, La.; Univ. of Texas at Dallas.

ADDRESS 1515 Hialeah Pl, Florissant, MO 63033.

Rosalind Kimball Moulton *PHOTOGRAPHER · TEACHER* Born November 25, 1941, in Buffalo, New York, Moulton studied privately with Minor White in 1966, earned a BFA from the School of the Art Institute of Chicago in 1971, and received an MFA from the State University of New York, Buffalo, in 1976.

She has been a photography instructor at Stephens College, Columbia, Missouri, since 1976 and was a visiting photography instructor at Purdue University, West Lafayette, Indiana, in 1971.

Moulton is a member of SPE (since 1973), Friends of Photography (since 1968), IMP/GEH (since 1971) and she founded the Women's Caucus for the Arts in Columbia in 1976.

The photographer works in silver and platinum processes.

PUBLICATIONS Anthologies: *Insights/Self-Portraits by Women*, Joyce Tenneson Cohen, ed., 1978; *Octave of Prayer*, Minor White, ed., 1972; *Vision & Expression*, Nathan Lyons, ed., 1969; *Light*[7], Minor White, ed., 1968. Periodical: *Fotografie, A German Quarterly for Creative Photography*, Aug 1979.

COLLECTIONS Apeiron Workshops, Millerton, N.Y.; Art Institute of Chicago; IMP/GEH, Rochester; MIT, Cambridge, Mass.; St. Louis Art Mus., Mo.

BUSINESS Dept. of Art, Stephens College, Columbia, MO 65201.

Jean Mounicq PHOTOGRAPHER Born September 30, 1931, in Pau, France, Mounicq has been a self-taught freelance photographer since 1958. He has also produced two animated films for Paris television.

In 1961 he won second place in the World Press Photo Contest in The Netherlands.

Working mostly in black-and-white in a variety of formats, Mounicq shoots landscapes, industrials, architecture and posed portraits.

PUBLICATIONS Books: *Londres*, n.d. (Editions Rencontre: Switzerland); *Les Toits dans le Paysage*, 1977 (Editions Claire: Paris). Periodicals: *Zoom*, no. 66, 1979 (France); *Arte Fotograáfico*, Mar 1971 (Spain); *L'Officiel de la Photo*, Jan 1968 (France); *Photography of the World*, 1961; *Camera*, Apr 1960.

COLLECTION Bibliothèque Nationale, Paris.

REPRESENTATIVE Anna Obolensky, 25 rue Pierre Brossolette, 94110 Arcueil, France.

ADDRESS 3 Avenue de Taillebourg, 75001 Paris, France.

Anita Ventura Mozley CURATOR·HISTORIAN·CRITIC Born August 29, 1928, in Washington, D.C., Mozley received a BA in Art from Northwestern University, Evanston, Illinois, in 1950. She then studied painting with Morris Kantor at the Art Students League in New York City (1950–51) and photography at the California School of Fine Arts in San Francisco (1951–52).

Mozley has been curator of photography at the Stanford University Museum of Art, Stanford, California, since 1972, and was registrar there (1970–78). Previously she was assistant curator and registrar at the San Francisco Maritime Museum (1963–68); film librarian for Sextant, Inc., New York City (1961–62); curatorial assistant at

the Guggenheim Museum, New York City (1961); and a designer, contributing editor and managing editor of *Arts* magazine in New York City from 1955 to 1960.

Mozley was a Bonbright Scholar at Northwestern University (1949–50) and received a scholarship from the Art Students League in 1950.

She writes about nineteenth-century photographers primarily, considering sociological and economic circumstances as well as photographic style. She is especially interested in Thomas Annan, but has also worked on twentieth-century photographers such as Imogen Cunningham, relating biography to the photographs and considering stylistic influences of particular periods.

PUBLICATIONS Books: *Eadweard Muybridge's Complete Animal Locomotion*, 1979; *Thomas Annan, Old Streets and Closes of Glasgow*, 1976. Anthology: *Paris/New York*, 1959. Catalogs: *American Photography, Past Into Present*, 1977 (Seattle Mus.: Wash.); *Mrs. Cameron's Photographs from the Life*, 1974 (Stanford Univ. Mus.: Calif.); *Eadweard Muybridge: The Stanford Years 1872–1882*, Stanford Art Book 14, 1973.

ADDRESS Stanford University Museum of Art, Stanford, CA 94305.

Claus Mroczynski PHOTOGRAPHER Born March 27, 1941, in Essen, West Germany, Mroczynski earned a degree in photography and design from Fach Hochschule in Dortmund, West Germany (1973), where he studied with Pan Walther. He continued his studies in 1973 at the Ansel Adams Workshop in Yosemite, California, under Adams, Wynn Bullock, Marie Cosindas and Paul Caponigro.

A freelance photographer, he has been affiliated with the Image Bank photo agency in New York City since 1979. Mroczynski has belonged to GDL since 1974.

PUBLICATIONS Book: *Ruhr Valley of West Germany*, 1972. Periodicals: *Popular Photography*, Dec 1976; *Progresso Fotografico*, Oct, June 1976; *Camera*, May 1975.

COLLECTIONS Denver Art Mus., Colo.; Smithsonian Inst., Wash., D.C.; Bibliothèque Nationale, Paris.

ADDRESS Box 265, Old Westbury, NY 11568.

Alphonse Marie Mucha GRAPHIC ARTIST·PAINTER·PHOTOGRAPHER Born August 24, 1860, in Ivancice, Moravia (now Czechoslovakia), Mucha died July 14, 1939, in Prague. He had his early education in Brno, Moravia, and then studied art in Munich (1883–88) and in Paris

(1888–89). He became friends with many artists and intellectuals, such as Paul Gauguin and August Strindberg.

Mucha first worked as a scene-painter in the theater at Brno. After his studies he remained in Paris and, in 1894, received a commission to design a poster advertising the performance of Sara Bernhardt in Sardou's *Gismonda*. This led to a six-year contract with Bernhardt, during which he designed more posters, along with her stage sets, costumes and even her jewelry. He also designed posters for several business firms and did illustrations for numerous magazines. Between the years of 1903 and 1922 he traveled to the U.S. on four occasions. After 1922 he returned to Czechoslovakia, where he designed the country's national banknotes and postage stamps. During his prime he had studios in France, America and Czechoslovakia.

Mucha was a celebrated artist of the Art Nouveau period. In addition to his renowned posters, his paintings—especially the "Slav Epic" series of twenty large oils—attracted a great deal of attention.

Although Mucha was noted more for his graphic art than for his photography, which he initially used as studies for his artwork, "many of his photographs provide a unique visual record of his surroundings, his home and studios, his family and friends. Whatever these more informal studies may lack in compositional sophistication . . . " writes Graham Ovenden *(Alphonse Marie Mucha)*, "all have a naturalness and spontaneity. . . . Mucha's photographs from his 1913 trip to Moscow and St. Petersburg . . . offer an historically important glimpse of Tsarist Russia, and they are one of the high points in the photographic oeuvre of a man who used the camera both for his art and for his diversion."

PUBLICATIONS Monographs: *Alphonse Mucha Photographs*, Graham Ovenden, 1974, *The Graphic Work of Alphonse Mucha*, Jiri Mucha & Marina Henderson, 1973, *Alphonse Mucha—Posters and Photographs*, Jiri Mucha, Marina Henderson & Aaron Scharf, 1971, rev. ed., *Alphonse Mucha*, 1974 (all Academy Editions: London). Book: *Lectures on Art*, 1975 (Academy Editions: London). Anthology: *The Invented Eye*, Edw. Lucie-Smith, 1975.

PORTFOLIO *Alphonse Marie Mucha: Settings & Models*, intro by Graham Ovenden, 1975 (Academy Editions, London/Graphics Internatl.: Wash., D.C.).

Grant Mudford PHOTOGRAPHER Born March 21, 1944, in Sydney, Australia, Mudford studied architecture in 1963–64 at the University of New South Wales, Sydney.

Between 1965 and 1974 Mudford worked as a commercial photographer in his own Sydney studio, served as a cinematographer on numerous short films and began to concentrate solely on his personal work (1971).

Mudford received an NEA Photographer's Fellowship in 1980, a grant (1977) and a travel grant (1974) from the Visual Arts Board of the Australia Council for the Arts. In 1971 he won a special award from Australian Film Awards for lighting of *The Widow*.

PUBLICATIONS Book: *Collecting Photographs: A Guide to the New Art Boom*, Landt & Lisl Dennis, 1977. Anthologies: *Australian Photography*, Laurence Le Guay, ed., 1979, 1976 (Sydney); *New Photography Australia*, Graham Howe, 1974 (Sydney). Catalogs: *Attitudes: Photography in the 70's*, 1979 (Santa Barbara Mus. of Art: Calif.); *Hirshhorn Museum and Sculpture Garden Catalogue*, 1979 (Smithsonian Inst.: Wash., D.C.); *Photographic Directions: Los Angeles, 1979*, 1979 (Security Pacific Bank: Los Angeles); *Aspects of Australian Photography*, Graham Howe, 1974 (Australian Centre of Photography: Sydney). Periodicals: "Gallery," Nancy Stevens, *American Photographer*, Sept 1979; *Camera*, Apr 1979; *Australian Photography*, May 1977; *Australian Camera and Cine*, Apr 1977; *Creative Camera*, Apr 1977; *Creative Camera Annual*, 1976; *Picture Magazine*, #3, 1976; "Grant Mudford," Nancy Stevens, *Popular Photography*, Sept 1976; *35mm Photography*, spring 1976.

COLLECTIONS IMP/GEH, Rochester; L/C, Wash., D.C.; MOMA, NYC; Graham Nash Cllctn., Los Angeles; Security Pacific Bank, Los Angeles; Univ. of Ala., University; Univ. of Louisville, Ky. Art Gall. of South Australia, Adelaide; Art Gall. of Tasmania, Hobart, Australia; Australian Centre for Photography, Sydney; Australian Natl. Gall., Canberra; Horsham Art Gall., Victoria, Australia; Natl. Gall. of Victoria, Melbourne, Australia; Phillip Morris Cllctn., Melbourne; Victoria & Albert Mus., London.

DEALERS Light Gall., 724 Fifth Ave, New York, NY 10019; Rosamund Felsen Gall., 669 N La Cienega Blvd, Los Angeles, CA 90069.

ADDRESS 5619 W 4th St #2, Los Angeles, CA 90036.

Bernis von zur Muehlen PHOTOGRAPHER · TEACHER Born April 10, 1942, in Philadelphia, Pennsylvania, von zur Muehlen received a BA in 1963 from the University of Pennsylvania, Philadelphia.

She has taught English, Russian, creative writing and film studies at James Madison High School in Vienna, Virginia, since 1963. The photographer won an award in 1975 from the Art Directors Club of Metropolitan Washington at their 27th Annual Exhibition.

Von zur Muehlen works in Tri-X and color, hand-paints photographs and does 35mm and 4 x 5 work with infrared film.

PUBLICATIONS Book: *The Story of American Photography: An Illustrated History for Young People*, Martin Sandler, 1979. Anthologies: *Family of Woman*, 1979; *SX-70 Art*, Ralph Gibson, ed., 1979; *In-Sights: Self-Portraits by Women*, Joyce T. Cohen, ed., 1978; *Women Photograph Men*, Dannielle B. Hayes, ed., intro. by Molly Haskell, 1977; *Women See Men*, Yvonne Kalmus et al., eds., intro. & text by Ingrid Bengis, 1977. Periodicals: *The Image Continuum Journal*, vol. 4, 1979; "Report from Washington," David Tannous, *Art in America*, July-Aug 1979; *Communications Arts Magazine Annual*, Nov/Dec 1975; *Lightwork*, Apr 1975.

COLLECTIONS Baltimore Mus. of Art, Md.; Corcoran Gall. of Art, Wash., D.C.; ICP, NYC; Wesleyan Univ., Davison Art Ctr., Middletown, Conn.

DEALERS Osuna Gall., 406 Seventh St NW, Washington, DC 20004; Susan Spiritus Gall., 3336 Via Lido, Newport Beach, CA 92663.

ADDRESS 3096 Cobb Hill Ln, Oakton, VA 22124.

Peter von zur Muehlen PHOTOGRAPHER·ECONOMIST Born in Germany on March 10, 1939, von zur Muehlen is a self-taught photographer. He received a PhD in Economics from Princeton University, New Jersey, in 1970.

Since 1968 he has been employed as an economist in Special Studies for the Federal Reserve Board, and before that as an economist for the U.S. Department of Agriculture (1966–68), both in Washington, D.C. He has belonged to the American Economic Association since 1973.

The photographer produces medium-format Type C color prints of urban environments. From 1976 to 1979 he did a series of SX-70 still lifes.

PUBLICATIONS Anthology: *One of a Kind*, 1979. Periodical: *Lightwork*, 1:2, 1975.

COLLECTIONS Corcoran Gall., Wash., D.C.; Va. Mus. of Art, Richmond.

DEALERS Osuna Gall., 406 Seventh St NW, Washington, DC 20004; Panopticon Gall., 187 Bay State Rd, Boston, MA 02215.

ADDRESS 2133 Colts Neck Ct, Reston, VA 22091.

David Josef Muench PHOTOGRAPHER Born June 25, 1936, in Santa Barbara, California, Muench studied at Rochester Institute of Technology, New York (1954–55), the University of California, Santa Barbara (1955–56), and Art Center School of Design in Los Angeles, where he took his BA in 1961.

A freelance since 1961, the ASMP member was commissioned in 1975 to provide photographs for thirty-three large murals depicting the Lewis and Clark expedition at the Jefferson Expansion Memorial in St. Louis, Missouri.

Working in 4 x 5, he produces color and black-and-white landscape photographs, primarily of the western United States. His goal is to "record the spirit of the land . . . to make what I see so stark and real visually that my photographs express a communication with a higher form of reality."

PUBLICATIONS Books: *Colorado*, 1978; *Lewis and Clark Country*, 1978; *Rocky Mountains*, 1975; *New Mexico*, 1974; *Utah*, 1973; *Arizona*, 1971.

DEALERS Steven White Gall., 835 La Cienega Blvd, Los Angeles, CA 90069; Keystone Gall., 1213 State St, Suite F, Santa Barbara, CA 93101.

ADDRESS POB 30500, Santa Barbara, CA 93105.

Robert Muffoletto PHOTOGRAPHER · CRITIC · TEACHER Born July 31, 1947, in Buffalo, New York, Muffoletto received a BS in Education from State University of New York (SUNY), Buffalo (1969), and an MFA from Visual Studies Workshop, SUNY, Buffalo (1973). He has studied photography with Nathan Lyons, John Upton, Robert Heinecken and Oscar Bailey.

As of this writing Muffoletto was publisher and editor of *Camera Lucida, The Journal of Photographic Criticism*. He has been a photography lecturer at the University of Wisconsin, Milwaukee, since 1978. Muffoletto founded and directed the Center for Exploratory and Perceptual Arts, Buffalo, from 1974 to 1977.

A member of SPE, he won Wisconsin Arts Board grants in 1978 and 1979. He was a founder and current board member of Perihelion Photographic Gallery, Milwaukee (since 1977), and has been on the board of directors of the Milwaukee Arts Alliance since 1977.

A photo critic published in a number of journals, Muffoletto also does his own work that involves video as well as silver prints and color type C prints.

PUBLICATIONS (selected) Monograph: *Metaphor I*, 1972 (self-pub.). Periodicals: "Of Snapshots and Art," *Wisconsin Photographer*, Aug 1979; *Review, New Art Examiner*, June 1978; "An Approach to the Criticism of Color Photography," *Philadelphia Photo Review*, Dec 1977.

PORTFOLIO *Visual Studies Workshop Portfolio* (group), 1972 (Rochester).

ADDRESS 2605 N Prospect, #1, Milwaukee, WI 53211.

George François Mugnier   PHOTOGRAPHER [See plate 28] Born ca. 1857 in Switzerland, Mugnier died in 1938 in New Orleans. He was a self-taught photographer.

The photographer opened a commercial studio in New Orleans in 1884 but closed it in 1888. He continued operating out of his home for several years, then went to work as an assayer's clerk at the New Orleans branch of the U.S. Mint until 1894, at which time he joined the Photo-Electric Engraving Company of New Orleans as a photographer. During the ensuing years he worked variously as an automobile mechanic, a machinist, and in the photo-engraving department of the *New Orleans Times-Democrat*.

Moving from the collodion wet-plate process to dry plates, Mugnier produced stereoscopic prints, panoramas, portraits, city scenes and landscapes. "Today Mugnier's work can be viewed as both an aesthetic and historical document of a period of Louisiana's history marked by social, political, and economic change," write John R. Kemp & Linda Orr King. "The variety and complexity of Louisiana's heritage are vividly reflected in the patrician mansions, laborers' cabins, and the rivers and bayous" contained in Mugnier's images.

PUBLICATIONS Monographs: *Louisiana Images, 1880–1920*, intro. by John R. Kemp & Linda Orr King, 1975; *New Orleans and Bayou Country: Photographs (1880–1910) by George François Mugnier*, Lester B. Bridaham, 1972. Catalog: *Mugnier: The Look of New Orleans, 1880–1910*, Mrs. Richard McCarthy, Jr., ca. 1960 (Louisiana State Mus.: New Orleans).

ARCHIVE Louisiana State Museum, 533 Royal St, New Orleans, LA 70130.

Thomas Minton B. Muir
See Alfred Henry Burton

Wardrop (Ward) Openshaw Muir   PHOTOGRA-PHER · WRITER Born in 1878 in Derby, England, he died June 9, 1927, in London. Muir was educated at Merchant Taylors School in Crosby and at Brighton College. The Impressionists influenced his work, as did his father J. J. Muir, a mi-croscopist who was skilled in botanical and scientific drawing.

After traveling abroad to Austria, Italy, France and Holland, Ward Muir took up photography about 1890, continuing his travels while photographing and writing for the press. He was a major force in the Practical Correspondence College, an association for "training photographers in the art of making the camera pay." A regular contributor to *Amateur Photographer*, he served with the Royal Army Medical Corps during World War I, editing their *Gazette*.

Elected to The Linked Ring in 1904, Muir was an early member of the London Salon of Photography. Aside from his photojournalism, he also wrote novels and short stories.

At the time of his death, the London *Times* wrote that Muir was "a valued contributor to a great variety of publications. He was a landscape photographer of taste and skill."

PUBLICATIONS Books: *The Bewildered Lover*, 1928 (John Lane: London); *No Fuss*, 1927 (Richards: London); *Jones in Paris*, 1925 (John Lane: London); *A Camera for Company*, 1923 (Selwyn & Blount: London); *Crossing Piccadilly Circus*, 1921 (Heinemann: London); *Adventures in Marriage*, 1920, *The Happy Hospital*, 1918, *Observations of an Orderly*, 1917 (Simpkin, Marshall, Hamilton & Kent: London); *Cupid Caterers*, 1914 (S. Paul: London).

Bertel Christian Budtz Müller   CHEMIST · PHO-TOGRAPHER Born December 26, 1837, in Mariager, Denmark, Müller died December 30, 1884, in Copenhagen, Denmark. He received a bachelor's degree in pharmacology.

Müller was employed at Swan Pharmacy in Copenhagen (1859) by Alfred Benzon, with whom he shared a photographic studio and supply business. He also taught photography. In 1870 he was photographer to the Royal Court. In cooperation with C. Ferslew, Müller was the first to do photolithography in Denmark.

During his life he published several photographic portfolios, and photographed the sculptures of Thorvaldsen as well as cartoons by Danish and foreign artists.

PUBLICATION Book: *Photographers in and from Denmark up till 1900*, Bjørn Ochsner, 1956, rev. ed. 1969.

COLLECTION Royal Lib., Copenhagen.

Andreas Müller-Pohle   PHOTOGRAPHER · EDI-TOR · CRITIC Born July 19, 1951, in Braunschweig, Germany, Müller-Pohle was influenced by Moholy-Nagy, Mondrian, Eisenstein and Steinert.

Currently editor of *European Photography*, he worked as a freelance photographer from 1978 to 1979.

Müller-Pohle has been a member of the DGPh since 1979.

PUBLICATIONS Periodicals: *Photographie*, 1979; *Printletter*, 1979; *Zoom*, 1979 (Munich); *Fotografie*, 1978.

COLLECTIONS Bibliothèque Nationale, Paris; Musée Cantini, Marseille, France; Museum für Kunst und Gewerbe, Hamburg, Germany; Polaroid Cllctn. (Europe), Amsterdam, The Netherlands.

DEALERS Benteler Gall., 3830 University Blvd, Houston, TX 77009; PPS Galerie, Feldstrasse/Hochhaus 1, D-2000 Hamburg 4, Germany; Work Gall., Trittligasse 24, CH-8001 Zurich, Switzerland.

ADDRESS Stargarder Weg 18, D-3400 Göttingen, W Germany.

Daniel Louis Mundy PHOTOGRAPHER Mundy flourished from 1858 to 1875 in New Zealand and London.

With a home base in Christchurch, New Zealand, the photographer roamed the countryside with his camera. He was commissioned by the Canterbury Museum to photograph its collection of moa skeletons, and he also photographed paleontologist Sir Richard Owen's specimens.

A member of the London Photographic Society, he was awarded a gold medal from the Emperor of Austria ca. 1875.

Mundy, in addition to his scientific photography, recorded various aspects of nature in New Zealand. He worked with wet-plate negatives.

PUBLICATIONS Book: *Rotomahana and the Boiling Springs of New Zealand*, 1875. Anthology: *19th Century New Zealand Photographers*, John B. Turner, 1970. Periodical: *The British Journal of Photography*, 1874.

COLLECTION Canterbury Mus., Christchurch, New Zealand.

Martin Munkácsi PHOTOGRAPHER Munkácsi was born May 18, 1896, in Kolozsvár, Hungary (now Cluj Napoca, Romania), and died in New York City on July 14, 1963. He was self-taught in the craft of photography.

Munkácsi moved to Budapest in 1912 at the age of sixteen. He wrote poetry and did reporting for the sports section of *Az Est*, also working for *Pesti Napló* and *Szinházi Élet*. In 1921 he began

his career as a sports photographer. Eventually he moved to Berlin, where he signed a three-year contract with Ullstein Verlag, publishers, and contributed to such magazines as *Illustrirte Zeitung*, *Die Dame*, *Koralle*, *Uhu* and *Die Woche*, receiving assignments that sent him traveling around the world. Contracted to work for *Harper's Bazaar* in 1934, he moved to New York, where he spent the rest of his life. From 1940 to 1946 he worked for *Ladies' Home Journal*, and also contributed to *Life*.

At the height of Munkácsi's reputation (1940) he was earning more than $100,000 per year—probably the highest salary or earnings by any photographer until that time. He continued writing his poetry and stories. In 1954 he was the cameraman and lighting designer for the animated puppet film *Hansel and Gretel* and directed the film *Bob's Declaration of Independence*.

He was also a noted fashion photographer. Munkácsi's work, says Colin Osman *(Spontaneity & Style)*, "was a subtle art of light, shadows, movement and inflections of mood." He was the first to take fashion photography out of the studio and its traditional conventions and breathe spontaneity and reality into the form.

PUBLICATIONS Monograph: *Nudes*, 1951. Books: *The World of Carmel Snow*, Carmel Snow w/Mary Louise Aswell, 1962; *Fool's Apprentice*, novel, 1945; *How America Lives*, 1941; *Knipsen*, text only, 1929 (Ullstein Verlag: Berlin). Anthologies: *The History of Fashion Photography*, Nancy Hall-Duncan, 1979; *The Magic Image*, Cecil Beaton & Gail Buckland, 1975; *The Studio*, Time-Life Series, 1971. Catalogs: *Spontaneity & Style: Munkácsi*, 1978 (ICP: NYC); *Fashion Photography—An Art of Democracy*, Gene Thornton, 1975 (Hofstra Univ.). Periodicals: *Creative Camera Internatl. Year Book*, 1977; "Munkácsi," Colin Osman, *Creative Camera*, 1977; "Photo-Journalism, the Legendary Twenties," Bernd Lohse, *Camera*, Apr 1967; "Martin Munkácsi," Richard Avedon, *Harper's Bazaar*, June 1964, repr. June 1967; "Glamour Portraits," P. F. Althaus, *Camera*, Nov 1965; "Martin Munkácsi," Gabriel P. Hackett, *Infinity: ASMP*, Sept 1963; *Ladies' Home Journal*, passim, 1955–59, 1948–53, & "How America Lives," column, 1940–46; "Must They Be Sharp?" *Photography*, text only, fall 1947; *Harper's Bazaar*, passim, Apr 1934–46; "How America Lives," *U.S. Camera*, May 1942; "Pictorial Analysis," Nicholas Ház, *The Camera*, Oct 1935; "Martin Munkácsi," Nicholas Ház, *Camera Craft*, July 1935; *Modern Photography Yearbook*, 1934/5, 1933/4, 1932/3;

Das Deutsche Lichtbild, yearbook, 1934, 1933, 1932; "Un Eugène Carrière de la Photographie: Munkácsi," Max Clary, *Le Miroir du Monde,* Oct 28, 1933; *Photographie,* yearbook, 1932.

COLLECTIONS Gibbs Art Gall., Charleston, S.C.; MOMA, NYC; Joan Munkácsi Cllctn., NYC.

Ralph Middleton Munroe PHOTOGRAPHER · YACHT DESIGNER · WRECKING AGENT Born April 3, 1851, in New York City, Munroe, who was most frequently referred to as The Commodore, died August 20, 1933, in Coconut Grove, Florida. He studied at Eagleswood Military Academy (1860–63) and took a course in drafting at the School of Mines, Columbia University, New York City.

Starting as a hobbyist, Munroe was a yacht designer from 1874 to 1924. He was Merritt and Chapman Wrecking Company's agent in South Florida from 1888 to 1912, and from 1890 to about 1895 he organized the Biscayne Bay Manufacturing Company. Munroe served as justice of the peace for Dade County, Florida, in 1890.

The founder and first commodore of the Biscayne Bay Yacht Club (1887–1909), his home, "The Barnacle," was designated as a historic site by the State of Florida, which purchased it in 1973. The city of Miami built the Commodore Ralph M. Munroe Marine Stadium in 1963. In 1885, Munroe designed the "Presto" type of boat hull and the Presto, or Munroe, topsail.

The yachtsman was one of the first known photographers of the Miami area, his work providing an invaluable record of southern Florida's early development and history through the 1920s. He used an 8 x 10 view camera made by the Blair Camera Company of Boston to photograph scenery and general subjects.

Vincent Gilpin said of Munroe's work in 1930 that it was "characterized by careful good taste in composition and lighting, exceptionally fine detail from excellent lenses carefully handled, and by chemical work, both in developing and in printing, far ahead of current practice today."

PUBLICATIONS Books: *The Forgotten Frontier,* Arva Moore Parks, 1977; *Historical Study for the Barnacle,* Arva Moore Parks, 1975; *The Commodore's Story,* autobio., Ralph M. Munroe & Vincent Gilpin, 1930.

COLLECTION Hist. Mus. of Southern Fla., Munroe Cllctn., Miami.

ARCHIVE Historical Association of Southern Florida, 3280 S Miami Ave, Bldg B, Miami, FL 33129.

Horst Reinhard Munzig PHOTOGRAPHER Born September 22, 1933, in Mindelheim, Germany, Munzig studied at the Franz-Lazi Photographic School in Stuttgart, Germany (1955), and names Herbert List as his mentor. He was also influenced by Werner Bischof, Henri Cartier-Bresson and Robert Frank.

He is currently a freelance photographer for the magazine *Geo* and other publications.

Munzig belongs to DGPh.

PUBLICATIONS Periodicals: *Camera,* Dec 1975, Oct 1972, Feb 1971; "Death of an Elephant," *Life,* Feb 26, 1971; *DU,* Mar 1967, Jan 1963, Dec 1961.

ADDRESS Bergwaldstrasse 2, 8948 Mindelheim, West Germany.

Nickolas Muray PHOTOGRAPHER · FENCER Born in Szeged, Hungary, in 1892, Muray died a U.S. citizen in New York City in 1965. He studied sculpture as a boy and apprenticed in engraving from 1904 to 1908, receiving an International Engraver's Certificate. About 1909 he studied color photoengraving in Germany and took an advanced three-year course in which he learned how to make color filters.

Muray worked part-time at engraving in the United States and shared a photo studio from 1918 to 1924. In 1924 he rented a large studio of his own and freelanced for magazines such as *Vanity Fair, Harper's Bazaar, Ladies' Home Journal* and *McCall's.* He was the official photographer for Wenner-Gren Foundation for Anthropological Research on an eight-month around-the-world expedition directed by Dr. Paul Fejos. Muray participated in the 1922 London exhibition.

The photographer was also renowned internationally as a fencer, competing for thirty years and noted as one of the greatest fencers in American history. He was U.S. Olympic Saber Champion in 1927–28 and participated in the 1932 Olympics. He also contended with épée and foil.

Muray additionally wrote magazine articles on dance.

The photographer specialized in portraiture of famed personalities in the artistic, literary, musical, theatrical and political worlds. He also used his highly naturalistic color style in advertising, fashion and other commercial photography.

PUBLICATIONS Books: *Muray's Celebrity Portraits of the Twenties and Thirties,* intro. by Marianne Fulton Margolis, 1978; *The Revealing Eye: Personalities of the 1920s,* Paul Gallico, 1967; *Pre-Columbian Art,* S. K. Lothrop, et al, 1959.

Anthology: *The Magic Image*, Cecil Beaton & Gail Buckland, 1975.

PORTFOLIO *Untitled*, intro. by Robert Sobieszek, printed by Michaeala Murphy, 1978 (IMP/GEH: Rochester & Prakapas Gall.: NYC).

COLLECTIONS IMP/GEH, Rochester; MOMA, NYC. RPS, London.

William R. Murchison *PHOTOGRAPHER · TEACHER* Born October 7, 1937, in Crockett, Texas, Murchison received an MS in Photography from Illinois Institute of Technology, Chicago, in 1972. His major influences were Arthur Siegel and Aaron Siskind.

As of this writing Murchison was director of the photography program at Odessa College, Odessa, Texas; he began developing the professional photography curriculum there in 1974. He also taught at the Winona School of Photography, Winona Lake, Indiana, in the summers of 1978 and 1977. Murchison was a photography teacher at Houston Technical Institute, Texas (1973–74), and at Sam Houston State University, Huntsville, Texas (1971–73).

A member of SPE and Professional Photographers of America, he edited *Texas Professional Photographer* for the organization of the same name in 1975–76.

A documentary photographer, Murchison usually works in medium format, often emulating the style of FSA photographers Russell Lee and Arthur Rothstein. One of his projects was a study of graffiti in Chicago.

PUBLICATION Book: *Colorado City, Texas*, 1976.

COLLECTIONS Colorado City Lib., Tex.; Stanton Lib., Tex.

ADDRESS Odessa College, Box 3752, Odessa, TX 79760.

Joan Murray *PHOTOGRAPHER · CRITIC · TEACHER* Born in Annapolis, Maryland, on March 6, 1927, Murray studied photography at California College of Arts and Crafts, Oakland, the San Francisco Art Institute, Ruth Bernhard Insight Studio and at University of California Extension. Wynn Bullock was a major influence on both her photography and writing.

Murray has been photography editor of *Artweek* since 1969 and an associate editor of *American Photographer* since 1978. She was also a critic for *Popular Photography* (1973–76). A teacher at University of California Extension, Berkeley, since 1970, she taught workshops with Wynn Bullock at the University's Santa Cruz Extension in 1974 and 1975. She also taught at

Ansel Adams Yosemite Workshop in 1974 and at San Francisco City College (1975–76).

Murray received an NEA Critics Grant in 1978.

COLLECTIONS IMP/GEH, Rochester; Oakland Mus., Calif.; San Francisco Mus. of Modern Art, Calif.

ADDRESS 120 Blair Ave, Piedmont, CA 94611.

Eadweard Muybridge *PHOTOGRAPHER* [See plate 26] Muybridge was born Edward James Muggeridge on April 9, 1830, and died May 8, 1904, in Kingston-on-Thames, England. He gave himself a pseudonym early in his career, "Helios —the Flying Studio." His motion studies were probably influenced by Oscar G. Rejlander.

Initially he worked in the family business, stationery and paper-making, and later found work with a book distributor. In 1852 he emigrated to the U.S.A., and by 1856 he had set up shop as a bookseller in San Francisco. Muybridge began taking landscape photographs in the mid-1860s, especially of the Yosemite region. His large-format images of Yosemite gained him his first recognition in 1869. In the employ of the U.S. government as director of photographic surveys along the coast of California, he also did surveys for Thomas Houseworth and accompanied General Halleck to Alaska. In May 1872 Muybridge came to the attention of ex-Governor Leland Stanford, president of Central Pacific Railroad. Stanford commissioned him to prove, photographically, that at some point during a horse's gallop all four of its legs are off the ground simultaneously. Due to the lack of a shutter that was fast enough, his first experiments were unsuccessful, but in 1877 he returned to prove Stanford's contention.

After being tried and acquitted for the murder of his wife's lover, he was in the employ of Stanford, photographing railroads during the interim years of 1872–77. He traveled to Mexico and Central America, where he recorded Panamanian ruins and Indian life and documented the Indian Modoc War (1873–74). During 1880–82 he traveled and lectured in Europe, then returned to the United States. At the request of Dr. William Pepper, president of the University of Pennsylvania, and artist Thomas Eakins, he continued his exploration of human and animal motion studies in 1884–85.

Muybridge invented one of the first shutters for a camera in 1869, and in 1880 he devised what he called a zoopraxiscope, or zoogyroscope. This was a machine that projected pictures on the screen in a rapid, sequential order and so he may be considered the inventor of the first projected animated photographs, the precursor of motion pictures. In 1893 Muybridge gave the first demonstration of the process at the California School of Fine Arts in San Francisco, and at the Chicago World's Fair, that same year, the Zoopraxographical Hall was erected for the sole purpose of projecting Muybridge's work. He returned to his birthplace in England in 1900. In 1929 Leland Stanford commissioned a bronze tablet to be dedicated to the memory of Muybridge at Stanford University in Palo Alto, California.

Homage to Muybridge (1965) and *Eadweard Muybridge, Zoopraxographer* (1975) are two color films about the artist.

In all of Muybridge's wide-ranging work, from his early albumen prints of Yosemite and California life to his views of San Francisco and Alaska, on to his motion studies, the prolific photographer retained a dramatic style.

PUBLICATIONS Monographs: *Muybridge: Man in Motion*, Robt. Bartlett Haas, 1976; *Eadweard Muybridge: The Father of the Motion Picture*, Gordon Hendricks, 1975; *Eadweard Muybridge: The Stanford Years, 1872–82*, intro. by Anita Ventura Mozley, 1972; *Eadweard Muybridge: The Man Who Invented the Moving Picture*, Kevin MacDonnell, 1972; *The Human Figure in Motion; an Electrophotographic Investigation of Consecutive Phases of Muscular Actions*, 1901, repr. w/intro. by Robert Taft, 1955; *Animals in Motion*, 1899, repr., Lewis S. Brown, ed., 1957; *Animal Locomotion: The Muybridge Work at the University of Pennsylvania*, 1888; *Animal Locomotion: An Electro-Photographic Investigation of Consecutive Phases of Animal Movement, 1872–85*, 11 vols, 1887; *The Horse in Motion*, J. D. B. Stillman, 1882; *The Attitudes of Animals in Motion*, 1881; *The Horse in Motion*, 1878; *The Pacific Coast of Central America and Mexico; the Isthmus of Panama, Guatemala; and the Cultivation and Shipment of Coffee*, 1877 (Pacific Mail Steamship Co.: San Francisco); *Panoramic San Francisco*, 1877. Books: *The Birth of Photography*, Brian Coe, 1976; *Pioneers of Photography*, Aaron Scharf, 1976; *Era of Exploration*, Weston J. Naef & James N. Wood, 1975; *The History of Photography*, Beaumont Newhall, 1964; *History of Photography*, Josef Maria Eder, 1945; *Photography and the American Scene*, Robt. Taft, 1938; *Descriptive Zoopraxography*, 1893; *Popular Zoopraxograph: The Science of Zoopraxography*, 1893; *Zoopraxography or the Science of Animal Locomotion*, 1891; *Yosemite: Its Wonders and Its Beauties*, John Shertzer Hittell, 1868. Anthologies: *The Photograph Collector's Guide*, Lee D. Witkin & Barbara London,

1979; *The Invented Eye*, Edw. Lucie-Smith, 1975; *The Magic Image*, Cecil Beaton & Gail Buckland, 1975; *Early Photographs & Early Photographers*, Oliver Mathews, 1973; *Picture Gallery Pioneers, 1850–1875*, Ralph W. Andrews, 1964. Periodicals: "Eadweard Muybridge," Timo Tauno Pajunen, *Camera*, Jan & Feb, 1973; "Les Allures du Cheval," Harlan Hamilton, *Film Comment*, 5:3, fall 1969; "Muybridge and the First Motion Picture," Beaumont Newhall, *Image*, Jan 1956; "Muybridge at the London Institute," W. P. Adams, *British Journal of Photography*, 36:826, 1889; "The Attitudes of Animals in Motion," *Journal of the Franklin Institute*, vol. 85, and *Proceedings of the Royal Institute of Great Britain*, 10:1, 1883; *Proceedings of the Royal Institute of Great Britain*, March 13, 1882; *The Scientific American Supplement*, no. 158, Oct 19, 1878.

PORTFOLIO *Yosemite Photographs, 1872*, intro. by Robt. Bartlett Haas, essay by Joel Snyder, printed by Doug Munson & Chas. B. Reynolds, 1977 (Chicago Albumen Works/Yosemite Natl. Parks: Calif.).

COLLECTIONS American Mus. of Natural History, NYC; Calif. Historical Soc., San Francisco; Calif. State Lib., Sacramento; Harvard Univ., Carpenter Ctr. for Visual Arts & Widener Memorial Lib., Cambridge; IMP/GEH, Rochester; L/C, Wash., D.C.; Metro. Mus. of Art, NYC; Univ. of N. Mex. Art Mus., Albuquerque; N.Y. Historical Soc., NYC; N.Y. Public Lib., NYC; Oakland Mus., Calif.; Philadelphia Mus. of Art, Penn.; Mus. of the Philadelphia Civic Ctr., Penn.; Free Lib. of Philadelphia, Penn.; Princeton Univ., N.J.; Smithsonian Inst., Wash., D.C.; Stanford Univ., Palo Alto, Calif; Univ. of Calif, Bancroft Lib., Berkeley; UCLA. Kingston-on-Thames Pub. Lib., England; Natl. Gall. of Canada, Ottawa, Ontario; RPS, London; Science Mus., London; Victoria & Albert Mus., London.

ARCHIVE Kingston-on-Thames Public Library, Kingston-on-Thames, England.

Carl Mydans PHOTOJOURNALIST · WRITER
Born in Boston, Massachusetts, Mydans earned a BS degree from Boston University School of Journalism in 1930 and a DH degree from the college in 1960.

A staff photographer for the Farm Security Administration (1935–36), Mydans served on the staff of *Life* magazine (1936–72).

He belongs to ASMP.

PUBLICATIONS Books: *China: A Visual Adventure*, w/Michael Demarest, 1979; *The Violent Peace*, w/Shelley Mydans, 1968; *More Than*

Meets the Eye, 1959. Anthology: *The Photograph Collector's Guide,* Lee D. Witkin & Barbara London, 1979.

ADDRESS 212 Hommocks Rd, Larchmont, NY 10538.

Joan Myers *PHOTOGRAPHER* Myers was born June 11, 1944. Her grandfather was Henry Wallace, Secretary of Agriculture and vice-president under Franklin D. Roosevelt. She earned a BA (1966) and an MA (1967) from Stanford University, Palo Alto, California, and studied photography with Robert Heinecken and Leland Rice in 1975.

Myers belongs to the Los Angeles Center for Photographic Studies, Friends of Photography and CCP.

She uses early photographic processes such as platinum and carbon with the addition of hand coloring.

PUBLICATIONS Anthology: *Platinum Print,* J. Hafey & Tom Shillea, 1979. Periodicals: *printletter,* July 1977; "Joan Myers," *Arts,* Feb 1977.

COLLECTIONS Delaware Art Mus., Wilmington; Denver Art Mus., Colo.; High Mus. of Art, Atlanta, Ga.; Newport Harbor Art Mus., Newport Beach, Calif.; N. Va. Community Coll., Annandale; Security Pacific Natl. Bank, Los Angeles; Seattle Art Mus., Wash.

DEALERS Marcuse Pfeifer, 825 Madison Ave, New York, NY 10021; Susan Spiritus Gall., 3336 Via Lido, Newport Beach, CA 92660.

ADDRESS 1710 Canyon Rd, Santa Fe, NM 87501.

N

Nadar (Gaspard Félix Tournachon)   *PHOTOG-RAPHER · CARICATURIST · WRITER · BALLOONIST*
[See plate 29] Born in Paris on April 5, 1820, with the name of Gaspard Félix Tournachon, he died in Paris in 1910. His pseudonym, Nadar, was derived from his nickname, "tourne à dard" (bitter sting), earned for his caricatures. His brother, Adrien Tournachon, was a photographer who signed his prints "Nadar Jeune." Nadar also had a son, Paul Nadar, who was a photographer. Nadar studied medicine in Lyons, France; he taught himself how to draw.

In 1842 he began selling caricatures to humor magazines. He became interested in photography about 1849, and opened a Paris portrait studio in 1853 with his brother. Their studio became a meeting place for the great artists and intelligentsia of the day and, in 1874, it held the first Impressionist exhibit. Nadar received a patent on October 29, 1858, for the taking of aerial photographs (from a balloon) for map-making and surveying. He operated a balloon passenger and postal service between Paris and Tours during the Franco-Prussian War (1870). Founder of the magazines *La Revue Comique* (1849) and *Paris Photographe* (1891, lasting only until 1893), he contributed articles and caricatures to myriad publications of the day, as well as writing novels, essays and satires.

Nadar took the first aerial photograph ever made from an enormous balloon he built around 1858. It was three times larger than any other made and carried a two-story gondola that could carry forty-nine men. Within the balloon itself he built a darkroom where he coated his wet plates. Nadar made several series of photographs of the catacombs and sewers beneath Paris in 1861–62, with the use of carbon arc lights. He was one of the first photographers to use electric lights, though he later switched to magnesium light. In 1886 he introduced the photo-interview via a series of portraits taken by his son during an interview between Nadar and scientist Michel-Eugène Chevruel on the occasion of his hundredth birthday.

Nadar is remembered as one of the best of the portraitists. André Jammes calls his work "utterly honest and most expressive." Making albumen prints in *cartes de visite* and large format, Nadar, at the hub of society's world of arts and letters, photographed scores of famous people—Franz Liszt, George Sand, Sara Bernhardt, Balzac, Delacroix, Rossini, etc. He used side-lighting, unusual in his day, and natural poses. Of his work, the artist said: "The portrait I do the best is that of the man I know the best."

PUBLICATIONS   Monographs: *Nadar*, Nigel Gosling, 1976; *Nadar: 50 Photographies de ses illustrés contemporains*, 1975 (Barret: Paris); *Nadar*, Jean Prinet & Antoinette Dillasser, 1966 (Colin: Paris); *Nadar*, 1965 (Bibliothèque Nationale: Paris). Books: *Quand j'étais Photographé*, preface by Léon Daudet, 1899 (E. Flammarion: Paris); *Le Mirroir due Alouettes*, 1883; *Le monde où on patague*, 1883; *L'Hôtellerie des Coquecigrus—Notes au crayon*, 1880 (E. Dentu: Paris); *A terre et en air, Mémoires du Géant*, autobio., w/ illus. by Honoré Daumier, 1864; *Le Cas des cloches, soumis par Nadar*, 1882 (Ménard: Chambéry); *Histoires buissonières*, 1877 (George Decaux: Paris); *Les Ballons en 1870*, 1870 (Chatelain: Paris); *Galerie des Contemporains*, 1870; *Le Droit au vol*, 1865, 3rd ed., w/preface by George Sand (Hetzel: Paris), U.K. ed., *The Right to Fly*, 1866 (Cassell: London); *Quand j'étais étudiant*, 1858; *Almanach Tintamarre pour 1855*, 1855 (Martinon: Paris); *Panthéon Nadar*, vol. 1, 1854; *Chants et chansons de la Bohème*, 1953 (J. Bryainé: Paris). Anthologies: *The Photograph Collector's Guide*, Lee D. Witkin & Barbara London, 1979; *The Julien Levy Collection*, Witkin Gallery, 1977; *Pioneers of Photography*, Aaron Scharf, 1976; *The Invented Eye*, Edw. Lucie-Smith, 1975; *The Magic Image*, Cecil Beaton & Gail Buckland, 1975; *Early Photographs & Early Photographers*, Oliver Mathews, 1973; *French*

Primitive Photography, André Jammes & Robt. Sobieszek, intro. by Minor White, 1969; *Masters of Photography*, Beaumont & Nancy Newhall, 1969; "Nadar," Berenice Abbott, "Nadar," Heinrich Schwarz, *Complete Photographer*, 1941–43; *Immortal Portraits*, Alex Strasser, 1941. Periodicals: *Camera*, entire issue, Dec 1960; "Ein Besuch in Nadar's Photographischen Atelier in Paris," J. M. Eder, *Photographische Korrespondenz*, 1887; *Les Hommes d'Aujord'hui*, Nov 1878.

PORTFOLIO *Portfolio No. 1*, intro. by Philippe Neagu, preface by André Jammes, printed by Claudine Sudre, 1978 (Claudine Sudre, Lacoste).

COLLECTIONS IMP/GEH, Rochester; Univ. of N. Mex. Art Mus., Albuquerque. In Paris: Archives Photographiques; Bibliothèque Nationale; Caisse Nationale des Monuments Historiques et des Sites; Société Française de Photographie. Provinciaal Museum voor Kunstambachten, Duerne (Antwerp), Belgium.

ARCHIVE Bibliothèque Nationale, 58 rue de Richelieu, 75002 Paris, France.

Paul Nadar *PHOTOGRAPHER* Born in Paris in 1856, Nadar died in France in 1939. He was taught photography and wholly influenced by his father, the photographer Nadar. His uncle, Adrien Tournachon, was also a photographer.

The young Nadar worked with his father in the elder's studio, doing portraits on his own as well. During Nadar's last years, Paul did his printing for him. He also photographed the acclaimed first photo-interview, conceived by his father, that took place between Nadar and scientist Michel-Eugène Chevruel. For several years around 1890, Paul was the Paris agent for George Eastman.

PUBLICATIONS Anthologies: *The Magic Image*, Cecil Beaton & Gail Buckland, 1975; *Early Photographs & Early Photographers*, Oliver Mathews, 1973.

See Nadar

Luis R. Nadeau *PHOTOGRAPHIC CONSERVATOR · WRITER* Born in 1951 in Quebec, Canada, Nadeau studied history and conservation of photographic materials in Canada, the United States, France and Spain.

Until recently, Nadeau spent several years as photographic conservator with the Provincial Archives of New Brunswick, Canada, in Fredericton. He occasionally lectures and gives workshops.

Nadeau belongs to the RPS and the National Association of Photographic Arts of Canada.

He owns and operates the only Fresson lab outside of France, which he acquired from José O. Echagüe. With the collaboration of several organizations, he conducts research on the improvement of archival printing techniques in monochrome and color, using pigment processes.

PUBLICATIONS Transcript: "The Quadrichromie Fresson Process," 1978 (ICP: NYC). Periodicals: "Michel St. Jean, Images de Québec," Dec 1977, "7th International Meeting of Photography in Arles," Dec 1976, "Archival Processing," Sept 1976, *Camera Canada*; "Restaurer des daguerréotypes," *Prestige de la Photographie*, June 1978; (Paris); "On Color Print Processes and Conservation," *printletter*, no. 8, Mar 1977; "Platinotipia," *Progresso Fotografico*, Nov 1978.

COLLECTIONS Bibliothèque Nationale, Paris; New Brunswick Art Bank, Fredericton, New Brunswick, Canada.

ADDRESS 647 Hanson St, Fredericton, New Brunswick, Canada E3B 4A1.

Weston J. Naef *CURATOR · PHOTOHISTORIAN · WRITER* Born January 8, 1942, in Gallup, New Mexico, Naef earned a BA from Claremont Men's College in California (1964) and an MA from Ohio State University, Columbus (1966). He studied at Brown University, Providence, Rhode Island (1966–69).

Naef is currently curator of photography at the Metropolitan Museum of Art in New York City and was previously its assistant curator (starting in 1971) and a staff member in the department of prints and photographs (1970). He directed the art gallery at Wheaton (Massachusetts) College in 1969 and was a visiting scholar at the Boston Public Library in 1968. Naef received a Kress Fellowship in 1968.

PUBLICATIONS (text only) Books: *Eliot Porter: The Intimate Landscapes*, 1979; *Georgia O'Keeffe*, Alfred Stieglitz, 1979; *The Collection of Alfred Stieglitz*, 1978; *Era of Exploration, The Rise of Landscape Photography in the American West 1860–1885*, 1975; *The Truthful Lens*, 1974; *The Painterly Photograph*, 1973; *Behind the Great Wall of China*, w/Cornell Capa, 1972. Anthology: *Pioneer Photographers of Brazil, 1839–1914*, 1976.

ADDRESSES Metropolitan Museum of Art, Fifth Ave & 82 St, New York, NY 10028; 155 Wooster St, New York, NY 10012.

Bent Næsby *PHOTOGRAPHER* Born November 1, 1934, in Copenhagen, Denmark, Næsby is a self-taught freelance photographer.

He has done work for Louisiana Museum of Modern Art, Humlebæk, Denmark (since 1976), publications for the Ministry of Foreign Affairs (since 1976) and photographs for *Scanorama* (SAS magazine—since 1974). He was the still photographer for Orson Welles' production of *The Process* in 1964.

A member of the Danish Photohistorical Society since 1979, Næsby won grants from the Foundation for Danish/Swedish Collaboration in 1979 and the Foundation for Danish/Finnish Collaboration in 1976.

The photographer has also directed and photographed two documentary films, *What Do You Believe in—God?* and *Sunday in Fælledparken.*

Næsby produces large-format silver prints.

COLLECTION   Royal Lib. Photo. Cllctn., Denmark.

ADDRESS   Overgaden Oven Vandet 54, DK 1514, Copenhagen, Denmark.

Patrick August Nagatani   PHOTOGRAPHER · TEACHER   Born August 19, 1945, in Chicago, Illinois, Nagatani received a BA from California State University, Los Angeles, in 1967 and in 1980 received an MFA from UCLA.

A teacher at Fairfax Community Adult School in Los Angeles from 1976 to the present, he has also done freelance photography since 1973 and taught at Hamilton High School since 1968. Nagatani was an art director for Orange Peel Graphics in Hollywood, California (1966–74).

A member of SPE and Friends of Photography since 1976, Nagatani has been a trustee for the Los Angeles Center for Photographic Studies since 1977. He won a Ford Foundation Travel Grant in 1979.

PUBLICATIONS   Catalog: *Spectrum: New Directions in Color Photography*, 1979 (Univ. of Hawaii: Manoa). Periodicals: *Color Foto*, Mar 1979; *Photography Annual*, 1979; "Patrick Nagatani: Isolating the Ephemeral Moment," *Petersen's Photographic Magazine*, Mar 1977.

ADDRESS   9130 Exposition Dr, Los Angeles, CA 90034.

John William Nagel   · PHOTOGRAPHER · TEACHER   Born October 31, 1942, in San Francisco, California, Nagel received a BA and MA from San Francisco State University (1970 and 1972). His major influences were Ansel Adams, Don Worth, Jack Welpott and Henry Holmes Smith.

Since 1974 Nagel has been assistant professor of photography at St. Louis Community College at Meramec, Missouri. In 1973 he was a factory worker and draftsman for Amana Refrigeration, Amana, Iowa, and from 1967 to 1972 he was an engineering photographer for Wildman & Morris, construction engineers in San Francisco. He worked for the city of Ukiah, California, for its Municipal Engineering Department in 1963–67 as a draftsman, surveyor and mapper.

Nagel received the James D. Phelan Award in Art in 1971.

His work has ranged from large-format landscapes to Minox images, his special interest being self-portraits utilizing a broad range of techniques, including photo silk screen, brownprint, cyanotype and carbon prints. He has also done extensive research in historically important photographic sensitizers.

PUBLICATIONS   Book: *Photo Art Processes*, 1979. Anthology: *Self-Portrayal*, 1979. Periodical: *Modern Photography*, Sept 1970.

COLLECTIONS   Art Inst. of Chicago; Oakland Mus., Calif; St. Louis Art Mus., Mo.; Univ. of Kans. Mus. of Art, Lawrence. Bibliothèque Nationale, Paris.

ADDRESS   229 S Old Orchard, Webster Groves, MO 63119.

Arthur Nager   PHOTOGRAPHER · TEACHER   Born January 29, 1949, in Jamaica, New York, Nager received a BA in 1970 (Psychology/History) from the University of Rochester, New York, and an MFA in 1975 from the Visual Studies Workshop, State University of New York at Buffalo, where he studied with Nathan Lyons and Syl Labrot.

Since 1973 he has been coordinator of photography (associate professor) at University of Bridgeport, Connecticut. He was a photography instructor in 1972–73 at both the Center of the Eye, Aspen, and for the Aurora Public School System, both in Colorado. In 1969–71 Nager was a museum assistant at IMP/GEH in Rochester.

A member of SPE since 1972, Nager received a grant from the Connecticut Commission on the Arts (with Fairfield Historical Society) in 1977 and a National Endowment for the Humanities grant in 1976.

His early work was in small-format black-and-white, but the photographer's latest work is large-format color, documenting urban landscapes.

COLLECTION   IMP/GEH, Rochester.

ADDRESS   35 Livingston St, Fairfield, CT 06432.

Masaaki Nakagawa   PHOTOGRAPHER   Born October 6, 1943, in Okayama, Japan, Nakagawa earned a BA in Japanese Literature from Konan University in Kobe, Japan, in 1966.

A freelance photographer since 1969, he has been a member of Japan Professional Photographers Society since 1973.

Most recently Nakagawa has been experimenting with a pinhole, 8 x 10 Polaroid format, using 40-minute exposures—"40 minutes being the unit of time used in Zen meditation."

PUBLICATIONS Periodicals: *Creative Camera*, Nov 1979; *Il Diaframma Fotografia Italiana*, Dec 1974; *Zoom*, Dec 1974 (France); *Camera Mainichi*, Nov 1974; *Asahi Camera*, Mar 1974.

COLLECTIONS Polaroid Gall., Boston. Bibliothèque Nationale, Paris; Canon Photo Gall., Amsterdam, The Netherlands; Stedelijk Mus., Amsterdam.

ADDRESS Itopia, #A-1401, Toyo 2–3–1, Koto-ku, Tokyo 135, Japan.

Rodolfo Namias CHEMIST · WRITER Born in 1867 in Modena, Italy, Namias died in 1938. He majored in chemistry at the Polytechnical School in Turin.

Namias worked in industry for a while after graduation, then became a professor of pure and applied chemistry in a technical institute. He later took charge of chemistry, photography and photomechanical reproduction at the School of Graphic Arts in Milan, where he stayed until 1905. In 1894 he established a laboratory for chemical research in Milan and founded the monthly periodical *Progresso Fotografico*, which his son continued to publish after Rodolfo's death. Namias' laboratory expanded into an educational establishment covering photochemistry, applied photography, photomicroscopy and other technical areas of photography. The chemist wrote many books on photography and photomechanical reproduction, including a manual on theoretical and practical photochemistry that was translated into French and German. He received numerous honors from European photographic and scientific organizations, including the silver medal of the Photographische Gesellschaft in Vienna for his book *Observations on the Relationship Between Thermochemistry and Photochemistry*.

Namias' first major photochemical discovery was the acid permanganate reducer (1899), and in 1892 he recommended the use of organic acids to increase the stability of photo papers. His 1909 work on mordanted dye photography aided the progress of color photography and cinematography.

PUBLICATIONS Books: *Quellendarstellungen zur Geschichte der Fotografie*, Wolfgang Baier, 1964; *History of Color Photography*, Joseph S.

Friedman, 1944; *Lexikon für Photographie und Reproduktionstechnik*, G. H. Emmerich, 1910. Anthology: *Photography's Great Inventors*, Louis W. Sipley, 1965. Periodicals: *Photographische Correspondenz*, 1939, 1900, 1894; *Il Progresso Fotografico*, 1921; *British Journal of Photography*, 1911, 1909, 1907; *Bulletin de la Société Française de Photographie*, 1903; *Penrose's Annual*, 1900; *Photography*, 1899; *Jahrbuch für Photographie und Reproduktionstechnik*, Eder, 1895, 1892.

Johsel Namkung PHOTOGRAPHER Born April 24, 1919, in Korea, Namkung received his BA in 1939 from the Tokyo Conservatory of Music, and his MA in 1951 from the School of Music, University of Washington, Seattle. He studied color photography with Chao-chen Yang and took workshops with Ansel Adams. He considers Paul Strand and Edward Weston his major influences.

Namkung has been a scientific photographer for the University of Washington since 1961.

He is a board member of Henry Gallery Association at the University of Washington (since 1972), Olympic Park Associates (since 1967) and Northwest School of Arts (since 1979). Namkung was a founding member of the Photography Council, Seattle Art Museum.

The photographer works in various large formats, printing 20 x 24. He does nature photography, mainly in color.

PUBLICATIONS Books: *An Artist's View of Nature*, 1978; *The Olympic Rain Forest*, w/Ruth Kirk, 1966. Periodicals: *Popular Photography*, Aug 1978; *Journal of Photography Council*, no. 1, 1978.

COLLECTIONS Oakland Mus., Calif.; U.S. Navy, Bangor, Wash. In Seattle: Bank of Calif.; Pacific Northwest Bell; Port of Seattle; Rainier Bank; Safeco Insurance Co.; Seattle Art Mus.; Univ of Wash., Henry Gall. Rainier Bank, London & Manila.

DEALER Foster/White Gall., 311½ Occidental Ave S, Seattle, WA 98104.

ADDRESS 3119 S King St, Seattle, WA 98144.

Hans Namuth PHOTOGRAPHER · FILM MAKER Born March 17, 1915, in Essen, Germany, Namuth studied with Joseph Breitenbach and Alexey Brodovitch at New York City's New School for Social Research after World War II. He was influenced by August Sander.

Namuth is a self-employed photographer and film maker. His photographs have appeared in *Life*, *Look*, *Fortune*, *Haper's Bazaar* and *Vogue*, among other publications.

He belongs to ASMP, VAGA and Artists' Equity.

Namuth made his first film, *Jackson Pollock,* in 1951 with Paul Falkenberg, and has since made seven others.

He is known for his portraits of over two hundred painters and sculptors, including John Cage, Alexander Calder, Joseph Cornell, Willem de Kooning, Helen Frankenthaler, Adolph Gottlieb, Hans Hofmann, Ad Reinhardt and Mark Rothko.

PUBLICATIONS Books: *L'Atelier de Jackson Pollock,* 1978 (MACULA: Paris); *Early American Tools,* 1975; *American Masters,* w/Brian O'Doherty, 1973. Anthologies: *Darkroom II,* 1978; *52 Artists,* 1973.

COLLECTIONS Cleveland Art Mus., Ohio; Los Angeles County Mus. of Art; Metro. Mus. of Art, NYC; MOMA, NYC; Tulane Univ., New Orleans; Va. Mus. of Fine Art, Richmond. Fondation de la Photographie, Lyon, France.

DEALER Castelli Graphics, 4 E 77 St, New York, NY 10021.

ADDRESS 157 W 54 St, New York, NY 10019.

Graham William Nash MUSICIAN · PHOTOGRAPHY COLLECTOR Born in Blackpool, Lancashire, England, in 1942, Nash gained an interest in photography from his father, William Nash, an avid amateur photographer.

Nash is currently a solo pop music performer, having previously been a member of the group Crosby, Stills and Nash (later Crosby, Stills, Nash and Young) from 1969 to 1971, and the British group The Hollies from 1963 to 1968. He has also been an environmental activist, affiliated with the Cousteau Society and the antinuclear groups MUSE and Alliance for Survival.

With Crosby and Stills, he won a Grammy Award in 1969 as Best New Artist of the Year.

Nash has put together a substantial collection of nineteenth- and twentieth-century photographs.

PUBLICATION Catalog: *The Graham Nash Collection,* ed. w/Susan Nash & Graham Howe, 1978 (The Nash Press: Los Angeles).

REPRESENTATIVE Segal & Goldman, 9200 Sunset Towers, Suite 1000, Los Angeles, CA 90069.

Paul Nash PHOTOGRAPHER · PAINTER · CRITIC Nash lived from 1889 to 1946 in England. He was influenced by Man Ray, Moholy-Nagy and the critic R. H. Wilenski, who was his friend.

Nash was an official war artist in England from 1938 through the end of World War II.

Using a No. 1A pocket Kodak, series 2, Nash made photographs that revealed shapes and textures generally passed over by most people. His work was often used in conjunction with printing and he frequently made watercolors directly from photographs. His style was evocative rather than descriptive, described by Andrew Causey as having "a near metaphysical quality attained through the very palpable presence of finely delineated machine forms versus the seeming endlessness of the sea and sky."

PUBLICATIONS Books: *Paul Nash's Photographs,* Andrew Causey, 1973 (Tate Gall.); *Fertile Image,* 1951, repr. 1975 (Faber: London); *Dorset Shell Guide,* 1936; *Outline: An Autobiography and Other Writings,* 1949.

COLLECTIONS Ashmolean Mus., Oxford, Great Britain; Durban Art Gall.; Graves Art Gall., Sheffield, Great Britain; Tate Gall., London; Town Hall, Warrambool, Victoria, Australia.

ARCHIVE Tate Gall., London, England.

Enrico Natali PHOTOGRAPHER Born August 10, 1933, in Utica, New York, Natali attended the U.S. Coast Guard Academy (1951–54), where he did photography for the school newspaper, magazine and yearbook. He also studied briefly at the School of Modern Photography and apprenticed with Anton Bruehl.

During the 1970–71 school year Natali was visiting associate professor of photography at the School of the Art Institute of Chicago. In Watertown, New York, he opened a studio in 1964 and also worked as a reporter/photographer for the Watertown newspaper. Before 1964 he lived for a period in New Orleans and, before that, in Chicago (1963). While in Watertown he was recalled to the U.S. Army (1962), in which he had served earlier (1956–58). In 1961 he traveled to England. He worked in the studio of William Syzdek in 1959.

Natali won a Guggenheim Fellowship in 1971.

Wrote Hugh Edwards, "One of Enrico Natali's principal talents is an ability to detect the personal and unique which still manages to exist within the most commonplace settings and happenings, and overall the American character is prevalent. He understands fully the worth of those areas that exist between the photographer, the camera, and the subject, and one enjoys the grateful absence of self-expression."

PUBLICATIONS Monograph: *New American People,* intro. by Hugh Edwards, 1972. Anthologies: *Photography in the Twentieth Century,* 1967; *American Photography: The Sixties,* 1966; *Photography '63,* 1963. Periodicals: *Modern Pho-*

tography Annual '71, 1970; *U.S. Camera World Annual 1970*, 1969; *Photography Annual 1961*, 1960.

COLLECTIONS Art Inst. of Chicago; IMP/GEH, Rochester; MOMA, NYC.

Rafael Navarro PHOTOGRAPHER · CRITIC Born October 8, 1940, in Zaragoza, Spain, Navarro began photographing at age twenty-eight.

A self-employed photographer, he has been a critic and writer for various publications since 1979. In 1979 he helped found the Centro Aragones de Investigación de la Imagen and in 1978 was named the Spanish representative of Consejo Latinoamericano de Fotografía. Together with Esclusa, Fontcuberta and Formiguera he founded the Grupo Alabern in 1977, and in 1976 was named AFIAP by the Fédération Internationale d'Art Photographique. Navarro served as President of the Sociedad Fotográfica de Zaragoza in 1974.

COLLECTIONS Sequentian Images, NYC. Bibliothèque Nationale, Paris; Canon Photo Gall., Geneva, Switzerland; Centro Hidalgo, Mexico; Foto Galerij Paule Pia, Antwerp, Belgium; Galerie Agathe Gaillard, Paris; Galeria Fotomania, Barcelona, Spain; Galeria Spectrum Canon, Zaragoza, Spain; Hartkamp Cllctn., The Netherlands; Il Diaframma, Milan; Musée Réattu, Arles, France; The Photographers Gall., London.

REPRESENTATIVE Michele Chomette, Vinci 1840, 240 bis Bd St. Germain, 75007 Paris, France.

ADDRESS Urb. Torres de San Lamberto 37-A, Zaragoza 11, Spain.

Carlo Naya PHOTOGRAPHER Born in Venice (date unknown), Naya died in 1873. The recipient of many awards, he earned a gold medal in the 1862 London Exposition, and a gold medal at the 1867 Universal Exposition in Paris for a series of views of Venice and the frescoes of Giotto and Mantegna. He was well known for his work on the city of Venice; approximately 8,000 of his negatives remain there.

PUBLICATIONS Books: *Venezia*, 1880 (Venice); *Ricordo di Venezia*, 1877 (Venice); *Vedute di Venezia 1866*, w/Carlo Ponti, 1867 (Venice); *Bassirilievi nella chiesa dei SS*, n.d. (Venice). Catalog: *Esposizione Universale di Vienna del 1873*.

Donald Lee Neal PHOTOGRAPHER · TEACHER Born August 4, 1948, in Aurora, Missouri, Neal received a Bachelor of Mechanical Engineering degree (1971) and a BFA (1973) from the University of Minnesota, Duluth. He then studied pho-

tography under Beaumont Newhall and Van Deren Coke at the University of New Mexico, Albuquerque, where he earned an MA (1975) and an MFA (1978).

Neal has taught history of photography at Minneapolis Community College, Minnesota, since 1979. He was an instructor and senior photographer at the University of Minnesota from 1975 to 1979, and a graduate teaching assistant at the University of New Mexico in 1975.

A member of SPE since 1971, Neal received a Horton Art Scholarship from the University of Minnesota in 1971, a research grant from the University of New Mexico in 1974, and an artist's grant from the Minnesota State Arts Board in 1976.

He uses large format and his style is "based on illusion, metaphor, and formal problems in direct observation of the world."

PUBLICATIONS Catalogs: *Metamorphose/Two*, 1976 (Minn. Mus. of Art: St. Paul); *Peculiar to Photography*, 1976 (Univ. of N. M.: Albuquerque). Periodical: *Progresso Fotografico*, Nov 1978.

COLLECTIONS Minneapolis Inst. of Arts, Minn.; Minn. Mus. of Art, St. Paul; Univ. of Kans., Lawrence; Univ. of N.M. Fine Arts Mus., Albuquerque.

ADDRESS 838 21 Ave SE, Minneapolis, MN 55414.

Charles Nègre PAINTER · PHOTOGRAPHER · INVENTOR Born in 1820 in Grasse, France, Nègre died in Nice, France, in 1879. He studied painting with Ingres and Delaroche in Paris.

Nègre operated a portrait studio in Paris, but also fulfilled outside commissions, such as that by Napoleon III to do a series on the Imperial Asylum at Vincennes. He spent his last years catering to the tourist trade on the Riviera in Nice.

An early experimenter in the process of metal plates, he undertook to transfer gelatine chromate images to zinc plates. He also explored the process of doing heliogravure on steel about 1853. Nègre was the first to experimentally produce halftone pictures in zincography (an example of which was printed in *La Lumière* in 1856), calling his method "gravure paniconographique en relief." According to Josef M. Eder, he also "invented the decorations for and on metal by photography." And, in 1867, he invented a process by which a steel plate was gold-plated in a galvanic bath. The artist also built a special lens with a wide opening and a sophisticated diaphragm that enabled him to make exposures in a matter of seconds.

Aside from his studio work, Nègre was noted for being one of the earliest street photographers. Particularly prized are his images of the various tradespeople of Paris. He also concentrated on monuments and landscapes. He sometimes produced calotypes and salt prints up to 20 x 29, as well as albumen prints. Nègre also experimented with photogravure, a process he mastered.

PUBLICATIONS Monograph: *Charles Nègre, Photographe*, André Jammes, 1963 (André Jammes: Paris). Books: *The Painter and the Photograph*, Van Deren Coke, 1964, rev. ed., 1972; *History of Photography*, Josef Maria Eder, 1945; *De la Gravure héliographique, son utilité, son origine, son application à l'étude de l'histoire, des arts et des sciences naturelles*, 1867 (Nice). Anthologies: *The Photograph Collector's Guide*, Lee D. Witkin & Barbara London, 1979; *The Invented Eye*, Edw. Lucie-Smith, 1975; *The Magic Image*, Cecil Beaton & Gail Buckland, 1975; *Early Photographs & Early Photographers*, Oliver Mathews, 1973 (Reedminster: London); *Great Photographers*, Time-Life Series, 1971; *French Primitive Photography*, André Jammes & Robt. Sobieszek, 1969. Catalogs: *Charles Nègre*, James Borcoman, 1976 (Natl. Gall. of Canada, Ottawa); *Charles Nègre, 1820–1880*, Max Heib & André Jammes, 1966 (Münchner Stadtmuseum, Munich); *Pioniere der Photographie: Edward Steichen, Charles Nègre*, Erike Billeter & Hans Finsler, 1963 (Kunstgewerbemuseum, Zurich). Periodicals: *La Lumière*, May 5, 1856, Sept 1853; *Bulletin Société Française Photographie*, 1856.

COLLECTIONS IMP/GEH, Rochester; Rhode Island School of Design, Providence; Smithsonian Inst., Wash., D.C. Bibliothèque Nationale, Paris; Natl. Gall. of Canada, Ottawa; Société Française, Paris.

Marjorie Neikrug GALLERY OWNER Born in New Rochelle, New York, Neikrug attended Sarah Lawrence College in Bronxville, New York.

She directs Neikrug Photographica Ltd. and also has taught at Parsons School of Design in New York City (1979) and New York University (1973–76).

Neikrug belongs to ASMP, Photographic Historical Society of New York and American Society for Picture Professionals. She is also a board member of SPE, Photographic Administrators, Inc., Volunteer Service Photographers and is a senior member and vice-president of the American Society of Appraisers.

Her gallery specializes in contemporary photography, photographica and rare books.

ADDRESS 224 E 68 St, New York, NY 10021.

Joyce Neimanas PHOTOGRAPHER · TEACHER Born January 22, 1944, in Chicago, Illinois, Neimanas earned her MFA at the School of the Art Institute of Chicago in 1969. She studied with Kenneth Josephson.

She has been associate professor at the School of the Art Institute of Chicago since 1971. She also taught photography at UCLA Extension in 1979, and in 1978 taught at Sun Valley Center for the Arts, Idaho, Visual Studies Workshop, Rochester, and California State University, Fullerton.

A board member of SPE since 1977, Neimanas won an NEA Individual Artist Grant in 1978.

Working in various formats, the photographer usually applies drawing and/or painting to the print surface.

PUBLICATIONS Anthology: *Eros and Photography*, Donna-Lee Phillips, ed., 1978. Catalogs: *Attitudes: Photography in the 1970's*, Fred Parker, ed., 1979 (Santa Barbara Mus. of Art: Calif.); *Forty American Photographers*, Roger Clisby, 1978 (E. B. Crocker Gall.: Sacramento, Calif.); *National Photography Invitational*, David Bremer, ed., 1975 (Anderson Gall., Va. Commonwealth Univ.: Richmond); *1971 Photography Invitational*, Murray Riss, ed., 1971 (Memphis Academy of Arts: Tenn.); *Into the Seventies*, Tom Muir Wilson, ed., 1970 (Akron Art Inst.: Ohio); *Vision and Expression*, Nathan Lyons, ed., 1966 (George Eastman House: Rochester).

COLLECTIONS Art Inst. of Chicago; Harvard Univ., Fogg Mus. of Art, Cambridge, Mass.; IMP/GEH, Rochester; Mus. of Contemporary Art, Chicago; Univ. of Neb., Sheldon Mem. Art Gall., Lincoln.

ADDRESS 2615 Southport, Chicago, IL 60614.

Janine Neipce JOURNALIST · PHOTOGRAPHER Born in Meudon, France, on February 12, 1921, Neipce earned art and archaeology degrees from the University of Paris. She is distantly related to Nicéphore Niepce.

She worked as a photographer for the Ministère des Affaires Etrangères (1960–68) and for the Commissariat au Tourisme (1948–55). Neipce belongs to Association des Gens d'Images, Association des Photographes Créateurs and Association des Journalistes Reporters Photographes.

PUBLICATIONS Books (all in France): *Ce Monde Qui Change*, 1970, *Réalité de L'Instant*, 1967 (Clairefontaine); *Les Jeunes Filles de Paris*, 1961 (Editions Bruna); *La Bourgogne*, 1959 (Editions Mondiales); *Le Livre de Paris*, 1957 (Arts et Métiers Graphiques). Periodicals: *Photo*, no. 5, 1968; *Photography Annual*, 1968; *Camera Annual*, 1965.

COLLECTIONS (in France) Bibliothèque Nationale, Paris; Chateau d'Eau, Toulouse; Historic Lib. of the City of Paris; Musée Nicéphore Niepce, Chalon-sur-Saône; Mus. of Arles, Toulon; Mus. of Dijon.

REPRESENTATIVE Agence Rapho, 8 rue d'Alger, 75001 Paris, France.

ADDRESS 19 rue Rousselet, 75007 Paris, France.

Helen Nestor PHOTOGRAPHER Born March 8, 1924, in San Mateo, California, Nestor received a BS in Public Health at University of California, Berkeley, in 1945. In the early 1960s she studied photography in workshops with Ansel Adams, Minor White and Morley Baer. She names Dorothea Lange as her mentor.

A freelance photographer, Nestor is a member of SPE.

She is basically a documentarian. Her subjects have included the Free Speech Movement in Berkeley, the Haight-Ashbury flower-child era in San Francisco, beginnings of busing in Berkeley and the hospital from the patient's point of view (a personal photographic journal). Recent projects have been shooting nontraditional family portraits and women in midlife.

PUBLICATIONS Monographs: *Equal Start (Beginnings of Busing in Berkeley)*, 1968; *On the Go*, 1968; *The Trouble in Berkeley (Free Speech)*, 1965. Book: *Field Trips*, w/Janet Nickelsburg, 1966.

COLLECTION Oakland Mus., Calif.

DEALER Focus Gall., 2146 Union St, San Francisco, CA 94123.

ADDRESS 3120 Lewiston Ave, Berkeley, CA 94705.

Bea Nettles MIXED-MEDIA PHOTOGRAPHER · TEACHER Born October 17, 1946, in Gainesville, Florida, Nettles earned her BFA from the University of Florida, Gainesville (1968), and her MFA from the University of Illinois, Chicago (1970).

She has taught at Rochester Institute of Technology, New York, since 1976, and also from 1971 to 1972. She taught at Tyler School of Art, Temple University, Philadelphia, Pennsylvania (1972–74), and at Nazareth College, Rochester (1970–71).

A member of SPE since 1972, she won an NEA Fellowship in Photography in 1979 and a CAPS grant in 1976.

She works in mixed media and nonsilver photography.

PUBLICATIONS Monographs: *Flamingo in the Dark*, 1979; *Breaking the Rules: A Photo Media*

Cookbook, 1977. Monographs (self-pub.): *Of Loss and Love*, 1976; *Dream Pages*, 1975; *Mountain Dream Tarot*, 1975; *Swamp Lady*, 1975; *A Is For Applebiting Alligators*, 1974; *The Elsewhere Bird*, 1974; *The Nymph of the Highlands*, 1974; *Events in the Sky*, 1973; *The Imaginary Blowtorch*, w/Grace N. Nettles, 1973; *Events in the Water*, 1972. Book: *Alternative Photographic Processes*, Kent Wade, 1978. Anthologies: *The Photograph Collector's Guide*, Lee D. Witkin & Barbara London, 1979; *In/Sights: Self Portraits by Women*, Joyce T. Cohen, 1978; *Women See Woman*, Cheryl Wiesenfeld, et al, eds., 1976. Periodicals: *Art in America*, May/June 1978; *Afterimage; VSW*, Feb 1978; *Village Voice*, Feb 1978. Reviews: *Petersen's Photographic Magazine*, June 1978; *Modern Photography*, May 7, 1978; *Art in America*, May/June 1978; *Camera 35*, Apr 1978; *Village Voice*, Feb 1978.

COLLECTIONS Baltimore Mus. of Art, Md.; CCP, Tucson; Colgate Univ. Gall., Hamilton, N.Y.; IMP/GEH, Rochester; Metro. Mus. of Art, NYC; Mus. of Fine Arts, Houston; Pomona Coll., Claremont, Calif.; St. Petersburg Mus. of Art, Fla.; Univ. of Colo. Libraries; Univ. of Kans. Mus., Lawrence; Vassar Coll. Mus., Poughkeepsie, N.Y. Natl. Gall. of Canada, Ottawa, Ontario.

DEALER Witkin Gall., 41 E 57 St, New York, NY 10022.

ADDRESS RIT Photo Dept, 1 Lomb Memorial Dr, Rochester, NY 14623.

Floris Michael Neusüss TEACHER · PHOTOGRAPHER Born in 1937 in Lennep, Germany, Neusüss attended several educational institutions: Werkkunstschule Wuppertal (1955–58), where he studied painting with Ernst Oberhoff; Bayerische Staatslehranstalt München (1958–60), where he studied photography with Hanna Seewald; and Hochschule für Bildende Künste Berlin (1960–62), where he studied photography with Hajek-Halke.

After freelancing for some years in Berlin, Vienna and Munich, Neusüss began teaching photography in Kassel, Germany, in 1966.

He belongs to DGPh, Bund Freier Fotodesigner and GDL.

He has participated in a number of German television films: *Künstlerportrait Floris M. Neusüss* (1979); *Aspekte der Fotografie, Floris M. Neusüss* (1978); *An der Wiege der Fotografie— Floris M. Neusüss und seine Studenten in Chalon-sur-Saône* (1978); *Aspekte: Interview im Bericht über das 8* (1977); and *Floris M. Neusüss —Experimentelle Fotografie* (1968).

PUBLICATIONS Monograph: *Fotografien 1957–*

1977, 1977 (Kassel: Germany). Books: *Berufsbild Foto-Design*, w/Volker Rattemeyer, 1977 (Bielefeld); *Einfuhrung in die Technologie der Schwarz-weiss-Fotografie*, 1974. Anthologies: *Die Geschichte der Fotografie im 20. Jahrhundert*, P. Tausk, 1977 (Cologne); *Malerei und Fotografie im Dialog*, E. Biletter, 1977 (Zürich); *Die Fotografie*, Honnef & Romain, 1976 (Frankfurt); *Generative Fotografie*, Jager & Holzhäuser, 1975 (Ravensburg); *Photography Without Camera*, P. Holter, 1972; *Das Deutsche Lichtbild*, Stuttgart, Otto Steinert & Wolfgang Strache, yearly since 1960. Catalogs: *Photography as Art—Art as Photography III*, 1979 (Dumont: Cologne); *Photography as Art—Art as Photography II*, text, 1977 (Foto-Forum: Kassel); *Fotografie an der Gesamthochschule Kassel, Arbeiten aus dem Studienschwerpunkt Fotografie*, text, 1976 (Kassel); *Photography as Art—Art as Photography*, text, w/Peter Böttcher, 1975 (Foto-Forum: Kassel). Periodicals: *Afterimage: VSW*, summer 1978; *Camera*, Jan 1978, Feb 1975, Feb 1971; *Zoom*, Aug/Sept 1977 (Paris); *Photo Revue*, July/Aug 1977; *Kunstforum International*, Apr 1976; *Fotografia*, Apr 1974; *Modern Photography*, May 1970; *Photo*, May 1965.

PORTFOLIO *Flugtraum und Körperauflösung*, 1977 (Kassel).

COLLECTIONS IMP/GEH, Rochester; Univ. of N. Mex. Art Mus., Albuquerque; Univ. of Tex., Gernsheim Cllctn., Austin; VSW, Rochester. Bibliothèque Nationale, Paris. In Germany: Folkwang Mus., Essen; Kestner Mus., Hannover; Mus. für Kunst und Gewerbe, Hamburg; Mus. Ludwig, Cologne.

REPRESENTATIVE Fotoforum, Gesamthochschule Kassel, Menzelstrasse 13, 3500 Kassel, Germany.

Beaumont Newhall   PHOTOHISTORIAN · WRITER · PHOTOGRAPHER · CURATOR · TEACHER Born June 22, 1908, in Lynn, Massachusetts, Newhall received an AB in Fine Arts from Harvard College in Cambridge, Massachusetts (1930), and an MA (1931) from Harvard's Graduate School of Arts & Sciences. He also studied at the Institut d'Art et d'Archéologie of the University of Paris (1933) and at Courtauld Institute of Art of the University of London (1934). His wife was Nancy Newhall (1908–74), a fellow photohistorian and writer.

Newhall has been professor of art at the University of New Mexico in Albuquerque since 1971. Previously he was curator (1948–58) and then director (1958–71) of the International Mu-

seum of Photography at George Eastman House in Rochester. He worked for the Museum of Modern Art in New York as a librarian (1935–42) and then curator of photography (1940–45), and in 1933–34 was assistant in the Department of Decorative Arts at the Metropolitan Museum of Art in New York City. Newhall has also been professor of art at State University of New York (SUNY), Buffalo (1968–71), lecturer on the history of American film at the Salzburg Seminar in American Studies in Austria (winter of 1958 & '59), a lecturer at Rochester Institute of Technology (1956–68), a lecturer at the University of Rochester (1954–56), an instructor at Black Mountain College in Black Mountain, North Carolina (summers of 1946 & '48), and a lecturer at the Philadelphia Museum of Art (1932–33).

A founding member (1967) of Friends of Photography in Carmel, California, and now on its advisory board, he also is an honorary fellow of RPS and the Photographic Historical Society of New York, a fellow of the American Academy of Arts and Sciences, an honorary master of photography in Professional Photographers of America and a corresponding member of DGPh. Newhall won the Claude M. Fuess Award from the Phillips Academy in Andover, Massachusetts (1979), an honorary Doctor of Arts degree from Harvard University (1978), the Progress Medal of RPS (1975) and the Kulturpreis of DGPh in 1970. The historian also won Guggenheim fellowships in 1947 and 1975.

PUBLICATIONS Books: *Frederick H. Evans*, 1975; *Airborne Camera*, 1969; *Latent Image: The Discovery of Photography*, 1967; *T. H. O'Sullivan*, w/Nancy Newhall, 1966; *The Daguerreotype in America*, 1961, rev. ed., 1968, 3rd ed., 1976; *The History of Photography from 1839 to the Present Day*, 1949, rev. ed., 1964; *Photography: A Short Critical History*, 1938. Anthologies: *Dialogue with Photography*, Thomas Cooper & Paul Hill, 1979; *Masters of Photography*, w/Nancy Newhall, 1969.

COLLECTIONS CCP, Tucson; Minneapolis Inst. of Art, Minn.; Mus. of Fine Arts, Houston. Sammlung Fotografis of the Oesterreichische Landesbank, Vienna; Victoria & Albert Mus., London.

ADDRESS Route 7, Box 126-C, Santa Fe, NM 87501.

Nancy Newhall   ART- AND PHOTOHISTORIAN · WRITER · PHOTOGRAPHER Born Nancy Lynne Parker in 1908 in Swampscott, Massachusetts, Newhall died in 1974 in Jackson Hole, Wyoming, from injuries suffered when a tree fell on the raft in which she and her husband were floating down the Snake River. Newhall studied drawing at the Museum of Fine Arts in Boston (1920) and graduated from Smith College, Northampton, Massachusetts (1930), having studied creative writing, drama and painting. She then went to New York to study painting and engraving at the Art Students League. Newhall was married to the photohistorian/writer/photographer Beaumont Newhall, and in 1933 began learning from him about photography. In 1936 she studied in the Louvre in Paris and the National Gallery in London.

Newhall served as acting curator of photography at the Museum of Modern Art in New York City while her husband was in the air corps (1942–45). She later served as a consultant on exhibitions and publications for George Eastman House in Rochester, and in 1967 was associate curator for the Exchange National Bank of Chicago Collection. Also in that year she was a founding member of Friends of Photography in Carmel, California, and served as trustee.

PUBLICATIONS Books: *P. H. Emerson: The Fight for Photography as a Fine Art,* 1975; *Edward Weston, Photographer—"The Flame of Recognition,"* ed., 1971; *The Tetons and the Yellowstone,* w/Ansel Adams, 1970; *Fiat Lux, The University of California,* w/Ansel Adams, 1967; *T. H. O'Sullivan,* w/Beaumont Newhall, 1966; *Brett Weston,* 1966; *". . . A More Beautiful America,"* ed., Lyndon B. Johnson, 1964; *Ansel Adams. Vol. I: The Eloquent Light,* 1963; *The Daybooks of Edward Weston: Vol. II, California,* ed., 1961; *This is the American Earth,* w/Ansel Adams, 1960; *Words of the Earth,* ed., Cedric Wright, 1960; *The Daybooks of Edward Weston: Vol. I, Mexico,* ed., 1957; *A Contribution to the Heritage of Every American: The Conservation Activities of John D. Rockefeller, Jr.,* 1956; *Death Valley,* w/Ansel Adams, 1954, 4th ed., 1970; *Mission San Xavier del Bac,* w/Ansel Adams, 1954; *The Pageant of History in Northern California,* w/Ansel Adams, 1954; *Time in New England,* w/Paul Strand, 1950. Anthology: *Masters of Photography,* w/Beaumont Newhall, 1958. Catalogs: *Brett Weston,* 1966 (Amon Carter Mus. of Western Art: Fort Worth, Tex.); *The Photographs of Edward Weston,* 1946 (MOMA: NYC); *Paul Strand Photographs, 1915–1945,* 1945 (MOMA: NYC). Periodical: "A Collection of Photographs [of the Exchange National Bank of Chicago]," *Aperture,* fall 1969.

PORTFOLIO *Alvin Langdon Coburn,* 1962 (GEH: Rochester).

Arnold Newman PHOTOGRAPHER [See plate 75] Born March 3, 1918, in New York City, Newman studied in the Art Department of the University of Miami (1936–38). He was influenced by Cubism, Surrealism, Dada, the avant-garde art of the 1930s and the Farm Security Administration photographers, particularly Walker Evans.

The photographer has maintained his own studio in New York City from 1946 to the present, having earlier operated his studio in Miami Beach, Florida (1942–46). In 1941–42 he worked independently in New York City after working there in commercial portrait studios from 1938 to 1941.

Newman is a member of ASMP. His many awards include ASMP's Life Achievement in Photography Award, 1975; The Fourth Biennale Internazionale Della Fotografic Gold Medal, Venice, Italy, 1963; University of Miami (Florida) Citation, 1963; The Newhouse Citation, Syracuse University, 1961; Philadelphia Museum College of Art Citation, 1961; First Annual Photojournalism Conference Award, University of Miami, 1957; and the Photokina Award, Cologne, Germany, 1951.

The photographer was the subject of a television film produced by Nebraska Educational Television Network: "The Image Makers—The Environment of Arnold Newman" (1977).

Newman's name has become synonymous with environmental and symbolic portraiture. Working in black-and-white and color, he has done commercial work that includes still lifes and portraits for publications such as *Life, Look* and *Travel and Leisure.* He is particularly known for his portraits of famous artists.

PUBLICATIONS Monographs: *Artists: Portraits from Four Decades,* 1980; *The Great British,* 1979 (Weidenfeld & Nicholson: London); *Faces USA,* 1978; *One Mind's Eye,* 1974; *Bravo Stravinsky,* 1967. Books: *The History of Photography from 1839 to the Present Day,* Beaumont Newhall, 1964; "Arnold Newman Biography," *The Encyclopedia of Photography,* 1964; *Famous Portraits,* L. Fritz Gruber, 1960. Anthologies: *The Photograph Collector's Guide,* Lee D. Witkin & Barbara London, 1979; *The Magic Image,* Cecil Beaton & Gail Buckland, 1975; *The Picture History of Photography,* Peter Pollack, 1969; *The Photographer's Eye,* John Szarkowski, 1966. Periodicals: *Popular Photography,* Dec 1979; *British Journal of Photography,* Apr 1975; "On Assignment with Arnold Newman," *Popular Photography,* May 1957.

COLLECTIONS Art Institute of Chicago; Detroit Art Mus., Mich.; IMP/GEH, Rochester; Metro. Mus. of Art, NYC; MOMA, NYC; Philadelphia Mus. of Art, Penn.; Phoenix Art Mus., Ariz.; Portland Mus. of Art, Ore.; Smithsonian Inst., Wash., D.C. Israel Mus., Jerusalem; Moderna Muséet, Stockholm, Sweden; Natl. Portrait Gall., London.

DEALER Light Gall., 724 Fifth Ave, New York, NY 10019.

ADDRESS 33 W 67 St, New York, NY 10023.

Richard Charles Newman PHOTOGRAPHER · TEACHER · PAINTER Born December 29, 1938, in North Tonawanda, New York, Newman earned a diploma in painting from Cleveland (Ohio) Institute of Art (1960) and a BFA from Cranbrook Academy of Art, Bloomfield Hills, Michigan (1962). He then took an MFA from Cornell University, Ithaca, New York (1964).

Since 1965 Newman has been chairman of the Art Department and the Creative Arts Division at Bradford College, Bradford, Massachusetts. Previous to that he was an art instructor at University of Washington, Seattle (1964–65).

He won the Painting Award at the 84th Art Annual in 1964 at the San Francisco Art Museum.

Working in small format with collage and assemblage, he is interested in exploring the relationship of photography with painting and sculpture processes.

PUBLICATIONS Book: *The Language Lens*, R. Brent Bonah & Sheila Shively, 1974. Periodicals: *Lightyear 1977*, 1977; *Bombay Duck*, #3 & 4, 1976; *Popular Photography*, Sept 1975.

COLLECTIONS Addison Gall. of Amer. Art, Andover, Mass.; Cornell Univ., Andrew Dickson White Art Mus., Ithaca, N.Y.; Middle Tenn. State Univ., Murfreesboro.

ADDRESS POB 162, Bradford, MA 01830.

Helmut Newton PHOTOGRAPHER Born in Berlin, Germany, in 1924, Newton, self-taught at age twelve, became apprenticed to Yva, a well known Berlin fashion photographer, in 1936. During World War II, he served in the Australian Army.

Starting after the war with a small fashion photography studio in Australia, he is presently a freelance photographer residing in Paris. Newton's photographs have appeared in such magazines as *Elle, Nova, Jardin des Modes, Stern, Playboy*, the French, Italian, English and American editions of *Vogue*, and others. He has been the recipient of several art director awards from Japan, Germany and France.

"Helmut Newton has become the grand couturier of fashion photography," writes Philippe Garner *(White Women)*. "There is a curious element of germanic perfectionism that attracts him towards a cleanliness of composition, a cool formal element that accentuates the cool control he exerts over his subjects."

PUBLICATIONS Monographs: *Special Collection/24 Photo Lithos*, 1979; *Sleepless Nights*, 1978; *White Women*, intro. by Philippe Garner, 1976. Anthologies: *The Magic Image*, Cecil Beaton & Gail Buckland, 1975; *Vogue Book of Fashion Photography 1919–1979*, Polly Devlin, w/ intro. by Alexander Liberman, 1979. Periodicals: "Fashion, Style and Art," Carter Radcliff, *Art in America*, July/Aug 1979; *Vogue*, Nov 1978; "Helmut Newton's Frankincense Monsters," Owen Edwards, *American Photographer*, Mar 1979; *Camera*, Sept 1978, Sept 1974, Mar 1974.

COLLECTIONS Marlborough Gall., NYC. Nikon Foto-Galeria, Zurich; Photographer Gall., London.

DEALER G. Ray Hawkins Gall., 7224 Melrose Ave, Los Angeles, CA 90046.

REPRESENTATIVE Xavier Moreau, Inc., 111 W 57 St, New York, NY 10019.

John Neil Newton PHOTOGRAPHER · PRINTMAKER Born October 30, 1933, in Montreal, Quebec, Canada, Newton studied at the St. Martins School of Art in London in 1953–55 and with Nathan Lyons (1973) and Arthur Kramer (1977) at VSW in Rochester. He earned the title Master Photographer from the Professional Photographers of America in 1969.

Currently he works with the Artists in the Schools Program sponsored by the Ontario Arts Council in Dunbarton, Ontario, Canada, and is a visiting artist through the Canada Council at the Atikokan Centennial Museum. In 1979 he was a visiting artist at the Emily Carr College of Art in Vancouver and at the University of Saskatchewan, Saskatoon, Canada. From 1976 to 1978 he served in the Artists with Their Work Program at the Art Gallery of Ontario.

He received grants in visual arts from the Ontario Arts Council in 1979, 1977, 1976 and 1974, and in photography in 1978, 1976, 1975, 1974 and 1971. He also received Canada Council grants in 1976, 1973 and 1971, and a travel grant to Sweden in 1978.

Using formats from 35mm to 8 x 10, Newton does personal work that "is of a romantic documentary style," he says, "with emphasis on the rural communities that surround my farm home.

Photographing working people is my main interest."

PUBLICATION Catalog: *Neil Newton Retrospective*, 1978 (Robert McLaughlin Gall.: Oshawa, Ontario, Can.).

COLLECTIONS VSW, Rochester. In Ottawa, Canada: Art Bank, The Canada Council; Dept. of External Affairs; Natl. Film Board of Canada; Natl. Gall. of Canada; Pub. Archives of Canada. Moderna Muséet, Stockholm, Sweden; Mt. St. Vincent Univ., Halifax, Nova Scotia, Canada; Ontario Arts Council, Toronto; Polaroid Corp. Ltd., Toronto; Robert McLaughlin Gall., Oshawa, Ontario; Tyrone Community Hall Board, Tyrone, Canada; York Univ., Toronto.

REPRESENTATIVE Miller Services, 45 Charles St, Toronto, Ontario, Canada.

ADDRESS RR#1, Enniskillen, Ontario, Canada LOB 1HO.

Dianora Niccolini PHOTOGRAPHER · FILM MAKER Born October 3, 1936, in Florence, Italy, Niccolini studied in three New York City schools: Hunter College (1955–61), Art Students League (1960), and Germain School of Photography (1961). Her mentor was Weegee.

As of this writing she was a photographer and photography teacher at the Germain School of Photography and the Camera Club of New York, as well as a contributing editor to *Functional Photography* and *Photo District News*. She created the photography department at St. Clare's Hospital and was its first medical photographer (1967–76), having filled the same role at Lenox Hill Hospital in New York City (1965–67).

Niccolini is a member of ASMP, American Society of Picture Professionals, Inc., Association of Independent Video and Filmmakers, Inc., Biological Photographic Association and Professional Women Photographers (coordinator).

Twenty-five of her surgical motion pictures are in the Library of the American College of Surgeons.

A freelance photographer specializing in medical photography and photo illustration, she does personal work that is experimental, often surrealistic or impressionistic.

PUBLICATIONS Anthologies: *Women Photograph Men*, Danielle Hayes, ed., 1977; *Women See Men*, Kalmus, Ripp, & Wiesenfeld, eds., 1977; *The History of the Nude in Photography*, Art Goldsmith, ed., 1975. Periodical: *Popular Photography*, Apr 1978. Reviews: *N.Y. Times*, Gene Thornton, Dec 7, 1975, A. D. Coleman, Sept 22, 1974.

COLLECTIONS Alternative Mus., NYC; Erie Art Ctr., Pa.; Floating Foundation of Photography, NYC; ICP, NYC.

DEALER Floating Foundation of Photography, 15 Greene St, New York, NY 10013.

ADDRESS 356 E 78 St, New York, NY 10021.

Horace Walter Nicholls PHOTOJOURNALIST Born in Cambridge, England, in 1867, Nicholls died in England in 1941. His father, Arthur, was a painter and photographic pioneer. The younger Nicholls attended school at Sandown on the Isle of Wight and was apprenticed to a chemist/photographer in Huddersfield (1884–86).

Nicholls worked as an assistant photographer in Chile between 1887 and 1888. From 1889 to 1892 he worked with the Cartland Photographic Studio in Windsor, occasionally taking photographs at the English Court. He moved to Johannesburg, South Africa, in 1892, joining the Goch studios and photographing the Boer War from 1899 to 1901. He permanently returned to England in 1901 and became a freelance photographer with premises in Ealing, London. An enlisted member of the Artists' Rifles during World War I, he was not sent overseas. In 1917–18 he was the photographer for the Department of Information, and from 1919 to 1932 he was on the staff of the Imperial War Museum in Crystal Palace, where he supervised the facility's darkroom and war-negative records. He continued his freelancing and his images were seen in such publications as the *Daily Mirror*, *Tatler*, *Bystander* and *Illustrated London News*.

Most noted for his "Women at War" series from the Boer War, Nicholls had a style that was "completely modern," according to Hopkinson in *Treasures of the Royal Photographic Society*. In South Africa the photographer recorded "unforgettable impressions" of the war, and his photographs of social and sporting occasions in England just before World War I "summon up Ascot, Derby Day, Henley as no one again will ever see them."

PUBLICATIONS Books: *Silver Images*, Dr. A. D. Bensusan, 1966 (Howard Timmins: Cape Town, South Africa); *Uitlanders and Colonists Who Fought for the Flag 1899–1900*, 1902 (pvt. pub.); *Johannesburg*, 1896; *Stirring Events in Johannesburg*, 1896. Anthology: *The Magic Image*, Cecil Beaton & Gail Buckland, 1975.

COLLECTIONS Bensusan Mus. of Photography, Johannesburg, South Africa; Imperial War Mus., London; RPS, London and Bath.

Joseph Nicéphore Niepce INVENTOR [See plate 1] Born March 7, 1765, in Chalon-sur-

Saône, France, Niepce died there on July 5, 1833. His brother Claude was a fellow inventor.

Niepce served in the French Army under Napoleon Bonaparte, but after being dismissed due to ill health he returned home and spent the rest of his life doing research.

In 1807 the brothers Niepce invented the Pyreolophore, an early version of a piston-and-cylinder internal-combustion engine. Joseph began experimenting with the then new process of lithography in 1813 and by 1816 made his first photographic experiments in a process he named "heliography," or sun-drawing. In 1822 he began working with bitumen of Judea, a substance which hardens when exposed to light, and in 1826 produced the first surviving permanent photograph—a view from the window of his house. That same year he also invented the first photomechanical reproduction process. Niepce began a collaboration with Daguerre in 1829 but didn't live to see the further advances of his work.

PUBLICATIONS   Books: *Joseph-Nicéphore Niepce: Correspondances, 1825–1829*, 1974; *Joseph-Nicéphore Niepce: Lettres, 1816–1817*, 1974; *Latent Image*, Beaumont Newhall, 1967; *The Truth Concerning the Invention of Photography: Nicéphore Niepce, His Life and Works*, 1935, repr. 1973; *Nicéphore Niepce: Inventeur de la Photographie*, A. Davanne, 1885 (Paris); *Les Inventeurs du Gaz et de la Photographie*, Baron A. A. Ernouf, 1877 (Hachette: Paris); *Historique et Description des Procédés du Daguerréotype et du Diorama*, 1839 (Giroux: Paris), repr. w/intro. by Beaumont Newhall, 1971. Anthologies: *The Photograph Collector's Guide*, Lee D. Witkin & Barbara London, 1979; *The Magic Image*, Cecil Beaton & Gail Buckland, 1975. Periodicals: "The 150th Anniversary of Photography," Helmut Gernsheim, *History of Photography*, Jan 1977; "Some Thoughts on the World's First Photography," Pierre G. Harmant & Paul Mariller, *Photographic Journal 107*, 1967.

COLLECTIONS   Univ. of Texas, Gernsheim Cllctn., Austin. Musée Nicéphore Niepce, Chalon-sur-Saône, France; Science Mus., London; Société Française de Photographie, Paris.

ARCHIVE   Musée Nicéphore Niepce, Chalon-sur-Saône, France.

(Claude Félix) Abel Niepce de St.-Victor

CHEMIST   Born in 1805 in St. Cyr, France, Abel Niepce de St.-Victor (as he was known), died in 1870. A cousin of Joseph Nicéphore Niepce, he graduated from the Military School of Saumur in 1827.

While stationed with the military at Montauban in 1842, he earned a transfer to the Garde Municipale in Paris because of his experiments to change and restore the color of faded uniforms. He then began devoting his spare time to photographic experiments. In 1847 he announced to the Académie des Sciences a process for making an albumen negative on a glass support, the first practical photographic process on glass. It was soon replaced by the wet collodion process for making negatives, but remained one of the most satisfactory processes in the nineteenth century for making positive glass lantern slides and glass stereograms. Niepce de St.-Victor lost his equipment in 1848 when his barracks laboratory was sacked and burned during the revolution, but the government later made him a captain and he set up another laboratory. In 1851 he developed a color photography process, but he could not fix the colors, and from 1853 to 1855 he developed improvements of his cousin's bitumen process on steel plates, enabling contact prints to be made in a few minutes, or in the camera with an exposure of 10–15 minutes. Among the twenty-six papers he presented to the Académie des Sciences from 1847 to 1862 were included the results of his experiments with uranium oxide in preparing photographic papers (1858). He was awarded the Legion of Honor in 1849 and made Commandant of the Louvre in 1854.

PUBLICATIONS   Books: *Quellendarstellungen zur Geschichte der Fotografie*, Wolfgang Baier, 1964; *Evolution of Rotogravure*, J. S. Mettle, 1957; *L. J. M. Daguerre*, 1956; *History of Photography*, Helmut & Alison Gernsheim, 1955; *Histoire de la Photographie*, Raymond Lécuyer, 1945; *History of Photography*, W. Jerome Harrison, 1887; *History and Handbook of Photography*, Gaston Tissandier, 1876. Anthologies: *Early Photographs and Early Photographers*, Oliver Mathews, 1973; *Photography's Great Inventors*, Louis W. Sipley, 1965. Periodicals: *Bild und Ton*, 1952, 1951; *Photographic Times*, 1894.

Lennart Nilsson

PHOTOGRAPHER   Born August 24, 1922, in Strängnäs, Nilsson received an honorary doctorate in Stockholm in 1976.

A pioneer in the field of medical photography, he was the first person to photograph the growth and development of the human embryo through all its fetal stages.

PUBLICATIONS   Monograph: *A Child Is Born*, 1965. Book: *Behold Man*, 1973.

ADDRESS   Stockholm, Sweden.

Niepce de St.-Victor

Frank E. (Pappy) Noel *PHOTOJOURNALIST*
Born 1905 in the United States, Noel died on November 29, 1966, in Gainesville, Florida.

Working for The Associated Press, Noel covered the Malayan jungle campaign as a reporter and photographer after the bombing of Pearl Harbor. Later he went to Burma and India. After the war he was assigned to the Mediterranean area for four years, with special emphasis on the Palestinian conflict. The following year he covered Berlin during the cold war. When the Korean War broke out, Noel volunteered to cover it. He was captured and held captive from 1950 to 1953, during which time he managed to photograph captured United Nations forces. He was apprehended during an attempted escape and spent seven weeks in solitary confinement. Upon his release by the North Koreans, he returned to New York. Then he was sent by AP to Tampa in 1958, and then to Tallahassee.

In 1943 Pappy Noel won the Pulitzer Prize for his picture of a seaman in a lifeboat, holding out his hand in silent supplication for water: when he took the photograph, Noel was adrift in another lifeboat on the Indian Ocean after his ship was torpedoed.

PUBLICATION Anthology: *Moments*, Sheryl & John Leekley, 1978.

Anne Noggle *PHOTOGRAPHER · TEACHER*
Born June 12, 1922, in Evanston, Illinois, Noggle received a BFA in Art History (1970) and an MA in Art (1976) from the University of New Mexico, Albuquerque. Her mentor was Van Deren Coke.

A lecturer in art at the University of New Mexico since 1970, she was also curator of photography at the Fine Arts Museum, Santa Fe, New Mexico (1970–76).

A member of SPE since 1970, Noggle has been on its board of directors since 1978. She won NEA fellowships in 1975 and 1978.

The photographer does "straight" work in small format, with a concern for "penetrating the surface of people, aging and time."

PUBLICATIONS Books: *History of Photography in New Mexico*, Van Deren Coke, 1979; *Is America Used Up?*, Judith M. Gutman, 1973; *Beautiful Southwest*, 1972; *Photography*, Phil Davis, 1972. Anthologies: *Self-Portrayal: The Photographer's Image*, 1978; *The Great West: Real/Ideal*, 1977. Catalogs: *Women of Photography*, w/Margery Mann, 1975 (San Francisco Mus. of Modern Art); *National Photography Invitational*, 1975 (Va. Commonwealth Univ.: Richmond). Periodicals: *Camera*, Feb 1980; *Exposure: SPE*, fall 1979; *Camera 35*, text & photos, Jan 1973; *Photogra-*

phy Italiana, Feb 1972; *Photography Annual*, 1972; *Modern Photography*, June 1972; *U.S. Camera Annual*, 1971; *Album #10*, text & photos, 1970.

COLLECTIONS Ariz. State Univ., Tempe; Crocker Art Gall., Sacramento, Calif.; Denver Art Mus., Colo.; Humboldt State Univ., Arcata, Calif; IMP/GEH, Rochester; Madison Art Ctr., Wisc.; Minneapolis Inst. of the Arts, Minn.; Mus. of N.M., Santa Fe; Pensacola Jr. Coll., Fla.; San Francisco Mus. of Modern Art; Smithsonian Inst., Wash., D.C.; Univ. of Mich., Ann Arbor; Univ. of N.M., Albuquerque. Natl. Gall. of Canada; RPS, London.

ADDRESS 1204 Espanola NE, Albuquerque, NM 87110.

Jeff Nolte *PHOTOGRAPHER* Born April 18, 1950, in Zanesville, Ohio, Nolte studied photography at Sheridan College, Oakville, Ontario, Canada (1969–70). He continued his photography studies (with Michael Semak, Jack Dale and Lawrence Weissman) at York University, Toronto, Ontario, where he received a BA in Fine Arts in 1975 and an MFA in Visual Arts in 1979.

Nolte was a photography instructor at York University (1978–79) and a teaching assistant there (1977–78).

He belongs to SPE, IMP/GEH and Friends of Photography. The photographer has received numerous grants from the Ontario Arts Council—in 1979, 1978, 1976, 1975, 1973 and 1972. He also received Ontario Arts Council Artist-in-schools funding in 1978 and 1976. The Canada Council awarded him short-term photography grants in 1977 and 1972, and he won a Faculty of Fine Arts in-course scholarship from York University in 1971.

Using small and large formats, Nolte does documentary work and extensive experimentation with nonsilver processes.

PUBLICATIONS Catalog: *Exposure, Contemporary Canadian Photography*, 1975 (Art Gall. of Ontario: Toronto). Periodical: *Camera Canada*, June 1977.

COLLECTIONS In Canada: Canada Council, Ottawa; Natl. Film Board of Canada, Ottawa; Ontario Arts Council, Toronto; York Univ. Archives, Toronto.

ADDRESS 45 McGlashan Rd, Toronto, Ontario, Canada M5M 2X6.

Kazuyoshi Nomachi *PHOTOGRAPHER* Born October 15, 1946, in Kochi, Japan, Nomachi is a freelance photographer.

A member of the Japan Professional Photographer's Society, Nomachi was awarded the Shin-jin-Sho by the Photographic Society of Japan in 1979.

PUBLICATIONS Books: *Sinai*, 1978 (Italy), 1979 (Japan, France, West Germany); *Crossing the Sahara*, 1977 (Japan); *Sahara*, 1977 (Italy), 1978 (Japan, France, England, U.S.A.).

REPRESENTATIVE Pacific Press Service, Tokyo C.P.O. Box 2051, Japan.

ADDRESS 3F Murata Bldg, 4-27-6 Yoyogi, Shibuya-ku, Tokyo, Japan.

Catherine Hanf Noren PHOTOGRAPHER · WRITER Noren was born April 5, 1938, in München-Gladbach, Germany. Her grandfather, Moritz Wallach (1879–1963), founded the Munich folk art museum, Wallachvolkskunsthaus. Noren received a BA in Literature from Bennington College in Bennington, Vermont, in 1959. She later studied photography with David Vestal, Garry Winogrand, Diane Arbus and Lisette Model, and was a darkroom apprentice to Sid Kaplan (1968–72).

Since 1972 she has been self-employed as a photographer and writer. Before that time she was employed as assistant to the director at Magnum Photo Archive (1971–72), and was head writer for Merv Griffin's "Jeopardy!" on NBC-TV (1964–70).

A member of ASMP, she received a grant from the International Fund for Concerned Photography in 1972.

Noren says of her work, "I'm something of an expert on the meaning, iconography, and psychological analysis of family photographs. And the same elements that draw me to family photographs are the concerns of my own work: love and other personal relationships, mystery, paradox, and humor."

PUBLICATIONS *The Camera of My Family*, 1976; *Photography—How to Improve Your Technique*, 1973.

DEALER Georges Borchardt, Inc., 136 E 57 St, New York, NY 10022.

REPRESENTATIVE Photo Researchers, 60 E 56 St, New York, NY 10022.

ADDRESS 143 E 13 St, New York, NY 10003.

Barbara Pugh Norfleet CURATOR · TEACHER · PHOTOGRAPHER Born in 1926 in Lakewood, New Jersey, Norfleet received a BA from Swarthmore College, Swarthmore, Pennsylvania (1947), and an MA and PhD from Harvard University/Radcliffe, Cambridge, Massachusetts (1950, 1951).

She has been a lecturer at Harvard since 1960, first in social sciences (until 1970) and then in visual and environmental studies. She is also curator of photography at Harvard's Carpenter Center for the Visual Arts (since 1972) and the organizer and director of Harvard's Photography Archive (since 1975).

Norfleet belongs to the American Psychological Association and to American Studies. She received NEA grants in 1978 and 1976, a National Endowment for the Humanities grant in 1975–77 and a Massachusetts Council of the Arts and Humanities grant in 1972.

Norfleet does straight photography in black-and-white and color, including documentary work. She curates shows for the Carpenter Center for the Visual Arts.

PUBLICATIONS Monographs: *The Champion Pig*, 1979; *Wedding*, 1979. Book: *The Head and the Heart*, E. Sekler, 1973.

COLLECTION MOMA, NYC.

ADDRESS 79 Raymond St, Cambridge, MA 02140.

Dorothy S. Norman WRITER · PHOTOGRAPHER · SOCIAL ACTIVIST Born March 28, 1905, in Philadelphia, Norman attended Smith College, Northampton, Massachusetts (1922–23), and University of Pennsylvania, Philadelphia (1923–25). Her major influences were Alfred Stieglitz, Indian art historian Ananda K. Coomaraswamy, curator Stella Kramrisch and Jawaharlal Nehru.

Best known for her writings on the life and work of Alfred Stieglitz, Norman worked for the *New York Post* (1942–49) and edited/published *Twice A Year, a Book of Literature, the Arts and Civil Liberties* from 1937 to 1948.

She worked in various civic and cultural organizations and movements in the 1920s and 1930s, including Planned Parenthood (with Margaret Sanger), N.Y. League of Women Voters, N.Y. Citizens Union and the first Civil Liberties Committee of the Women's City Club of N.Y. (chairwoman). Norman was a member of the board of directors of the National Urban League, City-Wide Citizens Committee on Harlem, N.Y. City Committee Against Discrimination in Employment, and Women's Archives. In the early 1950s she founded and was chairwoman of American Emergency Food Committee for India, American Citizens Committee for Economic Aid Abroad, and Citizens Committee to Support U.S. Economic Aid for India. She is an honorary trustee of the Philadelphia Museum of Art.

PUBLICATIONS Books: *Alfred Stieglitz, American Seer*, 1978; *The Hero: Myth/Image/Symbol*, 1969; *Civil Liberties and the Arts*, 1964; *Alfred Stieglitz, Introduction to an American Seer*,

1960; *Selected Writings of John Marin*, ed., intro., 1949; *America and Alfred Stieglitz*, co-ed., contributor, 1934; *Dualities*, poems, 1933.

COLLECTIONS Guild Hall, E. Hampton, N.Y.; MOMA, NYC; Philadelphia Mus. of Art.

DEALER Light Gall., 724 Fifth Ave, New York, NY 10019.

ADDRESS 124 E 70 St, New York, NY 10021.

Henry C. Norman PHOTOGRAPHER Born in Newnan, Georgia, in 1850, Norman died in 1913. His sons Earl, Burdette and Henry C. Norman, Jr., all became photographers. It is believed that Norman learned the basics of photography in 1870 from Henry Gurney in Natchez, Mississippi.

Gurney had worked as a photographer in Natchez since 1851, and left the town in the late 1870s or early 1880s. Norman was employed by Gurney from 1870 to 1876, then opened his own portrait studio in Natchez, where he worked from 1876 to 1913.

Besides his studio work, the photographer extensively shot street scenes and rural life and is especially known for his images of the Mississippi River and the famed steamboats that traveled its waterways.

PUBLICATION Book: *Norman's Natchez*, Joan W. & Thomas H. Gandy, 1978.

DEALER Myrtle Bank Galleries, 408 N Pearl St, Natchez, MS 39120.

ARCHIVE Thomas H. Gandy, M.D., 408 N Pearl St, Natchez, MS 39120.

Kenda North PHOTOGRAPHER · TEACHER Born May 13, 1951, in Chicago, Illinois, North earned a BA in Fine Arts from Colorado College, Colorado Springs, in 1972 after studying at the Institute for European Studies in Vienna, Austria (1970–71). She studied dye transfer printing with Larry McPherson in 1974 and received an MFA from the Visual Studies Workshop, Rochester, New York, in 1976.

She became a lecturer in photography at University of California, Riverside, in 1979. North was artist-in-residence and art coordinator at Colorado Mountain College, Breckenridge, in 1977–79 and a visiting artist/lecturer at the School of the Art Institute of Chicago, Illinois (1976–77).

A member of SPE, she was awarded a Photographer's Fellowship from NEA in 1977.

North's recent prints are hand-colored dye transfers. She is especially interested in researching contemporary color photography.

PUBLICATIONS Anthologies: *Darkroom Dy-namics*, Jim Stone, ed., 1979; *One of a Kind, Recent Polaroid Color Photography*, Belinda Rathbone, ed., 1979. Periodicals: *Artspace: Southwestern Contemporary Arts Quarterly*, interview by Katherine Chafee, fall 1978; *Camera Mainichi* 3, 1978; *Popular Photography Annual*, 1978; *Le Nouveau Photocinéma*, Dec 1976.

COLLECTIONS CCP, Tucson; Exchange Natl. Bank, Chicago; IMP/GEH, Rochester; Minneapolis Inst. of Art, Minn.; Polaroid Corp., Cambridge, Mass.; Sun Valley Ctr. for the Arts & Humanities, Sun Valley, Idaho; Univ. of Calif., Calif. Mus. of Photography, Riverside; Univ. of Colo., Boulder; Univ. of N. Mex. Art Mus., Albuquerque; VSW, Rochester.

DEALER G. Ray Hawkins Gall., 7224 Melrose Ave, Los Angeles, CA 90046.

ADDRESS c/o Dr. Irma H. North, 55 E Washington, Chicago, IL 60602.

Richard Alfred Northwood PHOTOGRAPHER Born in 1850, Northwood died in 1926. His two sons, Richard and Arthur Northwood, were both photographers.

Northwood set up a studio in Kohukohu, North Auckland, New Zealand, in the 1890s. Later his sons maintained additional studios in Kaitaia.

Together with his sons, Northwood specialized in documenting the kauri timber and kauri gum industries of the far north of New Zealand's North Island.

COLLECTIONS Kaitaia Pub. Lib., Kaitaia, New Zealand; Natl. Lib. of New Zealand, Alex. Turnbull Lib., Wellington.

Sonya Noskowiak PHOTOGRAPHER Born in 1900 in Leipzig, Germany, Noskowiak died in 1975 in Greenbrag, California. Raised in Chile, she settled in California in 1915.

When a receptionist at Johan Hagemeyer's photo studio in Los Angeles she met Edward Weston and worked as his darkroom assistant from 1929 to 1934. Noskowiak opened her own studio in San Francisco in 1935 and operated it through the 1940s.

Along with Weston and others, she was an organizing member of Group f.64 in 1932.

The photographer created landscapes and still lifes in the West Coast and Weston traditions, and she also did portraits of many well known people, among them John Steinbeck and Martha Graham.

PUBLICATION Monograph: *Sonya Noskowiak*, #9 1979 (CCP, Tucson).

COLLECTION CCP, Tucson.

ARCHIVE Center for Creative Photography, 843 E University Blvd, Tucson, AZ 85721.

Gabriele & Helmut Nothhelfer *PHOTOGRA-PHERS · TEACHERS* Both born in Germany, Gabriele on May 3, 1945, in Berlin and Helmut on March 6, 1945, in Bonn, they began joint studies of photography in 1967 at Folkwangschule für Gestaltung in Essen, Germany.

Both have been teaching photography since 1978 at the Freie Universität Berlin, where Helmut has been a staff photographer since 1971. Gabriele has been a staff photographer at the Technische Universität Berlin since 1972.

"Our photographs," they say, "were taken on the occasions of festive events. People are shown detached from their workaday life and are not captured in a snapshot-manner, not caught in the midst of an action, but observed at a moment of pause, of standstill, even of meditation."

PUBLICATIONS Monograph: *Gabriele und Helmut Nothhelfer*, 1980 (Galerie Breiting: Berlin). Catalogs: *Photographie als Kunst 1879–1979*, P. Weiermair (Innsbruck); *Sander Gallery Catalogue I*, 1979 (Washington, D.C.); *Berlin: a critical view*, 1978 (ICA: London); *Documenta 6*, 1977 (Kassel). Periodical: *Creative Camera*, 1977.

COLLECTIONS MOMA, NYC. Berlinische Galerie, Berlin, Germany; Bibliothèque Nationale, Paris; Folkwangmuseum, Essen, Germany; Stedelijk Mus., Amsterdam, The Netherlands.

DEALERS Sander Gall., 2604 Connecticut Ave NW, Washington, DC 20008; Jürgen Wilde, Auf dem Berlich 6, D 5000 Cologne 1, Germany; Galerie Breiting, Sächsische Strasse 1, D 1000, Berlin 15 Germany.

ADDRESSES Weimarer Strasse 32, D 1000, Berlin 12, Germany; Hammstrasse 14, D 53, Bonn Beuel 3, Germany.

William McFarlane Notman *PHOTOGRAPHER* Born in 1826 in Renfrewshire, Scotland, Notman died in 1891 in Canada. His sons, William McFarlane, Jr., and Charles, were also photographers.

Emigrating to Montreal, Canada, in 1856, Notman soon built up one of the most successful chains of photographic studios that Canada had known, with branches in Toronto, Montreal, Ottawa and Halifax. Later he opened additional branches of Notman Photographic Company in New York City, Albany (New York), Boston, and Newport (Rhode Island). In addition, Notman was the official Montreal photographer to the Queen. His sons continued operating the studios after their father's death.

With his company of photographers, Notman provided an unprecedented record of Canadian life that included portraits and genre scenes of Indians, hunters and trappers, local dignitaries and Canadian folk life. Using daguerreotypes, collodion wet-plate negatives, and (after 1880) gelatin dry-plate negatives, he produced albumen and platinum prints in formats ranging from stereographs to 16 x 20 enlargements. Notman also did some composite work. Though straightforward, his style showed an artistic flair.

PUBLICATIONS Monographs: *Portrait of a Period: A Collection of Notman Photographs, 1865–1915*, J. Russell Harper & S. Triggs, eds., 1967 (McGill Univ.: Montreal); *Notman's Photographic Selections*, 1965 (Notman: Montreal); *Photographic Selections by William Notman*, vol. 1, foreword by Vicount Monck, 1863 (John Lovell: Montreal). Books: *Early Photography in Canada*, Ralph Greenhill, 1965 (Oxford Univ. Press: Toronto); *48 Specially Selected Views of the Canadian Rockies on the Line of the Canadian Pacific Railway*, 1907 (Valentine: Montreal); *Through Mountains and Canyons: The Canadian Rockies...*, ca. 1900–1909 (MacFarlane: Toronto); *Royal Society of Canada*, 1891; *Our Birds of Prey*, Henry G. Vennor, 1876 (Dawson Bros.: Montreal); *Canadian Handbook & Tourist's Guide*, Henry Beaumont Small, 1866 (M. Longmoore: Montreal). Anthologies: *The Photograph Collector's Guide*, Lee D. Witkin & Barbara London, 1979; *The Invented Eye*, Edward Lucie-Smith, 1975; *The Magic Image*, Cecil Beaton & Gail Buckland, 1975; *Early Photographs & Early Photographers*, Oliver Mathews, 1973; *Great Photographers*, Time-Life Series, 1971.

COLLECTIONS Art Inst. of Chicago; Boston Pub. Lib.; IMP/GEH, Rochester; Smithsonian Inst., Wash., D.C. McGill Univ., McCord Mus., Montreal, Canada; Natl. Gall. of Canada, Ottawa, Ontario.

ARCHIVE Notman Archives, McCord Museum, McGill University, Montreal, Quebec, Canada.

Frank H. Nowell *PHOTOGRAPHER · BUSINESS-MAN* Born in Portsmouth, New Hampshire, on February 19, 1864, Nowell died in Seattle, Washington, in 1950. Beginning as a hobbyist, Nowell taught himself the craft. He traveled to North Platte, Nebraska, in 1878 to work with his brother on his father's small cattle ranch.

In 1886, with six cows and one bull, he shipped out on the S.S. *Ancon* to Juneau, Alaska, to start the first dairy ranch there. He then went into the mining business there with his father on Douglas Island. In 1894 he moved to the West Coast, living in several towns and operating as purchasing agent for his father's company. He returned to Alaska in 1900, starting a grocery store, the Miner's Supply Co., and then opened a photographic studio in Nome. By 1908 he was fairly settled in Seattle, where he was appointed the Official Photographer of the Alaska-Yukon Pacific Exposition (1909); there he opened a commercial studio, where he remained until his death.

Nowell was a member of the Benevolent and Protective Order of Elks and the Nome Pioneers, Igloo Number One. He started the first dray business in Alaska, and set up the first telephone used in Alaska, between Juneau and Silver Bow.

His work offers an extensive visual record of the people and activities of the time and places in which he lived. His work ranged from commercial portraits to ethnic studies of Eskimos and Indians, from scenic views to historical events.

PUBLICATIONS Books: *Photographers of the Frontier West*, Ralph Warren Andrews, 1965; *The Art Work of Seattle and Alaska*, 1907. Periodical: *Alaska Review*, Donald Deschner, fall/winter 1968/69.

COLLECTIONS State Historical Society, Olympia, Wash.; State of Alaska Lib. & Mus., Juneau; Univ. of Alaska Lib., Fairbanks; Univ. of Calif., Bancroft Lib., Berkeley; Univ. of Wash., Suzzallo Lib., Seattle.

Sandy Noyes *TEACHER · PHOTOGRAPHER* Born December 18, 1941, in New York City, Noyes received a BA in 1963 from Yale University, New Haven, Connecticut, studying painting with Bud Leak. The photographer also studied with Minor White, Paul Caponigro and George Tice from 1972 to 1974.

Since 1976 Noyes has been teaching printing at the International Center of Photography in New York City.

A member of SPE, the photographer was a co-recipient of a project grant from NEA.

Using landscapes and still-life interiors as subjects in both 5 x 7 and 11 x 14 negatives, the photographer produces silver and palladium prints.

PUBLICATIONS Book: *The Hudson River and Its Painters*, 1971. Catalog: *Seven Photographers: The Delaware Valley*, 1979 (New Jersey State Mus.: Trenton, N.J.).

COLLECTIONS Addison Gall. of Amer. Art, Andover, Mass.; Chase Manhattan Bank, NYC; High Mus. of Art, Atlanta, Ga.; N.J. State Mus.,

Trenton; Univ. of N.C., Weatherspoon Gall., Chapel Hill. Bibliothèque Nationale, Paris.

ADDRESS Star Rte, Peters Valley, Layton, NJ 07851.

Walter Nurnberg *PHOTOGRAPHER · AUTHOR · TEACHER* Nurnberg was born in Berlin on April 18, 1907. After a relatively short career in banking and business administration, he trained for photography and copywriting at the Reimann School of Art in Berlin (1931–32). He was strongly influenced by the works of Albert Renger-Patzsch and Selmar Lerski.

Nurnberg moved to London in 1934, establishing himself in the field of advertising photography and specializing in consumer goods. After serving in the British Army (1940–44), he turned to freelancing in industrial photography. He became a naturalized British subject in 1947. He lectured frequently, and from 1968 to 1974 was head of the Guildford School of Photography at the West Surrey College of Art and Design. In 1975 he was appointed contributing editor to the *British Journal of Photography*.

Sometimes referred to as "the father of British industrial photography," Nurnberg was awarded the Order of the British Empire in 1974. He is a member of The Institute of Incorporated Photographers and RPS.

Nurnberg looked upon his field "as a means of communication in the fields of marketing and industrial relations. He was also much concerned that photography could play a vital part in a fast-developing new era of internal and external industrial communications" (Kodak Ltd.). His images show not only the history and development of applied photography from the early 1930s until the present, but also a purely historic view of many industrial processes over the last thirty years.

PUBLICATIONS Books: *Lighting for Portraiture*, 1961; *Lighting for Photography*, 13th ed., 1957; *The Science and Technique of Advertising Photography*, 1940; *Industry in Focus*, Michael Colmer, n.d. (England). Catalog: *The Photography of Walter Nurnberg*, David Mellor, 1979 (Kodak Ltd: Hempstead; Science Mus.: London).

COLLECTION Science Mus., London.

ADDRESS 18 Cornwood Close, London N2 OHP, England.

Wallace Nutting *PHOTOGRAPHER · WRITER · CLERGYMAN* Born November 17, 1861, in Marlboro, Massachusetts, the Reverend Dr. Nutting died July 19, 1941, in Framingham, Massachusetts. He attended Harvard University, Cambridge, Massachusetts, Hartford (Connecticut) Theological Seminary and Union Theological Seminary, New York City.

Ordained in the Congregational ministry in 1888, Rev. Nutting occupied pulpits in Newark, New Jersey; St. Paul, Minnesota; Seattle, Washington; and Providence, Rhode Island. For many years he created prints of New England scenes, and retired from the ministry in 1905 to pursue photography. At about the same time he also started a furniture factory, Old America Co., in Framingham.

He received honorary degrees from Whitman College in Walla Walla, Washington, and from Washington and Jefferson College in Washington, Pennsylvania.

A collector of antique furniture, Rev. Nutting was considered an authority in the field and wrote several books on the subject.

His photographs were genre scenes of New England life, which he tinted, using his own coloring method, producing what were known as "Wallace Nutting Platinum Prints." The delicate pastel coloring became very popular. Nutting also wrote about and photographed antiques in Pennsylvania, Florida, Virginia, England and Ireland.

PUBLICATIONS Books ("State Beautiful" series, photos & text): *Connecticut*, 1935; *Pennsylvania*, 1935; *Virginia*, 1930, repr. 1935; *New York*, 1927; *Maine*, 1924, repr. 1935; *Massachusetts*, 1923; *New Hampshire*, 1923; *Ireland Beautiful*, n.d. Other books: *Furniture Treasury*, 3 vols., 1928–33, repr. 1949; *Photographic Art Secrets*, 1927 (Chapman & Hall, London); *Wallace Nutting Pictures*, 1915; *Furniture of the Pilgrim Century, 1620–1720*, 1910, rev. 1924, repr. 1965.

COLLECTION IMP/GEH, Rochester.

O

Johann Baptist Obernetter *CHEMIST* Born in Bavaria in 1840, Obernetter died in 1887. The son of an inspector in the Bavarian government printing plant, he studied chemistry at the University of Leipzig. Then in 1859–60 he studied photography in Professor Kayser's laboratory, where he worked.

In 1860 he began work for Josef Albert in Munich, seeking a printing process to substitute for the silver-positive one. He patented a ceramic enamel process in 1864 and, in 1867, introduced a commercial silver chloride collodion paper, and made improvements on Albert and Husnik's collotype printing process. By 1878 he had developed a reversal collodion-negative process, and in 1880 encouraged Otto Perutz to manufacture his silver bromide gelatin dry plate. Perutz later produced Obernetter's fast orthochromatic plate (1884), developed with Dr. Hermann Vogel's color-sensitizing processes and referred to as the Vogel-Obernetter Silver Eosin Plate.

Among the many honors he received were those from the Photographische Gesellschaft in Vienna and the Verein zur Foerderung der Photographie in Berlin.

PUBLICATIONS Books: *Quellendarstellungen zur Geschichte der Fotografie*, Wolfgang Baier, 1964; *Memoirs of a Photochemist*, Fritz Wentzel, 1960; *Perutz Jubilaeum 1880–1955*, 1955 (Denkschrift). Anthology: *Photography's Great Inventors*, Louis W. Sipley, 1965. Periodicals: *American Annual of Photography and Photographic Times Almanac*, 1888; *Jahrbuch für Photographie und Reproduktionstechnik*, 1888; *Photographische Correspondenz*, 1887; *Photographische Mittheilungen*, 1887; *British Journal of Photography*, 1886.

Michael O'Brien *PHOTOJOURNALIST* Born June 27, 1950, in Memphis, Tennessee, O'Brien received a BA from the University of Tennessee, Knoxville, in 1972.

Currently a freelance photographer in New York City, he was staff photographer for the *Miami News* (1973–79).

He is a member of ASMP and the NPPA.

O'Brien received the Special Recognition in World Understanding Award in 1977 and the Robert F. Kennedy Journalism Award in Photojournalism in 1977 and 1975.

PUBLICATIONS Periodicals: *Photo World*, Aug 1979; *Quest*, Feb 1979; *The Best of Photojournalism*, vol. 1, 1977, vol. 2, 1978, vol. 3, 1979.

COLLECTION ICP, NYC.

ADDRESS 22 W 85 St, New York, NY 10024.

Bjørn Ochsner *PHOTOHISTORIAN* Born April 4, 1910, in Frederiksberg, Denmark, Ochsner studied philosophy at the University of Berlin in 1931–33 and earned an MA in 1939 from the University of Copenhagen.

He has headed the Department of Maps, Prints and Photographs at the Royal Library in Copenhagen since 1944, and previously worked for the State Museum of Fine Arts in Copenhagen (1941–44).

Ochsner belongs to the Danish Cultural History Society and the National Commission for Collecting Old Photographs.

The historian has registered nearly all photographers at work in Denmark up to 1914, and has built up the photo collection of the Royal Library to over a million prints and as many negatives.

PUBLICATIONS Books: *Photography in Denmark, 1840–1940*, 1974; *Photography in 100 Years from a Danish Point of View*, 1962; *Photographs of Architecture and Views in Two Copenhagen Libraries*, 1957; *Photographs of Hans Andersen*, 1957; *Photographers in and from Denmark until the Year 1900*, 1956.

ADDRESS 25 Kildevej, DK-2960, Rungsted, Kyst, Denmark.

Starr Ockenga *PHOTOGRAPHER · TEACHER* [See plate 123] Born June 14, 1938, in Boston, Ockenga received a BA in English Literature from

Wheaton College in Wheaton, Illinois (1960), and an MFA from Rhode Island School of Design in Providence, where she studied with Harry Callahan and Aaron Siskind (1974).

An associate professor of photography and director of the Creative Photography Laboratory at MIT since 1978, she previously worked there as an assistant professor (1976–78). She was also photo editor and chief photographer for the Lawrence *Eagle Tribune* in Lawrence, Massachusetts (1974–76).

Ockenga is a member of SPE.

PUBLICATIONS Monographs: *Dress Up*, 1978; *Mirror After Mirror*, 1975. Anthologies: *Women See Men*, 1977; *Women See Woman*, 1976. Catalog: *Photographs*, 1977 (Sheldon Memorial Art Gall. Cllctns., Univ. of Nebr.: Lincoln). Periodical: *Photography Annual*, 1976.

COLLECTIONS Addison Gall. of American Art, Andover, Mass.; Humboldt State Univ., Eureka, Calif.; Panoptican Gall., Boston, Mass.; Rhode Island School of Design Mus. of Art, Providence; Univ. of Nebr., Sheldon Memorial Art Gall., Lincoln.

DEALER Robert Samuel Gall., 795 Broadway, New York, NY 10003.

ADDRESS 94 St. Botolph St, Boston, MA 02116.

Michael O'Cleary CIVIL SERVANT · PHOTOGRAPHER Born December 18, 1938, in England, O'Cleary cites Norman Hall, editor of *Photography* magazine, as his major influence.

A British civil servant, O'Cleary pursues photography on his own time.

He works in black-and-white, "guided by the belief that the best use of photography is to show, without technical contrivance, what has been seen."

PUBLICATIONS Periodicals: *Creative Camera*, 1972, 1967; *U.S. Camera Annual*, 1970; *British Journal of Photography Annual*, 1967.

COLLECTION Victoria & Albert Mus., London.

ADDRESS 15, Fairlawn Close, Hanworth, Middlesex, England.

Jeanne Marie O'Connor PHOTOGRAPHER · TEACHER Born December 17, 1945, in San Francisco, O'Connor earned a BA in Art (1967) and an MA in Painting/Drawing (1969) from the University of California, Berkeley. Her mentor was Imogen Cunningham.

As of this writing O'Connor was teaching at San Francisco City College (since 1979), Vista College in Berkeley (since 1978) and at the A.S.U.C. Studio at the University of California,

Berkeley (since 1978). She taught at California College of Arts and Crafts, Oakland, in 1978–79.

O'Connor joined the Center for Visual Arts in 1978 and SPE in 1979. She won a California Arts Council grant in 1980 and 1979 and first place in photography at the California State Fair in 1977.

Her work is chiefly portraiture and Kodalith collage, wherein a negative is printed on Kodalith, under which are built several layers of paint and collage.

PUBLICATIONS Book: *To Make a Difference*, 1978. Periodical: *Untitled 7/8*, 1974 (Friends of Photography: Carmel, Calif.).

COLLECTION Imogen Cunningham Trust, San Francisco.

DEALER Carol Arieff, Fine Arts Resources, 431 Bryant St, San Francisco, CA 94107.

ADDRESS 1736 9th St, Berkeley, CA 94710.

Georg Mirskij Oddner PHOTOGRAPHER · SCRIPTWRITER · FILM DIRECTOR Born October 17, 1923, in Stockholm, Oddner studied photography at Konstfack (art school) in Stockholm (until 1940). He worked as an assistant to Richard Avedon in New York City in 1950.

Oddner has been a photographer since 1950, a producer of television documentaries since 1965, and a script writer and director since 1971. He worked as a cinematographer in Copenhagen in (1963–65), and was a jazz musician in Stockholm (1946–50).

The photographer belongs to ASMP, Svenska Fotografernas Förbund and TIO in Stockholm (since 1958). He won a Swedish state scholarship for artists in 1972, the Malmö Culture Prize in 1971, VI magazine photojournalistic prize in 1967, Royal Libraries prize for graphic art in 1961, and the Åhlén & Åkerlunds photojournalistic prize in 1955.

Oddner was the cinematographer for the television film *Weekend* (1963) and wrote and directed the features *The Surprise* (1972) and *The Visiting Dreamer* (1978).

PUBLICATIONS Books: *To Spain*, w/Klaus Rifbjerg, 1971 (Gyldendals: Copenhagen); *A Concise History of Photography*, Helmut Gernsheim, 1965; *Creative Photography, Aesthetic Trends 1839–1960*, Helmut Gernsheim, 1962; *Good Morning South America*, w/P. Persson, 1956 (Bonniers). Periodicals: *Aktuell Fotografi*, May 1972; *Populär Fotografi*, June 1970; *Infinity: ASMP*, Sept 1968; *Vindrosen*, May 1962; *Photography*, July 1958; *Camera*, July 1957.

COLLECTIONS L/C, Wash., D.C. Bibliothèque Nationale, Paris; Malmoe Mus., Sweden; Photographic Mus., Helsinki, Finland; Photographic

Mus., Oslo, Norway; Photographic Mus., Stockholm.

REPRESENTATIVE TIO, Drottninggatan 88 c, 111 36 Stockholm, Sweden.

ADDRESS Herrestadsgatan 1A, 217 49 Malmö, Sweden.

Ken T. Ohara PHOTOGRAPHER Born August 13, 1942, Ohara studied photography at Nihon University in Tokyo (1961–62) and also attended the Art Students League in New York City (1963–65).

Since 1978 he has been technical director at Menken Selzer Studio in New York City, and from 1966 to 1970 he was an assistant to Richard Avedon and to Hiro in New York City. Ohara won a Guggenheim Fellowship in 1974.

His book *One* was made into a film that was broadcast on CBS-TV in 1974.

PUBLICATIONS Monograph: *One*, 1970 (Tsukiji Shokan: Tokyo). Book: *The City-American Experience*, Peter Bunnell, 1971. Catalog: *New Japanese Photography*, John Szarkowski, 1974 (MOMA: NYC). Periodicals: *Asahi Camera*, May 1979; *Camera Mainichi*, Apr 1979; *Harper's Bazaar*, May 1971; *U.S. Camera Annual*, 1971.

ADDRESS 335 Greenwich St, New York, NY 10013.

Yoichi Robert Okamoto PHOTOJOURNALIST Born July 3, 1915, in Yonkers, New York, Okamoto received a BS from Colgate University in Hamilton, New York, in 1938.

As of this writing Okamoto was a freelance photographer doing magazine and commercial photography. He worked as the personal photographer to President Lyndon B. Johnson at the White House (1964–69), as chief of the Pictures Branch of the U.S. Information Agency in Washington, D.C. (1958–64), and as a photo officer for the American Embassy in Vienna, Austria (1948–54).

A member of the White House News Photographers Association, Okamoto has received many awards, including a Special Citation from ASMP (1969), the Newhouse Citation from the School of Journalism, Syracuse University (1969), an Excellent Service Award from the U.S. Information Agency (1955), a silver medallion from Photographische Gesellschaft in Vienna (1955) and a Certificate of Commendation from the United States Forces in Austria (1946).

REPRESENTATIVE Photo Researchers, 60 E 56 St, New York, NY 10022.

ADDRESS Okamoto, Inc., 5602 Roosevelt St, Bethesda, MD 20034.

Tetsu Okuhara PHOTOGRAPHER Born in Los Angeles on March 3, 1940, Okuhara studied at the University of Chicago (1958–60) and at Cooper Union in New York City (1970).

A freelance photographer, the artist has been the recipient of two CAPS grants (1975, 1973) and a Guggenheim Fellowship (1974). In 1968 he was the cinematographer on the feature film *Sex Circus*.

PUBLICATION Anthology: *Mirrors and Windows*, John Szarkowski, ed., 1978.

COLLECTIONS Art Inst. of Chicago; ICP, NYC; MOMA, NYC; Chas. Rand Penney Fndn., Olcott, N.Y.; San Francisco Mus. of Modern Art; SUNY, Albany; UCLA, Wight Art Gall.; VSW, Rochester; Walker Art Ctr., Minneapolis, Minn. Natl. Gall. of Australia, Melbourne.

DEALER Witkin Gallery, 41 E 57 St, New York, NY 10022.

ADDRESS 202 E 42 St., New York, NY 10017.

Jenny Okun PHOTOGRAPHER · PAINTER · FILM MAKER · TEACHER Born October 3, 1953, in New York, Okun attended the Wimbledon School of Art (1971–72) and the Chelsea School of Art (1972–75), both in London, receiving a DipAD in Painting from the latter. She then did postgraduate work in experimental film and photography at the Slade School of Art in London (1975–77).

As of this writing she was teaching painting and drawing at the Central School of Art in London, and teaches film, television and photography at the London School of Printing. In 1978 she co-directed the London Filmmakers Co-op Workshop.

A member of the Stereoscope Society in London since 1975 and director of the London Filmmakers Co-op since 1978, she received an Arts Council of Great Britain grant in 1978.

Okun produces composite images on one negative by advancing the film gradually through her camera while making exposures, creating overlapping and superimposition. She has also made photographs from multiple slide projector images and photographed collages of end prints. The photographer works in 16mm filmmaking as well.

PUBLICATIONS Catalogs: *Contemporary Colour Photography*, 1980, *European Colour*, 1978 (Photographers Gall.: London).

COLLECTIONS Photographs: Victoria & Albert Mus., London. Films: Maryan Gall., Los Angeles; N.Y. Film Co-op; San Francisco Film Co-op. British Council, London Film Co-op.

DEALERS Zabriskie Gall., 29 rue Aubry Le Boucher, Paris, France; Daniel Wolf, Inc., 30 W

57 St, New York, NY 10019; G. Ray Hawkins Gall., 7224 Melrose Ave, Los Angeles, CA 90046; Photographers Gall., 8 Great Newport St, London WC2, England.

ADDRESS 21 Sudbourne Rd, London SW2, England.

Toby Old *PHOTOGRAPHER* Born October 12, 1945, in Stillwater, Minnesota, Old received a BS from Hamline University, St. Paul, Minnesota, in 1967 and a DDS from the University of Minnesota, Minneapolis, in 1971. He studied photography at Apeiron Workshops in Millerton, New York, in 1976.

A freelance magazine photographer since 1977, he has taken assignments for such publications as *The Washington Post, Rolling Stone* and *Penthouse International.* Old became a contributing photographer to the *Soho Weekly News* in 1979. From 1973 to 1976 he was an associate photographer for the Minnesota Geographic Society in Minneapolis.

Old won a CAPS grant in 1980 and a Coup Ville de Paris, Phot Univers in 1978.

For the past several years he has been documenting party night life at various New York City discos.

PUBLICATIONS Anthologies: *Contact Theory,* 1980; *SX-70 Art,* 1979. Periodicals: *Camera,* Sept 1979; *Flash,* 1:5, 1979.

COLLECTIONS Minn. Mus. of Art, St. Paul; Olden Camera Cllctn., NYC. French Mus. of Photography, Bièvres, France.

ADDRESS 342 Bowery, New York, NY 10012.

Arthur Ollman *PHOTOGRAPHER · TEACHER* Born March 6, 1947, in Milwaukee, Wisconsin, Ollman earned a BA in Art History from the University of Wisconsin in Madison (1969) and an MFA from Lone Mountain College, San Francisco (1977). He also studied at Columbia College, Chicago, in 1970, at VSW in Rochester in 1972, at San Francisco Art Institute in 1974 and briefly with Nathan Lyons. His major influences were Brassaï, Burchard and Johannes Itten.

Currently an instructor at Chabot College in Hayward, California (since 1977), Ollman has also taught at the San Francisco Museum of Modern Art (1976–78) and at Free University of Wisconsin (1967–69). He was artist-in-residence at Southwestern College in San Diego, California, under an NEA grant in the spring of 1978, and in that year became a founding member and president of the board of directors of Camerawork in San Francisco.

Ollman received an NEA Photographer's Fellowship and Arts Exhibition Aid grant in 1979, an NEA publications grant in 1978 and a grant from the California Arts Council in 1977 for a photohistory video project. In 1978 he won First Award in Photography from Cal Expo.

In the last several years the photographer has been working in color at night in urban environments around the world. He uses extended exposure, ambient light and occasional interactive flash.

PUBLICATIONS Book: *Eros and Photography,* 1978. Anthology: *SX-70 Art,* Ralph Gibson, ed., 1979. Catalogs: *Spectrum, New Directions in Color Photography,* 1979 (Univ. of Hawaii); *Contemporary California Photography,* 1978. Periodicals: *Popular Photography Annual,* 1979; *Aktuell Fotografi,* Nov 1979; *Pictures,* May 1979; *Zoom,* Mar 1979 (Paris); *Artforum,* Feb 1979; *American Photographer,* Nov 1978.

PORTFOLIO *New California Views* (group), 1979.

COLLECTIONS Atlantic Richfield Corp., Los Angeles; CCP, Tucson; Arnold Crane Clltn., Chicago; Delaware Art Mus., Wilmington; Denver Art Mus., Colo.; ICP, NYC; La Jolla Mus. of Contemp. Art, Calif.; Los Angeles County Mus. of Art; Metro. Mus. of Art, NYC; Minneapolis Inst. of Art, Minn.; MOMA, NYC; Museum of Fine Arts, Houston, TX; New Orleans Mus. of Art, La.; R.I. School of Design, Providence; San Francisco Mus. of Modern Art, Calif.; Santa Barbara Mus. of Art, Calif.; UCLA; Lee Witkin Cllctn., NYC. Centre Georges Pompidou, Paris; Tokyo Inst. of Polytechnics.

REPRESENTATIVE Grapestake Gall., 2876 California St, San Francisco, CA 94115.

ADDRESS 6509 Raymond St, Oakland, CA 94609.

Gustaf Lennart Eugen Olson *PHOTOGRAPHER · FILM MAKER* Born December 21, 1925, in Gothenburg, Sweden, Olson is a self-taught photographer. During the early fifties he was influenced by the nonfigurative arts, particularly the work of the painters connected with the Galerie Denise René in Paris.

Olson has been a freelance photographer since 1955, concentrating in the fields of architecture, industry and magazine photography. Since 1961 he has freelanced mainly for Swedish television, and has, over the years, produced and directed approximately fifty television films, including documentaries, theater plays and musicals.

A member of Tio Fotografer in Stockholm since 1958, he was the recipient of Swedish State Artist grants in 1978, 1968 and 1967.

The artist works primarily in black-and-white, and since 1978 has been working with the gumbichromate printing technique. Since 1950 the main subject of his work has been bridges. Trees have also been a major theme throughout his career.

PUBLICATIONS Book: *Photography Yearbook*, 1960. Periodical: *Camera*, 1962.

COLLECTIONS Art Inst. of Chicago; Harvard Univ., Cambridge, Mass.; IMP/GEH, Rochester; L/C, Wash., D.C.; MOMA, NYC. Bibliothèque National, Paris; National Museum, Stockholm, Sweden.

DEALER Camera Obscura, Kåkbrinken 5, S-111 27 Stockholm, Sweden.

REPRESENTATIVE Tiofoto, Drottninggatan 88c, S-111 36 Stockholm, Sweden.

ADDRESS Mariatorget 8, 2tr, S-116 48 Stockholm, Sweden.

Jane Louise O'Neal PHOTOGRAPHER Born in San Diego, California, on October 2, 1945, O'Neal earned a BA in Art from California State University, Fullerton, in 1973. She considers the paintings of Vermeer and Edward Hopper as major influences.

A freelance photographer since 1977, she taught color photography at University of California at Los Angeles Extension in 1978.

O'Neal has been a member of the Los Angeles Center for Photographic Studies since 1979.

The photographer produces 16 x 20 Cibachrome prints from small-format color transparencies. She explores "light, space, and graphics in the urban landscape and their intrinsic relationships to each other . . . isolating the elements within the ordinary to try to communicate the extraordinary."

PUBLICATIONS Periodicals: *Picture Magazine*, no. 7, 1978, no. 3, 1976. Reviews: *Artweek*, Apr 21, 1979; *New York Times Magazine*, Ada Louise Huxtable, Feb 12, 1978.

PORTFOLIO *L.A. Issue*, 1979 (Los Angeles Ctr. for Photographic Studies).

COLLECTIONS CCP, Tucson; Harvard Univ., Fogg Art Mus., Cambridge, Mass.; Los Angeles County Mus. of Art; Minneapolis Inst. of Art, Minn.; Santa Barbara Mus. of Art, Calif.; UCLA, Gruenwald Ctr. for Graphic Art; Univ. of Iowa Mus. of Art, Iowa City; Lee Witkin Cllctn., NYC.

ADDRESS 524½ N Sweetzer Ave, Los Angeles, CA 90048.

Elaine O'Neil PHOTOGRAPHER · TEACHER Born August 14, 1946, O'Neil received a BFA in Photography from Philadelphia College of Art in Pennsylvania (1968) and an MS in Photography at Illinois Institute of Technology, Institute of Design, in Chicago (1970).

As of this writing she was a visiting artist at California State College at Fullerton. O'Neil has also been an instructor at the School of the Museum of Fine Arts in Boston and at Tufts University in Medford, Massachusetts, since 1975. Between the years 1971 and 1975 she taught at College of the Dayton Art Institute, Sinclair Community College and Wright State University, all in Dayton, Ohio.

She was the recipient of a Ford Foundation grant in 1975.

O'Neil is the creator of Blueprint Postcards and Quilts. She also works in 35mm, producing 16 x 22 sepia-toned prints.

PUBLICATIONS Book: *Photo-Art Processes*, Nancy Howell-Kohler, ed., 1977. Anthology: *Women See Men*, Yvonne Kalmus et al, eds., intro. & text by Ingrid Bengis, 1977.

COLLECTIONS Brookdale Community Coll., Lincroft, N.J.; Corcoran Gall of Art, Wash., D.C.; Dayton Art Inst., Ohio; L/C, Wash., D.C.; New Orleans Mus. of Art; Standard Oil Co.; Univ. of Colorado Libs.

DEALERS Witkin Gall., 41 E 57 St, New York, NY 10022; The Gall. for Fine Photography, 5432 Magazine St, New Orleans, LA 70115; The Jeb Gall., 342 S Main St, Providence, RI 02901.

ADDRESS 33 Peter Parley Rd, Jamaica Plain, MA 02130.

Ferdinando Ongania PHOTOGRAPHER Ongania was born in Venice; his work flourished in the years 1870 to 1900. The winner of several prizes for his work on Venice, he was one of the first in Italy to use an elliptical process, invented by Ernest Edwards in London in 1869, to reproduce numerous art objects photomechanically, such as the San Marco Cathedral in Venice.

PUBLICATIONS Books: *Streets and Canals of Venice*, 1900; *Early Venetian Printing*, 1895. Catalogs: *Un secolo di fotografia della Collezione Gernsheim*, 1957 (Milan); *Details of Altars, Monuments, Sculptures, etc. in the Basilica of San Marco, Venice 1878–86, n.d.*

COLLECTION Humanities Resource., Gernsheim Cllctn., Univ. of Texas, Austin.

Susan V. Opotow PHOTOGRAPHER · TEACHER Born in New York City on November 21, 1943, Opotow earned a BA from Antioch College, Yellow Springs, Ohio, in 1965 and an MS from Bank

Street College in 1970. She studied photography with Lisette Model.

From 1972 to 1976 Opotow was adjunct professor of fine arts (photography) at C. W. Post College in Greenvale, New York, and in 1975 she taught photography at an alternative public school in New York City.

A member of SPE, she received grants from New York State in 1977 and Polaroid in 1975.

PUBLICATION Anthology: *Women See Woman*, Annie Gottlieb, Cheryl Wiesenfeld et al, eds., 1976.

ADDRESS 189 Claremont Ave, New York, NY 10027.

Suzanne Opton *PHOTOGRAPHER · TEACHER* [See plate 124] Born March 14, 1945, in Portland, Oregon, Opton earned a BA in Philosophy from Smith College, Northampton, Massachusetts (1967).

Currently a photography instructor at the School of Visual Arts in New York City (since 1979), she previously taught at Pratt Institute in New York City (1977–78). In 1977 she taught a workshop on "photo diaries" at Orange County Mental Health Center in Bradford, Vermont, and in 1976–77 taught a similar workshop privately in New York City. Her photographs have appeared in such magazines as *Life, Time, Esquire* and *Ms.*

A member of Professional Women Photographers in New York City, Opton received grants from the NEA in 1973 and from the Vermont Council on the Arts in 1975.

Her work falls into three categories: small-format black-and-white studies of unmarried brothers and sisters in Vermont who live together; small-format color self-portraits that are sequences and montages of dreams, relationships and states of mind; and medium-format black-and-white constructions on a wall using paper, ribbon, leaves, flowers, vegetables and "sometimes my baby Jules."

PUBLICATIONS Books: *Growing Old*, 1975; *Made with Oak*, Herbert H. Wise & Jeffrey Weiss, 1975. Anthologies: *Self-Portrayal*, Jim Alinder, ed., 1978; *The Family of Children*, 1977; *Women Photograph Men*, Danielle B. Hayes, ed., intro. by Molly Haskell, 1977; *Women See Men*, Yvonne Kalmus et al, eds., intro. & text by Ingrid Bengis, 1977. Periodicals: *35mm Photography*, spring 1978; *Popular Photography Annual*, 1977.

COLLECTION Portland Mus. of Art, Portland, Maine.

ADDRESS 652 Broadway, New York, NY 10012.

Ruth Orkin *PHOTOJOURNALIST · FILM MAKER* Born September 3, 1921, in Boston, Orkin was the daughter of the silent-film actress Mary Ruby; her husband was the photographer Morris Engel. Orkin is a self-taught photographer.

While working at MGM studios as a messenger in 1943 Orkin became fascinated with personalities and soon began photographing them. She moved to New York City in 1944 and began working as a freelance photojournalist. Her work has appeared in *Life, Look, Collier's, Ladies' Home Journal, Esquire* and *Cosmopolitan*.

A member of ASMP, she is also a member of the Academy of Motion Picture Arts and Sciences in California. Named one of the "Top Ten Women Photographers in U.S." by the Professional Photographers of America poll in 1959, she won the top prize, the Silver Lion of San Marco, for co-direction of a feature film entitled *Little Fugitive* at the Venice Film Festival in 1953.

Orkin works in a "candid, human, black-and-white" photojournalistic style.

PUBLICATIONS Monograph: *A World Through My Window*, 1978. Book: *Photography Workshop*, Peter Martin, 1953. Anthologies: *The Photograph Collector's Guide*, Lee D. Witkin & Barbara London, 1979; *Photographers on Photography*, 1978. Periodical: *Popular Photo*, June 1977.

COLLECTIONS Metro. Mus. of Art, NYC; MOMA, NYC.

DEALER Witkin Gall., 41 E 57 St, New York, NY 10022.

ADDRESS 65 Central Park West, New York, NY 10023.

Ted Orland *PHOTOGRAPHER · WRITER · TEACHER* Born in California in 1941, Orland earned a BS from the University of Southern California, Los Angeles, and an MA in Interdisciplinary Creative Arts from San Francisco State University in 1974. He studied with Wynn Bullock, Dave Bohn and Paul Caponigro.

Since 1973 he has been publisher and contributing editor of *The Image Continuum Journal* and an instructor with the University of California Extension. Orland taught a year at Stanford University in California (1979). Between 1972 and 1975 he was an assistant to Ansel Adams and printer of Adams' Special Edition Yosemite negatives. Prior to that he was a photographer for designer Charles Eames (1968–71).

A founding member of The Image Continuum in 1973, Orland is a member of SPE (since 1975) and Friends of Photography, where he served as an Advisory Trustee in 1976–77.

In 1978 Orland received an NEA Artist's Grant to photograph the Diablo Valley, and a National Park Service artist-in-residence award at Yosemite National Park. The NEA awarded him an artist-in-residence grant in 1976 at Volcanoes National Park in Hawaii.

Describing his art, Orland says; "Stylistically, my work is black-and-white medium-format, natural-light photography. Many of my prints are multiply-toned, and some are hand-colored. Overall, the prints fall within the 'West Coast tradition' of fine craftsmanship."

PUBLICATIONS Book: *Yosemite Reflections: The Words of John Muir, the Photographs of Ted Orland*, 1977. Anthologies: *Imogen Cunningham*, 1979; *Polaroid Land Photography*, Ansel Adams, 1979; *Self-Portrayal*, 1978. Catalog: *Diablo Valley in Focus*, 1979 (Walnut Creek Art Gall.: Calif.). Periodical: *Latent Image*, spring 1978.

PORTFOLIOS *Latent Image Portfolio* (group), 1978; *Out of State* (group), 1978 (San Francisco State Univ.).

COLLECTIONS CCP, Tucson; Graham Nash Cllctn., Los Angeles; Lee Witkin Cllctn, NYC; Oakland Mus., Calif.; Polaroid Corp., Cambridge, Mass.; San Francisco Mus., of Modern Art; Santa Barbara Mus. of Art, Calif.; Stanford Mus. of Art, Palo Alto, Calif.; Walnut Creek Civic Arts Gall., Walnut Creek, Calif.; Yosemite Natl. Park Mus., Calif.

DEALER Weston Gall., POB 655, Carmel, CA 93921.

ADDRESS 10061 Riverside Dr, Ben Lomond, CA 95005.

Mark Orlove PHOTOGRAPHER Born October 7, 1950, in Philadelphia, Pennsylvania, Orlove received a BA in Comparative Literature from Case Western Reserve University, Cleveland, Ohio, in 1972. He served a residence apprenticeship with Minor White in Arlington, Massachusetts, in 1972–73.

A commercial photographer since 1975, Orlove was a project photographer for an NEA-funded architectural survey in Providence, Rhode Island, in 1975 and a photolithographer for Pentacle Press in Carlisle, Massachusetts, in 1975–77.

He is a member of Photographic Resource Center.

Working primarily in color, Orlove employs all formats, especially greatly enlarged small-format negatives shot with a 110 camera. His visual concerns "engage a highly graphic compositional representation of the current ambience of modern society and the relationship of animate and inanimate, real and unreal."

PUBLICATIONS Books: *The New Zone System Manual*, Minor White & Richard Zakia, 1975; *Space Under Elevated Highways*, Gloria Root, 1975. Periodicals: *Lightyear*, 1978; *Sound Image*, 1975.

COLLECTIONS Addison Gall. of Amer. Art, Andover, Mass.; Amherst Coll., Mass.; Harvard Univ., Fogg Art Mus., Cambridge, Mass.; Mid-Tennessee State Univ., Murfreesboro; Minneapolis Inst. of Art, Minn.; Philadelphia Free Lib., Pa.; Princeton Univ., Minor White Archives, N.J.; Smithsonian Inst., Wash., D.C.; Worcester Art Mus., Mass. Bibliothèque Nationale, Paris.

DEALER Carl Siembab Gall., 162 Newbury St, Boston, MA 02116.

ADDRESS 791 Tremont St, E213, Boston, MA 02118.

José Ortiz Echagüe
See Echagüe

Wilhelm Ostwald CHEMIST · TEACHER Born in 1853 in Riga, Russia, Ostwald died in 1932. After studying at the Realgymnasium in Riga he attended the Landesuniversitaet in Dorpat, becoming a tutor there in 1876.

Ostwald returned to Riga to serve as a teacher at the Polytechnical Institute, later taking on a professorship in physical chemistry at the University of Leipzig (1887). He retired from teaching in 1907, setting up a laboratory (named Energie) in his country residence, close to Leipzig. He also traveled as a lecturer.

Ostwald suggested the redox potentials of a series of common reducing and oxidizing agents in the photochemical process (1892), and the next year he presented the "supersaturation theory" of development of the latent image, considered the best theory of development for many years. He described the Ostwald ripening process in 1900, which concerned the stable and metastable forms of mercuric oxide and iodide, and in 1902 he and C. Gros invented the Katatypie process for color prints. He considered his greatest work to be the development of a color theory and color atlas classifying all colors, which he began in 1914. Ostwald received the Nobel Prize for chemistry in 1909.

PUBLICATIONS Books: *Memoirs of a Photochemist*, Fritz Wentzel, 1960; *A Half Century of Color*, Louis W. Sipley, 1951; *The Theory of the Photographic Process*, C. E. K. Mees, 1944; *Lehrbuch der Allgemeinen Chemie*, 1893. Anthology:

Photography's Great Inventors, Louis W. Sipley, 1965. Periodicals: *Werkszeitschrift der Chemische Werke Huels,* 1960; *Journal of Chemical Education,* 1953; *More Business,* Nov 1937; *Photographische Correspondenz,* 1917, 1903; *Zeitschrift für physikalische Chemie,* 1900.

Timothy H. O'Sullivan PHOTOGRAPHER [See plate 23] Born ca. 1840 in New York City, O'Sullivan died on January 14, 1882, in Staten Island, New York. He learned photography while working at Mathew Brady's New York and Washington, D.C., galleries.

Initially in the employ of Mathew Brady, O'Sullivan later worked for Alexander Gardner. His numerous photographic missions, aside from that connected with the Civil War, included the Clarence King expedition along the fortieth parallel in Nevada, California and Utah (1867–69), on which he was the official photographer for the U.S. Geological Survey; Thomas O. Selfridge's expedition to Panama's Isthmus of Darien (1870); the George M. Wheeler expeditions to California, Nevada and Arizona (1871–75); and Lieutenant Wheeler's survey of the hundredth meridian (1870 and 1873–74). He was appointed chief photographer for the Department of the Treasury in 1880.

Known for his Civil War and western landscape photographs, O'Sullivan did work that was remarkable for its clarity and a modern aesthetic rare for his day. He used the collodion wet-plate and produced albumen prints in both small and large (11 x 14) formats.

PUBLICATIONS Monographs: *T. H. O'Sullivan: Photographer,* Beaumont & Nancy Newhall, 1966; *Timothy O'Sullivan: America's Forgotten Photographer,* James D. Horan, 1966. Books: *Era of Exploration,* Weston Naef & James N. Wood, 1975; *History of Photography,* Beaumont Newhall, 1964; *Photography and the American Scene,* Robert Taft, 1938; *Annual Report 1871–72: Photographs,* w/W. Bell, U.S. Army Corps of Engineers, ca. 1874; *Gardner's Photographic Sketch Book of the War,* 2 vols., Alexander Gardner, 1866, repr., 1 vol., 1959. Anthologies: *The Photograph Collector's Guide,* Lee D. Witkin & Barbara London, 1979; *The Invented Eye,* Edward Lucie-Smith, 1975; *The Magic Image,* Cecil Beaton & Gail Buckland, 1975; *Early Photographs & Early Photographers,* Oliver Mathews, 1973; *Great Photographers,* 1971, *Light and Film,* 1970, Time-Life Series; *Masters of Photography,* Beaumont & Nancy Newhall, 1969; *Picture Gallery Pioneers,* Ralph W. Andrews, 1965. Periodicals: "T. H. O'Sullivan," Hermine Baumhofer,

Image, Apr 1953; *Anthony's Bulletin of Photography,* 13:29, 1882.

COLLECTIONS Amer. Geological Soc., NYC; Art Inst. of Chicago; Boston Pub. Lib.; Harvard Univ., Carpenter Ctr. for the Visual Arts & Fogg Art Mus., Cambridge; IMP/GEH, Rochester; L/C, Wash., D.C.; Mus. of N. Mex., Santa Fe; Natl. Archives, Wash., D.C.; New Orleans Mus. of Art; N.Y. Hist. Soc., NYC; N.Y. Pub. Lib., Rare Book Rm., NYC; Princeton Univ., N.J.; UCLA; Univ. of Calif., Bancroft Lib., Berkeley, Calif. Natl. Gall. of Canada, Ottawa, Ontario.

Danuta Otfinowski PHOTOGRAPHER · TEACHER Born July 9, 1953, in Los Angeles, California, Otfinowski received a BFA in 1977 from San Francisco Art Institute. She also studied with Jack Fulton and Hank Wessels.

As of this writing Otfinowski has been on a stipend from University of California at San Diego for graduate work in the visual arts. She has worked as an instructor of photography at Grossmont College in El Cajon, California (1978–79), and as a freelance photographer in San Francisco (1977–78).

Otfinowski was the recipient of the Imogen Cunningham Award in 1980 and a Photographer's Fellowship from NEA in 1979.

The photographer says of her work: "My photographs are about the relationship between the place and its inhabitants.... I like to think of place in relation to its physical nature and its function.... The characters in my photographs are caught somewhere between the dictates of the place and their own humanness."

PUBLICATION Periodical: *Popular Photography,* Oct 1978.

COLLECTIONS Seagram Cllctn., NYC; Stanford Mus. of Art, Palo Alto, Calif. Bibliothèque Nationale, Paris.

DEALER Lowinsky & Arai, 228 Grant Ave, San Francisco, CA 94108.

ADDRESS 7852 Eads Ave, La Jolla, CA 92037.

Paul Outerbridge, Jr. PHOTOGRAPHER Born August 15, 1896, in New York, Outerbridge died October 17, 1959, in California. Educated at private schools, he studied sculpture at the Art Students League in New York in 1915 and, briefly, with Alexander Archipenko. He began photographing in 1917 while serving in the armed forces, and by 1921 had enrolled in a class at the Clarence H. White School of Photography in New York City.

Outerbridge taught aesthetics and composition at the Clarence White School, and his photographs appeared first in *Vanity Fair*, then in *Vogue* and *Harper's Bazaar*, among other publications. In 1925 he moved to Paris and became art director of Paris *Vogue*, establishing an advertising studio there as well. He returned to New York in 1929 and began experimenting in color photography, perfecting the three-color carbro process. The photographer moved to Hollywood in 1943, then to Laguna Beach, where he set up a small commercial color portrait studio. He traveled widely, using his photographs to illustrate travel articles, and wrote an occasional column on color photography for *U.S. Camera*.

Having studied film briefly in Berlin in 1928, Outerbridge worked as set adviser for E. A. Dupont's film *Variety* in London.

Howard De Vree *(New York Times)* wrote of an exhibit of Outerbridge's work: "The printing is almost beyond reproach. The clarity of the still lifes, the truly sculptural quality of the figures, the lighting and the compositional sense implicit in these photographs are altogether exceptional in the field."

PUBLICATIONS Book: *Photographing in Color*, 1940. Anthologies: *The Photograph Collector's Guide*, Lee D. Witkin & Barbara London, 1979; *Photography Rediscovered*, David Travis & Anne Kennedy, 1979; *Photography Year 1978*, Time-Life Books; *The Julien Levy Collection*, Witkin Gallery, 1977; *Photographs from the Julien Levy Collection*, David Travis, 1976; *Looking at Photographs*, John Szarkowski, 1973. Catalog: *Paul Outerbridge, Jr.*, Graham Howe, 1976 (Los Angeles Ctr. for Photographic Studies). Periodicals: "Outerbridge from Cubism to Fetishism," Graham Howe, *Artforum*, summer 1977; review, Howard De Vree, *New York Times*, Nov 24, 1935; "Paul Outerbridge, Jr.," M. Burcel, *Crea-tive Art*, Feb 1933; "Paul Outerbridge, Jr., " M. F. Agha, *Advertising Arts*, May 1931.

COLLECTIONS Boston Mus. of Fine Art, Mass.; Cleveland Mus. of Art, Ohio; Laguna Beach Mus. of Art, Calif.; L/C, Wash., D.C.; Metro. Mus. of Art, NYC.

William (Bill) Elmo Owens PHOTOGRAPHER [See plate 108] Born in San Jose, California, on September 25, 1938, Owens received a BA from Chico State College, California, in 1963. A self-employed photographer, Owens worked as a news photographer for the *Livermore Independent* in California between 1968 and 1978.

A member of SPE, ASMP and NPPA, Owens received NEA grants in 1978, 1977 and 1976. He was awarded a Guggenheim Fellowship in 1964.

The artist, who does documentary studies of American life-styles, including groups, social activities and people at work, says, "The heart of photography is the documentary image, as it is a record of people, places and events. The documentary photograph contains the symbols of our society and tells us something about ourselves."

PUBLICATIONS Monographs: *Publish Your Photo Book*, 1979; *Documentary Photography: A Personal View*, 1978; *Working: I Do It for the Money*, 1976; *Our Kind of People*, 1975; *Suburbia*, 1972. Anthology: *The Photograph Collector's Guide*, Lee D. Witkin & Barbara London, 1979. Periodicals: *Camera*, Mar 1974; *Camera 35 Annual*, 1972.

PORTFOLIO *Untitled*, 1977 (Bill Owens & John Bergurren Gall.: San Francisco).

COLLECTIONS MOMA, NYC; San Francisco Mus. of Modern Art. Bibliothèque Nationale, Paris.

ADDRESS Box 687, Livermore, CA 94550.

P

Fred Padula *PHOTOGRAPHER · FILM MAKER*
Born October 25, 1937, in Santa Barbara, California, Padula earned a BA in Music and an MA in Art (1965) from San Francisco State University. He studied with Jack Welpott, Don Worth and Wynn Bullock (who later became his close friend).

Currently self-employed, Padula taught photography and film-making at San Francisco State University (1963–79) and at the University of California, San Francisco (1966–71). He was also a visiting artist at the University of Minnesota, Minneapolis, in 1970, and has worked since college as a freelance film maker, carrying out projects for PBS, NET, NBC, KQED-TV, Pepsi-Cola, Lee Mendelson Films, Wolper Productions and Sesame Street.

Padula's first film, *Ephesus*, received first place in the San Francisco International Film Festival, and his latest work, *El Capitan* (1978), was funded by an American Film Institute grant and won the grand prize at the Trento International Film Festival in Italy (1978).

REPRESENTATIVE   Canyon Cinema Co-op, American Industrial Center, Ste 338, 2325 Third St, San Francisco, CA 94107.

ADDRESS   47 Shell Rd, Mill Valley, CA 94941.

Timothy John Page *PHOTOJOURNALIST* Born May 25, 1944 in Tunbridge Wells, Kent, England, Page is self-taught in photography, naming as his mentors Henri Huet, Steve Northup, Horst Faas and Larry Burrows.

As of this writing Page was freelancing (since 1979) in the United Kingdom for *Observer Magazine*, *Newsweek*, BBC and, in Paris, SIPA Press. He previously freelanced (1972–78) in the Los Angeles and San Francisco areas for *Rolling Stone*, *Crawdaddy/Feature* and *New Times*, among other journals. He was on contract to Time-Life in Rome in 1970–71, and from 1965 to 1969 photographed the war in Vietnam for Time-Life, *Look*, British newspapers and magazines,

UPI, AP and *Paris-Match*. He also shot documentary footage for BBC and CBC. He began his photographic career in Thailand and Laos in 1963–65, freelancing for UPI and AFP with images of the Laotian civil war and the activities of Hanoi-backed guerrillas in Thailand.

Page is best known for his work in the Vietnam war.

PUBLICATIONS Books: *Camera at War*, George Lewinski, 1979; *Life at War*, 1979; *Dispatches*, Michael Herr, 1978; *History of the Israeli Military*, 1974; *First Casualty*, Philip Knightley, 1973; *Two of the Missing*, Perry Deane Young, 1973; *Report or Distort*, MacDonald, 1971; *The Weary Falcon*, Tom Meyer, 1970; *And Or*, 1968; *Vietnam Vietnam Vietnam*, Felix Greene, 1966.

COLLECTION Victoria & Albert Mus., London.

REPRESENTATIVE SIPA Press, 14 rue Roquepine, Paris, France.

ADDRESSES 47 North Dr, Orpington, Kent, England; 1441½ Carroll Ave, Los Angeles, CA 90026.

Joshua Mann Pailet *GALLERY OWNER · PHOTOGRAPHER* Born June 30, 1950, in New Orleans, Louisiana, Pailet earned a BA in Economics (1972) and a BS in Accounting (1973) from Rice University, Houston, Texas. His mentor was Eve Sonneman.

Pailet has owned A Gallery for Fine Photography in New Orleans since 1974 and has been a freelance photographer since 1970. He was a photo instructor at Tulane University in New Orleans in 1978 and at Louisiana State University, Baton Rouge, in 1977.

He belongs to the Association of International Photography Art Dealers, Inc.

Pailet deals in contemporary and rare photographs. His own work is in small format, concentrating on street people.

PUBLICATION Monograph: *All Aboard America*, 1976.

COLLECTIONS La. Arts & Science Ctr., Baton Rouge; Menil Foundation, Houston, Tex. Bibliothèque Nationale, Paris.

ADDRESS A Gall. for Fine Photography, 5432 Magazine St, New Orleans, LA 70115.

Timo Tallno Pajunen PHOTOGRAPHER · TEACHER Born March 8, 1945, in Helsinki, Finland, Pajunen earned a BFA in 1970 from Art Center College of Design in Los Angeles and an MFA in 1971 from California College of Arts and Crafts in Oakland.

Since 1973 he has taught at the College of Marin in Kentfield, California. Pajunen has also taught at Diablo Valley College, Concord, California (1979, 1973), the University of Florida, Gainesville (1975), and Florida State University, Tallahassee (1972).

A member of the American Federation of Teachers, he won an NEA Photographer's Fellowship in 1980 and 1977.

PUBLICATIONS Catalog: *The Visual Dialogue*, 1972 (Friends of Photography: Carmel, Calif.). Periodicals: *Camera*, Jan 1973, July 1971.

COLLECTIONS Art Inst. of Chicago; CCP, Tucson; E. B. Crocker Gall., Sacramento, Calif.; Mus. of Fine Arts, St. Petersburg, Fla.; New Orleans Mus. of Art; Norton Simon Mus. of Art, Pasadena, Calif.; Oakland Mus., Calif.; San Francisco Mus. of Modern Art; St. Louis Art Mus., Mo.; Univ. of Nebr., Lincoln. El Museo Nacional de Historia, Museo Nacional de Antropologia, Mexico City, D.F., Mexico.

DEALER Fraenkel Gall., 55 Grant, San Francisco, CA 92110.

ADDRESS POB 638, Fairfax, CA 94930.

Daniela Palazzoli TEACHER · CONSULTANT · WRITER Palazzoli earned a Doctor of Fine Arts degree from the University of Milan, Italy.

Currently professor of theory and methods of mass media at the Academy of Brera, Milan, she contributes regularly to such magazines as *Bolaffi Arte* and *L'Europeo*. She also edits photographic books for Electa Publishing.

PUBLICATIONS Book: *Il Conte Primoli*, 1979 (Milan). Catalogs: *La Fotografia (Venezia '79)*, 1979 (Milan); *La Fotografia Italiana dell'800*, 1979 (Milan/Florence); *Fotomedia*, 1975 (Milan); *Combattimento per un immagine fotografi e pittori*, ed., 1973 (Turin, Italy).

ADDRESS Via Senato 12, 20121 Milan, Italy.

Marion Palfi PHOTOGRAPHER Born of Hungarian parents in Berlin, Germany, on October 21, 1917, Palfi died November 4, 1978, in Los Angeles, California. Her father was Victor Palfi, distinguished producer/director in Berlin and Hamburg, Germany, and her husband, Martin Magner, is a producer/director for stage and television. Palfi studied photography in a European studio and also received a general college education in Europe.

The late photographer taught at a variety of schools between the mid-1960s and mid-1970s: University of California at Los Angeles Extension, Chouinard–California Institute of the Arts, Inner City Cultural Center, the Woman's Building (all in Los Angeles). From 1959 to 1963 she was a faculty member of the New School for Social Research in New York City. Her images are found on the covers and in the pages of many magazines.

Palfi won an NEA fellowship in 1974, a Guggenheim Fellowship in 1967 and a Rosenwald Fellowship in 1946. Her photographs were used before the U.S. Congress and Senate to illustrate testimony on various programs and problems involving American children.

Palfi combined social research with photography, "not as a documentarian, but as a visual artist," writes Martin Magner. Working in black-and-white with a straightforward approach, in her photographs she dealt with minority groups, old people and other disadvantaged groups. Adds Magner, "She created her images . . . out of a deeply human knowledge and compassion for the people she dealt with."

PUBLICATIONS Monographs: *Invisible in America*, 1973; *Suffer Little Children*, 1952; *In These Ten Cities*, 1951. Anthology: *The Photograph Collector's Guide*, Lee D. Witkin & Barbara London, 1979.

COLLECTIONS MOMA, NYC; N.Y. Pub. Libs.; San Francisco Mus. of Modern Art; Univ. of Kans. Mus. of Art, Lawrence. Mus. of Port-au-Prince, Haiti.

DEALER Witkin Gall., 41 E 57 St, New York, NY 10022.

ARCHIVE Menninger Foundation, Verne B. Horne, Box 829, Topeka, KA 66601.

Tod Papageorge PHOTOGRAPHER · TEACHER Born in Portsmouth, New Hampshire, on August 1, 1940, Papageorge received a BA in English Literature from the University of New Hampshire in Durham in 1962.

Employed as a professor of photography at Yale University, New Haven, Connecticut, since 1978, Papageorge was a lecturer on visual studies at Harvard (1975–76) and a lecturer on photography at the Massachusetts Institute of Technology in Cambridge (1974–75). He served as visiting instructor in photography at Cooper Union in New York City and at Pratt Institute in New York City (both 1971–74).

The artist received two Guggenheim fellowships (1977, 1970) and two NEA fellowship grants (1976, 1973). He generally uses a 6 x 7 format to photograph a wide variety of subjects.

PUBLICATIONS   Book (text only): *Public Relations: The Photographs of Garry Winogrand*, 1977. Anthologies: *American Images*, 1979; *The Snapshot*, 1975. Catalog: *Fourteen American Photographers*, 1975 (Baltimore Mus.: Md).

COLLECTIONS   Art Inst. of Chicago; IMP/GEH, Rochester; MOMA, NYC; Mus. of Fine Arts, Boston; Mus. of Fine Arts, Houston, Tex; Natl. Exchange Bank, Chicago; Princeton Univ. Mus., N.J.; Seagram Cllctn., NYC; Univ. of Colorado, Boulder; Yale Univ., New Haven, Conn. Bibliothèque Nationale, Paris.

DEALER   Daniel Wolf Gall. 30 W 57 St, New York, NY 10019; Galerie Zabriskie, 29 rue Aubry-le-Boucher, 75002 Paris, France.

ADDRESS   50 White St, New York, NY 10013.

Esther Parada   *MIXED-MEDIA PHOTOGRAPHER*
Born May 10, 1938, in Grand Rapids, Michigan, Parada received a BA in History and Art History from Swarthmore College in Swarthmore, Pennsylvania (1960), an MFA in Painting and Drawing from Pratt Institute, Brooklyn, New York (1962), and an MS in Photography from Illinois Institute of Technology, Institute of Design, Chicago, where she studied with Joseph Jachna, Aaron Siskind and Arthur Siegel.

Parada has taught photography at the University of Illinois in Chicago since 1972, first as a lecturer (until 1975) and as of this writing as assistant professor of photography. Parada was a graphic designer for Science Research Associates in Chicago (1969–71) and for Chicago State University Publications Office (1967–69). She taught art at the University of St. Francis Xavier in Sucre, Bolivia, in 1964–66.

A member of SPE since 1976, the photographer won a research grant from the University of Illinois, Chicago Circle (1978), and a Ford Foundation Fellowship in International Development (1967).

Besides photography, Parada is also known for her sculptural macramé hangings.

Her current work is straight silver prints with darkroom manipulation at the film stage, thematically exploring "personal archaeology—layering or weaving images from different time periods." She previously created photo installation works, a series of modular units forming a large wall or hanging piece, done with mixed media.

PUBLICATIONS   Catalog: *Chicago, The City and Its Artists (1945–1978)*, 1978 (Univ. of Mich. Mus. of Art: Ann Arbor). Periodical: *Creative Communicator*, Nov 3, 1974.

COLLECTIONS   Columbia Coll.; Chicago Ctr. for Contemp. Photography; Humboldt Arts Ctr., Eureka, Calif.; Mus. of Contemp. Art, Chicago.

DEALER   Visual Studies Workshop Gall., 31 Prince St, Rochester, NY 14607.

ADDRESS   616 S Scoville, Oak Park, IL 60304.

Ann Parker   *PHOTOGRAPHER · GRAPHIC ARTIST*
Born March 6, 1934, Parker attended the Rhode Island School of Design, Providence, from 1952 to 1954. She earned a BFA from Yale University, New Haven, Connecticut, in 1956. In 1961 she studied with Lisette Model and Joseph Breitenbach at the New School in New York City. She considers her mentors to be Minor White, with whom she studied privately in 1954, and Nancy and Beaumont Newhall. Parker is married to Avon Neal, a graphic artist.

A freelance photographer and graphic artist who has worked with her husband for the last twenty years, Parker is a member of Friends of Photography. She received the American Institute of Graphic Artists 1979 Best Books Design Award. In 1976 she took first prize in the Americana Bicentennial Photo Contest. She won a Ford Foundation Fellowship in Arts and Humanities in 1962 and 1963.

Her style is "straight" imagery, producing silver prints. Parker does much magazine and commercial work in color. Her major emphasis is "to record with my own particular vision many aspects of folk arts and traditions. My long-term aim is to form an ever-expanding photographic archive of folk arts and traditions."

PUBLICATIONS   Books: *Scarecrows*, Avon Neal, 1978; *Molas, Folk Art of the Cuna Indians*, w/Avon Neal, 1977; *Ephemeral Folk Figures*, Avon Neal, 1969. Anthology: *Octave of Prayer*, Minor White, ed., 1972.

COLLECTIONS   (Selected)   Aldrich Rockefeller Folk Art Cllctn., Williamsburg, Va.; IMP/GEH, Rochester; Metro. Mus. of Art, N.Y.; MIT, Cambridge, Mass.; MOMA, NYC; Mus. of Fine Arts, Boston; Nelson Rockefeller Cllctn., Tarrytown, N.Y.; Princeton Univ., N.J.

DEALERS   Gall. of Graphic Arts, 1903 York

Ave, New York, NY 10028; Carl Siembab Gall., 162 Newbury St, Boston, MA 02116.

ADDRESS Thistle Hill, N Brookfield, MA 01535.

Fred R. Parker CURATOR · PAINTER · PHOTOG-RAPHER · TEACHER Born in Compton, California, on June 11, 1938, Parker earned a BA from San Francisco State College in 1964 and an MA from the University of California at Davis in 1966. In 1968 he received a fellowship to the Museum Training Program at the George Eastman International Museum of Photography in Rochester, New York. He has been influenced by Nathan Lyons, Jack Welpott, Robert Rauschenberg and Robert Heinecken.

As of this writing Parker was the director of the Sonoma State University Art Gallery; he is also curator of photography for the Santa Barbara Museum of Art (since 1977). Parker was assistant professor of art and art gallery director at the University of Wisconsin in Milwaukee in 1975, and in 1974 was a lecturer at the San Francisco Art Institute. Between 1972 and 1974 he was executive director for the Friends of Photography. At the same time he was also curatorial adviser for photography at the Pasadena Museum of Modern Art, having served as their exhibitions coordinator and curator of prints, drawings and photographs from 1969 to 1972. From 1966 to 1969 he was director of the Memorial Union Art Gallery at the University of California, Davis.

A member of SPE since 1969, Parker served as its national vice-chairman from 1973 to 1975. Most of his personal work is drawing and painting in the photo-realist style.

PUBLICATIONS Book: *Untitled*, ed., nos. 1–8, 1972–74. Catalogs (editor & designer): *Attitudes: Photography in the 1970s*, 1979 (Santa Barbara Mus. of Art: Calif.); *The Crowded Vacancy*, 1971, *Manuel Alvarez Bravo*, 1971 (Pasadena Mus. of Modern Art: Calif.); *California Photographers*, 1970 (Univ. of Calif.: Davis).

ADDRESS Santa Barbara Mus of Art, 1130 State St, Santa Barbara, CA 93101.

Olivia Parker PHOTOGRAPHER Born in Boston, Massachusetts, on June 10, 1941, Parker received a BA in Art History from Wellesley College, Massachusetts, in 1963. She worked with Kipton Kumler in 1975.

A member of SPE, the photographer received an Artists Foundation Fellowship in 1978.

Parker uses a view camera to produce still lifes and landscapes. She works in black-and-white contact prints on silver chloride paper, split-toned in selenium, and also in 8 x 10 color and 20 x 24 Polaroid.

PUBLICATIONS Monograph: *Signs of Life*, 1978. Book: *Darkroom Dynamics*, Jim Stone, ed., 1979. Periodicals: *American Photographer*, Feb 1980; *Modern Photography*, Mar 1980; *Popular Photography Annual*, 1980, 1978.

PORTFOLIO *Ephemera*, 1977 (Vision Gall.: Boston).

COLLECTIONS Addison Gall. of Amer. Art, Andover, Mass.; Art Inst. of Chicago; Boston Mus. of Fine Arts; Metro. Mus. of Art, NYC; MOMA, NYC; Phoenix College, Ariz.; Polaroid Cllctn., Boston; Portland Art Mus., Ore.

DEALER Vision Gall. of Photography, 216 Newbury St, Boston, MA 01216.

Gordon (Alexander Buchanan) Parks PHOTOG-RAPHER · WRITER · FILM DIRECTOR · COMPOSER Born November 30, 1912, in Fort Scott, Kansas, Parks was self-taught in photography. His son, Gordon Parks, Jr. (1935–79), was also a film director.

The senior Parks has been a film director since 1968. He was also editorial director of *Essence* magazine (1970–73) and a photographer for *Life* (1948–72). Previously Parks worked as a photographer for Standard Oil Co. of New Jersey (1945–48), the Office of War Information (1944) and the Farm Security Administration (1942–43).

His honors include the Spingarn Medal from the NAACP (1972), the Carr Van Adna Award (1970) and a Rosenwald Foundation fellowship (1942). In 1967, in an international vote conducted by Nikon, he was named the photographer/writer who had done the most to promote understanding among nations of the world.

He has directed the films *Leadbelly* (1975), *The Super Cops* (1974), *Shaft's Big Score* (1972), *Shaft* (1972) and *The Learning Tree* (1968). Parks was the subject of the film *The Weapons of Gordon Parks* (1968).

PUBLICATIONS Monographs: *Flavio*, 1978; *Moments Without Proper Names*, 1975; *Born Black*, 1971; *Gordon Parks: Whispers of Intimate Things*, 1971; *In Love*, 1971; *A Poet and His Camera*, 1968. Books: *A Choice of Weapons*, autobio., 1966; *The Learning Tree*, autobio. novel, 1963; *Camera Portraits: The Techniques and Principles of Documentary Portraiture*, F. Watts, 1948; *Flash Photography*, 1947. Anthology: *The Magic Image*, Cecil Beaton & Gail Buckland, 1975. Periodicals: *Creative Camera*, Apr 1976, Feb 1973, Mar 1971, June 1967, Dec 1966.

ADDRESS 860 United Nations Plaza, Apt 10B, New York, NY 10017.

Martin Parr PHOTOGRAPHER Born in 1952 in Epsom, London, England, Parr studied photography at Manchester Polytechnic, England (1970–73).

A freelance photographer, he taught photography at Oldham College of Art (1974–75) and worked as a photojournalist for Manchester Council for Community Relations (1973–74).

Parr received grants from the Arts Council of Great Britain in 1979, 1976 and 1975 and from Yorkshire Arts Association in 1978.

PUBLICATIONS Periodicals: *Creative Camera*, Feb 1975, June 1974.

COLLECTIONS Philadelphia Mus. of Modern Art, Pa.; Sam Wagstaff Cllctn., N.Y. In England: Arts Council of Great Britain, London; Castle Mus., York; Hebden Bridge Pub. Lib.; Victoria & Albert Mus., London. Bibliothèque Nationale, Paris.

DEALERS Photographer's Gall., 8 Great Newport St, London WC2, England; Neikrug Galls., 224 E 68 St, New York, NY 10021.

ADDRESS Albert St Workshop, 8 Albert St, Hebden Bridge, W Yorkshire, England.

Linda Parry PHOTOGRAPHER Born April 9, 1943, in Burlington, Vermont, Parry received a BA in Art and Graphic Design from Pennsylvania State University in 1968 and an MFA in Photographic Studies from State University of New York in Buffalo in 1974.

Since 1978 she has been employed by Leahy Press in Montpelier, Vermont. Prior to that she was employed by Goddard College in Plainfield, Vermont (1976–78), and the Visual Studies Workshop in Rochester (1971–76).

A member of SPE in 1975–77, Parry was the recipient of a CAPS grant in 1976.

COLLECTIONS IMP/GEH, Rochester; VSW, Rochester.

ADDRESS 13 Cross St, Montpelier, VT 05602.

Rondal Partridge PHOTOGRAPHER Born September 4, 1917, in San Francisco, Partridge studied at California State University in 1938, at the Cornish School of Music, Seattle, in 1947, and with Minor White at the San Francisco Art Institute in 1951. Prior to that he was apprenticed to Dorothea Lange (1934–37) and Ansel Adams (1937–39). He is the son of the noted late photographer Imogen Cunningham and etcher Roi Partridge.

Between 1971 and 1974 Partridge lectured extensively at California State University, Hayward; at the University of California, Santa Barbara; and at the Academy of Arts in San Francisco. A guest lecturer at the San Francisco Art Institute (1964, 1958) as well, since 1965 he has also been involved with the institute's television and film-making departments. Partridge's film-making credits include *Pave It and Paint It Green, They're Your Kids, Wayne Thiebaud* and *The Water Movie*. During World War II Partridge was a photographer with U.S. Navy Intelligence and with Edward Steichen's naval aviation photographic unit. In 1939 he was a photographer for the National Youth Administration, and from 1939 to 1940 was under contract to Black Star Publishing Company in New York City.

A freelance photographer, Partridge specializes in magazine, architectural, advertising and environmental work. He is also the printer for the Imogen Cunningham trust.

ADDRESS 12 Hillcrest Ct, Berkeley, CA 94705.

Bruce Patterson PHOTOGRAPHER Born November 8, 1950, in Dayton, Ohio, Patterson received his BA in 1973 from Haverford College, Haverford, Pennsylvania. In 1974 he studied with Arnold Newman, Stephen Shore and Garry Winogrand at Cooper Union in New York City, then earned his MA in 1976 from the University of New Mexico, Albuquerque.

Since 1976 Patterson has been vice-president of ferrous operations at Patterson Iron and Metal Co., Dayton.

In 1973 he won a Thomas A. Watson Fellowship.

Patterson "takes elements of traditional landscape photography and proceeds to destroy them by ripping, writing, and painting on the pictures." His work ranges from 4 x 5 drugstore prints to 8 x 10 Polacolor photographs to 30 x 40 black-and-white images.

PUBLICATIONS Catalogs: *Altered Landscapes*, 1979 (Florida School of the Arts); *Aesthetics of Graffiti*, 1978 (San Francisco Mus. of Modern Art). Periodicals: *Arts Magazine*, Jan 1978; *Exposure: SPE*, 1977.

COLLECTIONS IMP/GEH, Rochester; Polaroid Corp., Cambridge, Mass.; San Francisco Mus. of Modern Art; Univ. of Colorado, Boulder; Univ. of N. Mex. Art Mus., Albuquerque.

DEALER Robert Freidus Gall., 158 Lafayette St, New York, NY 10013.

Freeman W. Patterson PHOTOGRAPHER · WRITER · TEACHER Born September 25, 1937, in Saint John, New Brunswick, Canada, Patterson earned a BA in 1959 from Acadia University,

Wolfville, Nova Scotia, and a Master of Divinity degree in 1962 from Union Theological Seminary in New York.

A freelance photographer since 1966, Patterson edited *Camera Canada* from 1968 to 1978. Previously he was a photographer in the Still Photography Department, Berkeley Studio, United Church of Canada, Toronto (1965–66), and dean of religious education at Alberta College, Edmonton, Alberta, Canada (1962–65).

Patterson belongs to the National Association for Photographic Art, Colour Photographic Association of Canada (director, 1965–67) and Toronto Guild for Colour Photography (director, 1967–69; vice-president, 1969–70; president, 1970–71). He was named an Honorary Fellow of the Photographic Society of Southern Africa in 1976, received a grant in 1969 from the Province of Ontario Council for the Arts, and earned a National Film Board Gold Medal for Excellence in Photography in 1967. He also won a Rockefeller Fellowship in 1959, a World University Service of Canada Fellowship for summer study in Yugoslavia in 1957, and an I. B. Oakes Four-year Entrance Scholarship to Acadia University in 1955.

PUBLICATIONS Books: *Photography and the Art of Seeing*, 1979; *Photography for the Joy of It*, 1977.

COLLECTION Natl. Film Bd. of Canada, Still Photo. Div., Ottawa, Ontario.

ADDRESS Shamper's Bluff, Clifton Royal, New Brunswick EOG 1NO, Canada.

Marion L. Patterson PHOTOGRAPHER Born April 24, 1933, in San Francisco, Patterson earned a BA at Stanford University in Palo Alto, California (1955), then studied with Minor White, Dorothea Lange and Ansel Adams at the California School of Fine Arts in San Francisco (1956–58). She received an MA in 1970 from San Francisco State University, studying with Jack Welpott and Don Worth. She also studied with Jerry Uelsmann in 1969 at the University of Florida, Gainesville.

Since 1968 Patterson has taught at Foothill College, Los Altos Hills, California, and has done freelance photography since 1958. She served on the staff of *Sunset* magazine from 1961 to 1964, and from 1958 to 1961 worked in the studio of Virginia and Ansel Adams in Yosemite, California.

Patterson belongs to ASMP, SPE, Friends of Photography and Calif. Academy of Sciences.

PUBLICATIONS Anthologies: *Celebrations*,

Minor White & Jonathan Green, eds., 1974; *Being Without Clothes*, Minor White, ed., 1970; *Light⁷*, Minor White, ed., 1968.

COLLECTIONS MIT, Cambridge, Mass.; Oakland Mus., Calif.

ADDRESS POB 842, Menlo Park, CA 94025.

Thomas Edward Patton PHOTOGRAPHER · TEACHER Born May 17, 1954, in Sacramento, California, Patton studied commercial art at Oregon State University, Corvallis (1972–74), then took his BFA in Photography from the San Francisco Art Institute (1976). He received an MA in Photography from the University of New Mexico, Albuquerque, in 1977.

Patton has taught at the University of New Mexico (1977, 1978) and at Millersville State College, Millersville, Pennsylvania (1978).

Working in color and black-and-white, the photographer is primarily concerned with spatial interests. He says his images "all explore relationships between a focal point and its environment, using content devoid of specific social connotations."

PUBLICATIONS Monograph: *The Isolation and Intrusion Series*, 1979. Anthology: *The History of Photography in New Mexico, From the Daguerreotype to the Present*, Van Deren Coke, 1979. Periodicals: *Artweek*, Sept 15, 1979, Feb 10, 1979, Oct 15, 1977; *Spectrum Magazine of the Arts*, spring 1978.

COLLECTIONS Millersville State College, Pa.; San Francisco Mus. of Modern Art; Univ. of N. Mex. Art Mus., Albuquerque.

DEALERS Afterimage Gall., The Quadrangle No 151, 2800 Routh St, Dallas, TX 75201; Equivalents Gall., 1822 Broadway, Seattle, WA 98122.

ADDRESS Box 184, San Mateo, CA 94401.

Milan Pavić PHOTOGRAPHER Pavić was born in Daruvar, Yugoslavia, in 1914. He has been freelancing in Zagreb, Yugoslavia, since 1958. Prior to that he was employed as a photojournalist by the Photodocumentary Agency in Zagreb (1945–58), and spent the years 1935–45 working for various employers.

Pavić is a member of the Association of Plastic Artists–Applied Arts of Croatia, and an honorary member of the Fédération Internationale de l'Art Photographique (FIAP), Bern, Switzerland, and of the Austrian Federation of Photography (OGPh) in Vienna. Pavić has won thirty-eight prizes at international photo salons and fifty-four prizes at photo salons in Yugoslavia, among these: the "Golden Wings" of Technical Culture, Zagreb

(1974), Medal of Labor with a Golden Wreath (1971), the Silver Plaque of National Technics of Yugoslavia (1961) and the Gold Badge of the Photo Club of Zagreb (1956). He is one of the founders and leaders of the so-called Zagrebian photographic school.

Yugoslav critic Josip Depolo writes that Pavić has "achieved his own and new results through his manifold plans according to which he is building a new vision of urban agglomeration. . . . His basic interest keeps turning toward macro- and microstructures within which he sets apart and seeks 'abstract' forms."

PUBLICATIONS Catalog: *Milan Pavić*, intro. by Josip Depolo, 1976 (Mus. of Applied Arts: Belgrade). Periodical: "Exploring with a Camera" & "No Crisis for the Automobile," Review: *Yugoslav Monthly*, no. 12, 1975.

ADDRESS Marulićev Trg 8, 41000 Zagreb, Yugoslavia.

Henry Greenwood Peabody PHOTOGRAPHER · LECTURER · PUBLISHER Born in 1855 in the United States, Peabody died March 27, 1951 in Glendora, California. He graduated from Dartmouth College, Hanover, New Hampshire, in 1876. His daughter, Susie W. Peabody, also became a photographer.

Peabody was employed for a time by the Western Electric Company in Boston, then worked as a professional photographer in Boston (1886–1900). Concurrently he was the official photographer for the Boston and Maine Railroad. In 1900 he moved to California, and for the next twenty-five years traveled extensively, all the while lecturing and taking photographs.

In his earlier years Peabody specialized in marine, landscape and architectural photography. Once he moved to California, though, he concentrated more on landscapes of the Southwest. He was particularly noted for the lantern- and film-slides he produced, as well as movies he took for visual education.

PUBLICATIONS Monographs: *Bryce Canyon National Park*, 1932; *Mexican Scenery and Architecture*, 1932; *Zion National Park*, 1932; *Grand Canyon National Park*, 1930; *The Yellowstone National Park*, 1928; *In the Footsteps of Cortes*, 1918; *Colonial and Revolutionary Landmarks of Boston*, 1913; *The Grand Canyon of Arizona*, 1913; *Round About Yosemite Walls*, 1913; *Seashore of New England*, 1908; *Glimpses of the Grand Canyon*, 1900; *U.S. Squadron of Evolution*, 1891; *The Coast of Maine*, 1889; *Souvenir of the Isles of Shoals*, 1888. Books: *Spanish Colonial Architecture in Mexico*, Sylvester Baxter, 1901; *Representative American War Ships & Yachts*, notes by Geo. A. Stewart, 1898; *Representative American Yachts*, notes by Geo. A. Stewart, 1893; *Forty-six-foot Racing Yachts*, notes by Geo. A. Stewart, 1891.

Irving Penn PHOTOGRAPHER Born June 16, 1917, in Plainfield, New Jersey, Penn studied with Alexey Brodovitch at the Philadelphia Museum School of Industrial Art in the late 1930s.

Penn spent a year painting in Mexico and then returned to New York City to accept a job designing photographic covers for *Vogue* magazine in 1943. He eventually began photographing the covers himself and soon established himself in the area of fashion photography. Since 1943 Penn has been an editorial contributor to *Vogue* and has advertising and industrial clients in the U.S.A. and in Europe.

PUBLICATIONS Monographs: *Worlds in a Small Room*, 1974; *Moments Preserved*, 1960. Books: *Inventive Paris Clothes*, Diana Vreeland, 1977; *Photography Year*, 1975, *Great Photographers*, 1971, *The Studio*, 1971, *The Camera*, 1970, Time-Life Series. Anthologies: *The Photograph Collector's Guide*, Lee D. Witkin & Barbara London, 1979; *The Magic Image*, Cecil Beaton & Gail Buckland, 1975; *Looking At Photographs*, John Szarkowski, ed., 1973.

COLLECTIONS Art Inst. of Chicago; IMP/GEH, Rochester; Metro. Mus. of Art, NYC; MOMA, NYC; Smithsonian Inst., Wash., D.C.

DEALER Marlborough Gall., 40 W 57 St, New York, NY 10019.

ADDRESS Irving Penn Studios, Box 934 F.D.R. Station, New York, NY 10150.

Nissan Perez CURATOR · TEACHER Born in 1946 in Istanbul, Turkey, Perez studied psychology at Hebrew University in Jerusalem and served a one-year internship at the George Eastman House in Rochester.

Since 1977 he has been associate curator of photographs at the Israel Museum in Jerusalem, and in 1976 was the museum's photographer. He teaches history of photography at Bezalel Art School and Hadassah Vocational School in Jerusalem. In 1972 Perez was a freelance photographer in advertising and public relations.

Besides curating the Israel Musuem's collection of photographs and organizing exhibitions, Perez does research in nineteenth-century French photography and photography in the Middle East.

PUBLICATIONS Catalogs: *Auguste Salzmann*, 1980 (Galerie Octant, Paris); *Ben Dov, Photogra-*

pher, 1978 (Israel Mus.). Periodical: "Aimé Rochas, Daguerreotypist," *Image*, June 1979.

ADDRESS Israel Museum, Hakirya, Jerusalem 91000, Israel.

Abigail Perlmutter *PHOTOGRAPHER · REALTOR* Born in Miami, Florida, on May 18, 1950, Perlmutter earned a BA from Boston University and an MFA from the Rochester Institute of Technology, New York, in 1975.

As of this writing she was an instructor at Miami Dade Junior College, South Campus, where she has been since 1974. Before that she taught at the Metropolitan Museum and Art Center in Florida.

A member of CAA and SPE, Perlmutter received an award from the NEA in 1976.

Working in 20 x 24 format with black-and-white infrared images, she has produced a large body of work dealing with the evocation of sensation.

PUBLICATIONS Periodicals: "Invisible Light," *Popular Photography's 35 mm Photography*, spring 1979; *Popular Photography Annual*, 1977; *Creative Camera*, 1976.

COLLECTIONS IMP/GEH, Rochester; Metro. Dade County Public Lib. Systems, Miami, Fla.; Metro. Mus. & Art Cntrs., Miami, Fla.; MOMA, NYC; Murray State Univ., Ky.; NEA, Wash., D.C.; Rochester Inst. of Tech., N.Y.; Univ. of Miami, Lowe Mus., Fla.

ADDRESS 11361-C SW 109th Rd, Miami, FL 33176.

Stephen Perloff *PHOTOGRAPHER · CRITIC · TEACHER* Born April 5, 1948, in Kingston, Pennsylvania, Perloff earned a BA from the University of Pennsylvania, Philadelphia, in 1970 and from 1971 to 1976 did doctoral studies in modern European history at the university.

He has been a photography instructor and lecturer in photography history at Bucks County Community College, Newton, Pennsylvania, since 1977. He also is currently editor of (and a critic for) *Philadelphia Photo Review* (since 1976) and Philadelphia correspondent for *Afterimage: VSW*. He was previously a photography instructor at Cheltenham Art Centre, Cheltenham, Pennsylvania (1977–78); Delaware Valley Institute, Philadelphia (1976–78); and Gallery 3619, Philadelphia (1974–78). From 1971 to 1976 he was a teaching fellow and instructor in modern European history at the University of Pennsylvania.

Perloff has been chairperson of the photography committee of the Philadelphia Art Alliance since 1977.

As of this writing Perloff was doing a documentary on Philadelphia. His main photographic interest is black-and-white studies of architectural details.

COLLECTIONS In Pennsylvania: Free Lib. of Philadelphia; Lehigh Univ., Bethlehem; Philadelphia Mus. of Art.

ADDRESS POB 70, Arcola, PA 19420.

Bill A. Peronneau *PHOTOGRAPHER* Born April 28, 1946, in Philadelphia, Pennsylvania, Peronneau is a self-taught photographer. He names Daryl Johnson and Jerome Shestack as mentors.

Currently a photography instructor at Philadelphia College of Art, he was a photojournalist for the *Philadelphia Daily News* from 1972 to 1975.

Peronneau belongs to the Print Club and the Philadelphia Art Alliance. In 1979 the photographer won a Pennsylvania Council on the Arts grant.

PUBLICATIONS Anthology: *Photography Year 1977*, Time-Life Series, 1977. Periodical: *Afterimage: VSW*, Apr 1979.

COLLECTIONS Brooklyn Mus., N.Y.; Free Lib. of Philadelphia; Lehigh Univ., Bethlehem, Penn.; L/C, Wash., D.C.; Plummer-Miller Cllctn., Philadelphia; Sander Gall., Wash., D.C.

ADDRESS 503 S Melville St, Philadelphia, PA 19143.

Tony Perry *PHOTOGRAPHER · TEACHER · CRITIC* Born October 23, 1944, in Sydney, Australia, Perry studied at Photography Studies College, Melbourne, Australia, under John Cato.

Currently a teacher at Photography Studies College, he has been photography critic for *Age* magazine since 1978 and Australian correspondent for *printletter* since 1979. In 1978 Perry was associate editor of *Light Vision*.

The photographer received a grant from the Visual Arts Board of the Australia Council in 1979.

Working in small format, Perry considers his work an extension of the German photographic style of the 1920s (Sander, Patzsch, Lerski). He creates "a personal response to my immediate environment with a pictorial emphasis on still life and portraiture."

PUBLICATIONS Catalog: *Reflexions*, 1979 (Canon Photo Gall.: Amsterdam). Criticism: *Light Vision*, nos. 3–8, 1978.

COLLECTION Australian Natl. Gall., Philip Morris Cllctn., Canberra.

DEALER Photographers' Gall., 344 Punt Rd, S Yarra, 3141 Victoria, Australia.

ADDRESS 6/123 Alma Rd, E St Kilda, 3182 Victoria, Australia.

Robert S. Persky PUBLISHER · PHOTOGRAPHY DEALER Born January 5, 1930, in Jersey City, New Jersey, Persky received his BA in 1949 from New York University, New York City, and his JD in 1952 from Harvard Law School, Cambridge, Massachusetts.

He is currently the publisher of *The Photograph Collector*, a newsletter on "photography as an art and as an investment," and since 1976 has directed Images—A Gallery of Contemporary Photographic Art. Persky is a member of the Association of International Photography Art Dealers.

BUSINESS The Photograph Collector, 127 E 59 St, New York, NY 10022.

ADDRESS Box 1767, New York, NY 10150.

Otto Perutz CHEMIST · PHOTOGRAPHIC EQUIP-MENT MANUFACTURER Born in 1847 in Teplitz, Bohemia, Perutz died in 1922. He studied at the Technical High School in Dresden and earned a diploma in chemistry in 1868 at Zurich.

Perutz worked for a chemical manufacturing firm in Heufeld, Upper Bavaria (1870–76), becoming plant director in 1872. In 1880 he took over Dr. F. Schnitzer & Co. in Munich, a company that sold chemical products for medicine, pharmacy, chemistry, photography (mainly collodion materials) and other industries. He soon met Johann Baptist Obernetter and began to produce that chemist's silver-bromide gelatin dry plates. Perutz then manufactured the Perutz Vogel-Obernetter Silver Eosin Plate, combining Obernetter's fast orthochromatic plate with Dr. Hermann Vogel's discovery of the color-sensitizing effect of azalin and cosin. Perutz started to produce sensitized films on a celluloid base in 1892, and X-ray plates after Roentgen's discovery in 1895. He sold the business to Dr. Fritz Engelhorn of C. F. Boehringer & Soehne of Mannheim in 1897, but the firm retained the Perutz name.

He received numerous awards for his work, among them the first medal awarded for photographic chemicals from the Bavarian Landesausstellung in 1882.

PUBLICATIONS Books: *Quellendarstellungen zur Geschichte der Fotografie*, Wolfgang Baier, 1964; *Perutz Jubilaeum, 1880–1955*, 1955; Denkschrift, 1955; *Lexikon für Photographie und Reproduktionstechnik*, G. H. Emmerich, 1910.

Anthology: *Photography's Great Inventors*, Louis W. Sipley, 1965. Periodicals: *Bild und Ton*, 1961, 1959; *Jahrbuch für Photographie und Reproduktionstechnik*, 1892, 1891 (Eder); *Photographische Mittheilungen*, 1891, 1890, 1888.

Anders Petersen PHOTOGRAPHER Born in Stockholm, Sweden, in 1944, Petersen attended Christer Strömholm's Photography School (1966–68) and the Swedish Filmschool, Dramatiska Institutet (1973–74), both in Stockholm.

A freelance photographer, he taught at Christer Strömholm's Photography School in 1969–71.

Petersen belongs to PFK (Swedish press organization), SFF (Swedish photographers' organization) and MIRA (Swedish picture agency).

PUBLICATIONS Books: *Bistro d'Hambourg*, Roger Anderson, 1979 (Contrejour: Paris); *Cafe Lehmitz*, Roger Anderson, 1978 (Schirmer/ Mosel: Germany); *A Day at the Circus*, w/Mona Larsson & Stefan Lindberg, 1976 (Cavefors: Sweden); *Gyöna Lund—A Swedish Amusement Park*, Jan Stolpe, 1973 (Aktuell Fotolitteratur: Sweden).

COLLECTIONS Bibliothèque Nationale, Paris; Mus. of Modern Art, Stockholm.

ADDRESS Götgatan 29, 11621 Stockholm, Sweden.

Pierre Petit PHOTOGRAPHER Born 1832 in France, Petit flourished in the 1860s. He was the father of photographer Charles Petit.

Petit first began experimenting with the daguerreotype in 1849, and in 1854 traveled to Rome, where he produced paper photographs. He went into partnership with a M. Trinquart in Paris, eventually becoming sole proprietor of the studio in 1862 and continued operating at the same address throughout the century. In the 1870s he photographed the siege and burning of Paris, and in 1875 he covered the Universal Exposition and the construction of the Statue of Liberty. By 1875 he was appointed official photographer of the Faculté de Médecine, the Lycées et Ecoles de France, the Société des Gens de Lettres, the Chemin de Fer du Nord and, in 1876, to the Société Général du Credit Industriel. In 1880 he received commissions from the Ministère de l'Interieur and the Ministère de l'Instruction Publique.

Experimenting with permanent pigment processes, Petit collaborated with Alphonse Poitevin early in his career to produce carbon prints. He worked with Goupil et Cie, J. Marie and Lemercier at various times for aquatints, photolithographs, carbon prints and woodburytypes. One of the first to utilize electric light properly for portraiture, in 1880 he experimented with Liebert on its use.

Working from wet collodion negatives, Petit produced "magnificent portraits of the men of the day," according to Janet E. Buerger (*Pierre Petit: Photographer*, IMP/GEH). Unlike his contemporaries, Nadar and Adam Salomon, Petit frequently went to his client's home to produce straightforward portraits. "Of all the portraitists of the era, Petit was the most objectively naturalistic. He mastered a straight but controlled and sophisticated vision."

PUBLICATIONS Monographs: *Exposition Coloniale*, 1931 (Paris); *Guide-Recueil de Paris-Brulé, Evènements de Mai 1871*, 1871 (Paris); *Exposition Universelle de 1867: Vue Panoramique du Palais et du Parc*, 1867; *Galerie des Hommes du Jour*, n.d.; *Album des Maires et de la Commission Municipale de Paris*, 1863; *Album de l'Episcopat*, n.d. Books: *Le Biographe*, biography, Jean Prouvaire, 1876; *Simple Conseils*, n.d. Anthology: *Galerie Contemporaine, Littéraire, Artistique*, 1876–84. Catalogs: *Pierre Petit: Photographer*, 1981 (IMP/GEH, Rochester); *Pierre Petit*, Janet E. Buerger, n.d. (IMP/GEH: Rochester).

COLLECTION IMP/GEH, Rochester.

Josef Max Petzval *MATHEMATICIAN · INVENTOR* Born January 6, 1807, in Spišská Belá, Czechoslovakia, Petzval died on September 17, 1891. He received a doctorate from the University of Budapest in 1832, where he studied mathematics.

In 1835 Petzval became professor of higher mathematics at the University of Budapest, and in 1837 he took on a similar position at the University of Vienna, which he occupied until 1884. He published more than ninety papers on mathematics, optics and acoustics as a result of his scientific work.

In 1840 the mathematician calculated the Petzval objective, the first fast photographic lens, with an aperture of 1:3.5 and a focal length of 150mm. This lens reduced exposure time by 90 percent and marked the beginning of the photographic optic. The Voigtländer Company in Vienna manufactured the lens for use in the all-metal daguerreotype camera introduced in 1841, but later Petzval gave production rights to the firm of Dietzler in Vienna and others. He also designed a lens for landscape and reproduction work, which was produced in 1857 under the

name of Orthoskop. Petzval never completed the other optical calculations he started, and at the time of his death he had ceased his studies in photographic optics.

PUBLICATIONS Books: *Quellendarstellungen zur Geschichte der Fotografie*, Wolfgang Baier, 1964; *Focal Encyclopedia of Photography*, 1957, 1956 (Focal Press); *History of Photography*, J. M. Eder, 1945; *Photography Principles & Practice*, 3rd ed., C. B. Neblette, 1939; *Lexikon für Photographie und Reproduktionstechnik*, G. H. Emmerich, 1910. Anthology: *Photography's Great Inventors*, Louis W. Sipley, 1965. Periodicals: *Bild und Ton*, 1957, 1951, 1949; *Jahrbuch für Photographie und Reproduktionstechnik*, 1896 (Eder); *Photographische Correspondenz*, 1891.

ARCHIVE Petzval's Mus., Spišská Belá, Czechoslovakia.

Michael D. Peven *PHOTOGRAPHER · TEACHER* Born April 12, 1949, in Chicago, Peven received a BA in Photo Design from the University of Illinois at Chicago Circle (1971) and an MFA in Photography from the School of the Art Institute of Chicago (1977). His major influences have been Joseph Jachna, Kenneth Josephson, Harold Allen and Joyce Neimanas.

Since 1977 Peven has been assistant professor of art and director of the photography program at University of Arkansas in Fayetteville.

Peven belongs to SPE, VSW, Friends of Photography, Chicago Center for Contemporary Photography and Los Angeles Center for Photographic Studies. He won a Graham Foundation Grant in Architectural Design in Chicago in 1969.

PUBLICATION Monograph: *Snatches*, 1979 (self-pub.).

COLLECTIONS Art Inst. of Chicago; CCP, Tucson; Denver Art Mus., Colo.; Franklin Furnace, NYC; Gall. of Photographic Hist., Little Rock, Ark.; ICP, NYC; IMP/GEH, Rochester; MOMA, NYC; New Orleans Mus. of Art, La.; San Francisco Cameraworks Archive; Univ. of N. Mex. Mus. of Art, Albuquerque; Univ. of Tex., Austin; VSW, Rochester.

REPRESENTATIVE Visual Studies Workshop, 31 Prince St, Rochester, NY 14607.

BUSINESS Art Dept, 116 Fine Arts Bldg, Univ. of Arkansas, Fayetteville, AR 72701.

John Pfahl *PHOTOGRAPHER* Born February 17, 1939, in New York City, Pfahl attended Syracuse University in New York, where he received a BFA in 1961 and an MA in Communications in 1968.

He has been with Rochester Institute of Technology in New York since 1968 and is associate professor at its School of Photographic Arts and Science.

Pfahl is a member of SPE. He received CAPS grants in 1979 and 1975, and an NEA Photographer's Fellowship in 1977.

The artist works in color, producing 8 x 10 and 16 x 20 dye transfer prints.

PUBLICATIONS Anthology: *Time-Life Photography Year*, 1979. Periodical: *Afterimage: VSW*, Anthony Bannon, Feb 1979.

COLLECTIONS Albright-Knox Art Gall., Buffalo, N.Y.; Art Inst. of Chicago; Chase Manhattan Bank, N.Y.; Contemporary Art Mus., Houston; Denver Art Mus., Colo.; IMP/GEH, Rochester; Mus. of Fine Arts, Boston; Princeton Univ., N.J.; San Francisco Mus. of Modern Art; Smith Coll. Mus. of Art, Northampton, Mass.; Univ. of Arizona, Tucson; Univ. of Mass, Amherst; Univ. of N. Mex. Art Mus., Albuquerque. Australian National Gall., Canberra; Natl Gall. of Canada, Ottawa, Ontario.

DEALER Robert Freidus Gall., 158 Lafayette St, New York, NY 10013.

Marcuse Lucile Pfeifer GALLERY OWNER · DIRECTOR Born in Little Rock, Arkansas, on November 4, 1936, Pfeifer earned a BA from Sarah Lawrence College in Bronxville, New York, in 1958.

She has owned her own photographic gallery since 1976. Prior to that she worked for Robert Schoelkopf, running the photography section of his gallery from 1970 to 1976. Pfeifer was assistant to the director of the Art Center of the New School for Social Research in New York City (1966–70). From 1960 to 1963 she co-owned and ran the Greenhouse Gallery in Little Rock, Arkansas, which featured painting, sculpture and crafts. She worked for a year (1958) with the Museum of Modern Art in New York City.

Pfeifer is the first elected treasurer of the Association of International Photography Art Dealers (1979) and in 1980 was made president of that organization.

PUBLICATIONS Catalog: *The Male Nude*, 1978 (Pfeifer Gall.: NYC). Periodical: "The Photographs and Letters of Lewis Carroll to His Child Friends," *Book Forum*, 4:3, 1979.

ADDRESS Marcuse Pfeifer Gall., 825 Madison Ave, New York, NY 10021.

Joe Gwin Phillips PHOTOGRAPHER · TEACHER Born September 23, 1935, in McKenzie, Tennessee, Phillips earned a BA in 1957 and an MA in 1963 from Memphis State University, Tennessee. He studied with Jerry Uelsmann, Todd Walker and Douglas Prince.

As of this writing he was teaching photography at the University of Arkansas in Little Rock, also Phillips taught at the University of Central Arkansas (1976–78) and at Birmingham University School in Alabama (1969–73). He was with the United States Defense Department from 1964 to 1969.

A member of SPE since 1970, Phillips is treasurer for the South Central Region. He has been a member of Friends of Photography since 1969. The artist received an NEA/Florida Endowment for the Arts grant in 1977. He produces surreal, manipulated images in black-and-white silver prints, and he also prints with applied color.

PUBLICATION Anthology: *Self Portrayal*, 1978.

COLLECTIONS Bethel Coll., McKenzie, Tenn.; Birmingham Mus. of Art, Ala.; Ferrum Coll., Ferrum, Va.

ADDRESS 1224 Winfield St, Conway, AR 72032.

Nata Piaskowski PHOTOGRAPHER · LIBRARIAN Born in Lodz, Poland, January 5, 1912, Piaskowski emigrated to the United States in 1942. She received an honorary scholarship from the San Francisco Art Institute in 1949. Having studied with Minor White from 1948 to 1950, she considers him her major influence.

Piaskowski was photo librarian and historian of the Bechtel Corporation in San Francisco from 1954 to 1975, and took up the work again in 1979 on a part-time basis. She worked as a public school teacher in her native Poland in 1935.

The artist works in various formats. Shooting black-and-white prints since 1948, she has used color extensively since 1968, looking at "fragments of nature rather than vistas, and portraits. My photography is straightforward, non-manipulative, single exposures. I use color as light, as form, and for the expression of an emotion."

PUBLICATIONS Periodicals: *Light*[7], 14:1, 1968, *Perceptions*, 2:4, 1954 (Aperture: Millerton, N.Y.).

COLLECTIONS Mass. Inst. of Tech., Cambridge; Oakland Mus. of Art, Calif.

DEALER Allrich Gall., 2 Embarcadero Ctr, San Francisco, CA 94111.

ADDRESS 2143 Mason St, San Francisco, CA 94133.

Fred Picker PHOTOGRAPHER Born February 28, 1927, Picker attended the University of Vermont in Burlington. He is president of Zone VI Studios, Inc., which designs and manufactures specialized photo equipment, and director of Zone VI Workshops. He also publishes the *Zone VI Newsletter.*

Picker is a member of Friends of Photography and was on their advisory council in 1976. He is also an adviser to Polaroid Corporation and a panelist on the Vermont Council on the Arts.

Working in large format, Picker emphasizes natural subjects, landscapes and portraits. He is concerned with producing fine silver prints.

PUBLICATIONS Monograph: *Fred Picker,* 1979. Books: *The Fine Print,* 1974; *Rapa Nui,* w/Thor Heyerdahl, 1973; *The Zone VI Workshop,* 1972.

PORTFOLIO *The Iceland Portfolio,* 1976.

DEALER Prakapas Gall., 19 E 71 St, New York, NY 10021.

ADDRESS Rt 2, Putney, VT 05346.

Dale Woods Pickering *PHOTOGRAPHER* Born February 25, 1948, in San Francisco, Pickering earned a BFA from the University of British Columbia, Vancouver, in 1976.

A self-employed photographer, he is co-originator of the Blue Mule Gallery in Vancouver, British Columbia.

Pickering has belonged to "13 Cameras" since 1978. He received the Governor General Award for Artist of the Year in Canada in 1977 and won a 1975 grant from the Canadian government.

PUBLICATIONS Periodicals: *Arts Canada,* Aug/Sept 1979; *Photo Communique,* Mar/Apr 1979; *Arts West,* Jan/Feb 1979.

COLLECTION Natl. Film Board of Canada, Stills Div., Ottawa, Ontario.

ADDRESS 382 A Powell St, Vancouver, British Columbia, Canada.

Donato A. Pietrodangelo *PHOTOGRAPHER · MAGAZINE EDITOR · TEACHER* Born February 17, 1950, in New York City, Pietrodangelo received a BA and MA in Communications from Florida State University in Tallahassee (1972 and 1973). He studied photography since childhood under the direction of his photographer father, and in 1978 did an independent study at IMP/GEH, Rochester, on the history and criticism of color.

A freelance photographer since 1972, Pietrodangelo has also been teaching at the LeMoyne Art Foundation in Tallahassee since 1978, and edits the State of Florida *HRS Access Magazine* in the same city.

Pietrodangelo is a member of SPE, Friends of Photography and the LeMoyne Art Foundation, serving on the board of directors of the last as artist representative. He received an NEA/Florida Fine Arts Council Artists Fellowship in 1978.

He works exclusively in color. "My approach is straight, nonmanipulative medium- and large-format work. I have been researching and writing on the history and criticism of color photography."

PUBLICATIONS Periodicals: "Four Photographers," *Modern Photography,* July 1977; "Aesthetics of the Color Image," *Creative Camera,* Nov 1976.

PORTFOLIO *The Maine Series,* 1979 (self-pub.).

COLLECTION State Capitol Bldg., Tallahassee, Fla.

REPRESENTATIVE Aerugo Publishers, POB 5026, Tampa, FL 33675.

ADDRESS 1110 Albritton Dr, Tallahassee, FL 32301.

Oliver Gregory Pike *PHOTOGRAPHER · NATURALIST · FILM MAKER* Born October 1, 1877, in Enfield, Middlesex, England, Pike died October 17, 1963, in Luton, England. A self-taught photographer, he was educated at Enfield Grammar School.

Pike began taking photographs in 1890 and writing nature articles in 1899. A popular lecturer, he visited over 300 towns between 1898 and 1948. He served in the Royal Flying Corps during World War I (1917–19) and was an officer of the Home Guard during World War II.

A Fellow of RPS, Pike was on its council from 1924 to 1948.

As a film maker Pike produced more than thirty documentaries on British mammals, birds, pond life and other nature subjects, completing his first one in 1907.

He was considered one of the pioneers of nature photography, along with the Kearton brothers and Reginald B. Lodge. His chief subject matter was British flowers and birds' nests and eggs.

PUBLICATIONS Books: *Wild Animals in Britain,* 1950 (Macmillan: London); *Nature and My Cine Camera,* 1946; *Nature and Camera,* 1943; *The Nightingale,* 1932 (Arrowsmith: London); *Nature Photography,* 1931; *Rambles in Britain's Birdland,* 1930, *The Great Winding Road,* 1928 (Jenkins: London); *Birdland,* 1923? (RTS: London); *Bird Biographies and Other Bird Sketches,* w/Arthur Brook, 1915; *The Scouts Book of Birds,* 1913; *Farther Afield in Birdland,* 1911 (Stokes); *Wild Nature Wooed and Won,* 1911; *Through Birdland Byways with Pen and Camera,* 1909?; *Behind the Veil in Bird-land,* 1908, *Adventures in Bird-land,* 1907, both w/E. Richmond Paton

(Religious Tract Soc.: London); *Birdland Pictures*, 1906 (Crofton: London); *Home Life in Bird-land*, 1905 (RTS: London); *With the Birds on Hillside, Rock and Dale*, 1903; *Hillside, Rock and Dale*, 1902 (Hutchinson: London); *Woodland, Field and Shore*, 1901 (RTS: London); *In Bird-land with Field-glass and Camera*, 1900.

Ave Earl Pildas   PHOTOGRAPHER · DESIGNER
Born September 16, 1939, in Cincinnati, Ohio, Pildas studied at the University of Cincinnati School of Architecture (1957–59), and studied design at the Art Academy of Cincinnati from 1959 to 1963. He took graduate studies in design at Kunstgewerbeschule in Basel, Switzerland (1964–67).

A freelance photographer and designer since 1971, Pildas has taught at the California Institute of the Arts, Valencia, since 1978. He was an instructor at Art Center College of Design, Pasadena, California, in 1977–79, and a lecturer in the School of Architecture and Urban Planning at the University of California at Los Angeles in 1976. He was an art director for Capitol Records in 1971 and an assistant professor at Philadelphia College of Art, Pennsylvania, in 1969–71.

Pildas belongs to ASMP.

His work is self-described as "sequential, serial, conceptual." He is also interested in the "animal as icon" and in recording endangered architecture.

PUBLICATIONS Monograph: *Art Deco Los Angeles*, 1977. Periodicals: *Photo*, Sept 1978; *Picture*, Aug 1976; *Zoom*, Mar 1976 (Paris); *Creative Camera*, Aug 1975; *Fotografia Italiana*, Mar 1975; *Du*, Sept 1969, Dec 1975.

PORTFOLIO *Bijou*, 1975 (self-pub.).

COLLECTIONS Cincinnati Mus. of Art, Ohio; Los Angeles County Mus. of Art; Milwaukee Mus. of Art, Wisc.; New Orleans Mus. of Art, La.

DEALER Janus Gall., 8000 Melrose, Los Angeles, CA 90046.

ADDRESS 1231 Ozeta Terr, Los Angeles, CA 90069.

Sheila Pinkel   PHOTOGRAPHER · TEACHER
Born August 21, 1941, in Newport News, Virginia, Pinkel earned an MFA in 1977 from the University of California at Los Angeles, and considers Robert Heinecken to be her mentor.

She presently teaches at UCLA Extension, where she has been since 1975.

Pinkel has been a member of the Los Angeles Center for Photographic Studies since 1977 and serves as its vice-president and lecture-series coordinator. Awarded an NEA grant to individual artists in 1979, she also received a Mural Award from Park La Brea Towers (Los Angeles) in 1976.

Of her work she says; "I use the vehicles of light and light-sensitive paper to extend my understanding of the physical world and myself. In my sculpted paper lightworks I dimensionalize photographic paper, expose the sculpture to light and develop it. The result is a time/space paradox."

PUBLICATIONS Anthologies: *Time-Life Annual*, 1980; *Innovative Printmaking*, Thelma Newman, 1977. Catalogs: *Attitudes: Photography in the 1970's*, 1979 (Santa Barbara Museum of Art: Calif.); *Photographic Directions*, 1979 (Security Pacific Bank: Los Angeles).

PORTFOLIO *Silver See* (group), 1977 (Los Angeles Ctr. for Photographic Studies).

COLLECTIONS Fluor Corp., Irvine, Calif; Glendale Savings & Loan, Glendale, Calif.; Los Angeles County Mus. of Art; MOMA, NYC; Security Pacific Bank Cllctn., Los Angeles; UCLA, Frederick S. Wight Gall.; Univ. of N. Mex. Art Mus., Albuquerque.

ADDRESS 126 Hart St, Santa Monica, CA 90405.

Vesta Paige Pinnell, Jr.   PHOTOGRAPHER · TEACHER · COLLECTOR · DEALER Born October 11, 1944, in Macon, Georgia, Pinnell earned a BFA in 1967 from the University of Florida, Gainesville, and an MFA in 1971 from the University of New Mexico, Albuquerque. He names Jerry Uelsmann and Van Deren Coke as his mentors.

Self-employed as a photography dealer since 1978, Pinnell taught photography at the University of Florida in 1976–78 and was a curator at the Museum of New Mexico in Santa Fe from 1972 to 1976. He also directed the Center of the Eye Gallery in Aspen, Colorado, in 1975–76, and taught photography at Lane Community College, Eugene, Oregon (1971–72), and at University of New Mexico (1969–71).

Pinnell belongs to SPE and the Rising Sun Society.

He creates "serial overlapping images attempting to invoke a surrealism through expanding the time and space of a single photographic frame."

PUBLICATIONS Monograph: *Midnight Suite*, 1975. Catalog: *Van Deren Coke Cllctn.*, 1970 (Univ. of N. Mex.: Albuquerque).

PORTFOLIO *New Mexico Portfolio* (self-pub.).

COLLECTIONS Emory Univ. Cllctn., Atlanta, Ga.; High Mus. of Art, Atlanta, Ga.; Mus. of N. Mex, Santa Fe; Univ. of Fla. Gall., Gainesville;

Univ. of N. Mex. Gall., Albuquerque; Univ. of Ore., Eugene.

DEALER Andrew Smith, POB 1812, Santa Fe, NM 87501.

ADDRESS POB 2892, Santa Fe, NM 87501.

Andrew Pitcairn-Knowles *PHOTOJOURNALIST*
Born of Scottish parents on March 13, 1871, in Rotterdam, The Netherlands, Pitcairn-Knowles died in Hastings, England, in 1956. He attended the Sandhurst Academy as a cadet but gave up the idea of an army career and continued his education at Heidelberg University in Germany.

Working as a freelance photographer and journalist, Pitcairn-Knowles traveled widely in Europe, living at various times in Rotterdam, Brussels and Berlin. In 1895 he founded the illustrated magazine *Sport in Bild* in Berlin. During the next ten years he contributed to a number of magazines in America, France, Belgium, Holland, Italy and England, including Britain's *Wide World*. Taking up residence in England some time after 1906, he devoted the rest of his life to the study and practice of naturopathy, a healing method that had saved him from death. In Hastings he established a hydropathic spa, the Riposo.

Assisted by his son, Pitcairn-Knowles recorded the habits and customs of various European peoples from Holland, Flanders, France, Corsica, etc., penetrating out-of-the-way corners and little-traveled areas, investigating life-styles on an intimate basis.

ARCHIVE Pen and Picture, Riposo, St. Helen's Park, Hastings, England.

Matti A. Pitkänen *PHOTOGRAPHER* Born June 13, 1930, in Helsinki, Finland, Pitkänen studied at the Helsinki Lyseum.

A freelance studio photographer since 1956, he previously was a photographer for Finlandia Kuva Oy (1951–55) and a laboratory worker for Kuvanauha Oy (1946–50).

Pitkänen has belonged to Helsinki Camera Society since 1949, to RPS since 1959, to the Fédération Internationale d l'Art Photographique, and to the State Camera Art Commission since 1977. He received the Helsinki Prize in 1975, a three-year artist grant from Finland in 1974, a grant of the City of Helsinki in 1973, state awards for photographic art in 1971 and 1967, a grant from the Culture Foundation of Finland in 1966 and a PSA 5-Star Exhibitor award in 1963.

Pitkänen made the television programs "The Sea," in 1980, "The Fairy-tale Forest," "Autumn in Lapland," and "The Swamp" in 1979, and "Finland's National Parks," "The Lake" and "The Flower Meadow" in 1978.

PUBLICATIONS Books: *A Photographic Diary*, 1980; *Helsinki*, 1979; *The Winter Landscape*, 1979; *The Finnish Lake*, 1978; *Virrat*, 1977; *Finland's Beautiful Nature*, 1977; *Finnish Pictures*, 1975; *The Finnish Landscape*, 1973; *The Giant Pike-Perch*, 1972; *The Samoyed*, 1970; *Iltakirjamia*, 1968; *Land of the Midnight Sun*, 1966.

ADDRESS Topeliuksenkatu 15 A 16, 00250 Helsinki 25, Finland.

Terence Randolph Pitts *CURATOR · LIBRARIAN*
Born on February 5, 1950, in St. Louis, Missouri, Pitts earned a BA in English and an MLS in Library Science (1969–74) at the University of Illinois, Urbana.

Pitts has been curator and librarian at the Center for Creative Photography in Tucson since 1976. In 1979, with Sally Stein, he curated the exhibit "Photographs in Color by Harry Callahan" and in 1978, with Rene Verdugo, Pitts curated "Contemporary Photographers in Mexico."

A member of SPE, he received a museum travel grant through the Smithsonian Institution and the National Museum Act in 1979.

PUBLICATIONS Books: *George Fiske: Yosemite Photographer*, 1980; *Frederick Evans and George Bernard Shaw*, Dec 1979 (CCP: Tucson).

ADDRESS 843 E University, Tucson, AZ 85719.

Sylvia Plachy *PHOTOGRAPHER* Born May 24, 1943, in Budapest, Hungary, Plachy earned a BFA in 1965 from Pratt Institute, Brooklyn, New York.

She has been a staff photographer for the *Village Voice*, a weekly newspaper in New York City, since 1978, and was a photographer and picture researcher for that publication from 1974 to 1977 and for *New York* magazine in 1973. She has also worked as a freelance photographer since 1965.

Plachy won a Guggenheim Fellowship in 1977 and was first-prize winner of the Pratt Alumni Photo Contest in 1971.

The photojournalist's work frequently illustrates feature articles in the *Village Voice*.

COLLECTION MOMA, NYC.

ADDRESS 84–28 85 Rd, Woodhaven, NY 11421.

Joseph Antoine Ferdinand Plateau *MATHE-MATICIAN · PHYSICIST* Born in Brussels, Belgium, in 1801, Plateau died in 1883. He earned a Doctorate in Physical and Mathematical Sciences from the University of Liège in 1829.

Plateau's doctoral thesis, "Certain Properties of the Impressions Produced by Light upon the Organ of Sight," laid the basis for modern motion pictures, and he continued his researches as a teacher at the Royal College of Liège. Before 1829, Plateau discovered the principle of the anorthoscope, in which a distorted image on a revolving disc appears undistorted when viewed through slits in another revolving disc. In 1849 he attempted to project motion pictures with an instrument based on this principle.

Plateau discovered the laws of persistence of vision (the afterimage resulting from staring at certain objects), but during his experiments he gazed directly at the sun, which led to his total blindness by 1843. In 1833 he introduced the phenakistoscope, based on the persistence-of-vision principle, which consisted of a disc with a series of pictures drawn around the edges. As the disc was spun, the pictures viewed through the slits seemed to be in motion. (Independently at the same time, Simon Stampfer of Vienna invented a similar device, the stroboscope.)

"Plateau's Problem" was the name given his formulation of a "problem on minimal surface." He was particularly interested in physiological optics and molecular forces. One of the physicist's most famous nonphotographic experiments elucidated the theory of Kant and Laplace concerning the origin of the earth.

PUBLICATIONS Books: *Encyclopedia voor Fotografie en Cinematografie*, Elsevier, 1958; *Der Weg des Films*, F. von Zglinicki, 1956; *Histoire du Cinématographie*, G. Michel Coissac, 1925; *Cassell's Cyclopedia of Photography*, 1911, repr. 1973; *Living Pictures*, Henry V. Hopwood, 1899; *La Photographie Animée*, Eugene Trutat, 1899. Anthology: *Photography's Great Inventors*, Louis W. Sipley, 1965. Periodical: *Bild und Ton*, 1958.

Bernard Plossu PHOTOGRAPHER [See plate 129] Born February 26, 1945, in Da Lat, South Vietnam, Plossu studied philosophy in Paris, and was influenced by Renaissance and contemporary Italian painting as well as by the music of India.

A freelance photographer, he works mainly for European travel magazines.

Working in both black-and-white and color, he uses a 35mm camera with a 50mm lens and Tri-X film. He uses color for magazine illustration; his color prints for the last thirteen years have been made exclusively by the Fresson family in France. Plossu does straight, unmanipulated photography.

PUBLICATIONS Monograph: *Bernard Plossu 1965–1979*, Carlos Serrano, 1979 (Nueva Lente: Madrid, Spain). Books: *Egypt*, Carole Naggar, 1979 (Photoeil: Paris); *Le Voyage Mexicain*, Denis Roche, 1979 (Contrejour: Paris); *Go West*, Marc Saporta, 1976 (Du Chene: Paris); *Surbanalism*, Sergio Leone, 1972 (Du Chene: Paris). Periodicals: *Camera*, Dec 1975, July 1974, Mar 1972; *Creative Camera*, Apr 1973.

COLLECTIONS ICP, Tucson; IMP/GEH, Rochester. Australian Natl. Gall., Canberra; Royal Museums of Belgium; Stedelijk Mus., Amsterdam, The Netherlands. In France: Beaubourg Mus., Paris; Bibliothèque Nationale, Paris; Cantini Mus., Marseilles; Chateau d'Eau Photography Mus., Toulouse; Musée Réattu, Arles; Natl. Funds for Contemporary Arts, Paris; Nicéphore Niepce Mus., Chalon-sur-Saône; Paris Townhouse.

ADDRESS PO Box 5451, Santa Fe, NM 87502.

David Plowden PHOTOGRAPHER · WRITER · TEACHER Born October 9, 1932, in Boston, Massachusetts, Plowden earned a BA from Yale University, New Haven, Connecticut, in 1955. He studied with Minor White in 1959–60 and was a close friend of Walker Evans from 1960 to 1975.

He has been an associate professor at the Institute of Design, Illinois Institute of Technology, Chicago, since 1978.

Plowden belongs to ASMP and the Authors Guild.

The photographer was the recipient of the Wilson Hicks Award in 1977, a photographic grant from the Department of Transportation and the Smithsonian Institution in 1975, the Benjamin Barondess Award in 1971, a research grant from the Smithsonian Institution in 1970 and a Guggenheim Fellowship in 1968, among others.

Using both black-and-white and color, Plowden does documentary work concerned with the environment and rural and urban landscapes.

PUBLICATIONS Books (text & photos): *Tugboat*, 1976; *Commonplace*, 1974; *Bridges: The Spans of North America*, 1974; *Floor of the Sky: The Great Plains*, 1972; *The Hand of Man on America*, 1971; *Lincoln and His America*, 1970; *Farewell to Steam*, 1966. Books (photographs only): *Wayne County: The Aesthetic Heritage of a Rural Area*, 1979; *The Iron Road*, 1978; *Desert and Plain: The Mountains and the River*, 1975; *Cape May to Montauk*, 1973; *Nantucket*, 1970. Anthology: *The Photograph Collector's Guide*, Lee D. Witkin & Barbara London, 1979. Periodicals: *Modern Photography*, Jan 1977; *Photography Annual*, 1976; *Popular Photography*, June 1973, June 1971; *U.S. Camera Annual*, 1964, 1963.

COLLECTIONS MOMA, NYC; Smithsonian Inst., Wash., D.C.

DEALERS Witkin Gall., 41 E 57 St, New York, NY 10022; Gilbert Gall., 218 E Ontario St, Chicago, IL 60611.

ADDRESS 797 Walden Rd, Winnetka, IL 60093.

John Plumbe, Jr. *PHOTOGRAPHER · BUSINESSMAN* Born in July 1809, in Wales, Plumbe died May 30, 1857, in Dubuque, Iowa.

He came to the United States in 1821 with his family, and after attending school and becoming a naturalized citizen he worked as an assistant on a railroad survey across the Allegheny Mountains in Pennsylvania (1831–32). In 1832 Plumbe was appointed superintendent and manager of the railroad that stretched between Richmond, Virginia, and Roanoke, North Carolina. He migrated to the Wisconsin Territory in 1836 and became involved in land speculation, later owning a successful store in the town of Sinipee (1839) and becoming its postmaster. He moved to Washington, D.C., in 1839 and established what may have been "the first permanent daguerreotype gallery in Washington, D.C.," according to *Northlight Journal*.

Plumbe introduced the chain-studio concept. By 1845 he had a main office in New York and branches in Boston, Saratoga Springs, Philadelphia, Baltimore, Washington, Alexandria, Petersburg, Louisville, Cincinnati, St. Louis, Dubuque and Newport. He even claimed to have branches in Liverpool and Paris. Financial reversals caused him to sell his photographic interests and head out for the gold rush of 1849 in California, but he moved back to Dubuque in 1856, and the next year took his life.

Throughout Plumbe's diverse career he was dedicated to promoting his idea of a transcontinental railroad. Having conceived it as early as 1836, he formally proposed the idea to Congress on March 24, 1838, and was granted a $2,000 appropriation for a survey. His plan failed, however, and he never received credit for being the first person to conceive of a railroad to the Pacific.

PUBLICATIONS Books: *Photography and the American Scene*, Robert Taft, 1938; *Sketches of Iowa and Wisconsin*, 1839 (self-pub.). Pamphlet: *A Faithful Translation of the Papers Respecting the Grant Made by Governor Alvarado to Mr. J. A. Sutter*, 1850 (Sacramento, Calif.). Periodicals: "Photographer with a Vision," Cliff Krainik,

Northlight Journal, no. 1, 1974 (Photographic Historical Society); *The Plumbeian*, 1:1, Jan 1, 1847.

COLLECTIONS Mr. & Mrs. Cliff Krainik Cllctn.; N.Y. Pub. Lib. Rare Book Rm., NYC.

Alphonse Louis Poitevin *CHEMIST · ENGINEER · INVENTOR* Poitevin was born and died in Conflan, France (1819–82). He studied chemistry and mechanics at Ecole Centrale in Paris.

Poitevin became a chemical engineer in 1843, and in 1848 worked as a chemist for the Mines Nationales de l'Est. For several years he worked independently, then returned to engineering in 1869 at a silver mine at Kefoun-Theboul in Africa.

The chemist became interested in photography after the announcement of Daguerre's and Talbot's discoveries and began experimenting with daguerreotype plates. His experiments led to a method of photochemical engraving with silver or gold on metal plates, and his discovery of the action of light on bichromated gelatin laid the basis for photolithography, the carbon process and collotypy. His various patents, held in France and England, included those for collotype and carbon printing (1855–56) and for a direct positive process (1860, 1863).

Poitevin was awarded the Prix du Duc de Luynes in 1862 for his contributions to the carbon process and photolithography and in that year was named a Chevalier in the French Legion of Honor. He received the Prix Marquis d'Argenteuil from the Société d'Encouragement des Arts as well as their silver medal, and they helped him several times financially. In 1878 Poitevin received a gold medal for his work at the International Exposition of Paris.

PUBLICATIONS Books: *Quellendarstellungen zur Geschichte der Fotografie*, Wolfgang Baier, 1964; *Brevets d'Invention Français 1791–1902*, 1958; *March of Photography*, Erich Stenger, 1958; *Cassell's Cyclopedia of Photography*, 1911, repr. 1973; *Lexikon für Photographie und Reproduktionstechnik*, G. H. Emmerich, 1910; *Traité des impressions photographiques*, w/notes by Léon Vidal, 2nd ed., 1883 (Paris); *Notice sur la vie et les travaux de A. Poitevin*, M. A. Davanne, 1882; *A History & Handbook of Photography*, Gaston Tissandier, 1876; *Traité de l'Impression Photographiques sans Sel d'Argent*, 1862 (Paris). Anthologies: *Early Photographs and Early Photographers*, Oliver Mathews, 1973; *Photography's Great Inventors*, Louis W. Sipley, 1965. Periodicals: "Alphonse Louis Poitevin and His Work," J. Waterhouse, *Penrose's Annual*, no. 17,

485

1911–12; *Photographic Times*, 1894; *British Journal of Photography*, 1882; *Bulletin de la Société Française de Photographie*, 1882; *Photographische Correspondenz*, 1882.

ARCHIVE 171 rue St-Jacques, Paris 5, France.

Jacqueline Poitier PHOTOGRAPHER Born October 14, 1937, in Brighton, England, Poitier is a self-taught freelance photographer.

She earned a first-place award from San Francisco Women Artists in 1975 and a second place in the "E Pluribus Unum" Competition, Floating Foundation of Photography, New York City.

She does mainly dance photography in black-and-white.

PUBLICATIONS Anthologies: *Women See Men*, 1977; *Celebrations*, Minor White, 1975. Catalog: *Dance and Media*, 1978 (San Francisco Mus. of Modern Art).

ADDRESS 1239 21 Ave, San Francisco, CA 94122.

Richard Polak PHOTOGRAPHER Born in 1870 in Rotterdam, Polak died in 1957. He studied briefly with Karl Schenker in Berlin.

Polak began photographing in 1912, and exhibited his work in London in 1913. When he moved to Switzerland (1915) he gave up the craft.

In 1915 Polak was a member of the London Salon of Photography.

During his brief career as a photographer he concentrated on tableaus that imitated seventeenth-century Dutch paintings, producing platinum prints.

PUBLICATONS Book: *Photographs from Life in Old Dutch Costume*, intro. by F. J. Mortimer, 1923. Anthologies: *The Magic Image*, Cecil Beaton & Gail Buckland, 1975; *Early Photographs & Early Photographers*, Oliver Mathews, 1973.

COLLECTION RPS, London.

Kenneth Poli EDITOR · PHOTOJOURNALIST Born June 8, 1921, in Brooklyn, New York, Poli was educated at Goddard College in Plainfield, Vermont (1940), and studied photography with Joseph Lootens (1941).

Since 1970 he has been editor of *Popular Photography*, and also contributes to World Book Encyclopedia. Previously he was employed as editor of *Leica Photography* magazine (1954–65), and from 1946 to 1949 he worked as a writer and photographer for the public information office of the American National Red Cross at their New York area office.

Poli is a member of MENSA, the Society of Photographic Scientists and Engineers, Circle of Confusion, Photographic Administrators, Inc., the American Civil Liberties Union and NAACP.

ADDRESS 1 Park Ave, New York, NY 10016.

Prentice H. Polk PHOTOGRAPHER Born in Bessemer, Alabama, on November 25, 1898, Polk studied under C. M. Battey at Alabama's Tuskegee Institute. In 1922 he enrolled in a photography correspondence course in Chicago. After completing the course he served an apprenticeship with Fred Jensen (1924–26) of Chicago, who was his greatest influence.

Since 1939 Polk has owned and operated Polk's Studio, an arm of the Tuskegee Institute, for which he is official photographer. In 1938 he was freelancing in Atlanta, Georgia. From 1928 to 1938 he was an instructor of photography at Tuskegee; in 1933 he was appointed head of the department. From 1923 to 1927 he freelanced in Chicago.

Polk won six awards on three occasions at the Southeastern Photographers Convention (1931, 1930, 1928), and four awards at the National Photographers Association Convention in Chicago (1929). As a special honor he was designated Colonel of the State of Georgia by Governor George Busbee.

Polk's images "display an eerie tension between precise formality and X-ray vision," writes Kay Leigh Hagan. "The result is a compelling photographic style which stuns the viewer with an unexpected intimacy. The subjects of Polk's camera are looking at *you*" (*Art Voices South*, Nov/Dec 1980).

PUBLICATIONS Monograph: *P. H. Polk*, 1980. Periodicals: *Art Voices South*, Nov 1980; *Black Photographers Annual*, vol. 2.

DEALER Nexus Gall., 608 Forrest Rd NE, Atlanta, GA 30312.

ADDRESS POB 81, Tuskegee Inst., AL 36088.

Peter Pollack HISTORIAN · MUSEUM CURATOR · PHOTOGRAPHER Pollack was born March 21, 1909, in Wing, North Dakota, and died May 13, 1978. He studied at the University of Illinois in Chicago and at the Institute of Design in Chicago with Moholy-Nagy.

From 1962 until the time of his death Pollack was employed as an honorary curator of photography at the Worcester Art Museum in Massachusetts. He also was a lecturer on photography at the University of Southern Florida and the Fort Lauderdale Museum in 1970–71, as well as a visiting scholar in photography at Pratt Institute in

Brooklyn, New York, in 1969. Prior to that he had been director of the American Federation of Arts from 1962 to 1965, director of the World of Ancient Gold Exhibition at the New York World's Fair in 1965, an art consultant for the Guggenheim Museum in New York City, 1959–63, a curator of photography at the Art Institute of Chicago, 1945–57, and director of the Southside Community Art Center in Chicago, 1939–42.

PUBLICATIONS Books: *Understanding Primitive Art, Sula's Zoo*, text only, 1972; *Encyclopaedia Britannica*, contributor, 1968; *The Picture History of Photography*, text only, 1958, rev. 1970, abridged 1977.

COLLECTIONS CCP, Tucson; Worcester Mus. of Art, Mass.

ARCHIVE Mrs. Peter Pollack, 141 E 56 St, New York, NY 10022.

Carlo Ponti PHOTOGRAPHER Born in Venice, Italy, Carlo Ponti flourished between the years 1858 and 1875. He invented and constructed a device called the megalethoscope, which gained him the Grand Prize at the London Exposition of 1862.

A specialist in architectural photography, especially of the Piazza San Marco, Ponti was one of the few Italians who succeeded in competing with foreigners.

PUBLICATIONS Books: *Un Siècle de Photographie de Niepce à Man Ray*, 1965 (Paris); *Venezia*, 1862? (Venice); *Souvenir Photographique de Venise*, n.d. (Venice). Anthology: *Early Photographs and Early Photographers*, Oliver Mathews, 1973. Catalogs: *Vedute di Venezia 1866*, w/Carlo Naya, 1967; *Un Secolo di Fotografia dalla Collesione Gernsheim*, 1957 (Milan).

COLLECTIONS IMP/GEH, Rochester; Univ. of Texas, Humanities Resource Ctr., Gernsheim Cllctn., Austin.

Herbert George Ponting PHOTOGRAPHER · EXPLORER · INVENTOR Born in 1871, Ponting died on February 7, 1935, in London. A self-taught photographer, he was educated in England at Carlisle and Preston grammar schools and at Leyland.

Originally a rancher in California, Ponting joined a West Coast gold rush and became manager of a mine in 1898. In 1901 he was commissioned by *Leslie's Weekly* to do a tour of the Far East, recording his impressions with camera and pen. He photographed the conflict between Japan and Russia in 1903 for the *American Press*, and went out with the First Japanese Army in Manchuria for *Harper's Weekly*. After the war he traveled widely in the Far East, Spain and Switzerland, and in 1909 Captain Scott appointed Ponting the official photographer for Scott's expedition to the South Pole. In 1913 the photographer gave his famous lecture "With Captain Scott in the Antarctic" over 1,000 times in Philharmonic Hall. In 1918 he joined the Spitsbergen Expedition. During his Antarctic explorations Ponting also took motion pictures, which resulted in the documentary *93 deg. South* (1933).

Ponting was a Fellow of the Royal Geographical Society (RGS, London) and an honorary life member of the American National Geographic Society. He was awarded many medals during his lifetime, among them a Japanese medal for his service as a photojournalist, the first prize for telephotography in a world competition of 1900, a King George V Polar Medal and an RGS medal for Antarctic exploration.

His inventions included a portable projector called the Kinatome (1922) and the Variable Controllable Distortograph for photographic caricature (1933).

Captain Scott wrote in his journal: "Of the many admirable points about Ponting's work, the most notable are his eye for a picture and the mastery he has acquired of ice subjects. The composition of his pictures is extraordinarily good. He seems to know by instinct the exact value of foreground and middle distance, and of the introduction of 'life,' while with more technical skill he emphasizes the subtle shadows of the snow and reproduces its wonderfully transparent texture. He is an artist in love with his work."

PUBLICATIONS Books: *90 deg. South*, 1933 (London); *The Great White South*, 1921, repr. w/ intro by Lady Scott, 1950 (Duckworth: London); *With Captain Scott in the Antarctic . . .*, 1914? (London); *In Lotus-land Japan*, 1910, repr. 1922; *Japanese Studies*, 1906 (Ogawa: Yokohama); *Fuji San*, 1905 (Ogawa: Tokyo); *Another World*, n.d., repr. 1975.

COLLECTION British Mus., London.

Mungo Ponton INVENTOR Born in 1801 in Balgreen, Scotland, Ponton died in 1880 in Clifton, near Bristol, England.

Ponton was employed as the secretary of the Bank of Scotland in 1839, the year he announced his discovery of the action of light on potassium bichromate when coated on paper (the silver-salts process used in photoengraving). Ponton disclosed the process on May 29, 1839, to the Society of Arts for Scotland, an organization of which he was then vice-president. In 1849 he invented a process of photographically recording variation of temperature in a thermometer, but at the time of his death he had been disassociated from photographic activities for many years.

Ponton's discovery, coming in the same year that Daguerre's and Talbot's seminal work was publicized, was of great importance in the later development of permanent photographic and photochemical printing processes.

PUBLICATIONS Books: *March of Photography*, Erich Stenger, 1958; *The History of Photography*, Helmut & Alison Gernsheim, 1955; *Photo-Engraving*, A. J. Bull, 1934; *Cassell's Cyclopedia of Photography*, 1911, repr. 1973; *Chemistry of Photography*, W. Jerome Harrison, 1892; *Evolution of Photography*, John Werge, 1890. Anthology: *Photography's Great Inventors*, Louis W. Sipley, 1965. Periodicals: *British Journal of Photography*, 1885; *Photographic News*, 1880; *Edinburgh New Philosophical Journal*, July 1839.

Colin MacGarvey Poole   PHOTOGRAPHER
Born August 19, 1954, in Lagos, Nigeria, Poole attended Medway College of Design (1973–74) and Newport College of Art in England (1975); at the latter he studied under David Hurn.

A freelance since 1977, he worked for Camera Press Agency in London in 1976–77.

Poole won a Nikon Scholarship Photographic Award in 1976 to document crafts of the English countryside.

He primarily does documentary portraiture.

PUBLICATIONS Book: *New British Image*, 1977 (Arts Council of Great Britain: London). Periodical: *Creative Camera International Year Book*, 1978.

REPRESENTATIVE L. A. Poole, 12 Malt Kiln Rd, Plumley, nr Knutsford, Cheshire, England.

ADDRESS 11 Sunnyside, Childs Hill, London NW2 2QP, England.

Thomas David Porett   PHOTOGRAPHER ·
TEACHER · MUSICIAN   Born October 17, 1942, Porett received a BS from the University of Wisconsin in Madison in 1964 and an MS in Photography from the Institute of Design of Illinois Institute of Technology, Chicago, in 1966. He also studied synthesizer techniques and electronic music composition at Philadelphia Musical Academy, and attended an intensive workshop in holography at Lake Forest College in Illinois. He considers Aaron Siskind his mentor.

Since 1966 Porett has taught at the Philadelphia College of Art. Previously he taught at

Moore College of Art in Philadelphia from 1967 to 1970 and at Quetico Centre in Ontario, Canada, in spring of 1970 and summer of 1969.

Porett was the recipient of a Materials Grant from Polaroid Corporation in 1975 and a Guggenheim Fellowship in 1972. He was also the creator of a film entitled *Jesusday* (1969), commissioned by WCAU-TV and CBS in Philadelphia.

PUBLICATIONS Books: *Photography: A Handbook of History, Materials and Processes*, Charles Swedlund, 1974; *Frontiers of Photography*, 1972; *The Art of Photography*, 1971; *Vision and Expression*, Nathan Lyons, ed., 1969. Anthology: *Light*[7], Minor White, ed., 1968. Periodical: *Afterimage: VSW*, fall 1976.

ADDRESS 673 Aubrey Ave, Ardmore, PA 19003.

Allan Porter   EDITOR · AUTHOR · PHOTOGRAPHER · DESIGNER   Born April 29, 1934, in Philadelphia, Pennsylvania, Porter studied at Temple University in Philadelphia (1952–54) and at the Barnes Foundation (1953–55) before earning his BFA in 1957 from Philadelphia College of Art. His teachers included Franz Kline, Alexey Brodovitch and Sol Mednick.

Porter has been editor-in-chief of *Camera* since 1965, and previously was an art director and editor at *Seventeen* and *Holiday* magazines (1957–61). He served as design director for the American National Exhibition in Moscow in 1959, and was a tapestry designer from 1958 to 1963.

Porter belongs to DGPh and GDL. He won DGPh's Kulturpreis in 1979 and GDL's David Octavius Hill Medal in 1972.

In addition to his writing on photography, he has written a novel, poetry and plays and published two childrens' books: *A Child's Garden of Photography*, 1979 (C. J. Bucher) and *Sagittarius and the Mermaid*, 1969 (self-pub.).

As a critic, author and editor, Porter's expertise is in the field of nineteenth- and twentieth-century photography.

ADDRESS Weinmarkt 5, 6002 Lucerne, Switzerland.

Eliot Furness Porter   PHOTOGRAPHER · WRITER
[See plate 136] Born December 6, 1901, in Winnetka, Illinois, Porter received a BS from Harvard Engineering School, Cambridge, Massachusetts (1924), and an MD from Harvard Medical School (1929).

A self-employed photographer since 1944, he previously worked in the Radiation Laboratory at MIT, Cambridge (1942–44), as a tutor at Harvard

(1933–39), and as an instructor at Harvard Medical School (1930–33).

Porter is a life member of the American Ornithologist Union, Wilson Ornithological Society and Cooper Ornithological Society. He is also a life member of the Sierra Club, and served on its board of directors in 1965–71.

The photographer was named an Honorary Doctor of Fine Arts at Colby College, Waterville, Maine, in 1969 and became a Fellow of the American Academy of Arts and Sciences in 1971. He received a Department of the Interior Conservation Service Award in 1967 and a Country Life magazine International Exhibition of Wildlife Photography Silver Plaque in 1950.

Porter is a wildlife photographer, with an emphasis on birds and the natural landscape of geological and botanical subjects. He also has done extensive archaeological and architectural photography in Greece, Egypt and Mexico.

PUBLICATIONS Books: *Intimate Landscapes,* 1979; *Antarctica,* 1978; *Birds of North America,* 1975; *Appalachian Wilderness,* w/Edward Abbey, 1973; *The Tree Where Man Was Born,* w/ Peter Matthiessen, 1972; *Down the Colorado,* 1969; *Baja California,* 1969; *Galapagos—Flow of Wildness,* 1968; *Summer Island: Penobscot Country,* 1968; *The Place No One Knew, Glen Canyon on the Colorado,* 1963; *In Wildness Is the Preservation of the World,* 1962. Anthologies: *The Photograph Collector's Guide,* Lee D. Witkin & Barbara London, 1979; *The Magic Image,* Cecil Beaton & Gail Buckland, 1975.

PORTFOLIOS *Intimate Landscapes,* 1979 (Daniel Wolf Press, Inc.: NYC); *Birds in Flight,* 1979 (Bell Editions); *Portfolio II, Iceland,* 1975 (self-pub.); *The Seasons,* 1964 (Sierra Club).

COLLECTIONS Art Inst. of Chicago, Ill.; IMP/GEH, Rochester; Metro. Mus. of Art, NYC; MOMA, NYC; New Orleans Mus. of Art, La.; Worcester Art Mus., Mass.

DEALER Daniel Wolf Gall., 30 W 57 St, New York, NY 10019.

ADDRESS Rt 4, Box 33, Santa Fe, NM 87501.

Tim Porter PHOTOGRAPHER Born April 27, 1946, in Washington, D.C., Porter, as of this writing, was working on a Canada Council Arts Grant project (since 1978). He was previously a freelance.

A member of SPE, the photographer won arts grants from the Canada Council in 1972/73 and 1978/80 and short-term grants from the council in 1971 and 1977.

Porter's main photographic interest is Japan and Asia.

PUBLICATIONS Periodicals: *Camera Mainichi,* no. 2, 1979; *Asahi Camera,* no. 2, 1980, no. 11, 1978; *Grain Magazine,* no. 10, 1978.

COLLECTIONS Canada Council Art Bank, Ottawa, Ontario; Natl. Film Board of Canada, Ottawa, Ontario.

ADDRESS c/o Foreign Correspondents' Club of Japan, No. 7–1, Yurakucho, 1-chome Chiyoda-ku Tokyo, Japan.

W. A. Poucher PHOTOGRAPHER · CHEMIST · MOUNTAINEER Poucher was born November 22, 1891, in Horncastle, Lincolnshire, England.

He served as a captain in the Royal Army Medical Corps for five years during World War I, then was chief perfumer to Yardley for thirty years.

Poucher was elected to RPS in 1941 and was awarded their honorary fellowship in 1975. Known as "the father of British perfumery," Poucher won the gold medal of the Society of Cosmetic Chemists in 1954, and his three-volume textbook *Perfumes, Cosmetics and Soaps* is the industry's bible.

Poucher is also a prolific landscape photographer, having amassed some 20,000 black-and-white and 5,000 color photographs. His views of mountain scenery—in the Rockies, Alps, Dolomites, Snowdonia, Lake and Peak districts, Scottish Highlands, Cairngorms, Coolins and Isle of Skye—have been popular images in books and magazines for forty years.

PUBLICATIONS Books: *Scotland in Colour,* 1980; *The Peak and Pennines,* 1966, 3rd ed., 1979; *The Scottish Peaks,* 1965, 5th ed., 1979 (Constable, London); *Climbing with a Camera,* 1963; *The Welsh Peaks,* 1963, 7th ed., 1979, *The Lakeland Peaks,* 1960, 7th ed., 1979 (Constable: London); *West Country Journey,* 1957; *Journey into Ireland,* 1953; *Escape to the Hills,* 1952; *The Magic of the Dolomites,* 1951; *The Magic of Skye,* 1949; *The Surrey Hills,* 1949; *Wanderings in Wales,* 1949; *Over Lakeland Fells,* 1948; *A Camera in the Cairngorms,* 1947; *The Backbone of England,* 1946; *Peak Panorama,* 1946; *Lakeland Journey,* 1945; *Scotland Through the Lens,* 1943; *Snowdonia Through the Lens,* 1941; *Lakeland Through the Lens,* 1940.

ADDRESS c/o Constable & Co., Ltd, 10 Orange St, London WC2 H7EG, England.

Tage Poulsen PHOTOGRAPHER · JOURNALIST · LIGHTING DIRECTOR Born May 26, 1935, in Hjortshøj, Denmark, Poulsen studied photography with J. Juncker-Jensen in 1968 and was influenced by Peter Kinch and H. B. J. Cramer since 1965. He also studied with Stephen Ryan of the

Chicago Institute of Design at the Institute of Visual Communication, Academy of Art, Copenhagen (1971–72).

Currently a lighting director for TV-Denmark, he has also been co-editor of the Danish magazines *Foto* and *Smalfilm* since 1970, and regularly contributes photography criticism to both. Poulsen belongs to Danish Camera Pictorialists (since 1969) and AFIAP, an international photographers' federation (since 1972).

PUBLICATIONS Periodicals: *Hrymfaxe*, Dec 1978; *British Journal of Photography Annual*, 1977, 1976; *Foto*, Apr 1976, May 1974 (Poland).

COLLECTION Royal Lib., Copenhagen.

ADDRESS Katholmvej 1 b, DK 2720 Copenhagen-Vanløse, Denmark.

Mark Power PHOTOGRAPHER·TEACHER Born in 1937 in Washington, D.C., Power attended Bowdoin College in Brunswick, Maine (1956–57), Art Center College of Design in Pasadena, California (1960–61), and American University, Washington, D.C. (1961).

Power has taught at Corcoran School of Art in Washington, D.C., since 1971, first as instructor (1971–74) and then as assistant professor. He owned the Icon Gallery in Washington, D.C., in 1968–70, and freelanced there in 1968–69. He also freelanced in New York City (1967–68) and in Cambridge, Massachusetts (1963–67).

The photographer won Corcoran Workshop Program grants in 1973, 1972 and 1971.

Most recently Power has used dyes to hand-color his black-and-white images.

PUBLICATIONS Books: *Photography: Source & Resource*, Steven Lewis, James McQuaid & David Tait, 1973; *When Gloucester Was Gloucester*, Peter Anastas, 1973; *Glooskap's Children*, Peter Anastas, 1972. Periodicals: *Art in America*, Jan/Feb 1978; "Washington, D.C.: Man Ray, A Multi-Faceted Master," text only, May/June 1977, "Washington, D.C.: Capitol Photographs at the Corcoran," text only, Feb 1977, *Afterimage: VSW*; *Camera*, Jan 1978, Oct 1974, Sept 1969, June 1967; *Creative Camera*, May 1970.

COLLECTIONS Corcoran Gall. of Art, Wash., D.C.; Iowa Mus., Iowa City; L/C, Wash., D.C.; New Orleans Mus. of Art, La.; Norton Simon Mus. of Art, Pasadena, Calif.; Smithsonian Inst., Wash., D.C.; Sam Wagstaff Cllctn., NYC.

ADDRESS Corcoran School of Art, 17th & New York Ave NW, Washington, DC 20006.

Romualdas Požerskis PHOTOGRAPHER Born in Vilnius, Lithuanian SSR, on July 7, 1951, Pož-

erskis studied at the Politechnical Institute in Kaunas, Lithuanian SSR, from 1969 to 1975, where he specialized in power engineering. Then he joined the Faculty of Philosophy of the University of Marxism-Leninism during 1975–77.

Since 1975 Požerskis has worked with the Photography Art Society, Lithuania, in the Kaunas Department. He also works as a professional photographer. In 1977 he won the Prize of Spectators and Critics at the Festival of Young Photographers in Arles, France. In 1975 he won a Gold Medal at Poland's Foto Expo.

His work consists of reportage "closely connected to the traditions of Lithuanian national culture." In his images, Požerskis attempts to "combine the tragic and the humorous."

PUBLICATIONS Anthologies: *Photojahrbuch*, 1979, 1977 (VEB Fotokinoverlag: Leipzig, East Germany); *Photography Yearbook*, 1977 (Fountain Press: London). Periodicals: *Bolgarsko Foto*, July 1979 Apr 1978; *Fotografie*, Feb 1978, Mar 1977; *Foto*, Dec 1977 (Budapest, Hungary); *Sovietskoye Foto*, Jan 1977; *Foto*, July 1976 (Warsaw, Poland); *Valokuva*, no. 2, 1976.

COLLECTIONS Funds of Exhibitions of Arles Festival, France; Musée Française de la Photographie, Bièvres, France; Photography Mus., Šiauliai, Lithuanian SSR.

REPRESENTATIVE Photography Art Society, Pionieriu 8, 232600 Vilnius, Lithuanian SSR, USSR.

ADDRESS R. Armijos 47-5, Kaunas, Lithuanian SSR, USSR.

Craig Pozzi PHOTOGRAPHER Born November 18, 1942, in Pittsburgh, Pennsylvania, Pozzi earned an AB in 1964 from Brown University, Providence, Rhode Island, and a Bachelor of Professional Arts (BPA) in 1972 from Brooks Institute of Photography, Santa Barbara, California. He received an MFA in 1976 from California Institute of the Arts, Valencia.

Since 1976 he has been an instructor in the Graduate School of Architecture, University of Utah, Salt Lake City. Since 1978 he has also been an associate instructor in the school's Art Department.

Pozzi belongs to SPE and Friends of Photography. He received several grants in 1978: from the Utah Arts Council and the Utah Endowment for the Humanities to document the Salt Lake Valley, and from the University of Utah for his personal work.

The photographer's 16mm film *Shackles and Chains* won the Prix de la Chanson Filmée at the

Cannes International Amateur Film Festival in 1971.

Pozzi does primarily documentary work in small format. He also works in large format and SX-70. His major essays have been "Living in the Salt Lake Valley," "Living in Utah" and "The Leisure Landscape."

COLLECTIONS Brooks Inst., Santa Barbara, Calif.; Salt Lake Art Ctr., Salt Lake City, Utah; Utah State Cllctn. of Fine Arts, Salt Lake City.

REPRESENTATIVE Nancy Sullivan, 1883 S 20th E, Salt Lake City, UT 84108.

ADDRESS 584 Wall St, Salt Lake City, UT 84103.

Eugene Joseph Prakapas GALLERY OWNER · BOOK PUBLISHER Born July 29, 1932, in Lowell, Massachusetts, Prakapas earned his BA from Yale University, New Haven, Connecticut, in 1953 and his MA from Balliol College, Oxford University, England, in 1959.

Since 1976 Prakapas has been director of Prakapas Gallery in New York City. From 1973 to 1975 he was co-director of Carus Gallery in New York City, and from 1960 to 1971 he was vice-president and editor in chief of Trident Press and Pocket Books, divisions of Simon & Schuster, Inc., in New York City.

Prakapas has received numerous grants and awards, including a Fulbright grant to attend Oxford and a two-year fellowship to study Ikebana in Japan during the early 1970s.

ADDRESS Prakapas Gall., 19 E 71 St, New York, NY 10021.

Emanuele Prandi PHOTOGRAPHER Born in Rome, Italy, on December 8, 1948, Prandi earned a diploma in agricultural studies in Rome in 1966, then studied sociology at the Aichorn Institute in Germany in 1967–68. In 1969–70 he studied camerawork and film editing under Roberto Perpignani in Rome.

Since 1979 Prandi has concentrated on commercial freelancing and his personal work. Prior to that he was a news photographer for the DFP agency of Milan, a photographer for the State Bureaus of Fine Arts of Piedmont and Latium (1972–78) and an editor and cameraman for television documentaries and films (1969–72).

Among his accomplishments may be included videotaping for a socioanthropological study of Italian migrant workers in Switzerland and Germany (1979).

Prandi works in color, his main subject matter being architecture, landscapes and people.

PUBLICATIONS Books (in Italy): *Enciclopedia dell'Arte Italiana*, 1979 (Einaudi: Turin); *Federico II e l'Arte Italiana del '200*, 1979 (Congedo: Galatina); *La Basilica e il Convento di San Francesco in Assisi*, 1978 (Bretschneider: Rome); *Rieti e il suo territoria*, 1977 (C. Bestetti: Milan); *Roma e l'etá Carolingia*, 1977 (Multigrafica: Rome); *San Gemini e Carsulae*, 1977 (C. Bestetti: Milan).

COLLECTIONS Kodak Italiana, Milan, Italy; Polaroid, Amsterdam.

ADDRESS Via Nicola Fabrizi, II/B, 00153 Rome, Italy.

Charles Robert Pratsch PHOTOGRAPHER Born November 17, 1857, in Lancaster, Pennsylvania, Pratsch died in Aberdeen, Washington, in 1937. He learned photography ca. 1886 from an Aberdeen photographer named Tolman.

Pratsch moved from Pennsylvania to Iowa, then left Iowa in 1852 to homestead in Grays Harbor country (Washington). He built his own studio building in Aberdeen in 1890, and in later years was caretaker of the Laidlow Island duck preserve.

Pratsch was especially noted for his photographs of Grays Harbor, including portraits of local townspeople and various views of the area and its architecture.

PUBLICATION Book: *Grays Harbor, 1885–1913*, Robert A. Weinstein, 1978.

COLLECTION Wash. State Univ. Libs., Hist. Photograph Cllctns., Pullman.

Charles Pratt PHOTOGRAPHER Born April 13, 1926, in New York, Pratt died there in May 1976. He received a BA in 1948 from Yale University, New Haven, Connecticut, studying photography with Lisette Model.

From 1949 to 1956 Pratt was employed as stage manager for ten Broadway shows. During his freelance photographic career he contributed to many magazines, including *Natural History, Audubon, 35mm* and *American Heritage*, as well as appearing in several Time-Life anthologies. His photographs have been widely exhibited in the United States.

For a time the photographer served as director of the Council for a Livable World, headquartered in Washington, D.C. With L. Hururtze, Pratt made the film *Here at the Water's Edge* in 1962.

PUBLICATIONS Monographs: *The Garden and the Wilderness*, 1980; *Here on the Island*, 1974. Books: *Rocky Coast*, Rachel Carson, 1971; *A Sense of Wonder*, Rachel Carson, 1965; *At Night*,

Pratt

Phillip Ressner, 1965. Anthologies: *North East Coast*, 1972, *Photographing Children*, 1971, Time-Life Books; *Woman*, 1968. Periodicals: *Photography Annual*, 1969, 1968; *U.S. Camera Annual*, 1967; *Life*, Dec 1967; "Critic's Choice," David Vestal, *Popular Photography*, Dec 1966; *Infinity: ASMP*, July 1965; *Fortune*, May 1963.

COLLECTIONS   Metro. Mus. of Art, NYC; MOMA, NYC.

ARCHIVE   Julie Pratt, 242 E 68 St, New York, NY 10021.

Conrad J. Pressma   PHOTOGRAPHER   Born February 17, 1944, Pressma earned a BA in Art from Antioch College, Yellow Springs, Ohio (1967), and an MFA in Photography from Indiana University, Bloomington (1970), where he studied with Henry Holmes Smith. He also undertook special graduate studies in creative photography with Minor White at Massachusetts Institute of Technology, Cambridge, in 1967–68.

Since 1978 he has owned C. J. Pressma Productions, specializing in audiovisual presentations, and from 1970 to 1978 he was founding director of the Center for Photographic Studies, Inc., in Louisville, Kentucky. Pressma has also taught at the Advanced Workshop of Center of the Eye in Aspen, Colorado (summer 1973), at Indiana University (1969–70) and at MIT Art Association (1967–68).

The photographer belongs to SPE, IMP/GEH, and VSW and is a trustee of the Preservation Alliance of Louisville. He won an NEA Photographer's Fellowship in 1978.

PUBLICATIONS   Book: *Photography: Source and Resource*, Steven Lewis, James McQuaid & David Tait, 1973. Periodical: *Popular Photography Annual*, 1973.

COLLECTIONS   Cincinnati Art Mus., Ohio; New Orleans Mus. of Art, La.; Norton Simon Mus. of Art, Pasadena, Calif.; Rochester Inst. of Tech., N.Y.; Sam Houston State Univ., Huntsville, Tex.; J. B. Speed Art Mus. Louisville, Ky.; Univ. of Louisville Photographic Archives, Ky. Natl. Gall. of Canada, Ottawa, Ontario.

ADDRESS   432 W Ormsby, Louisville, KY 40203.

Pier Paolo Preti   CRITIC · JOURNALIST   Born July 16, 1940, in Modena, Italy, Preti earned a Doctorate in Modern Languages and Foreign Literatures from L. Bocconi University in Milan, Italy.

Since 1979 Preti has been communications manager of Ercole Marelli & Company. He also is editorial consultant and contributor to the

magazines *Il Fotografo* (Milan) and *Professional Camera* (Munich), and adviser to the publishing houses Selezione d'Immagini (Milan), Mahnert-Lueg (Munich) and RotoVision SA (Geneva).

Preti has been a member of the Ordine dei Giornalisti (Italian journalists' association) since 1970, and currently belongs to GUS (press office journalists' union).

He publishes his poems yearly (since 1966) in *La Trivèla* annual in Modena.

PUBLICATIONS   Books (text only): *Neue Wege der Photographie*, 1980 (Mahnert-Lueg); *Fotografare con David Lees*, 1978 (F. 11i Fabbri); *Modena, una città*, w/F. Fontana, 1971. Catalog: *The Photo-Novel*, 1978 (Photokina).

ADDRESS   Piazzale Lugano 9, 20158 Milan, Italy.

Paul Pretsch   PRINTER · INVENTOR   Born in Vienna in 1808, Pretsch died in 1873. He was trained as a book printer.

Pretsch went to work for the Imperial State Printing Office in Vienna in 1842, where he was promoted to manager. During his employment he applied himself to developing the process of photogalvanography, by which metal printing plates are produced from relief images obtained from exposed coatings of such substances as glue, potassium bichromate and gelatin. He edited the weekly *Der Erzähler* in 1845–46, and was sent to Paris in 1850 and to London to direct the Austrian printing exhibit at London's Crystal Palace Exhibition in 1851.

Pretsch left Vienna in 1854. He obtained patents for the processes he had developed and, in London, formed the Photo-Galvano-Graphic Company to print pictures; its first publication appeared in 1856. Commercially unsuccessful in his venture, he switched to stone lithography, and suffered from the harassment of Fox Talbot, who claimed patent infringement. Pretsch returned to Vienna in 1863 and was reinstated at the Imperial State Printing Office. Because of ill health he made no further advances with his photogalvanography.

PUBLICATIONS   Books: *Geschichte des Tiefdruckes*, vol. 1, Otto M. Lilien, 1959; *Photomechanical Halftone*, L. W. Sipley, 1958; *Evolution of Rotogravure*, J. S. Mertle, 1957; *Photographic Art Treasures*, 6 vols., 1956; *History of Photography*, Helmut & Alison Gernsheim, 1955; *Horgan's Halftone & Photomechanical Processes*, Stephen H. Horgan, 1913; *Cassell's Cyclopedia of Photography*, 1911, repr. 1973; *Lexikon für Photographie und Reproduktionstechnik*, G. H. Emmerich, 1910; *Die Photo-Galvanographie*, Ottomar Volkmer, 1894 (Halle); *Festschrift zur Enthüllungsfeier der Gedenktafel für Paul Pretsch*, G. Fritz, 1888 (Vienna). Anthologies: *Early Photographs & Early Photographers*, Oliver Mathews, 1973; *Photography's Great Inventors*, Louis W. Sipley, 1965. Periodicals: *Bild und Ton*, 1952; "Paul Pretsch and Photo-galvanography," J. Waterhouse, *Penrose's Annual*, vol. 16, 1910–11; *American Annual of Photography and Photographic Times Almanac*, 1899; *Photographische Correspondenz*, 1888, article by Joseph Leopold, 1874; article, Nov 15, 1880, "Photography Subject to the Press," 5:109, 1859, "Photo-galvanography or Nature's Engraving," 6:1, 1859, "Photogalvanography, or Engraving by Light and Electricity," 3:58, 1854, *Photographic Journal*.

Giuseppe Primoli   PHOTOGRAPHER   Born in 1851 or 1852 in Italy, Primoli died there in 1927. He was a direct descendant of Napoleon. His brother Luigi, who died in 1925, was also a photographer for a brief time.

Primoli was a count and was able to travel widely throughout Europe, mixing with the aristocracy, whom he photographed avidly.

For the most part Count Primoli used a casual snapshot approach with his Kinégraphe camera, although he sometimes took formal portraits. According to A. D. Coleman, in *The New York Times:* "Primoli can perhaps be best described as a cross between Eugene Atget and J. H. Lartigue. Like Atget, he was an insatiable recorder of all aspects of the life around him. . . . With Lartigue, Primoli shares a delightful lack of self-consciousness about his work, a frequent family-album atmosphere, and a celebrity-hound nature whose innocence is its saving grace." Coleman says of the 12,575 surviving prints taken between 1888 and 1905: "Their interest is not just their value as historic documents, but the grace and sensitivity with which Primoli saw and recorded the people and events of his time, and the spontaneity and freshness of his seeing."

PUBLICATIONS Book: *Un fotografo fin de siecle*, 1968 (Giulio Einaudi: Italy). Anthology: *The Magic Image*, Cecil Beaton & Gail Buckland, 1975. Periodical: Review, A. D. Coleman, *New York Times*, II:26, Aug 15, 1971.

ARCHIVE Fondazione Primoli, Rome.

Douglas Prince   PHOTOGRAPHER   Born in Des Moines, Iowa, in 1943, Prince studied at the University of Iowa, Iowa City, earning a BA in 1965 and an MFA in 1968. From 1968 to 1976 he was assistant professor of photography at the University of Florida, Gainesville, and since 1976 has been an assistant professor at the Rhode Island School of Design in Providence.

Prince received an NEA grant in 1977 and won Le Prix de la Ville d'Avignon, France, in 1972.

Prince works with sheets of positive transparent film sandwiched in plexiglass to create a three-dimensional photo sculpture. He also works in silver prints.

PUBLICATIONS Book: *Light & Lens*, Donald Werner & Dennis Longwell, 1973. Anthologies: *The Photograph Collector's Guide*, Lee D. Witkin & Barbara London, 1979; *Darkroom 2*, Jain Kelly, ed., 1978; *Mirrors and Windows*, John Szarkowski, ed., 1978. Catalogs: *Aspects of American Photography*, 1976 (Univ. of Missouri: St. Louis); *New Images in Photography*, 1974 (Univ. of Miami, Lowe Art Mus.: Fla.); *New Art from Photosensitized Materials*, Neal Spitzer, 1973 (Vassar College Art Gall: Poughkeepsie, N.Y.); *Young Photographers*, Van Deren Coke, 1968 (Univ. of New Mexico Art Mus.: Albuquerque). Periodicals: *Modern Photography*, July 1970; *Artscanada*, June 1970; "Photographs as Sculpture and Prints," Peter C. Bunnell, *Art in America*, Sept 1969; *Camera International*, Nov 1965.

COLLECTIONS Exchange Natl. Bank, Chicago; IMP/GEH, Rochester; Kansas City Art Inst., Mo.; Mus. of Fine Arts, St. Petersburg, Fla.; MOMA, NYC; Philadelphia Art Mus., Pa.; Princeton Univ. Art Mus., N.J.; Univ. of New Mexico Art Mus., Albuquerque; Worcester Art Mus., Mass.

DEALER Witkin Gall., 41 E. 57 St, New York, NY 10022.

Barry Pringle   PHOTOGRAPHER · GRAPHIC DESIGNER   Born March 17, 1943, in South Africa, Pringle studied at Guildford School of Art (1966) and Royal College of Art (1970), both in England. He is self-employed.

PUBLICATIONS Periodicals: *Foto*, May 1979 (Copenhagen), May 1973 (Copenhagen); *Foto Magazin*, Oct 1978 (Munich); *Camera*, Sept 1974, Sept 1973, Apr 1971; *The Image*, Sept 1973.

COLLECTIONS IMP/GEH, Rochester; L/C, Wash., D.C. Bibliothèque Nationale, Paris; Leiden Print Room, Leiden, The Netherlands; Kongelig Bibliotek, Copenhagen; Kunstindustri Muséet, Copenhagen; Moderna Muséet, Stockholm; Musée Cantini, Marseilles, France; Musée D'Ixelles, Brussels, Belgium; Musée Réattu, Arles, France; Stadtlisches Landesbestelle, Hamburg, Germany; Stedelijk Mus., Amsterdam, The Netherlands; Sterckshof Mus., Antwerp, Belgium; Victoria & Albert Mus., London.

Teglgaardsstraede 12 A, Mellemhus over Gaarden, 1452 Copenhagen K, Denmark.

Bonnie Allen Printz   *PHOTOGRAPHER* ·
TEACHER · PAINTER   Born in Luray, Virginia, in 1946, Printz earned a BFA from Virginia Commonwealth University, Richmond, in 1968, and an MA from Hunter College, New York City, in 1970, both as a painting major. She considers the major influences on her work to be the art community environment in New York City and her employment at the Museum of Modern Art there from 1968 to 1970. She is married to Daniel A. Gorski, painter and sculptor.

As of this writing she was employed at the Maryland Institute's College of Art in Baltimore, she has also taught at various times since 1971 at York College, York, Pennsylvania, and Harford Community College in Bel Air, Maryland.

In 1979 Printz received a Professional Fellowship in Photography from the Virginia Museum of Fine Arts in Richmond.

She works in Polaroid SX-70 and creates one-of-a-kind Polaroid images. She also produces prints in large-scale color and small black-and-white. Her subjects are autobiographical.

COLLECTIONS   Corcoran Gall. of Art, Wash., D.C.; Baltimore Mus. of Art, Md.

DEALER   Kathleen Ewing Gall., 3020 K St, Washington, DC 20007.

ADDRESS   RD 2, Box 297, Seven Valleys, PA 17360.

Richard V. Procopio   *PHOTOGRAPHER* ·
TEACHER   Born November 12, 1946 in Boston, Massachusetts, Procopio attended Boston College and received a BA in 1968. He earned an MFA in Photography from Ohio University, Athens, in 1973.

Since 1979 he has worked as assistant professor of photography at Western Connecticut State College in Danbury. He was photography instructor at Maine Photographic Workshops (1973–79) and at the University of Southern Maine (1975–79). Between 1968 and 1971 he taught communications in the Newton Public Schools in Massachusetts.

A member of SPE since 1973, Procopio is also a member of the American Association of University Professors. He earned a George X. Bernier Memorial Graphics Prize from the Farnsworth Art Museum, Rockland, Maine, 1978, and was awarded artist-in-residence status at Gardiner High School in 1974 by the Maine Council of Arts and Humanities.

The artist works in several formats: "My main interest is in the field of color photography. I have worked with all forms of color materials, including dye transfer and Polaroid materials."

COLLECTIONS   Daytona Beach Community Coll., Fla.; Maine Photographic Workshop, Rockport; Middle Tenn. State Univ., Murfreesboro; Portland School of Art, Maine; Univ. of N. Hamp., Durham; Univ. of Southern Maine, Gorham.

DEALER   Kathy Ewing Gall, 3020 K St NW, Washington, DC 20007.

ADDRESS   Western Connecticut State Coll., 181 White St, Danbury, CT 06810.

Sergei Mikhailovich Prokudin-Gorskii   *PHO-*
TOGRAPHER · CHEMIST · INVENTOR · EDITOR   Born in 1863 in St. Petersburg, Russia, Prokudin-Gorskii died in 1943. He attended the Imperial Alexander Lyceum and the Institute of Applied Technology, where he studied until 1889 under famed chemist D. I. Mendeleev.

After his schooling the scientist went abroad, lecturing at a technical school in Germany and continuing his work in chemistry at the laboratory of Edme Jules Maumene, who was doing research in color photography. He returned to Russia to teach photography and do photographic research, and from 1906 to 1910 he edited and contributed to *Fotograf-Liubitel*. In order to best show his laboriously produced positive slides he designed his own projector, which could house 3-color separations and project them simultaneously. With the support of the czar, Prokudin-Gorskii was provided with a specially modified Pullman railroad car and given permission to travel freely and use whatever official assistance was available; so equipped, he set out to document his country. From 1909 to 1914 he traveled thousands of miles by train and boat to do so, but after the revolution in 1917 he and his family emigrated to the West.

A straight documentarian, Prokudin-Gorskii worked with a small folding camera. Though most of his surviving work is scenic and architectural, he also made portraits and genre studies. Arthur Goldsmith writes that the photographer's 2,000 surviving images offer, "in gentle colors, nostalgic as a half-forgotten dream . . . the beautiful surface of Imperial Russia in the days of the Tsar: its rivers, hamlets, churches, peasants, and exotic corners. His work is a Russian Easter egg of visual delight" (*Camera Arts*, Nov/Dec 1980).

PUBLICATIONS   Books: *Fototekhnicheskodrelo* 1905; *O pechatanil . . . a negativov*, 1898. Catalog: *Guide to the Special Collections*, Paul Vanderbilt, 1955 (L/C: Wash., D.C.).

COLLECTION L/C, Prints & Photographs Div, Wash., D.C.

Josef Prošek *PHOTOGRAPHER* Born October 19, 1923, in Mšeno, Czechoslovakia, Prošek studied at the State Graphic School in Prague (1945–49) and was influenced by the work of Jaromír Funke and Man Ray.

A freelance photographer, he was picture editor for the journal *Květy* in 1950–55.

From 1948 to 1955 Prošek belonged to the Association of Fine Artists "Mánes," and in 1960–70 was a member of the art group "Radar." He has belonged to the Union of the Czechoslovak Fine Artists since 1949, and in 1968 won its award. In 1967 the photographer was honored by the publishing house Mladá Fronta for the book *Paříž v Paříži*.

PUBLICATIONS Monographs: *Czechoslovakia*, 1980 (Pressfoto: Prague); *Photographs*, 1962 (SNKL: Prague). Books (in Czechoslovakia): *Kuks*, 1978 (Pressfoto: Prague); *Radar, Anatomy of a Creative Group*, 1971 (Odeon); *Československo*, 1966 (Artia: Prague); *Sculptor J. Wielgus*, J. Řezáč, 1965 (Profil: Ostrov); *Sculptures of M. F. Braun*, E. Poche, 1965, *Kuks*, J. Neuman, 1956 (SNKL: Prague).

COLLECTIONS Bibliothèque Nationale, Paris; Mus. of Decorative Arts, Prague.

ADDRESS Na Dědince 13, CS-180 00, Prague 8, Czechoslovakia.

Jaydie Putterman *PHOTOGRAPHER* Born August 23, 1945, in New York City, Putterman received a Design Correlations certificate from Parsons School of Design in New York City (1969), a BFA from the New School for Social Research in New York City (1971) and a teaching certificate from Long Island University in Brooklyn, New York (1971).

A freelance photographer since 1968, he served as photography and design correlations coordinator for a program of the New York City Board of Education in 1971–72.

Putterman belongs to SPE. He won the Prix Nikon Photo Contest International in 1977, a Polaroid Corporation grant in 1976, a Fulbright-Hayes grant in 1975 and a MacDowell Colony grant in 1974.

PUBLICATIONS Periodicals: *Camera*, July 1978; *Popular Photography's Invitation to Photography*, 1973; *Camera 35*, Mar 1973, Sept 1971; *Invitation to Photography*, 1973; *Popular Photography's Woman*, 1970.

COLLECTIONS Minneapolis Inst. of Art, Minn.; MOMA, NYC. Bibliothèque Nationale, Paris.

ADDRESS 69 rue du Montparnasse, 75014 Paris, France.

Charles Puyo *PHOTOGRAPHER* Born in 1857 in France (and named Emile Joachim Constant), Puyo died there in 1933.

A major in the French Army artillery corps for many years, he took up photography about 1885. After retiring from the military in 1902 he devoted himself completely to photography.

Puyo belonged to the Photo-Club and, with Robert Demachy, René Le Bègue and Maurice Bucquet, co-organized the French Salon in 1894.

Using the gum-bichromate process and oil transfer, Puyo was a pictorialist, influenced by Impressionism. He produced images of graceful, feminine women as well as landscapes and street scenes.

PUBLICATIONS Monographs: *Mi parecer*, 1915; *Der Ölfarben-Kopierprozess nach Rawlins*, 1908 (Schmidt: Berlin); *Le procédé Rawlins à l'huile*, 1907, *Le procédé à la gomme bichromatée*, 1904, *Pour les débutantes*, 1904 (Photo-Club: Paris); *Notes sur la photographie artistique*, 1896 (Gauthier-Villars: Paris). Books: *The History of Photography*, Helmut & Alison Gernsheim, 1955; *Les Procédés d'art en Photographie*, w/Robert Demachy, 1906 (Paris); *Esthétique de la Photographie*, Paul Bourgeois, ed., text by Puyo et al, 1900 (Paris). Anthologies: *The Magic Image*, Cecil Beaton & Gail Buckland, 1975; *Early Photographs & Early Photographers*, Oliver Mathews, 1973. Periodical: *Camera Work*, Oct 1906.

COLLECTIONS Univ. of Tex., Gernsheim Cllctn., Austin. Société Française de Photographie, Paris.

Q

Herb Quick *PHOTOGRAPHER* Born November 7, 1925, in Manistique, Michigan, Quick attended the Art Center in Los Angeles, California, in 1946–48.

He has been a lecturer in photography at University of California, Riverside, since 1977 and has managed the college's photographic service since 1975 and been its staff photographer since 1964. Quick owned and operated Sirks' Camera Shop in Riverside from 1950 to 1958.

In 1979 Quick was commissioned to make a master set of negatives from the prints of Harry Ellis, a contemporary of Atget. In 1976–77 he printed platinum prints from original plates made by Karl Struss.

The photographer works in a traditional style, concentrating on landscapes and cityscapes in the manner of western American photography.

PUBLICATIONS Book: *The Face of California,* 1970. Anthology: *Photography in the Twentieth Century,* 1967. Periodicals: "Herb Quick," *Camera,* Nov 1979; *U.S. Camera Annual,* 1971; "Herb Quick Fundamentalist," C. W. Harrison, *U.S. Camera,* Sept 1959.

PORTFOLIO *Herb Quick's Christmas Portfolio,* 1970, ltd. ed. (Riverside, Calif.).

COLLECTIONS Adrian Coll., Adrian, Mich.; Fairmont Hotel Corp. San Francisco; IMP/GEH, Rochester; MOMA, NYC; Newport Harbor Art Mus., Newport Beach, Calif.; Oakland Mus. of Art, Calif.; Polaroid Corp., Cambridge, Mass.; San Francisco Mus. of Art; Seagram Cllctn., NYC; Security Pacific Natl. Bank, Los Angeles; Norton Simon Mus. of Art, Pasadena, Calif.; Univ. of Calif., Calif. Mus. of Photography, Riverside.

ADDRESS POB 2082, Riverside, CA 92516.

R

Vaughan Rachel *PHOTOGRAPHER · TEACHER*
Born May 15, 1933, in Oakland, California,
Rachel earned a BFA (1973) and MFA (1975) in
Photography from California Institute of the
Arts, Valencia, her mentor being Benjamin Lifson. She also studied painting at the Hans Hofmann School of Fine Art in New York City
(1954). Rachel's husband is conceptual artist
Allan Kaprow.

As of this writing Rachel was a photography
instructor at Otis/Parsons in Los Angeles and a
resident artist-photographer at the Los Angeles
Institute of Contemporary Art. She worked as a
photo assistant at Astra Image in Los Angeles (for
Startrek) in 1979. She taught photography at Ambassador College, Pasadena, California, in 1976
and was slide curator at California Institute of
the Arts from 1971 to 1975.

Rachel joined the Film Technicians Union, International Alliance of Theatrical and Stage Engineers, Local 683, in 1978. She also belongs to
the women artists' collective Double X (since
1978) and was its corresponding secretary in
1979.

Working in black-and-white, the photographer
documents the domestic environments of family
and friends. She says: "I look for the ephemeral
and fleeting moment, the in-between-times of
events in our daily lives."

PUBLICATIONS Monograph: *Thirteen Stories,*
1974 (self-pub.). Catalog: *Roy Lichtenstein at Cal
Arts,* 1977.

ADDRESS 4920 Echo St, Apt 14, Los Angeles,
CA 90042.

Jaroslav Rajzík *PHOTOGRAPHER · TEACHER*
Born May 3, 1940 in Hradec Králové, Bohemia
(Czechoslovakia), Rajzík graduated in 1964 from
the Film and TV Faculty, Academy of Arts,
Prague (FAMU), and took postgraduate work
there in 1977 in artistic photography.

Since 1966 he has been an assistant professor
at FAMU and has maintained a freelance studio
in Prague since 1970. The photographer belongs
to the Union of Czechoslovak Creative Artists
(since 1970).

His principal series of works are entitled "Philosophy of a Landscape," "Studies of Light," and
"Arches and Labyrinths."

PUBLICATIONS Anthologies: *Black and White
Creative Photography,* Petr Tausk, 1980 (Cologne, Germany); *Photography in the 20th Century,* Petr Tausk, 1977 (Cologne, Germany).

COLLECTIONS In Czechoslovakia: Moravian
Gall., Brno; Mus. of Art, Prague.

ADDRESS Kyselova 1186, 182 00, Prague 8,
Czechoslovakia.

Romualdas Rakauskas *PHOTOJOURNALIST*
Born in Akmené, Lithuanian SSR, on August 19,
1941, Rakauskas attended the University of Vilnius from 1959 to 1964. Currently head of illustration for *Nemanus* magazine in Kaunas, he was
previously (1965–67) photojournalist at the magazine *Mūsu Gamta* and (1963–65) at the weekly
Literatūra ir Menas.

Rakauskas has been a member of the Photography Art Society of Lithuanian SSR since 1970
and of the Journalist Union since 1964. He has
also been a member of the Fédération Internationale de l'Art Photographique (FIAP). He was
given the honorary title of Merited Journalist by
the Lithuanian Presidium of the Supreme Soviet
and has received two gold medals—one in
Plovdiv, Bulgaria, in 1977, and one in Yugoslavia,
in 1972. In 1976 he was awarded the Slupsko
Plenair grand prize and also the grand prize at the
"Man and Work" exhibit in Kapsukas; in 1973 he
received the grand prize at the "Man and Earth"
exhibit in Plateliai.

PUBLICATIONS Books: *Tarybu Lietuva,* 1977,
Salis Ta Lietuva Vadinas, w/A. Sutkus, 1970,
Vilniaus Šiokiadieniai, w/A. Sutkus, 1965 (Mintis: Vilnius); *Mūsu Kaunas,* 1976 (Sviesa). Anthologies: *Fotojahrbuch International,* 1977,
1973; *Photography Yearbook,* 1976, 1972.

COLLECTION Photography Mus., Šiauliai, Lithuanian SSR.
REPRESENTATIVE Photography Art Society, Pionieriu 8, 232600 Vilnius, Lithuanian SSR, USSR.
ADDRESS Urbšo 26–34, 233043 Kaunas, Lithuanian SSR, USSR.

Daniel Ranalli PHOTOGRAPHER·ARTS CONSULTANT Born in New Haven, Connecticut, on October 17, 1946, Ranalli earned a BA from Clark University, Worcester, Massachusetts, in 1968 and an MA from Boston University in 1971.

A self-employed consultant since 1979, he was director and artist-in-residence at the Artists Foundation in Boston from 1975 to 1979. He served as associate director of Beacon College, both in Boston and Washington, D.C., from 1973 to 1975, and from 1971 to 1973 was assistant program director for the North East Board of Higher Education in Wellesley, Massachusetts.

A member of the Boston Visual Artists Union since 1974, Ranalli was its vice-president in 1978, and was a member of the Massachusetts Alliance for Arts in Education from 1977 to 1979. He was recipient of an NEA Visual Arts in the Performing Arts Grant in 1978. Ranalli creates primarily large abstract photograms and combinations of photographs and photograms.

PUBLICATIONS Monograph: *Trail Pouch*, 1977. Anthology: *Darkroom Dynamics*, 1979. Catalog: *Patron's Choice*, 1977 (DeCordova Mus.). Periodical: *Afterimage: VSW* May/June 1977.
COLLECTIONS Amherst Coll., Mead Art Mus., Mass.; Boston Pub. Lib.; Franklin Furnace Artists Book Archive, NYC; Minneapolis Inst. of Arts, Minn.; Worcester Art Mus., Mass. Polaroid Europa, Amsterdam.
DEALERS Carl Siembab Gall., 162 Newbury St, Boston, MA 02116; Thomas Segal Gall., 73 Newbury St, Boston, MA 02116.
ADDRESS 76 Sumner St, Newton, MA 02159.

Herbert Eugene Randall PHOTOGRAPHER Born December 16, 1936, in Riverhead, Long Island, New York, Randall studied photography under Harold Feinstein in 1957–58.

Since 1974 he has been photographic consultant at the National Media Center Foundation, Inc., in Parksville, New York. He served as coordinator of photography in 1970–74 for the Multi-Media Project of the Board of Education, School District 5, in New York City, and in 1969–70 he taught photography at the Brooklyn Children's Museum, New York.

Randall won a CAPS grant in 1971 and a John Hay Whitney Fellowship for Creative Photography in 1964.
PUBLICATIONS Periodicals: *Popular Photography*, July 1975; *Reporter-Objectif*, Apr 1974; *Camera*, July 1966.
COLLECTIONS Catskill Art Soc., Catskill, N.Y.; Cornell Univ., Ithaca, N.Y.; IMP/GEH, Rochester; L/C, Wash., D.C.; Reva & David Logan Fndn., Chicago; Metro. Mus. of Art, NYC; MOMA, NYC; Charles Rand-Penney Fndn., Olcott, N.Y.; Vassar Coll. Art Gall., Poughkeepsie, N.Y.
ADDRESS Shinnecock Indian Reservation, Box 479, Southampton, NY 11968.

Susan Anne Rankaitis PHOTOGRAPHER · PAINTER Born in Cambridge, Massachusetts, on September 10, 1949, Rankaitis earned a BFA in Painting from the University of Illinois, Normal, in 1971, and an MFA from the University of Southern California, Los Angeles, in 1977. She has been greatly influenced by American abstract art of the 1930s and 1940s.

An instructor of photography at Orange Coast College in southern California since 1978, Rankaitis has also taught painting and art history at Chapman College in Orange County since 1977.

Rankaitis is a member of the CAA, the Los Angeles Institute of Contemporary Art and SPE. In 1977 she received a California State Fair Art Award.

She is interested in the linkages between painting and photography: "I use homemade photographic chemistry to, in a sense, 'paint' via multiple printing and intensive duotone solarization." Her work is abstract, with surfaces having a metallic quality.

PUBLICATIONS Periodicals (reviews): "Los Angeles: A Fantasy Life," Susan Larsen, *Artnews*, May 1979; "Between Photography and Painting," Mark Johnstone, *Artweek*, Nov 1978.
COLLECTIONS CCP, Tucson; ICP, NYC; Los Angeles County Mus.; Minneapolis Inst. of the Arts, Minn.; MOMA, NYC; Santa Barbara Mus. of Art, Calif.; Santa Monica Coll., Calif.; Seagram Cllctn., NYC; UCLA Grunwald Cllctn., Calif.; Univ. of Illinois, Normal.
ADDRESS 707 E Hyde Park Blvd, Inglewood, CA 90302.

Edward Ranney PHOTOGRAPHER · TEACHER Born March 4, 1942, in Chicago, Illinois, Ranney received a BA from Yale University, New Haven, Connecticut, in 1964. He is mostly self-taught in photography, having studied with David Plowden and being influenced by the work of Edward Weston and Paul Caponigro.

A freelance photographer since 1970, Ranney has taught at the Illinois Institute of Technology, Chicago (1974), and at East Hill School, Chester, Vermont (1966–70).

Ranney won a Guggenheim Fellowship in 1977 and a grant from Earthwatch, Inc., in the same year to work on the Martin Chambi archive in Cuzco, Peru. He received an NEA Photographer's Fellowship in 1975 and a Fulbright Fellowship to Cuzco in 1964.

Working in large format, mostly 5 x 7, Ranney photographs landscapes, archaeological sites (particularly of the Mayan and Incan cultures), contemporary townscapes and images of man's impact on land.

PUBLICATIONS Monograph: *Stonework of the Maya*, 1974. Anthologies: *History of Photography in New Mexico*, 1979; *Mirrors and Windows*, John Szarkowski, ed., 1978. Periodical: *Aperture*, 16:1, 1971.

COLLECTIONS Amon Carter Mus., Fort Worth, Tex.; Art Inst. of Chicago; Fine Arts Mus., Santa Fe, N. Mex.; MOMA, NYC; Polaroid Corp., Cambridge, Mass.; Princeton Univ. Art Mus., N.J.; Seagram Cllctn., NYC. Victoria & Albert Mus., London.

ADDRESS Rt 2, Box 299, Santa Fe, NM 87501.

Talbot Neal Rantoul *PHOTOGRAPHER · TEACHER* Born November 25, 1946, in Connecticut, Rantoul received a BFA (1971) and MFA (1973) from the Rhode Island School of Design, Providence, where he studied with Aaron Siskind and Harry Callahan.

He has been a teaching assistant at Harvard University, Cambridge, Massachusetts, since 1978, and has taught at the New England School of Photography in Boston since 1976. He has spent summers since 1978 teaching at the Maine Photographic Workshops in Rockport.

Rantoul belongs to the Photo Resource Center in Boston (since 1978) and SPE (since 1974).

He currently works with black-and-white infrared emulsion.

PUBLICATIONS Book: *Darkroom Dynamics*, Jim Stone, ed., 1979. Periodical: *British Journal of Photography*, 1977.

COLLECTIONS Addison Gall. of Amer. Art, Andover, Mass.; Princeton Univ. Mus., N.J.; R.I. School of Design Mus., Providence.

ADDRESS 1707 Cambridge St, Cambridge, MA 02138.

Victor Wilhelm Rasmussen *PHOTOGRAPHER · TV CAMERAMAN* Born March 23, 1909, Rasmussen died November 23, 1978.

A self-taught photographer, Rasmussen began his professional career in March 1950 and was the first TV cameraman on Danish television (June 15, 1952). He later became a press photographer at Denmark radio and TV, working there until his death.

A member of Amager Fotoklub and Danish Camera Pictorialists, he was appointed AFIAP (Artiste Fédération Internationale de l'Art Photographique).

Rasmussen grew from an amateur genre picture taker in the early 1940s to a serious artistic photographer in the late 1950s. Producing abstract nonfigurative black-and-white images, he described his photographs as "a kind of visual music."

PUBLICATIONS Book: *Dansk Fotografisk Tidsskrift*, 1951. Periodicals: *Fotomagasinet*, no. 1, 1960, no. 9, 1959, no. 5, 1956; *American Annual of Photography*, 1949.

COLLECTION Royal Lib., Copenhagen.

David Leigh Rathbun *PHOTOGRAPHER · EDUCATOR* Born February 28, 1943, in Denver, Colorado, Rathbun earned a BA in Literature from Wheaton College, Wheaton, Illinois, and later studied at Princeton Theological Seminary, New Jersey (1966–67), and Columbia Teachers College, New York City (1967–68). He served an apprenticeship to photographer Eliot Porter in Tesuque, New Mexico, from 1970 to 1975.

Since 1975 Rathbun has been assistant professor of photography at the Institute of Design, Illinois Institute of Technology, in Chicago. He worked for the Norman Kurshan Color Lab in New York City in 1969–70 and did freelance commercial photography in New York City in 1967–69.

Using color exclusively, the photographer works with a view camera and prints with the dye transfer process. His main concern is the effect of color upon visual perception.

DEALERS Douglas Kenyon, Inc, 155 E Ohio, Chicago, IL 60611; Hills Gall., 3113 E Third Ave, Denver, CO 80206.

ADDRESS 202 S Lake Ave, Michigan City, IN 46360.

William H. Rau *PHOTOGRAPHER* Born in 1855 in Philadelphia, Pennsylvania, Rau died in that city in 1920. His father, George Rau (fl. 1850–70) was a photographer, as was his father-in-law, William Bell.

Rau began his photographic career in 1877 in his father-in-law's stereograph company, which Bell had begun after a career as a government survey photographer. In 1878 Rau purchased the company, publishing stereo cards and lantern slides under his own name. In 1901 Underwood & Underwood acquired the business, continuing distribution of Rau's work until Griffith & Griffith took over that task. Rau worked briefly with William Henry Jackson in the 1880s, and in 1899 was hired by the Lehigh Valley Railroad to produce a portfolio of scenic views along the railroad line from Perth Amboy to Niagara Falls and Buffalo.

The photographer produced silver prints, stereographs and lantern slides showing scenic views of the Southwest and of railroad lines. He also did journalistic work, such as documenting the Johnstown, Pennsylvania, flood and the Baltimore fire of 1904.

PUBLICATIONS Books (in Philadelphia, Pa.): *Historical Pageant of Philadelphia, the Old Capitol of the United States*, 1912; *Photographs of Founders Week, October 4–10, 1908*, 1908; *Lantern Slides & Photographs*, 1902; *Spanish American War*, 1898. Anthology: *Photography Rediscovered*, David Travis & Anne Kennedy, 1979. Catalog: *Illustrated Catalog*, 1894 (Philadelphia). Periodicals: "How I Photograph Railroad-Scenery," *Photo Era*, June 1916; *Philadelphia Photographer*, 1881.

COLLECTION Samuel Wagstaff Cllctn., NYC.

Warren C. Rauhauser *TEACHER · ENGINEER · ARCHITECT · PHOTOGRAPHER* Born in Detroit, Michigan, on August 14, 1918, Rauhauser received a BAA degree from the University of Detroit in 1943.

Rauhauser has been a teacher at the Center for Creative Studies since 1970. In 1977–79 he lectured on the history of photography for the Detroit Institute of Arts; in 1975–76 he gave lectures on photography at the University of Michigan, Ann Arbor.

A member of SPE and the Engineering Society of Detroit, Rauhauser operated the first photography gallery in Detroit, Group 4 Gallery, beginning in 1964.

Working mostly as a documentary photographer, he has spent over twenty years preparing a comprehensive study of the city of Detroit.

PUBLICATION Anthology: *Family of Man*, 1955.

COLLECTIONS Archives of Amer. Art, Smithsonian Inst., Wash., D.C.; Detroit Inst. of Arts, Mich.; Kresge Fndn., Detroit, Mich.

ADDRESS 27735 Berkshire, Southfield, MI 48076.

Bill Ravanesi *PHOTOGRAPHER* Born June 18, 1947, in Boston, Massachusetts, Ravanesi received a BS from the University of Massachusetts, Amherst, in 1969. He studied at the Center for Visual Studies at Imageworks in Cambridge, Massachusetts, for a year in 1972, and earned an MA in 1978 from Goddard College in Plainfield, Vermont. He also attended workshops led by Kipton Kumler in 1975, Lisette Model in 1973 and Minor White in 1972 and 1973.

Ravanesi has been a freelance agricultural and industrial photographer since 1972.

He received an NEA Survey Grant in 1980 and a Ford Foundation Grant in 1979.

Working in large-format color, Ravanesi does landscapes and portraits, and documents farm labor.

PUBLICATIONS Periodicals: *Communication Arts Magazine*, Nov/Dec, July/Aug 1979; *Picture Magazine*, vol. 7, 1978; *Photographic Processing Magazine*, Sept 1975. Catalog: *Class of 1928 Photography Collection*, 1978 (Amherst Univ. Gall.: Amherst, Mass.).

COLLECTIONS Fine Arts Center, Amherst Univ. Gall., Amherst, Mass; Polaroid Corp., Cambridge, Mass.

ADDRESS 10 Selkirk Rd, Boston, MA 02146.

Gypsy Patricia Ray *PHOTOGRAPHER* Born March 22, 1949, in Kewanee, Illinois, Ray earned a BA in Art from the University of Iowa, Iowa City, in 1972 and an MA in Photography from Goddard College, Plainfield, Vermont, in 1978. She regards Laura Savakins as her mentor.

Currently senior photographer with the University of California, Santa Cruz Photo Lab (since 1976), she previously worked as an artist's model for six years at various universities and art schools.

Ray is a member of Friends of Photography.

She has concerned herself extensively with the male and female nude and says: "It is important to me to have my art have social implications." As of this writing her next project is an essay on farmers in Ireland.

PUBLICATIONS Anthology: *Eros and Photography*, 1978. Periodical: *Creative Camera*, Oct 1979.

COLLECTIONS Goddard Coll., Plainfield, Vt.; Univ. of Calif., Santa Cruz.

ADDRESS 134 Rincon St, Santa Cruz, CA 95060.

Tony Ray-Jones   PHOTOGRAPHER · TEACHER
Born in 1941 in Wells, Somerset, England, Ray-Jones died of leukemia on March 13, 1972, in London. He studied graphic design at London College of Printing (1957–61), then earned an MFA in 1964 from Yale University. He also studied with Alexey Brodovitch and Richard Avedon at the Design Laboratory in New York City (1962–63).

Ray-Jones first worked as associate art director to Alexey Brodovitch on *Sky* magazine (1964), then freelanced in America and England, publishing in such journals as *Album, Saturday Evening Post, Sunday Times Magazine* and *Horizon*. In 1971 he was appointed visiting lecturer to the San Francisco Art Institute's Department of Photography. His work has been widely exhibited internationally.

Ainslee Ellis in *A Day Off* wrote: "It is difficult to think of any other British photographer but Tony Ray-Jones whose pictures have that rare blend of humor and sadness which is born of both compassion and irony. This is something that springs from the depths of character and it is something that cannot be copied or faked. The imitation, the phoney baloney version of the mixture, as Tony would say, is a blend of sentiment and sarcasm, and is totally alien to his work and to his nature."

PUBLICATIONS Monograph: *A Day Off*, intro. by Ainslie Ellis, 1974, U.S. ed., 1977. Anthologies: *The Photograph Collector's Guide*, Lee D. Witkin & Barbara London, 1979; *The Magic Image*, Cecil Beaton & Gail Buckland, 1975; *The Art of Photography*, 1971, *The Great Themes*, 1970, *The Print*, 1970, Time-Life Series; *Vision and Expression*, Nathan Lyons, ed., 1969. Periodicals: *Creative Camera*, Oct 1974, Jan 1971, Oct 1968; *Album #3*, 1970; *British Journal of Photography Annual*, 1970.

PORTFOLIO *Untitled*, intro. by Pete Turner, 1975 (Photographic Cllctns.: London).

COLLECTIONS Dallas Mus. of Fine Arts, Tex.; IMP/GEH, Rochester; MOMA, NYC; Norton Simon Mus. of Art, Pasadena, Calif.; San Francisco Mus. of Modern Art; VSW, Rochester. In London: Arts Council of Great Britain; British Council; RPS; Victoria & Albert Mus. Bibliothèque Nationale, Paris.

ARCHIVE Photographic Collections Ltd, London.

Lilo Raymond   PHOTOGRAPHER   Born in Frankfurt, Germany, on June 23, 1922, Raymond studied with David Vestal from 1961 to 1963. As of this writing she was teaching at the School of Visual Arts in New York, having taught at the Maine Photographic Workshop during the summer of 1979, and at the International Center of Photography later that year.

Raymond works in 35mm, producing silver prints. She concentrates on the beauty and simplicity of everyday objects. Her photographs are "painterly" in style.

PUBLICATIONS Books: *Photographs: A Collector's Guide*, Richard Blodgett, 1979; *Classic Country Inns of America*, 1978; *Collecting Photographs*, 1977; *The Craft of Photography*, 1975; *Photographing Children, Special Problems*, 1971. Anthologies: *Family of Children*, 1977; *The Magic Image*, Cecil Beaton & Gail Buckland, 1975. Periodicals: *Popular Photography*, 1977; *35mm Photography*, summer 1979, winter 1975, summer 1973; *Popular Photography Annual*, 1971, 1968, 1967, 1964; *U.S. Camera Annual*, 1971, 1970, 1967, 1964.

PORTFOLIO *Still Life*, intro. by Cecil Beaton, 1976 (Helios Gall.: NYC).

COLLECTIONS Calif. Inst. of the Arts, Valencia; Univ. of Nebr., Lincoln. Bibliothèque Nationale, Paris.

DEALER Marcuse Pfeifer, 825 Madison Ave, New York, NY 10021.

ADDRESS 212 E 14 St, New York, NY 10003.

Jane Reece   PHOTOGRAPHER   Born June 18, 1868, in West Jefferson, Ohio, Reece died June 10, 1961 in Dayton, Ohio. She studied opera, piano and art, but was self-taught as a photographer. She was influenced by Clarence White and the Photo-Secessionists and, early in her career, by artist Howard Chandler Christy.

Reece set up her first studio in Dayton in 1904, where she devised a process of doing photographic silhouettes. In 1909 she traveled to New York and worked in the studio of Clarence White, returning to Dayton that same year to establish another studio, which she operated until 1917. Between 1919 and 1923 she traveled extensively, for a brief time setting up a studio in Paris. On returning to Dayton in 1924 she had a permanent studio built, which housed exhibits, concerts and a music/dance studio. She photographed until 1944, when dimming eyesight and loss of hearing caused her to stop.

Reece was a member of the New York Camera Club and the Photo-Secessionists, joining both groups in 1909. She received numerous awards and medals, among them: (in the U.S.) Cornell Camera Club, 1932; Photographers Association of America, 1907 & 1908; (in Germany) Amateur Photographers in Hamburg, 1911; Daguerre Memorial Institute, 1912 & 1913; (in England) Camera Club, 1929, London Salon of Photography, 1930; Photographic Society, 1927; (in Canada) M.A.A.A. Camera Club in Montreal, 1921 & 1922; International Exhibition at New Westminster, 1927; (in Spain) International Salon in Madrid, 1928 & 1930; Zaragoza award, 1928 & 1930.

She was also an accomplished painter in oils.

An ardent experimenter with the tools and materials of the photographer's art, Reece used a variety of papers—paladium, platinum, carbon, domestic chloride, linen, silk, even tissue. She was arduous in exploring the possibilities of controlling developer. She also experimented with the motion picture camera and in 1928 made an enlargement from 16mm film—unheard of at that time. In 1937 she revived a technique she had developed early in her career which she called "camera cameos" (photographic silhouettes), some of which were printed on fabric.

PUBLICATIONS Books: *Photo-Secession*, Robert Doty, 1960; *Photography: A Short Critical History*, Beaumont Newhall, 1938. Periodicals: "The Wonderful World of Photography," Helen L. Pinkney, *The Dayton Art Institute Bulletin*, Mar/Apr 1963; "Stieglitz & '291,'" Beaumont Newhall, *Art in America*, Feb 1963; "Jane Reece of the Rembrandt Studio," Mabel G. Martin, *Photographic Journal of America*, Jan 1915.

COLLECTIONS Dayton Art Inst., Ohio; Wright State Univ., Dayton, Ohio.

ARCHIVE Dayton Art Inst., Forest & Riverview Aves, POB 941, Dayton, OH 45401.

Roland Reed *PHOTOGRAPHER* Born in Fox River Valley, Wisconsin, Reed lived from 1864 to 1934. He was taught photography in 1893 by Daniel Dutro, a Civil War veteran, prospector and photographer.

At age eighteen, Reed set off to draw Indian faces in crayon and pencil. He served an apprenticeship with Dutro in 1893, and furnished Indian photographs to the Great Northern Railroad news department. In 1897 he signed on with Associated Press to photograph the Klondike gold rush. From 1900 to 1907 he operated a portrait studio in Bemidji, Minnesota, which he closed in order to continue his wide travels in Indian country. His work was published in *National Geography*, *The American West*, *Arizona Highways* and many newspapers.

The photographer won a gold medal at the Panama-California Exposition in San Diego in 1915.

Working with 11 x 14 glass-plate negatives, Reed produced a definitive photographic record of the North American Indian. His somewhat romanticized photographs evoked an idealized image of the proud people of the pre-reservation era. A meticulous planner and fine technician, Reed was called by one critic "a poet whose medium of expression is the camera."

PUBLICATION Periodical: "The Indian Photographs of Roland Reed," Patricia Condon Johnston, *The American West*, Mar/Apr 1978.

COLLECTION Kramer Gall., St. Paul, Minn.

ARCHIVE Kramer Gall., 229 E Sixth St, St Paul, MN 55101.

Arthur Reeder
See Art Siosabaugh

Katherine L. Reese *PHOTOGRAPHERS' AGENT · PICTURE EDITOR* Born in Chicago, Illinois, Reese received her BA cum laude in 1947 from Smith College, Northampton, Massachusetts.

Since 1971 she has directed Kay Reese and Associates, a photographic agency specializing in annual reports and advertising photography. She was director of the "Chicago Photo One" exhibit in 1972, and that same year created a research report, "Toward a National Photographic File," for the International Center of Photography in New York City.

Reese was executive editor for Rapho Guillumette Pictures in New York City from 1960 to 1970, executive director of the American Society of Magazine Photographers from 1955 to 1958 and editor of ASMP's *Infinity* magazine during that time as well.

ADDRESS 156 Fifth Ave, New York, NY 10010.

John Alexander Reeves *PHOTOGRAPHER* Born April 24, 1938, in Burlington, Ontario, Canada, Reeves graduated from the Ontario College of Art in Toronto. He names industrial designer Victor J. Papanek, typographer Alan R. Fleming and photographer Thomas Davenport as mentors.

A freelance photojournalist since 1962, Alexander has also been a freelance radio and television broadcaster and hosted the CBC AM broadcast "Toronto in Review" from 1968 to 1971.

He is a member of the Royal Canadian Academy of Art, Association of Canadian Radio and Television Artists, and the Royal Canadian Academy.

Reeves does general feature photography for magazines and location photography for corporations. He is known for his editorial portraits.

PUBLICATIONS Books: *Image 5*, 1969 (Natl. Film Board of Canada, Martlet Press); *Call Them Canadians*, 1967 (Natl. Film Board of Canada); *John Filion—Thoughts About My Sculpture*, 1968 (Martlet Press: Canada). Periodical: *Camera Canada*, June 1977, Nov 1972.

COLLECTION Natl. Film Board of Canada, Ottawa, Ontario.

DEALER Deja Vue Gall., 122 Scollard St, Toronto, Ontario, Canada.

ADDRESS 11 Yorkville Ave, Apt 602, Toronto, Ontario, Canada M4W 1L3.

Henri-Victor Regnault CHEMIST · PHYSICIST · PHOTOGRAPHER Born July 21, 1810, at Aachen, Germany, Regnault died in Auteuil, France, on January 19, 1878. He learned photography from Blanquart-Evrard, and studied chemistry with Justus von Liebig in Glessen, Germany. Regnault became professor of chemistry successively at the University of Lyons, the Ecole Polytechnique (1840) and the Collège de France (1841). From 1854 until 1871 he was director of the porcelain factory at Sèvres. His son, Henri Regnault, was a noted historical painter (d. 1870 or 1871).

A founding member of both the Société Héliographique (1851) and the Société Française de Photographie, he served as the latter's first president until 1868. He was also president of the Academy of Sciences in Paris.

Regnault discovered the developing action of pyrogallic acid. He also designed apparatus for taking a large number of physical measurements —such as an air thermometer that determined the absolute expansion of mercury—and he redetermined the specific heats of many solids, liquids and gases.

The photographer used paper negatives to produce his portraits and landscapes, and Regnault's "choice of subject matter and his marvelous use of light bear evidence of a certain influence of English romanticism. . . . His works suggest a synthesis of French and English tastes in landscape" *(French Primitive Photography)*. Weston Naef has written *(After Daguerre)*: "Regnault took advantage of the camera's ability to combine infinite detail into a single, cohesive image."

PUBLICATIONS *Correspondance de Henri Regnault*, Arthur Duparc, 1904 (Fasquelle: Paris); *Das Ausdehnungsgesetz der Gase*, 1894 (Engelmann: Leipzig, Germany); *Chemical Reports and Memoirs*, 1848 (Cavendish Soc.: London); *Cours de Chimie*, 4 vols., 1847 (Paris). Anthologies: *Early Photographs & Early Photographers*, Oliver Mathews, 1973; *French Primitive Photography*,

André Jammes & Robert Sobieszek, intro. by Minor White, 1970; *Photography's Great Inventors*, Louis W. Sipley, 1965. Catalogs: *A L'Origine de la photographie, le calotype*, Bernard Marbot, 1979, *Une Invention du XIXᵉ siècle: La photographie*, Bernard Marbot, 1976 (Bibliothèque Nationale: Paris); *De Niepce à Man Ray*, André Jammes & Laurent Roosens, 1965 (Musée des Arts Décoratifs: Paris); *Die Kalotypie in Franreich*, André Jammes, 1965 (Folkwang Mus.: Essen, Germany). Periodicals: *Bulletin de la Société Française de Photographie*, 1878, 1873, 1871, 1868, 1862, 1861, 1860, 1856, 1855; *Comptes rendus hebdomadaires des séances de l'Académie des sciences*, 1878, 1841; *Le Moniteur de la photographie*, 1866; *Revue photographique*, 1857, 1856; *La Lumière*, 1853, 1851.

COLLECTIONS Société Française de Photographie, Paris; Bibliothèque Nationale, Paris.

Vilém Reichmann PHOTOGRAPHER · CARTOONIST Born April 25, 1908, in Brno, Czechoslovakia, Reichmann studied architecture at Deutsche Technische Hochschule, Brno, Faculty of Architekture (1926–31).

Since 1945 he has been a freelance cartoonist and photographer. Previously he was clerk of a building office (1938–42) and a teacher (1932–38).

Reichmann belonged to the Union of Czechoslovak Fine Artists from 1950 to 1968, and from 1945 to 1948 he was a member of Group Ra, an association of painters and writers who were influenced by Surrealism.

PUBLICATIONS Monograph: *Vilém Reichmann*, Cykly, 1956 (Edition SNKLHU: Prague). Periodicals: *Revue Fotografie*, no. 3, 1976, no. 2, 1966, no. 4, 1962, no. 10, 1959; *Československá fotografie*, no. 8, 1970, no. 12, 1968, no. 9, 1967, no. 5, 1963, no. 10, 1958.

COLLECTIONS In Czechoslovakia: Moravian Gall., Brno; Northmoravian Mus., Opava; Southbohemian Gall., Hluboká.

ADDRESS Sady Osvobození 11, 602 00, Brno, Czechoslovakia.

Georg Reisner PHOTOGRAPHER Born December 9, 1911, in Breslau, Germany, Reisner died in December 1940 in Marseilles, France. After graduation from the Gymnasium in Breslau, he studied medicine and later law at the universities of Breslau and Freiburg. Because of his active involvement with German Socialists in the anti-Hitler struggle, he was unable to finish his studies and fled to France, where he studied photography (in Paris) in 1933 and 1934. Reisner was a friend and colleague of photographer Hans Namuth.

He started freelancing in 1934, traveling to Spain, Portugal and Morocco. In 1935 he opened a photographic studio with Hans Namuth in Mallorca, Spain, then another in Neuilly-sur-Seine, France. He covered the Spanish Civil War as a photojournalist in 1936–37, then did photojournalism in Paris until the outbreak of World War II, contributing to *Life* and other magazines. Jailed by the French in 1939, Reisner escaped to Marseilles, where he committed suicide in order to avoid internment at Les Milles, a French concentration camp.

Reisner joined the Association Professionelle de la Presse Etrangère en France in 1934.

The photographer was also a highly talented amateur musician, and in 1928 he completed a unique piano score of Mahler's Fourth Symphony which was lauded by the renowned German conductor Otto Klemperer.

An innovative photojournalist, Reisner had "technical brilliance" and a fine "sense of composition and style," according to Namuth, with whom he collaborated on his photographs of the Spanish Civil War. The photographer used Leica and Rolleiflex cameras.

PUBLICATIONS Catalog: *Photographs from the Spanish Civil War*, 1977 (Castelli Uptown: NYC). Periodicals: *Fotografie Annual*, 1938, 1937, 1936; "La Défense d'un République," *Vu*, 1936.

ARCHIVE c/o Hans Namuth, 157 W 54 St, New York, NY 10019.

Oscar Gustav Rejlander   PHOTOGRAPHER · PAINTER [See plate 10] Born in 1817, probably in Sweden, Rejlander died in England in 1875. First educated in Sweden, he then studied painting and sculpture in Rome, and learned photography from Nicholas Henneman in 1853 in England.

Rejlander was a portraitist and copyist in Rome, then left for England in 1841. He relocated several times before settling in Wolverhampton in 1846, and began his photography in 1853. Moving to London in 1860, he continued work as a photographer.

Initially using photography as a guide for his and others' paintings, Rejlander abandoned his painting career for the photographic art. He is especially noted for his "combination prints"— works achieved by combining several negatives. The most famous of these, "The Two Ways of Life," a sentimental allegory done in 1857, catapulted him to fame when Queen Victoria purchased a copy for Prince Albert.

PUBLICATIONS Books: *Father of Art Photography: O. G. Rejlander, 1813–1875*, Edgar Yoxall Jones, 1973; *The Expression of the Emotions in Man and Animals*, Charles Darwin, 1872 (John Murray: London); *The Two Ways of Life*, 1857. Anthologies: *The Photograph Collector's Guide*, Lee D. Witkin & Barbara London, 1979; *The Invented Eye*, Edward Lucie-Smith, 1975; *The Magic Image*, Cecil Beaton & Gail Buckland, 1975; *Great Photographers*, 1971; *The Camera*, Time-Life Series, 1970. Periodicals: "Cuthbert Bede and O. J. [sic] Rejlander," *History of Photography*, July 1977; "O. G. Rejlander: From Philistine to Forerunner," John Fuller, *Exposure: SPE*, Dec 1976; "On Photographing Horses," *The British Journal of Photography Almanac*, 1873.

COLLECTIONS IMP/GEH, Rochester; Smithsonian Inst., Wash., D.C.; Univ. of N. Mex. Art Mus., Albuquerque; Univ. of Tex., Gernsheim Cllctn., Austin. Edinburgh Photographic Soc., Scotland; Kodak Mus., Harrow, England; RPS, London.

Albert Renger-Patzsch   PHOTOGRAPHER [See plate 91] Born in 1897 in Wurzburg, Germany, Renger-Patzsch died in 1966 in Wamel Dorf, near Essen, Germany. He attended college in Sondershausen and later at Kreuzschule, Dresden, Germany, doing military service in 1916–18. He then studied chemistry at Technical College in Dresden.

Renger-Patzsch began photographing in his early teens, and by about 1920 he was directing the photographic department of Folkwang Publishing House in Hagen. He worked in a variety of jobs and moved around for several years before becoming director of the Department of Pictorial Photography at Folkwang College, about 1933. During World War II, Renger-Patzsch became a war correspondent and suffered the loss of 18,000 negatives when his studio at the Folkwang Museum was destroyed in a 1944 air raid.

The photographer was awarded the David Octavius Hill medal by the GDL in 1957.

A pioneer of realistic, straight photography, Renger-Patzsch produced large-format silver prints of nature, architecture and machinery, using Linhof and Felding cameras. Of his work Beaumont Newhall wrote in *History of Photography*, "Unlike the studio-bound painters of the time, [Renger-Patzsch] looked at the world and found it beautiful. He took his camera everywhere at a time when European artists in all media were avoiding contact with nature . . . he was exploring and interpreting the exterior world."

PUBLICATIONS Monographs: *Im Wald,* 1965 (Hermann Katelhöln: Wamel-Möhnesee); *Beständige Welt,* 1947 (Quell: Münster); *Land am Oberrhein,* 1944; *Deutsche Wasserburgen,* 1941 (Langewiesche: Königstein); *Eisen und Stahl,* foreword by Albert Vogler, 1931 (Reckendorf: Berlin); *Hamburg: Photographische Aufnah-men,* 1930 (Gebrüder Enoch: Hamburg); *Sylt-Bild einer Insel,* ca. 1930 (Bruckmann: Munich); *Lübeck,* 1928 (Wasmuth: Berlin); *Die Welt is schön,* intro. by Carl Georg Heise, 1928 (Wolff: Munich); *Die Halligen,* 1927 (Albertus: Berlin); *Das Gesicht einer Landschaft,* 1926; *Das Chorgestühl von Kappenberg,* 1925 (Auriga: Berlin). Books: *A Concise History of Photography,* Helmut & Alison Gernsheim, 1965. In Germany: *Hohenstaufenburgen in Suditalien,* Hanno Hahn, 1961 (Boehringer: Ingelheim am Rhein); *Oberrhein,* Michael Meier, 1959 (Deutscher Kunstverlag: Munich); *Dresden wie es war und wurde,* Friedrich Schnack, 1956 (Knorr & Hirth: Munich); *Leistungen deutscher Technik,* Albert Lange, 1935 (Seemann: Leipzig); *Norddeutsche Backsteindome,* Werner Burmeister, 1930 (Deutscher Kunstverlag: Berlin); *Das Münster in Essen,* Kurt Wilhelm-Kästner, 1929 (Fredebeul & Koenen: Essen); *Wegweisung der Technik,* Rudolf Schwarz, 1928 (Müller & Kiepenheuer: Potsdam). Anthologies: *The Photograph Collector's Guide,* Lee D. Witkin & Barbara London, 1979; *The Magic Image,* Cecil Beaton & Gail Buckland, 1975; *Great Photographers,* Time-Life Series, 1971; "Germany and the Bauhaus—Photography for Design," *The Picture History of Photography,* Peter Pollack, 1958. Catalog: *Fotografien 1925–1960 von Albert Renger-Patzsch,* Klaus Honnef, 1977 (Rheinisches Landesmus.: Bonn). Periodicals: *Untitled 12,* entire issue, Aug 1977; "Deutschland 1920–33," Allan Porter & Bernd Lohse, *Camera,* Apr 1967; "Albert Renger-Patzsch," Beaumont Newhall, *Image,* Sept 1959.
PORTFOLIO *Untitled,* 1977 (Galerie Wilde: Cologne).
COLLECTIONS Art Inst. of Chicago; Friends of Photography, Carmel, Calif.; IMP/GEH, Rochester; MOMA, NYC; Univ. of N. Mex. Art Mus., Albuquerque. Bibliothèque Nationale, Paris; Deutsche Staatliche Landesbildstelle, Germany; Mus. Ludwig, Cologne, Germany; Provinciaal Mus. voor Kunstambachten, Deurne (Antwerp), Belgium; RPS, London.

Eric Renner PHOTOGRAPHER Born November 6, 1941, in Philadelphia, Renner earned a BS in Design from the University of Cincinnati,

Ohio, in 1964 and an MFA from Cranbrook Academy of Art, Bloomfield, Michigan, in 1968.

He taught at Western New Mexico University, Silver City (1979), and prior to that was an instructor at Visual Studies Workshop in Rochester, New York (1975), Wright State University, Dayton, Ohio (1974), and State University of New York, Alfred (1968–70).

Renner received an NEA grant in 1980 and a Artist-in-the-Schools grant in 1976 with Laurie Klingensmith in Española, New Mexico.

He works mainly in pinhole photography.

PUBLICATIONS Monograph: *The Horsefetter,* 1978. Book: *Primitive Systems for Recycling Human Waste,* w/John Wood, 1969.
COLLECTIONS Cincinnati Mus. of Art, Ohio; Colgate Univ., Hamilton, N.Y.; MOMA, NYC; Mus. of Fine Art, Santa Fe, N. Mex.; Ohio-Wesleyan Univ., Delaware, Ohio; Univ. of N. Mex., Albuquerque; VSW, Rochester. Museo de Art de São Paulo, Brazil; Museo de Arte Moderno, Mexico City; Natl. Gall. of Canada, Ottawa, Ontario.
REPRESENTATIVE Visual Studies Workshop, 31 Prince St, Rochester, NY 14607.
ADDRESS Star Route 15, Box 1655, San Lorenzo, NM 88057.

Mark Edmund Rennie PHOTOGRAPHER · AD-MINISTRATOR · ATTORNEY Born May 23, 1949, in Baltimore, Maryland, Rennie received a BA from Ohio University, Athens (1971), and a law degree from the University of California, San Francisco, Hastings College of Law (1971). He studied photography under Arnold Gassan from 1969 to 1971.

A freelance photographer, Rennie is currently executive director (and founder) of Eyes and Ears Foundation, San Francisco, and is vice-president of Mega Arts Corporation, San Francisco and Richmond, Virginia. In 1973 he co-founded the Holographix Company, a holography studio in Emeryville, California.

Rennie obtained grants from the NEA in 1978 (Artists' Spaces) and 1979 (Photo Exhibition); from the California Arts Council in 1976 (Special Projects), 1977 and 1978 (Organization); and from the San Francisco Hotel Tax Fund in 1979. He belongs to MENSA and the California Bar Association (since 1974).

He is interested in large-scale environmental art works and as of this writing was curating a series of six 20-foot photographs displayed in a permanent outdoor location in San Francisco.

PUBLICATIONS Book: *Big Art,* Environmental Communications, 1977. Periodicals: *Artweek,*

Rennie

Oct 6, 1979, Nov 26, 1977; *Graphis,* Apr 1979; *Artnews,* Jan 1978.

COLLECTIONS Best Products, Inc., Richmond, Va.; Camerawork Gall., San Francisco; Internatl. Mus. of Science, Art & Tech., NYC; Public Art Fund, NYC; Sunlight Pictures Corp., Los Angeles.

ADDRESS 1209 Howard St, San Francisco, CA 94103.

Co Rentmeester *PHOTOGRAPHER* Born in Amsterdam, The Netherlands, on February 28, 1936, Rentmeester studied there until 1960. He continued his studies in the United States at the Art Center College of Design in Pasadena, California, from which he earned a BA in 1965. His mentor is John Bryson, a photojournalist.

Rentmeester was a staff photographer with *Life* magazine from 1966 to 1972, when *Life* stopped publishing as a weekly. Since then he has been a contract photographer with Time Inc. In 1974 he formed Co Rentmeester, Inc., which is still operating.

In 1979 this ASMP member was granted an award for two of his *Life* magazine stories by the University of Missouri, whose School of Journalism also named him Magazine Photographer of the Year in 1972 and granted him a special award for his coverage of the Watts riots in Los Angeles in 1965. Also in 1979 Rentmeester won an award from the World Press Photo in The Netherlands. In 1970 he was the recipient of the Penny-Missouri Award for his *Life* magazine essay "Snow Monkeys of Japan." In 1967 he won the grand prize in the World Photo Competition for a tank-crew photo in Vietnam.

Rentmeester has done many *Life* magazine essays, his subjects ranging from the Watts riot to the Vietnam war to human-interest stories. In the early part of his career he had a particular interest in Indonesia. "Co searches for jarring angles, points of conflict, compelling designs and peak moments. He often uses his camera to exaggerate, to underline, to emphasize. For me the single word that best sums him up as a photographer is 'bold' " (Philip B. Kunhart, Jr., editor, *Life* magazine.

PUBLICATION Monograph: *Three Faces of Indonesia,* 1972 (Elsevier Pub. Co.: Amsterdam).

COLLECTIONS Asia House, NYC; Smithsonian Inst., Wash. D.C. T.I.M., Jakarta, Indonesia; Vincent van Gogh Mus., Amsterdam.

Frank Forster Renwick *CHEMIST · INVENTOR* Born in London, England, in 1877, Renwick died in 1943. He studied science at City of London School, Central Technical College of the City, and Guilds of London Institute.

Renwick began professional research work with the Leathersellers Company, and in 1898 became a research chemist at Britannia Works Company Ltd, forerunner of Ilford. In 1922 he was hired by Dupont to direct the photographic research department at their Parlin, New Jersey, plant. He returned to England in 1925, rejoining Ilford and becoming research director there in 1930.

His earliest contributions to photographic technology were studies of light-absorbing and -scattering media. In 1912 he improved W. B. Ferguson's densitometer, named the Ferguson-Renwick bar photometer. With D. F. Benson's assistance in 1918, he further improved it, changing it from a two-lamp device to one lamp with mirrors. Before World War I, Renwick studied the underexposure curve of the Hurter and Driffield curves, pointing out that it was of greater significance than previously believed. During the war his researches on panchromatic emulsions led to the production of outstanding plates for aerial photography. While at Dupont he developed positive motion film emulsion, and in 1940 he produced what has been considered the first multicontrast paper. He also developed Kryptoscreen paper for use with X-rays.

Renwick's many honors included the Progress Medal of RPS in 1921 and the Péligot Medal of the Société Française de Photographie in 1938.

PUBLICATIONS Books: *Memoirs of a Photochemist,* Fritz Wentzel, 1960; *Photographic Chemistry,* 2 vols., Pierre Glafkides, 1960, 1958; *Focal Encyclopedia of Photography,* 1957, 1956; *Theory of the Photographic Process,* C. E. K. Mees, 1944; *Photography Principles and Practice,* 3rd ed., C. B. Neblette, 1939. Anthology: *Photography's Great Inventors,* Louis W. Sipley, 1965. Periodicals: *Photographic Journal,* 1945, 1943; "The Under-Exposure Period in Theory and Practice," 1913, *Photo Technique,* Oct 1940.

Susan Rebecca Ressler *PHOTOGRAPHER · TEACHER* Born in Philadelphia, Pennsylvania, on September 23, 1949, Ressler received a BA in English Literature from the University of Pittsburgh in Pennsylvania in 1971. She earned an MA in Art from the University of New Mexico, Albuquerque, in 1977, having studied under Van Deren Coke and Beaumont Newhall. She regards W. Eugene Smith as a major influence.

Presently an instructor of photography at Golden West College in Huntington Beach, California, and also at Cerritos College in Norwalk,

California, she taught at both the University of Akron and Cuyahoga Community College (at Parma) in Ohio in 1979. From 1976 to 1978 she taught photography at the University of New Mexico in Albuquerque.

A member of VSW, Rochester, New York, since 1975, Ressler has also been a member of SPE since 1976 and the Los Angeles Center for Photographic Studies since 1978. She received a Ford Foundation Grant, sponsored by the Art Department at the University of New Mexico, in 1978, and an NEA grant in 1979, sponsored by the Photographic Arts Museum in Los Angeles.

Ressler does documentary work with a 35mm camera, "making black-and-white images which describe the contemporary social environment."

PUBLICATIONS Periodicals: *Artweek*, Jan 27, 1979; *British Journal of Photography*, July 1978; *Artspace*, summer 1977.

COLLECTIONS Robert Freidus Gall., NYC; Univ. of New Mexico, Albuquerque. Natl. Film Board of Canada, Ottawa, Ontario.

ADDRESS 615 Hoyt Rd, Huntingdon Valley, PA 19006.

John Reuter MIXED-MEDIA PHOTOGRAPHER Born February 26, 1953 in Chicago, Illinois, Reuter received a BA in Studio Art from the State University of New York at Geneseo (1975), where he studied with Michael Teres, and an MA and MFA in Studio Art & Photography from the University of Iowa, Iowa City (1976, 1978), where he studied with John Schulze.

As of this writing, Reuter was a technical specialist and photographer for the Polaroid Corporation in Cambridge, Massachusetts, and taught photography at the University of Iowa in 1976–78. He directed "Refocus," the University's Photography Festival, in 1977, and was its photography programmer in 1976. From 1973 to 1975 the photographer was a technical assistant at SUNY, Geneseo, in Audio Visual Resources.

Reuter belongs to the Photographic Resource Center and Polaroid Collection Committee. He received a film grant from the Polaroid Corporation in 1977.

The photographer uses Polaroid materials "to explore the combination of the photographic medium with those of painting, drawing, and collage." Working primarily with SX-70 and Polacolor, he "breaks down the photographic image and reconstructs it in a multimedia image."

PUBLICATIONS Anthologies: *One of a Kind*, 1979; *SX-70 Art*, 1979. Periodical: *Zoom*, Nov 1978 (Germany). Reviews: *American Photographer*, Owen Edwards, Oct 1979; *Popular Photography*, Jim Hughes, Jan 1979.

COLLECTIONS State Univ. of N.Y., Geneseo; Univ. of Iowa School of Art, Iowa City. Polaroid Intl. Cllctn., Amsterdam.

REPRESENTATIVE Polaroid Intl, Publicity, 575 Technology Sq, Cambridge, MA 02139.

ADDRESS 8 Ransom Rd, #8, Brighton, MA 02135.

Nancy Louise Rexroth PHOTOGRAPHER · TEACHER Born June 27, 1946, in Washington, D.C., Rexroth attended Marietta (Ohio) College in 1964–65, then received a BFA in English from American University, Washington, D.C. in 1969. She earned an MFA in Photography from Ohio University, Athens, in 1971.

As of this writing, Rexroth was teaching at Wright State University in Dayton, Ohio; she previously taught at Antioch College (1977–79) and Ohio University (1975–76).

A member of SPE and the American Association of University Women, Rexroth won an NEA grant in 1972.

The photographer worked for six years with a Diana camera, creating "memory images." As of this date she works with the SX-70 transfer process, shooting landscapes as well as abstract images.

PUBLICATIONS Monographs: *The Platinotype 1977*, 1977; *Iowa*, 1976. Anthologies: *The Diana and the Nikon*, 1979; *Attitudes: Photography in the 1970's*, 1979; *The Platinum Print*, 1979; *Photography*, Phil Davis, 1979; *130 Years of Ohio Photography*, 1978; *Some Twenty Odd Visions*, 1978; *Aspects of American Photography 1976*, 1976; *The Snapshot*, 1975. Periodicals (reviews): *Camera 35*, A. D. Coleman, Apr & Aug, 1978.

COLLECTIONS CCP, Tucson; Corcoran Gall. of Art, Wash., D.C.; L/C, Wash., D.C.; MOMA, NYC; Smithsonian Inst., Wash., D.C.; Univ. of Mass., Amherst. Bibliothèque Nationale, Paris.

DEALER Light Gall., 724 Fifth Ave, New York, NY 10019.

ADDRESS 421 N. Stafford St, Yellow Springs, OH 45387.

Charles Barton Reynolds PHOTOGRAPHER · PAINTER · MUSICIAN Born January 8, 1935, in New Orleans, Louisiana, Reynolds studied at the Institute of Design, Chicago (1952–56), and at Columbia College, Chicago (1979). He names Aaron Siskind, Harry Callahan, Frederick Sommer and Richard Nickle as mentors.

Since 1978 Reynolds has been a member of the adjunct faculty of Columbia College, and since

1975 he has been a consultant to Chicago Albumen Works. He has also owned Charles Reynolds Photography since 1959.

Reynolds has played principal bassoon for the Northwest Indiana Symphony since 1974 and belongs to American Federation of musicians, Local 578.

The photographer has reactivated use of the Kallitype printing process and made copy negatives of a Muybridge portfolio to print on albumen paper. He also made the first modern albumen prints from Eugène Atget negatives, in association with Chicago Albumen Works and the Museum of Modern Art.

In his own photography Reynolds works with large-format negatives, using Kallitype printing and multiple exposures. He says he investigates "the beauties and mysteries of the natural scene, trying to look 'inside' reality."

PUBLICATIONS Catalogs: *Mirages of Memory: 200 Years of Indiana Art*, 1977 (Indianapolis Mus. of Modern Art/Notre Dame Univ.); *On the Job in Illinois: Then and Now*, 1976 (Ill. Labor Hist. Assoc.). Periodical: "Image Under Foot," *Infinity: ASMP*, 1959.

COLLECTIONS Continental Bank, Chicago; Exchange Natl. Bank, Chicago; Stein, Roe, & Farnham, Chicago; Sun First Natl. Bank, Orlando, Fla.; Anne Tucker Cllctn., Houston, Tex.

DEALER Jacques Baruch Gall., 900 N Michigan Ave, Ste 605, Chicago, IL 60611.

ADDRESS 1422 E Eighth St, Michigan City, IN 46360.

Marc Riboud *PHOTOGRAPHER* Born in 1923 in Lyons, France, Riboud earned a degree in engineering at Lyons in 1948, and is self-taught in photography. His wife, Barbara Chase-Riboud, is a sculptor and author, and they live in Paris.

Riboud joined Magnum Photos in 1954 at the invitation of Robert Capa and Henri Cartier-Bresson. Prior to starting his photographic career in 1952 Riboud worked as an industrial engineer.

The photographer won Overseas Press Club awards in 1970 and 1966.

Riboud has covered stories on almost every continent, from the exotic coronation of the King of Nepal, to the descent of the Swiss Mount Everest expedition, to the turmoil of the emerging African nations and Maoist China. He was the last European journalist to interview and photograph Ho Chi Minh.

PUBLICATIONS Books: *Bangkok*, 1972; *The Face of North Vietnam*, 1970; *The Three Banners of China*, 1966. Periodicals: *Camera*, Nov 1975; *Creative Camera*, Dec 1973, Feb 1973, June 1972,

Mar 1971, Mar 1969, May 1968, Apr 1968, Jan 1968, Aug 1967.

COLLECTIONS Metro. Mus. of Art, NYC; MOMA, NYC.

REPRESENTATIVE Magnum Photos, Inc, 15 W 46 St, New York, NY 10036.

Leland David Rice *PHOTOGRAPHER · TEACHER · CURATOR* Born in Los Angeles, California, on April 9, 1940, Rice received a BS from Arizona State University, Tempe, in 1964, where he studied with Van Deren Coke. He then studied at Chouinard Art Institute in Los Angeles (1964–65) and at California State University, San Francisco, where he received an MA in 1969. At the latter school he worked with Jack Welpott and Don Worth, also attending workshops conducted by Oliver Gagliani (1966) and Paul Caponigro (1968).

Rice was curator of photography and lecturer in art at Pomona College, California, in 1973–79. He was a visiting artist-in-residence at University of California at Los Angeles in 1972, and from 1969 to 1972 was an assistant professor at California College of Arts and Crafts in Oakland. He has also taught numerous short-term workshops, including the Ansel Adams Workshop in Yosemite (1978) and workshops at University of New Mexico, Albuquerque (1977), Tyler School of Art, Philadelphia (1976), and Penland School of Art, North Carolina (1974).

Rice joined the Council of the Center for Southern California Studies in the Visual Arts at California State University, Long Beach, in 1979. He was chairman of the exhibition committee of the Los Angeles Institute of Contemporary Art in 1978, and has been on the board of trustees of Friends of Photography since 1978. He founded and was first president of the Visual Dialogue Foundation in San Francisco (1969–72).

The photographer received an NEA Photographic Survey Grant in 1980, also a Guggenheim Fellowship in 1979, an NEA Photographer's Fellowship in 1978, and earned a commission from the Graphic Arts Council of the Los Angeles County Museum of Art in 1978.

Rice's black-and-white work "focused on environmental portraits of primarily women, then evolved into 'vacant interiors,' capturing the implications of human presence in an unoccupied room." In 1977 he began using color.

PUBLICATIONS Anthologies: *The Photography Collector's Guide*, Lee Witkin & Barbara London, 1979; *Mirrors and Windows*, John Szarkowski, ed., 1978; *Time-Life Annual of Photography*, 1978; *The Photographer's Choice*, 1975. Catalogs: *The Photographic Work of Leland Rice*, Charles W. Millard, 1977 (Hirshhorn Mus. & Sculpture Garden: Wash., D.C.); *Photography in America*, Robert Doty, 1974 (Whitney Mus. of Amer. Art: NYC); *Vision and Expression*, 1969 (IMP/GEH: Rochester); *The Visual Dialogue Foundation*, intro. by Jack Welpott, 1971 (Visual Dialogue Fdn. & Friends of Photography: Davis, Calif.). Catalogs (author): *Photographic Works of Herbert Bayer*, 1977 (MOMA: NYC); *Emerging Los Angeles Photographers*, 1976 (Friends of Photography: Carmel, Calif.); *The Photographs of Moholy-Nagy*, 1975 (Galls. of the Claremont Colls., Pomona Coll.: Calif.). Periodical: "Visual Dialogue Foundation: Members' Portfolio," *Album*, no. 10, 1970.

PORTFOLIO *Silver See*, 1977 (Los Angeles Ctr. for Photographic Studies).

COLLECTIONS Art Inst. of Chicago; CCP, Tucson; Hallmark Gall., NYC; Harvard Univ., Fogg Art Mus., Cambridge, Mass.; IMP/GEH, Rochester; Los Angeles County Mus. of Art; Metro. Mus. of Art, NYC; Minneapolis Inst. of Art, Minn.; MOMA, NYC; Mus. of Fine Arts, St. Petersburg, Fla.; Norton Simon Mus. of Art, Pasadena, Calif.; Oakland Art Mus., Calif.; Phoenix Coll., Ariz.; Pomona Coll., Claremont, Calif.; Princeton Univ. Art Mus., N.J.; San Francisco Mus. of Modern Art; UCLA; Univ. of Colo., Boulder; Univ. of Kans., Lawrence; Univ. of N. Mex., Albuquerque; Vassar Coll., Poughkeepsie, N.Y.; VSW, Rochester.

DEALERS Rosamund Felsen Gall., 669 N La Cienega, Los Angeles, CA 90069; Grapestake Gall., 2876 California St, San Francisco, CA 94115; Diane Brown Gall., 2028 P St NW, Washington, DC 20036.

ADDRESS POB 4188, Inglewood, CA 90309.

Eugene Richards PHOTOJOURNALIST Born April 25, 1944, in Boston, Massachusetts, Richards received a BA in English from Northeastern University, Chicago, Illinois, in 1967. He also studied with Minor White in 1968.

Currently a member of Magnum, Inc., in New York City, Richards was an artist-in-residence at the International Center of Photography, New York City, in 1978, and at the Maine Photo Workshop in 1977. In 1976–77 he conducted workshops and lectured on photography at Harvard University, Cambridge, and Andover Academy, both in Massachusetts, and at Yale University, New Haven, Connecticut. From 1974 to 1978 he was a freelance editorial photographer.

Richards received a Guggenheim Grant in 1980, also a grant from the Massachusetts Artists Foundation in 1978 and an NEA grant in 1974.

PUBLICATIONS Monographs: *Dorchester Days*, 1978; *Few Comforts or Surprises: The Arkansas Delta*, 1973. Anthologies: *Family of Children*, 1977; *Photographer's Choice*, K. Wise, ed., 1976.

COLLECTIONS Addison Gall. of Amer. Art, Andover, Mass.; Everson Mus. of Art, Syracuse, N.Y.; Harvard Univ., Fogg Art Mus., Cambridge, Mass.; Mus. of Fine Arts, Boston; Smithsonian Inst., Wash., D.C.; J. B. Speed Art Mus., Louisville, Ky. Folkwang Mus., Essen, West Germany.

REPRESENTATIVE Magnum Photos, 15 W 46 St, New York, NY 10036.

ADDRESS 251 Park Ave S, New York, NY 10010.

Arthur Rickerby PHOTOGRAPHER Born in New York City March 15, 1921, Rickerby died in Bethel, Connecticut, August 2, 1972. He earned his BA in Political Science from Duke University, Durham, North Carolina, in 1941 and did graduate work at New York University for two years.

Rickerby worked under the direction of Edward Steichen, then a naval captain, during World War II. In the U.S. Navy from 1942 to 1946, he then worked for UPI (1942–1960) and *Life* (1961–72) and freelanced for *Coronet, Parade, Paris-Match, Saturday Evening Post* and *Sports Illustrated*.

Rickerby won a variety of awards for his photography: first prize in magazine sports photography, University of Missouri School of Journalism, 1966; Picture of the Year, third prize in portrait or personality, 1962; Missouri School of Journalism annual award, 1951 and 1952; *Life* magazine award, 1952; National Headliners Award for best news feature picture, 1952; National Press Photographers Association, n.d.; U.S. Navy Photographic Institute citation "for exceptionally meritorious photography . . . showing the plight of the civilians on Okinawa . . . one of the great picture records of the war."

In honor of Rickerby, a dedicated environmentalist, the Ecology League of Connecticut established the Arthur Rickerby Memorial Award in 1972 to "recognize those in public service or journalism who have done distinguished work in protecting Connecticut's environment."

One of the first press photographers to experiment with 35mm, Rickerby was best known for his sports photographic essays and was nominated for a Pulitzer Prize for his part in bringing about more natural photojournalism.

COLLECTION MOMA, NYC.

ARCHIVE Time-Life Archives, 1271 Ave of the Americas, New York, NY 10020.

Heinrich Riebesehl *PHOTOGRAPHER* Born January 9, 1938, in Lathen, Germany, Riebesehl studied photography with Dr. Otto Steinert at the Folkwangschule, Essen, West Germany, in 1963–65.

A teacher of photography at the Fach Hochschule Hannover (West Germany) since 1968, he has also co-directed the Photogallery Spectrum at the Kunstmuseum, Hannover, since 1971.

Riebesehl belongs to GDL (since 1969) and DGPh (since 1970).

His work is documentary, being mainly landscapes and cityscapes in northern and central Germany.

PUBLICATIONS Monographs: *Heinrich Riebesehl: Agrarlandschaften,* intro. by Peter Sager, 1979 (Bremen); *Heinrich Riebesehl: Situationen und Objekte,* Jörg Krichbaum, 1978 (Riesweiler). Anthologies: *Photography as Art,* 1979 (Innsbruck); *In Deutschland, Aspekte gegenwärtiger Dokumentarfotografic,* 1979 (Bonn); *Exploring Photography,* 1978; *Kuntsforum International,* 1976 (Mainz); *Das Deutsche Lichtbild,* 1965–79. Periodicals: *Zoom,* July 1978 (Paris); *British Journal of Photography,* Mar 1976; *Creative Camera,* Nov 1975; *Leica Fotografie,* May 1975, Apr 1973; *Camera,* Jan 1976, July 1970, Mar 1966.

COLLECTIONS Boston Mus. of Fine Art; L/C, Wash., D.C.; New Orleans Mus. of Art, La.; Philadelphia Mus. of Art, Pa. Bibliothèque Nationale, Paris. In Germany: Folkwangmuseum, Essen; Mus. für Kunst und Gewerbe, Hamburg. Stedelijkmuseum, Amsterdam.

DEALERS Galerie Rudolf Kicken, Albertusstrasse 47–49, D-5000, Cologne 1, West Germany; Sander Gall., 2600 Connecticut Ave NW, Washington, DC 20008.

ADDRESS Am Kanonenwall 1, D-3000 Hannover 1, West Germany.

Leni Riefenstahl *FILM MAKER · PHOTOGRAPHER · ACTRESS* Riefenstahl was born in Berlin on August 22, 1902. She began her career as a ballet dancer with the Russian Ballet, having studied at the Mary Wigman School. Between 1923 and 1926 she toured Europe. She made her acting debut in *Der herlige Berg* in 1926. Eventually she became a film director. In 1931 she formed a company, Leni Riefenstahl-Produktion, and produced a number of films, including many documentaries that she also wrote, directed and edited.

Riefenstahl earned a gold medal from Germany's Art Director's Club in 1975, took first prize at the Fest der Volker and the Fest der Schönheit, and a gold medal at the Venice Biennale (1932) for *Das blaue Licht,* one of her best known films, in which she starred as well as co-wrote, produced, directed and edited. Her other films include *Sieg des Glaubens,* 1933; *Triumph des Willens,* 1936; *Olympische Spiele,* 1936. Many of these films suggested the superiority of the "Aryan" race and had the full support of Adolf Hitler. Because of this, Riefenstahl was blacklisted by the film industry after World War II and did not return to film work until 1952, when she worked as producer, screenwriter, and cinematographer of *Tiefland.*

In recent years Riefenstahl has concentrated on still photography. Her images have been published in such periodicals as *Stern* and the *Sunday Times Magazine.* Her devotion to the chronicling of the Nuba people of Kordofan, a province of the Sudan, has created a unique portrayal of this primitive people. She shoots in color, using a Leica.

PUBLICATIONS Monographs: *People of Kau,* 1976; *The Last of the Nuba,* 1973.

COLLECTION IMP/GEH, Rochester.

ADDRESS 20 Tengstrasse, Munich 40, Federal Republic of West Germany.

Jacob August Riis *PHOTOGRAPHER · WRITER · SOCIAL REFORMER · LECTURER* Born May 3, 1849, in Ribe, Denmark, Riis died May 26, 1914, in Barre, Massachusetts. Educated by his father, a teacher in the Latin School, he spent a four-year apprenticeship with a carpenter in Copenhagen after attending Ribe Katedralskole.

Riis learned about journalism when still a boy by helping his father prepare a weekly paper. He came to New York in 1870 and picked up various jobs as a laborer for three years. In 1873 he landed a job as a police reporter for the *New York Tribune,* and worked for the *Evening Sun* about 1888. He also did work for Associated Press.

Riis' photographs aided his work as a social reformer in putting through a statute providing for playgrounds. He was a leader in the tenement reform movement and helped establish Mulberry Bend Park and the Jacob A. Riis Neighborhood House. With the support of Theodore Roosevelt, then of the New York Police Commission, he was also instrumental in abolishing the police lodging-house system.

Riis never aimed for the aesthetic but nonetheless created an unequaled record of New York's slum life from about 1885 to 1902, including both its misery and its vitality. His dedication prompted Theodore Roosevelt in 1903 to call him "the ideal American." In his work as a police reporter on New York's Lower East Side, Riis employed the newly invented flashbulb technique to illuminate the dark hallways and drab squalor of tenement conditions, using gelatin dry-plate negatives and silver prints.

PUBLICATIONS Books: *Jacob A. Riis: Photographer and Citizen*, Alexander Alland, Jr., 1974; *Jacob A. Riis: Police Reporter, Reformer, Useful Citizen*, bio., Louise Ware, 1938; *Neighbors*, 1914; *Hero Tales of the Far North*, 1910; *The Old Town*, 1909; *Theodore Roosevelt, the Citizen*, 1904; *Is There a Santa Claus?*, 1904; *The Peril and the Preservation of the Home*, 1903; *Children of the Tenements*, 1903; *The Battle with the Slum*, 1902; *The Making of an American*, autobio., 1901, repr. 1970; *A Ten Years War*, 1900; *Out of Mulberry Street*, 1898; *Nibsy's Christmas*, 1893; *The Children of the Poor*, 1892; *How the Other Half Lives*, 1890. Anthology: *Christmas Stories*, 1923.

COLLECTIONS Mus. of the City of N.Y.; N.Y. Hist. Soc.; Univ. of Minn., Minneapolis.

Murray Riss *PHOTOGRAPHER · TEACHER* Born in Poland in February 1940, Riss received a BA in 1963 from City College of the City University of New York. He studied at Cooper Union School of Art in New York City from 1963 to 1966 and took his MFA at Rhode Island School of Design, Providence, in 1968.

A professor at the Memphis Academy of Arts (Tennessee), he has headed its Department of Photography since 1968. He has also been a visiting lecturer in photography and film at Southwestern University at Memphis since 1971.

Riss received an NEA Photographer's Fellowship in 1979.

PUBLICATIONS Book: *The Sleep Book*, w/Shirley M. Linde, 1974. Anthology: *Vision and Expression*, 1969. Periodicals: *Creative Camera*, Jan 1977; *Modern Photography*, June 1974, Nov 1972, June 1972; *Popular Photography's Invitation to Photography*, June 1974.

PORTFOLIO *Portfolio*, intro. by William Parker 1975 (Ctr. for Photographic Studies: Louisville, Ky.).

COLLECTIONS Art Inst. of Chicago; IMP/GEH, Rochester; L/C, Wash., D.C.; David Logan Fndtn., Chicago; Louisville Archives, Ky.; MOMA, NYC; New Orleans Mus. of Art; Opryland Hotel Cllctn., Nashville, Tenn.; Richmond Mus. of Art, Va.; Southwestern Univ. at Memphis, Tenn.; Tenn. State Mus., Nashville; Univ.

of Nebr., Sheldon Mem. Art Gall., Lincoln; Visual Studies Workshop, Rochester. Bibliothèque Nationale, Paris; Natl. Gall. of Canada, Ottawa, Ontario; Ryerson Polytechnic Inst., Ontario, Canada.

REPRESENTATIVE Visual Studies Workshop, 31 Prince St, Rochester, NY 14607.

ADDRESS 1306 Harbert Ave, Memphis, TN 38104.

Humberto Rivas *PHOTOGRAPHER · DRAFTSMAN · PAINTER · FILM MAKER* Born in Buenos Aires, Argentina, on July 14, 1937, Rivas names the photographer Anatole Saderman as his mentor. His wife, Maria Helguera, is a painter.

Working as a publicist photographer, he was photographer for Centro de Actividades e Investigaciones Artísticas, Xavier Corberó, Barcelona, Spain, in 1976–77, and a photography professor for Grup D'Art Fotografic, Barcelona, in 1977. Rivas served as photographer for the Investigation Center of Mass Communication, Art and Technology, in 1971–73, and was chief of the Cultural Center San Martín in Buenos Aires in 1970–71. From 1959 to 1970 he was chief of the photography department at Di Tella Institute in Buenos Aires.

Using medium and large format, the photographer shoots portraits and urban landscapes.

PUBLICATIONS Periodicals: *European Photography*, no. 2, 1980; *Flash Foto*, no. 69, 1980; *Nueva Mente*, Feb 1978; *Le Nouveau Photocinéma*, Apr 1977; *Fotografos Argentinos*, 1976.

COLLECTIONS MOMA, NYC. Bibliothèque Nationale, Paris; Museo de Arte Moderno de Buenos Aires, Argentina.

ADDRESS Avenida República Argentina, 162–2ºla, Barcelona 23, Spain.

LeRoy Robbins *PHOTOGRAPHER · FILM MAKER* Born June 14, 1904, in St. Louis, Missouri, Robbins was apprenticed to artist Oscar Thalinger while working as a photographer for the St. Louis (Missouri) Art Museum in 1922–27. He also studied at the Washington University School of Architecture, St. Louis, in 1924–27.

Currently a freelance photographer, Robbins worked in the motion picture industry from 1940 to 1973 as a documentary film director, cameraman and film editor in Hollywood. He worked in New York for the Office of War Information in 1943–45, for the Canadian Film Board in 1942–43 and as a freelance photographer and independent film producer in 1940–42. A WPA photographer in 1937–39, Robbins was a still photographer for motion picture studios in 1933–

36, and maintained a studio for architectural and advertising photography in 1927–31.

A member of NABET, Local 531, from 1950 to 1973, Robbins joined Friends of Photography in 1972 and Artists' Equity in 1974.

His films include *Even as You and I*, 1937; *Symphony in Stone* (Donal Hurd Sculpture, for the WPA), 1939; *The Big Inch*, 1943; and *Freedom to Learn* (on survival in the Aleutians, for the U.S. Air Force), 1944.

Working in black-and-white, Robbins describes his work as "illusions of reality seen as form."

PUBLICATIONS Catalogs: *New Deal Art—California*, 1976 (Univ. Santa Clara, De Saisset Art Gall.: Calif.); *A Pageant of Photography*, 1940 (Golden Gate Intl. Exposition: San Francisco). Periodical: *Popular Photography*, Oct 1975.

PORTFOLIO *Ancient Peru Today*, 1975 (self-pub.).

COLLECTIONS Oakland Mus., Calif.; MOMA, NYC; San Francisco Mus. of Modern Art; Univ. of Minn., Minneapolis.

DEALER Herbert B. Palmer, 9570 Wilshire Blvd, Beverly Hills, CA 90212.

ADDRESS 10210 Legend Rock Rd, Escondido, CA 92026.

Bruce Stuart Roberts   *PHOTOGRAPHER · EDITOR*   Born February 4, 1930, in Mt. Vernon, New York, Roberts received a BS from New York University in New York City and did postgraduate work in photojournalism at the University of Florida, Gainesville. His major influence was Charles Rado, founder of Rapho-Guillumette Agency.

The director of photography at *Southern Living Magazine* since 1978, Roberts became—and still is—an associate photographer with Rapho-Guillumette (now Photo Researchers) in 1963. Roberts was staff photographer with the *Charlotte Observer* (North Carolina) in 1959–61.

A member of ASMP, Roberts won five first-place awards in the NPPA Picture of the Year competitions between 1959 and 1961 and a *Look* magazine award for excellence in photography in 1959.

A photojournalist, he deals with "the human condition and life as it is in the American South."

PUBLICATIONS Books: *The Cape Hatteras Seashore*, w/David Stick, 1972; *Light of Many Suns*, 1972; *The Goodliest Land*, 1972; *Where Time Stood Still*, w/Nancy Roberts, 1970; *You Can't Kill the Dream*, 1968; *The Face of North Carolina*, 1962.

COLLECTIONS Boston Mus. of Science; Smithsonian Inst., Wash., D.C. World Exhibition of Photography Cllctn., Hamburg, Germany.

REPRESENTATIVE Photo Researchers, 60 E 56 St, New York, NY 10022.

ADDRESS 5018 Juiata Dr, Irondale, AL 35210.

Mark Dennis Roberts   *PHOTOGRAPHER · CURATOR*   Born on March 10, 1943, in Hermosa Beach, California, Roberts studied privately with Darius Milhaud (music) and Imogen Cunningham and Ansel Adams.

Roberts has been curator of the J. Hunt Galleries in Minneapolis, Minnesota, since 1974.

A member of SPE, he was voted architectural photographer of the year by the American Institute of Architects in 1977.

Roberts works in large format, primarily with 8 x 10 and 12 x 20 view cameras. His current work includes a series of male nudes, "Adam Without Eve," and some abstract images, mainly black-and-white.

PUBLICATIONS Periodicals: *European Photography*, no. 2, 1980; *Flash Foto*, no. 69, 1980; *Nueva Mente*, Feb 1978; *Le Nouveau Photocinéma*, Apr 1977; *Fotografos Argentinos*, 1976. Calif. Papal Cllctn., The Vatican, Rome.

ADDRESS J. Hunt Galls., 3011 E 25 St, Minneapolis, MN 55406.

Martin Roberts   *PHOTOGRAPHER · TEACHER · FILM MAKER*   Born on November 22, 1950, in Brighton, England, Roberts earned a diploma in creative photography from Derby College of Art, England (1972), where he studied with John Blakemore.

In 1980–81 Roberts was on a one-year sabbatical from Derby Lonsdale College; he is serving as a Photography Fellow (sponsored by the Arts Council of Great Britain) at Impressions Gallery in York, England, and at York University. He has been a lecturer at Derby since 1977.

A member of East Midlands Independent Filmmakers, Roberts won an East Midlands Arts Grant for film in 1979. He also received major awards from the Arts Council of Great Britain in 1977 and 1975.

The photographer produces 35mm and 4 x 5 color prints of urban landscapes and street scenes.

PUBLICATIONS Periodicals: *Creative Camera*, Apr 1980; *British Journal of Photography*, Oct 1978, Oct 1976.

COLLECTIONS Arts Council of Great Britain, London; Bibliothèque Nationale, Paris.

DEALER Impressions Gall. of Photography, 17 Colliergate, York, Yorkshire, England.

ADDRESS 7 Vincent Ave, Monton, Eccles, Manchester, Lancashire, M30 9GB England.

Selina M. Roberts ADMINISTRATOR · PHOTOGRAPHER Born October 8, 1948, in Philadelphia, Pennsylvania, Roberts received a BA in English from the University of Pennsylvania, Philadelphia (1970), and an MA in Photography from the University of Oregon, Eugene (1974).

In 1979 she became trust administrator of U.S. National Bank of Oregon, Portland, and from 1976 to 1979 was executive director of the Lane Regional Arts Council, Eugene, Oregon. Roberts was a photographer for Harvard University News Office, Cambridge, Massachusetts, from 1970 to 1972, and in 1972 she worked for WGBH-TV in Cambridge, providing slides for the evening news.

Working primarily in portraiture, Roberts uses medium-format black-and-white. Her main body of work is a group of photographs taken over a year's time in a small Oregon town.

PUBLICATIONS Anthologies: *Women See Men*, 1977; *Twelve Oregon Photographers*, 1974.

COLLECTIONS Coos Art Mus., Coos Bay, Ore.; Oakridge Art Mus., Ore.; Shado Gall., Oregon City, Ore.; State of Ore. Capitol Cllctn., Salem.

ADDRESS 1311 NW 24 Ave, Portland, OR 97210.

James Robertson PHOTOGRAPHER Robertson was born in England in the early 1800s; the date of his death is unknown.

He designed medals in the 1830s and was superintendent and chief engraver of the Imperial Mint at Constantinople ca. 1850. He was in partnership with Felice A. Beato from 1852 to 1865, and in 1857 was appointed official photographer to the British military forces in India. After his partnership with Beato was dissolved, Robertson remained in India and worked in association with the photographic firm of Shepherd in Simla.

Robertson and Beato's photographs of the aftermath of the seige of Lucknow in 1858, "are among the most terrifying documents of the ravages of war," according to Beaumont Newhall. Robertson worked with collodion wet-plate negatives made into both salt and albumen prints.

PUBLICATIONS Books: *En Egypte au temps de Flaubert*, Marie-Thérèse & André Jammes, ca. 1976 (Kodak-Pathé: Paris); *Photographic Views and Costumes of Japan*, 1868 (Yokohama); *Indian Mutiny*, 1857–58; *Scenes of the Mutiny*, 1857; *Photographic Views of the Antiquities of Athens*, 1854 (Joseph Cundall: London). Anthology: *The Photograph Collector's Guide*, Lee D. Witkin & Barbara London, 1979; *The Invented Eye*, Edward Lucie-Smith, 1975; *The Magic Image*, Cecil Beaton & Gail Buckland, 1975. Catalog: *19th Century Photographs from the Collection*, preface by Van Deren Coke, 1976 (Univ. of Santa Fe Art Mus.: N. Mex.). Periodical: "Robertson Beato & Co.: Camera Vision at Lucknow, 1857–58," Walter Chappell, *Image* 7, Feb 1958.

COLLECTIONS IMP/GEH, Rochester; MOMA, NYC; Univ. of N. Mex. Art Mus., Albuquerque. In London: Imperial War Mus.; Indian Records; Natl. Army Mus.; Victoria & Albert Mus.

Abby Robinson PHOTOGRAPHER Born November 7, 1947, in Connecticut, Robinson received a BA in Art and Architectural History from Barnard College, New York, in 1970. She earned an MFA in Photography from Pratt Institute, Brooklyn, New York, in 1974.

As of this writing Robinson was a contributing writer and photographer for the *Soho Weekly News*. She also teaches at the School of Visual Arts in New York City. A freelance photographer since 1973, Robinson taught at Rutgers University, New Jersey, in 1979, and was a consultant to the Center for Arts Information, New York, in 1977.

She received a Macdowell Fellowship in 1979.

Of her work Robinson says: "I work in black-and-white and have been concentrating on three series: body parts and gestures, small figures in landscapes (the figure as an intruder or visitor) and an ongoing self-portrait series."

PUBLICATIONS Anthologies: *Women Photograph Men*, 1977; *Women See Men*, 1977.

COLLECTION Droll Kolburt Gall., NYC.

ADDRESS 34 White St, New York, NY 10013.

Cervin Robinson PHOTOGRAPHER · AUTHOR Born May 18, 1928, in Boston, Massachusetts, Robinson received an AB from Harvard University, Cambridge, Massachusetts, in 1950.

Since 1957 he has been a freelance architectural photographer and American representative for *Architectural Review*. He also teaches a course in architectural photography at Columbia University Summer School in New York City and is a correspondent for *Werk/Archithese*, both since 1977.

A member of ASMP and the Society of Architectural Historians, Robinson won a Guggenheim Fellowship in 1971, was named a J. Clawson Mills Scholar in 1978 and directed an

NEA/New York State Council on the Arts-funded project in 1978.

He contributed background still photographs for the films *Superman the Movie* and *Superman II*.

PUBLICATIONS Books: *Skyscraper Style: Art Deco New York*, w/Rosemarie Haag Bletter, 1975; *Architecture of Frank Furness*, 1973. Periodicals: "County Courthouse Project: Group Work, Assigned Work," *Photograph*, July 1977; "Skyscraper Style: Art Deco New York," *Artforum*, Nov 1974.

ADDRESS 251 W 92 St, New York, NY 10025.

David Robinson *PHOTOGRAPHER · WRITER · TEACHER* Born in Cleveland, Ohio, on December 9, 1936, Robinson received a BA in History and English in 1959 from Dartmouth College, Hanover, New Hampshire. After pursuing graduate studies in African history and sociology at the University College of Ghana he returned to Boston University, Massachusetts, to complete an MA in African Studies in 1961. In 1967 he earned an EdM from Harvard University, Cambridge, Massachusetts, and an EdD from Harvard in 1976 in Educational Planning.

Director of the Urban Art Program of Boston's Institute of Contemporary Art in 1974, he has been a freelance photographer, writer and teacher since then.

Robinson is a member of VSW, Friends of Photography, International Center of Photography, Photographic Resource Center and SPE.

Robinson's color work includes dye transfer, Cibachrome and 20 x 24 Polaroid, as well as experimental computer work. He has done a series on Africa, on Yoga, and another on reflections.

PUBLICATIONS Monograph: *Reflections*, 1978. Book: *Beard's Roman Women*, w/Anthony Burgess, 1976. Periodicals: *Popular Photography*, Aug 1979; *The British Journal of Photography*, Sept 1978; *Camera 35*, Oct 1977; *Popular Photography*, Mar 1977; *Nuova Fotografia*, Feb 1974; *Fotografia Italiana*, Mar 1973.

COLLECTIONS AT&T, NYC; Chase Manhattan Bank, NYC; IBM, White Plains, N.Y.; Polaroid Cllctn., Cambridge, Mass.; Univ. of Texas, Gernsheim Cllctn., Austin. Bibliothèque Nationale, Paris.

DEALERS Weston Gall., POB 655, Carmel CA 93921; Boris Gall., 32 Landsdowne St, Boston, MA 02215; Jeb Gall., 342 S. Main St, Providence, RI 02901.

ADDRESS 159 W Canton St, Boston, MA 02118.

Henry Peach Robinson *PHOTOGRAPHER* [See plate 19] Born in 1830 in Ludlow, Shropshire, Robinson died in 1901 in Tunbridge Wells, England. He studied art, maintaining interests in etching, sculpture and literature, and was influenced by the Pre-Raphaelites and O. G. Rejlander's composite prints.

Robinson first worked as a clerk in a bookstore in Leamington, where he opened a portrait studio in 1857, having become interested in photography in 1852. In 1868 he worked in partnership with N. K. Cherrill in Tunbridge Wells where he built the Great Hall Studio in 1878. Robinson wrote eleven volumes on photography and had many articles published in the photographic journals of the day.

He was an honorary member of the London Photographic Society (1871) and a founder/member of The Linked Ring (1892). The photographer received more than 100 official honors and medals between the years 1860 and 1890, and his photography handbooks were for decades the most influential English-language works on the aesthetics and practice of photography.

Frequently recognized as the founder of the English pictorialist school, Robinson initially used the collodion wet-plate process, eventually changing to gelatin silver bromide plates. He is especially noted for his combination prints, created by piecing together various prints, blending the seams and rephotographing the assemblage. His subjects were anecdotal and often pastoral, though he created such scenes with the use of backdrops, props and costumes in his studio.

PUBLICATIONS Books: *The Elements of a Pictorial Photograph*, 1896, repr. 1973; *Art Photography in Short Chapters*, 1890, 5th ed., 1910 (London); *Photography as a Business*, 1890 (Percy Lund: Bradford, England); *Picture-Making by Photography*, 2nd ed., 1889 (London); *L'atelier du photographe*, 1888 (Gauthier-Villars: Paris); *Letters on Landscape Photography*, 1888, repr. 1973; *La Photographie en plein air*, 1886, *De l'effet artistique en photographie . . .* , 1885 (Gauthier-Villars: Paris); *The Studio and What to Do in It*, 1885, rev. ed. 1905 (Piper & Carter: London); *Picture-Making by Photography*, 1884, repr. 1973; *The Art and Practice of Silver Printing*, w/Capt. Abney, 1881, repr. 1973; *Pictorial Effect in Photography*, 1869, repr. 1971; *Yearbook of Photography*, 1871; *Die Momentphotographie*, 2nd ed., Josef Maria Eder, 1886. Anthologies: *The Photograph Collector's Guide*, Lee D. Witkin & Barbara London, 1979; *The Invented Eye*, Edward Lucie-Smith, 1975; *The Magic Image*, Cecil Bea-

ton & Gail Buckland, 1975; *Early Photographs &*
Early Photographers, Oliver Mathews, 1973; *The*
Camera, 1971, *Great Photographers*, 1970, Time-
Life Series; *Photographers on Photography*, Na-
than Lyons, ed., 1966. Periodical: *The Photo-*
graphic Times, autobio., 1897.

PORTFOLIO *Henry Peach Robinson*, 1830–
1901, intro. & notes by Margaret Harker, essay
by Ian Jeffrey, prntd. by Howard Grey, 1976 (Photographic Cllctns. & RPS: London).

COLLECTIONS IMP/GEH, Rochester; Smithsonian Inst., Wash., D.C.; Univ. of Tex., Gernsheim Cllctn., Austin. Natl. Gall. of Canada,
Ottawa, Ontario; RPS, London.

John R. Robinson *PHOTOJOURNALIST* Born
in 1907 in Des Moines, Iowa, Robinson died
there on September 28, 1972.

Robinson joined the staff of the *Des Moines*
Register and Tribune in 1927 and remained there
until his retirement on June 30, 1972. During
World War II, he served three years in the South
Pacific as a combat still and motion picture pho-
tographer for the Army Signal Corps.

The photographer was a member of Polk
County Men's Garden Club, the American Legion, the Iowa Press Photographers Association
and an honorary lifetime member of NPPA. He
won the Pulitzer Prize in 1952 for Best News
Photography. In the same year he won honorable
mention in the News Pictures of the Year competition sponsored by the University of Missouri
School of Journalism and the Encyclopaedia Britannica, an award from the Kappa Alpha Mu photographic fraternity, and the Graflex Diamond
award.

Though he specialized in sports pictures, Robinson covered everything from the 1929 Des
Moines University riot to a Billy Sunday revival
to Jean Piccard's balloon ascensions in the Midwest in the 1930s. His Pulitzer Prize-winning
sequence of photographs showed Drake University's black all-American halfback, Johnny
Bright, receive a deliberate blow to the jaw at a
football game in Stillwater, Oklahoma, with
what is now Oklahoma State University.

PUBLICATION Anthology: *Moments*, Sheryle
& John Leekley, foreword by Dan Rather, 1978.

Sue Carol Robinson *PHOTOGRAPHER · FILM*
MAKER · TEACHER Born December 28, 1944, in
Danville, Illinois, Robinson earned a BFA at the
University of New Mexico, Albuquerque (1967),
and an MFA from the University of Colorado,
Boulder (1973). Her early influences were Jack

Welpott and her association with Visual Dialogue Foundation.

Robinson has been an instructor of photography and film-making for the University of Colorado Fine Arts Department since 1973. She is a
founding member (1978) and currently co-chairperson of The Silver Source in Boulder.

An NEA grant recipient in 1978, Robinson has
produced three short 16mm color films: *Solar*
Film Journal (1979), *Brownian Movement* (1978)
and *Navigation Without Numbers* (1977).

The photographer's recent work involves inclusion of the written word and an additive process in which images are combined and altered
by chemical stains, hand-coloring and other techniques.

PUBLICATIONS Book: *Preparatory Notes and*
Drawings, 1976. Catalog: *California Photogra-*
phers, 1970 (Norton Simon Cllctn.). Periodical:
Combinations: Journal of Photography, vol. 1,
1977.

COLLECTIONS Denver Art Mus., Colo.; Norton Simon Mus., Pasadena, Calif.; Univ. of Colo.,
Boulder. Victoria & Albert Mus., London.

ADDRESS 216 Chautauqua, Boulder, CO
80302.

Alexander Mihailovich Rodchenko *PHOTOG-*
RAPHER · GRAPHIC ILLUSTRATOR · PAINTER Born
November 23, 1891, in St. Petersburg (now Leningrad), Rodchenko died on December 3, 1956.
He attended the School of Arts in Kazan, Russia,
from 1910 to 1914, then studied graphic arts at
the School of Applied Arts in Moscow (1915).
The artist was influenced by the Futurists, Cubism and Art Nouveau, and his mentor was Vladimir Tatlin.

Rodchenko's first job was as an assistant to
Tatlin at a 1916 Futurist exhibit in Moscow, at
which ten of Rodchenko's pictures were shown.
In 1918 Rodchenko helped found the Museum of
Artistic Culture and became its first director. By
1920 he was one of the most active members of
the Institut Khudozhestvennoy Kultury—also
known as Inkhuk—and he taught at Vkhutemas
(High-Grade Art—Technical Workshops). Beginning in 1918 he was active for several years with
the Committee of Applied Arts, a government
agency. In 1921–22 he did illustrative work in
theater, films, typography and advertising, and
continued throughout the 1920s to provide cover
designs for a remarkably wide range of publications—from the poet Mayakovsky's books
(1925–29) to scientific and technical literature
for Moscow publishers. He also designed the

cover of *Kino-Fot*, a periodical of the Russian Constructivists which began in 1922 and in which Rodchenko was regularly published.

He took up photography in 1924 and gave a short series of talks on the medium at Vkutein (Fine Arts Technical School) in the early 1920s. From 1920 to 1930 he taught at the newly organized Free Public Art Studio (formerly his alma mater, Stroganov School of Applied Arts), where he also served as dean of the faculty of metalwork. Rodchenko began photo-reporting in 1926, working for the magazines *Ogonok, Radioslushatel, Prozhektor, Krasnoye Studenchestvo, Dayosh, Za rubezhom, Smena, Borba klassov* and the daily *Vechernaya Moskva*, among others. In 1932 the photographer, whose work was—and still is—widely exhibited, began working in photomontage.

During his first and only trip abroad Rodchenko was awarded four silver medals at the Paris Exhibition of March 1925.

Also involved in the film world, Rodchenko shot a newsreel series directed by Dziga Vertov, originally called *Kino-Pravda* and later called *One-sixth of the World*, which was begun in 1922. Between 1927 and 1930 he was "constructor-artist" of the films *The Woman Journalist, Moscow in October, Albidum, The Puppet Millionaire* and *What Shall I be?*. He also directed the documentary *The Chemicalization of the Forest*. Seemingly unlimited in his versatility, Rodchenko was also involved in theater, designing the costumes and props for Glebov's *Pendulum* and *The Bed Bug* in 1929, and was one of Russia's foremost painters, collagists and poster artists.

A Constructivist, Rodchenko was one of the earliest photo-collagists. Some of his favorite themes were sports, the circus, festive processions and the Soviet way of life. He successfully experimented with close-up photography, and "the lens of his camera discovered objects of unusual architecture, rhythm, and plasticity" in objects removed from their usual surroundings. "The viewer who sees only a study in the picture of the glass jug illuminated from behind fails to appreciate the masterly composition, the noble purity of the lines, the rich plasticity of the form and consequently also the poetry and beauty of the picture, and still more important, its specifically photographic qualities" (Karginov, *Rodchenko*).

PUBLICATIONS Monographs: *Rodchenko*, German Karginov, 1975, 1979 (Thames & Hudson: London); *Alexander Rodchenko*, L. Volkov-Lannit, 1968 (Moscow); *Alexander Rodčenko*, L. Lin-

hart, 1964 (Prague). Books: *Rodchenko and the Arts of Revolutionary Russia*, David Elliott, ed., 1979; *Iz istoriy sovietskovo kostyuma*, T. Strizhenova, 1972 (Moscow); *Sovietsky reklamny plakat 1917–1932*, V. Lyakhov, 1972 (Moscow); *Az avantgardizmus (Avant-Gardism)*, M. De Micheli, 1969 (Gondolat: Budapest); *A Concise History of Modern Sculpture*, 1964, *A Concise History of Modern Painting*, 1959–74, H. A. Read; *A. M. Rodchenko*, Iskusstvo Knigi (Book Art), vol. 2, N. A. M. Khardzhiyev, 1961 (Moscow); *Puty sovietskoy zhivopisy 1917–1932*, M. Bush, 1933 (Moscow); *Sovietskoe iskusstvo za 15 let*, I. Matsa, L. Reingerndt & L. Rempely, eds., 1933 (Moscow); *About This*, Mayakovsky, 1932; *Agit i proiskusstvo*, B. Arvatov, 1930 (Moscow); *Iskusstvo i proizvodstvo*, B. Arvatov, 1926 (Moscow); *Ot molberta k mashinye*, N. Tarabukin, 1923 (Moscow); *Konstruktivizm*, A. Gan. 1922 (Tver); *Neue Kunst in Russland, 1914–1919*, K. Umansky, 1920 (Potsdam & Munich). Anthology: *The Magic Image*, Cecil Beaton & Gail Buckland, 1975. Catalog: *Masters of Soviet Photographic Art*, 1935 (Moscow). Periodicals: "A. M. Rodchenko," L. Zhadova, *Lettres Françaises*, Nov 10, 1966; "A. M. Rodchenko," A. Abramova, *Iskusstvo*, no. 11, 1966; "Ahizny, polnaya poiskov," V. Lapshin, *Tvorchestvo*, no. 9, 1962; *Novii Lef*, no. 6, 1927.

COLLECTIONS Sam Wagstaff Cllctn., NYC. Australian Natl. Gall., Canberra; Colin Osman Cllctn., London; Mus. of Modern Art, Oxford, England.

George Rodger PHOTOJOURNALIST Born in Cheshire, England, in 1908, Rodger began photographing while in the merchant marine.

Having gone around the world twice before he was nineteen, Rodger left the merchant marine and worked in America at many different jobs during the Depression. After seven years he returned to England and became a photographer for the BBC in London (1936–38). He then freelanced a year for the Black Star Agency before being hired as a *Life* staff photographer. Working in the magazine's London office, he covered the blitz and other war actions. His territory grew to encompass Morocco, China and over forty other countries.

Rodger was a founding member of Magnum in 1947, and he received an Arts Council of Great Britain grant in 1977.

PUBLICATIONS Monographs: *George Rodger*, 1975 (Gordon Fraser: London); *Le Village des Nubas*, 1955 (Robert Delpire: Paris); *Desert Journey*, 1944, *Red Moon Rising*, 1943 (Cresset Press:

London). Anthologies: *Dialogue with Photography*, Paul Hill & Thomas Cooper, 1979; *The Magic Image*, Cecil Beaton & Gail Buckland, 1975. Periodicals: *Creative Camera*, May 1972, Nov 1968, Feb 1968.

COLLECTIONS MOMA, NYC. Bibliothèque Nationale, Paris; Rijksmuseum, Amsterdam.

Wilhelm Conrad Roentgen PHYSICIST · TEACHER Born March 27, 1845, in Lennep, Prussia (now Remscheid, Germany), Roentgen died February 10, 1923, in Munich. Having moved to Apeldoorn, The Netherlands, at age three, he attended elementary and secondary schools there. He studied at the technical school in Utrecht from 1861 to 1864 and at the university there for a year. Roentgen completed his education at the university in Zurich, Switzerland, from 1865 to 1869.

The physicist taught at the agricultural academy in Hohenheim (1875), at the University of Strasbourg (1876–78), at the University of Giessen (1879–87), at the University of Würzburg (1888–89) and at the University of Munich (1900–23). During his career he presented some sixty scientific papers.

On November 8, 1895, Roentgen discovered X-rays, which proved to be invaluable in medicine, crystallography and industry. Originally they were called Roentgen Rays, and their discovery earned him the first Nobel Prize for physics, in 1901. Roentgen also did research on the action of fluids, absorption of heat by gases, conduction of heat in crystals, and absorptiopiezoelectricity. A museum was dedicated to him and his work in 1930 in the town of Remscheid-Lennep.

PUBLICATIONS Books: *Quellendarstellungen zur Geschichte der Fotografie*, Wolfgang Baier, 1964; *Lexikon für Photographie und Reproduktionstechnik*, G. H. Emmerich, 1910. Anthology: *Photography's Great Inventors*, Louis W. Sipley, 1965. Catalog: *Brochure by Roentgen Museum*, Aug 1961. Periodicals: *Bild und Ton*, 1961; *Image*, Mar 1960, Apr 1953; *Radiography and Clinical Photography*, 1945; *British Journal Photographic Almanac*, 1897; *Photographische Correspondenz*, 1896; *Photographic Times*, 1896.

Charles J. Roitz PHOTOGRAPHER · TEACHER Roitz earned a BS in English Literature, philosophy and administration from Regis College in Denver, Colorado (1961), and an MA in Art/Photography from San Francisco State University (1968).

Since 1970 Roitz has been associate professor of fine arts at the University of Colorado, Boulder. Previously he taught fine arts at Diablo Valley College, Concord, California (1969–70), at Phoenix College, Arizona (1968–69), and at California College of Arts and Crafts in Oakland (1968). He also worked as a motion picture specialist for Dow Chemical in Golden, Colorado (1963–64), and as a producer/director for KOA Television in Denver (1961–63).

Roitz is a founding member of The Silver Source (1977), Visual Dialogue Foundation (1968) and Colorado Center for Photographic Studies (1977), serving on the latter's executive committee. He is also a member of SPE (since 1968) and was the founding president of that group's regional chapter (1972). The photographer won an NEA fellowship in 1979.

PUBLICATIONS Book: *Innovative Printmaking*, Thelma R. Newman, 1977. Catalogs: *DAMXX*, 1977 (Denver Art Mus.); *The Great West, Real/Ideal*, 1977 (Univ. of Colo.: Boulder); *Photo/Synthesis*, Jason D. Wong, 1976 (Cornell Univ., Herbert F. Johnson Mus. of Art: Ithaca, N.Y.); *Charles Roitz, Photographs & Photosculptures*, 1974 (Denver Art Mus.); *Light and Substance*, Van Deren Coke, 1974 (Univ. of N. Mex. Art Mus.: Albuquerque). Periodicals: "Photography, Visual Dialogue in Carmel," Jan Murray, *Artweek*, Feb 19, 1972; *Album*, Sept 1971; "Photography into Sculpture," Peter Bunnell, *Artcanada*, June 1970; "Photography into Sculpture and Prints," Peter Bunnell, *Art in America*, Sept 1969.

COLLECTIONS Ctr. of the Eye, Aspen, Colo.; Chicago Art Inst.; Denver Art Mus.; Exchange Natl. Bank, Chicago; IMP/GEH, Rochester; Lange Cllctn., Boulder, Colo.; MOMA, NYC; Norton Simon Mus., Pasadena, Calif.; Oakland Mus., Calif.; San Francisco Mus. of Modern Art; San Jose State Coll., Calif.; UCLA; Univ. of Colo., Boulder; VSW, Rochester.

ADDRESS 1135 Jay St, Boulder, CO 80302.

Witold Romer PHOTOGRAPHER · SCIENTIST Romer was born in 1900 in Poland, where he died in 1967.

Beginning in 1931, Romer lectured on photography at Lwow Polytechnic, eventually transforming it into a scientific institute of photochemistry. A new technique he had developed, which he called "isohelia," was made public in 1932. During World War II he moved to London, where he worked for the Royal Air Force. In 1946 Romer returned to Poland and was appointed professor on the staff of Wrocław Polytechnic in Warsaw. Romer's photographic works were frequently exhibited.

PUBLICATIONS Periodicals: "Investigations on the Influence of Gelatin on the Recrystallization of Silver Bromide Suspensions," w/A. Sidorowicz, May/June 1967, "The Absorption Cross Section for Light of the Silver Grains in Photographic Deposits," w/T. Morawski, May/June 1963, "Part II: Further Experimental Results," Sept/Oct 1966, "Polish Research on Graininess and Granularity," Sept/Oct 1963, *Journal of Photographic Science;* "The Mechanism of Growth and the Structure of Microcrystals of the Silver Halides," May/June 1966, "Graininess of the Photographic Image," Nov/Dec, Sept/Oct, May/June 1960, *Zhurnal Nauchnoi I Prikladnoi Fotografii I Kinematografii;* Photographic Granularity and Graininess," *Science et Industrie Photographiques,* Jan 1959; "An Instrument for the Measurement of Graininess," w/E. W. H. Selwyn, *Photographic Journal,* no. 83, 1943.

COLLECTIONS Muzeum Narodowe we Wroctawiu, Warsaw, Poland.

Willy Ronis *PHOTOGRAPHER* Born in Paris, France, on August 14, 1910, Ronis earned a BA, but was self-taught in photography, beginning in 1926. His major influences have been drawing and music.

In 1932 Ronis joined his father's photo studio, working there until his father's death, in 1936. He then began a freelance career as an illustrator and reporter, which has continued until the present, interrupted only by World War II.

Ronis won the 1979 Grand Prix Nationale des Arts et Lettres, presented by the Culture and Communication Minister in France, and in 1975 received the Président d'Honneur of the Association Nationale des Reporters Photographes Illustrateurs.

Ronis does reportage, illustration and industrial photography. He used medium format until 1954, then switched to small format. He occasionally uses large format for advertising and fashion.

PUBLICATIONS Books: *Belleville-Menilmontant,* Arthaud, ed., text by Pierre MacOrlan, 1954; *Photo-Reportage et Chasse aux Images,* text & photos, Montel, ed., 1951.

COLLECTION Bibliothèque Nationale, Paris.

REPRESENTATIVE Rapho Agency, 8 rue d'Alger, 75001 Paris, France.

DEALER Agathe Gaillard Gall., 3 rue du Pont Louis Philippe, 75004 Paris, France.

ADDRESS 8 rue Ledru Rollin, 84800 l'Isle sur la Sorgue, France.

Laurent P. J. Roosens *WRITER · PHOTOHISTORIAN · ORGANIC CHEMIST* Born July 21, 1923, in Antwerp, Belgium, Roosens earned a Doctorate in Chemistry from the University of Basel, Switzerland, in 1950.

Since 1974 Roosens has been head of the Documentation and Information Department of Agfa-Gevaert, and previously held positions there in quality control (1958–73) and research (1950–57).

The chemist is a member of the board of trustees of the Sterckshof Museum in Deurne-Antwerp, Belgium (since 1972), and is currently president of the European Society for the History of Photography. He also belongs to DGPh, SPE, and RPS and is on the advisory board of the latter's Permanent Collection Committee. Roosens serves on the international advisory board of *History of Photography* magazine and is a permanent collaborator of *Misset Foto Magazine* in Brussels, Belgium.

Roosens holds fifteen patents in the field of organic chemistry and has authored some forty-five publications on organic chemistry and the history of photography.

PUBLICATIONS Books: *Encyclopedie voor Fotografie en Cinematografie,* 1971 (Elsevier: Amsterdam); *De Fotokunst in Belgie 1839–1940,* w/ Claude Magelhaes, 1970 (Sterckshof: Belgium). Anthology: *Fotofaszination,* J. Wilsberger & K. Opten Höfel, 1975 (Bertelsmann/Gutersloh).

ADDRESS Jaak Blockxstraat 39, B-2510, Mortsel, Belgium.

Nile Root *TEACHER · PHOTOGRAPHER* Born December 11, 1926, in Denver, Colorado, the self-taught photographer worked with Arnold Gasson, Walter Chappell and Syl Labrot in the 1950s and assisted Minor White in Denver workshops in the 1960s; he was also influenced by Edward Weston and Ansel Adams. In 1979 he received an MS from Rochester Institute of Technology (RIT), New York.

Root has been an associate professor of biomedical photographic communications at RIT since 1972, and previous to that was director of Photography for Science in Denver (1970–72). He was also director of the Department of Biomedical Photography at Children's Hospital, Denver (1970–71), and of the Department of Biophotography and Medical Illustration at General Rose Memorial Hospital in Denver (1960–70). From 1952 to 1960 Root was president of the Photography Workshop, Inc., in Denver.

The photographer has belonged to the American Association for the Advancement of Science since 1965, Astronomical Society of the Pacific since 1969, Biological Photographic Association since 1964 (he is a fellow, registered, and was on the board of governors in 1976–78), George Eastman House since 1972, SPE since 1972 and is a charter member of Friends of Photography.

Winner of thirty-five national and international awards in biomedical photography between 1965 and 1979, Root won a Faculty Fellowship Award from RIT in 1979 and directed a Department of Health, Education, and Welfare grant project at RIT from 1974 to 1977. He received five gold medal awards from the Art Directors Club in 1958.

Root works mainly with black-and-white medium- and large-format silver prints. His personal work is "straight" depictions of landscapes and designs and patterns in nature. His biological photography concentrates on the anatomy of the human brain and of the heart; he is also interested in astrophotography.

PUBLICATIONS Books: *Introductory Neuropathology*, J. Minckler, ed., 1974; *Introduction to Neuroscience*, J. Minckler, ed., 1972; *Human Heart*, B. Phibbs, ed., 1967. Catalog: *Photograph, USA*, 1967 (De Cordova Mus.: Lincoln, Mass.).

COLLECTIONS Biological Photographic Assoc., NYC; Colo. Photographic Arts Ctr., Denver.

ADDRESS 38 Kurt Rd, Pittsford, NY 14534.

Henry Enfield Roscoe *CHEMIST* Born in England in 1833, Roscoe died in 1915. He studied chemistry with Robert Wilhelm Bunsen at the University of Heidelberg, Germany, in the 1850s after 1852.

Roscoe began collaborating with Bunsen, and the two published a series of articles from 1854 to 1859 on the chemical action of light in photometry, actinometry and spectrum analysis. Considered by many historians to be the foundation of photochemistry, their work resulted in the formulation of the Bunsen and Roscoe Law, or the Reciprocity Law. It stated that the amount of a photochemical reaction depended upon the light energy absorbed, thus relating to the development of densities in a photographic emulsion. Later research by Schwarzschild, Sheppard, Mees and others found that the rule applied chiefly to moderate intensities of illumination. Bunsen and Roscoe also discovered that magnesium wire or ribbon could be used as a source of photographic light, and presented papers on this work in 1859 and 1864. They invented an apparatus for burning magnesium wire wound on spools and moved by clockwork, with the end of the wire being ignited by the flame of an alcohol lamp.

PUBLICATIONS Books: *Quellendarstellungen zur Geschichte der Fotografie*, Wolfgang Baier, 1964; *History of Photography*, Helmut & Alison Gernsheim, 1955; *Lexikon für Photographie und Reproduktionstechnik*, G. H. Emmerich, 1910. Anthology: *Photography's Great Inventors*, Louis W. Sipley, 1965. Periodicals: *Bild und Ton*, 1951, 1949; *Photographische Correspondenz*, 1899; *Photographic News*, 1864; *Poggendorffs Annalen der Physik und Chemie*, 1855–59.

Ann B. Rosen *PHOTOGRAPHER · BOOKMAKER · TEACHER* Born December 4, 1948, in Brooklyn, New York, Rosen received a BFA from State University of New York at Buffalo in 1971. She also received an MFA in 1978 from the Visual Studies Workshop of SUNY in Rochester, where she studied under Nathan and Joan Lyons, John Wood and Keith Smith. From 1971 to 1972 she attended Massachusetts Institute of Technology, studying with Minor White and Ron MacNeil.

Founder-manager of Hard Press since 1978, Rosen has also been publications co-ordinator at the Hallwalls Gallery since 1977. She has taught at SUNY (1979), the Educational Opportunity Center (1979) and Cepa Gallery (1976–79), all in Buffalo, and at VSW in Rochester (1975).

A recipient of a grant from the New York State Council on the Arts in 1979, Rosen was also awarded a Graduate Access Resource Development Corporation Grant for 1976–77.

The photographer describes her work as being "about combinations—an overlapping of mediums (words and images), a series of images (collage), color and textural patterns."

PUBLICATIONS Monographs: *Wenat-Chee Walla and Me*, 1980 (self-pub.); *Fog & Ice*, 1979 (self-pub.); *Tableaux Tablet*, 1978 (self-pub.); *Monolitto Mania*, 1977 (self-pub.); *Gospel According to Lilith*, 1976.

COLLECTIONS In N.Y.: Albright-Knox Art Gall. Lib., Buffalo; Burchfield Ctr., Buffalo; Niagara County Community Coll. Gall., Sanborn; Niagara Univ., Buscaglia Castellani Art Gall., DeVeaux Campus, Niagara Falls.

ADDRESS 417 E 64 St, Apt 4H, New York, NY 10021.

Walter Rosenblum *PHOTOGRAPHER · TEACHER* Born October 1, 1919, in New York City, Rosenblum attended College of the City of New York. He joined New York City's Photo League in 1937 and took a workshop led by Sid Grossman, later studying with Lewis Hine and Paul Strand (1939).

Rosenblum's photographs were first published by Ralph Steiner in the newspaper *PM*, and in 1939 he worked as assistant to *Life* photographer Eliot Elisofon. A staff photographer with the Agricultural Adjustment Administration in 1942, he became a professor in the Art Department at Brooklyn College, New York, in 1947, and has remained there to the present. He was also a professor at the Yale Summer School of Music and Art, New Haven, Connecticut (1952–78), and an adjunct instructor at New York City's Cooper Union (1949–59).

An active member of the Photo League from 1937 to 1952, Rosenblum served variously as its executive secretary, vice-president and president (1941), was chairman of the exhibition committee and edited *Photo Notes*. He has also served on the board of directors of Photographers Forum since 1952, and was a founding member of SPE in 1962.

The photographer won a Guggenheim Fellowship in 1979, an NEA fellowship in 1978, a working grant from the Institute for Art and Urban Resources in 1978 and a CAPS award in 1977.

His work is predominantly documentary, concerned with "man's relation to man." Working in black-and-white, he has photographed Manhattan's lower East Side, Haiti, Spanish refugee camps in France, and Spanish Harlem.

PUBLICATIONS Books: *The West Indies, Islands in the Sun*, Wilfred Carty, 1967; *Learning and Its Disorders*, Dr. I. N. Berlin, 1952. Anthologies: *The Photograph Collector's Guide*, Lee D. Witkin & Barbara London, 1979; *Documentary Photography*, Time-Life Series, 1972. Catalogs: *A Walter Rosenblum Retrospective*, intro. by Paul Strand, 1976 (Queens Mus.: Flushing, N.Y.); *Walter Rosenblum, Photographer*, intro. by Milton Brown, 1975 (Harvard Univ., Fogg Art Mus.: Cambridge, Mass.); *Walter Rosenblum*, intro. by Paul Strand, 1949 (Brooklyn Mus.: N.Y.). Periodicals: "Rare Dancer," Louis Stettner, Jan 1976, "Speaking Out," Louis Stettner, Dec 1974, "Famous Teachers Criticize Readers' Pictures," Barbara Ullman, June/July 1965, "Starting Your Photographic Career," Edna Bennett, Dec 1963, *Camera 35*; "Documentary Style, Human Expression," Stephen Perloff, *Philadelphia Photo Review*, Jan 1976; "Rosenblum Retrospective at Harvard," review, Jack Deschin, *The Photo Reporter*, Feb 1975; "Between Teacher and Student, Six Great Teachers Tell How They Work," Jack

Deschin, *35mm Photography*, summer 1974; "Educating the Young Photographer," *Infinity: ASMP*, Apr 1970; "Photographic Style," *Contemporary Photographer*, summer 1963; "The Art of Photography in College Teaching," Van Deren Coke, *College Art Journal*, summer 1960; "Teaching Photography," *Aperture*, 4:3; "Walter Rosenblum, Photographer in the Classic Tradition," Minor White, *Image*, Dec 1955; "Five Weeks with a Camera," Jan 1953, "Introducing Walter Rosenblum," Jerome Liebling, May 1951, "What Is Modern Photography," Mar 1951, *American Photography*.

COLLECTIONS Brooklyn Mus., N.Y.; IMP/ GEH, Rochester; MOMA, NYC; Queens Mus., Flushing, Queens, N.Y. Bibliothèque Nationale, Paris.

ADDRESS 21-36 33rd Rd, Long Island City, NY 11106.

Rachel Rosenfield CURATOR Born July 6, 1951, in New York City, Rosenfield earned a BA in English Literature from Northwestern University, Evanston, Illinois, in 1972 and an MA in Art History from the University of Massachusetts, Amherst, in 1974. She took postgraduate courses in art history at Harvard University, Cambridge, Massachusetts, in 1975–77.

In 1979 Rosenfield became associate curator in charge of twentieth-century art and photography at the Portland Art Museum, Oregon. She was an assistant curator there in 1978–79, and an administrative assistant at the Center for Conservation and Technical Studies, Fogg Art Museum, Harvard University, in 1975–77. Rosenfield taught art history in the Department of Continuing Education of the University of Massachusetts in 1974.

She is a member of CAA, American Association of Museums, Portland Center for the Visual Arts, Blue Sky Gallery of Photography and Contemporary Crafts Gallery.

PUBLICATIONS Catalogs (author): *Louis Bunce: A Retrospective*, 1979, *Frederic Littman: Themes and Variations*, 1978 (Portland Art Mus.: Ore.); "Catalogue of the Exhibition," *Wash and Gouache: A Study of the Development of the Materials of Watercolor*, 1977 (Ctr. for Conservation & Technical Studies, Fogg Art Mus., Harvard Univ., Cambridge, Mass.).

ADDRESS Portland Art Museum, 1219 SW Park Ave, Portland, OR 97205.

Ronald Rosenstock PHOTOGRAPHER · TEACHER Born in Monticello, New York, on August 5, 1943, Rosenstock studied with Minor

White from 1967 to 1969 and with Paul Caponigro from 1969 to 1971. In 1977 he received an MA in Photography from Goddard College in Plainfield, Vermont.

Since 1977 Rosenstock has been director of the Irish Photographic Workshops. He taught photography at Worcester Craft Center from 1968 to 1979, and from 1974 to 1979 taught at Clark University, also in Worcester, Massachusetts.

The photographer works in large-format black-and-white silver prints in the classical style, his main subjects being the seascapes, landscapes, early monasteries, ancient monuments, towns and people of Ireland.

PUBLICATIONS Monograph: *Photography: The Portrait*, 1978 (self-pub.). Periodicals: *Camera*, July 1972, Apr 1971, June 1970.

PORTFOLIO *Light of Ireland*, 1975.

COLLECTIONS MIT, Cambridge, Mass.; Univ. of Arizona, Tucson; Worcester Art Mus., Mass. In Ireland: Thoor Ballylee Mus., County Galway; Urban District Council, Castlebar, County Mayo.

ADDRESS 91 Sunnyside Ave, Holden, MA 01520.

Joseph J. Rosenthal *PHOTOJOURNALIST* Born October 9, 1911, in Washington, D.C., Rosenthal attended the University of San Francisco for one year.

The photojournalist recently retired from the *San Francisco Chronicle*, for which he had worked since 1946. Previously to that he was employed by the Associated Press (1941–46), New York Times Wide World Photos (1936–41), Acme Newspictures (1935–36), San Francisco News (1932–35) and Newspaper Enterprise Association (N.E.A.) Service Inc. (1930–32). Rosenthal also taught photojournalism at City College of San Francisco (1949–51).

He was director of the San Francisco Press Club in 1955 and 1956 and president in 1961 and 1979, winning the club's Photography Award in 1958. He also belongs to the San Francisco-Oakland Press Photographers Association, the American Newspaper Guild and ·Association· of Catholic Newsmen. Rosenthal won the Pulitzer Prize in 1945, and in the same year was awarded the International News Service Medal of Merit. In 1947 he received the Press Photographers of New York award.

While working as a war correspondent in the Pacific (1944–45), Rosenthal took the now famous picture of the Marines raising the U.S. flag on Iwo Jima, for which he subsequently won the Pulitzer Prize.

PUBLICATION Anthology: *Moments*, Sheryle & John Leekley, foreword by Dan Rather, 1978.

ADDRESS c/o San Francisco Chronicle, 901 Mission St, San Francisco, CA 94103.

Sanford H. Roth *PHOTOGRAPHER* Born August 10, 1906, in Brooklyn, New York, Roth died in Rome on March 5, 1962. His wife is author Beulah Roth. Roth earned a BA from New York University in 1928. He was influenced by André Kertész, Henri Cartier-Bresson, Robert Doisneau and Eugène Atget. He was a self-taught photographer.

Immediately after graduating, Roth began working for Reeds Millinery, a company with a large chain of stores, and eventually became executive supervisor. In 1946 he resigned and left for Paris, where he lived until about 1954. He then moved to Rome, where he stayed until his death.

In Europe Roth freelanced for every major magazine, including *Life, Look, Harper's Bazaar, Collier's, Paris-Match, Oggi, Elle* and others. He was frequently employed by major film studios to do portraits of their stars, and was attached to such motion pictures as *Giant, A Star Is Born, Billy Budd, The Sundowners, The Nun's Story, The Longest Day* and *Dial M for Murder*.

He was a founding member of ASMP.

Working only in small format and never using any artificial light, Roth photographed almost every famous personality in the arts of the 1950s. They included the painters Picasso and Chagall, writers such as Colette and Cocteau, film stars Jimmy Stewart, Peter Ustinov, Paul Newman, James Dean and Sophia Loren, and such other notables as Igor Stravinsky (on his eightieth birthday) and Albert Einstein. He did all his own darkroom work, leaving explicit instructions with all his negatives for posthumous printing.

PUBLICATIONS Monograph: *The French of Paris*, intro. by Aldous Huxley, w/Beulah Roth, 1954. Anthology: *The Family of Man*, prologue by Carl Sandburg, Edward Steichen, ed., 1955.

COLLECTION MOMA, NYC.

REPRESENTATIVES Rapho Agency, 8 rue d'Alger, 75001 Paris, France; Photo Researchers, 60 E 56 St, New York, NY 10022.

ARCHIVE Beulah Roth, 401 S Burnside Ave, Los Angeles, CA 90036.

S. Lee Rothschild *PHOTOGRAPHER · GALLERY DIRECTOR · PHOTO CRITIC* Born October 23, 1953, in Chicago, Illinois, Rothschild earned a BFA from the School of the Art Institute in conjunction with the University of Chicago in 1975.

He received an MFA in museology from the Rochester Institute of Technology, New York, in conjunction with the George Eastman House in 1977. As mentors he lists Lisette Model, Ruth Bernhard, Barbara Crane, sculptor William Brincka and rare book librarian Robert Volz.

A freelance photographer, Rothschild was photography critic for the *Windy City News* in 1979. In 1978 he co-directed Facets Gallery in Chicago, and was head of the platemaking division of the Black Box Collotype Studio. In 1976 he worked in sales, merchandising and exhibitions for Billy Hork Galleries in Chicago, and before that worked for two years as a conservation intern and archivist with the Rush Rhees Library at the University of Rochester in New York.

Rothschild is a member of CAA, SPE, Friends of Photography and VSW.

He has done 126 color landscapes that are collages with poetry or juxtapositions with poetry. He has also concentrated on extreme close-ups of people. He also works in 35mm black-and-white.

PORTFOLIO *Portfolio 77*, 1977 (Rochester Inst. of Tech: N.Y.).

COLLECTIONS IMP/GEH, Rochester; Southwest Cntr. of Photography, Austin, Tex. Mus. of Modern Art, Rio de Janeiro, Brazil; São Paulo Mus. of Art, São Paulo, Brazil.

ADDRESS 6338 N Kenmore Ave, Chicago, IL 60660.

Arthur Rothstein PHOTOGRAPHER [See plate 68] Born July 17, 1915, in New York City, Rothstein earned a BA from Columbia University in New York City in 1935, where he studied with Roy Stryker.

The director of photography at *Parade* magazine since 1972, he held the same position at *Look* magazine (1946–71). Rothstein was a photo officer in the U.S. Army Signal Corps (1943–46) and a picture editor for the U.S. Office of War Information (1941–43). From 1935 to 1940 he was a photographer for the U.S. Farm Security Administration, and in 1940–41 was a photographer for *Look*.

The photographer belongs to New York Press Photographers Association, NPPA, ASMP and Photographic Administrators. He is a fellow of RPS and the New York Photo Historical Society.

Rothstein developed a three-dimensional photographic and printing technique—Xograph—in 1963, for which he won a citation from Photographic Scientists and Engineers. He also won the NPPA Sprague Award in 1967 and the International Award from the Photographic Society of America in 1968.

Well known for his Farm Security Administration photographs, Rothstein works in documentary and photojournalism.

PUBLICATIONS Books: *Words and Pictures*, 1979; *The Depression Years*, 1978; *Color Photography Now*, 1970; *Look at Us, Let's See, Here We Are . . .*, William Saroyan, 1967; *Creative Color*, 1963; *Photojournalism: Pictures for Magazines & Newspapers*, 1956, rev. eds. 1965, 1969, 1974, 1979. Anthologies: *The Photograph Collector's Guide*, Lee D. Witkin & Barbara London, 1979; *The Magic Image*, Cecil Beaton & Gail Buckland, 1975.

COLLECTIONS IMP/GEH, Rochester; L/C, Wash., D.C.; MOMA, NYC; Smithsonian Inst., Wash., D.C. Bibliothèque Nationale, Paris; Centre Pompidou, Paris; RPS, London.

DEALER Witkin Gall., 41 E 57 St, New York, NY 10022.

ADDRESS 122 Sutton Manor, New Rochelle, NY 10805.

Robert D. Routh TEACHER · PHOTOGRAPHER Born in Chicago, Illinois, on September 10, 1921, Routh received a BA in Psychology and English from Whittier College, California, in 1949, and an MA in Instructional Media from California State University at Long Beach in 1970.

Since 1966 he has been associate professor of photography at Cal State Long Beach. From 1964 to 1966 Routh taught at Bellflower High School in Bellflower, California, and before that was owner/manager of a photo equipment store (1950–65).

Since 1968 he has been a member of the National Photography Instructors Association, acting as president, board member and editor of their monthly newsletter and magazine quarterly. He is vice-president of the International Visual Literacy Association, of which he has been a member since 1976. Since 1970 he has been a member of SPE and now serves as chairman of the Western region. Routh, who was elected an associate of the Photographic Society of America in 1967, has been chairman of their Education/Scholarship Committee since 1964. He has been a member of Friends of Photography since 1970.

Awarded the Clarence A. Bach Award for outstanding contributions to photography education (1973), he also won a Victor H. Scales Memorial Award from the Photographic Society of America in 1978.

Of his work he says, "My research has been mainly in graphic techniques and visual literacy. My work includes all types of graphics, alternative processes, as well as 'straight' photographic prints and slides in both black-and-white and color."

PUBLICATIONS Book: *Photographics*, 1976. Periodical: *Petersen's Photographic Magazine*, monthly column on photographic education, Nov 1974 to present.

ADDRESS 842 S Helena St, Anaheim, CA 92805.

William Henry Rowe *PHOTOGRAPHER · TEACHER* Born in Rockville, Long Island, New York, on June 11, 1946, Rowe earned a BFA from Pratt Institute, Brooklyn, in 1968.

Basically self-employed, as of this writing he was teaching at the School of Visual Arts in New York City (since 1978). He was an assistant to illustrator Norman Green in the early 1970s.

The photographer won a Canada Council Arts Award in 1977.

PUBLICATIONS Monographs: *William Rowe's Surreal Post Cards*, 1980; *Bird Fantasies*, 1978; *Nature Fantasies*, 1977; *Nurse Duck Takes a Walk, Fiestaware*, 1976 (VSW: Rochester); *Exotic Alphabet and Ornament*, 1974; *Original Art Deco Designs*, 1973.

COLLECTIONS Can. Council, Ottawa, Ontario.

ADDRESS c/o Keith Smith, 22 Cayuga St, Rochester, NY 14620.

Ted Rozumalski *PHOTOGRAPHER* Born June 26, 1931, in Milwaukee, Wisconsin, Rozumalski studied at Marquette University School of Journalism, Milwaukee, in 1957. He was influenced by Frank Scherschel, Robert Gilka and Angus MacDougal.

Since 1974 Rozumalski has been president and photographer for Visuals Plus, Incorporated. He worked as a photographer in the Chicago area for Black Star Publishing from 1967 to 1974, and was assigned to photograph the astronauts for World Book Science Service in Houston in 1966–67. A *Sunday Magazine* photographer for the *Houston Chronicle* (1962–66), he worked as a photographer for the *Milwaukee Journal* (1956–62).

Rozumalski was named Southwest U.S. News Photographer of the Year in 1964 and 1965 and National Newspaper Photographer of the Year in 1963 and 1964.

COLLECTION Metro. Mus. of Art, NYC.

REPRESENTATIVE Black Star Publishing, 450 Park Ave S, New York, NY 10016.

ADDRESS 810 N Plankinton Ave, Milwaukee, WI 53203.

Meridel Rubenstein *PHOTOGRAPHER · TEACHER* Born in Detroit, Michigan, on March

26, 1948, she received a BA from Sarah Lawrence College in Bronxville, New York, in 1970, studied with Minor White at the Massachusetts Institute of Technology, Cambridge, in 1972 and earned an MFA from the University of New Mexico (UNM), Albuquerque, in 1977.

As of this writing Rubenstein was a visiting lecturer at the University of Colorado at Boulder; she also teaches at the College of Santa Fe (since 1977). From 1976 to 1978 she taught photography and women's studies at UNM. Since 1977 she has also been the Southwest correspondent for *Afterimage: VSW*.

A member of SPE and Friends of Photography, she won an NEA Photography Survey Award in 1978, and an NEA Exhibition Aid in 1976. She received a Friends of Photography Ferguson Grant in 1977.

Her main concern "has always been how to distill visually the complexities and energies of a particular existence into a single image.... Landscape, writing, fragments and objects have variously been used as additive elements to reconstruct or extend the portrait, enhancing rather than distorting the reality of the subject." She uses a view camera, making silver bromide prints toned in ammonium sulfide.

PUBLICATIONS Monographs: *La Gente De La Luz*, 1977; *One Space, Three Visions*, 1979. Anthologies: *Photography for Collectors*, 1980; *Photography in New Mexico*, 1978; *The Great West: Real/Ideal*, 1977. Periodicals: *American Photographer*, text only, Nov 1979; *Untitled 14*, Apr 1978 (Friends of Photography: Carmel, Calif.).

COLLECTIONS Mus. of New Mex., Santa Fe; Univ. of Colorado, Boulder; Univ. of New Mex., Fine Arts Mus., Albuquerque.

ADDRESS Rt 2, Box 305A, Santa Fe, NM 87501.

Eva Rubinstein *PHOTOGRAPHER* [See photo 113] Born August 18, 1933, in Buenos Aires, Argentina, Rubinstein spent her early childhood in Paris before her family emigrated to the United States with the outbreak of World War II. She trained in dance as a child and later studied theater at University of California at Los Angeles. She studied photography with Sean Kernan, Lisette Model, Jim Hughes, Ken Heyman and Diane Arbus.

Rubinstein appeared in several on- and off-Broadway theater productions and in the European theater before turning to photography in 1968. She has since specialized in editorial, portrait and documentary work and, since 1977, has been teaching at the New School for Social Research in New York City.

PUBLICATIONS Monograph: *Eva Rubinstein*, 1974. Books: *Impossible Dreams*, Pati Hill, 1976; *The Leica Manual*, 1973. Anthologies: *The Photograph Collector's Guide*, Lee D. Witkin & Barbara London, 1979; *Photographers on Photography*, 1979; *The Family of Children*, 1977; *Women Photograph Men*, Danielle B. Hayes, ed., intro. by Molly Haskell, 1977; *Women See Woman*, 1976. Periodicals: *Camera 35*, Sept 1979, Nov 1972, Oct 1971; *Progresso Fotografico*, Apr 1977; *U.S. Camera Annual*, 1976, 1972; *Popular Photography*, Sept 1975, Dec 1971; *Photography Annual*, 1975, 1974; *35mm Photography*, summer 1974; *Camera*, Jan 1973; *Popular Photography's Woman*, fall 1972.

PORTFOLIOS *Venezia '79*, 1979 (Gruppo Editoriale Electa & Philip Morris); *Ten Photographers*, 1978 (Women's Campaign Fund: Wash., D.C.); *Portfolio #1*, intro. by John Vachon, 1975 (Neikrug Gall.: NYC).

COLLECTIONS ICP, NYC; L/C, Wash., D.C.; Metro. Mus. of Art, NYC. Bibliothèque Nationale, Paris; Israel Mus., Jerusalem; Musée Réattu, Arles, France; Mus. Sterckshof, Antwerp, Belgium.

REPRESENTATIVE Lee Gross, 366 Madison Ave, New York, NY 10001.

ADDRESS 145 W 27th St, New York, NY 10019.

Susan R. Rubinstein *PHOTOGRAPHER · TEACHER* Born May 17, 1946, in New York City, Rubinstein attended the Art Center College of Design in Pasadena, California (1969), having earned a BA in Art and Design from the American University in Washington, D.C. (1968). She spent a year at the School of Visual Arts in New York City (1967) and a year studying at the University of Florence, Italy, in 1966. She regards Arthur Secunda and John Lee as her mentors.

Currently an instructor at both the International Center of Photography (since 1979) and Marymount Manhattan College (since 1978) in New York City, she taught at Hunter College in 1978, and in the Learning to Read Through the Arts Program in Staten Island that same year.

A member of SPE since 1977, she is also a member of the Foundation for the Community of Artists. Rubinstein was artist-in-residence at the Apeiron Workshops in 1979, and in 1975 received an International Educational Exchange grant to live at the Cite International des Arts.

Her photographs explore reality and illusion. Using small and large format she is concerned with light, space and duality.

COLLECTIONS Atlantic Richfield Art Cllctn., L.A., Calif.; Denver Mus. of Art, Colo.; Exchange Natl. Bank of Chicago; Palm Springs Desert Mus. of Art, Calif.; Yale Univ. Art Gall., New Haven, Conn. Bibliothèque Nationale, Paris; Het Sterckhof Mus., Antwerp, Belgium; Mus. of Art & History, Fribourg, Switzerland.

DEALER Bertha Urdang Gall., 23 E 74 St, New York, NY 10021.

ADDRESS 155 Bank St, New York, NY 10014.

Paul Rudolph *OPTICIAN · INVENTOR* Born in Kahla, Sachsen-Altenburg, Germany, in 1858, Rudolph died in 1935. He studied at the Altenburg Gymnasium and at the universities in Munich, Leipzig and Jena.

After spending a few years teaching, Rudolph joined the Zeiss works in Jena in 1886 at the invitation of Ernst Abbe. While there, he developed a series of apochromatic lenses, patenting the first photographic lens corrected for astigmatism and curvature of the image field in 1890. Named Anastigmate by Dr. Adolf Miethe, the lens was the forerunner of the Protar, the Planare (1896), and the Unare (1899). Rudolph also patented a series of anamorphic lenses in 1899.

In 1900 Rudolph helped establish A. G. Camerawerk Palmos in Jena, a collaboration between Zeiss and Kamerafabrik Curt Benzin in Goerlitz, in order to build stable hand cameras that could use his fast lenses to best advantage. In 1902 he introduced the four-element Tessar lens, still considered one of the most efficient ever designed, and in 1920 he calculated the Double-Plasmat lens, manufactured by Meyer of Goerlitz. The inventor's many honors included the gold medal of the 1900 Paris Exhibition and the Progress Medal of RPS in 1905.

PUBLICATIONS Books: *Quellendarstellungen zur Geschichte der Fotografie*, Wolfgang Baier, 1964; *Die Photographische Kamera*, Josef Stuper, 1962; *Ernst Abbe*, Norbert Gunther, 1946; *Zeiss Werkzeitschrift*, #45. Anthology: *Photography's Great Inventors*, Louis W. Sipley, 1965. Periodicals: *Bild und Ton*, 1958; *Image*, Sept 1958; *Photographic Journal*, 1935; *Photographische Correspondenz*, 1902, 1897, 1893, 1890; *Jahrbuch für Photographie und Reproduktionstechnik*, Eder, 1896, 1895, 1894, 1891; *Photographic News*, 1890.

Michael Ruetz *PHOTOGRAPHER* Born April 4, 1940, in Berlin, Germany, Ruetz studied in

Germany at the Universities of Freiburg, Munich and Berlin from 1960 to 1965. He attended the Hochschule für bildende Kuenste (School for Fine Arts) in Berlin from 1965 to 1969; here he studied with Professor Heinz Hajek-Halke.

Since 1973 he has been a freelance photographer. His photos and photo stories have appeared in magazines such as *Geo, Time* and many others. He previously worked as a staff photographer with *Stern* magazine in Hamburg, Germany, from 1969 to 1973.

A member of DGPh, GDL and Bund freischaffender Fotodesigner, he was awarded the Otto Steinert Prize in 1979, given by the DGPh. He was the subject of a TV report in Berlin by Sender Freies entitled "Michael Ruetz, Photographer" in 1970.

PUBLICATIONS Books: *Berlin 1966–1969,* 1980 (Frankfurt); *The Other Germany,* 1979 (Munich); *Goethe in Switzerland,* 1979 (Zurich); *Nekropolis,* 1978 (Munich); *Auf Goethes Spuren,* 1978 (Zurich).

COLLECTIONS Bibliothèque Nationale, Paris. In Germany: Folkwangmuseum, Essen; Kunstverein, Hamburg; Photomuseum, Munich; Universitaet Kassel, Fotoforum.

DEALERS Focus Photographs, Schlueterstrasse 6, D-2000 Hamburg 20, Germany; PPS-Galerie, Feldstrasse, D-2000 Hamburg 4, Germany; Benteler Galls., Inc., 3830 University, Houston, TX 77005.

ADDRESS Gneisenaustrasse 5, D-2000 Hamburg 20, Germany.

Harald Rumpf PHOTOGRAPHER · JOURNALIST
Born June 26, 1955, in Reichenbach, Germany, Rumpf studied journalism at the Munich (Germany) Press Institution and photography at the Bavarian State School for Photography. He names Walker Evans, Harry Callahan, Robert Frank and Henri Cartier-Bresson as major influences.

Rumpf freelances as a journalist and photographer, as well as working for films and television as a camera assistant. He has been a member of the Bavarian Society for Journalists since 1976.

He defines his work as street photography, and since 1976 has taken theater photographs, documenting the Munich private theater scene.

PUBLICATION Monograph: *Gesichter—Gesten—Momente,* 1979 (self-pub.).

COLLECTIONS Bibliothèque Nationale, Paris; Fotomuseum of Munich, West Germany; Neue Sammlung, Munich, Germany.

DEALER Galerie Lange-Irschl, Türkenstrasse 54, D-8000, München 40, West Germany.

ADDRESS Rankestrasse 12, D-8000 München 40, West Germany.

Valter Kristian Runeberg PHOTOGRAPHER
Born November 28, 1934, in Helsinki, Finland, Runeberg studied photography at his father's studio in 1952. His great-great-grandfather was J. L. Runeberg, the national poet of Finland; his great-grandfather was sculptor Walter Runeberg; his grandfather, Nino Runeberg, was a writer, poet and translator; and his father, Fred Runeberg, was Valter's major influence as a photographer. He collaborates with his wife, Tutta Runeberg.

A freelance photographer since 1969, Runeberg has worked for such magazines as *Pirkka* and *Me Naiset* and for the Finnish Red Cross. Since 1979 his work has appeared in the Sunday pages of Finland's biggest newspaper, *Helsingin Sanomat.* He originally began freelancing in 1958, and from 1965 to 1969 was a founding member of Finnseven, a cooperative photographers' union.

Runeberg belongs to the Union of Journalists in Finland (SSL), the International Federation of Journalists in Brussels (since 1969) and the Finnish Press Photographers Society. He has received grants from the Ministry of Education (1973), the City of Helsinki (1973), the administrative district of Uudenmaan laani (1978, 1979).

PUBLICATIONS Books (all w/text by Tutta Runeberg): *Jugend,* 1975, *Paapuuri,* 1971, *Ravia ja laukkaa,* 1970 (Tammi: Finland).

COLLECTIONS Helsinki City Mus.; Mus. of Finnish Photographic Art, Helsinki.

REPRESENTATIVE TIOFOTO AB, Drottninggatan 88 C, 111 36 Stockholm, Sweden.

ADDRESS Siikakuja 2A, 02170 Espoo 17, Finland.

John Running PHOTOGRAPHER Born November 19, 1939, in Buffalo, New York, Running received a BA in Anthropology from Northern Arizona University, Flagstaff, in 1969. He also studied with photographer Walt Roeder.

Since 1970 he has operated his own freelance photography business, Running Productions. From 1965 to 1970 he was a cinematographer for the U.S. Geological Survey, Branch Surface Planetary Exploration.

Running belongs to ASMP and NPPA.

Working in small-format color and black-and-white, the photographer has a documentary style, most often photographing native peoples "with the concept that photography helps man understand man."

PUBLICATIONS Book: *Dancer,* 1980. Periodicals: "John Running, A Portfolio," *Plateau*, 51:3, 1979 (Mus. of Northern Ariz.: Flagstaff); "Faces of the Southwest," *Modern Photography*, Jan 1978.

PORTFOLIO *Navajo Portfolio*, 1978 (self-pub.).

COLLECTIONS Heard Mus., Phoenix, Ariz.; Northern Ariz. Univ., Flagstaff.

ADDRESS POB 1237, Flagstaff, AZ 86002.

Kosti S. Ruohomaa *PHOTOGRAPHER* Born in Quincy, Massachusetts, in 1914, Ruohomaa died November 5, 1961 in Rockland, Maine. He studied art in Boston.

First working as a commercial artist in Boston and New York, Ruohomaa then moved to Hollywood, where he did animation for Walt Disney Studios. During this period he took up photography, and soon devoted himself to it completely. He worked on the staff of *Life* magazine for a time, but in the 1940s turned to freelance assignments, represented by Black Star. During his career he had photographs published in such periodicals as *Collier's, Ladies' Home Journal, Down East, Yankee, Parade, This Week* and *How America Lives*, among others.

Ruohomaa worked with the simplest equipment—a Rolleiflex and a 35mm camera—yet produced photographs of "classical quality," according to Howard Chapnick. "He had a great sense of composition and mood and an ability to capture subtle nuances," Chapnick adds. Called "the Boswell of Maine characters" by one critic, Ruohomaa is best known for his brooding black-and-white Maine seascapes and New England scenes.

PUBLICATIONS Monograph: *Night Train at Wiscasset Station*, Lew Dietz, foreword by Andrew Wyeth, afterword by Howard Chapnick, 1977. Anthology: *Great Photographic Essays from Life*, Maitland Edey, 1978.

COLLECTIONS Farnworth Mus., Rockland, Maine; Life Picture Cllctn., NYC.

ARCHIVE Black Star, 450 Park Ave, New York, NY 10016.

A(ndrew) J(oseph) Russell *PHOTOGRAPHER · PAINTER* Born in 1830, he died in 1902 in the U.S.A.

Russell worked for Mathew Brady for a brief period of time, and then, a captain in the Union Army, he photographed for the U.S. Military Railroad Construction Corps (1861–65). He documented the construction of the transcontinental railroad for Union Pacific Railroad, and, on May 10, 1869, photographed the last spike, made of gold, that joined the Union Pacific with the Central Pacific Railroad at Promontory Point, Utah. He later opened a studio in New York City.

Working with albumen prints from collodion wet-plate negatives, Russell produced a variety of formats, including stereoscopic views and 10 x 13 plates. Of his work, notable for its sense of scale and its depiction of the vastness of the Old West, Barry Combs *(Westward to Promontory)* has written: "The quality of Russell's work is remarkable. . . . For negative quality and reproduction of detail, his photographs were unsurpassed by any photographer of his day."

PUBLICATIONS Monograph: *The Great West Illustrated*, 1869. Books: *Westward to Promontory*, Barry B. Combs, 1969; *Photography and the American Scene*, Robt. Taft, 1938; *Sun Pictures of Rocky Mountain Scenery*, Ferdinand Vandiveer Hayden, 1870. Anthologies: *The Photograph Collector's Guide*, Lee D. Witkin & Barbara London, 1979; *Photographs from the Coke Collection*, intro. by Van Deren Coke, 1973. Periodical: "The Pacific Railroad Rediscovered," E. D. Pattison, *Geographical Review*, 53:1, 1962.

COLLECTIONS Amer. Geographical Soc., NYC; Boston Pub. Lib.; L/C, Wash., D.C.; MOMA, NYC; Natl. Archives, Wash., D.C.; Oakland Mus., Calif.; Russell Cllctn., Wash., D.C.; Union Pacific Railrd. Cllctn; Univ. of N. Mex. Art Mus., Albuquerque.

Sura Ruth *PHOTOGRAPHER* Born December 21, 1942, in New York City, Ruth received a BFA from Pratt Institute, Brooklyn, New York. She has been influenced by scientific photography and visually abstract photography, including photograms.

A freelance photographer, she was assistant to the director of the Photographic Division, Navy and Marine Corps Exhibit Center, Washington Navy Yard, Washington, D.C., from 1967 to 1969.

Ruth has been a member of Professional Women Photographers since 1979, and won a CAPS grant in 1979.

She shoots small-format color slides and produces large Type C prints, her main subject matter being vegetables. Ruth says her photographs "allude to the unknown part of what we know."

PUBLICATIONS Anthology: *Women See Men*, 1977. Periodicals: *American Photographer*, Oct 1978; *U.S. Camera Annual*, 1967; *Popular Photography*, Aug 1966. Reviews: *Afterimage: VSW*, Meridel Rubenstein, Oct 1979; *Modern Photography*, Julia Scully, Jan 1978.

DEALER Ward-Nasse Gall., 178–131 Prince St, New York, NY 10012.

ADDRESS 87-15 37th Ave, Jackson Heights, NY 11372.

Joseph W. Ruther *PHOTOGRAPHER · PRINTER* Born December 15, 1932 in Charleston, South Carolina, Ruther studied with Robert W. Fichter in 1978 at Florida State University in Tallahassee and with George C. Floersch at Florida A & M University in Tallahassee in 1968.

Since 1970 Ruther has been a graphic arts instructor at the Lively Vocational-Technical Center in Tallahassee. He worked as an offset photographer at Florida State University in 1969, as a printer with the Florida State Geology Bureau in 1968 and with the Rose Printing Company, also in Tallahassee, from 1965 to 1969.

A member of SPE since 1976, he has also been a member of the Leon County Teachers Association since 1977 and the NEA since 1977.

He describes his work thus: "Beginning with the full-range black-and-white photograph and utilizing a variety of darkroom equipment and techniques, and working in conjunction with my own screenless process, I produce negatives for the planographic photo-offset lithographic plate. This, in turn, produces screenless continuous-tone images on offset printing paper in a wide range of colors, resulting in original photo-offset lithographic prints which are then incorporated in self-published, limited-edition art books." Subject matter is traditional and ranges from landscapes and nudes to still lifes.

PUBLICATIONS Monographs: *Color by Joseph*, 1976; *Joseph's Junk*, 1975.

COLLECTIONS CCP, Tucson; Harvard Univ., Fogg Art Mus., Cambridge, Mass.; Leon County Public Lib. Cllctn of Art, Tallahassee, Fla.

DEALER Weskim Art, S Monroe St, Tallahassee, FL 32301.

ADDRESS 3519 Estates Rd, Tallahassee, FL 32304.

Don Rutledge *PHOTOJOURNALIST* Born October 26, 1930, in Smithville, Tennessee, Rutledge graduated from the New York Institute of Photography. He has been a photographer for Black Star Picture Agency since 1960.

Rutledge belongs to ASMP (since 1959), NPPA (since 1967) and Photographic Society of America (since 1974).

PUBLICATIONS Books: *A Road to Reconciliation*, 1979; *Love With No Strings*, 1977; *The Human Touch*, 1975.

REPRESENTATIVE Black Star, Inc., 450 Park Ave S, New York, NY 10016.

ADDRESS Box 6597, Richmond, VA 23230.

Charles E. Rynd *GALLERY DIRECTOR* Born April 7, 1945, in New York City, Rynd earned a BS in Foreign Service from Georgetown University, Washington, D.C. (1967).

Since 1978 he has been director of Equivalents Gallery in Seattle, Washington, and from 1968 to 1978 worked as a financial analyst and adviser in New York, San Francisco and Seattle.

A member of the Seattle Art Museum Photography Council, he became its membership chairman in 1979.

ADDRESS Equivalents Gall., 1822 Broadway, Seattle, WA 98122.

S

Richard Gordon James Sadler *TEACHER · PHO-TOGRAPHER* Born November 8, 1927, in Coventry, Warwickshire, England, Sadler attended Coventry College of Art and Coventry Technical College between 1943 and 1948. He later completed advanced color process courses at Agfa in Germany, Gevaert in Belgium and Kodak and Ilford in England (1957–62). His major influences were European photographers, notably Horvat, Charbonier, Brassaï and the late Norman Hall, editor of *Photography Magazine* in the 1950s.

Since 1975 Sadler has been senior lecturer in the School of Photography, Derby Lonsdale College of Higher Education, Derby, England, and he also taught there (1969–72). From 1972 to 1975 he was a joint tutor in a course run with Trent Polytechnical College, and from 1962 to 1968 he taught at Coventry College of Art and Design and ran his own commercial studios in London and in Coventry.

A member of the Photography Advisory Panel of the Midland Group Gallery in Nottingham since 1977, Sadler was elected a fellow of the Royal Society of Arts in 1964. He won East Midlands Arts bursaries in 1978 and 1976 and in 1951 won a National Award for photographic printing from the Institute of Incorporated Photographers.

In the 1950s the photographer was mainly concerned with "the print and social documentation," but in the 1970s his interests expanded to include mixed-media images.

PUBLICATIONS Books: *Coventry Old and New*, 1974 (E. P. Publishing Ltd., Yorkshire, England); *Coventry Cathedral*, 1966 (Hodder & Stoughton, Ontario, Canada). Periodicals: *10 x 8 Magazine*, autumn 1979; *Fotografi*, Jan 1976; "Those who can, do," *British Journal of Photography*, Dec 1971; *Colour Photography*, Jan 1960; "Young Briton—Richard Sadler," *Photography Magazine*, 9:6, 1954; *Photography Year Book*, 1953.

COLLECTIONS East Midlands Arts Cllctn., England; West Midlands Arts Cllctn.; Herbert Art Gall. Mus. & Lib., Coventry.
DEALER The Photographers Gallery, 5 Great Newport St, London WC 2, England.
ADDRESS 2 Woodland Ave, Earlsdon, Coventry, CV5 6DB, England.

Linn Sage *PHOTOGRAPHER* Born in Baltimore, Maryland, on November 10, 1937, Sage earned a BA from Barnard College, Columbia University, New York City, in 1960. She also attended workshops given by Bruce Davidson, Lisette Model and Leo Manso, and lists as her major influences Lartigue, Cartier-Bresson and Ray Metzker. Kay Sage, the late surrealist painter, was Linn's distant cousin.

A freelance photographer since 1965, she was assistant to the cover editor at *Newsweek* in 1964–65 and art and photo editor of *Contact* magazine (Sausalito, California) in 1961–62.

A member of Soho Photo Gallery in New York City, Sage received a CAPS fellowship in 1974.

Using black-and-white with, primarily, a Leica camera, the photographer creates surreal and documentary images. She is "concerned with the significant moment . . . idea and form, the unexpected."

PUBLICATIONS Anthologies: *Women See Men*, 1977; *Contemporary Photography—Vision and Expression*, Nathan Lyons, ed., 1967.
COLLECTIONS IMP/GEH, Rochester; ICP, NYC.
DEALER Marcuse Pfeifer, 825 Madison Ave, New York, NY 10021.
ADDRESS c/o Rulon-Miller, 320 Central Park W, New York, NY 10025.

Robert Joel Sagerman *PHOTOGRAPHER* Born on August 18, 1947, in New York City, Sagerman received his BA at Goddard College, Plainfield,

Vermont, in 1975. He attended Yale University School of Drama, New Haven, Connecticut (1970–72), and studied photography there with Thomas A. Brown, Paul Caponigro, Emmet Gowin, Walker Evans and Minor White from 1969 to 1972.

He is currently a camera repair technician at New England Camera Service, Falmouth, Massachusetts, and a freelance photographer (since 1974). From 1972 to 1974 Sagerman was a theater technician.

In 1979 he received the Massachusetts Artists Foundation Fellowship.

Sagerman says, "I photograph landscape, still-life and constructions I have made for the camera's eye. I work with an 8 x 10 Deardorff view camera, and I print by the palladium printing process."

COLLECTIONS CCP, Tucson; Mus. of Fine Arts, Houston, Tex.

DEALERS The Cronin Gallery, 2008 Peden, Houston TX 77019; Kathleen Ewing Gallery, 3020 K St NW, Wash, DC 20007.

ADDRESS POB 246, Teaticket, MA 02536.

Mother St. Croix (Marie Souraut) NUN · PHOTOGRAPHER Born in Clermont-Ferand, France, ca. 1855, Mother St. Croix died in New Orleans in 1940. Her major influences were Reverend Albert Bieve and S. J. and E. Claudel.

She entered a convent about 1872–73 and came to New Orleans to join the Ursuline convent there in 1873. She first taught needlework, and in 1899 obtained her first camera from the Zion Company in Paris.

Working in large format from 4 x 5 lantern slides to approximately 16 x 20 plates, Mother St. Croix photographed the second and third Ursuline convents, a cloistered order at that time, including many images of the students. As of this writing the New Orleans Museum of Art was preparing a monograph on her work.

COLLECTIONS New Orleans Mus. of Art (glass plates & apparatus); Ursuline Convent, New Orleans (prints).

ARCHIVES New Orleans Museum of Art, Lelong Ave City Park, New Orleans, LA 70119; The Ursuline Convent, 2635 State St, New Orleans, LA 70897.

Toshio Sakai PHOTOJOURNALIST Born March 31, 1940, Sakai earned a BA in economics and political science in 1965 from Meiji University in Tokyo.

A freelance photographer since 1977, Sakai previously was UPI photo manager for Seoul (Korea) Bureau (1975–77) and UPI Newspictures editor for Southeast Asia (1973–75). From 1965 to 1975 Sakai worked for UPI as a staff photographer in the Tokyo Bureau. He belongs to NPPA.

In 1968 Sakai won the Pulitzer Prize in feature photography for his picture of an American GI wrapped in his poncho and trying to get some sleep during the Vietnam monsoon rain.

PUBLICATIONS Books: *Indochinese Refugees*, Kokusho Ltd., 1980 (Tokyo); *The Photo Book on the Vietnam War*, Eva Press, ed., 1979 (Kinokuniyashoten: Tokyo). Anthology: *Moments*, Sheryle & John Leekley, foreword by Dan Rather, 1978.

ADDRESS 15–17, Koenji Minami 2-chome, Suginami-Ku, Tokyo 166, Japan.

Roberto Salbitani PHOTOGRAPHER · WRITER · TEACHER Born June 7, 1945, in Padua, Italy, Salbitani studied foreign literature and languages at Venice University (1968–72).

As of this writing Salbitani was freelancing and writing for French magazines (since 1974). He was the photography writer for *Progresso Fotografico* in Milan, Italy, from 1972 to 1978. He also has taught workshops since 1977.

PUBLICATIONS Monograph: *The Invaded City*, 1978. Anthologies: *Premiere Triennale Internationale De Photographie*, 1980; *Iconic-City*, 1979; *Venezia '79—La Fotografia*, 1979; *The Naked Environment*, 1978. Periodical: *Popular Photography Annual*, 1978.

COLLECTIONS MOMA, NYC; Univ. of N. Mex. Art Mus., Albuquerque. Bibliothèque Nationale, Paris; Univ. of Parma, Centro Studi ed Archivio Della Comunicazione, Italy; Ville de Charleroi, Belgium.

ADDRESS Giudecca 700, 30100 Venice, Italy.

Joan A. Salinger PHOTOGRAPHER · TEACHER Born on March 20, 1951, in Detroit, Michigan, Salinger studied under Carl Toth at Cranbrook Academy of Art, Bloomfield Hills, Michigan, where she received an MFA (1976). She received her BFA, magna cum laude, from the University of Michigan, Ann Arbor (1973).

Salinger is currently a photography instructor in California at Orange Coast College, Costa Mesa, Otis Art Institute of Parsons School of Design, Los Angeles, Los Angeles Valley College, Van Nuys and Pasadena City College. She is a member of SPE, CAA, Los Angeles Center for Photographic Studies and the American Federation of Teachers. Salinger has been awarded grants from the Michigan Council for the Arts and NEA as well as from the Charles Stewart Mott Foundation as Artist In Schools, Flint, Michigan (1976–77).

The artist describes her work as experimental in technique. She works with Type C color film, often producing prints that are one of a kind. "Current work also plays tension between manipulated and unmanipulated areas of the image. It is also more specific in reference to the influence of Los Angeles on my feelings and attitude."

PUBLICATION Catalog: *Catalogue 1*, 1979 (Sander Gallery, Wash, D.C.).

COLLECTIONS Flint Community Schools, Mich.; Kresge–K-Mart Corp., Troy, Mich.; Michigan Art Education Assoc., Lansing; New Orleans Mus. of Art; Northern Virginia Coll., Alexandria.

DEALER Sander Gallery, 2600 Connecticut Ave NW, Washington, DC 20008.

ADDRESS 550 S. Barrington Ave, #1224, Los Angeles, CA 90049.

Erich Salomon PHOTOGRAPHER Born in Berlin in 1886, Salomon died at Auschwitz Concentration Camp in 1944. He studied mechanical engineering and law at the University of Munich, where he earned a doctorate in law.

Salomon was a prisoner of war for four years during World War I and after his release found employment with Ullstein Verlag, publishers. Salomon took up photography around 1927 and, subsequent to the great success he had with secret photographs taken during a controversial murder trial, began his professional career in 1928, contributing to such periodicals as *Berliner Illustrierte Zeitung* and the London *Graphic*.

One of the pioneers of the candid photograph, he was a master of the hidden camera. Salomon was a photojournalist who enjoyed entree into high places, thus obtaining many highly prized and rare scenes with the Ermanox he kept concealed in his briefcase (he later used an Er-Nox and, still later, a Leica). Aristide Briand, prime minister of France, once called him "le roi des indiscrets" (king of prying).

PUBLICATIONS Monographs: *Erich Salomon*, intro. by Peter Hunter, 1978; *Porträt einer Epoche*, 1963, U.S. ed, *Portrait of an Age*, 1967; *Berühmte Zeitgenoosen in unbewachten Augenblicken*, 1931 (J. Engelhorns: Stuttgart). Book: "Photography," *Quality*, Louis Kornenberger, ed., 1969. Anthologies: *The Photograph Collector's Guide*, Lee D. Witkin & Barbara London, 1979; *The Magic Image*, Cecil Beaton & Gail Buckland, 1975; *Looking at Photographs*, John Szarkowski, 1973; *Photojournalism*, 1971, *The Camera*, 1970, Time-Life Series; *Masters of Pho-* *tography*, Beaumont & Nancy Newhall, 1969; *The Picture History of Photography*, Peter Pollack, 1958, rev. 1969. Periodicals: "Dr. Erich Salomon," Peter Hunter, *Camera 35*, no. 4, 1958; "Salomon," Peter Hunter, *Photography*, Jan 1957; "Dr. Salomon," Kurt Safranski, *Popular Photography*, Aug 1948.

COLLECTIONS IMP/GEH, Rochester; Life Picture Cllctn., NYC; MOMA, NYC; New Orleans Art Mus.; Univ. of Tex., Gernsheim Cllctn., Austin. L. Fritz Gruber Cllctn., Germany; Peter Hunter Cllctn., Amsterdam; Provinciaal Museum voor Kunstambachten, Deurne (Antwerp), Belgium.

Ellen Salwen PHOTOGRAPHER · TEACHER Born on November 12, 1947, in Brooklyn, New York, Salwen studied with Walker Evans and Lee Friedlander. She received her MFA from Lone Mountain College, San Francisco, California (1978), studied at Apeiron Photographic Workshops, Millerton, New York (1974), and received her BS in Art Education from New York University, New York City, in 1970.

Salwen has been an instructor of photography at Chabot College, Hayward, Calif., University of California Extension, Berkeley, Calif., the San Francisco Museum of Modern Art, Lone Mountain College, San Francisco, and Maine Photographic Workshops, Rockport. She worked as a coordinator of art applicants for the John Simon Guggenheim Memorial Foundation, New York City.

She is a member of SPE.

The artist photographs the American landscape, using a 35mm camera and working in black-and-white.

PUBLICATION Catalog: *Contemporary California Photography*, 1978 (Camera Work Gallery).

DEALER Prakapas Gallery, 50 E 71 St, New York, NY 10021.

ADDRESS 31 Beulah St, San Francisco, CA 94117.

Auguste Salzmann PAINTER · PHOTOGRAPHER · ARCHAEOLOGIST Born in 1824 in Alsace (near Strasbourg), France, Salzmann died sometime after 1872–75. He studied painting under his brother, Henri-Gustave Salzmann, and developed a serious interest in archaeology about 1850.

The archaeologist traveled to the Holy Land in 1854 with the intent of confirming certain historical theories with regard to the dating of various monuments.

His paintings were first accepted in the Paris Salon in 1847, followed by exhibits there in 1849 and 1850.

As a photographer, Salzmann specialized in the recording of monuments and architecture of the Middle East, producing salted paper prints. André Jammes *(French Primitive Photography)* writes that he created documentary photography with a rare blend of "precision of detail and beauty of execution." Of his own work, Salzmann wrote, "Photographs are more than tales, they are facts endowed with convincing brute force."

PUBLICATIONS Books: *Nécropole de Camiros,* 1875 (Atlas: Paris); *Jérusalem,* 1856 (Gide & J. Baudry: Paris). Anthology: *French Primitive Photography,* André Jammes & Robt. Sobieszek, intro. by Minor White, 1969. Catalog: *The Painter as Photographer,* 1978 (Vancouver Art Gall.: Can.).

COLLECTIONS Akron Art Inst., Ohio; Harvard Univ., Fogg Art Mus., Cambridge, Mass.; IMP/GEH, Rochester. Natl. Gall. of Canada, Ottawa.

Laurence Salzmann PHOTOGRAPHER · FILM MAKER · PUBLISHER Born January 4, 1944, in Philadelphia, Pennsylvania, Salzmann studied film-making at the Institut des Hautes Etudes Cinématographiques in Paris (1964) and received an MA in anthropology from Temple University in Philadelphia (1974).

He is self-employed as a photographer, film maker and book distributor. A member of the Philadelphia Art Alliance and the Print Club of Philadelphia, Salzmann received an NEA film grant in 1979 and grants from the American Film Institute (1969) and the New York State Council on the Arts (for photography, 1970). For his work in Romania, he received a Jewish Memorial Foundation grant in 1979 and a Fulbright-Hays grant in 1974. Salzmann won a silver medal at the 1971 Venice Film Festival for his film *Scag.*

Working mostly with small format, the photographer is "concerned with [the] definition of culture and ethnography" through photography and film.

PUBLICATIONS Book: *La Baie,* 1980. Periodicals: *Creative Camera,* 1979; *Le Nouveau Photocinéma,* 1979; *Popular Photography,* Nov 1974; *Modern Photography Discovery,* 1971.

COLLECTIONS Albright Coll., Reading, Penn.; Corcoran Gall. of Art, Wash., D.C.; ICP, NYC; Lehigh Univ., Bethlehem, Pa.; MOMA, NYC; Philadelphia Art Mus. & Free Lib. Bibliothèque Nationale, Paris; Israel Mus., Jerusalem.

ADDRESS 3607 Baring St, Philadelphia, PA 19104.

Lucas Samaras SCULPTOR · PHOTOGRAPHER Born September 14, 1936, in Kastoria, Greece, Samaras received a BA from Rutgers University, New Brunswick, New Jersey, in 1959. He also attended Stella Adler Theatre Studio in 1960 and studied art history with Meyer Schapiro at Columbia University, New York City (1959–62).

Self-employed as a sculptor and photographer, Samaras taught at Brooklyn College, New York (1971–72), and gave an advanced sculpture seminar at Yale University, New Haven, Connecticut, in 1969.

In 1976 Samaras was commissioned by the General Services Administration to create a large-scale Cor-ten steel sculpture, which is permanently installed at Hale Boggs Federal Courthouse in New Orleans.

Beginning in 1969, the artist began working with the SX-70 process, manipulating images either with light and his body or with the Polaroid process itself. He generally uses his body, often nude, as subject and takes his photographs indoors.

PUBLICATIONS Monographs: *Lucas Samaras,* Kim Levin, 1975; *Lucas Samaras: Photo-Transformations,* Arnold B. Glimcher, 1975; *Samaras Album,* 1971. Books: *The Grotesque in Photography,* A. D. Coleman, 1977; *American Art of the Twentieth Century,* Sam Hunter, 1973. Anthologies: *The Photograph Collector's Guide,* Lee D. Witkin & Barbara London, 1979; *Mirrors & Windows,* John Szarkowski, ed., 1978; *The Magic Image,* Cecil Beaton & Gail Buckland, 1975; *Photography in America,* Robert Doty, 1974. Catalogs: *Lucas Samaras: Photo-Transformations,* 1974 (Pace Gall.: NYC); *Lucas Samaras,* 1972 (Whitney Mus. of Amer. Art: NYC); *Lucas Samaras' Boxes,* Joan Siegfried, 1971 (Mus. of Contemp. Art: Chicago). Periodicals: "Modernism Turned Inside Out: Lucas Samaras' 'Reconstructions,'" Carter Ratcliff, Nov 1979, "Samaras' Autopolaroids," Bruce Kurtz, Dec 1971/Jan 1972, *Arts Magazine; Camera Mainichi,* Shoji Yamagishi, July 1977; *Andy Warhol's Interview,* Richard Bernstein, Dec 1972; "Autopolaroids," *Art In America,* Nov/Dec 1970; "Samaras Bound," Kim Levin, *Artnews,* Feb 1969; "Conversations with Lucas Samaras," Alan Solomon, *Artforum,* Oct 1966; "The Obsessive Images of Lucas Samaras," Martin Friedman, Nov 1964, *Art and Artists.*

COLLECTIONS Albright-Knox Art Gall., Buffalo, N.Y.; Aldrich Mus. of Contemp. Art, Ridgefield, Conn.; Art Inst. of Chicago; City Art Mus. of St. Louis, Mo.; Dallas Mus. of Fine Arts, Tex.; Ft. Worth Art Ctr., Tex.; Gen. Services Admin. Fine Arts Cllctn., Hale Boggs Fed. Courthouse,

New Orleans; Guggenheim Mus., NYC; Harvard Univ., Fogg Art Mus., Cambridge, Mass.; Hirshhorn Mus. & Sculpture Garden, Wash., D.C.; Ind. Univ. Art Mus., Bloomington; Los Angeles County Mus. of Art; Miami-Dade Community Coll., Miami, Fla.; Minneapolis Inst. of Art, Minn.; MOMA, NYC; Mus. of Contemp. Art, Chicago; New Orleans Mus., La.; Philadelphia Mus. of Art, Pa.; Phoenix Art Mus., Ariz.; Princeton Univ. Art Mus., N.J.; Prudential Insurance Co. of Amer.; R.I. School of Design Mus. of Art, Providence; San Francisco Mus. of Art; Seattle Art Mus., Wash.; Wadsworth Atheneum, Hartford, Conn.; Walter Art Ctr., Minneapolis, Minn.; Whitney Mus. of Amer. Art, NYC. Australian Natl. Gall., Canberra.

DEALER Pace Gall., 32 E 57 St, New York, NY 10022.

ADDRESS 52 W 71 St, New York, NY 10023.

Pentti Ilmari Sammallahti   PHOTOGRAPHER
Born February 18, 1950, in Helsinki, Finland, Sammallahti is self-taught in photography.

He has taught photography at the University of Industrial Arts in Helsinki since 1974, and from 1974 to 1976 taught photography at the Lahti Art School in Finland. He joined the group Imago 6 in 1971.

Sammallahti won a three-year state artist's grant in 1978 and a one-year grant in 1975, as well as a state art prize in 1974. From the City of Helsinki he received artist's grants in 1971 and 1977.

His work mainly concerns "the relationship between man and nature."

PUBLICATIONS Monograph: *Cathleen ní Houlihan, An Irish Portfolio,* 1979 (Opus: Helsinki). Anthologies: *Finnish Photographic Yearbook,* 1976, 1975, 1974, 1973; *Fotoalmanach International,* 1969 (Germany); *Fotojahrbuch International,* 1970/71 (Germany). Catalog: *Photokina,* 1974 (Bilderschauen: Cologne). Periodicals: *Fotograficentrums Bildtidning* (Photography Center's Picture Magazine), Jan 1979; *Fotografie,* Apr 1975.

COLLECTIONS MOMA, NYC. Alvar Aaltomus., Jyväskylä, Finland; City of Helsinki, Finland; Lahti Art Mus., Lahti, Finland; Moderna Muséet, Stockholm; Photographic Mus., Helsinki; Victoria & Albert Mus., London.

ADDRESS Kristianinkatu 15 A 16, SF-00170 Helsinki 17, Finland.

Samuel Eli Samore   PHOTOGRAPHER · VIDEO
ARTIST Born in 1953 in Ann Arbor, Michigan,

Samore graduated magna cum laude from San Francisco State University with a BA degree in Broadcasting.

As of this writing Samore was teaching photography.

A recipient of an NEA Services to the Field grant in 1980 and an NEA Photographer's Fellowship in 1979, he was also awarded an NEA Artist's Fellowship in 1976. Samore also has produced the following videotapes: "Who's Famous?" and "Questioning Art," both in 1979; "A Videotape Catalogue: Photography and Language at Camerawork" and "On Fame" in 1978; and "Health Spa" and "McDonald's" in 1977.

Samore characterizes his work as "having moved from conceptual, idea-oriented arrangements and art-sniper attacks to visual statements concerned with line, form, color, mood and mystery. Rather than city/industrial scenes, these are more about natural, poetic still lifes."

PUBLICATIONS Monographs (self-pub.): *Selected Samore Letters: Correspondence 1974–1979,* 1979; *The Beginning,* 1977; *The Middle,* 1977; *The End,* 1977; *Untitled Lovers,* 1976; *Untitled Wedding,* 1976; *Untitled Child,* 1976; *Sunday Stroll,* 1975; *Zoo Visit,* 1975; *The Invasion From Mars Chronicles,* 1974; *It Turns Purple,* 1974; *My Curriculum Vitae,* 1974; *My Homage to that Weirdo Diane Arbus,* 1974; *My Own Suicide,* 1974; *The Sweet Smelling Behind Series,* 1974; *Where I Buried My Murdered Brother Eric,* 1974. Periodicals: *Popular Photography Annual,* 1980; *American Photographer,* June 1978.

COLLECTIONS IMP/GEH, Rochester; Madison Art Ctr., Wisconsin; MOMA, NYC; Oakland Mus., Calif.; San Francisco Mus. of Modern Art.

ADDRESS Route 2, POB 305A, Santa Fe, NM 87501.

Patricia Marie Sample   PHOTOGRAPHER ·
TEACHER Born August 15, 1949, in Scottsbluff, Nebraska, Sample received a BA and BFA from the University of Nebraska, Lincoln (1971, 1972), and an MFA from the University of Florida, Gainesville, in 1974.

As of this writing she was teaching photography at North Florida Evaluation and Treatment Center, Gainesville, and previously taught at the University of Illinois, Urbana-Champaign (1976–78), and at the University of Alabama, Tuscaloosa (1976).

Sample belongs to SPE and Friends of Photography.

The photographer received a University of Illinois Research Board grant in 1977 and won Ford Foundation grants in 1976 and 1977.

PUBLICATIONS Anthologies: *The Photographer's Choice*, Kelly Wise, ed., 1975; *Young American Photography*, 1974. Catalog: *The Invented Landscape*, 1979 (The New Museum, NYC). Periodicals: "Process Ideology and the Photographs of Tricia Sample," Michael Lonier, *Afterimage: VSW*, Sept 1977; *Popular Photography Annual*, 1974.

COLLECTIONS Lewis State Bank, Tallahassee, Fla.; Univ. of Ala. Art Gall., Tuscaloosa; Univ. of Neb., Sheldon Mem. Art Gall., Lincoln.

ADDRESS 514 SW 10 St, Gainesville, FL 32601.

August Sander PHOTOGRAPHER Born in Herdorf-am-der-Sieg, Germany, on November 17, 1876, Sander died in 1964 in Cologne. A self-taught photographer, he was influenced by progressive German artists, especially Franz Wilhelm Seiwart in the 1920s.

Sander started work as an iron miner's apprentice in 1889 and began photography in 1892 with a 13 x 18cm camera. He served in the German Army from 1896 to 1898 (and then again from 1914 to 1918) and bought his first photography studio, Studio Grief, in Linz, Austria, with Franz Stukenberg, ca. 1901–1902. The studio was renamed Studio Sander & Stukenberg and, finally, August Sander Studio for Pictorial Arts of Photography and Painting when he bought out Stukenberg in 1904. Sander also opened a studio in Cologne in 1910. His other work included a commission to photograph architecture for the Deutscher Werkbund exhibit in 1914.

A member of the German Photographic Society, which awarded him their Cultural Prize in 1961, Sander also received the Federal Order of Merit from the Federal Republic of Germany in 1960. Other honors included the Silver Medal (highest) at 1909 Linz Arts & Crafts Exhibition; first prize, Liepzig Book Fair, 1904; State Medal at Linz Arts & Crafts Fair, 1903; and gold medal and Cross of Honor for Arts & Sciences at Paris Exposition in the Palace of Fine Arts, 1904.

Sander produced and gave a series of lectures entitled "Nature & Development of Photography" for West German radio in 1931.

Sander's images, chiefly silver prints, were unpretentious, sympathetic portraits of everyday people, from cooks to artists, at their work. In his later photographs he concentrated on landscapes. Since Sander was influenced by Marxist socialism, many of his books were destroyed by the Nazis, but he saved his negatives, and most of his later years were spent assembling and printing them.

PUBLICATIONS Books: *August Sander*, intro.

by John von Hartz, 1977; *Rheinlandschaften*, Wolfgang Kemp, 1975 (Schirmer Mosel: Munich); *Menschen ohne Maske*, 1971, U.S. ed., *Men Without Masks: Faces of Germany*, 1910–1938, Gunther Sander, foreword by Golo Mann, 1973; *Land an Rhein und Ruhr*, 1955 (Umschau: Frankfort); *Das Siebengebirge*, 1934; *Die Mosel*, 1934; *Die Saar*, 1934; *Deutsche Lande, Deutsche Menschen, Bergisches Land*, 1933; *Die Eifel*, 1933; *Deutschenspiegel: Menschen des 20 Jahrhunderts*, intro. by Henrich Lützeler, 1929, repr. 1962 (Sigbert Mohn: Gütersloh, Germany); *Antlitz der Zeit* (Faces of Times), Alfred Doblin, 1929, repr. 1976 (Schirmer Mosel: Munich). Anthologies: *The Photograph Collector's Guide*, Lee D. Witkin & Barbara London, 1979; *The Magic Image*, Cecil Beaton & Gail Buckland, 1975. Periodicals: "Photographs in Context," Ulrich Keller, *Image*, Dec 1976; "The Uncanny Portrait: Sander, Arbus, Samaras," Max Kozloff, *Artforum*, June 1973.

COLLECTIONS IMP/GEH, Rochester; MOMA, NYC; New Orleans Mus. of Art, La.; Sander Gall., Wash., D.C.; Univ. of N. Mex. Art Mus., Albuquerque. Cologne Mus., Germany; Liepzig Mus., Germany; Mus. of Arts & Crafts, Berlin; Photogalerie Wilde, Cologne, Germany; RPS, London.

ARCHIVES Sander Gall., 2600 Connecticut Ave NW, Washington, DC 20008.

Charles W. Sanders PHOTOGRAPHER · TEACHER · INDUSTRIAL DESIGNER Born May 1, 1921, in Mason City, Iowa, Sanders earned a BFA from the University of Illinois, Urbana-Champaign (1949), and an MA from San Francisco State University (1971).

He has been a professor at San Jose State University, California, since 1964, and previously was an associate professor at the University of Illinois (1957–64). He served as a designer for Gibson Refrigerator Company from 1949 to 1957 and was in the U.S. Navy from 1942 to 1946.

A member of United Professors of California since 1965, he won a Faculty Research Grant from San Jose State University in 1968. He also received the Thomas A. Dooley Award for Dedicated Service in 1975, and the Time-Life Books Award for Outstanding Achievements in Photography in 1971.

PUBLICATIONS Anthology: *Octave of Prayer*, Minor White, ed., 1972. Catalog: *Young Photographers*, Van Deren Coke, 1968 (Univ. of N. Mex. Art Mus.: Albuquerque).

PORTFOLIO *12 Photographers* (group), 1972.

COLLECTIONS Home Savings & Loan Assoc.,

Los Angeles; Markham Gall., San Jose; Univ. of Santa Clara, De Saisset Art Gall., Calif.

DEALER   Markham Gall., 1940 The Alameda, San Jose, CA 95126.

ADDRESS   536 Curie Dr, San Jose, CA 95123.

Norman Sanders   PHOTOGRAPHER · LECTURER · AUTHOR · BUSINESSMAN   Born November 13, 1927, in New York City, Sanders earned a BS from New York University, New York City, in 1950.

He has been president of Sanders Printing Corporation since 1952 and an adjunct professor of art at Cooper Union in New York City since 1970. Sanders has also served the NEA as a lecturer and consultant to the Design Arts Program since 1977.

A member of ASMP and SPE, Sanders is also on the board of directors of the American Institute of Graphic Arts.

Working in medium and large format, Sanders produces "social and psychological photographic documents." He has developed an original system of applied sensitometry for black-and-white photography.

PUBLICATIONS   Monograph: *At Home*, 1977. Books: *Photography for Graphic Designers*, 1979; *Photographic Tone Control*, 1977.

ADDRESS   22 Meadowlark Dr, West Nyack, NY 10994.

Marni Sandweiss   CURATOR   Born in 1954 in St. Louis, Missouri, Sandweiss received a BA in 1975 from Harvard University, Cambridge, and an MA in History in 1977 from Yale University, New Haven, Connecticut.

She has been curator of photographs at the Amon Carter Museum, Ft. Worth, Texas, since 1979.

Sandweiss was a fellow at the Center for American Art and Material Culture at Yale in 1977–79 and a Smithsonian Institution Fellow through a National Endowment for the Humanities grant in 1975–76.

PUBLICATION   Catalog: *Pictures from an Expedition: Early Views of the American West*, 1978.

ADDRESS   Amon Carter Museum, POB 2365, Ft Worth, TX 76113.

Gary D. Saretzky   ARCHIVIST · PHOTOGRAPHER · EDUCATOR   Born June 26, 1946, in Newton, Massachusetts, he received a BA in 1968 and an MA in 1969 in American History from the University of Wisconsin in Madison. From 1973 to 1979 he studied photography with William Barksdale, Peter Bunnell, Frederick Sommer and Eva Rubenstein. He also studied photoconservation at Rochester Institute of Technology in New York and the New York State Historical Association.

Saretzky has been employed in New Jersey as an educational consultant at the Thomas Edison College, Princeton, since 1979, as an instructor at the Mercer County Community College since 1977 and as an archivist at the Educational Testing Service since 1969. He has also been a self-employed photographer since 1975.

A member of SPE since 1977 and the Society of American Archivists since 1969, he was awarded first prize at the Princeton Art Association photography exhibition in 1979.

The photographer's special interest and experience is in the history of photography, photographic conservation and the psychological interpretation of photographs.

PUBLICATION   Catalog: *New Jersey Photographers*, 1974 (New Jersey Art Assn.).

COLLECTIONS   In New Jersey: ETS Archives, Princeton; Hopewell Mus., Hopewell; Mercer County Cultural Comm., Trenton.

ADDRESS   3 W Broad St, Hopewell, NJ 08525.

Napoleon Sarony   PHOTOGRAPHER · DRAFTSMAN   [See plate 16]   Born in Quebec, Canada, in 1821, Sarony died in Manhattan on November 9, 1896. His brother, Olivier François Xavier Sarony (1820–79), was a portrait photographer.

Sarony apprenticed in his father's lithography business as a boy in Quebec. Much later he studied art and traveled in Europe for several years until in 1864, he began to study photography with his brother.

Sarony began work as a lithographer in New York City in 1833, then gained a reputation for his drawings on stone at Robertson & Co. He founded the firm of Sarony & Major, later known as Sarony, Major & Knapp and still later as Knapp Lithograph Co. Initially a draftsman, Sarony later branched into the production of theatrical posters.

He began work as a photographer in his own studio in Birmingham, England, in 1864 and was established as a master with his portrait of the famed actress Adah Isaac Menken as Mazeppa. In 1866 he returned to New York City and opened a photo studio.

A member of the Salmagundi, Kit-Kat and Lotus clubs, Sarony was reputed to have posed and photographed 30,000 to 40,000 actors and actresses and 200,000 of the general public, many of whom were famed personalities. Many of his crayon drawings (which were mainly of nudes) were donated to his clubs.

Sarony primarily did portraits using collodion wet-plate negatives and albumen prints. *The New York Times* called him "a master in composition, without a rival in the arrangement of subjects and settings."

PUBLICATIONS Books: *The Theatrical Photographs of Napoleon Sarony*, Ben L. Bassham, 1978; *Rip Van Winkle: A Legend of the Katskill Mountains*, Washington Irving, illus., 1970; *Sarony's Living Pictures*, 1894–95. Anthologies: *The Photograph Collector's Guide*, Lee D. Witkin & Barbara London, 1979; *The Invented Eye*, Edw. Lucie-Smith, 1975.

COLLECTIONS IMP/GEH, Rochester; Mus. of the City of N.Y.; Univ. of N. Mex., Albuquerque.

Olivier François Xavier Sarony PHOTOGRAPHER Born in 1820 near Birmingham, England, Sarony died in 1879 in Scarborough, England. His brother, Napoleon Sarony (1821–96), was also a photographer.

Sarony ran a portrait studio in Scarborough.

PUBLICATIONS Monograph: *The Beauties of England*, n.d. Anthology: *Early Photographs and Early Photographers*, Oliver Mathews, 1973.

Peter Sasgen PHOTOGRAPHER Born in Evanston, Illinois, on September 30, 1941, Sasgen earned a BFA in Graphic Arts from Philadelphia College of Art, Pennsylvania, in 1965. He names Francis Bacon, the Abstract Expressionists and John Coltrane as influential for his work.

Sasgen currently is a photographer and designer of books, portfolios and posters.

He describes his work as "highly subjective portraiture through which I have attempted to alter the traditional function of photographic portraits."

PUBLICATIONS Monographs: *Self Portraits, The Vision—A Journey in Two Parts, Encounters One, Encounters Two*, 1979 (self-pub.).

PORTFOLIO *Six Portraits*, 1979 (Paul Cava Gall.: Philadelphia).

COLLECTIONS Free Lib. of Philadelphia, Pa.; Ingersoll Cllctn., Philadelphia; L/C, Wash. D.C.; Philadelphia Mus. of Art.

DEALER Paul Cava Gall., 1715 Spruce St, Philadelphia, PA 19103.

ADDRESS 7816 Roanoke St, Philadelphia, PA 19118.

Jan Saudek PHOTOGRAPHER · FACTORY WORKER Born in 1935 in Prague, Czechoslovakia, Saudek received a Certificate of Photogra-

phy. He considers Edward Steichen and his "The Family of Man" exhibit a major influence.

He took up photography in 1952, using a Baby Brownie Kodak, switching in 1963 to a Flexaret VI, which he still uses. Saudek has been a factory worker since 1950 and a photographer in his spare time.

His work has been widely exhibited. His subject matter is "the people of my land, that forgotten land in middle Europe . . . the old and the young, children and mothers, lonely women and sensuous women, people alone and in relationship to others."

PUBLICATIONS Anthologies: *Family of Woman*, 1979; *Study of the Nude*, 1979. Catalog: *The World of Jan Saudek*, intro. by David Travis, 1979 (Jacques Baruch Gall., Chicago). Periodicals: "Jan Saudek," *Picture Magazine*, June/July 1979; "De Wereld van Jan Saudek," *Foto*, June 1979; "Jan Saudek: I'm Led by Instinct," Derek Bennett, Mar/Apr 1978, May/June, Mar/Apr 1977, *printletter*; "Jan Saudek," Giselle Freund, Oct/Nov, Aug/Sept 1977, *Zoom* (Germany); "Akt & Erotik," Ann Farova, *Fotografie*, vol. 4, 1977; "Allegories of Jan Saudek," *Midwest Art*, summer 1976.

COLLECTIONS Art Inst. of Chicago; Cincinnati Art Mus., Ohio; Exchange Natl. Bank, Chicago; Hopewell Fndn., NYC; IMP/GEH, Rochester; Kresge Art Ctr., Lansing, Mich.; L/C, Wash., D.C.; Mus. of Fine Arts, Boston; New Orleans Mus. of Art. Bibliothèque Nationale, Paris; Musée Nicéphore Niepce, Chalon-sur-Saône, France; Natl. Gall of Victoria, Melbourne, Australia; Photo Art, Basel, Switzerland; several private collections.

DEALER Jacques Baruch Gall., 900 N Michigan Ave, Chicago, IL 60611.

Charles Roscoe Savage PHOTOGRAPHER Born in England in 1832, Savage died in the United States in 1909. He came to New York in 1856, and in 1859 after some training in photography, set up a studio in Nebraska. In 1860 he moved to Salt Lake City, and then traveled in 1866 to San Francisco, where he spent time with Carleton E. Watkins. His firm, Savage & Ottinger, distributed the western scenes he photographed.

He is best remembered for his photograph of the joining of the Union Pacific and Central Pacific railroads at Promontory Point, Utah, 1869. Savage also documented the leaders of the Mormon Church. His other work concentrated on the architecture of Salt Lake City and its surrounding countryside.

535

PUBLICATIONS Books: *Era of Exploration: The Rise of Landscape Photography in the American West 1860–1885*, 1975; *Through Camera Eyes*, Nelson B. Wadsworth, 1975; *Photography and the American Scene*, Robert Taft, 1938; *Pictorial Reflex of Salt Lake City and Vicinity*, 1894; *Picturesque Utah*, Virginia M. Donaghé, 1888; *Views of Utah*, 1887; *Salt Lake City*, 1869; *Zion: Her Gates and Temple*, n.d. Anthology: *The Photograph Collector's Guide*, Lee D. Witkin & Barbara London, 1979. Periodicals: "A Photographic Tour of Near 9,000 Miles," *The Philadelphia Photographer*, Sept/Oct 1867.

PORTFOLIO *Gems of Utah Scenery*, 189? (self-pub.: Salt Lake City).

COLLECTIONS Boston Public Lib.; Church of Jesus Christ of the Latter-Day Saints, Office of the Historian, Salt Lake City, Utah; Harvard Univ., Carpenter Ctr, Cambridge, Mass.; IMP/GEH, Rochester; Univ. of New Mexico, Albuquerque.

Naomi Savage   PHOTOGRAPHER   Born June 25, 1927, in New Jersey, Savage took a course with Berenice Abbott at the New School in New York City in 1943, then studied at Bennington College, Vermont (1944–47). She apprenticed with her uncle, Man Ray (1947–48).

The photographer, who operates her own studio, won an NEA Fellowship in 1971 and a grant from the Cassandra Foundation in 1970. In 1971 she created a fifty-foot-long photoengraving mural of presidents' portraits for the Lyndon Baines Johnson Library in Austin, Texas.

Savage uses a variety of experimental techniques and materials in her work, including photoengraving, intaglio prints, solarization, collage, photograms, texture screens, gum-bichromate prints, photo ceramics and toners.

PUBLICATIONS Books: *The Photograph Collector's Guide*, Lee D. Witkin & Barbara London, 1979; *The Darkroom Handbook*, Curtin & London, 1979; *The Photography Catalog*, Norman Snyder, ed., 1976; *Photography: A Handbook of History, Materials, and Processes*, C. Swedlund, 1974; *Looking at Photographs*, John Szarkowski, 1973; *Frontiers of Photography*, 1972, *Color*, 1970, *The Print*, 1970, (Time-Life Series). Anthology: *Women See Woman*, 1976. Catalogs: *Art: A Woman's Sensibility*, Miriam Shapiro, ed., 1975 (Calif. Inst. of the Arts: Valencia); *Two Generations of Photographs: Man Ray and Naomi Savage*, 1969 (New Jersey State Mus.: Trenton). Periodicals: *Progresso Fotografico—Anno 83*, Dec 1976; *Ovo Photo*, Sept/Oct 1974; *Untitled*,

7/8, 1974; *Album*, no. 10, 1970; *Modern Photography*, Mar 1975, Jan 1970.

COLLECTIONS Harvard Univ., Fogg Art Mus., Cambridge, Mass.; LBJ Lib., Austin, Tex.; Madison Art Ctr., Wisconsin; MOMA, NYC; New Jersey State Mus., Trenton; Princeton Univ., N.J.; Mus. of Fine Arts, Houston; Ulster County Community Coll., N.Y.; Univ. of Ill., Urbana; Univ. of Kans., Lawrence; USTA Education & Research Ctr., Princeton, N.J.; Youth Tennis Fndn. of Princeton, N.J.

DEALER Witkin Gall., 41 E 57 St, New York, NY 10022.

ADDRESS 41 Drakes Corner Rd, Princeton, NJ 08540.

Constantin Savulescu   ENGINEER · WRITER · HISTORIAN   Born October 10, 1914, in Slănic Prahova, Romania, Savulescu graduated from engineering school in Bucharest, Romania, in 1934. He is employed as an engineer.

Savulescu has belonged to the Art Photographers Association of Romania since 1957 (directory board member since 1960), the Fédération Internationale d'Art Photographique in Switzerland since 1957, and is a member of the advisory board of *History of Photography* magazine. In 1962 he won a bronze medal from San Adrian de Besos in Barcelona, Spain.

He conducts research on the history of Romanian photography.

PUBLICATIONS Periodicals (text only): "Photography in the Independence War of Romania (1877–1878)," May/June 1977, "Photograph chronography of Romania, Period 1839–1916," no. 4-5, 1975, *Fotografia*; "Early photography in Eastern Europe—Romania," *History of Photography*, Jan 1977; "Carol Popp de Szathmary, first war photoreporter," *Magazin Istoric*, Dec 1973; "The First War Photographic Reportage," *Image*, Mar 1973.

ADDRESS Str. Agricultori 114, 73206 Bucharest, Of.39, Romania.

Kyoichi Sawada   PHOTOJOURNALIST   Born in Japan, Sawada was killed on October 28, 1970, while on assignment in war-torn Cambodia.

A combat photographer for UPI, Sawada covered the Vietnamese war, following ground action in isolated outposts and flying in helicopter missions. He was captured once, and narrowly escaped death innumerable times.

Time called him "the best, certainly the most daring photographer working for UPI in Indochina." Sawada won the Pulitzer Prize in 1966.

PUBLICATIONS Anthology: *Moments,* Sheryl & John Leekley, foreword by Dan Rather, 1978. Periodical: *Time,* obit w/photo., Nov 9, 1970.
COLLECTION IMP/GEH, Rochester.

Charles M. Sawyer PHOTOGRAPHER · WRITER Sawyer was born on July 2, 1941, in Concord, New Hampshire. His major influences were André Kertész, Henri Cartier-Bresson and Josef Sudek. He received his MS in physics at Case Institute of Technology, Cleveland, Ohio (1964), and his BS in physics from the University of New Hampshire, Durham (1962).

Sawyer currently works as a freelance writer and photographer. He was an associate professor of Humanities at New England College, Henniker, New Hampshire (1966–76), and a Yale University Fellow (1964–66). He is a member of the Authors Guild.

PUBLICATIONS Monograph: *Monograph: 18,* 1977. Periodicals (by Sawyer): "Masters Meet at the Press," *Camera 35,* Mar 1978; "Hang Loose, Hold Tight," *Revue Fotografie 76,* fall 1976; "Josef Sudek: The Czech Romantic," *Modern Photography,* Sept 1976; "Black Line Taboo," *Camera 35,* Nov 1975; "The Little Black Border and the Anti-Crop Taboo," *Photoreporter,* July 1973. About Sawyer: "Charles Sawyer," *Progresso Fotografico,* Apr 1978; "Of Postcards and Publishing," *Photograph,* spring 1977; "Charles Sawyer," *Nueva Lente Photographia,* Apr 1977.
COLLECTIONS MOMA, NYC. Bibliothèque Nationale, Paris.
ADDRESS 22 Laurel St, Somerville, MA 02143.

Egidio Scaïoni PHOTOGRAPHER Born in 1894 in Italy (possibly Milan), Scaïoni died in 1966 in Paris, France. A self-taught photographer, he was influenced by Edward Steichen and Baron Adolf de Meyer.

An accountant in Milan, Scaïoni moved to Paris in the late 1920s to photograph couturier collections and establish his career. In 1929 he formed a partnership with John de Forest Thompson, who took over the business aspects of Scaïoni's work. He later opened a studio in London and began publishing books with the firm Editions de Varenne. His images were published in various fashion magazines as well as *Time* and *Fortune,* among others.

A painter as well as a photographer, Scaïoni also developed formulas for perfumes.

Working with an 8 x 10 view camera, Scaïoni produced silver contact prints, using his own chemistry. He employed directional lighting and Art Deco backgrounds in his fashion work and set up distinctive stylized poses, often in silhouette. He also shot still lifes and nonfashion commercial photography, and was one of the first to use the Vivex color process.

PUBLICATIONS Books: *Meraviglie dei Fondi Marini,* Jacques Forest, 1955 & *Meraviglie della Flora Esotica,* Marcel Belvianes, 1955 (Novara Istituto Geografic De Agostino: Italy); *La Photographie de Nu,* 1950 (Editions Prisma: Paris). Anthology: *The History of Fashion Photography,* Nancy Hall-Duncan, 1979.
COLLECTION IMP/GEH, Rochester.

Francesco Scavullo PHOTOGRAPHER · DIRECTOR Scavullo was born on January 16, 1929, in Staten Island, New York.

He is a freelance photographer and television director. His photographs have appeared in such magazines as *Vogue, Harpers Bazaar, Cosmopolitan, Esquire, Newsweek* and *Time,* as well as on numerous record album covers. Scavullo belongs to the Director's Guild of America, American Federation of Television and Radio Artists, and to Screen Actors Guild.

Scavullo is known for his glamorous photographs of models and celebrities. In addition to still photography, he directed the 1979 CBS-television special, "The Crystal Gayle Show."

PUBLICATIONS Monographs: *Scavullo on Men,* 1977; *Scavullo on Beauty,* 1976. Periodical: *Camera 35,* Apr 1978.
COLLECTION Metro. Mus. of Art, NYC.
ADDRESS 212 E 63 St, New York, NY 10021.

Larry John Schaaf PHOTOHISTORIAN · TEACHER Born in Elgin, Illinois, on October 31, 1947, Schaaf received a BA in Journalism (1971) and an MA in Communication (1973) from the University of Texas, Austin. His major influence was the Gernsheim Collection.

An assistant professor in the Department of Journalism at the University of Texas, Austin, since 1973, he was a humanities-research associate at the Gernsheim Collection in 1972. Schaaf belongs to the NPPA.

He won a National Endowment for the Humanities summer stipend grant in 1978 and a special research grant from the University (of Texas) Research Institute in 1977. In 1972 Schaaf won the Martin Emmet Walter Fellowship in Journalism from the University of Texas.

His research interest is the history and development of nineteenth-century photography, with an emphasis on the interaction between technology and aesthetics in Britain.

Schaaf

PUBLICATIONS Books: *Paul Martin: Victorian Photographer*, w/Standish Meacham & Roy Flukinger, 1977; *Nineteenth Century Photographic Processes . . .*, 1973 (prvt. pub.). Periodicals: "Herschel, Talbot, and Photography," July 1980, "Charles Piazzi Smyth's 1865 Conquest of the Great Pyramid," Oct 1979, "Daguerreotype Portraiture" (review of book *Facing the Light: Historic American Portrait Daguerreotypes*), July 1979, "Sir John Herschel's 1839 Royal Society Paper on Photography," Jan 1979, *History of Photography*.

ADDRESS Dept. of Journalism, University of Texas, Austin, TX 78712.

John Paul Schaefer UNIVERSITY ADMINISTRATOR · PHOTOGRAPHER Born September 17, 1934, in New York City, Schaefer received a BS degree from the Polytechnic Institute of Brooklyn in New York City in 1955. He continued his education at the University of Illinois in Urbana, where he received a PhD in Chemistry in 1958, and at the California Institute of Technology in Pasadena, where he was made a Postdoctorate Fellow (1958–59).

Schaefer has been both president of the University of Arizona in Tucson since 1971 and professor of chemistry there since 1960.

He is a member of many national and international organizations, including United States-Israeli Bi-national Science Foundation, in which he also serves on the board of governors (1973–78), International Association of University Presidents (since 1974), Institute of International Education, National Association of State Universities and Land-Grant Colleges, Associated Western Universities, Navajo Health Authority, in which he serves as a member of the board of commissioners (since 1973), American Association for the Advancement of Science as a fellow (since 1972), American Association of University Professors (since 1972), Friends of Photography, in which he serves as a member of the advisory board, and he is also a trustee of the W. Eugene Smith Foundation. Schaefer was responsible for founding the Center for Creative Photography in Tucson, Arizona.

PUBLICATIONS Books: *Tarahumara, Where Night Is the Day of the Moon*, w/B. Fontana, 1979; *Bac—Where the Waters Rise*, 1977; *Research Techniques in Organic Chemistry*, w/R. Bates, 1971.

PORTFOLIO *Bac Portfolio*, 1977.

ADDRESS Univ. of Ariz., 843 E. University Blvd, Tucson, AZ 85721.

Deidi Von Schaewen PHOTOGRAPHER · CINEMATOGRAPHER · DESIGNER Born April 5, 1941, in Berlin, Von Schaewen attended the Hochschule für Bildende Künste in Berlin (1959–65).

A freelance, the photographer worked for Herb Lubalin in New York (1970–72) and for Harnden Bombelli in Barcelona, Spain (1966–68).

Von Schaewen made the 35mm film short *Murs (Walls)* in 1978.

Since 1962, the photographer has shot images of walls in Germany, France, Spain, England and the United States, as well as taking photos of constructions in the city. As of this writing von Schaewen was concentrating on "sequences of objects in the street."

PUBLICATION Monograph: *Walls*, 1977.

COLLECTION Beaubourg, Paris.

DEALER Emmy de Martelaere, Paris, France.

ADDRESS 148 rue du Temple, 75003 Paris, France.

David Scharf PHOTOGRAPHER · SCIENTIST Born December 17, 1942, in Newark, New Jersey, Scharf studied at Monmouth College, West Long Branch, New Jersey, from 1961 to 1963, majoring in physics.

A freelance photographer since 1975, he worked as an independent contractor in electronic engineering and vacuum physics from 1971 to 1975.

Scharf has belonged to ASMP since 1977.

His specialization is photography using a scanning electron microscope, and he has developed special techniques for photographing living biological subjects.

PUBLICATIONS Book: *Magnifications*, 1977. Periodicals: *Photo*, Feb 1980 (France); *Omni*, Apr 1979; *American Photographer*, Sept 1978; *Photography Annual*, 1977; *Scientific American*, July 1976; *Fotografia Universal*, Feb 1976; *Realités*, June 1975; *Popular Photography*, June 1975.

COLLECTIONS Adirondack Mus., New York; Mus. of Science & Industry, Los Angeles, Calif. Polaroid, Amsterdam, The Netherlands.

REPRESENTATIVES Peter Arnold, 1500 Broadway, New York, NY 10036; Harold Moskovitz (literary agent), 8961 Sunset Blvd, Los Angeles, CA 90069; Oxford Scientific Films Ltd, Long Hanborough, Oxford OX7 2LD, Great Britain.

ADDRESS 2100 Loma Vista Pl, Los Angeles, CA 90039.

Virginia Schau HOMEMAKER · AMATEUR PHOTOGRAPHER Born February 23, 1915, in Sacramento, California, Schau attended the University of the Pacific in Stockton, California (1934–37), receiving a degree of Bachelor of Music in 1937 and a BA in 1941.

·Schau is an amateur photographer. She is a member of Mu Phi Epsilon (honorary musical organization) and the American Association of University Women. She was awarded the Pulitzer Prize for Photography in 1954, having used a Kodak Brownie for the award-winning photograph of a truck that fell off a bridge, its driver suspended by a rescue rope. Schau was the first woman ever to win the award.

PUBLICATION Anthology: *Moments*, Sheryl & John Leekley, foreword by Dan Rather, 1978.

ADDRESS 7623 Oak Leaf Dr, Santa Rosa, CA 95405.

Alexander (Xanti) Schawinsky PHOTOGRA-PHER · PAINTER · DESIGNER Born in Basel, Switzerland, in 1904, Schawinsky died in Milan, Italy, in 1979. He studied at the Bauhaus beginning in 1924, where he worked under Kandinsky, Klee and Schlemmer. He also studied with Moholy-Nagy, who, along with Man Ray, was the greatest influence on his photography.

From 1924 to 1928 the artist was involved in theatrical experiments at the Bauhaus, the most famous being "Circus," which was performed in Weimar in 1924 and 1925. Schawinsky worked as a graphic designer for the city of Magdeburg (1928–33), then established a successful design office in Italy in 1933. After emigrating to the United States, he taught at Black Mountain College (1936–38), extending his experiments with "Spectodrama" that he had begun at the Bauhaus. He worked freelance in various artistic fields from 1938 on, eventually dividing his time between New York City and Oggebio, Italy.

Schawinsky worked with Man Ray in establishing the New Bauhaus in Chicago, Illinois.

Particularly active during the 1940s, the photographer experimented with optical transformations, photograms, solarizations, etc. His probing portraits and varied artistic talents warranted his inclusion among the small and significant circle of avant-garde photographers of his day.

PUBLICATIONS Books: *Graphic Work from the Bauhaus*, Hans M. Wingler, ed., 1969; *The Bauhaus: Weimar, Dessau, Berlin, Chicago*, Hans M. Wingler, 1969; *Bauhaus-Archiv*, Hans M. Wingler, 1963; *Das Bauhaus, 1919–1933, Weimar*, Hans M. Wingler, 1962. Catalog: *Ex Libris*, no. 2 (Ex Libris: NYC). Periodicals: *Form*, Sept 1968; "La Pubblicità," *L'Ufficio Moderno*," *Rivista Mensile*, Oct 1935.

COLLECTION Detroit Inst. of the Arts, Mich.

Sherie Scheer PHOTOGRAPHER Born February 15, 1940, in Estherville, Iowa, Scheer received a BA (1969) and MA (1971) in Environmental Design from University of California at Los Angeles (UCLA).

A freelance photographer, she belongs to the Los Angeles Center for Photographic Studies, SPE, Artists Equity, Artists for Economic Opportunity and the Los Angeles Institute for Contemporary Art.

Scheer created panoramic projections for the set of the play *Winter Dancers* at the Mark Taper Forum, Los Angeles, in 1978.

"The way I usually work," says Scheer, "is to make a lateral sweep of sequential images with a 35mm camera, print them in black-and-white, and butt them up against each other. Sometimes I rephotograph the resultant panorama with a large-format camera and print it again. Finally I paint the photograph with oil paint."

PUBLICATIONS Catalogs: *Photographic Directions, L.A. 1979*, 1979 (Security Pacific Bank, Los Angeles); *Untitled*, no. 11, 1976 (Friends of Photography). Periodicals: *Art in America*, Mar/Apr 1978; *Popular Photography*, Dec 1977.

PORTFOLIO *New California Views* (group), 1979 (Landwebber/Artists: Los Angeles).

COLLECTIONS Atlantic Richfield Corp., Los Angeles; CCP, Tucson; Denver Art Mus., Colo.; Robert Freidus Gall., NYC; Grapestake Gall., San Francisco; Harvard Univ., Fogg Art Mus., Cambridge, Mass.; Houston Mus. of Fine Arts; La Jolla Mus. of Art, Calif.; Miami-Dade Jr. Coll., Miami, Fla.; N. Mex. State Univ., Las Cruces; Newport Harbor Art Mus., Newport Beach, Calif.; Oakland Mus., Calif.; R.I. School of Design Art Mus., Providence; Security Pacific Natl. Bank, Los Angeles; Tyler Mus. of Art, Tex.; UCLA, Grunwald Ctr. for the Graphic Arts; Univ. of Calif., Calif. Mus. of Photography, Riverside; Univ. of Okla. Mus. of Art, Norman. Australian Natl. Gall., Canberra; Gallery Van, Haarlem, The Netherlands.

DEALERS Meghan Williams, 50 Los Patos Wy, Santa Barbara, CA 93108; Bertha Urdang Gall., 29 W 57 St, New York, NY 10019; Ufficio Dell'arte, 44 Rue Quincampoix, Paris 75, France.

ADDRESS 31 Park Ave, Venice, CA 90291.

David Edward Scherman PHOTOGRAPHER · WRITER · EDITOR · BUILDER Born March 2, 1916, in New York City, Scherman received a BA in 1936 from Dartmouth College, Hanover, New Hampshire. His major photographic influences were Carl Mydans, Otto Hagel, Hansel Mieth and

Edward Weston. Scherman's wife, Rosemarie Redlich, co-authored several books with him.

Currently a house-builder and contractor, Scherman also has been a book reviewer for the *New York Times Book Review* and the *Washington Post* since 1972. He worked for *Life* magazine from its inception in 1936 until its demise as a weekly in 1972, and continued under the employ of Time Inc., until 1976. He was a *Life* staff photographer (1939–47), associate editor in 1953, and senior editor (1963–72).

Scherman belongs to the American Newspaper Guild and is a member of the board of governors of the Willa Cather Pioneer Memorial Society in Nebraska. In addition to his photography, he produced a weekly TV show in 1949, "Preview—the Magazine of the Air," on CBS.

Scherman has been a news photographer, a war correspondent (1940–47) and, primarily, a scenic photographer since 1949.

PUBLICATIONS Books: *Life Goes to War*, 1976; *Life Goes to the Movies*, 1974; *The Best of Life*, ed., 1973; *Ford at Fifty*, 1953; *America, The Land and Its Writers*, w/Rosemarie Redlich, 1953; *Literary America*, w/Rosemarie Redlich, 1951; *The First of the Many*, w/Capt. John R. McCrary, 1944; *Literary England*, 1944.

ADDRESSES Collaberg Rd, Stony Point, NY 10980; Truro, MA 02666.

Karl Schinzel *CHEMIST · INVENTOR* Born in Edersdorf, North Moravia, Austria, in 1886, Schinzel died in Vienna in 1951. His father started him in a business career at age sixteen, but he managed to complete his secondary education through evening studies. Later he attended Vienna Technical University (1907–12), from which he graduated.

During World War I Schinzel worked as a chemist, and after the war joined J. M. Eder's staff at the Graphische Lehr- und Versuchsanstalt in Vienna. From 1922 to 1936 he worked in his own small research laboratory in Troppau, Bohemia, and was invited to the Eastman Kodak laboratories in Rochester in 1936 and 1937–38. Returning to Austria, he built a scientific laboratory in Baden, near Vienna, and worked there until 1942, when he joined the Zeiss-Ikon laboratory at Berlin-Zehlendorf. His research collection and apparatus were destroyed during World War II, so he moved to Vienna to continue his work.

Having become interested in color photography during his secondary studies, Schinzel developed the Katachromie color process in 1905, which included the first multilayer color film and the first proposal for making color prints based on the catalytic destruction of dyes through oxygen released from peroxide in contact with a silver image. It was the forerunner of modern color films. In his Troppau laboratory he made advances in the subtractive color process with multilayer films, and while at Eastman Kodak he made improvements in the production of Kodachrome. At the time of his death he was working on a comprehensive book on color photography. Schinzel obtained a total of 250 to 300 patents during his lifetime.

PUBLICATIONS Books: *Encyclopedie voor Fotografie en Cinematografie*, Elsevier, 1958; *The Focal Encyclopedia of Photography*, 1957, 1956 (Focal Press); *History of Color Photography*, Joseph S. Friedman, 1944; *History of 3-Color Photography*, E. J. Wall, 1925; *Lexikon für Photographie und Reproduktionstechnik*, G. H. Emmerich, 1910. Anthology: *Photography's Great Inventors*, Louis W. Sipley, 1965. Periodicals: *Bild und Ton*, 1953; *Photographische Correspondenz*, 1952; *Lichtbild*, July 1936–Sept 1937; *British Journal of Photography*, 1905; *Photographischen Wochenblatt*, no. 30, 1905.

Fee Schlapper *PHOTOGRAPHER* Born June 7, 1927, in Giessen, Germany, Schlapper earned a merit diploma (1952) and the title of master (1954) from the Bavarian State School of Photography in Munich. Her mentor was Dr. Otto Steinert.

A freelance photographer, Schlapper belongs to DGPh (since 1960), GDL (since 1956), VBK (Verband bildender Künstler Württemberg) and GEDOK (Gemeinschaft der Künstlerinnen & Kunstfreunde).

PUBLICATIONS Books: *Kindheit und Jugend*, 2 vols., 1978 (Thieme-Verlag); *Nymphenburg*, 1972 (Nymphenburger Verlagsanstalt); *Baden-Baden*, 1968 (Belser-Verlag); *Taha, Der Ägyptische Eselsjunge*, w/text, 1963 (Kosmos-Verlag). Anthology: *Family of Children*, 1977. Periodicals: *U.S. Camera Annual*, 1962, 1961, 1960, 1959, 1956.

ADDRESS Lenauweg 1, D-7570 Baden-Baden, West Germany.

Peter M. Schlessinger *PHOTOGRAPHER · TEACHER* Born in Cambridge, Massachusetts, on June 10, 1946, Schlessinger earned an MFA in 1972 from Rhode Island School of Design, Providence, where he studied under Harry Callahan and Aaron Siskind, and a BA in 1968 from Amherst College. In 1969 he was a student of Minor White and Paul Caponigro. He has been influenced by personal contacts with Robert Frank and Frederick Sommer.

Since 1971 he has been the director of Apeiron Workshops, Millerton, New York. From 1969 to 1970 he was editorial assistant of *Aperture* magazine.

PUBLICATIONS Anthology: *SX-70 Art*, Ralph Gibson, ed., 1979. Periodical: "Polishing the Mirror," *Photograph*, 1977.

COLLECTIONS Polaroid Corp., Cambridge, Mass.; Wesleyan Univ., Middletown, Conn.

ADDRESS Apeiron Workshops, Box 551, Millerton, NY 12546.

Michael Schmidt PHOTOGRAPHER Born October 6, 1945, in Berlin, Germany, Schmidt is a self-taught photographer and received a degree in Photo-design from Fach Hochschule Dortmund, Dortmund, Germany, in 1980.

A teacher of photography at Volkshochschule in Kreuzberg, Germany, since 1969, Schmidt has also taught at the Pädagogischen Hochschule in Berlin (1976–78) and at the Universität FB 4 in Essen (1979). From 1976 to 1977 he directed the Werkstatt für Fotografie der Volkshochschule in Kreuzberg.

The photographer has belonged to GDL since 1976 and DGPh since 1979.

Schmidt's main photographic theme is Berlin in its rebuilt stages after 1945.

PUBLICATIONS Books: *Berlin—Stadtlandschaft und Menschen*, 1978, *Berlin—Wedding*, 1978, *Berlin Kreuzberg*, 1973 (Berlin). Periodical: *Camera*, Mar 1979.

COLLECTIONS Berlinische Galerie, Berlin, West Ger.; Bibliothèque Nationale, Paris; Musée d'Art et d'Histoire, Fribourg, Switzerland; Stadtmuseum München, West Ger.

DEALERS Galerie Rudolf Kicken, Albertusstrasse 47/49, D-5000 Cologne 1, West Germany; Rudolf Springer Galerie, Fasanenstrasse 13, D-1000 Berlin 12, West Germany.

ADDRESS Wartenburgstrasse 16 a, D-1000 Berlin 61, West Germany.

Martin Schneider PHOTOGRAPHER · WRITER · FILM MAKER · ECOLOGIST Born September 23, 1926, in New York City. Schneider's father, Morris (1886–1965), was a sculptor. Martin majored in psychology and photography at the City University of New York from 1947 to 1951. He lists Walter Rosenblum and Louis Bernstein as his personal mentors, and W. Eugene Smith, Dorothea Lange and Lewis Hine among those who have influenced him.

Since 1965 Schneider has worked as a consumer advocate and public intervenor. He was a film maker for NBC-TV from 1970 to 1971 and a photojournalist for *Life* magazine from 1967 to 1969. He also was employed as an ecological consultant for the Environmental Protection Agency in New York City (1970), the U.S. Public Health Service (1965) and U.S. Senate (1965).

A member of ASMP, Schneider was awarded television's Franny Award "for practices on behalf of the American Consumer" (1974). He also received a CAPS grant in 1977.

Schneider worked as co-cinematographer on the following television documentaries: "Environment Crusade" and "The Poisoned Air," both CBS-TV (1970); "The Advocates" (1970) and "Pall Over Our Cities" (1966), both for WNET-TV. He was the cinematographer, director and writer of "Censorship of Pollution Solutions by Media & Government" (1973) for WNET and "Killers of the Environment" (1971) for NBC-TV.

Of his work, Schneider states: "In the tradition of sociologist Lewis Hine, whose crusading photography led to child labor laws, my ecological, engineering, photography and film work in public health and safety have been a basis for legislation, as well as consequent censorship, intimidation, blacklisting and seizure of my residence with all my possessions and my sabotaged mobile laboratory. However, where so many lives are at risk—where my work could make a difference—I can only be a concerned *participant*; never a superficial *spectator* of history."

PUBLICATIONS Books: *Eye of Conscience*, 1974; *New World or No World*, 1970. Contributor: *Encyclopaedia Britannica*, 1970. Periodicals: *N.Y. Times*, Apr 23, 1972, Oct 25, 1970; *Village Voice*, Feb 19, 1970; *Life*, Feb 1969; *Time*, Sept 1963, Aug 1962.

COLLECTIONS Art Inst. of Chicago; L/C, Wash., D.C.; MOMA, NYC.

ADDRESS 1501 Broadway, #2907, New York, NY 10036.

Donna F. Schneier ART DEALER Born March 30, 1938, in St. Louis, Missouri, Schneier earned a BA from Brandeis University in Waltham, Massachusetts, and an MFA from New York University in New York City.

She has been president of Donna Schneier, Inc., in New York City since 1973 and recently formed Una Donna Ltd. From 1977 to 1979 she was president of B&D Corporation and from 1966 to 1973 presided over Gallery 6M, both in New York City.

Schneier belongs to VSW, SPE, New York Historical Society, and the Association of International Photography Art Dealers.

Schneier deals in nineteenth- and twentieth-century vintage photographs.

ADDRESS Donna Schneier Fine Arts, 251 E 71 St, New York, NY 10021.

Volker Schöbel *GRAPHIC ARTIST · PHOTOGRAPHER* Born January 24, 1944, in Oelsa near Löbau, Saxony (now the German Democratic Republic), Schöbel studied graphic design at the Brunswick (Germany) College of Art, then served a retoucher's apprenticeship from 1963 to 1966. He carried out alternative service as a nurse in Gehrden Hospital near Hannover, Germany (1966–68), then continued his studies in graphic design and photography in Hannover from 1968 to 1971. His teachers included Grötzinger, Burkhard and Riebesehl.

A freelance graphic artist, photographer and photography teacher since 1975, Schöbel was a layout artist and book producer for Deutsche Verlagsanstalt in Stuttgart, Germany, from 1971 to 1975.

Using sepia toning, Schöbel creates photographs that "show events within my inner self."

PUBLICATIONS Book: *Jugendliche*, w/Gisela Schmeer, 1977 (Klett-Cotta: Stuttgart). Periodical: *Camera*, Aug 1971.

COLLECTIONS Bibliothèque Nationale, Paris; Neue Sammlung Mus., Munich, Germany.

DEALERS Fotogalerie Lange-Irschl, 54 Türkenstrasse, Munich 40, Germany; Photographers' Gall., 8 Great Newport St, London WC 2, England.

ADDRESS Danneckerstr. 27 B, 7000 Stuttgart 1, Germany.

Diana Lindsay Schoenfeld *PHOTOGRAPHER · TEACHER* Born September 3, 1949, in Knoxville, Tennessee, Schoenfeld earned a BVA in 1972 from Georgia State University, Atlanta, and an MA in 1974 from the University of New Mexico, Albuquerque. She names John McWilliams, Beaumont Newhall and Van Deren Coke as major influences.

She has directed the photography program at College of the Redwoods, Eureka, California, since 1976. From 1975 to 1976 she taught photography at Rio Hondo College in Whittier, California.

Schoenfeld has belonged to SPE since 1975.

Using a large-format camera and contact printing, the photographer organizes organic materials, botanical and biological specimens, found objects and objects of choice into highly stylized still-life arrangements.

PUBLICATIONS Monograph: *Illusory Arrange-*

ments, 1977. Anthologies: *Light and Substance*, text only, 1974; *Young American Photography*, vol. 1, 1974. Catalogs: *Attitudes: Photography in the 1970s*, 1979 (Santa Barbara Mus. of Art: Calif.); *Perception, Field of View*, 1979 (Los Angeles Ctr. for Photographic Studies); *Photoworks, 79*, 1979 (Bellevue Art Mus.; Wash.); *Interior Spaces*, 1978 (Univ. of Calif.: Davis). Periodicals: "New Mexico: Work by Women 'Outside the Mainstream,'" Meridel Rubenstein, *Afterimage: VSW*, Oct 1979; *Creative Camera*, Sept 1979; "Rediscovering a Process," Robert Mautner, *Artweek*, Feb 21, 1976.

COLLECTIONS Bellevue Art Mus., Wash.; CCP, Tucson; G. Ray Hawkins Gall., Los Angeles; Graham Nash Cllctn., Los Angeles; Los Angeles Ctr. for Photographic Studies; Ohio Wesleyan Univ., Delaware; Univ. of N. Mex. Art Mus., Albuquerque.

DEALERS G. Ray Hawkins Gall., 7224 Melrose Ave, Los Angeles, CA 90046; Neikrug Gall., 224 E 68 St, New York, NY 10021.

ADDRESS Creative Arts Dept, College of the Redwoods, Eureka, CA 95501.

Kathryn Schooley-Robins *PHOTOGRAPHER · TEACHER* Born April 16, 1948, in Kansas City, Missouri, Schooley-Robins earned a BFA in 1970 from the University of Florida, Gainesville, where she studied with Jerry Uelsmann and Douglas Prince. She took her MFA at Arizona State University, Tempe, in 1973.

As of this writing an instructor at Southern Illinois University, Carbondale, she was a visiting assistant professor at the University of Illinois, Urbana-Champaign, in 1978–79 and an instructor at Pima College, Tucson, Arizona, from 1973 to 1978.

The SPE member won an NEA Photographer-in-Residence Grant in 1980, an Illinois Arts Council Grant in 1979 and a Ford Foundation Allocations Grant in 1978.

Schooley-Robins produces blueprints, large-format brown Vandyke landscapes and hand-colored panoramic landscapes.

PUBLICATIONS Periodicals: *Combinations, A Journal of Photography*, winter 1976; *Florida Quarterly*, winter 1970, fall 1969.

COLLECTIONS Ariz. State Univ., Tempe; CCP, Tucson; Eastern Wash. State Univ., Cheney; Ill. State Mus., Springfield; La Grange Coll., La Grange, Ga.; L/C, Wash., D.C.; Phoenix Coll., Ariz.; Southern Ill. Univ., Carbondale.

DEALER Susan Spiritus, 3336 Via Lido, Newport Beach, CA 92663; Equivalents Gall., 1822 Broadway, Seattle, WA 98122.

Charles Schorre   *PAINTER · PHOTOGRAPHER*
Born March 9, 1925, in Cuero, Texas, Schorre earned a BFA from the University of Texas, Austin, in 1948.

He taught at Rice University, Houston, Texas (1960–72), and at Museum of Fine Arts, Houston (1950–55).

PUBLICATIONS   Periodicals: *Picture*, no. 12, 1979, 1:5, 1977, 1:3, 1977, 1:1, 1976; *Popular Photography Annual*, 1958, 1957; *Creative Photography #3*, 1959.

REPRESENTATIVE   Seashore Press, 5116 Morningside, Houston, TX 77005.

ADDRESS   2406 Tangley Rd, Houston, TX 77005.

Friedrich Otto Schott   *CHEMIST · GLASSMAKER · INVENTOR*   Born in 1851 in Witten, Westphalia, Germany, Schott died in 1935. Descended from glassworkers, he attended the Royal Provincial Trade School at Hagen and studied chemistry at Aachen, Würzburg and Leipzig. He earned a doctorate at Jena in 1875, then traveled in France and Belgium to study their glass industry.

From 1877 to 1880 Schott built a chemical factory and glassworks in Spain. In Witten, he conducted research into new kinds of glass, using previously unemployed elements. In 1879 he contacted Ernst Abbe at the Carl Zeiss works in Jena, which led to a series of test melts for optical glass. In 1882 Schott moved his laboratory to Jena to continue his experiments, and in 1884 he set up the glassworks of Schott und Genossen with Abbe, Carl Zeiss and Roderich Zeiss. Along with Abbe, Schott formed the Carl Zeiss Foundation in 1889, to which he deeded his Schott und Genossen shares in 1919. He succeeded Abbe as the foundation's manager, a post he held until 1927.

Starting in 1884, the Schott und Genossen glassworks began producing a new kind of optical glass, including the classic crown and flint glasses. They issued their first price list of forty-four kinds of glass in 1886, and added thirteen varieties in 1888.

PUBLICATIONS   Books: *Quellendarstellungen zur Geschichte der Fotografie*, Wolfgang Baier, 1964; *Odyssey of 41 Glassmakers*, Walther Kiaulehn, 1959; *March of Photography*, Erich Stenger, 1958; *Ernst Abbe*, Norbert Gunther, 1946. Anthology: *Photography's Great Inventors*, Louis W. Sipley, 1965. Periodicals: *Bild und Ton*, 1957,

1955, 1954; *Jahrbuch für Photographie und Reproduktionstechnik*, Josef Maria Eder, 1891; *Photografische Correspondenz*, 1890, 1887.

Victor Schrager   *PHOTOGRAPHER · TEACHER*
Born September 16, 1950, in Bethesda, Maryland, Schrager received a BA in History from Harvard College, Cambridge, Massachusetts (1972), and an MFA in Photography from Florida State University, Tallahassee (1975).

As of this writing Schrager was an instructor at New York University in New York City, he taught at the School of Visual Arts in New York City in 1978 and from 1975 to 1978 directed Light Gallery in New York City.

In 1980 Schrager received an NEA fellowship.

PUBLICATIONS   Anthology: *One of a Kind*, 1979. Catalog: *Cultural Artifacts*, 1979 (Florida School of the Arts).

COLLECTIONS   Cranbrook Academy Mus. of Art, Bloomfield Hills, Mich.; High Mus. of Art, Atlanta, Ga.; IMP/GEH, Rochester; L/C, Wash., D.C.; San Francisco Mus. of Modern Art; Univ. of Colo., Boulder.

ADDRESS   101 Wooster St, New York, NY 10012.

Michael George Schreier   *PHOTOGRAPHER · TEACHER*   Born February 19, 1949, in Vienna, Austria, Schreier is a Canadian citizen. He received a diploma in Photographic Arts in 1971 from Ryerson Polytechnical Institute in Toronto, Canada, and an MFA in 1975 from Concordia University, Montreal, Canada. He names artists David Heath and Jerome Krause as major influences.

Schreier has been an assistant professor at the University of Ottawa (Canada), Visual Arts Department, since 1972. In the summer of 1979 he taught workshops at Banff Centre of Fine Arts in Banff, Canada.

The photographer was a member of the Canada Council of the Arts Jury in 1975, and won grants from the Council in 1972, 1973, 1974, 1975, 1976, 1978 and 1980.

Since 1974 Schreier has taken "family snapshots" of family ceremonials, using small-format transparencies printed in Cibachrome. Since 1976 he has shot "anonymous space, anonymous individuals, portraits in transition" in 8 x 10 and 11 x 14 Cibachrome exposed directly.

PUBLICATIONS   Anthologies: *Time-Life Annual of Photography*, 1977; *Photographers Choice*, Kelly Wise, ed., 1975. Periodical (review): "Une Fleur, Un Arbre, Une Plante," Anne Thomas, *Arts Canada*, Oct/Nov 1977.

COLLECTIONS In Ottawa, Ontario: Art Bank, Canada Council; Natl. Archives of Canada; Natl. Film Board of Canada; Natl. Gall. of Canada.

DEALER Yashima Gall., 340 St Catherine St, Montreal, Quebec, Canada.

ADDRESS 59-3691 Albion Rd, Ottawa, Ontario, Canada KIT IP2.

Oliver A. Schuchard   PHOTOGRAPHER · TEACHER   Born in St. Louis, Missouri, on December 14, 1944, Schuchard earned a BFA in Painting in 1966 and an MFA in 1972 at Southern Illinois University in Carbondale. He has also studied at numerous photography workshops.

Since 1972 Schuchard has been a professor of photography at the University of Missouri in Columbia, and in 1975, he taught at the Ansel Adams Yosemite Workshop. Concurrent with his teaching assignments, Schuchard freelances.

The University of Missouri awarded the photographer grants to produce exhibition catalogs and traveling exhibits for "The Forests of Missouri" (1975) and "In Celebration" (1979).

Of his work Schuchard states, "My primary creative direction lies in interpretation of the landscape in the traditional style of West Coast photographers." He works in both medium and large formats.

PUBLICATIONS   Catalogs: *In Celebration*, 1979, *The Forests of Missouri*, 1975 (Univ. of Missouri: St. Louis).

COLLECTION   St. Louis Art Mus.

ADDRESS   Rte 1, Box 266B, Holts Summit, MO 65043.

Flip Schulke   PHOTOGRAPHER · CINEMATOGRAPHER   Born June 24, 1930, in St. Paul, Minnesota, Schulke graduated in 1953 from Macalester College, St. Paul, with majors in journalism, political science and sociology. He considers Wilson Hicks, executive editor of *Life* magazine, and Dr. Martin Luther King, Jr., as his mentors.

A freelance photojournalist with Black Star Agency since 1956, Schulke also worked for *Life* in 1966–69. He was a professor of art at Macalester College in 1976, assistant professor at the University of Missouri, Columbia, School of Journalism in 1974 and an instructor at the University of Miami, Florida, in 1953–56.

A member of ASMP, SPE and the NPPA, Schulke won a grant from the Minnesota State Arts Board in 1979.

In addition to his still photography, he has served as cinematographer on several documentaries and underwater films.

Nearly all of his photography, "including extensive underwater work, is 'humanist' in nature," says Schulke. He documented, in photos and words, the southern civil rights movement during the late 1950s, 1960s and early 1970s.

PUBLICATIONS   Books: *Underwater Photography for Everyone*, 1978; *Martin Luther King, Jr., A Documentary . . . Montgomery to Memphis*, 1976.

REPRESENTATIVE   Black Star, 450 Park Ave S, New York, NY 10016.

ADDRESS   POB 430760, Miami, FL 33143.

Emil Schulthess   ART DIRECTOR · PHOTOGRAPHER   Schulthess was born October 29, 1913.

Since 1957 he has been self-employed as a freelance photographer and art director, producing pictorial books. Prior to that he was picture editor and photographer of the Swiss monthly magazine *Du* in Zurich (1941–57), a freelance graphic artist (1932–37) and an apprentice graphic artist (1928–32).

Schulthess was the recipient of *U.S. Camera* awards in 1967 and 1950, a culture prize from the German Photographic Society in Cologne in 1964, a Prix Nadar in 1960 and an annual award from ASMP in 1958.

PUBLICATIONS   Books: *Lucerne*, 1978, *New York*, 1978 (Meridian Press: Zurich); *Matterhorn*, 1974, *Midnight Sun*, 1973 (Mill Publications Ltd.: Bern); *Soviet Union*, 1971 (Artemis-Verlag: Zurich); *Top of Switzerland*, 1970; *Africa III*, 1969, *China*, 1966, *The Amazon*, 1962, *Antarctica*, 1960 (Artemis-Verlag: Zurich); *Africa II*, 1959, *Africa I*, 1958, *USA*, 1955 (Manesse-Verlag: Zurich).

REPRESENTATIVE   Black Star, 450 Park Ave S, New York, NY 10016.

ADDRESS   Langacher 5, 8127 Forch, Zurich, Switzerland.

Myra Jo Schultz   PHOTOGRAPHER · DESIGNER · BOOKBINDER · TEACHER   Born September 1, 1953, in Chicago, Schultz received a BFA from the School of the Art Institute of Chicago in 1975, and an MFA from the University of Wisconsin in Madison in 1978. She studied with Barbara Crane, Harold Allen and Phil Hamilton.

Employed as an instructor at the University of Wisconsin Extension since 1977, Schultz is also the proprietor of Shutter Press, which produces limited-edition, handmade books, portfolios, graphics and typography.

She is a member of both SPE and Wisconsin Women in the Arts.

The photographer characterizes her work as "black-and-white silver prints, usually presented in a hand-bound book or portfolio with handset type. [The] images consist of ideas of space within people, between people and objects, and the textures and light created within these spaces."

PUBLICATIONS Periodicals: *Wisconsin Photographer*, Mar 1978; "Women Photographers," review, *New Art Examiner*, Oct 1974.

COLLECTIONS CCP, Tucson; City of Madison Clltn., Wis.; Scottsdale Community Coll., Ariz. Bibliothèque Nationale, Paris.

ADDRESS 744 Wellesley Ave, Kensington, CA 94707.

John Schulze PHOTOGRAPHER · TEACHER Born June 7, 1915, in Scottsbluff, Nebraska, he received an MFA in 1948 from the University of Iowa in Iowa City and a BS in 1940 from the Kansas State Teachers College of Emporia.

As of this date he is a professor of photography at the University of Iowa. Prior to that he was artist-in-residence at Sun Valley Center for the Arts in Idaho (August 1977, 1975), at SUNY Geneseo (November 1973), at Western Kentucky University in Bowling Green (October 1973), at Northwest Missouri State College (March 1972) and at Washburn University in Topeka, Kansas (February 1972).

A member of the CAA, Schulze was commissioned to do a sixty-foot photographic mural for the new science building at the University of Northern Iowa in Cedar Falls, which he completed in August 1972. He also made two films, *Fluid Image* in 1965 and *The Elusive Shadow* in 1964.

Schulze says of his work, "I mainly work in black-and-white, although I continue to be involved in color. A small percent of the black-and-white ends up as single-print photographs, while most of the images are put in collage compositions. Images are of the real world and of any conceivable subject."

PUBLICATIONS Book: *Photography: Source and Resource*, Lewis, McQuaid, & Tait, 1973. Anthology: *Light[7]*, Minor White, ed., 1968. Periodicals: *Photography Annual*, 1969; *Camera International*, Nov 1965.

COLLECTIONS Blanden Mus., Ft. Dodge, Iowa; Cedar Rapids Art Ctr., Iowa; Coe Coll. Print Archives, Cedar Rapids, Iowa; Educational Facilities Lab, NYC; Kansas State Teachers Coll., Emporia; Louisiana State Coll., Monroe; MIT, Hayden Gall.—Archival Prints, Cambridge; Oakland Mus., Calif.; Coll. of Saint Benedict, St. Jo-seph, Minn.; Sun Valley Ctr. for the Arts, Idaho; Univ. of Alabama, University; Univ. of Calif. at Davis; VSW, Rochester; Waterloo Municipal Galleries, Iowa; Western Illinois Univ., Macomb. Nihon University, Tokyo.

ADDRESS 5 Forest Glen, Iowa City, IA 52240.

Wilhelm Schürmann PHOTOGRAPHER Born August 12, 1946, in Dortmund, Germany, Schürmann is self-taught in photography.

He worked as a freelance newspaper photographer in the early 1970s before co-founding the gallery Schürmann & Kicken in 1973. Located in Aachen, Germany, he operated the gallery until 1978 and, since 1979, has freelanced and taught at the Aachen High School for Design.

A member of DGPh since 1977, the photographer received an Artist's Grant of Aachen in 1978.

Working in 8 x 10, Schürmann shoots architecture, portraits and still lifes, mostly about Belgium and West Germany.

PUBLICATIONS Book: *Klaus Honnef & Wilhelm Schürmann*, 1979. Catalog: *In Deutschland*, 1979 (Bonn, Germany). Periodicals: *Creative Camera*, Sept 1978, Apr 1976; *Zoom*, July 1978 (Paris); *Camera*, Apr 1978, Aug 1974.

COLLECTIONS IMP/GEH, Rochester; San Francisco Mus. of Modern Art; Seagrams Cllctn., NYC. Bibliothèque Nationale, Paris; Die Neue Sammlung, Munich, Germany; Landesmuseum, Bonn, Germany; Regionalmuseum, Xanten, Germany; Stadtmuseum, Munich.

DEALER Sander Gall., 2600 Connecticut Ave NW, Washington, DC 20008.

ADDRESS Haus-Heyden Str. 195, D5120, Herzogenrath-Kohlscheid, West Germany.

Mark Coffey Schwartz PHOTOGRAPHER · EXHIBITION DIRECTOR Born August 2, 1956, in Fall River, Massachusetts, Schwartz earned a BA in 1977 from Rutgers University, New Brunswick, New Jersey, and an MFA in 1979 from Ohio University, Athens. He also studied privately with Larry Fink and at Princeton University, Princeton, New Jersey, with Emmet Gowin (1975–77).

In 1979 Schwartz became assistant director of exhibitions at Ohio University.

A member of SPE and CAA, the photographer won an Ohio University Research Institute Grant and an Ohio Arts Council Fellowship in 1979.

He produces still lifes in color and platinum, using a 5 x 7 Deardorff. He also works with photo-booth images.

COLLECTIONS Bellevue Art Mus., Bellevue, Wash.; Kansas City Art Inst., Mo.; R.I. School of

Design, Providence; Rochester Inst. of Tech., N.Y.; Rutgers Univ., New Brunswick, N.J.

DEALER Light Gall., 724 Fifth Ave, New York, NY 10019.

ADDRESS 1251 Donald St, Lakewood, OH 44107.

Karl Schwarzschild ASTRONOMER · PHYSICIST Born October 9, 1873, in Frankfurt am Main, Germany, Schwarzschild died on May 11, 1916, in Potsdam, Germany, while serving with the German forces of World War I. He studied at his home town's Gymnasium and later at Strassburg and Munich. After 1896 he studied scientific photography at the Graphische Lehr- und Versuchsanstalt in Vienna.

Schwarzschild served as an assistant at the Kuffner observatory in Vienna-Ottakring in 1896, and began applying photography to his astronomical work. He joined the astronomy faculty at Göttingen in 1901 and, after the death of H. C. Vogel in 1901, assumed the directorship of the Royal Astrophysical Observatory in Potsdam.

In studying the Bunsen-Roscoe reciprocity law, Schwarzschild determined that it was partially incorrect and published a paper to that effect in 1899. His discovery is known as the Schwarzschild Effect or Law. It was modified in 1913 by his pupil, Erich Kron, and later by J. Hahn, based on the findings of C. E. K. Mees that the photographic emulsions best suited for astronomical use possess high sensitivity at low intensities of light. Schwarzschild's work in this field is considered by some to be the basis of modern sensitometry. In 1906 his work with W. Villiger resulted in the Schwarzschild-Villiger Effect, described in the paper "On the Distribution of Brightness of the Ultra-Violet Light in the Sun's Disk."

PUBLICATIONS Books: *Quellendarstellungen zur Geschichte der Fotografie*, Wolfgang Baier, 1964; *History of Color Photography*, Joseph S. Friedman, 1944; *Theory of the Photographic Process*, C. E. K. Mees, 1944; *Lexikon für Photographie und Reproduktionstechnik*, G. H. Emmerich, 1910. Anthology: *Photography's Great Inventors*, Louis W. Sipley, 1965. Periodicals: *Le Photographe*, 1963; *Bild und Ton*, 1962; *Photographische Correspondenz*, 1921, 1916, 1899; *Die Naturwissenschaften*, 1916; *Astrophysical Journal*, 1900; *Jahrbuch für Photographie und Reproduktionstechnik*, Josef Maria Eder, 1900.

Daniel K. Schweitzer HOLOGRAPHER Born December 22, 1946, in Bridgeton, New Jersey, Schweitzer earned a BA in Theater Arts from Ca-

tawba College, Salisbury, North Carolina. He also studied at the New York School of Holography in 1974; with Abe Rezny and Dr. Don White at Bell Laboratories in Murray Hill, New Jersey; and with Dr. Stephen A. Benton, both at Polaroid Corporation (1977) and in a master class at New York Holographic Laboratories in New York City (1979).

Since 1977 Schweitzer has co-directed the New York Holographic Laboratories. He also teaches there and is a lecturer and freelance consultant. He previously was associate director and an instructor at the New York School of Holography (1974–76).

A member of Optical Society of America, he received an NEA Research Grant in Holography in 1978 and New York State Council on the Arts grants for holography image research in 1978–79.

He co-directed and operated the camera for the videotape *Lipsink* for Manhattan Cable, and also made a documentary videotape for the Museum of Holography, *Holofame*.

Schweitzer's work includes holograms, white-light transmission, abstract narrative research in color control, and holographic optical animations.

COLLECTIONS Mus. of Holography, NYC. Matthias Lauk Cllctn., Palheim, Germany; Richard Payne Cllctn., London.

REPRESENTATIVE New York Holographic Laboratories, 34 W 13 St, New York, NY 10011.

Claire Schwob PHOTOGRAPHER Born February 12, 1948, in La Chaux-de-Fonds, Switzerland, Schwob studied photography in Fribourg (1964) and Lausanne (1965), Switzerland, then in Essen, Germany, at the Folkwangschule for two years under Dr. Otto Steinert. She also trained at an advertising and fashion studio in Hamburg, Germany. Schwob names Cartier-Bresson and W. Eugene Smith as major influences.

A freelance photographer since 1972, she worked for the agency Report in London and the agency Saftra in Stockholm in 1970.

She has been a member of the Arts Centre in London since 1972, and in 1973 obtained a grant from the Arts Council of Great Britain.

Primarily a photographic essayist, she also does portraits and landscapes.

PUBLICATIONS Book: *British Image 7*, 1975 (Arts Council of Great Britain: London). Periodical: *British Journal of Photography*, Apr 1976.

COLLECTIONS Arts Council of Great Britain, London; Photographic Gall., Southampton, Eng.

DEALER The Photographer's Gall., 8 Great Newport St, London WC2, England.

Ferdinando Scianna PHOTOGRAPHER · JOURNALIST Born April 7, 1943, in Bagheria, Sicily, Italy, Scianna studied letters and philosophy at the University of Palermo, Italy.

Since 1967 Scianna has been a journalist and photographer for the Italian weekly magazine *L'Europeo*. He previously worked freelance (1963–67). In 1966 Scianna won the Nadar Prize for the best book, *Feste Religiose in Sicilia*.

His photographs have been used in three films by Michele Gandin, *Bangla-Desh* (1973), *Terremoto* (1969) and *Feste in Sicilia* (1965).

PUBLICATIONS Books: *La Villa Dei Mostri*, 1977 (Einaudi: Torino); *Les Siciliens*, 1977 (Denoël: Paris); *Il Glorioso Alberto*, 1971 (Il Diaframma: Milan); *Feste Religiose in Sicilia*, 1965 (Leonardo da Vinci: Bari). Periodicals: *Progresso Fotografico*, Oct 1980; *Popular Photography Annual*, 1966.

COLLECTIONS Bibliothèque Nationale, Paris; Galleria d'Arte Moderna e Contemporanea, Bagheria, Italy; Salford Univ. Cllctn., Great Britain.

ADDRESS c/o Rizzoli, 280 Boulevard St. Germain, 75007 Paris, France.

Giuliana Scimè CRITIC Born May 2, 1939, in Milan, Italy, Scimè graduated with a professorship in 1976 from the Academy of Fine Arts "Brera" in Milan.

As a freelance critic, she has contributed regularly to *printletter* since 1979, *European Photography* from its inception and both *Foto* and *Fotozoom* (Mexico) since 1978. Scimè is also the curator of two cultural programs at RAI (Italian Broadcasting) and has been curator of the photographic department of Flaviana Gallery in Locarno, Switzerland, since 1979.

Scimè's main interests are "contemporary photography from the beginning of the century as well as painting, mixed media and video art. Several times I have investigated some critical problems concerning the arts of the past, but it's only an intellectual emotion. Contemporary art involves me totally although I also have a passion for archaeology. Contemporary art and archeology are the extremes of mankind's history. I don't make a distinction between abstractions or representative work; the true expression of creativity is what holds my interest."

PUBLICATIONS Books: *The Line in Movement*, 1980; *The Thin Line*, 1980. Catalog (text only): *19 Fotografos Italianos*, 1979 (Museo Carrillo Gil:Mexico City). Periodicals (text only): *printletter*, 5:4, 5:3, & 5:1, 1980, 4:2, 1979; *Progresso Fotografico*, no. 3, 1980, no 7/8, 1979; *Il Diaframma/Fotografia Italiana*, Oct/Nov 1980; *American Photographer*, Feb 1979; *Artes Visuales*, no. 19, autumn 1978, no. 16, winter 1977.

ADDRESS Via de Amicis 40, 20123 Milan, Italy.

David Lorne Scopick PHOTOGRAPHER · WRITER · TEACHER Born January 2, 1948, in Calgary, Alberta, Canada, Scopick received a BA from Ryerson Photographic Arts Center, Toronto, Canada, where he studied from 1967 to 1970 and 1974 to 1975. He also studied at the San Francisco Art Institute in California (1970–71) and at York University, Toronto (1973–74).

Since 1973 Scopick has been a lecturer at the Ontario College of Art in Toronto. Also in Toronto, he lectured at Seneca College from 1973 to 1977 after working as a freelance photographer (1972–73) and as an illustrative photographer for T.D.F. Artists (1971–72).

A member of SPE since 1976 and of the Historical Photographic Society in Toronto since 1978, the photographer won an Ontario College of Art Publications Grant in 1978 and an Ontario Arts Council Grant in 1974.

As of this date Scopick was researching stereo photographs and the Vectograph. He has also researched hand offset printing, color-separation techniques and the use of serigraphy with photomurals.

PUBLICATIONS *The Gum Bichromate Book*, 1978; *Ontario College of Art, Photography 1977*, 1977.

COLLECTION Ontario Arts Council, Toronto, Can.

ADDRESS c/o Ontario College of Art, 100 McCaul St, Toronto, Ontario, Canada M5T 1W1.

Julia Scully EDITOR Born February 9, 1929, in Seattle, Washington, Scully earned a BA from Stanford University in Palo Alto, California (1951), and an MA from New York University, New York City (1970).

Since 1966 Scully has been the editor of *Modern Photography*. She previously edited *Camera 35* (1961–66) and was associate editor for *U.S. Camera* (1956–61). She has taught at the New School for Social Research in New York City and at Ramapo College of New Jersey, Mahwah.

PUBLICATIONS Anthology: *The Family of Woman*, ed., 1979. Book: *Disfarmer: The Heber Springs Portraits, 1939–1946*, 1976.

ADDRESS Modern Photography, 825 Seventh Ave, New York, NY 10019.

William C. Seaman *PHOTOJOURNALIST* Born January 19, 1925, in Grand Island, Nebraska, Seaman is self-taught.

Since 1945 he has been a news photographer at the *Minneapolis Star.*

He belongs to the NPPA, the Twin City Press Association and the Newspaper Guild. A Pulitzer prize-winning photographer in 1959, Seaman won Honeywell's 25th Anniversary Photographic Award in 1975 and in 1956 received the National Headliner's Award.

PUBLICATIONS Anthologies: *The Instant It Happened*, 1972; *Moments*, Sheryle & John Leekley, foreword by Dan Rather, 1978.

COLLECTION Smithsonian Inst., Wash., D.C.

ADDRESS 8206 Virginia Circle So, St. Louis Park, MN 55426.

Brian Seed *PHOTOGRAPHER* Born May 27, 1929, in London, England, Seed learned photography while working as assistant to numerous *Life* magazine photographers, particularly Cornell Capa, during the years 1950–54.

Seed has been a freelance photographer since 1955, contributing to such publications as *Life, Time* and *Sports Illustrated.* Prior to that he was first an office boy, then a photographer's assistant at the London bureau of Time Inc. from 1946 to 1954.

A member of ASMP, he was named Photojournalist of the Year by the United Kingdom in 1966. He also was the creator of a film entitled *River Shannon* in 1971.

The photographer describes himself as being "initially a photojournalist working primarily with 35mm equipment." Of his work he says, "the scope is now much wider, but people, the human condition, our environment, the arts, remain of prime interest to me."

PUBLICATIONS Books (all Time-Life): *London*, 1976; *Africa*, 1970; *Spain-Portugal*, 1969; *Ireland*, 1963. Periodicals: *Le Nouveau Photocinéma*, Dec 1974; *British Journal of Photography*, Dec, Apr 1965; *Life*, Feb 28, 1964.

REPRESENTATIVE John Hillelson Agency, 145 Fleet St, London, England; Black Star Pub. Co., 450 Park Ave S, New York, NY 10016.

ADDRESS 7423 N Lamon Ave, Skokie, IL 60077.

Suzanne Seed *PHOTOGRAPHER* Born on March 8, 1940, in Gary, Indiana, Seed studied at the School of the Art Institute of Chicago from 1978 to 1980, received her BA in Fine Arts at Indiana University (1963) and had a Fellowship from Yale University Summer School of Music and Art in 1961.

Seed works as a freelance photographer and lecturer. She won the American Library Association Best Book of 1979 award and the Chicago Book Clinic Award (1979), as well as the Art Direction Magazine Creativity Award (1977). Seed is a member of ASMP and SPE.

The artist describes her work thus: "I use whatever techniques and tools best suit my subject, and combine older techniques—photography, film, drawing, sewing—with new tools—telecopier, electrostatic machines. I seek archetypal imagery for themes of accelerated evolution, violent growth, chaotic transformation and the hidden efforts of nature to right itself."

PUBLICATIONS Books: *Fine Trades*, 1979; *Saturday's Child*, 1974. Periodical: *Popular Photography*, Mar 1978.

COLLECTIONS Chase Manhattan Bank, NYC; Exchange Natl. Bank, Chicago; Mus. of Contemporary Art, Chicago.

DEALER Marjorie Neikrug Gallery, 224 E 68 St, New York, NY 10021.

ADDRESS 175 E Delaware, Chicago, IL 60611.

Norman Seeff *PHOTOGRAPHER · FILM MAKER · PHYSICIAN* Born March 5, 1939, in Johannesburg, South Africa, Seeff received his medical degree at Witwatersrand University in Johannesburg. As a photographer he is completely self-taught.

After having practiced medicine for three years, he left the profession to become a designer for Columbia Records in New York in 1971. In the years 1972–73 he was art director of United Artists Records in Los Angeles. In 1973 he formed Norman Seeff Enterprises and has been self-employed as its president ever since. The photographer has been a frequent contributor to *Life, Omni, Rolling Stone* and many other publications.

The Art Directors Club of New York awarded Seeff their Gold Medal for his book *Hot Shots.* Having produced and directed several short documentary films, as of this writing he was preparing a feature film entitled *The Creative Process.*

Initially having established himself as a designer and photographer of record album covers, Seef now concentrates on photographing people, especially public personalities. He is particularly interested in developing "techniques for enhancing intuition and spontaneity."

PUBLICATIONS Monographs: *Eye*, 1979; *Hot Shots*, 1974.

REPRESENTATIVE Bob Klewitz, 8165 Sunset Blvd, Los Angeles, CA 90046.

George Seeley   *PHOTOGRAPHER · PAINTER*
Seeley was born (1880) and died (1955) in Stockbridge, Massachusetts. He studied art at the Massachusetts Normal Art School in Boston.

The supervisor of art for the Stockbridge schools for many years, he was also associated with the *Springfield Republican* for a time. In his later years he became recognized as a fine painter of still lifes, particularly of brasses and coppers.

Seeley was a member of the Photo-Secession.

An authority on birds, he became involved with the Biological Survey of Washington, maintaining a landing station and reporting migratory patterns.

Seeley was known for the lyric quality of his outstanding pictorial photographs. Early in his career he was brought to the attention of Alfred Stieglitz by Alvin Langdon Coburn.

PUBLICATIONS Anthologies: *Pictorial Photography in Britain, 1900–1920*, Arts Council of Great Britain, 1978; *Camera Work: A Critical Anthology*, Jonathan Green, ed., 1973. Periodicals: *Camera Work*, Jan 1910, Oct 1907, July 1906; *Craftsman*, 1907.

J. Seeley *PHOTOGRAPHER* [See plate 125]
Born October 23, 1946, in Margaretville, New York, Seeley received a BS in 1969 from SUNY, Buffalo, and an MFA in 1971 from Rhode Island School of Design, Providence, where he studied with Harry Callahan.

Since 1972 he has been assistant professor of art at Wesleyan University, Middletown, Connecticut. He received Wesleyan project grants in 1979, 1978, 1977 and 1976, as well as Connecticut Commission on the Arts grants in 1978 and 1976 and first prize in the 1977 National Nikon Competition, College Teachers' Division.

Seeley shoots in black-and-white, creating photomontages involving nudes, still lifes, airplanes, video images, landscapes and striped fabric. He produces editions of serigraphs, offset lithographs and photographic contact prints and specializes in high-contrast photography.

PUBLICATIONS Books: *High Contrast*, 1980; "High Contrast Photography," *Darkroom Dynamics*, Jim Stone, ed., 1979. Periodicals: *Graphis*, 35:202 & 35:203, 1979/80; *Portfolio*, fall 1979; *Foto*, Apr 1979 (Sweden); *Fotographia*, Feb 1979; *Photographs*, 1979; *American Photographer*, Oct 1978; *Popular Photography Annual*, 1978, 1973; *Foto*, Dec 1977 (Germany); *Photographia*, Nov/Dec 1977; *Zoom*, no. 42, 1977 (France); *Petersen's Photographic Magazine*, Sept 1976, Nov 1973; *35mm Photography*, spring 1976; *Camerart*, Feb 1976, Sept 1974.

ADDRESS   RFD 1, South Rd, Portland, CT 06480.

Patrick Segal   *PHOTOJOURNALIST · WRITER*
Born in Magenta, France, on February 12, 1947, Segal graduated from physical therapy school in 1972.

As of this writing he worked in Paris as a freelance photojournalist, consultant reporter for television Channel 2: A2 and reporter for Radio 7. In 1976 he was a photojournalist for Sipa Press in Paris.

Segal made the film *Ama Dablang* in 1979.

His photojournalism has covered such things as the Vietnam War (1974), the war in Lebanon (1976–77), the Eritrean War and the Montreal Olympics of 1976.

PUBLICATIONS Books: *Cinq Ans Sous Les Etoiles*, 1979 (Denoël); *L'Homme Qui Marchait Dans Tête*, 1977; *Viens La Mort On Va Danser*, 1977 (Flammarion).

ADDRESS   33 rue Rennequin, 75017 Paris, France.

Eva Seid   *PHOTOGRAPHER · GRAPHIC DESIGNER*
Born July 29, 1950, in New York, Seid received a BFA in 1971 from Parsons School of Design in New York City. She names Lisette Model and Larry Fink as mentors.

To date she works for Brecker & Merryman in New York City (since 1977), having freelanced from 1973 to 1976. The photographer worked for Lord, Geller, Federico in New York City from 1971 to 1973.

Seid belongs to the Graphic Artists Guild, American Institute of Graphic Arts and International Women Photographers. She won a CAPS fellowship in photography in 1976.

She describes her work as documentary and environmental portraiture.

PUBLICATIONS Anthologies: *Self-Portrayal*, James Alinder, 1979; *Women Photograph Men*, Danielle B. Hayes, ed., intro. by Molly Haskell, 1977.

ADDRESS 85 South St, New York, NY 10038.

Peter Sekaer   *PHOTOGRAPHER* Born in Copenhagen, Denmark, on July 14, 1901, Sekaer died in 1950. He studied painting at the Art Students League in New York City from 1929 to 1934 and photography with Berenice Abbott at New York's New School in 1935. His friends included Walker Evans and Ben Shahn.

Sekaer worked for the U.S. Rural Electrification Administration (REA) and U.S. Housing Authority from 1936 to 1941, and was employed by the Bureau of Indian Affairs in 1940. His images appeared in several of their publications as well as in magazines such as *U.S. Camera* and *Vogue*. He also did the still photographs for REA's film, *Power and the Land*, in collaboration with Joris Ivens.

A member of the Art Students League of New York, Sekaer edited their magazine *The League* in 1932–33. He was the recipient of three of MOMA's "Image of Freedom" awards.

The photographer produced documentary images for the U.S. government on slum clearance, electrification of rural areas and Indian reservation life.

PUBLICATIONS Periodicals: *U.S. Camera Annual*, 1943, 1942, 1941.

COLLECTIONS MOMA, NYC; Natl. Archives, Wash., D.C.; Office of Indian Affairs, Wash., D.C.

DEALER Witkin Gall., 41 E 57 St, New York, NY 10022.

ARCHIVE Christina Sekaer, 19 W 69 St, Apt 1101, New York, NY 10023.

Giuseppe Venanzio Sella CHEMIST · PHOTOGRAPHER Born in Biella, Italy, in 1823, Sella died in 1876. A trip to Paris in 1851 exposed him to the use of chemistry in photography and precipitated his career in the combined fields.

Sella's book, *Plico del fotografo*, was the first book of photographic technique done in Italy and a great commercial success. It was subsequently translated into French and German.

PUBLICATIONS Books: *Giuseppe Venanzio Sella ed i suoi scritti*, Severino Pozzo, 1877 (Amosso: Biella); *Note Sopra l'industria della Lana*, 1873 (Biella); *Guide Théorique et Pratique du Photographe*, V. J. Sella, 1857 (E. De Valicourt: Paris); *Plico del fotografo*, 1856 (Paravia: Torino). Catalog: *Fotografi del Piemonte, 1852–1859*, 1977 (Torino). Periodicals: "G. V. Sella," L. Borlinetto, no. 11/12, 1884, "Il Plico del fotografo," O. Baratti, Dec 15, 1863, *La Camera Oscura*.

COLLECTION Univ. of Texas, Humanities Resource Ctr., Gernsheim Cllctn., Austin.

Michael William Semak PHOTOGRAPHER · TEACHER Born January 9, 1934, in Welland, Ontario, Canada, Semak graduated from Ryerson Polytechnical Institute in Toronto, Canada, in 1958, having studied architectural technology. He also received technical training at Kodak in Toronto, where his mentor was Lorraine Monk.

The photographer has taught at York University, Toronto, since 1969, and prior to that freelanced for ten years.

Semak won National Film Board of Canada grants in 1975 and 1971, as well as a Gold Medal in 1969; a Province of Ontario Council for the Arts grant in 1972, the Award of Excellence in Photojournalism from *Pravda*/Moscow in both 1972 and 1970; and the Arts Award Canada Council grant in 1971.

A photojournalist in the 1960s, Semak's current noncommercial work is small-format black-and-white, using available light. Among his favorite subjects are people around Toronto and nude women.

PUBLICATIONS Periodicals: *Creative Camera*, Jan 1979, Aug 1973, July 1970; *Camera*, July 1978, Nov 1970; *Photo Life*, Feb 1978; *Fotografia Italiana*, Nov 1976, Apr 1975; *Afterimage: VSW*, July/Aug 1976; *Photographer*, summer 1976; *Soviet Photo*, Nov 1975; *Canadian Photo Annual*, June 1975; *Camera Mainichi*, spring 1975; *Ovo*, spring 1975, Aug 1973; *35mm Photography*, Nov 1973, Mar 1970; *Foto News*, Aug 1973; *Nuova Fotografia*, Jan 1973; *Camera Canada*, fall 1971; *Popular Photography Italiana*, Aug, Apr 1971; *Popular Photography*, Nov 1970; *U.S. Camera Annual*, fall 1970.

COLLECTIONS Camerawork/Potrero Neighborhood House, San Francisco; IMP/GEH, Rochester; Internatl. Fund for Concerned Photography, NYC; James Van Derzee Inst., NYC; MOMA, NYC; New School for Social Research, NYC; Shado Gall., Oregon City, Ore. Bibliothèque Nationale, Paris; Deja Vue Gall., Toronto, Canada; Dept. of External Affairs, Ottawa, Canada; Il Diaframma Canon Gall., Milan, Italy; La Photogaleria Plaza de la Republica, Madrid, Spain; Mount Allison Univ., Owens Art Gall., Sackville, New Brunswick, Canada; Musée Nicéphore Niepce, Chalon-sur-Saône, France; Natl. Film Board of Canada, Stills Div., Ottawa; Natl. Gall. of Canada, Ottawa; Public Archives of Canada, Ottawa; Royal Canadian Academy of Art Resource Centre, Slide Lib., Toronto; United Nations Photo Archives, Geneva, Switzerland; Univ. of Parma Photo Mus., Italy; York Univ., Toronto.

ADDRESS 1796 Spruce Hill Rd, Pickering, Ontario, Canada L1V 1S4.

Sandra Ann Semchuk PHOTOGRAPHER Born in Meadow Lake, Saskatchewan, Canada, on June 16, 1948, Semchuk received her BFA from the University of Saskatchewan in Saskatoon (1971).

She is a founding member and director of the Photographers' Gallery, an artists cooperative, located in Saskatoon. A recipient of the Canada Council Arts Award "B," 1979, 1978 and 1975–

76, she also received the Saskatchewan Arts Board grants in 1977 and 1971.

The photographer's work is autobiographical, using the camera to explore her home town, family, friends and herself.

PUBLICATIONS Anthologies: *Self Portrayal*, Jim Alinder, ed., 1978; *The Feminine Eye*, 1975 (Natl. Film Board of Canada). Catalog: *Exposure*, 1975 (Art Gall. of Ontario).

COLLECTIONS In Canada: Art Bank, Canada Council, Ottawa, Ontario; Edmonton Art Gall., Alberta; Mendel Art Gall., Saskatoon, Saskatchewan; Photographers' Gall., Saskatoon.

ADDRESS RR6, Saskatoon, Saskatchewan, Canada S7K 3J9.

Robert Sennhauser *PHOTOGRAPHER · TEACHER · HOUSE PAINTER* Born June 14, 1940, in New York City, Sennhauser earned a BFA (1969) and MFA (1974) in printmaking from Ohio University, Athens. His mentor was Abner Jonas, and he was also influenced by Louis-Ferdinand Céline, Andy Warhol and black blues singers.

Since 1978 Sennhauser has been a visiting artist in printmaking at the School of the Art Institute of Chicago, and previously he was a visiting printmaking instructor at the University of Oklahoma, Norman (1977–78). Sennhauser belongs to the CAA. In 1980, with Klaus Schnitzer, he received an NEA Fellowship.

His primary interest is in narrative—"telling a story with words and photographs, both supplying information to make a greater whole."

PUBLICATIONS Book: *The Platinum Print*, John Hafey & Tom Shillea, 1979. Catalog: *Sequence Photography*, Fred R. Parker, 1980; *Attitudes: Photography in the 1970's*, Fred R. Parker, 1979 (Santa Barbara Mus. of Art: Calif.).

COLLECTION Ohio Univ., Athens.

ADDRESS 3543 N Fremont, Chicago, IL 60657.

Jiří Sever *CHEMIST · PHOTOGRAPHER · LITERARY ADVISER* Born Vojtěch Čech in 1904 in Brno, Czechoslovakia, Sever died in 1968 in Prague. He studied at the Technical University, Faculty of Chemical Technology, receiving an Ing. degree (similar to an MSc) and, in 1927, a doctorate. He was self-taught in photography.

In his activities as a chemist, he was known as Dr. Vojtěch Čech, but in all other endeavors as Jiří Sever, a name that related to his association with radio and jazz, of which he was a connoisseur. He also served as an adviser on French literature in a publishing house.

Petr Tausk said of Sever's photography, "The unique work of Jiří Sever was strongly influenced by the surrealism with which he came into touch with regard to his predilection for French poetry. Sever made from his images of various 'objets trouvés' closed cycles showing his admiration for the hidden poetry in the real world."

PUBLICATION Monograph: *Jiří Sever*, intro. by Ludvík Souček, 1968 (Odeon: Prague).

COLLECTIONS Moravian Gall., Brno, Czechoslovakia; Mus. of Decorative Arts, Prague.

Douglas G. Severson *PHOTOGRAPHER · CONSERVATOR* Born March 28, 1951, in Rochester, New York, Severson earned an MS in Photography from the Institute of Design at Illinois Institute of Technology, Chicago (1977). At this writing he was an MFA candidate in Museum Practice at Rochester Institute of Technology, New York.

In 1979 Severson worked as an intern in the Conservation Department at George Eastman House in Rochester and as a research assistant to James Reilly at Rochester Institute of Technology on a project to study the deterioration of albumen prints. He was an assistant in the Photography Department at the Art Institute of Chicago, Illinois, in 1978–79.

A member of SPE and Friends of Photography since 1976, Severson became an associate member of the American Institute for Conservation in 1979. In 1980 he was the recipient of a National Museum Act grant for work on photographic conservation at the Rochester Institute of Technology.

His research focuses on conservation of albumen and salted paper prints, while as a photographer he produces large-format, manipulated black-and-white landscapes.

PUBLICATIONS Book: *The Unseen Landscape*, 1977. Anthology: *Bumps and Flashes*, 1977. Periodical: "Oliver Wendell Holmes, Poet of Realism," *History of Photography*, July 1978.

COLLECTIONS Inst. of Design, Chicago, Ill.; Temple Univ., Philadelphia, Pa.; VSW, Rochester, N.Y.

ADDRESS 15 Harper St, Rochester, NY 14607.

John Sexton *PHOTOGRAPHER · TEACHER* Born May 22, 1953, in Maywood, California, Sexton earned an AA in Photography from Cypress College, California (1974), and a BA in Photography from Chapman College, Orange, California (1976). He also studied with Ansel Adams, Wynn Bullock and Paul Caponigro at Ansel Adams' Yosemite Workshops in 1973 and 1974.

Since 1980 Sexton has been director and instructor for Ansel Adams Workshops and has been Adams' technical assistant since 1979. He also is a staff instructor at Owens Valley (California) Photography Workshops (since 1976). Previously he taught photography at Cypress College (1976–79), and has led workshops at Friends of Photography in Carmel, University of California at Santa Cruz, and Maine Photographic Workshops.

A member of SPE and Friends of Photography, Sexton won a Cypress College Photography Department Scholarship in 1973.

Working with large-format cameras, he produces silver prints of "the utmost precision and subtlety." His subjects are primarily "the natural scene and found objects."

PUBLICATIONS Periodicals: *Popular Photography*, Nov 1980; *The Rangefinder*, Nov 1980; *Zoom*, no. 6, 1980; *Photo-Image*, 1:2, 1977.

COLLECTIONS CCP (Ansel Adams Archives), Tucson; Newport Harbor Art Mus., Newport Beach, Calif.; Polaroid Corp., Cambridge, Mass.

DEALERS Weston Gall., POB 655, Carmel, CA 93921; Susan Spiritus Gall., 3336 Via Lido, Newport Beach, CA 92633; Eloquent Light Gall., 145 S Livernois, Rochester, MI 48063.

ADDRESS 1199 Harrison St, Monterey, CA 93940.

David (Chim) Seymour PHOTOJOURNALIST Born November 20, 1911, in Warsaw, Poland, Seymour died November 10, 1956, near the Suez Canal, Egypt. He graduated from Leipzig Academie für Graphische Künst in 1931, where he studied graphic arts and photography. Then he studied at the Sorbonne in Paris. He was a multilinguist. His father was Benjamin Szymin, a renowned Hebrew and Yiddish publisher.

Seymour began his freelance career in Paris in 1933. From 1936 to 1938 he covered the Spanish Civil War and other major political events in North Africa, Czechoslovakia and throughout Europe. He traveled with Loyalist refugees to Mexico in 1939, recording their journey, and he voluntarily served in the U.S. Army (1942–45) as photo interpreter, rising to the rank of lieutenant. In 1948 he worked on assignment for UNESCO, creating a book on children in postwar Europe, and during that time he also covered the early development of Israel. Between 1949 and 1955 Chim worked on assignments for many American publications in Europe and Israel. While covering the war in Suez in 1956 he was killed by machine-gun fire.

Along with Cartier-Bresson, George Rodger and Robert Capa, Seymour co-founded the cooperative Magnum Photos, for which he served as president from 1954 to 1956. His name was engraved on the Honor Roll of the Overseas Press Club in New York City (1956), and in 1958 the Robert Capa–David Seymour Photographic Foundation was established in Israel "to promote the understanding and appreciation of photography as a medium for revealing the human condition." In 1966 the Fund for Concerned Photography was established "to foster the ideals and professional standards of these three men [Seymour, Capa and Werner Bischof] who died a decade ago while on photographic missions."

The photojournalist was mainly noted for his warm and compassionate photographs of people from all over the world, especially children. His series of Barcelona at war is one of his most memorable.

PUBLICATIONS Monographs: *David Seymour —Chim, 1911–1956*, Cornell Capa & Bhupendra Karia, eds., 1974; *David Seymour—"Chim,"* intro. by Judith Friedberg, 1966; *Little Ones*, 1957; *Children of Europe*, 1949 (UNESCO: Paris). Books: *Front Populaire*, w/Robert Capa, text by Georgette Elgey, 1976 (Chene/Magnum: Paris); *The Vatican*, Ann Carnahan, 1950. Anthologies: *The Magic Image*, Cecil Beaton & Gail Buckland, eds., 1975; *The Concerned Photographer*, Cornell Capa, ed., 1968; *The Picture History of Photography*, Peter Pollack, 1958, rev. ed., 1969. Periodicals: *Photorama*, Feb 1957; "Masters of the Leica: Life and Death of the Photographer, David Seymour," Robert d'Hooghe, *Leica Fotografie*, no. 2, 1957; "Chim, A Man of Peace," Judith Friedberg, *Camera*, Jan 1957; "Chim's Children," *Life*, Dec 17, 1956; *Vision*, Dec 7, 1956; "Magnum Opus," Horace Sutton, *Saturday Review*, Dec 1, 1956; "Chim . . . was Chim," John G. Morris, *Photography*, Dec 1956; "The World of David Seymour," *Infinity: ASMP*, spec. issue, 1956.

COLLECTIONS Art Inst. of Chicago; Boston Mus. of Fine Arts; Houston Mus. of Fine Arts; Metro. Mus. of Art, NYC; MOMA, NYC; Natl. Gall. of Art, Wash., D.C.

Ben Shahn PAINTER · PHOTOGRAPHER · ILLUSTRATOR Born September 12, 1898, in Kovno (now Kaunas), Lithuania, Shahn died March 14, 1969, in New York City. He attended New York University, City College of New York (1919–22) and the National Academy of Design (1922). Shahn was an admirer of the works of Cartier-Bresson, Atget, Mathew Brady and Lewis Hine. His wife, painter Bernarda Bryson, was especially active during the New Deal art projects of the 1930s in New York City.

Having worked as a lithographer's apprentice during his student years, Shahn then traveled to Europe and North Africa to study art (1925, 1927–29). Returning to New York, he shared a studio with photographer Walker Evans in 1930. In the early 1930s he painted scenes of social commentary, including a series on the Sacco and Vanzetti trial and Thomas Mooney. He assisted Diego Rivera on the Rockefeller Center frescoes in New York City (1932), then did a series of his own on the Prohibition era for the Public Works of Art Project in New York City (1933).

Shahn served as an artist and photographer for the Farm Security Administration (FSA) from 1935 to 1938, during which time he did his most famous photographic work. With his wife Shahn executed a series of panels for the Bronx, New York, post office in 1939, and also painted a mural for the Social Security Building in Washington, D.C. (1942). During World War II the artist designed posters for the Office of War Information and for the Congress of Industrial Organizations. He was appointed Norton Professor at Harvard University, Cambridge, Massachusetts, in 1956–57, and designed a mural for Syracuse (New York) University in 1965–66. Shahn's illustrations graced numerous books, magazines and posters.

Most of the silver prints Shahn produced were for the FSA, but he also photographed prison and street scenes and made studies for his paintings and illustrations. His photography is notable for its compassionate and humanistic approach—the same quality that marks his serigraphs, posters, paintings and prints.

PUBLICATIONS Monographs: *The Photographic Eye of Ben Shahn*, Davis Pratt, ed., 1975; *Ben Shahn, Photographer*, Margaret R. Weiss, ed. & intro., 1973; *Ben Shahn: The Passion of Sacco and Vanzetti* (paintings), Martin H. Bush, 1969; *Prints of Ben Shahn*, Kneeland McNulty, 1967; *Paintings of Ben Shahn*, James T. Soby, 1963; *Ben Shahn: His Graphic Art*, James T. Soby, 1957. Books: *A Vision Shared*, Hank O'Neal, 1976; *The Years of Bitterness and Pride*, Hiag Akmakjian, 1975; *In This Proud Land*, Roy Emerson Stryker & Nancy Wood, 1973; *Portrait of a Decade*, F. Jack Hurley, 1972; *Just Before the War*, Rothstein, Vachon & Stryker, w/Thomas E. Garver, ed., 1968; *Ecclesiastes*, illus., 1967; *Haggadah for Passover*, illus., trans. & notes by Cecil Roth, 1966; *The Alphabet of Creation*, illus., 1963; *Love and Joy About Letters*, 1963; *The Bitter Years*, Edward Steichen, ed., 1962; *A Partridge in a Pear Tree*, illus., 1959; *The Shape of Content*, 1957; *Portrait of the Artist as an American*,

Selden Rodman, 1951; *Poems of the Midwest*, illus., Carl Sandburg, 1946; *12 Million Black Voices*, R. Wright & Edward Rosskam, 1941; *The Face of America*, Sherwood Anderson, 1940; *Land of the Free*, Archibald MacLeish, ed., 1938. Anthology: *The Photograph Collector's Guide*, Lee D. Witkin & Barbara London, 1979.

COLLECTIONS FSA Cllctn., Wash., D.C.; Harvard Univ., Fogg Art Mus. & Carpenter Ctr. for the Visual Arts, Cambridge, Mass.; IMP/GEH, Rochester; L/C, Wash., D.C.; MOMA, NYC (paintings); R.I. School of Design Mus. of Art, Providence; San Francisco Mus. of Modern Art; Univ. of Louisville Photographic Archives, Ky.; Univ. of Minn., Minneapolis; Wadsworth Atheneum, Hartford, Conn. (painting).

Barbara Shamblin PHOTOGRAPHER · TEACHER Born May 21, 1951, Shamblin studied at Massachusetts Institute of Technology, Cambridge, in 1973 and in the same year earned a BA from Goddard College, Plainfield, Vermont. She received an MFA in 1977 from Rhode Island School of Design, Providence.

Since 1980 she has been an instructor of photography and design at Smith College, Northampton, Massachusetts. She was a visiting assistant professor of photography at Memphis Academy of Arts, Tennessee, in 1979. In 1978 Shamblin held the same position at the University of Alabama, Tuscaloosa, and in that year also was an artist-in-residence at Apeiron Photographic Workshops, Millerton, New York.

The photographer won an NEA Photographer's Fellowship in 1979 and a Rhode Island School of Design Full Teaching Fellowship award in 1976.

COLLECTIONS Addison Gall. of Amer. Art, Andover, Mass.; Apeiron Photographic Workshops, Millerton, N.Y.; High Mus. of Art, Atlanta, Ga.

REPRESENTATIVE Visual Studies Workshop Gall., 31 Prince St, Rochester, NY 14607.

ADDRESS 28 Tilden Ave, Newport, RI 02840.

Ronit Shany PHOTOGRAPHER · TEACHER Born November 24, 1950, in Haifa, Israel,. Shany received a diploma in photography from London College of Printing in 1973. His major influences have been David Lavendar and Bob Clerk.

Since 1977 Shany has been a teacher of photography at the State Art Teachers Training College in Ramat Hasharon, Israel. He has also been employed as a photojournalist for *Yediot Ahronot*, *Ha'aretz* and *At* (all newspapers) in Tel Aviv since 1975, previously working as a photojournalist for the *Evening Standard* in London (1973–75).

Shany has been a member of the Israel Press-Photographers Association in Tel Aviv, Israel, since 1975.

PUBLICATIONS Periodicals: *Musag*, Dec 1976; *British Journal of Photography*, June 1974.

COLLECTION Israel Mus., Jerusalem, Israel.

ADDRESS 33 Ma'ale Hazofim St, Ramat Gan, Israel 52483.

Hannah Shaviv PHOTOGRAPHER Born in Israel on January 16, 1949, Shaviv earned a BA in Geography and a BFA in Art from Haifa University, Israel (1973). She received a diploma in creative photography from the London College of Printing in 1976.

Since 1980 the director of Photo Workshop 39 in Jerusalem, Israel, she was an instructor at Bezalel Academy of Art, Jerusalem, and an assistant at Hank Londoner's Studio in New York City in 1979. Shaviv freelanced as a photographer in London from 1976 to 1978.

Shaviv says that her work's "mood and imagery shift from isolated and distorted figures within collapsing, destructing space to softly lit full forms within friendly rooms." She uses watercolor and photo oil to create the final image.

PUBLICATIONS Periodicals: *Camera 35*, Jan 1980; Review by Lucy R. Lippard, *Art in America*, Jan 1980; Review by Ellen Schwartz, *Artnews*, Jan 1980; *Hzilum*, 1977, July 1976; *British Journal of Photography Annual*, 1977; *British Journal of Photography*, Aug 6, 1976.

COLLECTIONS Photographer's Gall., London. In Israel: Tel Aviv Mus.; White Gall., Tel Aviv.

ADDRESS Cremieux St 6/A, German Colony, Jerusalem, Israel.

Lauren R. Shaw TEACHER · PHOTOGRAPHER Born April 2, 1946, in Atlanta, Georgia, Shaw earned a BVA from Georgia State University, Atlanta (1968), and an MFA in Photography from Rhode Island School of Design, Providence, where she studied with Aaron Siskind and Harry Callahan. She also undertook an independent study with Jack Welpott at San Francisco State College in 1969.

Since 1972 Shaw has been assistant professor of fine arts at Emerson College, Boston, and since 1977 has lectured at Essex Workshop in Essex, Massachusetts. She served on the staff of Apeiron Workshops in Millerton, New York, from 1974 to 1976.

PUBLICATIONS Anthologies: *Self-Portrayal*, 1979; *SX-70 Photographics*, 1979; *Art of the State/State of the Art*, 1978; *Women See Woman*, Annie Gottlieb, Cheryl Wiesenfeld et al, eds., 1976. Periodicals: *Popular Photography*, Jan 1977, Apr 1973.

PORTFOLIO *Rhode Island School of Design Portfolio* (group) 1972, 1971.

COLLECTIONS Apeiron Workshops, Millerton, N.Y.; Harvard Univ., Fogg Art Mus., Cambridge, Mass.; L/C, Wash., D.C.; Mus. of Fine Arts, Boston; Sam Wagstaff Cllctn., NYC; Wellesley Coll., Wellesley, Mass.

ADDRESS 18 Stanley Rd, Belmont, MA 02128.

Thomas O. Sheckell LAWYER · PHOTOGRAPHER · LECTURER Born in Nebraska in 1884, Sheckell died March 2, 1943, in East Orange, New Jersey. He earned a JD from the University of Indiana, Bloomington.

Sheckell was an executive of the New York Association of Credit Men. He was an attorney for the Intermountain Association of Credit Men in Utah, where he practiced law after his graduation. He moved to East Orange in 1928 and lectured widely on art and photography.

He won the national award of the American Forestry Association in 1933 for his image "In the Path of the Storm."

Sheckell was known for his landscape photography, and his work was described by *The New York Times* as showing "a loveliness and vigor, a majesty and homely suggestion, in all the rich enchantment of the wide American scene."

PUBLICATION Book: *Trees*, 1937.

Charles Sheeler PAINTER · PHOTOGRAPHER Born in Philadelphia, Pennsylvania, in 1883, Sheeler died on May 7, 1965, in Dobbs Ferry, New York. He studied from 1900 to 1903 at the School of Industrial Art in Philadelphia and from 1903 to 1906 at the Pennsylvania Academy of Fine Arts under William Merritt Chase. He then went abroad until 1910. Sheeler's major influences were Picasso, Braque and Alfred Stieglitz.

Sheeler began his professional photographic career in 1912, and in 1916 was commissioned by Marius de Zaya's Modern Gallery in New York to photograph works of art. He then freelanced for magazines such as *Fortune*, and in 1923 began doing portraiture and fashion, which he continued over the next eight years, for publications such as *Vogue*. Henry Ford commissioned Sheeler in 1927 to do a series of photos of the Ford plant at River Rouge, Michigan. In the early 1930s Sheeler gave up photography and devoted himself to his first love, painting, which he continued until he suffered a stroke in 1959.

Elected a member of the Department of Art of

the National Institute of Arts and Letters in 1963, Sheeler had won the Award of Merit (and $1,000) the previous year from the American Academy of Arts and Letters.

A noted painter of the precisionist school, Sheeler embodied in his paintings a poetic geometry of industrial forms and structures. They can be seen in most major museums in the United States. He also collaborated on a six-minute film with Paul Strand in 1921, *Manahatta* (sometimes called *New York the Magnificent*).

As with his paintings, Sheeler's photographs mainly recorded industrial and architectural images, although he also specialized in photographing artworks, Chinese jades, African masks, French cathedrals and still lifes as well as doing fashion work and portraiture. He most often produced silver prints, occasionally using sepia tone.

PUBLICATIONS Books: *Charles Sheeler: Paintings, Drawings, Photographs*, Martin Friedman, 1975; *Charles Sheeler: Artist in the American Tradition*, Constance Rourke, repr. 1969; *Charles Sheeler*, essays by Friedman, Hayes & Millard, 1968; *The Great King of Assyria*, 1946; *Egyptian Statues*, 1945; *Egyptian Statuettes*, 1945. Anthologies: *The History of Fashion Photography*, Nancy Hall-Duncan, 1979; *The Photograph Collector's Guide*, Lee D. Witkin & Barbara London, 1979; *Photography Rediscovered*, David Travis & Anne Kennedy, 1979; *The Collection of Alfred Stieglitz*, 1978; *Photographs from the Julien Levy Collection, Starting with Atget*, 1976; *The Magic Image*, Cecil Beaton & Gail Buckland, 1975; *The Painter and the Photograph*, Van Deren Coke, ed., 1964, rev. ed., 1972. Catalogs: *The Quest of Charles Sheeler*, 1963 (State Univ. of Iowa); *Charles Sheeler: Paintings, Drawings, Photographs*, intro. by William Carlos Williams, 1939 (MOMA: NYC). Periodicals: "Charles Sheeler: American Photographer," Charles W. Millard, *Contemporary Photographer*, 6:1, 1967; "Ford Plant Photos of Charles Sheeler," Samuel M. Kootz, *Creative Art*, no. 8, Apr 1931.

COLLECTIONS (selected) Addison Gall. of Art, Andover, Mass.; Ariz. State Coll., Tempe; Art Inst. of Chicago; Brooklyn Mus. of Art, N.Y.; Cincinnati Art Mus., Ohio; Cleveland Mus. of Art, Ohio; Columbus Gall. of Fine Arts, Ohio; Detroit Inst. of Art; Harvard Univ., Fogg Art Mus., Cambridge, Mass.; IMP/GEH, Rochester; Metro. Mus. of Art, NYC; MOMA, NYC; Mus. of Fine Arts, Boston; Newark Mus. Assoc., N.J.; Penn. Acad. of Fine Arts, Philadelphia; Philadelphia Mus. of Art, Pa.; Phillips Gall., Wash., D.C.; Princeton Univ., N.J.; R.I. School of Design Mus.,

Providence; Rutgers Univ., New Brunswick, N.J.; Santa Barbara Mus. of Art, Calif.; Smith Coll. Mus., Northampton, Mass.; Springfield Art Mus., Mo.; Springfield Mus. of Fine Arts, Mass.; Toledo Mus. of Art, Ohio; Univ. of Nebr., Lincoln; Univ. of N. Mex. Art Mus., Albuquerque; Walker Art Ctr., Minneapolis, Minn.; Wellesley Coll., Wellesley, Mass.; Whitney Mus. of Amer. Art, NYC; Worcester Art Mus., Mass. Tel Aviv Mus., Israel.

Rqael Shemtov PHOTOGRAPHER · TEACHER · PAINTER · SCULPTOR Born September 29, 1952, in Nahariya, Israel, Shemtov received a diploma from the Neri Bloomfield, Haifa, Community College School of Design in 1978 and a certificate in creative photography from Bezalel Academy of Arts and Design in Jerusalem in 1979 (both in Israel). From 1978 to 1980 she studied at State Art Teachers Training College, Ramat Hasharon, Israel.

Since 1979 she has been a photography teacher at Bezalel Academy of Arts and Design.

Shemtov won the Bezabel Academy's Agfa award in 1979 and its Halperin Award for Photography in 1978. In 1979 she also received grants from the Israeli Culture and Art Committee and the America-Israel Cultural Foundation.

Shemtov works in small-format black-and-white, staging certain situations for her photographs, then juxtaposing two prints. In 1978 she did a photographic documentation of Tel Aviv.

PUBLICATIONS Periodicals: *Hatzeelum*, Sept 1980, Oct 1978 (Israel).

COLLECTIONS In Israel: Bezalel Academy, Jerusalem; Tel-Aviv Mus.

ADDRESS 32 Mercaz Ba'Alei Hamlacha St, Tel Aviv, Israel.

Beth Shepherd PHOTOGRAPHER · WORKSHOP DIRECTOR · TEACHER Born September 25, 1949, in Bridgeport, Connecticut, Shepherd earned a BA in Fine Arts from Rider College, Lawrenceville, New Jersey, in 1971 and an MA in Photography from Goddard College in Plainfield, Vermont, in 1978. Her mother is photographer Carol Ruth Shepherd. She served an apprenticeship with Larry Colwell from 1970 to 1972.

Since 1971 Shepherd has been managing director and an instructor at Photo Graphics Workshop in New Canaan, Connecticut. She has also been a professor at the University of Bridgeport, Connecticut, since 1975.

The photographer works in a variety of formats, including 4 x 5 and SX-70. She uses black-and-white, except in her SX-70 photos, specializing in portraiture and documentation of her travels in the United States, Europe and the Middle East.

PUBLICATIONS Anthologies: *Family of Women*, 1979; *Women Photograph Men*, 1977. Periodical: *Lightwork Magazine*, Apr 1975.

COLLECTION Portland Mus. of Art, Maine.

REPRESENTATIVE Photo Graphics Workshop, 212 Elm St, New Canaan, CT 06840.

ADDRESS 705 Weed St, Apt B, New Canaan, CT 06840.

Carol Ruth Shepherd PHOTOGRAPHER Born on August 24, 1922, in Bridgeport, Connecticut, Shepherd received her BS from Cornell University in Ithaca, New York (1944). Her mentor was Larry Colwell. Her daughter Beth Shepherd is also a photographer.

Shepherd founded the Photo Graphics Workshop in New Canaan, Connecticut, in 1971 and served as its director until 1978. She is the current executive director. She was a member of ICP's board of trustees (1978–79) and belongs to the National League of American Pen Women.

The artist says of her work that she takes an "abstract and surrealistic approach to nature and found objects and subjects at home and abroad."

REPRESENTATIVE Photo Graphics Workshop, 212 Elm St, New Canaan, CT 06840.

ADDRESS 432 Frogtown Rd, New Canaan, CT 06840.

Samuel Edward Sheppard CHEMIST · INVENTOR · WRITER Born in 1882 in Hither Green, Kent, England, Sheppard died in 1948, probably in Rochester, New York. He attended preparatory school at Deal College and then went to St. Dunstan's College, earning his BS in 1903. He pursued doctoral studies for the next three years at University College in London, and from 1907 to 1910 he studied photochemistry at University of Marburg, Germany, and at the Sorbonne in Paris under a research scholarship from University College.

Returning to England in 1910, he joined the research laboratory of Wratten and Wainwright, which had been established by C. E. K. Mees, whom Sheppard had met at St. Dunstan's. They had collaborated on a BS thesis and had begun a lifelong association that continued when Sheppard left England to work for the newly established research department of Eastman Kodak Company in Rochester, supervised by Mees. The chemist remained with Kodak until his retirement in 1948. During his career he published, separately and collaboratively, 9 books and over 165 papers, and his name appeared on some 90 patents related to photography.

Among Sheppard's numerous awards were the Hurter and Driffield Medal, and the Progress Medal of RPS, in 1928.

In the joint BS thesis of Sheppard and Mees (1903) they introduced the idea of gamma infinity, and in 1907 they collected their numerous papers on photographic subjects into a book. In collaboration with R. T. Punnett in 1924, Sheppard made the important discovery of sulfur-containing constituents in gelatin, paving the way for increased emulsion sensitivity.

PUBLICATIONS Books: *From Dry Plates to Ektachrome Film*, C. E. K. Mees, 1961; *Focal Encyclopedia of Photography*, 1957, 1956; *History of 3-Color Photography*, E. J. Wall, 1956; *Theory of the Photographic Process*, C. E. K. Mees, 1944; *Photography Principles and Practice*, C. B. Neblette, 3rd ed., 1939; *Investigations of the Theory of the Photographic Press*, w/C. E. K. Mees, 1907. Anthology: *Photography's Great Inventors*, Louis W. Sipley, 1965. Periodical: "Obituary," C. E. K. Mees, *Photographic Journal*, Jan 1949.

Sonia Landy Sheridan PHOTOGRAPHER · PAINTER · SCULPTOR · TEACHER Born April 10, 1925, in Newark, Ohio, Sheridan received an AB in 1945 from Hunter College in New York City, and undertook graduate studies at Columbia University in New York City in 1946–47. She also studied at Taiwan Normal University, Tokyo, in 1957–59, then completed her MFA in 1960 at the California College of Arts and Crafts in Oakland.

She founded and has been professor and director of Generative Systems School of the Art Institute of Chicago since 1960. She taught at the California College of Arts and Crafts in 1960–61.

Sheridan belongs to SPE, the American Civil Liberties Union and the National Geographic Society. The photographer won an NEA Public Media grant in 1976, a grant from the Union of Independent Colleges of Art in 1975 and an NEA workshop grant in 1974; she was a Guggenheim Fellow in 1973.

She works in a wide variety of media, including painting, printing, sculpture and fabric, in addition to photography. Sheridan founded Generative Systems in 1969, "which laid out the field of contemporary still imaging and its links to former systems, thermography, electrostatics, photography, painting, etc."

PUBLICATIONS Catalogs: *Energized Art-Science*, 1976 (Mus. of Science & Industry: Chicago); *Arttransition*, 1974 (MIT: Cambridge, Mass.).

COLLECTIONS Art Inst. of Chicago; Mus. of the Univ. of Iowa, Iowa City; San Francisco Mus. of Art; VSW, Rochester.

REPRESENTATIVE Visual Studies Workshop, 31 Prince St, Rochester, NY 14607.

ADDRESS 718 Noyes, Evanston, IL 60201.

Shiro Shirahata PHOTOGRAPHER Born February 23, 1933, in Ohtsuk-Shi, Yamanashi-Ken, Japan, Shirahata served an apprenticeship under photographer Koyo Okada from 1951 to 1956. He has been a freelance photographer since 1958.

Shirahata helped organize the Nipon Alpine Photographer's Association in 1967 and belongs to the Photographic Society of Japan, Japanese Alpine Club, Rock Climbing Club II, and the "White Peak" Mountain Photographer's Group, of which he was president in 1975. He received the annual prize of the Photographic Society of Japan in 1977.

The photographer's main area of interest is photography of mountains, primarily Japanese and the European Alps; he is currently working on the Himalayas.

PUBLICATIONS Monographs: *The North Japan Alps*, 1980 (Yama-Kei Pubs.); *Les Alps*, 1979 (Denoël: France), U.S. ed., *The Alps*, 1980; *My Mountain*, 1979, *European Alps*, 1978 (Yama-Kei Pub.); *Mt. Fuji*, 1977, *My South Japan Alps*, 1976 (Asahi-Shinbun Sha); *Mt. Kitadake*, 1975 (Yama-Kei Pub.); *Oze*, 1974, *The South Japan Alps*, 1970 (Ashai-Shinbun Sha). Anthology: *Photography Year 1978*, Time-Life Series, 1978.

COLLECTION Bibliothèque Nationale, Paris.

ADDRESS No. 503 Shōseiso, 2 Funa-machi, Shinjuku-Ku, Tokyo, Japan.

Yoshikazu Shirakawa PHOTOGRAPHER · TEACHER Born January 28, 1935, in Kawanoe City, Japan, Shirakawa earned a BA from the College of Art at Nihon University in Japan in 1957.

A freelance photographer since 1960, Shirakawa previously worked as chief camera operator for Fuji Telecasting Company (1958–60) and as producer in the literature and art division of Nippon Broadcasting System (1957–58).

Shirakawa belongs to the Japanese Alpine Club, Nikakai Association of Artists, and Japan Professional Photographers' Society, of which he has been director since 1967. He won the Minister of Education Award and the 22nd Fine Art Grand Prix in 1972, the 13th Art Prize from the Mainichi Newspapers in 1972, the annual award of the Photographic Society of Japan in 1970, the Nika Prize at the 53rd Nika Exhibition in 1968, the special prize at the National Park Photo Con-

test in 1960 and annual Minister of Health and Welfare awards in 1956–61.

The theme of Shirakawa's work is "recovery of humanity through rediscovery of the earth."

PUBLICATIONS Monographs: *Kiristo no shogai*, 1980 (Nihon Kiristo Kyosho Hanbai); *Shinyaku Seisho no sekai*, 1978 (Shogakukan); *Kami-gami no za*, 1971 (Asahi Newspaper); *Yama*, 1971 (Chikuma Shobo); *Shiroi Yama*, 1960 (Hobundo). Books: *The Alps*, 1975; *Eternal America*, 1975; *The Himalayas*, 1973; *Sangaku-shashin no giho*, 1973 (Rikogakusha); *Roshutso no kimekata*, 1955, *Camera no Chishiki to ut-sushi-kata*, 1955 (Ikeda Shoten).

REPRESENTATIVE The Image Bank, 633 Third Ave, New York, NY 10017.

ADDRESS 2–12–15 Takanawa, Minato-ku, Tokyo 108, Japan.

Simcha Shirman PHOTOGRAPHER · TEACHER Born April 30, 1947, in Germany, Shirman received a BFA degree from the School of Visual Arts in New York in 1975 and an MFA from the Pratt Institute in New York in 1978. Her mentor and major influence has been Arthur Freed.

As of this writing Shirman was a coordinator of the Photography Department of the School of Art Teachers in Ramat Hasharon, Israel, she is also a teacher of photography at the Bezalel Academy of Arts and Design in Jerusalem.

Shirman was the recipient of a grant from the Council of Culture and Art in Tel Aviv in 1976.

The photographer says of her work: "The creation of a photograph involves a constant search for the meanings of shadow and light, space and time, new and old, knowledge and feelings, in transforming a three-dimensional world into a two-dimensional world."

PUBLICATIONS Periodicals: *Proza*, Sept 1980 (Tel Aviv, Israel); *The Photography*, July 1979 (Tel Aviv, Israel).

COLLECTION Israel Museum, Jerusalem.

ADDRESS 14 Hakim St, Ramat Aviv, Israel.

M. Melissa Shook PHOTOGRAPHER · TEACHER Born April 18, 1939, in New York City, Shook received a BA in 1969 from Goddard College, Plainfield, Vermont.

In 1979 Shook became an assistant professor in the Art Department of the University of Massachusetts Harbor Campus in Boston and artist-in-residence for Cornell University's Art Department. From 1974 to 1977 she was a lecturer and assistant professor in the Creative Photo Lab at MIT, Cambridge, Massachusetts, and in 1974 she lectured at the New School for Social Research in

New York City and at Kingsborough Community College in Brooklyn, New York. Shook belongs to SPE and the Word Guild in Boston.

Working in black-and-white, the photographer does photo-essays and autobiographical work. She has produced a twelve-year series on her daugher, Krissy, and as of this writing was photographing charismatic healing services.

PUBLICATIONS Book: *The Brain*, Time-Life Series, 1975. Periodicals: "Krissy," *Creative Camera*, Jan 1980; "Harry Callahan," interview, *Picture Magazine*, no. 12, 1979; interview w/ Steve Szabo, *Photograph*, 1:5, 1978; *Creative Camera*, Feb 1978, Nov 1974; "Personal Politics," *Camera 35*, Jan 1974; *Camera 35 Personal Pictures Annual*, 1974.

COLLECTIONS Metro. Mus. of Art, NYC; MOMA, NYC. In Stockholm: Fotografiska Muséet; Moderna Muséet.

ADDRESS 18 Short St, Brookline, MA 02146.

Stephen Shore PHOTOGRAPHER Shore was born October 8, 1947, in New York City.

The photographer won NEA fellowships in 1979 and 1974 and a Guggenheim Fellowship in 1975. He has served on the board of directors of Anthology Film Archives since 1969.

In the early 1970s Shore began working in large-format color. Known for his landscapes and cityscapes, he was one of the leading photographers in the "color movement" of the mid-1970s.

PUBLICATIONS Book: *Andy Warhol*, 1968 (Moderna Muséet: Stockholm). Anthologies: *American Images*, 1979; *The Photograph Collector's Guide*, Lee D. Witkin & Barbara London, 1979; *Court House*, Richard Pare, ed., 1978; *American Photographers*, Manfred Willmann, ed., 1977 (Graz, Austrai); *Photography Year/1977*, Time-Life Series, 1977; *New Topographics*, 1975. Periodicals: "The Framing of Stephen Shore," Tony Hiss, *American Photographer*, Feb 1979; *Camera*, Jan 1977; *Aperture*, vol. 77, 1976; *Artforum*, Jan 1975.

PORTFOLIO *Twelve Photographs*, 1976 (Metro. Mus. of Art: NYC).

COLLECTIONS CCP, Tucson; Delaware Art Mus., Wilmington; Everson Mus. of Art, Syracuse, N.Y.; IMP/GEH, Rochester; Metro. Mus. of Art, NYC; MOMA, NYC; Mus. of Fine Art, Houston, Tex.; Princeton Univ. Art Mus., N.J.; Seattle Art Mus., Wash.; Vassar Coll., Poughkeepsie, N.Y.; Yale Univ., New Haven, Conn.

DEALER Light Gall., 724 Fifth Ave, New York, NY 10019.

ADDRESS 3109 Lewiston Ave, Berkeley, CA 94705.

Kenneth Cooper Shorr PHOTOGRAPHER Born March 2, 1952, in Goodyear, Arizona, Shorr earned an MFA in 1978 from University of California at Los Angeles, where he studied with Robert Heinecken.

He is currently teaching at the School of the Art Institute of Chicago and since 1978 has also taught at the University of Illinois, Champaign-Urbana.

Shorr belongs to the American Dirigible Society. In 1979 he won an NEA Photographer's Fellowship.

PUBLICATIONS Anthologies: *Self-Portrayal*, 1979; *Young American Photographers*, 1974. Periodicals: *Combinations*, winter 1979; *Creative Camera*, Oct 1978.

COLLECTIONS Franklin Furnace Gall., NYC; Phoenix Coll., Ariz.; UCLA, Grunewald Cllctn.

ADDRESSES School of the Art Institute of Chicago, Photo Dept, Chicago, IL 60603; 109½ W University, #3, Champaign, IL 61820.

Thomas H. Shuler, Jr. PHOTOGRAPHER · TEACHER Born in Detroit, Michigan, on April 15, 1949, Shuler received a BA from Princeton University, New Jersey, in 1971 and an MA from the University of Delaware, Wilmington, in 1978. He also studied with Minor White at Hotchkiss Workshops, Lakeville, Connecticut, in 1973–74.

An assistant professor at Northern Virginia Community College in Annandale since 1976, he taught photography at the Smithsonian Institution in Washington, D.C., in 1975–76. Shuler has also done freelance commercial work since 1973.

A member of SPE, he won the Medaille de Verrières-le-Buisson from the Musée Française de la Photographie in 1978. In 1974 the photographer received a supply sponsorship from the Polaroid Foundation.

Although he has prevously worked with SX-70 and infrared film, Shuler currently deals primarily with platinum and palladium photographic processes.

PUBLICATIONS Anthologies: *1979 Time-Life Photography Annual*, 1979; *The Platinum Print*, Hafey & Shillea, eds., 1979; *SX-70 Art*, Ralph Gibson, ed., 1979. Catalog: *Places, Infrared Photographs, 1976–78*, 1978. Periodicals: *Camera 35*, Aug, June 1977.

COLLECTIONS Corcoran Gall. of Art, Wash., D.C. Musée Française de la Photographie, Bièvres, France.

ADDRESS 3626 Windom Pl NW, Washington, DC 20008.

Kay Shuper *PHOTOGRAPHER* Born July 19, 1947, in Colusa, California, Shuper earned a BA in 1971 from California State University, Northridge, and an MFA in 1975 from University of California at Los Angeles.

A freelance advertising photographer since 1978, she was artist-in-residence at the University of Kansas, Lawrence, in 1976.

PUBLICATION Catalog: *Emerging Los Angeles Photographers,* 1976 (Friends of Photography: Carmel, Calif.).

PORTFOLIO *Silver See* (group), 1977 (Los Angeles Ctr. for Photographic Studies).

COLLECTIONS Calif. State Univ., Los Angeles; MOMA, NYC; Univ. of Colo., Boulder; Univ. of Southern Calif., Los Angeles.

DEALER Witkin Gall., 41 E 57 St, New York, NY 10022.

ADDRESS 6084 W Pico, Los Angeles, CA 90035.

Irene Shwachman *PHOTOGRAPHER · TEACHER · CURATOR* Born July 30, 1915, in New York City, Schwachman attended New College of Columbia University in New York City from 1932 to 1935. She was self-taught in photography, guided by Berenice Abbott, Minor White and Robert Heinecken.

As of this writing, Shwachman was honorary curator of photographs at Brockton Art Museum, Massachusetts. She taught photography from 1966 to 1979 at the School of the Worcester Art Museum in Massachusetts. She was consultant in photography for the Wellesley (Massachusetts) Public Schools (1966–68), for the Boston Redevelopment Authority (1962–63) and for Carl Siembab Gallery in Boston (1959–61).

A member of SPE and the Society of Architectural Historians, Shwachman won Ford Foundation Faculty Enrichment grants from the School of the Worcester Art Museum in 1978, 1977 and 1976.

Especially concerned with architecture as a subject for photography and research, the photographer works in urban and rural social documentation. She creates multiple images from transparencies and with collage, many incorporating written texts.

COLLECTIONS Boston Athenaeum; Brockton Art Mus., Brockton, Mass.; Metro. Mus. of Art, NYC; MOMA, NYC; Mus. of Fine Arts, Boston; Soc. for the Preservation of New England Antiquities, Boston; State Lib., Commonwealth of Mass., Boston; Worcester Art Mus., Mass.

ADDRESS 33 Lakin St, Needham Heights, MA 02194.

Jeffery L. Shyshka *PHOTOGRAPHER · TEACHER* Born in San Francisco, California, on August 1, 1949, Shyshka studied art at San Jose State University, California, receiving his BA in Art in 1972 and his MA in Art in 1975.

Since 1971 he has been employed as a medical photographer at the Veterans' Administration Medical Center in Palo Alto, California. He was also employed as an assistant professor at San Jose State University in 1976–79, and has been cameraman on various 16mm medical films.

Shyshka joined the Biological Photographic Association in 1976.

PUBLICATIONS Monograph: *Duet,* w/Mike Beard, 1977. Anthology: *Photo-Erotica,* 1978. Periodicals: *Latent Image Quarterly,* 1:2, 1:3, 1979; *Aura Quarterly,* 1976.

COLLECTIONS Univ. of Santa Clara, De Saisset Art Gall., Calif.

ADDRESS 250 Fern Rock Way, Boulder Creek, CA 95006.

Michael H. Siede *PHOTOGRAPHER · FILM MAKER* Born September 29, 1952, in Hearne, Texas, Siede received a BFA in 1974 from Florida State University, Tallahassee, and an MFA in 1978 from Tyler School of Art at Temple University, Philadelphia, Pennsylvania.

As of this writing he was the gallery director at Atlanta College of Art, Georgia. Siede taught at both the Art Institute of Atlanta and Tyler School of Art in 1978.

He is a member of Access Atlanta, a nonprofit video production company.

In 1976 Siede directed and edited the film *Archaeology of the Grand French Battery.*

PUBLICATIONS Periodicals: *Quiver,* 1:4, 1979, Mar 1977; *Popular Photography,* Feb 1979; *Portfolio Magazine,* fall 1978.

COLLECTIONS High Mus. of Art, Atlanta, Ga.; New Orleans Mus. of Art; Norfolk Pub. Lib., Va. Bibliothèque Nationale, Paris.

DEALER Atlanta Gall. of Photography; 3077 E Shadowland Ave NE, Atlanta, GA 30305.

ADDRESS 872 Briarcliff Rd NE, Apt A-4, Atlanta, GA 30306.

Jeanloup Sieff *PHOTOGRAPHER* Born November 30, 1933, in Paris.

Currently a freelance photographer in Paris, Sieff began his career there in 1956–58 as a contributor of reportage and fashion to *Elle* magazine, and worked with the Magnum Agency in 1958–59. He also freelanced in New York in 1965.

Sieff is a member of ASMP and on the board of

the French Foundation of Photography. In 1959 he was awarded the Prix Niepce in Paris. In 1978 French Television showed a one-hour program on his work entitled *Death Valley*.

PUBLICATIONS Books: *Death Valley*, 1978, *La Photo*, 1977 (Ed. Denoge: Paris); *Le Ballet*, 1961 (Lausanne, Switzerland). Anthology: *The Magic Image*, Cecil Beaton & Gail Buckland, 1975.

COLLECTIONS In France: Bibliothèque Nationale, Paris; Musée Réattu, Arles.

ADDRESS 87 rue Ampère, 75017 Paris, France.

Adrian Siegel MUSICIAN · PHOTOGRAPHER · PAINTER Born July 17, 1898, in New York City, Siegel died December 5, 1978, in Philadelphia, Pennsylvania. Self-taught in painting and photography, he studied cello and other instruments privately and at the Curtis Institute of Music.

Siegel was a cellist and oboist with the Philadelphia Orchestra from 1922 to 1959 and also its official photographer from 1938 to 1976. He published his photographs in numerous American, European, South American and Japanese magazines.

Siegel belonged to the Musicians Union, Artists' Equity, Philadelphia Art Alliance, Woodstock (New York) Art Association and was a Fellow of the Royal Society of Art in England. He won the NeoGraphic Association gold medal in 1973, the Art Directors Club of New York gold medal in 1949 and the C. Hartman Kuhn Award in 1942.

Siegel took candid photographs of musicians, artists, dancers and actors.

PUBLICATIONS Books: *Concerto for Camera*, 1972, repr. 1979; *Those Fabulous Philadelphians*, Herbert Kupferberg, 1972.

COLLECTION Philadelphia Mus. of Art, Pa.

ARCHIVES c/o Mrs. Adrian Siegel, 1907 Pine St, Philadelphia, PA 19103.

Ed Sievers PHOTOGRAPHER · TEACHER Born June 26, 1932, in St. Louis, Missouri, Sievers received a BA in 1954 from Grinnell College in Grinnell, Iowa. He took his MFA in 1968 from the Rhode Island School of Design, Providence, where he studied with Harry Callahan.

Sievers has been an associate professor at California State University, Northridge, since 1968.

The photographer belongs to SPE.

He describes his work as "social landscape and color slides of light."

PUBLICATIONS Book: *People in My Corner*, 1973. Catalog: *Photo Media: Elements and Technics of Photography Experienced as an Artistic*

Medium, 1972 (Mus. of Contemporary Crafts: NYC).

COLLECTION Chicago Mus. of Art.

ADDRESS 515 W Quinto, Santa Barbara, CA 93105.

George Silk PHOTOGRAPHER Born November 17, 1916, Silk left school at age fourteen.

A freelance photographer since 1972, Silk was a staff photographer for *Life* magazine from 1943 to 1972. Since 1939 his photographic essays have also appeared in *Audubon*, *Smithsonian*, *Signature*, *Gourmet*, *Yachting* and *Sail*, among others. He covered the war in the Middle East and in the Pacific from 1939 to 1943 as a civilian photographer for the Australian Ministry of Information, and previously worked as a salesman in a photo store in Auckland, New Zealand (1934–39), and as a cowhand on a New Zealand ranch (1932–34).

Silk belongs to the NPPA (since 1960); Cedar Point Yacht Club of Westport, Connecticut (since 1957); the Westport Gourmet Society (since 1964) and ASMP (since 1948). He received the University of Rochester's Brehn Memorial Award in 1966, was named ASMP's Photographer of the Year in 1964 and earned a New York Art Directors gold medal in 1961. He received the title "Magazine Photographer of the Year" in 1964, 1963, 1962 and 1960 from the University of Missouri/NPPA.

Silk made a film about sailing in 1969, *The Many Moods of a Thistle*. Primarily a photojournalist, Silk is best known for his sports photographs, his war photographs of Rommel in the Middle East, and the fighting in New Guinea.

PUBLICATIONS Book: *War in New Guinea*, 1943 (F. H. Johnston Pub. Co.: Sydney, Australia). Anthology: *The Magic Image*, Cecil Beaton & Gail Buckland, 1975.

COLLECTIONS Baltimore Mus. of Art, Md. Auckland Inst. & Mus., New Zealand.

ADDRESS 27 Owenoke Park, Westport, CT 06880.

Jeffrey Kim Silverthorne TEACHER · PHOTOGRAPHER Born November 19, 1946, in Honolulu, Hawaii, Silverthorne earned a BFA (1969), an MA in Teaching (1970) and an MFA (1977) from the Rhode Island School of Design, Providence. He names Diane Arbus, Frederick Sommer, Harry Callahan and Man Ray as influences.

Since 1974 Silverthorne has taught at Newton North High School in Newtonville, Massachusetts, and previously taught at Wheelock College, Boston, Massachusetts (1972–73).

A member of the Massachusetts Teachers Association since 1978, he received a grant from the Massachusetts Artists Foundation in 1979.

The photographer uses medium and large formats to produce portraits, documentary work, nudes and landscapes.

PUBLICATIONS Periodicals: *Camera*, Oct 1974; *Modern Photography Annual*, 1969.

COLLECTIONS Boston Mus. of Fine Arts; IMP/GEH, Rochester; MOMA, NYC; Polaroid Corp., Cambridge, Mass.; R.I. School of Design Mus., Providence; Santa Barbara Mus. of Art, Calif; Vassar Coll., Poughkeepsie, N.Y.; Yale Univ., New Haven, Conn.

DEALERS Pfeifer Gall., 825 Madison Ave, New York, NY 10021; Visual Studies Workshop Gall., 31 Prince St, Rochester, NY 14607.

ADDRESS 59 Golden Ball Rd, Weston, MA 02193.

Camille Silvy PHOTOGRAPHER Silvy was born in France and was most active between the years 1857 and 1869. He worked as an amateur for several years when he was a French diplomat in London before opening his portrait studio in Porchester Terrace in that city. Silvy successfully ran the studio until 1869, when he sold it and, with the profits, retired to France. He returned to England in later years as a consul at Exeter.

A landscape photographer during his amateur years, Silvy turned to the popular *cartes de visite* when he opened his portrait studio, and was considered one of the most notable portraitists of his day. He worked with the collodion wet-plate process, producing albumen prints. Cecil Beaton called him "the Gainsborough of commercial photographers."

PUBLICATIONS Anthologies: *The Photograph Collector's Guide*, Lee D. Witkin & Barbara London, 1979; *Une Invention due XIXe siècle: Expression et technique la photographie*, Bernard Marbot, 1976 (Bibliothèque Nationale: Paris); *The Invented Eye*, Edward Lucie-Smith, 1975; *The Magic Image*, Cecil Beaton & Gail Buckland, 1975. Periodical: *Camera*, 1974.

COLLECTIONS Univ. of New Mexico Art Mus., Albuquerque. In London: Natl. Portrait Gall.; Victoria & Albert Mus. In Paris: Société Française; Bibliothèque Nationale.

Michael Simon PHOTOGRAPHER · TEACHER Born on June 20, 1936, in Budapest, Hungary, Simon studied at the Budapest Technical University (1954–56) and Pennsylvania State University in University Park (1957–58).

Since 1968 Simon has worked at Beloit College, Wisconsin. Previously he was a visiting art-ist at the School of the Art Institute of Chicago and an artist-in-residence at the University of Delaware, Newark. Simon was at the Center of the Eye, Aspen, Colorado, in 1969–70.

Simon has been the chairman of the board of SPE from 1979 to date. In 1980 he received a Photography Fellowship from the Wisconsin Art Board and an NEA Survey Grant. In 1977 he received a Mellon Grant for the study of the history of Hungarian photography.

From 1971 to 1974 Simon considered his work to be autobiographical. Since then he has been dealing with "questions of photographic truth and the limits of documentary fidelity."

PUBLICATIONS Book: *First Lessons in Black & White Photography*, w/Dennis Moore, 1978. Periodicals: "The Evolution of Photographic Styles," *Exposure: SPE*, Apr 1979; "Helyzetkép Az Egyesült A'llamokból, *Fotómüvészet*, Apr 1977.

COLLECTIONS IMP/GEH, Rochester; Univ. of Kansas, Lawrence; Minneapolis Inst. of Arts, Minn.; MOMA, NYC; Univ. of Nebr., Lincoln.

ADDRESS 925 Church St, Beloit, WI 53511.

Christopher John Simons PHOTOGRAPHER · TEACHER Born October 12, 1948, in Reno, Nevada, Simons earned a BA in 1971 from the University of Nevada, Reno, and an MFA in Photography in 1976 from Washington State University, Pullman. He names Ben Hazard, curator at the Oakland Art Museum, as his mentor.

Simons has been a photography instructor and head of the photography department at Shoreline Community College, Seattle, since 1977. In 1976 he was a visiting professor at Washington State University's Fine Arts Department, and in 1975–76 was a photographer and teaching assistant at the university. Simons worked as a photographer, producer and actor at the university's KWSU-TV station from 1974 to 1976.

PUBLICATIONS Catalogs: *Pullman Show*, 1977 (Foster/White Gall.: Seattle, Wash.); *In Touch*, 1976 (Portland Ctr. for the Visual Arts: Ore.). Periodical: *Art in America*, Aug 1976.

COLLECTION Rainier Bancorporation, Seattle, Wash.

DEALER Foster/White Gall., 311½ Occidental Ave So, Seattle, WA 98104.

ADDRESS 3873 E Bailey Rd, Clinton, WA 98236.

Mary Kay Simqu PHOTOGRAPHER · TEACHER Born June 13, 1947, in Pittsburg, Pennsylvania, Simqu received a BFA in Graphic Design in 1971 from Pennsylvania State University, University

Park, and an MFA in Photography at the Rhode Island School of Design, Providence, in 1973.

Since 1974 she has been employed in the Department of Design at Drexel University in Philadelphia, and also, since 1979, at the School of Visual Arts at Pennsylvania State University.

Simqu is a member of SPE.

PUBLICATIONS Anthologies: *Women Photograph Men*, 1977; *Women See Woman*, 1976. Periodicals: *Philadelphia Arts Exchange*, Jan/Feb 1978; *Exposure*, May 1977.

COLLECTIONS IMP/GEH, Rochester; Portland Mus. of Art, Maine. Museo de Arte Moderno, Mexico City.

ADDRESS 909 W Beaver Ave, State College, PA 16801.

Art Sinsabaugh (Arthur Reeder) *PHOTOGRAPHER · TEACHER* Born October 31, 1924, in Irvington, New Jersey, Sinsabaugh received a BS in 1949 from the Institute of Design, Chicago, Illinois, where he studied with Harry Callahan and Moholy-Nagy. He later took an MS (1967) from the Illinois Institute of Technology, Chicago, studying with Aaron Siskind.

As of this writing Sinsabaugh was head of the photography program at the University of Illinois, Champaign–Urbana, where he has taught since 1959. He became a professor there in 1969, and headed the Department of Photography and Cinematography from 1959 to 1977. The photographer founded and co-directed Visual Research Laboratory (1974–78). He was a visiting artist at Williams College, Williamstown, Massachusetts (1973), University of New Hampshire, Durham (1968), and University of Oregon, Eugene (1964). He taught at the Institute of Design of the Illinois Institute of Technology from 1949 to 1959. In 1943–46 Sinsabaugh served with the U.S. Army Air Corps, and in 1942–43 he was a photographer for the War Department.

A founding member of SPE, Sinsabaugh won an NEA fellowship in 1976 and a Guggenheim Fellowship in 1969.

He photographs urban and rural landscapes, using various formats, from 35mm through 12 x 20.

PUBLICATIONS Book: *6 Mid-American Chants/11 Midwest Photographs*, w/S. Anderson, 1964. Anthology: *The Print*, Time-Life Series, 1970. Periodical: *Camera*, June 1972.

COLLECTIONS Art Inst. of Chicago; Exchange Natl. Bank, Chicago; Guggenheim Fndn., NYC; IMP/GEH, Rochester; Ind. Univ., Bloomington; Metro. Mus. of Art, NYC; MOMA, NYC; Smithsonian Inst., Wash., D.C.; UCLA, Wight Art Gall.; Univ. of Nebr., Sheldon Mem. Art Gall., Lincoln; Williams College, Williamstown, Mass.

DEALER Daniel Wolf Inc., 30 W 57 St, New York, NY 10019.

ARCHIVE Indiana Univ. Art Mus., Bloomington, IN.

ADDRESS Box 322, Champaign, IL 61820.

Nancy Sirkis *PHOTOGRAPHER · PAINTER* Born August 22, 1936, in New York City, Sirkis received a BFA in 1958 from Rhode Island School of Design, Providence.

A staff member of the International Center of Photography since 1976, Sirkis belongs to Professional Women Photographers.

Using small, medium and large formats, the photographer works with nonsilver processes—photo-etching, Vandyke printing and palladium printing.

PUBLICATIONS Books: *Massachusetts: From the Berkshires to the Cape*, 1977; *Reflections of 1776: The Colonies Revisited*, 1974; *One Family*, 1971; *Boston*, 1964; *Newport: Pleasures and Palaces*, 1962.

ADDRESS 310 Riverside Dr, New York, NY 10025.

Petr Sirotek *PHOTOGRAPHER* Born May 13, 1946, in Prague, Czechoslovakia, Sirotek received a diploma from the Academy of Fine Arts Film and Television Faculty in Prague (1970).

A freelance photographer since 1972, he has also been director of photography at Krátký Film Prague since 1970.

Sirotek became a member of the Union of Czech Creative Artists in 1970. He won the prize of the Czech Ministry of Fine Arts in 1974 and a diploma from the UNESCO Commission—Photokina in 1968.

PUBLICATIONS Books: *In the Realm of Musical Instruments*, 1977 (Panton: Prague); *Mustang Rovaume tibetain interdit*, w/Michel Peissel, 1976, *The River with the Name of Red Morning-Sky*, 1975 (Olympia: Prague). Periodicals: *Revue Fotografie*, no. 1, 1978, no. 3, 1975, no. 2, 1962; *Fotografie*, no. 10, 1977, no. 5, 1966.

COLLECTIONS Moravian Gall., Brno, Czechoslovakia; Umprum Mus., Prague.

ADDRESS Záhořanského 4, Prague 2, 120 00, Czechoslovakia.

Aaron Siskind *PHOTOGRAPHER · TEACHER* [See plate 92] Born December 4, 1903, in New York City, Siskind received a BSS from the College of the City of New York in 1926. He is self-taught in photography.

Since 1971 Siskind has taught at the Rhode Island School of Design in Providence. Previously he taught at the Institute of Design of the Illinois Institute of Technology in Chicago, beginning in 1951. In 1961 he was appointed head of photography there. Siskind taught at Trenton Junior College in New Jersey in 1949–51, and taught English in New York City public schools from 1926 to 1949.

The photographer was a founding member of SPE in 1963 and joined the Film and Photo League in New York in 1930. He received the Gold Star of Merit from Philadelphia College of Art in 1971 and was named the Bingham Distinguished Professor in Humanities at the University of Louisville (Kentucky) in 1969. In 1966 he received a Guggenheim Fellowship.

PUBLICATIONS Mongraphs: *Places: Aaron Siskind Photographs*, 1976; *Photographs of Aaron Siskind in Homage to Franz Kline*, 1975; *Aaron Siskind: Photographer*, Nathan Lyons, ed., essays by Henry Holmes Smith & Thomas B. Hess, 1965; *Aaron Siskind: Photographs*, 1959. Books: *Poems*, J. Logan, 1976; *Bucks County*, 1974. Anthologies: *The Photograph Collector's Guide*, Lee D. Witkin & Barbara London, 1979; *Darkroom 2*, Jain Kelly, 1978; *The Magic Image*, Cecil Beaton & Gail Buckland, 1975; *Documentary Photography*, 1972, *The Art of Photography*, 1971, *Great Photographers*, 1971, Time-Life Series; *Photographers on Photography*, Nathan Lyons, ed. 1966. Catalogs: *Photographs*, 1977 (Univ. of Nebr., Sheldon Mem. Art Gall.: Lincoln); *New Images in Photography*, 1974 (Univ. of Miami, Lowe Art Mus.: Fla.); *American Photography: The Sixties*, 1966 (Univ. of Nebr., Sheldon Mem. Art Gall.: Lincoln). Periodicals: *Camera*, Dec 1979, Nov 1975, June 1973; *Creative Camera*, Aug 1968, Mar 1967.

COLLECTIONS Addison Gall. of Amer. Art, Andover, Mass.; Art Inst. of Chicago; Burpee Art Mus., Rockford, Ill.; CCP, Tucson; Detroit Inst. of Arts, Mich.; Exchange Natl. Bank, Chicago; Harvard Univ., Fogg Art Mus. & Carpenter Ctr., Cambridge, Mass.; High Mus. of Art, Atlanta, Ga.; IMP/GEH, Rochester; Kalamazoo Inst. of Arts, Mich.; Metro. Mus. of Art, NYC; Menil Fndn., Houston; Minneapolis Inst. of Arts, Minn.; MOMA, NYC; Mus. of Fine Arts, Houston; Mus. of Fine Arts, St. Petersburg, Fla.; Newark Mus., N.J.; New Orleans Mus. of Art; Oakland Mus., Calif.; Norton Simon Mus. of Art, Pasadena, Calif.; Philadelphia Mus. of Art, Pa.; Princeton Univ., N.J.; R.I. School of Design, Providence; San Francisco Mus. of Modern Art; Seagram Cllctn., NYC; Smith Coll. Mus. of Art,

Northhampton, Mass.; Smithsonian Inst., Wash., D.C.; UCLA; Univ. of Ill., Krannert Art Mus., Urbana; Univ. of Louisville, Photographic Archives, Ky.; Univ. of Mich., Mus. of Art, Ann Arbor; Univ. of Nebr., Sheldon Mem. Art Gall., Lincoln; Univ. of N. Mex., Albuquerque; Univ. of Okla., Mus. of Art, Norman; Virginia Mus. of Fine Arts, Richmond; VSW, Rochester; Yale Univ., New Haven, Conn. Bibliothèque Nationale, Paris; Natl. Gall. of Canada, Ottawa, Ontario.

ADDRESS 15 Elm Way, Providence, RI 02906.

Gail Skoff *PHOTOGRAPHER · TEACHER* [See plate 141] Born on September 27, 1949, in Los Angeles, Skoff studied at the San Francisco Art Institute, where she received her MFA (1979) and her BFA (1972). From 1969 to 1971 she attended Boston Museum School, Massachusetts, and from 1967 to 1969, University of California at Berkeley.

Skoff has worked as an instructor at the University of California Extension Division, Berkeley, since 1976, as well as at the Associated Students of the University of California (ASUC) Studio, also in Berkeley. She also works at the ASUC Studio as a darkroom supervisor.

Skoff, a member of SPE and the CAA, received an NEA Photographer's Fellowship in 1976.

The artist describes her work as hand-colored and toned silver photographs. Most recently she has been concentrating on landscapes and open spaces.

PUBLICATIONS Book: *Alternative Photographic Processes*, 1978. Anthologies: *The Photographer's Choice*, 1976; *Celebrations*, Minor White & Jonathan Green, 1974. Periodicals: *Picture Magazine*, no. 11, 1979; *Camera*, Sept 1973.

COLLECTIONS CCP, Tucson; Graham Nash Cllctn., Los Angeles; Oakland Mus., Calif.; Smith Coll. Art Gall., Northampton, Mass. Bibliothèque Nationale, Paris.

DEALER Lowinsky & Arai Gall., 228 Grant St, San Francisco, CA 94108.

ADDRESS 1718 Jaynes, Berkeley, CA 94703.

Neal Slavin *PHOTOGRAPHER* Born August 19, 1941, in Brooklyn, New York, Slavin earned a BFA from the Cooper Union School of Art and Architecture in New York City in 1963. In conjunction with his studies there he received a special scholarship to Oxford University's Lincoln College in 1961 to study Renaissance painting and sculpture.

Currently a freelance photographer in New York City, Slavin has taught photography at

Cooper Union, Queens College, Manhattanville College and the School of Visual Arts (all in New York City) from 1970 to 1973. He was a graphic designer for Macmillan Publishing Corporation in New York City in 1965.

A member of SPE, Slavin has won numerous awards: Art Directors Club of New York awards (1979, 1978); Mead Library of Ideas Award (1978); Communication Arts Magazine awards (1977, 1976); CAPS grant (1977); NEA grant through Mexican American Legal Defense and Educational Fund to document Mexican-American culture in the United States (1977); NEA fellowship (1972); and a Fulbright grant to photograph in Portugal (1968).

Slavin describes himself as "a documentarian who believes in doing whatever necessary in order to communicate to my viewer whatever is essential about the situation I am photographing. This often means posing, using artificial lights, formalism, etc., in any situation, so long as the idea of that situation will become clear and evident." Working in both large and small formats, he is known for his photographs of groups of people.

PUBLICATIONS Monographs: *When Two or More Are Gathered Together*, 1976; *Portugal*, 1971. Anthologies: *The Photograph Collector's Guide*, Lee D. Witkin & Barbara London, 1979; *Photography Year*, 1974, Time-Life Series. Periodicals: *Life*, text only, Feb 1979; *Photo*, Nov 1977 (France); "One Is Not Enough," Shelly Rice, *Village Voice*, Oct 19, 1976; "Looking at Groups, Defining America," Joan Murray, *Artweek*, Oct 9, 1976; "Photography in the U.S.A.," *Modern Photography*, July 1976; *Photo*, May 1976 (Italy); *Photo*, May 1976 (France); *Artnews*, Apr 1976; "New Frontiers in Color," Douglas Davis, *Newsweek*, Apr 19, 1976; "When Two or More Are Gathered Together," *Popular Photography*, Feb 1976; "America 76," entire issue, *Du*, Jan 1976; "The Coming to Age of Color," Max Kosloff, *Artforum*, Jan 1975; "New American Imagery," *Camera*, May 1974.

COLLECTIONS CCP, Tucson; Chase Manhattan Art Cllctn., NYC; Delaware Art Mus., Wilmington; Exchange Natl. Bank Cllctn., Chicago; ICP, NYC; Metro. Mus. of Art, NYC; MOMA, NYC; N.Y. Pub. Lib., Photography Archive, NYC; Oakland Mus., Calif; UCLA; Univ. of Maryland, Baltimore. Moderna Muséet, Stockholm; Neue Sammlung, West Germany; Stedelijk Mus., Amsterdam.

DEALER Light Gall., 724 Fifth Ave, New York, NY 10019.

REPRESENTATIVE Barbara von Schreiber, 315 Central Park West, New York, NY 10025.

ADDRESS 62 Greene St, New York, NY 10012.

Lynn Sloan-Theodore   *PHOTOGRAPHER · TEACHER · WRITER*   Born September 4, 1945, in San Angelo, Texas, Sloan-Theodore earned a BA in English Literature (1967) from Northwestern University, Evanston, Illinois, and an MS in Photography (1971) from the Institute of Design at the Illinois Institute of Technology, Chicago, where she studied with Aaron Siskind and Arthur Siegel.

Sloan-Theodore has been a photography instructor at Columbia College, Chicago, since 1972, and in 1975–77 she was photography reviewer for the *New Art Examiner*.

She belongs to SPE and Friends of Photography.

"My color work," says Sloan-Theodore, "explores the effects of light and spatial juxtapositions on our awareness of the world. I often work with grids, frontal arrangements and tight edge-to-edge picture organization and try to reveal, through this almost intellectual formalism, a level of meaning."

PUBLICATIONS Periodicals: *Modern Photography*, Nov 1980; *Camera*, July 1977; *Afterimage: VSW*, Nov 1976.

COLLECTIONS Art Inst. of Chicago; Burpee Art Mus., Rockford, Ill.; Exchange Natl. Bank, Chicago; Ind. Univ. Mus., Bloomington; Inst. of Design, Chicago; Mundelein Coll., Chicago; Univ. of Okla., Norman.

REPRESENTATIVE Susan Spiritus Gallery, 3336 Via Lido, Newport Beach, CA 92663.

ADDRESS 5459 N Lakewood, Chicago, IL 60640.

Kenneth B. Slosberg   *TEACHER · PHOTOGRAPHER*   Born November 27, 1944, in Gardiner, Maine, Slosberg earned an AB from Bowdoin College, Brunswick, Maine, in 1967 and a BFA from the San Francisco Art Institute, California, in 1972. He took his MFA from the Visual Studies Workshop, Rochester, New York, in 1974.

Since 1974 Slosberg has been assistant professor of photography at Orange Coast College, Costa Mesa, California. He taught at Memorial Art Museum at the University of Rochester in 1974 and at the Visual Studies Workshop in 1973–74.

The educator belongs to the American Federation of Teachers, SPE and Los Angeles Center for Photographic Studies.

He describes his photography as "an attempt to

reconcile the physical qualities of light on photo emulsion with an emotional experience of associative meanings."

PUBLICATION Anthology: *Emerging Los Angeles Photographers*, 1976.

PORTFOLIOS *L.A. Issue* (group), 1979 (Los Angeles Center for Photographic Studies); *Visual Studies Workshop*, 1974.

COLLECTIONS CCP, Tucson; IMP/GEH, Rochester; Los Angeles County Mus. of Art; Minneapolis Inst. of Arts, Minn.; VSW, Rochester.

ADDRESS Orange Coast College, 2701 Fairview Rd, Costa Mesa, CA 92626.

Rena Small *PHOTOGRAPHER · TEACHER · PAINTER* Born November 19, 1954, in Los Angeles, California, Small earned a BFA (1975) and an MFA in Art and Design from California Institute of the Arts, Valencia, California. She names sculptor Lynda Benglis and artist Michael McDonough as major influences.

As of this writing Small was teaching at the School of Visual Arts Photography Department in New York City. She was a photographer in 1979 for the architectural journal *VIA, Culture and the Social Vision*, published by the University of Pennsylvania and MIT Press. In 1979 she also worked as a photographer for Harcourt Brace Jovanovich, publishers, in New York City, and in 1978 photographed "Grid House," an architectural façade project by artist Michael McDonough in Boston, Massachusetts.

Small works in color and black-and-white, variously using an 8 x 10 view camera, SX-70, 20 x 24 Polaroids and painting in her photographs. With a current theme of "romance," her photography "reconstructs familiar subjects that are based on aspects of American lifestyles found in media, business, politics, work, and language."

PUBLICATIONS Anthology: *SX-70 Art*, Ralph Gibson, ed., 1979. Periodical: *Petersen's Photographic Magazine*, Dec 1979.

COLLECTIONS IMP/GEH, Rochester; Polaroid Cllctn., Cambridge, Mass.

DEALER G. Ray Hawkins Gall., 7224 Melrose Ave, Los Angeles, CA 90046.

Claudia Merin Smigrod *PHOTOGRAPHER · TEACHER* Born October 10, 1949, in New York City, Smigrod received a BFA in Photography (1971) from Alfred University, Alfred, New York, where she studied with and was influenced by John Wood. She then took an MFA in Photography (1978) from George Washington University, Washington, D.C.

Since 1975 Smigrod has been an assistant professorial lecturer at George Washington University, and has taught photography at the Smithsonian Institution in Washington, D.C., since 1979. In 1979 she also lectured on photography at Northern Virginia Community College, Annandale.

The photographer specializes in nonsilver photography, especially carbro and Vandyke brown prints. She uses all formats, from Diana to 5 x 7, and creates collages and contact prints.

PUBLICATION Book: *A Handbook of Photographic Alternatives for the Photographer and Surface Designer*, 1980.

COLLECTIONS Chrysler Mus., Norfolk, Va.; Corcoran Gall. of Art, Wash., D.C.; Intl. Communication Agency, Wash., D.C.

DEALER Kathleen Ewing Gall., 3020 K St NW, Washington, DC 20007.

ADDRESS 4270 S 35 St, Arlington, VA 22206.

Edwin Smith *PHOTOGRAPHER* Born in 1912 in London, Smith died in 1971. Trained as an architect, he was a self-taught painter and photographer.

Having taken up photography just prior to World War I, Smith soon became a regular contributor to *The Saturday Book*. He worked on assignment and traveled widely.

An architectural photographer, Smith worked with neither an assistant nor a light meter, producing black-and-white and color prints that were often dramatic and well detailed.

PUBLICATIONS Books: *Hatfield House*, 1973; *Rome, from Its Foundation to the Present*, Steward Perowne, 1971; *Reproducing Art*, w/John Lewis, 1969; *The English House Through Seven Centuries*, Olive Cook, 1968 (Nelson: London); *Scotland*, Olive Cook, 1968 (Thames & Hudson: London); *Great Interiors*, Ian Grant, ed., preface by Cecil Beaton, 1967 (Weidenfeld & Nicolson: London); *Ireland*, Olive Cook, 1966 (Thames & Hudson: London); *Prospect of Cambridge*, intro. by Olive Cook, 1965 (Batsford: London); *Athens, City of the Gods*, Angelo Procopiou, 1964; *The English Garden*, Edward Solomon Hyams, 1964 (Thames & Hudson: London); *Venice, the Masque of Italy*, Marcel Brion, 1962; *Great Houses of Europe*, Sacheverell Sitwell, 1961 (Weidenfeld & Nicolson: London); *English Abbeys and Priories*, Olive Cook, 1960; *All the Tricks*, 6th ed., 1957, rev. ed., 1973 (London); *Art Treasures of the British Museum*, intro. by Geoffrey Grigson, preface by Sir Thomas Kendrick, 1957, *English Parish Churches*, D. G. Hutton,

1957 (Thames & Hudson: London); *Phototips on Cats and Dogs, Not for Beginners Only,* w/Oswell Blakeston, 1938 (Focal Press: London). Anthology: *The Magic Image,* Cecil Beaton & Gail Buckland, 1975.

G. E. Kidder Smith ARCHITECT·AUTHOR·PHOTOGRAPHER Born October 1, 1913, in Birmingham, Alabama, Smith received a BA from Princeton University, New Jersey, in 1935, and an MFA from Princeton's Graduate School of Architecture in 1938.

Smith works as a self-employed architect. While in the navy he installed the "Power in the Pacific" exhibition at the Museum of Modern Art, New York City, for Captain Edward Steichen in 1945. He produced a traveling exhibition, "The Work of Alvar Aalto," in 1965, and another, "America's Architectural Heritage," in 1974, both for the Smithsonian Institution.

Smith is a member of the Society of Architectural Historians, the CAA and the American Institute of Architects. In 1975 and 1970 he received Ford Foundation grants, and in 1974 and 1967 he was the recipient of awards from the NEA and, in the same years, from the Graham Foundation for Advanced Studies in the Arts. He was awarded a Samuel H. Kress Foundation grant in 1967, and Fulbright Research fellowships to India in 1965, and to Italy in 1950. In 1949 Smith was a President's Fellow at Brown University, and in 1946 he was both a Guggenheim Fellow and an American-Scandinavian Fellow.

PUBLICATIONS *A Pictorial History of Architecture in America,* 1976; *The New Churches of Europe,* 1963; *The New Architecture of Europe,* 1961; *Italy Builds,* 1955 (Architectural Press: Italy); *Sweden Builds,* 1950, *Switzerland Builds,* 1950; *Brazil Builds* (photos only), 1943.

COLLECTIONS Metro. Mus. of Art, NYC; MOMA, NYC.

ADDRESS 163 E 81 St, New York, NY 10028.

Henry Holmes Smith PHOTOGRAPHER · WRITER · TEACHER Born October 23, 1909, in Bloomington, Illinois, Smith studied at Illinois State University in Normal (1927–32), the Art Institute of Chicago (1929–30), and Ohio State University, Columbus, where he received a BSEd in 1933. His influences were Bruguière, Edward Weston, Moholy-Nagy and Fred Sommer.

As of this writing Smith has been an emeritus professor (since 1977) at Indiana University Department of Fine Arts, Bloomington; he taught there from 1947 to 1977. Smith was associate editor of *Minicam Photography,* 1940–42, and taught at New Bauhaus in Chicago, in 1937–38.

He belongs to Friends of Photography (since 1974) and SPE (founding member, 1963, vice-chairman, 1963–70) and belonged to CAA until 1964. Awarded the Herman Frederick Lieber Distinguished Teaching Award in 1968 by Indiana University, he also received an Honorary Doctorate of Fine Arts from Maryland Institute College of Art in the same year.

The photographer states he produces "refraction images dealing with light play and themes from personal life and characters from mythology, translated into color prints derived from play of monochrome passages in the original positives and negatives generated from refraction work."

PUBLICATIONS Book: *Henry Holmes Smith: Selected Critical Articles,* Terence R. Pitts, ed., 1977. Anthologies: *The Photographer Collector's Guide,* Lee D. Witkin & Barbara London, 1979; *The Photographers' Choice,* Kelly Wise, ed., 1975. Catalogs: *Photographic Process as Medium,* Rosanne T. Livingston, 1975 (Rutgers Univ.: New Brunswick, N.J.); *Synthetic Color,* 1974 (Southern Ill. Univ.: Carbondale); *Henry Holmes Smith's Art,* 1973 (Ind. Univ. Art Mus.: Bloomington); *Photographers Midwest Invitations,* 1973 (Walker Art Ctr.: Minneapolis, Minn.); *Photography 1968,* 1968 (Lexington Camera Club: Lexington, Ky.); *Portfolio II,* 1949–72 (Center of Photographic Studies: Louisville, Ky.). Periodicals: "Critical Difficulties: Some Problems with Passing Judgment and Taking Issue," text only, *Afterimage: VSW,* summer 1978; "Henry Holmes Smith: Speaking with a Genuine Voice," Betty Hahn, *Image 16,* Dec 1973; "An Access of American Sensibility: The Photographs of Clarence John Laughlin," text only, *Exposure: SPE,* Nov 1973; "Photography: Henry Holmes Smith," Murray, *Afterimage: VSW,* Sept 1972; "Solarization Process," *Minicam Photography,* text & illus., Oct 1939.

PORTFOLIO *Colors* (group), 1975 (Florida State Univ.: Tallahassee).

COLLECTIONS CCP, Tucson; IMP/GEH, Rochester; MOMA, NYC; New Orleans Mus. of Art, La.; Univ. of N. Mex., Albuquerque.

DEALERS Susan Spiritus Gall., 3336 Via Lido, Newport Beach, CA 92660; The Gallery, 104 N Grant St, Bloomington, IN 47401.

ARCHIVE Indiana Univ., Bloomington, IN.

ADDRESS POB 3741, Incline Village, NV 89450.

J. Frederick Smith PHOTOGRAPHER · ILLUSTRATOR · PAINTER Born November 2, 1917, in

Pasadena, California, Smith studied for three years at the Chouinard School of Art in Los Angeles.

He has worked as a freelance since 1939 to the present day.

Smith describes his photography as having a "painterly quality—romantic, illustrative work dealing with people, beauty, fashion."

PUBLICATIONS Monographs: *Sappho by the Sea*, 1976; *J. Frederick Smith*, 1975; *Sappho, The Art of Loving Women*, 1975.

REPRESENTATIVE Nob Hovde, 829 Park Ave, New York, NY 10021.

ADDRESS 37 W 26 St, P.H. 1401, New York, NY 10010.

Keith A. Smith PHOTOGRAPHER · PRINTMAKER Born May 20, 1938, in Tipton, Indiana, Smith earned a BAE from the School of the Art Institute of Chicago in 1967 and an MS in Photography from the Institute of Design, Illinois Institute of Technology, Chicago, in 1968.

As of this writing Smith was teaching at Visual Studies Workshop in Rochester (since 1975), and previously taught at the Art Institute of Chicago (1971–75) and at University of California at Los Angeles (1970).

The photographer won an NEA Photographer's Fellowship in 1978, a CAPS grant in 1976 and a Guggenheim Photography Fellowship in 1972.

Smith produces portraits and multiple and serial imagery in various formats, using applied color, cliché verre, drawing, etching, 3M color and photo-etching.

PUBLICATIONS Monograph: *When I Was Two*, 1977. Anthologies: *The Art of Photography*, 1971, *The Print*, 1970, Time-Life Series.

COLLECTIONS Art Inst. of Chicago; CCP, Tucson; Harvard Univ., Fogg Art Mus., Cambridge; IMP/GEH, Rochester; MOMA, NYC; Mus. of Fine Art, Houston; Wellesley Coll. Mus., Mass. Gallerie Civica d'Arte Moderna, Torino, Italy; Mus. of Geelong, Victoria, Australia; Natl. Gall. of Canada, Ottawa.

DEALER Stuart Wilber, Inc, 2943 N Halsted St, Chicago, IL 60657.

ADDRESS 22 Cayuga St, Rochester, NY 14620.

Luther Smith PHOTOGRAPHER · TEACHER Born March 16, 1950, in Mississippi, Smith earned a BA from the University of Illinois, Urbana-Champaign, in 1972, where he studied with Art Sinsabaugh, Bart Parker, Reed Estabrook and Robert Flick. He received an MFA in 1974 from Rhode Island School of Design, Providence, where he studied with Aaron Siskind and Harry Callahan.

Since 1975 Smith has been an instructor at the University of Illinois, Urbana-Champaign, and since 1976 has freelanced as a photographer. He taught at the Rhode Island School of Design from 1972 to 1974.

Smith has won four University of Illinois Research Board grants for travel and materials since 1976 and has also received four Department of Art and Design Ford Foundation grants for materials (since 1974). In 1973 he earned a teaching fellowship from the Rhode Island School of Design, and in 1972 won first prize in the *Mademoiselle* magazine photo contest.

PUBLICATIONS Book: *Darkroom Dynamics*, Jim Stone, ed., 1979. Anthology: *Photography Year 1974*, Time-Life Series, 1974. Periodicals: *Camera*, Aug 1975; *Untitled 6*, 1974 (Friends of Photography).

PORTFOLIOS *Photographic Education Society Portfolio* (group), 1973 (R.I. School of Design, Providence); *1007: 1 Portfolio of Central Illinois Photographers*, 1972 (1007 Photographic Arts Gall., Urbana, Ill.).

ADDRESS POB 2961, Champaign, IL 61820.

Michael A. Smith PHOTOGRAPHER Born in 1942 in Philadelphia, Pennsylvania, Smith is a self-taught photographer.

Since 1974 he has supported himself through the sale of his fine art photography, and from 1966 to 1974 he taught private photography classes.

A member of SPE since 1970, Smith won an NEA Photographer's Fellowship in 1977.

Working within a traditional style and using 8 x 10 and 8 x 20 contact prints, Smith produces photographs of landscapes, urban landscapes and people.

PUBLICATION Periodical: "On Teaching Photography," *Exposure: SPE*, 14:1, 1976.

COLLECTIONS Amon Carter Mus. of Art, Fort Worth, Tex.; Art Inst. of Chicago, Ill.; CCP, Tucson; Delaware Art Mus., Wilmington; Exchange Natl. Bank, Chicago; Fort Lauderdale Mus. of Art, Fla.; Free Lib. of Philadelphia, Pa.; Harvard Univ., Fogg Art Mus., Cambridge, Mass.; High Mus. of Art, Atlanta, Ga.; IMP/GEH, Rochester; Kalamazoo Inst. of Art, Mich; Lehigh Univ., Bethlehem, Pa.; L/C, Wash, D.C.; Minneapolis Inst. of Arts, Minn.; MOMA, NYC; Mus. of Fine Arts, Boston, Mass.; New Orleans Mus. of Art; Norton Gall. of Art, West Palm Beach, Fla.; Ohio Wesleyan Univ., Delaware, Ohio; Philadelphia Mus. of Art, Pa.; Polaroid Corp., Cambridge,

Mass.; John & Mabel Ringling Mus. of Art, Sarasota, Fla.; Roswell Mus. & Art Ctr., Roswell, N. Mex.; St. Louis Mus. of Art, Mo.; Stanford Univ. Mus. of Art, Calif.; Toledo Mus. of Art, Ohio; UCLA, Frederick S. Wight Gall. of Art; Univ. of Kans. Mus. of Art, Lawrence; Univ. of Mass., Amherst; Univ. of Okla. Mus. of Art, Norman. Natl. Gall. of Canada, Ottawa.

ADDRESS Box 218, Bunker Hill Rd, Ottsville, PA 18942.

Michael P. Smith *PHOTOGRAPHER* Born June 15, 1937, in New Orleans, Louisiana, Smith earned a BA in English (1968) and did graduate studies (1968–70) at Tulane University, New Orleans.

Since 1974 he has been a staff photographer for Black Star Publishing Company.

Smith won NEA fellowships in 1976 and 1973.

PUBLICATION Book: *Photography for New Orleans Housing and Neighborhood Preservation Study,* 1974 (City of New Orleans).

COLLECTIONS Historic New Orleans Cllctn., La.; ICP, NYC; Jean Lafitte Natl. Historical Park, La.; Natl. Park Service, New Orleans; New Orleans Mus. of Art.

ADDRESS 1429-B Pine St, New Orleans, LA 70118.

Sharon Jean Smith *GRAPHIC DESIGNER · PHOTOGRAPHER · TEACHER* Born in Dallas, Texas, on June 25, 1951, Smith received a BA in Philosophy from Vanderbilt University, Nashville, Tennessee (1972), and studied photography in 1976 at Apeiron Workshops, Inc., in Millerton, New York. She names Peter Schlessinger (director of Apeiron Workshops), Don Ahn (Tai Chi Master) and Paul Vanderbilt (artist and philosopher) as important influences.

As of this writing Smith was a book designer for Ahn Tai Chi Studio in New York City. She coordinated Apeiron's Long Island Project in 1978 and was a director/teacher for Apeiron's Dutchess-Columbia Photographic Education Project in 1977.

A member of the Photography International Foundation, Inc., Smith received funding from NEA in 1978 for a photographic survey of Long Island.

Working with Polaroid materials, the photographer calls herself an "instant imagemaker" who uses a personal documentary style.

PUBLICATIONS Anthologies: *One of a Kind,* 1979; *SX-70 Art,* 1979. Periodical: "The Instant and Beyond," *Popular Photography,* 1979.

COLLECTIONS Apeiron Workshops, Inc., Millerton, N.Y.; Hofstra Univ. Lib., Hempstead, N.Y.; Polaroid Corp., Cambridge, Mass. Polaroid Europa, Amsterdam, The Netherlands.

DEALER Castelli Graphics, 4 E 77 St, New York, NY 10021.

ADDRESS 752 Greenwich St, #3A, New York, NY 10014.

W. Eugene Smith *PHOTOJOURNALIST* Born December 20, 1918, in Wichita, Kansas, Smith died October 15, 1978, in Tucson, Arizona. He studied at the University of Notre Dame in Notre Dame, Indiana, in 1936–37, on a special photography scholarship and was influenced by Pulitzer Prize-winning news photographer Frank Noel. Photographer Aileen Mioko, Smith's second wife, was his collaborator.

While still in high school Smith worked on assignment for the *Wichita Eagle* and *Wichita Beacon* (1935–36). He joined the staff of *Newsweek* in New York in 1937, but since he used 2¼" format, the magazine fired him for defying their nonminiature policy. Signing on with Black Star in 1938, Smith began doing freelance assignments for *Life, Collier's, American, Harper's Bazaar, New York Times* and other periodicals. In 1939 he joined the staff of *Life* and his on-and-off relationship with the magazine lasted through 1955 and, as a freelance, beyond that.

From 1942 to 1944 Smith was a war correspondent for Ziff-Davis Publishing *(Popular Photography, Flying, Radio News).* The photographer joined Magnum Photos in 1955, resigning in 1958. Commissioned by the American Institute of Architects to photograph contemporary American architecture for their centennial exhibition (1956–57), he produced a series of ten color transparencies, eighteen feet in length.

Smith began teaching at the New School for Social Research in New York City in 1958, and in 1960 he began to give private classes as well as to lecture and exhibit widely. In 1961 he traveled to Japan under commission to Hitachi Ltd., a Japanese industrial firm, to photograph their operations. Returning to the United States in 1963, he worked with Carole Thomas on the development of *Sensorium,* a magazine of photography and other arts, which was never published. From 1966 to 1969 Smith was the special editor for medical reportage of *Visual Medicine,* and was commissioned by the Hospital for Special Surgery in New York City to photograph its services. He also taught at the School of Visual Arts in New York City. In 1971 Smith and his wife Aileen moved to the village of Minamata, Japan, for three years, where they documented the plight of its mercury-poisoned citizens. In 1977 the photographer went to Tucson, Arizona, to work on his archives at the Center for Creative Photography.

A member of ASMP, Smith received its Third Annual Photojournalism Conference award in 1959. In that year he also won the Kappa Alpha Mu Photography Fraternity's Clif Edom Founders Award, and the year before that he was chosen one of the "World's 10 Greatest Photographers" by *Popular Photography*. Smith was appointed to the President's Committee on Photography in 1964, was awarded three Guggenheim fellowships (1956, 1958, 1969), and won an NEA grant and the Nikon World Understanding Award in 1975. The University of Wisconsin in Milwaukee named Smith an Honorary Doctor of Humane Letters.

Smith is best remembered for the numerous photo-essays he did for *Life* on such wide-ranging topics as the war in the South Pacific, Albert Schweitzer, a country doctor, a backwoods midwife and his own daughter. Robert Doty wrote (in *Photography in America*) that Smith's photography "has been a crusade for better human relations and a record of all that is noble in man." His work is remarkable for its sharp contrast and drama. Smith himself described it thus: "Through the passion I have put into my photographs—no matter how quiet those photographs —I want to call out, as teacher and surgeon and entertainer."

PUBLICATIONS Monograph: *W. Eugene Smith: His Photographs and Notes*, afterword by Lincoln Kirstein, 1969. Books: *Minamata*, w/Aileen M. Smith, 1975; *Minamata: Life—Sacred and Profane*, w/Aileen M. Smith, text by Michiko Ishimure, 1973 (Sojusha: Japan); *Hospital for Special Surgery*, 1966; *Pittsburgh*, Stefan Lorant, ed., 1964; "W. Eugene Smith," *Critica e Storia della Fotografia*, Piero Racanicchi, 1963 (Edizioni Tecniche: Milan); *Japan . . . A Chapter of Image*, w/ Carole Thomas, 1963, *Hitachi Reminder*, 1961 (Hitachi: Tokyo); *Universal Photography Almanac*, 1952; *Words and Pictures*, Wilson Hicks, 1952, repr. 1973; *Photography Is a Language*, John R. Whiting, 1946. Anthologies: *The Photograph Collector's Guide*, Lee D. Witkin & Barbara London, 1979; *Great Photographic Essays from LIFE*, Maitland Edey, 1978; *The Magic Image*, Cecil Beaton & Gail Buckland, 1975; *Looking at Photographs*, John Szarkowski, 1973; *Documentary Photography*, 1972, *Great Photographers*, 1971, *Photojournalism*, 1971, Time-Life Series; *Photographers on Photography*, Nathan

Lyons, ed., 1966; *ASMP Picture Annual*, 1957. Catalogs: *Photography by W. Eugene Smith*, intro. by Elizabeth Underhill, 1978 (Victoria & Albert Mus.: London); *Eugene Smith Photography*, 1954 (Univ. of Minn.: Minneapolis). Periodicals: *Album*, no. 2, 1970; "A Great Unknown Photographer," David Vestal, Dec 1966, "One Whom I Admire, Dorothea Lange," Feb 1966, "W. Eugene Smith," H. M. Kinzer, Feb 1965, "W. Eugene Smith Teacher Photographic Responsibility," Bill Pierce, Nov 1961, "How They Think About the Picture Story," June 1959, "The World's 10 Greatest Photographers," May 1958, "W. Eugene Smith: An Exclusive Portfolio of His Unpublished Photographs," Oct 1952, "Camera on a Carrier," John Whiting, June 1944, "The Kid Who Lives Photography," Peter Martin, July 1943, *Popular Photography*; "W. Eugene Smith," Jean Lattes, *Techniques Graphiques*, July/Aug 1965; "Pittsburgh," *1959 Photography Annual*, 1958; "Color/Be Exact As You Take It . . .," Sept 1955, "W. Eugene Smith's Spain," Jacquelyn Judge, Dec 1951, *Modern Photography*; "W. Eugene Smith," Lew Parrella, *U.S. Camera 1956*, 1955; "W. Eugene Smith," *Camera*, Apr 1954; "Photography Today," *Photography Annual 1954*, 1953; "Assignment in Studio 61," *Photography Workshop Number 3*, fall 1951; "A Spanish Village," *U.S. Camera Annual*, 1952, 1951; "Wonderful Smith," Tom Maloney, *U.S. Camera*, Aug 1945; *Life*, 1938–55, passim.

PORTFOLIO *Ten Photographs*, 1977 (Witkin-Berley: Roslyn Heights, N.Y.).

COLLECTIONS Art Inst. of Chicago; Boston Mus. of Fine Arts; CCP, Tucson; Dayton Art Inst., Ohio; Harvard Univ., Carpenter Ctr. for the Visual Arts, Cambridge, Mass.; IMP/GEH, Rochester; Life Picture Cllctn., NYC; MOMA, NYC; Univ. of Colo., Boulder; Univ. of Kans. Mus. of Art, Lawrence. Bibliothèque Nationale, Paris; Victoria & Albert Mus., London; Australian Natl. Gall., Canberra.

ARCHIVE Center for Creative Photography, Univ. of Ariz., 843 E University Blvd, Tucson, AZ 85721.

Ján Šmok *TEACHER·PHOTOGRAPHER* Born in Lučenec, Czechoslovakia, on December 30, 1921, Šmok received a diploma (1951) from the Film Department of the Akademie múzickyeh umění (FAMU) of Prague, where he has been head of the photography department since 1975. Before that he was with FAMU as a professor (1974), head of the film and TV department (1960–75) and assistant professor (1958).

Šmok is a member of DGPh, the Union of

Czech Photographers and the Fédération Internationale d'Art Photographique (FIAP).

PUBLICATIONS Books: *Artificial Lighting in Photography*, 1978 (SNTL: Prague); *Secrets of Photography*, 1975 (OSVETA: Martin); *Introduction on the Theory of Communication*, 1972 (SPN: Prague); *Nude in Photography*, 1969 (OSVETA: Martin).

ADDRESS Wilhelma Piecka 67, 130 00 Prague 3, ČSSR Czechoslovakia.

Charles Piazzi Smyth ASTRONOMER·PHOTOGRAPHER Born January 3, 1812, in Naples, Italy, Smyth died February 21, 1900, in Clova, near Ripon, Yorkshire, England.

At the age of sixteen he became an assistant at the Cape Royal Observatory, and in 1845 he was appointed Astronomer Royal for Scotland, a post he held for forty-two years. After his retirement he made many independent scientific expeditions, during which he photographed his observations.

A member of the Royal Society (he resigned in 1874) and a corresponding member of the Academies of Munich and Palermo, Smyth received an honorary LLD from the University of Edinburgh, Scotland.

As an astronomer he did his best work in the spectroscopic field. He gave the first detailed descriptions of the telluric bands in the solar spectrum and introduced the "end-on" mode of viewing vacuum tubes, among other innovations. The controversy raised by Smyth's interpretation of his measurements of the Great Pyramid and its relation to the decimal system of weight and measures led to his eventual resignation from the Royal Society.

Primarily an astronomical photographer, Smyth also photographed the inside of the Great Pyramid in 1865. His book *Teneriffe* may have been the first publication illustrated by stereoscopic photographs.

PUBLICATIONS Books: *On the Antiquity of Intellectual Man*, 1868 (Edinburgh); *Life and Work at the Great Pyramid*, 3 vols., 1867 (London); *Our Inheritance in the Great Pyramid*, 1864, 5th ed., 1890; *Three Cities in Russia*, 2 vols., 1862 (London); *Teneriffe, an Astronomer's Experiment*, 1858 (London).

Francis Sydney Smythe PHOTOGRAPHER · WRITER · MOUNTAIN CLIMBER Born in 1900, Smythe died June 28, 1949, near Horsham, England. He was educated at Berkhamsted School.

An electrical engineer at the Faraday House Engineering College from 1919 to 1926, he then served in the Royal Air Force from 1927 to 1929. He resigned because of a baffling illness that he caught in the Himalayas (which eventually killed him) and spent the rest of his life writing, photographing and mountain climbing.

He participated in the following famous mountain-climbing expeditions: Kanchenjunga, 1930; Mt. Kamet, 1931; Mt. Everest, 1933, 1936, 1938; Canadian Rockies, 1946, 1947.

Using a 3¼ x 2¼ format, Smythe extensively photographed his mountain-climbing expeditions, using the images to illustrate his many books. His accounts of these expeditions, widely praised, were published in *The New York Times*.

PUBLICATIONS Books: *Climbs in the Canadian Rockies*, 1950; *Behold the Mountains*, 1949; *Mountains in Color*, 1949 (Parrish: London); *Mountaineering Holiday*, 1948 (B. Arthaud: Grenoble, France); *Rocky Mountains*, 1948; *Swiss Winter*, 1948, repr. 1957, *Snow on the Hills*, 1946, *Alpine Ways*, 1942, *Over Welsh Hills*, 1941, *My Alpine Album*, 1940, *Peaks & Valleys*, 1938, *Camp Six*, foreword by Sir John Hunt, 1937, *An Alpine Journey*, foreword by Sir John Hunt, 1934, *Climbs and Ski Runs*, 1929, repr. 1957 (Adams & Charles Black: London); *Again Switzerland*, 1947 (Hodder & Stoughton: London); *The Mountain Top*, 1947 (St. Hugh's Press: London); *A Camera in the Hills*, 1946; *British Mountaineers*, 1942 (W. Collins: London); *The Mountain Vision*, 1941 (Hodder & Stoughton: London); *The Adventures of a Mountaineer*, 1940 (J. M. Dent: London); *Edward Whymper*, 1940, repr. 1947 (C. A. Reitzel: Copenhagen); *The Valley of the Flowers*, 1938, repr. 1949; *The Mountain Scene*, 1937; *The Spirit of the Hills*, 1937; *Over Tyrolese Hills*, 1936; *Kamet Conquered*, 1932, repr. 1947, *The Kanchenjunga Adventure*, 1930 (Gollancz: London).

Robert C. Snider TEACHER · EDITOR · WRITER · PHOTOHISTORIAN Born April 17, 1924, in Jamestown, North Dakota, Snider studied at the Winona School of Photography, Winona, Minnesota, in 1942, then took an MS in Visual Education in 1949 at Indiana University, Bloomington. He earned a PhD from the university's School of Education in 1956, his mentor being Henry Holmes Smith.

Snider has been on the professional staff of the National Education Association in Washington, D.C., since 1958, directing the publications unit of its Department of Audiovisual Education from 1965 to 1970. He served as book-review editor of *AV Communications Review* in 1970–73 and was on the Education Department faculty of the

University of Chicago, Illinois, from 1953 to 1958. Snider was director of visual education at Mankato State University, Minnesota, in 1949–51.

A member of SPE, Friends of Photography and the Society for the History of Technology, the educator won the Photojournalism Award from the Educational Press Association of America in 1969.

His major activities include writing, lecturing, collecting literature and doing research in the history of photography, photographic education and photographic criticism.

ADDRESS 105 Hesketh St, Chevy Chase, MD 20015.

Lord Snowdon (Antony Charles Robert Armstrong-Jones) *PHOTOGRAPHER* Born July 3, 1930, in London, England, Snowdon attended Eton College and Jesus College, Cambridge, both in England. He was married to Princess Margaret of England, sister of Queen Elizabeth, from 1960 to 1978.

A freelance photographer, Lord Snowdon has been artistic adviser to the British *Sunday Times* and Sunday Times Publications Ltd since 1962, consultative adviser to the Design Council of London since 1962 (and editorial adviser of *Design Magazine*) and constable of Caernarvon Castle, Wales, since 1963.

He is president of the Contemporary Art Society for Wales, the Civic Trust for Wales, the Welsh Theatre Company and the Greater London Arts Association. Snowdon is also a fellow of the Society of Industrial Artists and Designers (London), RPS and the Royal Society of Arts, London.

The photographer won the RPS Hood Award in 1979, the Society of Publication Designers Award of Excellence in 1973 and the Wilson Hicks Certificate of Merit for Photocommunication in 1971.

In addition to his still photography Snowdon has made the television films *Peter, Tina and Steve* (1977), *Burke and Wills* (1975), *Mary Kingsley* (1975), *Happy Being Happy* (1973), *Born to Be Small* (1971), *Love of a Kind* (1969) and *Don't Count the Candles* (1968, winner of two Emmys). He has also been a designer, creating the Snowdon Aviary for the London Zoo in 1965 and "The Chairmobile," an electricity-powered chair for the disabled, in 1972.

The photographer is primarily known for his portraiture and reportage.

PUBLICATIONS Books: *Personal View*, 1979; *Pride of the Shires*, w/John Oaksey, 1979; *Inchcape Review*, 1977; *Assignments*, 1972; *A View of Venice*, 1972; *Private View*, w/John Russell & Bryan Robertson, 1965; *London*, 1958; *Malta*, w/ Sacheverell Sitwell, 1958. Anthology: *The Magic Image*, Cecil Beaton & Gail Buckland, 1975.

ADDRESS 22, Launceston Pl, London W8, England.

Robert A. Sobieszek *CURATOR · PHOTOHISTORIAN · TEACHER* Born in Chicago on March 11, 1943, as of this writing Sobieszek is a doctoral candidate at Columbia University, New York City, where he received an MA in Philosophy in the field of Art History. He earned an MA in the same major at Stanford University in 1969 and a BFA with honors at the University of Illinois in Urbana in 1965. From 1961 to 1963 Sobieszek studied under Aaron Siskind at the Illinois Institute of Technology, Institute of Design, specializing in visual design and photography.

Presently the associate curator of nineteenth-century photography at International Museum of Photography at George Eastman House, Sobieszek joined Eastman House in 1968 to assist in the organization of its photographic collections. Prior to this he had been an intern there in 1967. He has been responsible for numerous exhibitions, among them "British Masters of the Albumen Print," "The Spirit of Fact: The Daguerreotypes of Southworth and Hawes," "Vedute della Camera: 19th-Century Views of Italy," and "An American Century of Photography, 1840–1940," among others. From 1971 to 1977 Sobieszek taught the history of photography in the Department of Fine Arts of the University of Rochester, and for the spring quarter of 1976 he was visiting lecturer at the University of California, Santa Barbara. He has lectured at the Center of the Eye in Aspen, Light Gallery in New York, the Oakland Museum, Philadelphia Museum of Art, Cooper Union in New York, Center for Creative Photography in Tucson, Kimbell Art Museum in Fort Worth, Indianapolis Museum of Art, the University of New Mexico and State University of New York, Purchase. He has also been chairman of several symposiums and conferences on photography. His articles appear abundantly in *Image* magazine.

Over the years Sobieszek has been the recipient of numerous awards and fellowships, among them: NEA grant (1971), Kress Foundation Fellowship (1968), Carnegie Corporation of New York Fellowship (1967), Newhouse Foundation Grant-in-aid (autumn 1967), Eastman House Intern Fellowship (summer 1967), Bourse de la Gouvernement Français (1966) and a Woodrow Wilson National Fellowship (1965).

PUBLICATIONS Books: *San Francisco in the 1850s*, G. R. Fardon, intro. only, 1977 (repr. of 1856 vol.); "The Art of Photography," *The Encyclopedia Americana*, 1977; *The Spirit of Fact*, w/ Odette M. Appel, 1976; "Photography and the Theory of Realism in the Second Empire," *A Hundred Years of Photography*, 1975; *One Mind's Eye*, intro. only, 1974; *The Incredible Case of the Stack O'Wheats Murders*, Les Krims, intro. only, 1972; *Pictorial Effect in Photography*, Henry Peach Robinson, intro. only, 1971 (repr. of 1869 vol.); *Beaumont Newhall*, Van Deren Coke, ed., biblio. only, w/Patricia Slahucka, 1971. Books (editor): *Two Pioneers of Color Photography: Cros and Du Hauron*, 1979; *The Prehistory of Photography*, 1979; *Early Experiments with Direct Color Photography*, 1979; *The Daguerreotype in Germany*, 1979; *The Sources of Modern Photography*, w/Peter C. Bunnell, 1979; *The Daguerreotype Process*, 1973; *The Collodion Process and the Ferrotype*, 1973; *The Literature of Photography*, w/Peter C. Bunnell, 1973. Anthology: *French Primitive Photography*, w/André Jammes & Minor White, 1969. Catalogs: "Mythological Structures and Du Hauron's Rooster," *Cultural Artifacts*, S. L. Berens, ed., 1979 (Florida School of the Arts: Palatka, Fla.); *An American Century of Photography, 1840–1940*, 1978 (C. J. Bucher, Ltd: Lucerne); *Nickolas Muray*, 1974, *Acquisitions 1970–73*, w/William Jenkins, 1973, *British Masters of the Albumen Print*, 1973, *Alexander Gardner's Photographs Along the 35th Parallel*, 1971 (IMP/GEH: Rochester); "A Celebration of the Female Sex Object," *Plastic Love Dream*, 1969 (Univ. of Calif. at Davis, Memorial Union Art Gall.). Periodicals: "Composite Imagery and the Origins of Photomontage, Part II: The Formalist Strain," Oct 1978, "Part I: The Naturalistic Strain," Sept 1978, *Artforum*; "Albert Sands Southworth and Josiah Johnson Hawes," *Camera*, Dec 1976; "Notes Concerning Photographic Exhibitions," *The Photographic Journal*, Sept 1975; "Conquest by Camera," Mar/Apr 1972, "Another Look at Walker Evans," Dec 1971, *Art in America*.
ADDRESS IMP/GEH, 900 East Ave, Rochester, NY 14607.

Adam Sobota CURATOR · ART HISTORIAN Born December 24, 1947, Sobota graduated from the University of Wrocław in 1971.

Since 1973 he has been the curator of the Photography Department at the Muzeum Narodowe. He is also a regular contributor to *History of Photography* magazine.

Sobota is a member of the Art Historians Society in Poland.
PUBLICATION Periodical: "Art photography in Poland 1900–1939," *History of Photography*, Jan 1980.
ADDRESS Muzeum Narodowe We Wrocłwin, 50–153 Wrocław, pl. Powstańców, Warszawy 5, Poland.

Howard J. Sochurek PHOTOGRAPHER Born November 27, 1924, in Milwaukee, Wisconsin, Sochurek attended Princeton University, New Jersey (1942–44), and was a Nieman Fellow at Harvard University, Cambridge, Massachusetts (1959–60). His grandfather, Dr. Aloys Sochurek, was a notable architect in Prague, Czechoslovakia, in the 1880s.

Self-employed since 1970, Sochurek served as a staff photographer for *Life* magazine from 1950 to 1970 and, before that, was a staff photographer for the *Milwaukee Journal* from 1945 to 1950.

He has been a member of ASMP since 1950 and also belongs to the Overseas Press Club and the Bronxville Field Club.

In 1957 the photographer won the New York Art Directors Award as well as being named Magazine Photographer of the Year by the University of Missouri. Sochurek received the Robert Capa Award from the Overseas Press Club in 1955.

He produced and photographed three ABC-TV documentaries: *Primary* (1961), *Yankqui No* (1962) and *X-Pilot* (1964).

His photographic work is mainly journalistic and scientific (ultrasound, thermography, computer graphics, image enhancement); he also does advertising illustration.
PUBLICATIONS Books: *The First Siberians*, 1973; *Lifelines for the New Frontier*, 1973; *The New Russians*, 1973; *Siberia at Work*, 1973.
COLLECTIONS ICP, NYC; K&L Gall. of Fine Photographic Art, NYC; Metro. Mus. of Art, NYC; Squibb Corp., Princeton, N.J.
DEALER K & L Gall. of Fine Art, 222 W 44 St, New York, NY 10036.
ADDRESS 680 Fifth Ave, Suite 2305, New York, NY 10019.

Frederick Sommer PHOTOGRAPHER · GRAPHIC ARTIST [See plate 81] Born in Angri, Italy, on September 7, 1905, Sommer earned an MA in Landscape Architecture from Cornell University, Ithaca, New York (1927), and an honorary Doctor of Fine Arts degree from the University of Arizona, Tucson (1979). He was influenced by Edward Weston, Charles Sheeler and Max Ernst.

In 1979 he was appointed Visiting Senior Fellow of the Council of the Humanities and Old Dominion Fellow in Visual Arts at Princeton University, Princeton, New Jersey. He previously served as coordinator of fine arts studies at Prescott College, Arizona (1966–71), and as photography lecturer at the Institute of Design in Chicago (1957–58). He won a Guggenheim Fellowship in 1974 and an NEA Photographer's Fellowship in 1973.

PUBLICATIONS Monograph: "Frederick Sommer Photographs: 1939–1962," *Aperture*, 10:4, 1962. Books: *The Poetic Logic of Art and Aesthetics*, w/Stephen Aldrich, 1972; *Masters of Modern Art*, 1954. Anthology: *The Photograph Collector's Guide*, Lee D. Witkin & Barbara London, 1979; *The Magic Image*, Cecil Beaton & Gail Buckland, 1975. Catalogs: *Venus, Jupiter and Mars*, John Weiss, 1980 (Delaware Art Museum, Wilmington, Del.); *Photographs*, Gerald Nordland, 1968 (Philadelphia Coll. of Art); *Frederick Sommer*, 1965 (Norton Simon Mus. of Art: Pasadena, Calif.). Periodicals: "An Extemporaneous Talk at the Art Institute of Chicago, October, 1970," 16:2, 1971, "Three Phantasts: Laughlin, Sommer, & Bullock," 9:3, 1961, *Aperture*.

COLLECTIONS Art Inst. of Chicago; CCP, Tucson; Dayton Art Inst., Ohio; Harvard Univ., Fogg Art Mus., Cambridge, Mass.; IMP/GEH, Rochester; MOMA, NYC; Norton Simon Mus., Pasadena, Calif.; R.I. School of Design Mus., Providence; Univ. of Ind. Art Mus., Bloomington; Univ. of N. Mex Art Mus., Albuquerque.

ARCHIVE Center for Creative Photography, University of Arizona, 843 E University Blvd, Tucson AZ 85721.

DEALER Light Gall., 720 Fifth Ave, New York, NY 10019.

ADDRESS POB 262, Prescott, AZ 86302.

Giorgio Sommer PHOTOGRAPHER Born in 1834 in Frankfurt, Germany, Sommer died in 1914 in Naples, Italy.

He began his photography career in Switzerland, producing a series of pictures documenting the feasiblity of opening new roads. In about 1860 Sommer went into business with the German photographer Edmund Behles in Rome. The next year he photographed the battle camps and forts of Gaeta after the siege, and documented, for the regional government, the suppression of highway robbers in the provinces. In 1873 he produced a catalogue of landscapes taken from the Alps to Malta, one of the most nearly complete works of the time. Sommer won the bronze medal at the Paris Exposition of 1867.

At the beginning of his long career the photographer occasionally did portraits, but his later work was almost exclusively landscapes and reproductions of art.

PUBLICATIONS Books: *Napoli*, 18–?, *Pompei*, 18–? (Naples). Anthology: *Early Photographs and Early Photographers*, Oliver Mathews, 1973. Catalogs: *Catalogo di fotografie d'Italia e Malta. Giorgio Sommer—Casa fondata nel 1857*, 1873 (Naples); *Cataloghi di fotografie d'Italia*, 1870 (Ferrante: Naples). Periodical: "Immagini di ieri," W. Settimelli, *Photography Italiana*, Oct 1968.

COLLECTION IMP/GEH, Rochester.

Eve Sonneman PHOTOGRAPHER · FILM MAKER Born January 14, 1946, in Chicago, Illinois, Sonneman received a BFA from the University of Illinois, Champaign, in 1967 and an MFA from the University of New Mexico, Albuquerque, in 1969.

Since 1975 she has taught at the School of Visual Arts in New York City. Sonneman has also taught at Cooper Union College of Art and Architecture, New York City (1975–78, 1970–71), City University of New York (1972–75) and Rice University, Houston, Texas (1971–72).

The photographer won an NEA fellowship in 1978 and 1971, a Polaroid Corporation grant for work in Polavision in 1978, a grant from the Institute for Art and Urban Resources of New York in 1977 and a Boskop Foundation Grant in the Arts in 1969.

She has appeared on several cable television specials: *Innertube* in 1978; a special on her exhibition at Castelli Gallery in 1976; and *Group Portrait: 3 Photographers of New York State*, produced by Cable Arts.

PUBLICATIONS Book: *Real Time*, 1976. Anthologies: *One of a Kind*, essay by Eugenia Parry Janis, 1979; *Mirrors and Windows*, John Szarkowski, 1978; *Photographers in New York*, 1973 (Seibundo Shindosha; Japan). Periodicals: "Windows," *Life*, 1979; "Eve Sonneman: l'instant et le moment," Michel Nuridsany, *Le Figaro*, Nov 21, 1977; *Photography Annual*, 1978; *Flash Art*, July/Aug 1977; *Modern Photography*, Aug 1977; *New York Times*, review by Gene Thornton, Aug 3, 1975; *Houston Chronicle*, review by John Scarborough, Jan 9, 1972.

COLLECTIONS Art Inst. of Chicago; Art Mus. of So. Tex., Corpus Christi; CCP, Tucson; IMP/GEH, Rochester; Metro. Mus. of Art, NYC; Menil Foundation, Houston; MOMA, NYC; Mus. of Contemporary Art, Chicago; Mus. of Fine Arts, Boston; Mus. of Fine Arts, Houston; Mus. of New Mex., Santa Fe; Natl. Archives,

Wash., D.C.; New Orleans Mus. of Art; Minneapolis Inst. of Arts, Minn.; Wadsworth Atheneum, Hartford, Conn.; Wellesley Art Mus., Mass. Bibliothèque Nationale, Paris; Natl. Gall. of Australia, Canberra.

DEALER Castelli Gall., 4 E 77 St, New York, NY 10021.

ADDRESS 98 Bowery, New York, NY 10013.

Emmanuel Sougez PHOTOGRAPHER · ART HISTORIAN Born in 1889 in Bordeaux, France, Sougez died in 1972. He studied painting at the Bordeaux School of Fine Arts, beginning in 1904, and started photographing around the same time.

Sougez traveled throughout Europe until World War I. He inaugurated a photographic department at *L'Illustration* in 1926, which he headed until the dissolution of that publication. The photographer also contributed to other journals, such as *Arts et Métiers graphiques* and *Camera*.

Using both large formats and the Rolleiflex, Sougez specialized in art and archaeological photography, also doing portraits, landscapes and nudes.

PUBLICATIONS Monographs: *Alphabet*, 1932 (Roche: Paris); *Notre-Dame de Paris*, 1932 (Tel: Paris); *Regarde!*, 193–? (Jonquières: Paris). Books: *La Photographie, son histoire*, 1968 (Paris); *La Sculpture contemporaine française et étrangère*, 1961; *La Sculpture au Musée du Louvre*, 1936–58, 1958; *Art de l'Amérique*, 1948; *Arts de l'Océanie*, 1948; *Arts de l'Afrique noire*, 1947; *La Chaise-Dieu*, w/Jean A. Fortier, 1946 (Cerf: Paris); *Histoire de la Photographie*, w/R. Lécuyer, 1945. Anthology: *The Magic Image*, Cecil Beaton & Gail Buckland, 1975.

COLLECTIONS In France: Bibliothèque Nationale, Paris; Musée Française de la Photographie, Bièvres.

William Stinson Soule PHOTOGRAPHER Born in 1836, Soule died in Maine in 1908. His brother, John P. Soule, was also a photographer.

Will Soule served in the Union Army during the Civil War and was severely wounded at Antietam in 1862, spending the rest of the war as a clerk in Washington, D.C. After the war he worked in a photographic studio in Chambersburg, Pennsylvania, then traveled to Fort Dodge, Kansas, in 1867 and secured employment as chief clerk at Tappin's Trading Co. He supplemented his income by doing photographic jobs with the equipment he had brought with him. Soule moved to Camp Supply in 1868, then in 1869 or 1870 to Fort Sill, Kansas, which was the Indian Agency and Military Control Headquarters for the Comanche, Kiowa, Kiowa-Apache, Wichita, Caddo and other tribes. He was evidently engaged by the U.S. Army to create a photographic log of the new fort's construction, and subsequently ran a photographic gallery there as well. Although records are vague, it seems Soule left the area in 1874–75 and returned to Boston, where he operated a studio until his retirement in 1902.

Working with the wet-plate collodion process on glass-plate negatives, Will Soule created portraits of American Indians from various tribes that provide invaluable documentation and "deserve very serious attention by photographers, historians, and ethnologists," say Belous and Weinstein in *Will Soule*.

PUBLICATIONS Monograph: *Will Soule*, Russell E. Belous & Robert A. Weinstein, 1969. Book: *Plains Indian Raiders*, 1968. Anthology: *The Invented Eye*, Edward Lucie-Smith, 1975. Periodical: *Harper's Weekly*, Jan 16, 1869.

COLLECTIONS Bur. of Amer. Ethnology, Wash., D.C.; Denver Pub. Lib., Colo.; Fort Sill Artillery & Missile Ctr. Mus., Kansas; Huntington Lib., Pasadena, Calif.; Los Angeles County Mus. of Natural Hist., Hist. Div.

ARCHIVE History Division, Los Angeles County Museum of Natural History, 900 Exposition Blvd, Los Angeles, CA 90007.

Marie Souraut
See Mother St. Croix

Albert Sands Southworth PHOTOGRAPHER Born on March 12, 1811, in West Fairlee, Vermont, Southworth died on March 3, 1894, in Charlestown, Massachusetts. Southworth attended Phillips Academy in Andover, Massachusetts. He learned daguerreotypy from François Gouraud, Daguerre's agent in America. His sister was Nancy Southworth Hawes, a hand-colorist at Southworth & Hawes. His brother-in-law and partner in daguerreotypy was Josiah Johnson Hawes.

Southworth was a pharmacist when he became interested in photography upon his first viewing of a daguerreotype in 1840. He purchased a camera from Samuel F. B. Morse and moved to Boston to open a studio with Joseph Pennell in the same year. The pair took Josiah Hawes in as a partner in 1841, but the firm was not named Southworth & Hawes until Pennell's death in 1845. In 1849 Southworth went to California to mine gold but failed in his pursuit. He returned home in ill health and retired.

During his active years, he, with Hawes, patented several photographic devices, such as a viewer for large, full-plate stereo daguerreotypes that they called a Grand Parlor Stereoscope. They also devised a method to reduce exposure time.

Southworth and Hawes were noted for their spontaneous and revealing portraits, which departed from the rather contrived poses of the day. They were daguerreotypists who also made scenes of Boston and its environs. Southworth did some scenes of San Francisco when he was on his gold-mining expedition in the 1850s.

PUBLICATIONS Books: *The Spirit of Fact*, Robert A. Sobieszek & Odette M. Appel, 1976; *Mirror Image: The Influence of the Daguerreotype on American Society*, Richard Rudisill, 1971; *The Daguerreotype in America*, Beaumont Newhall, 1961, rev. ed., 1968. Anthologies: *The Photograph Collector's Guide*, Lee D. Witkin & Barbara London, 1979; *The Invented Eye*, Edward Lucie-Smith, 1975; *The Magic Image*, Cecil Beaton & Gail Buckland, 1975; *Early Photographs and Early Photographers*, Oliver Mathews, 1973; *Great Photographers*, Time-Life Series, 1971; *Masters of Photography*, Beaumont & Nancy Newhall, 1969. Catalog: *The Hawes-Stokes Collection of American Daguerreotypes . . .*, I. N. Phelps Stokes, 1939 (Metro. Mus. of Art, NYC).

COLLECTIONS Boston Athenaeum; Bostonian Soc.; IMP/GEH, Rochester; Metro. Mus. of Art, NYC; Mus. of Fine Arts, Boston.

ARCHIVE Metropolitan Museum of Art, Fifth Ave & 82 St, New York, NY 10028.

Ted James Spagna, Jr. *FILM MAKER · PHOTOGRAPHER · ARCHITECT* Born on October 11, 1943, Spagna earned an MS in Film at Boston University in 1972 and a BA in Architecture at Cooper Union, where he studied with John Hejduk, in 1970. He went on to graduate studies in "cinéma vérité" under Richard Leacock at MIT (1971–72) and film animation at Harvard University, Cambridge (1971–72).

As of 1980 he began teaching Spatial Design/Architectonics at The School of the Museum of Fine Arts and Tufts University in Boston and Medford, Massachusetts, respectively. In 1976–77 Spagna lectured in visual and environmental studies at Harvard University. In 1976 he taught film production at The School of Visual Arts in New York City, and from 1974 to 1976 he taught film production and theory at State University of New York in Manhattan. He has freelanced in film and photography since 1977, collaborated on sleep research with Dr. Allan Hobson of Harvard Medical School since 1975, and was an associate designer for Spectrum Design Associates, Boston, in 1972–73. His images have appeared in such publications as *Vogue, Science News, Smithsonian, Psychology Today* and the *Japanese Journal of Architecture*.

A charter member of Zeiss Historica since 1978, Spagna also belongs to ASMP. He was awarded Massachusetts Council on the Arts grants in film in 1979 and 1976 and an NEA grant in film in 1977.

Among his several film credits are *Sleep Film* (1977), *Made in Japan* and *2 x 2* (1976), *Arabesque* and *The Miss Naked USA Contest* (feature length, 1974).

During the past four years Spagna has concentrated all his efforts, in both film and still photography, on documenting the sleep and dream research with which he is involved.

COLLECTIONS MOMA, NYC; Univ. of S. Carolina, Columbia (film).

ADDRESS 791 Tremont St #E-512, Boston, MA 02118.

Merle Spandorfer *PHOTOGRAPHER · TEACHER · VIDEO ARTIST* Born September 4, 1934, in Baltimore, Maryland, Spandorfer earned a BS in 1956 from the University of Maryland, College Park. She also studied at Syracuse University, New York (1954–56).

Currently teaching at the Tyler School of Art in Philadelphia, she has also taught at Cheltenham School of Fine Arts, Pennsylvania (since 1966), and at Philadelphia College of Textiles and Science, Philadelphia (1978).

A member of Artists' Equity Association in Washington, D.C., the photographer won awards from the Baltimore Museum of Art in 1969, 1970 (Governor's Prize) and 1971 (Maryland Institute of Art Award).

She works in experimental photo media, including gum-bichromate printing on paper and canvas, and also does video.

PUBLICATIONS Periodicals: *Flash Art*, Oct/Nov 1976; *Popular Photography*, Sept 1974; "Merle Spandorfer," review, Henry Gerrit, *Artnews*, May 1970.

COLLECTIONS Albion Coll., Mich.; Baltimore Mus. of Art, Md.; Calif. Coll. of Arts & Crafts, Oakland; Cornell Univ., Herbert J. Johnson Mus., Ithaca, N.Y.; L/C, Wash., D.C.; MOMA, NYC; Montclair Mus., N.J.; Penn. Academy of Fine Arts, Philadelphia; Philadelphia Mus. of Art; U.S. Info. Agcy., Japan.

DEALERS Ericson Gall., 23 E 74 St, New York, NY 10021; Marian Locks Gall., 1524 Walnut St, Philadelphia, PA 19102.

ADDRESS 8012 Ellen Lane, Cheltenham, PA 19012.

Howard Dean Spector *PHOTOGRAPHER · CU-RATOR · TEACHER* Born in Hartford, Connecticut, on October 26, 1946, Spector earned a BSCE in Civil Engineering in 1969 from the University of Connecticut, Storrs, and an MFA in Photography in 1978 from the Visual Studies Workshop (of the State University of New York) at Rochester.

He has been director of the Light Factory, Inc., in Charlotte, North Carolina, since 1978 and previously taught photography at the Rochester Museum and Science Center (1978), the Watford College Art Department in Watford, England (1977), and at VSW in Rochester (1976). He worked at the Photographers' Gallery in London, England, in 1976–77 and coordinated traveling exhibitions for the VSW Gallery from 1974 to 1976.

Spector is a member of SPE.

Working with medium format, the photographer is "currently investigating the idea of abstraction and multiplicity by multiple contact prints, photographic grids, minimal landscape. . . ."

PUBLICATIONS Periodicals: *Arts Journal*, 1979; *Fotografia Italiana*, May 1978; *British Journal of Photography Annual*, 1978.

COLLECTIONS VSW, Rochester. Bibliothèque Nationale, Paris; Photographers Gall., London.

ADDRESS Light Factory, 110 E Seventh St, Charlotte, NC 28202.

Terence Spencer *PHOTOJOURNALIST* Born in Bedford, England, on March 8, 1918, Spencer attended Birmingham University for two years before the start of World War II.

Since 1972 he has freelanced, mainly for Time-Life. He photographed for *Life* magazine from 1952 to 1972, covering the Black African continent and Southeast Asia until 1963, when he joined the magazine's London bureau. Prior to that he ran an aerial photographic business.

Spencer was awarded the Distinguished Flying Cross and the Belgian Croix de Guerre with Palms during World War II. He won the Picture of the Year award from the National Press Photographers Association (NPPA) in 1964 and an award from World Press Photo at The Hague in 1969.

His photojournalism, including aerial and underwater work, has appeared in such publications as *Smithsonian, Fortune, Sports Illustrated,* *Time* and *Paris-Match*. The photographer's essays for *Life* were on such topics as the Beatles, Abu Simbel, the 1967 Israeli war, Biafran starvation, Bobby Kennedy in the Ivory Coast, Vietnam and the Mau Mau in Kenya.

ADDRESS 133 North Hill, London N6 4DP, England.

Walter Baldwin Spencer *PHOTOGRAPHER · TEACHER · ETHNOGRAPHER · ANTHROPOLOGIST* Born June 23, 1860, in Lancashire, England, Spencer died July 14, 1929, in Patagonia, Argentina. He attended Manchester School of Art in 1880, then attended Oxford on a scholarship, graduating with honors in biology in 1884.

A professor of biology at Melbourne University, Australia, from 1887 to 1894, he organized the building of the school's new biology department. In 1887 he took expeditionary trips to unexplored areas of Victoria, Australia, during which he sketched and photographed. In 1894 he was the official photographer of the Horn Expedition to Central Australia, and between 1896 and 1898 he traveled to Alice Springs, where he studied the Arunta tribe, and to Lake Eyre, where he studied the Urabunna tribe. Both tribes initiated him into their ranks. Spencer then recorded the ceremonies and sacred rites of the Aborigines, and the countryside of Central Australia, using Edison's cine camera along with his own still equipment (1901). In 1912 he was made Special Commissioner and Special Protector of the Aborigines in Northern Australia. In order to compare Patagonian Indians with Australian Aborigines, Spencer set out in 1929 to follow Charles Darwin's voyage from England to Tierra del Fuego at the tip of South America, but he died of a heart attack en route.

With a clear, accurate style, Spencer was the first person to photograph native tribesmen in their natural environment in any land. He was also the first to photograph Ayers Rock and Central Gorges in Australia. Combining his anthropological work with his photographic abilities, he left important documents of tribal life-style in its natural habitat.

PUBLICATIONS Books: *The Arunta—A Study of Stone Age People*, ca. 1926; *Native Tribes of the Northern Territory of Australia*, 1912; *The Northern Tribes at Central Australia*, ca. 1901; *Native Tribes of Central Australia*, w/Frank Gillen, 1899.

COLLECTIONS In Australia: Natl. Mus. of Victoria; Royal Melbourne Inst. of Tech.; and many major museums in other countries.

Theodore Richard Spiegel PHOTOJOURNALIST Born June 15, 1934, in Newark, New Jersey, Spiegel earned an AB in 1954 from Columbia College, Columbia University, New York City. He also took photojournalism workshops at the University of Missouri in Columbia in 1960 and 1962.

As of this writing Spiegel was a visiting professor to the faculties of Communications and Architecture at Virginia Polytechnic Institute, Blacksburg. He has been associated with the Black Star agency since 1973 and was previously with Rapho Guillumette Pictures (1960–72). In 1976 Spiegel was a guest lecturer at ICP in New York City, and he was a photographer for the State of Washington in 1959–60.

A member of ASMP, the photographer won First Place for Feature Picture Story in the 1970 Pictures of the Year Competition.

PUBLICATIONS Books: *Western Shores*, 1975; *Columbia*, 1974; *Golden Isles of the Caribbean*, 1973; *The Vikings*, 1973; *Great Religions*, 1971; *Renaissance*, 1970; *Australia*, 1968; *Isles of the Caribees*, 1967. Periodicals: "Hudson River," Jan 1978, "George Washington and Kansas City," July 1976, *National Geographic*.

REPRESENTATIVES Black Star, 450 Park Ave S, New York, NY 10022; John Hillelson, 145 Fleet St, London, England; Agence Rapho, 8 rue d'Alger, Paris, France.

ADDRESS RD#2, Box 353A, South Salem, NY 10590.

Sean Sprague PHOTOGRAPHER · WRITER · TEACHER Born January 18, 1947, in Cardiff, Wales, Great Britain, Sprague earned a BA in Photographic Arts from the Polytechnic of Central London and a Teaching Certificate from Garnet College, London.

Currently a freelance photographer, he works for such organizations as Christian Aid International, Planned Parenthood Federation, Save the Children Fund, Action in Distress, Catholic Relief Services and Catholic Fund for Overseas Development.

A member of the National Union of Journalists in Great Britain, Sprague received an Arts Council of Great Britain grant in 1973 to photograph industrial landscapes in Britain.

Sprague is mainly a travel photographer, emphasizing development in third-world countries. His photojournalism includes images related to health, education, family planning, agriculture, industry and employment. He also maintains a library of some 50,000 photographs, available to researchers.

PUBLICATIONS Book: *Bali*, 1970. Periodicals:

"Samuel Bourne, photographer of India in the 1860s," Jan 1977, "Egerton in Spiti," Apr 1977, *British Journal of Photography*.

ADDRESS POB 290, Philo, CA 95466.

Bernhard J. Springer PHOTOGRAPHER · PUBLISHER · PAINTER Born February 16, 1907, in Germany, Springer died December 26, 1970, in New York. He studied law at the University of Göttingen, Germany. Self-taught as a photographer, he was influenced by famous photographers of the 1920s and 1930s. His father was a prominent German publisher, his mother an artist.

Springer came to the United States in 1937 and pursued his art. He established the Springer Publishing Company in New York in 1950.

Besides photography, the artist also painted in watercolor and acrylics and sculpted in wood, using an abstract style for both.

In his photography, Springer's major concerns were "visual beauty in nature, in architecture, in everyday objects, in the effects of shadow and light," writes his wife, Ursula, who has continued the publishing company.

PUBLICATION Monograph: *Shadow and Light*, 1975.

ARCHIVE Springer Publishing Co, 200 Park Ave S, New York, NY 10003.

Edward Wesley Stacey PHOTOGRAPHER Born February 10, 1949, in Sydney, Australia, Stacey attended design and drawing classes from 1959 to 1961 and sculpture classes from 1961 to 1963 in Sydney.

A freelance photographer since 1967, he previously worked as a graphics designer and photographer for television from 1964 to 1967.

Stacey was the founder of the Australian Centre for Photography, and is a member of the Australian Society of Authors. In 1973 he received the Silver Award from the Art Directors Club of Melbourne, Australia.

Working with small and medium format, and panoramic cameras, the photographer chooses as his main subjects landscape, environment, conservation and architecture.

PUBLICATIONS Books: *Mumbulla—Spiritual Contact*, 1980 (Australian National University); *Timeless Gardens*, 1977 (Pioneer Design Studio); *The Artist Craftsman in Australia*, 1973 (Pollard); *Historic Towns of Australia*, 1972 (Lansdowne); *The Australian Homestead*, 1971 (Lansdowne); *Rude Timber Buildings in Australia*, 1969 (Thames & Hudson).

COLLECTIONS In Australia: Australian Centre for Photography, Sydney; Natl. Gall., Canberra;

Natl. Gall. of New South Wales, Sydney; Natl. Gall. of Victoria; Philip Morris Cllctn.

DEALER Christine Godden, Australian Centre for Photography, Paddington, New South Wales 2021, Australia.

ADDRESS POB 4, Bermagui S, New South Wales, 2547 Australia.

Peter Stackpole PHOTOJOURNALIST Stackpole was born in San Francisco on June 15, 1913. His early mentor was Willard Van Dyke of the Group f.64. His father, Ralph Stackpole (1885–1973), was a sculptor, and his mother, Adele Stackpole (1885–1979), an artist.

Along with Alfred Eisenstaedt, Peter Stackpole was one of the first *Life* staff photographers, working for that magazine and Time Inc., from 1936 to 1960. He also wrote a column called "35mm Techniques" for *U.S. Camera* for fifteen years. The photographer covered the invasion of Saipan in 1945 as a war correspondent.

A member of the Circle of Confusion in New York City, Stackpole invented and built underwater equipment for still and movie photography between the years 1941 and 1974.

Working in various formats from 35mm to 4 x 5, the photographer was a pioneer in the development of U.S. photojournalism. His main subject concerns are people in relation to their environment.

COLLECTIONS Oakland Mus., Calif.; San Francisco Mus. of Mod. Art; Univ. of Calif., Bancroft Lib., Berkeley; Univ. of N. Mex., Albuquerque.

ADDRESS 1 Taurus Ave, Oakland, CA 94611.

Charles Stainback PHOTOGRAPHER · CURATOR Born July 12, 1952, in Somerville, Tennessee, Stainback received a BFA in 1974 from the Kansas City Art Institute, Missouri, and an MFA in 1979 from the Visual Studies Workshop, Rochester, New York, where he studied with Nathan Lyons.

The Director of Exhibitions at VSW since 1977, he served as the workshop's exhibitions preparator in 1976–77. Stainback was a teaching assistant at Kansas City Art Institute in 1974–75.

A member of SPE and the American Association of Museums, the photographer won a CAPS grant in 1978.

PUBLICATIONS Catalog: *Attitudes: Photography in the 1970's*, 1979 (Santa Barbara Mus. of Art, Calif.). Periodicals: *Modern Photography*, Apr 1980; *35mm Photography*, Sept 1977; *Popular Photography Annual*, 1976; *Camera*, Aug 1976.

COLLECTIONS Colgate Univ., Hamilton, N.Y.; VSW, Rochester, N.Y.

REPRESENTATIVE Richard Link Photography, Ltd., 225 W 20 St, New York NY 10011.

ADDRESS 246 Cedarwood Terr, Rochester, NY 14609.

Eric Staller PHOTOGRAPHER Born in Mineola, New York, in 1947, Staller earned a Bachelor of Architecture degree from the University of Michigan, Ann Arbor, in 1971.

A self-employed photographer, he won an NEA fellowship in 1977 and a CAPS grant in 1976. He has been an artist-in-residence at such schools as Maryland Institute College of Art, Baltimore; Coe College, Cedar Rapids, Iowa; and the University of Michigan.

His photographs capture the movement of light created by the photographer and his materials. Working mainly in color, he uses lengthy exposures (2–15 minutes) and has "animated 2- and 3-dimensional light constructions in space."

PUBLICATIONS Anthology: *A Book of Photographs*, The Sam Wagstaff Cllctn., 1978 (Gray Press). Periodicals: *American Photographer*, Jan 1980, Apr 1979; *Arts Magazine*, May 1975, Mar 1974; *Artforum*, Mar 1974.

COLLECTIONS Everson Mus. of Art, Syracuse, N.Y.; Hamilton Coll., Clinton, N.Y.; IMP/GEH, Rochester; ICP, NYC; Madison Art Ctr., Wisc.; MOMA, NYC.

ADDRESS 31 Walker St, New York, NY 10013.

Jan Evan Staller PHOTOGRAPHER Born May 27, 1952, in Mineola, New York, Staller received a BFA from the Maryland Institute in Baltimore in 1975.

Staller belongs to ASMP. In 1980 he received an NEA grant.

A freelance photographer, he shoots architecture, people, record album covers, and does various corporate photographic assignments. Using medium format, the photographer works in color, his main subjects being cityscapes, architecture and constructed objects.

PUBLICATIONS Anthology: *Time-Life Photography Annual 1979*. Periodicals: *Art Forum*, Mar 1980; *Popular Photography Color Annual*, 1980; *Popular Photography*, Sept 1979, Oct 1978.

COLLECTIONS Chase Manhattan Art Cllctn., NYC; Corcoran Gall., Wash., D.C.; Metro. Mus. of Art, NYC; Seagrams Cllctn., NYC.

DEALER Castelli Graphics, 4 E 77 St, New York, NY 10021.

ADDRESS 37 Walker St, New York, NY 10013.

Simon Stampfer *PHYSICIST* Born in the Tyrol, Austria, in 1792, Stampfer died in 1864.

A professor of practical physics at the Polytechnic Institute in Vienna in 1832, the scientist invented the "Wheel of Life," or, as he called it, the stroboscope. Concurrently but independently, Joseph Plateau of Belgium invented the similar phenakistoscope. Both devices placed serial images around the periphery of a disc; the images were reflected off a mirror and through slits in the disc and appeared to move as the disc revolved. Stampfer's device was patented in Austria on May 7, 1833, and he licensed a Vienna print shop to sell his "Optical Magic Disc." The independence of his discovery from Plateau's was verified by Poggendorf in 1834. Stampfer later improved on his invention by using two different discs and no mirror.

Unlike Plateau, Stampfer never realized the motion picture possibilities of his invention, but he is given credit for a major contribution in the development of modern cinematography.

PUBLICATIONS Books: *Der Weg des Films*, F. von Zglinicki, 1956; *Magic Shadows*, Martin Quigley, Jr., 1948; *Histoire du Cinématographie*, G. Michel Coissac, 1925; *Almanach der Kaiserlichen Akademie der Wissenschaft*, 1865 (Wien); *Annalen der Physik und Chemie*, Poggendorf, 1834. Anthology: *Photography's Great Inventors*, Louis W. Sipley, 1965. Periodical: *Bild und Ton*, 1952.

Ron Stark *PHOTOGRAPHER* Born June 27, 1944, in Sidney, New York, Stark studied with Minor White from 1962 to 1971.

A freelance photographer, he won a Virginia Museum of Art grant in 1974.

Stark produces 8 x 10 format still lifes of food, and gum prints of nudes.

PUBLICATIONS Book: *Delicacies*, 1978. Periodicals: *Camera*, Sept 1975, Nov 1973; *Popular Photography*, June 1974; *Profil*, Sept 1973; *Art Gallery*, Apr 1973.

COLLECTIONS Baltimore Mus., Md.; Beaumont Newhall Cllctn., Albuquerque, N. Mex.; Corcoran Gall. of Art, Wash., D.C.; Smithsonian Inst., Wash., D.C. Bibliothèque Nationale, Paris.

ADDRESS 6048½ Ramshorn Pl, McLean, VA 22101.

Ron Starr *PHOTOGRAPHER* Born May 25, 1947, in Cambridge, Massachusetts, Starr received a BA in Liberal Arts from Boston University (Massachusetts) in 1969. He studied with Pirkle Jones in 1972 and with Oliver Gagliani in 1976.

Since 1977 Starr has been workshop instructor at St. Mary's Art Center, Virginia City, Nevada. From 1972 to 1977 he did freelance photography, and in 1970–71 was a darkroom staff member at Center of the Eye in Aspen, Colorado.

PUBLICATION Anthology: *Octave of Prayer*, 1972.

COLLECTIONS Goddard Coll., Plainfield, Vt.; MIT, Hayden Gall., Cambridge, Mass.; Stanford Univ. Mus. of Art, Stanford, Calif.; Univ. of Calif. Art Mus., Berkeley. Victoria & Albert Mus., London.

DEALERS Silver Image Gall., 83 S Washington St, Seattle, WA 98104; Jeb Gall., 342 S Main St, Providence, RI 02901.

ADDRESSES 414 Seaside St, Santa Cruz, CA 95060; 19 Ardmore Rd, Scarsdale, NY 10585.

Randall States *PHOTOGRAPHER* Born May 31, 1955, in Boston, Massachusetts, States received his BFA in 1976 from Rochester Institute of Technology, New York, and his MFA in 1979 from Pratt Institute, Brooklyn, New York.

Currently a freelance, the photographer was a research assistant and writer for PhotoCollect gallery in New York City in 1979 and assistant to the curator of the New York Museum of Transportation in New York City from 1975 to 1978, of which museum he is an honorary life member.

He belongs to George Eastman House, CAA and SPE.

In September 1975 States designed and built a 4 x 12-foot-format portable camera. The achievement was noted in the October 1976 *Popular Photography*.

States works in color, emphasizing high-contrast lighting in landscape.

PUBLICATIONS Periodicals: *Photocollect Newsletter*, text only, Apr & May 1979; *Color Photography*, 1978; *Popular Photography*, Oct 1977.

COLLECTIONS N.Y. Mus. of Transportation, NYC; Pratt Inst., Brooklyn, N.Y.; Rochester Inst. of Technology, N.Y.

ADDRESS 331 Sackett St, #2L, Brooklyn, NY 11231.

Pavel Štecha *PHOTOGRAPHER · TEACHER* Born December 20, 1944, in Prague, Czechoslovakia, Štecha attended the Film Faculty of the Academy of Music Arts (FAMU) in Prague from 1967 to 1971. His mentors were Dr. Anna Fárová and Professor Ján Šmok.

In 1977 Štecha was a senior lecturer at FAMU in Prague; he had been an assistant lecturer there in 1975. He previously worked as a freelance photographer (1971–74).

He has been a member of the Union of Czech Artists' photography department since 1971. In 1968 he was recipient of the Youth Photography International Prize at Photokina in Cologne, Germany.

PUBLICATIONS Periodicals: *Camera*, July 1980; *Revue fotografiel*, Apr 1977; *Čs. fotografie*, June 1975, July 1974; *Creative Camera*, Nov 1973; "The Automobile," *OVO* Magazine, no. 30/31.

COLLECTION Mus. of Applied Art, Prague, Czechoslovakia.

ADDRESS Navrátilova 2, 110 00 Prague I, Czechoslovakia.

Christopher Steele-Perkins   PHOTOGRAPHER
Born July 28, 1947, in Burma, Steele-Perkins received a BSc in Psychology from Newcastle University, England.

A freelance photojournalist, Steele-Perkins was a lecturer at Polytechnic of Central London, England, in 1977–78.

The photographer has belonged to the National Union of Journalists since 1974 and was on the Photography Committee of the Arts Council of Great Britain from 1976 to 1979.

Steele-Perkins made the film *Harry* in 1972.

PUBLICATIONS Book: *The Teds*, w/Richard Smith, 1979 (London). Periodicals: *Photo*, 1978; *Creative Camera*, 1976.

COLLECTIONS Bibliothèque Nationale, Paris; Victoria & Albert Mus., London.

ADDRESS 5 Homer House, Rushcroft Rd, London SW2, England.

Edward Steichen   PHOTOGRAPHER · CURATOR ·
PAINTER · HORTICULTURIST   Born March 27, 1879, in Luxembourg and named Eduard Jean Steichen, he died March 25, 1973, in West Redding, Connecticut. The poet Carl Sandburg (1878–1967) was his brother-in-law, and his daughter, Mary Steichen Calderone (1904–   ), is a leading exponent of family planning and sex education.

The Steichen family moved to Hancock, Michigan, in 1882, and young Steichen was apprenticed as a designer to a commercial lithographic company in Milwaukee, Wisconsin, in 1894. Winning a prize for envelope design in 1897, he also studied painting in Milwaukee and organized the Milwaukee Art Students' League. Steichen learned photography from a local photographer and took his first photo in 1896. He was strongly influenced by Stieglitz around 1902,

and continued his painting studies in Paris in 1910.

Involved with the Little Galleries of the Photo-Secession ("291"), Steichen arranged exhibitions of many of the French avant-garde artists, beginning in 1905. He also designed galleries as well as the cover and typography for the Photo-Secessionists' quarterly, *Camera Work*. During World War I he commanded the Photographic Division of Aerial Photography in the American Expeditionary Forces, retiring as a lieutenant colonel in 1918. Steichen then operated a commercial studio in New York City from 1923 to 1938, during which time he became chief photographer for Condé Nast, his work appearing frequently in the pages of *Vogue* and *Vanity Fair*. He had earlier published his photos in *Art and Decoration* and, later, *Sketch*.

In 1942 he was commissioned as lieutenant commander in the U.S. Navy to organize a department to photograph the war at sea. Two exhibits resulted: "Road to Victory" in 1941 and "Power in the Pacific" in 1944, and Steichen retired with the rank of captain. He served as director of photography at the Museum of Modern Art from 1947 to 1962, during which time he curated the famed "Family of Man" exhibit (1955).

A member of The Linked Ring as of 1901, Steichen co-founded the Photo-Secession in 1902 and was named an Honorary Fellow of RPS in 1931. He won first prize in the 1903 Eastman Kodak Competition, the ribbon of Chevalier of the Legion of Honor from France in 1919, the Silver Medal from Annual Advertising Awards for Distinguished Service (1937), U.S. *Camera* Achievement Award for "Most Outstanding Contribution to Photography by an Individual" (1949), the Front Page Award from the Newspaper Guild for his "Family of Man" exhibit, a National Urban League award in 1955, the German Prize for Cultural Achievement in Photography from the Photographic Society of Germany (1960), the Silver Process Medal from RPS (1961) and John F. Kennedy's Presidential Medal of Freedom in 1963. He was also named to the ASMP honor roll in 1962, and was the first foreigner to receive an award from the Photographic Society of Japan.

Before the photographer relinquished his painting career, his canvases were exhibited in the United States and abroad. He was also a noted horticulturist. *Edward Steichen* (1958) and *This Is Edward Steichen* (1966) are black-and-white films about the artist.

Steichen's photographic work, which spanned a career of seventy-seven years, ranged from his early impressionistic and manipulated images to the straight documentary work of the war years. In between he was noted for fashion and advertising images as well as portraits of some of the most noted personalities and artists of his long lifetime. Additionally, his involvement as a curator helped promote photography to the status of art. In his earlier days Steichen produced platinum, palladium, gum-bichromate and pigment prints, but after the 1920s he worked chiefly with silver prints. He also made autochromes, Kodachrome transparencies and dye transfer prints.

PUBLICATIONS Monographs: *Edward Steichen*, 1978; *A Life in Photography*, w/bio. note by Grace Mayer, 1963; *Steichen the Photographer*, 1961; *Steichen the Photographer*, Carl Sandburg, 1929 (ltd. ed.). Books: *Edward Steichen*, intro. by Ruth Kelton, 1978; *Steichen: The Master Prints, 1895–1914. The Symbolist Period*, Dennis Longwell, 1978; *Alfred Stieglitz and the American Avant-Garde*, William Innes Homer, 1977; *Sandburg: Photographers View Carl Sandburg*, ed. & intro., 1966; *The History of Photography, from 1839 to the Present Day*, Beaumont Newhall, rev. ed., 1964; *The Bitter Years: 1935–1941. Rural America as Seen by the Photographers of the Farm Security Administration*, ed. 1962; *Photo-Secession—Photography as a Fine Art*, Robert Doty, 1960; "My Half-Century of Delphinium Breeding," *The Delphinium Society's Year Book*, 1959; *Once Upon a City*, Byron & Grace M. Mayer, foreword, 1958; *The Family of Man*, ed., 1955, repr. 1967; *The Blue Ghost: A Photographic Log and Personal Narrative of the Aircraft Carrier USS Lexington*, 1947; *U.S. Navy War Photographs: Pearl Harbor to Tokyo*, ed., 1946; *The Picture Garden Book and Gardener's Assistant*, Richard Pratt, 1942, repr. as *Gardens in Color*, 1944; *Walden, or Life in the Woods*, Henry David Thoreau, intro. by Henry S. Canby, 1936 (ltd. ed.); *The First Picture Book: Everyday Things for Babies*, Marcy Steichen Martin, 1930; *Photography as a Fine Art*, Charles M. Caffin, 1901. Anthologies: *The Photograph Collector's Guide*, Lee D. Witkin & Barbara London, 1979; *Photography Rediscovered*, David Travis & Anne Kennedy, 1979; *The Collection of Alfred Stieglitz*, Weston J. Naef, 1978; *Pictorial Photography in Britain 1900–1920*, Arts Council of Great Britain, 1978; *The Valiant Knights of Daguerre . . . by Sadakichi Hartmann*, Harry W. Lawton & George Know, eds., 1978; *The Invented Eye*, Edward Lucie-Smith, 1975; *The Magic Image*, Cecil Beaton & Gail Buckland, 1975; *Photography Year 1974*, *Great Photographers*, 1971, *The Studio*, 1971; *The Great Themes*, 1970, *The Print*, 1970,

Time-Life Series; *Picture History of Photography*, Peter Pollack, rev. 1970; *Masters of Photography*, Beaumont & Nancy Newhall, 1969; *Photographers on Photography*, Nathan Lyons, ed., 1966; *Wisdom: Conversations with the Elder Wise Men of Our Day*, James Nelson, ed., 1958; *America as Americans See It*, Fred J. Ringel, ed., ca. 1932. Periodicals: "Eduard Steichen as Painter and Photographer, 1897–1908," William Innes Homer, *American Art Journal*, Nov 1974; " 'De Lawd' of Modern Photography," Gilbert Millstein, *N.Y. Times Magazine*, Mar 22, 1959; *U.S. Camera*, Tom Maloney, ed., 1956; "The New Selective Lens," *Artnews*, Sept 1950; "The Fighting Photo-Secession," *Vogue*, June 15, 1941; "American Aerial Photography at the Front," *Camera*, July 1919; Oct 1913, Apr-July 1913, Apr-July 1911, Apr 1908, July 1907, July 1906, Apr 1906 (special Steichen supp.), Jan 1906, July 1905, Jan 1905, July 1904, Apr 1903, *Camera Work*; *Camera Notes*, 1897–1903, passim.

COLLECTIONS Art Inst. of Chicago; IMP/GEH, Rochester; L/C, Wash., D.C.; Metro. Mus. of Art, NYC; MOMA, NYC; New Orleans Mus. of Art. RPS, London.

Carla Steiger-Meister PHOTOGRAPHER · TEACHER Born March 27, 1951, in Chicago, Illinois, Steiger-Meister received a BA in Art History and Studio Arts from Oberlin College, Ohio, in 1974 and an MFA in Photography from the University of Minnesota, Minneapolis, in 1977. She names Gary Hallman and Kelly Wise as major influences.

As of this writing Steiger-Meister was a photography instructor for Continuing Education at Indiana University at South Bend. She was a visiting artist at Wright State University, Dayton, Ohio, in 1979. From 1977 to 1978 Steiger-Meister was assistant professor of photography at Kenyon College, Gambier, Ohio, and from 1975 to 1977 served as teaching assistant and lab manager in photography at the University of Minnesota. In 1974 she was a photographer and researcher for the *San Francisco Bay Guardian*.

The photographer won "Best in Show" at the 1977 North Shore Art League Photo Festival.

"I photograph small assemblages of old postcards, photos, flowers, ribbons and assorted bits that form dreamlike scenarios," she says. "The images are in color and conceptually relate to surrealistic painting of the 1920s and 1930s."

PUBLICATIONS Catalogs: *Photo-Art Processes*, Nancy Howell-Koehler, 1979; *130 Years of Ohio Photography*, 1978 (Columbus Gall. of Fine Arts, Oh.).

COLLECTIONS Corcoran Gall., Wash., D.C.; IMP/GEH, Rochester; K-Mart Corp., Troy, Mich.; Minneapolis Inst. of Art, Minn.; NDR Investments, Chicago, Ill.

DEALER Dobrick Gall., 216 E Ontario, Chicago, IL 60611.

ADDRESS 1721 E Jackson, Elkhart, IN 46514.

Harvey Stein PHOTOGRAPHER Born April 19, 1941, in Pittsburgh, Pennsylvania, Stein received a BS in 1962 from Carnegie-Mellon University in Pittsburgh and earned an MBA from Columbia University, New York, in 1968.

He has been an instructor of photography at the International Center of Photography in New York City since 1976.

A member of SPE since 1978, Stein is also a member of the American Society of Picture Professionals.

Stein works "within the documentary tradition, concentrating on producing extended photographic essays."

PUBLICATIONS Monograph: *Parallels: A Look at Twins*, 1979. Periodicals: *International Photography*, fall/winter 1979; *Camera 35*, Nov 1977; *Camera Magazine Quarterly*, summer 1977; *Popular Photography's 35mm Photography*, spring 1977; *Modern Photography*, May 1974; *Camera 35*, July/Aug 1973; *Print Magazine*, May/June 1973.

COLLECTIONS Addison Gall. of American Art, Andover, Mass.; Art Inst. of Chicago; Catskill Ctr. of Photography, Woodstock, N.Y.; Commodities Corp. Photography Cllctn., Princeton, N.J.; Exchange Natl. Bank, Chicago; Floating Fndn. of Photography, NYC; ICP, NYC; MIT, Cambridge, Mass.

REPRESENTATIVE Black Star Photography Agency, 450 Park Ave S, New York, NY 10016.

DEALER O. K. Harris Works of Art, 383 W Broadway, New York, NY 10016.

ADDRESS 41 W 74 St, New York, NY 10023.

Claire James Steinberg PHOTOGRAPHER · WRITER · TEACHER Born August 15, 1942, in Newport News, Virginia, Steinberg earned a BA in Art from University of California at Los Angeles in 1965.

As of this writing Steinberg was a writer for *Darkroom* magazine. She has been a freelance photographer, writer and teacher since 1972. She was a curator for the Craft and Folk Art Museum in Los Angeles in 1976 and picture editor for *Popular Photography* magazine and its annuals in 1969–71.

Steinberg has been vice-president of the West Coast chapter of ASMP since 1978.

The photographer works in photojournalism, portraiture and sequential images.

PUBLICATIONS Book: *Psychology & Human Experience*, 1974. Periodicals: "Steinberg's Peripatetic Eye," *Artweek*, June 14, 1975; "Alexi Brodovitch," *Popular Photography Annual*, 1972.

COLLECTIONS Los Angeles County Mus. of Art; Muckenthaler Mus., Fullerton, Calif. Paris Mus. of Modern Art, France.

ADDRESS 10434 Corfu Lane, Los Angeles, CA 90024.

Ralph Steiner PHOTOGRAPHER · EDITOR · WRITER · FILM MAKER [See plate 100] Born February 8, 1899, in Cleveland, Ohio, Steiner received an AB from Dartmouth in Hanover, New Hampshire, in 1921. He also attended the Clarence H. White School of Photography in New York City in 1922.

Steiner was employed as a photographer at Ruder & Finn, Inc. (1960–62) and was director of advertising at Strong, Cobb, Arner (1962–64). He was also the editor of the Sunday Photographic Section of the newspaper *P.M.* (1939–41).

Steiner was the recipient of a Guggenheim Fellowship in 1974 and Vermont Council on the Arts/NEA grants in 1974 and 1969. He also won a grant from the Carnegie Foundation in 1969.

Working as cameraman, Steiner was involved with the film series *The Joy of Seeing*, 1967, and the films *Surf and Seaweed*, 1931, *Pie in the Sky*, 1934, *The Plow that Broke the Plains*, 1935, *The City*, 1939, and *H20*, an abstract study of the patterns of light and shadow on water, in 1929.

PUBLICATIONS Monograph: *A Point of View*, intro. by Willard Van Dyke, 1978. Book: *Dartmouth*, 1922. Anthologies: *The Photograph Collector's Guide*, Lee D. Witkin & Barbara London, 1979; *Photography Rediscovered*, David Travis & Anne Kennedy, 1979.

COLLECTIONS Dartmouth Coll., Hanover, N.H.; Milwaukee Art Ctr., Wisc.; MOMA, NYC; Univ. of Mass., Amherst; Worcester Mus. of Art, Mass.

DEALERS Prakapas Gall., 19 E 71 St, New York, NY 10021; Harcus-Krakow, 7 Newbury St, Boston, MA 02116; Stephen Wirtz, 228 Grant Ave, San Francisco, CA 94108.

ADDRESS POB 75, Thetford Hill, VT 05074.

Otto Steinert PHOTOGRAPHER · TEACHER · PHYSICIAN Born in July 12, 1915, in Saarbrücken, Germany, Steinert died in Essen, Germany, in 1978. He studied medicine at various universities

(1934–39), taking his final examinations and degree in Berlin, 1939, at the surgical clinic of Charité.

Steinert was a medical officer during the war, then practiced privately until 1948. During his studies and early career he pursued an interest in modern art and photography, initially making photographs to support his medical career. Eventually he was engaged as a photography teacher at the Staatlichen Schule für Kunst und Handwerk in Saarbrücken. In 1952 he became headmaster of the school, and in 1954 he was made a full professor. In 1959 Steinert accepted a professorship at the Folkwangschule für Gestaltung in Essen-Werden, where he remained until his death. Concurrently he taught classes at the University of Essen's Gesamtechschule.

Internationally exhibited since 1951, in that year Steinert mounted his innovative exhibit "Subjektive Fotografie," which launched his career and established him as a pacemaker in the field of art photography. Since that time and until his death he won numerous awards, among them the Médaille Davanne, an award of Société Française de Photographie (1965) and the Kulturpreis from DGPh (1962). A member of Société Française since 1949 and of DGPh since 1951, he also served on the board of directors of DGPh from 1954 till his death. A member also of GDL from 1957 on, he served as its chairman in 1963–74 and as a jury chairman in 1958–65. He was organizer of the well known group "fotoform" (1949) and its leader till 1955.

Steinert's work is known for its formalistic severity in a decided, overintensified scale of black-and-white tones. A master of photographic technique in all its variations, he used the heritage of Renger-Patzsch and Moholy-Nagy to create a new style "emancipated from formalism and without any false attitude; in this way he emphasized the subjective pretension of the photograph," wrote Paul Vogt in *Otto Steinert*.

PUBLICATIONS Books (ed.): *Das Gesicht der deutschen Industrie*, w/Albert Oeckl, 1968, *Begegnung mit dem Ruhrgebiet*, Jürgen Lodemann, 1967 (Econ: Düsseldorf/Vienna); *Ereignisse in Stahl. Ein Bildband*, w/Helmuth Odenhausen, 1965 (Stahleisen mbH: Düsseldorf); *Das Deutsche Lichtbild*, w/Wolf Strache, 1960 (Verlag DSB); *Subjektive Fotografie 2. Ein Bildband moderner Fotografie*, 1955, *Subjektive Fotografie. Ein Bildband moderner europäischer Fotografie*, 1952 (Brüder Auer: Bonn). Books: *La Photographie et l'Homme*, Jean A. Keim, 1971 (Castermann: Belgium); *Düsseldorf, ja, das ist unsere Stadt*, Friedrich Tamms, 1966 (Econ: Düs-

seldorf); *A Concise History of Photography*, Helmut Gernsheim, 1965; *The History of Photography*, Beaumont Newhall, 1964. Anthologies: *Deutsche Fotografie nach 1945*, 1979 (Fotoforum, Universität Kassel: Kassel); *The Magic Image*, Cecil Beaton & Gail Buckland, 1975. Catalogs: *Die Kalotypie in Frankreich*, 1966, *Kunstphotographie um 1900*, 1964 (Mus. Folkwang: Essen); *Otto Steinert und Schüler*, 1962 (Göppinger Galerie: Frankfurt); *Otto Steinert en Leerlingen*, 1959 (Stedelijk van Abbe-Mus.: Eindhoven; Stedelijk Mus.: Amsterdam); *Otto Steinert—der Initiator einer fotografischen Bewegung*, J. A. Schmoll, 1959 (Folkwangschule für Gestaltung: Essen). Periodicals: "Otto Steinert—Stilist und Pädagoge," Fritz Kempe, no. 4, 1975, "Subjektive Fotografie," no. 7, 1975, "Subjektive Fotografie," Robert d'Hooghe, no. 5, 1951, "Über die freieren Möglichkeiten der Fotografie," Franz Roh, no. 1, 1951, *Leica-Fotografie*; "60 Aniversario de Otto Steinert," Vincente del Amo, *Arte Fotografico*, Nov 1975; "Otto Steinert zum Sechzigsten," Bernd Lohse, *Color Foto*, no. 7, 1975; "Eine Schule namens Otto Steinert—zu seinem 60. Geburstag," Fritz Kempe, July 1975, "fotoform," Dr. Schmoll, Mar 1951, "Sprache der Linien und Formen," Dr. Scholl, Feb 1950, *Photo-Magazin*; "Subjektive Photographie," Heinrich Freytag, July 1975, "Otto Steinert," Oct 1968, "Subjektive Fotografie (3)—nach einem Gespräch mit Professor Dr. Steinert," Otto Toussaint, Mar 1959, "Das Selbstportrait in der modernen Photographie," Otto Toussaint, Oct 1958, "Die photographische Abteilung der Staatlichen Schule für Kunst und Handwerk, Saarbrücken," Mar 1954, "Gute Fotobücher," Aug 1952, "Subjektive Fotografie," Franz Roh, Oct 1951, *Camera*; "Eine Orgel, gesehen von Otto Steinert GDL," Hermann Speer, Apr 1969, "Welt als Wille und Vorstellung—über Otto Steinert," Robert d'Hooghe, June 1965, "Problematik fotografischer Ausstellungen," no. 11, 1951, *Foto Prisma*; "Fris Waargenomen," Dick Boer, Feb 1968, "De inzending fotoform," no. 20, 1950, *Focus*; "Otto Steinert et la subjective photographie," Jean-Claude Gautrand, *Photo-Ciné-Revue*, Apr 1966; "Otto Steinert I Uczniowie," *Fotografia*, no. 11, 1965; "Otto Steinert en Alfred Eisenstaedt reçoirent à deux important Prix Culturel de la DGPh," *Phototribune*, no. 11/12 1962; "La obra de Otto Steinert por primera vez en España," *Afal-foto cine*, entire issue, Oct 1961; "Otto Steinert," Italo Zannier, *ferrania*, no. 8, 1960; "Otto Steinert," Louis van Beurden, *Foto*, no. 12, 1969 (Doetinchem); "La Subjektive Fotografie à la Photokina de Cologne," Dec 1958, "Le groupe fotoform,"

Mar 1952, *Photo Cinéma*; "Hommage au Docteur Steinert," Daniel Masclet, *ciné/photo magazin*, Sept 1956; "La Subjektive Fotografie et l'école de Sarrebruck," P. Sonthonnax, Feb 1955, "Otto Steinert," P. Sonthonnax, Oct 1954, *Photo Monde*; "Staatliche Schule für Kunst und Handwerk," *Foto*, no. 9, 1954 (Stockholm); "l'art de la photographie," Léon Degand, *Art d'aujourd'hui*, Oct 1952; "Photographes Allemands, fotoform," André Thevent, *Photo France*, May 1951.

COLLECTIONS In Germany: DGPh, Cologne; Fotografische Sammlung, Mus. Folkwang, Essen.

Alice Steinhardt PHOTOGRAPHER Born February 9, 1950, Steinhardt received a BA in English in 1972 from Florida University, Miami.

A freelance, she won a scholarship from the International Center of Photography in 1975.

Steinhardt paints in oils on black-and-white photographs.

PUBLICATIONS Anthology: *Self-Portrayal*, James Alinder, 1978. Catalog: *Attitudes: Photography in the 70s*, Fred Parker, 1979 (Santa Barbara Mus. of Art: Calif.). Periodicals: "New Mexico: Work by Women Outside the Mainstream," Meridal Rubenstein, *Afterimage: VSW*, Oct 1979; "Color by Hand," Hank Pitcher, *Artweek*, May 13, 1978.

COLLECTIONS Atlantic Richfield Corp., Los Angeles; CCP, Tucson; Corcoran Gall. of Art, Wash., D.C.; Security Pacific Bank, Los Angeles.

DEALERS G. Ray Hawkins Gall., 7224 Melrose Ave, Los Angeles, CA 90046; Barbara Gladstone Gall., 38 E 57 St, New York, NY 10022.

Judith H. Steinhauser PHOTOGRAPHER · TEACHER Born December 19, 1941, in Niagara Falls, New York, Steinhauser earned a BS in Art Education in 1963 from the State University of New York, Buffalo, where she studied photography with Oscar Bailey. She received an MS in Photography in 1967 from the Institute of Design, Illinois Institute of Technology, Chicago, studying with Aaron Siskind.

A teacher at Moore College of Art, Philadelphia, Pennsylvania, since 1974, Steinhauser also worked for South Carolina Educational Television in 1975–76. She taught at the University of South Carolina, Columbia (1971–74), and at Rochester Institute of Technology, New York (1967–71).

The photographer won an NEA fellowship in 1973.

She generally works "in areas where color can be manipulated extensively and arbitrarily to suit interpretation," such as gum printing, cyanoprint and hand-coloring.

PUBLICATIONS Periodicals: *Popular Photography Annual*, 1980; *British Journal of Photography*, Mar 1971.

COLLECTIONS Los Angeles Ctr. for Photographic Studies; Smithsonian Inst., Wash., D.C.; S.C. Arts Comm., Columbia; Univ. of Colo., Denver. Natl. Gall. of Canada, Ottawa.

DEALER Paul Cava Gall., 1715 Spruce St, Philadelphia, PA 19103.

ADDRESS c/o Moore College of Art, Photography Dept, 20 & Race Sts, Philadelphia, PA 19103.

Carl August von Steinheil PHYSICIST · INVENTOR · OPTICS MANUFACTURER Born in 1801 in Rappoltsweiler, Alsace, Germany, Steinheil died in 1870. He studied under the mathematician Gauss at Göttingen and with the astronomer Bessels at Königsberg. His son Hugo Adolf was his business partner and was also an inventor and writer.

After completing his studies Steinheil moved to Munich, where he became professor of physics and mathematics at the University of Munich in 1832. Pursuing research into telescopes and optical calculations, he constructed a photographic camera in 1839 and began photographic experiments with fellow professor Franz von Kobell. After Daguerre's discovery, Steinheil built another camera and began making the first daguerreotypes in Germany. In 1839 he also made a miniature camera to handle 8 x 11mm daguerreotype plates. The physicist then established a workshop in Munich, where he constructed a telegraph apparatus used in a telegraph system he installed in Austria in 1849–50 and in Switzerland in 1851. In 1855, along with his son, he established the Optical Workshop of C. A. v. Steinheil in Munich, which later became C. A. Steinheil Söhne. For ten years the business chiefly handled optics for astronomy, but in 1865 the Steinheils obtained a patent for a distortion-free symmetrical Periskop lens for photography. In 1866, the year he transferred the company's ownership to his sons, he designed a miniature camera with a plate-changing device.

Steinheil is also credited with the idea of using the earth as a return conductor in telegraphy.

PUBLICATIONS Books: *Quellendarstellungen zur Geschichte der Fotografie*, Wolfgang Baier, 1964; *Die Photographische Kamera*, Joseph Stuper, 1962; *Carl August von Steinheil*, Rudolf Loher, 1939; *Lexikon für Photographie und Reproduktionstechnik*, G. H. Emmerich, 1910. Anthology: *Photography's Great Inventors*, Louis

W. Sipley, 1965. Periodicals: *British Journal of Photography*, 1965; *Image*, 1960, 1958; *Bild und Ton*, 1954, 1953, 1952, 1949; *Jahrbuch für Photographie und Reproduktionstechnik*, J. M. Eder, 1895; *Photographische Correspondenz*, 1867.

COLLECTION Deutsches Mus., Munich, Germany.

Hugo Adolf Steinheil *INVENTOR · OPTICS MANUFACTURER* Born in Germany in 1832, Steinheil died in 1893. His father was Carl August von Steinheil, a physicist, inventor and founder of the company of which Hugo Adolf eventually took charge.

Along with his father, Hugo Adolf helped establish the Optical Workshop of C. A. v. Steinheil in Munich in 1855, later known as C. A. Steinheil Söhne. For ten years the business was devoted chiefly to astronomical optics, but in 1865 Carl and Hugo patented a distortion-free symmetrical Periskop objective (lens) for photographic use. The younger Steinheil constructed an achromatic rectilinear Aplanat objective lens in 1866 and in that year took over the company from his father. He also constructed a wide-angle lens for cartographic work (1871), an Aplanat for celestial photography (1872) and an Antiplanat (1881).

PUBLICATIONS Books: *Quellendarstellungen zur Geschichte der Fotografie*, Wolfgang Baier, 1964; *Die Photographische Kamera*, Joseph Stuper, 1962; *Carl August von Steinheil*, Rudolf Loher, 1939; *Lexikon für Photographie und Reproduktionstechnik*, G. H. Emmerlich, 1910; *Handbuch der Angewandten Optik*, w/Ernst Voit, 1891. Anthology: *Photography's Great Inventors*, Louis W. Sipley, 1965. Periodicals: *British Journal of Photography*, 1965; *Image*, 1960, 1958; *Bild und Ton*, 1954, 1953, 1952, 1949; *Jahrbuch für Photographie und Reproduktionstechnik*, J. M. Eder, 1895; *Photographische Correspondenz*, 1867.

Richard Houston Steinmetz *TEACHER · PHOTOGRAPHER · SCREENPRINTER* Born on September 15, 1947, in Lincoln, Nebraska, Steinmetz studied with Jim Alinder, Ellen Landweber, Doug Prince, Jerry Uelsmann and Todd Walker. He received his MFA in Photography at the University of Florida, Gainesville (1978), and a BA in Sociology at the University of Nebraska, Lincoln (1972).

Steinmetz currently is an instructor of photography in Florida at Daytona Beach Community College and The Casements Cultural and Civic Center.

He is a member of SPE, Florida Professional Photographers, Hogtown Original Graphics Society and Daytona Beach Community College Photographic Society.

The artist works with a photo-screenprint process and nonsilver light-sensitive systems and processes.

PUBLICATIONS Catalogs: *Pharos '78*, 15:2, 1978 (Mus. of Fine Arts: St. Petersburg, Fla.); *Photographs*, 1977 (Sheldon Memorial Art Gall., Univ. of Nebr.: Lincoln.). Periodical: *Florida Quarterly*, 6:2, 1976.

PORTFOLIOS *Silkpurse III*, 1979, *Silkpurse II*, 1978, *Silkpurse I*, 1977 (Hogtown Original Graphics Society).

COLLECTIONS Carneby Lib., Alexandria, Minn.; Univ. Gall., Univ. of Central Florida, Orlando; Univ. Gall., Univ. of Florida, Gainesville; High Mus., Atlanta, Ga.; Mus. of Fine Art, St. Petersburg, Fla.; Art Bank, Univ. of South Florida, Tampa; Southern Graphics Council Archives, Univ. of Mississippi, Oxford.

ADDRESS 137 North Hollywood Ave, Daytona Beach, FL 32018.

Louis John Stellman *PHOTOGRAPHER · WRITER · HISTORIAN* Born January 6, 1877, in Baltimore, Maryland, Stellman died June 20, 1961, in Carmel, California. Educated at a private school in Baltimore and public schools in Pittsburgh, Pennsylvania, he was a disciple of Arnold Genthe. His wife, Edith Kinney Stellman (1877–1957), was a painter.

Stellman began work as a telegraph operator in the San Francisco, Los Angeles, Bakersfield and Mojave (California) areas. He worked as a theatrical press agent in Los Angeles in 1901, then as a reporter for the *Herald*, the *Times* and the *Examiner* in Los Angeles. In 1902 he went to work for the *San Francisco News*, first as a reporter, then as editor and coast manager. Stellman switched to the *San Francisco Post* in 1909 and later became an editorial writer for the *San Francisco Globe*. He wrote many features and pieces of fiction for English and American magazines, and in the early 1940s wrote a weekly column for the *Oberlin Times* (Ohio). He moved to Carmel in 1947.

Stellman belonged to the Padre Trails Camera Club in Carmel and the Writer's Club of London and joined the San Francisco Press Club in 1903. He served as its librarian in 1904 and 1907–1908.

A California historian who specialized in the San Francisco area, he wrote several books and numerous articles on the subject.

Stellman's photography served as an accompaniment to his prolific writings on San Francisco. His images provide glimpses of the waterfront, the hills and odd nooks and corners that only an intimate of the city could know. His Chinatown photographs are among the best collections of their kind.

PUBLICATIONS Books: *Images of Chinatown*, Richard Dillon, 1976; *Sam Branna, Builder of San Francisco*, 1954; *Mother Lode*, 1934; *Mate o'Dreams* (verse), 1931; *Pot o'Gold*, 1922; *That Was a Dream Worth Building*, 1916; *The Vanished Ruin Era*, 1910; *Said the Observer*, 1903.

COLLECTION Calif. State Lib., Sacramento.

Carl Ferdinand Stelzner PHOTOGRAPHER · PAINTER [See plate 2] Born about 1805 in Hamburg, Germany, Stelzner died there in 1894. He studied painting in Paris with Isabey and others.

Starting off his career as a miniature painter, he learned daguerreotypy in Paris. In collaboration with Hermann Biow, he took some of the earliest news photographs, covering the great Hamburg fire of 1842, for example. Together they worked in a specially built glasshouse. He eventually went blind from the fumes of silver iodide and mercury used in his darkroom work.

"His portraits were among the best done by daguerreotype process," writes Gail Buckland (*Magic Image*); "they display a great sense of composition, awareness of background and props, and naturalness in pose and expression."

PUBLICATIONS Anthologies: *The Invented Eye*, Edward Lucie-Smith, 1975; *The Magic Image*, Cecil Beaton & Gail Buckland, 1975; *Early Photographs & Early Photographers*, Oliver Mathews, 1973.

COLLECTIONS IMP/GEH, Rochester. Staatliche Landesbildstell, Hamburg, Germany.

Jaromir Joseph Stephany PHOTOGRAPHER · TEACHER Born March 23, 1930, in Rochester, New York, Stephany earned a BFA in 1958 from Rochester Institute of Technology and an MFA in 1960 from Indiana University, Bloomington.

He has taught at the University of Maryland, Baltimore County (in Catonsville), since 1973, and prior to that taught at Maryland Institute College of Art, Baltimore (1967–70).

Stephany has been chairman of the mid-Atlantic region of SPE since 1976.

Stephany says he is especially noted for his work in "cliché-verre, a synthetic printed on conventional photographic material."

PUBLICATION Book: *The Developing Image*, 1978.

COLLECTIONS Fine Arts Mus., St. Petersburg,

Fla.; IMP/GEH, Rochester; Univ. of Md., Baltimore County, Catonsville.

ADDRESS 786 Creekview Rd, Severna Park, MD 21146.

Joseph Sterling PHOTOGRAPHER Born November 5, 1936, in El Paso, Texas, Sterling received a BS (1959) and an MS (1962) in Photography from the Institute of Design, Illinois Institute of Technology, Chicago. He studied with Aaron Siskind, Harry Callahan and Frederick Sommer. He has been a freelance photographer since 1962.

Sterling belongs to ASMP.

In 1964 the photographer completed a documentary study of American adolescents, "The Age of Adolescence." His later work has been experimental, relating to motion.

PUBLICATIONS Anthologies: *The Family of Children*, 1977; *This Fabulous Century 50–60*, 1970; *Photography Yearbook*, 1967, 1966, 1965; *Photography in the Twentieth Century*, 1967; *The Photographer's Eye*, 1966. Periodicals: *Photography*, June 1964; *Aperture* 9:2, 1961.

COLLECTIONS Art Inst. of Chicago; IMP/GEH, Rochester; MOMA, NYC.

ADDRESS 2216 N Cleveland Ave, Chicago, IL 60614.

Jane Stern WRITER · PHOTOGRAPHER Born in New York City on October 24, 1946, Stern received a BFA in 1968 from Pratt Institute, Brooklyn, New York, and an MFA in 1971 from Yale University, New Haven, Connecticut. Her husband, Michael Stern, is a writer.

She is self-employed. Stern has belonged to Writers Guild East since 1975.

While primarily a writer, she combined words and photographs in her book *Trucker*, which documents the life of American truck drivers. She has also made two documentary films for WNBC-TV, *The Dirty Side* (1975) and *42nd Street* (1976).

PUBLICATIONS Monograph: *Trucker: A Portrait of the Last American Cowboy*, 1975. Books (w/Michael Stern): *Friendly Relations*, 1979; *Amazing America*, 1978; *Auto Ads*, 1978; *Roadfood*, 1978.

REPRESENTATIVE Sterling Lord Agency, 660 Madison Ave, New York, NY 10022.

ADDRESS POB 282, Wilton, CT 06897.

Robert E. von Sternberg PHOTOGRAPHER · TEACHER Born January 19, 1939, in Glendale, California, von Sternberg received a BA in 1965 and an MA in 1970 from California State University at Long Beach.

Since 1971 he has been assistant professor of art at California State University, Northridge. Prior to that he was a lecturer for University of California at Los Angeles Extension (1971–76) and chairman of the Department of Art at Santa Ana College in Santa Ana, California (1970–71).

Von Sternberg defines his work as being documentary, concerned primarily with social landscape and architecture, with an emphasis on natural light. He also works in gum-bichromate.

COLLECTIONS   Art Inst. of Chicago; Florida State Univ., Tallahassee; Harvard Univ., Cambridge, Mass.; IMP/GEH, Rochester; Los Angeles County Mus. of Art; Minneapolis Art Inst., Minn.; MOMA, NYC; Mus. of Fine Arts, Houston, Tex.; Oakland Mus. of Art, Calif.; Univ. of Ariz., Tucson; UCLA, Los Angeles; Univ. of N. Mex., Albuquerque.

ADDRESS   30375 Morning View Dr, Malibu, CA 90265.

Joel Peter Sternfeld   PHOTOGRAPHER · TEACHER   [See plate 144] Born June 30, 1944, in New York City, Sternfeld received an AB from Dartmouth College, Hanover, New Hampshire, in 1965.

He is currently assistant professor of photography at Stockton College, Pomona, New Jersey.

A member of SPE, the photographer won a Guggenheim Fellowship in 1978.

Using color, Sternfeld does 8 x 10 landscapes and small-format street photography.

PUBLICATIONS   Anthology: *One of a Kind, Recent Polaroid Photography*, 1979. Periodicals: *Modern Photography*, Mar 1980; *Camera*, Nov 1977.

COLLECTION   MOMA, NYC.

ADDRESS   35 Perry St, New York, NY 10014.

Carol Linda Stetser   PHOTOGRAPHER · PUBLISHER   Born April 11, 1948, in Syracuse, New York, Stetser majored in theater at Smith College, Northampton, Massachusetts, from 1966 to 1969, then earned a BS in Film at Emerson College, Boston, Massachusetts, in 1970. She names Buddhist meditation master Chogyam Trungpa as a major influence.

Stetser founded and is editor of Padma Press, Oatman, Arizona (since 1966).

She has belonged to the Women's Caucus for Art since 1978.

The photographer's black-and-white images "attempt to show how the personal and cosmic order are interwoven." She also uses SX-70 color to "celebrate the desert environment."

COLLECTIONS   IMP/GEH, Rochester; Metro. Mus. of Art, NYC.

ADDRESS   POB 56, Oatman, AZ 86433.

Louis J. Stettner   PHOTOGRAPHER · WRITER   Born November 7, 1924, Stettner attended the Institut des Hautes Etudes Cinématographiques in Paris, then received a BA in Photography and Cinematography at the University of Paris.

A columnist for *Camera 35* since 1971, he has been a freelance photographer for numerous U.S. and European publications since 1949. From 1973 to 1979 Stettner taught photography as professor of art at C. W. Post Center, Long Island University, New York. In 1972–73 he taught photography at the High School of Art and Design, Brooklyn College, Queensboro College and Cooper Union (all in the boroughs of New York City).

The photographer won first prize at the Pravda International Photography Contest in 1975 and received grants from the NEA in 1974 and CAPS in 1973. In 1956–57 he won two fellowships to work in photography at Yaddo in Saratoga Springs, New York.

Brassaï described Stettner's portraits of men and women as "majestically simple and sculptural, as if they had been poured in bronze."

PUBLICATIONS   Monographs: *Surletas*, 1979 (Cercle d'Art, Paris); *Paris Street Stories*, w/intro. by Brassaï, 1949 (Raymond Cogniat, Beaux Arts: Paris). Books: *Weegee*, ed., 1977; *History of the Nude in American Photography*, 1966; *35mm Photography*, 1956. Periodicals: Apr 1972, Nov 1951, Dec 1949, *Camera*; *Photography Annual*, Sept 1953; *American Photography*, Aug 1953; *Photography*, Apr 1953; *Foto*, Apr, Feb 1950 (Sweden).

PORTFOLIO   *Workers, 24 photographs*, intro. by Jacob Deschin, 1974.

COLLECTIONS   Dartmouth Coll., Hanover, N.H.; IMP/GEH, Rochester; MOMA, NYC. Bibliothèque Nationale, Paris.

ADDRESS   172 W 79 St, New York, NY 10024.

Craig Stevens   PHOTOGRAPHER · TEACHER   Born on October 7, 1947, in Ware, Massachusetts, Stevens received his MFA at Ohio University, Athens, in 1975. While there he studied with Don Williams and Arnold Gassan. He also studied with Emmett Gowin at Apeiron Workshops, Millerton, New York (1972). Stevens received his MA in Communications at Fairfield University, Connecticut, studying there with Ruppert Williams (1971). He received a BA in Sociology at Colby College, Waterville, Maine (1969).

Since 1975 Stevens has been an associate director/resident instructor at Maine Photographic Workshops in Rockport.

He is a member of SPE and Maine Visual Artists. He received a grant from the Augusta, Maine, NEA to photograph that area (1977).

The artist says that he is "currently working with wide-field panoramic cameras, concentrating upon the natural landscape, primarily in silver prints."

PUBLICATION Periodicals: *Popular Photography*, May 1980; *Popular Photography Quarterly*, fall 1979.

COLLECTIONS Univ. of Southern Maine, Portland; L/C, Wash., D.C.; Soho Photo Gall., NYC.

REPRESENTATIVE Maine Photo Workshop, Rockport, ME 04856.

ADDRESS POB 183, Rockport, ME 04856.

James Arthur Stewart *TEACHER · PHOTOGRAPHER · AUTHOR* Born July 30, 1920, in Bassett, Nebraska, Stewart received his BA from Chadron State College, Chadron, Nebraska, in 1942. He studied at University of California at Los Angeles and Pepperdine University, Los Angeles, in 1965–66.

A professor of vocational art at Los Angeles Trade-Technical College in California since 1964, Stewart freelanced as a photographer and writer in Los Angeles from 1949 to 1964. From 1947 to 1949 he taught at the Fred Archer School of Photography in Los Angeles, and in 1947 taught at Southwest Photo-Arts Institute, Dallas, Texas. He served as a photographic officer in the U.S. Navy from 1942 to 1947, worked as a photographer/reporter for the *Omaha World Herald* in 1940–42 and was employed by the Waldschmidt Studio in Chadron from 1935 to 1940.

Stewart holds memberships in many organizations: the International Society of Political Psychology, the Silver Dollar Club, Book Publicists of Southern California, NPPA and Professional Photographers of America. An executive board member of the American Federation of Teachers, he is also a past president (1968–69) of ASMP, was chairman of the Faculty Senate at Los Angeles Trade-Technical College in 1969–70 and was elected an Associate of RPS in 1948.

The photographer received the Burt Williams Award in 1976 from the NPPA, the George Washington Honor Medal in 1971 from the Freedoms Foundation at Valley Forge and was awarded the degree of Master of Photography by Professional Photographers of America in 1961.

Stewart has also served as an interviewer for the Oral History Department at UCLA since 1967, and was technical editor, columnist and book reviewer for *The Rangefinder* from 1967 to 1978.

His life work has been directed toward the education of young photographers and to "recording the memoirs of old-time photographers for posterity" through the Oral History Department at UCLA.

PUBLICATIONS *The Photographer's Answer Book*, 1978; *Commercial Photographic Lightings*, Charles Abel, photos & articles, 1977; *Beautiful California*, 1963.

COLLECTIONS Professional Photographers of America, Des Plaines, Ill. RPS, London.

ADDRESS 3116 Fernwood, Los Angeles, CA 90039.

Miloslav Stibor *TEACHER · PHOTOGRAPHER* Born July 11, 1927, in Olomouc, Czechoslovakia, Stibor received a Professor of Fine Arts degree (1951) and a Doctor of Fine Arts degree (1952) from Palacky's University in Olomouc.

Since 1960 he has been director of the Popular School of Art, and since 1969 has also been associate professor of photography at Palacky's University.

Stibor belongs to the Union of Czechoslovak Artists (since 1966) and the Union of Czechoslovak Photographers (since 1969).

The photographer specializes in images of historical monuments; Egyptian, Greek and Roman sculpture; and, especially, nudes.

PUBLICATIONS Monographs: *Foto na LŠU*, 1979 (SPN: Prague); *Akt aktuel*, 1971 (EHAPA: Stuttgart); *Akty*, 1967 (Orbis: Prague). Book: *Guide to Figure Photography*, 1969. Periodicals: *Modern Photography Annual*, 1971; *Foto Canada*, no. 1, 1967.

REPRESENTATIVE Czechoslovak Agency DILIA, Vyšehradská ul. Prague, Czechoslovakia 110 00.

ADDRESS K sídlišti 8, Olomouc, 772 00, Czechoslovakia.

Robert William Stiegler *PHOTOGRAPHER · TEACHER · FILM MAKER* Born July 30, 1938, in Chicago, Illinois, Stiegler received his BS (1960) and MS (1970) in Photography from the Institute of Design, Illinois Institute of Technology, Chicago. He studied with Aaron Siskind, Harry Callahan, Fredrick Sommer and Arthur Siegel.

Since 1966 Stiegler has been associate professor in the School of Art of the University of Illinois, Chicago.

He is a member of SPE.

In 1980 Stiegler won an NEA Photographer's Fellowship.

In addition to his photography he has made a number of films, including *Full Circle* (1968), *Licht Spiel* (1966) and *Capitulation* (1965).

PUBLICATIONS Catalogs: *Illinois Photographers Invitational*, 1979 (Northern Ill. Univ.: DeKalb); *70's Wide View*, 1978 (Northwestern Univ.: Evanston); *The Photographer and the City*, 1977 (Mus. of Contemporary Art: Chicago); *Portrait of America*, 1975 (Smithsonian Inst.: Wash., D.C.). Periodical: *Camera*, May 1976.

COLLECTIONS Art Inst. of Chicago; Belleville Area Coll., Ill.; IMP/GEH, Rochester; L/C, Wash., D.C.; MOMA, NYC; Mundelein Coll., Chicago; Mus. of Contemporary Art, Chicago; Norton Simon Mus. of Art, Pasadena, Calif.; St. Xavier Coll., Chicago; Southern Illinois Univ., Edwardsville.

ADDRESS 1245 Carmen, Chicago, IL 60640.

Alfred Stieglitz PHOTOGRAPHER · EDITOR · CURATOR · COLLECTOR [See plates 33 and 135] Born January 1, 1864, in Hoboken, New Jersey, Stieglitz died July 13, 1946, in New York City. He was married to the renowned painter Georgia O'Keeffe (born 1887). Stieglitz studied at the Realgymnasium, Karlsruhe, Germany, in 1881, then at the Technische Hoschschule, Berlin, in 1882, where he first majored in mechanical engineering. He transferred to photochemistry under the tutelage of Herr Vogel after buying his first camera in 1883. He completed his studies in 1890 and then returned to the United States. During his European studies he was especially influenced by the modernist painters Picasso, Matisse, Braque and others.

Stieglitz worked in the photoengraving business in New York City from 1890 to 1895, concurrently writing for *American Amateur Photographer* and later becoming its editor. In 1897 he founded and became editor of *Camera Notes*, the journal of the New York Camera Club, and in 1903 he founded *Camera Work*, the journal of the newly formed Photo-Secession, which he edited until 1917. With an assist from Edward Steichen, in 1905 Stieglitz organized The Little Galleries of the Photo-Secession—known as "291"—and ran them until 1917. He organized the famed International Exhibition of Pictorial Photography at the Albright Art Gallery in Buffalo in 1910 and sponsored as well as co-edited "291" in 1915–16. The photographer directed the Intimate Gallery in 1925–29, then directed An American Place (1929–46), which mainly showed paintings by American artists.

A member of the Society of Amateur Photographers in 1891 (which became the N.Y. Camera Club in 1897), Stieglitz was the first American to be elected to The Linked Ring (1894). With twelve others he established the Photo-Secession, serving as director, in 1902. He received more than 150 medals and awards, among them the Progress Medal of RPS (1924), Townsend Harris Medal (1927), Honorary Fellowship of the Photographic Society of America (1940) and P. H. Emerson Award (1887).

Often called the father of modern photography, Stieglitz "broke down the barriers against photography in American art museums.... Almost single-handedly he launched his country into the twentieth-century art world, not only in the field of photography but in painting and sculpture as well," according to Doris Bry. His own work, says Bry, "was characterized by constant technical innovations, which at the time were believed impossible to achieve"—such as taking photographs in the rain or at night. Known for his straight, unmanipulated style, Stieglitz nonetheless advocated experimentation by other artists. His subjects varied widely, the most notable being his series of cloud images ("equivalents") and his portraits of Georgia O'Keeffe.

PUBLICATIONS Monographs: *Georgia O'Keeffe by Alfred Stieglitz*, text by O'Keeffe, 1979; *Alfred Stieglitz, 1864–1946*, Dorothy Norman, 1976; *Alfred Stieglitz: An American Seer*, Dorothy Norman, 1973; *Alfred Stieglitz: Photographer*, Doris Bry, 1965; *Alfred Stieglitz: Introduction to an American Seer*, Dorothy Norman, 1960; *Stieglitz Memorial Portfolio 1864–1946*, Dorothy Norman, ed., 1947; *Picturesque Bits of New York and Other Studies*, 1898. Books: *Stieglitz and the Photo-Secession*, Helen Gee, 1978; *Alfred Stieglitz and the American Avant-Garde*, William Innes Homer, 1977; *The Hieroglyphics of a New Speech*, Bram Dijkistra, 1969; *Alfred Stieglitz Talking: 1925–31*, Herbert Jacob Seligmann, 1966; *History of an American. Alfred Stieglitz: '291' and After*, 1945; *America and Alfred Stieglitz*, Waldo Frank et al, eds., 1934, repr. w/intro. by Dorothy Norman, 1977. Anthologies: *The Photograph Collector's Guide*, Lee D. Witkin & Barbara London, 1979; *Photography Rediscovered*, David Travis & Anne Kennedy, 1979; *Pictorial Photography in Britain 1900–1920*, 1978; *The Valiant Knights of Daguerre ...*, Sadakichi Hartmann, Harry W. Lawton & George Know, eds., 1978; *The Invented Eye*, Edward Lucie-Smith, 1975; *The Magic Image*, Cecil Beaton & Gail Buckland, 1975; *Camera Work: A Critical Anthology*, Jonathan Green, 1973; *Early Photo-*

graphs & Early Photographers, Oliver Mathews, 1973; Great Photographers, 1971, The Print, 1971, Time-Life Series; Masters of Photography, Beaumont & Nancy Newhall, 1969; Photographers on Photography, Nathan Lyons, ed., 1966; Photo-Secession: Photography as a Fine Art, Robert Doty, 1960, rev. ed., 1978; The Picture History of Photography, Peter Pollack, 1958. Catalogs: Exhibition of Photographs by Alfred Stieglitz, Doris Bry, 1958 (Natl. Gall. of Art: Wash., D.C.); Catalogue of the Alfred Stieglitz Collection for Fisk University, 1949 (Fisk Univ.: Nashville, Tenn.). Periodicals: Aperture, 3:4, 1955, 8:1, 1960; "His Pictures Collected Him," Georgia O'Keeffe, New York Times Magazine, Dec 11, 1949; "An American Collection," The Philadelphia Art Bulletin, May 1945; "Stieglitz—Old Master of the Camera," Thomas Craven, Saturday Evening Post, Jan 8, 1944; Twice A Year: A Semi-Annual Journal of Literature, the Arts, and Civil Liberties, Dorothy Norman, ed., 16 issues, 1938–48, passim; "The Lessons of Photography," C. Lewis Hind, Photographic Journal, vol. 63, 1923; Camera Work, pub. & ed., 50 issues, 1903–17, passim; Camera Notes, ed., 1897–1902, passim; American Amateur Photographer, ed., 1891–96, passim.

COLLECTIONS Art Inst. of Chicago; Cleveland Mus. of Art, Ohio; IMP/GEH, Rochester; L/C, Wash., D.C.; Metro. Mus of Art, NYC; MOMA, NYC; Mus. of Fine Arts, Boston; Natl. Gall. of Art, Wash., D.C.; Philadelphia Mus. of Art, Pa.; Princeton Univ. Art Mus., N.J.; San Francisco Mus. of Modern Art; Univ. of N. Mex. Art Mus., Albuquerque; Yale Univ., Beinecke Rare Book & Ms. Lib., New Haven, Conn. RPS, London; and many private collections.

ARCHIVE National Gallery of Art, Washington, DC.

Siggen Stinessen PHOTOGRAPHER Born in Oslo, Norway, on August 22, 1942, Stinessen earned a BA in 1973 from the Department of Furniture and Interior Design of the Royal College of Art in Oslo. He is a self-taught photographer.

Stinessen has been freelancing since 1975; from 1974 to 1978 he worked at the Halogaland Theater in Tromsø, Norway.

A member of Forbundet Frie Fotografer (FFF), Stinessen received a Norwegian government guaranteed lifetime income for artists in 1977.

Working in a subjective documentary style and using both small and large format, the artist chooses subject matter ranging from landscape and portraits to architecture.

PUBLICATIONS Anthology: Photography Year,

Time-Life Series, 1979. Periodicals: Foto Zoom, May 1979 (Mexico); Nye Foto (Vidar Askeland), no. 4, 1976.

COLLECTIONS In Norway: Norsk Kulturråd, Oslo; Preus Fotomuseum, Horten; Tromsø University, Tromsø.

REPRESENTATIVE Robert Meyer, POB 48-Kuerner, N-Oslo 1, Norway.

ADDRESS N-8310, Kabelvag, Norway.

Dennis Stock PHOTOGRAPHER · FILM MAKER Born in New York City in 1928, Stock apprenticed with Gjon Mili from 1947 to 1951.

He has been a member of Magnum since 1951, and also produces and directs films through his company, Visual Objectives, Inc.

PUBLICATIONS Books: California Coastline, 1974; Road People, 1973; The Seasons, 1973; The Sun, 1973; Estuary—The Edge of Life, 1972; National Park Centennial Portfolio, 1972; The Alternative, 1970; California Trip, 1970; Gelebte Zukunft Franz Von Assisi, 1970 (C. J. Bucher: Switzerland), English ed., 1972; The Happy Year, 1963; Jazz Street, 1960; Portrait of a Young Man, James Dean, 1956 (Dadakowa Shoten: Japan).

REPRESENTATIVE Magnum Photos, Inc, 15 W 46 St, New York, NY 10036.

ADDRESS Rt 1, Box 331, Woodstock, NY 12498.

John Stockdale PHOTOGRAPHER · PAINTER · PHYSICIST Born March 15, 1936, in Ipswich, Australia, Stockdale received an MS in 1957 from the University of Sydney, Australia, and a PhD in 1969 from the University of Tennessee in Knoxville, Tennessee. In 1975 he studied photography at New York University in New York City with Will Faller.

Since 1966 Stockdale has been employed at the Oak Ridge National Laboratory in chemical physics and photography. Previously he worked for the Australian Atomic Energy Commission in health physics (1958–66).

He has been a member of the American Physical Society since 1964 and the Professional Staff Association of Oak Ridge National Laboratory since 1972. Stockdale received a Guggenheim Fellowship in painting in 1970, and has published approximately forty papers in chemical physics, obtaining one U.S. patent.

PUBLICATIONS Periodicals: 35mm Photography, winter 1979; Artweek, Mar 1977; Popular Photography, June 1977.

COLLECTIONS Corcoran Gall. of Art, Wash., D.C.; Hunter Mus. of Art, Chattanooga, Tenn.;

San Francisco Mus. of Modern Art; Univ. of Calif. at Berkeley.

DEALER O. K. Harris Gall., 383 W Broadway, New York, NY 10012.

ADDRESS 907 W Outer Dr, Oak Ridge, TN 37830.

Philip Grenfell Stokes *PHOTOGRAPHER · TEACHER* Born July 8, 1932, in West Bromwich, England, Stokes received a BEd in Fine Arts and Philosophy and a PhD from the University of Exeter, England.

As of this writing Stokes was lecturing in photography at Trent Polytechnic in Nottingham, England (since 1978), and worked from 1968 to 1970 as a self-employed photographer in Plymouth, England.

A member of SPE and the Association of Art Historians, Stokes won the 1961 Darlington Award for studies in telephotography.

His photographic work concentrates on portraiture and images of places and objects, while his academic research centers on "photographic communication as language and in relation to verbal language."

PUBLICATIONS Periodicals: *British Journal of Photography*, July 1980; "Walker Evans," *Creative Camera*, Nov 1977; "Language and Photography," June 4, 1976, May 28, 1976, *British Journal of Photography*.

ADDRESS 2, Ferngill Close, Castle View, Nottingham NG2 1LB, England.

Erika Stone *PHOTOJOURNALIST* Born June 29, 1924, in Frankfurt, Germany, Stone studied in the 1950s at City College of New York and at the University of Wisconsin, Madison (journalism and photography). She also studied with Berenice Abbott and later with George Tice at the New School for Social Research in New York City.

A freelance photojournalist and illustrator since 1961, Stone previously owned and was a partner in a picture agency, Photo-Representatives (1953–60), and was a photographer for European Picture Service (1947–53).

The photographer was a member of the Photo League during the 1940s, and currently belongs to ASMP, ASPP and Professional Women Photographers. She won awards in the *Popular Photography* contests of 1952 and 1953.

She works in a documentary mode. Her main subjects are people and "children of the world."

PUBLICATIONS Book: *The Life of Man*, 1973. Anthology: *Women Photograph Men*, Dannielle

B. Hayes, ed., 1977. Periodicals: *U.S. Camera Annual*, 1956, 1955, 1954, 1952.

COLLECTIONS ICP, NYC; Maine Mus. of Fine Arts, Portland.

DEALERS Tanglewood Gall., 148 E 89 St, New York, NY 10028; Nassau Gall., Nassau St, Princeton, NJ.

ADDRESS 327 E 82 St, New York, NY 10028.

Jim Stone *PHOTOGRAPHER · TEACHER · EDITOR* Born December 2, 1947, in Los Angeles, California, Stone received an SB in Architecture (1970) from the Massachusetts Institute of Technology, where he studied with Minor White. He then earned an MFA in Photography (1975) from the Rhode Island School of Design, Providence, where he studied with Harry Callahan and Aaron Siskind.

As of this writing Stone was teaching at Boston College, Chestnut Hill, Massachusetts (since 1973), and at the New England School of Photography, Boston (since 1978, and also in 1975–76). He has taught at the Rhode Island School of Design in 1976–78, at the Art Institute of Boston in 1974 and at the Cambridge Center for Adult Education from 1970 to 1979.

A member of SPE, he has served on its Northeast Region governing board since 1978. He also belongs to the Boston Photographic Resource Center. The photographer received an artist-in-residence grant from the Alaska State Council on the Arts in 1977 and a Photographer's Fellowship from The Artist's Foundation (Massachusetts Arts and Humanities Foundation) in 1976.

PUBLICATIONS Book: *Darkroom Dynamics*, ed., 1979. Anthology: *Art of the State/State of the Art*, 1978. Periodicals: *American Photographer*, Feb 1979; *Philadelphia Photo Review*, Nov 1978.

COLLECTIONS Corcoran Gall. of Art, Wash., D.C.; Harvard Univ., Fogg Art Mus., Cambridge, Mass.; IMP/GEH, Rochester; Lehigh Univ., Bethlehem, Pa. Polaroid Europa Cllctn., Amsterdam, The Netherlands.

DEALER Carl Siembab Gall., 162 Newbury St, Boston, MA 02116.

ADDRESS 124 Ashmont St, Dorchester, MA 02124.

John Benjamin Stone *PHOTOGRAPHER · BUSINESSMAN · POLITICIAN* Born in Birmingham, England, Stone lived from 1836 to 1914. He was educated at King Edward VI Grammar School in Birmingham. His hobby of collecting photographs led to his becoming a photographer.

With his father Stone directed Stone, Faundry

& Stone, glassmakers of Birmingham. He served on the Birmingham Town Council in 1869 and was elected a Member of Parliament for East Birmingham, serving from 1895 to 1909.

The photographer belonged to many scientific and photographic organizations of his day: Geological Society (1863), Royal Astronomical Society (1894), Royal Photographic Society (1905), Society of Antiquaries (1905) and Birmingham Photographic Society (for which he served as president, 1889–90). Most significantly, Stone founded the National Photographic Record (1897–1910), an organization whose sole purpose was to document and safekeep records of life in England. He was knighted in 1892.

Referring to himself as a "history photographer," Stone voluminously depicted the manners, customs and people of England, which can be seen in his 20–30,000 surviving images. He made platinum prints from gelatin dry plates.

PUBLICATIONS Monographs: *Sir Benjamin Stone, Photographer*, intro. by Barry Lane, 1974 (Arts Council of Great Britain: London); *Customs and Faces: Photographs of Sir Benjamin Stone*, Bill Jay, 1972 (St. Martin: London); *Sir Benjamin Stone's Pictures: Records of National Life and History*, 2 vols., 1966 (Cassell: London). Books: *Sir Benjamin Stone, 1838–1914, and the National Photographic Record Association, 1897–1910*, Colin Ford, 1974 (Natl. Portrait Gall.: London); *On the Great Highway*, 1892; *Children in Norway*, 1884; *Traveller's Joy* (play), 1883; *Summer Holiday in Spain*, 1877; *A Tour with Cook Through Spain*, 1873; *History of Litchfield Cathedral*, 1869. Anthologies: *The Photograph Collector's Guide*, Lee D. Witkin & Barbara London, 1979; *The Magic Image*, Cecil Beaton & Gail Buckland, 1975; *Early Photographs & Early Photographers*, Oliver Mathews, 1973; *Documentary Photography*, Time-Life Series, 1972. Periodical: "Sir Benjamin Stone," *Album*, no. 1, 1970.

COLLECTIONS In England: Birmingham Reference Lib.; British Mus., London; Natl. Portrait Gall., London; House of Commons Lib., London.

ARCHIVE Birmingham Reference Library, Birmingham, England.

Michael Stone PHOTOGRAPHER · TEACHER Born April 5, 1945, in Detroit, Michigan, Stone earned a BA (1967), MA (1970) and MFA (1971) from University of California at Los Angeles. His teachers included Pat O'Neill, Robert Heinecken, Robert Fichter and Lee Friedlander.

A visiting artist with the Washington State Cultural Enrichment Program as of this writing, Stone was an artist-in-the-schools for the Wash-

ington State Arts Commission, Olympia, in 1979 and from 1975 to 1977. He was also an artist-in-the-schools for the Oregon Arts Commission, Salem, in 1977–78. He taught photography at Silver Image Gallery Photography Workshops, Seattle, Washington (1977), Camera's Eye Workshop, Port Townsend, Washington (1975), and at Yakima Valley College Adult Education, Ellensburg, Washington (1974–77).

Stone received a commission from the Washington State Arts Commission in 1979 to produce a series of photographs for a Washington school district.

The photographer works with nonsilver processes, hand-coloring, and photo sculpture, and his "preconceived and sometimes conceptual imagery is generally playful and can be looked at as having an aspect of political satire or commentary."

PUBLICATIONS Books: *Photo Art Processes*, Nancy Howell Koehler, 1979; *Faces*, Jack Sellack, 1972. Catalogs: *Trends: Contemporary Photography*, 1979 (Santa Barbara Art Mus.: Calif.); *Photography: The Permanent Collection*, 1977 (Univ. of Nebr., Sheldon Mem. Art Gall.: Lincoln); *Everson Museum Art Bulletin*, 1977 (Syracuse: N.Y.); *Work in Three Dimensions: Nine Northwest Sculptors*, 1977 (Central Wash. Univ.: Ellensburg); *Continuum*, 1970 (Downey Art Mus.: Calif.); *California Photographers 1970*, 1970 (Univ. of Calif.: Davis); *Recent Acquisitions*, 1969 (Pasadena Art Mus.: Calif.). Periodicals: *Artweek*, Jan 1977, June 1971; *Arts in Virginia*, 1971; *Photomethods in Industry*, Feb 1971; *Photographic Business and Product News*, July 1970; *Artscanada*, June 1970.

COLLECTIONS Indianapolis Mus. of Art, Ind.; Norton Simon Mus. of Art, Pasadena, Calif.; UCLA, Frederick S. Wight Art Gall.; Univ. of Nebr, Sheldon Mem. Art Gall., Lincoln; Wash. State Arts Commission, Art in New State Bldgs., Olympia.

ADDRESS 305 W Fourth St, Cle Elum, WA 98922.

Lou Stouman PHOTOGRAPHER · FILM MAKER · TEACHER · WRITER [See plate 70] Born in 1917 in Springtown, Pennsylvania, Stouman earned a BA from Lehigh University in Bethlehem, Pennsylvania, in 1939. In 1950 he did graduate work at the University of Southern California in Los Angeles. His major influences have been Alfred Stieglitz, Edward Weston, Paul Strand, Robert Capa and Gene Smith.

A war correspondent during World War II, he served on the staff of *Yank*, the army magazine, and did freelance work for New York's *P.M.* magazine. After the war he worked as a freelance photographer and journalist. Since 1966 Stouman has also taught film production at UCLA where he is a full professor.

The photographer is a member of SPE, AMPAS and the Los Angeles Center for Photographic Studies. He has been the recipient of two Academy Awards, one in 1957 for the best short documentary, *The True Story of the Civil War*, the other in 1964 for the best documentary feature, *Black Fox*.

Stouman describes himself as a street photographer "fascinated in finding miraculous aspects of ordinary things."

PUBLICATIONS Monographs: *Ordinary Miracles*, 1981; *Can't Agree with Sunrise*, 1975. Anthology: *Family of Man*, 1955. Periodicals: *Aperture*, no. 81, 1978; *U.S. Camera Annual*, 1947.

COLLECTIONS CCP, Tucson, Az.; ICP, NYC; MOMA, NYC; UCLA Art Gallery. Jerusalem Museum, Israel; Natl. Gall. of Canada, Ottawa, Ontario.

REPRESENTATIVES West Gallery, Box 655, Carmel, CA 93921; Stephen White Gallery, 835 N La Cienega Blvd, Los Angeles, CA 90069; Witkin Gallery, Inc, 41 E 57th St., New York, NY 10022.

ADDRESS 12015 Coyne St, Los Angeles, CA 90049

Dr. Wolf Strache PHOTOGRAPHER · AUTHOR · EDITOR Born October 5, 1910, in Greifswald, Germany, Strache studied at the Universities of Munich and Cologne, Germany.

A freelance photojournalist since 1934, he edited the German photography annual *Das Deutsche Lichtbild* from 1955 to 1979.

Strache belongs to GDL, DGPh, Deutscher Journalisten-Verband and Bund Freischaffender Foto-Designer. In 1979 he won the DPGh Kulturpreis.

PUBLICATIONS Books (selected): *100 Jahre Porsche—im Spiegel der Zeitgeschichte*, ed., 1975; *Die Grosse Ernte*, ed., 1961; *Le Golfe de Naples*, 1958; *Steinhausen—ein Lobgesang in Bildern*, 1958; *Japan—Fernes Land*, ed., 1957; *Forms and Patterns in Nature*, 1956; *Schopferische Kamera*, 1953; *Aesthetik der Bildgestaltung*, 1948; *Verwandelte Antlitz*, 1947.

ADDRESS Landhausstrasse 59, D-7000 Stuttgart 1, West Germany.

Ken Straiton PHOTOGRAPHER · CARPENTER Born in Toronto, Ontario, Canada, on February 9,

1949, Straiton earned a BA in Psychology in 1972 from the University of Waterloo, Ontario. He also studied at Simon Fraser University Film Workshop, Vancouver, Canada, from 1974 to 1976.

In 1979 he taught photography at Emily Carr College of Art in Vancouver and worked as a production manager and designer for Integra Construction, Ltd.

He received a Canada Council grant in 1979 and an Ontario Arts Council Grant in 1977.

Straiton has made two 16mm films: *Point of Departure* (1976) and *Windows* (1974).

He works in a 35mm format in both black-and-white and color. His main subject matter is landscape that contains "emotional and formal concerns."

PUBLICATIONS Anthology: *SX-70 Art*, Ralph Gibson, ed., 1979. Periodicals: *British Journal of Photography Annual*, 1980; *The Photographer*, fall 1976.

COLLECTIONS Art Bank, Ottawa, Ont., Canada; Polaroid Corp. Internatl., Amsterdam, The Netherlands.

REPRESENTATIVE Helene Faggianato, 42 Ave de Saxe, 75007 Paris, France.

ADDRESS 3650 W First Ave, Vancouver, British Columbia, Canada.

Paul Strand PHOTOGRAPHER · CINEMATOGRAPHER · WRITER [See plate 86] Born October 16, 1890, in New York City, Strand died on March 31, 1976, in Oregeval, near Paris, France. He studied at Ethical Culture High School in New York City, where, in 1907, he learned photography from Lewis W. Hine. Strand was strongly influenced by Stieglitz as well as by Picasso, Cezanne, Braque and the other modern painters exhibited at gallery "291."

The photographer set up a commercial studio in 1909, then served in the Army Medical Corps from 1917 to 1920 as an X-ray technician and a medical-film camera operator. He was appointed chief photographer and cinematographer for the Secretariat of Education of Mexico in 1933–34, and in 1937 he established and headed Frontier Films, a nonprofit documentary film production company that operated until 1942. Strand frequently published articles on the works of such artists as Georgia O'Keeffe, John Marin and Gaston Lachaise. He moved to France in 1950, where he continued to pursue his still photography.

A member of the New York Camera Club (joined 1908), Strand was chairman of the Committee of Photography of the Independent Voters Committee of the Arts and Sciences for Roose-

Strand

velt in 1943. He won the David Octavius Hill Medal of the GDL in Germany in 1967, was named to the ASMP honor roll in 1963 and won a prize for his film *Native Land* at the Czechoslovakia Film Festival in 1949.

As a film maker, Strand supervised and photographed the film *Redes* (released in the U.S. as *The Wave*) for the Mexican government in 1935. His company, Frontier Films, produced *Native Land* in 1942, a civil-rights documentary that he photographed. He also operated the camera on Pare Lorentz' documentary *The Plow That Broke the Plains* in 1936 and worked with Leo Hurwitz on *Heart of Spain* in the late 1930s. Strand's first film effort was *Manhatta* (also called *New York the Magnificent*), which he made with Charles Sheeler in 1921.

In his still photography Strand pioneered the use of abstract forms and patterns, yet he always relied on the camera's objectivity and used only the purest photographic methods. Working with platinum, palladium and silver prints, he did work that evolved to a laudable purity and simplicity, achieving a new awareness of natural forms, machines and architecture.

PUBLICATIONS Monographs: *Paul Strand: Sixty Years of Photographs*, profile by Calvin Tomkins, 1976; *Paul Strand: A Retrospective Monograph*, in 1- and 2-vol. eds., 1971; *Paul Strand*, Frantisek Vrba, 1961 (Prague, Czechoslovakia); *Paul Strand: Photographs 1915–1945*, Nancy Newhall, 1945; *Photographs of Mexico*, intro. by Leo Hurwitz, 1940, repr. as *The Mexican Portfolio*, preface by David Alfaro Siqueiros, 1967; *Paul Strand*, Elizabeth McCausland, 1933 (pvt. prntg.). Books: *Ghana: An African Portrait*, Basil Davidson, 1975; *Living Egypt*, James Aldridge, 1969; *Tir a'Mhurain, Outer Hebrides*, Basil Davidson, 1962, U.S. ed., 1968; *Un Paese*, Cesare Zavattini, 1955 (Einaudi: Turin, Italy); *La France de Profil*, Claude Roy, 1952 (La Guilde du Livre: Lausanne, Switzerland); *Time in New England*, w/Nancy Newhall, 1950; "A Statement," *Photographs of People by Morris Engel*, 1939; "Alfred Stieglitz and a Machine," *America and Alfred Stieglitz*, Waldo Frank et al, eds., 1934. Anthologies: *The Photograph Collector's Guide*, Lee D. Witkin & Barbara London, 1979; *The Collection of Alfred Stieglitz*, Weston J. Naef, 1978; *Pictorial Photography in Britain 1900–1920*, Arts Council of Great Britain, 1978; *Photography Year 1977*, 1973, Time-Life Series; *The Magic Image*, Cecil Beaton & Gail Buckland, 1975; *Camera Work: A Critical Anthology*, Jonathan Green, ed., 1973; *Documentary Photography*, 1972, The Art of Photography, 1971, *Great Photographers*, 1971, *The Print*, 1970, Time-Life Series; *Octave of Prayer*, Minor White, 1972; *Masters of Photography*, Beaumont & Nancy Newhall, 1969; *Photographers on Photography*, Nathan Lyons, ed., 1966. Catalogs: *Paul Strand: A Retrospective Exhibition of His Photographs, 1915–1968*, 1976 (Natl. Portrait Gall.: London); *Paul Strand*, 1969 (L'Administration Générale des Affaires Culturelles Françaises: Brussels, Belgium); *Paul Strand*, foreword by Siegfried Huth, 1969 (Haus der Heimat Kreismuseum: Freital, Germany); *Paul Strand, New Photographs*, Gaston Lachaise, 1929 (Intimate Gall.:NYC). Periodicals: "Paul Strand," Ian Jeffrey, Mar/Apr 1976, "Painting & Photography," July 1963, *The Photographic Journal*; "Un humaniste militant Photographe et Cinéaste," Marcel Martin & Marion Michelle, *L'Ecran*, Mar 1975; "Profiles: Look to the Things Around You," Calvin Tomkins, *The New Yorker*, Sept 16, 1974; "Speaking Out: Strand Unraveled," July/Aug 1973, "A Day to Remember: Paul Strand Interview," Oct 1972, both by Lou Stettner, *Camera 35*; "L'oeuvre de Paul Strand," *Le Nouveau Photocinéma*, Oct 6, 1972; "Meditations Around Paul Strand," Hollis Frampton, *Artforum*, Feb 1972; "Paul Strand, Catalyst and Revealer," Aug 1969, "Paul Strand: A Commentary on His New York," Sept 1953, both by Beaumont & Nancy Newhall, *Modern Photography*; "Manuel Alvarez Bravo," 13:4, 1968, "Paul Strand/Tir a'Mhurain: Outer Hebrides," Robert Koch, 11:2, 1964, "Letters from France & Italy: Paul Strand," Beaumont & Nancy Newhall, 2:2, 1953, *Aperture*; "Viewpoint—Paul Strand at 76," Jacob Deschin, Mar 1967, "Stieglitz, an Appraisal," July 1947, *Popular Photography*; "Paul Strand Portfolio," Milton W. Brown, *Photography Year Book 1963*, 1962; "Paul Strand, Traveling Photographer," Beaumont Newhall, *Art in America*, winter 1962; *U.S. Camera Yearbook 1955*, 1954; "Paul Strand," Walter Rosenblum, *American Annual of Photography*, 1951; "International Congress of Cinema, Perugia," spring 1950, "A Platform for Artists," fall 1948, "Paul Strand Writes a Letter to a Young Photographer," fall 1948, "Address by Paul Strand," Jan 1948, "An American Exodus by Dorothea Lange and Paul S. Taylor," Mar/Apr 1940, *Photo Notes*; "Paul Strand," *American Artist*, Oct 1945; "Paul Strand," *American Photography*, Sept 1945; "Photography to Me," *Minicam Photography*, May 1945; "An American Photographer Does Propaganda Movie for Mexico," *Life*, May 10, 1937; "Photographs by Paul Strand," Harold

Clurman, *Creative Art*, Oct 1929; "The Art Motive in Photography," *British Journal of Photography*, Oct 5, 1923; "John Marin," *Art Review*, Jan 1922; "Our Illustrations," Alfred Stieglitz, June 1917, "Paul Strand in 'Straight' Photos," Charles Caffin, Oct 1916, *Camera Work*.

PORTFOLIOS *Portfolio I: On My Doorstep, 1914–1973, Portfolio II: The Garden,* 1957–67, both printed by Richard Benson, 1976 (Aperture/Michael Hoffman: Millerton, N.Y.).

COLLECTIONS Boston Mus. of Fine Art; CCP, Tucson; Harvard Univ., Fogg Art Mus., Cambridge, Mass.; IMP/GEH, Rochester; Metro. Mus. of Art, NYC; MOMA, NYC; New Orleans Mus. of Art; Norton Simon Mus. of Art, Pasadena, Calif.; Philadelphia Mus. of Art, Pa.; San Francisco Mus. of Modern Art; St. Petersburg Art Mus., Fla.; Univ. of N. Mex. Art Mus., Albuquerque; Yale Univ., Beinecke Rare Book & Ms. Lib., New Haven, Conn. Bibliothèque Nationale, Paris; Musée Réattu, Arles, France; Natl. Gall. of Canada, Ottawa.

ARCHIVE Center for Creative Photography, Univ. of Arizona, 843 E University Blvd, Tucson, AZ 85721.

Liselotte Strelow PHOTOGRAPHER Born September 11, 1908, in Pommern, Germany, Strelow was tutored at home and then studied agriculture. She learned photography in Berlin beginning in 1930, first in the Lette-Verein and then as a certified assistant to Suse Byk (1933).

In 1933 Strelow was hired as an apprentice with Kodak in Germany, receiving her master's certificate by examination in 1936. She established a studio in 1938 in Berlin and a second in 1943 in Pommern, but the war forced her to abandon both, and she lost all but an old Rolleiflex. In 1950 she moved to Düsseldorf, using it as a base from which she traveled and continued her photographic work. In 1969 she moved to Munich but gave up photography soon after when she was stricken with cancer.

Strelow has also been actively involved in writing and making television films.

Her technically simple, straightforward portraits are unique and appealing in their composition and use of light, and are often quite revealing of the subject.

PUBLICATIONS Monograph: *Liselotte Strelow: Porträts 1933–1972,* 1977. Anthology: *Deutsche Fotografie nach 1945,* 1979 (Fotoforum, Universität Kassel: Kassel, Germany).

REPRESENTATIVES Rudolf Habelt Verlag,

GmbH, Bonn, Germany; Rheinisches Landesmuseum, Bonn, Germany.

Mark Strizic PHOTOGRAPHER · TEACHER Born April 9, 1928, in Berlin, Germany, Strizic is a self-taught photographer.

A freelance since 1957, he has been lecturer in charge of photography at Melbourne State College, Australia, since 1978. He was a part-time lecturer from 1975 to 1978.

Strizic won an Australia Council Crafts Board Grant in 1979, first prizes in nature and industry in the 1967 Pacific Photographic Competition, and in 1964 was commissioned by the World Bank to photograph in Japan and Thailand.

Using small format, the photographer did early work that commented on "urban aspects from a formal and socio-economic view." He later focused on "broader environmental themes—mostly civilization's incursion." Strizic has developed methods of converting black-and-white to color and has been investigating image modifications and nonsilver sensitizing techniques.

PUBLICATIONS Books: *The Other Side of the Fence,* 1972; *Living in Australia,* Robin Boyd, 1970 (Pergamon Press); *Involvement,* Andrew Grimwade, 1968 (Sun Books); *2000 Weeks,* Tim Burstall & Patrick Ryan, 1968 (Sun Books); *Design,* Colin Barrie, 1963; *Melbourne—A Portrait,* David Saunders, 1960 (Georgian House).

COLLECTIONS In Australia: Australian Natl. Gall., Canberra; Australian Natl. Univ., Canberra; Melbourne State Coll.; Monash Univ., Melbourne; Natl. Bank of Australia; Natl. Gall. of Victoria; Philip Morris Cllctn., Melbourne; Univ. of Melbourne.

DEALER Church Street Photographic Centre, 384 Church St, Richmond 3121, Australia.

ADDRESS 9 Belvedere, Kew, 3101 Victoria, Australia.

Bruce Stromberg PHOTOGRAPHER Born July 7, 1944, in Philadelphia, Pennsylvania, Stromberg graduated from Philadelphia College of Art in 1968. He has been a freelance photojournalist since 1970.

Stromberg belongs to SPE. He won the gold medal from the Philadelphia Art Directors Club in 1978 and the Award of Excellence from *Communication Arts Magazine* in 1974.

PUBLICATIONS Periodicals: *Professional Photographer,* Feb 1978; *Philadelphia Photo Review,* Apr 1977; *Communication Arts Art Annual,* 1976.

COLLECTIONS In Philadelphia, Pa.: Balch Inst.;

First Pa. Bank; Philadelphia Lib. Bibliothèque Nationale, Paris.

DEALER Witkin Gall., 41 E 57 St, New York, NY 10022.

ADDRESS 1818 Spruce St, Philadelphia, PA 19103.

Amy J. Stromsten PHOTOGRAPHER · WRITER Born December 5, 1942, in Detroit, Michigan, Stromsten received a BA in 1963 from the University of Michigan, Ann Arbor, where she studied with Keith Waldrup and X. J. Kennedy. She received a certificate from Cooper Union School of Art in New York City in 1969 and took graduate seminars in the history of photography at Princeton University, Princeton, New Jersey, in 1975–76. Stromsten then received an MFA from Rutgers University, New Brunswick, New Jersey, in 1977.

She has been an assistant professor since 1977 at Douglass College and the Mason Gross School of the Arts, both a part of Rutgers University. Stromsten was a visiting artist at Drew University, Madison, New Jersey, in the springs of 1976 and 1977, and was an instructor of photography and photo history at the New School for Social Research and Parsons School of Design, both in New York City, from 1973 to 1977. She also taught photography at the School of Visual Arts in New York City (1972–73) and directed the Art Center Program of the New Jersey Institute of Technology, Newark (1975). In 1967 she worked on art and public-relations projects for the New York City Department of Parks and Cultural Affairs Administration, and in 1974–75 she worked for Princeton Associates for Human Resources photographing a career education series.

Stromsten has belonged to SPE and CAA since 1977, the Art Workers Coalition since 1974 and was a member of the Womens Ad Hoc Group in New York City from 1972 to 1978. She received a Rutgers University Instructional Grant in 1979 and a research grant in 1977. The photographer was awarded New Jersey State Council on the Arts grants in 1979, 1977 and 1974, a National Park Service/American Craft Council grant in 1976, a Siggins Scholarship in 1962, the Hopwood Award in Creative Writing from the University of Michigan in 1960 and a Traub Art Award in 1959.

In 1973 Stromsten produced a documentary on Diane Arbus for WBAI radio in New York City.

She uses black-and-white for her documentary work, but also extensively uses the nonsilver cyanotype, Vandyke brown and Rockland emulsions.

PUBLICATIONS Books: *Home on Wheels*, Michael Rockland, 1980; *The Road Is Everywhere*, poetry by Rosemarie Waldrop, 1978; *From the Center*, Lucy Lippard, 1976; *Family Living*, 1974. Anthologies: *The Photography Catalogue*, 1976; *Light and Lens*, 1973.

COLLECTIONS Business Week Magazine, NYC; Gerald Freeman Inc., NYC; Time-Life, · NYC.

DEALER Neikrug Gall., 224 E. 68 St, New York, NY 10021.

ADDRESS 41 Washington St, Rocky Hill, NJ 08553.

Karl Struss CINEMATOGRAPHER · PHOTOGRAPHER [See plate 45] Born in New York City on November 30, 1886, Struss spent four years studying photography under Clarence White at Columbia University, New York City (1908–12).

He began photography in 1896. At age seventeen he went to work at his father's bonnet-wire factory, where he remained until 1914. In that year he received his first commission: he was hired by the Bermuda government to produce tourist pictures. Struss served in the armed forces during World War I, after which he set up his own studio in New York, from which he produced illustrations for such publications as *Vogue, Harper's Bazaar, Vanity Fair* and several newspapers and made some autochrome covers for the *American Journal of Photography*. After three years he closed his studio and moved to Hollywood, where he worked as a cameraman for Cecil B. DeMille (1919–22). Struss then freelanced as a cinematographer, working for Paramount Studios, United Artists, MGM and several independent producers as well, until his retirement in 1970.

Co-founder of Pictorial Photographers of America, Struss was also a member of Stieglitz's Photo-Secession, 1912–17. He also holds membership in the International Alliance of Theatrical Stage Employees (IATSE) and the American Society of Cinematographers, and was a founding member of the Academy of Motion Picture Arts and Sciences. In his early days as a still photographer he made the Struss Pictorial Lens (1909), publishing a descriptive and illustrative brochure about it in 1915. As a cinematographer he devised a special filter technique that was used in *Ben Hur* (1926) to visually transform lepers to health and in *Dr. Jekyll and Mr. Hyde* (1932) to change Jekyll into Hyde without optical cutaways. In 1928 Struss received an Academy Award for his work on the film *Sunrise*.

A few of his credits as a director of photography

include: *The Fly* (1958), *Limelight* (1952), *Rocketship XM* (1950), *The Great Dictator* (1940), *Anything Goes* (1936), *Island of Lost Souls* (1932), *Abraham Lincoln* (1930), *Taming of the Shrew* (1929) and *Fool's Paradise* (1921).

Although his cinematic career has tended to overshadow his still photography, Struss has continued to work on his images, of which he states: "Composition seems to be natural to me. Perhaps most of my images are gentle, but I do have dramatic ones, too. They have a luminous, rich quality—this is found both in the pictorial prints and on the motion picture screen."

PUBLICATIONS Anthology: *Pictorial Photography in Britain, 1900–1920*, Arts Council of Great Britain, 1978. Catalog: *Karl Struss: Man with a Camera*, 1976 (The Museum: Bloomfield Hills, Mich.). Periodical: *Camerawork*, Apr 1912.

COLLECTIONS IMP/GEH, Rochester; Los Angeles County Art Mus.; Metro. Mus. of Art, NYC; MOMA, NYC; Mus. of Art, Ann Arbor, Mich.; New Orleans Art Mus.

DEALER Stephen White Gallery, 835 N La Cienega Blvd, Los Angeles, CA 90069.

ADDRESS 1343 N Orange Grove Ave, Los Angeles, CA 90046.

Roy Emerson Stryker ADMINISTRATOR Born in 1882 in Great Bend, Kansas, Stryker died on September 27, 1975, in Grand Junction, Colorado. He graduated from Columbia University in New York City in 1924.

After serving in World War I, Stryker finished his education at Columbia and stayed on as an economics teacher. From 1935 to 1943 he was chief of the historical section of the Farm Security Administration (FSA) and directed the photographers who documented America during the Depression. He later headed similar projects for the Office of War Information, the Standard Oil Company of New Jersey, the University of Pittsburgh Photo Library, the Technical Cooperation Administration and the Jones & Laughlin Steel Company. Later he worked as an independent consultant.

Under Stryker's direction such stellar figures as Dorothea Lange, Ben Shahn, Arthur Rothstein, Russell Lee, Jack Delano, Marion Post Wolcott, John Vachon, Gordon Parks and Walker Evans produced a collection of 130,000 prints, some of which were exhibited in the 1955 "Family of Man" show and some in a 1962 show at the Museum of Modern Art. Several of the photographers called him "a great teacher and a demanding taskmaster, with a sense of mission," writes *The New York Times*. "He was impatient with pictures based on ignorance and misunderstanding, insisting that the photographer learn all about his subject before approaching the assignment."

PUBLICATIONS Books: *Roy Stryker: The Humane Propagandist*, James C. Anderson, ed., 1977; *In This Proud Land*, w/Nancy Wood, 1973; *Just Before the War*, w/Arthur Rothstein & John Vachon, 1968; *American Economic Life*, w/Rexford G. Tugwell, 193?.

COLLECTIONS N.Y. Pub. Lib., NYC; Univ. of Louisville Photographic Arch., Ky.

ARCHIVE L/C, Prints & Photographs Division, Washington, DC 20540.

Rodney Christopher Stuart PHOTOGRAPHER · ART CONSULTANT · TEACHER · CURATOR Born January 22, 1945, in Cleveland, Ohio, Stuart earned a BA in Photography (1972) and an MA in Arts Administration (1976) from San Franciso State University. He studied with Jack Welpott in 1973.

Since 1976 Stuart has owned and directed PhosGraPhos, an art consulting company. He was a curator for the Silver Image Gallery, Seattle, Washington, in 1977 and a curator for Friends of Photography, Carmel, California, in 1974–76. He directed the Cultural Arts programs for San Francisco State University in 1970–73.

A member of SPE since 1975, the photographer was a founding member of the Photography Council of the Seattle Art Museum in 1977 and its program chairman in 1979.

As a curator, Stuart specializes in nineteenth- and twentieth-century photographers of the Northwest and twentieth-century West Coast contemporary trends. In his photography he uses found paper and photo-collage.

PUBLICATIONS Catalogs (text only): *Jack Welpott, The Artist as Teacher, The Teacher as Artist*, 1976 (San Francisco Mus. of Modern Art); *Untitled 11, Emerging Los Angeles Photographers*, 1976 (Friends of Photography; Carmel, Calif.).

DEALER Erica Williams/Ann Johnson Gall., 317 E Pine St, Seattle, WA 98122.

ADDRESS PhosGraPhos, 1518 First Ave S, Seattle, WA 98134.

Jack H. Stuler PHOTOGRAPHER · TEACHER Born August 30, 1932, in Homestead, Pennsylvania, Stuler received a BA (1960) and an MFA (1963) from Arizona State University, Tempe. He studied with Van Deren Coke in 1961, and was influenced by his personal acquaintance with and by the work of Brett Weston, Minor White and Frederick Sommer.

Stuler has taught at Arizona State University since 1972, first as an associate professor (1972–75), then as a full professor of art.

A member of SPE, he won grants-in-aid from Arizona State in 1973 and 1968 and a first award from the Arizona Biennial of Photography at the Phoenix Art Museum in 1967.

Working in a medium-format black-and-white and color, Stuler frequently uses nature and family as subjects. He creates equivalent and collage images "which touch upon my fantasy world," he says.

PUBLICATIONS Anthology: *Celebrations*, 1974. Periodicals: "Jack Stuler," Rosemary Holusha, *Art Voices/South*, 2:1, 1979; *Camera*, Nov 1971; *Aperture*, 15:3, 1970; *Popular Photography's Woman*, fall 1970; *Photography Annual*, 1969.

COLLECTIONS Ariz. State Univ., Tempe; Glendale Coll., Glendale, Ariz.; IMP/GEH, Rochester; Mesa Community Coll., Ariz.; MIT, Cambridge, Mass.; Northlight Gall., Tempe; Phoenix Coll., Ariz.; Yuma Art Ctr., Ariz.

DEALER Southwest Gall., 4223 N Marshall Wy, Scottsdale, AZ 85251.

ADDRESS 1109 E Fairmont, Tempe, AZ 85282.

Edward Richard Sturr TEACHER · PHOTOGRAPHER Born on November 8, 1937, in Berwyn, Illinois, Sturr majored in art and philosophy at St. Ambrose College, Davenport, Iowa, where he received his BA (1959). He received an MS from the Institute of Design, Chicago (1964), and studied at the School of the Art Institute of Chicago (1966–67). In 1973 he received a Doctor of Education degree from Illinois State University College of Fine Arts in Normal.

Sturr has served as assistant professor of art at Kansas State University, Manhattan, since 1974. Prior to that he held the same position at Northeast Missouri State University, Kirksville (1973–74), and was instructor of photography at Morton College, Cicero, Illinois, from 1967 to 1970.

A member of SPE since 1963 and the National Art Education Association since 1973, Sturr was awarded first prize, Photography Division, "The Arena Art Open" National Exhibition, New York City (1978); first prize, "Photospiva 78," National Exhibition, Spiva Art Center, Missouri, and first prize, Invitational Photography Division, Chicago Arts Festival in 1973.

The artist describes his work as taking a technically "straight approach," formally concerned with spatial possibilities of image and "conceptually with metaphorical/expressive aspects of subject matter (most recently of landscape)."

PUBLICATIONS Anthology: *Photography in the Twentieth Century*, Nathan Lyons, 1967. Periodicals: "Photography in Contemporary Society," ed., *Kansas Quarterly*, fall 1979; "Teaching High School Photography," *The Professional Photographer*, Sept 1970; "Camera in the Classroom," Mildred A. Glueck, *PSA Journal*, Jan 1965; *Directions 64*, co-ed. w/Frank Utech, 1964.

COLLECTIONS Chicago Art Inst.; IMP/GEH, Rochester; La Grange Coll. Art Dept., Ga. Natl. Museums of Canada, Quebec.

ADDRESS RR 1, Box 158A, St George, KS 66535.

Josef Sudek PHOTOGRAPHER [See plate 111] Born March 17, 1896, in Kolin, Czechoslovakia, Sudek died September 15, 1976, in Prague. He studied photography at the School of Graphic Art in Prague with Professor Karel Novak (1922–23). A lifelong passion for music also influenced his life and work.

After being apprenticed to a bookbinder (1911–13) Sudek was inducted into the army (1915). While at the Italian front he was seriously injured and later suffered the loss of his right arm. Because of this handicap he could no longer be a bookbinder, so he turned to photography.

In 1920 Sudek joined the Club for Amateur Photographers in Prague, and in 1924, with Jaromire Funke and other avant-garde photographers, he founded the Czech Photographic Society. He was awarded the Order of Work by the Czech government in 1966 and received the title Artist of Merit in 1961, the first photographer so honored by the Czech government.

Known for lyrical images that show a fine eye for life's intimate details, Sudek once explained that "everything around us, dead or alive, in the eyes of a crazy photographer mysteriously takes on many variations, so that a seemingly dead object comes to life through light or by its surroundings. . . . To capture some of this—I suppose that's lyricism."

PUBLICATIONS Monographs: *Sudek*, Sonja Bullaty, 1978; *Janacek-Hukvaldy*, 1971 (Supraphon: Czechoslovakia); *A Musical Education*, Alojz Suchanek, 1970 (Statni Pedagogicke Nakladatelstvi: Czechoslovakia); *Sudek*, Jan Rezac, 1964 (Artia: Prague); *Charles Bridge*, Emanuel Poche, 1961; *Prague Panoramas*, 1959; *Josef Sudek Fotografie*, 1956 (State Pub. House of Literature, Music & Art: Prague); *Our Castle*, 1948 (J. R. Vilimek: Prague); *Praha—Josef Sudek*, 1948 (Svoboda: Prague); *Baroque Prague*, Arne Novak,

1947 (Czech Graphic Union); *Magic in Stone*, 1947 (Prager Pub. Ltd: London); *Prague Castle*, Rudolf Roucek, 1947 (Bohumil Janda Praha: Czechoslovakia). Books: *Prague Ateliers*, 1961 (Pub. House of the Czech. Graphic Artists: Prague); *Light and Shadow*, 1959 (Artia: Prague); *Prague Palaces*, 1946 (J. Pròchazka: Prague). Anthologies: *The Photograph Collector's Guide*, Lee D. Witkin & Barbara London, 1979; *Photography Year 1976*, Time-Life Series, 1977; *The Magic Image*, Cecil Beaton & Gail Buckland, 1975; *Octave of Prayer*, Minor White, ed., 1972; *Great Photographers*, Time-Life Series, 1971; *U.S. Camera Annual*, 1971. Catalogs: *Josef Sudek*, 1976 (Galerie Lichttropfen: Aachen, Germany); *Josef Sudek*, 1976 (Polygrafia: Czechoslovakia); *Five Photographers*, 1968 (Univ. of Nebr. Sheldon Mem. Art Gall.: Lincoln). Periodicals: *Camera*, Dec 1979, Apr 1976, Nov 1975, Oct 1974, June 1973, Dec 1972, July 1967, Mar 1966; "Josef Sudek: Photographs," Carter Ratcliffe, *Print Collector's Newsletter*, 8:4, 1977; *Zoom*, Aug/Sept 1977 (Paris); *British Journal of Photography*, Dec 1976; *Modern Photography*, Sept 1976; *Creative Camera*, Oct 1975; *Popular Photography*, Nov 1974; *Fotografie*, nos. 1 & 2, 1973, no. 3, 1971, no. 1, 1966, no. 4, 1961; *Life*, May 29, 1970; *Infinity: ASMP*, Dec 1969

PORTFOLIOS *Josef Sudek*, 1976 (Pressfoto: Prague); *Saint Vitus*, 1928 (Druzstevni Prace: Czechoslovakia).

COLLECTIONS IMP/GEH, Rochester; Univ. of N. Mex., Albuquerque. Mus. of Decorative Arts, Prague; RPS, London.

Jean-Pierre Sudre PHOTOGRAPHER [See plate 85] Born September 27, 1921, in Paris, Sudre studied at Ecole de Cinématographie in Paris and at Institut des Hautes Etudes Cinématographiques (1942–45).

As of this writing Sudre was teaching the history of photography at Ecole des Beaux-Arts in Marseille. Previously he was creator and animator of "Stage Experimental Photographique" in Paris (1968–72), and worked with the French magazines *Réalité*, *Connaissance des Arts* and *L'Oeil*, among others. From 1946 to 1948 he was an illustrative photographer.

Sudre belongs to SPE, Rencontres d'Arles in France, and Fondation Nationale de la Photographie in Lyon, France. He is honorary president of the Photo-Club des 30 x 40 in Paris. In 1968 Sudre won the Davanne Medal of the Société Française de Photographie.

From 1948 to 1950 the photographer worked in 30 x 40cm format, shooting still lifes. Since 1950

he has concentrated on such subjects as landscapes, suns and "apocalypses," all of which he describes as "matériographies."

PUBLICATIONS Books: *Photography of the 20th Century*, 1980; *Pralinne*, 1967; *Diamantine*, 1964; *Dictionnaire pittoresque de la France*, Arthaud, 1955. Catalogs: *Galérie du Château d'eau*, 1976 (Toulouse, France); *Musée N. Niepce*, 1976; *Apocalypse: La Demeure*, 1969 (Paris); *Musée Cantini*, 1968.

PORTFOLIOS *Porte-Folio de Nus*, 1978; *Douze Paysages Matériographiques*, 1972–75.

COLLECTIONS CCP, Tucson; MOMA, NYC; Univ. of Tex., Gernsheim Cllctn., Austin. In France: Bibliothèque Nationale, Paris; Musée Cantini, Marseilles; Musée Nicéphore Niepce, Chalon-sur-Saône; Musée Réattu, Arles. Fondation Veranneman, Courtrai, Belgium.

ADDRESS Le Mourre du Bes, Lacoste 84710, France.

Larry Sultan PHOTOGRAPHER Born in 1946 in New York, Sultan earned a BA in Political Science from the University of California at Santa Barbara (1968) and an MFA in Photography from San Francisco Art Institute (1973).

He has taught photography at San Francisco Art Institute since 1978 and previously taught photography and co-directed the photography programs at Lone Mountain College in San Francisco (1974–78). He has also been a photography instructor at the University of California, Berkeley Extension (1973–77), San Francisco Museum of Modern Art (1973–74) and School of Arts and Sciences, San Anselmo, California (1972–74).

The photographer won a California Arts Council Special Projects Grant in 1978, an NEA Photographer's Fellowship in 1980 and 1977 and an NEA Art in Public Places grant in 1976.

PUBLICATIONS Books: *Evidence*, w/Mike Mandel, 1977; *How to Read Music in One Evening*, w/Mike Mandel, 1974. Anthology: *Octave of Prayer*, Minor White, ed., 1972. Catalogs: *Attitudes: Photography in the 70s*, 1979 (Santa Barbara Mus. of Art: Calif.); *Project Interstate 5*, 1977 (San Jose State Univ.: Calif.). Periodicals: "Photographs as Symbols and Non-symbols," 16:4, 1978, "Evidence," Henri Man Barenose, 15:H, 1978, *Exposure: SPE*; "Open and Shut Case," Robert Heinecken, May/June 1977, "How to Read Music," Charles Desmarivs, 1975, *Afterimage: VSW*; review, Joan Murray, Apr 23, 1977, "Replaced, the Structure of Myth," Joe Czarnecki, Mar 15, 1975, "Immersion," Joan Murray, Nov 16, 1974, review, Joan Murray, July 27, 1974, "The Image World," Jaki Bershirs, Oct 28, 1972,

Artweek; "Evidence," Fred Gross, Photograph, 1:4, 1977; *Popular Photography*, Apr 1973; *Camera*, Oct 1972.

COLLECTIONS Atlantic Richfield Corp., Los Angeles; CCP, Tucson; MOMA, NYC; Univ. of Alaska, Fairbanks.

DEALER Light Gall., 800 N La Cienega Blvd, Los Angeles, CA 90069.

ADDRESS 119 Boardwalk, Greenbrae, CA 94904.

Ira E. Sumner *PHOTOGRAPHER* Born June 18, 1846, in McHenry County, Illinois, Sumner died there in 1918. He had received little formal education, studying daguerreotypy and tintype-making under the tutelage of an early photographer, Z. Roberts, in Red Wing, Minnesota.

Sumner went into partnership with Z. Roberts about 1868–69, dissolving it in 1872 when he married and moved to Northfield, Minnesota. There he set up Sumner Studio, which he operated from 1875 until his death.

Sumner was the recipient of several national and state awards, including one from the state of Minnesota.

Although his studio work consisted in the main of portraits as well as group poses for the nearby college, Sumner frequently did photojournalistic work. He is noted for his photographs of the notorious Younger brothers and of two shooting victims of Jesse James and the Younger brothers who were killed during the robbery of a Northfield bank in the early 1860s. Unfortunately, most of his well-preserved negatives were destroyed through negligence after his death.

COLLECTION Minnesota Historical Society.

ARCHIVE Grace Sumner Northrop, Sun Valley Lodge, 12415 N 103rd Ave, Sun City, AZ 85351.

Wolfgang Suschitzky *PHOTOGRAPHER · CINEMATOGRAPHER* Born in Vienna, Austria, Suschitzky studied at Graphische Lehr- und Versuchsanstalt in Vienna in 1933, then moved to London in 1935.

A freelance cinematographer, he works on features, documentaries, commercials and television shows. His films include *Falling in Love Again, Living Free, Get Carter, Entertaining Mr. Sloan, Ring of Bright Water* and *Ulysses*.

Suschitzky belongs to the Association of Cine and Television Technicians, the Zoological Society (Fellow), the British Kinematograph Sound and Television Society, the British Film Academy and the British Society of Cinematographers.

As a still photographer he specializes in animal images, but also does portraiture, geographical records and children. His "straight" photographs are mainly in black-and-white,

PUBLICATIONS Books: *Kingdom of the Beasts*, w/Julian Huxley, 1956; *Photographing Animals*, 1941, *Photographing Children*, 1940 (The Studio: London).

ADDRESS Flat 11, Douglas House, 6 Maida Ave, London W2 1TG, England.

Frank Meadow Sutcliffe *PHOTOGRAPHER · WRITER · CURATOR* [See plate 31] Born in 1853 in Headingly, Leeds, England, Sutcliffe died in 1941 in Whitby, England. His father, Tom Sutcliffe, was a painter, etcher, lithographer, printer and amateur photographer. Sutcliffe was influenced by P. H. Emerson and the early realist French painters.

Frank Sutcliffe took up photography around 1871, then established a studio in Whitby, a coastal town in Yorkshire, after having worked, briefly, for the large photographic firm of Francis Frith. He wrote a column that was originated by Horsely Hinton, "Photography Notes," for the *Yorkshire Weekly Post* from 1908 to about 1930. He also contributed articles to many newspapers and magazines, *Amateur Photography* among them. Sutcliffe was the curator of Whitby Literary and Philosophical Society from 1923 to 1940.

A founding-member of The Linked Ring in 1892, he was made an Honorary Fellow of RPS in 1941. Sutcliffe was widely exhibited; his was the first one-man show to be held by the Camera Club in 1888. He was the recipient of some sixty-two gold, silver and bronze medals from international exhibitions.

Although he worked commercially as a portrait and *carte de visite* photographer, Sutcliffe is best known for his personal work, in which he photographed small sea-town fishermen and farmers and their families at work and at play. He was noted especially for his naturalistic and spontaneous style, despite the fact that his early work was with unwieldy collodion wet plates. He produced many varieties of prints—albumen, silver, carbon and platinum and in his later years was absorbed with the new Kodak hand-held cameras.

PUBLICATIONS Monographs: *Frank Meadow Sutcliffe: A Second Selection*, Bill Eglon Shaw, ed., 1978; *Frank Meadow Sutcliffe*, Bill Eglon Shaw, ed., 1974; *Frank Sutcliffe: Photographer of Whitby*, Michael Hiley, 1974, U.S. ed., 1975; *The Pictorial Work of Frank M. Sutcliffe*, F. C. Lambert, 1908. Anthologies: *The Photograph Collector's Guide*, Lee D. Witkin & Barbara London, 1979; *The Invented Eye*, Edward Lucie-Smith,

1975; *The Magic Image*, Cecil Beaton & Gail Buckland, 1975; *Early Photographs & Early Photographers*, Oliver Mathews, 1973; *Photographing Children*, Time-Life Series, 1971; *Victorian Photography: Being an Album of Yesterday's Camera Work*, Alexander Strasser, 1942. Periodicals: "Sutcliffe of Whitby," Bill Eglon Shaw, *Creative Camera*, Mar 1968; "Frank M. Sutcliffe, Hon. F.R.P.S. Some Reminiscences," Irene Sutcliffe, Dec 1942, "The Frank M. Sutcliffe Memorial Lecture," J. L. Hankey, Aug 1942, *Photographic Journal*; "F. M. Sutcliffe of Whitby. An Appreciation and Some Examples of his Work," W. J. Warren, *The Amateur Photographer*, June 15, 1900; "Frank Sutcliffe," Charles Noel Armfield, *Sun Artists*, July 1891.

COLLECTIONS IMP/GEH, Rochester; Philadelphia Mus. of Art, Pa.; Univ. of New Mexico Art Mus., Albuquerque; Univ. of Texas, Gernsheim Cllctn., Austin; Yale Univ., Art Gall., New Haven, Conn. In England: Kodak Mus., Harrow; RPS, London; Sutcliffe Gall., Whitby; Whitby Gall. & Mus.; Whitby Literary & Philosophical Soc.

ARCHIVES The Sutcliffe Gall., Whitby, Yorkshire, England.

Antanas Sutkus PHOTOGRAPHER Born in the village of Kluoniškiai in the district of Kaunas, Lithuanian SSR, on June 27, 1939, Sutkus studied journalism at Vilnius State University (1958–63).

Currently president of the presidium of Photography Art Society of Lithuanian SSR, Vilnius has been very active with that organization since he became a member in 1969; he was vice-president for several years, beginning in 1974, and president of their Organizational Committee. From 1960 to 1962 Sutkus was on the staff of the weekly *Literatūra ir Menas* in Vilnius, and from 1962 to 1969 he was on staff of the magazine *Tarybinė Moteris*, Vilnius. Sutkus was a worker at Ežerėlis Peatery from 1956 to 1958.

He is a member of the Fédération Internationale d'Art Photographique (FIAP).

The artist concentrates on portraits and has been accumulating a series, "People of Lithuania," since 1976.

Sutkus has been awarded several prizes, among them FIAP's gold medal from Rabat, Morocco (1979), the "Man and His World" grand prize from Katowice, Poland (1973), the Michelangelo Gold Medal of Italy (1970) and the Fotoforum first prize from Ružomberock, Czechoslovakia (1970).

PUBLICATIONS Books (all pub. by Mintis: Vilnius): *Tarybu Lietuva*, 1977; *Tėviškės Spalvos*, 1976; *Lazdynai*, 1975; *Senojo Vilniaus Fragmentai*, 1975; Salis ta Lietuva Vadinas, w/R. Rakauskas, 1970; *Tėviškės Lauku Suvenyras*, 1969; *Vilniaus Siokiadieniai*, w/R. Rakauskas, 1965.

COLLECTIONS Prakapas Gall., NYC. Bibliothèque Nationale, Paris; Musée Français de la Photographie, Bièvres, France; Photography Mus., Helsinki, Finland; Photography Mus., Šiauliai, Lithuanian SSR.

REPRESENTATIVE Photography Art Society, Pionieriu 8, 232600 Vilnius, Lithuanian SSR, USSR.

ADDRESS Gajaus 38–7, Vilnius, Lithuanian SSR, USSR.

William Suttle PHOTOGRAPHER · TEACHER Born April 26, 1938, in Charlotte, North Carolina, Suttle earned a BA in Political Science from the University of North Carolina, Chapel Hill. He studied photography in 1964–65 at Rochester Institute of Technology, New York.

Since 1975 Suttle has been an assistant professor at the State University of New York, Purchase.

He won an NEA Photographer's Fellowship in 1975 and in 1971 and a CAPS grant in 1972.

COLLECTIONS Colgate Univ., Hamilton, N.Y.; Cornell Univ., Ithaca, N.Y.; IMP/GEH, Rochester; L/C, Wash., D.C.; Metro. Mus. of Art, NYC; MOMA, NYC.

ADDRESS 463 West St, New York, NY 10014.

Sir Joseph Wilson Swan CHEMIST · PHYSICIST Born in Sunderland, Durham, England, on October 31, 1828, Swan died on May 27, 1914, in Warlingham, Surrey, England. He graduated from Durham University with a DSc.

Beginning his career as a chemist's apprentice, he later became an assistant and then a partner in a company manufacturing photographic wet plates in Newcastle-upon-Tyne, England.

Sir Joseph served as president of the British Institute of Electrical Engineers, vice-president of RPS, president of the Society of Chemical Industry and president of the Faraday Society. He was vice-president of the Senate of University College, London, from 1899 to 1903, as well as a life governor of the college.

Knighted in 1904, Swan also was awarded the Progress Medal of RPS, the Hughes medal of the Royal Society, the Albert Medal of the Royal Society of Arts and the gold medal of the Society of Chemical Research.

Swan invented the dry plate in 1871, bromide paper in 1878, a primitive incandescent electric light in 1860 and a practical carbon-filament light bulb in 1878. He presented the latter to the Newcastle-upon-Tyne Chemical Society on December 18, 1878. Using nitrocellulose, he also developed the principles later used to manufacture the first synthetic fabric, rayon (1883). Outside of photography, Swan invented a miner's safety lamp, an electric meter and electric accumulators.

PUBLICATION Anthology: *Early Photographs & Early Photographers*, Oliver Mathews, 1973.

Joel Swartz *PHOTOGRAPHER · AUTHOR · TEACHER* Born December 9, 1944, in Rochester, New York, Swartz received a BFA from Rochester Institute of Technology in 1969 and an MFA in 1971 from the Visual Studies Workshop in Rochester, where he was influenced by Nathan Lyons.

Swartz has taught at the Visual Studies Workshop (1972–78), University of Rochester (1974–75), Empire State College, Saratoga Springs, New York (1973), and Nazareth College, Rochester (1971–73).

The photographer won CAPS grants in 1976 and 1974.

During the past few years Swartz has produced children's books, providing the photography and text as well as printing them. He has also conducted research in electrophotography for eleven years.

PUBLICATIONS Monographs: *Cathy Griffin Mussington*, 1979; *For Your Reading Pleasure*, 1978; *Something Different to Do*, 1976. Books: *Copy Art*, Firpo, Alexander, Katayangi & Ditlia, 1978; *The Making of American Society*, Edwin Rozwenc, 1973; *Is America Used Up . . .*, Judith Mara Gutman, 1974.

PORTFOLIO *CAPS Portfolio* (group), 1975 (New York).

COLLECTIONS Art Inst. of Chicago; Columbia Coll., Chicago; IMP/GEH, Rochester; Univ. of N. Mex., Albuquerque; VSW, Rochester; Xerox Corp., Rochester.

ADDRESS 237 Frost Ave, Rochester, NY 14608.

Juliana Swatko *PHOTOGRAPHER · TEACHER* Born October 10, 1952, Swatko received a BFA in Photography/Ceramics from Tyler School of Art, Temple University, Philadelphia, Pennsylvania (1974), and an MFA in Photography from the Visual Studies Workshop, State University of New York, Buffalo (1977).

In 1978–79 she worked with Light Work/Community Darkrooms at Syracuse University, Syracuse, New York, teaching workshops and setting up an "alternative imaging facility" under an NEA grant. In 1977 Swatko lectured at the Australian Center for Photography, Sydney; Tasmanian College for Advanced Education, Hobart, Tasmania, Australia; and at Rochester Institute of Technology, New York. She also lectured and demonstrated xerography at Colgate University, Hamilton, New York, and was assistant curator of the school's Fine Arts Slide Collection. In 1975 she taught a xerography workshop at Visual Studies Workshop in Rochester.

Working with a variety of copy machines, Swatko uses them to rephotograph and color her black-and-white images as well as to photograph objects placed on the machine. Her aim is to create imaginary environments and landscapes.

PUBLICATIONS Anthology: *Copy Art: The First Complete Guide to the Copy Machine*, Lester Alexander, 1978. Periodicals: *Popular Photography*, 1978; *35mm Photography*, 1978.

COLLECTION Rank Xerox Corp., Sydney, Australia.

ADDRESS 80 Candy Lane, Syosset, NY 11791.

Charles Swedlund *PHOTOGRAPHER · TEACHER* Born in Chicago, Illinois, in 1935, Swedlund earned a BS (1958) and MS (1961) in Photography from the Institute of Design, Illinois Institute of Technology, Chicago.

A teacher at Southern Illinois University, Carbondale, since 1971, he previously taught at the School of the Art Institute of Chicago (1970–71) and at the Institute of Design (1969–71).

Swedlund belongs to SPE, Friends of Photography and the New York Photographic Historical Society. The photographer won first prize in the Portrait of America National Photographic Competition in 1975, and also in that year received a Special Research Project grant from Southern Illinois University. He was given a grant-in-aid and fellowship in 1969 and a grant-in-aid in 1967 from the Research Foundation of the State University of New York.

In 1977 he made the films *Falling Waters* and *Olean*.

Swedlund creates multiple exposures and color separations in the camera and prints them by the dye transfer process. He also produces Kwik-Prints.

PUBLICATIONS Monograph: *Charles Swedlund Photographs*, 1973. Books: *Kwik-Print*, w/ Elizabeth Swedlund, 1978; *Photography: A Handbook of History, Materials, Processes*, 1974; *Photography, Source & Resource*, Louis et al, eds., 1973; *Views on Nudes*, Bill Jay, 1971; *A*

Guide to Photography, 1967; The History of the Nude in Photography, Peter Lacey, 1964. Anthologies: The Photographer's Choice, Kelly Wise, ed., 1976; Photography in the Twentieth Century, Nathan Lyons, 1967. Catalog: Repeated Images, 1975 (Eastern Tenn. Univ.). Periodicals: 35mm Photography, summer 1975; Petersen's Photographic Magazine, Jan 1974; "Be-ing Without Clothes," Aperture 15:3, 1970; Aperture 9:2, 1961.

PORTFOLIOS   Yearly portfolio, 1977 (School of the Art Institute of Chicago); Charles Swedlund Dye Transfers, 1976; Zoetrope Strips, 1976; Heather's Valentine, 1974; The Family That Bathes Together Stays Together, 1974; Rip-Off Portfolio, 1974 (VSW: Rochester).

COLLECTIONS   Art Inst. of Chicago; Columbia Coll. Gall., Chicago; Ill. State Mus., Springfield; IMP/GEH, Rochester; Kalamazoo Art Ctr., Mich.; Minneapolis Mus. of Art, Minn.; MOMA, NYC; Oakland Mus., Calif.; Ohio Wesleyan Univ., Delaware, Ohio; Purdue Univ., West Lafayette, Ind.; Smithsonian Inst., Wash., D.C.; UCLA Art Gall.; Univ. of Louisville Archives, Ky.; Univ. of South Fla., Tampa; VSW, Rochester. Natl. Mus. of Canada, Ottawa; Ryerson Polytechnical Inst., Canada; Bibliothèque Nationale, Paris.

ADDRESS   RFD 2, Box 126, Cobden, IL 62920.

Alex Sweetman   *PHOTOGRAPHER · TEACHER · WRITER*   Born December 8, 1946, in Greenlawn, New York, Sweetman received a BA in English Literature from New York University, New York City (1970), and an MFA from the Visual Studies Workshop State University of New York in Buffalo (1975).

Since 1976 Sweetman has been an assistant professor at the School of the Art Institute of Chicago. He has also taught at the Institute of Design, Illinois Institute of Technology, Chicago (1978, 1976), Columbia College, Chicago (1976), and at State University College of New York, Buffalo.

PUBLICATIONS   Monographs: Survivors, 1977; Time Pieces, 1973. Periodicals (selected): "American Snapshots," July 1978, "Photographica," Mar 1978, New Art Examiner; "Walker Evans: Photographs for the Farm Security Administration, 1935–38," May 1974, "Aaron Siskind: Thoughts and Reflections" (interview w/Siskind), Mar 1973, "Duane Michals' Disappointing Journey" (review of Michals' The Journey of the Spirit After Death), Oct 1972, "Death Is the Unconscious Goal" (review of Larry Clark's Tulsa), Apr 1972, Afterimage: VSW.

COLLECTIONS   Art Inst. of Chicago; IMP/GEH, Rochester; Ruth & Charles Levi Fndn., Chicago; Reva & David Logan Fndn., Chicago; Minneapolis Inst. of Art, Minn.; New Orleans Mus. of Art; Polaroid Corp., Cambridge, Mass.; San Francisco Mus. of Art; Sun Valley Ctr. for the Arts & Humanities, Idaho; Univ. of Ariz., Tucson; Univ. of N. Mex. Art Mus., Albuquerque; VSW, Rochester. Natl. Gall. of Canada, Ottawa.

ADDRESS   1118 W Patterson, Chicago, IL 60603.

Brian Joseph Swift   *PHOTOGRAPHER · TEACHER · PAPERMAKER*   Born August 27, 1948, in Elmira, New York, Swift received a BA in Photography (1975) from the University of Connecticut in Storrs, studying under James Baker Hall. He continued his photography studies at the Rhode Island School of Design with William E. Parker and Wendy MacNeil, receiving an MFA in 1979.

Since 1979 Swift has been self-employed, producing handmade photographic paper. He also is currently an adviser in photography at the College of the Atlantic in Bar Harbor, Maine. He was the head of photographic services at the Biology Department of the University of Connecticut from 1976 to 1978.

Swift, a member of SPE, received an award in 1976 from the Connecticut Commission on the Arts to produce a documentary film on playgrounds constructed from recycled materials, entitled Growing Your Own Playground. The commission also awarded him a grant in 1975 to create and coordinate a visual learning program for low-income-family children in Putnam, Connecticut.

The photographer's work is in the form of 35mm color-slide presentations involving shifts in vantage point and scale, and handmade photographic paper images from negatives of varying formats.

ADDRESS   POB 488, Bar Harbor, ME 04609.

Homer Warwick Sykes   *PHOTOGRAPHER*   Born January 11, 1948, in Vancouver, Canada, Sykes studied at London College of Printing and Graphic Arts in the late 1960s with Bill Jay and David Hurn. He became seriously interested in photography in 1967 and is now a freelance magazine photographer.

Sykes belongs to the National Union of Journalists in London, England. He won Arts Council of Great Britain grants in 1976 and 1974.

PUBLICATIONS   Book: Once a Year: Some Traditional British Customs, 1977 (Gordon Fraser:

London). Periodical: *Creative Camera Yearbook*, 1976.

COLLECTION   Arts Council of Great Britain, London.

REPRESENTATIVES   Woodfin Camp & Associates, 50 Rockefeller Plaza, New York, NY 10020; Viva Agence, 8 rue St Marc, 75002 Paris, France.

ADDRESS   19 Kenilworth Ave, London SW 19, England.

Stephen Lee Szabo   PHOTOGRAPHER · TEACHER Born July 17, 1940, in Berwick, Pennsylvania, Szabo studied at Pennsylvania State University in University Park and at Art Center School of Design in Los Angeles.

As of this writing Szabo was a photography instructor at the Corcoran School of Art in Washington, D.C. He was guest artist/lecturer at the Maine Photographic Workshops, Rockport in 1977–79.

In the early 1970s Szabo produced platinum photographs from 8 x 10 negatives, but in 1978 he began to take 11 x 14 view camera photographs of Washington, D.C.

PUBLICATION   Monograph: *The Eastern Shore*, 1976.

COLLECTIONS   Fine Arts Mus. of the South, Mobile, Ala.; ICP, NYC; IMP/GEH, Rochester; L/C, Wash., D.C.; Madison Art Ctr., Wisconsin; MOMA, NYC.

DEALER   Kathleen Ewing Gall., 3020 K St NW, Washington, DC 20007.

ADDRESS   Trenton Hall, Friendship, MD 20758.

John Thaddeus Szarkowski   CURATOR · PHOTOHISTORIAN · WRITER · PHOTOGRAPHER   Born in Ashland, Wisconsin, on December 18, 1925, Szarkowski earned a BS in 1948 from the University of Wisconsin, Madison. He also received honorary degrees from the Philadelphia College of Art (1972) and Minneapolis College of Art and Design (1974).

Since 1962 Szarkowski has been director of the Photography Department of the Museum of Modern Art in New York City. Previously he taught at the Albright Art School of the University of Buffalo, New York (1951–53), taught photography at the University of Minnesota, Minneapolis, in 1950 and worked as a photographer at the Walker Art Center in Minneapolis (1948–51).

Szarkowski won Guggenheim fellowships in 1961 and 1954.

PUBLICATIONS   Books: *Walker Evans*, 1971;

The Photographer and the American Landscape, 1963; *The Face of Minnesota*, 1958; *The Idea of Louis Sullivan*, 1956. Anthologies: *Mirrors and Windows*, ed., 1978; *From the Picture Press*, ed., 1973; *Looking at Photographs*, 1973; *The Photographer's Eye*, 1966. Catalog: *New Japanese Photography*, ed. w/Shoji Yamagishi, 1974.

ADDRESSES   Museum of Modern Art, 11 W 53 St, New York, NY 10019; 1165 Fifth Ave, New York, NY 10029.

Suzanne Szasz   PHOTOGRAPHER   Born October 20, 1919, in Budapest, Hungary, Szasz received a degree in foreign languages—including German, French and English—from Budapest University. She is self-taught in photography.

Currently Szasz is a self-employed photographer.

A member of ASMP and NPPA, she has been the recipient of numerous awards from the NPPA–Encyclopaedia Britannica Journalism contest, among them first prize for features in 1955 and first prize for picture stories in 1953 and 1952.

Szasz is best known for photographs of children. The artists says of her work that she "has used photography to illuminate and hold up for study the emotional world of children and parents."

PUBLICATIONS   Books: *The Body Language of Children*, foreword by Dr. B. Spock, 1978; *Modern Wedding Photography*, 1977; *Child Photography Simplified*, 1966; *The Silent Miaow*, Paul Gallico, 1964; *Young Folks' New York*, S. Lyman, 1960; *Helping Your Child's Emotional Growth*, A. Wolf, 1952. Periodicals: *Invitation to Photography*, 1971, 1970; *Popular Photography Woman Annual*, 1970.

ADDRESSES   Box 204, Westhampton, NY 11977; 15 W 46 St, Apt 9C, New York, NY 10036.

Karin Székessy   PHOTOGRAPHER   Born in Essen, Germany, on April 17, 1939, Székessy studied photojournalism in Munich from 1957 to 1959. She photographed for the German magazine *Kristall* in 1962–66 and taught fashion photography at the Hamburg Arts School from 1967 to 1970. She has been a freelance photographer since 1970.

PUBLICATIONS   Books: *Paul Wunderlich und Karin Székessy Correspondenzen*, Fritz J. Raddatz, 1976 (Belser: Zurich); *Medium Photographie*, 1975 (Kunsthalle: Kiel, Germany); *Les Filles dans l'atelier*, 1969 (Denoël: Paris). Anthology: *The Photograph Collector's Guide*, Lee D.

Witkin & Barbara London, 1979. Catalog: *Karin Székessy*, Fritz Kempe, 1975 (Galerie Levy: Hamburg).

PORTFOLIO *Pariser Zeichen*, 1978 (Grafik Internatl.).

COLLECTIONS Bibliothèque Nationale, Paris; Münchner Stadt Mus., Germany; Musée Royale Brussels, Belgium; Staedel, Frankfurt, Germany.

ADDRESS Wunderlich, Haynstrasse 2 D-2000 Hamburg 20, Germany.

T

Keiichi Tahara *PHOTOGRAPHER* Born August 21, 1951, in Kyoto, Japan, Tahara began learning photography at age twelve in the portrait studio of his grandfather, Y. Miyagawa, whom he names as his major influence.

A freelance photographer since 1973, Tahara worked as a lighting designer and photographer for the Japanese theater group Red Buddha on their European tour in 1971–72.

Tahara won the Kodak Award for La Critique Photographique in 1978, and the Young Photographers Award at the Rencontres Internationales de la Photographie in Arles, France, in 1977.

Working in black-and-white, Tahara photographs the windows of his apartments. "I consider many aspects of the window," he says. "The space that exists at the moment between the window and myself, the light, the landscape in the distance, etc."

PUBLICATIONS Anthology: *Japanese Photography and Its Origins*, 1979 (Inst. of Contemporary Arts: London). Catalog: *L'Album Photographique I*, 1979 (Centre Georges Pompidou: France). Periodicals: *Pentax Photography*, Mar 1979 (European ed.); *Yu*, no. 1002, 1978; *Asahi Camera*, Aug 1978; *Camera Mainichi*, Apr/June 1978; *Zoom*, no. 53, 1978 (Paris); *Clef*, no. 2, 1978; *Time-Life Photography Year*, 1978; *Fotografico Italiana*, no. 212, 1977; *Creative Camera*, no. 152, 1976; *Progresso Fotografico*, no. 82, 1975; *Nouveau Photocinéma*, no. 29, 1974.

COLLECTIONS Asahi Pentax Gall., Tokyo; Bibliothèque Nationale, Paris; Musée Réattu, Arles, France.

DEALERS UNAC Tokyo, Azabudai UniHouse 112, 1-1-20 Azabu Dai Minato-ku, Tokyo, Japan; Marcuse Pfeifer Gall., 825 Madison Ave, New York, NY 10021.

ADDRESS 21 Avenue Alphand, 94160 St Mande, France.

David B. Tait *PHOTOGRAPHER · ORCHARDIST* Born April 27, 1946, Tait earned a BA in Psychology from Pennsylvania State University, University Park, in 1968 and an MFA in Photography from Ohio University, Athens, in 1973. He considers Marshall Ritter his mentor.

Tait was senior research associate at the Institute for American Research, Columbus, Ohio, in 1973–79 and was a special consultant to IMP/GEH on their Oral History of Photography project in 1974–78.

He belongs to SPE and the Pennsylvania Vegetable Growers Association.

Tait uses "infrared materials combines with transcendent style and emphatically understated camera work to provide an incisive look at social posturing in America today."

PUBLICATION Book: *Photography: Source & Resource*, w/Lewis & McQuaid, 1973.

COLLECTIONS Minneapolis Inst. of Arts, Minn.; L/C, Wash., D.C.

DEALER O. K. Harris Gall., 383 W Broadway, New York, NY 10012.

ADDRESS RD Box 131, Centre Hall, PA 16828.

Henry Talbot *PHOTOGRAPHER · TEACHER* Born December 6, 1920, in Hindenburg, Germany, Talbot studied at the Reimann School, Berlin, Germany (1938–39), the College of Art, Birmingham, England (1939), and Melbourne Technical College, Australia (1946–47).

Since 1973 Talbot has been a lecturer in photography at the School of Art & Design, Preston Institute of Technology, Melbourne, Australia. In 1956 he became a partner in Helmut Newton & Henry Talbot Pty. Ltd, Photographic Studio, and in 1960 became the studio's governing director. From 1942 to 1946 Talbot served in the Australian Military Forces.

An Associate of the Institute of Australian

Photography and an Excellence in the Fédération Internationale de l'Art Photographique, Talbot won the Distinctive Merit Award from the Art Directors Club of Melbourne in 1968, the Award of Distinction in Professional Photography at the Pacific Photographic Fair in 1967, the 1965 A.P.R. Achievement in Photography Award from the Australian Photographic Society and that organization's C. S. Christian Trophy in 1962.

PUBLICATIONS Anthologies: *Australian Photography*, 1978, 1976, 1970, 1969, 1957.

COLLECTIONS In Australia: Art. Gall. of New South Wales, Sydney; Australian Photographic Soc., Melbourne; Natl. Gall. of Victoria, Melbourne; Phillip Morris Cllctn., Melbourne; State Coll. of Victoria, Melbourne.

REPRESENTATIVE Church St Photographic Centre, 384 Church St, Richmond, Victoria 3121, Australia.

ADDRESS 1 Miller Grove, KEW, Victoria 3101, Australia.

William Henry Fox Talbot *PHOTOGRAPHER · INVENTOR · LITERARY HISTORIAN* Born in Melbury, Dorset, England, Talbot lived from February 11, 1800, to September 17, 1877. He studied at Cambridge University in 1818–21 and received an MA in 1825. Sir John Herschel was a major, though unacknowledged, influence on Talbot's work.

Talbot was a Member of Parliament from 1833 to 1834. He became a Fellow of the Royal Society in 1832. He belonged to the Royal Astronomical Society since 1822 and was a member of its council in 1836.

As a historian Talbot deciphered Assyrian inscriptions and published papers in the journals of the Royal Society of Literature and the Society of Biblical Archaeology in 1854, 1857, 1860 and 1864. Along with Sir Henry Rawlinson and Dr. Edward Hincks, he was a pioneer in deciphering cuneiform inscriptions from Ninevah.

Sometimes called "the father of photography," Talbot invented the negative/positive process, devised a photogenic drawing process and invented the calotype (also known as the talbotype) in 1840. He produced the earliest negative (one inch square) in 1835 and published the first major book with photographic illustrations in 1844. Talbot also discovered a method for taking instantaneous pictures in 1851, invented a photoengraving process in 1852 and created a "traveller's" camera in 1854 (which combined a camera and two tanks, one for sensitizing wet plates and the other for developing prints).

Talbot used photogenic drawings, calotypes (talbotypes) and photoglyphic engravings to capture scenes in and around his home, Lacock Abbey, and environs. Much of his work consisted of simple documents of nineteenth-century life, although the composition and arrangement of some of it goes beyond factual records. Especially notable are his calotypes of chess players and of the construction of Nelson's column in Trafalgar Square. He also used photograms and photomicrographs to record botanical specimens, including enlargements of insect wings.

PUBLICATIONS Books pertaining to photography: *Annals of the Artists of Spain*, Sir William Stirling Maxwell, 4 vols., 1847; *The Talbotype Applied to Hieroglyphics*, 1846; *Sun Pictures of Scotland*, 1845; *The Pencil of Nature*, 1844–46. Other books: *Assyrian Texts*, trans., 1856; *English Etymologies*, 1847; *The Antiquity of the Book of Genesis*, 1839; *Hermes, or Classical and Antiquarian Researches*, 1838–39; *Legendary Tales in Verse and Prose*, 1830. Anthologies: *The Photograph Collector's Guide*, Lee D. Witkin & Barbara London, 1979; *The Invented Eye*, Edward Lucie-Smith, 1975; *The Magic Image*, Cecil Beaton & Gail Buckland, 1975. Periodicals: "Talbot's & Herschel's Photographic Experiments in 1839," Helmut Gernsheim, *Image*, no. 8, 1959; "H. Fox Talbot, Esq.," Beaumon & Newhall, *Modern Photography*, Dec 1952.

COLLECTIONS Art Inst. of Chicago; IMP/GEH, Rochester; L/C, Wash., D.C. (Prints and Photographs Div.); Metro. Mus. of Art, NYC; Princeton Univ., N.J.; Smithsonian Inst., Wash., D.C.; UCLA; Univ. of N. Mex. Art Mus., Albuquerque; Univ. of Tex., Gernsheim Cllctn. of Humanities Research Ctr., Austin; Wellesley Coll. Mus., Wellesley, Mass. Fox Talbot Mus., Lacock Abbey, Wiltshire, Great Britain; Natl. Gall. of Canada, Ottawa; RPS, London; Science Mus. of London.

ARCHIVE Fox Talbot Museum, Lacock Abbey, Wiltshire, England.

Akihide Tamura *PHOTOGRAPHER* Born March 13, 1947, in Tokyo, Tamura studied at the Tokyo College of Photography (1965–69).

In 1979 he became an instructor at Tokyo College of Photography, and he also teaches at Tokyo Zokei University (since 1972).

Tamura joined the Japan Professional Photographers Society in 1971.

PUBLICATIONS Monograph: *Photographs: Akihide Tamura*, 1978. Periodicals: *Nippon Camera*, Dec 1980, Aug 1975; *Asahi Camera*,

Sept 1970; *Camera Mainichi*, Sept 1970, Apr 1969, Feb 1969.

COLLECTION MOMA, NYC.

REPRESENTATIVE Zeit-Foto Co., Ltd, Yagicho-Bild. 5F, 1-4, Nihonbashi-Muromachi Chuo-Ku, Tokyo, Japan.

ADDRESS 3-13-12, Imaizumi-Dai, Kamakura, Kanagawa-Ken, Japan.

Chotoku Tanaka PHOTOGRAPHER Born May 31, 1947, in Tokyo, Japan, Tanaka received a BA from Nihon University.

A freelance photographer in Vienna, Austria, since 1973, he has taught at Salzburg College International Photo Workshop and International Summer Academy since 1978. From 1970 to 1973 Tanaka worked as a commercial photographer in the Japan Design Center.

He is a staff member of Japan Professional Photographers' Society.

Tanaka curated the traveling exhibit "New Photography from Japan," which was shown in Europe and Japan in 1976–79.

PUBLICATIONS Periodicals: *Camera*, Jan 1979, July 1970.

COLLECTIONS Polaroid Mus., Cambridge, Mass. In Vienna: Austria Lander Bank; Mus. of Modern Art; Mus. of 20th Century; Zentralsparkasse. Graz Kulturhaus, Austria; Salzburg Coll., Austria.

ADDRESS Chofushi Somechi 3-1-97, Tamagawa TO/10/101, Tokyo, Japan.

Kojo Tanaka PHOTOGRAPHER Born May 11, 1924, in Kambara-cho, Ihara-gun, Shizuoka Prefecture, Japan, Tanaka graduated from Hokkaido University's Department of Fisheries in Hakodate City, Hokkaido, Japan.

A freelance photographer since 1953, he has photographed wildlife all over the world.

Tanaka belongs to the Japanese Association for the Protection of Birds, the Mammalogical Society of Japan, Nature Photo Studio, Photographic Society of Japan and is a board member of Japan Photographers' Society. He was awarded the annual prize of the Photographic Society of Japan in 1971 and the Special Prize from the Japanese Society of Photographic Critics in 1964.

PUBLICATIONS Books: *Dobutsu ni Ai o Komete*, 1979 (Azuma Pub. Co.); *Sekai no Dobutsu o ou*, 1979 (Kodansha); *Sekai no Yasei Dobutsu*, 1978; *Galápagos Tankenki*, 1977 (Kokudo Sha); *Shakai Shiso Sha*, 7 vols., 1976/77; *Wildlife in the World Series*, 18 vols., 1975/77 (Komine Shoten); *Kori no Kuni no Dobutsu Tachi*, 1974 (NHK Press); *Zoku Dobutsu Kazoku*, w/Tetsuo Gyoda, 1974, *Dobutsu Kazoku*, w/Tetsuo Gyoda, 1970 (Asahi Shimbun Pub. Co.); *Yasei Dobutsu o ou—Sono Zuisoteki Satsuei-ho*, 1970 (Geijutsu Seikatsu Sha); *Wildlife in the World Series*, 5 vols., 1970/71 (Asahi Shimbun Pub. Co.); *Nihon no Yasei Dobutsu*, 1968 (Yama to Keikoku Sha); *Nihon Yasei Dobutsu Ki*, 1968 (Asahi Shimbun Sha).

ADDRESS Tanaka Kojo Office, Chateau Akasaka Rm. 405, 6-5-21, Akasaka, Minato-ku, Tokyo 107, Japan.

Paul Tanqueray PHOTOGRAPHER Born January 14, 1905, in Littlehampton, Sussex, England, Tanqueray studied at the Tonbridge School in England (1920–23). He was also a student at the studio of Hugh Cecil in London (1923–24).

After leaving Cecil's studio he set up his own and has ever since been self-employed as a photographer. His photographs have appeared many times in *Harper's Bazaar*.

During the 1930s Tanqueray was a member of the Institute of British Photographers.

He is known primarily for his portraits of such people as Gertrude Lawrence, Tallulah Bankhead and Cecil Beaton.

PUBLICATIONS Anthology: *The Magic Image*, Cecil Beaton & Gail Buckland, 1975. Catalog: *Monday's Children*, 1977 (Impressions Gall.: York, England).

ADDRESS London, England.

Takeyoshi Tanuma PHOTOGRAPHER · WRITER Born February 18, 1929, in Tokyo, Japan, Tanuma graduated from Tokyo Photography College in 1949. He names photographer Ihei Kimura as his mentor.

Currently a freelance, Tanuma was under contract with Time-Life from 1965 to 1972 and with Sincho-sha (a leading Tokyo publishing house) from 1951 to 1959. He served as a staff photographer for the Tokyo news agency Sun News Photos from 1949 to 1957.

Tanuma is a member of the Japan Photographers' Association and won its annual award in 1975. He also won the Children's Cultural Award, Mobil, in Japan in 1979.

He mainly photographs children, having traveled through sixty-five countries to do so.

PUBLICATIONS Books: *Bunshi*, 1979 (Sincho-sha: Tokyo); *These Marvelous Children*, 1979; *Playful Children*, 1978; *These Beautiful Children*, 1975; *Musashi Plains*, 1974 (Asahi Newspapers: Tokyo).

COLLECTIONS Baltimore Mus., Md.

ADDRESS 5-14-1 Higashi Nakano, Nakano-ku, Tokyo, Japan 164.

Sam Bejan Tata   *PHOTOJOURNALIST*   Born September 30, 1911, in Shanghai, China, of Indian parents, Tata studied at the University of Hong Kong in 1931–32 and began photographing in 1936. His friend Henri Cartier-Bresson was a major influence.

A self-employed photojournalist, he began practicing his profession full-time in 1956, after emigrating to Canada. He has contributed to *Maclean's*, *Chatelaine*, *Montrealer*, *Canadian Art* and *Time Canada*, among other journals.

A life member of RPS since 1948, he became a member of the Royal Canadian Academy in 1976. Tata won a gold medal at the All-India Exhibition in Bombay in 1947.

Using a small-format rangefinder camera, Tata takes candid photographs "in the streets of many cities in many countries," preferring black-and-white to color.

PUBLICATIONS   Books: *China the Great Unknown*, 1971 (Simon & Schuster: Canada); *Marcel Braitstein, Sculpteur*, Jean Simard, 1970 (Quebec Sculptors' Assn.: Montreal); *Call Them Canadians*, 1968 (Natl. Film Board of Canada: Ottawa); *Expo '67 Sculpture Dada-Nana*, 1967 (Tundra Books: Montreal); *Montreal*, Frank Lowe, 1963 (McClelland & Stewart: Toronto). Anthology: *Photography Yearbook*, 1979, 1976, 1965, 1964, 1953 (England). Periodicals: *Canadian Fiction Magazine*, no. 29, 1979; "Sam Tata, la lezione di Bresson," *Nuova Fotografia*, July/Aug 1976; *Camerart*, July 1974; "Sam Tata, l'artiste vu par l'artiste," Geoffrey James, *Vie des Arts*, spring 1973; *Image*, no. 6, 1970, no. 3, 1968, no. 2, 1967 (Natl. Film Board of Canada: Ottawa); review, John Linder, *Photoage*, Apr 1962; *Canadian Art*, Nov/Dec 1961; "Sam Tata's Rebellion," *Photography*, Oct 1956.

COLLECTIONS   MOMA, NYC. In Canada: Canada Council Art Bank, Ottawa; Concordia Univ., Montreal; Natl. Film Board of Canada, Ottawa; Natl. Gall., Ottawa; Public Archives, Ottawa.

ADDRESS   1750 Crevier, Apt 7, St Laurent, PQ, Canada H4L 2X5.

Henry William Taunt   *PHOTOGRAPHER · PUBLISHER*   Taunt (1842–1922) was born and died in Oxford, England. He was apprenticed to Edward Bracher, an early Oxford photographer, in 1856.

Taunt set up his own studio around 1868 and there published guidebooks and postcards. For many years he lectured at the University of Oxford's annual holiday program for children.

A Fellow of the Royal Geographical Society, Taunt was a sportsman, an excellent oarsman and a cyclist. He also was deeply involved in local civic affairs.

The photographer was known for his books, photographs and lantern slides of Oxford and the river Thames. Using a ladder for height, he photographed many races on the famed river.

PUBLICATIONS   Monograph: *A New Map of the River Thames*, 1872. Books: *The Scholar Gipsy*, *Thyrsis*, Matthew Arnold, n.d., *The Millenary of Oxford*, 1912?, *A Pretty Corner of Leafy Bucks*, 1910, Blenheim, Woodstock & Co., 1909, *Iffley Manor, Church and Village*, 1909?, *Iffley Mill and Its Story*, 1908?, *Oxford Illustrated by Camera and Pen*, 1908?, *Down the River to Nuneham and Avingdon*, 1907, *Charlbury, Oxon and Round It*, 1906?, *Dorchester (Oxon) and Its Abbey Church*, 1906?, *St. Giles Fair*, 1906, *The Boar's Head at Queen's College*, 1905, *Kirtlington, Oxon*, 1905?, *Godstow with Its Legend of Fair Rosamund . . .*, 1904?, *Photographs of Old Oxford*, 1901, *Fairford Church*, 189?, *Magdalen Tower on May Morning*, 1895, *The Rollright Stones: The Stonehenge of Oxfordshire*, 188? (all H. W. Taunt & Co., Oxford). Anthology: *The Invented Eye*, Edward Lucie-Smith, 1975.

Petr Tausk   *PHOTOHISTORIAN · WRITER · PHOTOGRAPHER*   Born January 24, 1927, in Prague, Czechoslovakia, Tausk earned a degree in chemistry in 1950 from Technical University in Prague, Faculty of Chemical Technology. He is self-educated in photography and photohistory.

Currently a scientific researcher in the Central Institute of Scientific, Technical and Economic Information in Prague, Tausk is also a visiting lecturer in the Department of Creative Photography of the Film and TV Faculty of the Academy of Musical Arts in Prague.

Tausk has been an associate member of the Union of Czechoslovak Creative Artists since 1967, registered in the Czech Fund of Creative Arts since 1979 and honorary secretary of the Czechoslovakian Committee of Fédération Internationale d'Art Photographique since 1969.

As a historian Tausk is concerned with the nature of creative photography and trends in twentieth-century photography. As a photographer he works in black-and-white and color, shooting landscapes, portraits and found objects.

PUBLICATIONS   Books: *Nestačí jen stisknout spoušť . . .*, 1978 (Práce: Prague); *Okamžitá fotografia, súčasnosť—možnosti—perspecktivy*, 1977 (Osveta: Martin); *Die Geschichte der Fotografie im 20 Jahrhundert*, 1977, repr. 1980

609

(DuMont Buchverlag: Cologne, Germany); *An Introduction to Press Photography*, 1976 (Internatl. Org. of Journalists: Prague); *Základy tvorivej farebnej fotografie*, 1973 (Osveta: Martin); *Oborová encyklopedia praktická fotografie*, 1972, *Fotografování s výměnnými objektivy*, w/B. Biskup, 1961 (SNTL: Prague).

COLLECTIONS Natl. Portrait Gall., London; Polaroid Cllctn., Amsterdam, The Netherlands.

ADDRESS Ondříčkova 9, CS-130 00 Prague 3, Žižkov, Czechoslovakia.

H. Arthur Taussig TEACHER · MIXED-MEDIA PHOTOGRAPHER · WRITER Born March 31, 1941, in Los Angeles, California, Taussig received a BS in Physics (1963) from University of California, Berkeley, and an MS in Biological Chemistry (1969) and a PhD in Biophysics (1971) at the University of California, Los Angeles. He studied photography with John Upton and Minor White.

From 1971 to the present Taussig has been an associate professor of photography, Department of Fine Arts, Orange Coast College in Costa Mesa, California. Since 1979 he has been both an instructor at Mr. Robert's Dance Studio in Newport Beach, California, and a contract instructor for Golden State Dance Teacher's Association in Downey, California. Taussig was director of the Orange Coast College Photography Gallery from 1975 to 1978; he was also acting head of its Photography Department and assistant division chairman of its Fine Arts Division from 1974 to 1976.

He is a member of several organizations: SPE, Los Angeles Graphic Arts Council, Friends of Photography, VSW, Los Angeles Institute of Contemporary Art and Los Angeles Center for Photographic Studies. Taussig has also done musical recordings, such as *Fate Is Only Once* (Talisman Records, Los Angeles, 1975) and *Contemporary Folk Guitar: Leo Kotke, Robbie Basho, John Fahey, Arthur Taussig* (Takoma Records, Berkeley, California, 1977).

Of his work Taussig states: "I have been concerned with printmaking, using photographic materials [and] . . . have worked with computer image generation, black-and-white and color prints, Xerox, animation, video, film, photobooths, book-making, etc. I am concerned with the issues and let the solutions select the specific medium for the expression of that solution."

PUBLICATIONS Periodicals: Review, "Arthur Taussig, An Interview With an Art Person," Marcia Wooding, *35mm Photography*, spring 1979; *Untitled #11*, 1976, *Untitled #9*, 1975 (Friends of Photography).

PORTFOLIOS *New California Views* (group), 1979 (Landweber/Artist: Los Angeles); *Silver See* (group), 1977 (Los Angeles Ctr. for Photographic Studies).

COLLECTIONS ARCO Ctr. for the Visual Arts, Los Angeles; Art Inst. of Chicago; CCP, Tucson; Harvard Univ., Fogg Art Mus., Cambridge, Mass.; IMP/GEH, Rochester; Los Angeles Ctr. for Photographic Studies; Los Angeles County Art Mus.; Metro. Mus. of Art, NYC; Mills College, Oakland, Calif.; Minneapolis Inst. of the Arts, Minn.; MOMA, NYC; Newport Harbor Art Mus., Newport Beach, Calif.; Oakland Mus. of Art, Calif.; Rochester Inst. of Technology; Security Pacific Bank, Los Angeles, Pomona, Santa Barbara, Calif.; Smith Coll. Mus. of Art, Northampton, Mass.; St. Louis Mus. of Art, Mo.; Stephen White Gall., Los Angeles; Susan Spiritus, Newport Beach, Calif.; Tyler Univ. Art Mus., Tex.; UCLA, Frederick Wight Art Mus., Los Angeles; Univ. of N. Mex. Art Mus., Albuquerque.

DEALER Robert Freidus Gall., Inc, 158 Lafayette St, New York, NY 10013.

ADDRESS 2404 Narbonne Way, Costa Mesa, CA 92627.

Patricia May Tavenner COLLAGE ARTIST · PHOTOGRAPHER · TEACHER Born March 22, 1941, in Doster, Michigan, Tavenner earned a BA from Michigan State University, East Lansing, and an MFA from California College of Arts and Crafts in Oakland.

Currently on the Art Faculty of University of California, Berkeley Extension in San Francisco, between 1972 and 1975 she taught variously at San Jose State University, San Francisco State University, San Francisco Art Institute and California College of Arts and Crafts.

Tavenner belongs to the Women's Caucus for Art.

The artist creates photo-collages, correspondence art and "meditation drawings." She also conducts workshops on exploring creative energy.

PUBLICATIONS Books: *Collaging With Paper*, G. Brommer, 1978; *Rubber Stamps*, Lori Thompson, ed., 1978; *Innovative Printmaking*, Thelma Newman, 1977; *Art et Comunication Marginale*, Herve Fisher, 1974 (Balland: Paris); *Collage and Assemblage*, Donna Meilach, 1973. Anthologies: *Women See Woman*, 1976; *Art: A Woman's Sensibility*, Miriam Shapiro, ed., 1975.

COLLECTIONS Cornell Univ., Herbert F. Johnson Art Mus., Ithaca, N.Y.; Kansas City Art Inst., Mo.; Oakland Mus. of Art, Calif.; Smith Coll.,

Amherst, Mass.; Wichita Art Mus., Kans. Simon Frazer Univ., Vancouver, Canada.

DEALER Artworks, 66 Windward Ave, Venice, CA 90291.

ADDRESS POB 11032, Oakland, CA 94611.

Brian D. Taylor *PHOTOGRAPHER · TEACHER*
Born in Tucson, Arizona, in 1954, Taylor received a BA in Visual Arts (1975) from the University of California, San Diego, an MA in Art Education (1976) from Stanford University, Stanford, California, and an MFA in Photography (1979) from the University of New Mexico, Albuquerque.

As of this writing Taylor was an assistant professor at San Jose State University, California. He taught at the University of New Mexico in 1978–79 and was an honorary teaching fellow at Stanford University in 1976.

Taylor belongs to SPE, CAA and Friends of Photography.

PUBLICATIONS Anthology: *Non-Silver Photography: Alternative Photographic Processes*, 1980. Catalogs: *Attitudes: Photography in the 1970's*, 1979 (Santa Barbara Mus. of Art, Calif.); *Translations: Photographic Images with New Forms*, 1979 (Herbert F. Johnson Mus. of Art, Cornell Univ., Ithaca, N.Y.); *New Photographics/78*, 1978 (Central Wash. Univ., Ellensburg). Periodical: *Artweek*, May 6, 1978.

COLLECTIONS Mus. of N. Mex., Santa Fe; Occidental Coll., Los Angeles; Seattle Art Mus., Wash.; Security Pacific Bank, Los Angeles; Stanford Univ., Calif.; Susan Spiritus Gall., Newport Beach, Calif.; Univ. of N. Mex. Art Mus., Albuquerque.

ADDRESS 60 Roberts Rd, #19, Los Gatos, CA 95030.

Harold Dennis Taylor *OPTICIAN* Born in 1862 in Huddersfield, England, Taylor died in 1943. He was educated at St. Peter's School in York.

His early interest in photographic optics led to his patenting of an exposure meter based on the use of a standard candle (1885) and an achromatic teleobjective (1892). But he received international fame—and stimulated the development of most modern anastigmat lenses—by his creation of triplet lenses in 1893. He continued to improve on them during the next ten years. Taylor also studied lens coating and, in 1904, patented a coating of ammonia and sulphuretted hydrogen, although it was another generation before the idea of lens coating became accepted.

Taylor received the Progress Medal of the RPS in 1935.

PUBLICATIONS Books: *Die Photographische Kamera*, Josef Stuper, 1962; *March of Photography*, Erich Stenger, 1958; *Focal Encyclopedia of Photography*, 1957, 1956 (Focal Press); *Photography Principles and Practice*, 3rd ed., C. B. Neblette, 1939; *A System of Applied Optics*, 1906. Anthology: *Photography's Great Inventors*, Louis W. Sipley, 1965. Periodicals: *Bild und Ton*, 1959; *Jahrbuch für Photographie und Reproduktionstechnik*, Josef Maria Eder, 1895; "A Simplified Form and Improved Type of Photographic Lens," *British Journal of Photography*, Dec 28, 1894.

Herb Taylor *PHOTOGRAPHER · WRITER · EDITOR* Born in Brooklyn, New York, on June 11, 1942, Taylor studied at City University of New York from 1970 to 1978.

He is currently the editor-in-chief of the *American Photographic Book Publishing Co.* (Amphoto), Garden City, New York.

In 1975 Taylor's book *The Lobster: Its Life Cycle*, was selected by the New York Academy of Sciences as one of the best science books for children published that year.

Taylor's documentary style depicts the ecology of different environments, and most of his work is in the field of underwater photography.

PUBLICATIONS Books: *Encyclopedia of Practical Photography*, ed., 1978; *Underwater with the Nikonos and Nikon Systems*, 1976; *The Lobster: Its Life Cycle*, 1975.

ADDRESS c/o Amphoto, 750 Zeckendorf Blvd, Garden City, NY 11530.

Jeremy Magee Taylor *PHOTOGRAPHER* Born March 11, 1938, in Montreal, Quebec, Canada, Taylor studied at the Instituto Allende, San Miguel de Allende, Guanajuato, Mexico. In 1959 he began photography studies with Pete Olwyler and Reva Brooks, and he attended Ansel Adams' Yosemite Workshop in 1969. Taylor names Edward Weston and Alfred Stieglitz as major influences. His father, Frederich B. Taylor (1906–   ), is a painter and sculptor.

Self-employed since 1962 as a photographer, Taylor specializes in architecture and portraiture. He also provides an archival printing service for such clients as the National Film Board of Canada, National Archives of Canada and individual photographers.

He belongs to Toronto Photographers Cooperative and the Canadian Natural Hygiene Society.

Primarily using a large-format camera and

long-scale black-and-white prints, Taylor "began photography concentrating on faces, objects, basic forms in nature." He now photographs "views of large spaces, sometimes with a single object dividing the field, emphasizing subtle differences on either side."

PUBLICATIONS Books: *Call Them Canadians*, 1967, *Canada/A Year of the Land*, 1967 (Natl. Film Board of Canada). Anthologies: *Image 6*, 1970, *Image 2*, 1968 (Natl. Film Board of Canada); *FIAP Yearbook*, 1969 (Fédération Internationale d'Art Photographique: Switzerland).

COLLECTIONS Natl. Film Bd. of Canada, Ottawa, Ontario; Natl. Gall. of Canada, Ottawa; Victoria & Albert Mus., London.

REPRESENTATIVE Baldwin Photography, 729 Carlaw Ave, Toronto, Ontario, Canada M4K 3K8.

ADDRESS 24 Kippendavie Ave, Toronto, Ontario, Canada M4L 3R4.

Liba Taylor PHOTOJOURNALIST Born May 30, 1950, in Prague, Czechoslovakia, Taylor earned a BA in Spanish and History of Art from the University of Bristol, England (1974), and a Certificate in Radio, Film and Television Studies (1975) from Bristol University, England.

A freelance photographer, she belongs to Xenon Photos in London. She won an Arts Council of Great Britain grant in 1977 to photograph Eastern religions in England.

Taylor shoots mainly in black-and-white in a documentary style. Her main photographic subjects are Eastern religions in England (Hare Krishnas, Western Buddhists, etc.) and people around the world.

PUBLICATION Anthology: *New British Image*, 1978 (Arts Council of Great Britain).

COLLECTION Arts Council of Great Britain.

DEALER The Photographers Gall., 8 Great Newport St, London WC2, England.

ADDRESS 142 Coleherne Ct, ld Brompton Rd, London SW5, England.

Paul Schuster Taylor ECONOMIST·PHOTOGRAPHER Born June 9, 1895, in Sioux City, Iowa, Taylor earned an AB from the University of Wisconsin, Madison, and an MA and PhD from the University of California, Berkeley. His wife was the late photographer Dorothea Lange.

Presently professor of economics emeritus at the University of California, Berkeley, Taylor was research director for the California Labor Federation in 1970. He was a consultant to the United Nations in 1963 and to the Agency for International Development at various times from 1955 to 1968. He consulted with the Department of Interior from 1943 to 1952, with the Export-Import Bank in 1952 and with the Social Security Board from 1936 to 1941. Taylor served as field director for the Division of Rural Rehabilitation of the California Emergency Relief Administration in 1935 and was regional labor adviser for the U.S. Resettlement Administration (later the Farm Security Administration) in 1935.

The economist was a member of the California State Board of Agriculture (1940–44) and the Governor's Commission on Reemployment in 1939. He won the Wagner Award from the California Historical Society in 1977 and a Guggenheim Fellowship in 1931.

Says Taylor, "I have used photography personally to document my field researches . . . in Arandas and Tateposco, Mexico, India, Pakistan and the Philippines."

PUBLICATIONS Books: *An American Exodus*, w/Dorothea Lange, 1939, rev. ed. 1969; *Making Cantaros in San Jose Tateposco*, 1932; *A Spanish-Mexican Peasant Community: Arandas in Jalisco, Mexico*, 1934.

COLLECTIONS (Dorothea Lange collections) L/C, Wash., D.C.; Natl. Archives, Wash., D.C.; Oakland Mus., Calif.

ADDRESS 1163 Euclid Ave, Berkeley, CA 94708.

Roger James Taylor TEACHER · WRITER · PHOTOGRAPHER Born October 31, 1940, in Cheshire, England, Taylor received a Diploma in Creative Photography, 1st Class, from Derby College of Art (1967) and an MA in Victorian Studies from the University of Leicester, England (1977).

Since 1968 he has been a senior lecturer in Photographic Studies at Sheffield City [England] Polytechnic. Taylor taught at Derby College of Art in 1966 and worked for commercial photographer Rex Lowden (1958–66). He has been chairman of the Photographic Advisory Committee, Yorkshire Arts Association, since 1979.

Taylor conducts research on nineteenth-century landscape photography, particularly on the photographer George Washington Wilson (1852–93). He has also compiled microfilm publications on the Royal Collection photographs at Windsor Castle and the photography archives of the Victoria and Albert Museum.

PUBLICATIONS Anthologies: *Photographs from the Victoria and Albert Museum*, 1980 (World Microfilms: London); *Photographs from the Royal Archives*, 1978 (World Microfilms: London); *Happy & Glorious*, 1977 (Angus and Robertson: London).

Theron Eldridge Taylor, Jr.   *PHOTOGRAPHER*
Born April 10, 1944, in Denver, Colorado, Taylor studied at the University of Colorado Denver Center in 1962–63 and at the Center of the Eye Photography Workshop in Aspen, Colorado, in 1969 and 1971. He names Gordon Parks, Minor White, Barbara Crane, Jack Welpott and Judy Dater as major influences.

Taylor has worked at the Photographic Center in Denver since 1978 and has been an audio/visual consultant since 1975. He directed the Denver Model City Cultural Center from 1968 to 1971 and was chief photographer for *The Denver Chronicle* in 1968–69.

The photographer creates mainly black-and-white environmental portraits using various formats and does some photojournalism. As of this writing he was experimenting with combining enlargements and photograms.

PUBLICATIONS   Anthologies: *Black Photographers Annual*, 1975, 1973; *Time/Life Yearbook*, 1974. Periodical: *Foto*, June/July 1972 (Sweden).

COLLECTIONS   Another View, Inc., NYC; Internatl. Photo Optical Show Assoc., Los Angeles; Van Der Zee Inst., NYC.

ADDRESS   8405 E Hampden, #3P, Denver, CO 80231.

Willard G. Taylor   *PHOTOGRAPHER*   Born July 21, 1938, in Richmond, Virginia, Taylor earned a BA in Philosophy (1973) and an MS in Media Technology (1975). His major influences were Dexter Oliver and Joseph "Tex" Gathings.

Currently he is president and founder of Visual Communication Concepts, Inc. (since 1978) and director of photography for the University of the District of Columbia Learning Resources Division (since 1978). He was president and co-founder of Educational Media and Systems Design in 1973–74, and a freelance photographer from 1968 to 1974.

Taylor belongs to the Capitol Press Club, National Academy of Television Arts and Sciences and Association for Educational Communications and Technology. He won First Place in Photography at the Expressions Art Festival in Richmond, Virginia, in 1977, a Cafritz Fellowship in 1973 and a Semester in Ghana Scholarship in 1972.

PUBLICATIONS   Books: *The Philosophical Foundations of the African Personality*, 1975; *Logic for Black Undergraduates*, 1974. Anthol-

ogy: *Photography Year 1977*, Time-Life Series, 1978. Periodical: *Black Photographers Annual*, 1974.

ADDRESS   POB 3037, Washington, DC 20010.

Helga Teiwes   *PHOTOGRAPHER*   Born in Meerbusch, near Düsseldorf, Germany, Teiwes received a BA in Art History in 1978 from the University of Arizona, Tucson. She also studied at the Hehmke-Winderer Studio in Düsseldorf for seven years with Erna Hehmke-Wagner.

Since 1965 Teiwes has been employed as a staff photographer for the Arizona State Museum in Tucson. She previously worked for the CCF Color Lab in New York City from 1962 to 1964 as a color transparency retoucher.

A member of the Professional Photographers of America from 1961 to 1963, and 1976 to the present, she was awarded a special University of Arizona Foundation grant to document the life of the Papago Indians in 1977. She also created two documentary films, entitled *Excavations at Snaketown* (1967) and *Mission San Xavier del Bac* (1969).

The photographer produces photographic documentation of the modern life of Indian groups from the greater Southwest, including northern Mexico.

PUBLICATIONS   Books: *The Material Culture of the Tarahumara Indians*, 1979; *The Hohokam: Desert Farmers and Craftsmen*, Haury, 1976; *Prehistoric Southwestern Craft Arts*, C. L. Tanner, 1976; *Indians of Arizona*, Thomas Weaver, 1974; *A Pima Past*, Anna Moore Shaw, 1974; *Saints of San Xavier*, R. E. Ahlborn, 1974; *The San Xavier Altarpiece*, R. C. Goss, 1974; *Mission San Xavier del Bac*, Teiwes, 1973; *Speaking of Indians*, Bernice Johnston, 1970.

COLLECTION   Univ. of Ariz. State Mus., Tucson.

ADDRESS   2611 N Teresa Ln, Tucson, AZ 85705.

John Telford   *PHOTOGRAPHER · TEACHER*
Born December 31, 1944, in Salt Lake City, Utah, the mainly self-taught photographer studied briefly with Ansel Adams and Wynn Bullock.

Since 1976 Telford has been director of Photographic Services at the University of Utah, Salt Lake City. From 1973 to 1976 he founded and directed Edison Street Gallery in Salt Lake City, and from 1969 to 1976 was a commercial photographer for Borge Andersen and Assoc., also in Salt Lake City.

A member of SPE since 1977, in 1975 Telford

founded and directed Light Source, a Utah photographers' organization.

Working with large-format black-and-white and color, he produces "straight" photographs, primarily of the natural landscape "with emphasis on the mysterious, surreal, and abstract forms in nature."

PORTFOLIO *Great Salt Lake Portfolio,* 1979 (self-pub.).

COLLECTIONS Univ. of Utah, Marriott Lib. & Medical Ctr., Salt Lake City; Utah Mus. of Fine Art, Salt Lake City; Utah State Univ., Logan.

REPRESENTATIVE Erica Wangsgard, 531 E Eighth S, Salt Lake City, UT 84102.

ADDRESS 2442 Charros Rd, Sandy, UT 84070.

Michael Jerome Teres PHOTOGRAPHER · TEACHER Born in Brooklyn, New York, on June 13, 1940, Teres earned a BA in Fine Arts from Hunter College in New York City (1962) and an MFA in Photography from the University of Iowa, Iowa City (1966). He names John Schulze as his mentor, and Man Ray and Jerry Uelsmann as major influences.

Teres has been an associate professor at State University of New York, Geneseo, since 1966. He belongs to the American Association of University Professors and SPE (since 1964). The photographer won a CAPS fellowship in 1975 and participated in Collaborations in Art, Science, and Technology, Inc. (CAST), in 1975 and 1978 (funded by the New York State Arts Council). He also won SUNY Faculty Research Committee grants in 1975 and 1978 and a Geneseo Foundation grant in 1974.

Teres produces "reticulated and manipulated imagery based on the figure and the landscape as subjects." He also studies the reticulation process as related to color manipulations.

PUBLICATIONS Books: "Reticulation," *Darkroom Dynamics,* Jim Stone, ed., 1979; *Photography: A Handbook of History, Materials and Processes,* Charles Swedlund, 1974. Catalog: *Horses and Hounds of the Genesee,* 1973 (W. F. Humphrey Press: Geneva, N.Y.). Periodical: *Creative Camera,* May 1976.

COLLECTIONS Art Inst. of Chicago; Chrysler Mus., Norfolk, Va.; Clemson Univ. Coll. of Arch., Clemson, S.C.; Greenville County Mus. of Art, Greenville, S.C.; IMP/GEH, Rochester; Metro. Mus. of Art, NYC; SUNY, Brockport; Univ. of Nebr., Lincoln.

REPRESENTATIVE Light Impressions, Box 3012, Rochester, NY 14614.

ADDRESS 4322 Reservoir Rd, Geneseo, NY 14454.

Edmund Teske PHOTOGRAPHER · TEACHER Born in Chicago on March 7, 1911, Teske credits his elementary school instructor, Mabel A. Morehouse, with being the most creative influence of his formative years. Morehouse taught him darkroom technique in 1923. In 1931 he attended evening classes at Huttle Art Studio in Chicago to study painting and drawing. During his residency in the theater department of the renowned Jane Addams Hull House, Teske learned about set design, acting and theatrical makeup. As a member of Frank Lloyd Wright's Taliesin Fellowship (1936), Teske began to photograph several of the houses Wright designed (1938). A guiding influence for his later work began in 1945 when he was first exposed to Vedantic thought through the teachings of the Hindu Swami Prabhavananda and learned about Hindu mythology and symbolism.

Since 1979 Teske has been a visiting professor at California State University in Los Angeles. Before that (1965–70), he held the same post at University of California in Los Angeles. In 1975 the photographer earned an NEA Fellowship and in 1969 received a Certificate of Recognition from the Photographic Society of America.

The artist is known for his multiple-image montages in which aspects of the Hindu mythology of Shiva (representing the male principle) and Shakhti (representing the female principle) are explored. Teske also developed a process called duotone solarization, which combines chemical toning and solarization.

PUBLICATIONS Anthologies: *The Photograph Collector's Guide,* Lee D. Witkin & Barbara London, 1979; *The Art of Photography,* Time-Life Series, 1971; *Be-ing Without Clothes,* Minor White, ed., 1970; *The Print,* Time-Life Series, 1970. Catalogs: *Edmund Teske,* Gerald Nordland, 1974 (Municipal Art Gall., Barnsdall Park: Los Angeles); *Light and Substance,* 1974 (Univ. of N. Mex. Art Mus.: Albuquerque); *Photography, U.S.A.,* 1967 (DeCordova Mus.: Lincoln, Mass.).

PORTFOLIO *Silver See* (group), 1977 (Los Angeles Ctr. for Photographic Studies).

COLLECTIONS Art Inst. of Chicago; CCP, Tucson, IMP/GEH, Rochester; MOMA, NYC; New Orleans Mus. of Art; Oakland Mus., Calif.; Norton Simon Mus. of Art, Pasadena, Calif.; Princeton Univ., N.J.; San Francisco Mus. of Modern Art; UCLA; Univ. of Ill., Krannert Art Mus., Urbana; Univ. of Nebr., Sheldon Memorial Art Gall., Lincoln; Univ. of N. Mex., Albuquerque; Virginia Mus. of Fine Arts, Richmond.

ADDRESS 1652 N Harvard Blvd, Los Angeles, CA 90027.

Ted Tessler *PHOTOGRAPHER · TEACHER · GRAPHIC ARTS CONSULTANT* Born April 22, 1919, in Philadelphia, Pennsylvania, Tessler studied at the Photo League (1946–51) with Walter Rosenblum, Don Weiner and Sid Grossman, and received a BS from New York University in 1950.

A freelance photographer since 1950, he has been a faculty member of the New School for Social Research in Manhattan since 1977 and since 1969 has been creative director of Sabine Press and Advertising in New York City. He has also taught photography at Queens College, Flushing, New York (1969), and at Cooper Union in New York City (1964–68).

Tessler has belonged to ASMP since 1956 and was a charter member of SPE.

The photographer's work includes photojournalism, in-depth studies of landscapes and shoreline forms, and photos of theater and public events.

COLLECTIONS ICP, NYC; IMP/GEH, Rochester. Natl. Gall. of Canada, Toronto.

DEALER Neikrug Gall., 224 E 68 St, New York, NY 10021.

ADDRESS 85 Arleigh Rd, Great Neck, NY 11021.

Ron Testa *PHOTOGRAPHER* Born October 31, 1942, in Youngstown, Ohio, Testa received a BFA in Photography from Cleveland Institute of Art (1965) and an MFA in Photography from VSW (of State University of New York), Rochester (1973). His major influences were Edward Hopper, Andy Warhol, Robert Frank and Nathan Lyons.

Testa has been head photographer at Field Museum, Chicago, since 1975 and previously taught photography at the Baldwin School in New York City (1973–75) and at Naples Mill School, Naples, New York (1972–73). In 1970 he was a photography salesman for Dodd Co., Cleveland, and from 1966 to 1970 he was a combat photographer on the U.S. Navy ship USS *Ticonderoga*.

Testa won a CAPS grant in 1973.

PUBLICATIONS Monograph: *Transient Places*, 1975. Anthology: *Vision and Expression*, 1968. Catalog: *Feather Arts Catalogue*, 1979 (Field Museum, Chicago). Periodicals: *Creative Camera*, Feb 1975; *Popular Photography*, summer 1973.

PORTFOLIO *Portfolio One* (group), 1972 (VSW, Rochester).

COLLECTIONS Cleveland Inst. of Art, Ohio; Cleveland Mus. of Art; Columbia Coll., Chicago; IMP/GEH, Rochester; MOMA, NYC; Mus. of Contemporary Art, Chicago; VSW, Rochester.

Amer. Arts Documentation Centre, Exeter, England.

ADDRESS 3313 N Hamilton St, Chicago, IL 60618.

Alfred B. Thomas, Jr. *PHOTOGRAPHER · ASSISTANT ENGINEER* Born December 30, 1925 in Easton, Pennsylvania, Thomas attended Lafayette College in Easton and studied photography under Otto Litzel.

He has been an assistant in the Engineering Department of the New York Telephone Company since 1948.

Thomas belongs to PSA, Volunteer Service Photographers, Inc., and is president of the Teaneck Camera Club.

PUBLICATIONS Periodicals: review, Fred McDarrah, *Village Voice*, June 4, 1979; *Camera 35*, Oct 1977, Feb 1976; *Popular Photography*, Nov 1976, Aug 1975.

COLLECTION Philadelphia Mus., Pa.

DEALER Alonzo Gall., 30 W 57 St, New York, NY 10019.

ADDRESS 52 Beverly Pl, Bergenfield, NJ 07621.

George Robert Thomas *PHOTOGRAPHER* Born 1887 in Washington, D.C., he died April 29, 1944, in New York City. He was known professionally as Tommy Vandamm. His wife, Florence Vandamm, also a photographer, was his partner.

Thomas worked with various engineering firms in New York City until World War I. Then, in 1915, he went to England to make small engine parts for the British Air Board. There he met and married Florence Vandamm, who was operating a portrait studio in London's West End. Thomas became interested in the profession, joined his wife, and the two added illustration and fashion photography to the portrait work. In 1923 they came to New York, establishing a business there that came to specialize in theatrical photography.

He was a member of The Players.

While Florence Vandamm conducted most of the studio work, Thomas was in the theaters, photographing the shows. During his sixteen years as a photographer, he documented more than 75 percent of Broadway's shows.

Lew Thomas *PHOTOGRAPHER · PUBLISHER · EDITOR · CURATOR* Born December 19, 1932, in San Francisco, Thomas earned a BA from the University of San Francisco in 1960.

He has managed the Legion of Honor Bookshop since 1963 and been the publisher of NFS Press since 1975, both in San Francisco.

Thomas belongs to the Artists Committee of the San Francisco Art Institute.

The photographer won an Artists Fellowship and a publications grant from the NEA in 1979 as well as an NEA Photographer's Fellowship in 1980 and 1975. He received a publications grant from the San Francisco Museum of Modern Art in 1976.

Thomas explores photography "as a system of information and reproduction," creating photographs, installations, collaborative projects and publications. Since 1971 he has combined "the practice of photography with ideas derived from language and philosophy."

PUBLICATIONS Books: *Structural(ism) & Photography*, 1979; *Photography & Ideology*, ed., 1977; *Eros & Photography*, co-ed., 1977; *Photography & Language*, ed., 1976; *8 x 10*, 1975. Catalog: *The Thinker*, 1974 (Fine Arts Museums of San Francisco).

COLLECTIONS Achenbach Fndn. for Graphic Arts, San Francisco; Fraenkel Gall., San Francisco; MOMA, NYC; Princeton Univ., N.J.; Univ. of Santa Clara, De Saisset Art Gall., Calif.; Wash. Proj. for the Arts, Wash., D.C.

DEALER Fraenkel Gall., 55 Grant Ave, San Francisco, CA 94108.

ADDRESS POB 31040, San Francisco, CA 94131.

Barbara G. Thompson *PHOTOGRAPHER* Born November 8, 1942, in Connecticut, Thompson received a BFA in Photography in 1974 from the San Francisco Art Institute, California, and an MFA in Photography in 1976 from Lone Mountain College, San Francisco. She also studied at Skidmore College, Saratoga Springs, New York, from 1960 to 1964.

She has taught photography at Dominican College, San Rafael, California, since 1977 and at Academy of Art College, San Francisco, since 1979. From 1976 to 1977 she was a photography instructor at the San Francisco Museum of Modern Art.

Thompson won a Lilly Foundation grant from Dominican College in 1979.

The photographer works in square format, producing color still lifes and studies of interiors. Her earlier work included cyanotypes, cloth pieces and cyanotype books.

PUBLICATION Anthology: *Self-Portrayal*, James Alinder, ed., 1978.

ADDRESS POB 196, Fairfax, CA 94930.

Dody (Warren Weston) Thompson *PHOTOG-RAPHER · AUTHOR · FILM MAKER* Born in New Or-leans, Louisiana, in 1923, Thompson studied at Tulane University (Newcomb) in New Orleans and at Black Mountain College in Asheville, North Carolina. She apprenticed with Edward Weston and served as assistant to Ansel Adams.

Self-employed, she belongs to the Los Angeles Center for Photographic Studies. In 1956 Thompson won the Albert M. Bender Award from the San Francisco Art Association.

She wrote the film *Prehistoric America*, produced by Camera Eye/McGraw-Hill, in 1960.

PUBLICATIONS Books: *The Great Themes*, Time-Life Series, 1970; *Photography of the World*, 1958 (Tokyo); *My Camera on Point Lobos*, text only, Edward Weston, 1950. Periodicals: *U.S. Camera Yearbook*, 1957; "Perceptions," text only, *U.S. Camera*, Aug 1954; "Brett Weston, Photographer," Sept 1952, article & photos, Jan 1951, *American Photography*, "Photography as Art," no. 3, 1952, 2:2, 1:3, *Aperture*.

PORTFOLIO *L.A. Issue* (group), 1979 (Los Angeles Ctr. for Photographic Studies).

COLLECTIONS CCP, Tucson; IMP/GEH, Rochester; Minneapolis Inst. of Art, Minn.; MOMA, NYC; Princeton Univ., McAlpin Cllctn., Princeton, N.J.; Univ. of N. Mex., Van Deren Coke Cllctn., Albuquerque; Lee Witkin Cllctn., NYC.

DEALERS Stephen White Gall., 835 N La Cienega Blvd, Los Angeles, CA 90069; Douglas Elliott Gall., 1151 Mission St, San Francisco, CA 94103.

ADDRESS 10520 Blythe Ave, Los Angeles, CA 90064.

John Thomson *PHOTOGRAPHER* [See plate 25] Born 1837 in Edinburgh, Scotland, Thomson died in 1921. He attended Edinburgh University, where he studied chemistry.

Thomson spent between five and ten years in the Far East, which he left in 1865. He established a studio in London and did some teaching of photography as well as publishing a short-lived periodical, *Street Life of London* (1877–78), with Adolphe Smith.

Thomson was a fellow of the Royal Geographical Society from about 1866 until his death. In 1876 he translated Gaston Tissandier's *Les Merveilles de la Photographie* into English.

Primarily noted as one of the earliest social documentarians, Thomson's series of photographs illustrating the working class made *Street Life in London* the first published social documentary illustrated with photographs. Working with collodion wet plates and albumen prints, he also documented much of life in the Far East.

PUBLICATIONS Books: *Through China with a*

Camera, 1898; *Through Cyprus with the Camera*, 2 vols., 1879; *Street Life in London*, Adolphe Smith, 1877, repr. 1969; *The Straits of Malacca, Indo-China and China*, 1875; *Illustrations of China and Its People*, 4 vols., 1873; *Foo Chew and the River Min*, 1872; *The Antiquities of Cambodia*, 1867. Anthologies: *The Photograph Collector's Guide*, Lee D. Witkin & Barbara London, 1979; *The Invented Eye*, Edw. Lucie-Smith, 1975; *The Magic Image*, Cecil Beaton & Gail Buckland, 1975; *Early Photographs and Early Photographers*, Oliver Mathews, 1973; *Documentary Photography*, 1972, *Great Photographers*, 1971, *Light and Film*, 1970, Time-Life Series.

COLLECTIONS Boston Pub. Lib.; IMP/GEH, Rochester; Univ. of N. Mex. Art Mus., Albuquerque. Royal Geographical Society, London; RPS, London.

Otmar Uwe Thormann PHOTOGRAPHER
Born September 26, 1944, in Graz, Austria, Thormann attended the Stockholm School of Photography.

A freelance photographer since 1970, he won artist scholarships from the Swedish state in 1979 and 1976.

Using a variety of large formats, Thormann produces still lifes, interiors, portraits, landscapes and experimental works.

PUBLICATIONS Monograph: *Otmar Thormann*, 1979 (Gall. Camera Obscura: Stockholm). Periodicals: *Protokolle*, no. 3, 1979, no. 2, 1976; *Foto*, no. 3, 1977, no. 10, 1972 (Sweden); *Fotografia Italiana*, no. 4, 1974; *Photography Year Book*, 1972 (Great Britain); *Photography of the World*, 1971–72; *Populär Fotografi*, no. 2, 1971; *Camera*, no. 8, 1970.

COLLECTIONS Moderna Muséet, Fotografiska Muséet, Stockholm, Sweden; Sammlung Fotografis, Vienna, Austria.

DEALERS Stephen White Gall., 835 N La Cienega Blvd, Los Angeles, CA 90069; Gallery·Rudolf Kicken, Albertusstrasse D-5000, Cologne 1, West Germany; Gall. Camera Obscura, Stockholm, Sweden.

ADDRESS Norr Mälarstrand 82, S112 35, Stockholm, Sweden.

Ruth Thorne-Thomsen PHOTOGRAPHER ·
TEACHER Born May 13, 1943, in New York City, Thorne-Thomsen earned a BFA in Painting from Southern Illinois University, Carbondale (1970), a BA in Photography from Columbia College, Chicago (1973), and an MFA in Photography from the School of the Art Institute, Chicago (1976).

She has been an adjunct professor at Columbia College since 1974, and served as staff photographer for the *Chicago Sun-Times* in 1978.

A member of SPE, she received an NEH summer seminar fellowship to Paris in 1979 and a John Quincy Adams Fellowship in 1976.

Thorne-Thomsen danced with the Sybil Shearer Dance Company in Northbrook, Illinois, in 1964–65.

Using a pinhole camera and paper negatives, the photographer produces 4 x 5 silver contact prints and mural-size enlargements of approximately 3 x 4 feet. She describes her work as "environmental collage."

PUBLICATIONS Anthology: *The Nude in Photography*, Arthur Goldsmith, 1975. Periodicals: *American Photographer*, June 1979; *Afterimage: VSW*, Feb 1977; *Photography Annual*, 1977.

COLLECTIONS Art Inst. of Chicago; Exchange Natl. Bank, Chicago; Graham Nash Cllctn., Los Angeles; Mus. of Contemporary Art, Chicago; San Francisco Mus. of Modern Art; Seagram Cllctn., NYC. Bibliothèque Nationale, Paris.

DEALER Frumkin Gallery Photographs Inc., 620 S Michigan Ave, Chicago, IL 60605.

ADDRESS 1924 N Halsted St, Chicago, IL 60614.

Finn Erik Thrane PHOTOGRAPHER · TEACHER
Born July 5, 1939, in Svendborg, Denmark, Thrane is mainly self-taught. He spent a semester at the Danish Film School in 1974.

Since 1972 he has taught photography at Askov Folk High School, and has also done freelance photography. Thrane joined the Danish Film Teachers Society in 1972.

In 1979 the photographer received a grant from the J. Th. Arnfred Foundation.

His early work was documentary in nature, but recently he is more interested in "pure expression." He attempts to "break the illusion of the 'realistic photograph' and introduce a 'psychological truth.'" Thrane attempts this by making series in rather small formats and bringing the viewer in close to the image.

PUBLICATIONS Periodicals: *Foto Og Smalfilm*, July/Aug 1978, Dec 1977, Jan 1974; *Kosmorama*, Dec 1971.

COLLECTIONS Lib. of the Academy of Fine Arts, Copenhagen; Royal Lib., Copenhagen.

ADDRESS Sydgården, Maltvej 15, Askov, 6600 Vejen, Denmark.

Jacqueline Beverly Thurston PHOTOGRAPHER·
PAINTER · TEACHER Born January 27, 1939, in

Cincinnati, Ohio, Thurston received a BFA (1961) from Carnegie-Mellon University, Pittsburgh, Pennsylvania, and an MFA (1962) from Stanford University, Stanford, California, both in Painting.

She has been professor of art at San Jose State University, California, since 1965.

A member of SPE, Thurston won NEA Photographer's Fellowships in 1976 and 1978.

The photographer has completed three major thematic groups of photos: "nocturnal" image prints, a medical series and a series on circus performers presented in portfolio format with notes and remembrances.

PUBLICATION Book: *Optical Illusions and the Arts*, 1965.

COLLECTIONS IMP/GEH, Rochester; L/C, Wash., D.C.; Newport Harbor Mus. of Art, Newport Beach, Calif.; Oakland Mus., Calif.; St. Louis Mus. of Art, Mo. Bibliothèque Nationale, Paris.

DEALER Susan Spiritus Gall., 3336 Via Lido, Newport Beach, CA 92663.

ADDRESS 1688 Woodhaven Wy, Oakland, CA 94611.

George A. Tice PHOTOGRAPHER [See plate 102] Born October 13, 1938, in Newark, New Jersey, Tice was first involved in camera clubs in his youth and was later influenced by the work of Fredrick Evans. He was a photographer in the U.S. Navy from 1956 to 1959.

A freelance photographer since 1969, Tice has also taught photography at the New School for Social Research in New York City since 1970. From 1960 to 1969 he was a home portrait photographer.

Tice won three awards in 1973: an NEA fellowship, a Guggenheim Fellowship and the Grand Prix du Festival d'Arles.

Working in platinum, palladium and silver prints, using formats from 35mm to 8 x 10, Tice photographs "man, nature and man's environment."

PUBLICATIONS Monographs: *Urban Landscapes*, 1976; *George A. Tice/Photographs/1953–73*, 1975; *Paterson*, 1972. Books: *Artie Van Blarcum*, 1977; *Fields of Peace*, w/Millen Brand, 1973; *Seacoast Maine*, w/Martin Dibner, 1973; *Goodbye, River, Goodbye*, w/George Mendoza, 1971. Anthology: *The Photograph Collector's Guide*, Lee D. Witkin & Barbara London, 1979.

COLLECTIONS Art Inst. of Chicago; L/C, Wash., D.C.; Metro. Mus. of Art, NYC; MOMA, NYC; N.J. State Mus., Trenton. Bibliothèque Nationale, Paris; Victoria & Albert Mus., London.

DEALER Witkin Gall., 41 E 57 St, New York, NY 10022.

ADDRESS 323 Gill La #9B, Iselin, NJ 08830.

Will Till PHOTOGRAPHER Born in 1893 in Johannesburg, South Africa, Till died there in 1971. A photohobbyist from an early age, he became a serious enthusiast in 1926 upon purchasing his first good camera.

Devoted to establishing photography as an art form in South Africa, Till lectured, demonstrated and did a great deal of executive work in photographic societies during his long career. For twenty-five years he was the South African correspondent for London's *Photograms of the Year*.

A member and one-time president of the Johannesburg Photographic Society, Till was also active in the Johannesburg Camera Club and chairman of the South African Salon of Photography. In 1937 he was appointed a member of the London Salon.

Till received the royal Belgian honor of the Cercle Royal d'Etudes Photographiques et Scientifiques d'Anvers in 1939. He was elected an Honorary Fellow of RPS, for which he served as South Africa's corresponding member, in 1937, and he won a large number of international salon awards.

Favoring a 2½ x 3½ Houghton Butcher single-lens reflex camera, the landscape photographer made images that "had an almost mystic quality . . . often enhanced by the 'oil and iodine' technique," according to Dr. A. D. Bensusan *(Silver Images)*.

PUBLICATION Book: *Silver Images*, Dr. A. D. Bensusan, 1966 (Howard Timmins: Cape Town, S. Africa).

COLLECTIONS In Johannesburg: Africana Mus.; Bensusan Mus. of Photography; Photographic Fndn. Mus.

Robert Title PHOTOGRAPHER Born August 12, 1936, in Toronto, Ontario, Canada, Title studied at the Instituto Allende, Guanajuato, Mexico, in 1958–59 and at the Germain School of Photography in New York City in 1960–61. He also attended Ansel Adams' Yosemite Workshop in 1966. He names Peter Olwyler, Carlyle Trevelyan and French Impressionist painting as his major influences.

A freelance photographer, Title taught at Vancouver Community College in Canada in 1975–76 and at Sheridan College of Applied Arts and Technology, Oakville, Ontario, Canada, from 1970 to 1975. He worked in his own Toronto photography studio from 1960 to 1975.

Title served as president of the North Vancouver Business Association in 1978–79. He won a project grant from the National Film Board of Canada in 1969 and a photography fellowship from the Instituto Allende in 1959.

Now working with Cibachrome, Title's work has primarily been black-and-white figurative and portraiture. He uses small and medium format and produces unmanipulated prints.

PUBLICATIONS Periodicals: *British Journal of Photography Annual*, 1975; *British Columbia Photographer*, winter 1975.

COLLECTIONS Dunant Cllctn., London, England; Natl. Film Board, Ottawa, Ontario, Canada; Bruno B. Sauermann Cllctn., Toronto, Ontario, Canada.

ADDRESS 102-4818 Fraser St, Vancouver, British Columbia, Canada V5V 4H4.

Ronald James Todd   *PHOTOGRAPHER* ·
TEACHER Born in Xenia, Ohio, on May 2, 1947, Todd studied at the School of the Art Institute of Chicago under Harold Allen, receiving an MFA degree in 1974. He received his BFA (1972) from the Dayton Art Institute in Ohio, where he studied with Emmet Gowin.

Presently an instructor of Photography and History of Photography in the Fine Arts Department at the University of New Orleans, he was previously employed as curator of photography at the New Orleans Museum of Art (1974–76).

Todd has been a member of SPE since 1969.

Underwater figure studies and studies of landscapes are the major concerns of his photographic work.

COLLECTIONS Calif. State Coll., Associated Students, Stanislaw; L/C, Wash., D.C.; New Orleans Mus. of Art; Ohio Arts Council.

DEALER A Gallery of Fine Photography, 5432 Magazine St, New Orleans, LA 70115.

ADDRESS 2527 Marengo St, New Orleans, LA 70115.

Terry N. Toedtemeier *PHOTOGRAPHER · CURA-
TOR* Born July 8, 1947, in Portland, Oregon, Toedtemeier received a BS from Oregon State University, Corvallis, in 1969. He names Robert Frank, Lee Friedlander and Emmet Gowin as major influences.

Most recently he served as interim curator for the Museum of Art at Washington State University, Pullman, and as consultant to the Washington Consortium of Art Museums and the Seattle Arts Commission. He co-founded and co-directed the Blue Sky Gallery in Portland, Oregon, for five years, beginning in 1975. Toedtemeier served as a consultant to the Oregon Arts Commission in 1977 and was on the Media Services staff at Evergreen State College, Olympia, Washington, in 1975.

A member of the Oregon Center for the Photographic Arts in Portland, the photographer won an NEA grant in 1979 to research the significant photographers of the Columbia River Gorge, 1865–1915. In 1978 he was artist-in-residence at Lewis and Clark College in Portland.

Working in small and large formats, Toedtemeier makes photographs that range from landscapes to gestural images in infrared. He also does research and lectures on nineteenth-century photography in the West and has curated numerous contemporary exhibitions.

PUBLICATIONS Anthologies: *American Snapshots*, 1977; *Drugstore Photographs*, 1976. Catalog: *Some Twenty Odd Visions*, 1978 (Blue Sky Gallery, Portland). Periodical: *Creative Camera*, Dec 1976.

COLLECTIONS Oregon State Capitol Cllctn. of Salem, Ore.; Portland Art Mus., Ore.; Springfield Art Mus., Ill.; Stanford University Art Mus., Stanford, Calif.; Univ. of Wash., Seattle.

DEALER Blue Sky Gallery, 117 NW Fifth Ave, Portland, OR 97209.

ADDRESS 8225 SE 37th Ave, Portland, OR 97202.

Shohmei Tohmatsu *PHOTOGRAPHER* Born January 16, 1930, in Nagoya-shi, Japan, Tohmatsu studied economics for four years at Aichi University, Toyohashi-shi, Aichi.

A self-employed photographer, he has been director of the Japan Professional Photographers Society since 1975.

He won the Most Promising Photographer Award in 1958, the Photographer of the Year Award in 1961, the Photographic Society of Japan Award for 1975, the Manich Art Award in 1976 and the Education Minister's Art Encouragement Award in 1976.

Tohmatsu also directed the television program "The Modern Aristocracy" in 1959 and produced the film *The Aeroplane* in 1960.

PUBLICATIONS (All Japan) Books: *A Brilliant Wind*, 1979 (Shueisha); *Kingdom of Mud*, 1978 (Asahisonorama); *I Am a King*, 1972 (Shashin Hyohronsha); *Après-guerre*, 1971 (Chuoh-Kohronsha); *Oh! Shinjuku*, 1969, *Okinawa Okinawa Okinawa*, 1969, *Salaam Aleikoum*, 1968, *Nihon*, 1967 (Shaken); *Nagasaki*, 1966 (Shashin Dohjinsha). Anthology: *A History of Japanese Photography*, ed., 1971 (Heibonsha).

COLLECTION MOMA, NYC.

Johan Georg Heinrich Ludwig Tönnies *POR-
CELAIN PAINTER · GLASSGRINDER · PHOTOGRAPHER*
Born May 5, 1825, in Grünenplan, Germany,
Heinrich Tönnies died December 11, 1903 in
Åalborg, Denmark. His son, Emil Tönnies, was a
photographer.

Tönnies emigrated to Konradsminde, near Nor-
lund, Denmark, to work as a porcelain painter
and glassgrinder. In 1855 he was employed at the
glass factory in Åalborg, and in 1856 he bought
Fritsches Studio and started his own photography
business. He became a Danish citizen in 1870.
Tönnies created a very large business, which was
taken over by his son Emil in 1899.

The photographer produced a great collection
of topographical recordings from the area around
Åalborg.

PUBLICATIONS Monograph: *Heinrich Tönnies,
Cartes-de-Visite Photographer Extraordinaire,*
Alexander Alland, Sr., n.d. (Camera Graphic
Press, Ltd.: NYC). Book: *Photographers in and
from Denmark, until 1900,* Bjørn Ochsner, 1956,
rev. ed. 1969.

COLLECTIONS (All Denmark) Åalborg Hist.
Archives; Åalborg Hist. Mus.; Royal Lib., Copenhagen.

Peeter Tooming *PHOTOGRAPHER · CINEMA-
TOGRAPHER · PRODUCER · JOURNALIST* [See plate
121] Born June 1, 1939, in Estonia (now in Rus-
sia), Tooming studied journalism at Tartu State
University from 1968 to 1974. His father, Osvald
Tooming, is a writer.

A member of the Society of Cinematographers
of USSR, Tooming has been director of photography at Tallinnfilm Film Studio in Estonia since
1963, where he does documentary work.

He has made approximately twenty documentary films, including *Moments* (1976), which
deals with the development of photography in
Estonia from 1850 to 1970.

Of his craft, the artist states, "A photographer
has the right to make use of the most diverse
means for expressing his thoughts and feelings.
An artistic photo is not only the recording of a
fact but also one of the forms of expression of an
artist."

PUBLICATIONS Monographs: *Fotolood (Pho-
tostories),* 1979; *Rakvere,* 1976, *25 Photos by P.
Tooming,* 1976 (Eesti Raamat: Tallinn).

COLLECTIONS Musée Français de la Photographie, Bièvres; Photography Mus., Šiauliai, Lithuania; Tow's Mus., Tallinn, Estonia.

ADDRESS 200001 Tallinn, Harju 1-7, Estonia,
USSR.

Stephanie B. Torbert *PHOTOGRAPHER* Born
May 31, 1945, in Wichita Falls, Texas, Torbert
attended the School for the American Craftsman
in Rochester, New York, in the summer of 1967
and earned her BFA the next year from the University of New Mexico, Albuquerque. She received an MFA from the Visual Studies
Workshop (State University of New York, Buffalo) in 1971. Torbert's mother, Marguerite (Meg)
Torbert, is a designer and writer.

A freelance photographer and consultant, she
taught photography at the Minneapolis College
of Art and Design in 1977–78, at North Hennepin
Community College, Brooklyn Center, Minnesota, in 1974–75 and at Urban Arts Program,
Minneapolis Institute of Art in 1970–71. She
headed the Art Department of the Southeast Alternatives Free School in Minneapolis in 1972–
73 and was head of Visual Communications at
Rochester Urban Center M.C.C. at SUNY, Buffalo, in 1969–70.

A member of SPE, Torbert won a Minneapolis
College of Art and Design Faculty Grant in 1978
and a Bush Foundation Fellowship for Artists in
1976. In that year she also won an NEA Minnesota Survey Grant and in 1974 received a grant
from the Minnesota State Arts Council.

The photographer works in Cibachrome color
and nonsilver processes.

COLLECTIONS CCP, Tucson; Dayton Hudson
Corp., Minneapolis, Minn.; Federal Reserve
Bank, Minneapolis; IMP/GEH, Rochester; Min-
neapolis Inst. of Art, Minn.; Mus. of N. Mex.,
Santa Fe; Univ. of Minn. Gall., Minneapolis.

ADDRESS 3824 Harriet Ave S, Minneapolis,
MN 55409.

Gaspard Félix Tournachon
See Paul Nadar

Neil Trager *PHOTOGRAPHER · TEACHER* Born
August 14, 1947 in Brooklyn, New York, Trager
earned a BA in psychology from City College of
New York in 1969. He was apprentice/assistant
to Anthony Nobile.

As of this writing he was teaching at Dutchess
Community College, Poughkeepsie, New York
(since 1978), and at State University of New
York, New Paltz (since 1979). He is also associate
curator of the Catskill Center for Photography in
Woodstock, New York. Previously, Trager taught
at La Guardia Community College, Long Island
City, New York (1976–78).

In 1980 Trager received a CAPS grant and a Photographer's Fund Grant from the Catskill Center for Photography.

Working with a view camera, Trager photographs people. "I am interested," he says, "in the presentation of self before the camera—the relationship between camera, subject, and photographer."

COLLECTIONS Catskill Ctr. for Photography, Woodstock, N.Y.; MOMA, NYC; Neuberger Mus., Purchase, N.Y.

DEALER O. K. Harris Gall., 383 W Broadway, New York, NY 10013.

ADDRESS POB 85, Rifton, NY 12471.

Philip Trager *PHOTOGRAPHER · ATTORNEY* Born February 27, 1935, in Bridgeport, Connecticut, Trager received a BA in 1956 from Wesleyan University, Middletown, Connecticut, and a JD in 1960 from Columbia University School of Law, New York City. He is self-taught in photography.

Since 1960 he has been a partner in the law firm Trager and Trager. In 1977 his book *Photographs of Architecture* was selected as one of the "Best Books of the Year" by the American Institute of Graphic Arts, the Association of the American University Presses and *The New York Times* Annual Review of Books.

Using 4 x 5 and 11 x 14 view cameras, the photographer mainly produces images of East Coast architecture. He also shoots landscapes and portraits.

PUBLICATIONS Monographs: *Photographs of Architecture*, 1977; *Echoes of Silence*, 1972. Anthologies: *The Photograph Collector's Guide*, Lee D. Witkin & Barbara London, 1979; *The Art of Photography*, Time-Life Series, 1971. Periodicals: *printletter*, Apr/May 1978; *Creative Camera*, Sept 1975.

COLLECTIONS Baltimore Mus. of Art, Md.; Metro. Mus. of Art, NYC; MOMA, NYC; Smith Coll. Mus. of Art, Northampton, Mass.; Smithsonian Inst., Natl. Mus. of Hist. & Tech., Wash., D.C.; St. Petersburg Mus. of Fine Arts, Fla.; Univ. of Conn., Wm. Benton Mus. of Art, Storrs; Wesleyan Univ., Middletown, Conn.; Yale Univ. Gall. of Art, New Haven, Conn.

DEALER Witkin Gall., Inc., 41 E 57 St, Suite 802, New York, NY 10022.

ADDRESS 1305 Post Rd, Fairfield, CT 06430.

Barbara Lynn Traisman *PHOTOGRAPHER* Born January 24, 1945, in Chicago, Illinois, Traisman received her BS in 1968 from the University of Wisconsin, Madison.

A freelance photographer, she participated in a documentary project called "Workers" in 1976, supported by a CETA grant.

Traisman has frequently taken portraits of people in their work environments and as of this writing was producing "less conventional" portraits using double negatives and double exposures "to modify the apparent passage of time."

PUBLICATIONS Anthology: *Witness to Our Times*, 1977. Periodicals: *Combinations, A Journal of Photography*, 1978; *Camera 35*, Jan 1977.

COLLECTIONS Calif. Historical Soc. Archive, San Francisco; Oakland Mus., Calif.; San Francisco Mus. of Modern Art.

ADDRESS 16 Hillcrest Court, Berkeley, CA 94705.

Charles H. Traub *PHOTOGRAPHER · TEACHER · GALLERY DIRECTOR* Born in Louisville, Kentucky, on April 6, 1945, Traub earned a BA (1967) from the University of Illinois, Urbana-Champaign, then attended the Humanities Master's Program at the University of Louisville, Kentucky (1967–69). He received an MS in Photography in 1971 from the Institute of Design, Illinois Institute of Technology, Chicago, where he studied with Aaron Siskind and Arthur Siegel.

Traub was director of Light Gallery in New York City from 1978 to 1980. He also lectures at the International Center for Photography in New York City. From 1971 to 1977 he taught photography at Columbia College, Chicago.

A member of SPE and CAA, Traub initiated the founding of and chaired the Chicago Center for Contemporary Photography.

PUBLICATIONS Monograph: *Beach*, 1978. Books: *Court House*, Richard Pare, ed., 1978; *Photographing Children*, Time-Life Series, 1971. Catalog: *Photographer and the City*, 1977 (Mus. of Contemporary Art, Chicago). Periodicals: *Picture Magazine*, summer 1979; *Creative Camera*, Dec 1978; "Currents," *Modern Photography*, Nov 1978.

COLLECTIONS Art Inst. of Chicago; Harvard Univ., Fogg Art Mus., Cambridge, Mass.; IMP/GEH, Rochester; MOMA, NYC; VSW, Rochester.

ADDRESS 39 E Tenth St, New York, NY 10003.

Alex Traube *PHOTOGRAPHER · TEACHER* Born June 5, 1946, in New York City, Traube received an MA in Photography at Ohio University in Athens in 1970 and a BA in Government and Literature from American University in Washington, D.C., in 1968. Traube studied with Minor White as a private student in Boston (spring 1970) and at the Center of the Eye in Aspen, Colorado (1969 and 1970). His main influences have been Emmet Gowin, Minor White, Jerry Uelsmann and Henry Miller.

Currently Traube lectures at universities, colleges and art schools in the United States and Canada as well as doing freelance commercial photography. Previously he was employed at the Center for Photographic Studies in Louisville, Kentucky, as associate director and full-time faculty member from 1971 to 1974.

He was a recipient of an NEA Individual Fellowship in still photography in 1976.

"The main thrust of my work since 1976," Traube says, "has been toward sequential work, often accompanied by text. Much of the work is autobiographical, but there is a large body of lesser known work which is quiet and highly formal. From 1978 to the present, I have been working on a project involving major league baseball."

PUBLICATIONS Anthology: *Family of Woman*, 1979. Catalogs: *Aesthetics of Graffiti*, 1978 (San Francisco Mus. of Modern Art); *American Narrative/Story Art: 1967–1977*, 1978 (Contemporary Arts Mus.: Houston). Periodicals: *Arts Magazine*, Jan 1980; *Photo Ovo*, Jan/Feb 1975.

PORTFOLIOS *The New Mexico Portfolio*, 1976 (Ctr. of the Eye Photography Collaborative); *Portfolio One*, 1971 (Ctr. for Photographic Studies: Louisville).

COLLECTIONS Addison Gall. of American Art, Andover, Mass.; Cincinnati Art Mus., Ohio; Indiana Univ. Art Mus., Bloomington; IMP/GEH, Rochester; J. B. Speed Art Mus.; Minneapolis Art Inst.; Mus. of Fine Arts, Houston; Mus. of N. Mex., Santa Fe; New Orleans Mus.; Norton Simon Mus. of Art, Pasadena, Calif.; Rochester Inst. of Technology; Sam Houston State Univ., Huntsville, Tx.; San Francisco Mus. of Modern Art; Univ. of Louisville Photo Archives, Ky.; Univ. of N. Mex. Art Mus., Albuquerque; Univ. of Okla. Fred Jones Memorial Art Ctr.; Univ. of Wis. Madison Art Ctr.; VSW, Rochester; Wesleyan Univ., Macon, Ga. Natl. Gall. of Canada.

DEALER Robert Freidus Gall., 158 Lafayette St, New York, NY 10013.

ADDRESS 4200 Lime Kiln Ln, Louisville, KY 40222.

David Travis CURATOR·AUTHOR Born January 31, 1948, in Omaha, Nebraska, Travis received a BA in Art History in 1971 from the University of Chicago, Illinois.

Since 1977 he has been curator of photography at the Art Institute of Chicago, before which he was its assistant curator (1974–77) and photog-

raphy lecturer (1972–74). In 1972 he held a Research Fellowship from the Smithsonian Institution in Washington, D.C.

PUBLICATIONS (text only) Book: *Photographs from the Julien Levy Collection: Starting With Atget*, 1976. Catalogs: *Photography Rediscovered: American Photographs 1900–1930*, 1979; *The First Century of Photography from the Collection of André Jammes*, ed., 1977.

ADDRESS Art Institute of Chicago, Collection of Photography, Michigan Ave at Adams St, Chicago, IL 60603.

Arthur Tress PHOTOGRAPHER Born November 24, 1940, in Brooklyn, New York, Tress received a BFA from Bard College in Annandale-on-Hudson, New York, in 1962. He studied art history and the ancient cultures in Mexico, Japan, India and Europe from 1963 to 1966. In recent years he has been influenced by the writings of Jung and Eliade.

A freelance photographer, Tress worked as an ethnographic photographer recording several primitive tribal groups (1967–68) and as a documentary photographer for U.S. government agencies preparing studies of ethnic poverty groups (1969–70).

Tress has been the recipient of grants from the New York State Council on the Arts in 1976 and 1971, as well as from the Reva and David Logan Foundation in 1974 and NEA in 1972.

Arthur Tress is concerned with the creation of visual symbols for the deep-rooted fears within all of us. Described by A. D. Coleman in the *Village Voice* as "psychic Rorschachs," his images are photographic interpretations of actual children's dreams as recounted to him.

PUBLICATIONS Monographs: *Facing Up*, 1980; *Rêves*, 1979 (Edition Complexe: Brussels); *Theater of the Mind*, 1976; *Shadow*, 1975; *The Dream Collector*, 1973. Books: *Open Space and the Inner City*, 1970; *Songs of the Blue Ridge Mountains*, 1968. Anthology: *The Photograph Collector's Guide*, Lee D. Witkin & Barbara London, 1979. Periodicals: *Photo*, Oct 1979, Feb 1978, Oct 1975, May 1975; *35mm*, summer 1978; *Progresso Fotografico*, Mar 1976, Oct 1974; *Photo Revue*, July 1975; *Fotografia Italiana*, June 1975, Oct 1969; *Foto Technique*, Oct 1974, Oct 1968, Dec, Oct 1967; *Camera Mainichi*, Jan 1973; *Modern Photography Annual*, 1973, 1971; *Popular Photography Annual*, 1972, 1971, 1970; *Fototribune*, Sept 1971; *Creative Camera*, Oct, Mar 1970; *Fotografisk Arsbok*, 1970, 1968; *Popular Fotografi*, Feb 1967.

COLLECTIONS IMP/GEH, Rochester; Metro.

Mus. of Art, NYC; MOMA, NYC. Bibliothèque Nationale, Paris; Stedlik Mus., Amsterdam, The Netherlands.

ADDRESS 2 Riverside Dr, New York, NY 10023.

Aadu Treufeldt PHOTOGRAPHER Born in 1874 in Turi, Estonia, he died in 1956 in Hagudi, near Tallinn, Estonia, USSR.

Raised in the village of Turi, Treufeldt often photographed local events (weddings and village parties), at which he also would sing. He opened a studio in Pilistvere, and then, in 1906, journeyed to Pogranichnaya on the frontier of China, where he was employed at the studio of R. Gottlieb. He returned to Turi in 1909, where he frequently shared the studio of Avelinius Tonisson. He moved to Hagudi, near Tallinn, in his later years, where he died.

Aside from his photographs of village events, Treufeldt produced images of the Russian railwaymen, Chinese and Japanese villagers on the Russia-China frontier, and notably, two prints of the beheading of a band of "hunhuus" (robbers) on June 17, 1909.

PUBLICATION Periodical: *History of Photography*, "Aadu Treufeldt," Peeter Tooming, Jan 1978.

Paul Trevor PHOTOGRAPHER · WRITER Born August 29, 1947, in London, England, Trevor studied photography, painting and sculpture at Sir John Cass School of Art in London (1972–74).

A freelance photographer since 1974, he was a part-time lecturer in photography for City of London Polytechnic in 1979 and for North East London Polytechnic (1974–77). Trevor worked as an accountant from 1969 to 1974.

The photographer is a founder-member of Exit, a photographers' group (since 1973), a member of the Half Moon Photography Workshop Collective (since 1973) and he belongs to the National Union of Journalists (since 1979), all located in London. As a member of Exit he won grants from the Calouste Gulbenkian Foundation in London in 1974, 1976 and 1978, and also received bursaries from the Arts Council of Great Britain in 1978 and 1979.

PUBLICATIONS Book: *Down Wapping*, 1974 (London). Anthology: *Reading Photographs*, 1977 (London). Catalog: *Personal Views: 1860–1977*, 1978 (British Council, London). Periodical: *Camerawork*, May 1979.

COLLECTIONS In London: Arts Council of Great Britain; British Council; Calouste Gulbenkian Fndn.; Victoria & Albert Mus.

ADDRESS 7 Philip House, Heneage St, London E1, England.

Linda Troeller PHOTOGRAPHER · TEACHER Born February 26, 1949, in New Jersey, Troeller received her MFA in Photography from the School of Art, Syracuse University, New York, in 1975; she also received an MS degree in Public Relations (1972). Prior to that she attended West Virginia University in Morgantown, receiving a BS degree in Journalism (1971).

Currently teaching at Otis/Parsons Institute of Art & Design, Los Angeles, and Orange Coast College, Costa Mesa, California, she previously worked as a teacher at Stockton State College, Pomona, New Jersey (1977–79), a visiting lecturer on photography at the Indiana University Art Department, Bloomington (1976–77), and as a UPI Photographer for the Sailing Olympics, in Kiel, Germany (1972).

She has been a member of SPE and Friends of Photography since 1974. A recipient of the Rose McGill Fund Fellowship in 1978, she also received a New York State Council on the Arts Grant in 1974.

As of this writing Troeller was working on "Birds and Baths," a series of black-and-white murals of men, women and birds in spas and near bodies of water. She is also working on a novella illustrated with her photographs.

PUBLICATION Anthology: *Self-Portrayal*, March 1979.

PORTFOLIO *Greenhouse and Beyond*, 1974 (self-pub.).

ADDRESS 4846 Rosewood Ave, #28, Los Angeles, CA 90004.

Charlotte Pendleton Trolinger PHOTOGRAPHER · TEACHER Born on September 28, 1949, in Baltimore, Maryland, Trolinger received her MS in Photography from the Institute of Design, Illinois Institute of Technology, Chicago, in 1978, where she also received a BS degree (1973) in the field of architecture. Her mentor and adviser was Arthur Siegel.

Trolinger has been teaching at the Old Town Triangle Art Center in Chicago since 1979, and has been an artist-in-residence at the Chicago Council on Fine Arts in Photography since 1978. Previously she worked at Columbia College, Chicago, as a photo instructor from 1978 to 1979 and as a freelance photographer in Chicago, from June 1977 through September 1978.

A member of the SPE, she is also a member of Friends of Photography.

Working primarily in large format, she concentrates on architectural photographs in black-and-white and color in a formal style. She also works in small format.

PUBLICATION Periodical: *Popular Photography Annual*, 1979.

COLLECTIONS Bureau of Architecture, Chicago; Chicago Council on Fine Arts, Artist-in-Residence Archives & "Art Bank" Cllctn.

ADDRESS 2619 N Southport, Chicago, IL 60614.

Arthur James Trory PHOTOGRAPHER · PHARMACIST · BUSINESSMAN Trory was born May 4, 1879, in Lyons, Ohio; he died November 26, 1967, in Kent, Ohio. He studied pharmacy, and worked as a pharmacist throughout his life. He was also involved in various business ventures, including a shop called Bookstore and Refinishing Room.

Trory's work ranged from tintypes to albumen prints and blueprints, and later to color and Polaroid. He focused on the local side of life—family and friends. His style ranged from photojournalism to genre realist to mood.

PUBLICATION Monograph: *The Arthur J. Trory Photograph Collection: The Early Years, 1895–1927*, 1976.

COLLECTION American Hist. Research Center, Kent State Univ. Library, Ohio.

ARCHIVE Kent State Univ. Lib., Kent, OH 44240.

Karen Truax PHOTOGRAPHER · TEACHER Born in Vermillion, South Dakota, on May 17, 1946, Truax received a BFA Summa Cum Laude from Arizona State University, Tempe (1974), where she studied with Jack Stuler and Eric Kronengold. She earned an MFA in 1975 from the University of New Mexico, Albuquerque.

Truax taught at the University of New Mexico in 1977–78 and currently teaches photography at the University of California in Los Angeles. She is a member of the Los Angeles Center for Photographic Studies.

PUBLICATIONS Anthologies: *Photography and Eros*, 1977; *Women See Woman*, Annie Gottlieb, Cheryl Wiesenfeld, et al, eds., 1976. Catalogs: *Attitudes: Photography in the 70's*, 1979 (Santa Barbara Mus. of Art: Calif.); *Photographic Directions: Los Angeles, 1979*, 1979 (Security Pacific Bank: Los Angeles); *Photokina*, 1976 (Cologne, Germany); *Women in Photography: An Historical Survey*, 1975 (San Francisco Mus. of Modern Art). Periodicals: "How to Hand-Color Photographs," *Modern Photography*, Feb 1979; *Popular Photography Annual 1979; Popular Pho-*

tography, Dec 1977; *Nye Foto*, June 1977; *Creative Camera International Yearbook 1977*; "Colors of My Hand," *Camera 35*, May 1976; *Camera*, Sept 1973.

COLLECTIONS Albuquerque Arts Council, N. Mex.; Evergreen State Coll., Olympia, Wash.; Intermont Coll., Bristol, Va.; Kalamazoo Inst. of the Arts, Mich.; Mus. of N. Mex., Santa Fe; Phoenix Coll., Ariz.; Portland Mus. of Art, Maine; Univ. of N. Mex. Art Mus., Albuquerque; Yale Univ. Art Mus., New Haven, Conn.

DEALER G. Ray Hawkins Gall., 7224 Melrose, Los Angeles, CA 90046.

Hiromi Tsuchida PHOTOGRAPHER Born December 20, 1939, in Fukui Prefecture, Japan, Tsuchida received a BS in 1963 from Fukui University. He studied with, and was influenced by, Koen Shigemori at the Tokyo Institute of Photography in 1966.

Tsuchida is a freelance photographer and teaches at the Tokyo Institute of Photography. A member of the Japan Professional Photography Society, he won the Nobuo Ina Award in 1978 and the Taiyo Magazine Grand Prize in 1971.

Working in black-and-white, the photographer explores changing attitudes in Japan: "First I worked on traditional customs. Then I recorded the changes in the lives of the atom bomb victims in Hiroshima—how they live in the world today and the significance this holds for us."

PUBLICATIONS Monographs: *Hiroshima: 1945–1978*, 1979 (Asahi Sonorama Co.: Tokyo); *Zokushin—The Gods of Earth*, 1976 (Ottos Books: Yokohama). Periodicals: *American Photographer*, Apr 1979; *Zoom*, Mar 1977 (Paris); *Modern Photography*, May 1976; *Camera*, Sept 1970.

COLLECTIONS MOMA, NYC. Japan Professional Photography Soc., Tokyo; Tokyo-Sogo Inst. of Photography, Yokohama, Jap.

ADDRESS 8-18-405 Sakonyama Danchi, Asahi-ku Yokohama, Japan 241.

Anne Tucker CURATOR · PHOTOHISTORIAN · CRITIC Born October 18, 1945, in Baton Rouge, Louisiana, Tucker earned a BA in Art History from Randolph-Macon Woman's College, Lynchburg, Virginia (1967), an AAS in Photographic Illustration from Rochester Institute of Technology, New York (1968), and an MFA in the History of Photography from VSW (of State University of New York), Rochester (1972).

A curator at the Museum of Fine Arts, Houston, Texas, since 1976, Tucker also served as an affiliate artist at the University of Houston from

1976 to 1979. She was a visiting lecturer at Philadelphia College of Art (1973–75) and directed the photography lecture series at Cooper Union Forum in New York City (1972–75).

A member of CAA and SPE, she served on the latter's national board from 1976 to the present and was its secretary from 1977 to 1979.

As historian and critic, Tucker specializes in twentieth-century American photography.

PUBLICATIONS Anthology: *The Woman's Eye,* ed., 1973. Catalogs: *The Anthony G. Cronin Memorial Collection,* ed., 1979 (Mus. of Fine Arts: Houston); *Contemporary American Photographers: Curator's Choice,* 1979 (Rizzoli: NYC); *The Target Collection of American Photography,* w/Wm. C. Agee, 1977 (Mus. of Fine Arts: Houston); *Rare Books and Photographs, Catalogue 1,* 1973 (Witkin Gall.: NYC). Periodical: "Photographs of Women," ed. & intro., *Camera,* Feb 1972.

ADDRESS Museum of Fine Arts, 1001 Bissonnet, Houston, TX 77005.

Kay Tucker *PHOTOGRAPHER* Born in Chicago, Illinois, on January 26, 1918, the artist was a student of Josepha Haveman in Berkeley, 1967–73. She also was an apprentice to Vories Fisher from 1941 to 1943, in Chicago and received a BA degree in 1939 from Manhattanville College in Purchase, New York.

Presently retired, Tucker was formerly a free-lance photographer.

Tucker is a member of SPE, as well as The Image Circle in Berkeley and The Friends of Photography.

Working in large and medium format, the artist concentrated mostly on found objects in nature in a black-and-white traditional "West Coast" style.

PUBLICATIONS Monographs: *Kay Tucker, Images and Reflections,* Patrick J. Hansen, 1977. Pamphlets: *The Educated Innocent Eye,* 1972, 2nd prntg., 1974 (Image Circle, Berkeley, Calif.). Periodicals: "Sadakichi's Impact on Photography," *Sadakichi Hartmann Newsletter,* summer 1974.

COLLECTION Oakland Museum, Calif.

DEALER Focus Gallery, 2146 Union Street, San Francisco, CA 94123.

ADDRESS 2 Yankee Beach Way, Carmel, CA 93923.

Toba Tucker *PHOTOGRAPHER* Born July 1, 1935, in the Bronx, New York City, Tucker is a self-taught photographer who names Harold Feinstein as her mentor.

She has taught photography at the International Center of Photography in New York City since 1978 and previously worked in the education department of the Whitney Museum of American Art in New York City (1971–76).

A member of SPE, Tucker won a CAPS grant in 1979 and first prize from the Musée Française de la Photographie in 1978.

She currently works in medium-format black-and-white, creating documentary portraiture emphasizing direct confrontation.

PUBLICATIONS Periodicals: *Modern Photography,* Apr 1980; *Camera Art,* Oct 1980.

COLLECTION Musée Français de la Photographie, Bièvres, France.

ADDRESS 476 Broome St, New York, NY 10013.

Jane Tuckerman *PHOTOGRAPHER · TEACHER* Born June 11, 1947, in Boston, Massachusetts, Tuckerman attended the Art Institute of Boston from 1968 to 1971 and earned her MFA in Photography from the Rhode Island School of Design, Providence, where she studied with Aaron Siskind and Harry Callahan.

An assistant professor of art at Harvard University since 1978, she directs the school's photography program. In 1977–78 she taught at Harvard's New England School of Photography and from 1971 to 1975 organized photography programs for juvenile delinquents at reform and alternative schools. Tuckerman served as photography critic for *Boston After Dark* in 1971–72 and was a photographer at MGM Studios in Los Angeles in 1970.

She works with infrared black-and-white, and also produces watercolored carbro prints.

PUBLICATIONS Books: *Lightworks,* 1980; *Darkroom Dynamics,* Jim Stone, ed., 1979; *Criticism of Photography,* 1978; *Art From Dreams,* 1975. Anthologies: *SX-70 Art,* Ralph Gibson, ed., 1979; *Self-Portrayal,* 1978.

COLLECTIONS Addison Gall. of American Art, Andover, Mass.; Metro. Mus. of Art, NYC; Minneapolis Inst. of Arts, Minn.; Polaroid Cllctn., Cambridge, Mass.; Univ. of Mass., Amherst.

DEALERS Carl Siembab Gall., 162 Newbury St, Boston, MA 02116; Equivalents Gall., 1822 Broadway, Seattle, WA 98122; Jeb Gall., 342 S Main, Providence, RI 02901.

ADDRESS 116 Commonwealth Ave, Boston, MA 02116.

Deborah Turbeville *PHOTOGRAPHER* Born July 6, 1938, in Medford, Massachusetts, Turbeville studied at Parsons School of Design in New York City (1955–57).

A freelance photographer, she was fashion editor for *Mademoiselle* (1966–71) and for *Harper's Bazaar* in 1963–65. She won a CAPS grant in 1976.

Her work evolved from fashion assignments in the U.S. and abroad for such magazines as *Vogue.* "The exhibited work," she says, "is always in collage now with some text, and the print quality has a slightly scratched and faded look."

PUBLICATIONS Monograph: *Wallflower*, 1978. Books: *Women on Women*, 1978 (London); *Photography Year 1976*, Time-Life Series, 1976. Anthology: *The History of Fashion Photography*, Nancy Hall-Duncan, 1979. Periodical: *Camera*, Sept 1978.

DEALER Sonnabend Gall., 420 W Broadway, New York, NY 10012.

ADDRESS c/o Janice Goodman, 36 W 44 St, Rm 1212, New York, NY 10036.

John B. Turner PHOTOGRAPHER · TEACHER · WRITER · EDITOR · CURATOR Born October 11, 1943 in Porirua, Wellington, New Zealand, Turner considers himself a self-taught photographer.

Since 1971 he has been a senior lecturer in photography at the University of Auckland, School of Fine Arts, and has also been the editor of *Photo-Forum* in New Zealand since 1974. Previously he worked as a photographer for the National Museum in Wellington, New Zealand (1967–70), and for South Pacific Photos Ltd. in Wellington, doing both news and commercial photography (1965–67).

A member of Professional Photographers Association of New Zealand (1968–79), he was a founder of Photo-Forum, Inc. (1973) and also served as its president (1977–78). Turner was awarded the Queen Elizabeth II Arts Council of New Zealand Fellowship Grant in 1979.

Turner says of his involvement with photography, "Increasingly over the past years my activity as an expressive photographer has become secondary to my work as a teacher, editor and curator. I have a wide-ranging interest in the history and criticism of photography, particularly that of New Zealand, Australia and the Pacific."

PUBLICATIONS Catalogs (text only): *David Moore, Retrospective Exhibition 1940–1976*, ed., 1977 (Auckland City Art Gall.); *Three New Zealand Photographers: Baigent, Collins & Fields*, ed., 1973 (Auckland City Art Gall.); *Nineteenth Century New Zealand Photographs*, ed., 1970 (Govett-Brewster Art Gall.: New Plymouth, New Zealand). Periodicals (text only): "Recent Australian Photography," *Photo-Forum*, 31:12, 1976; "New Zealand Photography Since 1945," *printletter*, Sept/Oct 1979; "Joseph D. Jachna: Door County Landscapes," *Photo-Forum*, 26:3, 1975; *New Zealand Camera*, 21:5, 1974; "Large Format Photography," *Photo-Forum*, 21:14, 1974; "Paul Strand," *New Zealand Studio*, 6:3, 1971; "M. E. Brugsch: The Treasure of Deir-El-Bahari," *Creative Camera*, Sept 1970.

COLLECTIONS Auckland City Art Gall., Auckland, New Zealand; Natl. Art Gall., Wellington, New Zealand.

ADDRESS 43 Woodside Rd, Mt. Eden, Auckland 3, New Zealand.

Pete Turner PHOTOGRAPHER Born May 30, 1934, in Albany, New York, Turner earned a BA in 1956 from Rochester Institute of Technology, New York.

He has been a freelance photographer since 1956. His work has appeared in numerous magazines, such as *Look, Life, Esquire* and *Playboy.*

He belongs to ASMP, and in 1966 won the German Art Directors Club Award.

Working in 35mm color, Turner ascribes part of his style to the fact that he's "an avid science-fiction reader."

PUBLICATIONS Anthology: *Photography Year 1974*, Time-Life Series. Periodicals: *American Photographer*, Nov 1980; *Il Fotografo*, Dec 1979; *Foto Magazin*, Oct 1979; *Photographer's Forum*, Aug/Sept 1979; *Camera 35 Photo World*, Aug 1978; *Photographie*, Mar 1977; *Zoom*, Jan/Feb 1977 (Paris); *Camera 35*, Dec 1976, Apr/May 1962; *Photo*, Oct 1976, Sept 1976, Apr 1975, July 1973, June 1969; *Modern Photography Annual*, 1973; *Photo*, Jan 1973; *Foto*, Sept 1972 (Germany), June/July 1972 (Stockholm); *Look*, Jan 1971; *Popular Photography*, Mar 1967, Aug 1959.

COLLECTION IMP/GEH, Rochester.

REPRESENTATIVE Gene O'Rourke, 200 E 62 St, #8C, New York, NY 10021.

DEALER The Space Gall., 154 W 57 St, New York NY 10019.

ADDRESS 154 W 57 St, New York, NY 10019.

Peter Nicolas Turner PUBLISHER · PHOTOGRAPHER · AUTHOR · EDITOR Born February 3, 1947, in London, England, Turner studied at the Guildford School of Art of Surrey, England, where he took a diploma in photography in 1968 and a City & Guilds Certificate in Photography in 1967.

Turner has been director of Travelling Light

Publishers in London since 1978 and co-editor of *Creative Camera International Yearbook* since 1975. He previously served as artist-in-residence at Prahran College of Advanced Education, Melbourne, Australia (1977), taught at Antioch Center for British Studies in London (1975) and co-edited *Creative Camera* magazine (1969–78). His writing has been widely published in photography magazines.

Currently a member of the Visual Arts Panel of the Greater London Arts Association (having received their Visual Arts Award in 1978), he served on the Photography Committee of the Arts Council of Great Britain (1973–78). He won the Arles Festival of Photography prize for *Creative Camera International Yearbook 1975.*

His photography, writing and teaching are concerned with "how the objects that make up the urban and rural sprawl can be transformed into 'pictures' [and] what those pictures (my own & others') might mean."

PUBLICATIONS Book: *P. H. Emerson, Photographer of Norfolk,* co-author, 1974 (Gordon Fraser: London). Catalogs: *Bill Brandt—Early Photographs,* 1976 (London); *Remnants & Prenotations,* 1975 (Bristol); *Tony Ray-Jones—The English Seen,* 1974, *Peter Henry Emerson,* 1974, *Serpentine Photography '73,* 1973 (London). Periodicals: *Untitled 14,* 1979; *Camera,* Dec 1975, Aug 1972; *Creative Camera,* Mar 1970.

COLLECTIONS Bibliothèque Nationale, Paris; Dept. of the Environment Cllctn., London.

ADDRESS 14 Cromford Rd, London SW18 1RU, England.

Giuseppe Turroni *CRITIC · WRITER* Turroni was born April 12, 1929, in Meldola (Forlì), Italy.

Since 1952 he has been the film critic of *Filmcritica* magazine and photography critic for the magazines *Fotografia* and *Popular Photography Italiana* since 1955. He has also written about photography for *Corriere Della Sera* since 1975.

Turroni joined the Sindacato Nazionale Critici Cinematografici Italiani in 1965 and the Fédération Internationale de l'Art Photographique (FIAP) in 1973.

PUBLICATIONS Books: *Guida Alla Critica Fotografica,* 1972, 1962 (Il Castello); *Cento Capolavori Della Fotografia,* w/Massimo Casolaro, 1969 (Clic); *Il Nostro Amico Gatto,* w/Marigold, 1967, *Come Realizzare Un Film Documentario,* 1966 (Il Castello); *Fotografiamo Insieme,* 1966 (Touring Club Italiano: Ferrania); *Il Nome Della Pietra,* 1965 (Rebellato); *L'Arte E La Tecnica Nel Film,* 1965, *Guida All'Estetica Della Fotografia*

A Colori, 1963 (Il Castello); *Nuova Fotografia Italiana,* 1959 (Schwarz). Periodicals: "Franco Grignani," Mar 1978, "James Abbe," Apr 1977, *Fotografia Italiana.*

ADDRESS Via Attilio Deffenu, #7, 20133 Milan, Italy.

Karen Tweedy-Holmes *PHOTOGRAPHER · EDITOR · WRITER* Born September 21, 1942, in Columbus, Ohio, Tweedy-Holmes received a BA in Art History from Barnard College, Columbia University, New York City, in 1964. She names Ralph M. Hattersley, Jr., as her mentor and was also influenced by Eugène Atget, W. Eugene Smith, Roman Vishniac and Dorothea Lange.

A freelance photographer and editor since 1975, she has been coordinating editor for Avon Products, Inc., in New York City since 1978. She served as humanities editor for Columbia University Press (1971–75) and was staff photographer and copy and production editor for Conover-Mast, Inc., in New York City (1967–69).

Tweedy-Holmes has belonged to Professional Women Photographers since 1977.

The photographer won Best in Show, first and third prizes in the New York Morgan Horse Society Photo Contest in 1979 and first prize in photography in the 1979 Avon Art Show. She also won first and second prizes in photography in the 1978 Avon Show and the Neil Design Award for Photography in 1968.

Shooting black-and-white and printing without manipulation, Tweedy-Holmes makes her subjects the human face and body, animals, architecture, New York City, Paris and still lifes. She uses color for macrophotography of insects.

PUBLICATIONS Anthologies: *Apple of My Eye,* H. Hanff, 1978; *Women See Men,* Yvonne Kalmus, et al, eds., intro & text by Ingrid Bengis, 1977; *Women Photograph Men,* Danielle B. Hayes, ed., intro. by Molly Haskell, 1977; *The Nude in Photography,* A. Goldsmith, 1975; *Discover Your Self Through Photography,* R. M. Hattersley, 1971; *Be-ing Without Clothes,* Minor White, ed., 1970. Periodicals: *Popular Photography Annual,* 1974; *Feminist Art Journal,* fall 1973; *Popular Photography's Woman,* fall 1972 (includes interview), spring 1972, spring 1971, fall 1970, spring 1970; *Popular Photography,* Mar 1972, Oct 1967.

COLLECTIONS Cooper-Hewitt Mus., NYC; ICP, NYC.

REPRESENTATIVES Animals Animals, 203 W 81 St, New York, NY 10024; Corporate Art Alternatives, Inc., 160 E 84 St, New York, NY 10028.

ADDRESS   180 Claremont Ave, Apt 51, New York, NY 10027.

William Tyree   *PHOTOGRAPHER*   Tyree had a flourishing career between 1878 and 1895 in New Zealand and died in Sydney, Australia, sometime between 1914 and 1918. His brother, Frederick Tyree, was also a photographer.

William Tyree established a studio at Nelson, New Zealand, in 1878. The studio grew to be one of the largest in New Zealand, employing six professional assistants by the turn of the century. Initially his brother Frederick was his partner, but left the business in 1889. In 1895 Tyree moved to Sydney, where he remained until his death.

He was responsible for a fine series of 8 x 10 coaching scenes in the Nelson, Blenheim and Buller districts of New Zealand, made on behalf of Newman & Canning's Coach Service in the 1890s. He also photographed coal miners.

COLLECTION   Natl. Lib. of New Zealand, Alex Turnbull Lib., Wellington.

Mellon Tytell   *PHOTOGRAPHER · WRITER*   Born in New York City, Tytell earned a BA at the New School for Social Research in New York City and also studied at Le Grand Berger in Lausanne, Switzerland. She worked for Weegee during the last year of his life, and she names Jay Maisel and Ernst Haas as mentors.

She has been freelance photographer since 1972. Her work has appeared in such magazines as *Stern, Geo* and *Natural History*.

The ASMP member won the Silver Medal Award from the Philadelphia Art Directors Club in 1975.

Her "first love" as a photographer is recording the lives of primitive peoples, but she also does surrealistic and erotic photography. Ernst Haas has described her work as "stylized reportage."

PUBLICATIONS   Book: *The Beat Book*, Arthur Knight, ed., n.d. Anthology: *Ecstasy*, 1976.

DEALERS   Neikrug Gall., 224 E 68 St, New York, NY 10021; Gamma-Liaison, 150 E 58 St, New York, NY 10022.

ADDRESS   69 Perry St., New York, NY 10014.

U

Shoji Ueda *PHOTOGRAPHER* Born in Sakai-minato City of the Tottori Prefecture in Japan on March 27, 1913, Ueda attended Oriental Photographic College in Tokyo in 1933. Currently a professor in the photography department at Kyushyu Industrial College, he previously taught at Shimane University.

A member of the Nika Photography Society and the Professional Photographers Society, Ueda earned the Prize of Cultural Merits in 1978 and the Nika Award at the 1955 Nika Exhibition.

PUBLICATIONS Books (all Japan): *Sand Dunes*, 1978 (Asahi Sonorama); *Children the Year Round*, 1971 (Chuokoron-sha); *Memory Without Sound*, 1974 (Nippon Camera-sha); *The Legend of Izumo*, 1974 (Mainichi Newspapers); *Oki*, 1967, *Izumo Myths*, 1965 (Tanko-sha do).

COLLECTIONS Asahi Pentax Gall., Tokyo; Bibliothèque Nationale, Paris; Nikon Salon, Tokyo.

REPRESENTATIVE Zeito-Foto Co. Ltd., Yagicho Bldg., 5th fl., 1–4 Muromachi, Nihonbashi, Chuo-ku, Tokyo, Japan.

ADDRESS 82 Suehiro-cho, Sakaiminato-shi, Tottori Pref., Japan.

Jerry N. Uelsmann *PHOTOGRAPHER · TEACHER* [See plate 131] Born June 11, 1934, in Detroit, Michigan, Uelsmann earned a BFA from Rochester Institute of Technology in 1957 and an MS and MFA (1960) from Indiana University, Bloomington. He studied with Ralph Hattersley, Minor White and Henry Holmes Smith.

Uelsmann has taught at the University of Florida, Gainesville, since 1960. He has been a graduate research professor since 1974, was a professor (1969–74), an associate professor (1966–69), assistant professor (1964–66), an instructor (1962–64) and an interim instructor (1960–62).

He is a founding member and serves on the board of SPE, and is also a board member of Friends of Photography.

The photographer was named Teacher Scholar of the Year in 1975 at the University of Florida, and won a faculty development grant from the school in 1971. He was named a Fellow of RPS in 1973, won an NEA fellowship in 1972, and in 1967 was honored with a Guggenheim Fellowship.

Known for his surreal combination prints, Uelsmann, through a complicated process often utilizing several enlargers, creates a visually perfect blending of the manipulated and unmanipulated areas of the print.

PUBLICATIONS Monographs: *Jerry N. Uelsmann: Silver Meditations*, intro. by Peter Bunnell, 1975; *The Criticism of Photography as Art*; *The Photographs of Jerry N. Uelsmann*, 1970; *Eights Photographs*, intro. by William E. Parker, 1970; *Jerry N. Uelsmann*, intro. by Peter Bunnell, 1970, rev. ed., 1973. Book: *The Persistence of Vision*, Nathan Lyons, ed., 1967. Anthologies: *The Photograph Collector's Guide*, Lee D. Witkin & Barbara London, 1979; *The Great West: Real/Ideal*, 1977; *Darkroom 1*, Eleanor Lewis, ed., 1976; *Photography Year 1976*, 1976, Time-Life Series; *The Magic Image*, Cecil Beaton & Gail Buckland, 1975; *The Photographers' Choice*, Kelly Wise, ed., 1975; *Looking at Photographs*, John Szarkowski, 1973; *Octave of Prayer*, Minor White, 1972; *The Art of Photography*, 1971, *The Camera*, 1970, *Color*, 1970, *The Print*, 1970, Time-Life Series; *Light*[7], Minor White, ed., 1968. Catalogs: *Photographs*, 1977 (Univ. of Nebr., Sheldon Mem. Art Gall.: Lincoln); *New Images in Photography*, 1974 (Univ. of Miami, Lowe Art Mus.: Fla.); *Private Realities: Recent American Photography*, Clifford S. Ackley, 1974 (Mus. of Fine Arts: Boston); *Synthetic Color*, 1974 (Southern Ill. Univ.: Carbondale); *Light & Lens*, 1973 (Hudson River Mus.: N.Y.); *Photography into*

Art, 1972 (Arts Council of Great Britain: London); *Photography Invitational,* 1971 (Arkansas Arts Ctr.: Little Rock); *Into the 70's,* 1970 (Akron Art Inst.: Ohio); *Photography U.S.A.,* 1967 (De Cordova Mus.: Lincoln, Mass.); *American Photography: The Sixties,* 1966 (Univ. of Nebr., Sheldon Mem. Art Gall.: Lincoln). Periodicals: *Creative Camera,* May 1976, May 1975, July 1972, May 1972, June 1969, Feb 1969; *Camera,* Dec 1975, Jan 1967; "Jerry Uelsmann," May 1972, "Notes on Uelsmann's Invented World," William E. Parker, Feb 1967, *Infinity: ASMP.*

COLLECTIONS Addison Gall. of Amer. Art, Andover, Mass.; Arizona State Univ., Tempe; Art Inst. of Chicago; CCP, Tucson; Ctr. for Photographic Studies, Louisville, Ky.; Cleveland Mus. of Art, Ohio; Denver Art Mus., Colo.; Detroit Inst. of Arts, Mich.; Exchange Natl. Bank of Chicago; Harvard Univ., Fogg Art Mus., Cambridge, Mass.; High Mus. of Art, Atlanta, Ga.; ICP, NYC; Kalamazoo Inst. of Arts, Mich.; L/C, Wash., D.C.; Metro. Mus. of Art, NYC; Minneapolis Inst. of Arts, Minn.; MOMA, NYC; Mus. of Fine Arts, Boston, Mass.; Mus. of Fine Arts, Houston; Mus. of Fine Arts of St. Petersburg, Fla.; New Orleans Mus. of Art; Norton Simon Mus. of Art, Pasadena, Calif.; Philadelphia Mus. of Art, Penn.; Princeton Univ., N.J.; R. I. School of Design, Providence; John & Mable Ringling Mus. of Art, Sarasota, Fla.; Smithsonian Inst., Wash., D.C.; Southern Ill. Univ., Carbondale; Univ. of Ala., Tuscaloosa, Ala.; UCLA; Univ. of Calif., Berkeley; Univ. of Fla., Gainesville; Univ. of Ill., Krannert Art Mus., Urbana; Univ. of Kans., Lawrence; Univ. of Louisville, Ky.; Univ. of Nebr., Sheldon Mem. Art Gall., Lincoln; Univ. of Ok., Norman; Univ. of S. Fla., Tampa. Natl. Gall. of Canada, Ottawa, Ontario.

DEALERS Susan Spiritus Gall., 3336 Via Lido, Newport Beach, CA 92663; Silver Image Gall., 83 S Washington, Seattle, WA 98104; Stephen White Gall., 835 La Cienega Blvd, Los Angeles, CA 90069; Witkin Gall., 41 E 57 St, New York, NY 10022; Atlanta Gall. of Photography, 3077 E Shadowlawn Ave NE, Atlanta, GA 30305.

ADDRESS 5701 SW 17 Dr, Gainesville, FL 32608.

Doris Ulmann *PHOTOGRAPHER* Born in New York City in 1884, Ulmann died there on August 28, 1934. During her marriage she was briefly known as Doris Jaeger. She attended Ethical Culture School, then Columbia University, both in New York City, and she studied photography with Clarence White in 1914.

Ulmann began her photography career as a por-traitist in 1918. Her interest in American handicrafts took her to Appalachia around 1925, where she became taken with the people. For the rest of her life she spent six to eight months a year traveling through the mountains and back roads of the South with her companion John Jacob Niles.

Ulmann joined Pictorial Photographers of America in 1918.

Despite the fact that she in no way hid her tremendous family wealth, Ulmann produced straightforward, unpretentious and respectful photographs of the Appalachian people, who remained unself-conscious before her camera's eye. In New York she photographed professional people.

PUBLICATIONS Monographs: *The Darkness and the Light,* Robert Coles & Wm. Clift, 1974; *The Appalachian Photographs of Doris Ulmann,* John Jacob Niles & Jonathan Williams, 1971; *A Portrait Gallery of American Editors,* Louis Evans Shipman, 1925; *Portraits of the Medical Faculty of the Johns Hopkins University,* 1922; *The Faculty of the College of Physicians and Surgeons,* Columbia University, foreword by Samuel W. Lambert, 1918. Books: *Handicrafts of the Southern Highlands,* Allen Hendershott Eaton, 1937; *Roll, Jordan, Roll,* Julia Peterkin, 1933. Anthologies: *The Photograph Collector's Guide,* Lee D. Witkin & Barbara London, 1979; *Photography Rediscovered,* David Travis & Anne Kennedy, 1979; *The Magic Image,* Cecil Beaton & Gail Buckland, 1975; *Women of Photography,* Margery Mann & Ann Noggle, eds., 1975.

COLLECTIONS Berea Coll., Berea, Ky.; IMP/GEH, Rochester; L/C, Wash., D.C.; Univ. of N. Mex. Art Mus., Albuquerque; Univ. of Ore. Lib., Eugene; Van Deren Coke Cllctn.

ARCHIVE University of Oregon Library, Eugene, OR.

David A. Ulrich *PHOTOGRAPHER · TEACHER* Born in Akron, Ohio, on April 18, 1950, Ulrich received an MFA from the Rhode Island School of Design in Providence in 1977. Before that he received a BFA degree from Tufts University, School of the Museum of Fine Arts, Boston. He also studied photography from 1970 to 1975 with Minor White and from 1970 to 1973 with Nicholas Hlobeczy.

Ulrich has been assistant chairman of the Photography Department, Art Institute of Boston since 1979, as well as a full-time instructor of photography at the Institute since 1977. He previously worked for Ohio University in Athens as a teaching assistant in photography from 1975 to 1976, was employed by Minor White in 1975 and was gallery director for the Prospect Street Photo Co-op/Gallery, Inc., Cambridge, Massachusetts.

He has been a member of SPE since 1977, and of the Photographic Resource Center, Boston, Massachusetts, from 1976 to the present.

The artist's work focuses on black-and-white landscapes in large format.

PUBLICATIONS Anthologies: *Celebrations*, 1974; *Octave of Prayer*, Minor White, 1972. Catalogs: *Nine Photographers*, 1975 (Akron Art Institute, Ohio).

COLLECTIONS MIT, Cambridge, Mass.; Photogenesis Gallery, Columbus, Ohio; Photography Place, Strafford, Penn.; Rhode Island School of Design, Providence, R.I.

DEALER Panopticon, Inc., 187 Bay State Rd, Boston, MA 02215.

ADDRESS 278 Concord Rd, Wayland, MA 01778.

Donald Theodore Ultang PHOTOJOURNALIST · AVIATOR Born March 23, 1917, in Fort Dodge, Iowa, Ultang attended Iowa State University, Ames (1935–36), and received a BA in Economics from the University of Iowa, Iowa City, in 1939. He studied journalism under Frank Luther Mott.

Since 1979 Ultang has been a lecturer in photojournalism at Drake University, Des Moines, Iowa, as well as freelancing in photography. He was an insurance executive (1959–79), managed the news photo department of the *Des Moines Register and Tribune* (1953–59) and was staff photographer and company pilot for that newspaper (1946–59).

Ultang was the co-winner (with John Robinson) of the Pulitzer Prize in 1952. He also won First Place in the Sequence Category of the NPPA "Great Pictures" contest of 1954 and First Place for Spot News in their 1951 contest. In 1949 the photographer was First Place winner and *Detroit Daily News* Feature Award winner from the Kent State University School of Journalism.

According to Tom Maloney in *U.S. Camera Annual*, Ultang shows the "ability to make one picture representative of all similar situations." He specializes in photojournalism and aerial photography.

PUBLICATIONS Anthology: *Moments*, Sheryle & John Leekley, foreword by Dan Rather, 1978. Periodicals: *Popular Photography Annual*, 1954; *U.S. Camera Annual*, 1954.

ADDRESS 10 SW 34 St, Des Moines, IA 50312.

Umbo (Otto Umbehr) PHOTOGRAPHER · TEACHER Born Otto Umbehr on January 18, 1902, in Düsseldorf, Germany, Umbo died May 13,

1980, in Hannover. He studied at the Bauhaus in Weimar under Walter Gropius, Johannes Itten, Wassily Kandinsky, Paul Klee, Lionel Feininger and Oscar Schlemmer in the years 1921 to 1923.

Moving to Berlin in 1923, he worked as a production assistant to film maker Kurt Bernhardt. Later he was camera assistant to Walter Ruttmann (until 1926). From 1928 on, his photographs appeared in many German publications, such as *Berliner Illustrierte Zeitung*, *Münchner Illustrierte Presse*, *Uhu*, *Scherl's Magazin*, *Dame*, *Neue Linie*, *Koralle*, *Es Kommt der Neue Fotograf*, *Foto-Auge*, as well as the annuals of *Arts et Métiers Graphiques*. He took assignments in North Africa (1941) and in Italy (1942). From 1943 to 1945 he served in his country's army, during which time he lost all his photographs and negatives. He continued freelancing after the war, publishing in such journals as *Picture Post*, *Quick* and *Der Spiegel*. He traveled to the United States in 1952 and, until 1974, taught photography at several schools in and around Hannover.

A founding member of Dephot, the first photo agency anywhere, Umbo served as its studio director from 1928 until 1933, when it was dissolved. During those five years Dephot represented such photographers as Robert Capa, Felix H. Mann, Kurt Hutton, Andreas Feininger and Hans Reinke.

Essentially a photojournalist, Umbo specialized in theater, dance and film. He was a versatile photographer and used several cameras, especially the light and portable Ermanox and Leica.

PUBLICATIONS Monograph: *Umbo: Photographien 1925–1933* (Spectrum Photogalerie, Kunst Mus.: Hannover). Catalog: *Photographs from the Julien Levy Collection*, David Travis, 1976 (Art Inst. of Chicago).

COLLECTION Art Inst. of Chicago, Julien Levy Cllctn.

DEALER Galerie R. Kicken, Albertusstrasse 47/49, 5000 Cologne 1, West Germany.

Bert Elias Underwood PHOTOGRAPHER · BUSINESSMAN Born 1862 in Oxford, Illinois, Underwood died December 27, 1943, in Tucson, Arizona. His brother, Elmer Underwood (1860–47), also a photographer, was his partner; and his nephew, C. Thomas Underwood, was the one-time head of Underwood & Underwood's New York illustration studios. Self-taught as a photographer, he attended the Ottawa University in Ottawa, Kansas.

In 1882 he began selling stereoscopic photographs in Kansas and with his brother Elmer, formed the firm of Underwood and Underwood. Within two years the firm extended its activities to the Pacific coast. In 1886 an office was opened in Baltimore, followed by others in New York, Chicago, Toronto and other foreign countries. As early as 1896 Underwood began providing pictures with news interest to *The Illustrated London News* and *Harper's Weekly*. During World War I, with a major's commission, he commanded the photographic division of the Signal Corps.

Actively involved in his community and the Presbyterian Church, he was a member of the following organizations: Mayor's Committee, American Legion, Sons of the American Revolution, Masons and Lake Placid (New York) Club.

Working as a news photographer, Bert Underwood covered the Greco-Turkish War, and made the only pictures of Edward VII and Queen Alexandra wearing their coronation crowns and robes. He traveled to many parts of the world to gather material.

PUBLICATION Book: *A Stereograph Record of William McKinley*, 1901.

See also Elmer Underwood

Elmer Underwood PHOTOGRAPHER·BUSINESS-MAN Born in 1860 in Fulton County, Illinois, Underwood died August 18, 1947, in St. Petersburg, Florida. Completely self-taught, he was influenced in his work with stereoscopes by Oliver Wendell Holmes' essays on the apparatus in *The Atlantic Monthly*. Underwood's brother Bert (1862–1943) was also a photographer and his partner; his son, C. Thomas, at one time headed Underwood and Underwood's New York illustration studios.

Beginning work on an Ohio dairy farm at age eleven, Underwood entered the printing trade at fourteen, serving as an apprentice and journeyman for six years. In 1877 he established his own printing firm in Ottawa, Kansas, specializing in periodicals. Five years later he and his brother formed the photographic firm Underwood and Underwood, which moved to Baltimore and, in 1897, to New York, where it remains today (as U&U News Photos).

Underwood and his brother eventually built up a worldwide organization, with branches and agencies in many foreign countries. By 1901 the firm was producing 25,000 photos a day. Just before World War I the brothers established portrait and commercial photo departments; they discontinued the sale and manufacture of stereoscopes in 1921. The company reorganized into four separate firms in 1931.

Elmer Underwood is credited by many as having introduced the first news pictures in 1897—a stereoscopic record of the Greco-Turkish War. Despite opposition, he persuaded *The Illustrated London News* to publish the war pictures.

A pioneer in the development of news pictures, Underwood traveled throughout the world taking photographs of royalty, famous personalities and major news events. He was also the official photographer for several U.S. presidents, and among his well-known pictures was the last photograph of the dramatist Henrik Ibsen. Underwood was known as the father of the rather short-lived stereoscope industry.

See also Bert Elias Underwood

Howard A. Unger PHOTOGRAPHER·TEACHER·WRITER Born October 13, 1944, in Mt. Vernon, New York, Unger studied painting and drawing at the Art Students League in New York City in 1960–61. He received a BFA (1966) and an MA (1968) in Graphic Design from Kent State University, Kent, Ohio, then took an MEd (1972) from Teachers College, Columbia University, New York City. In 1975–76 he studied photography with Jerry Uelsmann at the School of Visual Arts in New York City, and studied holography in 1976 at New York Institute of Holography. In 1978 Unger attended a postdoctoral seminar on educational administration at Teachers College.

He presently teaches educational technology and is photography coordinator at Teachers College (since 1976) and is associate professor in visual communications technology at Ocean County College, Toms River, New Jersey. He was a photographic critic for the *Village Voice* (1976–77) and a photography columnist for *SoHo Weekly News* (1977–78).

A member of SPE and the National Education Association, Unger received an honorarium from Teachers College for the development and implementation of a course in experimental photography.

He directed the 1974 16mm color film *The Life of V. I. Lenin as portrayed by Soviet Artists*.

PUBLICATIONS Books: *Printmaking: A Beginner's Handbook*, w/Wm. Maxwell, 1977; *The Fourth R*, Steward Kranz, 1971. Periodicals: "Holography Is Not a Four Letter Word," Jan 3, 1977, "Let Us Now Praise the F.S.A.," Nov 15, 1976, "A Man a Plan a Canal Panama," Sept 20, 1976, *Village Voice*; *Visual Communications Magazine*, text only, spring 1968.

COLLECTIONS Kent State Univ., Kent, Ohio; Mus. of Holography, NYC (hologram); Ocean

County Coll., Toms River, N.J. (painting); Teachers Coll., Columbia Univ., NYC.

ADDRESS 437 E 76 St, New York, NY 10021.

Rosi M. Urbine *PHOTOGRAPHER · AUDIOVISUAL SPECIALIST* Born July 11, 1952, in Ft. Belvoir, Virginia, Urbine took a BA in Journalism from Loyola University, New Orleans, Louisiana, in 1977.

From 1976 to 1979 she worked as an audiovisual specialist for Kitchenaides, Inc., Harahan, Louisiana, and before that was a photographer/research assistant for St. Charles Parish School Board, Luling, Louisiana (1975–76). Urbine served as staff photographer for the Festival of Women in the Arts in New Orleans in 1978, and from 1976 to 1978 taught photography for the New Orleans Recreation Department.

The photographer uses color to explore movement and peripheral vision, especially with photomicrography and infrared color films. Most recently she has been experimenting with laser art prints.

PUBLICATIONS Book: *The Infrared Book Project*, 1980. Catalogs: *Legacy, The Documenting of Louisiana Traditions and Folk Life*, 1979 (Xavier Univ., New Orleans); *Celebration of the Creative Woman*, 1978 (Festival for Women in the Arts, New Orleans).

DEALER Kathleen Ewing Gall., 3020 K St NW, Washington, DC 20007.

ADDRESS 33 Peter Parley Rd, Jamaica Plain, MA 02130.

Jesús Sánchez Uribe *PHOTOGRAPHER* [See plate 110] Born August 24, 1948, in Mexico, Uribe earned a BA in Architecture from Universidad La Salle in 1967 and later studied photography with Alejandro Parodi (1971–74). He was also influenced by Manuel Alvarez Bravo.

Currently a freelance photographer (since 1977), he previously worked for the Instituto Mexicano del Seguro Social in the department of photo-ophthalmology (1975–77).

PUBLICATIONS Periodicals: *Creative Camera*, July 1979; *Camera*, Oct 1978; *Fotozoom*, Mar 1978; *Mexicana de Cultura*, Sept 1977; *Artes Visuales*, Oct 1976; *Bellas Artes*, May 1975; *Fotoguía*, Dec 1974.

COLLECTIONS CCP, Tucson. Consejo Mexicano de Fotografía; Fototeca Casa del Lago, National University of Mexico, Mexico City; Museo de Arte Moderna de Guatemala.

REPRESENTATIVE Rene Verdugo, POB 5187, Tucson, AZ 85703.

ADDRESS Av. Fresnos #10-A, Jardínes de San Mateo, Edo. de México, México.

"Nick" Ut
See Ut Cong Huynh

Burk Uzzle *PHOTOGRAPHER* Born in Raleigh, North Carolina, on August 4, 1938, Uzzle is a self-taught photographer. His mentor was Gjon Mili, and his major influence has been Magnum photographers. Motorcycle racing is his hobby.

Uzzle worked as a contract photographer with *Life* magazine from 1962 to 1968, and also freelanced with Black Star in Chicago, Houston and Atlanta.

A member of Magnum Photos since 1967, he has been president since 1979. Uzzle was recipient of an NEA Fellowship-Grant in 1975, and received the Page One Award from the Newspaper Guild of New York in 1970 for an essay on U.S. Marines.

The artist concentrates on "contemporary themes, people and their environment, social and emotional themes, the traditional photojournalistic concerns tempered and influenced by a very personal vision and love for photography."

PUBLICATIONS Monograph: *Landscapes*, 1973. Anthologies: *The Photograph Collector's Guide*, Lee D. Witkin & Barbara London, 1979; *Vision and Expression*, Nathan Lyons, ed., 1969. Catalog: *Album Photographique 1*, 1979 (Centre Georges Pompidou: Paris). Periodicals: *Photography Annual*, 1979; *Zoom*, Dec 1978, Apr 1976 (Paris); *Photo*, Apr 1978, Oct 1976; *Camera Mainichi*, 1978; "The Hustle Comes of Age," J. B. Hall, *Aperture*, no. 77, 1976; *Creative Camera*, Jan 1976; *Camera*, Nov 1973, Oct 1970; *Modern Photography Annual*, 1972.

PORTFOLIO *Triptych: The Second Apeiron Portfolio* (group), 1978 (Apeiron Workshops: Millerton, N.Y.).

COLLECTIONS Art Inst. of Chicago; Detroit Inst. of Art, Mich.; Harvard Univ., Fogg Art Mus., Cambridge, Mass.; ICP, NYC; IMP/GEH, Rochester; Metro. Mus. of Art, NYC; MOMA, NYC; Richmond Mus. of Art, Va.; Santa Barbara Mus. of Art, Calif.; Smithsonian Inst., Wash., D.C. Bibliothèque Nationale, Paris; Stedelijk Mus., Amsterdam, The Netherlands.

REPRESENTATIVE Magnum Photos, 15 W 46 St, New York, NY 10036.

V

John Felix Vachon *PHOTOGRAPHER* [See plate 69] Born in St. Paul, Minnesota, in 1914, Vachon died in New York on April 21, 1975. He graduated from the College of St. Thomas in St. Paul in 1935 and also attended Catholic University of America.

Vachon was an assistant messenger for the Farm Security Administration (FSA) in Washington, D.C., in 1935, then became a photographer for FSA (1935–42). He later worked as a photographer for Standard Oil of New Jersey (1943–44), the U.N. Relief Fund in Poland (1946) and for *Look* magazine (1947–71).

Vachon won a Guggenheim Fellowship in 1973.

Producing chiefly silver prints, Vachon, like the other FSA photographers, captured the hardships being suffered by Americans of the Depression era in their homes, at work and in the fields.

PUBLICATIONS Books: *Just Before the War*, w/ Arthur Rothstein & Roy Stryker, Thomas E. Garver, ed., 1968; *The Bitter Years*, Edward Steichen, ed., 1962; *12 Million Black Voices*, Richard Wright & Edwin Rosskam, 1941. Periodical: "John Vachon—A Remembrance," Brian Vachon, *American Photographer*, Oct 1979.

COLLECTIONS L/C, Wash., D.C.; N.Y. Pub. Lib.

ARCHIVE Brian Vachon, 4 Pinewood, Montpelier, VT 05602.

Roger Vail *PHOTOGRAPHER · TEACHER* Born in Chicago in 1945, Vail earned an MFA from the Art Institute of Chicago in 1969.

An instructor at California State University, Sacramento, since 1970, he also taught at the Art Institute of Chicago in 1977 and 1973.

PUBLICATIONS Periodicals: *Afterimage: VSW*, Apr 1979; *Modern Photography*, Nov 1973; *Camera*, Oct 1972.

COLLECTIONS Art Inst. of Chicago; E. B. Crocker Art Mus., Sacramento; Exchange Natl. Bank of Chicago Cllctn.; Ill. Arts Council; MOMA, NYC; Mus. of Art, Iowa City, Iowa; Purdue Univ., West Lafayette, Ind.; Univ. of N. Mex., Albuquerque. Galerie Delpire, Paris.

DEALERS Douglas Kenyon, 155 E Ohio, Chicago, IL 60611; Keystone Gall., 1213 State St, Santa Barbara, CA 93101.

ADDRESS 2689 13 St, Sacramento, CA 95818.

Eduard Valenta *CHEMIST · INVENTOR · WRITER* Born in Vienna in 1857, Valenta died in 1937. He attended the Schottenfelder Realschule and studied chemistry at the Technische Hochschule in Vienna.

Valenta served as chemist and then director of F. Fischer's chemical factory in Unterlaa, near Vienna (1884–92), then became a professor of photochemistry at Graphische Lehr- und Versuchsanstalt in Vienna (1892). While there he headed the research department of scientific and applied photography and photomechanical reproduction. In 1899 he took over the photochemistry chair at Technische Hochschule in Charlottenburg after the death of Professor Hermann Vogel, and upon J. M. Eder's retirement in 1923 Valenta became director of the Graphische Lehr- und Versuchsanstalt.

The chemist began his published contributions to photography in 1880 with an article co-written with Eder on iron oxalate and its salts. In 1894 he published a book on color photography, emphasizing the Lippmann color process and Valenta's improvements on it. He and Eder next collaborated on studies in the new field of X-ray, publishing a treatise on Roentgen photography in 1896. In the same year Valenta developed the first stereo X-rays and published a book on printing-out papers. His other work included the discovery of the use of glycin red and ethyl violet as sensitizing dyes (1898–99); spectral analysis of hundreds of aniline dyes and their suitability as light filters and printing inks (recorded in a 1904 volume co-written with Eder and in a 1911 atlas); and research on photomechanical reproduction that led to two volumes on photochemistry in the graphic arts and three volumes on the raw materials of printing.

Valenta received many honors during his lifetime, such as Knight of the Order of Franz Joseph, Officer of the Academy, Honorary Member of the Photographische Gesellschaft in Wien and Honorary Member of RPS.

PUBLICATIONS Books: *Quellendarstellungen zur Geschichte der Fotografie*, Wolfgang Baier, 1964; *Focal Encyclopedia of Photography*, 1957, 1956 (Focal Press); *History of Photography*, J. M. Eder, 1945; *History of 3-Color Photography*, E. J. Wall, 1925; *Lexikon für Photographie und Reproduktionstechnik*, G. H. Emmerich, 1910. Anthology: *Photography's Great Inventors*, Louis W. Sipley, 1965. Periodicals: *Photographische Correspondenz*, 1963, 1937, 1932, 1892; *Bild und Ton*, 1962; *Photographic Times*, 1897; *Jahrbuch für Photographie und Reproduktionstechnik*, J. M. Eder, 1896, 1895.

Arthur Van Blarcum MECHANICAL ASSEMBLER · PHOTOGRAPHER Born in Newark, New Jersey, on July 4, 1925, Van Blarcum attended the Suburban School of Photography in East Orange, New Jersey, in 1947.

Since 1968 he has been employed by the Walter Kidde Company and from 1950 to 1968 worked for Federal Radio and Television Company, both in New Jersey. He belongs to the electrical workers union (I.U.E.C.I.O.), Veterans of Foreign Wars and the Tri-County Camera Club in Nutley, New Jersey.

The photographer is a pictorialist.

PUBLICATIONS Book: *Artie Van Blarcum: An Extended Portrait*, bio., George A. Tice, 1977.

COLLECTION CCP, Tucson.

DEALER George Tice, 323 Gill Lane, #9b, Iselin NJ 08330.

ADDRESS 10 Cedar St N., Arlington NJ 07032.

Florence Vandamm PHOTOGRAPHER Born in 1882 in London, Vandamm died March 15, 1966, in New York City. She studied art at the Royal Academy, and married George R. Thomas (died 1944), her photographic partner, who was known professionally as Tommy Vandamm.

First attracted to photography as an adjunct to her painting of portraits and miniatures, she established a portrait photography studio in the West End of London in 1908. Its immediate suc-

cess established Vandamm's Studio as a salon for painters, actors, musicians and writers. In 1918 she married and formed a partnership with her husband, adding illustration and fashion work to her repertoire. Florence and Tommy migrated to New York (he was from Washington) in 1923 and established a successful studio that received many newspaper and magazine assignments. She retired in 1951.

Vandamm was a member of RPS.

Noted as a stage photographer, Vandamm provided an invaluable contribution to the documentation of the Broadway stage, particularly from 1925 to 1950, during which time she covered more than 2,000 professional theater productions. Her subjects—Broadway personalities —included Paul Muni, Burgess Meredith, Dame Judith Anderson and Sir John Gielgud. While her husband was alive Vandamm mainly did studio work, and he photographed the stage, but after his death she finally stepped onto the stage with her camera.

COLLECTION N.Y. Pub. Lib. at Lincoln Ctr., Theater Cllctn., NYC.

ARCHIVE Vandamm Cllctn., Theater Cllctn., Lib. & Mus. of Performing Arts, N.Y. Pub. Lib. at Lincoln Ctr., 111 Amsterdam Ave, New York, NY 10023.

Tommy Vandamm
See George Robert Thomas

Eduard Van der Elsken PHOTOGRAPHER Van der Elsken was born March 10, 1925, in Amsterdam, The Netherlands.

Since 1947, Van der Elsken has worked as a freelance photographer and cinematographer. He lived in Paris (1950–55), then returned to The Netherlands. Van der Elsken received a Dutch National Film award in 1971.

One critic described the photographer's work as portraying "the adventure of life dramatically, but devoid of aestheticism." He is most notable for the form of his picture books, in which only a few words appear, and then only to indicate direction. "Van der Elsken uses this demanding medium like a novelist, describing a cast of characters, a place, a mood, time, plot, and dramatic development . . . he does not pose or direct the subjects; there is nothing faked in his story," writes Peter Pollack.

PUBLICATIONS Monographs: *Sweet Life*, 1966; *Jazz*, 1959; *Bagara*, 1958; *Love on the Left Bank*, 1956. Anthology: *Picture History of Photography*, Peter Pollack.

ADDRESS   Zeevangszeedijk 4, Edam, The Netherlands.

James Augustus Joseph Van Der Zee   PHOTOGRAPHER · MUSICIAN   [See plate 47]   Born on June 29, 1886, in Lenox, Massachusetts, Van Der Zee was self-taught in photography. He was awarded an honorary doctorate by Seton Hall University, South Orange, N.J., in 1976 and another by Haverford College, Pa., in 1980. Around 1906 he studied music at the Carlton Conservatory. He died in New York on May 15, 1983.

A self-employed photographer for most of his life, he opened his first studio in 1918 in Harlem, New York City. Before that he was the darkroom man for Gertz Department Store in New York City.

Van Der Zee is an Honorary Fellow for Life of the Metropolitan Museum of Art. He has been the recipient of many awards, including the International Black Photographers Award and the Living Legacy Award, both presented by President Jimmy Carter at a White House ceremony in 1979. He also received the Pierre Touissaint Award in 1978, presented by Cardinal Cooke at St. Patrick's Cathedral. Van Der Zee's photographs were the basis of a film done in 1975 entitled *Uncommon Images*.

Van Der Zee's documentation of life in Harlem at the height of its cultural glory is of tremendous historical significance. The bulk of his work consists of portraits that are sensitive, respectful and warmly understanding of their subjects.

PUBLICATIONS   Monographs: *James Van Der Zee the Picture-Takin' Man*, Jim Haskins, 1979; *The Harlem Book of the Dead*, w/Owen Dodson & Camille Billops, 1978; *James Van Der Zee*, 1973; *The World of James Van Der Zee*, 1969; *Harlem on My Mind*, 1968. Anthology: *The Photograph Collector's Guide*, Lee D. Witkin & Barbara London, 1979.

PORTFOLIO   *Eighteen Photographs*, 1974 (James Van Der Zee Inst., NYC).

COLLECTIONS   Delaware Art Mus., Wilmington; High Mus., Atlanta, Ga.; Metro. Mus. of Art, NYC; New Orleans Mus. of Art; San Antonio Mus. of Art, Tex.

REPRESENTATIVE   Ms. Donna Mussenden, 220 W 93 St, New York, NY 10025.

ADDRESS   220 W 93 St, New York, NY 10025.

Willard Van Dyke   PHOTOGRAPHER · FILM MAKER · TEACHER · FILM HISTORIAN   Born on December 5, 1906, Van Dyke was influenced by and learned from his friends Edward Weston from 1929 to 1957, Ralph Steiner from 1935 to the present, and Ansel Adams since 1931.

As of this date employed as adjunct professor at State University of New York College at Purchase, New York, he worked as director for the Museum of Modern Art, Department of Film, in New York City from 1965 to 1973. He has been self-employed for most of his life, and also worked as film director for the U.S. government during World War II.

Van Dyke served as president of International Film Seminars from 1965 to 1972, president of Screen Directors International Guild from 1960 to 1962 and president of the New York Film Council in 1947. He was co-founder of Group f.64 in 1932. A recipient of a Ford Foundation Grant in Ireland in 1979, Van Dyke was also awarded a citation and silver cup from George Eastman House in 1978.

In 1939, in collaboration with Ralph Steiner, he photographed and directed *The City*, a black-and-white film.

Working almost entirely with 8 x 10 contact prints, he creates portraits and rural and urban landscapes in both black-and-white and color.

PUBLICATIONS   Periodicals: *Image*, 21:2, 1978; *Photograph*, 1:4, 1977; *Film Comment*, 3:2, 1965.

COLLECTIONS   Houston Mus. of Fine Arts; IMP/GEH, Rochester; MOMA, NYC; Neuberger Mus., Purchase, N.Y.; Oakland Mus., Calif.; San Francisco Mus. of Modern Art; St. Louis Art Mus., Mo.

DEALERS   Witkin Gall., 41 E 57 St, New York, NY 10022; Stephen Wirtz Gall., 228 Grant Ave, San Francisco, CA 94108.

ADDRESS   47A Beach St, New York, NY 10013.

Albert van Rheede van Oudtshoorn   PHOTOGRAPHER · ASTRONOMER   Born in 1894 in Aberdeen, on the Cape, South Africa, van Oudtshoorn died on April 29, 1959, in Maritzburg, South Africa. His early forebear, the Earl of Athlone, a seventeenth-century loyalist to William of Orange, was chosen to be one of seventeen privileged families of Holland in which the title is still handed down to every child. His eighteenth-century ancestor Pieter van Reede van Oudtshoorn came to South Africa in 1745 as second-in-command to the governor of the Cape, and a village in the Cape bears the family name.

Albert became a civil servant in Cape Town, rising to the position of assistant registrar of deeds for Natal province when he moved to Pietermaritzburg years later. He served in the Ninth Infantry Regiment during World War I. In his later years he ceased photographing and turned his attention to astronomy.

A member of the Cape Town Photographic Society as of 1926, he served on its council as vice-president and as president for thirteen years (from 1930). He became a Fellow of RPS in 1928 and Honorary Fellow in 1937. He also received honorary life memberships from the Amsterdam Focus Salon (1936), Pietermaritzburg Photographic Society (1948), Western International Photographic Salon, Bristol (1934), for which he was overseas vice-president, and the Cape Town Photographic Society (1943). In 1925 van Oudtshoorn won his first bronze medal, awarded by the Cape Peninsula Publicity Association, and subsequently received close to 300 awards for his images. The *American Annual of Photography* rated him fourth in the world in 1935, and between the years 1926 and 1939 he had 450 prints accepted at approximately 150 salons spread over five continents.

In the *American Annual of Photography* Frank Fraprie describes the pictorialist as "one of the world's greatest exponents of land and seascape photography." Favoring a quarter-plate camera of unknown vintage and a 3½ x 2½ rolliefilm reflex, the incorrigible tinkerer built his own enlarger as well as several darkroom gadgets. "Dodging was his main stock-in-trade," said Eric Vertue of van Oudtshoorn in *Camera News.*

PUBLICATIONS Book: *Silver Images,* Dr. A. D. Bensusan, 1966 (Howard Timmins: Cape Town, South Africa). Periodical: "Photographic Personalities," Eric Vertue, *Camera News,* Feb 1958.

COLLECTIONS In Johannesburg, South Africa: Bensusan Mus. of Photography; Photography Fndn. Mus.

Carl Van Vechten PHOTOGRAPHER · CRITIC · AUTHOR · COLLECTOR Born June 17, 1880, in Cedar Rapids, Iowa, Van Vechten died December 21, 1964, in New York City. He was educated at the University of Chicago ca. 1899–1902.

Van Vechten began his journalism career as a crime reporter for Hearst's *Chicago American* (1903–1905), then moved on to *The New York Times,* where he became music critic and, briefly, Paris correspondent (ca. 1906). By 1920 he was probably the city's foremost music critic, but he quit the job in 1921, declaring that at forty a man experiences "intellectual hardening of the arteries" and is thus unfit for criticism. Van Vechten took up novel writing, which he quit in 1933 to become a portrait photographer. Until his death he used his camera to capture celebrities in the art, theater, music and literary worlds.

He was also well known as one of the first exponents of civil rights and as a collector of blacks' contributions to American life as recorded in photos, manuscripts, phonograph records, letters, etc. His holdings formed the basis of the James Weldon Johnson Memorial Collection, which Van Vechten contributed to Yale University in 1950. Collections of his photos of artists and intellectuals are also held at Fisk and Howard universities. Van Vechten was a prolific correspondent, and his letters are held in collections at the New York Public Library, Princeton and, mainly, Yale.

PUBLICATIONS Books (nonfiction): *Keep A-Inchin' Along,* 1979; *Contributions of Carl Van Vechten to the Negro Renaissance, 1920–1930,* Leon Duncan Coleman, 1969; *Carl Van Vechten and the Irreverent Decades,* Bruce Kellner, 1968; *The Lens of Carl Van Vechten* (photos), 1968; *Carl Van Vechten,* Edward G. Lueders, 1965; *Fragments,* autobio., 1955; *The Tiger in the House,* 1950; *Sacred and Profane Memories,* autobio., 1932; *Parties, Scenes from Contemporary New York Life,* 1930; *Excavations: A Book of Advocacies,* 1926; *A Bibliography of the Writings of Carl Van Vechten,* Scott Cunningham, 1924; *Peter Whiffle,* bio., 1922, repr. 1929; *In the Garret,* 1920; *The Merry-Go-Round,* 1918; *The Music of Spain,* 1918; *Interpreters and Interpretations,* 1917, rev. 1920; *Music and Bad Manners,* 1916; *Music After the Great War, and Other Studies,* 1915. Editor: *Selected Writings of Gertrude Stein,* also intro. & notes, 1962; *Gertrude Stein: Last Operas and Plays* intro., 1949; *Lord of the Housetaps: Thirteen Cat Tales,* also preface, 1930. Fiction: *Spider Boy,* 1928; *Nigger Heaven,* 1926; *Firecrackers,* 1925; *The Tattooed Countess,* 1924; *The Blind Bow-Boy,* 1923.

COLLECTIONS Fisk Univ., Nashville, Tenn.; Howard Univ., Wash., D.C.; Yale Univ., New Haven, Conn.

Vivian Varney TEACHER · PHOTOGRAPHER · AUTHOR Born in Lynn, Massachusetts, in 1935, Varney received a BA from Bates College, Lewiston, Maine (1957), and an MA from New York University Institute of Fine Arts, New York City (1965). She also studied photography, painting and drawing at Pratt Institute, Brooklyn, New York (1963–65), and earned her PhD at Ohio State University, Columbus, in 1980.

As of this date chairman of the Education Department of Dayton Art Institute in Ohio, Varney previously served as assistant professor of fine arts and director of the Sordoni Art Gallery at Wilkes College in Wilkes-Barre, Pennsylvania

(1973–76). From 1965 to 1973 she was a university professor of fine arts at Tyler School of Art, Temple University, Philadelphia, and at the University of Rochester, New York, and Illinois State University, Normal.

PUBLICATIONS Books: *The Photographer as Designer*, 1977, *Design in Nature*, 1970 (Davis Publications).

ADDRESS c/o Davis Publications, Printer's Bldg, 50 Portland St, Worcester, MA 01608.

Magda Vasillov TEACHER · COLLECTOR Born January 23, 1934, Vasillov earned a BA from Wellesley College, Wellesley, Massachusetts, and an MA from New York University in New York City. Her late husband, Wasil Vasillov, was a photographer.

Since 1970 Vasillov has taught photography and history of art at Hostos Community College of the City University of New York. Previously she was assistant to the president of Magnum Photos, Inc. (1968–70). To date she is compiling the photographic illustrations to Charles Darwin's *Expression of the Emotions in Man and Animals*, including the unknown works of Rejlander and other photographers which Darwin collected.

Vasillov belongs to SPE and Wellesley Friends of Art.

Her extensive collection of vintage photographs, inherited from her late husband, includes the work of George Platt Lynes and of photographers who participated in Vogue Studios during the late 1940s and early 1950s.

ADDRESS 325 E 77 St, New York, NY 10021.

Wasil (Bill) Vasillov PHOTOGRAPHER Born in 1914 in Burwick, Pennsylvania, Vasillov died in 1961 in New York City. His wife, Magda Vasillov, is a photography teacher and collector.

Vasillov served in the U.S. Army Corps of Engineers from 1940 to 1946, then worked as an assistant to George Platt Lynes in 1950–55. His interest in photography pre-dated World War II, and his special interest in Horst B. Horst led to an invitation by Horst to come to *Vogue*'s New York studios, where he worked with Irving Penn, Leslie Gill and eventually Henry Clark. Vasillov set up his own fashion photography studio in 1958, which he operated until his death. His work has appeared in such magazines as *Vogue*, *Baby Talk* and *Parents*.

Vasillov was a member of ASMP.

PUBLICATION Book: *New York City Ballet Book*, 1958.

COLLECTIONS Metro. Mus. of Art, NYC; MOMA, NYC.

ARCHIVE Magda Vasillov, 325 E 77 St, New York, NY 10021.

Paul Vathis PHOTOGRAPHER Vathis was born in Jim Thorpe, Pennsylvania, on October 18, 1925. He served in the U.S. Marine Corps in World War II until 1945.

He joined the Associated Press (AP) in Philadelphia as a copy boy in January 1946, was promoted first to a wirephoto operator, and then a staff photographer in 1949, when he transferred to their Pittsburgh bureau. In 1950 he again transferred, this time to Harrisburg, Pennsylvania, where, to date, he still worked for AP.

A member of both the American Newspaper Guild and the Society of Professional Journalists, Vathis won the Pulitzer Prize for news photography in 1962.

PUBLICATION Anthology: *Moments*, Sheryle & John Leekley, foreword by Dan Rather, 1978.

REPRESENTATIVE Associated Press, 408 Payne Shoemaker Bldg, Third & Pine Sts, Harrisburg, PA 17101.

David Vestal PHOTOGRAPHER · WRITER · TEACHER · EDITOR Born March 21, 1924, in California, Vestal studied at the Art Institute of Chicago (until 1944) and with Sid Grossman in New York City at various times from 1947 to 1955.

A contributing editor to *Popular Photography* since 1975, Vestal also teaches and writes criticism of photography.

He won Guggenheim fellowships in photography in 1966 and 1973.

Vestal shoots in small-format black-and-white, his style being largely "straight." He has also done some craft-oriented study of black-and-white photography, mainly in regard to image quality and permanence.

PUBLICATIONS Book: *The Craft of Photography*, 1975. Catalog: *Vision & Expression*, 1969 (GEH: Rochester). Periodicals: *Popular Photography*, text only, Apr 1969, Dec 1967; *Photography Annual*, 1962.

COLLECTIONS Art Inst. of Chicago; High Mus., Atlanta, Ga.; IMP/GEH, Rochester; MOMA, NYC; Mus. of N. Mex., Santa Fe; Univ. of N. Mex., Art Mus., Albuquerque.

DEALER Marcuse Pfeifer Gall., 825 Madison Ave, New York, NY 10021.

ADDRESS POB 309, Bethlehem, CT 06751.

Grey Villet PHOTOJOURNALIST Born August 16, 1927, in South Africa, Villet studied for one year in medical school. He is self-taught in photography.

A freelance since 1973, Villet served on the *Life* magazine staff from 1955 to 1973.

In 1956 Villet was named Magazine Photographer of the Year by the *Encyclopaedia Brittanica.*

PUBLICATIONS Book: *Those Whom God Chooses,* w/Barbara Villet, 1965. Anthologies: *Great Photographic Essays from Life,* Maitland Edey, 1978; *Best of Life,* 1976. Periodicals: "N.Y. Subways' Terror," June 1979, "Threatened Wilderness," 1971, "Nurse," 1967, "4 Essays on an American Family," Nov-Dec 1966, "Nuns," 1963, "Essay on Synanon," 1962, "Lash of Success," Nov 1961, *Life.*

ADDRESS RFD #1, Shushan, NY 12873.

Peter Vincent PHOTOGRAPHER · TEACHER · DE-SIGNER Born April 11, 1945, in Salt Lake City, Utah, Vincent received a BS in Architecture from Idaho State University in Pocatello in 1973. He attended workshops led by Ansel Adams and Brett Weston, and was also influenced by Peter de Lory and the painter Robert Motherwell.

Employed as a lecturer in photography at Idaho State University since 1977, he also taught at the Sun Valley Center for the Arts and Humanities in 1978 and 1979, and worked as artist, photographer and assistant production manager for Eastern Idaho Television Corporation from 1974 to 1976.

Vincent has been a member of SPE since 1978 and of Friends of Photography since 1976. His work was the subject of a PBS documentary aired by KBGL in November 1979 in Pocatello, Idaho.

Working primarily in black-and-white, he uses large format and 35mm to create abstracts and prints that question reality through the experimental use of hand-coloring techniques.

PUBLICATIONS Periodicals: *Popular Photography,* Aug 1979; *Artweek,* May 12, 1979.

COLLECTIONS In Idaho: Alexander House, Boise; Coll. of S. Idaho, Twin Falls; Idaho Bank & Trust Co., Pocatello; Sun Valley Center for the Arts & Humanities, Sun Valley.

REPRESENTATIVES Sun Valley Ctr. for the Arts & Humanities, POB 656, Sun Valley ID 83353; Corporate Art Directions, 41 E 57 St, New York, NY 10022.

ADDRESS 650 N Tenth, Pocatello, ID 83201.

Paolo Gasparini Viola PHOTOGRAPHER Born March 15, 1934, in Gorizia, Italy, Viola is self-taught in photography. He names Paul Strand as his "friend and master" during a stay in Orgeval, France, in 1956.

Most recently Viola worked for UNESCO as an architectural photographer in Latin America (1970–72). In 1962–65 he worked for the Consejo Nacional de Cultura in Havana, Cuba, and in 1961–62 he worked on the newspaper *Revolución* in Havana.

Viola belongs to Consejo Venezolano de Fotografía in Caracas (since 1978) and to Consejo Latinoamericano de Fotografía in Mexico.

Viola considers his work "essay photography," and he is interested in "contradictions (social, historic) and the emotional inner self." He has photographed mainly in Latin America.

In 1980 he made the film short *San Salvador de Paúl, mina de diamantes* in Venezuela.

PUBLICATIONS Books: *Panorámica de la Arquitectura Latinoamericana,* Damian Bayón, 1977 (Blume/UNESCO); *Para Verte Mejor, América Latina,* Edmundo Desnoes, 1972 (Siglo XXI: Mexico); *La Ciudad de las Columnas,* Alejo Carpentier, 1970 (Lumen: Barcelona).

COLLECTIONS IMP/GEH, Rochester; MOMA, NYC; Polaroid Corp., Cambridge, Mass. Casa de las Americas, Havana, Cuba; Galería de Arte Nacional, Caracas, Venezuela.

DEALER Fototeca, apartado 929, Caracas 1010, Venezuela.

ADDRESS Apartado 3305, Caracas 1010, Venezuela.

Šonta Virgilijus ENGINEER · PHOTOGRAPHER Born in Panevėžys, Lithuanian SSR, on February 16, 1952, Virgilijus studied power engineering at the Polytechnical Institute in Kaunas, Lithuanian SSR (1970–76).

A professional fine-art photographer since 1980, he previously worked as a photographer for the Photography Art Society of Lithuanian SSR, Kaunas Department (1978–80), and as a photojournalist at Lithuanian Telegram Agency (ELTA) from 1976 to 1978.

A member of Photography Art Society of Lithuanian SSR since 1974, Virgilijus won the Prix de la Mere in Bièvres, France, in 1978 and the grand prize at the Man and Earth exhibition in Plateliai, Lithuanian SSR, in 1974.

His early works were landscapes of Lithuania, with special attention to light. In his "flight" series he "tried to convey the state of a human being in flight," and in his most recent group of photographs, "things and forms," he is concerned with "the interrelations between object and space."

PUBLICATIONS Periodicals: *Damont Foto,* no. 2, 1980 (Cologne); *Foto,* no. 2, 1980 & no. 12, 1978 (Budapest, Hungary); *Fotografie,* no. 9,

1980; *Fotojahrbuch International 1980/1981*, 1980 & *1979/1980*, 1979; *Photo 78*, 1980.

COLLECTIONS Bibliothèque Nationale, Paris; Musée Français de la Photographie, Bièvres, France; Photography Mus., Šiauliai, Lithuanian SSR.

REPRESENTATIVE Photography Art Society of Lithuanian SSR, Pionieriu 8, 232600 Vilnius, Lithuanian SSR.

ADDRESS Rotušés I, 233000 Kaunas, Lithuanian SSR.

Zdeněk Virt GRAPHIC ARTIST · PHOTOGRAPHER Born November 2, 1925, in Prague, Czechoslovakia, Virt attended the College of Decorative Arts in Prague (1945–50), studying under Dr. Tichý.

A freelance photographer and graphic artist, he lectures on nude photography at High School of Decorative Arts (FAMU) in Prague.

PUBLICATIONS Monographs: *Vision*, 1973, *Op Art Akte* (Muller und Kiepenheuer: Hanau, Germany).

ADDRESS U akademie 11, Prague 7, Czechoslovakia.

Roman Vishniac PHOTOGRAPHER · MICROBIOLOGIST · FILM MAKER · INVENTOR Vishniac was born in Russia, near St. Petersburg (now Leningrad), on August 19, 1897. His son, Wolf Vishniac, has been chairman of the Biology Department at the University of Rochester, New York. Vishniac studied at Shanyavsky University in Moscow from 1914 to 1920, earning a Doctorate in Zoology. In 1917 he enrolled in a three-year course in medicine, sponsored by the Russian government, and received a medical degree.

He moved to Berlin in 1918, where he worked at odd jobs and studied Oriental art at the University of Berlin. In 1920 he returned to Shanyavsky University, having been appointed assistant professor of biology.

For four years, beginning in 1936, Dr. Vishniac traveled throughout eastern Europe photographing the Jewish people. He left for France just prior to World War II, and was interned there for three months in a Vichy concentration camp.

In 1940 Vishniac sailed for the United States. He took up freelance portrait photography, but gave that up in 1950 when an opportunity to pursue his interests in photomicrography made it possible for him to freelance in that field. Then, in 1957, he was appointed research associate at the Albert Einstein College of Medicine in New York. In 1960 he was project director for the "Living Biology" film series, a project financed by a National Science Foundation grant, wherein a total of forty 16mm sound-color films for high school and college use would be produced. Vishniac was also involved in films of the series "The Vanished World of Central Europe Jewry." In 1961–62 he taught biology education at Yeshiva University in New York. Most recently he has been professor of creativity at Pratt Institute, New York University and Rhode Island School of Design.

Vishniac is former president of the New York Entomological Society and a Fellow of the New York Academy of Sciences, the Royal Microscopical Society (British) and the Biological Photographic Association. He is a member of the American Society of Limnology and Oceanography, the American Society of Protozoologists and the National Association of Biology Teachers.

Vishniac earned a gold medal from Eastman Kodak and the best-of-show award three years in a row (1952–54) at the annual exhibition of the New York Chapter of the Biological Photographic Association. In 1956 he received ASMP's Memorial Award for "showing mankind the beauty of the world it cannot see"; he also won grand prize in art in photography at "Art in U.S.A.: 1959." He received the gold lens from ASFA and has earned many other awards in many fields. In 1959 he was the subject of a film entitled *The Worlds of Dr. Vishniac* that covered his research into the physiology of protozoa, employing his own cinematographic techniques.

In 1915 Vishniac invented time-lapse cinematography, presenting in rapid review the sequential processes of growth or reproduction. He took the first photograph since 1885 of the world as seen through the eye of an insect—in this case a firefly.

He is one of the world's foremost photomicrographers, his chief subjects of interest being the physiology of ciliates, plasma circulation in unicellular plants and unsolved issues in microbiology. At the age of seven he fitted the lens of his camera over the eyepiece of a small microscope and took his first important picture, a photomicrograph of a cockroach's leg. The basic technique he has developed essentially involves the use of polarized light—ordinary light that has been passed through a calcite prism to make it vibrate in one plane (i.e., one color) only. Calling the technique "colorization," he passes the colors through devices that speed up some wave lengths and slow down others. The result is that the detail and the color of the image that reach the eye are greatly intensified. In his work Vishniac is adamant about preserving the natural colors of microscopic organisms, emphasizing the third dimension, and, unlike many of his colleagues, will photograph microscopic animals only alive and in their free-swimming state. It takes extraordinary patience and time to accomplish these goals, but Vishniac's determination is apparent in his words: "Everything made by human hands looks terrible under magnification —crude, rough, and unsymmetrical. But in nature every bit of life is lovely. The more magnification that we use, the more details are brought out, perfectly formed."

PUBLICATIONS Monographs: *Roman Vishniac*, Eugene Kinkead, 1974; *Building Blocks by Vishniac*, 1971; *Polish Jews: A Pictorial Record*, Abraham Joshua Heschel, 1942, repr. 1965. Books: *The Concerned Photographer 2*, Michael Edelson, 1972; *A Day of Pleasure*, Isaac Bashevis Singer, 1969. Anthologies: *The Photograph Collector's Guide*, Lee D. Witkin & Barbara London, 1979; *The Magic Image*, Cecil Beaton & Gail Buckland, 1975; *Looking at Photographs*, John Szarkowski, 1973. Periodicals: "The Photomicrographic World of Roman Vishniac," Francene Sabin, *Omni*, Oct 1978; *Creative Camera*, July 1975, Feb 1973, Mar 1971.

COLLECTIONS L/C, Wash., D.C.; MOMA, NYC; Smithsonian Inst., Wash., D.C. Amsterdam Mus., The Netherlands; British Mus., London; Louvre, Paris; Victoria & Albert Mus., London.

ADDRESS 219 W 81 St, New York, NY 10024.

Julius Vitali PHOTOGRAPHER · PAINTER Born July 1, 1952, in New Hyde Park, New York, Vitali is a self-taught photographer. He was influenced by André Breton, Julien Levy and Nicolas Calas.

Currently a freelance, Vitali was a CETA artist with the town of Oyster Bay, New York, in 1977–79.

Vitali received a Polaroid grant in 1979. His film *Hot Logarithms* was shown in the 1977 Atlanta Film & Video Festival.

He describes himself as a surrealist, often photographing food, light switches and other objects in puddles of water in order to juxtapose them with reflections.

PUBLICATIONS Periodicals: *Lens on Campus*, Nov 1979; *Grazia*, Sept 1979; *Petersen's Photographic Magazine*, Apr 1979.

COLLECTIONS Julien Levy Cllctn., Bridgewater, Conn. Creatis Gall., Paris.

DEALER Sea Cliff Photography Co, 310 Sea Cliff Ave, Sea Cliff, NY 11579.

ADDRESS 201 Maple Ave, Sea Cliff, NY 11579.

Carol Vitz PHOTOGRAPHER Born April 20, 1941, in Minneapolis, Minnesota, Vitz received a BA in Psychology from Mills College in Oakland, California, in 1963 and did graduate work at the Department of International Relations at Claremont Graduate School, California, in 1964. From 1967 to 1968 she studied at the Mannes Conservatory of Music in New York City. She began her study of photography at the Reitveld Academy of Art, Amsterdam (1970–72), and in 1975 studied with Robert Heinecken in a master's course in photography at University of California at Los Angeles.

Vitz worked as a filmstrip producer from 1978 to 1979 at Montage Audio Visuals in Los Angeles, having freelanced from 1975 to 1979.

She is a member of the Friends of Photography and the Los Angeles Center for Photographic Studies. In 1979 she won both the Dukane Gold Camera Award and the Gold Camera Award at the Industrial Film Festival.

PUBLICATIONS (The Netherlands) Book: *Timothy Leary*, 1972. Periodicals: *Avenue*, Feb, Apr 1972, July, Nov 1971.

COLLECTIONS Capital Research Corp., Los Angeles; Fluor Corp., Irvine, Calif.; Kresges Corp., Troy, Mich.; Security Pacific Natl. Bank, Los Angeles. Bibliothèque Nationale, Paris.

DEALERS Modernism, 236 Eighth St, San Francisco, CA 94103; William M. Lyons Gall., 3041 Grand Ave, Coconut Grove, FL 33133; Cirrus, 542 S Alameda, Los Angeles, CA 90013.

ADDRESS 445 28th Ave, Venice, CA 90291.

František Vobecký FASHION DESIGNER · PAINTER · PHOTOGRAPHER Born November 9, 1902, at Trhový Štěpánov, near Prague, Czechoslovakia, Vobecký studied at the Academie de la Grande Chaumière and Academie de la Model in Paris (1926–27). His major influence was Surrealism.

Retired since 1965, he had been a fashion designer at a prominent salon in Prague and director of its design department for twenty years. From 1955 to 1975 he lectured part-time at the School of Applied Art and Design in Prague.

Vobecký has belonged to the Czechoslovak Art Union since 1952 and to the Union of Creative Artists, "Mánes," since 1931.

He is a painter as well as a photographer, and his paintings were reproduced in the Prague periodical *Volné směry* during the years 1931–50.

Working in black-and-white, Vobecký creates "poetical photomontages and assemblages of diverse objects."

PUBLICATIONS Periodicals: *Creative Camera*,

June 1974; *Fotografický obzor*, no. 11, 1940; *Fotografie*, no. 19, 1938, no. 10, 1936.

COLLECTIONS Sander Gall., Wash., D.C. In Prague: Mus. of Applied Art; Natl. Gall. of Czechoslovakia.

REPRESENTATIVE Art Centrum, V Jámě 10, Prague 1, Czechoslovakia.

ADDRESS Kubánova 736/30, Prague 4, Háje, Czechoslovakia.

Hermann Wilhelm Vogel CHEMIST · WRITER
Born in 1834 in Dobrilugk, Niederlausitz, Germany, Vogel died in 1898. He entered Free Mason Institute in Friedrichstadt near Dresden in 1846, and in 1851 began trade school at Frankfurt an der Oder. The next year he started chemistry and physics studies at Vocational Academy in Berlin, eventually earning his doctorate there.

After initial forays as a mechanic, farmer, merchant, sailor and waiter in a wine tavern, Vogel became an industrial chemist. In 1860 he joined the instructional faculty at the Vocational Academy and became interested in photography. He founded the Berlin Photographische Verein in 1863, and in 1864 was appointed to the chair of photochemistry at the Academy, which he continued to hold after the school became the Technische Hochschule. In 1864 Vogel founded the journal *Photographische Mittheilungen*, and by the end of the decade had published one of the major photographic textbooks of the century, *Lehrbuch der Photographie*. The chemist also took part in many solar-eclipse expeditions and wrote numerous articles.

Vogel's doctoral dissertation, "The Light Sensitivity of Chloride, Bromide and Iodide of Silver," marked the beginning of his photo researches. In 1873 he discovered the technique of dye sensitization of photographic plates, later to be of great use in the development of orthochromatic, panchromatic and color photography. In 1884, with Otto Perutz and J. B. Obernetter, he developed the first orthochromatic dry plate, and he also introduced Azaline, a combination of quinoline red and cyanine, as a sensitizer. Vogel undertook important studies in spectrum analysis and in color photography and reproduction, the latter carried out with Ulrich of Berlin and his son Ernst Vogel.

PUBLICATIONS Books: *Quellendarstellungen zur Geschichte der Fotografie*, Wolfgang Baier, 1964; *Perutz Jubilaeum 1880–1955*, 1955 (Denkschrift); *History of Photography*, J. M. Eder, 3rd ed., 1905, repr. 1945; *History of 3-Color Photography*, E. J. Wall, 1925; *Lexikon für Photographie und Reproduktionstechnik*, G H. Emmerich,

1910. Anthology: *Photography's Great Inventors*, Louis W. Sipley, 1965. Periodicals: *Foto Magazin*, Jan 1959 (Munich); *Bild und Ton*, 1956, 1954; *Photographische Correspondenz*, 1899; *Photographische Mittheilungen*, 1899; *Photographic News*, 1864.

Walter Vogel PHOTOGRAPHER Born October 18, 1932, in Düsseldorf, Germany, Vogel studied with Dr. Otto Steinert at Folkwangschule in Essen-Werden from 1963 to 1968. He is a freelance photographer.

Vogel won a World Press award in 1964.

PUBLICATIONS Periodicals: *Popular Photography Annual*, 1976, 1970, 1967, 1964; *Photography Italiana*, 1970; *U.S. Camera Annual*, 1969.

ADDRESS Eppsteiner Strasse 43, 6000 Frankfurt 1, Germany.

Christian Vogt PHOTOGRAPHER Born April 12, 1946, in Basel, Switzerland, Vogt is a self-trained photographer.

He has freelanced out of his own studio since 1970.

PUBLICATIONS Monograph: *Christian Vogt/ Photographs*, 1980. Anthology: *SX-70 Art*, Ralph Gibson, ed., 1979. Periodicals: *Picture Magazine*, no. 10, 1979, no. 8, 1978; *Camera*, Dec 1975, Sept 1975, Mar 1974, Sept 1973, Oct 1972, Sept 1971, Feb 1971, Aug 1970.

COLLECTIONS Bibliothèque Nationale, Paris; Moderna Muséet, Stockholm; Polaroid Cllctn., Amsterdam. In Switzerland: Hoffman Stiftung, Basel; Swiss Fndn. for Photography, Zurich.

ADDRESS Augustinergasse 3, CH-4051, Basel, Switzerland.

Peter Wilhelm Friedrich Voigtländer PHOTOGRAPHIC EQUIPMENT MANUFACTURER · INVENTOR
Born in 1812 in Vienna, Voigtländer died in 1878. His grandfather, Johann Christoph Voigtländer, established a shop in 1756 to manufacture microscopes, compasses and other optical instruments. Peter's father, Johann Friederich, continued the family business and in 1823 invented and patented the opera glass. Peter studied with his father and took advanced courses at the Polytechnic Institute of Vienna.

Voigtländer traveled and worked in Germany, France and England, and in 1837 he took over the family business, then ranked among the finest of European optical-goods manufacturers. Based on Josef Petzal's calculation, the company manufactured the first objective (lens) designed exclusively for photographic use. Reportedly sixteen times faster than the lens used by Daguerre, it reduced exposure times from minutes to seconds. Voigtländer also developed the first all-metal daguerreotype camera in 1841. By 1849 business was good enough to encourage construction of another factory in Braunschweig, Germany, his wife's hometown. In 1857 the company produced the achromatic Orthoskop objective, and in 1862 produced objective #10,000.

Voigtländer received many honors during his lifetime, including a hereditary peerage from the Emperor of Austria in 1868.

PUBLICATIONS Books: *Quellendarstellungen zur Geschichte der Fotografie*, Wolfgang Baier, 1964; *Die Photographische Kamera*, Josef Stupor, 1962; *Objective Einst und Heute*, Voigtländer A.G., 1956; *Cassell's Cyclopedia of Photography*, 1911, repr. 1973. Anthologies: *Early Photographs and Early Photographers*, Oliver Mathews, 1973; *Photography's Great Inventors*, Louis W. Sipley, 1965. Periodicals: *Tradition*, Ilse Erdmann, Apr 1, 1962; *Bild und Ton*, 1956; *Photographische Mittheilungen*, 1878; *Photographische Correspondenz*, 1865.

Chris Von Wangenheim   PHOTOGRAPHER Born February 21, 1942, in Germany, Von Wangenheim died in an automobile crash on St. Martin island in the Caribbean on March 9, 1981.

Von Wangenheim studied architecture at the University of Munich, Germany, in 1961, and became a self-employed fashion photographer with his own studio. At the time of his death he was working on a book entitled "Women Alone." The photographer had resided with his wife and daughter in Washington Depot, Connecticut.

In Von Wangenheim's *New York Times* obituary Alexander Liberman, editorial director of Condé Nast Publications, said the photographer "was able to bring to a picture a European sophistication, and he combined an admirable love of women, a sensuous feeling, with a modern image."

PUBLICATIONS Books: *Fashion Theory*, Ralph Gibson, 1980; *SX-70 Art*, Ralph Gibson, ed., 1979; *Vogue Book of Fashion Photography 1919–1979*, Polly Devlin, 1979; *History of Fashion Photography*, Nancy Hall-Duncan, 1978. Periodical: *Camera*, Jan 1970.

REPRESENTATIVE Jan & Jack Garten, 50 Riverside Dr, New York, NY 10022.

Gerhard Vormwald   PHOTOGRAPHER Born March 6, 1948, in Heidelberg, Germany, Vormwald was educated at the Academie of Arts in Mannheim, Germany (1965–70), where he studied painting, graphics and sculpture.

Vormwald works as a freelance photographer. He has been a member of Bund Freischaffender Fotodesigner (BFF) since 1975.

Working mainly with Polaroid prints, the photographer also does reportage and theater photography. For his portraits and still lifes Vormwald builds sets in his studio or in the open air.

PUBLICATION Book: *Cemeteries of Europe*, 1977.

COLLECTIONS Polaroid Corp., Amsterdam; Polaroid Corp., Frankfurt, Germany.

REPRESENTATIVES Hugo Mayer Nouten Group, Kufsteiner Platz 5, 8000 Munich, Germany; The Compagnie, Agathenstrasse 7, 2000 Hamburg, Germany; Ingrid Thardieu, 5 Blvd Edgar Quinet, Paris 75, France.

ADDRESSES Tullastrasse 14, 6800 Mannheim, Germany; 75 rue Henri-Barbusse, 2ᵉ Etage, 92 Paris-Clichy, France.

Zdeněk Voženílek   PHOTOGRAPHER Born January 23, 1929, in Běchovice, Czechoslovakia, Voženílek attended Architectural Technical School in Prague (1944–48) and studied photography at the Academy of Arts in Prague (1962).

A freelance photographer, he served as chief of the photo studio at the Prague Planning Institute from 1958 to 1978.

Voženílek has been a member of the Union of Czech Fine Artists since 1963, and won first prize from the National Committee of Prague in 1961.

PUBLICATIONS Books: *Photography Year Book*, 1973, 1970, 1966, 1965, 1963, 1962 (London); *The Art of Photography*, Time-Life Series, 1971. Periodicals: "Photographer and Architecture," Karel Dvořák, *Czechoslovak Photography*, Jan 1972; review, Petr Tausk, *Slovaque photography*, no. 2, 1970.

COLLECTIONS Seattle Art Mus., Wash. Bibliothèque Nationale, Paris; Moravian Gall., Brno, Czechoslovakia.

ADDRESS Hvozdíková 7–106 00, Prague 10, Czechoslovakia.

Adam Clark Vroman   PHOTOGRAPHER · LECTURER · WRITER [See plate 37] Born April 15, 1856, in La Salle, Illinois, Vroman died July 24, 1916, in Alta Dena, California.

Vroman began taking photographs about 1892. He worked for the Chicago, Burlington & Quincy Railroad in 1874, and eventually moved to Pasadena, California, where, with J. S. Glasscock, he opened a bookstore which prospered. In 1895 he witnessed a Hopi Indian snake ceremony, which influenced several photographic trips to the Indian territory of the Southwest during the next ten years.

He wrote and lectured on the Indian way of life, in which he was extremely interested, and also amassed one of the most important collections of Indian arts and crafts.

Working in large format with both a hand view and view camera, Vroman produced platinum prints (from gelatin dry plates) that captured, with directness and honesty, the Hopi and Navaho life-styles. He also photographed California missions and landscapes of Yosemite and other areas of the Southwest. The Natural History Museum of Los Angeles County housed the artist's work in the Vroman Gallery from 1960 to 1973.

PUBLICATIONS Monographs: *Dwellers at the Source*, William Webb & Robert A. Weinstein, 1973; *Photographer of the Southwest*, Ruth I. Mahood, ed., w/Robert A. Weinstein, intro. by Beaumont Newhall, 1961. Books: *Untitled 2/3* (Friends of Photography), 1972–73; *Ramona*, intro. by Helen Hunt Jackson, 1913; *The Genesis of the Story of Ramona*, w/T. F. Barnes, 1899; *Mission Memories*, 1898. Anthologies: *The Photograph Collector's Guide*, Lee D. Witkin & Barbara London, 1979; *Photography Rediscovered*, David Travis & Anne Kennedy, 1979; *The Magic Image*, Cecil Beaton & Gail Buckland, 1975; *Great Photographers*, Time-Life Series, 1971.

COLLECTIONS Friends of Photography, Carmel, Calif.; IMP/GEH, Rochester; MOMA, NYC; Natural History Mus. of Los Angeles County; Pasadena Pub. Lib., Calif.; Smithsonian Inst., Natl. Anthropological Archives, Wash., D.C.; Southwest Mus., Los Angeles.

W

Alison Ehrlich Wachstein *PHOTOJOURNALIST·*
AUTHOR Born April 22, 1947, in New Jersey,
Wachstein received a BA from Northwestern
University, Evanston, Illinois, in 1969. She has
taken workshops with Paul Caponigro, Cornell
Capa, Minor White and Arnold Gassan and has
attended the Columbia Photojournalism Work-
shop of the University of Missouri in 1970.

A freelance and portrait studio photographer
since 1971, Wachstein also was an adjunct assistant professor of photography at Seton Hall University in South Orange, New Jersey (1976–79),
and a photography instructor at Fairleigh Dickinson University, Teaneck, New Jersey (1976–
77).

Wachstein belongs to NPPA, Connecticut
Press Women, Professional Women Photographers and the New Jersey Press Photographers
Association. She won first prize awards from the
latter in the life-style category (1977) and for spot
news (1976).

Her photojournalism includes images of preg-
nancy and childbirth, and she specializes in mul-
tigenerational family portraits and candid
photography albums.

PUBLICATIONS Monograph: *Pregnant Moments*, 1979. Anthologies: *Family of Woman*,
1979; *Choices in Childbirth*, 1978; *Women Photograph Men*, Danielle B. Hayes, ed., intro. by
Molly Haskell, 1977; *Help Your Community . . .
Through Photography*, 1973; *Wilderness USA*,
1973.

COLLECTION ICP, NYC.

ADDRESS 5 Jana Dr, Weston, CT 06883.

Kent E. Wade *PHOTOGRAPHER · WRITER ·*
TEACHER Born January 22, 1944, in Portland,
Oregon, he received an MBA in Marketing from
Portland State University in Oregon in 1970, as
well as a BBA in Marketing in 1966. Wade is a
self-taught photographer.

Currently he is the owner of Photographic
Glassworks, a company specializing in the photo
transfer of images or intricate designs to glass and
metal surfaces; he also does freelance photography. Since 1978 he has taught several photographic workshops in the Portland area, and in
1970–71 he did freelance photography in Australia.

Wade is a member of SPE and Friends of Photography. In 1977 he was artist-in-residence at
Grant High School in Portland, and in 1976 art-
ist-in-community-residence with Metropolitan
Arts Commission of Portland, Oregon.

Wade says: "For the last several years I have
been exploring photographic processes which enable me to integrate my images on or in media
such as metal, glass, clay, etc. These materials
enable me to break the two-dimensional plane of
the traditional photograph."

PUBLICATIONS Books: *Alternative Photographic Processes*, 1978; *Asia by Over-
land**Cheap!*, 1973 (self-pub.). Periodical: *Glass
Studio*, Jan 1979.

ADDRESS 1925 SW Broadway Dr, Portland, OR
97201.

Robert S. Wade *PHOTOGRAPHER · TEACHER ·*
SCULPTOR Born January 6, 1943, in Austin,
Texas, Wade received a BFA from the University
of Texas, Austin (1965), and an MA from the University of California, Berkeley, in 1966. He
names artist/writer Robert Smithson and actor
James Dean as major influences.

A self-employed artist since 1977, Wade was
assistant professor of art at North Texas State
University, Denton, from 1973 to 1977 and director of Northwood Art Institute in Dallas in 1972–
73. He served as artist-in-residence at Northwood
Institute in Cedar Hill, Texas, in 1970–72, and
taught art at McClennan Community College in
Waco, Texas, from 1966 to 1970.

Recipient of NEA artists fellowships in 1973 and 1974, Wade won North Texas State University Faculty Research grants from 1973 through 1977.

Wade's nonphotographic achievements include the 1979 sculpture "Biggest Cowboy Boots in the World" for Washington (D.C.) Art Site, "Giant Iguana" sculpture for Artpark in New York (1978) and videotape (1979) and participation in the 1975 film *Jackalope,* by Ken Harrison, documenting Texas artists.

Using small and large format, the photographer produces large-scale black-and-white photos on sensitized linen, hand-colored with photo oils. His main subject matter is "indigenous Americana of the Southwest."

PUBLICATIONS Monograph: *Bob Wade's Texas,* 1976 (self-pub.). Catalogs: *Fire Show,* 1979 (Contemporary Arts Mus.: Houston); *Malerei und Photographie im Dialog,* 1977 (Kunsthaus: Zurich, Switzerland); *Texas Artists,* 1977 (Amer. Cultural Ctr., Paris); *Photo Process as Media,* Rosanne Truxes, 1976 (Rutgers Univ. Art Gall., N.J.). Periodicals: "Bob Wade's Texas Artifacts," Jim Moisan, *Artweek,* May 6, 1978; "Texas," Janet Kutner, summer 1975, "Contemporary Art in Texas," Henry Hopkins, May 1973, *Artnews;* "The Young Texans," Jan Butterfield, *Arts,* Mar 1973; *Artforum,* review, Robert Pincus-Witten, Dec 1971.

COLLECTIONS In Texas: Dallas Mus. of Fine Arts; Fort Worth Art Mus.; Waco Art Ctr., Waco; Witte Mus., San Antonio. CCP, Tucson; Chase Manhattan Bank, NYC; IT&T, Chicago. Archive Sohm, Markgroningen, Germany; Beaubourg Mus., Pompidou Ctr., Paris; Groningen Mus., The Netherlands.

DEALERS Lone Star Gall., 61 Fifth Ave, New York, NY 10003; Delahunty Gall., 2611 Cedar Springs, Dallas, TX 75201.

ADDRESS 5110 Lemmon Ave, Dallas, TX 75209.

Catherine Wagner PHOTOGRAPHER · TEACHER Born January 31, 1953, in San Francisco, Wagner earned a BA (1975) and MA (1977) from San Francisco State University. She also studied at Instituto del Arte in San Miguel de Allende, Mexico (1970–71), San Francisco Art Institute (1971) and the College of Marin in Kentfield, California (1972–73).

Since 1978 Wagner has taught art and photography at Mills College in Oakland and at San Francisco State University. In 1978 she taught at the University of California Extension in Berkeley, Diablo Valley College in Pleasant Hill, California, and at College of San Mateo, California.

She is a member of SPE.

Wagner's current works are urban landscapes.

PUBLICATIONS Periodicals: *Picture Magazine,* May 1979; *Popular Photography's 35mm Photography,* winter 1979; *Untitled #14,* 1978 (Friends of Photography: Carmel, Calif.); review, *Artforum,* Sept 1978.

COLLECTIONS CCP, Tucson; Delaware Art Mus., Wilmington; ICP, NYC; Houston Mus. of Fine Arts; Los Angeles County Mus. of Art; Minneapolis Inst. of the Arts, Minn.; Graham Nash Cllctn., Los Angeles; Oakland Mus. of Art, Calif.; San Francisco Mus. of Modern Art; UCLA. Bibliothèque Nationale, Paris; Tokyo Inst. of Polytechnics.

DEALER Lowinsky & Arai Gall., 228 Grant Ave, San Francisco, CA 94108.

ADDRESS 28 Precita Ave, San Francisco, CA 94110.

Yasuhiro Wakabayashi
See Hiro

Max Waldman PHOTOGRAPHER Born June 2, 1919, Waldman died in New York City on March 8, 1981. He had earned an MA in Fine Arts in 1945 from Teachers College at Columbia University, New York City. He had been a freelance photographer since 1949.

In 1976 and 1971 Waldman won CAPS grants and in 1972 he was awarded an NEA fellowship.

Waldman specialized in black-and-white images of the performing arts.

PUBLICATIONS Books: *Waldman on Dance,* intro. by Clive Barnes, 1977; *Waldman on Theatre,* intro. by Clive Barnes, 1971; *Zero on Mostel,* Zero Mostel, 1965. Anthology: *The Photograph Collector's Guide,* Lee D. Witkin & Barbara London, 1979. Periodicals: *Popular Photography Annual,* 1977; *Photo,* Dec 1975, Jan 1974, May 1971; *Life,* Dec 17, 1972, Oct 22, 1974, Oct 16, 1972, Apr 9, 1971, Jan 12, 1971, Dec 12, 1969; *Zoom,* Oct 1972 (Paris); "Artistry of Max Waldman," R. Hattersley, *Popular Photography,* Jan 1970; *Aperture,* spring 1967.

COLLECTIONS Brooklyn Acad. of Music, N.Y.; Catskill Art Soc., N.Y.; Colgate Univ., Hamilton, N.Y.; Cornell Univ., Ithaca, N.Y.; IMP/GEH, Rochester; L/C, Wash., D.C.; Reva & David Logan Fndn., Chicago; Metro. Mus. of Art, NYC; MOMA, NYC; Port Authority of N.Y.; Pratt Inst. Lib., Brooklyn, N.Y.; St. Bonaventure Univ., Bonaventure, N.Y.; Vassar Coll., Poughkeepsie, N.Y.

DEALER Witkin Gall., 41 E 57 St, New York, NY 10022.
ADDRESS 21 W 17 St, New York, NY 10011.

(Harold) Todd Walker PHOTOGRAPHER · TEACHER Born September 25, 1917, in Salt Lake City, Utah, Walker was educated at Glendale Junior College in California, 1939–40, and at Art Center School in Los Angeles, 1939–41.

Walker has been professor of art at the University of Arizona in Tucson since 1977, assistant professor of art in printmaking and photography at the University of Florida in Gainesville (1970–77), associate professor of art at California State University at Northridge (1970), instructor of photography at University of California at Los Angeles Extension (1969–70) and teacher of photography at the Art Center College of Design in Los Angeles (1966–70). He owned his own studios in Los Angeles and Beverly Hills from 1946 to 1970. Before that he worked in Hollywood as a photographer for Tradefilms, Inc. (1941–43) and in the Scenic Department of RKO Studios (1934–42).

Walker was the recipient of a fellowship from the Florida Council of the Arts in 1976 and an individual grant from the National Foundation for the Arts in 1971.

The photographer uses a variety of processes, such as gum-bichromate, lithographs, silver prints, collotypes and silk screens. Generally using solarization or posterization processes, the female nude is his most common subject.

PUBLICATIONS Monographs: *See*, 1978; *A Few Notes*, 1977; *Edge of the Shadow*, 1977; *Three Soliloquies*, 1977; *For Nothing Changes*, 1976; *Twenty-Seven Photographs*, 1975; *Melancholy*, 1968; *How Would It Feel to Be Able to Dance Like This?*, 1967; *John Donne*, 1966; *The Story of an Abandoned Shack in the Desert*, 1966; *8 Shakespeare's Sonnets*, 1965. Books: *The Grotesque in Photography*, A. D. Coleman, 1977; *Object and Image*, George Craven, 1975; *Photography in America*, Robert Doty, ed., 1974. Anthologies: *The Photograph Collector's Guide*, Lee D. Witkin & Barbara London, 1979; *Photographers' Choice*, Kelly Wise, 1975; *Mirrors and Windows*, John Szarkowski, 1960. Periodicals: *American Photographer*, Dec 1978; *Afterimage: VSW*, Mar 1974; *Popular Photography Annual*, 1974, 1973; *Modern Photography*, Nov 1975; *Creative Camera*, May 1973; *U.S. Camera*, Apr 1964; *Camera*, Dec/Jan, 1971/1972.

PORTFOLIOS *Portfolio III*, 1974; *John Donne*, 1968; *An Abandoned Shack*, 1967.

COLLECTIONS CCP, Tucson; Colgate Univ., Picker Art Gall., Hamilton, N.Y.; Columbia Coll. Gall., Chicago; E. B. Crocker Art Gall., Mus. of City of Sacramento, Calif.; Harvard Univ., Fogg Art Mus., Cambridge, Mass.; Houston Mus. of Art, Tex.; IMP/GEH, Rochester; Minneapolis Inst. of Art, Minn.; Mint Mus. of Art, Charlotte, N.C.; MOMA, NYC; Mus. of Fine Art, St. Petersburg, Fla.; New Orleans Mus. of Art; Northern Ky. State Coll., Highland Heights, Ky.; Norton Simon Mus., Pasadena, Calif.; Notre Dame Univ., South Bend, Ind.; Oakland Art Mus., Calif.; Philadelphia Mus. of Art, Pa.; Phoenix Coll., Phoenix, Ariz.; San Diego State Univ., Calif.; Southern Ill. Univ., Carbondale; Univ. of Alabama, Birmingham; UCLA; Univ. of Nebr., Sheldon Art Gall., Lincoln; Univ. of Northern Iowa, Cedar Falls; Univ. of Virginia, Charlottesville; Utah State Univ., Logan; Virginia Mus. of Fine Arts, Richmond. Bibliothèque Nationale, Paris; Natl. Gall. of Canada, Ottawa, Ontario; Ryerson Polytechnical Inst., Toronto, Canada.
ADDRESS 2890 N Orland Ave, Tucson, AZ 85712.

Edward John Wall CHEMIST · PUBLISHER · TEACHER Born in 1860 in England, Wall died October 13, 1928, in Boston.

He published a technical photographic journal in London in 1889, *The Photographic Answers*, and, beginning in 1896, he published *Photographic News*. Later he taught 3-color photography at the London Council School of Photo-Engraving. Active in the photographic industry, Wall emigrated to the United States in 1910 to work for the Fire-Proof Acetylcellulose Company in Rochester. Later he worked for Technicolor Motion Picture Company in Boston, and while in that city became assistant editor of *American Photography* and built up an important and influential photographic publishing house. In his earlier years the publisher translated into English J. M. Eder's *Photographie mit Bromsilbergelatine*, Fritz's *Lithographie*, E. König's *Farbenphotographie* and Mayer's *Bromöldruck*.

Wall's most singular contribution to photography was the theoretical introduction of the bromoil process in 1907, by which pictures are obtained by bleaching and pigmenting bromide prints.

PUBLICATIONS Books: *Photographic Darkroom*, 1933; *Photographic Emulsions*, 1929; *Collected Papers on Photography, 1901–1928*, 1928; *Intensification & Reduction*, 1927; *History of Three-Color Photography*, 1925; *Photographic*

Facts & Formulas, 1924; *Practical Color Photography*, 1922; *Cassell's Cyclopedia of Photography*, 1911, repr. 1973; *History of Photography*, Josef Maria Eder, 3rd ed. 1905, repr. 1945; *The ABC of Photography*, 190?; *Beginner's Guide to Photography*, n.d. (Perken: London); *Everyone's Guide to Photography*, 1898; *The Imperial Textbook of Photography*, 1897 (Imperial Dry Plate Co.: Cricklewood, England); *Carbon Printing*, 1894, *Dictionary of Photography*, 1889, repr. 1941 (Hazell, Watson & Viney: London). Anthology: *Early Photographs & Early Photographers*, Oliver Mathews, 1973. Periodical: *Photographic News*, Apr 12, 1907.

John Wall TEACHER · ARCHIVIST Born September 16, 1928, in Middlesbrough, Yorkshire, England, Wall earned a Bachelor of Divinity degree from Manchester University and Hartley-Victoria Theological College (1952), an MA from Bristol University, England (1966), and a PhD from London University (1975).

Currently head of Religious Education and the Humanities Department at New College, Durham, England, Wall has directed the National Photographic Record in England since its inception as a department of the RPS in 1973. He headed the Department of Religious and Social Studies at Middleton St. George College of Education in Durham from 1968 to 1979 and was a lecturer in divinity at Edge Hill College of Education, Lancashire, England (1966–68).

Wall became a Fellow of the RPS in 1976 and belongs to its Collections Advisory Committee as well as being an Associate of the Royal Historical Society.

Having a special interest in the permanency of color photography archives, Wall developed and patented a video recording system for the storage and reconstitution of color photographic images. His field of research is cataloging and classifying systems for photographs as well as ongoing studies in the permanency of color photographic archives.

PUBLICATIONS Book: *The Directory of British Photographic Collections*, 1977 (Heinemann: London). Periodicals: "Full-Colour (Polychromatic) Photosensitive Glass," *Journal of Photographic Science*, Sept/Oct 1978; "The Video Recorder as a Colour Transparency Store," *Television Society Journal*, winter 1967/68; "Overcoming the Problem of Permanency in Colour Archives," *Photographic Journal*, Apr 1967.

ADDRESS 46 The Meadows, Sedgefield, Stockton on Tees, Cleveland County, TS21 2DH, England.

John Walmsley PHOTOGRAPHER Born March 11, 1947, in Harrow, Middlesex, England, Walmsley received a diploma in photography in 1968 from Guildford Art School, Surrey, England.

A freelance photographer since 1968, he worked as a part-time lecturer at the Architectural Association School of Architecture in London from 1973 to 1979.

Walmsley has belonged to the National Union of Journalists since 1968. He has been the recipient of awards from the Scottish Arts Council (1979) and from the Arts Council of Great Britain (1974).

The photographer works "in the reportage tradition," mainly capturing images of people, which are used largely by educational book publishers in Great Britain and the U.S.

PUBLICATIONS Books: *Snaps*, w/Leila Berg, 1977 (Macmillan, England); *Neill & Summerhill: A Man and His Work*, 1969 (Penguin: England). Periodicals: *Camera*, Mar 1970, Feb 1969; *Creative Camera*, Apr 1969.

COLLECTIONS Bibliothèque Nationale, Paris; Hertfordshire County Cllctn., England; Natl. Portrait Gall., London.

ADDRESS 58, Lawrence Rd, Biggleswade, Bedfordshire SG18 OLS, England.

J. C. (John Cimon) Warburg PHOTOGRAPHER Born in 1867 in the Paddington section of London, England, Warburg died in 1931 in London's Kensington district. Educated at home because of ill health, he was first attracted to photography by an exhibit of James Craig Annan's work.

The child of a wealthy family, Warburg pursued many interests: music, linguistics and entomology. He took up photography about 1880 and was soon writing numerous articles for German and English publications. He was a member of the advisory committee for the Hamburg International Jubilee Exhibition of 1903.

Joining RPS in 1895, he was elected to its council in 1913 and to fellowship in 1916, also serving on several committees. He joined the Postal Camera Club in 1899 and was a founder-member of the Pictorial Group in 1921.

Warburg worked in the pictorial style, chiefly using platinum and gum-bichromate processes. He also produced many autochrome transparencies (1907). Although his earlier work was realistic (1880s), he worked in an Impressionist style for the remainder of his career.

PUBLICATIONS Anthologies: *Pictorial Photography in Britain, 1900–1920*, Arts Council of Great Britain, 1978; *Camera Work: A Critical*

Anthology, Jonathan Green, ed., 1973. Periodical: *Camera Work*, 1903.

Fred Ward PHOTOGRAPHER · WRITER Born in Huntsville, Alabama, on July 16, 1935, Ward received a BA in Political Science (1957) and an MA in Journalism and Communications (1959) from the University of Florida, Gainesville.

He has been a freelance photographer/writer since 1960, previously having taught in the Radio-TV-Film Department of St. Petersburg Jr. College in Florida (1959–60). He also taught photography at the University of Florida (1958–59) and was a film director for WKNO-TV in Memphis, Tennessee (1959).

Ward has been a member of the White House News Photographers Association since 1962, winning first prizes in their 1975 and 1966 contests. He has also belonged to the U.S. Senate Press Photographers Gallery since 1962 and the NPPA since 1958, winning the latter's first prize in a contest jointly sponsored with the University of Missouri in 1970.

The photographer directed and photographed a film on biological control in 1978 entitled *Why Spray*, and he produced and directed two films for the National Endowment for the Humanities in 1970: *La Raza: The Story of Mexican Americans* and *Mexico: 12,000 Years of History*.

PUBLICATIONS Books: *Inside Cuba Today*, 1978; *The Home Birth Book*, w/Charlotte Ward, 1977; *Portrait of a President*, w/Hugh Sidey, 1975; *Golden Islands of the Caribbean*, 1972. Periodicals: "Fiber Optics," Oct 1979, "Diamonds," Jan 1979, "Cuba," Jan 1977, "Cree Indians," Apr 1975, "Japan," Mar 1974, "Everglades," Jan 1972, "Rhode Island," Sept 1968, *National Geographic*.

COLLECTION Metro. Mus. of Art, NYC.

REPRESENTATIVE Black Star, 450 Park Ave S, New York, NY 10016.

ADDRESS 7106 Saunders Ct, Bethesda, MD 20034.

John Frederick Ward PHOTOGRAPHER Born March 23, 1943, in Washington, D.C., Ward received a BA in 1964 from Harvard University, Cambridge, Massachusetts, and a PhD in 1971 from the University of Colorado, Boulder. Ansel Adams and Eliot Porter were major influences.

A self-employed photographer since 1972, Ward was assistant professor of physics at Lawrence University, Appleton, Wisconsin, in 1971–72.

He belongs to the American Physical Society.

"My principal concern," says the photographer, "is with design and texture in landscape, extending from abstract detail to broad panorama, including both natural subjects and the relics of man." He uses 4 x 5 and 8 x 10 formats in both color and black-and-white.

COLLECTIONS Allen State Bank, Allen, Tex.; Amoco Oil Co., Denver, Colo.; Brunswick Corp., Chicago; Detroit Inst. of Arts, Mich.; K-Mart Corp., Troy, Mich.

DEALERS Afterimage Gall., Quadrangle #151, 2800 Routh St, Dallas, TX 75201; Douglas Kenyon, 155 E Ohio St, Chicago, IL 60611; Eclipse Gall., 2012 Tenth St, Seattle, WA 98166; Gallery of Photographic Arts, 26777 Lorraine Rd, North Olmsted, OH 44070; Halsted Gall., 560 N Woodward, Birmingham, MI 48011; Hills Gall., 3113 E Third Ave, Denver, CO 80206; Silver Image Gall., 83 W Washington, Seattle, WA 98104.

ADDRESS 907 Ninth St, Boulder, CO 80302.

John Lawrence Ward TEACHER · ART CRITIC · PAINTER Born February 6, 1938, in East Orange, New Jersey, Ward received a BA in Music (1960) from Hamilton College, Clinton, New York, an MA in Art History (1962) from Yale University, New Haven, Connecticut, and an MFA in Painting (1964) from the University of New Mexico, Albuquerque. As of this writing he was PhD candidate at Boston University.

Ward has been a professor of art history and art at the University of Florida, Gainesville, from 1966 to the present, and before that from 1962 to 1964.

He belongs to the CAA.

PUBLICATIONS Book: *The Criticism of Photography as Art: The Photographs of Jerry Uelsmann*, 1970. Periodicals: "Historical Survey of Approaches to Criticism," *Photo Communique*, May/Jun–Sept/Oct 1979; "The Nature of Photography as Art," *Visual Dialog*, 1:4, 1976.

ADDRESS Art Dept, FAA, University of Florida, Gainesville, FL 32611.

Leon Warnerke INVENTOR · PHOTOGRAPHER · CIVIL ENGINEER Born in 1837 in Russia, Warnerke died October 7, 1900, in Geneva, Switzerland.

He left St. Petersburg, Russia, in 1870 for London, where he started a photochemical company. Having invented a film-roll holder in 1875, he also experimented with the production of silver bromide collodion emulsion, producing silver bromide films on gelatinized paper and becoming the first to use "stripping films" with a roller dark-slide. In 1889 Warnerke produced gelatin silver chloride paper, calling it "the printing process of the future." He devised the sensitometer in 1880—the first practical device for measuring exposures—and in 1885 introduced and patented a negative paper coated on both sides. Warnerke lectured frequently before the photographic societies of England, France, Belgium and Germany. He returned to St. Petersburg and founded a photographic firm there in 1880 as well as a technical journal, then retired to Geneva around 1898–99.

The inventor received a prize from the Association Belge de Photographie in 1877, and the Progress Medal of RPS in 1881.

PUBLICATIONS Books: *Ausführliches Handbuch der Photographie*, Josef Maria Eder, 1:3, 1912 ed., & 2:2, 1927 ed.; *Cassell's Cyclopedia*, 1911, repr. 1973; *History of Photography*, Josef Maria Eder, 1905, repr. 1972. Periodicals: *International Photographer*, Jan 1958; *Photographic News*, nos. 876 & 877, 1875.

Julianne Bussert Baker Warren *PHOTOGRAPHER* Born May 8, 1916, in Lima, Ohio, Warren is married to the editorial cartoonist L. D. Warren. She was taught and influenced by her father, who was a professional photographer. In 1936 she started working seriously at photography.

Currently a self-employed photographer, Warren previously worked as a staff photographer at the *Cincinnati Post* in Ohio from 1952 to 1968. She was employed in Cincinnati as a photographer and promotion manager for radio station WSAI from 1950 to 1952 and as a plant manager of a photo-finishing plant from 1941 to 1948.

Warren is a member of the Association of American Editorial Cartoonists and in 1971 was elected historian of that organization.

PUBLICATIONS Books: *Cincinnati in Color*, w/ Dr. Walter C. Langsam, 1978; *The World and Warren's Cartoons*, Walter C. Langsam, 1976; *Press Photography*, Robert B. Rhode, 1961.

COLLECTIONS Hamilton County & Cincinnati Pub. Lib., Ohio; Smithsonian Inst., Washington, D.C.; Truman Lib., Austin, Tex.

DEALERS Closson's Gall., Fourth & Race Sts, Cincinnati, OH 45202; L'Idee Art Concepts, B. Alden Olson, POB 3098, Cincinnati, OH 45201.

ADDRESS 1815 William H. Taft Rd, Apt 203, Cincinnati, OH 45206.

(Henry) Bradford Washburn, Jr. *PHOTOGRAPHER · MOUNTAIN CLIMBER · MUSEUM DIRECTOR · TEACHER* Born June 7, 1910, in Cambridge, Massachusetts, Washburn received an AB in 1933 and an AM degree in 1960, both from Harvard University in Cambridge. He also had two years of graduate study at Harvard's Institute of Geographical Exploration in 1934–35.

Since 1939 Washburn has been director of the Museum of Science in Boston. From 1971 to 1975 he did field work for a map of the Grand Canyon, published by the National Geographic Society and the Museum of Science, Boston. Beginning in 1926 and continuing until 1955, he led several mountain-climbing expeditions. He is best known for the National Geographic Society expeditions to Alaska that resulted in a mapping out of Mount McKinley and the surrounding area. From 1935 to 1942 Washburn was an instructor at Harvard University's Institute of Geographical Exploration.

Washburn became a member of the national advisory board of the World Center for Exploration in 1969 and was named an Honorary Fellow of the American Geographical Society in 1961. He joined the American Association for the Advancement of Science in 1960, the Royal Geographical Society (London) in 1936 and the Explorers Club in 1931. He was awarded a grant from the National Geographic Society in 1972, received the Richard Hopper Day Medal from the American Academy of Arts and Sciences in 1966 and earned the Burr Prize from the National Geographic Society for "outstanding exploration" in Alaska in 1940.

Washburn is known for high-altitude aerial photographs of remote regions, which are used for the purpose of cartographic research, and for the photographs resulting from his mountain-climbing expeditions.

PUBLICATIONS Book: *A Tourist Guide to Mount McKinley*, 1971. Periodicals: *The Mountain World*, 1964–65, 1960–61, 1956–57; *Look*, Dec 9, 1947; *Life*, Aug 20, 1956, Sept 2, 1946, Mar 19, 1943, Jan 20, 1941, Sept 23, 1937; *National Geographic*, Aug 1953, July 1938, June 1936, Mar 1935.

ADDRESS Museum of Science, Science Park, Boston, MA 02114.

Cary Robert Wasserman *PHOTOGRAPHER · CRITIC* Born November 27, 1939, in Los Angeles, California, Wasserman received a BA in English Literature and Criticism in 1961 and an MA in 1963 from the University of California at Los Angeles. He also studied with Henry Holmes Smith (1967–70), and his major influences have been Eugène Atget, Henri Cartier-Bresson and Edward Weston.

Wasserman has been employed as an instructor of photography at the University of Lowell in Massachusetts since 1978, and in 1979 taught at Phillips Academy summer session in Andover.

Previously he was an instructor at the University of Maine in Portland-Gorham in 1976–77.

A member of Boston Visual Artists Union, he was founding vice-president of their credit union in 1976. He was also a founding member of the Art Consultants Group in 1974 and a member of SPE (1975–76). In 1975 he was awarded a grant from the Cambridge Arts Council, and in 1974 he received one from the Polaroid Corporation.

Wasserman works with all photographic formats. "People and their gestural relationships, explorations with the formal and expressive properties of color and the interrelationships of time and space," he says, are the focus of his work.

PUBLICATIONS Books: *New Blues*, Che Du Puich, 1976. Anthologies: *Creative Camera International Yearbook 1977*, Peter Turner, ed., 1976 (London); *The Photographer's Choice*, Kelly Wise, ed., 1975; *Private Realities: Recent American Photography*, Clifford S. Ackley, ed., 1974. Catalogs: *The Color Photography of Cary Wasserman*, Susan Dodge Peters, 1978; *Points of View*, Susan Channing/John Snyder, eds., 1972. Periodicals: Reviews, "Man Ray," May 1979, "Duane Michaels," Apr 1979, *New Age Journal*; reviews, "Edward Weston Nudes," "On Photography," Oct 1978, "Steichen: the Master Prints," Dec 1978, *Boston Visual Arts Union Newsletter*; "Steichen: The Master Prints," Oct 1978, "Brugiere," June 1978, "Photographs of Architecture" (Philip Trager), Apr 1978, reviews, *New Age Journal*; "SX-70 Manipulation," *Petersen's Photographic Magazine*, Dec 1976; *Zoom*, May 1975 (Paris).

COLLECTIONS Mus. of Fine Arts, Boston; Polaroid Corp. Cllctn, Cambridge, Mass.; Portland Mus. of Art, Maine; Smith Coll. Mus. of Art, Northampton, Mass.; Wellesley Coll. Mus. of Art, Wellesley, Mass.

ADDRESS 6 Porter Rd, Cambridge, MA 02140.

Carleton Eugene Watkins   PHOTOGRAPHER
[See plate 20] Born November 11, 1829, in Oneonta, Otsego County, New York, Watkins died June 23, 1916, at Napa State Hospital, Imola, California. He was taught the daguerreotype method by Robert H. Vance in San Francisco in 1854.

Watkins left New York for the California gold rush sometime between 1849 and 1851. He first worked in a bookstore, then as an operator for Robert H. Vance's daguerrean gallery in San Francisco. He set up his own gallery, eventually called the Watkins Yosemite Art Gallery, which he owned or operated (others owned it during difficult financial periods) until April 16, 1906. On that date the great San Francisco earthquake and fire destroyed his studio and most of his life's work. During his active years Watkins made many trips to Yosemite Valley, to the Northwest and to the Southwest. He was a member of numerous surveys and excursions, such as the 1866 Geological Survey of California, and his work was widely exhibited.

The photographer won a medal at the 1868 Paris International Exposition, a silver medal at the Eighth Industrial Exhibit of the Mechanics Institute in the San Francisco Bay Area (1871) and a medal of progress at the Vienna International Exhibition of 1873.

He was especially noted for his mammoth-plate landscape views of Yosemite Valley and Mariposa Grove. Over his fifty-year career he also took views of cities, towns, mining camps, missions, orchards, ranches and engineering works. Oliver Wendell Holmes has described his Yosemite photographs as "clear, yet soft, vigorous in the foreground, delicately distinct in the distance, in a perfection of art which compares with the finest European work" (*Atlantic Monthly*). Watkins produced stereo views as well as 16 x 20s, and even constructed his own stereo camera.

PUBLICATIONS Monograph: *Yosemite*, 1867. Books: *Era of Exploration*, Weston J. Naef & James N. Wood, 1975; *Photography and the American Scene*, Robert Taft, 1938; *Bentley's Hand-book of the Pacific Coast*, William R. Bentley, 1884; *Pictorial of California*, Edward Vischer, 1870; *Catalogue of Photographic Views of Scenery on the Pacific Coast*, 1869; *The Yosemite Book*, J. D. Whitney w/W. Harris, 1868; *Gems of California Scenery*, w/Weed, 1866. Anthologies: *The Photograph Collector's Guide*, Lee D. Witkin & Barbara London, 1979; *Early Photographs & Early Photographers*, Oliver Mathews, 1973; *Picture Gallery Pioneers*, R. W. Andrews, 1964. Periodicals: "Carleton E. Watkins," Paul Mickman, *Northlight*, Jan 1977; "The Early Pacific Coast Photographs of Carleton E. Watkins," J. W. Johnson, *Water Resources Center Archives*, Feb 1960; "Carleton E. Watkins," H. S. Giffen, *Eye to Eye*, Sept 1954; *Yosemite Nature Notes*, Apr 1953, Mar 1936; "An Early California Photographer," C. B. Turrill, *News Notes of California Libraries*, Jan 1918; "Photographic Mining Views," *Scientific Press of San Francisco*, Nov 4, 1871; "Photography in California," *Photographic Press*, Oct 11, 1867.

PORTFOLIO *Yo-Semite Valley: Photographic Views of the Falls and Valley*, 1863 (self-pub.: San Francisco).

COLLECTIONS Amer. Geological Soc., NYC; Ariz. Pioneers' Hist. Soc., Tucson; Boston Pub. Lib.; Buffalo & Erie County Pub. Lib., Buffalo, N.Y.; Calif. Hist. Soc., San Francisco; Calif. State Lib., Sacramento; CCP, Tucson; Harvard Univ. Libs., Cambridge, Mass.; Huntington Lib., San Marino, Calif.; IMP/GEH, Rochester; L/C, Wash., D.C.; Metro. Mus. of Art, NYC; MOMA, NYC; Nev. State Mus., Carson City; N.Y. Pub. Lib., Rare Bk. Rm., NYC; Soc. of Calif. Pioneers, San Francisco; Stanford Univ. Lib., Palo Alto, Calif.; UCLA; Univ. of Calif., Hearst Mining Bldg. & Bancroft Lib., Berkeley; Univ. of Tex., Humanities Research Ctr., Austin; U.S. Geological Survey, Photography Lib., Denver, Colo.; Utah State Hist. Soc., Salt Lake City; Yale Univ., Western Americana Cllctn., New Haven, Conn.; Yosemite Mus., Yosemite Natl. Park, Calif.

Albert Mackenzie Watson   PHOTOGRAPHER
Born August 6, 1942, in Edinburgh, Scotland, Watson received a BA in Graphic Design from Duncan of Jordanstone College of Art in Dundee, Scotland, in 1966 and an MA in Film from the Royal College of Art in London, England, in 1970.

Since 1970 Watson has been a freelance photographer, contributing fashion and beauty photography to *Vogue* magazine in the U.S., United Kingdom, France and Germany (since 1976), and *Harper's Bazaar* (since 1974).

He has been a member of ASMP since 1972, and was the recipient of a grant from the British Film Institute in 1969 and an IBM Traveling Fellowship in 1966. Watson's film *Milian* (1969) was shown at the Edinburgh International Festival in 1969.

PUBLICATIONS Periodicals: *Photographers Annual*, 1974 through 1979.

REPRESENTATIVE Peter Schub, 37 Beekman Pl, New York, NY 10022.

ADDRESS 237 E 77 St, New York, NY 10021.

Tom Watson   PHOTOGRAPHER   Born March 16, 1863, in Whitby, Yorkshire, England, Watson died in 1957. He was a self-taught photographer.

Watson began his professional career in 1892 in the general practice of photography, doing portraits, views, postcards and albums in Scandinavia, France, Spain, Portugal, the U.S. and particularly in the village of Lythe of Whitby, Yorkshire, England. He was the personal photographer of the Marquis of Normanby, who was also his patron. While his surviving work is in the form of glass negatives and modern prints of local topographical interest, there is also a smaller collection of original prints in existence. A large portion of his work is missing.

He was a member of the Institute of Incorporated Photographers in Great Britain.

Curator Ken Baird describes Watson's work as "topographical views of historical value, in land use and environmental change." There are 2,000 of his topographical views of Yorkshire from glass-plate negatives in existence. Photographs taken after the turn of the century have the visual characteristics of current twentieth-century topographical photography.

PUBLICATIONS Monograph: *Thomas Watson 1863–1957*, 1979 (Tindale: Whitby). Book: *Sunley's Daughter: The Ways of a Yorkshire Dale*, 1974 (London).

ARCHIVE Whitby Museum, Pannet Park, Whitby, North Yorkshire, England.

Jane Rachel Wattenberg   PHOTOGRAPHER · IL-LUSTRATOR · BEEKEEPER   Born April 19, 1949, in Norwalk, Connecticut, Wattenberg received her MFA in Photography in 1974 from the Rochester Institute of Technology and a BA in Art History from Simmons College, Boston, in 1971. She also studied at the International Museum of Photography at the George Eastman House with Robert Sobieszek in 1972, and was an intern at the Guggenheim Museum, New York City, in 1970.

Since 1975 Wattenberg has been a freelance photographer. She has been an instructor in color photography at the University of California Extension Center in San Francisco from 1978 to the present, and was previously an instructor of photography at the San Francisco Museum of Modern Art from 1976 to 1978.

A member of SPE since 1977, Wattenberg broadcast a biweekly radio show, *Asparagus Fern Presents*, in Rochester in 1972.

The artist says: "My special style of work is photographic montage, consisting of cut and reworked color photographs of my own taking. Much of my work is fictional narrative, mysterious, edging toward superrealism."

PUBLICATIONS Books: *While the Sun Was out Moonlighting*, 1972; *Snip Snap Snout Snatch*, illus., 1971.

COLLECTIONS IMP/GEH, Rochester; Rochester Inst. of Technology; VSW, Rochester.

ADDRESS 73 Waltham St, San Francisco, CA 94110.

Gregory Charles Wayn   PHOTOGRAPHER · IN-DUSTRIAL DESIGNER · TEACHER   Born December 22, 1950, in Devonport, Tasmania (Australia),

Wayn received his Diploma of Education in 1974 at the State College of Victoria at Hawthorn, in Melbourne, Australia, and received his Diploma of Industrial Design in 1971 from the Royal Melbourne Institute of Technology.

He has been employed as a teacher in the Art Department of Victoria's Lalor Technical School from 1975 to date.

Wayn is a member of the Technical Teachers Union of Victoria since 1975 and is also a member of the Friends of the Earth.

He usually works in medium format and his general photographic direction is that of landscape, both urban and country. Some images are abstractions of space, form, texture and light, while others are metaphorical.

PUBLICATIONS Catalog: *Australian Photographers*, Philip Morris Cllctn, 1979. Periodical: *Light Vision*, nos. 6 & 7, 1978.

COLLECTION Philip Morris Cllctn, Natl. Gall., Canberra, Australia.

DEALER The Photographers Gallery, 344 Punt Rd, South Yarra 3141, Victoria, Australia.

ADDRESS 48 View St, Alphington, Melbourne 3078, Victoria, Australia.

John Stephen Webb *PHOTOGRAPHER* Born in London, England, on October 7, 1950, Webb studied photography at Medway College of Design, Kent, England, from 1970 to 1973.

A freelance photographer in Sweden since 1976, he works for *Aktuell Fotografi*, a monthly Swedish photo magazine. Before moving to Sweden in 1974 he freelanced as an assistant photographer, a city gardener, a road sweeper and a film technician.

A member of Svenska Fotografernas Förbund, Webb won grants from the Swedish Authors fund (Författarfonden) in 1979, Arts Council of Great Britain in 1978 and Swedish Arts Council (Konstnärsnämnden) in 1976.

Working mostly in black-and-white, 4 x 5 format, the photographer shoots landscapes (urban and rural) and portraits.

PUBLICATIONS Monograph: *Still Movements*, 1977. Periodicals: *printletter*, May/June 1979; *Schweden Hente*, no. 2, 1978; *Sweden NOW*, no. 5, 1978; *Nueva Lente*, Nov 1978; *Aktuell Fotografi*, Dec 1974; *British Journal of Photography*, May 17, 1974; *Creative Camera*, May 1974.

COLLECTIONS Arts Council of Great Britain; Dept. of Environment, Great Britain; Malmö Mus., Sweden; Moderna Muséet/Fotografiska Muséet, Stockholm.

DEALER Photographers Gall., 8 Gt Newport St, London WC2, England.

ADDRESS Erik Dahlbergs Gata 34 E, 252 39 Helsingborg, Sweden.

Spider Webb *PAINTER · PHOTOGRAPHER · TATTOO ARTIST* Born in New York City on March 3, 1944, the artist received an MFA degree from Yale University in 1972 and a BFA from the School of Visual Arts in 1970.

He has been president of Spider Webb Studios, Ltd, since 1972.

A member of the Tattoo Club of America since 1974, Webb is currently president of that organization.

PUBLICATIONS Books: *Pushing Ink*, 1979; *Bisexual Dragons*, 1978; *X-1000*, 1977; *Heavily Tattooed Men & Women*, 1976.

COLLECTIONS Metro. Mus. of Art, NYC; MOMA, NYC; Whitney Mus. of Art, NYC.

DEALERS Leo Castelli, 4 E 77 St, New York, NY 10021; Neikrug Gall., 224 E 68 St., New York, NY 10021.

ADDRESS 112 W First St, Mt Vernon, NY 10550.

Roland Weber *TEACHER · PHOTOGRAPHER* Born November 15, 1924, in Tunis, Tunisia, Weber received a BA degree in Education at the Université de Montréal in 1962.

He has been teaching photography at the Université du Québec à Montréal since 1969, and before that he was the initiator of the photo program at the Institut des Arts Graphiques (1959–69).

A member of SPE, Weber was awarded a grant from the Canadian Council for research on solarization in 1973. In 1971 he received a Diplôme d'Honneur at the 12th Salon International in Nantes, France.

Weber describes his work as a "black-and-white reportage approach to subjects of which people are the pivot. I search for formal relationships that open doors for interpretation or establish a surreal or dreamlike quality." His color work is mostly devoted to nature.

PUBLICATIONS Books: *Je développe mes photos*, 1973, *Je prends des photos*, 1972 (Editions de l'Homme: Montreal, Canada). Periodicals: *Hasselblad*, no. 2, 1976; *International Photography*, 1974.

COLLECTIONS L/C, Wash., D.C. Musée d'Art Contemporain, Montréal, Canada; Musée d'Art et d'Histoire, Fribourg, Switzerland.

REPRESENTATIVE Image Bank of Canada, 2 Carlton St, Toronto, Ontario, Canada M5B IJ3.

ADDRESS 2455 Edouard Montpetit, #2, Montréal, Québec, Canada H3T 1J5.

Thomas Wedgwood   *INVENTOR*   Born in Stoke-upon-Trent on May 14, 1771, Wedgwood died July 11, 1805. His father, Josiah Wedgwood, was the famous potter, and his nephew was the naturalist Charles Darwin.

Wedgwood attended Edinburgh University from 1786 to 1788. He spent much time with Alexander Chisolm, his father's secretary and chemical assistant, and was also influenced by the Lunar Society, a select group of scholars and engineers that met monthly at his father's home.

Wedgwood experimented with thermometers and light, heat and silver nitrate (1790 to 1792). By 1800 he was working with colored glasses and the microscope. In June 1802 he announced to the public that he had invented a process of developing an outline of images on white paper or white leather with nitrate of silver. This account was recorded by Sir Humphry Davy in the *Journals of the Royal Institution*. Wedgwood also discovered the varying effects of color on development—red having the least action, blue and violet the most. At this same time he discovered the physical law that solid bodies have the same temperature at the point of incandescence. (Some historians say this was his father's discovery.) During his experiments Wedgwood was influenced by the Reverend J. B. Reade, who, some forty years later, experimented with gallic acid by applying tannin solution to paper.

Sometimes referred to as "the first photographer," Wedgwood was "the first person who conceived and put in practice the idea of using the agency of light to obtain a representation of an object," according to his biographer, R. B. Litchfield. Wedgwood's process was similar to what is commonly called a photogram. Unfortunately he was never able to make the image permanent.

PUBLICATIONS   Book: *Tom Wedgwood: The First Photographer*, R. B. Litchfield, 1903, repr. 1973. Periodical: *Journal of the Royal Institution*, June 1802.

Weegee (Arthur Fellig)   *PHOTOGRAPHER*   [See plate 78]   Born June 12, 1899, in Zloczew, Austria (now Poland), Weegee died on December 26, 1968, in New York City.

The self-taught photographer quit school at fourteen to help support his family. He worked first as a tintype operator, then as an assistant to a commercial photographer. Hiring a pony he nicknamed "Hypo," Weegee became a street photographer, taking portraits of children astride the pony. After three years as a passport photographer Weegee joined Acme Newspicture (now UPI) around 1924, working first as a darkroom technician, then as a news photographer until 1935. Freelancing again, he set up a post in Manhattan Police Headquarters for ten years and, with an officially authorized police radio in his car, was often at the scene of a crime before the police—let alone his competitors. Weegee worked on the staff of the tabloid *P.M.* in 1940 and later on the staff of *Vogue*. He also contributed photographs to *Holiday, Life, Look* and *Fortune*. Besides being a photographer, he was an amateur violinst.

Weegee made three film shorts: *Weegee's New York*, 1948; *The Idiot Box*, ca. 1965; and *Cocktail Party*, ca. 1950. He has been the subject of two films, Lou Stoumen's feature *The Naked Eye*, 1957, and *Weegee in Hollywood*, a short by Erven Jourden and Esther McCoy, ca. 1950.

Working strictly in black-and-white with a 4 x 5 Speed Graphic, Weegee prowled the streets of New York capturing incidents of violence and catastrophe in his stark, graphic style. Many of his better known photos are humorous, often the results of a multiple printing technique. He also did some fashion and advertising work, as well as more ordinary genre scenes of New York life.

PUBLICATIONS   Monographs: *Weegee: Täter und Opfer*, John Coplans, 1978; *Weegee*, Louis Stettner, 1977; *Weegee's Creative Photography*, w/Gerry Sheck, 1964 (Ward, Lock: London); *Weegee by Weegee*, 1961; *Weegee's Creative Camera*, 1959; *Naked Hollywood*, w/Mel Harris, 1953; *Weegee's Secrets of Shooting with Photo Flash*, w/Mel Harris, 1953; *Weegee's People*, 1946; *Naked City*, 1945. Anthologies: *The Photograph Collector's Guide*, Lee D. Witkin & Barbara London, 1979; *The Magic Image*, Cecil Beaton & Gail Buckland, 1975. Periodicals: "Weegee the Famous," John Coplans, *Art in America*, Sept/Oct 1977; "Weegee the Famous," Judith Goldman, *Quest/77*, Sept/Oct 1977; "Night Light: Brassaï and Weegee," Colin Westerbeck, *Artforum*, Dec 1976; "Naked Weegee," Gretchen Berg, *Photograph*, summer 1976; "Weegee: A Lens on Life 1899–1968," Fondiller, Rothschild & Vestal, *Popular Photography*, Apr 1969.

COLLECTIONS   CCP, Tucson; ICP, NYC; IMP/GEH, Rochester; Metro. Mus. of Art, NYC; MOMA, NYC. Bibliothèque Nationale, Paris.

William Wegman   *PHOTOGRAPHER·VIDEO ARTIST*   Born December 2, 1942, in Holyoke, Massachusetts, Wegman received a BFA from Massachusetts College of Art in Boston in 1965 and an MFA from University of Illinois at Urbana-Champaigne in 1967.

Currently Wegman is a self-employed photographer.

He was awarded a CAPS grant for video in 1979.

Wegman is known for his photographs and video tapes that often use his dog "Man Ray" as his subject. His recent work includes 20 x 24 color Polaroid prints.

PUBLICATIONS Catalogs: *American Portraits of the Sixties and Seventies*, 1979 (Aspen Ctr. for Visual Arts: Aspen, Colo.); *Images of the Self*, 1979 (Hampshire Coll. Gall.; Amherst, Mass.); *Born in Boston*, 1978 (DeCordova Mus.: Lincoln, Mass.); *Small Is Beautiful*, 1978 (Freedman Gall., Albright Coll.: Reading, Pa. & Center Gall., Bucknell Univ.: Lewisburg, Pa.). Periodicals: "William Wegman at Holly Solomon," Paul Stimson, Sept 1979, review, Apr/May 1973, *Art in America*; "Shared Humor and Sophistication," Louise Lewis, *Artweek*, May 1978; review, Jim Collins, review, Bruce Boice, 1973, "Place and Process," Willoughby Sharp, Nov 1969, *Artforum*; review, Rosemary Matthias, 1972, "Los Angeles," Melinda Terbell, May 1971, "Subject-Object Body Art," Sept/Oct 1971, *Arts Magazine*.

COLLECTIONS IMP/GEH, Rochester; Los Angeles County Mus. of Art; MOMA, NYC; Whitney Mus. of American Art, NYC. Mus. of Modern Art, Paris.

DEALER Holly Solomon Gall. Inc, 392 W Broadway, New York, NY 10012.

ADDRESS 27 Thames St, New York, NY 10007.

Daniel L. Weingrod PHOTOGRAPHER · TEACHER Born September 25, 1954, in Chicago, Illinois, Weingrod attended Antioch College, Yellow Springs, Ohio (1972–74), and the Center for Photographic Studies in Louisville, Kentucky (1974), where he studied with Alex Traube and C. J. Pressma. He earned a BA in Anthropology from Brandeis University, Waltham, Massachusetts.

Since 1979 Weingrod has been instructor of photography at Bezalel Academy of Art and Design in Jerusalem, Israel.

A member of VSW, the photographer won a photography research fellowship from the America-Israel Cultural Foundation in 1980 and a Photography Fellowship from Massachusetts Artists Foundation in 1978.

His work focuses on three major areas: documentation in Israel, diptych and triptych photographs and photographic constructions.

PUBLICATIONS Book: *Clearing*, w/Anthony Petruzzi, 1979 (self-pub.). Periodical: *Rolling Stone*, Mar 8, 1979.

ADDRESS PO 10129, Jerusalem, Israel.

Michael Weisbrot PHOTOGRAPHER Born April 14, 1944, in New York City, Weisbrot received a BA and BBA in 1966 from Pace University in New York City.

Weisbrot is a freelance photographer in a family business, and has been a teacher at C. W. Post College in New York and Long Island University in New York City since 1977. Prior to that he was an instructor at LaGuardia Community College in New York City (1975–78). He has also worked with the Sponsor in Arts Apprenticeship Program for the New York City Department of Cultural Affairs.

Weisbrot is a member of American Society Picture Professionals, the Black Star Photo Agency in New York City and the Lensman Photo Agency in Washington, D.C. In 1977 he won a CAPS grant from the New York State Council on the Arts.

The artist describes his work as "a continuing personal diary of life and the lives of those I love. After time, the diary images make up stories—for example, the eight-year-long struggle of my nephew and his family as they deal with his illness and society's failure to heal its own. Also my mother's last ten years, in which she is alone as a widow and finds new identity and love."

PUBLICATIONS Monograph: *Street Kids, New York*, 1978. Periodicals: *American Photographer*, June 1980; *Invitation to Photography*, 1973.

ADDRESS 505 Eighth Ave, Brooklyn, NY 11215.

Eva Diane Weiss PHOTOGRAPHER Born January 18, 1950, Weiss earned a BFA at Rochester Institute of Technology, New York, in 1971.

Weiss is a freelance photographer in New York City.

Weiss won the *Ms.* magazine Photo Competition in 1979 and was awarded a CAPS grant in 1976.

The photographer hand-colors her images with oils. Her themes usually involve dreams or fantasies, and recent photographs utilize street scenes and still life. "My work deals mostly with portraits or alter-ego portraits," she says.

PUBLICATION Anthology: *Women See Men*, 1977.

COLLECTIONS Kenan Ctr., Lockport, N.Y.; Mancini Gall., Philadelphia, Pa., & Houston, Tex.; William Lyons Gall., Coconut Grove, Fla.

DEALER Mancini Gall., 1728 Spruce St, Philadelphia, PA 19103.

ADDRESS 1919 Gates Ave, Ridgewood, NY 11385.

John Weiss PHOTOGRAPHER · TEACHER Born January 31, 1941, in Philadelphia, Pennsylvania, Weiss earned a BS from Temple University in Philadelphia (1963) and an MFA from Rhode Island School of Design, Providence, in 1973. He names Minor White, Frederick Sommer and Luis Tiant as mentors.

Weiss has taught at the University of Delaware, Newark, since 1975, first as an assistant professor and since 1979 as an associate professor. He has also been coordinator of photography at the school since 1976. He served in the position of artist-in-the-schools in New Castle, Delaware, in 1974–75, and taught in the MIT Creative Photography Program from 1969 to 1973.

Weiss belongs to SPE.

PUBLICATIONS Book: *Venus, Jupiter and Mars —The Photographs of Frederick Sommer*, ed., 1980. Anthology: *Celebrations*, Minor White & Jonathan Green, 1974. Periodicals: *Popular Photography Annual*, 1978; "A Darkroom Philosophy," *Camera 35*, Sept 1977; "Creative Photography at the University of Delaware," *Philadelphia Photo Review*, June 1977; *Modern Photography*, June 1977.

COLLECTIONS Addison Gall. of Amer. Art, Andover, Mass.; Del. Art Mus., Wilmington; MIT, Cambridge, Mass.; Princeton Univ., Minor White Archive, N.J.; MOMA, NYC.

ADDRESS 721 Swarthmore Dr, Newark, DE 19711.

Murray Weiss PHOTOGRAPHER · GALLERY DIRECTOR · TEACHER Born on February 20, 1926, in New York City, Weiss earned a diploma from the School of Modern Photography in New York City (1951) and a BA from City University of New York, Brooklyn College (1952), where he studied with Walter Rosenblum. In 1952–53 he worked and studied with Ralph Steiner in New York City. Weiss names Paul Strand, along with his two teachers, as major influences.

Most recently the photographer has been a visiting artist at the University of Wisconsin, Oshkosh, and at Viterbo College, La Crosse, Wisconsin. Since 1975 he has directed and presided over the Milwaukee Center for Photography (Wisconsin), which he co-founded. In 1977 Weiss was appointed photography instructor-in-residence at Yale-Norfolk Summer Art School in Norfolk, Connecticut, and in 1974 he was a lecturer in the history of photography at the University of Wisconsin Art History Department, Milwaukee. In that year he also founded and directed Creative Photography Workshops in Milwaukee (until 1975). An instructor of photography at Philadelphia College of Art, Pennsylvania, from 1955 to 1972, he became an associate professor of art there in 1961 and director of the Photography/Film Department in 1970. In 1969–72 Weiss also lectured on the history of photography at Brooklyn College in New York City.

Weiss produced and moderated *Art and Artists* for WUHY-FM Educational Radio in Philadelphia in 1967–68.

The photographer produces black-and-white prints from 35mm and 8 x 10 negatives. He shoots the natural landscape, architecture, people and environments in Greece, Cape Breton, Mexico and the United States.

PUBLICATIONS Books: *Rodin*, 1976; *Sculpture of a City: Philadelphia's Treasures in Bronze and Stone*, 1974.

COLLECTIONS Milwaukee Art Ctr., Wisc.; Philadelphia Mus. of Art, Pa. Instituto Mexican Norteamericano de Relaciones, Mexico City.

DEALERS Photopia Gall., 1728 Spruce St, Philadelphia, PA 19103; Milwaukee Art Ctr, 750 N Lincoln Memorial Dr, Milwaukee, WI 53202.

ADDRESS 2605 E Hartford Ave, Milwaukee, WI 53211.

James Booker Blakemore Wellington PHOTOGRAPHER · SCIENTIST Born in 1858 in Lansdown, Bath, Wellington died in 1939 in Elstree, Hertfordshire, England. He studied architecture but took up photography before completing his studies. The paintings of John Constable and Thomas Gainsborough influenced the photographer's work.

Wellington was sent to New York to work under George Eastman in 1890, returning to England to become the manager of the new Kodak Works in Harrow (1891–93). He later worked for Elliot & Sons, Barnet, then founded Wellington & Ward in Elstreet with his brother-in-law H. H. Ward, serving as scientific and technical director. The firm later merged with Ilford Ltd.

A member of The Linked Ring, Wellington joined RPS in 1887 and was elected an Honorary Fellow in 1935.

Among other innovations, he developed the Iso-Wellington photographic plate (a fast, fine-grain emulsion) and the Silver Intensifier (1889), which helped control density. He further improved upon his own formula in 1911 by inventing a process that did not stain or dissolve the emulsion of some plates as the original had.

Though his major contributions to photography were in the laboratory, Wellington was an accomplished pictorial photographer as well, depicting genre scenes of the Edwardian leisure class.

PUBLICATIONS Monograph: *The Pictorial Work of J. B. B. Wellington*, F. C. Lambert, 1904 (Practical Photographer Series: London). Book: *Sun Artists*, 1899. Anthologies: *Pictorial Photography in Britain, 1900–1920*, 1978 (Arts Council of Great Britain); *The Magic Image*, Cecil Beaton & Gail Buckland, 1975.

COLLECTION RPS, London.

Lynton Wells PHOTOGRAPHER Born October 21, 1940, in Baltimore, Maryland, Wells received his BFA from Rhode Island School of Design in Providence in 1962 and his MFA from Cranbrook Academy of Art in Bloomfield Hills, Michigan, in 1965.

Wells works as a freelance photogapher.

He was the recipient of grants from the New York State Council on the Arts in 1977 and 1973, and won an NEA grant in 1975.

PUBLICATIONS Catalog: *Lynton Wells, Paintings 1971–78*, Peter Bunnel, 1979 (Princeton Univ. Art Mus: N.J.). Periodicals: Review, John Yau, *Art in America*, May/June 1979; "Working Between Photography and Painting," James Welling, 1978, "A Painter's View in Photographic Perspective," Leland Rice, 1976, *Art Week*; "Lynton Wells," Joseph Dreiss, *Arts Magazine*, Oct 1975; review, Bruce Boice, *Artforum*, May 1973; Lord Barry, *Arts Canada*, June 1970; *Modern Photography*, June 1970; Margery Mann, *Popular Photography*, June 1970; "Photography into Sculpture," Peter Bunnell, *Creative Camera*, June 1970.

COLLECTIONS Arnot Art Mus., Elmira, N.Y.; Cornell Univ., H. F. Johnson Mus. of Art, Ithaca, N.Y.; Dallas Mus. of Fine Arts, Tex.; Indianapolis Mus. of Art, Ind.; MOMA, NYC; Princeton Univ. Art Mus., N.J.; Univ. of N. Mex. Art Mus., Albuquerque; Univ. of Va. Art Mus., Charlottesville; Vassar Coll. Art Gall., Poughkeepsie, N.Y.; Virginia Mus. of Fine Arts, Richmond; Walker Art Ctr., Minneapolis, Minn. Power Inst. of Fine Arts, Sydney, Australia.

DEALER Holly Solomon Gall. Inc, 392 W Broadway, New York, NY 10012.

Alisa Wells-Witteman PHOTOGRAPHER Born in Erie, Pennsylvania, in 1929, the photographer studied in workshops with Nathan Lyons (1965–66 and 1961–62) and with Ansel Adams (1961).

She was employed as an assistant to Nathan Lyons, director of Visual Studies Workshop in Rochester, New York, from 1969 to 1972, and prior to that was associate curator of George Eastman House (1962–69).

A recipient of the Western States Art Foundation Fellowship in 1975, Wells-Witteman also received an NEA Fellowship Grant and a CAPS award in 1972.

Art critic Alfred Barr said of her work: "Many cannot relate to her work because her photographs are too personal. Her work is so autobiographical that it is for many viewers too intimate to encounter."

PUBLICATIONS Anthologies: *Women of Photography*, 1975; *The Woman's Eye*, Anne Tucker, ed., 1973; *The Art of Photography*, 1971, *The Print*, 1970, Time-Life Series; *The Photograph as Object, 1843–1969*, 1969 (Natl. Gall. of Canada). Periodical: *Fotografia Italiana*, Dec. 1972.

COLLECTIONS N. Mex. Fine Art Mus., Santa Fe; New York Univ. at Alfred; Pasadena Art Mus., Calif.; UCLA; Univ. of N. Mex., Albuquerque; Vassar Art Mus., Poughkeepsie, N.Y.; VSW, Rochester. Natl. Gall. of Canada, Ottawa, Ontario.

ADDRESS Rt 7, Hyde Park, Aztec Springs, Santa Fe, NM 87501.

Jack Welpott PHOTOGRAPHER·TEACHER [See plate 117] Born in Kansas City, Kansas, on April 27, 1923, Welpott studied at Indiana University, receiving a BS (1949), an MS (1955) and an MFA (1959). Henry Holmes Smith was his most important teacher. Welpott was formerly married to photographer Judy Dater.

He has been a professor of art at San Francisco State University since 1959, and has also conducted many workshops in the U.S., Japan and Europe.

Welpott is a member of Friends of Photography and serves on their board of trustees. He was a recipient of an NEA award in 1979.

PUBLICATIONS Books: *Women & Other Visions* w/Judy Dater, 1975. Anthologies: *The Photograph Collector's Guide*, Lee D. Witkin & Barbara London, 1979; *Faces: A Narrative History of the Portrait*, 1977; *The Photographer's Choice*, Kelly Wise, ed., 1975; *Photography in America*, 1974; *Photography in the 20th Century*, 1967. Catalogs: *Jack Welpott: The Artist as Teacher, the Teacher as Artist*, 1975 (San Francisco Mus. of Modern Art); *California Photographers*, 1970, 1969; *American Photography: The*

60's, 1966 (Univ. of Nebr., Sheldon Memorial Art Gall.). Periodical: *Camera*, May 1975.

COLLECTIONS CCP, Tucson; Chicago Art Inst.; Graham Nash Cllctn., Los Angeles; IMP/ GEH, Rochester; MOMA, NYC; San Francisco Mus. of Photography; Whitney Mus., NYC. Bibliothèque Nationale, Paris; Tokyo Coll. of Photography.

DEALER Witkin Gall., 41 E 57 St, New York, NY 10022.

ADDRESS 28½ Prelita Ave, San Francisco, CA 94110.

Ulrike Welsch PHOTOGRAPHER Born in Bonn, West Germany, Welsch served an apprenticeship as a druggist in her homeland and took up photography as a hobby, her father being an avid photographer. She began her serious photographic career after coming to the United States in 1964.

Since 1972 Welsch has been a staff photographer with the *Boston Globe,* for which she also writes a monthly photography column, and since 1966 has also been a staff photographer for the *Boston Herald Traveler*. In addition, she teaches photojournalism at Essex Photographic Workshop in Essex and at Harvard University Center for Lifelong Learning in Cambridge, both in Massachusetts.

Welsch was named Press Photographer of the Year in New England in 1974 by the Boston Press Photographers Association.

The photographer describes her work as creative photojournalism. She likes to photograph people in common places and portray a touch of life. In 1978–79 she spent seven months in South America photographing the people of the Andes.

PUBLICATIONS Monograph: *The World I Love to See*, 1977. Book: *Kids of Colombia*, Jessie Sargent, 1974.

ADDRESS 42 Elm St, Marblehead, MA 01945.

Eudora Welty WRITER · PHOTOGRAPHER [See plate 66] Born April 13, 1909, in Jackson, Mississippi, Welty attended Mississippi State College for Women in Columbus (1925–27) and earned a BA in 1929 from the University of Wisconsin, Madison. She studied advertising at Columbia University in New York City in 1930–31.

Predominantly known as a novelist and short-story writer, Welty has also been active in photography.

For her fiction Welty won the Howells Medal in 1955 and the American Academy of Arts & Letters Award in 1944.

PUBLICATIONS Monographs: *Eudora Welty:*

Twenty Photographs, 1980; *One Time, One Place*, 1971. Books: *Images of the South: Visits with Eudora Welty and Walker Evans*, Bill Ferris, 1978; *A Pageant of Birds*, 1974. Fiction: *The Bride of the Innisfallen*, 1955; *The Ponder Heart*, 1954; *The Golden Apples*, 1949; *Music from Spain*, 1948; *Delta Wedding*, 1946; *The Wide Net*, 1943; *The Robber Bridegroom*, 1942; *A Curtain of Green*, 1941. Periodical: *Vogue*, Aug 1944.

COLLECTION CCP, Tucson.

ARCHIVE Mississippi Dept of Archives & History, 100 S State St, Jackson, MS 39205.

Jane Brooke Wenger PHOTOGRAPHER · TEACHER Born January 24, 1944, in New York City, Wenger earned a BFA from Alfred University, Alfred, New York (1966), where she studied with John Wood and Daniel Rhodes. She then studied with Aaron Siskind and Arthur Siegel at the Institute of Design, Illinois Institute of Technology, Chicago (1967–69), and in 1980 received an MFA from the University of Illinois at Chicago Circle. The photographer names René Magritte and Bill Brandt as major influences.

A freelance since 1969, Wenger has taught photography part-time at the University of Illinois, Chicago Circle, and at the Art Institute of Chicago since 1975.

The photographer is an SPE member (since 1977) and won an Illinois Arts Council Project Completion Grant in 1979.

PUBLICATIONS Book: "The Nude—The Compelling Image," Yale Joel, *Creative Camera Techniques*, 1979. Periodical: "Jane Wenger: The Dialectics of Sexuality," *Afterimage: VSW*, Dec 1979.

COLLECTIONS Indianapolis Mus. of Art, Ind.; Lehigh Univ., Bethlehem, Pa.; Milwaukee Art Ctr., Wisc.; MOMA, NYC; Mus. of Contemporary Art, Chicago; Southern Ill. Univ. at Edwardsville.

DEALER Allan Frumkin Photographs, 620 N Michigan Ave, Chicago, IL 60611.

ADDRESS 1509 N Wicker Park, Chicago, IL 60622.

Robert E. Werling PHOTOGRAPHER Born May 9, 1946, in San Francisco, California, Werling earned a BPA in 1970 from Brooks Institute, Santa Barbara, California, having previously studied commercial art at the College of San Mateo, California (1965–66), under Robert Coyne. He names Edward Weston and Ansel Adams as major influences.

Werling has been a photography instructor at the University of California, Santa Barbara, since

1978. In that year he was also guest curator of an exhibit of contemporary Japanese photography at the Santa Barbara Museum of Art, and in 1977 he conducted photo workshops for the museum.

A member of Friends of Photography since 1968, Werling belonged to the Photography Advisory Committee at the Santa Barbara Museum of Art in 1976. Under a 1975 NEA grant he produced a portfolio of prints from the negatives of W. Edwin Gledhill.

Using 4 x 5 and 8 x 10 formats, the photographer produces gelatin silver prints of landscapes and abstract images.

PUBLICATIONS Monograph: *Bob Werling: Selected Photographs*, 1977. Periodical: *Pentax Family*, 1974.

PORTFOLIO *The Sierra Nevada* (self-pub.), 1980.

COLLECTIONS IMP/GEH, Rochester; Metro. Mus. of Art, NYC; MOMA, NYC; Santa Barbara Mus. of Art; Univ. of Ariz., Ansel Adams Cllctn., Tucson. Pentax Camera Corp., Tokyo.

DEALERS Weston Gall., Dolores & Lincoln Sts, Carmel, CA 93921; Keystone Gall., 1213 State St, Santa Barbara, CA 93101.

ADDRESS 2758 Las Encinas Rd, Santa Barbara, CA 93105.

Donald L. Werner EXHIBITIONS & GRAPHICS DESIGNER · PHOTOGRAPHER Born February 2, 1929, in Fresno, California, Werner received a BA degree in Art and Art Education in 1952 from Fresno State College in Fresno, California, where he studied photography with Ella Odorfer. He also studied at the Chouinard Art Institute in Los Angeles.

Since 1978 Werner has been the exhibitions and graphics designer for the Museum of the American Indian in New York City. Prior to that he designed photo exhibitions for the Neikrug Galleries in New York City (1976), and did exhibitions and graphics design for the Hudson River Museum (1969–76).

Working in black-and-white, the photographer is interested in "images of strong graphic character and poetry, communication of ideas and man in his landscape."

PUBLICATION Book: *Reflections of Winter*, w/ Joyce T. Garrett, 1979.

DEALER Neikrug Gall., 224 E 68 St, New York, NY 10021.

ADDRESS 65 W 92 St, New York, NY 10025.

Neite Werner LIBRARIAN · PHOTOHISTORIAN Born September 22, 1920, in Potsdam, Germany,

Werner studied psychology and history at the University of Cologne (1956–58) and the University of Bonn, receiving a diploma in psychology from the latter (1961).

Since 1962 Werner has been scientific collaborator and librarian for the Cologne Historical Museum. Previously the photohistorian worked as a teacher and librarian (1955–62).

Werner belongs to the European Society for the History of Photography (since 1978), DGPh (since 1974) and Maximilian-Gesellschaft (since 1971).

Werner is interested in "visual communication and the early years of photography in Germany."

PUBLICATIONS Book: "Die Frühzeit der Photographie in der Rheinprovinz," *Kunst des 19. Jahrhunderts im Rheinland*, vol. 3, 1979 (Dusseldorf). Catalog: "Die frühen Jahre der Photographie-Dokumentarisches zu den Anfängen in Deutschland, *In unnachahmlicher Treue*, 1979 (Cologne). Periodicals: "The Cologne Diorama," no. 3, 1979, "G. Schauer, Photograph- und Kunstverleger in Berlin," no. 1, 1977, *History of Photography*; "Das Diorama in Köln," no. 48, 1977, "Die Photographie in Köln 1839–1870," no. 46, 1975, *Jahrbuch Kölnischen Geschichtsvereins*; "Der Kölner Dom als erstes Bauwerk der frühen deutschen Architekturphotographie," *Kölner Domblatt*, no. 36/37, 1973.

ADDRESS Hermann Pflaume Strasse 27, 5 Cologne 41, West Germany.

Sigwart Wilhelm Theodor Werner PHOTOGRAPHER · BUSINESSMAN Born June 13, 1872, in Frederiksberg (Taarbaek), Denmark, Werner flourished between the years of 1927 and 1940. The date of his death is unknown. He graduated from Brocks School of Commerce in 1893, and was influenced by the philosopher Aage Werner.

Licensed as a wholesale dealer in 1989, Werner was co-owner of the T. M. Werner Company until 1927, when he resigned.

A member of Denmark's Association of Nature Preservation in 1919, he was also a member of the council, and was made a member of honor in 1936.

The photographer is described by Bjørn Ochsner as "a solid photographic technician who sensitively recorded the intimate relationship between Danish nature and ancient architecture."

PUBLICATIONS Books: *Eastern Jutland*, 1940; *Western Jutland*, 1939; *Western Sealand*, 1938; *Copenhagen*, 1937; *Lolland Falster and Möen*, 1936; *Djursland and Samsoe*, 1935; *The Southern Sealand*, 1934; *Southern Jutland*, 1933; *The Islands of Fyn*, 1932; *Northern Jutland*, 1931;

Northern Sealand, 1930; *Bornholm*, 1929; *Rebild and Rold*, 1928; *The Deer Forest*, 1927.

COLLECTION Royal Lib., Copenhagen, Denmark.

Henry Wessel, Jr. *PHOTOGRAPHER* Born July 28, 1942, in Teaneck, New Jersey, Wessel earned a BA in 1965 from Pennsylvania State University in University Park and an MFA in 1972 from Visual Studies Workshop at State University of New York, Buffalo.

In 1977 Wessel was a visiting lecturer at California College of Arts and Crafts in Oakland and a visiting artist at the University of California, Davis. He served as assistant professor at San Francisco State University in 1974 and has also taught at the San Francisco Art Institute (1973), University of California, Berkeley (1973), and Center of the Eye in Aspen, Colorado (1973).

Wessel won Guggenheim fellowships in 1978 and 1971 and NEA Photographer's Fellowships in 1976 and 1974.

PUBLICATIONS Anthologies: *The Photograph Collector's Guide*, Lee D. Witkin & Barbara London, 1979; *Mirrors and Windows*, John Szarkowski, ed., 1978; *The Great West: Real/Ideal*, Sandy Hume et al, eds., 1977; *Snapshot*, Jonathan Green, ed., 1974; *Looking at Photographs*, John Szarkowski, 1973; *Vision and Expression*, Nathan Lyons, ed., 1969. Catalogs: *Photographs*, 1977 (Univ. of Nebr., Sheldon Mem. Art Gall.: Lincoln); *Henry Wessel, Jr.*, intro. by Ben Lifson, 1976 (Grossmont Coll. Art Gall.: El Cajon, Calif.); *New Topographics*, William Jenkins, 1975 (IMP/GEH: Rochester). Periodicals: *Camera*, May 1974; *Modern Photography*, July 1973; *Afterimage: VSW*, 3:1, 2:8.

COLLECTIONS IMP/GEH, Rochester; MOMA, NYC; Norton Simon Mus. of Art, Pasadena, Calif.; Philadelphia Mus. of Art, Pa.; Seagram Cllctn., NYC; Univ. of Maine, Orono; Univ. of Nebr., Sheldon Mem. Art Gall., Lincoln; VSW, Rochester. Amer. Arts Documentation Ctr., Exeter, England; Natl. Gall. of Canada, Ottawa, Ontario.

REPRESENTATIVE Visual Studies Workshop, 31 Prince St, Rochester, NY 14607.

ADDRESS Box 475, Point Richmond, CA 94807.

Bruce West *PHOTOGRAPHER* Born February 16, 1953, in Baltimore, Maryland, West received a BA in Philosophy in 1975 and an MFA in Photography in 1978, both from Pennsylvania State University, University Park. His major influ-

ences have been Stieglitz, Weston, Caponigro and Atget.

Since 1979 he has been a resident artist in the Artist-in-the-Schools Program of the Pennsylvania Council on the Arts, and an instructor of photography at the Pennsylvania State University's Continuing Education Program. He also worked as a freelance industrial photographer in 1978–79.

West has been a member of the CAA since 1977 and of the Philadelphia Print Club since 1979. A Ford Foundation of the Arts Fellowship was awarded to him in 1977.

The photographer says: "My work is a celebration of what is. Through my work I hope to realize a relationship with nature that is ecstatic, embracing, and erotic."

PUBLICATIONS Book: *A Study of the Identification with Nature of Selected Writers and Photographers of the 19th and 20th Centuries*, 1978. Catalog: *Invisions Catalogue*, 1978 (Penn. State Univ.).

DEALER Brindl Gall., 13A Wood St, Camden, ME 04843.

ADDRESS 211 E King St, 3rd Floor, Lancaster, PA 17602.

Edward West *PHOTOGRAPHER · TEACHER · WRITER · PHOTOHISTORIAN* Born September 25, 1949, in New York City, West earned a BA in Art History from Lake Forest College, Lake Forest, Illinois (1971), and an MFA in Photography from Rochester Institute of Technology, New York (1973).

He has taught at the School of the Art Institute of Chicago since 1973, and in 1977–79 served as chairman of the Photography Department as well as assistant professor. In 1973 he taught both at Columbia College in Chicago and at the University of New Mexico, Albuquerque.

West received an NEA Services to the Field grant in 1979, a Union of Independent Colleges of Art Research and Development grant in 1975, an SPE grant in aid in 1975, the Rockford Art Association's Radius Award in 1974, National Teaching Fellowships in 1974 and 1973 and the Ellington Award for Scholarship in 1972.

PUBLICATIONS Periodicals: "A Question of Identity," fall 1979, Feb 1975, *Exposure: SPE*; *New Art Examiner*, text only, May 1974; *Camera*, July 1973; *Black Photographers' Annual*, 1973.

PORTFOLIOS (group) *Underware*, 1976 (Photography Dept., School of the Art Inst. of Chicago); *Radius*, 1974 (Burpee Art Mus.: Rockford, Ill.).

COLLECTIONS Art Inst. of Chicago; Burpee Art

Mus., Rockford, Ill.; CCP, Tucson; Friends of Photography, Carmel, Calif.; Governors State Univ., Park Forest South, Ill.; IMP/GEH, Rochester; James Van Der Zee Inst., NYC; Ruth & Charles Levy Fndn., Chicago; Reva & David Logan Fndn., Chicago; Milwaukee War Memorial, Wisc.; Minneapolis Inst. of Art, Minn.; MOMA, NYC; Polaroid Corp., Boston; Rochester Inst. of Tech., N.Y.

ADDRESS 2529 N Sawyer, Chicago, IL 60647.

Colin L. Westerbeck, Jr. *FILM & PHOTOGRAPHY CRITIC* Born April 17, 1941, in St. Louis, Missouri, Westerbeck received a BA from Amherst College, Amherst, Massachusetts (1963), and a PhD in English and Comparative Literature from Columbia University, New York City (1972). His mentors were teacher/critic Benjamin DeMott, critic Pauline Kael, John Szarkowski and Joel Meyerowitz.

As of this writing Westerbeck was a photography critic for *Artforum* and *Aperture*. He has been a film critic for *Commonweal* since 1970, and has taught film and photography at Fordham University, New York City, since 1977. He also taught literature and film at City University of New York from 1970 to 1976.

Westerbeck has belonged to the National Society of Film Critics since 1973 and was its president in 1978. He won an NEA Art Critic's Fellowship in 1978 and a General Research Grant in the same year (jointly, with Joel Meyerowitz) from the National Endowment for the Humanities.

"In my writing," he says, "I am trying to chronicle the cultural history of photography, to see this medium in the context of others I have studied. I don't see any essential difference between my tasks as a critic of new work in my columns and as an historian of the past."

PUBLICATIONS Periodicals: "American Images" & "Helen Levitt," May 1980, *Artforum;* "Last Call for Pictorialism," May 1979, "John Thomson," Sept 1978, *American Photographer;* "China Is Near," Nov 1978, "On Sontag," Apr 1978, "Night Light: Brassaï and Weegee," Dec 1976, *Artforum.*

ADDRESS 601 West End Ave, New York, NY 10024.

Brett Weston *PHOTOGRAPHER* [See plate 126] Born in Los Angeles on December 16, 1911, Weston learned photography from his father, the famed photographer Edward Weston. His brother, Cole Weston, is a photographer, film maker and lecturer.

Weston began to photograph at age thirteen while on a trip to Mexico with his father. He served an apprenticeship in his father's Glendale (then Tropico), California, studio in 1925–27, then shared a studio with him in San Francisco (1928), in Carmel (1929) and in Santa Monica (1935).

Brett Weston won a Guggenheim award in 1945.

Mainly influenced by his father, he produces large-format silver prints. His images usually have more of a "graphic" hard-edged tonality than his father's. His subjects are mainly abstracts of nature and landscapes.

PUBLICATIONS Monographs: *Brett Weston: Voyage of the Eye,* 1975; *Brett Weston: Photographs,* 1966; *Brett Weston: Photographs,* Merle Armitage, 1956. Anthologies: *Dialogue with Photography,* Thomas Cooper & Paul Hill, 1979; *The Photograph Collector's Guide,* Lee D. Witkin & Barbara London, 1979; *The Great West: Real/Ideal,* Sandy Hume et al, eds., 1977; *Interviews with Master Photographers,* James Danziger & Barnaby Conrad III, 1977; *The Julien Levy Collection,* Witkin Gall., 1977; *The Magic Image,* Cecil Beaton & Gail Buckland, 1975; *Looking at Photographs,* John Szarkowski, 1973; *A Collection of Photographs,* Beaumont & Nancy Newhall, 1969. Catalogs: *Photographs,* 1977; *American Photography: The Sixties,* 1966 (Univ. of Nebr., Sheldon Mem. Art Gall.: Lincoln). Periodicals: *Camera,* Oct 1979, Nov 1975, Oct 1974, Feb 1973, Dec 1972; *Creative Camera,* Aug 1976, May 1976, Feb 1971; *Art Journal 32,* summer 1973; *Aperture,* 7:4, 1959; *American Photography,* Sept 1952; *Camera Craft,* Mar 1940.

PORTFOLIOS (all self-pub.: Carmel, Calif.) *Twenty Photographs 1970–1977,* 1977; *Portraits of My Father,* 1976; *Oregon,* 1975; *Europe,* 1973; *Japan,* 1970; *Baja California,* 1967; *Ten Photographs,* 1958; *New York,* 1951; *White Sands,* 1949; *San Francisco,* 1938.

COLLECTIONS Amon Carter Mus., Fort Worth, Tex.; Ariz. State Univ., Tempe; Art Inst. of Chicago; Bowdoin Coll. Mus. of Art, Brunswick, Maine; Burpee Art Mus., Rockford, Ill.; CCP, Tucson; Cleveland Mus. of Art, Ohio; Exchange Natl. Bank, Chicago; Harvard Univ., Carpenter Ctr. & Fogg Art Mus., Cambridge, Mass.; IMP/GEH, Rochester; Kalamazoo Inst. of Arts, Mich.; L/C, Wash., D.C.; Minneapolis Inst. of Arts, Minn.; Mus. of Fine Arts, Houston, Tex.; MOMA, NYC; Mus. of Fine Arts, St. Petersburg, Fla.; New Orleans Mus. of Art; Norton Simon Mus., Pasadena, Calif.; Oakland Mus., Calif.; Philadelphia Mus. of Art, Pa.; Polaroid Corp.,

Cambridge, Mass.; Princeton Univ., N.J.; San Francisco Mus. of Mod. Art; Seagrams Cllctn., NYC; Univ. of Louisville, Ky.; Univ. of Mich., Ann Arbor; Univ. of Nebr., Sheldon Mem. Art Gall., Lincoln; Univ. of N. Mex., Albuquerque; Univ. of Ore., Eugene; Univ. of Tex., Austin; VSW, Rochester; Wadsworth Athenaeum, Hartford, Conn.; Worcester Art Mus., Mass.; Yale Univ., New Haven, Conn.

ADDRESS 228 Vista Verde, Box 694, Carmel Valley, CA 93924.

Cole Weston *PHOTOGRAPHER · THEATRICAL DIRECTOR · FILM MAKER* Born in Los Angeles in 1919, Weston majored in theater arts at the Cornish School in Seattle (1940). His father is photographer Edward Weston and his brother is photographer Brett Weston.

When Edward Weston requested his son's assistance in 1946, Cole joined his father in Carmel, California, where he worked with the elder Weston until the latter's death in 1958. Prior to that Cole had photographed for *Life* magazine after beginning his photographic career in the U.S. Navy (1946). He is also executor of the Edward Weston Estate.

Working strictly in large format, Weston has produced color landscapes "that stand solidly within the tradition of American landscape painting," according to Ben Maddow *(Eighteen Photographs)*. He has been working in large-format color for more than thirty years.

PUBLICATIONS Books: *Not Man Apart*, Robinson Jeffers, 1965; *The Sea Around Us*, Rachel Carson, 1954. Anthology: *Darkroom 2*, Jain Kelly, ed., 1978.

COLLECTIONS Harvard Univ., Fogg Art Mus., Cambridge, Mass.; Philadelphia Mus. of Art, Pa.

DEALERS Susan Spiritus, 3336 Via Lido, Newport Beach, CA 92663; Weston Gall., Box 655, Carmel, CA 93921; Witkin Gall., 41 E 57 St, New York, NY 10022.

Edward Weston *PHOTOGRAPHER* [See plate 51] Born on March 24, 1886, in Highland Park, Illinois, Weston died on January 1, 1958, at his home, Wildcat Hill, in Carmel, California, after a ten-year bout with Parkinson's disease. Weston's first son, Brett (born 1911), is a photographer and worked with his father in the 1930s and 1940s. Another son, Cole (born 1919), is also a photographer and a printer of Weston's negatives from the time of his father's illness to the present day. Weston, in his early years, was greatly influenced by modern painters and photographer/companion Margrethe Mather. He later collabo-

rated with both his second wife, Charis Wilson, and Tina Modotti, his companion for many years. Weston attended Illinois College of Photography from 1908 to 1911.

After working as an errand boy at Marshall Fields in Chicago for three years, Weston moved to California, where he did surveying for the railroads and peddled photographs door-to-door. Having made his first photographs in 1902, he opened his first studio in Tropico (now Glendale), California, in 1911. Weston moved the studio to the Pasadena/Hollywood area when he formed a partnership of sorts with Margrethe Mather; it was still operating in the early 1920s. In 1928 he moved to Carmel, which was to become his permanent home, and opened a studio there. Prior to that he had run a studio with Tina Modotti in Mexico City (1923–25) and in San Francisco with Johan Hagemeyer in 1925. He worked briefly for the U.S. government Public Works of Art Project in 1933.

In 1917 Weston was elected to the London Salon and in 1932, with Ansel Adams and Willard Van Dyke, he formed Group f.64. During his early years he won many prizes and awards in the pictorial salons of the day (1914–17). He was the first photographer to receive a Guggenheim Fellowship (1937), which was extended in 1938.

Weston was the subject of the 1948 motion picture *The Photographer*, directed by his friend Willard Van Dyke. He was also represented in the films *The Naked Eye*, by Louis Clyde Stoumen (1957), and in *The Daybooks of Edward Weston*, Parts I & II (1965), produced by KQED TV, San Francisco.

Although in his earliest years Weston emulated the pictorialists, once he set his sights on realism he worked steadfastly toward that goal. Always working in large format, he strived to achieve the greatest possible depth of field and resolution of detail. He made only contact prints, chiefly silver and platinum, although he did some color. One of the most influential photographers of the twentieth century, Weston remarked in 1931, "My work has vitality because I have helped, done my part in revealing to others the living world about them, showing to them what their own unseeing eyes have missed."

PUBLICATIONS Monographs: *Edward Weston: Nudes*, note by Charis Wilson, 1977; *Edward Weston: Fifty Years*, Ben Maddow, 1973; *The Daybooks*, vol. 2: *California 1927–34*, intro. by Nancy Newhall, 1966, vol. 1: *Mexico*, intro. by Beaumont Newhall, foreword & note by Nancy Newhall, 1961, vols. 1 & 2 repr. 1971; *The Flame of Recognition*, 1965, rev. ed., 1971; *My Camera* on *Point Lobos*, Ansel Adams, ed., 1950, repr. 1968; *Fifty Photographs: Edward Weston*, designed & ed. by Merle Armitage, 1947; *The Photographs of Edward Weston*, Nancy Newhall, 1946; *California and the West*, Charis Wilson, 1940, rev. ed., 1978; *Seeing California with Edward Weston*, 1939; *The Art of Edward Weston*, designed & ed. by Merle Armitage, 1932. Books: *Accent on Life*, Merle Armitage, 1965; *The Wind That Swept Mexico*, Anita Brenner, 1943; *Leaves of Grass*, Walt Whitman, 1942, repr. w/intro. by Richard Erlich, 1972; *Death Valley, A Guide, Federal Writers' Project of the WPA of Calif.*, 1939; *Fit for a King*, Merle Armitage, 1939; *Modern Dance*, Merle Armitage, ed., 1935; *Photography*, Enjoy Your Museum Series, 1934; *Idols Behind Altars*, w/Tina Modotti, text by Anita Brenner, 1929. Anthologies: *The Photograph Collector's Guide*, Lee D. Witkin & Barbara London, 1979; *Photography Rediscovered*, David Travis & Anne Kennedy, 1979; *Pictorial Photography in Britain 1900–1920*, Arts Council of Great Britain, 1978; *The Magic Image*, Cecil Beaton & Gail Buckland, 1975; *Celebrations*, Minor White & Jonathan Green, preface by Gyorgy Kepes, 1974; *Looking at Photographs*, John Szarkowski, 1973; *Octave of Prayer*, Minor White, 1972; *Great Photographers*, 1971, *The Great Themes*, 1970, Time-Life Series; *Masters of Photography*, Beaumont & Nancy Newhall, 1969; *The Photographer and the American Landscape*, 1963; "Edward Weston: A New Vision," *The Picture History of Photography*, Peter Pollack, 1958. Catalog: *Deutsche Werkbund Exhibition Film und Foto*, foreword, 1929 (Stuttgart, Germany). Periodicals: "Edward Weston: A Chronological Bibliography," Bernard Freemesser, *Exposure: SPE*, Feb 1977; "Review of the Daybooks," Ansel Adams, *Contemporary Photographer*, winter 1962; "Edward Weston, Master Photographer, 1886–1958," Tom Maloney, *U.S. Camera*, May 1958; "Edward Weston: Photographer," Nancy Newhall, *Aperture*, 6:1, 1958; "Special Weston Issue," Lew Parella, ed., *Camera*, Apr 1958; "Color as Form," Dec 1953, "Edward Weston and the Nude," Nancy Newhall, June 1952, *Modern Photography*; "Edward Weston in Retrospect," Beaumont Newhall, *Popular Photography*, Mar 1946; "Seeing Photographically," Jan 1943, "Portrait Photography," Dec 1942, *Complete Photographer*; "Of the West: A Guggenheim Portrait," w/ Charis Wilson Weston, *U.S. Camera Annual*, 1940, "What Is Photographic Beauty," vol. 46, 1939, "Photography—Not Pictorial," July 1930, *Camera Craft*; "From My Day Book," *Creative Art*, Aug 1928.

PORTFOLIOS *Six Nudes of Neil*, 1925, intro. by Neil Weston, note & printed by George A. Tice, 1977 (Witkin Gall.: NYC); *Desnudos*, intro. by Charis Wilson, printed by Cole Weston, 1972 (Cole Weston: Carmel, Calif.); *Edward Weston Portfolio*, intro. by Wynn Bullock, foreword & printed by Cole Weston, 1971 (Witkin-Berley: Roslyn Heights, N.Y.); *50th Anniversary Portfolio*, printed by Brett Weston, 1952 (pvt. prntg., Carmel, Calif.).

COLLECTIONS Amon Carter Mus. of Western Art, Fort Worth, Tex.; Art Inst. of Chicago; Henry E. Huntington Lib., San Marino, Calif.; IMP/GEH, Rochester; Los Angeles Pub. Lib.; MOMA, NYC; Mus. of Fine Arts, Houston; Oakland Mus., Calif.; Univ. of Ill., Krannert Art Mus., Urbana; Univ. of N. Mex. Art Mus., Albuquerque. Museo de Arte Moderno, Mexico City; RPS, London; and most major collections.

ARCHIVE Cole Weston, Box 22155, Carmel, CA 93921.

Marla Katz Westover CURATOR Born May 3, 1951, in Roslyn, New York, Westover received a BA in 1974 from Arizona State University, Tempe, and as of this writing was an MA candidate at the University of California, Davis. She served an internship at the Guggenheim Museum in New York City in 1975.

Since 1977 she has been a curatorial associate at University Art Museum, Berkeley, California. She worked for Gallery Paule Anglim in San Francisco in 1977, was a conservator for the California State Railroad Museum in Sacramento in 1976, and co-directed The Gallery, Memorial Union at the University of California, Davis, in 1976.

Westover belongs to CAA, SPE and Friends of Photography.

Her major curatorial interests are photographs by women, interiors, color photography and Bay Area photography.

PUBLICATIONS Catalogs: *Wright Morris: Matrix/Berkeley 27*, 1979 (Univ. Art Mus.: Berkeley); *Interior Spaces: Photographs by Lawrie Brown, JoAnne Leonard, Helen Nestor, Irene Poon & Diana Schoenfeld*, 1978 (The Gallery, Univ. of Calif.: Davis); *Marion Post Wolcott: FSA Photographs*, 1978 (Univ. Art Mus.: Berkeley).

ADDRESS 860 Mandana Blvd, Oakland, CA 95610.

Jerome L. Wexler PHOTOGRAPHER Born in New York City on February 6, 1923, Wexler is a self-employed photographer.

His books have won numerous awards, including being named Best Books for Young Adults by the American Library Association and Outstanding Science Trade Books for Children by the National Science Teachers Association.

Wexler photographs plants, animals and insects, mostly in close-up ten to twenty times life size. He describes his style as "straightforward, scientific, poster effect."

PUBLICATIONS Books: *Find the Hidden Insect,* 1979; *A Fish Hatches,* 1978; *Mimosa, The Sensitive Plant,* 1978; *Play With Plants,* 1978; *The Amazing Dandelion,* 1977; *A Chick Hatches,* 1976; *Popcorn,* 1976; *A Calf Is Born,* 1975; *The Harlequin Moth,* 1975; *Bulbs, Corms, and Such,* 1974; *Rock Tumbling, From Stones to Gems to Jewelry,* 1974; *The Apple and Other Fruits,* 1973; *My Puppy Is Born,* 1973; *Vegetables From Stems and Leaves,* 1972; *The Carrot and Other Root Vegetables,* 1971; *The Tomato & Other Fruit Vegetables,* 1970; *Peanut,* 1969; *Maple Tree,* 1968; *Milkweed,* 1967.

ADDRESS 4 Middle Ln, Wallingford, CT 06492.

Charles Wheatstone   PHYSICIST · INVENTOR Born February 6, 1802, in Gloucester, England, Wheatstone died October 19, 1875, in Paris. Educated at a private school, he later made a study of the laws of sound and their application to music, then a study of light.

Initially, Wheatstone was in the manufacture of musical instruments. Devoting himself mainly to the principles of their construction, he invented the concertina in 1829. In 1834 he was appointed professor of experimental philosophy at King's College. During his career, Wheatstone contributed many impressive papers to the *Journal of the Royal Institution* and *Philosophical Magazine.*

Specializing in electrical science, he, with Sir William Fothergill Cooke, patented an early five-needle telegraph in 1837. He later developed the alphabet dial telegraph (1840), the type-printing telegraph (1841), the improved magnetic-alphabetic dial telegraph (between 1858 and 1860) and the automatic telegraph (between 1858 and 1867). He also invented the chronoscope, a device for electrically recording the velocity of projectiles, and a telegraph thermometer for ascertaining temperatures at high altitudes. His last work was to contrive a new recording instrument for submarine cables that was fifty-eight times more sensitive than any recorder previously employed. Most notable among his achievements is a device known as the Wheatstone bridge (1843), that accurately measures electrical resistance. It became widely used in laboratories the world over. It was

Wheatstone who first suggested a "unit" measurement of electricity.

Elected a fellow of the Royal Society in 1836, a Chevalier of the Legion of Honor in 1855 and a Foreign Member of the Institute of France in 1873, he was awarded at least thirty-four distinctions or diplomas by various universities, governments and learned societies. Wheatstone was also an active member of the London Phrenological Society. He received the honor of knighthood in 1868 in recognition of his scientific discoveries.

Sir Charles' contribution to the field of photography was his invention of the stereoscope, along with his studies of binocular vision. Although the stereoscope (a device for observing pictures three-dimensionally) no longer enjoys the immense popularity that it once did, it is still in use in viewing X-rays and aerial photographs.

PUBLICATIONS Books: *Abhandlungen zur geschichte des stereoskops von Wheatstone, Brewster, Riddel, Helmholtz, Wenham, d'Almeida und Harmer,* Louis O. M. Rohr, 1908 (W. Engelmann: Leipzig); *Letters Respecting the Original Invention of the Stereoscope,* W/D. Brewster, 1856 (Liverpool); *New Experiments in Sound,* 1823. Anthologies: *Early Photographs & Early Photographers,* Oliver Mathews, 1973; "Photometry," Cargill Gilston Knott, *Encyclopaedia Britannica,* 11th ed., vol. 21. Periodicals: "Contributions to the Physiology of Vision: Part I. On Some Remarkable and Hitherto Unobserved Phenomena of Binocular Vision," 1838, Part II, 1852, *Philosophical Transactions of the Royal Society of London;* "On Binocular Vision; and on the Stereoscope . . . ," *British Association Report,* 1838; "Experiments on Audition," & "Description of the Kaleidoscope," *Quarterly Journal of Science,* 1827.

Clarence Hudson White   PHOTOGRAPHER · TEACHER Born on April 8, 1871, in West Carlisle, Ohio, White died on July 8, 1925, in Mexico City. A self-taught photographer, White was influenced by Whistler and by Japanese art.

White was head bookkeeper in a wholesale grocery firm in Newark, Ohio, from 1890 to 1906 and took up photography around 1893. He launched a commercial career in photography when, in 1906, he moved to New York and established a studio. From 1907 until his death he lectured at Columbia University Teachers College.

In 1910 he, with the assistance of Fred Holland Day, Gertrude Käsebier and Max Weber, began the Summer School in Photography in Seguinland, Maine. From 1908 to 1921 he taught at the

Brooklyn Institute of Arts and Sciences, and in 1914 he founded the Clarence White School of Photography in New York, which his wife and friends continued to run after his death until 1943.

White helped organize the Newark (Ohio) Camera Club, 1898, and was elected to The Linked Ring in 1900. In 1899 he was made an honorary member of the New York Camera Club and was a founder-member of the Photo-Secession, 1902. In 1915 he helped found the Pictorial Photographers of America, of which he was the first president (1916).

A pictorialist, White made platinum, palladium and gum-bichromate prints. He also made use of artificial light. He chose varied subjects, showing a partiality toward women and children. He was a teacher of considerable influence; some of his pupils were Karl Struss, Margaret Bourke-White, Dorothea Lange, Doris Ulmann, Ralph Steiner, Paul Outerbridge and Anton Bruehl.

PUBLICATIONS Monographs: *Clarence H. White*, intro. by Maynard P. White, Jr., 1977; *Symbolism of Light: The Photographs of Clarence H. White*, Wm. Innes Homer, ed., text by Maynard P. White, Jr., 1977; *Photographs of Clarence H. White*, Jerald C. Maddox, 1968; *Newport the Maligned*, Clara Morris, 1908; *Beneath the Wrinkle*, Clara Morris, 1904; *Eben Holden*, Irving Bacheller, 1901. Anthologies: *The Photograph Collector's Guide*, Lee D. Witkin & Barbara London, 1979; *Photography Rediscovered*, David Travis & Anne Kennedy, 1979; *The Collection of Alfred Stieglitz*, Weston J. Naef, 1978; *Pictorial Photography in Great Britain 1900–1920*, Arts Council of Great Britain, 1978; *The Valient Knights of Daguerre . . . by Sadakichi Hartmann*, Harry W. Lawton & Geo. Know, eds., 1978; *The Magic Image*, Cecil Beaton & Gail Buckland, 1975; *Camera Work: A Critical Anthology*, Jonathan Green, ed., 1973; *Early Photographs & Early Photographers*, Oliver Mathews, 1973; *Great Photographers*, 1971, *The Print*, 1970, Time-Life Series; *The Picture History of Photography*, Peter Pollack, 1958, rev. ed., 1969. Periodicals: "Clarence H. White," Peter C. Bunnell, *Camera*, Nov 1972; *Camera Work*, Oct 1910, July 1909, July 1908, Jan 1905, July 1903.

COLLECTIONS Cleveland Mus. of Art, Ohio; IMP/GEH, Rochester; L/C, Wash. D.C.; Metro. Mus. of Art, NYC; MOMA, NYC; Princeton Univ. Art Mus., N.J.; Univ. of Kansas Mus. of Art, Lawrence. RPS, London.

ARCHIVE The Clarence H. White Family Collection, Princeton Univ. Art Mus., Princeton, NJ 08540.

Henry White   SOLICITOR · PHOTOGRAPHER
Born in 1819 in England, White died there in 1903.

He combined photography with the legal profession until he gave up the former in 1861. He won prizes at the Paris Universal Exhibition of 1855 and at the Universal Exhibition of Photography at Brussels in 1856.

Regarded as a fine landscape photographer, White produced "pastoral landscapes—from rivered woodlands to rural architecture and farmed fields—delicately composed by the arrangement of light and of tonal values" (Cropley/Dawson/Elliott).

PUBLICATION Anthology: *Early Photographs & Early Photographers*, Oliver Mathews, 1973.

DEALER Cropley/Dawson/Elliott, 20 Hanway St., London WC1, England.

Minor Martin White PHOTOGRAPHER · EDITOR · WRITER [See plate 74] Born July 9, 1908, in Minneapolis, Minnesota, White died June 24, 1976, in Boston, Massachusetts. An early interest in photography was encouraged by his grandfather, an amateur photographer, who gave White his equipment. White received a BS in Botany from the University of Minnesota in Minneapolis in 1933. At various times in his life, White was influenced by Catholicism, Meyer Schapiro's psychological approach to creativity and art, Zen, Gestalt, and, most influential of all, the teachings of the mystic G. I. Gurdjieff. Close personal friendships with Edward Weston, Alfred Stieglitz and Ansel Adams influenced and shaped him as a photographer.

White was hired as a creative photographer for the government's Works Progress Administration (WPA) in Portland, Oregon (1938), then became director of photography at La Grande Art Center, La Grande, Oregon (1940–41). After a stint in the U.S. Army (1942–45) he started teaching at the California School of Fine Arts (now the San Francisco Art Institute) and remained there until 1953. With Beaumont and Nancy Newhall, Ansel Adams, Dorothea Lange and others, White founded *Aperture* in 1952 and served as its editor until 1975. During those years he also was Beaumont Newhall's assistant curator at GEH (1953–57), taught at Rochester Institute of Technology (1956–59) and was a professor (1965–74) and senior lecturer (1975) at MIT.

He was a founding member of SPE in 1962, and was made a fellow of MIT Council of the Arts in 1975. In 1970 White received a Guggenheim Fellowship.

The photographer is known for sharply focused

black-and-white prints of visual realism and tonal beauty that function as metaphors for personal inner experience.

PUBLICATIONS Monographs: *Minor White: Rites and Passages,* James Baker Hall, 1978; *Mirrors Messages Manifestations,* 1969. Books: *The New Zone System Manual,* w/Richard Zakia & Peter Lorenz, 1976; *Zone System Manual,* 1961, 3rd ed., 1967; *Exposure with the Zone System,* 1956. Anthologies: *Dialogue with Photography,* Paul Hill & Thomas Cooper, 1979; *The Photograph Collector's Guide,* Lee D. Witkin & Barbara London, 1979; *The Great West: Real/Ideal,* Sandy Hume, et al, eds., 1977; *Interviews with Master Photographers,* James Danziger & Barnaby Conrad, 1977; *Photography Year 1977,* Time-Life Series, 1977; *The Magic Image,* Cecil Beaton & Gail Buckland, 1975; *100 Years of Photographic History,* Van Deren Coke, ed., 1975; *The Photographers' Choice,* Kelly Wise, ed., 1975; *Celebrations,* 1974; *Octave of Prayer,* 1972; *The Art of Photography,*1971, *Great Photographers,* 1971, Time-Life Series; *Be-ing Without Clothes,* 1970; *The Great Themes,* 1970, Time-Life Series; *Light⁷,* 1968; *Photographers on Photography,* Nathan Lyons, ed., 1966. Catalogs: *Photograph, U.S.A.,* 1967 (DeCordova Mus.: Lincoln, Mass.); *American Photography: The Sixties,* 1966 (Sheldon Mem. Art Gall., Univ. of Nebr.: Lincoln). Periodicals: *Camera,* Dec 1979, Nov 1975, July 1975, Dec 1972, Jan 1972, Aug 1959; *Camera 35,* June 1977; "Viewpoint: Clout and Metaphysics," Walter Klink, Feb/Mar 1974, "Debate: A. D. Coleman vs. Minor White," Nov 1973, "Minor White, 1908–1976," David Vestal, Oct 1976, "Photography: An UNdefinition," Apr 1962, *Popular Photography;* "Minor White (1908–1976): The Significance of Formal Quality in His Photographs," Janet E. Buerger, no. 19, 1976, "The Whiff of a New Trend," no. 5, 1956, "Lyrical and Accurate," no. 5, 1956, *Image; Aperture,* ed., passim, 1975–1952; "On the Invention of Photographic Meaning," Alan Sekula, *Artforum,* Jan 1975; "Latent Image: Scattered Shot and Gathered Prints," A. D. Coleman, Feb 22, 1973, "Latent Image: Smith/White," A. D. Coleman, Apr 2, 1970, *Village Voice;* "How Creative Is Color Photography?" *Popular Photography Color Annual,* 1957; "Your Concepts Are Showing: How to Judge Your Own Photographs," *American Photography,* May 1951.

PORTFOLIOS *The First Portfolio,* 1975 (Apeiron Workshops: Millerton, N.Y.); *Jupiter Portfolio,* 1975 (Light Gall.: NYC); *Invitational Portfolio #1,* 1973 (Ctr. for Photographic Studies: Louisville, Ky.); *Sequence 6,* 1951 (self-pub.).

COLLECTIONS Art Inst. of Chicago; Harvard Univ., Fogg Art Mus., Cambridge; IMP/GEH, Rochester; Kalamazoo Inst. of Arts, Mich.; L/C, Wash., D.C.; New Orleans Mus. of Art, La.; N.Y. Pub. Lib., NYC; Norton Simon Mus., Pasadena, Calif.; Oakland Mus., Calif.; Ore. Hist. Soc., Portland; Philadelphia Mus. of Art, Pa.; John & Mabel Ringling Mus. of Art, Sarasota, Fla.; San Francisco Mus. of Modern Art; UCLA; Univ. of Louisville, Ky.; Univ. of N. Mex., Albuquerque; Univ. of Ore., Eugene. Natl. Gall. of Canada, Ottawa, Ontario.

ARCHIVE Princeton University Art Museum, Princeton N.J.

Stephen Leon White GALLERY OWNER · PHOTOHISTORIAN · WRITER Born May 4, 1938, in Jacksonville, Florida, White received a BA in History from San Francisco State College (1962) and an MFA in Film from University of California at Los Angeles (1968).

After working in the corrections field for the better part of eight years, White opened his own photography gallery in 1975. He also made documentaries and did news reporting for King TV in Seattle, Washington (1969–70), and taught photographic history at Orange Coast College, Costa Mesa, California, in 1976. In 1980 he became president of the Association of International Photography and Art Dealers.

White received a grant from the California Law Enforcement Assistance Administration in 1969 to make a training film for the Parole Department. He also made *Film Geel* for Swedish Television.

BUSINESS Stephen White Gallery, 835 N La Cienega Blvd, Los Angeles, CA 90069.

ADDRESS 111 N Gardner St, Los Angeles, CA 90036.

Ray Henry Whiting PHOTOGRAPHER · TEACHER Born September 26, 1942, in Denver, Colorado, he received an MFA degree in Photography from Ohio University, Athens, in 1973 and a BFA from the University of Denver (Colorado) in 1964 in Painting. He worked and studied with Brett Weston and Don Ross from 1964 to 1967.

Since 1976 he has been co-chairman of the Department of Photography at the Community College of Denver, and from 1962 to 1975 he worked as a freelance photographer, industrial designer and art director. He was also photographic illustrator and art director of *The Camera Craftsman,* published by National Camera Schools from 1962 to 1965.

He was given a graduate assistantship at Ohio

University (1971–73), and won a Department of Art Scholarship at Denver University (1960–64).

Working with an 11 x 14 view camera, he specializes in landscape photography.

COLLECTIONS Amoco Prod. Co., Denver, Colo.; Continental Illinois Natl. Bank, Chicago; Littleton Historical Mus., Colo.; Mountain Bell, Denver, Colo.

DEALERS Eclipse Photographics, 2012 Tenth St, Boulder, CO 80302; Hills Gall., 3113 E Third Ave, Denver, CO 80206; Keystone Gall., 1213 State St, Santa Barbara, CA 93101; Douglas Kenyon, Inc., 155 E Ohio St, Chicago IL 60611.

ADDRESS 6456 S Crocker, Littleton, CO 80120.

Robert Alan Widdicombe *TEACHER · PHOTOGRAPHER* Born August 11, 1949, in Ft. Wayne, Indiana, he received an MA degree in Photography from the University of New Mexico in Albuquerque (1978) and a BA degree from Michigan State University in East Lansing in Communications (1974). His most important teachers were Van Deren Coke, Thomas Barrow, Betty Hahn and Beaumont Newhall.

From 1979 to the present he has been an instructor in photography at the University of Texas in Austin. Previously he had been a teaching assistant (1978–79) and director of the ASA Gallery (1977–78) at the University of New Mexico.

A member of SPE, he was awarded a Photographer's Fellowship grant from NEA in 1979.

Currently he is producing 20 x 24 Ektacolor RC prints, using artificial light, that deal with cultural aspects of man-made environments, specifically in the southwest United States and in Mexico.

PUBLICATIONS Periodicals: *Darkroom*, July, Aug 1979; *Artweek*, review, May 5, 1979.

COLLECTIONS Mus. of N. Mex., Santa Fe; Univ. of N. Mex. Art Mus., Albuquerque.

ADDRESS 4908 West Park, Austin, TX 78731.

Gwen Widmer *PHOTOGRAPHER · TEACHER* Born March 10, 1945, in Chicago, Illinois, Widmer earned a BA from Goshen College, Goshen, Indiana (1967), and an MFA from the School of the Art Institute of Chicago (1973). Her husband is photographer Reed Estabrook.

She has been assistant professor of art at the University of Northern Iowa, Cedar Falls, since 1976, and previously taught at the University of Illinois, Champaign/Urbana (1972–74).

A member of SPE, Widmer won an Iowa Arts Council Grant in 1978 and an NEA Photographer's Fellowship in 1980 and 1975.

Her large hand-colored photographs sometimes include writing and drawing.

PUBLICATIONS Monograph: *Personal Erotic Drawings*, 1975. Books: *Broadside*, 1979; *Darkroom Dynamics*, Jim Stone, ed., 1979; *Portraits and Other Disclosures*, 1979; *Lines*, 1977. Anthologies: *Color*, Time-Life Series, 1980; *Self-Portrayal*, 1978. Catalog: *Photographers Midwest Invitational*, 1973 (Walker Art Ctr., Minneapolis, Minn.). Periodicals: *The New Art Examiner*, 3:9, 1976; *Popular Photography*, 75:2, 1974.

COLLECTIONS Humboldt State Univ., Arcata, Calif.; J. B. Speed Art Mus., Louisville, Ky.; Kalamazoo Inst. of Arts, Mich.; Madison Art Ctr., Wisc.; State of Iowa, Des Moines.

ADDRESS 703 Iowa St, Cedar Falls, IA 50613.

Leigh A. Wiener *PHOTOGRAPHER* Born August 28, 1929, in New York, Wiener studied political science and geography at University of California at Los Angeles from 1948 to 1952.

Self-employed since 1957, he worked as a staff photographer for the *Los Angeles Times* from 1950 to 1957, with a break from 1952 to 1954 to serve in the U.S. Army.

A member of the Los Angeles Press Photographers Association, Wiener won an Emmy in 1975 for the television series he produced, "Talk About Pictures," and an Eddy award in 1967 for his TV documentary, "A Slice of Sunday."

Working as an editorial and illustration photographer, Wiener does special assignments that have included photographing Senator John F. Kennedy on his presidential campaign, three atomic bomb tests and the high-altitude hydrogen bomb tests (for *Life*).

PUBLICATIONS Books: *Not Subject to Change*, 1969; *Letters of Robinson Jeffers*, Ann Ridgeway, 1967; *Here Comes Me*, 1965; *Range of Research*, 1961. Anthologies: *Life Goes to the Movies*, 1975; *Best of Life*, 1973.

COLLECTIONS Cedars-Sinai Medical Ctr., Los Angeles; Security Pacific Bank Cllctn., Los Angeles.

ADDRESS 2600 Carman Crest Dr, Los Angeles, CA 90068.

Leif Wigh *CURATOR · WRITER* Born December 26, 1938, in Stockholm, Sweden, Wigh attended the School of Photography in Stockholm (1963–65) and, since 1976, has undertaken advanced studies in psychology.

Wigh became associate curator at Fotografiska

Muséet in Stockholm in 1977 and, from 1973, did freelance work for the photography museum. He is also a critic for the magazines *Fotonyheterna* and *Aktuell Fotografi*. From 1963 to 1972 he did freelance photography, and from 1972 to 1977 was photographer and information officer at the Swedish National Theatre Center and the Birgit Culberg Ballet Company. He taught at the School of Photography in Stockholm (1965–69).

A member of the European Society for the History of Photography, Wigh is chairman of the board of Konstföreningen på Mälaröarna. He won a grant from the Swedish government's culture department in 1975 and one from the city of Stockholm in 1970.

PUBLICATIONS Catalogs (all Fotografiska Muséet: Stockholm): *Josef Sudek, tjeckoslovakisk fotograf*, 1978; *Bill Brandt*, w/Åke Sidwall, 1978; *Den fantastiska fotografin i Europa*, w/Åke Sidwall, 1977; *Ansel Adams*, 1977; *Imogen Cunningham*, 1976; *Ralph Gibson*, 1976; *Walker Evans*, 1976; *Four Swedish Photographers*, w/Åke Sidwall, 1975; *Dokumentärbilder från Japan och Kuba*, w/Åke Sidwall, 1974.

ADDRESS Fotografiska Muséet, Box 16382, S-103 27, Stockholm, Sweden.

Terry Wild PHOTOGRAPHER · TEACHER Born January 18, 1947, in Wilmington, Delaware, Wild earned a BA in English (1968) from Lycoming College, Williamsport, Pennsylvania, and a BFA in Still Photography (1971) from Art Center College of Design, Los Angeles.

He has operated his own photography studio since 1971, and has taught photography part-time since 1972 at Lycoming College. Since 1973 he has also been chairperson of the Photography Department at the Pennsylvania Governors' School for the Arts, Bucknell University, Lewisburg, Pennsylvania.

Primarily using black-and-white in a traditional "straight" manner, Wild photographs people and environments with an "emphasis on presences within the landscape . . . clarity, value, form and texture."

PUBLICATIONS Anthologies: "Emerging L.A. Photographers," *Untitled II*, 1978; *Photography Year*, Time-Life Series, 1974; *Color Photography*, 1972. Catalog: *The Crowded Vacancy*, 1971 (Pasadena Art Mus.). Periodical: *Camera*, no. 8.

COLLECTIONS IMP/GEH, Rochester; Portland Mus. of Art, Maine; Santa Barbara Mus. of Art, Calif.; Univ. of Ariz., Northlight Gall., Tempe; Univ. of Calif., Memorial Union Art Gall., Davis. Bibliothèque Nationale, Paris.

ADDRESS RD3 Box 141, Williamsport, PA 17701.

(Karl Friedrich) Jurgen Wilde PHOTOGRAPHER · ART HISTORIAN · WRITER Born August 20, 1937, in Geldern, Germany, Wilde worked in industry as an apprentice machinist (1957–59), but left to study at the Technische Hochschule, Stuttgart (1959–61). He worked for Agfa-Gevaert in Leverkusen (1962), then studied art history at Cologne University and photography at the High School for Photography in Cologne (1963–65).

A collector of photographs and historical material about photographers since 1966, Wilde founded the first gallery of photography in Germany, Galerie Wilde, in 1972. He has been producing photographic portfolios since 1974.

Wilde is a member of the Bauhaus Archive, Berlin.

PUBLICATIONS Books: *The Art Director's Index to Photographers*, co-ed., nos. 1, 2, & 3. Catalogs: *Photokina Catalogues*, co-author, 1968, 1966.

ADDRESS Galerie Wilde, Auf dem Berlich 6, D-5000 Cologne 1, West Germany.

Roy Wilfred
See Roloff Beny

Stephen Guion Williams PHOTOGRAPHER Born in New York in 1941, he graduated with a BS in Journalism from the University of Kansas, Lawrence, in 1965.

Since 1971 Williams has been co-director of The Photography Place in Philadelphia, Pennsylvania. He was a teaching assistant at the Ansel Adams Workshop in Tucson, Arizona, in 1976; an instructor at the University of Delaware at Newark, New Jersey, in 1974; and a lecturer in the Arts Division at Rosemont College in Rosemont, Pennsylvania (1973–77). He was an assistant director in the CBS-TV Film Department (1967–68).

For his work *Chosen Land*, Williams was awarded "Cover 75" by the American Institute for Graphic Arts, and Time-Life selected it as one of the "twelve most important photographic books" of 1975. In 1969 he produced a documentary film, *We Hold These Truths*.

PUBLICATIONS Monograph: *Chosen Land*, 1975. Periodical: "Inhabitants," *Camera*, Aug 1973.

COLLECTIONS Free Lib. of Philadelphia; Philadelphia Natl. Bank; Shaker Mus. Fndn., Old Chatham, N.Y.

William Willis *INVENTOR* Born in 1841 in Kent, England, Willis died March 31, 1923. His father, William Willis, was a noted engraver of landscapes and inventor of the aniline printing process in 1864.

The younger Willis worked as a practical engineer at Tangyes, Birmingham, and later joined the staff at Birmingham and Midland Bank. He then went into business with his father, later founding the Platinotype Company, which first offered platinum papers for sale in 1880.

Willis received the Progress Medal of the London Photographic Society in 1881 and the gold medal of the International Inventions Exhibition in 1885. He invented the platinotype, patented in England on June 5, 1873, and made several improvements on it during the following years. In 1878 he added lead salts to the iron platinum mixture; in 1880 he eliminated the lead salts from the sensitive layer and increased the content of the platinum salt. He later worked out alternative processes, helping to circumvent the high cost of platinum: satista paper, a silver-platinum paper, and palladiotype paper, the substance of which was palladium.

PUBLICATIONS Books: *Cassell's Cyclopedia of Photography*, 1911, repr. 1973; *The History of Photography*, Josef Maria Eder, 1905, repr. 1972. Anthology: *Early Photographs & Early Photographers*, Oliver Mathews, 1973.

Gustav Wilmanns *CHEMIST* Born in Bremen, Germany, in 1881, Wilmanns died in 1965. He studied chemistry at Bonn, Heidelberg and Hannover in Germany.

After a short stint as an academic assistant, Wilmanns joined the scientific laboratory of Agfa in Berlin (1905). He transferred to Agfa's new Wolfen film factory in 1910 to manage film-coating and to develop a serviceable emulsion. From 1931 on, he developed Agfa's Technico-Scientific Department at Wolfen, organizing a project in 1934 to develop a multilayer color film based on Rudolf Fischer's color-coupler proposal.

He received such honors as the Gold Medal of Photographische Gesellschaft in Vienna, the Oska Messter Medal and the Kulturpreis of DGPh.

In his early work, Wilmanns came up with an emulsion formula using albumen that eliminated fog and was adopted in the manufacture of photographic papers. His discoveries in the following years included a high-sensitive cooked emulsion replacing ammonia that paved the way to the development of a practical motion picture film negative emulsion; a way to stabilize photographic emulsions for years rather than months; and the first panchromatic emulsion in Europe. The multilayer color film developed by Wilmanns and Dr. W. Schneider consisted of a protective coating, a blue-sensitive emulsion, a yellow filter, a green-sensitive emulsion, a separation layer, a red-sensitive emulsion, and an antihalation coating—all on a cellulose support 0.023mm in thickness. In 1936 Wilmanns and his associates developed a color negative and color paper prints.

PUBLICATIONS Books: *Quellendarstellungen zur Geschichte der Fotografie*, Wolfgang Baier, 1964; *Photographic Chemistry*, vol. 2, Pierre Glafkides, 1960 (Fountain Press); *Der Weg des Films*, F. von Zglinicki, 1956. Anthology: *Photography's Great Inventors*, Louis W. Sipley, 1965. Periodicals: *Monatliche Fototechnische Mitteilungen*, 1961; *Photographische Correspondenz*, 1961; *Bild und Ton*, 1960, 1958; *Foto Prisma*, 1956.

Valerie Sybil Wilmer *JOURNALIST · PHOTOGRAPHER* Born December 7, 1941, in Harrogate, Yorkshire, England, Wilmer attended the School of Photography at Regent Street Polytechnic in London (1959–60).

Wilmer is a documentary photographer and writer, and works as a freelance photojournalist, "specializing in the field of African–American music."

A member of the National Union of Journalists, she was the recipient of awards from the Arts Council of Great Britain in 1974 and 1976.

PUBLICATIONS Books: *As Serious as Your Life*, 1977, *Jazz People*, 1970 (Allison & Busby: London); *The Face of Black Music*, 1976. Periodical: *Creative Camera*, July 1973.

COLLECTION Victoria & Albert Mus., London.

ADDRESS 10 Balham Pk Mansions, Balham Pk Rd, London SW128DY, England.

George Washington Wilson *PHOTOGRAPHER* Born in 1823 at Aberdeen, Scotland, Wilson died in 1893.

Wilson established a studio in Aberdeen in 1852, and soon became a popular portrait photographer. In 1860 he was appointed Photographer to Her Majesty Queen Victoria in Scotland, and by the 1880s he had become one of the world's largest photographic publishers.

Producing consistently fine stereoscopic views, *cartes de visite* and albumen prints, Wilson made images consisting of landscapes and genre scenes as well as portraits. He is best remembered for having been an early practitioner of stop-action, or instantaneous, stereographs, having achieved an exposure time of less than one second.

PUBLICATIONS Monographs: *Photographs of English and Scottish Scenery—Glasgow*, 1868; *Photographs of English and Scottish Scenery—The Caledonian Canal*, 1867; *Gloucester Cathedral*, 1866; *Photographs of English and Scottish Scenery—English Cathedrals York and Durham*, 1865. Books: *The Birth of Photography*, Brian Coe, 1976 (Ash & Grant, London); *Queen Victoria, A Biography in Word and Picture*, Helmut & Allison Gernsheim, 1959; *Poetical Works*, Sir Walter Scott, 1886; *Ruined Abbeys and Castles of Great Britain and Ireland*, Wm. & Mary Howitt, 1862; *The Sunbeam*, 1859. Anthologies: *The Magic Image*, Cecil Beaton & Gail Buckland, 1975; *Early Photographs & Early Photographers*, Oliver Mathews, 1973. Periodicals: "G.W.W.," Gerda Peterich, *Image*, Dec 1956; *Literary Gazette*, Apr 13, 1839.

Harry Wilson   PHOTOGRAPHER · TEACHER
Born June 18, 1943, in Seattle, Washington, Wilson received an MFA in 1970 and a BFA in 1966 from the San Francisco Art Institute. He has been influenced by Geraldine Sharpe, Blair Stapp, Jerry Burchard and Jack Welpott.

Since 1971 he has been photography professor at Bakersfield College in California. Previously he was a photography instructor at the University of California Extension in Berkeley (1971) and at the San Francisco Photography Center (1966–71).

Wilson is a member of VSW.

From 1970 to the present, his themes have been the tourist landscape and the man-altered landscape. Prior to that, his themes were a spoof of the snapshot/family album (1969–74), and the social landscape (1965–69).

PUBLICATIONS Anthologies: *Self-Portrayal*, Jim Alinder, ed., 1978; *Photography and Language*, 1976.

COLLECTION Oakland Art Mus., Calif.

ADDRESS 3316 McCourry, Bakersfield, CA 93304.

Helena Chapellin Wilson   PHOTOGRAPHER ·
INTERIOR ARCHITECT/DESIGNER   Born in Caracas, Venezuela, Wilson attended Academia De Dibujo Tecnico y Architectura in Caracas and studied art at the Universities of Florence and Perugia, Italy. She received a BA in Photography from Columbia College, Chicago, in 1976.

A self-employed photographer and interior design consultant, she had worked since 1974 as coordinator of interior design for the Chicago Board of Education. Before coming to the United States in 1971 she owned an art gallery and conducted an interior design business in Caracas. She was also the chief designer for the Venezuelan Presidential Palace and of several government offices and the Venezuelan Presidential country house. In 1970 she was chief designer for the Venezuelan government-owned hotels. Wilson has been a member of Professional Women Photographers since 1975.

For the last seven years she has been working exclusively in black-and-white multiples of one-of-a-kind gum-bichromate prints.

PUBLICATIONS Anthology: *Women Photograph Men*, 1977. Periodicals: *Midwest Art Quarterly*, summer 1977; *The New Art Examiner*, June 1977; *Popular Photography Annual*, 1975.

COLLECTIONS Exchange Natl. Bank of Chicago; Friedman & Koven Cllctn., Chicago; Ill. State Mus., Springfield; ICP, NYC; Metro. Mus. of Art, NYC. Galería de Arte National, Caracas; Muséo de Ciudad Bolivar en el Correo del Orinoco, Venezuela.

DEALER Adler/Castillo Gall., 55 E 86 St, New York, NY 10028.

ADDRESS Unit No A-9, 5555 S Everett Ave, Chicago, IL 60637.

Wallace Wilson   PHOTOGRAPHER · TEACHER
Born June 10, 1947, in Dallas, Texas, Wilson received a BA from the University of Texas at Austin in 1970, and an MFA in 1975 from the School of the Art Institute of Chicago. He also studied privately with Ralph Eugene Meatyard (1971–72).

Since 1979 Wallace has been an assistant professor in the Art Department of the University of Florida in Gainesville. He has previous teaching experience as assistant professor in the Art Department of the University of Delaware in Newark (1975–79) and at the College of Architecture of the University of Kentucky in Lexington (1970–75).

He was the recipient of a University of Florida Faculty Research Grant in 1980 and a grant from the University of Delaware Research Foundation in 1978.

The photographer describes his work as being "constructed color photographic reliefs."

PUBLICATIONS Periodicals: *Exposure: SPE*, Dec 1977; *Light Places*, 1977; *Village Voice*, Oct

10, 1977; *Art Week*, Oct 9, 1976; *Camera*, July 1973.

COLLECTIONS Art Inst. of Chicago; Baltimore Mus. of Art, Md.; MOMA, NYC; New Orleans Mus. of Art, La.; Oakland Mus., Calif.; Univ. of N. Mex., Albuquerque. City Mus. of Munich, W. Germany.

DEALERS O. K. Harris, 383 W Broadway, New York, NY 10012; Zabriskie Gall., 29 W 57 St, New York, NY 10019 & 29 rue Aubry le Boucher, Paris, France; Afterimage, The Quadrangle #151, 2800 Routh St, Dallas, TX 75201; David Mancini Gall., 5020 Montrose Blvd, Houston, TX 77006 & 1728 Spruce St, Philadelphia, PA 19103.

ADDRESSES 604 SW 43 Terr, Gainesville, FL 32607; Art Dept, Univ. of Fla., Gainesville, FL 32611.

Alan D. Winer PHOTOGRAPHER · TEACHER Born January 29, 1945, in Oakland, California, Winer earned an MFA in Photography from the Visual Studies Workshop of State University of New York at Buffalo, Rochester, New York (1977).

Since 1978 he has been a photography instructor and coordinator of photographic programs at VSW.

Winer belongs to SPE.

He works in multiple photographs and combinations of photographs and drawing.

PUBLICATIONS Catalog: *Attitudes: Photography in the 1970's*, 1979 (Santa Barbara Mus. of Art: Calif.). Periodical: *Art in America*, Apr 1980.

COLLECTIONS Art Inst. of Chicago; IMP/GEH, Rochester; Rochester Inst. of Tech.; Soc. for Critical Exchange, Inc., Seattle, Wash.; VSW, Rochester.

DEALER Visual Studies Workshop Gall., 31 Prince St, Rochester, NY 14607

ADDRESS 104 Rockingham St, Rochester, NY 14620.

Merry Morr Winnett PHOTOGRAPHER Born November 24, 1951, in Newport News, Virginia, Winnett studied at Michigan State University, East Lansing (1969–72), on a Michigan Higher Education Authority Scholarship and a Creative Arts Scholarship. She took her BA from the University of South Florida, Tampa, in 1975, and studied photography with Oscar Bailey.

From 1978 to the present Winnett has been a freelance graphic artist and photographer.

A member of SPE, VSW, and Associated Photographers of Winston-Salem, North Carolina, she won individual photographers fellowships in

1978 and 1979 from the Fine Arts Council of Florida.

The photographer uses selective chemical toning on black-and-white prints or employs Kwik-Print emulsion with applied hand stitching, dried flowers, sequins, or other objects such as ribbons and fabrics.

PUBLICATIONS Book: *Innovative Printmaking*, 1977. Periodicals: *Combinations—A Journal of Photography*, spring 1979, winter 1977; *The Photographic Image*, spring 1976; *Invitation to Photography*, spring 1976; *Petersen's Photographic*, May 1976.

COLLECTIONS Andromeda Gall., Buffalo, N.Y.; Chrysler Mus., Norfolk, Va.; *Combinations* Archives, Greenfield Ctr., N.Y.; Floating Fndn. of Photography, NYC; Southwest Ctr. of Photography, Austin, Tex.; Univ. of S. Florida, Tampa.

DEALERS Gallery 25, 620½ W Fourth St, Winston-Salem, NC 27101; Atlanta Gall. of Photography, 3077 E Shadowlawn NE, Atlanta, GA 30305.

Geoff Winningham PHOTOGRAPHER Born March 4, 1943, in Jackson, Tennessee, Winningham earned a BA in English in 1965 from Rice University in Houston, Texas, and an MS in Photography in 1968 from Illinois Institute of Technology in Chicago, where he studied with Aaron Siskind.

Since 1978 he has been a professor of art and photography at Rice University, previously serving as an associate professor of photography at the school (1969–78). In 1968–69 he was assistant professor of photography at the University of St. Thomas in Houston.

The photographer won NEA fellowships in 1977 and 1975, a Guggenheim fellowship in 1972 and an award from the Corporation for Public Broadcasting in 1972.

PUBLICATIONS Monographs: *Geoff Winningham: Photographs*, 1974; *Going Texan: The Days of the Houston Livestock Show & Rodeo*, 1972; *Friday Night in the Coliseum*, 1971. Anthologies: *The Photograph Collector's Guide*, Lee D. Witkin & Barbara London, 1979; *Mirrors and Windows*, John Szarkowski, ed., 1978; *The Great West: Real/Ideal*, Sandy Hume, et al, eds., 1977; *Photography Year 1973*, Time-Life Series; *Vision & Expression*, Nathan Lyons, ed., 1969. Catalog: *Photography Invitational 1971*, 1971 (Ark. Arts Ctr.: Little Rock). Periodicals: *Camera*, Aug 1977; *35mm Photography Annual*, 1973, 1968.

COLLECTIONS Boston Mus. of Fine Arts, Mass.; Harvard Univ., Carpenter Ctr., Cambridge, Mass.; IMP/GEH, Rochester; MOMA, NYC; Mus. of Fine Arts, Houston; Princeton Univ., Princeton, N.J.

DEALER Cronin Gall., 2008 Peden St, Houston, TX 77019.

ADDRESS Dept of Art, Rice University, Houston, TX 77001.

Garry Winogrand PHOTOGRAPHER [See plate 98] Born January 14, 1928, in New York City, Winogrand studied at City College of New York (1947–48), Columbia University (1948) and with Alexey Brodovitch at the New School for Social Research (1951), all in New York City. His mentors were Robert Frank and Walker Evans.

Currently a freelance photographer, Winogrand taught at the Institute of Design, Illinois Institute of Technology (1971–72), the University of Texas, Austin (1973), Cooper Union in New York City, School of Visual Arts in New York City and Art Institute of Chicago.

He received Guggenheim fellowships in 1978, 1969 and 1964, an NEA fellowship in 1975 and a grant from the New York State Council on the Arts in 1971.

PUBLICATIONS Monographs: *Public Relations*, 1977; *Women Are Beautiful*, 1975; *The Animals*, John Szarkowski, 1969. Anthologies: *The Photograph Collector's Guide*, Lee D. Witkin & Barbara London, 1979; *Mirrors & Windows*, John Szarkowski, 1978; *The Great West: Real/Ideal*, Sandy Hume et al, eds., 1977; *The Magic Image*, Cecil Beaton & Gail Buckland, 1975; *Photography Year 1974, Documentary Photography*, 1972, Time-Life Series. Catalogs: *Photographs*, 1977 (Univ. of Nebr., Sheldon Mem. Art Gall.: Lincoln); *Aspects of American Photography*, 1976 (Univ. of Mo.: St. Louis); *Peculiar to Photography*, 1976 (Univ. of N. Mex.: Albuquerque); *14 American Photographers*, Renato Danese, 1974 (Baltimore Mus. of Art: Md.); *New Images in Photography*, 1974 (Univ. of Miami, Lowe Art Mus.: Fla.); *New Documents*, John Szarkowski, 1967 (MOMA: NYC); *Contemporary Photographers: Toward a Social Landscape*, Nathan Lyons, 1966 (GEH: Rochester). Periodicals: *Creative Camera*, Sept 1977, Dec 1972, May 1972, Aug 1969; *Image 15*, July 1972; *Camera*, Feb 1972.

PORTFOLIO *Fifteen Photographs*, 1974 (Double Elephant Press: N.Y.).

COLLECTIONS Baltimore Mus. of Art, Md.; CCP, Tucson; IMP/GEH, Rochester; Kalamazoo Inst. of Arts, Mich.; L/C, Wash., D.C.; MOMA, NYC; Mus. of Fine Arts, Houston, Tex.; Princeton Univ., Princeton, N.J.; Seagram Cllctn.,

NYC; UCLA; Univ. of Mich., Ann Arbor; Univ. of Nebr., Sheldon Mem. Art Gall., Lincoln; Va. Mus. of Fine Arts, Richmond. Natl. Gall of Canada, Ottawa, Ontario.

DEALER Light Gall., 724 Fifth Ave, New York, NY 10019.

Kelly Wise TEACHER · PHOTOGRAPHER · AUTHOR · EDITOR Born December 1, 1932, in New Castle, Indiana, Wise received an MA degree in Contemporary Literature from Columbia University, New York City, in 1959, and a BS degree in Creative Writing from Purdue University, West Lafayette, Indiana, in 1955.

He has been an instructor of English since 1966 at the Phillips Academy in Andover, Massachusetts, and chairman of the English Department there since 1978; he also served as residential dean at the academy from 1969 to 1973. Prior to that he taught English at Mount Hermon School (1960–66).

PUBLICATIONS Books: *Still Points*, 1975; *Lotte Jacobi*, 1975; *Private Realities*, 1974. Anthology: *The Photographer's Choice*, ed., 1975. Periodical: *Creative Camera*, Jan 1977.

COLLECTIONS Addison Gall. of American Art, Andover, Mass.; Harvard Univ., Fogg Art Mus., Cambridge, Mass.; IMP/GEH, Rochester; L/C, Wash., D.C.; Mus. of Fine Arts, Boston; Mus. of Fine Arts, Houston; Polaroid Corp., Cambridge, Mass.; Univ. of Maryland, Baltimore County; Univ. of Nebr., Lincoln; Yale Univ., New Haven, Conn. Bibliothèque Nationale, Paris.

DEALERS Witkin Gallery, 41 E 57 St, New York, NY 10022; Vision Gallery, 216 Newbury St, Boston, MA 02116.

ADDRESS 22 School St, Andover, MA 01810.

Eugen Wiškovský PHILOLOGIST · PHOTOGRAPHER · PHOTOHISTORIAN Born September 20, 1888, in Dvůr Králové, Czechoslovakia, Wiškovský died January 15, 1964, in Prague. He studied languages at universities in Prague and Geneva, but was self-taught in photography.

Wiškovský taught languages at secondary schools in Kolín nad Labem and Prague. He published ten important articles in various photographic journals about the problems of creative photography, and also translated some of Freud's work into Czech.

According to Petr Tausk, "Although Wiškovský was an amateur photographer, he influenced considerably the evolution of Czechoslovak photography since his own photographic work was highly innovative. He was a typical intellectual photographer who confirmed his theoretic opinions by his own praxis. In his photographic work there is evident the influence of 'New Objectivity' with regard to keen views on modern architecture and in some cases even [the] slight influence of surrealism in his approach toward the depicting of 'objets trouvés.'"

PUBLICATION Monograph: *Eugen Wiškovský*, intro. by A. Fárová, 1964 (SNKLU: Prague).

Joel-Peter Witkin PHOTOGRAPHER Born September 13, 1939, in Brooklyn, New York, Witkin earned a BFA in Sculpture (1975) from Cooper Union in New York City and an MA in Photography (1977) from the University of New Mexico, Albuquerque, where he is a candidate for an MFA in Photography.

Currently a photography instructor at the University of New Mexico, Witkin won an NEA grant in 1980 and a CAPS grant in 1975.

PUBLICATIONS Book: *Infinity*, 1968. Anthologies: *Eros and Photography*, 1978; *Famous Photographers Annual*, 1970.

COLLECTIONS MOMA, NYC; San Francisco Mus. of Modern Art; Syracuse Univ., N.Y.; Univ. of N. Mex., Albuquerque.

DEALER Robert Samuel Gall., 795 Broadway, New York, NY 10011.

ADDRESS 222 Amherst NE, Albuquerque, NM 87100.

Lee D. Witkin GALLERY OWNER · WRITER Born in East Orange, New Jersey, in 1935, Witkin earned a BA from New York University, New York City, in 1958.

He owns Witkin Gallery in New York City, which he founded in 1969. He also serves as a consultant to Time Inc., for their photographic archive, and is an adviser and appraiser for major museums and private collectors. From 1959 to 1969 Witkin was a writer, photographer and manager at *Constructioneer* magazine, and in 1967 was an editor of *Popular Science*.

PUBLICATIONS Anthologies: *A Ten Year Salute*, 1979; *The Photograph Collector's Guide*, w/ Barbara London, 1979; *The Julien Levy Collection*, 1977.

ADDRESS Witkin Gallery, 41 E 57 St, New York, NY 10022.

(George Benjamin) Ben Wittick PHOTOGRAPHER · ETHNOLOGIST Born January 1, 1845, in Huntingdon, Pennsylvania, Wittick died August 30, 1903, in Ft. Wingate, New Mexico. He learned photography from E. E. Mangold, a local photographer in Moline, Illinois, about 1863. Wittick served in the U.S. Army (1861–63),

then operated a studio in Moline before moving (about 1878–79) to Santa Fe, New Mexico, where he worked for the Atchison, Topeka & Santa Fe Railroad. He began a partnership with R. W. Russell about 1880 that lasted until 1884. Russell managed the studio's operation (in Albuquerque from 1881) while Wittick traveled and photographed for the Atlantic & Pacific Railroad and participated in the Stevenson Expedition in Arizona territory (1882). Wittick then operated a studio in Gallup, New Mexico, from 1884 to 1900, with a second studio in Ft. Wingate, where he established a permanent residence in 1900. A rattlesnake he captured for a gift to the Hopi Indians caused his death.

The photographer produced a large body of work that included stereo views, lantern slides and large-format (11 x 14) negatives and prints. Aside from his work for the railroads, he was an ardent recorder of Indian life, and made images of the Hopi Snake Dances in Arizona through the 1880s and 1890s. During that time he made many trips to the Grand Canyon, Zuñi Pueblo, and other parts of Arizona.

PUBLICATIONS Monographs: *The Wittick Collection*, Arthur Olivas, vol. 1, 1971; *Southwest 1880, with Ben Wittick, Pioneer Photographer*, Gar & Maggy Packard, 1970. Books: *Photography in New Mexico from the Dageurreotype to the Present*, Van Deren Coke, 1979; *The Railroad Collection*, vol. 1, Vernon Glover, 1977; *Photographers of the New Mexico Territory 1854–1912*, Richard Rudisill, 1973. Periodicals: "An 1883 Expedition to the Grand Canyon—Pioneer Photographer Ben Wittick Views the Marvels of the Colorado," Tom Wittick, *The American West*, Mar 1973; "Ben Wittick Views the Pueblos," summer 1966, "A Ben Wittick Item, 1883," Tom Wittick, June 1958, *El Palacio: Journal of the Museum of New Mexico*; "Ben Wittick, Pioneer Photographer of the Southwest," Richard van Valkenburgh, *Arizona Highways*, Aug 1942; "Indian Types of Beauty," R. W. Shufeldt, *The American Field*, 36, 1891.

COLLECTIONS Ariz. Hist. Soc., Tucson; El Paso Pub. Lib., Tex.; Ft. Larned Cllctn., Kans.; Hubbell Trading Post Natl. Monument, Ariz.; L/C, Wash., D.C.; Mus. of N. Mex., Santa Fe; Science Mus. of Minn., St. Paul; Univ. of Tex., El Paso Centennial Mus., Austin.

ARCHIVE Museum of New Mexico, Box 2087, Santa Fe, NM 87503.

Ronald W. Wohlauer PHOTOGRAPHER · TEACHER Born July 1, 1947, in Akron, Colorado, Wohlauer earned a BA (1969) and MA (1970) in

History from the University of Colorado, Boulder. He also took an MA in Photography from the University of Oregon (1973) and studied with Brett Weston (1972–74).

Wohlauer has been chairperson of the Photography Department of Community College of Denver since 1975 and director of the Darkroom Gallery in Denver since 1974. He taught photography at Metropolitan State College, Denver, in 1973–74.

A member of SPE since 1975, the photographer worked on the NEA-funded "From This Land Survey Project" in 1978 and received a First Place Award for Photography from Colorado Celebration of the Arts in 1975.

"I attempt to capture the effects of light on the myriad forms and designs on the landscape and man's temporary imprint upon it," says Wohlauer. He produces large-format black-and-white landscapes, environmental details, portraits and nudes.

PUBLICATIONS Anthology: *The Great West: Survey of Western American Photography Since 1950*, 1977. Periodicals: *The Image Continuum*, May 1976; *Camera*, Sept 1975.

COLLECTIONS Amer. Oil Co. Fine Art Cllctn., Denver; Atlantic Richfield Corp. Print Cllctn., Denver, Colo.; Calumet Photographic Corp., Elk Grove Village, Ill.; Denver Art Mus.; Exeter Corp., Denver; MOMA, NYC.

DEALER Douglas Kenyon, 155 E Ohio St, Chicago, IL 60611.

ADDRESS 4301 E 13 Ave, Denver, CO 80220.

Marion Post Wolcott *PHOTOGRAPHER* Born June 7, 1910, in Montclair, New Jersey, Wolcott studied at the New School for Social Research (1928) and at New York University (1929), both in New York City, before taking her BA in 1934 from the University of Vienna, Austria. In 1935 she studied photography with Ralph Steiner in New York City.

Most recently a teacher in American schools in Iran and Pakistan (1960, 1962, 1963), Wolcott worked in the Documentary Photography Section of the U.S. Farm Security Administration (FSA) (1938–41). Previous to that she had been a staff photographer for the *Philadelphia Evening Bulletin* (1936–38) and a freelance photographer in New York City (1935).

She has been a member of the Newspaper Guild since 1936 and also belongs to the New York Photo League, ACLU, Art Affiliates of the University of California at Santa Barbara and Friends of Photography.

Wolcott participated in a documentary film about the FSA photography project in 1979.

Her FSA photography documented the New Deal era, especially the conditions of rural life, small towns and migrants. She emphasized the contrast between "the fertility and beauty of the U.S., the affluent and the middle class with the areas of poverty." Wolcott currently works in color.

PUBLICATIONS Anthologies: *The Photograph Collector's Guide*, Lee D. Witkin & Barbara London, 1979; *A Vision Shared*, Hank O'Neal, 1976; *In This Proud Land*, Roy E. Stryker & Nancy Wood, 1973.

COLLECTIONS Art Inst. of Chicago; Brooklyn Mus., N.Y.; IMP/GEH, Rochester; L/C, Wash., D.C.; Metro. Mus. of Art, NYC; MOMA, NYC; Mus. of Fine Arts, Houston; Portland Mus. of Art, Ore.; Santa Barbara Mus. of Art, Calif.; Smithsonian Inst., Wash., D.C.; Univ. of Minn., Minneapolis. Natl. Gall. of Can., Ottawa, Ontario.

DEALERS Witkin Gall., 41 E 57 St, New York, NY 10022; Lowinsky-Arai Gall., 228 Grant Ave, San Francisco, CA 94108; Focus Gall., 2146 Union St, San Francisco, CA 94123.

ADDRESS 2265 Broadway, Apt 9, San Francisco, CA 94115.

Ole Woldbye *PHOTOGRAPHER* Born July 23, 1930, in Copenhagen, Woldbye studied at the University of Copenhagen (1949–54) and received his photographic education at the National Museum in Copenhagen (1954–58).

Since 1962 Woldbye has been a freelance photographer, working for museums in Copenhagen, such as the Museum of Decorative Art, Copenhagen Town Museum and Thorvaldsen's Museum.

He belongs to the Danish Photographic Society (MDFF). In 1977 he won a grant from the National Art Fund (Statens Kunstfond).

The photographer's main interests are nineteenth-century sculpture, Venice, the North Sea region. He works in medium and large format.

PUBLICATIONS Books: *En Københavnsk Porcelænsfabriks Historie*, E. Lassen, 1978; *Piazza Navona*, Knud Voss, 1975; *Dansk Glas*, E. Lassen, 1975; *Amalienborg*, Viggo Sten Møller, 1973; *Arkitekten Nikolaj Eigtved*, Knud Voss, 1971; Dansk Lertøj, Louis Ehlers, 1967; *Møbelkunsten*, Ole Wanscher, 1966; *Henning Koppel*, V. W. Møller, 1965; *Dansk Keramik*, M. Bodelsen, 1960; *Patrick Nordstrøm*, M. Bodelsen, 1956.

COLLECTIONS Mus. Boymans-van Beuningen, Rotterdam, The Netherlands; Mus. of Decorative

Art, Copenhagen; Royal Lib., Copenhagen; Statens Kunstfond, Denmark; Thorvaldsen Mus., Copenhagen; Willumsen Mus., Frederikssund, Denmark.

ADDRESS Kunstindustrimuseet, Bredgade 68, DK 1260, Copenhagen K, Denmark.

Richard Woldendorp *PHOTOGRAPHER* Born on January 1, 1927, in Utrecht, The Netherlands, Woldendorp is a freelance photographer and a member of the Institute of Australian Photographers (IAP).

Working in 35mm with color transparencies, the artist makes abstract images of nature.

PUBLICATIONS Books: *Perth: 150 Years*, 1979; *Looking West*, 1977; *Walkabout*, 1974; *Indonesia*, 1972; *A Million Square*, 1969; *The Hidden Face of Australia*, 1968.

COLLECTION Philip Morris Cllctn., Melbourne, Australia.

DEALER Church St Gallery, 384 Church St, Richmond, Victoria 3121, Australia.

ADDRESS 2 Binbrook Pl, Darlington 6070, Western Australia.

Daniel Wolf *DEALER · GALLERY OWNER* Born March 29, 1955, in Cheyenne, Wyoming, Wolf received a BFA in 1975 from Bennington College, Vermont.

He is currently president of Daniel Wolf Gallery, Inc., and Daniel Wolf Press, Inc. He also became vice-president of the Association of International Photographic Art Dealers in 1979.

PUBLICATIONS Periodicals: "The Pictorial Ideal," *Modern Photography*, Aug 1979; "The Golden Age of Landscape Photography," *American Art and Antiques*, Mar/Apr 1979; "Portrait of the Dealer as a Young Collector," *Village Voice*, Dec 4, 1978; "Viewpoint by Jacob Deschin," *Popular Photography*, Feb 1978.

ADDRESS 30 W 57 St, New York, NY 10019.

Linda Ann Wolf *PHOTOGRAPHER* Born in Los Angeles on March 17, 1950, Wolf studied at L'Institut Americain in Aix-en-Provence, France, and at L'Ecole Expérimentale Photographique in La Coste, France.

A freelance photographer since 1978, she also worked for Los Angeles Citywide Mural Project and for the Social and Public Art Resource Center in Venice, California (1978–79). Wolf was employed by Prolab Photographic Lab in Los Angeles (1976–78) and taught for UCLA Extension in 1976.

She won grants in 1980 from the Center for Visual Arts in Oakland, California, and in 1978 from the California Arts Council in Sacramento and the Bench Ad Company, Los Angeles.

In her work the photographer strives to "exalt people, to show them with dignity and integrity," and "to celebrate the common ordinariness which unites all people regardless of race or national boundaries, age or sex. . . ."

PUBLICATIONS Anthologies: *Bachy*, 13, winter 1978, 11, spring 1978 (Papa Bach Pubs., Los Angeles). Periodicals: "Art on the Streets," review, Gail Stavitsky, *Artweek*, Sept 8, 1979; *Petersen's Photographic Magazine*, May 1977, May 1976; review, Burt Prelutsky, *Los Angeles Times*, July 1976.

COLLECTIONS est Fndn., San Francisco; Oakland Mus., Calif.; Steve White Cllctn., Los Angeles. Bibliothèque Nationale, Paris; Musée Cantini, Marseille, France; Musée Het Sterkshof, Belgium.

ADDRESS 2243 22 St, Santa Monica, CA 90405.

Bernard Pierre Wolff *PHOTOGRAPHER · GRAPHIC DESIGNER* Born November 26, 1930, in Connérré, France, Wolff was assistant to Henri Langlois and Charles Harbutt for five years. He also worked with Henri Cartier-Bresson in India.

Since 1969 Wolff has been a freelance photographer and graphic designer for UNICEF and other United Nations agencies, as well as the Foreign Policy Association in New York City. His work has taken him on extensive travels to developing countries in Asia, Africa and Latin America on United Nations photo missions. From 1959 to 1968 he worked as art director for the Foreign Policy Association.

Working in 35mm black-and-white, Wolff characterizes himself as a "street photographer." His main subjects are "characters in the urban landscape, the marginal, unconventional, outcast or bizarre, the cultural confusion of the streets in the world's great cities: New York, Delhi, Benares, Quito, Rome and the towns of industrialized and developing countries." He makes use of "lines, curves and shadows to emphasize the intrinsic design of socially disorganized subjects. [There is a] strong element of social metaphor."

PUBLICATIONS Book: *Friends and Friends of Friends*, 1978. Periodicals: *Zoom*, Sept/Oct 1979, June/July 1976 (France); *The British Journal of Photography Annual*, 1977; *Progresso Fotografico*, Jan 1977; *Modern Photography*, Nov 1975.

COLLECTION Bibliothèque Nationale, Paris.

REPRESENTATIVES Magnum Photos, 251 Park

Ave S, New York, NY 10017; Photo Researchers, 60 E 56 St, New York, NY 10022.

ADDRESS 310 E 46 St, Apt 4N, New York, NY 10017.

Myron Gilmore Wood PHOTOGRAPHER Born December 11, 1921, in Wilson, Oklahoma, he received a BFA degree in music in 1943. He studied with Edward Weston in 1948 and 1949 and later with Roy Stryker from 1967 to 1973.

Since 1961 he has been self-employed. From 1960 to 1963 he was a photographer for the Ford Foundation Education Project in Colorado, and from 1951 to 1961 a photographer and assistant curator for the Colorado Springs Fine Arts Center. Prior to 1951 Wood worked as a pianist (until 1947) and freelance photographer.

He was a member of ASMP from 1962 to 1966, and the Musicians Union from 1947 to 1950. In 1979 he was awarded a grant from the Waco Foundation to photograph Waco, Texas, and surrounding McLennan County. He was also the recipient of a grant from the Bonfils Foundation in 1966.

PUBLICATIONS Books: *Hollering Sun*, w/ Nancy Wood, 1972; *Colorado, Big Mountain Country*, 1969; *Little Wrangler*, w/Nancy Wood, 1966; *Durango*, 1964; *Central City*, 1963. Anthology: *Vision & Expression*, 1969.

COLLECTIONS Colo. Springs Fine Arts Ctr., Colo.; Denver Art Mus., Colo.; IMP/GEH, Rochester; Metro. Mus. of Art, NYC; MOMA, NYC; Pikes Peak Regional Lib., Colo. Springs; Pueblo Regional Lib., Colo.; Univ. of Louisville Photographic Archives, Ky.; Univ. of Nebr., Sheldon Memorial Art Gall., Lincoln.

ADDRESS 20 W Columbia, Colo. Springs, CO 80907.

Nancy Wood WRITER · PHOTOGRAPHER Wood was born in Trenton, New Jersey, on June 20, 1936. Her mentor was Roy Stryker (1962–74).

A self-employed author and photographer, she is a member of the Author's Guild. In 1977 Wood received a grant in photography from the Colorado State Historical Society and in 1976 she received a grant from the Colorado Centennial/Bicentennial Commission for photographic work.

PUBLICATIONS Books Fiction: *When Buffalo Free the Mountains*, 1980; *War Cry on a Prayer Feather*, 1979; *The Man Who Gave Thunder to the Earth*, 1977; *The King of Liberty Bend*, 1976; *Many Winters*, 1975; *The Last Five Dollar Baby*, 1973; *Hollering Sun*, 1972; *Little Wrangler*, 1966. Non-fiction books: *The Grass Roots People*,

1978; *In This Proud Land*, w/Roy Stryker, 1974; *Clearcut: the Deforestation of America*, 1973; *Colorado: Big Mountain Country*, 1969.

COLLECTION Heritage Ctr., Denver, Colo.

ADDRESS 825 Paseo, Colorado Springs, CO 80907.

Roger Wood PHOTOGRAPHER · CONSULTANT · JOURNALIST Born August 6, 1920, in Madras, India, Wood studied photography at Harrow Technical School and Bolt Court, London, England, and was awarded the City and Guilds of London's Diploma in Photography.

A self-employed proprietor since 1947, he previously was assistant editor of *The Amateur Photographer* magazine in London and assistant production controller for film finishing at Kodak Ltd., Harrow, England.

Wood has been a member of the National Union of Journalists since 1953 and was named a fellow of RPS in 1951 and of the Royal Society of Arts in 1978. He received three fellowships from the Institute of British Photographers in 1951 and an Encyclopaedia Britannica Press Award in 1955.

PUBLICATIONS Books: *An Introduction to the Antiquities of Saudi Arabia*, w/Prof. Abdullah Masry, 1975 (Riyadh); *Persia/Iran*, 1970; *Roman Africa in Colour*, w/Sir Mortimer Wheeler, 1966; *Egypt in Colour*, w/Margaret Drower, 1964; *Shakespeare at the Old Vic*, w/Mary Clarke, 3 vols., 1956, 1955, 1954; *The D'Oyly Carte Album*, 1953; *The New York City Ballet*, w/B. Manchester, 1953; *The Theatre Ballet of Sadlers Wells*, 1952; *The Sadlers Wells Ballet*, 1951; *Katherine Dunham*, w/Richard Buckle, 1949 (London).

COLLECTIONS Dance Archive, Lincoln Ctr., NYC. Natl. Mus. of Oman, Muscat; Natl. Mus. of Qatar, Doha; Natl. Mus. of Saudi Arabia, Riyadh.

ADDRESS 293 Liverpool Rd, London N1 1NF, England.

Walter Bentley Woodbury PHOTOGRAPHER · INVENTOR Born in Manchester, England, in 1834, Woodbury died in 1885. Apprenticed as a youth in a Manchester patent office, he early on took pleasure in building camera obscuras from cigar boxes and spectacle lenses.

Woodbury joined the Australian gold rush in 1851 only to find on his arrival in Melbourne that the diggings were being abandoned. He worked at odd jobs for several years, eventually becoming a draftsman in the engineering department of the Melbourne waterworks. He started using a second-hand camera he had bought, photographing the construction of the waterworks and other buildings in the city. Woodbury then moved to Java, doing much photography there, and returned to England in 1859. The next year he went back to Java and established a photographic business for a few years until ill health forced his return to England once again. He then put his efforts into photomechanical inventions.

Woodbury's most famous invention (1864) was the woodburytype, a continuous-tone carbon photomechanical printing process that allowed low-cost, permanent reproductions. In the next twenty years he continued to improve the process, which was used extensively for book illustrations during the rest of the nineteenth century. His other inventions included a camera for use in unmanned balloons, transparencies and special photographs, sensitized films and improvements in optical lanterns and stereoscopes. Woodbury is also remembered for his documentary photographs of London's poor.

PUBLICATIONS Books: *Evolution of Rotogravure*, J. S. Mertle, 1957; *History of Photography*, J. M. Eder, 3rd ed. 1905, repr. 1945; *History and Handbook of Photography*, Gaston Tissandier, 1876; *Treasure Spots of the World*, 1875 (Ward. Lock & Tyler: London); *Science at Home*, 188? (London). Anthology: *Photography's Great Inventors*, Louis W. Sipley, 1965. Periodicals: *Image*, 1957; *Bild und Ton*, 1955; *Photographic Times*, 1893; *Philadelphia Photographer*, 1885, 1870; *British Journal of Photography*, 1884.

Don Worth *PHOTOGRAPHER · TEACHER* [See plate 120] Born in Hayes Center, Nebraska, on June 2, 1924, Worth earned a BA (1949) and MA (1951) in Music from Manhattan School of Music in New York City. He is self-taught in photography.

Worth has been a professor of art at San Francisco State University since 1962. He received an NEA Fellowship in 1980 and a Guggenheim Fellowship in 1974.

PUBLICATIONS Catalogs: *Photographs*, 1977 (Univ. of Neb., Sheldon Mem. Art Gall.: Lincoln); *Plants, Photographs by Don Worth*, 1977 (Friends of Photography: Carmel, Calif.); *Don Worth, Photographs*, 1973 (San Francisco Mus. of Modern Art).

PORTFOLIO *Out of State* (group), 1978 (San Francisco State Univ.).

COLLECTIONS Addison Gall. of Amer. Art, Andover, Mass.; Art Inst. of Chicago; CCP, Tucson; IMP/GEH, Rochester; MOMA, NYC; New Orleans Mus. of Art; Norton Simon Mus. of Art, Pasadena, Calif.; Oakland Mus., Calif.; San Francisco Mus. of Modern Art; UCLA; Univ. of Nebr., Sheldon Mem. Art Gall., Lincoln. Bibliothèque Nationale, Paris.

ADDRESS Art Dept, San Francisco State Univ, 1600 Holloway Ave, San Francisco, CA 94132.

Frederick Charles Luther Wratten *INVENTOR · PHOTOGRAPHIC EQUIPMENT MANUFACTURER* Born in 1840, Wratten died in 1926.

Starting his career as a schoolteacher and organist, he moved to London at age twenty-one to become a clerk in the photographic and optical warehouse of Joseph Solomon. Stimulated to begin his own experiments by news of the discovery of gelatin as an emulsion for sensitization, Wratten invented the use of alcohol in drying gelatin emulsion and removing unwanted silver nitrate (1876). In 1877, with Henry Wainwright, he formed Wratten & Wainwright in order to manufacture and sell photographic supplies for the collodion and new gelatin dry processes. One of the first firms in England to offer commercially successful dry plates, Wratten & Wainwright is also credited with introducing the process of "noodling" gelatin emulsions before washing (1878). Wratten continued the business after Wainwright's death in 1892. In 1906 S. H. Wratten, his son, and C. E. Kenneth Mees joined the business; together they soon introduced the first English panchromatic plates and filters. In 1907 Mees and the company patented a color-screen process. The company was sold to George Eastmen in 1912 and Wratten joined Kodak Ltd. in Harrow, where the manufacturing processes were transferred.

PUBLICATIONS Books: *From Dry Plates to Ektachrome Film*, C. E. K. Mees, 1961; *Memoirs of a Photochemist*, Fritz Wentzel, 1960; *Theory of the Photographic Process*, C. E. K. Mees, 1944; *History of 3-Color Photography*, E. J. Wall, 1925; *History of Photography*, W. Jerome Harrison, 1892. Anthology: *Photography's Great Inventors*, Louis W. Sipley, 1965. Periodicals: *Photographic Journal*, 1939; *British Journal Photographic Almanac*, 1926, 1878; *Photographische Mittheilungen*, 1879, 1878; *British Journal of Photography*, 1878; *Photographic News*, 1878, 1877.

Henry Wright *PHOTOGRAPHER · BUSINESSMAN* Born in the south of England in 1844, Wright died in Wellington, New Zealand, in 1936.

Until 1877 Wright worked in the Auckland province of New Zealand as a storekeeper, mine manager, company secretary and commercial agent, also serving as accountant on the Auckland City Council. He moved to Wellington in 1877, working at several posts and becoming active in community affairs. The photographer was also a horticulturist and a pioneer in the meat-freezing industry.

Wright co-founded the Wellington Employers Association in 1890 and was appointed landscape photographer to Lord Onslow during the latter's term of office, 1889–92. At the New Zealand Exhibition of 1889, Wright was awarded a special prize for his collection of twenty-six photographs.

Generally working in a 6 x 8 format with dry plates, he photographed landscapes, ethnographic images, made family shots and some portrait studies. He traveled widely in the North Island of New Zealand, making notable photos of the timber-trading ports of the far north as well as of the city and environs of Wellington. Of his work, 360 images survive.

PUBLICATIONS Book: *Little Barrier Island*, W. M. Hamilton, 1961 (Wellington, N.Z.). Periodical: "The Henry Wright Collection of Photographic Negatives," John Sullivan, *The Alexander Turnbull Library Record*, May 1979.

ARCHIVES Alexander Turnbull Library, POB 12-349, Wellington, New Zealand.

Willie Anne Wright   PHOTOGRAPHER · PAINTER   Born June 6, 1924, in Richmond, Virginia, Wright earned a BS in Psychology from the College of William and Mary in Williamsburg, Virginia (1945), and an MFA in Painting from Virginia Commonwealth University, Richmond (1964). She studied photography at the latter school from 1972 to 1976 and at the Visual Studies Workshop in Rochester, New York, in 1974.

Wright has been a freelance photographer, painter, printmaker and lecturer since 1964. Working mainly with pinhole cameras, she has designed a number of cameras since 1972 that accept both paper and film negatives. She has also developed a system for using Cibachrome for direct color exposures.

She has belonged to the Virginia Society for the Photographic Arts since 1976.

PUBLICATION Periodical: "Willie Anne Wright at Deja Vue," *Art-Magazine*, Nov-Dec 1979.

COLLECTIONS All in Virginia: Bank of Va., Richmond; First & Merchants Bank, Richmond; 14th District Federal Reserve, Richmond; Mary Baldwin Coll., Staunton; Philip Morris Cllctn., Richmond; Richmond Pub. Schools; Va. Mus., Richmond; Walter Cecil Rawls Mus., Surry.

DEALERS Deja Vue Gall. of Photographic Art, 122 Scollard St, Toronto, Canada; Scott-McKennis Fine Art, 3465 W Cary St, Richmond, VA 23221; Afterimage Gall., The Quadrangle #151, 2800 Routh St, Dallas, TX 75201.

ADDRESS 205 Strawberry St, Richmond, VA 23220.

Dazhen Wu   MUSICIAN · PHOTOGRAPHER [See plate 132] Born June 25, 1944, in Chunchen, Szechuan, Peoples Republic of China, Wu received a BA from Central Music College in Peking (1967). As of this writing he was studying at the University of Arizona, Tucson.

Wu played clarinet for the Peking Ballet Symphony Orchestra. His photographs have appeared in *Chinese Photographer* and *China Popular Photographer* (1978–79). He belongs to the Chinese Association of Photographers and Peking April Photographers.

The photographer creates landscapes "closely related to the style of Chinese traditional paintings of mountains, lakes, gardens." He also takes "quick, spontaneous photographs of activities in the streets, the markets and public places."

COLLECTIONS CCP, Tucson. Peking Mus. of Art.

ADDRESS 4259 N Limberlost Place, Tucson, AZ 85705.

Charles L. Wyrick, Jr.   MUSEUM DIRECTOR · PHOTOGRAPHER · WRITER   Born May 5, 1939, in Greensboro, North Carolina, Wyrick received an MFA from the University of North Carolina at Greensboro, and a BA from Davidson College in 1961. Primarily self-taught as a photographer, he studied in workshops with Emmet Gowin and Duane Michals.

Presently he is the director of Gibbes Art Gallery in Charleston, South Carolina. Prior to that he was director of the Delaware Art Museum in Wilmington (1973–79), president of Research & Restoration, Inc., in Richmond, Virginia (1970–73), art and architecture critic for the *Richmond News Leader* in Virginia (1970–73), and executive director for the Association for the Preservation of Virginia Antiquities, in Richmond (1968–70).

Wyrick is a member of the Association of Art Museum Directors, the American Association of Museums, the Society of Architectural Historians and SPE.

Working in 35mm and 4 x 5 in both black-and-white and color, he focuses on landscape, genre and portraiture. He also does research, writes about and exhibits works by young American photographers.

PUBLICATIONS (text only) Books: *The 17th Street Market*, w/David H. White, 1973. Catalogs: *Gertrude Kasebier*, 1979 (Univ. of Delaware); *Clarence White*, 1978 (Univ. of Delaware).

ADDRESS c/o Gibbes Art Gallery, 135 Meeting St, Charleston, SC 29401.

Y

Michiko Yajima *GALLERY DIRECTOR* Born February 28, 1937, in Tokyo, Japan, Yajima graduated from Toyo Eiwa College in Tokyo (1957) and New York School of Interior Design (1959). She studied photography at Loyola College in Montreal, Canada, in 1969–70.

Since 1974 Yajima has directed Yajima/Galerie. She belongs to the Association of International Art Photography Dealers.

Her gallery specializes in twentieth-century photographs, vintage and contemporary prints.

ADDRESS Yajima/Galerie, 307 Ste Catherine St W, Suite 515, Montreal, Quebec H2X 2A3, Canada.

John Yang *PHOTOGRAPHER · ARCHITECT* Born April 16, 1933 in China, Yang received a BA in 1954 from Harvard University, Cambridge, Massachusetts, and a BA in 1957 from the University of Pennsylvania, Philadelphia. He studied with Minor White at the San Francisco Art Institute in 1951.

Having retired as an architect in 1977, Yang has since been self-employed as a photographer. He belongs to the Sierra Club, N.Y.–N.J. Trail Conference, the Palisades, New Jersey Nature Association, and is a patron of the Mohonk Trust.

Yang won the Excellence in Design Medal in 1957 from the University of Pennsylvania and a John Harvard Honorary Scholarship in 1953.

Using black-and-white 8 x 10 negatives, he shoots landscapes in the northeastern United States.

PUBLICATIONS Anthology: *Photographing Children*, 1971. Periodicals: *Popular Photography*, Nov 1978; *Infinity Magazine*, July 1968.

DEALER Marcuse Pfeifer Gall., 825 Madison Ave, New York, NY 10021.

ADDRESS 325 E 51 St, New York, NY 10022.

Steve Yates *CURATOR · PHOTOGRAPHER · PAINTER* Born November 14, 1949, in Chicago, Illinois, Yates received a BFA from the University of Nebraska, Lincoln (1972), and an MA (1975) and MFA (1978) from the University of New Mexico, Albuquerque.

Currently Curator of Photography and Prints at the Museum of Fine Arts, Santa Fe, New Mexico, he taught photography, history, drawing and painting from 1975 to 1979 at the University of New Mexico. Yates worked as a curatorial assistant at the University of New Mexico Art Museum in 1974–75 and at Sheldon Memorial Art Gallery (University of Nebraska, Lincoln) in 1973–74.

He received a Ford Foundation Fellowship in 1977.

Yates adds painting with acrylics, drawing and abrasions to his color photographs.

PUBLICATIONS Catalogs: *Altered Landscapes*, 1979 (Florida School of the Arts: Palatka); *Construction Series*, 1978, *Photographs*, 1977 (Sheldon Mem. Art Gall., Univ. of Nebr.: Lincoln).

COLLECTIONS Los Angeles Ctr. for Photographic Studies; Mus. of Fine Arts, Santa Fe; Univ. of Nebr., Sheldon Mem. Art Gall., Lincoln; Univ. of N. Mex. Art Mus., Albuquerque.

ADDRESS Museum of Fine Arts, POB 2087, Santa Fe, NM 87503.

Max Yavno *PHOTOGRAPHER* Born April 26, 1911, in New York City, Yavno earned a BSS in 1932 from City College of New York, then attended the Graduate School of Business Administration (1932–33) and the Graduate Faculty of Political Science (1933–34) at Columbia University in New York City. He roomed with Aaron Siskind from 1939 to 1942, and later studied cinematography at University of California in Los Angeles (1972–75).

Currently concentrating on his personal work,

Yavno operated his own commercial photography studio in Los Angeles (1954–75). Previously he worked on the WPA (1936–42) and as a social worker for the New York City Home Relief Bureau (1935). He was president of the Photo League in 1938–39.

PUBLICATIONS Monographs: *The Los Angeles Book*, w/Lee Shippey, 1950; *The San Francisco Book*, w/Herb Caen, 1948. Book: *The Wine Book*, w/M. K. Fisher, 1962.

COLLECTION MOMA, NYC.

DEALER G. Ray Hawkins, 7224 Melrose Ave, Los Angeles, CA 90046.

ADDRESS 7207 Melrose Ave, Los Angeles, CA 90046.

Francis Rowland Yerbury PHOTOGRAPHER Born in October 1885, Yerbury died in July 1970, in London.

In 1901 he was an office boy at the Architectural Association (AA), where he was promoted to secretary in 1911. His efforts contributed to the success of that lively association (he served as secretary for twenty-six years), and he helped create one of the finest schools of architecture in the country, The Building Centre, of which he was co-founder and director from 1932 to 1961.

Yerbury was awarded an Order of the British Empire and was elected an Honorary Associate of the Royal Institute of British Architects (1924).

He made a considerable contribution to modern architecture by his photography of new buildings in Scandinavia, Germany and Holland. He was considered brilliant with a camera, and "had an eye for composition and detail second to none among the architectural photographers of his time" *(London Times)*.

PUBLICATIONS Monographs: *One Hundred Photographs*, foreword by James Bone, 1935 (Jordon-Gaskell: London); *Modern Dutch Buildings*, 1931; *Eighteenth Century Bath*, 1930; *Small Modern English Houses*, 1929 (Gollancz: London); *Modern European Buildings*, 1928; *Georgian Details of Domestic Architecture*, 1926 (E. Benn: London); *The Human Form and Its Use in Art*, intro. by G. Montague Ellwood, 1924. Books: *Modern Homes Illustrated*, ed., 1947 (Odhams: London); *The Old Bank of England*, w/H. Rooksby Steele, 1930; *Examples of Modern French Architecture*, w/Howard Robertson, 1928; *Modern Danish Architecture*, ph. & ed. w/ Kay Fisker, 1927; *Roedean School*, w/L. Cofe Cornford, 1927 (E. Benn: London); *Dutch Architecture*, w/J. P. Mieras, 1926; *Lesser Known Architecture of Spain*, 1925–26; *Modern English Houses and Interiors*, ed. w/C. H. James, 1925 (E.

Benn: London); *Old Domestic Architecture of Holland*, intro. by Dr. Ir. D. F. Slothouwer, 1924 (Architectural Press: London); *Small Houses for the Community*, w/C. H. James, 1924 (Lockwood: London); *Architectural Students' Handbook*, 1922 (Technical Journals: London); *Studies of the Human Figure*, w/G. M. Ellwood, 1918 (Batsford: London).

Becky Young PHOTOGRAPHER Born March 18, 1939, in Springfield, Massachusetts, Young earned a BFA in 1961 from the Rhode Island School of Design, Providence.

Since 1975 she has been on the faculty of the University of Pennsylvania, Philadelphia, and in 1976 she also taught at the University City Arts League in Philadelphia. From 1964 to 1967 Young belonged to the faculty of the Boston Center for Adult Education, and from 1961 to 1964 she was an assistant to Harry Callahan at Rhode Island School of Design.

She has photographed the nude since 1967, first in black-and-white and recently in color. Originally she defined nudes "classically as pure form," she says, but her newer work "transcends surface realities and captures the private selves of women and men alone or interacting with others in their environment."

PUBLICATION Periodical: "Waiting for Becky," *American Photographer*, Oct 1979.

DEALERS Graham Gall., 1014 Madison Ave, New York, NY 10021; Marion Locks Gall., 1524 Walnut St, Philadelphia, PA 19102.

ADDRESS 230 S 20 St, Philadelphia, PA 19103.

Cheryl Gwen Younger PHOTOGRAPHER · TEACHER Born December 26, 1946, in Jennings, Missouri, Younger earned a BS in Business (1970) from the University of Missouri, St. Louis. She then took an MA in Art and Art History/Photography (1976) and an MFA in Art (1977) from the University of Iowa, Iowa City, her major influences being John Schulze and Peter Feldstein. Younger served assistantships in 1974 and 1975 at Ansel Adams Gallery Spring Workshop. ·

She has taught at Bemidji State University, Bemidj, Minnesota, since 1978, and previously was student activities adviser from 1973 to 1978 at the University of Iowa.

Younger belongs to CAA and the National Women's Studies Organization, and is a board member of North Country Arts Council. She serves as Midwest regional president of SPE.

Younger won a University of Iowa Staff Council Tuition Grant in 1976 and a Staff Tuition Grant in 1974.

PUBLICATIONS Books: *Poems for a Revolution*, Annette Van Dyke, 1979; *Individ og Autoritet. Drom, drift, fortrangning*, 1978 (Gags Forlag: Denmark). Anthology: *In-Sights: Self-Portraits by Women*, Joyce T. Cohen, ed., 1978. Periodicals: *American Photographer*, Dec 1979; "Creative Photography," *Northlight*, Nov 1979; *Northwest Photographer*, Sept 1978; *Popular Photography Annual 78*, Sept 1977.

COLLECTIONS St. Louis Art Mus., Mo.; Univ. of Iowa, Iowa City.

DEALER Yuen Lui Gall., 906 Pine St, Seattle, WA 98101.

ADDRESS 921 Lake Blvd, Bemidji, MN 56601.

Z

Richard D. Zakia *TEACHER · SCIENTIST* Born in 1925 in Rochester, New York, Zakia earned a BS in Photographic Science from Rochester Institute of Technology (1956) and an EdD in Educational Psychology from the University of Rochester (1970).

He has been coordinator of MFA photography at Rochester Institute of Technology since 1976, from 1970 to 1976 was the school's director of instructional research and development and was a professor of photographic science there from 1958 to 1969. Zakia served as a photographic engineer for Eastman Kodak from 1956 to 1958.

He belongs to SPE, Society for Aesthetics and Visual Literacy Association.

PUBLICATIONS Books: *Perceptual Quotes for Photographers*, 1980; *Visual Concepts for Photographers*, 1980; *The New Zone System Manual*, w/Minor White & Peter Lorenz, 1976; *Perception & Photography*, 1974; *Zone Systemizer*, w/John Dowdell, 1973; *Color Primer I & II*, w/Hollis N. Todd, 1974; *101 Experiments in Photography*, w/Todd, 1969; *Photographic Sensitometry*, w/Todd, 1969.

ADDRESS Rochester Institute of Technology/ Photography, 1 Lomb Dr, Rochester, NY 14623.

Carl Zeiss *INDUSTRIALIST · OPTICAL MANUFACTURER* Born September 11, 1816, in Weimar, Germany, Zeiss died December 3, 1888, in Jena, Germany. He completed the sixth form at the Weimar Gymnasium, then apprenticed to the mechanic Dr. Frederick Koerner. He also traveled and worked in places such as Vienna, Berlin, Stuttgart and Darmstadt, as was customary for one's education in those days.

Zeiss established a workshop in 1846 in Jena, where he manufactured magnifying glasses and microscopes. He began to make compound microscopes in 1858, a wasteful and time-consuming task at that time. Ernst Abbe was enlisted to develop the required optics to ease the process, which he achieved in 1871, guaranteeing the worldwide fame of Zeiss. In 1880 Abbe began to help Friedrich Otto Schott develop a technique for making optical glass, and in 1884 the Glass Technical Laboratory of Schott & Genossen at Jena was established. Abbe, by now a partner in the Zeiss works, Schott and Zeiss (with his son Roderich) each owned a third of the firm, which became the world's most famous producer of glass for photo lenses. In 1886, Zeiss hired Paul Rudolph, who developed anastigmat lenses for the company.

PUBLICATIONS Books: *Odyssey of 41 Glassmakers*, Walter Kiaulehn, 1959; *Ernest Abbe*, Norbert Gunther, 1946; *Zur Geschichte der Zeissischen Werkstaette biszum Tode Ernst Abbes*, Moritz von Rohr, 1936; *Zeiss Werkzeitschrift*, no. 50. Anthology: *Photography's Great Inventors*, Louis W. Sipley, 1965. Periodical: *Bild und Ton*, 1963, 1952, 1951.

Marilyn Zimmerman *TEACHER · PHOTOGRAPHER* Born February 4, 1952, in Gary, Indiana, Zimmerman received a BA from Purdue University in West Lafayette, Indiana, in 1974, where she studied under Steve Sprague, an associate professor, photographer and film maker. In 1979 she received an MFA from the School of the Art Institute of Chicago, studying under Barbara Crane, Ken Josephson and Joyce Neimanas.

Zimmerman has been employed as an assistant professor of art at Austin Peay State University in Clarksville, Tennessee, since September 1978.

She has been a member of SPE since 1978, and, since 1979, a member of the United Teaching Profession and the National Education Association/Tennessee Education Association. In 1979 she was the recipient of Bryon Lathrop Traveling Fellowship from the School of the Art Institute of Chicago.

Working with silver prints and Type C color, the photographer describes her work as "formally composed images of fabric camouflaged in natural environments."

PUBLICATIONS Periodicals: *Showcase*, Sept 1978; *Lightworks*, summer 1977.

COLLECTIONS Art Inst. of Chicago, Illinois; IMP/GEH, Rochester; San Francisco Art Mus., Calif.; Univ. of Arkansas, Fayetteville; Univ. of N. Mex., Albuquerque.

ADDRESS POB 8324 Austin Peay State Univ., Clarksville, TN 37040.

Philip B. Zimmerman PRINTMAKER · PHOTOGRAPHER · GRAPHIC DESIGNER Zimmerman was born in Bangkok, Thailand, on January 24, 1951, and received his BFA from Cornell University, Ithaca, New York (1973). He received an MFA at VSW (of State University of New York), Rochester, in 1980. His major influences have been Keith Smith, Gary Frost, John Wood and Joan Lyons.

For two years he taught photo-silk screen at Allofus Art Workshop in Rochester and in the VSW Summer Institute.

Zimmerman has belonged to SPE since 1977.

Especially interested in the book format, he uses printmaking mediums such as photo-offset and photo-silkscreen "as a tool for expression rather than merely as a way of reproducing photographs."

PUBLICATIONS Books: *C-Commercial*, 1979; *The Rusty Plate*, w/Tim Ahern, 1979; *Spine*, w/ Joan Lyons, 1979; *The Cure*, 1977, *Excerpts From Alphaville*, 1977 (self-pub.); *Calles i Reculls*, 1975 (G. Gili Editorial: Barcelona, Spain).

COLLECTIONS Cornell Univ., Johnson Art Mus., Ithaca, N.Y.; Franklin Furnace Archive, NYC; VSW Research Ctr., Rochester. Bibliothèque Nationale, Paris.

ADDRESS 29 Wellesley St, Rochester, NY 14607.

Harvey S. Zucker PHOTOGRAPHER · WRITER · EDITOR Zucker was born September 7, 1931, in the Bronx, New York City.

Currently the operator of A Photographers Place in New York City, he was previously technical editor of *Penthouse Photo World* magazine (1977) and a contributing editor of *Popular Photography*. He also once operated a commercial photographic studio in the New York area.

A member of SPE, Zucker is a founding member and fellow of the Photographic Historical Society of New York and was its president in 1971–72.

The photographer both works and conducts research in early photographic processes such as daguerreotype and tintype. He also researches the history of photography.

PUBLICATION Anthology: *Photography Year*, Time-Life Series, 1975.

COLLECTIONS IMP/GEH, Rochester; Smithsonian Inst., Wash., D.C.

ADDRESS 13 Dongan St, Staten Island, NY 10310.

Museums

UNITED STATES

ALABAMA

Birmingham Museum of Art
2000 Eighth Ave N
Birmingham 35203

Fine Arts Museum of the South
Langan Park
Mobile 36608

University Art Gallery
University of Alabama
Tuscaloosa 35486

ARIZONA

Art Gallery
Northern Arizona State University
Flagstaff 86001

Phoenix Art Museum
1625 N Central Ave
Phoenix 85004

Photography Southwest
4223 N Marshall Way
Scottsdale 85251

Arizona State University Art Collections
Tempe 85281

Northlight Gallery
Arizona State University
Tempe 85281

Center for Creative Photography
University of Arizona
843 E University Blvd
Tucson 85721

University of Arizona Museum of Art
Olive & Speedway
Tucson 85721

ARKANSAS

Fine Arts Gallery
University of Arkansas
Fayetteville 72701

Union Gallery
University of Arkansas
Fayetteville 72701

Arkansas Arts Center
MacArthur Park
POB 2137
Little Rock 72203

CALIFORNIA

The Bancroft Library
University of California at Berkeley
Berkeley 94720

Friends of Photography
Sunset Center
San Carlos & Ninth
Carmel 93921

Pomona College Art Gallery
Montgomery Art Center
Claremont 91711

Hippolyte Bayard Memorial Photo Gallery
Orange Coast College
2701 Fairview Rd
Costa Mesa 92626

Helen Euphrat Gallery
De Anza College
21250 Stevens Creek Rd
Cupertino 95104

Memorial Union Art Gallery
University of California at Davis
Davis 95616

Fresno Arts Center
3033 E Yale Ave
Fresno 93703

Brand Library & Art Center
1601 W Mountain St
Glendale 91201

University Art Gallery
California State University
25800 Hilary St
Hayward 94542

Laguna Beach Museum of Art
307 Cliff Dr
Laguna Beach 92651

La Jolla Museum of Contemporary Art
700 Prospect St
La Jolla 92037

Arco Center for Visual Arts
505 S Flower St
Los Angeles 90017

Fine Arts Gallery
California State University at Los Angeles
5151 State University Dr
Los Angeles 90032

Los Angeles County Museum of Art & Natural
  History
5905 Wilshire Blvd
Los Angeles 90036

Malone Art Gallery
Loyola Marymount University
7101 W 80 St
Los Angeles 90045

Southwest Museum
Highland Park
Los Angeles 90042

University Galleries
University of Southern California
University Park
Los Angeles 90007

University of California at Los Angeles
  Research Library
Dept of Special Collections
Boni Collection on the History of Photography
405 Hilgard Ave
Los Angeles 90024

Newport Harbor Art Museum
850 San Clemente Dr
Newport Beach 92660

Fine Arts Gallery
California State University at Northridge
Northridge 91324

Norton Simon Museum of Art
Colorado & Orange Grove Blvds
Pasadena 91105

Pasadena Public Library
285 E Walnut St
Pasadena 91101

California Museum of Photography
University of California at Riverside
Riverside 92502

California State Library
Library-Courts Bldg
POB 2037
Sacramento 95809

College Art Gallery
California State University at San Bernardino
5500 State College Pkwy
San Bernardino 92407

California Historical Society
2090 Jackson St
San Francisco 94109

California Palace of the Legion of Honor
Lincoln Park
San Francisco 94121

M. H. de Young Memorial Museum
Golden Gate Park
San Francisco 94118

San Francisco Museum of Modern Art
McAllister St & Van Ness Ave
San Francisco 94102

The Huntington Library
Art Gallery-Botanical Gardens
1151 Oxford Rd
San Marino 91108

Art Galleries
University of California at Santa Barbara
Santa Barbara 93106

Santa Barbara Museum of Art
1130 State St
Santa Barbara 93101

De Saisset Art Gallery & Museum
University of Santa Clara
Santa Clara 95053

Mary Porter Sesnon Art Gallery
University of California at Santa Cruz
College Five
Santa Cruz 95064

Art Gallery
Allan Hancock College
800 S College Dr
Santa Maria 93454

Department of Special Collections
Stanford University Libraries
Stanford 94304

Stanford University Museum of Art
Museum Way & Lomita
Stanford 94305

Art Gallery
College of the Pacific
University of the Pacific
Stockton 95211

The Oakland Museum
1000 Oak St
Oakland 94607

California Institute of Arts
Art Department
Valencia 91355

Mendocino County Museum
400 E Commercial
Willits 94590

COLORADO

Colorado Center for Photographic Studies
University of Colorado
Boulder 80302

Western Historical Collections
University of Colorado
Fine Arts Bldg
Boulder 80302

Fine Arts Gallery
Colorado Mountain College
POB 2208
Breckenridge 80424

Colorado Historical Society
The Colorado Heritage Center
1300 Broadway
Denver 80203

Colorado State Museum
State Historical Society of Colorado
200 14th Ave
Denver 80203

Works on Paper Gallery
Denver Art Museum
100 W 14th Ave Pkwy
Denver 80204

Historical Museum & Institute of Western
    Colorado
Fourth & Ute Sts
Grand Junction 81501

CONNECTICUT

Artworks Gallery
Asylum Hill Artist Coop
94 Allyn St
Hartford 06103

Wadsworth Atheneum
600 Main St
Hartford 06103

Davison Art Center
Wesleyan University
301 High St
Middletown 06457

American Literature Collection
Yale University
New Haven 06520

Beinecke Rare Book & Manuscript Library
1603A Yale Station
New Haven 06520

New Haven Colony Historical Society
114 Whitney Ave
New Haven 06510

Western Americana Collection
Yale University
New Haven 06520

Yale University Art Gallery
Chapel St at York
2006 Yale Station
New Haven 06520

Aldrich Museum of Contemporary Art
258 Main St
Ridgefield 06877

Mattatuck Museum
Waterbury 06701

DELAWARE

Delaware Art Museum
230 Kentmere Pkwy
Wilmington 19806

Eleutherian Mills Historical Library
Hagley Foundation Inc
Barley Mill Rd & Brandywine Crk
POB 3630 Greenville
Wilmington 19807

DISTRICT OF COLUMBIA

Corcoran Gallery of Art
17 St & New York Ave NW
Washington 20006

Georgetown University
Special Collections Division
37 & O Sts NW
Washington 20007

Joseph H. Hirshhorn Museum & Sculpture
    Garden
Eighth St & Independence Ave SW
Washington 20560

Library of Congress
Prints & Photographs Division
10 First St SE
Washington 20545

National Air & Space Museum
Smithsonian Institution
Independence Ave & Seventh St SW
Washington 20560

National Archives & Record Service
General Services Administration
Pennsylvania Ave & Eighth St NW
Washington 20408

National Collection of Fine Arts
Eighth & G Sts NW
Washington 20560

National Gallery of Art
Constitution Ave & Sixth St NW
Washington 20565

National Museum of History and Technology
Smithsonian Institution
Constitution Ave & 12 St NW
Washington 20560

National Museum of Natural History
Smithsonian Institution
Constitution Ave & Tenth St NW
Washington 20560

National Portrait Gallery
Eighth & F Sts NW
Washington 20560

Smithsonian Institution
Hall of Photography
1000 Jefferson Dr SW
Washington 20560

The Phillips Collection
1600 21 St NW
Washington 20009

United States Dept of Interior
C St betw 18 & 19 Sts NW
Washington 20240

FLORIDA

Broward Community College Art Gallery
Davie Rd
Fort Lauderdale 33314

University Gallery
University of Florida
Gainesville 32601

Jacksonville Art Museum
4160 Boulevard Center
Jacksonville 32207

Polk Public Museum
800 Palmetto
Lakeland 33801

John and Mabel Ringling Museum of Art
Box 1838
Sarasota 33578

Museum of Fine Arts
255 Beach Dr N
St Petersburg 33701

Florida Center for the Arts
University of South Florida
4202 E Fowler Ave
Tampa 33620

GEORGIA

High Museum of Art
1280 Peachtree St NE
Atlanta 30309

Columbus Museum of Arts & Sciences Inc
1251 Wynnton Rd
Columbus 31906

ILLINOIS

University Museum
Southern Illinois University
Carbondale 62901

Art Institute of Chicago
Michigan Ave & Adams St
Chicago 60603

Chicago Historical Society
Chicago 60614

Exchange National Bank
LaSalle & Adams Sts
Chicago 60690

Museum of Contemporary Art
237 E Ohio St
Chicago 60611

University of Chicago
Goodspeed Hall
5845 S Ellis
Chicago 60637

Ward Gallery
University of Illinois at Chicago Circle
650 S Halsted
POB 4348
Chicago 60680

Gallery of Photographic Art
Elgin Community College
1700 Spartan Ave
Elgin 60121

Western Illinois University Art Gallery
Macomb 61455

Center for the Visual Arts Gallery
Illinois State University
Normal 61761

Krannert Art Museum
University of Illinois
500 Peabody Dr
Urbana 61820

INDIANA

Indiana University Art Museum
Bloomington 47401

Institute for Sex Research
Morrison Hall 416
Indiana University
Bloomington 47401

Ball State University Art Gallery
Muncie 47306

Art Gallery
University of Notre Dame
Notre Dame 46556

IOWA

Sioux City Art Center
513 Nebraska St
Sioux City 51101

KANSAS

Museum of Art
University of Kansas
Lawrence 66045

Kansas State Historical society
120 W Tenth St
Topeka 66612

Ulrich Museum of Art
Wichita State University
Wichita 67208

KENTUCKY

Berea College
Berea 40403

Barnhart Gallery
University of Kentucky
Reynolds Bldg #1
627 S Broadway
Lexington 40508

Photographic Archives
University Library
University of Louisville
Louisville 40208

LOUISIANA

New Orleans Museum of Art
Box 19123 Lelong Ave
New Orleans 70179

MAINE

Bowdoin College Museum of Art
Walker Art Bldg
Brunswick 04011

University of Maine Art Gallery
Carnegie Hall
Orono 04473

Portland Museum of Art
111 High St
Portland 04101

Colby College Art Museum
Waterville 04901

MARYLAND

Baltimore Museum of Art
Art Museum Dr at Wyman Park
Baltimore 21218

University of Maryland
Baltimore County Library
5401 Wilkens Ave
Baltimore 21228

MASSACHUSETTS

Addison Gallery of American Art
Phillips Academy
Andover 01810

Boston Athenaeum
10½ Beacon St
Boston 02108

Boston Public Library
Print Dept
666 Boylston St
Boston 02117

Massachusetts College of Art
C-10 Gallery
364 Brookline Ave
Boston 02215

MIT Creative Photography Gallery
120 Massachusetts Ave
Boston 02115

Museum of Fine Arts
465 Huntington Ave
Boston 02115

Museum of Science
Science Park
Boston 02114

Carpenter Center for Visual Arts
Harvard University
19 Prescott St
Cambridge 02138

Clarence Kennedy Gallery
770 Main St
Cambridge 02139

Fogg Art Museum
Harvard University
32 Quincy St
Cambridge 02138

Hayden Gallery
MIT
265 Massachusetts Ave, Room 7-145
Cambridge 02139

Houghton Library
Harvard University
Harvard Yard
Cambridge 02138

MIT Historical Collections
265 Massachusetts Ave, Room N52-260
Cambridge 02139

MIT Permanent Collections
Committee on the Visual Arts
MIT
265 Massachusetts Ave
Room N52-260
Cambridge 02139

Semitic Museum
Harvard University
6 Divinity Ave
Cambridge 02138

Widener Memorial Library
Harvard University
Harvard Yard
Cambridge 02138

Museum of Our National Heritage
33 Marrett Rd
Lexington 02173

Newton Free Library
414 Center St
Newton Corner 02158

Smith College Museum of Art
Northampton 01063

Norwood Historical Society
93 Day St
Norwood 02062

The Berkshire Museum
39 South St
Pittsfield 01201

Peabody Museum of Salem
161 Essex St
Salem 01970

Brandeis University
Waltham 02154

Jewett Arts Center
Wellesley College Museum
Wellesley 02181

Williams College Museum of Art
Lawrence Hall
Williamstown 01267

American Antiquarian Society
185 Salisbury St
Worcester 01609

Worcester Art Museum
55 Salisbury St
Worcester 01608

MICHIGAN

Jessee Besser Museum
491 Johnson St
Alpena 49707

Alumni Memorial Hall
University of Michigan
State St & S University
Ann Arbor 48104

Michigan Historical Collection
Bentley Historical Library
1150 Beal St
Ann Arbor 48109

Detroit Institute of Arts
5200 Woodward Ave
Detroit 48202

Flint Institute of Arts
DeWaters Art Center
1120 E Kearsley
Flint 48503

Kalamazoo Institute of Arts
314 S Park St
Kalamazoo 49006

MINNESOTA

University Gallery
110 Northrup Memorial Auditorium
84 Church St SE
Minneapolis 55455

Minneapolis Institute of Arts
2400 Third Ave S
Minneapolis 55404

Walker Art Center
Vineland Pl
Minneapolis 55403

Plains Art Museum
521 Main Ave
Moorhead 56560

MISSOURI

St Louis Art Museum
Forest Park 63110

William Rockhill Nelson Gallery of Art
Atkins Museum of Fine Arts
4525 Oak St
Kansas City 64111

Springfield Art Museum
1111 E Brookside Dr
Springfield 65807

Missouri Historical Society
Jefferson Memorial Bldg
Lindell & De Balivière
St Louis 63112

NEBRASKA

Plainsman Museum
Aurora 68818

Sheldon Memorial Art Gallery
University of Nebraska
Lincoln 68588

Joslyn Art Museum
2280 Dodge St
Omaha 68102

NEW HAMPSHIRE

Hopkins Center Art Galleries
Dartmouth College
Hanover 03755

NEW JERSEY

Rider College
Student Center Gallery
Box 6400
Lawrenceville
08648

Newark Museum
49 Washington St
Newark 07107

Art Museum
Princeton University
Princeton 08540

Firestone Library
Princeton University
Princeton 08540

New Jersey State Museum
205 W State St
Trenton 08625

NEW MEXICO

University Art Museum
University of New Mexico
Albuquerque 87131

Museum of New Mexico
Photographic Archives
Box 2087
Santa Fe 87501

Southwest Center of Photography
Box 3018
Taos 87571

NEW YORK

University Art Gallery
State University of New York at Albany
FA 101
1400 Washington Ave
Albany 12222

Brooklyn Museum
Eastern Pkwy & Washington Ave
Brooklyn 11238

Long Island University
Brooklyn Center
Zeckendorf Campus
Brooklyn 11201

Albright-Knox Art Gallery
1285 Elmwood Ave
Buffalo 14222

Picker Art Gallery
C A Dana Creative Arts Center
Colgate University
Hamilton 13346

Emily Lowe Gallery
Hofstra University Museum
Hempstead 11550

Johnson Museum of Art
Cornell University
Ithaca 14850

American Geographical Society
Broadway & 156 St
New York 10032

American Museum of Natural History
Central Park West & 79 St
New York 10024

Archives of American Art
41 E 65 St
New York 10021

Avery Architectural and Fine Arts Library
Columbia University
New York 10027

Fashion Institute of Technology Library
227 W 27 St
New York 10001

International Center of Photography
1130 Fifth Ave
New York 10028

Jewish Museum
1109 Fifth Ave
New York 10028

Metropolitan Museum of Art
Dept of Prints & Photographs
Fifth Ave & 82 St
New York 10028

Museum of the City of New York
1220 Fifth Ave
New York 10029

Museum of Modern Art
11 W 53 St
New York 10019

Library & Museum of Performing Arts
Lincoln Center
New York Public Library
111 Amsterdam Ave
New York 10023

Photography Archive
New York Public Library
Fifth Ave & 42 St
New York 10018

Pierpont Morgan Library
29 E 36 St
New York 10016

Whitney Museum of American Art
945 Madison Ave
New York 10021

Vassar College Art Gallery
Taylor Hall
Poughkeepsie 12601

International Museum of Photography
George Eastman House
900 East Ave
Rochester 14607

Rush Rhees Gallery
201 C Wilson Commons
University of Rochester
Rochester

Visual Studies Workshop
31 Prince St
Rochester 14607

Staten Island Historical Society
302 Center St
Staten Island 10306

Schenectady Museum
Nott Terrace Heights
Schenectady 12308

Everson Museum of Art
401 Harrison St
Syracuse 13202

Hudson River Museum
511 Warburton Ave
Trevor-Park-on-Hudson
Yonkers 10701

NORTH CAROLINA
University of North Carolina
Chapel Hill 27514

Mint Museum of Art
501 Hempstead Pl
POB 6011
Charlotte 28207

Duke University Art Museum
Box 6877 College Station
Durham 27708

OHIO
Akron Art Museum
69 E Market St
Akron 44308

Cincinnati Art Museum
Eden Park
Cincinnati 45202

Cleveland Museum of Art
11150 East Blvd
Cleveland 44106

Columbus Museum of Art
480 E Broad St
Columbus 43215

Rinhart Collection
Ohio State University
Columbus 43210

Dayton Art Institute
Forest & Riverview Aves
Dayton 45405

Ohio Wesleyan University
Humphries Art Hall
Delaware 43015

The Antique Camera Museum
1065 Jer Les Dr
Milford 45150

Gallery for Photographic Arts
26777 Loraine Rd
North Olmstead 44070

Allen Memorial Art Museum
Oberlin College
Oberlin 44704

Butler Institute of American Art
524 Wick Ave
Youngstown 44502

OKLAHOMA

Gardner Art Gallery
Department of Art
Oklahoma State University
Stillwater 74074

OREGON

The Library
University of Oregon
Eugene 97403

The Library
Special Collections
University of Oregon
Eugene 97403

Oregon Historical Society
1230 SW Park Ave
Portland 97205

Portland Art Museum
1219 SW Park Ave
Portland 97205

Portland Center for Visual Arts
117 NW Fifth
Portland 97209

PENNSYLVANIA

Academy of Natural Sciences of Philadelphia
19 St & B Franklin Pkwy
Philadelphia 19103

Free Library of Philadelphia
Print & Picture Dept
Logan Square
Philadelphia 19103

Museum of the Philadelphia Civic Center
34 & Civic Center Blvd
Philadelphia 19104

Philadelphia Museum of Art
Alfred Stieglitz Center
26 St & B Franklin Pkwy
Philadelphia 19130

Tyler School of Art
Temple University
Beech & Penrose Aves
Philadelphia 19126

Museum of Art
Carnegie Institute
4400 Forbes Ave
Pittsburgh 15213

Reading Museum
500 Museum Rd
Reading 19611

RHODE ISLAND

Main Gallery
College of Arts & Sciences
University of Rhode Island
Kingston 02881

Museum of Art
Rhode Island School of Design
224 Benefit St
Providence 02903

Anyart Contemporary Arts Center
5 Steeple St
Providence 02903

SOUTH CAROLINA

Gibbes Art Gallery
135 Meeting St
Charleston 29401

TENNESSEE

Hunter Museum of Art
10 Bluff View
Chattanooga 37403

The Tennessee Valley Authority
Graphics Dept
400 Commerce Ave
Knoxville 37902

University of Tennessee
School of Journalism
Knoxville 37916

Brooks Memorial Art Gallery
Overton Park
Memphis 38112

Middle Tennessee State University
Photography Gallery
Box 305
Murfreesboro 37132

Carl Van Vechten Gallery of Fine Arts
Fisk University
Nashville 37203

TEXAS

Southern Light Gallery
Photography Department
Amarillo College Box 447
Amarillo 79178

Humanities Research Center
Photography Collection
Box 7219
University of Texas at Austin
Austin 78712

Corpus Christi Museum
1919 N Water St
Corpus Christi 78401

Dallas Museum of Fine Arts
Fair Park
Dallas 75226

Amon Carter Museum
POB 2365
3501 Camp Bowie Blvd
Fort Worth 76113

Fort Worth Art Museum
1309 Montgomery St
Fort Worth 76107

Rosenberg Library
2310 Sealy Ave
Galveston 77550

Menil Foundation Inc
3363 San Felipe Rd
Houston 77019

Museum of Fine Arts
1001 Bissonnet St
Houston 77005

San Antonio Museum of Art
3801 Broadway
San Antonio 78209

UTAH

Utah State Historical Society
603 E So Temple
Salt Lake City 84102

VIRGINIA

Friends of Photography of the
  Chrysler Museum at Norfolk
Olney Rd & Mowbray Arch
Norfolk 23510

Valentine Museum
1015 E Clay St
Richmond 23219

Virginia Museum of Fine Arts
Boulevard & Grove Ave
Richmond 23221

WASHINGTON

Fine Arts Center
Washington State University
Pullman 99163

Seattle Art Museum
Volunteer Park
Seattle 98112

University of Washington Libraries
Seattle 98195

Tacoma Art Museum
12 & Pacific Ave
Tacoma 98402

WISCONSIN

Madison Art Center
720 E Gorham St
Madison 53703

Cudahy Gallery of Wisconsin Art
Milwaukee Art Center
750 N Lincoln Memorial Dr
Milwaukee 53202

FOREIGN

Public Archives of Canada
395 Wellington St
Ottawa K1A ON3

Agnes Etherington Art Centre
Queen's University
Kingston

York University Art Gallery
4700 Keele St
Downsview, Toronto M3J 1P3

Quebec

Musée d'Art de Joliette
145 rue Wilfred-Corbeil
Joliette

McCord Museum
McGill University
690 Sherbrooke St W
Montreal H31 1E9

Montreal Museum of Fine Arts
1379 Sherbrooke St W
Montreal H3G 1K3

Musée d'Art Contemporain
Cité du Havre
Montreal H3C 3R4

Saidye Bronfman Centre of the YM/YWCA
5170 Cote St
Montreal

Sir George Williams University
1455 DeMaisonneuve Blvd
Montreal H3G 1M8

La Bibliothèque Nationale du Quebec
1700 Rue St Denis
Quebec H3C 150

CZECHOSLOVAKIA

Museum of Decorative Arts
Prague

DENMARK

Royal Academy of Fine Arts Library
Charlottenborg
1 Kongens Nytorv
Copenhagen 2550

Royal Library
Dept of Prints, Maps, Photographs
8 Christians Brygge
Copenhagen 1219

Thorvaldsen Museum
Copenhagen K-1213

Danmarks Tekniske Museum
N Strandvej 23
Helsingør DK-3000

ENGLAND

Birmingham Reference Library
Birmingham

Midland Arts Centre
Cannon Hill Park
Birmingham 12

Cambridge University
Cambridge

Stonyhurst College
Clitheroe

University Exeter Library
Exeter

Kodak Museum
Kodak Ltd
Headstone Dr
Harrow, Middlesex

Ipswich Museum
Civic Center
Civic Dr
Ipswich 1P1 2EE

Libraries & Museums Dept
Central Library
Fairfield Rd
Kingston upon Thames
Surrey KT1 2Ps

Fox Talbot Museum
Lacock, Wiltshire SN15 2LG

Municipal Art Gallery
Leeds

Liverpool City Libraries
Liverpool

Arts Council of Great Britain
4 St James's Sq
London SW1

British Council
10 Spring Gardens
London SW1

British Museum
Great Russell St
London WC1B 3DG

Ealing College of Higher Education
St Mary's Rd
London W5 5RF

Earlsfield Library
Magdalen Rd
London

House of Commons Library
London SW1

Imperial War Museum
Lambeth Rd
London SE1

India Office Library & Records
Foreign & Commonwealth Office
197 Blackfriars Rd
London SE1 8NG

Mansell Collection
42 Linden Gardens
London W2 4ER

National Army Museum
Royal Hospital Rd
London SW3 4HT

National Portrait Gallery
2 St Martin's Pl
London WC2H OHE

The Photographer's Gallery Ltd.
8 Great Newport St
London WC2

Radio Times Hulton Picture LIbrary
35 Marylebone High St
London W1M 4AA

Royal Geographical Society
1 Kensington Gore
London SW7 2AR

Royal Photographic Society of Great Britain
14 S Audley St
London W1Y 5DP

Royal Photographic Society Science Museum
South Kensington
London SW7 2DD

Science Museum
Exhibition Rd
London SW7 2DD

Victoria & Albert Museum
Cromwell Rd
London SW7 2RL

North Western Museum of Science & Industry
97 Grosvenor St
Manchester M1 7HF

Libraries of Local History
Central Library
Bethel St
Norwich NR2 1NJ

Museum of Modern Art
30 Pembroke St
Oxford

Museum of English Rural Life
Reading University
Reading

Whitby Literary & Philosophical Society
Whitby

Royal Library
Windsor Castle
Windsor Park

FINLAND

Helsingin Kaupunginmuseo
Kuva-arkisto
Fabianinkatu 9
Helsinki 13, 00130

Museovirasto
Historical & Ethnological Collections
Nervanderinkatu 13
Helsinki 10, 00100

Photographic Museum of Finland
Korkeavuorenkatu 2bF72
Helsinki 14, 00140

Keski-Suomen museo
Ruusupuisto
Jyväskylä 60, 40600

Kuopion museo
Kappakatu 23
Kuopio 10, 70100

Turun Kaupungin historiallinen museo
Kalastajankatu 4
Turku 10, 20100

FRANCE

Musée Réattu
rue du Grand-Prieure de Malte
Arles

Musée Marey à Beaune
Beaune

Musée Français de la Photographie
Musée Départemental de l'Essonne
Agrée et Contrôlé par l'Etat
78 rue de Paris
Bièvres 91570

Musée Nicéphore Niepce
28 quai des Messageries
Chalon-sur-Saône 71100

Maison Européene de la Photographie
26 quai des Messageries
Chalon-sur-Saône F-7100

Foundation Nationale de la Photographie
25 rue du Premier Film
Lyons 69372

Mulhouse Textile Museum
3 rue des Bonnes-Gens
Mulhouse

Académie des Beaux Arts
Archives
Paris

Archives Photographiques
3 rue du Valois
Paris 75042 (Sedex 01)

Bibliothèque Historique de la Ville de Paris
2 Av Octave Créard
Paris

Bibliothèque Nationale
Dept des Estampes/Photographie
58 rue de Richelieu
Paris 75084

Caisse Nationale des Monuments Historiques et
    des Sites
Archives Photographiques
1 rue Valois
Paris

Centre d'Art Contemporain
Georges Pompidou Centre
Plateau Beaubourg
Paris 75004

La Galerie du Photo-Club de Paris
28ter rue Gassendi
Paris 75014

Musée des Arts Décoratifs
107-109 rue de Rivoli
Palais du Louvre
Paris

Musée Carnavalet
23 rue Sévigné
Paris 75003

Musée du Conservatoire National des Arts et
    Métiers
292 rue St Martin
Paris 75003

Le Musée Lartique
au Grand-Palais
Champs-Elysées
Paris

Le Musée d'Orsay
Musée du Louvre
Quai Anatole France
Paris

Pompidou Centre
35 Blvd de Sabastopol
Paris 75004

Société Française de Photographie
Pavillon d'Orléans
Paris 75020

Pavillon de la Photographie
Hôtel des Sociétés Savantes
190 rue Beauvoisine
Rouen 76000

Kodak-Pathe
Bureau de Rechèrches
30 rue des Gignerons
Vincennes

GERMANY, WEST

Archiv für Kunst und Geschichte
34 Prinz-Friedrich-Leopold-Strasse
1 Berlin 38

Kupferstichkabinett
Fabeckstrasse 18/20
Berlin 33 (Dahlem) D-1000

Nationalgalerie
Staatliche Museen
Berlin

Rheinisches Landemuseum
Colmanstrasse 14-16
Bonn 53

Museum Ludwig
L Fritz Guber Collection
Cologne 5 1

Wallraf-Richartz Museum
An der Rechtschule
Cologne

Fotographische Sammlung
Museum Folkwang
Bismarkstrasse 64-66
Essen 4300

Museum für Kunst und Gewerbe
1 Steintorplatz
Hamburg 2 1

Staatliche Landesbildstelle Hamburg
171 Kielerstrasse
Hamburg 2000

Agfa-Gevaert Foto-Historama
Leverkusen

Schiller Nationalmuseum
Schillerhohe
Marbach 7142

Deutsches Museum von Meisterwerkend
der Naturwissenschaft und Technik
1 Museumsinsel
Munich 26

Munchner Stadtmuseum
1 St-Jakobs-Platz
Munich 2

Neue Sammlung
3 Prinzregentenstrasse
Munich 8 22

GERMANY, EAST

Akademie der Kunste der DDR
58/59 Hermann-Matern Strasse
E Berlin 104

Museum der Photographie
14 Lewickistrasse
Dresden a21

Polytechnisches Museum Dresden
15 Friedrich-Engels Strasse
Dresden 806

IRELAND

Gallery of Photography
37/39 Wellington Quay
Dublin 2

ISRAEL

Israel Museum
Hakirya St
Jerusalem 9100

ITALY

Museo del Cinema
2 Piazza San Giovanni
Turin

JAPAN

National Museum of Modern Art
3 Kitanomaru Koen
Chiyoda-ku, 102
Tokyo

Pentax Museum
3-21-20 Mishiazabu
Mirato-ku
Tokyo 106

MEXICO

Museo de Arte Moderno
Bosque de Chapultepec
Mexico City

THE NETHERLANDS

Stedelijk Museum
13 Paulus Potterstraat
Amsterdam

Print Room
University of Leiden
65 Rapenburg
Leiden

NEW ZEALAND

Auckland City Art Gallery
E Wellesley St
Auckland 1

Auckland Institute & Museum
The Domain
Auckland 1

Dunedin Public Art Gallery
Box 566 Logan Park
Dunedin

The Hocken Library
University of Otago
Box 56
Dunedin

Nelson Provincial Museum
Hardy St
Nelson

Manawatu Art Gallery
Grey & Carroll Sts
Palmerston North

Alexander Turnbull Library
Box 12-349
Wellington

National Museum
Buckle St
Wellington 1

NORWAY

Preus Fotomuseum
82 Langgt
Horten 3190

POLAND

Museum Sztuki
36 ul. Wieckowskiego
Lodz 90-734

Muzeum Narodowe we Wroclawiu
50-153 Wroclaw
Plac Powstancow
Warsaw 5

PORTUGAL

Museu Nacional de Arte Antiga
Largo 9 de Abril
Lisbon

REPUBLIC OF SOUTH AFRICA

National Museum
Bloemfonten
POB 266
Bloemfontein 9300

Africana Museum
Market Square
Johannesburg 2001

Bensusan Museum of Photography & Library
17 Empire Rd
Parktown (Johannesburg) 2001

Government Archives
Union Bldg
Pretoria 0136

South African National Museum of Military
    History
POB Posbus 52090
Saxonwold
Transvaal 2132

SCOTLAND

Edinburgh Photographic Society
Edinburgh

Edinburgh Public Library
Edinburgh

Royal Scottish Museum
Dept. of Technology
Chambers St
Edinburgh EH1 1JF

Scottish National Portrait Gallery
1 Queen St
Edinburgh EH2 1JD

Scottish United Service Museum
The Castle
Crown Square
Edinburgh EH1 2YT

Mitchell Library
Glasgow

Fotografiska Muséet
Moderna Muséet
Skeppsholmen Box 16382
S-10327 Stockholm

Tekniska Muséet
Museivagen
7 Gen
Stockholm

Kunsthaus Zurich
Heinplatz-1
CH-8001 Zurich

Kunstgewerbemuseum der Stadt Zurich
60 Ausstellungsstrasse
Zurich 5

Museu de Bellas Artes
Parque Sucre
105 Los Caobos
Caracas

Photographic Galleries

ARIZONA

Fifth Avenue Gallery of Photography
6960 Fifth Ave
Scottsdale 85251

Stable Art Gallery at the Zocalo
7610 E McDonald Dr
Scottsdale 85253

Kay Bonfoey Gallery
1157 S Swan Rd
Tucson 85711

ARKANSAS

Camera Works Gallery
219 N Block St
Fayetteville

CALIFORNIA

Ameka
1507 G St
Arcata 95521

Photographic Gallery
211 H St
Bakersfield 93304

Friends of Photography
San Carlos & Ninth Ave
Carmel 93921

The Print Gallery
Delores & Sixth St
Carmel 93921

The Weston Gallery Inc
Box 655
Carmel 93921

Photo-Synthesis
64 Shaw Rd
Clovis 93612

Photo-Arts of Cupertino
10025 Mann Dr
Cupertino 95014

Orlando Gallery
17037 Ventura Blvd
Encino 91316

Mills House Art Gallery
12732 Main St
Fullerton 92640

309 Walden Gallery
309 Walden Ave
Fullerton 92632

Danny Ball Gallery
147 N Franklin
Hemet 92343

BC Space
235 Forest Ave
Laguna Beach 92651

Lang Photography Gallery
1450-A S Coast Hwy
Laguna Beach 92651

G Ray Hawkins Gallery
7224 Melrose Ave
Los Angeles 90060

Nicholas Wilder Gallery
8225½ Santa Monica Blvd
Los Angeles 90046

Stephen White's Gallery of Photography Inc
835 N La Cienega Blvd
Los Angeles 90069

Steps into Space
7518 Melrose Ave
Los Angeles 90046

Susan Spiritus Gallery
3336 Via Lido
Newport Beach 92663

Alpha Photo Gallery
560 20 St
Oakland 94612

Gallery House
538 Ramona St
Palo Alto 94303

Smith Andersen Gallery
200 Homer St
Palo Alto 94301

Cityscape Photo Gallery
97 E Colorado Blvd
Pasadena 91105

Tanega Maher Gallery
214 Avenida del Norte
Redondo Beach 90277

Library Gallery
E B Crocker Art Gallery
216 "O" St
Sacramento 95814

Gallery Graphics
3847 Fifth Ave
San Diego 92103

Berggruen Gallery
228 Grant Ave
San Francisco 94108

Camerawork
70 12 St
San Francisco 94103

Cannon House Gallery
776 Market St
San Francisco

Douglas Elliot Gallery
1151 Mission St
San Francisco 94103

80 Langton Street Gallery
80 Langton St
San Francisco 94103

Focus Gallery
2146 Union St
San Francisco 94123

Fraenkel Gallery
55 Grant Ave
San Francisco 94108

Grapestake Gallery
2876 California St
San Francisco 94115

Hansen-Fuller Gallery
228 Grant Ave
San Francisco 94108

John Howell Books
434 Post St
San Francisco 94102

Lawson de Celle Gallery
54 Kissling St
San Francisco 94103

The North Point Gallery
872 North Point
San Francisco 94109

Phoenix Gallery
257 Grant Ave
San Francisco 94108

Secret City Gallery
306 Fourth Ave
San Francisco 94118

Simon Lowinsky Gallery
228 Grant Ave
San Francisco 94108

Stephen Wirtz Gallery
345 Sutter Ave
San Francisco 94108

Thackrey & Robertson Gallery
2266 Union St
San Francisco 94123

Floating Wall Gallery
215 N Broadway
Santa Ana 92701

The Keystone Gallery
1213 State St
Santa Barbara 93102

The Visible Light Gallery
729 Chapala St
Santa Barbara 93101

Exposure/Neary Gallery
1326 Pacific Garden Mall
Santa Cruz

Gallery 115
115 Maple St
Santa Cruz 95060

Annex Photo Gallery
604 College Ave
Santa Rosa 95404

Camera Work Gallery
14501-B Big Basin Way
Saratoga 95070

Living Room Gallery
13025 Ventura Blvd
Studio City 91604

Janus Gallery
21 Market St
Venice 90291

Ansel Adams Gallery
Box 455
Yosemite National Park 95389

COLORADO

Eclipse Photographics
2012 Tenth St
Boulder 80302

Colorado Photographic Arts Center
1301 Bannock St
Denver 80204

Cosmopolitan Art Gallery
701 S Milwaukee St
Denver 80209

Hill's Gallery
3113 E Third Ave
Denver 80206

CONNECTICUT

Photo Graphics Workshop
212 Elm St
New Canaan 06840

Archetype Photographic Gallery
159 Orange St
New Haven 06510

Charles B Wood III, Inc
The Green
South Woodstock 06281

DISTRICT OF COLUMBIA

Diane Brown Gallery
2028 P St NW
Washington 20036

Colorfax Photo Gallery
5511 Connecticut Ave NW
Washington 20015

Kathleen Ewing-Quindacqua Ltd
3020 K St NW
Washington 20007

Lunn Gallery
3243 P St NW
Washington 20007

Osuna Gallery
406 Seventh St NW
Washington 20004

Sander Gallery
2604 Connecticut Ave NW
Washington 20008

Smith-Mason Gallery
1207 Rhode Island Ave NW
Washington 20005

Street Corner Gallery Ltd
4932 Wisconsin Ave NW
Washington 20016

Washington Gallery of Photography
216 Seventh St SE
Washington 20003

FLORIDA

Frank D. Guarino
POB 89
DeBary 32713

Gallery Gemini
245 Worth Ave
Palm Beach 33480

Gulf Coast Photographic Gallery
3941 W Kennedy Blvd
Tampa 33609

Gates & Tripp
150 S Market Bldg
Boston 02109

Vision Gallery
216 Newbury St
Boston 02116

Voices Gallery
220 North St
Boston 02113

Cambridge Photo Co-op
188 Prospect St
Cambridge 02139

Cambridge Public Library
The Gallery
449 Broadway
Cambridge 02138

Clarence Kennedy Gallery
770 Main St
Cambridge 02139

Creative Photography Gallery
120 Massachusetts Ave
Cambridge 02115

Project's Photographic Gallery
141 Huron Ave
Cambridge 02138

Prospect Street Photo Co-op & Gallery
188 Prospect St
Cambridge 02139

Temple Bar Bookshop Gallery
9 Boylston St
Cambridge 02138

Craft Resource Center
Newburyport Public Library
91 State St
Newburyport 01950

Image Gallery
Main St
Stockbridge 01262

Exposure
Main St
Wellfleet 02667

MICHIGAN

Art World's Photo Gallery
213½ S Main St
Ann Arbor 48104

Blixt Gallery
229 Nickols Arcade
Ann Arbor 48106

Union Gallery
530 State St
Ann Arbor 48104

The Halstead 831 Gallery
560 N Woodward
Birmingham 48011

MINNESOTA

Hanson-Cowles Gallery
331 Second Ave N
Minneapolis 55401

J. Hunt Gallery
3011 E 25 St
Minneapolis 55406

Lightworks
25 University Ave E
Minneapolis 55414

Peter M. David Gallery Inc.
920 Nicollet Mall
Minneapolis 55402

Oxman's Gallery
639 Second Ave N
Minneapolis 55403

Tidepool Gallery
3907 W 50 St
Saint Edna 55424

MISSISSIPPI

The Northgate Gallery
4436 N State St
Jackson 39206

MISSOURI

Columbia Gallery of Photography
1015 E Broadway
Columbia 65201

13 x 15 Photo Gallery
118 E Lockwood Ave
Webster Groves 63119

Floating Foundation of Photography
15 Greene St
New York 10013

Focus II Gallery
163 W 74 St
New York 10023

Foto
492 Broome St
New York 10013

Fourth Street Gallery
67 E Fourth St
New York 10003

Genesis Gallery
41 E 57 St
New York 10022

Gombinski Gallery of Art
46 Walker St
New York 10013

Hansen Galleries
41 E 57 St
New York 10022

Images Inc
11 E 57 St
New York 10022

International Arts Inc
28 E Fourth St
New York 10003

International Center of Photography
1130 Fifth Ave
New York 10028

Janet Lehr
45 E 85 St
New York 10028

John Gordon Gallery
37 W 57 St
New York 10019

K & L Gallery
222 E 44 St
New York 10017

Kimmel/Cohn Photography Arts
41 Central Park West
New York 10023

Lee Nordness Galleries
252 W 38 St
New York 10018

Light Gallery
724 Fifth Ave
New York 10019

Louis K Meisel Gallery
141 Prince St
New York 10012

Marcuse Pfeifer Gallery
825 Madison Ave
New York 10021

M Knoedler & Co Inc
21 E 70 St
New York 10021

Marlborough Gallery
40 W 57 St
New York 10019

Modernage Gallery
319 E 44 St
New York 10017

Multiples
55 E 80 St
New York 10021

Neikrug Photographica Ltd.
224 E 68 St
New York 10021

Nikon House
c/o Charles E Kurtak
Gilbert, Felix & Sharf
566 Seventh Ave
New York 10018

Noho Gallery
542 La Guardia Pl
New York 10012

O K Harris
383 W Broadway
New York 10012

Pace Gallery
32 E 57 St
New York 10022

Parsons-Dreyfuss Gallery
24 W 57 St
New York 10019

Portogallo Gallery
72 W 45 St
New York 10036

Prakapas Gallery
19 E 71 St
New York 10021

Rinhart Galleries Inc
710 Park Ave
New York 10020

Robert Freidus Gallery Inc
158 Lafayette St
New York 10013

Robert Samuels Gallery
795 Broadway
New York 10003

Robert Schoelkopf Gallery
825 Madison Ave
New York 10021

Sidney Janis Gallery
6 W 57 St
New York 10019

Soho Photo Gallery
34 W 13 St
New York 10011

Soho 20
99 Spring St
New York 10012

Sonnabend Gallery
420 W Broadway
New York 10012

The Space
154 W 57 St
New York 10019

A Street Corner Gallery
15 W 84 St., #10
New York 10024

Studio 505 Gallery
141 Greene St
New York 10013

Terrain Gallery
Aesthetic Realism Foundation Inc
141 Greene St
New York 10012

Theatre Gallery
961 Madison Ave
New York 10021

Timothy Baum
40 E 78 St
New York 10021

Ward-Nasse Gallery
178 Prince St
New York 10012

William L Schaeffer/Photographs
450 W 20 St
New York 10011

Witkin Gallery
41 E 57 St
New York 10022

Zabriskie Gallery
29 W 57 St
New York 10019

Light Impressions Gallery
8 S Washington St
Rochester 14614

The Workshop Gallery
Visual Studies Workshop
31 Prince St
Rochester 14607

Sea Cliff Photograph Co
310 Sea Cliff Ave
Sea Cliff 11579

Light Work Gallery
316 Waverly Ave
Syracuse 13210

Catskill Center for Photography
59A Tinker St
Woodstock 12498

NORTH CAROLINA

Light Factory
110 E Seventh St
Charlotte 28202

OHIO

Nova Gallery
1290 Euclid Ave #207
Cleveland 44115

Herbert Ascherman Gallery
1785 Coventry Rd
Cleveland Heights 44118

Gallery 200
200 W Mound
Columbus 43215

Jackson Street Gallery
205 Jackson St
Columbus 43206

Photogenesis Gallery
4930 N High St
Columbus 43214

Vista Gallery of Contemporary Photography
164 S Market St
East Palestine 44413

Gallery of Photographic Arts Inc
Community National Bank Bldg
26777 Lorain Rd #214
North Olmstead 44070

OKLAHOMA

Clubb Gallery
Philbrook Art Center
2272 S Rockford
Tulsa 74114

OREGON

Pearl Street Gallery
410 Pearl St
Eugene 97401

Blue Sky Gallery
117 NW Fifth Ave
Portland 97209

The Shado Gallery
2910 SE Lambert St
Portland 97202

PENNSYLVANIA

David Mancini Gallery
1728 Spruce St
Philadelphia 19103

Hahn Gallery
8439 Germantown Ave
Philadelphia 19118

Janet Fleisher Gallery
211 S 17 St
Philadelphia 19103

London Gallery
23 & Fairmont Ave
Philadelphia

Paul Càva Gallery
1715 Spruce St
Philadelphia 19103

The Photography Place
132 S 17 St
Philadelphia 19103

Photopia
1728 Spruce St
Philadelphia 19103

Print Club
1614 Latimer St
Philadelphia 19103

Soho Photo Gallery
162 N Third St
Philadelphia 19106

RHODE ISLAND

Jeb Gallery
342 S Main St
Providence 02901

Lenore Grey Gallery
15 Meeting St
Providence 02903

SOUTH CAROLINA

Silver Eye Studio
401 W Croft St
Greenville 29609

TENNESSEE

Photographic Gallery
Middle Tennessee State University
Murfreesboro 37130

TEXAS

The Afterimage
The Quadrangle #151
2800 Routh St
Dallas 75201

Allen Street Gallery
2817 Allen St
Dallas 75204

Contemporary Gallery
2425 Cedar Springs
Dallas 75201

Benteler Gallery Inc
3830 University
Houston 77005

The Cronin Gallery
2424 Bissonnet
Houston 77005

Sol Del Rio
1020 Townsend
San Antonio 78209

UTAH

Edison Street Gallery
231 Edison St
Salt Lake City 84111

VERMONT

Photo Garden Gallery
115 S Winooski Ave
Burlington 05401

Mr & Mrs Tom Burnside
Pawlet 05761

VIRGINIA

Fuller & Albert Gallery
3170 Campbell Dr
Fairfax 22030

Photoworks
204 N Mulberry St
Richmond 23220

Scott-McKennis Fine Art
3465 W Cary St
Richmond 23221

WASHINGTON

Equivalents
1822 Broadway
Seattle 98122

Phos Graphos
108 S Jackson
Seattle 98104

Photo Printworks
114 W Elliott
Seattle 98119

Silver Image Gallery
83 W Washington
Seattle 98104

Yuen Lui Gallery
906 Pine St
Seattle 98101

WISCONSIN

Sunprint Gallery
638 State St
Madison 53703

Hayes Gallery
2520 E Capitol Dr
Milwaukee 53211

Infinite Eye Gallery
2553 N Downer Ave
Milwaukee 53211

Milwaukee Center for Photography
207 E Buffalo St
Milwaukee 53202

Peter J. Kondos Art Galleries
2233 N Prospect Ave
Milwaukee 53202

FOREIGN

AUSTRALIA

Hogart Galleries
7-9 McLaughland Pl
Paddington (Sydney)
New South Wales

The Image Gallery
42 Gurner St
Paddington (Sydney)
New South Wales

Realities Gallery
Orange Rd
Toorak
Queensland

Church Street Photographic Centre
384 Church St
Richmond (Melbourne)
Victoria 3121

Pentax-Brummels Gallery of Photography
95 Toorak Rd
South Yarra (Melbourne)
Victoria

Photographer's Gallery & Workshop
344 Punt Rd
South Yarra (Melbourne)
Victoria 3141

AUSTRIA

Fotogalerie im Forum Stadtpark
Stadtpark 1
Graz 8010

Fotogalerie "Klo"
Prokopigasse 16/1
Graz

Fotogalerie Schillerhof
Cafe Schillerhof
Schillerplatz
Graz

Kulturhaus
Stadt Graz
Graz 8010

Innsbrucker Fotoschau
Hohenstrasse 17 a/1
A-6020 Innsbruck

P P Galerie
Linz 4020

Galerie die Brucke
Backerstrasse 5
Vienna 1010

Kodak Galerie
4 Albert Schweitzer-Gasse
Vienna 1148

BELGIUM

Paule Pia Photo Galerij
Kammenstraat 57
Antwerp 2000

Aspects
72 rue du President
Brussels 1050

Galerie & Fils
105 Blvd Brand Whitlock
Brussels

Galerie Spectrum
15 rue de la Chapelle
Brussels

Ilford Gallery
180 Terkamerenstraat
Brussels

Museum voor Fotografie en Cinematographie
Revensteinstraat 23
Brussels

Het Sterckshof, Provincial Museum voor
    Kunstambachten
Hooftvunderlei 160
B-2100
Deurne

Photogalerie 5.6
St Michielsplein 14
Ghent 9000

Kreatief Camera Galerie
68 Nieuwstraat
Herentals 2410

BRAZIL

Sociedade Fluminense de Fotografia
CP 118
Niteroi 24000

CANADA

Alberta

Walter Phillips Gallery
The Banff Centre
Banff

Edmonton Art Gallery
2 Sir Winston Churchill Sq
Edmonton T5J 2C1

Southern Alberta Art Gallery
601 Third Ave S
Lethbridge T1J OH4

British Columbia

Gallery of Photography
3619 W Broadway
Vancouver

Nova Gallery
1972 W Fourth
Vancouver V6J 1M5

Photographic Art Dealers
4574 Langara Ave
Vancouver

Vancouver Art Gallery
1145 W Georgia St
Vancouver

Secession Gallery of Photography
Open Space
510 Fort St
Victoria

Manitoba

Winnipeg Art Gallery
300 Memorial Blvd
Winnipeg R3C 1V1

Ontario

Photo Image 33
33 Brock St
Kingston

Canada Council-Visual Arts
255 Albert St
Ottawa

Gallery Graphics
521 Sussex Dr
Ottawa K1N 6Z6

National Film Board of Canada
Photo Gallery
150 Kent St
Ottawa

Saw Gallery
72 Rideau St
Ottawa K1N 5W9

Art Gallery of Ontario
Grange Park
Toronto M5T 1G4

Baldwin Street Gallery
38 Baldwin St
Toronto 130

David Mirvish Gallery
596 Markham St
Toronto

Deja-Vue Galleries Ltd
122 Scollard
Toronto M5R 1G2

Isaacs Gallery
832 Yonge St
Toronto M4W 2H1

Jane Corkin Gallery Suite
144 Front St W, Suite 620
Toronto M5J 1G2

Marlborough Godard Gallery
22 Hazelton Ave
Toronto

A Moment in Time
398 King St E
Toronto M5A 1K9

Photo Artists Canada
398 King St E
Toronto M5A 1K9

Photowork
239 Gerrard St E
Toronto

A Space Exhibition
352 Spadina Ave
Toronto

Yarlow/Salzman Gallery
211 Avenue Rd
Toronto

Quebec

Art 45
2175 Crescent
Montreal

Galerie Mira Godard
1490 Sherbrooke St W
Montreal

Galerie Optica
453 St Francois Xavier
Montreal

Gallery Notkin
1650 Sherbrooke St W
Montreal

Gallery Photo Progressio
1417 MacKay St
Montreal

Le Maison Sauvegard
160 Notre Dame E
Montreal

Power House Gallery
3738 St Dominique
Montreal H2X 2X8

Vehicule Art
61 St Catherine W
Montreal

Workshop
7308 Sherbrooke St W
Montreal

Yajima/Galerie
307 St Catherine St W, Suite 515
Montreal H2X 2A3

La Chambre Blanche
531 St Jean
Quebec

Université Concordia
The Main Sprinkler Valve Gallery
1230 Mountain St
Quebec H3C 1S0

Saskatchewan

Mendel Art Gallery
Saskatoon Gallery & Conservatory Corporation
950 Spadina Crescent E
Box 569
Saskatoon S7K 3L6

Photographers' Gallery
The Dowding Bldg
234 Second Ave S
Saskatoon

Image
Mejlgarde 6
Aarhus DK-8000

Gallery Huset
Magstraede 14
Copenhagen 1204

Art Gallery
Market Place
Batley

Arnolfini
Narrow Quay
Bristol BS1 4QA

Art Facult Concourse
Kedleston Rd
Derby

Albert Street Workshop
8 Albert St
Hebden Bridge HX7

Bluecoat Gallery
School Lane
Liverpool L13BX

Open Eye Gallery
90 Whitechapel
Liverpool L1 6EN

Aberbach Fine Art Gallery
17 Savile Row
London W1

Anderson & Hershkowitz Ltd
90 Wigmore St
London

Asahi Pentax Gallery
6 Vigo St
London W1X 1AH

Battersea Arts Centre
Lavender Hill
London SW11

Box Room of Photography
125 Shaftsbury Ave
London

Creative Camera Gallery
19 Doughty St
London WCIN 2 PT

Gallery of Photography
112 Pricedale Rd
London W11

Half Moon Gallery
27 Alie St
London E1

Hayward Gallery
South Bank
London

Howard Ricketts Ltd
180 New Bond St
London

I.C.A.
Nash House
12 Carlton House Terrace
London SW1

Kettering Gallery
Sheep St
London

Kodak Photo Gallery
246 High Holborn
London WC1

Marlborough Fine Art Ltd
6 Albermarle St
London W1X 3HF

P & D Colnaghi
14 Old Bond St
London W1X 4JL

The Photographer's Gallery
8 Great Newport St
London WC2

Robert Self Ltd Gallery
48-50 Earlham St
London WC2

Russ Anderson
59 Montholme Rd
London

Serpentine Gallery
Kensington Gardens
London W2

York Library
Wye St
London

Grass Roots Photography Gallery
1 Newton St
Manchester M1 1HW

Side Gallery
9 Side
Newcastle-upon-Tyne NE1 3JE

Spectro Photography
Bells Court
Pilgrim St
Newcastle-upon-Tyne NE1 6RH

Midland Group Gallery
24-32 Carlton St
Nottingham

Inner Gallery
St Edmund's Art Trust
Salisbury

The Photographic Gallery
The University
Southampton SO9 5NH

The Sutcliffe Gallery
1 Flowergate
Whitby YO21 3BA

Impressions Gallery of Photography
17 Colliergate
York

FINLAND

Waino Aaltosen
Itainen Rantakatu
Turku

FRANCE

Atelier 6
22 rue Richard Coeur de Lion
Agen

FNAC-Strasbourg
Plate Kléber
Bas-Rhin

Galerie Nicéphore
8 rue de la Gare
Bollwiller 68540

Collection Kahn
5 Quai du 4-Septembre
Boulogne 92100

Galerie Amerin Vie
1 rue Grasset
Nantes 4400

FNAC-Lille
9 Place Charles-de-Gaulle
Nord

Agathe Gaillard
3 rue de Pont-Louis-Philippe
Paris 75004

Centre International de Sejour de Paris
Club Photographique
6 Av Maurice Ravel
Paris 75012

Editions de la Tortue
11 rue Jacob
Paris 75006

FNAC-Étoille 22
Ave Wagram (8ᵉ)
Paris

FNAC-Montparnasse
136 rue de Rennes
Paris 75006

Galerie Arpa à Bordeaux
17 rue Candale
Paris

Galerie Canon
Plateau Beabourg (4ᵉ)
Paris

Galerie Contrejour
19 rue de l'Ouest
Paris 75014

Galerie Delpire
13 rue de l'Abbaye
Paris

Galerie Demi Teinte
159 bis, Blvd Montparnasse (6ᵉ)
Paris

Galerie Gérard Levy
17 rue de Beaune
Paris 75014

Galerie Jean Dieuzaide
4 Place St Etienne
Paris

Galerie Nikon
1 rue Jacob
Paris 75006

Galerie Octant
8-10 rue du 29 Juillet
Paris 75001

Galerie Sonnabend
12 rue Mazarine
Paris

Odeon-Photo
110 blvd St. Germain
Paris

L'Oeil du Diaph
2 place Jean-Zay
Paris 75014

La Photogalerie
2 rue Christine
Paris 75006

Photo 'Oeil/Galerie 11
11 rue Boyer-Barret (14ᵉ)
Paris

Le Remise du Parc
2 Impasse des Bourdonnais
Paris 75001

Ufficio Dell'arte/Creatis
44 rue Quincampoix (4ᵉ)
Près du Centre Pompidou
Paris

Vinci et Niepce
7 rue Martignac
Paris 75007

Viviane Esders Gallery
12 rue Saint Merri
Paris 75004

Zabriskie Gallery
29 rue Aubry-le-Boucher
Paris

FNAC-Lyon
62 rue de la République
Rhône

Galerie Jean Dieuzaide
4 Place St-Etienne
Toulouse

Voir
42 rue Pargaminières
Toulouse

GERMANY, WEST

Fotogalerie Lichttropfen
Kockerellstrasse 19
Aachen

Galerie Lichttropfen
Mauerstrasse 7
Aachen 5100

Galerie an der Neupforte
9 Neupforte
Aachen 51

Folkwangschüle für Gestaltung
43 Essen-Werden
Abtei

Stadtgalerie Altena
Lennestrasse 93
Altena 5990

Galerie A Nagel
Fasanenstrasse 42
Berlin 15 D-1800

Galerie Breiting
Sächsische Strasse 1
Berlin 15 D-1000

Galerie Mikro
Carmerstrasse 1
Berlin

Landesbildstelle Berlin
Photographic Center
Berlin

Trockenpresse
Schlüterstrasse 70
Berlin

Werkstatt für Photographie
210 Friedrichstrasse
Berlin 1 61

Kunsthaus
Bielefeld

Galerie M
Hause Weitmar
Bochum 463

Galerie Jollenback
Lindenstrasse 18
Cologne

Galerie Rudolf Kicken
Albertusstrasse 47/49
Cologne 1 D-5000

Galerie Wilde
Auf dem Berlich 6
Cologne 1 D-5000

Camera Galerie
49 Bolkerstrasse
Düsseldorf 4

Galerie im Riek
Ruhrstrasse 44
Essen-Kettwig 4307

Fotogalerie f/32
Erkastrasse 89
Hamburg

Galerie Levy
Magdalenenstrasse 26
Hamburg

Photogalerie
Kielerstrasse 171
Hamburg

PPS Gallery
1 Feldstrasse/Hochhaus
Hamburg 4 D-2000

Galerie Spectrum
Holzmarkt 6
Hannover 3000

Galerie Z
Silberstrasse 30
Hannover 3051

Spectrum Photogalerie
Karmarschshstrasse 44
Hannover 1 D-3000

Galerie Krebaum
8 Im Faudenbuhl
Heddesheim 6805

Fotoforum
Gasamthochschule Kassel
Kassel 350

Fotogalerie Nune
Masseldieksdammer Uleg 9
Kiel

Agfa-Gevaert AG
Leverkusen

Galerie Arnoldi-Livie
Maximilianstrasse 36
Munich

Galerie Walter Kober
Leopoldstrasse 13
Munich

Photogalerie Lange-Irschl
Türkenstrasse 54
Munich 40 D-8000

Galerie Deko-Art
Ohechausee 15
Norderstedt D-2000

Gallerie im Kettenladle
Paulinenstrasse 53
Stuttgart

Kunstkabinett G A Richter
Konigstrasse 33
Stuttgart

GREECE

Photographic Center of Athens
Sina 52
Athens 135

Photothiki
Mitropolitou Iosif St
Thessaloniki

ISRAEL

The White Gallery Ltd
4 Habima Sq
Tel Aviv

ITALY

Galleria Fossati
Via Legnano 5
Alessandria

Galleria dell-Immagine
Piazza Vecchia 4
Bergamo 24100

Figura
Via Marconi 5
Biella

Fotografis
Via Bocca di Lupo 4
Bologna

Il Diaframma
Piazza Duomo ang.
Via Trieste 3
Brescia

Il Cupolone
Via del Servi 12r
Florence 50122

Antra Studio
Via Fiori Chiari 8
Milan

Il Diaframma/Canon
Via Brera 10
Milan

Luciano Inga-Pin
Via Pontaccio 12/A
Milan

Galleria Fotografica
Piazza Grande 28
Modena

Lucio Amelio
Piazza del Martiri 58
Naples

Galleria Grandangolo
Via Crescini 102
Padua

Galleria Fotografica Nadar
Vicolo dei Tidi 26
Pisa 56100

Galleria Pan
Via del Fiume 3a
Rome

Galleria Rondanini
Piazza Rondanini
Rome

Il Fotogramma
Via Ripetta 153
Rome

Agorà
Via Pastrengo 9/d
Turin

Foto-Grafia
Via Peschiera 11
Treviso

Nuova Galleria Fotografia
Piazza Giustinian 14
Treviso

Galleria Documenta
Via Santa Maria 2
Turin

Ikona Photo Gallery
San Marco 2084
Venice

JAPAN

Asahi Pentax Gallery
21-20, 3-chome
Nishi-Azabu, Minato-ku
Tokyo

Canon Salon
9-9, 3-chome
Ginza, Chou-ku
Tokyo

Eikoh Hosoe
5 Aizumi-cho, Shinjuku-ku
Tokyo

Nantenshi
3-11 Kyobashi
Chuo-ku
Tokyo

Nikon Salon
5-6, 3-chome
Ginza, Chou-ku
Tokyo

Shadai Gallery
Tokyo Institute of Polytechnics
2-9-5, Honcho, Nakano-ku
Tokyo

MEXICO

Galeria de Fotografia
Casa del Lago, UNAM
Bosque de Chapultepec
Mexico City

THE NETHERLANDS

Canon Photo Gallery
Reestraat 19
Amsterdam

Galeri Fiolet
Herengracht 86
Amsterdam

NEW ZEALAND

Real Pictures Ltd
POB 7195
Auckland

Snaps: A Photographer's Gallery
30 Airedale St
Auckland 1

NORWAY

Gallerie for Fri Fotografi
49 Pilestredet
Oslo

PERU

Galeria Secuencia
1130 Conquistadores
Lima 27

POLAND

Union of Polish Art Photographers
Plac Zamkowy 8
Warsaw 00-277

REPUBLIC OF SOUTH AFRICA

Duggan Cronin Bantu Art Gallery
POB 316
Kimberley 8300

Pentax Gallery
Baker Square
Rosebank
Johannesburg 2196

SCOTLAND

David Webster of Oban Gallery of Photography
15/19 Stafford St
Oban, Argyll

SPAIN

Fotomania
Granduxer, 26
Barcelona 21

Galleria Spectrum/Canon
Balmes, 86
Barcelona 8

Spectrum Art Photographic Gallery
Balmes, 86
Barcelona

La Photo Galeria
Plaza de la Republica Argentina, 2
Madrid 6

SWEDEN
Malmo Konsthall
Johannesgatan 7
Malmo

Camera Obscura
Hall & Cederquist AB
Strandvagen 5A
Stockholm 114 51

Fotografiecentrum
Malmskillnadsgatan 45
Stockholm

SWITZERLAND
Galerie Handschin
Baumleingasse 16
Basel

Photo Art Basel
St Albans-Vorstadt 10
Basel 4059

Galerie de Photographie
25 rue de Pont-Neuf
Carouge

Canon Photo Galerie
3 rue Saint-Léger
Geneva 1206

Galerie Rivolta
rue de la Mercerie
Geneva

Galerie Sonnabend
14 rue Etienne-Dumont
Geneva

Soft Art Galerie
31 rue Centrale
Geneva

Galerie Rivolta
1 rue de la Mercerie
Lausanne 1003

Galerie Media
29 rue des Moulins
Neuchâtel 2000

St Galler Fotogalerie
6 Webergasse
Saint Gallen 9000

Claudia Tadini
Clausuisstrasse 64
Zurich

Galerie Form
2 Predigerplatz
Zurich 8001

Galerie 38
38 Kirchgasse
Zurich 8001

Gallery Tolgge im Cafe Drahlschmidli
Juggenhaus
Wasserwerk Strasse 17
Zurich 8006

Nikon Foto-Galerie
3 Schoffelgasse
Zurich 8001

Photogalerie Kunsthaus Zurich
Heimplatz 1
Zurich 8001

Picture Gallery
Fortunagasse 20
Zurich

VENEZUELA
Fototeca
929 Apartado
Caracas

YUGOSLAVIA
Galerie Spot/Galerije grada Zagreb
2 Katerinin Trg
Zagreb 4100

Fotogalerija Focus
Podhod Zvezda
Ljubljana 6100

Photo Credits

The authors gratefully acknowledge the following for supplying the photographs reproduced herein; the numbers refer to plates.

Courtesy of Fotogram Agence, Paris: 1

Courtesy of IMP/GEH: 3, 4, 7, 9, 10, 11, 12, 13, 14, 15, 16, 22, 25, 26, 27, 29, 31, 32, 41, 53, 134, 135

Courtesy of California Museum of Photography at Riverside: 5, 6, 8, 17, 21, 23, 24, 30, 36, 37, 91, 93

Courtesy of Gernsheim Collection, Humanities Research Center, University of Texas at Austin: 19

Courtesy of Staatliche Landesbildstelle, Hamburg: 2

Courtesy of Center for Creative Photography, University of Arizona at Tucson: 20, 33, 34, 35, 39, 40, 42 (© 1981 Imogen Cunningham Trust), 44 (© 1981 Jacques Henri Lartigue), 45, 46 (© 1981 Board of Regents, University of Arizona), 47 (© 1981 James Van Der Zee), 48, 50, 51 (© 1981 Board of Regents, University of Arizona), 52 (© 1981 Anton Bruehl), 54 (© 1981 Florence Henri), 57 (© 1981 Brassaï), 62 (© 1981 Lisette Model), 66, 70 (© 1981 Lou Stouman), 72 (© 1981 Amon Carter Museum), 74 (© 1981 Estate of Minor White), 76 (© 1981 Wright Morris), 77 (© 1981 Manuel Alvarez Bravo), 78, 79 (© 1981 Robert Doisneau), 81 (© 1981 Frederick Sommer), 82 (© 1981 Gisele Freund), 83 (© 1981 Harold Edgerton), 84 (© 1981 Roy DeCarava), 86 (© 1981 Estate of Paul Strand), 87 (© 1981 Yousuf Karsh), 88 (© 1981 Harry Callahan), 89 (© 1981 Elliot Erwitt), 90 (© 1981 Edna Bullock), 92 (© 1981 Aaron Siskind), 94 (© 1981 Eve Arnold), 98 (© 1981 Garry Winogrand), 99 (© 1981 William Klein), 100 (© 1981 Ralph Steiner), 101 (© 1981 Danny Lyon), 102 (© 1981 George Tice), 103 (© 1981 Paul Caponigro), 106 (© 1981 Doon Arbus), 110 (© 1981 Jesus Sanchez Uribe), 116 (© 1981 Arno Minkkinen), 117 (© 1981 Jack Welpott), 120 (© 1981 Don Worth), 122 (© 1981 Jo Ann Callis), 126 (© 1981 Brett Weston), 132 (© 1981 Dachen Wu)

Courtesy of New Orleans Museum of Art: 43, 56, 63, 111

Courtesy of the Library of Congress, Prints and Photographs Division, Washington, D.C.: 18, 60, 61, 67, 68, 69, 71

Courtesy of Louisiana State Museum Collection: 28

Courtesy of Walt Burton Gallery, Cincinnati: 38

Courtesy of the Mortensen Estate Collection: 58 (© Mortensen Estate Collection)

Courtesy of the Chambi Family: 59

Courtesy of Clarence Laughlin © 1949, 1981: 80

Courtesy of the National Museum of African Art, Eliot Elisofon Archives, Smithsonian Institution: 137

Courtesy of the Daniel Wolf Gallery, New York City: 136

Courtesy of the artist: 49, 55 (Copyright Felix H. Man), 64, 65, 73, 75 (© Arnold Newman), 85, 95 (Copyright Ruth Bernhard), 96, 97, 104 (© Lucien Clergue), 105 (Copyright Vilem Kriz), 107, 108, 109 (© 1971 Jay Dusard), 112 (© 1975 Kipton C. Kumler), 113 (© Eva Rubinstein), 114, 115, 118 (© 1974 Robert Cumming), 119, 121, 123, 124, 125 (© 1977 J. Seeley), 127 (© 1977 Robert Adams), 128, 129, 130, 131 (Copyright Jerry N. Uelsmann), 133, 138, 139, 140, 141, 142, 143, 144